Principles of Demography

Principles of Demography

DONALD J. BOGUE, *1918–*

Professor of Sociology and Director,
Community and Family Study Center,
University of Chicago

John Wiley and Sons, Inc.   *New York · London · Sydney · Toronto*

Library of Congress Catalog Card Number: 68–26847
SBN 471 08620 7
Printed in the United States of America

TO

William Gum

AND

Betty Bogue

Preface

Principles of Demography is intended to be a comprehensive treatise covering the entire field of population study. It was designed to serve a dual purpose: as a textbook and as a reference work. Four goals have been pursued in its preparation:

1. *To present demography as a systematic discipline.* Despite the fact that they have been leaders in social science research, students of population has insisted on giving their general treatises a "social problems" perspective. The "population problems" approach should follow, rather than precede, the learning of fundamental facts and principles. The view supported here is that population would be worthy of scientific study even if there were no "population explosion" or "maldistribution of people." The present work discusses these problems, and the proposed remedies, but only after a systematic groundwork has been established.

2. *To assemble and formulate generalizations and principles* that have emerged and are emerging from demographic research and to present them as a set of quasi theories or theories. Far too much of demography has been simple decription (recitation of facts from censuses) and extrapolation (projection of past time series into the future). Demography must launch into the activities of prediction and control, as have all other "mature" sciences. These efforts at population prediction must do more than simply hold a mirror to the past in order to foresee the future. Instead, an effort must be made to identify the processes at work, and the forces that underlie them, and then armed with this understanding, to try to predict the future. Chapter 20 attempts this, making predictions that are consistent with demographic principles but are flatly contradicted by recent population trends.

3. *To promote an international approach to demography.* Few if any branches of social science have developed so high a sense of professional international fraternity as has demography. The International Population Union for the Scientific Study of Population Problems is one of the finest international social science organizations. The United Nations, through the activities of its Population Division and the publication of the *Demographic Yearbook*, has sponsored the philosophy that the concerns of demography are of worldwide importance and significance. Demographers have participated in two World Population Conferences in which differences in economic systems, religions, stages of economic development, and other realities or ideologies were played down in the interests of exchanging scientific information. Each year the research and experience that take place in the developing nations, in countries with a Communistic form of government, or in developed non-Christian nations such as Japan contribute as much or

more to the development of demography as a science as does the activity of American and European demographers. Yet, it is easy for a scholar to become so engrossed in the census materials for particular nations, states, or even municipalities that they can become provincial and chauvinistic in their outlook. This book tries to reflect the spirit of international goodwill and objective scholarship that now exists. It is hoped that younger readers will appreciate this situation and will absorb it as a part of their developing professional value system.

4. *To integrate demography with the other social sciences.* In order to "explain" most demographic events it is necessary to make use of hypotheses and theories derived from other sciences—psychology, social psychology, psychiatry, history, and political science, as well as sociology, economics, geography, anthropology, and biology. On the other hand, demography has a great deal to offer the other disciplines—both in providing essential data and in providing essential principles. Strong biases against any of the social sciences, as they pertain to population events, have been consciously avoided in an effort to show the interdependence with all of them. If there is over-emphasis or bias in this respect, it is in urging the greater use of theories of attitudes, motives, and other psychological and sociopsychological principles in research on demographic change—especially in the study of fertility and migration.

This work was undertaken because no book with these specifications existed. There is no scarcity of splendid individual research studies that have these traits, but the beginning student and the intelligent layman in search of demographic information need to have a review of all of demography from these perspectives within one set of covers.

It will be all too evident to the critical reader that these ambitious goals have been only partially achieved. Already the field has grown to such a size that it defies the capacity of a single person to review all of the important literature. In the present case, this difficulty was complicated by my near-complete occupation with research to improve or evaluate international programs of fertility reduction. In a very genuine sense, this book was "moonlighted," and many of its deficiencies and incompletenesses stem from the fact that despite six years of effort there was insufficient time to follow out all of the topics in the detail required by the blueprint. Another handicap is that it is difficult for a writer of a systematic treatise to rise above the general state of the discipline. Though dramatic progress has been made, there are still many large gaps in demographic research, and theorizing and principle-formulation are only in their early stages. Despite these limitations, if the present work helps to establish demography as a unique systematic discipline and to shake it out of its historic "population problems" mold, its primary objectives will have been achieved. The oncoming generations of bright young demographers all over the world have plenty of time to complete the task, or to redo it completely, with improvements.

It is essential to add, as a footnote, that the goals announced for this book have been present in some combination in previous writings. The eight years of very pleasant association with Professor Warren S. Thompson at Scripps Foundation have left an imprint that is clearly visible in the organization and presentation of the materials—even though this book arrives at a very different conclusion. Also, I have long admired the writings of A. M. Carr-Saunders and would like to imagine that if he were writing today —with the facts now at our disposal—his book would have taken a form somewhat along the lines of this one.

THE TEXTBOOK FUNCTION

Each chapter has been written as a more or less self-contained essay, so that the material may be presented in almost any sequence desired by the teacher. Numerous subdivisions of the chapters have been made, with more or less esoteric (hence optional) topics placed in separate sections and late in the chapter. Teachers who believe that labor force, marriage and family status, and socioeconomic status are topics that lie outside the realm of demography may simply omit the chapters dealing with them. By selection of chapters and sections of chapters it should be possible for a teacher to find suitable reading material for a course in demography, ranging from a very simple introduction to a rather sophisticated and comprehensive review of the field and its research. Wherever weakness or inadequacy in the presentation is sensed, the teacher will almost inevitably have in mind a supplementary set of readings that can be assigned to repair the deficiency.

A conscious effort has been made to have a clear and readable exposition with a minimum of technical material that could confuse the beginner. This has been done for two reasons. (1) I believe that demography has an obligation to make its findings widely available in langauge that is understood by those who have not had special demographic training. Therefore, the fewest possible technical terms have been used. Where it has been necessary to use the terminology of technical demography, these terms have been defined, explained, and illustrated in nonmathematical language before using them in the analysis. (2) In collaboration with Dr. Evelyn M. Kitagawa, I am preparing a companion volume, *A Manual of Demographic Research Techniques,* which is almost wholly a methodological treatise. When the two volumes are available as a set, the teacher can select the appropriate methodological sections as supplementary readings to the present book.

THE REFERENCE WORK FUNCTION

The individual chapters of the volume are intended to represent the major subfields of demography. Each chapter is designed to be a comprehensive treatment of that particular subfield. Wherever possible, key data are presented to verify or support the generalizations and principles stated. When assembled, the book is supposed to be a source of quick information on almost any topic of demography. In a sense, it is a "demographic encyclopedia," organized a little more along topic lines than is the usual encyclopedia. The index has been prepared with this use in mind.

There are several sets of population statistics that are of interest and use to persons from many disciplines. Unluckily, many of these data are scattered in the censuses of many nations, in many issues of the *Demographic Yearbook,* and in many monographs, special reports, and articles. Many other tables have been derived from raw data at the expense of considerable effort and ingenuity by the world's demographers. These derived tables now are available only to those few who possess a library of monographs, technical journals, and demographic raw data. In preparing this book, the policy has been adopted of selecting the most important of these statistics and publishing them in full. Arrangements were made with the publisher to use photographic reproduction for publishing the statistical materials, to keep the cost of printing within reasonable limits. At first, these large tables may frighten the beginning student, unless he realizes that he is not expected to read them in their entirety, but only to read their titles and to know where to go when he needs specific facts at a later date. As the years pass, these tables will need updating; nevertheless, they will remain as an inventory of basic data as of about 1965 and may assume greater than less importance as a baseline for measuring change.

At the end of each chapter there is a selected bibliography. This is also intended as a reference source for persons who wish to pursue the topic of the chapter further and wish to have a guide for further reading. The Population Index, published by the Princeton Office of Population Research, is an unexcelled bibliographic source. However, it is so thoroughly complete that it can bewilder the beginner. The selected bibliographies of the present book are intended to guide the reader to high-priority items. These lists can be of use to departments that wish to improve their demographic libraries.

INADEQUACIES

The original outline called for two additional chapters—"Population and Economic Development" and "Eugenics: The Transition from Concern about Quantity to Concern for Quality." The pressure of work led to the decision to publish the completed portion and to leave two important missing topics to a possible later edition.

Chicago, Illinois
May 1968

Donald J. Bogue

Acknowledgments

Several parts of this book summarizes research that I did in collaboration with others. Footnotes at the appropriate locations do not adequately acknowledge the very great debt owed to these colleagues. Margaret Jarman Hagood, Calvin L. Beale, Henry S. Shryock, Jr., Wilson H. Grabill, Gladys K. Bowles, Sigfried Hoermann, Walter Mertens, Lee Jay Cho, and James Palmore all contributed to this volume through earlier collaborative research, and it is a pleasure to acknowledge this debt. To Dr. Cho I am especially indebted for the supervision and actual participation in the preparation of many of the statistical tables. Mr. Robert Yaspin and Beverly Wilder have patiently labored over census volumes to extract needed summaries.

Many of the data assembled especially for this book were compiled by electronic computation. In several chapters it was necessary to launch into rather extensive research projects to produce the materials needed to deal with a particular topic. Elizabeth J. Bogue, my wife, wrote the computer programs and carried out the data processing necessary to produce the needed tabulations and computations. Thus I am deeply indebted to her for both professional and sentimental reasons. As in all of my other publications, her participation has made this a family enterprise in which my indebtedness goes far beyond the usual domestic chore of encouragement and forbearance at the incursions of writing on family time.

The statistical tables were typed for direct photocopy by Mrs. Carmen Fernandez. Her patience and care have made possible the assembly of the many large tables which make this a useful reference work.

Finally, I wish to acknowledge with special thanks the catalytic role of William Gum, the sociology editor for the publisher. It was he who stimulated the undertaking. He ceaselessly encouraged and urged its completion. When the demands of other work slowed progress, he exercised motivation by telephone, letter, telegram, and personal visit. For half a decade, the typists have referred to this work not by its title, but simply as "The Gum Book." Because his encouragement and expressions of confidence in its ultimate utility far outran his duties and any material gain he might receive, I have taken the liberty of dedicating it to him. Had it not been for him, I am afraid this project would have died of neglect in favor of fertility control research. I sincerely hope his judgment was sound.

D. J. B.

Contents

CHAPTER 1

Introduction to the Study of Demography

1.1. Demography as a Field of Study

Demography is the empirical, statistical, and mathematical study of human populations. This rather overinclusive definition may be narrowed by enumerating the principal topics of demographic study. It focuses its attention on three rather commonplace and readily observable human phenomena: (*a*) change in population size (growth or decline), (*b*) the composition of the population, and (c) the distribution of population in space.[1] It is interested not only in size, composition, and distribution of the population at the present time, but also in changes in these aspects over time. Moreover, it is concerned with seeking explanations of why a particular combination of population conditions exist at a given time and why the conditions are changing in exactly the way they are and at the rate of change they exhibit. Therefore, the field of demography may be defined as the description of current status and of changes over time in the size, composition,

[1] This definition of the field is well established. For example, Warren S. Thompson, whose *Population Problems* has been a leading demographic treatise since 1930, opens the 1953 edition with the following statement: "The aspects of population growth and change to which the discussion in this book will be devoted may be indicated by three questions. . . . 1. What changes are taking place in the size of populations, and how are changes in size effected? What is the significance of these changes from the standpoint of human welfare? . . . 2. Where are people found, and what changes in their distribution in communities and areas are taking place? . . . 3. What kind of people are found in any given population group, and how do those in one group differ from those in another?" Warren S. Thompson, *Population Problems* (New York: McGraw-Hill, 1953), p. 1.

and distribution of populations, and the development of scientific explanations of these events.

Demography can also be defined as the quantitative study of five "demographic processes": fertility, mortality, marriage, migration, and social mobility (change in social status or condition). The five processes are continuously at work within a population, determining size, composition, and distribution. And if there is a change in size, composition, or distribution, these are the components or mechanisms by which the change occurs. In fact, even the "static" condition with no change is, in reality, only a temporary equilibrium among these five very dynamic processes. Although this definition is useful for emphasizing the components or forces that demographers study, it is overly inclusive. Scholars in other disciplines also engage in the quantitative study of the same processes. This may range all the way from medical studies of the process by which the human egg is fertilized to socio-psychological studies of the status aspirations of teenagers in comparison with the status aspirations that parents have for their teenage children. Yet this definition is useful, because it identifies those processes that are of most interest to the demographer.

A third and more precise definition is as follows: *Demography is the statistical and mathematical study of the size, composition, and spatial distribution of human populations, and of changes over time in these aspects through the operation of the five processes of fertility, mortality, marriage, migration, and social mobility. Although it maintains a continuous descriptive and comparative analysis*

1

of trends, in each of these processes and in their net result, its long-run goal is to develop a body of theory to explain the events that it charts and compares. Three examples of demographic work will help to clarify the definition.

Example 1. The National Population Census and Its Interpretation for the Public. Once every ten years most nations of the world conduct a national population census. The census is of vital concern to all branches of government and business and has many practical as well as academic uses. The new census count is used to redistrict states for representation in the national and state legislatures, to allocate tax benefits to local governments, and for many other purposes. It provides key information for setting production schedules and marketing quotas in industry. It helps to orient plans for the future in organizations of many types. Its results, therefore, are anxiously awaited and widely studied.

At census time every household or other dwelling place is contacted and the name of every resident recorded. Military installations, merchant ships in port, hospitals, prisons, college dormitories, and other institutional places of residence are all included in the census inquiry. As each name is recorded, certain additional information about the person is also written down. The following is usually considered to be a minimum list of population characteristics about which information is to be collected, either from the entire population or from a very sizeable sample:

sex
age
race or ethnic origin
marital status
number of children ever born (by married
　women)
literacy or educational attainment
place of birth
work status
occupation

As later chapters illustrate, some censuses, including that of the United States, gather information for a much larger list of characteristics.

As they enumerate the population, the census takers make a record of where each person is living, which provides the basis for later studies of population distribution.

The roster of names assembled by the census forms the basis for a head count for finding the total population size. This count may be compared with the corresponding count from preceding censuses to determine how much change in total population size has taken place. Thus the simple roster of names supplies the demographer with data about population size, and very intensive research may be undertaken to explain exactly how and why certain observed changes in size have occurred.

The information about personal characteristics is pooled and tabulated to show the makeup or composition of the population in terms of sex, age, race, marital status, and so on. Do females outnumber males and if so, by how much? Is the percentage of persons in their late teens who are married greater at the new census than at the preceding census? How much has the educational level of the foreign-born population changed since the last census, and has the differential in educational level between natives and the foreign-born widened or narrowed? These and many other questions about the composition of the population, and change in that composition, can be answered from the census tabulations of population characteristics.

The recording of the place of residence (place of enumeration) permits the census to make tabulations for each of the numerous territorial subdivisions of the nation. Thus not only is it possible to report the total population size and the population composition for the entire nation, but also for each state, province, municipality, and even segments of communities. Changes in the territorial pattern of distribution from one census to another can be noted, and research programs to explain them may be attempted.

The demographer is a key figure in making census results easily comprehensible to the general public. He is the statistical gold miner who screens the mountain of statistics turned out by the census, sorting out the nuggets of useful information. And the years immediately after a census become a veritable "gold rush" for demographers. Articles and monographs on a wide variety of population topics appear. Textbooks in many branches of social science are revised to incorporate the new demographic output. In a very real sense, the demographer is responsible for rendering a public professional service in digesting and interpreting census results.

Example 2. The Annual Registration of Births and Deaths. Most nations have laws that make it compulsory to register each birth and death shortly after they occur. A certificate of birth is issued to the parents of each newborn child for future use as proof of citizenship, age, birthplace, and parentage. Similarly, a certificate of death is drawn up for legal use in distributing the property of the deceased, in making claims for life insurance payment, or in obtaining survivors' social security benefits. In addition to these uses as legal documents, certificates of birth and death may serve an important statistical function. By compiling the information that they contain into statistical tables it is possible to derive data about the collective effect of births in increasing the population and the collective effect of deaths in tending to decrease it. Thus, by studying vital statistics (as statistics of birth and death are termed), the process of population growth can be broken into its component parts and each part studied separately. Statistical compilations of births and deaths are made annually, and the amount and rate of growth due to the operation of the vital processes can be stated for a nation and for each of its major subdivisions. Comparisons with similar measures for earlier years are made, and explanations of why the rates have changed as they have may be undertaken.

Demographers are the statistical technicians who compile vital statistics and analyze and interpret them. Sets of birthrates and death rates are computed for many different places and population groups for each year. Places and groups with unusually high or unusually low rates are noted, and explanations are developed of why these variations have occurred. The rates for each new year are compared with those for preceding years; if there has been a change, efforts are made to understand how and why it has occurred. To be sure, medical and public health researchers, called biostatisticians, also do much analysis of this type, and it is often difficult to state at what point demographic analysis of births and deaths ends and biostatistical and medical analysis begins. Many biostatisticians belong to the professional organizations of demographers, and vice versa.

Example 3. Population Projections for Economic and Social Planning. Suppose that a national planning agency is making long-range plans for economic welfare. It wishes to reduce unemployment and underemployment, to eliminate jobs that are economically submarginal and degrading to human dignity, and to increase the amount of income that each family receives. To make its plans, the agency must have a wide array of information. Three of the most important items are: (*a*) facts about employment, unemployment, and underemployment at the time in the population—how many workers, what kinds of workers, and their location; (*b*) the current size and rate of growth, and the probable size of the work force and its probable composition in future years, under various assumptions about population growth; (*c*) the current and probable future number of dependents that must be supported by the economy—the number of youngsters who must be educated, the number of oldsters who must be pensioned, and so on. This set of facts calls for a model of how the population will grow in future years. To obtain it, the planners usually approach a demographer and ask him to make estimates. If he is an honest demographer, he will reply that this is a very difficult task and one that is beset with the dangers of making sizeable errors. The planners assert that running the risk of making moderate errors is better than having no information at all, and assure the demographer that his best judgment, utilizing his knowledge of the history of population change in other parts of the world and of recent population changes in his own locality, together with his assessment of the forces that underlie these changes, should provide a better basis for the estimates than mechanical extrapolation or pure guess. The demographer obliges and prepares the estimates. To warn users that the estimates are too crude and inexact to be taken literally as precise estimates or predictions of what will actually materialize, he labels them "population projections" or illustrations of what would happen if the combination of demographic events that he envisions were to materialize. Usually he is very reluctant to assert with any confidence that the assumptions he makes about the future will actually take place in the pattern that his model projections specify.

Together, these three examples paint a fairly representative picture of the research activity that comprises demographic analysis. Many who pursue it find great personal satisfaction in one of its outstanding characteristics—a widespread appreciation for and almost immediate use of its research findings. It also explains why demographers are feared and abused by dictators, corrupt politicians, and charlatans who earn a living by making unwarranted, exaggerated, or speculative claims about population matters. As one of the nation's leading fact finders, the demographer is an integral part of the team that strives, with professional integrity, to "keep the record straight" about many topics of fundamental public concern. Thus dangerous myths and rumors about racial, religious, and ethnic groups are routinely dispelled by factual statistical evidence assembled by demographers. Demographers have also been in the forefront of movements to solve national social problems. For example, it is the data from the official national censuses, compiled by demographers, that have persistently shown the extent of discrimination to which particular ethnic and racial groups in the United States have been subjected. By adhering to his facts, the demographer often performs the latent function of keeping his colleagues in other branches of social science in touch with social reality; this is especially true where social scientists are inclined to indulge to facile and deceptively plausible flights of speculative fancy on the basis of a few flimsy impressions. Equally often he pricks the public conscience.

1.2. "Demography" versus "Population Study"

In earlier years an effort was made to maintain **a** difference of meaning between the terms "population study" and "demography," but with little apparent success. Demography, or even "formal demography," was supposed to refer to the study of vital processes (birth and death), with a grudging admission of migration. Demographers were said to be interested primarily in population growth and reproduction from a mathematical or quasi-actuarial point of view in that their study was in terms of the components of change. Population study, on the other hand, was regarded as a broader term, encompassing not only what was called demography, but also the less mathematical study of population composition and distribution. Some have used the term "social demography" (in contrast with "formal demography") to denote the broader field of population study. Thus demography was formerly considered a part of population study—the mathematically more precise part.[2] Apparently this terminology divided the population pie into too many pieces, for in recent years monographs, articles, and books have used the terms "population study" and "demography"

[2] An example of a recent statement of this distinction may be found in Philip M. Hauser and Otis Dudley Duncan, *The Study of Human Population* (Chicago: University of Chicago Press, 1959), pp. 2–3, 33–35. The same distinction is endorsed by William Petersen in his *Population* (New York: Macmillan, 1961), p. 3, with the added connotation that people who do population analysis are comparatively less sophisticated in their use of methodology, whereas demographers have a higher order of analytical skill. Most Americans still seem to prefer to use the term "population" when speaking very broadly. "Demography" is more widely used outside the United States and by the United Nations. For example, the population publication of the United Nations is called *Demographic Yearbook,* and the United Nations has established Demographic Training Centers in Bombay and Santiago. The official journal of the International Population Union is called *Le Démographe.* In contrast, the official demographic society in the United States is called the Population Association of America; its official publication is called *Population Index,* and the older leading research organizations have the word "population" rather than "demography" in their titles. The title of this book was chosen deliberately to conform to international usage and to try to hasten the wider adoption of a more elegant name for one of social science's more elegant disciplines.

interchangeably. Possibly this amalgamation of terminology was stimulated by the wider use of mathematics in all branches of social science and by the discovery that vital processes are highly interrelated with population composition and even social science in general. In this book "demography" is preferred as the name of the discipline. "Population" is used to refer to the raw data of census statistics and to the aggregates of people to which the data refer.

1.3 Demography in Relation to the Other Social Sciences

Demography enjoys a very enviable status among the social sciences: it interacts freely with all and finds itself incompatible with none. Although it neither competes directly with nor duplicates the work of any of the other social sciences, it makes extensive use of the principles employed by all of them. Simultaneously, it contributes directly to their research and theory. In addition to the popularity of demography among practical people, as already described, trends in population size, composition, and distribution are of interest to all other social sciences. Researchers in the other disciplines rely on demographers to "keep them posted" about demographic conditions. In their short-run analyses the economist, the political scientist, and others tend to regard demographic facts as basic forces over which there is little control and which are therefore among the fundamental explainers or determinants of economic and political events in the near future.

Example 3 of Section 1.1 illustrates the attitude of many social scientists toward demography. To them, an understanding of such processes as population growth, composition, and distribution requires specialized study beyond their ken. They would prefer to depend on the results of a demographic analysis of high quality and to accept the results as "basic data" for their own research. They are not uncritical in this division of labor, however, and when demographers fail to deliver a needed analysis, or seem to commit errors of interpretation, it is not uncommon for economists or political scientists to undertake the work themselves.[3] An increasing number of professional training programs include demography in their curricula, and an increasing number of graduate students are encouraged to elect such courses. Schools of public health, social work, medicine, and public administration are among those that have recently placed much greater emphasis on giving basic demographic education to their students.

Demography is no less dependent on the other social sciences than they are on it. Despite the fact that demography is highly mathematical and is a leader in the construction of mathematical models, it has few unique concepts and theories that would explain "why" a particular demographic situation exists at a particular moment or what forces underlie an observed change in demographic status. Most of the variables and theories that "explain" demographic events come from other social science disciplines, and "demographic theory" is an organized synthesis of inferences and principles extracted from economics, sociology, social psychology, psychiatry, political science, anthropology, and geography. A familiar example is the use of the findings of agronomy, soil science, and agricultural economics in explaining the phenomenon of food shortage and its impact on population events. Another example may be cited from fertility study. No demographer interprets the phenomenon of changing birthrates as being due to autonomous principles or forces. Instead, he regards birthrates as a response to changes in economic conditions, cultural definition, psychological states, and political conditions. Fertility analysis is currently using the full range of social science in its search for explanations of observed changes and trends. A similar statement can also be made for the processes of marriage, migration, and (to a lesser extent) mortality.

Thus we have the anomalous situation that demographic factors are treated as explanatory variables by many social scientists, where-

[3] For a very interesting example see the article by Joseph S. Davis, "The Population Upsurge in the United States," which protests the unwillingness of demographers to admit that a fundamental change in fertility patterns had taken place shortly after 1940. War-Peace pamphlet No. 12 (Stanford, Calif.: Stanford University Food Research Institute, 1949).

as demographers treat the same factors as variables *to be explained*.

As part of their inventory and appraisal of the field of demography, Hauser and Duncan elicited the cooperation of a group of experts to explore the interaction and interdependency between demography and other disciplines. Seven essays that analyze the field of demography with respect to general ecology, human ecology, geography, physical anthropology, genetics, economics, and sociology comprise a complete unit in their report. Each of the essays is listed in the bibliography at the end of this chapter and is recommended to the reader.[4]

1.4. The World Population Crisis

As every adult who keeps informed on current events knows, within the past 300 years there has been a remarkable acceleration in the rates of growth among the human population, and within the past 25 years even the pace of acceleration has increased. This has occurred through man's steady progress in reducing his death rate, while making much smaller, and tardier, reductions in his birthrate. Many nations are undergoing severe political and economic crises in which a very rapid population growth threatens to nullify or even outrun the gains that they are making in industrializing and modernizing their economies. Also, a combination of rapid migration and high fertility among a small part of the population is creating similar problems at particular sites in North America and Europe. Consequently, much is being written in a highly dramatic, fright-provoking language of the type that orators use to describe the horrors of atomic warfare. "The population bomb" and "the population explosion" are, in fact, favorite phrases of many essayists on the population crisis. The changes under way are so great, and their implications for the future even one or two decades away so urgent, that scientific reserve is abandoned and highly colorful outpourings that reveal profound concern and strong value judgments are substituted. Following is an ex-

ample of such writing. As Chapter 20 will make clear, this is not the view-point taken in this book.

"Preface" to *The Future Growth of World Population*[5] by the United Nations

"When told that the world's population may rise from 2,500 million to 4,000 million during the next twenty-five years, we think at once of the direct practical consequences in the economic and social sphere. And yet such a statement should stimulate even more profound thought; we should do well to ponder the significance of this development in terms of the destiny of our species.

"These next twenty-five years form part of a process which began some 200,000 years ago and which is about to culminate in man's full possession of the earth.

"Two hundred thousand years ago, an extraordinary event occurred, as important perhaps in its outcome as the appearance of the first living cell: a creature which morphologically probably hardly differed from the other primates surrounding it, crossed the threshold of deliberate reflection; man had quietly entered the scene.

"The consequences of this event were not at once apparent; moreover, this first man was a mere semblance of what man is today. Palaeontology traces the stages of that evolution, and we now have a fairly clear idea of the process whereby, during these 200,000 years, the *homo faber* of the early quaternary age developed into the *homo sapiens* of today's demography. Palaeontology is concerned with periods of the order of two hundred thousand years and, though man eventually emerges as the dominant figure in that evolution, he does not appear, at least at the outset, to have materially altered the rate of change in the varying forms of life.

"Yet, while it took 200,000 years for the world's human population to reach 2,500 mil-

---

[4] Hauser and Duncan, *op. cit.*, Part IV, Population Studies in Various Disciplines.

[5] United Nations, *The Future Growth of World Population*, Population Studies, No. 28, Population Branch of the Department of Economic and Social Affairs (New York, 1958).

lion, it will now take a mere thirty years to add another 2,000 million. With the present rate of increase, it can be calculated that in 600 years the number of human beings on earth will be such that there will be only one square metre for each to live on. It goes without saying that this can never take place; something will happen to prevent it.

"We are now speaking of 600 years, whereas just now we were talking of periods 200 times as long. Six hundred years is a little more than the time that has elapsed since the discovery of the New World. We have left paleontology for history; the natural evolution of man is virtually completed. A new process is about to begin, or has perhaps already started, and the first signs of that "socialization" of the world which appear on the horizon may be significant in this connection. Our previous view that the crossing of the "threshold of thought" had not altered the rate of evolution no longer holds. Deliberate thinking, in fact, has so increased this rate that the very nature of the evolutionary process has been thereby changed and that it seems imperative having created the means of accelerating it, to find also the means of slowing it down and recovering equilibrium. Yet the danger of such remedial action is obvious. As long as it was a question of increasing the population, we were part of the stream followed by evolution during millions of years. Faced with the problem of checking this growth, we are swimming against the tide and, in extremity, having discovered how to increase the flood waters we now also possess the means of arresting them. It now depends on us whether this awakening of consciousness within the stream of life ends in failure or success. If tomorrow mankind loses the desire to live, or more correctly, to survive, the history of life on earth will have lost all meaning. This explains why those who have undertaken to be the custodians of man's moral heritage are questioning his moral preparedness to govern his own destiny.

"The growth of world population during the next twenty-five years, therefore, has an importance which transcends economic and social considerations. It is at the very heart of the problem of our existence."

In the present book we postpone the consideration of crises and problematic aspects of population events until later chapters, after reviewing the processes and forces involved and assessing the resources for resolving the world's population problems. In this way, we hope, the reader will acquire the opinion, if he does not already hold it, that all is not lost and that population "bombs" are not immune to "defusing" by prompt, well-planned action. The conclusion is a mobilizing call to action by the application of social science, *now*. Few nuclear scientists have remained unmoved by the potential destructive power of atomic weapons or have refused to urge a program to prevent atomic wars. In like manner, few demographers today can maintain an impassive air while discussing the implications of possible and probable future population trends, or belittle programs aimed at slowing down population growth. This does not mean, however, that their fears for the future of the human race need derange their scientific and analytic faculties. It is important for the flow of emotion to start only after the full facts and their implications have been assessed.

1.5. Other Population Problems

The population crisis created by runaway growth is only one of several contemporary social problems that have an important population component. Brief statements of some of these problems follow. All of them will be discussed in more detail in later chapters.

Urban Agglomeration. All over the world the population is urbanizing rapidly. A larger and larger share of mankind is being compressed into densely settled urban areas. Congestion, social disorganization incident to rapid influx of new ethnic and cultural groups, and other problems associated with urban life are apparent. The urbanization movement has become so vast that some demographers now devote all of their research energies to studying it, and we can properly speak of urban demography as a subfield. Demographic research furnishes a substantial part of the information needed to launch programs of urban renewal and, as later chapters show, provides a factual backdrop for the study of all social problems.

Rural Depopulation. A consequence of rapid urbanization has been a mass exodus of people from rural areas. Some rural communities have lost one half or more of their population in one decade, and others have so shrunk in size that not enough people remain to maintain many of the basic enterprises and institutions. Certain areas have become so sparse that it has been necessary to purchase the remaining farmland and other enterprises, to evacuate these submarginal rural territories, and to convert them to national forest land. In others, extensive retrenchment by the closing of post offices, the consolidation of schools, and the withdrawal of branch establishments of major corporations has taken place.

The populations that remain in such communities exist in a chronically depressed condition and constitute a major national welfare problem. Almost every technologically advanced nation has at least one such region. Programs to alleviate the economic hardship of these areas inevitably invoke the participation of demographers, who study the vital process, the migration pattern, and the social and (or) economic composition of these populations. Almost invariably these areas of mass exodus are also areas of economic stagnation—little new industry is developing to replace the dying establishments. A state of economic depression settles over the territory, and mass poverty develops. As we shall see later, such "distress areas" are not all rural; suburbanization is creating a similar condition in the central cities. These phenomena are worldwide. It is of interest to note that in 1963 the famous Institut National d'Études Démographiques (I.N.E.D.) in Paris launched a large and comprehensive program for the study of "les populations maladaptées" (maladjusted populations).

Differential Adjustment or Well-Being of Minority Ethnic Groups. Almost every nation contains one or more minority groups that in comparison with the population at large remain unadjusted, lower in status, and deviant in behavior. Often this status is perpetuated or aggravated by prejudice and discrimination on the part of the majority group, rendering assimilation painfully long. Negroes in the United States, scheduled castes in India, Negroes in South Africa, Indians in Latin America, and Gypsies in Europe are examples of this situation. Demographers have performed a highly useful service by maintaining a factual record of the social and economic conditions under which these groups live and by attempting to measure statistically the extent of the social injustice that they suffer. Demographers have also charted the progress of adjustment and assimilation of that part of these groups which has been allowed to join the mainstream of the society and economy. Perhaps more than any other branch of social science, demography has emphasized the importance of "economic opportunity" in facilitating the rapid adjustment of minority ethnic, religious, and cultural groups.

The Eugenic Problem. Many biologists, who have ample opportunity to observe the transmission of traits—both favorable and unfavorable—through the mechanism of biological inheritance, are profoundly concerned that the vital processes as they now operate may be tending to cause the segments of the population that have less desirable combinations of genes (from the viewpoint of the dominant values of the society) to grow at a faster rate than do those that have the "best" genes. For example, some psychologists have raised the question whether the genetic factors involved in intelligence are not deteriorating under the impact of high fertility among the less intelligent and low fertility among the more intelligent. All species of living organisms exhibit a wide variation in their ability to achieve or perform in certain ways that are deemed "good" or "desirable" from the point of view of human society at large. The human species is no exception. The exact extent to which this variation is inherited and the extent to which it is due to an unusually great opportunity for some individuals and to a comparatively small opportunity for others to develop their aptitudes, remain a major research problem.

1.6. A Short History of Demography [6]

Modern demography dates from about 1925, when Alfred J. Lotka developed a mathematical model for the study of reproduction.

Most of the materials synthesized in this book are taken from writings since this date. Nevertheless, demography has existed as a systematic empirical discipline for more than three centuries.

The Founding Fathers: John Graunt and William Petty. John Graunt, a haberdasher, who seems to have been a very active participant in the lively intellectual life in mid-seventeenth-century London, is generally regarded as the father of demography. He carried out a numerical analysis of births and deaths, arrived at a set of limited generalizations about mortality, fertility, migration, and marriage as interrelated population processes, and visualized clearly many facets of population research. He obtained his data from the "Bills of Mortality," which were weekly reports of burials (containing also information on christenings) compiled by parish clerks. These reports had been initiated during the great plagues of the late sixteenth and early seventeenth centuries and continued in an almost unbroken series for several decades. From this mass of detail he undertook to discover regularities and uniformities in vital events that would enable him to formulate "laws" about the growth of populations. Graunt's study, published in 1662, was entitled *Natural and Political Observations . . . Made Upon the Bills of Mortality.* He discovered that in London of that day deaths exceeded births, whereas in rural areas the reverse was true. He discovered the biological phenomena that at birth the number of male infants exceeds the number of female infants and that there is a distinctive age pattern to deaths. He classified deaths by cause and learned that the causes of death vary from place to place and from year to year. He is credited with constructing a crude mortality table that adumbrated the modern life table.

---

[6] The materials in this and the next two sections have been taken primarily from secondary sources, which are cited at the end of this chapter. The student who is interested in pursuing this topic further should begin by reading the essay by Frank Lorimer, "The Development of Demography." His selected bibliography of historically important writings, arranged in chronological order, will be found to be very useful.

He undertook to estimate the trend of growth and size of London's population and correctly identified migration, fertility, and mortality as the components of growth. Moreover, he set the precedent for one of demography's oldest traditions—to evaluate the data used in any research to learn the extent, types, and probable causes of errors and to devise adjustment and correction factors to remove biases in statistical measures computed from the data. Above all, he established as a leading goal of population study the development of explanations for the underlying regularities observed.

Graunt's work was partially inspired and greatly encouraged by his friend, William Petty, who is honored for his many insights into how statistical measures can be used to help to solve problems of national economy and government policy. Petty's work, *Political Arithmetick* (published posthumously in 1690), had a substantial impact on the subsequent development of demography. Although he was not so skilled in compiling and analyzing data as Graunt, Petty generated many original and stimulating ideas about population. In commenting on his work, Durand states:

"It is remarkable how many questions Petty tackled, with which demographers and statisticians are still wrestling today, particularly in studies of the problems of under-developed countries. Among other things, he was concerned with population projections, the economics of urbanization, population structure and the labor force, unemployment and underemployment, and the measure of national income."[7]

In tracing the history of demography, Lorimer and Durand both note that "scholarly speculation" about population matters has been made by almost all of civilization's great thinkers; they mention especially Aristotle, Plato, Confucius, ibn-Khaldun (fourteenth century), and a Jesuit, Giovanni Botero (sixteenth century). But the empirical research of Graunt,

[7] John Durand, "Demography's Three Hundredth Anniversary," *Population Index,* **28** (4) (October 1962), 334.

supplemented by the insights of Petty, marks the emergence of demography as a scientific discipline. The accomplishment of these men is all the more remarkable because they had only a fraction of the data needed for an adequate testing of their ideas, and even this fraction was not of good quality.

During the century or so following Graunt, progress in population study was slow. Edmund Halley constructed the first empirical life table (1693). In response to a growing interest in population matters in the British Parliament, Gregory King developed population estimates for England from tax records and partial enumerations (1696). The influence of Graunt and Petty spread to France and later to Germany and other European countries, and during the eighteenth century there was an awakening of interest in population study. This often took the form of compiling as many facts as possible about the nation or parts thereof and led to early census enumeration or the starting of vital registration.

Johann Süssmilch, a Lutheran clergyman in Germany, was the leading demographic researcher in the mid-eighteenth century. In his book of 1741, *Die Göttliche Ordnung* ("The Divine Order"), he undertook to demonstrate that the orderliness that underlies vital events is an expression of a divine mind. In his efforts to establish this proposition, he was led to search widely and make many splendid comparative analyses in order to produce instances of orderliness in population events. He studied the changing pattern of sex composition with advancing age, made numerous computations of birth, death, and marriage rates both in urban and rural populations, and studied the trends in marriages and births over time.

In evaluating the work of these "founding fathers" of demography, Lorimer writes: "The critical characteristics that gave their efforts a cumulative force were their enthusiasm for the discovery of previously unknown relations— especially quantitative relations—in the processes of life and death and their respect for empirical observations."[8]

Thomas R. Malthus. It has been customary to give Thomas R. Malthus a place of top honor

in the history of demography. It is the opinion of the present writer that although his writings have attracted worldwide attention and have dominated the thinking of many students of population, his contribution to the development of demography as a science was rather modest. In 1799 this clergyman published a brochure, *An Essay on the Principle of Population as it Affects the Future Improvement of Society.* . . . It was his main thesis that inasmuch as man's capacity to increase his food supply and other means of subsistence is much smaller than his capacity to reproduce himself, population growth necessarily always tends to continue until it presses upon the limits of subsistence. Man, like all other forms of life, is capable of very rapid reproduction. If death does not intervene, an average healthy couple starting a family at about age twenty can easily produce ten or more children before the woman reaches menopause. Malthus used this phenomenon as the foundation on which to build his famous "principle of population," namely, that unlimited growth is prevented only by war, famine, pestilence, premature death, and other forms of misery and vice. He believed that most populations had reached the point where they were being held in check by these forces; the large numbers of poverty-stricken proletarians, living in misery in Malthus's day, he accepted as convincing proof. From this principle it was easy for political leaders and economists to deduce that poverty and destitution are a natural and ordained phenomenon of nature against which governments and systems for allocating national wealth are virtually powerless. Therefore, any form of relief or welfare program aimed at improving the lot of the poor is doomed to failure and is a waste of the nation's resources. Many economists, and apparently Malthus himself, accepted this view, with the result that his *Essay* stirred up a great storm of controversy that involved morals and politics as well as economics. When challenged, Malthus did a great deal of fact-collection in an effort to document his thesis. His *Essay* went through seven editions, and became somewhat more moderate in the process. Even in its final form, however, he defended his "principle of population" and asserted that there was little that man could do,

[8] Frank Lorimer, *op. cit.*, p. 131.

except to abstain from marriage or to abstain within marriage, to escape the dilemma. He refused to admit birth control, in forms then known, as a moral solution to the problem.

Those who defend Malthus as having more than historical relevance for demographic theory often take refuge in an accusation that those who do not accept him have not read him. To obviate this charge for the reader, the full detail of the Malthusian argument has been carefully pieced together, in Malthus's own words, and reproduced below. This has been accomplished by assembling extracts from his essay, "A Summary View of the Principle of Population," written and published in 1830. It is believed that this represents rather accurately the position that he held toward the end of his career, after more than three decades of discussion of his first edition of the *Essay*.[9]

"In taking a view of animated nature, we cannot fail to be struck with a prodigious power of increase in plants and animals. But whether they increase slowly or rapidly, if they increase by seed or generation, their natural tendency must be to increase in a geometrical ratio, that is, by multiplication. . . .

"Elevated as man is above all other animals by his intellectual faculties, it is not to be supposed that the physical laws to which he is subjected should be essentially different from those which are observed to prevail in other parts of animated nature. . . . Food is equally necessary to his support; and if his natural capacity of increase be greater than can be permanently supplied from a limited territory, his increase must be constantly retarded by the difficulty of procuring the means of subsistence. . . .

". . . [Human] population, when unchecked, increases in a geometrical progression of such a nature as to double itself every twenty-five years.

"If, setting out from a tolerably well-peopled country such as England, France, Italy, or

⁹ An earlier version of this essay had appeared previously in the 1824 Supplement to the *Encyclopaedia Britannica*. The 1830 version has been recently reprinted in a paperback book, *Three Essays on Population*, Frank W. Notestein, ed. (New York: New American Library of World Literature, 1960).

Germany, we were to suppose that by great attention to agriculture, its produce could be permanently increased every twenty-five years by a quantity equal to that which it at present produces, it would be allowing a rate of increase decidedly beyond any probability of realization. . . . Yet this would be an arithmetical progression and would fall short, beyond all comparison, of the natural increase of population in a geometrical progression. . . .

"Whatever temporary and partial relief . . . may be derived from emigration . . . it is quite obvious that, considering the subject generally and largely, emigration may be fairly said not in any degree to touch the difficulty. And whether we exclude or include emigration— whether we refer to particular countries, or to the whole earth—the supposition of a future capacity in the soil to increase the necessaries of life every twenty-five years by a quantity equal to that which is at present produced must be decidedly beyond the truth.

"But if the natural increase of population, when unchecked by the difficulty of procuring the means of subsistence or other peculiar causes, be such as to continue doubling its numbers in twenty-five years, and if the greatest increase of food which, for a continuance, could possibly take place on a limited territory like our earth in its present state, be at the most only such as would add every twenty-five years an amount equal to its present produce then it is quite clear that a powerful check on the increase of the population must be almost constantly in action.

"Consequently, it follows necessarily that the average rate of the *actual* increase of population over the greatest part of the globe, obeying the same laws as the increase of food, must be totally of a different character from the rate at which it would increase if unchecked. The great question, then, which remains to be considered, is the manner in which this constant and necessary check upon population practically operates.

". . . The difficulty of procuring in adequate plenty the necessaries of life should either indispose . . . persons to marry early, or disable them from rearing in health the largest families. Its effect would be either to discourage early marriages, which would check the rate of increase by preventing the same proportion of births, or to render the children unhealthy from bad and insufficient nourishment, which would check the rate of increase by occasioning a greater proportion of deaths.

"The first of these checks may, with propriety, be called the *preventive* check to population; the second, the *positive* check; and the absolute necessity of their operation in the case supposed is as certain and obvious as that man cannot live without food.

". . . In civilized and improved countries, the accumulation of capital, the division of labour, and the invention of machinery will extend the bounds of production; but . . . the effects of these causes . . . are very much less efficient in producing an increase of food. . . . The increased quantity of the necessaries of life so obtained can never be such as to supersede, for any length of time, the operation of the preventive and positive checks to population.

"If in any country the yearly earnings of the commonest labourers determined, as they always will be, by the state of the demand and the supply of necessaries compared with labour, be not sufficient to bring up in health the largest families, one of the three things before stated must happen; either the prospect of this difficulty will prevent some and delay other marriages; or the diseases arising from bad nourishment will be introduced and the mortality be increased, or the progress of population will be retarded, partly by one cause, and partly by the other.

". . . It is unquestionably true that the laws of private property, which are the grand stimulants to production, do themselves so limit it as always to make the actual produce of the earth fall very considerably short of the *power* of production. On a system of private property no adequate motive to the extension of cultivation can exist unless the returns are sufficient not only to pay the wages necessary to keep up the population, which at the very least must include the support of a wife and two or three children, but also afford a profit on the capital which has been employed. This necessarily excludes from cultivation a considerable portion of land which might be made to bear corn. If it were possible to suppose that man might

be adequately stimulated to labour under a system of common property such land might be cultivated, and the production of food and the increase of population might go on till the soil absolutely refused to grow a single additional quarter, and the whole of the society was exclusively engaged in procuring the necessaries of life. But it is quite obvious that such a state of things would inevitably lead to the greatest degree of distress and degradation. And if a system of private property secures mankind from such evils, which it certainly does in a great degree by securing to a portion of the society the leisure necessary for the progress of the arts and sciences, it must be allowed that such a check to the increase of cultivation confers on society a most signal benefit.

"It makes little difference in the actual rate of the increase of population, or the necessary existence of checks to it, whether that state of demand and supply which occasions an insufficiency of wages to the whole of the labouring classes be produced prematurely by a bad structure of society and an unfavourable distribution of wealth, or necessarily by the comparative exhaustion of the soil. The labourer feels the difficulty nearly in the same degree, and it must have nearly the same results, from whatever cause it arises; consequently, in every country with which we are acquainted where the yearly earnings of the labouring classes are not sufficient to bring up in health the largest families, it may be safely said that population is actually checked by the difficulty of procuring the means of subsistence, and, as we well know that ample wages, combined with full employment for all who choose to work, are extremely rare . . . it follows that the pressure arising from the difficulty of procuring subsistence is not to be considered as a remote one which will be felt only when the earth refuses to produce any more, but as one which not only actually exists at present over the greatest part of the globe, but, with few exceptions, has been almost constantly acting upon all the countries of which we have any account.

"It is to the laws of nature, therefore, and not to the conduct and institutions of man, that we are to attribute the necessity of a strong check on the natural increase of population.

"Though man has but a trifling and temporary influence in altering the proportionate amount of the checks to population or the degree in which they press upon the actual numbers, yet he has a great and most extensive influence on their character and mode of operation.

"It will be found that all (of the population checks) are resolvable into *moral restraint, vice,* and *misery.* And if, from the laws of nature, some check to the increase of population be absolutely inevitable, and human institutions have any influence upon the extent to which each of these checks operates, a heavy responsibility will be incurred if all that influence, whether direct or indirect, be not exerted to diminish the amount of vice and misery.

"Moral restraint, . . . may be defined to be abstinence from marriage, either for a time or permanently, from prudential considerations, with a strictly moral conduct towards the sex in the interval. And this is the only mode of keeping population on a level with the means of subsistence which is perfectly consistent with virtue and happiness. All other checks, whether of the preventive or the positive kind, though they may greatly vary in degree, resolve themselves into some form of vice or misery.

"The remaining checks of the preventive kind are the sort of intercourse which renders some of the women of large towns unprolific; a general corruption of morals with regard to the sex, which has a similar effect; unnatural passions and improper acts to prevent the consequences of irregular connections. These evidently come under the head of vice.

"The positive checks to population include all the causes which tend in any way prematurely to shorten the duration of human life, such as unwholesome occupations, severe labour and exposure to the seasons, bad and insufficient food and clothing arising from poverty, bad nursing of children, excesses of all kinds, great towns and manufactories, the whole train of common diseases and epidemics,

wars, infanticide, plague, and famine. Of these positive checks, those which appear to arise from the laws of nature may be called exclusively misery; and those which we bring upon ourselves, such as wars, excesses of all kinds, and many others which it would be in our power to avoid, are of a mixed nature. They are brought upon us by vice, and their consequences are misery.

"Some of these checks, in various combinations and operating with various force, are constantly in action in all the countries with which we are acquainted and form the immediate causes which keep the population on a level with the means of subsistence.

"But if the preventive check on population —that check which can alone supersede great misery and mortality—operates chiefly by a prudential restraint on marriage, it will be obvious . . . that direct legislation cannot do much. Prudence cannot be enforced by laws without a great violation of natural liberty and a great risk of producing more evil than good.

"Each individual has, to a great degree, the power of avoiding the evil consequences to himself and society resulting from it (the principle of population), by the practice of a virtue (abstinence) dictated to him by the light of nature and sanctioned by revealed religion. And, as there can be no question that this virtue tends greatly to improve the condition and increase the comforts both of the individuals who practice it, and through them, of the whole society, the ways of God to man with regard to this great law are completely vindicated."

It is difficult to point to anything original, either methodological or substantive, in the writings of Malthus that can be cited as a major contribution of lasting influence in shaping either theory or research. His "principle of population" proved invalid for Europe and North America, since by dint of the industrial revolution man's capacity to increase his subsistence has far exceeded his tendency to reproduce. Contrary to the Malthusian assumption, the *capacity* to increase without limit until stopped by checks was not translated into reality on an historic scale. Instead, the birthrate began to decline in the industrializing nations. (In fact, the decline was already under way during the time that Malthus was studying population.) Because the very phenomenon about which he was generalizing failed to conform to either term of his famous dilemma, the Malthusian principle actually materialized in no nation of Europe or North America. Instead, the level of living has risen and poverty has greatly diminished.

Scholars have tried conscientiously to evaluate Malthus's contribution to social thought in general and to population theories in particular, with varying results. D. E. C. Eversley, after carefully reviewing thinking on population matters both before and after Malthus, concludes:

"As to observations of the contemporary British scene, Malthus' work bears almost no evidence. . . . There is no sign that even at the end of his life he knew anything in detail about industrialization. His thesis was based on the life of an agricultural nation, and so it remained long after the exports of manufactures had begun to pay for the imports of large quantities of raw materials. If not much corn came in, the increase of volume of foreign trade in his own lifetime was at least so startling that it escaped no one else. Fond as he was of mathematical methods of forecasting population, he never allowed that even in his period the rate of increase of population was already slackening. The results of the 1831 Census were out before he died, yet he never came to interpret them. Statistics apart, the main charge against him must be that he was a bad observer of his fellow human beings." [10]

In an essay, "Malthus and the Limitation of Population Growth," David Glass has pointed out that Malthus was a poor prophet, because only one nation of Europe (Ireland) actually followed the historical path prescribed by him —population control through drastic postponement of marriage, with incidental famine— while placing no reliance on artificial checks

to family size. He also reminds us that a large bloc of nations of Northwest Europe did accept Malthusian theory in the sense that they practiced late marriage. However, by mass adoption of contraception they abandoned Malthus. Glass contrasts what actually happened in history with the Malthusian prescriptions thus:

"The development of the birth control movement in nineteenth century England represented an explicit acceptance of Malthusian theory and a complete abandonment of Malthus' rules of conduct. . . . This very spread of family limitation has itself destroyed an important part of Malthus' argument. . . . The ability easily to limit one's family has not, as Malthus feared, reduced individuals to indolence or society to stagnation. On the contrary, it has been one of the ways through which new incentives and aspirations have been able to work with effect." [11]

Until recently many demographers assumed that even though Malthusian principles may have failed in Europe, they would succeed in Asia and probably eventually also in Latin America and Africa. [12] As later chapters will undertake to demonstrate, this is a gross oversimplification of the events that are taking place in these regions and is useless as a "theory" of population trends or as a guide to national or international population policy. Alan T. Peacock has noted that if we were to transfer the nineteenth-century Malthusian view to the twentieth century and apply it to the developing nations, we would have a policy somewhat as follows: Inasmuch as the distribution of wealth from richer to poorer population tends to defeat its own ends because the rise in living standards automatically stimulates population growth which merely swallows up the increase in the disposable national product, such redistribution should not be attempted and investments in raising living standards of the poor should be minimized in the interests of industrialization. Similarly, it

[10] D. E. C. Eversley, *Social Theories of Fertility and the Malthusian Debate* (Oxford: Clarendon Press, 1959), pp. 256–257.

[11] David V. Glass (ed.), *Introduction to Malthus* (New York: Wiley, 1953), pp. 47–50.

[12] For example, see Warren S. Thompson, *Population and Peace in the Pacific* (Chicago: University of Chicago Press, 1946), pp. 210, 234, 257.

could be argued that the redistribution of wealth from rich to poor countries would defeat its own ends, for it would simply accentuate the population problem through pronounced declines in mortality rates.[13] The national governments of Asia, Latin America, or Africa are not acting on this set of premises. The richer nations also have not invoked Malthusian-type thinking in their behavior toward poorer nations; instead there has been an outpouring across national boundaries of financial and technical assistance of a generosity and magnitude unprecedented in history, in which the nations of Europe and America led by the United Nations have acted in concert despite wide differences in political ideology.

The events of history and the results of empirical research gradually are relegating the "principle of population" to the scientific trash heap of theories that are inconsistent with the data. Malthus's work illustrated the rules in social science that (a) one cannot reliably predict the behavior of men in reasoning by analogy from the behavior of animals, (b) man's behavior in the historical past is not an infallible predictor of his future adjustments, and (c) generalizations about the lower class made by members of the middle and upper classes often are based on ignorance of how the lower class thinks and feels.

The controversy that Malthus generated brought the population problem to the attention of the entire scholarly world. But even this service was not an unmixed blessing. Lorimer asserts: "There is considerable evidence to the effect that the Malthusian controversy tended to inhibit the progress of demography as a science." He cites David Glass as being of the opinion that the comparative neglect of the study of fertility by eighteenth-century statisticians was due in part to the fact that it was a controversial topic, with uninviting political overtones which were almost certain to press a scientist studying fertility to join or be relegated to one political camp or another.[14]

[13] Alan T. Peacock, "Malthus in the Twentieth Century," in David Glass, ed. *Introduction to Malthus, op. cit.,* pp. 69–70.

[14] Frank Lorimer, *op. cit.,* p. 141.

This evaluation of Malthus is not universally accepted. For example, a contrary view has been recently expressed by William Petersen, who writes: "Malthus' results were not all new and were not all true; but his work has the merit of being the first thorough application of the inductive method to social science. . . . He is still worth reading today because he forcefully posed a few important questions, but his answers to them are inadequate by today's standards."[15]

Karl Marx. Karl Marx, the most powerful critic of Malthus, may also be dismissed as being largely irrelevant to the mainstream of modern empirical demography. Some writers have accorded him a high status in the development of demography. It is difficult, however, to trace any lasting methodological or theoretical development to his influence, either directly or indirectly. His refutations of Malthus consisted of declaring that the pressure of man upon resources and the existence of a large body of unemployed or underemployed workers are unique and inevitable consequences of the capitalist mode of production.

Instead of citing the writings of antagonists and protagonists, we shall, as we did with Malthus, return directly to Marx's own words. His argument concerning population is pieced together in the following excerpts:

"Since the demand for labour is determined not by the amount of capital as a whole, but by its variable constituent alone, that demand falls progressively with the increase of the total capital, instead of, as previously assumed, rising in proportion to it. It falls relatively to the magnitude of the total capital, and at an accelerated rate, as this magnitude increases. With the growth of the total capital, its variable constituent or the labour incorporated in it, also does increase, but in a constantly diminishing proportion. The intermediate pauses are shortened, in which accumulation works as simple extension of production, on a given technical basis. It is not merely that an accelerated accumulation of total capital, accelerated

[15] William Petersen, *The Politics of Population* (Garden City, N.Y.: Doubleday, 1964), pp. 44–45.

in a constantly growing progression, is needed to absorb an additional number of labourers, or even, on account of the constant metamorphosis of old capital, to keep employed those already functioning. In its turn, this increasing accumulation and centralisation becomes a source of new changes in the composition of capital, of a more accelerated diminution of its variable, as compared with its constant constituent. This accelerated relative diminution of the variable constituent, that goes along with the accelerated increase of the total capital, and moves more rapidly than this increase, takes the inverse form, at the other pole, of an apparently absolute increase of the labouring population, an increase always moving more rapidly than that of the variable capital or the means of employment. But in fact, it is capitalistic accumulation itself that constantly produces, and produces in the direct ratio of its own energy and extent, a relatively redundant population of labourers, *i.e.*, a population of greater extent than suffices for the average needs of the self-expansion of capital, and therefore a surplus-population. . . .

"The labouring population therefore produces, along with the accumulation of capital produced by it, the means by which itself is made relatively superfluous, is turned into a relative surplus population; and it does this to an always increasing extent. This is a law of population peculiar to the capitalist mode of production; and in fact every special historic mode of production has its own special laws of population, historically valid within its limits alone. An abstract law of population exists for plants and animals only, and only in so far as man has not interfered with them.

"But if a surplus labouring population is a necessary product of accumulation or of the development of wealth on a capitalist basis, this surplus population becomes, conversely, the lever of capitalistic accumulation, nay, a condition of existence of the capitalist mode of production. It forms a disposable industrial reserve army, that belongs to capital quite as absolutely as if the latter had bred it at its own cost. Independently of the limits of the actual increase of population, it creates, for the changing needs of the self-expansion of capital, a mass of human material always ready for exploitation. . . .

"Even Malthus recognizes over-population as a necessity of modern industry, though, after his narrow fashion, he explains it by the absolute over-growth of the labouring population, not by their becoming relatively supernumerary. . . .

"After Political Economy has thus demonstrated the constant production of a relative surplus-population of labourers to be a necessity of capitalistic accumulation, she very aptly, in the guise of an old maid, puts in the mouth of her beau ideal of a capitalist the following words addressed to those supernumeraries thrown on the streets by their own creation of additional capital: We manufacturers do what we can for you, whilst we are increasing that capital on which you must subsist, and you must do the rest by accommodating your numbers to the means of subsistence!"[16]

The Marxian argument is a set of specific assertions about how economies, and groups of people in them, behave. The quotations are not a scientifically valid summary of any epoch in human history since the industrial revolution, just as the assertions of Malthus are not. History simply refused to behave in the pattern they predicted for it.

The intensity of Marx's dislike of Malthusianism is revealed in this vitriolic footnote:

"If a reader reminds me of Malthus, whose 'Essay on Population' appeared in 1798, I remind him that this work in its first form is nothing more than a school-boyish, superficial plagiary of De Foe, Sir James Steuart, Townsend, Franklin, Wallace, etc., and does not contain a single sentence thought out by himself. The great sensation this pamphlet caused, was due solely to party interest. . . . Malthus, hugely astonished at his success, gave himself to stuffing into his book materials superficially compiled and adding to it new matter, not discovered but annexed by him."[17]

[16] Karl Marx, *Das Kapital* (Chicago: Charles H. Kerr and Co., 1907), I, pp. 690–696.
[17] *Ibid.*, p. 676.

Marx's theory of the process by which "population pressure" develops was not based on research. Research refutes it, and so do the events of history both before and since the industrial revolution. Moreover, Marx's assumption that all population problems will disappear under a communist mode of production is as invalid as Malthus's population principle. Marxian writers have also declared that population is not a matter of very great concern because under a communist economy birthrates will automatically decline because of rising levels of living and decreasing child labor. This is an assertion of faith, rather than an explanation of the process that takes place when a technologically advanced society, under any form of economy, adjusts its fertility to its lowered mortality. Actually, the process seems to involve a fundamental social reorganization in capitalist and communist nations alike. Its course is influenced by political and economic ideologies, but it does not originate in them nor can it be stopped by them. It is an historical fact that before 1950 both capitalist and communist nations officially frowned on birth control and declared it to be an outright evil or else a private matter for individual decision. Yet both made available the various means of contraception as they were developed and did not punish those who used them. Their official and unofficial positions have been impressively similar and equally ambiguous. It remained for Japan and other developing nations to acknowledge demographic planning as a part of total national, economic and social development.

Like Malthus, Marx created acrimonious debates without stimulating objective scientific research. And, like Malthus, he appears to have discouraged scientific population study. Even today some otherwise well-qualified demographers believe that they must produce research that appears either to support a Marxian position or to attack Malthusianism; this distracts their attention from the multitude of more fundamental research problems that transcend this controversy.

It is academically fashionable to try to rescue shreds of contemporary validity for both Malthus and Marx and even to both justify

and reconcile their views.[18] The result usually is to attribute to them rather minor insights that they shared with many, such as "Both Marx and Malthus described the present conditions of the proletariat as miserable, and they differed only on the means to alleviate this misery."[19]

The work of these two men is mentioned here so that it may be largely dismissed from consideration in the remainder of this book. The author would like to propose a slogan: "Demographers of the world unite—in burying the population theories both of Malthus and of Marx."

1.7.   Demography in Europe in the Nineteenth and Early Twentieth Centuries

A new era in demographic science began during the nineteenth century with the simultaneous development of the mathematical study of probability, of the taking of national censuses in Europe and America, and of systems of birth and death registration. Actuarial science entered the field of mortality study and carried the preparation of life tables to a high level of precision and sophistication, making use of probability theory. Census-taking became an established activity of national governments. Sweden was completely enumerated in 1751, and her system of parish population registers has provided reliable vital statistics and population counts for two centuries. The United States had its first complete census in 1790; England and France followed in 1801. Thereafter the number of nations taking a census increased slowly until during the period from 1945 to 1951, according to an inventory made by the United Nations, sixty-five nations covering roughly 80 percent of the world's population took censuses. As census-taking developed, the scope of the censuses widened to include more topics. The tabulations of the data also became more elaborate, with more

[18] William Petersen, *The Politics of Population* (Garden City, N.Y.: Doubleday, 1964) and Nathan Keyfitz, "History of Population Theories," background paper for United Nations World Population Conference, Belgrade, 1965.

[19] Keyfitz, *ibid.*, p. 25.

detailed cross-classification of variables. The quantity of empirical research greatly increased.

British, French, Italian, and German demographers have grounds for dispute over comparative leadership and originality of thinking in the development of demography during the nineteenth century. Achille Guillard, a French writer, is credited with coining the term "demography" in 1855 in his *Eléments de statistique humaine ou démographie comparée*. Historians of social thought are able to find rough forerunners of modern demography also in Italian writings (just as Italian scholars had anticipated the formulations of Malthus).[20] However, leadership in formulating the theoretical viewpoint of modern demography, in launching objective empirical research, in developing new research methodologies, and in elevating demography to membership in the fraternity of "hard data" sciences clearly rests with English scholars.

William Farr. Outstanding among the names of this period is that of William Farr, a distinguished vital statistician and England's first Register-General, who held office from 1839 to 1880. In addition to designing and launching the British system of census-taking and vital registration, he developed the first official life tables and conducted numerous statistical inquiries of death and the causes of death. He made the construction of life tables a major venture in actuarial science, preceded by painstaking evaluation and adjustment of the available data. Grebenick calls him a pioneer in the study of occupational mortality (the study of differences in rate of death from various causes between occupational groups).[21] The Register-General Office today continues to be a superior technical center, which not only produces data of high quality but also leads in developing research methodology and maintaining a continuous interpretation of population trends.

A somewhat puzzling characteristic of demographic research in England before 1900 is its very great preoccupation with mortality and its comparative neglect of fertility. Although it is understandable that public concern with conquering epidemics and infectious diseases, the hopes aroused by the progress then being made in surgery and medicine, and the great expansion in the business of insuring lives and operating pension schemes would stimulate a major program of mortality study, this need not have precluded a simultaneous interest in fertility. There were ample intellectual resources to support major programs of both fertility and mortality analyses. It would appear that there was a clear disinclination to study childbearing. As noted above, this seems to have been an unfortunate consequence of the Malthusian controversy. Fertility analysis may also have been further suppressed by the public furor over the emergence of the birth control movement.

The Movement for Birth Control and its Effect on Demographic Study. In 1823 a series of handbills appeared, advocating birth control (by *coitus interruptus* and the sponge) to the working people. Their authorship has been attributed to Francis Place, founder of the birth control movement in England. The bills aroused intense indignation in many quarters and were known as the "diabolical handbills." Place campaigned energetically for the principle that they advocated and for the right to make the information available. He was supported by liberal thinkers of the time; similar tracts prepared by Robert Dale Owens and others were sold in surprisingly large quantities in both Europe and America. For nearly half of the century these materials were circulated rather freely with little objection. In 1876 a Bristol bookseller was arrested for selling an illustrated edition of *Fruits of Philosophy*, which advocated birth control. Thereupon two crusaders, Mr. Bradlaugh and Mrs. Besant, had an edition of the tract printed and openly displayed for sale. They were prosecuted, tried, and sentenced to six months' imprisonment amid great publicity. Although their sentence was not carried out, proponents of birth control were thereafter in frequent trouble with the law. There ensued a long series of legal battles and heated public and private debate

[20] Alessandro Constanzo, "Contributions of Italy to Demography," in Hauser and Duncan, *op cit.,* Chapter 10.

[21] E. Grebenik, "The Development of Demography in Great Britain," in Hauser and Duncan, *op. cit.,* p. 192.

over whether such communication was an obscene and immoral act or a public welfare service necessary to preserve the health, standard of living, and social well-being of members of individual families and of the community at large. The movement spread to other countries; trials and/or imprisonment took place in America, Australia, India, and Belgium. Prosecution seemed only to encourage the propagandists, and the great excitement and publicity that accompanied the arrests and trials aroused the public's curiosity to learn much more about the subject than they otherwise would have. Meanwhile, the risks of providing birth control information to the poor were so great that only the more fanatic and dedicated dared to continue.

Under these conditions, a statistician whose intellectual curiosity might have led him to study fertility scientifically would have found himself in double jeopardy—he would have been suspected of being either a Malthusian or anti-Malthusian on the one hand and of having dubious morals on the other.[22] The birth control movement was not a scholarly activity, but it has influenced the course of development of demography. If in the nineteenth century its effect was to discourage the study of fertility, in the mid-twentieth century it has greatly stimulated demographic research, as will be shown later.

Birth of the Eugenics Movement. One of the Register-General's accomplishments was to achieve a high level of precision in birth registration by about 1875. The data for the last quarter of the nineteenth century gave unmistakable proof that birthrates were declining in England. This became a matter of substantial concern. Sir Francis Galton, Karl Pearson, and other scientists interested in heredity studied the fertility decline in terms of differences between social and economic groups. There emerged a widespread fear of the eugenic consequences of the fertility decline; if the poor and illiterate segments of society had higher birthrates than the more educated and wealthy, it was asserted, the "unfit" would gradually outbreed the "fit" and create biological deterioration and a decline in the national level of intelligence. This concern and an awakening general interest in fertility led to the inclusion of special fertility inquiries in the census of 1911 and to the establishment of a national commission to study fertility.

In general, from 1800 to 1925 population theories were dominated by a biological viewpoint, the instinct theory, and a dispute over the Malthusian doctrine. Consequently, demographic research was primarily a search for the discovery of fixed interrelationships that, once discovered, would be valid and unchanging for all time. But dissident voices had already begun to be heard before 1925, pointing out that demographic events are influenced by their social context and suggesting that the theoretical outlook of population experts needed to be widened.

A. M. Carr-Saunders. In 1922, A. M. Carr-Saunders published *The Population Problem: A Study in Evolution,* which signaled the change from the biological to the social science approach to population. His work was a systematic statement of the problems both of population size and growth and of the eugenics question. It brought together many different pieces of historical, anthropological, and biological as well as demographic information and organized them in such a way as to make it clear that the study of population was a separate and new discipline with roots in social as well as biological science. The book opens with the following passage:

"Problems of population fall into two main groups—those connected with the quantity and those connected with the quality of the population. Considerations of the population problem are commonly devoted to one of these chief aspects to the exclusion of the other, with the result that the relation between them is seldom appreciated."[23]

---

[22] For a highly interesting account of this controversy, see Part V, Norman E. Himes, *Medical History of Contraception* (Baltimore: The Williams and Wilkins Company, 1936). (Reprinted by Gamut Press, New York, 1963.)

[23] A. M. Carr-Saunders, *The Population Problem: A Study in Human Evolution* (Oxford: The Clarendon Press, 1922), p. 17.

According to Carr-Saunders, all population problems have a single common root—the need and efforts of human societies to adjust their numbers and composition to the environment. He sees two mechanisms for such change—modification of the genetically determined factors and modification of social factors (which he calls "tradition"), the latter having been by far the more powerful force since the dawn of civilization. He asserts that all societies, at all times, are trying to achieve such an adjustment. By implication, their population problem is a social problem on the one hand and a social science research problem on the other.

Carr-Saunders attacks Malthus and the biologic-deterministic view of population growth and supplants it with a social science perspective:

". . . From the first period of history onwards—from the time, that is to say, that it began to be possible for man to reap the benefits of co-operation—it was of the utmost importance for every group to approximate to the optimum number. This is the number which—taking into consideration the nature of the environment, the degree of skill employed, the habits and customs of the people concerned, and all other relevant facts—gives the highest average return per head. This number is not fixed once and for all. On the contrary, it is constantly varying as the conditions referred to vary, and, as skill has tended to increase throughout history, so has the number economically desirable tended to increase. The errors underlying the wholly different exposition given by Malthus have been indicated; for him there was no such thing as overpopulation. In his view population had at any one time increased up to the possible limit and was in process of being checked. In the modern view numbers may approximate to the desirable level, may not reach it, or they may exceed it and if either of the two latter positions arise, the return per head will not be as high as it might be.

"The quantitative problem (problem of desirable population size) presents itself to all races at all times. There is no escaping it. The common notion that it only presents itself at certain times and in certain places is based upon a failure to grasp the strength of fecundity. Almost without exception those factors, which incidentally restrict increase and produce elimination (normal death and migration), are insufficient so to reduce fertility as to keep numbers down to the optimum level. There thus arises the need for factors which directly restrict fertility and cause elimination; among primitive races these factors take the form of abortion, infanticide, and prolonged abstention from intercourse. There is no correlation between these factors and the economic stage reached, and therefore we have no grounds for assuming any one factor to have been prevalent at any one stage in prehistory, though we must assume that one or more of these factors was always at work. This assumption is confirmed by the fact that, whenever we can catch sight of the emergence of prehistoric races into the light of history, we find one or more of these factors to have been present. Further there is every reason to suppose that normally such of these factors as are in use are effective and that therefore in the first and second periods (prehistory and history before the modern era) some approximation to the optimum number was normally attained.

"The third period (modern era) is in many respects different from those that preceded it. In the first place the number desirable has been constantly increasing, so much so that increasing numbers are taken as being a normal feature of human society whereas in fact, numbers throughout human history as a whole have been stationary. It may be that we are nearing a time when numbers will be again normally stationary, for though increase may remain economically desirable, it may cease to be so from a wider point of view of human welfare, when, that is to say, facts other than income per capita are taken into account. In the second place, there have been frequent failures to attain the optimum number owing to the many disturbing influences at work. Chief among them are the fluctuation in the number desirable, the erratic action of certain causes of elimination, such as war and disease and migration.

"Regarding the quantitative problem as a

whole, it is evident that the necessity of solving it has been the most profound effect upon all societies at all times. It bears directly upon the relation between the sexes—around which so largely centres human welfare—and upon the most intimate and most valued aspects of the life of every adult—those connected with the family. In the past the solution has been unconsciously or semi-consciously achieved; it has now come within the power of mankind after a due consideration of the position deliberately to decide what the best solution may be."[24]

With respect to population quality and eugenics, he concludes:

"No one problem should be considered without reference to its bearing both upon quantity and quality. At the present day, for instance, differential fertility is almost always considered solely from the point of view of quality; it is forgotten that the reduction in the birth rate may be that which economic conditions demand and that it may of necessity have to begin among the upper classes. Though, therefore, differential fertility by producing unfavourable germinal changes is to be to that degree deplored, yet we have to remember that, so far as quantity is concerned, failure to meet economic requirements might be a much greater misfortune."[25]

These viewpoints are very similar to those of modern demography, and Carr-Saunders's contribution on the theoretical side may be taken to be as significant as were those of the English statisticians on the methodological and analytical side. We have divided the development of demography into three major periods:

1. Graunt to the advent of census-taking (about 1800).
2. Advent of census-taking to the modern era 1920-1925).
3. The modern era.

Carr-Saunders's work is the substantive and theoretical bridge between the second and third periods.

[24] *Ibid.*, pp. 476–477.
[25] *Ibid.*, pp. 475–476.

1.8. The Modern Era

Several factors characterize demography in the modern era. First, demography has been established as an independent discipline and forms a significant part of scholarly work in all major nations of the world. Although demography is not sufficiently large to be an independent department and is usually housed in sociology, economics, or public health departments, systematic training in demography and demographic techniques is now a standard part of the curricula of most major universities.

Second, a great expansion in sociological economic, and psychological research into demographic events has taken place. One evidence of this is the transfer of demographic work to departments of sociology and economics. The process of interpenetration and infusion of social science into the field of demography is still incomplete, however. Yet a possible unfortunate consequence of this swing may well be that the isolation from biological science has become too complete, and the next decades may see a closer interaction that better reflects the facts in both disciplines.

Third, the volume of demographic research being undertaken has increased greatly and has been extended into many new fields. Political science, housing, market research, labor economics, social service (welfare) work, and national and local planning are only a few of the fields.

Finally, there has been a flowing together of theory and research, so that the demographic statistician, instead of being a "theoretically naïve raw empiricist," is becoming increasingly well-read in social science theories.

England.[26] Systematic research in modern demography was given great impetus during the 1930s at the University of London by a group comprised of Lancelot Hogben, R. R. Kuczynski, and Enid Charles. In 1936 a Population Investigation Commission was established to study the phenomenon of declining birth rates and related matters, with A. M.

[26] For a more complete statement see E. Grebenik, "The Development of Demography in Great Britain," in Hauser and Duncan, *op. cit.*, Chapter 8.

Carr-Saunders as chairman and David V. Glass as research secretary. Since 1947 this group has published a journal, *Population Studies,* which enjoys a large international circulation and is a leading forum for the exchange of research findings.

During World War II, concern about England's postwar population prospects led the British government to set up, in 1943, a Royal Commission on Population. The Commission has sponsored some large-scale demographic surveys. Its Report (1949) and published working papers have served to organize thinking about demography as well as to stimulate further research. The members of the Population Investigation Commission have been very active in the work of the Royal Commission. Today, the University of London has a demographic training program and an ongoing research program. The technical staffs of the Register-General Office, the Population Investigation Commission, and the universities together are causing demography to make rapid progress in England.

France. Before World War II there was considerably less vigor and rigor in the demographic research output of France than in that of England. However, there was great interest in the then sharply declining birthrates and in research that might reverse this trend. Also, the mass exodus of French peasants to the major cities created concern about rural depopulation. A great deal of writing on these two problems had appeared. Shortly after World War II the *Institut National d'Études Démographiques* was established. The background for this action has been described by its first director, Alfred Sauvy:

"After World War II a profound change occurred, basically caused by the collapse of 1940. During four years of occupation and humiliation, France had felt, somewhat vaguely, that this collapse had resulted from a decrease in vitality which had accompanied the excessive sterility of families and the aging which had continued for the past century and a half. In the optimistic atmosphere of the liberation a new national consciousness developed, and with it came the desire for a deliberate population policy. These considerations

prompted the formation of the Institut National d'Études Démographiques, a scientific organization charged with studying all the phenomena of population, in the broadest sense of the word."[27]

More than thirty monographs have been published by this organization. It also publishes a journal, *Population,* which reports the results of research and thinking not only of its own staff but also of demographers throughout the world writing in the French language. The I.N.E.D. also works closely with the staff of the University of Paris, and university faculties often use its facilities.

Italy.[28] During the modern period several general treatises on population have appeared. Several of them link the study of population to biometry (bodily measurements and classification). There have been numerous high-quality empirical studies both of mortality and of fertility. Corrado Gini and M. Boldrini have been the most widely acclaimed scholars, and their studies have covered a wide variety of topics, including differential mortality according to body type, sex ratios of births and conceptions, differential fertility, and the preparation of life tables by single causes of death.

Germany. After Süssmilch, nineteenth-century demographers writing in German produced rather formally descriptive statistical digests of census and vital statistics, with comparatively little theory.[29] As mathematics flourished and data collection improved, the preparation of actuarial and statistical compendia of population facts became an established branch of applied mathematics. The comparative scarcity of explanatory research may have been due to the fact that theorists in Germany also were preoccupied in arguments over the Malthusian dilemma. In the twentieth century the declining birthrate attracted attention to the systematic study of growth, as it had in England and France. Frederik Burgdörfer and

[27] Alfred Sauvy, "Development and Perspectives of Demographic Research in France," in Hauser and Duncan, *op. cit.,* p. 180.

[28] See Alessandro Costanzo, "Contributions of Italy to Demography," *ibid.,* Chapter 10.

[29] Hermann Schubnell, "Demography in Germany," in Hauser and Duncan, *op. cit.,* p. 204.

H. Harmsen both produced systematic treatises, which undertook to state the socioeconomic consequences of population trends. After World War I there was much political concern, especially on the part of the totalitarian Hitler regime, with overpopulation and with *Lebensraum* for the excess and greatly unemployed or underemployed population. Demographic research and demographers were exploited to justify and carry out programs of territorial expansion and racist fanaticism; the efficiency with which Jews were exterminated in some sections was due in part to the use of demographic methods for detecting and locating persons of Jewish birth. Consequently, after World War II demography was in disrepute in Germany and, as a group, German demographers were suspected of having Nazi leanings. A new team of statisticians and scholars have since attacked the postwar census and other data in an effort to study Germany's monstrous population problems, and the scientific tradition is slowly reasserting itself. Through G. Mackenroth's systematic treatise, *Bevölkerungslehre: Theorie, Soziologie, und Statistik der Bevölkerung* (1953), demography regained much of its lost scholarly and scientific prestige. In 1953 a professional association, *Deutsche Akademie für Bevölkerungswissenschaft,* was established, and a growing volume of objective demographic research is now under way at several universities and at the numerous state and municipal statistical offices. This research covers the entire range of population topics. One of the primary research concerns has been the impact on German economy of the many thousands of refugees who have fled from East Germany and the Soviet satellites. West Germany's feat of receiving and rehabilitating this horde of destitute and desperate humanity, while itself rising from abject physical and economic prostration to the present unprecedented prosperity, is a demographic as well as an economic miracle worthy of prolonged and intensive research, with fundamental implications for economic development elsewhere in the world.

United States. John Durand is probably correct in declaring that "Walter Wilcox was the first real demographer in America," although it has been customary to honor Benjamin Franklin for an essay, "Observations Concerning the Increase of Mankind, the Peopling of Countries, etc.," written in 1775.[30] Rupert Vance calls Wilcox "the father of American Demography."[31] Yet in bestowing this accolade we must not overlook Lemuel Shattuck, a leading figure in public health work who established a good vital registration system for Massachusetts and then moved on to improve greatly the Federal census of 1850. Francis A. Walker, an economist interested in migration, supervised the census of 1880, which he greatly expanded in scope and detail over preceding censuses, and prepared numerous colorful reports, interpretations, and comments on the results. J. W. Glover, an actuarial mathematician, also deserves honorable mention for constructing the United States life tables of 1890, 1901, and 1910 after careful demographic analysis of the scanty data then available. However, it remained for Wilcox, with his statistical study of divorce in 1891, to establish firmly a tradition of empirical statistical research in demography in America. As chief statistician at the census office, he wrote numerous interpretative reports based on data of the census and the developing vital registration system. A selection of abstracts and revisions of these reports, *Studies in American Demography*, attests to his strong influence in stimulating systematic demographic research.[32] As a professor at Cornell University, he influenced the development of several of America's present generation of demographers.

The 1920s witnessed the firm establishment of demography as a science in the United States. In 1925 Louis I. Dublin and Alfred J. Lotka published the first complete statement of the stable population model.[33] E. W. Scripps, a scholarly journalist-philanthropist, established

---

[30] John Durand, *op. cit.*

[31] Rupert B. Vance, "The Development and Status of American Demography," in Hauser and Duncan, *op. cit.*, Chapter 14, p. 292.

[32] Walter F. Wilcox, *Studies in American Demography* (Ithaca, N. Y.: Cornell University Press, 1940.

[33] Louis I. Dublin and Alfred J. Lotka, "On the True Rate of Natural Increase, As Exemplified by the Population of the United States, 1920," *Journal of the American Statistical Association,* **20** (1925), 305–339.

in 1922 the Scripps Foundation for Research in Population Problems at Miami University, Oxford, Ohio. Warren S. Thompson, the director, and P. K. Whelpton, his associate, teamed up to turn out a steady stream of high-quality interpretative and methodological articles and monographs. In 1933 Thompson and Whelpton published a monograph, *Population Trends in the United States,* that has served as a prototype for the systematic study of national populations all over the world.[34] Whelpton had already developed in America the components method of population projection[35] (the method most widely accepted today), and the monograph combined this method with past trends to link the past and the future. In the same year Raymond Pearle published a systematic statement of his studies of logistic aspects of population growth.[36] R. R. Kuczynski published the first volume of *The Balance of Births and Deaths,*[37] Edgar Sydenstricker published his study of differential fertility,[38] Woodbury made the important methodological contribution of "expected cases" while contributing to a more fundamental understanding of the social and economic causes of infant mortality,[39] and Dorothy Thomas pointed out clearly that fluctuations in demographic events are correlated with variations in the business cycle.[40]

The 1920s, active as they were, were only the foundation for even greater activity during the 1930s and after. The Population Association of America was organized in 1931; today it has nearly 1500 members. The Office of Population Research was established in 1937 at Princeton University under the directorship of Frank W. Notestein. This office recruited and trained a group of students who now constitute a substantial portion of professional American demographers. In addition to a sustained program of research that turns out a series of monographs of front-rank importance in the field, both in terms of information and in terms of research methodology, it publishes *Population Index,* a quarterly publication that lists and annotates publications throughout the world in demography and in many related fields. It enables demographers all over the world to keep in touch with one another's progress. One of the significant contributions of the Office of Population Research was to produce a series of monographs on the demography of particular nations or regions. Among the best known are studies of Europe,[41] India,[42] Japan,[43] and Puerto Rico.[44]

At the University of Chicago, William F. Ogburn established a program of population research. A Population and Research Training Center was founded there in 1954, with Philip M. Hauser as director. This center has specialized in studies of urban demography, internal migration, and more recently in the study of socioeconomic differentials in mortality. In 1961 this activity was supplemented by active experiments in reducing birthrates in low-income populations, initiated by the Community and Family Study Center and directed by the writer. The latter organization collaborated with the Population Association of America to launch the journal *Demography,* which since 1963 has been a major publisher of the results

[34] Warren S. Thompson and P. K. Whelpton, *Population Trends in the United States* (New York: McGraw-Hill, 1933).

[35] P. K. Whelpton, "Population of the United States, 1925–1957," *American Journal of Sociology,* 34 (1928), 253–271.

[36] Raymond Pearl, *The Biology of Population Growth* (New York: Knopf, 1925).

[37] R. R. Kuczynski, *The Balance of Births and Deaths* (New York: Macmillan, 1929), I.

[38] Edgar Sydenstricker, *Differential Fertility According to Economic Status,* U. S. Public Health Reports, Hagerstown Morbidity Study No. 11, 1929.

[39] Robert M. Woodbury, *Causal Factors in Infant Mortality: A Statistical Study Based on Investigations in Eight Cities,* Washington, D.C.: United States Children's Bureau, No. 142, 1925.

[40] Dorothy S. Thomas, *Social Aspects of the Business Cycle* (New York: E. P. Dutton, 1925).

[41] Dudley Kirk, *Europe's Population in the Inter-War Years* (Geneva: League of Nations, 1946). Also Frank W. Notestein and Ansley Coale, *The Future Population of Europe and the Soviet Union: Population Projections, 1940–1970* (Geneva: League of Nations, 1944).

[42] Kingsley Davis, *The Population of India and Pakistan* (Princeton, N.J.: Princeton University Press, 1951).

[43] Irene Taeuber, *The Population of Japan* (Princeton, N.J.: Princeton University Press, 1958).

[44] Paul K. Hatt, *Backgrounds of Human Fertility in Puerto Rico: A Sociological Survey* (Princeton, N.J.: Princeton University Press, 1952).

of scientific research on population. Population study centers with major programs are located at Universities of Michigan, Wisconsin, California, North Carolina, Pennsylvania, Florida, Georgia, and Washington. George Washington University, Columbia, Cornell, Brown, and Georgetown should be added to this list.

Not a little of this burgeoning of population study has been due to generous and well-administered foundation support. Since the late 1920s the Milbank Memorial Fund of New York City has been highly interested in demography and under the leadership of Clyde V. Kiser has financed a great deal of population research. The *Milbank Quarterly* has published the results of much demographic research. In sponsoring research and action in public health around the world, the Rockefeller Foundation quickly realized that rapid population growth follows on the heels of successful health and medical programs and as a result began, more than three decades ago, to sponsor basic research in fertility and then in general demography. Since 1960 the Ford Foundation has joined in support of demographic research and its Population Division, directed by Dr. Oscar Harkavy, is now sponsoring some massive programs of research and experimentation in population control. The Population Council, Inc., was founded in 1952, under a grant from the Rockefeller family, to administer a program of recruiting and training demographers from less developed countries, to stimulate and sponsor basic research pertaining to the world's population problem, and to act as a source of technical assistance to nations desiring help in establishing a national program of population control. Its first director, Frederick Osborne, established it at a high level of technical competence that continued until 1968 under the directorship of Frank W. Notestein. Dr. Bernard Berelson is the present director.

The United States Bureau of Census has been a major force in the development of American demography. Since 1940, especially, it has accumulated an ever-increasing number of technicians who have been encouraged to specialize in the study and improvement of particular parts of the total program. The result has been steady revision in techniques of collecting, processing, and publishing data and in devising new tabulations and new topics for study. Several members publish research and methodological articles in scientific journals. Although the staff of the Vital Statistics Division of the Department of Health, Education, and Welfare (which collects and tabulates registration data) is smaller, its professional qualifications and activities are similar to those of the census. Both the Bureau of Census and the Vital Statistics Division are cosponsors of major programs to generate research monographs from the results of their tabulations. Systematic demographic research has been extended to other departments of the Federal government. Units studying population statistics are found in the Labor Department, Department of Agriculture, the State Department, U. S. A.I.D., Social Security Administration, Defense Department, Bureau of Public Roads, Housing and Home Finance Agency, and others. Very large programs to promote fertility control are now sponsored by U.S. A.I.D., the Department of Health, Education and Welfare, and the Office of Economic Opportunity.

It is clear that in America demography now is an integral part of the scholarly life of higher education, that it is one of the most active of the social sciences, and that it is a discipline that maintains a host of interdisciplinary and international ties.

Other Nations. Since space does not permit a description of the population study programs in all other nations, we simply present a list, (possibly incomplete) of major demographic research organizations, including those mentioned earlier.

International Institutions

Caribbean Commission, Trinidad, West Indies
Commission for Technical Cooperation for Africa South of the Sahara, London and Bukavu, Belgian Congo
Economic Commission on Asia and the Far East, United Nations, Bangkok, Thailand
Food and Agricultural Organization of the United Nations, Rome, Italy
Interamerican Statistical Institute, Pan American Union, Washington, D. C., United States
International Catholic Institute for Social-Cultural Ecclesiastical Research, The Hague, Netherlands

International Labour Office, Geneva, Switzerland

International Statistical Institute, The Hague, Netherlands

Latin American Demographic Centre (CELADE), Santiago, Chile

The Milbank Memorial Fund, New York, United States

North African Demographic Centre (United Nations), Cairo, Egypt

Population Branch, Bureau of Social Affairs, United Nations, New York, United States

The Population Council, Inc., New York, United States

Research Group for European Migration Problems, The Hague, Netherlands

South Pacific Commission, Noumea, New Caledonia

Statistical Office, United Nations, New York, United States

United Nations Economic Commission for Africa, Addis Ababa, Ethiopia

United Nations Economic Commission for Asia and the Far East, Bangkok, Thailand

United Nations Economic Commission for Latin America, Santiago, Chile

United Nations Educational, Scientific, and Cultural Organization, Paris, France

World Health Organization, Geneva, Switzerland

National Institutions

Department of Demography, Research School of Social Science, Australian National University, Canberra, Australia

Centre D'Études Démographiques, Institut de Sociologie Solvay, Brussels, Belgium

Faculty of Hygiene and Public Health, University of São Paulo, São Paulo, Brazil

Laboratório de Estatística, Consejo Nacional de Estatística, Instituto Brasileiro de Geografia e Estatística, Rio De Janeiro, Brazil

Department of Economics, Commerce, and Statistics, University of Rangoon, Burma

Department of Demography, University of Montreal, Canada

Department of Sociology, University of Western Ontario, London, Canada

Instituto de Estadística, Universidad de Costa Rica, Costa Rica

Department of Demography, National University, Bogotá, Colombia

Department of Demography, University of the Andes, Bogotá, Columbia

Divisiónde Estudios de Población, Asociación Colombiana de Facultades de Medicina, Bogotá, Colombia

Population Policy Research Institute, Helsinki, Finland

Institut D'Études Démographiques de l'Université de Bordeaux, Bordeaux, France

Institut D'Études de la Population, Lyons, France

Institut de Démographie de l'Université de Paris, Paris, France

Institut National D'Études Démographiques, Paris, France

Institut National de la Statistique et des Économiques, Paris, France

Department for Population Studies, Munster University, Dortmund, Germany

Institut für Weltwirtschaft, University of Kiel, Kiel, Germany

Deutsche Adakemie für Bevölkerungswissenschaft, University of Hamburg, Hamburg, Germany

Demographic Training and Research Centre, Chembur, Bombay, India

All-India Institute of Hygiene and Public Health, Calcutta, India

Demographic Research Unit, Jadavpur University, Calcutta, India

Demographic Research Centre, Delhi School of Economics, University of Delhi, Delhi, India

Demographic Research Centre, Patna University, Patna, India

Department of Anthropology, University of Lucknow, Lucknow, India

Demographic Research Centre, University of Kerala, Trivandrum, India

Family Planning Institute, New Delhi, India

Gokhale Institute of Politics and Economics, Poona, India

Indian Institute for Population Studies, Madras, India

Indian Statistical Institute, Calcutta, India

Institute of Social Studies and Research, University of Tehran, Iran

Department of Statistics and Demography, Hebrew University, Jerusalem, Israel

Instituto di Demografia Della Facolta' de Scienze Statistiche Demografiche e Attuariali, University of Rome, Rome, Italy

Instituto di Statistica Dell'Universita di Bologna, Bologna, Italy

Instituto di Statistica e Demografia, Florence, Italy

Department of Statistics, Kingston, Jamaica

Institute of Social and Economic Research, University College of the West Indies, Jamaica, West Indies

Foundation-Institute for Research of Population Problems, Tokyo, Japan

Institute of Population Problems, Ministry of Health and Welfare, Tokyo, Japan

The Population Problems Research Council, Mainichi Newspapers, Tokyo, Japan

Institute of Population Problems, Seoul National University, Seoul, Korea

Division of Statistics, University of Malaya, Kuala Lumpur, Malaya

Center for Economic and Demographic Studies, Colégio de Mexico, Mexico City, Mexico

Foundation for Population Studies, Mexico City, Mexico

Department of Economics and Statistics, University of Amsterdam, Amsterdam, Netherlands

Department of Rural Sociology, University of Wageningen, Wageningen, Netherlands

Sociological Institute, University of Leyden, Leyden, Netherlands

Population Study Center, University of Abadan, Abadan, Nigeria

Academy for Village Development, Comilla, East Pakistan

Institute of Family Planning, Karachi, Pakistan

Social Sciences Research Centre, University of the Panjab, Lahore, Pakistan

Institute of Development Economics, Karachi, Pakistan

Centro de Estudios de Población y Dessarrollo, University of San Marcos, Lima, Peru

Population Institute, University of the Philippines, Manila, Philippines

Research Institute for Mindanao Culture, Xavier University, Philippines

Institute of Demography, Varsovie, Poland

Central School of Planning and Statistics, Warsaw, Poland

Department of Economics, University of Singapore, Singapore

Instituto Nacional de Estadística, Madrid, Spain

Statistical Institute, Gothenburg, Sweden

Population Research and Training Center, Chulalongkorn University, Bangkok, Thailand

Hacettepe Institute of Population Studies, Hacettepe, Ankara, Turkey

Comité National pour les Études de Population, Cairo, United Arab Republic

Faculty of Commerce, Cairo University, Cairo, United Arab Republic

Social Research Centre, The American University at Cairo, Cairo, United Arab Republic

Agricultural Economics Research Institute, University of Oxford, Oxford, United Kingdom

Department of Social Studies, University of Leeds, Leeds, United Kingdom

Department of Statistics, University of Aberdeen, Aberdeen, Scotland, United Kingdom

The Population Investigation Committee, University of London, London, United Kingdom

Department of Sociology, University of California at Santa Barbara, Santa Barbara, California, United States

Department of Sociology, University of Southern California, Los Angeles, California, United States

Department of Sociology, University of California at Los Angeles, Los Angeles, California, United States

Department of Demography, University of California, Berkeley, California, United States

Farm Population and Rural Life Branch, Agricultural Economics Division, United States Department of Agriculture, Washington, D. C., United States

The Catholic University of America, School of Social Science, Washington, D. C., United States

Center for Population Research, Georgetown University, Washington, D. C., United States

Division of Manpower and Employment Statistics, Bureau of Labor Statistics, Washington, D. C., United States

Population Reference Bureau, Washington, D. C., United States

Population Study Programs, Department of Sociology, The American University, Washington, D. C., United States

Department of Sociology and Anthropology, University of Florida, Gainesville, Florida, United States

Department of Sociology, Florida State University, Tallahassee, Florida, United States

Department of Sociology, University of Georgia, Athens, Georgia, United States

Department of Sociology, University of Hawaii, Honolulu, Hawaii, United States

Department of Sociology, University of Iowa, Iowa City, Iowa, United States

Community and Family Study Center, University of Chicago, Chicago, Illinois, United States

Population Research and Training Center, University of Chicago, Chicago, Illinois, United States

Department of Economics, University of Indiana, Bloomington, Indiana, United States

Department of Sociology, University of Kentucky, Lexington, Kentucky, United States

Department of Demography, Johns Hopkins University, Baltimore, Maryland, United States

Center for Population Studies, Harvard University, Cambridge, Mass., United States

Population Studies Center, University of Michigan, Ann Arbor, Michigan, United States

Department of Sociology, University of Massachusetts, Amherst, Mass., United States

Sociology Department, University of Mississippi, State College, Mississippi, United States

Social Science Institute, Washington University, St. Louis, Missouri, United States

Department of Sociology, Rutgers University, Newark, New Jersey, United States

Office of Population Research, Princeton University, Princeton, New Jersey, United States

Bureau of Applied Social Science, Columbia University, New York, United States

International Institute for the Study of Human Reproduction, Columbia University, New York, United States

Department of Political Philosophy, Fordham University, New York, United States

International Population Program, Cornell University, Ithaca, New York, United States

Metropolitan Life Insurance Company, New York, United States

Department of Rural Sociology, North Carolina State College, Raleigh, North Carolina, United States

Carolina Population Center, University of North Carolina, Chapel Hill, North Carolina, United States

Population Studies Program, Duke University, Durham, North Carolina, United States

Scripps Foundation for Research in Population, Miami University, Oxford, Ohio, United States

Sociology Department, University of Oregon, Eugene, Oregon, United States

Population Studies Center, University of Pennsylvania, Philadelphia, Pennsylvania, United States

Department of Sociology, Pennsylvania State University, State College, Pa., United States

Department of Sociology, Brown University, Providence, Rhode Island, United States

Population Research Center, University of Texas, Austin, Texas, United States

Bureau of Population and Economic Research, University of Virginia, Charlottesville, Virginia, United States

Office of Population Research, University of Washington, Seattle, Washington, United States

Department of Sociology, University of Wisconsin, Madison, Wisconsin, United States

Department of Demography, University of Caracas, Caracas, Venezuela

Centre de recherches démographiques de l'Institut des sciences sociales, Belgrade, Yugoslavia

Federal Statistics Institute, Belgrade, Yugoslavia

Institute of Statistics of the Faculty of Economics, University of Ljubljana, Ljubljana, Yugoslavia

To this list should be added the official census and vital statistics organizations of all of the major nations. The professional staffs of these offices do a great deal of demographic research.

International Organizations. A World Population Conference was held in Geneva in 1927. Margaret Sanger, the founder of the American birth control movement, was a leader in planning and organizing this conference. In the next year an international professional organization was organized in Paris—the International Union for the Scientific Study of Population Problems. Raymond Pearl was its first president. The International Union has sponsored conferences, usually in conjunction with the meetings of the International Statistical Institute because of the substantial overlap in membership. The organization has done much to stimulate the international flow of research findings and to establish demographic research in new places. It was cosponsor with the United Nations of a second World Population Conference in Rome in 1954 and a third World Population Conference in Belgrade in 1965.

The League of Nations maintained a substantial interest in population problems and undertook to make international compilations of population data a part of its statistical services. It also promoted research in population to the extent of its limited resources. The early monographs of the Office of Population Research were produced under League sponsorship.

When the United Nations was formed, a Population Commission became part of the legislative organization, and a Population Division within the Department of Social Affairs was made a permanent part of the administrative organization. The Population Division has fostered the development of the scientific study of population throughout the world. It sponsored a World Population Conference in Rome in 1954, the proceedings of which were published in eight large volumes. It has prepared a long series of population studies which, in terms of research methodology and in examples of research, have established prototypes of needed work throughout the world.

The United Nations has established three Demographic Research and Training Centers—in Santiago, Chile, in Bombay, India, and in Cairo, Egypt. Others are being planned.

Other branches of the United Nations also maintain a steady interest in demographic matters. The World Health Organization is greatly interested in improving the quality of registration of births and deaths and is working with demographers to achieve this goal. The UNESCO is interested in obtaining statistics on population composition in order to conduct comparative studies of education and literacy, economic well-being, labor force, urbanization, and other topics of special concern to it. The ECAFE (Economic Commission on Asia and the Far East), from its headquarters in Bangkok, makes extensive studies of population trends in the nations of its region for purposes of helping to formulate plans for economic development. The Pan American Health Organization, with headquarters in Washington, D. C., is promoting population research throughout Latin America.

In addition to the United Nations, several other bodies maintain an international interest in population statistics. The International Statistical Institute sponsors the publication of comparative international statistics in which population data are conspicuously emphasized. The Inter-American Statistical Institute of the Pan American Union is especially interested in demographic research and works industri-

ously to help get censuses of good quality taken and tabulated in Latin American countries. The World Bank maintains a research unit in which world population trends and demographic conditions in particular places are studied.

CONCLUSION

It has been the purpose of this introductory chapter to define demography, to illustrate the nature of demographic research, to show the interrelationships between demography and other social sciences, to describe in broad outlines the nature of the world population crisis and the part demography is playing in keeping the nations of the world informed of it, to describe briefly some other important population problems, to give a brief history of the origin and development of demography as a science, and finally to provide familiarity with the organizations around the world currently engaged in demographic research. With this background information we may now proceed to a systematic study of the content of demography as a branch of social science.

QUESTIONS AND TOPICS FOR DISCUSSION

1. What are some of the uses that the following types of organizations might make of population information? What specific population facts do they need?

(a) A national planning commission in Asia, mapping out a five-year program of economic development

(b) A state superintendent of schools

(c) A university president

(d) The political parties in a nation

(e) The marketing division of a manufacturer producing:

    Diamond rings
    Television sets
    Athletic equipment
    Hair-straightening solutions
    Lawn mowers
    Hearing aids
    College textbooks

(f) The Bureau of Public Roads

(g) The president of a labor union

(h) The National Association for the Advancement of Colored People (United States)

(i) The social security pension system of a nation

(j) The national housing authority planning an urban renewal program

(k) A stock market broker or investment adviser

(l) The national department of labor

(m) The military establishment of a nation, wanting to know:

    About the population of the nation it must defend

    About the population of other nations against which it may need to defend itself

2. List some of the hypotheses that involve population information which each of the following types of professional persons might formulate.

(a) An economist studying business cycles

(b) A political scientist trying to understand a legislature's pattern of voting on a bill to reduce taxes

(c) A historian trying to discover what factors determined victory in a war during the eighteenth century

(*d*) A geographer studying the pattern of distribution of rice culture

(*e*) A geneticist tracing the tendency toward inheritance of a rare disease

(*f*) A biometrician trying to learn whether there is a linkage between smoking and lung cancer

(*g*) A psychiatrist faced with determining whether or not the incidence of mental disease is rising

(*h*) A criminologist studying the social factors in crime

(*i*) An anthropologist studying the family system in a preliterate society

(*j*) A sociologist trying to find out whether

social mobility is increasing or decreasing in a particular nation

(*k*) A psychologist studying differences in intelligence between persons of various types

3. In your opinion, should demography be set up as a separate department in a university and taught as a special subject, should it be a special program operated cooperatively by several departments, or should it be lodged in one department, say sociology or economics? What reasons do you have for your recommendation?

4. Do you agree with the exposition of what constitutes "explanation" of demographic events presented in this chapter? If not, what alternative formulation would you make?

BIBLIOGRAPHY

Ackerman, Edward A. "Geography and Demography," in Philip M. Hauser and Otis Dudley Duncan (eds.). *The Study of Population*. Chicago: University of Chicago Press, 1959, pp. 717–727.

American Assembly. *The Population Dilemma*. Hauser, Philip M. (ed.). New York: Prentice Hall, 1963.

American Medical Association. "William Farr (1807-1833)—Vital Statistician," *Journal of the American Medical Association,* **192** (9) (May 31, 1965), pp. 779–780.

Balfour, Marshall C. "The Population Problem," *American Journal of Public Health and Nation's Health,* **54** (4) (April 1964), pp. 644–648.

Carr-Saunders, A. M. *The Population Problem*. Oxford: The Clarendon Press, 1922.

Chandrasekaran, C. "Survey of the Status of Demography in India," in Philip M. Hauser and Otis Dudley Duncan (eds.). *The Study of Population*. Chicago: University of Chicago Press, 1959, pp. 249–258.

Cold Spring Harbor Laboratory of Quantitative Biology. *Human Genetics*. (Cold Spring Harbor Symposia on Quantitative Biology, Vol. 29, 1946) Cold Spring Harbor, N. Y., 1965.

Constanzo, Alessandro. "Contributions of Italy to Demography," in Philip M. Hauser and Otis Dudley Duncan (eds.). *The Study of Population*. Chicago: University of Chicago Press, 1959, pp. 217–234.

Cox, Peter R. *Demography* (3rd ed.). Published for the Institute of Actuaries and the Faculty at the University Press, Cambridge, England, 1959.

Davis, Kingsley. "The Sociology of Demographic Behavior," in Robert Merton et al. (eds.).

Sociology Today. New York: Basic Books, 1959, pp. 309–333.

Dublin, Louis I. *Factbook on Man, From Birth to Death* (2nd ed.). New York: Macmillan, 1965.

Durand, John D. "Demography's Three Hundredth Anniversary," *Population Index,* **28** (4) (October 1962), pp. 333–338.

Eversley, David E. C. *Social Theories of Fertility and the Malthusian Debate*. Oxford: Clarendon Press, 1959.

Frank, Peter W. "Ecology and Demography," in Philip M. Hauser and Otis Dudley Duncan (eds.). *The Study of Population*. Chicago: University of Chicago Press, 1959, pp. 652–678.

Freedman, Ronald (ed.). *Population: The Vital Revolution*. Garden City, N. Y.: Anchor Books, Doubleday, 1964.

Glass, David V. *Introduction to Malthus*. London: Watts and Co., 1953.

Glass, David V., and David E. C. Eversley (eds.). *Population in History: Essays in Historical Demography*. London: Edward Arnold, 1965.

Bourgeois-Pichat, J. "The General Development of the Population of France Since the Eighteenth Century," pp. 474–506.

Chevalier, Louis. "Towards a History of Population," pp. 70–78.

Goubert, Pierre, "Recent Theories and Research in French Population Between 1500 and 1700," pp. 457–473.

Hajnal, J. "European Marriage Patterns in Perspective," pp. 101–143.

Henry, Louis, "The Population of France in the Eighteenth Century," pp. 434–456.

Grebenik, E. "The Development of Demography in Great Britain," in Philip M. Hauser and Otis Dudley Duncan (eds.). *The Study of Popula-*

tion. Chicago: University of Chicago Press, 1959, pp. 190–202.

Hauser, Philip M., *Population Perspectives*. New Brunswick, N. J.: Rutgers University Press, 1961, 1960.

Hauser, Philip M., and Otis Dudley Duncan (eds.). *The Study of Population: An Inventory and Appraisal*. Chicago: University of Chicago Press, 1959. Part I. Demography as a Science.

Kallmann, Franz J., and John D. Reiner. "Genetics and Demography," in Philip M. Hauser and Otis Dudley Duncan (eds.). *The Study of Population*. Chicago: University of Chicago Press, 1959, pp. 759–790.

Kirk, Dudley. "Some Reflections on American Demography in the Nineteen Sixties," *Population Index*, **26** (4) (October 1960), pp. 305–310.

Landis, P. H., and P. K. Hatt. *Population Problems: A Cultural Interpretation*. New York: American Book Company, 1954.

Landry, Adolphe. *Traité de Démographie*. Paris: Payot, 1945.

Lorimer, Frank. "The Development of Demography," in Philip M. Hauser and Otis Dudley Duncan (eds.). *The Study of Population*. Chicago: University of Chicago Press, 1959, pp. 124–179.

Lorimer, Frank, and Frederick Osborne. *Dynamics of Population*. New York: Macmillan, 1934.

Malthus, T. R. *Principles of Population* (7th ed.). London: J. Johnson, 1798.

Moore, Wilbert E. "Sociology and Demography," in Philip M. Hauser and Otis Dudley Duncan (eds.). *The Study of Population*. Chicago: University of Chicago Press, 1959, pp. 832–855.

Mortara, Giorgio. "Demographic Studies in Brazil," in Philip M. Hauser and Otis Dudley Duncan (eds.). *The Study of Population*. Chicago: University of Chicago Press, 1959, pp. 235–249.

Notestein, Frank W. (ed.). *Three Essays on Population*. New York: New American Library of World Literature, 1960.

PEP (Political and Economic Planning). *World Population and Resources*. London: Political and Economic Planning, 1955.

Petersen, William. *The Politics of Population*. Garden City, N. Y.: Doubleday, 1964.

Pressat, Roland. *L'Analyse Démographie*. Paris: Presses Universitaires de France, 1961.

Ryder, N. B. "Notes on the Concept of a Population," *American Journal of Sociology*, **69** (5) (March 1964), pp. 447–463.

Sauvy, Alfred. *Theorie Generale de la Population*. Paris: Presses Universitaires de France, 1952.

Sauvy, Alfred. "Development and Prospects of Demographic Research in France," in Philip M. Hauser and Otis Dudley Duncan (eds.). *The Study of Population*. Chicago: University of Chicago Press, 1959, pp. 180–189.

Schubnell, Hermann. "Demography in Germany," in Philip M. Hauser and Otis Dudley Duncan (eds.). *The Study of Population*. Chicago: University of Chicago Press, 1959, pp. 203–216.

Spengler, Joseph J. "The Aesthetics of Population," *Population Bulletin*, **13** (4) (June 1957), pp. 61–75.

Spengler, Joseph J. "Economics and Demography," in Philip M. Hauser and Otis Dudley Duncan (eds.). *The Study of Population*. Chicago: University of Chicago Press, 1959, pp. 791–832.

Spengler, Joseph J. "The Population Problem: Yesterday, Today, Tomorrow," *Southern Economic Journal*, **27** (3) (January 1961), pp. 194–208.

Spengler, Joseph J., and Otis Dudley Duncan (eds.). *Demographic Analysis: Selected Readings*. Glencoe, Ill.: The Free Press, 1956.

Spiegelman, Mortimer. *Introduction to Demography*. Society of Actuaries' Textbook. Chicago: The Society of Actuaries, 1955.

Spuhler, J. N. "Physical Anthropology and Demography," in Philip M. Hauser and Otis Dudley Duncan (eds.). *The Study of Population*. Chicago: University of Chicago Press, 1959, pp. 728–758.

Taeuber, Irene B. "Demographic Research in the Pacific Area," in Philip M. Hauser and Otis Dudley Duncan (eds.). *The Study of Population*. Chicago: University of Chicago Press, 1959, pp. 258–285.

Thompson, Warren S., and David T. Lewis. *Population Problems* (5th ed.). New York: McGraw-Hill, 1965.

Thomlinson, Ralph. *Population Dynamics*. New York: Random House, 1965.

United Nations, Department of Social Affairs, Population Division. "History of Population Theories." Chapter 3 in *The Determinants and Consequences of Population Trends*. New York, 1953.

United Nations, Department of Social Affairs, Population Division *Report on world population projects, as assessed in 1963*. New York, 1964.

Vance, Rupert B. "The Development and Status of American Demography," in Philip M. Hauser and Otis Dudley Duncan (eds.). *The Study of Population*. Chicago: University of Chicago Press, 1959, pp. 286–316.

Wrigley, E. A. (ed.). *An Introduction to English Historical Demography from the Sixteenth to the Nineteenth Century*. (Cambridge Group for the History of Population and Social Structure, Publication No. 1.) London: Weidenfeld and Nicolson, 1966.

Wrong, Dennis H. *Population*. Random House Studies in Sociology, 15. New York: Random House, 1956.

CHAPTER 2

Population Change and Its Components

2.1. The Significance of Population Change

One of the most important single demographic facts about a population is its rate of growth.[1] The rate at which a population is changing affects not only its size and numerical increase, but also (as will be shown later) its composition. Various people attach different meanings to population growth, but almost no one ignores it. The businessman may regard each infant born as a potential customer for a new television set, a new automobile, or a new house. The politician may regard each newborn infant as a potential voter who twenty-one years hence will vote for or against his party. A political dictator may translate figures of growth into potential armies. The school administrator may see a bumper crop of babies in terms of the number of additional classrooms and teachers needed to accommodate them in grade schools, high schools, and colleges. The municipal official translates population growth into miles of new watermains, streets, and sidewalks or into hundreds of extra policemen and firemen who must be added to the payroll and paid out of taxes that must be collected. Scarcely any establishment or institution in a community or nation is unaffected by the rate of population growth; a very high

[1] Because most populations are increasing in size, demographers regularly use the word "growth" to mean "change." The reader should keep in mind that "growth" as used by demographers can be negative, that is, it can represent a population decline. The absence of any sign in front of a growth statistic signifies positive growth—an increase in size—whereas a minus sign denotes negative growth.

percentage of them are aware of this fact and therefore actively seek information about it.

Like the farmer who is never pleased with the weather, almost no one seems to be satisfied with the current rate of population growth. If a population's growth becomes slower, as in the nations of Europe and North America during the 1930s, there is concern about insufficient growth. On the other hand, if a population begins to grow very rapidly, as in many nations around the world at present, there is grave concern about excessive growth—not only on the part of the nations themselves, but also on the part of their neighbors and friends.

We shall begin the systematic study of demography by studying the phenomenon of change in total size. When followed into all of its detailed ramifications, the subject becomes complex. In this chapter we attempt only to provide a general foundation, leaving to later chapters a more intensive probing of the details. However, this foundation will permit us, in the next chapter, to gain an overview of total world population and its growth trends and potentials.

2.2. How Population Change Is Measured

Most nations measure population change by comparing the results of two censuses, taken 10 years or so apart. The simplest measure of population growth is the intercensal change, or the population of the earlier census subtracted from the population of the later census. For example, India took a population census in 1951 and again in 1961 and discovered an astounding growth:

Year	Census population
1961	434,807,245
1951	356,879,394
Change	77,927,851

(These data do not include estimates for Goa, Daman and Diu which are added to current official census figures.)

In contrast, Japan in the census of 1960 discovered a much smaller intercensal growth:

Year	Census population
1960	93,418,501
1950	83,199,637
Change	10,218,864

This procedure enables the demographer to learn the *absolute amount* of population change that has taken place. If there was an incomplete count in the earlier census or an overcount in the later one, this procedure yields an overestimate of growth. Conversely, if the later census has a more incomplete count than the earlier one, the amount of growth is understated. Before accepting the results of this calculation, the demographer must evaluate the relative completeness of the two censuses. If both were overenumerated or underenumerated by the same amount, the estimate of growth is unaffected. But if there has been improvement or deterioration in quality between one census and the next, the extent of this change and its effect on the data must be estimated and an adjustment made to one census count or the other before growth is estimated. There are small fluctuations in the completeness of count even in the most modern censuses, and in working with older census materials or with censuses from countries where census-taking has not yet become a tradition, it may be necessary to make an adjustment of 5 to 10 percent or more in the count for one census before growth can be estimated. *Population growth is never measured directly; it is a residual (difference) or net balance between two censuses including the net balance of all errors of enumeration.*[2] Fortunately, errors in

[2] It can also be measured as a residual from National Population registers in counties where an accurate record of births, deaths, and migration is kept. (See Section 2–5.)

census coverage are sufficiently small or are sufficiently alike to permit direct measurements of intercensal growth in most nations. For example, most European, American, Australian, Japanese, and Indian researchers can use this procedure to compute growth during the last decade with little fear of a major error.

2.3. The Intercensal Percent Change

Estimates of the absolute amount of growth suffer from a major deficiency—they do not take into account the size of the population that caused the growth. Because India's population is about 4½ times that of Japan, it is quite logical to expect India to have a larger growth. In other words, what is desired is a measure of growth *relative* to the size of the population. Demographers employ a very simple measure, the intercensal percent change, for this purpose. This is simply the amount of intercensal increase divided by the population at the earlier census, the result multiplied by 100 to convert it to a percent. The computations for India and Japan from our examples are:

$$\text{India} = \frac{77,927,851}{356,879,394} \times 100 = 21.8 \text{ percent}$$

$$\text{Japan} = \frac{10,218,864}{83,199,637} \times 100 = 12.3 \text{ percent}$$

The population of India is growing at the rate of 21.8 percent every 10 years, while that of Japan is growing at the much lower rate of 12.3 percent every 10 years. A simpler way to compute this measure, obtaining the same results, is to divide the later census by the earlier, multiply the result by 100, and subtract 100.

These operations can be expressed in symbols as follows:

$$\text{intercensal percent change} = \frac{P_t - P_0}{P_0} \times 100$$

$$= 100\frac{P_t}{P_0} - 100$$

$$(2.1)$$

where P_0 is the census count for the earlier census and P_t is the census count for the later

Table 2-1 Growth History of India and Japan:
1900–1901 to 1960–1961

Year of census	Population (thousands)		Intercensal percent change	
	India	Japan	India	Japan
1960–61......	439,235	93,419	21.6	12.3
1950–51......	361,130	83,200	13.3	14.7
1940–41......	318,701	72,540	14.2	13.6
1930–31......	279,015	63,872	11.0	15.3
1920–21......	251,352	55,391	-0.3	10.1
1910–11......	252,122	50,297	6.7	12.3
1900–01......	236,281	44,770	....	....

Source: Data for India: Census of India, 1961, Paper No. 1
of 1962, Final Population Totals, Data for Japan
1900 and 1910 estimated from Table 9, and from
1920-40 transcribed from Table 20 of Irene Taeuber,
The Population of Japan, Princeton, Princeton
University Press, 1958; data for 1950 and 1960
taken from United Nations Demographic Yearbook,
1960.

census. This measure shows the percent change over the intercensal period, usually 10 years. Insofar as possible, demographers reserve the term "rate" to refer to the frequency of occurrence *per year* of some event; hence this measure is not a true rate in this sense. It is an index of the rate of growth, but in the literature it is often referred to as the "intercensal growth rate."

The intercensal percent change can be used to chart the trend in growth over time of a nation or a part of a nation. For example, Table 2-1 gives the intercensal percent change figures for India and Japan for the past seven decades. (In order to preserve comparability of figures, the data for India include the population of Kashmir and Jammu, claimed by both India and Pakistan.) Note the different growth histories of the two nations. Famines, epidemics, and sustained high death rates wiped out growth in India before 1920, so that her population was almost stationary. In recent years modernization and technical aid have moderated the effect of these sources of attrition on population growth in India and as a result growth has accelerated. Japan, on the other hand, has grown less rapidly in the last decade than in the 1930–1940 period.

In using the intercensal percent change, it must be remembered that the figures can be compared only if the length of the intercensal period is the same. In our example all intercensal periods are 10 years apart. (If the exact date of the census is changed, so that the censuses fall slightly less or more than exactly 10 years apart, for highly precise work an adjustment is necessary.) In many nations, including the United States, there has been a census every 10 years for several decades, so that it is possible to compare growth trends over time and for various parts of the country quite satisfactorily. It must be emphasized that this measure cannot be used to compare the relative growth between places that have different intervals between censuses. For example, we cannot use the intercensal percent change to compare the rates of growth in India, Argentina, and Thailand, because each of these countries has a different interval between censuses. Even shifting the date of the census to a different month within the census year affects comparability.

2.4. The Annual Rate of Population Change

Where the interval between censuses varies, as in the example just cited, it is useful to express growth in terms of *percent change per year,* or as an *annual rate*. The procedure and the formulas for the computation are the same as in the preceding section, except that the interval refers to exactly one year: the annual rate of change is the population increase during the year divided by the population at the beginning of the year. If P_0 is the population at the beginning of the year and P_t the population at the end of the year, Equation 2.1 becomes the formula for the annual rate of population change. Usually it is not possible to use this equation to compute annual growth rates, however, because data are not available for single years; the census taken at 10-year intervals is the only source of information. In this case, it is possible to use the data for two successive censuses to estimate an *average annual growth rate* for the intercensal period. This is accomplished by using the compound interest formula from business arithmetic:

$$P_t = P_0 (1 + r)^t \, 100 \qquad (2.2)$$

or

$$r = \left(\sqrt[t]{\frac{P_t}{P_0}} - 1 \right) \times 100$$

where

P_0 = the census count for the earlier census
P_t = the census count for the later census
r = the average annual rate of growth (it is usually multiplied by 100 in order that it may be expressed as a percent)
t = the interval in years or decimal fractions thereof between the two censuses

For the details of computing this measure, the student is referred to Chapter 2 of the *Manual of Demographic Research Techniques.*

To illustrate the usefulness of this measure, let us compare the growth rate of Argentina with that of Japan. The data for Japan, given previously, cover an exact 10-year interval, from November 1, 1950, to November 1, 1960, whereas the data for Argentina cover an interval of 13 years and 143 days, as follows:

	Date of census	Population
Later census	September 30, 1960	20,008,945
Earlier census	May 10, 1947	15,893,827
Difference	13 years, 143 days	4,115,118

Clearly, an intercensal percent change for the two countries would give a very erroneous picture of their rates of growth. But by substituting the census information into Equation 2.2, with $t = 13^{143}\!/_{365} = 13.4$ years, and establishing an average annual growth rate, we can make the comparison:

$$\log (1 + r) = \frac{1}{13.4} (\log 20,008,945 - \log 15,893,827)$$

$$r = 1.7 \text{ (after multiplication by 100)}$$

A similar calculation for Japan yields a value of $r = 1.2$. Although it is clear that Argentina is growing more rapidly than Japan, the difference is not nearly so great as would be suggested by the improper comparison of their intercensal percent changes.

2.5. The Demographic Significance of Growth Rates

Beginning students of demography often are surprised at the great importance attached to small differences in growth rates and at the great concern shown for growth rates that in other realms of life would appear quite small. Table 2-2 offers a rating scale that may be used as an approximate guide in interpreting the significance of population growth rates. The significance of these apparently small numbers is better appreciated when their analogy to the compounding of interest on a savings account in the bank is recalled. Each year's growth is added to the "principal" (population size) to which the rate is applied, so that the rate applies to a number that becomes steadily larger and larger. The right-hand column of Table 2-2 reports the number of years required for the population to double in size if it grew continuously at the rate indicated. In the next chapter we shall learn that the world currently is growing at the rate of about 2 percent per year. Beginning with a population of 3 billion

Table 2-2 Rating of the Levels of Population Growth and the Number of Years Required for the Population to Double in Size

Rating	Annual rate of growth	Number of years required for the population to double in size
Stationary population........	No growth	......
Slow growth.................	less than 0.5 percent	more than 139 years
Moderate growth.............	0.5 to 1.0 percent	139 to 70 years
Rapid growth................	1.0 to 1.5 percent	70 to 47 years
Very rapid growth...........	1.5 to 2.0 percent	47 to 35 years
"Explosive" growth..........	2.0 to 2.5 percent	35 to 28 years
" "	2.5 to 3.0 percent	28 to 23 years
" "	3.0 to 3.5 percent	23 to 20 years
" "	3.5 to 4.0 percent	20 to 18 years

in 1960 and assuming that this growth rate continues indefinitely, we use Equation 2.2 to calculate the population in future years by substituting various values of t in the equation $P_t = 3(1 + 0.02)^t$. Table 2-3 reports the results. It is a computation of this type that caused the United Nations to declare (in the statement quoted in Chapter 1) that at the present rate of increase the number of human beings on earth would within only 600 years reach the density of one person per square meter. And it is the possibility of such a result that causes us to classify an average annual rate of 2 percent as "explosive."

As later chapters will try to amplify, almost every aspect of national life is conditioned by the rate of growth. At the present moment most social scientists tend to regard both a condition of stationary population and a condition of fast or very fast growth as undesirable because

Table 2-3 Projected Population of the World, Assuming Average Annual Increase of 2 Percent per Year, for Selected Future Dates.

Year	Estimated population (billions)
1960..................	3.0
1970..................	3.7
1980..................	4.5
2000..................	6.7
2050..................	17.8
2100..................	47.9
2200..................	430.6

each tends to bring with it social problems. Historically, a declining population has been associated with a listless economy. Such a population tends to have an older age composition. It tends to be conservative, is thought to have below-average amounts of initiative and daring, and lives in dread of being overrun by a more rapidly growing neighbor who needs living space. Very rapid growth, on the other hand, is associated with (a) hordes of children to educate, (b) a perennial threat of unemployment or underemployment (because it is difficult to provide jobs for the increasing flow of great masses of new workers into the labor force), (c) concern about the nation's ability to produce enough food to feed the population, and (d) worry that certain critical natural resources will become exhausted through quick exploitation. Nations undergoing economic development are striving to lower their birthrates in order to hasten their climb into higher per capita levels of living. Modern warfare gives a very great advantage to the nation that is technologically advanced and has a literate and skilled labor force. Self-defense rests on skill and knowledge rather than on quantity of flesh in uniforms. Consideration of these facts leads us to agree with Carr-Saunders that, in theory at least, at any given stage of technological and social development and under any specified system of value there is an optimum size for the population at any given time. There may also be an optimum rate of growth if the optimum size has not yet been attained. As we shall see, it is very diffi-

Table 2-4 Growth of the Urban and Rural
Population of the United States: 1950–1960.

Residence	Population (thousands)		Increase 1950-60 (thousands)	Intercensal percent change
	1960	1950		
Total.....	179,323	151,326	27,997	18.5
Urban........	125,269	96,847	28,422	29.3
Rural........	54,054	54,479	-425	-0.8

Source: United States Census of Population: 1960. Number
         of Inhabitants, United States Summary, Table 3.

cult to estimate what the optimum is for any particular population, but luckily it seems to fall within a rather broad range. Table 2-3 makes one fact very clear: *A condition of zero growth must become the normal demographic state of all nations of the world within less than one century.* Almost none can afford to support an increase at even an annual rate of 1.0 percent for this long.

2.6 Differential Growth

In addition to total or overall rate of growth, there is also concern about *differential* growth. Differential growth is the comparative rate at which the various parts of the population are growing. Is one region growing faster than another? How fast are the urban and rural populations growing in relation to each other? Are the illiterate outbreeding the literate? Are Catholics outbreeding Protestants? Is the manufacturing segment of the labor force growing as fast as the retail trade segment? At what rate is the number of divorced persons increasing? Questions such as these raise the problem of differential growth. Thus the study of population trends deals not only with global overall totals but also with measuring growth of parts.

Table 2-4 is a typical compilation made to study differential growth. It reports, for the 1950-1960 decade, the intercensal percent change for urban and rural areas in the United States; a very striking growth differential is revealed. In this decade of unprecedented growth all of the growth accrued to urban areas. In fact, rural territory lost population slightly. As will be discussed in a later chapter,

a similar differential now exists in most countries of the world and on all continents.

2.7. The Components of Population Growth

Population growth is a dynamic equilibrium between forces of increment and forces of decrement. Continuously the population is being increased by the birth of infants, but it is simultaneously being diminished by the death of persons of all ages. Meanwhile, a similar situation holds for migration: immigrants are arriving and emigrants are departing. The size of the population may be likened to the level of water in a great tank that is being filled by two pipes (births and immigration) and is at the same time being emptied by two drains (death and migration). The level will rise if the inflow is greater in volume than the outflow, and vice versa. If anything happens to slacken the inflow without altering the outflow, the level will fall, but if the outflow is restricted the level will rise. Thus we quickly see that population growth is not a simple unitary phenomenon, but is comprised of four major components: fertility, mortality, in-migration, and out-migration. The balance between births and deaths is called "reproductive change" or "natural increase."[3] The balance of in-migration and out-migration is called "net migration." Thus it can also be said that there are only two ways in which a population can change

[3] In this book we use the term "reproductive change" rather than "natural increase." We do not believe that migration, even by implication, is any less "natural" than the reproductive processes, and certainly the net resultant is not always an increase.

Table 2-5 Estimates of Population Change and of the Components, United States: 1950 to 1960.

A. SUMMARY (In thousands)

```
Population April 1, 1960................................. 179,323
Population April 1, 1950................................. 151,326
```

Net increase... +27,997

Components of change:

```
Births (corrected for under-registration)............... 40,963
Deaths.................................................. 15,608
Net movement of aliens and citizens..................... +2,695
Net movement of Armed Forces abroad..................... -330
```

Expected net increase.. +27,720

Error of closure... +277

B. DETAILS OF MIGRATION
(Figures may not add to totals because of rounding)

Class of migrant	Net movement	Total	
		Arrivals	Departures
1. Alien immigrants and emigrants..............	+2,249	2,500	251
2. Alien nonimmigrants and nonemigrants........	-10	3,459	3,469
3. Citizen passengers arriving and departing...	-	NA	NA
4. Movement to and from Puerto Rico and other outlying areas..........................	+455	3,725	3,269
5. Total.......................................	+2,695	NA	NA

Source: U.S. Bureau of Census.

in size—through reproductive change and through net migration.

If we know the population count as of a particular date and keep track of the number of occurrences of each of these four components of growth, we can calculate the population at any later date. One of the simplest yet most often used formulas in the study of population growth is the *demographic book-keeping equation,* which summarizes the above set of ideas:

$$P_t = P_0 + (B - D) + (M_i - M_0) \qquad (2.3)$$

where

P_t and P_0 are defined as in Equation 2.1

B denotes births during the interval between P_0 and P_t

D denotes deaths during the interval between P_0 and P_t

M_0 denotes out-migration during the interval between P_0 and P_t

M_i denotes in-migration during the interval between P_0 and P_t

Table 2.5 presents the components of growth, in bookkeeping form, for the United States during the decade 1950-1960. This method of keeping track of population growth is called "demographic bookkeeping" because it sets up a sort of population ledger for a nation or any other area, inserting births and in-migration on the debit side of the account and entering deaths and out-migration on the credit side. When a net balance of the increments and decrements is taken and added to the balance on hand at the beginning of the transaction (initial population), we have an estimate of present net worth (present population). The reader should note the close analogy between birth and in-migrants on the one hand and death and out-migrants on the other.

It is readily apparent that the estimate of the population for April 1, 1950, derived from the components of growth, was amazingly close to the actual 1960 census count, for the "bookkeeping" estimate of the 1960 population failed to match the actual census count of 179.3

million by only 277,000, or by less than two hundredths of 1 percent. Demographers call this difference the "error of closure." Although this is an unusually close estimate, demographers in most nations where the registration of vital events is reasonably complete and where even moderately accurate records of migration are maintained are able to predict the results of the next census within 1 percent or less of the official total.

Wherever possible, demographers seek to analyze population growth in terms of its components, for only when each of the components is known, can the growth process be understood. All too often growth from migration is mistaken for growth due to reproductive change, and vice versa.

The first step in analyzing growth is to subdivide total growth into the major components of reproductive change and net migration. The second step is to subdivide each of the major components into their subcomponents, if this is possible. As later chapters will explain, it is often possible to estimate the component of reproductive change and the component of net migration with reasonable accuracy without being able to determine exactly what the true values of the subcomponents are.

"Open" and "Closed" Populations. In many nations the quantity of migration, either into or out of the nation, is so small that for all practical purposes the migration component is zero. Therefore, the problem of studying growth is greatly simplified, for growth is determined entirely by reproductive change. Such populations are termed "closed" populations. An "open" population is one in which migration is present in significant quantities. If a population has a substantial quantity of in-migration exactly balanced by out-migration to yield zero net migration, the population is nevertheless "open" because of the possibility that the migration will affect age, sex, and other compositional aspects.

In the study of entire nations the migration component is almost always much smaller than the component of reproductive change. Table 2.4 is an excellent illustration. During the decade 1950-1960 the United States accepted 2.5 million immigrants. This is more than any other nation of the world accepted during this period. Yet net migration for the decade was less than 10 percent of the total net increase. In the study of differential growth *within* a nation or region, however, this is not necessarily true. Great streams of internal migration often flow within national boundaries and cause some places to grow explosively and others to become almost depopulated. Table 2.4 shows evidence of such a major migratory process. If there were no migration between rural and urban areas, the rural areas would show a *greater* rate of growth than the urban areas, for birthrates are higher in rural than in urban areas and death rates are about equal. Thus all of the differential growth reported in Table 2.4 must be attributed to the effect of migration. The parts of a nation are almost always "open" populations, irrespective of whether or not international movement is zero.

2.8. The Components of Change Expressed as Rates

Each of the components of change is usually measured as a rate. The simplest rates are the "crude" rates: crude birth, death, and migration rates. A crude rate is simply the number of events of a given type that occur in a year divided by the midyear population. Usually this ratio is multiplied by 1000 to show the number of events per 1000 people. For example, the crude birthrate is the number of births that occur during the year divided by the population as of July 1 of that year; similarly the crude death rate is the number of deaths in a year divided by the July 1 population. In algebraic terms the crude birth and death rates are:

$$CBR = \frac{\text{total births}}{\text{midyear population}} \times 1000 \qquad (2.4)$$

$$CDR = \frac{\text{total deaths}}{\text{midyear population}} \times 1000 \qquad (2.5)$$

The crude rate of reproductive change is the balance of births and deaths divided by the midyear population. In other words, it is simply the crude birthrate minus the crude death rate.

rate of reproductive change

$$= \frac{\text{total births} - \text{total deaths}}{\text{midyear population}} \times 1000$$

$$= \text{CBR} - \text{CDR} \qquad (2.6)$$

In a similar way, the crude in-migration rate is the number of in-migrants divided by the midyear population. The crude out-migration rate is the number of out-migrants divided by the midyear population.

$$M_i = \frac{\text{total in-migrants}}{\text{midyear population}} \times 1000 \qquad (2.7)$$

$$M_0 = \frac{\text{total out-migrants}}{\text{midyear population}} \times 1000 \qquad (2.8)$$

The net migration rate by analogy is the difference between the in-migration and the out-migration rates.

rate of net migration

$$= \frac{\text{total in-migrants} - \text{total out-migrants}}{\text{midyear population}} \times 1000$$

$$= M_i - M_0 \qquad (2.9)$$

It is possible to take the algebraic sum of reproductive change and net migration to arrive at an estimate of the annual rate of growth described in Section 2.2.[4]

annual rate of increase = rate of reproductive change + rate of net migration

An example of the computation of the rates for the components of reproductive change is

[4] It should be pointed out that the rates presented in this section are computed with the midyear population as denominator, whereas for the average annual rate of growth described in Section 2.2 the population at the *beginning* of the year is taken as the denominator. For much work in demography the two may be used interchangeably when the period of time is one year because the difference is small. The rates of Equations 2.4, 2.5, and 2.6 are termed "central growth rates" (based on midyear populations). If desired, by estimating procedures the average annual growth rate may be converted to a central rate, and vice versa. For a more detailed discussion see the *Manual of Demographic Research Techniques*, Chapter 2.

provided in Table 2.6. It lists three nations that fall toward the slow-growth end of the scale and three nations in the "explosive growth" category and gives the data required to compute their birth and death rates and rates of reproductive change. The population is the estimated midyear population of 1960, and the births and deaths are the counts for the calendar year 1960:

column 5 = column 2 divided by column 1
column 6 = column 3 divided by column 1
column 4 = column 5 minus column 6 divided by 10

Although demographers have devised highly refined and special rates and techniques for measuring mortality, fertility, and migration, they have never abandoned this basic system of components expressed in terms of crude rates. Despite the several shortcomings that these measures have, they are a very important medium of exchange of demographic information around the world. They are easy to compute; their meaning is widely understood by those who have little demographic training; and despite their simplicity, they are amazingly efficient in detecting and measuring fairly accurately differences and changes in population growth. Often they can be calculated or estimated in situations where the other more refined measures have not yet been established.

2.9.   The Explanation of Population Growth

In a sense, a population change has been "explained" when it has been subdivided into its major components and subcomponents. However, this is not a fundamental explanation; it states *how* a population change has come about, but not *why*. In other words, the study of population change in terms of its components is a study of the *mechanisms* by which change takes place, but not of the forces that operate the mechanism. It is like explaining the operation of a watch by outlining in detail how the various wheels and gears combine to cause the hands to move without mentioning the driving power of the tension in the mainspring. This is not to say that the component analysis is not important; it is an *essential* but

Table 2-6 Birth and Death Rates of Reproductive Change for Selected Nations: 1960.

Nation	Number			Rate		
	Population (thousands)	Births	Deaths	Reproductive change	Births	Deaths
	(1)	(2)	(3)	(4)	(5)	(6)
Low rates of growth						
Sweden................	7,480	102,088	74,968	0.36	13.6	10.0
England and Wales......	45,862	782,700	526,300	0.56	17.1	11.5
Hungary...............	9,999	146,436	101,539	0.44	14.6	10.2
High rates of growth						
Singapore.............	1,634	61,775	10,203	3.16	37.8	6.2
China (Taiwan)........	10,612	419,442	73,715	3.26	39.5	6.9
British Honduras.......	90	4,016	730	3.67	44.8	8.1

Source: United Nations: Population and Vital Statistics Report, (Series A, Vol. XIII, No. 3), and Demographic Yearbook, 1961.

intermediate step in arriving at an explanation of population growth.

The intermediate question of how population change occurs may be extended and elaborated into an examination of how each element exerts its effect, in terms of its constituent elements. For example, if the birthrate declines, we can perform research to find out whether it was younger or older women who have had lower birthrates. We can look to see whether there had been a rise in the average age at marriage, a rise in childlessness among married couples, or a fall in the percentage of couples in their late thirties who are bearing a fourth or fifth child. Similarly, if the death rate falls, a study can be undertaken to determine what causes of death have become less potent and whether the change occurred at the infant, young adult, or older ages, was confined to women of a particular racial group, or was spread among both sexes and all groups. If there is a change in the migration rate, special studies could be made to learn what kinds of people are migrating with greater or lesser frequency than formerly—from where they come, where they go, what are their socioeconomic traits, whether they move as persons or as families, and whether they settle down quickly or make several moves. It is essential for demographers to understand and accept the notion that this type of research is still *intermediate* in nature:

it is the study of the mechanisms by which the components exert their effect; it is a very intensive and detailed study of how change takes place, but not why.

The study of mechanisms of population change is a fairly accurate description of what is sometimes called "formal demography." This very important type of research must precede any effort to develop a more fundamental explanation that involves the driving forces behind population change, for the driving forces —whatever they are—always manifest themselves in the form of action through one or more of the mechanisms. For example, much of the fall in death rates from 1937 to 1955 may be attributed, mechanistically, to a decline in deaths from infection. One of the major underlying forces or "causes" was the development and extensive use of sulpha drugs, penicillin, and other antibiotics.

The field of demography has been criticized for being atheoretical, or weak in theory. To the extent that this is true, it consists in large part in a shortage of testable hypotheses and generalizations concerning the driving forces behind the mechanisms of population change. Probably there is no discipline in the entire field of social science that has explored as fully and with more precision the mechanisms involved in the behavior it studies as has demography. Insofar as the criticism mentioned above is valid, the next decade may witness a great flowering of theory about the *why* of population change, because an excellent foundation for it has been laid in the form of intermediate explanations of the *how* of population dynamics.

CONCLUSION

In this chapter we have undertaken to prepare the student to think clearly about the phenomenon of population growth. We define it, describe how it is measured, and provide simple techniques for comparing the growth tendencies in populations over time and in space. Total growth is shown to consist of two major components—reproductive change and net migration. Each of these, in turn, consists of two subcomponents—births and deaths and in-migration and out-migration, respectively. The first step in studying a population change is to break it into its components and, if possible, into its subcomponents. Then an explanatory analysis of the forces acting on each component or subcomponent should be undertaken.

With this background, we are now prepared to look at the world population situation.

QUESTIONS AND EXERCISES

1. Compute the most recent intercensal percent change for your (*a*) country, (*b*) state or province, (*c*) home community. Calculate the average birth and death rates for the intercensal period or for a year at midcensal interval. Repeat for the preceding intercensal period if possible. Write an essay on the growth tendency in your home community in comparison with that in the state and nation. Develop some explanations of why you think the differences exist.

2. From the census report "Estimates of the Components of Population Change by Color" (see Bibliography) and from Table 137 of the 1960 Census report *General Social and Economic Characteristics* complete the table below. Make a scattergram of the relationship between migration and family income and write a short essay on the results.

3. From the *Statistical Abstract of the United States* obtain the percent intercensal change for each of the geographic divisions listed in Exercise 2 and the birth and death rate for each in 1950 and 1960. Using an average birthrate and death rate for the decade, estimate what the rate of intercensal change would be in each division if it had a closed population. Compare the results with the actual rate. Interpret the differences in the light of the information about income given in Exercise 2.

4. Obtain the data for differential growth among the regions of some nation other than the United States. Write a short essay describing the pattern and developing hypotheses to explain the observed differences. If data are available for one of your explanatory hypotheses, make a simple scattergram or table to test it.

	Net migration rate	Median family income
United States		
New England states		
Middle Atlantic states . . .		
East North Central states		
West North Central states		
South Atlantic states		
East South Central states		
West South Central states		
Mountain states		
Pacific states		

5. In Exercise 1, can you think of a way of estimating net migration for the intercensal period if no migration statistics were available? Using this principle, calculate the net migration rate of California and South Dakota and compare the results. Why is this procedure limited to counties or combinations of counties?

BIBLIOGRAPHY

Arretx, G. Carmen, and Jorge L. Samoza. "Survey Methods, Based on Periodically Repeated Interviews, Aimed at Determining Demographic Rates," *Demography*, **2**, pp. 289–302.

Barclay, George W. "Rates and Ratios" and "Growth of Population," Chapters 2 and 7 in *Techniques of Population Analysis*. New York: John Wiley and Sons, 1958.

Bogue, Donald J. *Components of Population Change, 1940–50: Estimates of Net Migration and Natural Increase for Each Standard Metropolitan Area and State Economic Area.* Scripps Foundation Studies in Population Distribution, No. 12. Oxford, Ohio: Scripps Foundation for Research in Population Problems, Miami University, and Population Research and Training Center, University of Chicago, 1957.

Bogue, Donald J., and Evelyn M. Kitagawa. "Population Dynamics," Chapter 2 in *A Manual of Demographic Research Techniques*. New York: John Wiley and Sons, in press.

Carr-Saunders, A. M. "Natural Increase," Chapter 5 in *World Population*. Oxford: Clarendon Press, 1936.

El-Badry, M. A. "Trends in the Components of Population Growth in the Arab Countries of the Middle East: A Survey of Present Information," *Demography*, **2**, pp. 140–186.

Hyrenius, Hannes. "Population Growth and Replacement," in Philip M. Hauser and Otis Dudley Duncan (eds.). *The Study of Population*. Chicago: University of Chicago Press, 1959, pp. 472–485.

Kuczynski, R. R. *The Balance of Births and Deaths,* Vol. 1. New York: Macmillan, 1928.

Pressat, Roland. "Les Taux en Démographie," Chapter 2 in *L'Analyse Démographique*. Paris: Presses Universitaires de France, 1961.

Ryder, Norman B. "Components of Canadian Population Growth," in Bernard R. Blishen et al. (eds.). *Canadian Society: Sociological Perspectives*. Toronto: Macmillan Company of Canada, Ltd., 1961.

Stolnitz, George J. "The Demographic Transition: From High to Low Birth Rates and Death Rates," in Ronald Freedman (ed.). *Population: The Vital Revolution*. Garden City, N.Y.: Anchor Books, Doubleday, 1964.

United Nations, "Historical Outline of World Population Growth," Chapter 2 in *The Determinants and Consequences of Population Trends*. New York: United Nations, 1953.

U. S. Bureau of the Census. "Estimates of the Population of the United States and Components of Change: 1940 to 1967," *Current Population Reports–Population Estimates*. Washington, D.C.: U. S. Government Printing Office, June 27, 1967.

U. S. Bureau of the Census. "Estimates of the Components of Population Change by Color, for States: 1950–60," *Current Population Reports–Population Estimates*, Series P-25, No. 247. Washington, D.C.: U. S. Government Printing Office, April 1962.

U. S. Bureau of the Census. "Components of Population Change 1950–1960, for Counties, Standard Metropolitan Statistical Areas, State Economic Areas, and Economic Subregions," *Current Population Reports–Population Estimates*, Series P-23, No. 7. Washington, D. C.: U. S. Government Printing Office, November 1962.

CHAPTER 3

The Growth of the World's Population and the Theory of Demographic Regulation

3.1. Present Size and Rate of Growth of the World's Population

It is estimated that as of mid-1965 the population of the world stood at about 3.3 billion. This figure is derived by carrying forward the official estimates of the United Nations based on the results of the most recent censuses of the various nations taken between 1950 and 1961. As nearly as can be determined, the world's population is *increasing* at the rate of 62 to 63 million persons per year, which is 170,000 to 172,000 persons per day, 7000 to 7200 persons per hour, or 117 to 120 persons per minute! Never before in human history has the human race increased by such amounts. Perhaps the magnitude of this expansion may be better appreciated if we consider the time that would be required for the current rate of growth to produce a population equivalent in size to those of certain well-known places:

Rio de Janeiro 18-19 days
Moscow (metropolitan area) 36-37 days
All of Australia 62-63 days
New York City (metropolitan area) 81-83 days
All of France 270-272 days
All of Africa 4.2 years

This, it should be remembered, is not births, but population *increase*—the net *gain* in population after all deaths have been replaced.

When it is realized that growth of this magnitude is taking place around the clock, month after month, year after year, it is easy to understand why demographers use colorful phrases such as "population explosion" to describe it.

Oddly enough, the vital processes that underlie this astounding growth look innocuous. The annual crude birthrate of the world is estimated at 34 per thousand population, the crude death rate at 16 per thousand, and the annual rate of growth at 1.9 per year. This growth rate may not seem impressively high until we realize that it applies to a very huge population: 1.9 percent times 3.3 billion is 62.7 million per year. Those who are studying this phenomenon are quick to point out another fact: each year's net growth is added to the preexisting population, so that even if the rates should remain constant, the *amounts* of population growth will go on increasing by ever-enlarging amounts. Hence the amounts of increase per year, per day, and so forth quoted above represent the situation only at the years 1964-1965; for later dates and at the same rates the amounts will be progressively even larger. Therefore, even if we wish merely to "hold the line" and have no more than the same *amount* of population growth each year as at present, it is necessary for the rate to decline in such a way that each year it is only about 98 percent of the rate for the preceding year. A marked slackening in the amount of growth would require a fall in the rate of growth greater than this. Inasmuch as death rates in most of the rapidly growing nations are not likely to rise in the near future, if a slackening of population growth is to occur, it must be accomplished, of course, by lowering the birthrate.

Table 3-1 World Population, Vital Rates, Distribution, and Density by Continents, Divisions, and Regions: 1966

Major divisions and regions of the world	Estimated population 1966		Vital statistics 1960-66		Percent distribution		Density per square kilometer 1966
	Mid-year population (millions)	Annual rate of growth	Crude birth rate	Crude death rate	World's population	World's land area	
WORLD TOTAL............	3,356	1.9	34	16	100.0	100.0	25
AFRICA.........	318	2.3	46	23	9.5	22.3	11
Western Africa.............	100	2.3	50	27	3.0	4.5	16
Eastern Africa.............	88	2.4	45	21	2.6	4.6	14
Northern Africa............	76	2.4	43	19	2.3	6.2	9
Middle Africa..............	33	1.9	42	23	1.0	4.9	5
Southern Africa............	21	2.5	42	17	0.6	2.0	8
AMERICA........	470	2.2	32	11	14.0	30.9	11
NORTHERN AMERICA.....	217	1.5	22	9	6.5	15.8	10
LATIN AMERICA.......	253	2.8	41	13	7.5	15.1	12
Tropical South America......	135	2.9	43	14	3.9	10.1	10
Middle America.............	59	3.5	45	10	1.8	1.8	24
Temperate South America.....	36	1.8	28	10	1.1	3.0	9
Caribbean.................	23	2.4	38	14	0.7	0.2	99
ASIA..........	1,868	2.0	38	18	55.7	20.3	68
EAST ASIA.........	864	1.4	33	19	25.7	8.6	73
Mainland region............	710	1.4	35	21	21.1	8.2	64
Japan.....................	99	1.0	17	7	3.0	0.3	267
Other East Asia............	55	2.8	40	12	1.6	0.2	214
SOUTH ASIA........	1,004	2.5	43	18	30.0	11.7	64
Middle South Asia...........	681	2.5	43	18	20.4	5.0	101
South East Asia.............	255	2.6	43	17	7.6	3.3	57
South West Asia............	68	2.4	42	18	2.0	3.4	15
EUROPE..........	449	0.9	18	10	13.4	3.6	91
Western Europe.............	145	1.2	18	11	4.3	0.7	147
Southern Europe............	124	0.8	21	9	3.7	1.0	94
Eastern Europe.............	101	0.6	17	9	3.0	0.7	102
Northern Europe............	79	0.7	16	11	2.4	1.2	48
OCEANIA........	17.9	2.1	26	11	0.5	6.3	2
Australia and New Zealand...	14.3	2.0	22	9	0.4	5.9	2
Melanesia..................	2.5	2.4	44	20	0.1	0.4	5
Polynesia and Micronesia....	1.1	3.0	40	10	....	....	36
U.S.S.R........	233	1.4	22	7	6.9	16.5	10

Source: United Nations. Demographic Yearbook, 1966, Table 1.

3.2. Population Size and Growth in World Regions

The United Nations has prepared estimates of world population and growth for each continent and for world regions (subdivisions of the continents). Data for each continent and region are reported in Table 3-1. (Data for nations within each region are reported in Table 3-4.) From this table, and from the first paragraph in Section 3.1 it is readily seen that more than one half of the earth's inhabitants (56 percent) live in Asia (excluding USSR). Europe comprises a little less than one seventh of the world population, as do the

Americas combined. Africa, USSR, and Oceania together comprise the remaining one sixth. Columns 5 and 6 of Table 3-1 give the percentage of the population and the land area of each continental region.

A glance at column 3 of Table 3-1 reveals a very surprising fact. With respect to fertility behavior the world is divided into two distinct groups: the European region, which has moderately low birthrates—16 to 21 per thousand population—and the Afro-Asian-Latin American group, which has high birthrates—35 to 50 per thousand population. In this grouping, North America, the USSR, and Oceania tend to fall between the two clusters at 22 to 26 per thousand. This is closer to the European than to the Asian—African-Latin American group. It is a very surprising fact that at the present time there are no regions where the birthrates fall in the high 20's or low 30's. In other words, birthrates tend to be either very high or moderately low, with no regions falling in between.

To summarize, if we group the world regions according to their level of birthrates, we have the following division:

Low-Birthrate Regions

Europe (all regions)
Northern America
USSR
Oceania

High-Birthrate Regions

Asia
Africa
Middle America
South America

We see immediately that this list also rather neatly divides the world along economic lines into the "economically underdeveloped" and the "economically developed" or industrialized nations.[1] (Inasmuch as nearly all of the nations in the former group are in a highly dynamic condition of rapid economic development, we shall call them "developing" rather than "underdeveloped" nations.) The following

[1] There are, however, some outstanding exceptions. Argentina, Japan, Israel, Cyprus, and the Ryukyu Islands are now quite industrialized and resemble the European group more than they do the region in which they are located. For details, see the later sections of this chapter where the growth trends within each region are discussed.

social and economic characteristics are commonly associated with these two types of economies:

Industrialized Economies

High level of literacy and educational attainment
Material comfort: high per capita income
Predominantly urban
Dominant occupations: white collar, skilled, and government
Much communication and transportation
Much spatial mobility
Much use of electricity and fuel
Intensive medical care: high ratio of doctors and hospitals to population

Developing Economies

Low level of literacy
Poverty: low per capita income
Predominantly rural
Dominant occupations: farming, labor, and service
Low development of communication and transportation
Low spatial mobility
Low consumption of electricity and fuel
Insufficient medical care: low ratio of doctors and hospitals to population

We arrive, therefore, at the following generalization: at the present stage in the world's history there is a very strong inverse relationship between the level of economic development and the birthrate; *in the less developed nations the birthrates are high, whereas in the industrialized nations they are low.*

Let us weight the vital rates as of 1960-1966 for these regions by population size and compute a set of weighted average rates for the industrialized and the developing regions:

Rate	Developing regions (high birthrate) (A)	Industrialized regions (lower birthrate) (B)	Difference (A minus B)
Crude birthrate	39.3	20.1	19.2
Crude deathrate	18.1	9.0	9.1
Rate of reproductive change	21.2 per thousand	11.1 per thousand	10.1 per thousand

Like the birthrate, the death rates in the developing countries are much higher (more than twice as high as in the industrialized areas), and the rate of growth is also higher.

The reason why the developing nations are growing faster than the industrialized nations is that their death rates have fallen quickly, while their birthrates have remained higher or have declined only slightly. As will be shown in more detail later, high death rates may be reduced very quickly and at very moderate cost, whereas much more effort, time, and cost are required to lower birthrates. Inasmuch as the death rates in the developing nations are still quite high and inasmuch as all these nations have ambitious programs for improving sanitation, public health, and medical care, there is every reason to believe that in the years immediately ahead the death rates will continue to decline in this group. Unless the birthrates of the developing nations also begin to decline, and soon, the rate of world population growth will rise even higher!

The great demographic problem in the modern world may now be stated: *A disproportionate share of the current population growth in the world is concentrated in the poorer regions and is inundating them just as they are making a major effort to improve their economic condition. Thus not only is the world growing at an explosive pace, but its growth is concentrated in exactly those spots where it can be afforded least (from the point of view of reducing world poverty and raising levels of living).*

3.3. The History of World Population Growth

Any attempt to trace the history of population growth around the world must necessarily be based on very scanty and widely scattered shreds of evidence and a great deal of conjecture. It is difficult enough to arrive at good estimates of these facts for the present time, and as one goes backward in time even a mere half century the portion of the globe for which there is no census count at all increases very rapidly, and the data that are available very often are of dubious value. Only 150 years ago official national censuses were a rare and recent innovation, so that any effort to estimate the population for any part of the world for dates earlier than this must be based completely on scholarly sleuthing. The number and quality of clues available vary widely from one part of the earth to another. Nevertheless, this is a problem that has intrigued demographers from the time of Graunt, and much work has gone into compiling estimates of population size for

various parts of the earth for which there was no census.

The United Nations has carefully reviewed the information available for the period since 1920 and has prepared estimates for the world, by major regions, as shown in Table 3-2. For the period 1650 to 1900 a careful and scholarly review of the evidence available has been made by Walter F. Wilcox and A. M. Carr-Saunders (see references at end of chapter). Their estimates are almost identical for Northern America, Latin America, Europe, and Oceania and differ significantly (and then only by modest amounts) for Asia and Africa. Inasmuch as both estimates are widely accepted and there appears to be little basis for preferring one over the other, in order to present a single coherent picture we have averaged the Wilcox–Carr-Saunders estimates for the period 1650 to 1900. The consolidated figures are shown in the second panel of Table 3-2. These statistics pertain to the span of time that we commonly refer to as the industrial revolution. For a better understanding of the world trends, the regions have been grouped according to their present status as "industrialized" and "developing."

From Table 3-2 we learn that during the 310 years since 1650 the world has multiplied its population sixfold, from 0.5 billion to 3 billion. This is a phenomenal achievement, which stands in sharp contrast to the situation that must have existed during the many thousands of years of man's existence on the earth before this time. If we accept the United Nations conjecture that there were only 200 to 300 million persons on earth at the beginning of the Christian era, the growth from A.D. to 1600 could only have been very slow for the population to require 16 centuries to double. In the three centuries since 1650 the world population has doubled twice and, if current trends continue, will have doubled again by about 1980 to reach 4 billion, or eight times its size in 1650. In other words, *the rapid increase in the world's population began only recently.*

When the rates of growth over the past three centuries in the industrialized regions are compared with those in the developing

Table 3-2 Estimates of World Population by Regions: 1650 to 1960

Source of estimate and year	World total	Industrialized regions				Developing regions			
		Total	Europe and USSR	Northern America	Oceania	Total	Asia	Latin America	Africa
A. ESTIMATED POPULATION (millions)									
United Nations estimates									
1960................	3008	857	640	200	16.5	2151	1685	211	255
1950................	2509	756	576	267	13.0	1753	1384	162	207
1940................	2249	730	573	146	11.3	1519	1212	131	176
1930................	2015	671	532	135	10.4	1338	1072	109	157
1920................	1811	613	487	117	8.8	1198	966	91	141
Carr-Saunders-Wilcox estimates									
1900................	1590	510	423	81	6	1079	886	63	130
1850................	1131	302	274	26	2	829	698	33	98
1800................	912	200	192	6	2	712	596	21	95
1750................	711	147	144	1	2	564	456	10	98
1650................	507	106	103	1	2	402	292	10	100
B. IMPLIED AVERAGE ANNUAL RATES OF GROWTH									
1950-1960...........	1.83	1.26	1.06	1.82	2.41	2.07	1.99	2.68	2.11
1940-1950...........	1.10	0.35	0.05	1.35	1.41	1.44	1.34	2.15	1.64
1930-1940...........	1.11	0.85	0.75	0.79	0.83	1.28	1.24	1.86	1.15
1920-1930...........	1.07	0.91	0.89	1.44	1.68	1.11	1.05	1.82	1.08
1900-1920...........	0.65	0.92	0.71	1.86	1.93	0.52	0.43	1.86	0.41
1850-1900...........	0.68	1.05	0.87	2.30	2.22	0.53	0.48	1.30	0.57
1800-1850...........	0.43	0.83	0.71	2.98	0.00	0.31	0.32	0.91	0.06
1750-1800...........	0.50	0.62	0.58	3.65	0.00	0.47	0.54	1.50	-0.06
1650-1750...........	0.34	0.33	0.34	0.00	0.00	0.34	0.45	0.00	-0.02

Source: Data for 1920-1960 from United Nations, Demographic Yearbook, 1962, Table 2. Data for 1650-1900 are based on average of estimates by Carr-Saunders-Wilcox, as modified by United Nations and reported in The Determinants and Consequences of Population Trends, page 11.

48

Table 3-3   Comparison of Rates of Growth and Distribution of Population and Population Growth between Industrialized and Developing Regions of the world: 1650 to 2000

Interval	Average annual rate			Percent of world population in developing regions (A)	Percent of growth in population in developing regions (B)
	Industrialized regions (B)	Developing regions (A)	Difference (B–A)		
Estimated future:					
1975–2000.............	0.97	2.30	-1.33	79.4	88.7
1950–1975.............	1.16	1.94	-0.78	73.6	81.1
Estimated past:					
1950–1960.............	1.26	2.07	-0.81	69.9	79.8
1940–1950.............	0.35	1.44	-1.09	67.5	90.0
1930–1940.............	0.85	1.28	-0.43	66.4	77.3
1920–1930.............	0.91	1.11	-0.20	66.1	68.6
1900–1920.............	0.92	0.52	0.40	67.9	53.8
1850–1900.............	1.05	0.53	0.52	73.3	54.5
1800–1850.............	0.83	0.31	0.52	78.1	53.4
1750–1800.............	0.62	0.47	0.15	79.3	73.6
1650–1750.............	0.33	0.34	-0.01	79.3	79.4

Source: Table 3-2.   Estimated future derived from United Nations population projections.

regions, it becomes apparent that there has been another inversion: *during the earlier phase, and until 1900, the industrialized regions were growing at a faster rate than the developing regions, but since 1920 the developing nations have been growing faster than the industrialized nations.* Table 3-3 has been prepared to bring out the full extent of this change.

Even more important than past events are the estimates of probable future events. In 1958 the United Nations performed the monumental service of publishing estimates of the population of the world and its various regions by the year 2000, provided that recent trends continue, modified by only slight declines in fertility.[2] Table 3-3 reports these estimates for the industrialized and developing regions. These estimates were revised in *World Population Projects as Assessed in 1963*, Population Studies, No. 41 (New York: United Nations, 1966). Later discussions will make use of the revised projections, which differ only slightly from the totals shown in Table 3-3.

[2] United Nations, *The Future Growth of World Population*, Population Studies, No. 28 (New York: United Nations, 1958).

Unless there is some very drastic alleviation in the course of world population growth, the average annual amount of population increase will rise to unprecedented high levels in the developing countries, and this growth will be increasingly concentrated in the developing nations. The struggling economies of these nations will receive annual amounts of increase that will dwarf in size even the very great increments now accruing to them.

The growth curves of Figures 3-1 and 3-2 illustrate the great transformation that has taken place since 1650 and reveal just how swiftly population will grow if the current pace continues for more than a few decades. Demographers are reluctant even to speculate about the situation more than 40 years from now, because extending the current rate very much further than this yields results that seem almost nonsensical: no known present or presently foreseeable technology would be able to support the very large population that these estimates predict even at bare animallike subsistence.

All observers of this dramatic "demographic revolution" agree that a change is inevitable. But how this change will occur and what form

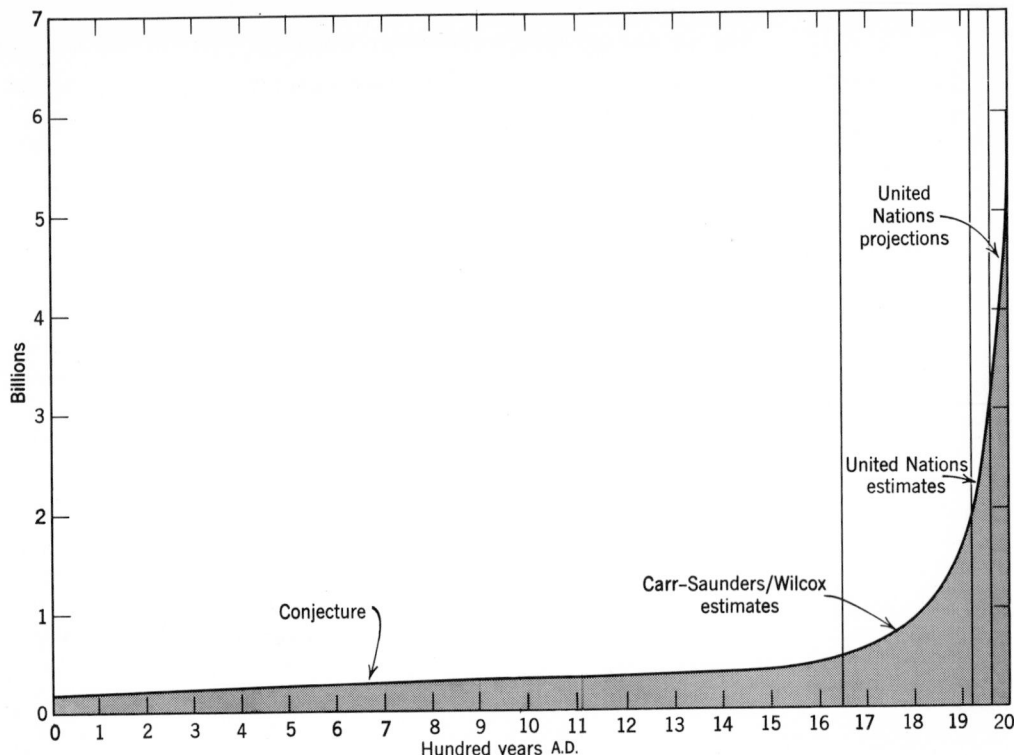

Figure 3-1 Trend of World Population Growth since the Beginning of the Christian Era.

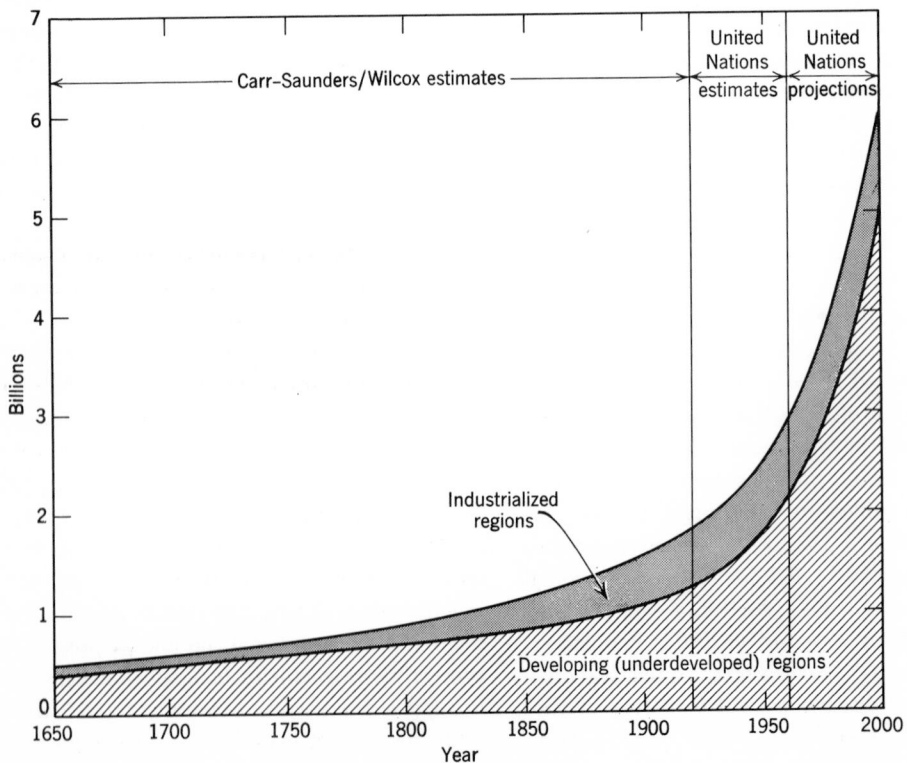

Figure 3-2 Trend of Population Growth in World Regions Currently Classified as "Industrialized" or "Developing (Underdeveloped)."

it will take—peaceful or other—is still a matter of conjecture. The inexorable demographic bookkeeping equation tells us that we can suspend growth only in two ways:

(a) by decreasing fertility or

(b) by increasing mortality.

To a steadily increasing share of the world's statesmen and intellectual and moral leaders the first of these alternatives appears to be a much simpler and more humane resolution of the probem, and more in accordance with the morals, aspirations, and beliefs of the great religions of the world. Men everywhere seek protection from premature and unnecessary death, and it is immoral to condone such death, even implicitly. Man is widely advertised in all his books about himself, both in biological and in social science, as being a highly flexible and adaptable creature who is capable of intelligently foreseeing dangers and taking appropriate action to avoid them without actually having to undergo them. We would expect the human race, when faced with this problem, to tamper with its birthrate and to lower fertility by some readjustment of its social system. This in fact appears to be the case. The tendency for a population to curtail fertility in order to avoid the unpleasant necessity of having growth curtailed by mortality may be called "the theory of demographic regulation."

3.4. The Theory of Demographic Regulation

This theory may be stated as follows: *Every society tends to keep its vital processes in a state of balance such that population will replenish losses from death and grow to an extent deemed desirable by collective norms. These norms are flexible and readjust rather promptly to changes in the ability of the economy to support population.* Almost everywhere this adjustment takes the form of first minimizing death rates to the greatest extent possible under the given state of technology and then regulating birthrates in such a way that the desired balance or rate of growth is accomplished. In societies where death rates are high there is comparatively little need for regulation of fertility, except to conform to the desires of individual couples,

because high fertility is required to offset high mortality. In technologically advanced societies, where death rates have been brought to a very low level, high birthrates come to be perceived by the collectivity as dysfunctional because they cause the size of the family to be larger than that deemed desirable by the prevailing norms. As a consequence, in such societies the regulation of fertility comes to be identified with group (as well as individual) welfare and becomes a positive good and a part of the culture. The steps by which this process of adjustment through fertility regulation takes place as death rates decline are such that fertility regulation inevitably lags behind mortality regulation (see below). As a direct result, during the period of adjustment there is a phase of rapid population growth. This growth may not be anticipated or desired by the group.

In a sense, this theory is merely an extension to man of the principle of the "balance of nature" as enunciated by Charles Darwin, but it is a sociological version of that principle. It has two facets that are missing in the balance-of-nature principle as it exerts its force on other forms of life: (a) the theory of demographic regulation asserts that the species itself has a norm that implies, at any given time, what constitutes "good" or "desirable" population trends and that this norm can and does change with changes in demographic conditions; (b) whereas the balance of nature is *imposed* by the rigors of the environment on other forms of life by the action of death rates, human societies tend to avoid this drastic type of control through starvation and the action of "fang and claw" by *imposing upon themselves* the desired balance by regulation of the birth rate. The avoidance of death is everywhere a social value; with only minor exceptions all societies readily accept practices that reduce mortality. Almost no society imposes death on members as a means of controlling growth, except by occasional use of infanticide and except for the indirect effects of war. Adaptive action has consisted primarily of attempting to change fertility behavior. The extent of this type of regulative action has increased steadily as populations have increased in size and density; and the intensity of the desire for strict regulation rises rapidly as a state of social maladjustment that threatens the standard of life, or life itself, is reached.

The phase of rapid population growth that emerges during the period of readjustment and regulation following mortality reduction is of extraordinary concern to demographers. Their studies have taught them that this phase is inevitable whenever death rates fall. In every such case the decline in the birthrate lags behind the decline in the death rate. This happens for two major reasons. First, the mortality reduction occurs first in time; it is the stimulus to which fertility regulation is a response. A finite *response time,* or demographic reaction time, is involved. Second, the adjustment of fertility to reduced mortality is not a simple automatic reflex, but is an entire *process* of social change, which consists of several different steps or phases. If death rates fall, the population must sense the fact by realizing that average family size is increasing. Merely attaining this awareness would require a period of several years, in the absence of demographic research that would announce the fact. Next, the implications of this change for individual and group welfare must be appreciated, and defined as undesirable. Finally, some socially acceptable solution (mode of fertility control) must be devised, diffused throughout the population, and adopted as socially acceptable behavior. Even under the most favorable circumstances substantial time would be required for a population to go through these steps. If there are strong forces resisting the regulation of fertility, the process is slowed even more. Resistance may exist either in the form of active opposition or in the form of cultural or bureaucratic inertia.

The amount by which the population grows during this phase is determined by the extent of the disparity between the birthrate and the death rate and by the number of years the disparity persists.

The theory of demographic regulation is premised on the assertion that every society has a set of norms that guide population growth. *These norms are not explicit opinions about desired population size or the optimum rate of growth. Instead, they are opinions concerning what constitutes the ideal size of completed family, or the number of surviving children a couple ought to have when it reaches the end of the reproductive period.* Completed family size is an entity that may be translated directly into population growth and is therefore a cultural value reflecting the "demographic cultural policy" of the society. Any society whose average members believe that it is good or desirable to have four or more surviving children either will grow rapidly or must face very high mortality. A society whose members agree to bear no more than two children is one that expects to suspend further growth, and expects very low mortality. Recent studies have demonstrated that these attitudes of ideal family size definitely exist and can be clearly verbalized by all but a small minority of the adult population.[3] Opinions about family size vary from person to person, so that the norm at any one time is an average about which there is a substantial amount of dispersion.

The effort required to achieve a particular average size of desired completed family varies with the mortality condition that exists. If death rates are high, many of the children will die before they reach adulthood, and a couple must "overbear" in order to attain the ideal family size. If death rates are very low, the couples need bear only the number of children they desire in their family of ideal size.

Readjustment to a condition of lower mortality therefore requires a double change in social attitudes:

1. A lowering of the ideal size of completed family to match the growth rate indicated by the present conditions.

2. A lowering of the estimated amount of "overbearing" of children necessary to overcome mortality and attain the desired family size.

Such a double adjustment cannot be arrived at instantaneously. It involves the solution by trial and error of what is actually a rather complex set of demographic calculations, and a

[3] For details of this phenomenon and a summary of recent research pertaining to it, see the chapters on fertility and family planning.

modification of the customs, attitudes, and outlook to conform to the new pattern. Moreover, the social organization itself must change to facilitate the carrying out of the changed ideals. For example, fertility control must be admitted as a normal part of health and medical services, and medical and health organizations must become prepared, technologically and psychologically, to offer such services. On the other hand, there is nothing in the situation that would prevent a rather rapid adjustment in the course of a very few years, or even months. The speed with which the change can take place depends on many factors, not the least of which are the intensity and the degree of uniformity of the old fertility attitudes and the extent of communication, discussion, and social consensus.

It may be presupposed that such a change can be accomplished today in much shorter time than in any previous period, because of the existence of several new factors that were not previously acting:

1. Modern demographic science can and does keep the national leadership fully informed of its present and prospective future population. As a result, there is a widespread social consciousness of the demographic balance and the need for regulation.

2. Modern methods of communication make it possible to circulate new ideas rapidly through the population. Awareness of the need for regulation can be rapidly diffused throughout the society. Information about how this regulation may be achieved can be diffused just as rapidly.

3. Social change has permeated society to such an extent that entire nations are now growing accustomed to making changes almost continuously. Resistance to change is being lowered everywhere.

4. The techniques for limiting fertility (contraception) are now numerous, varied, and cheap, so that every couple has available at least one method that will be both effective and acceptable to it. Further technological progress along these lines may be expected in the very near future.

5. Major and powerful institutional groups are placing the weight of their prestige and influence in favor of fertility regulation. They include medical groups, economic planners, religious groups, and political leaders and educators. The resistance to fertility regulation is rapidly becoming identified with an outmoded way of thinking and behaving.

Because of the combined action of these forces, it may be supposed that the efficiency and degree of success with which a population can realize its ideals in practice are much greater today than ever before and will increase even more as further advances are made in contraceptive technology and experience in its use. Within our lifetime we may see fertility control become an integral part of the morals and culture, with highly developed social organizations for maintaining it, in all societies of the world. In other words, the theory of demographic regulation is a positive assertion that nations, when faced with serious overpopulation, will undergo adaptive social change to lower fertility rates and in so doing will invent and adopt a technology of contraception. Moreover, this theory asserts that *modern man is able to foresee demographic catastrophe long before it arrives and takes adaptive action long before it is forced on him by the brute forces of nature.*

3.5. Population Growth in the Ancient World

During the many thousands of years of man's existence on the earth before the beginning of civilization, the population problem facing most communities was that of survival—to offset successfully the terrible attrition of death on their numbers. Under the conditions of life that must have prevailed before 3000 B.C., it was probably not unusual for more than one half of all infants to perish during the first year of life and for men of all ages to have substantially higher death rates than those found anywhere in the world today. When population did manage to grow, there was always the threat of famine, war, and epidemics. Such a situation is the only conjecture that is consistent with the facts. It has been reported in *Determinants and Consequences of Population Growth* that if man has lived on the earth for 100,000 years as supposed, the entire population of the world today can be the offspring of a mere half-dozen couples reproducing in such a way as to grow at the slight rate of 0.002 percent per year (1/100 of today's rate).[4] We are forced, therefore, to conclude that the human race has been required by circumstances of high mortality to reproduce at near-biological capacity and that a whole system of fertility-promoting practices has evolved as an integral part of every culture.

It is quite possible that food supply was a major factor limiting growth in ancient times, because primitive agriculture was almost certain to suffer from low productivity and frequent calamity because of climatic fluctuations. Not until ten to three centuries B.C. did the exploitation of productive agricultural land in fertile areas, such as the lower Nile, the lower Mesopotamian, Yellow River, and Indus valleys, make it possible for populations to grow rapidly, and it is probably at about this time that the human race could begin to be numbered in terms of millions. These ancient civilizations expanded and, despite many catastrophes of pestilence and war, managed to total the 200 to 300 million already reported as the estimated world population at the beginning of the Christian era. It is thought that at this time the Roman Empire had 50 to 55 million persons, India 100 to 140 million, and China about 60 million, with unestimated but small numbers in the largely unsettled areas of the Americas, Northern Europe, Oceania, and Northern Asia.

A recent study, *Histoire Générale de la Population Mondiale*, devotes nine chapters to reviewing population growth from prehistoric times to the year 1600. Although many discrete bits of informative demographic fact are assembled from a wide variety of sources, including summaries of work by other scholars, the authors did not and apparently were not able to synthesize the material into a systematic and integrated set of estimates for particular times and places.[5]

The specific facts and figures that are avail-

able from ancient records are often inconsistent with other data; ancient historians do not qualify as expert statisticians or demographers. Inasmuch as this field of scholarship has now been explored rather fully for at least a century, by historians of several different nationalities, it appears that the statistical study of world population must perforce begin about 1650. Estimates for particular nations or cities, especially for several in Europe, are available for earlier dates than this, but are too incomplete in their coverage to permit a precise charting of trends. Historical demography is a very strong branch of population study, and as this type of research accumulates we shall gradually learn more of the details of population events between the fifteenth century and the modern era. The bibliography at the end of this chapter cites several of the more recent explorations in historical demography.

It would be incorrect to leave the impression that in the ancient world there was no need for or attempts at demographic regulation. As has already been noted, the high death rates were in effect often related to a shortage of food. Since the dawn of history mankind seems to have been almost universally aware that pregnancy results from coitus. In a condition of chronic food shortage and frequent famine, it is not surprising that human reason would deduce that one solution to the problem would be to regulate the number of mouths to be fed. Numerous practices, many of them ceremonial with apparently little direct intent to reduce fertility, were extant in the most ancient of cultures. Anthropologists have reported in detail on similar practices in preliterate societies studied over the past two centuries. In addition to these ceremonies and indirect customs, there have been, almost universally throughout recorded history, conscious and deliberate efforts to avoid pregnancy or prevent birth.

Norman Himes opens his book, *Medical History of Contraception*, with the blunt assertion that "Man's attempts to control the increase in his numbers reach so far back into the dim past that it is impossible to discern their real origin. Some forms of limitation on the rate of increase are undoubtedly as old as the life history of man."[6] He notes that infanticide was widely practiced among a great many peoples

---

[4] United Nations, *Determinants and Consequences of Population Trends* (New York: United Nations, 1953), p. 5.

[5] Marcel R. Reinhard and Andrè Argengaud, *Histoire Générale de la Population Mondiale* (Paris: Editions Montchrestien, 1961).

of antiquity and that abortion is a very ancient art with practitioners all over the globe. *Coitus interruptus* also appears to have been known and used on all continents, long before Biblical times when Onan was slain by the Lord for practicing it. He also points out that delayed marriage, celibacy, sex taboos, limitations on the time and frequency of coitus, prepuberty coition, sex perversions, and prolonged lactation were a part of many primitive cultures, either singly or in combination, and tended to lower fertility whether or not practiced for this purpose. Himes was also able to cite groups that used tampons made of seaweed or other vegetable matter (or even of animal dung) and inserted into the vagina to block the entrance of semen into the uterus. He also finds in very ancient cultures the beginning of chemical contraception in the insertion into the vagina of salty, acidic, greasy, or gummy substances that have the effect of destroying sperm or diminishing their motility. Each tribe appears to have had a great multiplicity of recipes, many of which were useless because they were either of a magical nature or ineffective. Moreover, knowledge of the techniques that were reliable seems to have been limited to a small part of the population. Medical prescriptions for contraceptives, consciously concocted and employed to avoid conception or to achieve indefinite sterility, have been found in fragments of written medical lore from ancient Egypt, Palestine, Greece, and Rome. Himes dedicates his book to Soranos, a Roman gynecologist who practiced medicine in the second century of our era and wrote prescriptions that, if known and accepted by a modern population, would permit it to attain a moderately low birthrate. Even in China, India and Japan—where great stress is placed on the bearing of sons, the extended family, and ancestor worship—there is evidence that the desire for fertility limitation and efforts to accomplish it extend far back into ancient times.[7] The situation in which a wife attains the age of about thirty and finds herself in frail and failing health as a direct

result of closely spaced childbearing creates a desire to avoid further childbearing and a very intense longing for sterility or contraception. This situation is recognized in the most ancient of manuscripts, and it has spontaneously arisen in all cultures and all human history. In concluding his review of contraception before the eighteenth century Himes observes:

"The persistence of the folk practices detailed above suggests additional proof of the main thesis of this book: that the human race has in all ages and in all geographical locations *desired* to control its own fertility; that while women have wanted babies, they have wanted them when they wanted them. And they have wanted neither too few nor too many. . . . What is new is not the desire for prevention, but effective harmless means of achieving it on a grand scale. The older effective techniques were never until recently democratically diffused; and even that process is still going on."[8]

3.6. The Process of Demographic Transition

When viewed from the perspective of the history described above, it appears that each of the world's populations is being called upon to undergo a process that demographers term "the demographic transition." In this process death rates are lowered through conquest of disease, and then fertility rates are readjusted by lowering them in order to avoid runaway population growth. Before the transition begins there is an initial condition of high birthrates counterbalanced by high death rates, and the population is in a state of stationary numbers or at best very slow growth. As public health and medical technology brings about a fall in the death rate the population begins to grow more rapidly, because birthrates lag behind and remain at their former high level. Eventually by the process of demographic regulation, described in the preceding section, the birthrate is lowered and again brought into balance with the death rate. This transition from a condition of high vital rates to that of low vital rates is one of the phenomena of greatest research interest to demographers and is beyond any doubt one of the great events of human history. As we shall see, *the entire*

[6] Norman E. Himes, *Medical History of Contraception* (New York: Gamut Press, 1936, reprinted in 1963).
[7] *Ibid.*, pp. 88–92.

[8] *Ibid.*, p. 185.

world is in its grip; there is no major population on earth that has not entered upon or already passed through the early stages of this process. As yet there are only two or three major populations on earth that may be said to have entirely completed it.

In discussing the demographic transition, demographers have spoken of "phases" or "stages." Although there has been some divergence in meaning, they have referred essentially to the demographic balance of vital rates that exists (*a*) *before,* (*b*) *during,* and (*c*) *after* the transition. Thus we may categorize all populations of the world according to this threefold classification, recognizing substages of the middle stage.

I. *Pretransitional*—little regulation or control either of death rates or of birthrates, with a consequent condition of high vital rates but almost zero growth.

II. *Transitional*—death rates and birthrates in process of being lowered, with death rates lower than birthrates, resulting in moderate-to-rapid growth. Three types of situations may be recognized:

(*a*) *Early transitional*—death rates are being lowered but birthrates remain high; in fact, they may rise even higher because of the improved health of the childbearing population.

(*b*) *Midtransitional*—death rates and birthrates both are being lowered, with birthrates higher than death rates.

(*c*) *Late transitional*—death rates are low and unchanging or declining only slightly, and birthrates are moderate to low and fluctuating or declining. Knowledge of contraceptive methods is widely diffused throughout the population.

III. *Posttransitional*—death rates and birthrates both are low; knowledge of contraceptive methods is almost universally diffused and used as needed to keep vital rates in near balance; growth is nearly zero or quite low on a long-term basis.

The abstract formulation of the general pattern of demographic transition was developed independently by Warren S. Thompson and Frank W. Notestein, and the term "demographic transition" has been taken from the writings of the latter. In the *American Journal of Sociology,* in 1929, and again in his book *Plenty of People* Thompson listed three classes of nations, according to the degree of control they had achieved over their vital rates. The order of his ranking is the reverse of the outline above:

Class I. Nations where there is a large measure of control over both death rates and birthrates.

Class II. Nations where both birthrates and death rates have been declining in recent decades, but the death rate has declined more rapidly than the birthrate.

Class III. Nations where neither the death rate nor the birthrate has come under reasonably secure control.[9]

In a classic article, "Population—The Long View," Frank W. Notestein outlined a similar typology of populations (also ranked in the reverse order to the system outlined above), defined as follows:[10]

Type I. *Incipient decline*—populations in which fertility has fallen below the replacement level or is near and rapidly approaching that level.

Type II. *Transitional growth*—populations in which birth and death rates are still high and growth is rapid, but the decline in the birthrate is well established. (Professor Notestein presumes a prior decline in the death rate.)

Type III. *High growth potential*—populations in which mortality is high and variable, while fertility is high and has shown no evidence of downward trend. In these populations rapid growth is to be expected just as soon as technical developments make possible a decline in mortality.

Although the theory of the process of demographic transition sounds highly plausible, before accepting it uncritically we should examine some of the empirical evidence on which it is

[9] Warren S. Thompson, "Population," *American Journal of Sociology,* **34** (May 1929), pp. 959–975; *Plenty of People* (Lancaster, Pa.: The Jacques Cattell Press, 1944), pp. 89–98.

[10] Frank W. Notestein, "Population—the Long View," in Theodore W. Schultz (ed.), *Food for the World* (Chicago: University of Chicago Press, 1945), pp. 36–57.

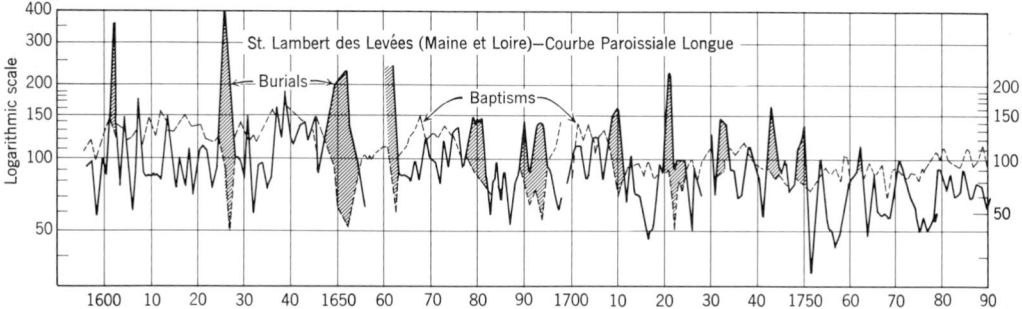

Figure 3-3   Number of Baptisms and Burials for the French Parish of St. Lambert des Levées during the Seventeenth and Eighteenth Centuries. SOURCE: Adapted from Marcel R. Reinhard and André Armengaud, *Histoire Général de la Population Mondiale* (Paris: Editions Montchrestien, 1961), p.126.

based. In other words, we need to ask ourselves, how well does it fit the facts?

Unfortunately, reliable population statistics do not extend far enough into history to permit a full documentation of the process in its first stages. Instead, we must rely on fragmentary data and deduction. Data about pretransitional populations are especially scanty: by the time a reliable system of vital registration is established in a population, death rates invariably are already in the process of decline in that population. This occurs because the technology of data collection comes at a later stage in economic development and follows well behind the introduction of public health and a minimal amount of modern medical care.

Almost the only source of information for such populations are the ancient parish registers of baptisms and burials that were sometimes kept with extraordinary care by religious clerks. In Italy, Spain, and France some of these registers extend backward into the Middle Ages. In parishes where there is little net migration the count of christenings and burials can give a rough indication of the demographic conditions that must have prevailed. Since the degree of completeness of these records is directly proportional to the degree of interest that particular religious administrators maintained in them as well as to the completeness with which entries were made for persons of all social ranks, there is much latitude for defects in quality and for fluctuations in quality over time. There is also the matter of variations in the method of recording birth and death of infants who live only a few hours or a few days, especially for

the large mass of serfs and peasants. Figure 3-3 shows the baptismal and burial data for a small French parish, St. Lambert des Levées, which span two centuries from 1590 to 1790, reported by Reinhard and Armengaud.[11] We may study these bits of data as an indication of the demographic situation in Europe during the pretransitional and early transitional stages. This long-time series indicates the following outstanding facts:

1. Births and deaths were about equal in number when averaged over several years. This means that population growth fluctuated about zero.

2. The number of deaths fluctuated widely from year to year, presumably because of periodic epidemics and famines.

3. The annual number of births and deaths remained almost constant when averaged over a span of several years. This signifies in still another way that the population was stationary in size, for if it had been growing, the number of vital events would have gradually risen, even though the rates may have remained constant.

Figure 3-3 is thought to be a typical representation of demographic conditions in pretransitional populations. Similar conditions must have existed over the entire earth for many thousands of years before the dawn of civilization.

Attempts to explain the wide year-to-year fluctuations in such data have almost always pointed to food shortage or outright famine

[11] Marcel R. Reinhard and André Armengaud, *Histoire Générale de la Population Mondiale* (Paris: Editions Montchrestien, 1961).

and to outbreaks of epidemics as the major causes. For example, in presenting the data of Figure 3-3, Reinhard and Armengaud note that there is a rough correlation between the level of the death rate and the price of grain. During years of poor harvest there was much speculation in grain, and prices rose. It is during years of high grain prices that death rates also tend to be high. The decimating effect of the great plagues during the seventeenth century also contributed to the wide fluctuations in deaths in this period.

A close study of the graph reveals also that deaths are unusually few in the year or years immediately following a peak in mortality. This effect, widely observed also in modern times, seems to result from the premature removal from the population of people in poor health ("impaired lives" in the language of actuaries). It means that the long-run effect of sudden mortality is smaller than it would seem at first glance. The sweeping away of impaired lives during times of hunger or epidemic makes the surviving population younger in age composition and more vigorous on an average. But famine and hunger themselves tend to impair lives, so that the effect is only temporary.

Birthrates also tend to fluctuate inversely with mortality, with a lag of a year or slightly less. Epidemics and famines are no respecters of pregnant women, and deaths of pregnant women obviously reduce fertility. Also, certain types of epidemics tend to cause a substantial increase in the number of miscarriages, spontaneous abortions, and stillbirths. Finally, during times of mass sickness or hunger we could expect a slackening of sex activity and a possible reduction in the rate of conceptions. Consequently, we can regard the pretransitional stage of demographic conditions as one of highly fluctuating death rates with a tendency toward a corresponding inverse fluctuation in the birthrate, with a short lag.

It would be incorrect to claim that the situation depicted in Figure 3-3 existed uniformly over the world until about 1650. Even in very ancient times there appear to have been rather long periods when mortality remained lower than fertility and population grew rapidly—only

to be nullified later by famine or epidemic and especially by the direct and indirect effects of war. During the span from 2000 B.C. to the beginning of our era the settlements of Mesopotamia, Egypt, Greece, China, India, and Rome appear to have enjoyed an adequate food supply for sustained periods, during which population grew by impressive amounts. Invasion and conquest from without rather than population collapse within were major forces in the fall of particular dynasties. A very good case can be constructed for claiming that the true beginning of the transitional stage of demographic balance coincides with the dawn of civilization and that civilization itself —the invention of bronze and iron tools, the domestication of animals, the practice of agriculture, and the use of the sailing ship for trade in fixed settlements—ushered in the first elements of what we call the early transitional stage.

More and more war and its sequelae became responsible for keeping down population growth in Asia Minor, North Africa, and Europe. Although famine was not unknown and food shortages were chronic occurrences, the food supply was more adequate and better assured even in feudal Europe than it could have been in the collection and hunting economies of prehistory. Moreover, the first inroads on mortality were made by these ancients through the beginnings of medicine, controlled water supplies, and other crude public health regulations. Although the impact of technology on the death rate was small and often completely ineffectual, it was nevertheless significant. The delicate balance between birth and death need be tipped only ever so slightly against mortality for a small but cumulatively significant thrust of population growth to ensue. And the first tipping of the balance through technological advance was made at least 5000 years ago. From this perspective, which we believe to be valid, *the demographic transition is coterminous with civilization,* and the task of achieving and maintaining a *peaceful* balance between birth and death rates is a problem that is much older than the industrial revolution.

However, it cannot be emphasized too

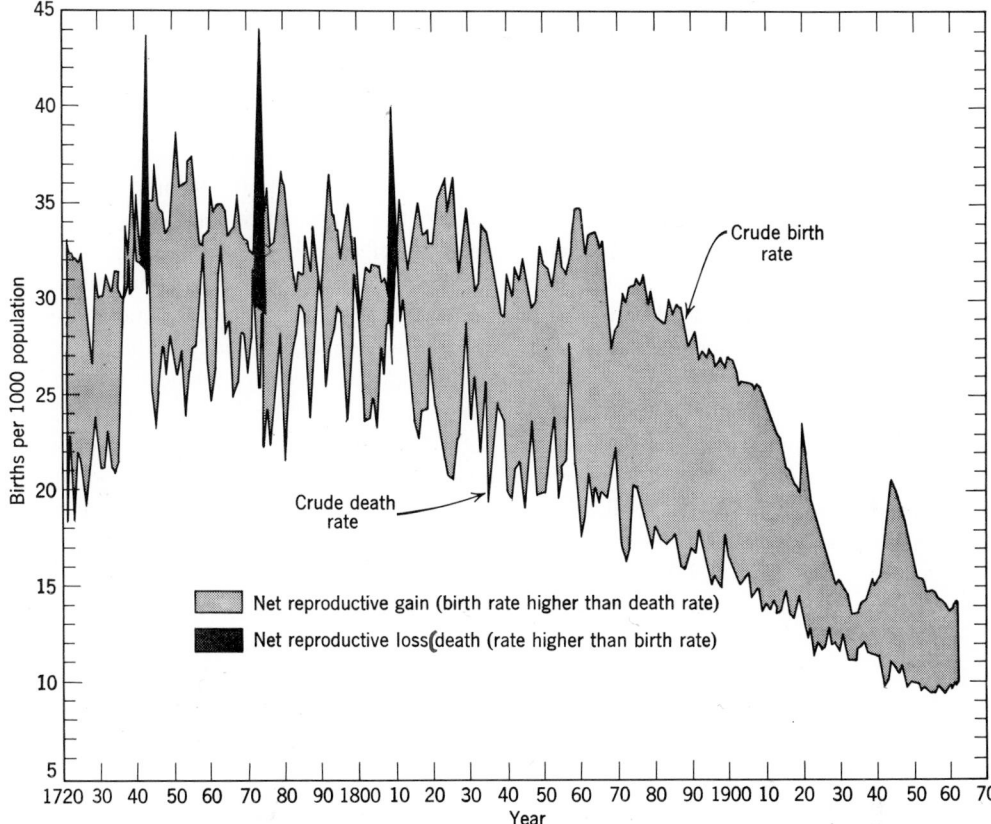

Figure 3-4   Crude Birthrates and Crude Death Rates for Sweden: 1720 to 1962.
SOURCE: *Historisk Statistik för Sverige, Befolkning: 1720–1950.* (Stockholm: Statistiska
Centralbyrän, 1955). United Nations, *Demographic Yearbook, 1962.*

strongly that the industrial revolution, which swept over Europe in the seventeenth and eighteenth centuries, had the incidental side effect of greatly accelerating the pace of population growth by reducing mortality. The harnessing of science to improve the physical conditions of life became a major cultural trait of Western and Northwestern Europe. The year-to-year fluctuations in deaths diminished, and the death rates themselves began to fall. Meanwhile, conditions for fertility may have improved because the population was healthier, so that birthrates may even have risen somewhat. A close examination of the right-hand portion of Figure 3-3, for the years following 1750, reveals a marked change in the historic pattern that had persisted for a century and a half. Deaths have clearly fallen below births and are showing less violent fluctuations; births, on the other hand, appear to be rising—

connoting population growth. Although these are data for only one tiny village for which parish records happen to be available, they illustrate the marked change in the pace of the demographic transition that took place between 1700 and 1800.

More reliable evidence of the impact of the industrial revolution on population growth is provided in Figure 3-4, which reports birth and death rates for Sweden from 1720 to the present. Fortunately, remarkably complete parish registers were kept in Sweden, and from them it has been possible to compile a long, unbroken chain of statistics spanning nearly two and one-half centuries. By 1720 Sweden was enjoying the benefits of her maritime commerce and industries. Population clearly was growing rapidly in most years, with birthrates in the low 30's and average death rates in the low 20's. Nevertheless, the chart shows just how incomplete the control over death rates was in the early years of the industrial revolution. There are frequent peaks of high mortality, which result in a greater number of deaths than of births in isolated years. Presumably, if we were able to extend these data backward to 1600, the farther back we could go the more erratic would be the death rate, the more frequent the years when deaths exceeded births, and the narrower the range between the birth and death rates, on an average. Throughout the nineteenth century death rates declined much more rapidly than birthrates, with the result that the size of the population increased much more rapidly than before. (Most of this growth was drained off by emigration to the New World.) Following the classification that has been presented, we can say definitely that from 1800 until 1925 Sweden was in the midtransitional phase and that since 1925 she has been in the late transitional phase.

As nearly as can be determined, a similar chain of events took place in France, England, Belgium, and the other nations of Western and Northern Europe. In fact, every nation in this region, and even the overseas descendants of these nationality groups, has followed approximately the same demographic pattern. As is shown in the next section, Central Europe and Southern Europe also have traveled the same demographic route, as have nations in Asia, Latin America, and Africa. *It is this uniformity that makes it seem highly plausible that the hypothesis of demographic transition is valid.* The conditions under which the various nations of Europe entered the modern scene were quite diverse, yet demographically speaking the end results were amazingly similar. As we have tried to indicate, we do not regard this as evolutionary predestination, but as a predictable sociological adjustment to an inexorable force. It would seem wholly appropriate to apply this set of concepts to the developing nations today and to presume that they are in the midstream of a similar process and will eventually achieve a new equilibrium. The hypothesis of the demographic transition thus appears to be a valid perspective from which to view the entire sweep of the demographic history of the world, and of every population group within it, *provided one presupposes the operation of the more basic process of demographic regulation.*

The beginning of very rapid population growth about 1650 seems to be closely linked in time and causally to the beginning of manufacture, trade, commerce, and burgeoning technology. Ability to buy, sell, and transport food greatly reduced famines and malnutrition. Sanitation and vaccines against infectious diseases reduced epidemics, especially in the nineteenth century. More recently, medical science has removed most of the hazards of childbirth, both for mother and child, and greatly increased the proportion of females who survive through the childbearing period. The net result of these improvements in medical science has been to cause the death rate to decline steadily and rather swiftly, especially between 1850 and 1950. During the half century 1880 to 1930 births fell just as rapidly.

By making this demographic readjustment, Europe avoided an explosion in population growth. Growth was quite rapid, but it did not destroy economic advancement. Emigration to the New World provided a safety valve, but it may also have greatly lengthened the span of time required for birthrates to decline. Fertility control started early and paralleled each step of economic development. Today birth and death rates are nearly equal and the rate of growth is slow. As yet no nation, with the possible exception of Sweden, Romania, Hungary, Belgium, Bulgaria, and Japan, has entered the posttransitional phase, where deaths and births are equal in number on a long-term basis and population growth over the next generation is destined to be zero. The nations mentioned above are very close to this state, if they have not already achieved it, and several others are approaching it.

Limitations of the Demographic Transition Hypothesis. It must be emphasized that the theory of demographic transition is not intended to be a detailed and refined "law of population growth," but is only an empirical generalization of the world's demographic history. In later chapters we present evidence that there has been much variation between countries in the details by which birthrates and death rates have changed in relation to each other and with respect to time. Consequently, there are no useful averages. There is no "typical" length of time required for the transition. There is no typical amount of average lag in the birthrate behind the death rate. There is no absolute level to which mortality must fall—nor any absolute time that it must remain there—to "trigger" a fall in fertility. Not only is there great variation among these measurements for the nations of Europe and Northern America, but there is a great difference in trend between populations that were in the early stages of the transition in 1770 and those that are in the early stages of the transition two centuries later, in 1970. Many factors are operating today that were almost absent in the earlier period, and many forces that were very strong in the earlier period are quite weak or absent today.

In like fashion, efforts to arrive at a single set of "causes" for the decline in mortality and fertility (especially the latter) are likely to end in disappointment. It is not yet clear what were the necessary and the sufficient conditions for fertility decline in Europe and North America—and what conditions were simple time-correlated epiphenomena. It is not yet clear which (if any) of the factors that may prove to have been "causal" in the case of the Western nations will also be equally effective in the developing nations. It is not impossible that other factors, not previously considered important, may be highly effective in reducing fertility in nations with high birthrates.

Finally, there is no assurance that the demographic transition, as stated, will travel all of the way and directly to the posttransitional phase. It is quite possible for war or revolution to cause a population to return to an earlier stage. As many nations have recently learned, it is also quite possible for a population that is in the late transitional stage to undergo a lengthy "baby boom." It is even possible for a posttransitional population to revert suddenly to the transitional type by increasing its birthrate in response to some change in its economic, social, or psychological climate. In fact, inasmuch as no population can as yet be said

to be irrevocably in the posttransitional stage and inasmuch as there is such wide variation in population behavior—both over time and between nations at the same time—the process of demographic transition becomes only a general assertion of faith that ultimately every population must bring its birth and death rates into balance and that if it does not do this voluntarily, it will be done for it by external forces. Although the factual evidence now available supports this general assertion, as yet there is no neat theory specifying how this is to be done at any particular time or place or predicting the speed and the means by which it may be done.

THE CURRENT POPULATION GROWTH SITUATION IN EACH OF THE WORLD REGIONS

With the twin theories of demographic regulation and demographic transition established, we can proceed to take a closer look at current and recent population growth in each nation of the world. Table 3-4 reports the following basic measures for every nation for which reliable data are available or an approximate estimate can be made:

1. Estimated midyear population in 1965
2. Average annual rate of growth
3. Crude birthrate
4. Crude death rate
5. Rate of reproductive change
6. Density per square kilometer

The table is divided into sections by the world regions reported in Table 3-1 and here arranged in alphabetical order. This rather lengthy table brings together a great mass of information that is widely scattered in several sources and incorporates estimates that are intended as substitutes for deficient statistics. It is intended to be as nearly a complete, accurate, and succinct report of current international growth conditions as can be assembled with information now available. It should be used as a source of reference in reading later chapters.

In studying Table 3-4 the reader should keep in mind that the vital rates reported are *crude* rates and that differences in age composition between nations will account for at

Table 3-4   Current Population Growth Rates in Major Nations of the World.

Nations	Estimated midyear population 1965 (in thousands)	Average annual rate of growth	Vital rates — Crude birth rates	Vital rates — Crude death rates	Vital rates — Rate of repro-ductive change	Density per square kilometer 1965
WESTERN EUROPE						
Austria......................	7,255	0.5	17.9	13.0	4.9	87
Belgium......................	9,464	0.6	16.4	12.1	4.3	310
France.......................	48,922	1.3	17.7	11.1	6.6	89
Germany, F. Rep..............	56,839	1.3	17.9	11.2	6.7	229
Luxembourg...................	331	0.9	16.0	12.3	3.7	128
Netherlands..................	12,292	1.4	19.9	8.0	11.9	366
Switzerland..................	5,945	1.9	18.8	9.3	9.5	144
West Berlin..................	2,202	-0.1	11.8	18.0	- 6.2	4578
NORTHERN EUROPE						
Channel Islands..............	114	0.8	18.8	12.7	6.1	585
Denmark......................	4,758	0.8	18.0	10.1	7.9	110
Finland......................	4,612	0.8	16.9	9.6	7.3	14
Iceland......................	192	1.9	24.7	6.7	18.0	2
Ireland......................	2,873	0.1	22.1	11.5	10.6	41
Norway.......................	3,723	0.8	17.5	9.1	8.4	11
Sweden.......................	7,734	0.6	15.9	10.1	5.8	17
United Kingdom...............	54,595	0.7	18.3	11.5	6.8	224
England and Wales............	47,884	0.8	18.1	11.5	6.6	317
Northern Ireland.............	1,471	0.7	23.1	10.6	12.5	104
Scotland.....................	5,239	0.1	19.3	12.1	7.2	67
EASTERN EUROPE						
Bulgaria.....................	8,200	0.9	15.3	8.2	7.1	74
Czechoslovakia...............	14,159	0.7	16.4	10.0	6.4	111
Eastern Germany..............	16,000	-0.2	16.5	13.4	3.1	148
Hungary......................	10,148	0.4	13.1	10.7	2.4	109
Poland.......................	31,496	1.3	17.3	7.4	9.9	101
Romania......................	19,027	0.8	14.6	8.6	6.0	80
East Berlin..................	1,100	(-0.7)	(17.0)	(16.6)	(- 0.4)	2730
SOUTHERN EUROPE						
Albania......................	1,865	3.1	35.2	9.0	26.2	65
Greece.......................	8,551	0.6	17.7	7.9	9.8	65
Italy........................	51,576	0.7	19.2	10.0	9.2	171
Malta........................	319	-0.1	17.6	9.4	8.2	1010
Portugal.....................	9,199	0.8	22.9	10.3	12.6	100
Spain........................	31,604	0.8	21.3	8.7	12.6	63
Yugoslavia...................	19,508	1.1	20.9	8.7	12.2	76
UNION OF SOVIET SOCIALIST REPUBLICS	230,600	1.6	18.4	7.3	11.1	10
WESTERN AFRICA						
Cape Verde Islands...........	232	2.5	41.5	10.3	(29.2)	58
Dahomey......................	2,365	2.9	(55.0)	(27.0)	(28.0)	21
Gambia.......................	330	2.0	....	....	....	29
Ghana........................	7,740	2.7	(53.5)	....	....	32
Guinea.......................	3,500	2.7	(54.3)	36.0	(10.0)	14
Ivory Coast..................	3,835	3.1	(49.1)	(33.3)	(22.8)	12
Liberia......................	1,070	1.6	....	....	....	10
Mali.........................	4,576	2.2	(56.0)	(28.0)	(28.0)	4
Mauritania...................	1,050	1.6	....	....	....	1
Niger........................	3,328	3.2	(59.0)	(32.0)	(27.0)	3
Nigeria......................	57,500	2.0	(50.7)	....	....	62
Portugese Guinea.............	527	0.2	(47.0)	....	....	15
Senegal......................	3,490	2.3	(43.3)	(16.7)	(26.6)	18
Sierra Leone.................	2,290	2.1	....	....	....	32
Togo.........................	1,638	2.7	(55.0)	(29.0)	(26.0)	29
Upper Volta..................	4,858	2.5	(49.0)	(30.5)	(18.6)	18

Table 3-4 (Continued)

Nations	Estimated midyear population 1965 (in thousands)	Average annual rate of growth	Vital rates			Density per square kilometer 1965
			Crude birth rates	Crude death rates	Rate of repro- ductive change	
EASTERN AFRICA						
Burundi..........................	3,210	2.0	(46.6)	(17.4)	(29.2)	115
Comoro Islands...................	220	2.7	....	....	....	101
Ethiopia.........................	22,600	1.7	....	....	....	18
French Somaliland................	81	...	....	....	....	4
Kenya............................	9,365	2.9	(49.7)	....	....	16
Madagascar.......................	6,420	3.3	(42.8)	....	....	11
Malawi...........................	3,940	2.4	....	....	....	33
Mauritius........................	741	2.8	35.5	8.6	26.9	397
Mozambique.......................	6,956	1.3	(47.0)	....	....	9
Reunion..........................	397	3.3	42.5	9.5	33.0	158
Rwanda...........................	3,110	3.1	(52.0)	(13.7)	(38.3)	118
Somalia..........................	2,500	3.4	....	....	....	4
Southern Rhodesia................	4,260	3.2	(56.8)	(32.2)	(24.6)	11
Uganda...........................	7,551	2.5	(47.5)	(20.0)	(22.0)	32
United Republic of Tanzania......	10,515	1.9	(47.0)	(25.0)	(22.0)	11
Zambia...........................	3,710	2.9	....	....	....	5
NORTHERN AFRICA						
Algeria..........................	11,871	1.9	(46.5)	....	....	5
Libya............................	1,617	3.7	(43.0)	....	....	1
Morocco..........................	13,323	2.8	(47.0)	....	....	30
Spanish North Africa.............	158	0.8	(20.0)	(7.3)	(12.7)	4943
Sudan............................	13,540	2.8	(54.9)	(18.5)	(33.2)	5
Tunisia..........................	4,414	1.2	45.1	(10.7)	(32.5)	27
United Arab Republic.............	29,600	2.6	(42.3)	(20.0)	(25.0)	30
MIDDLE AFRICA						
Angola...........................	5,154	1.4	(49.0)	....	....	4
Cameroon.........................	5,229	2.2	(44.0)	....	....	11
Central African Republic.........	1,352	2.2	(48.0)	(30.0)	(18.0)	2
Chad.............................	3,307	1.5	....	....	....	3
Congo (Brazzaville)..............	840	1.6	(47.7)	(27.0)	(20.0)	2
Congo (Democratic Republuc of)...	15,627	2.1	(42.8)	(20.0)	(23.0)	7
Equatorial Guinea................	267	1.9	....	....	....	10
Gabon............................	463	1.5	(38.0)	(28.0)	(10.0)	2
SOUTHERN AFRICA						
Basutoland (now Lesotho).........	838	2.9	(49.5)	(23.0)	(17.0)	28
Bechuanaland (now Botswana)......	559	3.0	....	....	....	1
South Africa.....................	17,867	2.4	46.1	15.8	30.3	15
South West Africa................	574	2.0	....	....	....	1
Swaziland........................	375	...	....	....	....	22
AUSTRALIA AND NEW ZEALAND						
Australia........................	11,360	2.1	19.6	8.8	10.8	1
New Zealand......................	2,640	2.1	22.8	8.7	14.1	10
British Solomn Islands...........	137	2.0	....	....	....	5
New Caledonia....................	91	2.7	(35.2)	....	....	5
New Guinea.......................	1,576	2.3	32.2(a)	4.6(a)	27.6(a)	7
New Hebrides.....................	68	2.9	....	....	....	5
Papua............................	573	2.5	32.1(a)	2.2(a)	29.9(a)	3
POLYNESIA AND MICHONESIA						
American Samoa...................	21	...	(40.6)	(5.3)	(37.1)	109
Cook Islands.....................	21	3.1	40.8	7.0	33.8	90
Fiji Islands.....................	464	3.4	35.9	...	...	26
French Polynesia.................	88	2.3	(43.0)	(10.5)	(32.5)	22
Gilbert and Ellice Island........	52	2.5	....	....	....	59
Guam.............................	77	2.0	33.0	4.4	28.6	139
Pacific Islands..................	91	3.0	(42.3)	(5.3)	(31.9)	51
Tonga............................	73	2.8	(42.3)	....	....	104
Western Samoa....................	126	2.9	(48.6)	....	....	44

Table 3-4   *(Continued)*

Nations	Estimated midyear population 1965 (in thousands)	Average annual rate of growth	Vital rates			Density per square kilometer 1965
			Crude birth rates	Crude death rates	Rate of repro- ductive change	
NORTHERN AMERICA						
Bermuda..........................	48	1.7	23.1	7.4	15.7	913
Canada...........................	19,604	2.0	21.4	7.6	13.8	2
Greenland........................	40	4.2	(40.9)	(9.9)	(37.7)	0
United States (including Hawaii)	194,572	1.5	19.4	9.4	10.0	21
TROPICAL SOUTH AMERICA						
Bolivia..........................	3,697	1.4	(43.6)	(26.0)	(17.0)	3
Brazil...........................	82,222	3.0	(44.6)	(20.6)	(22.4)	10
Guyana...........................	647	2.8	39.7	7.6	32.1	3
Colombia.........................	18,068	3.2	(42.1)	....	....	16
Ecuador..........................	5,084	3.2	(45.2)	(22.0)	(22.0)	18
French Guinea....................	36	2.4	(50.0)	(15.0)	(35.0)	0
Peru.............................	11,650	3.0	(45.9)	(26.0)	(20.0)	9
Surinam..........................	335	4.4	(44.5)	(8.2)	(36.3)	2
Venezuela........................	8,722	3.6	(45.8)	(12.0)	(33.0)	10
MIDDLE AMERICAN (Mainland)						
British Honduras................	106	3.1	(44.7)	(7.8)	(36.9)	5
Canal Zone......................	54	3.2	12.8	2.9	9.9	38
Costa Rica......................	1,433	4.2	40.5	8.1	32.4	28
El Salvador.....................	2,928	3.4	46.5	10.5	36.0	137
Guatemala.......................	4,438	3.1	43.5	16.8	26.7	41
Honduras........................	2,284	3.3	(50.8)	(9.5)	(35.8)	20
Mexico..........................	42,689	3.4	44.2	9.5	34.7	22
Nicaragua.......................	1,655	3.2	(44.8)	....	....	13
Panama..........................	1,246	3.2	39.4	(8.2)	(33.1)	16
TEMPERATE SOUTH AMERICA						
Argentina.......................	22,352	1.6	21.5	8.2	13.3	8
Chile...........................	8,567	2.3	(35.4)	(11.7)	(22.8)	11
Paraguay........................	2,030	2.7	(39.8)	(19.0)	(24.0)	5
Uruguay.........................	2,715	1.4	22.0	(9.0)	(13.0)	15
CARIBBEAN						
Antigua.........................	57	1.1	30.4	8.4	22.0	130
Bahama Islands..................	136	4.1	32.7	6.4	26.3	12
Barbados........................	244	1.0	26.1	7.8	18.3	567
Cuba............................	7,631	2.2	(33.9)	(12.1)	(21.0)	67
Dominica........................	66	1.9	42.7	8.9	33.8	88
Dominican Republic..............	3,619	3.6	(44.8)	(10.0)	(34.0)	74
Grenada.........................	96	1.2	30.9	8.6	22.3	279
Guadeloupe......................	316	2.9	33.2	7.6	25.6	178
Haiti...........................	4,396	1.9	(42.7)	(25.5)	(20.0)	158
Jamaica.........................	1,788	1.9	39.0	7.9	31.1	163
Martinique......................	321	2.7	32.7	7.8	24.9	291
Nertherlands Antilles...........	208	1.4	(39.4)	....	....	216
Puerto Rico.....................	2,633	2.0	30.2	6.6	23.6	296
St. Kitts-Nevis and Anguilla....	60	1.3	(49.8)	(12.0)	(22.5)	168
St. Lucia.......................	103	1.6	42.4	8.9	33.5	166
St. Vincent.....................	87	1.8	(49.8)	(12.5)	(36.1)	224
Trinidad and Tobago.............	975	3.1	28.9	6.1	22.8	190
Virgin Islands (US).............	43	5.4	(35.2)	(9.0)	(29.4)	126
EAST ASIA						
China (mainland)................	700,000	1.5	(39.3)	(11.0)	(23.0)	73
Hong Kong.......................	3,804	4.2	26.9	4.6	22.3	3686
Macau...........................	175	0.2	(30.0)	(18.0)	(24.0)	10938
Mongolia........................	1,104	3.0	(39.0)	(23.0)	(10.0)	1
Japan...........................	97,960	1.0	18.6	7.1	11.5	265
OTHER EAST ASIA						
China (Taiwan)..................	12,429	3.4	32.7	5.5	27.2	346
South Korea.....................	28,377	2.8	(42.0)	(17.0)	(27.0)	288
Ryukyu Islands..................	931	1.4	21.7	5.3	16.4	424

Table 3-4 (*Continued*)

Nations	Estimated midyear population 1965 (in thousands)	Average annual rate of growth	Vital rates			Density per square kilometer 1965
			Crude birth rates	Crude death rates	Rate of reproductive change	
MIDDLE SOUTH ASIA						
Afghanistan......................	15,051	1.8	(51.7)	(19.0)	(26.0)	23
Bhutan...........................	770	2.4	....	....	....	16
Ceylon...........................	11,232	2.6	(40.0)	....	....	171
India............................	483,000	2.3	(41.0)	(19.0)	(19.3)	159
Iran.............................	23,428	2.5	(45.5)	(25.0)	(20.0)	14
Maldive Islands..................	98	2.0	....	....	....	328
Sikkim...........................	176	1.8	(28.8)	(15.9)	(12.9)	25
Pakistan.........................	102,876	2.1	(50.8)	(30.0)	(15.0)	109
Nepal............................	10,100	1.8	....	....	....	72
SOUTH-EAST ASIA						
Brunei...........................	101	4.1	41.5	6.6	34.9	18
Burma............................	24,732	2.0	(43.0)	(35.0)	(15.0)	36
Cambodia.........................	6,115	2.5	(49.7)	(19.7)	(22.7)	34
Indonesia........................	104,500	2.2	(47.9)	(20.0)	(20.0)	70
Laos.............................	2,000	2.3	(46.0)	(28.0)	(18.0)	8
Malaysia (West).[b]..............	8,039	3.1	(43.6)	(9.2)	(33.7)	61
Philippines......................	32,345	3.3	(48.5)	(31.0)	(19.0)	108
Portuguese Timor.................	554	1.5	....	....	....	37
Thailand.........................	30,591	3.0	(45.5)	(20.0)	(22.0)	60
South Viet-Nam...................	16,124	3.2	(45.0)	(28.0)	(19.0)	94
SOUTH-WEST ASIA						
Aden.............................	240	3.3	(46.6)	(10.9)	(35.7)	1237
Bahrain..........................	185	4.1	....	....	....	309
Cyprus...........................	594	0.9	(25.8)	....	....	64
Gaza Strip (Palestine)...........	428	2.9	....	....	....	1132
Iraq.............................	8,262	3.3	(50.6)	....	....	18
Israel...........................	2,563	3.6	25.8)	6.4	19.4	124
Jordan...........................	1,976	3.2	(46.3)	....	....	22
Kuwait...........................	467	11.6	(40.3)	....	....	29
Lebanon..........................	2,405	2.7	....	....	....	231
Muscat and Oman..................	565	0.4	....	....	....	3
Protectorate of South Arabia.....	...	...	....	....	....	...
Qator............................	70	8.3	....	....	....	3
Saudi Arabia.....................	6,750	1.7	....	....	....	3
Syria............................	5,300	3.0	....	....	....	29
Trucial Oman.....................	111	3.7	....	....	....	1
Turkey...........................	31,086	2.6	(48.2)	....	....	40
Yemen............................	5,000	1.8	....	....	....	26

(a) Non-indigenons population.
(b) Excluding Sabah, Sarawak.

Source: United Nations Demographic Yearbook, Figures in parentheses are estimates as of about 1960. Most of the estimates reported were for birth rates were prepared by Dr. Lee Jay Cho of the Community and Family Study Center.

least a small part of the differences in their birth and death rates. More refined measures will be presented in the chapters on fertility and mortality. Meanwhile, the crude rates are sufficiently exact to permit us to sketch the general world picture of population growth nation by nation, taking one world region at a time.

3.7. The Economically Developed Regions

Northern and Western Europe. If a birthrate below 20 may be taken as evidence that a nation has entered the late transitional stage, it can be claimed that all of the nations in this so-called cradle of the industrial revolution either have definitely entered it or are on the verge of entering it. Only two sizable populations—the Dutch and the Irish—had crude birthrates above 20 in 1965, and both were only slightly above the mark. Together the populations with birthrates above 20 (Ireland, Netherlands, North Ireland, and Iceland) comprise only 16 million out of the total of 143 million for this region. On the other hand, in Sweden, Belgium, Denmark, France, and Luxembourg the gap between the birthrate and the death rate is quite narrow and population growth is slow. The current rate of growth in the region as a whole is only 0.7 percent per year, and in several of the nations it is down to 0.1 percent per year. It is quite possible that within a decade we may witness the emergence of a situation of stationary population in this major world region.

Moreover, population growth in this region has been very slow for more than three decades. During the economic depression of the 1930s birthrates sank to the same low level as at present. World War II removed all of the population growth of the 1940s. By reaching the late transitional stage first, and hovering there for such a prolonged time, this world region also qualifies as the "cradle of the demographic transition."

Eastern Europe. At the present time the growth situation in *Eastern* Europe is almost identical to that in Western and Northern Europe. All but one tiny nation have a crude birthrate below 17, and the average for the region is only slightly lower than for Northern

and Western Europe. Hungary appears now to have the honor of the lowest birthrate in the world (although perhaps for rather unusual reasons), with Romania and Bulgaria only a step behind. These developments have come more recently and much more swiftly than they did in Northern and Western Europe, but it seems very likely that in the future there will be comparatively little difference in their growth rates. The growth trend of Poland (birthrate of 17.3 in 1965) is especially impressive, for only 13 years earlier, in 1952, the crude birthrate was 30 per thousand!

It is to be doubted whether this recent lowering of growth is caused by World War II, because in that case the rates would tend to rise as the effects of the war recede into history; instead the rates have been falling as the nations have recovered.

Southern Europe. Except for Albania, the only European nation with a truly high birthrate, the nations of this region appear to be in the process of leaving the midtransitional and entering the late transitional stage. In some nations the current pace of change is very rapid:

	1952	1963-1964	Nine-year percent change
Bulgaria	21.2	16.4	−22.6
Romania	24.8	15.2	−38.7
Yugoslavia	29.7	20.8	−30.0

In Italy, Greece, and Spain also fertility has declined substantially since World War II. In several of these nations the completeness of registration has improved, which tends to mask declines in fertility. These developments in Southern European countries are of great significance in our effort to comprehend the world population problem for at least three reasons. First, most of the nations are of the Roman Catholic faith, and these developments suggest, as do recent demographic events in other parts of the world, that when the necessity for demographic readjustment becomes critical, religious resistance may be a temporary but certainly not an insuperable barrier.

A second significance in these developments is that about one half of these nations lie behind the Iron Curtain and have the Communist type of economy and political organization; the others are of the "free world," have two-party democracies, and follow an economy of capitalism, or free private enterprise. Despite these differences, both sets of nations have had a common pattern of growth in recent years. This is evidence (to supplement other evidence from other parts of the world) that when the need for demographic readjustment reaches a certain critical level of intensity, it will occur irrespective of the political or economic system.

Still a third important lesson can be learned from a careful study of this region. Inasmuch as it is the most recent of the regions of Europe to enter the midtransitional phase and pass into the late transitional phase, we should be especially interested in noting the length of time required for the transition. Data to be presented below will show that the time required for the change in this region is much shorter than it was in the other two regions of Europe. This leads us to the hypothesis that under appropriate circumstances it is possible for the demographic transition to be completed in a much shorter time today than in the second half of the nineteenth century.

In interpreting growth trends it must be kept in mind that actual rates of population growth in this region are lowered somewhat by a steady flow of out-migration to South America and other parts of the world. It is also well known that after World War II there was a large exodus of refugees from this region into other parts of Europe. Despite the fact that it contains many nations with religious, political, and economic systems that differ vastly from those in the rest of Europe, Southern Europe seems to be only a short step behind Central and Northwestern Europe in the demographic transition.

Northern America. All but a tiny fraction of the population of this region is in the United States and Canada. These nations clearly are in the midtransitional phase of demographic transition. Their death rates are among the world's lowest and their birth rates are still moderately high, with the result that population growth averaged about 1.7 percent per year in 1965. In addition, the two nations are

among the very few in the world that still welcome voluntary immigrants in large numbers.

During the depression of the 1930s the birthrate in both the United States and Canada sank to a low level, but after World War II there was a fertility upsurge that was substantially greater and more prolonged than the corresponding development in Europe (see Section 3.8). But in recent years the rate has been falling again, so that these nations appear to be approaching the late transitional stage. It is important to note however, that their birthrates and their rates of reproductive increase are clearly above those of almost all of Europe.

Because of the special interest that many readers of this book will have in the United States, a detailed analysis of its growth is made in a later chapter. At this point we are interested only in fitting it into the world demographic picture.

Union of Soviet Socialist Republics. Taken as a whole the population of the USSR may be placed demographically in almost exactly the same stage as the United States and Canada, namely, toward the terminal part of the midtransitional phase. Death rates are quite low and birthrates are moderately low, with a rate growth of about 1.4 percent per year about 1960.

Oceania. The overall statistics for this region place it toward the lower end of the midtransitional stage: average death rates are very low, and average birthrates are still moderately high. These characteristics are determined by the two very large population masses of European origin—Australia and New Zealand. In these two nations population growth is very similar to that of the United States, Canada, and the USSR.

On the many small islands, however, the native populations have very high birthrates and very low death rates and as a consequence are experiencing very rapid population growth. One of the most dramatic examples is American Samoa, with a crude birthrate of 40.6 and a crude death rate of 5.3. This tiny island has one of the fastest rates of reproductive change in the world, namely 4.0 percent per year. Most of the native populations of these Pacific Islands have birthrates in the high 30's or low 40's, with very low death rates, which qualifies them for placement in the early transitional phase of the demographic transition.

3.8.   The Developing Regions

Tropical and Temperate South America. All nations of South America except three fall squarely in the early transitional stage of demographic balance. Birthrates for the region as a whole are 40 per thousand or higher and show little if any evidence of recent decline. The death rates have been declining for several decades, although they are still moderately high in comparison with industrialized nations. Precise data are not available, since most nations lack either accurate vital registration or a good census, or both. Nevertheless, the data of Table 3-4 suggest that there is a very substantial nation-to-nation variation in the rate of growth, probably caused primarily by differences in death rates. Among the nations with extraordinarily high birthrates are French Guiana, Ecuador, Venezuela and Peru. All nations that have substantial segments of Indian populations have high birthrates. Throughout much of South America these high rates of reproductive increase are being augmented by substantial amounts of immigration.

Argentina and Uruguay are outstanding exceptions to this picture of high fertility. These nations have vital rates that would place them either with Australia or with North America—in the late midtransitional period.

Chile is one of the few nations of the world with a birthrate in the mid-30's. This country seems to have started to reduce birthrates more recently than Argentina and Uruguay and has not yet progressed as far.

What interpretation should be placed on the demographic situation in South America? Some point to this region as a great underdeveloped "empty continent" capable of carrying a far greater population; others point to its vast mountain, arid, tropical rain forest, and waste areas and claim that if all of the present population (which currently lives at a very low average level of comfort) were to be raised to a comfortable level, little room would remain for population expansion. The case of Brazil especially is a topic for demographic and economic debate. Is it a land of great underexploited opportunity, needing only large quantities of capital investment and technological know-how to raise its per capita productivity? Or is it a country that has already pushed to the limits of its carrying capacity and must now retreat from an overextension of population into semidesert and other territories that are submarginal both for agriculture and industry?

Middle America and the Caribbean. In comparison with South America, Middle America has somewhat lower birth and death rates and therefore seems to be a pace or two farther along in the demographic transition. This is indeed fortunate, because the density of the population per square kilometer is far higher in Middle America than in South America and in several instances seems to be reaching a level that will make long-run efforts to improve the economic condition of the population very difficult. Within the regions there are significant differences in the level of fertility. El Salvador, Costa Rica, Dominica, British Honduras, Guatemala, Haiti, Mexico and Nicaragua appear to have unusually high fertility. In contrast, birthrates appear to be falling in Barbados, Cuba, Puerto Rico, Trinidad and Tobago, and the Bahamas. There seems to be a very good prospect that within the next decade several nations of this region will begin to move more rapidly toward the low-fertility or late transitional stage. As in the case of Southern Europe, this demographic readjustment is being made despite religious opposition.

Middle South Asia. It may come somewhat as a surprise to many readers to discover that the great population mass of India and Ceylon, which together make up a very substantial majority of this region, have birthrates that are almost identical to those of Latin America. We have become so accustomed to being frightened by stories about Asia's "teeming millions" that we sometimes assume that the birthrates there are somewhere near the biological capacity of the human species to reproduce. Actually, they are only about 70 percent as high as this capacity. This is clear evidence that demographic regulation has been developing as the population has grown. In the absence of modern inexpensive methods these populations have adopted indirect though only insufficiently effective methods. But it would be a mistake to fail to credit this region with a substantial amount of demographic regulation—spontaneously initiated and carried out even before it became the beneficiary of international technical assistance.

On the other hand, Pakistan, Nepal, and possibly Afghanistan, which appear to have very high birthrates that only recently, if at all, have begun to decline substantially, may definitely be placed in the early transition stage. This difference between India and Ceylon on the one hand and Pakistan, Nepal, and Afghanistan on the other may reflect religious values. Apparently the Moslem culture so far has been somewhat more resistant to the notion of fertility limitation than have been Hindu and Buddhist nations.

Because death rates are still quite high in some Middle South Asian nations, the rate of reproductive change is lower than it is in Latin America, where death rates are now low. The higher Asian death rates are no accident. Much of the population lives in a state of chronic nutritional deficiency because of poverty and food shortage. It is impossible for the magic of modern public health and medicine to bring to an underfed nation a death rate as low as in well-fed populations. It is unlikely that death rates in Southern Asia can sink to the levels of those in Latin America until modern medicine is accompanied by a genuine rise in the level of living.

East Asia. This region contains more than one fourth of the world's population, but for every nation except Japan and Taiwan our knowledge of the vital processes is scanty indeed. What data are available suggest that here, too, birthrates are well below the biological capacity of the human species. Demographic readjustment has taken place to such an extent that the birthrate is 40 percent or more below this maximum almost everywhere. In other words, these countries have equaled or surpassed India's spontaneous demographic re-

adjustment. The epithet "uncontrolled fertility" certainly is not warranted.

Japan, in this region, is an outstanding demonstration that rapid demographic readjustment is possible in the modern era. As Table 3-6 shows, Japan's birthrate has literally plummeted since World War II, from a point that was clearly above that of Northern American nations to a point that places her with the most advanced nations of Europe. The Ryukyu Islands with a crude birthrate of 22 are also a dramatic example of inducing low fertility quickly among rural populations.

As yet very little is known about the populations of Mainland China and Mongolia. On the other hand, fairly complete data are available for the islands of Taiwan and Hong Kong. Among both of these Chinese populations, fertility regulation is unmistakably under way and is steadily becoming more effective, as will be demonstrated elsewhere. In this region, only Korea may be said to have an outstandingly high level of fertility; because of inadequate statistics, we do not know whether this is a temporary situation related to the war or a long-standing cultural trait.

South East Asia. This is a region of very high fertility. Birthrates are often near a biological maximum; the Philippines, Burma, Cambodia, North Borneo, and possibly Indonesia have rates of nearly 50. Throughout most of this region death rates are also moderately high but are declining as a result of malaria control and other health and medical programs. The region is fortunate in that almost everywhere there is a food surplus, and food is exported to obtain foreign currency for industrial equipment. Settlement of the region is recent in comparison with East and Middle South Asia; as a consequence, the density is lower in relation to arable land. Nevertheless, population now is growing so rapidly that it is beginning to press upon the land and threaten economic development, and we may expect that pressures for demographic readjustment will rise rapidly in the years immediately ahead.

In two populations the fertility is definitely lower than the regional total and seems to be falling quite rapidly—in Singapore and in Malaya. Fertility limitation seems to be definitely on the increase among these populations, and their birthrates are falling. So far the fertility decline in Singapore is unmistakable, though in Malaya it has been as yet only modest.

South West Asia. South West Asia shares with Africa the dubious honor of being one of the most inadequately enumerated regions of the world; hence only the scantiest, most inadequate data are available for most of the populations in this area. The information that exists, however, indicates that it is one of the most fertile populations of the world and has progressed least in the demographic transition. This may be attributed in part to the Moslem religion, but probably much more important is the fact that industrialization and modernization have only very recently begun to have even a modest impact on the rural areas. For part this could well be the result of prejudices by Christian nations, dating back to the Crusades, which have tended to inhibit empathy with this important world region. Density is low, but much of the territory is desert wasteland. There are far too few data to permit a discussion of differences between nations in birthrates and growth rates. However, we should note that save for Cyprus and Israel they are in the early transitional stage. Cyprus and Israel are deviant in South West Asia, just as Argentina and Japan are deviant in their regions.

Northern Africa. As a region, Northern Africa has fertility rates that are high but definitely lower than those of tropical Africa, discussed next. These populations are descended from very ancient civilizations. In addition, they have had a prolonged and a more intimate contact with European culture than the other populations of Africa. As a result, the demographic progress of this region is reflected in a substantial amount of demographic regulation. Nevertheless, birthrates are high—about 45 per thousand. The rate of population growth is extremely rapid, because death rates have been lowered substantially. Although these nations are in the early transition stage, they appear to be moving in a direction that will soon shift them to the next lower stage. Egypt, especially, seems to be manifesting the beginnings of a fertility decline.

Tropical and Southern Africa. Taken as a whole, this is by far the most "demographically backward" region of the world. Birthrates still show comparatively little evidence of demographic regulation—rates of 50 and above are quite common and are, in fact, almost the rule. Death rates are also still high, although they seem to be declining, according to the small amount of data available. Nevertheless, the average crude death rate in Western and Middle Africa is 20 percent, or higher than that in any other region of the world. Inasmuch as population data for this region are among the most inadequate, the amount of information is too small and too unreliable to permit much international comparison. Nevertheless, there do seem to be several instances where demographic regulation has begun to take place, even in this region. Madagascar, Mauritia, Réunion, Senegal, Tanganyika, Cameroon, and Gabon, for example, all appear to have birthrates of 45 or below. In contrast to nations with birthrates of 50 or above, this suggests a significant beginning of demographic regulation.

3.9.   Recent Birthrate Trends: The World "Baby Boom"

We have so far emphasized the recent or current demographic status of particular regions or nations, with only incidental attention to recent trends or changes that have brought about this status. In this section we consider data that show recent trends in the birthrate over the past 40 years.

The trend in births since 1920 is reported in Table 3-5 for two groups of nations—the industrialized nations and the developing nations. A summary of this information is charted in Figure 3-5. Unfortunately, reliable data on births are available for only a few of the developing nations, hence we must use these data as illustrative rather than as exact measurements. We obtain the following information:

1. The crude birthrates of the developing and the industrialized nations have been separated by 10 to 15 points, or more, throughout almost all of the entire span of time for which information is available. The gap in 1962 is

Table 3-5   Crude Birthrate for World Regions: 1920 to 1962

Year	Indus-trial-ized coun-tries	Devel-oping coun-tries	Industrialized nations					Developing nations		
			Europe			U.S. and Canada	Austral-ia and New Zealand	South* America	Middle* America	Asia*
			Northern Western Europe	Central Europe	South Europe					
1962......	21.3	32.7	18.3	17.3	22.5	24.0	24.2	26.9	40.6	30.5
1961......	21.7	34.8	18.1	17.6	23.3	24.6	25.0	36.4	36.6	31.4
1960......	21.9	37.0	18.0	17.7	24.0	25.2	24.4	35.9	42.0	33.2
1959......	22.1	37.4	18.1	18.2	23.9	25.8	24.6	36.9	41.4	33.9
1958......	22.3	37.5	18.0	18.6	24.2	25.9	24.6	37.0	40.5	34.9
1957......	22.6	38.0	18.3	19.2	24.1	26.6	24.6	37.1	41.6	35.4
1956......	22.7	38.3	18.3	19.6	24.8	26.4	24.2	37.1	41.1	36.7
1955......	22.9	38.4	18.3	19.9	25.7	26.4	24.4	36.9	42.0	36.4
1954......	22.9	38.6	18.4	20.1	25.1	26.8	24.2	36.6	42.3	36.8
1953......	22.9	38.5	18.6	20.0	25.1	26.4	24.2	37.0	41.3	37.1
1952......	22.9	38.0	18.9	20.0	24.9	26.3	24.6	35.9	40.6	37.6
1951......	22.8	38.5	18.8	20.3	25.0	25.6	24.3	36.0	40.6	38.7
1950......	23.3	37.4	19.4	20.9	26.4	25.3	24.6	34.9	40.5	36.8
1949......	23.5	37.3	20.1	20.7	26.7	25.6	24.5	34.4	40.0	37.4
1948......	23.9	36.7	21.0	21.3	26.4	25.8	25.0	34.2	40.5	35.4
1947......	24.3	37.3	22.3	21.0	25.1	27.4	25.9	33.1	42.7	36.2
1946......	23.7	34.3	22.5	19.6	25.9	25.2	25.4	33.3	39.7	30.0
1945......	21.6	34.2	20.0	18.7	24.1	21.8	23.2	32.7	40.4	29.5
1944......	21.7	34.7	19.9	20.6	23.9	22.0	22.0	31.4	39.9	32.8
1943......	21.3	34.2	19.0	19.4	24.6	22.8	20.9	31.1	39.7	31.7
1942......	20.8	34.5	17.7	18.8	24.0	22.1	24.6	30.9	39.2	33.5
1941......	20.4	34.6	17.0	19.6	23.3	20.5	21.5	30.9	39.1	33.9
1940......	20.5	35.3	16.6	20.4	25.8	19.7	20.2	31.6	39.7	34.6
1939......	19.7	34.8	17.2	19.4	24.2	18.8	18.9	30.9	38.1	35.3
1938......	19.7	34.8	17.3	18.1	26.3	19.1	17.8	29.8	39.9	34.8
1937......	19.6	34.8	16.9	17.9	27.0	18.6	17.4	30.0	38.7	35.8
1936......	19.6	35.4	16.9	18.4	27.9	18.4	16.6	30.0	39.8	36.5
1935......	19.8	34.9	16.9	18.8	28.2	18.6	16.4	29.7	38.4	36.5
1934......	18.3	34.4	17.1	19.3	29.6	18.9	16.4	29.1	38.5	35.5
1933......	20.4	34.4	16.9	19.6	29.8	18.8	16.7	29.7	38.0	35.4
1932......	21.4	34.4	17.9	21.0	31.3	20.0	17.0	29.7	39.2	34.4
1931......	21.9	35.4	18.2	21.5	30.8	20.6	18.4	30.0	40.9	35.2
1930......	23.0	36.3	18.9	22.8	32.3	21.4	19.4	32.2	41.6	35.1
1960-61...	21.8	36.0	18.1	17.6	23.7	24.9	24.7	36.2	40.9	30.9
1955-59...	22.5	39.6	18.2	19.1	24.4	26.2	24.4	37.8	41.2	39.8
1950-54...	23.0	37.4	18.8	20.3	25.3	26.1	24.4	36.1	38.8	37.4
1945-49...	23.4	36.1	21.2	20.2	25.6	25.2	24.8	34.0	40.4	33.8
1940-44...	21.0	35.4	18.2	19.7	24.3	21.6	21.2	32.4	39.6	34.1
1935-39...	19.8	35.4	17.1	18.5	26.7	18.8	18.0	31.4	39.0	35.7
1930-34...	21.4	35.8	17.8	20.8	30.6	19.9	17.8	32.0	39.8	35.7
1925-29...	23.6	36.9	19.6	23.7	31.8	22.3	20.8	33.8	40.4	36.4
1920-24...	26.6	36.6	22.6	26.8	34.4	25.5	23.7	34.0	40.8	35.1

* Data are available for a few selected nations only.

neither wider nor narrower than it was 40 years earlier.

2. The rates for the developing nations appear to have traveled on a high plateau until 1946 (perhaps depressed slightly by the war) and then to have suddenly increased by several points to reach a higher level in 1954-1955 than in any previous year for which data are available. Thus, in the 15 years from 1946 to 1961, "underdeveloped countries" experienced a very pronounced "baby boom." Only in 1961-1962 did this sudden acceleration in the birthrate show signs of slackening.

3. The rates for the industrialized countries reacted very strongly to the great World Economic Depression of the 1930s and reached a point below 20 per thousand in 1933. As the economic recession retreated, the rate rose gradually. With the ending of World War II, the industrialized nations experienced a "baby boom" similar to that in the developing nations. It seems to have begun about one year earlier and reached a peak in 1946-1947, after which the fertility rate began to decline slowly. By 1962 the birthrates in the developing nations had returned to a point where they had been in the early 1930s. Inasmuch as this point in the 1930s represented economic hardship, whereas the present level has been attained under conditions of economic prosperity, we may tentatively conclude that the fertility level in the industrialized nations has reached a

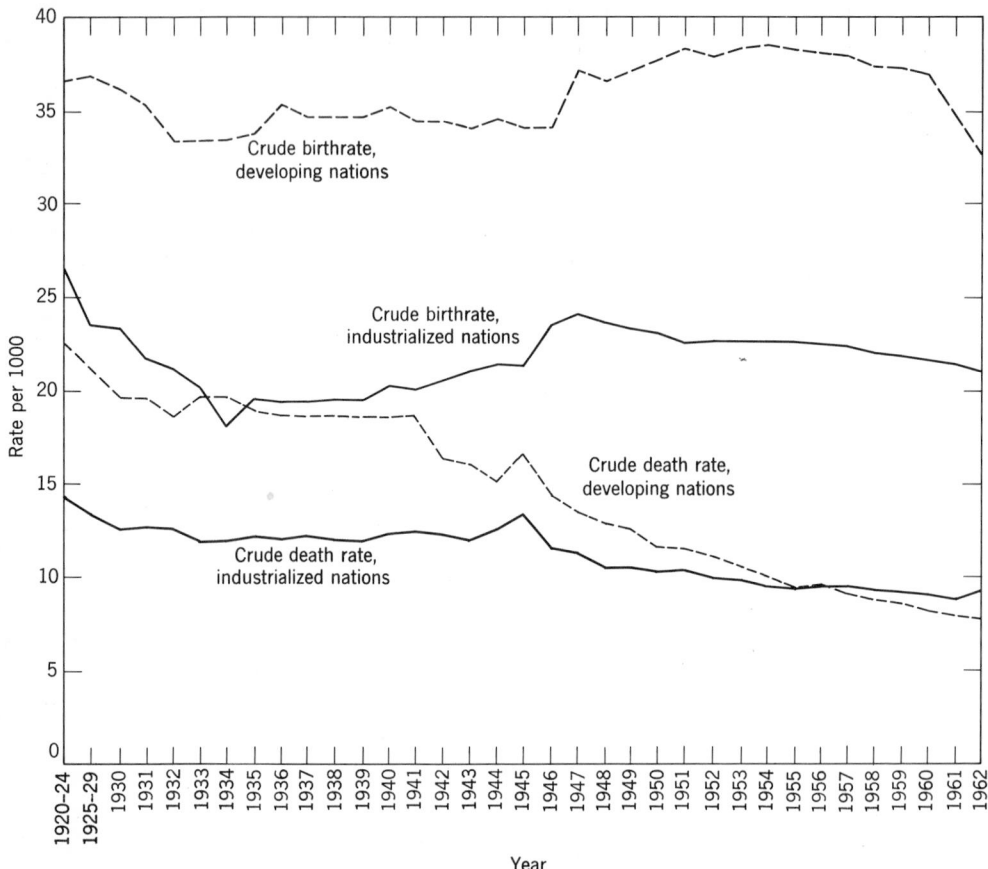

Figure 3-5 Trend in the Crude Birthrate and Death Rate in Industrialized and Developing Nations: 1920 to 1962.

lower "normal" level than at any previous time in human history; presumably a very severe economic depression could drive it to extremely low levels and perhaps temporarily below the point where births are sufficient to replace deaths. Figure 3-4 illustrates the onset of the baby boom in Sweden, where there was no major military action during World War II.

4. The "baby boom" in the industrialized countries appears to have been a reaction to the war: demobilization of armies resulted in the reunion of couples and in a large number of weddings that had been postponed. The unprecedented economic prosperity that the war brought to many countries may also have served to accelerate fertility during this period above what it otherwise would have been. But once this phase of "catching up" was completed, the rates began to drift down slowly, to the present point. Inasmuch as a very large

proportion of the populations of the industrialized countries practice contraception, the trend in the birthrate in these nations may be taken to represent a reflection of public attitude with respect to family size. More detailed information on this point is given in the chapters on fertility and family planning.

The "baby boom" in the developing countries is less easy to explain. Because a much smaller percentage of the populations practice contraception, we must search for other explanations for the sudden rise in fertility after World War II. One explanation is that the rising level of health (as indicated by falling death rates) resulted in fewer miscarriages, fewer instances of widowhood, and less illness among couples in the reproductive years. The making up of postponed marriages undoubtedly is a factor in this sudden rise in fertility. This force tending to raise fertility could have been

Table 3-6 Crude Birthrates for Selected Nations of World Regions Where Reliable Data Are Available: 1920 to 1962 (*Continued on pages 74-77*)

Year	Northern and Western Europe									
	Belgium	Denmark	Finland	France	Ireland	Nether-lands	Norway	Sweden	England and Wales	Scotland
1962........	16.8	16.8	18.1	17.8	21.8	20.8	17.3	14.2	18.0	20.1
1961........	17.0	16.6	18.4	18.2	21.3	21.2	17.5	13.9	17.6	19.5
1960........	16.9	16.6	18.5	18.0	21.4	20.8	17.3	13.7	17.2	19.6
1959........	17.4	16.3	18.9	18.4	21.1	21.3	17.7	14.1	16.5	19.2
1958........	17.1	16.5	18.6	18.2	20.9	21.1	17.9	14.2	16.4	19.3
1957........	17.0	16.8	20.1	18.5	21.2	21.2	18.0	14.6	16.1	19.1
1956........	16.8	17.2	20.8	18.5	21.0	21.2	18.5	14.8	15.7	18.6
1955........	16.8	17.3	21.2	18.6	21.1	21.3	18.5	14.8	15.0	18.1
1954........	16.8	17.3	21.5	18.9	21.3	21.5	18.5	14.6	15.2	18.1
1953........	16.6	17.9	22.0	18.9	21.2	21.7	18.7	15.4	15.5	17.8
1952........	16.7	17.8	23.1	19.4	21.9	22.3	18.8	15.5	15.3	17.7
1951........	16.4	17.8	23.0	19.7	21.3	22.2	18.4	15.6	15.5	17.7
1950........	16.9	18.6	24.5	20.7	21.3	22.7	19.1	16.4	15.9	18.0
1949........	17.2	18.9	26.1	21.1	21.5	23.7	19.5	17.4	16.7	18.5
1948........	17.6	20.3	27.5	21.2	22.1	25.3	20.5	18.4	17.8	19.4
1947........	17.8	22.1	28.0	21.4	23.2	27.8	21.4	18.9	20.5	22.0
1946........	18.3	23.4	27.9	20.9	23.0	30.2	22.6	19.7	19.2	20.2
1945........	15.7	23.5	25.5	16.6	22.6	22.6	20.0	20.4	15.9	16.8
1944........	15.3	22.7	21.3	16.3	22.2	24.0	20.4	20.6	17.7	18.4
1943........	15.0	21.4	20.5	15.8	21.9	23.0	18.9	19.3	16.2	18.2
1942........	13.2	20.4	16.6	14.5	22.3	21.0	17.7	17.7	15.6	17.5
1941........	12.2	18.5	24.2	13.1	19.0	20.3	15.3	15.6	13.9	17.4
1940........	13.6	18.3	17.8	13.8	19.1	20.8	16.1	15.1	14.1	17.1
1939........	15.5	17.8	21.2	14.7	19.1	20.6	15.8	15.4	14.8	17.4
1938........	16.0	18.1	21.0	14.9	19.4	20.5	15.4	14.9	15.1	17.7
1937........	15.4	18.0	19.9	15.0	19.2	19.8	15.0	14.4	14.9	17.6
1936........	15.4	17.8	19.1	15.3	19.6	20.2	14.5	14.2	14.8	17.9
1935........	15.5	17.7	19.6	15.5	19.6	20.2	14.3	13.8	14.7	17.8
1934........	16.2	17.8	19.1	16.4	19.5	20.6	14.6	13.7	14.8	18.0
1933........	16.6	17.3	18.4	16.4	19.4	20.8	14.7	13.7	14.4	17.6
1932........	17.8	17.9	19.8	17.5	19.1	22.0	16.0	14.5	15.3	18.6
1931........	18.4	18.0	20.7	17.7	19.5	22.2	16.3	14.8	15.8	19.0
1930........	18.9	18.7	21.8	18.2	19.9	23.1	17.0	15.4	16.3	19.6
1960-61......	17.0	16.6	18.4	18.1	21.4	21.0	17.4	13.8	17.4	19.6
1955-59......	17.0	16.8	19.9	18.4	21.1	21.2	18.1	14.5	15.9	18.8
1950-54......	16.7	17.9	22.8	19.5	21.4	22.1	18.7	15.5	15.5	17.9
1945-49......	17.3	21.6	27.0	20.3	22.5	25.9	20.8	19.0	18.0	19.4
1940-44......	13.8	20.3	20.1	16.3	20.9	21.8	17.7	17.7	15.5	17.7
1935-39......	15.8	17.9	20.2	15.1	19.4	20.3	15.0	14.5	14.9	17.7
1930-34......	17.6	17.9	20.0	17.5	19.5	21.7	15.7	14.4	15.3	18.6
1925-29......	18.9	19.8	22.8	18.5	20.3	23.4	18.5	16.3	17.1	20.3
1920-24......	21.1	22.6	25.4	19.9	20.5	26.7	23.5	20.3	21.3	24.3

greater for several years before 1946, but the war would have hidden at least some of its effect.

Table 3-6 furnishes detailed rates for those nations for which reasonably reliable data are available and which have provided the data for Table 3-5 and Figure 3-5. It may be seen that a similar pattern has been followed in a great many nations, although it is much more pronounced in some than in others. The conclusion certainly seems warranted, however, that *between 1946 and 1960 the entire world was in the grip of a great rise in birthrates in complete defiance of prewar trends.* Only in recent years (since 1960) has there been evidence of a return to the pattern of demographic transition described above. As yet we have very incomplete information and almost no

fully satisfactory theories that would explain these events.

Figure 3-6 provides information about trends in the crude birthrates for four of the industrialized regions of the world. Northwestern Europe, it is clear, led the parade toward lower birthrates during the 1920s and 1940s. It temporarily enjoyed a "baby boom" in 1946-1948, but its birthrate sank again rather promptly and has remained on a low plateau for the last decade. A similar pattern can be seen in Central Europe, especially since 1948; before 1940 Central Europe had higher fertility rates than Northwestern Europe.

The other two regions charted in Figure 3-6 are quite divergent from these European regions. Northern America (United States and Canada) followed a pattern very similar to

Table 3-6　(Continued)

Year	Central Europe					Southern Europe				
	West Germany	Czecho-slovakia	Hungary	Poland	Swit-zerland	Austria	Albania	Bulgaria	Italy	Portugal
1962.........	18.1	15.7	12.9	19.6	18.7	18.6	38.7	16.4	18.9	24.7
1961.........	18.3	15.8	14.0	20.7	18.1	18.6	41.2	17.4	18.8	24.5
1960.........	17.8	15.9	14.7	22.3	17.6	17.8	43.4	17.8	18.4	24.2
1959.........	17.7	16.0	15.2	24.7	17.7	17.6	41.9	17.6	18.4	24.2
1958.........	17.0	17.4	16.0	26.3	17.6	17.1	41.8	17.9	17.9	24.3
1957.........	17.0	18.9	17.0	27.6	17.7	17.0	39.1	18.4	18.1	24.3
1956.........	16.5	19.8	19.5	28.0	17.4	16.6	41.9	19.5	18.1	23.4
1955.........	16.0	20.3	21.4	29.1	17.1	15.6	44.5	20.1	18.1	24.3
1954.........	16.1	20.6	23.0	29.1	17.0	14.9	40.8	20.2	18.2	23.0
1953.........	15.8	21.2	21.6	29.7	17.0	14.8	40.9	20.9	17.7	23.7
1952.........	16.0	22.2	19.6	30.2	17.4	14.8	35.2	21.2	17.9	24.7
1951.........	16.0	22.8	20.2	31.0	17.2	14.8	38.5	21.1	18.4	24.5
1950.........	16.5	23.3	20.9	30.7	18.1	15.6	38.8	25.2	19.6	24.4
1949.........	17.2	22.4	20.6	29.5	18.4	16.3	36.8	24.7	20.3	25.5
1948.........	17.0	23.4	21.0	29.3	19.2	17.7	36.5	24.6	21.9	26.7
1947.........	16.5	24.2	20.6	26.5	19.4	18.6	34.5	24.0	22.2	24.5
1946.........	16.4	22.7	18.7	23.6	20.0	15.9	35.1	25.6	23.0	25.4
1945.........	16.0	19.5	18.7	23.1	20.1	14.9	32.6	24.1	18.3	26.0
1944.........	17.6	22.1	20.5	25.4	19.6	18.6	32.3	22.0	18.3	25.3
1943.........	16.0	21.5	18.4	23.5	19.2	18.0	33.2	21.8	19.9	25.1
1942.........	14.9	19.7	19.9	22.7	18.4	17.1	32.8	22.7	20.5	23.9
1941.........	18.1	20.1	19.0	23.7	16.9	20.1	27.8	21.9	20.9	23.8
1940.........	20.0	20.6	20.0	24.6	15.2	21.8	30.9	22.2	23.5	24.3
1939.........	19.0	18.6	19.4	23.3	15.2	20.7	27.7	21.4	23.6	26.2
1938.........	18.5	16.7	19.9	24.3	15.2	13.9	34.5	22.8	22.8	26.6
1937.........	18.3	16.3	20.0	24.9	14.9	12.8	33.8	24.3	22.9	26.7
1936.........	18.9	16.6	20.3	26.2	15.6	13.1	33.7	25.9	22.4	28.1
1935.........	19.2	17.0	21.1	26.1	16.0	13.1	33.1	26.4	23.4	28.2
1934.........	19.7	17.8	21.8	26.6	16.3	13.6	34.7	30.1	23.5	28.4
1933.........	20.0	18.4	21.9	26.5	16.4	14.3	34.9	29.2	23.8	29.0
1932.........	21.4	20.1	23.4	28.9	16.7	15.2	36.7	31.5	23.8	29.9
1931.........	22.0	20.6	23.7	30.2	16.7	15.9	36.5	29.5	24.9	29.7
1930.........	23.3	21.8	25.4	32.5	17.2	16.8	38.3	31.4	26.7	29.7
1960-61......	18.0	15.8	14.4	21.5	17.8	18.2	42.3	17.6	18.6	24.4
1955-59......	16.8	18.5	17.8	27.1	17.5	16.8	41.8	18.7	18.1	23.6
1950-54......	16.1	22.0	21.1	30.1	17.3	15.0	38.9	22.7	18.4	24.1
1945-49......	16.3	22.4	19.9	26.4	19.4	15.7	35.1	24.6	21.1	25.6
1940-44......	17.3	20.8	19.3	24.0	17.9	19.1	31.4	22.1	20.8	24.5
1935-39......	18.8	17.1	20.1	25.0	15.4	14.7	32.6	24.1	23.2	27.1
1930-34......	21.3	19.7	23.2	28.9	16.7	15.1	36.2	30.3	24.5	29.3
1925-29......	23.7	22.9	26.6	32.9	17.8	18.4	31.8	34.2	27.2	31.7
1920-24......	26.8	26.8	30.2	34.3	20.0	22.6	34.4	39.6	30.1	33.0

that of Northwestern and Central Europe until 1948. It experienced a very extraordinary rise during the "baby boom" phase and, to the amazement of the entire demographic world, remained for several years at the higher plateau of 25 per thousand instead of sinking to the typical level of 15-18 per thousand that would be regarded as "normal" for nations in the late transitional stage. Since 1958 the birthrate in Northern America has been declining. Chapter 6 discusses this unusual development in more detail.

Southern Europe has been passing from the midtransitional to the late transitional stage during the past four decades; the graph of its birthrate shows a steady downward drift from 35 in the early 1920s to about 22 in 1962. World War II affected this trend—by hastening it in the war years and retarding it shortly after the war—but the long-run pattern is clear. It may surprise some readers to learn that the birthrate in the United States recently has been higher than the birthrates of Italy and Spain, nations that long have been regarded as high-birthrate nations because of a combination of economic backwardness and religious beliefs opposing contraception.

3.10.　Recent Death Rate Trends: Big Declines in Developing Nations

A necessary condition for a nation to have reached the late transitional stage of population adjustment is to have lowered its death rate to a point where it cannot be lowered further except by great expenditures of effort and money. At the present stage of medical science,

Table 3-6 (*Continued*)

Year	Southern Europe			Northern America		South America				Middle America
	Romania	Spain	Yugo-slavia	Canada	United States	Argentina	Chile	Surinam	Venezuela	Barbados
1962.........	16.4	20.0	22.2	25.5	22.4	16.5	25.5	32.9	32.8	31.2
1961.........	17.5	21.3	22.6	26.0	23.3	22.4	34.5	44.5	44.4	28.6
1960.........	19.1	21.9	23.5	26.7	23.7	22.5	34.2	41.8	45.2	33.8
1959.........	20.2	21.8	23.3	27.4	24.1	23.3	35.8	45.5	42.9	29.8
1958.........	21.6	21.9	24.0	27.5	24.3	23.6	36.0	45.9	42.4	30.3
1957.........	22.9	21.9	23.9	28.1	25.0	24.2	36.9	44.3	42.9	31.7
1956.........	24.2	20.7	26.0	28.0	24.9	24.5	36.0	44.5	43.5	31.0
1955.........	25.6	20.6	26.9	28.2	24.7	24.3	35.1	43.7	44.3	33.2
1954.........	24.8	20.0	28.6	28.5	25.0	24.6	33.5	43.8	44.4	33.6
1953.........	23.8	20.6	28.4	28.1	24.7	25.2	34.6	44.0	44.3	33.1
1952.........	24.8	20.8	29.7	27.9	24.7	24.9	32.7	43.5	42.6	33.6
1951.........	25.1	20.1	27.0	27.2	24.1	25.2	33.9	41.0	43.8	31.8
1950.........	26.2	20.2	30.2	27.1	23.5	25.5	34.0	37.6	42.6	30.7
1949.........	27.6	21.7	30.0	27.3	23.9	25.1	34.7	36.4	41.2	32.0
1948.........	23.9	23.3	28.1	27.3	24.2	25.3	35.3	37.2	39.2	32.5
1947.........	22.4	21.5	26.6	28.9	25.8	25.0	36.0	33.3	38.2	32.7
1946.........	23.8	21.6	27.1	27.2	23.3	24.7	36.2	34.7	37.6	31.9
1945.........	19.6	23.2	25.1	24.0	19.5	25.2	33.3	36.1	36.2	32.3
1944.........	21.7	22.6	24.9	23.8	20.2	25.2	33.2	31.7	35.5	32.4
1943.........	23.4	23.0	25.6	24.1	21.5	24.2	33.1	30.9	36.1	32.3
1942.........	21.4	20.3	26.7	23.4	20.8	23.3	33.1	31.5	35.6	31.0
1941.........	23.0	19.7	25.9	22.2	18.8	23.7	32.6	32.0	35.3	32.3
1940.........	26.5	24.5	28.6	21.5	17.9	24.0	33.4	33.1	36.0	32.4
1939.........	28.3	16.6	25.9	20.4	17.3	23.6	33.3	30.7	35.9	31.1
1938.........	29.6	20.1	26.7	20.6	17.6	23.7	32.1	29.7	33.7	30.5
1937.........	30.8	22.7	28.0	20.0	17.1	23.8	32.3	30.2	33.7	32.8
1936.........	31.5	24.9	29.1	20.2	16.7	24.1	33.5	30.7	31.9	34.8
1935.........	30.7	25.9	29.9	20.4	16.9	24.7	33.3	33.0	27.8	31.6
1934.........	32.4	26.4	31.6	20.6	17.2	24.9	33.2	31.3	27.0	32.4
1933.........	32.1	27.9	31.5	21.0	16.6	25.4	33.1	32.3	27.9	32.5
1932.........	35.9	28.3	32.9	22.5	17.4	25.8	34.0	30.5	28.4	33.5
1931.........	33.4	28.1	33.6	23.2	18.0	26.2	34.6	30.9	28.1	30.4
1930.........	35.0	29.5	35.5	23.9	18.9	27.8	39.8	31.3	29.7	35.2
1960-61......	18.3	21.6	23.0	26.4	23.5	22.4	34.4	43.2	44.8	31.2
1955-59......	22.9	21.4	24.6	27.9	24.6	23.6	35.5	44.8	47.1	31.2
1950-54......	24.9	20.3	28.8	27.8	24.5	25.1	33.8	42.1	43.5	32.6
1945-49......	23.5	22.2	27.4	27.0	23.4	25.1	35.7	36.6	38.5	32.1
1940-44......	23.2	22.0	26.4	23.2	19.9	24.1	36.4	33.5	35.7	32.1
1935-39......	30.2	21.9	27.9	20.4	17.2	24.0	36.6	32.4	32.7	32.2
1930-34......	33.7	27.5	33.0	22.2	17.6	26.8	40.5	32.3	28.2	32.8
1925-29......	35.4	28.7	33.9	24.5	20.1	29.9	44.9	31.9	31.4	34.5
1920-24......	37.6	30.0	35.3	28.1	22.8	32.0	42.4	31.8	29.9	35.5

this low point is 7 to 12 per thousand, depending on the age composition of the population. Once this level is reached, it is extremely difficult to make further reductions in mortality, which would necessitate conquest of the chronic diseases of older people: heart disease, cancer, and degenerative disorders of all kinds.

In contrast, modern medicine finds it comparatively easy to make big inroads on high mortality conditions. By spraying the breeding places of mosquitoes with DDT for a few years it is possible to control malaria. By vaccinating it is possible to eradicate smallpox, cholera, yellow fever, and typhoid. By boiling water or otherwise ensuring the purity of drinking water and cleanliness in handling food it is possible to reduce greatly deaths from digestive infections of all kinds—especially

among infants. Antibiotics are capable of cutting deaths from infectious diseases to a small fraction of the former toll. Since all of the developing nations want health and escape from premature death, it is only to be expected that programs of public health and medical care would be one of the first goals of modernization. This, in fact, is exactly what has happened, and the death rates of the developing nations have literally plummeted because of it. Table 3-7 presents statistics of mortality trends for selected regions of the world. Figure 3-5 shows the trend since 1920 in the death rates of the industrialized and the developing nations. We see that in the industrialized nations the rates have been low since 1930 and have been declining very slowly, as if they were approaching a lower limit. Death rates

Table 3-6 (Continued)

Year	Middle America (continued)								Asia	
	Costa Rica	El Salvador	Guatemala	Jamaica	Mexico	Panama	Puerto Rico	Trinidad and Tobago	China (Taiwan)	Malaya
1962.........	50.5	45.3	46.8	40.6	44.7	42.2	31.4	32.7	37.4	36.1
1961.........	43.2	46.1	49.9	41.0	44.9	41.3	31.0	32.0	38.3	37.2
1960.........	47.5	46.5	49.5	43.1	46.0	41.0	31.7	38.9	39.5	40.9
1959.........	48.2	45.9	49.8	41.1	46.9	40.8	32.3	37.4	41.2	42.2
1958.........	46.4	47.3	48.7	38.1	44.0	39.3	33.2	37.6	41.7	43.3
1957.........	47.7	48.9	49.4	37.9	46.6	40.5	33.7	37.7	41.4	46.2
1956.........	49.0	47.0	48.8	37.2	46.1	39.3	34.8	37.0	44.8	46.7
1955.........	49.8	47.9	48.8	36.2	45.9	39.4	34.6	41.9	45.3	44.0
1954.........	50.9	48.1	51.5	35.3	46.0	39.0	35.2	41.4	44.6	44.6
1953.........	49.6	47.9	51.1	34.4	44.7	37.9	35.3	37.7	45.2	44.4
1952.........	48.6	48.7	50.9	33.3	43.6	36.1	36.1	34.6	46.6	45.0
1951.........	47.6	48.8	52.3	34.0	44.6	32.5	37.6	36.7	50.0	44.0
1950.........	45.9	48.5	50.9	33.1	45.5	33.3	39.0	37.5	43.3	42.3
1949.........	44.1	46.2	51.6	32.3	44.7	32.8	39.0	37.2	42.4	43.8
1948.........	44.5	44.6	51.9	30.7	44.6	35.6	40.2	39.9	39.7	40.4
1947.........	57.0	47.2	52.2	31.9	45.3	37.2	42.2	38.3	39.7	43.0
1946.........	45.0	40.8	48.2	30.8	42.9	37.0	41.6	38.8	33.0	35.0
1945.........	45.9	42.9	48.7	30.0	44.9	37.7	41.9	39.5	32.4	34.4
1944.........	43.3	42.2	46.6	33.2	44.2	37.8	40.6	39.0	36.1	38.3
1943.........	43.4	42.2	47.9	31.5	45.5	37.7	38.7	38.5	40.7	43.1
1942.........	42.6	42.6	46.4	32.7	45.5	37.0	40.2	34.7	40.9	40.5
1941.........	44.6	43.8	45.7	31.4	43.5	37.4	39.8	33.5	41.8	38.0
1940.........	44.6	45.7	48.2	30.8	44.3	38.0	38.6	34.7	43.7	40.7
1939.........	44.2	44.5	47.4	32.3	44.6	27.9	39.6	31.1	44.4	42.0
1938.........	45.0	43.7	46.4	33.3	43.5	45.5	38.6	33.0	43.9	41.2
1937.........	43.9	41.7	46.5	31.5	44.1	38.0	38.2	31.6	45.5	39.0
1936.........	44.8	43.4	47.8	32.9	43.0	38.5	39.6	33.1	44.2	40.4
1935.........	44.7	40.1	48.1	34.1	42.3	32.0	39.5	33.0	45.7	37.8
1934.........	43.8	41.5	47.0	31.7	44.3	37.1	39.1	29.8	45.4	37.1
1933.........	43.2	40.9	47.5	33.4	42.2	33.6	37.4	31.1	45.1	37.6
1932.........	44.3	40.1	50.3	32.7	43.3	38.6	41.1	29.0	44.8	36.1
1931.........	45.7	45.3	54.7	35.3	43.8	41.5	41.5	30.0	46.7	37.2
1930.........	46.4	45.8	56.8	37.5	49.4	31.6	40.6	31.4	45.7	37.1
1960-61.......	45.4	46.3	49.7	42.0	45.4	41.2	31.4	35.4	38.9	....
1955-59.......	47.7	47.4	49.1	37.7	45.9	39.9	33.7	38.3	42.8	44.4
1950-54.......	48.7	48.4	51.4	34.0	44.9	35.8	36.6	37.7	45.9	44.1
1945-49.......	45.5	44.4	50.6	31.3	44.4	36.0	40.8	38.7	37.4	39.3
1940-44.......	44.9	43.3	47.2	31.5	44.2	37.5	39.6	36.2	40.6	40.1
1935-39.......	45.0	42.7	47.7	32.2	43.5	36.4	39.1	32.4	44.7	40.2
1930-34.......	45.7	43.3	51.6	33.6	44.5	36.5	40.6	30.3	45.5	37.0
1925-29.......	46.6	44.7	58.7	35.6	33.3	38.4	40.4	31.5	44.0	36.4
1920-24.......	43.4	45.9	62.6	37.6	31.4	37.4	40.8	32.5	41.8	35.1

for developing nations, in contrast, have been sinking very rapidly, from a point well above 20 in 1920 to a point well below 10 in 1960. (The reader must keep in mind that reliable death rates are available for only a few of the developing nations—and the more prosperous and advanced ones at that. For this reason, the *level* of rates shown in Figure 3-5 is misleading, although the *trend* is typical. Reference to Table 3-1 reminds us that in developing nations as a whole the death rate is still 18 to 25 per thousand; Table 3-4 reports even higher estimates for particular nations.)

Table 3-8 lists the crude death rates in recent years for particular nations. The experiences of Taiwan, Ceylon, and Malaya is very impressive: in the 15 years between 1945 and 1960 their registered death rate was cut almost

in half. This is an unprecedented rate of progress in mortality reduction. If we refer to Figure 3-5, we note that it took only 23 years for the developing nations reported there to pass from a death rate of 20 to a death rate of 10. It took Sweden 53 years (from 1859 to 1912) to accomplish this.

Much of the responsibility for this mortality reduction must be attributed to the industrialized nations themselves. During and after World War II they sponsored (both financially and operationally), either as military or as "good neighbor" projects, the programs of disease eradication that have been most instrumental in saving lives. Under the auspices of the United Nations or as direct nation-to-nation foreign aid they have shipped millions of tons of food into areas of chronic undernourishment

Table 3-6 (Continued)

Year	Asia (continued)				Oceania			Union of Soviet Socialist Republics
	Hong Kong	Israel	Japan	Singapore	American Samoa	Australia	New Zealand	
1962.........	32.8	25.4	17.0	34.1	41.0	22.2	26.2	22.5
1961.........	34.2	25.2	16.9	36.5	42.4	22.8	27.1	23.8
1960.........	36.0	26.8	17.2	38.7	42.8	22.4	26.5	24.9
1959.........	35.2	26.8	17.6	40.3	42.4	22.6	26.5	25.0
1958.........	37.4	26.7	18.1	42.0	40.1	22.6	26.6	25.3
1957.........	35.8	28.2	17.3	43.4	37.8	22.9	26.2	25.4
1956.........	37.0	28.8	18.5	44.4	40.6	22.5	26.0	25.2
1955.........	36.3	29.2	19.4	44.3	39.7	22.6	26.1	25.7
1954.........	36.6	29.2	20.1	45.7	39.7	22.5	25.9	26.6
1953.........	33.6	32.1	21.5	45.8	37.3	22.9	25.4	25.1
1952.........	32.0	33.0	23.5	45.4	42.0	23.3	26.0	26.5
1951.........	34.0	34.1	25.4	45.0	45.5	23.0	25.6	27.0
1950.........	26.8	34.7	28.2	45.4	43.5	23.3	25.9	26.7
1949.........	29.5	28.6	32.8	47.1	43.6	22.9	26.1	....
1948.........	26.4	26.3	33.7	46.2	42.7	23.1	26.8	....
1947.........	24.3	30.1	34.3	45.9	41.7	24.1	27.7	....
1946.........	20.1	28.6	25.3	38.1	40.7	23.6	27.1	....
1945.........	19.7	29.9	23.2	37.4	37.4	21.7	24.6	....
1944.........	21.9	29.7	29.2	41.6	35.4	21.0	23.0	....
1943.........	24.6	28.6	30.3	46.8	33.6	20.6	21.2	....
1942.........	23.1	22.5	30.3	44.0	34.0	19.0	23.1	
1941.........	27.5	20.4	31.1	44.7	34.6	18.9	24.1	....
1940.........	25.2	23.5	29.4	45.0	32.7	17.9	22.6	....
1939.........	28.1	23.1	26.6	47.6	30.4	17.6	20.2	....
1938.........	25.2	26.3	27.1	44.9	28.7	17.5	18.0	....
1937.........	27.2	26.7	30.8	45.8	28.0	17.4	17.3	....
1936.........	27.7	29.7	30.0	46.6	26.7	17.1	16.1	....
1935.........	27.7	30.8	31.7	45.2	26.4	16.6	16.2	....
1934.........	26.9	30.2	30.0	43.3	26.6	16.4	16.5	....
1933.........	26.9	29.2	31.5	41.9	26.9	16.8	16.6	....
1932.........	25.9	29.2	32.9	35.8	27.4	16.9	17.1	....
1931.........	26.7	32.2	32.2	36.4	29.6	18.2	18.5	....
1930.........	26.6	33.0	32.4	36.0	31.2	19.9	18.8	....
1960-61......	35.1	26.0	17.0	37.6	42.6	22.6	26.8	24.4
1955-59......	38.3	27.9	18.2	42.8	40.1	22.6	26.3	....
1950-54......	32.6	32.5	23.7	45.5	40.7	23.0	25.8	26.4
1945-49......	24.0	29.0	30.1	42.9	41.2	23.1	26.5	....
1940-44......	24.5	25.1	30.1	44.4	34.1	19.5	22.8	....
1935-39......	27.2	27.1	29.2	46.0	28.0	17.2	18.8	....
1930-34......	30.9	30.6	31.8	38.5	28.3	17.6	17.5	....
1925-29......	36.4	34.3	34.0	33.2	....	21.6	20.0	....
1920-24......	35.1	34.5	35.0	28.9	....	24.4	23.0	....

and have thus kept alive and healthy many millions of people who otherwise would have suffered premature death. They have trained thousands of physicians and nurses and have helped build a modern drug industry as a top priority item in economic development. Thus the program of economic development itself has been a major factor in creating the present population problem.

3.11. The Inverse Correlation between National Wealth and Fertility

At the present time in world history there exists a rather clear-cut inverse correlation between the level of economic comfort of a nation and the nation's birthrate. That is, the poorer nations have high birthrates and the wealthier nations have lower birthrates. Empirical dem-

onstration of this generalization is presented in Figure 3-7. The gross domestic product is a generally accepted measure of the average amount of goods and services produced by a nation, and inasmuch as almost all of a nation's product is consumed by its citizens, this measure becomes a measure of total national consumption. When it is converted to a per capita basis by dividing by the national population, it suggests the average amount of goods and services available to each person. Figure 3-7 is a scattergram in which this measure has been plotted against the crude birthrate of the nation, for those nations for which reasonably accurate measures both of fertility and per capita domestic product are available. The curve, sketched in by hand, illustrates that the two sets of data are correlated and that

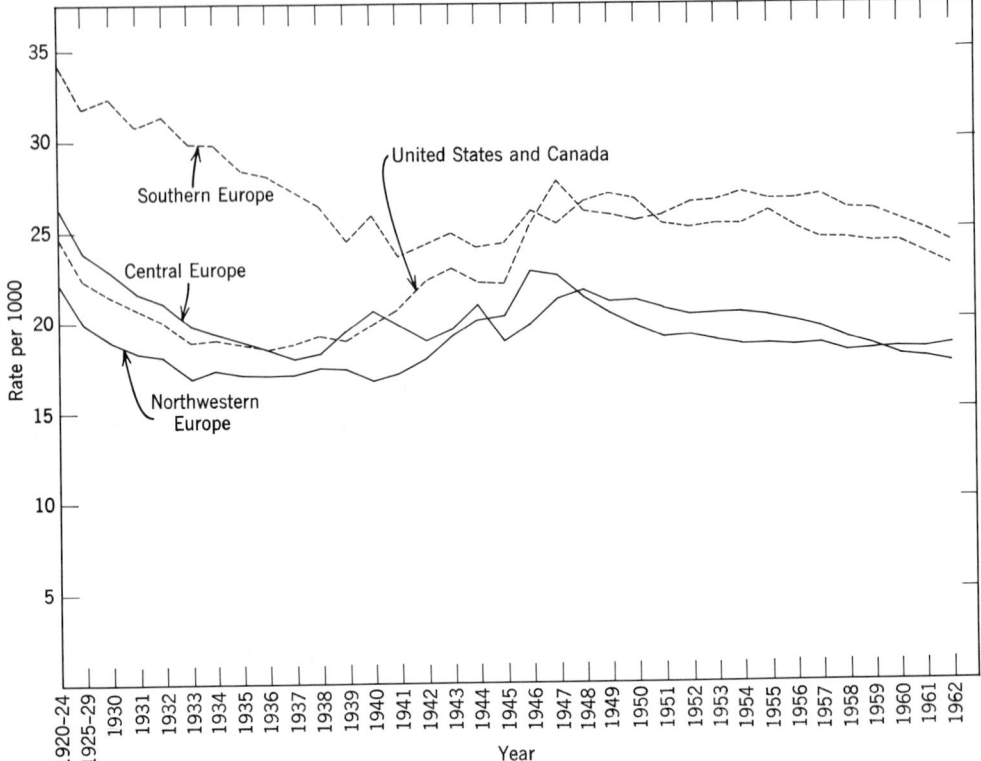

Figure 3-6   Trend in the Crude Birthrates in Four Industrialized World Regions: 1920 to 1962.

the relationship is inverse: high fertility occurs with low level of material comfort and low fertility is associated with high level of material comfort. However, we must be cautious in interpreting this correlation:

1. The existence of a correlation between two variables does not necessarily mean that there is a direct cause-and-effect relationship between them. We cannot declare, without further research, that high birthrates are either a *cause* or an *effect* of a low level of living in a nation. The "explanation" either of national per capita productivity or of the level of the crude birthrate is highly complex and involves many different factors. Here we only wish to point out that this relationship exists and leave to later chapters the task of exploring its implications and the processes that have brought it about.

2. Although the correlation is substantial, there is much "scatter" or deviation of individual nations away from the trend line that expresses the average relationship. For ex-

ample, there are several rather poor nations that have low crude birthrates. This can be partly a result of incomplete fertility data, but it may also serve as a warning that *reducing the national birthrate will not alone bring economic prosperity*. On the other hand, it is clear that no high-birthrate nation has a high per capita productivity; although some high-birthrate nations are more prosperous than others, all are "poor" in comparison with the lower-birthrate nations. Perhaps we may be permitted to conclude, pending a more detailed study of the problem later, that *fertility reduction is a necessary, but not a sufficient condition for raising the economic well-being of a poorer nation*. Sometimes students of population become so convinced of the absolute necessity for fertility control that they appear to suggest that this alone will bring prosperity. On the other hand, they sometimes turn this around and in despair claim that birthrates cannot fall until a rise in the level of living is accomplished. It is important to recognize that either

Table 3-7   Crude Death Rates for Selected Regions: 1920 to 1962

Year	Industrialized countries	Developing countries	Industrialized nations					Developing nations		
			Europe			U.S. and Canada	Australia and New Zealand	South* America	Middle * America	Asia *
			Northern Western Europe	Central Europe	South Europe					
1962.......	9.6	8.4	10.7	10.4	9.7	8.6	8.8	8.6	9.9	6.8
1961.......	9.3	8.4	10.4	9.8	9.2	8.5	8.8	8.7	9.7	6.8
1960.......	9.5	8.7	10.4	10.1	9.5	8.7	8.7	9.0	10.0	7.0
1959.......	9.6	9.1	10.3	10.3	9.8	8.7	9.0	9.4	10.5	7.3
1958.......	9.4	9.4	10.3	10.0	9.1	8.7	8.7	9.3	11.1	7.7
1957.......	9.9	10.0	10.4	10.7	10.4	8.9	9.1	10.2	11.5	8.4
1956.......	9.9	9.7	10.4	10.5	10.6	8.8	9.0	9.8	11.1	8.2
1955.......	9.9	10.2	10.4	10.4	10.8	8.8	9.0	10.2	12.0	8.3
1954.......	9.9	10.2	10.3	10.7	10.6	8.7	9.0	10.0	11.7	8.8
1953.......	10.1	10.9	10.4	11.0	11.2	9.1	9.0	10.4	13.0	9.2
1952.......	10.3	11.4	10.4	10.9	11.8	9.2	9.4	10.5	13.7	9.9
1951.......	10.8	11.9	11.0	11.6	12.4	9.3	9.7	11.4	13.4	10.9
1950.......	10.6	11.9	10.8	11.2	11.8	9.4	9.6	11.4	13.5	10.9
1949.......	10.8	12.6	11.0	11.4	12.9	9.5	9.4	12.7	14.1	11.0
1948.......	10.9	13.1	10.6	11.3	13.1	9.6	9.7	12.9	14.8	11.5
1947.......	11.6	13.9	11.7	12.1	14.6	9.8	9.7	13.3	15.6	12.8
1946.......	11.9	14.5	11.7	13.1	14.7	9.7	10.1	13.2	15.9	14.4
1945.......	13.6	16.8	13.1	19.2	15.2	10.1	10.4	14.2	16.6	19.7
1944.......	12.9	15.5	14.0	14.5	15.5	10.2	10.3	15.4	17.6	13.4
1943.......	12.4	16.3	12.5	12.8	15.2	10.5	11.0	15.2	18.7	15.1
1942.......	12.5	16.5	12.6	13.0	15.1	10.1	11.5	15.0	19.7	14.9
1941.......	12.7	18.2	13.7	12.8	16.2	10.3	10.6	14.7	18.6	21.2
1940.......	12.7	18.1	14.1	13.5	15.6	10.3	9.8	15.6	18.7	20.0
1939.......	12.2	18.1	12.3	13.2	15.6	10.2	9.8	16.3	19.0	19.0
1938.......	12.3	18.4	12.0	13.0	16.4	10.2	10.0	16.6	19.2	19.3
1937.......	12.5	18.2	12.5	12.9	16.8	10.9	9.5	16.3	19.5	18.9
1936.......	12.3	18.7	12.4	12.9	16.2	10.8	9.4	16.6	19.7	19.9
1935.......	12.3	19.0	12.2	13.4	16.6	10.4	9.1	16.4	20.6	19.9
1934.......	12.1	19.8	11.9	12.9	16.4	10.3	9.1	17.1	21.5	20.7
1933.......	12.1	19.6	12.3	13.1	16.5	10.2	8.6	17.4	21.9	19.5
1932.......	12.7	18.7	12.5	14.3	17.6	10.5	8.5	16.1	20.8	19.1
1931.......	12.8	19.9	12.9	14.2	17.8	10.7	8.6	16.7	22.6	20.4
1930.......	12.6	19.6	12.4	13.8	17.0	11.1	8.6	17.0	21.2	20.6
1960-61....	9.4	8.5	10.4	10.0	9.3	8.6	8.8	8.9	9.8	6.9
1955-59....	9.7	10.2	10.4	10.4	10.1	8.8	9.0	9.8	11.2	9.6
1950-54....	10.3	11.9	10.6	11.1	11.5	9.1	9.4	10.8	13.0	11.9
1945-49....	11.6	15.1	11.5	13.4	13.8	9.7	9.8	13.2	15.4	16.6
1940-44....	12.6	18.1	13.4	13.3	15.5	10.3	10.6	15.2	18.7	20.3
1935-39....	12.3	18.4	12.3	13.1	16.4	10.4	9.3	16.4	19.6	19.3
1930-34....	12.4	20.8	12.1	13.6	17.0	10.5	8.7	16.8	21.6	24.1
1925-29....	13.5	21.1	12.8	15.3	19.0	11.5	9.0	18.6	23.6	21.0
1920-24....	14.5	22.8	13.4	17.5	20.4	12.0	9.4	21.5	23.9	23.1

* Data are available for a few selected nations only.

of these views is an unwarranted cause-and-effect inference from a correlation. We shall argue later that for economic prosperity a nation must have *both* a program of economic development and a program of fertility control and that for ultimate success they both can and should proceed together.

In studying Figure 3-7 the reader should note the anomolous position of the United States. As the nation with the highest per capita gross product, it falls well above the average trend line. According to the typical pattern it would be expected to have a birthrate of 14 or 15 per thousand, as does Sweden and several other nations in Europe. This illustrates in still another way that despite its

wealth it is less advanced in the process of demographic transition than several other nations of the world. It also adds a point to the argument that the association between fertility and national level of living is not a simple one.

3.12.   The Future Growth of World Population and Its Implication for National and International Policy

Our appreciation of the world population problem would be greatly enhanced if we could somehow quantify the trends discussed above and arrive at an estimate of what the population of the world will be in the years 1975 and 2000 if recent trends continue, with a moderate amount of demographic readjustment

Table 3-8 Crude Death Rates for Selected Nations of World Regions Where Reliable Data Are Available: 1920 to 1962

Year	Northern and Western Europe									
	Belgium	Denmark	Finland	France	Ireland	Nether-lands	Norway	Sweden	England and Wales	Scotland
1962.........	12.5	9.8	9.5	11.5	11.9	7.9	9.3	10.1	11.9	12.2
1961.........	11.7	9.4	9.1	10.9	12.4	7.6	9.1	9.8	12.0	12.3
1960.........	12.4	9.5	9.0	11.4	11.5	7.6	9.1	10.0	11.5	11.9
1959.........	11.4	9.3	8.8	11.3	12.0	7.6	8.9	9.5	11.6	12.2
1958.........	11.7	9.2	8.9	11.2	12.0	7.5	9.0	9.6	11.7	12.1
1957.........	12.0	9.3	9.4	12.1	11.9	7.5	8.7	9.9	11.5	11.9
1956.........	12.2	8.9	9.0	12.5	11.7	7.8	8.7	9.6	11.7	12.1
1955.........	12.3	8.7	9.3	12.2	12.6	7.6	8.5	9.5	11.7	12.1
1954.........	11.9	9.1	9.1	12.1	12.1	7.5	8.6	9.6	11.3	12.0
1953.........	12.1	9.0	9.6	13.1	11.7	7.7	8.5	9.7	11.4	11.5
1952.........	11.9	9.0	9.5	12.4	11.9	7.3	8.5	9.6	11.3	12.1
1951.........	12.6	8.8	10.0	13.5	14.3	7.5	8.4	9.9	12.4	12.9
1950.........	12.5	9.2	10.1	12.8	12.7	7.5	9.1	10.0	11.7	12.5
1949.........	12.9	8.9	11.3	13.7	12.7	8.1	9.0	10.0	11.6	12.2
1948.........	12.6	8.6	11.2	12.5	12.2	7.4	8.9	9.8	10.8	11.8
1947.........	13.3	9.7	11.9	13.2	14.8	8.1	9.5	10.8	12.3	13.2
1946.........	13.6	10.2	11.8	13.6	14.0	8.5	9.4	10.5	12.0	13.0
1945.........	14.9	10.5	13.1	16.3	14.5	15.3	9.7	10.8	12.7	13.3
1944.........	16.0	10.3	18.9	19.2	15.3	11.8	10.7	11.0	12.7	13.6
1943.........	13.6	9.6	13.3	16.3	14.8	10.0	10.4	10.2	13.0	14.0
1942.........	14.8	9.6	15.1	16.9	14.1	9.5	10.7	9.9	12.3	13.3
1941.........	14.7	10.3	19.8	17.3	14.6	10.0	10.8	11.3	13.5	14.7
1940.........	16.2	10.4	19.4	18.9	14.2	9.9	10.9	11.4	14.4	14.9
1939.........	13.9	10.1	14.3	15.6	14.2	8.6	10.1	11.5	12.1	12.9
1938.........	13.2	10.3	12.8	15.8	13.6	8.5	9.9	11.5	11.6	12.6
1937.........	13.2	10.8	12.8	15.4	15.3	8.8	10.4	12.0	12.4	13.9
1936.........	12.9	11.0	13.6	15.6	14.4	8.7	10.4	12.0	12.1	13.4
1935.........	12.9	11.0	12.7	16.0	14.0	8.7	10.3	11.7	11.7	13.2
1934.........	12.3	10.4	13.1	15.4	13.2	8.4	9.9	11.2	11.8	12.9
1933.........	13.3	10.5	13.6	16.1	13.7	8.8	10.1	11.2	12.3	13.2
1932.........	13.3	11.0	13.3	16.1	14.6	9.0	10.6	11.6	12.0	13.5
1931.........	13.4	11.4	14.1	16.5	14.6	9.6	10.9	12.5	12.3	13.3
1930.........	13.4	10.8	14.0	15.9	14.2	9.1	10.5	11.7	11.4	13.3
1926-1930....	13.7	11.1	14.8	16.8	14.4	9.9	11.0	12.1	12.1	13.6
1921-1925....	13.4	11.3	15.1	17.2	14.6	10.4	11.5	12.1	12.2	13.9
1911-1913....	15.3	13.0	17.3	19.0	16.4	13.1	13.3	13.9	13.9	15.3
1905-1909....	16.2	14.1	17.7	19.5	17.2	14.7	14.1	14.6	15.1	16.3
1960-61......	12.0	9.4	9.0	11.2	12.0	7.6	9.1	9.9	11.8	12.1
1955-59......	11.9	9.1	9.1	11.8	12.0	7.6	8.8	9.6	11.6	12.0
1950-54......	12.2	9.0	9.7	12.8	12.5	7.5	8.6	9.7	11.6	12.2
1945-49......	13.4	9.6	11.8	13.9	13.7	9.4	9.3	10.4	11.5	12.3
1940-44......	15.1	10.0	17.3	17.7	14.6	10.2	10.7	10.8	13.2	14.1
1935-39......	13.3	10.7	13.3	15.6	14.3	8.7	10.2	11.7	12.0	13.2
1930-34......	13.2	10.8	13.6	16.0	10.9	9.0	10.4	11.7	12.0	13.2
1925-29......	13.8	11.1	14.9	17.3	11.7	10.0	11.1	12.1	12.2	13.7
1920-24......	13.7	11.4	15.6	17.3	14.3	11.0	11.8	12.4	12.2	14.0

in the meantime. The United Nations performed this monumental task in 1958 and again in 1966.[12] After a careful estimate of the population in each of the world regions as of 1950, of the growth rate in 1950-1960, and of the level of fertility and mortality, each region and major nation is fitted into a population growth "model," which predicts how the growth trend will be modified in future years from that currently observed. For example,

[12] United Nations, *The Future Growth of World Population*, Population Studies, No. 28 *World Population Projects*, Population Studies, No. 41. (New York: United Nations Department of Economic and Social Affairs, 1958, 1966.)

under the model of "moderate growth" those nations that currently have high birth and death rates are expected to show a steady decline in mortality beginning promptly but a slow and moderate decline in fertility only after 1980, whereas nations with moderate fertility are expected to continue a slow decline and nations with low fertility to remain at about their present level. All nations are expected to make steady progress in mortality reduction, so that by the year 2000 a life expectancy at birth of about 70 years will be a worldwide average. By applying this model to each major nation the United Nations arrives at an estimate for the years 1980 and 2000.

Table 3-8 (Continued)

Year	Central Europe						Southern Europe			
	West Germany	Czecho-slovakia	Hungary	Poland	Swit-zerland	Austria	Albania	Bulgaria	Italy	Portugal
1962.........	11.1	10.0	10.8	7.9	9.8	12.7	10.0	8.5	9.9	10.9
1961.........	11.0	9.2	9.6	7.6	9.3	12.1	9.3	7.9	9.4	11.2
1960.........	11.4	9.2	10.2	7.5	9.7	12.7	10.4	8.1	9.7	10.8
1959.........	10.8	9.7	10.5	8.6	9.5	12.5	9.8	9.5	9.3	11.1
1958.........	10.8	9.3	9.9	8.4	9.5	12.2	9.3	7.9	9.4	10.5
1957.........	11.3	10.1	10.5	9.5	10.0	12.8	11.8	8.6	10.0	11.7
1956.........	11.2	9.6	10.5	9.0	10.2	12.4	11.5	9.4	10.3	12.3
1955.........	11.0	9.6	10.0	9.6	10.1	12.2	15.1	9.1	9.3	11.5
1954.........	10.6	10.4	11.0	10.3	10.0	12.1	13.1	9.2	9.2	11.1
1953.........	11.2	10.5	11.7	10.2	10.2	12.0	13.7	9.3	10.0	11.4
1952.........	10.6	10.6	11.3	11.1	9.9	12.0	15.6	11.6	10.1	11.8
1951.........	10.7	11.4	11.7	12.4	10.5	12.7	15.2	10.7	10.3	12.4
1950.........	10.5	11.5	11.4	11.6	10.1	12.4	14.1	10.2	9.8	12.2
1949.........	10.2	11.9	11.4	11.6	10.7	12.9	14.9	11.8	10.5	14.1
1948.........	10.5	11.5	11.6	11.2	10.8	12.1	15.3	12.6	10.7	13.0
1947.........	11.6	12.1	12.9	11.4	11.4	13.0	17.0	13.4	11.5	13.5
1946.........	12.3	14.1	15.0	12.4	11.3	13.4	17.3	13.7	12.1	14.9
1945.........	18.3	17.8	23.4	18.5	11.6	25.6	17.9	14.9	13.6	14.4
1944.........	13.3	15.0	17.1	13.5	12.0	16.0	18.3	13.7	15.3	15.0
1943.........	12.2	14.1	13.5	12.3	11.0	13.8	17.9	13.0	15.2	15.4
1942.........	12.4	14.3	14.6	12.5	10.9	13.3	14.2	13.0	14.3	16.2
1941.........	12.2	14.0	13.2	12.3	11.1	14.0	16.6	12.7	13.9	17.4
1940.........	12.9	14.0	14.3	13.0	12.0	14.8	16.4	13.4	13.6	15.7
1939.........	12.6	13.3	13.5	12.7	11.8	15.3	15.0	13.4	13.4	15.3
1938.........	11.4	13.2	14.3	13.7	11.6	14.0	17.7	13.7	14.1	15.4
1937.........	11.6	13.1	14.1	14.0	11.3	13.3	19.5	13.6	14.3	15.8
1936.........	11.6	13.0	14.2	14.2	11.4	13.2	16.6	14.3	13.8	16.2
1935.........	12.0	13.3	15.2	14.0	12.1	13.7	17.0	14.6	14.0	17.0
1934.........	11.6	13.0	14.5	14.4	11.3	12.7	16.7	14.1	13.3	16.6
1933.........	11.8	13.5	14.7	14.2	11.4	13.2	16.8	15.6	13.7	17.1
1932.........	12.8	13.9	17.9	15.0	12.2	13.9	18.0	16.3	14.7	17.1
1931.........	12.7	14.1	16.6	15.5	12.1	14.0	18.2	17.0	14.8	16.8
1930.........	12.3	13.9	15.5	15.7	11.6	13.5	16.3	16.2	14.1	17.1
1926-1930....	11.8	15.3	17.0	16.8	12.1	14.4	....	....	....	....
1921-1925....	13.3	16.1	19.9	18.5	12.5	15.8	....	....	....	....
1911-1913....	14.8	20.4	22.9	21.7	14.8	18.8	....	....	....	....
1905-1909....	18.3	24.1	25.7	....	16.5	....	....	....	....	....
1960-61......	11.2	9.2	9.9	7.6	9.5	12.4	9.8	8.0	9.6	11.0
1955-59......	11.0	9.7	10.3	9.0	9.9	12.4	11.4	8.9	9.6	11.2
1950-54......	10.7	10.9	11.4	11.1	10.1	12.2	14.3	10.2	9.9	11.8
1945-49......	12.6	13.5	14.8	13.0	11.1	15.3	16.5	13.3	11.7	14.0
1940-44......	12.6	14.3	14.5	12.7	11.4	14.4	16.7	13.2	14.5	15.9
1935-39......	11.8	13.2	14.3	14.0	11.6	13.9	17.2	13.9	13.9	15.9
1930-34......	12.2	13.7	15.8	15.0	11.7	13.5	17.2	15.8	14.1	16.9
1925-29......	15.3	15.2	17.3	17.0	12.2	14.7	....	18.5	16.6	18.7
1920-24......	17.5	16.5	20.9	20.6	12.9	16.7	....	21.3	17.5	21.5

The estimates for each world region for these dates are reported in Table 3-9.

The result of this exercise yields predictions of almost unbelievably rapid population expansion. The 3 billion persons of 1965 are expected to more than double in 35 years, so that by the year 2000 there will be 6.3 billion persons on earth. Moreover, this growth is expected to occur primarily in the developing (underdeveloped) nations of Asia, Latin America, and Africa. Whereas the industrialized nations will grow only at slightly less than 1 percent per year in the last quarter of this century, the developing nations are expected to be growing by 2.3 percent per year.

In making its report, the United Nations does not claim to predict what actually will happen. In fact, this research seems to have been done to show what will happen if something constructive by way of a fertility control program is not done—and quickly. Is it possible to more than double in such a short time the populations of already overcrowded nations like India, Pakistan, Ceylon, China, El Salvador, Costa Rica, and Haiti without bringing economic collapse? If such doubling does take place, what will happen to the programs of economic development? Does it make impossible the plans for raising the level of living that all of these nations have?

Table 3-8   (*Continued*)

Year	Southern Europe			Northern America		South America				Middle America
	Romania	Spain	Yugo-slavia	Canada	United States	Argentina	Chile	Surinam	Venezuela	Barbados
1962........	9.4	9.0	9.9	7.6	9.5	7.9	11.6	8.1	6.9	10.9
1961........	8.7	8.6	9.0	7.7	9.3	8.0	11.7	8.2	7.0	10.2
1960........	8.7	8.9	9.9	7.8	9.5	8.2	12.5	8.2	7.2	9.2
1959........	10.2	9.0	9.9	8.0	9.4	8.4	12.7	8.4	8.0	8.7
1958........	8.7	8.8	9.3	7.9	9.5	8.3	12.2	8.0	8.7	9.8
1957........	10.2	10.0	10.7	8.2	9.6	9.0	12.9	9.5	9.3	10.7
1956........	9.9	9.9	11.2	8.2	9.3	8.3	12.1	9.4	9.3	10.6
1955........	9.7	9.4	11.4	8.2	9.3	8.8	13.0	9.2	9.6	12.6
1954........	11.4	9.2	10.8	8.2	9.2	8.4	12.8	9.2	9.6	11.2
1953........	11.6	9.7	12.4	8.6	9.6	8.9	12.4	10.7	9.5	13.6
1952........	11.7	9.7	11.8	8.7	9.6	8.6	13.0	9.8	10.5	14.7
1951........	12.8	11.6	14.1	9.0	9.6	8.9	15.0	10.5	11.1	14.1
1950........	12.4	10.9	13.0	9.1	9.6	9.0	15.0	10.8	10.9	12.8
1949........	13.7	11.6	13.5	9.3	9.7	9.0	17.3	12.6	11.9	14.6
1948........	15.6	11.1	13.5	9.3	9.9	9.4	16.7	12.7	12.8	15.7
1947........	22.1	12.1	12.8	9.4	10.1	9.9	16.1	13.7	13.4	16.3
1946........	18.9	13.0	13.1	9.4	10.0	9.6	16.6	12.1	14.7	17.0
1945........	20.0	12.3	13.5	9.5	10.6	10.3	19.3	12.0	15.0	16.9
1944........	19.6	13.1	13.8	9.8	10.6	10.2	18.9	15.3	17.0	18.3
1943........	18.1	13.4	13.5	10.1	10.9	10.1	19.3	15.6	15.9	17.1
1942........	19.5	14.8	13.8	9.8	10.3	10.3	19.9	13.8	16.2	18.2
1941........	19.3	18.8	14.9	10.1	10.5	10.4	19.4	12.6	16.4	21.8
1940........	19.1	16.6	14.2	9.8	10.7	10.7	21.3	13.6	16.6	18.5
1939........	18.6	18.5	15.0	9.7	10.6	10.7	22.9	12.8	18.7	19.1
1938........	19.2	19.3	15.6	9.7	10.6	11.8	23.1	13.3	18.3	21.4
1937........	19.3	19.0	16.0	10.4	11.3	11.5	22.7	13.0	18.1	20.3
1936........	19.8	16.8	16.1	9.9	11.6	11.3	24.0	13.6	17.4	20.3
1935........	21.1	15.8	16.9	9.9	10.9	12.5	23.9	12.5	16.6	22.0
1934........	20.7	16.1	17.1	9.5	11.1	11.1	25.7	13.4	18.1	25.1
1933........	18.7	16.5	17.0	9.7	10.7	11.3	26.0	13.7	18.5	21.9
1932........	21.7	16.5	19.2	10.0	10.9	11.4	22.2	13.7	17.1	20.6
1931........	20.9	17.3	19.8	10.2	11.1	11.9	21.5	15.0	18.4	28.2
1930........	19.4	16.8	19.0	10.8	11.3	12.2	24.1	14.3	17.2	24.9
1960-61.....	8.7	8.8	9.4	7.8	9.4	8.1	12.1	8.2	7.1	9.7
1955-59.....	9.7	9.4	10.4	8.1	9.4	8.3	12.5	8.9	9.7	10.5
1950-54.....	12.0	10.2	12.4	8.7	9.5	8.8	13.6	10.2	10.6	13.3
1945-49.....	16.1	12.0	13.3	9.4	10.0	9.6	17.2	12.6	13.5	16.1
1940-44.....	19.1	15.3	14.0	9.9	10.6	10.3	19.8	14.2	16.4	18.8
1935-39.....	20.0	17.9	15.9	9.8	11.0	11.6	23.7	12.4	17.9	20.6
1930-34.....	20.3	16.5	18.4	10.0	11.0	11.6	23.9	13.6	17.9	24.1
1925-29.....	21.6	18.4	20.0	11.2	11.8	13.0	25.5	16.2	19.5	28.1
1920-24.....	24.0	21.0	17.1	11.9	12.0	14.0	30.2	20.1	21.7	30.2

As discouraging as these estimates are, the United Nations hastens to point out that according to its model of growth by the year 2000 more than one half of the world's population will still be growing moderately rapidly, so that another doubling can be expected by the year 2050 or so. It is beyond our comprehension that the density of Europe, Asia, and the other world regions could quadruple, even under the most optimistic expectations about the miracles of technology, without creating an economic situation of bare subsistence. And world thinkers who like to think in terms of centuries are wondering what to expect after 2050.

Inasmuch as the "moderate growth" estimates have a small amount of fertility decline

built in, they show what might be expected to happen if things are "just allowed to take their course" and normal processes of demographic readjustment are allowed to take care of things. These estimates therefore show, in cold arithmetic, that the nations of the world must accelerate the process of demographic readjustment and achieve low birthrates much more quickly than did the nations of Europe. The trends of the past clearly cannot continue for more than just a few decades before some kind of a drastic readjustment, peaceful or other, will be made.

Table 3-9 may very profitably be employed in conjunction with Table 3-4 to obtain a full picture of recent and expected future growth trends in the major nations of the world. Al-

Table 3-8 (Continued)

Year	Middle America (continued)								Asia	
	Costa Rica	El Salvador	Guate- mala	Jamaica	Mexico	Panama	Puerto Rico	Trinidad and Tobago	China (Taiwan)	Malaya
1962........	8.5	10.8	17.2	9.0	10.4	8.0	6.7	7.7	6.4	8.7
1961........	7.9	10.5	16.3	8.8	10.6	8.2	6.7	7.9	6.7	8.7
1960........	8.6	11.0	17.5	8.9	11.5	8.4	6.7	7.8	6.9	9.5
1959........	9.0	11.9	17.3	10.6	11.7	9.1	6.8	9.1	7.2	9.7
1958........	9.0	13.5	21.3	9.1	12.3	8.7	7.0	9.2	7.6	11.0
1957........	10.1	14.0	20.6	8.9	13.0	9.3	7.1	9.5	8.5	12.4
1956........	9.6	12.4	19.8	9.4	11.9	9.2	7.4	9.6	8.0	11.6
1955........	10.5	14.2	20.6	9.9	13.6	9.2	7.2	10.4	8.6	11.7
1954........	10.6	15.0	18.4	10.7	13.0	8.8	7.6	9.8	8.2	12.4
1953........	11.7	14.7	23.1	10.4	15.8	9.2	8.2	10.7	9.4	12.6
1952........	11.6	16.3	24.2	11.5	14.9	8.4	9.2	12.1	9.9	13.8
1951........	11.7	15.1	19.6	12.1	17.3	8.7	10.0	12.0	11.6	15.4
1950........	12.2	14.7	21.8	11.9	16.2	9.6	9.9	12.1	11.5	15.9
1949........	12.7	15.4	21.8	12.3	17.6	9.8	10.6	12.2	13.1	14.2
1948........	13.2	16.9	23.5	13.2	16.7	10.2	12.0	12.2	14.3	16.3
1947........	14.9	17.2	24.7	14.1	16.4	11.7	11.8	13.4	15.3	19.4
1946........	13.9	17.6	24.7	13.3	19.1	11.2	12.9	13.8	17.0	20.0
1945........	15.5	18.2	24.5	14.9	19.2	11.8	13.7	14.5	22.4	26.3
1944........	16.7	19.7	26.5	15.1	20.3	12.3	14.4	15.0	15.3	18.0
1943........	17.7	22.6	31.1	14.1	22.2	13.0	14.3	16.6	19.0	20.9
1942........	21.0	22.8	31.5	14.3	22.6	12.8	16.2	17.7	18.0	20.6
1941........	18.1	18.4	25.1	14.4	22.0	13.3	18.3	16.1	16.5	28.8
1940........	18.1	19.1	25.0	15.4	23.2	14.6	18.3	15.8	19.7	20.7
1939........	19.3	19.6	29.6	15.1	23.0	11.4	17.7	16.1	20.1	19.1
1938........	17.7	19.1	26.3	16.8	22.9	14.2	18.7	15.9	20.0	20.4
1937........	19.2	20.5	24.4	15.6	24.4	13.1	20.9	17.4	20.1	20.9
1936........	21.0	21.2	24.7	17.7	23.5	12.7	20.0	16.3	20.1	22.0
1935........	22.9	25.1	27.4	18.0	22.6	11.9	18.0	17.5	20.7	22.3
1934........	18.6	25.3	30.6	17.3	23.8	15.7	18.9	18.6	20.9	23.4
1933........	21.7	23.6	27.3	19.7	25.7	15.6	22.3	19.6	20.1	21.1
1932........	22.9	21.9	23.6	17.4	26.1	15.8	22.0	17.1	20.7	20.1
1931........	24.7	22.4	24.3	18.9	25.9	16.4	22.5	20.1	21.7	21.1
1930........	22.5	21.6	24.7	17.3	26.6	13.1	21.2	19.1	19.8	21.3
1960-61.....	8.2	10.8	16.9	8.8	11.0	8.3	6.7	7.8	6.8	9.1
1955-59.....	9.6	13.2	19.9	9.4	12.5	9.1	7.1	9.6	8.0	11.3
1950-54.....	11.5	15.2	21.4	11.3	15.4	8.8	9.0	11.3	10.0	14.0
1945-49.....	14.0	17.0	23.8	13.5	17.8	10.9	12.2	13.2	16.4	19.2
1940-44.....	18.3	20.5	27.8	14.7	22.1	13.2	16.3	16.2	17.7	21.8
1935-39.....	20.0	21.1	26.5	16.6	23.3	12.7	19.0	16.6	19.8	20.8
1930-34.....	22.0	23.0	26.2	18.1	25.6	15.4	21.1	18.9	20.6	21.6
1925-29.....	23.2	24.4	29.9	20.4	25.5	17.1	23.6	20.2	22.8	....
1920-24.....	22.3	24.3	25.7	24.4	25.1	17.1	23.9	22.3	25.8	....

though the United Nations emphasizes that their projections for individual nations are highly approximate, they perform the very valuable service of warning all who read of the magnitude of population size and the growth rate to anticipate in the coming decade.

Before we succumb to despair and predict demographic doom for the developing nations we need to review very carefully the prospects for accomplishing fertility control at a more rapid rate than has taken place in any of the nations of Europe or Northern America. This is undertaken in Chapters 20 and 21, where the United Nations estimating procedure is reviewed very carefully and where an intensive study is made of the changes in fertility that have taken place around the world since 1960.

CONCLUSION

This overview of population trends around the world has tried to present the world population problem in a distinctly social science, as contrasted with a biological, perspective. We have seen how every nation that has not already achieved it is racing toward a point at which its death rate will be 10 per thousand or less. This is being accomplished by modern medical and public health technology and modern methods of producing and distributing food and other essentials of life. Under modern conditions, and often with a helping hand from more prosperous nations, the less developed nations of the world are succeeding in conquering the problem of the death rate in less

Table 3-8   (Continued)

Year	Asia (continued)				Oceania			Union of Soviet Socialist Republics
	Hong Kong	Israel	Japan	Singapore	American Samoa	Australia	New Zealand	
1962	6.0	6.0	7.5	5.9	6.1	8.7	8.9	7.5
1961	5.9	5.8	7.4	6.0	5.3	8.5	9.0	7.2
1960	6.2	5.7	7.6	6.3	5.4	8.6	8.8	7.1
1959	6.8	5.9	7.5	6.5	5.3	8.9	9.1	7.6
1958	7.2	5.8	7.5	7.0	7.1	8.5	8.9	7.2
1957	7.1	6.5	8.3	7.4	10.6	8.8	9.4	7.8
1956	7.4	6.6	8.1	7.5	7.4	9.1	9.0	7.6
1955	7.7	6.1	7.8	8.1	6.5	8.9	9.0	8.2
1954	8.5	6.8	8.2	8.6	6.4	9.1	9.0	8.9
1953	8.1	6.7	8.9	9.7	5.3	9.1	9.0	9.1
1952	8.6	7.3	8.9	10.7	10.6	9.4	9.5	9.4
1951	10.2	6.7	10.0	11.6	9.6	9.7	9.7	9.7
1950	8.2	6.9	10.9	12.0	9.7	9.6	9.5	9.7
1949	8.8	6.8	11.6	11.8	7.5	9.5	9.4	....
1948	7.5	6.6	12.0	12.4	9.0	10.0	9.4	....
1947	7.6	6.5	14.6	13.3	11.0	9.7	9.7	....
1946	10.7	6.3	17.6	14.8	11.5	10.1	10.1	....
1945	14.1	6.7	29.2	19.5	11.8	10.3	10.4	....
1944	9.6	7.1	17.4	13.3	11.7	10.3	10.3	....
1943	11.2	7.7	16.3	15.5	12.5	11.5	10.5	....
1942	11.0	8.6	15.8	15.2	13.0	12.0	11.0	....
1941	37.4	7.9	15.7	20.8	12.0	10.6	10.5	....
1940	34.2	8.2	16.4	20.9	11.1	9.8	9.7	18.3
1939	29.9	7.7	17.8	19.5	11.2	9.9	9.8	....
1938	28.1	8.2	17.7	21.4	11.5	9.6	10.5	....
1937	25.6	7.8	17.0	22.0	10.8	9.4	9.6	....
1936	26.9	8.8	17.5	24.2	10.7	9.4	9.3	....
1935	26.9	8.6	16.8	24.3	10.3	9.5	8.7	....
1934	28.0	9.5	18.1	24.1	10.3	9.3	8.9	....
1933	26.4	9.3	17.7	22.5	9.9	8.9	8.4	....
1932	25.8	9.7	17.7	20.4	9.6	8.6	8.4	....
1931	27.1	9.6	19.0	24.2	9.9	8.7	8.6	....
1930	27.4	9.5	18.2	27.6	9.8	8.6	8.6	....
1960-61	6.0	5.8	7.5	6.2	5.4	8.6	8.9	7.2
1955-59	7.6	6.2	7.8	7.3	7.4	8.8	9.1	....
1950-54	8.7	6.9	9.4	10.4	8.1	9.4	9.3	....
1945-49	9.7	6.5	16.8	14.4	10.2	9.9	9.8	....
1940-44	20.7	7.9	16.3	17.1	12.1	10.8	10.4	....
1935-39	27.5	8.2	17.4	22.1	10.9	9.6	9.0	....
1930-34	26.9	9.5	18.1	23.8	9.9	8.8	8.6	....
1925-29	....	12.6	19.8	29.0	....	9.4	8.6	....
1920-24	....	13.0	23.0	30.5	....	9.8	9.0	....

than one-half the time that it required in Europe and Northern America. The pace has been so fast that birthrates, always less responsive to changed conditions, have scarcely moved from their high levels in many of these developing nations. We have, as a result, the anomalous situation of having late transitional death rates and early transitional birthrates in the same population. The consequence of this situation is more rapid rates of growth than attained ever before in human history on a sustained basis.

Many people have been greatly frightened by this development. The basis of their fright is that it will take several decades, perhaps generations, to bring the birthrates into line with the lowered death rates. Projecting population growth into the future, assuming gradual decline in fertility, produces estimates of future population that are truly astronomical and lead almost to intellectual despair.

The present book undertakes to challenge the major premise of this dilemma: *Is it really inevitable that so long a time is required to reduce birthrates?* Why cannot it be done effectively in 10 or 15 years, if we launch large-scale and scientifically based programs of fertility control to match our programs of mortality control? The foregoing review of world population history has emphasized that throughout the history of civilization there has been a tendency toward regulation of demographic processes by social or group controls. What evidence we have suggests that the tendency toward such regulation has grown steadily stronger as population density mounts.

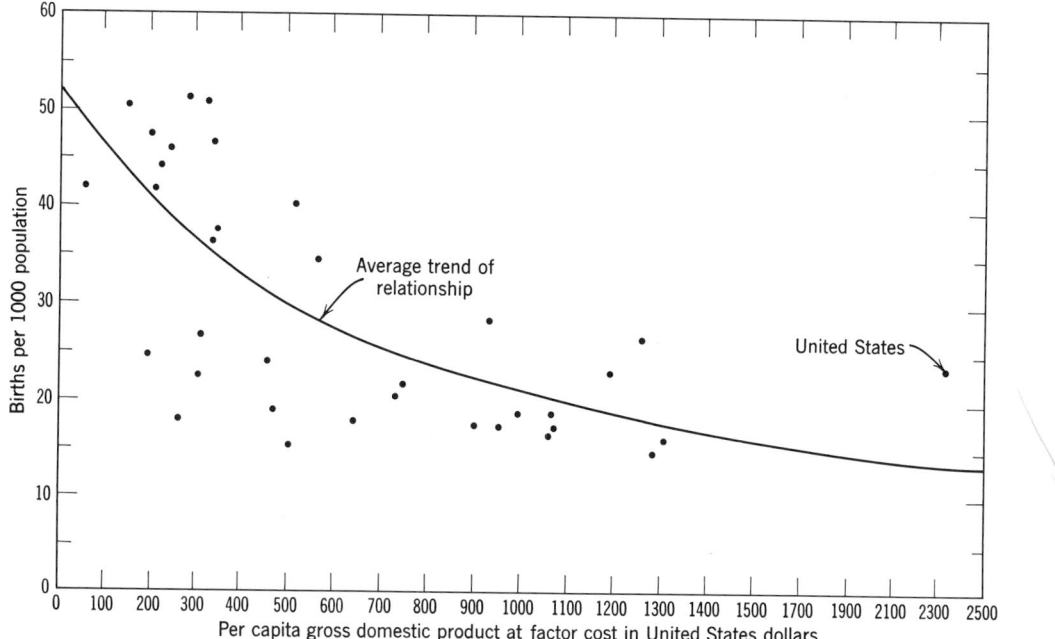

Figure 3-7   Scattergram of Per Capita Gross Domestic Product Plotted against the Crude Birthrate for Selected Nations of the World: 1960.

SOURCE: United Nations.

It is inherent in all cultures and in the social institutions of all societies. In other words, the notion of fertility control is not alien to any culture. One of the major themes, to which we return in almost every chapter, is the question, How can social science theories and research reinforce and speed the process of demographic regulation, in order that the transition from uncontrolled to fully controlled vital processes may be accomplished in less time?

It is not improbable that this question is one of the most important research topics of the second half of the twentieth century, ranking with the harnessing of atomic energy and the conquest of space. And the timetable for raising the per capita income and the level of living of poverty-stricken populations depends on the timetable for fertility reduction. We believe that fertility reduction in these populations can and will be achieved much faster than it was in Northwest Europe and Northern America.

QUESTIONS AND TOPICS FOR DISCUSSION

1. From the data on trends in crude birth and death rates compute an index for each year, 1920-1924 = 100. Compare the change in the value of this index number for developing and industrialized nations, both for birth and death rates. Write an essay interpreting your findings.

2. Repeat the procedure for selected pairs of nations. Examples of contrasting nations are France and Poland, Albania and Bulgaria, Argentina and Chile, Costa Rica and Puerto Rico, and Malaya and Japan.

3. If we presume that the developing na-

tions have a much younger age composition than the industrialized nations, would you say that the crude birthrates presented here minimize or exaggerate differences in fertility levels between developing and industrialized nations? Would you make the same inference concerning differences in mortality levels?

4. What would be the birthrate of India in 1980 if it succeeded in reducing birthrates by the same number of points each year as did Romania between 1950 and 1960? Repeat the estimate, using Hungary, Poland, and Bulgaria. Assume that the average of these four countries

Table 3-9   Projected Future Population in 1975 of World Regions and Selected Nations; and Estimated Percent Change: 1965 to 1980

World region and nation	Population in 1980	Percent change 1970-80
WORLD TOTAL (IN MILLIONS)..	4,330	20.4
INDUSTRIALIZED REGIONS (IN MILLIONS).......	1,194	10.4
NORTHERN AND WESTERN EUROPE	233,225	4.7
Austria...................	7,275	0.8
Belgium...................	10,100	5.4
Denmark...................	5,200	6.3
Finland...................	5,250	8.7
France...................	53,250	7.6
German Fed. Rep...........	58,500	3.4
Ireland...................	2,860	0.7
Netherlands...............	14,050	10.2
Norway...................	4,250	9.0
Sweden...................	8,375	5.7
Switzerland...............	6,250	5.6
United Kingdom...........	57,250	3.9
EASTERN EUROPE.......	113,597	7.8
Bulgaria.................	9,275	8.2
Czechoslovakia...........	15,800	7.7
East Germany.............	17,600	1.1
Hungary.................	10,700	3.6
Poland...................	38,000	13.1
Romania.................	22,250	9.6
SOUTHERN EUROPE	132,569	5.5
Greece...................	9,500	6.5
Italy...................	56,400	6.6
Portugal.................	9,750	4.6
Spain...................	36,000	8.8
Yugoslavia...............	22,750	10.2
NORTHERN AMERICA	261,629	15.4
Canada...................	26,300	21.3
United States.............	240,893	16.1
OCEANIA	22,556	20.5
Australia.................	14,571	18.5
New Zealand...............	3,666	24.5
New Guinea...............	1,985	21.1
U.S.S.R.........	277,800	13.1
DEVELOPING REGIONS, TOTAL (IN MILLIONS).......	3,136	24.9
ASIA, TOTAL..........	2461,355	24.2
SOUTH CENTRAL ASIA......	953,709	27.7
Afghanistan...............	22,100	25.6
Ceylon...................	18,300	36.9
India...................	682,300	25.6
Nepal...................	14,100	25.9
Pakistan.................	183,000	36.6
SOUTH ASIA	603,272	28.7
Burma...................	35,000	26.9
Cambodia.................	9,810	33.8
Indonesia.................	152,750	29.2
Viet-Nam.................	46,400	20.5
Thailand.................	47,516	30.9
Philippines...............	55,750	45.1
Malaya...................	12,693	36.5

Table 3-9   *(Continued)*

World region and nation	Population in 1980	Percent change 1970-80
EAST ASIA........	1287,270	14.3
China (Mainland)..........	843,000	13.6
China (Taiwan)............	17,180	24.9
Japan....................	111,064	9.5
Korea...................	60,837	29.6
Hong Kong.................	5,500	26.4
SOUTH WEST ASIA	102,239	32.8
Iran....................	33,050	29.9
Iraq....................	13,800	42.3
Israel...................	3,141	20.1
Jordan...................	3,350	42.6
Lebanon.................	3,100	31.9
Saudi Arabia.............	9,400	26.2
Syria...................	9,250	43.4
Turkey...................	48,478	32.4
Yemen...................	6,900	26.6
SOUTH AMERICA	255,727	32.7
Argentina.................	28,998	17.0
Bolivia.................	6,000	28.8
Brazil...................	123,716	31.8
Chile...................	12,378	26.9
Colombia.................	27,691	35.0
Ecuador.................	7,981	37.2
Paraguay.................	2,981	33.5
Peru....................	17,560	32.3
Uruguay.................	3,126	11.6
Venezuela.................	14,857	42.5
MIDDLE AMERICA	122,710	36.6
Costa Rica...............	2,419	40.8
Cuba....................	10,034	20.8
Dominican Rep.............	6,174	44.4
El Salvador...............	4,585	37.0
Guatemala.................	6,878	36.7
Haiti...................	6,912	31.5
Honduras.................	3,656	41.0
Jamaica and Dependencies...	2,080	13.0
Mexico...................	70,581	43.2
Nicaragua.................	2,791	41.0
Puerto Rico...............	3,117	13.2
Panama...................	2,023	38.8
Trinidad & Tobago..........	1,450	29.5
NORTHERN AFRICA	116,369	34.2
Egypt (UAR)...............	46,750	35.5
Algeria.................	19,500	34.5
Morocco.................	22,400	40.0
Tunisia.................	6,450	25.9
TROPICAL AND SOUTHERN AFRICA	332,500	28.7

Source: World Population Prospects, 1963, Table A3.2, A3.6, A3.8.

have been achieved when the birthrate is 15 per thousand)? What are your reasons for supposing it will not happen?

5. Study the differences in estimated birthrates for the various nations of Africa and Latin America. Are these differences genuine or simply unsystematic variations in bad data? Which differences are genuine and which are due only to poor data? What causes the genuine differences?

6. The hypothesis of demographic transition presumes that death rates fall faster than birth-

represents the rate of fertility reduction that could be achieved under a well-organized program of family planning. How many years would be required to bring the population of India to a growth rate of zero (assume this to

rates. Study the trend in the birthrates of Eastern Europe between 1950 and 1960 and compare it with the change in death rates. Search the mortality tables to find instances where

death rates have fallen as rapidly as birthrates did in Eastern Europe between 1950 and 1960. How do you interpret this?

BIBLIOGRAPHY

I. POPULATION GROWTH AS A WORLDWIDE PROBLEM

Ady, P. H., et al. *Oxford Regional Economic Atlas.* (In series) Oxford Regional Atlases. Oxford: Clarendon Press, 1965, **60** (iv).

Bates, Marston. *Expanding Population in a Shrinking World.* Public Affairs Pamphlets, for the American Library Association in cooperation with Public Affairs Committee, Inc. Reading for an Age of Change, No. 4, New York, 1963.

Carr-Saunders, A. M. *World Population: Past Growth and Present Trends.* Oxford: Clarendon Press, 1936.

Cook, Robert C. "How Many People Have Ever Lived on Earth?" *Population Bulletin,* **18** (1) (February 1962), 1–19.

Dorn, Harold F. "World Population Growth: An International Dilemma," *Science,* **135** (January 26, 1962), 283–290.

DuBois, Cora A. "Socio-Cultural Aspects of Population Growth," in Roy O. Greep (ed.). *Human Fertility and Population Problems.* Proceedings of the seminar sponsored by the American Academy of Arts and Sciences with the support of the Ford Foundation. Cambridge, Mass.: Schenkman Publishing Co., 1963, pp. 251–265.

El-Badry, M. A. "Population Projections for the World, Developed and Developing Regions: 1965–2000," *Annals of the American Academy of Political and Social Science,* **369** (January 1967), 9–15.

Freedman, Ronald. "The Transition from High to Low Fertility: Challenge to Demographers," *Population Index,* **31** (4) (October 1965), 417–429.

Ginsburg, Norton, et al. *Atlas of Economic Development.* Department of Geography Research Paper, No. 68. Chicago: University of Chicago Press, 1961.

Kirk, Dudley. "Prospects for Reducing Natality in the Underdeveloped World," *Annals of the American Academy of Political and Social Science,* **369** (January 1967), 48–60.

Mackenroth, Gerhard. *World Population and World Economy.* Prepared for publication by Erik Boettcher. *Zeitschrift fuer die Gesamte Staatswissenschaft* (Tuebingen), **112** (1) (1956), 115–130.

Paltridge, T. B. "World Population and the World Food Supply," *World Crops,* **15** (September 1963), 286–300, 402.

Ryder, Norman B. "The Character of Modern Fertility," pp. 26–36 in *Annals of the American Academy of Political and Social Science,* **369** (January 1967).

Stamp, L. Dudley. *Our Developing World.* London: Faber and Faber, 1960.

Thompson, Warren S. "The Spiral of Population," in William L. Thomas, Jr. (ed.). *Man's Role in Changing the Face of the Earth.* International Symposium, Wenner-Gren Foundation for Anthropological Research, Princeton, N. J., 1955. Chicago: University of Chicago Press, 1956, pp. 970–986.

United Nations. Department of Economic and Social Affairs. *World Population Prospects as Assessed in 1963.* Population Studies, No. 41. New York: United Nations, 1966.

United Nations. *The Determinants and Consequences of Population Trends.* New York: United Nations, 1953.

United Nations. *The Future Growth of World Population.* Population Studies, No. 28. New York: United Nations, 1958.

United Nations. Population Division. *World Population: Challenge to Development.* Summary of the highlights of the World Population Conference, Belgrade, Yugoslavia, August 30-September 10, 1965. New York; United Nations, 1966.

United Nations. Social Commission. *Report on the World Social Situation.* Item (3) of the provisional agenda, fifteenth session. (In 3 parts), New York, March 1963.

II. AFRICA — GENERAL

Africa Institute. *Africa: Maps and Statistics.* In 12 parts. No. 1. Pretoria, July 1962.

Barbour, Kennth H., and R. M. Prothero. (eds.). *Essays on African Population.* London: Routledge and Kegan Paul, 1961.

International Union for the Scientific Study of Population. *Problems in African Demography: A Colloquium,* Paris, August 20–27, 1959. Problèmes de démographie en Afrique: colloque de Paris, 20 au 27 Août, 1959. Paris

1960, IV. Duplicate text in English and French.

Lorimer, Frank. "The Population of Africa," in Ronald Freedman (ed.). *Population: The Vital Revolution*. Garden City, N.Y.: Anchor Books, Doubleday, 1964, pp. 206–214.

Murdock, George P. *Africa: Its Peoples and Their Culture History*. New York: McGraw-Hill, 1959.

Smith, T. E., and J. G. C. Blacker. *Population Characteristics of the Commonwealth Countries of Tropical Africa*. University of London, Institute of Commonwealth Papers, 9. London: University of London, Athlone Press for the Institute of Commonwealth Studies, 1963.

Stephens, Richard W. *Population Pressures in Africa South of the Sahara*. Population Research Project. Washington, D. C.: George Washington University, 1958.

United Nations. Economic Commission for Africa. *Fertility, Mortality, International Migration and Population Growth in Africa*. Prepared by the Economic Commission for Africa with the cooperation of the Population Branch of the Bureau of Social Affairs.

United Nations. Economic Commission for Africa. *Economic Commission for Africa Seminar on Population Problems in Africa*. October 29-November 10, 1962, Cairo, United Arab Republic.

United Nations. Economic Commission for Africa. "Demographic Factors Related to Social and Economic Development in Africa," *Economic Bulletin for Africa* (Addis Ababa), **2** (2) (June 1962), 59–81.

Van de Walle, Etienne. "Future Growth of Population and Changes in Population Composition: Tropical Africa." Paper contributed for the United Nations World Population Conference, August 30-September 10, 1965. Office of Population Research, Princeton University.

III. WESTERN AFRICA

Acquah, Ioné. *Accra Survey: A Social Survey of the Capital of Ghana,* formerly called the Gold Coast, undertaken for the West African Institute of Social and Economic Research, 1953–1956. London: University of London Press, 1958.

Eke, I.I.U. "Population of Nigeria: 1952–1965," *Nigerian Journal of Economic and Social Studies* (Ibadan, 8 (2) (July 1966), 289–309.

Henry, Louis. "Données sur la population de la Guinée," (Data on the Population of Guinea) *Population* (Paris), **11** (3) (July-September 1956), 554–560.

Hunter, J. M. "Regional Patterns of Population Growth in Ghana, 1948–60." Pp. 272–290 in J. B. Whittow, and P. D. Wood (eds.). *Essays in Geography for Austin Miller*. Reading, Pa.: University of Reading, 1965.

Spengler, Joseph J. "Population Movements and Economic Development in Nigeria," in Robert O. Tilman, and Taylor Cole (eds.). *The Nigerian Political Scene*. Durham, N.C., and London. Published for the Duke University Commonwealth Studies Center by the Duke University Press and the Cambridge University Press, 1962, pp. 147–197.

IV. EASTERN AFRICA

Baker, S. J. K. "The Population Geography of East Africa," *East African Geographical Review* (Kampala), **1** (April 1963), 1–6.

Blacker, J. G. C. "The Demography of East Africa," in E. W. Russell (ed.). The Natural Resources of East Africa. Nairobi: D. A. Hawkins, Ltd. in association with East African Literature Bureau, June 1962, pp. 22–36.

Blacker, J. G. C. "Population Growth in Kenya," *Inter-American Labour Institute Bulletin*, **12** (2) (May 1965), 246–255, 256–266.

Brookfield, H. C. "Mauritius: Demographic Upsurge and Prospect," *Population Studies*, **11** (2) (November 1957), 102–122.

Chevalier, Louis. *Madagascar: Population and Resources.* (Madagascar: Population et Ressources.) Institut National d'Études Démographiques, Travaux et Documents, Cahier No. 15. Paris: Presses Universities de France, 1952.

Institut National de la Statistique et des Études Économiques. Service de Cooperation. *Population Projections in the French-speaking African Countries and Madagascar*. Paris, December 1963.

Morgan, W. T. W., and N. Manfred Shaffer. *Population of Kenya: Density and Distribution*. Nairobi, Oxford University Press, 1966.

Rhodes-Livingston Institute. "The Distribution of African Population in Southern Rhodesia," *Rhodes-Livingston Communication*, 28. Lusaka, 1964.

V. NORTHERN AFRICA

Assouline, Albert. *Évolution Naturelle de la Population et Développement Économique au Maroc,* Paper contributed for the United Nations World Population Conference, August 30-September 10, 1965.

Good, Dorothy. "Notes on the Demography of

Algeria," *Population Index,* **27** (1) (January 1961), 3–32.

Seklani, Mahmoud. *Le Cout de la Croissance Démographique d'Après le Plan de Developpement de la Tunisie* (1962–1971). Paper contributed for the United Nations World

Population Conference, August 30-September 10, 1965.

United Nations Educational, Scientific and Cultural Organization. "Nomades et Nomadisme au Sahara" (Nomads and Nomadism in the Sahara) Claude Bataillon (ed.). *Recherches sur la Zone Aride,* 19. Paris, 1963.

VI. MIDDLE AFRICA

Congo. Service de la Statistique. *Enquête Démographique,* 1960–61 (*Demographic Survey,*

1960–61). Brazzaville, 1965.

VII. SOUTHERN AFRICA

Badenhorst, L. T. "Prospects for Future Population Changes in South Africa," *Proceedings of the World Population Conference: 1954,* 3. New York, 1955.

Holleman, J. F. (ed.). *Experiment in Swaziland,* Report of the Swaziland Sample Survey 1960

by the Institute for Social Research, University of Natal, for the Swaziland Administration. London: Oxford University Press, 1964.

Houghton, D. Hobart. *The South African Economy.* Cape Town: Oxford University Press, 1964.

VIII. NORTHERN AMERICA

Bladen, V. W. (ed.). *Canadian Population and Northern Colonization.* Symposium presented to the Royal Society of Canada in 1961. Royal Society of Canada, Studia Varia, 7. Toronto: University of Toronto Press, 1962. Duplicate in French.

Dominion Bureau of Statistics, Health and Welfare Division. *Canadian Vital Statistics Trends, 1921–1954.* Reference Paper No. 70. Ottawa: Queen's Printer, 1956.

Henripin, Jacques. *The Population of Canada at the Beginning of the 18th Century: Nuptiality, Fertility, Infant Mortality. (La Population Canadienne au Debut du 18 Siècle: Nuptialité, Fecondité, Mortalité Infantile.)* Paris: Presses Universitaires, 1954.

Keyfitz, Nathan. "The Changing Canadian Population," in S. D. Clark (ed.). *Urbanism and the Changing Canadian Society.* Toronto: University of Toronto Press, 1961, pp. 3–19.

Keyfitz, Nathan, and Jacques Henripin. "Trends in Canadian Population," in U. S. Congress, House Committee on the Judiciary, Subcommittee 1. *Study of Population and Immigration Problems.* Special Series, No. 1. (Transcripts of hearings.) Washington, D.C.: 1962.

LeNeveu, A. H., and Y. Kasahara. "Demographic Trends in Canada, 1941–56, and Some of Their Implications," *Canadian Journal of Economics and Political Science* **24** (1) (February 1958), 9–20.

IX. UNITED STATES (SEE BIBLIOGRAPHY, CHAPTER 6).

X. LATIN AMERICA — GENERAL

Collver, Andrew O. *Birth Rates in Latin America.* University of California, Berkeley. Institute of International Studies, Research Series 7, Berkeley, 1965.

Davis, Kingsley. "The Place of Latin America in World Demographic History," in *Demography and Public Health in Latin America.* Proceedings of the 40th Annual Conference of the Milbank Memorial Fund, New York, September 17–18, 1963. *Milbank Memorial Fund Quarterly,* **42** (2, Part 2), 3–357.

ECLA. "La Situacion Demográfica en America Latina," *United Nations Economic Bulletin for Latin America,* **6** (2). Santiago, 1961.

Interamerican Statistical Institute. Instituto Interamericano de Estadística. *La Estructura Demográfica de la Naciones Americanas: Analisis Estadisticocensal de los Resultados Obtenidos*

Bajo el Programa del Censo de las Américas de 1960, Washington, D.C., 1965.

Miró, Carmen A. "The Population of Latin America," *Demography* 1 (1964), 15–41.

Mortara, Giorgio. *Characteristics of the Demographic Structure of the American Countries.* Inter-American Statistical Institute. Special Document 4480. Washington, D.C.: Pan American Union, 1964.

Pan-American Union, Department of Estadística and Instituto Interamericano de Estadística. *America in Figures, 1960* (in 8 parts). Washington, D.C., 1961.

Sauvy, Alfred. "The Population of Latin American Countries. Overall View of Their Current State and Growth," *Population,* **18** (1) (January-March 1963), 49–64.

Smith, T. Lyon. "The Population of Latin America," in Ronald Freedman (ed.). *Population: The Vital Revolution*. Garden City, N.Y.: Anchor Books, Doubleday, 1964.

Steward, Julian H., and Louis C. Faran. *Native Peoples of South America*. New York, Toronto, London: McGraw-Hill, 1959.

United Nations. Economic Commission for Latin America. "The Demographic Situation in Latin America," *Economic Bulletin for Latin America* (Santiago), **6** (2) (October 1961), 13–52.

United Nations. Population Branch. *The Population of South America, 1905–1980. Future Population Estimates by Sex and Age, Report II. Population Studies* No. 21. New York, 1955.

XI. TROPICAL SOUTH AMERICA

Bertram, G. C. L. "The Indians of British Guiana," *Population Review* (Madras), **6** (July 1962), 114–117.

Brazil. Conselho Nacional de Estadística (IBGE). Laboratório de Estadística. *Contribuicoes para o Estudo da Demografiia de Brasil (Contributions to the Study of Demography of Brazil)*. Estudos de Estadistica Teorica e Aplicada. Rio de Janeiro, 1961.

Carvalho, Alceu Vincente W. de. *The Brazilian Population (Study and Interpretation)*. Rio de Janeiro: Conselho Nacional de Estadística, 1960.

Cataldi, Alberto. *Reconstruction de las Tendencies del Crecimiento de la Poblacion de Uruguay Para Periodos Anteriores al Censo de 1963*. Paper contributed for the United Nations World Population Conference, August 30-September 10, 1965.

Costa Pinto, L. A., and Waldemiro Bazzanella. "Economic Development, Social Change, and Population Problems in Brazil," *The Annals of the American Academy of Political and Social Science*, 316 (March 1958,) 121–126.

Ford, Thomas R. *Man and Land in Peru*. Gainesville, Fla.: University of Florida Press, 1955.

López, José E. "The Demographic Growth of Venezuela," *Revista Geográfica* (Merida, Venezuela), 3 (8) (November, 1961-April 1962), 195–275.

Michalup, Erich. "Some Demographic Aspects of the Population of Venezuela," *Bulletin de l'Institut International de Statistique* (Rio de Janeiro), 35 (3) (1957), 325–331.

Mortara, Giorgio. "The Development and Structure of Brazil's Population," *Population Studies*, 8 (2) (November 1954), 121–139.

Romero Rojas, Bernardo. "Apuntes Sobre la Poblacion de Colombia" (Remarks on the Population of Colombia), *Bulletin de l'Institute International de Statistique* (Rio de Janeiro), 35 (1957), 401–420.

Saunders, J. V. D. "The People of Ecuador: A Demographic Analysis," *Latin American Monograph*, 14. Gainesville, Fla.: University of Florida Press, 1961.

Siagnes, Miguel Acosta. "La Estructure Demografica de Venezuela" (The Demographic Structure of Venezuela), *Sociología* (Caracas), 1 (April 1961), 27–43.

Smith, T. Lynn. *Brazil: People and Institutions* (revised edition). Baton Rouge, La.: Louisiana State University Press, 1954.

United Nations. Economic Commission for Latin America. *Algunos Aspectos del Crecimiento Demográfico en Colombia*. Santiago: CEPAL, November 1962 (mimeographed).

XII. MIDDLE AMERICA

Arias, B. Jorge. "Aspectos Demográficos de la Población Indígena de Guatemala," (Demographic Aspects of the Indian Population of Guatemala), *Boletin Estadístico* (Guatemala, C.A.), 1–2 (January-February 1959), 18–38.

Beñitez, Zenteno Raúl. *Analysis of the Population of Mexico*. Instituto de Investigaciones Sociales, Biblioteca de Ensayos Sociológicos, Cuadernos de Sociología. Mexico, D. F.: Universidad Nacional, 1961.

Bénitez Zenteno, Rául, and Gustavo Cabrera Acevedo. "La Poblacíon Futura de México—Total, Urbana y Rural" ("The future Population of Mexico—Total, Urban and Rural"), *El Trimestre Económico* (Mexico, D. F.), 33, 2 (130) (April-June 1966), 163–170.

Cook, Sherburne F., and Borah, Woodrow. "The Rate of Population Change in Central Mexico, 1550–1570," *Hispanic American Historical Review*, 37 (4) (November 1957), 463–470.

Ducoff, Louis J. "The Future Population and Labor Force of Mexico, Central America and Panama: Some Implications for Economic Development," *Estadística* (Washington, D.C.), 17 (63) (June 1959), 315–324.

Ducoff, Louis. *Los Recursos Humanos de Centroamérica, Panamá y México en 1950–1980, y Sus Relaciones con Algunos Aspectos del Desarrollo Economico (The Human Resources of Central America, Panama, and Mexico, 1950–1980, and Their Relations with Some Aspects of Economic Development)*. Mexico, D.F. United Nations Economic Commission for Latin America, 1960.

Durán Ochoa, Julio. "Principales Aspectos Demograficos de Mexico," *Bulletin de l'Institute In-*

ternational de Statistique (Rio de Janeiro), **35** (3) (1957), 313–324.

Durán Ochoa, Julio. "The Demographic Explosion," reprinted from *Mexico: Fifty Years of Revolution, 2. Social Life.* Mexico, D. F. 1963.

León-Portilla, Miguel. "Panorama de la Población Indígena de Mexico," *América Indígena* (Mexico, D.F.), **19** (1) (January 1959), 43–73.

Loyo, Gilberto. "Algunos Problemas Demográficos de Mexico y América Latina (Some Demographic Problems of Mexico and Latin America), *Cuadernos Americanos* (Mexico, D. F.), **26** (January-February 1967), 41–64.

Loyo, Gilberto. "The Population of Mexico: Present State and Tendencies," in *Instituto Mexicano de Recursos Naturales Renovables*, pp. 1–187.

Ministerio de Educación Publica. *Situación Demográfica, Económica, Social y Educativa de Guatemala.* Guatemala City, 1963.

Miró, Carmen A. "Principales Características Demográficos de la República de Panamá," *Bulletin de l'Institute International de Statistique* (Rio de Janeiro), **35** (3) (1957), 421–435.

Nunley, Robert E. *The Distribution of Population in Costa Rico.* National Research Council Publication 743. National Research Council, Division of Earth Sciences, Foreign Field Research Program, Report No. 8. Washington, D.C.: National Academy of Sciences—National Research Council, 1960.

Panama. Contraloría General. "Algunos Aspectos de la Situación Demográfica y Económica de Panama" (Some Aspects of the Demographic and Economic Position of Panama), pp. 1-A to 39-A in *Informe del Contralor General de la República, 1 de Octubre de 1963 (Report of the Controller General of the Republic, October, 1963).* Panama, 1963.

Population Reference Bureau. "Mexico: The Problem of People," *Population Bulletin*, **20** (7) (November 1964), 173–203.

United Nations. *Population of Central America (including Mexico), 1950–1980.* Population Studies, No. 16. New York: United Nations, 1954.

Whetten, Nathan L. *Guatemala: The Land and the People.* Caribbean Series 4. New Haven, Conn.: Yale University Press, 1961.

XIII. TEMPERATE SOUTH AMERICA

Arevalo, Jorge V. *La Poblacíon Futura de la Republica Argentina.* Paper contributed for the United Nations World Population Conference, August 30-September 10, 1965.

Barral Souto, José. "Caracteristicas Demográficas de la Republica Argentina" (Demographic Characteristics of the Argentine Republic), *Bulletin de l'Institut International de Statistique* (Rio de Janeiro), **35** (3) (1957), 369-381.

Cabello, Octavio. "The Demography of Chile," *Population Studies*, **9** (3) (March 1956), 237–350.

Cataldi, Alberto. *La Situación Demográfica de Uruguay en 1957 y Projecciones a 1982.* Santiago: Centro Latinoamericano de Demografia, 1963 (unpublished manuscript.)

Sadie, Johannes L. *Poblacion y Mano de Obra de Chile, 1930-1975.* Santiago: Centro Latinoamericano de Demografíe, 1962.

XIV. CARIBBEAN

Cumper, G. E. "Population Movements in Jamaica, 1830–1950," *Social and Economic Studies* (Mona, Jamaica), **5** (3) (September 1956), 261–280.

Francis, O. C. *The People of Modern Jamaica.* Kingston, Jamaica: Department of Statistics, November 1963.

Geisert, Harold L. *The Caribbean: Population and Resources.* Washington, D.C.: Population Research Project, George Washington University, 1960.

Harewood, Jack. "Population Growth in Trinidad and Tobago in the Twentieth Century," *Social and Economic Studies* (Mona, Jamaica), **12** (1) (March 1963), 1–26.

Hatt, Paul K. *Backgrounds of Human Fertility in Puerto Rico.* Princeton, N.J.: Princeton University Press, 1952.

Kuczynski, Robert R. *Demographic Survey of the British Colonial Empire,* Vol. III. *West Indian*

and American Territories. London and New York: Oxford University Press, 1953.

Lowenthal, David. "The Population of Barbados," *Social and Economic Studies* (Mona, Jamaica), **6** (4) (December 1957), 445–501.

Roberts, G. W. "The Caribbean Islands," *The Annals of the American Academy of Political and Social Science*, 316 (March 1958), 127–136.

Roberts, G. W. *The Population of Jamaica.* Cambridge, England: published for the Conservation Foundation at the University Press, 1957.

Roberts, G. W. "Prospects for Population Growth in the West Indies," *Social and Economic Studies* (Mona, Jamaica), **11** (4) (December 1962), 339–350.

Roberts, G. W. "Recent Demographic Trends in Cuba, Haiti and the British Caribbean," *Population Bulletin of the United Nations*, No. 5, July 1956, pp. 42–50.

XV. ASIA — GENERAL

Belshaw, Horace. *Population Growth and Levels of Consumption with Special Reference to Countries of Asia.* New York: Institute of Pacific Relations, 1956.

Kono, Shigemi. *Forecasts in Some Asian Areas During Recent Years: Criticism and Suggestions.* Paper contributed for the United Nations World Population Conference, August 30-September 10, 1965.

Olin, Ulla. *Population Growth and Problems of Equipment in Asia and the Far East.* Paper contributed for the United Nations World Population Conference, August 30-September 10, 1965.

Paltridge, T. B. "Population and Food Supply in the Far East," *World Crops,* 15 (December 1963), 413–423.

Taeuber, Irene B. "Asia's Increasing Population," *The Annals of the American Academy of Political and Social Science,* 318, pp. 1–7.

United Nations Department of Economic and Social Affairs. Population Branch. *Future Population Estimates by Sex and Age. Report IV. The Population of Asia and the Far East.* Population Studies, No. 31. New York: United Nations, 1959.

United Nations Economic Commission for Asia and the Far East. *Economic Survey of Asia and the Far East, 1963.* New York: United Nations, 1964.

XVI. MAINLAND EAST ASIA

Aird, John S. "The Present and Prospective Population of Mainland China," in *Population Trends in Eastern Europe, the U.S.S.R. and Mainland China. Milbank Memorial Fund Quarterly,* New York, 1960, pp. 93–133.

Barclay, George W. "Population and the Future in Taiwan," in *The Interrelations of Demographic, Economic and Social Problems in Selected Underdeveloped Area. Milbank Memorial Fund Quarterly,* New York, 1954, pp. 32–54.

Bruk, Solomon I. *Peoples of China, Mongolian People's Republic, and Korea.* U. S. Joint Publications Research Service Report, p. 3710. New York, August 16, 1960.

Clark, Colin. "L'Accroissement de la Population de la Chine" (Population Growth in China), *Population* (Paris), 19 (3) (June-July 1964), 559–568.

Clark, Colin. "Le Population de la Chine depuis 1915" ("China's Population since 1915"), *Population* (Paris), 21 (6) (November-December 1966), pp. 1191–1200, 1289–1290, and 1292–1293.

Durand, John D. "The Population Statistics of China A.D. 2–1953," *Population Studies,* 13 (3) (March 1960), 209–256.

Etienne, Gilbert. "Quelques Données Récentes sur la Population de la Chine" (Recent Data on the Population of China), *Population* (Paris), 17 (3) (July-September 1962), 459–464.

Ho, Ping-ti. *Studies on the Population of China, 1368–1953.* Cambridge, Mass.: Harvard University Press, 1959.

Lal, Amrit. "Population Growth in Mainland China: Some Aspects," *Eugenics Review,* 56 (1) (April 1964), 29–34.

Orleans, Leo A: "The Population of Communist China," in Ronald Freedman (ed.). *Population: The Vital Revolution.* Garden City, N. Y.: Anchor Books, Doubleday, 1964, pp. 227–239.

Pan, Chia-Lin. "An Estimate of the Long-Term Crude Birth Rate of the Agricultural Population of China," *Demography,* 3 (1) (1966), 204–208.

Pressat, Roland. *Etát Present et Avenir de la Population Chinoise.* Paper contributed to the United Nations World Population Conference, August 30–September 10, 1965.

Pressat, Roland. "La Population de la Chine et son Economie" (China's Population and Economy), *Population* (Paris), 13 (4) (October-December 1958), 569–589. With comment by Albert Sauvy.

Taeuber, Irene B., and Leo A. Orleans. "A Note on the Population Statistics of Communist China," *Population Index,* 22 (4) (October 1956), 274–276.

Taeuber, Irene B., and Nai-Chi Wang. "Population in the Ch'ing Dynasty," *Journal of Asian Studies,* 19 (4) (October 1956), 403–417.

Taeuber, Irene B., and Nai-chi Wang. "Questions on Population Growth in China," in *Population Trends in Eastern Europe, the U.S.S.R. and Mainland China. Milbank Memorial Fund Quarterly,* New York, 1960, pp. 263–302.

U. S. Bureau of the Census. "The Population of Manchuria," by Waller Wynne, Jr. *International Population Statistics Reports* Series P-90, No. 7. Washington, D.C.: U.S. Government Printing Office, 1958.

U. S. Bureau of the Census. "The Size, Composition and Growth of the Population of Mainland China," by John S. Aird. *International Population Statistics Reports* Series P-90, No. 15. Washington, D.C.: U. S. Government Printing Office, 1961.

XVII. MIDDLE SOUTH ASIA

Agarwala, S. N. (ed.). *India's Population: Some Problems in Perspective and Planning.* Bombay and London: Asia Publishing House, 1961.

Arasteh, A. Reza, and Josephine Arasteh. *Man and Society in Iran.* Leyden: E. J. Brill, 1964.

Coale, Ansley J., and Edgar M. Hoover. *Population Growth and Economic Development.* Princeton N. J.: Princeton University Press, 1958.

Colombo. Department of Census and Statistics, Government Press, 1956. *Fertility Trends in Ceylon.* 1953 Census (1 percent sample). Monograph No. 8.

Etienne, Gilbert. "L'Inde, Economie et Population." (India, Economy and Population). *Études d'Histoire Economique, Politique et Sociale,* 16. Geneva: Librairie E. Droz, 1955.

Ghosh, A. "A Study of Demographic Trends in West Bengal During 1901-1950," *Population Studies,* 9 (3) (March 1956), 217–235.

Hashmi, Sultan S., et al. *The People of Karachi: Data from a Survey.* Pakistan Institute of Development Economics, Statistical Papers, 2. Karachi, June 1964.

India. Cabinet Secretariat. *Preliminary Estimates of Birth and Death Rates and of the Rate of Growth of Population.* Fourteenth Round, July 1958–July 1959. The National Sample Survey, 48. Calcutta and Delhi, Manager of Publications, Civil Lines, 1961.

India. National Council of Applied Economic Research, New Delhi, 1962. *Long Term Projections of Demand for and Supply of Selected Agricultural Commodities, 1960–61 to 1975–76.*

International Labour Office. "Protection and Integration of Tribal Populations of Pakistan,"

International Labour Review (Geneva), **75** (1) (January 1957), 68–77.

Jain, S. P. "Indian Fertility—Our Knowledge and Gaps," *Journal of Family Welfare* (Bombay), 10 (June 1964), 16–32.

Kohli, B. R. "Components of Population Growth in India During the Decade 1951-1961," *AICC Economic Review* (New Delhi), **14** (23) (May 1, 1963), 20–22.

Mauldin, W. Parker. "The Population of India," in Ronald Freedman (ed.). *Population: The Vital Revolution.* Garden City, N. Y.: Anchor Books, Doubleday, 1964, pp. 191–205.

Pant, Y. P. "Nepal's Population Growth," *Far Eastern Economic Review* (Hong Kong), **37** (11) (September 13, 1962), 499–504.

Poti, S. J. "A Study of the Indian Population Growth," *Indian Population Bulletin* (New Delhi), **1** (1) (April 1960), 82–128.

Sarkar, N. K. *The Demography of Ceylon.* Colombo: Government Press, 1957.

Sarkar, N. K. "Population Trends and Population Policy in Ceylon: A Summary of Findings," *Population Studies,* 9 (3) (March 1956), 195–216.

Selvaratnam, S. "Some Implications of Population Growth in Ceylon," *Ceylon Journal of Historical and Social Studies (Peradeniya),* 4 (1) (January-June 1961), 33–49.

Sovani, N. *The Population Problem in India: A Regional Approach.* Gokholi: Institute of Politics and Economics, 1962.

Trewartha, Glenn T., and Gurdev Gosal. "The Regionalism of Population Change in India," in *Cold Spring Harbor Symposia on Quantitative Biology,* 22, 1957.

XVIII. SOUTHEAST ASIA

Adams, Edith. "New Population Estimates for the Philippines 1948-1962," *The Philippine Statistician* (Manila), **7** (3) (September 1958), 134–166.

Aromin, Basilio B. "Considerations for a Philippine Population Policy," *The Philippine Statistician* (Manila), **12** (December 1963), 122–144.

Das Gupta, Ajit, and Suranjan Sen Gupta. *Population Projections for Thailand and a Study of the Elements and Criteria.* Paper contributed to the United Nations World Population Conference, August 30-September 10, 1965.

Delvert, Jean. *Le Paysan Cambodgien (Peasants of Cambodia).* Paris and The Hague: Mouton, 1961.

Hauser, Philip M., and Evelyn M. Kitagawa. "Demographic Glimpses into Burma," in *The Interrelations of Demographic, Economic and Social Problems in Selected Underdeveloped*

Areas. Milbank Memorial Fund Quarterly, New York, 1954, pp. 103–129.

Hock, Saw Swee. "The Changing Population Structure in Singapore During 1824-1962," *Malayan Economic Review* (Singapore), **9** (1) (April 1964), 90–101.

Horstmann, Kurt. "Indonesien; Bevölkerungsproblem und Wirtschaftsentwicklung" (Indonesia; The Population Problem and Economic Development), *Geographisches Taschenbuch; Jahrweiser zur Deutschen Landeskunde,* 1958/9 (Stuttgart), 1958, pp. 410–423.

Hunter, A. "Notes on Indonesian Population," *Bulletin of Indonesian Economic Studies* (Canberra), (4), (June 1966), 36–49.

Ingram, James C. *Economic Change in Thailand Since 1850.* Issued under the Auspices of the International Secretariat, Institute of Pacific Relations. Stanford, Calif.: Stanford University Press, 1955.

Jones, L. W. *The Population of Borneo: A Study of the People of Sarawak, Sabah and Brunei.* London: Athlone Press (for) University of London, 1966.

Jupp, Kathleen M. "Patterns of Population Change in the Philippines, 1939 to 1957," *Central Bank News Digest* (Manila), **13** (October 10, 1961), 2–9. Reprinted from *The Philippine Statistician*, March 1960.

Keyfitz, Nathan. "Indonesia's Population Prospects," *Proceedings of the World Population Conference: 1954.* New York, 1965, Vol. III.

Lee, Y. L. "The Population of British Borneo," *Population Studies,* **15** (3) (March 1962), 226–243.

Lee, Y. L. "The Population of Sarawak," *Geographical Journal,* **131** (3) (September 1965), 344–356.

Madigan, Francis C., S.J. "Estimated Trends of Fertility, Mortality, and Natural Increase in the North Mindanao Region of the Philippine Islands, 1960–1970," *Philippine Sociological Review* (Quezon City), **13** (October 1965), 260–267.

Madigan, Francis C., S. J. "Some Recent Vital Rates and Trends in the Philippines: Estimates and Evaluation," *Demography,* **2,** 309–316.

Mendoza-Pascual, Elvira. "Reinvestigation of Birth and Death Statistics in the Philippines," *The Philippine Statistician* (Manila), **9** (4) December 1962.

Neville, R. J. W. "Singapore: Recent Trends in the Sex and Age Composition of a Cosmopolitan Community," *Population Studies,* **17** (2) (November 1963), 99–112.

Purcell, Victor. *The Chinese in Southeast Asia* (2nd ed.). Issued under the auspices of the Royal Institute of International affairs. London: Oxford University Press, 1965.

Ramachandran, K. V., et al. "Population Projections for the Philippines, 1960-1980," *The Philippine Statistician* (Manila), **12** (December 1963), 145–169.

Smith, T. E. "Prospects for Future Population Change in Malaya," *Proceedings of the World Population Conference: 1954.* New York, 1955, Vol. III.

Sundrum, R. M. *Population Statistics of Burma.* Economics Research Project, Statistical Paper No. 3. Rangoon: University of Rangoon, Economics, Statistics and Commerce Departments, December 1957.

Taeuber, Irene B. "The Bases of a Population Problem: The Philippines," *Population Index,* **26** (2) (April 1960), 97–114.

United Nations Department of Economic and Social Affairs. *Future Population Estimates by Sex and Age. Report III. The Population of South-East Asia (including Ceylon and China: Taiwan) 1950-1980.* Population Studies, No. 30. New York, 1958.

United Nations Department of Economic and Social Affairs. *Population Growth and Manpower in the Philippines.* A joint study by the United Nations and the Government of the Philippines, National Economic Council of the Philippines, Manila. Population Studies, No. 32. New York, 1960.

United Nations Economic Commission for Asia and the Far East. "Evaluation of the Population Census Data of Malaya," *Economic Bulletin for Asia and the Far East* (Bangkok), **13** (2) (September 1962), 23–44.

XIX. JAPAN AND OTHER EAST ASIA ISLANDS

Ohkawa, Kazushi, and Henry Rosovsky. "Recent Japanese Growth in Historical Perspective," *American Economic Review,* **53** (2) (May 1963), 578–588.

Tachi, Minoru (ed.). *Annual Reports of the Institute of Population Problems,* 12. Tokyo: Institute of Population Problems, 1967.

Tachi, Minoru. *The Problem of Population and National Development.* Tokyo: Institute of Population Problems, English Pamphlet Series No. 59, 1964.

Taeuber, Irene B. "Japan's Demographic Transition Re-examined," *Population Studies,* **14** (1) (July 1960), 28–39.

Taeuber, Irene B. *The Population of Japan.* Princeton, N. J.: published under the editorial sponsorship of the Office of Population Research, Princeton University, by the Princeton University Press, 1958.

Taeuber, Irene B. "The Population of Japan," in Ronald Freedman (ed.). *Population: The Vital Revolution.* Garden City, N. Y.: Anchor Books, Doubleday, 1964, pp. 215–226.

Taeuber, Irene B. "The Population of the Ryukyu Islands," *Population Index,* **21** (4) (October 1955), 233–263.

Thompson, Warren S. *Population and Progress in the Far East.* Chicago: University of Chicago Press, 1959.

XX. SOUTHWEST ASIA

Adams, Doris G. "Current Population Trends in Iraq," *Middle East Journal,* **10** (2) (Spring 1956), 151–165.

Cyprus. Department of Statistics and Research. *Demographic Report.* Nicosia: Printing Office of the Republic of Cyprus, published annually.

El-Badry, M. A. "Trends in the Components of Population Growth in the Arab Countries of the Middle East: A Survey of Present Information," *Demography*, **2**, 140–186.

Hasan, M. S. "Growth and Structure of Iraq's Population 1867-1947," *Bulletin of the Oxford University Institute of Statistics*, **20** (4) (November 1958), 339–352.

Holler, Joanne E. *Population Growth and Social Change in the Middle East*. Population Research Project of George Washington University Publication. Washington, D.C., 1964.

Population Reference Bureau. "Israel: Land of Promise and Perplexities," *Population Bulletin*, **21** (5) (November 1965), 101–34.

Rubio-Garcia, Leandro. "Demografía, Sociedad y Economía en la Turquia Contemporanea" (Demography, Society and Economy in Present Day Turkey), *Revista Internacional de Sociología* (Madrid), **21** (81) (January-March 1963), 61–85.

Russell, Josiah C. "Late Medieval Balkan and Asia Minor Population," *Journal of the Economic and Social History of the Orient*, 3 (1960), 265–274.

Taeuber, Irene B. "Cyprus: The Demography of a Strategic Island," *Population Index*, **21** (1) (January 1954), 4–20.

Taeuber, Irene B. "Population and Modernization in Turkey," *Population Index*, **24** (2) (April 1958), 101–122.

XXI. EUROPE — GENERAL

Centre European d'Études de Population. *Studies of European Population. Labor Force, Employment, Migration. Situation and Prospects. (Études Européennes de Population. Main d'oeuvre, Emploi, Migrations. Situation et Perspectives.)* Paris: Institut National d'Études Démographiques, 1954.

Dewhurst, J. Frederic, et al. *Europe's Needs and Resources: Trends and Prospects in Eighteen Countries*. New York: Twentieth Century Fund; London: Macmillan, 1961.

Glass, D. V., *Population Policies and Movements in Europe*. Oxford: Clarendon Press, 1940.

Glass, D. V., and D. E. C. Eversley (eds.). *Population in History: Essays in Historical Demography*. London: Edward Arnold, 1965.

Kirk, Dudley. *Europe's Population in the Interwar Years*. Geneva: League of Nations, 1946.

Kulischer, E. M. *Europe on the Move: War and Population Changes, 1917-1947*. New York: Columbia University Press, 1948.

National Center of Scientific Research. *Studies and Notes on Historical Demography, 1964*. (Work published in conjunction with National Center of Scientific Research.) Paris, 1964.

Notestein, Frank W., et al. *The Future Population of Europe and the Soviet Union*. Geneva: League of Nations, 1944.

Petersen, William. "The Population of Europe," in Ronald Freedman (ed.). *Population: The Vital Revolution*. Garden City, N. Y.: Anchor Books, Doubleday, 1964.

Russell, Josiah C. "Late Ancient and Medieval Population," *Transactions of the American Philosophical Society*, New Series, Vol. 48, Part 3.

XXII. WESTERN EUROPE

Biraben, Jean-Noel, et al. "La Situation Démographique de l'Europe Occidentale" (Demographic Situation of Western Europe), *Population* (Paris), **19** (3) (June-July 1964), 439–484.

Chevalier, Louis (ed.). *Le Cholera: La Premiere Epidemie du 19eme Siecle (Cholera: The Prime Epidemic of the Nineteenth Century)*. Paris: La Société d'Histoire de la Revolution de 1848, 1958.

Damas, Henriette. "Le Mouvement Naturel de la Population Belge: Son Évolution de 1846 à 1960" (The Balance of Births and Deaths of the Belgian Population: The Trend from 1846 to 1960), *Population et Famille* (Brussels), 2 (April 1964), 64–120.

Deniel, Raymond, and Louis Henry. "La Population d'un Village du Nord de la France, Sainghin-en-Mélantois, de 1665 à 1851" ("Population of a Village from the Northern Part of France"), *Population* (Paris), **20** (4) (July-August 1965), 563–602.

Edding, Friedrick. *The Refugees as a Burden: A Stimulus and a Challenge to the West German Economy*. Kiel: Kieler Studien, Forschungsberichte des Institutes fuer Weltwirtschaft, 12, 1951.

France. Institut National de la Statistique et des Études Économiques. By C. Piro. "La Situation Démographique en 1961" (The Demographic Position in 1961), *Études Statistiques: Supplément Trimestriel du Bulletin Mensuel de Statistique*, **13** (4) (October-December 1962), 343–378.

France. Institut National d'Études Démographiques. *Vital Statistics: International Statistics, 1906-1936 (Le Mouvement Naturel de la Population: Statistiques Internationales de 1906 a 1936)*. Paris, 1954.

Ganiage, Jean. *Trois Villages d'Ile-de-France au XVIII Siécle. Étude Démographique. (Three Villages of Ile-de-France in the XVIII Century. A Demographic Study)*. I.N.E.D. Cahier 40. Paris: Presses Universitaires, 1963.

Harmsen, Hans, and Karl Christian von Loesch. *Die Deutsche Bevölkerungsfrage im Europäischen Raum.* Berlin: Grunewald, K. Vowenckel, 1929.

Henry, Louis, and Claude Levy. "Quelques Données sur la Région Autour de Paris au XVIII Siècle" (Some Data on the Region around Paris in the 18th Century), *Population* (Paris), **17** (2) (April-June 1962), 297–326.

Henry, Louis, and Roland Pressat. "Growth of the Population of France to 1970," *Population* (Paris), **10** (1) (January-March 1955), 9–56.

Huber, Michel. *La Population de la France.* Paris: Hachette, 1955.

Kirk, Dudley. "Economic and Demographic Development in Western Germany," *Population Index,* **24** (1) (January 1958), 3–21.

Leridon, Francoise. "La Population Allemand Depuis 1939" (The German Population since 1939), *Population* (Paris), **13** (3) (July-September 1958), 441–456.

Mayer, Kurt B. *The Population of Switzerland.* New York: Columbia University Press, 1952.

Monatsberichte des Oesterreichischen Institutes fuer Wirtschaftsorshung, Vienna, 1962, pp.
496–503. "Growth Trends of the Population of Austria."

Petersen, William. "The Demographic Transition in the Netherlands," *American Sociological Review,* **25** (3) (June 1960), 334–347.

Pressat, Roland. "The Population of France at the 1962 Census: First Results," *Population* (Paris), **17** (4) (October-December 1962), 627–644.

Pressat, Roland. "Demographic Conditions," *Population* (Paris), **15** (3) (June-July 1960), 517–543.

Pouthas, Charles H. *La Population Francaise pendant la Premiere Moitie du XIX Siècle.* Paris: Presses Universitaires de France, 1956.

Reinhard, Marcel. "La Population Française au XVII Siècle" (The French Population in the 17th Century), *Population* (Paris), **13** (4) (October-December 1958), 619–631.

Spengler, Joseph J. *France Faces Depopulation.* Durham, N. C.: Duke University Press, 1938.

Terrisse, Michel. "Un Faubourg de Havre: Ingouville" (A Suburb of Le Havre: Ingouville), *Population* (Paris), **16** (2) (April-June 1961), 285–300. Commentary by Louis Henry, pp. 294–296.

XXIII. SOUTHERN EUROPE

Boldrini, M. "Un Secolo de Sviluppo della Poplazione Italiana" (A Century of Growth of the Italian Population), in *The Italian Economy from 1861 to 1961.* Studies of the first century of Italian unity. Biblioteca della Rivista "Economia e Storia": 6. Milan: Casa Editrice Dott. Antonino Giuffre, 1961.

Campo, Salustiano del. "Componentes del Crecimiento de la Población de España, 1940-1950" (Components in the Growth of the Population of Spain, 1940-1950), *Revista de Estudios Politicos* (Madrid), 95 (September-October 1957) 149–176.

Casa Nova, Antonio. "Aspectos Demográficos da Populaçao Portuguesa: Estudo Comparativo de Populações Predominantemente Urbanas e Rurais" (Demographic Aspects of the Portuguese Population: A Comparative Study of Predominantly Urban and Rural Populations). Centro de Estudos Demográficos, *Revista* (Lisbon), 10 (1956-1957), 7–30.

Common, R. "Some Recent Developments in Greece," *Tijdschrift voor Economische en Sociale Geografie* (Rotterdam), **49** (12) (December 1958), 253–266.

Fernandes, L. Santos, and V. A. Pinto Nunes. "Alguns Aspectos do Crescimento da População Portuguesa no Periódo de 1920 a 1950" (Some Aspects of the Growth of Population in Portugal in the Period 1920-1950), *Colectânea de Estudos* (Lisbon), 17 (1962), 115–127.

Macura, Milos. "The Population of Yugoslavia and
the Conditions of its Development," *Population* (Paris), **10** (2) (April-June 1955), 295–316.

Meo, Giuseppe de. *Saggi de Statistica Economica e Demografica sull' Italia Meridionale nei Secoli XVII e XVIII (Essays on the Economic and Population Statistics of Southern Italy in the 17th and 18th Centuries).* Rome: Instituto di Statistica Economica dell' Universita di Roma, 1, 1962.

Milenko, Ban. "Population Structure and Trends," *Yugoslav Survey* (Belgrade), 3 (1962), 1073–1084.

United Nations. Bureau of Social Affairs and Technical Assistance Administration, in cooperation with the Government of Greece. *Seminar on Population Studies in Southern European Countries, Athens, September 15–26, 1958.*

U. S. Bureau of the Census. *The Population of Yugoslavia,* by Paul F. Myers and Arthur A. Campbell. International Population Statistics Reports, Series P-90, No. 5. Washington, D.C.: U. S. Government Printing Office, 1954.

Valaoras, Vasilios G. "A Reconstruction of the Demographic History of Modern Greece," *Milbank Memorial Fund Quarterly,* **38** (2) April 1960, 115–139.

Wise, M. J. "Population Pressure and National Resources: Some Observations Upon the Italian Population Problem," *Economic Geography,* **30** (2) (April 1954), 114–156.

XXIV. EASTERN EUROPE

Billig, Wilhelm. *Population Trends in the Socialist Countries.* Paper contributed for the United Nations World Population Conference, August 30-September 10, 1965.

Combs, Jerry W., Jr. "Demographic Changes in Eastern Europe," in *Population Trends in Eastern Europe, the U.S.S.R. and Mainland China.* Milbank Memorial Fund Quarterly, New York, 1960, pp. 11–29.

Czechoslovakia. Akademie Ved. *Statistika a Demografie III (Statistics and Demography, Vol. 3).* Frantisek Egermayer (ed.). Prague: Nakladetelstvi CSAV, 1963.

Czechoslovak State Population Committee. *Czechoslovak Population Problems.* Prague, 1965.

Jaho, Dibra, and Vako Pakso. "La Population de l'Albania, d'Après les Recensements de 1955 à 1960" (The Population of Albania, According to the 1955 and 1960 Censuses), *Population* (Paris), (March, 1965), 253–268.

Moore, Wilbert E. *Economic Demography of Eastern and Southern Europe.* Geneva: League of Nations, 1945.

Poland. Glówny Urzad Statystyczny. *Ludność w latach 1954-1965* (Population of Poland in the Period 1945-65). Edited by Eugenia Krzeczkowska et al. Studie i Prace Statystycne, 1. Warsaw, 1966.

Rosset, Edward. "Przeobrazenia Demograficzne w Polsce i ich Konsekencje dla Nauka i Gospodarki Narodowej" (Demographic Change in Poland and Consequences for Science and the National Economy), *Studia Demograficzne* (Warsaw), **2** (4) (1964), 3–36.

Roubiček, Vladimir. *Demograficka Statistika (Demographic Statistics).* Prague: Státní Pedagogické Nakladatelstvi, 1958. For a review of this book by Jan Sveton, see *Demografie* (Prague), **1** (3) (1959), 171–172.

Srb, Vladimir. "Population Development and Population Policy in Czechslovakia," *Population Studies,* **16** (2) (November 1962), 147–159.

Szabady, Egon, et al. "La Population des Pays Socialistes Européens" ("The Population of the European Socialist Countries"), in 2 parts, *Population* (Paris), **21** (5) (September-October 1966), 939–1012.

Szulc, S. "Demographic Problems of Poland," *International Social Science Bulletin* (Paris), **9** (2) (1957), 165–174.

U.S. Bureau of the Census. *Projections of the Population of Hungary, by Age and Sex: 1958-1976.* International Population Reports, Series P-91, No. 7. Washington, D. C.: U.S. Government Printing Office, July 1958.

U.S. Bureau of the Census. *Projections of the Population of Rumania, by Age and Sex: 1960-1976,* by James W. Brackett. International Population Reports, Series P-91, No. 10. Washington, D.C.: U.S. Government Printing Office, June 1960.

U.S. Bureau of the Census. *Projections of the Population of the Soviet Zone of Germany and the Soviet sector of Berlin, by Age and Sex: 1960–1976,* by James W. Brackett. International Population Reports, Series P-91, No. 11. Washington, D.C.: U.S. Government Printing Office, September 1960.

U.S. Bureau of the Census. *The Population of Hungary,* by Jacob S. Siegel. International Population Statistics Reports, Series P-90, No. 9. Washington, D.C.: U.S. Government Printing Office, 1958.

XXV. NORTHERN EUROPE

Aagesen, Aage. "The Population of Denmark, 1955–1960," *Geografisk Tidsskrift* (Copenhagen), **63** (2) (December 1964), 191–202.

Aalen, F. H. A. "A Review of Recent Irish Population Trends," *Population Studies* (London), **17** (1) (July 1963), 73–78.

Backer, Julie E. "Future Population Prospects in the Scandinavian Countries," *Proceedings of the World Population Conference: 1954.* New York, 1955, Vol. III.

Carr-Saunders, A. M., Caradog D. Jones, and C. A. Moser. *A Survey of Social Conditions in England and Wales as Illustrated in Statistics.* Oxford: Clarendon Press, 1958.

Charles, Enid. *The Effect of Present Trends in Fertility and Mortality Upon the Future Population of England and Wales.* London: The Royal Economic Society, 1935. Special Memorandum No. 40.

Cole, G. D. H. *The Postwar Condition of Britain.* London: Routledge and Kegan Paul, 1956.

Drake, Michael. "The Growth of Population in Norway 1735–1855," *Scandinavian Economic History Review* (Copenhagen), **13** (2) (1965), 97–142.

Eversley, D. E. C. "A Survey of Population in an Area of Worcestershire from 1660–1850 on the Basis of Parish Records," *Population Studies,* **10** (3) (March 1957), 253–279.

Great Britain. General Register Office, England and Wales. *The Registrar General's Statistical Review of England and Wales.* Part III. Commentary. London: H. M. Stationers Office (annual).

Great Britain. Royal Commission on Population. *Report of the Royal Commission on Population.* London: H. M. Stationers Office, 1949.

Historical Statistics of Sweden. I. Population, 1720–1950. Historik Statistik for Sverige. I. Befolkning, 1720–1950. Stockholm, 1955. English and Swedish text. In Sweden: Statistiska Centralbyran, Stockholm, 1955. English and Swedish text.

Holmans, A. "Current Population Trends in Britain," *Scottish Journal of Political Economy,* **11** (1) (February 1964), 31–56.

Honohan, W. A. "The Population of Ireland," *Journal of the Institute of Actuaries,* **86** (1372) (1960), 30–49.

Johnson, James H. "Population Changes in Ireland, 1951–1961," *Geographical Journal,* **129** (2) (June 1963), 167–174.

Krause, J. T. "Changes in English Fertility and Mortality, 1781–1850," *Economic History Review,* **11** (1) (August 1958), 52–70.

Lawton, R. "Recent Trends in Population and Housing in England and Wales," *Sociological Review,* **11** (3) (November 1963), 303–322.

Lunde, A. S. *Norway: A Population Study.* Ann Arbor, Mich.: University of Michigan Microfilms, 1955.

Marsh, David C. *The Changing Social Structure of England and Wales, 1871–1951.* International Library of Sociology and Social Reconstruction. London: Routledge and Kegan Paul; New York: Humanities Press, 1958.

McKeown, Thomas, and R. G. Brown. "Medical Evidence Related to English Population Changes in the Eighteenth Century," *Population Studies,* **9** (2) (November 1955), 119–141.

Population and Economic Planning. *Population Policy in Great Britain.* PEP. London, 1948.

Razzell, P. E. "Population Change in Eighteenth-Century England: A Reinterpretation," *Economic History Review* (2nd series), **18** (2) (August 1965), 312–333.

Russell, Josiah C. *British Medieval Population.* Albuquerque, N.M.: University of New Mexico Press, 1948.

Sogner, Sölvi. "Aspects of the Demographic Situation in Seventeen Parishes in Shropshire, 1711–1760. An Exercise Based on Parish Registers," *Population Studies,* **17** (2) (November 1963), 126–146.

Törnquist, Leo W. *The Post-War Population Development of Finland Compared with Predictions Made After the War.* Paper contributed for the United Nations World Population Conference, August 30-September 10, 1965.

Tucker, G. S. L. "English Pre-industrial Population Trends," *Economic History Review,* 2nd series, **16** (2) (December 1963), 205–218.

Utterström, Gustaf. "Population and Agriculture in Sweden, circa 1700–1830," *Scandinavian Economic History Review* (Uppsala), **9** (2) (1961), 176–194.

Utterström, Gustaf. "Some Population Problems in Pre-Industrial Sweden," *Scandinavian Economic History Review* (Stockholm), **2** (2) (1954), 103–165.

Väestöpoliittinen Tutkimuslaitos (Population Research Institute). *Väestöntutkimuksen vo Vuosikirja, VII, 1961–1962 (Yearbook of Population Research in Finland, Vol. 7, 1961–1962).* Helsinki, 1962. English summaries for principal papers; English titles for remainder.

Webb, John W. "The Natural and Migrational Components of Population Changes in England and Wales, 1921–1931," *Economic Geography,* **39** (2) (April 1963), 130–148.

Widén, Lars, and Rune Tryggveson. "Sveriges Befolkning 1962–1980" (The Population of Sweden, 1962–1980), *Statistisk Tidskrift* (Stockholm), **11** (9) (September 1962), 523–532. English summary, 629–630.

XXVI. OCEANIA

Beaglehole, Ernest. "The Maori in New Zealand: A Case Study in Socio-Economic Integration," *International Labour Review* (Geneva), **76** (2) (August 1957), 103–123.

Bleakley, J. W. *The Aborigines of Australia: Their History, Their Habits, Their Assimilation.* Brisbane: Jacaranda Press, 1961.

Borrie, Wilfred D., and Ruth Rodgers. *Australian Population Projections, 1960–1975.* Canberra: Australian National University, Department of Demography, Institute of Advanced Studies, 1961.

Borrie, W. D., and Geraldine Spencer. *Australia's Population Structure and Growth* (2nd rev. ed.). Melbourne: Committee for Economic Development of Australia, 1965.

Borrie, Wilfred D. "The Maori Population: A Microcosm of a New World." Reprinted from *Anthropology in the South Seas,* 1959, pp. 247–262.

Borrie, Wilfred D. "The Growth of the Australian Population with Particular Reference to the Period Since 1947. Part I. The Role of Immigrants," *Population Studies,* **13** (1) (July 1959), 4–18.

Borrie, Wilfred, et al. "The Population of Tikopia, 1929 and 1952," *Population Studies,* **10** (3) (March 1957), 229–252.

McArthur, Norma. *The Populations of the Pacific Islands.* Canberra: The Australian National University, Department of Demography, 1955.

McArthur, Norma. "Population and Social Change: Prospect for Polynesia," *Journal of the Polynesian Society* (Wellington, New Zealand), **70** (4) (December 1961), 393–400.

Pirie, P., and W. Barrett. "Western Samoa: Population Production and Wealth," *Pacific Viewpoint* (Wellington, New Zealand) (March 1962), 63–95.

Smith, T. E. "The Cocos-Keeling Islands: A Demographic Laboratory," *Population Studies,* **14** (2) (November 1960), 94–129.

Taeuber, Irene B. *Demographic Instabilities in Island Ecosystems.* Paper given in the symposium, "Man's Place in the Island Ecosystem," at the Tenth Pacific Science Congress. Honolulu, n.d., pp. 226–252.

Ward, R. Gerard. "The Population of Fiji," *Geographical Review,* **49** (3) (July 1959), 322–341.

XXVII. USSR

Brackett, James W. "Population Dynamics in the U.S.S.R.," *American Statistician,* **13** (1) (February 1959), 16–19.

Eason, Warren W. "The Population of the Soviet Union," in Ronald Freedman (ed.). *Population: The Vital Revolution.* Garden City, N. Y.: Anchor Books, Doubleday, 1964, pp. 240–255.

Kantner, John F. "Recent Demographic Trends in the U.S.S.R.," in *Population Trends in Eastern Europe, the U.S.S.R. and Mainland China.* Milbank Memorial Fund Quarterly, New York, 1960, pp. 35–63.

Myers, Robert J. "Analysis of Mortality and Fertility Data of the Soviet Union," *Public Health Reports,* **74** (11) (November 1959), 975–981.

Myers, Robert J. "Further Analysis of Soviet Data on Mortality and Fertility," *Public Health Reports,* **77** (2) (February 1962), 177–182.

Newth, J. A. "The Soviet Population: Wartime Losses and the Postwar Recovery," *Soviet Studies,* **15** (3) (January 1964), 345–351.

Pavlovskii, E. N. (ed.). "Geografiia Naseleniia v SSSR" (The Geography of Population in the USSR). Akademiia Nauk USSR, *Geograficheskoe Obshchestovo Soiuza SSR.* Moscow, 1964.

Pisarev, Innokentii IU. *The Population of the U.S.S.R.; a Socioeconomic Survey.* Translated from the Russian by B. Bezey. Moscow: Progress Publishers, 1962, 157 pp.

Roof, Michael K. "The Russian Population Enigma Reconsidered," *Population Studies,* **14** (1) (July 1960), 3–16.

Roof, Michael K. "Soviet Population Trends," *Eugenics Quarterly,* **8** (3) (September, 1961), 123–134.

Sauvy, Alfred. "La Population de l'Union Soviétique: Situation, Croissance et Problemes Actuels." (The Population of the Soviet Union: Situation, Growth, and Present Problems), *Population* (Paris), **11** (3) (July-September 1956), 461–480.

Shimkin, Demitri B. "Demographic Changes and Socio-economic Forces Within the Soviet Union, 1939–1959," in *Population Trends in Eastern Europe, the U.S.S.R. and Mainland China.* Milbank Memorial Fund Quarterly, New York, 1960, pp. 224–258.

U. S. Congress, Joint Economic Committee. *Current Economic Indicators for the U.S.S.R.* 89th Congress, 1st session, Joint Committee Print. Washington, D.C.: U. S. Government Printing Office, 1965.

USSR. Akademiia Nauk SSSR. *Sibirskoe Otdelenie.* Institut Geografii Sibiri i Dal'nego Vostoka. Geografiia Naselniia Vostochnoi Sibiri (The Population Geography of Eastern Siberia). Moscow, 1962.

CHAPTER 4

The Raw Materials
of Demographic Research

4.1. Sources of Demographic Data

Demography obtains most of its research data from three main sources: *national censuses; national registers* of birth, death, marriage, divorce, and migration; and special *sample surveys*. Working either with the official statistical publications or with special statistical retabulations of the original observations of the censuses, surveys, and registers, demographers study the research problems that are of special concern to them. Over several decades they have developed a body of research techniques for working with these data that has come to be known as the "demographic methodology." This chapter discusses the sources of data with which demographers work; the next chapter discusses the research methods that they use. Both chapters are intended only to equip the student to study the materials that follow. A more detailed presentation of the sources of demographic data is given in Chapters 5, 6, and 7 of the *Manual of Demographic Research Techniques* (see also the suggested readings).

I. NATIONAL POPULATION CENSUSES

4.2. The National Population Census as a Demographic Inventory

Demographers in most nations are fortunate, in that they have more extensive and reliable data than does any other branch of social science. This happy state arises from the fact that in order to function properly, national governments must periodically take a national population census—an "inventory," so to speak.

The nation needs to find out how many people it has, how many there are of every kind, and where they are to be found. Without a count of population, a picture of how population is distributed, and other basic population facts, government administrators are unable to appreciate current and impending problems.

The national census not only provides the demographer with a rich opportunity for scientific analysis, but also involves him in research to establish a sound basis for administrative decisions. This results from the fact that a more refined type of demographic analysis is often necessary to extract from census data the findings and implications for the future that administrators are anxious to obtain. Several professional analytical demographers are usually found on the staff of experts that designs and supervises the taking of a census, because the very government that authorizes or finances a census usually expects a rather prompt official analysis and interpretation. Demography goes far beyond this public service function, however, and carries out scientific analysis for its own sake, irrespective of whether the new knowledge about population processes is of any immediate use to government or business.

Inasmuch as all demographers rely heavily on census data, and because census data can be used properly only if the concepts, definitions, and procedures followed are known and understood, it behooves every demographer to become familiar with the process of planning and taking censuses and to have actual census experience if at all possible. Moreover, it is becoming more and more common for independent investigators to carry out special sample surveys for specific research projects. Ability to design and supervise the collection and tabulation of special demographic surveys should be one of the skills of every research demographer and can best be acquired by actual experience with a census organization.

4.3. Fundamental Definitions

Strange though it may seem, demographers find it difficult to agree on a definition of "population" that will fit all needs. Should the count include citizens living overseas? Should it include the crews of vessels on the high seas? Should it include aliens residing in the country? What criteria should be used to separate temporary visitors from immigrants? For tabulations of particular topics the problem can take many forms, depending on the topic of a particular tabulation. Are soldiers, sailors, and military air force members to be considered a part of the labor force? Should prisoners be included in the labor force?

Most censuses avoid these problems by publishing several totals, thus permitting the user to choose the one that best fits his needs:

total population—including citizens overseas
total home population—excluding citizens overseas
total civilian population—excluding members of the armed forces
total noninstitutional population—excluding civilians confined in certain categories of prisons and in mental institutions and hospitals that house patients with long-term illnesses

Another difficulty arises in specifying the population of particular communities. Should the count take in all persons who are in the community on a particular day (including all visitors and excluding all regular residents who are temporarily absent) or all regular residents irrespective of where they temporarily are at the date of enumeration? A *de facto* population count takes the first approach and counts the population according to where it happens to be on the census night (*de facto* location is the place where the person slept during the night preceding enumeration). A *de jure* population count allocates the persons to their regular place of residence. Some censuses are taken on a strictly *de facto* basis, others on a *de jure* basis, and some on both. The United States census, for example, uses the *de jure* (usual abode) definition in the official counts, but collects also *de facto* statistics. The proponents of *de facto* enumeration believe that it enhances completeness of coverage and reduces errors of duplication, whereas the proponents of the *de jure* definition point out that the population of certain vacation and resort places fluctuates widely with the seasons and that birth and death rates are more valid when computed from *de jure* data.

4.4. How a National Census is Taken[1]

In most nations, provision for taking a census is made by a census law, and every citizen's cooperation is mandatory. Arrest with fine or imprisonment could result from refusal to furnish information. The law also fixes the responsibility in a particular department of government and outlines the organization that will perform the work. In modern nations there is need to take not only a census of population, but also censuses of housing, agriculture, manufactures, wholesale trade, retail trade, service industries, and special organizations such as governmental units, religious bodies, schools, and institutions. Consequently, there is a need for a more or less permanent census-taking organization, working according to a fixed schedule in such a way that one census or another is always in the process of being planned or carried out. Many nations have a permanent central statistical office for which census-taking is one of its responsibilities.

The United States census establishment may be used as an illustration of a national organization for census-taking. The census is the responsibility of the Secretary of Commerce,

[1] The United Nations has prepared some superb guides for the planning and conducting of censuses: *Principles and Recommendations for National Population Censuses*, Statistical Papers Series M, No. 27, 1958; and *Handbook of Population Census Methods*, Vol. I, "General Aspects of a Census," Vol. II, "Economic Characteristics of the Population" (1958), Vol. III, "Social Characteristics of the Population" (1959). *Principles and Recommendations for the 1970 Population Censuses*, Statistical Papers, Series M, No. 44, 1967.

and a separate Bureau of Census has been set up within the Commerce Department. The population census is only one of several censuses taken by this bureau. It is planned and sponsored by the Population Division, an organization of professional demographers and their statistical assistants. The actual field enumeration is done by the Field Division, and the data processing is done by the Operations Division. The entire census-taking operation is carried out according to a plan that is developed jointly by the Population, Field, and Operations Divisions and aims at statistical objectives worked out by the Population Division in consultation with the Census Director, Deputy Director, Assistant Directors, and panels of technical and nontechnical advisers both inside and outside government.

Determination of Content. The first step in taking a census is to determine the content—the items of information to be obtained. The following items are so standard that they appear on almost every census of the world:

A. *Geographic items*
    1. Location at time of census and/or place of usual residence
B. *Household or family information*
    2. Relationship to head of household or family
C. *Personal characteristics*
    3. Sex
    4. Age
    5. Marital status
    6. Place of birth
    7. Citizenship
D. *Economic characteristics*
    8. Type of activity
    9. Occupation
    10. Industry
    11. Status (as employer, employee, etc.)
E. *Cultural characteristics*
    12. Language
    13. Ethnic or nationality characteristics
F. *Educational characteristics*
    14. Literacy
    15. Level of education
    16. School attendance
G. *Fertility data*
    17. Children—total live-born
H. *Topics derived from the questionnaire*
    18. Total population
    19. Population by size of locality
    20. Urban-rural classification
    21. Household or family composition

In fact, the United Nations lists these as the minimum essentials for a census.[2] Most nations desire to go beyond this, however, and collect additional information. The need for this information may be urged by government, by business, or by private professional organizations. For the United States Census of 1960, the Bureau of Census and the Budget Bureau jointly canvassed every government department and many dozens of nongovernmental users of census data to obtain recommendations for content of the census. In addition to the standard items, the following were included in that census:

birthplace of parents
migration—place of residence five years ago
income (personal and family)
family status (relationship to the family head)
place of work
mode of transportation to work
number of times married
date of marriage
age at marriage

Additional topics about which the censuses of other nations have made inquiries are:

religion
caste
number of living children
age at birth of first child
languages spoken

Development of Census Schedule. Once the content of the census has been established, the next step is to perfect a questionnaire or census schedule that will obtain reliably the information desired about each person. Standard questions must be formulated which, when answered, will yield the desired information. Questions must be so worded that their meaning is completely clear both to the interviewer and to the respondents. To make certain that this has been accomplished, the proposed question should be pretested on a variety of population groups and then revised to avoid the most common misinterpretations or misunderstandings. The questions must then be arranged on a field enumeration form (schedule) in such a way that the information can be filled

[2] *Principles and Recommendations for the 1970 Population Censuses, op. cit.,* pp. 40–41.

in quickly and easily and with a minimum of error and omissions. This also must be pre-tested. It is especially important that this pre-testing include the most difficult situations under which the census must later be taken—slum neighborhoods, hostile subpopulations (if any), and groups that may be predisposed to refuse to give particular types of information, such as ethnicity or income. A sufficient number of censuses have now been taken, by many different field approaches, all over the world to provide many examples of good and poor question wording and schedule layout. A demographer designing a new census should study as many of them as possible.[3] It is highly important that the program for processing the data be planned beforehand and that the schedule be laid out in such a way that office processing as well as field enumeration are made easy.

Field Enumeration. There are two major approaches to obtaining census data: direct enumeration and householder enumeration. In the first case, a corps of enumerators is hired, trained, and sent into the field; each enumerator is assigned to a particular enumeration area to obtain by direct personal interviews information about every person living within the assigned boundaries. The enumerator locates a reliable informant in each household and obtains the information from him. Under householder enumeration, the census schedule is mailed or delivered by hand to each household or living quarters, and the household head is responsible for reporting for every person in the household, or getting each person to report for himself. Both systems have been in use successfully for more than two centuries. Each has its advantages and its drawbacks. Under either system it is highly important to have strict supervision and quality control to detect poor work promptly and correct it.

Editing, Coding, and Preparing Data for Tabulation Input. When the completed schedules are received in the census office, they

must be edited. Obvious errors must either be changed to entries of "no information" or corrected, if possible, by using other items of information on the schedule. (In censuses prepared on electronic computers, much of the editing and adjusting are done by the computer.) Complex items such as occupation, industry, place of birth, migration status, relationship to head, and family income must be specially coded, because judgment, reasoning, and decisions are involved. After the special hand coding is completed, the cards are punched if the tabulation is to be by machine using punched cards. Items that have a few clearly reported categories, such as sex, age, and marital status, can be coded by a punch operator. One card is punched for each person enumerated, but in lengthy censuses or sample surveys two cards for each person may be required. Often a family or household card is prepared for tabulations according to the characteristics of families or households.

Tabulation. When the topics for a census are selected, plans about the information to be reported for each topic are also made. This is reviewed and made more specific until it becomes a set of "dummy" table outlines, showing the statistical tables exactly as they will appear in the final publication, complete with titles and captions for each row and column, and with only the statistics missing. Specifications are then prepared for tabulation runs that will yield the data necessary to fill in the blank columns of the "dummy" table outlines. With modern electronic tabulation equipment, it is possible to program the printing-out equipment to prepare the tables exactly in the form needed for publication, so that typing is eliminated.

Editing and Publication. Once the tables have been set up, they must be carefully reviewed for errors by experts in the subject fields and then prepared for publication. Derived figures (percents, rates, ratios, averages, medians, etc.) must be calculated if they have not already been computed during the tabulating process. The tables are then typed and organized into a publication. This step concludes our greatly oversimplified description of the census-taking process.

---

[3] *The United Nations Handbook of Population Methods,* Vol. I, reproduces the actual census questionnaire used in 12 countries. Most censuses reproduce the questionnaire as a part of one of the volumes reporting the results.

4.5.   Errors in Census Data

Because national censuses are such monumental and official undertakings, the legend has developed that they are almost completely free of errors and that their data are so accurate as to have only a negligible degree of imperfection. This notion is largely unfounded. Several censuses in the world have managed to attain a very high degree of precision, but a significant amount of error is always present. The censuses of some nations are so untrustworthy as to be almost worthless for research (or any other) purposes. The majority fall between these extremes. Before approaching a research problem in population and beginning to assemble data for this task, the researcher not only must determine whether the data he needs are available from the censuses, but must also evaluate the quality of the data that are available. This is often a major research project in itself and often requires very complex methods. To be able to recognize inconsistent and improbable results, the researcher must be familiar with the data from several reliable censuses. Chapter 7 of the *Manual of Demographic Research Techniques* discusses this topic in considerable detail and describes tests for measuring census accuracy.

There are two main classes of error in census and other survey data: errors of *coverage* and errors of *classification*. Errors of coverage arise from failure to enumerate all of the population or from counting some of the population twice. Errors of omission usually far outnumber errors of duplicate counting. Such errors occur because of (a) failure to contact every household (missing whole households) because of failure to cover the entire enumeration area thoroughly and (b) failure to enumerate every member of a household. It often happens that very young children are overlooked in reporting the household membership. In some nations there seems to be a tendency to forget to report women, especially if not the spouse of the household head. The nature and extent of coverage errors vary from nation to nation and may change quite dramatically for better or worse between consecutive censuses in a particular nation. Only the utmost care and thoroughness in enumeration, with unfail-

ing quality check on every phase of data collection, can reduce this error, and even then there is no assurance of complete coverage. For example, it is thought that despite very elaborate precautions the census of the United States in 1960 failed to enumerate about 3.5 million persons, or about 2 percent of the population.[4]

Errors of classification arise from recording incorrectly the age, marital status, occupation, or other population characteristics that are enumerated. Such errors occur in many ways. The respondent may give a false report, and the enumerator may fail to ask a question and will later guess and write in the answer himself, or he may obtain information about a person from an ill-informed household member or a neighbor. When data with errors of classification are tabulated, it is often discovered that, to a surprisingly large extent, the errors cancel out. For example, about as many people are reported as being older than they actually are as are reported as being younger. This leads to two measures of error: the *gross* error rate and the *net* error rate. The gross error rate is a measure of the proportion of persons in a classification of a whole statistical table that are in the wrong cell. This rate, whenever measured with reasonable accuracy, is found to be discouragingly high—sometimes as great as 30 to 40 percent; gross error rates of 10 to 15 percent are common. The net error rate is the net difference between a correct and a given count, permitting errors to offset each other to the extent to which they can do so. Although still substantial, net error rates are usually less than one-half or one-fourth the gross error rate. Often there is a complacency about high gross error rate, because of this self-cancelling tendency. This is unwarranted for two reasons: (a) Although overall net errors may be low, the net errors for a particular category may be very high. (b) A high rate of gross error tends to distort the analysis of relationships, especially if several variables are involved; when cross-classified with other variables, the self-cancelling fea-

[4] Conrad Taeuber and Morris H. Hansen, "A Preliminary Evaluation of the 1960 Census of Population," *Demography*, **1** (1964), 2–16.

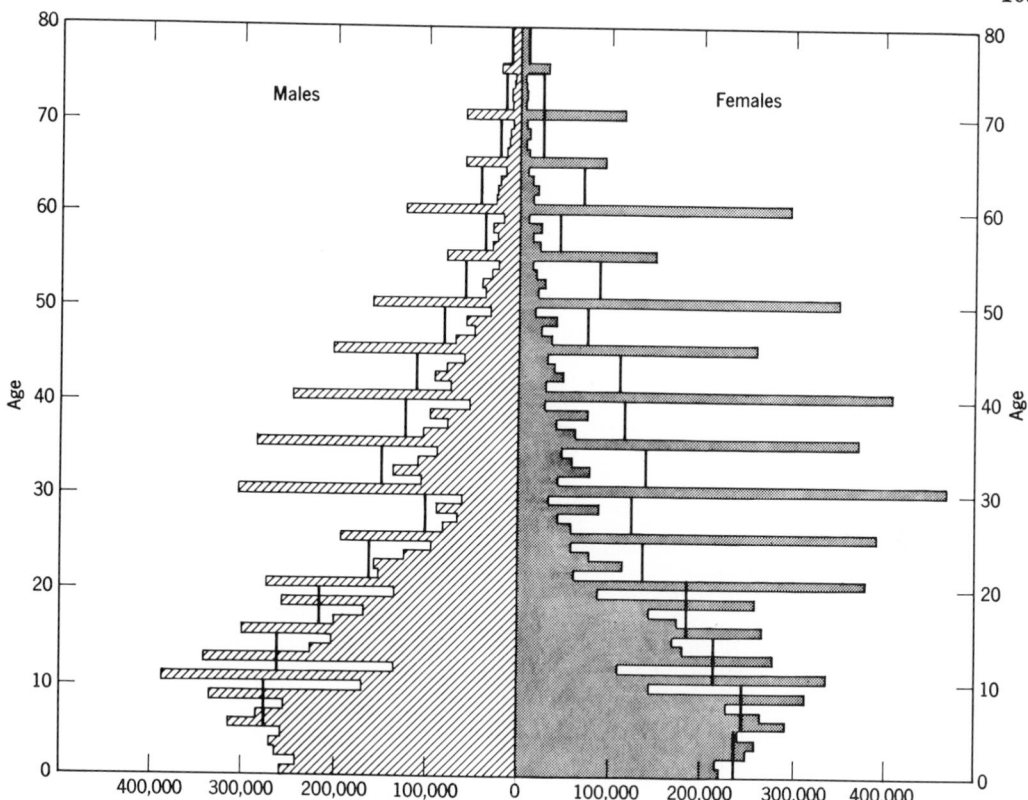

Figure 4-1 Population of Turkey, 1945, by Sex, by Single Years of Age, and by 5-Year Age Groups, according to Census.

SOURCE: United Nations, *Methods of Appraisal of Quality of Basic Data for Population Estimates,* Population Studies, No. 23, 1955, p.34.

ture may not carry over in all parts of the multiple cross-classification.

The magnitude of error that can occur in a census is illustrated in Figure 4-1, which portrays the reporting of age in the 1945 census of Turkey. Note the great tendency to "heap" ages at digits ending in 0 and 5 and the seeming undercount of children under 5. The student of demography should be very cautious in claiming significance and meaning for small differences, especially in detailed cross-classification of statistics for small areas.

Errors of sampling, in addition to the errors of classification and incomplete coverage, are another reason for caution.

There is no perfect way to measure the amount of census error. One technique is to reenumerate a sample of the population, using highly trained, specially selected, unusually well-paid, and elaborately supervised workers with instructions to be exhaustively thorough.

Even this procedure is liable to errors, so that a reenumeration survey only measures the improvement that could be obtained. Other methods of measuring coverage and classification involve an item-by-item comparison with registration records, such as birth certificates, social security records, internal revenue records, and population registers. Since such records also contain errors of coverage and classification, any cross-checks give a useful indication but are a precise measure of the errors only insofar as they approach perfection in coverage and classification.

These comments are intended to provoke an attitude of caution, but not to discourage the student from using census data. Each year some highly reliable and important principles or findings are extracted from data that are incomplete or inaccurate. Demographers have developed ingenious ways of adjusting and correcting the data for known or estimated errors. Censuses that are inadequate in one respect or for one topic often are found to be remarkably useful for another.

We may conclude this brief overview of census errors by stating that census data must be terribly inaccurate before a skilled demographer cannot extract some information from them, and they must be most extraordinarily precise before he can fail to find deficiencies of sufficient size to make it necessary to qualify his conclusions at least somewhat.

4.6 Special Sample Surveys and Their Errors

Special sample surveys are undertaken more and more routinely to obtain demographic information at more frequent intervals and on special topics not included in the national census. In fact, a growing number of nations have an official national sample survey that is taken once each month, each quarter, or each year. In addition, information of great value has been produced from special one-time surveys of fertility, migration, health, employment, and other topics.

The procedures for conducting such surveys are similar to those outlined in Section 4.4 for censuses, with the additional step that the sampling design must be worked out with great care and precision. This topic is too large and specialized to be discussed here, but several excellent books about it are available.[5]

It should be pointed out that sample surveys also contain errors of coverage and classification, *plus* the error of sampling. Because abler and better-trained persons are usually employed for this work, the total error, including the sampling error, may not be very much greater than it is for a census and may sometimes actually be less for broad national totals. Nevertheless, tests made on the quality of survey data, especially so-called "attitude" or

"open end" questions, show that the errors of classification usually are very high.

In some nations sample surveys are so widely used and have become so precise that a national census serves less to provide national totals of population composition than to provide data about smaller areas—states, cities, counties, townships, census tracts, and similar minor civil divisions—and to permit more detailed breakdown into refined categories and more elaborate cross-classifications of characteristics than do the sample surveys.

II. REGISTRATION

4.7. Registration as a Record of Demographic Events[6]

Whereas a census is a static cross-sectional view of the population at a given moment of time, a registration system undertakes to measure movement by making a record of important demographic events as birth, death, marriage, divorce, and migration. The most complete, best organized, and most accurate registration systems in the world are those in the Scandanavian countries and the Netherlands. Unfortunately, for most of the world population registration either does not exist at all or is very inadequate. For example, in Asia (excluding Japan and Taiwan) only about two thirds of the births and deaths get registered, and statistics for marriage, divorce, and internal migration either do not exist or are even less complete. Two major objectives of demographers are (a) to raise the quality of registration to a point of near completeness and (b) to measure the errors of registration in order to adjust the statistics so as to approximate their true values.

A vital event is registered by filling out an official document that certifies that the event has taken place. The legal purpose of registration is not the collection of statistics, but the creation of an official record that serves as evidence of citizenship, marital status, and death. The certificate of birth, death, or marriage is a standard form that is filled out and deposited

---

[5] One of the best known is Morris H. Hansen, William N. Hurwitz, and William G. Madow, *Sample Survey Methods and Theory* (2 vols.), John Wiley and Sons, 1953. See also United Nations, *A Short Manual on Sampling*, Studies in Methods, Series F, No. 9, 1960. *Handbook of Household Surveys*, Studies in Methods, Series F, No. 10, 1964. Leslie Kish, *Survey Sampling*, John Wiley, 1967.

[6] For a more detailed exposition see United Nations, *Handbook of Vital Statistics Methods*, Studies in Methods, Series F, No. 7, 1957.

with the registrar. Statistics of these events are then obtained by tabulating the information contained on the certificates. The statistical tables that can be constructed are limited to the information contained on the certificate.

The following information is given on most certificates, and it constitutes the principal variables of analysis:

Birth Certificate
Race
Age of mother
Age of father
Legitimacy
Date of marriage
Order of birth
Occupation of husband
Place of birth
Place of residence

Death Certificate
Race
Age of deceased
Place of birth
Occupation
Marital status
Place of residence
Cause of death

Marriage Certificate
Race
Age of bride
Age of bridegroom
Place of birth of bride and bridegroom
Occupation of bridegroom
Place of residence

The accuracy of the data is determined by the accuracy of the responses given by the persons who furnished the data on the certificate. In general, the person furnishing the information is well acquainted with the situation and the persons involved, so that the reporting tends to be accurate. Careless registrars may fail to obtain or to record items of information that they do not regard as important. The major deficiency, however, is coverage. If people do not consider it important to register in order to have official proof of birth, death, or marriage, it is very difficult to compel them to go to the bother of doing it. Perhaps the major forces behind the comparatively complete registration of vital events in Europe and North America are the needs to prove citizenship and age by birth certificate in order to enjoy employment rights, social security benefits, and other privileges and to prove death in order to settle insurance claims.

4.8.   How Statistics Are Produced from Registration Certificates

Before each certificate is filed for possible future reference, arrangements are made for statistical processing. One common way of doing this is to prepare a microfilm copy of each certificate as it is made. At the end of each month or each quarter these microfilm records are transmitted to central statistical units for editing, coding, card punching, and tabulation. The process is similar to that for censuses, except that the flow is continuous. Since reports must be made for each calendar year, data for the current year are prepared for tabulation while data for the preceding year are tabulated. A period of six months or more is required to assemble all records for a given calendar year from all offices, so that even under conditions of utmost efficiency usually one full year or more elapses before the report for a given calendar year appears. This time gap often is filled with interim reports based on samples.

The vital statistical tabulation in some countries is based on a sample of the records rather than on every record. Because tabulations are needed for small areas, the sample must be a very large one—about 50 percent. Sampling saves processing time, reduces costs, and hastens the appearance of the reports. It is more appropriate to use samples with birth and marriage statistics than with death statistics, for the latter require very detailed tabulations according to cause of death (with more than 100 categories) and the age and sex of the deceased; a great deal of special attention is also being focused on many comparatively rare types of diseases as causes of death. Under such circumstances, it is important to have as many cases in each category as possible, and sampling is inappropriate. Inasmuch as each year's vital events may be regarded as a sample from a larger universe, it is not uncommon to combine two or three consecutive years' experience in order to obtain a large total number of cases for studying causes of death. In fact, for small areas or rare diseases a few studies have pooled death records for five or ten years.

III. OTHER SOURCES OF DEMOGRAPHIC DATA

4.9. Population Data from Administrative Operations

In order to administer certain national programs it often is necessary to collect information that can be tabulated to produce usable demographic information. These data usually refer only to a segment of the population, but for certain specialized demographic studies this need not be a limitation. National social security schemes, for example, routinely collect information about almost all workers in the labor force and about persons who have been pensioned under the scheme. Military conscription requires all men between certain ages to register and furnish information about themselves. Food rationing, voter registration, school enrollment, automobile licensing, collection of income taxes, church affiliation, telephone installation, taking out life insurance, joining a medical care insurance program, submitting notices of change of address to the post office, and even being arrested by the police generate a set of records that can be tabulated to obtain population statistics.

Many of these potential sources of data are not exploited because of the great expense of transferring the information to punched cards or otherwise preparing it for tabulation. However, all of these administrative operations are increasingly being computerized, with the result that the records can be summarized for statistical purposes much more readily. Also, the administrators who operate these programs are rapidly becoming sensitive to the need for obtaining more information about the people whom they serve or care for and are stepping up the fact-gathering phase of their work. The alert demographer will discover highly useful untapped bodies of data pertaining to specific types of population events.

Even when the data provided by the administrative operations are limited, they may provide an ideal sampling frame for carrying out special surveys. For example, it is very costly to find, by routine interviewing of randomly selected households, representative samples of migrants, divorced persons, members of particular religious or ethnic groups, or couples with two children. The records kept for administrative purposes may provide a comparatively complete or representative set of names and addresses, which can then be sampled for intensive interviewing.

The national welfare system, which cares for the poor, indigent, and disabled, maintains a very elaborate set of records that may be used to great advantage in demographic studies pertaining to these special groups.

CONCLUSION

In this chapter we have examined the sources from which the demographer obtains his data. He is an expert at "secondary analysis," since he digests the output of the national census and vital registration system and often the data from other administrative operations. To an increasing extent, however, demographers are engaging in "primary analysis." They do this in two ways: by taking a very active hand as advisers in the design and tabulation of census and vital statistics and by designing and carrying out special sample surveys to obtain the information required to test particular research propositions.

QUESTIONS FOR DISCUSSION AND EXERCISES

1. Read the "Introduction" to the latest census of your own nation and of at least two other nations. Compare the definitions used and write a short essay explaining how the differences in definition might affect the comparability of the results.

2. Perform Exercise 1 for the vital statistics publications of your country and two other countries. Try to find out how reliable the vital statistics are and what caused the errors that exist. What must be done to achieve greater precision in registration?

3. If you were designing a new census, would you plan for the collection of data by the householder or the enumerator method? Would you make your count on a *de facto* or a *de jure* basis? Give your reasons for the choice.

4. Many nations complain that use of the definitions recommended by United Nations lead to data that are not the best needed for solving their own national problems. For example, the international definitions make very little provision for occupational classifications appropriate in many developing economies. In such countries, should the census sacrifice international comparability to its own welfare, submerge its own needs in the interest of international comparability, or make some compromise? What are some of the compromises that it might make?

5. If you examine the list of topics recommended for census enumeration, you will find many economic items—labor force status, occupation, industry, and so on. Sociologists, psychologists, anthropologists, and political scientists are almost unrepresented on the census schedule. Is this as it should be? What items of information for each of these unrepresented disciplines might be included in the census? Why is this not done? Do you think that the data you suggest might be made a part of a continuing national sample survey?

6. Each new census gives an opportunity to change the definitions of the various items. Any change lessens comparability with previous censuses, even though it may improve the quality of the data for current analytical use. In your opinion, is it more important to have data that reflect as precisely as possible the actual situation by continuously revising definitions or to preserve comparability even at the expense of having classifications that are a little out of focus with current reality? What compromises might be made? Use the following examples in discussing this problem: classification of population according to urban or rural residence; literacy; marital status in Latin American countries or in American slums; and occupational classification in the face of rapid technological change.

BIBLIOGRAPHY

Arias, B. Jorge. "Algunos Errores en la Declaracíon de Edad en los Censos de Población de 1950 en Centro América y México," (Some Errors in Age Declarations in the Population Censuses of 1950 in Central America and Mexico), *Estadística* (Washington, D. C.), **14** (52) (September 1956), 403–425. With English summary.

Arretx, G. Carmen. *Metodo Para Estimar Tasas Demograficas en Regiones Donde no se Dispone de Estadisticas Vitales y Censales. Ensayos Realizados en Guanabara (Brasil) y Cauquenes (Chile.)* Paper contributed for the United Nations World Population Conference, August 30-September 10, 1965.

Bachi, Roberto. "Measurement of the Tendency to Round Off Age Returns," *Bulletin of the International Statistical Institute,* **34** (3) (1954), 129–138.

Benjamin, Bernard. "The Quality of Response in Census-Taking," *Population Studies,* **8** (3) (March 1955), 288–293.

Benjamin, Bernard. "Statistical Problems Connected with the 1961 Population Census," *Journal of the Royal Statistical Society,* Series A, **123** (4) (1960), 413–426.

Benjamin, Bernard, and N. H. Carrier. "An Evaluation of the Quality of Demographic Statistics in England and Wales," *Proceedings of the World Population Conference: 1954.* New York, 1955, Vol. IV.

Blacker, J. G. C. *Use of Sample Surveys to Obtain Data of Age Structure of the Population Where Respondents in a Regular Census Enumeration Cannot Give Accurate Data (Some Kenya Experiments).* Paper contributed for the United Nations World Population Conference, August 30-September 10, 1965.

Bogue, Donald J., and Edmund M. Murphy. "The Effect of Classification Errors Upon Statistical Inference: A Case Analysis with Census Data," *Demography,* **1** (1) (1964), 42–55.

Bourgeois-Pichat, Jean. "Un Essai d'Évaluation de la Précision des Statistiques Démographiques d'un Pays Sous-développé: La Thailande" (An Attempt to Appraise the Accuracy of the Demographic Statistics of an Underdeveloped Country: Thailand), *Population,* **15** (1) (January-March 1960), 131–135.

Brass, William. *Methods of Collecting Demographic Statistics in Africa,* in United Nations Economic Commission for Africa Seminar on Population Problems in Africa. October 29-November 10, 1962. Cairo, U.A.R.

Brichler, Marcel. "Classification of the Population by Social and Economic Characteristics: the French Experience and International Recommendations," *Journal of the Royal Statisti-*

cal Society, Series A, **121** (2) (1958), 162–195.

Brivkalne, Mirdza. "Kontrollundersökningen i samband med 1960 års folkräkning" (The Control Study Made in Connection with the 1960 Census of Population), *Statistisk Tidskrift,* 3rd series, **2** (2) (1964), 105–117. English summary.

Bunle, Henri. "Sur les Erreurs Entachant les Statistiques et des Recensements de la Population et de l'État Civil" (Errors Marring the Statistics of Population Censuses and of Civil Status), *Bulletin de l'Institut International de Statistique* (Rio de Janeiro), **35** (3) (1957), 283–288. With English summary.

Carrier, N. H., and A. M. Farrag. "The Reduction of Errors in Census Population for Statistically Under-developed Countries," *Population Studies,* **12** (3) (March 1959), 240–285.

Cavanaugh, Joseph A. *Research and Data Collection Techniques for Developing Areas.* Paper contributed for the United Nations World Population Conference, August 30-September 10, 1965.

Coale, Ashley J. "The Design of an Experimental Procedure for Obtaining Accurate Vital Statistics," in International Union for the Study of Population. Session 10. *International Population Conference, New York, 1961* (Proceedings). Vol. 2. London, 1963, pp. 339–437.

Coale, Ansley J., and Frederick F. Stephan. "The Case of the Indians and the Teenage Widows," *Journal of the American Statistical Association,* **57** (298) (June 1962), 338–347.

Depoid, Pierre. "Degree of Accuracy of Demographic Data" (Le Degré de Précision des Données Démographiques), *Bulletin of the International Statistical Institute,* **33** (4) (1954), 1–6.

Drake, Michael. "An Elementary Exercise in Parish Register Demography," *Economic History Review,* 2nd series, **14** (3) (April 1962), 427–445.

Eckler, A. Ross, and Leon Pritzker. "Measuring the Accuracy of Enumeration Surveys," *Bulletin of the International Statistical Institute,* **33** (4) (1954), 7–24.

El-Badry, M. A., and Frederick F. Stephan. "On Adjusting Sample Tabulations to Census Counts," *Journal of the American Statistical Association,* **50** (271) (September 1955), 738–762.

Eldridge, Hope T. *The Materials of Demography: A Selected and Annotated Bibliography.* Published by the International Union for the Scientific Study of Population and Population Association of America. New York: Columbia University Press, 1959.

Fasteau, Herman H., et al. "Control of Quality of Coding in the 1960 Censuses," *Journal of the American Statistical Association,* **59** (305) (March 1964), 120–132.

Fellegi, Ivan P. "Response Variance and its Estimation," *Journal of the American Statistical Association,* **59** (308) (1964), 1016–1041.

Fellegi, Ivan P. "Some Sampling Techniques Applied by the Dominion Bureau of Statistics," *Estadística* (Washington, D.C.), **21** (80) (September 1963), 532–534.

Frumpkin, G. "Appraisal of the Quality of Demographic Statistics," *Proceedings of the World Population Conference: 1954.* New York, 1955, Vol. IV.

Gear, H. S., et al. "International Work in Health Statistics, 1948-1958. 2. Nature and Extent of the Problem," *World Health Organization Chronicle* (Geneva), **13** (5) (May 1959), 214–221.

Grebenik, E. "The Sources and Nature of Statistical Information in Special Fields of Statistics. Population and Vital Statistics," *Journal of the Royal Statistical Society,* Series A (General), **118** (4) (1955), 452–462.

Gutman, Robert. *The Accuracy of Vital Statistics in Massachusetts, 1842–1901.* University Microfilms, Publication No. 16,281. Ann Arbor, Mich.: University of Michigan Microfilms, 1956.

Hansen, Morris, et al. "Measurement Errors in Censuses and Surveys," *Bulletin de l'Institut International de Statistique* (Tokyo), **38** (2) (1961), 359–374.

Hansen, Morris, and Joseph Steinberg. "Control of Errors in Surveys," *Biometrics,* **12** (1956), 462–474.

Henry, Louis. "D'un Problème Fondamental de l'Analyse Démographique," *Population* (Paris), **14** (1) (January-March 1959).

Henry, Louis. "Réflections sur l'Observation en Démographie" (Reflections on Observation in Demography), *Population* (Paris), **18** (2) (April-June 1963), 233–362.

Hollingsworth, T. H. *Methods of Using Old Documents to Study Population Trends in the Past.* Paper contributed for the United Nations World Population Conference, August 30-September 10, 1965.

Indian Statistical Institute. *The Use of the National Sample Survey in the Estimation of Current Birth and Death Rates in India,* pp. 395–402. In International Union for the Study of Population. Session 10. New Methods of Obtaining Vital Statistics in Underdeveloped Countries. *International Population Conference, New York, 1961* (Proceedings). Vol. 2. London, 1963, pp. 339–437.

Jaffe, A. J. "Demographic Analysis in the Absence of Official Census and Vital Statistics," *Proceedings of the World Population Conference: 1954.* New York, 1955, Vol. IV.

Kappes Barrientos, Hector, and Eli S. Marks.

"Evaluation of the Accuracy of the 1960 Censuses of Chile," *Estadística* (Washington, D.C.), **19** (72) (December 1961), 689–704.

Keyfitz, Nathan, and Edmund M. Murphy. *Comparative Demographic Computations Based on Official (Unadjusted) Data for 69 Selected Countries and Regions*. Chicago: University of Chicago, Population Research and Training Center, June, 1964.

Keys, A., et al. "Effect of Misclassification on Estimated Relative Prevalence of a Characteristic. I. Two Populations Infallibly Distinguished. II. Errors in Two Variables," *American Journal of Public Health,* **53** (October 1963), 1656–1665.

Khan, Muhammad K. H. *Some Difficulties in Utilizing Survey Methods for the Determination of Vital Rates*. In International Union for the Study of Population. Session 10. *International Population Conference, New York, 1961* (Proceedings). Vol. 2. London, 1963, pp. 339–437.

Krieger, Konrad. "Evaluation of Quality of Demographic Statistics," *Proceedings of the World Population Conference: 1954*. New York, 1955, Vol. IV.

Krótki, Karol J. *The Problem of Estimating Vital Rates in Pakistan*. Paper contributed for United Nations World Population Conference, August 30-September 10, 1965.

Linder, Forrest E. *The Increased Scope of Demographic Investigations Through the Use of Sampling Surveys*. Paper contributed for the United Nations World Population Conference, August 30-September 10, 1965.

Lorimer, Frank. *Demographic Information on Tropical Africa*. Boston: Boston University Press, 1961.

Mahalanobis, P. C., and D. B. Lahiri. "Analysis of Errors in Censuses and Surveys with Special Reference to Experience in India," *Bulletin de l'Institut International de Statistique* (Tokyo), **38** (2) (1961), 401–433.

Mandel, B. J., et al. *Coordination of Old-Age and Survivors Insurance Wage Records and the Post-Enumeration Survey*. In National Bureau of Economic Research. Studies in Income and Wealth, Vol. 23, by the Conference on Research in Income and Wealth. Princeton, N.J.: Princeton University Press, 1958.

Marks, Eli S. "Techniques of Sampling and Statistical Evaluation for Census Work," *Estadística* (Washington, D.C.), **21** (80) (September 1963), 551–556.

Martin, C. J. "The Collection of Basic Demographic Data in Under-developed Territories," *Bulletin of the International Statistical Institute,* **34** (3) (1954), 17–27.

Mauldin, W. Parker. "Comments on Possible National and International Standards for the Determination and Indication of Degree of Ac-

curacy of Demographic Statistics," *Proceedings of the World Population Conference: 1954*. New York, 1955, Vol. IV.

Mendoza-Pascual, Elvira. "Reinvestigation of Birth and Death Statistics in the Philippines," *The Philippine Statistician* (Manila), **11** (4) (December 1962), 171–189.

Midzuno, H. "On the Post Enumeration Survey," *Bulletin de l'Institut International de Statistique* (Tokyo), **38** (2) (1961), 435–441.

Miró, Carmen A. *A. 6. Algunos Problemas Relativos a la Evaluación de los Resultados de los Censos de Población (Some Problems in Evaluating the Results of Population Censuses)*, 1959. In United Nations. Centro Latinoamericano de Demografía (CELADE) Publicaciones. Series A. Santiago, 1962.

Moser, C. A. "Recent Developments in the Sampling of Human Populations in Great Britain," *Journal of the American Statistical Association,* **50** (272) (December 1955), 1195–1214.

Muhsam, H. V. "Population Estimates Based on Census Enumeration and Coverage Check," *Population Studies,* **13** (3) (March 1960), 278–281.

Mukherjee, P. K. *Economic Surveys in Under-developed Countries: A Study in Methodology* (2nd ed.). London: Asia Publishing House, 1960.

Newcombe, H. B. et al. "Automatic Linkage of Vital Records," *Science,* **130** (3381) (October 16, 1959), 954–959.

Powell, Barbara A., and Leon Pritzker. "Effects of Variations in Field Personnel on Census Results," *Demography,* **2** (1965), 8–32.

Prothero, R. Mansell. "The Population Census of Northern Nigeria, 1952: Problems and Results," *Population Studies,* **10** (2) (November 1956), 166–183.

Sabagh, Georges, and Christopher Scott. *An Evaluation of the Use of Retrospective Questionnaires for Obtaining Vital Data: The Experience of the Moroccan Multi-Purpose Sample Survey of 1961–1963*. Paper contributed for the United Nations World Population Conference, August 30-September 10, 1965.

Simmons, Walt R., and George A. Schnack. *Use of Current Surveys as an Aid to Constructing Post-Censal Population Estimates*. Paper contributed for United Nations World Population Conference, August 30-September 10, 1965.

Sirken, Monroe G. "Research Uses of Vital Records in Vital Statistics Surveys," *Milbank Memorial Fund Quarterly,* **41** (3) (July 1963), 309–316.

Som, Ranjan Kumar. *On Recall Lapse in Demographic Studies*, in International Union for the Scientific Study of Population, Vienna, 1959, pp. 50–61.

Som, Ranjan Kumar. *Response Biases in Demographic Enquiries*. Paper contributed for the

United Nations World Population Conference, August 30-September 10, 1965.

Somoza, Jorge, et al. "Examen Critico de Algunas Estadísticas de Población de la Argentina: Posibilidades para el Análisis Demográfico" (Critical Examination of Some Population Statistics of Argentina: Possibilities for a Demographic Analysis), *Desarrollo Económico* (Buenos Aires), **2** (2) (1962), 85–141.

Taeuber, Conrad. *New Concepts in Census Methodology.* Paper contributed for the United Nations World Population Conference, August 30-September 10, 1965.

Taeuber, Conrad, and Morris H. Hansen. "A Preliminary Evaluation of the 1960 Censuses of Population and Housing," *Demography*, **1** (1) (1964), 1–14.

Taeuber, Conrad, and Morris H. Hansen. "Self Enumeration as a Census Method," *Demography*, **3** (1966), 289–295.

Ullman, Morris B. *The 1939 U.S.S.R. Census of Population: Organization and Methodology: With Notes on Plans for the 1959 Census of Population.* U.S. Bureau of the Census. Foreign Manpower Research Office. Washington, D.C.: U. S. Government Printing Office, 1959.

United Nations. Centro Latinoamericano de Demografia (CELADE) Publications. Series A. "Experimental Demographic Survey of Guanabara," Santiago, 1962.

United Nations Department of Economic and Social Affairs. Population Studies No. 36. *National Programmes of Analysis of Population Census Data as an Aid to Planning and Policy Making.* New York, 1964.

United Nations Economic Commission for Africa. Seminar on Vital Statistics. *Technical Paper on Non-Sampling Errors and Biases in Retrospective Demographic Enquiries.* Addis Ababa, December 14-19, 1964.

United Nations Population Commission. *United Nations Seminar on Evaluation and Utilization of Population Census Data in Latin America.* (Working Papers). New York, September 16-December 18, 1959.

United Nations Population Division. "Some Attempts to Measure the Accuracy of International Population Statistics." *Proceedings of the World Population Conference: 1954.* New York, 1955, Vol. IV.

United Nations Statistical Commission, 12th Session, Item 9 of the Provisional Agenda. *Methodology and Evaluation of Continuous Population Registers (Report of the Secretary-General).* New York, February 7, 1962.

United Nations Statistical Office. *Compendium of Social Statistics 1963* (Data available as of November 1, 1962). United Nations Statistical Papers, Series K, No. 2. New York, 1963.

United Nations Statistical Office. *Enumeration in Population Censuses.* New York, August 20, 1957.

United Nations Statistical Office. *Handbook of Statistical Organization.* Studies in Method, Series F, No. 6. New York, 1954.

United Nations Statistical Office. *Handbook of Vital Statistics Methods.* Studies in Method, Series F, No. 7. New York, 1955.

United Nations Statistical Office. *Handbook of Population Census Methods, Vol. 1. General Aspects of a Population Census.* Studies in Method, Series F, No. 5. New York, 1958.

United Nations Statistical Office. *Handbook of Population Census Methods. Vol. III. Demographic and Social Characteristics of the Population.* Studies in Method, Series F, No. 5. New York, 1959.

United Nations Statistical Office. Statistical Papers, Series M, to No. 27. *Principles and Recommendations for National Population Censuses.* New York, June 1958.

U. S. Bureau of the Census Technical Paper No. 2. *The Accuracy of Census Statistics With and Without Sampling.* Washington, D.C.: U. S. Government Printing Office, 1960.

U. S. Bureau of the Census. *Evaluation and Research Program of the 1960 Censuses of Population and Housing (Reports),* Series ER-60. No. 1. Washington, D.C.: U. S. Government Printing Office, 1963.

U. S. Bureau of the Census Working Paper No. 8. Foreign Manpower Research Office. *Materials on the Preparation and Conduct of the U.S.S.R. All-Union Population Census of 1959.* Washington, D.C.: U. S. Government Printing Office, 1959.

U. S. Bureau of the Census. The Post-Enumeration Survey: 1950 (Bureau of the Census Technical Paper No. 4; Washington, D.C., 1960).

U. S. Bureau of the Census, Censuses of Population and Housing: Procedural History, Washington, D.C.: Government Printing Office, 1966.

U. S. Bureau of the Census. *United States Censuses of Population and Housing, 1960. Enumeration Time and Cost Study.* Washington, D.C.: U. S. Government Printing Office, 1963.

U. S. National Health Survey. *Concepts and Definitions in the Health Household-Interview Survey.* Series A-3. Washington, D.C., September 1958.

Valaoras, Vasilios G. *Testing Deficiencies and Analytical Adjustments of Vital Statistics.* Paper contributed for the United Nations World Population Conference, August 30-September 10, 1965.

World Health Organization. *Annual Epidemiological and Vital Statistics, 1956.* Geneva, 1959.

World Health Organization. "Summary of Demographic and Health Statistics Published by National Authorities on Vital and Health

Statistics. *Epidemiological and Vital Statistics Report,* **20** (3) (1967), 169–310.

Zarkovíc, S. S. "Some Remarks on Coverage Checks in Population Censuses," *Population Studies,* **9** (3) (March 1956), 271–275.

Zelnik, Melvin. "Age Reporting Based on 'Date of Birth,'" *Population Index,* **23** (4) (October 1957), 305.

Zelnik, Melvin. "Errors in the 1960 Census Enumeration of Native Whites," *Journal of the American Statistical Association,* **59** (306) (June 1964), 437–459.

Zobel, Don C., and Gustavo R. Avila. "Estudio de Enumeración Post-censal del Censo de Población y Viviende de Honduras, 1961" (Study of the Postcensal Enumeration of the 1961 Census of Population and Housing of Honduras), in *Dirección General de Estadística y Censos.* Honduras, May 1962.

CHAPTER 5

Basic Demographic Methodology

5.1. Introduction to Demographic Methods

It is important that discussions of methods in population research not overemphasize the uniqueness of demographic techniques. Demography may be regarded as one of the fields of applied statistics, and many of the research techniques used by demographers are merely well-known and well-established procedures of statistical methodology and applied mathematics. On the other hand, it would be incorrect to say that familiarity with general statistics and mathematics is sufficient preparation for doing demographic research. The nature of the problems studied, the nature of the data to be handled, and the uses to which the findings are put all help to determine which procedures a researcher will use in a particular research study. Because these factors tend to be common over a broad range of topics, every science gradually accumulates a body of methodological lore that becomes a part of its "organized body of knowledge." Particular procedures, principles, and styles of reasoning may be greatly emphasized in one branch of research while receiving only incidental attention in conventional courses in statistics. *Moreover, it is necessary for each discipline to define its basic concepts in terms that make quantitative analysis possible.* The numerous variables must be defined in terms of the computations or operations that must be performed on the results of censuses, registrations, or special surveys to derive measures that correspond as closely as possible to the theoretical meaning of the concepts or variables with which they are equated. This applies to the *dependent variables* (population events whose explanation is being sought) and the *independent variables* (factors that are thought to be explanatory). Such data-linked definitions comprise a major part of the methodology of each discipline, and demography has an especially large body of such methodology.

As stated in the Preface, the present volume has a companion book, *A Manual of Demographic Research Techniques.* Whereas the present volume emphasizes research findings, principles, and implications, the *Manual* undertakes to make a detailed exposition of methodology. Therefore, this chapter is intended to be only a brief overview to prepare the student to read the remaining chapters of this book and other simple demographic literature without having to do extensive collateral reading in the *Manual.* Some later chapters contain additional methodological materials, also presented in simplified form, to prepare the student to understand the topics under discussion. Neither this chapter nor the methodological sections in later chapters should be used as a guide in computing demographic measures without further study, since almost all of the finer points, qualifications, and adjustments have been omitted and technical detail has been suppressed in favor of informational content.

5.2. The Analysis of Population Composition

Most of the composition characteristics, or "population traits," with which demographers deal may be expressed as a set of categories. The basic method of analysis consists of four steps.

1. *Description of Composition.* In this step the population distribution according to the categories is shown. An example is a tabulation of the entire population of marriageable age according to a trait such as marital status to

Table 5-1   Marital Status of the Female Population of
the United States, 14 Years and Over, 1960

Marital Status	Number persons 14+ years old (thousands)	Percent distribution
Total.....................	64,914	100.0
Single....................	12,380	19.1
Married (not separated)....	41,443	63.8
Married (separated)........	1,306	2.0
Widowed...................	7,945	12.2
Divorced..................	1,839	2.8

Source: U. S. Census of Population: 1960.

show how many people are single, married, widowed, or divorced. Table 5-1 illustrates this step.

2. Comparison of Composition of Different Populations. In this step the distribution of two or more populations, or subdivisions of a given population, according to the categories is examined. A comparison of the marital status composition for several different nations, for the urban and rural parts of the same nation, or even for the various sections of a city or metropolitan area would be an example. In each case, the composition of the population occupying one particular segment of territory is compared with the composition of the population occupying another segment.

The differences noted by this procedure are commonly known as *spatial differentials* in composition. Table 5-2 illustrates a statistical table from which an analysis of this type can be made. The data in the top panel of the table are difficult to interpret because they are the original census numbers; since the totals of the various rows and columns are all different, it is not easy to compare them. By computing a percent distribution for each column of the table, the raw census numbers are reduced to a form in which they can be compared. This is accomplished by dividing each figure in a column by its column total, which has been done to obtain the lower panel of Table 5-2. We note that the percentage of

Table 5-2   Marital Status of the Female Population in Urban and
Rural Areas of the United States: 1960 (Thousands of Persons)

Marital Status	Total females 14 years old and over	Urban-Rural residence		
		Urban	Rural nonfarm	Rural farm
Total.....................	64,961	46,846	13,613	4,502
Single....................	12,320	9,072	2,347	901
Married (not separated).....	41,587	29,110	9,307	3,170
Married (separated)........	1,318	1,096	188	33
Widowed...................	7,881	5,988	1,529	364
Divorced..................	1,855	1,579	242	34
	Percent Distribution			
Total.....................	100.0	100.0	100.0	100.0
Single....................	19.0	19.4	17.2	20.0
Married (not separated).....	64.0	62.1	68.4	70.4
Married (separated)........	2.0	2.3	1.4	0.7
Widowed...................	12.1	12.8	11.2	8.1
Divorced..................	2.9	3.4	1.8	0.8

Source: U. S. Census of Population: 1960, Detailed Characteristics.
United States Summary, Table 176.
The totals differ slightly from those of Table 5-1 because the present
table is based on a 25 percent sample of the population whereas Table 5-1
is based on a complete count.

Table 5-3   Marital Status of the Female Population of the United States at Selected Ages: 1960 (Thousands of Persons)

Marital Status	Total females 14 yrs. and over	Age				
		14 years	18 years	30-34 years	45-49 years	85 yrs. + over
Total.....................	64,961	1,345	1,249	6,111	5,554	531
Single....................	12,320	1,330	945	423	363	51
Married (not separated)....	41,587	13	286	5,249	4,441	42
Separated.................	1,318	1	11	174	139	2
Widowed...................	7,881	+	1	74	373	432
Divorced..................	1,855	+	6	191	238	4
			Percent distribution			
Total.....................	100.0	100.0	100.0	100.0	100.0	100.0
Single....................	19.0	98.9	75.6	6.9	6.5	9.6
Married (not separated)....	64.0	1.0	22.9	85.9	80.0	7.9
Separated.................	2.0	0.1	0.9	2.9	2.5	0.3
Widowed...................	12.1	...	0.1	1.2	6.7	81.4
Divorced..................	2.9	...	0.5	3.1	4.3	0.8

Source: U. S. Census of Population: 1960. Detailed Characteristics, United States Summary, Table 176.

people who are married decreases progressively in Table 5-2 from rural-farm through the rural-nonfarm to the urban category. But we must keep in mind that we are noting *relative* and *proportionate* size. The number of married people living in cities is much greater than of those living in rural areas simply because nearly three quarters of the population is urban.

3. *Comparison of Composition of Categories of Population.* In the first two steps, the composition of whole population clusters is studied. Further refinement calls for a comparison of types of population. In other words, the population is classified according to a second characteristic such as age, educational attainment, or income, and the compositions *within* each of the various categories of this classification are compared. An example would be a comparison of the marital status composition of each of several age groups in a population. For such an analysis, the population is "cross-classified" simultaneously according to the two traits of marital status and age, as in Table 5-3. Here the comparison is between categories of population wherein people who share a particular trait (e.g., are of the same age) are placed in the same category. The basic question is whether or not there is any difference in marital status composition between the various age groups of people. This type of analysis usually is called the study of "Age Differences in .... Composition," with the

characteristic according to which composition is compared being inserted in the blank; for instance, "Age Differentials in Marital Status Composition."

This process may be readily extended to simultaneous cross-classification for several categories. For example, a table similar to Table 5-3 could be prepared for males, and we could then compare the marital status compositions of the male and female populations at each age.

4. *Explanation and Interpretation of Compositional Differences.* After the compositional differences between different types of spatially delimited populations or between different categories of population classified according to presence or absence of some trait are noted and measured, the final task is to explain how these differences have arisen and to assess their implication for other population events. This requires that the researcher introduce other additional information (perhaps the findings of other research investigations) to explain how or why differential composition of a given type exists and persists. For example, the differences in Table 5-2 may be explained partly in terms of differences in the marriage habits of urban and rural populations and partly in terms of selective migration. In rural areas there may be a much greater social pressure upon females to marry, and the proportion of divorced persons may be less because the

Table 5-4 Percentage Point Differences and Index of Relative Composition between "Total" and Each "Urban-Rural Residence" Category, Female Population of the United States: 1960

Marital Status	Urban	Rural non-farm	Rural farm
Percentage point differences			
Total......................	0.0	0.0	0.0
Single......................	+0.4	-1.8	+1.0
Married (not separated)......	-1.9	+4.4	+6.4
Separated...................	+0.3	-0.6	-1.3
Widowed.....................	+0.7	-0.9	-4.0
Divorced....................	+0.5	-1.1	-2.1
Index of dissimilarity.......	1.9	4.4	7.4
Index of relative composition			
Single......................	+2.11	-9.47	+5.26
Married (not separated)......	-2.97	+6.88	+10.00
Separated...................	+15.00	-30.00	-65.00
Widowed.....................	+5.79	-7.44	-33.06
Divorced....................	-17.24	-37.93	-72.41

rural family is more stable than the urban family. But it is also plausible that single, widowed, or divorced females migrate from rural to urban areas where they are better able to obtain employment and to work out a set of interpersonal relations that is much more satisfying than rural society could provide.[1] Selective migration of this type would reduce the percentage of single, widowed, and divorced women in rural areas and increase the proportions in these categories in urban areas. Thus the explanation of the observed compositional differences may involve further, more detailed compositional analysis, such as studying the marital status composition of urban women cross-classified by age and migration status.

5.3. Percentage Point Differences

Sometimes the mental gymnastics of comparing every percent distribution in a table with every other percent distribution becomes so involved that it is impossible to keep all of the comparisons in mind. This difficulty can be reduced greatly by computing a set of percent-

age point differences. When we compare two percent distributions, we are mentally subtracting one set of figures from the other and noting how much larger or smaller one is than the other. By selecting one percent distribution as a standard of comparison (say the total column) and successively subtracting it from all of the other columns, recording only the differences, we obtain a set of percentage point differences. Table 5-4 illustrates the results of this process, using the data of Table 5-2. (Note that the sum of the percentage point differences in any column is zero.) Each difference shows whether the category has a relative surplus or deficit of population of that status in comparison with the distribution used for making the comparison. The upper panel of this table shows very clearly which populations have a comparative deficit of single, married, widowed, or divorced persons. There are numerous qualifications and fine points to this procedure, which are spelled out in full in Chapter 1 of the *Manual*.

Index of Dissimilarity. Often it is desired to know how different the composition of one population is in comparison with that of another, without specifying in what way the compositions differ. This measure may be expressed easily by the "index of dissimilarity," which is simply the sum of the percentage point differences of like sign (taking either the positive or the negative differences, since they are equal in size). This measure is reported in the center row of Table 5-4.

Some useful extensions of these measures to summarizing differences in entire cross-classifications or to populations simultaneously cross-classified by several variables are discussed in Chapter 1 of the *Manual*.

Index of Relative Composition. The critical student who has carefully followed the process by which Table 5-4 is derived from Table 5-2 will have been left unsatisfied on one important point. He will have noted that some of the differences that look rather small in percentage point size are actually quite large when we consider that they are derived from very small percentages. For example, take the category of "divorced" females. In the total population 2.9 percent of the females are di-

---

[1] The figure of 20 percent single persons among the farm females in Table 5-2 appears to contradict this statement. This is caused by a disproportionate concentration of females in the ages 14 through 17 because of higher fertility in farm areas.

vorced, whereas in the rural-farm population only 0.8 percent of the females are divorced. The difference of −2.1 percentage points is quite small in comparison with some other differences shown in the table. But we see that it is very large when we consider the small proportion of the total population on which it is based upon to begin with. In fact, we begin to suspect that it is one of the most outstanding and significant differences in the table. This leads us to generalize that *the size of the percentage point differences is related to the size of the percentages from which they are derived, and the meaningfulness of the differences is proportional to the size of the base percent that was subtracted in obtaining the differences.* We can see that if we end the analysis with a table of percentage point differences, merely searching for the largest differences and neglecting the smaller ones, we could easily miss some of the most meaningful findings. By dividing each percentage point difference by the base percent that was used in establishing it, "and multiplying by 100," we can develop a whole new set of indices that measure *relative differences in composition.* This set of measures is illustrated in the bottom part of Table 5-4. The meaning of this measure is as follows: The index of relative difference in composition shows the percentage by which the share of a subpopulation that falls in a given category exceeds or falls short of the share of the base (comparison) popula-

easy to understand and one that demographers use often.

A comparison of the upper and lower panels of Table 5-4 will show that although the *signs* of the differences are the same, the magnitudes are quite different. One will arrive at the same general conclusions using either measurement, but the index of relative difference in composition reveals a different and important aspect, namely, the relative importance of the difference with respect to the specific subcategories of population being compared. For a full interpretation of composition, *both* types of measurement are important. In using the second type of measure, care must be taken not to be too impressed by very large differences based on very small percentages. Inaccuracies and biases in the data can often create large indices of relative difference in composition, based on small percents, which may look impressive but represent no major demographic or social changes. For example, suppose that we compare the marital status of 15-year-old girls in two successive censuses, as shown below. The impressiveness of the 300 percent increase in the proportion of 15-year-old girls who are married is obviously negated by the information in the first column that 99.6 percent of the 15-year-old girls are still single, so that much, if not all, of the increase could be due to processing errors, differences in enumeration procedures, and other factors not related to marriage trends at all.

Marital status	1960	1950	Percentage point difference	Index of relative composition
Total	100.0	100.0	. . .	. . .
Single	99.6	99.9	−0.3	−0.3
Married	0.4	0.1	+0.3	300.0

tion that falls in the same category. For an example on divorces, we can say that "the population of divorced women in the rural-farm population is 72 percent less than in the national population generally" and that "the population of widowed women in urban areas is 6 percent greater than among the national population generally." Although the language is a little cumbersome, the idea is one that is

To summarize: A full analysis of differential composition requires a study of percentage point differences and their size relative to the percentages from which they are derived. The index of relative composition shows how extreme a difference this is when allowance is made for the share of population involved.

It is not necessary for an experienced statistician to go through all of these steps formally, and certainly measures of differences are seldom published. Usually only the percent distributions and perhaps indices of dissimilarity are reported and analyzed. Table 5-4 may be regarded as a record of the mental comparisons the analyst could (and should) make in making a complete digest. It could also be the work sheet he actually computes and uses, just to make sure that he does not miss anything and is correct in his interpretation, even though it is not published.

5.4. The Analysis of Population Dynamics

A compositional analysis is a static comparative study of composition at a given point of time. A different set of methods is required on the measurement of population dynamics, or the occurrence of population events over time. Whereas compositional analysis asks the question, "How *prevalent* is this trait?" dynamic analysis asks "What is the *incidence* (rate of fresh occurrence) of this event?" Particular interest focuses on four classes of events: birth, death, marriage, and migration. For each of these events the ideal basic measure is the same:

concept of "life years" or "person years." One life year is equal to 12 months of life, and the total life years for a population are comprised of the sum of all the whole years and fractions of years lived by the population. If the vital events are uniformly distributed throughout the year, the midyear population is equal to the number of life years lived during the year. (For proof, see the *Manual.*) Hence most birth, death, marriage, and divorce rates are expressed as ratios of the event to the midyear population and are therefore called "central rates." Usually this rate is multiplied by 1000, so that the rate is "x per thousand." Crude birth and death rates expressed in this way have already been introduced in Chapters 2 and 3.

Specific rates. Very often a single rate for an entire population, such as a crude death rate, is not adequate for demographic analysis. There is need to compute rates for particular *subgroupings* of the population. For example, a death rate can be computed separately for males and females, for each of several age groups, or for each of various racial or ethnic groups. These are called *specific* rates. Thus

$$\text{rate of incidence} = \frac{\text{number of events that occur during a time interval}}{\text{population exposed to risk of the event during that interval}}$$

Thus the death rate is the number of deaths that occur during a time interval divided by the number of people who were exposed to the possibility of dying during that period. The numerator of this rate can be obtained from registration statistics of birth and death, and the denominator must be provided from another source such as population census or an estimate.

Since most populations change in size during the period of a year, it is not obvious what the correct count of "exposed" population is. Some members are exposed for only a small fraction of the year because they were born or moved in sometime during the year, or died or moved out sometime during the year. Demographers get around this by creating the

a set of age-specific death rates would consist of a death rate for each age group in the population. The process of computing would be as follows:

age-specific death rate

$$= \frac{\text{deaths to persons of age } x}{\text{midyear population of age } x} \times 1000$$

The corresponding measure for fertility is

age-specific fertility rate

$$= \frac{\text{births to women of age } x}{\text{midyear female population of age } x} \times 1000$$

Table 5-5 Illustrative Computation of Age-Specific Birthrates for El Salvador, 1961, and Spain, 1960

Age	El Salvador			Spain		
	Births to women of age	Females of age	Age specific fertility rate	Births to women of age	Females of age	Age specific fertility rate
Total 15-49 years.....	123,080	584,570	210.5	646,497	7,821,352	82.7
15 - 19 years.........	17,601	123,080	143.0	11,210	1,229,677	9.1
20 - 24 years.........	36,339	112,390	323.3	115,423	1,102,866	104.7
25 - 29 years.........	29,685	93,760	316.6	232,040	1,252,616	185.2
30 - 34 years.........	20,983	79,230	264.8	166,023	1,183,897	140.2
35 - 39 years.........	13,603	72,000	188.9	91,219	1,158,575	78.7
40 - 44 years.........	4,106	58,770	69.9	27,734	964,636	28.8
45 - 49 years.........	763	45,340	16.8	2,848	929,085	3.1

Source: United Nations Demographic Yearbook. 1961, 1962.

Rates may be made specific for two or more traits simultaneously. Thus a set of age-sex-race-specific mortality rates would be the rate of death to persons of each combination (age, sex, and race) divided by the midyear population of each corresponding combination of age, sex, and race multiplied by 1000. Instead of being computed for each single year of age, the rates are often computed for 5-year groupings of age. Table 5-5 illustrates the computation of age-specific fertility rates for Spain and El Salvador.

A similar procedure is used to calculate specific rates for marriage, divorce, and migration. The particular measures used for each are discussed in later chapters where each of these topics is taken up in detail. The intent here is to present the methodological and conceptual principles common to all.

A set of specific rates, one for each of several categories that together represent a population characteristic, is called a *schedule* of rates. Thus columns 3 and 6 of Table 5-5 are schedules of age-specific fertility rates. It should be noted that the total or overall rate of a schedule of specific rates is a weighted average of the specific rates, the weight for each specific rate being determined by the relative size in the population composition of the group to which it refers. Thus the overall death rate, which is the crude rate of deaths to persons

of all ages divided by the midyear population of all ages, is a weighted average of the age-specific death rates. The number of births to women of all ages divided by the total midyear female population of childbearing age is a weighted average of the age-specific birth rates, the weight being determined by the number of women in each of the childbearing ages. This measure is called the general fertility rate:

$$\text{general fertility rate} = \frac{\text{births to women 15-49 (all childbearing ages)}}{\text{midyear female population aged 15-49}} \times 1000$$

Comparison of Rates. Rates are used in research in the same sequence of steps specified above for the statistics of compositions:

1. Description.
2. Measurement of differences between spatially distinct populations.
3. Measurement of differences between categories of people.
4. Explanation and interpretation of observed differences.

The procedure is somewhat similar to that described for the study of composition. Here, however, we speak of *rate differences* rather than *percentage point differences*. Let us, for example, compare the age-specific fertility rates of males and females. Table 5-6 shows the procedure. We may accept the fertility of Spain as the basis of comparison (we could also use the age-specific fertility rates of the world or of El Salvador as a base of compari-

Table 5-6 Illustrative Computation of Differences and
Relative Differences between Schedules of Fertility Rates:
El Salvador, 1961, and Spain, 1960

Age	Age-specific birth rates		Differences	Relative difference
	Spain	El Salvador		
	(1)	(2)	(3)	(4)
Total 15-49 years...	82.7	210.5	127.8	155
15 - 19 years.......	9.1	143.0	133.9	1471
20 - 24 years.......	104.7	323.3	218.6	209
25 - 29 years.......	185.2	316.6	131.4	71
30 - 34 years.......	140.2	264.8	124.6	89
35 - 39 years.......	78.7	188.9	110.2	140
40 - 44 years.......	28.8	69.9	41.1	143
45 - 49 years.......	3.1	16.8	13.7	442

Source: Derived from Table 5-5.
Column (3) equals column (2) minus column (1)
Column (4) equals column (3) divided by column (1) times 100

son) and show the rate differences for each age group. It is clear that at every age the fertility rate for El Salvador exceeds that of Spain.

Here also we very quickly discover that the size of the rate difference is influenced by the size of the rates on which it is based and that some rather small rate differences seem quite large in comparison with the rates on which they are based. The difference between El Salvador and Spain is relatively smaller at the ages of peak fertility than at the higher ages when the birthrates of both are quite low. A relative measure can be made, as Table 5-6 illustrates, by dividing each of the rate differences by the base rate that was subtracted in obtaining the difference and multiplying by 100. This shows us by what percentage each rate for El Salvador is greater in comparison with the rate for Spain. For example, the rate for El Salvador at the age 45-49 is 442 percent greater than the corresponding rate for Spain. Although the rate difference is small in absolute size, the *relative* difference is much greater than at intermediate ages where the rate differences are much greater in absolute size but are referred to a higher rate.

There is another dimension of comparison that should not be overlooked. This is the comparison between the rate for the population as a whole and the rate for each of the specific subpopulations. For example, it could be meaningful to compare the death rate of each specific age group with the average death rate for the total population and to compute the rate difference and the relative difference for each age group. The interpretation is as follows: The total rate is a mean of the *specific* rates in the population. The comparison shows how much greater and smaller the risk is, in comparison with the average, for particular subgroups of the population. By subtracting the average rate from each specific rate in the schedule of rates, we can show how the *pattern of rates* varies among the specific categories. Columns 3 and 4 of Table 5-7 illustrate this procedure. Often we wish to compare the pattern of differences for several populations, eliminating the effect of the differences in the level of the rates and noting only the relative similarities and differences in the pattern; this may be facilitated by dividing the differences by the average rate used to establish them. This is illustrated in columns 5 and 6 of Table 5-7. The student who grasps thoroughly the operations illustrated in Tables 5-5, 5-6, and 5-7 will have no difficulty in interpreting demographic rates.

5.5. Standardization

Specific rates are often cumbersome to interpret because they are so numerous. Instead of one number there are several: one for each age, sex, or other group. Very often there is need for a single overall rate that applies to a whole population. Although crude rates are

Table 5-7 Illustrative Computations of Differences Between an
Average Rate and a Schedule of Rates: Age-Specific Birthrates of
El Salvador and Spain

Age	Age specific rates		Difference between average rates and specific rates		Ratio of difference to average rate	
	Spain	El Salvador	Spain	El Salvador	Spain	El Salvador
Total.......	82.7	210.5	0.0	0.0		
15-19 years......	9.1	143.0	-73.6	-67.5	-0.89	-0.32
20-24 years......	104.7	323.3	+22.0	112.8	+0.27	+0.54
25-29 years......	185.2	316.6	+102.5	106.1	+1.24	+0.50
30-34 years......	140.2	264.8	+57.5	54.3	+0.70	+0.26
35-39 years......	78.7	188.9	-4.0	-21.6	-0.05	-0.10
40-45 years......	28.8	69.9	-53.9	-140.6	-0.65	-0.67
45-49 years......	3.1	16.8	-79.6	-193.7	-0.96	-0.92

Source: Derived from Table 5-5

often used for this purpose, they are not fully adequate. The major weakness of using crude rates of birth, death, and marriage for comparisons between populations lies in the fact that *hidden differences in population composition may account (in whole or in part) for the differences that are observed.* For example, if we try to compare the death rate in a new suburban community inhabited largely by young couples and their young children with the death rate for an old industrial suburb established a half century ago and containing a large share of elderly people, we become uncomfortably aware that there are *two* possible explanations: (*a*) the compositional force of mortality in terms of conditions of health, sanitation, medical care, and other factors and (*b*) the comparative age composition of the two populations. Now, in the study of population dynamics we are usually interested in studying the pure force of mortality, level of fertility, proclivity toward marriage, or rate of migration. Extraneous factors that affect the measures of these movements, such as age or sex composition, are simply research nuisances that should somehow be controlled or held constant. The problem could be resolved by comparing the schedules of age or other specific rates for the two populations, as described in the preceding section. But there is need for a single statistic that measures the force of mortality or fertility while holding compositional factors constant. In other words, the demographer wants to write a single figure that

will allow him to claim that "Holding constant the factors of age and sex, the death rate in area A is *x* percent lower than in area B." This then leaves him free to explore what factors *other* than age and sex could be at work to cause these differences.

One of the most widely used procedures for accomplishing this is "standardization" of rates. In its simplest and most straightforward form it consists in establishing a standard population composition and then applying a set of specific rates to it in order to note what the general rate *would be* if a particular population had the same composition as the standard. Table 5-8 illustrates the procedure for standardization of the fertility rate for El Salvador. The estimated age composition of the world is used as a standard. The steps are spelled out at the foot of the table. The standard population is simply a total of 1 million females distributed according to the estimated age composition of the world as of 1960. The age-specific birthrates of El Salvador in 1961 are multiplied by these numbers in order to estimate how many births would occur in a population of this composition if the force of fertility expressed by the age-specific rates were to be in effect for one year. The total of births divided by the total of the standard population yields an overall rate of fertility. If the rates for several populations were standardized in this way, they would be directly comparable. One of the best ways to use standardized rates is to express them as a ratio

Table 5-8   Illustrative Example of Direct
Standardization: Age Specific Fertility Rates of
El Salvador, 1961

Age	Standard composition (world)	Age specific rate for El Salvador	Expected births
	(1)	(2)	(3)
15–19 years.......	195,827	143.0	28,003
20–24 years......	174,739	323.3	56,493
25–29 years......	153,801	316.6	48,693
30–34 years......	139,763	264.8	37,009
35–39 years......	125,761	188.9	23,756
40–44 years......	111,878	69.9	7,820
45–49 years.......	98,231	16.8	1,650
Total.........	1,000,000	210.5	203,424

Standardized rate = Sum of Column (3) ÷ Sum of
Column (1) X 1000 = 203,424/1,000,000 = 203.4

of the corresponding rate for the standard population itself. Thus the age-standardized birthrate of the El Salvador population is 1.31 times as large as the estimated birthrate of the world as of 1960 (203.4/155.7 = 1.31).

This procedure is known as *direct standardization.* It requires a schedule of age-specific rates for the population for which a standardized measure is desired. Often such a schedule is not available. For example, age-specific rates usually are not available for small areas such as individual cities. An alternative procedure, *indirect standardization,* which tends to approximate the results of direct standardization, is often employed in these circumstances. The computational sequence is shown at the foot of Table 5-9, which uses the age-specific fertility rates to obtain an indirectly standardized general fertility rate for El Salvador. By this procedure a set of rates is accepted as standard and weighted by the composition of the population for which a standard rate is desired. A cross-multiplication yields an expected number of events (births). The sum of these expected births divided by the female population 15 to 49 is the expected general fertility rate if the population were to have its own composition and the specific rates of the standard. The actual general fertility rate for the population is then expressed as a ratio of the expected general fertility rate, and this is multiplied by the general fertility rate of the standard population.

The logic of this procedure is as follows:

if the expected general fertility rate is different from the actual general fertility rate, the ratio is above or below 1, and since the *same composition* was used in calculating the actual and expected rates, the difference is presumed to be due to a difference in fertility level. Therefore, this rate tends to show how much greater or smaller than the standard population the fertility level in the population tends to be.

Because composition is not strictly held constant by indirect standardization (the weights change from population to population), it is less valid than direct standardization as a technique for controlling composition. In the range of most demographic applications the two procedures yield sufficiently close results to permit their use almost interchangeably. Chapter 8 of the *Manual* contains a rather full discussion of standardization. Students interested in pursuing this topic further are encouraged to consult it.

5.6.   The Measurement of Change as a Continuous Process

Some more abstract and mathematical applications of demographic analysis call for the calculation of the rate of growth in terms that recognize that growth is a continuous process. The average annual rate, described in Section 2.4, assumes that a particular rate is in effect for one full year and that the population growth accumulated during the year is added to the population at the year's end. It is similar to a bank's compounding interest once

Table 5-9   Illustrative Example of Indirect Standardization: Age-Specific Fertility Rates, El Salvador, 1961

Age	Composition of El Salvador	Standard age-specific rates for the world	Expected births
	(1)	(2)	(3)
15-19 years......	123,080	78.5	9,662
20-24 years......	112,390	246.0	27,648
25-29 years......	93,760	283.3	26,562
30-34 years......	79,230	212.3	16,805
35-39 years......	72,000	132.1	9,511
40-44 years......	58,770	56.1	3,344
45-49 years......	45,340	10.9	494
Total......	584,570	155.7	94,026

Indirectly standardized rate $= \dfrac{A}{E} \times S$, where:

E = Expected Rate
    = Sum of column (3) ÷ Sum of column (1)
A = Actual General Fertility Rate of each population
    (El Salvador)
S = General Fertility Rate of Standard population
    (world)

Expected Rate = 94,026/584,570 = 160.8
Actual Rate = 210.5
Standardized Rate $= \dfrac{A}{E} \times S = \dfrac{210.5}{160.8} \times 155.7$
               $= 1.31 \times 155.7 = 204.0$

each year and adding it to the principal. An alternative formula, which compounds continuously, is as follows:

$$\frac{P_1}{P_0} = e^{rn}$$

where e is the base of the natural (or Naperian) system of logarithms, r is the continuous rate of growth, and n is the interval of time over which the rate is computed.

Instead of using natural logarithms in the computation, it is easier to use tables of exponential functions, e^x, which are easily available.[2] To illustrate the procedure we use the same example for Argentina as was used in Chapter 2.

$$\frac{P_1}{P_0} = \frac{20,008,945}{15,893,827} = 1.258913$$

We now look up the value 1.258913 in the e^x column of the table of exponential functions

[2] For example *Standard Mathematical Tables*, published by the Chemical Rubber Publishing Company, Cleveland, Ohio.

to obtain the corresponding value in the x column. (For precision we interpolate between values.) The result, 0.232476, is equal to rn, or the rate of growth times the interval of time. We solve for r by dividing by n (13.4 years in this case):

$$r = \frac{0.232476}{13.4} = 1.7 \text{ percent per year}$$

If the calculations are carried out to several decimals it will be noted that the continuous rate of growth, computed by this method, is slightly smaller than the average annual rate of growth computed by the compound interest formula.

This measure is used in mathematical models of demographic processes because it is an abstract expression that lends itself well to mathematical analysis and evaluation, whereas the compound interest formula is an empirical expression that is too cumbersome and clumsy for easy mathematical manipulation. For empirical work the two equations may be regarded as equivalent, because they give almost identical results except for very rapid rates of growth over long periods of time.

5.7. Other Items of Demographic Methodology

Demographers make extensive use of several other methodological techniques. Among them are procedures for interpolating values along a curve; for smoothing data to estimate the underlying distributions; for preparing life tables, nuptiality tables, and population projections; for estimating the current population of small places between census dates, using symptomatic indicators of population change; for estimating net migration; and for estimating birth and death rates from census data where vital registration is inadequate. In addition there are numerous procedures for evaluating the extent of error and bias in census and vital registration data. These involve more complex considerations and are described in the *Manual* and the other references cited at the end of this chapter.

QUESTIONS FOR DISCUSSION AND EXERCISES

1. Discuss the uses each of the following demographic techniques might have in *(a)* economic research, *(b)* sociological research, *(c)* social psychological research, and *(d)* research in political science.

    Age-specific rates

    Standardization

    Index of differential composition

2. From the latest census of your own country develop a statistical table for males and females corresponding to the data in Table 5-2. Compute appropriate percent distributions and indexes of differential composition. Write a brief essay on sex differentials in marital status, by urban and rural residence. Try to formulate hypotheses that explain how these differences arise. If data are available, repeat for an earlier period and note the changes that have taken place.

3. Using the data of Table 5-2, compute a set of percent distributions horizontally. What is the question you can answer with the data arranged in this way? What would you say to the joke that "Demographers interested in population distribution merely run their percentages the wrong way"?

4. From current vital statistics reports for your country compute the schedule of age-specific death rates separately for males and females. Then compute an index of relative difference for each age group. Write a short essay comparing the mortality differences between males and females, developing hypotheses to explain the result. If data are available, repeat for an earlier decade and note the changes that have taken place.

5. Think about the problem of *multiple* characteristics. How would you go about holding constant two or three factors while studying the effect of a particular factor? For hints, see the *Manual*.

BIBLIOGRAPHY

Barclay, George W. *Techniques of Population Analysis.* New York: John Wiley and Sons, London: Chapman and Hall, 1958.

Benjamin, Bernard. *Elements of Vital Statistics.* London: Allen and Unwin, 1959.

Bogue, Donald J., and Beverly Duncan. *A Composite Method for Estimating Postcensal Population of Small Areas by Age, Sex, and Color,* in U. S. National Office of Vital Statistics. Vital Statistics, Special Reports Vol. 47. Selected Studies, Washington, D.C., 1957.

Bogue, Donald J., and Evelyn M. Kitagawa. *Manual of Demographic Research Techniques* (in preparation.)

Buechley, Robert W. "A Reproducible Method of Counting Persons of Spanish Surname," *Journal of the American Statistical Association,* **56** (293) (March 1961), 88–97.

Cox, Peter R. *Demography.* Cambridge, England: University Press, 1959.

Duncan, Otis Dudley, et al. *Statistical Geography: Problems in Analyzing Areal Data.* Glencoe, Ill.: Free Press, 1961.

El-Badry, M. A. "Some Demographic Measurements for Egypt Based on the Stability of the Census Age Distribution," *Milbank Memorial Fund Quarterly,* 33 (3) (July 1955), 268–305.

Hajnal, J. "Mathematical Models in Demography," in *Cold Spring Harbor Symposia on Quantitative Biology,* Vol. XXII (1957), 97–103.

Henry, Louis. "D'un Problème Fondamental de l'Analyse Démographique" (A Basic Problem in Population Analysis), *Population* (Paris), **14** (1) (January-March 1959), 9–32.

Hofsten, Erland V. "Population Registers and Computers: New Possibilities for the Production of Demographic Data," *Review of the International Statistical Institute* (The Hague), **34** (2) (1966), 186–194.

Hyrenius, Hannes. *Demographic Simulation Models With the Aid of Electronic Computers*. Paper contributed for the United Nations World Population Conference, August 30-September 10, 1965.

Jaffe, A. J. *Handbook of Statistical Methods for Demographers*. Washington, D.C., U. S. Bureau of the Census, 1951.

Keyfitz, Nathan. *Introduction to Mathematical Demography*. Reading, Mass.: Addison-Wesley (1968).

Keyfitz, Nathan. "Matrix Multiplication as a Technique of Population Analysis," *Milbank Memorial Fund Quarterly* **42** (4, Pt. 1) (October 1964), 68–84.

Kitagawa, Evelyn M. "Standardized Comparisons in Population Research," *Demography,* **1** (1) (1964), 296–315.

Ledermann, Sully. *Les Modeles en Démographie*. Paper contributed for the United Nations World Population Conference, August 30-September 10, 1965.

Milbank Memorial Fund. *Emerging Techniques in Population Research*. Proceedings of a Round Table at the 39th Annual Conference of the Milbank Memorial Fund, September 18-19, 1962, at the Carnegie Endowment International Center, New York, 1963.

Pressat, Roland. *L'Analyse Démographique: Méthodes, Résultats, Applications (Demographic Analysis: Methods, Findings, Applications)*. Paris: Presses Universitaires de France, for the Institut National d'Études Démographiques, 1961.

Smith, T. M. F. "Ratios of Ratios and Their Applications," *Journal of the Royal Statistical Society,* Series A, **129** (1966), 531–533.

Spiegelman, Mortimer. *Introduction to Demography*. Chicago: The Society of Actuaries, 1955.

Tarver, James D. *A Component Method of Estimating and Projecting State and Subdivisional Populations*. Norman, Okla.: Oklahoma State University, Agricultural Experiment Station, Miscellaneous Publication MP-54, December 1959.

United Nations. *Handbook of Population Census Methods. Studies in Methods, Series F, No. 5*. New York, 1954.

United Nations Department of Economic and Social Affairs. *The Future Growth of World Population*. Population Studies, No. 28, Series A. New York, 1958.

United Nations Population Branch. *Manuals on Methods of Estimating Population, Manual II*. Population Studies, No. 23, Series A, October 1955. New York, 1956.

United Nations Population Branch. *Manuals on Methods of Estimating Population, Manual III*. Population Studies, No. 25, Series A, August 1956. New York, 1956.

United Nations Population Branch. *Manuals on Methods of Estimating Population, Manual IV*. Population Studies, No. 42, Series A. New York, 1967.

Wolfenden, Hugh H. "On the Theoretical and Practical Considerations Underlying the Direct and Indirect Standardization of Death Rates," *Population Studies,* **16** (2) (November 1962), 188–190.

Wolfenden, Hugh H. *Population Statistics and Their Compilation*. Chicago: University of Chicago Press, 1954.

Zitter, Meyer, and Henry S. Shryock, Jr. "Accuracy of Methods of Preparing Postcensal Estimates for States and Local Areas," *Demography,* **1** (1) (1964), 227–241.

CHAPTER 6

Population Growth in the United States

6.1. The United States in the Current World Demographic Situation

It is expected that most readers of this book will be residents of the United States and will be seeking detailed and specific information about demographic events in the United States. To satisfy this need, this and the succeeding chapters provide as full and detailed an account of the United States as is possible without sacrificing the principal goal of making a truly international presentation. The materials for the United States are presented *after* the general international discussion. The reader whose demographic interests are centered in a different nation can profitably substitute a reading of the account of population growth for his own country for a reading of this chapter. Fortunately, a good statement of population growth trends now is available for almost every part of the world. The most recent or best citation may be obtained by writing to the statistical or census office of the particular country. The reader may also find it profitable to study the United States materials for comparison with the materials for his own nation.

From the preceding chapters we know the following facts about population growth in the United States:

1. At the 1960 census, the population count was 179.3 million. It is estimated that in late 1967 the population passed the 200 million mark.

2. Death rates in 1960 were very low, but birthrates were still moderately high, after having experienced an upsurge during and after World War II. In 1960 the death rate was only 9.5 per thousand population, but the birthrate was 23.7 per thousand, which is more than 25 percent higher than the birthrate of

Europe (Albania was the only populous nation of Europe to have a higher rate).

3. As a consequence of this moderately high birthrate, the rate of reproductive change was quite high: 1.4 percent per year. In addition, the United States is still accepting immigrants in substantial numbers, so that the overall annual rate of growth as of 1960 was 1.7 percent per year. This is almost equal to the rates at which India, Pakistan, and other developing nations were growing at about the same time and substantially higher than those reported or estimated for the nations of Europe and for several less developed nations such as Argentina, Uruguay, Puerto Rico, Burma, and the West Indies.

4. In recent years the birthrate has shown evidence of declining, so that the growth pattern appears to be approaching more closely that of Europe.

We now supplement this general information with a more detailed review of the country's population history.

6.2. The Period before Independence

In the late fifteenth century, when Europeans first became aware of the Americas, Northern America was inhabited by a population that had established settlements from coast to coast and from above the Arctic Circle past the Rio Grande deep into Central and South America. For the next 300 years the nations of Northwestern Europe proceeded to occupy and colonize this territory. During this process the colonial population grew extremely rapidly, while the American Indian population declined as a result of attrition from being in a continuous state of warfare in defense of their traditional lands and because of unusual hardships

Table 6-1 Estimated Population of American Colonies: 1630 to 1780 (in Thousands)

Colony	1780	1770	1760	1750	1740	1730	1720	1710	1700	1690	1680	1670	1660	1650	1640	1630
Total........	2,780.4	2,148.1	1,593.6	1,170.8	905.6	629.4	466.2	331.7	250.9	210.4	151.5	111.9	75.1	50.4	26.6	4.6
Percent change....	29.4	34.8	36.1	30.0	43.9	35.0	40.5	32.2	19.3	38.9	35.4	49.1	49.0	89.1	473.3	....
Maine (counties).....	49.1	31.3	....	....	....	....	....	....	....	....	....	....	....	1.0	0.9	0.4
New Hampshire.......	87.8	62.4	39.1	27.5	23.3	10.8	9.4	5.7	5.0	4.2	2.0	1.8	1.6	1.3	1.1	0.5
Vermont...........	47.6	10.0	....	....	....	....	....	....	....	....	....	....	....	....	....	....
Plymouth & Mass....	268.6	235.3	222.6	188.0	151.6	114.1	91.0	62.4	55.9	56.9	46.2	35.3	22.0	15.6	10.0	0.9
Rhode Island........	52.9	58.2	45.5	33.2	25.3	17.0	11.7	7.6	5.9	4.2	3.0	2.2	1.5	0.8	0.3	....
Connecticut........	206.7	183.9	142.5	111.3	89.6	75.5	58.8	39.4	26.0	21.6	17.2	12.6	8.0	4.1	1.5	....
New York...........	210.5	162.9	117.1	76.7	63.7	48.6	36.9	21.6	19.1	13.9	9.8	5.8	4.9	4.1	1.9	0.4
New Jersey.........	139.6	117.4	93.8	71.4	51.4	37.5	29.8	19.9	14.0	8.0	3.4	1.0	....	....	....	....
Pennsylvania.......	327.3	240.1	183.7	119.7	85.6	51.7	31.0	24.4	18.0	11.4	0.7	....	....	....	....	....
Delaware...........	45.4	35.5	33.2	28.7	19.9	9.2	5.4	3.6	2.5	1.5	1.0	0.7	0.5	0.2	....	....
Maryland...........	245.5	202.6	162.3	141.1	116.1	91.1	66.1	42.7	29.6	24.0	17.9	13.2	8.4	4.5	0.6	....
Virginia...........	538.0	447.0	339.7	231.0	180.4	114.0	87.8	78.3	58.6	53.0	43.6	35.3	27.0	18.7	10.4	2.5
North Carolina......	270.1	197.2	110.4	73.0	51.8	30.0	21.3	15.1	10.7	7.6	5.4	3.8	1.0	....	....	....
South Carolina......	180.0	124.2	94.1	64.0	45.0	30.0	17.0	10.9	5.7	3.9	1.2	0.2	....	....	....	....
Georgia............	56.1	23.4	9.6	5.2	2.0	....	....	....	....	....	....	....	....	....	....	....
Kentucky...........	45.0	15.7	....	....	....	....	....	....	....	....	....	....	....	....	....	....
Tennessee..........	10.0	1.0	....	....	....	....	....	....	....	....	....	....	....	....	....	....

Source: U.S. Bureau of Census, Historical Statistics of the United States. Washington: Government Printing Office, 1960. Table Z 1-19, p. 756.

and disease brought about by the colonial and frontier movement. There is little doubt that before the colonial period the American Indian population had been growing moderately rapidly.

We can trace only in a sketchy way the growth of the European population from the time of the landing of the first colonists to the establishment of the Republic. No systematic records of immigration and emigration were kept, and reliable censuses were difficult to take. Several efforts at population counts were made, but most appear to have been failures—in part because the colonists stoutly resisted enumeration.[1] Using the reports of colonial officials, those census reports that seem reasonably reliable, tax lists, militia lists, and estimates of unknown basis by contemporary observers, a very rough picture of population increase during each decade 1630 to 1780 for each colony has been pieced together by historians, which is shown in Table 6-1. These data suggest that by about 1745 the territory that now comprises the United States contained about 1 million inhabitants.[2] The population was growing so rapidly that it doubled in only about 23 years—to 2 million persons. During the earliest years of settlement, immigration was necessarily the major component of growth. However, it is known that birthrates were extremely high and that reproductive change quickly began to add to the population numbers. As a result, throughout most of the colonial period after 1650 population grew very rapidly because of the combined impact of high rates of immigration and reproductive increase. Living conditions in Colonial America involved many hardships and hazards to life and health, but there was an ample supply of food and the population was rather widely dispersed over the land. Thus epidemics, when they occurred, could wipe out only small segments of the population, which helped to keep death rates moderately low. The colonies managed to grow at the average annual rate of about 3 to 3.5

percent throughout most of this time. Figure 6-1 undertakes to guess, in a very crude way, what the comparative weights of reproductive change and of immigration from Europe must have been during this period. First the average annual rates of population change, using the data of Table 6-1, were computed. Then, from estimates by Thompson and Whelpton (see below) it was surmised that the *difference* between the birth and death rates, whatever their level, was about 3 per thousand. In those decades when the average annual rate of growth exceeded 3 percent there is an implied net immigration from abroad. In those decades when the average annual rate of growth was below 3 percent, a net migration loss is implied. The periods of estimated net migration gain and migration loss, and the percent of gain or loss implied, are charted in Figure 6-1. Before 1660, the implied rates of immigration are very high and range from 6 to 20 percent per year. After about 1670, reproductive change was the major source of growth. By this time the colonial population numbered 100,000. By their natural fertility they were able to produce an estimated 3000 additional population each year. This seems to have been much more than were delivered from Europe by ship. Figure 6-1 suggests that net migration may have been almost zero for the century preceding the American Revolution, taken as a whole. If this is true, the equivalent of all population growth from 1690 to 1790 was due to reproductive increase alone. This line of reasoning leads us to conclude that *immigration played a comparatively minor part in the growth of the American population from 1680 to 1840.* If the correct rate of reproductive increase is lower than we have estimated, say around 2.5 percent per year instead of 3, a somewhat more generous allowance could be made for the role of immigration, but the general conclusion would still be the same— after a very few decades of initial settlement, the major force behind population growth in this nation has been an excess of births over deaths.

This line of reasoning has been based entirely on estimates by Thompson and Whelpton that at the end of the eighteenth century the

[1] U.S. Bureau of Census, *A Century of Population Growth in the United States: 1790–1900* (Washington, D.C.: Government Printing Office, 1909), p. 4.

[2] *Ibid.*

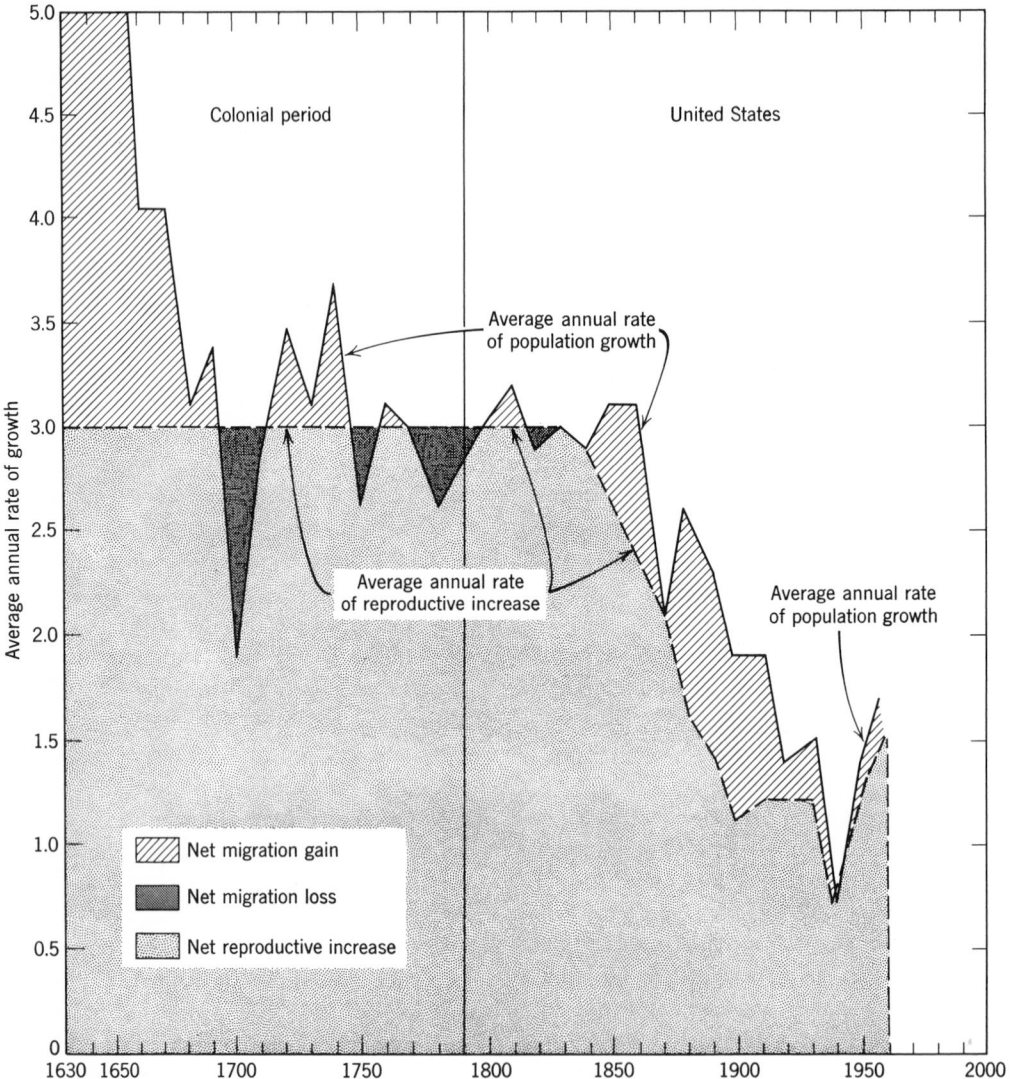

Figure 6-1 Estimated Components of the Growth Rate in Territory of the United States: 1630 to 1960.

birthrate was about 55 per thousand and the death rate about 25 per thousand, which implies an annual net reproductive gain of 30 per thousand.[3] If this performance is compared with the historical trend in Sweden (Chapter 3), which is more or less typical of European countries, it may be seen at once that Northern America in 1800 was growing much faster. In fact, the United States was exhibiting a demographic behavior that is common in the de-

[3] Warren S. Thompson and P. K. Whelpton, *Population Trends in the United States* (New York: McGraw-Hill, 1933), p. 263.

veloping nations of the world today, namely, combining very high birthrates with moderately low death rates. This growth attracted a great deal of attention among scholars in Europe. Among them was Thomas Malthus, who saw in the American growth rate the proof to his proposition that the human species tends to grow by geometric progression.

This period ends with the formation of the Union. Inasmuch as the Constitution of the United States specifies that a census should be taken and used as the basis for apportionment of Congressional representatives, one of the

Table 6-2 Population and Land Area of the United States: 1790 to 1960

Census date	United States				
	Population	Increase over preceding census[1]		Land area in square miles	Population per square mile [2]
		Number	Percent		
1960 (April 1).........	179,323,175	27,997,377	18.5	3,548,974	50.5
1950 (April 1).........	151,325,798	19,161,229	14.5	3,552,206	42.6
1940 (April 1).........	132,164,569	8,961,945	7.3	3,554,608	37.2
1930 (April 1).........	123,202,624	17,181,087	16.2	3,551,608	34.7
1920 (January 1)......	106,021,537	13,793,041	15.0	3,546,931	29.9
1910 (April 15).......	92,228,496	16,016,328	21.0	3,547,045	26.0
1900 (June 1)..........	76,212,168	13,232,402	21.0	3,547,314	21.5
1890 (June 1).........	62,979,766	12,790,557	25.5	3,540,705	17.8
1880 (June 1).........	50,189,209	[3]11,630,838	[3]30.2	3,540,705	14.2
1870 (June 1)[3]........	38,558,371	7,115,050	22.6	3,540,705	10.9
1860 (June 1)..........	31,443,321	8,251,445	35.6	2,969,640	10.6
1850 (June 1)..........	23,191,876	6,122,423	35.9	2,940,042	7.9
1840 (June 1).........	17,069,453	4,203,433	32.7	1,749,462	9.8
1830 (June 1)..........	12,866,020	3,227,567	33.5	1,749,462	7.4
1820 (August 7).......	9,638,453	2,398,572	33.1	1,749,462	5.5
1810 (August 6).......	7,239,881	1,931,398	36.4	1,681,828	4.3
1800 (August 4).......	5,308,483	1,379,269	35.1	864,746	6.1
1790 (August 2).......	3,929,214	...	....	864,746	4.5

[1] Percentage increases are computed on basis of change in population since preceding census date, and period covered therefore is not always exactly 10 years. Adjustments for differences in census dates must be made if strictly comparable figures are desired for each decade.

[2] Figures given for various census years represent the area of all land within the present boundaries of the United States and conterminous United States which was under the jurisdiction of the United States on the date in question, including in some cases considerable areas of land not then organized or settled and not covered by the census. In 1870, for example, Alaska was not covered by the census. Area figures for conterminous United States for the years 1790 through 1920 have been revised since publication of 1950 reports to bring them in agreement with remeasurements made in 1940.

[3] Revised figure of 39,818,449 for the 1870 population includes adjustments for underenumeration in the Southern States. On the basis of the revised figure, the population increased by 8,375,128, or 26.6 percent, between 1860 and 1870, and 10,370,760 or 26.1 percent, between 1870 and 1880.

first projects of the new nation, in 1790, was to undertake a census. It revealed that the United States had slightly fewer than 4 million inhabitants, occupying the territory that it then claimed at the very sparse density of 4.5 persons per square mile.

6.3. Early Nineteenth Century

Since 1790 a census has been taken once every ten years. Table 6-2 reports the total population count at each of the 18 decennial censuses, including the first one. Figure 6-2 charts the pattern of growth in population size between 1790 and 1960. Information about the components of the very large growth that has taken place is given in Figures 6-3 and 6-4, which should be studied with the discussion that follows. Figure 6-3 reports the estimated crude birth and death rates that have prevailed since 1800, and Figure 6-4 reports the number of immigrants that came to the United States during

each year from 1820 to 1962. Figure 6-1 undertakes to break down each decade's rate of growth for three centuries, 1630 to 1960, into its components of reproductive increase and net immigration. With these data, which are highly approximate for the earlier periods, we can build up a reasonably detailed picture of the demographic process that took place.

In the years just before and after independence, immigration from abroad apparently was much less voluminous in comparison to population size than it had been earlier. Figure 6-4 shows that in 1820 the annual number of entrants was only about 8000 or 9000. It is likely that the immigration data for this period are very incomplete. However, it is also plausible to place some reliance on them and to suppose that separation from the mother country, the interruption of trade and commerce, and the generally uncertain political future of the new nation temporarily made it less at-

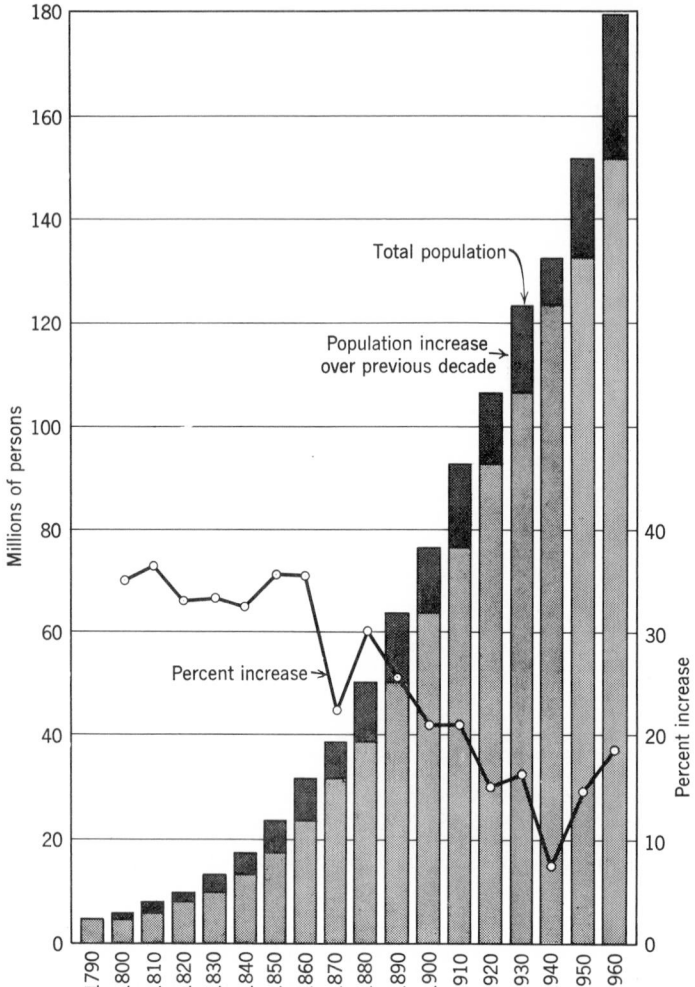

Figure 6-2 Total Population, Decennial Population Increase, and Percent of Increase: 1790 to 1960.

tractive to potential immigrants from Europe. The War of 1812 and the events leading up to it probably prolonged this uncertainty. It therefore appears that most of the population growth from 1790 to about 1830 was provided by reproductive increase. Figure 6-1 confirms the interpretation.

During this time the reproductive increase was very large. Rough estimates, based on rather shaky age statistics, suggest that the birthrate was declining gradually—from about 55 in 1800 to about 50 in 1835. The exact course of the death rate is not known, but it is almost certain to have fluctuated between 22 and 25 per thousand, perhaps declining by almost the same amount as the birthrate, to

maintain a continuous growth of about 3 percent per year. The very large growth through reproduction that was characteristic of this period is illustrated in Figure 6-1.

6.4. Mid-Nineteenth Century

Beginning about 1832, immigration into the United States began to flow in much larger amounts. The nation was expanding its commercial and industrial activities, as well as settling large areas of arable land in the interior. There were many opportunities for employment for new arrivals from abroad. The new government followed a liberal policy of making land available to those who would settle in the wilderness and bring it into productivity.

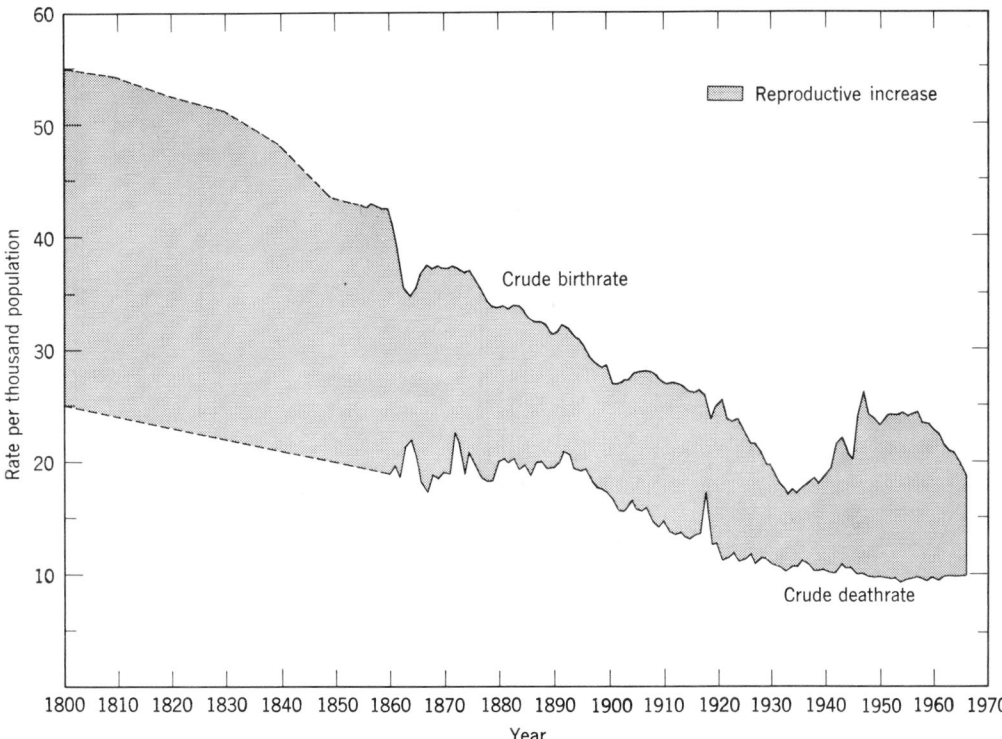

Figure 6-3   Crude Birth and Death Rates in the United States: 1800 to 1963.

SOURCE: Births: 1800 to 1850, W. S. Thompson and P. K. Whelpton, *Population Trends in the United States*; 1855 to 1940, Ansley J. Coale and Melvin Zelnik, *The Enumeration of the White Population of the United States and Its Fertility*; 1940 to 1966, official reports of National Vital Statistics Division.

This period of growth and settlement happened to coincide with political upheaval in Europe. From 1845 to 1860 the volume of inflow was very great and undoubtedly dwarfed all previous migrations in human history in terms of the combined number of persons who moved and the distances spanned. Irish and German newcomers were especially numerous. During these years the United States grew by nearly 1 percent per year from immigration alone.

Meanwhile, the birthrate appears to have begun to decline somewhat more rapidly, so that by 1860 it was in the low 40's instead of the low 50's, as previously. In fact, it appears to have declined more rapidly than the death rate; hence the rate of growth due to reproductive increase was somewhat lower than it had been during the earlier period, although still amazingly large in comparison with events to be observed elsewhere in the world.

When these two components are combined,

it is not surprising to learn, from Table 6-2, that the rate of increase during most decades of this period was between 33 and 36 percent. The increased immigration made up for any slackening of growth that may otherwise have resulted from the 20 percent decline in birthrates that appears to have taken place during the first half of the nineteenth century.

6.5.   The Civil War Period

The Civil War brought a short interim of very great economic and social disorder, which caused a sudden drop in population growth. Figure 6-3 shows that not only did the death rate rise, but the birthrate also fell precipitously. (The reader should note that the birthrates are estimates for the entire nation, prepared by Ansley J. Coale and Melvin Zelnick from census data, while the death rates are simply those for the State of Massachusetts, inserted to show the general trend. Deaths

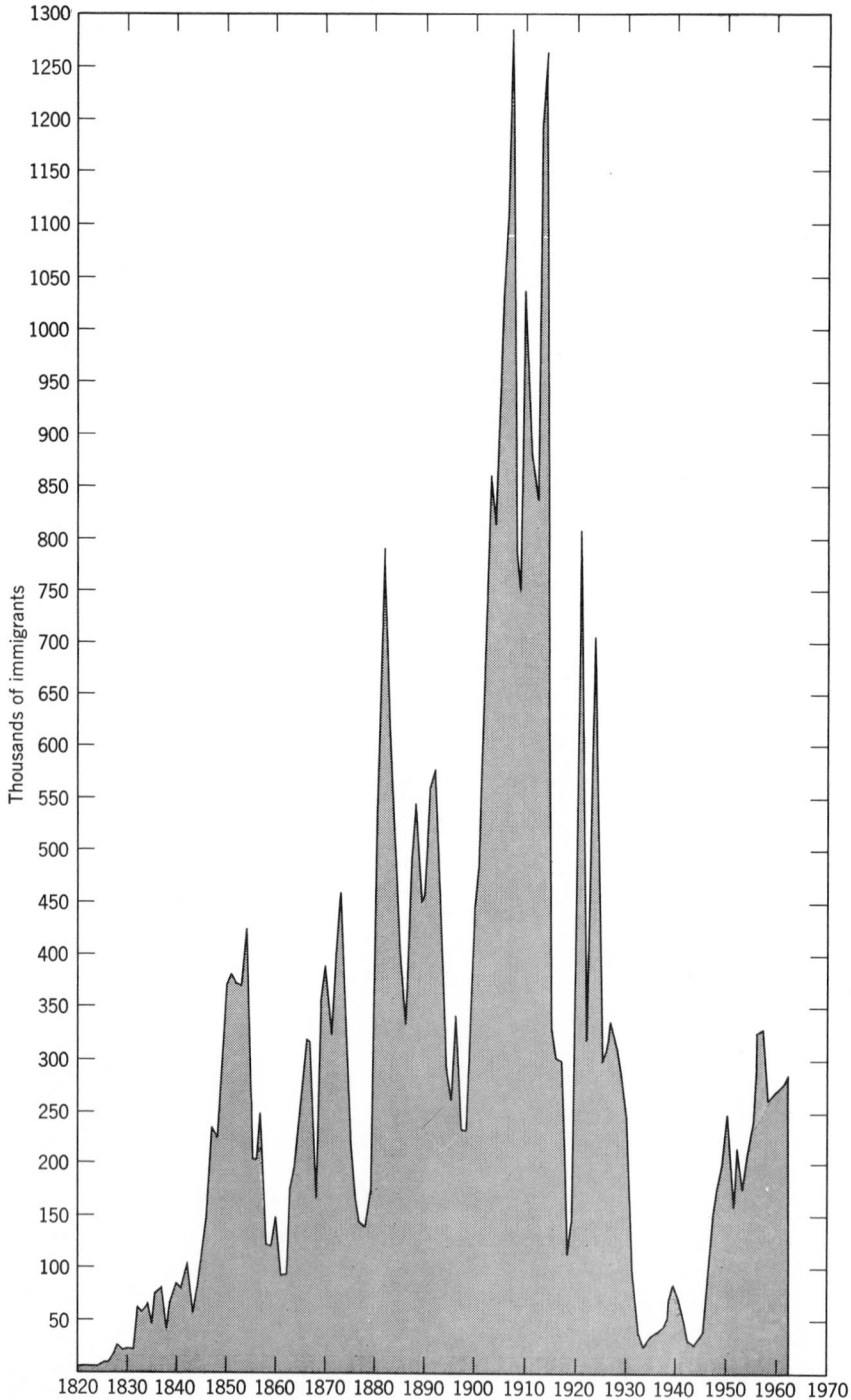

Figure 6-4 Number of Immigrants to the United States, Single Years from 1820 to 1962.

SOURCE: U. S. Bureau of Census, *Historical Statistics of the United States*, Washington, D. C., 1960. Table C88-114; *Statistical Abstract of the United States: 1963*, Table 123.

from combat and war-connected hardships certainly are inadequately reflected in this graph, and it is very likely that the drop in reproductive change was much sharper than suggested.) Figure 6-4 shows that the Civil War period was one of a very great drop in immigration; the annual flow was only one-fourth as great as it had been only a few years earlier. It is difficult to know exactly how great the decline in growth was, because the census of 1870 is thought to have been incomplete in the South. The footnotes to Table 6-2 provide estimates of the deficiency; when adjustments are made for this undercount, the national growth rate shows a sudden slump from 35.6 during the 1850-1860 decade to 26.6 during the 1860-1870 decade.

The Civil War brought many economic and social changes, which had consequences that persist even today. It is not clear to what extent demographic events were affected. Certainly the effect on immigration was only temporary; immigration from abroad rebounded quickly to the heights that had prevailed before the war, and death rates returned to their prewar levels. However, the birthrate did not return to its prewar level of about 40 per thousand, but instead proceeded on a plateau some 10 percent lower, at about 36 per thousand. This may have been a result of the great industrialization engendered by the war. It is even possible that a fertility decline was retarded by increased marriages immediately before the war, and that when viewed in the broad perspective of the entire century the Civil War period was one of only a short-term deviation from the general secular trend.

6.6. Late Nineteenth Century

From 1865 into the early twentieth century, the flow of immigration from Europe was huge. Figure 6-4 shows that with the exception of two slumps, 1876 to 1880 and 1894 to 1899, the flow of immigrants was very great. There are substantial year-to-year fluctuations, which reflected business conditions both in the United States and on the Continent. During the short but often very severe financial panics that developed immigration tended to slacken, only to resume when prosperity returned. It is be-

lieved that the cycle of business conditions in Europe had an inverse effect on migration; when times were good people tended to stay in their homeland instead of migrating. From 1865 to 1880 the flow came primarily from England, Ireland, Germany, and Scandinavia. A great many Canadians began to migrate to the States after the Civil War; it is not known what proportion were simply people from Europe arriving by way of Canada. During this period (especially between 1868 and 1883) there was a substantial flow of Chinese immigrants. This was the first voluntary arrival, in large numbers, of any but white immigrants, and it began to arouse concern about possible effects of unrestricted immigration, both in terms of the numbers that could arrive and apprehensions about its effect on the economic and social life.

In the latter part of the century people began to arrive in increasing numbers from Southern and Eastern Europe, especially from Poland and Italy. Meanwhile, the rate of reproductive change declined steadily and even more sharply during this period than it had done previously. Death rates seemed to remain nearly unchanged, fluctuating about a crude rate of 20 per thousand. It was not until about 1893, toward the very end of the century, that the death rate really began to fall steadily and by large amounts. But the birthrate fell from about 37 in 1870 to 27 in 1900; this was a decline of about 1 percent per year, for a period of 30 years. At the end of the century, the death rate stood only 8 points below the 25 estimated for the start of the century, but the birthrate was 28 points below where it had been at the outset. This represented an overall decline of 50 percent. The decline was accomplished during a time when scientific methods of contraception were almost unknown, and the ones that were available were extremely crude. Delaying the age at marriage, the widespread practice of withdrawal, and contraception by use of the douche or vaginal tampon seem to have been primarily responsible.

6.7. Early Twentieth Century

If the waves of immigrants that had entered the United States during the late nineteenth century had seemed large, those that began to arrive shortly after the turn of the century were a flood, dwarfing all previous events. A glance at Figure 6-4 will give the picture. A total of 1,285,000 immigrants entered in 1907, and very nearly as many came in each of the years 1913 and 1914. During the 10-year period between 1905 and 1915, 10 million immigrants (an average of 1 million per year) flowed in. The streams from Southern and Eastern Europe, which had begun to grow in the last decade of the nineteenth century, now became tremendous. To this was added a greatly increased flow of immigrants from Japan and Mexico. Meanwhile, immigration from Northwestern Europe was no larger than it had been and showed signs of declining. There was much public discussion of this great immigration as a threat to the prosperity of the nation. Many of the proposals for regulation clearly reflected the racial and ethnic prejudices of the majority population of white Protestant ancestry. World War I intervened and curtailed immigration, but immediately after the war the flow was resumed. In 1920 a quota system, limiting both the total number of immigrants and the number that could be admitted from each nation, was placed into effect. This quota undertook to limit immigration to 150,000 per year.

Whereas the preceding waves of immigration had proceeded primarily to the Western Frontier and had contributed to the building up of the Midwestern and Western sections, the immigrants who arrived after the turn of the twentieth century concentrated largely in the cities. Every major industrial city of the Northeast acquired large ethnic communities of Italian, Polish, Czech, or other immigrant groups who worked in the factories and mines and as laborers for industrial and commercial expansion. A major factor in this shift was that the last of the arable frontier land had been claimed by the homesteaders, and the frontier phase of American development had come to an end.

During this period the birthrate declined, but the decline appears to have been somewhat more gradual than during the 1890 period. It is quite plausible to suppose that its descent was counterbalanced by the high fertility among the arriving immigrants. A high propor- tion of them were from peasant societies in Eastern and Southern Europe, where religious beliefs strongly supported a pronatalist attitude and were antagonistic to fertility control. Figure 6-3 reports that there was a rise in the birthrate from 1901 to 1907. The estimates are too approximate to permit us to determine whether this actually was the case. In any event, with high volume of immigration, a falling death rate, and a somewhat revived birthrate, the period from 1900 to World War I was one of moderately rapid growth.

6.8. World War I and the 1920s

World War I appears to have created a sharp but highly temporary fluctuation in population growth trends in the United States. As has been noted, the great flood of immigrants ceased when ocean passage became dangerous and shipping was controlled. Birthrates fell during 1918 and 1919 as a result of sending an army overseas. Shortly after demobilization, the birthrate recovered and compensated somewhat for the fertility losses of the preceding two years. However, after this temporary upsurge the birthrate began to fall and fell more rapidly than at any previous time. In the seven years from 1922 to 1929 the birthrate fell by 5 points, or nearly 25 percent. This occurred during a time when the nation was enjoying unprecedented prosperity.

This decline in the American birthrate between 1922 and 1930 had a profound impact on the thinking of American demographers. It is important for the newer generation to understand the full significance of this short seven-year span of time in order to interpret demographic writings before 1950. Demography as a vigorous research discipline was born about 1922 and began to develop in years immediately following. It is during this time that Warren S. Thompson, P.K. Whelpton, Frank W. Notestein, Frank Lorimer, Clyde Kiser, and others of the "founding fathers" began their research careers. It is also during this time that the first useful registration data for deaths, and then for births, became available. As their explorations led them to discover that the birthrate had been declining almost continuously for the preceding 120 years and that it was continuing to fall very rapidly during the prosperous 1920s, they concluded that the population was barely reproducing itself, even in 1929. Fear of insufficient population growth was the subject for public concern in America as well as in Europe. *There were no theories and no data to warn demographers about the great fertility uprising to come.*

The imposition of immigration quotas in 1920 had the effect of suppressing immigration. In the second half of the 1920-1930 decade the annual flow of immigrants was about the same as it had been during the 1850-1860 decade, just before the Civil War.

This slackening of the birthrate and of immigration substantially slowed down population growth. Despite the fact that it was a decade of peace and prosperity, the nation grew only by 16 percent between 1920 and 1930. This is very slow indeed when we recall that between 1820 and 1830 the rate of growth was more than twice this amount.

6.9. The Great Economic Depression

The stock market crash in 1929 ushered in a phase of such economic hardship as the population of the United States had not witnessed before. Previous economic setbacks, which often were very severe and created panic, had been brief, ending within a year or two. But this one persisted for almost a full decade. At its nadir, one man out of four was without a job. There was no frontier to which to flee to make a living. During this time birthrates continued to decline, until in 1933 they reached a level of 18 per thousand. For six or seven years they fluctuated at this low plateau, rising gradually as the economy began to recover. Meanwhile death rates continued to drift down gradually. Important medical discoveries (sulfa and other antibiotic drugs) were made during this period, and medical services were extended to low-income groups, which previously had been very inadequately served. These developments tended to offset the inability of middle- and upper-income populations to afford the quantity of medical services they had previously enjoyed.

During the 1930s, net immigration declined to zero or slightly below. As Figure 6-4 shows, the number of arrivals was at the same low ebb as during the early days after independence in 1800-1810. Foreign-born citizens returning to their homeland equaled in number the new arrivals from abroad, so that net immigration actually was zero. The great economic depression destroyed, at least temporarily, the international image of the United States as a land of opportunity.

This period ended with a gradual easing of unemployment due to the success of the programs to induce economic recovery. After 1937, the effort to build up a defense organization because of the outbreak of war in Europe also stimulated employment. Military mobilization began in 1939, which also helped to put to work many thousands of men who had been unemployed for prolonged periods of time.

When the 1940 census was taken it was discovered that the United States had grown more slowly than at any time in its history—7.2 percent. This low growth rate applied to such a large population, however, that the population gain for the decade was 8 million persons.

6.10. World War II

Beginning in 1940 the United States birthrate began to rise rather rapidly. Figure 6-5 shows the pattern of events that followed. Table 6-3 reports the rates for each of the components of population change from 1940 to 1965. At first this recovery did not surprise demographers. They interpreted it as being a "making up" of births that had been postponed during the depression, when economic insecurity had caused couples to have fewer children than they really desired. It was hypothesized that couples who had postponed childbearing proceeded to complete their families when better times returned. The birthrate rose for four years, until 1944, but fell back in 1945 as a result of several million American servicemen having been shipped to overseas combat zones in 1944. With the cessation of hostilities, millions of men were discharged from military service in late 1945 and through 1946. This demobilization brought a great increase in marriages that had been previously postponed, and many couples that had been unable or un-

Table 6-3   Annual Rates of Net Growth, Births, Deaths, and Net
Immigration: 1940 to 1965 (Rate per 1000 of the Midyear Population
Including Armed Forces Abroad)

Year or period	Net growth rate	Rate of reproductive change	Birth rate	Death rate	Net civilian immigration rate
Calendar year:					
1965..................	12.1	10.2	19.6	9.4	1.9
1964..................	13.6	11.8	21.2	9.4	1.8
1963..................	14.3	12.3	21.9	9.6	2.0
1962..................	15.1	13.2	22.6	9.4	2.0
1961..................	16.4	14.2	23.5	9.3	2.1
1960..................	16.3	14.4	23.8	9.5	1.9
1959..................	16.5	14.9	24.3	9.4	1.6
1958..................	16.7	15.0	24.5	9.5	1.7
1957..................	17.2	15.7	25.2	9.5	1.6
1956..................	18.1	15.8	25.1	9.3	2.3
1955..................	17.6	15.6	24.9	9.3	2.0
1954..................	17.8	16.0	25.2	9.1	1.8
1953..................	17.0	15.3	24.9	9.6	1.6
1952..................	16.9	15.4	25.0	9.6	1.5
1951..................	17.4	15.1	24.8	9.7	2.2
1950..................	16.3	14.3	23.9	9.6	2.0
1949..................	17.1	14.8	24.5	9.7	2.2
1948..................	17.2	15.0	24.8	9.9	1.9
1947..................	18.3	16.4	26.5	10.1	1.6
1946..................	15.3	14.2	24.1	9.9	1.1
1945..................	10.4	9.4	20.5	11.0	1.2
1944..................	11.5	9.9	21.3	11.4	1.5
1943..................	13.1	11.8	22.7	10.9	1.1
1942..................	12.7	11.8	22.2	10.4	0.6
1941..................	10.3	9.7	20.3	10.6	0.4
1940..................	9.2	8.6	19.4	10.8	0.6
Annual average:					
1960-1965[1]...........	14.6	12.7	22.1	9.4	2.0
1955-1959.............	17.2	15.4	24.8	9.4	1.8
1950-1954.............	17.1	15.2	24.8	9.5	1.8
1945-1949.............	15.7	14.0	24.1	10.1	1.6
1940-1944.............	11.4	10.4	21.2	10.8	0.8

[1] 6-year period.

Source: U.S. Bureau of the Census Current Population Reports, P-25, No. 331
          March, 1966.

willing to start their families during wartime now proceeded to have children. The result was that in 1947 the crude birthrate reached a high point of 26.5 per thousand. It had not been this high since 1920-1921, immediately following World War I. The sudden leap from a low of 18 per thousand in 1933 to nearly 27 per thousand in 1947 was a very great one indeed. Yet even this postwar upsurge in fertility of 1946 failed to occasion more than mild surprise among demographers. They pointed out that the proportion of men in the child-bearing years that had been sent overseas was much greater than during World War I and that the average duration of their stay away from home had been much longer. It was therefore only to be expected that there should

be a rather dramatic rise in fertility upon their demobilization. What amazed all observers, however, was that the high birthrate did not subside within a year or two as it had after World War I, but continued at a high plateau of about 25 per thousand. Although demographers had expected a swift return to the condition of near replacement that had developed in the late 1920s, or even a continuation of the decline in the birthrates, they were confronted by a new situation where the population was growing at a rate that had not been witnessed since the days before World War I. Moreover, this rate now applied to such a huge population base that the numerical increase each year was astounding. It was difficult for demographers to convince themselves that a

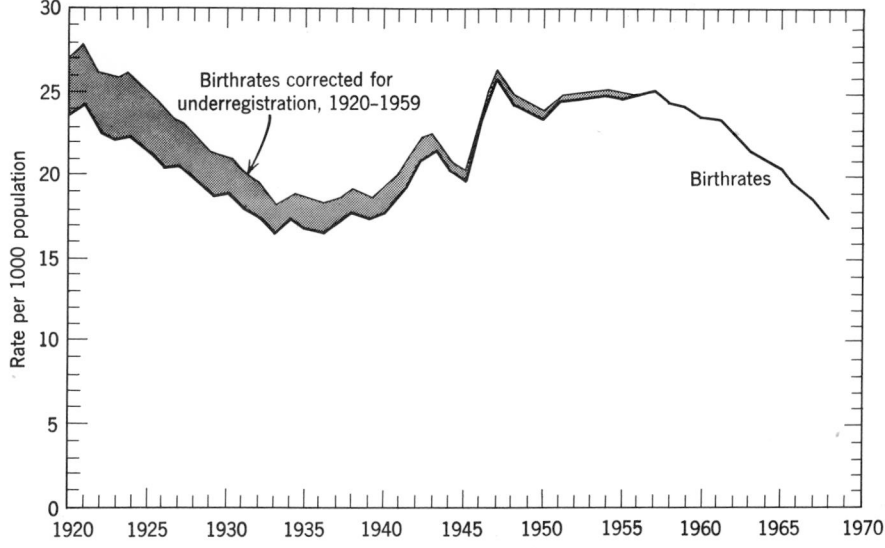

Figure 6-5 Vital Statistics Rates: 1920 to 1966.

SOURCE: Chart Prepared by Department of Commerce, Bureau of the Census. Data from Department of Health, Education, and Welfare, Public Health Service.

trend of a century and a half had been reversed and that a completely new and unanticipated pattern of fertility had developed. Now, after two decades, the picture is clearer. The World War II phase must be interpreted as the period that reversed the long-term downward trend in the birthrate and brought about a resurgence in growth in the American population. This new growth through reproductive increase was greatly augmented by the arrival, through special legislation modifying immigration restrictions, of large numbers of political refugees from Europe. During World War II, there was comparatively little immigration. As in World War I, the hazards of war and restrictions upon shipping had reduced immigration to a very low point.

Although combat losses during World War II were moderately large in terms of the number of men lost, the population from which they were drawn numbered so many millions that on an overall basis these losses had only a slight dampening effect, which could scarcely be noticed in the overall growth occasioned by the upswing of fertility. When the census of 1950 was taken, it revealed that during the World War II years and immediately after, the growth rate was double that of the previous decade. Instead of leveling off, as the demog-

raphers had predicted it would at about this time, the nation grew by 19.3 million persons. This was a larger numerical gain than during any decade in the nation's history. Moreover, there was no evidence that the "baby boom" would end soon.

6.11. Post-World War II Era

In the years following 1946-1947 the birthrates in the United States continued to be moderately high—25 per thousand or slightly below —with a death rate of 8 or 9 per thousand. As Figure 6-5 shows, this condition persisted for a full decade, until 1957. Since 1957 the rates have been drifting downward, at first gradually and then more swiftly. In 1964 and 1965 they turned down sharply. By January of 1966 it was clear that a major new trend was under way and that the "baby boom" had ended. By 1968 the birthrate had fallen almost to the low level of 1933, which was achieved under great economic hardship. The fact that this decline took place during a time of uninterrupted prosperity is highly significant. A genuine shift in desired family size appears to be in the making. What the future will bring is not predictable with the knowledge at hand. It is possible that under conditions of continuing high prosperity, the desire for moderately large

Table 6-4 Estimates of the Components of Population Change for the United States Including Armed Forces Abroad by Annual and Semiannual Periods: 1940 to 1966 (Number in Thousands. Includes Alaska and Hawaii in All Years)

Period	Population at beginning of period	Net change during year or period		Components of change during year or period			
		Number	Percent[1]	Births[2]	Deaths[3]	Net civilian immigration	Other[4]
Calendar year:							
1966..............	195,832	(X)	(X)	(X)	(X)	(X)	(X)
1965..............	193,483	2,348	1.21	3,806	1,828	368	+2
1964..............	190,871	2,612	1.37	4,070	1,799	340	+1
1963..............	188,160	2,712	1.44	4,142	1,815	384	+1
1962..............	185,333	2,827	1.53	4,213	1,758	373	(Z)
1961..............	182,326	3,007	1.65	4,317	1,703	391	+1
1960..............	179,386	2,940	1.64	4,307	1,708	340	+1
1959..............	176,447	2,939	1.67	4,313	1,663	292	-2
1958..............	173,533	2,915	1.68	4,279	1,655	292	(Z)
1957..............	170,571	2,961	1.74	4,332	1,641	272	-1
1956..............	167,513	3,058	1.83	4,244	1,572	387	-1
1955..............	164,588	2,925	1.78	4,128	1,537	337	-2
1954..............	161,690	2,898	1.79	4,102	1,489	287	-2
1953..............	158,973	2,717	1.71	3,989	1,531	261	-1
1952..............	156,309	2,663	1.70	3,933	1,512	242	(Z)
1951..............	153,622	2,688	1.75	3,845	1,501	335	+9
1950..............	151,135	2,486	1.65	3,645	1,468	299	+11
1949..............	148,580	2,556	1.72	3,667	1,452	323	+18
1948..............	146,047	2,533	1.73	3,655	1,453	280	+52
1947..............	143,394	2,653	1.85	3,834	1,455	238	+35
1946..............	141,229	2,165	1.53	3,426	1,409	151	-3
1945..............	139,767	1,462	1.05	2,873	1,549	162	-24
1944..............	138,170	1,597	1.16	2,954	1,582	202	+23
1943..............	136,371	1,799	1.32	3,118	1,503	148	+36
1942..............	134,657	1,714	1.27	3,002	1,407	83	+36
1941..............	133,275	1,382	1.04	2,716	1,415	60	+21
1940..............	132,054	1,221	0.92	2,570	1,432	77	+6

X Not applicable. "Z less than 500."

[1] Percent of population at beginning of period.

[2] Adjusted for underregistration.

[3] Deaths occurring in the United States plus estimated deaths occurring to Armed Forces abroad.

[4] Infant deaths adjusted to underregistration through March, 1960.

Source: U.S. Bureau of Census. Current Population Reports, "Estimates of the Population of the United States and Components of Change: 1940 to 1966," Series P-25, No. 331, March 22, 1966

families will continue and that the birthrate could level off at about 18 for a sustained period of time. On the other hand, it is possible that the two-child family will become the norm and that birthrates will sink close to 15-16 per thousand and bring about a near cessation of population growth. The critical factor, not as yet known, is whether couples will continue to want three or four children or whether they will be content with two.

Meanwhile, during the postwar era a new development has taken place in the field of mortality. Death rates have stopped declining. Despite the fact that huge quantities of money have gone into programs of research and con-

struction for improving health and medical services to the population, despite the fact that medical insurance has been extended from the upper class to the middle class and down to include a very large share of the total population, and despite the fact that free medical services are provided in almost all states to persons on welfare, the death rate in 1960 (after adjustment for changes in age composition) stands almost exactly where it was in 1950. The reasons for this are numerous and somewhat complex and will be discussed further in the chapter on mortality. At present we need only to note that during the 1950-1960 decade the mortality component com-

Table 6-5   Components of Population Change, by Type of Population: 1940 to 1950, 1950 to 1960, and 1960 to 1966 (Includes Alaska and Hawaii in All Periods)

Type of population and component of change	April 1, 1960, to Jan. 1, 1966	April 1, 1950 to 1960	April 1, 1940 to 1950	Percent[1]		
				April 1, 1960, to Jan. 1, 1966	April 1, 1950 to 1960	April 1, 1940 to 1950
TOTAL POPULATION INCLUDING ARMED FORCES ABROAD						
Population at beginning of period............	180,007,000	151,718,000	132,288,000	(X)	(X)	(X)
Net change.................................	15,824,000	28,289,000	19,429,000	8.8	18.6	14.7
Births[2].................................	23,817,000	40,963,000	32,064,000	13.2	27.0	24.2
Total deaths[3]............................	10,138,000	15,653,000	14,638,000	5.6	10.3	11.1
Net civilian immigration...................	2,139,000	2,975,000	1,789,000	1.2	2.0	1.4
Inductions less discharges abroad..........	6,000	8,000	12,000	(Z)	(Z)	(Z)
Error of closure..........................	(X)	-3,000	202,000	(X)	(Z)	0.2
Population at end of period.................	195,832,000	180,007,000	151,718,000	(X)	(X)	(X)
TOTAL RESIDENT POPULATION						
Population at beginning of period............	179,323,175[4]	151,325,798[4]	132,166,000[4]	(X)	(X)	(X)
Net change.................................	15,594,000	27,997,000	19,160,000	8.7	18.5	14.5
Births[2].................................	23,817,000	40,963,000	32,064,000	13.3	27.1	24.3
Deaths occurring in United States[3].........	10,131,000	15,608,000	14,294,000	5.6	10.3	10.8
Net civilian immigration...................	2,139,000	2,975,000	1,789,000	1.2	2.0	1.4
Net movement of Armed Forces to posts abroad	231,000	330,000	602,000	0.1	0.2	0.5
Error of closure..........................	(X)	-3,000	202,000	(X)	(Z)	0.2
Population at end of period.................	194,918,000	179,323,175[4]	151,325,798[4]	(X)	(X)	(X)
CIVILIAN RESIDENT POPULATION						
Population at beginning of period............	177,472,000	150,219,000	131,859,000	(X)	(X)	(X)
Net change.................................	15,470,000	27,253,000	18,360,000	8.7	18.1	13.9
Births[2].................................	23,817,000	40,963,000	32,064,000	13.4	27.3	24.3
Civilian deaths[3].........................	10,113,000	15,570,000	14,221,000	5.7	10.4	10.8
Net civilian immigration...................	2,139,000	2,975,000	1,789,000	1.2	2.0	1.4
Inductions less discharges in United States.	374,000	1,112,000	1,475,000	0.2	0.7	1.1
Error of closure..........................	(X)	-3,000	202,000	(X)	(Z)	0.2
Population at end of period.................	192,942,000	177,472,000	150,219,000	(X)	(X)	(X)

X Not applicable.   Z Less than 0.05 percent.
[1] Percent of population at beginning of period.
[2] Adjusted for underregistration.
[3] Infant deaths adjusted for underregistration through March,1960. Estimates of deaths differ according to type of population as a result of inclusion or exclusion of deaths of Armed Forces at home and abroad.
[4] Census counts. Figure for April 1, 1940, includes an estimate for Alaska of 74,000; census count of Alaska as of October 1, 1939, was 73,024.

Source: U.S. Bureau of Census. Current Population Reports, "Estimates of the Population of the United States and Components of Change: 1940 to 1966," Series P-25 No. 331., March 22, 1966.

pleted the demographic transition in the United States—at least from the point of view of medical science as it is now known. Today mortality levels stand at a point where further improvements will likely be small and uncertain.

Meanwhile the immigration flow to the United States has continued at a moderately high level. The nation has only recently returned to the quota system that had been established after World War I (now liberalized to admit nationals from Asian countries in small numbers). Throughout much of the time since World War II the immigration quotas have been liberalized to admit emergency-entry refugees.

Table 6-4 reports the components of population change for each year from 1940 to 1965. This is a very valuable table, and its construction cost the Bureau of Census much demographic labor. Table 6-5, which summarizes the data by decades, is a succinct statement of population growth trends in the United States. During the 10-year period 1950-1960 the population increased by nearly 30 million. This is a volume of increase that has not been matched in the nation's history. An excess of births over deaths was responsible for 25.3 million of this increase. The remaining 11 percent (3 million persons) was created by the net arrival of persons from abroad. Because of lowered fertility, it is certain that the growth during the 1960-1970 decade will be below that of the 1950-1960 decade, despite the fact that the rates apply to a much larger population and that the level of immigration is higher.

6.12.   What Can We Learn from the Growth History of the United States?

A survey of the history of United States population growth, in terms of its components, reveals the amazing fact that most of the historic decline in fertility took place during the nineteenth century, before contraception became easy, rather than inconvenient and annoying. Of the total of 34 or 35 points by which the birthrate appears to have fallen in the 165 years since 1800, not less than 27 points (80 percent) of decline was accomplished in the nineteenth century before the advent of modern contraception. Birthrates in the United States in 1965 were only about 7 or 8 points below their level of 1900, despite the invention and almost universal diffusion throughout the population of new and more acceptable methods of fertility control. Sociologically speaking, this is clear evidence that demographic readjustment will be attempted when a population senses the need for it—even though the available means may be crude and unpleasant. Modern family planning experts who are today formulating programs for bringing about rapid fertility reduction in the developing countries would do well to review this century of fertility decline in the United States (as well as in Europe). The United States population of the nineteenth century, in terms of level of living, level of education, and level of industrialization, was not unlike the populations in most of the developing countries today. It was predominantly rural, and the level of literacy was low. Moreover, it was steeped in the belief that fate controlled all events in life; belief in predestination pervaded the thinking of rural America, and mysticism was rampant on the frontier. Yet these people brought about a reduction in birthrates under conditions of great personal inconvenience. We need to know what were the elements in the social climate of nineteenth-century America that facilitated this fertility decline.

In like fashion, we need to know what "motives" stimulated a highly urban, highly educated, and highly sophisticated population that knew all about birth control to launch itself on a quarter-century fertility spree such as that of the period 1940 to 1965. This type of reversal is something that cannot be explained by the theories of demographic readjustment developed in Chapter 3. At least it is not easy to point to any sudden mass demographic "need" that was satisfied by the "baby boom." A few observers interpret it as a subconscious response of the population to the so-regarded threat of world Communism so as to ensure numerical equality with the USSR in the current state of great world tensions. Others interpret it as a personal reaction of many millions of persons born during the 1920s to dissatisfaction with having been reared in a family of only one or two children. Some suggest that our culture still contains important elements of high-fertility values, engendered on the one hand by our rural and frontier heritage and on the other by our great urban population of Roman Catholic belief, so that when great prosperity increases purchasing power, one of the commodities Americans want to buy is children. Thus it is not difficult to fabricate explanations from psychiatry, anthropology, economics, and sociology. What has been lacking so far is the research needed to submit them to test. The help of other branches of social science is needed in order to do this.

6.13. Implications for the Future

National leaders of all types are seriously concerned about the future implications of the population upsurge for the American economy and the American people. Never before has the nation grown at the rate of 3 million persons per year for a whole decade—not even during the years of the great inflooding of immigrants from abroad. If 1960-1965 birth and death rates were to continue, this annual growth will get larger and larger as the size of the base population to which they apply gets larger. Even if a moderate fertility decline occurred, very great increases would still be possible. Table 6-6 reports population projections prepared by the U.S. Bureau of Census, which show the population of the nation at various dates in the future under varying conditions of fertility. If fertility remained at the 1962-1965 level (Series A), we could expect a population of 273 million by 1985. The Series D projections shown in Table 6-6 assume that birthrates will decline sharply. This yields an estimated population of nearly 240 million in 1985. (Although the Census Bureau regards Series D as the lower extreme, it is here re-

Table 6-6 Annual Estimates and Projections of the Population and of the Components of Population Change, for the United States: 1950 to 1985 (Numbers in Thousands. Figures Include Armed Forces Abroad. For a Description of the Assumptions Underlying the Four Series Shown, See Text)

Series and year (July 1 to June 30)	Population at beginning of year	Net change during year[1]		Births		Deaths	
		Amount	Percent[2]	Amount	Rate[3]	Amount	Rate[3]
Series A							
1965-1966..............	194,583[4]	2,426	1.25	3,911	20.0	1,885	9.6
1966-1967..............	197,009	2,699	1.37	4,213	21.2	1,194	9.6
1967-1968..............	199,708	2,877	1.44	4,420	22.0	1,943	9.7
1968-1969..............	202,585	3,056	1.51	4,628	22.7	1,972	9.7
1969-1970..............	205,641	3,232	1.57	4,833	23.3	2,001	9.7
1970-1971..............	208,874	3,404	1.63	5,034	23.9	2,030	9.6
1971-1972..............	212,278	3,571	1.68	5,229	24.4	2,058	9.6
1972-1973..............	215,849	3,729	1.73	5,414	24.9	2,085	9.6
1973-1974..............	219,577	3,878	1.77	5,590	25.2	2,112	9.5
1974-1975..............	223,455	4,019	1.80	5,758	25.5	2,138	9.5
1975-1976..............	227,474	4,154	1.83	5,918	25.8	2,164	9.4
1976-1977..............	231,629	4,282	1.85	6,071	26.0	2,189	9.4
1977-1978..............	235,911	4,400	1.87	6,213	26.1	2,213	9.3
1978-1979..............	240,311	4,508	1.88	6,344	26.2	2,236	9.2
1979-1980..............	244,819	4,603	1.88	6,462	26.2	2,259	9.1
1980-1981..............	249,421	4,684	1.88	6,565	26.1	2,281	9.1
1981-1982..............	254,106	4,750	1.87	6,653	25.9	2,303	9.0
1982-1983..............	258,855	4,798	1.85	6,724	25.7	2,325	8.9
1983-1984..............	263,654	4,831	1.83	6,779	25.5	2,348	8.8
1984-1985..............	268,485	4,853	1.81	6,823	25.2	2,371	8.8
1985-1986..............	273,338	(NA)	(NA)	(NA)	(NA)	(NA)	(NA)
Series D							
1965-1966..............	194,583[4]	2,058	1.06	3,535	18.1	1,877	9.6
1966-1967..............	196,641	1,871	0.95	3,366	17.0	1,895	9.6
1967-1968..............	198,512	1,870	0.94	3,388	17.0	1,918	9.6
1968-1969..............	200,383	1,873	0.93	3,415	17.0	1,942	9.6
1969-1970..............	202,256	1,883	0.93	3,449	17.0	1,966	9.7
1970-1971..............	204,139	1,903	0.93	3,493	17.0	1,990	9.7
1971-1972..............	206,042	1,935	0.94	3,549	17.1	2,014	9.7
1972-1973..............	207,977	1,979	0.95	3,617	17.3	2,038	9.8
1973-1974..............	209,956	2,037	0.97	3,699	17.5	2,062	9.8
1974-1975..............	211,993	2,107	0.99	3,793	17.8	2,086	9.8
1975-1976..............	214,100	2,188	1.02	3,898	18.1	2,110	9.8
1976-1977..............	216,288	2,277	1.05	4,011	18.4	2,134	9.8
1977-1978..............	218,565	2,371	1.08	4,128	18.8	2,157	9.8
1978-1979..............	220,937	2,465	1.12	4,245	19.1	2,180	9.8
1979-1980..............	223,402	2,557	1.14	4,359	19.4	2,202	9.8
1980-1981..............	225,959	2,643	1.17	4,467	19.7	2,224	9.8
1981-1982..............	228,602	2,721	1.19	4,566	19.9	2,245	9.8
1982-1983..............	231,323	2,786	1.20	4,653	20.0	2,267	9.7
1983-1984..............	234,109	2,833	1.21	4,722	20.1	2,289	9.7
1984-1985..............	236,942	2,861	1.21	4,773	20.0	2,311	9.7
1985-1986..............	239,804	(NA)	(NA)	(NA)	(NA)	(NA)	(NA)

NA Not available.

[1] Includes annual net immigration of 400,000, not shown separately, in future years.
[2] Percent of population at beginning of fiscal year.
[3] Rate per 1,000 population at middle of fiscal year.
[4] Current estimate for July 1, 1965.

Source: U.S. Bureau of Census. Current Population Reports, "Revised Projections of the Population of the United States by Age and Sex to 1985". Series P-25, No. 329, March 10, 1966.

garded as higher than the most likely trend.) From these projections we may make two inferences:

1. The United States population has become so large that small differences in the birthrate (hence in the rate of growth) can produce very large differences in the population size in only a few years.

2. If the United States population growth is to be slowed down to a point where numbers remain nearly stationary or increase only gradually, birthrates must fall to a point much lower than those that have prevailed since 1946. Until this happens, the annual increments to the national population will be very large.

Moreover, whereas immigrants arrived as adults, ready to go to work, the arrivals that constitute this new population growth are infants that must be reared, educated, and absorbed into national life as they mature. The process of absorption is growing to large proportions in the 1960s. During 1955-1965 the nation was plagued with rising levels of unemployment, especially among younger people. The military conscription of 1965-1968 appears to have alleviated it at least temporarily. There have been large increases in the number of juvenile delinquents. Even though we have enjoyed unprecedented economic prosperity, we have been unable to absorb and eliminate the last remnants of poverty. Instead, the number of persons who become public dependents has been increasing.

The large increase in the number of infants in the population has placed a tremendous strain on our public school system. Some declare that the quality of American education has been declining, both absolutely and relative to the needs of our rapidly increasing technical society. Population growth has created housing shortages, which appear to have made it difficult if not impossible to demolish slums and raise the quality of housing as quickly as would be desired and might otherwise be possible. Our great cities are becoming more congested, so that living conditions seem to be deteriorating. Air pollution, inadequate pure water supply, intolerably long commuting journeys, traffic congestion, and other problems associated with great size and rapid growth are plaguing municipal officials. *Yet it can fairly be said that so far only the first tremors have been felt of this great demographic earthquake.* The dysfunctional impact of the 1946-1957 era will sweep over the nation in full force between 1970 and 1980. As such problems become more acute and as legislatures are called on to vote increasingly larger appropriations to pay for the burden of bearing them, some questions are asked more and more persistently: To what extent are these problems a by-product of the "baby boom" that we created after World War II? To what extent can they be eased or eliminated by slowing down population growth? Is a birthrate of 22 to 25 good for America or would a birthrate of 12 or 14 be better? A few years ago we were concerned about underpopulation. Until 1966 America was concerned equally seriously about the overly rapid growth of population. It is a topic about which we read regularly in the newspapers and news magazines. It was discussed on television and radio forums, and there was open agitation from many different directions to initiate programs of public family planning to slow down population growth (especially among the poor) to a point that would permit our economy to absorb the increases more systematically. In other words, Americans came to see their own recent population trends as being different in degree but not in kind from those that are faced by the developing nations of the world.

Since the sharp downturn in birthrates in 1965-1968, rumbles of fear about population stagnation again have been heard—especially from the business community. Chapter 21 evaluates these very recent developments in more detail, viewing them in their world perspective.

Ultimately, our nation must learn to have prosperity for a stationary population. Perhaps we are sufficiently wise in economics to achieve it now. If not, perhaps we must substitute bravery for wisdom and learn on the way.

QUESTIONS AND EXERCISES

1. From the library, consult the most recent monthly and annual reports of the Vital Statistics Division of the U.S. Public Health Service to determine what the birth and death rates are at the present time. Write a short essay on population trends in the United States since the last year for which data were available when this book was written. Make whatever explanatory analysis you care to make. Divide the growth into reproductive change and net immigration.

2. Using data from Chapter 3 and from the

most recent issue of the United Nations *Demographic Yearbook*, chart on a graph the fertility trends of the United States, Taiwan, Poland, Sweden, and Japan, taking an average for five-year intervals. What conclusions can you draw concerning the speed over time with which birthrates decline? Is there an average amount per decade to which all nations tend to conform? Can you note any difference between nations in which the decline has been recent and those in which the decline began early in the nineteenth century?

3. Repeat Exercise 1 with respect to death rates.

4. Read up on business cycles and identify the dates at which high points and low points occurred in business conditions in the United States. Compare these with the fluctuations in immigration shown in Figure 6-2. Write a short paragraph about the interrelationship between migration flow and business conditions.

Does migration appear to respond promptly to changing business conditions or is there a lag?

5. Read all you can about the American Indian population, from the earliest estimates to the present time. How do the birthrates of American Indians compare today with those of Indians in Asia and Latin America?

6. Repeat Exercise 5 for the Negro, Japanese, and Spanish-speaking populations.

7. Consult the most recent population projections of the U.S. Bureau of Census. Consult also the vital statistics for current and recent years. Compare both with Table 6-6. Write an essay on the discrepancies between predicted and actual population growth between 1965 and the time you are writing.

8. Urbanism is supposed to have a retardative effect on population growth. Yet the "baby boom" took place during a period of unprecedented urbanization and metropolitanization. How do you account for this?

BIBLIOGRAPHY

Balestra, Pietro, and N. Koteswara Rao. *Basic Economic Projections, United States Population, 1965-1980. (Estimates).* Menlo Park, Calif.: Stanford Research Institute, 1964.

Beale, Calvin L., and Donald J. Bogue. "Recent Population Trends in the United States with Emphasis on Rural Areas," *Agricultural Economic Report,* **23**, in U.S. Department of Agriculture Economic Research Service. Washington, D.C.: U. S. Government Printing Office, January 1963.

Bogue, Donald J. "Population Growth in the United States," Chapter 5 in Philip M. Hauser (ed.). *The Population Dilemma.* New York: Prentice-Hall, 1963.

Bogue, Donald J. *The Population of the United States.* (With a special chapter on fertility by Wilson H. Grabill.) Glencoe, Ill.: The Free Press, 1959.

Bogue, Donald J., and Reynolds Farley. "Population Growth, Problems and Trends in the United States," *American Journal of Public Health,* **56** (1) (January 1966).

Bogue, Donald J., D. Misra Bhaskar, and D. P. Dandekar. "A New Estimate of the Negro Population and Negro Vital Rates in the United States, 1930-60," *Demography,* **1** (1964), 341–348.

Brown, Harrison. "Life in the Americas During the Next Century," *The Annals of The American Academy of Political and Social Science,* **316** (March 1958), 11–17.

Clawson, Marion, et al. *Land for the Future.* Balti-

more, Md.: Published for Resources for the Future, Inc., by the Johns Hopkins Press, 1960.

Coale, Ansley J., and Melvin Zelnick. *The Enumeration of the White Population of the United States and Its Fertility.* Princeton, N. J.: Princeton University Press, 1964.

Davis, Kingsley (ed.). "A Crowding Hemisphere: Population Change in the Americas," *The Annals of the American Academy of Political and Social Science,* **316** (March 1958), 1–136.

Davis, Kingsley, "Recent Population Trends in the New World: An Over-All View," *The Annals of the American Academy of Political and Social Science,* **316** (March 1958), 1–10.

Dewhurst, J. F., et al. *America's Needs and Resources: A New Survey.* New York: Twentieth Century Fund, 1955.

Drucker, Peter F. *America's Next Twenty Years.* New York: Harper and Bros., 1957.

Easterlin, Richard A. "The American Baby Boom in Historical Perspective," *American Economic Review,* **60** (5) (December 1961), 869–911.

Easterlin, Richard A. "Long Swings in the United States Demographic and Economic Growth: Some Findings in Historical Pattern", *Demography,* **2** (1965), 490–507.

Eblen, Jack E. "An Analysis of Nineteenth-Century Frontier Populations," *Demography,* **2** (1965), 399–413.

Farley, Reynolds. "The Demographic Rates and Social Institutions of the Nineteenth-Century Negro Population: A Stable Population Analysis," *Demography,* **2** (1965), 386–398.

Greville, T. N. E. "Illustrative United States Population Projections," *Actuarial Study No. 46.* Washington, D.C., May 1957.

Hansen, Marcus Lee. "The Peopling of the Colonies," Ch. 2 in *The Atlantic Migration, 1607-1860.* Cambridge, Mass., Harvard University Press, 1940.

Hutchinson, Edward P. "Immigration Policy since World War I," *The Annals of the American Academy of Political and Social Science,* **262** (1949), 15–21.

Kuznets, Simon. "Notes on the Pattern of U. S. Economic Growth," in Edgar O. Edwards (ed.). *The Nation's Economic Objectives.* Chicago: Published for William Marsh Rice University by University of Chicago Press, 1964, 15–35.

Landsberger, Hans H., Leonard L. Fishman, and Joseph L. Fisher. *Resources in America's Future.* Baltimore, Md.: Johns Hopkins Press, 1965.

Linder, F. E., and R. D. Grove. *Vital Statistics Rates in the United States, 1900-1941.* Washington, D.C.: U. S. Government Printing Office, 1943.

Ryder, Norman B. "The Reproductive Renaissance North of the Rio Grande," *The Annals of The American Academy of Political and Social Science,* **316** (March 1958), 18–24.

Shryock, Henry S., Jr. "Population Distribution and Population Movements in the United States," in *U. S. National Academy of Sciences—National Research Council. Highway Research Board.* Presented at the 42nd Annual Meeting, January 7-11, 1963, pp. 65–78. Washington, D.C., 1963.

Siegel, Jacob S., et al. "Projections of the Population of the United States, By Age and Sex: 1964-1985, With Extensions to 2010," in *Current Population Reports.* Series P-25. U. S. Bureau of the Census Population Estimates. No. 1. Washington, D.C.: U. S. Government Printing Office, July 1964.

Taeuber, Conrad, and Irene B. Taeuber. *The Changing Population of the United States.* (A volume in the Census Monograph Series.) New York: John Wiley and Sons; London: Chapman and Hall; for the Social Science Research Council in cooperation with the U. S. Department of Commerce Bureau of the Census, 1958.

Taeuber, Irene B. "Migration, Mobility and the Assimilation of the Negro," *Population Bulletin,* **14** (7) November 1958), 127–151.

Taeuber, Irene B. "The Population of the Forty-Ninth State," *Population Index,* **25** (2) (April 1959), 93–113.

Thompson, Warren S., and P. K. Whelpton. *Population Trends in the United States,* New York: McGraw-Hill, 1933.

U. S. Bureau of the Census. *Americans at Mid-Decade,* Series P-23, No. 16, January 1966.

U. S. Bureau of the Census. *A Century of Population Growth in the United States, 1790-1900.* Washington, D. C. Government Printing Office, 1909.

U. S. Bureau of the Census. *Current Population Reports,* "Estimates of the Population of the United States and Components of Change: 1940 to 1966," Series P-25, No. 331, March 22, 1966.

U. S. Bureau of the Census. *Current Population Reports,* "Revised Projections of the Population of the United States by Age and Sex to 1985," in *Current Population Reports,* Series P-25, No. 329, March 10, 1966.

U. S. Bureau of the Census. "Estimates of the Population of the United States and Components of Population Change: 1940 to 1962," in *Current Population Reports.* Series P-25, Population Estimates. Washington, D.C.: U. S. Government Printing Office, No. 331, March, 1966.

U. S. Bureau of the Census. *U. S. Census of Population: 1960. Number of Inhabitants, United States Summary.* Washington, D.C.: U. S. Government Printing Office, 1961.

Yasuba, Yasukichi. *Birth Rates of the White Population of the United States, 1800-1861: An Economic Study.* The Johns Hopkins University Studies in Historical and Political Science. Series 79, No. 2. Baltimore, Md.: The Johns Hopkins University Press, 1962.

CHAPTER 7

Population Composition: The Demographic Variables

7.1. Introduction

In Chapter 1 we divided the field of population study according to three main lines of analysis: the study of population composition, the study of population dynamics, and the study of population distribution. Population composition was subdivided into four parts: demographic, social, household-family, and economic characteristics of the population. In this chapter we begin the study of population composition by focusing on the so-called "demographic traits"—age and sex. These variables are so named because of the very intimate relation they have to the study of population growth. Later chapters will discuss the other aspects of population composition. The age-sex composition of the population at a given instant has a substantial influence on the capacity or potential for population growth in future years. For example, in a population that has an extraordinarily high share of members aged over 45 we would expect low birthrates and high death rates—and slow growth. Similarly, an extraordinarily great preponderance of one sex would tend to result in a lowered fertility and slower growth. Such imbalances also affect the social, family-household, and economic composition of the population, as we shall see.

Thus population composition can be viewed as an active factor that determines or conditions population growth. Yet it is equally valid to regard composition as an *effect*. This is true because the present age-sex composition of the population is greatly influenced by the growth trends of the past and may be said to be in part a residue of past demographic processes.

This twofold relationship, wherein demographic composition is simultaneously a cause and an effect, is quite intricate. In this chapter, therefore, we concentrate on the first point of view and study composition as an active factor, leaving to the chapters on fertility and reproduction a more detailed explanation of the processes that modify composition.

Because age and sex variables are intensively studied by demographers, other social scientists tend to dismiss them as being of lesser importance for anthropological, sociological, or sociopsychological analysis. Actually, this is a mistake. *Almost any measurement that can be taken of human beings or of groups of human beings will show substantial variation by sex and age.* It is essential, therefore, in comprehending almost any social phenomenon to know the population composition in terms of these traits and how other phenomena are related to them. Sex and age composition can and does vary significantly from population to population. Also, the demographic structure of a particular population may change to a surprising extent within only a few years. It is therefore important to know what the typical range of variation is in each of the demographic variables and the conditions that are associated with unusual age and sex composition.

I. AGE COMPOSITION

7.2. Statistics concerning Age Composition

Almost every census in the world collects data on age. Age, of course, is a continuous variable that flows by ever-increasing amounts from

Table 7-1 Estimated Age Composition of the World and of the Industrialized and Developing (Underdeveloped) Regions of the World: 1960

Age group	World	Develop- ing nations	Indus- trial- ized nations	Percent- age point differ- ence	Index of rela- tive compos- ition
Total.................	100.0	100.0	100.0	...	...
0 - 4 years.........	14.2	16.1	9.5	6.6	69
5 - 9 years........	11.9	13.0	9.2	3.8	41
10 - 14 years........	10.7	11.2	9.0	2.2	24
15 - 19 years........	9.6	9.9	8.4	1.5	18
20 - 24 years........	8.5	9.2	7.3	1.9	26
25 - 29 years........	7.5	7.9	6.8	1.1	16
30 - 34 years........	6.9	6.8	7.1	-0.3	- 4
35 - 39 years........	6.2	5.8	7.0	-1.2	- 17
40 - 44 years........	5.4	5.0	6.6	-1.6	- 24
45 - 49 years........	4.7	4.1	6.0	-1.9	- 32
50 - 54 years........	4.0	3.4	5.5	-2.1	- 38
55 - 59 years........	3.3	2.7	4.8	-2.1	- 44
60 - 64 years........	2.6	2.0	4.2	-2.2	- 52
65 - 69 years........	1.9	1.4	3.3	-1.9	- 58
70 - 74 years........	1.3	0.8	2.4	-1.6	- 67
75 - 79 years........	0.8	0.4	1.6	-1.2	- 75
80 - 84 years........	0.4	0.2	0.9	-0.7	- 78
85 and over.....	0.1	0.1	0.4	-0.3	- 75

Source: United Nations. The Future Growth of World Population. Population Studies No. 28. New York: United Nations, 1958. Tables 18-19 pp. 36-37. The industrialized regions are defined as those of Northern America, Europe, Oceania, and U.S.S.R.; the developing regions are defined as those of Africa, Latin America, Asia.

birth until death. It should be reported in terms of completed whole years, or *age at last birthday*. Thus, in a census enumeration that takes place on October 1 of a particular year, a respondent who is aged 31 and due to become 32 on October 2 because it is his next birthday would nevertheless report himself as aged 31. Some older censuses (and a few contemporary surveys and censuses) mistakenly report age to the nearest birthday; this creates analytical difficulties and damages the conception of age as a continuous variable.

Wherever possible, age data should be collected by asking actual date (month and year) of birth and then subtracting from the census date to get actual completed years. If people are asked to report their ages directly, those with less education and those who wish to hide their age tend to give a biased answer or to round their age to the nearest digit ending in 0 or 5 (40, 50, etc.) (Figure 4-1 provides an extreme example of this phenomenon). It is more difficult for them to misrepresent their age if the actual date of birth is requested. However, in populations with a low level of

literacy comparatively few people may know their birth date or may guess at a year of birth with results that are even less reliable than a guess at their ages. In some nations there may be two or even three different calendars in use by the population; there are even cultural differences in the way age is reported. A Chinese infant, for example, is considered to be one year of age at birth according to traditional reckoning and has a birthday at the next New Year. In this way it is possible for an infant only one week old to be recorded as being two years old. The *Manual of Demographic Research Techniques* discusses the deficiencies of age statistics and how they may be adjusted for demographic analysis.

7.3. Age Composition in Developing Nations and in Industrialized Nations

Age composition is most conveniently studied in the form of a percent distribution, in which the total population of all ages is equal to 100 percent and the relative share of the population falling in each age group is expressed as a percent of the total. Table 7-1 illustrates such

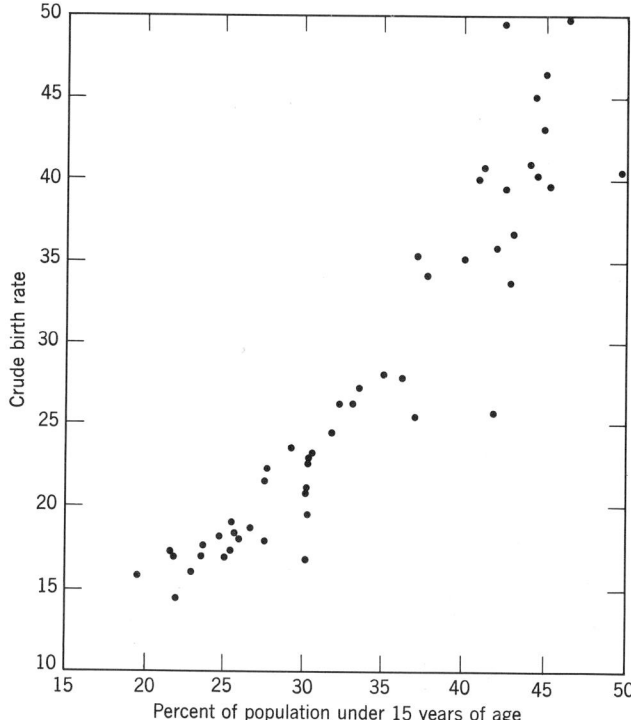

Figure 7-1 Scattergram Showing the Relationship between Age Composition and Fertility; 50 Nations with Reliable Statistics, 1960.

distributions and shows the estimated age composition of the developing and the industrialized nations. In the developing nations more than 40 percent of the population is comprised of children under 15 years of age, whereas in the industrialized nations only slightly more than one fourth of the population falls in this group. At the other extreme, the industrialized nations have substantially more persons in the middle-age and old-age groups. The index of relative composition, in the right-hand column of Table 7-1, shows how great the deviation is.

Despite great differences at the extreme ages, the proportion of the total population in the prime working ages (and the ages of greatest fertility)—20 to 44 years—is almost identical for the two populations:

Industrialized nations	34.8 percent
Developing nations	34.7 percent

This is a characteristic feature of almost all populations: about 35 percent fall in the interval between 20 and 44 years, irrespective of their detailed age composition.

Age Composition and Fertility. As is shown in more detail in later chapters, differences in birthrates are the principal explanation for differences in age composition; nations with high birthrates have young age composition, whereas nations with low birthrates have older age compositions. This relationship is quite consistent and uniform. Figure 7-1 illustrates it. Here the crude birthrate for nations of the world with reliable birth statistics and a good census is plotted against the proportion of the population in the same nation under 15 years of age. Considering that the effect of migration is not controlled, that fertility is measured only in an approximate way, and that there may be errors in the measurement of age (especially in the tendency to undercount young children), the relationship is amazingly consistent.

7.4. Age Composition and the Life Cycle

Age statistics are of fundamental importance in demographic as well as in all social science analysis in that they reflect changes in behavior at various stages of the life cycle. Like other species, man is subject to the processes of bodily growth, maturation to adulthood, slow decline in vigor, and eventual death. This physiological life cycle is paralleled by a rather elaborate set of cultural prescriptions of behavior that are appropriate for each of the physiological stages. Throughout history every society has placed its own interpretation on the social meaning of the life cycle. There is a socially appropriate age at which to leave the parental household, to enter the working force, to end formal schooling, to marry, or to retire from the work force. To a certain extent, the limitations of strength and physical and mental agility determine the social prescriptions. But to a very substantial extent, they are cultural, that is, determined by tradition or administrative rules, and may vary from society to society or from one era to another within the same society. For example, in the United States the normal age for civil servants to retire from government service is about 65, whereas in India it is 55. The cultural differences greatly affect the rate at which a population grows, principally through the age at marriage and the age pattern of childbearing. In some populations very little childbearing takes place after age 35, whereas in other populations it persists at a moderately high level to age 40 or 45.

Because age does have this dual significance of physiological and sociological life cycle patterns, almost any aspect of human behavior may be expected to vary with age. For example, political attitudes of liberalism or conservatism, patterns of expenditure and income, the amount of income received, number and type of group membership and recreational activities, and a wide variety of other behaviors, statuses, and characteristics may be expected to vary with the life cycle, hence with age. For this reason, age is one of the primary factors to be controlled in all branches of research that study the behavior of human beings. Very often it is necessary to consider and control the age factor before the effect of other factors can be assessed.

Many demographers illustrate the life cycle process of aging by use of the *population pyra-* mid. The population pyramid (see Figure 7-2) is constructed by computing a percentage distribution of a population, simultaneously cross-classified by sex and age. The percent that each female age group is of the total is plotted on the right, as in the figure, and the corresponding percents for males are plotted on the left. Sometimes a population pyramid is intended to provide a quick overall comprehension of age structure in a population. A population whose pyramid has a broad base and relatively small shares at the upper ages may be identified as a high-fertility population.

Dr. Paul C. Glick, a leader in the study of the life cycle of the individual and the family, identified the following stages for the family: first marriage, birth of first child, birth of last child, first marriage of last child, and death of one spouse. These events mark major transitions in the family. By calculating the median age at which each of these events takes place in the population, it is possible to specify when each of the stages is reached in the typical family. Glick made these calculations for data covering half a century, to study trends. His major results are charted in Figure 7-3. There has been a long-term trend for first marriage, birth of children, and marriage of children to occur at younger ages, while the breakup of the marriage by the death of one spouse has been advanced to much higher ages.

7.5. Age Composition and the Cohort Principle

Another way of viewing the population pyramid and the life cycle is to think in terms of cohorts. A cohort is a population group that enters on some stage of the life cycle simultaneously, hence may be looked upon as a group of people traveling through life together. For example, 1000 babies all born in the same calendar year are a "birth cohort." Similarly, 1000 couples all married for the first time in the same calendar year are a "marriage cohort," and 1000 mothers who bear their third child in the same year are identified by demographers as a "cohort of third-parity women." Birth cohorts are of special interest to demographers, for by following groups of people through the various stages of the life cycle it is possible to

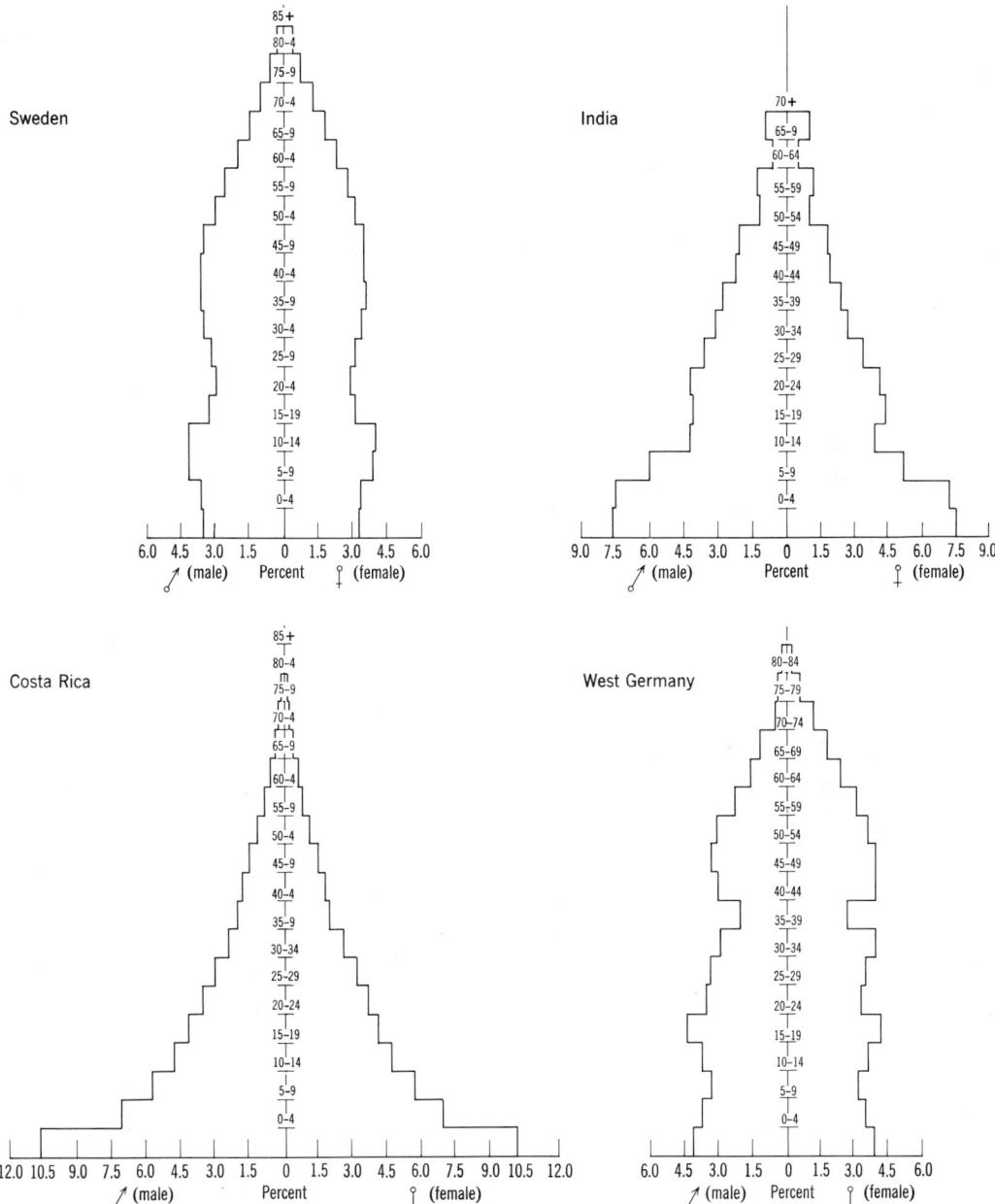

Figure 7-2 Population Pyramids for Selected Nations of the World.

obtain a much clearer picture of the processes involved and of the differences between generations. Various physiological and social forces exert their effect on the cohort at each age. Some members of the group die and disappear from the population. Among those who survive to each age there will emerge a typical pattern of behavior that may be taken to characterize the group. There will be an average amount of schooling completed, an average age at first marriage, an average age at bearing the first child, and so on. Yet some of the members will complete their schooling at a very early age, marry unusually early, or enter the labor force before they are 15 years old. Others may remain in school until age 30 or beyond; some

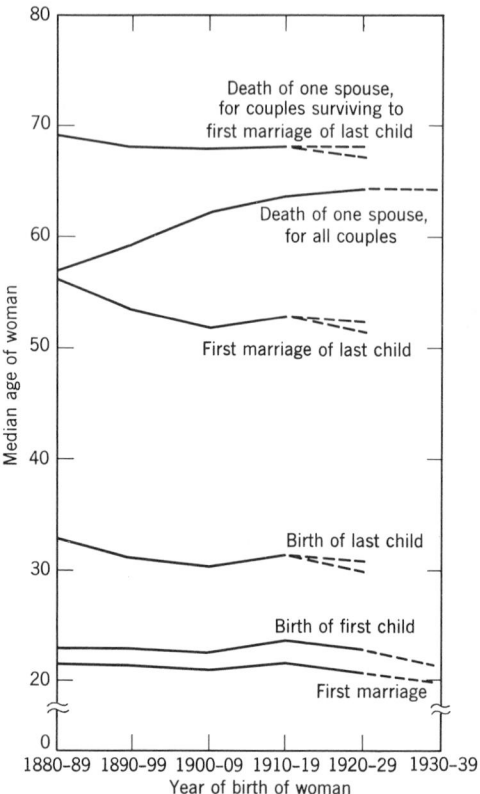

Figure 7-3 Stages of the Family Life Cycle, for Women Born from 1880 to 1939.

SOURCE: Paul C. Glick and Robert Parke, Jr., "New Approaches in Studying the Life Cycle of the Family," *Demography* **2** (1965) p. 189.

is to construct an "hypothetical cohort" based on age statistics for a given instant of time. If we are willing to assume that each age group in the population is behaving generally in a way that is typical of the culturally and biologically prescribed patterns at that particular stage of the life cycle, we are justified in constructing a generalized pattern of the life cycle by piecing together, or linking together, the age patterns for the successive age groups. Thus to find the age pattern for marriage we may take a thousand or a million members of a real, live population at about age 10, when all of them are never-married persons, and follow them through life, noting how many marry at each age, until all have died. By this procedure, we can compute a marriage rate at each age and a proportion of the group that never married. On the other hand, if we are willing to assume that the marriage behavior of each age group in a population at a given year is typical of what would happen if we were to follow a real cohort through time, we are constructing the typical life cycle marriage pattern for a hypothetical cohort.

The study of real cohorts is of substantial significance in interpreting age composition. A sudden rise or fall in the birthrate may produce a correspondingly large or small crop of children in particular calendar years. A war may remove a large proportion of young males in a nation. As the cohorts affected by these events, be they large or small, age through time, they constitute a wave or a trough in the age structure. At successive censuses, this fluctuation will pass into successively older age groups until finally it dies out at the top of the age pyramid. The United States is an excellent example of such a population, having experienced rather violent cohort fluctuations in the recent past. Figure 7-4 shows the number of persons in the United States population at each year of age in 1960. The period of very low fertility in the 1930s is clearly manifested by a sharp trough in the age interval between 30 and 40 in 1960. The subsequent "baby boom" is clearly manifested in the sharply increased number of persons in the younger ages, and the preceding era of high fertility is illustrated by the hump in the

may marry for the first time at age 45, and some may even obtain employment at their first full-time job at about age 35. Thus, although there may be a typical life cycle pattern, there is inevitably a great deal of variation within the population with respect to adherence to this pattern. Demographers are interested as much in the variations, or pattern of distribution through the cycle, as in the average itself.

Demographers are able to study the life cycle through cohort analysis in two ways. (1) They may study *real* cohorts by following groups of actual populations of the same age through time and observing the distribution of events to them. Usually this is a very costly process because of the necessity of keeping a sustained observational watch over the group for many years. (2) The alternative procedure

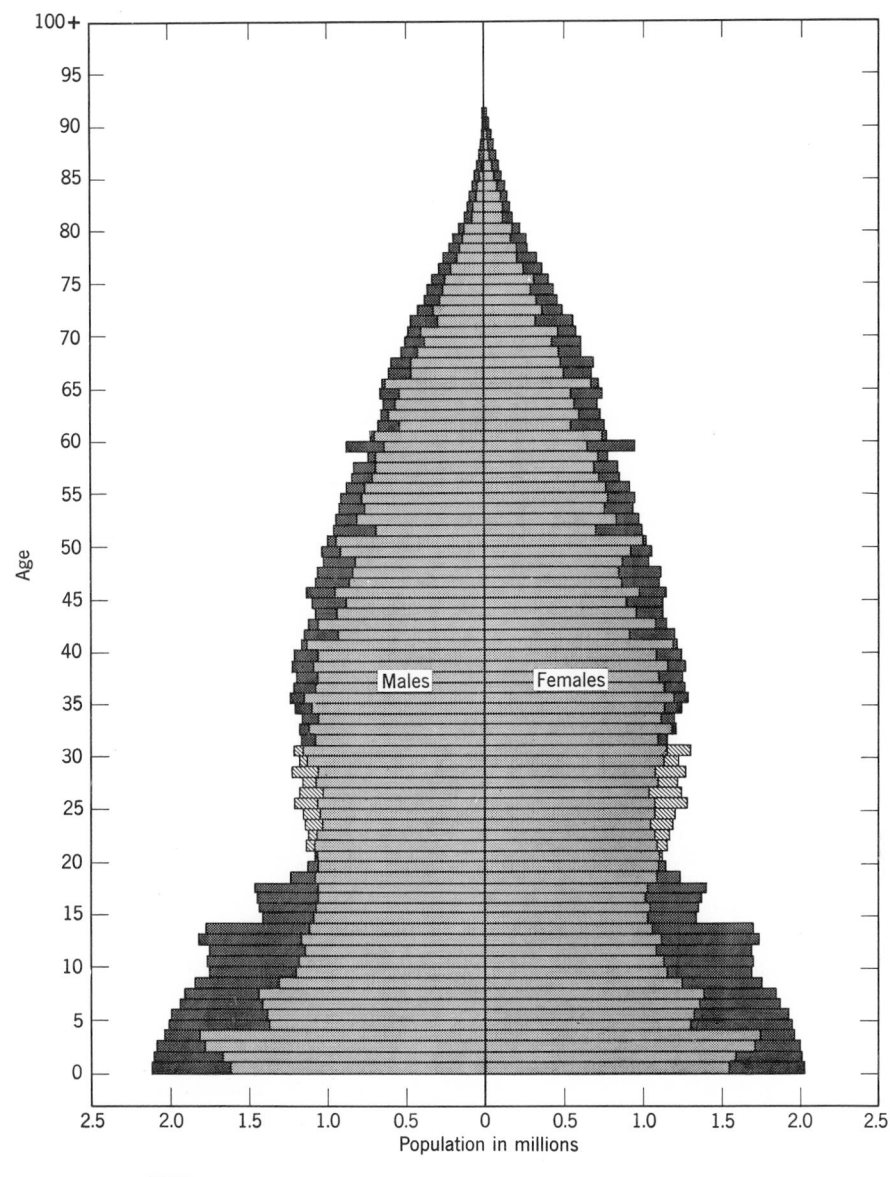

Figure 7-4 Population of the United States, by Single Years of Age and Sex: 1960 and 1950.

SOURCE: U. S. Census of Population: 1960. *Detailed Characteristics, U.S. Summary,* p. xi.

ages above 45. Rather substantial fluctuations of this type may be introduced into the age composition by catastrophes, such as an epidemic that strikes a particular age group of population or a war that kills a large number of young men. Such catastrophes leave a trough in the age structure, which will persist until the generation has died out.

We may generalize the preceding comments to arrive at the following principles, which may prove useful in interpreting age statistics.

1. Whenever birthrates fall, in comparison with a previous level, children constitute a smaller proportion of the total population than formerly. As a result, the population pyramid

has a comparatively smaller base. The base, in fact, may appear smaller than do the older age groups, and the pyramid has a "Christmas tree" effect. A sudden rise in birthrates has the opposite effect on the age pyramid. The proportion of people in the younger age group increases, and the pyramid assumes a much broader appearance at the base.

2. A sudden decline in death rate at any age tends to pass on to the higher age classes a larger proportion of the individuals who have already been born. Where death rates are extremely high, only a very small proportion of the people succeed in attaining the upper rung of the population pyramid. A decline in the death rate enables the pyramid to become broader toward the top. Thus a decline in the death rate at a particular age has the tendency to increase the percentage of population at that age and at all later ages. If death rates rise, the effects on the age composition is reversed.

3. It has already been suggested that the age structure is affected by the survival of persons to the age of reproduction. If death rates are high at the ages of infancy and early childhood, only a small percentage of the population is able to survive to reproduce. Lowering the death rates at the younger ages has the effect of increasing survivorship to the ages of 20 to 45—the reproductive ages—and, as a result, creates an indirect increment to the base of the population pyramid.

4. Migration streams all over the world tend to contain a preponderance of young adults. The effect of migration is to add members to those cohorts that are represented in the migration stream. The typical effect on the population pyramid is to make it fatter in the middle if the migration is inward and to make it lean if there is more out-migration.

By utilizing these principles, it is possible to study the age composition of a population, and to infer some of the fertility, mortality, and migration events over the past several decades. The experienced demographer who has studied the age composition for many different nations over the earth and has observed changes in age composition in many different populations is able to estimate within fairly narrow limits what the general rates of birth, death, and net migration are for a particular population using only data for age composition. His success in doing this depends, of course, on the detail and reliability of the age data at his disposal.

7.6. The Age Composition of the World's Continents

Table 7-2 reports the estimated age composition by 5-year age groups of the population of the various continents and of the United States (right-hand column). The continent of Africa has the youngest age composition, while Europe has the oldest. If we contrast the two in terms of broad age groups, we can observe just how unlike they are:

Age Group	Europe	Africa	Difference
Total	100.0	100.0	
0 to 14 years	25.6	40.9	−15.3
15 to 44 years	42.8	44.8	− 2.0
45 to 64 years	22.1	11.7	10.4
65 years and over	9.5	2.6	6.9

The other continents fall between these extremes, but in two clusters. In one group is the industrialized section of the world—Northern America, the USSR, and Oceania, as well as Europe. In the other group fall Latin America, Asia, and Africa. Asia's population is somewhat younger than that of Latin America, the USSR has a slightly younger age composition than Northern America, and Oceania falls between them.

These statistics point to a very important demographic implication for economic development. The developing nations must carry a tremendous burden of dependency of young persons, although they have a comparative scarcity of older and more experienced members in their labor force.

7.7. The Dependency Ratio

Demographers often employ a simple statistic, the dependency ratio, to measure the impact of age composition on the livelihood activity of the population. It is assumed that the age group 20 to 64 years is the "productive" segment of the population and that youth under

Table 7-2 Estimated Age Composition of the World's Population, by Continents: 1960

Age	World total	Northern America	Latin America	Europe	Asia	Africa	Oceania	U.S.S.R.	United States
All ages........	100.0	100.0	100.0	100.0	100.0	100.0	100.0	100.0	100.0
0 - 4........	14.2	9.4	16.0	8.5	16.2	16.2	10.9	11.3	11.1
5 - 9........	11.9	9.4	13.2	8.5	12.9	13.1	10.3	10.1	10.4
10 - 14........	10.7	9.4	11.4	8.6	11.4	11.6	9.8	9.5	9.4
15 - 19........	9.6	8.3	9.9	8.0	10.2	10.3	8.6	9.2	7.4
20 - 24........	8.5	6.4	8.5	6.9	9.0	9.1	6.9	8.7	6.0
25 - 29........	7.5	5.9	7.3	6.7	7.9	7.9	6.2	8.1	6.1
30 - 34........	6.9	6.5	6.4	7.1	6.8	6.8	6.5	7.5	6.7
35 - 39........	6.2	6.8	5.6	7.2	5.9	5.8	6.5	6.8	7.0
40 - 44........	5.4	6.6	4.9	6.9	5.0	4.9	6.2	6.0	6.5
45 - 49........	4.7	6.2	4.2	6.4	4.1	4.0	5.8	5.3	6.1
50 - 54........	4.0	5.8	3.6	5.9	3.4	3.3	5.3	4.6	5.4
55 - 59........	3.3	5.2	2.9	5.3	2.6	2.5	4.7	3.9	4.7
60 - 64........	2.6	4.5	2.3	4.5	1.9	1.9	4.0	3.1	4.0
65 - 69........	1.9	3.7	1.7	3.6	1.3	1.3	3.2	2.4	3.5
70 - 74........	1.3	2.7	1.1	2.7	0.8	0.8	2.4	1.7	2.6
75 - 79........	0.8	1.8	0.6	1.8	0.4	0.4	1.5	1.1	1.7
80 - 84........	0.4	1.0	0.3	1.0	0.2	0.1	0.8	0.5	0.9
85 years +.....	0.1	0.4	0.1	0.4	0.0	0.0	0.4	0.2	0.5
Index of dissimilarity..		14.0	4.1	15.2	5.2	5.8	10.1	6.3	12.2

Source: United Nations. The Future Growth of World Population, population Studies No. 28. (New York: United Nations, 1958) Table 19, p.37. U.S. Census of Population: 1960, General Population Characteristics, U.S. Summary, Table 45, p. 146.

20 and older persons aged 65 years or over are the "dependent" segment. A rough measure of the dependency load that the productive population must bear is the ratio of the population under 20 and 65 or over to the population 20 to 64, multiplied by 100:

It is important to note that the dependency ratio can be computed *in parts*, one part measuring the dependency load of youth and the other part the dependency load of the aged. This is done by expressing singly each term of the numerator as a ratio of the denominator

$$\text{dependency ratio} = \frac{\text{population under 20 years} + 65 \text{ years and over}}{\text{population 20 to 64 years}} \times 100$$

The ratio purports to measure how many dependents each 100 persons in the productive years must support. This, of course, is only an approximate measure. Not all of the persons between 20 and 64 are actually engaged in breadwinning (especially among females), and a substantial fraction of teen-age and retirement-age persons are economically active. (In the chapter on the working force we shall learn how to compute a more refined measure of the average number of dependents per worker.) Nevertheless, this ratio is highly useful because it requires only age statistics and can therefore be calculated for many nations or parts of nations for which employment statistics are not available. Moreover, it points out fairly precisely the same differences and reports their comparative magnitude in about the same way as does a more refined measure.

and then multiplying by 100. The sum of the youth dependency ratio and the old-age dependency ratio equals the total dependency ratio.

Table 7-3 reports the dependency ratio, by parts, for the world and the continents. According to this measure, there are about 103 "dependents" for each 100 persons in the productive ages. The majority of these are children and youth (94); only a few (9) are in the old-age category.

The industrialized continents have a much lower dependency load than do the developing continents of Asia, Africa, and Latin America. In fact, *the total dependency load of the "underdeveloped" areas is roughly 40 percent greater than that of the industrialized continents. The difference is entirely in the youth portion of the dependency ratio.*

Table 7-3   Estimated Dependency Ratios for the World and the United States Population, by Continents: 1960

Continent	Dependency ratio		
	Total	Youth	Old age
World total.....	103	94	9
Northern America.....	86	68	18
United States........	91	73	18
Latin America........	118	110	8
Europe..............	76	59	17
Asia................	114	108	6
Africa..............	117	111	6
Oceania.............	92	76	16
U. S. S. R..........	85	74	11

Source: Table 7-2.

The industrialized nations are forced to carry a heavier load of old-age dependency than the developing nations because of lower birth and death rates. In the developing areas there are only 6 to 8 older persons per 100 production workers, whereas in the industrialized areas the number is 16 to 18. Yet this is a small price to pay, for the old-age dependency load is very small in comparison with the youth dependency load created by high fertility. Economists sometimes complain about the "economic drag" of the large number of unproductive elderly workers who are retired and living on pensions in the industrialized nations. This drag is quite small in comparison with the drain created by the need to rear large numbers of children to adulthood—especially when there already is a surplus of humanity that cannot be employed effectively under current conditions. Where death rates are high in the early years of life, a large percentage of youths do not survive to make a contribution to the national welfare. The elderly retired worker, living on a social security pension and on income from his lifetime savings, represents the maximum of success in achieving a high level of material comfort. Society at large, which has paid for his education and other expenses of upbringing, succeeds in getting a full lifetime of productive service from him. A sufficiently large amount of his earnings were saved during his working years to permit him to be a small investor. The wastage of needless mortality

during the vigorous working years has been cut to a minimum. The goal of every economic system could well be that of maximizing this condition, while not jeopardizing the long-run ability of the population to maintain its numbers.

Therefore, there is invariably a gain in economic efficiency, in terms of reducing the dependency load, to lower both birthrates and death rates. The minimum dependency load, in the long run, is that obtained when the population is barely replacing itself at the lowest possible combination of mortality and fertility. Population growth always implies a higher dependency load than do stationary numbers. Where a population adopts fertility control, an immediate lessening of the total dependency load results, through a lowering of youth dependency. In fact, there is a temporary situation in which the dependency load is extraordinarily light, for there are fewer children and many adults, but no great increase in the proportion of persons in the older ages. After a few decades of the process of aging, the dependency ratio will rise, assuming that fertility remains low. *It will never rise as high as it was before the fertility reduction, however.* (Theoretically, if birthrates sank far below the replacement level such a situation could develop, but it would be very unlikely to happen in a real population.)

The sharp reader will inquire why the population of Northern America, which generally has higher birthrates, should have as high an old-age dependency load as Europe. This is due in large part to the sudden reaching of retirement age of the several millions of immigrants who came between 1890 and 1915 and to the fact that in the 1930s the American birthrate was nearly as low as those that prevail in Europe today.

7.8.   Age Composition of Nations of the World

Within each major region of the world there is a certain amount of variation in age composition, from nation to nation. Table 7-4 reports statistics of age composition for those nations of the world for which data on age are available. This is shown in two forms: as a percent

Table 7-4 Age Composition of Nations of the World for Which Data are Available

Country	Date of Census	Percent distribution by age						Dependency ratio			Sex ratio
		0–14 years	15–24 years	25–34 years	35–49 years	50–64 years	65 and over	Total	Youth	Old age	
NORTH AFRICA											
Sudan..........	1956	46.7	19.5	13.4	12.3	6.0	2.0	146.4	141.4	5.0	102.2
Tunisia..........	1956	40.8	17.4	13.9	14.7	13.1		...	...	...	98.6
United Arab Republic..........	1960	42.7	15.2	13.7	16.0	8.9	3.5	119.8	112.2	7.6	101.1
TROPICAL & SOUTHERN AFRICA											
Congo (Leopoldville)..........	1955-57	39.4	14.6	18.2	...	...	...	...	...	...	94.4
Gabon..........	1960-61	28.8	13.0	17.1	25.8	11.0	4.3	63.5	56.5	7.0	89.0
Ghana..........	1960	44.5	16.8	16.0	13.4	6.1	3.2	126.0	118.8	7.2	102.2
Guinea..........	1955	42.1	16.6	14.6	16.2	7.1	3.4	111.0	104.1	6.9	90.8
Ivory Coast..........	1961	42.7	...	...	...	...	...	...	...	...	102.7
Madagascar..........	1959	40.0	15.8	15.7	17.4	8.6	3.5	99.1	92.1	7.0	99.4
Mauritius..........	1961	44.4	16.5	13.5	15.0	7.6	3.1	130.1	123.1	7.0	102.2
Reunion..........	1960	44.2	17.8	12.9	14.1	7.5	3.4	130.7	123.0	7.7	95.2
St. Helena..........	1956	43.6	13.9	9.0	14.3	12.2	6.9	148.4	131.2	17.2	92.0
Seychelles..........	1960	38.5	16.0	13.3	15.2	10.7	6.3	113.1	99.7	13.4	96.0
South West Africa..........	1960	39.6	16.4	15.8	15.7	7.3	5.1	113.5	102.6	10.9	101.8
Tanganyika..........	1957	42.5	19.5	15.2	14.3	6.5	2.0	121.0	116.6	4.4	92.6
Togo..........	1958-60	46.9	13.9	14.9	13.9	6.2	4.1	133.5	123.9	9.6	91.9
Uganda..........	1959	41.4	17.5	15.7	16.0	7.3	2.1	110.3	105.9	4.4	100.9
Union of South Africa..........	1960	32.5	16.4	13.4	18.4	12.6	6.7	92.4	79.5	12.9	99.3
Upper Volta..........	1960	40.9	16.4	15.9	16.2	7.2	3.4	109.2	102.1	7.1	100.8
NORTHERN AMERICA											
Bermuda..........	1960	33.4	15.3	15.7	17.9	11.8	5.9	88.6	77.5	11.1	99.2
Canada..........	1961	33.6	14.3	13.7	18.7	11.8	7.7	97.8	82.7	15.1	102.2
Greenland..........	1955	42.8	18.4	15.2	13.9	7.3	2.4	120.4	115.2	5.2	100.1
St. Pierre & Miquelon..........	1962	32.6	16.6	13.3	17.2	13.2	7.1	93.8	80.1	13.7	95.7
United States..........	1961	31.4	13.7	12.3	19.3	14.0	9.3	92.8	74.9	17.9	97.7
MIDDLE AMERICA											
Barbados..........	1961	37.2	17.8	11.7	15.1	12.7	5.4	108.4	97.1	11.3	84.9
Costa Rica..........	1960	46.4	17.8	13.5	12.7	6.9	2.7	141.5	134.9	6.6	100.4
Dominica..........	1960	44.7	16.4	10.6	13.2	9.5	5.5	144.7	131.2	13.5	88.7
Dominican Republic..........	1960	44.6	20.6	12.9	12.7	6.3	2.9	138.6	131.7	6.9	102.0
El Salvador..........	1961	44.8	17.9	13.1	13.6	7.3	3.3	135.8	128.1	7.7	97.2
Granada..........	1960	47.7	15.8	10.5	11.8	9.0	5.2	160.8	147.2	13.6	84.7
Guadeloupe..........	1960	41.8	17.2	13.0	14.9	8.6	4.5	124.5	114.5	10.0	96.5
Honduras..........	1961	48.1	18.1	12.7	12.2	6.4	2.6	153.4	146.8	6.6	99.1
Jamaica..........	1960	41.2	16.8	12.7	15.5	9.5	4.3	119.7	110.2	9.5	92.5
Martinique..........	1960	42.6	14.5	13.2	15.5	9.4	4.8	123.6	113.0	10.6	93.7
Mexico..........	1960	44.4	18.6	13.1	13.0	7.5	3.4	138.0	129.8	8.2	99.5
Montserrat..........	1960	42.7	16.8	7.5	12.4	12.4	8.2	161.1	139.7	21.4	80.0

Table 7-4 (Continued)

Country	Date of Census	Percent distribution by age						Dependency ratio			Sex ratio
		0-14 years	15-24 years	25-34 years	35-49 years	50-64 years	65 and over	Total	Youth	Old age	
MIDDLE AMERICA (continued)											
Netherlands Antilles..........	1960	41.4	15.8	12.7	15.3	9.9	4.8	121.6	110.8	10.8	97.0
Nicaragua....................	1961	44.5	18.8	13.4	13.1	6.9	3.3	138.4	130.6	7.8	100.2
Panama......................	1962	43.3	18.4	13.1	14.3	7.3	3.6	132.3	123.9	8.4	103.0
Puerto Rico.................	1960	42.7	17.8	11.2	14.6	8.5	5.2	140.4	127.9	12.5	98.0
St. Kitts Nevis & Anguilla..	1960	45.7	14.9	9.9	14.3	10.1	5.0	147.7	135.3	12.4	85.6
St. Lucia...................	1960	44.2	17.5	11.2	13.8	8.4	4.8	143.0	131.4	11.6	89.6
St. Vincent.................	1960	49.2	16.7	10.4	11.8	7.7	4.2	166.7	155.4	11.3	88.6
Trinidad & Tobago...........	1960	42.4	17.6	12.3	15.2	8.3	4.1	128.5	119.2	9.3	98.8
Virgin Islands (U.S.).......	1960	39.8	16.0	12.0	15.6	9.6	6.9	126.7	111.1	15.6	98.5
Virgin Islands (U.K.).......	1960	47.9	15.9	9.9	12.6	8.0	5.7	170.2	154.8	15.4	98.5
SOUTH AMERICA											
Argentina...................	1961	29.9	16.7	16.5	19.2	12.5	5.2	77.0	67.8	9.2	102.9
British Guiana..............	1960	46.3	16.8	12.2	13.5	7.9	3.4	143.2	135.0	8.2	99.3
Chile.......................	1960	39.8	18.0	13.6	15.2	9.2	4.3	116.1	106.9	9.2	96.3
Ecuador.....................	1962	45.1	18.0	13.3	13.1	7.2	3.3	138.3	130.5	7.8	100.9
Paraguay....................	1960	38.5	21.3	14.5	14.0	7.3	4.2	118.8	109.6	9.2	95.3
Peru........................	1961	43.5	18.1	13.7	13.3	7.5	3.9	133.6	124.6	9.0	97.8
Venezuela...................	1961	44.8	17.6	14.1	13.7	7.0	2.8	132.6	126.2	6.4	103.3
SOUTH WEST ASIA											
Cyprus......................	1960	36.7	16.5	13.2	15.8	11.9	5.9	103.8	91.7	12.1	96.7
Iran........................	1956	42.2	15.4	15.3	14.4	8.7	4.0	115.7	107.1	8.6	103.6
Iraq........................	1957	44.9	14.2	13.4	13.3	9.1	5.1	137.7	125.5	12.2	101.0
Israel......................	1961	36.1	15.0	13.0	17.6	13.0	5.2	97.9	87.6	10.3	103.0
Kuwait......................	1957	31.3	21.7	22.2	15.4	6.4	3.0	74.5	70.3	4.2	176.5
Turkey......................	1960	41.3	16.7	15.7	12.9	9.9	3.7	113.9	106.1	7.8	104.6
SOUTH CENTRAL ASIA											
Ceylon......................	1955	40.7	18.4	15.0	16.4	7.6	1.9	109.4	105.4	4.0	110.6
India.......................	1961	41.0	16.7	15.4	15.1	8.7	3.1	109.6	103.1	6.5	106.3
Pakistan....................	1961	44.5	15.9	14.2	13.8	11.6		...	....	...	111.1
SOUTH EAST ASIA											
Brunei......................	1960	46.6	15.6	13.8	13.7	7.6	2.8	133.6	127.0	6.6	108.6
Cambodia....................	1959	44.6	18.0	13.5	14.1	7.6	2.3	131.2	125.9	5.3	99.8
Federation of Malaya........	1957	43.8	18.0	12.9	14.4	8.0	2.8	129.1	122.8	6.3	106.5
North Borneo................	1960	43.5	16.8	15.5	15.4	6.5	2.2	118.6	113.8	4.8	108.6
Philippines.................	1960	45.7	19.5	13.0	13.1	6.0	2.7	142.8	136.2	6.6	101.8
Sarawak.....................	1960	44.5	16.2	13.6	14.7	8.0	3.0	129.5	122.6	6.9	101.9
Singapore...................	1957	42.8	17.6	13.9	15.6	7.9	2.1	119.0	114.3	4.7	111.6
Thailand....................	1960	43.2	18.8	14.6	13.3	7.3	2.8	124.8	118.5	6.3	100.4

Table 7-4 (Continued)

Country	Date of Census	Percent distribution by age						Dependency ratio			Sex ratio
		0-14 years	15-24 years	25-34 years	35-49 years	50-64 years	65 and over	Total	Youth	Old age	
EAST ASIA											
China (Taiwan)	1961	45.6	15.5	14.2	14.8	7.4	2.5	130.5	124.8	5.7	105.0
Hong Kong	1961	40.8	11.8	16.5	19.4	8.8	2.8	95.5	90.0	5.5	105.8
Japan	1962	28.6	18.9	16.9	17.6	11.9	6.0	79.6	68.9	10.7	96.5
South Korea	1960	41.5	17.7	13.4	14.8	8.7	3.9	123.6	114.9	8.7	96.3
Macau	1960	40.3	12.7	12.5	18.1	11.0	5.3	110.8	99.5	11.3	98.2
Mongolia	1956	30.4	17.1	14.5	18.4	10.4	9.2	94.5	76.5	18.0	98.8
Ryukyu Islands	1960	41.6	16.3	14.5	13.4	8.8	5.5	122.9	110.7	12.2	91.9
NORTHERN AND WESTERN EUROPE											
Belgium	1960	23.6	12.2	13.9	19.3	19.1	12.0	70.8	50.4	20.4	96.2
Denmark	1960	25.2	14.9	12.3	20.0	16.9	10.6	78.9	60.0	18.9	98.4
Finland	1960	30.1	15.4	13.4	18.5	15.1	7.4	84.8	71.2	13.6	93.0
France	1961	25.4	12.9	14.1	17.7	17.7	12.1	79.6	57.8	21.8	94.7
Iceland	1960	34.8	14.7	13.6	16.7	12.1	8.1	103.9	87.5	16.4	102.1
Ireland	1956	30.0	14.2	11.9	18.6	14.3	10.9	96.0	74.6	21.4	102.0
Luxembourg	1959	19.5	13.0	16.6	21.1	19.3	10.5	56.7	40.3	16.4	103.0
Netherlands	1961	29.7	15.4	13.1	18.2	14.5	9.1	89.2	71.9	17.3	99.2
Norway	1960	25.9	13.0	12.1	21.2	16.9	10.9	78.4	58.9	19.5	99.3
Scotland	1961	25.5	14.1	13.1	19.4	17.5	10.4	76.1	57.7	18.4	93.7
Sweden	1961	21.9	14.4	12.0	21.2	18.5	11.9	72.4	51.8	20.6	99.6
England and Wales	1961	22.9	13.3	12.6	20.6	18.7	11.9	71.7	51.2	20.5	94.2
CENTRAL EUROPE											
Czechoslovakia	1961	27.3	14.1	13.6	18.5	17.8	8.8	77.8	62.2	15.6	95.2
West Germany	1960	21.7	16.0	13.7	18.6	19.5	10.6	65.5	48.0	17.5	89.3
Hungary	1961	25.1	14.4	14.4	19.3	17.6	9.3	71.9	56.0	15.9	93.3
Poland	1960	34.3	12.3	15.6	17.3	14.5	6.0	86.0	74.9	11.1	90.0
Switzerland	1961	23.3	15.5	14.8	19.1	16.9	10.3	71.2	53.5	17.7	96.9
SOUTHERN EUROPE											
Bulgaria	1961	25.8	14.9	16.4	19.9	15.3	7.7	69.9	56.8	13.1	99.7
Gibraltar	1961	25.0	13.4	14.4	22.1	16.6	8.5	67.0	52.9	14.1	92.0
Greece	1961	26.7	16.0	17.2	17.6	14.4	8.2	73.1	58.9	14.2	95.7
Italy	1960	24.7	15.4	15.7	19.4	15.6	9.2	70.0	54.4	15.6	96.1
Malta and Gozo	1961	36.0	16.3	12.5	15.3	12.6	7.2	112.8	97.4	15.4	91.4
Portugal	1960	29.0	16.4	15.6	18.1	13.2	7.6	81.1	67.4	13.7	92.8
Romania	1956	27.0	18.2	16.8	17.7	13.4	6.4	75.3	64.1	11.2	94.6
Spain	1960	27.4	15.2	15.7	19.0	14.4	8.2	77.2	62.6	14.6	94.2
Yugoslavia	1961	31.5	16.0	17.2	15.7	13.6	6.1	81.8	70.8	11.0	94.9

Table 7-4 (Continued)

Country	Date of Census	Percent distribution by age						Dependency ratio			Sex ratio
		0-14 years	15-24 years	25-34 years	35-49 years	50-64 years	65 and over	Total	Youth	Old age	
OCEANIA											
American Samoa...........	1960	49.6	18.1	11.3	12.6	5.7	2.7	171.6	164.3	7.3	102.8
Australia................	1960	30.1	14.0	13.6	20.1	13.6	8.5	85.4	69.7	15.7	102.2
British Solomon Islands..	1959	44.3	18.4	14.8	12.9	9.6		....	....	...	111.9
Cook Islands.............	1961	48.6	17.8	11.7	12.1	6.8	3.0	159.0	151.1	7.9	105.9
Fiji Islands.............	1961	45.2	19.3	13.4	12.9	6.1	3.2	143.2	135.5	7.7	105.6
Guam....................	1960	40.6	17.5	18.2	16.7	5.4	1.6	98.8	95.6	3.2	140.9
New Caledonia...........	1956	36.5	17.6	14.5	18.2	9.4	3.8	98.8	91.3	7.5	111.2
New Zealand.............	1960	32.8	14.1	12.8	18.4	13.2	8.7	96.9	79.9	17.0	101.0
Niue....................	1961	47.7	15.5	10.8	12.2	8.8	5.1	152.3	139.5	12.8	93.9
Pacific Islands.........	1958	44.0	14.8	12.9	14.8	8.7	4.7	128.9	118.2	10.7	106.3
Tokelau Islands.........	1961	46.0	14.6	12.8	13.3	8.7	4.6	141.9	130.8	11.1	87.8
Tonga Islands...........	1956	44.0	19.4	14.0	12.2	6.8	3.7	139.6	130.8	8.8	103.7
Western Samoa...........	1961	50.2	17.6	12.3	11.5	5.6	2.7	167.5	160.2	7.3	105.6

Source: United Nations, Demography Yearbook, 1965, 1964, 1963, 1962.

distribution in terms of six broad age groups and as the dependency ratio with its two components of youth and old age. Although the data are not reliable in all cases, the following places appear to have the youngest age composition among the nations of the world:

Country	Percent of population under 15 years of age
Western Samoa	50.2
American Samoa	49.6
St. Vincent	49.2
Cook Islands	48.6
Honduras	48.1
Virgin Islands (U.K.)	47.9
Niue	47.7
Grenada	47.7
Sudan	46.7
Brunei	46.6
Costa Rica	46.4
British Guiana	46.3
Tokelau Islands	46.0
St. Kitts, Nevis, and Anguilla	45.7
China (Taiwan)	45.6
Fiji Islands	45.2

In all of these countries, one half or more of the population is 16 or 17 years of age or younger. In all of them the dependency load is very heavy; there is an average of 1.5 dependents or more per adult. Almost all of this very high dependency is due to the very large number of children; old-age dependency comprises a very small part of the total dependency. This condition, of course, is the direct result of very high birthrates.

In contrast with the above are the nations of the world with the oldest average-age composition. In the following countries, at least 1 person in 10 is at the age of retirement or older.

Country	Percent of population 65 years old or over
France	12.1
Belgium	12.0
England and Wales	11.9
Sweden	11.9
Norway	10.9
Ireland	10.9
Denmark	10.6
West Germany	10.6
Luxembourg	10.5
Scotland	10.4
Switzerland	10.3

These are the nations of the world where birthrates have fallen to their lowest point and have remained there for a prolonged time, while death rates have also been lowered to their lowest possible point.

Despite the fact that nearly 1 person in 8 in France, Belgium, England, and Sweden is of retirement age, the total dependency load of these nations is far less than that of the first group with young populations. In fact, their dependency ratios are among the very lowest in the world. Only a few places with highly unusual age compositions distorted by war and migration have lower dependency ratios than they.

The situation with respect to dependency can be made clear if we compare the dependency pattern of two nations, taken from near the center of each array:

Dependency ratio total	Honduras	Norway	Difference
	153	78	−75
Youth	147	59	−88
Old age	6	20	14

Even though the dependency load for old age in Norway is more than two times greater than it is in Honduras, the total dependency load of Norway is only about one-half that of Honduras. This illustrates once again the comparative advantage of fertility reduction to any nation that wishes to minimize the ratio of dependents to workers in its population.

All of the remaining nations of the world are arrayed between these two extremes, their rank corresponding rather closely to their level of fertility. The pattern of distribution by age is rather monotonously uniform. The only cases that are really interesting, from a demographic point of view, are nations where there has been a recent, sudden decline in fertility. Among such nations are Japan, Bulgaria, Portugal, Italy, Romania, and Spain. In these nations the proportion of the population that is 15 to 44 is higher than would be expected on the basis of current fertility levels alone.

Another group of nations that are of demographic interest are those that have experienced severe out-migration or heavy in-migration. The former tend to have a deficit of persons in the central ages, while the latter tend to have a comparative surplus of persons in such ages. Ireland is a country from which there is very steady out-migration to other parts of Europe and the world. Australia, on the other hand, is an example of a nation that has a substantial amount of immigration. If we compare their age composition, we obtain the following results:

Age	Ireland	Australia	Difference
Total	100.0	100.0	0.0
Under 15 years	30.0	30.1	+0.1
15 to 24 years	14.2	14.0	−0.2
25 to 34 years	11.9	13.6	+1.7
35 to 49 years	18.6	20.1	+1.5
50 to 64 years	14.3	13.6	−0.7
65 years and over	10.9	8.5	−2.4

The effect of immigration is to decrease the proportion of the population in the vigorous adult ages in the areas of origin and to increase the proportion in these ages at the area of destination.

This brief introduction to world age composition should make it clear that it is of utmost importance for economic planning to understand the problem of age dependency and its intimate relationship to other demographic processes, especially fertility. Good age data for a nation can assist greatly in measuring the current level of fertility, mortality, and migration. Age data, when cross-tabulated by other population characteristics, can assist in the discovery of the life-cycle pattern of other events and statuses, such as marriage, school attendance, and labor force participation.

7.9. The Age Composition of the United States in Comparison with the World

At the present moment the United States has one of the most extraordinary age compositions in the world. Moreover, it has undergone a very great transformation in the past two decades. A glance at Figure 7-4 (a population pyramid by single years of age as of 1950 and 1960) will verify these statements. Because of the long historic decline in fertility, described in Chapter 6, the pyramid is long and narrow at the top, showing that there is a large elderly

population above retirement years. The very sharp decline in fertility, which took place in the 1920s and 1930s, causes the pyramid to be constricted in the age group 20 to 35. Finally, the "baby boom," which reversed this fertility restriction trend, has caused the base of the pyramid to broaden suddenly. Never in the history of the world has a nation acquired such a distorted age distribution as a result of fluctuations in fertility. Only a devastating war or wholesale migration has been known to cause greater deviations. Distortions of this type can arise only where knowledge of fertility control is widely dispersed throughout the population and this knowledge is used or not used in response to changing social and economic climates.

Utilizing the principles of cohort analysis, it should be evident that the population of the United States is destined to have an hourglass shape for several decades to come. The constricted middle portion will rise gradually higher at each succeeding census. For example, in 1970 the maximum constriction will occur at about 37 years, in 1980 it will be at 47 years, in 1990 at 57 years, and so on until it passes out of the picture at the very peak. Meanwhile, if the recent high fertility had continued the 1960 broad base would have risen higher and higher. However, it now appears that birthrates are taking another sharp readjustive downward trend, as in the late 1920s. As a result, at the 1970 census the pyramid will exhibit a second constriction, below the first, so that the pyramid will have a definitely wavy appearance.

The net effect of the recent fluctuations in the American birthrate has been to increase the dependency load for youth and to cause the dependency load for old age to stabilize or decline. Table 7-5 reports the dependency ratios for the United States from 1820 to 1980.

Table 7-5 Trend in the Dependency Ratio for the United States: 1820 to 1960, with Estimates to 1980

Year	Dependency ratio		
	Total	Youth	Old Age
1980 (est)...	94.5	75.2	19.4
1970 (est)...	94.3	75.7	18.6
1960........	91.2	73.6	17.7
1950........	72.7	58.5	14.2
1940........	70.4	58.6	11.8
1930........	79.1	69.4	9.7
1920........	83.5	74.9	8.6
1910........	86.2	78.2	8.0
1900........	94.2	86.2	8.0
1890........	100.0	92.2	7.8
1880........	106.2	99.2	7.0
1870........	111.4	105.1	6.3
1860........	117.2	111.3	5.9
1850........	122.4	116.7	5.8
1840........	133.1	127.3	5.8
1820........	153.4	146.6	6.8

Changing Age Structure of the United States in Terms of the Life Cycle. Let us specify the stages of the life cycle as it seems to exist in the American culture and trace the changing age structure of the United States population since 1880 in terms of it. In Table 7-6 the life-

span has been subdivided into four major stages, each with two or more subdivisions. Each stage is identified by an interval of years that represents average conditions as they exist now. We have arbitrarily imposed these definitions on all of the censuses since 1880, despite the fact that children may have been considered to have become adult at a somewhat earlier age then than they are now. The data of Table 7-6 permit us to gain a much more detailed picture of the changing age structure of the nation than would be possible with the dependency ratios.

In 1960, about 20 percent of the United States population was comprised of children; not quite 10 percent consisted of people in their old age; slightly more than one half were adults; and about one sixth were youths. From 1880 until 1940 there was a steady decline in the proportion of the population at the younger ages. This was associated with the steady fall in fertility and the falling death rate that allowed larger proportions of the population to rise higher in the age pyramid. This fall in the proportion of children was compensated for by a steady increase in the proportion of people in adulthood and old age. Immigration from abroad, comprised primarily of younger

Table 7-6 Age Composition of the United States Population in Terms of the Life Cycle: 1950 (Statistics for 1950 Based on a 20 Percent Sample)

Stages in the life cycle	Age span (years)	Percent distribution								
		1960	1950	1940	1930	1920	1910	1900	1890	1880
All ages..........	...	100.0	100.0	100.0	100.0	100.0	100.0	100.0	100.0	100.0
Childhood............	0–8	19.8	18.0	14.4	17.5	19.7	20.2	21.6	22.1	24.4
Infancy............	Under 1	2.3	2.1	1.5	1.8	2.1	2.4	2.5	2.5	2.9
Early childhood.....	1–5	11.3	10.5	8.1	9.6	11.0	11.4	11.9	12.2	13.6
Late childhood......	6–8	6.2	5.4	4.8	6.2	6.5	6.4	7.1	7.4	7.9
Youth................	9–17	16.0	13.2	16.1	17.5	17.5	17.7	18.8	19.7	19.4
Preadolescence......	9–11	5.8	4.6	5.1	6.0	6.1	5.9	6.6	6.6	7.0
Early adolescence...	12–14	5.5	4.4	5.5	5.8	6.0	6.0	6.2	6.8	6.7
Late adolescence....	15–17	4.7	4.2	5.6	5.7	5.4	5.8	6.0	6.3	5.7
Adulthood............	18–64	55.0	60.6	62.5	59.5	58.0	57.6	55.3	54.1	52.8
Early maturity......	18–24	8.7	10.5	12.6	12.6	12.3	13.9	13.6	14.1	14.4
Maturity...........	25–44	26.2	29.9	30.1	29.4	29.6	29.2	28.0	26.9	25.8
Middle age..........	45–64	20.1	20.2	19.8	17.4	16.1	14.6	13.7	13.1	12.6
Old age..............	65–over	9.2	8.2	6.8	5.4	4.7	4.3	4.1	3.8	3.4
Early old age.......	65–74	6.1	5.6	4.8	3.9	3.3	3.0	2.9	2.7	2.4
Advanced old age....	75–over	3.1	2.6	2.0	1.5	1.4	1.2	1.2	1.1	1.0
Not reported.........	...	...	...	...	0.1	0.1	0.2	0.3	0.3	...

Source: Compiled from U. S. Census of Population: 1960.

adults, helped to swell the percentage of persons between the ages of 18 and 64. The percentage of population at the oldest ages increased steadily, thanks to progress in medicine and public health, as well as to an aging effect as the larger cohorts born in the 1920s or earlier are passing into the upper age brackets.

The "baby boom" of 1946-1957 reversed this trend, so that by 1960 the proportion of population in the childhood ages was very nearly the same as it had been in 1910. Sometime about 1980 or 1990 the percentage of population in the old-age group should decline substantially as the small cohorts of children born in the 1930s reach retirement age.

Some demographers may think that it is too much work to construct tables reflecting the life cycle as precisely as has been done in Table 7-6. It should be kept in mind, however, that by appropriate methods of interpolation it is possible to construct a table such as this for almost any nation in the world. It is our opinion that if age data throughout the world were grouped by categories such as these, especially for cross-tabulations of social and economic characteristics, the significance of the age variable would be more widely appreciated.

7.10. Long-Term Trends in Age Composition

Age data from several censuses are available for only a comparatively few nations of the earth, and these are concentrated largely in Europe and North America. Sufficient data are available from other countries of the world, however, to permit us to state rather dogmatically that the age composition of a population tends to remain comparatively unchanged so long as its fertility rates and migration rates remain unchanged. If the fertility rate falls, the base of the population pyramid tends to shrink, and the proportion of population in the younger ages tends to decline. If, for any reason, there is a reversal in the birthrate and an increase occurs, the reverse happens, as has just been noted for the United States. The long-term trend in age composition for most nations of Europe and the United States and Canada therefore has been one of a rather steady decline in the percentage of population below age 20 (until the interruption of the

"baby boom") and a corresponding increase in the percentages in the adult years and the years of old age. In nations where there has been prolonged high fertility the trend has been one of a continuous young age composition, with 40 percent or more of the population being under 15 years of age.

7.11. Urban-Rural Differences in Age Composition

In general, urban populations tend to have an older age composition than rural populations. Although there are exceptions, this is the general situation in most countries of the world. This is due in large part to the fertility factor: rural populations tend to have higher fertility rates than urban populations. But it is also affected by migration. The current trend toward out-migration from rural areas into urban areas tends to remove young adults and add them to the urban population. This exchange may tend to lower the average age of the rural population and raise the average age of the urban population. Table 7-7 illustrates this combination of circumstances for the United States population. There is also some evidence that urban centers become collecting points for older persons who are disabled, retired, or in poor health. Apparently, many people who are physically unable to participate in the rural economy tend to move to the urban centers where they can obtain medical care, secure employment that requires less physical activity, or withdraw from the labor force and enjoy life to the extent permitted by their physical condition. For example, it is well known that widows tend to move to villages or cities from farm areas shortly after they lose their farmer-husbands.

7.12. Regional Differences in Age Composition

Within a given country, there tend to be regional differences in age composition. As in the case of urban-rural differences, the two most important factors are the regional differences in fertility and regional differences in the pattern of net in- or out-migration. A region that has a high level of fertility will tend to have a young age composition. A region that is

Table 7-7 Age Composition of the Urban and Rural Population of the United States and of the South by Color

Age and color	U. S. total	Urban-rural residence			The South		
		Urban	Rural-nonfarm	Rural-farm	Total	Urban	Rural
Total.........	100.0	100.0	100.0	100.0	100.0	100.0	100.0
0 - 14 years...	31.1	30.0	40.0	32.5	32.6	33.6	31.7
15 - 34 years...	26.2	26.4	26.7	22.7	27.3	27.4	27.1
35 - 49 years...	19.6	20.0	18.1	18.9	18.7	18.5	18.9
50 - 64 years...	14.2	14.4	12.4	16.4	13.1	12.8	13.4
65 and over.....	9.1	9.1	8.8	9.4	8.3	7.7	8.9
White.........	100.0	100.0	100.0	100.0	100.0	100.0	100.0
0 - 14 years...	31.0	29.3	33.0	31.0	31.9	32.1	31.6
15 - 34 years...	26.4	26.1	26.7	22.4	26.9	27.5	26.4
35 - 49 years...	18.7	20.2	18.4	19.7	18.4	18.1	18.8
50 - 64 years...	14.5	14.8	12.8	17.2	13.7	13.5	13.8
65 and over.....	9.4	9.4	9.1	9.8	9.0	8.7	9.3
Nonwhite......	100.0	100.0	100.0	100.0	100.0	100.0	100.0
0 - 14 years...	37.5	35.0	40.3	44.4	39.3	40.6	38.0
15 - 34 years...	27.4	28.3	27.0	24.7	26.4	26.0	26.7
35 - 49 years...	17.5	19.3	14.6	13.6	16.2	15.7	16.8
50 - 64 years...	11.5	11.7	10.7	11.1	11.2	11.0	11.4
65 and over.....	6.1	5.7	7.4	6.2	6.9	6.6	7.1

Source: U.S. Census of Population: 1960, United States Summary, Tables 52 and 65.

experiencing a high rate of out-migration will tend to have a deficit of persons aged 15-34. A region that has a low birthrate, or is experiencing a substantial amount of net immigration of adults, will tend to have a deficit at ages 0-14 and a surplus at older ages. Very often these regional differences are associated with differences in urban-rural composition of the regions. Thus the more urbanized regions tend to have a deficit of children and the more rural regions tend to have a surplus. This pattern of regional differences has persisted for many decades in the South of the United States, which has tended to have a younger population, while the regions of the Northeast, North Center, and West have had an older age composition. Table 7-7 illustrates these differences for 1960.

Regional differences in age composition may be expected to be minimal in those countries where interregional differences in fertility are small and where there is comparatively little interregional migration. Both of these situations tend to characterize many of the countries undergoing economic development, with the result that there is a much more uniform age composition than is found in many regions of nations of Europe and North America. If one studies trends in regional differences in age composition, over time, he will find that for

most industrialized nations the regional differences tend to converge toward the national average. This is an indirect reflection of the fact that interregional differences in fertility have tended to diminish as urban-rural differences in fertility have declined.

II. SEX COMPOSITION

7.13. Demographic and Social Significance of Sex Composition

In most populations the numbers of males and females tend to be nearly equal, with males outnumbering the females at the younger ages and females outnumbering the males at the older ages. From the demographic point of view a situation of near equality assures that each sex has an adequate supply of mates so that the population can replenish its losses from mortality. It does appear to be true that social, economic, and community life are affected in many ways by large imbalances in sex composition, but large imbalances tend to be unusual and temporary. Where a war has removed a large proportion of the males, leaving large numbers of adult women with no eligible mates, or where a new region is being first settled, as the American West, large sex imbalances do exist and influence profoundly the nature of the society. One of the most obvious effects is that normal family life is impossible for a substantial proportion of the adults, with the result that a great deal of deviant behavior with respect to sex, recreation, and community life occurs. Where the supply of one sex is scarce, occupations that traditionally are filled by persons of the sex in short supply are filled by persons of the sex in surplus. But most nations of the earth do not have sufficiently large sex imbalances to bring about such problems; where they do occur, they tend to be removed by the passing of generations. However, sex imbalances often are found in particular communities, or even in particular neighborhoods of a community, so that the problem is more often a local than a national one. One of the outstanding examples of a massive sex imbalance in modern times has been Germany, which suffered severe military losses in two world wars. (To the extent that modern warfare destroys whole populations rather than military installations it does not have the marked effect on sex composition that it formerly had.) There seems to be little correlation between the sex composition of a population and its "national character." Nations that appear to extol virility and tend to be highly aggressive in their relations with their neighbors and those that appear to be more effeminate do not differ significantly in their sex compositions.

7.14. The Sex Ratio as a Measure of Sex Composition

Demographers have two methods of expressing sex composition:

1. Percent of population that is male (or female).

2. The sex ratio—number of males per 100 (or per 1000) females. A sex ratio of 100 means equality of the sexes, a sex ratio above 100 indicates a larger number of males than of females, and a sex ratio below 100 indicates a majority of females. The sex ratio can be computed for any subgroup of the population. The sex ratio is used more often than percent male, although the latter is a much better measure for use in correlation and regression analysis.

The sex composition of a population is determined by three factors:

1. Ratio among infants at time of birth.

2. Differences between the sexes in death rates.

3. Differences between the sexes in net migration rates.

Sex Ratio at Birth. The sex ratio among newborn infants is about 105 or 106. This means that there is a slight preponderance of males over females at the start of life. This seems to be a tendency among all human populations. Although one frequently hears claims that particular populations have sex ratios at birth that are much higher than this, or lower, it is difficult to establish that such differences exist or that if they do exist they are due to genetic factors. If there is a tendency to register the birth of male infants and to neglect to register the birth of female infants, the official statistics could show an exaggerated sex ratio at birth. It is also known that a disproportionately high percentage of male fetuses are miscarried or stillborn, so that a population in a poor nutritional state or in poor health may be expected to have a lower sex ratio at birth, other things being equal. The sex ratio at birth among the American Negro population is about 103, and it is not yet known whether this lower ratio is due to differences in level of living or to other factors.

Sex Composition and Mortality. A later chapter will discuss in detail differences in mortality rates between males and females. Here we need only to note that in most populations from the first instant of life onward death rates for males are higher than those for females. This seems to be due to constitutional factors: males are more susceptible to most diseases than females and have higher death rates at every age. As a result, the excess of males that exists at birth is gradually dissipated, until by ages 30 to 50 the numbers of males and females are about equal and beyond age 50 females definitely outnumber males. The result is that in most populations there is a slight majority of females. This is not a universal condition, however, for in some societies males apparently get better care than do females, who tend to be neglected. In some

Table 7-8   Sex Ratio by Age of Selected Nations of the World: 1960

Age	United States	Taiwan	Mexico	Poland	India
All ages	97.7	105.0	99.5	90.0	106.3
0-4	103.6	105.5	103.4	104.3	102.7
5-9	103.4	105.4	103.6	103.4	
10-14	103.3	106.0	105.2	102.8	114.1
15-19	102.6	106.4	96.8	95.2	107.6
20-24	100.2	*69.5	91.1	71.4	95.1
25-29	98.5	104.8	91.4	95.1	102.7
30-34	97.3	113.4	96.8	92.8	107.6
35-39	95.9	120.9	99.8	84.7	114.7
40-44	96.1	125.2	98.1	86.1	112.2
45-49	96.8	130.1	98.0	83.1	117.0
50-54	96.8	117.7	98.4	88.2	114.5
55-59	95.5	111.0	102.7	84.6	116.2
60-64	91.1	99.0	99.8	75.6	103.2
65-69	86.8	87.9	96.6	68.2	104.0
70-74	84.1	72.8	93.7		
75-79	79.4	57.6	94.3	56.7	94.1
80-84	72.0	40.8	82.1		
85-over	63.7		91.8		

*Excluding armed forces and foreigners
Source: Demographic Yearbook   Table 55

societies girls are definitely a financial liability because of the necessity of furnishing a dowry, whereas a son is an asset because he will receive money upon marriage. It is said that in some cultures if the member of the family who falls ill is a male, the doctor is sent for much more readily than if the patient is female. Thus by comparative neglect it is possible for a population to affect its sex composition. It has even been asserted that in some societies where food is scarce mothers often starve themselves in order that their children and husbands may eat more. South Asia, and especially India, has appeared to exhibit this unusual differential of greater mortality among females.

In considering the sex ratio at various ages it must be kept in mind that until very recently females were subject to attrition from death during childbearing, and this additional hazard has tended to reduce the number of females in the population. Once this extra risk of death is removed, women prove to be less prone to die at a young age than men.

Table 7-8, showing the sex ratio at the various age intervals for selected nations around the world, illustrates the near universality of the age pattern described above.

The sex balance of a population can be altered quite rapidly if migration tends to drain off or bring in large numbers of persons of one sex. The high sex ratio in frontier areas, in mining and lumbering settlements, and at the sites of industry requiring large amounts of manual labor (such as building railroads or dams) illustrates this. In industrialized nations women tend to migrate from rural areas to cities more readily and at an earlier age than males, so that rural areas tend to have a masculine and the cities a feminine balance. However, in some cities of Asia one finds the opposite situation: males migrate to the city in search of work and leave their wives and families in the village with relatives, so that the cities have a much higher sex ratio than the rural areas. In migrations that span long distances or involve risk or hardship, men tend to outnumber women. For this reason, the foreign-born population in most nations tends to be predominantly male, but even this has its exceptions. For example, the tendency for American servicemen stationed overseas to marry abroad and then bring their spouses to live in the States has helped to cause the foreign-born population at the younger ages to have a low sex ratio, although the sex ratio at the older ages remains high.

7.15.   Sex Composition of the Nations of the World

Given a preponderance of males at birth and a tendency for females to outlive males, especially under conditions of good medical care, it would be expected that the economically developed nations should tend to have a larger proportion of females (lower sex ratio) than the developing nations where fertility is still high and there is still much maternal mortality. Table 7-4, which in its right-hand column reports the overall sex ratio for nations of the world where this information is available, supports this hypothesis.

War tends to depress the sex ratio by decimating the ranks of young males. Out-migration to other nations tends to have the same effect if it is selective of males, as it often is. Some nations of Europe such as Germany, Poland, and France have extraordinarily low sex ratios because they have suffered a combination of all the factors that tend to cause females to outnumber males.

Only a very few countries in the world have a sex ratio as high as 105:

Country	Sex ratio
Kuwait	177
Guam	141
Singapore	112
Ceylon	111
Pakistan	111
North Borneo	109
Brunei	109
India	106
Federation of Malaya	106
Fiji Islands	106
Western Samoa	106
Pacific Islands	106
Taiwan	105
Albania	105
Turkey	105

High fertility with consequent young age composition, possible underenumeration of females in the census, comparative neglect of the health of females, and in-migration of males appear to be the factors that cause this predominance of males in these countries. In each of the countries listed, probably two or three if not all of the factors are operating simultaneously.

The following nations have the lowest sex ratios:

Montserrat	80
U.S.S.R.	83
Grenada	85
Barbados	85
St. Kitts	86
Austria	88
West Germany	89
Dominica	89
St. Vincent	89
Poland	90

All reflect the effect of war or out-migration that is selective of males. The vast majority of the nations have sex ratios that range between 94 and 102. This is really a very small margin. A sex ratio of 94 indicates that 48.5 percent of the population is male; a sex ratio of 102 indicates that 50.5 percent is male. Both of these are comparatively small deviations from the 50-50 balance of exactly equal numbers of each sex. One of the disadvantages of the sex ratio as a measure of sex composition is that it may suggest a much greater degree of imbalance than actually exists.

7.16. Sex Composition of the United States

In 1960, the sex ratio for the United States population was 97. This is "normal" for a population of this fertility level and mortality rates. Although it is depressed slightly by combat losses in World War II and the Korean conflict, the two major factors causing it to be below 100 are the moderate birthrate and a very large differential in death rates that favor the survival of females, especially after age 65.

The data of Table 7-9 report that the sex composition of the nation appears to have been one of net males outnumbering net females until the census of 1950. Heavy immigration from Europe, comprised predominantly of males, and a young age composition supported by high birthrates appear to have been the major forces keeping the sex ratio above 100. The sex ratios in the right-hand column of Table 7-9 appear to be almost unbelievably high until it is appreciated that the Chinese and Japanese immigrants to the United States were almost entirely male in the initial migrations, and that only a comparatively few Oriental women were admitted until the "Japanese war bride" era following World War II. The high sex ratio among immigrants is indicated by the very high

Table 7-9   Trend in the Sex Ratio in the United States
Population by Nativity and Race: 1860 to 1960

Year	All classes	Native white	Foreign born white	Negro	Indian Japanese Chinese other
1960............	97.0	97.5	94.2	93.3	111.5
1950............	98.6	98.6	103.8	94.3	131.7
1940............	100.7	100.1	111.1	95.0	140.5
1930............	102.5	101.1	115.8	97.0	150.6
1920............	104.0	101.7	121.7	99.2	156.6
1910............	106.0	102.7	129.2	98.9	185.7
1900............	104.4	102.8	117.4	98.6	185.2
1890............	105.0	102.9	118.7	99.5	182.5
1880............	103.6	102.1	115.9	97.8	362.2
1870............	102.2	100.6	115.3	96.2	400.7
1860............	104.7	103.7	115.1	99.6	260.8

Source: U.S. Census of Population: 1960, U.S. Summary, Tables 44, 158.

sex ratios reported for the foreign-born population. The high sex ratios for the native white population is a function of high birthrates (and possibly of some foreign-born citizens reporting themselves as natives).

The Negro population had a sex ratio of only 93.3 reported for it in 1960. This is probably in part a reflection of the lower sex ratio at birth. But it is also suspected that there is a serious undercount of Negro males at ages 20 to 40 in the U.S. Census, and this depresses the reported sex ratio even further. It should be noted that at no time during the past century has the Negro sex ratio for the Negro population been above 100. At the present time, all ethnic and racial segments of the population save the Oriental appear to be definitely in a situation where females outnumber males.

The urban areas have a preponderance of females, while rural areas have a preponderance of males. This is shown, by age, in Table 7-10. The decline in the sex ratio over recent decades has been concentrated in urban areas; the rural areas have maintained the same high sex ratio for nearly half a century. Apparently, as the surplus of women has developed, it has been drawn into the cities. It is well known that rural areas afford comparatively few employment opportunities to women. Women who find it necessary to enter the labor market must therefore migrate to the city.

Within the United States one can still find small areas where unusually high sex ratios exist. Areas of lumbering, mining, and military installations and those where large quantities of farm labor are required tend to have a masculine balance. Alaska, for example, reports 132 males for each 100 females in 1960. On the other hand, there are localities where the sex ratio is very heavily overbalanced in favor of females. Especially noteworthy are metropolises where large quantities of clerical workers are required. The District of Columbia exemplifies such conditions: a sex ratio of 88 was reported there at the 1960 census. Significant differences in sex ratios may be found between the various cities of the different regions. The requirements of the labor force appear to cause a substantial share of these differences.

CONCLUSION

This first foray into the topic of population composition has revealed that populations around the world may differ substantially in their demographic (age and sex) characteristics. Age and sex composition can change rather quickly within a nation. The United States, in fact, is a dramatic example of rapid change in both of these demographic traits. At the present moment, the United States has one of the most distorted age compositions of all

Table 7-10   Sex Ratio of the Population by Age, Nativity, Color, and
Urban-Rural Residence—United States and the South: 1960

Age, Nativity & Race	Total	Urban-rural residence			The South		
		Urban	Rural-Nonfarm	Rural-farm	Urban	Rural-Nonfarm	Rural-farm
Native white							
0-19	103.7	101.9	106.7	109.9	101.5	107.3	110.3
20-34	97.7	95.7	102.8	102.7	95.8	105.4	100.9
35-49	96.7	94.4	102.8	100.5	94.8	101.9	95.5
50-64	93.7	89.3	100.6	111.9	86.9	97.5	105.9
65-over	77.5	68.9	90.8	115.9	69.7	90.5	108.7
Foreign white							
0-19	99.7	98.3	108.1	115.6	97.2	108.8	110.9
20-34	76.8	75.8	67.9	206.4	54.9	61.2	191.6
35-49	88.5	88.0	85.9	124.6	78.0	73.3	161.8
50-64	98.1	96.5	106.7	132.3	94.4	110.5	138.3
65-over.......	99.0	95.8	116.6	141.3	105.6	135.6	137.7
Negro							
0-19	99.8	98.1	103.9	104.2	98.3	102.9	104.1
20-34	86.7	81.9	109.3	94.2	81.4	99.7	94.0
35-49	88.2	86.5	96.8	88.8	83.3	92.4	88.6
50-64	91.4	89.2	94.2	108.2	85.7	91.4	107.6
65-over	86.2	81.2	93.1	114.7	78.5	91.3	114.2

Source: U.S. Census of Population: 1960. U.S. Summary Tables 158 and 233

nations throughout all history. This age composition threatens to become even more distorted in the future. Therefore an understanding of the demographic variables must precede and underlie any analysis of trends in other variables that are related to age and sex compositions.

A close linkage between age composition and fertility levels was established. It may be expected that as nations with high fertility bring about a fall in their birthrates, their age composition will change promptly and substantially. The significance and implications of these changes need to be appreciated—both by demographers and by others.

The cohort and the life cycle, introduced in this chapter, are basic demographic principles and will be followed systematically throughout the chapters that follow.

QUESTIONS AND EXERCISES

1. After learning the relationship between age composition and fertility, illustrated in Figure 7-3, write a short paragraph describing the direction of bias that the crude birth and death rates will have in (a) high-fertility and (b) low-fertility populations. Also, describe the nature of the bias that will take place if within any nation there is (a) a sudden rise in birthrates and (b) a sudden fall in birthrates.

2. The anthropologists have written a great deal about age-grading and about the changing social status of the individual as he changes in age. Read one or more of these accounts carefully and draw out a typical life cycle status pattern for that society. Compare it with the categories of Table 7-6. What, in general, are the leading differences in life cycle patterns between preliterate and literate societies and between developing nations and industrialized nations?

3. At the present time colleges and universities all over the United States are in considerable turmoil. Students are restless and prone to mass demonstrations over issues that, in preceding generations, would have caused a much milder reaction. Is this due to the fact that these students are the "baby boom generation" and throughout their lives have been forced to attend overcrowded schools where the chances for interaction with teachers and other adults were less, or is it due to other factors?

4. In a later chapter we shall discover that differences in death rates have only a modest effect on age composition. You have seen in this chapter that birthrates affect age composition markedly. Why should fertility affect age composition so much and mortality affect it so little?

5. From the estimates of the future population of the United States (Table 6-6) it was claimed that the Series D estimates anticipated a sharp drop in birthrates. Yet, if you study this table carefully, you will note that the crude birthrate is expected to fall to a low of 17 in 1970 and then to rise to 20 in 1985. Is this due to changing age composition? How could this apparent inconsistency actually come about?

6. From the *Demographic Yearbook* obtain data on the crude death rate. Make a scattergram showing the proportion of the population over 65 years of age plotted against the crude death rate. Interpret the results. Compare the results with Figure 7-3 and account for the difference.

7. Find a metropolitan area that grew rapidly during the preceding decade. Compare its age composition with that of a metropolitan area that grew slowly. Compare the age composition of Mississippi (an area of out-migration) with the age composition of California (an area of in-migration). Interpret the differences.

8. Trace the age composition of France, Sweden, or some other nation for which age data are available for a long series of censuses. From the trends, what inferences can you make about the birthrate? Calculate the dependency ratio for a long series of censuses and interpret the trend in youth dependency and old-age dependency.

BIBLIOGRAPHY

Agarwala, S. N. "A Method for Correcting Reported Ages and Marriage Durations," *Indian Population Bulletin* (New Delhi), **1** (1) (April 1960), 129–164.

Bachi, Riccardo. "The Tendency to Round Off Age Returns: Measurement and Correction," *Bulletin of the International Statistical Institute,* **33** (4) (1954), 195–222.

Berent, Jerzy. "Aging of Population: Future Trends," *Proceedings of the World Population Conference: 1954.* New York, 1955, Vol. III.

Carrier, N. H. "A Note on the Measurement of Digital Preference in Age Recordings," *Journal of the Institute of Actuaries,* **85** (1, 369) (1959), 71–85.

Coale, Ansley J. "How the Age Distribution of a Human Population is Determined," *Cold Spring Harbor Symposia on Quantitative Biology,* Vol. XXII, 1957, pp. 83–89.

Colombo, Bernardo. "On the Sex Ratio in Man," *Cold Spring Harbor Symposia on Quantitative Biology,* Vol. XXII, 1957, pp. 193–202.

Das Gupta, Ajit. "Accuracy Index of Census Age Distributions," *Proceedings of the World Population Conference: 1954.* New York, 1955, Vol. IV.

Edwards, A. W. F. "A Factorial Analysis of Sex-Ratio Data," *Annals of Human Genetics,* **25** (4) (May 1962), 323–346.

Edwards, A. W. F., and M. Fraccaro. "Distribution and Sequences of Sexes in a Selected Sample of Swedish Families," *Annals of Human Genetics,* **24** (3) (1960), 245–252.

Florence, P. Sargent. "A Note on Recent Age-Pyramids in Underdeveloped Countries," *Eugenics Review,* **56** (3) (October 1964), 143–145.

Goodman, Leo. "Population Growth of the Sexes," *Biometrics,* **9** (1953).

Grauman, John V. "Effects of Population Trends upon Age Structure, with Application to the Americas," *Estadística* (Washington, D.C.) **14** (51) (June 1956), 271–287.

Hawley, Amos H. "Population Composition," in Philip M. Hauser, and Otis Dudley Duncan (eds.). *The Study of Population: An Inventory and Appraisal.* Chicago: University of Chicago Press, 1959.

Hopkins, Keith. "On the Probable Age Structure of the Roman Population," *Population Studies,* **20** (2) (November 1966), 245–264.

Indian Department of Economic Affairs. The National Sample Survey, No. 12. *A Technical Note on Age Grouping.* Prepared by the Demography Section of the Indian Statistical Institute, under the direction of Ajit Das Gupta. Calcutta and Delhi, 1958. Also published in *Sankhya* (Calcutta), **21** (1-2) (March 1959) 55–90.

Karpinos, Bernard D. "Age Distributions as Affected by Changes in Fertility and Mortality," *Milbank Memorial Fund Quarterly,* **35** (1) (January 1957), 95–96.

López, Alvaro. "Dos Aplicaciones Demográficas del Diagrama de Lexis-Vincent" (Demographic Applications of the Lexis-Vincent Diagram) *Estadística* (Washington, D. C.), **15** (54) (March 1957), 24–35. With English summary.

Michalup, Erich. "The Enumeration of Age," *Proceedings of the World Population Conference: 1954.* New York, 1955, Vol. IV.

Moore, P. G. "Variations in the Sex-Ratio at Birth," *Journal of the Institute of Actuaries,* **84** (I, 366) (1958), 92–96.

Morita, Yuzo. "The Accuracy of Age-Reporting in the Population Census," *Bulletin de l'Institut International de Statistique* (Stockholm), **36** (2) (1958), 183–189.

Myers, Robert J. "Accuracy of Age Reporting in the 1950 United States Census," *Journal of the American Statistical Association,* **49** (268) (December 1954), 826–831.

Parsons, Talcott. "The Aging in American Society," in *Law and Contemporary Problems,* **27** (1) (Winter 1962), 1–156.

Renkonen, K. O. "Decreasing Sex-Ratio by Birth Order," *Lancet,* **1** (January 5, 1963), 60.

Renkonen, K. O., et al. "Factors Affecting the Human Sex Ratio," *Annales Medicinae Experimentalis et Biologiae Fenniae* (Helsinki), **39** (2) (1961), 173–184.

Sheldon, Henry D., and Clark Tibbitts. *The Older Population in the United States.* A volume in the Census Monograph Series. Published for the Social Science Research Council in cooperation with the U. S. Bureau of the Census. New York: John Wiley and Sons; London: Chapman and Hall, 1958.

Spengler, Joseph J. "Aging Populations: Mechanics, Historical Emergence, Impact," pp. 2–21 in *Law and Contemporary Problems,* **27** (1) (Winter 1962), 1–156.

Stockwell, Edward G. "Some Notes on the Changing Age Composition of the Population of the United States," *Rural Sociology,* **29** (1) (March 1964), 67–74.

Stolnitz, George J. "Vital Trends and Age Distribution: An Added Note," *Milbank Memorial Fund Quarterly,* **35** (3), 307–308.

Tibbitts, Clark, and Wilma Donahue (eds.). *Social and Psychological Aspects of Aging.* One of four volumes in *Aging Around the World: Proceedings of the Fifth Congress of the International Association of Gerontology* (San Francisco, 1960). New York and London: Columbia University Press, 1962.

Turner, Stanley H. "Patterns of Heaping in the Reporting of Numerical Data. (Age Reporting in U. S. Censuses, 1880-1950)," in *American Statistical Association Proceedings of the Social Statistics Section.*

United Nations Department of Economic and Social Affairs. *The Aging of Populations and Its Economic and Social Implications.* Population Studies, No. 26, Series A. New York, December 1956.

United Nations. Economic Commission for Europe. *Population Structure in European countries: Tables and Pyramids Showing the Distribution of Population by Sex, Age and Marital Status.* New York, 1966, 115 pp.

U. S. Bureau of the Census. *Americans at Mid-decade,* Series P-23, No. 16, January 1966.

U. S. Bureau of the Census. *Current Population Reports,* "Revised Projections of the Population of the United States by Age and Sex to 1985," Series P-25, No. 329, March 10, 1966.

Valaoras, Vasilios G. "Young and Aged Populations," *Annals of the American Academy of Political and Social Science,* **316** (March 1958), 69–83.

You, Poh Seng. "Errors in Age Reporting in Statistically Underdeveloped Countries (with special reference to the Chinese population of Singapore)," *Population Studies,* **13** (2) (November 1959), 164–182.

Zelnik, Melvin. "Age Heaping in the United States Census: 1880-1950," *Milbank Memorial Fund Quarterly,* **39** (3) (July 1961), 540–573.

CHAPTER 8

Population Composition:
Ethnic and Social Characteristics

8.1. The Significance of Ethnic and Social Traits

Almost every census in the world collects information about selected social characteristics of the population. Nation of birth, race, or ethnic origins, citizenship, the level of literacy or educational attainment, religious affiliation, and class or caste are items most commonly enumerated. Such data are significant and meaningful for a wide variety of purposes because they are indexes of cultural background and legal or social status differences within the population of interest or concern at the local, regional, national, or international level. The classifications of the population according to whether persons are citizens or noncitizens or native-born or foreign-born is useful for research, planning, or administration only insofar as there are differences in political, legal, or social status, in cultural traits, or in behavior between one group and another. To the extent that a classification does not reveal significant differences in citizenship rights, birthrate, death rate, occupational composition, income level, unemployment rate, or some other topic of interest, it ceases to have any usefulness.

The topics for which data are collected and the categories employed to report these social traits must be appropriate to the particular population being studied in order to reveal the maximum of variability and to isolate the distinctive social and cultural groupings within specific populations. Since the categories employed must represent the distinctions that are current in the particular population, nationwide and international comparability is often difficult to achieve without glossing over distinctions that are highly significant at the local level. To the extent that some social problems and some social distinctions (such as educational attainment) transcend national boundaries, it is possible by adjustment and estimation to reconcile differences between censuses in classifications.

I. RACE AND ETHNICITY

8.2. Race, Caste, and Color as an Index of Cultural and Social Composition

Even expert anthropologists and physiologists have been unable to devise a refined scheme of racial classification by which all members of a population can be categorized. It is too much to expect, therefore, that a census enumeration could do more than subdivide the population into a few "racial" groups that are currently recognized throughout the population and that represent significant social distinctions. Skin color is one of the easiest bases for such distinction, so that the population can be sorted into categories of black (Negroes), brown (Indo-Asian), yellow (Mongoloid), red (American Indian), and white (Caucasian). Since within any one nation usually only two or three such groups are present, the race classification is abbreviated in some way. For example, in many African censuses the population is subdivided into "indigenous peoples" and those of "European descent." The same distinction is maintained in the U. S. Census in the form of a white-nonwhite classification. Sometimes nationality is used as a racial classification. In Malaya, for example, the Chinese, the Malayans, and the Indians are regarded as distinct

Table 8-1 Nationality of Major Foreign Born Groups Residing in Each Nation

Nation and date	Percent foreign born total	Sex ratio of foreign born	Most populous foreign born groups Nationality	Percent of total population	Second most populous foreign born groups Nationality	Percent of total population	Third most populous foreign born groups Nationality	Percent of total population
NORTHERN & WESTERN EUROPE								
Finland (31.XII.60)	0.7	-	-		-		-	
France (7.III.62)	8.2	122	North America	5.7	Algeria	1.4	Tunisia	0.4
Netherlands (31.V.60)	3.9	69	Indonesia	1.8	Germany	1.1	Belgium	0.3
Norway (1.XI.60)	1.7	32	United States	0.2	Canada	0.02	Africa	0.01
Sweden (1.XI.60)	4.0	82	Finland	1.4	Germany	0.5	Norway	0.5
CENTRAL EUROPE								
Switzerland (1.XII.60)	13.5	89	-		-		-	
SOUTHERN EUROPE								
Portugal (15.XII.60)	0.4	72	-		-		-	
Yugoslavia (31.III.61)	0.8	76	-		-		-	
NORTHERN AMERICA								
Canada (1.VI.61)	15.6	107	England & Wales	3.6	United States	1.6	Italy	1.4
United States (1.IV.60)	5.4	96	Italy	0.7	Germany	0.6	Canada	0.5
OCEANIA								
Australia (30.VI.1961)	16.9	125	England & Wales	5.4	Italy	2.2	Germany	1.0
Fiji Islands (27.IX.1956)	6.3	179	India	3.6	Other	1.1	Oceania	0.8
New Zealand (17.IV.56)	14.2	114	England & Wales	6.9	Scotland	2.1	Australia	1.6
Western Samoa (25.IX.61)	3.0	115	American Samoa	1.2	Oceania	1.0	Other	0.8
SOUTH AMERICA								
Argentina (30.Ix.60)	12.8	110	-		-		-	
Ecuador (25.XI.62)	0.6	118	-		-		-	
Venezuela (26.II.61)	7.4	157	Spain	2.4	Italy	1.6	Colombia	1.4
MIDDLE AMERICA								
Barbados (7.IV.60)	4.2	67	North America	2.5	Other	1.6	Unknown	1.5
Jamaica (7.IV.60)	1.3	108	United Kingdom	0.3	Cuba	0.3	North America	0.2
Mexico (8.VI.60)	0.6	116	United States	0.3	Spain	0.1	North America	0.03
Netherland Antil. (27.VI.61)	14.8	32	Unknown	12.5	North America	1.8	Venezuela	0.2
Panama (11.XII.60)	4.2	140	Colombia	0.9	Jamaica	0.7	Costa Rica	0.3
Puerto Rico (1.IV.60)	2.7	112	United States	2.2	United Kingdom	0.1	Unknown	0.1
Trinidad & Tobago (7.IV.60)	10.0	101	North America	7.5	Other	2.5	-	

Table 8-1 (*Continued*)

Nation and date	Percent foreign born total	Sex ratio of foreign born	Most populous foreign born groups		Second most populous foreign born groups		Third most populous foreign born groups	
			Nationality	Percent of total population	Nationality	Percent of total population	Nationality	Percent of total population
SOUTH CENTRAL ASIA								
Pakistan (1.II.61)	7.0	121	India	6.9	Burma	0.008	Iran	0.008
EAST ASIA								
Hong Kong (7.III.61)	52.3	107	China & Macau	-	Other	0.9	Other (Asians)	0.9
Korea, Rep. of (1.XII.60)	0.7	-	Japan	0.4	Other	0.2	China	0.1
SOUTH EAST ASIA								
Fed. of Malaya (17.VI.57)	15.1	156	China	8.9	India	3.9	Indonesia	-
Philippines (15.II.60)	0.04	-	China (Mainland)	-	-	-	-	-
Sarawak (14.VI.60)	7.6	137	China	5.8	Indonesia	0.6	Ceylon	0.3
Singapore (17.VI.57)	35.7	133	China	19.1	Fed. of Malaya	8.6	India	4.6
Thailand (23.II.56)	2.0	182	China	1.6	Other	0.3	India	0.02
SOUTH WEST ASIA								
Aden (7.II.55)	62.0	-	Yemen	34.2	South Arabia	13.0	French Somaliland	6.0
Cyprus (11.XII.60)	5.4	99	United Kingdom	2.8	Turkey	0.7	Greece	0.5
Iran (1-15.XI.56)	0.2	-	U.S.S.R.	0.1	Iraq	0.05	Turkey	0.01
Iraq (12.X.57)	1.3	141	Iran	0.5	Other (Asians)	0.3	Turkey	0.2
Israel (22.V.61)	62.2	102	U.S.S.R.	16.5	Morocco & Tunisia	8.1	Romania	8.0
Turkey (in Asia) (23.X.60)	3.4	108	Bulgaria	1.0	Greece	0.9	Yugoslavia	0.9
NORTHERN AFRICA								
Sudan (17.I.56)	2.4	117	Other (Asians)	-	-	-	-	-
United Arab Rep. (20.IX.60)	0.8	109	Other (Asians)	0.4	Unknown	0.3	Syria	0.05
TROPICAL & SOUTH AFRICA								
Basutoland (8.IV.56)	65.5	101	South Africa	37.7	United Kingdom	7.3	Canada	6.4
Cameroon (15.I.57)	88.7	139	France	65.6	Unknown	16.2	Greece	3.2
Ghana (20.III.60)	8.3	171	-	-	-	-	-	-
Kenya (15.VIII.62)	44.1	119	-	-	-	-	-	-
Mauritius (1.VII.62)	1.9	135	-	-	-	-	-	-
Northern Rhodesia (15.V.63)	6.7	117	Nyasaland	1.9	Angola	1.7	Tanganyika	1.5
Nyasaland (26.IX.61)	57.8	116	India	21.0	United Kingdom	18.7	Unknown	11.7
Southern Rhodesia (26.IX.61)	61.8	101	South Africa	24.5	United Kingdom	24.4	India	1.3
Swaziland (17.VII.56)	4.1	106	Unknown	3.9	United Kingdom	0.2	-	-
Tanganyika (20.II.57)	48.9	133	-	-	-	-	-	-
Togo (XI-58:XII-60)	4.3	97	-	-	-	-	-	-
Zanzibar (19.III.58)	13.8	196	Tanganyika	8.5	India	1.3	Muscat & Oman	1.2

Source: United Nations. Demographic Yearbook, 1963.

Table 8-2   Racial Composition of the United States Population: 1860 to 1960

Subject and year	Total	White	Negro	Indian	Japanese	Chinese	Filipino	All Other
Number (000)								
1960........................	178,464	158,455	18,860	509	260	199	106	75
1950.....................	150,698	134,942	15,042	343	142	118	62	49
1940.....................	131,671	118,215	12,866	334	127	78	46	5
1930.....................	122,775	110,287	11,891	332	139	75	45	6
1920.....................	105,711	94,821	10,463	244	111	62	6	4
1910.....................	91,972	81,732	9,828	266	72	72	–	3
1900.....................	75,995	66,809	8,834	237	24	90	–	–
1890.....................	62,947	55,101	7,489	248	2	107	–	–
1880.....................	50,155	43,403	6,581	66	–	105	–	–
1870.....................	38,558	33,589	4,880	26	–	63	–	–
1860.....................	31,444	26,923	4,442	44	–	35	–	–
Percent distribution								
1960.....................	100.00	88.78	10.57	0.29	0.15	0.11	0.06	0.04
1950.....................	100.00	89.55	9.98	0.23	0.09	0.08	0.04	0.03
1930.....................	100.00	89.83	9.69	0.27	0.11	0.06	0.04	0.005
1900.....................	100.00	87.92	11.62	0.31	0.03	0.12	–	–
1880.....................	100.00	86.54	13.12	0.13	–	0.21	–	–
1860.....................	100.00	85.62	14.13	0.14	–	0.11	–	–
Percent change								
1950-60..............	+18.43	+17.42	+25.38	+48.40	+83.10	+68.64	+70.97	+53.06
1940-50..............	+14.45	+14.15	+16.91	+ 2.69	+11.81	+51.28	+34.78	+880.00
1930-40..............	+ 7.24	+ 7.19	+ 8.20	+ 0.60	– 8.63	+ 4.00	+ 2.22	– 16.67
1900-60..............	+134.84	+137.18	+113.49	+114.77	+983.33	+121.11	(NA)	(NA)
Sex ratio								
1960.....................	97.0	97.3	93.3	101.1	91.6	139.4	172.4	131.1
1950.....................	98.6	99.0	94.3	108.7	117.7	189.6	296.8	122.3
1930.....................	102.5	102.9	97.0	105.1	143.3	394.7	1437.7	435.3
1900.....................	104.4	104.9	98.6	101.5	2369.6	1887.2	–	–
1880.....................	103.6	104.0	97.8	104.8	–	2106.8	–	–
1860.....................	104.7	105.3	99.6	119.0	–	1858.1	–	–
Urban-rural residence, 1960								
Urban.................	69.9	69.5	73.2	27.8	82.1	95.5	73.6	68.7
Rural.................	30.1	30.5	26.8	72.2	17.9	4.5	26.4	31.3

Source: U.S. Census of Population: 1960. United States Summary. General Population Characteristics, Table 44.

socioethnic groups. Some Latin American censuses have attempted to separate populations of Indian extraction from populations of Spanish descent. Because this topic is much too vast to cover adequately for all nations, with the exception of Table 8-1 and the subsection that follows the presentation is confined to the United States. The reader interested in race, ethnicity, or nationality composition of other nations should consult *Population Index* for citations of research on these topics.

Foreign Populations around the World. Table 8-1 undertakes to report, for each nation where data on the presence of foreign ethnic groups were reported, the three leading foreign ethnic groups in the population. This table also reports the proportion that each of the groups constitutes of the total population, and the sex ratio of the foreign-born population. It is apparent that Europeans, Chinese, and Indians are the wanderers of the world. Yet with only a few exceptions, these foreign groups comprise

a small fraction of the total population of the countries where they have settled. In all but a very few nations the sex ratio is strongly masculine; males, therefore, must outnumber females by a substantial majority in overseas migration.

Table 8-1 is not intended to be a complete inventory of foreign populations around the world. Many important nations with a substantial foreign-born population are not included for lack of data. Among them are several nations of Latin America, such as Brazil, Chile, and Argentina. The table is intended only to point out that substantial foreign populations reside in many nations and to illustrate how important it is that more comprehensive worldwide tables of this type be built up.

8.3. Race Composition of the United States

The U. S. Census recognizes four major nonwhite races, as shown in Table 8-2. (It should be noted in passing that persons of Mexican ancestry are classified as white by the census.) As of 1960, one ninth of the population was nonwhite, and 92 percent of this nonwhite population was Negro. In other words, 10 percent of the United States population is Negro; American Indians, Japanese, Chinese, Filipinos, and all other races together comprise only about 1 percent.

Sex Composition of the Races. In the United States the Negro population has a lower sex ratio (number of males per 100 females) than the white population. All of the other nonwhite races have a high sex ratio, with a predominance of males. This is an especially outstanding characteristic of Asiatic populations (except the Japanese) and reflects the immigration of large numbers of males into this country.

The tendency for military personnel on duty in Japan to marry Japanese girls has contributed remarkably to lowering the sex ratio of the United States Japanese population. It reverses an earlier tendency toward a high sex ratio among Japanese Americans. In 1950 the sex ratio of the Japanese population was 118, and in 1940, before World War II, it was 131. Of course the dying-out of older foreign-born Japanese with their replacement by native-born Japanese with a balanced sex ratio has also been a major factor. It is interesting to note that near the turn of the century large numbers of male Asians were in the United States with almost no females of the same race. Thus in 1900 the sex ratio among Filipinos was 1438. The immigration of women following the men and the gradual predominance of native-born over foreign-born members of these groups are steadily causing the high sex ratios for Asians to decline, and at future censuses they will be even lower.

Rate of Increase of the Races. Between 1950 and 1960 the nonwhite population grew 55 percent faster than the white population. As will be shown in the chapter on fertility, this was created by a wide disparity between the birthrates of the two populations. Until recently, the immigration of large numbers of white persons and a comparatively high mortality rate among Negroes have kept the white and nonwhite races growing at about the same rate. In fact, from 1790 to 1930 there was a ten-

dency for the Negro population to grow more slowly than did the white population, and it is only since 1930 that the proportion of nonwhites has begun to rise.

Urban-Rural Residence of the Races. Except for American Indians, the nonwhite races are all more urbanized than the white population. Both Chinese and Japanese populations are highly urbanized. The Filipinos, because many of them are employed on sugarcane and pineapple plantations in Hawaii, are less urbanized. A great preponderance of American Indians still live on reservations in rural areas, and for this reason only 28 percent were reported in urban areas in 1960. The census count of American Indians is thought to be very incomplete.

The urbanization of Negroes is a trend that has been underway for many decades but it has greatly accelerated since 1940. As the chapter on internal migration will show, this is associated with a most dramatic depopulation of farms and rural villages in the South.

Racial Composition of the Regions. In the South the percentage of Negro population is much higher than in any other region. In both urban and rural areas of the South, more than one fifth of the total population is Negro, whereas in none of the other regions does the share reach 10 percent. Outside the South, Negroes are almost nonexistent in rural areas, and even in the South nearly 60 percent of the Negroes live in urban areas. The urban-rural and regional distribution of the races will be analyzed in more detail in Chapter 14.

8.4. Nativity and Ethnic Origin as a Measure of Cultural Pluralism

In any nation that has received large contingents of immigrants from other nations or that has been settled jointly by two or more distinctive cultural groups, the census almost invariably contains questions pertaining to nativity and ethnic origin. In its simplest form, the nativity question inquires only about the birthplace of each respondent and classifies him according to whether he is "native-born" or "foreign-born". If the question, "Where was this person born?" elicits a response naming a foreign country, the respondent is classified as foreign-born. If a state or province within the nation is named, he is classified as native-born. Persons born overseas to native parents who are temporarily living abroad usually are classed as native-born. Additional questions about the birthplace of the father and mother of each respondent (parentage) permit a classification of persons into the following categories:

Native-born of native parents
Native-born of mixed parentage
    (*a*) Father foreign, mother native
    (*b*) Mother foreign, father native
Native-born of foreign parents
Foreign-born (of foreign parents)

In special surveys the procedure may be extended to include a question about the birthplace of grandparents, so that even more elaborate classifications are possible.

These categories are useful for measuring the extent to which a population is culturally homogeneous and the extent to which there is "cultural pluralism." In the United States and in many other parts of the world, native-born persons whose parents were also native-born may be expected to be well integrated into the national culture. Not only would the national language be their native tongue, but a high percentage of them would not be literate in the other (another) language. This is not universal; some native-born offspring of a migrant group have remained unassimilated (or have not been permitted to join the native cultures) even after one or two centuries of settlement.

A person with one foreign-born parent may be thought to be influenced to a significant extent by a foreign culture, while a native-born person with two foreign-born parents may be thought to be truly a "marginal man" with his home life in one cultural context and his community life in another. The foreign-born person represents the maximum separation from the local culture. This classification, of course, is unable to specify the extent to which the foreign-born have rejected or abandoned the cultural ways of their homeland and have adopted the ways of the country into which they have immigrated. For this reason, the classification can measure *relative* cultural plu-

ralism, to the extent that it exists, but not the *absolute* extent of cultural pluralism.

Many sociologists and others are not satisfied with the nativity classification alone, because it does not specify *how many, how divergent,* and *which particular* cultures are involved. For the United States to have a high percentage of English-speaking citizens who were born in Canada would be quite a different thing, culturally speaking, from having a high percentage of Spanish-speaking citizens who were born in Cuba. To obtain additional detail, the population is tabulated according to the country of birth of the person and of his parents. To simplify the tabulation problem, all foreign-born persons and all persons of foreign or mixed parentage may be pooled as a single group called "the foreign stock," from which a nation-of-origin tabulation is then made. Native persons whose foreign-born parents are from different nations may be classified according to the nationality of the father.

8.5. Nativity and Parentage of the United States Population

Only one person in twenty was a first-generation American (foreign-born) in 1960, and four out of five were third-generation (or more) Americans (native-born of native parentage). This represents a marked shift toward cultural homogeneity, from a situation of very great cultural pluralism a half century ago. Table 8-3 shows that in 1910, when the great international migration flow was at its peak, one sixth of the population was first-generation and an additional one fourth was second-generation (foreign or mixed parentage), so that 40 percent of the population was of "foreign stock." The slackening of immigration has led to a steady decline not only of the foreign-born but also of the native-born of mixed parentage. As the definition requires, the foreign-born group has declined earlier and more rapidly than the mixed-parentage group: now only about 28 percent of the foreign stock is foreign-born, whereas in 1910 this proportion was about 40 percent. The slight decline in the percentage of the native white population between 1900 and 1910 was caused by an exceptionally large immigration from Southern and Eastern Europe

Table 8-3 Nativity and Parentage of the United States Population by Color: 1900 to 1960

Place and date	Total	Native			Foreign born
		Total	Native parentage	Foreign or mixed parentage	
U.S. 1960, total........	100.0	94.6	81.0	13.6	5.4
White	100.0	94.1	79.1	15.0	5.9
Nonwhite..........	100.0	97.8	95.2	2.6	2.2
Coterminous U.S. white					
1960	100.0	94.1	79.1	15.0	5.9
1950	100.0	92.5	75.0	17.5	7.5
1940	100.0	90.4	70.9	19.5	9.6
1930	100.0	87.3	63.8	23.5	12.7
1920	100.0	85.5	61.6	23.9	14.5
1910	100.0	83.7	60.6	23.1	16.3
1900	100.0	84.7	61.3	23.4	15.3
Percent change, coterminous U.S. white					
1950-60	+17.83	+19.94	+24.44	+0.67	-8.08
1930-40	+ 7.63	+11.40	+19.49	-10.60	-18.34
1920-30	+16.31	+18.73	+20.50	+14.18	+1.97
1910-20	+16.01	+18.60	+18.05	+20.05	+2.75
1900-10	+22.34	+20.83	+20.85	+20.78	+30.66
1900-60	+137.18	+163.59	+206.34	+51.71	-9.15

Source: U.S. Census of Population; 1960. General Social and Economic Characteristics, U.S. Summary, Table 66.

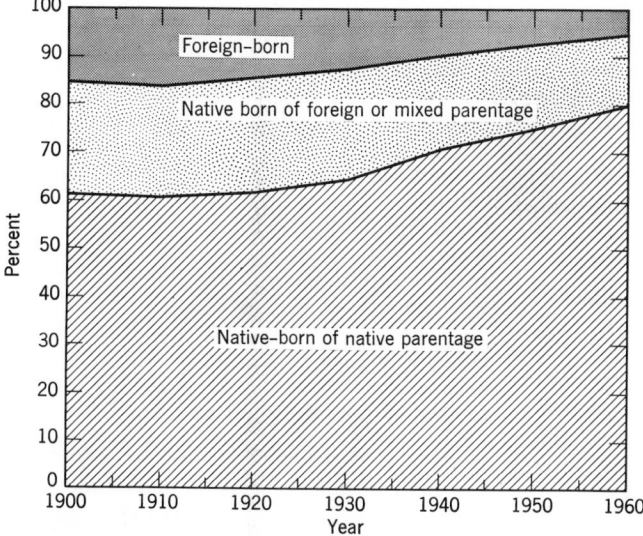

Figure 8-1 Trends in the Nativity Composition of the United States Population: 1900 to 1960.

SOURCE: Table 8-3.

Table 8-4　Country of Origin of the Foreign Stocks, for the United States, Urban and Rural, 1960, and of the Foreign White Stocks, for Coterminous United States, 1940

Country of Origin	Number 1960 (000)	Percent distribution 1960	Percent urban 1960	Percent rural farm 1960	Coterminous U.S. foreign white stocks, 1940
Total...............	34,050	100.0	83.6	3.7	100.0
United Kingdom.................	2,885	8.5	82.1	2.6	9.2
Ireland (Eire)................	1,773	5.2	90.6	1.3	7.0
Norway.......................	775	2.3	65.7	12.8	2.7
Sweden.......................	1,047	3.1	74.2	7.9	3.8
Denmark.......................	399	1.2	70.2	10.4	1.3
Netherlands...................	399	1.2	71.2	10.8	1.1
Switzerland...................	263	0.8	70.9	10.2	0.9
France.......................	352	1.0	82.3	3.0	1.0
Germany.......................	4,321	12.7	76.0	7.7	15.0
Poland.......................	2,780	8.2	89.4	1.9	8.3
Czechoslovakia................	918	2.7	78.6	6.0	2.8
Austria......................	1.099	3.2	85.9	2.3	3.6
Hungary......................	702	2.1	87.4	1.9	1.9
Yugoslavia...................	449	1.3	85.0	2.2	1.1
U.S.S.R......................	2,290	6.7	90.9	2.8	7.4
Lithuania....................	403	1.2	89.2	1.4	1.1
Finland......................	241	0.7	65.5	6.9	0.8
Rumania......................	234	0.7	93.1	1.4	0.7
Greece.......................	379	1.1	93.4	0.6	0.9
Italy.......................	4,544	13.3	91.7	0.8	13.2
Portugal.....................	277	0.8	80.2	6.3	0.7
Other Europe.................	492	1.4	84.3	3.8	1.1
Asia.........................	1,142	3.4	86.4	2.3	1.0
Canada.......................	3,181	9.3	78.8	3.2	8.5
Mexico.......................	1,736	5.1	81.4	4.1	3.1
Other America................	581	1.7	93.0	0.6	0.4
All other....................	140	0.4	82.5	2.0	0.7
Not reported.................	251	0.7	83.6	3.2	0.7

Source:　U.S. Census of Population: 1960. United States Summary,　Table 69.

during the decade. Figure 8-1 illustrates the changed nativity composition over the half century 1910-1960.

8.6.　Country of Origin of the Foreign Stock

Table 8-4 reports the country of origin of the foreign stock. Although there are substantial numbers of immigrants from every country of Europe, the following groups comprise the major foci of cultural pluralism in the United States population, ranked in order of size.

Percent of All Foreign Stock

United Kingdom and Canada	17.8
German and Austrian	15.9
Italian	13.3
Eastern European, except Polish	8.7
Polish	8.2
USSR (primarily Jewish)	6.7
Scandinavian	6.6
Irish (except those from the United Kingdom)	5.2
Mexican	5.1
Other European	6.6
Asian	3.4
Central and South American	1.7

The data of Table 8-4 must be interpreted only as indicators of general magnitude rather than as precise measurements. Although persons were asked to report the place of birth of themselves and their parents according to the international boundaries of 1960, it is very likely that many persons reported nationalities in terms of the boundaries that existed at the time of birth or emigration or in accordance with their feelings of national loyalty.

In the U.S. Census, Puerto Ricans are reported as native-born; hence the above tables do not report the additional cultural diversity created by the presence in the mainland United States of the 892,513 persons who reported that they or one of their parents was born in Puerto Rico.

Later in this chapter, and in the chapters that follow, the outstanding differences between the major racial and ethnic groups in the United States in demographic, social, and economic status are discussed.

II. EDUCATION

8.7. Education in Relation to Technological, Cultural, and Political Progress

It is widely assumed that before a nation can benefit from the natural blessings of modern technology and science, or enjoy an active cultural life of art, literature, and music, a very large share of its population must be literate and a substantial proportion must have secondary and college training. There is no direct cause-and-effect relationship here; education programs alone cannot induce economic development. Yet it is equally clear that lack of literacy and education can retard economic development. Not only must there be enough college graduates to be the engineers, physicians, scientists, and other professionals that are necessary to manage and improve a national economy, but there must also be a vast population with an intermediate level of education that can keep books, read blueprints and technical specifications, measure in fractions and decimals, and make judgments based on written instructions. A certain minimum level of literacy seems to be required in order for a population to break out of the vicious circle of a subsistence economy into full participation in the modern world economy based on complex technology and intricate systems of specialization and exchange.

Moreover, a democratic form of government in which political leaders are responsive to the needs and will of the people, in contrast to a military junta enriching itself in the traditional feudal lord-serf pattern, presupposes literacy and informed opinion about national and political problems. Once the serf awakens and refuses to be a serf any longer, the education process must be intensified to equip him not only for a more productive occupation, but also for participation in making decisions that formerly were made by his master.

For these reasons, the educational level of a population is of great interest and concern. Moreover, within a given population there is a very great disparity between the social and economic status of the well-educated and the poorly educated. As a result, "years of schooling completed" becomes a trait that is highly useful in studying internal diversity.

The rate of school attendance at each age today will determine the level of education among the adult population in future years. In fact, the process of eliminating illiteracy and low education is a lengthy one because large cohorts of well-educated youngsters must be produced on a sustained basis over many years to replace gradually the uneducated older workers as they retire from the work force. Although it is theoretically possible to reduce illiteracy and raise educational levels among adults, it has had only limited success where it has been tried, for only a small fraction of the adult population will spend more than just a few days or weeks at acquiring more formal education. Except for the few college students pursuing advanced professional study, to all intents and purposes the educational process is completed by the time age 25 is reached, and thereafter educational attainment remains fixed for life.

Most censuses of the world contain an inquiry about either literacy (the ability to read and write simple messages) or the level of educational attainment, or both. Because the educational systems of nations throughout the world differ in grading their schools, only very approximate comparisons can be made.

8.8. Level of Educational Attainment Around the World

The educational picture for the world is not a very encouraging one, for as yet only about one half of the earth's inhabitants are literate. Table 8-5 reports the level of educational at-

Table 8-5   Educational Attainment in Nations of the World for Which Data are Available

Country	Year	Percent of population 15 years of age and over, unable to read and write			Percentage distribution of population 25 years of age and over, by educational attainment							
					Male				Female			
		Total	Male	Female	Less than 1st level	1st level primary	2nd level secondary	3rd level higher	Less than 1st level	1st level primary	2nd level secondary	3rd level higher
NORTHERN & WESTERN EUROPE												
Belgium	1947	3.0	3.0	3.0	....	....	....	....	....	....	....	....
Finland	1950	....	....	....	31.0	62.0	3.5	3.6	33.0	59.0	5.9	2.5
France	1946	¹4.0	3.0	4.0	49.0	42.0	5.7	3.3	53.0	39.0	7.1	0.7
Iceland	1950	....	....	....	....	75.0	← 25.0 →		....	89.0	← 11.0 →	
Norway	1950	....	....	....	....	89.0	8.9	2.4	....	91.0	8.4	0.2
United Kingdom												
England & Wales	1950	....	....	....	....	80.0	18.0	1.7	....	76.0	23.0	1.3
Scotland	1951	....	....	....	....	83.0	15.0	2.0	....	76.0	21.0	2.4
CENTRAL EUROPE												
Hungary	1960	3.0	3.0	4.0	8.2	²80.0	7.4	4.1	11.0	84.0	4.8	1.1
Poland	1960	5.0	3.0	6.0	48.0	37.0	11.0	3.7	55.0	34.0	9.0	1.4
SOUTHERN EUROPE												
Albania	1955	³28.0	20.0	37.0	19.0	68.0	9.4	3.8	37.0	54.0	7.6	1.2
Bulgaria	1956	15.0	7.0	22.0	⁴29.0	57.0	11.0	3.4	60.0	33.0	6.1	0.7
Greece	1961	20.0	8.0	30.0	58.0	35.0	4.3	2.5	68.0	29.0	3.1	0.5
Italy	1951	14.0	11.0	17.0	....	....	....	....	....	....	....	....
Malta & Gozo	1948	42.0	40.0	45.0	77.0	18.0	3.3	1.6	86.0	12.0	1.7	0.3
Portugal	1950	44.0	35.0	52.0	5.7	85.0	5.5	3.6	8.5	86.0	3.9	1.4
Romania	1956	11.0	6.0	16.0	26.0	68.0	4.8	1.5	30.0	67.0	3.0	0.2
Spain⁵	1960	13.0	8.0	18.0	23.0	61.0	14.0	2.3	52.0	40.0	7.2	0.3
Yugoslavia⁶	1961	23.0	12.0	34.0	....	....	....	....	....	....	....	....
NORTHERN AMERICA												
Canada	1951	....	....	....	12.0	47.0	38.0	3.1	8.6	43.0	48.0	1.2
United States	1959	2.0	2.0	2.0	⁷12.0	55.0	25.0	7.3	10.0	54.0	31.0	5.2
OCEANIA												
Fiji Islands	1946	36.0	29.0	43.0	....	....	....	....	....	....	....	....
Western Samoa	1951	14.0	23.0	6.0	....	....	....	....	....	....	....	....
U.S.S.R.⁸	....	2.0	1.0	2.0	....	....	....	....	....	....	....	....

Table 8-5 (*Continued*)

Country	Year	Percent of population 15 years of age and over, unable to read and write			Percentage distribution of population 25 years of age and over, by educational attainment							
					Male				Female			
		Total	Male	Female	Less than 1st level	1st level primary	2nd level secondary	3rd level higher	Less than 1st level	1st level primary	2nd level secondary	3rd level higher
SOUTH AMERICA												
Argentina..........	1947	[9]14.0	12.0	15.0	[10]37.0	58.0	3.6	1.4	40.0	55.0	4.8	0.2
Bolivia............	1950	68.0	58.0	77.0	[11]81.0	15.0	3.2	1.0	88.0	9.5	2.2	0.1
Brazil.............	1950	51.0	45.0	56.0	78.0	17.0	3.2	1.4	81.0	15.0	3.1	0.1
British Guiana.....	1946	24.0	18.0	29.0	...	...	...	...	...	...	...	...
Chile..............	1952	20.0	18.0	21.0	21.0	56.0	19.0	3.4	26.0	54.0	19.0	1.4
Colombia...........	1951	38.0	35.0	40.0	55.0	37.0	6.0	2.0	50.0	44.0	6.1	0.2
Ecuador............	1950	44.0	38.0	50.0	...	23.0	2.1	0.7	...	16.0	0.8	0.1
Paraguay...........	1950	34.0	24.0	43.0	75.0	...	...	...	83.0	...	...	...
Venezuela..........	1950	48.0	43.0	53.0	...	...	...	...	...	...	...	...
MIDDLE AMERICA												
Bahamas[12]........	1953	15.0	15.0	15.0	...	...	...	...	...	...	...	...
Barbados...........	1946	9.0	7.0	10.0	...	...	...	...	...	...	...	...
Costa Rica........	1950	21.0	20.0	21.0	62.0	33.0	2.9	2.0	63.0	33.0	2.7	1.0
Cuba..............	1953	22.0	24.0	20.0	53.0	43.0	3.0	1.2	52.0	45.0	3.2	0.3
Dominican Republic.	1950	57.0	55.0	59.0	[13]89.0	10.0	0.4	0.2	90.0	9.8	0.4	0.0
El Salvador.......	1950	61.0	56.0	64.0	85.0	10.0	3.3	0.8	89.0	8.6	2.4	0.1
Guadeloupe........	1954	35.0	34.0	36.0	89.0	←—11.0—→		0.0	89.0	←—11.0—→		0.0
Guatemala.........	1950	71.0	66.0	76.0	87.0	11.0	1.0	0.8	90.0	9.4	0.9	0.1
Haiti.............	1950	89.0	87.0	92.0	92.0	5.6	1.8	0.1	95.0	4.4	0.5	0.0
Honduras[14]......	1961	55.0	52.0	59.0	84.0	13.0	2.3	0.8	86.0	12.0	1.9	0.1
Jamaica[15].......	1953	23.0	26.0	20.0	...	...	...	...	...	...	...	...
Martinique........	1954	26.0	27.0	25.0	86.0	←—14.0—→		...	85.0	←—15.0—→		...
Mexico............	1960	35.0	30.0	39.0	[16]40.0	54.0	4.9	1.8	52.0	43.0	4.2	0.5
Nicaragua.........	1950	62.0	62.0	61.0	84.0	14.0	1.4	0.9	85.0	15.0	0.7	0.1
Panama............	1950	30.0	29.0	31.0	[17]52.0	40.0	6.3	1.0	50.0	42.0	6.8	0.5
Puerto Rico.......	1960	19.0	17.0	22.0	[18]41.0	42.0	13.0	4.3	47.0	40.0	10.0	2.7
Trinidad and Tobago	1946	26.0	22.0	31.0	...	...	...	...	...	...	...	...
SOUTH CENTRAL ASIA												
Ceylon............	1953	32.0	19.0	47.0	...	...	...	...	...	...	...	...
India.............	1961	[19]76.0	66.0	87.0	[20]96.0	2.3	1.2	0.5	99.0	0.6	0.2	0.1
Nepal.............	1952–54	95.0	90.0	99.0	...	...	...	...	...	...	...	...
Pakistan..........	1951	81.0	75.0	88.0	[21]86.0	8.5	3.8	1.5	96.0	2.8	0.7	0.2
Portuguese India..	1950	78.0	72.0	84.0	...	...	...	...	...	...	...	...

183

Table 8-5 (*Continued*)

		Percent of population 15 years of age and over, unable to read and write			Percentage distribution of population 25 years of age and over, by educational attainment							
					Male				Female			
Country	Year	Total	Male	Female	Less than 1st level	1st level primary	2nd level secondary	3rd level higher	Less than 1st level	1st level primary	2nd level secondary	3rd level higher
EAST ASIA												
China (Taiwan)	1956	46.0	30.0	63.0	40.0	47.0	6.8	5.8	76.0	20.0	2.7	0.8
Hong Kong	1961	29.0	10.0	48.0	[22]17.0	66.0	12.0	5.0	52.0	39.0	6.6	2.0
Japan	1960	2.0	1.0	3.0	1.5	63.0	25.0	11.0	4.4	68.0	26.0	2.3
Korea, Republic of	1955	23.0	13.0	33.0	....	....	....	....	....	....	....	....
Macau	1950	[23]47.0	33.0	63.0	....	....	....	....	....	....	....	....
Ryukyu Islands	1950	25.0	17.0	32.0	30.0	61.0	7.4	1.7	44.0	53.0	2.6	0.2
SOUTH EAST ASIA												
Burma	1954	[24]42.0	17.0	66.0	[25]71.9	←27.5→		0.6	81.1	←18.8→		0.1
Cambodia	1958	69.0	42.0	95.0	....	....	....	....	....	....	....	....
Federation of Malaya	1957	53.0	34.0	73.0	80.0	18.0	1.4	0.4	95.0	4.9	0.5	0.1
North Borneo	1960	76.0	66.0	87.0	[26]66.0	....	2.8	3.4	74.0	22.0	1.6	2.0
Philippines	1958	25.0	22.0	28.0	82.0	17.0	0.8	0.4	95.0	4.5	0.3	0.1
Sarawak	1960	79.0	69.0	88.0	....	....	....	....	....	....	....	....
Singapore	1957	50.0	32.0	71.0	....	....	....	....	....	....	....	....
Thailand	1960	32.0	21.0	44.0	52.0	43.0	4.2	0.5	70.0	29.0	1.3	0.2
SOUTHWEST ASIA												
Aden	1946	79.0	70.0	95.0	....	....	....	....	....	....	....	....
Bahrain	1959	[27]15.0	66.0	87.0	52.0	41.0	3.8	2.6	82.0	15.0	1.8	1.1
Cyprus	1946	39.0	22.0	56.0	91.0	7.0	1.6	0.1	97.0	2.2	0.4	0.0
Iran	1956	85.0	78.0	93.0	....	....	....	....	....	....	....	....
Iraq	1947	[28]87.0	81.0	96.0	[29]40.0	33.0	22.0	6.1	47.0	31.0	20.0	2.8
Israel	1948	6.0	3.0	10.0	....	....	....	....	....	....	....	....
Kuwait	1957	66.0	59.0	78.0	[30]74.0	18.0	6.1	1.9	92.0	6.1	2.0	0.3
Turkey	1955	61.0	44.0	79.0	....	....	....	....	....	....	....	....
NORTHERN AFRICA												
Algeria	1954	92.0	88.0	97.0	....	....	....	....	....	....	....	....
Libya	1954	87.0	77.0	99.0	35.0	49.0	14.0	2.7	48.0	49.0	2.5	0.8
Spanish North Africa	....	[31]93.0	....	....	[32]78.0	19.0	←2.1→		97.0	2.3	←0.4→	
Sudan	1956	84.0	90.0	97.0	....	....	....	....	....	....	....	....
Tunisia[33]	1956	84.0	....	....	....	....	....	....	....	....	....	....
United Arab Republic	1947	80.0	69.0	91.0	....	....	....	....	....	....	....	....

Table 8-5 (*Continued*)

Country	Year	Percent of population 15 years of age and over, unable to read and write			Percentage distribution of population 25 years of age and over, by educational attainment							
					Male				Female			
		Total	Male	Female	Less than 1st level	1st level primary	2nd level secondary	3rd level higher	Less than 1st level	1st level primary	2nd level secondary	3rd level higher
TROPICAL & SOUTHERN AFRICA												
Angola....................	1950	97.0	96.0	98.0	....	....	....	....	....	....	....	....
Basutoland................	1946	65.0	71.0	60.0	[34] 87.0	13.0	....	←0.3→	79.0	21.0	....	←0.1→
Bechuanaland..............	1946	80.0	....	....	[35] 95.0	4.8	....	←0.1→	94.0	5.9	....	↓0.0→
Cameroun.[3][6]...........	1952–53	93.0	000	....	....	....	....	....	....	....	....	....
Cape Verde Islands........	1950	79.0	70.0	87.0	....	....	....	....	....	....	....	....
Ghana.....................	1948	....	....	....	[37] 96.0	2.4	....	←1.6→	....	....	....	....
Mauritius.................	1952	58.0	50.0	64.0	39.0	54.0	5.9	0.7	64.0	30.0	5.5	0.8
Mozambique................	1950	96.9	94.8	98.6	....	....	....	....	....	....	....	....
Nigeria...................	1952–53	89.0	....	....	....	....	....	....	....	....	....	....
Portuguese Guinea.........	1950	98.2	97.4	98.8	....	....	....	....	....	....	....	....
Reunion...................	1954	61.0	63.0	58.0	....	....	....	....	....	....	....	....
South Africa.............	1946	72.0	72.0	73.0	....	....	....	....	....	....	....	....
Swaziland................ [38]	.....	77.0	....	....	....	....	....	....	....	....	....	....
Uganda [27]...............	1959	75.0	63.0	86.0	85.0	14.0	....	←1.8→	96.0	3.7	....	←0.3→

[1] 14 years old and over.
[2] Percentage of 20 and over.
[3] Population 9 years and over.
[4] 1951.
[5] All ages.
[6] 10 years old.
[7] 1950.
[8] Population aged 9-49 years.
[9] Population 14 years and over.
[10] 20 years and over.
[11] 5 years and over.
[12] Population 5 years and over.
[13] All ages.
[14] Population 10 years and over.
[15] 10 years and over.
[16] 1950
[17] 1960
[18] 7 years and over
[19] Population all ages.

[20] 1951 population.
[21] All ages.
[22] 15 years and over.
[23] Population all ages.
[24] 1953 population of 252 towns and 2131 village areas.
[25] Population in 2131 village tracts. 1953
[26] 1948 sample survey covering 6,500 households.
[27] Population 16 years and over.
[28] Population 5 years and over.
[29] 1954 sample survey.
[30] 1950.
[31] Population 5 years old and over.
[32] 20 years and over.
[33] Population 10 years old and over.
[34] All ages.
[35] All ages.
[36] Population 7 years and over.
[37] All ages. Data refer to male and female population.
[38] Population 10 years and over.

Source: United Nations, Compendium of Social Statistics: 1963: Tables 59, 60

tainment of the nations for which data are available. (Among nations for which no data are collected illiteracy tends to be very high.) As with all data assembled from many national censuses, there are serious problems of comparability. This table, and Table 8-6 on school attendance, may be used to arrive at broad general findings, but not to measure small differences between specific nations. Except for a few "islands" of high literacy—in Northwestern and Central Europe, USSR, Northern America, Japan, Argentina, and Australia and New Zealand—illiteracy still handicaps a large share of most populations. Even in Southern and Eastern Europe, substantial fractions of the population are still unable to read or write. Portugal appears to be the most backward of the major nations of Europe in this respect, and in Albania, Yugoslavia, and Greece also 20 percent or more of the population is illiterate.

Most Latin American nations fall in the range where 30 to 60 percent of the population is illiterate. In a few nations such as Argentina, Chile, Costa Rica, Cuba, and the Islands of the Caribbean 75 percent or more of the population is literate. Among this group Argentina is outstanding, with an illiteracy proportion of 14 percent reported for 1947; today it must be much lower. In contrast, in Haiti 89 percent and in Guatemala 71 percent were reported illiterate in 1950.

It is in Asia and Africa, however, that illiteracy is as yet most firmly entrenched. In India and Pakistan, three fourths or more of the population are unable to read and write. The literacy level in Mainland China cannot be determined, but if we suppose it to be near that of Taiwan or slightly below, we would place it at 50 percent. In Africa the illiteracy rates are even higher than in Asia.

Not all of Asia and Africa must be declared to be illiterate, however. In Japan, the Philippines, Thailand, Burma, Israel, Hong Kong, and Korea, two thirds or more of the population now is literate. In Japan and Israel the illiteracy rates are so low as to be equal to those of Europe.

Ability to read and write is not an adequate test of the educational level of a population however. A better measure is one that shows the *amount* of formal schooling the adult population has obtained. The United Nations has attempted to collect such data from the various nations and to reconcile them in three levels, as follows:

First level—elementary school, primary school, or equivalent.
Second level—middle school, secondary school, high school, vocational school, teacher-training school, or equivalent.
Third level—university, teachers' college, higher professional school, or equivalent.

Table 8-5 reports data showing the proportion of the population 25 years or older that has completed each of these levels of education for nations of the world where data are available. According to these statistics, Japan and the United States have the highest general educational level. In much of Europe we find the pattern in which a very high percentage of the population completes the first level, but comparatively small proportions go on to the second and third levels. Even in the most advanced nations of the world, only 2 to 4 percent of the male population complete the third level. In the developing nations, a comparative lack of college graduates to provide scientific and technical leadership is a great handicap. The data for India, which are quite reliable, reveal clearly the educational plight of the developing nations:

Level of education	Percent of population 25 and over having amount of education indicated
Did not complete first level	96.0
Completed first level only	2.3
Completed second level only	1.2
Completed third level	0.5
	100.0

A third-level education seems to be much more prevalent among the Chinese populations than the other populations of Asia. In Taiwan and Hong Kong, more than 5 percent of the population has completed the third level of education.

8.9. School Attendance around the World

Rapid strides are being made all over the world to improve the rather poor record of literacy and educational attainment just reviewed. Table 8-6 undertakes to report the rate of school attendance at various levels. This is an even more difficult task than trying to compile comparable educational attainment statistics. In order to do this, the following ratios have been devised by the United Nations:

Rate of attendance at first level—ratio of enrollment at first level to population 5 to 14 years of age.

Rate of attendance at second level—ratio of enrollment at second level to population 15 to 19 years of age.

Rate of attendance at third level—ratio of enrollment at third level to total population, multiplied by 100,000.

These measures are reported in Table 8-6 for as many nations as data were made available. This table also shows what percentage of the students at each level are female. To portray recent changes, data are given for both 1950 and 1960.

All over the world school attendance is on the increase. With the exception of only a few nations, the attendance rates at all levels have improved, and some of the greatest improvements have been made in nations where literacy previously was at a very low level. Some changes are very dramatic indeed. For example, the population of Cambodia in 1959 was reported to be 69 percent illiterate, with literacy confined almost entirely to males. (Only 5 percent of females were reported to be literate.) In 1960 the rates of school attendance for 1950 and 1960 were reported to have changed as follows:

	1950	1960
First level	13	41
Second level	0	5
Third level	2	18

The following developing nations are reported to have made similar improvements: India, Mainland China, Taiwan, Hong Kong, Burma, Indonesia, Laos, Iraq, Jordan, Turkey, Algeria, United Arab Republic, and most of the nations throughout Tropical and Southern Africa. In fact, the drive to wipe out illiteracy appears to be a great social movement. It is being pushed as a major goal by Communist and non-Communist nations alike and may be expected to have an increasingly great impact in the decades immediately ahead.

The sex ratios for school enrollees shown in Table 8-6 indicate that the traditional pattern of educating males and not educating females is also rapidly crumbling. Throughout Latin America the number of girls attending at the primary and secondary levels is very nearly equal to the number of boys, and often is greater. In those nations of Asia and Africa where illiteracy is highest, this equality of educational opportunity does not exist for girls, but progress to admit girls to schools is being made. At the highest level, university study, males are still highly predominant, all over the world. But here, too, the proportion of students who are female is rising.

This campaign to raise the educational level of the world, especially in the developing nations, has been one of the major programs of the United Nations. It is also receiving strong emphasis in the international technical assistance program of the United States. Some of its critics feel that it has been waged too vigorously and without discrimination; the national economies cannot yet provide adequate employment for some of the posts for which its citizens have been educated. Whatever the evaluation may be, it is clear that in all of these nations the political and social life of the next generation will be very different from that of the past generations. If blind adherence to folk tradition is a major obstacle to progress, this obstacle is being removed, for the time has already arrived when the new leadership—even in the more rural settlements—has passed out of the hands of the illiterate into the custody of the literate. In the years immediately ahead the average amount of education that this leadership possesses will rise steadily. The im-

Table 8-6 Rates of School Attendance for Nations of the World for Which Data Are Available

Nations	Level of education-Rates						Proportion of students female					
	First		Second		Third		First level		Second level		Third level	
	1950	1960	1950	1960	1950	1960	1950	1960	1950	1960	1950	1960
NORTHERN AND WESTERN EUROPE												
Belgium	72	70	59	79	234	536	49	49	41	46	16	26
Denmark	61	71	63	74	402	570	49	49	49	42	23	26
Finland	69	68	40	74	359	529	48	47	57	..	37	46
France	79	76	76	75	325	667	50	49	55	51	34	..
Iceland	58	80	70	109	431	445	..	..	..	..	19	32
Ireland	102	89	34	42	296	362	50	50	51	51	29	..
Luxembourg	65	58	17	38	33	36	49	49	36	27	..	31
Netherlands	71	62	44	82	603	923	49	48	44	48	25	26
Norway	71	78	40	51	217	258	49	49	47	46	..	27
Sweden	68	74	42	65	346	438	49	..	54	..	23	32
United Kingdom												
England & Wales	69	63	72	122	209	484	48	49	50	49	36	23
Northern Ireland	79	75	31	70	238	329	49	49	49	48	34	36
Scotland	67	69	60	74	382	..	49	49	50	46	34	..
CENTRAL EUROPE												
Austria	80	61	35	55	358	546	50	50	37	38	21	23
Berlin, East	84	36	..	70	560	1248	49	49	49	49	23	22
Berlin, West	88	91	16	21	302	493	..	49	..	55	..	37
Czechoslovakia	..	57	..	49	150	401	..	..	39	45	23	32
Germany, Eastern	81	71	77	77	257	528	49	49	43	53	20	24
Germany, Federal Rep.	83	80	14	32	264	403	49	49	43	50	25	35
Hungary	77	77	10	44	477	534	48	49	55	50	25	35
Poland	..	..	..	..	..	..	..	49	..	45	..	..
Switzerland	67	65	31	39	341	398	49	49	45	45	13	17
SOUTHERN EUROPE												
Albania	77	78	5	10	11	192	46	45	29	29	33	18
Bulgaria	61	76	26	42	381	768	..	48	..	51	33	41
Greece	64	62	29	35	..	320	..	48	29	41	25	25
Italy	54	50	29	48	520	362	47	48	39	40	25	28
Malta & Gozo	67	104	9	37	79	142	48	49	41	39	7	41
Portugal	40	53	11	30	161	272	45	48	38	40	25	30
Romania	59	70	21	32	299	391	..	47	37	37	32	33
Spain	54	75	17	30	267	258	50	51	36	35	10	18
Yugoslavia	50	82	53	22	369	757	46	47	39	37	33	29
NORTHERN AMERICA												
Canada	84	86	43	64	594	645	48	48	51	50	29	24
United States	88	83	60	76	1511	1983	49	48	51	49	36	37

Table 8-6 (Continued)

Nations	Level of education—Rates: First (1950)	First (1960)	Second (1950)	Second (1960)	Third (1950)	Third (1960)	Proportion of students female: First level (1950)	First level (1960)	Second level (1950)	Second level (1960)	Third level (1950)	Third level (1960)
OCEANIA												
Australia	79	78	57	75	441	856	49	49	49	48	..	27
British Solomon Islands	..	50	..	1	..	..	..	42	..	..	..	..
Fiji Islands	71	78	5	15	106	109	44	46	35	32	..	11
New Guinea (Aust.)	33	38	..	2	..	..	39	39	14	14	..	..
New Zealand	91	86	41	64	742	839	49	48	49	49	30	34
Papua	45	55	2	5	..	..	39	42	14	10	..	..
Western Samoa	103	99	4	13	242	67	49	50	36	43	..	0
U.S.S.R.	81	71	16	27	689	1118	..	..	..	..	..	43
SOUTH AMERICA												
Argentina	66	68	21	32	480	827	48	49	48	52	18	32
Bolivia	24	38	7	10	166	..	..	..	39	47	..	..
Brazil	26	46	10	18	98	132	49	48	45	47	22	28
British Guiana	80	85	4	16	10	27	48	50	41	48	40	49
Chile	66	67	18	34	..	257	48	47	50	44	..	37
Colombia	28	45	7	16	94	296	49	46	43	44	..	44
Ecuador	41	50	9	14	127	193	45	..	43	43	15	18
Paraguay	51	62	9	13	121	188	46	48	40	50	29	31
Peru	44	48	..	16	193	253	40	49	36	..	23	21
Surinam	76	77	15	32	..	109	47	49	38	48	..	10
Uruguay	62	64	17	38	484	541	49	49	52	50	18	41
Venezuela	40	62	6	22	137	355	50	49	45	46	..	29
MIDDLE AMERICA												
Bahamas	100	73	7	53	..	..	50	46	48	53	..	..
Barbados	55	75	58	58	29	24	50	49	46	56	26	36
Costa Rica	49	66	7	29	192	326	..	48	..	49	..	44
Cuba	49	78	9	19	..	258	51	..	..	..	..	..
Dominican Republic	40	66	7	7	106	..	49	49	43	..	..	..
El Salvador	31	49	4	13	65	89	51	48	43	46	11	19
Guadeloupe	78	85	9	32	..	..	43	50	50	57	..	..
Guatemala	22	32	7	7	84	135	39	43	47	42	..	9
Haiti	15	28	..	5	28	29	54	44	..	31	..	12
Honduras	22	42	3	8	57	78	51	49	50	44	5	16
Jamaica	68	70	6	13	10	42	49	51	51	56	26	36
Martinique	88	99	12	36	197	86	48	50	47	54	19	49
Mexico	39	54	4	10	111	258	50	47	36	..	..	..
Netherlands Antilles	77	..	6	..	..	..	..	51	..	24	..	..
Nicaragua	23	34	3	4	81	110	49	48	..	34	..	17
Panama	54	60	24	35	190	371	49	..	55	53	46	44
Puerto Rico	60	..	80	..	550	1192	48	49	48	..	44	50
Trinidad & Tobago	83	80	16	27	33	61	48	49	43	50	52	42

189

Table 8-6 (Continued)

Nations	First 1950	First 1960	Second 1950	Second 1960	Third 1950	Third 1960	First level 1950	First level 1960	Second level 1950	Second level 1960	Third level 1950	Third level 1960
SOUTH CENTRAL ASIA												
Afghanistan	3	5	..	1	3	12	4	11	4	16	8	9
Bhutan	..	..	..	..	..	..	..	..	..	..	..	..
Ceylon	21	32	15	22	57	56	7	..	15	..	12	17
India	..	..	..	..	112	220	..	23	..	..	5	15
Nepal	17	22	15	16	..	56	..	..	8	16	4	..
Pakistan	18	..	21	..	93	165	..	..	..	..	..	..
Portuguese India	..	..	..	..	31	30	..	..	..	..	..	..
Sikkim	..	..	..	..	..	..	..	..	..	..	..	..
Kashmir, Jammu	..	..	..	..	..	..	..	..	..	..	..	..
EAST ASIA												
China (Mainland)	21	57	3	..	25	..	39	47	27	34	11	23
China (Taiwan)	48	67	15	37	88	329	40	43	36	40	30	36
Hong Kong	24	55	13	28	43	176	46	49	48	48	9	20
Japan	61	62	86	95	470	750	..	45	..	26	..	..
Korea, North	..	..	..	..	..	..	..	..	..	..	..	..
Korea, Republic of	53	60	20	32	177	397	37	42	19	43	11	17
Macau	..	86	..	30	..	..	..	..	..	..	..	..
Mongolia	..	..	..	..	..	..	..	..	..	..	..	..
Ryukyu Islands	..	96	..	88	80	505	49	49	..	47	17	31
SOUTH EAST ASIA												
Burma	9	29	3	17	18	63	45	..	48	34	23	28
Cambodia	13	41	0.0	5	2	18	9	43	25	10	..	26
Federation of Malaya	45	58	1	25	5	475	33	43	..	..	..	15
Indonesia	28	42	2	13	8	62	..	32	13	30	..	..
Laos	11	22	1	2	..	4	20	37	..	..	..	..
North Borneo	22	42	1	9	..	..	29	..	..	..	..	..
Philippines	74	56	21	25	1397	976	..	..	..	..	..	..
Portuguese Timor	5	7	0.2	0.4	..	..	..	..	..	..	..	..
Sarawak	29	52	11	13	184	437	33	39	..	33	26	29
Singapore	55	67	7	48	138	251	47	44	32	38	17	28
Thailand	52	54	..	27	..	..	32	48	30	38	..	..
Viet Nam, North	..	..	..	..	..	..	..	..	..	..	17	..
Viet Nam, Republic	..	..	..	..	..	83	..	40	24	31	..	31
West New Guinea, West India	17	23	1	2	..	39	..	44	..	21	..	28

Table 8-6 (*Continued*)

Nations	Level of education—Rates — First 1950	First 1960	Second 1950	Second 1960	Third 1950	Third 1960	Proportion of students female — First level 1950	First level 1960	Second level 1950	Second level 1960	Third level 1950	Third level 1960
SOUTHWEST ASIA												
Aden	25	44	5	15	..	..	28	36	7	22	..	..
Bahrain	10	26	2	9	..	..	20	28	..	12	..	..
Cyprus	63	60	29	42	40	78	46	48	31	37	39	29
Gaza Strip	..	..	5	14	..	..	26	32	21	..	..	..
Iran	16	28	6	21	34	90	26	32	21	29	..	4
Iraq	16	43	20	36	91	173	24	27	19	22	..	23
Israel	77	80	6	35	445	700	47	46	46	51	50	..
Jordan	18	51	..	13	..	..	21	36	16	24	..	..
Kuwait	..	61	..	28	..	..	..	42	..	31	..	..
Lebanon	..	64	..	..	..	345	..	43	30	..	..	28
Muscat & Oman	2	..	0.2	2	..	..	..	..	..	..	..	..
Saudi Arabia	..	6	..	..	..	6	..	..	..	..	..	..
Syria	35	37	11	17	89	223	26	29	24	23	20	18
Turkey	33	46	6	18	118	255	37	38	24	25	20	21
Yemen	..	..	..	..	..	..	..	..	..	..	..	..
NORTHERN AFRICA												
Algeria	15	28	6	10	57	70	33	40	..	44	31	30
Ethiopia	1	3	0.1	0.4	..	5	..	..	9	..	..	..
Libya	..	46	..	10	..	49	14	16	10	6	..	14
Morocco	1	27	0.2	7	15	40	..	28	22	26	..	9
Somalia	..	5	..	1	..	..	11	21	..	..	..	..
Spanish North Africa	..	..	..	..	..	..	..	..	..	..	..	..
Sudan	6	11	0.4	5	4	34	..	27	..	19	..	5
Tunisia	18	36	9	18	51	64	27	33	30	29	16	17
United Arab Republic	26	40	7	19	164	399	36	39	15	27	7	13
TROPICAL & SOUTHERN AFRICA												
Angola	1	9	1	3	..	..	44	29	1	40	..	..
Basutoland	59	78	2	5	..	..	67	62	40	51	18	22
Bechuanaland	22	40	1	2	..	24	63	58	41	48	..	..
Burundi	..	..	..	..	..	..	..	..	..	..	..	..
Cameroon	19	42	0.5	4	..	..	..	..	..	18	..	..
Cape Verde Islands	21	17	6	7	..	..	12	30	..	36	..	..
Central African Rep	..	22	..	2	..	..	6	38	29	39	..	..
Chad	..	.8	..	0.5	..	..	7	19	1	..	..	..
Comoro Islands	6	10	1	1	..	..	..	11	..	9	..	..
Congo (Brazzaville)	..	..	..	6	..	..	15	16	41	..	..	..
Congo (Leopoldville)	33	53	1	4	..	..	..	29	..	39	..	..
Dahomey	..	18	..	2	..	4	28	27	26	27	..	12
Gabon	..	49	..	6	..	..	22	38	4	21	..	..
Gambia	5	10	2	5	..	..	12	31	36	26	..	..
Ghana	19	29	..	26	4	29	25	35	..	26	7	11

191

Table 8-6 (*Continued*)

Nations	First level rate 1950	First level rate 1960	Second level rate 1950	Second level rate 1960	Third level rate 1950	Third level rate 1960	Female First level 1950	Female First level 1960	Female Second level 1950	Female Second level 1960	Female Third level 1950	Female Third level 1960
TROPICAL & SOUTHERN AFRICA (Continued)												
Guinea	..	13	..	3	..	..	14	..	14	17	..	14
Ivory Coast	..	26	..	3	..	4	17	25	11	14	..	14
Kenya	27	49	3	4	..	5	27	32	20	32	..	..
Liberia	10	17	1	2	..	..	..	27	25	16	..	..
Madagascar	23	35	1	6	2	21	39	44	..	32	23	22
Mali	..	5	..	1	..	..	19	..	8	5	..	..
Mauritania	..	6	..	1	..	..	6	18	..	..	..	..
Mauritius	51	77	8	34	6	14	42	46	31	33	..	..
Mozambique	12	27	2	2	..	..	35	38	27	35	..	..
Niger	..	3	1	0.4	1	4	17	29	6	16	4	7
Nigeria	16	34	1	5	..	..	22	37	11	21	..	..
Portuguese Guinea	3	10	4	3	..	..	..	..	..	..	38	..
Reunion	78	83	..	7	11	3	54	52	25	47	..	..
Rhodesia & Nyasaland	11	..	0.4	1	..	..	22	31	16	35	..	..
*Rwanda & Burundi	..	23	..	1	..	..	17	33	..	27	..	..
Senegal	7	17	1	4	..	55	29	34	30	30	29	18
Sierra Leone	..	14	1	3	11	19	..	49	..	..	25	24
South Africa	..	60	..	..	174	189	..	..	..	..	..	27
Southwest Africa	..	..	..	..	..	..	..	..	..	..	..	..
Spanish Equator & Region	29	46	0.4	3	..	..	53	40	27	16	..	..
Swaziland	29	53	2	6	..	9	..	50	55	45	..	..
Tanganyika	10	20	1	2	..	..	28	34	20	32	..	..
Togo	16	29	..	2	5	..	19	28	15	23	..	7
Uganda	18	31	2	6	..	14	26	30	21	19	..	..
Upper Volta	..	6	..	1	..	..	24	29	9	27	2	..
Zanzibar & Pemba	13	26	3	5	..	..	28	40	16	33	..	..

* Former Ruanda–Urundi. Rwanda and Burundi became independent states from Ruanda–Urundi respectively on 1 July, 1960.

Source: United Nations Compendium of Social Statistics: 1963.

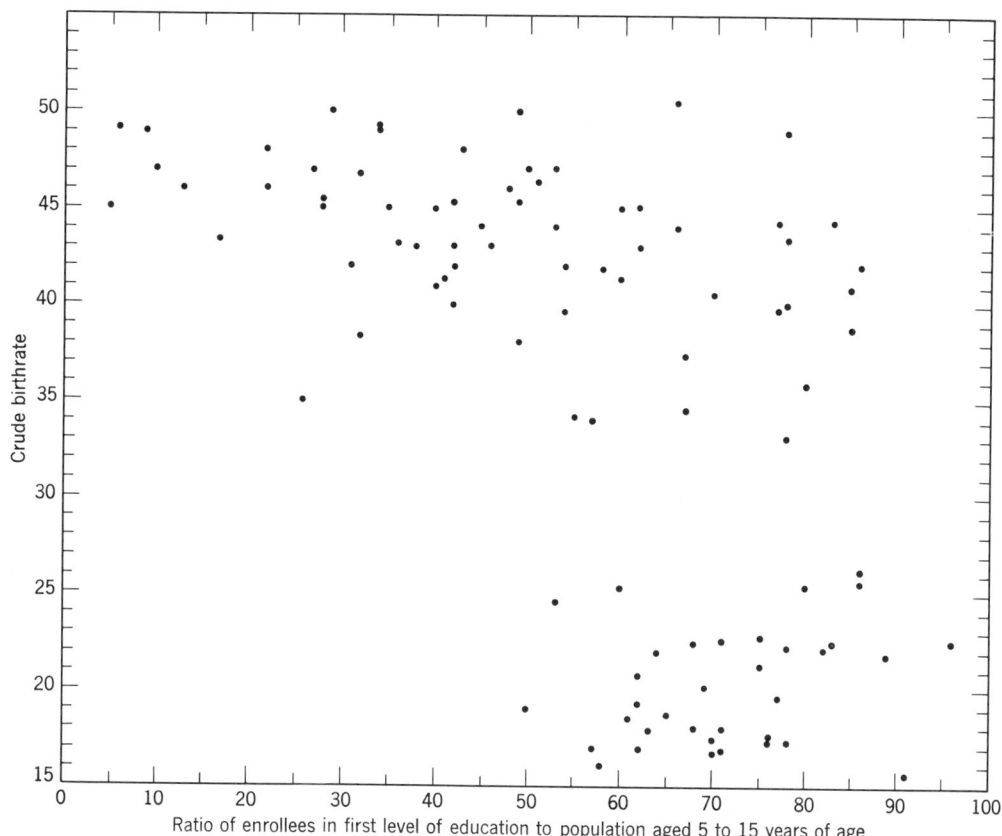

Figure 8-2 Scattergram of Crude Birthrate Plotted against Ratio of Children Enrolled in First Level of School to Population Aged 5 to 15 Years for Selected Nations of the World.
SOURCE: United Nations.

pact of education on the quality of local as well as national social life is certain to be very great. Even now, it is only the inexperienced and uninformed who equate "economically underdeveloped" with "untrained and incompetent leadership." Developing nations are progressively being led by well-trained corps of administrators and by well-organized sets of specialists who are keenly aware of the social and economic facts of their nations in relation to the world.

Nations with high birthrates are having to run very fast to educate the vast numbers of children being born. The effort required to attain literacy is much greater in a high-fertility population than in a low-fertility population, because the ratio of children to earners and taxpayers is much greater in the former. Figure 8-2 illustrates the inverse relationship that exists throughout the world between birthrate

and the rate of school enrollment at the elementary school level. The nations of Europe, with their low birthrates, have high rates of school attendance, while the nations of Asia, Latin America, and Africa, with high birthrates, have low rates of school attendance. This inverse correlation is not exact, however. A few nations with high birthrates are making a very determined effort to educate all of the children born, while several nations with lower birthrates appear to be doing less than they might to educate their offspring.

One of the first and most important results of reducing fertility is to make the goal of high literacy and high educational level attainable. It is doubtful whether a high level of attendance even at elementary school can be sustained so long as the birthrate of a nation remains over 35 per thousand. It could also be postulated that a high rate of attendance at

Table 8-7 Educational Attainment of Young Adult Population in Nations of the World (Ages 25-24, 25-29, or 15-19 in Priority Order of Availability)

Country	Age group	Percent of age group in level indicated				Sex ratio				Percent of adult population who have completed	
		Less than 1 year	Primary level	Secondary level	Higher level	Less than 1 year	Primary level	Secondary level	Higher level	Primary level	Secondary or higher
Central Europe											
Czechoslovakia............	25-34	0.4	74.6	20.8	4.2	76.1	91.8	107.7	295.8	82.3	10.5*
Hungary..................	25-34	1.7	83.5	9.7	5.1	78.4	89.3	110.4	269.0	70.6	8.5
North America											
Canada	25-34	0.7	36.3	55.3	7.7	113.0	118.7	85.8	167.5	35.6	13.0
United States	25-34	0.7	18.8	58.3	22.2	125.9	122.3	77.0	137.9	28.3	40.8
Middle America											
Honduras.................	25-34	57.6	38.0	4.2	0.2	79.2	112.7	102.5	...⁺	8.2	1.2
Jamaica	25-34	13.0	79.1	7.4	0.5	131.0	76.2	75.5	220.9	48.3	3.1
Mexico	15-29	33.2	56.8	8.9	1.1	79.6	110.8	101.9	225.5	11.2	1.4
Panama	25-34	19.6	56.6	20.1	3.6	105.4	102.9	96.1	150.4	27.4	5.4
Puerto Rico.............	25-34	9.3	51.5	26.4	12.9	61.3	71.7	109.9	109.1	29.8	14.2
South East Asia											
Malaya	25-34	47.1	42.1	9.0	1.8	35.2	225.2	325.1	397.0	24.3	4.7
Philippines	15-19	10.7	62.2	22.9	4.2	102.8	93.3	108.8	75.9	24.5	11.8
Sabah	25-34	77.8	17.0	4.8	0.3	80.3	343.1	376.9	374.0	8.4	1.1
Sarawak	25-34	79.7	14.2	5.7	0.3	70.9	243.8	282.7	355.4	7.4	0.9
Thailand	25-34	22.4	70.6	6.2	0.8	57.9	107.0	236.4	197.2	38.8	3.6
Southwest Asia											
Jordan	25-29	65.9	21.2	11.8	1.1	50.0	356.8	281.4	478.4	10.5	4.3
Tropical and South Africa											
Seychelles	25-34	33.2	60.2	6.0	0.6	108.9	80.9	119.2	190.9	29.7	2.6

*Includes persons having completed 3 or more years.
⁺Less than 100 females in category.
Source: U.N. Demography Yearbook Table 14.

Table 8-8 Years of School Completed by Persons 25 Years Old and Over by Color and Sex for the United States: 1960

Educational Attainment	Both sexes	Male			Female		
		Total	White	Non-white	Total	White	Non-white
Total	100.0	100.0	100.0	100.0	100.0	100.0	100.0
None.	2.3	2.4	2.0	6.8	2.2	1.9	4.6
Elementary school							
1 to 4 years	6.1	7.0	5.5	21.0	5.2	4.1	15.1
5 or 6 years	7.5	7.8	7.1	14.6	7.1	6.3	14.5
7 years	6.4	6.8	6.6	8.4	6.0	5.6	9.2
8 years	17.5	17.8	18.4	12.3	17.3	17.8	13.3
High school							
1 to 3 years.	19.2	18.7	18.9	17.0	19.7	19.6	20.1
4 years	24.5	21.2	22.1	12.0	27.7	29.2	15.2
College							
1 to 3 years.	8.8	8.6	9.1	4.4	9.0	9.5	4.4
4 years or more. . .	7.7	9.7	10.3	3.5	5.8	6.0	3.6
Median school years completed.	10.6	10.3	10.7	7.9	10.9	11.2	8.5

Source: U.S. Census of Population: 1960 General Social or Economic Characteristics, U.S. Summary, Table 76.

the secondary level can be achieved only after the birthrate dips below 30 per thousand, and a high rate of college attendance is possible only when it falls below 25 per thousand. The future course of the level of literacy and educational attainment in the developing nations may very well be determined as much by the future course of their birthrates as by the magnitude of their efforts to provide more educational facilities. Complete success can be achieved only by a monumental effort on both fronts: in education and in fertility control.

One of the most revealing ways to study the current educational status of a nation is to examine the level of educational attainment of its young adults. Table 8-7 presents data for selected nations of the world, to show that very great diversity exists within most of the world regions, as well as between them. It is very unfortunate that data of this type are not available for all nations.

8.10. Educational Attainment in the United States

In the 1960 U.S. Census the following question was asked: "What is the highest grade of regular school this person has ever attended? Did he *finish* the highest grade he attended?" Similar questions were asked in the 1950 and 1940 censuses. (Prior censuses had a question on literacy, which was abandoned because the amount of illiteracy had declined to very small proportions.) Table 8-8 shows the results that this question yielded at the 1960 Census, by sex and color. It may be seen that the median grade of schooling completed was 10.6 years. Only 2.3 percent of the population had never attended school, and 8 percent could be classed as "functionally illiterate" by reason of not having completed 4 years of school. One fourth of the population had completed high school, and an additional 15 percent had gone on to college. About 8 percent (equal to the percent of functional illiterates) had graduated from college.

In general, males tend to be both less-educated and more-educated than females. The percentage of males with less than 8 years of elementary school is substantially higher than for females. (24 versus 20.5 percent.) On the other hand, the percentage of males who have graduated from college is much higher than the corresponding percentage for females (9.7

Table 8-9   Trends in Educational Attainment in the Coterminous
United States, by Color: 1940 to 1960

Educational Attainment	White			Nonwhite		
	1960	1950	1940	1960	1950	1940
Total............	100.0	100.0	100.0	100.0	100.0	100.0
None....................	1.9	2.1	3.1	5.5	6.8	10.5
Elementary school						
1 to 4 years.......	4.8	6.8	7.8	18.0	25.8	31.3
5 or 6 years.......	6.7	8.4	10.6	14.7	18.7	21.5
7 years...........	6.1	6.8	6.8	8.9	9.6	8.4
8 years...........	18.1	21.7	29.8	12.8	11.9	11.9
High school						
1 to 3 years.......	19.3	17.8	15.8	18.8	13.5	8.7
4 years...........	25.8	22.0	15.3	13.4	8.4	4.5
College						
1 to 3 years.......	9.3	7.8	5.9	4.4	3.0	1.9
4 years or more....	8.1	6.6	4.9	3.5	2.2	1.3
Median school years........	10.9	9.7	8.7	8.2	6.9	5.8

Source: U.S. Census of Population: 1960,   General Social and Economic
Characteristics, United States Summary, Table 76

versus 5.8 percent). In other words, women tend to be unusually diligent about school until they complete high school, but a larger share of males who do complete high school continue their education and go on to complete college.

The nonwhite population is much more poorly educated than the white. Not only is there still a very substantial proportion of functional illiteracy (almost one fourth), but there is also a comparative shortage of high school and college students. The percentage of Negroes who have completed college is less than one-half that of whites. Negro women have made considerably more educational progress than Negro men, for a higher proportion of them have graduated from grammar school and high school, and the proportion that has graduated from college is equal to that for nonwhite men.

Table 8-9 shows the change in the level of educational attainment that took place between 1940 and 1960. For both the white and the nonwhite population the improvement has been quite dramatic. In both groups the proportion that failed to complete eighth grade has diminished remarkably, while the proportion that has completed high school has under-

gone a marked increase. This shift has been substantially greater among the nonwhite than among the white population. This has occurred despite the much better facilities for education, the greater freedom to remain in school rather than join the labor force, and the greater encouragement and support for going to college that children from white families have enjoyed in comparison with Negro children. It can truthfully be said that in 1960 Negroes stood educationally almost where the white population had been only twenty years earlier and that the segment of the Negro population that is truly incompetent to participate in modern urban society for lack of sufficient schooling has diminished rapidly.

Table 8-10 reveals the generational aspect of education by reporting, separately for sex and color, the median years of schooling that each age group has obtained. (The reader who desires to study the full educational distribution for the age groups should consult the very informative census table from which Table 8-10 is extracted.) Note that the greatest differential between the white and the nonwhite population occurs at the *oldest* ages and that in both groups the functionally illiterate are highly

Table 8-10   Median School Years Completed by the United States Population by Age, Sex, and Color: 1950 and 1960

Age	1960 by sex			1960 males by color		1950 males by color	
	Total	Male	Female	White	Nonwhite	White	Nonwhite
14 years..........	8.1	8.0	8.2	8.0	7.1	7.8	6.5
15...............	9.0	8.9	9.1	8.5	7.6	8.7	7.3
16...............	10.0	9.9	10.1	9.0	8.2	9.6	8.0
17...............	10.9	10.8	11.1	9.8	9.0	10.5	8.5
18...............	11.7	11.6	11.9	11.6	9.9	11.4	8.7
19...............	12.3	12.2	12.3	12.1	10.5	12.1	8.8
20...............	12.3	12.3	12.4	12.2	10.7	12.2	8.7
21...............	12.4	12.3	12.4	12.2	10.8	12.1	8.7
22...............	12.3	12.3	12.4	13.3	10.7	12.1	8.6
23...............	12.3	12.3	12.3	12.3	10.7	12.1	8.6
24...............	12.3	12.3	12.3	12.3	10.6	12.1	8.6
25 to 29..........	12.3	12.3	12.3	12.4	10.5	12.4	7.4
30 to 34..........	12.2	12.1	12.2	12.2	9.7	11.9	7.8
35 to 39..........	12.1	12.1	12.2	12.2	8.9	10.7	7.1
40 to 44..........	11.8	11.6	12.0	12.0	8.3	9.9	6.5
45 to 49..........	10.6	10.3	10.8	10.7	7.4	8.9	6.0
50 to 54..........	9.7	9.4	10.1	9.8	6.8	8.7	5.6
55 to 59..........	8.8	8.7	9.0	8.8	6.0	8.5	5.1
60 to 64..........	8.6	8.5	8.7	8.6	5.5	8.3	4.7
65 to 69..........	8.4	8.3	8.5	8.4	4.7	8.2	4.0
70 to 74..........	8.3	8.1	8.4	8.2	4.4	8.1	3.9
75 and over.......	8.2	8.0	8.3	8.1	3.9	8.1	3.1

Source: U.S. Census of Population: 1960 , Detailed Characteristics, United States Summary, Table 173- U.S. Census Population: 1950 Vol. II, U.S. Summary, Table 115.

concentrated in the older ages (65 and over). As these generations die off in the next decade or two and are replaced by younger generations with greater education, the educational level of the population will be raised still higher. However, the table demonstrates clearly that *even at the present time there is a serious discrepancy between the white and the nonwhite population in educational attainment.* The discrepancy lies in a tendency for the nonwhite (Negro) population not to complete high school and attend college—the famous "dropout" problem about which there has been much concern. Many of the people who talk gloomily about the high dropout rate among the Negro population fail to appreciate the tremendous improvement that has taken and is taking place in this group. This is indicated in the four right-hand columns of Table 8-10. Note that between

1950 and 1960 educational attainment at each age below 34 (the younger generation) changed comparatively little for whites, but improved tremendously for the nonwhite group. Before 1950 it was not even customary for Negroes to aspire to attend high school, and it was not expected of them—even in the big cities of the North. Now that times have changed, Negroes are accepting the new pattern. The progress that they made during the 10-year period, 1950-1960, is truly impressive. There is much evidence that this progress is being continued during the 1960s, at least in the tendency to complete high school. Negroes find it more difficult to complete college at the same rate as the white population, in large part probably because of the comparatively inferior quality of their preparation for college. It is well known that even in the Northern

Table 8-11 Median School Years Completed by the Male Population of Various Ethnic Groups of the Population, at Selected Ages: 1960

Ethnic Group	Total	Selected Ages		
		20 to 24 years	35 to 44 years	65 years and over
Total in United States..............	10.3	12.3	12.0	8.2
Native white of native parentage.................	11.0	12.4	12.1	8.3
Native of foreign or mixed parentage............	10.8	12.6	12.1	8.3
Foreign born...................................	8.4	12.0	11.3	7.0
Foreign stocks: Northern or Western Europe.......	9.7	12.7	12.3	8.3
Foreign stocks: Central or Eastern Europe........	10.3	12.9	12.1	6.2
Foreign stocks: Southern Europe..................	9.2	12.3	11.4	4.2
Foreign stocks: Mexico, Latin America...........	7.7	10.2	8.3	3.1
Foreign stocks: Canada, Australia, New Zealand...	10.6	12.5	12.2	8.4
Foreign stocks: Other...........................	11.4	13.1	12.3	6.7
Puerto Rican total..............................	----	9.4	8.1	3.9
Born in Puerto Rico......................	----	9.1	8.0	3.8
Born in United States....................	----	11.6	10.0	6.9
Persons of Spanish surname (California)..........	----	10.8	9.0	3.9
Native of native parentage................	----	11.7	10.5	7.0
Native of foreign mixed parentage.........	----	11.4	9.7	6.4
Foreign born.............................	----	5.5	6.2	2.3
Nonwhite Population by Race				
Negro...	----	10.8	8.5	4.2
Indian..	----	10.0	8.7	4.3
Japanese..	----	12.9	12.4	8.1
Chinese...	----	13.3	12.1	1.5
Filipino..	----	12.5	9.0	2.6

Source: U.S. Census of Population : 1960 . Subject Reports. School Enrollment, Persons of Spanish Surname; Puerto Ricans in the United States; Nonwhite Population by Race.

cities grammar schools and high schools in Negro neighborhoods are distinctly inferior in quality to the schools in the all-white suburbs. Some educators maintain that Negroes in the segregated schools have accepted with resignation the philosophy that they should not even aspire to college, and that only by desegregation can their level of aspiration be raised to that of the general population. Lack of income to pay tuition and living expenses is another major factor that keeps Negroes out of college.

The various ethnic groups in the United States population differ substantially from each other in the level of educational attainment. Table 8-11 reports data for such groups—both total figures and figures for three selected ages. We see that foreign stock and foreign-born from Northwest Europe have never been inferior in educational attainment to native whites of native parentage, when taken age-for-age. Immigrants from Southern and Eastern Europe, however, had substantially less education than the native Americans. However, among the younger generation this discrepancy has entirely disappeared; there are essentially no differences among the white ethnic groups of European ancestry in the amount of schooling they have received. In like manner, the stock of younger generations of Canadian, Japanese, Chinese, and Filipino ancestry has kept fully abreast of the educational progress of the native Americans. Those who have lagged behind are Negroes and those of Mexican, other Latin American, Indian, and Puerto Rican ancestry. But even in these more retarded groups there has been much improvement in the past decade or two, as indicated by the higher level of educational attainment for age groups 20 to 24 in comparison with age groups 35 to 44 years.

Table 8-12 Trends in School Enrollment of Males in the United States, by Age and Color: 1920 to 1960

Age	Total Males					Nonwhite Males	
	1960	1950	1940	1930	1920	1960	1950
5 years............	44.8	33.9	17.5	19.5	18.3	42.0	24.8
6 years............	83.0	76.4	68.2	65.5	62.8	78.0	70.2
7 years............	96.9	94.2	92.2	89.0	83.1	94.5	90.7
8 years............	97.8	95.6	94.7	94.0	88.3	96.3	93.5
9 years............	97.9	96.0	95.5	95.4	90.3	96.6	94.5
10 years............	97.8	95.9	95.6	96.9	92.9	96.4	94.2
11 years............	97.7	96.1	95.8	97.4	93.8	96.2	94.4
12 years............	97.4	95.6	95.3	96.9	93.0	95.6	94.2
13 years............	96.9	95.7	94.6	96.4	92.4	94.7	93.5
14 years............	95.4	94.7	92.2	92.9	86.2	92.0	91.2
15 years............	93.1	91.5	87.3	84.8	71.9	88.4	85.7
16 years............	86.6	80.6	75.7	65.8	48.2	80.0	72.2
17 years............	76.3	67.9	60.5	47.1	32.1	67.1	55.0
18 years............	54.6	42.4	38.1	31.1	20.5	48.5	32.4
19 years............	37.3	27.8	23.2	20.8	14.0	30.9	20.1
20 years............	27.9	21.2	14.4	14.6	9.3	19.3	13.7

Source: U.S. Census of Population: 1960, Detailed Characteristics U.S. Summary, Table 166.

From whatever angle viewed, it is clear that a completed high school education, or its equivalent in a vocational school, has become a cultural norm in the United States and that the younger generations are all conforming to it irrespective of race or ethnicity. To the extent that there are shortcomings, it is not unlikely they may be attributed more to lack of opportunity and inferior facilities than to lack of achievement motivation.

8.11. School Enrollment in the United States

The age-specific rate of school attendance is defined as the ratio of the number of students of a given age who are in school to the total number of children of that age in the population. Table 8-12, which presents such rates for single years for each census from 1920 to 1960 for males, reveals the following outstanding facts:

1. At the present time, the rate of attendance is almost 100 percent for ages 7 to 14 (the elementary school years of compulsory attendance).

2. The rate of attendance declines beginning with age 15 and drops precipitously be-

tween the ages of 17 and 19, so that by age 20 only slightly more than one fourth of the male population is still attending school.

3. There has been a very great improvement in the rates of school attendance, especially at ages above 14. There seem to have been two episodes of major improvement: (a) between 1920 and 1930 in high school attendance—ages 15 to 18—and (b) between 1950 and 1960 in college attendance—ages 18 and above.

4. At the elementary school ages the rate of attendance for the nonwhite population is very nearly equal to that of the white, but at ages 15 and above there is a steadily widening discrepancy between the two. Despite the fact that the rate of attendance for Negroes increased remarkably at ages above 15 during the 1950-1960 decade, the progress of the white population was equally great or greater, so that the differential was not narrowed. Although a much higher percentage of Negroes in their late teens are attending school now than ever before, *in comparison with whites they are in about the same or slightly worse position they were a decade ago*. Table 8-13 shows in full detail the race differential in

Table 8-13 School Enrollment by Single Years of Age by Color and Sex for the United States: 1960

Age	Both sexes	Male			Female		
		Total	White	Nonwhite	Total	White	Nonwhite
5 years..............	44.9	44.8	45.1	42.7	45.1	45.4	43.5
6 years......... ...	83.3	83.0	83.8	78.4	83.5	84.2	79.1
7 years..............	97.0	96.9	97.3	94.5	97.1	97.4	95.0
8 years..............	97.8	97.8	98.0	96.3	97.9	98.1	96.5
9 years..............	98.0	97.9	98.1	96.6	98.0	98.4	96.9
10 years..............	97.9	97.8	98.0	96.5	97.9	98.1	96.7
11 years..............	97.8	97.7	97.9	96.2	97.8	98.0	96.6
12 years..............	97.5	97.4	97.7	95.6	97.6	97.8	96.1
13 years..............	97.0	96.9	97.2	94.8	97.0	97.3	95.0
14 years..............	95.3	95.4	95.8	92.1	95.3	95.7	92.5
15 years..............	92.9	93.1	93.8	88.6	92.7	93.4	87.9
16 years..............	86.3	86.6	87.4	80.4	86.1	86.9	79.9
17 years..............	75.6	76.3	77.5	67.6	74.9	76.0	66.5
18 years..............	50.6	54.6	55.5	48.7	46.6	46.9	44.4
19 years..............	32.7	37.3	38.1	30.9	28.4	28.5	28.1
20 years..............	23.5	27.9	29.1	19.4	19.3	19.6	16.9
21 years..............	18.7	23.6	24.8	14.6	13.9	14.1	12.4
22 years..............	12.5	17.9	18.8	11.1	7.2	7.1	8.0
23 years..............	9.7	14.7	15.4	10.1	4.8	4.6	5.9
24 years..............	8.3	12.9	13.5	8.4	4.0	3.9	5.2

Source: U.S. Census of Population: 1960. Detailed Characteristics. United States Summary, Table 165.

school attendance, by sex. Note that nonwhite females compare very favorably with white females above age 18 and even surpass them at ages above 22. The differential between the races is very great for males, and for teen-age males is at a maximum at age 17.

It is difficult to determine the current comparative educational attainment of various subgroups of the population because of the problem of retardation. For example, the percentage of Negroes who have completed high school by age 18 cannot be used as a measure of the current rate of getting a high school education, for many Negroes of 19, 20, or even older are working part-time and will graduate from high school in the future. A rough but fairly informative measure is the "grade-attainment rate"—the number of persons enrolled in a given grade divided by the total number of persons who *would* be in that grade if all entered school at age 6 and progressed through every grade without retardation. It measures

the extent to which the various groups are succeeding in eventually attaining each grade, disregarding the factor of retardation. Table 8-14 reports such rates for the first 16 grades of schooling, by sex and color. This table is presented here for one highly important finding: the nonwhite population is falling far short of the white population in its rate of attaining college entrance and of progressing through college. If we compare Table 8-14 with Table 8-15, which reports similar information for 1950, it is possible to obtain a measure of improvement in recent years. This comparison shows very great progress for the white population in attaining college-level enrollment, but much more modest progress for the nonwhite population. It does emphasize, however, the very great improvement in high school attendance by the nonwhite population and the substantial improvement in entering the first two years of college.

What are the factors that influence school

Table 8-14 Estimated Grade Attainment Rates for the United States Population, by Sex and Color, 5 to 29 Years Old: 1960

Year of school	Total	Color		Males		Females	
		White	Nonwhite	White	Nonwhite	White	Nonwhite
Elementary School							
Grade 1	106.2	105.1	113.0	107.1	115.8	103.1	110.3
Grade 2	104.1	103.1	110.6	104.5	113.9	101.6	107.4
Grade 3	104.9	103.1	113.9	103.7	116.2	102.5	111.6
Grade 4	102.2	101.4	106.8	102.6	109.1	100.3	104.6
Grade 5	100.8	100.7	101.4	101.4	102.8	100.1	99.9
Grade 6	99.9	100.2	98.0	101.0	98.0	99.4	98.1
Grade 7	98.4	99.1	93.2	99.7	92.7	98.5	93.7
Grade 8	87.7	87.7	87.8	87.6	87.1	87.7	88.6
High School							
Grade 1	95.3	96.3	88.4	96.5	87.0	96.1	89.7
Grade 2	87.6	89.1	77.8	88.6	75.7	89.6	79.9
Grade 3	80.4	82.0	68.6	81.6	65.1	83.0	72.3
Grade 4	77.1	78.9	63.9	79.0	60.5	78.8	67.4
College							
Year 1	34.0	36.1	19.0	41.4	18.1	30.7	19.8
Year 2	28.9	30.8	15.8	39.0	17.4	22.9	14.4
Year 3	21.6	23.1	11.0	30.2	12.2	16.2	10.0
Year 4	19.9	21.3	9.9	28.8	10.8	13.9	9.2

Source: U.S. Census of Population: 1960, Detailed Characteristics, U.S. Summary, Tables 165 and 168

Note: The rate for Grade 1 is the number of persons enrolled in Grade 1 divided by the population 6 years of age; the rate for grade 2 is the number of persons enrolled in grade 2 divided by the population 7 years of age; and so on progressively. The rate for college, year 4, is the number of persons enrolled in the fourth year of college divided by the population 21 years of age.

enrollment of young people? This is a complex question that cannot be answered fully here. However, just to "advertise" the rich array of data that the U.S. Census provides for exploring this problem, Table 8-16 has been prepared. This table shows the percent of youth 18 and 19 years of age enrolled in school according to selected social and economic characteristics of the home. The ages 18 and 19 are taken because they are critical in measuring dropout from high school and entrance into college. The table provides statistics for all youths of these ages and for the nonwhite youth, by sex. From it we can derive the following generalization about family differences in young people completing high school and starting college:

1. *The rate is highest when both parents are present in the home and when the mother as well as the father is in the labor force.* Having a working mother appears to be conducive to sending the young son or daughter on to college, or encouraging him to complete high school.

2. *The rate is lowest for youngsters living in a family where neither parent is present, and is low where there is only one parent and that parent is not working.*

3. *The amount of education attained by the parents affects greatly the tendency for the youngster to complete high school or enter college.* Where both father and mother have less than an eighth grade education, the rate is only about one-half that where both parents have attended college. The effect of each parent upon this is very great. They influence the school attendance both of the son and of the daughter.

Table 8-15 Estimated Grade Attainment Rate for United States Population by Sex and Color: 1950

Year of school	Total	Color		Males		Females	
		White	Nonwhite	White	Nonwhite	White	Nonwhite
Elementary School							
Grade 1........	109.6	106.6	131.6	108.8	138.0	104.4	125.2
Grade 2........	100.2	97.8	118.4	99.5	123.1	96.1	113.8
Grade 3........	102.4	100.4	116.7	102.5	121.3	98.2	112.2
Grade 4........	103.6	101.8	116.6	103.2	121.7	100.3	111.5
Grade 5........	98.2	97.9	99.5	99.4	99.9	96.4	99.1
Grade 6........	100.4	100.2	101.8	100.9	99.6	99.4	104.1
Grade 7........	91.1	92.5	81.2	93.2	78.9	91.8	83.4
Grade 8........	92.8	94.9	78.7	95.6	77.0	94.2	80.3
High School							
Year 1........	80.8	82.9	66.4	81.6	63.9	84.3	68.8
Year 2........	76.5	79.1	57.4	78.3	54.5	80.0	60.3
Year 3........	66.0	69.3	43.3	68.1	41.2	70.6	45.2
Year 4........	76.7	81.5	42.1	83.2	40.5	79.7	43.7
College							
Year 1........	26.6	28.5	13.1	34.4	13.5	22.6	12.7
Year 2........	24.6	26.1	12.6	35.0	14.4	17.6	10.9
Year 3........	18.8	20.2	8.5	29.3	10.5	11.7	6.8
Year 4........	19.7	21.2	8.0	32.0	9.5	10.6	6.7

4. *When the amount of education of parents is controlled, the nonwhite population appears to be encouraging its youth to complete school even more than the white population.* It has been observed in other contexts that white parents who did not finish high school place only secondary importance upon their children finishing high school. These statistics indicate that after allowance is made for the lower educational status of Negro parents, and the fact that many Negro homes are broken homes where the child must go to work, *Negro parents are trying harder than white parents to get their children to stay in school and are succeeding better.*

5. *The income of the family has much less to do with continuing in school than the education of the parents.* There is tendency for young people from families where the income is above $5000 per year to have a higher rate of school attendance, but the income difference is small in comparison with the difference associated with the educational level of the parent.

6. *Where the occupation of the parent is farmer, operative, or laborer, the school attendance is much lower than where the father is a white-collar worker or skilled worker.* When the parent is a professional or managerial worker, the attendance rate is highest. Parents who wish to see their children hold a similar high status appear to exert extra effort to keep their children in school. Much of the occupational difference is a reflection of the education difference, described above.

8.12   The Future Educational Level of the United States Population

By making reasonable assumptions about the rates of school attendance that will probably occur in the future, it is possible to predict what the educational level of the population will be. As each year passes, an older generation of less well-educated persons is replaced by a new generation of better-educated persons, so that we may look forward to a further substantial improvement in the educational level of the adult population. An original ef-

Table 8-16   Percent of Youth 18 and 19 Years of Age Enrolled in School by Characteristics of the Home and Color: 1960

Characteristics of the home	Total		Nonwhite	
	Male	Female	Male	Female
Total persons 18 or 19 years old............	46.6	37.7	40.1	36.5
A. LABOR FORCE PARTICIPATION				
Both parents present:				
Father in labor force, mother not in labor force	50.1	42.9	44.4	46.3
Both parents in labor force:..............	54.7	44.8	49.3	45.7
Mother in labor force, father not in labor force	42.1	37.6	38.9	46.1
Neither parent in the labor force..............	35.8	35.9	42.7	39.6
One parent present:				
Parent in labor force.........................	44.0	35.9	42.1	36.7
Parent not in labor force.....................	36.1	33.7	37.6	37.4
Neither parent present:				
Living in a family............................	22.8	10.5	30.1	18.3
Not in a family..............................	49.9	73.6	33.4	57.9
B. EDUCATION OF PARENTS				
Total living with both parents..............	50.9	43.2	46.5	45.8
Father less than 8 years				
Mother less than 8 years........................	34.4	35.1	39.8	42.2
Mother 8 years or more..........................	42.9	37.7	46.8	45.2
Father 8 to 11 years				
Mother less than 8 years........................	40.2	35.1	46.8	48.0
Mother 8 to 11 years............................	45.9	45.8	60.6	49.7
Mother 12 years or some college.................	56.6	45.8	60.6	49.7
Father 12 years				
Mother less than 12 years.......................	55.1	39.7	56.3	49.5
Mother 12 years................................	63.7	50.6	63.8	52.5
Mother some college............................	74.1	65.9	----	----
Father some college				
Mother less than college.......................	70.7	59.8	67.0	57.1
Mother some college............................	81.8	76.8	83.1	79.7
C. EDUCATION AND INCOME OF PARENTS				
Parent's Education:........................	49.5	42.0	44.6	43.1
Less than 8 years school				
Income under $3,000.......................	36.5	39.9	41.2	43.5
Income $3,000 to $4,999....................	37.3	37.4	43.0	40.5
Income $5,000 to $6,999....................	39.1	35.8	38.9	38.4
Income $7,000 and over....................	36.9	28.3	41.1	32.4
8 to 11 years of school				
Income under $3,000.......................	44.1	41.9	47.5	44.0
Income $5,000 to $6,999....................	49.1	40.4	45.6	44.1
Income $7,000 or more.....................	46.5	34.4	44.9	42.8
12 years or more				
Income under $3,000.......................	61.8	55.7	60.1	51.1
Income $3,000 to $4,999....................	60.6	51.9	55.6	48.4
Income $5,000 to $6,999....................	63.5	54.2	57.1	54.1
Income $7,000 or more.....................	67.7	54.4	65.5	56.7
D. MAJOR OCCUPATION GROUP OF FATHER..............	51.9	43.7	47.4	46.4
Professional: technical,or kindred workers......	74.5	63.6	69.1	68.1
Farmers and farm managers......................	42.4	47.5	46.2	53.0
Managers, officials and proprietors............	67.4	56.3	66.5	59.9
Clerical and kindred workers...................	58.4	44.2	50.9	57.7
Sales workers.................................	65.3	51.8	66.6	----
Craftsmen, foremen, and kindred workers	50.7	39.6	51.2	47.3
Operatives and kindred workers.................	44.9	36.9	47.0	44.0
Services workers	49.2	38.3	49.5	45.0
Farm laborers or foremen.......................	34.4	37.7	37.0	43.9
Laborers etc. farm and mine...................	39.7	37.8	43.2	43.1

Source: U.S. Census of Population: 1960 Subject Reports, School Enrollment, Tables 3,4,5, and 6.

fort to examine this process and to foresee this particular bit of the future has been made by Mary G. Powers and Charles Nam of the Education Branch of the U.S. Bureau of the Census. Table 8-17 summarizes the results of their efforts to make projections until the year 1985. There are three sets of projections. One set (Series X) anticipates no increase in the rate of school attendance after 1965 and measures the process of generational replacement only.

Table 8-17 Projections of Educational Attainment, 1970 to 1985, for the Male Population of the United States 25 Years of Age and Over.

| Year and type of estimate | Total | Years of school completed | | | | | | | | | |
| | | None | Elementary school | | | High school | | College | | |
			1 to 4 years	5 to 7 years	8 years	1 to 3 years	4 years	1 to 3 years	4 years	5 or more years
1960 (census)........................	100.0	2.4	7.0	14.6	17.8	18.7	21.2	8.6	5.2	4.4
1965 (sample survey).................	100.0	2.0	5.9	13.1	16.0	19.5	22.9	9.2	6.2	5.2
1970: Series A--Increase in rate of change of past trends........	100.0	1.5	4.8	11.3	13.8	20.3	24.8	9.9	7.4	6.0
Series B--Continuation of rate of change in past trends.....	100.0	1.5	4.8	11.4	13.9	20.3	24.7	9.9	7.4	6.0
1975: Series A--Increase in rate of change of past trends........	100.0	1.1	3.8	9.5	11.6	20.7	26.9	10.7	8.8	6.9
Series B--Continuation of rate of change in past trends.....	100.0	1.2	3.9	9.7	11.8	20.6	26.8	10.7	8.6	6.8
1980: Series A--Increase in rate of change of past trends........	100.0	0.8	2.9	7.8	9.5	20.8	28.8	11.6	10.1	7.8
Series B--Continuation of rate of change in past trends.....	100.0	0.9	3.1	8.1	9.8	20.6	28.6	11.5	9.8	7.6
1985: Series A--Increase in rate of change of past trends........	100.0	0.7	2.2	6.4	7.7	20.4	30.4	12.3	11.3	8.6
Series B--Continuation of rate of change in past trends.....	100.0	0.7	2.5	6.7	8.0	20.3	30.2	12.2	11.0	8.5

Source: U.S. Bureau of the Census, "Projections of Educational Attainment in the United States: 1965 to 1985", Current Population Reports--Population Estimates, Series P-25, No. 305, April 14, 1965

A second set (Series B) assumes that the rate of improvement in school attendance rates will continue at the same rate as between 1940 and 1950. The third series (Series A) assumes that the rate of improvement over the past two decades will improve by a plausible amount. This yields a "low," a "medium," and a "high" set of estimates. Data for 1960 and 1965 are presented to show the trend more clearly. These estimates were prepared for each sex and by age; the interested student is referred to the original report for these additional details. Unfortunately, projections were not made separately for the white and nonwhite population.

The Powers-Nam medium projections anticipate that by 1985 nearly 20 percent of all males will be college graduates and that nearly 62 percent of the population will be high school graduates. By this time the percentage of the population with less than 4 years of schooling will have shrunk to only slightly less than 1 percent. Figure 8-3 graphically summarizes this anticipated future change in relation to past trends.

An incidental contribution of Table 8-17 is that it shows the very substantial improvement in educational attainment that has taken place since 1960 and thus demonstrates that the trends discussed above have continued.

8.13. Religious Composition

Another important social characteristic of the population is its religious composition. Significant cultural differences are associated with the major religious groups of the world, and some nations contain mixtures of these groups in substantial proportions. Table 8-18 reports the religious composition of selected nations for which data are available. For example, we can see that Mauritius is 49 percent Hindu, 34 percent Christian, and 16 percent Moslem.

Within each of the great religious classifications there are subdivisions of importance. The division of Christians into Roman Catholics and Protestants, for example, may be expected to yield significant differences on many demographic as well as cultural items. Unfortunately, the U. S. Bureau of the Census has not included religious affiliation as one of its questions on a decennial census. As a result, our knowledge of the religious composition of the United States population is meager. In a survey taken in 1957, the U.S. Bureau of the Census found the religious composition of the United States population to be as follows:

Religion	*Percent of population 14 years of age or over*
Total	100.0
Protestant	66.2
White	57.4
Nonwhite	8.8
Roman Catholic	25.7
Jewish	3.2
Other religoin	1.3
No religion	2.7
Religion not reported	0.9

Denomination	*Percent of population 14 years of age or over*
Total	66.2
Baptist	19.7
Methodist	14.0
Presbyterian	5.6
Lutheran	7.1
Episcopal	2.8
Other Protestant	17.0

The nearly two-thirds of the population that was Protestant was distributed among denominations as follows:

When the item of religious affiliation is obtained in demographic surveys, care must be exercised not to interpret the crude differences between religious groups as being due solely to

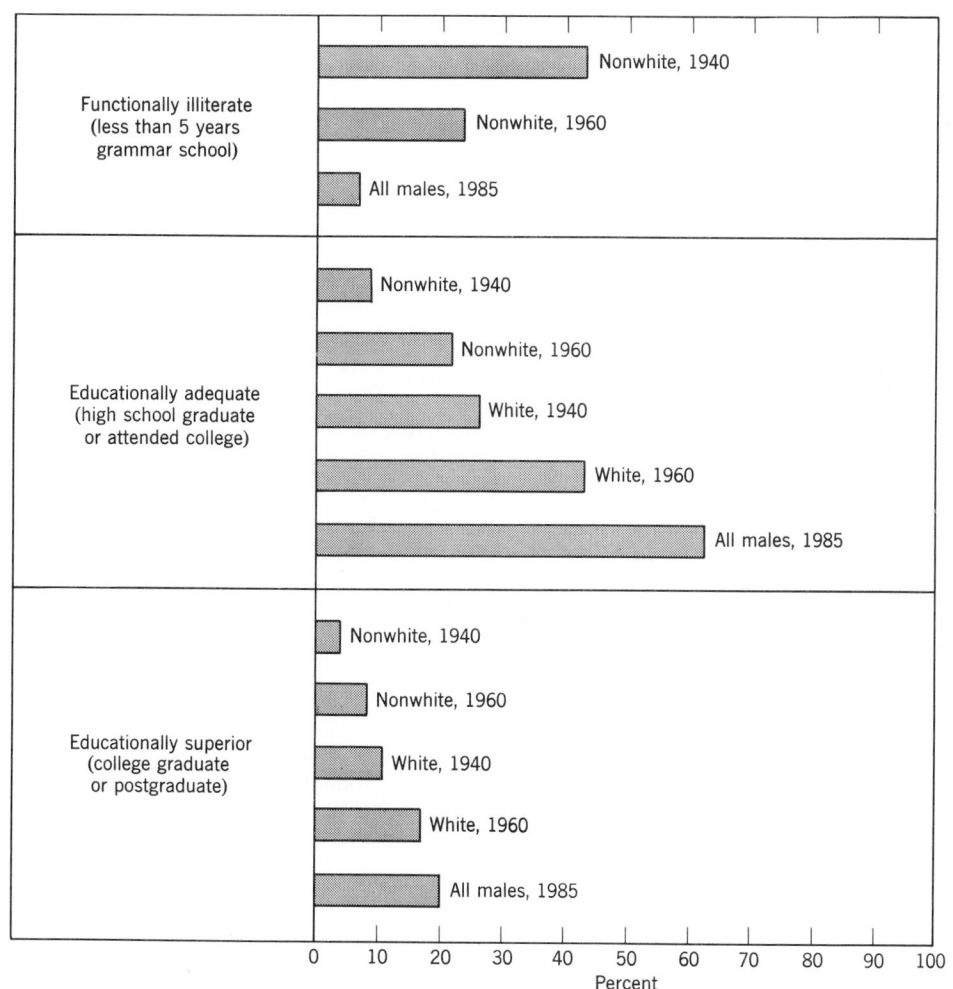

Figure 8-3 Trends in Educational Attainment in the United States: 1940 to 1985.

SOURCE: U. S. Bureau of the Census, "Projections of Educational Attainment in the United States: 1965 to 1985, *Current Population Reports—Population Estimates,* Series P-25, No. 305, 1965.

Table 8-18   Religious Composition of Selected Nations of the World

Country and Region	Leading Religion		Second		Third	
	Name	%	Name	%	Name	%
NORTHERN & WESTERN EUROPE						
Finland 1960	Christian	94.1	Unknown & other	5.8		
Luxembourg 1960	Christian	95.4	Unknown & other	4.1	No Religion	0.2
Netherlands 1960	Christian	81.4	No Religion	18.3	Jew	0.1
United Kingdom 1961 . .	Christian	93.1	Unknown & other	6.9		
CENTRAL EUROPE						
Berlin, West 1961	Christian	85.8	No Religion	12.5	Unknown & other	1.5
Germany, Fed. Rep. 1961	Christian	96.7	No Religion	2.4	Unknown & Other	0.8
Switzerland 1960.	Christian	98.6	No Religion	0.5	Jew	0.4
SOUTHERN EUROPE						
Portugal 1960	Christian	98.3	No Religion	1.7		
NORTHERN AMERICA						
Canada 1961.	Christian	97.0	Other	1.6	Jew	1.4
OCEANIA						
Australia 1961	Christian	88.2	Unknown & other	10.8	Jew	0.6
British Solomon Is. 1959.	Christian	96.1	Unknown & other	3.3	Pagan	0.6
Fiji Islands 1956. . . .	Christian	51.5	Hindu	39.7	Moslem	7.3
New Zealand 1956	Christian	88.3	Ratana	0.9	Other	0.7
SOUTH AMERICA						
British Guiana 1960 . .	Christian	56.7	Hindu	33.4	Moslem	8.8
MIDDLE AMERICA						
Barbados 1960.	Christian	94.6	No Religion, Unknown & other	5.2	Moslem	0.1
Jamaica 1960	Christian	82.0	No Religion	11.4	Unknown & other	6.5
Mexico 1960	Christian	98.1	Unknown & other	1.0	No Religion	0.6
Netherlands Antilles 1960	Christian	95.5	Unknown & other	4.2	Jew	0.4
Trinidad and Tobago 1960	Christian	70.4	Hindu	23.0	Moslem	6.0

religious membership. The various religious groups differ significantly in the level of their educational attainment, in urban-rural residence, and in occupational and income distributions. It is quite possible that differences in these other traits, rather than religion as such, accounts for much of the differences in demographic behavior (such as birthrates or migration rates) that may be observed between Protestants and Catholics or among the various Protestant denominations. For an illustration of an exploration of this area, see Chapter 23, "Religious Affiliation," in the author's *Population of the United States.*

CONCLUSION

This brief treatment of ethnicity, education, and religion should demonstrate to the reader that a national census can assemble data that will illuminate and reveal the major forces at work in a wide variety of social circumstances that may be of national concern. In the United States, the progress of the Negro population toward gaining economic and social equality is due in no small part to the courage of the U.S. Bureau of the Census to persist in collecting data on the basis of race and to present refined cross-tabulations that reveal the full extent of the penalties and inequities Negroes suffer because of discrimination. Irrefutable statistical facts of this type furnish a more powerful lever for social progress than public demonstrations and riots.

The educational attainment variable is one that has been greatly underestimated and neglected in demographic analysis. As we undertake to demonstrate in a later chapter, it has explanatory power fully equal to that of occupation and other social status measures that are more widely used.

The refusal of the U.S. Census to ask a question on religious affiliation, in view of the worldwide precedence illustrated in Table 8-18, is a discredit both to the American Congress and the Bureau of Census.

Table 8-18 (*Continued*)

Country and Region	Leading Religion		Second		Third	
	Name	%	Name	%	Name	%
SOUTH CENTRAL ASIA						
Pakistan 1961	Moslem	88.1	Hindu	10.7	Christian	0.8
Macau 1960	Other	71.0	No Religion	17.0	Christian	12.0
SOUTH EAST ASIA						
Sabah 1960	Other	45.5	Moslem	37.9	Christian	16.6
Sarawak 1960	Other	60.8	Moslem	23.4	Christian	15.8
Philippines 1960	Christian	92.9	Moslem	4.9	Other, No Religion & Unknown	2.1
Thailand 1960	Buddhist	93.5	Moslem	3.9	Confucian	1.8
SOUTH WEST ASIA						
Aden 1955	Moslem	91.1	Christian	4.0	Hindu	3.4
Bahrain 1959	Moslem	94.8	Christian	3.4	Other	1.6
Cyprus 1960	Christian	78.8	Moslem	18.3	Other	2.8
Iran 1956	Moslem	98.4	Christian	0.3	Unknown & others	0.6
Iraq 1957	Moslem	95.5	Christian	3.2	Yazedea	0.9
Israel 1961	Jew	88.7	Moslem	7.8	Christian	2.3
Jordan 1961	Moslem	93.6	Christian	6.4		
Kuwait 1957	Moslem	94.4	Christian	4.7	Other	.9
NORTHERN AFRICA						
Algeria 1960	Moslem	88.2	Unknown & others	11.8		
Tunisia 1960	Moslem	92.0	Unknown & others	6.5	Jew	1.5
United Arab Rep. 1960 .	Moslem	92.6	Christian	7.3		
TROPICAL AND SOUTHERN AFRICA						
Basutoland 1956	Christian	71.0	No Religion & other	29.0		
Mauritius 1962	Hindu	48.8	Christian	33.6	Moslem	16.2
Senegal 1961	Moslem	89.7	Christian	5.7	No Religion	2.6
South Africa 1960	Christian	58.8	Unknown & others	23.7	Bantu Churches	13.7
Swaziland 1956	Christian	61.1	Heathen & No Religion	38.9		
Uganda 1959	Christian	57.3	Other	37.4	Moslem	5.2

Source: Table 11, U.N. Demographic Yearbook

QUESTIONS AND EXERCISES

1. What causes the apparently low sex ratio at birth among the nonwhite population? Is it some genetic or physiological difference between the races or could it be caused by social and medical factors?

2. Compare the nations of Europe with respect to the level of their educational attainment. What accounts for the differences? What effect have the differences had on the level of economic development of the country? Is the level of educational attainment an independent factor that influences economic development or is it simply a reflection of the level of economic development that has been attained?

3. Note the nations where there is a lag in the education of females. What kinds of nations are they? Why does this difference persist? Can you see any evidences of "matriarchal," "patriarchal," and "equalitarian" societies around the world in this respect?

4. In Table 8-7, compare the educational attainment of the younger generations with the educational attainment of the total adult population, reported in Table 8-5. On the basis of this comparison, predict what the general level of education in these nations may be 20 years from now. What information must you have to make such predictions?

5. Calculate the deficit of college-trained men and women among the nonwhite population as of 1960. How many thousands of men and women is it? Suppose that a special university were set up with the sole purpose of making up this deficit. How many graduates must it produce each year in order to eliminate the deficit within 10 years? Can you estimate the amount of deficit that probably accumulated between 1960 and 1970? What would be the size of the graduating classes if there were to be equality of educational attainment between the races by 1970? Look up in *Statistical Abstract of the United States* the number of college degrees that are currently being awarded each year. If the task of removing the nonwhite deficit were to be divided proportionately among the universities, how much of an increase in their size would be required?

6. Suppose that you wish to use census data on grade of enrollment cross-classified by age to measure the extent of acceleration and retardation in school. Develop an appropriate measure, remembering that the census is taken in April and that a child must normally be 6 years of age by September 1 to enter the first grade. What proportion of children of each age would normally be in each grade, assuming that an equal proportion is born each month? After

your formula has been developed, go to the most recent census and apply it to various populations to see if there are differences.

7. Read the report "Projections of Educational Attainment in the United States: 1965-1985," cited in Table 8-17. See if you can construct a work sheet that shows how the basic calculations were made. What might be the biases or unwarranted assumptions of this mode of population forecasting?

8. Consult *Population Index* to get a list of studies that show socioeconomic differences among religious groups. Write an essay on these differences, summarizing and interpreting them. Based on this information, what groups do you think lobby in Congress to keep the item of religion off the decennial censuses?

BIBLIOGRAPHY

I. RACE AND ETHNIC GROUPS

Awad, Mohammed. "The Assimilation of Nomads in Egypt," *Geographical Review*, **44** (2) (April 1954), 240–252.

Azevedo, Thales de. "Panorama Demográfico dos grupos étnicos na América Latina" (A Demographic Panorama of the Ethnic Groups in Latin America), *América Indígena* (México, D. F.), **17** (2) (April 1957), 121–139. With English summary.

Beale, Calvin L. "American Triracial Isolates: Their Status and Pertinence to Genetic Research," *Eugenics Quarterly*, **4** (4) (December 1957), 187–196.

Beegle, J. Allan. "Demographic Characteristics of the United States-Mexican Border," *Rural Sociology*, **25** (1) (March 1960), 107–162.

Blalock, H. M. "Economic Discrimination and Negro Increase," *American Sociological Review*, **21** (5) (October 1956), 584–588.

Bogue, Donald J. "Color-Nativity-Race-Composition." Chapter 7 in *Population of the United States*. New York: Free Press, 1959.

Bogue, Donald, et al. "A New Estimate of the Negro Population and Negro Vital Rates in the United States, 1930-1960," *Demography*, **1** (1) (1964), 339–358.

Borah, Woodrow W., and Sherburne F. Cook, *The Aboriginal Population of Central Mexico on the Eve of the Spanish Conquest*. Ibero-Americana: **45**. Berkeley, Calif.: University of California Press, 1963.

Broom, Leonard. "The Social Differentiation of Jamica," *American Sociological Review*, **19** (2) (April 1954), 115–125.

Browning, Harley L., and S. Dale McLemore. *A Statistical Profile of the Spanish-surname*

Population of Texas. University of Texas, Bureau of Business Research, Population Series 1. Austin, Texas, 1964.

Burma, John H. *Spanish-speaking Groups in the United States*. Durham, N.C.: Duke University Press, 1954.

California Department of Industrial Relations. *Californians of Spanish Surname: Population, Education, Employment, Income*. Division of Fair Employment Practices. San Francisco, May 1964.

Claude, Inis L. *National Minorities: An International Problem*. Harvard Political Studies Series. Cambridge, Mass.: Harvard University Press, 1955.

Coughlin, R. J. "The Chinese in Bangkok: A Commercial-oriented Minority," *American Sociological Review*, **20** (3) (June 1955), 311–316.

Cowhig, James D., and Calvin L. Beale. "Socioeconomic Differences Between White and Non-white Farm Populations of the South," *Social Forces*, **42** (3) (March 1964), 354–362.

Dey, Mukul K. "The Ethnic Groups of Malaya: A Population Study," *Population Review* (Madras), **6** (2) (July 1962), 131–136.

Douglass, Joseph H. "The Urban Negro family," in John P. Davis, *The American Negro Reference Book*. Englewood Cliffs, N.J.: Prentice-Hall, 1966.

Driver, Harold E. *Indians of North America*. Chicago: University of Chicago Press, 1961.

Duncan, Otis Dudley, and Stanley Lieberson. "Ethnic Segregation and Assimilation," *American Journal of Sociology*, **64** (4) (January 1959), 364–374.

Geschwender, James A. "Social Structure and the Negro Revolt: An Examination of Some Hypotheses," *Social Forces,* **43** (2) (December 1964), 248–256.

Ginzberg, Eli, et al. *The Negro Potential.* New York: Columbia University Press, 1956.

Gist, Noel P. "Caste Differentiation in South India," *American Sociological Review,* **19** (2) (April 1954), 126–137.

Glenn, Norval D. "Some Changes in the Relative Status of American Non-whites, 1940 to 1960," *Phylon,* **24** (2) (Summer 1963), 109–122.

Handlin, Oscar. *The American People in the Twentieth Century.* The Library of Congress Series in American Civilization. Cambridge, Mass.: Harvard University Press, 1954.

Hardley, J. Nixon. "Demography of the American Indians," in George E. Simpson, and J. Milton Yinger (eds.). *American Indians and American Life. Annals of the American Academy of Political and Social Science,* Vol. 311, May 1957, 1–165.

Hayes, Marion. "A Century of Change: Negroes in the U.S. Economy, 1860–1960," *Monthly Labor Review,* **85** (12) (December 1962), 1359–1365.

Hillery, George H., Jr. "The Negro in New Orleans: A Functional Analysis of Demographic Data," *American Sociological Review,* **22** (2) (April 1957), 183–188.

Huyck, Earl E. "White-Nonwhite Differentials: Overview and Implications," *Demography* 3 1966), 548–565.

Johnston, Denis F. *Analysis of Sources of Information on the Population of the Navaho.* American Ethnology Bureau Bulletin 197. U.S. Congress, House Document 235, 89th Congress, 1st Session. Washington, Government Printing Office, 1966.

Khalid, Ashraf. *Tribal People of West Pakistan: A Demographic Study of a Selected Population.* Peshawar, Peshawar University, 1962.

Lieberson, Stanley. *Ethnic Patterns in American Cities.* New York: Free Press of Glencoe, 1963.

Mayo, Selz C., and C. Horace Hamilton. "The Rural Negro Population of the South in Transition," *Phylon,* **24** (2) (Summer 1963), 160–171.

Mühlmann, Wilhelm E. "Social Mechanisms of Ethnic Assimilation," in *International Congress of Sociology,* 14th, Rome, 1950. Vol. II, Rome, 1953.

Newman, Dorothy K. "The Negroes in the United States: Their Economic and Social Situation," *U.S. Bureau of Labor Statistics Bulletin 1511,* Washington, D.C.: Government Printing Office, 1966.

Noble, Jeanne L. "The American Negro woman," in John P. Davis, *The American Negro Refer-*

ence Book. Englewood Cliffs, N.J.: Prentice-Hall, 1966.

Rubin, Ernest. "Les Esclaves aux Etats-Unis de 1790 à 1860. Données sur leur Nombre et leurs Caractéristiques Démographiques" (The Slaves in the United States: 1790–1860. Data on Their Number and Demographic Characteristics), *Population* (Paris), **14** (1) (January-March 1959), 33–46.

Ryder, Norman B. "The Interpretation of Origin Statistics," *Canadian Journal of Economics and Political Science,* **21** (4) (November 1955), 466–479.

Schmid, Calvin F., and Charles E. Nobbe. "Socioeconomic Differentials Among Non-white Races in the State of Washington," *Demography,* **2**, 549–566.

Schmid, Calvin F., and Charles E. Nobbe. "Socioeconomic Differentials among Non-White Races," *American Sociological Review,* **30** (6) (December 1965), 909–922.

Smith, T. Lynn. The Racial Composition of the Population of Colombia, *Journal of Inter-American Studies,* **8** (2) (April 1966), 212–235.

Spicer, Edward H. *Cycles of Conquest: The Impact of Spain, Mexico, and the United States on the Indians of the Southwest, 1533–1960.* Tucson, Ariz.: University of Arizona Press, 1962.

Taeuber, Karl E., and Alma F. Taeuber. *Negroes in Cities.* Chicago: Aldine Press, 1965.

Taeuber, Karl E., and Alma F. Taeuber. "The Negro Population in the United States," in John P. Davis (ed.). *The American Negro Reference Book.* Englewood Cliffs, N.J.: Prentice-Hall, 1966, 96–160.

U. S. Bureau of the Census. "Negro Population: March 1965," *Current Population Reports: Population Characteristics,* Series P-20, No. 145, December 27, 1965.

U. S. Public Health Service. *Indians on Federal Reservations in the United States: A Digest.* Oklahoma, Kansas, Mississippi, North Carolina, South Carolina, Florida, Washington, D.C. Publication No. 615, Part 5, June 1960.

United Nations Educational, Scientific and Cultural Organization. "Recent Research on Racial Relations – II," *International Social Science Journal* (Paris), **13** (2) (1961), 175–299.

Vallee, Frank G., et al. "Ethnic Assimilation and Differentiation in Canada," *Canadian Journal of Economics and Political Science,* **23** (4) (November 1957), 540–549.

Westoff, Charles F. *Population and Social Characteristics of the Jewish Community of the Camden Area, 1964.* Cherry Hill, N.J.: Jewish Federation of Camden County, 1965.

Winnie, William W., Jr. "The Spanish Surname Criterion for Identifying Hispaños in the

Southwestern United States: A Preliminary Evaluation," *Social Forces* 38 (4) (May 1960), 363–366.

II. EDUCATION AND SCHOOL ATTENDANCE

Akhtar, Jamila. "Literacy and Education: Fifth Release from the 1961 Census of Pakistan," *Pakistan Development Review* (Karachi), 3 (3) (Autumn 1963), 424–442.

Bangnee, Alfred Liu. *Some Demographic Factors Associated With the Development of School Enrollment*. Paper contributed for the United Nations World Population Conference, August 30-September 10, 1965.

Bogue, Donald J. "School Enrollment and Educational Attainment." Chapter 12 in *Population of the United States*. New York: Free Press, 1959.

Cowhig, James D. *School Dropout Rates Among Farm and Non-farm Youth: 1950 and 1960*. Agricultural Report 42. U. S. Department of Agriculture Economic Research. Washington, D.C.: U. S. Government Printing Office, 1963.

Folger, John K., and Charles B. Nam. "Educational Trends from Census Data," *Demography*, 1 (1) (1964), 247–257.

Golden, Hilda H. "Literacy and Social Change in Underdeveloped Countries," *Rural Sociology*, 20 (1) (March 1955), 1–7.

Gosal, Gurdev S. "Literacy in India: An Interpretative Study," *Rural Sociology*, 29 (3) (September 1964), 261–277.

Jillani, M. S. "Changes in Levels of Educational Attainment in Pakistan: 1951–1961," *Pakistan Development Review* (Karachi), 4 (1) (Spring 1964), 69–92.

Karpinos, Bernard D. "The Mental Test Qualification of American Youths for Military Service and Its Relationship to Educational Attainment," *1966 Proceedings of the Social Statistics Section of the American Statistical Association*. Washington, 1966.

Liu, B. A. "Measuring Progress of Literacy in the General Population," *Proceedings of the World Population Conference: 1954*. New York, 1955, Vol. IV.

Liu, B. A., and A. Pineda-Espinosa. "Measuring the Educational Level of the Population: A Methodological Study," *Bulletin de l'Institut International de Statistique* (Brussels), 37 (2) (1960), 161–174.

Low, Seth. *America's Children and Youth in Institutions, 1950-1960-1964: A Demographic Analysis*. (U.S. Children's Bureau, Publication 435.) Washington, D.C.: Government Printing Office, 1965.

Nam, Charles B. *Factors Associated with the Historical Decline of Illiteracy in the United States*. Paper contributed for the United Na-

tions World Population Conference, August 30-September 10, 1965.

Nam, Charles B. "Impact of the 'GI Bills' on the Educational Level of the Male Population," *Social Forces*, 43 (1) (October 1964), 26–32.

Nam, Charles B., and John K. Folger. "Factors Related to School Retention," *Demography*, 2 (1965), 456–462.

Pan American Union. "Aspectos Sociales de la Población en América Latina" (Social Aspects of Population in Latin America). *Revista Interamericana de Ciencias Sociales* (Washington, 2nd series), 3(3) (1965), 1–148.

Perkin, H. J. "Middle-class Education and Employment in the Nineteenth Century: A Critical Note," *Economic History Review* (Utrecht), 2nd Series, 14 (1) (August 1961), 122–130.

Rogers, Everett M., and William Herzog. "Functional Literacy among Colombian peasants," *Economic Development and Cultural Change*, 14 (2) (January 1966), 190–203.

Sadie, Johannes L. A. *1. Análisis Demográfico del Estado de la Educación en la América Latina (Demographic Analysis of the Educational Situation in Latin America)*. United Nations Centro Latinoamericano de Demografía (CELADE) Publications. Series A. (Reports on Investigations by CELADE). Santiago, 1962.

Schmid, Calvin F. *Logic, Techniques, Interpretations, Applications and Limitations of Enrollment Forecasts*. Paper contributed for the United Nations World Population Conference, August 30-September 10, 1965.

Schwartzberg, Joseph E. "Observations on the Progress of Literacy in India, 1951–61," *Indian Population Bulletin* (New Delhi), (2) (August 1961), 295–300.

Stockwell, Edward G., and Charles B. Nam. "Illustrative Tables of School Life," *Journal of the American Statistical Association*, 58 (304) (December 1963), 1113–1124.

United Nations Educational, Scientific and Cultural Organization. "World Illiteracy at Mid-century: A Statistical Study," *Monographs on Fundamental Education*, 10. Paris, 1957.

United Nations General Assembly. *The Eradication of Illiteracy*. July 12, 1957.

U. S. Bureau of the Census. *Current Population Reports*. Series P-23, No. 6. *Estimates of Illiteracy, By States: 1950*. Washington, D.C.: U. S. Government Printing Office, November 1959.

U. S. Bureau of the Census. *Current Population*

Yuan, D. Y. "Chinatown and Beyond: The Chinese Population in Metropolitan New York," *Phylon*, 27(1966), 321–332.

Reports. Series P-23. Technical Studies, Nos. 1-8. No. 9. *Estimates of Median Age at High School and College Graduation: 1960 and 1950.* Washington, D.C.: U. S. Government Printing Office, November 8, 1963.

U. S. Bureau of the Census. "Educational Attainment," *Current Population Reports.* Series P-20. Washington, D.C.: U.S. Government Printing Office, February 7, 1963.

U. S. Bureau of the Census (Mary G. Powers and Charles B. Nam). "Projections of Educational Attainment in the United States: 1965 to 1985," *Current Population Reports: Population Estimates.* Series P-25, No. 305, April 14, 1965.

U. S. Department of Health, Education and Welfare. "Limited Educational Attainment: Extent and Consequences," *Health, Education and Welfare Indicators.* Washington, D.C.: U.S. Government Printing Office, April 1962.

U. S. Office of Education. *Projections of Educational Statistics to 1973–74* (1964 edition). Circular 754. Washington, D.C.: U.S. Government Printing Office, 1964.

Windle, Charles. "The Accuracy of Census Literacy Statistics in Iran," *Journal of the American Statistical Association,* 54 (287) (September 1959), 578–581.

Zitter, Meyer. *Forecasting School Enrollment.* Paper contributed for the United Nations World Population Conference, August 30-September 10, 1965.

III. RELIGIOUS AFFILIATION

Bogue, Donald J. "Religious Affiliation," Chapter 23 in *Population of the United States.* New York: The Free Press of Glencoe, 1960.

Cowhig, James D., and Leo F. Schnore. "Religious Affiliation and Church Attendance in Metropolitan Center," *American Catholic Sociological Review,* 23 (2) (Summer 1962), 113–127.

Demerath, N. J., III. *Social Class in American Protestantism.* A publication from the Research Program in the Sociology of Religion, Survey Research Center, University of California, Berkeley. Chicago: Rand McNally, 1965.

Erskine, Hazel G. "The Polls: Organized Religion," *Public Opinion Quarterly,* 29 (2) (Summer 1965), 326–337.

Gaustad, Edwin S. *Historical Atlas of Religion in America.* New York: Harper and Row, 1962.

Goldberg, David, and Harry Sharp. "Some Characteristics of Detroit Area Jewish and Non-Jewish Adults," in Marshall Sklare (ed.). *The Jews: Social Patterns of an American Group.* Glencoe, Ill.: The Free Press, 1958.

Goldberg, Nathan. "Demographic Characteristics of American Jews," in Jacob Fried (ed.). *Jews in the Modern World.* New York: Twayne, 1962, 638–717.

Good, Dorothy. "Questions on Religion in the United States Census," *Population Index,* 25 (1) (January 1959), 3–16.

Houtart, Fr. "A Sociological Study of the Evolution of the American Catholics," *Social Compass* (The Hague), 2 (5/6) (1955), 189–216.

Horowitz, C. Morris. "Estimated Jewish Population of New York, 1958: A Study in Techniques," *Jewish Journal of Sociology,* 3 (2) (December 1961), 243–253.

Klausner, Samuel Z. "Methods of Data Collection in Studies of Religion," *Journal for the Scientific Study of Religion,* 3 (2) (Spring 1964), 193–203.

Landis, Benson Y. "Trends in Church Membership in the United States," *Annals of the American Academy of Political and Social Science,* Vol. 332, November 1960, 1–8.

Lazerwitz, Bernard. "A Comparison of Major United States Religious Groups," *Journal of the American Statistical Association,* 56 (295) (September 1961), 568–579.

Lenski, Gerhard E. *The Religious Factor: A Sociological Study of Religion's Impact on Politics, Economics and Family Life.* Garden City, N.Y.: Doubleday, 1961.

National Council of Churches of Christ in the United States of America. *Churches and Church Membership in the United States.* September 1956-November 1957. Enumeration and Analysis by Counties, States, and Regions (80 Bulletins): Series A, Major faiths by regions, divisions and states; Series B, Denominational Statistics by regions, divisions and states; Series C, Denominational Statistics by states and counties; Series D, Denominational Statistics by standard metropolitan areas; Series E, Analyses of socio-economic characteristics. New York, 1958.

Nixon, J. W. "Some Demographic Characteristics of Protestants and Catholics in Switzerland," *Revue de l'Institut International de Statistique* (The Hague), 29 (3) (1961), 13–28.

Petersen, William. "Religious Statistics in the United States," *Journal for the Scientific Study of Religion,* 1 (2) (April 1962), 166–177.

Pfautz, Harold W. "The Sociology of Secularization: Religious Groups," *American Journal of Sociology,* 61 (2) (September 1955), 121–128.

Rosenswaike, Ira. "The Utilization of Census Tract Data in the Study of the American Jewish

Population," *Jewish Social Studies,* **25** (1) (January 1963), 42–56.

United Nations Educational, Scientific and Cultural Organization. *Sociology of Religions.* A trend report and bibliography prepared for the International Sociological Association with the support of the International Committee for Social Sciences Documentation. *Current Sociology* (Paris), **5** (1) (1956), 3–87.

U. S. Bureau of the Census. *Religion Reported by the Civilian Population of the United States: March, 1957. Current Population Reports,* No. 79. Series P-20. Population Characteristics. Washington, D.C.: U.S. Government Printing Office, February 2, 1958.

Zelinsky, Wilbur. "An Approach to the Religious Geography of the United States: Patterns of Church Membership in 1952," *Annals of the Association of American Geographers,* **51** (2) (June 1961), 139–193.

CHAPTER 9

Economic Characteristics: The Economically Active Population

9.1. Introduction: Economic Characteristics and Demographic Study

There are economic questions that are so fundamental for any community or nation that they transcend the domain of the economists and are of basic concern to all branches of social science. These are:

1. Size of work force and proportion of the adult population actively engaged in economically gainful pursuits.

2. Number of unemployed or underemployed persons and their proportion of the total work force.

3. "Structure" or composition of the work force:

    (a) Industry composition—types of industries and the number of persons each employs.

    (b) Occupation composition—types of occupations and the number of workers in each.

4. Regularity of employment—the extent to which employment is only part-time, both in terms of the workweek and of the year.

5. Income level and distribution—the average amount of income generated per worker and the pattern by which it is distributed. Facts with which to answer these questions are collected as a part of population censuses. Although the professional technicians who direct the collection and publication of this information are primarily economists, usually they are also professional demographers. The same tends to be true of those who are most directly interested in research pertaining to work force and income distribution. Thus a substantial sub-group of demographers are interested primarily in studying the economic characteristics of the population; hence they form a bridge between demography and economics.

The reasons for the widespread interest in these questions are reasonably self-evident. The economic and social well-being of a nation or a community is influenced by the number of earners, their qualifications, the regularity of their employment, and the amounts they earn. A great deal can be inferred about the social life of a nation or a community if we know its industry composition, its occupation composition, and other basic facts about its work force. Do its youngsters enter the labor force too young to obtain a good basic education? How many of its elderly people are forced by circumstances of poverty to remain in the labor force long after the normal retirement age? How many women are employed, and to what extent is their employment an expression of ambition and to what extent is it a result of inability of their families to gain an adequate livelihood from the earnings of the male workers alone? To what kinds of jobs are women, children, and elderly persons put and what are their hours of work? How much are they able to earn? Are they being exploited by their employers and are they engaged in work that is physically injurious or highly unremunerative? How much does seasonality of employment reduce the annual earnings of workers and create hardship? To what extent are women or persons of particular castes, classes, or races being excluded from particular industries or occupations without regard to their qualifications? To what extent is there inequity in income distribution according to race, caste, or class? These are only a few of the questions that can be answered unambiguously by well collected and carefully tabulated statistics on the work force and its characteristics.

There is a direct reciprocal relationship between demographic forces and economic forces; each influences the other. From one point of view, demographic events may be regarded as *dependent* on economic events—during times of prosperity birthrates and migration rates tend to rise, whereas in times of economic depression they tend to fall, and so forth. From another point of view, the reverse is true: economic events are dependent on demographic events. The size of the labor force and its age, sex, and other composition is conditioned in very large part by demographic trends over the preceding several decades—by the number of births, deaths, and migrants.

This is the first of three chapters that undertake to deal with the entire topic of "economic demography" or "demographic economics." It begins by discussing fundamental concepts of work force study, then launches into a comparative analysis of the work force of the world's nations, and ends with an intensive study of the labor force in the United States. These chapters are written with the intent that they may be used as an introduction to labor force study by social scientists of any field of interest.

9.2. Definition of the Economically Active Population

Those who engage in this field of study try to dichotomize the total population into the "economically active" and the "economically inactive." To the first group belong the workers who are producers of economic goods or services, hence are said to be gainfully employed. They are the breadwinners or livelihood earners. Other terms such as "work force," "gainfully employed," or "labor force" are used to refer to the "economically active" portion of the population. The student must learn to be cautious in using these terms, because (as described below) each tends to be identified with a particular way of defining what constitutes the earners and the dependents. The term "economically active" is used by the United Nations and it generally subsumes all other definitions. To the other group belong the nonworkers, who consume but do not produce in the economic sense.

Farmers, wage or salary workers in offices, factories, or at other work sites, and self-employed professionals, proprietors, artisans, or others performing services for a fee are all economically active. Even the unpaid son, daughter, or wife of the farmer, shopkeeper, or other manager of an enterprise is considered to be a part of the economically active population, provided that he or she devotes a certain minimum specified amount of time per week, per month, or per year to gainful work. Excluded, however, are workers whose activity is not primarily oriented toward economic production or working for gain. Although the housewife performs essential services that would cost a substantial sum of money if performed by a hired servant, her activities are defined as being oriented primarily toward consumption—food preparation, and so on. However, a farmwife who does major chores or fieldwork that directly contributes to the production of food or incomes or a city wife who types for a self-employed husband, keeps his accounts, or helps in the family establishment is considered to be economically active, irrespective of whether or not she is paid.

In every economy there are some workers whose work force status is somewhat ambiguous, or marginal. A wife or an elderly person may not have a regular job, but may be available to help out occasionally when there is a rush task or an emergency. An elderly lady or a teenager may baby-sit for neighbors occasionally. A small boy may have a paper route with a few customers. Children may attend school during most of the year, but do odd jobs during the summer. Children may work a short time before or after school at some minor task. The exclusion or inclusion of these marginal workers makes a very great difference in the size of the enumerated work force because it involves a substantial share of the population. It is true that marginal workers often represent only a small fraction of the total productive work performed, but their numbers comprise a significant fraction of the economically active population. It is essential, in the study of changes and trends, that the definitions used be the same. International comparisons may be extremely hazardous because of differences in the definitions used. One way of limiting the number of marginal child workers is to set a minimum age at which a child can be considered to be economically active. In many nations it is as low as 10 years, to take cognizance of the fact that in agricultural communities many boys of 10 years of age help in the fields. The usual way of limiting the number of older marginal workers is to establish a minimum amount of work per week, per month, and so on that they must perform in order to be considered economically active.

Another form of marginality is seasonal or other cyclical employment of short duration. A fisherman in Bombay or Karachi may be idle during the months of the monsoon. The Asian farmer will be highly active plowing and planting his rice during the monsoon, but may be economically inactive during much of the dry season. In other words, the size and characteristics of the work force may vary widely with the season of the year. An important problem is to get both the farmer and the fisherman counted in the economically active population in a way that is useful. Work force statistics reported by a given census are influenced by the time of the year at which the census is taken, as well as by the definitions used of what constitutes the economically active population.

In any given moment there is a substantial number of adults who are not employed but are looking for work. Most experts agree that they should be considered as a part of the work force, even though they may be new workers who have never held a job before.

There is much turnover in the work force. Persons are continuously entering and leaving the status of being economically active. Young people graduate or leave school and begin to search for work. Wives quit their jobs to have a family or enter the work force when their children are all in school or grown. Middle-aged and elderly people retire for reasons of health or on attaining compulsory retirement age. At all ages there are a few persons who tend to be sporadic or irregular in their work habits or who enter or quit the work force for personal reasons.

It may be concluded that there is no one definition of the work force that can clearly separate workers from nonworkers. It is difficult to formulate a definition that satisfies all needs and all points of view. The size and characteristics of the work force depend on the length of the time span used. We could classify people according to their work activity *at a given instant of time* or during a very short span of time such as one week, or according to their work activity during a longer span of time such as three months, six months, or one year. Or, we could specify no time span and classify people according to their *usual* activity in the recent past, indefinitely specified. The advantage of setting an arbitrary time interval is twofold. It prevents workers from reporting a status they may have held several years ago but have lost, and it permits a measurement of unemployment—those in the work force but without a specific job. Its weakness is that it may classify the seasonal worker or the worker temporarily laid off according to a fill-in activity that is atypical for him, or may fail to include him in the work force at all. The "usual activity" approach avoids this, but grossly understates the amount of unemployment, and gives an opportunity for the respondent to report to the census the best job he has ever held, which may have been several years in the past. It may also inflate the size of the work force by including persons who may have worked in the recent past but no longer participate in the work force. If the cost were not prohibitive, the best census inquiry of the economically active population would ask for a report of type and amount of economic activity during each of the 12 months preceding the census date.

9.3. Work Force Participation and Unemployment

Once a definition of what constitutes membership in the economically active population is established, the entire population may be classified as being "active" or "inactive" in the work force. As has been mentioned, a lower age limit is also fixed. It may be age 10, 12, 14, or even older—depending on the extent to which a significant number of children engage in gainful work. Since it is customary in farm communities for children to begin work at an early age, the lower limit of work force participation is lower in the economically less advanced nations. Being economically active often is termed "work force participation" or "participation in the labor force." Since many persons remain in the labor force until their death, irrespective of age, usually no upper age limit is set to work force participation.

The work force participation rate is defined as that percentage of the total population of work force age which is economically active. The United Nations uses the term "activity rate" for this concept. It is the ratio of all those actually in the work force to all those eligible to be in it, multiplied by 100. This measure can be computed not only for a population as a whole, but also for parts of the population. It can be computed separately for males and females, for each age group, and for regions, provinces, states, and individual local areas.

If a reasonably short span of time is used in defining work force status, it is possible to obtain a count of persons in the work force but unemployed (without a job). This leads directly to the calculation of an unemployment rate. *The rate of unemployment is defined as that percentage of the total work force which is without a current job.* It is the number of unemployed members of the work force divided by the total work force and multiplied by 100. It can also be computed for sex, age, or locality subdivisions of the population.

The problems of defining the labor force have been receiving increasingly systematic review. Two provocative reviews were presented at the World Population Conference of 1965 by Dr. Asok Mitra, Registrar General of India,[1] and by Dr. Yuki Miura of the United Nations Economic Commission for Africa.[2] Dr. Miura reviewed more than 60 population censuses and surveys conducted in African and

Asian countries during the period 1955-1964. The differences among the concepts and definitions used in these studies were classified into eight groups:

1. Definition of "work" or "economic activity."

2. Formulation of questions on the questionnaire.

3. Reference time period.

4. Limit of amount of time worked above which a person may be classified as economically active.

5. Age limits in enumerating the economically active population.

6. Treatment of certain population groups (e.g., unpaid family workers).

7. Priority phasings (persons with more than one activity status, e.g., students who work).

8. Treatment of inactive employed and unemployed persons.

This inventory showed wide variation among the nations in all eight of these aspects and suggested that the differences are of such magnitude as to affect substantially the comparability of results. Undoubtedly, some of the differences reflect the unique needs of individual nations, but many others seem to reflect only the tastes of individual research groups and could easily be eliminated by international agreements in the interest of promoting the cumulation of scientific knowledge.

In his report, Dr. Mitra assesses the problems of applying labor force concepts in the developing nations. He writes:

". . . The feature of illiteracy common to so many Asian and African countries reduces very considerably the worth or usefulness of concepts and definitions of dependency, work, occupation, industry, time reference, employment, underemployment and unemployment. It is not what the census designer wants to put across, however elaborately or precisely, but what the head of the household is capable of making out in his own way in the space of a few minutes for each member of his household that ultimately matters. In such a situation hair-splitting nuances, which might be good for investigations in depth in small surveys, could prove futile. A second feature common to most

[1] Asok Mitra, "Indian Experience in Recording Economically Active Population: 1961 Population Census," paper submitted to the United Nations World Population Conference, Belgrade, 1965.

[2] Yuki Miura, "A Comparative Analysis of Operational Definitions of the Economically Active Population in African and Asian Statistics," paper submitted to the United Nations World Population Conference, Belgrade, 1965.

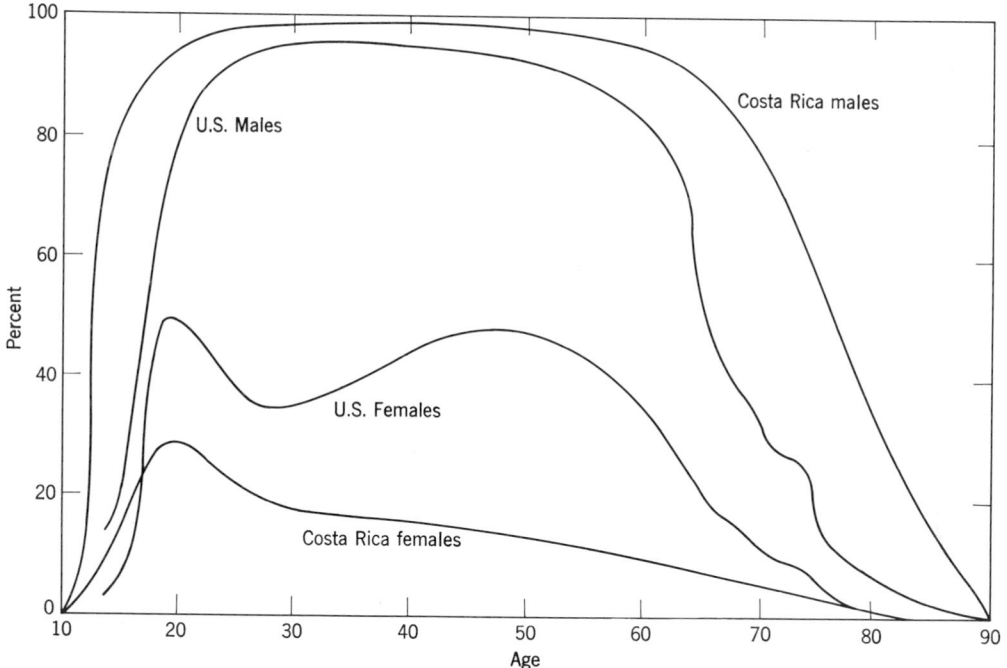

Figure 9-1   Labor Force Participation Rates by Age and Sex for an Industrialized and a Developing Nation, United States and Costa Rica: 1960.

SOURCE: Costa Rica: United Nations, *Human Resources of Central America, Panama, and Mexico: 1950-1960* (New York: United Nations Economic Commission for Latin America, 1960), p. 138.

Asian and African countries would be the multiplicity in the stages of economic development between one part of the country and another. This renders difficult uniform applications of concepts and definitions. To this may be added the multiplicity of social and cultural levels and values. Work to some communities is a matter of pride, to some others still a matter of disdain. The situation thus is one which seems to defy application of uniform concepts and units of measurement. Then again, since we are all guided by the U. N. recommendations and concepts which are written in the European languages, difficulties arise in achieving correct and uniform nuances in their translation into native tongues."

9.4. Age and Sex Differentials in Work Force Participation Rates

In most societies, men are the principal breadwinners. As soon as they complete their schooling and/or become physically strong enough to perform some gainful task, boys and young men are expected to join the ranks of the economically active population. They remain in this status until retirement or ill health removes them, whichever comes first. Figure 9-1 reports the age-specific participation rates for workers in Costa Rica and the United States. This example permits a comparison between an industrialized and a developing nation. Although the shape of the curve is very similar for males in the two nations, there are three major differences:

1. Rates of participation are much lower among youth in industrialized nations. In such nations youth are expected to remain in school longer, so that they are older on an average when they join the work force.

2. At the ages of peak adult participation, a slightly larger proportion of the males in the developing nations than in the industrialized nations are in the labor force. This may be a consequence of the fact that in the developing nations there is less provision for taking care of disabled persons, so that it is necessary for men

who are in ill health to remain economically active. It may reflect the greater opportunity in the more agricultural societies for disabled men to have some gainful work instead of being wholly excluded from participation.

3. Participation rates at the older ages are much higher in the developing nations than in the industrialized nations. At the older ages, men in the industrialized nations have the privilege of retiring from the work force and spending their last years supported by a pension and income from savings. In contrast, much less security in old age forces a high percentage of older men in developing countries to remain in the work force as long as their health permits.

The three generalizations that have just been made apply to industrialized and developing nations generally, and not just to the United States and Costa Rica, which are used only as examples.

Participation rate for females is always and everywhere much lower than that for men. This is a consequence of the fact that much of the work performed by females falls completely outside the scope of the definition of the economically active population. Figure 9-1 reports the participation rates for women in Costa Rica and the United States. Again we may make a series of comparisons:

1. The participation rate for females in industrialized nations is slightly higher than the participation rate for females in developing nations. The principal explanation is that there are more opportunities for gainful employment in urbanized and industrialized economies. Yet this rule is not an invariant one; many agricultural societies make very extensive use of females as unpaid family workers in farming work, especially at ages 10 to 19. A carefully conducted inventory may very well show that some of the highest work force participation rates for females in the world are to be found among certain highly rural cultures in South Asia or Africa where women are expected to do extensive work in the fields and in tending farm animals.

2. The participation rate for females tends to reach a peak in the late teens or early twenties, just before marriage or the onset of childbearing. After age 25 the rate tends to decline as the necessity for household work and caring for children makes participation in the work force less and less possible.

3. In industrialized societies, the greater participation of women (where it occurs) manifests itself in the premarital ages and the ages after 35. In the latter case, when their children are mature enough to be in school, women tend to reenter the labor force. The explanation for this may be as much sociological as economic. Female earners may be helping to earn money to put the children through college, to save for old age, or to complete payments on a house. But they may also be seeking meaningful activity and a sense of self-worth after their children no longer are dependent on them.

4. In industrialized nations, the rates of participation of females at ages younger than 15 and at ages beyond 75 are definitely below those for the developing nations, and probably reflect the same types of economic pressures that operate to bring males of these ages into the work force. At the intervening ages, the participation rate for females depends on whether or not the culture permits the use of women as agricultural laborers—and the exact wording of the definition used.

As in the case of males, these differences tend to be characteristic of industrialized and developing nations generally, hence are valid beyond the United States and Costa Rica.

The foregoing set of differences should warn us that simple overall comparisons of the participation rates for two nations may be very misleading if we do not know the pattern of age-sex differences involved. If we are to understand fully how the work force of one population differs from that of another, we must compare the full array of participation rates separately for each sex by age. Overall or general participation rates that have not been standardized for age and sex can lead to improper inferences.

9.5. International Comparisons of Activity Rates of Males

Because of differences in definitions and procedures for enumeration it is difficult to make precise measurements of international differences in the proportion of population of work-

Table 9-1A Average Activity Rates by Regions:
Recent Population Censuses
(Percentage Economically Active among Population of
All Ages of Given Sex)

Region	Both sexes	Males	Females
WORLD	42.5	58.3	27.2
Africa......................	35.8	56.8	14.5
North America..	39.7	58.2	21.3
Middle America[1]	35.2	56.6	14.2
South America...............	35.2	57.3	13.1
Asia[2].......................	42.5	56.4	28.1
Europe[2]....................	45.1	64.1	27.6
Oceania.....................	40.1	61.2	18.5
Union of Soviet Socialist Republics................	47.5	54.8	41.4

[1] The Central American Republics, Mexico and countries
   and territories in the Caribbean.

[2] Excluding the USSR.

Source: United Nations, Sex and Age Patterns of Participation in Economic Activities (op. cit.), p.3.
   Computed from data derived from censuses and
   surveys carried out between 1946 and 1959. Figures
   are weighted means.

ing age that is defined as economically active.
Even within a given population, differences in
concepts and definitions, and even differences
in the census procedure for applying the same
definition, tend to create problems of comparability. Unfortunately, the application of what
appears to be essentially the same set of concepts and definitions not infrequently leads to
differences that seem to reflect the mode of
enumeration rather than genuine differences in
"way of life" of the population. Hence in making international comparisons of work force
participation rates it is necessary to be constantly on guard in order to distinguish
between genuine differences and statistical artifacts. There is most urgent need for international standardization of definitions and procedures in this area of census-taking, insofar
as national needs permit it.

In 1962 the United Nations undertook to organize and draw some general findings from
the large amount of data concerning employment and work force that had been accumulated by the nations of the world. Most of the
information presented below is drawn from this
report, *Sex and Age Patterns of Participation in
Economic Activities*,[3] supplemented with materials from other less comprehensive studies.
Table 9-1A, extracted from that report, presents estimated overall rates of participation

for workers in the work force by world regions.
In this table we observe a very interesting inversion: despite the fact that at every single
age the rate of participation for men is higher
in developing nations than in industrialized
nations, the average overall rate of participation is higher in industrialized nations than in
developing nations. The explanation of this apparent inconsistency, of course, is differences in
age composition. The developing nations have
very large proportions of population in the extremely young ages 10 to 19, where rates are
lower. This tends to lower the average rates for
developing countries to a point slightly below
that for the industrialized countries. For example, the rates of participation for North
America, Europe, and Oceania are well above
those for Africa, Asia, and Middle and South
America. The USSR rate for males appears to
be an exception for an industrialized nation. Although full data are not available, the effect of
the war on the age composition of the Soviet
Union may account for much of the deviation.

[3] United Nations, *Demographic Aspects of Manpower. Report I. Sex and Age Patterns of Participation in Economic Activities* (New York: United
Nations, 1962). (See also United Nations, *Human
Resources of Central America, Panama and Mexico, 1950–60*, New York Economic Commission for
Latin America, 1960.)

Table 9-1B   Labor Force Participation Rates of the Areas by Sex and Different Age Groups

Regions	Age groups							
	10–14 a/	15–19	20–24	25–34	35–44	45–54	55–64	65+
Male								
Less developed:								
Africa......................	31.7	63.7	89.0	96.3	97.4	95.6	90.4	65.2
Asia b/.....................	31.5	68.8	89.0	96.8	97.4	96.5	89.7	66.5
Latin America c/..............	19.4	70.5	93.3	97.1	97.6	96.9	94.1	79.6
More developed:								
Europe......................	7.1	65.4	87.9	95.5	97.1	94.8	81.7	32.1
North America...............	2.3	43.2	86.2	94.8	95.5	93.3	84.3	30.4
Temp. South America d/........	11.8	61.7	91.6	97.3	96.4	90.9	80.6	51.4
Australia and New Zealand......	1.2	68.8	94.8	98.4	98.3	96.5	86.0	25.6
Japan.......................	....	51.6	87.9	97.3	97.7	96.6	86.9	54.4
Female								
Less developed:								
Africa......................	13.0	28.7	35.3	37.4	37.8	35.2	14.9	8.8
Asia........................	21.2	33.8	38.1	40.0	42.1	39.1	34.0	20.2
Latin America................	4.3	19.0	22.7	19.0	19.9	21.6	22.4	19.7
More developed:								
Europe......................	4.5	46.6	55.9	35.8	41.9	37.4	27.9	10.1
North America...............	0.9	28.2	45.3	34.8	41.7	45.6	34.2	10.1
Temp. South America..........	3.9	23.5	32.5	25.9	22.4	20.5	15.4	7.9
Australia and New Zealand......	1.2	64.3	50.6	24.7	27.1	27.5	17.9	4.2
Japan.......................	....	49.7	69.4	50.7	55.8	54.4	43.3	20.9

Note: The population of countries having census data on economically active population by sex and age as a percentage of total population in each is as follows: More developed regions, 63 percent; North America, 100 percent; Australia and New Zealand, 100 percent; Europe, 72 percent; Temperate South America, 22 percent; and Japan, 100 percent. Less-developed regions, 47 percent; Asia, 52 percent; Asia, excluding Mainland China, 90 percent; Africa, 26 percent; and Latin America, 38 percent.

a/ Economically active population below age 15 years is related to the age group 10-14.

b/ Excludes Japan which is a developed country.

c/ Excludes Temperate South America.

d/ Rates are for Chile only.

Source: "An Aspect of Global View of Labour Force Growth" by G.S. Revankar, Population Branch, United Nations. Paper presented to the United Nations World Population Conference, Belgrade, 1965.

One of the impressive things to observe in Table 9-1A is the *similarity* of rates for males around the world. The range of differences between the lowest and highest rate is quite small and would be even smaller if country-to-country differences in age composition were controlled.

When we look at the male labor force participation rates by age groups, we see that for the central working ages 25 to 55, the rates all over the world are nearly 100 percent, with small differences between one nation and another. Table 9-1B illustrates this. Table 9-2 illustrates the points, inferred from Table 9-1B that in the developing nations the participation rate for children in their early teens is much higher than in the industrialized countries. The developing nations also have a low rate of school attendance. Thus there is a positive correlation between low rates of school attendance and early entrance into the economically active population. Those nations where lack of edu-

cational facilities makes it impossible for young males to attend school are the nations with the highest rates of work participation for boys 10 to 14 years of age and 15 to 19 years of age. The fact that the nations with low rates of school attendance are also predominantly ru-

Age	Less developed nations	Industrialized nations
All ages.........	54.5	61.7
10-14 years............	27.8	63.3
15-19 years............	75.8	69.0
20-24 years............	91.9	90.1
25-34 years............	96.9	96.7
35-44 years............	97.5	97.4
45-54 years............	96.0	95.8
55-64 years............	89.6	84.9
65 years and over......	67.0	32.9

Source: Prepared by Dr. Edith Adams, Population Division, United Nations Conference on Demographic and Economic Trends in Developing Countries. Derived from U.N. Report. Demographic Aspects of Manpower, 1962

Table 9-2   Work Force Participation Rates for Males in Developing and Industrialized Nations by Age

ral societies that readily press out-of-school youth into service as unpaid family workers helps to explain this relationship. One of the major problems of the developing nations is that of getting larger proportions of rural youth to obtain more education so that the quality of the work force in future years can be improved.

Agricultural employment also helps to account for the high rates of participation reported for males of retirement age in the developing nations. Industrialized and urbanized communities tend to have definite retirement policies and arrangements, whereas in small-scale agricultural enterprises there is nothing to prevent an elderly man from working as long as he chooses or feels he must.

Within each country for which data are available there is a distinct tendency for the rate of participation for males to be higher in rural areas than in urban, and the differences appear to be due largely to the greater participation of young boys and old men in rural areas.

Although we often hear rumors about developing nations where the men loaf and the women do all of the productive work, the census statistics available do not support this as a characteristic for any nation with work force statistics. Everywhere male labor force participation rates are higher than are those for women. Throughout the world, young boys are expected to go to work if they are not in school. Men are expected to stay in the work force until forced out by compulsory retirement or ill health. This is an international cultural definition for which the nation-to-nation variations seem to be rather minor. The major source of international differences in overall labor force participation rates for males are largely noneconomic in nature; they result from differences in the percentage of the population that is 10 to 19 years of age.

9.6. International Comparisons of Participation Rates for Females

If valid and reliable data were available, an international comparison of participation rates for women would offer great opportunities for research into cultural differences in the socio-economic status of women in various societies.

As mentioned above, the task of researching this problem is rendered especially difficult because of differences in the way the large group of unpaid female family workers, who help in the fields and with the animals in agricultural societies, are treated in the census enumeration procedure.

If we arbitrarily declare that in nations where 10 percent or more of all women who are in the work force (exclusive of unpaid family workers) are "active," it is possible to classify societies and cultures according to whether or not their women appear to be active. Using this definition we may classify the nations as follows:

Developing Nations

Females comparatively active	*Females comparatively inactive*
Ghana	Algeria
Ceylon	Egypt
Federation of Malaya	Iran
India	North Borneo
Philippines	Sarawak
Bolivia	Taiwan
Colombia	Thailand
Costa Rica	Turkey
Ecuador	Brazil
El Salvador	Guatemala
Panama	Nicaragua
	Honduras

These differences must be used cautiously; in some nations it appears that large numbers of housewives have been classified as being in the labor force with little reference to their participation in gainful activity.

In almost all nations, the participation rates for married women are much lower than those for single women. For this reason, the age at marriage and the proportions ever-marrying by particular ages exert a substantial influence on the number of women who are economically active.

9.7. International Trends in Participation Rates

Reliable data, collected consistently by constant definitions, are available for so few countries that almost no empirical data can be presented to describe international trends in participation rates. However, the evidence that is available suggests that as economic development takes place, the participation rates for young males 10 to 19 years and for both males and females 65 and over decline, and may be expected to do so in the future. Industrialization tends to shrink the employment of women and children as unpaid family workers and to promote the employment of young and middle-aged women (especially single women) as wage or salary workers.

Underemployment. A much-discussed problem of the working force is the phenomenon of underemployment. If the participation of a worker in the work force makes a contribution to the national economy that is nearly zero (because his services are a duplication of services already plentifully performed, are so small as not to maintain him, or are not of utility, hence are not used, etc.), he may be said to be underemployed.

Most developing nations are faced with this problem in acute form. It is also found in the depressed regions of many industrialized nations and in the slums of all of the world's metropolises. The International Labour Office has undertaken to clarify the problem of definition by recognizing two forms of underemployment:

"(*a*) *Visible underemployment,* which involves persons involuntarily working parttime or for shorter than normal periods of work.

"(*b*) *Invisible underemployment,* which exists when a person's working time is not abnormally reduced but whose employment is inadequate in other respects such as (1) when his job does not permit full use of his highest existing skill or capacity; (2) when his earnings from employment are abnormally low; (3) when he is employed in an establishment or economic unit whose productivity is abnormally low."[4]

[4] Quoted by Kailas C. Doctor, of the International Labour Office, in a paper, "Recent Progress in Underemployment Statistics and Analysis," submitted to the World Population Conference, Belgrade, 1965.

Visible underemployment may be measured with comparative ease, but invisible underemployment must be inferred indirectly. In an effort to help quantify this phenomenon, Elizaga has suggested that agricultural workers who till less than two hectares of cultivable land are underemployed, and that where agricultural production per worker is less than half the national average for all workers, there is evidence of rural underemployment.[5] For nonagricultural workers he suggests that earning an income below a designated minimum amount is indirect evidence of invisible underemployment. On this basis he estimates that in 1958 nearly one fourth of the male workers of Greater Santiago, Chile, were underemployed, using data from a special survey.

In nations that are largely agricultural, unemployment is comparatively low but underemployment, as represented by full-time work during only a few weeks in the year, may be very high. In nations such as India the implications of underemployment may be tremendous:

"Provisional calculations have shown that in India a planned decrease in dependence on agriculture from 70 percent in 1961 to 60 percent in 1976 will still mean an addition of another 23 million to labour force in agriculture. This is a challenging picture requiring a tremendous organizational effort for the following reasons:

"(*a*) The transfer of male population from agricultural activity has been so small in 1951-61 that it is difficult to conceive of the proposed reduction in dependence on agriculture.

"(*b*) To absorb 23 million persons at a higher level of efficiency in agriculture will mean substantial investment in agriculture.

"(*c*) The Indian economy is still in the process of building the infra-structure for development. In the non-agricultural sector where about 47 million may have to find employment in 1961-76, this would mean that the capital employment ratio will continue to be adverse.

[5] Juan C. Elizaga, "The Demographic Aspects of Unemployment and Under-Employment in Latin America," paper submitted to the United Nations World Population Conference, Belgrade, 1965.

"(d) An increase in employment in the non-agricultural sector will require development of sufficient technical skills."[6]

The prospect of having to absorb an additional 23 million workers into the already saturated Indian agricultural economy while trying to find nonagricultural employment for an additional 47 million workers (plus trying to absorb the unemployed and improve the lot of the underemployed) who are of low education and without skills is very discouraging. Such a feat would also be unprecedented. Datar reports that "India's Second Plan (1956-61) started with the assumption that the development activity could be so organized as would enable India to hold the unemployment line. . . . [instead] It seems there will be a fresh gap of about 4 million by the end of the Third Plan. . . . Thus the situation by the end of the Third Plan is likely to be more difficult than what it was when the plan was initiated."

This tragedy, as it unfolds, will not register so much as unemployment as invisible underemployment. A very large proportion of the world's hungry people are underemployed rather than being outright unemployed. In many developing nations both categories are growing rapidly, and are destined to grow for at least two decades because the persons involved are already born.

9.8. The Labor Force of the United States

In the United States the work force is known as the "labor force." The definition used is one that refers to a short specific time—one week. The labor force is comprised of two major groups: (1) those who are employed and (2) those who are unemployed.

The *employed* comprise all persons 14 years of age and over who during a particular specified week were (a) at work—those who did any work for pay or profit or worked without pay for 15 hours or more on a family farm or in a

family business—or (b) "with a job but not at work"—those who did not work and were not looking for work but had a job or business from which they were temporarily absent because of bad weather, industrial dispute, vacation, illness, or for other personal reasons.

The *unemployed* are persons 14 years of age and over who are not at work but looking for work. A person is considered as looking for work not only if he actually tried to find work during the specified week but also if he had made such efforts recently (within the last 60 days) and was awaiting the results of these efforts. Registration at a public or private employment office, meeting or telephoning prospective employers, being on call at a personal office, union hall, or professional register, writing letters of application, or placing or answering work advertisements would be considered as looking for work. Persons waiting to be called back to a job from which they have been laid off or furloughed are also counted as unemployed.

There are several sources of work force data. The leading source of current information is the Current Population Survey (CPS), a monthly survey of a representative probability sample of the population. This survey is a sensitive barometer of both total employment and unemployment.

The decennial census is a second source of data. Although it is available only once every ten years, it furnishes detailed information about the work force of individual communities (even census tracts within cities) that are unobtainable with the sample used for the CPS.

Very important but sometimes overlooked sources of work force data are the reports that employers routinely turn in. Such reports of employment are made routinely to the Bureau of Labor Statistics and to the Social Security Administration. State employment offices keep statistics of registrants for unemployment compensation.

The sequence of questions asked at the 1960 census was as follows:

1. Did this person work at any time last week? Include part-time work such as a Satur-

---

[6] B. N. Datar, "Demographic Aspects of Unemployment and Under-Employment with Particular Reference to India," paper submitted to the United Nations World Population Conference, Belgrade, 1965. (Shri Datar is Chief of Labour and Employment, Planning Commission, Government of India.)

day job, delivering papers, or helping without pay in a family business or farm. Do *not* count own housework.

A. IF YES:

2. How many hours did he work *last week* (at all jobs)? (If exact figures not known, give best estimates.)

1 to 14 hours	40 hours
15 to 29 hours	41 to 48 hours
30 to 34 hours	49 to 59 hours
35 to 39 hours	60 hours or more

3. Was this person looking for work, or on layoff from a job?

4. Does he have a job or business from which he was temporarily absent all last week because of illness, vacation or other reasons?

The sequence of questioning used in the Current Population Survey is very similar.

From the data yielded by these questions each member of the population aged 14 and over was classified as follows:

A. In the labor force
1. Employed
2. Unemployed
B. Not in the labor force

Despite the fact that the Current Population Survey is only a sample, it is generally conceded to yield more reliable results than the decennial census. The reason is that the CPS enumerators are very carefully selected, are given thorough training, and have the experience of performing enumeration month after month. They know the basic objectives, concepts, and definitions and are able to apply them with better judgment than the more hastily recruited and less thoroughly trained field employee of the decennial census. Where self-enumeration is used, the trained interviewer is more capable of applying the definitions correctly than the untrained respondent.

Labor Force Participation Rate. The labor force participation rate is defined as the percentage of the population 14 years of age and over that is in the labor force.

The labor force participation rate in the United States is about 55 percent. This is a weighted average of a much higher rate for males (77 percent) and a much lower rate for females (35 percent). There is also a very interesting set of sex-color differentials:

Color	Both sexes	Males	Females
Total	55.3	77.4	34.5
White	45.2	78.0	33.6
Nonwhite	56.3	72.1	41.8

Nonwhite females have a *higher* labor force participation rate than white females. But nonwhite males have a *lower* labor force participation rate than white males. Tables 9-3 reports trends in labor force size and participation rate, with projection to 1975, on the presumption that past trends of participation will continue. It is clear that in the immediate future the American labor force is due to undergo a very rapid expansion in size, even though there will be only modest changes in the participation rates.

Age Patterns and Race of Labor Force Participation. Males and females have a very unlike age pattern of labor force participation. This is shown by Table 9-4 and Figure 9-1. By age 16, nearly one third of the males are in the labor force. These represent school dropouts and part-time workers. From age 16 to 20 the rate rises sharply, and by age 25 more than 90 percent of the males are employed. The rate rises to about 95 percent at age 28. It remains on this high plateau through age 45 and then begins to decline gradually. At age 65 it drops sharply as enforced retirement and ill health cause withdrawal.

Among women the participation rate is very low before age 17, but then rises very swiftly to about age 22. Then marriage and childbearing begin and cause withdrawal from the labor force. The rate sags lower until about age 35, at which age it again rises and remains high until age 55; then it declines again. This age pattern for females is especially pronounced among the white population.

Nonwhite males have lower rates of labor force participation than white males at every age from 14 to 70. This is a differential of long standing, and one that is not easily explained. One explanation is that it represents hidden unemployment; some unemployed Negroes are

Table 9-3   The Work Force of the United States: 1820 to 1975

Year	Gainful workers (000)	Total labor force			Percent of total population	Percent of workers female	Participation rate		
		(000) Total	(000) Male	(000) Female			Total	Male	Female
	(1)	(2)	(3)	(4)	(5)	(6)	(7)	(8)	(9)
1820	2,881	...	...	...	29.9	...	...	...	...
1830	3,932	...	...	...	30.6	...	...	...	...
1840	5,420	...	...	...	31.8	...	...	...	...
1850	7,697	...	...	...	33.2	...	...	...	...
1860	10,533	...	...	...	33.5	...	...	...	...
1870	12,925	12,557	10,699	1,858	31.5	14.8	51.5	86.2	15.5
1880	17,392	16,896	14,328	2,568	33.7	15.2	52.5	87.3	16.3
1890	23,318	22,653	18,757	3,896	36 0	17.2	54.2	87.3	19.2
1900	29,073	28,282	23,168	5,114	37.2	18.1	55.0	87.7	20.4
1910	37,371	...	...	...	...	...	...	...	...
1920	42,434	42,660	33,957	8,703	38.7	20.4	55.8	85.9	24.1
1930	48,830	50,080	39,062	11,018	39.5	22.0	54.6	83.4	25.1
1940	...	56,030	41,870	14,160	42.5	25.3	55.9	83.9	28.2
1941	...	57,380	42,740	14,640	43.1	25.5	56.6	84.8	28.7
1942	...	60,230	44,110	16,120	45.0	26.8	58.8	86.6	31.3
1943	...	64,410	45,600	18,810	48.0	29.2	62.2	88.7	36.1
1944	...	65,890	46,520	19,370	49.6	29.4	63.1	89.8	36.8
1945	...	65,140	45,870	19,270	49.2	29.6	61.8	88.0	36.2
1946	...	60,820	43,980	16,840	43.4	27.7	57.2	83.7	31.3
1947	...	61,608	44,694	16,915	42.9	27.5	57.3	84.4	31.0
1948	...	62,748	45,150	17,599	43.0	28.0	57.8	84.6	31.9
1949	...	63,571	45,524	18,048	42.8	28.4	58.0	84.5	32.4
1950	...	64,599	45,919	18,680	42.7	28.9	58.3	84.4	33.1
1951	...	65,832	46,524	19,309	42.9	29.3	58.8	84.8	33.8
1952	...	66,426	46,868	19,559	42.6	29.4	58.7	84.6	33.9
1953	...	67,362	47,692	19,668	42.5	29.2	58.5	84.4	33.6
1954	...	67,818	47,847	19,970	42.1	29.4	58.4	83.9	33.7
1955	...	68,896	48,054	20,842	41.9	30.3	58.7	83.6	34.8
1956	...	70,387	48,579	21,808	42.1	31.0	59.3	83.7	35.9
1957	...	70,746	48,649	22,097	41.5	31.2	58.7	82.7	35.9
1960	...	73,372	49,751	23,621	41.3	32.2	58.1	80.7	36.5
1965	...	79,442	52,536	26,906	41.7	33.9	57.9	78.7	38.2
1970	...	86,604	56,213	30,391	42.3	35.1	58.3	77.9	39.8
1975	...	93,705	60,104	33,601	42.3	35.9	59.0	77.9	41.1

Source: Bogue, Population of the United States, p. 423.

reported as not in the labor force. This certainly seems to be a plausible explanation for the very large differences at ages 14 to 20. At these ages the rate of school attendance for Negroes is much lower than for whites, yet at the same ages Negroes have lower participation rates. This means that a very large number of Negro youths are out of school but not in the labor force. The fact that they are not reported as seeking work may reflect the fact that they know that no work is available for them.

Negro girls also experience difficulty in obtaining employment. Until age 22 the participation rates for Negro females are below those of white females. For all ages thereafter the participation rates for nonwhite females surpass those for white females.

It is generally conceded that the higher participation of nonwhite women in the United States is related to the low economic status of this group. In an effort to supplement the family income a large portion of nonwhite married women, even those with small children, must seek employment.

9.9.   Ethnic Factors in Labor Force Participation

Table 9-5 reports the labor force participation rate for the United States: population classified by parentage and nativity as well as by race. This has been done separately for males and females, by age. The reader will note that only 66.8 percent of the male foreign-born population age 14 and over was reported as being in the labor force in 1960. This is not because foreign-born men are lazy, but because they are so highly concentrated in ages above 65 that the overall rate is low. On an age-specific basis, they tend to have higher rates of participation. In fact, it appears that although all male race and ethnic groups in the labor force have high rates of labor force participation for

Table 9-4   Labor Force Participation Rates by Sex and Color for Single Years of Age: 1960

Single years of age	Male			Female		
	Total	White	Nonwhite	Total	White	Nonwhite
14	13.9	14.4	10.2	5.7	5.9	4.4
15	18.2	18.7	14.6	8.2	8.4	6.4
16	30.1	31.0	22.9	15.7	16.4	10.5
17	43.5	44.6	34.8	25.9	27.0	17.6
18	60.7	61.9	52.0	43.1	44.0	30.7
19	72.8	73.6	66.5	49.7	51.2	39.2
20	79.6	80.1	75.6	49.2	50.0	43.9
21	83.4	83.7	80.5	47.1	47.4	45.1
22	87.3	87.9	83.2	45.7	45.6	46.3
23	89.8	90.5	84.8	42.5	42.0	45.9
24	91.2	91.9	86.3	39.6	38.6	46.4
25	92.2	92.9	87.1	37.5	36.1	46.6
26	93.3	94.0	87.8	35.5	33.9	45.7
27	94.0	94.9	87.5	34.5	32.5	47.2
28	94.7	95.5	88.1	34.0	32.2	46.9
29	95.2	96.0	88.7	33.7	31.8	47.2
30	95.5	96.3	88.8	34.3	32.1	49.5
31	95.7	96.5	89.1	34.7	32.7	49.3
32	95.7	96.5	89.0	35.2	33.2	49.6
33	96.0	96.7	89.3	36.0	34.0	51.2
34	95.9	96.7	89.4	37.4	35.4	52.2
35	95.9	96.7	89.5	38.3	36.5	53.1
36	95.8	96.4	90.0	38.7	37.1	52.1
37	95.9	96.6	90.4	40.0	38.1	55.1
38	95.6	96.3	89.2	41.4	39.8	54.8
39	95.8	96.5	89.4	42.4	40.8	55.7
40	95.6	96.2	90.0	43.9	42.1	57.4
41	95.2	95.8	90.0	44.9	43.4	57.2
42	95.4	96.0	89.6	45.3	44.0	56.5
43	95.5	96.0	90.0	46.1	44.9	57.6
44	95.2	95.7	90.1	46.7	45.5	57.3
45	95.1	95.6	90.0	46.9	45.8	56.4
46	94.8	95.3	89.0	47.5	46.5	57.2
47	94.4	94.9	89.4	47.6	46.5	57.2
48	94.3	94.8	89.1	47.4	46.4	56.5
49	93.9	94.4	89.0	47.7	46.7	55.5
50	93.0	93.7	86.6	47.2	46.4	54.5
51	92.7	93.4	85.8	47.0	46.3	53.1
52	92.1	92.7	86.7	46.0	45.2	53.5
53	91.3	91.8	85.3	44.8	44.2	51.0
54	90.7	91.4	84.8	44.2	43.7	49.6
55	89.9	90.4	84.9	42.5	41.9	48.2
56	89.0	89.6	82.9	40.7	40.0	47.3
57	87.8	88.6	80.4	39.7	39.1	45.6
58	86.7	87.4	80.4	38.7	38.2	43.6
59	85.0	86.1	76.7	37.0	36.6	40.9
60	82.9	83.7	75.4	34.9	34.5	39.5
61	80.6	81.2	72.3	32.3	31.9	37.0
62	78.3	79.0	70.2	29.2	28.7	34.9
63	75.2	76.0	65.9	26.3	25.9	30.8
64	70.4	71.5	60.2	24.3	23.9	38.0
65	53.5	54.0	48.9	20.3	19.9	24.2
66	46.0	46.3	42.5	17.7	17.4	20.9
67	41.9	42.2	38.8	16.1	15.9	18.4
68	38.9	39.1	36.3	14.7	**14.5**	16.7
69	36.2	36.5	33.2	13.2	13.0	15.7
70	33.2	33.3	31.3	11.7	11.5	14.3

Source: U.S. Census of Population: 1960 Subject Report, Employment Status and Work Experience, Table 1.

ages 50 to 64, the foreign-born population tends to have a higher rate of participation than the native-born. A similar difference is observable for the native-born of foreign-born or mixed parentage.

Among women, there appear to be no major differences among the white ethnic groups in labor force participation when the factor of age is controlled. However, for all ages above 20 years Negro women have a higher rate of labor force participation than any of the white ethnic groups.

Marital Status and Labor Force Participation Rate. It is to be expected that the labor force participation rate for females would be influenced markedly by their marital status. That

Table 9-5 Labor Force Participation Rate of the United States Population by Race, Nativity, Parentage, Age, and Sex: 1960

Age and Sex	White			Negro	Other Nonwhite
	Native of native parentage	Native of foreign or mixed parentage	Foreign born		
MALE, TOTAL	77.8	83.4	66.8	72.1	73.1
14 to 17 years	27.4	27.1	26.4	20.7	18.2
18 and 19 years.....	67.6	66.8	68.4	59.1	51.9
20 to 24 years	86.9	85.9	84.3	82.7	73.9
25 to 29 years	94.6	95.0	94.1	88.2	84.9
30 to 34 years	96.4	97.1	96.4	89.0	90.3
35 to 39 years	96.2	97.3	97.2	89.4	92.8
40 to 44 years	95.6	96.9	96.6	89.8	91.1
45 to 49 years	94.5	96.2	96.1	89.2	90.3
50 to 54 years	91.9	94.0	94.3	85.6	87.9
55 to 59 years	87.3	90.3	90.9	80.7	81.9
60 to 64 years	77.0	81.3	80.8	68.4	72.9
65 to 69 years	44.1	46.0	43.2	40.6	39.4
70 to 74 years	29.5	31.0	25.1	28.2	29.8
75 and over	16.3	17.0	12.9	15.8	17.1
FEMALE, TOTAL	33.7	35.9	28.3	42.1	36.8
14 to 17 years	14.5	16.7	16.9	9.4	9.8
18 and 19 years	47.3	55.7	52.6	34.5	36.7
20 to 24 years	43.9	51.1	49.1	45.7	45.3
25 to 29 years	32.9	34.5	38.2	47.8	36.5
30 to 34 years	33.6	32.6	36.8	51.6	38.5
35 to 39 years	38.6	37.6	40.3	55.0	44.3
40 to 44 years	43.8	44.0	45.9	57.6	51.6
45 to 49 years	45.8	47.5	47.7	57.0	48.7
50 to 54 years	44.7	46.8	44.7	52.9	44.1
55 to 59 years	38.7	41.5	37.5	45.2	40.8
60 to 64 years	28.9	31.0	26.1	34.4	30.0
65 to 69 years	16.4	78.3	13.5	19.5	17.7
70 to 74 years	9.6	10.9	7.7	11.4	12.2
75 and over	4.3	5.0	3.4	5.6	5.3

Source: U.S. Census of Population: 1960 Subject reports, Employment Status and Work Experience, Table 3

this is true is shown in the bottom panel of Table 9-6. Among women who are single, the rate of labor force participation corresponds rather well to that for males. In fact, from ages 18 to 70 the labor force participation rate for single males and single females is very similar. In sharp contrast to this, females who are married and living with their husbands have much lower participation rates at each age group. Where the woman is married, but the husband is absent, the participation rates tend to be substantially higher. They tend to be higher still if the woman is widowed and yet higher if she is divorced. The participation rates for divorced women at each age tend to be very nearly equal to those for single women.

The pattern of differences in labor force participation rate according to marital status is similar for nonwhite females to that for whites, with a few important modifications. First, the tendency for women to remain in the labor force even though married and living with their husbands is much greater in the nonwhite than in the white population. Similarly, the participation rate is higher if the woman is married but the spouse is absent. In contrast, the labor force participation rates for single, nonwhite women of all ages are significantly *lower* than those for single white women. This is probably due to two forces: (1) the greater difficulty that single, nonwhite women experience in gaining employment and (2) the fact that a substantial proportion of single, nonwhite females have borne children and are caring for them in the home.

For males, marital status has a completely different relationship to labor force participation than for females. First, its significance is a much smaller one. Second, the relationships tend to be the reverse of those for females. Being married and living with the spouse tend to generate the very highest participation rate

Table 9-6   Labor Force Participation Rates of the United States Population by Marital Status: 1960

Age and sex	White					Nonwhite				
	Single	Married, spouse present	Married, spouse absent	Widowed	Divorced	Single	Married, spouse present	Married, spouse absent	Widowed	Divorced
MALE, TOTAL	55.8	88.6	69.8	35.3	73.1	50.7	87.0	70.1	44.4	73.4
14 - 17 years	27.0	82.8	35.1	29.9	40.6	20.1	69.8	36.7	....	....
18 and 19 "	65.1	95.7	79.4	51.3	86.7	56.2	92.1	71.2	....	....
20 - 24 "	79.0	96.4	85.4	75.0	87.2	74.9	95.1	76.9	67.6	78.9
25 - 29 "	85.2	97.9	82.4	80.0	88.6	75.9	96.3	74.7	81.0	81.3
30 - 34 "	85.7	98.8	83.3	86.4	87.3	74.6	96.4	74.3	70.4	79.6
35 - 44 "	81.6	98.4	81.3	86.2	85.7	72.6	95.9	75.2	76.8	81.3
45 - 54 "	76.6	96.5	78.1	84.0	81.5	70.6	92.9	76.0	78.1	79.7
55 - 64 "	65.6	87.8	66.9	70.2	69.8	62.3	82.1	65.4	62.3	67.1
65 - 69 "	34.1	47.5	33.0	33.8	34.0	32.8	44.9	35.8	30.9	37.5
70 - 74 "	22.0	31.7	21.4	21.3	22.5	20.2	32.5	26.8	20.2	28.9
75 and over	14.2	19.0	11.7	10.7	14.5	14.5	19.0	16.9	11.4	17.7
FEMALE, TOTAL	43.9	29.8	44.9	26.9	71.0	35.6	40.6	56.2	35.5	69.4
14 - 17 years	14.6	16.2	20.3	26.7	38.0	8.8	18.0	21.5	....	....
18 and 19 "	55.9	29.6	42.4	46.2	63.2	37.6	25.6	34.2	....	49.2
20 - 24 "	75.7	30.8	48.9	50.3	73.4	59.8	34.0	47.6	47.3	58.9
25 - 29 "	82.0	25.7	47.1	51.1	77.2	67.1	38.2	53.7	54.2	68.7
30 - 34 "	81.7	27.6	48.9	55.7	78.2	68.4	43.1	60.3	58.0	72.4
35 - 44 "	79.6	35.4	55.3	65.3	81.6	68.4	48.9	66.1	63.3	77.0
45 - 54 "	77.0	38.6	56.5	66.4	79.4	66.2	47.3	65.0	61.6	76.4
55 - 64 "	65.9	24.8	42.8	45.4	65.7	49.7	33.7	49.7	43.3	60.8
65 - 69 "	37.5	8.9	18.3	20.0	33.0	34.8	14.7	23.9	20.3	29.9
70 - 74 "	22.1	4.8	9.6	10.0	18.9	17.9	8.7	16.2	11.5	22.4
75 and over	10.1	2.9	4.4	3.7	9.3	14.3	6.5	11.0	4.6	9.2

Source: U.S. Census of Population : 1960. Subject Reports - Employment Status and Work Experience, Table 4.

level among males instead of the lowest as for females. At all ages, the tendency to remain in the labor force is somewhat lower for widowed, divorced, or single men than for those who are responsible for a wife. This is true for both the nonwhite and the white population.

Other things being equal, the more children under age 18 a woman has living in the household, the less likely she is to participate in the labor force. Table 9-7A shows this to be true for women of all marital statuses and for both white and nonwhite women. (Note that Table 9-7 is in four parts, one for each major marital status.)

Moreover, when the youngest child is under 6 years of age, the participation rate tends to be lower than if the child is of school age. In addition, the younger the child the lower the rate of labor force participation tends to be. In contrast, the labor force participation rate tends to be highest when the youngest child is of high school age (12 to 17 years). This relationship also tends to be true for all marital statuses and for both white and nonwhite women.

Inasmuch as all of these factors tend to be true simultaneously, the women with the lowest

labor force participation rate are currently married white women with four or more children under 18, with the youngest under 3 years of age.

In contrast, the ever married women with the highest rates of labor force participation are divorced, nonwhite women with one child under 18, that child being under 5 or 12 years of age or older (80 percent). Table 9-7 is remarkable for the consistency with which all of the factors of color, presence of husband, number of children, and age of children influence the rate of participation of ever-married women with children and the average amount of time worked per week.

Part-time employment. When they are at the peak of labor force vigor, about 95 percent of employed males but only 85 percent of employed females are able to have work that keeps them busy for 35 hours or more per week. A small fraction are engaged in part-time work, that is, they work less than a full workweek. Table 9-8, which reports this information for ages 14 to 34 for males and females, shows that part-time work is highly concentrated among younger workers, among nonwhite workers, and among female workers. The young person

Table 9-7A Labor Force Participation Rates of Women by Number and Ages of Children—Married Women, Husbands Present: 1960

Number and age of own children	White			Nonwhite		
	Labor force participation rate	Percent worked 15 or more hrs. per week	Percent worked 50 or more weeks	Labor force participation rate	Percent worked 15 or more hrs. per week	Percent worked 50 or more weeks
1 own child under 18......	33.8	72.1	35.1	44.9	66.4	34.7
12-17................	42.6	75.0	45.2	52.5	65.1	42.2
6-11................	36.3	74.0	41.2	51.5	67.0	40.6
Under 6 years old.....	23.2	64.5	20.4	37.0	67.3	26.1
5 years old........	32.2	69.7	38.9	48.9	70.1	38.9
3 and 4...........	29.8	68.6	37.0	45.9	62.6	37.0
Under 3...........	20.6	62.3	14.8	32.6	68.9	19.9
2 own children under 18....	27.4	68.9	32.0	40.7	64.0	33.7
Younger 12-17..........	43.8	74.1	42.7	52.6	59.0	43.4
Younger 6-11:						
None 12-17..........	31.5	69.5	33.3	52.2	65.8	40.8
One 12-17..........	36.2	73.0	37.4	51.3	70.5	42.0
Younger 5 years old....	24.7	66.8	33.2	46.1	67.4	35.0
Younger 3 and 4........	21.7	64.8	30.3	41.1	63.2	37.6
Younger under 3........	15.2	59.2	16.0	28.7	61.7	19.8
3 own children under 18...	22.2	66.6	28.1	36.2	62.8	29.7
Youngest 6-17.........	34.8	70.8	34.8	47.7	65.0	37.9
12-17..............	41.4	74.3	41.8	48.8	64.3	42.2
6-11:						
None 12-17......	130.1	69.9	28.3	46.4	72.7	39.2
1 or more 12-17.	34.5	70.3	34.6	47.7	63.5	36.2
Youngest 5 years old..	24.2	64.9	31.3	42.0	66.9	35.4
Youngest 3 and 4......	19.9	65.6	28.6	39.9	64.2	35.6
Youngest under 3......	13.1	59.9	16.8	27.1	58.5	18.7
4 or more under 18........	17.6	65.4	25.8	29.6	60.2	23.9
Youngest 6-17.........	32.1	70.9	33.4	44.2	62.4	34.3
12-17..............	39.4	72.1	39.3	40.7	51.3	27.8
6-11:						
None 12-17......	29.5	63.6	27.0	44.1	56.9	40.8
1 or more 12-17.	31.9	71.2	33.4	44.4	63.2	34.2
Youngest 5 years old..	24.6	64.5	31.0	39.7	63.7	30.2
Youngest 3 and 4......	19.5	63.8	28.2	35.6	62.1	30.2
Youngest under 3......	11.9	62.6	18.9	23.6	58.0	17.4

Source: U.S. Bureau of the Census; 1960 Subject Reports. Employment Status and Work Experience, Table 8.

only 14 to 16 years of age who is not enrolled in school, but who nevertheless is in the labor force is able to find full-time employment in only slightly more than half the cases. With increasing age, this proportion rises steadily until it reaches a peak at about age 20 for females and age 35 for males. At each age group the proportion of nonwhite workers who are able to obtain full-time employment is less than that for whites. This differential is greater among female workers than among male workers. In other words, the most disadvantaged person in the effort to get full-time employment is the nonwhite female worker who is under 25 years of age.

Although data are not shown here, a similar pattern exists at the older ages at and beyond

retirement. Another important group of part-time workers are elderly people who supplement pensions or other similar incomes by part-time employment.

Among married women with children, the most likely to have part-time work are those who have several children, who have young children, and whose husbands are present. This is indicated by column 2 of Table 9-7.

Part-Year Employment. Just as many workers are not able to work a full week, many workers are unable to work a full year. In fact, if working 50 to 52 weeks can be defined as working full-time, then even at maximum employment only a little more than three fourths of all white male workers get a full work year. The corresponding proportion for nonwhite

Table 9-7B   Labor Force Participation Rates of Women by Number and Ages of Children—Married Women, Husbands Absent: 1960

Number and age of own children	White			Nonwhite		
	Labor force participation rate	Percent worked 15 or more hrs. per week	Percent worked 50 or more weeks	Labor force participation rate	Percent worked 15 or more hrs. per week	Percent worked 50 or more weeks
1 own child under 18.......	55.8	72.7	40.8	63.9	69.1	43.8
12-17..................	68.4	72.9	54.6	76.4	71.3	49.8
6-11..................	62.8	76.1	51.5	69.6	66.0	49.4
Under 6 years old......	44.2	70.6	23.5	52.2	68.9	34.4
5 years old........	61.2	65.4	41.3	70.4	79.2	47.3
3 and 4............	58.6	73.4	37.9	64.9	79.5	48.1
Under 3............	39.2	70.2	17.1	44.8	62.1	25.0
2 own children under 18....	49.4	76.0	38.8	57.7	67.4	40.8
Younger 12-17..........	64.5	74.6	50.0	66.1	59.7	49.3
Younger 6-11:						
None 12-17.........	55.7	76.2	42.2	65.2	66.9	46.0
one 12-17.........	62.7	76.8	48.6	71.3	65.4	53.8
Younger 5 years old....	47.2	74.9	42.7	62.1	64.3	46.9
Younger 3 and 4........	49.3	77.0	39.4	61.1	68.0	40.5
Younger under 3........	34.1	75.9	20.8	45.3	73.2	26.9
3 own children under 18....	42.2	68.0	34.8	49.4	61.5	39.5
Youngest 6-17..........	53.0	65.6	45.7	63.0	57.3	49.0
12-17...............	55.0	71.3	50.4	63.3	49.9	52.3
6-11:						
None 12-17.......	54.5	61.1	39.0	59.4	43.7	46.7
1 or more 12-17..	52.1	65.6	46.1	62.7	63.1	48.6
Youngest 5 years old...	44.3	69.8	34.6	54.6	70.7	43.4
Youngest 3 and 4......	40.3	74.4	30.9	50.5	61.0	44.6
Youngest under 3.......	30.8	68.3	22.3	38.5	64.8	27.2
4 or more under 18........	29.7	67.8	27.5	41.4	60.1	33.5
Youngest 6-17..........	43.2	70.1	37.5	52.5	68.0	45.9
12-17...............	51.3	66.1	28.9	64.9	79.4	25.1
6-11:						
None 12-17.......	38.4	57.1	30.3	38.6	100.0	57.2
1 or more 12-17..	43.1	71.5	38.3	53.2	66.5	46.2
Youngest 5 years old...	35.3	69.0	31.0	48.0	69.5	40.0
Youngest 3 and 4.......	30.4	70.7	29.2	45.3	67.1	39.6
Youngest under 3.......	23.4	65.4	19.6	36.8	54.4	26.5

Source: U.S. Bureau of the Census; 1960 Subject Reports.   Employment Status and Work Experience, Table 8.

males is only about 60 percent. Among women, the proportion is even lower. Thus, on an overall basis, only slightly more than one half of the total work force works a full year. This part-year employment is caused by seasonal or other layoffs, unemployment, entering and leaving the labor-force, and job-changing. Some of it is voluntary, but much is not.

Part-time employment is more highly concentrated at the younger and older ages for both sexes. Again, the most disadvantaged person is the nonwhite female and especially the nonwhite elderly female.

Table 9-9 shows the proportion of people working less than half-time and those working an intermediate amount of time—27 to 49 weeks. The workers with the very short employment duration for the year are, as is to be expected, those who are nonwhite, those who are female, and those who are young. The most disadvantaged are those having all three of these traits. Even married women with children are more inclined toward part-year work than are other women in age bracket 20 to 55. Those with several children, those with very young children, and those whose husbands are in the home are most inclined to work only part of the year.

In interpreting the data of Table 9-9, it should not be inferred that all of the part-time work is involuntary. Many women are able to participate in the labor force only because they

Table 9-7C Labor Force Participation Rates of Women by Number and Ages of Children—Widowed: 1960

Number and ages of own children	White			Nonwhite		
	Labor force participation rate	Percent worked 15 or more hrs. per week	Percent worked 50 or more weeks	Labor force participation rate	Percent worked 15 or more hrs. per week	Percent worked 50 or more weeks
1 own child under 18......	62.0	72.0	49.6	58.9	63.4	44.8
12-17.................	64.0	71.9	50.8	59.1	60.9	46.9
6-11.................	57.9	73.0	47.5	61.4	68.5	43.6
Under 6 years old.....	51.3	67.9	39.9	60.4	68.9	36.7
5 years old........	57.0	71.4	50.9	66.7	72.7	28.4
3 and 4...........	51.4	55.4	41.7	64.0	73.9	36.8
Under 3...........	48.4	74.5	33.0	54.5	60.2	40.7
2 own children under 18...	56.9	72.7	44.8	56.9	65.9	45.8
Younger 12-17........	61.9	72.5	50.7	56.7	65.6	46.0
Younger 6-11:						
None 12-17........	58.8	69.2	41.3	58.7	59.6	43.6
One 12-17........	57.1	75.0	41.9	56.6	69.0	49.9
Younger 5 years old...	49.4	66.2	37.0	68.3	60.8	47.4
Younger 3 and 4.......	44.0	68.0	36.8	57.0	76.0	40.7
Younger under 3.......	34.5	76.8	25.7	51.6	63.1	40.9
3 own children under 18...	47.2	70.5	41.2	49.8	60.5	35.4
Youngest 6-17........	52.1	72.0	43.9	53.3	53.2	36.1
12-17.............	57.3	75.7	46.6	57.0	75.0	40.2
6-11:						
None 12-17......	40.2	60.3	36.9	54.0	63.5	25.1
1 or more 12-17.	51.5	71.4	43.5	51.6	43.2	35.6
Youngest 5 years old..	45.1	69.2	40.6	48.6	86.8	28.7
Youngest 3 and 4......	38.9	61.8	34.4	48.2	75.9	30.2
Youngest under 3......	29.2	71.0	27.2	41.8	68.5	39.3
4 or more under 18........	34.1	67.1	33.4	42.2	60.6	29.8
Youngest 6-17........	41.5	67.8	35.1	45.2	54.5	30.2
12-17.............	50.7	55.3	48.4	58.3	67.2	40.1
6-11:						
None 12-17......	50.0	80.0	31.4	40.8	100.0	24.9
1 or more 12-17.	40.4	68.2	34.2	44.5	51.3	29.7
Youngest 5 years old..	37.6	75.7	36.1	44.8	77.0	34.3
Youngest 3 and 4......	29.7	72.3	31.4	48.2	62.4	32.0
Youngest under 3......	24.9	55.3	29.4	37.0	60.6	27.6

Source: U.S. Bureau of the Census; 1960 Subject Reports. Employment Status and Work Experience, Table 8.

have jobs that require them to work only a few hours per week or only part of the year. If they were forced to accept full-time or full-year work, they would withdraw from the labor force. On the other hand, much of this differential is involuntary and represents a discriminatory operation of the labor market. The seasonality of industry that enforces a prolonged layoff during each year is a major cause of poor utilization of manpower and loss of purchasing power in the population. The fact that it affects 25 percent or more of the white workers in the most vigorous working ages is a rough measure of its seriousness. The fact that it affects nearly twice this many nonwhite workers is a measure of the hardship it causes among Negroes.

9.10. Unemployment in the United States

In an industrialized nation the rate of unemployment is one of the sensitive measures of economic well-being. A certain amount of unemployment is inevitable in a free economy. Young people just entering the labor force must search for a job, and if they dislike their first job, they leave it and search for another. New firms are continuously being born, and others die. Often the dying firms represent units whose production methods and equipment are obsolete or that produce a product no longer in demand. The employees of such firms suffer a period of unemployment (and receive unemployment compensation) while they seek work with a new firm. If these workers are older, have little education, and have a skill that can-

Table 9-7D   Labor Force Participation Rates of Women by Number and Ages of Children—Divorced: 1960

Number and ages of own children	White			Nonwhite		
	Labor force partici-pation rate	Percent worked 15 or more hrs. per week	Percent worked 50 or more weeks	Labor force partici-pation rate	Percent worked 15 or more hrs. per week	Percent worked 50 or more weeks
1 own child under 18.......	82.2	75.0	60.9	77.6	70.2	53.7
12-17..................	85.7	75.5	66.3	80.6	71.2	57.6
6-11..................	83.0	75.9	64.5	80.4	68.3	54.0
Under 6 years old......	75.0	73.0	46.2	69.7	71.3	46.6
5 years old........	81.8	91.2	62.1	83.2	81.2	63.5
3 and 4............	79.3	66.0	55.3	70.0	70.5	45.5
Under 3............	69.5	72.0	32.0	63.9	67.6	39.4
2 own children under 18....	77.3	74.9	56.6	70.5	69.3	50.2
Younger 12-17..........	84.8	78.3	65.0	77.8	63.1	50.7
Younger 6-11:						
None 12-17..........	78.5	74.6	57.8	77.9	77.4	58.7
One 12-17..........	81.0	74.7	61.8	78.7	74.1	55.6
Younger 5 years old....	75.4	78.1	56.6	70.6	60.0	56.5
Younger 3 and 4........	72.8	66.6	52.0	67.3	89.5	47.2
Younger under 3........	63.6	75.7	33.9	52.9	49.9	33.5
3 own children under 18....	67.2	73.9	50.1	58.6	60.1	42.4
Youngest 6-17..........	73.8	75.8	58.1	71.4	71.3	52.2
12-17..............	74.3	73.7	63.2	77.6	79.8	48.2
6-11:						
None 12-17.......	72.0	80.0	51.5	67.8	66.7	55.1
1 or more 12-17..	74.2	75.2	58.4	70.9	70.9	52.6
Youngest 5 years old...	68.3	77.1	47.6	60.3	60.6	39.2
Youngest 3 and 4......	62.9	68.2	46.3	48.1	55.2	23.4
Youngest under 3......	54.7	71.6	32.0	47.5	46.9	34.7
4 or more under 18........	49.6	77.4	39.3	47.6	50.9	41.0
Youngest 6-17..........	61.7	81.6	48.9	61.6	61.0	58.2
12-17..............	60.6	100.0	42.8	62.8	53.8	26.9
6-11:						
None 12-17.......	55.8	100.0	54.2	45.2	....	80.0
1 or more 12-17..	62.2	79.5	48.9	62.6	61.4	58.3
Youngest 5 years old...	52.5	71.7	53.7	59.8	37.3	33.1
Youngest 3 and 4......	51.2	73.1	34.0	50.2	54.8	48.6
Youngest under 3......	36.7	76.4	26.0	39.1	45.7	29.5

Source: U.S. Bureau of the Census; 1960 Subject Reports. Employment Status and Work Experience, Table 8.

not be easily converted to another use (such as an elderly textile mill worker in New England), the period of unemployment may be quite long unless there is planned retraining and transfer to other work.

Unfortunately, no way has yet been devised to completely eliminate seasonality in employment—especially in the construction, agricultural, forestry, fishing, mining, railway maintenance, and tourist industries. During a part of the year workers in these industries are feverishly busy and then have enforced idleness for several weeks or months during which time they are unemployed. Competition in the world market can cause certain industries to become less active and force a layoff. An ex-

ample of this is the sudden rise in ready-to-wear clothing manufacturing in Japan, Hong Kong, and other nations with a labor surplus, forcing American garment workers to seek other jobs.

These two forms of unemployment are termed "frictional" and "structural."

Frictional unemployment results from the adjustment or readjustment of individual workers as they enter and leave the labor force for personal or individual reasons not connected with technological change or fluctuation in the business cycle. It is termed "frictional" because the readjustment cannot be made instantaneously; it takes time to find a job. Unemployment caused by secular trends and technologi-

Table 9-8 Percent of Employed Persons at Work Not Enrolled in School and Working 35 Hours or More, by Sex, Color, and Single Years of Age

Age	Male			Female		
	Total	White	Nonwhite	Total	White	Nonwhite
14	51.5	50.7	53.9	59.1	62.4	46.4
15	52.8	53.2	51.4	58.1	60.1	49.7
16	58.4	58.6	57.4	58.7	59.8	50.3
17	63.7	63.8	63.2	64.1	65.0	56.6
18	78.7	79.8	70.9	83.5	84.9	66.6
19	84.8	86.3	76.5	86.2	87.9	69.6
20	87.9	89.1	79.7	86.4	88.0	72.3
21-22	90.4	91.3	83.7	85.1	86.6	73.1
23-24	92.1	92.9	86.4	81.9	83.3	73.5
25-29	93.7	94.3	88.2	77.4	78.4	72.0
30-34	94.3	91.1	89.0	73.6	74.2	70.3

Source: U.S. Bureau of the Census. 1960 Census of Population, Detailed Characteristics: U.S. Summary - Table 197.

cal changes is called "structural" because it is caused by fundamental changes in the structure of the economy.

"Frictional" and "structural" unemployment are difficult to separate from each other, but both are regarded as normal events in a healthy economy undergoing improvement.

Economists are not in agreement concerning what the minimum rate of unemployment due solely to frictional and structural causes would be, but place it at 2 to 3 percent. When unemployment rises to 5 percent, it is regarded as a clear sign that the economy is failing to provide full employment to its work force.

A major share of unemployment arises from causes other than personal and technological. Business cycle fluctuations are a major cause of such unemployment. Even minor business fluctuations can create a rise in unemployment in particular segments of the economy or in particular types of industries.

Unemployment can persist and become chronic in particular places because of prejudice. Otherwise qualified people may be denied all but low-level employment because they are of a particular race, caste, nationality, or religion. Where ethnic or other prejudice and discrimination in employment exist, a high level of unemployment or underemployment is also almost always found. Whole regions of

a nation can sink into a state of chronic unemployment when the single industry on which they depend becomes depressed, provided that the population is too immobile to emigrate elsewhere. Examples are forested areas after the timber has been exhausted and mining areas where modernization has greatly reduced the need for large amounts of manpower. For this reason, unemployment analysis is conducted at provincial, regional, and local levels, as well as at the national level. Finally, many economists believe that full employment (reduction of unemployment to the frictional level) is not consistent with maximum profits, and that in the effort to maximize profits employment is allowed to sag to a point where a substantial fraction of the labor force is continuously seeking work.

Psychologists point out that a certain fraction of the population is unemployable or are such poor workers that they are discharged repeatedly and are more or less continuously seeking work. Persons of low intelligence, persons who are emotionally unstable or neurotic, chronic alcoholics, persons who are willing to work but suffer from partial disability or have severe physical handicaps such as blindness or cerebral palsy are examples. Although many persons in this group are so disabled that they would be classed as not in the labor force, a

Table 9-9   Percent of Full-Time and Part-Time Workers, by Age, Sex, and Color, for the United States: 1960

Age and sex	White			Nonwhite		
	50 to 52 weeks	27 - 49 weeks	Less than 26 weeks	50 to 52 weeks	27 - 49 weeks	Less than 26 weeks
MALE, TOTAL	66.4	22.3	11.3	52.1	23.0	24.9
14 to 19 years.....	20.3	20.7	59.0	17.6	22.4	60.0
20 to 24 "	52.2	28.3	19.5	44.2	23.3	32.5
25 to 29 "	70.6	22.4	7.0	55.8	23.1	21.1
30 to 34 "	77.1	18.9	4.0	59.1	23.0	17.9
35 to 39 "	77.8	18.4	3.8	60.0	23.0	17.0
40 to 44 "	77.0	18.9	4.1	59.3	23.1	17.6
45 to 54 "	74.1	20.6	5.3	57.7	23.1	19.2
55 to 59 "	70.6	21.9	7.5	55.3	23.2	21.5
60 to 64 "	67.7	22.5	9.8	53.6	23.1	23.3
65 to 79 "	51.8	23.5	24.7	42.8	22.9	34.3
70 to 74 "	47.2	22.6	30.2	39.0	22.7	38.3
75 and over	47.7	21.9	30.4	36.5	22.6	40.9
FEMALE, TOTAL	42.4	22.7	34.9	37.4	23.0	39.6
14 to 19 years.....	14.1	19.2	66.7	11.0	31.8	57.2
20 to 24 "	36.4	27.2	36.4	27.6	22.9	49.5
25 to 29 "	38.7	26.8	34.5	35.5	23.1	41.4
30 to 34 "	41.9	25.9	32.2	39.7	23.1	37.2
35 to 39 "	45.9	26.4	27.7	43.4	23.1	33.5
40 to 44 "	49.0	27.5	23.5	44.6	23.1	32.3
45 to 54 "	51.7	28.5	19.8	44.2	23.2	32.6
55 to 59 "	52.8	28.4	18.8	42.2	23.1	34.7
60 to 64 "	50.3	28.4	21.3	40.5	23.0	36.5
65 to 70 "	41.4	28.0	30.6	34.4	22.7	42.9
70 to 74 "	39.9	26.6	33.5	33.6	22.5	43.9
75 and over	41.4	24.8	33.8	32.8	22.3	44.9

Source: U.S. Summary Detailed Charateristics Table 199.   See Table 8.

substantial share are marginally employable and would continue to seek work and would work when a job became available.

Many elderly men continue to seek work after age 65 when they have been retired from their regular occupation. If they have little skill to offer, their chances of getting work are small, and employer prejudice against hiring elderly pensioners is widespread. Even men 45 to 64 years of age who are factory operatives experience difficulty in finding a new job if they are laid off and lose their seniority in a firm.

For all these reasons, the level of unemployment is always above the theoretically attainable frictional minimum. Despite very large and comprehensive programs of unemployment compensation and State employment services, there is a substantial and fluctuating amount of economic hardship prevalent today.

In the mid-1960s, roughly 5 percent of the civilian labor force was unemployed. The rate was somewhat higher for women than for men, and was very much higher among nonwhite

than among white workers, as the following tabulation for 1964-1965 shows:

Sex	Total	White	Nonwhite
Total	5.1	4.7	8.7
Male	5.0	4.6	8.8
Female	5.4	4.9	8.5

Among nonwhite population, males suffered a greater rate of unemployment than females, whereas the reverse was true among the white population. In 1966 the unemployment rates of the nation dipped sharply as a result of military conscription and stepped-up employment related to the conflict in Vietnam. By mid-1966 the unemployment rates had fallen to about 3 percent—the lowest in several years. It remained low throughout 1967.

Unemployment rates tended to be lowest among the rural-farm and highest among the rural-nonfarm population, as the following rates for 1960 show:

Sex and color	Urban	Rural-nonfarm	Rural-farm
White male	4.5	5.9	2.4
White female	4.8	5.8	4.4
Nonwhite male	9.3	8.8	3.4
Nonwhite female	8.5	8.7	7.8

Farm operators are seldom unemployed, although they may be seriously underemployed; there are enough chores and miscellaneous tasks to be done throughout the year so that they will perform at least some gainful work each week. However, the situation is quite different in rural villages, where lack of economic expansion often coincides with high fertility. As successive generations of small-town youths mature, they have almost no alternative but to migrate to a large city in search of work. The "push" for emigration is a high rate of unemployment. The tragic economic toll that race prejudice is taking annually in the United States can begin to be appreciated when it is recognized that one nonwhite male worker in 12 is unemployed and that, as they flee from the subsistence livelihood that they are no longer permitted on the land and crowd into cities, they are being absorbed so slowly that the unemployment rate in the cities is as high as it was in the villages. For a Negro youth in an American slum, the problem of finding a reasonably permanent and life-sustaining "niche" in the economy may be no less difficult than the similar problem faced by a member of a low caste in India.

Unemployment Rate by Age. Rates of unemployment are highest among the very young and among older workers. At each age they are higher among nonwhite than among white workers and higher among females than among males. This consistent pattern of differentials is revealed in Table 9-10. Because these factors can exist simultaneously, the very highest rates of unemployment are found among nonwhite females in the youngest age groups. These rates are astoundingly high. For example, in 1960 fully 20 percent of the nonwhite girls 17 to 19 years of age and in the labor force were unemployed. And even at ages 20 to 24 an average of nearly 13 percent was unemployed.

Among young male nonwhite workers the rates were only slightly less discouragingly high: 17 percent for youths 17 to 19 years of age and 12 percent for youths 20 to 24 years of age. Under conditions of high economic prosperity that prevailed in 1960 it was "normal" for one nonwhite worker in 12 to be unemployed, and to obtain even this level of security the average nonwhite worker had to be 25 years old or over. Thus the task of even entering the labor force with any kind of a job is an extremely difficult one for the nonwhite youth.

White youth experience a similar period of difficulty in entering the labor force, but it is far less severe and ends earlier than for the nonwhite population.

At age 65 the unemployment rate takes a sudden jump for workers of all classes. This represents the effort of persons who have been retired from one job to continue to seek work and relocate themselves in another job. Those who succeed continue working; those who fail tend to withdraw from the labor force. With advancing age, the rate of unemployment tends to remain level or even to decline slightly at the very oldest ages. Nevertheless, at all ages 65 and above, the level of reported unemployment is higher than at ages 55 to 60.

Older foreign-born workmen, (40 years of age or over) suffer from unemployment to a somewhat greater extent than the native-born population of the same age. This is shown to be true for both males and females in Table 9-11. Furthermore, the table shows that the other nonwhite races tend to suffer from high rates of unemployment, nearly as high as those to which the Negro workers are subjected. This is especially true for younger Chinese, Japanese, Indian, and Filipino workers.

Marital Status and Unemployment. Just as labor force participation rates are related to marital status, so are unemployment rates. Among males these rates are lowest for men who are married and living with their spouse. They are highest for men who are divorced. Thus the man who cannot find a job he likes will tend to accept any job if he is responsible for dependents, whereas men who have no dependents are freer to remain unemployed and search for a position they really wish. On the other side of the picture, firms who find that they must lay off a certain proportion of their

Table 9-10 Unemployment Rates by Sex and Color for Single Years of Age

Single years of age	Male			Female		
	Total	White	Nonwhite	Total	White	Nonwhite
All Ages - 14 and over	5.0	4.6	8.8	5.4	5.0	8.6
14	5.7	5.2	10.6	7.8	6.5	18.2
15	8.2	8.2	13.9	9.0	8.3	16.3
16	12.2	11.9	15.3	12.4	11.6	21.9
17	11.7	11.1	17.8	11.3	10.5	20.2
18	12.0	11.3	17.2	9.3	8.4	19.2
19	11.1	10.6	15.2	8.2	7.2	18.2
20	10.0	9.4	14.4	7.7	6.8	14.6
21	9.1	8.4	13.8	7.0	6.0	14.9
22	8.0	7.4	12.4	6.3	5.5	12.4
23	7.3	6.8	11.5	6.2	5.4	11.6
24	6.3	5.7	10.4	6.5	5.6	11.4
25	5.7	5.2	9.8	6.3	5.5	10.3
26	5.0	4.6	8.5	6.2	5.7	9.1
27	4.8	4.3	8.9	6.0	5.1	9.8
28	4.3	3.9	8.1	6.1	5.3	10.2
29	4.0	3.5	8.0	6.1	5.4	9.5
30	4.1	3.6	8.5	6.0	5.2	9.7
31	4.0	3.5	8.4	5.5	4.9	8.6
32	3.9	3.4	8.0	5.9	5.1	9.6
33	3.8	3.4	7.9	5.4	5.0	7.4
34	3.9	3.5	8.5	5.5	5.0	8.4
35	3.8	3.3	8.4	5.3	4.9	7.4
36	3.6	3.1	8.0	5.3	4.9	8.1
37	3.9	3.5	7.3	5.1	4.5	7.9
38	3.6	3.2	7.5	4.9	4.6	6.7
39	3.8	3.3	7.6	4.8	4.4	7.2
40	3.7	3.3	7.4	5.0	4.6	7.1
41	3.7	3.3	7.4	4.9	4.6	6.8
42	3.8	3.5	7.1	4.7	4.4	7.1
43	3.8	3.4	7.4	4.6	4.2	6.9
44	4.0	3.6	8.0	4.7	4.5	6.4
45	3.8	3.5	7.0	4.3	4.1	7.4
46	4.0	3.7	7.1	4.4	4.1	6.9
47	4.1	3.7	7.3	4.6	4.3	6.3
48	4.1	3.9	6.6	4.2	4.0	5.3
49	4.2	3.9	6.8	4.3	4.0	6.2
50	4.2	3.8	7.3	4.0	3.8	5.5
51	4.1	3.7	8.0	4.0	3.9	5.5
52	4.4	4.1	8.0	4.2	3.9	5.9
53	4.5	4.2	7.9	4.2	3.9	6.4
54	4.5	4.2	7.5	4.4	4.2	5.8
55	4.6	4.3	7.7	4.1	4.0	5.3
56	4.6	4.4	6.3	4.0	3.8	5.8
57	4.9	4.6	8.3	3.9	3.8	5.0
58	4.8	4.6	7.4	3.9	3.7	5.6
59	5.2	4.9	7.7	4.3	4.1	5.3
60	5.0	4.7	8.4	3.9	3.9	4.7
61	5.1	4.9	7.5	3.9	3.7	5.6
62	5.1	4.8	9.4	4.1	3.9	6.6
63	5.5	5.0	7.7	4.2	4.0	5.3
64	5.3	5.1	8.3	4.0	3.7	6.5
65	6.9	6.7	8.8	4.4	4.2	6.1

Source: U.S. Bureau of the Census: 1960. Subject Reports, Employment Status and
Work Experience, Table 2.

workers, may tend to keep those who are married and are responsible for supporting a family and selectively discharge those without dependents. The upper panel of Table 9-12 reveals an interesting inversion: the rate of unemployment among nonwhite men who are married and living with their spouse is much lower than for the white population that is single, widowed, or divorced. The great rate of unemployment among nonwhite males is due in part to very high rates of unemployment among widowed, divorced, and single nonwhite males. The fact that the proportion of nonwhite workers that falls in these other categories is large helps to account for the higher overall rate of unemployment for nonwhites than for whites.

Table 9-11   Unemployment Rates among the United States
Population by Race, Nativity, Parentage, Age, and Sex: 1960

Age and Sex	White			Negro	Other non-white
	Native parentage	Foreign mixed parentage	Foreign born		
MALE, TOTAL	4.7	4.1	4.8	9.0	6.9
14 to 17 years....	9.8	11.1	9.1	15.3	16.2
18 + 19 "	11.0	10.5	8.3	16.2	15.6
20 to 26 "	7.4	7.7	5.8	12.3	14.0
25 to 29 "	4.2	4.3	4.0	8.8	6.8
30 to 34 "	3.4	3.5	3.4	8.5	5.3
35 to 39 "	3.3	3.1	3.1	8.0	5.1
40 to 44 "	3.4	3.2	3.6	7.6	5.0
45 to 49 "	3.8	3.4	4.1	7.1	5.0
50 to 54 "	4.0	3.8	4.1	7.9	5.8
55 to 59 "	4.6	4.3	4.5	7.6	6.2
60 to 64 "	4.7	4.7	5.4	8.4	6.1
65 to 69 "	4.8	5.9	7.9	7.8	8.4
70 to 74 "	4.3	5.0	7.2	7.2	6.6
75 years old and over............	3.7	4.4	6.2	7.4	5.4
FEMALE, TOTAL	4.9	4.9	5.9	8.7	6.5
14 to 17 years....	10.1	10.5	11.2	20.2	14.4
18 + 19 "	7.9	6.8	6.4	19.0	13.4
20 to 26 "	6.0	5.3	6.1	13.4	7.4
25 to 29 "	5.4	5.1	6.1	10.0	7.0
30 to 34 "	4.9	5.4	6.1	9.0	6.2
35 to 39 "	4.4	5.3	5.2	7.6	5.8
40 to 44 "	4.2	5.1	5.6	7.0	5.2
45 to 49 "	3.8	4.5	5.8	6.1	5.9
50 to 54 "	3.6	4.2	5.7	5.8	5.4
55 to 59 "	3.4	4.0	5.7	5.5	3.6
60 to 64 "	3.3	4.1	5.7	5.7	4.6
65 to 69 "	3.7	4.3	6.5	5.7	5.4
70 to 74 "	3.6	4.2	7.1	6.0	5.7
75 years old and over............	4.3	2.9	3.7	5.8	8.2

Source: U.S. Census Population: 1960.   Subject Reports - Employment
Status and Work Experience, Table 4.

Female unemployment does not show very great differences by marital status. This may be another way of saying that if women are in the labor market, they are neither favored nor discriminated against because of their marital status. There is a slight overall tendency toward the unemployment rate to be higher among women who are married and especially married with the spouse absent than among other female workers. This may result from the fact that it is more difficult for this group to find employment because they may have children at home and must seek employment that must meet additional conditions in order that they may meet their family obligations.

Other Characteristics of the Unemployed.
Labor force experts are interested in a wide variety of additional characteristics of the un-employed—their educational attainment, the type of occupation they had last, the industry

that employed them last, the rate of pay they held on their last job, and of course the forces or factors at work that cause the unemployment. Later chapters in this book dealing with economic composition will present some of this material. However, for a full treatment of it, the reader is referred to monographs that deal with labor force in greater detail than is possible here.

9.11.   The Length of Working Life

Demographic as well as social and economic changes have a dramatic effect on the labor force. Decreases in the death rate have the effect of causing fewer members of the labor force to die while they are still in the productive years. The result is a great saving in the nation's investment in education and socialization, and a preservation of valuable experience and skills. Decreases in infant and child mor-

Table 9-12   Unemployment Rate by Marital Status

Age and sex	White					Nonwhite				
	Single	Married, spouse present	Married, spouse absent	Widowed	Divorced	Single	Married, spouse present	Married, spouse absent	Widowed	Divorced
MALE, TOTAL	9.3	3.3	8.6	6.9	10.5	14.5	6.4	11.9	10.4	12.2
14 to 17 Yrs	9.9	10.9	11.6	0.0	15.5	15.5	12.4	13.6	0.0	20.4
18 + 19 "	11.4	6.7	15.7	10.3	14.9	16.7	10.0	19.8	0.0	24.7
20 - 24 "	10.0	4.7	13.8	9.2	13.8	15.7	8.2	14.3	8.3	16.2
25 - 29 "	7.9	3.2	9.2	8.2	9.9	13.6	6.2	12.7	10.9	13.6
30 - 34 "	7.5	2.7	8.2	7.0	10.1	13.3	6.4	12.2	10.8	15.0
35 - 44 "	8.0	2.7	7.5	8.4	10.1	13.6	6.0	12.1	12.1	12.0
45 - 54 "	8.0	3.2	7.8	7.1	10.9	10.7	6.2	10.6	10.5	11.2
55 - 64 "	8.6	4.0	8.4	7.3	10.5	10.2	6.6	11.0	10.7	10.3
65 - 69 "	8.6	5.2	7.8	7.2	10.1	12.2	6.6	11.0	9.3	15.8
70 - 74 "	7.9	4.7	5.7	5.8	9.4	8.8	6.3	10.6	9.4	5.4
75 + "	5.3	4.0	4.5	4.8	10.1	10.9	6.3	12.4	7.4	3.5
FEMALE, TOTAL	4.8	4.8	7.8	4.7	5.7	11.1	7.7	9.7	7.0	7.2
14 to 17 Yrs	9.6	17.2	16.9	16.5	10.9	19.0	23.8	29.2	0.0	14.5
18 + 19 "	6.9	9.9	15.2	15.0	14.9	17.5	21.7	22.6	16.3	27.5
20 - 24 "	4.2	6.9	11.2	6.9	8.4	11.8	13.4	15.7	15.4	10.6
25 - 29 "	3.1	5.8	8.8	4.7	7.3	8.0	9.6	11.6	14.8	10.4
30 - 34 "	3.0	5.2	7.7	6.7	6.0	8.3	8.4	10.3	9.5	8.6
35 - 44 "	3.0	4.5	6.9	4.9	5.6	7.0	6.6	8.2	9.2	7.1
45 - 54 "	2.7	3.9	6.2	4.9	5.0	5.1	5.7	6.9	6.4	5.2
55 - 64 "	2.5	3.8	4.8	4.4	4.6	4.0	5.2	6.4	5.8	5.7
65 - 69 "	3.2	3.8	6.1	5.0	4.1	4.2	5.7	10.2	5.4	4.1
70 - 74 "	2.4	4.6	6.0	4.6	7.4	4.4	5.7	5.3	6.4	4.7
75 + "	2.4	3.8	2.2	4.5	4.0	8.7	5.2	5.1	5.6	7.6

Source: U.S. Census Population: 1960. Subject Reports – Employment Status and Work Experience, Table 4.

tality cause less wastage of potential manpower after substantial investments have already been made in providing a livelihood and education to dependent oncoming generations. On the other hand, rising prosperity and the establishment of Social Security systems cause elderly members to retire from the labor force at ages 60 to 65, instead of remaining workers until death or disabling illness removes them.

Labor force demographers have devised a systematic way of showing the average effect of these changes, in terms of the typical worker. They compute what is called a "table of working life." Table 9-13, for example, is such a table for United States males as of 1960. The table of working life is derived from the ordinary life table (see Chapter 15). It has 10 columns. One of the "inventors" of these tables, and a world expert, is Stuart Garfinkle. He explains the tables as follows: [7]

"The table of working life starts with a group of 100,000 male babies, and follows them through life until the age when the last person

[7] Stuart Garfinkle, "The Lengthening of Working Life and its Implications," paper submitted to the United Nations World Population Conference, Belgrade, 1965.

has died. The table of working life differs from an ordinary life table. It reflects not only the effects of death on a group of 100,000 males born alive, but also the effects of labor market activities. The following is a brief description of the meaning of each of the columns shown in a Table of Working Life:

"(1) *Year of age (x to x + 1).* All of the variables in the table are expressed in terms of the exact birthday (x) or of the interval between successive birthdays $(x$ to $x + 1)$, in accordance with standard life table practice.

"(2) *Number living in year of age* (L_x). This is the "stationary population" or number of persons who would be living in any age interval under the assumption of 100,000 live births annually, subject throughout life to the specified mortality rates.

"(3) *Number in labor force in year of age* (Lw_x). The "stationary labor force" shows the number in labor force status in each year of age under conditions of labor force participation prevailing in the reference year.

"(4) *Percent of population in labor force in year of age* (W_x).

"(5) *Accessions to labor force (1,000 A_x).* This column shows the net accessions to the

Table 9-13   Table of Working Life, Males: 1960

Year of age	Number living of 100,000 born alive			Accession to the labor force (per 1,000 in population)	Separations from the labor force (per 1,000 in labor force)			Average number of remaining years of:	
	In population	In labor force			Due to all causes	Due to death	Due to retirement	Life	Labor force participation
		Number	Percent of population						
(1)	(2)	(3)	(4)	(5)	(6)	(7)	(8)	(9)	(10)
X	L_x	Lw_x	w_x	$1000\ A_x$	$1000\ Q_x$	$1000\ Q_x^d$	$1000\ Q_x^r$	$\overset{o}{e}_x$	$\overset{o}{ew}_x$
	(In year of age)				(Between years of age)			(At beginning of year of age)	
14........	96,102	14,800	15.4	52.0	.9	.9	....	55.2	48.3
15........	96,020	19,780	20.6	119.9	1.1	1.1	....	54.2	47.3
16........	95,918	31,269	32.6	143.8	1.2	1.2	....	53.3	46.3
17........	95,800	45,026	47.0	177.8	1.4	1.4	....	52.3	45.4
18........	95,666	61,992	64.8	116.8	1.5	1.5	....	51.4	44.4
19........	95,523	73,075	76.5	63.9	1.5	1.6	....	50.5	43.5
20........	95,374	79,065	82.9	33.9	1.7	1.7	....	49.6	42.6
21........	95,211	82,167	86.3	26.0	1.8	1.8	....	48.6	41.6
22........	95,039	84,490	88.9	18.9	1.8	1.8	....	47.7	40.7
23........	94,865	86,137	90.8	14.0	1.8	1.8	....	46.8	39.8
24........	94,692	87,306	92.2	11.0	1.8	1.8	....	45.9	38.9
25........	94,526	88,193	93.3	9.0	1.8	1.8	....	45.0	37.9
26........	94,360	88,887	94.2	8.0	1.7	1.7	....	44.1	37.0
27........	94,197	89,487	95.0	7.0	1.7	1.7	....	43.1	36.1
28........	94,033	89,990	95.7	5.9	1.7	1.7	....	42.2	35.1
29........	93,869	90,396	96.3	5.0	1.8	1.8	....	41.3	34.2
30........	93,697	90,699	96.8	2.0	1.9	1.9	....	40.4	33.2
31........	93,522	90,716	97.0	1.0	1.9	1.9	....	39.4	32.3
32........	93,341	90,634	97.1	1.0	2.0	2.0	....	38.5	31.4
33........	93,151	90,543	97.2	1.0	2.2	2.2	....	37.6	30.4
34........	92,948	90,438	97.3	....	3.4	2.4	1.0	36.7	29.5
35........	92,728	90,132	97.2	....	3.6	2.5	1.1	35.7	28.6
36........	92,493	89,811	97.1	....	3.8	2.8	1.0	34.8	27.7
37........	92,238	89,471	97.0	. ..	4.0	.0	1.0	33.9	26.8
38........	91,960	89,109	96.9	....	4.3	3.3	1.0	33.0	25.9
39........	91,659	88,726	96.8	....	4.7	3.6	1.1	32.1	25.0
40........	91,326	88,312	96.7	....	5.0	4.0	1.0	31.2	24.1
41........	90,964	87,871	96.6	....	5.4	4.4	1.0	30.3	23.2
42........	90,568	87,398	96.5	....	5.9	4.8	1.1	29.5	22.3
43........	90,131	86,886	96.4	....	6.3	5.3	1.0	28.6	21.4
44........	89,654	86,337	96.3	....	7.1	6.1	1.0	27.7	20.6
45........	89,106	85,720	96.2	....	7.5	6.4	1.1	26.9	19.7
46........	88,534	85,081	96.1	....	9.2	7.1	2.1	26.0	18.8
47........	87,904	84,300	95.9	....	10.0	7.9	2.1	25.2	18.0
48........	87,206	83,456	95.7	....	12.0	8.9	3.1	24.4	17.2
49........	86,428	82,452	95.4	....	13.8	9.6	4.2	23.6	16.4
50........	85,596	81,316	95.0	....	16.4	11.2	5.2	22.8	15.6
51........	84,637	79,982	94.5	....	18.6	12.4	6.2	22.1	14.8
52........	83,591	78,492	93.9	....	20.8	13.4	7.4	21.3	14.0
53........	82,468	76,860	93.2	....	22.8	14.3	8.5	20.6	13.3
54........	81,283	75,105	92.4	....	25.1	15.4	9.7	19.9	12.6
55........	80,020	73,218	91.5	....	27.0	16.2	10.8	19.2	11.9
56........	78,717	71,239	90.5	....	28.3	17.3	11.0	18.5	11.2
57........	77,344	69,223	89.5	....	32.1	18.8	13.3	17.8	10.5
58........	75,881	67,003	88.3	....	35.2	20.6	14.6	17.1	9.8
59........	74,306	64,646	87.0	....	41.1	22.9	18.2	16.4	9.1
60........	72,588	61,990	85.4	....	47.8	24.7	23.1	15.8	8.5
61........	70,774	59,026	83.4	....	54.0	26.8	27.2	15.2	7.8
62........	68,820	55,837	81.1	....	61.8	29.0	32.8	14.6	7.2
63........	66,820	52,387	78.4	....	87.3	30.8	56.5	14.0	6.7
64........	64,699	47,813	73.9	....	263.7	29.6	234.1	13.4	6.1

life table labor force per 1,000 population between successive years of age.

"(6) *Probability of separations due to all causes (1,000 Q_x^s)*. The probability of separation is defined as the net separations from the

life table labor force between successive ages of those in the stationary labor force in the base year.

"(7) *Probability of separations due to death (1,000 Q_x^d)*

Table 9-13 (Continued)

Year of age	Number living of 100,000 born alive			Accession to the labor force (per 1,000 in population)	Separations from the labor force (per 1,000 in labor force)			Average number of remaining years of:	
	In population	In labor force			Due to all causes	Due to death	Due to retirement	Life	Labor force participation
		Number	Percent of population						
(1)	(2)	(3)	(4)	(5)	(6)	(7)	(8)	(9)	(10)
x	L_x	Lw_x	w_x	$1000 A_x$	$1000 Q_x$	$1000 Q_x^d$	$1000 Q_x^r$	$\overset{o}{e}_x$	$\overset{o}{e}w_x$
	(In year of age)				(Between years of age)			(At beginning of year of age)	
65........	62,533	35,206	56.3	....	170.1	34.1	136.0	12.8	6.3
66........	60,246	29,219	48.5	....	122.5	37.6	84.9	12.3	7.0
67........	57,879	25,640	44.3	....	98.4	41.0	57.4	11.8	7.1
68........	55,438	23,118	41.7	....	102.6	44.1	58.5	11.2	7.0
69........	52,923	20,746	39.2	....	106.4	46.8	59.6	10.7	6.7
70........	50,374	18,538	36.8	....	111.7	50.8	60.9	10.2	6.4
71........	47,733	16,468	34.5	....	116.5	54.6	61.9	9.8	6.1
72........	45,046	14,550	32.3	....	121.5	58.5	63.0	9.3	5.9
73........	42,325	12,782	30.2	....	129.7	62.5	67.2	8.8	5.6
74........	39,586	11,124	28.1	....	133.6	68.5	65.1	8.4	5.3
75........	36,785	9,638	26.2	....	145.2	71.7	73.5	8.0	5.1
76........	34,047	8,239	24.2	....	152.3	77.1	75.2	7.5	4.8
77........	31,320	6,984	22.3	....	164.1	82.8	81.3	7.1	4.6
78........	28,617	5,838	20.4	....	173.3	89.4	83.9	6.7	4.3
79........	25,946	4,826	18.6	....	190.8	99.6	91.2	6.3	4.1
80........	23,245	3,905	16.8	....	200.8	105.5	95.3	6.0	3.9
81........	20,669	3,121	15.1	....	220.4	115.0	105.4	5.6	3.7
82........	18,159	2,433	13.4	....	243.3	125.6	117.7	5.3	3.6
83........	15,734	1,841	11.7	....	256.9	139.1	117.8	5.0	3.6
84........	13,408	1,368	10.2	....	265.4	140.4	125.0	4.7	3.6
85 years and over.	55,525	4,386	7.9	....	....	....	....	4.5	3.6

"(8) *Probability of separations due to retirement (1,000 Q_x^r).*

"(9) *Average number of remaining years of life* ($\overset{o}{e}_x$). The total life expectancy function is identical with that shown in the conventional life tables.

"(10) *Average number of remaining years of working life* ($\overset{o}{e}w_x$). This function shows the average remaining years of working life for men in the labor force.

"Between 1900 and 1960 the number of man-years of work expected increased from 32 to 41 years for men; for women, from 6 to 20 years.

Average Number of Man-Years of Work
Expected Per Persons Born Alive

Year	Men	Women
1900	32	6
1940	38	12
1950	42	15
1960	41	20

"This increase has occurred as a result of the lengthened life expectancy and despite longer schooling prior to a work career and more years in retirement. The work life potential of women has also increased as a result of the trend toward longer life, but this trend has been accelerated by an increased tendency for women to work outside the home. However, work life potential does not reflect the full gain in productive capacity because it does not allow either for the greater education and training of workers or for changing technology. Both of these have combined to increase our productive capacity per worker more than is indicated by the ratio of productive population to total population. ...

"Work life expectancy for a 20-year-old man rose from 39 years in 1900 to 43 years by 1960 largely as a result of longer life expectancy. Retirement as it is known today was relatively uncommon in 1900 and the difference between life expectancy and work life expectancy was only 3 years. The longer range effects of the decline in opportunities for self-employment in agricultural as well as nonagricultural industries, the recent availability of public and private pension plans, and the effects of discrimination against older workers in layoff and hiring practices, are evident from a comparison of 1900 and 1960 working life patterns. For 60-year-old men, life expectancy rose moderately by almost a year and a half but work life expectancy declined by 3 years as a result of a long-run trend toward earlier retirement.

9.12. Estimating Entrants to and Separations from the Labor Force

"In recent years concern has been expressed about the increasing number of young people who can be expected to enter the labor force as a result of population growth in the young ages. The number of babies born during and after World War II reached phenomenally high levels. These youngsters are now reaching ages when they typically begin a work career. One can observe the effects of this development in the rising number of young people both in the population and in the labor force. Estimates of the gross number of men who can be expected to begin a work career in the years ahead can be made by applying annual labor force accession rates from Tables of Working Life, by age, to the projected population at corresponding ages. Similar approximations can be made for entry into the labor force of women at young ages.[8] These numbers should be regarded as approximations, however, since economic conditions and other considerations may increase or decrease the number of young persons seeking to begin a work career in any one year.

"At the opposite end of the working life span, the "Tables of Working Life" provide a measure of separation from the labor force resulting from death or retirement. Separation rates from Tables of Working Life provide a basis for measuring expected losses from certain occupations due to death and retirement. These rates applied to the age distribution of workers in specified occupations indicate roughly the number of persons who must be trained

in those occupations if the demand for the occupational skills remains unchanged. These estimates assume that separation rates for each age group in the labor force apply to corresponding age groups in each occupation.

9.13. Estimates of Lifetime Job Changes

"Tables of Working Life have also been adapted to provide an estimate of the number of times a man can be expected to change jobs during his working life as well as the length of time he can be expected to stay on each job.[9]

"A recent study of job mobility prepared by the Bureau of Labor Statistics[10] provided data on the number of job changes that were made during 1961 by men in each age group. If it is assumed that the 1961 age patterns of job changing will remain constant, it is possible to estimate the number of job changes (defined as a change of employer) that men at each age can be expected to make during the rest of their working life. If the number of different jobs is divided into the remaining years of work life, it is also possible to derive an estimate of the average length of time that men at each age can be expected to remain on one job.

"Under conditions prevailing at the beginning of the 1960s the average 20-year-old man in the work force could be expected to change jobs about 6 or 7 times, and spend about 5½ years on each job during his remaining working life of about 43 years. Despite their shorter overall work life expectancy of only 12 years, the length of time 55-year-old men can be expected to stay on a job is over 7 years—1½ years longer than for young men of 20 because more workers who change jobs in their fifties can be expected to work on their new job until they die or retire.

"Tables of Working Life have been prepared for several countries using either the same or similar techniques that were used by the Bureau of Labor Statistics. When historical comparisons can be made, such as in the United States, the development from a predominantly agricultural to an industrial econ-

[8] BLS *Bulletin 1204, Tables of Working Life for Women*, 1950.

[9] *Manpower Report No. 10, Job Changing and Manpower Training*.

[10] *Special Labor Force Report No. 35, Job Mobility in 1961*.

omy has been accompanied by a lengthening of life expectancy, of work life expectancy and a lengthening of the period of life spent outside the work force.[11] Similarly, when agricultural and industrialized countries are compared at the same approximate dates, life expectancy, work life expectancy and years outside the labor force are longer in industrialized countries.[12] These changing relationships have many implications for national well-being. The number of years spent in productive work by 100,000 persons born alive, as they live out their lives, increases greatly as sanitation and medical advances reduce death rates at all ages. Usually this type of development accompanies industrialization and the development of advanced technology.

"Many analysts have measured social and economic development of various countries in terms of some variant of the ratio of productive population to total (productive plus nonproductive) population. A more complete evaluation of this situation should consider that the lengthening of life prior to entry into the work force has made it possible to greatly increase the amount of education and training provided to the work force. And the lengthening of working life has permitted the more intensively trained workers to spend more man-years at work. These two features coupled with advanced technology have added greatly to productive capacity. It is, of course, impossible to separate the effects of the greater education and training of our work force from the development of technology in assessing the greater productive capacity of industrialized countries. But any appraisal should not be limited to the increasing ratio of productive to total population. Ideally it should be possible to synthesize these developments in a single measure of man-years of productive capacity by combining a measure of working life with a measure of the more intensive training of our work force, and/or with a measure of the

increasing output per man-year to give more perspective to international comparisons of industrial and social development."[13]

CONCLUSION

This chapter has undertaken to present the basic concepts of work force analysis, especially the concepts of work force participation rate and rate of unemployment. It has been demonstrated that both of these measures vary markedly but systematically with age, sex, race, nativity, marital status, number of children in the family, and other factors. The review of data for the United States demonstrates that sociological and demographic factors interact with economic factors to influence the level of labor force participation. The severest of the social problems of the nation are traced to the difficulties that members of minority groups have in attaining employment, especially employment that pays a living wage. Fluctuations of the business cycle affect the economic well-being of all segments of the labor force, but act with extraordinary severity on these minority groups.

Women are entering the labor force in increasing numbers. Their participation is lessened by family obligations, but once these are discharged, they tend to seek gainful work. Much of their work is part-week and part-year.

In developing nations youths enter the labor force at an earlier age and withdraw at an older age than in the industrialized nations. Despite the fact that in the industrialized nations males enter the labor force much later and retire earlier, the average length of working life is considerably longer than in the developing nations—thanks to lower mortality rates. The Table of Working Life is a useful technique for summarizing the net impact of the various components of labor force dynamics, and facilitates greatly the making of international as well as internal national comparisons and the study of trends at both international and national levels.

[11] S. Wolfbein, *Employment and Unemployment in the United States,* Chapter 7.

[12] *Demographic Aspects of Manpower Report 1, Sex and Age Patterns of Participation in Economic Activities,* United Nations, 1962.

[13] *Ibid.*

QUESTIONS AND EXERCISES

1. Look up the age-specific labor force participation rates for specific developed and industrialized nations. Note the differences within each group as well as between the two groups. Undertake to explain these intragroup differences. Are the intragroup differences as large as the intergroup differences?

2. Look up the age-specific labor force participation rates for two or more censuses for nations undergoing economic development and for nations already industrialized. Note the changes that have taken place within each nation. Are the changes for the developing nations the same as for the industrialized nations? Develop an explanation for each type of change.

3. Read the references to Bancroft and some of the most recent releases of the *Current Reports on the Labor Force* to obtain information about the characteristics of persons with (*a*) short-term unemployment and (*b*) long-term unemployment. Write an essay contrasting the characteristics of the employed and the unemployed and the characteristics of those with prolonged unemployment in comparison with those unemployed only a brief time. Obtain data for such characteristics as educational attainment, last occupation, industry, and income.

4. Find out what you can about the characteristics of the small group of males between the ages of 25 and 64 who are not in the labor force. Develop some hypotheses that would explain their lack of participation.

5. Find out what you can about the participation of the elderly population of retirement age (65 and over). To what extent is their participation due to lack of income and the need to continue earning in order to avoid poverty, and to what extent is it a desire to work to avoid the monotony and isolation of retirement? How does your hypothesis differ according to race? sex? age? occupation before age 65?

6. Investigate more thoroughly the relationship between the participation of women in the labor force and their educational attainment. For example, how does the labor force participation of women with college degrees differ from that of women who graduated from high school, when the spouse is present in the household and there are small children? Write a term paper or class report on the "career woman" in modern America. What proportion of women who are college graduates exhibit the "career woman" syndrome?

7. Investigate the work participation of older men whose major occupation had been as a professional person. Compare it with the activity of men who had been business managers, craftsmen, operatives, and so on. Do you find evidences of involuntary retirement and acceptance of low-paying posts just to keep in contact with the professional and business world, or do most white-collar men appear to accept retirement gladly. Try to supplement your demographic data with social psychological studies in this area.

8. Look up the annual average income of a male worker who has a college education. Find the same item of information for a male worker who graduated only from high school. Can you use the Table of Working Life to estimate how much more money the university graduate will make during his lifetime? What is the money value of a college education? (Do not forget to make allowance for the cost of going to college and the years spent out of the labor force while doing so.)

9. Assume that a man is 50 years of age and plans to retire at the time normal for his age group. He will get Social Security, but wants to supplement it with enough savings and investment (yielding an average of 5 percent per year) to have an annual income of $10,000. (He wants to give the principal to his heirs.) How much must he have saved by the time he reaches retirement?

BIBLIOGRAPHY

Adams, Edith. "A Comparison of Recent Census Statistics on the Economically Active Population," *Proceedings of the World Population Conference: 1954*. New York, 1955, Vol. IV.

Andrews, Edith W. *Labor in Indonesia,* in U. S. Bureau of Labor Statistics. Labor in BLS Reports, Nos. 243, 246, 251, 261. (Parts in a series on labor in selected countries prepared by the Bureau for the Agency for International Development.) Washington, D.C.: U.S. Government Printing Office, 1963.

Bailey, Donald. "Note on British Unemployment Statistics," *Applied Statistics,* 9 (1) (March 1960), 51–59.

Bancroft, Gertrude. *The American Labor Force: Its Growth and Changing Composition.* A volume in the Census Monograph Series. Published for the Social Science Research Council in cooperation with the U. S. Bureau of the Census. New York: John Wiley and Sons. London: Chapman and Hall, 1958.

Bancroft, Gertrude. "Some Illustrative Indexes of Employment and Unemployment," *Monthly Labor Review,* 85 (2) (February 1962), 167–174.

Barclay, George W. "Demographic Aspects of Manpower in the Far East," pp. 28–33 in *Population Bulletin of the United Nations,* No. 5, July, 1956.

Basilio B., Aromin. *Population and Labour Force Growth in Selected Countries of Asia and the Far East.* Paper contributed for the United Nations World Population Conference, August 30-September 10, 1965.

Bauer, Peter T., and B. S. Yamey. *The Economics of Under-developed Countries.* The Cambridge Economic Handbooks. Chicago: University of Chicago Press, 1957.

Baum, Samuel. *Population, Manpower, and Economic Development of Eastern Europe.* Washington, D.C., George Washington University, Population Research Project, 1961.

Baum, Samuel. "The World's Labour Force and Its Industrial Distribution, 1950 and 1960," *International Labour Review* (Geneva), 95 (1–2) (January-February 1967), 96–112.

Bean, Lee L., et al. "The Labour Force of Pakistan: A Note on the 1961 Census," *Pakistan Development Review* (Karachi), 6 (4) (Winter 1966), 589–591.

Berthoud, Denise. "La Situation de la Femme dans la Vie Economique" (The Position of Women in Economic Life), *Schweizerische Zeitschrift fur Volkswirtschaft und Statistik* (Basel), 92 (3) (September 1956), 346–357.

Bhattacharjee, J. P. "Underemployment Among Indian Farmers: An Analysis of Its Nature and Extent Based on Data for Bihar," *Artha Vijñana* (Poona), 3 (3) (September 1961), 246–279.

Bogue, Donald J. "The Labor Force and its Composition," Chapter 16, "Unemployment and Characteristics of the Unemployed," Chapter 19 in *The Population of the United States,* Glencoe: the Free Press, 1959.

Bourque, Philip J. "Regional Patterns of Seasonality in the Labor Force and Its Components," *Quarterly Journal of Economics and Business,* 2 (4) (November 1962), 53–67.

Bowen, William G., and T. Aldrich Finegan. "Educational Attainment and Labor Force Participation," *American Economic Review,* 56 (2) (May 1966), 567–582.

Bowman, Raymond T., and Margaret E. Martin. Special Report on Unemployment Statistics: Meaning and Measurement," *American Statistician,* 16 (4) (October 1962), 14–22.

Bruntz, Francois. "The Part-Time Employment of Women in Industrialised Countries," *International Labour Review,* 86 (5) (November 1962), 425–442.

Cain, Glen G. "Married Women in the Labor Force: An Economic Analysis," *Studies in Economics of the Economics Research Center of the University of Chicago.* Chicago: University of Chicago Press, 1966.

Canada. Dominion Bureau of Statistics. *Unemployment in Canada.* Catalogue No. 71–503, Occasional. Ottawa: Queen's Printer, April 1962.

Collver, Andrew, and Eleanor Langlois. "The Female Labor Force in Metropolitan Areas: An International Comparison," *Economic Development and Cultural Change,* 10 (4) (July 1962), 367–385.

Cormier, Gerard H., and Louise E. Butt. *Labor in Brazil.* U. S. Bureau of Labor Statistics Report 191. Published in cooperation with the Agency for International Development. Washington, D.C.: U.S. Government Printing Office, January 1962.

Debeauvais, Michel. "Manpower Planning in Developing Countries," *International Labour Review* (Geneva), 39 (4) (April 1964), 317–338.

Dernburg, Thomas, and Kenneth Strand. "Hidden Unemployment 1953-62: A Quantitative Analysis by Age and Sex," *American Economic Review,* 56 (1) (March 1966), 71–95.

de Wolff, P. *Employment Forecasting by Professions.* Paper contributed for the United Nations World Population Conference, August 30-September 10, 1965.

Dodge, Norton T. *Women in the Soviet Economy: Their Role in Economic, Scientific, and Technical Development.* Baltimore: Johns Hopkins Press, 1966.

Ducoff, Louis J. *Population Growth in Relation to the Agricultural Labor Force in Developed and Some Developing American Countries.* Paper contributed to United Nations World Population Conference, August 30-September 10, 1965.

Ducoff, Louis J., and Margaret J. Hagood. "The Meaning and Measurement of Special and Disguised Unemployment," in *The Measurement and Behavior of Unemployment.* A conference of the Universities-National Bureau Committee for Economic Research. A report of the National Bureau of Economic Research, New York. Special Conference Series, 8. Princeton, N. J.: Princeton University Press, 1957.

Duncan, Beverly. *Population Distribution and Economic Activity: The Non-metropolitan United States in 1950.* Chicago: Department of Photo-Duplication, University of Chicago Library, 1957.

Durand, John D. "Population Structure as a Factor in Manpower and Dependency Problems of Underdeveloped Countries," *Population Bulletin of the United Nations,* (3) (October 1953), 1–16.

Eason, Warren W. "Labor Force," pp. 38–95 in Abram Bergson and Simon Kuznets (eds.). *Economic Trends in the Soviet Union.* Cambridge, Mass.: Harvard University Press, 1963.

Elfvengren, Elisabeth *"Finlands Arbetskraft; Struktur och Utvecklingstendenser." (Finland's Labor Force; Structure and Development Trends).* Helsinki: Taloudellinen Tutkimuskeskus-Ekonomiska Utredningsbyran, 1955. With English summary.

Elfvengren, Elisabeth. "The Finnish Labour Force," *International Labour Review* (Geneva), 73 (4) (April 1956), 358–376.

El Shafei, Abdel M. N. "The Current Labour Force Sample Survey in Egypt (U.A.R.)," *International Labour Review* (Geneva), 82 (5) (November 1960), 432–449.

European Economic Community. *The Trend of Employment in the Member States (1954-58).* Brussels, 1961.

Farrag, Abdelmegid M. "The Occupational Structure of the Labour Force: Patterns and Trends in Selected Countries," *Population Studies,* 18 (1) (July 1964), 17–34.

Fei, John C. H., and Gustav Ranis. "Unlimited Supply of Labor and the Concept of Balanced Growth," *Pakistan Development Review* (Karachi), 1 (3) (Winter 1961), 29–58.

Fischlowitz, Estanislau. "Manpower Problems and Prospects in Latin America," *Monthly Labor Review,* 83 (9) (September 1960), 900–916.

Flanagan, R. J. "Disguised Unemployment and the Structural Hypothesis," *Industrial Relations,* 5 (1) (October 1965), 23–36.

Fornaciari, M. L. "Osservazioni sull'Andamento del Lavoro Feminile in Italia negli Ultimi 50 Anni" (Notes on the Growth of the Female Labor Force in Italy in the Past Fifty Years), *Rivista Internazionale di Scienze Sociali* (Rome), 27 (3) (May-June 1956), 222–240.

Galenson, Walter, and Arnold Zellner. "International Comparisons of Unemployment Rates," with comment by Gladys L. Palmer and Angus

McMorran, in *The Measurement and Behavior of Unemployment.* A conference of the Universities-National Bureau Committee for Economic Research. A report of the National Bureau of Economic Research, New York. Special Conference Series, 8. Princeton, N. J.: Princeton University Press, 1957.

García-Frías, and O. Alexander de Moraes. "Determination of the Economically Active Population for the Purpose of International Comparability." *Proceedings of the World Population Conference: 1954.* New York, 1955, Vol. IV.

Garfinkle, Stuart. "Changes in Working Life of Men, 1900-2000," *Monthly Labor Review,* 78 (March 1955), 297–300.

Garfinkle, Stuart. "Table of Working Life for Men, 1960," *Monthly Labor Review,* 86 (7) (July 1963), 820–823.

Garfinkle, Stuart. "Tables of Working Life for Women, 1950," *Bureau of Labor Statistics Bulletin,* No. 1204. Washington, D.C.: U. S. Government Printing Office, 1962.

Garfinkle, Stuart. "Tables of Working Life for Women, 1950," *Monthly Labor Review,* 79 (6) (June 1956), 654–659.

Garfinkle, Stuart. "Tables of Working Life for Women, 1950. II. Work Life Expectancy and Accession and Separation Rates," *Monthly Labor Review,* 79 (8) (August 1956), 901–907.

Garfinkle, Stuart. "Tables of Working Life for Women, 1950. III. Changes in Patterns of Working Life, 1940 and 1950," *Monthly Labor Review,* 79 (10) (October 1956), 1152–1158.

Garfinkle, Stuart H. *The Length of Working Life for Males, 1900-1961.* Office of Manpower, Automation and Training, Manpower Report No. 8. Washington, D.C.: U. S. Manpower Administration, 1963.

Garfinkle, Stuart. *The Lengthening of Working Life and Its Implication.* Paper contributed for the United Nations World Population Conference August 30-September 10, 1965.

Gendell, Murray. *Swedish Working Wives: A Study of Determinants and Consequences.* Totowa, N. J.: Bedminster Press, 1963.

Gibbs, Jack P., and Walter T. Martin. "Mortality Rates and Participation in Sustenance Activities: An Ecological Analysis," *Journal of Health and Human Behavior,* 3 (Summer 1962), 112–120.

Goldstein, Harold. *Population and Labor Force Projections, 1960-1975.* U. S. Bureau of Labor Statistics, 1961, 6, processed. Paper presented at a conference on forecasting and the business community, American Statistical Association, San Franciso, October 16, 1959.

Gordon, Margaret S. "Work and Patterns of Retirement." University of California, Institute of Industrial Relations Reprint 170. Berkeley, 1961. Reprinted from *Aging and Leisure: A Research Perspective Into the Meaningful Use of Time*. Robert W. Kleemeier (ed.). New York: Oxford University Press, 1961, 15–53.

Gordon, R. A. "Has Structural Unemployment Worsened?" *Industrial Relations*, 3 (3) (May 1964), 53–77. Also issued as Reprint 234, Berkeley, Calif., Institute of Industrial Relations, 1964.

Great Britain. Ministry of Labour and National Service. *The Length of Working Life of Males in Great Britain*. Studies in Official Statistics, No. 4. London: H. M. Stationers Office, 1959.

Guelaud-Leridon, Françoise. *Le Travail des Femmes en France (Female Labor in France)*. Institút National d'Études Démographiques Cahiers de "Travaux et Documents," 42. Paris, 1964.

Habibullah, M., and A. Farouk. *The Pattern of Agricultural Unemployment. A Case Study of an East Pakistan Village*. Dacca University, Bureau of Economic Research, 1962.

Harewood, Jack. "Overpopulation and Unemployment in the West Indies," *International Labour Review* (Geneva), 82 (2) (August 1960), 103–137.

Harewood, Jack. *Some Views on the Collection, Analysis and Utilization of Current Employment Statistics in an Economically Less Developed Country*. Paper contributed for the United Nations World Population Conference, August 30-September 10, 1965.

Howes, Amy. "Women Part-time Workers in the United States," *International Labour Review* 86 (5) (November 1962), 443-452.

Horstmann, K. "Bevölkerung und Arbeitspotential" (Population and Labor Potential), in *Wandlungen der Wirtschaftsstruktur in der Bundesrepublik Deutschland* (Changes in the Economic Structure of the German Federal Republic), Schriften des Vereins für Sozialpolitik; Gesellschaft für Wirtschafts- und Sozial-wissenschaften, neue Folge, Band 26. Berlin: Duncker und Humblot, 1962.

Hovne, Avner. *The Labor Force in Israel*. Jerusalem: The Falk Project for Economic Research in Israel, 1961.

Hunter, Thelma. "The Employment of Women in Australia," *Journal of Industrial Relations* (Sydney), 3 (2) (October 1961), 94–104.

India. Cabinet Secretariat. *Tables With Notes on Employment and Unemployment in Urban Areas*, by Sudhir Bhattacharyya et al. The National Sample Survey, No. 63. Prepared by the Indian Statistical Institute. Delhi: Manager of Publications, 1962.

India. Department of Economic Affairs. *Report on*

Some Characteristics of the Economically Active Population, by Ranjan Kumar Som and Ajit Das Gupta. The National Sample Survey, No. 14. Prepared by the Indian Statistical Institute. Calcutta and Delhi, 1958–1959.

International Labour Office. "The Active Population of the U.S.S.R.," *International Labour Review* (Geneva), 84 (3) (September 1961), 198–203.

International Labour Office. "Agricultural Labour in India," *International Labour Review* (Geneva), 85 (2) (February 1962), 148–162.

International Labour Office. "A Survey of Employment, Unemployment and Underemployment in Ceylon," *International Labour Review* (Geneva), 87 (3) (March 1963), 247–257.

International Labour Office. "Demographic Trends in Western Europe and Their Implications for the Employment Market," *International Labour Review* (Geneva), 75 (2) (February 1957), 137–142.

International Labour Office. *Labour Survey of North Africa*. Studies and Reports, New Series, No. 60. Geneva, 1960.

International Labour Office. "The Measurement of Underemployment," *International Labour Review* (Geneva), 76 (4) (October 1957), 349–366.

International Labour Office. "Manpower Planning in Eastern Europe," *International Labour Review* (Geneva), 86 (2) (August 1962), 95–127.

International Labour Office. "Population and Labour Force in Africa," *International Labour Review* (Geneva), 84 (6) (December 1961), 499–514.

International Labour Office. "The Population and Labour Force of Asia, 1950-80," *International Labour Review* (Geneva), 86 (4) (October 1962), 348–368.

International Labour Office. "The Problem of the Employment of Older Workers," *International Labour Review*, 69 (6) (June 1954), 594–618.

International Labour Office. "Projections of Population and Labour Force," *International Labour Review* (Geneva), 83 (4) (April 1961), 378–399.

International Labour Office. "Recent Trends in Employment and Unemployment," *International Labour Review* (Geneva), 73 (1) (January 1956), 58–76.

International Labour Office. "Recent Trends in Employment and Unemployment," *International Labour Review* (Geneva), 78 (3) (September 1958), 291–315.

International Labour Office. "Unemployment and Underemployment in India, Indonesia, Pakistan, and the Philippines," *International Labour*

Review (Geneva), 86 (4) October 1962), 369–387.

International Labour Office. *Why Labour Leaves the Land. A Comparative Study of the Movement of Labour Out of Agriculture.* Studies and Reports, New Series, No. 59. Geneva, 1960.

International Labour Office. "Women in Employment in India," *International Labour Review* (Geneva), 79 (4) (April 1959), 440–444.

International Labour Office. "Women in the Labour Force," *International Labour Review* (Geneva), 77 (3) (March 1958), 254–272.

International Labour Office. "Women Workers in a Changing World," *Sixth Item on the Agenda, International Labour Conference,* 48th session, 1964 Report VI (1). Geneva, 1963.

International Labour Office. "Women Workers in Japan: Employment Trends and Conditions of Work in 1960," *International Labour Review* (Geneva), 85 (6) (June 1962), 632–636.

International Labour Office. "The World's Working Population. Some Demographic Aspects," *International Labour Review,* 73 (2) (February 1965), 152–176.

International Labour Organisation. *African Labour Survey.* Studies and Reports, New Series, No. 48. Geneva, 1958.

International Labour Organisation. *The Age of Retirement.* Geneva, 1954.

Islam, Nurul. "Concepts and Measurement of Unemployment and Underemployment in Developing Economies," pp. 240–256 in International Institute for Labor Studies. "Problems of Employment in Economic Development," *International Labour Review* (Geneva), 89 (3) (March 1964), 213–285.

Jaffe, A. J. and L. E. Quesada. *Assessment of Underemployment in Non-agricultural Industries of the Less Developed Countries.* Paper contributed for the United Nations World Population Conference, August 30-September 10, 1965.

Jaffe, A. J. "Economic Development and the Growth of the Male Working Force of Panama, 1950-60," *American Journal of Economics and Sociology,* 25 (3) (July 1966), 297–306.

Jaffe, A. J. "From New Entries to Retirement: The Changing Age Composition of the U.S. Male Labor Force by Industry," *Demography,* 4 (1967), 273-282.

Jaffe, A. J. *People, Jobs and Economic Development: A Case History of Puerto Rico, Supplemented by Recent Mexican Experiences.* A report of the Bureau of Applied Social Research of Columbia University. Glencoe, Ill.: The Free Press, 1959.

Jaffe, A. J. "Working Force," pp. 604–620 in Philip M. Hauser, and Otis Dudley Duncan (eds.). *The Study of Population.* Chicago: University of Chicago Press, 1959.

Jones, G. W. "The Growth and Changing Structure of the Indonesian Labour Force, 1930-81," *Bulletin of Indonesian Economic Studies* (Canberra), (4) (June 1966), 50–74.

Kailas, C. *Recent Progress in Underemployment Statistics and Analysis.* Paper contributed to United Nations World Population Conference, August 30-September 10, 1965.

Kelsall, R. K., and Sheila Mitchell. "Married Women and Employment in England and Wales," *Population Studies,* 13 (1) (July 1959), 19–33.

Knoellinger, F. C. E. *Labor in Finland.* Cambridge, Mass.: Harvard University Press, 1960; London: Oxford University Press, 1961.

Kono, Shigemi. "Abridged Working Life Table for Japanese Males: 1930, 1950 and 1955," *Archives of the Population Association of Japan,* No. 4. English edition. Tokyo, 1963, 1–17.

Kreps, Juanita M. "Aggregate Income and Labour Force Participation of the Aged," pp. 52–66 in Hans W. Baade (ed.). *Law and Contemporary Problems,* 27 (1) (Winter 1962), 1–156.

Kuptzin, Harold. "Chronic Labor Surplus Areas, Experience and Outlook," in U.S. Bureau of Employment Security, *Bureau of Economic Security No. R-182.* Washington, 1959.

Lacroix, Henri P. *Les Statistiques de la Main D'-Oeuvre.* Paper contributed to the United Nations World Population Conference, August 30-September 10, 1965.

Lebergott, Stanley. "Annual Estimates of Unemployment in the United States, 1900-1950," with comment by Martin R. Gainsbrugh, in *The Measurement and Behavior of Unemployment.* A conference of the Universities-National Bureau Committee for Economic Research. A report of the National Bureau of Economic Research, New York. Special Conference Series, No. 8. Princeton, N. J.: Princeton University Press, 1957.

Lebergott, Stanley. *Manpower in Economic Growth: The American Record Since 1800.* New York: McGraw-Hill, 1964.

Lebergott, Stanley. "Measuring Unemployment," *Review of Economics and Statistics,* 36 (4) (November 1954), 390–500.

Lebergott, Stanley. "Population Change and the Supply of Labor," comment by James N. Morgan and John Durand, pp. 377–422 in *National Bureau of Economic Research.* Princeton, N. J., 1960.

Leser, C. E. V. "Trends in Women's Work Participation," *Population Studies,* 12 (2) (November 1958), 100–110.

Livingston, Robert G. "Yugoslavian Unemployment Trends," *Monthly Labor Review*, **87** (7) (July 1964), 756–762.

Long, Clarence E. "The Labor Force Under Changing Income and Employment," *National Bureau of Economic Research*, General Series, No. 65. Princeton, N. J.: Princeton University Press, 1958.

Lux, André. *Le Marché du Travail en Afrique Noire (The Labor Market in Negro Africa)*. Publications de l'Université Lovanium de Leopoldville, 10. Louvain, Institut de Recherches Economiques Sociales et Politiques; Editions Nauwelaerts, 1962.

Mathur, Ashok. "The Anatomy of Disguised Unemployment, "*Oxford Economic Papers,* n.s., **16** (2) (July 1964), 161–193.

Miller, Ann R. "Components of Labor Force Growth," *Journal of Economic History*, **22** (1) (March 1962), 47–58.

Miller, Ann R. "Trends in Labour Force Participation Rates, United States, 1890-1950: Analysis of State Rates in Their Relation to Migration and Population Growth," *Proceedings of the World Population Conference: 1954*. New York, 1955, Vol. II.

Mitra, Asok. *Indian Experience in Recording Economically Active Population: 1961 Population Census*. Paper contributed for the United Nations World Population Conference, August 30-September 10, 1965.

Moore, Wilbert E. "The Adaptation of African Labor Systems to Social Change," pp. 277–297 in *Economic Transition in Africa*. Northwestern University African Studies, 12. Melville J. Herskovits and Mitchell Harwitz (eds.). Evanston, Ill.: Northwestern University Press, 1963.

Moore, Wilbert E. "Population and Labor Force in Relation to Economic Growth," pp. 231–240 in Simon Kuznets et al. (eds.). *Economic Growth: Brazil, India, Japan*. Durham, N. C.: Duke University Press, 1955.

Myers, Robert J., and John H. Chandler. "International Comparisons of Unemployment," *Monthly Labor Review*, **85** (9) (August 1962), 857–864.

Myers, Robert H., and John H. Chandler. "Toward Explaining International Unemployment Rates," *Monthly Labor Review*, **85** (9) (September 1962), 969–974.

National Bureau of Economic Research. *The Measurement and Interpretation of Job Vacancies: A Conference Report of the National Bureau of Economic Research*. New York: Columbia University Press, 1966.

Neef, Arthur. "Labor in Mexico," in U. S. Bureau of Labor Statistics. *Bureau of Labor Statistics Reports*, Nos. 243, 246, 251, 261. Washington, D. C., 1963.

Okita, Saburo. "Manpower Policy in Japan," *International Labour Review* (Geneva), **90** (1) (July 1964), 45–58.

Organisation for Economic Cooperation and Development. *Manpower Statistics 1950-1962*. Paris, 1963.

Palmore, Erdman. "Retirement Patterns Among Aged Men: Findings of the 1963 Survey of the Aged," *Social Security Bulletin*, **27** (8) (August 1964), 3–10.

Palmore, Erdman. "Work Experience and Earnings of the Aged in 1962: Findings of the 1963 Survey of the Aged," *Social Security Bulletin*, **27** (6) (June 1964), 3–14.

Penniment, K. J. *The Influence of Cultural and Socio-economic Factors on Labour Force Participation Rates*. Paper contributed for the United Nations World Population Conference, August 30-September 10, 1965.

Philippine Social Security Bulletin. "Our Economically Active Population," by Virgina M. Moscoso. *Philippine Social Security Bulletin* (Manila), **4** (3) (March 1962), 60–67.

Population Problems Research Council. "Various Forms of 'Invisible' Unemployment in Agricultural Districts," *Population Problems Series*, No. 2, 1950.

Population Problems Research Council. "Japanese Economy and Problems of Employment," *Population Problems Series*, No. 10, 1954.

Pressat, Roland. "La Population Active en France. Premiers Résultats du Recensement de 1962" (The Working Population in France: First Results of the 1962 Census), *Population* (Paris), **18** (3) (July-September 1963), 473–488. English and Spanish summaries.

Pressat, Roland. "La Prévision de l'Emploi: Apercus Méthodologiques" (The Projection of Employment: Methodological Survey), *Cahiers de l'Institut de Science Economique Apliquée: Economie du Travail* (Paris), Series BB, **122** (2) (February 1962), 127–240.

Rees, Albert. "The Meaning and Measurement of Full Employment," with comment by Elmer C. Bratt, in *The Measurement and Behavior of Unemployment*. A conference of the Universities-National Bureau Committee for Economic Research. A report of the National Bureau of Economic Research, New York. Special Conference Series, 8. Princeton, N.J.: Princeton University Press, 1957.

Roof, Michael K., and Allen Hetmanek. "The Soviet Labor Force: Implications of New Data," *Monthly Labor Review*, **81** (12) (December 1958), 1393–1398.

Salz, Beate R. "The Human Element in Industrialization. A Hypothetical Case Study of Ecuadorean Indians," *American Anthropologist*, **57** (6) (1955), Memoir No. 85. Published jointly with the Research Center in Economic Development and Cultural Change, University of

Chicago, appearing as Vol. IV, No. 1, Part 2 (October 1955) of *Economic Development and Cultural Change*.

Sarkar, N. K. "A Method of Estimating Surplus Labour in Peasant Agriculture in Over-populated Under-developed Countries," *Journal of the Royal Statistical Society*, Series A (General), **120** (2) (1957), 209–214.

Saw Swee-Hock. "Malaya: Tables of Male Working Life, 1957," *Journal of the Royal Statistical Society*, Series A (General), **128** (3) (1965), 421–438.

Schiffman, Jacob. "Characteristics of the Long-term Unemployed," *Monthly Labor Review*, **80** (10) (October 1957), 1233–1236.

Schwarzweiller, Harry K. "Education, Migration, and Economic Life Chances of Male Entrants to the Labor Force from a Low-income Rural Area," *Rural Sociology*, **29** (2) (June 1964), 152–167.

Spain. Instituto de Cultura Hispánica. "La Población Activa Española de 1900 a 1957" (The Economically Active Population of Spain from 1900 to 1957), *Estudios Hispánicos de Desarrollo Económico*, Monografía No. 1. Madrid, 1957.

Stabile, Blanca. "The Working Women in the Argentine Economy," *International Labour Review* (Geneva), **85** (2) (February 1962), 122–128.

Stein, Robert L. "Married Women and the Level of Unemployment," *Monthly Labor Review*, **84** (8) (August 1961), 869–870.

Stein, Robert L. "Work History, Attitudes, and Income of the Unemployed," reprint 2430 from *Monthly Labor Review*, **86** (12) (December 1963), 1405–1413. Supplementary Pages A-1 to A-7 in U. S. Bureau of Labor Statistics, *Special Labor Force Reports*, No. 1-. Washington, D.C., 1960.

Stolper, Wolfgang F. "The Labor Force and Industrial Development in Soviet Germany," *Quarterly Journal of Economics*, **71** (4) (November 1957), 518–545.

Szabady, Egon. *Demographic Aspects of the Changes in the Structure of the Population by Economic Activity in Hungary*. Paper contributed to the United Nations World Population Conference, August 30-September 10, 1965.

Taeuber, Irene B. "Population and Labor Force in the Industrialization of Japan, 1850–1950," pp. 316–359 in Simon Kuznets et al. (eds.). *Economic Growth: Brazil, India, Japan*. Durham, N.C.: Duke University Press, 1955.

Taira, Koji. "The Characteristics of Japanese Labor Markets," *Economic Development and Cultural Change*, **10** (2, Part 1) (January 1962), 150–168.

Thorner, Daniel, and Alice Thorner. *The Working Force in India, 1881–1951*. Census of 1961

Project. Bombay: Indian Statistical Institute, 1960, in 5 parts.

Tilak, V.R.K. "The Future Manpower Situation in India, 1961–1976," *International Labour Review* (Geneva), **87** (5) (May 1963), 435–446.

Tilak, V.R.K. *Some Problems in Projecting the Economically Active Population*. Paper contributed for the United Nations World Population Conference, August 30-September 10, 1965.

Turner, H. A. "Measuring Unemployment," *Journal of the Royal Statistical Society*, **118** (1) (1955), 28–50.

Ullman, Joseph C. "How Accurate Are Estimates of State and Local Unemployment?" *Industrial and Labor Relations Review*, **16** (3) (April 1963), 434–445.

United Nations Centro Latinoamericano de Demografia (CELADE). *Population and Labor Force of Chile, 1930–1975*. Publications, Series A. Reports on investigations by CELADE. Santiago, 1962.

United Nations Department of Economic and Social Affairs. "Demographic Aspects of Manpower. Report I. Sex and Age Patterns of Participation in Economic Activity," *Population Studies* 33, Series A.

United Nations Department of Economic and Social Affairs. *Population Growth and Manpower in the Sudan*. A joint study by the United Nations and the Government of the Sudan, Department of Statistics, Council of Ministers, The Republic of the Sudan, Khartoum. *Population Studies* 37, Series A.

United Nations Economic Commission for Latin America. "Changes in Employment Structure in Latin America, 1945–1955," *Economic Bulletin for Latin America* (Santiago, Chile), **2** (1) (February 1957), 15–42.

United Nations Latinoamericano Centre de Demografia. *The Demographic Aspects of Unemployment and Underemployment in Latin America*. Paper contributed to United Nations World Population Conference, August 30-September 10, 1965.

United Nations Population Division. "Factors Affecting the Size of the Economically Active Population," *Proceedings of the World Population Conference: 1954*. New York, 1955, Vol. III.

United Nations Statistical Office. *Handbook of Population Census Methods*. Vol. II. Economic Characteristics of the Population. Studies in Methods, Series F, No. 5, Rev. 1. New York, 1958.

Uribe Romo, Emilio. "The Labor Force of Mexico: an Analysis of its Structure, Characteristics, and Development" (La Fuerza de Trabajo de Mexico: un Analisis de su Estructura, sus Caracteristicas y su Evolución), *Estadística*

(Washington, D. C.), **47** (13) (June 1955), 185–210.

U. S. Bureau of the Census. "Family Characteristics of Working Wives: March, 1957," *Current Population Reports.* Series P-50. Labor Force. Washington, D.C., 1947-.

U. S. Bureau of the Census. Foreign Demographic Analysis Division. "The Labor Force in Czechoslovakia: Scope and Concepts," by Andrew Elias. *International Population Reports,* Series P-95, No. 61. Washington, D.C., 1963.

U. S. Bureau of the Census. Foreign Manpower Research Office. "The Labor Force in Bulgaria," by Zora Prochazka. *International Population Statistics Reports,* Series P-90, No. 16. Washington, D.C., 1962.

U. S. Bureau of the Census. Foreign Manpower Research Office. "The Labor Force of Hungary," by Samuel Baum. *International Population Statistics Reports,* Series P-90, No. 18. Washington, D.C., 1962.

U. S. Bureau of the Census. Foreign Manpower Research Office. "The Soviet Statistical System: Labor Force Record-keeping and Reporting Since 1957," by Murray Feshbach. *International Population Statistics Reports,* Series P-90, No. 17, Washington, D.C., 1962.

U. S. Bureau of the Census. "The Labor Force of Czechoslovakia," by James N. Ypsilantis. *International Population Statistics Reports,* Series P-90, No. 13, Washington, D.C., 1960.

U. S. Bureau of the Census. "The Labor Force of Poland," by Zora Prochaska and Jerry W. Combs, Jr. *International Population Statistics Reports, Series* P-90, No. 20, Washington, D.C., 1964.

U. S. Bureau of Employment Security. "Family Characteristics of the Long-term Unemployed: A Report on a Study of Claimants Under the Temporary Extended Unemployment Compensation Program, 1961–1962," *TEUC Report Series,* 1-. Washington, D.C., 1961.

U. S. Bureau of Employment Security. "Sources of Data for Manpower Projections," *Employment Security Research Methods Handbook Series,* R-199. Washington, D.C., March 1961.

U. S. Bureau of Labor Statistics. "Labor in Colombia," study prepared by Kurt Braun. *Bureau of Labor Statistics* Report 222. Washington, D.C., March 1962.

U. S. Bureau of Labor Statistics. "Labor Force and Employment Trends in Canada, 1950–1960," *Monthly Labor Review,* **85** (6) (June 1962), 668–672.

U. S. Bureau of Labor Statistics. "Labor in Nigeria," in *BLS Reports,* No. 243, 246, 251, 261. Washington, D.C., 1963.

U. S. Bureau of Labor Statistics. "Labor in Peru," in *BLS Reports,* No. 262. Washington, D.C., February 1964.

U. S. Bureau of Labor Statistics. *Special Labor Force Reports.* No. 1-. Washington, D.C., February 1960.

U. S. Central Intelligence Agency. *Comparison of U.S. and Soviet Population and Manpower.* CIA/RRER 60–38. Washington, D.C., November, 1960.

Labor Supply and Employment in the USSR, 1950–1965. Prepared by Philip Grossman. Washington, D.C., October 1960.

Soviet Manpower 1960–1970. Washington, D.C., 1960.

U. S. Congress. Joint Economic Committee. Subcommittee on Economic Statistics. *Unemployment: Terminology, Measurement, and Analysis.* Report of the Sub-Committee of the Committee, 87th Congress, 1st session. Washington, D.C.: U. S. Government Printing Office, 1961.

U.S. Department of Agriculture. Economic Research Service. *Characteristics of the Population of Hired Farmworker Households.* By Gladys K. Bowles and Calvin L. Beale. Agricultural Economic Report 84. Washington, (August 1965).

U.S. Department of Agriculture. Economic Research Service. *Potential Supply and Replacement of Rural Males of Labor Force Age, 1960-70.* Statistical Bulletin 378. Washington, October 1966.

U. S. Department of Labor. "Manpower Resources and Use," *Monthly Labor Review,* **86** (3) (March 1963), 237–254.

U. S. Department of State. Agency for International Development. Communications Resources Division. *Demographic Techniques for Manpower Planning in Developing Countries.* Prepared by the United States Employment Service, Bureau of Employment Security, U. S. Department of Labor, for the Agency for International Development. Washington, D.C.: U.S. Government Printing Office, 1963.

U. S. Office of Manpower, Automation and Training. "Selected Manpower Indicators for States," *Manpower Research Bulletin* 4. Washington, D.C.: U. S. Government Printing Office, 1963.

U. S. President's Committee to Appraise Employment and Unemployment Statistics. *Measuring Employment and Unemployment.* Washington, D.C.: U.S. Government Printing Office, 1962.

U. S. President's Task Force on Manpower Conservation. *One-Third of a Nation: A Report on Young Men Found Unqualified for Military Service.* Washington, D.C., 1964.

U. S. Women's Bureau. "Women Workers in 1960: Geographical Differences," *Women's Bureau Bulletin* 284. Washington, D.C.: U. S. Government Printing Office, 1962.

von Hofsten, Erland. *Projections of the Economi-*

cally Active Population. Paper contributed for the United Nations World Population Conference, August 30-September 10, 1965.

Widstam, Ture. "Married Women Economically Active. II. A Special Investigation Based on the Population Sample Register," *Statistiks Ridskrift* (Stockholm), **7** (1) (January 1958), 32–39.

Wilkinson, Thomas O. *The Urbanization of Japanese Labor 1868-1955.* Amherst, Mass.: University of Massachusetts Press, 1965.

Wolfbein, Seymour L. "The Changing Length of Working Life," reprinted from *Proceedings of the 7th Annual Meeting,* Industrial Relations Research Association. Madison, Wis., 1955.

Wolfbein, Seymour L. *Employment and Unemployment in the United States: A Study of the American Labor Force.* Chicago: Science Research Associates, 1964.

Wonnacott, Paul. "Disguised and Overt Unemployment in Underdeveloped Economies," *Quar-*
terly Journal of Economics, **76** (May 1962), 279–297.

Woodsmall, Ruth F. *Women and the New East.* Washington, D.C., Middle East Institute, 1960.

Yong, Sam Cho. *"Disguised Unemployment" in Underdeveloped Areas with Special Reference to South Korean Agriculture.* Publications of the Bureau of Business and Economic Research, University of California, Los Angeles. Berkeley and Los Angeles: University of California Press, 1963.

Yuki, Miura. *A Comparative Analysis of Operational Definitions of the Economically Active Population in African and Asian Statistics.* Paper contributed to the United Nations World Population Conference, August 30-September 10, 1965.

Zeisel, Joseph S. "Comparison of British and United States Unemployment Rates," *Monthly Labor Review,* **85** (5) (May 1962), 489–500.

CHAPTER 10

Occupational and Industrial Composition of the Work Force

10.1. The Structure of the Work Force and Reasons for Studying It

Studying the trends in the size of the work force, in work force participation rates, and in rates of unemployment constitutes only the first round of investigation in work force analysis. In a sense, Chapter 9 only circumscribed the problem but did little to study its internal pattern. The second round of investigation consists in subdividing the work force into its constituent parts and studying the changes in these parts. The two most fundamental ways of subdividing the total work force is by occupation and industry. The occupational classification of a person refers to the *type of job* that he holds. The industrial classification refers to the *type of organization or firm* for which he works.

Occupational Composition. It would be difficult to overemphasize the importance of the occupational classification of the individual for general social science analysis. This significance was stated succinctly a quarter century ago by Dr. Alba M. Edwards in his famous study of comparative occupations.

"The most nearly dominant single influence in a man's life is probably his occupation. More than anything else, perhaps, a man's occupation determines his course and his contribution in life. And when life's span is ended, quite likely there is no single set of facts that will tell so well the kind of man he was and the part he played in life as will a detailed chronological statement of the occupation, or occupations, he pursued. Indeed, there is no other single characteristic that tells so much about a man and his status—social, intellectual, and economic—

as does his occupation. A man's occupation not only tells, for each workday, what he does during one-half of his waking hours, but it indicates, with some degree of accuracy, his manner of life during the other half—the kind of associates he will have, the kind of clothes he will wear, the kind of house he will live in, and even, to some extent, the kind of food he will eat. And, usually, it indicates, in some degree, the cultural level of his family.

"In similar manner there probably is no single set of closely related facts that tell so much about a nation as do detailed statistics about the occupations of its workers. The occupations of a people influence directly their lives, their customs, their institutions—indeed, their very numbers. In fact, the social and the economic status of a people is largely determined by the social and economic status of its gainful workers. And, were the figures available, the social and industrial history of a people might be traced more accurately through detailed statistics of the occupations of its gainful workers than through the records of its wars, its territorial conquests, and its political struggles.

"With present-day interest in social problems and in their statistical measurement, it has become quite evident that statistics which show the actual life conditions of 40 percent of the population for one-third of each workday, and which give at least a rough index of the life conditions of those dependent upon them, are far too important to be neglected." [1]

[1] Alba M. Edwards, "Preface" to *Comparative Occupation Statistics for the United States: 1870 to 1940.* U.S. Census of Population: 1940, p. xi.

While appreciating the above quotation, it should be kept in mind that Edwards ascribes to occupation all of the attributes that a person has as a correlate of his participation in the work force. In the next chapter we shall challenge this view in behalf of the variable of income. It is not at all improper, however, to consider the income paid to those who participate in a particular occupation as an attribute of that occupation. When accepted in this sense, Edwards' view is sound. Certainly, those who undertake to study life styles, attitudes, and social organization without reference to the occupational structure of the community or the nation are failing to appreciate one of the most fundamental axes around which social life is organized.

Industrial Composition. The Industrial composition of an economy is its "economy base." Industrial composition provides knowledge about the integration of occupations into firms, plants, or other establishments. They show how the activities of people with various skills are integrated in the economy to provide the total range of products and services that the community needs. Another reason for beginning the study of the labor force in terms of industrial units is that these are the units of employment. Workers are employed by firms that are engaged in particular types of industry. Hence as new products emerge, new types of industry may emerge; as old products fall out of favor or are replaced by better ones, the establishments that produce these products also decline and tend to die out. When a community grows or declines in the size of its labor force, it is usually because a particular industry or group of industries has expanded or contracted its employment in that area.

The study of industrial composition may be pursued either at the national level or at the level of the local community economic base— the goods that the community produces in excess of its own needs to trade with other communities in order to import the goods and services that it cannot provide for itself locally. Thus to the human ecologist who is interested in how communities sustain themselves in their physical and socioeconomic environment, statistics of industrial composition are of unusual-

ly great interest. Sociologists have adopted a somewhat ambiguous position in the study of work force structure. On the one hand, they have tended to exaggerate the effect of occupation on other aspects of social life. On the other hand, they have tended to underestimate and underuse the available data. The exaggeration consists of seizing upon a few broad classifications such as "white collar" versus "blue collar" and using these as stereotypes with far-reaching theoretical implications to subdivide the work force along lines that were much more significant a century or so ago than they are today. At the same time, sociologists have not taken full advantage of the opportunities to delve into the detailed empirical facts of occupations as they exist at the present time and to dig out the actual relationships between occupations and other social statuses and events. The present chapter undertakes to encourage further research in this important area.

10.2. Industrial Composition around the World

Statistics for industry are collected in response to a question of the following type: "For whom did he work (name of company, business, organization, or other employer)? What kind of business or industry was this? (Describe activity at location where employed.)" The International Labour Office has developed a standard classification of industries with which to categorize the responses to this question. This classification has three levels—a "general," an "intermediate," and a "detailed" set of categories. Table 10-1 summarizes the industrial composition of the comparatively few nations of the world for which data are available, using the general categories of ILO.

It is immediately apparent from Table 10-1 that in the industrialized nations of the world agriculture employs a minority of the work force, whereas in the so-called underdeveloped nations of the world the agriculture industry is the major source of employment. In fact, we could accept as a simple rule that the degree of economic development that a nation exhibits is inversely proportional to the percentage of its working force employed in an

Table 10-1   Industrial Composition of the Economically Active Population

Country and Region	Year	Male				Female			
		Agri-culture	In-dustry	Service	Not classi-fiable	Agri-culture	In-dustry	Service	Not classi-fiable
NORTHERN AND WESTERN EUROPE									
Belgium............	1947	13.6	51.8	31.5	3.1	7.4	38.7	51.8	2.1
Denmark............	1950	29.0	39.0	30.9	1.1	17.5	22.0	59.4	1.1
Finland............	1950	46.2	32.4	19.6	1.8	45.7	20.9	32.6	0.8
France.............	1954	27.5	42.0	29.2	1.3	28.0	25.6	45.2	1.2
Iceland............	1950	37.9	35.7	26.3	0.1	34.4	21.9	43.5	0.2
Ireland............	1951	46.0	26.0	26.9	1.1	20.8	19.7	58.3	1.2
Luxembourg.........	1947	21.4	50.4	27.9	0.3	37.3	12.5	48.7	1.5
Netherlands........	1959	13.7	46.8	22.6	16.9	4.9	24.4	27.2	43.5
Norway.............	1950	31.4	39.7	28.3	0.6	8.2	26.1	65.4	0.3
Sweden.............	1950	25.3	46.2	27.8	0.7	6.4	25.2	67.6	0.8
United Kingdom:									
England & Wales...	1951	6.2	53.6	39.8	0.4	1.6	39.2	58.7	0.5
Scotland...........	1951	9.5	54.6	35.2	0.7	2.2	36.4	60.6	0.8
CENTRAL EUROPE									
Austria............	1951	24.9	46.8	26.7	1.6	43.5	21.6	33.4	1.5
Berlin, East.......	1950	1.5	53.1	45.4	0.0	2.4	40.5	57.1	0.0
Berlin, West.......	1950	2.0	50.0	46.7	1.3	2.1	33.8	61.0	3.1
Czechoslovakia.....	1947	29.6	43.2	27.0	0.2	52.7	26.5	20.2	0.6
Germany, Eastern....	1950	20.2	54.2	25.5	0.1	34.8	32.2	32.6	0.4
Germany, Western....	1950	16.4	52.1	29.9	1.6	35.2	24.8	36.8	3.2
Hungary............	1960	34.8	35.0	19.9	10.3	35.9	25.1	26.1	12.9
Switzerland........	1950	21.5	51.0	26.7	0.8	4.7	36.2	58.2	0.9
SOUTHERN EUROPE									
Greece.............	1951	49.5	18.3	26.0	6.2	42.1	24.2	27.4	6.3
Italy..............	1951	27.2	54.5	8.6	9.7	8.1	42.5	9.8	39.6
Malta & Gozo.......	1957	10.5	43.1	45.7	0.7	11.0	16.4	72.1	0.5
Portugal...........	1950	52.9	25.2	21.7	0.2	32.8	24.2	42.7	0.3
NORTHERN AMERICA									
Canada.............	1951	23.5	38.5	36.5	1.5	3.2	24.7	70.6	1.5
Greenland..........	1951	58.3	10.5	26.5	4.7	30.4	6.3	29.4	33.9
United States......	1950	15.4	40.2	42.0	2.4	3.7	25.0	68.0	3.3
OCEANIA									
Australia..........	1954	16.1	43.8	39.1	1.0	3.8	27.9	67.1	1.2
Fiji Islands.......	1946	59.4	15.6	14.6	10.4	1.9	0.3	86.5	11.3
New Zealand........	1956	19.7	39.5	40.3	0.5	4.7	23.7	71.1	0.5
SOUTH AMERICA									
Argentina..........	1947	29.7	27.5	36.8	6.0	6.8	31.9	55.8	5.5
Bolivia............	1950	68.5	20.4	9.1	2.0	75.7	10.3	13.3	0.7
Brazil.............	1950	65.7	12.6	21.4	0.3	30.3	15.5	53.9	0.3
British Guiana.....	1946	48.2	26.4	23.5	1.9	39.2	15.8	43.8	1.2
Chile..............	1952	36.8	30.3	27.4	5.5	7.7	24.9	63.7	3.7
Colombia...........	1951	63.2	16.0	17.0	3.8	13.3	25.0	59.0	2.7
Ecuador............	1950	61.9	17.9	16.0	4.2	17.6	48.7	28.8	4.9
Venezuela..........	1950	47.7	18.6	25.2	8.5	11.9	17.4	62.6	8.1
MIDDLE AMERICA									
Barbados...........	1946	30.1	37.0	29.5	3.4	26.8	18.2	52.5	2.5
Costa Rica.........	1950	62.6	16.2	17.7	3.5	11.3	15.9	72.2	0.6
El Salvador........	1950	73.3	13.0	10.7	3.0	12.3	23.0	59.9	4.8
Haiti..............	1950	86.5	5.5	5.6	2.4	79.7	5.7	11.5	3.1
Honduras...........	1950	83.1	7.4	6.8	2.7	....	....	....	....
Mexico.............	1950	57.8	15.8	21.3	5.1	....	....	....	....
Nicaragua..........	1950	76.9	13.8	9.3	0.0	11.3	23.6	65.1	0.0
Panama.............	1950	59.2	12.3	18.8	9.7	14.2	12.0	62.3	11.5
Puerto Rico........	1950	47.0	19.3	30.9	2.8	2.9	39.3	53.5	4.3
Trinidad & Tobago...	1946	29.3	33.3	31.0	6.4	19.8	21.3	53.4	5.5

agricultural industry. If we were to use this definition, we could classify the following nations as being the most industrialized in the world: Belgium, Netherlands, United Kingdom, East Germany, West Germany, United States, Australia, New Zealand, Hong Kong, and Singapore. Among those nations for which data

are available we would classify the following as the most underdeveloped nations in the world: El Salvador, Haiti, Honduras, Nicaragua, North Borneo, Thailand, and Algeria.

Table 10-1 reports that in the industrialized nations female employment tends to be heavily concentrated in the service industry, to a lesser

Table 10-1 (*Continued*)

Country and Region	Year	Male				Female			
		Agri-culture	In-dustry	Service	Not classi-fiable	Agri-culture	In-dustry	Service	Not classi-fiable
SOUTH CENTRAL ASIA									
Ceylon..............	1953	50.5	12.5	30.0	7.0	60.2	13.3	21.0	5.5
EAST ASIA									
China (Taiwan)......	1956	53.8	17.6	27.9	0.7	63.9	12.3	23.3	0.5
Hong Kong..........	1961	6.6	51.2	40.8	1.4	9.2	49.4	40.0	1.5
Japan..............	1960	26.0	35.6	38.3	0.0	43.5	20.2	36.2	0.0
Ryukyu Island.......	1950	54.1	11.0	11.9	22.9	68.1	3.4	17.3	11.2
SOUTH EAST ASIA									
Federation of Malaya	1957	51.6	14.4	31.1	2.9	75.8	7.1	15.3	1.8
North Borneo.......	1960	76.6	8.4	15.0	0.0	89.4	3.2	7.5	0.0
Phillipines.........	1958	67.8	12.1	16.7	3.4	39.0	21.6	32.1	7.3
Singapore..........	1957	6.7	21.4	69.9	2.0	16.0	16.6	64.6	2.8
Thailand...........	1954	83.9	3.8	11.9	0.3	92.1	1.3	6.4	0.2
SOUTH WEST ASIA									
Turkey in Asia......	1955	63.6	12.7	13.7	10.1	95.6	2.3	1.5	0.5
NORTHERN AFRICA									
Algeria.............	1948	83.5	5.5	7.7	3.3	95.7	1.5	2.7	0.1
Morocco...........	1952	65.2	11.3	22.3	1.1	83.8	8.7	6.8	0.7
Tunisia............	1956	60.6	11.7	14.8	12.9	80.6	5.0	4.9	0.6
United Arab Rep.....	1947	58.7	11.9	23.9	5.5	66.6	6.5	25.8	1.1
TROPICAL AND SOUTHERN AFRICA									
Ghana..............	1960	59.6	16.8	17.1	6.5	55.2	10.0	29.6	5.2
Swaziland..........	1956	66.1	17.8	1.3	14.9	68.8	3.8	1.6	25.7

Source: U.N. Compendium of Social Statistics: 1963 Table 67.

extent in manufacturing industries, and least in agriculture. Outside of the less developed countries, only in Finland, Austria, Czechoslovakia, Greece, Germany, Hungary, and Poland does a substantial share of the female population find employment in agriculture. All over the world, with the exception of Central Europe, agriculture tends to provide disproportionately less employment for females than for males. If we compare the percentage of males and females in each industry employed in agriculture, we find that in all but a very few countries of Central and Southern Europe, Asia, and Africa the proportion for males is higher than for females. Thus, as economic development proceeds and females are able to obtain employment, they tend to do so in the fields of business and service rather than in agriculture. This tendency is especially pronounced in Latin America (with the exception of Bolivia and Haiti, which are among those for which data are available). In interpreting the statistics for females, it must be kept in mind that Table 10-1 does not report the extent to which employment of any kind is available to females (it shows only the industrial distribu-

tion of those females who do find employment), and it also does not fully control international differences in definition of when a female is in the labor force and when she is simply engaged in normal household work.

10.3. Occupational Composition around the World

Most census statistics on occupation are collected in the form of responses to a question of the type "what kind of work does he do?" In replying to this question, the person is supposed to report a specific occupation or describe his work in such a detailed way that it can be properly categorized. Inasmuch as the modern industrial nations have a work force performing from 10,000 to 50,000 different kinds of tasks, it would be impossible to produce statistics for each of these jobs. It is necessary to arrive at some classification or set of categories of occupations.

There is substantial disagreement among the nations of the world and even within nations about the exact nature of classification that should be used for occupations. It would be

Table 10-2 Occupational Composition of the Economically Active Population of the World

Region and Nation	Year	Profes- sional & Tech- nical	Manageri- al adminis- tratives clerical	Sales	Farmers fisherman lumberman etc	Mine quarry & related occu- pation	Operating Transport occu- pation	Craftsmen production workers & laborers	Service workers	Armed Forces	Not class- fiable
NORTHERN & WESTERN EUROPE											
Denmark...................	1950	4.7	9.6	7.2	28.8	0.2	7.2	38.1	2.7	0.4	1.1
Finland...................	1950	4.8	3.1	3.5	45.9	0.3	9.2	28.7	3.0	0.8	0.7
Sweden....................	1960	11.2	6.7	6.7	17.7	0.6	8.8	43.7	3.6	0.8	0.2
United Kingdon											
England & Wales..........	1951	5.5	12.2	6.0	7.0	4.2	8.7	48.2	4.2	...	4.0
Northern Ireland........	1951	4.4	7.4	8.7	23.7	0.7	7.4	41.1	3.8	1.9	0.9
Scotland.................	1951	5.0	9.1	6.1	10.0	5.4	9.2	48.8	3.9	2.0	0.5
CENTRAL EUROPE											
Austria...................	1951	5.3	10.3	2.2	25.1	1.8	6.4	41.3	5.0	....	2.6
SOUTHERN EUROPE											
Malta & Gozo..............	1957	5.8	15.9	3.5	10.2	1.5	7.9	40.9	9.2	4.2	1.7
Yugoslavia................	1961	5.2	4.2	3.1	50.5	....	4.0	26.5	3.0	2.4	1.1
NORTHERN AMERICA											
Canada....................	1951	4.6	16.5	4.9	23.1	1.6	6.2	35.4	4.5	1.7	1.5
United States............	1950	6.2	16.8	6.1	14.9	1.4	5.7	38.2	6.3	2.2	2.2
OCEANIA											
Australia.................	1947	3.3	14.7	7.4	17.9	...	47.3	....	4.5	1.6	3.3
Fiji Islands.............	1956	3.9	52.5	3.4	15.7	2.1	2.7	12.9	4.6	0.5	1.7
New Zealand..............	1956	6.6	13.3	6.6	20.1	0.9	8.6	38.1	4.0	1.5	0.3
SOUTH AMERICA											
Brazil....................	1950	1.4	6.4	3.6	64.1	0.7	3.0	14.3	2.8	1.1	2.6
British Guiana...........	1946	2.5	6.9	3.3	47.2	3.0	3.7	27.4	4.4	0.6	1.0
Chile.....................	1952	3.2	13.1	2.5	35.3	3.8	3.2	26.0	5.0	...	7.9
Colombia..................	1951	1.8	8.1	1.4	62.5	1.1	2.4	15.6	2.7	1.2	3.2
Ecuador...................	1950	1.5	6.2	1.7	62.3	0.5	1.6	18.7	2.9	....	4.6
Paraguay..................	1950	2.0	7.2	1.2	62.5	0.1	2.3	15.0	2.9	....	6.8
Venezuela.................	1950	2.3	9.7	3.0	42.2	0.3	4.5	19.7	2.9	1.3	14.1

desirable to have one standard set of occupational categories that could be universally employed around the world. Unfortunately, this is not yet available.

The standard classification of occupations that is employed by the United Nations, and recommended for use by other nations, was developed by the International Labour Office; its major categories are reported in Table 10-2. Critics of this system of classification point out that it is a mixture of occupation and industry rather than a pure occupational classification. They also point out that in developing the general categories the desirable principle of socioeconomic homogeneity, which is so well described in the quotation from Edwards, is often needlessly violated. Its defendants maintain that it seems to fit the comparative occupational situation around the world rather well. Certainly, it is useful in accomplishing our purpose here—to discover the major occupational differences between the industrialized and economically developing nations. When we compare the occupational composition of the nations of Northern and Western Europe, Central Europe, Southern Europe, and North America with those of Asia and Africa, we immediately note two outstanding characteristics:

1. In the industrialized nations at least 35 percent or more of the labor force is engaged in craft production or other industrial, nonagricultural work, whereas in the developing countries more than 50 percent of the labor force is engaged in farming.

2. In the industrialized nations a very substantial percentage of the work force is employed in professional, technical, managerial, administrative, or clerical work. Usually this is at least 15 percent of the work force. In contrast, in the developing nations only a tiny fraction of the work force is engaged in this type of work. Instead, the nonagricultural segment of the work force in developing nations seems to be disproportionately concentrated in sales. Economists have written much about the tendency for the work force in developing countries to dissipate much of its economic energy in duplicating sales endeavors in the form of small-shop and street vendors, rather than channeling this effort into basic technical and production processing. This comparatively large sales force in the developing nations is often regarded as a form of disguised unemployment or underemployment.

Another difference between the industrialized nations and the developing nations is that a substantially larger percentage of the work force in the industrialized nations is engaged

Table 10-2 (*Continued*)

Region and Nation	Year	Professional & Technical	Managerial administratives clerical	Sales	Farmers fisherman lumberman etc.	Mine quarry & related occupation	Operating Transport occupation	Craftsmen production workers & laborers	Service workers	Armed Forces	Not classifiable
MIDDLE AMERICA											
Barbados	1946	2.5	6.1	3.9	29.3	0.7	5.5	41.4	6.2	1.8	2.6
Costa Rica	1950	1.8	7.3	3.4	62.0	0.3	2.1	16.2	....	3.4	3.5
Cuba	1953	2.6	11.3	6.5	46.4	0.4	5.0	21.7	4.2	....	1.9
Dominican Republic	1050	1.0	4.0	2.0	65.4	....	1.4	10.4	1.3	....	14.5
El Salvador	1950	1.2	4.1	1.0	72.8	0.2	1.4	14.5	3.0	....	1.8
Guadeloupe	1954	1.9	6.7	1.3	54.1	....	2.2	30.9	1.9	0.9	0.1
Guatemala	1950	1.1	2.7	2.7	75.3	0.3	1.4	13.6	1.9	0.7	0.3
Haiti	1950	0.7	0.9	0.8	87.1	....	0.6	5.0	2.6	....	2.3
Honduras	1950	0.9	2.1	0.7	83.0	0.4	0.9	9.0	3.0	....	....
Martinique	1954	2.4	6.4	1.1	51.2	....	2.8	30.8	1.9	2.2	1.2
Panama	1950	2.4	5.7	2.8	57.9	0.1	3.6	14.2	5.1	....	8.2
Puerto Rico	1950	2.7	10.5	5.9	46.0	0.3	5.0	20.9	5.1	1.2	2.4
Trinidad & Tobago	1946	2.8	9.1	4.5	27.2	1.5	6.6	39.2	5.4	1.5	2.2
SOUTH CENTRAL ASIA											
Ceylon	1953	3.6	5.4	8.7	49.1	0.6	3.4	....	13.0	15.0	1.2
India	1951	1.5	0.4	5.9	69.4	0.5	1.9	9.5	....	10.9	....
Pakistan	1951	1.0	2.4	4.7	76.4	....	0.9	11.4	3.2	....	....
EAST ASIA											
China (Taiwan)	1956	3.1	8.7	8.2	53.3	1.3	2.6	16.0	4.4	....	2.4
Japan	1960	5.2	14.5	10.1	25.9	1.3	4.7	34.0	3.5	0.8	....
Republic of Korea	1960	2.7	5.0	6.9	59.9	0.1	4.5	9.7	3.9	....	7.3
Ryukyu Islands	1955	3.4	7.2	6.6	48.3	0.2	5.2	23.4	5.7	....	....
SOUTH EAST ASIA											
Federation of Malaya	1957	2.9	5.0	10.0	49.0	0.1	4.0	17.7	....	8.9	2.4
North Borneo	1960	1.8	0.6	4.0	72.0	0.1	3.2	12.5	3.2	2.6	....
Sarawak	1960	2.5	0.5	5.8	74.0	0.1	2.3	10.1	2.6	2.1	....
Singapore	1957	3.7	13.4	19.7	6.9	....	9.7	32.2	10.6	2.1	1.7
Thailand	1954	1.4	2.0	3.7	84.1	0.1	1.2	4.8	1.2	....	1.5
SOUTH WEST ASIA											
Iran	1956	1.4	3.3	6.4	58.5	1.0	2.6	16.4	6.5	....	3.9
Israel	1948	8.7	15.1	8.9	11.4	0.2	5.8	44.0	2.9	0.3	2.7
Turkey	1955	1.9	2.9	3.8	63.4	0.7	2.4	13.5	3.6	....	7.8

Table 10-2 (*Continued*)

Region and Nation	Year	Profes-sional & Technical	Manageri-al adminis-tratives clerical	Sales	Farmers fisherman lumberman etc.	Mine quarry & related occu-pation	Operating Transport occu-pation	Craftsmen production workers & laborers	Service workers	Armed Forces	Not class-fiable
NORTHERN AFRICA											
Sudan..............	1956	1.4	0.7	2.5	86.8	....	0.9	4.9	1.9	0.5	0.4
Tunisia............	1946	1.8	....	11.0	63.5	....	....	23.0	....	....	0.7
TROPICAL & SOUTHERN AFRICA											
Ghana..............	1960	2.9	3.1	4.0	58.8	1.9	3.0	17.5	2.3	*	6.5
Mauritius..........	1952	1.9	3.0	9.7	41.5	....	8.0	26.4	5.2	2.8	1.5
Reunion............	1954	1.3	7.7	1.2	56.9	....	1.7	20.8	2.0	0.7	7.7
South Africa.......	1946		7.2		47.0	12.4	6.0	17.8	5.3	0.7	3.6
Southwest Africa...	1951	1.4	3.7	0.9	57.3	9.4	1.1	19.4	5.1	....	1.7
Zanzibar & Pemba...	1948	0.6	0.3	4.9	60.6	....	1.6	6.1	5.1	0.4	20.4

* Classified together with the civilian economically active population.

Source: U.N. Compendium, Table 68.

in operating transport activities. The full extent of this differential is not revealed by occupational statistics alone because it is the type of transportation operated as well as the volume of employment in transportation that makes the difference. Even in the most underdeveloped countries there is a substantial amount of employment in transportation in the form of operating rickshaws or similar vehicles capable of transporting only small quantities of goods or passengers per worker employed.

The category "service worker" in Table 10-2 has a different meaning in the industrialized countries than it does in the developing countries. In the industrialized nations service workers are employed outside households, primarily in laundries, barbershops, and other establishments that provide business and personal services to the population. In the developing nations, on the other hand, a substantial percentage of the service workers are household servants. For this reason there are no large or consistent differences between the developing nations and the industrialized nations in the proportion of the work force classified as service workers.

If we wish to make a simple, yet somewhat arbitrary, definition of what constitutes economic development or the "take-off point" in the process of economic development, we can formulate the following rule: a country has become industrialized when it has reached the point where less than 50 percent of its work force is engaged in agriculture and at least 15 percent are professional and managerial workers.

Table 10-2 reports occupational data for only a small fraction of the major nations of the world—both economically developed and underdeveloped. The importance of collecting detailed economic statistics that are internationally comparable has only recently been appreciated.

Before leaving this brief comparison of the occupation composition of nations, we should note that there is a great deal of variation among the nations of the world, with a substantial number of countries apparently just standing on the threshold of entering the state of being economically developed or techno-

logically advanced. These are nations where the percentage of the total work force engaged in agriculture is nearing 50 percent or has already dipped slightly below it, where the proportion of professional or managerial workers has risen as high as 10 percent or more, and where one fourth or more of the work force could be classified as craftsmen or production workers and production laborers. Among the leading nations of the world that seem to stand on this "threshold" are Chile, Venezuela, Cuba, Puerto Rico and Tobago, Ryukyu Island, and Mauritius. It can be expected that within the next decade almost all of Latin America will move to this threshold position or beyond it and that most, if not all, of Asia will be rapidly approaching it.

10.4. The Industrial Composition of the United States Labor Force

Before making an inquiry concerning the occupational composition for the United States work force, let us first ask the question, How does the United States earn its living? By this we mean, What are the combinations of establishments or businesses or enterprises that the various communities of the country have set up to obtain a living from their environment? This information is reported in the statistics of industrial composition. As noted above, these statistics are obtained by classifying whole establishments into a set of categories that describe the nature of the economic activity carried out. To make certain that the statistics on industrial composition reported by various agencies are comparable, a federal interagency committee has developed what is called a Standard Industrial Classification for use in publishing official statistics. This classification is made at three levels: major industrial classification, 13 categories; and a detailed industrial classification of 161 categories. The intermediate categories represent combinations of the detailed categories, and major categories represent combinations of intermediate categories. Which set of categories one uses, therefore, depends on the amount of detail one wishes to present. Table 10-3 shows the industrial composition of the employed labor force in the United States

Table 10-3   Industrial Composition of the Employed Labor Force in the United States: 1940 to 1960

Industry group	Percent distribution			Percent change	
	1960	1950	1940	1950 to 1960	1940 to 1960
Total employed	100.0	100.0	100.0	14.5	43.4
Agriculture	6.6	12.2	18.8	-38.4	-49.6
Forestry and fisheries	0.1	0.2	0.2	-25.4	-15.1
Mining	1.0	1.6	2.0	-29.7	-28.8
Construction	5.9	6.1	4.6	10.4	82.8
Manufacturing	27.1	26.1	23.7	19.3	64.1
Furniture and lumber and wood products	1.7	2.1	2.0	-10.8	18.1
Primary metal industries	1.9	2.1	3.4	3.4	67.0
Fabricated metal industries	2.0	1.5		52.5	
Machinery, except electrical	2.4	2.2	1.5	25.1	126.9
Electrical equipment, machinery, supplies	2.3	1.5	0.9	72.7	253.4
Motor vehicles and motor vehicle equipment	1.3	1.5	1.3	- 1.7	47.8
Transportation equipment, except motor vehicle	1.5	0.9	0.7	100.8	217.3
Other durable goods	2.1	1.9	1.7	27.1	82.2
Food and kindred products	2.8	2.7	2.7	23.0	51.5
Textile mill products	1.5	2.2	2.6	-22.3	-18.2
Apparel and other fabricated textile products	1.8	1.9	1.7	8.7	47.9
Printing, publishing, and allied products	1.8	1.5	1.4	32.2	78.9
Chemical and allied products	1.3	1.1	0.9	35.6	115.7
Other nondurable goods	2.7	3.0	2.9	5.9	31.5
Railroad and railway express service	1.5	2.5	2.5	-32.3	-17.2
Trucking service and warehousing	1.4	1.2	1.1	30.6	84.1
Other transportation	1.4	1.5	1.2	2.6	58.0
Communications	1.3	1.3	0.9	15.4	107.8
Utilities and sanitary services	1.4	1.4	1.2	14.4	61.9
Wholesale trade	3.4	3.5	2.7	12.6	83.9
Food and dairy products stores	2.6	3.0	3.0	1.4	23.1
Eating and drinking places	2.8	3.0	2.5	6.5	61.1
Other retail trade	9.4	9.2	8.5	17.4	60.1
Finance, insurance and real estate	4.2	3.4	3.3	40.4	82.7
Business services	1.2	0.6	0.5	12.6	209.1
Repair services	1.3	1.7	1.4	-10.6	33.3
Private households	3.0	2.8	5.1	19.7	-14.8
Other personal services	3.0	3.3	3.7	4.2	17.3
Entertainment and recreation services	0.8	0.9	0.9	1.9	26.8
Educational services: Government	3.9	2.7	2.7	64.2	107.0
Private	1.3	0.9	0.8	60.6	151.8
Welfare, religions, and nonprofit membership	1.3	1.0		45.4	
Hospitals	2.6	1.8	4.0	70.1	129.4
Other professional and related services	2.5	2.1		40.6	
Public administration	5.0	4.5	3.1	27.4	126.3
Industry note reported	4.0	1.5	1.6	209.3	257.5

Source: U.S. Census of Population: 1960.   General Social and Economic Characteristics, U.S. Summary, Table 92.

in 1940, 1950, and 1960, and the percent change between the censuses. If we look at the composition of 1960, we find the following significant facts: (1) The nation is fed (agricultural industry) by only a tiny fraction of the nation's work force—6.6 percent. This reflects the highly mechanized state of farming at the present time. Only one worker in 100 is re-

quired to dig coal, drill for oil, and perform other work related to mining raw materials for our industries. (2) By far the largest proportion of the workers are engaged in manufacturing—27 percent. These are distributed widely through a great variety of types of manufacturing establishments. (3) Retail and wholesale trade constitute the second largest single type of industry in the economy; about one worker in 6 is engaged in distributing the product of the industrial system to the consumer. (4) Some important though reasonably small (only about 5 percent each) segments of the work force comes next. These are: (*a*) business and business services represented by finance, insurance, and real estate and services to business corporations; (*b*) transportation and communication, including railway, highway, and water transport, and professional and related services representing the activities of physicians, lawyers, and other professionals; (*c*) educational services at all levels from elementary school through university; and (*d*) public administration. The percentage composition shown for the United States in 1960 may be regarded as the more or less typical industrial composition of a self-sufficient, industrialized nation at the current stage of technological advancement. It has an industrial composition that is more or less a prototype at which the developing nations aim when they seek to reduce the percentage of persons employed in agriculture and other extractive industries and increase the proportion of workers in manufacturing and technologically advanced industries.

We should hasten to point out, however, that achieving a state of "economic development" does not necessitate having such an extremely small proportion of workers in agriculture as was reported for the United States in 1960. If we look at the composition for 1940 reported in Table 10-3, we note that at that time nearly one fifth of all workers were employed in agriculture and yet the nation was considered to be highly industrialized. It is a mistake to presume that a reasonably high level of living cannot be achieved without shrinking the agriculture population to a very low point. In fact it is quite possible that almost all of the benefits of technology required to provide adequate comfort for an entire population can be achieved with as much as one third of the working force employed in agriculture.

If we look at the recent changes in industrial composition in the United States (Table 10-3), we note that there have been sharp declines in all of the extractive types of industry, in agriculture, in forestry and fishing, and in mining. There have been substantial increases in the professional services, educational services, welfare and related services, finance, insurance and real estate, and, in particular, such lines of manufacturing as those of chemicals, transportation equipment, electrical machinery, and fabricated metal products. Certain other manufacturing industries have declined rather sharply because of technological change. For example, employment has declined in textile mills and in the railroad and railway express service because of new processes or equipment that requires less manpower per unit of product.

Table 10-4 subdivides the labor force according to industry, using a more detailed set of categories, and reports characteristics of the workers in each industrial grouping. For example, we can identify those industries in which Negroes are employed in disproportionately large numbers and those industries from which they appear to be comparatively excluded. Negro males are apparently in surplus in the following industries:

agriculture
forestry
logging
sawmill work
primary iron and steel industry
manufacture of motor vehicles and motor vehicle equipment
manufacture of meat products
manufacture of miscellaneous nondurable goods
operators of vehicles on street railways and bus lines
deckhands on ships and water transportation
truck drivers and other drivers of land motor vehicles
laborers in sanitary service (garbage collection, etc.)
workers in eating and drinking places
workers in automotive repair service stations and garages
workers in private households
workers in hotels and lodging places
workers in laundering and dry cleaning establishments
workers in medical and other health services
workers in entertainment and other recreational services
workers in the postal service and in federal public administration

Table 10-4   Industry of the Experienced Labor Force, and Unemployment Rate, by Color and Sex: 1960

Industry	Male					Female				
	Percent of total	Percent of employed Negro	Percent unemployed White	Nonwhite	Median age	Percent of total	Percent of employed Negro	percent unemployed White	Nonwhite	Median age
	1	2	3	4	5	6	7	8	9	10
Female, male, 14 years old & over ..	100.0	8.4	4.5	8.4	40.6	100.0	11.6	4.7	7.9	40.4
Agriculture, forestry & fisheries .	8.9	11.8	3.0	5.8	44.7	2.0	21.1	4.5	15.3	43.5
Agriculture..........	8.7	11.9	2.8	5.6	44.7	2.0	21.3	4.4	15.2	43.5
Forestry and fisheries	0.2	9.8	9.5	16.4	41.6	0.0	8.6	8.1	23.7	40.1
Mining..........	1.5	3.0	8.6	12.4	41.2	0.1	1.1	3.6	7.4	35.6
Construction..........	9.1	8.8	11.1	16.0	40.8	0.7	3.4	4.5	13.6	39.7
Manufacturing...........	30.1	7.1	4.3	8.5	39.6	21.4	5.0	7.7	14.1	39.4
Durable goods	18.7	7.3	4.8	9.0	39.8	8.4	3.9	7.7	13.5	38.2
Logging	0.4	28.4	15.3	7.9	37.2	0.0	14.4	9.3	6.6	36.9
Sawmills, planing mills, mill work & miscellaneous wood pro't	1.1	18.5	7.1	6.7	40.7	0.2	12.3	7.6	9.0	39.3
Furniture & fixtures	0.7	7.6	5.3	8.1	38.7	0.3	6.6	8.2	11.5	39.0
Stone, clay, & glass products ..	1.2	8.5	5.2	7.8	39.4	0.5	2.7	7.3	12.5	37.9
Primary iron & steel industry ..	2.0	13.3	4.4	8.4	41.6	0.2	3.2	4.2	9.6	36.9
Primary nonferrous industries ..	0.6	7.7	4.8	10.1	40.9	0.2	2.2	8.2	12.5	38.1
Fab'd metal industry (incl. not specific metal)	2.5	5.0	4.8	9.0	39.5	1.1	3.7	7.8	13.1	38.7
Machinery, except electrical ...	3.1	2.7	3.5	9.7	40.5	1.0	1.5	5.6	12.3	38.2
Electrical machinery equipment and supplies	2.3	3.1	3.1	6.8	37.4	2.5	3.6	7.8	12.5	37.2
Motor vehicles & motor vehicle equipment	1.8	9.3	5.4	14.5	40.3	0.5	4.9	9.6	16.9	39.4
Aircraft & parts	1.2	2.9	5.1	9.5	38.7	0.5	2.0	9.3	16.7	37.6
Other transportation equipment .	0.7	8.9	7.1	8.7	42.4	0.1	5.0	6.0	7.1	39.3
All other durable goods	1.1	3.6	3.5	8.7	39.8	1.3	5.9	8.4	16.6	39.4

Table 10-4 (*Continued*)

	1	2	3	4	5	6	7	8	9	10
Nondurable goods	11.3	6.8	3.6	7.5	39.3	12.9	5.6	7.6	14.4	40.2
Meat products	0.6	14.1	4.5	9.3	39.5	0.4	12.8	10.3	12.2	39.5
Bakery products	0.6	7.0	3.3	6.5	38.6	0.5	5.2	6.1	8.7	40.9
Other food industries	2.1	7.8	4.7	9.4	39.9	1.3	8.1	14.6	21.3	40.5
Knitting mills	0.1	4.8	5.1	7.9	39.8	0.7	3.6	8.4	13.0	38.4
Yarn, thread, & fabric mills ..	0.8	6.4	3.5	3.8	40.9	1.2	1.6	7.0	7.9	41.4
Other textile mill products ...	0.2	6.9	4.4	6.6	41.4	0.2	4.5	7.9	12.0	41.2
Apparel & other fab'd textile products	0.7	7.5	6.3	9.4	42.3	4.0	7.5	7.4	10.6	41.1
Paper & allied products	1.0	6.8	2.7	5.1	38.4	0.6	4.0	6.1	12.5	38.7
Printing, publishing, & allied industries	1.9	3.7	2.5	5.5	34.2	1.4	3.8	4.0	8.8	39.5
Chemical & allied products	1.6	6.9	2.1	5.6	39.7	0.8	2.9	4.8	10.3	37.1
Petroleum & coal products	0.6	4.3	2.0	5.9	41.9	0.2	1.4	2.2	7.3	34.0
Rubber & miscellaneous plastic products	0.6	6.8	3.8	6.3	39.7	0.5	4.0	9.5	17.4	39.3
Footwear, except rubber	0.3	1.7	5.8	7.7	40.6	0.7	1.5	7.6	10.7	40.7
All other nondurable goods	0.2	14.7	5.5	14.6	41.2	0.4	14.0	8.6	33.3	40.8
Not specified manufacturing industries	0.1	10.8	6.0	12.0	40.0	0.1	12.7	8.5	13.1	41.5
Transportation, communication, & other public utilities	8.3	8.2	3.6	7.3	41.6	3.6	3.2	3.1	5.8	34.0
Railroads & railway express service	2.0	8.3	4.0	9.7	47.3	0.2	6.0	4.4	10.7	45.3
Street railways & bus lines ...	0.6	11.2	1.7	2.2	45.6	0.1	8.2	2.5	5.6	41.2
Trucking service & warehousing	1.9	7.7	4.9	9.4	38.8	0.3	2.6	4.5	12.4	36.6
Water transportation	0.4	15.4	10.1	11.4	43.8	0.0	3.2	4.2	10.7	37.6
Air transportation	0.3	5.3	2.0	4.1	35.6	0.2	2.1	2.7	3.2	27.3
All other transportation	0.4	11.6	4.3	5.5	44.9	0.1	6.7	4.2	8.5	38.9
Communications	0.9	2.3	1.3	4.3	35.5	2.2	2.7	3.0	3.7	31.9
Electric & gas utilities	1.2	3.5	1.6	3.3	40.6	0.4	2.0	1.8	1.8	33.6
Water supply sanitary services & other utilities	0.6	20.1	2.8	4.6	43.4	0.1	5.0	1.9	5.1	40.5

Industries from which Negroes appear to be comparatively excluded, inasmuch as a disproportionately small percentage are employed, are:

mining
fabricated metal industry
the manufacture of machinery
electrical machinery
aircraft
knitting yarn, thread, and fabric mills
printing establishments
petroleum and petroleum product establishments
manufacture of footwear
air transportation
communication
electric and gas facilities
banking, insurance, and real estate business services
legal, engineering, and other professional services
state and local public administration

By studying Table 10-4 the reader can select those industries in which there is a comparative surplus and deficit of Negro females.

There is a fair amount of variation between industries in the average age of the workers. The following industries tend to have a concentration of older workers:

agriculture
manufacture of apparel and fabricated textile products
railroad and railway express service
workers on street railways and bus lines
workers in water transportation
workers in sanitary services, water supply, and other utilities
workers in eating and drinking places
workers in insurance and real estate
workers in all branches of personal service
workers in medical and other health services, welfare, religious, and similar activities
workers in state and local administration

In contrast, industries where workers tend to be younger on the average are:

logging
manufacture of electrical machinery, equipment, and supplies
manufacture of aircraft and aircraft parts
printing and publishing industry
manufacture of paper and allied products
trucking and warehousing

Table 10-4 (*Continued*)

	1	2	3	4	5	6	7	8	9	10
Wholesale & retail trade..........	16.9	6.8	3.7	8.0	39.2	20.9	5.6	5.2	10.5	40.7
Wholesale trade.................	4.0	6.2	2.9	7.8	40.6	2.1	3.8	5.2	12.9	38.6
Retail trade....................	12.9	7.0	3.9	8.0	38.7	18.8	5.8	5.2	10.3	40.9
Food & dairy products stores, & milk retail..................	2.7	5.0	3.4	6.8	34.6	2.6	3.7	3.9	6.5	40.5
General merchandise & retail price variety stores..........	1.1	7.0	4.2	8.4	38.2	5.2	4.0	5.5	10.8	41.7
Apparel & accessories stores....	0.6	5.8	3.3	7.3	42.6	1.9	5.1	4.5	8.9	45.5
Furnitures, home furnish, & equipment stores.............	0.8	5.8	3.4	8.0	40.0	0.6	4.0	4.2	10.5	41.9
Motor vehicles & accessories retailing....................	1.6	7.3	2.8	7.1	38.7	0.4	1.5	3.9	9.7	36.9
Gasoline service stations......	1.4	6.8	4.7	7.4	32.3	0.1	4.1	3.0	7.9	40.9
Drug stores....................	0.4	8.0	2.4	7.7	35.8	0.9	4.7	4.3	11.3	37.5
Eating & drinking places.......	1.7	11.8	6.5	9.5	42.0	5.2	10.9	7.1	11.5	38.7
Hardware, farm implement, bldg. material retail...............	1.2	6.5	3.7	7.1	41.3	0.4	1.4	3.6	7.2	42.2
All other retail trade.........	1.4	5.9	3.3	8.4	42.4	1.5	3.3	3.9	7.4	44.1
Finance, insurance & real estate.	3.3	4.3	1.6	4.2	43.2	5.7	2.8	2.2	4.3	34.2
Banking & other finance........	1.0	2.5	1.3	3.1	41.0	2.5	1.4	2.0	3.1	30.8
Insurance & real estate........	2.3	5.1	1.7	4.5	44.0	3.2	3.9	2.4	4.7	37.1
Business & repair services.......	2.9	7.0	3.6	8.9	39.2	1.6	4.2	4.9	11.2	38.5
Business services.............	1.1	5.3	3.6	9.4	39.2	1.4	4.0	5.2	10.6	38.1
Automobile repair services & garages......................	1.1	10.5	3.7	9.0	38.2	0.1	7.4	3.6	14.4	39.0
Miscellaneous repair services..	0.7	4.0	3.5	7.6	40.9	0.1	3.2	3.8	11.9	41.4
Personal services..............	2.5	18.9	4.5	7.7	45.2	13.2	40.1	4.6	6.4	44.2
Private households............	0.4	39.8	9.1	9.2	45.7	8.3	52.0	4.8	6.1	45.3
Hotels & lodging places........	0.6	16.3	7.0	9.7	47.0	1.5	20.4	6.5	10.6	46.6
Laundering, cleaning & dying services...................	0.6	17.8	3.3	6.1	42.5	1.7	28.9	5.4	7.7	42.0
All other personal services....	0.9	10.8	1.5	4.0	45.9	1.7	12.3	2.1	3.4	41.2
Entertainment & recreation service services......................	0.8	10.5	9.4	10.2	39.3	0.8	6.9	8.2	12.3	36.9

air transportation
communication
workers in food and dairy products stores and
  general products stores
workers in gasoline service stations
drugstores
repair services and garages
educational services

This group represents industries that are newer and expanding, hence more able to offer employment to new workers just entering the labor force. They also represent industries that tend to require youth and vigor for their successful conduct.

10.5. Occupational Composition of the United States Labor Force

Because modern industrial processes involve a highly elaborate division of labor and a subdivision of operations into tasks, each task presided over by a separate worker, the number of different occupations is very great, perhaps 25,000 or more. Clearly, it is impossible for the U.S. Census to report statistics for each of these occupations. To resolve the problem, three sets of classifications have been made by a federal committee on occupational classification. These are more or less standard and are used throughout both the federal system and nonfederal organizations in classifying occupations. (1) The *detailed occupation classification* contains 479 categories; of these 297 are specific occupation categories and the remainder are subgroups (mainly on the basis of industry) of the occupation categories. (2) The *major occupation classification*, in which the detailed classification has been grouped into 12 major occupation categories. (3) The *intermediate occupational classification*. For many purposes the detailed classification is too elaborate and detailed, yet more detail is desired than the 12 major occupational categories can give. For such purposes various groupings of the detailed classification are made.

Because of rapid technological change, the occupational composition of the labor force changes rapidly between censuses. It is necessary that each census reflect the new developments that have occurred since the last cen-

Table 10-4   (*Continued*)

	1	2	3	4	5	6	7	8	9	10
Professional & related services...	6.7	7.9	1.5	3.4	40.8	20.8	9.5	1.6	3.7	41.6
Medical & other health services.	1.7	12.3	1.6	4.1	42.6	8.2	11.9	2.3	4.7	39.5
Educational services, government	2.1	8.0	0.9	1.8	38.3	7.3	9.5	0.9	1.9	43.7
Educational services, private...	0.7	6.9	1.6	3.8	37.5	2.4	6.2	1.0	3.1	41.9
Welfare, religious, & membership organizations.................	1.0	8.4	2.0	4.2	44.9	1.8	7.4	2.1	5.6	45.0
Legal, engineering, & misc. professional services.........	1.2	1.2	1.6	3.9	40.6	1.1	1.5	2.3	5.8	37.3
Public administration............	5.2	8.9	3.0	5.2	41.8	4.2	9.6	2.2	4.5	41.8
Postal service..................	1.2	14.8	2.5	4.9	41.6	0.3	11.0	3.6	12.9	47.1
Federal public administration...	1.8	10.0	4.9	6.5	41.4	2.1	11.5	2.2	4.0	40.1
State & local public administration......................	2.2	5.2	1.7	3.3	42.3	1.8	7.3	1.9	3.3	43.2
Industry not reported............	3.8	16.8	7.8	12.1	38.0	5.0	17.5	7.3	11.3	40.0

Source: U.S. Census of Population: 1960,   Detailed Characteristics, Tables 212, 213.

sus. To achieve this, the system of occupational classification must be overhauled and revised for each census. New occupational titles must be created and old ones that are disappearing must be dropped. Others that have diminished greatly in importance may be combined. The result is that the detailed and intermediate occupational classifications tend to change from census to census. Even the major occupational categories may change in definition slightly. The task of tracing occupational trends over a long span of time is one that requires intimate knowledge of the changing economy.

Table 10-5 shows the occupational composition of the employed labor force of the United States in the last three censuses classified by the 12 major occupation categories, with a few subdivisions of the major categories. The reader is encouraged to study the statistics of this table carefully and thoroughly.

About one fifth of the employed workers are skilled craftsmen, foremen, mechanics, and so on, and another one fifth are semiskilled operatives who operate machines, drive trucks, and so forth. Together these two groups perform most of the productive work in the technical sector of the economy. Their labors are directed by a group of managers, officials, and proprietors who together comprise about 10 percent of the population. Thus roughly 50 percent of the total employed labor force is engaged in occupations pertaining to the performance of technical, nonagricultural tasks that result in the production of some good or service desired by the population.

Another outstanding trait is the presence of

a very large professional and technical group of persons whose task it is to provide the population with professional services, to teach the oncoming generations, and to sustain a continuing stream of research to maintain progress. One person in 10 was in this category in 1960.

Two other groups of substantial size are the record keepers—clerical workers—and the service workers who provide services to businesses and persons. In this hierarchy the numbers of farmers, farm laborers, and common laborers are comparatively minor. Together all three comprised only 15 percent in 1960.

The above description applies to males. The employment of females follows a similar pattern with greater emphasis on clerical and professional work and much less emphasis on farm labor and craft occupations. In other words, female workers are highly concentrated in the white-collar occupations that do not involve managerial or proprietorship tasks and in blue-collar operations that do not involve skill.

In the two decades between 1940 and 1960, the occupation composition of the nation changed dramatically. The major shifts were as follows:

1. The agricultural work force diminished by more than 50 percent.

2. There was more than 100 percent increase in the number of professional and technical workers. The increase was especially great among engineers.

3. There was a great increase in female workers.

4. There was a very large increase in clerical workers and managers.

Table 10-5 Occupational Composition of the Employed Labor Force of the United States: 1940 to 1960

Occupation group and sex	Percent distribution			Percent change	
	1960	1950	1940	1950 to 1960	1940 to 1960
MALE					
Total employed.....................	100.0	100.0	100.0	6.9	28.3
Professional, technical, kindred workers.......	10.3	7.3	6.1	50.8	115.1
Engineers, technical.....................	2.0	1.3	0.8	64.3	209.8
Medical and other health workers..........	1.2	1.1		18.8	
Teachers, elementary and secondary schools.	1.0	0.5	5.3	89.3	100.7
Other professional, technical, workers	6.1	4.4		50.0	
Farmers and farm managers.....................	5.5	10.4	14.7	-43.1	-52.2
Managers, officials, proprietors, exc. farm....	10.7	10.7	9.6	6.3	42.8
Salaried.................................	6.7	5.3	N.A.	34.1	N.A.
Self employed	4.0	5.4	N.A.	-21.2	N.A.
Clerical workers.............................	6.9	6.5	6.0	13.9	49.3
Sales workers	6.9	6.3	6.7	15.8	31.4
Retail trade	2.9	3.1	N.A.	-0.4	N.A.
Other than retail trade	4.0	3.2	N.A.	31.1	N.A.
Craftsmen, foremen, and kindred workers........	19.5	18.6	14.9	11.9	68.1
Foremen (n.e.c.).........................	2.5	1.9	1.4	41.1	126.0
Mechanics and repairmen	5.1	4.2	2.4	28.6	164.4
Metal craftsmen, exc. mechanics	2.5	2.7	2.8	0.4	17.9
Construction craftsmen	5.5	5.8	8.3	2.1	46.3
Other craftsmen	3.9	4.0		2.6	
Operatives and kindred workers	19.8	20.1	17.9	6.0	42.7
Drivers and deliverymen	5.2	4.7	4.4	19.6	52.5
Other operatives					
Durable goods manufacturing	6.3				
Nondurable goods manufacturing	3.7	15.4	13.5	.1.8	39.6
Nonmanufacturing industries	4.6				
Private household workers	0.1	0.2	0.3	-16.8	-47.0
Service workers, exc. private households	6.0	5.8	5.8	9.3	31.9
Protective service workers	1.5	1.4	1.3	17.3	47.2
Waiters, bartenders, cooks and counter-workers	1.2	1.3	1.3	-5.2	14.1
Other service workers	3.3	3.1	3.2	11.9	32.9
Farm laborers and farm foremen	2.8	4.9	8.3	-38.9	-57.3
Laborers, except farm and mine................	6.9	8.1	9.0	-9.4	-1.2
Construction	1.5	N.A.	N.A.	N.A.	N.A.
Manufacturing	2.3	N.A.	N.A.	N.A.	N.A.
Other industries	3.1	N.A.	N.A.	N.A.	N.A.
Occupation not reported......................	4.6	1.1	0.7	332.3	710.5
FEMALE					
Total employed.....................	100.0	100.0	100.0	34.2	89.4
Professional, technical, kindred workers	13.0	12.4	13.4	41.1	83.9
Medical and other health workers	3.7	3.6	N.A.	37.9	N.A.
Teachers, elementary and secondary school .	5.2	5.2	N.A.	34.5	N.A.
Other professional and technical workers ..	4.1	3.6	N.A.	54.0	N.A.
Farmers and farm managers	0.6	0.7	1.4	0.9	-22.5
Managers, officials, proprietors exc. farm.....	3.7	4.3	3.5	14.6	99.4

5. There was a very large increase in the number of craftsmen in manufacturing industries.

6. There was a substantial decrease in the number of unskilled workers.

The following occupations grew at about the average rate between 1940 and 1960:

service workers
craftsmen engaged in the construction industry
sales workers
salaried managers and officials
sales workers in retail trade

On an overall basis the change has been in the direction of abandoning the less desirable unskilled and blue-collar occupations, of emphasizing the occupations that require technical training, and of more education for work in an office rather than at machines. The employ-

Table 10-5 *(Continued)*

Occupation group and sex	Percent distribution			Percent change	
	1960	1950	1940	1950 to 1960	1940 to 1960
Managers, officials (Con't)					
Salaried	2.3	2.2	N.A.	41.2	N.A.
Self employed	1.4	2.1	N.A.	-12.2	N.A.
Retail trade	0.9				
Other than retail trade	0.5				
Clerical and kindred workers	29.7	27.3	21.1	46.0	166.3
Secretaries, stenographers, typists	10.3	9.6	8.8	44.5	120.0
Other clerical workers	19.4	17.7	12.3	46.9	199.8
Sales Workers	7.8	8.5	7.3	24.5	104.0
Retail trade	6.8	7.6	N.A.	20.9	N.A.
Other than retail trade	1.0	0.9	N.A.	56.4	N.A.
Craftsmen, foremen, and kindred workers	1.2	1.5	1.1	6.8	105.8
Operatives and kindred workers	15.4	19.2	18.1	7.6	60.7
Durable goods manufacturing	4.0	4.2	N.A	28.6	N.A.
Nondurable goods manufacturing	8.3	10.8	N.A.	2.6	N.A.
Nonmanufacturing industries	3.1	4.2	N.A.	-0.6	N.A.
Private household workers	7.9	8.5	17.7	24.4	-15.8
Service workers, except private household	13.4	12.2	11.0	48.2	131.3
Waiters, bartenders, cooks, counter workers	5.7	5.0	4.3	52.6	150.7
Other service workers....................	7.7	7.2	6.7	45.1	118.8
Farm laborers and farm foremen...............	1.1	2.9	2.9	-46.2	-25.3
Laborers, except farm and mine...............	0.5	0.7	1.0	-14.0	2.3
Occupation not reported	5.7	1.8	1.5	322.4	590.9

Source: U.S. Census of Population: 1960. General Social and Economic Characteristics, United States Summary, Table 89.

ment of women has also undergone very extensive changes in the 1940-1960 period. It will be remembered that the employment rate for women was raised phenomenally during this period, resulting in a rate of growth in employment that was nearly three times that for men. This growth took place in craft and service occupations outside private households. Employment of women as farmers and farm managers, private household workers, farm laborers and farm foremen, and unskilled laborers either declined or increased by a tiny fraction. The increase in professional occupations was roughly proportional to the overall increase in female employment, which in itself represents a very impressive growth. Thus, on an overall basis, during these two decades female workers managed to rise higher in the occupational hierarchy that had previously been reserved for men.

How does this picture compare with the long-range trends in occupational composition? Table 10-6 reports the occupational composi-

tion of the labor force from 1900 to 1960. During this time the proportion of workers in the professional categories increased two and one-half times. The proportion classified as farmers and farm managers sank to less than one-eighth its earlier share. The proportion classified as managers and officials nearly doubled. The number classified as clerical and kindred workers nearly quintupled. The proportion classified as sales workers increased only slightly. The proportion classified as operatives increased only slightly. The number classified as private household workers increased only slightly. The proportion classified as service workers outside private households increased 50 percent. The proportion classified as farm laborers and farm foremen declined to less than one-fourth its earlier share, and the proportion classified as unskilled laborers was reduced by one half. Thus the trends we have observed for the 1940-1960 period appear to represent a continuation of a longer sweep that is of at least 60 years' duration.

Table 10-6 Occupational Composition of the Experienced Labor Force: 1900 and 1960

Occupation	1960	1940	1900	Change 1940 to 1960	Change 1900 to 1960
Total	100.0	100.0	100.0	. . . .	. . . .
Professional, technical workers	11.8	7.5	4.3	4.3	7.5
Farmers and farm managers	4.1	10.4	19.9	-6.3	-15.8
Managers, officials, proprietors	8.8	7.3	5.8	1.5	3.0
Clerical and kindred workers	15.1	9.6	3.0	5.5	12.1
Sales workers	7.5	6.7	4.5	0.8	3.0
Craftsmen, foremen	14.2	12.0	10.5	2.2	3.7
Operatives and kindred workers	19.4	18.3	12.8	1.0	6.6
Private household workers	2.8	4.8	5.4	-2.0	-2.6
Service workers exc. private household .	8.9	7.0	3.6	1.9	5.3
Farm laborers and foremen	2.4	7.0	17.7	-4.6	-15.3
Laborers exc. farm and mine	5.0	9.4	12.5	-4.4	-7.5

Source: Data for 1900 derived from "Occupational Trends in the United States, 1900 to 1950" By David L. Kaplan and M. Claire Casey. Data for 1960 from U.S. Census of 1960: Detailed Characteristics. United States Summary. Table 202.

10.6. Detailed Occupational Analysis of the United States Labor Force

The study of the labor force in terms of major occupational groupings fails to provide full insight into the occupational composition of the nation. Tables 10-7 and 10-8, in showing selected characteristics of the work force classified by detailed occupation, provide data with which to do this. Space does not permit a full analysis and interpretation of these tables. They are reproduced here to provide reference to the reader in his future work. They represent an assembly and synthesis of a very great amount of statistics gathered through several different tabulations of the census. In order to encourage further study of these tables, we point out the following highlights:

1. Although the quantity of employment in each of the detailed occupational categories varies substantially, no one occupation comprises more than a comparatively small fraction of the total labor force. If we look at column 2 of Table 10-7, we note that only a very few of the categories comprise as much as one half of 1 percent of the total employed labor force and that even fewer comprise as much as 1 percent.

Percent of the total work force

Technical engineers	1.33
Elementary and secondary school teachers	2.35
Farm owners and tenants	3.84
Managers and officials in manufacturing industries	1.00
Managers and officials in retail trade	1.55
Bookkeepers	1.44
Secretaries	2.26
Salesmen and sales clerks in retail trade	4.03
Carpenters	1.27
Foremen in manufacturing industries	1.15
Mechanics and repairmen in automobile industry	1.06
Truck and tractor drivers	2.41
Private household workers	1.88
Farm laborers and wage workers	1.76
Laborers in manufacturing industries	1.33
Laborers in nonmanufacturing industries	2.41

In other words, a modern, technologically advanced economy involves an elaborate division of labor in which a few people with special skills provide a service for a very

Table 10-7 Detailed Occupation of the Experienced Labor Force: 1960

Detailed Occupation	Total employed (000)	Percent distribution	Percent change 1950-60			Percent female		Urban-rural distribution		
			Total	Male	Female	1960	1950	Percent Urban	Percent rural-Nonfarm	Percent Rural-farm
	Col 1	Col 2	Col 3	Col 4	Col 5	Col 6	Col 7	Col 8	Col 9	Col 10
Total employed..........	64,639,256	100.00	14.5	6.9	34.2	32.8	27.9	71.0	20.4	8.6
Professional, technical & kindred workers...............	7,232,410	11.19	47.0	50.8	41.1	38.1	39.6	83.0	15.5	1.4
Accountants and auditors.........	471,302	0.73	24.7	21.8	41.1	16.8	14.8	90.3	8.9	0.8
Actors...............	9,200	0.01	-37.5	-37.6	-37.3	34.7	34.6	95.1	4.6	0.3
Airplane pilots & navigators......	26,976	0.04	92.2	93.7	-14.1	0.6	1.4	80.5	17.3	2.2
Architects	30,261	0.05	27.8	29.7	-18.4	2.5	4.0	88.9	10.4	0.7
Artists & art teachers.........	101,852	0.16	31.1	37.1	21.3	35.3	38.2	89.0	10.5	0.6
Athletes	4,224	0.01	-63.6	-64.3	-52.4	8.0	6.1	82.3	15.8	1.9
Authors	27,806	0.04	77.2	115.7	16.3	25.4	38.8	87.9	11.4	0.7
Chiropractors	14,320	0.02	10.9	16.7	-23.9	9.8	14.3	82.9	16.1	1.0
Clergymen............	200,999	0.31	19.6	21.7	-31.2	2.3	4.1	67.7	31.1	1.2
College president, professors, & instructors. (n.e.c.)	177,739	0.27	42.2	44.7	34.0	21.9	23.2	86.4	12.8	0.8
Dancers & dancing teachers	20,432	0.03	25.9	-1.9	37.1	77.6	71.2	94.2	4.8	1.0
Dentists	83,003	0.13	10.1	10.6	-5.9	2.3	2.7	86.4	12.6	1.0
Designers	65,856	0.10	137.2	206.8	17.9	18.3	36.9	88.7	10.6	0.6
Dietitians & nutritionists	26,119	0.04	16.2	40.2	14.7	92.8	94.0	84.3	14.5	1.3
Draftsmen............	213,369	0.33	60.3	61.8	39.4	5.5	6.3	87.6	11.6	0.8
Editors & reporters	100,717	0.16	41.7	42.7	39.9	37.2	37.6	88.5	10.7	0.8
Engineers & technical............	860,949	1.33	63.6	64.3	11.0	0.8	1.2	85.6	13.5	0.8

Table 10-7 (*Continued*)

	(1)	(2)	(3)	(4)	(5)	(6)	(7)	(8)	(9)	(10)
Engineers & technical (Continued)										
Aeronautical	51,703	0.08	192.9	193.9	144.1	1.6	1.9	88.9	10.6	0.5
Chemical	41,026	0.06	26.1	27.3	-38.4	0.9	1.9	86.2	13.2	0.6
Civil	155,173	0.24	24.9	26.2	-54.7	0.6	1.6	83.5	15.1	1.5
Electrical	183,887	0.28	73.7	74.3	19.1	0.8	1.2	86.8	12.7	0.6
Industrial	97,458	0.15	142.0	139.5	358.8	2.1	1.1	85.6	13.8	0.7
Mechanical	158,188	0.24	40.7	40.9	-8.7	0.3	0.5	85.2	13.9	0.9
Metallurgical, & metallurgists	18,459	0.03	49.5	51.0	-25.7	1.0	2.0	85.0	14.2	0.8
Mining	12,084	0.02	-14.6	-14.3	-61.5	0.3	0.8	80.3	18.9	0.8
Sales	56,836	0.09	129.8	129.1	-	0.3	-	89.1	10.6	0.3
Not elsewhere classified	86,135	0.13	105.5	108.7	-31.4	0.8	2.3	84.4	14.5	1.0
Entertainers (n.e.c.)	10,982	0.02	-26.9	-19.8	-44.3	22.1	29.0	75.9	19.9	4.2
Farm & home management advisors	13,417	0.02	9.1	14.0	4.2	47.0	49.3	53.1	39.9	7.0
Foresters & conservationists	32,115	0.05	22.4	23.4	-6.3	2.4	3.2	36.1	53.0	10.9
Funeral directors & embalmers	36,981	0.06	-6.3	-5.6	-14.8	6.1	6.7	79.9	19.3	0.8
Lawyers & judges	212,408	0.33	16.9	16.9	18.5	3.5	3.5	89.3	9.6	1.1
Librarians	83,881	0.13	50.9	90.3	45.8	85.6	88.6	89.5	9.7	0.8
Musicians & music teachers	191,884	0.30	24.6	8.3	40.4	57.1	50.7	85.3	13.8	0.9
Natural scientists	149,330	0.23	27.7	30.0	10.4	9.9	11.4	84.3	14.4	1.2
Agricultural scientists	7,895	0.01	27.3	27.6	23.3	5.2	5.3	70.4	24.3	5.4
Biological scientists	13,937	0.02	51.2	56.6	38.2	26.7	29.2	78.5	20.1	1.3
Chemists	83,420	0.13	11.8	13.5	-3.6	8.6	10.0	85.1	13.8	1.1
Geologists & geophysicists	18,551	0.03	75.0	81.1	-27.3	2.3	5.6	90.3	9.1	0.6
Mathematicians	7,527	0.01	345.1	428.1	209.8	26.5	38.0	84.8	14.7	0.5
Physicists	13,941	0.02	87.7	92.5	20.2	4.2	6.5	84.5	15.0	0.6
Miscellaneous natural scientists	4,059	0.01	-43.3	-39.1	-65.1	9.8	15.9	83.7	15.4	0.9
Nurses, professional	582,379	0.90	45.5	50.6	45.4	97.5	97.6	81.1	16.8	2.1
Nurses, student professional	57,340	0.09	-25.0	-49.1	-24.5	98.6	97.9	89.8	10.3	-
Optometrists	16,044	0.02	9.6	11.4	-19.9	4.2	5.7	87.5	11.9	0.6
Osteopaths	3,940	0.01	-23.6	-20.7	-39.7	12.0	15.2	79.7	19.5	0.8
Personnel & labor relations workers	97,870	0.15	86.7	81.3	100.2	30.9	28.8	87.9	11.2	0.9
Pharmacists	92,115	0.14	4.3	4.9	-2.3	7.7	8.3	86.0	13.4	0.6
Photographers	51,567	0.08	-2.3	4.0	-32.4	12.0	17.3	88.9	10.4	0.7
Physicians & surgeons	228,926	0.35	18.9	18.1	32.0	6.8	6.1	87.6	11.6	0.8

Table 10-7 (*Continued*)

	(1)	(2)	(3)	(4)	(5)	(6)	(7)	(8)	(9)	(10)
Public relations men & publicity writers	30,363	0.05	63.5	40.7	257.8	23.1	10.5	90.6	8.7	0.7
Radio operators	28,441	0.04	69.8	67.6	91.4	10.4	9.2	84.5	14.5	1.1
Recreation & group workers	36,355	0.06	124.5	121.2	129.1	42.6	41.8	89.3	10.1	0.6
Religious workers	56,338	0.09	34.7	66.3	20.9	62.3	69.4	74.2	24.8	1.1
Social & Welfare workers, exc. group	96,696	0.15	27.4	54.0	15.5	62.7	69.2	85.9	12.5	1.6
Social scientists	56,580	0.09	60.1	77.2	24.2	25.1	32.3	90.6	8.8	0.6
Economists	19,132	0.03	117.7	128.0	71.8	14.5	18.4	91.2	7.9	0.9
Psychologists	12,040	0.02	150.2	206.8	77.5	31.1	43.8	88.4	11.3	0.2
Statisticians & actuaries	21,885	0.03	18.7	28.5	1.2	30.6	35.9	92.0	7.5	0.5
Miscellaneous social scientists	3,523	0.01	6.9	15.2	-10.4	27.1	32.4	85.5	13.7	0.8
Sports instructors & officials	76,888	0.12	70.3	53.0	122.9	32.4	24.8	74.6	23.3	2.1
Surveyors	43,565	0.07	70.1	69.7	79.0	3.9	3.7	69.1	25.5	5.4
Teachers:										
Elementary Schools	1,003,576	1.55	48.7	132.1	40.3	85.7	90.9	67.8	27.2	5.0
Secondary schools	518,014	0.80	40.8	72.5	16.6	47.0	56.7	69.2	27.5	3.3
Teachers (n.e.c.)	150,324	0.23	80.7	-12.5	435.6	61.6	20.8	75.6	22.0	2.4
Technicians:										
Medical & dental	138,162	0.21	80.2	56.2	98.6	62.4	56.7	86.8	12.1	1.0
Electrical & electronic	91,463	0.14	679.2	643.1	-	4.6	-	84.3	14.9	0.8
Other eng. & physical sciences	183,609	0.28	101.8	114.7	43.0	12.8	18.0	80.0	18.3	1.8
Technicians (n.e.c.)	65,723	0.10	253.2	309.4	144.7	23.6	34.1	75.1	19.7	5.2
Therapists and healers (n.e.c.)	36,654	0.06	48.9	35.9	62.2	53.9	49.5	87.2	11.7	1.0
Veterinarians	14,819	0.02	10.5	15.4	-63.4	2.1	6.2	58.7	35.0	6.3
Professional, technical, & kindred workers (n.e.c.)	308,497	0.48	256.5	286.9	173.1	20.4	26.7	86.4	12.5	1.1
Farmers & farm managers	2,505,684	3.88	-41.9	-43.1	0.9	4.7	2.7	5.1	12.9	82.0
Farmers (owners & tenants)	2,481,202	3.84	-42.0	-43.2	2.3	4.7	2.7	5.0	12.7	82.3
Farm managers	24,482	0.04	-30.3	-27.9	-67.7	2.9	6.3	18.8	30.5	50.8
Managers, officials, & propr., exc. farm	5,409,543	8.37	7.4	6.3	14.6	14.4	13.5	79.2	18.7	2.1
Buyers & department heads, store	233,974	0.36	64.2	69.5	48.6	23.0	25.4	88.2	10.9	1.0
Buyers & shippers, farm products	17,353	0.03	-38.5	-38.4	-41.2	2.0	2.1	49.3	35.1	15.6

Table 10-7 (*Continued*)

	(1)	(2)	(3)	(4)	(5)	(6)	(7)	(8)	(9)	(10)
Conductors, railroad	43,810	0.07	-21.5	-21.2	-64.8	0.3	0.6	82.2	16.4	1.4
Credit men	46,657	0.07	41.5	35.6	62.7	25.0	21.7	91.2	8.2	0.7
Floormen & floor managers, store ...	10,850	0.02	0.1	-6.4	7.6	49.7	46.2	89.7	9.4	0.9
Inspectors, public administration .	75,542	0.12	32.0	32.1	29.6	3.9	4.0	80.2	16.8	3.0
Federal public administration & postal service	40,706	0.06	45.3	44.5	70.6	3.5	3.0	80.3	17.3	2.3
State public administration ...	13,395	0.02	40.2	39.3	63.0	4.4	3.8	69.5	25.0	5.5
Local public administration ...	21,441	0.03	9.2	10.5	-13.6	4.3	5.5	86.7	10.7	2.6
Managers & superintendent, building	52,887	0.08	-19.9	-23.6	-12.6	37.2	34.1	94.2	5.3	0.5
Officers, pilots pursers & engineers	34,058	0.05	-11.6	-9.4	-85.3	0.5	2.9	77.2	21.4	1.5
Officials & administrators (n.e.c.) public administration	198,632	0.31	28.3	25.2	43.5	19.1	17.1	76.0	19.4	4.6
Federal public administration & postal service	67,704	0.10	35.1	33.8	46.0	11.6	10.8	86.1	12.3	1.6
State public administration ...	36,375	0.06	55.9	54.4	67.1	13.0	12.1	69.1	26.9	4.1
Local public administration ...	94,553	0.15	16.2	9.5	39.1	26.8	22.4	70.5	22.0	7.4
Officials, lodge, society, union, etc.	33,235	0.05	24.1	25.1	15.3	10.1	10.8	87.6	10.9	1.5
Postmasters	36,671	0.06	-5.8	-1.4	-11.7	40.4	43.1	34.3	57.6	8.1
Purchasing agents & buyers (n.e.c.)	103,368	0.16	63.5	62.9	68.7	9.4	9.1	85.8	12.7	1.5
Managers, officials, & proprietors (n.e.c.)--salaried	2,554,314	3.95	42.4	40.7	55.2	13.0	12.0	82.9	15.7	1.5
Construction	142,542	0.22	65.8	63.9	145.5	3.4	2.3	77.0	20.2	2.9
Manufacturing	646,084	1.00	54.0	53.9	56.1	6.7	6.6	84.1	14.7	1.2
Transportation	117,844	0.18	22.3	21.2	52.4	4.5	3.6	86.4	12.5	1.0
Communications, utilities, & sanitary service	102,353	0.16	30.2	34.9	1.5	10.9	14.0	80.2	18.4	1.4
Wholesale trade	199,954	0.31	26.9	25.2	55.6	7.0	5.7	84.0	14.4	1.6
Retail trade	605,904	0.94	19.0	18.8	19.9	15.4	15.2	81.0	17.6	1.4
Food & dairy products stores	104,838	0.16	9.6	13.3	-18.1	8.7	11.7	81.9	17.0	1.2
Eating & drinking places .	71,884	0.11	4.2	1.0	12.2	30.4	28.2	87.8	11.6	0.6
General mdse. & ltd. price variety stores	87,194	0.13	46.0	41.3	62.6	24.8	22.3	85.1	14.0	0.9
Apparel & accessories stores	50,018	0.08	18.8	17.2	22.2	33.1	32.2	93.2	6.6	0.3

Table 10-7 (*Continued*)

	(1)	(2)	(3)	(4)	(5)	(6)	(7)	(8)	(9)	(10)
Retail trade (Con't)										
Furniture, housefurnishing & equipment stores	31,085	0.05	12.3	10.5	30.2	10.6	9.2	86.5	12.8	0.7
Motor vehicles & accessories retailing	85,801	0.13	51.7	50.0	98.8	4.4	3.4	79.1	19.5	1.4
Gasoline service stations	43,293	0.07	21.9	22.7	-20.7	1.1	1.8	72.2	25.6	2.2
Hardware, farm equipment building material retail	53,790	0.08	23.0	22.2	44.4	4.2	3.6	69.3	28.0	2.7
Other retail trade	78,001	0.12	-1.5	-2.6	4.1	17.9	17.0	79.3	18.3	2.4
Banking & other finance	203,190	0.31	70.6	66.4	107.5	10.4	12.6	83.3	15.3	1.4
Insurance & real estate	140,062	0.22	99.3	97.7	107.3	17.2	16.5	89.5	9.7	0.8
Business services	64,559	0.10	150.9	146.6	168.6	21.1	19.7	90.9	8.5	0.6
Automobile repair services & garages	20,984	0.03	-11.7	-13.9	115.2	4.1	1.7	81.2	17.2	1.6
Miscellaneous repair services	7,218	0.01	66.3	64.0	107.9	6.6	5.3	86.2	12.5	1.3
Personal services	76,633	0.12	17.5	16.1	20.2	34.2	33.4	85.0	14.1	0.8
All other industries (incl. not reported)	226,987	0.35	65.0	48.8	117.6	31.1	23.6	78.4	19.1	2.5
Managers, officials proprietors (n.e.c.)--self-employed	1,968,192	3.04	-22.1	-23.2	-15.2	14.6	13.4	73.4	23.8	2.9
Construction	225,256	0.35	12.4	12.4	9.0	1.3	1.3	74.4	23.0	2.6
Manufacturing	170,372	0.26	-30.2	-30.9	-19.4	6.9	6.0	75.2	20.7	4.2
Transportation	39,312	0.06	-24.0	-25.0	-3.7	6.0	4.7	72.0	25.1	2.8
Communications, utilities & sanitary service	5,038	0.01	-25.3	-28.4	52.3	7.9	3.9	70.4	27.9	1.7
Wholesale trade	134,428	0.21	-24.2	-24.9	-8.1	5.1	4.2	81.5	16.1	2.3
Retail trade	999,863	1.55	-29.3	-30.2	-25.2	18.2	17.2	70.4	26.8	2.9
Food & dairy products stores	218,121	0.34	-44.7	-45.6	-40.7	19.4	18.1	66.7	29.5	3.9
Eating & drinking places	208,244	0.32	-28.1	-33.1	-14.3	31.4	26.3	76.2	22.3	1.5
General mdse. & ltd. price variety stores	45,736	0.07	-41.9	-45.7	-24.8	23.3	18.0	57.1	37.8	5.0
Apparel & accessories stores	56,559	0.09	-33.5	-36.4	-26.8	33.7	30.7	89.2	10.2	0.6
Furniture, housefurnishing & equipment stores	49,269	0.08	-28.0	-28.7	-21.1	9.1	8.3	80.3	18.3	1.4
Motor vehicles & accessories retailing	56,128	0.09	-6.3	-6.4	-2.5	2.7	2.6	72.4	25.2	2.4

Table 10-7 (Continued)

	(1)	(2)	(3)	(4)	(5)	(6)	(7)	(8)	(9)	(10)
Self-employed (Con't)										
Gasoline service stations	150,551	0.23	2.6	3.6	-25.3	2.7	3.7	62.9	34.1	3.0
Hardware, farm equipment bldg. material	67,055	0.10	-21.2	-21.3	-19.0	5.1	4.9	61.9	33.9	4.2
Other retail trade	148,200	0.23	-28.3	-30.4	-18.9	20.9	18.5	76.1	21.0	2.9
Banking & other finance	22,228	0.03	1.2	0.7	11.6	5.2	4.7	86.5	12.0	1.5
Insurance & real estate	49,589	0.08	10.2	8.8	19.2	14.3	13.2	86.0	12.4	1.6
Business services	36,778	0.06	11.6	9.9	21.6	15.8	14.5	89.0	10.2	0.8
Automobile repair services & garages	38,143	0.06	-36.8	-37.6	5.0	3.0	1.8	71.5	26.6	1.8
Miscellaneous repair services	19,975	0.03	-32.8	-33.2	-23.4	5.1	4.4	77.1	20.9	2.0
Personal services	130,402	0.20	-10.0	-17.2	9.3	33.1	27.3	73.5	24.6	1.9
All other industries (incl. not reported)	96,808	0.15	-1.0	-9.6	49.4	22.1	14.6	68.8	25.7	5.5
Clerical & kindred workers	9,306,896	14.40	33.8	13.9	46.0	67.6	61.9	84.6	13.4	2.0
Agents (n.e.c.)	160,262	0.25	28.9	25.0	49.9	18.1	15.6	84.7	13.0	2.3
Attendants & assistants, library	32,257	0.05	162.4	131.5	173.1	77.3	74.2	92.3	7.3	0.4
Attendants, physicians & dentists office	70,655	0.11	72.5	-16.3	77.2	97.6	95.0	84.0	13.6	2.5
Baggagemen, transportation	5,467	0.01	-31.0	-32.0	22.2	3.4	1.9	91.8	7.5	0.7
Bank tellers	129,190	0.20	101.2	12.1	211.1	69.2	44.8	83.2	14.7	2.0
Bookkeepers	913,231	1.41	26.2	-10.0	37.0	83.7	77.1	79.7	17.3	3.0
Cashiers	468,950	0.73	102.7	114.6	99.6	78.5	79.7	83.5	14.4	2.1
Collectors, bill & account	30,573	0.05	30.2	20.3	87.4	21.2	14.7	85.8	12.8	1.4
Dispatchers & starters, vehicle	57,802	0.09	84.3	85.5	74.7	11.0	11.6	86.0	12.9	1.1
Express messengers & railway mail clerks	6,598	0.01	-64.7	-65.4	-16.5	3.5	1.5	85.1	13.0	1.9
File clerks	131,367	0.20	23.7	30.7	22.6	85.5	86.3	89.8	8.9	1.3
Insur. adjusters, examiners, & investigators	55,177	0.09	72.4	56.7	561.4	12.0	3.1	89.1	10.2	0.8
Mail carriers	196,728	0.30	19.0	18.9	22.0	2.1	2.1	77.3	18.5	4.1
Messengers & office boys	58,833	0.09	5.8	6.2	4.2	18.0	18.3	93.0	6.3	0.7
Office machine operators	307,828	0.48	116.2	216.9	94.6	74.0	82.3	90.3	8.7	1.0
Payroll & timekeeping clerks	106,874	0.17	66.5	20.2	125.4	59.6	44.0	83.2	15.0	1.8
Postal clerks	209,385	0.32	15.1	7.3	70.3	18.2	12.3	88.1	10.6	1.3
Receptionists	134,121	0.21	125.7	53.0	128.1	97.8	96.7	91.3	8.0	0.7

274

Table 10-7 (*Continued*)

	(1)	(2)	(3)	(4)	(5)	(6)	(7)	(8)	(9)	(10)
Secretaries	1,463,958	2.26	80.1	-13.6	85.8	97.2	94.2	87.2	10.7	2.2
Shipping & receiving clerks	280,214	0.43	-1.6	-3.0	17.2	8.3	7.0	83.8	14.0	2.1
Stenographers	270,179	0.42	-36.3	-23.9	-36.7	95.7	96.4	89.1	9.7	1.2
Stock clerks & storekeepers	325,869	0.50	40.9	34.0	100.0	15.0	10.5	83.5	14.5	2.0
Telegraph messengers	4,074	0.01	-43.5	-40.3	-71.0	5.4	10.6	94.5	5.1	0.4
Telegraph operators	20,075	0.03	-41.6	-42.6	-39.1	22.6	21.7	66.6	30.9	2.6
Telephone operators	356,916	0.55	-0.5	-6.9	-0.2	95.8	95.5	82.5	15.7	1.7
Ticket, station, & express agents	72,058	0.11	6.8	-6.0	106.0	22.0	11.4	79.3	19.4	1.2
Typists	522,203	0.81	45.2	-4.1	49.1	95.1	92.6	88.2	10.3	1.5
Clerical & kindred workers (n.e.c.)	2,916,772	4.51	27.4	11.4	41.4	59.2	53.3	85.5	12.6	1.9
Sales workers	4,638,985	7.18	18.7	15.8	24.5	35.8	34.1	82.8	15.3	1.9
Advertising agents & salesmen	33,901	0.05	4.4	4.8	2.1	13.8	14.1	89.1	10.2	0.7
Auctioneers	4,052	0.01	-23.3	-17.8	-81.4	2.1	8.6	50.6	32.5	16.9
Demonstrators	24,225	0.04	80.9	-23.9	104.0	92.4	81.9	81.3	17.0	1.7
Hucksters & Peddlers	54,584	0.08	143.5	18.1	899.2	58.4	14.2	81.1	16.0	2.9
Insurance agents, brokers & underwriters	364,557	0.56	33.7	32.9	41.4	9.7	9.2	83.6	14.7	1.7
Newsboys	190,408	0.29	97.4	96.7	114.6	4.4	4.0	85.3	14.1	0.7
Real estate agents and brokers	193,104	0.30	37.0	21.8	126.7	23.9	14.4	85.7	12.6	1.7
Stock & bond salesmen	28,617	0.04	160.1	170.3	68.3	6.4	9.9	88.6	10.4	1.1
Salesmen & sales clerks (n.e.c.)	3,745,537	5.79	13.1	9.2	19.4	40.3	38.2	82.2	15.7	2.1
Manufacturing	464,770	0.72	41.7	36.3	114.5	10.4	6.9	87.6	11.4	1.1
Wholesale trade	495,405	0.77	22.3	21.8	33.9	4.1	3.7	86.9	11.8	1.2
Retail trade	2,607,410	4.03	6.4	-3.4	16.7	53.6	48.9	78.3	18.9	2.8
Other industries (incl. not reported)	177,952	0.28	37.8	34.3	49.3	25.0	23.1	84.3	13.9	1.8
Craftsmen, foremen, & kindred workers	8,741,292	13.52	11.8	11.9	6.8	2.9	3.0	73.5	23.4	3.1
Bakers	108,367	0.17	-9.9	-14.5	25.0	16.2	11.7	89.4	9.7	0.9
Blacksmiths	20,030	0.03	-54.2	-54.2	-49.8	0.5	0.5	53.0	40.6	6.4
Boilermakers	23,754	0.04	-33.4	-32.9	-87.1	0.2	0.9	79.3	18.5	2.1
Bookbinders	27,015	0.04	-13.5	-12.5	-14.3	55.6	56.2	89.0	10.0	1.0
Brickmasons, stonemasons, & tile setters	185,909	0.29	12.0	12.2	-23.2	0.4	0.6	71.2	25.4	3.4
Cabinetmakers	65,669	0.10	-10.6	-10.5	-16.4	1.4	1.5	73.8	22.9	3.3
Carpenters	818,835	1.27	-10.9	-10.7	-45.3	0.3	0.5	59.1	34.2	6.7

Table 10-7 (*Continued*)

	(1)	(2)	(3)	(4)	(5)	(6)	(7)	(8)	(9)	(10)
Craftsmen, foremen, & kindred workers (Con't)										
Cement & concrete finishers	40,767	0.06	37.9	38.4	-46.2	0.2	0.6	79.2	18.3	2.4
Compositors & typesetters	179,552	0.28	2.1	-0.3	36.7	8.5	6.3	85.6	13.3	1.1
Cranemen, derickmen, & hoistmen	123,991	0.19	19.6	19.8	-16.1	0.5	0.8	71.9	25.3	2.8
Decorators, & window dressers	50,939	0.08	17.3	-10.0	80.7	46.3	30.0	89.0	9.8	1.1
Electricians	337,147	0.52	8.3	8.3	8.5	0.7	0.7	75.0	22.7	2.2
Electrotypers & sterotypers	9,178	0.01	-22.0	-19.7	-83.5	0.8	3.7	87.9	10.9	1.2
Engravers, exc. photoengravers	11,269	0.02	15.6	9.5	58.0	17.3	12.7	87.6	11.7	0.6
Excavating, grading, & road machinery operators	198,802	0.31	88.6	88.8	37.9	0.3	0.5	46.8	44.9	8.3
Foremen (n.e.c.)	1,175,112	1.82	39.0	41.1	15.0	6.7	8.1	76.1	21.7	2.2
Construction	96,477	0.15	63.4	63.8	-23.4	0.2	0.5	65.8	29.9	4.3
Manufacturing	744,011	1.15	44.9	48.3	13.6	7.7	9.8	78.0	20.0	2.0
Metal industries	129,068	0.20	54.9	55.8	11.4	1.5	2.1	81.4	17.1	1.5
Machinery, including electrical	132,624	0.21	65.4	66.4	48.8	5.3	5.9	81.5	17.0	1.6
Transportation equipment	81,357	0.13	62.6	63.3	24.3	1.3	1.7	82.8	15.5	1.7
Other durable goods	100,481	0.16	33.0	35.4	2.9	5.7	7.4	67.9	28.9	3.2
Textiles, textile products, & apparel	74,365	0.12	7.8	6.7	10.5	31.3	30.5	69.1	28.4	2.6
Other nondurable goods, (incl. not specific mfg.)	226,116	0.35	45.5	49.7	10.9	8.1	10.7	78.7	19.2	2.1
Railroads & railway express service	35,875	0.06	-33.6	-33.4	-77.4	0.2	0.5	68.5	29.6	2.0
Transportation, exc. railroad	27,099	0.04	36.0	36.0	32.3	1.1	1.2	84.5	14.1	1.3
Communications & utilities & sanitary service	57,579	0.09	42.7	43.6	5.1	1.8	2.5	80.3	18.2	1.5
Other industries (incl. not reported)	214,071	0.33	35.0	36.4	21.9	9.1	10.1	73.5	24.1	2.4
Forgemen & hammermen	11,698	0.02	-10.9	-12.2	53.8	3.4	2.0	77.4	19.7	3.0
Furries	3,283	0.01	-70.2	-70.5	68.7	15.1	14.4	93.4	6.1	0.5
Glaziers	14,987	0.02	45.4	47.9	-30.2	1.5	3.2	86.1	12.6	1.4
Heat treaters, annealers, & temperers	19,568	0.03	10.2	10.2	14.9	1.5	1.4	79.6	17.7	2.7
Inspectors, scalers, & graders, log & lumber	19,661	0.03	2.3	2.0	8.1	4.1	3.8	41.5	52.1	6.4
Inspectors (n.e.c.)	98,193	0.15	2.2	3.6	-15.8	5.8	7.0	78.1	19.4	2.5

Table 10-7 (Continued)

	(1)	(2)	(3)	(4)	(5)	(6)	(7)	(8)	(9)	(10)
Craftsmen, foremen, & kindred workers (Con't)										
Construction	14,854	0.02	83.2	83.9	-	0.7	1.0	68.0	27.1	4.9
Railroads & railway express service	29,361	0.05	-20.2	-20.1	-52.2	0.3	0.4	79.0	18.8	2.2
Transportation exc. R.R. comm., other pub. utilities	14,458	0.02	15.4	18.0	-48.7	1.7	3.9	84.9	13.7	1.4
Other industries (incl. not reported)	39,520	0.06	2.3	5.0	-12.6	13.3	15.5	79.0	18.8	2.2
Jewellers, watchmakers, goldsmiths & silversmiths	36,762	0.06	-19.8	-20.2	-13.1	5.8	5.4	84.2	14.6	1.2
Job setters, metal	39,718	0.06	62.5	63.2	7.3	0.8	1.2	80.0	17.6	2.4
Linemen & servicemen, telegraph, telephone, & power	274,621	0.42	28.6	29.0	11.0	2.0	2.3	75.7	22.2	2.1
Locomotive engineers	56,630	0.09	-22.4	-22.1	-80.3	0.2	0.6	80.8	17.4	1.8
Locomotive firemen	37,087	0.06	-31.7	-31.6	-46.9	0.3	0.4	77.0	20.6	2.4
Loom fixers	23,889	0.04	-21.2	-21.0	-38.8	0.9	1.1	52.8	43.2	4.0
Machinists	498,688	0.77	-3.1	-2.8	-20.6	1.3	1.6	78.8	18.9	2.3
Mechanics & repairmen	2,223,358	3.44	28.5	28.6	24.5	1.2	1.2	72.1	24.8	3.1
Air conditioning, heating, & refrigeration	61,997	0.10	42.1	41.8	-	0.2	-	78.1	19.9	2.1
Airplane	114,181	0.18	60.0	60.3	44.8	1.5	1.6	83.0	15.3	1.7
Automobile	682,103	1.06	4.2	4.6	-45.2	0.3	0.6	67.4	29.2	3.4
Office machine	29,262	0.05	-5.7	-5.9	16.7	1.0	0.8	87.4	11.7	0.9
Radio & television	102,829	0.16	36.5	37.9	-16.8	0.3	0.5	75.7	21.9	2.4
Railroad & car shop	39,020	0.06	-17.9	-17.8	-49.8	0.3	0.5	74.6	22.9	2.5
Not elsewhere classified	1,193,966	1.85	48.0	48.0	51.0	1.7	1.6	72.7	24.0	3.3
Millers, grain, flour, feed, etc.	9,059	0.01	-5.7	-5.7	-	0.7	0.7	40.2	43.9	15.9
Millwrights	64,348	0.10	11.0	11.4	-66.8	0.1	0.4	68.2	28.6	3.2
Molders, metal	48,929	0.08	-19.2	-20.7	117.7	3.0	1.1	75.4	21.7	2.9
Motion picture projectionists	17,559	0.03	-33.0	-33.2	-19.9	2.2	1.9	81.3	16.8	1.9
Opticians, lens grinders, & polishers	20,349	0.03	6.0	3.7	20.9	1.5	13.1	89.4	9.7	0.9
Painters, construction & maintenance	370,660	0.57	-5.4	-5.4	-5.2	2.1	2.1	77.5	20.2	2.3
Paperchangers	10,181	0.02	-51.4	-51.5	-50.5	14.3	14.0	82.4	16.0	1.7
Pattern & model makers, exc. paper	38,939	0.06	8.2	10.1	-46.6	1.7	3.4	83.0	15.7	1.2

Table 10-7 (Continued)

	(1)	(2)	(3)	(4)	(5)	(6)	(7)	(8)	(9)	(10)
Craftsmen, foremen, & kindred workers (Con't)										
Photoengravers & lithographers	25,015	0.04	-12.4	-13.8	23.2	5.2	3.7	91.5	8.0	0.5
Piano & organ tuners & repairmen	6,011	0.01	-22.6	-21.9	-42.9	2.5	3.5	84.9	13.7	1.5
Plasterers	46,169	0.07	-23.9	-23.2	-67.9	0.3	0.8	79.0	18.8	2.2
Plumbers & pipe fitters	304,459	0.47	8.9	9.4	-53.5	0.3	0.7	74.5	23.0	2.5
Pressmen & plate printers, printing	73,914	0.11	50.0	50.1	46.9	4.2	4.3	87.8	11.0	1.2
Rollers & roll hands, metal	29,655	0.05	-2.3	-2.9	21.7	2.7	2.2	80.4	18.1	1.6
Roofers & slaters	47,980	0.07	7.9	8.2	-54.9	0.2	0.5	79.9	18.1	2.1
Shoemakers & repairers, exc. factory	36,188	0.06	-36.8	-36.7	-38.7	3.7	3.8	85.1	14.0	0.9
Stationary engineers	269,743	0.42	25.5	25.6	8.7	0.6	0.7	73.7	23.5	2.8
Stone cutters & stone carvers	6,102	0.01	-29.9	-29.6	-41.6	2.2	2.6	58.9	36.3	4.8
Structural metal workers	58,223	0.09	17.7	17.9	-11.9	0.4	0.5	76.2	21.2	2.7
Tailors	41,021	0.06	-50.5	-51.9	-44.6	21.8	19.5	96.6	3.2	0.3
Tinsmiths, coppersmiths, & sheet metal workers	135,315	0.21	9.8	9.7	22.3	1.1	0.9	80.8	17.2	2.0
Toolmakers, & die makers & setters	182,345	0.28	19.4	19.5	6.5	0.6	0.7	81.4	16.7	1.9
Upholsterers	59,370	0.09	-3.1	-4.2	8.3	9.5	8.5	78.5	18.8	2.6
Craftsmen & kindred workers (n.e.c.)	105,279	0.16	52.6	52.6	52.0	1.6	1.6	80.0	17.7	2.3
Former members of the Armed Forces	-	-	-	-	-	-	-	-	-	-
Operatives & kindred workers	11,897,601	18.41	6.4	6.0	7.6	27.4	27.1	70.4	25.2	4.3
Apprentices	82,537	0.13	-28.5	-28.5	-30.4	2.7	2.8	82.2	16.0	1.8
Auto mechanics	1,771	-	-52.4	-51.0	-86.4	1.1	3.9	75.6	21.0	3.4
Bricklayers & masons	2,802	-	-54.4	-54.4	-	0.4	0.4	77.8	19.0	3.2
Carpenters	5,159	0.01	-48.4	-48.2	-	0.4	0.8	78.1	19.0	2.9
Electricians	9,117	0.01	2.6	2.7	-	0.7	0.9	82.7	15.8	1.6
Machinists & toolmakers	15,183	0.02	-0.8	-1.3	41.5	1.5	1.0	81.5	16.6	1.9
Mechanics, exc. auto	3,567	0.01	-43.5	-40.2	-85.3	1.9	7.3	76.9	20.5	2.5
Plumbers & pipe fitters	7,742	0.01	-35.2	-32.4	-93.6	0.4	4.5	82.8	16.3	0.9
Building trades (n.e.c.)	2,250	-	-43.8	-44.6	-	2.3	0.8	84.1	14.9	1.0
Metalworking trades (n.e.c.)	5,415	0.01	-18.4	-19.1	-	1.9	1.1	84.9	13.9	1.2
Printing trades	11,343	0.02	-25.6	-25.4	-32.7	2.3	2.6	86.6	11.8	1.6
Other specified trade	8,411	0.01	-33.5	-36.8	49.2	8.6	3.8	82.1	16.3	1.7
Trade not specified	9,777	0.02	-33.4	-34.4	-13.6	6.4	4.9	81.8	16.4	1.8
Asbestos & insulation workers	18,086	0.03	27.1	26.3	55.3	3.5	2.8	78.5	19.3	2.2

Table 10-7 (*Continued*)

Operatives & kindred workers (Con't)	(1)	(2)	(3)	(4)	(5)	(6)	(7)	(8)	(9)	(10)
Assemblers..............	614,347	0.95	62.6	50.5	81.0	44.1	39.6	77.7	18.4	3.9
Attendants, auto service & parking .	351,826	0.54	48.6	49.8	6.7	2.0	2.8	68.3	27.4	4.3
Blasters & powdermen	6,370	0.01	-41.9	-42.1	-	1.1	0.9	39.2	54.5	6.3
Boatmen, canalmen, & lock keepers ..	6,779	0.01	-16.8	-15.8	-52.2	1.4	2.5	52.8	43.5	3.7
Brakemen, railroad	61,670	0.10	-21.6	-21.4	-59.9	0.2	0.4	75.7	22.3	1.9
Bus drivers	181,794	0.28	16.8	8.5	268.4	10.1	3.2	63.8	24.0	12.2
Chainmen, rodmen, & axmen, surveying	9,639	0.01	36.0	33.5	137.3	4.1	2.3	63.9	29.5	6.7
Checkers, examiners, & inspectors, mfg.	480,092	0.74	44.7	71.0	21.6	44.8	53.3	78.7	18.6	2.7
Conductors, bus, & street railway ..	4,237	0.01	-62.4	-62.5	-57.2	2.1	1.8	98.4	1.3	0.3
Deliverymen & routemen	419,651	0.65	75.1	73.7	152.3	2.6	1.8	80.5	17.1	2.3
Dressmakers & seamstresses, exc. factory	119,217	0.18	-16.2	3.6	-16.8	96.7	97.3	88.0	10.4	1.5
Dyers	18,411	0.03	-24.0	-23.7	-30.0	4.0	4.3	62.2	33.6	4.3
Filers, grinders, & polishers, metal	148,424	0.23	0.4	-0.3	16.3	5.3	4.5	77.2	19.9	2.9
Fruit, nut, and vegetable graders & packers exc. factory	220,060	0.03	-23.3	-39.0	-13.0	68.3	60.2	62.2	29.3	8.5
Furnacemen, smeltermen, & pourers ..	53,343	0.08	-3.7	-3.2	-27.7	1.7	2.2	77.9	19.5	2.6
Graders & sorters, mfg.	34,446	0.05	-17.5	-21.7	-15.1	65.5	63.7	68.7	26.3	5.0
Heaters, metal	7,657	0.01	-17.4	-15.5	-58.8	2.2	4.5	81.6	16.8	1.6
Knitters, loopers, & toppers, textile	44,039	0.07	-45.4	-63.5	-28.0	67.2	51.0	57.0	37.4	5.5
Laundry & dry cleaning operatives ..	386,873	0.60	-10.1	-22.5	-4.0	71.7	67.2	87.0	11.9	1.1
Meat cutters, exc. slaughter and packing house	180,755	0.28	5.6	4.5	56.8	3.0	2.0	79.4	18.3	2.3
Milliners	3,826	0.01	-69.0	-72.5	-68.6	90.6	89.4	87.2	12.8	-
Mine operatives & laborers (n.e.c.).	290,148	0.45	-49.5	-49.3	-75.3	0.4	0.8	36.2	58.1	5.7
Coal mining	116,263	0.18	-67.9	-67.9	-79.7	0.2	0.4	20.3	74.9	4.8
Crude petroleum & natural gas extraction.............	91,468	0.14	-10.9	-10.8	-27.9	0.4	0.4	52.7	41.0	6.3
Mining & quarrying, exc. fuel .	82,417	0.13	-24.6	-23.1	-80.6	0.7	2.7	40.3	53.4	6.3
Motormen, mine, factory, logging camp., etc	12,747	0.02	-46.4	-46.4	-69.2	0.5	0.9	36.0	61.4	2.6
Motormen, street, subway, & elevated railway	7,436	0.01	-72.0	-72.0	-72.6	1.3	1.3	97.4	2.5	0.2
Oilers & greasers, exc. auto	51,364	0.08	-13.3	-12.9	-44.1	1.0	1.6	63.2	32.5	4.3

Table 10-7 (*Continued*)

	(1)	(2)	(3)	(4)	(5)	(6)	(7)	(8)	(9)	(10)
Packers & wrappers (n.e.c.)	438,140	0.68	34.1	49.5	25.5	60.0	64.1	76.3	19.5	4.1
Painters exc. construction & maintenance	138,053	0.21	18.1	20.6	-1.9	9.5	11.4	75.0	21.6	3.4
Photographic process workers	41,262	0.06	46.4	51.1	40.6	42.7	44.5	91.2	7.9	0.9
Power station operators	26,707	0.04	23.4	21.7	65.7	5.1	3.8	66.9	30.7	2.4
Sailors & deck hands	32,748	0.05	-19.8	-18.9	-69.3	0.7	1.9	82.8	15.8	1.4
Sawyers	86,704	0.13	-8.5	-9.0	13.0	2.5	2.0	34.6	53.6	11.8
Sewers & stitchers, mfg.	568,495	0.88	20.5	3.5	21.7	94.0	93.0	79.8	17.3	2.9
Spinners, textile	48,776	0.08	-39.7	-49.4	-36.4	79.0	75.0	51.4	43.3	5.3
Stationary firemen	87,887	0.14	-28.3	-28.1	-54.1	0.6	0.9	68.1	28.0	3.9
Switchmen, railroad	57,778	0.09	-5.8	-5.4	-50.8	0.4	0.8	82.8	15.4	1.8
Taxicab drivers & chauffeurs	162,499	0.25	-20.1	-20.9	26.1	2.7	1.7	90.9	8.3	0.8
Truck & tractor drivers	1,556,837	2.41	17.2	17.3	-4.3	0.5	0.6	64.2	29.7	6.0
Weavers, textile	62,691	0.10	-36.0	-38.1	-32.8	41.4	39.4	54.4	40.9	4.8
Welders & flame cutters	360,630	0.56	38.0	36.7	72.5	4.5	3.6	70.8	25.4	3.8
Operatives & kindred workers (n.e.c.)	4,610,610	7.13	2.3	3.6	-0.9	28.7	29.7	71.9	24.1	4.0
Manufacturing	3,977,886	6.15	2.7	4.1	-0.3	30.7	31.6	71.8	24.2	4.0
Durable goods	1,890,974	2.93	7.3	8.2	3.9	20.5	21.2	72.8	23.3	3.9
Sawmills, planing mills, & misc. wood products	132,383	0.20	-24.5	-25.8	-4.2	7.8	6.1	42.2	48.6	9.2
Sawmills, planing mills, & mill work	96,874	0.15	-30.2	-30.1	-33.9	3.4	3.6	38.0	52.2	9.8
Miscellaneous wood products	35,509	0.05	-2.6	-7.1	21.4	19.8	15.9	56.0	37.0	7.0
Furniture & fixtures	99,493	0.15	-7.6	-1.7	-31.4	14.8	19.9	60.0	33.7	6.4
Stone, clay, & glass products ..	157,920	0.24	1.1	7.5	-24.6	14.9	20.0	64.3	31.4	4.4
Glass & glass products	50,658	0.08	-6.0	-1.7	-25.0	14.9	18.7	68.7	27.8	3.4
Cement, concrete, gypsum & plastic products	32,726	0.05	19.4	21.8	-54.8	1.2	3.2	60.1	34.6	5.2
Structural clay products ..	19,054	0.03	-5.6	-1.8	-28.0	11.3	14.8	52.4	41.5	6.1
Pottery & related products ..	20,088	0.03	-36.1	-33.3	-40.0	39.4	41.9	64.4	32.3	3.3
Misc. nonmetallic mineral & stone products	35,394	0.05	52.7	56.1	36.2	15.5	17.3	68.9	26.9	4.2
Metal industries	498,499	0.77	11.0	12.6	0.9	12.4	13.6	78.4	18.9	2.7

Table 10-7 (*Continued*)

	(1)	(2)	(3)	(4)	(5)	(6)	(7)	(8)	(9)	(10)
Primary metal industries ..	233,327	0.36	-3.8	-4.3	7.4	4.9	4.4	77.0	20.4	2.6
Blast furnaces, steel works & rolling & finishing mills	94,991	0.15	-18.6	-18.6	-22.2	1.5	1.6	80.4	18.1	1.5
Other primary iron & steel industries	60,272	0.09	-2.3	-0.5	-35.6	3.4	5.1	76.1	21.0	2.9
Primary nonferrous ind.	78,064	0.12	22.0	20.1	41.6	10.1	8.7	73.3	22.9	3.7
Fab'd metal ind. (ind. not spec. metal).............	265,172	0.41	28.4	37.7	-0.5	19.0	24.5	79.8	17.4	2.8
Cutlery, hand tools & other hardware..............	30,727	0.05	11.0	-11.1	97.1	36.3	20.4	77.5	19.1	3.5
Fabricated structural metal products...........	59,510	0.09	6.2	13.4	-46.7	6.0	12.0	79.2	18.0	2.8
Misc. fabricated metal products...............	173,569	0.27	45.4	68.7	-5.5	20.4	31.4	80.4	16.9	2.7
Not specified metal ind....	1,366	-	-60.7	-59.5	-64.6	21.3	23.6	74.0	22.0	3.9
Machinery, exc. electrical.....	262,510	0.41	18.0	23.2	-10.4	11.7	15.5	74.6	21.6	3.7
Farm machinery & equipment	21,023	0.03	-40.4	37.1	-72.8	4.3	9.3	67.4	25.3	7.2
Office, computing & accounting machines........	24,514	0.04	-7.5	16.8	-34.7	33.2	47.1	76.6	21.1	2.4
Miscellaneous machinery ...	216,973	0.34	35.0	37.4	16.9	10.0	11.6	75.2	21.3	3.5
Electrical machinery, equip. & supplies	289,671	0.45	36.0	38.7	33.1	47.6	48.7	78.9	18.0	3.1
Transportation equipment	262,798	0.41	2.6	6.5	-21.6	10.6	13.9	77.9	18.5	3.6
Motor vehicles & motor vehicle equipment	157,934	0.24	-20.8	-16.2	-46.3	10.4	15.3	77.8	18.5	3.6
Aircraft & parts	70,369	0.11	144.9	136.7	215.6	13.4	10.4	82.2	15.6	2.2
Ship & boat building & repairing...............	18,297	0.03	39.4	39.0	49.6	4.5	4.2	74.3	21.0	4.7
Railroad & misc. transportation equip.......	16,198	0.03	8.6	11.4	-16.9	7.4	9.6	66.2	26.4	7.4
Professional & photographic equipment & watches.......	61,561	0.10	18.3	39.2	-5.3	37.6	46.9	84.5	14.0	1.4
Professional equip. & supplies...........	41,973	0.06	47.9	61.0	30.5	37.8	42.9	84.5	14.0	1.6
Photographic equip. & supplies...........	10,857	0.02	24.2	77.9	-40.8	21.6	45.2	84.1	14.8	1.1
Watches, clocks, clock-work-oper. devices	8,731	0.01	-41.5	-42.3	-40.8	56.2	55.6	85.8	12.9	1.3

Table 10-7 (*Continued*)

	(1)	(2)	(3)	(4)	(5)	(6)	(7)	(8)	(9)	(10)
Misc. manufacturing ind.	126,139	0.20	-3.7	-14.9	14.0	45.8	38.7	80.6	17.0	2.5
Nondurable goods	2,077,693	3.21	-0.8	-0.4	-1.4	40.0	40.2	70.7	25.2	4.1
Food & kindred products	419,061	0.65	16.7	11.2	34.1	27.8	24.2	71.1	23.3	5.6
Meat products	123,621	0.19	38.6	17.0	205.8	25.3	11.5	73.2	21.2	5.6
Dairy products	54,983	0.09	-3.0	-1.9	-16.0	6.8	7.9	60.2	31.7	8.1
Canning & preserving fruits, vegetables, & sea foods	68,465	0.11	38.4	19.8	56.2	57.8	51.3	60.8	32.7	6.5
Grain-mill products	28,034	0.04	1.7	9.7	-49.1	6.8	13.6	53.3	35.2	11.5
Bakery products	41,051	0.06	37.6	62.8	8.0	36.1	46.0	87.6	10.8	1.6
Confectionery & related products	23,505	0.04	-1.0	3.5	-5.3	48.9	51.1	84.6	13.4	2.1
Beverage industries	43,697	0.07	-9.4	-5.5	-31.7	11.1	14.7	84.2	13.2	2.7
Misc. food preparations & kindred products	31,749	0.05	5.9	15.2	-18.0	21.8	28.1	72.1	24.2	3.7
Not specified food ind.	3,956	0.01	-9.1	-20.4	10.6	44.3	36.4	76.4	19.8	3.7
Tobacco manufactures	35,424	0.05	-28.7	-15.1	-35.6	60.0	66.4	68.8	26.3	4.9
Textile mill products	347,218	0.54	-23.5	-23.9	-23.0	47.2	46.9	53.3	41.1	5.5
Knitting mills	57,210	0.09	138.1	200.7	124.6	77.7	82.3	64.5	30.5	5.1
Dye'g. & fin. text., exc. wool & knit gds.	23,137	0.04	-4.6	0.9	-23.4	18.1	22.5	60.1	35.5	4.4
Floor covering, exc. hard surface	11,259	0.02	-42.2	-33.3	-51.4	41.4	49.3	52.0	40.2	7.8
Yarn, thread, & fabric mills	235,062	0.37	-34.4	-32.1	-37.0	43.8	45.6	49.4	44.8	5.8
Miscellaneous textile mill products	19,550	0.03	-26.2	-2.0	-48.5	36.4	52.1	74.5	22.1	3.4
Apparel & other fabricated textile products	400,261	0.62	1.0	-18.5	10.7	73.3	66.9	83.6	13.5	2.9
Apparel & accessories	362,477	0.56	0.1	-21.4	10.7	74.7	67.7	83.8	13.2	2.9
Misc. fabricated textile products	37,784	0.06	10.8	5.5	14.5	60.5	58.5	82.2	15.3	2.5
Paper & allied products	217,741	0.34	9.0	17.9	-13.7	22.2	28.1	67.4	29.2	3.4
Pulp, paper, & paperboard mills	106,621	0.16	10.1	11.7	-3.8	8.8	10.1	59.5	36.5	4.0
Paperboard containers & boxes	65,212	0.10	18.1	47.1	-17.2	31.7	45.1	79.9	17.5	2.6
Misc. paper & pulp prod.	45,908	0.07	-3.6	5.0	-14.1	39.9	44.8	74.6	22.6	2.8

Table 10-7 (*Continued*)

	(1)	(2)	(3)	(4)	(5)	(6)	(7)	(8)	(9)	(10)
Printing, publishing, & allied industries	91,960	0.14	34.8	44.3	21.5	37.5	41.6	88.6	10.1	1.3
Newspaper publishing & printing	10,832	0.02	80.5	72.9	118.5	20.2	16.7	83.8	14.5	1.7
Printing, publishing, & allied ind. exc. newspapers	81,128	0.13	30.4	40.2	17.9	39.8	44.0	89.5	9.3	1.2
Chemicals & allied products	185,925	0.29	14.7	20.8	-12.3	14.1	18.5	70.6	25.9	3.4
Synthetic fibers	22,125	0.03	-13.5	-13.8	-13.0	32.5	32.4	39.9	51.1	9.0
Drugs & medicines	16,820	0.03	36.4	87.4	-7.6	36.3	53.6	79.6	17.9	2.5
Paints, varnishes, & related products	16,429	0.03	5.9	9.1	-20.9	8.0	10.7	89.0	10.2	0.7
Misc. chemicals & allied products	130,551	0.20	20.1	24.8	-13.1	8.9	12.3	71.3	25.5	3.2
Petroleum & coal products	48,826	0.08	0.3	1.7	-48.6	1.5	2.9	77.8	19.9	2.2
Petroleum refining	43,461	0.07	2.8	4.7	-62.6	1.0	2.8	77.2	20.5	2.3
Misc. petroleum & coal products	5,365	0.01	-16.6	-18.0	16.7	5.5	3.9	83.5	15.2	1.3
Rubber & miscellaneous plastic products	150,403	0.23	14.5	15.0	13.1	26.7	27.0	77.2	19.4	3.4
Rubber products	103,150	0.16	-0.2	2.2	-7.9	21.9	23.7	76.9	19.4	3.7
Misc. plastic products	47,253	0.07	68.8	74.5	59.9	37.2	39.3	77.9	19.3	2.8
Leather & leather products	180,874	0.28	-19.7	-27.8	-8.3	47.1	41.3	72.2	23.7	4.1
Leather: tanned, curried, & finished	16,605	0.03	-41.6	-39.3	-53.8	12.9	16.3	71.0	25.8	3.3
Footwear, exc. rubber	136,777	0.21	-15.1	-24.3	-3.5	50.5	44.4	69.2	26.0	4.8
Leather products, exc. footwear	27,492	0.04	-23.3	-29.7	-15.9	51.3	46.8	88.6	9.7	1.6
Not specified manufacturing industries	9,219	0.01	-41.8	-7.9	-62.3	40.2	62.2	78.6	17.3	4.1
Manufacturing industries (ind. not reported)	632,724	0.98	-0.3	1.3	-8.1	16.3	17.7	72.2	23.6	4.2
Construction	89,530	0.14	34.9	36.4	-32.3	1.1	2.1	65.9	29.4	4.7
Railroads & railway express service	52,483	0.08	-42.3	-42.0	-62.6	0.8	1.3	72.8	24.1	3.1
Transportation, exc. railroad	33,357	0.05	16.2	19.7	-17.5	6.6	9.3	76.6	19.9	3.5
Communications, & utilities & sanitary service	48,650	0.08	-4.6	-0.7	-61.3	2.6	6.4	76.1	21.5	2.4

Table 10-7 (*Continued*)

	(1)	(2)	(3)	(4)	(5)	(6)	(7)	(8)	(9)	(10)
Wholesale & retail trade........	202,143	0.31	-4.9	-1.7	-12.6	26.5	28.9	74.3	21.2	4.5
Business & repair services......	67,091	0.10	42.9	-43.1	41.3	11.9	12.0	77.2	20.0	2.8
Personal services..............	13,936	0.02	-26.3	-21.3	-30.7	50.7	53.9	76.2	21.7	2.1
Public administration	43,668	0.07	-9.4	-8.2	-18.9	9.8	10.9	71.1	24.6	4.3
All other industries (ind. not reported).....................	81,866	0.13	14.8	12.9	19.2	30.8	29.6	65.6	27.1	7.3
Private household workers.......	1,725,826	2.67	22.3	-16.8	24.4	96.5	94.8	73.5	22.9	3.6
Baby sitters, private household	327,781	0.51	367.4	330.5	368.4	97.5	97.3	75.8	21.6	2.6
Housekeepers, private household	145,391	0.22	3.9	-60.2	6.4	98.6	96.2	76.0	19.8	4.1
Living in	55,431	0.09	5.0	5.3	5.0	98.9	98.9	82.5	14.0	3.5
Living out	89,960	0.14	3.3	-68.1	7.3	98.3	94.6	73.4	22.2	4.4
Laundresses, private household	39,754	0.06	-44.1	-68.4	-43.6	98.2	96.9	81.0	14.9	4.1
Living in.............	210	-	-67.4	-	-67.2	100.0	99.2	-	-	-
Living out............	39,544	0.06	-44.1	-68.3	-43.4	98.2	96.9	81.0	14.9	4.1
Private household workers (n.e.c.) ...	1,212,900	1.88	7.4	-21.5	9.1	95.9	94.3	72.9	23.4	3.8
Living in.............	103,309	0.16	-36.7	-44.8	-36.1	93.6	92.7	76.4	17.8	5.8
Living out............	1,109,591	1.72	14.8	-16.2	16.6	96.1	94.6	72.3	24.2	3.4
Service workers, exc. private household	5,444,962	8.42	26.7	9.3	48.2	52.3	44.7	83.4	14.9	1.7
Attendants hospital & other institutions.........	391,800	0.61	90.9	23.9	136.9	73.6	59.3	74.6	22.2	3.2
Attendants profess. & personal serv. (n.e.c.) ...	70,246	0.11	71.5	71.7	71.4	70.4	70.5	80.5	17.0	2.5
Attendants recreation & amusement ..	55,423	0.09	-6.4	-11.3	48.5	12.9	8.1	80.4	17.5	2.1
Barbers	178,968	0.28	1.0	-2.1	-	3.1	-	78.0	20.1	2.0
Bartenders	171,901	0.27	-11.4	-15.5	43.6	11.3	6.9	81.9	17.0	1.1
Boarding & lodging house keepers	29,250	0.05	1.0	-56.7	22.3	88.4	73.0	79.8	19.0	1.2
Bootblacks	9,417	0.01	-32.2	-32.7	-18.2	4.1	3.4	89.4	9.6	1.0
Chambermaids & maids, exc. private household	165,195	0.26	36.0	203.9	34.7	98.3	99.3	88.3	10.7	1.0
Charwomen & cleaners	179,691	0.28	50.5	20.7	70.1	68.3	60.5	80.9	17.0	2.1
Cooks, exc. private household......	562,062	0.87	28.6	3.4	48.7	64.4	55.7	86.4	12.4	1.2
Counter & fountain workers.........	157,514	0.24	81.3	6.6	151.8	71.5	51.4	89.4	9.6	0.9
Elevator operators	71,882	0.11	-19.4	-21.4	-14.7	32.0	30.2	93.7	5.5	0.8

Table 10-7 (*Continued*)

	(1)	(2)	(3)	(4)	(5)	(6)	(7)	(8)	(9)	(10)
Hairdressers & cosmetologists	301,020	0.47	45.4	109.8	39.9	88.7	92.2	90.4	8.8	0.8
Housekeepers & stewards, exc. private household	146,000	0.23	37.1	22.2	41.2	80.6	78.3	84.9	13.8	1.3
Janitors & sextons	593,757	0.92	29.8	28.0	43.9	13.0	11.8	78.2	19.4	2.4
Kitchen workers (n.e.c.) exc. private household	304,023	0.47	48.9	57.6	43.4	59.1	61.4	87.5	11.6	1.0
Midwives	922	-	-45.4	-25.5	-49.4	76.9	83.1	72.3	18.8	8.9
Porters	142,194	0.22	-12.2	-11.9	-27.2	1.9	2.2	95.9	3.8	0.3
Practical nurses	205,974	0.32	50.9	57.1	50.6	95.7	95.9	71.8	24.2	4.0
Protective service workers	689,562	1.07	19.9	17.3	158.4	4.0	1.8	83.6	14.6	1.8
Fireman, fire protection	137,884	0.21	24.6	24.8	-26.2	0.2	0.4	92.9	6.3	0.7
Guards, watchmen, & doorkeepers	244,486	0.38	2.9	2.1	39.4	3.0	2.2	75.8	21.0	3.2
Marshals & constables	5,909	0.01	-9.7	-10.6	22.3	3.8	2.8	52.8	44.2	3.0
Policemen & detectives	252,194	0.39	30.6	29.4	92.8	2.7	1.8	88.0	11.1	0.8
Government	235,888	0.36	36.1	34.8	129.2	2.3	1.4	88.1	11.0	0.8
Private	16,306	0.03	-18.1	-20.2	16.6	8.1	5.7	86.8	12.1	1.1
Sheriffs & bailiffs	23,930	0.04	29.4	28.2	57.7	5.0	4.1	69.4	26.5	4.1
Watchmen (crossing) & bridge tenders	25,159	0.04	195.5	68.6	2427.3	46.0	5.4	82.7	16.2	1.2
Ushers, recreation & amusement	14,265	0.02	-39.2	-36.2	-45.1	30.8	34.2	91.9	7.3	0.8
Waiters	825,606	1.28	23.5	-7.6	30.3	86.6	82.1	89.0	10.1	0.9
Service workers, exc. private household (n.e.c.)	178,290	0.28	-1.8	-14.1	19.9	44.2	36.2	87.1	11.8	1.2
Farm laborers & foremen	1,444,807	2.24	-40.2	-38.9	-46.2	16.8	18.7	15.4	36.3	48.2
Farm foremen	24,963	0.04	38.9	39.5	15.1	2.1	2.5	23.1	36.9	40.0
Farm laborers, wage workers	1,135,800	1.76	-23.1	-24.5	-9.1	10.5	8.9	17.0	40.2	42.8
Farm laborers, unpaid family workers	278,826	0.43	-69.4	-73.8	-61.3	44.1	34.9	3.3	10.6	86.1
Farm service laborers, self-employed	5,218	0.01	-42.7	-37.2	-88.2	2.2	10.8	34.8	44.5	20.6
Laborers, exc. farm & mine	3,107,531	4.81	-9.6	-9.4	-14.0	3.5	3.7	67.9	27.4	4.8
Carpenters' helpers, exc. logging & mining	36,306	0.06	-37.5	-38.1	-	0.9	-	53.4	37.3	9.2
Fisherman & oystermen	35,769	0.06	-50.5	-50.5	-55.4	1.3	1.5	40.9	55.5	3.6
Garage laborers & car washers & greasers	82,746	0.13	26.7	27.2	12.1	3.0	3.4	78.2	18.8	3.1

Table 10-7 (*Continued*)

	(1)	(2)	(3)	(4)	(5)	(6)	(7)	(8)	(9)	(10)
Gardeners, exc. farm and ground keepers	196,446	0.30	34.3	35.3	-8.4	1.5	2.3	73.2	23.8	2.9
Longshoremen & stevedores	55,780	0.09	-14.0	-13.5	-55.6	0.5	1.0	93.2	6.1	0.7
Lumbermen, raftsmen, & wood choppers	117,551	0.18	-31.8	-31.7	-41.7	0.8	0.9	14.1	69.7	16.1
Teamsters	19,657	0.03	-7.2	-6.2	-76.8	0.4	1.5	31.4	54.4	14.2
Truck drivers' helpers	29,675	0.05	-34.6	-35.2	-	0.9	-	85.9	12.4	1.7
Warehousemen (n.e.c.)	113,338	0.18	66.6	64.3	-	1.4	-	83.5	14.2	2.3
Laborers (n.e.c.)	2,420,263	3.74	-11.1	-10.9	-15.3	4.1	4.3	69.1	26.4	4.5
Manufacturing	862,417	1.33	-19.5	-19.5	-20.6	6.2	6.3	67.2	28.3	4.5
Durable goods	553,747	0.86	-18.5	-18.5	-18.7	4.4	4.4	66.4	29.2	4.4
Sawmills, planing mills & miscellaneous wood products	99,289	0.15	-36.1	-36.2	-32.2	2.7	2.5	32.9	57.2	10.0
Sawmills, planing mills & mill work	87,607	0.14	-37.0	-37.0	-33.2	1.8	1.7	30.0	59.6	10.3
Misc. wood products	11,682	0.02	-28.3	-28.0	-30.8	9.4	9.8	55.8	37.1	7.1
Furniture & fixtures	16,408	0.03	-12.5	-12.9	-6.7	8.0	7.5	57.6	35.7	6.7
Stone, clay, & glass products	74,334	0.11	-4.4	-3.8	-17.9	3.4	3.9	57.8	37.6	4.6
Glass & glass products	12,175	0.02	-8.3	-5.6	-34.3	6.8	9.4	62.6	33.9	3.5
Cement, & concrete, gypsum & plaster products	25,248	0.04	10.7	11.0	-20.8	0.6	0.8	61.6	34.0	4.4
Structural clay products	23,243	0.04	-12.7	-13.1	1.1	2.9	2.5	49.4	45.1	5.5
Pottery & related products	4,135	0.01	-34.7	-38.0	-7.9	15.7	11.2	59.2	36.4	4.4
Miscellaneous nonmetallic mineral & stone products	9,533	0.01	9.8	10.4	-11.6	2.3	2.9	61.6	34.1	4.3
Metal industries	223,696	0.35	-14.2	-14.1	-17.5	3.0	3.1	79.0	18.9	2.0
Primary metal industries	168,635	0.26	-17.8	-17.5	-38.7	1.0	1.4	79.2	19.0	1.8
Blast furnaces, steel works & rolling & finishing mills	108,655	0.17	-18.0	-17.7	-48.5	0.7	1.1	81.9	16.9	1.2
Other primary iron & steel ind.	37,281	0.06	-21.7	-21.4	-43.4	1.2	1.6	76.3	20.9	2.7
Primary nonferrous industries	22,699	0.04	-9.1	-9.1	-7.8	2.4	2.4	71.0	25.9	3.1
Fab'd metal ind. (ind. not spec. metal)	55,061	0.09	-0.8	-0.3	-5.9	8.9	9.3	78.4	18.7	2.9
Cutlery, hand tools, & other hardware	4,145	0.01	-50.3	-47.3	-60.7	18.2	22.9	75.3	20.4	4.2
Fabricated structural metal products	17,745	0.03	6.9	10.5	-51.5	2.6	5.8	78.3	19.3	2.5

Table 10-7 (*Continued*)

	(1)	(2)	(3)	(4)	(5)	(6)	(7)	(8)	(9)	(10)
Miscellaneous fabricated metal products	32,840	0.05	10.5	6.4	60.9	11.1	7.6	78.8	18.2	3.0
Not specified metal industries	331	-	-61.6	-63.0	-	10.0	6.5	79.2	18.1	2.7
Machinery, exc. electrical	40,996	0.06	-20.2	-19.9	-29.2	3.4	3.9	73.3	22.6	4.1
Farm machinery & equipment	5,993	0.01	-53.7	-53.7	-53.7	3.0	3.0	68.6	25.5	6.0
Office, computing & accounting machines	1,704	-	5.3	5.8	-	8.0	8.4	76.3	20.8	2.9
Miscellaneous machinery	33,359	0.05	-9.7	-9.1	-25.4	3.3	3.9	74.0	22.2	3.8
Electrical machinery, equipment & supplies	29,806	0.05	-5.5	-8.0	7.9	17.7	15.5	75.0	20.8	4.2
Transportation equipment	54,890	0.08	-17.5	-16.7	-35.1	3.2	4.0	79.3	17.7	3.0
Motor vehicles & motor vehicle equipment	31,956	0.05	-30.3	-29.1	-53.5	3.2	4.8	81.6	15.5	2.9
Aircraft & parts	5,568	0.01	56.8	56.9	55.7	5.4	5.4	75.6	21.7	2.7
Ship & boat building & repairing	12,292	0.02	-0.7	-1.2	42.1	1.8	1.2	80.3	17.1	2.6
Railroad & miscellaneous transportation equipment	5,074	0.01	6.6	5.5	46.4	4.0	2.9	66.2	28.8	5.0
Professional & photographic equipment, & watches	3,980	0.01	-9.1	-11.1	0.5	19.1	17.2	80.3	17.7	2.0
Professional equipment & supplies	2,836	-	13.4	12.2	19.4	18.7	17.7	80.1	18.0	1.9
Photographic equipment & supplies	842	-	-19.8	-23.5	7.2	15.9	11.9	81.6	15.5	2.8
Watches, clocks, clockwork-oper. devices	302	-	-63.5	-67.8	-48.7	31.8	22.6	78.2	21.8	-
Miscellaneous manufacturing industries	10,348	0.02	-23.9	-19.9	-38.2	17.6	21.7	72.1	23.9	4.0
Nondurable goods	306,611	0.47	-19.9	-19.9	-20.5	9.6	9.7	68.5	26.6	4.8
Food & kindred products	119,409	0.18	-18.9	-18.8	-20.1	7.4	7.5	69.3	24.9	5.9
Meat products	26,504	0.04	-22.4	-22.7	-19.6	9.5	9.1	73.8	20.5	5.8
Dairy products	16,534	0.03	-25.6	-25.6	-26.9	3.0	3.1	63.7	28.4	7.9
Canning & preserving fruits vegetables & sea foods	17,809	0.03	2.1	6.6	-17.4	15.2	18.8	57.9	35.2	6.9
Grain--mill products	15,823	0.02	-8.1	-8.1	-4.5	1.6	1.6	59.1	31.9	9.1
Bakery products	8,624	0.01	81.6	112.1	-13.7	11.5	24.3	85.2	13.3	1.6

Table 10-7 (*Continued*)

	(1)	(2)	(3)	(4)	(5)	(6)	(7)	(8)	(9)	(10)
Confectionery & related products........	3,063	-	-16.4	-15.4	-22.1	-	16.1	74.2	22.4	3.4
Beverage industries........	15,017	0.02	-19.9	-19.2	-37.4	2.9	3.7	81.1	15.8	3.1
Misc. food preparations & kindred products........	14,726	0.02	-45.8	-46.9	-8.7	5.2	3.1	69.5	25.8	4.7
Not specified food ind.....	1,309	-	-29.7	-22.9	-50.8	-	24.4	68.9	25.8	5.3
Tobacco manufactures........	5,395	0.01	5.7	22.1	-27.7	22.6	33.0	77.7	17.4	5.0
Textile mill products.......	36,704	0.06	-33.5	-33.8	-31.4	15.6	15.2	54.5	39.3	6.1
Yarn, thread, & fabric mills............	27,926	0.04	-33.7	-34.0	-32.3	15.7	15.3	51.3	42.2	6.5
Other textile mill products	8,778	0.01	-32.6	-33.3	-28.6	15.4	14.5	64.7	30.2	5.1
Apparel & other fabricated textile products	9,831	0.02	-5.3	-10.9	4.2	41.0	37.3	71.0	23.9	5.1
Paper & allied products	36,741	0.06	-16.6	-15.9	-26.5	6.2	7.1	64.3	31.5	4.2
Pulp, paper, & paperboard mills	23,395	0.04	-14.1	-13.4	-36.9	2.1	2.9	58.1	37.3	4.6
Paperboard containers & boxes............	8,660	0.01	-3.1	0.9	-25.9	11.4	14.9	77.7	19.1	3.2
Miscellaneous paper & pulp products	4,686	0.01	-40.8	-43.9	-18.9	17.0	12.4	74.1	22.1	3.8
Printing, publishing, & allied industries........	11,768	0.02	5.5	3.0	27.3	12.8	10.6	88.6	9.9	1.5
Chemicals & allied products ...	44,861	0.07	-12.5	-10.7	-43.7	3.3	5.2	68.5	27.5	4.0
Synthetic fibers	2,391	-	-21.8	-20.4	-40.4	5.2	6.8	39.8	53.2	7.0
Drugs & medicines	1,892	-	0.6	7.0	-31.6	11.3	16.6	75.0	21.3	3.8
Paints, varnishes, & related products	2,850	-	-36.7	-36.2	-46.7	4.6	5.5	87.7	10.4	1.9
Miscellaneous chemicals & allied products	37,728	0.06	-9.8	-8.0	-45.7	2.7	4.5	68.5	27.5	4.0
Petroleum & coal products	15,893	0.02	-36.4	-36.3	-42.7	1.1	1.2	76.8	20.7	2.5
Petroleum refining........	13,372	0.02	-40.3	-40.2	-46.4	0.9	1.0	75.6	21.8	2.6
Miscellaneous petroleum & coal products	2,521	-	-2.6	-1.6	-	2.2	3.2	83.7	14.8	1.5
Rubber & misc. plastic products	16,521	0.03	-17.4	-19.0	-3.6	12.3	10.5	76.7	19.8	3.4
Leather & leather products	9,488	0.01	-30.6	-33.1	-20.7	22.6	19.7	67.8	27.5	4.7
Not specified manufacturing ind.	2,059	-	-77.3	-77.2	-77.6	11.1	11.3	75.7	20.8	3.5

Table 10-7 (Continued)

	(1)	(2)	(3)	(4)	(5)	(6)	(7)	(8)	(9)	(10)
Nonmanufacturing industries (ind. not reported)	1,557,846	2.41	-5.6	-5.5	-8.2	3.0	3.1	70.2	25.3	4.5
Construction	612,465	0.95	1.2	1.4	-22.5	0.6	0.8	65.9	28.3	5.8
Railroads & railway express service	121,052	0.19	-54.0	-53.9	-56.5	2.3	2.5	65.9	30.6	3.5
Transportation, exc. railroad	81,419	0.13	0.4	1.7	-48.4	1.4	2.6	82.2	15.1	2.7
Communications, & utilities & sanitary service	116,287	0.18	-7.1	-6.8	-26.6	1.0	1.2	77.5	19.8	2.7
Wholesale & retail trade	334,991	0.52	31.9	33.2	9.8	4.9	5.9	74.0	22.0	4.0
Business & repair services	21,037	0.03	45.2	68.6	-62.5	4.6	17.9	78.0	19.7	2.2
Personal services	67,205	0.10	-4.8	-3.2	-21.8	7.2	8.8	67.7	29.0	3.4
Public administration	70,937	0.11	-22.5	-22.5	-24.5	2.7	2.8	79.2	18.4	2.4
All other industries (ind. not reported)	132,453	0.20	-8.7	-12.4	46.2	10.0	6.3	65.0	29.4	5.6
Occupation not reported	3,183,719	4.93	328.5	332.3	322.4	38.1	37.6	79.8	16.2	4.0

large population. The fact that they are small in numbers does not diminish their importance to the economy, but merely reflects the complexity of the economy. For example, only 27,000 airline pilots and navigators, 12,000 engineers, and 14,000 physicists provide highly specialized services that are just as essential to the economy as those of the 1,464,000 secretaries or the 1,557,000 truck and tractor drivers. Thus the listing of occupations in Table 10-7 may be regarded as a breakdown of the ways in which labor is divided in industrialized nations and an indication of how a comparatively few specialists can serve a large population.

2. There is wide diversity between the detailed occupations in the extent of female employment. In 1960 roughly one third of all employed workers were women. However, there were almost no women employed in the following occupations:

airplane pilots and navigators
engineers of all types
railroad conductors
officers
pilots and engineers aboard ship
blacksmiths
boilermakers
brickmasons or stonemasons
carpenters
cement or concrete finishers
cranemen
derrickmen and hoistmen
electricians
electrotypers
excavating
grading and road machine operators
construction foremen
foremen on railroad and railway express service
locomotive engineers and firemen
mechanics in a wide range of activities
millers
plasterers
plumbers and pipefitters
roofers and slaters
railroad switchmen and brakemen
truck and tractor drivers
firemen and firefighters
longshoremen
stevedores
lumbermen
raftsmen and woodchoppers
truck drivers' helpers
laborers at blast furnaces

laborers in petroleum refining plants
mine operatives
sailors and deckhands

These are all occupations in which 1 percent or less than 1 percent of the total employees are female. It is clear that women have managed to enter all occupations that do not involve arduous labor or some physical danger. However, there is a very long list of more or less desirable occupations in which women are comparatively underrepresented.

In contrast to this, there are some occupations in which women far outnumber men. Examples are:

Percent of work force female

Librarians	85.6
Professional nurses	97.5
Elementary school teachers	85.7
Attendants in physicians' and dentists' offices	97.6
Bookkeepers	83.7
File clerks	85.5
Receptionists	97.8
Secretaries	97.2
Stenographers	95.7
Telephone operators	95.8
Typists	95.1
Sales demonstrators	92.4
Milliners	90.6
Private household workers of all types	96.0
Boarding and lodging housekeepers	88.4
Chambermaids and maids outside private households	98.0
Housekeepers	80.6
Practical nurses	95.7

These occupations tend to be those dealing with young children or performing tasks that involve some amount of responsibility, but no major decision-making. A careful study of column 6 in Table 10-7 will reveal that women tend to be underrepresented in the major professional and technical occupations where great responsibility and highly specialized training are required.

Differential Growth in Employment among Occupations. Some occupations are being born or expanding while others are on the decline. Although the overall increase in employment in the 1950-1960 decade was 14.5 percent, employment in many of the professional and technical occupations increased by more than 100 percent. The following is a list of occupations in which there was a 100 percent or more increase in the number of persons during the decade:

designers
aeronautical engineers
industrial engineers
sales engineers
mathematicians
recreation and group workers

Clearly, the widely advertised inroads of mechanization and automation on the unskilled and semiskilled occupations are very genuine. Prospects for employment in the next generation for workers who are qualified only to work as operatives or laborers or even as certain low-category skilled workers are very unpromising indeed.

Race Composition. Much has been said about the exclusion of Negroes from participation in certain occupations. Columns 4 and 5 of Table 10-8 report what percentage of employees in each of the detail occupations were Negro in 1960 and 1950 respectively. This permits an analysis of the extent of underrepresentation of Negroes in the occupations and trends in the recent past. It is clear the Negroes are underrepresented in the white-collar group. This is due in part, of course, to the lesser degree of education that Negroes have. It is also due in part to outright discrimination. In all occupations requiring a high degree of technical training or responsibility, Negroes are underrepresented, and they tend to be overrepresented in occupations that are uncomfortable, dangerous, poorly paid, or otherwise undesirable.

Yet it must be pointed out that during the 1950-1960 decade very significant strides toward admitting Negroes to the upper socioeconomic strata appear to have been made. The following occupations seem to have a significantly higher percentage of Negro incumbents in 1960 than in 1950:

accountants and auditors
chemists
designers and draftsmen
engineers of all types
social welfare and recreation workers

elementary and secondary school teachers
medical and dental technicians
managers and officials in manufacturing and wholesale trade industries
bookkeepers
mail carriers
sales workers in retail trade
bakers
trainmen
derrickmen and hoistmen
foremen in manufacturing industries
linemen and servicemen for telegraph and telephone lines
mechanics and repairmen of automobiles
radio and television repairmen
airplane repairmen
skilled workers in the building trade and in the metal working industries

In fact, the progress toward removing outright discrimination, after allowance has been made for differences in education and technical preparation, was probably greater in the 1950-1960 decade than in any preceding half century. This is a movement that is still under way, and it is to be expected that by the 1970 census the statistics will show even more improvement as younger generations of better educated and better qualified Negroes enter the work force and seek employment in occupations that heretofore have been closed to them.

Age of Workers in the Various Occupations. Some occupations are held primarily by young workers; in other occupations older workers predominate. Table 10-8 shows the percentage of workers that fall in these broad age groups.

The following occupations tend to have extremely young workers:

sales workers
retail and door-to-door selling
private household workers
parking lot attendants
packers and wrappers
farm laborers
laborers outside manufacturing industries

The following occupations have a concentration of older workers:

clergymen
dentists
lawyers and judges
pharmacists
farmers and farm managers and officials of all types
real estate agents and brokers

Table 10-8 Detailed Occupation of the Experienced Male Labor Force (or Employed) by Selected Characteristics

Occupation	Age composition Median age Col 1	Age composition Percent under 20 Col 2	Age composition Percent 45 & over Col 3	Percent Negro 1960 Col 4	Percent Negro 1950 Col 5	Unemployment rate Total Col 6	Unemployment rate White Col 7	Unemployment rate Nonwhite Col 8	Percent self-employed Col 9	Median earnings Col 10	Percent worked 50 to 52 weeks Col 11
Total Male, employed	40.6	5.7	39.4	8.4	8.6	4.9	4.5	8.4	15.7	4,621	68.8
Professional, technical, & kindred workers	38.2	1.2	31.6	2.5	2.5	1.4	1.4	2.3	15.2	6,619	77.4
Accounts & Auditors............	40.1	0.5	36.5	0.6	0.3	1.0	1.0	1.0	13.0	6,611	88.6
Architects	41.5	0.3	39.9	0.8	0.6	0.8	0.7	1.0	42.2	8,753	87.4
Artists and art teachers	37.7	1.2	29.7	1.7	1.2	2.5	2.4	2.9	23.5	6,143	71.1
Authors, editors & reporters ...	39.1	1.5	34.7	0.9	0.8	2.2	2.2	4.7	12.6	6,833	80.4
Chemists	36.9	0.5	25.4	2.0	1.0	1.0	1.0	1.8	1.7	7,163	87.4
Clergymen	43.0	0.3	45.1	7.1	11.3	0.4	0.3	1.2	10.2	4,020	87.8
College pres., prof'rs & instr's (n.e.c.).........	39.6	0.3	34.2	2.5	2.6	0.4	0.4	0.7	0.6	7,207	58.4
Dentists.................	46.1	0.04	52.2	2.5	2.1	0.2	0.2	0.3	91.7	10,000 +	59.9
Designers & draftsmen	32.4	2.6	18.7	1.1	0.4	2.4	2.3	4.1	3.7	5,958	81.1
Engineers: aeronautical	36.0	0.1	15.8	0.6	0.2	1.9	1.8	3.2	0.2	9,059	90.3
Civil	40.2	0.5	37.6	0.8	0.4	1.8	1.8	2.6	5.4	7,701	86.7
Electrical	36.2	0.2	23.0	0.7	0.3	0.7	0.7	1.1	1.2	8,613	89.6
Mechanical............	38.8	0.2	29.3	0.4	0.3	1.3	1.3	2.6	2.3	8,437	88.8
Other technical engineers	38.7	0.2	28.4	0.3	0.2	1.1	1.0	2.5	4.2	8,304	89.9
Lawyers & judges	45.3	0.03	50.8	1.0	0.8	0.3	0.3	0.3	64.8	10,000 +	86.5
Musicians & Music teachers ...	35.8	6.7	29.5	7.0	7.4	4.7	4.3	9.5	22.7	4,653	42.6
Natural scientists (n.e.c.)	35.2	0.5	19.2	1.5	1.4	1.2	1.2	1.8	5.8	7,658	87.2
Pharmacists	45.4	0.3	50.8	1.7	1.4	0.5	0.5	1.5	39.2	7,202	86.6
Physicians & surgeons	43.2	0.05	44.9	2.0	2.1	0.2	0.2	0.3	66.7	10,000 +	77.6
Social scientists	38.1	0.4	29.6	1.6	1.3	0.9	0.9	0.3	5.6	7,674	85.2
Social, welfare, & recreation workers	36.2	4.7	30.0	9.8	6.3	2.5	2.5	2.6	1.0	4,961	74.1
Teachers: Elementary school	34.5	0.3	24.1	9.4	-	0.5	0.5	1.0	0.4	5,220	42.5
Secondary school	37.0	0.1	29.9	5.4	-	0.4	0.4	0.6	0.2	5,827	47.1
Teachers (n.e.c.)	37.6	1.9	30.9	4.5	6.6	1.4	1.3	1.8	6.1	5,359	59.2

Table 10-8 (*Continued*)

	1	2	3	4	5	6	7	8	9	10	11
Technicians: Medical and dental	34.6	3.3	24.3	8.0	3.8	1.9	1.8	2.3	11.0	4,503	78.7
Electrical & electronic	31.1	1.5	12.4	1.8	-	1.7	1.7	3.4	0.4	5,921	82.6
Other professional, technical& kindred workers	36.5	2.5	27.3	2.4	2.7	2.4	2.3	3.9	12.0	5,848	76.5
Farmers & farm managers	49.2	1.8	60.7	6.5	11.1	0.8	0.7	1.7	99.0	2,169	79.4
Managers, offices & proprietors exc. farm	45.4	0.4	51.0	1.4	1.6	1.4	1.4	2.9	37.1	6,664	87.4
Officials & insp's state & local administration	49.7	0.2	62.5	1.4	0.9	1.2	1.2	2.2	-	5,554	87.7
Other specified managers & officials	44.2	0.7	47.6	1.6	1.6	1.9	1.9	2.8	7.2	6,613	86.6
Mgrs., offs., & propr's (n.e.c) --salaried	43.3	0.6	44.8	0.9	1.0	1.4	1.3	3.4	-	7,389	90.1
Manufacturing	44.0	0.3	46.7	0.4	0.3	1.1	1.1	3.5	-	9,156	92.7
Wholesale & retail trade	41.3	1.0	39.3	0.9	1.1	1.4	1.3	3.5	-	6,067	89.6
Finance, insurance & real estate	43.5	0.1	46.0	1.0	0.9	0.6	0.6	1.3	-	7,971	92.7
Other industries (incl. not reported)	44.6	0.6	48.8	1.3	1.7	2.0	1.9	4.1	-	7,282	86.9
Mgrs., offs., & propr's (n.e.c) --self employed	48.1	0.2	59.3	1.9	1.9	1.3	1.2	2.7	99.7	5,764	84.1
Construction	44.5	0.1	48.3	1.8	1.7	2.4	2.4	6.0	99.9	6,577	68.4
Manufacturing	48.4	0.2	60.3	0.8	0.5	1.0	0.9	2.8	99.8	8,076	85.3
Wholesale trade	49.0	0.2	62.5	2.0	1.5	1.0	0.9	4.8	99.8	7,541	85.8
Eating & drinking places	48.4	0.2	60.8	3.8	4.0	2.0	2.0	2.2	99.5	4,886	83.1
Retail trade, exc. eating & drinking places	48.4	0.2	60.3	1.5	1.6	0.9	0.8	1.8	99.8	5,223	89.6
Other industries (ind. not reported)	49.1	0.2	62.0	2.7	2.8	1.2	1.1	2.3	99.6	5,907	83.0
Clerical & kindred workers	38.0	7.1	34.4	5.9	4.1	3.4	3.2	5.6	1.4	4,785	76.4
Bookkeepers	38.8	4.1	38.1	1.0	0.5	2.5	2.4	4.6	4.2	4,444	79.2
Mail carriers	40.4	1.3	33.9	10.4	7.5	2.5	2.3	3.9	-	5,289	85.9
Other clerical & kindred wrks.	37.7	7.7	34.2	5.9	4.1	3.5	3.3	5.8	1.3	4,736	75.6
Sales workers	39.2	11.3	36.7	1.6	1.5	2.5	2.5	5.6	16.7	4,987	75.4
Insurance agents, brokers, & underwriters	40.2	0.3	36.6	1.5	2.0	1.2	1.1	2.6	19.3	6,173	84.0
Real estate agents & brokers	50.5	0.2	63.3	1.7	1.7	1.3	1.3	3.1	47.8	5,978	74.4
Other specified sales workers	17.3	62.9	17.2	3.2	3.7	3.4	3.2	6.8	12.0	783	59.6

Table 10-8 (Continued)

	1	2	3	4	5	6	7	8	9	10	11
Sales workers (Con't)											
Salesmen & sales clerks (n.e.c)	39.7	7.6	37.3	1.4	1.2	2.7	2.6	5.9	14.9	4,982	76.0
Manufacturing	40.2	1.2	35.9	0.5	0.4	1.7	1.7	6.7	4.9	6,719	84.0
Wholesale trade	41.2	1.0	39.2	0.5	0.4	1.6	1.6	4.2	15.8	6,037	84.7
Retail trade	38.6	12.7	37.0	2.1	1.7	3.4	3.3	6.0	18.0	3,894	69.9
Other industries (incl. not reported)	40.5	3.8	38.2	1.0	1.0	3.1	3.1	6.4	14.1	5,548	75.2
Craftsmen, foremen, & kindred wkrs	41.8	1.9	41.1	4.2	3.6	5.4	5.2	8.3	9.4	5,240	67.9
Bakers	42.5	4.1	44.6	7.7	5.7	3.6	3.5	5.1	13.1	4,552	75.3
Blacksmiths, forgemen, & hammermen	47.9	1.3	57.1	4.9	4.6	5.4	5.5	4.9	19.2	4,655	59.9
Boilermakers	44.7	0.3	49.0	2.8	2.2	11.6	11.7	7.4	1.6	5,496	51.8
Cabinetmakers & patternmakers	42.5	2.1	43.5	1.9	2.2	4.3	4.2	9.5	14.6	5,142	68.2
Carpenters	43.4	2.2	45.8	4.4	3.8	11.4	11.3	12.0	20.8	4,164	38.9
Compositors & typesetters	40.2	3.7	39.6	2.2	1.4	1.6	1.6	3.1	6.8	5,758	82.2
Cranemen, derrickmen, & hoistmen	42.2	0.6	41.6	9.3	4.5	6.1	6.2	5.9	0.8	5,251	52.7
Electricians	40.8	1.0	37.9	1.5	1.1	5.1	5.1	5.2	7.6	5,959	70.1
Foremen (n.e.c.)	44.5	0.3	48.3	1.5	1.1	1.9	1.8	3.5	-	6,616	88.3
Manufacturing, durable goods	43.8	0.2	45.8	0.9	0.8	1.3	1.3	3.0	-	7,347	90.1
Mfg. nondurable goods, (incl. not specific manufacturing)	44.4	0.4	48.3	1.3	1.0	1.4	1.4	3.3	-	6,404	91.2
Nonmanufacturing ind. (incl. not reported)	45.3	0.3	50.9	2.2	1.5	2.7	2.7	3.7	-	6,107	84.6
Linemen & servicemen, telegraph, telephone, & power	33.7	0.9	18.4	1.2	0.9	1.3	1.2	3.5	-	6,000	91.0
Locomotive engineers	53.9	0.09	72.1	0.4	0.5	1.8	1.8	1.4	-	7,667	73.3
Locomotive firemen	39.3	0.9	31.7	2.3	4.1	5.2	5.2	4.8	-	5,983	61.7
Machinists & job setters	42.2	1.4	41.9	2.3	1.5	3.1	3.0	5.6	1.1	5,498	75.4
Masons, tile setters & stone cutters	37.9	2.3	31.1	11.4	10.4	10.3	10.1	11.7	19.0	4,793	31.0
Mechanics & repairmen:											
Airplane	37.9	0.6	24.4	2.9	1.5	3.7	3.6	5.0	0.7	5,898	86.2
Automobile	38.4	4.2	31.6	6.5	5.9	3.0	2.8	4.8	16.4	4,298	73.9
Radio & TV	35.8	4.4	23.2	3.8	3.3	3.1	2.9	5.8	34.7	4,304	76.6
Other mechanics & repairmen, & loan fixers	42.0	2.4	41.9	4.9	3.4	3.5	3.4	5.2	4.9	4,836	75.0
Millnights	44.8	0.2	49.2	1.7	1.7	5.2	5.1	8.2	0.3	5,995	62.8

Table 10-8 (*Continued*)

	1	2	3	4	5	6	7	8	9	10	11
Mechanics & repairmen (Con't)											
Molders, metal	41.0	1.4	38.0	22.3	18.2	6.1	5.0	9.8	0.6	4,759	63.2
Painters (const.) paperhangers, & glaziers	45.2	3.0	50.4	6.8	5.4	10.7	10.6	12.2	32.6	3,727	38.6
Plasterers & cement finishers	39.8	1.8	35.9	21.7	19.3	13.5	12.8	16.0	17.5	4,646	30.4
Plumbers & pipe fitters	42.2	1.1	41.9	3.3	3.0	8.0	8.1	6.5	15.0	5,593	61.6
Printing craft, exc. compos. & typesetters	38.6	3.1	34.6	2.2	1.2	1.8	1.8	3.6	2.8	6,208	81.7
Shoemakers & repairers, except factory	51.8	3.5	66.2	12.1	9.3	1.8	1.5	3.9	63.1	2,899	75.5
Stationary engineers	44.0	0.6	47.3	1.7	1.9	2.1	2.0	3.8	1.0	6,296	85.2
Structural metal workers	41.1	1.2	37.5	3.9	2.4	12.0	12.1	9.5	1.8	5,543	46.2
Tailors & furriers	56.4	0.7	73.0	6.9	6.2	4.6	4.7	3.0	31.5	4,060	65.1
Tinsmiths, coppersmiths, & sheet metal workers	39.4	1.7	33.2	1.8	1.1	6.9	6.9	4.8	4.0	5,485	67.8
Toolmakers, & die makers & setters	42.1	0.6	40.6	0.8	0.3	2.3	2.2	4.5	1.7	6,527	77.7
Other craftsmen & kindred workers	40.9	2.6	39.0	4.6	3.9	9.4	9.1	13.9	10.3	4,800	60.7
Operatives & kindred workers	38.4	5.8	33.5	10.3	9.1	6.4	6.2	8.2	3.9	4,299	62.5
Apprentices	22.9	24.8	2.2	2.2	1.8	5.8	5.8	7.6	-	3,486	52.3
Assemblers	36.9	5.2	30.2	6.8	-	8.6	8.1	14.2	0.3	4,491	56.1
Attendants, auto service & parking	25.8	27.5	18.5	9.2	8.9	6.9	6.8	7.7	5.9	2,296	51.4
Brakemen & switchmen, railroad	41.1	0.7	38.4	2.8	2.6	4.2	4.1	7.4	-	5,642	65.5
Bus drivers	44.7	3.7	49.1	10.1	3.9	1.7	1.7	1.9	2.3	4,411	65.2
Checkers, examiners, & inspectors, mfg.	40.5	2.0	37.9	3.2	-	4.5	4.4	8.2	0.1	5,240	70.5
Fillers, grinders, & polishers, metal	41.7	2.0	40.8	7.5	5.9	6.2	5.6	12.6	2.9	5,051	62.0
Furnacemen, smeltermen & pourers	41.8	1.2	40.8	22.8	19.4	6.0	5.0	9.2	0.3	5,096	48.3
Laundry & dry cleaning operatives	41.1	7.1	41.0	33.3	31.7	5.4	5.1	5.9	16.8	2,948	68.7
Meat cutters, exc. slaughter & packing house	41.1	4.5	41.3	3.6	3.7	2.7	2.6	5.4	14.2	4,644	79.1
Mine operatives & laborers (n.e.c)	40.2	2.4	37.1	4.6	6.5	12.3	12.2	14.0	2.7	4,240	45.0
Packers & wrappers (n.e.c.)	32.4	19.4	27.1	15.4	-	8.5	8.0	10.8	0.5	3,333	56.1
Painters, exc. construction & maintenance	38.5	4.7	34.2	10.3	7.1	6.4	6.1	9.0	4.2	4,245	62.5

Table 10-8 (*Continued*)

	1	2	3	4	5	6	7	8	9	10	p 11
Operatives & kindred workers (Con't)											
Power station operators	44.0	0.5	47.2	1.3	0.7	1.3	1.3	1.6	0.6	6,238	89.8
Sailors & deck hands	38.8	3.9	33.2	10.5	10.8	19.5	20.0	16.3	0.3	4,294	36.0
Lawyers	40.5	3.9	39.7	17.8	22.1	8.3	8.4	7.7	6.3	2,775	47.6
Spinners and weavers, textile	40.6	3.8	39.9	1.1	0.7	4.3	4.3	7.3	0.8	3,599	71.4
Stationary firemen	47.3	0.6	56.1	12.3	13.8	5.0	4.8	5.8	0.1	4,800	75.2
Taxicab drivers & chauffeurs	45.6	1.0	51.7	18.3	14.6	4.9	4.8	5.1	12.6	3,272	61.2
Truck drivers & deliverymen	37.1	5.3	28.5	12.7	11.2	5.9	5.8	6.8	7.3	4,221	65.1
Welders & flame- cutters	39.9	1.6	33.8	5.6	3.7	6.5	6.2	11.3	3.8	5,026	60.5
Other spec. operatives & kindred workers	40.5	4.9	39.7	7.6	6.7	8.1	8.1	8.1	2.4	4,240	57.3
Operatives & kindred workers (n.e.c.)	38.7	4.9	34.6	10.3	8.6	6.3	6.0	8.9	1.8	4,374	64.0
Manufacturing	38.6	4.4	34.3	9.5	.7.9	6.1	5.8	8.7	1.0	4,447	64.4
Durable goods	38.9	3.7	34.4	9.8	8.2	6.7	6.4	9.4	1.0	4,542	‐60.2
Saw & planing mills, & misc. wood products	38.9	5.3	37.0	18.8	22.8	6.7	6.8	6.2	3.0	3,067	56.2
Furniture & fixtures	37.1	7.0	33.6	9.3	6.9	6.6	6.4	8.7	1.6	3,229	60.9
Stone, clay & glass products	38.4	3.2	33.3	10.2	7.5	6.3	6.1	7.9	1.4	4,542	64.3
Primary metal industries	40.7	1.7	37.9	15.0	13.0	6.3	6.0	8.4	0.2	4,821	48.9
Fabricd metal ind. (incl.not specific)	38.0	4.0	32.1	8.0	5.5	7.4	7.2	9.7	0.9	4,512	63.4
Machinery, except electrical	39.5	3.8	35.5	4.2	2.6	5.9	5.6	11.4	0.7	4,795	64.7
Electrical machinery equipment & supplies	37.1	4.1	29.8	5.4	2.7	4.9	4.7	8.2	0.2	4,802	71.4
Motor vehicles & motor vehicle equipment	39.4	2.1	34.6	14.0	9.6	8.6	7.5	14.5	0.1	4,994	43.1
Transportation equipment except motor vehicle	39.2	3.0	33.9	8.0	5.0	8.7	8.6	10.5	0.2	4,951	67.7
Other durable goods	38.9	5.5	35.4	6.1	4.0	6.1	5.9	9.6	3.7	4,118	67.0
Nondurable goods	38.3	5.1	34.1	9.1	7.6	5.3	5.0	7.8	0.9	4,316	69.6
Food & kindred products	38.2	6.1	34.4	14.7	12.6	7.0	6.5	9.4	1.9	4,248	68.1
Yarn, thread, & fabric mills	39.0	6.1	36.4	5.0	3.6	4.0	4.0	4.4	0.2	3,155	71.5
Knitting & other text mill prod	39.0	5.6	36.5	7.3	3.7	5.9	5.7	7.9	0.5	3,493	65.4
Apparel & other fab'd textile products	41.4	6.4	42.9	7.3	5.2	8.6	8.4	9.9	1.9	3,804	52.2

Table 10-8 (Continued)

	1	2	3	4	5	6	7	8	9	10	11
Nondurable goods (Con't)											
Paper & allied products	35.7	3.2	27.4	6.7	6.4	3.0	2.9	5.0	0.2	4,920	76.6
Chemicals & allied products	38.4	1.9	30.9	9.6	12.5	3.0	2.7	5.7	0.3	5,306	80.5
Other nondurable goods	38.5	6.0	34.7	7.6	8.9	5.3	5.1	7.7	0.6	4,541	67.9
Not specified manufacturing ind's	34.5	7.6	27.9	19.9	10.4	10.8	10.6	11.8	1.9	3,543	58.4
Nonmanufacturing industries (incl. not reported)	38.8	7.5	36.0	14.6	12.7	7.6	7.2	9.4	6.2	3,950	61.9
Transportation, communication & other public utilities	43.2	2.1	45.6	11.5	10.7	5.1	4.7	7.8	0.7	4,669	74.0
Wholesale & retail trade	36.8	10.9	33.2	17.2	13.2	6.9	6.5	8.8	4.4	3,443	62.1
Other industries (incl. not reported)	37.4	8.2	32.7	14.7	13.8	9.2	8.9	10.4	10.0	3,698	55.7
Private Household workers	47.2	19.6	54.1	44.7	49.3	6.1	5.8	6.4	0.6	1,078	47.0
Service workers except private household	43.4	9.2	47.0	19.5	19.6	5.3	4.9	7.1	8.0	3,310	66.1
Barbers	48.8	1.3	58.7	8.7	8.5	1.0	0.9	1.7	56.2	3,716	71.1
Charwomen, janitors & porters	48.5	8.3	57.6	37.2	40.6	5.5	4.8	6.5	1.6	2,756	64.6
Cooks except private household	42.8	7.3	45.4	21.5	22.9	7.3	7.4	6.9	9.9	3,397	62.1
Elevator operators	52.2	3.5	65.7	21.4	19.1	5.4	5.3	5.9	-	3,359	71.7
Firemen, fire protection	38.6	0.3	29.0	1.9	1.3	0.8	0.7	4.1	-	5,469	93.2
Guards & watchmen	52.8	1.4	68.6	5.4	4.2	5.3	5.3	5.6	0.2	3,950	73.3
Policemen, sheriffs, & marshals	38.7	0.1	31.6	3.4	1.9	1.1	1.1	1.5	0.6	5,210	89.5
Waiters, bartenders, & counter workers	40.8	12.7	41.4	12.2	12.4	6.9	6.6	8.6	15.8	2,975	55.6
Other service workers, except private household	33.5	23.0	33.3	22.1	21.1	8.2	7.7	9.5	5.6	2,062	50.5
Farm laborers and foreman	31.2	26.0	30.2	21.4	18.5	6.8	6.6	7.4	0.4	1,066	42.2
Farm laborers:											
Unpaid family workers	18.3	63.9	9.3	12.6	19.4	2.0	1.8	3.3	-	649	51.1
Except unpaid, & farm foremen	34.2	20.4	33.4	22.7	18.1	7.5	7.4	7.7	0.5	1,124	41.8
Laborers, except farm & mine	37.4	13.1	34.9	24.9	25.2	12.0	11.8	12.5	4.7	2,948	44.7
Fishermen & oystermen	42.9	5.7	45.6	8.0	8.2	12.8	11.1	24.1	58.9	2,395	32.4
Longshoremen & stevedores	44.8	1.4	49.6	34.5	34.2	8.0	6.9	9.8	0.4	4,710	42.8
Lumbermen, raftsmen, & wood choppers	36.6	8.9	31.5	30.8	25.4	13.7	16.0	8.4	23.9	1,748	28.5
Other specified laborers	36.7	16.2	35.5	23.7	25.4	9.6	9.3	10.5	8.7	2,566	48.1

Table 10-8 (*Continued*)

	1	2	3	4	5	6	7	8	9	10	11
Farm laborers (Con't)											
Laborers (n.e.c.)	37.3	13.1	34.4	24.8	25.4	12.4	12.1	13.1	2.2	3,049	45.0
Manufacturing	37.5	6.6	33.4	23.7	24.7	10.0	9.9	10.2	0.2	3,623	49.4
Durable goods	38.1	5.4	34.4	23.7	25.4	10.3	10.3	10.4	0.2	3,668	43.7
Furniture, saw & planing mills & miscellaneous wood products ..	37.2	7.9	34.4	30.0	36.0	9.8	10.6	8.1	0.5	2,395	44.7
Stone, clay, & glass products ..	36.5	5.0	30.6	19.7	18.4	10.4	10.7	9.0	0.4	3,705	52.5
Primary metal industries	39.0	2.9	35.5	26.4	27.2	9.8	9.6	10.2	-	4,040	31.5
Fabric'd metal industries (ind. not specified)	37.7	5.8	33.9	18.0	15.8	12.0	12.2	11.3	0.2	3,779	50.3
Machinery including electrical	37.7	7.4	34.9	13.4	11.6	9.7	9.3	12.1	0.1	3,962	55.6
Transportation equipment	39.5	4.1	36.3	27.9	26.8	12.3	10.9	15.6	0.1	4,218	44.3
Other durable goods	36.0	12.4	32.8	12.5	11.0	9.6	9.4	10.9	0.3	3,345	56.2
Nondurable goods	36.3	9.0	31.5	23.5	23.7	9.3	9.1	9.8	0.2	3,533	60.3
Food & kindred products	35.8	10.3	31.1	21.8	20.6	11.7	11.4	12.7	0.2	3,368	56.2
Textile mill products & apparel	36.3	12.8	33.7	22.7	20.3	7.5	7.9	6.0	0.1	2,639	60.2
Chemicals & allied products	37.2	4.3	31.0	30.2	34.5	6.9	6.8	7.2	0.1	3,987	63.9
Other nondurable goods	36.5	8.2	31.2	22.7	23.1	7.9	7.6	9.2	0.1	4,071	64.0
Not specified manufacturing industries	34.4	6.8	28.0	35.1	22.3	17.0	15.6	19.4	-	3,129	52.5
Nonmanufacturing industries (incl. not reported)............	37.2	16.5	35.0	25.4	25.7	13.6	13.3	14.5	3.2	2,680	42.8
Construction................	38.6	7.4	35.6	25.9	25.3	18.4	18.1	19.4	3.8	2,965	34.8
Railroads & railway express service	48.1	1.0	59.0	27.8	27.9	11.3	10.9	12.3	0.1	4,024	60.9
Transportation except railroad	36.7	7.1	30.7	21.0	20.4	10.1	9.5	12.3	3.0	3,714	53.8
Communication, & utilities & sanitary service	40.2	4.1	39.0	30.7	24.0	5.6	5.8	5.2	3.3	3,433	71.0
Wholesale & retail trade	21.6	46.4	18.9	17.9	20.5	9.9	9.6	11.4	0.9	1,318	38.7
Other industries (incl. not reported)	40.2	16.6	41.6	31.2	32.1	11.5	11.5	11.4	6.1	1,841	44.2
Occupation not reported	37.8	9.7	35.2	15.5	11.1	7.8	7.1	11.3	2.1	4,114	63.4

Source: U.S. Census of Population: 1960. Detailed Characteristics, U.S. Summary, Tables 204, 205, 206, 208.

blacksmiths and hammermen
locomotive engineers
painters
paperhangers and glaziers
shoemakers and repairmen
tailors and furriers
taxi drivers
private household workers
barbers
charwomen
elevator operators
guards and watchmen
laborers in railroad and railway express service

Some of the occupations in which elderly people are found are those that are dying out because of technological change. Others are jobs that older men and women who are drawing retirement pensions can hold part-time, or full-time as a supplement to their income.

Self-Employment. The various occupations differ widely in the extent to which they permit the person to be self-employed. Column 9 of Table 10-8 reports the percentage of those in each occupation that are self-employed. It may be surprising to discover that only 15 percent of all professional and technical workers are self-employed and that even in some of the occupations that are widely regarded as being manned by persons who work entirely for themselves a high percentage are not self-employed. For example, only two thirds of lawyers and judges are self-employed, two-thirds of physicians and surgeons, 42 percent of architects, and 39 percent of pharmacists. The only groups of self-employed persons remaining in the economy are farmers and farm managers and managers of private businesses in wholesale and retail manufacturing, trade construction, and other industries.

On the other hand, self-employment has not disappeared from any of the major occupational groups: 16.7 percent of all sales workers, 9.4 percent of all craftsmen, and even some categories of operatives are self-employed. Self-employment is found even among the labor group: 59 percent of fishermen and oystermen and 24 percent of lumbermen, raftsmen, and woodchoppers are self-employed. The desire to "go into business for oneself" is still very widely dispersed throughout the economy. However, the trend in business organization has been one that has steadily increased the proportion of wage and salary workers and decreased the proportion of those who are self-employed.

Full-Time and Part-Time Work. Some occupations provide full-time employment, whereas others furnish their incumbents with only part-time work. The following is a list of occupations in which less than one half of the workers had full-time employment (50 to 52 weeks) during the year preceding the 1960 census:

musicians and music teachers
elementary school teachers
carpenters
masons
tile setters and stonecutters
painters
paperhangers and glaziers
structural metal workers
furnacemen
smeltermen and pourers
mine operatives and laborers
sailors and deckhands
operatives in primary metal industries
private household workers
farm laborers and foremen

In the unskilled, nonfarm categories the occupations in which persons were unable to obtain full-time employment were many. Thus these occupations not only were among the lowest-paid in the economy, but also among those that provide much part-time work. Tables 10-7 and 10-8 give information about the urban and rural distribution and the income of these various occupations. These data will be discussed in a later chapter.

Unemployment. The extent to which workers in each of the occupations become unemployed varies widely. In the 1960 census, 4.9 percent of all workers were reported as being unemployed. Yet the rate of unemployment among the professional, technical, and white-collar occupations was very low indeed, whereas among occupations low in scale it was very high. Among the skilled workers, only certain categories of occupations had high rates of unemployment, and in general these represented occupations connected with technical obsolescence or seasonal employment. Unemployment rates of 10 percent or more were found among the following occupations:

boilermakers
carpenters

masons
printers
plasterers
structural metal workers
mine operatives and laborers
sailors and deckhands

There is also a long list of occupations in the operative and labor category that have above-average unemployment rates.

Table 10-8 reports the rate of unemployment for white and nonwhite workers separately. Much has been written about the high rate of unemployment among the nonwhite workers. This table permits us to gain some insight into the extent to which this high rate of unemployment is due to apparent racial discrimination and the extent to which it is due to the fact that nonwhite workers tend to be concentrated in occupations low in the socio-economic scale where the rate of unemployment is high irrespective of the race of the worker. If there were no discrimination, the rate of unemployment shown in column 7 of Table 10-8 would be approximately equal for white and nonwhite workers in each of the detailed occupations. When we go down the list making this comparison, we arrive at the finding that although the rate of unemployment for the nonwhite worker is higher than that for the white worker in all but a few instances, the difference is much smaller than one would be led to expect by the overall difference in unemployment rates for white and nonwhite. In a few instances, such as sailors and deckhands, the rate of unemployment among the nonwhite is lower than among the white population. *In fact, if we study the table carefully, we are led to the conclusion that the rate of discrimination as reflected in unemployment is relatively higher in the upper occupational strata than in the lower.* Nevertheless, the fact remains that for most of the detailed occupational categories, nonwhite workers suffer from a significantly higher rate of unemployment than the white workers. This may be due in part to the fact that they have less education, less skill, possibly less experience, and less seniority. It is apparent, however, that racial discrimination, either overt or covert, is also a factor. The following are occupations in which the rate of

unemployment for nonwhite workers is more than twice that for white workers:

authors
editors and reporters
clergymen
mechanical engineers
musicians and music teachers
pharmacists
elementary school teachers
electrical and electronic technicians
farmers and farm managers
managers and officials in manufacturing industries
managers and officials in wholesale and retail trade
finance, insurance, and real estate managers
self-employed officials and proprietors
clerical and sales workers of all types
cabinetmakers
telephone and telegraph linemen
radio and television repairmen
tool and diemakers
grinders and polishers
meat cutters
operatives of machinery in factories manufacturing machinery
operatives in factories manufacturing chemicals and allied products
charwomen and janitors
firemen

It must be emphasized again that at the very bottom of the labor category the high rate of unemployment applies almost equally to whites and nonwhites. For example, for laborers taken as a whole the unemployment rate was 11.8 percent for white, 12.5 percent for nonwhite. We conclude therefore that much but not nearly all of the higher rate of unemployment among nonwhites is due to their concentration in occupations where there is a decline in employment opportunities.

10.7. Occupational Mobility

In most economies the individual is free to terminate his employment at one establishment and negotiate for work at another. As a consequence, there is much job-changing, or "labor force turnover." It includes not only the shifting of work force participants from one job to another, but also the entrance of new workers into the work force and the withdrawal of old workers. The study of job-changing by individuals is an important branch of work force analysis which, as will be illustrated below, is of fundamental importance for some lines of research that normally are not considered a part of demography. The labor economists call it the study of "labor mobility," but the sociologists tend to equate it with the phenomenon of "social mobility."

Labor mobility, of course, involves both industries and occupations. A person's first occupation on entering the labor force marks the status at which he began. This occupation may be either an old post that was previously occupied by a retiring worker or a new post created because of new economic growth. If it is an old post, its filling probably is not one of direct replacement, but takes the form of a chain reaction. If the vacated post is one that is high in the occupational hierarchy, it will be filled with an experienced worker who had been working at a level slightly below. This will leave a vacancy which, in turn, will be filled by someone who was still lower in the scale. By such successive promotions one departure can generate a substantial amount of occupational shifting.

Occupational mobility, therefore, is the changing of individual workers from one occupational classification to another. Social scientists are keenly interested in this phenomenon for several reasons, independently of its implications for work force study.

1. *As a measure of social change.* Occupational mobility is a sensitive indicator of social change. If people abandon a given occupation and rush to enter another, it is indicative of a major change in economic structure. If a new generation obtaining first employment enters occupations radically different from those in the established occupational structure, this also is indicative of social change.

2. *As a measure of intragenerational mobility.* Occupational mobility is a good index of the changing social status of individuals or their "social mobility." Persons who move from low-status occupations to higher-status occupations usually experience a corresponding favorable change in esteem within the community at large. Conversely, a person who experiences a sharp fall from a high-status occupation to a low-status one, suffers socially to a corresponding degree. This type of mobili-

ty is called "intragenerational" (personal) mobility and is measured by comparing the occupational status of the same persons at two different dates. For example, the first full-time occupation of the individual when he first enters the work force may be compared with his present occupation.

3. *As a measure of intergenerational mobility and "social inheritance."* Successful parents seek to impart to their offspring as much of their own social status as possible, while less successful parents strive to help their children arrive at a much higher position than they were able to attain. If the first group is successful, a disproportionately large proportion of their offspring will also be of high status, while if the second group is unsuccessful, a disproportionately large share of their offspring will have the low status of their parents. High-status parents seek to perpetuate their high status across generations by the transfer of wealth or by gaining favorable consideration for their child to climb rapidly into an occupational position of high status. Low-status parents seek to obtain a college or postgraduate education in a professional school for their child, in order that he may have the qualifications necessary to enter a high-status post. High-status families provide their children with superior education at famous schools in order to assist in the inheritance process. The success or failure that various social strata experience in transmitting their status or in helping their children to climb to a higher status is usually measured by comparing the occupation of sons with the occupation of their fathers and then computing measures of "intergenerational mobility."

It would not be appropriate here to review the very substantial sociological and psychological literature pertaining to social mobility. It is, however, the objective of this section to point out that *occupational mobility has been and still is used as the principal indicator of social mobility.* For this reason, it is of interest and significance far beyond the limits of the fields of labor economics and economic demography. When demographers explore this phenomenon, they are helping to build a foundation for a major branch of social research. (Oftentimes, the sociologists and psychologists who become interested in the problem of social mobility are so poorly informed about work force statistics and the contents of the occupational classification that they naïvely make assumptions about the data and interpretations of results that are not warranted. For this reason, the study of social mobility needs a continuously strong demographic element.)

4. *As a dimension of personality study.* Persons who rise from a very low to a very high position within a short time are thought to be of a different personality structure than are those who begin at a particular level and spend their entire lifetime at that level. And both are thought to have different personalities than does the person who sinks in the occupational status scale from a high to a low level. It has been hypothesized that the person who is highly mobile upwardly will sacrifice many normal human values in the interests of "getting ahead." He may postpone marriage to a late age, have few children, and neglect his homelife in order to gain promotions as rapidly and as large as possible. Conversely, the man who is failing at his occupational career may find consolation and compensation in fathering a large family, in being an extraordinarily strong supporter of his local community or neighborhood, in being a strong church member, and so on. Or he may be embittered and withdrawn. Research in this area requires a combination of occupational mobility analysis and psychological testing and measurement techniques for assessing personality differences. Here, also, the demographer must lay the factual foundation.

Unfortunately, the systematic study of occupational mobility is of comparatively recent origin. Such studies require data showing not only the present occupation of individuals, but also their occupation at some earlier date. For studies of occupational inheritance, the occupation of the father at the time the son was 16 to 18 years of age must be known. For studies of "intragenerational" (lifetime) social mobility, at least the occupation of the first full-time job and the present occupation, but preferably a complete occupational history, must

be known. Data of this type were collected under the sponsorship of the Social Science Research Council shortly after World War II as the Six-City Labor Mobility Study. Other sample surveys were taken of individual places, such as Oakland, California. Individual researchers had extracted data on occupational mobility from records, such as marriage records where the occupations of the person and of his parent were recorded. Since the war, studies have been made in England and other nations around the world as well as in the United States.

Nationwide data on social mobility, both intergenerational and intragenerational, were first obtained in March 1962 by the U.S. Bureau of the Census as a supplement to its Current Population Survey. The enumeration of father's occupation at the time the son was 16 years of age and of the first full-time occupation of males was made by the Census on behalf of a research project sponsored by the National Science Foundation and directed by Otis Dudley Duncan and Peter M. Blau. The basic occupational mobility tabulations from this survey are reported in Tables 10-9, 10-10, and 10-11.

If occupational mobility were zero, all of the statistics in the three mobility tables would fall in the diagonal, and would be 100 percent. The cells above the diagonals in these tables represent workers who are currently in a lower-status occupation than the one they occupied formerly (or was occupied by their father). For this reason, the portion of the tables above the diagonal represents *downward* social mobility. The portion of the tables below the diagonal represents *upward* social mobility. (By temporal analogy, the same argument holds for Table 10-11.) It is clear that there is a great deal of occupational inheritance and immobility at all levels, because a disproportionately large share of the members of every occupational category had their origin (either intergenerationally or intragenerationally) in the same category. But it is equally evident that there is a very substantial amount of upward and downward mobility. A major share of the mobility is between occupations that lie near each other in the array, although not an

Table 10-9 Current Occupation by Father's Occupation—Noninstitutional Male Population 25 to 64 Years Old, for the United States: March 1962 (Percent Distribution)

Father's occupation	Total population 25 to 64 years old	Current occupation										
		Professional, technical, and kindred workers	Managers, officials, and propr's, except farm	Sales workers	Clerical and kindred workers	Craftsmen, foremen, and kindred workers	Operatives and kindred workers	Service workers, including private household	Laborers, except farm and mine	Farmers and farm managers	Farm laborers and foremen	Not in experienced civilian labor force
Total..............	100.0	11.6	14.9	4.7	6.1	19.2	17.5	5.5	6.4	5.2	1.7	7.2
Professional, technical, and kindred workers..........	100.0	38.9	16.7	8.6	6.6	8.3	9.8	2.9	1.9	1.2	0.4	4.7
Managers, officials, and proprietors, except farm...	100.0	20.3	32.1	8.5	6.6	13.1	8.0	2.4	1.8	0.9	0.3	6.0
Sales workers.........	100.0	18.3	28.3	14.1	5.8	11.2	9.8	3.0	1.9	1.6	0.1	5.9
Clerical and kindred workers	100.0	25.7	16.3	7.2	8.8	15.5	8.4	5.6	2.8	1.3	-	8.4
Craftsmen, foremen, and kindred workers...........	100.0	12.1	15.3	4.4	7.2	27.3	16.2	4.8	4.5	0.7	0.3	7.2
Operatives and kindred workers..............	100.0	10.8	11.3	4.1	6.1	22.0	23.8	5.5	7.0	0.9	0.9	7.6
Service workers, including private household.........	100.0	9.5	13.4	5.4	9.0	19.8	19.8	10.5	5.9	1.0	0.2	5.5
Laborers, except farm and mine..............	100.0	5.5	7.4	3.4	7.4	21.0	24.6	8.5	13.2	1.1	1.1	7.0
Farmers and farm managers...	100.0	4.9	10.6	2.3	4.3	18.1	18.9	4.8	7.8	16.4	3.9	8.0
Farm laborers and foremen..	100.0	2.1	6.7	1.8	3.5	18.8	24.0	7.5	12.3	5.7	9.4	8.0
Occupation not reported.....	100.0	7.9	13.1	3.3	6.2	18.9	19.7	9.7	10.1	2.1	1.6	7.4

- Entry represents zero.

Table 10-10 Current Occupation by Occupation of First Job—Noninstitutional Male Population 25 to 64 Years Old, for the United States: March 1962 (Percent Distribution)

Occupation of first job	Total population 25 to 64 years old	Current occupation										
		Professional, technical, and kindred workers	Managers, offi'ls, and pro- prietors, except farm	Sales workers	Clerical and kindred workers	Crafts- and foremen, and kindred workers	Opera- tives and kindred workers	Service workers, including private household	Laborers, except farm and mine	Farmers and farm managers	Farm laborers and foremen	Not in exper- ienced civilian labor force
Total.................	100.0	11.6	14.9	4.7	6.1	19.2	17.5	5.5	6.4	5.2	1.7	7.2
Professional, technical, and kindred workers......	100.0	62.6	16.7	3.3	4.6	3.8	2.3	0.9	0.5	0.9	0.2	4.2
Managers, officials, and proprietors, except farm...	100.0	17.1	48.3	7.4	5.3	7.6	5.1	1.8	2.2	1.7	0.3	3.2
Sales workers..........	100.0	11.4	29.5	15.5	10.1	10.6	12.6	3.0	2.3	0.9	-	4.1
Clerical and kindred workers...............	100.0	14.6	22.7	9.1	17.6	11.5	9.8	4.4	2.8	1.2	0.2	6.1
Craftsmen, foremen, and kindred workers......	100.0	8.6	17.4	3.8	3.9	38.5	11.8	3.4	3.9	1.8	0.5	6.4
Operatives and kindred workers...............	100.0	6.1	13.4	3.9	5.4	24.8	25.6	5.3	6.2	2.0	0.8	6.5
Service workers, including private household......	100.0	7.6	11.1	2.6	5.0	16.0	20.9	19.8	8.3	0.4	0.5	7.8
Laborers, except farm and mine...............	100.0	5.8	10.1	3.3	4.9	21.5	23.4	6.7	14.2	1.9	1.2	7.0
Farmers and farm managers...	100.0	2.6	6.3	3.0	3.0	15.6	13.4	4.6	5.0	36.1	5.0	5.4
Farm laborers and foremen....	100.0	1.9	7.1	1.8	2.7	17.1	19.8	5.8	9.5	19.2	7.0	8.1
Occupation not reported....	100.0	7.4	11.9	3.2	2.9	14.4	14.2	10.7	5.7	1.9	1.9	25.8

- Entry rounds to zero.

Table 10-11 Occupation of First Job by Father's Occupation—Noninstitutional Male Population 25 to 64 Years Old, for the United States: March 1962 (Percent Distribution)

Father's occupation	Total population 25 to 64 years old[1]	Occupation of first job									
		Professional, techn'l, and kindred workers	Managers, off'ls, and proprietors, except farm	Sales workers	Clerical and kindred workers	Craftsmen, foremen, and kindred workers	Operatives and kindred workers	Service workers, including private household	Laborers, except farm and mine	Farmers and farm managers	Farm laborers and foremen
Total..............	100.0	8.3	1.9	6.3	11.0	9.6	27.1	4.0	13.7	3.3	14.9
Professional, technical, and kindred workers..........	100.0	34.3	3.7	8.7	14.6	9.3	16.2	3.1	7.4	0.7	2.0
Managers, officials, and proprietors, except farm...	100.0	17.9	7.0	14.3	15.8	9.9	20.9	3.0	8.9	0.4	1.9
Sales workers.............	100.0	16.5	4.1	18.1	19.0	6.3	21.7	2.0	8.5	0.4	3.4
Clerical and kindred workers	100.0	19.1	2.6	6.2	22.7	9.8	23.5	3.2	10.9	0.7	1.3
Craftsmen, foremen, and kindred workers.............	100.0	6.6	0.8	6.4	14.1	17.5	31.3	4.7	14.0	0.6	4.0
Operatives and kindred workers..............	100.0	5.2	1.3	5.1	11.5	9.1	44.7	4.5	14.7	0.3	3.6
Service workers, including private household.........	100.0	4.7	1.7	5.5	14.2	11.3	31.9	10.4	15.4	0.7	4.2
Laborers, except farm and mine.................	100.0	4.3	0.3	5.1	8.5	6.8	31.0	6.1	30.3	0.6	7.0
Farmers and farm managers...	100.0	3.7	0.7	2.7	4.3	6.0	18.8	2.2	12.0	10.5	39.1
Farm laborers and foremen...	100.0	0.9	0.5	1.4	2.4	4.7	18.0	2.9	11.8	1.6	55.8
Occupation not reported......	100.0	5.1	1.4	5.9	12.5	9.3	29.0	5.4	17.2	1.9	12.3

[1]Excludes persons not reporting on occupation of first job.

insignificant share of workers either climb or slip down two, three, or even more "rungs" on the occupational ladder—in comparison both with their fathers' occupation and with their own first full-time job.

Detailed techniques for analyzing occupational mobility data to gain exact measures of status change form a specialized branch of social research. It is necessary to take into account the relative size of the occupational category in the total labor force at the time the data were collected. It is also necessary to take into account the changing occupational structure of the national economy within which mobility occurs, and this is not easily done. It is also necessary to give some consideration to the changing content over time of the various occupational categories. The reader who is interested in pursuing this topic further should begin by reading the studies by Duncan, Blau, Rogoff, Palmer, Lipset-Bendix, and Glass and then go on to the other studies of occupational mobility research that are cited in the Bibliography at the end of this chapter.

CONCLUSION

The systematic study of occupational composition with its socioeconomic implications and its implications for demography is only beginning to develop around the world. The statistics presented here clearly reveal that the data for making international comparison suffer not only from lack of detailed and consistent definition, but also from lack of availability of data for many nations. Although we could not discuss this fully here, the data that are reported in the U.S. Census for the detailed occupations are seriously deficient in accuracy and precision, and the cross-tabulations in many cases are made from samples that are much too small to support the refined analysis that would be desirable. The research needs to weigh the quality of the data available. We would like to emphasize again that the analyst who confines himself only to the study of the ten or twelve major occupational groups of a country is almost certainly performing a superficial analysis. It is only when the occupational data are tabulated at the level of intermediate or detailed occupational classifications and are cross-classified with other social, demographic, and economic characteristics that the full structure and dynamics of the labor force begin to emerge. A similar set of comments can be made with respect to industrial composition. It is to be hoped that one of the lines of demographic analysis that will expand greatly in the coming years will lie in the direction of greatly improving the quality of the data and the multiplying use of data for occupations and industry.

QUESTIONS AND EXERCISES

1. Obtain a copy of the most recent projection of the future size of the labor force for any nation, subdivided according to occupations and industry. (For example, see *Special Labor Force Reports*, U.S. Bureau of Labor Statistics.) Write an essay on the probable future changes in the occupational and industrial composition of the national work force.

2. Select three "underdeveloped" nations and make a careful comparative study of their occupational and industrial structure. Note the amount of difference and similarity between them. Try to account for the differences.

3. Select three "industrialized" nations (excluding the United States) and make a careful comparative study of their occupational and industrial structure. Note the amount of difference and similarity between them. Try to account for the differences.

4. Study the occupational and industrial structure of some nations recently industrialized (Japan, Argentina, Israel, Yugoslavia, etc.). Try to construct what you would regard as the minimal occupational structure for a modernizing nation. Apply this to selected industrializing nations of the world, such as India, Pakistan, or Ecuador, and measure the amount of occupational and industrial mobility that must take place before their economic goal can be reached.

5. Sociologists have often used occupations as a measure of the assimilation of immigrants as minority groups into the general population. To what extent is this valid? What biases or intervening factors might distort the relationship? On the basis of information presented in this chapter, how well integrated into American society do Negroes appear to be? How much improvement in their integration has taken place between 1940 and 1960? Name some "key" occupations at all levels of the occupational scale that, if occupied by Negroes, would be indicative of increasing integration. Look up the data for these occupations and check your hypotheses.

6. Using the procedure of Question 5, try to trace the cultural assimilation in the United States of (a) German, (b) Irish, (c) Italian, (d) Mexican, and (e) Puerto Rican immigrants.

7. Write an essay on "How Surplus Population Gains Its Livelihood: Population Pressure from the Working Force Perspective." Use the references as an aid in collecting information.

8. Suppose that you are asked to measure invisible underemployment in (a) the plantations of Malaya, (b) a regional city in South America, and (c) the slums of an American metropolis. Develop the interview schedule you would use, the coding and tabulating procedures you would follow, and the procedures you would use to identify underemployed persons and their characteristics.

9. Studies of occupational mobility sometimes use only two categories, "white-collar" and "blue-collar" occupations. Other studies use six categories. Conceivably it would be possible to use the 300 or more categories of the detailed occupational classification. What would be the effect of using such a detailed classification? What advantages would it have? What disadvantages?

10. From data tabulated in tables such as Table 10-10 it is possible to classify persons into three categories:

Upwardly mobile

Immobile

Downwardly mobile

It has been said by some that this is a useful way to classify people, whereas others maintain that it makes little sense unless the *starting point* from which mobility was measured is specified. Do you consider this a valid claim, and if so, why?

BIBLIOGRAPHY

Allen, Patrick. "Occupations et Origines Ethniques: I. Analyse des Occupations Primaries et Secondaires dans le Québec, 1931 a 1951" (Occupations and Ethnic Origins: I. Analysis of Primary and Secondary Occupations in Quebec, 1931-1951), *Actualité Économique* (Montreal), **38** (1) (April-June 1962), 20–55.

Anderson, C. Arnold. "Employment, Occupation, and Socio-economic Status of Swedish Wives in Relation to Occupation and Status of Husbands," *Statistisk Tidskrift* (Stockholm), **6** (1) (January 1957), 3–15.

Anderson, C. Arnold. "Lifetime Inter-occupational Mobility Patterns in Sweden," *Acta Sociologica: Scandinavian Review of Sociology* (Copenhagen), **1** (3) (1956), 168–202.

Anderson, H. Dewey, and E. Percy Davidson. *Occupational Mobility in an American Community.* Stanford, Calif.: Stanford University Press, 1937.

Bancroft, Gertrude, and Stuart Garfinkle. "Job Mobility in 1961," Preprint 2421 from the *Monthly Labor Review*, **86** (8) (August 1963), 897–906. Supplementary material, pp. A–5–A–14, in U. S. Bureau of Labor Statistics. *Special Labor Force Reports*, No. 1-. Washington, D.C., February 1960-.

Barraclough, Solon L., and Arthur L. Domike. "Agrarian Structure in Seven Latin American Countries," *Land Economics*, **42** (4) (November 1966), 391–424.

Barry, Carol A. "White-collar Employment: I— Trends and Structure," *Monthly Labor Review*, **84** (1) (January 1961), 11–18.

Baum, Samuel, et al. "The Hired Farm Working Force of 1961," *Agricultural Economic Report* 36. By U. S. Department of Agriculture. Economic Research Service. Economic and Statistical Analysis Division.

Bellerby, J. R. "The Distribution of Manpower in Agriculture and Industry, 1851-1951, *Farm Economist*, **9** (1) (1958), 1–11.

Benjamin, B. "Inter-generation Differences in Occupation: A Sample Comparison, in England and Wales, of Census and Birth Registration Records," *Population Studies*, **11** (3) (March 1958), 262–268.

Blau, Peter M., and Otis Dudley Duncan. *The American Occupational Structure.* New York: John Wiley and Sons, 1967.

Blau, Peter M. "The Flow of Occupational Supply and Recruitment," *American Sociological Review*, **30** (4) (August 1965), 475–490.

Blumen, Isadore, et al. "The Industrial Mobility of

Labor as a Probability Process," *Cornell Studies in Industrial and Labor Relations,* Vol. VI. Ithaca, N. Y.: Cornell University Press, 1955.

Bogue, Donald J. "Occupational Composition and Occupational Trends, Chapter 17 and "Industrial Composition," Chapter 18, in *Population of the United States.* New York: The Free Press of Glencoe, 1959.

Bogue, Donald J. *A Methodological Study of Migration and Labor Mobility in Michigan and Ohio, 1947.* Oxford, Ohio: Scripps Foundation for Research in Population Problems, 1952.

Canada. Department of Labor. "Occupational Trends in Canada, 1931 to 1961," by Noah M. Meltz. *Research Program on the Training of Skilled Manpower,* Report 11. Ottawa, 1963.

Caplow, Theodore. "The Principles of Occupational Distribution," *Revista Mexicana de Sociologia,* 15 (3) (1953), 363–374.

Carlson, Gösta. *Social Mobility and Class Structure.* Lund, CWK Gleeruys, 1958.

Carpenter, Howard S. "The International Classification of Occupations for Migration and Employment Placement," *International Labour Review,* 59 (2) (February 1954), 111–125.

Crespi, Irving. "Occupational Status and Religion," *American Sociological Review,* 28 (1) (February 1963), 131.

Duncan, Otis Dudley. "Methodological Issues in the Analysis of Social Mobility," in N. J. Smelser and S. M. Lipset (eds.). *Social Structure and Social Mobility in Economic Development.* Chicago: Aldine Press, 1966.

Duncan, Otis D. "Occupational Trends and Patterns of Net Mobility in the United States," *Demography,* 3 (1966), 1–17.

Duncan, Otis Dudley. "The Trend of Occupational Mobility in the United States," *American Sociological Review,* 30 (4) (August 1965), 491–498.

Edwards, G. Franklin. "Occupational Mobility of Negro Professional Workers," pp. 443–458 in Ernest W. Burgess and Donald J. Bogue (eds.). *Contributions to Urban Sociology.* Chicago: University of Chicago Press, 1964.

Erickson, Charlotte. "American Industry and the European Immigrant, 1860-1885," *Studies in Economic History.* Cambridge, Mass.: Harvard University Press, 1957.

Farber, David J. "Measuring Wage and Employment Changes as Workers Age by Use of Cohort Data," in American Statistical Association. Social Statistics Section. *Proceedings of the Social Statistics Section,* 1962. Washington, D. C., 1962.

Frenkel, Izaslaw. "Employment Problems in Polish Agriculture," *International Labour Review* (Geneva), 83 (2) (February 1961), 156–177.

Gibbs, Jack P. "A Note on Industry Changes and

Migration," *American Sociological Review,* 29 (2) (April 1964), 266–270.

Glass, David V. (ed.). *Social Mobility in Britain.* New York: The Free Press of Glencoe, 1960.

Glenn, Norval D. "Changes in the American Occupational Structure and Occupational Gains of Negroes During the 1940's," *Social Forces,* 41 (2) (December 1962), 188–195.

Glick, Paul C. "Educational Attainment and Occupational Advancement," pp. 183–193 in International Sociological Association. *Transactions of the Second World Congress of Sociology . . . ,* Vol. 2. London, 1954.

Gnanasekaran, K. S. "Interrelations between Industrial and Occupational Changes in Manpower, United States, 1950-1960." Analytical and Technical Reports, 6. Philadelphia: Population Studies Center, University of Pennsylvania, June 1966.

Goldstein, Sidney. "Patterns of Migration and Occupational Mobility, pp. 82-97 in Sidney Goldstein et al. *The Norristown Study: an Experiment in Interdisciplinary Research Training.* Philadelphia: University of Pennsylvania Press, 1961.

Gyulay, Ferenc. "Adatok a Szovjetunió Népességének Foglalkozási Megoszlásárol" (Data About the Occupational Pattern of the Population in the Soviet Union), *Demográfia* (Budapest), 4 (3) (1961), 342–347. Russian and English summaries.

Gross, Edward. "The Occupational Variable as a Research Category," *American Sociological Review,* 24 (5) (October 1959), 640–649.

Hare, Nathan. "Recent Trends in the Occupational Mobility of Negroes, 1930-1960: An Intracohort Analysis," *Social Forces,* 44 (2) (December 1965), 166–173.

Heasman, M. A., et al. "The Accuracy of Occupational Vital Statistics," *British Journal of Industrial Medicine,* 15 (3) (July 1958), 141–146.

Hedberg, Magnus. "The Turnover of Labour in Industry: an Actuarial Study," *Acta Sociologica* (Copenhagen), 5 (3) (1961), 129–143.

Henderson, John P. "Changes in the Industrial Distribution of Employment, 1919-1959," *University of Illinois Bulletin,* 59 (3). *Bureau of Economic and Business Research Bulletin Series* 87. Urbana, August 1961.

Hock, Saw Swee, and Ronald Ma. "The Economic Characteristics of the Population of Singapore, 1957," reprinted from *The Malayan Economic Review,* 5 (1) (April 1960), 31–51.

Hodge, Robert, and Otis Dudley Duncan. "Education and Occupational Mobility: A Regression Analysis," *American Journal of Sociology,* 68 (6) (May 1963), 629–644.

Hodge, Robert, and Patricia Hodge. "Occupational Assimilation as a Competitive Process," *Ameri-*

can *Journal of Sociology*, **71** (3) (November 1965), 249–264.

Hodge, Robert W. "Occupational Mobility as a Probability Process," *Demography*, **3** (1966), 19–34.

Hoselitz, Bert F. "Population Pressure, Industrialization and Social Mobility," *Population Studies*, **11** (2) (November 1957), 123–135.

Houghton, D. Hobart. "Men of Two Worlds: Some Aspects of Migratory Labour in South Africa," *The South African Journal of Economics* (Johannesburg), **28** (3) (September 1960), 177–190.

Hutchinson, Edward P. "Immigrants and Their Children, 1850-1950," *Census Monograph Series*. New York: John Wiley and Sons, for the Social Science Research Council in cooperation with the U. S. Department of Commerce, Bureau of the Census, 1956.

Ianni, Francis A. J. "Residential and Occupational Mobility as Indices of the Acculturation of an Ethnic Group," *Social Forces*, **36** (1) (October 1957), 65–72.

Inter-American Statistical Institute. Secretariat. Focal Point for Statistical Information. "Activity of the Population of the American Nations According to the Most Recent Census," *Estadística* (Washington, D. C.), **16** (58) (March 1958), 98–110.

International Labour Office. "Employment Characteristics of the Labour Force in India: Preliminary Results of a Sample Survey," *Industry and Labour* (Geneva), **23** (3) (February 1, 1960), 90–95.

International Labour Office. "The World's Working Population: Its Distribution by Status and Occupation," *International Labour Review*, **74** (2) (August 1956), 174–192.

International Labour Office. "The World's Working Population: Its Industrial Distribution," *International Labour Review*, **73** (5) (May 1956), 501–521.

Jaffe, A. J. "Suggestions for a Supplemental Grouping of the Occupational Classification System," *Estadística* (Washington, D. C.), **15** (54) (March 1957), 13–23. With Spanish summary.

Jaffe, A. J., and R. O. Carleton. *Occupational Mobility in the United States, 1930-1960*. New York: King's Crown Press, Columbia University, 1954.

Jefferys, Margot. *Mobility in the Labour Market*. London: Routledge and Kegan Paul, 1954.

Kahl, Joseph A. "Urbanicao e Mudancas Ocupacionais no Brazil" (Urbanization and Occupational Changes in Brazil), *América Latina* (Rio de Janeiro), **5** (4) (October-December 1962), 21–30. Spanish, French, and English summaries.

Klinger, András. "Some Characteristics of Social Mobility in Budapest," *Demografia* (Buda-pest), **5** (4) (1962), 477–485. Russian and English summaries.

Kuznets, Simon. "Quantitative Aspects of the Economic Growth of Nations. III. Industrial Distribution of Income and Labor Force by States, United States, 1919-1921 to 1955," *Economic Development and Cultural Change*, **6** (4) (July 1958), Part II.

Lipset, S. M., and R. Bendix. *Social Mobility in Industrial Society*. Berkeley, Calif.: University of California Press, 1959.

Ma, Ronald, and Poh Seng You. "Economic Characteristics of the Population of the Federation of Malaya, 1957," *Malayan Economic Review*, **5** (2) (October 1960), 10–45.

Makower, H., J. Marschak, and H. W. Robinson. "Studies in Mobility of Labor," *Oxford Economic Papers*, Nos. 1, 2, 3. Oxford: Clarendon Press, 1938, 1939.

Matras, Judah. "Some Data on Integrational Occupational Mobility in Israel," *Population Studies*, **17** (2) (November 1963), 167–186.

McElveen, Jackson V. "Family Farms in a Changing Economy," U. S. Agricultural Research Service, *Agricultural Information Bulletin*, No. 171. Washington, D. C.: U. S. Government Printing Office, 1957.

McKellar, Neil. "Some Aspects of the International Standard Classification of Occupations," *International Labour Review*, **74** (1) (July 1956), 56–73.

McLoughlin, Peter F. M. "The Sudan's Three Towns: a Demographic and Economic Profile of an African Urban Complex. Part 3. Labor Force Occupations. Occupational Income, Income Distribution," *Economic Development and Cultural Change*, **12** (3) (April 1964), 286–304.

Meltz, Noah M. "Changes in the Occupational Composition of the Canadian Labour Force, 1931-1961," Department of Labour, Canada, *Economics and Research Branch Occasional Paper*, 2. Ottawa: Queens Printer, 1965.

Miller, S. M. "Comparative Social Mobility," *Current Sociology*, **9** (1) (1960).

Moore, Wilbert E. "A Preliminary Functional Classification of Activities," *Proceedings of the World Population Conference: 1954*. New York, 1955, Vol. IV.

Myrdal, Gunnar. *An International Economy: Problems and Prospects*. New York: Harper, 1956.

Nicol, Helen O., and Merci L. Drake. "Negro Women Workers in 1960," U. S. *Women's Bureau Bulletin* 287. Washington, D. C.: U. S. Government Printing Office, 1964.

Nixon, J. W. "Classification of the Population by Economic Activities," *Journal of the Royal Statistical Society*, Series A (General), **124** (4) (1961), 526–542.

Organization for Economic Cooperational Development. *The Position of the Agricultural*

Hired Worker. A survey carried out in eight European countries by Dr. P. Von Blanckenburg on behalf of the Agrarsoziale Gesellschaft. Paris, 1963.

Palmer, Gladys L. *Labor Mobility in Six Cities.* New York: Social Science Research Council, 1954.

Palmer, Gladys, with Carol P. Brainerd. *Labor Mobility in Six Cities. A Report on the Survey of Patterns and Factors in Labor Mobility, 1940-1950.* Prepared for the Committee on Labor Market Research, Social Science Research Council. New York, 1954.

Parnes, Herbert S. *Research Labor Mobility; an Appraisal of Research Findings in the United States.* New York: Social Science Research Council, 1954.

Pihlblad, C. T., and Dagfinn Aas. "Residential and Occupational Mobility in an Area of Rapid Industrialization in Norway," *American Sociological Review,* **25** (3) (June 1960), 369–375.

Pourcher, Guy. "Un Essai d'Analyse par Cohorte de la Mobilité Géographique et Professionnelle en France"), ("An Attempt at Cohort Analysis of Geographical and Occupational Mobility in France"), *Acta Sociologica* (Copenhagen), **9** (1-2) (1965), 137–151.

Rao, V. K. R. V. (ed.). "Agricultural Labour in India," Institute of Economic Growth, Delhi, *Studies in Economic Growth* 3. Bombay, etc.: Asia Publishing House, 1962.

Raup, P. M. "Economic Aspects of Population Decline in Rural Communities," pp. 95–106 in *Labor Mobility and Population in Agriculture.* Papers assembled and published under the sponsorship of the Iowa State University Center for Agricultural and Economic Adjustment. Ames, Iowa: Iowa State University Press, 1961.

Reiss, Albert J., and O. D. Duncan. *Occupations and Social Status.* New York: The Free Press, 1961.

Reynolds, Lloyd G. *The Structure of Labor Markets.* New York: Harper, 1951.

Rocher, Guy. "Les Recherches sur les Occupations et la Stratification Sociale" (Research on Occupations and Social Stratification), pp. 173–184 in Fernand Dumont and Yves Martin (eds.). "Situation de la Recherche sur le Canada Français" (The Position of Research on French Canada), *Recherches Sociographiques* (Quebec), **3** (1-2) (January-August 1962), 7–294.

Rogoff, Natalie. *Recent Trends in Occupational Mobility.* With a foreword by Herbert Goldhamer. Glencoe, Ill.: Free Press, 1953. (In Marion County, Ind.)

Rutzick, Max, and Sol Swerdloff. "The Occupational Structure of U. S. Employment, 1940-

60," *Monthly Labor Review,* **85** (11) (November 1962), 1209–1213.

Schultz, T. W. "A Policy to Redistribute Losses From Economic Progress," pp. 158–168 in *Labor Mobility and Population in Agriculture.* Papers assembled and published under the sponsorship of the Iowa State University Center for Agricultural and Economic Adjustment. Ames, Iowa: Iowa State University Press, 1961.

Scudder, Richard, and C. Arnold Anderson. "Migration and Vertical Occupational Mobility," *American Sociological Review,* **19** (3) (June 1954), 329–334.

Shannon, L. W. "Occupational and Residential Adjustment of Rural Migrants," pp. 122–150 in *Labor Mobility and Population in Agriculture.* Papers assembled and published under the sponsorship of the Iowa State University Center for Agricultural and Economic Adjustment. Ames, Iowa: Iowa State University Press, 1961.

Shannon, Lyle W., and Elaine M. Krass. "The Economic Absorption of In-migrant Laborers in a Northern Industrial Community," *American Journal of Economics and Sociology,* **23** (1) (January 1964), 65–84.

Slotkin, James S. *From Field to Factory: New Industrial Employees.* Publications of the Research Center in Economic Development and Cultural Change (University of Chicago). Glencoe, Ill.: Free Press, 1960.

Sperling, H. "Zur Theorie und Methode der Berufsklassifizierung" (Theory and Method in Occupational Classification), *Schmollers Jahrbuch* (Berlin), **81** (6) (1961), 65–80.

Sundrun, R. M. *A Note on Comparisons or Occupational Data in the 1921 and 1931 Censuses.* Economics Research Project, Economics Paper 4. Rangoon: University of Rangoon, Departments of Economics, Statistics and Commerce, December 1957.

Svalastoga, Kaare. *Prestige Class and Mobility.* Copenhagen, Glydendal, 1959.

Sweden. Statistiska Centralbyrån. "Förvarvsverksamhet, Bostadsförhållanden m.m. Enligt 1960 års Folk-och Bostadsräkningar" (Economic Activity, Housing Conditions, etc. According to the 1960 Censuses of Population and Housing. Preliminary data.) By G. B-d and B. H-dt. *Statistisk Tidskrift,* **11** (6) (1962), 379–392.

Szabady, Egon. "A Tarsadalmi-Foglakozási Atrétegezó-dés és Demográfia Hatásai" (Socio-occupational Restratification and its Demographic Impacts), *Demográfia* (Budapest), **5** (40) (1962), 494–500. Russian and English summaries.

Thomas, Brinley. "Trends in the International Migration of Skilled Manpower," *Migration*

(Geneva), **1** (3) (July-September 1961), 5–20.

Tulder, J. J. M. van. *De Beroepsmobiliteit in Nederland van 1919 tot 1954 (Sociale Stijging en daling in Nederland III) [(Occupational Mobility in the Netherlands from 1919 to 1954. (Social Rigidity in Decline in the Netherlands. 3. A Social-statistics study)].* Leiden: H. E. Stenfert Kroese, N. V., 1962.

United Nations. Statistical Office. Handbook of Population Census Methods. Vol. II. *Economic Characteristics of the Population.* Studies in Methods, Series F, No. 5, Rev. 1. New York, 1958.

U. S. Bureau of the Census. *Current Population Reports.* Series P-23. Technical studies. No. 1-. Washington, 1949-. No. 11. "Lifetime Occupational Mobility of Adult Males, March 1962." May 12, 1964.

U. S. Bureau of the Census. *Occupational Trends in the United States, 1900-1950.* By David L. Kaplan and M. Claire Casey. Working Paper, No. 5. Washington, 1958.

U. S. Bureau of the Census. Foreign Demographic Analysis Division. "Comparison of U. S. and U. S. S. R. Employment in Industry: 1939-1958," by Murray S. Weitzman. *International Population Reports,* Series P-95, No. 60. Washington, 1963.

U. S. Bureau of Labor Statistics. Special Labor Force Reports. No. 1-. Washington, February 1960-. No. 28. Employment projections, by industry and occupation, 1960-75. Reprint 2412 from the *Monthly Labor Review,* **86** (3) (March 1963), 240–250.

U. S. Bureau of Labor Statistics. "Techniques of Preparing Major Bureau of Labor Statistics Statistical Series," *Bureau of Labor Statistics Bulletin* 1168. Washington, D. C.: U. S. Government Printing Office, December 1954.

U. S. Bureau of Labor Statistics. *The Long-range Demand for Scientific and Technical Personnel: a Methodological Study Prepared for the National Science Foundation.* Washington, D. C.: U. S. Government Printing Office, 1961.

Walter, Emil J. "Population and Occupational Censuses of Geneva in the Eighteenth Century" (Genfer Volks- und Berufszählungen des 18. Jahrhunderts), *Schweizerische Zeitschrift für Volkswirschaft und Statistik (Revue Suisse d'Economie Politique et de Statisque),* **90** (3) (September 1954), 337–345.

Woodbury, Robert Morse. "Demographic Changes in Age and Occupation, with Special Reference to the United States, 1910 to 1950," *Proceedings of the World Population Conference: 1954.* New York, 1955, Vol. III.

CHAPTER 11

Marital Status

11.1. Marital Status as a Key Sociodemographic Variable

Almost all cultures of the world recognize four marital statuses and have highly elaborate descriptions of appropriate behavior for the persons in each status:

single (never-married)
married
widowed
divorced

Each status has deep religious and legal as well as general social significance. Legal permission must be obtained to acquire the status of being married or divorced. Most religions solemnize changes in status with a ceremony or declaration. In most populations the act of obtaining a divorce either is forbidden by the church and results in loss of religious status or is permitted only after the local religious authorities have attempted to effect a reconciliation. It is to be expected, therefore, that the marital status composition of the population would influence national and local community life in a great many ways, and the study of population composition should include it.

In view of this central importance for sociology and anthropology of marital status, it may seem odd that demographers perform much if not most of the systematic research concerning it. There are two principal reasons for this:

1. Marital status is a social characteristic that is very easy to enumerate in the national censuses of most countries, and therefore most population censuses make it an integral part of their routine work. Demographers analyze and interpret the results as a normal part of the study of population composition.

2. Marital status affects population growth directly. There can be little doubt that a major reason for the great legal and religious concern about marital status is its implication for group survival through childbearing. It is not simply the number of fertile females, as such, that influences the level of fertility in a population, but the number of cohabiting fertile females. In most societies all but a small fraction of childbearing is done by persons who are married. Where pregnancy occurs outside marriage, marriage usually follows rather promptly, because of the aforementioned sanctions. Hence, in the eyes of the demographer, marriage and the dissolution of marriage are vital processes and statistics of marriage and divorce are vital statistics. The proportion of the population that marries, the age at which it marries, and the extent to which marriages are dissolved by death and divorce (and the age at which dissolution occurs) all can affect the birthrate. Moreover, death rates and migration rates both vary substantially according to marital status, so that marital status conditions all aspects of population dynamics. Marital status also affects labor force participation, school attendance, urban-rural residence, and almost every other topic in which demographers are interested. It is this fact that causes demographers to treat it as one of the fundamental variables of their discipline. The fact that they do so, of course, does not preclude marital status from being fundamental to other lines of social science study. Because demographers are concerned, however, they have been the group of researchers that has kept informed and has informed others concerning the marital status of the population and the trends in marital status.

David V. Glass has summarized the importance of this variable for demographers in the following terms:

"It is through the intervening variable of marriage that replacement indices become sociologically meaningful. In the more developed societies, recent changes in the level and trend of fertility owe much to changes in the amount of, and age at, marriage.

"The study of marital patterns and trends in less developed societies is of still greater importance. . . . The existing *de facto* familial arrangements have important bearings upon fertility and so too will any tendency to a more widespread legalised relationship.

"With divorce replacing death as a factor in the dissolution of marriage in the childbearing period, more attention should be given to the study of divorce, and with the growth of interest in the spread of new norms of family size in many of the less developed countries, the study of those aspects of marriage which most strongly condition what is regarded as desired or acceptable from the point of view of family size, is greatly to be desired."[1]

In making studies of marital status, demographers sometimes combine the basic fourfold classification into two categories:

never-married (single)
ever-married (married, widowed, divorced)

On the other hand, they often attempt to expand the category of "married" to show the present status more precisely:

married, spouse present
married, separated (estranged)
married, spouse absent (other)

For studies of marital discord, the separated and divorced may be combined. (The category "married, spouse absent—other" covers cases where the spouse is in a military camp, is in an institution, is working at a job too far from home to live with his family, etc.)

In some nations, especially in Latin America, there is a somewhat unique status of the married category that is termed "consensual

union" or "conviviente" (living together). It is similar to common-law marriage but may be less enduring. Braithwaite and Roberts have found a threefold family typology useful in discussing mating patterns among Negro populations in Trinidad: married, common-law, and "visiting."[2] On the basis of a sample survey they found that less than one half of the cohabiting women of age 25 (as an example) were living in regular marriage unions. Instead they found the marital status to be as follows:

	Percent
Not in a union	30.3
In a visiting union	21.2
In a common-law union	21.1
In married union	27.4
Total	100.0

They regard these as representing three different levels of intensity of exposure to the risk of childbearing. On the one hand, women in legal marriages are continuously at risk. On the other hand, those in the "visiting" category are least exposed to childbearing because of the intermittent nature of the sexual contact of the participants. The common-law type is midway between these two. The authors also found that the type of union affects fertility. The visiting type of union produces fewer children than the married or common-law. It predominates in rural areas where people have lower educational status and where women are employed as unskilled and domestic workers. Catholic women were found to be less likely than Protestant to enter visiting unions, although the difference between the two was not great.

The Braithwaite-Roberts study emphasizes both that data on marital status are important and that in every society an accurate portrayal of the actual marital status composition is difficult to obtain from those members of the population who live together as man and wife without having been married by either a re-

[1] David V. Glass, "Introductory Comments," Session on Nuptiality, *Proceedings of the World Population Conference: 1954* (New York: United Nations, 1955), Vol. IV, pp. 141.

[2] L. Braithwaite and G. W. Roberts, "Mating Patterns and Prospects in Trinidad," *Proceedings of International Population Conference*, International Union for the Study of Population (London, 1963), Vol. 2, pp. 173–181.

ligious or a civil ceremony. In most censuses, common-law marriages, "conviviente," or other arrangements are classified as married or single according to the way in which the reporting person declares, with little effort on the part of census officials to challenge or probe the responses. Women who have borne an illegitimate child, whether in a common-law marriage or not, may tend to report themselves as widowed, separated, or divorced if they are not currently living with a man. Women who have lived in a common-law marriage that has since been dissolved may tend to report themselves as single rather than ever-married if there are no children. Lemieux has observed that common-law or *de facto* marriages may be much less durable than is commonly asserted, with the result that the international comparability of marital status statistics is less than is commonly belived.[3] These problems are confounded by the fact that there are no internationally accepted clear definitions of how these problem cases should be enumerated.

In reading the materials that follow, it should be kept in mind that marital status is a net result of the action of three processes, all of which are acting continuously upon the population:

nuptiality (marriage)
widowhood
separation and divorce

Each of these processes has a rate of incidence, and each of these rates varies with age and social and economic characteristics. In Chapter 16 we shall study each process in terms of family formation and dissolution. At present, however, we are not interested in the incidence of these processes, but in the comparative *prevalence* of the statuses that result from their joint action in marital status composition.

As yet many nations of the world have made insufficient use of the marital status variables in exploring the socioeconomic implication of marital status; they have been content to make only a few basic calculations that show how

[3] Omer A. Lemieux, "Analysis of Marital Status Statistics in some Recent Censuses," *Proceedings of the World Population Conference* (New York: United Nations, 1955), Vol. IV, pp. 715–727.

persons in each status are distributed by age and sex in various parts of their country. Because of the demands made by sociologists and others interested in family life, the census of the United States is unusually rich in materials that reveal social and economic differentials by marital status. This chapter exploits a part of these materials not only to inform United States readers about their national population, but also to illustrate the great usefulness that can emerge from expanding this line of demographic inquiry in any nation.

11.2. Marital Status and Age

Marital status varies sharply with age:

Children and adolescents tend to be single.
Young adults and adults tend to be married.
Divorce tends to be greatest at the adult ages 35 to 40.
Widowhood is concentrated at the older ages.

Although these generalizations tend to apply to all populations, there is much variation between populations in the proportions that are in each status at each age. The typical pattern for marriage is for the proportion married to rise very swiftly between ages 18 and 22 for girls (20 to 25 for males) and then to slacken. As some of these marriages are dissolved, the proportion of divorced persons increases. Finally, rising mortality at ages beyond 50 tends to create a rapid rise in the proportion that is widowed.

Figure 11-1 graphs data about the proportion that is single by age for females in Ireland, France, India, and the United States. It is presented to illustrate the fact that marriage-age curves, although distinctive in various populations, are all of the same general form. Within each population there may be expected to be an equal or greater amount of variation, indicating distinctive patterns associated with the major ethnic, social, and economic groups of the nation, but also following the general form.

In studying marriage patterns according to age, we need to make use of two basic concepts:

proportion ever marrying
age at marriage

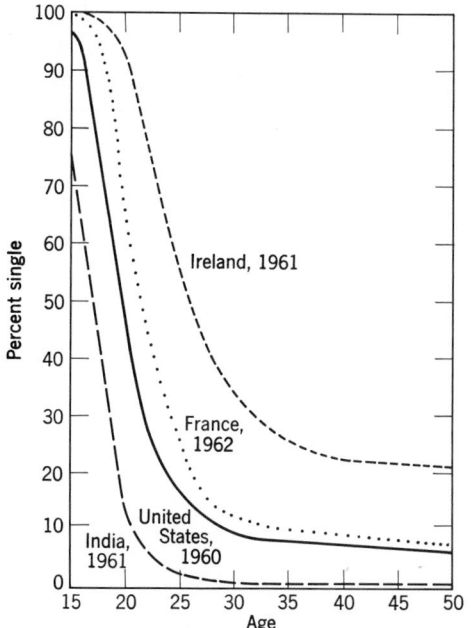

Figure 11-1 Percent of Population Single, by Age, Selected Nations of the World.

Proportion Ever Marrying. A certain percentage of the population never marries but completes the life cycle still in the status of being single. This proportion may vary from population to population and may change over time within the same population. Comparatively few women marry for the first time after age 45 or 50; hence the proportion married by this age may be taken as an estimate of the proportion ever marrying. Figure 11-1 shows that Ireland is an example of a population where a very substantial percentage of the women never marry, whereas India exemplifies a situation where almost every woman marries at some time during her life. Figure 11-1 also reports the proportion never marrying; the proportion ever marrying is, of course, this proportion subtracted from 100. In general, the best indicator of the proportion of the population ever marrying at the current time is provided by data for age group 45 to 49. Data for ages older than this may represent patterns of ever marrying for older generations and data for ages younger than this refer to cohorts that still are getting married.

Pattern of Age at First Marriage. Among the major portion of the population that does mar-

ry, a few marry at an extraordinarily young age. As suggested above, a very large fraction of the females marry within a span of a few years between ages 18 and 22, and most of the remainder marry before age 30. The specific ages at which the greatest rush to get married takes place may vary substantially from one nation to another or from one subgroup of a population to another within the nation. The pattern of age at marriage may be inferred by noting the proportions married at each of the younger ages. In Figure 11-1, India is an example of a nation where the age pattern of marriage is an extraordinarily young one. Ireland, on the other hand, exemplifies an unusually old pattern of age at marriage. France illustrates the pattern now current in Europe. Although the pattern of age at marriage for the United States appears to be intermediate between these extremes, in comparison with those of most nations of the world it would be considered a "young" one.

As the proportion of the population that is single (never-married) declines with increasing age, the proportion of the population that is ever-married rises by a corresponding amount. However, the forces of widowhood and divorce are at work, so that the married population becomes smaller and smaller and the proportion divorced or widowed rises. At no age in any population does the percentage that is divorced reach more than 2 to 4 percent. After age 50, widowhood begins to rise very substantially, so that at the advanced ages we find a comparatively small percentage of the population married and a very substantial percentage widowed. (See Sections 11-5 and 11-6 for further discussion of divorce and widowhood.) We cannot make use of conventional census data on marital status to compute the proportion of couples ever divorced or ever widowed because many widows and divorcees remarry and at the time of the census report their current status rather than their previous marital status.

A complete comparison of the marital status patterns of two populations would involve a comparison of the proportions at each age that are single, married, widowed, or divorced. When a single overall figure is required to summarize the marriage pattern, usually the median age at first marriage is used. The average age at first marriage, however, is an equally appropriate measure. Demographers have devised techniques for estimating these measures from census data if data are not available from a register of marriages.[4]

India and Ireland, whose marital status patterns are charted in Figure 11-1, represent nearly the extremes that the life cycle pattern of marital status may take. Widowhood at the younger ages is at a near maximum in India because death rates are high and there are taboos against remarriage of widows that are still widely observed. At the present time, the United States represents the upper limit in divorce, for divorce rates are higher in the United States than in almost any other nation. Ireland has long been noted for its combining late marriage with a high percentage of persons who never marry. Each nation of the world seems to have its own somewhat unique combination of age patterns for first marriage, divorce, widowhood, and remarriage—with the result that each tends to have a unique set of marital status characteristics. Within each nation there may also be variations in the marriage pattern according to region, urban-rural residence, ethnic origin, religion, and socioeconomic status.

11.3. International Differences in Age Patterns of Marriage for Females

Age at First Marriage. It is possible to classify the nations of the world into four groups:

Category	Median age of females at first marriage
Child marriage	Less than 18 years
Early marriage	18 or 19 years
Marriage at maturity	20 or 21 years
Late marriage	22 years and over

Differences in the marital status patterns among the world's populations—and changes in those patterns—are not very well known because until recently the data have been widely

scattered, and often are noncomparable because of differences in age grouping. A special program to assemble these materials permits us to offer, in Table 11-1, a rather comprehensive tabulation of the proportion of the female population that is single at selected ages from 16 to 50 for almost all nations for which this information has been tabulated. Moreover, trends since 1900 are available for many of these nations. This table also reports the estimated median age at first marriage for both males and females. In interpreting this table it must be kept in mind that there may be wide differences in the quality of the data; hence small differences must be accepted cautiously. Also, for some nations data do not exist, and estimates of median age at first marriage have been made for them on the basis of similar cultures.

The data for Table 11-1 were obtained by correspondence by the author with census offices around the world. Most of the data obtained were reported in five-year age groups. These were interpolated to single years by Dr. Walter Mertens. Dr. Mertens has in preparation a monograph, "World Nuptiality Patterns: A Comparative Study Based on Nuptiality Tables," which is based on these and other data.[5] The data presented here are simple osculatory interpolations of census data. By special techniques, Dr. Mertens adjusts these data for deficiencies in enumeration and from his refined tabulations is developing a comprehensive analysis of marriage patterns around the world.

The following nations may tentatively be said to have such an unusually early age at marriage that they can probably be termed "child marriage" nations:

Africa	Asia
Congo	Afghanistan
Ghana	India
Guinea	Pakistan
Ivory Coast	Nepal
Nigeria	
Tunisia	
Upper Volta	
Zanzibar	

[4] U. S. Bureau of the Census, *Current Population Reports*, Series P-20, No. 122, "Marital Status and Family Status: March, 1962" (Washington, D. C., 1963).

[5] This monograph is to be published by the Community and Family Study Center, University of Chicago.

Table 11-1 Median Age at Marriage, by Sex, and Proportion Single by Age for Females, Nations of the World for Which Data Are Available, Selected Dates

Country	Median age at marriage — Male	Median age at marriage — Female	Percent single at specified ages — 16	17	18	19	20	21	22	23	24	25	26	27	28	29	30	35	40	45	50	55
N. & W. Europe																						
Belgium																						
1960	25.3	22.6	99.2	97.8	93.4	86.8	73.8	64.3	55.4	47.8	41.2	34.5	27.7	22.4	19.2	17.3	16.0	11.8	10.5	10.2	10.1	
1947	25.4	22.8	99.2	97.9	94.7	88.5	75.9	67.2	58.7	51.2	44.4	37.4	30.4	25.0	21.8	20.2	18.8	15.3	14.4	13.7	12.8	
1930	26.3	24.4	99.7	99.1	97.0	93.4	82.7	76.0	69.3	62.8	56.6	50.3	43.9	38.5	34.5	31.6		19.6	16.5	15.7	14.7	12.7
1920	25.8	24.0	99.7	99.1	96.4	91.8	82.4	75.8	68.7	61.3	53.9	46.5	38.9	35.1	31.5	29.4	27.3	20.3	17.7	16.8	16.4	14.7
1910	26.0	24.2	99.9	99.8	96.6	92.4	83.9	78.0	71.9	64.7	57.2	49.7	42.0	39.2	35.4	32.9	30.5	22.6	19.0	17.4	16.6	15.1
1900			99.6	98.7																		
Denmark																						
1960	25.0	21.7	99.6	98.0	92.3	81.9	69.7	55.8	43.2	33.1	25.3	19.6	16.2	14.0	12.0	10.9	10.2	8.4	7.8	8.8	10.4	
1950	25.6	22.0	99.8	98.4	93.6	85.0	73.9	61.6	50.0	39.3	32.5	26.9	22.7	19.6	16.9	15.0	13.3	11.2	11.8	14.0	14.7	
1945	26.1	22.6	99.9	98.9	95.5	88.6	79.8	69.2	58.8	49.0	40.0	33.4	28.2	24.3	21.6	19.4	17.9	15.4	15.7	15.8	15.2	
1940	26.3	22.9	99.9	99.2	96.2	90.1	77.7	69.2	60.9	53.2	46.2	39.1	31.8	29.1	23.2	21.8	20.6	17.6	17.3	16.1	15.4	
1935	26.8	24.0	100.0	99.4	97.0	92.4	82.5	75.8	68.7	61.3	53.9	46.5	38.9	32.9	29.3	27.4	25.6	19.7	17.5	16.2	15.7	
1930	27.3	24.4	99.9	99.3	97.8	93.8	84.6	78.6	71.9	64.7	57.2	49.7	42.0	35.7	31.8	29.3	27.0	19.8	17.9	16.6	15.7	
1921	26.7	24.6	99.9	99.1	97.7	94.2	85.1	79.3	72.9	65.8	58.4	51.0	43.4	37.3	33.3	30.8	28.3	20.4	18.2	16.6	15.5	
1911	26.6	24.7	99.5	99.1	97.5	94.2	85.2	79.5	73.2	66.3	59.0	57.7	44.3	38.2	34.2	31.7	29.2	20.9	17.9	16.2	14.3	
1901	26.7	24.9	99.9	99.5	98.0	95.2	89.7	82.7	74.6	66.2	59.1	51.6	46.1	41.1	30.0	32.5	30.0	20.4	12.4	13.9	12.6	
England & Wales																						
1961																						
1951	25.0	21.3	99.8	98.5	94.1	86.2	75.0	61.3	49.6	40.3	33.4	28.1	24.1	21.3	18.9	17.0	15.6	13.6	13.0	13.0	13.0	12.4
1921	25.9	24.7	99.9	99.5	97.8	93.9	85.2	79.4	73.0	66.3	59.4	52.4	45.3	37.4	35.3	32.6	29.9	21.7	18.6	17.1	16.2	
1911	26.4	25.2	100.0	99.5	98.5	95.7	87.4	82.3	76.5	69.7	62.5	55.3	48.0	41.8	37.5	34.5	31.5	22.5	18.9	17.0	15.8	
Finland																						
1960	25.0	25.0	99.6	97.6	92.4	84.4	73.2	63.6	52.7	43.7	36.2	30.7	26.7	23.6	21.1	19.2	17.9	14.9	13.4	13.7	15.3	17.2
1950	25.3	22.4	99.7	98.3	93.8	86.8	78.0	67.4	57.6	49.3	41.3	35.7	31.9	28.6	25.6	23.2	21.5	17.8	17.6	18.5	19.6	19.3
1940	26.9	24.1	100.0	99.2	97.0	92.5	83.6	77.4	71.1	64.8	58.6	52.5	46.2	41.1	37.8	35.8	33.8	27.8	25.5	24.0	22.6	
1930	27.3	25.5	100.0	99.2	96.9	93.4	86.4	81.3	75.7	69.8	63.6	57.9	51.6	45.7	42.1	39.7	37.3	29.1	25.2			
1920	27.6	25.3	100.0	99.2	97.2	93.8	86.8	81.8	76.3	70.3	64.2	57.9	51.6	46.1	42.2	39.4	36.6	26.4	21.3	18.0	16.0	
1910	26.8	24.6	99.7	98.2	91.2	91.2	86.8	81.8	76.1	70.1	64.2	57.7	51.6	45.1	41.0	36.1	33.5	21.9	17.9	15.5	13.8	
1900	26.4	24.0	99.5	98.1	94.7	89.4	81.2	74.5	67.9	61.6	55.6	49.6	43.4	38.4	34.9	32.6	30.4	22.2	18.4	15.9	14.8	
France																						
1962	25.1	21.6	98.9	96.4	91.0	81.9	67.0	55.1	44.8	37.4	32.1	26.6	21.1	16.9	14.5	13.3	12.5	10.3	9.2	8.7	8.6	
1954	25.0	22.0	99.3	97.5	92.5	84.2	73.0	60.8	49.7	39.4	32.1	26.2	22.4	19.8	17.6	16.0	14.6	11.1	9.7	9.7	9.7	
1946	26.1	22.9	98.7	97.2	93.4	86.9	78.2	68.7	59.2	50.1	41.7	34.3	29.8	25.5	22.5	18.0	18.6	13.6	12.4	11.8	11.8	
1936	25.2	21.6	98.2	94.3	88.2	80.2	67.8	56.5	46.8	40.0	35.3	30.3	25.3	21.6	19.2	18.0	17.1	14.6	13.7	12.4	10.9	
1931	25.9	21.8	98.6	95.6	90.1	82.1	68.3	57.8	53.5	46.7	37.0	31.9	26.9	23.0	20.6	19.3	18.3	15.4	12.9	11.5	11.0	
1901	25.7	22.9	98.3	95.5	90.5	83.3	73.6	65.1	57.1	50.4	44.7	38.8	32.8	28.1	25.0	23.0	21.2	15.6	13.3	12.0	11.3	
Iceland																						
1950	25.5						57.2					29.7					20.4	18.5	19.8	21.1	20.3	10.5
Ireland																						
1961	27.8	24.7	99.8	99.4	98.1	96.1	91.9	85.9	78.8	70.0	62.0	54.8	49.6	44.5	39.8	37.1	33.8	25.2	22.7	22.1	24.4	
1951	30.4	25.9	99.8	99.4	98.4	96.4	91.9	88.3	82.8	76.8	70.7	65.2	58.4	53.9	49.4	45.4	41.5	31.0	26.8	26.5	25.8	
1946	31.1	26.4	99.8	98.7	97.8	95.4	90.8	87.3	83.2	78.3	72.9	67.5	62.0	56.9	52.4	48.5	44.6	33.8	28.9	26.6	25.3	
1936	31.6	27.8	99.8	99.5	98.6	97.1	93.3	90.5	87.1	83.0	78.2	73.4	68.5	63.8	59.3	55.2	51.1	36.2	28.5	25.9	25.9	
1926	31.5	27.4	99.9	99.6	99.0	97.7	94.1	91.6	88.2	83.4	77.9	72.3	66.5	61.2	56.5	52.4	48.2	35.1	28.2	24.6	23.7	

317

Table 11-1 (*Continued*)

Country	Median age at marriage — Male	Female	Percent single at specified ages — 16	17	18	19	20	21	22	23	24	25	26	27	28	29	30	35	40	45	50	55
N. & W. Europe (cont'd.)																						
Luxembourg 1960	25.3	21.1	99.5	97.2	93.4	85.4	75.7	59.9	48.7	39.0	29.1	26.1	21.4	18.6	17.1	15.6	13.4	11.2	11.2	11.2	11.2	12.7
Netherlands 1960	25.8	23.1	99.6	98.5	95.8	90.9	84.1	74.6	62.6	49.9	39.4	30.3	24.2	20.0	16.9	15.0	13.4	10.9	9.8	9.7	9.7	
Netherlands 1950	26.7	24.4	99.8	99.0	97.2	94.0	88.6	81.2	71.8	62.6	52.8	43.8	36.5	30.7	26.0	21.7	19.3	14.1	13.8	13.7	13.1	
Netherlands 1947	26.8	24.4	99.8	98.9	96.7	92.8	79.3	56.0	77.0	64.7	56.0	47.3	43.0	35.7	31.4	28.4	25.6	18.0	14.8	14.8	14.8	
Netherlands 1930	26.6	24.8	99.8	99.2	97.7	95.0	87.6	83.0	77.0	69.2	60.5	51.8	43.0	35.7	31.1	31.1	28.4	20.3	16.5	15.6	14.8	
Netherlands 1920	26.5	24.9	99.8	99.4	97.9	94.7	86.9	81.9	75.8	68.6	60.6	52.7	44.6	38.0	33.7	33.1	30.2	21.0	17.5	15.9	15.0	
Netherlands 1909	26.7	25.3	100.0	99.7	98.1	96.1	88.9	84.5	78.9	71.7	63.6	55.5	47.3	40.4	35.9	34.5	31.4	21.6	17.8	16.1	17.7	
Netherlands 1899	26.9	25.3	99.9	99.5	98.6	96.5	89.6	85.4	80.0	73.0	65.0	57.1	49.0	42.2	37.6				17.8	15.0	13.8	
Northern Ireland 1951	26.6																					
Norway 1960	25.3	21.8	99.7	97.9	92.3	82.5	71.4	58.5	47.2	37.4	30.3	23.8	20.2	17.1	15.3	13.7	12.3	10.9	10.6	10.6	10.6	
Norway 1950	27.0	23.3	99.8	98.8	95.9	90.8	83.2	74.7	65.2	56.7	49.8	42.6	33.2	30.9	28.7	25.8	22.7	17.5	17.0	17.0	17.0	
Norway 1930	27.0	25.1	99.9	99.6	98.6	94.6	90.7	86.0	82.4	76.5	69.8	63.1	56.3	50.4	45.8	41.0	38.8	28.3	24.9	23.2	21.6	
Norway 1920	27.3	25.1	99.9	99.6	98.1	94.5	87.5	82.6	77.1	70.9	64.4	57.8	51.2	45.1	41.8	39.2	36.7	28.2	24.1	21.8	20.6	
Norway 1910	27.6	25.6	99.7	99.1	97.5	94.5	88.2	83.7	78.6	72.7	66.5	60.2	54.9	49.2	43.9	40.6	37.4	27.5	23.7	21.5	19.8	
Norway 1900	27.2	25.3	99.8	99.4	97.8	94.5	87.3	82.4	76.9	70.3	64.6	58.2	51.7	46.2	44.6	38.6	38.1	27.2	25.2	19.3	20.0	
Scotland 1951	25.5	22.6	99.8	98.8	95.3	88.7	79.0	69.1	58.8	50.5	42.9	36.5	32.2	28.8	25.0	22.9	20.7	17.2	17.8	20.0	20.4	20.6
Scotland 1931	27.2	25.4	99.8	99.0	96.2	93.2	87.3	82.7	77.5	71.9	65.9	60.0	53.9	48.5	44.3	40.8	37.5	27.6	24.0	22.2	21.3	
Scotland 1921	26.7	25.1	99.9	99.2	97.1	93.2	86.3	81.2	75.7	69.9	64.0	58.1	52.1	46.9	42.8	39.8	36.8	27.5	23.6	21.5	20.7	
Scotland 1911	27.4	25.6	100.0	99.7	98.1	96.1	88.4	83.9	78.7	75.3	68.8	60.8	54.6	50.1	45.9	41.6	38.4	29.7	23.3	21.5	20.7	
Scotland 1901	27.0	25.3	100.0	99.4	97.8	94.5	87.3	82.4	76.9	70.9	64.6	58.2	51.7	50.2	42.2	39.2	36.3	27.2	23.1	20.4	18.8	
Sweden 1960	25.5	24.1					57.5					20.7					11.9	10.0	9.5	11.0	13.7	16.9
Sweden 1950	26.1	25.3					59.7					26.4					15.9	14.4	15.8	18.5	19.8	20.4
Sweden 1945	26.5	25.7					63.6					30.4					20.4	19.0	20.4	20.4	21.0	21.7
Sweden 1940	27.6	25.6	100.0	99.7	97.8	93.9	84.5	78.0	72.0	65.0	57.8	50.6	43.3	37.1	33.8	31.8	29.8	25.0	23.6	22.5	21.8	
Sweden 1935	28.9	25.8	100.0	99.9	98.5	95.7	88.9	84.4	79.2	73.0	66.3	59.6	52.8	47.1	43.2	40.5	39.4	24.7	24.7	23.3	24.7	
Sweden 1930	29.0	26.0	100.0	99.9	98.8	96.2	90.1	86.0	80.7	75.4	69.1	62.7	56.2	50.5	46.2	42.8	39.5	23.7	25.2	23.4	22.3	
Sweden 1920	28.4		100.0	99.9	98.8	96.1	89.7	85.5	81.2	74.7	68.1	61.6	54.9	49.2	45.4	42.4	39.7	29.7	25.2	23.2	22.1	
Sweden 1910	28.2		100.0	99.7	98.5	96.1	90.0	86.1	81.1	75.3	68.8	62.4	55.8	50.1	45.9	42.8	39.9	29.2	25.2	22.5	20.5	
Sweden 1900	28.1		100.0	99.6	98.4	96.0	90.1	86.1	81.3	75.5	69.0	62.5	55.9	50.2	46.0	43.0		28.9	23.7	20.3	18.5	
Central Europe																						
Austria 1961	25.6	22.7	99.2	97.0	92.3	84.6	74.3	65.9	57.6	49.7	42.4	35.0	27.5	21.8	18.9	17.8	16.8	14.6	13.1	11.7	11.7	
Austria 1951	26.4	23.7	99.5	98.4	95.3	89.9	82.7	74.4	65.8	58.0	51.0	44.1	40.0	35.9	31.4	27.1	23.2	17.7	14.4	14.1	14.0	
Austria 1934	29.5	26.1	99.7	99.4	98.3	96.2	90.5	87.0	82.4	76.3	69.5	62.6	55.0	49.4	44.7	41.0	37.8	25.3	20.7	18.5	16.7	
Austria 1910		25.9	99.6	99.4	98.3	96.2	92.0	86.4	81.7	76.9	68.8	62.6	55.6	49.4	44.4	40.9	37.4	26.1	21.5	19.4	18.8	
Austria 1900		26.2	99.5	99.1	98.1	96.1	92.6	87.0	82.5	76.9	70.6	64.3	57.8	51.9	46.7	42.2	37.8	24.6	20.7	20.0	19.5	
Czechoslovakia 1961	24.2	20.6	99.5	97.2	86.4	70.8	53.1	39.4	29.7	21.7	16.6	13.5	11.0	9.5	8.4	8.0	7.3	6.5	5.9	6.7	6.4	
Czechoslovakia 1947	25.7	22.5	99.0	96.7	91.5	83.7	71.6	61.8	52.8	45.3	39.1	32.7	26.3	21.2	17.9	16.0	14.3	10.1	9.7	9.6	9.1	
Germany, West 1961	25.5	22.4	99.4	98.0	94.0	86.3	72.5	62.9	53.7	45.6	38.4	31.2	23.9	18.4	15.6	14.6	13.9	12.6	11.6	9.7	9.2	
Germany, West 1950	26.5	23.0	99.8	99.0	96.6	91.7	84.8	76.1	67.4	59.0	51.5	45.3	39.4	34.1	29.2	25.1	21.4	13.8	11.4	11.4	11.4	
Germany, West 1939	26.5	23.2	99.8	99.1	97.7	92.0	87.0	82.2	76.4	69.1	61.0	48.7	44.8	38.0	33.5	30.6	27.7	17.2	15.8	14.4	12.8	
Germany, West 1933	27.7	25.2	99.8	99.1	97.7	95.0	87.0	82.2	76.4	75.3	61.0	53.0	41.8	38.0	30.3		25.8	18.7	15.5	12.8	11.0	
Germany, West 1900												51.0	41.8					17.1	13.0	11.1	10.2	

Table 11-1 *(Continued)*

Country	Median age at marriage — Male	Female	16	17	18	19	20	21	22	23	24	25	26	27	28	29	30	35	40	45	50	55
Germany, West (cont'd.)																						
1910	26.7	24.4	99.9	99.4	98.0	94.7	84.7	76.8	71.6	63.5	54.8	46.1	37.3	30.2	25.9	23.6	21.3	14.5	12.5	11.4	10.6	
1900	25.7	23.5	100.0	99.6	98.1	94.6	85.0	79.0	72.1	64.3	55.9	47.6	39.1	32.2	27.8	25.2	22.6	15.0	12.5	10.9	10.1	
Hungary																						
1960	24.0	20.3	96.3	89.1	77.2	63.2	52.1	38.2	27.2	21.1	18.4	15.3	12.5	10.5	9.3	8.5	8.3	7.8	7.5	7.3	7.2	
1949	25.7	21.4	96.7	91.2	83.2	72.8	63.7	53.3	44.4	38.1	33.6	29.0	24.5	20.9	18.4	16.8	15.5	11.4	9.8	8.8	8.2	
1941	26.6	27.2	97.7	93.5	85.9	75.7	68.7	59.7	51.4	44.5	38.8	33.0	27.2	22.7	20.0	18.6	17.4	12.9	10.6	9.1	7.9	
Switzerland																						
1960	26.2	23.1	100.0	99.6	97.6	93.3	85.9	75.7	65.2	54.3	45.3	37.4	31.5	27.3	23.8	21.8	19.8	16.0	14.8	14.2	14.2	
1950	27.0	24.2	100.0	99.8	98.6	95.8	90.5	83.2	74.3	65.3	56.5	48.7	42.0	36.5	31.9	28.7	26.0	20.6	18.3	18.3	18.3	
1941	28.2	25.3	100.0	99.8	99.1	97.0	90.5	86.7	81.5	74.4	66.2	58.1	49.8	42.9	38.4	35.6	32.7	24.7	22.1	20.5	19.5	
1930	27.8	25.8	100.0	99.9	99.2	97.6	92.2	89.0	84.2	77.4	69.3	61.3	53.0	46.1	41.4	38.2	35.0	25.4	21.9	19.5	17.6	
1920	27.8	25.9	100.0	99.9	99.1	97.4	94.1	89.0	82.2	75.1	67.5	60.8	53.9	48.2	43.1	38.6	35.3	25.8	20.0	18.0	17.6	
Southern Europe																						
Bulgaria																						
1956	23.0	20.0	93.4	84.4	71.5	56.6	47.3	33.6	23.0	17.5	15.4	13.0	11.0	9.4	7.8	6.5	5.7	3.8	2.7	2.2	2.0	
Greece																						
1951	29.0	25.0	98.2	96.0	92.5	88.3	82.0	76.3	70.1	63.5	56.4	49.3	42.2	36.0	31.5	28.0	24.7	12.0	7.2	5.5	4.9	
1928	27.1	22.9	97.9	94.8	89.1	81.6	71.8	63.0	54.7	47.8	41.8	35.7	29.6	24.4	20.4	17.2	14.4	6.9	4.7	3.9	3.7	
1920	29.1	24.6	98.1	96.2	93.1	88.9	81.0	74.9	68.1	60.4	52.2	44.0	35.8	28.7	23.6	19.8	16.2	6.1	4.0	3.2	3.0	
Italy																						
1951	27.6	24.0	98.9	97.5	94.7	90.4	84.0	76.5	67.5	59.0	51.0	44.2	38.8	33.8	29.9	26.3	23.5	18.1	15.9	15.2	14.7	14.4
1931	26.6	24.0	99.0	97.2	94.3	89.7	83.1	74.9	65.8	57.5	50.1	43.4	37.9	34.0	30.7	28.0	25.9	20.0	16.1	13.4	12.5	11.2
1921	27.1	24.4	99.4	97.8	94.3	89.2	80.9	74.2	67.5	61.2	55.2	49.2	43.1	37.8	33.9	30.5	27.5	18.2	14.6	11.5	11.5	
1911	26.2	23.1	99.3	97.4	93.2	86.6	76.1	67.7	59.7	52.7	46.4	40.0	33.6	28.4	25.2	23.4	21.7	15.8	13.3	11.7	10.7	
Malta & Gozo																						
1957							57.7					33.9					25.3	20.3	22.7	24.2	25.9	25.5
Portugal																						
1960	25.5	23.1	97.7	96.7	93.0	86.7	79.9	70.7	61.9	52.6	45.4	39.7	34.9	30.9	28.6	25.4	25.4	19.7	18.6	17.0	18.1	
1950	25.9	23.5	99.1	97.5	94.2	89.0	81.5	73.2	65.6	56.5	49.3	43.4	38.5	33.9	32.0	27.4	28.4	22.5	22.0	19.2	19.7	16.7
1940	26.2	24.1	99.1	97.8	94.9	89.3	81.9	76.0	69.0	61.1	53.9	47.6	43.4	39.7	36.8	32.9	33.8	24.8	24.3	20.5	21.6	16.8
1930	25.9	24.1	99.1	97.6	94.9	95.6	81.8	75.2	68.5	62.0	55.7	49.4	42.9	37.7	34.3	32.1	30.2	22.7	20.0	18.0	16.8	17.8
1920	26.0	24.5	98.4	97.6	95.5	91.1	82.6	76.5	70.2	63.9	57.7	51.5	45.7	40.0	36.6	34.5	32.4	24.3	20.9	19.2	15.8	
1911	26.0	24.2	98.2	97.1	95.1	90.5	81.5	74.9	68.3	62.0	56.0	49.9	43.7	38.7	35.4	33.3	31.4	23.3	20.7	19.7	15.5	
1900	26.7	24.2	98.2	97.1	94.8	90.4	81.8	75.4	68.9	62.7	56.7	50.7	44.5	39.5	36.4	34.5	32.8	24.5	21.8	21.7	16.8	
Spain																						
1960	28.7	25.6	99.8	99.4	98.3	96.2	89.5	85.3	79.9	73.1	65.2	57.5	49.5	42.7	37.8	34.2	30.6	20.0	17.0	14.5	13.3	
1940							40.5					15.4					10.5	9.2	8.9	9.5	10.4	
Northern America																						
Canada																						
1961			98.3	94.8	88.3	78.9	66.8	55.9	46.4	39.4	34.1	28.7	23.3	19.2	16.7	15.5	14.7	12.5	12.3	12.0	11.2	10.5
1951			98.7	96.2	91.6	84.8	75.6	67.6	60.1	53.6	47.9	42.1	36.3	31.6	28.3	26.1	24.1	17.4	13.9	12.0	11.2	
1941			98.5	96.6	92.7	86.8	77.6	70.1	62.7	55.8	49.4	42.9	36.3	30.9	27.1	24.6	24.1	14.8	13.9	11.7	10.5	
1931			98.0	95.4	90.3	82.9	72.7	63.9	55.8	49.1	43.6	37.9	32.1	27.5	24.2	23.3	22.2	13.9	11.9	10.6	9.9	
1921			97.8	94.9	89.8	82.8	74.2	66.2	58.7	52.4	46.9	41.4	35.8	31.2	27.9	25.6	23.5	16.9	12.1	11.5	11.5	
1911																			14.2	12.4	11.7	

Table 11-1 (Continued)

Country	Median age at marriage		Percent single at specified ages																			
	Male	Female	16	17	18	19	20	21	22	23	24	25	26	27	28	29	30	35	40	45	50	55
Northern America (cont'd.)																						
U.S.A.																						
1960........	22.3	20.2	94.0	86.2	74.8	61.2	51.5	38.6	28.4	22.8	20.2	17.3	14.8	12.8	11.3	10.2	9.6	8.4	8.3	8.2	7.8	
1950........	23.0	21.5	95.9	90.6	82.6	72.7	63.8	53.7	45.0	38.8	34.4	29.8	25.4	21.8	19.3	17.7	16.5	12.1	10.0	8.9	8.3	
1940........	24.7	21.4	95.2	89.3	80.9	70.8	62.6	52.6	44.0	37.9	33.4	28.8	24.4	20.8	18.2	16.5	15.0	11.0	9.7	9.3	8.7	
1930........	24.3																					
Oceania																						
New Zealand																						
1956........	25.1	21.9	99.6	98.2	94.4	86.5	74.9	61.3	47.8	37.5	29.8	24.7	20.5	19.1	16.4	14.8	14.1	11.1	10.7	10.7	10.7	
Maori........	24.3	21.0	97.4	91.6	82.2	69.7	58.3	45.3	34.9	28.9	25.7	22.3	19.0	16.3	14.0	12.0	10.6	6.8	5.8	4.5	3.2	
1951........	25.3	22.3	99.7	98.6	96.4	90.7	83.6	73.3	62.9	52.0	43.5	36.6	31.7	27.3	23.8	20.6	19.1	14.9	13.7	13.3	12.6	
Maori........	24.1	23.5	99.2	98.4	96.6	93.0	84.6	78.9	72.6	65.4	57.7	50.1	42.4	36.0	31.8	29.2	26.6	18.3	15.5	14.0	13.2	
1945........	25.8	24.3	100.0	99.1	96.6	92.4	83.7	77.7	70.9	63.3	55.4	47.4	39.3	32.8	29.0	27.0	25.0	18.4	15.2	14.3	14.2	
1936........	27.2	24.2	100.0	99.8	96.9	92.1	82.6	75.7	68.7	61.9	55.3	48.6	41.9	36.2	32.2	29.3	26.7	18.9	16.4	15.4	14.7	
1926........	25.7	24.4	100.0	99.5	96.8	92.3	83.4	77.1	70.4	63.4	56.4	49.3	42.0	36.1	32.0	29.3	26.6	19.5	17.1	15.4	13.2	
1921........	26.8	25.0	100.0	99.7	97.0	92.5	84.4	78.5	72.2	65.5	58.7	51.8	44.8	39.0	35.0	32.2	29.5	21.7	17.2	13.6	10.5	
1916........	26.2	25.5	100.0	99.2	96.4	92.0	84.9	79.2	73.1	66.8	60.5	54.2	47.6	42.1	38.0	35.1	32.1	21.3	15.2	10.8	7.8	
1911........	28.2	26.1	100.0	99.3	97.0	93.4	87.0	82.0	76.3	70.1	63.4	56.7	49.9	43.9	39.1	35.4	31.7	18.8	12.1	7.9	5.9	
1906........	28.3																					
1901........	28.2																					
U.S.S.R.																						
1926........	22.4	20.4	96.6	90.4	79.0	64.1	50.1	34.7	22.8	16.8	14.8	12.4	10.3	8.7	7.2	6.1	5.6	4.2	3.8	3.7	3.6	

Table 11-1 (Continued)

Country	Median age at marriage		Percent single at specified ages																			
	Male	Female	16	17	18	19	20	21	22	23	24	25	26	27	28	29	30	35	40	45	50	55
South West Asia																						
Cyprus 1960	24.0	21.3	97.6	93.6	85.8	75.2	62.9	51.1	41.1	34.4	29.9	25.2	20.6	17.0	14.5	12.8	11.6	7.3	5.9	5.2	4.7	—
Cyprus 1946	24.8	22.6	95.7	90.7	83.4	74.8	67.	58.9	51.0	44.8	39.7	34.5	29.4	25.0	21.6	19.0	16.6	9.2	6.1	4.5	4.0	—
Iraq 1957	25.0	18.5	83.4	66.8	50.4	36.7	35.1	33.6	27.0	22.8	20.1	17.6	15.4	13.6	11.8	10.2	9.0	5.4	4.6	3.8	2.7	—
Israel 1961	25.0	20.8	97.5	92.7	83.2	70.0	55.3	40.9	29.3	22.5	19.0	15.1	11.4	8.7	6.8	5.5	4.9	3.3	2.6	2.6	2.4	
Israel 1948	26.2	21.0	97.4	92.4	83.0	70.6	58.1	45.0	34.4	28.0	24.5	20.6	16.9	14.0	12.0	10.6	9.7	6.7	5.2	4.5	4.0	
Jordan 1961	24.0	19.0	87.9	74.5	59.0	44.4	42.9	31.9	23.3	18.6	16.6	14.4	12.7	11.2	9.6	7.9	6.9	3.7	2.8	2.8	2.8	—
Palestine 1931	26.0						30.1					11.8					5.9	4.5	4.1	4.3	3.9	4.9
Turkey 1960	22.5	18.0	81.3	62.0	41.5	23.7	14.3	17.6	9.7	6.5	6.5	4.7	6.3	6.1	6.0	5.8	2.7	2.4	1.7	1.7	1.9	1.8
Turkey 1955	19.6						20.6					6.5					5.4	3.4	2.3	2.3	2.0	—
Turkey 1945	22.9						18.8					5.9					3.4	2.6	2.6	2.6	3.0	2.8
South Central Asia																						
Ceylon 1953	25.8	19.3	89.2	78.0	65.0	52.0	48.7	38.3	29.9	24.4	21.1	17.7	14.6	12.2	10.4	9.2	8.4	5.9	5.1	4.9	3.8	—
Ceylon 1946	26.0	19.7	89.4	77.9	64.0	50.1	46.3	35.1	26.2	21.0	18.5	15.8	13.4	11.5	9.9	8.5	7.6	4.8	4.1	3.9	3.6	—
Ceylon 1921	25.9	19.1	87.3	74.1	59.6	45.9	45.7	35.9	28.2	23.7	21.4	19.1	17.2	15.6	14.3	13.2	12.5	10.1	9.1	7.8	7.0	—
Ceylon 1911	26.0						27.1					15.4					12.3	9.9	10.0	8.0	8.4	7.3
Ceylon 1901	23.0	16.4					10.1	10.1	10.1	10.1	10.1	10.1	10.1	10.1	10.0	10.0	10.0	10.0	9.9	9.8	9.6	—
India 1961	18.9	17.2	74.1	48.7	26.0	10.1	5.9					1.9					1.0	.7	.6	.5	.5	.4
India 1941	18.5						4.1					1.4					.9	.9	.9	1.0	.9	.9
India 1931	18.5	17.0					6.2					2.4					1.9	1.4	1.3	1.1	1.0	1.0
India 1921	18.5						5.1					2.5					1.9	1.5	1.4	1.3	1.2	1.2
India 1911	18.4	17.1					4.4					2.2					1.7	1.4	1.3	1.1	1.1	1.2
India 1901	18.4	17.1					5.1					3.0					2.2	2.0	1.4	1.3	1.1	1.4
Pakistan 1961	22.1	17.1					5.8					2.5					1.5	1.3	1.0	1.0	.7	.8
South East Asia																						
North Borneo 1960	24.0						20.8					4.8					2.8	1.8	1.9	1.7	1.6	2.1
Philippines 1960	24.2	21.3	95.4	89.8	81.3	70.9	61.9	51.1	42.0	35.6	31.2	26.6	22.1	18.5	16.1	14.5	13.3	8.9	7.6	7.5	6.4	—
Sarawak 1960	23.3						25.5					7.9					4.2	2.7	2.7	2.9	2.9	2.3
Sarawak 1947	24.3						21.3					7.1					4.3	2.8	3.1	2.5	3.1	—
East Asia																						
China 1956	23.0	20.3	97.7	92.6	82.4	68.3	52.6	37.3	24.9	17.7	14.1	10.1	6.3	3.7	2.2	1.6	1.6	1.6	1.4	1.1	.9	—
Hong Kong 1961	28.1						48.6					15.5					6.0	5.0	5.9	7.4	8.2	6.9

Table 11-1 (Continued)

Country	Median age at marriage		Percent single at specified ages																			
	Male	Female	16	17	18	19	20	21	22	23	24	25	26	27	28	29	30	35	40	45	50	55
East Asia (Cont'd)																						
Japan																						
1960.......	27.0	24.3	100.0	100.0	99.0	95.6	84.4	78.3	70.4	60.2	48.8	37.5	25.9	17.2	13.2	12.2	11.2	6.5	3.8	2.2	1.7	–
1955.......	<20.4	24.2	100.0	99.7	98.1	94.1	82.9	76.2	68.1	58.2	47.3	36.5	25.4	17.0	12.8	11.4	10.0	4.7	2.7	1.9	1.4	–
1950.......	25.8	23.0	100.0	98.9	95.2	88.3	74.4	64.7	55.0	45.7	36.9	28.1	19.1	12.3	8.9	7.8	6.9	3.5	2.2	1.6	1.6	–
1940.......	26.5	22.8	99.7	98.1	94.0	86.7	72.8	63.0	53.1	43.8	35.0	26.1	17.1	10.5	7.3	6.6	5.9	3.3	2.2	1.7	1.4	–
1935.......	25.8	21.8	98.7	95.5	89.0	79.3	65.3	53.6	43.0	34.7	27.9	21.0	14.0	8.9	6.2	5.2	4.5	2.6	1.9	1.6	1.4	–
1930.......	25.3	21.1	97.4	92.7	84.1	72.3	58.8	45.9	34.8	27.1	21.8	16.2	10.7	6.7	4.7	4.0	3.7	2.6	2.0	1.6	1.4	–
1925.......	24.8	20.2	96.3	89.9	78.8	64.6	51.4	38.6	25.2	18.7	15.8	12.5	9.5	7.2	5.5	4.4	3.8	2.5	2.0	1.8	1.6	–
1920.......	24.7	20.4	93.8	85.6	73.9	60.4	51.0	38.3	27.9	21.6	18.2	14.5	11.0	8.4	6.6	5.3	4.6	2.9	2.3	2.0	1.8	–
Korea																						
1960.......	26.0	–	–	90.0	77.4	60.8	45.0	27.8	14.8	8.8	7.4	5.5	4.0	2.9	1.8	.7	.4	.3	.3	.2	.1	–
1955.......	24.5	20.2	96.6																			–
Ryukyu Islands																						
1960.......	25.5	23.4	99.5	99.1	97.4	93.9	83.5	77.2	69.8	60.9	51.2	41.5	31.7	23.6	18.3	14.9	11.6	3.4	2.0	1.4	1.2	–
1955.......	24.9	23.6	100.0	98.8	95.4	88.8	74.8	65.4	55.7	46.1	36.7	27.3	17.8	10.6	7.1	6.0	5.1	2.0	1.2	.9	.7	–
1950.......	23.0	21.3	99.4	96.5	89.2	77.8	62.0	48.6	37.2	29.5	24.5	19.2	13.9	10.0	7.8	6.8	6.2	3.7	2.6	2.5	1.8	–
Middle America																						
Costa Rica																						
1950.......	23.0	20.4	93.4	87.1	78.9	69.3	63.3	54.6	47.3	42.4	39.2	35.9	32.8	30.1	27.9	26.0	24.5	20.2	18.9	18.6	18.3	–
Curacao																						
1960.......							63.7					38.3					25.8	21.8	23.1	23.1	26.1	26.8
El Salvador																						
1950.......	23.5						47.3					32.0					26.5	24.9	26.7	27.4	29.1	28.6
Guatemala																						
1950.......	22.8						32.5					20.5					17.5	16.1	16.6	17.9	19.6	19.4
Haiti																						
1950.......	26.8						62.6					33.8					22.0	17.5	19.1	20.8	26.1	26.4
Honduras																						
1961.......	24.0						39.4					24.5					20.6	19.8	21.8	24.1	28.3	30.5
Nicaragua																						
1950.......	24.8						49.2					34.1					28.8	25.0	26.1	26.7	30.3	29.0
Panama																						
1960.......	24.1						42.2					25.8					19.6	18.5	20.3	22.6	25.6	30.0
1950.......							40.3					24.9					21.0	20.3	22.7	25.3	26.3	27.4
Puerto Rico																						
1960.......	23.6	20.8	93.0	84.6	74.1	62.7	56.4	46.1	37.4	31.2	26.8	22.4	18.1	14.8	12.4	10.9	9.8	6.4	5.5	5.6	5.3	–
1950.......	24.3																					
South America																						
Bolivia																						
1950.......	23.0	21.0	94.4	88.1	79.3	68.9	61.6	51.7	43.4	38.0	34.7	31.1	27.7	24.9	22.5	20.6	19.1	14.4	12.9	12.1	9.8	–
Chile																						
1920.......	25.8	23.0	96.6	93.1	88.5	82.6	77.8	72.0	66.5	61.9	57.9	53.8	49.7	46.2	43.5	41.4	39.4	31.4	27.3	23.9	22.3	–

322

Table 11-1 (Continued)

Country	Median age at marriage		Percent single at specified ages																			
	Male	Female	16	17	18	19	20	21	22	23	24	25	26	27	28	29	30	35	40	45	50	55
South America (cont'd.)																						
Ecuador																						
1950......	23.6											25.4					20.0	18.2	18.6	17.5	18.3	17.1
Paraguay																						
1962......	24.7											33.2					26.0	22.2	25.1	27.1	27.3	32.6
1950......	25.8											39.5					31.8	29.9	30.3	32.1	33.4	34.6
Peru																						
1940......	25.0	21.1	93.3	87.2	78.8	68.5	59.6	52.8	48.7	43.5	40.7	38.9	34.8	32.5	31.4	26.7	27.2	23.4	20.8	19.1	17.2	15.9
Venezuela																						
1961......	25.2	19.1																				
1950......	25.5	25.6	86.6	78.4	70.9	62.5	53.9	50.0	46.1	42.2	39.3	36.6	34.3	32.2	31.5	29.3	28.0	26.7	26.7	26.7	26.7	
1941......	29.4	24.3	95.3	91.8	88.7	84.1	83.2	79.9	77.1	75.2	73.7	72.3	70.9	69.5	68.1	66.7	65.4	60.7	58.3	49.4	44.2	
1936......	30.5		96.7	94.1	91.7	87.8	86.1	83.0	80.2	77.8	75.9	73.8	71.8	70.1	68.6	67.5	66.4	60.7	58.0	56.4	52.6	
Northern Africa																						
Algeria (Moslem)																						
1948......	25.0	18.2	85.1	69.1	51.8	36.2	31.9	27.7	19.7	15.6	14.0	12.4	11.3	10.3	8.8	7.3	6.3	3.8	2.8	2.5	2.3	
Egypt																						
1960......	24.7	19.2	89.7	77.8	62.8	47.2	41.7	28.8	18.8	13.7	11.8	9.6	7.9	6.6	5.3	4.2	3.6	2.2	1.7	1.7	.5	
1947......	24.8	18.1	83.1	65.6	47.3	31.3	28.0	24.7	16.9	12.5	10.6	8.7	7.3	6.2	5.0	2.9	3.4	1.9	1.3	1.0	.8	
Morocco (Indg. Pop.)																						
1952......							8.3					3.3					1.8	1.7	1.9	1.5	1.9	1.8
Tunisia (Moslem)																						
1946......	26.1						28.6					13.1					7.4	6.0	4.3	4.3	3.6	3.8
Tropical & Southern Africa																						
Guinea																						
1955......	24.1	16.3					1.8					.7					.3	.2	-	-	-	-
Libya																						
1954......	25.7																					
Seychelles																						
1960......	27.0	24.6	98.3	96.5	93.8	89.1	84.1	79.5	74.8	70.1	65.6	61.0	56.3	52.5	50.0	48.4	43.9	39.3	33.3	31.2	30.3	
South Africa 1960																						
Asian..	25.6	21.9	96.5	90.7	82.3	72.5	64.7	55.0	46.4	39.8	34.6	29.3	24.1	19.9	17.1	15.2	13.7	7.7	3.8	2.5	2.2	1.8
Colored..	25.2	22.8	98.5	96.1	91.1	83.6	73.4	64.6	56.5	49.9	44.5	38.8	33.2	28.6	25.2	22.7	20.6	14.5	11.9	10.0	8.9	
1951																						
Asian..	25.1	20.2	93.0	84.4	72.9	60.3	53.1	41.6	32.1	26.2	22.5	18.7	15.1	12.2	10.0	8.3	7.0	3.4	2.2	1.8	1.5	
Colored..	25.7	23.0	98.8	96.6	91.8	84.7	75.0	66.6	58.8	52.5	47.2	41.7	36.3	31.8	28.7	26.5	24.6	17.7	14.4	12.5	11.8	
White..	25.1	23.0	98.4	94.4	86.1	75.0	62.9	49.8	37.8	29.1	23.1	18.8	15.4	13.6	11.2	10.3	9.9	7.7	7.7	7.7	7.7	

Table 11-1 (Continued)

Country	Median age at marriage Male	Female	\multicolumn{20}{c}{Percent single at specified ages}

Country	Male	Female	16	17	18	19	20	21	22	23	24	25	26	27	28	29	30	35	40	45	50	55
South Africa (cont'd.)																						
1946																						
Asian....	24.4	19.3	90.4	79.4	65.8	51.5	46.0	34.0	24.4	18.8	16.0	13.0	10.3	8.3	6.5	5.2	4.4	3.1	2.8	1.9	.6	
Colored.	26.2	23.2	99.2	97.1	92.6	85.6	75.5	67.1	59.1	52.1	46.0	39.8	33.5	28.3	24.9	22.7	20.7	14.3	11.3	9.7	8.9	
Eur. Pop.	25.6	21.5	98.3	94.8	88.3	78.6	65.7	54.5	44.6	37.2	31.7	26.0	20.3	16.1	13.7	12.6	11.9	10.5	10.5	10.0	8.7	
1941																						
White....	25.8	21.8	98.3	94.0	87.1	78.2	66.8	56.3	47.0	40.2	35.1	29.8	24.6	20.6	18.1	16.9	15.9	13.0	11.3	9.8	8.2	
1936																						
Colored..	26.6	22.9	98.4	95.5	90.0	82.4	73.0	64.4	56.5	49.9	44.4	38.8	33.1	28.5	25.1	22.8	20.8	14.3	10.5	8.8	8.2	
1926	27.0	23.6	98.3	96.1	92.3	86.6	77.3	70.1	62.6	55.0	47.6	40.2	32.7	26.5	22.5	19.9	17.5	11.5	9.8	8.5	8.0	
1921																						
Asian....	26.7	23.5	99.7	98.1	94.1	87.7	76.9	68.4	60.3	53.2	47.0	40.6	34.1	29.0	25.8	23.9	22.2	15.7	12.6	10.4	6.6	
Colored	25.5	22.7	99.2	97.1	92.2	84.6	73.0	63.6	54.8	47.6	41.4	35.1	28.7	23.7	20.3	18.2	16.3	11.1	9.0	8.0	8.1	
1911																						
White	27.7	22.3	98.9	96.2	90.6	82.3	70.9	61.1	52.2	45.3	39.7	34.0	28.3	23.7	20.4	18.2	16.4	11.4	9.7	8.7	8.3	

The list of nations that may be said to have "early marriage" patterns is much longer:

Africa	Asia	Latin America and South America	Northern America
Algeria	Brunei	British Guiana	United States (white population)
Kenya	Burma	Colombia	
Sudan	Ceylon	Cuba	
Swaziland	Indonesia	Ecuador	
Togo	Iraq	Guatemala	*Europe*
Tanganyika	Iran	Honduras	Hungary
Uganda	Jordan	Mexico	
United Arab Republic	Kuwait	Nicaragua	
	Malaya	Panama	
	Mongolia	Salvadore	*Oceania*
	North Borneo	Trinidad and Tobago	
	Sarawak	Venezuela	Fiji Islands
	Singapore		New Caledonia
	Thailand		Solomon Islands
	Turkey		

Perhaps some readers will be surprised to discover that in 1960 the United States white population fell within this "early marriage" group. Among all of the industrialized nations of the world, this population is the only one that falls in this category; all other highly industrialized nations are in the "maturity" or "late" marriage category.

Almost all of the "industrialized nations" have patterns of marriage at maturity, but they share this pattern with many less developed nations:

Africa	Europe and USSR	Northern America	South America
Basutoland	Albania	Barbados	Bolivia
Dominion of South Africa	Bulgaria	Bermuda	Brazil
	Cyprus	Canada	Paraguay
Madagascar	Czechoslovakia	Costa Rica	Peru
Mauritius	Denmark	Dominican Republic	Puerto Rico
Sierra Leone	England and Wales	Guadalupe	
	France	Martinique	*Oceania*
Asia	Gibraltar	Montserrat	
	Hungary	Netherlands Antilles	Australia
Cambodia	Iceland	St. Kitts	Guam
China	Luxembourg	St. Lucia	New Zealand
Hong Kong	Malta	United States (nonwhite population)	Pacific Islands
Israel	Norway	Virgin Islands	Western Samoa
Korea	USSR		
Philippines	Yugoslavia		
South Vietnam			

The nations that fall in the "late marriage" pattern are primarily European or Central and South American. It is not known to what extent "conviviente" marriage and deficiency in the data allow some of the Latin American and some small countries to fall in this category. Japan is an outstanding exception to the pattern of early marriage in Asia. The census data that indicate late marriage for nations are as follows:

Europe	Northern America	South America
Austria	Dominica	Argentina
Belgium	Granada	Chile
Finland	Greenland	Venezuela
Greece	Haiti	
Ireland	St. Pierre and Miquelon	Oceania
Italy	St. Vincent	
Netherlands		Niue
Pharoah Islands	Africa	Tonga Island
Portugal		
Scotland	Seychelles	
Spain	South Africa (colored)	
Sweden		
Switzerland	Asia	
West Germany		
	Japan	
	Macau	
	Ryukyu Islands	

By noting the countries that fall in each of the three categories, we can develop a few hypotheses pertaining to the factors that promote early and late marriage. Apparently, a low level of literacy and a low level of industrial development tend to be associated with early marriage. A high level of industrialization and literacy have tended to be associated with late marriage. But as we can clearly see, these relationships are very general, with many exceptions. We have already noticed, on the one hand, that the white population of the United States falls in the "early marriage" group. On the other hand, we must note that some of the nations with a very late pattern of marriage—Ireland, Greece, Italy, Spain—are not among the more highly industrialized and urbanized nations of the world. In some nations where there is much common-law marriage and "living together" the median age at first marriage

Bachelorhood-Spinsterhood Unusually Scarce

Africa	Asia	Europe	Oceania
Algeria	Afghanistan	Bulgaria	American Samoa
Congo	Brunei	Romania	Cook Islands
Ghana	Burma		Fiji Islands
Guinea	Cambodia		Niue
Ivory Coast	Ceylon		Solomon Islands
Kenya	China		Western Samoa
Libya	Cyprus		
Madagascar	Federation of Malaya		
Mauritius	India		
Morocco	Indonesia		
Nigeria	Iran		
Reunion	Iraq		
South Africa (Asia)	Israel		
Togo	Japan		
Tunisia	Jordan		
Upper Volta	Kuwait		
United Arab Republic	Mongolia		
Zanzibar	North Borneo		
Sudan	Pakistan		
	Ryukyu Islands		
	Sarawak		
	South Korea		
	South Vietnam		
	Thailand		
	Turkey		

tends to be late, and may reflect census definitions. Clearly, much research needs to be done before an adequate theory is developed that would explain differences in marriage patterns between the nations of the world.

But we must not dismiss lightly the cultural elements that underlie marriage patterns. For example, migrants from India have found their way to many parts of the world—Burma, Thailand, Africa, Malaya, and even the Caribbean. Despite generations of separation from their homeland and despite the fact that it usually is disapproved or "deviant behavior" in the country to which they have migrated, they have persisted in child marriage.

Proportions Ever Marrying. Another way of viewing the nations of the world is to note whether the proportion ever marrying is high,

intermediate, or low. A high proportion ever marrying, of course, indicates a low level of bachelorhood or spinsterhood, whereas a low proportion ever marrying indicates high prevalence of bachelorhood and spinsterhood. If we establish for females the limit of 95 percent and above as representing low spinsterhood, 90 to 95 percent as representing "normal" spinsterhood, and below 90 percent as representing unusually great spinsterhood, we can classify the nations again. In order to avoid repeating a very long list of nations that fall in the "normal" group, we present only the two extreme groups: nations where an unusually high proportion (20 percent or more) never marry and nations where a very low proportion (5 percent or less) never marry.

Bachelorhood-Spinsterhood Unusually Prevalent (20 Percent or More)

Africa	*Middle America*	*South America*	*Europe*
Seychelles	Barbados	Argentina	Iceland
St. Helena	Costa Rica	Brazil	Ireland
	Cuba	British Guiana	Malta and Gozo
	Dominican Republic	Chile	Scotland
	Dominica	Colombia	
	El Salvador	Ecuador	*Oceania*
	Guadalupe	Paraguay	
	Guatemala	Peru	Pacific Islands
	Grenada	Venezuela	
	Haiti		
	Honduras		
	Jamaica		
	Martinique		
	Montserrat		
	Netherlands Antilles		
	Nicaragua		
	Panama		
	St. Kitts		
	St. Lucia		
	St. Vincent		
	Tobago		
	Trinidad		
	Virgin Islands		

To a substantial degree, the high apparent proportion of spinsters in many of the countries of Middle and South America is due to the "conviviente" or consensual union arrangement described above. Many such unions have been dissolved by age 45, even where they are recognized as marriages in official national censuses or are not so reported by the respondents.

In general, early marriage tends to be accompanied by low levels and late marriage by a high prevalence of bachelorhood and spinsterhood. This is graphed in Figure 11.2. The relationship is only a rather general one, however. Each nation of the world seems to have its own unique pattern of age at marriage and prevalence of bachelorhood. As was true for

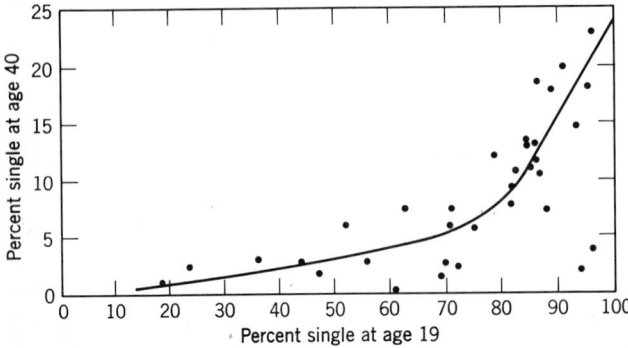

Figure 11-2 Scattergram of Percent of Females Single at Age 40 Plotted against Percent of Females Single at Age 19, Selected Nations of the World: Circa 1960.

SOURCE: Table 11-2.

the age-at-marriage pattern, there seems to be no adequate explanation of such variation in bachelorhood around the world. One possible explanation is religion: wherever the Christian religion is predominant, avoidance of marriage tends to be more prevalent than where the religion is Muslim, Hindu, Buddha, African, or other.

Consensual Unions in Latin America. Any review of international marriage patterns must pay special attention to the institution of "consensual" or "conviviente" unions common in Latin America and to the cohabitation arrange-

ments of Negro populations all over the world. Unfortunately, these quasi-institutionalized marital statuses have received insufficient research attention from both demographers and sociologists. Mortara has undertaken to make international comparisons, despite weaknesses in and poor comparability of the data.[6] Table 11-2, taken from his report, demonstrates that consensual unions are an integral part of the culture in several nations. His tabulation shows

[6] Giorgia Mortara, "Les Uniones Consensuelles dans l'Amérique Latine," *Proceedings of the International Population Conference* (New York, 1961).

Table 11-2 Proportions of the Population in Consensual Unions and Ratio of Such Unions to Marriages, Selected Nations of Latin America: 1940 to 1950

Country	Percent of men 15 years and over:		Percent of women 15 years and over:		Persons in consensual union per 100 persons married:	
	Married	In cons. union	Married	In cons. union	Men	Women
Mexico................	50.4	12.2	49.9	12.9	24.1	25.8
Guatemala............	18.9	40.3	19.4	41.5	213.2	213.1
El Salvador..........	26.4	24.9	25.1	26.2	94.5	104.3
Honduras.............	22.6	22.4	22.7	22.3	98.9	98.0
Nicaragua............	29.6	21.1	28.5	21.6	71.4	76.1
Costa Rica...........	44.2	7.6	43.2	7.4	17.2	17.2
Panama...............	23.9	27.9	25.2	31.8	116.6	126.4
Cuba.................	36.1	18.2	38.9	21.3	50.5	54.7
Jamaica..............	27.9	19.1	26.2	17.4	68.5	66.5
Haiti................	13.7	37.8	12.8	40.2	276.6	314.7
Rep. Dominican.......	26.5	24.0	26.3	28.3	90.7	107.5
Puerto Rico..........	43.9	13.2	44.8	14.6	30.0	32.6
Trinidad & Tobago....	31.0	26.9	31.5	28.2	86.7	89.7
Colombia.............	39.9	9.0	38.8	9.5	22.4	24.4
Venezuela............	29.3	18.3	28.5	20.5	62.4	71.9
Ecuador..............	44.2	12.4	42.8	13.2	28.1	30.9
Peru.................	37.2	17.2	32.7	18.4	46.4	56.3
Bolivia..............	50.3	9.6	46.2	10.3	19.1	22.4
Paraguay.............	34.9	15.2	31.9	14.3	43.6	44.7
Chile................	48.8	3.4	46.8	3.4	7.0	7.3

Source: Mortara, Giorgio, "Les uniones consensuelles dans l' Amérique Latine" International Population Conference: New York, 1961. (Proceedings)

that as of about 1950 in five Latin American countries the number of persons living in consensual unions was larger than the number living in normal marriages—in Guatemala, Panama, Haiti, Dominican Republic, and El Salvador. In eight others there were more than 50 consensual unions per 100 regular marriages— in Honduras, Nicaragua, Cuba, Jamaica, Trinidad, Tobago, Venezuela, and Peru. Only Chile and Costa Rica in the group of nations studied had fewer than 20 consensual unions per 100 marriages. Mortara's table reveals that in most of the nations more women than men report themselves as living in consensual unions; this indicates in yet another way the deficiencies in marital status data.

"Conviviente" marriages are declining in many Latin American nations. Technical, economic, and social developments are causing this institution to yield to legally approved unions. Inasmuch as we suspect that the Braithwaite-Roberts finding that irregular unions tend to lower fertility is a general principle of demography, this trend toward legal unions may constitute a slight force to increase still further the already high birthrates of Latin America.

11.4. International Differences between Male and Female Patterns in Age at Marriage and Proportions Marrying

All over the world males tend to marry at an age that averages 1 to 5 years older than for females. As a consequence, the proportion of never-married young males is universally larger than that of females. Table 11-3 reports the differences in the proportion that is single between females and males (proportion of females of a given age who are single subtracted from proportion of single males at the same age). By adding the differences in Table 11-3 to the proportions in Table 11-1 it is possible to derive for males a table matching Table 11-1 for females.

This disparity between the sexes in marital status begins with the earliest ages of marriage and continues through age 30 or 35. From zero it rises to a maximum at age 22 or 23 and then gradually declines to zero again after age 30. At its maximum point it almost always involves 20 percent or more of the population, that is, at least 20 percent more of females than of

males are married at this age.) In a few nations the disparity becomes very large:

Maximum Disparity

Country	Age	Amount (%)
Ceylon	22	56
Israel	22	47
Korea	22	54
Egypt	22	58
Czechoslovakia	22	47
Hungary	22	49

In most of the industrialized nations maximum disparity is between 25 and 30 percentage points and occurs at age 23 about as often as at age 22.

There are some substantial differences between nations in this disparity. In most European populations the median age at first marriage is 2.7 to 3.7 years greater for males than for females. In general, the older the median age of bride at marriage, the smaller the discrepancy tends to be. This is another way of stating that the institution of child marriage of males occurs almost nowhere in the world, and that international differences in age at marriage for males are smaller than for females. Consider, for example, India, Pakistan, and the other child marriage nations for which data are available; in all cases the median age at first marriage for grooms is 6 years or more older than that for brides. But age disparity of marriage partners is not completely explained in this fashion; there seem to be genuine cultural differences and preferences in this respect. (See Exercises 1 and 2.)

In most nations there is also a substantial difference between the sexes in the proportions ever marrying by age 45 or 50. Usually a higher proportion of males than of females ever marry. This can result from the combined action of several factors:

1. Never-married men continue to marry at ages beyond 40, whereas women who have not married by this age tend not to marry at all. Often these older men marry a widow or a divorced woman instead of a never-married woman.

2. Men may migrate to other countries, leaving behind women who thus cannot find a mate.

Table 11-3 Difference between Males and Females in Median Age at First Marriage and Proportions Marrying at Each Age, Nations of the World for Which Data Are Available: 1900 to 1961

Country	Med. age at mar-riage	Percentage point difference at specified age 16	17	18	19	20	21	22	23	24	25	26	27	28	29	30	35	40	45	50
N. & W. Europe																				
Belgium																				
1960	2.7	.8	2.1	5.7	10.6	16.0	21.3	24.2	23.5	20.3	17.4	14.3	11.5	9.7	8.4	6.9	3.1	1.9	-.5	-2.4
1947	2.6	.7	1.9	4.8	9.9	15.7	20.9	23.8	22.9	19.6	16.7	13.5	10.5	8.3	6.5	4.5	-2.0	-3.4	-2.9	-2.8
1930	1.9	.3	.9	2.6	5.1	10.2	13.7	15.8	15.6	13.8	12.1	10.9	8.6	7.1	5.8	4.3	.3	-.1	-.9	-1.9
1920	1.8	.3	1.2	2.3	7.1	11.2	15.0	17.3	17.0	14.8	13.0	10.4	9.1	7.6	6.5	5.2	1.0	.8	-1.9	-2.1
1900	1.8	.4	1.3	3.1	6.8	10.3	13.6	15.7	15.4	13.6	12.0	10.4	8.7	7.5	6.4	5.2	.8	.3	-.9	-.9
Denmark																				
1960	3.3	.4	2.0	7.5	16.2	20.4	30.2	36.6	37.4	34.3	29.2	21.5	15.0	12.3	11.4	10.0	4.8	3.0	1.0	-1.0
1950	3.6	.2	1.6	6.2	14.1	19.1	28.4	34.7	36.4	33.4	28.9	22.6	17.0	14.2	12.8	10.9	3.2	0.0	-3.6	-5.3
1945	3.5	.1	1.1	4.3	10.8	14.8	23.0	28.8	28.4	25.4	22.8	22.0	17.5	14.7	13.2	10.9	1.4	-2.7	-5.2	-6.3
1940	3.4	-.1	.8	3.7	9.5	17.9	24.5	28.5	28.4	25.4	22.9	20.0	17.0	14.2	11.7	8.8	-.6	-4.3	-6.1	-6.3
1935	2.8	-.1	.4	2.7	7.1	14.4	19.7	23.1	21.2	23.4	21.6	18.2	16.0	13.4	10.6	7.5	-2.2	-5.7	-5.7	-6.2
1930	2.5	.1	.5	2.2	6.0	13.1	17.9	21.1	21.6	19.4	17.7	16.0	13.8	11.0	8.1	4.9	-4.0	-6.0	-6.0	-6.8
1921	2.1	.1	.9	2.2	5.5	11.2	15.3	17.7	17.6	15.8	14.1	12.4	10.3	8.2	6.1	3.9	-4.4	-5.6	-6.0	-5.6
1911	1.9	.5	.9	2.2	5.1	10.9	14.9	17.2	16.9	14.9	13.1	11.1	8.9	6.6	4.3	1.9	-4.4	-5.7	-6.0	-5.5
1901	1.8	.1	.5	1.9	4.6	6.8	12.1	16.3	17.5	15.4	13.9	10.0	6.8	11.7	4.5	2.2	-3.0	-.6	-4.6	-4.6
England & Wales																				
1961	3.7	.2	1.4	5.3	11.9	19.9	27.1	28.3	25.9	22.9	18.9	15.7	12.8	10.7	8.4	6.5	1.2	-1.2	-2.9	-4.0
1921	1.2	.2	.4	1.8	4.5	7.3	9.9	11.3	10.6	8.7	7.0	5.1	3.3	1.9	.6	-.7	-4.0	-4.3	-4.3	-4.4
1911	1.2	0.0	.3	1.3	3.5	7.3	10.0	11.6	11.4	9.9	8.6	7.0	5.6	4.4	3.4	2.3	-1.8	-3.0	-3.7	-3.9
Finland																				
1960	2.8	.3	2.1	6.4	11.7	14.5	19.2	23.9	24.9	23.4	30.6	14.7	10.6	8.9	8.8	8.1	2.7	-1.0	-3.9	-5.5
1950	2.9	0.0	1.4	5.2	9.7	12.2	19.0	23.1	23.4	21.9	18.1	12.3	7.7	5.7	5.1	3.8	-2.1	-4.6	-6.4	-7.9
1940	2.8	0.0	.7	2.7	6.1	12.8	17.6	20.4	20.5	18.7	16.9	15.1	13.1	11.2	9.4	7.4	0.0	-3.5	-3.5	-5.2
1930	2.2	0.0	.8	2.8	5.6	10.2	13.7	16.0	16.1	14.7	13.5	12.3	10.7	9.0	7.1	5.1	-1.3	-3.7	-	-
1920	2.3	.3	1.5	2.4	4.8	9.3	12.6	14.7	15.0	13.7	12.8	11.6	10.4	9.3	7.7	5.8	-1.9	-1.9	-1.9	-3.4
1910	2.2	.5	1.9	3.8	7.2	10.9	14.5	16.6	16.7	15.2	13.9	12.5	10.9	7.7	5.9	5.9	0.0	-1.8	-2.5	-2.5
1900	2.2			4.7	8.8	11.6	15.2	17.3	17.2	15.6	14.1	12.5	10.8	9.6	8.4	7.1	2.3	-0.1	-.8	-1.5
France																				
1961	3.5	1.1	3.5	8.1	14.9	23.2	31.1	35.4	34.0	28.9	24.1	19.0	14.8	12.6	11.8	10.4	5.3	2.7	1.4	1.1
1954	3.0	.7	2.3	7.0	13.6	16.5	24.3	29.1	30.5	27.4	23.1	16.4	10.7	8.2	7.5	6.6	3.2	2.8	1.5	0.0
1946	3.2	1.3	2.7	5.6	13.1	13.1	19.0	23.5	23.5	26.0	25.3	21.5	18.7	16.7	15.0	13.4	5.7	1.4	-1.3	-3.3
1936	3.6	1.8	5.6	11.0	17.3	23.4	31.1	35.0	32.9	36.9	21.4	15.5	10.7	8.5	7.8	6.6	.5	-2.6	-3.3	-2.4
1931	3.4	1.6	4.0	9.2	15.6	22.1	28.6	31.9	27.7	24.8	19.9	14.6	10.2	7.7	6.3	4.6	-1.5	-2.1	-2.0	-1.9
1911	3.5	.7	4.4	8.0	15.5	26.1	34.8	39.4	35.8	31.8	26.4	20.7	8.1	6.0	4.9	3.6	2.4	.4	-.1	-.6
1901	2.8	1.6	4.4	9.1	15.5	24.6	32.5	36.9	35.8	30.9	26.6	22.0	17.6	14.4	12.0	9.3	2.1	.5	-.6	-.8
Iceland																				
1950																				
Ireland																				
1961	3.1	.2	.5	1.6	3.3	5.9	11.0	15.6	19.8	21.7	22.9	21.9	21.5	22.1	21.5	21.4	16.8	12.5	9.4	4.8
1951	4.5	.2	.5	1.4	3.2	6.7	9.5	13.3	16.2	18.2	19.6	22.2	22.5	23.1	23.3	23.4	18.2	11.8	6.5	4.7
1946	4.7	.2	.9	2.1	4.0	7.5	10.1	12.6	15.8	17.2	19.4	21.5	23.0	23.6	23.6	23.6	18.3	12.0	8.2	6.0
1936	3.8	.2	.5	1.3	2.6	5.6	7.7	9.8	11.8	13.8	15.7	17.5	18.9	19.6	19.8	19.9	17.4	13.6	10.1	8.3
1926	4.1	.1	.4	.9	2.1	5.0	6.9	8.9	11.0	12.9	14.9	17.0	18.5	19.6	20.2	20.8	19.0	15.3	11.2	7.0

Table 11-3 *(Continued)*

Percentage point difference at specified age

Country	Med. age at marriage	16	17	18	19	20	21	22	23	24	25	26	27	28	29	30	35	40	45	50
Central Europe (cont'd.)																				
Germany, West																				
1961	3.1	.6	1.8	5.7	12.4	18.8	24.7	28.2	27.6	24.5	21.5	18.3	15.0	11.9	9.0	5.8	4.0	-5.8	-4.8	-4.3
1950	3.5	.2	1.0	3.2	7.4	8.4	14.0	18.0	19.4	18.4	16.2	13.4	11.1	10.2	9.8	8.9	1.0	-2.1	-4.1	-5.6
1939	3.6	.2	.9	3.1	7.7	19.7	27.3	31.9	32.0	29.0	26.4	23.3	20.1	16.9	13.7	10.1	-1.5	-6.4	-7.8	-7.0
1933	2.5	.9	.9	2.2	4.7	10.9	13.7	16.7	15.8	17.6	17.2	10.7	8.6	6.1	10.0	6.5	4.8	-7.6	-6.5	-5.2
1925	1.5	.2	.5	1.3	3.5	9.9	13.7	16.0	15.8	14.0	12.3	10.7	8.6		3.5	.9	.3	-4.7	-4.2	-3.7
1910	2.3	.1	.6	1.9	5.1	14.1	21.5	23.2	23.6	21.8	20.3	18.6	16.6	14.0	11.3	8.4	.3	-1.9	-2.5	-2.5
1900	2.2	0.0	.4	1.9	5.0	13.6	18.9	22.3	22.3	20.2	18.3	16.2	14.0	11.7	9.5	7.1	0.0	-1.7	-1.8	-1.7
Hungary																				
1960	3.7	3.7	10.7	21.4	32.2	37.5	45.7	48.7	37.7	26.9	19.2	14.7	11.1	7.9	6.2	4.4		-2.2	-2.0	-1.9
1949	4.3	3.0	8.3	15.7	23.4	24.0	29.4	32.3	31.5	28.4	25.2	21.9	18.6	15.7	13.0	10.1	2.3	0.0	-1.3	-2.6
1941	4.4	2.3	6.4	13.6	22.1	27.5	35.1	29.4	38.6	34.2	30.1	25.7	21.4	18.0	15.0	11.7	2.2	-1.2	-2.4	-2.4
Switzerland																				
1960	3.1	0.0	.4	2.3	6.1	9.4	17.5	23.7	27.0	26.4	24.9	21.1	16.9	14.4	12.1	9.7	.7	-1.7	-2.2	-2.4
1950	2.8	0.0	.2	1.4	3.9	7.1	13.3	18.8	21.2	21.3	20.5	18.4	15.9	14.2	12.4	9.9	.1	-2.4	-4.4	-5.5
1941	2.9	0.0	.2	.7	2.8	8.7	12.0	14.6	16.3	17.1	17.9	18.7	18.3	16.3	13.1	10.0	-.5	-4.6	-6.0	-6.4
1930	2.0	0.0	.1	.7	2.2	6.9	9.5	11.6	12.6	12.9	13.1	13.5	12.8	10.8	8.0	5.1	-3.7	-5.3	-4.5	-4.1
1920	1.9	0.0	.1	.8	2.3	4.2	8.4	12.3	13.7	13.7	12.9	12.1	10.6	9.6	8.9	7.0	-.5	-1.8	-2.8	-3.3
Southern Europe																				
Bulgaria																				
1956	3.0	2.9	13.4	21.4	27.5	30.3	36.9	39.1	35.4	27.8	20.6	12.9	6.9	4.3	3.8	2.8	-.3	-.3	-.2	-.2
Greece																				
1951	4.0	1.7	3.5	5.9	8.0	12.8	16.4	19.6	22.1	23.8	25.6	27.3	27.8	26.2	23.6	20.8	11.1	5.4	2.7	1.3
1928	4.2	1.7	3.9	6.8	9.5	18.0	25.5	29.8	30.9	29.8	28.8	27.7	26.3	24.7	23.2	21.2	11.6	6.7	4.3	2.8
1920	4.5	1.5	2.8	3.5	3.9	11.7	17.6	24.3	27.5	29.8	32.1	34.2	35.1	33.8	31.3	28.5	17.2	9.2	5.4	4.1
Italy																				
1951	3.6	.9	2.6	4.8	8.5	13.6	20.1	25.9	28.1	27.8	26.3	23.3	20.5	18.1	16.5	13.9	-4.0	-3.7	-5.4	-6.4
1931	2.6	.9	2.6	5.1	8.9	13.6	20.4	25.7	26.7	24.5	21.8	17.7	13.0	9.9	7.7	4.7	-4.0	-4.0	-3.0	-3.2
1921	2.7	.5	2.0	4.9	8.6	13.2	17.5	20.2	20.4	19.0	17.6	16.1	14.4	12.8	11.1	9.1	2.3	-.4	-1.0	-1.1
1911	3.1	.6	2.5	6.2	11.8	19.3	25.9	29.7	29.0	25.5	22.3	18.7	15.5	13.1	11.1	8.8	2.6	1.0	.3	-.3
Malta & Gozo																				
1957	3.1	.2	.5	1.5	3.1	9.4	12.9	15.8	17.6	18.7	19.6	20.7	20.3	17.8	14.1	10.3	-.3	-3.9	-4.5	-4.8
Portugal																				
1960	2.4	1.3	3.0	5.9	10.8	12.1	18.1	21.6	22.6	19.7	15.5	10.1	5.8	3.5	3.4	.4	-3.3	-5.3	-5.1	-7.1
1950	2.4	.7	2.1	5.0	9.2	12.3	18.1	21.0	22.3	19.7	16.1	11.1	7.5	3.9	5.0	.3	-4.1	-6.9	-6.3	-8.6
1940	2.1	.8	2.1	3.8	9.0	12.1	15.5	18.7	18.2	17.0	14.5	9.6	5.7	3.4	3.8	-.1	-3.6	-8.2	-7.9	-10.1
1930	1.8	.8	1.8	3.8	7.2	11.6	15.5	17.5	16.2	13.0	9.9	6.8	3.9	2.0	.8	.8	-4.6	-5.5	-5.6	-5.8
1920	1.5	1.6	2.2	3.7	7.0	10.8	14.3	16.0	14.9	12.5	9.3	6.3	3.8	2.1	.8	.5	-3.8	-4.9	-6.0	-4.2
1911	1.8	1.5	2.3	4.2	7.7	11.5	15.9	17.2	16.4	13.8	10.2	7.3	3.8	3.0	1.8	.3	-2.9	-4.8	-6.6	-3.9
1900	2.5	1.7	2.5	4.1	6.9	11.4	15.1	17.2	16.4	13.8	11.4	8.9	6.5	4.5	2.8	.8	-3.1	-4.8	-7.5	-4.0
Spain																				
1960	3.1														14.1	10.3		-3.9	-4.5	-4.8
1940																				
Northern America																				
U.S.A.																				
1950	2.8	5.6	12.4	20.7	28.2	24.7	28.7	30.1	27.5	22.6	17.9	12.7	8.7	6.8	6.3	5.5	2.3	.9	.8	.7
1940	3.2	3.9	8.7	15.1	21.6	21.6	26.0	28.1	26.7	22.8	19.3	15.3	12.1	10.3	9.3	8.0	4.5	3.4	2.7	2.7
1930	2.9	4.6	10.0	16.7	23.3	21.8	25.7	27.6	26.4	23.3	20.3	16.9	14.1	12.5	11.4	10.3	5.7	4.0	3.0	2.5

Table 11-3 *(Continued)*

Country	Med. age at mar- riage	Percentage point difference at specified age																		
		16	17	18	19	20	21	22	23	24	25	26	27	28	29	30	35	40	45	50
Oceania																				
New Zealand																				
1951......	3.4	.4	1.7	5.2	12.1	16.5	26.5	34.4	36.1	33.5	28.4	22.2	15.2	12.7	11.5	9.2	3.6	1.0	- .3	- .3
Maori......	3.1	2.2	7.7	14.8	23.4	22.9	28.4	31.1	29.6	25.6	21.6	17.5	14.1	12.2	11.5	10.3	7.3	4.9	3.8	4.7
1945......	2.5	.3	1.3	3.2	8.0	8.5	15.4	20.7	24.4	24.2	22.5	18.6	15.5	13.8	13.3	11.1	2.9	- .3	- .8	- .5
1936......	3.7	.7	1.5	3.0	5.9	12.3	16.7	19.6	20.7	20.4	20.1	19.7	18.7	16.8	14.2	11.6	4.1	1.0	.4	.6
1926......	1.4	-.1	.8	3.0	6.4	12.2	16.4	19.5	20.5	20.0	19.7	19.3	18.3	16.3	13.8	11.2	3.9	2.2	1.4	.9
1921 (Exc. Maori)..	2.6	-.1	.1	2.9	6.7	12.5	17.2	20.5	21.2	20.4	19.7	18.8	17.7	16.3	14.8	13.0	7.0	3.6	2.8	3.1
1916 (Exc. Maori)..	1.8	0.0	.5	3.2	7.2	12.0	16.3	19.0	19.2	17.7	16.4	15.0	13.6	12.7	12.0	11.2	6.3	3.8	4.5	5.8
1911......	3.2	0.0	.2	2.9	7.1	13.3	18.1	21.7	23.5	24.0	24.7	25.2	24.9	23.4	21.4	19.1	10.4	7.4	7.4	9.3
1906......	2.8	-.1	.7	3.4	7.6	12.9	17.6	21.0	22.4	22.4	22.5	22.6	22.0	21.0	19.3	17.8	11.6	10.3	11.5	12.6
1901......	2.1	-.1	.6	2.8	6.4	11.0	15.0	18.1	19.5	19.9	20.4	20.8	20.6	19.9	18.6	17.3	13.7	14.0	14.9	15.4
U.S.S.R. 1926......	.1	2.8	7.5	14.2	20.2	20.8	26.7	27.8	25.6	20.7	15.9	10.8	6.9	5.0	4.4	3.5	.5	- .6	-1.1	-1.3

Table 11-3 (Continued)

Country	Med. age at marriage	Percentage point difference at specified age																		
		16	17	18	19	20	21	22	23	24	25	26	27	28	29	30	35	40	45	50
Middle America																				
Costa Rica 1950	2.6	6.4	12.2	18.9	25.6	23.3	26.7	28.0	25.9	21.6	17.4	12.8	9.1	7.1	6.3	5.1	-.5	-3.7	-5.7	-6.1
Puerto Rico 1960	2.8	6.6	14.0	21.3	26.3	22.4	25.0	25.7	23.9	20.4	16.9	13.2	10.3	9.2	9.1	8.7	7.6	5.7	3.9	3.2
South America																				
Bolivia 1950	1.8	5.0	10.0	14.9	18.0	14.7	16.1	16.2	14.5	11.5	8.6	5.5	3.0	1.8	1.4	.8	-1.5	-2.9	-4.0	-2.4
Chile 1920	2.8	3.2	6.4	9.9	13.3	13.0	15.2	16.4	16.0	14.6	13.2	11.7	10.3	9.3	8.6	7.7	5.1	2.3	1.4	.1
Peru 1940	3.9	6.2	11.9	18.3	24.8	24.9	25.8	23.6	22.1	18.1	13.0	10.1	6.5	3.4	5.2	1.8	-4.3	-6.0	-7.1	-6.4
Venezuela																				
1950	6.4	12.9	20.5	25.8	31.1	33.8	33.2	32.2	30.6	27.7	24.6	21.0	17.9	14.7	13.9	12.2	3.0	-1.4	-3.6	-4.5
1941	3.8	4.4	7.8	10.7	14.6	13.0	14.7	15.5	14.8	13.4	11.9	10.2	8.8	7.6	6.7	5.7	2.4	-1.5	2.0	2.5
1936	6.2	3.2	5.7	7.9	11.3	11.1	13.0	14.1	14.2	13.4	12.7	11.8	10.7	9.6	8.3	7.0	3.5	-1.8	-5.3	-6.4
Northern Africa																				
Algeria 1948	6.3	14.3	28.8	41.5	48.9	49.1	47.2	48.8	46.2	41.0	35.8	30.0	25.0	22.0	20.0	17.6	8.5	4.8	3.1	1.6
Egypt																				
1960	6.0	10.0	21.4	34.3	46.1	46.0	54.3	58.4	55.6	48.5	41.7	34.3	27.7	23.2	20.0	16.4	5.1	2.0	.8	1.5
1947	6.9	16.3	32.4	46.3	54.6	55.7	54.0	55.7	52.7	46.5	40.2	33.4	27.3	23.2	20.4	17.0	6.4	3.0	1.5	1.0
Tropical & Southern Africa																				
Guinea 1955	7.0																			
Seychelles 1960	2.4	1.6	3.3	5.9	8.9	9.9	12.0	13.1	12.8	11.4	10.2	9.0	7.5	5.9	4.3	3.6	1.7	.3	-4.0	-4.8
South Africa																				
1960																				
Asian	3.6	3.4	9.0	16.5	24.6	27.1	33.7	36.7	34.3	28.5	22.9	17.0	12.0	8.9	7.2	5.0	-.3	.6	1.1	0.0
Colored	2.4	1.5	3.7	8.0	13.6	14.8	18.6	20.6	19.7	16.7	14.2	11.3	8.9	8.0	7.9	7.4	5.0	4.0	3.2	2.1
1951:																				
Asian	4.5	6.8	15.1	25.2	34.7	33.6	39.9	42.7	40.2	34.1	28.3	22.1	16.8	13.5	11.6	9.3	2.6	1.0	.8	1.1
Colored	2.7	1.1	3.2	7.3	12.8	15.7	20.2	22.8	22.3	19.6	17.3	14.6	12.3	11.0	10.4	9.4	5.9	4.1	3.1	3.0
White		1.5	5.5	13.5	23.4	27.6	26.7	42.5	42.0	37.1	30.6	22.9	15.8	13.0	11.2	8.8	2.7	.5	.1	-1.2
1946:																				
Asian	4.1	1.7	5.1	11.2	19.6	26.6	34.6	39.1	38.1	33.3	28.8	24.1	19.7	16.7	14.4	11.7	2.7	-1.0	-2.1	-1.4
Colored	4.6	9.3	19.7	31.3	41.6	36.9	42.4	44.4	41.0	34.1	27.4	20.3	14.4	11.4	10.1	8.3	2.4	.7	.9	2.0
White	3.0	.7	2.7	6.5	11.7	16.7	21.9	25.2	25.5	23.7	22.0	20.3	18.4	16.3	14.3	12.1	5.9	4.1	4.3	4.1
1941 White	4.0	1.7	5.9	12.5	20.8	26.4	34.0	38.2	36.9	31.9	27.3	22.3	17.8	14.8	12.5	9.9	1.2	-1.0	-1.1	-1.1
1936	3.7	1.7	4.3	9.7	16.4	21.7	28.0	31.7	31.3	28.1	25.1	22.0	18.8	16.1	13.7	11.0	2.5	.5	.1	.4
1926	3.4	1.7	3.8	7.5	12.6	19.6	25.4	29.3	30.2	28.9	27.7	26.4	24.6	22.1	19.4	16.3	6.4	3.1	2.9	2.7
1921	4.1	.8	2.8	7.6	14.6	22.9	30.4	35.4	35.9	33.6	31.6	29.4	26.7	23.9	20.9	17.7	5.4	4.3	4.3	2.9
1911 White	5.4	1.1	3.8	9.1	16.7	26.0	34.4	40.0	41.1	39.1	37.4	35.4	33.0	31.0	28.9	26.3	15.7	9.5	5.6	3.8

Table 11-3 (*Continued*)

Percentage point difference at specified age

Country	Med. age at marriage	16	17	18	19	20	21	22	23	24	25	26	27	28	29	30	35	40	45	50
N. & W. Europe (cont'd.)																				
Luxemburg																				
1960	4.2																			
Netherlands																				
1960	2.7	.4	1.4	3.8	7.5	11.6	19.4	26.7	30.5	29.4	27.2	21.6	16.1	13.0	11.2	8.7	-.1	-1.6	-2.2	-2.2
1950	2.3	.2	1.0	2.6	5.1	8.9	15.1	20.8	22.6	22.7	22.1	19.6	16.5	14.0	12.4	8.8	-1.1	-3.5	-4.4	-4.8
1947	2.4	.1	1.1	2.8	5.9	11.4	15.3	18.1	19.1	18.7	18.5	18.1	17.0	14.6	11.5	8.4	-.5	-5.1	-4.3	-4.7
1930	1.8	.2	.7	2.1	4.2	10.0	13.5	15.8	16.3	15.3	14.5	13.5	12.1	9.7	6.9	4.0	-3.7	-5.1	-4.6	-4.0
1920	1.6	.1	.6	1.9	4.5	9.2	12.5	14.7	14.7	13.6	12.5	11.4	9.9	7.9	5.7	4.1	-2.2	-3.1	-3.1	-3.3
1909	1.4	0.0	.3	1.2	3.3	7.9	10.8	12.7	12.9	11.9	11.1	10.1	8.9	7.5	5.8	4.1	-2.8	-2.5	-2.7	-2.2
1899	1.6	.1	.5	1.2	2.8	7.1	9.9	11.7	12.0	11.4	10.9	10.3	9.3	7.9	6.3	4.6	0.0	-1.0	-.9	-1.2
Northern Ireland																				
1951																				
Norway																				
1960	3.5	.2	2.0	7.0	14.5	19.0	27.9	33.6	35.7	33.7	31.2	25.6	21.2	18.2	17.0	15.5	8.1	4.8	3.0	2.7
1950	3.7	.2	1.1	3.8	8.0	12.5	19.2	25.0	27.4	26.5	26.1	27.6	22.7	19.1	17.1	15.3	5.1	.5	-1.2	-2.0
1930	3.0	.1	.4	1.2	3.4	8.0	11.7	13.2	14.3	14.5	14.8	15.1	14.4	12.7	10.1	7.5	-1.9	-5.9	-7.4	-8.1
1920	2.2	.1	.3	1.8	4.1	8.6	11.0	13.6	13.7	12.4	11.3	10.0	8.5	6.7	4.8	8.4	-3.7	-6.7	-6.7	-8.7
1910	2.1	.2	.6	2.0	4.1	7.3	9.8	11.4	11.6	10.7	10.0	9.2	8.0	6.3	4.2	3.0	-4.6	-7.2	-8.2	-8.3
1900	–	.1	.7	1.8	4.2	4.2	8.5	11.2	12.1	11.3	10.1	8.4	6.3	2.9	4.1	-.2	-5.7	-9.5	-7.3	-9.4
Scotland																				
1951	2.9	.2	1.1	4.2	9.6	12.2	18.3	23.2	23.8	22.3	19.8	14.8	10.7	9.7	8.9	8.1	1.6	-2.8	-6.2	-7.6
1931	1.8	.2	.9	2.9	5.4	8.6	11.2	12.6	12.5	11.2	9.9	8.7	7.1	5.3	3.6	1.6	-5.0	-6.5	-5.7	-5.2
1921	1.6	.1	.7	2.4	5.0	6.5	9.9	11.3	11.1	9.8	8.5	7.2	6.8	4.5	3.1	1.7	-2.2	-3.1	-3.3	-4.0
1911	1.8	0.0	.2	1.6	4.1	7.3	9.9	11.6	11.7	10.8	9.9	9.0	7.9	7.0	6.0	4.8	-2.3	-1.6	-3.5	-5.0
1901	1.7	-.1	.5	1.8	4.6	8.0	10.8	12.5	12.4	11.1	10.0	8.8	7.4	6.2	5.2	3.9	-1.2	-3.0	-4.1	-4.6
Sweden																				
1960	3.5	0.0	.3	2.2	5.9	13.5	18.4	22.0	23.1	22.6	22.2	21.7	20.5	18.4	15.8	13.1	2.9	-2.1	-4.9	-6.1
1950	3.6	0.0	.1	1.5	4.2	9.1	13.8	16.7	18.2	18.6	19.1	19.5	18.9	17.1	14.4	11.6	1.9	-3.2	-5.9	-6.7
1945	3.3	0.0	.1	1.2	3.7	9.3	12.9	15.3	16.1	15.6	16.7	16.8	16.2	14.4	12.1	9.7	.3	-4.6	-6.1	-6.9
1940	2.8	0.0	.1	1.3	3.9	8.9	12.3	14.6	14.9	14.0	15.2	14.8	13.7	11.7	9.2	6.6	-1.3	-4.7	-6.1	-7.2
1935	2.4	0.0	.3	1.5	3.8	8.0	11.0	12.9	13.2	12.3	13.2	12.2	10.9	9.3	7.3	5.2	-1.6	-5.3	-6.3	-6.5
1930	2.1	0.0	.4	1.6	3.9						11.6	10.7	9.5	7.8	5.8	3.8	-2.4	-4.9	-5.7	-6.2
1920																				
1910																				
1900																				
Central Europe																				
Austria																				
1961	2.9	.8	2.7	7.2	13.1	18.4	23.9	27.0	26.4	23.2	20.3	17.2	14.2	11.6	9.4	7.0	-1.9	-4.3	-3.8	-3.8
1951	2.7	.5	1.6	4.3	8.9	10.7	16.1	20.2	21.0	19.7	17.6	13.8	10.4	9.3	9.4	9.0	-.1	-2.1	-3.6	-5.1
1934	3.4	.3	.5	1.7	3.6	8.7	11.6	14.1	15.9	16.9	17.9	18.9	18.8	17.1	14.4	11.1	-.1	-5.1	-5.9	-5.6
1910																				
1900																				
Czechoslovakia																				
1961	4.1	.5	2.7	12.8	26.0	35.3	44.4	47.2	45.0	38.2	29.6	20.0	12.3	8.9	7.9	7.0	2.3	.8	-1.1	-1.2
1947	3.2	.9	3.1	8.0	14.8	22.8	30.1	34.6	34.8	32.0	29.4	26.7	23.4	19.7	15.8	11.7	1.6	-1.2	-3.2	-4.0

Table 11-3 (Continued)

Country	Med. age at marriage	Percentage point difference at specified age																		
		16	17	18	19	20	21	22	23	24	25	26	27	28	29	30	35	40	45	50
South West Asia																				
Cyprus 1960	2.7	2.2	5.8	12.2	19.5	17.6	21.3	23.0	21.4	17.9	14.4	10.7	7.5	5.4	4.1	2.5	-.9	-1.2	-1.1	-.7
1946	2.2	4.1	8.5	14.0	18.9	18.9	22.5	24.3	23.4	20.8	18.3	15.6	13.1	11.2	9.6	8.0	2.6	1.6	2.3	2.4
Iraq 1957	6.5	15.2	28.6	35.0	32.2	33.3	34.2	40.2	38.8	35.6	32.2	28.5	25.4	23.6	22.7	21.4	14.4	8.3	4.6	3.1
Israel 1961	4.2	2.4	6.8	14.9	25.2	32.4	42.1	47.1	44.8	37.8	31.4	24.4	18.6	15.4	14.0	11.8	4.8	2.6	1.4	.8
1948	5.2	2.5	7.2	15.4	25.1	32.3	41.7	47.2	46.6	42.0	37.8	33.2	28.9	25.6	23.2	20.1	8.8	3.5	1.4	.4
Jordan 1961	5.0	11.8	24.4	37.5	47.1	37.3	40.7	41.3	37.6	31.1	24.8	17.8	12.4	9.6	8.8	7.4	3.4	2.2	1.1	.7
Turkey 1955	1.6	16.2	29.8	33.2	22.6	24.3	25.9	32.5	34.3	27.6	21.1	14.8	9.9	6.9	5.3	4.2	2.1	2.1	1.6	1.2
South Central Asia																				
Ceylon 1953	6.5	10.7	21.5	33.4	44.2	44.4	52.3	56.2	54.4	48.6	43.1	37.0	31.4	27.4	24.2	20.5	8.3	4.2	3.0	3.5
1946	6.3	10.5	21.6	34.3	46.0	44.7	52.4	56.2	54.1	47.9	42.0	35.6	30.0	26.3	24.0	21.1	10.3	5.9	4.1	4.8
1921	6.8	12.4	25.3	38.3	49.5	45.4	52.4	55.0	52.7	47.0	41.4	29.8	29.8	27.0	25.6	23.8	11.8	5.5	4.2	3.6
1901	6.6	24.9	48.2	64.3	68.6	66.3	59.3	52.4	46.1	40.2	34.3	28.3	23.3	19.9	17.4	15.1	7.4	3.9	3.0	3.1
South East Asia																				
Philippines 1960	2.9	4.2	9.0	14.6	19.5	19.1	22.7	24.0	22.1	18.0	14.1	9.8	6.4	4.3	3.2	1.9	-1.7	-3.0	-4.1	-3.4
East Asia																				
China 1956	2.7	2.2	6.6	14.7	24.6	28.3	36.2	40.3	38.0	31.7	25.8	19.4	14.6	13.2	13.7	13.7	9.6	7.2	5.4	4.0
Japan 1960	2.7	-.1	.1	.9	4.0	15.1	20.8	25.3	27.5	28.0	28.6	29.3	27.8	22.9	16.3	9.5	-2.7	-1.5	-.8	.6
1955	2.2	0.0	.2	1.8	5.2	16.0	22.2	26.4	27.4	26.2	25.2	24.2	21.9	18.0	13.1	8.1	-1.3	-.8	-.8	.3
1950	2.8	-.1	1.0	4.3	10.0	19.7	26.9	31.4	31.4	28.4	25.7	22.9	19.6	15.9	12.2	8.0	-.2	-.1	0.0	.1
1940	3.7	.2	1.8	5.5	12.0	24.8	33.5	42.3	42.7	39.4	36.4	33.3	29.2	24.4	18.9	13.2	1.4	.8	.3	.3
1935	4.0	1.2	4.4	10.4	18.8	29.6	39.4	44.9	43.8	38.5	33.5	28.3	23.2	18.9	15.3	11.1	1.7	.8	.4	.2
1930	4.2	2.5	7.0	14.6	24.2	33.3	43.4	48.6	46.2	38.8	32.0	24.7	18.4	14.4	12.0	9.0	1.6	.8	.4	.2
1925	4.3	3.5	9.5	18.9	29.6	35.5	45.2	49.8	46.5	37.9	30.0	21.4	14.5	10.8	9.3	7.1	1.2	.5	.2	.1
1920	4.3	5.9	13.3	22.4	30.9	34.3	41.8	45.3	42.2	34.8	27.9	20.5	14.4	11.0	9.6	7.5	1.7	.8	.4	.3
Korea 1955	4.3	2.6	7.5	14.8	22.1	36.1	47.7	53.8	51.2	43.0	35.4	27.3	20.3	15.8	13.0	9.5	.9	.2	.3	.2
Ryukyu Islands 1960	2.1	.5	.8	2.4	5.2	13.2	18.0	21.2	22.1	21.3	20.6	19.9	18.4	15.9	12.9	9.7	1.6	.6	.7	.5
1955	1.3	0.0	1.2	4.1	9.3	16.9	23.0	26.4	25.8	22.4	19.4	16.1	13.0	10.4	8.3	5.8	.8	.8	.6	.6
1950	1.7	.4	2.8	8.1	15.4	18.9	24.9	27.8	25.6	20.1	15.0	9.7	5.5	3.6	3.3	2.6	.8	.7	.2	.6

3. Large losses of men in time of war can also promote spinsterhood. (See Table 11-3 for Germany, 1939.)

4. Higher death rates among males than among females may lead to a deficit of potential husbands, although in most populations this effect does not become significant until after age 50.

5. Differences may exist between the sexes in the way they report their marital status at the time of the census. Estranged males may tend to claim to be single, whereas their former spouses may claim to have been married.

Italy, Portugal, and Finland are examples of nations with a large proportion of middle-aged spinsters in comparison with middle-aged bachelors. Ireland and Greece are outstanding as nations where a higher proportion of males than of females remain unmarried.

11.5. Recent International Trends in Proportions Married

We have so far implicitly presumed that marital status patterns are more or less stable around the world. This is not true; some very remarkable changes have recently occurred and are occurring in many nations. At the risk of oversimplification we can summarize these changes as follows: *In the economically advanced nations marriage is tending to occur earlier, and in the developing nations it is tending to occur later.* Consider, for example, recent changes in the median age at marriage in Ceylon and Ireland.

Median Age at Marriage

Ireland:	Males	Females	Change	
1961	27.8	24.7	−3.7	−2.7
1926	31.5	27.4		

Ceylon:				
1953	25.8	19.3	+2.8	+2.9
1901	23.0	16.4		

Thus there appears to be a tendency toward convergence of the world's marriage patterns.

The data of Table 11-1 reveal that since 1940 in almost all European nations there has been a rather sharp reduction in the median age at marriage. This was not just a return to a former pattern after the disturbances of World War II. Instead it is a new pattern that had not manifested itself in most European nations before 1945, although in some of them there had been a gradual downward drift in the median age at marriage from 1900 onward. (See data for Netherlands, Sweden, and Denmark.)

This phenomenon was studied and placed in historical perspective two decades and a half ago by John Hájnal in a classic article, "The Marriage Boom," in *Population Index*, April 1953. Hájnal found that most of the countries of Northwest Europe experienced "a marriage boom" during the period 1935-1950 and that this caused in part the better-known "baby boom." He found that the timing of the "marriage boom" differed in different countries; nations who were belligerents in the war experienced sharper fluctuations in the marriage rate than nonbelligerent nations such as Sweden. The net effect on marital status was a substantial decline in the proportion single, especially at the younger ages. Hájnal assembled data for proportions single at such ages for long spans of time for European countries and discovered that the recent "marriage boom" is largely unprecedented in history, both in its scope and in its suddenness. He based these findings on data for Denmark, Sweden, France, Great Britain, Switzerland, and the United States. The proportion single at the younger ages had been greater throughout the nineteenth and twentieth centuries than it was in the postwar era.

Hájnal discovered that the pattern of very late marriage in Ireland appears to have developed in the latter part of the nineteenth century, because the proportion single rose substantially between 1861 and 1891.

By 1951 neither France nor Ireland appeared to have participated in this decline in the proportion single. France had experienced such a decline earlier in the late 1930s. Hájnal found that the proportion single, especially among men, was less in Eastern Europe (Bulgaria, Russia, Yugoslavia) than in Western and Central Europe.

Table 11-4 Historical Series for Proportions Single at Specified Ages in Selected Countries

Country	Year	Men			Women		
		20-24	25-29	45-49	20-24	25-29	45-49
Denmark	1787	.80[a]		.09[b]	.64[a]		.09[b]
	1801	.80[a]		.12[b]	.63[a]		.09[b]
	1840	.82[a]		.09[b]	.70[a]		.09[b]
	1880	.76[a]		.10[b]	.64[a]		.12[b]
	1901	.70[a]		.10[b]	.59[a]		.15[b]
	1930	.71[a]		.10[b]	.55[a]		.16[b]
	1945	.65[a]		.11[b]	.43[a]		.16[b]
	1950	.61		.14	.37		.21
	1960	.56		.10	.31		.09
France	1881	.87	.49	.13	.60	.32	.13
	1901	.90	.48	.11	.58	.30	.12
	1911	.89	.44	.11	.55	.27	.11
	1936	.79	.36	.10[b]	.49	.23	.13[b]
	1949	.81	.39	.12[b]	.54	.22	.11[b]
	1954	.81	.37	.12	.57	.23	.10
	1962	.84	.38	.11	.56	.20	.09
Great Britain	1851	.80	.45	.12	.70	.41	.14
	1871	.78	.40	.10	.66	.37	.13
	1911	.86	.50	.13	.76	.44	.17
	1931	.86	.48	.12	.74	.42	.17
	1951	.77	.35	.10	.53	.22	.16
	1961						
Ireland [c]	1861	.91	.66	.16	.76	.49	.14
	1891	.96	.78	.20	.86	.59	.17
	1936	.96	.82	.34	.86	.64	.25
	1946	.95	.80	.33	.83	.57	.26
	1951	.95	.77	.34	.82	.55	.34
	1961	.93	.67	.31	.78	.45	.22
Netherlands	1830	.89	.56	.11	.81	.49	.14
	1849	.94	.65	.13	.87	.57	.15
	1879	.90	.54	.13	.78	.43	.14
	1909	.89	.51	.13	.78	.42	.16
	1930	.90	.49	.11	.75	.38	.15
	1951	.89	.48	.09	.71	.31	.13
	1960	.86	.39	.08	.63	.21	.11
Norway	1801	.73[a]		.09[b]	.64[a]		.15[b]
	1875	.76[a]		.13[b]	.67[a]		.17[b]
	1910	.73[a]		.14[b]	.64[a]		.22[b]
	1930	.80[a]		.16[b]	.67[a]		.23[b]
	1946	.75[a]		.17[b]	.56[a]		.22[b]
	1950	.71		.19	.49		.28
	1960	.60		.14	.34		.12
Sweden [d]	1750	.84	.42	.06	.73	.43	.10
	1800	.87	.50	.07	.78	.48	.12
	1850	.92	.59	.09	.84	.51	.12
	1870	.94	.62	.10	.84	.54	.16
	1910	.93	.62	.15	.80	.51	.22
	1930	.94	.67	.17	.80	.52	.23
	1945	.87	.52	.17	.64	.30	.21
	1950	.85	.51	.20	.60	.22	.26
	1960	.82	.41	.15	.57	.21	.11
Switzerland	1860	.93	.68	.20	.83	.55	.20
	1880	.90	.59	.18	.77	.44	.20
	1910	.92	.58	.15	.78	.43	.18
	1930	.93	.60	.14	.82	.48	.19
	1950	.86	.50	.13	.66	.31	.19
United States	1890	.81	.46	.09[e]	.52	.25	.07[e]
	1910	.75	.43	.11[e]	.48	.25	.09[e]
	1930	.71	.37	.11[e]	.46	.22	.09[e]
	1950	.52	.20	.08[e]	.31	.11	.07[e]

[a] Age group 20-29.
[b] Age group 40-49.
[c] Figures for 1861 include Northern Ireland. Subsequent years relate to territory of the Republic of Ireland only.
[d] Years 1750-1850: Estimates
[e] Age group 45-54.

Source: John Hahval, "The Marriage Boom," Population Index, April, 1953 (updated).

Hájnal comments that "the widespread impression that the special pattern of Western Europe late age at marriage is due to the rise of urban industrial civilization is demonstrably false. It seems to be based largely on the view that the marriage used to occur at a very much earlier age in Western Europe. Such statistical data as exist for the eighteenth and early nineteenth centuries indicate that the marriage pattern in Northwest European countries has not changed much substantially between that time and the 1930's. Moreover, it has not been true within Western experience that the agricultural population is married to a greater extent or earlier than urban population. In fact, on the whole both nineteenth and twentieth century statistics show the reverse, at least for the male population. A special pattern of marriage (relatively late marriage and high proportions never marrying) has apparently characterized for centuries the civilization which gave rise to modern industrial society."[7]

Table 11-4 reproduces the historical series that Hájnal constructed, updated to include the round of censuses taken since then. It is clear that the "boom" of which he spoke continued throughout the 1950s and in fact dwarfed in size the changes that had so impressed him. Moreover, as our Table 11-1 shows, the "marriage boom" had spread to additional nations, including France, Ireland, and countries in Eastern Europe.

In another comprehensive study of marital status trends, Jean-Claude Chasteland and Roland Pressat investigated marriage trends in France over one hundred years from 1821 to 1921.[8] They found an irregular and small but nevertheless definite *downward* drift in the average age at first marriage, with the differences between the ages of the spouses remaining nearly constant at about three years. They also found a steady decline in spinsterhood and bachelorhood from about 1830 onward, with irregularities created by wars (which force spinsterhood upon particular cohorts of women).

Together, these two studies leave little doubt that child marriage was not a cultural trait of preindustrial Europe, and this represents a fundamental demographic difference between the industrialized and many of the developing nations.

As nations in Asia and Latin America have undergone economic development, there has been a tendency for young adults to prolong the status of being never married beyond the "child marriage" stage to an older age. Perhaps the most dramatic example is Japan, where the median age at marriage advanced by an average age almost one year per decade, from 1920 to 1960, as follows:

Median Age at Marriage

Year		Males	Females
1960	....	27.0	24.3
1950	....	25.8	23.0
1940	....	26.5	22.0
1930	....	25.3	21.1
1920	....	24.7	20.4

The greatest advance occurred during the period 1950-1960 when Japan truly emerged as a leading industrial and commercial world power.

Agarwala has charted a similar trend for India. Using the methods developed by Hájnal, he estimated the mean age at marriage in India since 1900.[9] He notes, however, that girls who marry before age 15 do not actually enter the state of being in a fertile union until about age 15. He has estimated the mean age at entry into the fertile union in column 2 of Table 11-5. Because death rates are high, the withdrawal from fertile unions created by widowhood is substantial. Column 3 of Table 11-5 reports the estimated mean age at leaving fertile unions. Finally, the last column shows the mean duration of fertile unions for each age. He finds that the mean entry age into fertile unions did not change substantially during the first half of the twentieth century. But because of declining mortality the mean

---

[7] John Hájnal, "The Marriage Boom," *Population Index,* April 1953.

[8] Jean-Claude Chasteland and Roland Pressat, "La Nuptialité des Generations Françaises Depuis un Siècle," *Population,* **17** (1962), pp. 215-40.

[9] S. N. Agarwala, "Mean Ages at Marriage and Widowhood in India," *Proceedings of the International Population Conference,* 1963 (London: International Union for the Study of Population, 1963), Vol. 2, pp. 141–147.

Table 11-5 Mean Age at Marriage in India: 1901 to 1951

Year	Mean age at marriage	Mean age at entry into fertile union	Mean age at leaving fertile union (a)	Mean duration at fertile unions
1901-11........	13.0	17.1	40.6	23.5
1911-21........	13.5	17.0	37.9	20.9
1921-31........	12.5	17.1	42.6	25.5
1931-41........	14.9	17.1	38.9	21.8
1941-51........	15.4	17.0	44.1	27.1

(a) Mean age at leaving the fertile union by age 50 when the minimum age at entry is 15 years.

Source: S. N. Agarwala, "Mean Ages at Marriage and Widowhood in India," Proceedings of the International Population Conference, New York, 1961. Longon, International Population Union, 1963

duration of fertile unions had increased by about three and a half years. Almost all of this increase occurred after 1941.

Even though Hájnal has demonstrated that European nations did not undergo a dramatic change in age at marriage as they became industrialized (because they already had a late age at marriage), it may turn out that one of the prices that the developing nations of Asia and Africa must pay to achieve economic development is to abandon the custom of marriage of females before at least average age 20 —both as a fertility control measure and as a measure to facilitate national capital accumulation for new investment.

Meanwhile, the "marriage boom" remains an unexplained social and demographic phenomenon. A speculative theory, which might be called the "wealthy nation" hypothesis of early marriage, is advanced in Section 11-7 to account for this change.

11.6. Prevalence of Marital Disruption around the World

Persons who are widowed, divorced, or separated from their spouse comprise that fraction of the ever-married population who are living in a state of marital disruption. They can lose this status only by remarrying or dying. For studies of fertility, social welfare, and national insurance plans, as well as for sociological studies of the family, the proportion of adults who are in this status is an important demographic parameter. Unfortunately, a complete and unbiased measurement of marital disruption exists for almost no nation of the world. Many nations do not recognize divorce or have

laws that severely limit it; estranged couples must either seek an annulment or separate without divorce. National censuses often fail to obtain statistics on separation, with the result that the total prevalence of marital disruption cannot be known. This represents an important area for international standardization of definitions and of data collection practices. Unless information is obtained for each of the three disruption statuses—widowhood, divorce, and separation—a severe underestimate and biased picture of marital disruption will result.

Table 11-6A presents international data on divorce, and Table 11-6B presents data on widowhood. Both refer to the female population only. Statistics on separation are available in only a few censuses, so that the generalizations must be rather broad and tentative.

Divorce. In most nations of the world, less than 1 or 2 percent of the adult female population is found in the status of being divorced. This testifies to the fact, not adequately appreciated, that the family is one of the most stable and universally accepted aspects of social organization. In Communist and non-Communist countries, in industrialized and developing countries, and in Christian, Hindu, Muslim, and Buddhist countries only a comparatively small fraction of the marriages are broken by formal divorce. Where divorce does occur, it very often is followed by remarriage. Thus a common world cultural trait is the tradition that marriage should last until death.

A few nations of the world have higher proportions divorced, but even here the fraction is a small one. Following is a list of nations, for which there are data, where more than 3 per-

Table 11-6A Proportion of the Population Divorced at Specified Ages for Selected Nations of the World: 1900 to 1960

Country	Year	Percent divorced at selected ages									
		20	25	30	35	40	45	50	55	60	65
NORTHERN AFRICA											
Algeria.............	1948	2.7	2.5	2.1	1.7	1.7	1.6	1.4	1.3	1.1	.9
Morocco.............	1952	4.7	3.3	3.4	3.5	4.1	4.2	4.1	4.3	4.3	2.6
Egypt..............	1960	2.5	2.4	2.4	2.0	2.4	2.0	2.3	1.7	1.7	1.3
	1947	3.1	2.8	2.6	2.1	2.4	2.0	2.2	1.6	1.6	1.3
TROPICAL & SOUTHERN AFRICA											
Guinea.............	1955	.9	1.2	1.0	1.0	.5	.7	1.1	1.0	.5	.0
Libya..............	1954	5.6	5.0	4.2	3.6	3.9	4.4	5.3	5.4	5.5	5.4
Seychelles..........	1960	.0	.7	1.0	1.5	.9	.5	1.2	.4	1.0	.8
NORTHERN AMERICA											
	1961	.2	.4	.6	.7	.8	.9	.9	.7	.6	.4
	1951	.1	.4	.6	.7	.8	.7	.6	.4	.3	.2
Canada.............	1941	.0	.2	.3	.4	.4	.3	.2	.2	.1	.1
	1931	.0	.1	.2	.2	.2	.1	.1	.1	.1	.1
	1921	.1	.1	.2	.2	.2	.2	.2	.2	.2	.1
	1911	.0	.1	.1	.1	.2	.2	.2	.2	.2	.2
MIDDLE AMERICA											
Costa Rica.........	1950	.2	.4	.6	.7	.7	.5	.7	.8	.5	.2
Curacao............	1960	.5	1.4	2.1	3.0	3.4	3.4	3.6	3.5	3.3	1.5
El Salvador........	1950	.2	.4	.5	.6	.7	.6	.7	.6	.5	.5
Guatemala..........	1950	.3	.4	.6	.7	.6	.7	.5	.6	.4	.4
Haiti..............	1950	.0	.0	.1	.1	.1	.1	.2	.1	.1	.1
Nicaragua..........	1950	.4	.4	.5	.6	.7	.8	.8	.8	1.1	1.1
Panama.............	1950	.3	.7	1.3	1.4	1.5	1.1	1.1	.8	.8	.6
	1960	.3	.6	1.1	1.3	1.7	1.9	1.7	1.1	.9	.7
SOUTH AMERICA											
Bolivia............	1950	.3	.5	.7	.8	.7	.7	.5	.5	.3	.3
Ecuador............	1950	.3	.5	.7	.7	.7	.7	.6	.6	.4	.4
Paraguay...........	1962	.3	.2	.5	.9	.9	.9	1.1	.4	.7	1.2
	1950	0.6	1.0	1.2	1.7	2.1	2.2	2.3	2.4	2.1	1.9
Peru...............	1940	.1	.2	.2	.3	.3	.3	.3	.3	.3	.2
Venezuela..........	1961	.6	1.0	1.6	1.3	1.5	1.9	1.0	1.8	...	...
	1950	.4	.8	.9	.9	.9	.8	.6	.6	.4	.4
	1941	.14	.34	.49	.51	.52	.41	.42	.41	.43	...
SOUTH WEST ASIA											
Cyprus.............	1960	.3	.6	.9	1.1	1.1	.9	.9	.7	...	...
	1946	.8	1.2	1.3	1.4	1.7	1.2	1.3	.9	1.1	...
Iraq...............	1957	.8	1.4	1.1	1.1	1.4	1.5	2.4	2.3	1.5	1.3
Israel.............	1961	1.0	1.8	2.1	2.3	2.7	2.9	3.1	3.0	2.8	2.2
	1948	.5	1.4	1.8	2.4	2.8	2.9	2.5	1.9	1.3	.7
Palestine..........	1931	.6	.6	.8	.8	.9	1.1	1.2	1.1	1.1	.9
Turkey.............	1960	.7	.9	.7	.9	1.3	1.3	1.2	1.2	1.2	...
	1955	.8	.8	.9	1.1	1.2	1.4	1.5	1.7	1.5	...
	1945	.6	.6	.7	.8	.7	.8	.7	.8	.5	.4
SOUTH CENTRAL ASIA											
Ceylon.............	1953	.5	.3	.6	.6	.6	.6	.5	.5	.4	...
	1946	.4	.4	.4	.4	.4	.4	.3	.3	.3	...
India..............	1961	.9	1.0	1.0	1.0	1.0	.9	.7	.7	.5	.5
Pakistan...........	1961	.8	.7	.6	.6	.6	.6	.6	.6	...	...
SOUTH EAST ASIA											
North Borneo.......	1960	2.3	1.9	2.0	2.0	2.4	2.3	2.9	2.7	2.8	2.6
Philippines........	1960	.6	.9	.9	.9	.9	.9	.9	.9	.9	...
Sarawak............	1960	4.1	3.4	3.1	2.9	3.3	3.1	4.0	3.3	4.5	3.4
	1947	6.1	4.9	4.2	3.5	4.0	4.0	4.3	...	...	...
EAST ASIA											
China..............	1956	.7	1.0	1.2	1.3	1.4	1.3	1.4	1.2	1.0	0.7
Hong Kong..........	1961	0.2	0.4	0.6	0.7	0.7	0.8	1.0	1.0	1.2	1.1

Table 11-6A (*Continued*)

Country	Year	Percent divorced at selected ages									
		20	25	30	35	40	45	50	55	60	65
EAST ASIA (continued)											
Japan.............	1960	.4	1.5	3.0	4.2	3.9	3.3	3.0	2.5	2.1	1.8
	1955	.8	2.4	3.5	3.4	3.0	2.7	2.4	2.0	1.7	1.4
	1950	1.6	3.0	3.0	2.6	2.4	2.3	2.0	1.9	1.7	1.5
	1930	1.8	2.3	2.3	2.3	2.3	2.5	2.5	2.4	2.0	1.6
	1935	1.3	2.3	2.4	2.3	2.3	2.3	2.3	2.3	2.1	1.7
Korea.............	1920	2.84	2.95	2.70	2.77	2.89	2.92	2.80	2.51	2.28	1.79
	1955	2.07	2.52	2.21	1.80	1.55	1.38	1.21	1.06	.89	.85
Ryukyu Islands......	1960	1.58	4.92	6.94	6.41	5.78	5.12	4.38	4.06	3.41	3.27
	1955	4.09	7.48	7.55	6.96	5.68	4.97	4.48	3.94	3.43	2.86
	1950	5.75	7.55	7.34	7.15	6.58	5.96	6.15	5.31	4.12	3.09
U.S.S.R.............	1926	2.14	2.99	1.55	1.18	.97	.66	.49	.36	.27	.20
NORTHERN & WESTERN EUROPE											
Belgium............	1930	.01	.26	.64	.88	1.27	1.28	1.10	.93	.78	...
	1920	.02	.12	.41	.57	.67	.66	.71	.68	.46	...
	1910	.02	.10	.33	.49	.52	.61	.51	.59	.44	...
	1947	.03	.63	1.57	1.89	1.86	1.68	1.49	1.29	1.26	...
Denmark............	1960	.26	1.93	2.85	3.54	4.80	5.11	5.26	4.73	4.45	....
	1950	.17	1.41	2.72	3.42	3.46	3.56	3.78	3.57	3.69	....
	1945	.10	1.10	1.90	2.23	2.61	2.83	2.96	2.92	2.70	....
	1940	.07	.61	1.23	1.80	2.25	2.53	2.87	2.48	2.58	....
	1930	.02	.51	.97	1.33	1.59	1.84	1.93	1.82	1.56	....
	1921	.02	.51	.97	1.33	1.59	1.84	1.93	1.82	1.56	....
	1911	.03	.11	.30	.58	.66	.76	.54	.61	.48	....
	1901		.06	.14	.33	.48	.52	.50	.50	.43	....
Finland............	1960	.14	.93	1.86	2.87	3.48	4.06	4.13	3.74	3.24	....
	1950	.08	.92	2.02	2.54	2.87	2.66	2.72	2.58	2.24	....
	1940	.02	.23	.72	1.10	1.47	1.63	1.77	1.43	1.47	....
	1930	.01	.11	.39	.74	.83	.81	.93	.75	.72	.....
	1920	.01	.09	.18	.31	.35	.48	.42	.34	.32	....
	1910	...	.04	.10	.17	.25	.27	.30	.19	.14	...
	1900	.004	.02	.09	.10	.20	.16	.11	.14	.10	...
France.............	1962	.08	.69	1.70	2.50	3.90	5.10	4.70	3.90	3.00	...
	1954	...	.71	2.13	4.47	4.47	3.96	3.15	2.64	2.24	...
	1946	.10	.99	1.83	2.03	2.22	2.22	2.02	1.88	1.85	...
	1936	.09	.79	1.42	1.73	1.79	1.89	1.80	1.52	1.26	...
	1931	.14	.69	1.20	1.44	1.71	1.75	1.51	1.26	1.06	...
	1911	.22	.59	.88	1.04	1.04	.95	.78	.58	.40	.26
Iceland............	1950	.35	.91	1.63	1.63	2.03	2.62	2.48	3.01	1.53	2.37
Ireland............	1951	.02	.21	.34	.27	.26	.31	.18	.12	.11	.97
Netherlands........	1960	.14	.54	.84	1.17	1.64	1.98	2.25	1.94	2.01	...
	1950	.09	.72	1.36	1.75	2.05	1.91	2.02	1.76	1.77	...
	1947	.09	.91	1.56	1.69	1.63	1.63	1.66	1.75	1.56	...
	1930	.03	.32	.69	.93	1.07	1.05	1.16	1.07	.92	...
	1920	.04	.24	.43	.59	.74	.78	.69	.79	.77	...
	1909	.02	.14	.28	.46	.52	.57	.63	.59	.56	...
	1899	...	.09	.20	.29	.42	.45	.39	.51	.39	...
Norway.............	1960	.12	.76	1.09	1.43	1.82	2.39	2.51	2.51	2.63	...
	1950	.02	.50	1.19	1.52	1.60	1.93	2.25	2.16	1.95	...
	1930	.04	.36	.97	1.29	1.56	1.50	1.64	1.48	1.21	...
	1920	.09	.33	.60	.83	.97	1.08	1.02	.95	.75	...
	1910	.01	.04	.16	.27	.24	.33	.37	.26	.16	...
	1900	.02	.02	.03	.07	.13	.08	.10	.14	.09	...
Scotland...........	1951	.01	.29	.83	.89	.71	.72	.67	.54	.44	...
	1931	.00	.04	.15	.25	.23	.22	.18	.15	.11	...
	1921	.01	.17	.12	.12	.15	.08	.09	.06	.08	...
Sweden.............	1960	.51	1.97	2.92	3.80	4.35	4.58	4.35	3.92	3.67	3.42
	1950	.44	1.48	2.13	2.58	2.70	2.83	3.00	3.04	3.01	2.88
	1945	.30	.98	1.41	1.73	2.08	2.43	2.65	2.35	2.59	2.33
England & Wales.....	1951	.03	.41	1.25	1.37	1.36	1.17	.01	.73	.56	...
	1921	.01	.05	.08	.10	.12	.09	.08	.07	.05	...

Table 11-6A *(Continued)*

Country	Year	Percent divorced at selected ages									
		20	25	30	35	40	45	50	55	60	65
CENTRAL EUROPE											
Austria............	1961	.51	1.97	3.25	4.38	5.52	5.86	5.32	4.89	4.38	...
	1951	.26	1.84	3.99	4.76	4.15	4.25	4.41	4.04	3.35	...
	1934	.13	1.04	2.84	4.13	4.30	4.21	3.55	3.01	2.31	...
Czechoslovakia......	1947	.45	1.02	1.25	1.39	1.45	1.41	1.21	.99	.77	.50
	1961	.32	1.78	2.74	3.29	3.78	3.91	3.54	3.30	2.85	...
	1900	.04	.19	.39	.50	.59	.62	.58	.51	.44	.36
West Germany........	1961	.21	1.23	1.85	2.73	3.70	4.04	3.72	3.34	2.95	...
	1950	.17	1.38	3.16	3.22	2.95	2.60	2.50	2.21	1.88	...
	1939	.12	.71	1.40	2.00	2.62	2.71	2.59	2.22	1.82	...
	1933	.05	.54	1.31	1.96	2.07	2.06	1.82	1.56	1.24	...
	1925	.03	.49	.98	1.29	1.34	1.27	1.16	.96	.82	...
	1910	.02	.17	.45	.65	.72	.73	.70	.66	.52	...
Hungary............	1960	.65	2.22	2.98	3.30	3.66	3.60	3.62	3.36	3.14	...
	1949	.28	1.18	2.02	2.11	2.18	2.47	2.53	2.21	1.75	...
	1941	.19	.80	1.57	2.09	2.48	2.40	2.07	1.73	1.38	...
Switzerland........	1960	.06	.97	1.98	2.61	3.57	3.78	4.05	4.07	3.71	...
	1950	.05	.90	1.83	2.30	2.92	3.44	3.50	3.67	3.56	...
	1941	.02	.65	1.51	2.12	2.65	2.98	3.03	3.24	3.33	...
	1930	.02	.50	1.26	1.67	1.98	2.30	2.50	2.69	2.60	...
	1920	.02	.38	.90	1.38	1.62	2.08	2.24	2.25	2.02	...
SOUTH EUROPE											
Bulgaria............	1956	1.21	1.64	1.71	1.60	1.36	1.23	1.03	.92	.71	.46
Greece..............	1951	.31	.75	1.09	1.04	1.03	.82	.70	.56	.42	.27
Italy..............	1951	...	.01	.01	.01	.01	.01	.02	.02	.02	...
	1931	...	.01	.02	.03	.03	.03	.03	.02	.02	...
	1960	.02	.13	.31	.48	.75	.89	1.00	.93	.96	...
	1950	.03	.16	.44	.73	.93	.96	1.04	.91	.81	...
	1940	.06	.17	.40	.52	.82	.99	.88	.90	.58	...
Portugal............	1930	.09	.26	.50	.68	.76	.74	.64	.57	.45	.34
	1920	.08	.21	.34	.44	.45	.45	.42	.38	.31	.25
	1900	.01	.03	.06	.09	.11	.12	.10	.12	.12	.13
	1911	.06	.14	.23	.30	.33	.31	.28	.30	.26	.22

Source: United Nations Demographic Yearbooks and censuses of the nations

cent of the population at some age is reported as divorced:

		Maximum Prevalence of Divorce	
Nation		*Age*	*Percent*
Austria, 1961		45	5.9
Czechoslovakia, 1961		45	3.9
Denmark, 1960		50	5.3
Finland, 1960		50	4.1
France, 1960		45	4.5
Hungary, 1960		50	3.6
Israel, 1961		50	3.1
Japan, 1960		35	4.2
Libya, 1954		60	5.5
Morocco, 1952		60	4.3
Ryukyu Islands, 1960		30	6.9
Sarawak, 1960		60	4.5
Sweden, 1960		45	4.6
Switzerland, 1960		55	4.1
United States, 1960		45	4.1
West Germany, 1961		45	4.0

At the ages at which divorce is at a maximum, 90 percent or more of the population is ever-married. Thus even in those nations where the prevalence of divorce is greatest only 4 to 7 percent of the ever-married population is divorced. Moreover, divorce reaches its maximum prevalence at the very end of the child-bearing period, or even later. For this reason the effect on birthrates of divorce is comparatively minor, although its effects on child-rearing may be substantial.

There are at least two hypotheses that are advanced to explain above-average divorce rates—the "physiological sterility" hypothesis and the "sociological sterility" hypothesis. Some cultures of the world, especially Japanese and Muslim populations, have long approved of the dissolution of marriages that have not produced offspring. Usually the wife is held responsible and is divorced by the husband. Inasmuch as 5 to 10 percent of couples all over the world are unable to bear children, a rather high prevalence of divorce among women can result from this cause alone. (In some cultures the husband may merely take a second wife without divorcing the first.) A high prevalence of divorce, in such populations, may be indicative of traditionalism. In many of the modernized nations great emphasis has come to be placed on companionship in marriage, and each partner expects strong emotional support and affection from the other. Where these are not forthcoming, the culture approves of the dissolution of the marriage, on the grounds that it is sociologically "sterile." The above list of high-divorce-rate nations contains examples of both types of explanations. The maximum prevalence of divorce for physiological reasons (e.g., Libya or Ryukyu Islands) is as high as for sociological reasons (Denmark, France, United States).

Separation. As already noted, statistics on separation are available for very few nations. Where they are available, they suggest that separation may be nearly as prevalent as divorce. This is illustrated by data for four nations.

	Maximum Proportion Separated	
Nation	*Age*	*Percent*
Costa Rica	50	4.6
Denmark	40	1.4
Haiti	60	4.3
United States	50	3.2

One hypothesis assumes an inverse relationship between the stringency of divorce laws and the proportion of persons separated. In nations where divorce is not permitted or is very costly to the male, estranged couples merely live apart. Also, where there is much common law marriage estrangement tends to end in separation rather than divorce. In nations where divorce is more easily obtained, estranged couples tend to get a divorce rather than merely separate.

Widowhood. The proportion of the population that is widowed is a function of male and female age-specific death rates, the ages at which males and females marry, and the rates at which widowed persons remarry. With only minor exceptions, the death of one spouse is randomly distributed with respect to the death of the other. As a result, where death rates are low, widowhood is postponed to advanced ages. But where death rates are high, it is found in substantial proportions at younger ages. Wherever death rates fall, the prevalence of widowhood also falls.

At all ages and almost everywhere a larger proportion of women are widowed than of men. The reasons are that women are two to five years younger than their husbands, that in most nations women have lower death rates than men at all ages, and also that widowed men remarry much more readily than widowed women.

The following data for India and Norway illustrate how widowhood has declined as death rates have fallen, both in industrialized and in developing nations. Table 11-6B provides numerous additional examples.

Age	Proportion widowed			
	India		Norway	
	1901	1961	1900	1960
30	18.5	6.4	2.1	0.5
35	25.8	11.2	3.5	0.9
40	40.2	20.7	5.8	1.4
45	46.4	28.9	9.1	3.1
50	63.2	45.5	13.3	5.7
55	62.6	50.3	18.3	9.0
60	82.5	69.7	24.3	15.4

When death rates are high, widowhood occurs to a very substantial proportion of women in the reproductive ages. Even now in India roughly one tenth of females in the fertile ages 30 years and over are widowed and, by custom, removed from childbearing. Where death rates are low, as in Norway, widowhood occurs only to a very small segment of the population before age 45. Thus one of the incidental by-products of lowering the death rates is to increase fertility rates by prolonging the exposure to childbearing of women who otherwise would have become widows. It is of interest to note that in Norway and all developed nations the rise in proportions divorced is smaller than the decreases in proportions

Table 11-6B Proportion of the Population Widowed at Specified Ages for
Selected Nations of the World: 1900 to 1960

Country	Year	Percent widowed at selected ages							
		30	35	40	45	50	55	60	65
NORTHERN AFRICA									
Algeria..............	1948	7.3	11.7	19.7	30.3	45.9	56.5	70.6	77.9
Morocco.............	1952	5.4	9.9	19.8	30.7	46.7	55.7	67.2	73.1
Tunisia.............	1946	7.8	10.5	16.2	22.4	33.5	37.2	....	....
Egypt...............	1947	6.3	9.3	21.7	24.1	49.8	43.1	72.0	67.0
	1960	4.4	7.1	16.2	20.6	40.6	40.5	66.7	68.2
TROPICAL & SOUTHERN AFRICA									
Guinea..............	1955	2.7	4.6	8.7	16.6	24.7	37.7	48.5	59.2
Libya...............	1954	3.1	5.1	10.3	16.1	26.7	32.4	48.0	54.2
Seychelles..........	1960	1.0	2.7	5.4	8.1	11.7	16.2	23.8	31.1
NORTH AMERICA									
	1961	.8	1.6	3.2	5.9	9.5	15.8	24.4	34.2
	1951	1.2	2.1	3.7	6.5	11.0	16.7	24.4	34.0
Canada..............	1941	1.3	2.7	4.8	7.7	11.7	16.9	24.1	33.7
	1931	1.9	3.6	5.7	8.1	11.9	17.1	25.1	35.4
	1921	2.8	4.0	5.7	8.4	12.9	18.3	26.9	36.8
	1911	2.0	3.4	5.6	8.6	13.1	18.8	27.1	36.5
MIDDLE AMERICA									
Costa Rica.........	1950	2.3	4.2	8.0	12.5	20.4	27.2	37.6	43.0
El Salvador........	1950	2.5	4.1	8.4	11.6	17.8	22.7	31.0	36.0
Guatemala..........	1950	2.7	4.8	10.0	13.7	21.5	23.7	35.5	40.5
Haiti..............	1950	.7	1.4	.28	4.4	7.3	8.9	13.0	16.1
Curacao............	1960	.7	1.6	2.9	4.8	7.9	11.2	20.0	28.3
Nicaragua..........	1950	2.4	4.4	8.1	11.6	17.5	21.7	31.1	35.6
Panama.............	1960	.9	1.8	3.2	5.6	10.2	15.9	23.6	31.0
	1950	1.5	2.7	5.9	9.0	16.3	21.7	29.3	35.9
SOUTH AMERICA									
Bolivia............	1950	4.5	8.2	13.6	19.7	27.1	30.0	40.7	43.9
Chile..............	1920	5.6	8.6	14.1	19.1	26.9	31.2	41.2	43.8
Ecuador............	1950	3.2	5.2	9.1	12.8	20.1	24.9	36.5	40.5
Paraguay...........	1962	.7	1.4	3.3	5.2	8.4	11.8	20.2	22.9
	1950	1.5	2.9	5.5	7.6	9.9	12.9	19.5	25.8
Peru...............	1940	3.8	6.2	11.1	16.6	25.2	30.3	43.3	....
	1961	1.6	3.0	4.6	9.8	15.8	22.2	....	....
Venezuela..........	1950	2.4	4.3	8.1	12.1	18.4	23.7	30.0	34.7
	1941	3.3	5.0	10.0	11.5	16.6	18.0	23.7	....
	1936	4.0	6.2	10.8	13.4	19.5	22.2	28.7	....
SOUTH WEST ASIA									
Cyprus.............	1960	1.8	2.7	5.4	7.9	14.3	20.7	....	....
	1946	2.5	4.0	6.3	10.4	17.7	24.3	35.7	....
Iraq...............	1957	3.6	5.7	12.1	17.7	29.9	41.8	50.1	55.2
Israel.............	1948	2.6	3.7	6.4	10.4	17.8	26.4	39.2	50.9
	1961	1.3	2.4	5.1	7.9	14.5	22.8	36.9	48.8
Palestine..........	1931	4.5	8.2	16.9	25.2	40.6	45.6	60.9	65.8
Jordan.............	1961	2.9	5.3	10.3	15.9	26.4	31.6	47.1	....
Turkey	1960	2.0	3.6	8.2	11.8	19.4	27.3	46.8	....
	1955	2.7	5.0	9.3	14.1	24.0	33.1	52.9	....
	1945	4.3	7.1	13.7	20.8	36.9	47.6	65.0	71.9
SOUTH CENTRAL ASIA									
Ceylon.............	1953	4.1	7.5	13.6	21.1	32.3	40.5	53.0	....
	1946	5.9	9.8	17.1	24.8	34.8	42.4	53.4	59.0
	1921	10.9	17.4	27.3	35.4	45.7	53.5	66.0	71.4
	1911	10.6	16.5	27.1	34.4	45.3	52.5	66.2	70.6
	1901	14.0	24.0	31.5	42.4	48.5	62.5	....	....
India..............	1961	6.4	11.2	20.7	28.9	45.5	50.3	69.7	71.9
	1941	13.4	22.3	31.7	45.3	54.1	67.9	74.6	81.1
	1931	15.6	28.2	36.0	51.6	58.1	71.2	76.2	81.1
	1921	18.4	25.8	38.7	46.1	61.9	63.6	79.6	77.8
	1911	17.0	24.5	38.8	46.6	63.4	64.9	81.3	80.0
	1901	18.5	25.8	40.2	46.4	63.2	62.6	82.5	....

widowed, so that even with greater divorce for sociological reasons there is now less overall marital disruption than at any previous time in their history, and less marital disruption than in most of the developing nations.

11.7. Trends in the Marital Status Composition of the United States Population

It has already been demonstrated that in comparison with other industrialized nations of the world the United States population tends to

Table 11-6B (Continued)

Country	Year	Percent widowed at selected ages							
		30	35	40	45	50	55	60	65
SOUTH CENTRAL ASIA (continued)									
Pakistan............	1961	6.1	10.7	20.9	28.2	42.3	47.4	....	....
SOUTH EAST ASIA									
North Borneo........	1960	6.2	14.2	20.5	34.6	44.2	59.6	64.3	....
Philippines.........	1960	2.7	4.6	8.3	11.8	19.1	23.9	37.8	....
Sarawak	1960	3.3	5.1	10.7	16.1	28.8	35.8	51.2	56.6
	1947	5.9	8.3	16.7	22.2	37.4	....	....	....
EAST ASIA									
China..............	1956	2.8	6.3	11.7	19.6	30.9	43.4	57.9	71.0
Hong Kong..........	1961	2.0	4.3	8.8	16.2	26.8	36.3	46.0	51.6
	1960	1.5	4.6	11.3	17.8	22.4	30.8	41.1	56.4
	1955	3.3	9.3	14.3	17.3	23.4	32.7	45.1	59.1
	1950	8.1	11.8	13.5	17.8	24.8	35.1	47.7	60.9
Japan..............	1940	5.9	8.6	12.5	18.5	26.9	37.8	50.0	63.4
	1930	3.2	6.0	10.4	16.7	24.9	35.7	49.7	62.4
	1935	3.4	6.0	10.3	16.5	24.9	35.3	48.2	63.0
	1930	3.7	6.4	10.3	16.0	25.0	34.8	47.7	60.8
Korea..............	1955	7.4	10.9	16.8	24.8	34.5	43.9	55.6	66.6
	1960	2.9	8.7	18.9	28.6	35.6	42.5	48.0	56.1
Ryukyu Islands	1955	7.1	16.1	25.9	32.1	38.1	42.9	50.9	61.6
	1950	13.8	20.9	26.2	29.9	33.4	39.4	49.0	59.5
U.S.S.R............	1926	7.7	12.8	18.8	25.2	34.4	41.0	52.6	60.1
NORTHERN & WESTERN EUROPE									
Belgium............	1947	1.6	2.4	3.8	6.2	9.7	14.9	21.8	....
	1930	1.2	2.1	3.8	6.1	9.1	14.1	21.8	....
	1920	2.4	3.3	4.5	6.6	10.4	16.6	25.0	....
	1910	1.2	2.3	3.9	7.0	11.1	18.5	27.0	....
Denmark............	1960	.6	.8	1.9	3.5	6.2	10.5	17.0	....
	1950	.8	1.3	2.3	3.9	6.7	11.9	18.0	....
	1945	.9	1.4	2.6	4.9	7.7	12.7	19.7	....
	1940	.7	1.4	2.9	5.2	8.8	13.5	20.7	....
	1930	.9	2.0	3.8	6.1	9.1	14.0	21.5	....
	1921	1.9	3.0	4.6	6.9	10.7	16.8	25.1	....
	1911	1.2	2.7	4.7	7.8	13.4	18.9	26.7	....
	1901	1.3	3.0	5.7	8.7	13.5	19.5	28.8	....
Finland............	1960	.8	1.6	3.6	7.5	12.4	17.7	26.7	....
	1950	1.8	4.4	6.9	9.5	13.8	21.3	30.8	....
	1940	3.1	3.9	5.7	9.3	14.5	23.1	31.8	....
	1930	1.9	4.0	6.9	11.5	16.6	24.1	32.1	....
	1920	3.5	5.8	8.5	11.9	16.0	23.5	31.9	....
	1910	2.1	4.3	6.5	10.1	16.0	21.6	30.4	....
	1900	2.1	3.9	6.6	9.5	14.8	22.3	31.8	....
France.............	1901	4.3	7.1	10.8	15.5	21.6	28.8	38.8	49.2
	1962	.6	1.4	2.7	5.4	9.3	14.8	23.4	....
	1954	.8	2.1	4.0	6.8	11.1	17.7	27.7	....
	1946	3.0	4.0	5.8	9.3	14.6	23.6	33.3	....
	1936	1.9	3.6	6.6	12.7	18.9	24.1	31.6	....
	1931	2.0	4.3	9.5	14.4	17.7	22.9	31.9	....
	1911	3.3	5.7	9.4	14.3	20.9	28.9	39.0	49.9
Iceland............	1950	1.3	2.7	4.5	6.1	9.8	16.0	24.0	31.6
	1951	1.4	2.4	4.0	6.8	11.7	17.7	26.2	34.7
	1961	.4	1.1	2.6	4.9	9.2	13.4	22.2	....
Ireland............	1951	.8	1.6	3.3	5.6	11.0	16.5	23.5	....
	1946	.9	1.9	3.7	7.0	11.8	17.5	24.9	....
	1936	1.0	2.1	4.5	7.1	12.0	16.7	24.6	....
	1926	1.6	3.0	6.3	9.2	15.1	18.8	28.8	....

Table 11-6B (*Continued*)

Country	Year	Percent widowed at selected ages							
		30	35	40	45	50	55	60	65
NORTHERN & WESTERN EUROPE (continued)									
Netherlands.........	1960	.4	.7	1.6	3.2	5.7	9.8	15.8	....
	1950	.6	1.4	2.4	4.2	6.9	10.4	15.9	....
	1947	1.2	1.9	2.8	4.5	6.9	10.8	16.6	....
	1930	.6	1.3	2.7	4.3	7.0	11.6	18.8	....
	1920	1.1	2.0	3.1	5.3	8.9	13.9	21.7	....
	1909	1.0	1.9	3.7	6.3	10.2	16.0	24.9	....
	1899	1.3	2.7	4.6	7.8	11.8	18.4	26.2	....
Norway..............	1960	.5	.9	1.4	3.1	5.7	9.0	15.4	....
	1950	.8	1.5	2.5	3.8	7.3	11.6	18.0	....
	1930	1.1	2.5	4.4	7.0	10.4	16.2	22.5	....
	1920	2.1	3.3	4.9	8.4	11.9	17.2	24.4	....
	1910	1.7	3.6	5.7	8.2	12.0	17.7	24.6	....
	1900	2.1	3.5	5.8	9.1	13.3	18.3	24.3	....
Scotland...........	1951	1.3	2.3	3.5	5.5	9.7	15.9	24.3	....
	1931	1.2	3.0	5.8	8.4	11.3	16.7	24.6	....
	1921	3.3	4.7	6.3	8.4	13.1	18.2	27.1	....
	1911	2.0	4.0	7.0	11.2	17.0	24.4	33.6	44.4
	1901	2.5	4.9	8.4	13.2	19.9	27.2	37.1	45.9
Sweden.............	1960	.6	1.1	2.1	3.7	6.5	11.1	18.2	27.2
	1950	.8	1.5	2.6	4.6	8.2	13.2	20.5	29.3
	1945	.9	1.6	3.0	5.5	9.0	14.4	21.1	29.7
England & Wales......	1951	1.1	2.0	2.9	4.6	8.5	13.9	23.0	....
	1921	3.5	5.1	6.4	8.2	12.5	17.6	26.8	....
	1911	1.5	2.9	5.7	9.1	14.9	20.6	30.9	....
CENTRAL EUROPE									
Austria............	1961	.9	1.8	6.2	12.3	16.2	19.9	26.9	....
	1951	4.8	8.5	9.9	10.3	13.4	18.9	27.5	....
	1934	1.2	2.9	5.1	9.4	14.9	22.0	30.7	....
	1910	2.1	4.2	6.7	10.5	15.5	22.8	31.5	....
	1900	1.9	3.4	6.6	9.9	15.3	20.8	30.7	....
Czechoslovakia.......	1947	3.3	4.7	7.2	11.5	17.9	27.9	38.6	49.6
	1961	1.0	1.9	4.1	7.0	11.3	18.2	27.8	....
	1900	2.3	4.5	8.3	13.9	21.0	29.9	40.4	51.9
West Germany.........	1961	.7	1.5	6.0	13.8	18.3	20.2	25.9	....
	1950	5.7	9.9	10.5	9.8	12.3	17.6	27.1	....
	1939	.8	1.8	3.8	7.2	13.4	19.7	27.3	....
	1933	1.0	2.3	4.9	9.9	14.0	18.9	26.4	....
	1925	1.7	5.1	8.2	10.2	13.2	19.7	29.5	....
	1910	1.4	3.0	5.6	9.7	15.9	24.4	35.2	....
Hungary.............	1960	.9	2.2	6.6	10.3	14.0	19.4	28.0	....
	1949	5.8	7.1	8.5	11.0	16.0	24.8	37.7	....
	1941	1.7	3.2	5.7	10.7	19.0	27.4	36.9	....
Switzerland.........	1960	.6	1.0	2.0	3.7	6.5	10.6	17.8	....
	1950	.7	1.5	2.3	4.0	7.4	13.0	21.4	....
	1941	.6	1.4	3.1	5.6	9.8	16.0	24.8	....
	1930	.9	2.0	4.4	7.1	11.8	18.3	26.9	....
	1920	2.1	3.3	5.3	8.8	13.3	20.3	30.4	....
SOUTHERN EUROPE									
Bulgaria............	1956	1.5	2.8	4.7	7.1	11.0	18.3	28.2	41.9
Greece..............	1951	4.8	7.6	11.2	16.8	25.6	34.8	46.7	56.2
Italy..............	1951	1.9	3.7	5.1	7.7	12.1	17.9	27.0	....
	1931	1.8	4.0	8.6	12.3	15.6	21.1	29.7	....
Malta & Gozo.........	1957	1.1	2.0	4.3	6.9	12.1	18.3	27.8	38.8
Portugal............	1960	1.1	1.9	3.9	5.9	10.3	15.2	25.6	....
	1950	1.6	3.0	5.5	8.8	14.4	20.2	30.9	....
	1940	2.3	4.0	7.3	10.9	17.1	22.4	34.6	....
	1911	3.4	5.5	9.3	13.0	19.9	25.1	35.6	41.2
	1930	3.2	5.6	8.8	13.2	18.9	25.8	35.7	44.7
	1920	4.3	6.5	9.9	13.6	19.8	25.4	35.1	41.0
	1900	3.5	5.9	9.4	13.2	19.9	25.0	35.5	42.2

Source: United Nations <u>Demographic Yearbooks</u> and censuses of the nations

Table 11-7 Marital Status and Median Age at Marriage of the United States Population, by Sex: 1890 to 1964

Year	Median age at first marriage		Percent distribution by marital status [1]							
			Female				Male			
	Female	Male	Single	Married	Widowed	Divorced	Single	Married	Widowed	Divorced
1890................	22.0	26.1	34.1	54.8	10.6	0.4	43.6	52.1	3.8	0.2
1900................	21.9	25.9	33.3	55.2	10.9	0.5	42.0	52.8	4.5	0.3
1910................	21.6	25.1	31.8	57.1	10.3	0.6	40.4	54.2	4.4	0.5
1920................	21.2	24.6	29.4	58.9	10.8	0.8	36.9	57.6	4.6	0.6
1930................	21.3	24.3	28.4	59.5	10.8	1.3	35.8	58.4	4.5	1.1
1940................	21.5	24.3	27.6	59.5	11.3	1.6	34.8	59.7	4.2	1.2
1950................	20.3	22.8	20.0	65.8	11.8	2.4	26.4	67.5	4.1	2.0
1960................	20.3	22.8	19.0	66.0	12.2	2.9	24.9	69.6	3.4	2.1
1963................	20.5	22.8	20.0	64.9	12.3	2.8	25.9	68.8	3.3	2.1
1964................	20.5	23.1	20.3	64.4	12.3	3.0	26.4	68.1	3.3	2.1
Index (1890=100)										
1890................	100	100	100	100	100	100	100	100	100	100
1900................	100	99	98	101	103	125	96	101	118	150
1910................	98	96	93	104	97	150	93	104	116	250
1920................	96	94	86	107	102	200	85	111	121	300
1930................	97	93	83	109	102	325	82	112	118	550
1940................	98	87	81	109	107	400	80	115	111	600
1950................	92	87	59	120	111	600	61	130	108	1000
1960................	92	87	56	120	115	725	57	134	89	1050
1963................	93	87	59	118	116	700	59	132	87	1050
1964................	93	85	60	117	116	750	61	131	87	1050

[1] The index reported in the lower panel is based upon percent distribution standardized for age, using the 1950 age composition as standard.

Source: Statistical Abstract of the U.S., 1963, Table 31, 1964, Historical Statistics of U.S. 1960, p. 15
U.S. Census of Populations: 1960, Detailed Characteristics, United States Summary, Table 177.

have a pattern of early marriage at the present time, with a low level of bachelorhood and a high prevalence of divorce. However, this is a comparatively recent development that occurred only during and immediately following World War II. Table 11-7 presents measures of marital status and median age at first marriage from 1890 to 1964. From this table it can be seen that the median age of marriage of females in 1890 was 22 years, whereas in 1960 it was 20.3 years. For males, the change was from 26.1 in 1890 to 22.8 in 1960. Thus in 1890 the United States population fell almost in the "late marriage" category, spent more than half a century in the "marriage at maturity" category, and only in 1950 to 1960 did it turn toward the "early marriage" end of the range. A similar development occurred for males.

If we look closely at these statistics, we see that although there had been a gradual downward drift in the age at marriage and in the proportion single, the really dramatic change occurred between 1940 and 1950. In this 10-year period a veritable revolution in the marital status pattern of the nation occurred.

Throughout the 1890-1960 span, the proportion divorced increased more than tenfold for males and more than sevenfold for females.

Here again the largest single increase occurred between 1940 and 1950.

Among males widowhood tended to remain nearly constant over the 70-year span, whereas it increased steadily although slightly among females. Actually, two counteracting forces are at work, which tend to cancel each other. On the one hand, death rates at younger ages have fallen steadily. This tends to reduce the proportion of the population that is widowed. However, an increasing proportion of the population has fallen into the ever-married group because of decline in bachelorhood, which exposes a larger segment of the population to the possibility of widowhood. Inasmuch as greater improvement in mortality control has taken place for females than for males, wives tend to outlive their husbands, with the result that a higher proportion of them tend to be classified as widows.

The bottom portion of Table 11-7 is of unusual importance. It consists of indexes in which the data for 1890 are allowed to equal 100. The eight righthand columns represent sets of percent distributions by marital status that have been standardized for age (using the 1960 census age composition as a standard and then letting the percentages for 1890 represent

Table 11-8 Trends in Marital Status Composition for Selected Age Groups
by Sex, United States: 1890 to 1960

Sex marital status and age		Year							
		1960	1950	1940	1930[1]	1920	1910	1900	1890
MALE									
Single,	15 - 19 years....	96.1	96.7	98.3	98.0	97.7	98.3	98.8	99.4
	20 - 24 years....	53.0	59.1	72.2	70.8	70.7	74.9	77.6	80.7
Single,	35 - 39 years....	8.8	10.1	15.3	15.4[2]	16.1	16.7	17.0	15.3
	40 - 44 years....	7.3	9.0	12.6	13.1				
Divorced	45 - 49 years....	3.0	2.9	2.0	1.7	1.0	0.8	0.6	0.4
	50 - 54 years....	3.1	3.0	2.0	1.6				
Widowed	55 - 59 years....	3.8	5.9	7.4	8.4	11.2	11.7	11.9	10.2
	60 - 64 years....	6.5	9.6	11.1	12.4				
FEMALE									
Single,	15 - 19 years....	83.9	82.9	88.1	86.6	87.0	87.9	88.7	90.3
	20 - 24 years....	28.4	32.3	47.2	46.0	45.6	48.3	51.6	51.8
Single,	35 - 39 years....	6.1	8.4	11.2	10.4	11.4	11.4	11.1	9.9
	40 - 44 years....	6.1	8.3	9.5	9.5				
Divorced	45 - 49 years....	4.3	3.6	2.4	1.7	1.0	0.8	0.6	0.5
	50 - 54 years....	4.2	3.3	2.0	1.5				
Widowed	55 - 59 years....	17.9	20.5	22.4	23.4	29.5	30.0	32.3	33.3
	60 - 64 years....	27.6	29.7	31.3	33.1				

[1]/ 1890 to 1930 Reports include persons whose age not reported.

[2]/ 1890 to 1920 age groups are: 35-44, 45-54, 55-64, 65 and over.

Source: U.S. Census of Population: 1960 Detailed Characteristics, U.S. Summary,
Table 177.

100). These indexes are extremely useful because they reveal the change that has taken place, holding constant the changing age composition of the population. These indexes show that, holding age composition constant, spinsterhood has declined by nearly 50 percent, widowhood among females has increased slightly, and divorce has increased about sevenfold. For males the change has been even more extreme—bachelorhood has been cut almost in half, the proportion married has increased by one third, the proportion divorced has been multiplied ten-fold, and widowhood has been reduced substantially. These indexes reveal, even more clearly, how great the changes were between 1940 and 1950 in comparison with preceding and succeeding years.

The extraordinary changes that have occurred since 1940 have been accomplished in two ways: (a) the younger generation has entered marriage at an earlier age than ever before in recent history, and (b) a higher proportion of persons in middle age (including widowed or divorced) have married. Table 11-8 reports the trends in marital status composition for selected age groups for each sex from 1890 to 1960. Whereas in 1890 more than

one half of all women 20 to 24 were still unmarried, by 1960 the never-married percentage of this age group was only 28 percent. A similar drop is indicated for males. In both cases most of the change occurred in the 10 years between 1940 and 1950, with a modest continuation of the same trends between 1950 and 1960. Simultaneously with the declining age at marriage has come a reduction in the prevalence of spinsterhood and bachelorhood. Whereas in 1890 one tenth of all women 35 to 44 were spinsters, by 1960 the percentage had fallen to only 6 percent—a 40 percent reduction. Among males the decline in bachelorhood was almost 50 percent. Almost all of this decline in bachelorhood and spinsterhood seems to have occurred since 1920, with more than three fourths of the change having occurred in the 20 years between 1940 and 1960.

This sudden and unforeseen revolution in marriage pattern has had a very dramatic effect on many aspects of social life of the country. Especially, as we shall see in a chapter on fertility, it greatly altered the fertility trends in this country. As yet, sociologists have not produced an adequate explanation of the forces that created this shift to early marriage.

At the time it was taking place it was usual to blame it on World War II and the postwar readjustment. Now this explanation seems inadequate. As was noted in the international comparisons of Section 11-3, the United States is somewhat unique among the industrialized nations of the world in having such a low age at marriage and such a high proportion of the population married. From one point of view, this may be interpreted as a symptom that we are still an underdeveloped or frontier country that, we feel, can tolerate unlimited population growth. *On the other hand, this may represent the emergence of a new marriage pattern for all industrialized nations.* When a nation attains a condition of wealth and prosperity, people assign priorities to the things that they wish to purchase with their wealth. Health and freedom from disease and death will always be at the top of this list. Next comes the desire for a certain amount of improvement in material comfort, but clearly a third category is the ability to establish a home and begin regular sexual relations with social approval at the earliest appropriate time. From one point of view it is an anomaly that the richer a nation is, the more it has demanded that young people postpone the beginning of sexual life to a point far beyond that to which their biological nature predisposes them. It has seemed almost as if prolonged sexual abstinence were a price that the industrialized nations have paid in order to achieve their prosperity. It is difficult to visualize why this should continue to be so indefinitely. If a nation is wealthy and is free to expend its wealth in any way it sees fit, there is no reason why it should not place a high priority on permitting young people to marry as soon as they are physiologically mature—especially if the situation is one where fertility is under control and runaway population growth does not result. Often it has been maintained that young adults in the industrialized, more wealthy, urbanized nations have not wished to marry and that the postponement of marriage was not dictated by economic necessity but by conscious avoidance. The "marriage boom" is explained in terms of increased sexual activity among teenagers, with increased prevalence of premarital

pregnancy. Although this is very likely a powerful factor, we prefer also to believe that the younger generation of Americans is highly conventional and compliant in its outlook on marriage and enters this status because it wishes to do so.

The revolutionary change in marriage pattern that occurred after World War II with the great increase in child marriage appears to have about run its course, having reached a peak about 1959 or 1960. The median age at marriage has remained constant since then or has tended to rise a little, and when data are standardized for age, a slight reversal of the trend toward earlier marriage is shown for recent years. The following data show that little change has taken place since 1960:

Year	Median Age	
	Male	Female
1960	22.8	20.3
1961	22.8	20.3
1962	22.7	20.3
1963	22.8	20.5
1964	23.1	20.5
1965	22.8	20.6
1966	22.8	20.5

Figure 11-3 graphs these recent trends in marital status distribution.

This overview of trends in marital status in the United States may be summarized by stating that at the present moment the population of the United States appears to have reached the end of a revolutionary change that began in the 1940s and is now in a state of near equilibrium. We do not know enough to predict what the future course will be. It is entirely possible that the present pattern could be maintained for a long period of time, that there could be a return to the former pattern caused by a rise in the prevalence of spinsterhood and bachelorhood both at the younger and at the more advanced ages, or that with continuing prosperity the practice of early marriage could spread to even larger segments of oncoming generations. It may be that we are witnessing the convergence of two opposing trends. On the one hand, we attempt to prolong the period of childhood by prolonging training. On the other hand, we may be mak-

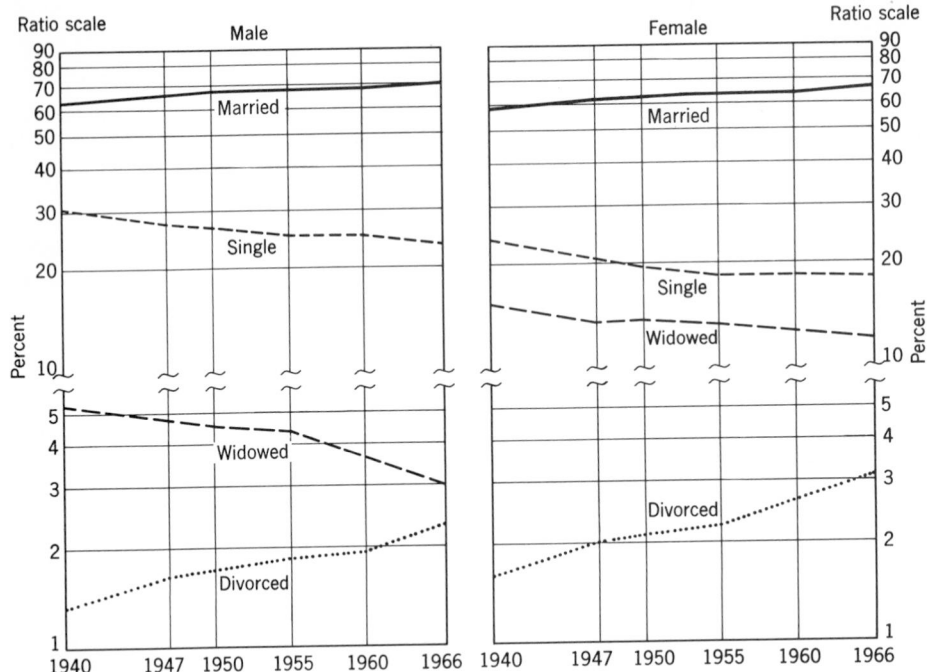

ing it possible to obtain all of the privileges of adulthood almost overnight, without having to work, plan, and save, so that the transition from one to the other can be made abruptly and at a comparatively early age. One group of youths may follow one pattern and another group the other, with the result that marriage may be spread more evenly over the years 18 to 30.

11.8. Differentials in Marital Status Composition within the United States Population according to Race

A detailed picture of the marital status of the United States population, by sex and color, is provided in Table 11-9. For the white population the principal elements of the marriage pattern may be summarized in a few points. (1) The earlier age at marriage of women causes the proportion single to shrink much more rapidly with advancing age for females than for males. After age 18 the proportion married and living with the spouse rises rapidly and reaches a peak at ages 40-44 for males and 30-34 for females. (2) During the early years about 2.5 percent of the couples are separated from each other because of work, military service, or other factors. (3) A signifi-

cant amount of estrangement manifests itself quickly, for after about age 23 between 1 and 1.5 percent of the couples are separated for reasons of incompatibility. (Reconciliations and divorces prevent this from accumulating to higher values.) (4) The proportion divorced increases gradually with age, so that by age 35 more than 2 percent of the men and 3 percent of the women are divorced. (Remarriage of divorced persons prevents this proportion from cumulating to very high values.) The proportion divorced reaches a peak of 3.1 percent of men at ages 50-59 and 4.1 percent for women at ages 45-54. Widowhood remains at infinitesimally small levels until about age 30 for women and age 45 for men. As death dissolves marriages at older ages, the proportion widowed rises steadily. For women it becomes the dominant marital status after age 70. Three factors account for this: greater longevity of women, younger ages of wives, and a greater propensity for widowed men than for widowed women to remarry.

Beyond a doubt the greatest differential in marital status within the United States population is that between the white and nonwhite (primarily Negro) groups. The bottom panel (second page) of Table 11-9 provides informa-

Table 11-9   Marital Status of United States Population, by Sex and Color: 1960

Age and color	Male								Female							
				Married								Married				
					Spouse present	Spouse absent							Spouse present	Spouse absent		
	Total	Single	Total married		Separated	Other	Widowed	Divorced	Total	Single	Total married		Separated	Other	Widowed	Divorced
WHITE	100.0	24.4	70.3	67.5	1.0	1.8	3.2	2.1	100.0	18.6	66.7	63.7	1.3	1.7	11.9	2.8
14 years............	100.0	99.4	0.6	0.1	...	0.4	...	...	100.0	98.9	1.0	0.5	...	0.5	...	...
15 years............	100.0	99.4	0.6	0.2	...	0.4	...	...	100.0	97.7	2.2	1.5	0.1	0.6	...	0.1
16 years............	100.0	99.1	0.9	0.4	...	0.5	...	...	100.0	94.3	5.5	4.3	0.2	1.0	...	0.1
17 years............	100.0	98.1	1.8	1.2	0.1	0.6	...	0.1	100.0	88.0	11.7	9.7	0.4	1.6	0.1	0.2
18 years............	100.0	94.5	5.3	4.2	0.2	1.0	...	0.1	100.0	75.5	23.9	20.8	0.7	2.4	0.1	0.5
19 years............	100.0	87.0	12.7	10.7	0.3	1.7	...	0.3	100.0	59.4	39.6	35.4	1.0	3.1	0.1	0.9
20 years............	100.0	75.6	23.8	20.8	0.6	2.4	0.1	0.6	100.0	45.2	53.3	48.6	1.4	3.4	0.2	1.3
21 years............	100.0	63.0	36.2	32.8	0.8	2.6	0.1	0.8	100.0	33.7	64.4	59.7	1.5	3.3	0.2	1.7
22 years............	100.0	51.1	47.8	44.0	0.9	2.8	0.1	1.1	100.0	24.5	73.3	68.7	1.5	3.1	0.3	1.9
23 years............	100.0	39.8	58.8	54.3	1.0	3.4	0.1	1.3	100.0	18.3	79.3	75.1	1.5	2.7	0.3	2.1
24 years............	100.0	32.5	65.9	61.8	1.0	3.1	0.1	1.5	100.0	14.6	82.9	78.9	1.6	2.4	0.3	2.2
25 years............	100.0	27.0	71.2	67.6	1.1	2.6	0.1	1.7	100.0	12.2	85.0	81.3	1.5	2.3	0.4	2.4
26 years............	100.0	22.6	75.6	72.2	1.0	2.3	0.1	1.7	100.0	10.5	86.5	83.0	1.5	2.1	0.5	2.5
27 years............	100.0	18.9	79.1	75.9	1.0	2.2	0.2	1.8	100.0	9.4	87.6	84.2	1.5	1.9	0.5	2.5
28 years............	100.0	16.7	81.4	78.3	1.0	2.1	0.2	1.8	100.0	8.7	88.2	84.9	1.4	1.9	0.6	2.5
29 years............	100.0	15.1	82.8	79.7	1.0	2.1	0.2	1.9	100.0	8.2	88.6	85.3	1.6	1.8	0.6	2.6
30 – 34 years........	100.0	11.3	86.4	83.5	1.0	1.9	0.2	2.1	100.0	6.6	89.6	86.5	1.5	1.7	0.9	2.9
35 – 39 years........	100.0	8.3	89.0	86.1	1.0	1.8	0.4	2.3	100.0	5.9	89.0	85.9	1.5	1.6	1.8	3.4
40 – 44 years........	100.0	7.1	89.6	86.8	1.1	1.7	0.7	2.6	100.0	6.0	86.7	83.6	1.6	1.5	3.4	3.8
45 – 49 years........	100.0	7.0	88.9	86.1	1.1	1.7	1.2	2.9	100.0	6.6	83.3	80.2	1.6	1.5	6.0	4.1
50 – 54 years........	100.0	7.5	87.5	84.5	1.2	1.8	1.9	3.1	100.0	7.8	77.9	74.7	1.6	1.6	10.2	4.1
55 – 59 years........	100.0	8.0	85.5	82.4	1.3	1.8	3.4	3.1	100.0	8.4	70.9	67.8	1.4	1.6	16.8	3.9
60 – 64 years........	100.0	7.6	83.5	80.2	1.3	2.0	6.0	2.9	100.0	7.9	62.3	59.4	1.3	1.6	26.5	3.3
65 – 69 years........	100.0	7.8	80.0	76.7	1.3	2.0	9.6	2.7	100.0	8.2	52.4	49.6	1.1	1.6	36.7	2.7
70 – 74 years........	100.0	7.9	73.5	70.1	1.2	2.1	16.2	2.4	100.0	8.7	39.6	37.1	0.9	1.7	49.6	2.1
75 – 79 years........	100.0	8.1	65.0	61.3	1.2	2.5	24.9	2.1	100.0	9.1	27.8	25.4	0.7	1.7	61.6	1.5
80 – 84 years........	100.0	7.6	53.7	49.6	1.0	3.0	37.1	1.6	100.0	9.9	16.3	14.1	0.4	1.8	72.7	1.1
85 – and over........	100.0	7.2	38.3	33.9	0.8	3.5	53.0	1.4	100.0	10.0	8.1	6.3	0.3	1.5	81.0	0.8

Table 11-9 (Continued)

	Male								Female							
			Married								Married					
					Spouse absent								Spouse absent			
Age and color	Total	Single	Total married	Spouse present	Separated	Other	Widowed	Divorced	Total	Single	Total married	Spouse present	Separated	Other	Widowed	Divorced
NONWHITE	100.0	30.4	62.6	53.0	5.4	4.2	4.5	2.4	100.0	22.0	60.6	48.6	8.4	3.6	13.8	3.6
14 years	100.0	99.4	0.5	0.2	0.1	0.2	...	0.1	100.0	98.6	1.3	0.7	0.2	0.4	0.1	...
15 years	100.0	99.3	0.7	0.2	0.1	0.3	0.1	...	100.0	97.1	2.8	1.8	0.4	0.6	0.1	...
16 years	100.0	98.9	1.0	0.5	0.1	0.4	0.1	0.1	100.0	93.2	6.6	4.6	0.7	1.3	0.1	0.1
17 years	100.0	97.9	2.0	1.2	0.3	0.6	0.1	...	100.0	86.4	13.3	9.6	1.3	2.3	0.1	0.2
18 years	100.0	94.7	5.1	3.3	0.5	1.3	0.1	0.1	100.0	76.4	23.0	17.0	2.4	3.7	0.2	0.3
19 years	100.0	88.0	11.8	8.4	0.8	2.6	0.1	0.1	100.0	61.7	37.5	28.8	3.7	4.9	0.3	0.6
20 years	100.0	77.2	22.3	16.8	1.7	3.8	0.1	0.3	100.0	51.4	47.4	36.1	5.4	5.8	0.4	0.9
21 years	100.0	66.4	33.0	25.7	2.5	4.9	0.2	0.5	100.0	41.3	56.7	43.6	6.9	6.2	0.6	1.4
22 years	100.0	55.8	43.3	34.3	3.4	5.6	0.2	0.6	100.0	33.7	63.9	49.6	7.8	6.5	0.7	1.7
23 years	100.0	45.3	53.6	43.8	3.7	6.2	0.2	0.8	100.0	27.0	69.8	54.4	9.1	6.3	0.9	2.3
24 years	100.0	39.8	58.8	47.4	4.5	6.8	0.3	1.2	100.0	23.3	73.3	57.2	10.2	5.9	1.1	2.4
25 years	100.0	34.5	63.9	52.9	5.0	6.0	0.3	1.3	100.0	15.7	78.9	62.3	11.6	5.4	1.2	3.0
26 years	100.0	30.8	67.3	56.0	5.0	6.3	0.4	1.5	100.0	19.8	76.0	59.8	10.7	5.3	1.6	3.2
27 years	100.0	26.0	71.7	59.7	5.5	6.4	0.5	1.8	100.0	15.2	79.4	62.5	11.7	5.2	1.8	3.7
28 years	100.0	24.1	73.6	61.4	6.1	6.2	0.5	1.8	100.0	13.5	80.7	64.1	11.8	4.7	2.0	3.9
29 years	100.0	22.7	74.7	62.4	6.2	6.1	0.5	2.2	100.0	12.7	80.7	63.4	12.6	4.6	2.9	4.2
30 – 34 years	100.0	17.2	79.1	66.3	7.0	5.8	0.8	2.9	100.0	9.6	82.3	65.1	12.9	4.3	3.3	4.8
35 – 39 years	100.0	12.7	82.4	69.7	7.7	5.1	1.4	3.5	100.0	7.6	81.7	65.3	12.7	3.7	5.2	5.5
40 – 44 years	100.0	9.7	84.2	71.8	7.9	4.5	2.3	3.8	100.0	6.4	79.0	64.0	11.6	3.4	8.7	5.8
45 – 49 years	100.0	8.8	83.9	71.7	7.8	4.4	3.4	3.9	100.0	5.9	75.1	61.3	10.5	3.4	13.2	5.8
50 – 54 years	100.0	9.2	81.5	70.0	7.2	4.3	5.4	3.8	100.0	6.1	68.9	56.7	9.1	3.2	19.8	5.2
55 – 59 years	100.0	10.6	77.8	66.6	6.8	4.4	8.1	3.5	100.0	6.9	60.7	50.2	7.5	3.0	28.2	4.3
60 – 64 years	100.0	7.9	76.5	66.0	6.0	4.5	12.3	3.2	100.0	4.7	52.0	44.0	5.5	2.5	39.9	3.3
65 – 69 years	100.0	7.1	72.9	63.8	5.4	3.7	17.2	2.9	100.0	4.3	42.5	35.9	4.3	2.4	50.6	2.5
70 – 74 years	100.0	6.4	68.0	60.2	4.4	3.5	23.2	2.4	100.0	4.4	32.4	27.3	3.2	2.0	61.2	2.0
75 – 79 years	100.0	6.2	61.2	54.2	3.8	3.2	30.5	2.1	100.0	4.4	22.9	18.8	2.3	1.8	71.3	1.4
80 – 84 years	100.0	5.9	53.6	47.1	3.3	3.1	38.4	2.1	100.0	4.5	14.8	11.3	1.6	1.9	79.6	1.1
85 – and over	100.0	6.1	42.9	36.4	3.0	3.5	49.7	1.3	100.0	4.3	9.3	6.5	1.2	1.6	85.4	1.0

Source: U.S. Census of Population: 1960, Detailed Characteristics, United States Summary, Table 176.

tion that permits us to examine these differences carefully. Although the general pattern is similar to that for the white population, several differences are outstanding. (1) Child marriage is more common among the nonwhite population than among the white, but the difference is very slight:

Male

	White	Nonwhite	Difference
Percent married at age 17	1.9	2.1	+0.2
Percent married at age 19	13.0	12.0	−1.0

Female

	White	Nonwhite	Difference
Percent married at age 17	12.0	13.6	+1.6
Percent married at age 19	40.6	38.3	−2.3

At age 17 a slightly higher proportion of nonwhite males and females have ever married, but by age 19 the balance is reversed and a higher proportion of the white males and females have ever married in comparison with nonwhites. Actually the differences are so small that for all practical purposes the age pattern at marriage is identical for white and nonwhite youngsters up to age 19. (2) At age 19 and above there is a greater tendency among the nonwhite than among the white population not to marry but to remain single. Contrary to popular belief, *the adult nonwhite population postpones marriage to a greater extent than the white, and the proportion that passes entirely through the reproductive ages without marrying is significantly greater for the nonwhite than for the white population.* This is shown by the following summary of the proportions that remain single at mature ages:

Male

	White	Nonwhite	Difference
Percent single at ages 30-44	11.3	17.2	+5.9
Percent single at ages 40-44	7.1	9.7	+2.6

Female

	White	Nonwhite	Difference
Percent single at ages 30-44	6.6	9.6	+3.0
Percent single at ages 40-44	6.0	6.4	+0.4

Thus the marital status differential is one that would tend to depress the fertility of the nonwhite population in relation to the white, if other factors were equal. A part of this difference is offset by the greater propensity of Negroes to bear children out of wedlock. These differences are probably understatements, especially for nonwhite females, because of the tendency to report erroneously widowhood or divorce status at the older ages. (3) Almost immediately after marriage, nonwhite marriages begin to suffer greater disintegration than do white marriages. At the youngest ages this takes the form of greater proportions separated. Nonwhite women in particular appear to be victims of abandonment and divorce, and by age 30 one nonwhite woman in eight is separated in addition to the substantial proportion divorced. (4) Furthermore, a substantially larger share of nonwhite marriages are temporarily disrupted for reasons of work, institutionalization, military service, and so on. Nonwhite males appear to claim separation for these reasons as a substitute to admitting estrangement. (5) Contrary to the usual opinion that the nonwhite population separates and does not bother to divorce, beyond age 23 for females and age 30 for males the proportion divorced is higher among the nonwhite than among the white population. The peak prevalence for the status of divorce is at ages 40-49. The devastating impact on the nonwhite population of the combined forces of separation and divorce is revealed in the following summary:

Divorced, ages 45-49	White	Nonwhite	Difference
Male	2.9	3.9	+1.0
Female	4.1	5.8	+1.7

Separated, ages 30-34			
Male	1.0	7.0	+6.0
Female	1.5	12.9	+11.4

Separated and divorced, ages 35-39			
Male	3.3	11.2	+7.9
Female	4.9	18.2	+13.3

(6) Because of higher death rates, the phenomenon of widowhood sets in at an earlier age for both nonwhite males and females, but especially for females.

Thus all possible forces conspire against marriage in the nonwhite population: bachelorhood, mortality, divorce, and separation. As a consequence, the proportion of the nonwhite population classed as "married spouse present" is much smaller than that of the white population, as the following comparison demonstrates:

Percent of females married with spouse present, by age	White	Nonwhite	Difference
20-24 years	66	62	− 4
25-29 years	84	62	−22
30-34 years	87	65	−22
35-39 years	86	65	−21

Clearly the smaller prevalence of marriage and greater prevalence of marital dissolution in the nonwhite population leads to a situation where the proportion of the white population married with spouse present is at least 30 percent greater than that of the nonwhite population.

Although above age 65 marital status statistics are less reliable in indicating historical trends (situations that have existed in the past) because of the memory factor and of the influence of widowhood, Tables 11-8 and 11-9 nevertheless clearly shows that the white and nonwhite differences that are indicated above have persisted for a substantial number of years. At all ages, right up to age 85, the proportion separated is three to five times as great among the nonwhite as among the white population. Moreover, throughout most of this age span the proportion divorced is higher among the nonwhite than among the white population. It is clear that a greater prevalence of family disorganization has long been a characteristic of the latter group.

Remarriage. About 15 percent of the white population and more than 20 percent of the nonwhite population have been married more than once (Table 11-10). The proportion rises very steadily with increasing age. Up to about age 40 a higher proportion of women than of men have been remarried. Because women have married earlier, they have more years of exposure to marital dissolution and eligibility to remarry than have men. At each age the proportion of the nonwhite population that has remarried is higher than that of the white.

Beyond age 65 the proportion of males that have remarried tends to be greater than that of females. This seems to result from the fact that elderly widowers tend to remarry more frequently than elderly widows. Differential death rates provide progressively fewer eligible partners for the elderly widow, whereas the elderly male has an ample supply of widows,

Table 11-10 Percent of Ever-Married Population That Has Been Married More Than Once, by Age, Color, and Sex, United States: 1960

Age	Male White Married spouse present	Other	Male Nonwhite Married spouse present	Other	Female White Married spouse present	Other	Female Nonwhite Married spouse present	Other
Total.....	12.7	17.3	22.2	20.8	12.5	16.7	19.5	22.7
18.......	.7	2.0	1.0	2.3	2.0	2.7	1.6	1.6
19.......	.9	2.1	1.4	2.4	2.5	3.4	2.6	2.2
20.......	1.3	2.6	1.3	1.8	3.1	4.7	2.8	2.6
21.......	1.7	2.9	1.8	2.4	3.8	6.2	3.4	3.1
22.......	2.1	3.7	2.3	2.9	4.4	7.4	3.9	4.0
23.......	2.7	4.3	3.2	2.9	4.9	8.8	4.2	4.8
24.......	3.3	5.7	3.4	3.6	5.8	9.7	5.6	5.2
25.......	4.0	7.9	4.7	5.3	6.7	12.3	7.7	7.2
26.......	4.7	8.9	5.6	6.8	7.2	13.8	8.6	8.1
27.......	5.3	9.7	6.2	7.6	7.7	14.5	10.2	9.5
28.......	5.6	10.9	7.4	6.9	8.2	16.3	10.6	10.3
29.......	6.3	11.3	8.7	8.2	8.6	16.2	11.7	10.5
30 – 34.....	8.1	14.5	12.1	10.6	10.6	19.1	15.3	13.8
35 – 39.....	10.5	17.9	17.3	15.4	13.1	22.0	20.0	19.1
40 – 44.....	12.4	20.4	21.9	18.7	14.1	21.9	23.1	22.3
45 – 49.....	13.9	21.4	26.3	22.7	15.1	21.5	26.2	25.6
50 – 54.....	15.6	21.9	29.6	25.1	16.1	20.5	29.4	27.5
55 – 59.....	17.0	21.3	33.2	26.9	16.3	18.7	31.0	28.8
60 – 64.....	18.1	20.0	36.5	28.8	16.1	17.2	31.8	29.6
65 – 69.....	19.3	18.6	40.4	31.8	16.0	16.2	32.4	31.7
70 – 74.....	20.8	17.1	43.0	33.6	16.1	15.0	33.0	31.3
75 – 79.....	22.5	16.8	44.4	34.0	16.3	14.1	31.9	30.6
80 – 84.....	24.7	15.9	46.9	34.5	17.1	13.0	31.9	29.6
85 – over...	27.8	16.5	49.9	37.0	19.2	12.5	31.3	28.4

Source: U.S. Census of Population: 1960, Detailed Characteristics U.S. Summary, Table 176.

spinsters, and divorcees from which to choose. Almost one half of elderly nonwhite males and more than one fourth of elderly white males who are living with a spouse are living with a second or third wife.

Trends in Marital Status. As has already been shown and as will be demonstrated further in later chapters, the nonwhite population has made revolutionary advances in social and economic status since 1940, especially in the decade between 1950 and 1960. An important question arises: to what extent was this dramatic improvement reflected in changing marital patterns? Table 11-11 provides information with which to answer this question. (1) Whereas the white population continued the trend toward younger age at marriage, the nonwhite population showed a distinct trend in the opposite direction. A smaller proportion of extremely young nonwhite males and females were married in 1960 than in 1950. This occurred at all ages from 15 to 25. *Thus the continuation of the trend toward younger marriage during the 1950-1960 decade was entirely a*

phenomenon of the white population. In other words, it appears that spinsterhood and bachelorhood have been becoming more rather than less popular among the nonwhite population. (2) A net result is that a smaller percentage of the nonwhite than of the white population are now in the category "percent married, spouse present." (3) There appears to have been a modest improvement in the stability of both the white and nonwhite marriage in the 1950-1960 decade if the statistics of Table 11-11 are valid. This improvement seems to have been greater for males than for females, and greater for white females than for nonwhite females. Within most age groups the percentage of the ever-married population now in the status of having a disrupted marriage was slightly smaller in 1960 than in 1950. The greatest improvement seems to have been effected at the younger and older age groups. Among the younger age groups this improvement seems to have been a result of a decrease in the proportion of couples who are separated, although this is counterbalanced by a slight

Table 11-11 Change in Marital Status Composition of White and Nonwhite Population, by Sex and Selected Age Groups, United States: 1950 to 1960

Age	Male				Female			
	White		Nonwhite		White		Nonwhite	
	1960	1950	1960	1950	1960	1950	1960	1950
Percent single								
16.........	99.1	99.0	98.9	99.2	94.3	94.2	93.2	90.7
17.........	98.1	98.5	97.9	97.5	88.0	87.5	86.4	81.3
18.........	94.5	96.3	94.7	94.1	75.5	76.4	76.4	68.8
19.........	87.0	91.2	88.0	86.9	59.4	63.2	61.7	56.1
20.........	75.6	82.5	77.2	75.7	45.2	50.5	51.4	44.4
21.........	63.0	71.7	66.4	63.5	33.7	39.2	41.3	36.7
22.........	51.1	59.6	55.8	54.3	24.5	30.4	33.7	30.3
23.........	39.8	47.7	45.3	44.6	18.3	24.0	27.0	24.6
24.........	32.5	38.9	39.8	37.2	14.6	19.4	23.3	20.8
Percent married spouse present								
15-19........	2.9	2.4	2.4	3.2	13.5	14.9	11.8	16.3
20-24........	42.6	37.1	33.4	35.9	66.0	62.8	48.7	52.6
25-29........	74.8	71.4	58.4	60.6	83.8	80.9	62.3	64.7
30-34........	83.5	81.7	66.3	69.5	86.5	83.9	65.1	68.0
35-39........	86.1	84.1	69.7	72.2	85.9	83.1	65.3	67.0
40-44........	86.8	84.2	71.8	72.7	83.6	80.6	64.0	63.9
45-49........	86.1	83.1	71.7	71.9	80.2	77.5	61.3	59.8
Percent of ever married with disrupted marriage								
15-19........	5.7	10.1	12.1	13.6	5.4	5.2	12.5	15.3
20-24........	4.2	4.4	9.4	17.3	4.9	4.8	16.2	18.1
25-29........	3.7	3.9	10.8	12.4	5.0	5.2	20.6	20.7
30-34........	3.8	3.9	13.1	13.2	5.7	6.1	23.6	22.2
35-39........	4.1	4.4	14.7	14.5	7.1	7.8	25.8	25.1
40-44........	4.7	5.4	15.7	15.4	9.4	10.3	28.5	29.4
45-49........	5.6	6.7	16.8	17.0	12.5	14.0	31.6	34.4
Percent of married who are separated								
15-19........	3.1	4.4	9.0	10.8	3.0	2.9	10.3	13.2
20-24........	1.9	2.0	7.6	14.6	2.1	2.0	12.9	14.3
25-29........	1.3	1.3	8.1	9.5	1.7	1.6	15.0	15.1
30-34........	1.2	1.2	9.1	9.6	1.7	1.6	16.1	14.7
35-39........	1.1	1.3	9.6	9.9	1.7	1.8	15.9	14.7
40-44........	1.2	1.4	9.6	9.6	1.8	2.0	15.1	14.5
45-49........	1.3	1.6	9.5	9.5	1.9	2.2	14.2	13.7
Percent of ever married who are divorced								
15-19........	2.1	3.1	1.8	1.1	2.1	1.9	1.4	1.3
20-24........	2.2	2.3	1.6	1.9	2.5	2.4	2.7	2.8
25-29........	2.2	2.3	2.4	2.3	2.8	2.8	4.3	3.9
30-34........	2.4	2.4	3.5	2.8	3.1	3.2	5.3	4.3
35-39........	2.5	2.6	4.1	3.0	3.6	3.7	6.0	4.6
40-44........	2.8	3.0	4.2	3.1	4.1	4.0	6.3	4.3
45-49........	3.1	3.3	4.3	3.0	4.4	4.0	6.2	3.9
Percent of ever married who are widowed								
15-19........	.6	3.0	1.6	2.0	.4	.5	.9	1.1
20-24........	.2	.3	.5	1.1	.4	.5	1.1	1.7
25-29........	.2	.3	.6	.9	.6	.9	2.2	2.7
30-34........	.3	.3	1.0	1.3	1.0	1.4	3.7	4.5
35-39........	.4	.6	1.6	2.1	1.9	2.4	5.7	7.6
40-44........	.7	1.1	2.6	3.3	3.7	4.5	9.5	13.1
45-49........	1.2	1.9	3.8	5.3	6.4	8.1	14.2	20.1

Source: U.S. Census of Population: 1960 Detailed Characteristics, U.S. Summary, Table 176, 177, 178. Census of Population: 1950 Vol. II. Characteristics of the Population Part I U.S. Summary Table 104.

Table 11-12 Marital Status Composition of Selected Ethnic Groups in Comparison with the White Population, Female United States Population: 1960

Marital status and age	White population	Ethnic groups						
		Negro	American Indian	Japanese	Chinese	Filipino	Puerto Rican	Spanish surname
Female, All ages (14 and over)	100.0	100.0	100.0	100.0	100.0	100.0	100.0	100.0
Single	19.2	21.7	29.1	21.1	22.0	27.7	21.9	24.6
Ever married	80.8	78.3	70.9	78.9	78.0	72.3	78.1	75.4
Married more than once	11.3	16.7	14.6	5.4	4.5	9.9	8.7	10.6
Married, spouse present	61.8	47.7	51.6	65.9	66.0	60.5	57.8	58.8
Married more than once	8.0	9.7	9.9	3.9	3.6	8.1	6.1	7.6
Separated	1.4	8.9	3.2	.5	.5	1.2	6.1	8.2
Other married spouse absent	1.7	3.6	3.5	3.1	2.9	5.7	6.8	2.8
Widowed	12.6	14.3	9.5	7.7	7.0	2.9	3.6	2.4
Divorced	3.3	3.7	3.1	1.7	1.6	2.0	3.7	3.3
Female, age 14 to 19 years	100.0	100.0	100.0	100.0	100.0	100.0	100.0	100.0
Single	86.7	86.1	86.3	96.8	95.1	87.4	80.6	84.2
Ever married	13.3	13.9	13.7	3.2	4.9	12.6	19.4	15.8
Married more than once	.3	.3	.4	.1	.1	.2	.4	.4
Married spouse present	11.1	10.0	10.8	2.6	4.1	10.2	16.0	13.0
Married more than once	.3	.2	.3	.1		.2	.4	.3
Separated	.4	1.4	.7	.1	0.1	.4	1.0	.8
Other married spouse absent	1.4	2.2	1.9	.4	.7	1.9	2.1	1.6
Widowed	0.1	.1	.1				0.1	0.1
Divorced	.3	.2	.2	.04	0.1	0.1	.3	.4
Female, age 35 to 44 years	100.0	100.0	100.0	100.0	100.0	100.0	100 0	100.0
Single	6.8	7.0	7.5	7.7	5.6	5.5	5.3	6.5
Ever married	93.2	93.0	92.5	92.3	94.4	94.5	94.7	93.5
Married more than once	14.1	20.3	21.6	6.7	6.9	16.5	15.1	15.8
Married spouse present	82.9	63.3	74.2	84.9	86.8	83.3	72.8	79.0
Married more than once	11.8	14.1	16.8	5.9	6.1	13.6	11.4	12.6
Separated	1.8	13.0	5.0	.5	.7	1.2	8.7	3.6
Other married spouse absent	1.5	3.6	3.3	2.5	2.4	5.1	3.7	2.4
Widowed	2.7	7.2	5.1	1.8	2.5	2.0	3.7	3.6
Divorced	4.3	5.9	4.8	2.5	2.1	2.9	5.9	4.8

Source: See Table 11-12.

increase in the proportion who are divorced. At the older age groups the improvement seems to have been due entirely to a decline in widowhood as a result of falling death rates. In part this improvement may indicate quicker remarriage of divorced persons, but it also appears to represent a small but genuine decline in the practice of separation without divorce, especially among the nonwhite population. It is entirely possible that the new prosperity that is coming to the Negro population is leading to an increase in marital stability. We must await future censuses in order to determine whether this change constitutes a trend.

11.9. Ethnic Differences

There are significant differences in marital status between the various ethnic groups in the population, as Tables 11-12 and 11-13 show. In comparison with the white population, spinsterhood and bachelorhood is higher among all of the nonwhite population—but American Indians and Filipinos, both male and female, appear to be especially inclined in this direction. Negroes and Puerto Ricans, on the other hand, show a pattern more similar to that of the white population. Marital disruption is far more prevalent among the Negro than among any of the other ethnic groups, especially in their tendency to be separated. American Indians, Filipinos, and Puerto Ricans tend to have a greater prevalence of separation or divorce or both. Marital disruption is clearly lower in the Japanese and Chinese populations than in the rest of the ethnic groups and than in the white population.

Tables 11-12 and 11-13 provide data for an extremely young and for an older age group in order to control for the factor of age. Marriage at extremely young ages is more prevalent among the Puerto Rican than among any other population, followed by persons of Spanish surname. Among the Japanese and Chinese populations, on the other hand, child marriage is almost unknown.

Among populations 35-44 years of age, bachelorhood is highest among the Chinese, Japanese, Filipino, and American Indian males. The differences in spinsterhood are comparatively small among the ethnic groups, although

Table 11-13 Marital Status Composition of Selected Ethnic Groups in Comparison with the White Population, Male United States Population: 1960

Marital status, and age	White population	Ethnic groups						
		Negro	American Indian	Japanese	Chinese	Filipino	Puerto Rican	Spanish surname
Male, All ages (14 and over)	100.0	100.0	100.0	100.0	100.0	100.0	100.0	100.0
Single........................	24.4	29.6	40.3		35.1	40.3	31.1	31.2
Ever married..................	75.6	70.4	59.7	65.8	64.9	59.7	68.9	68.8
Married more than once......	10.0	16.0	11.8	3.9	5.4	8.2	7.6	8.9
Married, spouse present......	67.5	53.5	46.3	58.5	46.1	37.7	58.1	57.7
Married more than once......	8.5	12.4	8.9	3.3	4.1	6.0	6.4	7.4
Separated.....................	1.0	5.7	2.2	.5	2.0	2.5	2.6	1.4
Other married spouse absent...	1.8	4.1	3.8	2.7	11.6	11.2	5.3	5.0
Widowed.......................	3.2	4.6	4.4	3.1	3.6	3.9	1.5	2.7
Divorced......................	2.1	2.4	2.9	1.2	1.2	4.4	1.5	2.0
Male, Age 14 to 19 years	100.0	100.0	100.0	100.0	100.0	100.0	100.0	100.0
Single........................	96.7	96.7	97.2	99.0	98.3	97.6	94.9	94.7
Ever married..................	3.3	3.3	2.8	1.0	1.7	2.4	5.1	5.3
Married more than once......	0.1	0.1	.1			0.1	0.1	.1
Married, spouse present......	2.4	2.1	1.9	.4	.8	1.6	3.7	3.6
Married more than once......			0.1			0.1	0.1	0.1
Separated.....................	.1	.3	0.1				.2	.3
Other married, spouse absent..	.7	.8	.8	.4	.7	.6	1.1	1.2
Widowed.......................				.1	.2			
Divorced......................	0.1	0.1	.1			.2	.1	0.1
Male, Age 35 to 44 years	100.0	100.0	100.0	100.0	100.0	100.0	100.0	100.0
Single........................	7.7	10.9	13.7	14.2	16.1	18.6	8.7	9.3
Ever married..................	92.3	89.1	86.3	85.8	83.9	81.4	91.3	90.7
Married more than once......	11.0	17.7	16.1	3.6	5.4	9.3	11.7	12.4
Married, spouse present......	86.5	70.4	71.2	81.2	70.8	53.7	78.9	78.3
Married more than once......	9.9	14.4	13.0	3.3	4.5	7.2	10.2	10.9
Separated.....................	1.0	8.4	3.4	.4	1.5	2.2	1.6	3.2
Other married, spouse absent..	1.8	4.7	4.9	2.2	8.4	19.7	7.3	6.3
Widowed.......................	.5	1.9	2.0	.5	1.0	1.2	.9	.7
Divorced......................	2.5	3.7	4.7	1.6	2.2	4.6	2.6	2.2

Source: U.S. Census of Population: 1960, Subject Reports, <u>Nonwhite Population Race</u>, Tables 19-23. Subject Reports Persons of Spanish Surname, Tables 3, 7. Puerto Rican in the United States Tables 2,6 . <u>Detailed Characteristics, U.S. Summary</u>, Table 176.

American Indian, Japanese, and Negro women tend to have above-average spinsterhood while the Puerto Ricans, Filipinos, Chinese, and persons of Spanish surname tend to be slightly below average in spinsterhood.

At the intermediate ages family disruption is essentially the same as that described for all age groups combined. Negroes far exceed all other ethnic groups in the extent of family disruption, with a surprisingly high amount of separation and divorce among the Puerto Rican population. Japanese and Chinese couples show high stability of marriage, and American Indians show a level of separation intermediate between those of the white and the Puerto Rican populations.

Intermarriage among Ethnic Groups in the United States Population. One widely used index of the extent to which two populations have assimilated into a common society is the extent to which they intermarry. The U.S. Census provides tabulations of the nativity and parentage of the wife, cross-classified by the nativity and parentage of the husband, for the white population. This provides the basis for a crude measure of the extent to which the various ethnic groups in the United States have intermarried. Table 11-14 presents the data. In the preparation of this table a calculation was made of the number of persons that would be expected to intermarry on the basis of chance selection alone, that is, if men and women of each ethnic group were to choose mates on a purely random basis without reference to ethnicity of the partner. The actual number of intermarriages were then divided by this expected number, and the ratio of the actual to expected intermarriages is recorded in the various cells of Table 11-14. A ratio of 1 or greater indicates affinity of two ethnic groups for intermarriage, and a ratio of less than 1 indicates a comparative deficit of intermarriage between two or more groups. Each line of this table shows the extent to which men of a particular ethnicity have intermarried with women of the same or other ethnicity, and each column of the table shows the extent to which women of a given ethnicity have

Table 11-14   Ratio of Actual Number of Marriages between Persons of Various Ethnic Origins to the Number That Would be Expected on the Basis of Selection by Chance Alone: United States: 1960

Area, nativity, parentage and country of origin of husband	Native or native parentage		Foreign born or native of foreign or mixed parentage by country of origin								
	Total	Puerto Rican	Total	United Kingdom	Ireland	Germany	Poland	U.S.S.R.	Italy	Canada	Other
Native or native parentage........	1.18	1.25	0.46	0.72	0.60	.062	0.28	0.21	0.30	0.67	0.44
Puerto Rican......	1.26	313.00	0.22	0.12	....	0.09	....	....	0.23	....	0.44
Foreign or mixed parentage.......	0.51	0.33	2.44	1.74	2.09	2.00	2.92	3.11	2.89	1.90	2.48
United Kingdom ...	0.74	....	1.75	8.60	2.72	1.43	0.70	0.81	0.53	2.31	0.97
Ireland...........	0.64	....	2.06	2.62	22.93	1.36	0.79	0.29	0.82	2.14	0.74
Germany..........	0.68	0.08	1.94	1.38	1.48	8.60	1.06	0.72	0.37	0.91	1.16
Poland...........	0.34	0.11	2.93	0.76	0.57	0.97	19.09	3.88	0.78	0.73	1.44
U.S.S.R...........	0.28	....	3.10	0.98	0.29	0.78	3.66	24.40	0.35	0.60	1.67
Italy.............	0.36	0.27	2.86	0.70	1.06	0.53	0.95	0.42	15.73	0.66	0.75
Canada...........	0.68	....	1.94	2.22	2.12	0.94	0.67	0.51	0.55	12.14	0.80
Other...........	0.49	0.71	2.49	0.96	0.72	1.20	1.45	1.65	0.71	0.84	5.15

Source: U.S. Census of 1960. Special Reports, Families, Table 62.

intermarried with men of the same or other ethnicity.

The most striking factor in this table is that there is clearly a tendency for people of the same ethnic group to marry each other. This is indicated by the diagonal of the table in which all diagonal cells have ratios well in excess of 1. Because the size of a ratio that goes into each cell is influenced in part by the comparative size of the categories in the total population, we cannot take the ratios as an unbiased measure of the extent of the intensity of intermarriage. Nevertheless, it seems clear that persons of Puerto Rican, Irish, Polish, USSR, and Italian extraction have a very strong propensity to marry within their own group (have a ratio of 15 or greater). A second point that stands out clearly is that the male of most ethnic groups has a greater propensity to intermarry with other ethnic groups than do females.

It is clear from Table 11-14 that persons from Northwest Europe, if they do not marry other persons of the same national origin, have an affinity for marrying other people from Northwestern Europe or Canada. For example, persons of the United Kingdom show a positive affinity for marrying Irish, German, Canadian, and "other" persons (which includes Scandinavian countries). The Irish, on their part, show a preference for marrying people of the United Kingdom, Germany, or Canada.

There are some examples of disaffinities or apparent rejection of each other as potential marriage partners among the various ethnic groups. Among these are:

USSR and Irish
Polish and Irish
Italian and German
Canadian and USSR
Canadian and Polish
Italian and USSR
Italian and United Kingdom

It must be pointed out that our discussion and Table 11-14 refer to all age groups and marriages of all durations. Many of the disaffinities reflect prejudices that are of long standing and may now be greatly diminished. Also, many of them, such as the Puerto Rican, may reflect the fact that marriage was contracted prior to the time of migration. However, it is clear that in the past, if not in the present, there has been substantial prejudice among people of Northwestern European ancestry and among native Americans of native parentage against intermarriage with persons of Eastern or Southern European ancestry. It is improper to attribute all of these disaffinities to a rejection of the minority group by the dominant group. In many cases (especially in the case of Jewish and Catholic parents) there is a strong cultural drive to maintain identity by preventing intermarriage of children with the dominant Protestant group.

The Marital Status of Second-Generation

Table 11-15 Percentage Never Married by Age and Sex for the Urban White Population, Urban Native White Population of Foreign or Mixed Parentage, and Urban White Population of 13 Second-Generation Ethnic Groups, for the United States; April 1950 (Standardized percentages shown for groups of persons under 45 years old, observed percentages shown for groups of persons 45 years and over. Ethnic groups arranged in descending order of percentage never married)

14 to 24 years		25 to 44 years		45 years and older	
Group	Standardized percentage	Group	Standardized percentage	Group	Observed percentage
Males		**Males**		**Males**	
Total, urban white population	78.5	Total, urban white population	14.4	Total, urban white population	8.3
Total, urban native white of foreign or mixed parentage	84.7	Total, urban native white of foreign or mixed parentage	18.9	Total, urban native white of foreign or mixed parentage	10.4
Austria	88.9	Ireland	26.7	Ireland	17.1
Ireland	88.0	Austria	22.4	Poland	12.7
Poland	87.7	Poland	21.6	Austria	11.0
U.S.S.R.	86.8	Czechoslovakia	20.2	Sweden	10.1
Czechoslovakia	86.2	Italy	18.2	Italy	10.0
Italy	85.9	Canada-French	17.4	Czechoslovakia	9.9
Norway	82.5	U.S.S.R.	16.9	Norway	9.9
Sweden	82.2	Canada-Other	16.2	Canada-French	9.1
Canada-Other	81.6	Norway	16.1	Germany	9.1
England & Wales	81.6	Sweden	16.0	Mexico	8.8
Canada-French	81.2	Mexico	15.9	Canada-Other	8.6
Germany	80.9	Germany	15.4	U.S.S.R.	8.2
Mexico	76.9	England & Wales	14.1	England & Wales	7.7
Females		**Females**		**Females**	
Total, urban white population	61.2	Total, urban white population	11.6	Total, urban white population	9.6
Total, urban native white of foreign or mixed parentage	69.6	Total, urban native white of foreign or mixed parentage	14.8	Total, urban native white of foreign or mixed parentage	13.0
Ireland	78.0	Ireland	23.5	Ireland	23.2
Italy	72.7	Canada-French	16.7	Canada-French	14.2
Austria	71.1	Italy	16.1	Sweden	13.5
Czechoslovakia	70.4	Austria	15.2	Canada-Other	12.1
Poland	70.1	Czechoslovakia	14.3	Germany	11.7
Canada-French	69.6	Sweden	14.2	Norway	11.5
U.S.S.R.	67.2	Poland	13.9	England & Wales	11.4
Germany	66.8	Canada-Other	13.1	Austria	9.8
Sweden	66.2	Germany	13.1	Czechoslovakia	9.3
England & Wales	66.0	U.S.S.R.	13.1	Poland	9.2
Canada-Other	65.9	England & Wales	12.3	U.S.S.R.	8.0
Norway	64.7	Norway	12.2	Italy	7.6
Mexico	61.9	Mexico	11.5	Mexico	7.0

Source: David M. Heer, "Derived from 1950 Census of Population Reports."

Americans. David M. Heer has discovered that in 1950 there was a substantial variation in the marital status of second generation Americans, that is, the children of persons who are foreign-born.[10] After standardizing for age, he finds that the proportion who have never married is higher for all second-generation men and women than for men and women of the total white population (including the native-born). He also finds that for all second-generation men

[10] David M. Heer, "The Marital Status of Second Generation Americans," *American Sociological Review,* **26** (1961), 233-241.

and women under 45 the tendency to marry late or never to marry at all is greater than for the total white population. Men and women of Irish descent are the least likely to marry, whereas men and women of Mexican descent are the most likely to marry. His findings are summarized in Table 11-15. To explain this set of differences, Heer hypothesizes that the proportion who never marry varies directly with the degree of emphasis on obtaining high socioeconomic status and inversely with permissiveness of their religion and culture with respect to the use of birth control.

Table 11-16 Labor Force Participation Rate of Population by Marital Status, Sex, Age, and Color, United States Urban Population: 1960

Age	Male						Female						
	Total	Single	Married, wife present	Married, wife absent	Widowed	Divorced	Total	Single	Married, husband present Total	With children under 6	Married, husband absent	Widowed	Divorced
White													
14 – 15...	16.6	16.5	71.2	18.4	20.7	29.7	7.4	7.3	16.4	12.0	12.4	18.3	33.8
16 – 17...	38.8	38.4	86.9	47.0	35.2	59.2	24.4	24.4	18.4	11.6	25.8	36.3	47.9
18 – 19...	65.8	63.1	95.4	80.3	54.3	83.2	51.0	57.7	32.7	16.0	45.7	48.8	65.9
20 – 24...	85.5	76.5	96.0	83.7	72.3	89.2	48.3	76.9	33.2	19.6	52.2	55.2	76.4
25 – 29...	94.9	86.4	97.8	85.6	81.7	90.9	35.2	85.8	26.8	18.2	50.4	56.3	79.2
30 – 34...	97.1	88.3	98.9	85.9	86.5	90.2	35.2	86.1	27.9	17.2	52.8	57.6	80.7
35 – 39...	97.1	86.0	98.9	84.8	87.7	89.1	40.4	85.1	33.6	17.8	57.0	65.1	83.4
40 – 44...	96.6	83.2	98.5	83.5	88.7	87.4	46.5	83.9	39.7	18.9	60.3	70.4	83.7
45 – 49...	95.8	81.0	98.0	81.9	87.4	85.5	49.7	83.1	42.0	20.7	61.4	71.8	83.1
50 – 54...	93.8	78.0	96.3	78.7	84.9	82.8	48.7	81.2	39.2	25.9	59.1	68.2	79.7
55 – 59...	89.7	72.4	92.9	74.2	78.4	77.5	42.7	75.2	31.1	24.2	51.1	58.2	73.0
60 – 64...	80.1	61.9	84.2	62.5	66.4	65.4	32.0	65.4	19.8	19.8	38.8	40.9	59.4
65 – 69...	44.4	33.4	47.7	34.0	34.2	35.3	17.9	40.3	9.4	11.2	20.1	21.2	34.2
70 – 74...	27.9	20.8	31.0	21.9	20.6	24.3	10.2	23.1	5.0	8.1	10.1	10.9	19.2
75+...	14.8	12.7	18.1	11.2	10.3	14.5	4.5	10.3	3.0	13.1	4.3	3.8	9.3
Nonwhite													
14 – 15...	11.1	10.9	50.6	20.3	9.5	13.6	4.8	4.5	19.8	17.8	17.4	21.9	31.0
16 – 17...	27.2	26.6	71.3	40.7	30.4	35.6	15.0	14.2	19.6	16.6	24.0	34.1	35.1
18 – 19...	59.6	57.0	91.1	72.0	22.2	72.5	39.0	42.9	28.3	22.6	37.2	37.0	44.3
20 – 24...	83.5	75.8	95.6	80.9	64.9	84.0	48.8	64.9	36.3	29.4	50.4	48.1	63.1
25 – 29...	89.8	79.2	96.5	79.9	70.9	86.5	49.8	72.1	41.1	32.7	55.5	54.6	69.1
30 – 34...	91.3	79.1	96.8	79.9	77.1	86.1	53.2	72.0	46.0	35.0	60.8	58.6	74.9
35 – 39...	91.7	78.3	96.6	80.3	79.7	85.5	58.0	74.0	50.8	36.4	67.3	64.8	78.7
40 – 44...	91.3	76.6	95.9	80.5	82.1	84.3	60.9	73.7	53.8	37.7	70.4	68.6	79.6
45 – 49...	90.3	75.8	94.7	80.3	81.2	83.5	60.7	72.9	53.5	39.8	69.7	66.9	79.2
50 – 54...	87.3	73.9	92.3	76.9	76.4	80.2	56.7	69.6	48.6	39.9	65.2	62.6	75.5
55 – 59...	82.1	70.0	87.8	72.6	69.8	75.1	48.3	58.1	40.7	33.1	55.5	52.0	66.4
60 – 64...	70.2	56.9	76.7	61.2	56.4	62.1	37.4	50.6	30.8	24.9	44.2	39.1	53.2
65 – 69...	39.8	31.7	44.7	35.7	29.8	36.9	22.0	34.8	17.7	21.7	25.5	22.2	34.1
70 – 74...	26.1	22.8	30.2	25.0	18.1	24.5	13.0	23.9	10.9	11.9	16.7	12.3	20.9
75 +	15.6	17.5	19.0	16.7	10.7	18.0	6.2	15.5	6.9	24.1	10.1	5.2	12.2

Source: 1960 U.S. Census: U.S. Summary Detailed Characteristics PC(1) –2D Table 196 P. 1–503.

11.10. Marital Status Differentials according to Economic Characteristics

Labor Force Participation. This topic has been discussed in rather full detail in Chapter 9. Table 11-16 provides detailed labor force participation rates for persons of each marital status by age, sex, and color as a summary of data presented earlier.

Occupation and Age at Marriage. A report by the U.S. Public Health Service based on data from a current population survey of the U.S. Census provides unique statistics pertaining to the median age at marriage by major occupation groups of the husband. White-collar workers tend to marry at a later age than blue-collar workers (see Table 11-17). The brides of professional workers and white-collar workers tend to be above average age, whereas those of blue-collar workers tend to be younger than average. At the time of the survey 38.8 percent of all of the wives who had married in the last three and a half years were employed. The wives of farmers and managers and of officials and laborers were less inclined to be employed than others, whereas the wives of professional, clerical, and service workers tended to be employed in above-average proportions. However, the deviation in employment status rates from the average for the group was not large in any case. Where the marriage was a second one either for the husband or the wife or both, a higher proportion of the wives were found to be working. The study also found that the tendency toward divorce and remarriage appears to be higher than average among professional and clerical workers, whereas managers, craftsmen, service workers, and husbands not in the labor force tend to be married only for the first time. Husbands in the operative and laborer occupations were overrepresented among the remarried couples if the wife was in the labor force, but tended to be in the "married only once" category if the wife was not in the labor force. It was also found that the percentage of wives in the labor force was above average among couples where the husbands were not in the labor force.

CONCLUSION

It seems clear that in almost all major nations of the world significant changes in marital status composition are taking place. Nations with early marriage are tending toward an older age at marriage. Nations with late marriage are tending toward earlier marriage. Divorce seems to be on the increase nearly

Table 11-17 Median Age at Marriage, by Major Occupation Group of Husband at Survey Date and Marriage Order of Husband and of Wife, United States: January 1955 to June 1958

Major occupation group of husband	Marriage order			
	Husband		Wife	
	First marriage	Remarriage	First marriage	Remarriage
	Median age			
All occupation groups..........	23.4	39.1	20.4	34.6
Professional, technical, and kindred workers............................	24.1	36.5	21.6	31.0
Farmers and farm laborers..............	22.4	43.4	19.2	36.4
Managers, officials, and proprietors, except farm...........................	24.3	42.2	20.8	36.5
Clerical and kindred workers...........	23.5	36.3	21.0	28.4
Sales workers..........................	24.1	39.2	21.3	34.1
Craftsmen, foremen, and kindred workers.	23.8	38.3	20.4	33.6
Operatives and kindred workers.........	22.5	31.5	19.6	32.7
Service workers........................	23.6	41.9	20.8	32.8
Laborers, except farm and mine.........	22.4	38.5	19.5	36.6
Husband not in labor force.............	23.2	50+	20.8	40+

Source: "Demographic Characteristics of Persons Married Between January, 1955 and June, 1958," National Center for Health Statistics Series 21, No. 2, April, 1965.

everywhere and seems to be an inevitable concomitant of granting equal legal and social status to women and of basing marriage more on personal choice and companionship and less on obligation to the extended family. As mortality rates decline, widowhood at young ages is becoming much less prevalent.

Variations in marriage arrangements are very great, but appear to be converging. In Latin America consensual unions are on the decline, and in the United States the widespread family disorganization that has beset the Negro population appears to be diminishing somewhat. In Asia and Africa the custom of child marriage and prohibition of remarriage of widows is changing toward the world average.

Space and scarcity of data did not permit an international comparison of population composition according to marital status, but a review of the data for the United States showed that marital status varies greatly among the various socioeconomic groups. This is because marital statuses are categories of major social, legal, and economic significance. Like occupation, education, and income they are one of the major axes around which all personal and communal life is arranged.

Sociologists formerly hinted that industrialization and modernization would lead to a decline in marriage and family life; the reverse appears to be happening. In most nations of the world the proportion of the adult population that is married and living with spouse is at an all-time high. Because of declines in widowhood, in bachelorhood and spinsterhood, and in postponing marriage to advanced

maturity and because of greater permissiveness in the remarriage of those whose marriages have been dissolved, the percentage of the population that is acutely maladjusted vis-à-vis matrimony is now at an all-time low in many if not most of the nations of the world. Being forced to pass from maturity to old age without having been married or being forced to live alone as a widow or divorcee is defined in most societies as a serious social problem. The net balance of the current changes therefore appears to be one of progress. Morality may be changing, but it does not appear to be on the decline, since young people seem to be more anxious than at any previous time in the recent past to gain social approval for their sexual conduct by rushing at unprecedentedly early ages into the state of "holy matrimony" and by attempting it again if it fails the first time. It is even possible that the higher divorce rate, by freeing unhappy persons from each other's presence and giving them a chance to remake their lives, is contributing toward an eventual better state of marital adjustment among the population.

The demographic effect of most current marriage trends is to promote more rapid population growth. Modern marriage exposes the female to a longer period of risk of pregnancy. Declining common-law and consensual marriages make the risk more intense and more continuous. To the extent that marriage improves health it promotes longevity. Although the growth-boosting effects of these changes may be modest, they very possibly account for much of the fertility increases that have been recorded since World War II in several nations.

QUESTIONS AND EXERCISES

1. Study Tables 11-1 and 11-2 in the light of the hypothesis that differences between male and female age at marriage are influenced by:

Religion (Christianity, Muslim, Hindu, etc.)

Branch of Christianity (Catholicism versus Protestantism)

Degree of economic development

Emancipation of women

Write an essay on the factors that influence international differences in marriage patterns. Develop additional hypotheses of your own to supplement those suggested above.

2. Search the reports of the U. S. Bureau of the Census since 1960 to evaluate the trends in the stability of the Negro family. For example, *Current Population Survey Reports*, Series P-20, No. 135, April 28, 1965, provided evidence that the improvement in stability of

nonwhite families, reported in Table 11-11, had continued. Search for an even later report, calculate the measures of Table 11-11, and write an essay on trends in Negro family stability. Go to the library and look up a report by Thomas Moynihan, *The Negro Family* (U. S. Department of Commerce, 1965). How do you reconcile the opposite conclusions of the Moynihan monograph and the present chapter?

3. Write an essay on "Child Marriage in the United States." Find as many data as you can about the characteristics of youngsters who marry before age 20, and especially before age 18.

4. Write an essay on "Spinsterhood and Bachelorhood in My Country." Find as many data as you can about the characteristics of persons who arrive at age 45 having never married. Develop hypotheses to explain this phenomenon. To what extent is it influenced by imbalances in the sex ratio?

5. If men prefer to marry women about two years younger than they are, this would mean (since most populations are growing) that, on an average, when women reach the age where it is normal for them to marry, the men of the same age are not yet ready to marry. Therefore, the girls must seek their mates from an older and somewhat smaller cohort of men. Do you think that this might account for some of the spinsterhood data presented in this chapter?

6. Continuing along the line of reasoning used in Question 5, let us recall that the "baby boom" began in 1946. The unusually large cohort of girls born in that year began seeking mates in 1966 and thereafter. Each year after 1966 there will be a tremendous increase in the number of marriageable girls for whom the eligible mates (two years older) are in short supply. What do you predict will happen? Will spinsterhood rise or will women begin marrying men more nearly their own age? Search the latest census and vital statistics data to see if you can answer this question.

7. By a strange oversight, data showing marital status by educational attainment, by age, and by color were not included in the regular census tabulations of 1960 in the United States. Look up these data for 1950 and write an essay on the relationship between educational attainment and marital status. Try to find more recent data in order to discover trends. A U. S. Census Bureau *Current Population Survey Report* for 1957 contains some data; see if more recent information can be had.

8. At the time this book was written, comparatively little detailed information concerning marital status was available from the international censuses. Select a topic such as one of the following and see how much comparative information you can obtain.

(*a*) Trends in consensual unions in Latin America and the characteristics of men and women who live in consensual unions.

(*b*) Trends in child marriage in India, Pakistan, and Ceylon and the characteristics of persons who marry before age 15.

(*c*) The changing pattern of differences in age and socio-economic characteristics of the families of the bride and bridegroom.

(*d*) The labor force participation of married women.

(*e*) The unemployment rates among young unmarried women.

9. It has been claimed that premarital pregnancy is responsible for the trend toward earlier marriage. See if you can find research evidence on this hypothesis. Design a research study that would make an unambiguous test of this hypothesis.

10. One of the interesting phenomena of the "marriage boom" is the sudden increase in young people who married while still students. Write a report on this subject, describing the trend and the characteristics of the students who marry. Can you find out whether this trend has been reversed and there is now a tendency to return to the former pattern of postponing marriage until after completing undergraduate school? Have the trends been the same for graduate and undergraduate students or have they differed?

BIBLIOGRAPHY

Agarwala, S. N. "Mean Ages at Marriage and Widowhood in India," pp. 148–156 in International Union for the Study of Population (Session) 9. Marriage, divorce and widowhood. *International Population Conference,* *New York, 1961* (Proceedings). Vol. 2. London, 1963, pp. 141–147.

Akers, Donald. "The Marriage Squeeze," *Demography,* **5** (1968).

Braithwaite, L., and G. W. Roberts. "Mating Patterns and Prospects in Trinidad," International Union for the Study of Population. *International Population Conference, New York, 1961* (Proceedings). Vol. 2. London, 1963, pp. 173–181.

Canada. Dominion Bureau of Statistics. *Nuptiality, 1950-1964.* Ottawa, 1967.

Carter, Hugh, et al. "Some Demographic Characteristics of Recently Married Persons: Comparison of Registration Data and Sample Survey Data," *American Sociological Review,* **20** (2) (April 1955), 165–172.

Carter, Hugh, and Paul C. Glick. "Trends and Current Patterns of Marital Status Among Nonwhite Persons," *Demography,* **3** (1) (1966), 276–288.

Chambliss, Rollin. "Median Age at First Marriage in Sweden, 1881-1953," *Milbank Memorial Fund Quarterly,* **35** (3) (July 1957), 280–286.

Chasteland, Jean-Claude, and Roland Pressat. "La Nuptialité des Générations Francaises Depuis un Siècle" (The Nuptiality of the French Generations Over a Century), *Population* (Paris), **17** (2) (April-June 1962), 215–240.

Dandekar, Kumudini. "Widow Remarriage in Six Rural Communities in Western India," pp. 191–207 in International Union for the Study of Population (Session) 9. Marriage, divorce and widowhood. *International Population Conference, New York, 1961.* (Proceedings). Vol. 2. London, 1963, pp. 141–337.

Day, Lincoln H. "Patterns of Divorce in Australia and the United States," *American Sociological Review,* **29** (4) (August 1964), 509–522.

Erlich, Vera St. *Family in Transition: A Study of 300 Yugoslav Villages.* Princeton: Princeton University Press, 1966.

Falzon, Norbert. "Notes on the Comparability of Marital Status Data Obtained from Population Censuses," *Proceedings of the World Population Conference: 1954.* New York, 1955, Vol. IV.

Glick, Paul C. "First Marriages and Remarriages," *American Sociological Review,* **14** (December 1949), 726–734.

Glick, Paul C., and Hugh Carter. "Marriage Patterns and Educational Level," *American Sociological Review,* **23** (3) (June 1958), 294–300.

Glick, Paul C., and Emmanuel Landau. "Age as a Factor in Marriage," *American Sociological Review,* **15** (August 1950), 517–529.

Great Britain, Royal Commission on Marriage and Divorce. *Report, 1951-55.* Presented to Parliament by Command of Her Majesty, March, 1956. Cmd, 9678. London: H. M. Stationers Office, 1956.

Grebenik, E., and Griselda Rowntree. "Factors Associated with the Age at Marriage in Britain, pp. 178–198, discussion pp. 198–202 in

Royal Society of London. A discussion on demography. Arranged by P. B. Medawar and D. V. Glass. *Proceedings of the Royal Society of London,* Series B., Biological Sciences, **159** (974) (March 17, 1964), 1–255.

Hájnal, John. "Age at Marriage and Proportion Marrying," *Population Studies,* **7** (November 1951), 111–113.

Hájnal, John. "Analyses of Changes in the Marriage Pattern by Economic Groups," *American Sociological Review,* **19** (3) (June 1954), 295–302.

Hájnal, John. "Differential Changes in Marriage Patterns," *American Sociological Review,* **19** (2) (April 1954), 148–154.

Hájnal, John. "Population of Singulate Mean Age at Marriage," *Population Studies,* **7** (2) (November 1953).

Heer, David M. "The Marital Status of Second-generation Americans," *American Sociological Review,* **26** (2) (April 1961), 233–241.

Hocking, W. S. "A Method of Forecasting the Future Composition of the Population of Great Britain by Marital Status," *Population Studies,* **12** (2) (November 1958), 131–148.

Kephart, William M. "The Duration of Marriage," *American Sociological Review,* **19** (3) (June 1954), 287–295.

Lemieux, Omer A. "Analysis of Marital Status Statistics in Some Recent Censuses," *Proceedings of the World Population Conference: 1954,* pp. 715–727. New York, 1955.

Majumdar, Murari. "Ages at Marriage and Marriage Rates in India," pp. 236–242 in International Union for the Study of Population (Session) 9. Marriage, divorce and widowhood. *International Population Conference, New York, 1961* (Proceedings). Vol. 2. London, 1963, pp. 141–337.

Metropolitan Life Insurance Company. "The American Widow," *Statistical Bulletin,* **43** (November 1962), 1–4.

Monohan, Thomas P. "Is Childlessness Related to Family Stability?" *American Sociological Review,* **20** (4) (August 1955), 446–456.

Monohan, Thomas P. *The Pattern of Age at Marriage in the United States.* Philadelphia: Stevenson Brothers, 1951.

Mortara, Giorgio. "Les Unions Consensuelles dans l'Amerique Latine" (Consensual Unions in Latin America), pp. 264–273 in International Union for the Study of Population (Session) 9. Marriage, divorce and widowhood. *International Population Conference, New York, 1961* (Proceedings). Vol. 2. London, 1963, pp. 141–337.

Notestein, F. W. "Differential Age at Marriage According to Social Class," *American Journal of Sociology,* **38** (1) (July 1931), 22–49.

Ortmeyer, Carl E. "Educational Attainment as a Selective Factor in Marital Status Transitions in the United States," *Demography,* 4 (1967), 108–125.

Parke, Robert, Jr., and Paul C. Glick. "Prospective Changes in Marriage and the Family," *Journal of Marriage and the Family,* 29 (1967), 249–256.

Population Reference Bureau. "Spotlight on Marriage," *Population Bulletin,* 17 (4) (June 1961), 61–79.

Rosset, Edward. "Wiek Nowozénców w Polsce" (Age at Marriage in Poland), *Studia Demograficzne* (Warsaw), 1 (3) (1963), 3–37. Russian and English summaries.

Rosset, Edward. "Malzenstwa w Polsce" (Marriages in Poland), *Studia Demograficzne* (Warsaw), 1 (2) (1963), 3–32. Russian and English summaries.

Ryder, N. B. "Measures of Recent Nuptiality in the Western World," pp. 293–301 in International Union for the Study of Population (Session) 9. Marriage, divorce and widowhood. *International Population Conference, New York, 1961* (Proceedings). Vol. 2. London, 1963, pp. 141–337. French and English summaries.

Smith, T. Lynn. "A Demographic Study of Widows," pp. 311–318 in International Union for the Study of Population (Session) 9. Marriage, divorce and widowhood. *International Population Conference, New York, 1961* (Proceedings). Vol. 2. London, 1963, pp. 311–315. French and English summaries.

Smith, W. "Marriage, Widowhood and Divorce in the Federation of Malaya," pp. 302–319 in International Union for the Study of Population (Session) 9. Marriage, divorce and widowhood. *International Population Conference, New York, 1961* (Proceedings). Vol. 2. London, 1963, pp. 141–337. French and English summaries.

Tietze, Christopher, and Patience Lauriat. "Age at Marriage and Educational Attainment in the United States," *Population Studies,* 9 (2) (November 1955), 159–166.

Udry, J. Richard. "Marital Instability and Income Based on 1960 Census Data," *American Journal of Sociology,* 72 (1967), 673–674.

Udry, J. Richard. "Marital Instability by Race, Sex, Education, and Occupation using 1960 Census Data," *American Journal of Sociology,* 72 (2) (September 1966), 203–209.

United Nations Department of Economic and Social Affairs. "Trends in Nuptiality Affecting Fertility," pp. 44–56 in *Recent Trends in Fertility in Industrialized Countries.* New York, 1958.

United Nations Population Branch. "Survey of Legislation on Marriage, Divorce and Related Topics Relevant to Population," March 9, 1956. New York, 1956.

U. S. Bureau of the Census. "Marital Status and Family Status, March, 1966," *Current Population Reports.* Series P-20. January 1967.

U. S. Department of Health, Education, and Welfare, Public Health Service. "Demographic Characteristics of Persons Married Between January, 1955 and June, 1958," *National Center for Health Statistics.* Series 21, No. 2, April 1965.

U. S. Public Health Service. National Vital Statistics Division. *Marriage and Divorce: Selected Bibliography of Statistically Oriented Studies.* Washington, D. C., National Center for Health Statistics, July 1963 (2).

Vukovich, G. "Some Characteristics of Hungarian Nuptiality," pp. 319–326 in International Union for the Study of Population (Session) 9. Marriage, divorce and widowhood. *International Population Conference, New York, 1961* (Proceedings). Vol. 2. London, 1963, pp. 319–326. French and English summaries.

Wyon, John B., et al. "Delayed Marriage and Prospects for Fewer Births in Punjab Villages," *Demography,* 3 (1) (1966), 209–217.

CHAPTER 12

Families, Households, and Housing Conditions

12.1. The Study of Residential Population Groupings

Throughout the preceding chapters we studied members of a population as *individuals*. We also studied population composition in terms of individual traits—sex, age, race, employment status, and so on. In a sociological sense, this is an abstract and incomplete way of viewing the population. It is well known that human adaptation involves participation in *groups*. It is important, therefore, that the study of population include a study of human groupings. Unfortunately, so much of demography is focused on the study of individuals that the study of groups is comparatively neglected. The distinction between a population *category* and a human *group* is a very important one. In the former, similarity of characteristics is the criterion for classification. In the latter, the criterion is a more or less enduring social, economic, or psychological interaction or interdependency. There has been a tendency to correct this oversight in recent censuses, but the study of groups still represents one of the major areas for demographic research development.

Perhaps the single, most important human grouping that can be of concern in a population census is the *residential* group—a cluster of people who occupy a residence together. Every member of a population must have some dwelling place and a set of living arrangements. Within any community, there is a finite or limited supply of dwelling places—houses, apartments, or other living units. To achieve a satisfactory residential adjustment, the individual citizen must make formal arrangements

to occupy one of these dwelling places—through purchase, rental, gift, or work in lieu of rent. In a high proportion of instances it is not possible for a single person to claim sole occupancy of a living unit. For social reasons, he usually also does not desire to live alone. Thus the most frequently encountered residential grouping is the nuclear family where husband and wife occupy the living unit together with any offspring they might have.

There are two approaches to the study of residential groupings. One, which is primarily economic, concentrates on the *household* or *living unit* as a unit of economic consumption. The other, more sociological in its emphasis, concentrates on the *family*. Unfortunately, group statistics pertaining to households that are tabulated for the economist, the city planner, and the student of consumption do not fully satisfy the needs of the sociologist. Similarly, family statistics that may be tabulated to satisfy the needs of sociologists and anthropologists cannot answer many of the questions posed by the economist. Demographers who undertake to study residential groupings must be familiar with both modes of approach and must be cognizant of the strength and the shortcomings of each.

12.2. Basic Definitions

Household. A household consists of all of the persons who occupy a housing unit as a collectivity. A house, an apartment, or even a single room, if occupied as separate living quarters, is considered a household. Separate living quarters are those whose occupants do not live and eat with any other persons in the structure. Usually, persons who have separate living quarters in a structure have a separate entrance and separate kitchen or cooking equipment for their exclusive use. Each household has a head, who usually is the husband of the family or the chief breadwinner. The number of households is equal to the number of household heads; it is also equal to the number of residential units. Thus the household is an economic, ecological, or livelihood unit. It consists of those persons who, so to speak, put their feet under the same table or otherwise join together in an arrangement to provide food, shelter, and other basic residential necessities. For this reason housing experts, market analysts, public untility companies, and architects tend to look at residential patterns in terms of households and household composition. Many commodities, such as telephones, gas, sewer, and electricity, are distributed primarily to household units. Several other major durable items, such as washing machines, television sets, air-conditioners, dishwashers, and refrigerators, are installed and used in terms of household units. In designing new housing units—apartments or single-family homes—the market demand for housing is determined in large part by the household pattern.

Not all members of the population live in private residential dwelling units. Persons who live in military barracks, students in college dormitories, inmates of institutions—prisons, hospitals, sanatoriums, homes for the aged, orphanages, training centers, detention homes—and occupants of certain types of public residential accommodations such as missions, flophouses, convents and monasteries, and migratory workers' camps or barracks cannot be treated as members of households. Even the large rooming or boarding house fails to conform to the definition given above. Some arbitrary point must be established at which a rooming house ceases to be a private household and becomes group quarters. In the U.S. Census this is the presence of five or more persons unrelated to the person in charge.

Once the basic definitions of households and group quarters have been established, it is possible for the census to identify all residential units in the nation and to classify them ac-

cording to size, type, and many other characteristics. Two of the most widely quoted statistics are the average size of households and the average number of persons per room. These are obtained simply by dividing the total population by the total number of household units or by the total number of rooms contained in household units to obtain measures of average household size and of crowding, respectively.

Family. Most sociologists would define a family as consisting of two or more persons who are related to each other by blood, marriage, or adoption, living together in the same household. All of the persons living in one household who are related to each other would be regarded as constituting a "primary family." (A primary family is a family that includes among its members the head of the household.) Thus a family is a set of relatives occupying a housing unit together.

It is clear that not all households contain families, because a household may be occupied by two friends who are not related to each other or even by a single person. Also, a household may contain two or more families. For example, if a house servant or a lodger has children and lives in the household of the employer or landlord without separate living quarters, this is an example of two families living in one household. Such families, which do not include among its members the head of the household, are called "secondary families."

Because the family (the husband-wife family) is the unit of reproduction, statistics on families are of extraordinary importance for studies of fertility. Demographers need to know the total number of husband-wife families where the wife is of childbearing age, the number of such families that are formed each year through marriage, and the number that disappear through death or through the process of aging. In addition, many persons engaged in community welfare work have a keen interest in family statistics. Welfare workers need to know the number of families in which there are preschool children or adolescent children. They want to know the number of families in which there is no male head, where the income is inadequate for the number of members, or where mothers with small children are working.

Household and Family Status. Although we have decided in this chapter to study population in terms of groups, we should not lose sight of the individual completely. Within the household or within the family, each individual has a status. This status is readily identifiable and should be spelled out in the study of household and family composition. The relationship of every other member of the household can be categorized in terms of his relationship to the head. The following categories are widely used in classifying members according to their household status:

head of household
wife of head
child of head
other relative of head
nonrelative of head—lodger
nonrelative of head—employee

Within the family, each person also stands in a definite relation to the family head. In classifying status the following categories are commonly used:

head of family
wife of family head
child of family head
parent of head
grandchild of head
other relative of head

(Children-in-law or parents-in-law are categorized as "children" or "parents" in this classification.) It is clear that if a living unit is occupied solely by a family and no persons are present who are not related to the head, then the household status and the family status are identical. It is only where the household is occupied by persons unrelated to the head that differences arise.

Not infrequently, we find "families within families" living in a household. This is the familiar extended family where married sons and daughters may continue to live in the household of their parents with their own spouse and perhaps children. As indicated above, the "primary family" is the family of the household head and all of the persons related to him. If one of these persons is in turn married, and is living in the primary family with his spouse and/or children, this person together with the spouse and/or children constitutes a "subfamily." In other words, a subfamily is a married couple with or without children or one parent with one or more own single children under 18 years of age living in a household and related to the head of the household or his wife. A married son or daughter living with parents and a divorced or widowed daughter and child living in her parents' house are examples of subfamilies.

Statistics on household and family status may be obtained very readily at a national census simply by inserting the following question in the schedule: "What is the relationship of each person in the household to the head of this household?" Family status can be coded from the entries for households.

12.3. International Comparisons of Households

The *Demographic Yearbook* provides some data on households and housing conditions around the world, which are summarized in Table 12-1. Perhaps the most important fact to be recognized is that *the nuclear family (husband-wife-children) is the predominant living arrangement almost everywhere in the world.* The so-called "extended family," where three or four generations (often a family head and his sons with their wives and children and possibly grandchildren) live together under one roof or within one compound, is a part of the cultural standards of many countries (especially in South, Central, and East Asia), but occurs in fact primarily among the upper and upper-middle classes. The vast mass of the population in such countries either cannot or does not follow this prescription. That this is the case is evident from statistics on average size of households: households are too small to be of the extended-family type. In only one country (Mexico) for which data are available is the average size of household greater than 6 persons. A true extended-family unit may be expected to have a minimum of about 7 persons, and under the ideal prototype it would have 10 to 20 persons. In a situation where a high percentage of the population is married,

Table 12-1 Comparative International Statistics for Households

Country	Average size of households persons	Percent of dwelling units with following number of rooms:				Average number of persons per room	Percent of dwelling units having:		
		1-2	3-4	5-6	7 or more		Pipe water	Electricity	Flush toilet
Northern & Western Europe									
Belgium.............	3.0	25.5	44.7	22.0	7.9	0.8	55.7	95.4	....
Denmark.............	2.9	4.8	56.3		38.9	0.7	....	98.4	73.6
Finland.............	3.4	48.7	41.8	8.1	1.4	1.3	....	88.6	35.4
France.............	3.1	38.8	45.7	12.4	3.0	1.0	81.5	93.0	86.5
Iceland.............	3.8	6.6	54.0	29.8	9.6	1.0	92.7	89.2	78.1
Ireland.............	4.0	8.8	51.6	29.9	9.6	0.9	51.0	83.0	....
Luxembourg..........	3.5	11.0	41.8	33.3	13.9	0.8	99.0	100.0	51.1
Netherlands.........	3.7	5.4	28.3	49.8	16.5	0.8	89.6	98.1	67.5
Norway.............	3.1	13.0	49.2	28.2	9.5	0.8	92.8	....	57.9
Sweden.............	2.8	25.2	55.5	16.5	2.9	0.8	91.4	....	75.8
United Kingdom.......	3.2	7.3	40.9	44.0	7.8	0.8	....	....	92.3
Central Europe									
Austria.............	3.1	26.3	53.9	14.8	5.0	0.9	100.0	98.3	....
Czechoslovakia.......	3.1	44.3	50.5	4.9	0.3	1.3	60.5	97.3	39.5
Germany, Eastern.....	...	52.0	42.7		5.3	1.2	....	....	....
Germany, Fed. Rep. of	2.9	10.0	60.5	23.2	6.2	0.9	....	99.4	75.3
Hungary.............	3.1	62.7		37.3		1.1	29.3	74.0	22.5
Poland.............	3.5	58.1	37.7		4.2	1.7	....	....	....
Switzerland..........	3.6	....	....	....	....	0.8	....	....	....
Southern Europe									
Bulgaria.............	3.7	60.6	35.6	3.4	0.4	1.8	....	....	....
Greece.............	...	63.9	29.5	5.4	1.2	1.5	70.4	28.7	....
Italy.............	4.0	42.3	38.4	13.3	6.1	1.3	44.2	80.9	40.5
Malta & Gozo.........	4.1	38.3	46.5	12.0	3.2	1.3	....	70.4	88.3
Portugal.............	3.9	30.3	47.7	15.0	7.0	1.1	....	40.5	23.2
Spain...............	3.7	20.7	42.3	26.1	10.9	1.1	....	80.5	....
Northern America									
Canada.............	4.1	6.7	29.7	39.2	24.4	0.7	....	87.0	68.3
United States........	3.3	6.4	32.4	45.1	16.1	0.7	93.9	....	89.7
Oceania									
Australia.............	...	4.6	23.1	58.8	13.5	0.7	....	96.2	....
New Guinea...........	...	8.5	42.4	41.5	7.7	0.7	....	78.0	....
New Zealand..........	3.6	5.1	31.9	54.3	8.7	0.8	99.5	....	88.4

where fertility rates are high, and where the average size of household is only slightly more than 5.2 persons, as in India, there is no alternative but to conclude that the nuclear family is the typical or usual living arrangement. To be sure, there may be very elaborate patterns of mutual aid and family solidarity extending over larger kinship groups, but where it exists, it is primarily an interhousehold and not a single residential unit arrangement.

When we consider the average size of household, we must think of families living at all stages of the life cycle: newly married with no children, young adults with two or more children who are still of school age, middle-aged adults who have some children still single and other children married, and elderly couples whose children are grown-up. It is impossible to construct a typical extended family as a composite of three or more nuclear families

without exceeding the median size of household as measured by a recent census. Therefore, only a rather small proportion of the households around the world can be said to be of the extended-family type. Where three generations occur together in a single household, it may be more of an expression of inability of aged parents to maintain themselves economically from savings or pensions, especially when the elderly parent is widowed.

With the joint family seen as a sociological tradition more than as a statistical reality, we can infer that four major factors are responsible for determining the average size of households in a population:

1. The level of fertility.

2. The extent to which elderly relatives, especially parents, are able to maintain themselves financially and can afford to live apart from their children in their own households.

Table 12-1 (*Continued*)

Country	Average size of households persons	Percent of dwelling units with following number of rooms:				Average number of persons per room	Percent of dwelling units having:		
		1-2	3-4	5-6	7 or more		Pipe water	Electri- city	Flush toilet
South America									
Argentina............	...	67.2	27.4	7.2	2.7	1.8	46.7	59.7	....
Brazil...............	...	12.5	44.1	28.7	14.7	...	....	24.6	....
British Guinea........	4.9	57.1	37.8	4.5	0.7	1.0	....	....	....
Chile................	5.4	46.6	34.3		19.2	1.7	56.1	....	44.8
Colombia.............	5.8	39.5	38.6	12.7	9.2	...	28.4	25.5	21.0
Ecuador..............	5.1	83.2	11.5		5.3	...	....	....	....
Venezuela............	5.6	37.3	39.0	15.8	7.9	1.6	....	78.4	49.5
Middle America									
Barbados.............	4.0	33.2	52.6	12.0	2.2	1.2	....	....	....
Cuba.................	...	37.9	45.4	13.3	3.4	...	55.2	55.6	40.4
Dominican Republic....	5.0	58.6		41.4		1.7	18.2	15.5	9.6
Guadeloupe...........	3.9	72.7	22.0	4.3	1.0	1.7	7.1	14.6	....
Honduras.............	...	67.8	26.5	4.3	1.5	2.4	25.1	4.5	10.6
Jamaica..............	4.0	76.6	16.3		7.0	...	71.0	....	....
Martinique...........	4.0	60.1	31.8	6.5	1.6	1.5	12.4	20.8	....
Mexico...............	6.8	80.1	13.9	3.5	2.5	2.9	32.3	....	....
Panama...............	4.8	77.0	18.0	3.8	1.1	2.4	....	44.0	38.4
Puerto Rico..........	4.8	29.7	44.9	19.0	6.4	1.4	69.9	80.0	37.2
Trinidad & Tobago.....	...	57.1	35.5	6.3	1.1	1.8	31.5	37.8	16.1
South Central Asia									
Ceylon...............	4.9	67.7	25.2	4.4	1.6	2.2	....	....	....
India................	5.2	76.5	17.4		6.1	2.6	....	....	....
Pakistan.............	5.4	82.5	14.5	2.3	0.7	3.1	....	....	....
Sikkim...............	5.6	83.5	12.7		3.7	3.1	....	....	....
East Asia									
Japan................	4.9	30.6	42.8	19.4	7.1	1.4	....	....	....
Korea, Rep. of........	5.6	68.6	28.2	2.7	0.5	...	....	....	....
South West Asia									
Cyprus...............	3.9	51.5	36.1	10.7	1.6	1.5	....	43.1	....
Jordan...............	5.5	69.2	19.9	5.7	5.2	...	....	5.5	30.7
Northern Africa									
Algeria..............	...	57.2	36.1	4.9	1.7	...	....	....	73.0
Mauritius............	4.5	74.0	18.4	5.2	2.4	2.0	....	....	....
Reunion..............	4.4	68.4	23.4	5.9	2.3	1.8	22.9	13.1	....
Senegal..............	...	60.0	36.3		3.6	1.5	....	96.4	....

Source: United Nations *Yearbook*, 1963.

3. The extent to which unmarried persons leave home and establish "bachelor households," either alone or with one or more friends of the same sex.

4. International differences of definition of what constitutes a household.

In nations where fertility is low, where parents tend to live apart, and where bachelor living arrangements are common, the average size of household tends to be small—3.2 persons or fewer. Examples of such nations are:

Belgium
Denmark
Sweden
Federal Republic of Germany
France
Norway
United Kingdom

Austria
Czechoslovakia
Hungary

Where the reverse set of conditions occur, households are large—5 persons or more:

Chile
Colombia
Ecuador
Venezuela
Dominican Republic
Mexico
India
Korea
Pakistan
Jordan

(These listings are not complete; they are simply nations for which data happen to be available.) From the listings and from Table

12-1 we can infer that the average size of household not only varies from nation to nation, but tends to vary inversely with the level of economic development and level of living; the higher the level of living of a nation, the smaller the average size of household tends to be.

Number of Rooms and Persons per Room. Households vary widely in size, and there is great international variation in this respect. Thus in Ecuador, Pakistan, and Mexico 80 percent of the households contain only 1 or 2 rooms, whereas in the following nations one half or more of the households have at least 5 rooms:

Netherlands
United Kingdom
Canada
United States
Australia
New Zealand

Again, we may make a rough generalization that the higher the standard of living in a nation, the larger the average number of rooms in the housing units.

To measure crowding, it is necessary to calculate the number of persons per room. In general, 1 person or fewer per room is regarded as desirable and 1.51 or more persons per room may be defined as "crowded" housing. By this definition, the following nations may be defined as "crowded" as of a comparatively recent census:

Bulgaria	Trinidad
Poland	Ceylon
Argentina	India
Venezuela	Pakistan
Dominican Republic	Chile
Honduras	Guadeloupe
Mexico	Mauritius
Panama	

A detailed examination of the figures leads us to the generalization that the lower the level of living in a nation, the higher the degree of residential crowding.

Household Utilities. For modern living, it is necessary that each living unit have piped running water, electricity, and flush toilet. Table 12-1 undertakes to report for several nations the proportion of units having these facilities.

In Europe, Northern America, and Oceania a high percentage of homes have modern facilities, whereas in Asia, Africa, and Latin America they tend to be absent in all but a comparatively small fraction of homes.

Thus in the developing countries households tend to consist of a large number of persons crowded at high density into a few rooms, without running water, electricity, or flush toilets. Rapid strides are being made to electrify rural areas and otherwise improve housing quality in many nations, but adequate housing is one of the needs that economic development is intended to provide. As we shall see when we consider the United States in detail, there is much inadequate and substandard housing in the industrialized nations also.

12.4. Types of Households and Families in the United States

According to the results of the Census Bureau's Current Population Survey, there were 57.3 million households in the United States in March 1965.[1] Of these, nearly three fourths (72.6 percent) were occupied by conventional families where the head is a married man and his wife is present (Table 12-2). An additional 10.7 percent were occupied by incomplete families where the head did not have a spouse present. The remaining 17 percent of the households were nonfamily households, where the heads were living alone or with nonrelatives only. Households increased about 900,000 per year between 1960 and 1965. Figure 12-1 illustrates the type-of-household distribution by color.

About 8 out of 10 "incomplete family" households have a female head. Among the nonwhite population this ratio is much greater; 22 percent of all nonwhite families are incomplete families, and of these 9 out of 10 had female heads in 1965.

It is important to appreciate that 1 household in 6 contains no family at all, but is simply a single person living alone or with persons not related to him. In about one third of the cases the head of such households is male and in

[1] U.S. Bureau of the Census, "Households and Families, by type: 1965," *Current Population Reports,* Series P-20, No. 140, July 1965. Table 1.

Table 12-2 United States Households by Type of Occupancy and Color, 1965, and Percent Change, 1960 to 1965

Type of household	All households		1965 households	
	1965	Percent change 1960-65	White	Nonwhite
All households.........	100.0	8.4	100.0	100.0
Occupied by families............	83.4	6.3	83.6	81.2
Husband - wife families.......	72.6	5.9	74.1	59.5
Incomplete families...........	10.7	8.5	9.5	21.7
Female head...............	8.7	12.3	7.5	19.1
Male head.................	2.0	- 4.9	2.0	2.6
Nonfamily households............	16.6	20.7	16.4	18.8
Female heads..............	10.9	20.9	10.9	11.1
Male heads................	5.7	20.4	5.5	7.7

Source: U.S. Bureau of Census. "Households and Families by Type: 1965" Current Population Reports, Series P-20 No. 140, July 2, 1965.

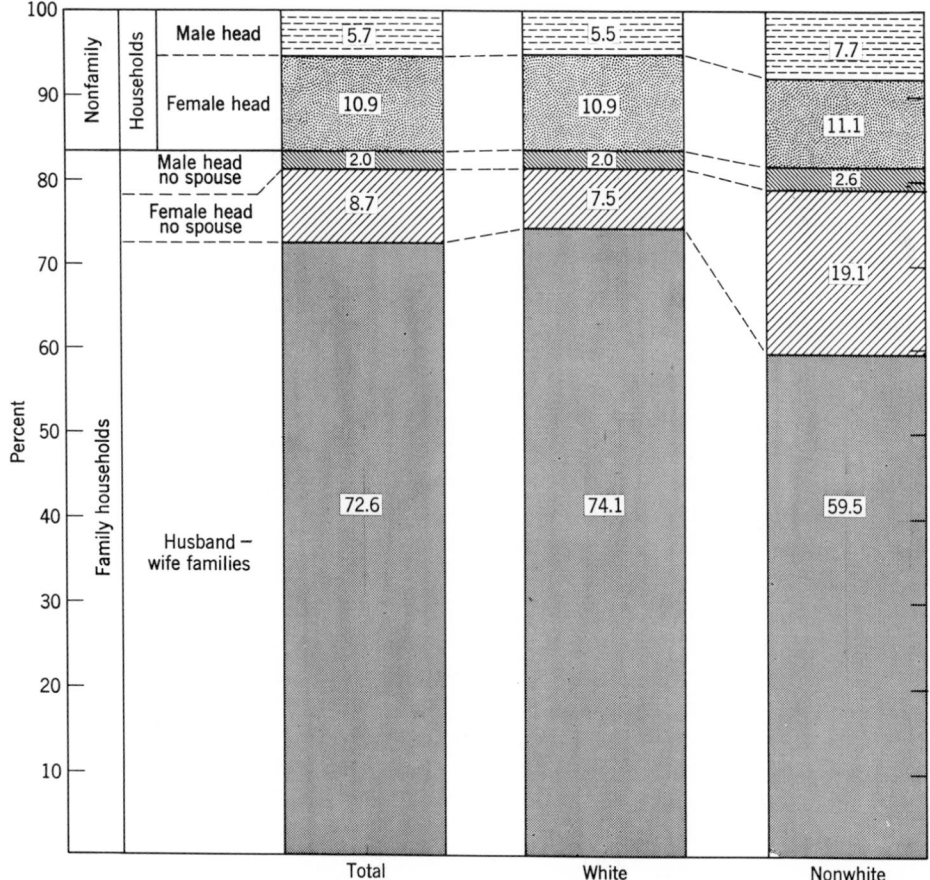

Figure 12-1 Type of Household Composition, by Color, United States Population: 1965.

SOURCE: "Households of Families by Type," *Current Population Reports,* (140) (July 1965), 20.

Table 12-3   Age and Sex of Household Heads by Color

Sex and age of households head	Total	White	Nonwhite
Total	100.0	100.0	100.0
Husband-wife household..........	74.7	76.1	61.3
Under 25 years.................	4.0	4.1	3.4
25 to 29 years.................	7.0	7.1	6.2
30 to 34 years.................	8.8	8.9	7.6
35 to 44 years.................	18.6	18.9	15.6
45 to 54 years.................	15.9	16.2	13.1
55 to 64 years.................	11.3	11.6	8.8
65 years and over.............	9.0	9.3	6.5
Male head-other marital status...	8.0	7.6	11.5
Under 45 years.................	2.6	2.4	4.4
45 years and over.............	5.4	5.2	7.1
Female head-other marital status.	17.2	16.2	27.2
Under 45 years.................	4.5	3.7	11.7
45 years and over.............	12.8	12.5	15.4

Source: U.S. Census of Population 1960:   Subject Report. Families,
          Table 2.

about two thirds of the cases it is female. If family and nonfamily households are combined, we may note that 18 percent of all white households are headed by females, whereas among the nonwhite population this proportion is 31 percent.

Age of Household Heads. A surprising proportion of household heads in the United States are middle-aged or older (Table 12-3). Among the husband-wife households, 9 percent of household heads were past retirement age in 1960. In addition, there was a substantial proportion of households with elderly female heads, the result of widowhood. On the other hand, only a comparatively small fraction (4 percent) of all husband-wife households had as heads husbands who were under 25 years of age. A high level of economic prosperity, the extension of social security to the entire population, and the greater incidence of private pension and savings schemes have made it possible for elderly couples to maintain a separate household after retirement and for widows to live apart from their children after the death of the father to a much greater extent than ever before. This is demonstrated in the fact that 12.8 percent of all households were headed by females aged 45 or over. Be-

cause they tend to be outsurvived by their wives, middle-aged and elderly males are less frequent heads of incomplete households than are females. Table 12-3 shows that although the proportion of incomplete households is higher for nonwhites than for whites—for both male and female heads and for both young and older heads—the really dramatic difference between the two is that *the proportion of nonwhite households where the head is female and under 45 is 2½ times as great as among the white population.* This phenomenon of households with female heads is so outstanding that a separate section is devoted to a more detailed analysis (Section 12.5).

Size of Household. The typical household in the United States contains only 2 or 3 persons (Table 12-4). The single-person household is very common, and the household with 6 or more persons is comparatively uncommon. The large households tend to be husband-wife households with the husband between 30 and 54 years of age and are primarily a result of couples with high fertility. Where the head is younger than this, there tend to be comparatively few children born yet; where the head is older than this, at least some of the children tend to have grown up and left the house.

Table 12-4 Size of Households by Sex, Age and Color of Head

Color and size of households	All house-holds	Husband – wife households by age of head			Other households	
		Under 30	30 – 54 years	55 and over	Male head	Female head
WHITE Head........	100.0	100.0	100.0	100.0	100.0	100.0
1 person..............	14.7	...	...	...	69.8	57.7
2 persons.............	28.2	23.0	16.4	65.0	17.2	21.8
3 persons.............	18.7	29.9	20.1	20.2	7.0	10.6
4 persons.............	17.5	26.7	26.7	7.9	3.1	5.1
5 persons.............	11.0	13.2	18.7	3.5	1.6	2.5
6 persons or more......	10.0	7.2	18.1	3.5	1.4	2.3
NONWHITE head	...	...	...	...	...	...
1 person	18.2	...	...	...	71.1	36.9
2 persons..............	23.1	16.9	21.3	46.8	12.0	19.1
3 persons.............	15.7	22.8	16.6	20.1	6.3	13.5
4 persons.............	12.3	22.1	15.2	10.8	3.6	9.5
5 persons.............	9.5	16.2	12.8	6.8	2.4	7.1
6 persons or more......	21.2	22.1	34.1	15.5	4.5	13.9

Source: U.S. Census of Population: 1960 Subject Report, Table 2.

Large households with 6 or more persons living in them are much more common among the nonwhite population than among the white. Although the pattern by age of head is the same as that for the white household, large households are prevalent among the non-white population under all circumstances. This is because nonwhite households tend to contain nonrelatives and distant relatives living in the household, added to the children brought by high birthrates. It is a highly significant fact for persons interested in households and family life that even in these days of moderately high fertility, in 80 percent of cases for the white families, the typical household contains only 1 to 4 persons. And even in the nonwhite households there are 4 persons or less in 70 percent of the cases.

For the white population, in a majority of households where the head is a female or a male not living with a wife, the household consists of one person living alone. This is not true, however, in the case of households where the head is a Negro female. In two thirds of the cases where a female nonwhite person is the head of the household, the household is also occupied by 2 or more persons, and in more than 30 percent of the cases, there are 4 or more persons in the household. These are children of the female head in most cases. High fertility, and low income, characterized a substantial proportion of the 6+ person husband-wife households and the 4+ person incomplete-family households.

Marital Status of Household and Family Heads. Single persons are household heads in comparatively few cases (6 percent). Table 12-5 reports that in incomplete households with a female head in slightly more than one half of the cases the head is widowed and in about one fourth of the cases she is estranged from her husband (separated or divorced). Where males are heads of an incomplete household, they are single, widowed, or estranged from a wife in roughly equal proportions. In about five percent of the incomplete households, the spouse is absent for reasons of work, being in the armed forces, or being in an institution—absences not related to estrangement.

A more intensive study of marital status and living arrangements is provided by Table

Table 12-5   Marital Status of Family Head, by Sex, Color, and Age, for the United States: 1960

Category	All Ages	Age of family head								
		14-19	20-24	25-29	30-34	35-39	40-44	45-54	55-64	65 and over
WHITE, All Families	100.0	100.0	100.0	100.0	100.0	100.0	100.0	100.0	100.0	100.0
Male head................	92.0	89.1	95.1	95.7	95.1	93.9	93.0	91.8	90.7	84.8
Married, wife present.....	89.2	84.6	93.6	94.4	93.6	92.2	90.9	89.1	87.2	79.0
Separated................	0.1	0.1	0.1	0.1	0.1	0.1	0.2	0.2	0.1	0.1
Wife absent, other........	0.4	0.6	0.3	0.3	0.3	0.3	0.3	0.4	0.4	0.4
Widowed..................	1.0	0.0	0.0	0.0	0.1	0.2	0.3	0.6	1.5	4.0
Divorced.................	0.3	0.1	0.0	0.1	0.2	0.3	0.4	0.4	0.3	0.2
Single...................	1.0	3.7	1.1	0.8	0.8	0.8	0.9	1.1	1.2	1.1
Female head..............	8.1	10.9	4.8	4.2	4.8	6.0	7.0	8.1	9.4	15.3
Separated................	0.8	2.1	1.2	1.0	1.0	1.1	1.0	0.8	0.4	0.2
Husband absent, other.....	0.6	3.2	1.3	0.9	0.8	0.8	0.7	0.5	0.3	0.3
Widowed..................	4.2	0.4	0.3	0.4	0.8	1.4	2.5	4.2	6.6	12.6
Divorced.................	1.5	1.3	1.2	1.5	1.8	2.2	2.1	1.6	0.8	0.4
Single...................	1.0	3.9	0.8	0.4	0.4	0.5	0.7	1.0	1.3	1.8
NONWHITE, All Families	100.0	100.0	100.0	100.0	100.0	100.0	100.0	100.0	100.0	100.0
Male head................	79.1	63.5	78.6	79.2	78.5	79.6	79.8	81.1	79.6	75.0
Married, wife present.....	74.9	53.4	75.4	76.4	75.6	76.6	76.3	76.7	74.3	67.6
Separated................	0.8	0.1	0.3	0.6	0.8	0.9	1.0	1.0	0.7	0.5
Wife absent, other........	0.6	0.7	0.6	0.6	0.5	0.5	0.6	0.7	0.7	0.6
Widowed..................	1.5	0.0	0.0	0.1	0.2	0.4	0.7	1.4	2.7	5.5
Divorced.................	0.4	0.1	0.1	0.2	0.3	0.4	0.4	0.6	0.5	0.3
Single...................	0.9	9.2	2.2	1.3	1.1	0.8	0.8	0.7	0.7	0.5
Female head..............	20.8	36.4	21.3	20.9	21.3	20.4	20.2	18.9	20.3	24.9
Separated................	6.3	10.3	8.6	10.1	10.2	8.8	7.2	4.8	2.7	1.0
Husband absent, other.....	1.5	4.8	2.7	2.2	2.1	1.9	1.5	1.2	0.9	0.5
Widowed..................	8.4	1.3	1.0	1.6	2.7	4.1	6.2	9.3	14.4	21.9
Divorced.................	2.4	1.6	1.8	2.7	3.4	3.6	3.5	2.3	1.3	0.5
Single...................	2.2	18.4	7.2	4.3	2.9	2.0	1.8	1.3	1.0	1.0

Source: U.S. Census of Population, Subject Reports, Families, Table 6.

12-5, which summarizes the marital status of family heads by age, sex, and color as of 1960. This table brings out the following points:

1. Single persons are almost never heads of (incomplete) families; when they are household heads, it is almost a nonfamily household.

2. Female heads are found with greatest relative frequency at the very youngest (14 to 19 years) or at the oldest (65 and over) ages.

3. At every age, the proportion of households with a female head is much higher among the nonwhite than among the white population. The difference is greatest for years 20 to 29—the childbearing years. For these ages, less than 5 percent of white households are female, whereas in the nonwhite population the proportion is 20 percent or more.

4. Widowhood is by far the major cause of incomplete households where the head is 45 years or older; at ages younger than this divorce and separation are the major causes.

5. The very high prevalence of nonwhite female heads during the reproductive years results primarily from separation; although divorce is a substantial contributing factor, it is involved in less than one fourth of the instances.

Children in the Household. Nearly one half of all households in the United States in 1960 did not contain children under 18 years of age (Table 12-6). In fact, nearly 40 percent of the conventional husband-wife households did not contain children under 18 years of age. These are married couples who have not yet started a family or elderly couples whose children have grown up and moved out of the household. Only about one third of all households contain two or more children under 18 years of age. Since the stereotyped idea of the typical American household is that of a father and mother living together with one or more children, we find to our surprise that slightly less than one half of the households fit this description and that slightly more than one half either lack children, lack a parent, or do not even contain a family at all.

Where the household is occupied by a husband-wife family, three out of five households contain children under 18 years of age (Table 12-6). These are almost equally divided among

Table 12-6   Households by Type: 1960

| Type of household | Total | Race of head | | | | |
| | | White | | | Negro | Other races |
		Total	Native	Foreign born		
All households (000)	52809	47759	43303	4456	4777	273
All households (percent)	100.0	100.0	100.0	100.0	100.0	100.0
No related children under 18....	49.1	49.4	47.2	71.7	45.6	42.8
1 related child under 18........	16.6	16.7	17.2	12.4	15.2	14.9
2 related children under 18.....	15.9	16.3	17.1	8.6	12.1	15.9
3 or more under 18..............	18.4	17.5	18.5	7.3	27.1	26.3
Male heads	100.0	100.0	100.0	100.0	100.0	100.0
Married, wife present						
No related children under 18....	38.7	39.0	36.9	62.7	35.4	26.3
1 related child under 18........	19.3	19.5	19.8	15.7	17.4	18.4
2 related children under 18.....	19.5	19.9	20.7	11.5	14.2	20.9
3 or more under 18..............	22.5	21.6	22.6	10.1	33.0	34.3
Male head	100.0	100.0	100.0	100.0	100.0	100.0
Other marital status						
No related children under 18....	89.9	90.7	90.3	93.4	84.1	91.1
1 related child under 18........	4.8	4.6	4.8	3.7	6.1	4.0
2 related children under 18.....	2.7	2.5	2.6	1.7	3.7	2.2
3 or more under 18..............	2.6	2.1	2.3	1.2	6.1	2.7
Female head total	100.0	100.0	100.0	100.0	100.0	100.0
No related children under 18....	75.0	79.0	77.7	88.2	52.7	54.9
1 related child under 18........	10.3	9.6	10.1	6.6	14.1	13.7
2 related children under 18.....	6.7	5.9	6.3	3.1	10.7	10.8
3 or more under 18..............	8.0	5.5	5.9	2.1	22.4	20.6

Source: U. S. Census of Population: 1960, Subject Report Families. Table 1.

households with one, two, three, or more children. In husband-wife households where the head is foreign-born, children are present much less frequently, because a large proportion of the foreign-born population is elderly. The Negro husband-wife families, on the other hand, tend to have children and many of them; in one third of such households there are three or more children under 18. A similar situation exists for "other races" (American Indian, Filipino).

When the head of the household is a male with no wife present, children under 18 are present in only about 10 percent of the cases. However, one fourth of all households with a female head have children under 18 years. Among Negro households this proportion is nearly one half. One fifth of all Negro households with female heads have three children or more.

Table 12-7 reports the change in households during the years 1940-1960, according to the race and nativity of the head and the number of children. Throughout this time there was a

50 percent increase in households. However, the number of native-white households with three or more children increased by 104 percent and of those with 2 children by 87 percent! Meanwhile the number of one-child households increased by only 27 percent. A similar rate of increase occurred among the Negro population. Households with foreign-born heads and where there were children under 18 declined by about one half because of aging. This overall spurt in households containing two and three children is, of course, a direct result of the higher fertility rates that have prevailed since 1945.

Trend in Marital Status of Households. Between 1940 and 1960 both the white and the nonwhite populations experienced an increase in the proportion of households headed by females. As Table 12-8 shows, this increase was rather slight among the white population and seems to be due primarily to small increases in the proportion of single and divorced women being household heads (there was a decrease in the prevalence of white households headed

Table 12-7   Percent Change in Households by Type: 1940 to 1960

Number of related children in households	Total	Race of head				
		White			Negro	Other race
		Total	Native	Foreign born		
All households (000)	17722	15944	16818	-874	1626	152
All households (Percent)	50.5	50.1	63.5	-16.4	51.6	125.2
No related children under 18	51.0	48.0	60.4	11.5	43.4	136.9
1 related child under 18	17.3	16.1	27.4	-47.2	30.0	95.8
2 related children under 18	65.4	65.8	86.5	-47.2	55.9	151.2
3 or more under 18	81.1	80.4	103.8	-52.8	84.3	113.0

Source: U.S. Census of Population: 1960, Subject Report, _Families_. Table 1.

by a widow or a married woman with an absent husband.

Among the nonwhite population, the increase in households with female heads was rather substantial (from 22.6 to 27.2 percent). Most of this was caused by an increase in the proportion of Negro households with a divorced or separated female as head. There was a small decline in the proportion of widowed women as household heads. Possibly a part of this was caused by the urbanization of the Negro population during these years; it was possible for separated, divorced, or widowed persons to move from the rural household of a relative to their own household in the city.

Increased economic prosperity, Social Security, and welfare programs have apparently made it possible for a larger population of single, widowed, and divorced women to maintain a separate household. This is especially

true for the nonwhite population. Whether or not there has been a relative increase in marital stability among the nonwhite (principally Negro) population is a question that was considered in the preceding chapter and is discussed further in the next section.

Other Children in the Household. An index of family disruption and disorganization is the presence of "other related children" under 18 years of age in households. These are grandchildren, nephews, nieces, or cousins of the head, who have been taken in because the parents are separated, divorced, or otherwise unable to care for them. Table 12-9 reports the ratio of such children to own children under 18 years of age, by race, sex, and marital status of the head and by urban-rural residence. Only 3 percent of children under 18 years of age in white husband-wife families (Table 12-9) are "other related children." Among nonwhite households, however, the rate is nearly five

Table 12-8   Sex and Marital Status of Households Heads: 1960 and 1940

Sex and marital status of household heads	1960			1940		
	Total	White	Nonwhite	Total	White	Nonwhite
Total..............	100.0	100.0	100.0	100.0	100.0	100.0
Male heads, total...........	82.7	83.8	72.8	84.7	91.2	77.4
Married, wife present............	74.7	76.1	61.3	75.8	82.1	65.4
Married, wife absent.............	1.4	1.1	3.8	1.3	1.2	3.1
Widowed.........................	2.3	2.2	3.2	3.3	3.5	4.2
Divorced........................	1.1	1.1	1.3	0.6	0.6	0.5
Single..........................	3.2	3.2	3.3	3.8	4.0	4.2
Females heads, total........	17.3	16.2	27.2	15.3	15.5	22.6
Married, husband absent..........	2.4	1.7	8.5	2.2	2.0	5.7
Widowed.........................	9.6	9.3	12.2	9.4	9.6	13.2
Divorced........................	2.3	2.3	3.1	1.1	1.2	1.1
Single..........................	3.0	2.9	3.3	2.6	2.7	2.7

Source: U.S. Census of Population: 1960. Subject Report, _Families_, Table 3.

Table 12-9 Ratio of Other Children under 18 Years of Age to Own Children in Household: 1960 (Per 1000)

Sex and marital status	White				Nonwhite			
	Total	Urban	Rural nonfarm	Rural farm	Total	Urban	Rural nonfarm	Rural farm
Male head........	32.5	29.3	36.5	45.9	152.8	133.1	182.0	218.7
Wife present..........	29.1	26.1	33.4	40.1	139.2	121.1	165.0	201.3
Other...............	400.4	381.7	362.7	664.3	724.3	627.9	918.0	976.1
Female head......	178.6	163.0	206.0	397.6	365.3	304.5	600.4	677.6
Separated............	60.8	58.1	71.0	99.9	162.2	149.5	240.0	230.5
Other................	51.3	49.9	50.1	87.4	190.4	165.3	276.3	269.7
Widowed.............	394.5	377.1	402.3	592.2	962.3	900.1	1057.4	1173.7
Divorced............	71.0	68.4	80.6	137.6	221.6	210.7	322.1	324.6
Single...............	744.5	787.8	605.0	764.3	266.9	204.6	507.6	712.6

Source: U.S. Census of Population: 1960. Special Reports, Families, Table 6.

times as high (14 percent). Among incomplete households where the head is a male with no wife, the ratio of other related to own children is 40 per 100 for white and 72 per 100 for nonwhite households.

Where the head is a female, the ratio of other children to own children is very high, for all categories of marital status. Widowed women are especially prone to be found caring for the dependent children of relatives. Among the nonwhite population this pattern is indeed very pronounced. It is said that many Negro women who bear an illegitimate child or are deserted by their husbands leave their children with the grandmother (often in the rural South) in order that they may continue to work.

12.5. Families with Female Heads

From the preceding analysis it has emerged that the number of households with a female head has increased dramatically in recent years. Table 12-10 reports that the increase has been 68 percent for the white population and 85 percent for the nonwhite population. These high rates of increase have *not* been due to widowhood, to any great extent, nor to the tendency for girls to live in "bachelor apartments" (the "marriage boom" has absorbed much of this group). This great acceleration in families with female heads can be attributed largely, if not entirely, to increased divorce among the white population and to a high prevalence of separation and divorce among

Table 12-10 Marital Status of Households with Female Heads: 1940 to 1960

Marital status	Percent distribution: 1960		Percent change 1940-60	
	U.S. Total	South	U.S. Total	South
White, total	100.0	100.0	67.9	90.7
Married, husband absent........	10.8	12.1	38.9	78.1
Widowed.....................	57.4	60.2	56.4	73.9
Divorced....................	13.9	13.7	206.6	250.0
Single.....................	17.9	14.0	69.9	97.2
Nonwhite, total	100.0	100.0	85.2	44.7
Married, husband absent........	31.4	28.1	132.7	79.8
Widowed.....................	44.8	53.0	42.5	25.1
Divorced....................	11.5	8.7	327.4	164.9
Single.....................	12.3	10.2	94.0	29.7

Source: U.S. Census of Population: 1960. Subject Report, Families, Table 3.

Table 12-11 Family Composition of Household with Female Head by Nativity of Race and Age: 1940 to 1960

	Total all households	White			Negro		Other
		Total	Native	Foreign born	All U.S.	South	
Total, 1960.......	100.0	100.0	100.0	100.0	100.0	100.0	100.0
Under 45 years........	25.8	22.7	24.5	9.3	42.9	36.4	52.8
No related children.	10.8	10.4	11.1	5.2	13.2	9.7	23.8
1 related child.....	4.7	4.3	4.6	1.7	6.8	5.4	7.5
2 related children..	4.3	3.8	4.2	1.3	6.8	5.6	7.0
3 or more related children..........	6.0	4.2	4.6	1.1	16.1	15.6	14.5
45 years and over.....	74.2	77.3	75.5	90.7	57.1	63.6	47.2
No related children.	64.0	68.5	66.7	82.9	39.5	41.5	31.1
1 related child.....	5.7	5.4	5.4	5.0	7.3	8.7	6.2
2 related children..	2.4	2.1	2.1	1.8	4.0	4.9	3.9
3 or more related children..........	2.1	1.3	1.3	1.0	6.3	8.6	6.0
	Percent change: 1940-60						
Total, 1960.......	70.3	67.9	81.0	9.9	83.4	44.1	185.1
Under 45 years........	53.4	50.0	58.3	-25.1	61.4	11.3	274.3
No related children.	30.1	36.1	39.4	.2	5.0	-35.7	396.7
1 related child.....	38.2	40.0	49.9	-40.0	30.0	-12.8	209.7
2 related children..	80.6	74.9	90.6	-41.1	99.0	34.8	258.1
3 or more related children..........	120.2	86.3	105.2	-49.9	200.4	117.8	193.9
45 years and over.....	77.1	74.0	90.0	15.5	104.3	73.3	125.2
No related children.	96.9	94.1	109.4	35.8	128.5	94.7	200.7
1 related child.....	8.1	1.0	16.6	-51.1	52.4	27.7	46.8
2 related children..	3.7	- 6.6	9.9	-59.6	53.3	32.6	104.7
3 or more related children..........	13.5	-15.7	- .6	-66.2	92.6	73.9	33.6

Source: U.S. Census: Families. Table 1.

the nonwhite population. The nonwhite population especially has appeared to have suffered from these disorganizing forces. Often it is common to blame the traditional Negro culture (a culture of matriarchy) for this tendency for Negro families to have female heads. Table 12-10 shows that evidences of disorganization are greater for the United States as a whole than for the South. This suggests that perhaps we should look more closely to the *contemporary* situation rather than to Negro history, Negro culture, and Negro marriage traditions for an explanation. Table 12-11 reports the number of children in households with female heads, according to age, race, and nativity—and the percent change in each of these categories in 1940-1960. The greatest rate of increase has occurred in the households of nonwhite females with three or more children. *This dramatic increase in the number of Negro households headed by females who are married but whose husband is absent appears to be*

a comparatively new pattern, centered in urban areas—not an ancient Negro cultural trait. John Beresford pointed out this fact in 1964.[1] It deserves special study by sociologists of the family. Some observers have declared that the provisions of the Federal Aid to Dependent Children laws are such that by abandoning their families Negro males who have suffered prolonged unemployment or low wages perform the altruistic act of improving the level of living of their family by making them eligible for assistance. Aid to Dependent Children may also, consciously or subconsciously, be construed as a form of "employment" or "unemployment compensation" to young Negro females who (as we saw in Chapter 9) suffer fantastically high rates of unemployment. It is unmistakable that despite rapid urbanization, up until 1960 comparatively little progress had

[1] John Beresford and Alice M. Rivlin, "Characteristics of 'Other' Families," *Demography*, **1** (1964), pp. 242-246.

been made toward eliminating the broken family among the Negro population. It is quite possible that discrimination in employment, inflation, rising standards of living, and the peculiar way in which social welfare legislation affects Negro families have had the combined effect of retarding or impeding progress in this direction.

12.6. Educational Attainment and Household Characteristics

It is generally assumed that the educational attainment of the household head conditions many other aspects of family life. Tables 12-12 and 12-13 are tabulations of the white and nonwhite heads of families according to educational status of the head and his wife (of husband-wife family) and a selected set of characteristics. Several interesting points emerge from this table.

1. Although there is a general tendency for spouses to be drawn from the same educational level, the degree of educational homogamy in American families is not overwhelmingly great. For example, about 38 percent of the white males who are college graduates have married women with no college education; among nonwhites the percentage is 27 percent. College-educated women, in turn, marry men with much less education in a substantial share of cases.

2. The tendency for a higher proportion of nonwhite than white women to be family heads persists at all educational levels.

3. The tendency to have three or more children is much lower where the head is female and either college-graduated or with some college education. Below the college level, however, there appears to be no systematic difference in number of children and educational attainment. Couples with less than high school education do not tend to have more children under 18 than couples with high school education. Column 2 of Tables 12-12 and 12-13 do not measure fertility accurately. There is no control on age, and only children under 18 living at home are counted. The small percentage of households where both husband and wife have no education and where there are 3 or more children under 18 is not due to

the low fertility of such couples so much as to the fact that such couples tend to be older, with their children grown and away from home.

4. Family income is related to the level of education of *both* the wife and the husband. The higher the level of education of husbands, the smaller the percentage of families with incomes of less than $6000. A similar, though smaller effect, is found for wives. Thus the most well-to-do couples are those where both husband and wife are college graduates, and the least well-to-do are those where neither has completed high school. This relationship is even sharper for nonwhite than for white families. At all educational levels, families with female heads have a much smaller average income than families with male heads.

12.7. Employment of Wife or Female Head and Family Characteristics

The five right-hand columns of Tables 12-12 and 12-13 present data for families where the wife or female head is employed. The following points emerge:

1. The greater the educational level of women, the greater their tendency to be employed, holding constant the educational level of the husband. This is true of both white and nonwhite families. When added to the greater propensity for nonwhite population to be employed this results in a situation where a very high percentage of nonwhite wives with a college education are employed.

2. However, when no children under 18 are present in the family, women of all educational levels tend to be employed. In 1960 an average of 47 percent of such women were employed, and a very large share of those who were not employed were beyond 65 years of age.

3. When the woman has one or more children under 6 in the family, the tendency to be employed is greatly reduced—to an average of 8.6 percent in 1960. Moreover, among families with small children, wives with a college degree or some college education are more likely to be found working than are women with less education, holding constant the education of the husband.

Table 12-12 Educational Status of White Family Heads and Their Spouses by Selected Socioeconomic Characteristics: 1960

Educational status	Percent distribution by education of head	Percent with 3 or more own children under 18	Percent with income less than $6,000	Families where wife or female head is employed				
				Total	Percent with no own children under 18	Percent with own children under 6 only	Percent with children 6-17 some below modal attainment	Percent with children 6-17 some above none below modal attainment
All families..........	100.0	19.7	51.3	100.0	47.1	8.5	4.7	3.7
Head a college graduate......	10.0	24.0	21.6	9.3	48.1	10.8	1.7	3.8
Wife a college graduate........	3.0	24.1	16.1	3.4	46.5	12.8	1.5	4.0
Wife some college, not a graduate......	2.6	26.7	21.2	2.1	46.1	12.3	1.6	3.4
Wife no college.......	3.8	24.8	23.1	2.7	47.6	9.7	2.0	4.0
Female head, or no wife.....	.6	6.3	41.5	1.0	58.9	4.4	1.8	3.2
Head some college, not a graduate...	9.4	20.2	36.1	10.7	47.7	10.8	2.3	3.6
Wife a college graduate........	.8	18.8	22.7	1.2	49.0	11.4	1.4	3.5
Wife some college, not a graduate......	2.1	20.8	31.7	2.5	49.3	11.9	1.8	3.3
Wife no college.......	5.6	21.9	35.6	5.5	46.6	11.5	2.6	3.6
Female head, or no wife.....	.9	8.7	61.8	1.4	48.3	5.6	3.0	4.2
Head no college..........	8.1	13.5	33.5	10.7	53.9	6.4	2.4	3.7
Wife a college graduate........	1.2	15.0	28.0	2.2	51.7	7.4	1.9	3.5
Wife some college, not a graduate......	4.1	18.8	39.9	5.5	47.7	8.8	2.7	3.4
Wife no college.......	1.9	6.9	18.5	2.0	59.6	1.4	2.5	5.3
Female head, or no wife.....	.9	1.5	43.9	1.0	83.4	.6	1.4	2.1
Head a high school graduate......	20.3	23.9	47.6	21.7	39.8	11.6	3.4	4.0
Wife a high school graduate........	12.0	25.4	41.5	12.6	39.7	13.3	2.5	3.8
Wife some high school, not a graduate.....	4.2	26.0	48.7	3.8	37.4	11.5	4.3	4.1
Wife no high school.....	2.1	20.8	55.3	1.7	48.1	6.6	5.5	4.0
Female head, or no wife.....	2.0	13.4	73.8	3.6	38.6	8.3	4.6	4.6
Head, some high school, not a graduate.	17.8	22.4	54.0	18.9	42.0	9.2	5.3	4.2
Wife a high school graduate........	5.9	25.1	45.3	7.0	39.2	11.8	3.5	4.1
Wife some high school, not a graduate.....	6.4	23.7	52.7	6.2	41.6	9.0	5.3	4.4
Wife no high school.....	3.6	19.6	58.4	3.1	49.4	5.3	7.4	4.1
Female head, or no wife.....	1.9	14.3	78.0	2.7	41.2	7.0	7.7	4.4
Head, no high school......	34.4	16.1	69.1	28.7	52.9	4.8	8.1	3.5
Wife a high school graduate........	4.8	22.3	56.2	5.6	44.5	8.4	4.8	3.6
Wife some high school, not a graduate.....	6.6	21.2	61.9	6.7	46.9	6.3	7.5	3.8
Wife no high school......	18.5	14.7	72.6	13.0	58.1	3.0	9.4	3.2
Female head, or no wife.....	4.5	8.0	78.6	3.5	57.8	3.0	9.8	3.3

Table 12-13 Educational Status of Nonwhite Family Heads and Their Spouses by Selected Socioeconomic Characteristics: 1960

Educational status	Percent distri- bution by education of head	Percent with 3 or more own children under 18	Percent with income less than $6,000	Families where wife or female head is employed				
				Total	Percent with no own children under 18	Percent with own children under 6 only	Percent with children 6-17 some below modal attainment	Percent with children 6-17 some above none below modal attainment
All families..............	100.0	27.8	81.2	100.0	46.4	10.2	10.6	11.9
Head a college graduate.......	3.2	17.1	41.2	4.5	43.8	18.1	2.0	7.0
Wife a college graduate.......	1.2	15.4	24.8	2.1	40.1	20.3	1.6	7.1
Wife some college, not a graduate.....	.5	21.5	37.6	.6	42.5	19.8	1.8	6.9
Wife no college..............	.9	23.1	49.5	.9	45.6	16.9	2.5	6.5
Female head, or no wife.......	.6	7.2	66.5	1.0	50.9	13.4	2.7	7.0
Head some college, not a graduate.....	4.2	24.3	61.0	5.1	41.5	16.7	3.1	6.3
Wife a college graduate.......	.4	15.2	31.4	.8	41.9	20.3	1.0	7.2
Wife some college, not a graduate.....	.8	25.9	52.7	1.0	38.7	22.3	2.6	6.1
Wife no college..............	2.2	27.6	62.5	2.2	42.7	15.7	3.7	6.1
Female head, or no wife.......	.8	18.9	79.7	1.1	41.6	11.1	4.0	6.6
Head no college..........	6.4	16.6	55.6	8.2	52.5	11.3	3.7	6.4
Wife a college graduate.......	1.1	13.9	45.1	2.1	49.5	14.6	2.1	6.7
Wife some college, not a graduate.....	2.4	24.2	63.4	3.1	44.0	16.9	3.9	6.4
Wife no college..............	1.7	14.6	43.1	1.8	55.8	4.5	5.1	7.5
Female head, or no wife.......	1.2	6.2	67.4	1.3	73.3	2.6	3.6	4.7
Head, a high school graduate	11.0	29.3	74.9	11.9	36.9	16.6	5.9	6.8
Wife a high school graduate.....	4.4	27.7	64.4	4.7	37.1	20.3	3.7	6.4
Wife some high school, not a graduate.....	2.4	34.8	75.9	2.1	37.3	17.8	6.1	6.2
Wife No high school.........	1.4	29.7	78.4	1.3	51.6	8.4	9.9	5.2
Female head, or no wife.......	2.8	26.8	88.6	3.7	31.1	14.2	7.0	8.2
Head, some high school, not a graduate	17.4	34.9	82.1	17.7	37.4	13.6	9.4	7.0
Wife a high school graduate.....	3.3	32.2	70.8	3.7	37.2	19.0	4.7	7.1
Wife some high school, not a graduate.....	5.6	37.4	79.1	5.0	38.5	15.9	8.3	6.4
Wife no high school.........	3.3	33.3	82.0	3.1	48.8	8.7	10.5	5.0
Female head, or.no wife.......	5.1	35.0	92.7	5.9	30.7	10.7	12.7	8.6
Head, no high school........	57.8	27.5	88.6	52.6	51.4	6.1	14.5	5.0
Wife a high school graduate.....	4.0	33.1	77.4	4.4	44.1	12.1	7.7	5.7
Wife some high school,not a graduate.....	8.7	36.8	84.3	8.7	44.1	9.1	11.3	6.2
Wife no high school	30.5	27.3	89.2	26.1	55.6	4.6	15.4	4.4
Female head, or no wife.......	14.6	21.0	93.1	13.4	50.2	5.0	17.2	5.0

Source: U.S. Census of Population, Subject Reports, Families, Tables 25 and 26.

4. Where the male head himself is a college graduate or has some college, there is also a greater tendency for women with preschool children to be employed. Thus the employment of women with small children is highest where both husband and wife have some college and smallest where neither has attended college.

5. Labor force participation of wives declines when there are children of school age (6 to 17 years) in the house. In families where the head or the wife has some college education, the lower the tendency toward participation during these years and the lower the educational status of the couple, the greater the labor force participation of the wife—both among the white and nonwhite population. Thus the employment of women with school age children may be more closely linked to augmenting family income and less closely linked to "self-realization" than is the employment of women with no children or with only preschool children.

6. Where a child is "retarded" in school, in comparison with his age group, women with some college education tend to remain outside the labor force—possibly to provide additional care and training for the child. Conversely, when there are children who are accelerated ahead of their age group, there is a greater tendency for mothers of school age children to be employed, provided that they have some college education.

At the lower educational levels, these relationships are exactly reversed: a higher percentage of women with less than a high school education who are employed tend to have children who are below model educational attainment. It is not possible to say whether their employment promotes below-average performance of the children in school or whether economic necessity requires that they continue working despite the poorer academic performance of one or more of their children.

12.8. The Life Cycle of the Family

One of the major contributions of demography to the study of family life has been the development of the concept "life cycle of the family" and a set of definitions that facilitate comparable research internationally as well as intranationally. As was pointed out in Chapter 9, Dr. Paul E. Glick of the U.S. Bureau of the Census has pioneered in this development, and his excellent methodological summary should be read in conjunction with the presentation.[2] The basic idea is that families go through a definite sequence of stages, and that with appropriately tabulated demographic data it is possible to specify at what point in the life of the family each stage occurs. The stages in the family cycle specified by Glick and Parke are:

1. Family formation: first marriage.
2. Start of childbearing: birth of first child.
3. End of childbearing: birth of last child.
4. "Empty nest": marriage of last child.
5. Family dissolution: death of one spouse.

Additional stages have also been recognized:

1. "Baby" stage: oldest children in the family are of preschool age.
2. "Pre-teen" stage: oldest children in the family are of grammar school age.
3. "Teenage" stage: oldest children in the family are of high school age.
4. "Put to pasture" stage: retirement of chief family breadwinner.
5. "Third-generation" stage: birth of first grandchild.

The data required for quantifying the time at which each of these events or stages begins are derived either from census tabulations (directly or indirectly) or from direct census questions. Usually, the *median age* at which each event occurs is taken as the average time at which each stage occurs in the family life cycle. By repeatedly taking these observations at each census, it is possible to measure changes in the life cycle of the family. Thus Figure 9-1 portrays changes in the life cycle pattern of United States population for women born from 1880 to 1939. The time at which each of these stages in the life cycle occurs varies by a substantial amount according to differences in customs of marriage, fertility levels, longevity, and other factors. Culver, for example, has compared the family cycles in India (Benares) and in the United

[2] Paul C. Glick, and Robert Parke, Jr., "New Approaches in Studying the Life Cycle of the Family," *Demography,* **2** (1965), 187–202.

States, to point out the much earlier age at marriage in India,[3] earlier birth of first child, and earlier age of one spouse at the dissolution of the marriage.

Lansing and Kish have demonstrated that for some types of analyses the family cycle classifications may be used as an explanatory variable of considerable power.[4]

For many sociological studies, they believe, the family life cycle has greater explanatory power than age. It is well known that changes occur in people's attitudes and behavior as they grow older. Many of these changes may be associated less with the biological process of aging than with the changes that are taking place in the individual's family membership. To understand an individual's social behavior, they claim, it may be more relevant to consider which stage in the life cycle he has reached than how old he is. They propose seven stages in the life cycle:[5] young-single; young-married, no children; young-married, youngest child under 6; young-married, youngest child 6 or older; older-married with children; older-married, no children; older-single; others, not ascertainable.

They discover that for several variables, such as home ownership, indebtedness, working wives, income level, and purchase of new car or television set, the family life cycle explains more of the total variance than do age categories. As Lansing and Kish point out, "This result is consistent with social theory since the family life cycle should be a better reflection than age of the individual's social role. Advantages of the family life cycle over age probably can be shown from many economic, social, political and psychological variables as well as for the few shown here. . . . We believe that the life cycle should be adopted more widely as an independent variable to be used in place of or parallel to age."[6]

[3] A. Collver, "The Family Cycle in India and the United States, *American Sociological Review*, 28 (1963), 86–96.

[4] John B. Lansing, and Leslie Kish, "Family Cycle as an Independent Variable," *American Sociological Review*, October 1957.

[5] *Ibid.*, p. 513.

[6] *Ibid.*, p. 518.

12.9. Social Change, Family Structure, and Demography

Anthropologists and sociologists have emphasized differences between cultures in family structure, and that family structure may be expected to change drastically when a nation becomes modernized. The question of what effect modernization, urbanization, and industrialization have on family structure is a topic that currently is of worldwide interest. It has been hypothesized that in the preindustrial society the joint family was predominant and that industrialization brings about a breakdown in family structure with a great increase in family disorganization, by weakening the duties and obligations that spouses feel toward each other and toward the community. Finally, after some time, there may be a restabilization of the family along norms and customs that correspond to modern needs and conditions.

Demography has a major responsibility for research in the sociology of family life, because the empirical data with which to test these theories are available from censuses and demographic surveys. For example, family disorganization, if it exists, will be manifest in a high proportion of persons divorced or separated and in many children being born out of wedlock. If the institution of marriage itself is falling into disrepute, we may expect persons to marry later and larger proportions not to marry at all. An adequately collected and tabulated set of household and family statistics can provide precise data on each of these aspects of family structure. If unwanted children are being left with grandparents or if there are many divorced or separated women living with young children, these facts also can be known. In other words, a good census is a more comprehensive source than anthropological observation or special field studies, because by appropriate cross-tabulation it is possible to know the pattern at all social and economic levels. Moreover, change over time can be detected and measured by making intercensal comparisons. Census enumeration is always carried out with the household as the unit of enumeration. One or two very simple questions, supplemented by appropriate coding in the census office, can yield a very precise picture of family organization. Detailed tabulations, supplemented by sociological data and careful analysis and interpretation, can provide insights and perspectives that otherwise might not be achieved. Following is an example of basing sociological analysis on demographic data concerning families.

Impact of Industrialization on the Family in Yugoslavia. In a study of changes in families in Yugoslavia, Pusic finds that the size of family has declined steadily since 1930.[7] The number of women in the labor force has increased from its prewar level (by about 24 percent). Industrialization has brought rapid urbanization and an end to the self-sufficient rural family economy. He concludes that, enigmatically, rapid industrialization does not necessarily mean the breakup of the two-generation family. He finds that housing conditions in the town have been so acute that often members of three generations are forced to live together and married couples more often than not must live with one of their parents. Upon balance the modification of the family is much less than

[7] M. Pusic, "Structure of the Family in Yugoslavia," paper presented at World Population Conference, Belgrade, 1965.

might have been expected. Pusic states, "The violent process of change—during the war and after—effected radically the whole political and economic structure of Yugoslavia society and has pushed the Yugoslav family further in its development from the traditional rural large family towards the modern urban small type of family. That development is not surprising, what is surprising is its moderate rate as compared with general environmental changes. It seems as if the family has reacted chiefly by absorbing and softening the shock of change, by creating adaptive forms and generally reacting much less on the changes in its environment."

CONCLUSION

This chapter undertakes to develop the thesis that the study of households and families is a branch of demography that needs to be developed internationally. It is a study for which the U.S. Bureau of Census has published much data that have been comparatively neglected—both by American demographers and by sociologists studying the family. Demographic studies have much to contribute to the understanding of the family life of any nation in both its social and its economic aspects.

QUESTIONS AND EXERCISES

1. Compute a scattergram and a coefficient of correlation between crude birthrate (Chapter 3) and the average number of persons per household (Table 12-1), using nations as the unit of observation. How close is the relationship? Identify any extreme deviations; how do you account for them? What factors other than fertility seem to account for large or small average size of households?

2. Locate statistics in the U. S. Census that show families classified by the occupation of the head. Write an essay on "Similarities and differences between White-Collar and Blue-Collar Families."

3. Repeat Exercise 2, but use data for the education of the head. Write an essay on "Similarities and Differences between Families Where the Head Is a High School Dropout

and Families of College Graduates." Which set of data gives the largest differences, the data for occupation in Exercise 2 or the data for education in Exercise 3? What implication does this have?

4. Go to the census tract statistics for any major metropolitan area. Identify the 10 tracts with the lowest median family income where the population is 80 percent or more white. Identify the 10 tracts with the highest median family income where the population is white. Assemble as much household, housing, and family data as you can for the two groups of tracts. Write a paper on "Family and Household Characteristics of White High- and Low-Income Neighborhoods in (city)."

5. The present chapter has emphasized that families where the head is a female in the

childbearing years tend to be Negro. However, the number of such families among the white population is not insubstantial. Assemble as much information as you can about white families with female heads. Write an essay contrasting these families with the corresponding nonwhite families.

6. In traditional societies it is customary for elderly parents to remain in the household of a child. Consult the Bibliography and other sources and write a paper on "The Family and Household Status of Elderly People in My Country."

7. The statistics on households and families have the category "other relative." Explore the data to find out what relationships the "other relatives" hold to the head and why they are living in the household of a somewhat distant relative. Base your judgment on characteristics of the other relatives, the types of areas in which they are most commonly found, and the characteristics of the households where they are most concentrated.

8. Cynics of the Aid-to-Dependent Children program assert that many Negro girls living in Northern cities bear illegitimate children for whom they receive ADC monthly stipends. However, instead of caring for the child, they take it to the home of their mother in Alabama, Mississippi, or Georgia and leave it there. They collect ADC money both in the South and the North. (The grandmother is supposed to claim the child in the South.) When it is time for the Northern social worker to check up, they rush home for a visit, pick up the child, and then return it when the coast is clear. Examine the family and household statistics for the North and the South to see if you can find evidence to substantiate this claim.

9. There is a common misbelief that all Negroes live in slums. From census tract statistics for a Northern city in the United States, identify the 10 tracts with highest median family income where the residents are 80 percent or more Negro. Assemble as much family and household information as you can about these tracts. Write an essay contrasting these households with the "typical American household." If you did not have the information on race, would you be able to detect that these were not white neighborhoods? What differences, if any, persist that would suggest Negro occupancy?

10. City planners and many business firms wish to make predictions about the number of households there will be at particular future dates and the number of new households and families that will be formed each year. (This is a prediction of future markets and service load.) Without doing any preliminary reading, sit down with a pencil and paper and develop a procedure for making such forecasts. Then go to one of the official forecasts, cited in the Bibliography, and check the procedure you worked out against the methods used by the experts.

11. One of the favorite hypotheses of sociology is the hypothesis of "social disorganization"—that there are neighborhoods in the city where a very high proportion of the families are disorganized and deviant subcultures take over control. Examine the data for marital status, family and household status, and housing and labor force status and try to put together a quantitative "Index of Social Disorganization." Test it out by scoring ten high and ten low census tracts and then try to find the incidence of delinquency or some other disorganization-related phenomenon.

BIBLIOGRAPHY

Aldous, Joan. "Urbanization, the Extended Family, and Kinship Ties in West Africa," *Social Forces*, 41 (1) (October 1962), 6–11.

Benjamin, B. "Household and Family Composition Analysis in the 1961 Census of Great Britain," pp. 166–178 in International Union for the Study of Population (Session) 2. Families and households. *International Population Conference, New York, 1961* (Proceedings). Vol. 1. London, 1963, pp. 153–284.

Beresford, John C., and Alice M. Rivlin. "Charac-teristics of Other Families," *Demography*, 1 (1) (1964), 242–246.

Bernard, Jessie. *Marriage and Family among Negroes.* Englewood Cliffs, N.J.: Prentice-Hall, 1966.

Breznik, Dusan. "Recherches sur la Structure Familiale des Ménages en Yougoslavie" (The Study of Family Structure of Households in Yugoslavia), pp. 187–197 in International Union for the Study of Population (Session) 2. Families and households. *International Popu-*

lation Conference, New York, 1961 (Proceedings). Vol. 1. London, 1963, pp. 153–284. French and English summaries.

Buchholz, Ernst W. "The Importance of the Family and the Family Structure for Economic Studies—Some Methodological Considerations," pp. 198–205 in International Union for the Study of Population (Session) 2. Families and households. International Population Conference, New York, 1961 (Proceedings). Vol. 1. London, 1963, pp. 153–284.

Burgess, Ernest W. "The Older Generation and the Family," in Wilma Donahue and Clark Tibbitts (eds.). The New Frontiers of Aging. Ann Arbor, Mich.: University of Michigan Press, 1957.

Caldwell, J. C. "The Erosion of the Family: A Study of the Fate of the Family in Ghana," Population Studies, 20 (1) (July 1966), 5–26.

Calhoun, Arthur W. A Social History of the American Family. New York: Barnes and Noble, 1960. (In 3 vols.)

Calot, Gérard, and Maurice Febvay. "L'Analyse de la Composition des Ménages dans le Recensement Francais de 1954" (An Analysis of the Composition of Households in the French Census of 1954), pp. 206–216 in International Union for the Study of Population (Session) 2. Families and households. International Population Conference, New York, 1961 (Proceedings). Vol. 1. London, 1963, pp. 153–284. French and English summaries.

Camp, Wesley D. Marriage and the Family in France since the Revolution: An Essay in the History of Population. New York: Bookman Associates, 1961.

Carter, Hugh, et al. (No. 12) "Socio-economic Characteristics of Persons who Married Between January, 1947 and June, 1954: United States," September 9, 1957, pp. 271–354 in U. S. National Office of Vital Statistics. Vital Statistics—Special Reports. Vol. 45. Selected studies. Washington, 1956.

Clarke, Edith. My Mother who Fathered Me; a Study of the Family in Three Selected Communities in Jamaica. London: G. Allen and Unwin, 1957.

Coale, Ansley J., et al. Aspects of the Analysis of Family Structure. Princeton, N.J.: Princeton University Press, 1965.

Collver, Andrew. "The Family Cycle in India and the United States," American Sociological Review, 28 (1) (February 1963), 86–96.

Corredor, Berta. "La Familia en América Latina" (The Family in Latin America), Estudios Latino-americanos, 4. Fribourg, Switzerland, and Bogota, Colombia, Centro Internacional de Investigaciones Sociales de FERES: Departmento Socio-economico, 1962.

Elder, Glen H., Jr. "Family Structure and Educational Attainment: a Cross-National Analysis,"

American Sociological Review, 30 (1) (February 1965), 81–96.

Elizaga, Juan C. A. 2. Formas de Asentamiento de la Poblacion en la América Latina (Types of Residence among the Population of Latin America), 1963, in United Nations. Centro Latinoamericano de Demografía (CELADE) Publications. Series A (Reports on investigations by CELADE). Santiago, 1962.

Forsyth, F. G. "The Relationship Between Family Size and Family Expenditure (with discussion)," Journal of the Royal Statistical Society, Series A, 123 (4) (1960), 367–397.

Gendell, Murray. The Influence of Family-Building Activity on Women's Rate of Economic Activity. Paper contributed for the United Nations World Population Conference, August 30-September 10, 1965.

Glass, D. V., and E. Grebnik. A Report on the Family Census of 1946. Summary chapter from the trend and pattern of fertility in Great Britain. London: H. M. Stationers Office, June 1954.

Glick, Paul C. "The Life Cycle of the Family," Proceedings of the World Population Conference: 1954. New York, 1955, Vol. VI.

Glick, Paul C. "Analysis Demográfico y Comportamiento de la Familia (cont.)" (Demographic Analysis and Family Behavior, continued), Estadística (Washington, D. C.), 22 (82) (March 1964), 72–95.

Glick, Paul C. "Demographic Analysis of Family Data," in Harold T. Christensen., (ed.). Handbook of Marriage and the Family. Chicago: Rand, McNally, 1964.

Glick, Paul, et al. "Family Formation and Family Composition: Trends and Prospects" (Washington, D. C., U. S. Bureau of the Census, 1963). Published in Marvin B. Sussman (ed.). Sourcebook in Marriage and the Family, 2nd ed. Boston: Houghton Mifflin, 1963.

Glick, Paul C., and David M. Heer. "Joint Analysis of Personal and Family Characteristics," pp. 217–228 in International Union for the Study of Population (Session) 2. Families and households. International Population Conference, New York, 1961 (Proceedings). Vol. 1. London, 1963, pp. 153–284.

Glick, Paul C., and Robert Parke, Jr. "New Approaches in Studying the Life Cycle of the Family," Demography, 2 (1965), 187–202.

Goldberger, Arthur S., and Lee Lin Lee Maw. "Toward a Microanalytic Model of the Household Sector," American Economic Review, 52 (2) (May 1962), 241–251. Discussion, pp. 252–258.

Goode, William J. Industrialization and Family Change. The Hague: Mouton, 1963.

Goode, William J. World Revolution and Family Patterns. New York: Free Press of Glencoe, 1963.

Graham, Henry M., and Juanita K. Graham. Some

Changes in Thai Family Life; a Preliminary Study. Bangkok: Institute of Public Administration, Thammasat University, 1961.

Gutkind, Peter C. W. "African Urban Family Life," *Cahiers d'Etudes Africaines* (Paris), **3** (10) (1962), 127, 149.

Gutkind, Peter C. W. "La Famille Africaine et son Adaptation à la Vie Urbaine. Quelques Aspects du Problème d'après une Etude Effectuée à Kampala, Ouganda, Afrique Orientale Britannique" (The African Family and its Adaptation to Urban Life. Some Aspects of the Problem According to a Study Carried out at Kampala, Uganda, British East Africa), *Diogène* (Paris), **37** (January-March 1962), 93–112.

Hadden, Jeffrey K., and Edgar F. Borgatta. "Family Growth in Metropolitan America: a Reanalysis," *Marriage and Family Living,* **24** (4) (November 1962), 352–357.

Heer, David M., and Judith G. Bryden. "Family Allowances and Population Policy in the U.S.S.R., *Journal of Marriage and the Family,* **28** (4) (November 1966), 514–519.

Hellström, Inger. "The Chinese Family in the Communist Revolution. Aspects of the Changes Brought About by the Communist Government," *Acta Sociologica* (Copenhagen), **6** (4) (1962), 256–277.

Hill, Reuben. "A Critique of Contemporary Marriage and Family Research," *Social Forces,* **33** (3) (March 1955), 268–280.

Hill, Reuben. "New Knowledge About the Family: a Review of Family Research in Europe and America," *Social Compass* (Brussels), **11** (1) (1964), 5–22.

International Sociological Association. Vol. IV. Changes in the Family. Changements dans la Famille. "Factors in Changing Family Patterns" (6 papers); "The Western Family" (16 papers); "The Oriental Family" (8 papers). *Transactions of the Third World Congress of Sociology.* Amsterdam, 22-29 August, 1956, London, International Sociological Association, 1956. In 7 Vols.

International Sociological Association. "The Sociology of the Family," Opatija seminar. Impact of urbanization and industrialization on the family. Prepared . . . with the support of UNESCO. *Current Sociology* (Geneva), **12** (1) (1963–64), i-vi, 1–121.

    Goode, William J. "The Process of Role Bargaining in the Impact of Urbanization and Industrialization on Family Systems," pp. 1–13.

    Delcourt, Jacques. "L'influence de L'urbanisation aux Diverses Phases du Cycle de Developpement d'une Famille," pp. 34–45.

International Union for the Study of Population (Session) 2. "Families and households," *International Population Conference, New York, 1961* (Proceedings). Vol. 1. London, 1963, pp. 153–284.

Italy. Servizio Informazioni. "Aspeti di Alcuni Fenomeni Demografici: i Nuclei Familiari Italiani dal 1860 al 1960" (Aspects of Some Demographic Phenomena: the Nuclear Italian Family from 1860 to 1960), *Document di Vita Italiana,* **11** (120–121) (November-December 1961), 9515–9520.

Lamser, Václav. "Rodina a Společnost" (Families and Society), *Demografie* (Prague), **6** (1) (1964), 34–39. Russian and English summaries.

Levy, Marion J., Jr. "A Strategy of Analysis of Variations in Family Structure: Actual Convergence and Ideal Patterns," *American Statistical Association.* Proceedings of the Social Statistics Section, 1964. Washington, 1965, pp. 80–81.

Maisel, Sherman J. "Changes in the Rate and Components of Household Formation," *Journal of the American Statistical Association,* **55** (290) (June 1960), 268–283.

Marriage and Family Living. "The family in (name of country or region)" *Marriage and Family Living,* **16** (4) (November 1954), 293–404.

Martinson, Floyd M. "Value Assumptions in Family Research with Reference to Population," in Roy G. Francis (ed.). "A Symposium on Values in Demographic Research," *Sociological Quarterly,* **2** (4) (October 1961), 259–297.

Orcutt, Guy H. "Microanalytic Models of the United States Economy—Need and Development," *American Economic Review,* **52** (2) (May 1962), 229–240.

Parke, Robert, Jr., and Paul Glick. "Interim Revised Projections of Number of Households and Families, 1965–80," U. S. Bureau of the Census *Current Population Reports.* Series P-20. April 11, 1963.

Pratt, William F. "Profile of American Families, 1940–57," *Public Health Reports,* **74** (3) (March 1959), 189–194.

Shanas, Ethel. "Family and Household Characteristics of Older People in the U. S. A.," in International Congress of Gerontology, Sixth. *Age with a Future: Proceedings of the Sixth International Congress of Gerontology,* Copenhagen, August 11-16, 1963. Edited by Per F. Hansen. Copenhagen: Munksgaard, 1964.

Smith, Raymond T. "Culture and Social Structure in the Caribbean; Some Recent Work on Family and Kinship Studies (Review article)," *Comparative Studies in Society and History,* **6** (1) (October 1963), 24–46.

Taback, Matthew. "Family Studies in the Eastern Health District. Family Structure and Its Changing Pattern," *Milbank Memorial Fund Quarterly,* **32** (4) (October 1954), 343–382.

Thirring, Louis (Lajos). "Family Statistics. Work Done in the Scope of Hungarian Population Censuses," pp. 260–267 in International Union for the Study of Population (Session) 2. Families and households. *International Population Conference, New York, 1961* (Proceedings). Vol. 1. London, 1963, pp. 153–284.

Ueda, Masao. "Families and Households in Japan," pp. 268–276 in International Union for the Study of Population (Session) 2. Families and households. *International Population Conference, New York, 1961* (Proceedings). Vol. 1. London, 1963, pp. 153–284.

United Nations General Assembly. Committee on Information from Non-Self-Governing Territories. "Development and Problems of the Urban Family in Africa South of the Sahara," *Report by the United Nations Educational, Scientific, and Cultural Organization.* New York, March 31, 1958.

U.S. Department of Labor. Office of Policy Planning and Research. *The Negro Family: The Case for National Action.* Washington, D.C.: Government Printing Office, 1965.

CHAPTER 13

Economic Status and Income

Of the compositional aspects of population, one of the most important and one that shows high correlations with all other compositional characteristics is material comfort or economic well-being. The term "economic status" is used here to refer to this variable. It is assumed to be a continuous variable, which takes on substantive meanings at points along the scale:

destitution
poverty
deprivation
minimum adequacy
adequate
economic comfort
affluence
wealth

These statuses refer to the degree to which an individual or a family can have access first to the physical necessities, then to the amenities, and finally to the luxuries of life.

Economic status is a variable of fundamental importance in all branches of social science research. Any tendency to regard it as being the private property of the science of economics is indeed a narrow-minded and unfortunate viewpoint.

The sociological importance of income has been nicely stated by Ogburn and Allen:

"A higher material standard of living is one of the great desiderata of mankind and ranks with better health, more education, happiness, the spiritual values of religion, and the belief in a life after death. Indeed, in a monetary economy a larger per capita income helps us to get more education and to obtain better health, though it may be of little aid in our search for happiness and spiritual peace. The struggle of organized labor is largely for more income, and most of those in business are there to make

money. The peoples of the Far East and Southeast Asia have developed five-year plans largely to obtain for themselves more of the good material things of life, that is, a higher standard of living." [1]

This chapter undertakes to deal with the variable of economic status from the viewpoint of demography and population research.

13.1. Income and Economic Status

There is only one set of statistics that can adequately determine the level of material comfort in a population. This is income statistics. Within any given nation, the amount of income that individuals and families receive is the most sensitive and most direct measure of economic well-being. This is true because it measures directly the resources that the family possesses in order to provide itself with the necessities of life—food, shelter, and so on. To be sure, some families may squander their income on nonessentials and live at a level of poverty, and other families may reduce themselves to a very low level of living in order to save as much as possible of their income in the hope of achieving some future economic goal. But on an average, income that is received is expended in a more or less patterned way to provide the necessities of life and to care for both current and prospective future needs. Income distribution is, therefore, the most adequate measure available of economic status.

Calculation or estimation of income is not an easy task. In highly urbanized and industrialized societies, income may be received in

[1] William F. Ogburn and Francis R. Allen, "Technological Development and Per Capita Income," *American Journal of Sociology*, 65 (1959) p. 127.

a variety of ways: from wages or salary, from profits or return from investments, from gifts or inheritance, and from pensions and other "transfer" payments made by the government or by private organizations to individuals. Income may be received in money form, or it may come in the form of indirect benefits or services that are given to persons as a result of their having some particular claim. The person who owns his house is not required to pay rent and enjoys additional income as a result. In agricultural societies, income is no less difficult to determine, because farm families obtain a large part of their income in the form of food, shelter, clothing, and other necessities that they produce themselves without need of purchasing them in the open market. Estimating income requires placing a money value on these "home-produced" items and adding it to the cash income received. The importance of income is so great that the effort required to generate income statistics is fully justified and no nation should be without a good set of income statistics.

There are two major approaches to the estimation of income. The so-called national accounts approach organizes the entire economy of a nation as a set of accounts that may be summarized by a balance sheet, similar to that of a large corporation.[2] One by-product of the national accounts approach is the estimation of the amount of income that the population at large has for the purpose of purchasing goods. This is sometimes termed "personal disposable income." It may be approximated also by the category "net national product." This figure changes from year to year in each country, but usually an annual estimate can be made. One measure of the average level of the economic well-being in the population, therefore, may be derived simply by dividing the total disposable

[2] For a summary statement of the national accounts, estimates, and definitions of concepts see "National Income, 1954" in *Survey of Current Business* for July, published by the Department of Commerce. The July issue of this publication updates the series annually. See also the introduction to the section on "Income, Expenditures, and Wealth" in each annual issue of the *Statistical Abstract of the United States,* U.S. Bureau of Census.

personal income for the nation as a whole by the total number of persons in the population. This yields a statistic that might be termed "per capita disposable personal income." It states the number of dollars or other monetary units that are available for each man, woman, and child to be spent for self-maintenance, education, recreation, and any other goods and services that may be needed or desired. Economists have become highly skilled in estimating this statistic for countries for which only scanty data are available.

The second approach to the measurement of income is to ask questions at the time of a census with which to determine the approximate income of each earner or family during the year preceding the census. If this is not or cannot be done as a part of the census, special sample surveys can be made to obtain national or regional estimates of the annual income received by persons or families. This approach has a tremendous advantage over the first—it permits the preparation of statistics showing the *distribution* of the income, whereas the first approach can yield only an *average*. It can also show what percentage of the population is living in great wealth, what percentage is living at some medium adequate level of living, and what percentage is living in poverty. Moreover, if this question is asked at successive censuses or surveys, it is possible to trace changes in the distribution of income.

Neither of these approaches can completely replace the other; both are highly essential in the study of the economic well-being of the population. Unfortunately, there has been a tendency throughout the world to rely on the first type of statistics and neglect the collection and tabulation of the second. The U. S. Bureau of the Census has been a pioneer in the collection of statistics concerning income received by individuals and families. The major portion of this chapter is devoted to the analysis of selections from the extensive data that have been produced under this program. This analysis may be used to illustrate the type of information that could be generated in any nation if a similar procedure were made a part of the national census program.

13.2. The Average Income Level of Nations of the World

Using the national accounts approach, Table 13-1 undertakes to report two sets of facts for all nations of the world for which income estimates are available: (1) the average level of living of the population as of a recent date as indicated by average per capita income; (2) recent changes in per capita income in order to show progress in improving the level of living in each of several nations of the world. In order to facilitate international comparison, the first of these indexes is expressed in United States dollars. The procedure by which these estimates are derived is a complex one, based on several assumptions that are not fully tested. Converting the results of this estimate to a single national currency involves further assumptions, so that the results of column 1 of this table should be interpreted with caution and should be used only to indicate general orders of magnitude. Also, to simplify the problem of showing trends, each country's currency has been used in estimating recent changes but the data have been reduced to an index number with the earlier year representing 100. Again, there are great variations between nations in the precision of the estimate, so that inferences that one country is progressing more rapidly than another should be made very cautiously. Finally, the statistics reported are for per capita gross domestic product, which is only a rough index of net individual disposable income.

Despite their many limitations and inadequacies, the data of Table 13-1 reveal just how great is the disparity between the "have" and "have-not" nations of the world. In the United States the average Gross National Product is in excess of $2690 per person per year. In contrast, in most of the underdeveloped nations of Asia, this figure is less than $300 per year. In other words, as nearly as economists can estimate, the average American citizen has 30 times as much income at his disposal to spend on himself as the average Asian. This raises the important question: "What represents adequate income goals for economic develop-

ment?" It is quite possible that much of the expenditures that Americans make may represent trivial luxuries or purchase of nonessential items that do not contribute much toward a high level of intellectual or social life. It might be a mistake for someone from Latin America to infer that economic development in his country will not have been achieved until the per capita level of income in the United States has been equaled. If we note the per capita income for other nations where the level of living is known to be adequate and high, such as Sweden, it may be seen that true economic development can be acquired at rather modest income levels.

Economists who specialize in planning for accelerating economic development emphasize that raising the per capita income of a population involves saving a certain amount of the national income for investment in new factories and other production facilities that will provide additional income in the future. In other words, industrialization will take place only by forcing a certain amount of the national income into the construction of new production facilities of a technologically advanced nature. Such investment can be made only after the essential expenditures required to sustain the population at least at a subsistence level of living have been made. Therefore, expenditures made to sustain today's population must be treated as a drain upon the potentials for economic development and improved standard of living.[3] One of the expenditures that these economists regret is the necessity for providing food, clothing, education, and other benefits to large quantities of oncoming generations that really are not needed. For example, in developing nations, where there is already a problem of serious underemployment and outright unemployment, the struggling economy is forced to spend a great share of its scarce funds to

[3] See, for example, Ansley J. Coale and E. M. Hoover in *Population Growth and Economic Development in Low Income Countries,* Princeton, Princeton University Press, 1958. Simon Kuznets, "Quantitative Aspects of the Economic Growth of Nations," *Economic Development and Cultural Change,* 1963.

Table 13-1   Estimates of Per Capita Gross Domestic Product for Selected
Nations of the World, Expressed in United States Dollars: 1953, 1958, 1962

Country	1953	1958	1962	Percent change	
				1953-58	1958-62
AFRICA					
Total - Africa.............	...	130	...	....	....
Algeria..........................	133	208	229	56.4	10.1
Angola...........................	43	56	...	30.2	....
Basutoland.......................	...	...	...	....	....
Bechuanaland.....................	...	...	...	....	....
Cameroon.........................	50	64	62	28.0	- 3.1
Central African Republic...........	69	77	78	11.6	1.3
Chad.............................	49	51	60	4.1	17.6
Congo (Brazzaville)..............	70	92	107	31.4	16.3
Congo (Leopoldville).............	92	110	100	19.6	- 9.1
Dahomey..........................	83	97	80	16.9	-17.5
Ethiopia.........................	38	46	51	21.1	10.9
Gabon............................	114	182	203	59.6	11.5
Ghana............................	135	170	187	25.9	10.0
Guinea...........................	61	52	...	-14.8	....
Ivory Coast......................	83	129	143	55.4	10.9
Kenya............................	75	84	85	12.0	1.2
Libya............................	...	147	186	....	26.5
Madagascar.......................	68	75	70	10.3	- 6.7
Mali.............................	71	74	79	4.2	6.8
Mauritania.......................	70	83	75	18.6	- 9.6
Mauritius........................	181	197	210	8.8	6.6
Morocco..........................	158	151	159	- 4.4	5.3
Mozambique.......................	25	37	...	48.0	....
Niger............................	67	64	57	- 4.5	-10.9
Nigeria..........................	98	95	86	- 3.1	- 9.5
Rhodesia & Nyasaland.............	158	173	178	9.5	2.9
Senegal..........................	162	178	165	9.9	- 7.3
Somolia..........................	...	48	...	....	....
South Africa.....................	429	496	554	15.6	11.7
Sudan............................	62	66	72	6.5	9.1
Swaziland........................	...	...	...	....	....
Tanganyika.......................	50	57	68	14.0	19.3
Togo.............................	80	78	73	- 2.5	- 6.4
Tunisia..........................	154	145	...	- 5.8	....
Uganda...........................	66	65	60	- 1.5	- 7.7
United Arab Republic.............	138	155	156	12.3	0.6
Upper Volta......................	34	42	43	23.5	2.4
Others...........................	...	80	...	....	....
NORTH AMERICA					
Total - North America.......	...	1775	...	...	...
Barbados.........................	206	264	323	28.2	22.3
Canada...........................	1475	1692	1887	14.7	11.5
Costa Rica.......................	227	251	260	10.6	3.6
Cuba.............................	246	303	...	23.2	....
Dominican Republic...............	161	188	214	16.8	13.8
El Salvador......................	...	121	134	....	10.7
Guatemala........................	120	155	166	29.2	7.1
Haiti............................	83	78	93	- 6.0	19.2
Honduras.........................	160	177	194	10.6	9.6
Jamaica..........................	235	398	418	69.4	5.0
Mexico...........................	228	321	361	40.8	12.5
Nicaragua........................	...	192	...	....	....
Panama...........................	287	348	429	21.3	23.3
Puerto Rico......................	405	581	825	43.5	42.0
Trinidad & Tobago................	305	486	650	59.3	33.7
United States...................	2080	2324	2691	11.7	15.8
Other............................	...	431	...	....	....

Table 13-1   (*Continued*)

Country	1953	1958	1962	1953-58	1958-62
SOUTH AMERICA					
Total - South America......	...	247	...	....	....
Argentina.........................	390	465	462	19.2	- 0.6
Bolivia...........................	...	84	...	....	....
Brazil............................	116	145	179	25.0	23.4
British Guiana....................	271	276	...	1.8	....
Chile.............................	364	405	422	11.3	4.2
Colombia..........................	204	248	285	21.6	14.9
Ecuador...........................	139	165	188	18.7	13.9
Paraguay..........................	83	97	86	16.9	-11.3
Peru..............................	133	152	173	14.3	13.8
Uruguay...........................	...	435	...	....	....
Venezuela.........................	474	650	701	37.1	7.8
Other.............................	...	230	...	....	....
ASIA					
Total - Asia...............	...	111	...	....	....
Afghanustan.......................	25	54	61	116.0	13.0
Burma.............................	42	55	57	31.0	3.6
Cambodia..........................	52	65	68	25.0	4.6
Ceylon............................	108	122	137	13.0	12.3
China (Taiwan)....................	78	97	121	24.4	24.7
Federation of Malaya..............	...	186	207	....	11.3
Hong Kong.........................	130	142	188	9.2	32.4
India.............................	65	70	73	7.7	4.3
Indonesia.........................	60	73	73	21.7	0.0
Iran..............................	97	130	153	34.0	17.7
Iraq..............................	100	115	162	15.0	40.9
Israel............................	558	905	1232	62.2	36.1
Japan.............................	217	337	551	55.3	63.5
Jordan............................	101	153	223	51.5	45.8
Korea, Republic of...............	77	103	110	33.8	6.8
Laos..............................	57	65	68	14.0	4.6
Lebanon...........................	197	182	225	- 7.6	23.6
Nepal.............................	...	50	...	....	....
Pakistan..........................	56	64	74	14.3	15.6
Philippines.......................	90	113	125	25.6	10.6
Saudi Arabia......................	174	206	225	18.8	9.2
Singapore.........................	...	323	336	....	4.0
Syria.............................	117	120	119	2.6	- 0.8
Thailand..........................	91	84	106	- 7.7	26.2
Turkey............................	210	254	272	21.0	7.1
Viet-Nam Rep.of...................	...	59	68	....	15.3
Other.............................	...	205	...	....	....
EUROPE					
Total - Europe.............	...	950	...	....	....
Austria...........................	476	743	850	56.1	14.4
Belgium...........................	831	1040	1239	25.2	19.1
Denmark...........................	965	1177	1492	22.0	26.8
Finland...........................	442	576	770	30.3	33.7
France............................	861	1168	1437	35.7	23.0
Germany, Fed. Republic of........	751	1122	1439	49.4	28.3
Greece............................	210	297	374	41.4	25.9
Ireland...........................	513	576	755	12.3	31.1
Italy.............................	496	689	917	38.9	33.1
Luxembourg........................	1060	1345	1543	26.9	14.7
Netherlands.......................	780	1038	1250	33.1	20.4
Norway............................	1066	1313	1608	23.2	22.5
Portugal..........................	205	271	352	32.2	29.9
Spain.............................	...	372	...	....	....
Sweden............................	1177	1512	1833	28.5	21.2

Table 13-1   (*Continued*)

Country	1953	1958	1962	Percent change	
				1953–58	1958–62
EUROPE--continued					
Switzerland.....................	1173	1510	1951	28.7	29.2
United Kingdom..................	1028	1254	1454	22.0	15.9
West Berlin.....................	653	1075	1372	64.6	27.6
Other...........................	...	716	...	....	....
OCEANIA					
Total - Oceania.............	...	1200	...	....	....
Australia.......................	1127	1413	1843	25.4	30.4
New Zealand.....................	1324	1615	1860	22.0	15.2
Other...........................	...	156	...	....	....
Grand Total.............	...	493	...	....	....

Source: United Nations, Yearbook of National Accounts Statistics, 1963, New York:
United Nations, 1964.

support large quantities of infants and young-sters many of whom, when they mature, will be considered to be superfluous and unneeded workers. A great deal has been written about the need to reduce the birthrate in order to be able to channel scarce investment money into investment in the future into new production facilities. Figure 13-1 illustrates the nature of this problem. It is a scatter diagram showing the average per capita income charted against the percentage of the population under 15 years of age in the developing countries. It will be recalled from Chapter 7 on age distribution that there is a very close correlation between the proportion under 15 and the birthrate. Figure 13-1 illustrates the tremendous load of supporting large quantities of young dependents that the developing nations with

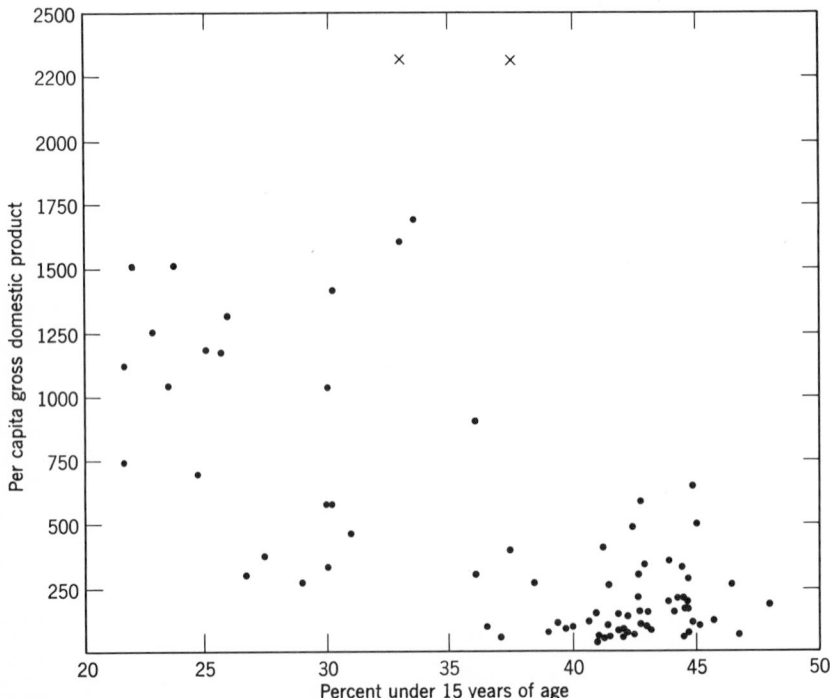

Figure 13-1   Scattergram of Per Capita Gross Domestic Product for Selected Nations, Plotted against Percent of Population under 15 Years of Age: 1958 to 1960.

low levels of living at the current time must bear.

Throughout the world, the level of material comfort appears to be rising rather steadily, even if slowly. Comparatively few of the countries report a retrogression in the trend of per capita national product. Nevertheless, many of the nations are progressing at a rate far slower than desired by their national leaders, and many believe that in the long run their programs will stagnate if the load of youth dependency is not somehow reduced. As later chapters will indicate, the prospect for fertility reduction seems to be reasonably good, so that the overall picture for the eventual success of the program to improve the world's level of living permits cautious optimism. It is quite likely that during the next half century the worst ravages of poverty will be eliminated from around the world and the benefits of scientific technology will lead to adequate levels of living for all of the world's inhabitants. This, of course, presumes that many problems of social organization both between and within nations will somehow be resolved in the meantime.

13.3. The Distribution of Economic Status among Individuals and Families

The phenomenon of wealth and poverty, coexisting side by side within communities all over the world (irrespective of political ideology), is of importance both as a phenomenon to be explained and as a factor that explains many other aspects of human behavior. This chapter concentrates on the second of these points of view: economic status is treated as a compositional trait of the population. The goal is to show the pattern of distribution of economic status among the population, and how economic status is interrelated with other compositional characteristics. Explanations of *why* economic status is distributed in the way it is, and what forces are at work to cause this pattern to change, lie within the fields of economics and social organization rather than demography. For this reason, only brief mention will be made here to the forces that influence income distribution.

Economic status may be regarded as an attribute that adheres to every person by virtue of his status either as breadwinner or as a member of a family that shares the income of the breadwinner(s). As asserted above, the best measure of this status is annual income. This may be the income of individual earners or of families. By appropriate cross-tabulation it is possible to learn how the economic status of individuals and families is related to other social, economic, and demographic characteristics. The definitions and procedures used by the U. S. Census illustrate the approach and the type of results that can be obtained.

To obtain information about the income of individuals and families, the 1960 Census included three questions: (1) "How much did this person earn in 1959 in wages, salary, commission or tips from all jobs?" This is to include income before deductions for taxes, bonds, dues, or other items that are made from the paycheck by the employer. (2) "How much did he earn in 1959 in profits or fees from working in his own business, professional practice, partnership, or farm?" This is supposed to be net income after business expenses. (3) "Last year (1959) did this person receive any income from Social Security, pensions, veteran payments, rent (minus expenses), interest, dividends, unemployment insurance, welfare payments, any other sources not already reported?" If the answer to the third item is yes, the amount received from these supplementary sources is also to be reported.[4] These questions were asked of every person 14 years old and over who fell in the 25 percent sample of respondents of households from which this information was collected. Not included as income in this definition is the value of food produced and consumed in the home, the economic benefits of home ownership, and the consumption of funds from savings, borrowed money, tax refunds, gifts and lump sum inheritances, and insurance benefits.

The three questions asked by the census lead directly to three types of income: (1) wage

[4] "Introduction," *U. S. Census of Population: 1960: Detailed Characteristics. U. S. Summary* (Washington, D.C.: Government Printing Office, 1962), p. xxxxix.

Table 13-2 Percent Distribution of Income Received by Individuals, by Sex and Color: 1950 and 1960

Sex and income	Total		White		Nonwhite	
	1960	1950	1960	1950	1960	1950
MALE						
Total with income	100.0	100.0	100.0	100.0	100.0	100.0
$1 to $499 and less...	7.2	10.5	6.6	9.6	20.6	10.5
$500 to $999.........	7.5	10.4	6.9	9.6	18.1	10.4
$1,000 to $1,499......	6.8	9.7	6.5	9.0	11.2	9.7
$1,500 to $1,999......	5.1	9.2	4.8	8.7	8.3	9.2
$2,000 to $2,499......	5.8	11.7	5.3	11.5	8.9	11.7
$2,500 to $2,999......	4.7	10.7	4.5	11.0	5.9	10.7
$3,000 to $3,499......	6.1	19.2	5.8	20.4	6.6	19.2
$3,500 to $3,999......	5.2		5.2		4.3	
$4,000 to $4,499......	6.8	8.4	6.8	9.2	5.0	8.4
$4,500 to $4,999......	5.8		6.0		2.9	
$5,000 to $5,999......	12.6	4.1	13.2	4.5	4.5	4.1
$6,000 to $6,999......	8.7	1.8	1.3	2.0	1.8	1.8
$7,000 to $9,999......	10.9	2.0	11.8	2.2	1.4	2.0
$10,000 and over......	6.6	2.1	7.2	2.3	0.4	2.1
Median income.......	$4,103	$2,434	$4,319	$2,573	$1,502	$973
FEMALE						
Total with income	100.0	100.0	100.0	100.0	100.0	100.0
$1 to $499............	22.9	30.5	21.9	28.4	30.4	45.5
$500 to $999.........	19.3	18.7	18.7	17.9	23.9	24.9
$1,000 to $1,499......	11.0	13.1	10.7	13.2	12.9	12.7
$1,500 to $1,999......	7.9	12.3	7.8	12.9	8.5	7.7
$2,000 to $2,499......	8.3	11.0	8.4	11.9	7.5	4.8
$2,500 to $2,999......	6.1	6.1	6.3	6.6	4.2	2.2
$3,000 to $3,499......	6.7	5.1	7.0	5.6	4.1	1.4
$3,500 to $3,999......	4.7		5.0		2.5	
$4,000 to $4,499......	4.4	1.4	4.6	1.5	2.5	0.3
$4,500 to $4,999......	2.6		2.7		1.1	
$5,000 to $5,999......	3.2	0.6	3.4	0.7	1.3	0.1
$6,000 to $6,999......	1.4	0.3	1.5	0.3	0.5	0.1
$7,000 to $9,999......	1.2	0.3	1.3	0.4	0.4	0.1
$10,000 and over......	0.6	0.4	0.7	0.5	0.1	0.1
Median income.......	$1,357	$1,029	$1,441	$1,138	$909	$590

Source: U.S. Census of Population: 1960. Detailed Characteristics. U.S. Summary, Table 219.

or salary income; (2) self-employment income; (3) income from sources other than earnings. The first two types of income, added together, may be termed total money earnings. The total money income of the individual may be estimated by adding together the three sources of income.

Family income is the total income received by all persons in the family during 1959 from all sources. Thus, with this set of census inquiries, it is possible to obtain statistics on the income of the individual, of families, or of both.

Table 13-2 reports the income distribution of individuals among the United States population at the 1950 and 1960 censuses by sex and color.

It is clear from this table that the range of variations in individual income is very great indeed. Persons who receive an income of less than $1000 per year at the present time in the United States are subject to very severe economic deprivation. Yet more than one seventh of the population that did receive income fell in this bracket in 1960, and more than one third of the nonwhite population was in this unfortunate circumstance. At the other extreme, receiving an income of $7000 or more clearly denotes economic comfort, and more than one sixth of the population found itself in this status in 1960.

Economists have developed a variety of techniques for comparing the income distribution of two populations. One of the most widely used is the ogive, or cumulative frequency distribution, as illustrated in Figure 13-2. This curve is plotted by cumulating two percent distributions—income recipients and income—and plotting one against the other. If income were equally distributed, 10 percent of the

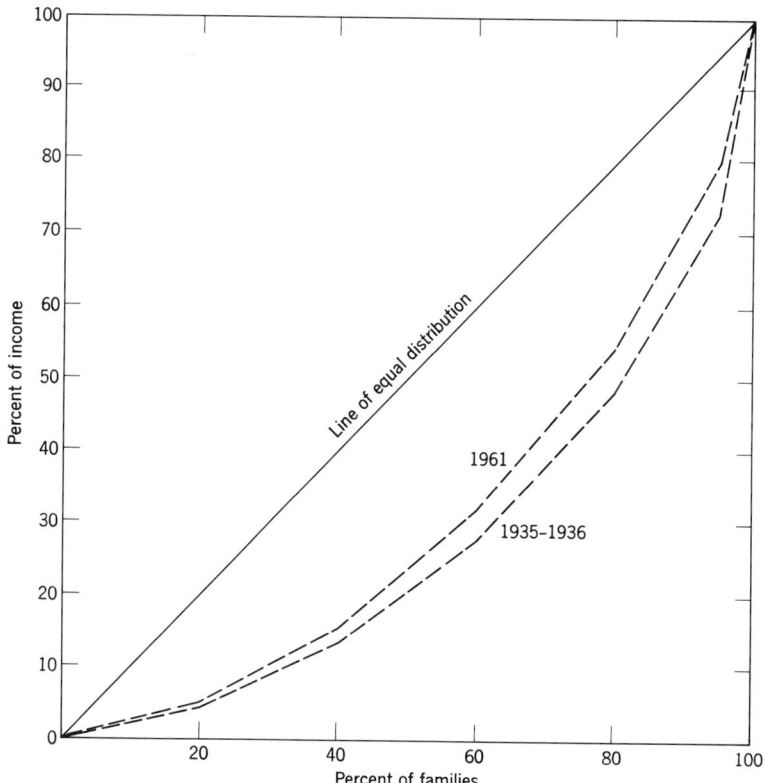

Figure 13-2   Cumulative Percentage of Families Receiving Specified Amounts of Income, Plotted against the Proportion of All Family Income That They Receive.

population would receive 10 percent of the income, 20 percent would receive 20 percent of the income, and so forth. The ogive would then be a straight line forming the diagonal of the figure. To the extent that the ogive forms a curve that deviates from the diagonal, it indicates inequality in income distribution. Thus Figure 13-2 shows that in 1961 the wealthiest 5 percent of families received 20 percent of the income, the wealthiest 10 percent of the families received 30 percent of the income, and so forth. The area between the diagonal and the curve of income distribution measures the degree to which income is unequally distributed; the greater the deviation from the diagonal, the greater the inequality of distribution. This may be given rather precise expression by calculating what percentage of the total area beneath the diagonal lies between the diagonal and the curve.[5] The resulting concentration ratio may vary in theory, from 0 to 100. It must be kept in mind that it states nothing

about differences in income levels; it only compares the extent of concentration of distribution of whatever income is available. From Table 13-2 and Figure 13-2 we may compare the income distribution of the population at 1950 and 1960, adjusted for change in the purchasing power of the dollar. During the recent past there has been a very clear upward shift in the average income level of the population, even after allowances are made for the changing value of the purchasing power of the dollar.

Table 13-2 shows also that there are very substantial differences between subgroups of the population in the level of economic status and in the pattern of income distribution. Two of the greatest differentials are those related to sex and color. The following summary of median income brings out the picture sharply:

[5] S. Andic and A. T. Peacock, "The International Distribution of Income," *Journal of the Royal Statistical Society*, **124** (1961).

	Total	*White*	*Nonwhite*
Male	$4103	$4319	$1502
Female	1357	1441	909

Women who receive income take in only about 35 percent as much as men, and male non-white recipients of income receive only about 35 percent as much as white males. The sex differential is sharper among the white population than among the nonwhite population.

13.4. Causes of Disparity in Income Distribution

What are the causes of this wide disparity in income that people receive? Social scientists assert that at least six factors are involved:

1. People differ widely in their ability, training, and drive to earn. As a result, some people are capable of creating much more value in the form of goods or services than others, and are rewarded accordingly. Nations all over the world agree that the persons who work hard, who stay in school to obtain special skills, and who are capable of outstanding, original, or highly skilled contributions should receive a greater monetary reward for their efforts than persons who perform the jobs that require little skill or intelligence.

2. Various types of work command a different price in the labor market. Certain types of work are paid handsomely, while other types of work, even though they may involve a great deal of skill, are much more poorly paid. For example, few people are capable of composing music or painting pictures, yet the average income received by artists and music composers is quite small. In contrast, persons in certain other occupations, such as physicians or dentists, receive very high incomes. Also, occupations involving business management are highly rewarding in wealth or power.

3. Inheritance of wealth, prestige, or influence is widely asserted to be the major explanation for the receipt of unusually large incomes. Parents in all societies attempt to transfer a part or all of their wealth and influence to their offspring. Much of this transfer may take the form of superior education and careful upbringing to hold a high-status occupation. But the transfer from generation to

generation of material wealth permits some persons to have much higher economic status than they could achieve in the open labor market on the basis of their education and work abilities alone.

4. Labor turnover and part-time and part-year employment are responsible for many small incomes. Most workers are able to work continuously throughout the year, but some are laid off for several weeks or months because of seasonal or other fluctuations. Among those who suffer greatly from part-year work are forestry workers, lumbermen, workers in the construction industry, and in many countries farmers. Many jobs are offered to people on a part-time basis, allowing them to work only a few days a week. The mining industry is an example of this. Other examples are part-time jobs that students hold while attending school, baby-sitting work, and the work that older men frequently do as night watchmen or "handymen" in an office or a business establishment. Still other workers are unable to get in a full work year because of labor turnover. Persons who are just entering the labor force or who have recently left the labor force may have worked only for a portion of a year and may have a low annual income for this reason.

5. The system of social organization, with its accompanying power structure and traditions, also influences the pattern of income distribution. The way in which the total personal disposable income of a nation is divided among the population is determined not completely by economic laws but to a large extent by the structure of the society and by customs and traditions. The amount of income to be awarded to each participant is to a certain extent determined by past history and by widely accepted standards of what constitutes "economic justice." Also involved is the "bargaining power" of the various groups. Among the factors of custom and tradition are laws concerning inheritance of wealth; the dominance over the economy achieved by either management or workers in an industry by virtue of the fact that they are organized into unions or associations that further the economic interests of the members; the general social status and esteem that people who hold a particular occupation

(such as physicians) have in the society; the political philosophy that a society holds concerning the degrees of income differential that are morally allowable; the comparative willingness of a society to close its eyes to the economic suffering of those who are destitute; and the prevalence of humanitarian sentiments to share income in order to put a floor under human deprivation. The tax structure of the national, state, and local governments also affects income distribution; if the rate of taxation gets progressively greater as income rises, the effect is to redistribute income after taxes more evenly among the taxpayers.

6. The physical and mental health of workers is also an important factor influencing income. Workers who are undernourished, who have physical impairments, or who are otherwise in poor health are able to earn less. Workers vary widely in the state of their health. This is especially true after age 40 is reached. Many workers receive modest incomes because they have impaired health and must hold jobs that represent less than the attainment they would otherwise have. Many other workers suffer from neurosis or other mental disorders, and for this reason are unable to hold jobs for which they are otherwise qualified. Inability to work cooperatively with others, alcoholism, outbursts of temper, and other behaviors that interfere with the work routine force the mentally ill person to accept menial jobs that pay low wages.

Table 13-2 is the net resultant of the operation of all six of these forces. At the lowest end of the income scale should be the workers who were employed only part-time or a part of the preceding year, who are of the lowest order of skill, intelligence, ability, and initiative, whose parents were able to give them no financial assistance in life, who are employed at jobs having the lowest market value, and whose degree of bargaining power was least, and whose health is poorest. At the other extreme, in the high-income groups, we would expect to find people of high average intelligence, training, and ability employed at jobs commanding high prices in the labor market, who worked a full 52 weeks and full workweeks during the preceding year, who succeeded in obtaining a great deal of supplemental income through investments resulting from the inheritance of money, who wield unusually great economic power by virtue of belonging to associations that help maximize the share of the income they obtain, and who are in sound physical condition.

13.5. Income Distribution in Developing Nations Compared with Industrialized Nations

Students of economic development would like to know how the pattern of income distribution in the developing nations compares with that in the industrialized nations and how the two are changing. This subject has been studied by Simon Kuznets, who undertook to compare the income distributions of selected nations of the world in the late 1940s and early 1950s. His statistics are summarized in Table 13-3.[6] On the basis of this evidence, Kuznets concludes that "the shares of the upper-income group are distinctly larger in the underdeveloped than in the developed countries. The top 5 percent of family or spending units in most underdeveloped countries receives 30 percent of total income or more. The shares of the corresponding groups in the developed countries range from 20-25 percent" (p. 16). Kuznets also finds that the share of the lowest income groups is somewhat lower in the underdeveloped countries than in the developed countries, but the differences are rather small and may not be significant. Thus the lowest 60 percent of the population receive 21 to 30 percent of the income in the underdeveloped countries and 29 to 33 percent in the developed countries. An implication of these two findings is that underdeveloped countries have a small "middle class" in comparison with industrialized nations. In overall terms the inequality of income distribution is greater in the underdeveloped than in the developed countries. Kuznets computes the concentration ratio for a group of underdeveloped countries and obtains a ratio of 0.44. A similar measure for six developed countries was 0.37.

[6] Simon Kuznets, "Quantitative Aspects of the Economic Growth of Nations," *Economic Development and Cultural Change*, 1963.

Table 13-3   Shares of Ordinal Groups of Income Units (Families or Tax Returns), Selected Countries: Late 1940s and Early 1950s

Country and year	Shares of ordinal groups							
	0–20 (percent)	21–40 (percent)	41–60 (percent)	0–60 (percent)	61–80 (percent)	81–90 (percent)	91–95 (percent)	Top 5 (percent)
	(1)	(2)	(3)	(4)	(5)	(6)	(7)	(8)
India, 1950.............	7.8	9.2	11.4	28.5	16.0	12.4	9.6	33.4
India, 1955/56.........	n.a.	n.a.	14.8	33.5	19.7	13.6	9.6	23.6
Ceylon, 1952/53........	5.1	9.3	13.3	27.7	18.4	13.3	9.6	31.0
Northern Rhodesia, 1946.	n.a.	n.a.	n.a.	n.a.	n.a.	n.a.	n.a.	45.3+(1.4%)
Southern Rhodesia, 1946.	n.a.	n.a.	n.a	n.a.	n.a.	n.a.	n.a.	65.3 (5%)
Kenya, 1949............	n.a.	n.a.	n.a.	n.a.	n.a.	n.a.	n.a.	50.9+(2.9%)
Mexico, 1950...........	6.1	8.2	10.3	24.6	15.6	10.8	9.0	40.0
Mexico, 1957...........	4.4	6.9	9.9	21.2	17.4	14.7	9.7	37.0
Colombia, 1953.........	n.a.	n.a.	n.a.	31.4	12.2	8.0	6.8	41.6
El Salvador, 1946......	n.a.	n.a.	n.a.	32.2	15.7	8.5	8.1	35.5
Guatemala, 1947/48.....	n.a.	n.a.	13.2	28.8	15.8	11.6	9.3	34.5
Barbados, 1951/52......	3.6	9.3	14.2	27.1	21.3	17.4	11.9	22.3
Puerto Rico, 1953......	5.6	9.8	14.9	30.3	19.9	16.9	9.5	23.4
Italy, 1948...........	6.1	10.5	14.6	31.2	20.4	14.4	10.0	24.1
Great Britain, 1951/52..	5.4	11.3	16.6	33.3	22.2	14.3	9.3	20.9
West Germany, 1950......	4.0	8.5	16.5	29.0	23.0	14.0	10.4	23.6
Netherlands, 1950.......	4.2	9.6	15.7	29.5	21.5	14.0	10.4	24.6
Denmark, 1952..........	3.4	10.3	15.8	29.5	23.5	16.3	10.6	20.1
Sweden, 1948...........	3.2	9.6	16.3	29.1	24.3	16.3	10.2	20.1
United States, 1950.....	4.8	11.0	16.2	32.0	22.3	15.4	9.9	20.4

Source: Simon Kuznets, "Quantitative Aspects of the Economic Growth of Nations" _Economic Development and Cultural Change_, 1963.

After examining inequalities between industries in developed and underdeveloped countries and between geographic regions in developed and underdeveloped countries, Kuznets reaffirms this conclusion. The explanation of this inequality is complex, he reports. He attributes it to the fact that ownership of income-yielding assets may be more concentrated in the less developed than in the developed countries and that the less developed countries have less legislation tending to redistribute and equalize income in the form of progressive taxation and transfer payments by way of social insurance schemes. He also concludes that "the very low income level of the underdeveloped countries means a weaker economic position of the lower income groups and a greater possibility of persisting monopoly of the wealthy few than in the developed countries" (p. 47).

After studying income inequality between the agricultural and nonagricultural sectors of nations, Kuznets concludes that in both underdeveloped and most developed countries income within the agricultural sector is distributed less unequally than income within the nonagricultural sector. He says that this is a plausible conclusion if we consider that there is a wider range of occupations and industries in the nonagricultural sector and that many of the occupations have a wide range of income by age, degrees of education, and success in capital accumulation. In underdeveloped countries the distribution of income within the nonagricultural sector may be made relatively more unequal by the concentration of low-income migrants from the countryside at the lower end and by the concentration of economic and financial elite at the upper end (p. 54). Kuznets attempts to find whether there is movement or change in this respect. He discovers that the pattern of greater inequality that now characterizes the less developed countries also characterized the presently developed nations only a few decades ago and that the change to the present pattern occurred rather rapidly. He concludes that there is a variety of forces at work now, tending to bring about a similar narrowing of income inequalities in the developing countries (pp. 64-66).

13.6.   Differential in Income Distribution in the United States

In the United States there is inequality of income distribution associated with almost every other social, economic, and demographic characteristic of the population. If data were avail-

Table 13-4 Median Income in 1959 of Persons by Age, Color, and Sex

Age	Male			Female		
	Total	White	Nonwhite	Total	White	Nonwhite
Total	4,111	4,337	2,317	1,415	1,510	920
14 to 19 years.........	720	725	674	696	704	624
20 to 24 years.........	2,573	2,705	1,733	1.672	1,815	902
25 to 34 years.........	4,823	5,039	2,911	1,848	2,002	1,295
35 to 44 years.........	5,465	5,680	3,215	2,039	2,195	1,307
45 to 54 years.........	5,097	5,324	2,812	2,185	2,370	1,011
55 to 64 years.........	4,380	4,601	2,249	1,611	1,747	827
65 to 74 years.........	2,024	2,144	1,155	813	832	640
75 and over...........	1,229	1,289	743	732	746	587

Source: U.S. Census of Population: 1960 Detailed Characteristics, U.S. Summary, Table 219.

able for other nations, this would probably be found to be a universal condition.

Of special interest in demographic studies is the age differential in income distribution. Table 13-4 reports the median income in 1959 of income recipients according to their age. There is a very definite age pattern to the income. It is similar in shape for males and females and for white and nonwhite workers, though it differs in detail for each. In this pattern the income is very modest during the early years of participation in the labor force, rises steadily, and reaches a peak at about 35 to 44 years of age, after which it declines.

Figure 13-3 illustrates this curve in the United States population in 1959. This age differential in income is again a combined result of the factors that we have enumerated previously. Very young workers are often engaged in part-time and part-year work. They work at jobs that require low skill and little training and have a low market value. After leaving school and entering the labor force, workers gradually acquire work experience and become more valuable employees; they also acquire seniority rights and gain promotion on the job, so that their wages and salaries gradually rise. In addition, they may manage to save funds,

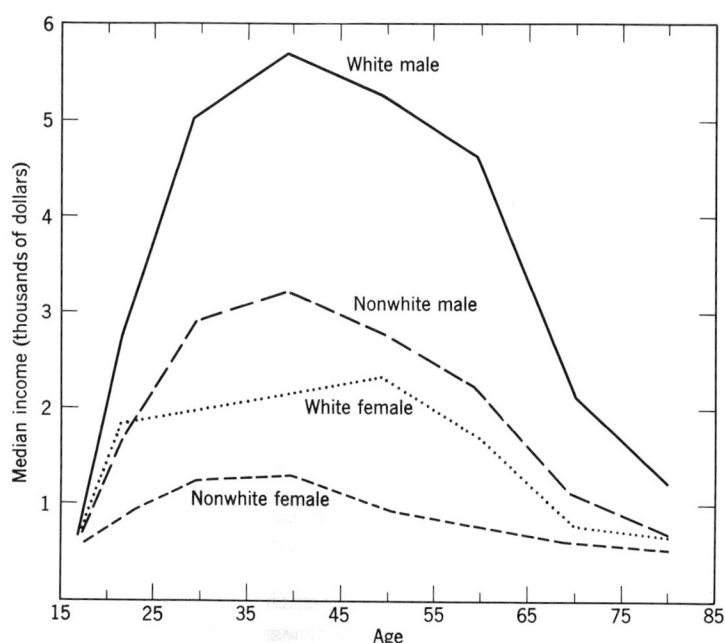

Figure 13-3 Median Income Received by Individuals at Each Age Group, by Sex and Color, United States: 1959.

which they may invest and thereby obtain supplemental income. However, as they reach middle age, the health of some begins to fail, and they are forced either to accept jobs that do not pay well or to withdraw from the labor force. This is especially true of factory workers whose jobs require great physical exertion; as they pass their physical prime, they may be shifted to jobs that pay lower wages. After retirement the worker is forced to live on the returns from his life savings and on the social security pension. If he has not been provident and saved for his old age, he must live on whatever payments the welfare system will allow him. Thus we find that at ages 75 and over the incomes of the population are very modest indeed.

There is undoubtedly also a generational aspect to the age curve of income distribution. Older workers are employed at jobs that are obsolescent; they have less education; they were "settled in their jobs" when new technological advances opened new and higher-paying areas of economic activity. As a result, younger generations tend to flow into the avenues that lead to higher salaries, leaving the traditional lower-paying posts to the older generation.

However, the age curve of income itself is changing radically as Table 13-5 reports. The

national program of social security payments, the prolonged period of economic prosperity which has permitted savings, the introduction of minimum wage legislation, have all combined to extend the period of higher income into older ages. Despite this fact, the greatest income gains have been made by workers 25-44 years of age.

13.7. Family Income

Statistics for income of individuals can grossly understate the economic status of a population. It is incorrect to assume that each income recipient must support a family on his earnings, for many families have two or even three or more earners. The economic status of the family is determined, of course, by the total income it receives from all sources. On the other hand, many recipients of income are not members of a family and are required to support only one individual, themselves, from their earnings. A substantial proportion of the very small incomes received by individuals are the incomes of wives, children, or elderly persons working only part-time or intermittently to supplement the family income—the major share of which is contributed by a principal earner —and such regular payments as the pension. Table 13-6 shows how prevalent the phenomenon of multiple earners is in the United States and what an important impact it has had on the income level of the family. Nearly 45 percent of white families and 50 percent of nonwhite families had two or more earners in 1960. A second earner increased the income of the white family by an average of nearly 30 percent and of the nonwhite family by an average of nearly 50 percent. Figure 13-4 compares the curve of income distribution for individuals and families. The curve for families shows a very heavy concentration of incomes at the middle-income range. This curve approaches the normal curve in shape, somewhat skewed toward the upper end because of the presence of a small percentage of families that receive very large incomes.

Income varies sharply according to the type of family and the color and age of the head. Families with female heads and families where the head is elderly tend to be poor families. This is demonstrated in Table 13-7.

Table 13-5 Median Income of Persons, by Age and Sex, in 1959 and 1949, United States

| Age | Median income | | |
	1959	1949	Percent change
Males, all ages........	4111	3001	36.7
14 to 19 years.......	720	792	-5.4
15 to 24 years.......	2573	2081	23.6
25 to 34 years.......	4823	3345	44.2
35 to 44 years.......	5465	3774	44.8
45 to 54 years.......	5097	3645	39.8
55 to 64 years.......	4380	3151	39.0
65 years and over....	1766	1406	25.6
Females, all ages......	1415	1260	12.3
14 to 19 years.......	696	785	-11.4
20 to 24 years.......	1672	1530	9.3
25 to 34 years.......	1848	1600	15.5
35 to 44 years.......	2039	1665	22.5
45 to 54 years.......	2185	1630	34.0
55 to 64 years.......	1611	1232	30.7
65 years and over....	784	817	-4.0

Income for 1949 converted to value of dollar in 1959

Source: U.S. Census of Population: 1960, Detailed Characteristics, U.S. Summary, Table 219

Table 13-6 Number of Earners Per Family and Median Family Income: 1960

Number of earners	Percent distribution		Media income	
	White	Nonwhite	White	Nonwhite
Total	100.0	100.0	5,893	$3,161
No earner..................	7.7	10.2	1,577	973
One earner.................	49.0	40.9	5,379	2,757
Two earners................	34.7	36.8	6,911	4,099
Three earners or more........	8.6	12.1	9,152	5,357

Source: U.S. Census of Population: 1960, Detailed Characteristics, Table 227.

The highest median income for families in 1960 was that for husband-wife families where the head was between the ages of 35 and 64 and there were three persons in the family. The lowest family income was for families where the head was a female, under 35 years of age, and there were three or more persons in the family, or where the head was a female 65 or more years of age.

13.8.   Race and Income

Tables 13-6 and 13-7 outline sharply one of the greatest social problems of the United States: the abysmally low economic status of the nonwhite population in comparison with the white. It is generally accepted as a rough rule of thumb that $3000 represents the poverty line, and that families receiving less than this are definitely living in a state of poverty. (Families with income of $3000 to $5000 are living in a state of deprivation.) Table 13-6 shows that nearly one half of all nonwhite families were poverty-stricken in 1960, and that it required two or more earners in the family to rise above this level in a high proportion of cases. The median income for all nonwhite families with female heads (which, as we have seen, comprise a large percentage of nonwhite families) is below the poverty line. The median income for conventional husband-wife nonwhite families was only one-half (52 percent) as large as that of white families in

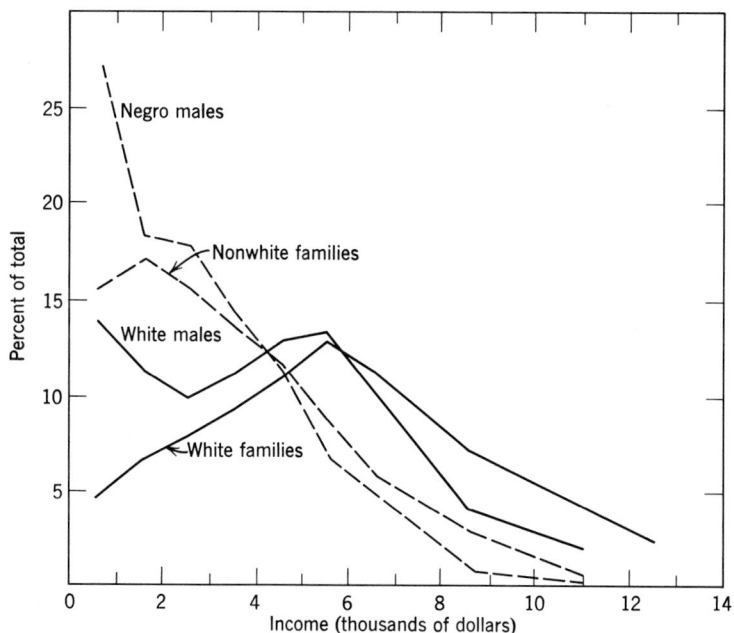

Figure 13-4 Percent Distribution of Income in 1959 of Persons and Families, by Color, for the United States.

Table 13-7 Median Family Income by Size and Type of Family, Color, and Age of Head

Age and number of persons in family	White			Nonwhite		
	Husband wife	Other male head	Female head	Husband wife	Other male head	Female head
All families	7,022	5,334	3,532	3,637	3,178	1,757
Head under 35................	5,680	5,429	2,441	3,622	3,527	1,509
2 persons................	5,863	5,158	2,530	3,718	3,452	1,576
3 persons................	5,384	5,653	1,956	3,681	3,481	1,481
4 persons or more........	5,755	5,898	1,838	3,583	3,684	1,497
Head 35 to 64................	6,954	5,745	3,895	3,955	3,467	1,947
2 persons................	5,247	5,525	3,802	3,528	3,090	1,761
3 persons................	7,062	6,350	4,054	4,222	3,768	1,939
4 persons or more........	7,002	6,220	3,938	4,108	3,730	2,136
Head 65 and over............	3,185	4,228	3,692	1,820	2,127	1,654
2 persons................	2,710	3,293	2,822	1,533	1,626	1,385
3 persons................	5,082	5,504	5,253	2,036	2,439	1,830
4 persons or more........	6,570	6,964	6,602	2,739	3,025	2,226

Source: U.S. Census of Population: 1960, Sources and Structure of Family Income, Subject Reports PC(2)-4c, Table 1.

1960. During the childrearing phase of the family cycle the nonwhite couples had only 57 percent as much money with which to support their children, despite the fact that they had a considerably larger number of children to support.

An aspect of the race differential in income that has concerned economists and which is manifesting itself in such demonstrations as "the poor people's march on Washington" by predominantly Negro participants is that the trend in income distribution during the early 1960's was to *widen* the differential rather than to narrow it. Following is the median income of white and nonwhite families over recent years, and the ratio of nonwhite to white income:

	Median family income		
Year	White	Non-white	Ratio nonwhite to white
1950	3445	1869	0.54
1955	4605	2549	0.55
1960	5835	3233	0.55
1961	5981	3191	0.53
1962	6237	3330	0.53
1963	6548	3465	0.53
1964	6858	3839	0.56
1965	7251	3994	0.55
1966	7722	4628	0.60

Apparently the "war on poverty" programs had begun by 1966 to ameliorate the disparity slightly, or at least to keep the gap from widening further.

Another way of viewing this problem is to note the percentage of individuals who fall below the "poverty line" of $3000 annual income, and the trend in this proportion for white and nonwhite persons:

Year	Percent below poverty line		
	Total	White	Nonwhite
1959	22	18	55
1961	21	16	55
1963	19	15	51
1965	17	13	46
1966	15	11	41

The income position of the Negro seems to have begun to improve slowly after 1961. But in 1966 nearly one third of the poor were nonwhite, despite the fact that they comprised less than ⅛ of the population.

13.9. Income and Education

The higher the educational attainment of an individual, the higher his income tends to be. This is shown in Table 13-8.

This educational differential is one of the most consistent and fundamental aspects of

Table 13-8 Median Income of Persons 25 Years of Age and Over, by Years of School Completed, Color, and Sex, for the United States: 1960

Educational attainment	Males			Females		
	Total	White	Nonwhite	Total	White	Nonwhite
Total	4,617	4,851	2,610	1,533	1,635	959
No school completed..........	1,439	1,569	1,042	687	711	622
Elementary: 1 to 4 years....	1,844	1,962	1,565	734	771	668
5 to 7 years....	3,062	3,240	2,353	898	929	796
8 years.........	3,885	3,981	2,900	1,111	1,131	967
High school: 1 to 3 years....	4,847	5,013	3,253	1,616	1,692	1,199
4 years.........	5,437	5,529	3,735	2,186	2,232	1,707
College: 1 to 3 years....	5,980	6,104	4,029	2,402	2,422	2,119
4 years.........	7,646	7,779	4,840	3,751	3,758	3,708

Source: U.S. Census of Population: 1960. 1960 Detailed Characteristics. U.S. Summary, Table 223.

income distribution. It holds for both males and females, for both white and nonwhite individuals, and for persons in all age groups. The increments to income with each increment of education are very substantial, especially for graduation from grammar school, high school, or college. Although this set of relationships is one of the most consistent to be found in social science, it should not be generalized too far with reference to individuals. Some persons with much education have very small incomes. Roman Catholic priests are an example of this. On the other hand, a few persons of low education have large incomes. Many successful businessmen, athletes, and entertainers fall into this category. It should be kept in mind that for each educational attainment level there is a *distribution* of income. Table 13-9 presents this distribution for the male labor force. Note that one college graduate in 11 could be defined as "poor" in 1960,

while about 4 percent of the "functionally illiterate" (persons with less than five years of schooling) received incomes that classified them as affluent.

The implications of educational attainment have been explored by Paul C. Glick and Herman T. Miller.[7] By studying data on average income by years of school completed for men 25 to 50 years old, Glick and Miller found that not only does the average income increase progressively with each additional increment of education attained, but the increment itself tends to become larger in the higher levels of education. For example, they found that in 1949 an additional year of grammar school was worth about $150 per year in earnings; whereas completing the senior year in college or going one year beyond college was equivalent

[7] Paul C. Glick and Herman C. Miller, Education-al Level and Potential Income," *American Sociological Review*, June 1956.

Table 13-9 Income in 1959 of the Experienced Male Labor Force by Educational Attainment

Years of school completed	Total	Less than $1000	1,000 to 1,999	2,000 to 2,999	3,000 to 3,999	4,000 to 4,999	5,000 to 5,999	6,000 to 6,999	7,000 to 9,999	10,000 to 14,999	15,000 and over
Total	100.0	9.2	8.4	10.0	12.3	14.4	14.9	10.3	12.8	4.7	3.0
Grammar school											
Less than 5 years..	100.0	22.2	19.3	18.3	14.6	11.3	7.3	3.2	2.7	0.7	0.4
5-7 years.........	100.0	12.9	12.4	15.3	16.4	15.9	12.8	6.7	5.8	1.2	0.6
8 years...........	100.0	9.4	9.4	12.0	14.8	17.1	15.9	9.3	9.1	2.1	1.1
High school											
1-3 years.........	100.0	13.1	7.6	9.3	12.6	15.5	16.2	10.6	11.1	2.7	1.4
4 years...........	100.0	4.6	6.4	8.1	12.0	15.5	17.9	13.1	15.6	4.6	2.3
College											
1-3 years.........	100.0	6.2	7.2	6.9	8.8	11.6	14.3	12.2	18.8	8.6	5.3
4 years...........	100.0	1.9	3.3	3.1	5.9	8.7	11.8	11.9	25.0	16.1	11.2
5+ years..........	100.0	2.0	3.4	4.0	4.9	6.9	9.7	10.5	23.9	17.5	17.1

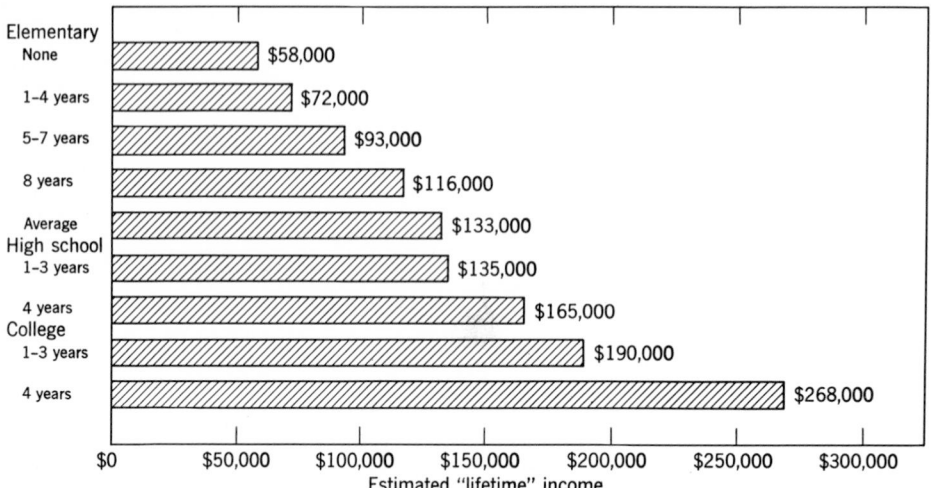

Figure 13-5 Estimated "Lifetime" Income For Men by Amount of Education.

SOURCE: Paul C. Glick and Herman C. Miller, "Educational Level and Potential Income," *American Sociological Review*; June 1956, p. 310; derived from 1950 Census of Population, Vol. IV, Special Reports, PE, No. 5B, Education, Table 12.

to an increase in salary of nearly $1000 per year. The statistics on educational differentials in incomes are even more impressive when converted to lifetime earnings. Their results are shown in Figure 13-5. These lifetime estimates are obtained by applying current earning rates to a representative life table. They are based on wage levels that prevailed in 1950 and include adjustments for illness, disability, unemployment, and inflation. Glick and Miller estimated that the total cost of obtaining a college education, including loss of earnings, was about $9000. On this basis, the additional lifetime income that results from completing college is about eight times that of the cost of attending college. They discovered that completion of a given level of school—elementary, high school, or college—provides especially large bonuses in income. They found, however, that these bonuses were much more modest for nonwhite than for the white population.

More recently Miller has retraced this ground thoroughly in Chapter 6, "Income and Education," of his book, *Income Distribution in the United States*, a monograph published by the U.S. Census in 1966. The following statistics from this source reveal the status at the time of the 1960 census:

Years of school completed	Lifetime earnings (thousands of dollars)		
	White	Non-white	Nonwhite as percent of white
Total	241	122	51
Elementary			
Under 8 years ..	157	95	61
8 years	191	123	64
High school			
1 to 3 years	221	132	60
4 years	253	151	60
College			
1 to 3 years	301	162	54
4 years or more .	427	215	50

This table, for males 18 to 64 years of age, reveals the following:

1. Lifetime earnings increased for all groups between 1950 and 1960.

2. The lifetime earnings of the average Negro are one-half those of the average white.

3. Although the Negro gained by increasing his education, the "payoff" for him continued to be smaller than for whites (even though it improved between 1950 and 1960).

4. The average Negro college graduate could look forward to slightly less lifetime

Table 13-10   Median Income in 1959 of Experienced Labor Force by Major
Occupation Group Educational Attainment and Sex: United States

Major occupation group and sex	Total	Elementary school		High school		College	
		Less than 8 years	8 years	1-3 years	4 years	1-3 years	4 or more years
Males, total							
Professional and technical workers............	6,622	4,284	5,194	5,652	6,073	6,108	7,338
Farmers and farm managers....................	2,174	1,287	2,186	2,460	3,053	3,503	4,142
Managers, officials, proprietors.............	6,651	4,266	5,393	5,951	6,582	7,393	9,297
Clerical and kindred workers.................	4,787	4,135	4,601	4,531	4,913	4,831	5,660
Sales workers................................	4,983	2,789	3,537	3,838	5,316	5,799	7,033
Craftsmen, foremen and kindred workers........	5,239	4,253	5,026	5,314	5,630	5,827	7,241
Operatives and kindred workers...............	4,302	3,643	4,419	4,388	4,699	4,545	5,102
Private household workers....................	1,058	1,033	1,272	792	1,689	1,884	.....
Service workers except private household......	3,323	2,746	3,330	3,222	4,216	3,499	4,048
Farm laborers and foremen....................	1,070	973	1,369	841	1,885	1,828	3,523
Laborers, except farm and mine..............	2,949	2,615	3,370	2,687	3,607	2,890	3,825
Females, total							
Professional and technical workers............	3,625	1,969	2,425	2,480	3.033	3,133	4,365
Farmers and farm managers....................	825	716	826	840	948	1,006	1,344
Managers, officials, proprietors.............	3,339	1,820	2,400	2,820	3,582	3,989	4,785
Clerical and kindred workers.................	3,014	2,483	2,918	2,767	3,054	3,078	3,422
Sales workers................................	1,502	1,510	1,692	1,201	1,599	1,649	2,364
Craftsmen, foremen and kindred workers........	2,908	2,468	2,893	2,906	3,097	3,094	3,372
Operatives and kindred workers...............	2,320	2,195	2,410	2,320	2,373	2,253	2,308
Private household workers....................	684	662	718	659	737	730	878
Service workers, except private household......	1,384	1,313	1,486	1,239	1,492	1,470	2,164
Farm laborers and foremen....................	600	568	645	592	715	.671	.....
Laborers, except farm and mine..............	1,896	1,738	2,169	1,727	2,068	1,738	.....

Source: U.S. Census of Population: 1960. Subject Reports. Occupation by Earnings and Education.

earnings than the average white dropout from high school.

Miller interprets these figures as follows: "Nonwhite men earn less than whites with the same number of years of schooling for at least two reasons: first, they are employed in lower paid jobs; and second, they are paid less even when they are doing the same kind of work."

13.10.   Income and Occupation

Professional and managerial occupations stand well above all others in the level of income that they provide (Table 13-10). Laborers, both farm and nonfarm; farmers; and private household workers receive a small income that damns the vast majority of them to perpetual poverty or destitution. Between these extremes the other occupations are spaced. Craftsmen stand above the lower-level white-collar groups, while semiskilled operatives stand below. There is a general relationship between occupation and income that may be summarized as follows:

Occupation	*Average economic status*
Professionals and managers	Affluent or wealthy
Craftsmen, clerical, and sales	Economic comfort
Operatives	Minimum adequacy
Service workers, except household	Deprivation
Farmers, nonfarm laborers	Poverty
Farm laborers, private household workers	Destitution

Table 13-10 reveals that there is a wide range of income within each of the general occupation groups and that this variation is highly associated with the level of education. In fact, education appears to be a very powerful factor in influencing income. For example, craftsmen who have a college degree receive an average income almost equal to that of professional persons, and managers with a college degree have an average income that stands far above that of professionals. Even a laborer with a college education receives 50 percent more pay than a laborer with less than a grammar school education. This, of course, is an indirect way of asserting that there is a wide variety of specific occupations within each of the broad occupation groups (as was emphasized in Chapter 10) and that each of these specific occupations carries with it educational or skill prerequisites and a pay scale.

13.11.   Sex and Occupation

Table 13-10 demonstrates that category-for-category women receive less pay than men for the same work. The differential is very substantial in all occupational categories. It is as pervasive at the higher educational levels as at the lower. This is explained in part by the fact that a high percentage of women work only part-time. However, the median incomes of males and females living in urban areas who worked a full year in 1959 (52 weeks) were as follows (from 1960 Census of Population, *Detailed Characteristics,* Table 221)

Males $5634
Females $3271

It is clearly evident that if female workers were dependent entirely upon their own earnings for a livelihood, the vast majority would be living in poverty or severe deprivation. The economic position of widowed or divorced women who must support a family tends to be of this type.

If statistical adjustments were made simultaneously for occupation, level of education, weeks worked per year, and hours worked per week, it is quite plausible that much of the sex differential in income would disappear. However, the differential is so very great in its crude form that almost certainly it would still be substantial if all of these alternative explanatory factors were controlled.

13.12. Poverty in the United States and Redistribution of Income

The continued existence of the phenomenon of poverty, especially in industrialized nations, has come to be regarded as a condition of social pathology which should be eradicated. This task is now considered to be a responsibility of government, both in taking short-range remedial steps and in taking longer-range ameliorative steps. The developing nations are adopting a similar philosophy. It has become a part of the world culture that for the welfare of children, for humanitarian reasons, and for national welfare, there should be a minimum economic status below which families and individuals should not be allowed to sink.

The population census, if it includes data on income, is the major single source of information about poverty. Demography-oriented economists who analyze this material are able to arrive at generalizations concerning poverty that provide a starting point for more detailed studies. In June 1965 the U.S. Bureau of the Census released a report entitled "Low-Income Families and Unrelated Individuals in the United States," based on data from the 1963 Current Population Survey.[8] For purposes of this report, families with incomes of less than $3000 were defined as low-income (poverty) families. Adults not living in families who received incomes of less than $1500 were defined as low-income (poor) persons. It was found that 8,883,000 families (19 percent of all families) fell in the low-income category. Among nonfamily persons 4,940,000 (44 percent) were classified as poor. It was found that low-income families tend to have one or more of the following demographic characteristics:

family is Negro
head is 65 years of age or older
head is a female
family lives on a farm
family has no earner and is not in labor force
head has not completed grammar school
family lives in the South
head is employed as a semiskilled worker, service worker, or farmer or farm laborer

This report finds that some families live on very low incomes; 1,770,000 (20 percent) of the low-income families received less than $1000. Thus despite a very high average per capita income in comparison with other nations a substantial proportion and a disturbingly large number of American families live in great absolute as well as relative deprivation, and not a few are destitute.

The Census report gives the encouraging information that progress is being made to eliminate poverty. The proportion of low-income families dropped from 31 percent in 1947 to 19 percent in 1963. However, certain groups did not share fully in this progress. The nonwhite family, the family with a female head,

[8] U. S. Bureau of the Census, "Low-Income Families and Unrelated Individuals in the United States: 1963," *Current Population Reports, Consumer Income,* Series P-60, No. 45, June 18, 1965.

and the family with an elderly head did not improve in economic status as much as other families. At the present time, the "hard core" of American poverty is concentrated in families with these three characteristics:

negro family—25 percent of all low-income
    families
female head—26 percent of all low-income
    families
elderly head—35 percent of all low-income
    families

The poorest families are those that combine two or more of these characteristics, especially Negro families with a female head or Negro families with an elderly head.

Several excellent overall analyses and interpretations have been made of the current poverty situation in the United States. In a report on income distribution to the Arden House Conference on Population, Simon Kuznets[9] reviews the changes that have occurred since 1929. He finds that the average income per family in constant prices has grown by more than 60 percent between 1929 and 1959 and that during this time the inequalities in the distribution of income by size have been substantially reduced. Also during this time the proportion of income earned as wage and salary or as transfer payments has risen (p. 21). Kuznets points out, however, that a part of the rise in the real level of income is illusory. The provision of food, shelter, sanitation, transportation, and other amenities at the same level of satisfaction requires far more resources (for additional processing, transportation, distributions, etc.) in the cities, particularly the larger ones, than in the countryside. Because of greatly increased urbanization, some allowance should be made for the higher cost of living under urban conditions.

Kuznets estimates that at the turn of the century income was earned in the following ways: wages and salaries, 55 percent; income to farm proprietors, 15.5 percent; income to other proprietors, 8.5 percent; income through property in the form of rent, 9 percent; in-

[9] Simon Kuznets, "Income Distribution and Changes in Consumption," in *The Changing American Population,* Hoke S. Simpson, editor, 1962.

come in interest, 7 percent; income in dividends, 5 percent; income from transfer payments, negligible. In contrast, the income during the 1951-1960 period, according to Department of Commerce estimates, was earned as follows: wages and salaries, 70 percent; farm proprietors, 4 percent; other proprietors, 9.5 percent; rent, 5.4 percent; interest, 5.4 percent; dividends, 3.5 percent; transfer payments, 4.3 percent. There has been a large relative decline in proprietor income, in farming income, and in property income from all sources. The emergence of transfers as a component of personal income is a natural consequence of Social Security, spread of private pensions, and retirement pay and welfare programs. Kuznets measures inequality by determining the proportion of all income received by the lowest one fifth of the population and by the top 5 percent. He then computes the average per unit income received by each of these two groups and expresses it as percent of the national average. He then divides the ratio for the richer group by the index for the poorer group. By following this procedure he discovers that after federal income taxes, the relative range between the rich and poor declined by more than one half from 1929 to 1951. But he also finds no change after 1951.

Kuznets continues to find out how this income is spent. He asserts that the pattern of consumer expenditures has changed as real income has risen. For example, the percentage of income spent on food has declined from about 35 percent in 1909 to about 27 percent in 1950-1960. There have also been declines in the proportion spent on clothing—14 to 11 percent—and on housing—19 to 13 percent. Increases have taken place in expenditures for medical care, insurance, transportation, recreation, and education. Kuznets reports: "With the marked rise in consumer expenditures from the 1920s to the 1950s, the shares of clothing, domestic service, public transportation, and possibly housing declined; the shares of medical care, certain types of house furnishings, passenger automobiles, recreation and education rose. The share of personal care, and surprisingly, the share of food, remained constant" (p. 50).

A report, "Poverty and Deprivation in the United States," prepared by the Conference on Economic Progress, also expresses alarm that progress in reducing poverty appears to have slackened and almost stopped.[10] It concludes:

". . . during the years 1953-60, marked by very low economic growth and chronically rising idleness of manpower and plants, the average annual rate of reduction in the total number of Americans living in poverty dropped to 1.1 percent. There was no reduction in the number of families with incomes less than half the amount needed to place them above poverty, and there was practically no reduction in the number of unattached individuals living in poverty. Moreover, in this period of 1953-60 the distribution of income has worsened. The shares of total personal income flowing to the lowest income fifth of all consumer units, to the second lowest and to the third lowest all declined. Meanwhile the shares flowing to the two highest income fifths rose. In 1960 the highest 5 percent of all consumer units received about 20 percent of total personal income or very much more than the 15.5 percent of income received by the lowest 40 percent of all consumer units."

This report emphasizes that income not only is related to education, but also has a close interrelationship with health (see Figure 13-6):

"Among families with money incomes under $2,000 in 1958, 16.5 percent of all persons were either disabled or limited in their major activities by chronic ill health. The figure was about 8 percent among families with incomes ranging from $2,000 to $3,999; 4.8 percent among families with incomes ranging from $4,000 to $6,999, and only 4.3 percent among families with incomes of $7,000 and over."

The report continues to point out that massive pockets of poverty create social environ-

ments that feed social problems for both the present and the future:

"Poverty, dependency and deprivation are responsible for the fact that millions of people still live in urban and rural slums because they do not earn enough to live better. Meanwhile the slums help to perpetuate poverty and deprivation because they are hurtful to health and morale, and generate many social aberrations that impede family and individual economic progress. There are now about 9.5 million seriously deficient dwelling units in the United States or about one-sixth the total of 58 million units. About 5 million of these are in metropolitan areas. An additional 6.2 million units need repair and alteration, including modernization. According to the data from the U. S. Census Bureau of 1956 National Housing Inventory, more than one-half of the rented units were occupied in that year by families with incomes below $2,000 and almost a third of those rented by families with incomes below $2,000 and $4,000 were substandard" (See Figure 13-7).

Although these analyses of census materials are highly useful, they need to be supplemented by special intensive studies. An excellent contribution of this type was made by Morgan, David, Cohen, and Brazer in a report entitled *Income and Welfare in the United States*.[11] This book supplements census materials with a detailed analysis of the processes by which families obtain their income in terms of the following factors: the hours worked; the weeks worked per year; the rates of pay received by the principal breadwinner and by supplemental breadwinners such as wife and children; the extent to which families are able to accumulate savings and obtain capital income from investments and savings; home ownership as a source of income; and the part that "transfer income" (veterans' benefits, unemployment compensation, social security, free medical care, gifts from institutions, private re-

[10] Conference on Economic Progress, *Poverty and Deprivation in the United States*, 1965.

[11] James N. Morgan, Martin H. David, Wilbur J. Cohen, and Harvey E. Brazee, *Income and Welfare in the United States* (New York: McGraw-Hill, 1962).

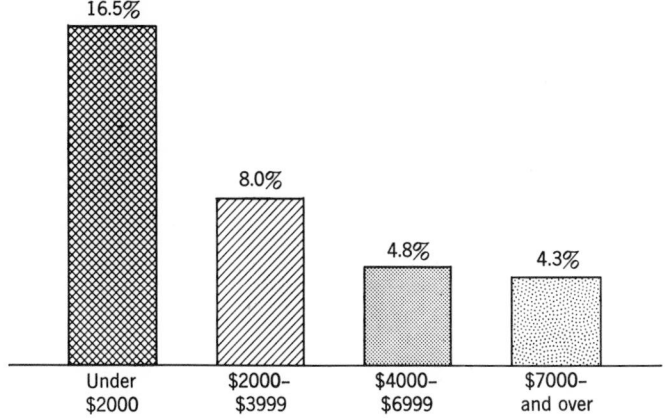

LOW INCOME AND ILL HEALTH ARE LINKED
Percent of persons, grouped by family money income, who are disabled
or whose major activity is limited by chronic ailment, 1958

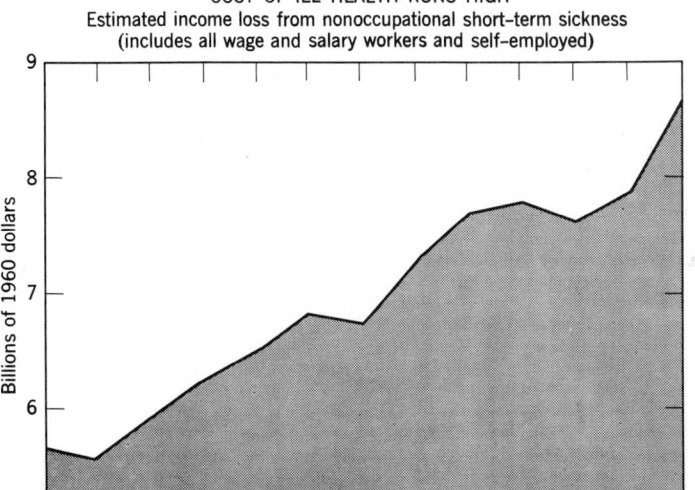

COST OF ILL HEALTH RUNS HIGH
Estimated income loss from nonoccupational short-term sickness
(includes all wage and salary workers and self-employed)

Figure 13-6 Relationships between Income and Health.

SOURCE: "Poverty and Deprivation in the United States," a report
by the Conference on Economic Progress, 1965. Data: Department
of Health, Education, and Welfare.

tirement pensions, alimony, gifts, other public
welfare) play in the income of various types
of families according to the total size of income. A special section on the low-income
families in the United States seeks to isolate
the major causes of poverty and finds them to
be as follows: age, disability, inability to obtain employment, part-time employment, being nonwhite, being a self-employed small-
scale businessman or farmer, being unmarried
with children. This volume gives insights of a

type that are badly needed. It analyzes the
status of being poor—how this status developed and why the families cannot rise above
it. The authors also present invaluable materials on the attitudes of the poor and on the
aspirations that they have for their children.
They find that a great preponderance of low-
income families have expectations that their
children will rise to heights that will place
them well above the poverty line. They also
inventory the attitudes of the general public

PERCENT OF VARIOUS INCOME GROUPS LIVING IN SUBSTANDARD HOUSING

Percent of various income groups[1]
living in substandard rented units

Percent of various income groups[1]
living in substandard owned units
(Owner-occupied)

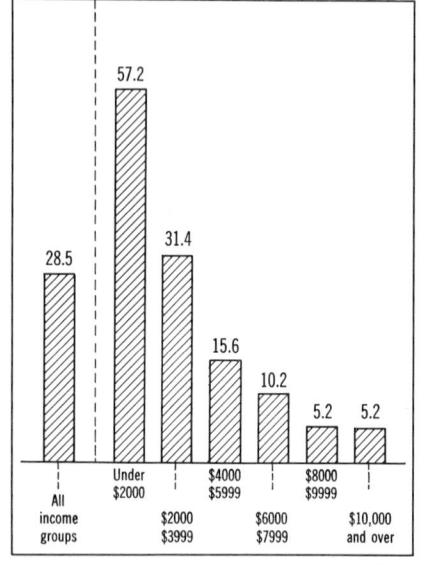
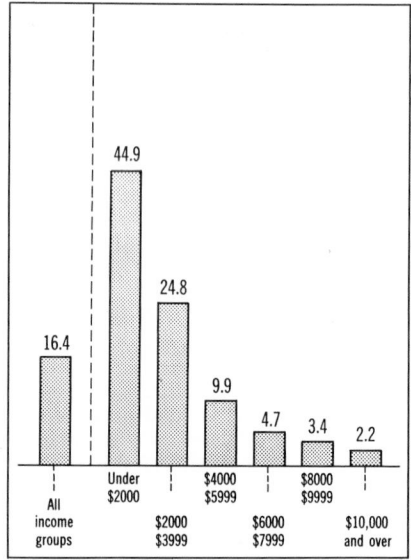

PERCENT OF SUBSTANDARD HOUSING OCCUPIED BY VARIOUS INCOME GROUPS

All substandard rented units
shown by income of renter[1]

All substandard owned units
shown by income of owner[1]
(Owner-occupied)

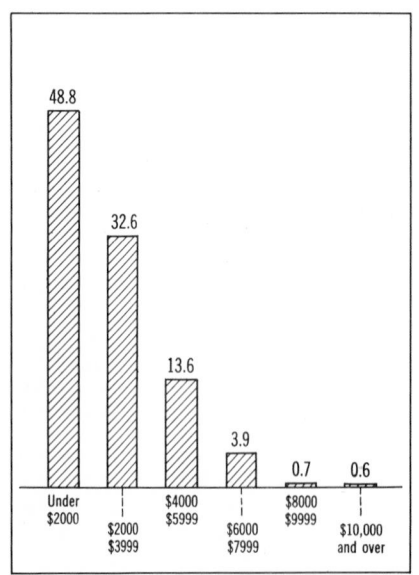
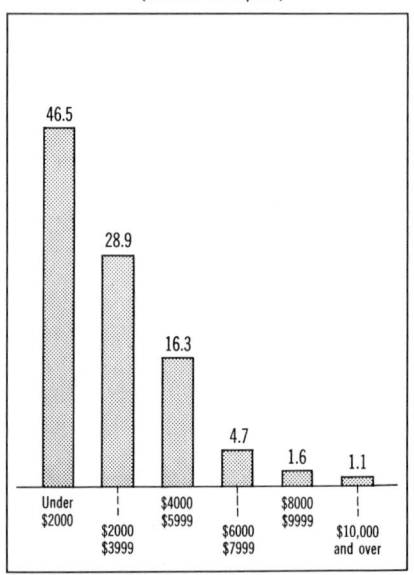

[1] Income shown is total money income before taxes, of occupying family or individual.

Figure 13-7   Relationships between Income and Housing Quality.

SOURCE: U. S. Bureau of Census, National Housing Inventory, 1956.

toward the amelioration of poverty through welfare programs and find widespread public approval for poverty eradication.

Another recent study, *Characteristics of the Low Income Population,* prepared by the special Federal Subcommittee on Low-Income Families, find that the "hard core" of poverty in the United States contains two groups that cannot easily be aided by programs of education and improved employment opportunities.[12] These are (1) the family with a female head who has school-age children to care for and (2) the family where the head is elderly. The first of these has been rather fully discussed in Chapter 12. The present status of the second group, the aged, has been well summarized by Leonore A. Epstein. Writing in the *Social Security Bulletin,* she reports:[13]

"In the 10-year period between June, 1948 to June, 1958, while the aged population increased by 3.6 million, the number receiving benefits under social insurance and related programs jumped by more than 8 million. The number estimated to be without money or to have income solely from sources other than employment, social insurance or assistance, declined almost 2 million. The 50 percent increase in the proportion having some income from employment or social insurance represents a remarkable gain in economic security for one decade" (p. 3).

Although substantial improvement has occurred in the size of incomes that older people receive, it still tend to be very small. Epstein estimates that not less than 40 percent of the aggregate income of all aged persons in 1958 was derived from social insurance, public assistance, and other transfer payments. She concludes that "there can be no question as to the importance of these programs to the welfare of the aged. At the same time it is clear that the public income maintenance programs play a more significant role in terms of the

number of persons for whom they provide a regular source of income than in terms of the amount they contribute to the total income of the aged" (p. 11).

In a second article, "Living Arrangements and Income of the Aged," [14] Epstein finds that elderly people who are not married (single, widowed, or divorced) tend to live alone in a higher percentage of cases when they have a higher income than when they are poorer. Thus she found that among men receiving less than $1000, 47 percent were living alone, whereas 58 percent who received $3000 were living alone. For women the corresponding percentages were 39 and 62 percent. She also found that this tendency toward living alone of the elderly couples increased remarkably between 1952 and 1960. For example, whereas 41 percent of nonmarried women were living alone or with nonrelatives in 1952, 47 were living alone or with nonrelatives in 1960. She concludes: "In terms of purchasing power the median income more than doubled from 1951 to 1959 for nonmarried women, increased two-thirds for couples, and advanced more than 50 percent for nonmarried men" (p. 6).

The situation of low-income elderly Negroes has been clearly portrayed by Orshansky.[15]

"Thanks to Old Age Survivors and Disability insurance and other public programs that help support so many persons aged 65 or more, the Negro in his old age may find his income more closely approximating that of his white fellow American than often was the case during his working years.

"Public programs are administered without respect to race and, though limited in what they pay, are relatively more generous to the aged whose previous earnings were lowest or whose current need is greatest. In contrast, earned income of young families is very imbalanced between white and nonwhite, nor is there yet adequate public provision for young families who may be in need — not even to the limited extent that there is for the aged. Ac-

[12] Federal Subcommittee on Low-Income Families, *Characteristics of the Low Income Population* (Washington, D. C. Government Printing Office, 1965).

[13] Leonore A. Epstein, "Money Income of Aged Persons: A Ten Year Review," *Social Security Bulletin,* June 1959.

[14] Leonore A. Epstein, "Living Arrangements and Income of the Aged, 1959," *Social Security Bulletin,* **26** (September 1953), 3–8.

[15] Mollie Orshansky, "The Aged Negro and his Income," *Social Security Bulletin,* February 1964.

cordingly, the Negro family, though larger than the white, generally must get along on little better than half as much income. The Negro man earns little more than half that of the employed white worker, even when both work full time. Among those aged 65 or older, however, the nonwhite couples average two-thirds as much income as do the white couples and nonmarried nonwhite persons about three-fourths the income of white persons. By and large, racial differences in income are less among aged persons drawing Old-Age, Survivors, and Disability insurance benefits than among those not benefiting from this income-support program.

"To be sure, the Negro in old age does not lose the underprivileged economic status of his younger years: Simply because he fares somewhat better, he does not fare well. It is perhaps not so much that his lot improves as that the income of the generally more fortunate drops proportionately more in retirement than does his own." (p. 3)

Formerly, economists and the public at large regarded the phenomenon of poverty as inevitable and even good and necessary. By providing large quantities of cheap docile labor, it facilitated production at low cost and accumulation of profits and capital for expansion, and kept down worker discontent. As tangible evidence of what happens to those who do not work, it served as a stimulus and motivating force. This philosophy is dying out today. In its place we find the philosophy that the economic welfare of a society is influenced by the level of productivity of its workers and that economic growth is retarded by having large masses of workers of low productivity. Chronic unemployment or underemployment represents a loss in productivity and a burden that the economy must carry without profit. Therefore, extraordinary efforts are made to transform submarginal workers into more productive members of the community. The social processes that produce these workers—whether they be the second-rate school systems of the rural South or of the big-city slums, the prejudice and discrimination of a dominant white racial group, or a culture of hopelessness and low level of initiative and aspiration engendered by having been born and reared in a state of destitution—must be altered if the goal of poverty reduction is to be achieved. This calls for intervention by social scientists of many disciplines. The practitioners of these disciplines, no less than the economists, are continuously being surprised at how fundamentally and yet rapidly the austere, calculating discipline of economics is being warmed by radiations from sociology, psychology, political science, geography, and demography. As the principles of these disciplines penetrate, the generalizations that economists make about income, and especially about income distribution and poverty, will become progressively less precise and more valid.

13.13. Adjustment of Income for Family Size and Composition

Statistics on income are often criticized because they do not take into account the number and type of persons who must be supported from the income. Thus two men each earning $5000 per year are in very different economic statuses if one is a bachelor with no dependents and the other must support five children and care for an elderly parent who is chronically ill. Experts on consumer statistics have devised systems for adjusting income statistics to take into account these factors. In preparing a special report on *Sources and Structure of Family Income*, based on the 1960 census, the U. S. Bureau of the Census undertook to adjust its statistics. Table 13-11 provides data on family income by characteristics of the head and of the family. The procedure by which the regular family income data were adjusted is described by the Census Bureau as follows:

"Indices that measure the relative income required by families of different size and composition to maintain the same level of material well-being constitute an important tool in studies of family living. For example, other things being equal, a four-person family will require a larger amount of income to achieve a given level of well-being than a two-person family, and a four-person family with teenage children will require somewhat more income than a four-person family with younger children. A number of indices that measure the relative income required by families of different size and age to maintain equal levels of living are available. The most extensive index of this type is the scale of equivalent income for urban families prepared by the Bureau of Labor Statistics of the Department of Labor, which is based on data obtained in the BLS survey of Consumer Expenditures in 1950. This scale has been adapted for use in adjusting the income of urban families tabulated by selected family characteristics in . . . this report.

". . . Each family's income was divided by the appropriate factor in Table A, to obtain its adjusted income. The factors shown are the ratios of the average amount of income required for equivalent levels of living by a family of the specified type to the average amount required by a four-person family with its head 35 to 54 years of age.

"Table A shows, for example, that on the average a two-person family with head under 35 years of age requires 59 percent of the income of the standard family to purchase the same level of material well-being. It follows from this that an income of $3,000 for the younger two-person family is equivalent to an income of $5,085 for the older four-person family. Thus, both types of family are included in the same adjusted income class ($5,000 to $5,999) . . . ."[16]

Table 13-11 provides adjusted statistics for all families and Table 11-13B provides identical data for nonwhite families, subdivided according to the type of family and characteristics of the family head. If we accept $3000 as the cutting point for poverty and $10,000 as the cutting point for affluence, we can obtain a much clearer picture of the "true" prevalence of rags and riches in the nation. According to these data, one family in 9 is definitely poor, and only slightly more than one fourth are affluent. Poverty is shown again to be concentrated in families of the following types:

large families—six persons or more
families with elderly heads
families where the head has low educational attainment—8 years or less
families where the head is a laborer
families where there is no earner
families where the male head is not married
families where the head is a female
families where the head is Negro

However, if the statistics of Table 13-11 are compared with the unadjusted family income data from which they are derived, it is found that *adjustment brightens the picture somewhat*. For most categories, the adjustment shows a smaller fraction of families living in poverty than the unadjusted data imply. Whereas the unadjusted statistics report 5.2 million families in urban areas living in poverty, the adjusted statistics report 3.8 million such families, out of a total of 31.9 million families. However, the adjustment reveals that families with four or more members are definitely worse off financially than the size of the income they receive would indicate. The student who is interested in studying more closely the differences between the adjusted and unadjusted income figures should consult Table 4 of the source publication.

Throughout this chapter the nonwhite population has been mentioned only in the context of poverty. Table 13-11 offers an opportunity

[16] U.S. Bureau of Census. *Sources and Structure of Family Income:* 1960 Census of the U.S.

Table A   Adjustment Factors for Urban Family Income

Size of family	Age of head (years)			
	Under 35	35 to 54	55 to 64	65 and over
2 persons	0.59	0.62	0.63	0.56
3 persons	0.68	0.85	0.87	0.78
4 persons	0.82	1.00	1.08	0.97
5 persons	1.02	1.15	1.25	1.11
6 persons or more	1.18	1.31	1.40	1.20

Table 13-11A   Family Income in 1959 of All Families Adjusted for Family Size and Age of Head, for Urban Areas: 1960

Type of family	Total	Under $3000	$3000–$5999	$6000–$9999	$10000+	Median
All families...........................	100	11.9	26.2	33.5	28.5	$7258
Husband-wife families..................	100	8.9	26.3	34.9	29.8	7493
Size of family:						
2 persons........................	100	10.7	18.6	27.2	43.4	9052
3 persons........................	100	6.4	19.8	39.0	34.8	8372
4 persons........................	100	5.3	25.6	45.3	23.8	7414
5 persons........................	100	8.2	38.3	36.1	17.4	6183
6 persons or more...............	100	16.0	45.6	27.6	10.7	5218
Age of head:						
Under 25 years..................	100	13.7	33.6	35.1	17.6	6247
25-34..........................	100	6.8	28.2	39.5	25.5	7266
35-54..........................	100	6.5	26.0	36.3	31.2	7721
55-64..........................	100	8.8	18.3	32.5	40.5	8791
65 and over....................	100	20.6	30.9	23.9	24.6	5835
Years of school completed by head:						
Elementary: Less than eight years.	100	21.5	34.5	28.3	15.6	5425
8 years..............	100	10.7	30.3	34.6	24.4	6923
High school:1-3 years............	100	7.6	29.7	36.7	26.0	7192
4 years..............	100	4.6	25.6	39.6	30.2	7725
College: 1-3 years............	100	4.3	19.0	36.5	40.2	8809
4 years or more.......	100	2.8	11.0	31.2	55.0	10754
Earner status and occupational group of head:						
Head an earner.................	100	6.2	25.5	36.6	31.7	7777
Professional, managerial and kindred, except farm............	100	2.7	14.0	32.6	50.7	10109
Salaried........................	100	1.8	12.9	35.5	49.9	9984
Self employed...................	100	5.3	17.2	24.5	53.1	10616
Clerical, sales and kindred......	100	3.2	23.1	38.4	35.2	8257
Carftsmen, operatives and kindred.	100	6.0	28.9	40.3	24.8	7304
Service workers, including private household..............	100	11.1	35.9	34.8	18.2	6288
Laborers, except mine............	100	20.0	38.6	29.2	12.2	5294
Head worked 50-52 weeks..........	100	3.5	23.0	38.1	35.3	8273
Head not an earner.............	100	37.3	34.5	17.9	10.3	3847
Number of earners in family:						
None............................	100	46.9	35.7	10.6	6.8	3179
One.............................	100	9.0	32.0	36.2	22.8	6819
Two or more.....................	100	4.3	19.4	36.5	39.7	8831
Other male head......................	100	13.7	21.6	30.3	34.3	7899
Size of family:						
2 persons........................	100	13.6	18.5	30.2	37.7	8436
3 persons........................	100	11.9	21.8	31.4	34.9	8331
4 persons........................	100	12.9	27.1	31.2	28.8	7096
5 persons........................	100	15.5	31.7	29.7	23.1	6302
6 persons or more...............	100	23.1	34.3	25.2	17.4	5282
Age of head:						
Under 25 years..................	100	23.8	28.1	27.1	21.0	5820
25-34..........................	100	10.2	19.3	31.2	39.3	8614
35-54..........................	100	11.1	21.0	33.2	34.7	8157
55-64..........................	100	13.5	20.7	29.9	35.9	8056
65 years and over...............	100	18.0	23.5	26.2	32.3	7252
Earner status and occupational group of head:						
Head an earner.................	100	8.2	20.4	32.6	38.8	8610
Professional, managerial and kindred, except farm............	100	3.5	10.7	24.4	61.4	11567
Salaried........................	100	2.6	9.0	25.3	63.1	11633
Self-employed...................	100	6.1	15.3	21.8	56.8	11294
Clerical, sales and kindred.......	100	4.2	16.5	35.7	43.6	9295
Craftsmen, operatives, and kindred	100	6.9	21.5	36.8	34.9	8350
Service, including private household......................	100	16.7	30.4	31.2	21.7	6325
Laborers, except mine............	100	19.6	30.9	30.5	19.0	5950
Head worked 50-52 weeks..........	100	3.9	17.1	34.0	45.1	9442

Table 13-11A   (Continued)

Type of family	Total	Under $3000	$3000–$5999	$6000–$9999	$10000+	Median
Head not an earner..............	100	31.0	25.7	22.9	20.3	5116
Number of earners in family:						
None..........................	100	59.4	26.7	8.3	5.6	2478
One...........................	100	12.6	26.3	36.0	25.1	7190
Two or more...................	100	5.4	15.6	28.8	50.2	10030
Female Head	100	36.4	26.4	22.0	15.3	4441
Size of family:						
2 persons.....................	100	27.5	25.9	26.7	19.9	5591
3 persons.....................	100	35.3	28.9	21.3	14.5	4443
4 persons.....................	100	45.7	27.5	17.0	9.8	3384
5 persons.....................	100	56.3	23.9	12.9	6.9	2604
6 or more.....................	100	62.8	22.4	10.2	4.5	2266
Age of head:						
Under 25......................	100	67.2	20.1	8.6	4.0	1953
25–34.........................	100	57.9	24.5	12.9	4.7	2521
35–54.........................	100	35.7	29.5	22.6	12.2	4347
55–64.........................	100	24.4	25.1	27.3	23.2	6063
65 years and over.............	100	26.2	24.0	25.3	24.6	5975
Earner status and occupational group of head:						
Head and earner...............	100	36.4	37.2	19.4	6.9	3929
Professional, managerial and kindred, except farm.............	100	14.5	36.3	32.8	16.3	5934
Salaried......................	100	12.5	37.2	34.6	15.7	6029
Self employed.................	100	25.9	31.7	22.4	20.0	5223
Clerical, sales, and kindred.......	100	22.6	46.7	23.1	7.6	4947
Craftsmen, operatives, and kindred.	100	35.9	40.0	18.9	5.2	3824
Service, including private household.....................	100	61.7	26.2	9.6	2.5	2386
Laborers, except mine.............	100	62.8	25.8	8.0	3.4	2255
Head worked 50–52 weeks...........	100	24.0	43.9	23.7	8.5	4625
Head not an earner.............	100	57.6	23.9	12.2	6.3	2445
Number of earner in family:						
None..........................	100	87.2	9.3	2.1	1.3	1376
One...........................	100	47.1	39.6	10.9	2.4	3174
Two or more...................	100	17.9	34.2	32.3	15.7	5819

Source: U.S. Census of Population.   Source and Structure of Family Income.   Table 4.

to look at the other side of the picture: by migrating to cities Negroes have made very substantial economic progress. By 1950 nearly 40 percent of the families were above the $5000 mark (adjusted), which would provide a minimum comfortable level of living. This is a status they could never have attained as sharecroppers in rural areas. Fully 10 percent had passed into the "affluent" or "wealthy" class. Thus, while we are pointing out the social and economic problems of the Negro, we should never forget that in comparison with where he stood only a few decades ago, he has made tremendous progress and is continuing to do so.

13.14.   Income by Occupation and Education

In earlier sections it was clearly demonstrated that income varies by occupation and also by the educational attainment of the individual. The question has often arisen concerning the manner in which these three variables are interrelated. Does difference in income between occupations disappear when education is held constant? Do differences in income between educational levels disappear when occupation is held constant? Table 13-12 provides information for males concerning this topic. This table is of fundamental importance, for it provides the foundation which the next chapter is built. Several important points may be gleaned from an analysis of these data:

1. Income varies according to educational attainment within each of the occupational categories. Therefore, educational attainment influences income within each occupation.

Table 13-11B   Family Income in 1959 of Nonwhite Families, Adjusted for Family Size and Age of Head, for Urban Areas; 1960

Type of family	Total	Under 3000	3000-5999	6000-9999	10000+	Median
All families..........................	100	35.1	34.8	20.7	9.4	$4101
Husband-wife families..................	100	26.8	38.5	23.8	10.9	4638
Size of family:						
2 persons.........................	100	22.6	29.7	29.6	18.1	5755
3 persons.........................	100	20.3	37.0	28.5	14.2	5394
4 persons.........................	100	20.9	42.1	27.8	9.3	4968
5 persons.........................	100	29.5	46.0	18.7	5.8	4136
6 persons or more.................	100	40.0	44.0	12.7	3.3	3483
Age of head:						
Under 25 years....................	100	35.3	41.8	17.2	5.7	3855
25-34.............................	100	24.1	40.4	23.5	12.0	4754
35-54.............................	100	23.3	39.5	25.4	11.8	4872
55-64.............................	100	29.1	34.4	26.0	10.4	4660
65 and over......................	100	44.2	31.7	16.3	7.8	3407
Years of school completed by head:						
Elementary: Less than eight years.	100	37.1	38.8	18.7	5.4	3785
8 years..............	100	25.5	40.8	24.3	9.5	4653
High school:1-3 years.............	100	23.5	41.1	24.9	10.5	4779
4 years..............	100	16.1	39.2	29.6	15.1	5566
College: 1-3 years.............	100	12.7	33.0	32.4	21.8	6456
4 years or more.......	100	7.0	19.9	32.1	41.0	8854
Earner status and occupational group of head:						
Head an earner.................	100	22.6	40.0	25.5	11.9	4894
Professional, managerial and kindred, except farm............	100	11.4	25.1	30.1	33.3	7637
Salaried........................	100	8.6	23.7	32.7	35.0	8040
Self employed....................	100	18.5	28.6	23.8	29.1	6411
Clerical, sales and kindred......	100	10.1	35.8	33.0	21.1	6428
Carftsmen, operatives and kindred.	100	21.0	41.4	26.8	10.8	4958
Service workers, including private household...............	100	25.4	42.8	23.9	8.0	4555
Laborers, except mine............	100	32.8	41.8	19.6	5.8	3984
Head worked 50-52 weeks...........	100	15.9	41.2	28.6	14.3	5405
Head not an earner...............	100	65.0	24.7	7.8	2.5	2274
Number of earners in family:						
None.............................	100	80.4	16.9	2.0	0.6	1740
One..............................	100	33.3	45.1	18.0	3.6	3878
Two or more......................	100	17.2	35.6	30.0	17.2	5756
Other male head:.....................	100	29.6	33.0	23.6	13.6	4703
Size of family:						
2 persons.........................	100	26.9	28.2	28.1	16.8	5438
3 persons.........................	100	27.2	35.3	23.8	13.7	4877
4 persons.........................	100	31.9	36.6	21.1	10.3	4376
5 persons.........................	100	33.6	38.6	16.7	11.0	4169
6 persons or more.................	100	39.5	40.0	13.8	6.8	3616
Age of head:						
Under 25 years....................	100	35.0	32.5	19.8	12.8	4289
25-34.............................	100	23.2	30.0	25.6	21.2	5668
35-54.............................	100	26.8	34.8	26.0	12.4	4912
55-64.............................	100	32.5	32.3	22.7	12.5	4456
65 years and over................	100	38.5	32.9	18.1	10.6	3857
Earner status and occupational group of head:						
Head an earner.................	100	21.6	34.8	27.4	16.2	5414
Professional, managerial and kindred, except farm............	100	11.2	25.7	27.4	25.7	7959
Salaried........................	100	8.6	24.8	30.0	36.6	8316
Self-employed....................	100	17.9	28.1	20.7	33.3	6695
Clerical, sales and kindred.......	100	8.3	27.0	27.1	27.6	7599
Craftsmen, operatives, and kindred.	100	18.4	35.2	30.1	16.3	5657
Service, including private household....................	100	29.0	37.0	23.5	10.5	4619
Laborers, except mine............	100	29.0	38.9	22.7	9.4	4539
Head worked 50-52 weeks..........	100	13.5	35.0	31.4	20.1	6170
Head not an earner............	100	57.4	27.2	10.7	4.8	2564

Type of family	Total	Under 3000	3000-5999	6000-9999	10000+	Median
Number of earners in family:						
None............................	100	86.4	11.2	2.0	0.3	1492
One.............................	100	33.7	40.8	20.9	4.6	4041
Two or more.....................	100	14.6	30.7	30.4	24.2	6546
Female Head:.....................	100	63.8	22.7	10.1	3.4	2243
Size of family:						
2 persons.......................	100	53.5	26.9	14.3	5.3	2790
3 persons.......................	100	60.4	25.1	10.8	3.7	2437
4 persons.......................	100	68.4	20.6	8.2	2.8	2091
5 persons.......................	100	74.9	17.4	6.0	1.6	1768
6 persons or more...............	100	75.0	17.7	5.9	1.5	1780
Age of head:						
Under 25........................	100	80.5	13.6	4.4	1.5	1628
25-34...........................	100	73.4	18.4	6.6	1.6	1900
35-54...........................	100	60.3	25.0	11.1	3.7	2412
55-64...........................	100	55.1	25.8	14.2	4.9	2667
65 and over.....................	100	56.2	25.5	12.5	5.8	2664
Earner status and occupational group of head:						
Head and earner................	100	55.0	27.5	13.0	4.5	2704
Professional, managerial and kindred, except farm............	100	17.7	34.1	30.3	17.9	5851
Salaried........................	100	15.3	34.9	31.6	18.3	5990
Self employed...................	100	34.5	29.0	21.7	14.9	4375
Clerical, sales and kindred......	100	26.4	35.8	26.6	11.2	4900
Craftsmen, operatives, and kindred	100	41.7	36.8	16.4	5.1	3499
Service, including private household.......................	100	65.4	23.9	8.6	2.1	2168
Laborers, except mine...........	100	71.4	19.8	6.5	2.3	1815
Head worked 50-52 weeks.........	100	44.4	33.1	16.7	5.9	3404
Head not an earner.............	100	76.8	15.6	5.8	1.8	1763
Number of earner in family:						
None............................	100	93.1	6.1	0.6	0.2	1385
One.............................	100	66.0	25.2	7.4	1.4	2135
Two or more.....................	100	36.9	32.8	21.5	8.9	4279

Source: Source and Structure of Family Income: Table 4.

2. Similarly, occupation influences income independently of education. Persons with a college degree earn twice as much income if they are managers or officials than if they are farmers. Education does not do a great deal to improve income within the ranks of clerical workers, operatives, service workers, or laborers. These appear to be occupations where education beyond a certain minimal point is not of much additional benefit to the holder. In contrast, professional, managerial, and craft workers appear to benefit incomewise with each increment in education.

3. In all of the occupational groups, having less than a grammar school education leads to unusually low income; the economy has become so advanced technologically that persons with less than a grammar school education are marginal workers even as unskilled laborers.

4. There is a great deal of variation in receipt of income, even when both education and occupation are held constant. It might have been expected that when these two variables are both controlled simultaneously, there would be a distinct tendency for all income recipients to fall into a very narrow range of income classes. In no case does this happen, although there are marked reductions in the variation of income distribution when the data are cross-tabulated in this fashion. There are very few professional persons with less than 8 years of elementary education who are earning $15,000 or more, and there are comparatively few managers or proprietors who have a college education who earned less than $3000 per year. Nevertheless, a few instances of these combinations are found, and much more numerous cases of deviation from

Table 13-12   Occupation by Education by Income for Males

Occupation by educational attainment	Median income (dollars)	Percent distribution by income of persons with income in 1959										
		0 to 999	1,000 to 1,999	2,000 to 2,999	3,000 to 3,999	4,000 to 4,999	5,000 to 5,999	6,000 to 6,999	7,000 to 7,999	8,000 to 9,999	10,000 to 14,999	15,000 and over
Total, experienced labor force.......	147149	100.0	100.0	100.0	100.0	100.0	100.0	100.0	100.0	100.0	100.0	100.0
Professional, technical, and kindred wkrs												
Less than 8 years of elementary school.	4284	10.7	10.4	12.0	13.0	13.8	13.2	9.2	5.8	5.7	4.4	1.9
Elementary school, 8 years............	5194	5.9	6.6	7.9	12.1	14.7	14.8	12.8	8.3	8.7	6.1	2.2
High school: 1 to 3 years............	5652	7.3	5.0	6.2	8.9	12.5	15.5	14.3	10.5	10.6	6.7	2.5
High school: 4 years................	6073	2.7	3.6	4.7	8.2	12.6	17.0	16.6	11.9	12.6	7.7	2.5
College: 1 to 3 years............	6108	5.2	6.1	5.5	7.2	10.6	13.8	14.1	11.4	12.9	9.4	3.7
College: 4 years or more..........	7338	2.1	4.1	3.9	5.3	8.2	11.0	11.7	10.6	15.1	16.1	11.8
Farmers and farm managers												
Less than 8 years of elementary school.	1287	43.0	24.5	12.9	7.2	4.4	2.7	1.5	0.9	1.2	1.0	0.6
Elementary school, 8 years............	2186	24.1	22.7	17.5	12.0	8.5	5.2	2.9	1.7	2.1	2.1	1.2
High school: 1 to 3 years............	2460	23.1	19.3	16.5	13.2	8.5	5.8	3.5	2.1	2.7	3.3	1.4
High school: 4 years................	3053	14.6	16.4	18.1	15.9	10.6	7.3	4.5	2.6	3.5	4.0	2.5
College: 1 to 3 years............	3507	14.9	14.4	13.6	14.1	11.1	8.5	5.3	3.1	4.5	5.9	4.5
College: 4 years or more..........	4142	12.5	11.9	11.5	12.5	11.2	9.3	6.7	4.7	5.1	6.8	7.7
Managers, officials and proprietors, except farm												
Less than 8 years of elementary school.	4266	9.9	11.7	12.1	13.2	11.6	11.4	7.4	4.9	6.3	6.2	5.2
Elementary school, 8 years............	5393	5.4	6.9	8.0	11.5	13.0	13.4	9.8	7.7	8.9	8.7	6.8
High school: 1 to 3 years............	5951	3.4	4.3	6.2	9.6	12.6	14.5	11.5	8.9	10.5	10.6	7.7
High school: 4 years................	6582	1.9	2.9	4.0	7.6	11.1	15.0	12.9	10.5	12.5	12.6	9.0
College: 1 to 3 years............	7393	2.0	3.0	3.3	5.6	8.5	11.9	11.7	10.2	13.4	16.5	13.9
College: 4 years or more..........	9297	1.3	2.3	2.3	3.1	4.8	8.3	9.4	9.3	14.2	21.8	23.2
Clerical and kindred workers												
Less than 8 years of elementary school.	4135	7.8	8.1	12.7	18.2	23.1	18.4	6.5	2.9	1.3	0.7	0.2
Elementary school, 8 years............	4601	6.5	5.9	8.8	15.3	22.5	23.8	9.4	4.0	2.5	1.1	0.2
High school: 1 to 3 years............	4531	12.7	6.8	7.6	12.6	19.5	22.7	9.5	4.4	2.8	1.2	0.3
High school: 4 years................	4913	4.7	5.7	7.5	13.2	20.7	25.5	11.7	5.6	3.7	1.4	0.4
College: 1 to 3 years............	4831	7.6	8.6	7.5	11.7	17.5	21.9	11.6	5.9	4.5	2.5	0.7
College: 4 years or more..........	5660	3.6	5.2	5.7	7.9	14.1	20.3	14.8	9.7	9.3	7.1	2.2
Sales workers												
Less than 8 years of elementary school.	2789	26.3	13.4	13.1	13.7	11.0	7.9	4.6	2.7	3.0	2.8	1.6
Elementary school, 8 years............	3537	25.2	8.3	9.6	12.8	12.8	10.7	6.5	4.0	3.9	3.9	2.3
High school: 1 to 3 years............	3838	26.4	7.5	7.1	10.6	11.9	11.8	7.7	4.9	5.0	4.4	2.5
High school: 4 years................	5316	5.0	6.0	7.2	11.9	14.9	16.0	11.7	7.9	8.2	7.5	3.9
College: 1 to 3 years............	5799	5.9	7.1	6.5	8.5	11.4	13.3	11.6	8.0	9.8	10.7	6.4
College: 4 years or more..........	7033	2.8	3.7	4.0	5.6	8.3	12.5	13.5	11.1	12.9	15.5	10.9

what one might consider a strict occupation-income determination of income abound. Thus *the contention that income is distributed strictly according to the market worth of the individual and his qualifications to participate in a modern technologically advanced society is incorrect.* Conversely, educators cannot claim that merely graduating from college qualifies one to receive a salary of $10,000, nor does employment at a job that the census lists as "professional" assure one of economic comfort. Evidently, many high school and college graduates are very poorly educated, and probably many professional and managerial employees are incompetent, inefficient, and really without specialized abilities—and are paid accordingly by their employers. A truly refined analysis of the relationship should shift to a more refined breakdown of occupations. This is done in the next chapter.

CONCLUSION

The economic well-being of the population conditions every aspect of demography, as it does all other aspects of social life. In later chapters we shall demonstrate that the demographic processes—mortality, fertility, nuptiality, and migration—vary according to economic status, just as do the various compositional traits considered here. As the best single measure of economic well-being, statistics on income are of fundamental importance in the study of population composition. They are needed to measure the distribution of income and differential income distribution according to age, sex, race, educational attainment, occupation, and other characteristics. If income data are not obtainable from a national census, they should be obtained by special sample surveys. When comparable income data are available for two or more dates, it becomes possible to trace changes in economic status and changes in income differentials.

The phenomena of poverty and of unusual wealth—and of the gap between these extremes—are currently of great interest in many parts of the world. Data for the United States show that despite the fact that it has the highest

Table 13-12 (Continued)

Occupation by educational attainment	Median income (dollars)	Percent distribution by income of persons with income in 1959										
		0 to 999	1,000 to 1,999	2,000 to 2,999	3,000 to 3,999	4,000 to 4,999	5,000 to 5,999	6,000 to 6,999	7,000 to 7,999	8,000 to 9,999	10,000 to 14,999	15,000 and over
Total, experienced labor force........	117241	100.0	100.0	100.0	100.0	100.0	100.0	100.0	100.0	100.0	100.0	100.0
Craftsmen, foremen and kindred workers												
Less than 8 years of elementary school.	4253	7.7	9.1	12.3	16.3	18.1	16.9	9.7	5.0	3.5	1.1	0.3
Elementary school, 8 years............	5026	4.3	5.7	8.0	13.2	18.3	20.4	13.9	7.9	6.1	1.9	0.3
High school: 1 to 3 years............	5314	4.5	4.7	6.7	11.3	16.2	20.5	15.9	9.8	7.5	2.4	0.4
High school: 4 years................	5640	2.5	3.7	5.5	10.1	15.2	20.5	18.1	11.6	9.3	3.1	0.5
College: 1 to 3 years............	5827	4.0	4.9	5.5	8.5	12.6	17.5	17.1	12.3	11.0	5.4	1.1
College: 4 years or more.........	7241	2.3	3.3	4.1	5.5	7.9	11.1	13.0	11.8	·18.0	17.9	5.1
Operatives and kindred workers												
Less than 8 years of elementary school.	3643	9.2	11.5	17.2	18.9	18.4	13.9	6.3	2.7	1.5	0.4	0.1
Elementary school, 8 years............	4419	5.8	7.0	11.4	16.9	21.5	19.5	10.0	4.4	2.6	0.8	0.3
High school: 1 to 3 years............	4388	10.2	7.3	10.5	14.9	18.5	18.7	10.9	5.0	3.0	0.9	0.3
High school: 4 years................	4699	5.1	6.9	9.9	14.7	19.1	20.3	12.4	6.3	3.7	1.2	0.3
College: 1 to 3 years............	4545	8.6	10.0	10.3	12.3	16.1	17.4	12.2	6.6	4.2	1.7	0.5
College: 4 years or more.........	5102	5.8	7.9	8.5	11.3	14.8	16.9	13.4	8.1	7.0	4.3	2.0
Private household workers												
Less than 8 years of elementary school.	1033	49.2	23.7	15.9	7.7	2.2	0.7	0.2	....	0.2	0.2	....
Elementary school, 8 years............	1272	44.9	18.6	18.7	11.6	4.5	1.0	0.3	....	0.2	0.2	....
High school: 1 to 3 years............	792	63.1	12.9	10.4	8.2	3.1	1.5	0.6	0.1	0.1	....	....
High school: 4 years................	1689	33.6	23.8	17.9	11.7	5.0	4.5	2.1	0.6	....	0.3	0.6
College: 1 to 3 years............	1884	29.2	23.5	17.9	12.3	7.9	2.7	3.6	....	....	0.9	....
College: 4 years or more.........		13.4	30.3	16.5	10.3	3.3	....	....	3.3	3.3	9.8	9.8
Service workers, except private household												
Less than 8 years of elementary school.	2746	15.4	17.7	22.7	20.9	13.5	5.8	2.1	0.8	0.6	0.4	0.2
Elementary school: 8 years............	3330	13.5	12.6	16.9	21.3	18.0	10.0	4.1	1.6	1.3	0.5	0.2
High school: 1 to 3 years............	3222	22.8	10.7	12.9	16.5	15.4	11.6	5.7	2.1	1.4	0.7	0.2
High school: 4 years................	4216	9.4	8.8	11.6	16.0	19.3	17.3	9.7	4.0	2.4	1.1	0.3
College: 1 to 3 years............	3499	18.0	15.4	10.5	12.2	13.3	12.7	9.1	4.0	3.1	1.4	0.3
College: 4 years or more.........	4048	11.6	13.3	12.2	12.3	11.5	10.7	9.2	6.6	5.9	5.9	0.8
Farm laborers and foremen												
Less than 8 years of elementary school.	973	51.4	26.6	13.3	5.7	1.8	0.6	0.3	0.1	0.1	0.1	0.0
Elementary school, 8 years............	1369	41.6	22.9	17.5	10.3	4.4	1.9	0.7	0.2	0.3	0.2	0.1
High school: 1 to 3 years............	841	59.5	14.9	11.0	7.9	3.4	1.6	0.8	0.4	0.2	0.2	0.2
High school: 4 years................	1885	30.9	21.5	18.9	14.2	6.5	3.8	1.7	0.7	0.7	0.5	0.3
College: 1 to 3 years............	1828	31.6	22.3	14.4	12.3	7.0	4.8	3.0	1.5	1.1	1.4	0.5
College: 4 years or more.........	3523	16.3	14.9	11.2	14.5	11.3	11.0	9.3	4.6	2.3	3.5	1.1
Laborers, except farm and mine												
Less than 8 years of elementary school.	2615	20.2	17.8	19.5	17.5	14.2	7.0	2.3	0.8	0.5	0.2	0.1
Elementary school, 8 years............	3370	16.1	11.9	15.2	18.5	18.9	11.7	4.4	1.7	1.0	0.4	0.2
High school: 1 to 3 years............	2687	29.0	12.4	12.6	14.2	14.9	9.8	4.0	1.6	1.0	0.4	0.2
High school: 4 years................	3607	13.3	12.3	14.1	17.1	19.0	13.3	5.9	2.5	1.6	0.7	0.2
College: 1 to 3 years............	2890	19.9	18.6	12.9	13.6	13.6	10.5	5.1	2.6	1.6	0.8	0.6
College: 4 years or more.........	3825	13.3	14.6	11.3	13.1	16.5	12.1	5.9	3.6	4.3	3.1	2.2

per capita income, a substantial fraction (one person in seven) of United States population are poverty-ridden and a smaller fraction (but nevertheless a very large number of people) are even now living at the level of destitution. This unhappy situation is a chronic condition over large portions of Asia, Latin America, and Africa. Progress toward improving the economic status of people is apparently being made in almost all nations of the world. If population growth rates in these nations were lower, this progress would undoubtedly be faster.

QUESTIONS AND EXERCISES

1. We saw that adjusting family income data for size of family and age of head had the effect of reducing the number and proportion of families reported to be in the poverty class and increasing the number and proportion at higher income levels. Go to the source from which these data were taken and develop an explanation of why and how this is the effect that the adjustment has. Would such adjustment have the same effect in other nations and for other cultures? Under what circumstances would you expect the adjustment to reveal that poverty is even more prevalent than regular statistics for family income indicate? Does this adjustment improve the picture for the non-white population more than for the white, or is the effect about equal? Develop an explanation of why this inequality should exist.

2. Look up the income statistics for detailed occupations. Prepare a list of occupations that appear to offer only poverty-level incomes. Find out as much as you can about the indus-

tries that have these occupations, the kinds of people who hold these occupations, and the reasons why they persist in a modern industrialized society. Is it fair to assert that the practice of having household servants at current wages is a modern form of exploitation of man by man? From the wages paid agricultural workers, would you say that urbanites are exploiting this group?

3. Look up the income statistics for males and females in the detailed occupations. By matching specific occupations in which both males and females commonly participate, try to obtain a more refined measure of sex discrimination in income. Repeat the same procedure for race. Do you get differentials of the same size as appear on the gross level of comparison?

4. Compute the quartile points for income for 1950, 1960, and the most recent sample survey of the Bureau of the Census. Has the range between the lower quartile and the upper quartile diminished or increased? Has it changed as much, per year, since 1960 as it did between 1950 and 1960?

5. Look up the incomes of persons according to marital status, holding age constant. Do never-married men earn as much income as married men? What accounts for the difference? Can you find tabulations in the Census to test your hypothesis?

6. Look up the incomes received by divorced women who are mothers of a child under 18 years of age, separately for the white and nonwhite population. Does obtaining a divorce appear to cause women to sink to a lower livelihood status than they would have if they continued to live with their husbands? How great a role does economic dependency play in keeping marriages intact, especially after children are born to the marriage?

7. There has been a general improvement in family income in the United States in recent years. There has been a much greater participation of married women in the labor force during this time. Can you devise an estimate of what proportion of the improvement of family income has been caused by the increased proportion of families with two earners and what proportion has been caused by a more even distribution of income among income recipients?

8. It has been stated in this chapter that additional schooling causes a smaller increment in income among the nonwhite than among the white population. Conduct a small research study to find out how this takes place. Is it because they are not able to enter occupations that make full use of their education or is it because they get differential pay in a given occupation? By comparing data for 1950 and 1960, can you note any improvement in the income rewards to nonwhite workers for obtaining additional education?

9. Since 1965 there have been a variety of "war on poverty" programs. The goal of these programs is to reduce the percentage of families receiving extremely small incomes. Look up income statistics to find out whether there has been any observable change—especially for the nonwhite population. Read any evaluation studies you can find and write an essay on the subject.

10. A guaranteed minimum annual income has been proposed for the United States. What do you think would be the demographic consequences (impact on birth, death, marriage, migration, socioeconomic composition) of such a program?

BIBLIOGRAPHY

Adams, F. Gerard. "The Size of Individual Incomes: Socio-economic Variables and Chance Variation," *Review of Economics and Statistics*, **40** (4) (December 1958), 390–398.

Batchelder, Alan B. "Decline in the Relative Income of Negro Men," *Quarterly Journal of Economics*, **78** (November 1964), 525–548.

Beresford, John C., and Alice M. Rivlin. "Privacy, Poverty, and Old Age," *Demography*, **3** (1) (1966), 247–258.

Bogue, Donald J. "Income and Population Composition." Chapter 20 in *The Population of the United States*. Glencoe, Ill.: The Free Press, 1959.

Booth, E. J. R. "Interregional Income Differences," *Southern Economic Journal*, **31** (July 1964), 44–51.

Bowman, Mary Jean. "Human Inequalities and

Southern Underdevelopment," *Southern Economic Journal*, **32** (1, Part 2) (July 1965), 73–102.

Brady, Dorothy S. "Research on the Size Distribution of Income," *Studies in Income and Wealth*, Vol. 13. National Bureau of Economic Research, New York, 1951.

Brown, Bonnar, and Janet H. Tate. *Income Trends in the United States Through 1975: Personal Income, Spendable Income, 9 Census Divisions, 11 Western States*. Menlo Park, Calif.: Stanford Research Institute, 1957.

Coale, Ansley J., and Edgar M. Hoover. *Population Growth and Economic Development in Low Income Countries*. Princeton, N. J.: Princeton University Press, 1958.

Cohen, Wilbur J., and Eugenia Sullivan. "Poverty in the United States," *Health, Education, and Welfare Indicators* (February 1964), 6–22.

Conference of European Statisticians. *Statistics of Consumers Expenditures in Different Systems of National Accounts and Balances*. Geneva, United Nations, 1963.

Conference on Economic Progress. *Poverty and Deprivation in the United States. The Plight of Two-fifths of a Nation*. Washington, D.C., April 1962.

Conference on Research in Income and Wealth. *An Appraisal of the 1950 Census Income Data: A Report of the National Bureau of Economic Research*. Princeton, N.J.: Princeton University Press, 1950.

Conference on Research in Income and Wealth. *Regional Income*. Princeton, N.J.: Princeton University Press, 1957.

Creamer, Daniel B. *Personal Income During Business Cycles*. Princeton, N.J.: Princeton University Press, 1956.

Davis, Kingsley. "Some Demographic Aspects of Poverty in the United States." Pp. 299–319 in Margaret S. Gordon (ed.). *Poverty in America*. Proceedings of a national conference held at the University of California, Berkeley, February 16-28, 1965. San Francisco: Chandler Publishing Company, for the Institute of Industrial Relations, University of California, Berkeley, 1965.

Dodge, Robert E. "Purchasing Habits and Market Potentialities of the Older Consumer," pp. 142–156 in *Law and Contemporary Problems*. Problems of the aging. (A group of articles). *Law and Contemporary Problems*, **27** (1) (Winter 1962), 1–156.

Dornbusch, Sanford M. "Correlations Between Income and Labor-force Participation by Race," *American Journal of Sociology*, **61** (4) (January 1956), 340–344.

Economic Council of Canada. *Interregional Disparities in Income*, Staff Study No. 1, Ottawa, 1966.

Ferber, Robert. "A Study of the Comparative Financial Position of Older People in the United States," in International Congress of Gerontology, Sixth. *Age with a Future: Proceedings of the Sixth International Congress of Gerontology*, Copenhagen, August 11-16, 1963. Edited by Per F. Hansen. Copenhagen, Munksgaard, 1964.

Fisher, Janet A. "Measuring the Adequacy of Retirement Incomes," pp. 103–113 in Harold L. Orbach and Clark Tibbitts (eds.). *Aging and the Economy*. Ann Arbor, Mich.: University of Michigan Press, 1963.

Forsyth, F. G. "The Relationship Between Family Size and Family Expenditures," *Journal of the Royal Statistical Society*, **123** (1960), 367–397.

Goldsmith, Selma P. "Changes in the Size Distribution of Income," *American Economic Review*, **47** (Papers and Proceedings, May 1957), 504–518.

Hagood, Margaret J., et al. *Farm-operator Family Level-of-living Indexes for Counties of the United States, 1945, 1950, and 1954*. U.S. Agricultural Marketing Service, Statistical Bulletin No. 204. Washington, D.C., March 1957.

Hanoch, Giora. "Income Differentials in Israel," pp. 35–130 in *Falk Project for Economic Research in Israel*. Fifth Report 1959 and 1960. Jerusalem, 1961.

Harris, C. P. "Interregional Variations in Levels and Rates of Increase of Per Capita Personal Income," *Yorkshire Bulletin of Economic and Social Research*, **18** (1966), 95–108.

India. National Council of Applied Economic Research. *Urban Income and Saving*. New Delhi, 1962.

India Planning Commission. *Distribution of Income and Wealth and Concentration of Economic Power*: Report of the Committee on Distribution of Income and Levels of Living, Part 1. New Delhi: Manager of Publications, 1965.

Kleiman, E. "Age Composition, Size of Households, and the Interpretation of Per Capita Income," *Economic Development and Cultural Change*, **15** (1) (October 1966), 37–58.

Kreps, Juanita M. "Aggregate Income and Labor Force Participation of the Aged," pp. 52–66 in *Law and Contemporary Problems*. Problems of the aging. (A group of articles). *Law and Contemporary Problems*, **27** (1) (Winter 1962), 1–156.

Kuznets, Simon. "Economic Growth and Income Inequality," *American Economic Review*, **45**

(1) (March 1955), 1–28.

Lakdawala, D. T., et al. University of Bombay. *Work Wages and Well-being in an Indian Metropolis: Economic Survey of Bombay City.* Series in Economics No. 11. Bombay, 1963.

Lebergott, Stanley. "The Shape of the Income Distribution," *American Economic Review,* 49 (June 1959), 328–347.

Leven, Maurice. *The Income Structure of the United States.* Washington, D.C.: The Brookings Institution, 1938.

Lininger, Charles A. "Some Aspects of the Economic Situation of the Aged: Recent Survey Findings," pp. 71–90 in Harold L. Orbach and Clark Tibbitts (eds.). *Aging and the Economy.* Ann Arbor, Mich.: University of Michigan Press, 1963.

Mayer, Thomas. "The Distribution of Ability and Earnings," *Review of Economics and Statistics,* 42 (May 1960), 189–195.

Miller, Herman P. "Annual and Lifetime Income in Relation to Education, 1939-59," *American Economic Review,* 50 (December 1960), 962–986.

Miller, Herman P. "Changes in the Number and Composition of the Poor." Pp. 81–101 in Margaret E. Gordon (ed.). *Poverty in America.* Proceedings of a national conference held at the University of California, Berkeley, February 26-28, 1965. San Francisco: Chandler Publishing Company, for the Institute of Industrial Relations, University of California, Berkeley, 1965.

Miller, Herman P. "Lifetime Income and Economic Growth," *American Economic Review,* 55 (September 1965), 834–844.

Miller, Herman P. *Income of the American People.* New York: John Wiley and Sons, 1955.

Miller, Herman P. *Rich Man, Poor Man: a Study of Income Distribution in the U.S.A.* New York: Crowell, 1964.

Miller, Herman P. "Trends in Income of Families and Persons in the United States, 1947–1960," in U.S. Bureau of the Census. *Technical Papers No. 8,* 1963.

Morgan, James N. "Measuring the Economic Status of the Aged," in Per F. Hansen, (ed.), Sixth International Congress of Gerontology. *Age with a Future: Proceedings of the Sixth International Congress of Gerontology,* Copenhagen, August 11-16, 1963. Copenhagen, Munksgaard, 1964.

Morgan, James N., David H. Martin, Wilbur J. Cohen, and Harvey E. Brazer. *Income and Welfare in the United States.* New York: McGraw-Hill, 1962.

Muhsam, H. V. "Revision of the Concept 'The Money Value of a Man,' " pp. 106–111 in *International Union for the Scientific Study of Population.* Vienna, 1959.

Orshansky, Mollie. "Counting the Poor: Another Look at the Poverty Profile," *Social Security Bulletin,* 28 (1) (January 1965), 3–29.

Orshansky, Mollie. "More about the Poor in 1964," *Social Security Bulletin,* 29 (5) (May 1966), 3–38.

Orshansky, Mollie, "Recounting the Poor—a Five year Review," *Social Security Bulletin,* 29 (4) (April 1966), 20–37.

Orshansky, Mollie. "The Poor in City and Suburb, 1964," *Social Security Bulletin,* 19 (12) (December 1966), 22–37.

Orshansky, Mollie. "Who's Who Among the Poor: A Demographic View of Poverty," *Social Security Bulletin,* 28 (7) (July 1965), 3–27.

Peacock, Alan T. (ed.). *Income Redistribution and Social Policy.* London: Jonathan Cape, Ltd., 1954.

Pearson, D. S. "Income Distribution and the Size of Nations," *Economic Development and Cultural Change,* 13 (4, Part 1) (July 1965), 472–478.

Pethe, Vasant P., and B. D. Kanethkar. "Urban Income Structure in India." Reprinted from *AICC Economic Review* (Delhi), 14 (16-17) (February 15, 1963).

Pigou, Arthur C. *Income: an Introduction to Economics.* London: Macmillan and Co., 1946.

Radomski, Alexander, and Anita V. Mills. *Family Income and Related Characteristics Among Low-income Counties and States.* Washington, D. C.: U. S. Department of Health, Education and Welfare, Welfare Division of Research, 1964.

Reid, Margaret G. *Housing and Income.* Chicago: University of Chicago Press, 1962.

Ross, Myron H. *Income: Analysis and Policy.* New York: McGraw-Hill, 1964.

Schmid, Calvin F., and Charles E. Nobbe. "Socioeconomic Differentials Among Nonwhite Races in the State of Washington," *Demography,* 2 (1965), 549–566.

Schultz, T. Paul. *The Distribution of Personal Income: A Study of the Size and Distribution of Personal Income in the United States.* Washington, D.C.: U.S. Government Printing Office, 1965.

Steiner, Peter O., and Robert Dorfman. *The Economic Status of the Aged.* A publication of the Institute of Industrial Relations, University of California. Berkeley and Los Angeles: University of California Press, 1957.

Striner, Herbert E. "The Capacity of the Economy to Support Older People," pp. 17–28 in Harold L. Orbach and Clark Tibbitts (eds.). *Aging and the Economy.* Ann Arbor, Mich.: University of Michigan Press, 1963.

Thernstrom, Stephan. *Poverty and Progress: So-*

cial Mobility in a Nineteenth Century City. Cambridge, Mass.: Harvard University Press, 1964, xii, 286 pp.

Townsend, Peter. "Measuring Poverty," *British Journal of Sociology,* **5** (a) (June 1954), 130–137.

U.S. Bureau of Labor Statistics. "Family Income Distribution in the United States," *Monthly Labor Review,* **78** (6) (June 1955), 671–672.

U.S. Bureau of Labor Statistics. "Techniques of Preparing Major Bureau of Labor Statistics Statistical Series," *Bureau of Labor Statistics Bulletin 1168.* Washington, D. C.: U. S. Government Printing Office, December 1954.

U.S. Bureau of the Census. *Current Population Reports.* Series P-60. Consumer Income. Income of Families and Persons in the United States: (annual). Washington, D. C., 1948-.

U.S. Bureau of the Census. *Income Distribution in the United States.* By Herman P. Miller. A 1960 Census Monograph, prepared for and in cooperation with the Social Science Research Council. Washington, D.C.: Government Printing Office, 1966, vii, 306 pp.

U. S. Bureau of the Census. *Long Term Economic Growth, 1860-1965.* Statistical Compendium ES 4-No. 1. Washington, D.C.: October 1966, iv, 256 pp.

U.S. Congress. Joint Committee on the Economic Report. *Characteristics of the Low-income Population and Related Federal Programs.* Selected materials assembled by the staff of the subcommittee on low-income families 84th Congress, 1st Session. Joint Committee Print. Washington, D.C.: U. S. Government Printing Office, 1955.

U.S. National Resources Committee. *Consumer Incomes in the United States: Their Distribution in 1935-36.* Washington, D. C.: U. S. Government Printing Office, 1938.

U.S. Social Security Administration. Division of Program Research, *Social Security Programs Throughout the World 1961.* Washington, D. C.: U. S. Government Printing Office, 1961.

Vannutelli, C. "Occupazione e Salari dal 1861 al 1961" ("Occupations and Wages from 1861 to 1961"), in *The Italian Economy from 1861 to 1961.* Studies on the first century of Italian unity. Biblioteca della Rivista "Economia e Storia": 6. Milan: Casa Editrice Dott. Antonino Giuffre, 1961.

Wahlbeck, L. *Om Inkomstnivåns Geografi i Finland år 1950. (The Geography of the Income Level in Finland in 1950).* In 2 vols. Helsinki: Söderströms, 1955. With English summary and titles.

Wedgwood, Josiah. *The Economics of Inheritance.* London: G. Routledge and Sons, 1929.

Weisbrod, Burton A. (ed.). *The Economics of Poverty: An American Paradox.* Englewood Cliffs, N. J.: Prentice-Hall, 1965.

CHAPTER 14

Socioeconomic Achievement:
A System for Measuring Social Status
and Social Mobility*

14.1 The Study of Social Status and Social Mobility as a Subfield of Demography

One of the newer branches of social research in which demographers are major participants is the study of social status and social mobility. Although it may be disputed whether this branch of study should be considered a subfield of demography, there is a very strong demographic component in this line of research. The position taken in this chapter is that this is an interdisciplinary field of great interest to many demographers; hence it is not inappropriate to include it as a part of this book. This contention is supported by two arguments: (a) the variables used are population variables and the data collected are obtained by population census counts or from population sample surveys; (b) much if not most of the rigorous and vigorous work in this area in recent years has been done by demographers—among them David V. Glass, Otis Dudley Duncan, Kingsley Davis, Charles Nam, Robert Hodge, and others.

Still another reason for emphasizing the close dependence of this field on demography is that its methodology is very much akin to the methodology of one of the main branches of demography—the study of population distribution and human migration. To an amazing ex-

tent, the rates, models, and even the theories propounded in the study of social status and social mobility are adaptations or parallel formulations of similar work already performed in this well-established field of demographic research.

The present chapter, unlike the others in this book, is not intended to be a general synthesis of an entire field. Instead, it adopts a particular theme and undertakes to develop it. This theme is to challenge the established premise of most social mobility research that occupational data are the "key" to research progress in this field. Professors who find the material presented here too controversial may wish to omit the chapter, or else to prepare their own rebuttal. They will be assisted in this by materials from the excellent monograph, *The American Occupational Structure*, by Peter M. Blau and Otis Dudley Duncan (see Bibliography). In using this monograph, however, they should distinguish carefully between the chapters written by Blau and those written by Duncan. The latter author, it is believed, would agree with much of the material presented here.

Despite its apparently controversial nature, this chapter is nevertheless intended as an introduction and statement of basic principles, in the same way as the other chapters. By listing the specifications to which measures used in this line of study should conform, it hopes to prepare the student for a more careful and insightful study of the readings listed in the Bibliography.

---

* This chapter was written by Donald J. Bogue and Elizabeth J. Bogue. It is an expansion of a paper presented to the annual spring meeting of the Society for Social Research, University of Chicago, May 1966.

14.2 Are Occupations the Best Indicators of the "Life Style," "Social Condition," or "Social Status" of the Population?

Sociologists and economists studying the phenomenon of socioeconomic status and social mobility have placed very strong reliance upon *occupation* as a sensitive indicator of status. This viewpoint is well expressed by Leonard Reissman, who states that occupations "seem to catch and concretize the impressions that most people have of the class structure." [1] It has prestigious roots in the writings of Herbert Spencer on social differentiation, Emile Durkheim on the division of labor, and Max Weber on class and status. Durkheim observed that "Classes . . . probably have no other origin nor any other nature; they arise from the multitude of occupational organizations. . . ." [2] Max Weber also accepted the view that broad occupational groups form the basis for social classes: ". . .the most important source of the development of distinct strata is . . . the development of a peculiar style of life including, particularly, the type of occupation pursued." [3] This is a point about which Talcott Parsons and Pitirim Sorokin agreed. Parsons stated that, ". . . Broadly speaking there are two fundamental elements in the dominant American scale of stratification. We determine status very largely on the basis of achievement within an occupational system which is in turn organized primarily in terms of universalistic criteria of performance and status within functionally specialized fields." [4] ". . . In our own society, apart from hereditary groups at the top in certain sections of the country, the main criteria of class status are to be found in the occupational achievements of men. . . ." [5] Sorokin asserted: "Neither individual conduct and psychology, nor group behavior and characteristics, nor social antagonisms and solidarity, nor processes of social reconstruction and revolution, nor almost any important social change or irregularity, can be accounted for satisfactorily without the occupational factors. [6] ". . . Vertical mobility of individuals and their placement at different social strata is controlled by a complex machinery of social testing, selection, and distribution of individuals within the society. This machinery is composed of social institutions of the family, church, and school, which test the general intelligence and character of individuals, *and of different occupational institutions which retest the results of the family, church, and school testing,* and especially test the specific ability of individuals necessary for a successful performance of definite occupational functions. [italics ours] . . . From this it follows that the population of different social strata is selective." [7]

The occupational basis of social status is a principle that both human ecologists and culturologists have accepted. The "functional basis of stratification" hypothesis, proposed by Davis and Moore, is, upon closer observation, based upon this same view that persons occupying particularly vital occupations are accorded especially high status. [8] In recent years there has been a tendency to reify this relationship, so that social status has been *equated* with occupation. Most of the major empirical studies of social mobility have defined social mobility in terms of occupational mobility. This is true of the work of Rogoff, Glass, Bendix and Lipset, Dudley Duncan, and Peter Blau. (See studies by these authors listed in the Bibliography.)

It is the intent of this paper to challenge this hypothesis as being obsolescent as a viewpoint for studying social status in modern in-

[1] Leonard Reissman, *Class in American Society* (Glencoe, Ill.: The Free Press, 1959), p. 141.

[2] Emile Durkheim, *Division of Labor in Society,* translated by George Simpson (Glencoe, Ill.: The Free Press, 1947), p. 182.

[3] Max Weber, *The Theory of Social and Economic Organization,* translated by A. M. Henderson and Talcott Parsons (Glencoe, Ill.: The Free Press, 1947), p. 429.

[4] Talcott Parsons, *Essays in Sociological Theory* (Glencoe, Ill.: The Free Press, 1954), p. 79.

[5] *Ibid.,* p. 83.

[6] Pitirim Sorokin, *Contemporary Sociological Theories* (New York: Harper and Brothers, 1928), p. 718.

[7] *Ibid.,* p. 751.

[8] Kingsley Davis and Wilbert E. Moore, "Some Principles of Stratification: A Critical Analysis," *American Sociological Review,* **10** (April 1945), 242–249.

dustrialized societies. We agree that the occupation-equals-status assumption was undoubtedly valid in the days of Durkheim and Weber. But times have changed, and it is becoming increasingly evident that technological advances and increasing democratization have seriously weakened occupations as indicators of status and social mobility. In fact, except for the obviously prestigious gulf separating professional and managerial categories from the remainder of the industrialized occupational categories and the gulf separating servile and pariah occupations (which are preindustrial in character) from the great bulk of modern employment, we regard the study of status in terms of occupations at best to be inefficient and at worst to be misleading. We believe this criticism is valid irrespective of whether occupations are studied in terms of a dozen or so broad categories or in terms of the much more numerous detailed occupational categories, although it is much more cogent in the former than in the latter case. However, it should be emphasized that occupational data have lost none of their utility for ecological studies of how a population earns its livelihood and the interrelationships between livelihood activity and other aspects of social life. It also remains true that each occupation tends to have its own tiny "culture": unique attitudes, customs, traditions, language, and terminology. We do hypothesize, however, that for studies of general social status and social mobility, sociologists today are emphasizing the wrong variables, possibly out of veneration for the "founding fathers."

He who would refuse to venerate a tradition should be prepared to offer a substitute. This also is attempted here. A measure termed "socioeconomic achievement," (SEA), derived from data on income and educational attainment, is proposed as an alternative measure to occupation for studies of status and mobility. It is claimed that it more sensitively measures small differences in status and changes in status of particular individuals. It escapes many of the methodological difficulties with which occupational analysis is beset. Its technological base is also advantageous, for it separates the phenomenon of prestige and esteem attached

to a few particularly high social statuses from the general phenomenon of status, and permits explicit research on esteem independently of general socioeconomic status. The meaning of the SEA measure does not change over time and may be made comparable from place to place, so that historical and cross-cultural studies may be more comparable. Instead of *assuming* that stratification (class boundaries) exist, it provides a comparatively exact measure with which to make *tests* for the existence of such boundaries. Finally, it makes it possible to measure absolute as well as relative social mobility.

14.3. Specifications for a Status-Mobility Measure

Many if not most researchers who study social status probably would agree that an "ideal" yardstick for measuring social status should possess the following attributes:

1. The measure should have a sound basis in social theory; the components of which it is constructed should be sensitive indexes of status.

2. It should be a continuous measure, capable of expressing small differences in status.

3. It should be a ratio scale with zero as a theoretical lower limit and with a meaningful upper limit. A convenient form would be a scale ranging from 0 to 100. Only by such a scale can the concept "social distance" have rigorous meaning. The status scale must measure in absolute terms the absolute size of the social distance between individuals.

4. The system should be capable of detecting class boundaries if they exist, and of simultaneously considering categories of status and continuity of status within categories.

5. The system should be capable of operationalizing all of the concepts related to stratification theory, such as status crystallization, status consistency, level of aspiration, and so on.

6. It should be capable of use for classifying all of the peers of a person as well as the social milieu in which the person resides.

7. It should be comparable over time.

8. It should be able to portray dispersion of statuses from average values for the group. In fact, it should be able to portray the frequency

distribution of statuses, in order to permit a "status profile" to be constructed for groupings and subgroupings of the population.

9. The units in which it is expressed should be translatable into cultural definitions of status. As cultural definitions change, it should be possible for the "cutting points" along the scale to be altered without destroying comparability with the past.

10. It should be expressed in measures that would permit cross-cultural comparisons.

11. The units should be independent of technological change and economic fluctuations, except insofar as such changes and fluctuations affect the status system in a meaningful way.

12. The system should be capable of measuring both individual and family status, and of comparing the two.

13. The system should be capable of tracing both intragenerational and intergenerational social mobility, and should facilitate mathematical treatment of each.

14. The system should be capable of determining what is a statistically significant change in status and what is a change that could be due only to chance variation in measurement.

15. The system should be capable of measuring the status of neighborhoods, entire cities, regions, or nations—and yet be applicable to individuals within these same groupings. Such a system would be of immense importance in measuring "structural effects" and "overachieving" or "underachieving" individuals.

16. The system should accommodate the study of social status and social mobility of females as well as males.

17. The system should be equally sensitive and meaningful at the low as well as the high end of the continuum.

18. The system should be compatible with other methods of measuring status and mobility, so that two or more measures may be used simultaneously to supplement each other. In particular, it is anticipated that the scale proposed here would be supplemented with a "prestige scale" for the study of elite groups and with a "disesteem scale" for the study of pariah groups.

19. The system should furnish data in a form that permits the use of the more powerful styles of mathematical and statistical analysis.

20. The system of scores should be capable of being extended backward in time to permit historical studies of mobility, and of being maintained as a series in the future.

21. The system should be compatible with status research being done in other branches of social science, and the elements of similarity and difference with other measures of status should be capable of explicit study.

The Index of Socioeconomic Achievement attempts to meet all of these specifications.

14.4. A Critique of Occupations as Indicators of Status

Throughout the eighteenth and nineteenth centuries, occupations were comparatively few in number and probably were rather widely known and rather uniformly graded. Each occupation tended to carry with it its own mode of life and unique social orientations. It is quite plausible to presuppose that dress, recreation, manners, patterns of association, speech, educational level, and other aspects of "life style" varied rather sharply and in disjunctive fashion between one occupational level and another. Inasmuch as the number of levels was comparatively small, distinctive social strata could be observed. Undoubtedly, it was this comparatively simple occupational structure that permitted nineteenth-century thinkers to dichotomize the population into two warring classes or otherwise think of it in terms of a few simple strata. The hypothesis of congruity between status and occupation certainly is a major theme in studies of preindustrial societies; studies of the Middle Ages, the Roman and Greek epochs, and the caste system of India; and innumerable studies of "primitive" peoples have verified and reverified it many times.

Modernization is changing this. At the present time the division of labor has become so minute that the number of different occupations runs into the tens of thousands. These occupations no longer fall neatly into categories that represent distinctive work activities, styles of life, or modes of behavior. Instead, *they form a gradation or hierarchy that proceeds from high to low by steps that are so small as to be almost imperceptible.* Our general occupational classifications are highly heterogeneous internally and often are not especially distinctive from each other externally. *It is difficult to find distinctive modes of behavior or thinking that can be traced directly to the work context and which are also significant enough to permit us to identify them as distinctive social strata.* With modern methods of automated and assembly line production, the great masses can share as consumers in life styles that formerly were confined to the elite. Sports cars, ranch house–suburban living, private swimming pools, golfing, sailboating, annual vacations, color television sets, college education for children, participation in the arts, stylish dress and hair arrangements— even the wearing of jewels—are no longer identified as occupational symbols. Moreover, there has been a substantial corruption of occupation-based modes of economic behavior. Educators, professional welfare workers, and even physicians and nurses now organize into unions and threaten to strike or withhold service in order to obtain economic objectives, while labor unions accumulate capital and invest their savings as independent entrepreneurs. Some "blue-collar" workers perform tasks that require a college education plus great intelligence, judgment, and skill. Many "white-collar" occupations, in contrast, are little more than domestic chores performed in an office, and require very little special training, skill, or special ability; those who hold them are accorded comparatively little esteem. For example, the operators of the huge cranes that transfer molten steel in a steel mill may shower and change to street clothes and drive away from the plant undistinguishable from the personnel officer who hired them, and their salary may be substantially greater than his. The two types of workers may live in the same subdivision, send their children to the same public school, attend the same church, and even share many a friend.

As a result, knowing the general category into which a person's occupation falls today may reveal much less about his personality, his social life, and his social status than it did even a decade ago.

Moreover, *as automation and modernization progress rapidly, there is every prospect that this trend will continue and accelerate.* If true, we can only look forward to further deterioration of general occupational type as a social indicator.

Occupational information is deficient for the study of status on other grounds. It is impossible to study the social status of persons who are not in the labor force—persons who are on public welfare, retired, or living from investment income. Moreover, the meaning of occupational categories changes over time, so that a concept applied today may have only limited comparability with the same concept applied a decade hence. If there is an improvement or deterioration of the status of some occupations, either absolutely or relatively, it is not detected.

An even more serious deficiency is that there is a great deal of movement *within* occupations that cannot be measured by occupational data. A physician can move from being an intern to chief surgeon and a lawyer can rise from being a low-salaried legal assistant to a famous trial lawyer without these facts showing in most available occupational data. Moreover, the full range of efforts that a person makes to better his station in life is not reflected in occupation statistics. By "moonlighting," by saving, and by wise investment a person can accumulate position and status not available to a fellow worker in the same occupation who spends all as he earns it. In other words, the use of broad occupation classifications probably seriously understates the amount of intragenerational mobility (both up and down) that actually takes place. Each individual is given credit only for the *average* status of his role and as a result his *actual performance* in the role may be drastically understated or exaggerated.

As serious as the shortcomings listed above is the fact that the use of occupation as the sole or primary index of social status has been justified only on rather common-sense and highly informal grounds, with very little of what one might call rigorous theoretical foundation. Social stratification has been defined as ". . . the differential ranking of the human individuals who compose a given social system and their treatment as superior and inferior relative to one another in certain socially important respects."[9] The concepts of "respect," "esteem," or "prestige" have been used to identify the particular moral basis by which one person is declared to be superior or inferior to another. Max Weber defines it thus: "The term of 'social status' will be applied to a typically effective claim to positive or negative privilege with respect to social prestige so far as it rests on one or more of the following bases: (a) mode of living, (b) a formal process of education which may consist in empirical or rational training and the acquisition of the corresponding modes of life, or (c) on the prestige of birth, or of an occupation."[10]

It is difficult to find an explicit theoretical statement of how and why occupations are better able than any alternative measure to rank individuals as inferior or superior to each other, or to specify the amount of esteem or prestige each person in a group is to receive, in accordance with the above definitions. In the context of nineteenth century society, perhaps the superiority of occupation (or the complete absence of alternative data) caused this point to seem too trivial to require justification. When we attempt to apply these classic ideas to the contemporary scene, however, the matter is much less unambiguous and self-evident. If, instead of arbitrarily *defining* status as equivalent to occupation, we ask the question "What is the basis of social status and stratification in the modern world?" we find that there are at least four major answers, which might be termed the *components* of status. We must next not only enumerate each of these components, but also evaluate the adequacy with which occupational data measure it. Following this, we shall undertake to devise a system of status measurement that accomplishes the task more effectively than can be done with occupations.

Component 1: Livelihood (Economic) Status —Plane of Material Comfort in Living. This is the system of stratification discussed in the

preceding chapter. Every society has, in some form, the strata of livelihood status presented below, where each livelihood status is matched by an appropriate social status label:

Livelihood status	Equivalent social status
Wealth	Upper-upper class
Affluence	Lower-upper class
Economic comfort	Upper-middle class
Minimum decency	Lower-middle class
Poverty	Upper-lower class
Destitution	Lower-lower class

As any sociologist worthy of his badge will hasten to point out, the correspondence between the livelihood statuses and the social statuses is only approximate; there are many individual exceptions. Yet, on an empirical basis, the correlation is very high—much higher in fact than most of the correlations with which we deal in social science. Where an individual is misclassified, it will usually be by one class interval only: for example, an "upper-upper" class person of great prestige may be affluent but not wealthy, but not poor. However, errors of two intervals may occur: a "lower-lower" class person who is a petty thief may be found to be living with "minimum decency," and a very wealthy person may be classified only as "upper-middle class" because of other factors. It is by considering the other components that these misclassifications can be corrected. Errors of three or more intervals are probably so rare as to comprise only a small percent of the population in the United States at the present time.

The major determinant of this status, of course, is income. The "cutting points" between one class and another will vary from society to society, as will the proportion of the total population that falls in each class. To the extent that occupations are a superior measure of this component, it must be demonstrated that occupations are able sensitively to divide the various livelihood classes from each other. In order for this to be valid it must be shown that the members of particular occupational categories are heavily concentrated in particular livelihood categories. The evidence currently available indicates that income does this more effectively than occupation.

[9] Parsons, *op. cit.*, p. 69.
[10] M. Weber, *op. cit.*, p. 428.

Component 2: General Cultural-Technical Status—Plane of Intellectual Life and Participation in Modern Social and Cultural Life. It is widely appreciated that in order to participate fully in modern scientific-technical-rational societies a substantial amount of general acculturation and preparation is necessary. The person who is not equipped to understand at least some modern technological processes is incapable of participating in the labor force except at tasks that have remained unchanged by industrialization. As the above quotation from Sorokin emphasizes, one must be *qualified* to join a social stratum. If a person is to participate at the highest levels in the intellectual and cultural life, he must possess extraordinary knowledge and skill; it is no longer enough simply to have been "born to it." Inasmuch as the art, culture, and science upon which modern social living is based are taught formally in educational institutions rather than informally in the home, *educational attainment is the major determinant of the capacity of a person to participate on a high or only on a low level. Hence educational attainment is the major determinant of this component.* Whether a person reads *Newsweek* magazine, listens to classical music on the radio, watches discussion programs on television, and patronizes the local efforts at drama in his community depends more upon his own educational attainment and the educational attainment of his parents than upon his occupation or the occupation of his father. The "cutting points" between one class and another will vary from society to society, and will be highly sensitive to the level of technological development. We may tentatively allocate the American population as of the 1960s as follows:

Educational status	Approximate equivalent cultural status	Equivalent social class
College postgraduate doctoral level	Leaders and innovators in art, science, and technology	Upper-upper class
College graduate (4 years) and postgraduate M.A. level	Professional practitioners in art, science, and technology	Lower-upper class
High school graduate, college dropout	Artisans skilled in specialized applications of art, science, and technology; consumers of popular culture with intellectual content	Upper-middle class
Grammar school graduate, high school dropout	Semiskilled mass-producers and assistants to technicians; consumers of popular culture with primarily affective content	Lower-middle class
Barely functionally literate, (grammar school 5-7 years)	Operators of simple machines or workers where technical processes are simple and require little skill or training; consumers of popular culture with almost entirely affective content	Upper-lower class
Functionally illiterate (grammar school 1-4 years or no schooling whatsoever)	Workers at preindustrial tasks; consumers of folk culture, adherents to folk rather than popular culture	Lower-lower class (depending on income)

The evidence currently available indicates that educational attainment measures this component more effectively than does occupation.

Component 3: Unique Cultural Traits, Interests, and Pattern of Life of Members of the Individual Social Strata. Where classes are present, the members of each stratum share certain interests and live according to a particular pattern that is more or less unique to them. They have a common tradition, a common set of cultural traits that spring from their position. Each stratum is a self-conscious minority, developed through social interaction among its own members as well as with members of other strata. Perhaps the castes of India may be taken as a clear example of this phenomenon; the priestly, merchant, or warrior caste each had an elaborate body of culture that could readily be comprehended as being something added to, or in addition to, the general livelihood status or the general educational status. There tends to be endogamy, tight in-group interaction, and social segregation (either self-imposed or imposed by the majority). This is the "essence," of a truly stratified society, and if a society is strongly stratified, it will be found to be stratified along these lines of "subcultures."

If occupations are to be a sensitive measure of this component, it must be shown that the unique subcultures of the society are organized principally around occupations as were the castes of India, or if the strata are organized along some other lines, that those lines are in turn also lines of relatively sharp occupational demarcation.

Whether or not occupations function effectively in modern industrialized societies as a measure of this component, especially when the first two components already mentioned are held constant, is questionable. Below we submit evidence that the phenomenon of residential segregation according to occupation largely disappears when the factors of income and education are held constant. There seems to be little evidence of occupational endogamy or other proof that occupations are functioning as viable social strata. In view of the highly specialized nature of modern occupations, the comparatively small numerical size of each particular occupation, and the comparative lack of opportunity for the members of a particular occupation to interact as a social group and build up a tight social system of a caste-nature, it does not seem plausible that subcultures based upon modern occupations can be regarded as important elements in stratification. A possible exception (numerically minor

when viewed from total societal perspective) may be a tendency for members of the highest prestige professional and managerial occupations to segregate themselves from the balance of the population, to interact primarily with those of their own occupation to the exclusion of others, and to develop unique cultural traits, interests, and styles of life that may be said to reflect occupation as well as education and income. However, prolonged residence in a community, given high income and high education, is adequate to bring about elite status in these groups, irrespective of specific occupation—excluding, of course, illegal occupations. Every modern society has subcultural strata, but occupation does not appear to be the major factor. Income and education are powerful stratifying forces. In addition to these there is stratification along the lines of race, ethnicity, religion, or political beliefs—or some combination of these factors.

Component 4: Prestige, Esteem, Respect, or Power. The phenomenon of deference, prestige, esteem, respect, or power (in the sociological sense) is one manifestation of status. The ideal prototype at the upper extreme is the monarch. At some intermediate point the variable must change from one of esteem to disesteem, so that at the lower extreme we have the untouchable pariah or the despised. At this point we must emphasize that each of the three first components mentioned may be thought of as a *source* of status, a functional explanation of *why* status and stratification exist in the modern world. By appropriate classification of the three components we are able to arrive at operational definitions of social classes. This fourth component is of an entirely different nature; instead of being a source it is a *result*, a by-product, a *symptom* of status. It is an emotional state that individuals experience when they perceive status; or the capacity of persons with given status to provoke these emotions in others. It is a psychological form of "payoff" for success in status striving.

If occupations are to be a highly sensitive measure of this component, it must be shown that prestige and disesteem are distributed in society according to occupational categories, and that the prestige of particular individuals is measured adequately by specifying the occupation that they hold.

In recent studies of social status, the element of prestige has received strong emphasis.[11] However, prestige has not been defined directly but only as an attribute of occupations, and then only in such a way that it has been interpreted to *include* both livelihood status and general social status as well as "intrinsic prestige." Thus the "prestige" of an occupation has been defined in terms of status derived from all economic and all noneconomic attributes. The attempts to measure prestige quantitatively have distorted the meaning of the term so as to give it a different meaning; a prestigious occupation is simply a job with a "good standing" and other desirable traits. In fact, a recent study used the term "prestige" as a summary index of twenty different traits of occupations that might be termed desirable.[12]

At this point we come face-to-face with the realization that we have a choice of alternative strategies for measuring social status: (*a*) a more or less "objective" approach via the first three functional components and (*b*) a more afunctional "subjective" approach via prestige-disesteem measurement. If both approaches were equally reliable and valid, they would yield identical results, except that the functional approach would be more useful in identifying strata. If one approach were more reliable within a particular range than another, it would succeed in measuring statuses that the other would fail to detect.

The strategy that we have followed in developing the SEA indexes is to accept the functional components approach to the measurement of social status. We recommend that those interested in studying elites supplement the ratings of the upper 10 percent with a

prestige-measurement approach to see if it can succeed in improving upon the classification obtained by the functional components approach. If it does succeed in discriminating among elite statuses at the very top levels, we can speak of "pure esteem" apart from that attributable to the components. We recommend this procedure for two reasons. First, we are of the opinion that with objective indexes of education and income we can measure differences throughout the range of social rank in social status of individual persons with far greater precision than could ever be achieved by the occupation-prestige approach. We believe that the method we propose may fail to discriminate with the desired precision among the statuses of the elite or upper 10 percent of a society, and that for those interested in making such a discrimination, special supplementary data must be collected. (For a very high percentage of persons in an elite status the SEA scores will rank individuals correctly and show their approximate "social distance" from each other.) We believe that elite occupations are one index of such status, but alone are no more definitive than are income and education. By adopting this strategy it is possible to construct an index that conforms well to the long list of specifications for a status measurement that were enumerated above. Second, we believe that the concept of prestige is *not* a sensitive measure of status except at the extreme upper end of the status range. In other words, except for the most elite statuses, we believe that "prestige" is nothing more than a subjective measurement of the income-education components.

In support of the above position it may be plausibly contended that in the modern world the concept of "prestige" in its "pure" definition may be applied in a meaningful way only to the upper 10 percent or so of the population, and that it becomes progressively less meaningful as one progresses down the social scale. In fact, comparatively little prestige or esteem adheres to many of the categories in the "professional" or "managerial-proprietor" groups, for example, chiropractors, embalmers, osteopaths, healers, managers of small laundry, shoe repair, or repair shops, of small bars, filling

[11] C. C. North and P. I. Hatt, "Jobs and Occupations: A Popular Evaluation," *Public Opinion News,* 9 (September 1947), 3–13; Robert W. Hodge, Paul M. Siegel, and Peter H. Rossi, "Occupational Prestige in the United States, 1925-63," *American Journal of Sociology,* November 1964; A. F. Davies, "Prestige of Occupations," *British Journal of Sociology,* 3 (June 1952), 132–147.

[12] A. P. Garbin and Frederick L. Bates, "Occupational Prestige and its Correlates: A Re-examination." *Social Forces,* 44 (March 1966), 295–302.

stations, or restaurants, or railroad conductors. As one passes the midpoint of the status system and continues toward the bottom, it is necessary to abandon the concept of prestige and switch to "negative prestige" or degrees of degradation or of contempt (disesteem) generally felt toward persons earning their living in particular lowly occupations. The notion that every occupation is endowed, to some variable degree, with an attribute "prestige" independently of the economic emoluments it receives may itself be a hangover from the guild system or the earlier phases of the industrial revolution. Certainly, there is comparatively little research evidence to support the hypothesis. For example, when North and Hatt constructed their famous scale of occupational prestige, only a tiny fraction of the respondents apparently used pure prestige in making their ranking. When asked the basis for their rank, the responses were as follows:

	Percent
The *income* that holders of the occupation receive	18
The service to humanity	16
The *education*, preparation required to hold it	14
The social prestige the job carries	14
High moral standing, responsibility involved	9
Intelligence, ability required	9

These responses suggest both that a number of attributes other than prestige are involved in ranking the position and that prestige when it is used as a major criterion is brought into play only to measure social distance between persons in the very upper social strata. One would suspect that almost all of the responses involving prestige referred principally to professional and managerial occupations. It is quite possible that prestige is almost nonexistent as a criterion in ranking workers in the clerical, craft, operative, service, and laborer categories. Instead, it is more plausible that the wage or salary paid becomes progressively more powerful in ranking lower-level occupations the lower one descends in the scale. Also, at the very lowest end of the scale it may well be that there are positions to which negative prestige (disesteem) is

attached so that a money reward must be paid to get persons to occupy them. If this is true, then special measurements must be taken to delimit precisely the lower strata of society.

Thus there are not only empirical but also theoretical reasons why the monopoly of the occupational approach in the study of social status and social mobility should be reexamined. *If we are to continue to use occupations as a measure of status, we should identify the components of status in mutually exclusive terms and undertake to measure each separately, or at least to find a suitable index for each.* The SEA index purports to measure the level of livelihood and the general cultural components for each occupation and leaves the way open for supplemental independent measures of prestige for elite occupations and of disesteem for pariah occupations. We hypothesize that for the vast number of occupations between these two extremes, the components of livelihood and culture, as measured by income and education, measure the status of occupations in the precise theoretical meaning of the term "status" with about as much precision as is possible in the context of the present state of highly minute specialization of occupation.

14.5. Education and Income: Indexes of the Basic Components of Socioeconomic Achievement

We have argued above that there are two indicators, widely available, that together may be used to construct a comparatively sensitive measure of social status. They are *education* and *income*. It has been hypothesized that a person's social status at any given moment may be regarded as a function of two principal components: a plane of livelihood (economic) component and a plane of social life (interests) component.

The livelihood component may be validly and reliably measured by income. The income that is paid to an individual is determined by a wide variety of forces—his skill, his productivity, the "bargaining power" that he commands as a member of a labor union, and the scarcity of the supply of workers of his type in relation to demand or need. The normal processes of the labor market assign to each person an "economic worth" or an economic rank in the form of a wage or salary rate. Therefore, the annual income, including income from savings and investments, gauges rather sensitively the functional status of the person in the livelihood system of the community or society. Thus income may be adopted as a measure of *ecological* social status. The dynamism of the income-determining process should not be underestimated. The individual strives earnestly to increase his income and devotes a great deal of planning and strategy to achieve this goal. Competition for top-quality workers among potential employers; discharge or failure to give salary increases to indolent, inefficient, or careless workers tends to rank individuals. Thus we may adopt the view that the labor market ranks workers continuously and that a comparatively reliable and valid up-to-date ranking of the ecological status of an individual is his annual rate of income receipt. Income from inherited wealth is included in this, of course.

To no small extent, esteem or prestige is also expressed in monetary terms. The Supreme Court justice, the prosecuting attorney, or a world-famous university professor of law each tends to receive a salary that is substantially higher than that received by less prestigious persons in the "attorney" occupation.

The social component may be measured by educational attainment: the number of years of formal schooling of the individual. It is an index of the amount of preparation that the individual has undergone to participate in the intellectual, cultural, and technical activities of the society. It is also an index of the interest and potential to participate in the intellectual and "cultural" activities of the modern community. Education is widely and correctly heralded as the avenue by which one qualifies to climb higher in the status scale and justifies his claim to a high position. The person with a high level of education has a high potential for climbing to the upper levels; the person with no education can hope only for modest status. Children from high-status families are forced to get education to justify the inheritance of their parents' status. Children from low-status families seek advanced education in order to fulfill the prerequisites for upward

mobility. Thus education is a sensitive component of both intragenerational and intergenerational mobility.

Moreover, if one were to search for an indicator of social esteem that operates at all status levels, the variable of education would be a strong contender. Diplomas and degrees are widely used as prestige and ranking symbols. In the United States at the present time, a person who did not graduate from grammar school suffers a depressed social status while graduation from high school is a prerequisite to being genuinely "middle-class." A college degree is a necessary, though not sufficient, condition for entrance to higher levels. In many Asian countries, not only college degrees but even the awarding institutions are listed in the signature to letters and on other prestige-designating occasions. A vast amount of research findings have accumulated to show that a wide variety of attitudes, values, and behaviors vary systematically with the educational attainment of the holder. Thus "life styles" appear to be linked rather sensitively to educational attainment, and these distinctive life styles appear to reflect the status system, in which the better educated occupy high positions on the social status ladder and the poorly educated remain on the lower rungs.

The Income-Education Amalgam as an Index of Socioeconomic Achievement. If income is taken as a measure of the ecological position that an individual holds and education is taken as a measure of the social position that he occupies, his socioeconomic achievement at any particular moment may be considered to be the composite of these two components. It requires very little experimentation to discover that inasmuch as the two measures are highly correlated, a person's ranking is influenced comparatively little by varying the weights in which the two components are combined. In the absence of better information they may be given equal weight.

In amalgamating the two components, there is a tendency for one component to compensate for the deficiencies of the other. For example, the income component obviously fails to measure the status of Roman Catholic priests, while it exaggerates the status of wealthy but undereducated national sports

Table 14-1 Income in 1959 of the Experienced Labor Force by Educational Attainment

Years of school completed	Total	Less than $1,000	$1,000 to $1,999	$2,000 to $2,999	$3,000 to $3,999	$4,000 to $4,999	$5,000 to $5,999	$6,000 to $6,999	$7,000 to $9,999	$10,000 to $14,999	$15,000 and over
Total......	100.0	9.2	8.4	10.0	12.3	14.4	14.9	10.3	12.8	4.7	3.0
Grammar school											
Less than 5 years	100.0	22.2	19.3	18.3	14.6	11.3	7.3	3.2	2.7	0.7	0.4
5-7 years........	100.0	12.9	12.4	15.3	16.4	15.9	12.8	6.7	5.8	1.2	0.6
8 years..........	100.0	9.4	9.4	12.0	14.8	17.1	15.9	9.3	9.1	2.1	1.1
High school											
1-3 years........	100.0	13.1	7.6	9.3	12.6	15.5	16.2	10.6	11.1	2.7	1.4
4 years..........	100.0	4.6	6.4	8.1	12.0	15.5	17.9	13.1	15.6	4.6	2.3
College											
1-3 years........	100.0	6.2	7.2	6.9	8.8	11.6	14.3	12.2	18.8	8.6	5.3
4 years..........	100.0	1.9	3.3	3.1	5.9	8.7	11.8	11.9	25.0	16.1	11.2
5+ years........	100.0	2.0	3.4	4.0	4.9	6.9	9.7	10.5	23.9	17.5	17.1

idols such as boxers. The rich businessman receives credit for his success, but his status is moderated if he lacks education. Thus *the Socioeconomic Achievement Index is based on the premise that income and education each is a moderately sensitive measure of status, that each measures a somewhat different aspect of status (but with much overlapping), that one tends to compensate for the inadequacies of the other, and that together they are able to provide a comparatively sensitive measure of the status level that individuals or groups have achieved.* We believe that in addition to measuring the social and economic components, they measure the components of prestige moderately well except for a very few of the highest-status elite positions. In other words, we believe *the SEA index conforms more closely to the theoretical definitions of social status of Weber and Parsons than do the various occupational prestige indexes.*

Money as the Unit of Measurement. How may we average income and education when they are expressed in different units? It is here proposed to measure them both in terms of the same unit—money. This is accomplished by converting educational attainment into its average income-producing equivalent. Table 14-1 reports the average income that persons of each educational level received in 1959. It is clear that the higher the educational level, the higher was the income. The income distribution associated with each educational level may therefore be accepted as a schedule of weights that may be used in estimating the amount of status that a population may be *expected* to receive on the basis of its education (social status).

Its *actual* income may then be compared with this expected income to note the degree to which the group actually receives in economic terms (ecological status) the income that it should expect on the basis of education alone.

At first, some sociologists and social psychologists may be offended at the notion of evaluating social status in monetary units. A little study, however, reveals the great advantage of making this transformation. Economists have devised highly effective systems to express change over time in monetary units and to adjust these units for secular changes in the purchasing power of the dollar. By adopting monetary values as the unit of measure it is possible to capitalize on their research techniques, time series, and knowledge of trends. It is possible to make cross-national comparisons through conversion of monetary units to a common base. It is possible to sidestep many of the thorny problems of changes in occupational titles between censuses and of differences between cultures and between generations. It transforms the education variable, which is not truly a continuous variable, into a continuous form. In fact, almost all of the traits listed above for an "ideal" social status measure can be quite closely approximated by accepting this conversion of education into equivalent dollars.

14.6. Operational Definition of Socioeconomic Achievement

The definition proposed here for socioeconomic status, therefore, takes the following steps: (1) calculate the income that would be *expected* on the basis of educational attainment alone;

(2) enumerate the *actual* income that is received; (3) average the two to arrive at a combined index; (4) if data are collected for several different dates, convert to "constant dollars" by adjusting for purchasing power; (5) convert to an index value by dividing the above results by $20,000 and multiplying the result by 100 (see next section).

Mean versus Median Income and Education. In the system here proposed it is held that the proper measure of the income position for a group is *mean* income, and that the proper measure of the educational position for a group is *mean* education. This is supported on the following grounds:

1. For a great many of the subpopulations for which research will be undertaken (neighborhoods, occupations, census tracts, ethnic groups, etc.), the distribution tends toward the normal distribution, which makes the arithmetic mean the most appropriate single measure. In such subpopulations the typical distribution tends to be only moderately skewed.

2. From statistical theory it is known that the standard error of means is quite normally distributed even when computed from markedly skewed distributions.

3. The mean is a more sensitive measure of status difference than is the median. There is basis for argument that in the presence of moderate skewness the mean is a superior measure to the median because it is more sensitive to the concentration of upper-class members.

4. The use of the arithmetic mean leads directly to the calculation of measures of dispersion: standard deviation and standard error. This permits the introduction of the ideas of sampling theory into the study of social stratification and social mobility. The inability to use sampling theory in most of the previous research has constituted a major weakness.

The $20,000 Upper Reference Point. There are some advantages to be gained by converting the amalgam of education and income obtained by the preceding definition into a scale ranging between 0 and 100 points. For the scale proposed here, the value $20,000 has been allowed to represent a score of 100. This procedure was followed for the following reasons:

1. In 1960, an income of $20,000 represents

the point at which a family begins to live in wealth in the United States. At this income level the family can afford a wide variety of consumption items—modern housing; the purchase annually of a new automobile; overseas vacations; full and complete insurance against ill health and death; savings against retirement and for education of the children; furnishing of the home with a wide variety of luxury appliances such as color television, high-fidelity stereo radio, air-conditioners, dishwashers, and clothes washers and dryers. It also is the income level at which community leadership is concentrated.

2. Although well below the upper limit that many elite families actually achieve, this is roughly the socioeconomic goal toward which the population generally aspires. Permitting the income of $20,000 (1960 dollars) to have a scale value of 100, therefore, provides a meaningful reference point. The person or group that has a scale value of 55, for example, may be said to be 55 percent of the way toward this goal.

3. This procedure also has certain statistical advantages. Expressing high socioeconomic values as a ratio of the average would tend to create a curvilinear distribution which complicates analysis, whereas the procedure suggested here avoids this problem in all but the most extreme cases.

Age Control. In calculating the SEA index, differences in age composition offer a source of bias. Low education among the young population often means lower income than a correspondingly low education among the older population. In all of the applications proposed here, the index has been fully adjusted for age composition. A special table, showing the income distribution for each of eight educational levels was prepared for each of eight age groups (64 age-education distributions). Each individual is assigned to one of these 64 categories according to his combination of age and educational attainment. In order to obtain the SEA status for a group, this procedure is repeated for each member and the results are accumulated and averaged. This has been programmed for computation on electronic computers and therefore is readily accomplished.

Use of Individual or Family Income. If the

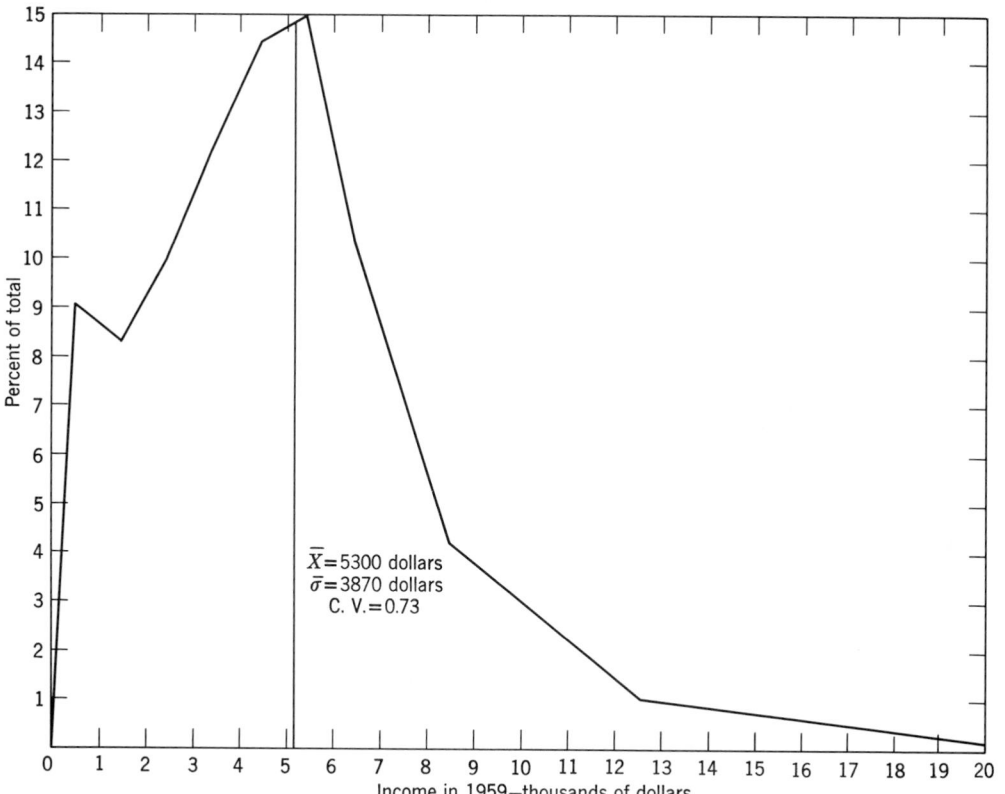

$\bar{X}$=5300 dollars
$\bar{\sigma}$=3870 dollars
C. V.=0.73

Income in 1959—thousands of dollars

Figure 14-1 Income Distributions of Male Experienced Civilian Labor Force: 1960.

index is being computed for an individual, the educational attainment and income of that individual (if an adult earner) would be used. If the index is being computed for families, the educational attainment of the family head and the actual family income would be used. Each member of the family would then receive the status of the family. Where family income is higher than individual income, it measures directly the extent to which the population improves its status by the practice of having multiple earners in the family.

14.7. Some Illustrations and Applications

The SEA system provides a standard yardstick against which we can measure the status of any individual or group for which educational attainment and income data are available. The following examples illustrate some of the uses to which it may be put.

The Socioeconomic Status Profile of a Nation. It is a characteristic of this system that the socioeconomic profile for a nation is exactly equal to its overall income distribution. This is

true because the national income distribution is used to convert educational attainment to monetary units; therefore, for the national population the educational attainment and the income distributions are identical when educational attainment is expressed in monetary units. Rather than being regarded as a fault, this is held to be a valid and useful insight. *At this generalized level, the shape of the income curve for individuals in the experienced labor force is asserted to outline faithfully the shape of the social status distribution.* A nation with an income distribution of the type shown in Figure 14-1 for the United States in 1960 is a nation with a large middle class. A nation with an income distribution that is a sharp "reverse J" pattern is a nation with a large peasant or proletarian population. The relative size of the elite group is indicated by the proportion of the population falling in the right tail, while the relative size of the bottom-rung group is indicated by the proportion of the population falling in the left tail. The standard deviation and the coefficient of variation indicate the amount

Table 14-2　SEA Indexes for Major Occupation Groups

Major occupation group	SEA index	Standard deviation	Coefficient of variation	Income base SEA	Education base SEA
Professional, technical and kindred workers..........................	39	25	64	40	38
Managers, officials and proprietors except farm.......................	37	25	67	42	32
Farm managers.......................	20	18	88	16	24
Clerical and kindred workers........	26	17	64	25	27
Sales workers......................	29	22	77	30	27
Craftsmen, foremen and kindred workers...........................	27	15	58	27	26
Operatives and kindred workers......	23	14	62	22	23
Service workers except private household......................	20	15	73	18	23
Private household workers..........	14	14	103	9	19
Laborers except farm...............	18	13	75	16	20
Farm laborers......................	12	12	100	8	16

of distance that separates the poor from the wealthy and the presence or absence of a middle class. A status curve that is leptokurtic is one where near equality in income prevails, while a platykurtic status curve indicates great disparity in income distribution. A curve that is badly skewed toward the upper end of the income scale represents a population that is being economically exploited by its elite group, while a curve that approaches the normal curve represents a society where income is distributed more nearly in accordance with abilities and productivity.

International comparison of status profiles is possible. Income distributions are becoming available for an increasing number of nations around the world; these distributions should be used as the entering wedge for international comparison of status systems.

The SEA Values of the General Occupational Categories. Table 14-2 reports the SEA scores for each of the major occupation groups. In contrast to previous scores of this type, these scores are based upon a ratio scale with a zero point, so that we may validly talk of absolute and relative differences among the categories. For example, professional workers have a score of 39, while farm laborers have a score of only 12. Not only may we claim that professional workers are 27 units more advanced along the scale than laborers, but that their status is 3.2 times that of farm laborers.

From Table 14-2 we learn that the American Dream of complete economic comfort and afflu-

ence is far from realization even among professional and managerial workers; the average scores of 39 and 37 for these groups indicate that they are only slightly more than one third of the way toward the attainment of this goal.

Table 14-2 teaches us a very important principle: the differentials in status among the occupational categories are unequal. Moreover, they are not ranked in the conventional manner. The broad occupational categories tend to fall into groups, as follows:

SEA score

Professional workers	39
Managers	37
Sales	29
Craftsmen	27
Clerical	26
Operatives	23
Service workers	20
Farmers and farm managers	20
Laborers	18
Farm laborers	12
Private household workers	14

At the top, managers and professionals stand apart from the rest by a rather wide margin. At the bottom, farm laborers and private household workers are separated from the balance of the workers by a substantial amount. The intermediate occupation groups are clustered in an array in such a way that the average difference between categories is only 2 or 3 points.

This finding has some important implications for the study of social mobility. Mobility studies that make use of occupational categories in studying movement give equal weight in the movement from one occupational category to another. The data of Table 14-2 suggest that this is a gross procedure. The farm laborer or private household worker who moves to the position of operative, for example, is improving his status by almost 100 percent, while the operative (blue-collar) worker who manages to become a clerical worker is improving his status by only 13 percent. The fact that craftsmen (traditionally classed among the blue-collar workers) have a status equal to that of sales and clerical workers should not be overlooked. Also, the small differential between craftsmen and operatives suggests that technological change, unionization, and automation have caused the difference between these two groups to shrink to a fraction of its former size. Finally, we must note that the relative difference between professional and managerial workers from the balance of the occupations is substantial—more than 30 percent.

If there are distinctive class boundaries in American society, we may identify at least three strata, where there is substantial disjunction, as follows:

1. Industrial and technological leaders: professional and managerial.

2. Industrial and technological followers: sales, craft, clerical, operatives, service, farmers, and laborers.

3. Preindustrial occupations: farm laborers and private household workers.

Within the second group there are slight indications of four substrata.

In summary, it is believed that the SEA scores provide fresh insight into the nature of occupational stratification in modern America. With a ratio scale we can reevaluate the traditional categories and cease to treat them as if they were an equal-interval or a simple rank system.

Detailed Occupation Categories. One way of refining the study of occupational status and occupational mobility is to compute an index of socioeconomic status for each of the detailed occupational groups published by the Census. This has been done previously by

Duncan[13] and Bogue[14], making use of the 1950 census. An SEA score has now been computed for each of the detailed occupation categories of the 1960 census (more than 400 items). Table 14-3 provides indexes for each detailed occupation as of 1960.

The SEA scores for detailed occupations permit the emphatic statement that the broad occupation groups are highly heterogeneous internally: the average value for the broad occupation group is only an average of a wide range of values for detailed occupations within the group. The following tabulation, showing the range of scores for detailed occupations within each of the major occupation groups, illustrates the point: in most cases there is a deep overlap between occupation groups. The highest-scoring detailed occupation in one category often is above the average for the highest group. In fact, the range of scores within each of the major occupation groups is, in every group, equal to almost 100 percent of the average score for the group. This is indeed a very high level of heterogeneity. This illustrates, with data, the generalization that technological advance has created such a multiplicity of occupations that it is almost impossible to group them into a few internally homogeneous categories that refer to the type of work performed.

Occupation group	SEA scores for detailed occupations within the group		
	SEA score	Highest	Lowest	Range
Professional	39	58	17	41
Managers ..	37	53	25	28
Clerical	26	34	13	21
Sales	29	41	18	23
Craft	27	38	15	23
Operatives .	23	31	11	20
Services ...	20	29	10	19
Laborers ...	18	25	11	14

[13] Otis Dudley Duncan, "A Socio-economic Index for All Occupations," in Albert J. Reiss, Jr., *et al.*, Occupations and Social Status (New York: Free Press, 1961).

[14] Donald J. Bogue, "Socioeconomic Scores for Detailed Occupational Groups," Appendix to *Skid Row in American Cities* (Chicago: Community and Family Study Center, 1962).

Table 14-3   Socioeconomic Achievement Index—Male Experienced Civilian Labor Force: 1960

Detailed occupation	Code number (1)	SEA index average (2)	Standard deviation (3)	Coefficient of variation (4)	Standard error (5)	Sample number (6)	Education based SEA index (7)	Income based SEA index (8)
United States Total	000	26	19	73	.0026	2236372	..	..
Professional, technical, and kindred wkrs..	001	39	25	64	.0105	224305	38	40
Accountants and auditors.....................	002	38	22	59	.0316	19734	37	39
Actors....................................	003	35	27	74	.2565	395	34	36
Airplane pilots and navigators...............	004	46	28	62	.1537	1361	35	57
Architects.................................	005	47	27	58	.1421	1478	43	52
Artists and art teachers....................	006	35	23	65	.0781	3348	34	36
Athletes..................................	007	30	25	81	.3532	193	25	36
Authors...................................	008	38	24	63	.1527	995	37	39
Chiropractors.............................	009	41	27	65	.2165	620	44	39
Clergymen.................................	010	32	24	75	.0499	9393	42	22
College presidents, prof'rs, & instr's (n.e.c)	011	43	26	61	.0643	6775	45	41
College presidents and deans...............	012	53	28	52	.3435	267	52	55
Professors and instructors:								
Agricultural sciences....................	013	45	25	56	.3984	158	48	42
Biological sciences.....................	014	43	26	60	.2924	310	46	41
Chemistry...............................	015	42	26	63	.2958	315	44	40
Economics...............................	016	45	26	58	.4069	168	47	43
Engineering.............................	017	46	26	58	.2392	487	44	47
Geology and geophysics..................	018	42	26	63	.6043	75	44	39
Mathematics.............................	019	39	25	65	.2597	383	41	37
Medical sciences........................	020	56	31	55	.3928	242	28	31
Physics.................................	021	41	28	64	.3012	293	41	40
Psychology..............................	022	44	25	56	.3854	164	46	43
Statistics..............................	023	46	30	66	1.8166	11	43	49
Natural sciences (n.e.c.)...............	024	43	27	63	1.1569	22	43	43
Social sciences (n.e.c.)................	025	45	26	57	.1698	915	48	43
Nonscientific subjects..................	026	41	25	60	.1523	1046	47	35
Subject not specified...................	027	42	27	64	.1225	1919	44	40
Dancers and dancing teachers................	028	23	20	86	.2721	219	24	22
Dentists...................................	029	56	31	55	.0956	4236	48	64
Designers..................................	030	37	22	59	.0831	2738	34	40
Dietitians and nutritionists................	031	27	19	69	.3855	96	31	24
Draftsmen..................................	032	29	17	57	.0328	10224	28	30
Editors and reporters......................	033	38	24	63	.0852	3222	37	40
Engineers, technical.......................	034	42	23	54	.0218	42965	39	46
Aeronautical.............................	035	44	23	51	.0896	2531	39	49
Chemical.................................	036	45	24	53	.1061	2011	41	48
Civil....................................	037	40	23	56	.0508	7921	38	42
Electrical...............................	038	42	22	52	.0467	9045	38	46
Industrial...............................	039	40	21	52	.0610	4727	38	43
Mechanical...............................	040	42	22	53	.0497	7961	38	46
Metallurgical, and metallurgists.........	041	43	24	55	.1549	936	40	47
Mining...................................	042	44	25	56	.2018	606	40	48
Sales....................................	043	44	24	53	.0871	2946	39	49
Not elsewhere classified.................	044	42	23	55	.0704	4281	38	46
Entertainers (n.e.c.).......................	045	26	22	87	.2094	451	25	26
Farm and home management advisors...........	046	38	21	57	.2325	335	42	32
Foresters and conservationists.............	047	29	20	68	.0970	1634	32	26
Funeral directors and embalmers.............	048	36	25	69	.1177	1753	36	38
Lawyers and judges.........................	049	54	31	57	.0618	10040	47	60
Librarians.................................	050	29	23	80	.1908	602	35	23
Musicians and music teachers...............	051	30	23	77	.0699	4206	33	26
Natural scientists.........................	052	41	23	57	.0567	6751	41	41
Agricultural scientists..................	053	36	22	63	.2292	377	39	32
Biological scientists....................	054	39	23	58	.2046	487	43	35
Chemists.................................	055	40	23	56	.0734	3760	40	40
Geologists and geophysicists.............	056	46	25	54	.1585	979	43	48
Mathematicians...........................	057	39	23	59	.2703	297	37	42
Physicists...............................	058	45	25	56	.1925	680	41	49
Miscellaneous natural scientists.........	059	40	22	54	.3312	173	40	40
Nurses, professional.......................	060	29	21	72	.1598	706	33	26
Nurses, student professional...............	061	17	18	105	.5565	43	20	14
Optometrists...............................	062	48	27	57	.1966	771	45	50
Osteopaths.................................	063	53	31	59	.4677	181	49	58
Personnel and labor relations workers........	064	41	23	56	.0791	3457	39	43
Pharmacists................................	065	42	25	61	.0773	4227	40	43
Photographers..............................	066	31	20	66	.0860	2270	30	32
Physicians and surgeons....................	067	58	34	58	.0657	10653	48	68
Public relations men and publicity writers....	068	43	26	60	.1492	1193	39	48
Radio operators............................	069	30	17	56	.0908	1346	28	31
Recreation and group workers...............	070	26	21	82	.1294	1119	30	23
Religious workers..........................	071	27	24	88	.1599	892	34	20

Table 14-3 (Continued)

Detailed occupation	(1)	(2)	(3)	(4)	(5)	(6)	(7)	(8)
Social and welfare workers, except group......	072	34	22	64	.1065	1739	39	30
Social scientists...........................	073	43	25	58	.1106	2059	41	45
Economists...............................	074	46	26	57	.1853	802	42	50
Psychologists............................	075	44	25	56	.2444	406	45	43
Statisticians and acturies...............	076	40	24	60	.1759	719	38	41
Miscellaneous social scientists..........	077	40	24	60	.4199	132	43	37
Sports instructors and officials.............	078	32	22	67	.0848	2537	35	29
Surveyors....................................	079	25	17	67	.0714	2213	26	24
Teachers, elementary schools.................	080	34	22	63	.0517	7022	41	28
Public...................................	081	35	22	62	.0543	6365	41	28
Private..................................	082	30	21	72	.1670	656	36	23
Teachers, secondary schools.................	083	38	23	60	.0389	13529	43	32
Public...................................	084	38	23	60	.0407	12339	43	32
Private..................................	085	35	23	66	.1347	1190	41	28
Teachers (n.e.c.)............................	086	33	22	66	.0823	2842	38	29
Technicians: Medical and dental.............	087	27	19	68	.0721	2632	29	26
Electrical and electronic.......	088	29	16	53	.0467	4446	27	31
Other engineer'g & physical sciences.....................	089	29	17	58	.0370	8233	28	30
Technicians (n.e.c.).........................	090	27	18	66	.0703	2574	28	26
Therapists and healers (n.e.c.)..............	091	36	25	68	.1699	852	39	33
Veterinarians...............................	092	48	28	59	.2069	746	45	51
Professional, technical & kindred wkrs (n.e.).	093	36	24	67	.0430	12225	35	37
Farmers and farm managers..............	094	20	18	88	.0106	113681	24	16
Farmers (owners and tenants).................	095	20	18	88	.0107	112524	24	16
Farm managers...............................	096	27	20	74	.1164	1157	29	25
Managers, Officials, & propr's exc. farm	097	37	25	67	.0104	232087	32	42
Buyers and department heads, store...........	098	37	23	64	.0487		32	41
Buyers and shippers, farm products..........	099	29	22	76	.1499	848	27	30
Conductors, railroad........................	100	32	16	50	.0680	2244	28	37
Credit men..................................	101	34	19	58	.0914	1797	33	34
Floormen and floor managers, store..........	102	28	18	66	.2135	293	28	28
Inspectors, public administration...........	103	32	17	54	.0574	3620	32	32
Federal public administration & postal ser..	104	34	17	51	.0777	1966	33	35
State public administration.................	105	30	17	57	.1351	654	32	28
Local public administration.................	106	30	17	56	.1071	1001	31	29
Managers and superintendents, building.......	107	25	20	78	.0973	1636	27	24
Officers, pilots, pursers, & engineers, ship..	108	34	22	64	.1005	1894	27	41
Officials & administrators (n.e.c.), public administration...........................	109	37	22	60	.0495	7973	36	38
Federal public administration and postal service..................................	110	41	22	54	.0812	2991	39	44
State public administration.................	111	37	22	60	.1103	1553	36	37
Local public administration.................	112	33	21	66	.0731	3429	32	33
Officials, lodge, society, union, etc........	113	36	22	61	.1127	1523	31	41
Postmasters.................................	114	33	18	55	.1083	1110	33	33
Purchasing agents and buyers (n.e.c.)........	115	37	21	56	.0602	4724	34	40
Managers, off'ls, & propr's (n.e.c)--salaried.	116	40	25	64	.0151	111916	34	46
Construction................................	117	38	14	61	.0559	7077	32	45
Manufacturing...............................	118	45	28	60	.0315	30481	36	55
Transportation..............................	119	38	22	58	.0588	5660	32	44
Communications, & utilities & sanitary ser..	120	41	23	58	.0691	4598	35	46
Wholesale trade.............................	121	41	26	64	.0533	9445	34	47
Retail trade................................	122	32	21	64	.0259	25915	30	35
Food and dairy products stores...........	123	30	18	59	.0516	4770	28	32
Eating and drinking places..............	124	29	20	68	.0771	2580	29	29
Gen. merchandise & Ltd. price variety stores..................................	125	36	24	66	.0818	3325	32	39
Apparel and accessories stores...........	126	34	22	63	.1060	1662	31	38
Furniture, housefurnishings, & equip. stores..................................	127	37	23	63	.1232	1403	32	41
Motor vehicles and accessories retailing..	128	34	20	60	.0628	4154	31	37
Gasoline service stations................	129	25	15	62	.0671	2096	26	24
Hardware, farm equip., & bldg. material retail..................................	130	35	22	63	.0867	2639	32	3
Other retail trade.......................	131	34	22	65	.0776	3287	32	37
Banking and other finance...................	132	42	26	63	.0553	8883	35	48
Insurance and real estate...................	133	43	26	60	.0694	5666	37	50
Business services...........................	134	45	28	63	.1126	2504	37	53
Automobile repair services and garages......	135	30	18	60	.1143	1006	29	31
Miscellaneous repair services...............	136	36	22	60	.2392	323	32	40
Personal services..........................	137	32	23	71	.0892	2557	31	33
All other industries (incl. not reported)...	138	39	26	67	.0585	7812	36	42
Mgrs., off'ls, & propr's (n.e.c.)--self employed.................................	139	35	26	74	.0179	83318	30	40
Construction................................	140	37	26	71	.0493	11262	30	43
Manufacturing...............................	141	41	30	72	.0670	7822	32	51
Transportation..............................	142	26	26	73	.1237	1790	20	30
Communications, & utilities & sanitary services................................	143	38	27	69	.3629	216	32	45
Wholesale trade.............................	144	40	29	73	.0733	6296	31	49

Table 14-3   (Continued)

Detailed occupation	(1)	(2)	(3)	(4)	(5)	(6)	(7)	(8)
Retail trade................................	145	32	23	73	.0230	40507	29	34
Food and dairy products stores............	146	27	21	75	.0445	8592	27	28
Eating and drinking places................	147	29	22	74	.0517	7026	28	31
Gen. merchandise & Ltd. price variety stores.................................	148	33	25	75	.1169	1797	30	35
Apparel and accessories stores............	149	39	27	69	.1256	1823	32	46
Furniture, housefurnishings, & equip, stores.................................	150	38	26	69	.1092	2256	32	43
Motor vehicles and accessories retailing..	151	40	28	70	.1070	2682	32	48
Gasoline service stations.................	152	27	18	66	.0423	7388	28	27
Hardware, farm equip., & bldg material retail.................................	153	37	27	69	.0913	3159	32	42
Other retail trade........................	154	34	25	73	.0651	5784	31	37
Banking and other finance.................	155	53	34	64	.2116	1025	37	68
Insurance and real estate.................	156	46	31	68	.1367	2090	35	58
Business services........................	157	41	29	69	.1457	1542	35	48
Automobile repair services and garages......	158	30	22	71	.0999	1867	28	32
Miscellaneous repair services..............	159	30	22	74	.1440	916	29	30
Personal services........................	160	31	24	75	.0719	4280	30	33
All other industries (incl. not reported)	161	36	28	78	.0916	3707	31	40
Clerical and kindred workers............	162	26	17	64	.0085	154731	27	25
Agents (n.e.c.)...........................	163	34	21	60	.0507	6601	34	35
Attendants and assistants, library...........	164	14	15	109	.1542	373	18	09
Attendants, physician's and dentist's office..	165	24	22	91	.4546	91	25	22
Baggagemen, transportation...................	166	26	14	55	.1768	261	26	26
Bank tellers...............................	167	24	15	63	.0694	1965	26	23
Bookkeepers...............................	168	26	17	65	.0391	7730	29	24
Cashiers.................................	169	19	16	85	.0442	5164	20	17
Collectors, bill and account...............	170	25	17	69	.0942	1323	27	23
Dispatchers and starters, vehicle...........	171	28	15	53	.0579	2591	28	28
Express messengers and railway mail clerks....	172	29	15	52	.1687	331	30	29
File clerks................................	173	19	15	78	.0944	997	22	16
Insurance adjusters, examiners and investigators.................................	174	33	19	57	.0755	2457	35	31
Mail carriers..............................	175	28	14	52	.0291	9841	29	26
Messengers and office boys...................	176	14	14	97	.0553	2875	16	12
Office machine operators.....................	177	24	14	59	.0452	4048	24	24
Payroll and timekeeping clerks..............	178	28	16	57	.0665	2208	29	26
Postal clerks..............................	179	29	15	52	.0317	9030	31	27
Receptionists..............................	180	22	17	78	.2722	161	25	19
Secretaries...............................	181	33	23	71	.1021	2066	31	34
Shipping and receiving clerks................	182	23	13	59	.0232	13236	24	21
Stenographers.............................	183	31	21	68	.1724	594	29	33
Stock clerks and storekeepers..............	184	21	15	69	.0242	14540	23	20
Telegraph messengers.......................	185	13	12	98	.1848	181	14	11
Telegraph operators........................	186	27	14	52	.0992	798	27	27
Telephone operators........................	187	25	17	69	.1227	775	26	24
Ticket, station, and express agents...........	188	29	16	55	.0604	2819	29	29
Typists..................................	189	21	15	71	.0840	1322	24	19
Clerical and kindred workers (n.e.c.).........	190	27	17	64	.0138	60757	28	26
Manufacturing.............................	191	28	16	59	.0228	20873	28	28
Transportation, commun., & other public utilities.................................	192	27	15	56	.0291	10793	28	27
Wholesale and retail trade.................	193	23	17	71	.0398	6981	25	22
Finance, insurance, and real estate.........	194	26	18	70	.0536	4757	27	26
Professional and related services..........	195	23	20	86	.0815	2328	26	19
Public administration......................	196	29	18	61	.0363	9664	31	27
Other industries (incl. not reported).......	197	24	18	76	.0495	5362	26	22
Sales workers.........................	198	29	22	77	.0114	147959	27	30
Advertising...............................	199	36	23	66	.1237	1424	33	38
Auctioneers...............................	200	31	24	77	.3331	204	28	34
Demonstrators.............................	201	25	18	73	.3895	88	26	24
Hucksters and peddlers.....................	202	21	17	83	.1028	1127	24	17
Insurance agents, brokers, and underwriters...	203	35	23	64	.0352	16563	33	38
Newsboys.................................	204	06	09	156	.0221	6935	07	04
Real estate agents and brokers..............	205	37	27	72	.0613	7509	33	41
Stock and bond salesman....................	206	41	29	69	.1524	1422	35	48
Salesmen and sales clerks (n.e.c.)............	207	29	21	73	.0125	112686	28	30
Manufacturing.............................	208	36	23	63	.0315	21000	33	40
Wholesale trade...........................	209	34	22	64	.0281	23986	31	37
Food and related products.................	210	31	19	62	.0589	4152	30	32
Other wholesale trade.....................	211	35	22	64	.0316	19834	32	38
Retail trade..............................	212	24	18	77	.0149	60898	25	23
Food and dairy products stores	213	18	15	84	.0264	13510	20	16
General merchandise retailing..............	214	23	17	74	.0451	5887	25	21
Limited price variety stores..............	215	18	18	102	.1912	368	20	16
Apparel and accessories...................	216	23	19	83	.0517	5275	24	21
Motor vehicles and accessories retailing..	217	28	18	66	.0351	10868	28	28
Other retail trade........................	218	25	19	76	.0244	24992	26	25
Other industries (incl. not reported).......	219	31	22	69	.0521	6801	30	32

Table 14-3 (*Continued*)

Detailed occupation	(1)	(2)	(3)	(4)	(5)	(6)	(7)	(8)
Craftsmen, foremen, and kindred workers..	220	27	16	58	.0047	445010	26	27
Bakers...................................	221	24	15	62	.0427	4616	24	24
Blacksmiths..............................	222	22	14	66	.0883	1064	23	21
Boilermakers.............................	223	27	14	52	.0765	1323	26	28
Bookbinders..............................	224	25	15	58	.1150	648	24	26
Brickmasons, stonemasons, and tile setters····	225	25	15	60	.0295	10176	24	25
Cabinetmakers............................	226	24	15	62	.0510	3363	25	23
Carpenters...............................	227	23	15	64	.0140	45461	24	22
Cement and concrete finishers............	228	23	14	61	.0581	2400	23	24
Compositors and typesetters..............	229	28	16	56	.0346	8342	27	30
Cranemen, derrickmen, and hoistmen...........	230	26	13	52	.0332	6500	25	27
Decorators and window dressers..............	231	27	18	68	.0960	1424	27	26
Electricians.............................	232	29	15	52	.0231	17669	28	31
Electrotypers and stereotypers..............	233	32	16	51	.1533	453	27	37
Engravers, except photoengravers..............	234	29	18	61	.1627	465	26	31
Excavating, grading, & road machinery opers...	235	25	14	57	.0271	10961	24	26
Foremen (n.e.c.)..........................	236	32	17	53	.0146	55637	29	36
Construction..........................	237	30	16	54	.0454	5045	27	33
Manufacturing.........................	238	34	17	52	.0188	34593	30	38
Metal industries....................	239	35	18	51	.0458	6299	30	41
Machinery, except electrical..............	240	34	17	49	.0587	3283	30	39
Electrical machinery, equipment & supplies	241	36	18	50	.0643	3049	31	40
Transportation equipment..................	242	37	18	49	.0569	4083	31	44
Motor vehicles & motor vehicle equipment	243	37	18	49	.0815	1975	31	44
Other transportation equipment.........	244	38	19	49	.0794	2108	32	43
Other durable goods......................	245	31	17	54	.0480	4783	28	33
Textiles, textile products, & apparel.....	246	28	16	57	.0627	2685	27	30
Other nondurable goods (incl. not specific manufacturing)..................	247	33	17	52	.0334	10410	30	36
Railroads & railway express service.........	248	29	15	50	.0693	1768	27	31
Transportation, except railroad.............	249	31	16	50	.0855	1344	28	34
Communications, & utilities & sanitary service................................	250	34	16	49	.0613	2877	30	37
Other industries (incl. not reported).......	251	31	17	56	.0344	10010	29	33
Forgemen and hammermen.......................	252	27	14	54	.1235	550	25	29
Furriers.................................	253	29	17	60	.2810	153	27	31
Glaziers.................................	254	26	15	56	.1044	779	24	28
Heat treaters, annealers and temperers........	255	27	14	50	.0854	1006	25	28
Inspectors, scalers, & graders, log & lumber..	256	23	15	62	.0928	981	25	22
Inspectors (n.e.c.)...........................	257	28	15	54	.0441	4847	28	28
Construction..........................	258	28	16	58	.1178	767	29	27
Railroads and railway express service.......	259	27	13	49	.0662	1581	26	28
Transportation except R.R., communication, and other public utilities.................	260	29	15	51	.1094	743	28	30
Other industries (incl. not reported).......	261	29	17	57	.0795	1757	30	28
Jewelers, watchmakers, goldsmiths, silversmiths.............................	262	26	17	64	.0809	1714	27	25
Job setters, metal.......................	263	28	13	47	.0595	1935	26	29
Linemen & servicemen, telegraph, t'phone & power...................................	264	29	14	47	.0233	13513	27	30
Locomotive engineers.........................	265	33	17	51	.0637	2894	27	39
Locomotive firemen.......................	266	29	14	50	.0651	1971	27	31
Loom fixers..............................	267	22	11	52	.0647	1249	23	21
Machinists...............................	268	27	14	52	.0177	25275	26	28
Mechanics and repairmen......................	269	25	14	58	.0086	112349	25	24
Air conditioning heating, & refrigeration...	270	27	15	57	.0527	3286	26	27
Airplane..............................	271	29	15	50	.0387	5699	28	31
Automobile............................	272	23	14	60	.0151	34646	24	22
Office machine........................	273	26	14	55	.0766	1415	26	26
Radio and television..................	274	25	16	64	.0439	5160	27	23
Railroad and car shop..................	275	25	13	51	.0571	2027	25	25
Not elsewhere classified	276	25	14	57	.0118	60116	25	25
Construction........................	277	26	15	59	.0485	3888	25	26
Manufacturing.......................	278	26	14	53	.0176	25412	26	27
Transportation, communication & other public utilities.......................	279	27	14	51	.0351	6197	27	27
Wholesale and retail trade..............	280	23	14	61	.0318	7959	25	22
Business and repair services.............	281	24	16	67	.0474	4448	25	22
Public administration....................	282	26	14	55	.0466	3590	26	20
Other industries (including not reported).	283	22	15	67	.0320	8622	24	20
Millers, grain, flour, feed, etc..............	284	22	15	65	.1345	470	23	21
Millwrights..............................	285	29	14	49	.0479	3429	27	31
Molders, metal...........................	286	24	13	54	.0507	2546	24	24
Motion picture projectionists.................	287	23	17	74	.1159	888	23	24
Opticians, and lens grinders and polishers....	288	28	18	64	.1225	875	27	29
Painters, construction and maintenance........	289	22	15	68	.0211	20214	24	20
Paperhangers.............................	290	21	16	75	.1459	465	24	18
Pattern and model makers, except paper........	291	31	16	51	.0718	1965	28	35

Table 14-3   (Continued)

Detailed occupation	(1)	(2)	(3)	(4)	(5)	(6)	(7)	(8)
Photoengravers and lithographers.............	262	32	17	53	.0986	1194	28	37
Piano and organ tuners and repairmen.........	293	24	18	77	.2020	332	27	21
Plasterers....................................	294	25	15	62	.0602	2563	24	26
Plumbers and pipe fitters....................	295	28	15	56	.0240	16441	26	29
Pressmen and plate printers, printing........	296	29	15	53	.0498	3699	26	31
Rollers and roll hands, metal................	297	27	15	55	.0753	1508	25	29
Roofers and slaters..........................	298	21	14	66	.0533	2739	22	20
Shoemakers and repairers, except factory.....	299	19	15	77	.0708	1733	22	17
Stationary engineers.........................	300	33	19	59	.0334	13511	31	35
Stone cutters and stone carvers..............	301	23	15	65	.1645	330	24	22
Structural metal workers.....................	302	27	14	52	.0496	3293	26	29
Tailors......................................	303	22	15	69	.0736	1611	22	21
Tinsmiths, coppersmiths, and sheet metal wkrs.	304	27	14	52	.0334	7135	26	28
Toolmakers, and die makers and setters.......	305	31	15	49	.0321	9199	28	34
Upholsterers.................................	306	23	14	62	.0536	2784	23	22
Craftsmen and kindred workers (n.e.c.).......	307	27	15	57	.0408	5496	25	28
Formers members of the armed forces..........	308	16	13	84	.0894	871	20	12
Operatives and kindred workers........	309	23	14	62	.0041	456051	23	22
Apprentices..................................	310	17	11	66	.0353	4088	17	18
Auto mechanics............................	311	11	10	88	.2212	79	12	10
Bricklayers and masons....................	312	16	11	67	.1722	159	16	16
Carpenters................................	313	15	11	70	.1174	321	15	15
Electricians..............................	314	20	11	54	.1024	422	19	20
Machinists and toolmakers.................	315	19	11	60	.0840	702	18	20
Mechanics, except auto....................	316	18	12	65	.1827	173	18	19
Plumbers and pipe fitters.................	317	18	11	62	.1079	428	18	18
Building trades (n.e.c.)..................	318	14	10	71	.1821	123	14	14
Metalworking trades (n.e.c.)..............	319	19	11	60	.1347	277	18	19
Printing trades...........................	320	17	11	66	.0954	551	17	17
Other specified trades....................	321	16	11	72	.1161	390	16	16
Trade not specified.......................	322	16	12	74	.1137	464	17	16
Asbestos and insulation workers..............	323	27	15	54	.0941	992	25	30
Assemblers...................................	324	23	13	57	.0191	18601	24	22
Attendants, auto service and parking.........	325	16	13	85	.0199	17751	18	13
Blasters and powdermen.......................	326	23	14	59	.1509	326	24	23
Boatmen, canalmen, and lock keepers..........	327	25	15	60	.1600	348	25	25
Brakemen, railroad...........................	328	28	14	50	.0497	3319	27	30
Bus drivers..................................	329	23	15	62	.0321	8302	25	21
Chainmen, rodmen, and axmen, surveying.......	330	17	14	79	.1265	476	19	15
Checkers, examiners, and inspectors, mfg.....	331	27	14	54	.0245	13980	27	27
Conductors, bus and street railway...........	332	26	13	49	.1768	215	27	25
Deliveryman and routemen	333	22	15	69	.0212	20893	23	22
Dressmakers and seamstresses, except factory..	334	22	16	71	.2278	194	24	21
Dyers..	335	21	13	64	.0874	939	22	20
Filers, grinders, and polishers, metal.......	336	25	14	54	.0316	7448	24	26
Fruit, nut, & veg. graders & packers except factory.............................	337	15	13	86	.1328	397	19	12
Furnacemen, smeltermen, and pourers..........	338	25	14	54	.0516	2831	24	26
Graders and sorters mfg......................	339	21	14	65	.1110	609	22	20
Heaters, metal...............................	340	27	14	51	.1382	401	25	30
Knitters, loopers, and toppers, textile......	341	21	12	58	.0887	772	23	20
Laundry and dry cleaning operatives..........	342	20	14	74	.0384	5666	23	17
Meat cutters, except slaughter and packing house..................................	343	25	15	60	.0312	8926	25	24
Milliners....................................	344	26	18	71	.7929	21	24	27
Mine operatives and laborers (n.e.c.)........	345	22	14	62	.0218	16191	23	22
Coal mining..............................	346	21	13	64	.0318	6836	22	19
Crude petroleum and natural gas extraction .	347	24	15	60	.0417	5015	24	25
Mining and quarrying, exc. fuel..........	348	22	13	60	.0405	4340	23	21
Motormen, mine, factory, logging camp, etc....	349	23	13	56	.0960	692	23	22
Motormen, street, subway, and elevated railway	350	27	13	47	.1343	366	27	27
Oilers and greasers, except auto.............	351	23	13	55	.0492	2790	23	24
Packers and wrappers (n.e.c.)................	352	18	13	73	.0274	9279	19	17
Painters, except construction and maintenance.	353	22	13	60	.0325	6745	23	22
Photographic process workers.................	354	24	17	69	.0951	1230	24	24
Power station operators......................	355	31	15	50	.0852	1286	29	32
Sailors and dock hands.......................	356	23	14	61	.0643	1963	24	23
Sawyers......................................	357	19	13	70	.0393	4436	21	16
Sewers and stitchers, mfg....................	358	20	13	64	.0596	1894	21	19
Spinners, textile............................	359	20	12	60	.1016	534	22	18
Stationary, firemen..........................	360	24	14	57	.0406	4587	24	24
Switchmen, railroad..........................	361	27	13	49	.0492	2951	26	28
Taxicab drivers and chauffeurs...............	362	22	14	67	.0317	8222	25	18
Truck and tractor drivers....................	363	23	14	63	.0100	81731	23	22
Weavers, textile.............................	364	20	12	58	.0548	1856	22	19
Welders, and flame-cutters...................	365	25	13	53	.0198	18461	25	26

Table 14-3   (*Continued*)

Detailed occupation	(1)	(2)	(3)	(4)	(5)	(6)	(7)	(8)
Operatives and kindred workers (n.e.c.).......	366	23	14	60	.0065	173342	23	22
Manufacturing...............................	367	23	13	59	.0070	145413	23	23
Durable goods............................	368	23	13	57	.0095	80014	23	23
Sawmills, planing mills, & misc.. wood products.........................	369	19	13	69	.0332	6304	21	17
Sawmills planing mills misc. wood prods.......	370	19	13	68	.0381	4809	21	18
Miscellaneous wood products.............	371	19	13	71	.0677	1495	21	16
Furniture and fixtures..................	372	19	12	65	.0371	4438	21	17
Stone, clay, and glass products........	373	23	13	57	.0311	7205	23	23
Glass and glass products..............	374	25	14	55	.0570	2327	24	26
Cement, & concrete, gypsum, & plaster product.........................	375	22	13	58	.0604	1789	22	22
Structural clay products..............	376	20	12	60	.0831	862	21	19
Pottery and related products..........	377	23	14	59	.1058	654	23	23
Miscellaneous nonmetallic mineral & stone products......................	378	24	13	54	.0652	1574	24	24
Metal industries.......................	379	24	13	55	.0172	23184	24	24
Primary metal industries...............	380	24	13	54	.0241	11782	24	25
Blast furnaces, steel works, and rolling and finishing mills........	381	25	13	53	.0382	4864	29	25
Other primary iron & steel inds.....	382	23	13	55	.0460	3100	23	24
Primary nonferrous industries.......	383	25	13	53	.0417	3819	24	25
Fabr'd metal ind. (inc. not spec. metal).............................	384	23	13	57	.0245	11402	23	23
Cutlery, hand tools & other hardware	385	23	13	57	.0782	1079	23	22
Fabricated structural metal prods...	386	23	13	57	.0471	3037	23	22
Misc. fabricated metal products.....	387	23	13	56	.0310	7230	23	23
Not specified metal industries......	388	22	13	60	.3568	55	24	20
Machinery, except electrical...........	389	24	13	56	.0242	12442	24	24
Farm machinery and equipment..........	390	24	13	55	.0770	1177	24	24
Office, computing and accounting machines.............................	391	25	13	52	.0879	887	25	25
Miscellaneous machinery...............	392	24	14	56	.0266	10378	24	24
Electrical machinery, equipment, & supplies.............................	393	24	14	55	.0304	7957	24	24
Transportation equipment...............	394	25	13	54	.0234	12907	24	25
Motor vehicles & motor vehicle equipment..........................	395	25	13	53	.0295	7797	24	25
Aircraft and parts...................	396	27	14	52	.0481	3290	26	27
Ship and boat building and repairing..	397	22	13	61	.0849	979	23	21
Railroad & misc. transportation equipment..........................	398	22	13	59	.0890	841	23	21
Profess'l & photographic equip., & watches..............................	399	25	14	57	.0648	1989	25	26
Professional equipment and supplies.....	400	24	14	57	.0755	1370	25	24
Photographic equipment and supplies.....	401	29	15	54	.1457	443	26	31
Watches, clocks, clockwork - oper. devices....	402	24	15	61	.2213	175	25	23
Miscellaneous manufacturing industries....	403	21	13	65	.0447	3588	22	19
Nondurable goods...........................	404	23	13	60	.0106	65102	23	22
Food and kindred workers..................	405	22	14	62	.0214	15974	22	21
Meat products.........................	406	23	14	59	.0394	4862	23	24
Dairy products........................	407	23	14	60	.0531	2639	23	22
Canning & pres. fruits, veg., & sea foods..............................	408	18	13	71	.0619	1676	20	16
Grain-mill products...................	409	22	13	62	.0719	1373	22	21
Bakery products.......................	410	19	13	65	.0691	1311	20	18
Confectionery and related products......	411	21	13	62	.1055	606	22	20
Beverage industries...................	412	23	14	59	.0604	2005	23	23
Misc. food preparations & kindred prods.	413	21	13	62	.0717	1369	22	21
Not specified food industries...........	414	21	14	66	.2431	132	23	20
Tobacco manufactures....................	415	20	12	60	.0862	747	21	18
Textile mill products...................	416	19	12	63	.0242	9777	21	17
Knitting mills........................	417	20	13	67	.1018	659	21	18
Dyeing & fin. text., except wool & knit gds..........................	418	21	13	60	.0793	1002	22	19
Floor covering, except hard surface.....	419	18	11	62	.1235	336	21	16
Yarn, thread, and fabric mills.........	420	18	11	63	.0277	6825	20	16
Miscellaneous textile mill products.....	421	21	12	59	.0969	656	22	20
Apparel & other fabricated textile prods..	422	22	14	66	.0375	5640	22	21
Apparel and accessories................	423	22	14	65	.0408	4849	22	21
Miscellaneous fabricated textile prods..	424	20	13	66	.0945	791	21	20
Paper and allied products................	425	24	13	53	.0272	8701	23	25
Pulp, paper, and paperboard mills.......	426	25	13	51	.0363	4964	24	26
Paperboard containers and boxes........	427	22	12	55	.0508	2354	22	22
Miscellaneous paper and pulp products...	428	23	13	54	.0675	1383	23	24
Printing, publishing, and allied inds.....	429	23	15	65	.0543	3001	22	24
Newspaper publishing, and printing.....	430	16	15	96	.1447	452	16	16
Printing, publishing, and allied inds., except newspapers....................	431	24	14	60	.0573	2549	23	25

Table 14-3 (Continued)

Detailed occupation	(1)	(2)	(3)	(4)	(5)	(6)	(7)	(8)
Chemicals and allied products..........	432	26	14	53	.0302	8241	25	27
Synthetic fibers.....................	433	24	12	51	.0912	747	25	24
Drugs and medicines..................	434	26	14	52	.1146	569	26	27
Paints, varnishes, and related prods..	435	24	13	57	.0929	824	24	24
Miscellaneous chemicals & allied prods	436	27	14	52	.0355	6101	25	28
Petroleum and coal products...........	437	30	15	49	.0598	2431	28	33
Petroleum refining...................	438	31	15	47	.0637	2152	28	34
Miscellaneous petroleum & coal prods..	439	23	13	55	.1543	280	23	24
Rubber and misc. plastic products......	440	24	13	55	.0350	5814	24	25
Rubber products.....................	441	26	13	52	.0407	4224	24	27
Misc. plastic products..............	442	21	13	62	.0660	1591	22	21
Leather and leather products..........	443	20	12	63	.0349	5076	21	18
Leather, tanned, curried, & finished..	444	22	13	68	.0887	812	23	21
Footwear, except rubber.............	445	19	12	64	.0413	3521	21	17
Leather products, except footwear.....	446	19	13	66	.0928	743	21	17
Not specified manufacturing industries....	447	19	13	66	.1479	296	21	18
Nonmanufacturing industries (incl. not reported).................................	448	21	14	67	.0171	27929	23	20
Construction.......................	449	22	15	66	.0416	5014	23	22
Railroads & railway express service.......	450	24	13	53	.0484	2754	25	23
Transportation, except railroad...........	451	23	14	62	.0705	1644	24	23
Communications, and utilities & sanitary service...................................	452	25	14	57	.0573	2397	25	24
Wholesale and retail trade.............	453	20	14	71	.0317	7664	21	18
Business and repair services..........	454	20	14	71	.0522	3024	22	19
Personal services...................	455	16	14	86	.1362	404	20	12
Public administration...............	456	24	14	57	.0618	2005	25	23
All other industries (incl. not reported).	457	19	15	81	.0548	3024	21	16
Private household workers..............	458	13	14	103	.0518	3027	19	9
Baby sitters, private household..............	459	6	9	149	.0966	363	9	4
Housekeepers, private household...........	460	16	17	105	.3039	122	22	10
Living in..................................	461	15	15	102	.5105	35	22	7
Living out................................	462	17	17	105	.3729	87	23	11
Laundresses, private household...........	463	14	14	98	.4345	43	19	10
Living out...............................	464	14	14	98	.4345	43	19	10
Private household workers (n.e.c))...........	465	15	14	97	.0575	2500	20	9
Living in.................................	466	17	14	87	.1570	337	23	11
Living out................................	467	15	14	99	.0617	2163	20	9
Service workers, exc. private household.	468	20	15	73	.0082	133645	23	18
Attendants, hospital and other institution....	469	19	14	70	.0379	5224	24	15
Attendants, professional & personal service (n.e.c.).................................	470	19	15	82	.0946	1050	21	16
Attendants, recreation and amusement.........	471	12	14	117	.0543	2540	14	10
Barbers...............................	472	23	15	67	.0329	8673	24	22
Bartenders............................	473	24	16	67	.0354	8011	26	21
Boarding and lodging house keepers............	474	22	19	87	.3081	156	26	19
Bootblacks............................	475	11	12	109	.1141	138	15	7
Chambermaids and maids, exc. private household	476	17	14	83	.2314	150	22	12
Charwomen and cleaners...............	477	17	14	83	.0503	3010	19	15
Cooks, except private household..............	478	21	15	70	.0282	10590	23	19
Counter and fountain workers................	479	14	14	98	.0545	2221	17	12
Elevator operators..........................	480	20	13	67	.0520	2605	22	17
Hairdressers and cosmetologists..............	481	26	18	71	.0884	1703	26	26
Housekeepers and stewards, exc. private household..................................	482	24	17	71	.0888	1481	26	22
Janitors and sextons......................	483	18	14	75	.0169	26671	21	15
Kitchen workers (n.e.c.) exc. private household..................................	484	13	12	95	.0305	6353	16	9
Midwives.................................	485	20	13	63	.6014	18	22	19
Porters.................................	486	17	13	74	.0298	7428	21	14
Practical nurses........................	487	21	16	75	.1499	437	26	16
Protective service workers....................	488	26	15	56	.0161	33724	27	25
Firemen, fire protection...................	489	29	14	48	.0331	6909	28	29
Guards, watchmen, and doorkeepers..........	490	23	15	64	.0266	12283	24	21
Marshals and constables....................	491	25	16	64	.1743	323	27	23
Policemen and detectives...................	492	28	14	51	.0259	12353	29	28
Public..................................	493	28	14	50	.0266	11440	29	28
Private.................................	494	27	16	60	.1069	913	27	26
Sheriffs and bailiffs......................	495	28	16	58	.0934	1159	28	26
Watchmen (crossing) and bridge tenders......	496	20	14	72	.1081	698	22	18
Ushers, recreation and amusement.............	497	7	10	132	.0883	492	9	6
Waiters.................................	498	17	15	88	.0390	5648	21	13
Service workers, exc. private household (n.e.c)	499	14	13	97	.0377	5021	17	10
Farm laborers and foremen..............	500	12	12	100	.0102	56818	16	8
Farm foremen.............................	501	24	17	70	.0949	1218	25	22
Farm laborers, wage workers.............	502	12	12	98	.0106	52233	16	8
Farm laborers, unpaid family workers.........	503	8	10	124	.0363	3080	11	6
Farm service laborers, self-employed.........	504	23	19	83	.2286	288	24	22

Table 14-3 (*Continued*)

Detailed Occupation	(1)	(2)	(3)	(4)	(5)	(6)	(7)	(8)
Laborers, except farm and mine........	505	18	13	75	.0066	164236	20	16
Carpenters, helpers, exc. logging and mining..	506	14	12	84	.0523	2125	18	11
Fishermen and oystermen.....................	507	19	15	82	.0701	1939	21	16
Garage laborers, and car washers and greasers.	508	14	12	86	.0377	4086	17	12
Gardeners, exc. farm, and groundskeepers......	509	15	14	91	.0275	10092	18	12
Longshoremen and stevedores..................	510	23	14	60	.0522	2883	23	24
Lumbermen, raftsmen, and wood choppers	511	16	14	86	.0341	6513	19	13
Teamsters....................................	512	18	14	81	.0868	1081	20	15
Truck drivers, helpers......................	513	16	12	78	.0622	1613	18	14
Warehousemen (n.e.c.)........................	514	23	13	57	.0346	5905	24	22
Laborers (n.e.c.)............................	515	18	13	73	.0074	127998	20	16
Manufacturing...............................	516	20	13	64	.0120	44023	21	18
Durable goods...............................	517	20	13	63	.0148	28927	21	19
Sawmills, planing mills, & misc. wood products..............................	518	17	12	75	.0343	5237	19	14
Sawmills, planing mills, and mill work	519	17	12	75	.0366	4664	19	14
Miscellaneous wood products..........	520	16	12	74	.0986	573	19	13
Furniture and fixtures...................	521	16	12	70	.0799	829	19	14
Stone, clay, and glass products........	522	20	12	61	.0390	3937	21	19
Glass and glass products.............	523	21	13	60	.0994	664	22	21
Cement, & concr., gypsum, & plaster products...........................	524	20	12	61	.0655	1367	21	19
Structural clay products.............	525	19	12	62	.0685	1234	21	18
Pottery and related products.........	526	18	12	67	.1809	174	20	16
Misc. nonmetallic mineral & stone prod	527	20	12	60	.1082	498	22	19
Metal industries.......................	528	21	12	59	.0229	11806	22	20
Primary metal industries.............	529	21	12	58	.0260	9034	22	21
Blast furnaces, steel works, and rolling and finishing mills........	530	22	12	58	.0327	5826	22	21
Other primary iron and steel inds...	531	21	12	58	.0534	2022	22	20
Primary nonferrous industries.......	532	22	13	58	.0727	1186	23	21
Fabr'd metal ind. (incl. not specified metal)...............................	533	20	13	62	.0476	2771	21	19
Cutlery, hand tools, and other hardware..........................	534	20	12	61	.1776	192	21	19
Fabricated structural metal prods...	535	20	12	62	.0803	946	21	18
Misc. fabricated metal products.....	536	20	13	62	.0631	1615	21	20
Not specified metal industries......	537	15	11	73	.5114	18	18	12
Machinery, exc. electrical.............	538	20	13	62	.0548	2170	21	19
Farm machinery and equipment.........	539	21	13	60	.1368	339	21	21
Office, computing, and accounting machines...........................	540	21	13	60	.2461	73	22	20
Miscellaneous machinery..............	541	20	13	63	.0610	1758	21	19
Electrical machinery, equipment, & supplies............................	542	21	13	61	.0691	1322	22	19
Transportation equipment...............	543	21	13	60	.0466	2995	22	20
Motor vehicles & motor vehicle equip..	544	22	13	57	.0618	1701	23	22
Aircraft and parts...................	545	23	13	56	.1597	256	24	22
Ship and boat building and repairing..	546	20	12	64	.0914	745	21	18
Railroad & misc. transportation equip.	547	20	13	64	.1504	293	23	17
Profess'l & photographic equipment, & watches..............................	548	22	14	67	.2170	175	22	21
Professional equipment and supplies...	549	21	15	70	.2500	135	22	20
Photographic equipment and supplies...	550	25	14	55	.4674	35	25	26
Watches, clocks, & clockwork-operators devices.............................	551	20	10	48	.0000	5	21	20
Miscellaneous manufacturing industries..	552	18	13	73	.1219	457	20	16
Nondurable goods..................	553	19	13	66	.0208	14988	21	18
Food and kindred workers...............	554	19	13	69	.0329	6118	20	17
Meat products........................	555	21	13	63	.0709	1361	21	20
Dairy products.......................	556	20	13	67	.0934	814	21	19
Canning & pres. fruits veg., & sea foods...............................	557	16	12	75	.0781	929	19	13
Grain-mill products..................	558	20	13	65	.0874	820	21	18
Bakery products......................	559	16	13	84	.1291	406	17	14
Confectionery and related products....	560	18	13	75	.2329	134	19	17
Beverage industries..................	561	19	13	68	.0936	786	20	19
Misc. food preparations & kindred products...........................	562	18	12	67	.0861	789	20	16
Not specified food industries.........	563	17	13	74	.2828	78	20	14
Tobacco manufactures..................	564	16	12	72	.1413	266	20	12
Textile mill products..................	565	16	11	70	.0561	1667	19	14
Yarn, thread, and fabric mills........	566	16	11	70	.0629	1275	19	13
Other textile mill products.........	567	18	12	68	.1220	392	20	15
Apparel & other fabricated textile prods	568	14	12	82	.1292	323	17	11
Paper and allied products.............	569	21	12	58	.0574	1806	22	20
Pulp, paper, and paperboard mills.....	570	21	12	57	.0697	1214	22	21
Paperboard containers and boxes.......	571	20	12	63	.1229	400	21	18
Miscellaneous paper and pulp products.	572	21	12	58	.1742	192	22	20
Printing, publishing, and allied ind....	573	17	14	80	.1203	529	18	17

Table 14-3   (Continued)

Detailed occupation	(1)	(2)	(3)	(4)	(5)	(6)	(7)	(8)
Chemicals and allied products............	574	21	13	61	.0537	2213	22	20
Synthetic fibers.......................	575	20	12	58	.2328	99	22	18
Drugs and medicines....................	576	22	13	58	.2645	94	23	21
Paints, varnishes, and related prods....	577	21	12	56	.1859	163	22	20
Miscellaneous chemicals & allied prods..	578	21	13	61	.0591	1857	22	20
Petroleum and coal products.............	579	24	13	53	.0870	861	24	24
Petroleum refining.....................	580	25	13	52	.0973	693	24	25
Misc. petroleum and coal products......	581	21	12	58	.1884	168	21	21
Rubber and misc. plastic products........	582	22	13	56	.0906	768	22	22
Leather and leather products.............	583	18	12	69	.1184	438	20	16
Not specified manufacturing industries.....	584	18	12	68	.2310	108	20	15
Nonmanufacturing industries (incl. not rptd)..	585	17	13	78	.0092	83975	19	15
Construction.............................	586	19	13	72	.0140	36176	21	16
Railroads and railway express service.......	587	21	12	60	.0308	6507	22	19
Transportation, except railroad............	588	20	14	67	.0409	4410	22	19
Communications, & utilities & sanitary serv.	589	20	13	65	.0326	6101	21	18
Wholesale and retail trade.................	590	12	12	100	.0189	16360	14	10
Business and repair services	591	16	14	85	.0850	1081	19	14
Personal services.........................	592	11	12	114	.0426	3368	15	6
Public administration.....................	593	21	13	62	.0439	3624	24	19
All other industries (incl. not reported)...	594	15	14	90	.0340	6348	19	11
Occupation not reported...................	595	24	18	77	.0113	103210	24	24

Two of the right-hand columns of Table 14-3 report the education and the income components separately which, when averaged together, form the average index for each occupation. The education component is obtained by computing the income level that would be expected for the holders of a given occupation on the expectation that they receive income in accordance with the amount of education they have completed, and the age composition of those in the occupation. In other words, the education component reports what the income level in an occupation would be if people employed in that occupation were paid according to their education attainment and age, using the average income received by each age-education group as a basis for payment. It may be surprising to find that for a majority of occupations the value of the education component differs very little from the income value. This means that many of the attributes that we have been attributing to occupations in the past may be nothing more than the attributes associated with the educational and income level of the people who hold that occupation, and that most workers are paid average salaries that are considered "normal" for persons of their educational level, irrespective of what occupation they hold. The following values for major occupational categories illustrate this point:

Occupation	Component Education	Income
Professional, technical, and kindred workers	38	40
Clerical and kindred workers	27	25
Sales workers	27	30
Craftsmen, foremen, and kindred workers	26	27
Operatives and kindred workers	23	22
Service workers, except private household	23	18

It is most impressive to see how nearly perfectly the educational component alone can "predict" the income distribution for such diverse occupations as professionals and operatives.

However, this generalization does not apply to all occupations. The remaining categories in the major occupational classifications show a substantial disparity for the components:

Occupation	Component Education	Income
Managers, officials, proprietors	32	42
Private household workers	19	9
Farmers and farm managers	24	16
Farm laborers and foremen	16	8
Laborers, exc. farm and mine	20	16

Within this group we have two situations. (1) A group that receives *more* income than its educational level would lead us to suspect. These are the leaders of business—managers, officials, and proprietors. (2) A group that receives *less* income than its educational level would lead us to suspect. Farmers, laborers, and private household workers fall in this group. On the one hand we may be tempted to label the first group "overpaid" and the second group "underpaid." Yet we must remember that not all grammar school, high school, and college graduates have equal abilities and that there is a process of selection in which the more able persons are placed in the better positions with higher pay and the less able are given lesser jobs and poorer pay. Thus if laborers appear to be underpaid in relation to the amount of education they claim to have completed, it may be that laborers are persons who, when in school, made inferior grades and were found unqualified for the better jobs. Although data are unavailable, it is quite plausible to suppose that this accounts for much of the phenomenon of apparent "overpayment" and "underpayment."

Another explanation is the amount of education actually received. The category "5 years of college or more" gives equal income expectation to those with M.A. and Ph.D. degrees, overvaluing the one and undervaluing the other.

Economic Dominance and Relative Deprivation. It is doubtful whether differences in academic accomplishment can account for all of the large differentials between the education and the income components for particular occupations. We can hypothesize that two additional forces—"economic dominance" and "economic subordination"—are at work to pay some members a disproportionately large share of the disposable net product and others a disproportionately small share. The phenomenon of economic dominance arises where individuals are in a unique position to divert the flow of income to themselves and the phenomenon of economic subordination arises where the individual is comparatively less powerful and is unable even to command his proportionate share of income. Individuals stand in one of

three positions with respect to the amount of income they actually receive in comparison with their "fair share" as measured by educational attainment:

Economic dominant—persons who receive significantly more money income than one would expect on the basis of educational preparation alone.

Full participant—persons who receive the amount of money income that one would expect on the basis of educational preparation alone.

Economic subordinant ("relatively deprived")—persons who receive significantly less money income than one would expect on the basis of education alone.

If the indexes for the education were fully sensitive to differences in technical preparation, persons could be easily classified into one of the three categories simply by dividing the economic component by the education component. Values greater than 1 would then indicate economic dominance, while values smaller than 1 would indicate economic subordination.

In order to isolate cases of unmistakable dominance and subordination, an allowance of $1000 discrepancy (5 points on the SEA scale) has been allowed. Table 14-4 lists the occupations that appear to be economically dominant because their recipients receive, on an average, at least $1000 more income per year than one would expect on the basis of their educational attainment and age. Similarly, Table 14-5 lists occupations that appear to be economically subordinate because those who hold them receive at least $1000 per year less than one would expect on the basis of educational attainment and age. All of the manager, proprietor, and official categories are in the dominant group, as are physicians, dentists, lawyers, and engineers. Some of these differentials are very large indeed, as the components for physicians, bank managers, and lawyers illustrate:

Component	Physician	Bank	Lawyer
Educational	48	37	47
Income	68	68	60
SEA score	58	53	54

Table 14-4 List of Occupations That Are Economic Dominants: Average Income Paid Exceeds Amount Expected on Basis of Education by $1000 per Year or More

Occupation	Education based index	Income based index
Professional workers		
Airplane pilots and navigators	35	57
Architects	43	52
Athletes	25	36
Professors: statistics	43	49
Dentists	48	64
Designers	34	40
Engineers: technical	39	46
Lawyers and judges	47	60
Natural scientists: geologists and geophysicists	43	48
Natural scientists: mathematicians	37	42
Natural scientists: physicists	41	49
Osteopaths	45	50
Personnel and labor relations workers	9	58
Physicians and surgeons	48	68
Public relations men and publicity writers	39	48
Social scientists: economists	42	50
Veterinarians	45	51
Proprietors, managers, officials		
Buyers and department heads	32	41
Conductors, railroad	28	37
Officials: Federal public administration and postal	39	44
Officials: Lodge society, union, etc.	31	41
Purchasing agents and buyers	34	40
Managers, officials and proprietors--salaried	34	46
Managers, officials, and proprietors--self employed	30	40
Advertising agents and salesmen	33	38
Insurance agents, brokers, and underwriters	33	38
Real estate agents and brokers	33	41
Stocks and bond salesmen	35	48
Salesmen and sales clerks (n.e.c.)	28	30
Craft workers		
Electrotypers and stereotypers	27	37
Engravers, except photoengravers	26	31
Foremen (n.e.c.)	29	36
Locomotive engineers	27	39
Pattern and model makers, except paper	28	35
Photoengravers and lithographers	28	37
Pressmen and plate printers, printing	26	31
Tool makers and die makers and setters	28	34
Asbestos and insulation workers	25	30
Operatives		
Operatives: manufacture of photographic equipment	26	31
Operatives: manufacture--petroleum refining	28	33
Operatives: manufacture of miscellaneous petroleum and coal products	28	34

Table 14-5, listing the economically subordinate occupations, demonstrates that intellectual and moral leaders and those devoted to serving their fellowman—either intellectually, commercially, or personally—are relatively deprived economically. Clergymen, teachers from the university level to the grammar school level, welfare workers, nurses and medical attendants, are all in this category. It is well known that a professor teaching zoology, a sociologist concerned with social change, a social worker attending to the needs of poor families, a nurse attending the sick, and the like, have had more technical training and would probably score higher on an intelligence test or a general test of knowledge than would a department head or buyer in a department store or the manager of a real estate or insurance office, yet they all earn significantly less when full allowance is made for their additional special training.

In addition there is a large body of service workers, operatives, farmers, and laborers who receive lower incomes than the level of their education would indicate, and the reason seems to be only that they are economically less powerful. Within each of these groups

Table 14-5 List of Occupations That Are Economically Subordinate ("Relatively Deprived"); Average Income Paid is $1000 per Year Less Than the Amount Expected on the Basis of Educational Attainment and Age of the Members: 1960

Occupation	Education based index	Income based index
Professional and technical workers		
Chiropractors..	44	39
Clergymen..	42	22
Professors: agricultural science....................	48	42
Professors: biological sciences....................	46	41
Professors: geology and geophysics................	44	39
Professors: social sciences (n.e.c.)...............	48	43
Professors: nonscientific subjects................	47	35
Dieticians and nutritionists.......................	31	24
Farm and home management advisers..................	42	32
Foresters and conservationists.....................	32	26
Librarians...	35	23
Musicians and music teachers.......................	33	26
Agricultural scientists............................	39	32
Natural scientists: biological scientists.........	43	35
Nurses, professional...............................	33	26
Nurses, student professional.......................	20	14
Recreation and group workers.......................	30	23
Religious workers..................................	34	20
Social and welfare workers.........................	29	30
Miscellaneous social scientists....................	43	37
Sports instructors, officials......................	35	29
Teachers: elementary schools......................	41	28
Teachers: secondary schools.......................	43	32
Teachers: n.e.c...................................	38	29
Therapists and healers.............................	39	33
Farmers and farm managers		
Farmers (owners and tenants).......................	24	16
Clerical and kindred workers		
Attendants and assistants, library.................	18	09
File clerks..	22	16
Secretaries..	25	19
Typists..	24	19
Clerical (n.e.c.): professional....................	26	19
Sales workers		
Hucksters and peddlers.............................	24	17
Craftsmen, foremen, etc.		
Paperhangers.......................................	24	17
Piano and organ tuners.............................	27	21
Shoemakers and repairers, except factory...........	22	17
Former members of armed forces.....................	20	12
Operatives		
Attendants: Auto service and parking..............	18	13
Fruit, nut and vegetable graders...................	19	12
Laundry and dry cleaning operatives................	23	17
Sawyers..	21	16
Truck and tractor drivers..........................	25	18
Manufacture of miscellaneous wood products.........	21	16
Manufacture of textiles: floor covering...........	21	16
Operatives: personal services....................	20	12
Nonmanufacturing industries: religious, other.....	21	16

there are categories of workers who receive their full share of income: mine workers, stevedores, barbers, railroad brakemen, machinists in factories, laborers in glass, metal, machinery, and meat processing industries, and others. A strong labor union seems to be the major distinguishing trait between these occupations that are full participants in the economy and those that are economically subordinate. Following are some examples of extreme relative deprivation that are so severe that they appear to border on economic exploitation:

Table 14-5   (continued)

Occupation	Education based index	Income based index
Private household workers (all classes)	19	9
Service workers	23	18
Attendants: hospitals and other institutions.............	24	15
Attendants: professional and personal services..........	21	16
Bartenders..	26	21
Boarding and lodging house keepers.......................	26	19
Bootblacks...	15	7
Chambermaids and maids, except private house..............	22	12
Counter and fountain workers.............................	17	12
Elevator operators.......................................	22	17
Janitors and sextons.....................................	21	15
Kitchen workers (n.e.c.) except household.................	16	9
Porters...	21	14
Practical nurses...	26	16
Waiters...	21	13
Service workers (n.e.c.) except private household.........	17	10
Farm laborers and foremen		
Farm laborers: wage workers.............................	16	8
Farm laborers: unpaid family workers....................	11	6
Laborers, except farm and mine		
Carpenter's helpers......................................	18	11
Fishermen and oystermen..................................	21	16
Garage laborers and car washers..........................	17	12
Gardeners and groundskeepers.............................	18	12
Lumbermen, raftsmen and wood choppers.....................	19	13
Teamsters...	20	15
Laborers: sawmills.......................................	19	14
Laborers: canning and preserving fruits, vegetable and sea foods....................................	19	13
Laborers: tobacco manufactures...........................	20	12
Laborers: textile mills..................................	19	14
Laborers: manufacturing industries, type not specified ...	20	15
Laborers: construction industries........................	21	16
Laborers: business and repair services...................		
Laborers: personal services..............................	15	6
Laborers: public administration..........................	24	19

Occupation	Component Education	Income	Index of relative deprivation
Nurses	33	26	.79
Teachers: elementary	41	28	.68
Library attendants	18	9	.50
Fishermen and oystermen	21	16	.76
Hospital attendants	24	15	.63
Kitchen workers	16	9	.56
Farm owners and tenants	24	16	.67
Laborers: canning food ..	19	13	.68
Farm laborers	16	8	.50

Clergymen, equally seriously deprived, have been omitted from the table because of the vow of poverty that many must take.

In each of the cases listed above, the occupation is an important and essential one without which the economy could not operate smoothly. It could be predicted that there will be a movement toward stronger unionization in each in coming years, for workers who are receiving only one-half to three-fourths of what would appear to be their "fair share" may be expected to undertake to alter the situation. If the society is sincere about its vow to end poverty, it must be prepared to pay to those who perform these functions a salary or wage that will permit them to live above the poverty line. The fact that this would increase the price of food, education, hospital care, housekeeping service, and a wide variety of personal services is simply another way of saying that poverty cannot be eliminated without some redistribution of wealth.

In considering the above data it should be kept in mind that they refer to males only; the entire range of female employment, when viewed in these terms, is portrayed as subject to severe relative economic deprivation. It should also be remembered that many cases of severe relative deprivation (watchmen, ushers, newsboys, etc.) are not reported in Table 14-5 because although the relative differential is large, the absolute differential does not quite attain the $1000 gap that was set to identify economic dominants and subordinates.

The Study of the Status and Mobility of Persons. It is believed that the SEA system of measuring status offers fresh opportunities to conduct special studies of status and social mobility, making use of samples. If, for each respondent in the sample, we collect the following information for himself, his father, and his grandfather, we can compute status and change in status on both an absolute and a relative basis:

educational attainment
occupational history
income history

Even though the data for the preceding generations may be very crude indeed, with this system we can greatly improve upon previous measures of status and mobility. We can compute both intergenerational and intragenerational mobility. But we can go much further: we can pinpoint in time the changes in status and relate them to events that are present hypotheses of "cause." We can, for example, compare the mobility history of men who married early and bore large families with those of men who married late and bore small families, holding constant factors such as father's status.

Another feature of the SEA scores that should help clarify research in this area is their ability to rate persons as "overachievers" and "underachievers" in relation to their level of education. The educational level of the person may be converted to "expected" income, according to his age. This may be compared with the actual income of the person. An "overachiever" is a person whose actual income is above the expected income, while the "underachiever" is a person in the reverse situation. Also, it is possible to compute two SEA scores for a person: one based on his education and income and the other based on his detailed occupation classification. He may be declared

to be an "overachiever" or "underachiever" by comparing his occupation SEA with his income-education SEA. Studies of status inconsistency and status crystallization may be made much more specific and explicit by these procedures. The fact that the SEA scores measure absolute as well as relative differences and are available for more than one decade makes it possible to compare interoccupational differences and trends over time in overachieving and underachieving. Moreover, researchers can collect data pertaining to the attitudes, prejudices, and behavior of individuals to be correlated with the degree to which they have overachieved or underachieved status in accordance with their expected status.

The Status Meaning of SEA Scores. All of the evidence presented thus far, and data to be presented below, tends to deny that sharp castelike strata exist in the American population along the lines of occupation-education-income. Instead, there seems to be more or less a continuum of status, with layer upon layer gradually merging from one set of conditions to another. Under such circumstances, the process of establishing strata is more one of selecting meaningful "cutting points" than one of discovering rigid boundaries of disjunction in social life. A system of layers, widely used and quite useful when not taken seriously as a sharp demarking class boundaries, is the six-category classification of W. Lloyd Warner and Paul S. Lunt.[15]

To interpret SEA scores more meaningfully, it is useful to have some generalized system of status categories against which to refer the numbers, in order that they may be more adequately interpreted. Therefore, we make use of the Warner-Lunt categories, but give them class boundaries in terms of SEA scores. The recommended translation is as shown in Table 14-6. If these ranges of the SEA score are given this general interpretation, it is believed that the correct meaning attached to most groups and individuals will be significant and will correspond to usage in other research. At the risk of unnecessary repetition, we empha-

[15] W. Lloyd Warner and Paul S. Lunt, *The Social Life of a Modern Community* (New Haven, Conn.: Yale University Press, 1941), pp. 88.

Table 14.6 Approximate Range of SEA Values Associated with Social Strata, Their Meaning in Terms of Income-Education Units, and Distribution of the Population among Status Categories: 1960

Social status category	Range of SEA scores	Equivalent in Income-education dollars	Equivalent in livelihood status	1960 Distribution of U.S. population,	
				Individuals	Families
Upper-upper	50+	$10,000 and over	Wealth	7.7	15.1
Lower-upper	35.0-49.9	7,000 to 9,999	Affluence	12.8	20.1
Upper-middle	25.0-34.9	5,000 to 6,999	Economic comfort	25.2	23.0
Lower-middle	15.0-34.9	3,000 to 4,999	Minimum decency	26.7	19.5
Upper-lower	5.0-14.9	1,000 to 2,999	Poverty	18.4	15.8
Lower-lower	0.1- 4.9	Under $1,000	Destitution	9.2	5.6

size again that the upper-upper category contains the elite members of a society as well as many persons who are not endowed with more than a high level of education and income. In order to separate the elite from the nonelite, and to rank the elite members and show the real as well as social distance between members of the elite, special prestige-measuring procedures must be introduced. It is not believed that the use of occupational categories alone can accomplish this, no matter how detailed and refined they may be.

Another point of fundamental importance must be kept in mind in making use of the status intervals. The data refer to the "real world" and not to "ideal types." Thus the rather modest ranking for college presidents and deans is based on the educational attainment and income of the presidents of state teachers' colleges, small religious colleges, and community junior colleges—as well as upon the data for the presidents of the Ivy League, Big Ten, and other leading universities. As a result, some findings that may be offensive to sociological prejudices may appear.

Such discordant results should not be taken as automatic proof that the system of SEA scores is incorrect. Instead, these results may provide an opportunity to learn just how high or low is the socioeconomic position that groups about which we may be more prejudiced than familiar have succeeded in attaining in the society. The results for osteopaths, airline pilots, and others are examples.

Another point that must be mentioned here is that the system for collecting data for occupations is itself highly defective and in need of overhaul. We can compute an SEA index only for those occupational categories that have been established by the U. S. Bureau of the Census. This occupational classification system is very weak for the purpose of measuring status, because it fails to identify and code separately many unique and meaningful occupations. Examples are members of state and national legislatures, presidents and vice-presidents of corporations, and other categories that would reflect the occupational structure of modern corporations. In other cases, highly unique and unlike occupations are tossed into a single category that ruins both for studies of mobility. Examples are "lawyers and judges," "college presidents and deans," and "editors and reporters."

The Study of the Social Status of Residential Populations. It is possible to compute SEA scores for a city, a state, a county, or a census tract. Table 14-7 illustrates such computations for selected metropolitan areas and for selected census tracts in the Chicago Standard Metropolitan Area. It is possible to compute such indexes for each decade, and thereby to measure the change in social status of the residents. The standard deviation and coefficient of variation for the tract or the SMA provides a measure of the degree of dispersion away from the average score. As Table 14-7 illustrates, it is possible to compute the SEA distribution for a tract on the basis of its reported occupational composition. These indexes based on occupation yield results almost identical with the educational component in

Table 14-7 Illustrative SEA Indexes for Areas

Area	SEA index	Standard deviation (index)	Coefficient of variation	Family income	Education component	Occupation component
Chicago						
City Total..................	32	20	64	38	26	26
City tract 125 (Gold coast)..	56	28	50	77	36	35
City tract 506 (Italian).....	30	17	59	35	24	25
City tract 120 (Negro slum)..	18	12	71	14	22	22
Suburb tract NTT 007.........	61	26	42	85	39	36
Suburb tract EVC 14..........	54	28	58	56	33	33
Suburb tract BRT 021-B.......	23	17	73	23	23	23
Standard metropolitan areas						
Los Angeles.................	34	22	64	40	29	29
Chicago.....................	35	22	63	41	28	28
Philadelphia................	32	21	65	37	27	28
Detroit.....................	33	21	64	38	27	27
Boston......................	34	22	64	39	29	29
Pittsburgh..................	31	20	66	34	27	28
Washington D.C..............	36	23	63	43	31	29
Seattle.....................	34	21	63	39	30	29
Dallas......................	32	22	69	35	28	29
Atlanta.....................	31	22	70	34	27	27
Indianapolis................	33	21	64	37	28	28
Richmond....................	31	21	67	35	27	28
Augusta.....................	26	19	74	26	26	27

most cases. In general, the education-income SEA scores for local areas may be expected to portray the status situation adequately, and the occupation scores only corroborate them. In calculating the scores for Table 14-7, the occupation and education components were each given a weight of ¼ and the income data were given a weight of ½.

Table 14-7 demonstrates that there are significant differences between areas in their SEA levels. For example, it is demonstrated that within the suburbs there are tracts that have almost as low a SEA level as the poorest tracts within Chicago central city. It also demonstrates that within the suburbs there are particular tracts where the SEA level is very high. The SEA scores open up a wide range of new opportunities for studies in human ecology, for it permits the scoring of a wide range of populations.

The Study of Group Effects on the Individual. Because the SEA system computes values with equal ease for residential, classificatory, or functional groups as well as for individuals, it offers excellent opportunities to study individuals in their group context. For example, if a sample of individuals are identified according to the census tracts of their residence, their

SEA scores can be compared with the scores for the neighborhoods in which they live. If high-status persons living in low-status areas may be expected to behave differently from high-status persons living in high-status areas, this system will permit explicit and unambiguous tests to be made, for it permits a measurement of the status difference between an individual and his group.

CONCLUSION

This chapter is intended only as a descriptive introduction to a system. Because the components from which this index is constructed are variables that normally constitute a part of a regular population census, and because the approach taken here is that of the route of an objective index derived from education-income-occupation data, which are widely analyzed and exploited as a part of the field of population composition, the entire subject of the functional measurement of social status is here defined to be a subfield of demography. This needs to be supplemented for the elite class by prestige studies. However, it is emphatically denied that prestige ratings alone can ever provide adequate basis for the study of social status, social stratification, or social mobility. Furthermore, it is emphatically denied that occupation is the appropriate basis from which to begin the study of social status—even for the study of prestige. Occupation is only one facet of the position of the social status of an individual, and a facet that is overshadowed in most instances by considerations of income, education, race or ethnicity, and duration of residence in present community. Occupations, being scored as group averages, waste much valuable information about the status achievement of individuals, which is saved by shifting to an amalgam of education and income. The amount of variation in income and education that characterizes even the detailed occupational categories is truly amazing. The variation effectively destroys any hope of erecting a valid scheme for the study of social status based on occupations. It is more efficient and meaningful to go directly to the components which are functional measures of social status.

QUESTIONS AND EXERCISES

1. There has been a great deal of discussion of whether social strata are really strata or only layers of status distributed along a more or less even continuum of prestige or status. Write an essay on the methodology for determining which of these views is correct in a particular society at a particular time. Plan a research study to make an empirical test. For an unbiased test, will it be necessary to make the measures of status along a continuous scale, as asserted in this chapter?

2. Sociologists studying status have been concerned primarily about relative status: the position of one person with respect to another. They have neglected absolute changes in status. Thus there have been arguments concerning whether ours is becoming a closed society (little upward social mobility) or whether it remains open. Chapter 13 showed that the economic position of the population has improved markedly in the past generation. Chapter 8 reported a similar change with respect to educational attainment. It is clear, by the premises of this chapter, that there has been a very substantial absolute rise in the socioeconomic status of the entire population. Should this fact be considered in the discussion of "open" and "closed" societies?

3. It has been asserted that the SEA scores may be used to measure social mobility, but no effort was made to demonstrate this fact. Write a methodological essay on the appropriate procedures for measuring social mobility with these sources. Design a research study for measuring social mobility by this procedure. Do you think you will find more intragenerational mobility and less intergenerational mobility by this procedure than would be reported by the occupational procedure, or would the reverse tend to be true?

4. Read the articles on "Status Crystallization" and "Status Consistency" by Lenski, Hodge, and Landecker cited in the Bibliography. Does the system of SEA scores provide an opportunity to improve upon measures of status crystallization? How would you define status crystallization in terms of SEA scores? With the SEA system, can you develop quantitative measures of several types of status inconsistencies? Does the fact that the SEA scores are measured along a ratio scale justify the assertion that with them it is possible to measure absolute as well as relative inconsistency? Does the fact that the SEA scores have a standard error attached to each clarify thinking concerning what is and what is not an inconsistent pair of statuses?

5. It has been asserted that the SEA system could be used for making international comparisons, yet no illustration of this fact was given. Write a methodological essay on this subject. Design the procedure for setting up SEA scores for another nation. How would you generalize this procedure as a recommendation to the United Nations and International Labour Office as a program for the international measurement of social status and social mobility throughout the world?

6. In Chapter 13 it was pointed out that income data need to be adjusted for the size and type of family that they support. Is the fact that no such adjustment was made here for income statistics a qualification on the meaningfulness and utility of the SEA indexes?

7. It was stated that either individual or family income could be used in computing SEA scores. Would it be meaningful and useful to calculate how many points of SEA status a woman can add to her family by entering the labor force?

8. Would it be easier or more difficult to measure intergenerational mobility with SEA scores based on the education and income of the two generations than by the use of occupations? List the arguments in favor of and against each procedure. On balance, how would you proceed to measure intergenerational mobility with greatest precision?

9. As often measured, intragenerational mobility and intergenerational mobility are not mutually exclusive. How might this problem be resolved?

10. No measures of the SEA scores for women are presented in this chapter. What procedure do you think should be followed in compiling such scores? Can differences in scores for men and women be a realistic measure of differences in their status? When should we undertake to compute an SEA score for women and when should women simply be given the score of their family or their husband or father?

BIBLIOGRAPHY

Barber, Bernard. *Social Stratification.* New York: Harcourt, Brace and Company, 1957.

Bendix, Reinhard, and Seymour Martin Lipset (eds.). *Class, Status and Power: A Reader in Social Stratification.* Glencoe, Ill.: The Free Press, 1957.

Blau, Peter M., and Otis Dudley Duncan. *The American Occupational Structure.* New York: John Wiley and Sons, 1967.

Bogue, Donald J. "Socioeconomic Scores for Detailed Occupational Groups." Appendix to *Skid Row in American Cities.* Chicago: Community and Family Study Center, 1962.

Blumer, Isadore, Marvin Kogan, and Philip J. McCarthy. *The Industrial Mobility of Labor as a Probability Process.* Ithaca, N. Y.: Cornell University Press, 1955.

Caicedo Reinaldo, Torres. *Los estratos socioeconómicos del Ecuador: un ensayo de cuantificiatión (Socioeconomic Strata in Ecuador: An Attempt at Qualification).* Quito: Junta Nacional de Planificación y Coordinación Económica, 1960.

Centers, Richard. *The Psychology of Social Classes.* Princeton, N. J.: Princeton University Press, 1949.

Clerc, Paul. "Changement dans la structure socio-professionnelle de la France entre 1954 et 1962" ("Changes in the Structure of Social Status Categories in France Between 1954 and 1962"), *Population* (Paris), **19** (4) (August-September 1964), 683–706.

Cole, G. D. H. "La structure de classes de la Grande-Bretagne en 1951" ("The Class Structure of Great Britain in 1951"), *Cahiers Internationaux de Sociologie* (Paris), N.S. **1** (16) (1954), 87–117.

Cole, G. D. H. *Studies in Class Structure.* London: Routledge and Kegan Paul, 1955.

Counts, George S. "Social Status of Occupations," *School Review,* **33** (January 1925), 16–27.

Davies, A. F. "Prestige of Occupations," *British Journal of Sociology,* **3** (June 1952), 134–147.

Davis, Kingsley, and Wilbert E. Moore. "Some Principles of Stratification: A Critical Analysis," *American Sociological Review,* **10** (April 1945), 242–249.

Deeg, M. E., and D. G. Paterson. "Changes in Social Status of Occupations," *Occupations,* **25** (1947), 205–208.

Dollard, John. *Caste and Class in a Southern Town.* New Haven, Conn.: Yale University Press, 1937.

Duncan, Otis Dudley. "A Socioeconomic Index for All Occupations," pp. 109–138 in Albert J. Reiss, *et al. Occupations and Social Status.* New York: Free Press of Glencoe, 1962.

Duncan, Otis Dudley, and Beverly Duncan. "Residential Distribution in Occupational Stratification," *American Journal of Sociology,* **60** (March 1955), 493–503.

Duncan, Otis Dudley. "Occupation Trends and Patterns of Net Mobility in the United States, *Demography,* **3** (1966), pp. 1–17.

Edwards, Alba M. "A Social Economic Grouping of the Gainful Workers in the United States," *Journal of the American Statistical Association,* **28** (December 1933), 377–387.

Garbin, A. P., and Frederick L. Bates. "Occupational Prestige and its Correlates: A Re-examination," *Social Forces,* **44** (March 1966), 295–302.

Gusfield, Joseph R., and Michael Schwartz. "The Meanings of Occupational Prestige: Reconsideration of the NORC Scale," *American Sociological Review,* **28** (April 1963), 265–271.

Hatt, Paul K. "Occupations and Social Stratification," *American Journal of Sociology,* **55** (April 1950), 533–543.

Hodge, Robert W., Paul M. Siegel, and Peter H.

Rossi. "Occupational Prestige in the United States, 1925-63," *American Journal of Sociology* (November 1964), 282–306.

Hodge, Robert W. "Occupational Mobility as a Probability Process," *Demography*, 3 (1966), 19–34.

Hodges, Harold M., Jr. *Social Stratification: Class in America.* Cambridge, Mass.: Schenkman Publishing Company, 1964.

Inkeles, Alex. "Social Stratification and Mobility in the Soviet Union: 1940-50," *American Sociological Review,* 15 (August 1950), 465–479.

Inkeles, Alex, and Peter H. Rossi. "National Comparisons of Occupational Prestige," *American Journal of Sociology,* 61 (January 1956), 329–339.

International Sociological Association. *Transactions of the Third World Congress of Sociology.* Vol. III. "Changes in Class Structure." (Amsterdam, 22–29 August, 1956.) London: International Sociological Association, 1956.

Kahl, Joseph A. *The American Class Structure.* New York: Rinehart and Company, 1957.

Kahl, Joseph A., and James A. Davis. "A Comparison of Indexes of Socio-economic Status," *American Sociological Review,* 20 (June 1955), 317–325.

Lasswell, Thomas E. *Class and Stratum: An Introduction to Concepts and Research.* Boston: Houghton Mifflin Company, 1965.

Lenski, Gerhard E. "American Social Classes, Statistical Strata or Social Groups," *American Journal of Sociology,* 58 (September 1952), 139–144.

Lenski, Gerhard E. "Status Crystallization: A Non-Vertical Dimension of Social Status," *American Sociological Review,* 19 (August 1954), 405–413.

Matras, Judah. "Comparison of Intergenerational Occupational Mobility Patterns: An Approach Application of the Formal Theory of Social Mobility," *Population Studies,* 14 (1960), 163–169.

Moser, C. A., and J. R. Hall. "The Social Grading of Occupations," in D. V. Glass (ed.). *Social Mobility in Britain.* London: Routledge and Kegan Paul, 1954, pp. 29–50.

Nam, Charles B., *et al.* "Socioeconomic Characteristics of the Population," *Current Population Reports.* Series P-23. Technical Studies No. 1. Washington, D.C.: U.S. Bureau of the Census, 1964.

Nam, Charles B., and Mary G. Powers. "Variations in Socioeconomic Structure by Race, Residence, and the Life Cycle," *American Sociological Review,* 30 (1) (February 1965), 97–103.

North, C. C., and P. I. Hatt. "Jobs and Occupations: A Popular Evaluation," *Public Opinion News,* 9 (September 1947), 3–13.

Prais, S. J. "Measuring Social Mobility," *Journal of the Royal Statistical Society,* Series A, 118 (1955), 55–66.

Prais, S. J. "The Formal Theory of Social Mobility," *Population Studies,* 9 (1955), 72–81.

Reiss, Albert J., Jr., and Otis Dudley Duncan. *Occupations and Social Status.* New York: Free Press, 1961.

Reissman, Leonard. *Class in American Society.* Glencoe, Ill.: The Free Press, 1959.

Rogoff, Natalie. *Occupational Mobility.* New York: The Free Press, 1953.

Rogoff, Natalie. "Social Stratification in France and the United States," *American Journal of Sociology,* 58 (April 1953), 347–357.

Schnore, Leo F. "Social Mobility in Demographic Perspective," *American Sociological Review,* 26 (3) (June 1961), 407–423.

Shah, S. A. "A Statistical Estimate of the Class Structure of Contemporary India," *Science and Society,* 28 (Summer 1964), 275–285.

Smith, Mapheus. "An Empirical Scale of Prestige Status of Occupations," *American Sociological Review,* 8 (April 1943), 185–192.

Spengler, Joseph J. "Changes in Income Distribution and Social Stratification," *American Journal of Sociology,* 59 (1953), 247–259.

Warner, W. Lloyd, Marchia Meeker, and Kenneth Eels. *Social Class in America.* Chicago: Science Research Associates, 1949.

CHAPTER 15

Population Distribution
and Urban-Rural Residence*

15.1. The Phenomenon of Distribution
Patterns of Population

Population distribution is a branch of demography that studies the way in which populations are arranged within the physical space that is available to them for exploitation and settlement. As they use this land for agriculture, forestry, mining, manufacturing, commerce, and residence, they create *patterns* of distribution that reflect the type of adjustment they have made to the environment and to each other, using the technology at their disposal. This spatial patterning of population takes three different forms:

1. *Differential density of settlement.* The globe is very unevenly inhabited. Some territories (Northern Alaska, the Sahara, Northern Siberia, Southern Chile, Central Australia, etc.) are almost uninhabited or only very sparsely settled. Other territories (Java, the valleys of the Ganges and Yangtze rivers, and highly urbanized places such as Hong Kong, Singapore, and the Netherlands) have a density of several hundreds, or even thousands, of persons per square kilometer. Within each nation there are also very great differences in density.

2. *Differential population composition.* As

* The materials representing new research for this chapter were prepared as part of a research program, "Basic Demographic Research," under a grant from the Rockefeller Foundation. The materials presented for Economic Regions are derived from a special retabulation of the 1960 census summary tapes which are the basis for a forthcoming monograph, *New Data for Economic Areas: 1960-1969.*

has been demonstrated in the preceding chapters, the demographic, social, and economic characteristics of the earth's inhabitants vary widely from nation to nation. For example, very substantial differences in composition with respect to age, sex, ethnicity, religion, marital status, educational attainment, occupation, and income may be observed among the inhabitants of the several continents. Within each nation there is a similar variation.

3. *Differential rates at which the vital processes are functioning.* Birthrates, death rates, and rates of population growth differ markedly from place to place. This is true also for rates of marriage and divorce and for rates of morbidity or mortality due to particular diseases. Migration rates show perhaps the greatest place-to-place variation of any of the components of population dynamics.

The task of the demographer who is interested in the study of population distribution is twofold. First, he must *discover and describe* the spatial differentials in density, composition, and dynamics. The description should include, if possible, a portrayal of the changes that have taken place in the spatial patterns over past decades. Second, he should develop an *explanation* of why the pattern exists, why it takes a particular form, and why it is changing in a particular way.

There is another aspect to the study of population distribution. This is a study design of a particular type that is popularly known as "ecological correlation." A separate section of this chapter is devoted to the procedures and principles of research designs that employ ecological correlations.

15.2. Systems of Area Classification for Distributional Studies

The unique aspect of distributional studies is that the entire population is subdivided into subareas, according to some criterion, and the population that inhabits each of the categories of a subarea is subjected to demographic analysis as a separate entity. The procedure for delimiting the subareas is established in the census office. Censuses are taken in terms of small parcels of territory known as "enumeration districts." Enumeration districts may be compared to a child's set of building blocks: they may be combined in a great variety of ways to construct desired units of territory.

There are two types of criteria that may be used to arrive at subareas for distributional analysis:

1. *Homogeneity* of the physical environment or of the population that inhabits it.

2. *Functional integration* of the population into organized units.

Homogeneous Areas. When areas are delimited according to the criterion of homogeneity, the classification strives to combine areas (enumeration districts) in such a way as to maximize the homogeneity within each area delimited. This simultaneously has the effect of maximizing the differences between areas. Each area is then internally homogeneous and distinctively different from all surrounding areas. The specific criterion for homogeneity may be similarity of topography, climate, natural resources, any population characteristic, any demographic rate, or, in fact, any trait that may be attributed either to the physical environment or the population that inhabits it. Clearly, the possible delimitations number in the hundreds or even thousands. It is, of course, impossible for the census to tabulate population data according to all of the possible area delimitations of homogeneity. It has long been observed that population tends to be distributed in such a way that particular *combinations* of traits tend to be concentrated together in space, so that it is possible to develop a *general classification* that *maximizes simultaneously several environmental and population traits.*

In the two most recent censuses of the United States, for example, the census enumeration districts have been grouped into the following hierarchy of homogeneous areas:

1. Enumeration districts.
2. Census tracts (in metropolitan areas only).
3. Individual cities and minor civil divisions of rural area.
4. Counties.
5. Metropolitan areas.
6. Economic areas.
7. Economic subregions.
8. Economic regions.

With minor exceptions (cities lying in two counties), each type of area is obtained by grouping units of the type immediately above it in the list. As a consequence, there is decreasing homogeneity in the system.

At level 4, the census is compelled (as are all censuses) by needs of governmental administration to group counties into states. Unfortunately, in most nations the states or provinces are inefficient units for distributional study because internally they usually are quite heterogeneous.

The boundaries between areas tend to be fuzzy, as one combination of traits changes to another combination, with a zone of intermingling between them. It is not correct to assume, however, that the zone of transitions is so broad that one should think of a continuity of environmental conditions. Because of this zone of intermixed traits, reasonably homogeneous large areas can be established by grouping counties or similar small civil divisions. The system of economic areas, described below, makes use of this principle.

Functionally Integrated Areas. The criterion for this type of area is that it represent some system of interdependency or interaction, wherein the area enclosed within the boundaries functions more or less as a unit. The zone of commuting around a metropolis, the retail trade territory of a city, and the zone within which a newspaper has its circulation are examples of such types of areas. Almost invariably, areas that are functionally integrated are integrated around some central point such as a seaport, a source of power, a source of raw materials, the junction of rivers with main over-land transportation routes, or the intersection of principal highways. At such points, there tends to be a concentration of manufacturing, freight handling, storage, and markets (both for raw materials and finished goods). At the center of the integrated area, therefore, almost always there is a city larger in population than any other place in the area. These types of units have been termed "nodal" areas.

The criterion for the delimitation of functionally integrated areas is therefore some type of activity or flow of goods, services, and communication, rather than homogeneity with respect to some trait. Delimitation consists in identifying the node, or center about which the activity is organized, and then establishing the line at which the integration ceases and the population is organized with respect to an adjoining center. It is possible to delimit such areas with respect to each of a great many activities. Also, it is possible to establish a set of general areas, on the premise that the boundaries for a great many functions are more or less identical. The territory of "Greater Metropolitan Tokyo" or any other metropolis, for example, is a generalized functionally integrated area.

The U.S. Census has recognized officially only one classification of functionally integrated areas. These are the standard metropolitan statistical areas (see below).

Sometimes there is a tendency to regard the two systems of area classification as mutually contradictory between which a researcher must choose. This is not correct; each approach is able to reveal spatial patterns that the other cannot, and very often it is highly useful to use both approaches simultaneously.

15.3. The Urban-Rural Classification

There is one system of land classification that is simultaneously a homogeneous area and a functionally integrated area. This is the urban-rural classification. Using a variety of criteria (either traits or interdependency), it is possible to identify areas that are "urban." These include cities and the built-up territory surrounding them. The remaining area that is not urban is, by definition, rural. In the United States, where

farmers live on their land rather than clustering in villages, the rural population is further subdivided into rural-farm and rural-nonfarm. This is done by identifying the rural-farm population and defining the rural-nonfarm population as the residue after the urban and rural-farm populations have been separated.

The urban-rural classification is a very important one. Although often it is difficult to state the specific criteria for delimitation, the conceptual differences between the two are well known and appreciated. Urban areas are densely populated areas where manufacturing, commerce, administration, and a great variety of specialized services are available. Rural areas are more sparsely populated and tend to be specialized in agriculture, forestry, or other exploitation of resources. Small towns that provide services to those who pursue rural industries are also a part of the rural area, as are nonagricultural aggregations of population that are too small or too dispersed to be classed as urban. The physical environment, the mode of life, and economic and political conditions in urban areas usually are distinctively different from those in rural areas. For this reason, it is a basic distinction that every census must make. As we shall see, this difference tends to diminish as nations become more modernized.

Each nation defines the urban (hence the rural) population by a more or less unique set of criteria that conforms to its particular administration. Below is quoted the official definition of the urban population in the United States in 1960.[1]

"In general, the urban population comprises all persons living in urbanized areas and in places of 2,500 inhabitants or more outside urbanized areas. More specifically, according to the definition adopted for use in the 1960 Census, the urban population comprises all persons living in (a) places of 2,500 inhabitants or more incorporated as cities, boroughs, villages, and towns (except towns in New England, New York, and Wisconsin); (b) the

[1] U. S. Census of Population, 1960, *Detailed Characteristics. United States Summary*, "Area Classifications," pp. vii–x in the Introduction (Washington, D. C.: Government Printing Office, 1963).

densely settled urban fringe, whether incorporated or unincorporated, of urbanized areas (for definition of urbanized areas see section below); (c) towns in New England and townships in New Jersey and Pennsylvania which contain no incorporated municipalities as subdivisions and have either 25,000 inhabitants or more or a population of 1,500 to 25,000 and a density of 1,500 persons or more per square mile; (d) counties in States other than the New England States, New Jersey, and Pennsylvania that have no incorporated municipalities within their boundaries and have a density of 1,500 persons or more per square mile; and (e) unincorporated places of 2,500 inhabitants or more.

"This definition of urban is substantially the same as that used in 1950. . . . The most important component of the urban territory in both definitions is the group of incorporated places having 2,500 inhabitants or more. A definition of urban territory restricted to such places, however, excludes a number of equally large and densely settled places merely because they are not incorporated places.

"To improve its measure of urban population, the Bureau of the Census adopted in 1950, the concept of the urbanized area and defined the larger unincorporated places as urban. All of the population residing in the urban-fringe areas and in unincorporated places of 2,500 or more is classified as urban. . . .

"*Urbanized Areas* . . . correspond to what are called 'conurbations' in some countries. An urbanized area contains at least one city which had 50,000 inhabitants or more in 1960, as well as the surrounding closely settled incorporated places and unincorporated areas that meet the criteria listed below. An urbanized area may be thought of as divided into the central city, or cities, and the remainder of the area, or the urban fringe. All persons residing in an urbanized area are included in the urban population.

"In addition to its central city or cities, an urbanized area also contains the following types of *contiguous* areas, which together constitute its urban fringe:

"1. Incorporated places with 2,500 inhabitants or more.

"2. Incorporated places with less than 2,500 inhabitants, provided each has a closely settled area of 100 housing units or more.

"3. Towns in the New England States, townships in New Jersey and Pennsylvania and counties elsewhere which are classified as urban.

"4. Enumeration districts in unincorporated territory with a population density of 1,000 inhabitants or more per square mile (the areas of large nonresidential tracts devoted to such urban land uses as railroad yards, factories, and cemeteries, were excluded in computing the population density of an ED).

"5. Other ED's, provided that they serve one of the following purposes:

    a. To eliminate enclaves.

    b. To close indentations in the urbanized areas of one mile or less across an open end.

    c. To link outlying ED's of qualifying density that were no more than 1½ miles from the main body of the urbanized area."

Other nations use cities of different sizes as the lower limit of population. These range all the way from 50,000 in Japan to 1000 persons in Iceland. In some countries, urban places are defined by their assigned legal status—more or less independently of their size and function. Many very large settlements may be unincorporated, hence defined as rural, while very often the boundaries of places that are incorporated as cities may extend far out into the countryside and embrace much territory that, by its economy and characteristics, is rural.

Once urban places are identified, they can be classified further by other criteria, such as size, type of economy, type of population composition, or region of location.

A unique problem encountered in the study of urban-rural distribution is that between censuses parcels of territory may shift from one classification to another. For example, an incorporated town in the United States may have 2499 inhabitants at one census and 2500 at the next, and thereby shift from rural to urban. Also, cities tend to annex built-up territory around their edges. Thus, in addition to any

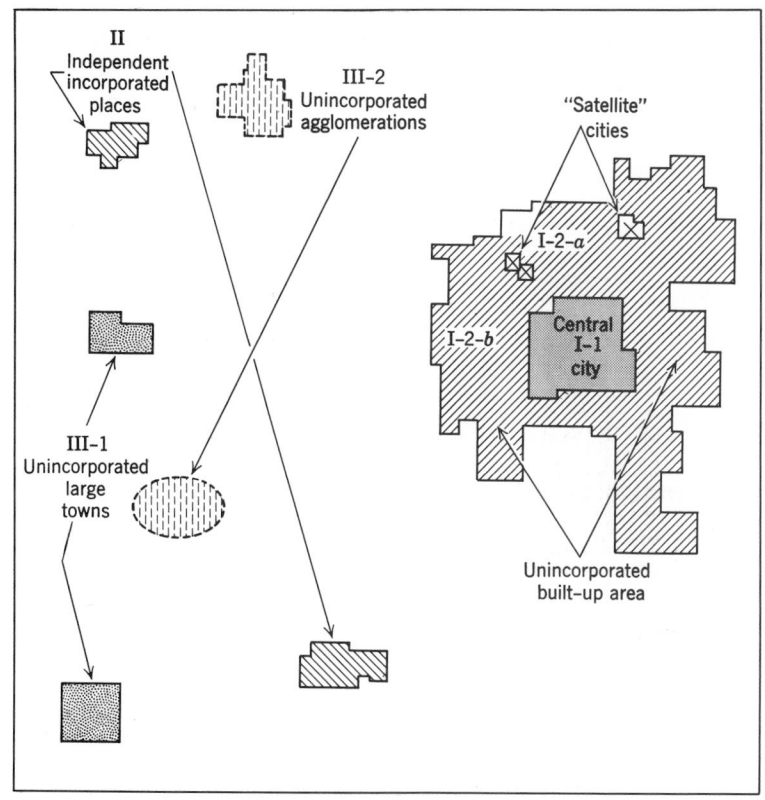

I. Urbanized areas:
  1. Central cities—cities of 50,000 or more inhabitants
  2. Urban fringe—densely settled territory surrounding the central city:
    (a) "Satellite cities"—incorporated suburban places of 2500 or more inhabitants
    (b) Unincorporated built up area
II. Incorporated places of 2500 to 49, 999 (outside orbit of central cities)
III. Urban agglomerations not incorporated
  1. Large towns or densely settled places (especially in New England)
  2. Unincorporated agglomerations of 2500 or more inhabitants

Figure 15-1 Diagrammatic Illustration of Definitions of Urban Population in the United States.

growth that may result from a positive net migration balance, there is a double encroachment of the urban upon the rural population.

15.4. Urban-Rural Composition of the World's Population and World Urbanization

By making a reasonably valid reconciliation of international differences in definitions of the urban population, the United Nations has made estimates of the urban-rural composition of the earth's inhabitants, by countries, continents, and world regions. These estimates are reported in Table 15-1. Table 15-2 reports an estimate of the change in urban-rural distribution, and rate of change, for the period 1950-1960. These data show that when taken as a whole, the world's population is still more rural than urban, but there are very sharp differences between world regions. Three of the world regions are highly urbanized:

Northwest Europe
Central Europe
Northern America

Five of the regions have an intermediate level of urbanization:

Table 15-1   Urban-Rural Composition and Sex Composition in Urban and Rural Areas of Nations of the World: 1963 and 1964

Country and region	Years	Percent urban	Sex Ratio		Percent under 15 years of age	
			Urban	Rural	Urban	Rural
NORTHERN and WESTERN EUROPE						
Belgium..........................	1964	50.0	82.0	92.9	....	....
Denmark..........................	1963	74.1	93.3	114.1	23.8	28.9
Finland..........................	1963	55.9	86.2	102.4	28.4	32.2
France...........................	1963	63.0	92.0	99.1	29.3	25.7
Ireland..........................	1963	46.1	88.9	112.7	31.7	30.6
Luxembourg.......................	1964	62.2	95.1	101.6	20.8	22.4
Netherlands......................	1963	80.0	97.7	103.4	28.0	32.5
Norway...........................	1963	48.7	92.0	108.3	23.8	27.6
Sweden...........................	1963	72.8	95.0	112.6	22.1	21.6
Northern Ireland.................	1964	54.0	89.0	102.6	27.8	30.2
Scotland.........................	1964	70.4	89.9	97.5	25.5	26.7
Channel Islands..................	1964	33.6	88.3	95.7	27.6	25.1
CENTRAL EUROPE						
Austria..........................	1964	50.0	82.0	92.9	....	....
Czechoslovakia...................	1963	47.6	92.8	97.5	26.3	28.1
Hungary..........................	1963	39.7	91.0	99.6	22.4	27.4
Poland...........................	1964	47.7	90.1	93.0	31.5	35.9
Switzerland......................	9164	51.3	91.6	101.6	20.1	27.0
SOUTHERN EUROPE						
Albania..........................	1963	27.5	119.0	100.4	34.7	40.4
Bulgaria.........................	1963	33.6	99.8	99.5	25.8	27.0
Greece...........................	1964	43.2	95.6	93.7	23.0	30.1
Italy............................	1963	47.7	....	....	....	....
Malta and Gozo...................	1964	63.8	91.3	83.6	37.3	37.8
Portugal.........................	9164	22.7	83.6	94.3	23.1	30.9
Romania..........................	1963	31.3	96.2	93.9	22.5	29.8
Yugoslavia.......................	1964	28.3	94.9	95.2	28.0	32.3
Monaco...........................	1962	100.0	81.6	....	12.6	....
NORTHERN AMERICA						
Canada...........................	1963	69.6	98.2	112.2	32.2	38.0
United States...................	1963	69.6	99.0	104.2	30.1	33.4
OCEANIA						
Australia........................	1963	81.4	98.7	118.4	29.3	34.8
New Zealand......................	1963	63.6	95.3	110.4	30.0	
U.S.S.R..........................	1964	47.9	82.5	81.4	....	....
SOUTH AMERICA						
British Guiana...................	1964	15.5	86.6	101.8	37.3	47.9
Chile............................	1964	68.2	88.9	113.3	37.7	43.7
Ecuador..........................	1963	35.8	93.3	105.4	44.2	44.7
Peru.............................	1964	47.7	99.2	98.6	41.3	45.1
Uruguay..........................	1964	82.2	93.4	131.9	27.1	31.2
MIDDLE AMERICA						
Barbados.........................	1964	4.9	76.6	83.6	30.7	38.6
Costa Rica.......................	1964	34.5	88.0	107.4	....	....
El Salvador......................	1964	38.5	87.7	103.4	....	....
Honduras.........................	1964	23.2	89.8	102.4	....	....
Jamaica..........................	1963	29.5	83.1	96.7	39.8	43.8
Martinique.......................	1964	41.7	....	....	....	....
Mexico...........................	1963	50.7	94.6	104.8	43.0	45.5
Netherlands Antilles.............	1963	32.1	91.3	96.8	39.1	42.9
Nicaragua........................	1964	40.8	86.4	106.5	46.5	49.6
Panama...........................	1963	41.5	92.9	110.8	38.2	47.2
Puerto Rico......................	1963	44.1	92.1	102.9	37.8	46.6
SOUTH CENTRAL ASIA						
India............................	1964	18.0	18.4	103.8	39.0	41.5
Nepal............................	1963	2.8	111.5	96.5	....	....
Pakistan.........................	1963	13.6	128.9	108.6	41.3	45.0

Table 15-1   (*Continued*)

Country and region	Years	Percent Urban	Sex Ratio		Percent under 15 years of age	
			Urban	Rural	Urban	Rural
EAST ASIA						
Hong Kong..........................	1963	73.2	....	....	39.1	45.1
Japan..............................	1964	63.5	97.5	94.7	28.1	32.8
Korea (Republic).................	1963	24.5	101.6	99.5	41.7	43.6
Mongolia..........................	1963	40.8	111.9	93.1	....	....
SOUTH EAST ASIA						
Indonesia.........................	1963	14.9	100.1	96.8	40.1	42.9
North Borneo (Sabah).............	1963	14.9	113.3	107.8	44.1	43.4
Philippines......................	1964	29.9	96.6	104.0	....	....
Sarawak...........................	1963	15.0	103.8	101.6	45.4	44.3
Thailand..........................	1964	18.2	103.6	99.7	....	....
SOUTH WEST ASIA						
Cyprus............................	1964	35.9	98.9	95.5	39.6	37.9
Iran..............................	1963	31.4	106.5	102.3	40.2	43.0
Iraq..............................	1964	39.2	106.9	97.3	42.0	46.0
Israel............................	1963	77.9	101.9	107.1	33.9	43.8
Jordan............................	1963	43.9	109.6	98.9	45.0	45.7
Syria.............................	1964	38.7	106.4	105.0	44.4	47.4
Turkey in Asia...................	1964	26.3	119.5	99.2	33.6	43.9
NORTHERN AFRICA						
Morocco...........................	1964	29.3	98.9	100.5	41.4	45.5
U.A.R.............................	1963	38.0	103.7	99.7	43.6	42.3
TROPICAL and SOUTHERN AFRICA						
Angola............................	1964	10.6	126.3	101.3	....	....
Congo (Leopoldville).............	1963	22.0	115.8	89.1	39.5	39.3
Gambia............................	1964	8.8	108.9	103.6	37.4	37.6
Ghana.............................	1963	23.1	106.2	101.0	41.6	45.4
Guinea............................	1963	8.3	96.9	90.3	40.3	42.2
Kenya.............................	1963	5.3	163.2	95.0	34.1	52.2
Southern Rhodesia...............	1964	18.0	173.3	95.6	35.2	52.5

Source: 1963 Demographic Yearbook, Table 5.

Southern Europe
USSR
Latin America
Northern Africa
Oceania

The remaining three regions of the world are preponderantly rural:

Asia, excluding Mainland China
Mainland China
Sub-Sahara Africa

Table 15-2 demonstrates one of the most important current demographic events: *a process of very rapid urbanization is under way everywhere in the world.* Whereas the rural population has been growing at the rate of about 1.4 percent per year, the urban population has been growing more than twice as fast. Moreover, some of the greatest differentials between urban and rural growth rates are found in those regions of the world that are predominantly rural. An exception to this is Asia, excluding

mainland China. India, Pakistan, Ceylon, and Southeast Asia are urbanizing at a slower rate than any region of the world except the three regions that already are highly urbanized. Urbanization is proceeding fastest in Sub-Sahara Africa and in Latin America. It is progressing least rapidly in Northwestern Europe, which appears to be approaching an equilibrium in urban-rural distribution as the overall population growth rate approaches zero.

The mechanism by which this phenomenal change is taking place is, of course, a massive exodus of people from rural to urban areas. In a later chapter we shall study this migratory movement in some detail; presently we are interested only in its redistributional effects.

This generalized picture of urbanization of the world's population fails to bring out some of the very dramatic and dynamic (and some very tragic) events that are taking place. At the World Population Conference of 1965 several demographers presented papers giving some

Table 15-2   Average Annual Percent Rate of Increase for Total, Urban, and Rural Population for the World, Continents, and Regions: 1950 to 1960

Continent and region	Average annual percent rate of increase			
	Total	Urban	Rural	Difference, Urban-Rural
World total.........	1.7	2.9-3.3	1.4-1.3	1.5-2.1
Africa......................	2.1	5.4	1.7	3.7
Sub-Sahara Africa..........	2.1	6.3	1.7	4.6
Northern Africa............	2.3	4.4	1.6	2.8
America...........	2.3	3.6	1.5	2.1
Northern America.............	1.8	2.5	1.3	1.2
Latin America...............	2.7	5.3	1.7	3.6
Argentina, Chile, Uruguay....	2.0	3.8	0.1	3.7
Rest of Latin America........	2.8	5.8	1.9	4.0
Asia.............	1.8	2.9-4.1	1.6-1.4	1.3-2.7
Excluding China (Mainland)....	2.0	3.4	1.7	1.8
China (Mainland)..............	1.5	1.5-5.7	1.5-0.9	--4.8
Europe[2]...........	0.8	1.6	0.3	1.2
North-Western Europe..........	0.7	1.0	0.3	0.7
Central Europe...............	0.9	1.8	0.3	1.5
Southern Europe..............	0.9	2.4	0.4	2.1
Oceania......................	2.1	3.6	0.1	3.5
USSR........................	1.8	3.4	1.0	2.4

[1]   Data do not include population in countries of less than 250,000 inhabitants.   Urban population is defined as population in localities of 20,000 inhabitants and over; rural population as population in localities of less than 20,000 inhabitants.

[2]   Regions of Europe comprised of countries as classified in United Nations Demographic Yearbook 1963.

Source: Prepared by the United Nations Population Branch, based on population estimate given in United Nations Provisional Report on World Populations Prospects, as Assessed in 1963, ST/SOA?ser.R/7 (1964).

of these details. From these reports we can gain a deeper insight into what is happening.

The following statement by an official of the United Nations reflects the drama and immense social problems that lie behind world urbanization, especially in the developing nations, but present everywhere:

"The current explosive growth of cities and metropolitan agglomerations is a new phenomenon. The world is now rapidly changing from an agricultural and rural to a highly urbanized society; and industry is becoming the chief source of livelihood for progressively larger populations. Everywhere people are on the move in pursuit of better life that science and technology made possible, that high productivity and better health and nutrition made probable and, universal education and mass media of communication, an aspiration common to all mankind. In our time, the city embodies the basic conditions for the fulfillment of

this aspiration. Consequently, it attracts with elemental force populations that insufficient land and conditions of tenure could barely sustain in the past and whom new agricultural technology has now made superfluous.

"As a consequence, the 'push' away from the country and the 'pull' to the city generate a rapidly swelling stream of migration. At the same time, however, industry, transport, commerce and most other sectors also need fewer people to make more and better implements of work and of better life. The more conspicuous symptoms of this situation in the pre-industrialized and in many industrial countries are inadequate shelter and communal services in many cities, frequent absence of safe water and sanitation, filth and squalor in ever-expanding areas, and a growing rate of disease and mortality. The intense physical congestion and social tension in metropolitan slums and shanty towns of the pre-industrialized countries, however, are rapidly approaching the state of a crisis which may not only distort the projected patterns of the economics but also delay or even reverse their development. The newcomer rarely finds in the city employment sufficient to improve his condition. In fact, he may shift from rural subsistence to urban living below the humblest concept of human decency. Almost never does he become a full member of his chosen community nor do its institutions serve him well.

"In many metropolitan areas, squatter settlements and shanty towns already shelter one-quarter to one-half of their total population. Slum and shanty town dwellers grow at the staggering (annual) rate of 12.0 to 15.0 percent. An inevitable consequence of the current urban explosion is a further decline of their lowest income groups, the slum dwellers and squatters.

"The slum dwellers in the industrialized countries are hardly better off. Here, due to fundamental economic and social changes associated with automation of industry, mechanization of agriculture, expansion of service sectors, computer programming and multiplication of power, the remaining rural people and those living in the stagnating small towns, move to great metropolitan belts, or they shift from one metropolis to another. As conditions deteriorate, industries, businesses and higher income families move to new suburban communities in search of a more congenial environment; and the labouring migrant and newcomer take over the decaying central areas abandoned by the more affluent citizens.

"The outlook at the beginning of the second half of the twentieth century is indeed grim. Many highly industrialized countries are slow to use their resources for developing an environment desirable as a place to live in, and conducive to economic growth. The developing countries, on the other hand, lack the necessary resources to do so. But failure to act has already brought about an urban crisis in every part of the world, threatening to human progress. In many areas, rapid growth of population and slow economic progress are causing a galloping expansion of blight and decay which with delinquency, vice and social maladjustment have become the urban

setting for "marginal" populations. The cities with 100,000 inhabitants or more have grown from 15 million to nearly 314 in 1950, or over 20 times in 150 years. In the year 2000 about 60 percent of the world population will probably be urban. Thus, a tolerable urban environment will have to be provided in five decades for thirteen times as many people as was built in the previous 150 years; or, the rate of construction in the next 50 years must average almost 40 times that of the past; a task hardly conceivable with the resources and productivity of the developing countries." [2]

We may accept Weissman's article as an accurate portrayal of the facts and still maintain that were migrants to remain in rural areas, a solution to their problem might be even more remote. Their collection into urban places (albeit with great misery) dramatizes the need for increased employment and reduced fertility, and assembles the population in an environment where tradition has less control and fertility reduction may be more easily achieved. The destitute economic outcasts become a political influence, demanding remedy. They communicate their misery to each other and form a worldwide social movement for great social change. This movement is not the monopoly of any political or economic bloc: it is as apparent in Mainland China as in the Negro slums of Chicago and the shantytowns of Africa and Asia. Refugees to the city from the decadent village economy hope for their children if not for themselves; were they to remain in rural areas, dispersed and also living as serfs at the starvation level, the world's population crisis possibly would be prolonged and ultimately reach more tragic proportions than it has now.

15.5. Differences in Composition of the Urban and Rural Population

Differences in population composition between urban and rural areas may be rather substantial. Tables 15-3 to 15-15 report com-

[2] Ernest Weissman, "Population, Urban Growth, and Regional Development," a paper contributed to the United Nations World Population Conference, Belgrade, 1965.

Table 15-3   Age Composition of the Urban and Rural Population, United States: 1960

Age	Urban	Rural nonfarm	Rural farm
Total.........	100.0	100.0	100.0
Under 15 years........	30.1	33.7	32.5
15-24 years...........	13.2	14.1	13.7
25-34 years...........	13.2	12.6	9.0
35-44 years...........	13.9	12.5	12.2
45-54 years...........	11.7	10.4	13.0
55-64 years...........	9.0	7.7	10.2
65 years and over.....	9.1	8.9	9.3

Source: U.S. Census of Population: 1960, Detailed Characteristics, United States Summary, Table 158.

Table 15-4   Sex Composition by Age of the Urban and Rural Population, United States: 1960

Age	Sex ratio		
	Urban	Rural nonfarm	Rural farm
Total.........	94.0	102.9	107.7
Under 15 years........	102.9	104.8	106.0
15-24 years...........	92.2	112.7	120.4
25-34 years...........	95.1	98.5	95.1
35-44 years...........	93.3	100.9	96.3
45-54 years...........	93.2	104.1	108.0
55-64 years...........	89.1	98.6	114.3
65 years and over.....	75.6	93.4	117.4

Source: U.S. Census of Population: 1960, Detailed Characteristics, United States Summary, Table 158.

positional data for the United States urban, rural-nonfarm, and rural-farm population for 1960 in order to illustrate this point. Many of the same differences will be found in other nations, but each population may be expected to have its own unique pattern of compositional differences. One of the major tasks of demographers after each national census is to identify these differences, show if they have changed since the last census, and to explain why they exist.

Age Composition. Because of lower fertility, the proportion of the population that is under 15 is lower in urban than in rural areas (See Table 15-3). However, because of rapid rural-to-urban migration of young people, the city has a comparative surplus of people aged 25 to 44 years, while rural areas (especially rural-farm areas) have a comparative deficit in these ages. Because rural-nonfarm areas include much rapidly growing suburban territory, they have a comparatively smaller proportion of elderly persons. Rural-farm areas, on the other hand, have an unusually large share of elderly people: because they are less mobile, they stay behind when youth migrates.

Sex Composition. In rural areas (especially in rural-farm areas) the sex balance favors males; in urban areas females predominate. (This generalization applies rather uniformly to Europe and Northern America; some cities in Asia have a strong predominance of males because wives and children remain in the village while the husbands work in the cities and send home a portion of their wages.) In

the United States the sex ratios for 1960 were:

Urban 94.0
Rural-nonfarm 102.9
Rural-farm 107.7

The variation in sex composition by age is very different in urban and rural areas, as Table 15-4 shows. In urban areas, the sex ratio decreases rather uniformly with increasing age, because cities accumulate spinsters, widows, and divorced women. In rural-farm areas there is a great surplus of males at ages 14 to 24, because females tend to begin migrating to cities at a younger age than do males. There is also a comparative surplus of males on farms at ages 45 and above—presumably because older widowed and unmarried males are less inclined to move to the city than are females at these ages and because they have greater employment opportunities as farm laborers.

Nativity and Race. Foreign-born white populations are concentrated in the cities, while native white populations are somewhat less urbanized (Table 15-5). During the days of the American frontier, immigrants from Europe poured into the new lands of the Midwest and West, but after 1900 they poured into the industrial cities. The foreign-born population of the frontier period is now largely deceased, with the result that the comparatively small foreign-born population that remains is found largely in urban areas. The immigrants arriving today almost all settle in urban areas.

The minority nonwhite races (Negroes,

Table 15-5 Race and Nativity Composition of the Urban and Rural Population, United States: 1960

Race and nativity	Total	Urban	Rural nonfarm	Rural farm
White, total.........	100.0	69.5	23.0	7.5
Native..............	100.0	68.4	23.8	7.8
Foreign born........	100.0	87.5	10.0	2.5
Nonwhite, total.......	100.0	72.5	19.6	7.9
Negro..............	100.0	73.1	19.0	7.9
Other..............	100.0	60.9	30.0	9.1

Source: U.S. Census of Population: 1960, Detailed Characteristics, United States Summary, Table 158.

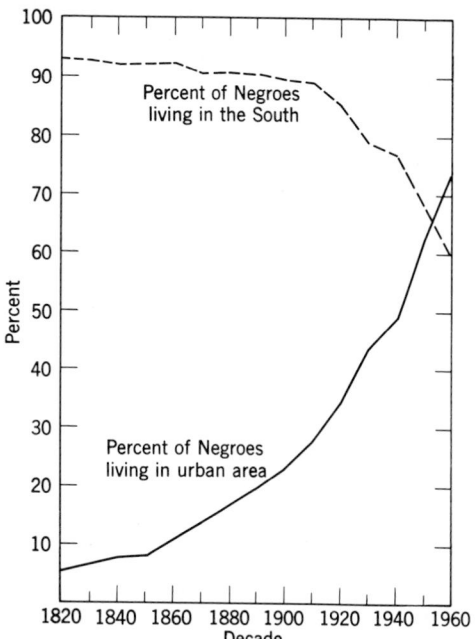

Figure 15-2 Trend in Percent of Negroes Living in Urban Areas and Percent of Negroes Living in the South.

Japanese, and Chinese) tend to be concentrated in urban areas. An exception is American Indians who, because of the reservation system, tend to have a more rural distribution. The preponderance of Negroes living in urban areas is a comparatively recent phenomenon, as is shown by the time series of Figure 15-2; a century ago the Negro population was even less urbanized than the white population.

School Attendance. In urban areas the proportion of young people attending school is higher at each age than in rural areas (Table 15-6). At the younger ages (below 16 years) the differences are rather small, but at the young adult ages the differences become very

Table 15-6 School Enrollment (Percent Enrolled in School) of the Urban and Rural Population by Age and Color, United States: 1960

Age	Urban		Rural nonfarm		Rural farm	
	White	Nonwhite	White	Nonwhite	White	Nonwhite
6 years..............	87.7	83.7	77.2	67.9	73.6	66.1
7 years..............	97.6	95.7	96.7	92.8	96.8	92.0
8 years..............	98.2	96.9	97.7	95.3	97.9	95.3
9 years..............	98.3	97.1	97.8	96.1	98.1	95.8
10 years.............	98.2	96.9	97.7	96.0	98.0	95.8
11 years.............	98.1	96.7	97.6	95.7	97.9	95.6
12 years.............	97.9	96.4	97.4	94.8	97.7	95.0
13 years.............	97.5	95.6	96.7	93.6	97.0	93.3
14 years.............	96.2	93.4	94.9	90.2	95.2	90.6
15 years.............	94.4	90.0	91.8	85.3	92.6	85.4
16 years.............	88.2	82.0	84.6	76.9	86.9	77.0
17 years.............	77.8	68.1	72.9	64.5	79.5	66.4
18 years.............	53.7	46.0	43.8	46.1	50.5	50.5
19 years.............	38.1	29.4	21.7	28.2	21.3	32.9
20 years.............	29.0	18.9	13.1	15.7	10.7	17.4

Source: U.S. Census of Population: 1960, Detailed Characteristics, United States Summary, Table 165.

Table 15-7   Median Years of School Completed by Males 25 Years of Age and Over by Color, for Urban and Rural Areas, United States: 1960

Age	Urban		Rural nonfarm		Rural farm	
	White	Nonwhite	White	Nonwhite	White	Nonwhite
Total................	11.2	8.5	9.3	5.8	8.7	4.8
25 to 29 years.........	12.5	11.1	12.1	8.7	12.1	7.0
30 to 34 years.........	12.4	10.3	11.5	7.8	11.0	6.2
35 to 39 years.........	12.3	9.7	11.4	7.2	10.5	5.7
40 to 44 years.........	12.1	8.7	10.6	6.4	9.2	5.2
45 to 49 years.........	11.3	8.1	9.4	5.6	8.8	4.9
50 to 54 years.........	10.4	7.4	8.8	5.1	8.6	4.7
55 to 59 years.........	9.1	6.7	8.5	4.4	8.4	4.3
60 to 64 years.........	8.8	6.1	8.4	4.1	8.3	4.1
65 to 69 years.........	8.5	5.3	8.2	3.6	8.2	3.8
70 to 74 years.........	8.3	5.0	8.0	3.4	8.1	3.7
75 years and over......	8.2	4.4	7.7	3.0	7.8	3.3

Source: U.S. Census of Populations: 1960, Detailed Characteristics, United States Summary, Table 173.

large. At age 20, for example, the proportion of urban youths still in school is more than twice that of rural youths. At these ages, rural-farm youths are much less likely to be in school than are rural-nonfarm youths. This set of differences is due in part to the fact that colleges and universities tend to be located in urban areas, and rural youths who desire to get a higher education must migrate to the city (hence be counted in the city population). Table 15-6 shows that attendance rates of the nonwhite population are somewhat lower than those for whites in urban as well as rural areas, although the discrepancies are greater in rural than in urban areas. The higher rate of school attendance of the rural nonwhite population in comparison with the white, reported in Table 15-6 for ages 19 and 20, may be due to retardation in completing high school.

Educational Attainment. The level of educational attainment among adults is significantly higher in urban than in rural areas (Table 15-7). Persons who have very little education are concentrated in the rural areas, and persons who have attended college are concentrated in urban areas. The rural-farm population is less educated than is the rural-nonfarm population. This pattern is even greater for

the nonwhite than for the white population, with the result that racial differences in educational attainment are much smaller in the city than in rural areas. The great difference in urban-rural distribution according to educational attainment is emphasized in Figure 15-3, which depicts the proportion of males of various educational levels living in cities.

Marital Status and Living Arrangements. Among the white population, rural-farm girls marry at a somewhat later age than city girls, but rural-nonfarm girls marry much earlier than either (Table 15-8). Among the nonwhite population, early marriage is concentrated in the city, with latest marriage at older ages occurring in the rural areas. However, women who do not marry tend to migrate to the city, so that after age 22 for white women and age 35 for nonwhite women the proportion of never-married women is greater in cities than in rural-nonfarm or rural-farm areas. As is shown by Table 15-9, broken marriage is much more common in urban than in rural areas, both for white and nonwhite populations. Note that the differences between whites and nonwhites are much greater in urban than in rural areas. Table 15-9 makes it very clear that although broken marriage is a serious problem of the Negro family in rural-farm as well as

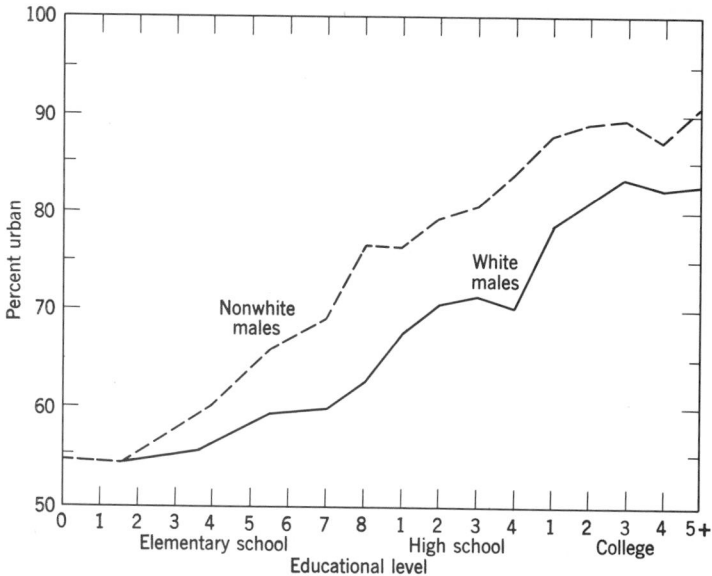

Figure 15-3 Percent of Male Population Living in Urban Areas, by Educational Attainment, White and Nonwhite Males: 1960.

in urban areas, it is in the urban areas that it reaches its peak. Throughout most of the child-bearing years, in 1960 one fifth of the Negro females were separated or divorced. It is difficult, under these conditions, to attribute this problem to a "hangover from slavery." For this theory to be valid, it would be necessary to declare that the slavery culture is now stronger in the cities than in rural areas, or that those who are most intensively imbued with it have migrated to the city, leaving in rural areas the families with values more like those of the white

culture. It would seem to be more logical to look at the contemporary scene for forces that are tending to sustain disorganization in the Negro family, that concentrate disorganized families in the city, and that are acting to generate greater disorganization in the city than had previously existed in rural areas.

The living arrangements of the population in urban and rural areas are portrayed in Table 15-10A (for males) and Table 15-10B (for females). From these tables it is clear that with the exception of rural-farm men 20

Table 15-8 Proportion of Females Who Have Ever Married, by Age and Color, for Urban and Rural Residence, United States: 1960

Age	White				Nonwhite			
	Total	Urban	Rural nonfarm	Rural farm	Total	Urban	Rural nonfarm	Rural farm
15 years...............	2.3	2.1	2.8	1.9	2.9	2.9	3.0	2.6
16 years...............	5.7	5.4	7.0	4.1	6.8	7.2	6.5	5.4
17 years...............	12.0	11.5	14.8	8.0	13.6	14.3	13.3	10.3
18 years...............	24.5	22.6	32.6	20.0	23.6	24.7	22.5	18.1
19 years...............	40.6	37.2	53.0	40.2	38.3	39.3	37.0	33.4
20 years...............	54.8	51.1	68.4	54.5	48.6	49.7	47.1	41.3
21 years...............	66.3	62.9	78.7	66.7	58.7	59.7	57.3	50.2
22 years...............	75.5	72.8	84.5	76.4	66.3	67.1	65.6	58.0
23 years...............	81.7	79.6	88.8	81.1	73.0	73.5	72.6	67.4
24 years...............	85.4	83.5	91.2	86.1	76.7	77.2	76.5	70.4
25 to 29 years.........	90.2	88.8	94.3	91.4	84.3	84.5	84.2	80.7
30 to 34 years.........	93.4	92.5	96.0	95.1	90.4	90.5	90.1	90.1
35 to 39 years.........	94.1	93.3	96.3	96.2	92.4	92.3	92.6	94.1
40 to 44 years.........	94.0	93.1	96.0	96.5	93.6	93.5	93.4	95.8
45 to 49 years.........	93.4	92.5	95.4	96.5	94.1	93.9	94.5	95.8
50 to 54 years.........	91.9	91.2	94.5	91.5	93.9	93.7	93.9	95.7

Source: U.S. Census of Population: 1960, <u>Detailed</u> <u>Characteristics</u>, <u>United</u> <u>States</u> <u>Summary</u>, Table 176.

Table 15-9   Proportion of Ever-Married Females Who Are Separated or Divorced, by Age and Color, for Urban and Rural Residence, United States: 1960

Age	White				Nonwhite			
	Total	Urban	Rural nonfarm	Rural farm	Total	Urban	Rural nonfarm	Rural farm
15 to 19 years.........	5.0	5.5	4.1	4.2	11.4	12.5	8.4	9.1
20 to 24 years.........	4.6	5.1	3.3	3.3	14.9	16.1	10.2	11.8
25 to 29 years.........	4.4	5.1	2.8	2.0	18.0	19.7	11.6	11.1
30 to 34 years.........	4.7	5.5	2.9	1.5	19.6	21.5	12.5	9.3
35 to 39 years.........	5.2	6.1	3.3	1.2	19.7	21.9	12.5	7.8
40 to 44 years.........	5.8	6.9	3.7	1.1	18.7	21.0	11.8	6.2
45 to 49 years.........	6.1	7.3	4.1	1.2	17.3	19.9	10.5	5.2
50 to 54 years.........	6.2	7.3	4.1	1.3	15.2	17.4	9.7	4.6
55 to 59 years.........	5.8	6.8	3.9	1.3	12.6	14.5	8.2	4.0
60 to 64 years.........	5.0	5.8	3.5	1.2	9.3	10.7	6.3	3.5

Source: U.S. Census of Population: 1960, Detailed Characteristics, United States Summary, Table 176.

to 39 tending to remain in the parent's household as a child, living arrangements among the white population are quite similar in urban and rural areas. In contrast, in urban areas the Negro population has a pattern very different from that for rural areas. The phenomenon of the nonwhite household with a female head is much more common in urban than in rural (especially rural-farm) areas. The nonwhite urban household is much more likely to contain adult relatives (brother, sister, other relatives) or lodgers than is the rural-farm

household. The presence of grandchildren in nonwhite households is even more characteristic of rural than of urban households. It has been noted in an earlier chapter that nonwhite migrants who have migrated North and have suffered a broken marriage are said to bring back their children to live with the grandparents in the South. Table 15-10 suggests that there is a factual basis to this contention.

Labor Force Status. Males participate in the labor force in about equal proportions in rural

Table 15-10A   Relationship of Males in Households to Household Head, by Age and Color, for Urban and Rural Areas, United States: 1960

Relationship to household head	White				Nonwhite			
	0 to 19 years	20 to 39 years	40 to 64 years	65 years and over	0 to 19 years	20 to 39 years	40 to 64 years	65 years and over
URBAN, TOTAL	100.0	100.0	100.0	100.0	100.0	100.0	100.0	100.0
Head of household................	0.6	80.2	93.3	86.9	0.4	67.6	84.2	80.0
Child of head....................	95.4	13.8	2.1	0.1	83.8	15.4	2.4	0.2
Grandchild of head..............	2.4	0.2	0.0	0.0	9.1	0.8	0.0	0.0
Parent of head..................	0.0	0.0	0.5	7.0	0.0	0.0	0.8	7.0
Son or daughter-in-law...........	0.0	1.0	0.4	0.1	0.1	1.7	0.5	0.1
Brother or sister...............	0.3	1.3	1.5	1.9	0.7	3.8	2.7	2.3
Other relative..................	0.8	0.8	0.6	1.3	4.4	3.7	2.2	2.7
Lodger.........................	0.5	2.7	1.6	2.7	1.5	6.9	7.0	7.5
Resident employee..............	0.0	0.0	0.0	0.0	0.0	0.1	0.2	0.2
RURAL-NONFARM, TOTAL	100.0	100.0	100.0	100.0	100.0	100.0	100.0	100.0
Head of household	0.5	82.5	93.9	88.5	0.3	62.4	87.8	87.5
Child of head	94.0	13.4	2.3	0.1	79.6	24.4	3.4	0.2
Grandchild of head..............	2.9	0.2	0.0	0.0	14.0	1.7	0.0	....
Parent of head	0.0	0.0	0.5	6.3	....	0.0	0.7	4.9
Son or daughter-in-law...........	0.0	1.1	0.3	0.1	0.1	2.8	0.6	0.1
Brother or sister...............	0.3	1.0	1.5	1.8	0.6	2.7	2.4	2.1
Other relative..................	0.9	0.7	0.5	1.3	4.4	3.1	1.8	2.1
Lodger.........................	0.5	1.1	0.9	1.8	1.0	2.8	3.2	3.0
Resident employee..............	0.0	0.0	0.1	0.1	0.0	0.1	0.2	0.1
RURAL-FARM, TOTAL	100.0	100.0	100.0	100.0	100.0	100.0	100.0	100.0
Head of household...............	0.3	66.0	91.7	86.3	0.2	51.5	90.6	85.7
Child of head...................	94.0	28.2	3.4	0.1	78.7	35.5	2.5	0.2
Grandchild of head..............	3.5	0.4	0.0	....	15.3	2.0	....	....
Parent of head..................	....	0.0	0.3	7.4	....	0.0	0.5	7.0
Son or daughter-in-law...........	0.1	1.6	0.4	0.1	0.1	2.7	0.4	0.1
Brother or sister...............	0.2	1.2	2.2	2.5	0.5	2.6	2.3	1.8
Other relative..................	1.0	1.0	0.6	1.7	4.2	3.2	1.5	2.6
Lodger.........................	0.7	1.0	0.8	1.5	0.9	2.1	1.8	2.2
Resident employee..............	0.2	0.6	0.6	0.4	0.1	0.4	0.4	0.4

Source: U.S. Census of Population: 1960, Detailed Characteristics, United States Summary, Table 181.

Table 15-10B Relationship of Females in Households to Household Head, by Age and Color, for Urban and Rural Areas, United States: 1960

Relationship to household head	White				Nonwhite			
	0 to 19 years	20 to 39 years	40 to 64 years	65 years and over	0 to 19 years	20 to 39 years	40 to 64 years	65 years and over
URBAN, TOTAL	100.0	100.0	100.0	100.0	100.0	100.0	100.0	100.0
Head of household...............	0.2	7.1	18.4	39.9	0.2	18.2	30.2	43.9
Wife of head....................	2.3	79.0	72.1	33.4	1.5	57.3	53.6	23.2
Child of head...................	93.0	9.8	2.7	0.2	81.9	12.2	2.5	0.3
Grandchild of head..............	2.3	0.1	0.0	0.0	8.7	0.5	0.0	....
Parent of head..................	0.0	0.0	2.3	17.2	0.0	0.1	3.8	19.1
Son or daughter-in-law..........	0.2	0.6	0.2	0.0	0.2	1.2	0.2	0.0
Brother or sister...............	0.3	0.9	2.2	4.1	0.8	3.1	3.1	3.6
Other relative..................	0.9	0.6	0.7	2.5	4.9	2.7	2.1	5.0
Lodger..........................	0.6	1.7	1.0	2.2	1.6	3.9	3.4	4.4
Resident employee...............	0.0	0.2	0.4	0.5	0.1	0.8	1.1	0.5
RURAL-NONFARM, TOTAL	100.0	100.0	100.0	100.0	100.0	100.0	100.0	100.0
Head of household...............	0.1	3.4	12.8	36.2	0.1	9.6	24.7	44.8
Wife of head....................	2.5	86.2	79.9	41.7	1.4	62.5	63.5	32.9
Child of head...................	92.4	7.7	2.3	0.2	78.7	18.7	3.5	0.3
Grandchild of head..............	2.8	0.1	0.0	....	13.4	1.0	....	....
Parent of head..................	0.0	0.0	1.8	14.7	....	0.1	2.3	13.4
Son or daughter-in-law..........	0.3	0.9	0.2	....	0.4	2.1	0.3	....
Brother or sister...............	0.3	0.6	1.4	3.1	0.6	2.0	2.2	3.0
Other relative..................	0.9	0.4	0.6	2.2	4.4	2.0	1.5	3.6
Lodger..........................	0.5	0.5	0.6	1.4	0.9	1.5	1.2	1.5
Resident employee...............	0.1	0.1	0.4	0.5	0.1	0.5	0.8	0.5
RURAL-FARM, TOTAL	100.0	100.0	100.0	100.0	100.0	100.0	100.0	100.0
Head of household...............	....	0.9	5.7	21.1	....	4.2	12.5	25.0
Wife of head....................	1.3	82.8	87.4	51.4	1.1	60.3	76.7	40.0
Child of head...................	93.2	12.4	2.5	0.2	78.6	25.2	3.0	0.4
Grandchild of head..............	3.4	0.1	....	....	14.6	1.1	....	....
Parent of head..................	....	....	1.0	18.6	....	0.1	2.2	22.2
Son or daughter-in-law..........	0.4	2.1	0.3	....	0.5	3.5	0.3	0.0
Brother or sister...............	0.2	0.6	2.0	4.6	0.5	2.2	2.5	4.1
Other relative..................	0.9	0.6	0.5	2.6	4.0	2.2	1.3	5.1
Lodger..........................	0.5	0.3	0.3	0.9	0.7	0.9	0.8	1.8
Resident employee...............	0.1	0.2	0.3	0.5	....	0.3	0.6	0.5

Source: U.S. Census of Population: 1960, Detailed Characteristics, United States Summary Table 181.

and urban areas. Females, however, appear to have much better employment opportunities in cities than in rural areas (Table 15-11). Fewer women living on farms are in the labor force than are rural-nonfarm women. Negro women have higher labor force participation rates than white women at all except the youngest ages in both rural and urban areas.

The differential is much greater in urban than in rural areas, however.

Unemployment. Unemployment rates are highest in rural-nonfarm areas and lowest in rural-farm areas. It is widely observed that agricultural populations frequently suffer from underemployment, but that comparatively few adults in such areas are completely without

Table 15-11 Labor Force Participation Rate of Females, by Age and Color, for Urban and Rural Areas, United States: 1960

Age	Urban		Rural nonfarm		Rural farm	
	White	Nonwhite	White	Nonwhite	White	Nonwhite
Total 14 and over....	36.2	45.8	28.5	31.5	22.7	24.4
14 to 19 years.......	27.7	19.3	19.2	14.1	16.6	12.2
20 to 24 years.......	48.3	48.8	34.9	35.7	35.2	30.1
25 to 29 years.......	35.9	49.8	27.9	37.0	24.3	31.1
30 to 34 years.......	35.2	53.2	30.4	40.3	25.2	30.9
35 to 39 years.......	40.4	58.0	35.1	44.9	28.0	33.1
40 to 44 years.......	46.5	60.9	39.8	47.2	29.9	34.5
45 to 49 years.......	49.7	60.7	41.3	46.3	30.0	33.8
50 to 54 years.......	48.7	56.7	39.2	42.6	27.7	32.3
55 to 59 years.......	42.7	48.3	32.6	36.1	22.6	28.2
60 to 64 years.......	32.0	37.4	23.2	26.2	16.3	21.7
65 to 69 years.......	17.9	22.0	12.7	13.7	10.3	13.5

Source: U.S. Census of Population: 1960, Detailed Characteristics, United States Summary. Table 194.

Table 15-12 Occupational Composition of the Employed Male Population, by Urban and Rural Residence, United States: 1960

Occupation	Total	Urban	Rural nonfarm	Rural farm
Total......................................	100.0	100.0	100.0	100.0
Professional, technical, and kindred workers............	10.3	12.0	7.8	1.7
Farmers and farm managers................................	5.5	.4	3.5	52.6
Managers, officials, and proprietors, except farm........	10.7	11.9	9.7	2.7
Clerical and kindred workers...........................	6.9	8.3	4.6	1.6
Sales workers...	6.9	8.0	5.1	1.6
Craftsmen, foremen, and kindred workers.................	19.5	20.2	22.4	7.0
Operatives and kindred workers.........................	19.8	19.7	24.6	10.0
Private household workers..............................	.1	.2	.2	.1
Service workers, except private households.............	6.0	7.0	4.4	1.2
Farm laborers and foremen.............................	2.8	.6	4.9	15.6
Laborers, except farm and mine........................	6.9	6.6	9.2	3.8
Occupation not reported...............................	4.6	5.1	3.6	2.1

Source: U.S. Census of Population: 1960, Detailed Characteristics, United States Summary, Table 203.

employment. Unemployment rates in rural-nonfarm areas reflect lack of economic opportunities in small towns throughout the nation, and especially in the South.

The following summary reports the unemployment rates of rural and urban areas in 1960:

Area	Males	Females
Urban	5.0	5.3
Rural-nonfarm	6.1	6.1
Rural-farm	2.4	4.8

These rates, derived from the census, are somewhat below the rates obtained by the *Current Population Survey.*

Major Occupation Classification. In urban areas the employed labor force is much more heavily concentrated in the "white-collar" occupations than is the rural-nonfarm population (Table 15-12). The rural-farm population, of course, is heavily employed as farmers or farm laborers, although a surprisingly high proportion of persons living on farms are employed at other occupations—especially as craftsmen and operatives. This reflects the high degree to which suburbanization and long-distance commuting has intermingled urbanlike population with rural communities. The rural-nonfarm population tends to have a concentration of operatives, craftsmen, and

nonfarm laborers in comparison with other areas. It is semiurban also in that it contains substantial proportions of white-collar workers.

Class of Worker. In the cities, nearly nine out of 10 employed males work as wage or salary workers either for private industry or for government. In rural-nonfarm areas the proportion is nearly as high (85 percent). However, in rural-farm areas more than one-half (57 percent) of the males are self-employed. The independent farm operator is still the predominant class of worker in rural-farm areas.

Industry Classification. In both urban and rural-nonfarm areas, manufacturing, commerce, and professional services are the principal means of livelihood. Among rural-farm residents, agriculture and manufacturing are the leading types of industries. Finance, insurance, real estate, business services, and personal services are also much more concentrated in urban places than are other types of industry. These tend to be very specialized enterprises which, by locating in central places, can serve both urban and rural populations. Urban populations consume a much greater amount of such services than do rural populations. (See Table 15-13.)

Transportation to Work. Rural-farm residents tend to work at home and therefore have minimum travel to work. Rural-nonfarm people tend to be commuters and place great reliance

Table 15-13   Industry Composition of the Employed Population (Both Male and Female) by Urban and Rural Residence: 1960

Industry	Urban	Rural nonfarm	Rural farm
Industry groups (males and females)	100.0	100.0	100.0
Agriculture, forestry, fisheries, mining....	1.7	10.6	61.1
Construction..............................	5.5	8.2	3.7
Manufacturing.............................	28.2	28.7	12.0
Transportation, communication, utilities....	7.6	6.2	2.4
Retail and wholesale trade.................	19.7	17.4	6.9
Finance, insurance, real estate............	4.9	2.4	1.0
Business and repair services...............	2.7	2.3	0.8
Private household service..................	3.0	3.3	2.0
Other personal service....................	3.4	2.5	0.8
Professional service--education, welfare, medical, recreational....................	13.5	11.3	5.2
Public administration.....................	5.5	4.2	1.9
Industry not reported.....................	4.5	3.0	2.1

Source: U.S. Census of Population: 1960, Detailed Characteristics, United States Summary, Table 211.

on the automobile. In urban places also the private automobile is the principal means of getting to work, but public rapid transit plays a significant role, as indicated in Table 15-14.

Income. The average income paid to individuals is much higher in cities than in rural areas (Table 15-15). Rural-farm populations are much poorer than are rural-nonfarm and urban populations. The nonwhite population is poorer than the white population in both rural and urban areas, but the income level of the nonwhite population in rural areas is so low as to be at the subsistence level. The low incomes reported for the rural-farm population do not include food grown at home and

housing sometimes provided as a part of the tenancy of the land. Yet even when a rather generous allowance is made for these items (often of much less monetary value than might be presupposed), the incomes of farm residents are distressingly low. Undoubtedly, this is one of the major reasons for the precipitous drop in the farm population during the past quarter century. The median income of only $773 per year for Negro males in the South is a national disgrace.

Summary. Space prevents a more detailed analysis of urban-rural differentials. A complete treatment would trace each differential over several decades, noting the amount and direc-

Table 15-14   Means of Transportation to Work of the Employed Population, by Urban and Rural Residence: 1960

Means of transportation to work	Urban	Rural nonfarm	Rural farm
Means of transportation to work	100.0	100.0	100.0
Private automobile or car pool...	64.2	72.5	37.0
Railroad, subway, or elevated....	5.2	0.3	0.1
Bus or streetcar.................	10.9	1.2	0.5
Walked to work..................	10.0	11.1	5.8
Other means.....................	2.2	3.6	2.6
Worked at home..................	2.9	7.7	50.9
Not reported....................	4.6	3.5	3.2

Table 15-15 Income of White and Negro Males in the South and Remainder of United States, by Urban-Rural Residence: 1959

Income	Northeast, North Center, West				South			
	Total	Urban	Rural nonfarm	Rural farm	Total	Urban	Rural nonfarm	Rural farm
WHITE MALES								
Total..........	100.0	100.0	100.0	100.0	100.0	100.0	100.0	100.0
Less than $1,000...........	12.1	10.6	14.9	21.5	17.4	13.1	21.1	31.0
$1,000 to $1,999...........	10.5	9.4	12.1	18.3	13.6	10.6	16.1	22.6
$2,000 to $2,999...........	8.9	7.9	10.2	15.8	12.4	10.8	14.6	15.3
$3,000 to $3,999...........	10.4	9.8	12.3	12.9	12.6	12.2	14.1	10.5
$4,000 to $4,999...........	13.2	13.1	14.3	10.2	11.7	12.6	11.5	7.0
$5,000 to $5,999...........	14.2	15.1	13.2	7.3	10.4	12.2	8.8	4.8
$6,000 to $6,999...........	10.1	11.1	8.4	4.3	7.1	8.8	5.3	2.8
$7,000 to $9,999...........	12.9	14.4	9.6	5.5	8.8	11.5	5.5	3.3
$10,000 and over...........	7.7	8.7	5.0	4.0	6.0	8.2	3.0	2.7
Median income (dollars)	4614	4939	4035	2646	3524	4262	2877	1841
NEGRO MALES								
Total..........	100.0	100.0	100.0	100.0	100.0	100.0	100.0	100.0
Less than $1,000..........	15.4	14.4	30.0	45.1	35.7	25.0	46.1	64.7
$1,000 to $1,999..........	13.0	12.5	21.8	23.1	22.3	20.7	25.2	22.8
$2,000 to $2,999..........	14.4	14.3	16.1	13.7	19.9	23.9	16.4	7.6
$3,000 to $3,999..........	18.4	18.8	13.3	8.4	11.3	15.2	6.7	2.5
$4,000 to $4,999..........	18.1	18.7	9.4	3.9	6.4	8.8	3.3	1.4
$5,000 to $5,999..........	12.2	12.7	5.1	3.1	2.7	3.9	1.3	0.5
$6,000 to $6,999..........	4.7	4.9	2.2	1.1	0.9	1.3	0.5	0.2
$7,000 to $9,999..........	3.0	3.1	1.6	1.1	0.6	0.9	0.3	0.2
$10,000 and over..........	0.7	0.7	0.5	0.6	0.2	0.3	0.1	0.1
Median income (dollars)	3391	3468	1917	1212	1641	2180	1155	773

Source: U.S. Census of Population: 1960, Detailed Characteristics, United States Summary, Table 262.

tion of change as well as the status at the most recent census. There is need for international comparisons of urban and rural differentials in population composition, especially between the populations of industrialized and developing nations. The international differences in definitions need not be a barrier to such study, although they make precision difficult.

15.6. The System of Economic Areas

The system of economic areas is a delimitation of the land area of the United States according to the criterion of general socioeconomic homogeneity. The "building blocks" from which it is constructed are counties; similar counties are grouped together to form homogeneous units of territory. The complete system has four levels of such grouping. Each grouping consists of combinations of the next lower level of units:

	Number of areas
Economic provinces	5
Economic regions	13
Economic subregions	121
State economic areas	607

In other words, economic provinces are combinations of similar economic regions. Econom-

ic regions, in turn, are combinations of similar economic subregions. Economic subregions are combinations of similar state economic areas. State economic areas are groupings of similar counties lying within the same state. Figure 15-4 presents the boundaries of the provinces and regions, Figure 15-5 outlines the 121 economic subregions, and Figure 15-6 outlines the state economic areas.

This system of areas was delimited under the sponsorship of the U.S. Bureau of the Census for use in the censuses of 1950 and 1960. The work of grouping together similar counties to form the state economic areas and then of grouping similar SEA's into the successively larger units of territory was carried out over a period of a year by a demographer-ecologist and a geographer working in collaboration and with their work under review by a Census Statistical Areas Committee.[3] Inasmuch as the delimitation was a general-purpose one, a great many different series of statistical data were taken into account in maximizing the homogeneity of the areas (64 statistical indexes were employed, with the weight given to each index

[3] Donald J. Bogue and Calvin L. Beale. *Economic Areas of the United States* (Glencoe, Ill.: The Free Press, 1959).

Figure 15-4 Outline Map of the Economic Regions and the Economic Provinces of the United States

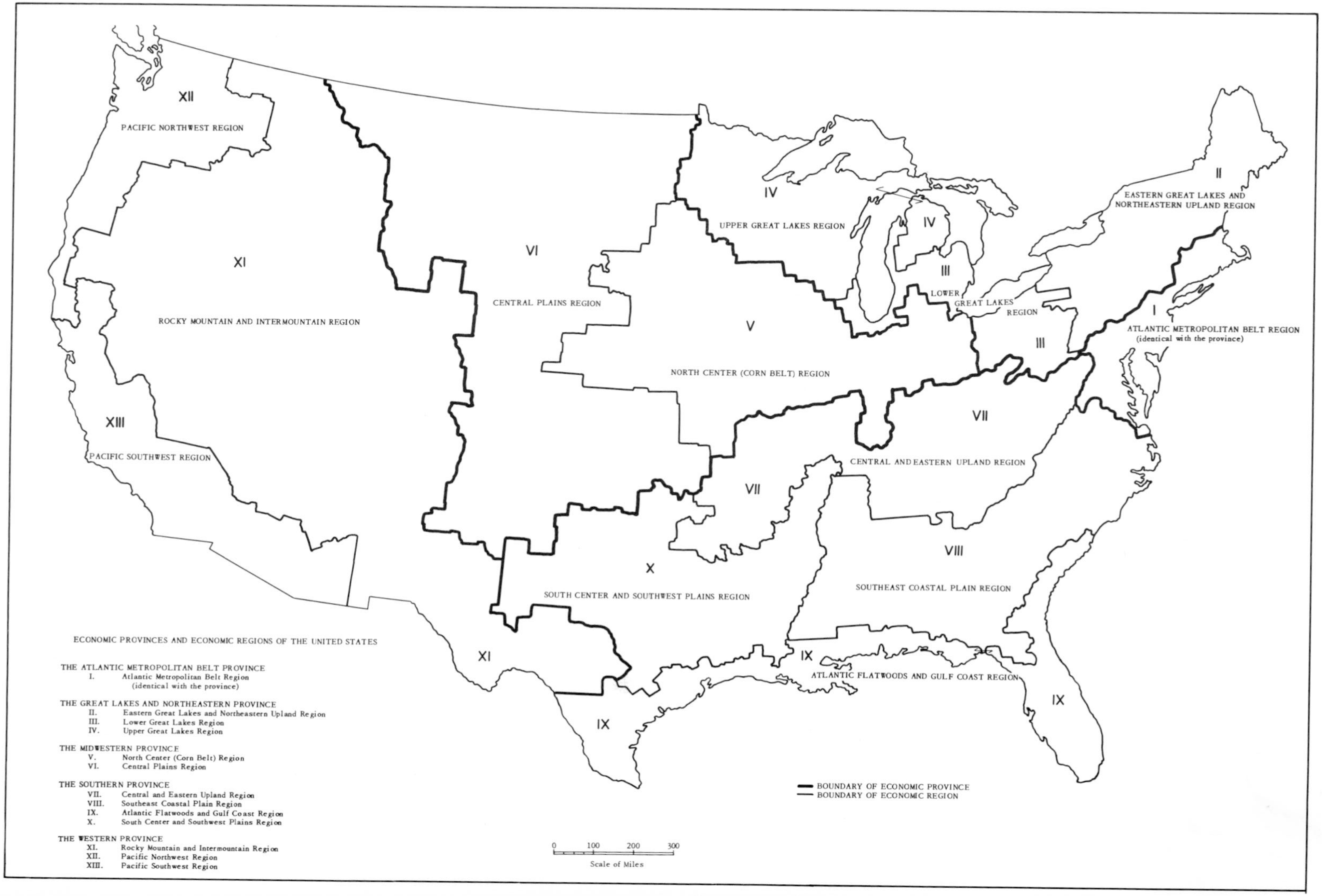
XII
PACIFIC NORTHWEST REGION
XI
ROCKY MOUNTAIN AND INTERMOUNTAIN REGION
XIII
PACIFIC SOUTHWEST REGION
VI
CENTRAL PLAINS REGION
V
NORTH CENTER (CORN BELT) REGION
IV
UPPER GREAT LAKES REGION
IV
III
LOWER GREAT LAKES REGION
III
II
EASTERN GREAT LAKES AND NORTHEASTERN UPLAND REGION
I
ATLANTIC METROPOLITAN BELT REGION
(identical with the province)
VII
CENTRAL AND EASTERN UPLAND REGION
VII
VIII
SOUTHEAST COASTAL PLAIN REGION
X
SOUTH CENTER AND SOUTHWEST PLAINS REGION
IX
ATLANTIC FLATWOODS AND GULF COAST REGION
IX
IX
XI
BOUNDARY OF ECONOMIC PROVINCE
BOUNDARY OF ECONOMIC REGION
0 100 200 300
Scale of Miles
ECONOMIC PROVINCES AND ECONOMIC REGIONS OF THE UNITED STATES
THE ATLANTIC METROPOLITAN BELT PROVINCE
I. Atlantic Metropolitan Belt Region
(identical with the province)
THE GREAT LAKES AND NORTHEASTERN PROVINCE
II. Eastern Great Lakes and Northeastern Upland Region
III. Lower Great Lakes Region
IV. Upper Great Lakes Region
THE MIDWESTERN PROVINCE
V. North Center (Corn Belt) Region
VI. Central Plains Region
THE SOUTHERN PROVINCE
VII. Central and Eastern Upland Region
VIII. Southeast Coastal Plain Region
IX. Atlantic Flatwoods and Gulf Coast Region
X. South Center and Southwest Plains Region
THE WESTERN PROVINCE
XI. Rocky Mountain and Intermountain Region
XII. Pacific Northwest Region
XIII. Pacific Southwest Region

Figure 15-5 Outline Map of the Economic Subregions of the United States.

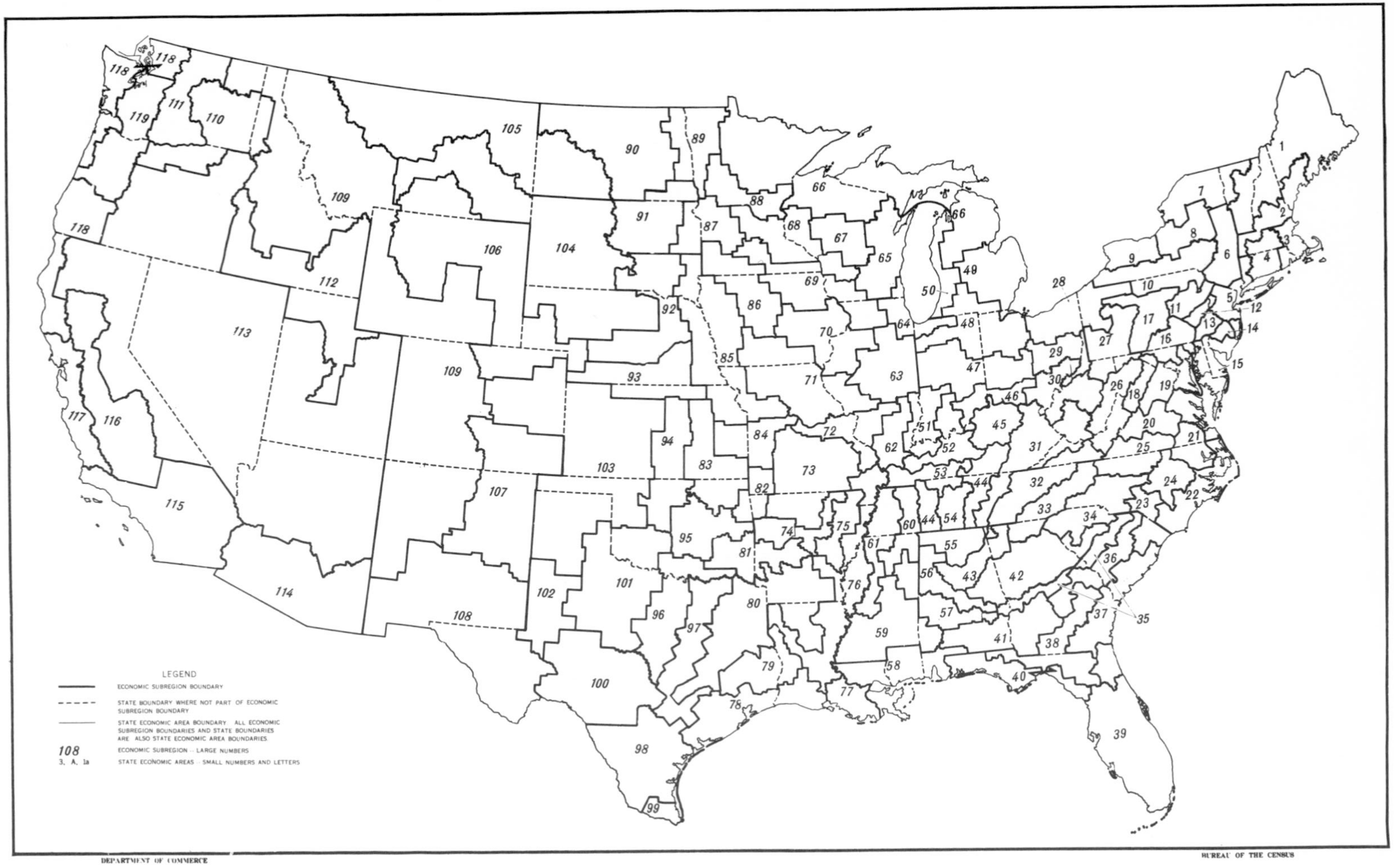

LEGEND

ECONOMIC SUBREGION BOUNDARY

STATE BOUNDARY WHERE NOT PART OF ECONOMIC
SUBREGION BOUNDARY

STATE ECONOMIC AREA BOUNDARY   ALL ECONOMIC
SUBREGION BOUNDARIES AND STATE BOUNDARIES
ARE ALSO STATE ECONOMIC AREA BOUNDARIES.

108   ECONOMIC SUBREGION - LARGE NUMBERS AND LETTERS

3, A, 1a   STATE ECONOMIC AREAS - SMALL NUMBERS AND LETTERS

DEPARTMENT OF COMMERCE

BUREAU OF THE CENSUS

being allowed to change in relation to its importance in the entire economy characterizing the areas). The detailed procedure by which this was accomplished has been stated in an appendix to the basic report on this delimitation. Upon the completion of the system, a monograph was written which describes each of the areas in some detail and specifies the traits that distinguish each area from other areas.

Each of the 13 economic regions represents a distinctive environmental type. If one were to undertake to describe the major environmental components of the nation, it is believed that it could be most parsimoniously done with these units. The economic subregions of each region are regarded as variations on the regional theme, while the state economic areas are, in turn, variations on the subregional themes.

It requires a great deal of study to comprehend the full range of environmental diversity within a nation. However, each student of demography should become at least generally familiar with the distinctive regions of his nation, and appreciate the range of variation between these regions in their demographic characteristics. A very brief description of each of the 13 economic regions of the United States is presented below in order to assist American students with this task.

Region 1. The Atlantic Metropolitan Belt Region. The word "megapolis" characterizes this region. Along the Atlantic Coast from Boston, Massachusetts, to Norfolk, Virginia, the metropolitan areas crowd against each other so closely that more than 90 percent of the inhabitants live within a standard metropolitan statistical area (SMSA). Density of settlement is very high. There is comparatively little open-country rural territory left; even the "rural" areas are only suburbs, and "farms" tend to be no more than specialized food factories or exurban residences or summer homes. This is the region where American commerce and industry were born and from which they have spread. Almost all of the flow of economic goods between Europe and the United States passes through the ports of New York, Boston, Baltimore, Philadelphia, and the smaller coastal SMSA's of this region. Here are concentrated the leading national centers of government, finance, and cultural activities. Manufacturing, using raw materials imported from overseas or from the interior of the continent, is a leading source of employment; emphasis is on consumer goods and nondurables, although the diversity of articles produced is very great. Incomes are high, and there is less economically depressed population than in most other regions.

Region 2. Eastern Great Lakes and Northeastern Uplands Region. Low mountains and extensive forests have made this region the summer and winter playground of the metropolitan of Region 1. The Appalachian, Green, White, Catskill, Adirondack, and other mountains and uplands that comprise this region form a long uplands barrier sandwiched between the Metropolitan Belt Region and Canada. Despite the region's more rugged terrain and comparative lesser accessibility to world and national markets, its economy is moderately industrialized and urbanized. Much of the land is too steep, rocky, and infertile for prosperous crop farming; the population depends primarily on commerce and industry for a livelihood. In the eastern portion, the manufacture of textiles, apparel, shoes, and other nondurable goods tends to predominate. On the western side, the presence of coal and availability of minerals lead to greater emphasis on metal industries and the manufacture of machinery. Many of the largest industries were established in the nineteenth or early twentieth century, hence are old in comparison with other regions. Dairying and special-crop growing for the metropolitan market utilize all land that can be made agriculturally productive and is not claimed for other purposes. The natural resources have been rather fully exploited, including summer tourism and winter sports. Because economic growth in this region now is slow, population growth has been moderate. Some industries, such as lumbering and coal mining, have suffered very sharp curtailment. Other industries such as textiles have suffered from the competition of younger firms with more modern facilities located in other regions. Economic growth is not completely stagnant, however, and efforts are being made to modern-

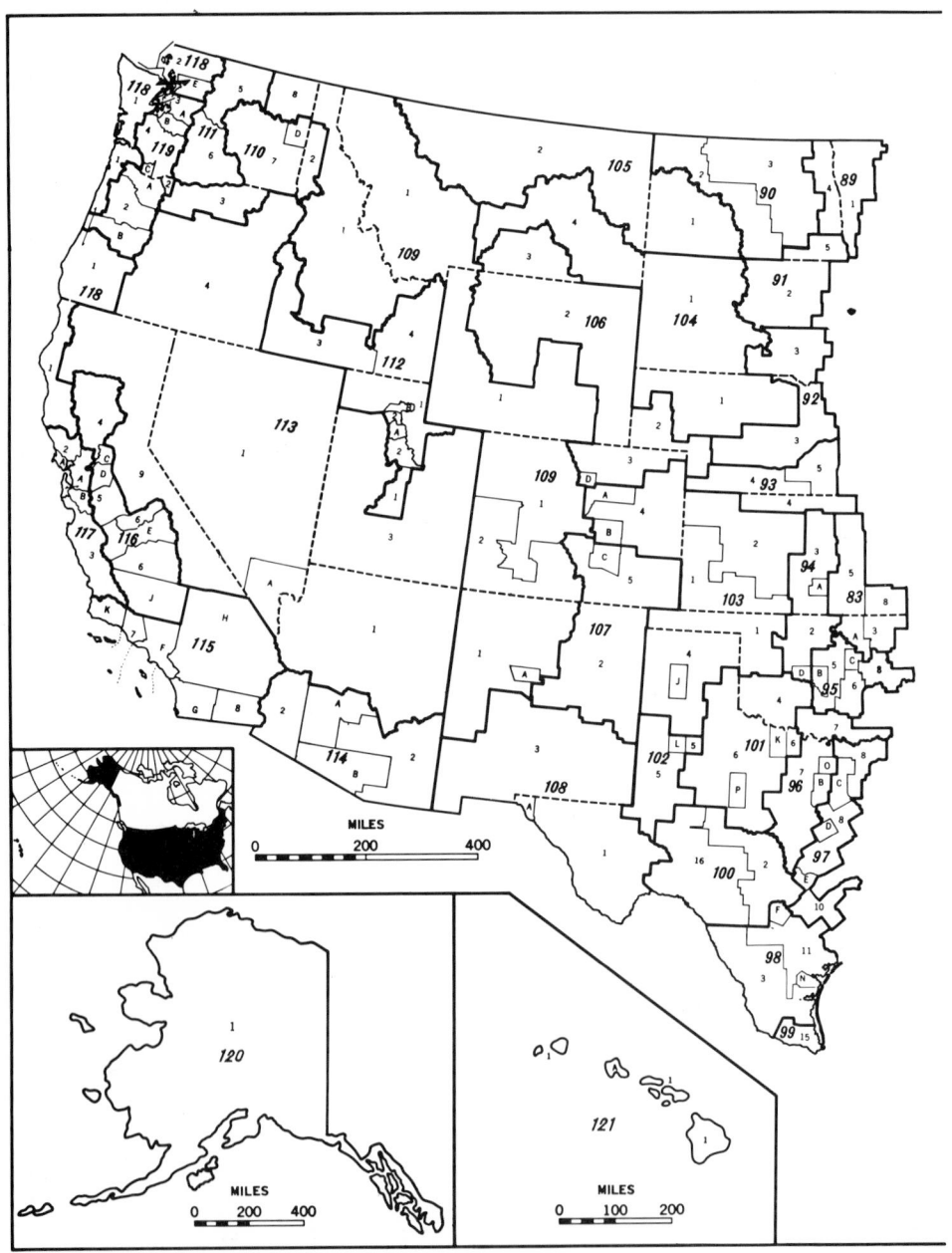

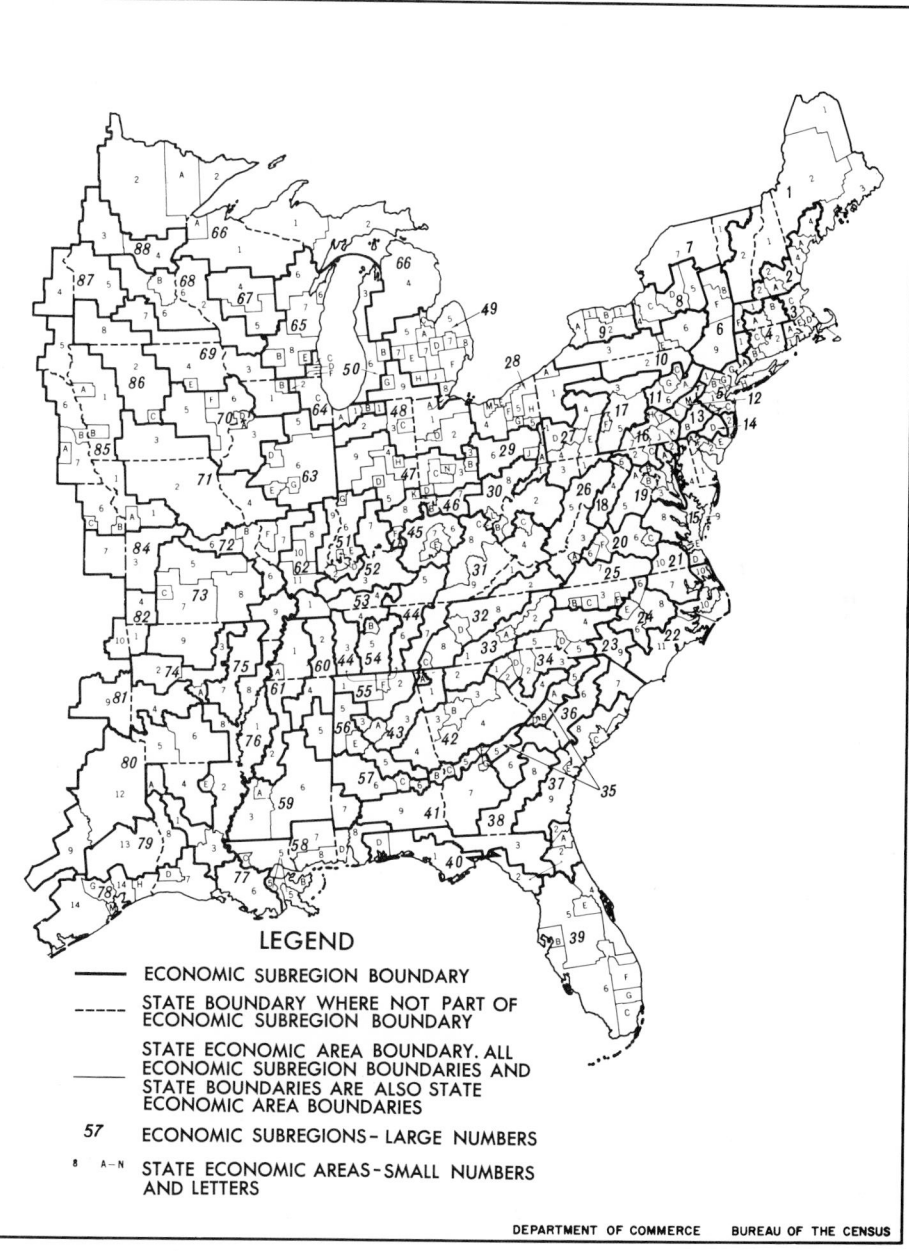

LEGEND

―――― ECONOMIC SUBREGION BOUNDARY

----- STATE BOUNDARY WHERE NOT PART OF
ECONOMIC SUBREGION BOUNDARY

―――― STATE ECONOMIC AREA BOUNDARY. ALL
ECONOMIC SUBREGION BOUNDARIES AND
STATE BOUNDARIES ARE ALSO STATE
ECONOMIC AREA BOUNDARIES

57 ECONOMIC SUBREGIONS - LARGE NUMBERS

8   A-N STATE ECONOMIC AREAS - SMALL NUMBERS
AND LETTERS

DEPARTMENT OF COMMERCE   BUREAU OF THE CENSUS

Figure 15-6   Outline Map of the State Economic Areas, and Economic Subregions, of
the United States.

ize the economy. The level of living is moderately high, although unemployment is severe in some of the places that have suffered most from out-migration of industry.

Region 3. Lower Great Lakes Region. Region 3 is symbolized by the steel mill and the gigantic assembly line. The nation's heavy industry is concentrated here. Chicago, Pittsburgh, Detroit, Cleveland, and a number of smaller metropolitan areas are specialized in the production of iron and steel motor vehicles, machinery (both electrical and nonelectrical), and fabricated metal products. Inland water transportation is highly developed for the movement of bulk materials and cargo from overseas. Coal is mined in great quantities and is merged at the steel mills with iron ore brought by boat from Region 4. Railroads from all over the nation converge upon this region, to haul away industrial products and to bring agricultural products for processing. The area is highly urbanized. Except for slums in the large cities, the level of prosperity is high, both in urban and rural areas. Agriculture is limited in amount and is highly suburbanized and oriented toward adjoining metropolitan markets. Dairying, truck farming, cattle feeding, and special-crop farming are tucked in between suburban subdivisions and behind the string-residential developments along major highways.

Region 4. Upper Great Lakes Region. Forests, mines, and big dairy farms characterize this region. Here is mined the iron ore that feeds the steel mills of Region 3. Extensive woodlands provide the raw materials for a large pulp, paper, and lumber industry. Much of the land makes excellent pasture, and for this reason it is often called the "Dairy Belt." Milk and cheese are produced by the ton. Because large expanses of land are stony or sandy as a result of glacial action, much of the land is of little use for purposes other than forestry. Lakes are numerous, and tourism and sports provide an important part of the economic base. Like Region 2, this region lies between Canada and a very active industrial-commercial region and lies in somewhat of an economic backwater. The industrial towns are comparatively small and most are growing only slowly. Much of the

growth that is occurring is centered in the Minneapolis–St. Paul and the Madison, Wisconsin, SMSA's.

Region 5. The North Center (Corn Belt) Region. America's ability to feed its own population well and yet ship food to hungry nations in Asia centers in this region. An extraordinary combination of favorable soil and climatic conditions together with modern scientific agricultural practices has led to unmatched levels of agricultural productivity. Ancient glaciers leveled the land and laid down a layer of fertile and highly tillable topsoil. The annual rainfall, length of growing season, and summer temperatures are almost ideal for the growing of corn and a wide variety of vegetable and field crops. Stretching from central Ohio westward to central Nebraska and from the Dakotas to Oklahoma there are 270,000 square miles of this combination of fertile prairie and ideal climate for tilled crops.

Farmers in this region are technicians who make use of fertilizers, especially prepared to match the soil and the crop to be grown. Tilling is done with elaborate combinations of machinery. Farm animals are superior species, the result of genetic selection. Many of the farm families have very comfortable incomes and are able to have homes and a level of living not unlike that of suburbanites.

Less well known is that much manufacturing takes place in this agricultural zone—not only at Omaha and Kansas City, but also in smaller SMSA's and small cities. Although this manufacturing is quite diversified, much of it is related to farming—the production of machinery or equipment for farming, the processing of farming, or the processing of farm products.

For several decades the farm industry has been undergoing intensive modernization, which has resulted in fewer but much larger farms, operated by machinery with less manpower. The result has been great shrinking of the farm population. This, in turn, has caused a decline in the village population that earns its livelihood by providing goods and services to farmers. Because industrial growth has been only moderate, the overall increase in population recently has been comparatively small.

Region 6. The Central Plains Region. The

economic symbols of this region are tall grain elevators and cattle pens located on the western plains in small whistle-stop towns along transcontinental railways. Manufacturing is only a small part of the economy. It is a region heavily dependent on agriculture, yet without the bountiful resources of the Corn Belt. Soil conditions are favorable, but rainfall is much less plentiful. In fact, most of the region is semiarid, and there is much annual variation in rainfall. As a result, wheat and other crops requiring less moisture than corn are grown wherever possible. Where crops cannot be grown, cattle are grazed, often on ranches with several thousands of acres of grazing land. There are only two sizeable SMSA's and only a comparatively few moderate-size cities. Because the agricultural industry requires no additional manpower, and nonagricultural activities are expanding slowly, population growth has been only moderate in recent decades.

Region 7. The Central and Eastern Upland Region. Many people refer to this region as "the Southern Mountains." The outstanding traits are that most of the land is too rough and broken for farming, cities are comparatively few, small, and unindustrialized, and the people are poor. Public attention has been often directed toward the Southern Appalachian mountains of West Virginia, Tennessee, and eastern Kentucky, which lie in this region. But this is only a part of the picture; this combination of economic events also blankets southern Ohio, southern Illinois, southern Indiana, southern Missouri, and a large portion of Arkansas and Oklahoma. Mining, a leading source of nonagricultural employment in widely scattered localities, has been mechanized and automated in recent years, stranding thousands of families.

Subsistence farming on badly eroded mountain farms or on small patches of tobacco land is the way of life of large segments of the population. Commercially profitable tillage farming can be conducted only on limited amounts of valley lands between mountains or high hills. The few exceptional areas, such as the Kentucky Bluegrass, contain only a small fraction of the 15 million inhabitants.

There are some large and important industrial centers in the region: Cincinnati, Louis-

ville, and St. Louis are the largest. Economic expansion has been slow in comparison with other regions, despite large programs to aid this economically depressed region, such as the Tennessee Valley Authority, which promotes economic development through developing water resources for electric power.

Birth rates in this region are high; because of restricted economic opportunities there has been a mass exodus to Northern industrial centers. This is the well-known "hillbilly" or "Southern white" migration. This is a region of rural white poverty; Region 8, to be described next, is a region of rural Negro poverty.

Region 8. The Southeast Coastal Plain and Piedmont Region. The stereotyped portrait of the "Old South" of Civil War days—plantations, slaves, tall pillared mansions—had its origin in this region. The post-Civil War stereotype of the South as the Negro sharecropper in a cotton-tobacco-peanut economy dedicated to WASP (White Anglo-Saxon Protestant) supremacy also was born here. Today, in a rapidly changing economic and social situation, it is the scene of the largest single concentration of Negro poverty in the nation, of rapid urbanization, and of social and political turmoil, including Civil Rights demonstrations. About one third of the population is Negro—a higher proportion than in any other region. It is the most rural of the regions and also the poorest. Agriculture is the leading single industry. However, the economy is changing rapidly. Much of the cotton lands have been converted to pasture, and cattle and dairying are on the increase. This process has swept many thousands of Negro farmers off the land and into the cities—both in the South and in the North. Manufacturing has been moving into the region; foremost has been the textile industry. Large military installations have assisted greatly in the process of economic growth.

Because of its milder winter climate the region is becoming an attractive site for elderly couples in retirement. The revolution in agriculture is causing the rural areas to lose population rapidly, but because the cities are industrializing, urban areas are growing. In recent decades, literally millions of Negroes have abandoned this region to move to the North, and the process appears to be continuing. Levels of living are rising.

Region 9. The Gulf Coast and Atlantic Flatwoods Region. Stretching along the South Atlantic Coast and the coast of the Gulf of Mexico, this is one of the most rapidly growing regions of the nation. The region has suddenly come alive and is receiving a great variety of new industries. The mild subtropical climate has made it attractive for winter tourism and year-round residence. The port cities have enjoyed new commerce and have acquired many new factories. Discovery and exploitation of large resources of crude oil and natural gas are also contributing to the rapid development of the region. Agricultural developments in the direction of making this a "winter garden" to supply the North with food when its own gardens are bare are also under way. This region is a favorite site for military bases. Some of these installations (for example, Cape Kennedy) are very large and employ many thousands of civilians as well as military personnel. For these varied reasons, the area increased by nearly 50 percent between 1950 and 1960.

Region 10. The South Center and Southwest Plains Region. Mechanized cotton production, huge petroleum fields, cattle ranching on a grand scale, and rapidly growing metropolises are the dominant characteristics of this region. It is the "New Cotton Belt" of the South and Southwest, where the plantation system did not have a chance to develop because the broad prairie lands encouraged early mechanization of agriculture. Excellent grazing lands are found in this region, and cattle ranching is a leading type of agricultural production. Oil and gas wells are scattered at many points throughout the region. In recent years there has been very rapid industrialization. Dallas, Fort Worth, and Oklahoma City are the leading centers, but numerous smaller places such as Lubbock, Austin, and Waco have leaped into metropolitan status with a wide range of industry. Military installations have also provided a large stimulus to the economic growth and urbanization of the region. Originally, the processing of cotton, cattle, and petroleum comprised much of the economic base, but in recent years, as industry has moved southward and westward, the metropolitan centers are becoming very diversified; it is not improper to speak now of the "Southwest Manufacturing Belt."

Region 11. The Rocky Mountain and Intermountain Region. Mountains and deserts too barren for settlement are the outstanding traits of this region. Population density is very low —only one-tenth the average for the nation. Vast tracts are completely uninhabited. Where water can be brought to valley lands, rich crops can be produced. Mining (copper, silver, lead, uranium, coal) is an important activity. The 5 million persons who live in this region are found clustered in small valleys where land can be irrigated or on plateaus where dry-land farming is possible. A few live on huge ranches where only a few cattle can be allocated to each square mile of semidesert range. There are only three metropolitan areas (El Paso, Albuquerque, and Salt Lake City) and only a comparatively few medium-size cities. Cities tend to be marketing and service centers rather than places of manufacture. Forestry and tourism are important secondary industries. A large proportion of the American Indian population lives in this region. Oil and gas fields are numerous, although less productive than in Region 10.

Las Vegas and Reno in Nevada, specializing in divorces, gambling, and entertainment, are among the most unique cities of the world.

Region 12. The Pacific Northwest Region. The Pacific Coast from Northern California to the Canadian border, extending inland to the Rocky Mountains, comprises this region. It is a territory of lumbering, irrigated farms, and extensive dry-land wheat farming. The nation's best timber resources are found here. Water for irrigation is comparatively abundant, and large tracts of valley lands can be irrigated. With plentiful supplies of raw materials, several industrial centers such as Seattle, Portland, Spokane, and Tacoma have grown rapidly. Although it is a prosperous region, it is less fabulous than Southern California and has grown rapidly but not explosively in recent decades. It is now appropriate to refer to this region as the "Pacific Metropolitan Belt" region. Alaska is also included in this region.

Region 13. The Pacific Southwest Region. A

Table 15-16A Demographic, Social and Economic Characteristics of the Economic Regions of the United States: 1960

Subject	U.S. Total	Regions												
		1	2	3	4	5	6	7	8	9	10	11	12	13
Total population............	100.0	100.0	100.0	100.0	100.0	100.0	100.0	100.0	100.0	100.0	100.0	100.0	100.0	100.0
White:														
Native of native parentage...	70.1	56.3	73.0	64.6	75.3	85.3	82.2	87.5	67.2	68.0	75.5	80.0	76.5	66.8
Native of foreign or mixed parentage..	13.3	22.2	18.4	18.6	19.5	8.8	11.5	3.4	1.1	8.5	3.0	11.2	14.6	15.4
Foreign born................	5.2	10.3	6.3	7.0	3.9	1.8	2.5	1.0	0.5	3.9	0.8	3.9	5.0	7.5
Nonwhite....................	11.4	11.3	2.3	9.8	1.2	4.1	3.8	8.1	31.2	19.7	20.7	5.0	3.9	10.3
AGE														
White, all ages...........	100.0	100.0	100.0	100.0	100.0	100.0	100.0	100.0	100.0	100.0	100.0	100.0	100.0	100.0
Under 15 years...........	30.3	27.8	29.7	30.7	32.6	30.8	32.2	30.8	30.5	31.7	30.2	34.8	31.0	30.2
15 to 19 years...........	7.3	6.7	7.3	6.9	7.5	7.3	7.7	8.1	8.4	7.4	8.0	8.0	7.4	7.1
20 to 24 years...........	6.0	5.6	5.5	5.6	5.7	5.9	6.1	6.1	6.9	6.2	6.4	6.4	6.0	6.3
25 to 34 years...........	12.7	12.9	12.0	12.8	11.6	12.2	12.6	12.1	13.5	13.3	12.6	12.8	12.1	13.4
35 to 44 years...........	13.6	14.5	13.3	14.1	12.2	12.6	12.7	12.7	13.6	13.3	12.8	12.7	13.5	14.5
45 to 64 years...........	20.7	22.7	21.5	21.0	20.2	20.3	19.3	20.5	19.3	19.4	20.6	18.0	20.3	19.7
65 years and over.......	9.4	9.7	10.7	9.0	10.2	10.8	9.4	9.6	7.8	8.7	9.4	7.3	9.7	8.8
Nonwhite, all ages........	100.0	100.0	100.0	100.0	100.0	100.0	100.0	100.0	100.0	100.0	100.0	100.0	100.0	100.0
Under 15 years...........	37.5	33.6	35.2	36.8	38.2	35.2	39.4	35.1	40.7	38.9	40.9	43.1	39.0	35.5
15 to 19 years...........	7.9	6.8	7.3	6.5	7.6	7.1	7.8	7.6	9.6	8.0	8.9	8.8	7.4	7.1
20 to 24 years...........	6.5	6.9	8.0	6.2	7.1	6.5	7.2	5.9	6.2	6.7	5.6	8.1	7.8	6.8
25 to 34 years...........	13.0	15.3	16.8	14.9	14.1	13.7	13.7	11.8	10.5	12.8	9.8	13.6	14.6	15.4
35 to 44 years...........	12.3	14.5	13.1	13.9	11.5	12.6	11.0	11.8	10.4	11.7	9.5	10.0	12.6	14.3
45 to 64 years...........	16.8	17.6	15.4	16.9	15.4	17.7	14.9	19.6	15.9	16.2	17.4	11.9	14.0	16.3
65 years and over.......	6.1	5.2	4.1	4.7	6.2	7.3	6.1	8.3	6.8	5.7	8.7	4.5	4.6	4.5
DEPENDENCY RATIO														
Total:														
White....................	.89	.79	.91	.87	1.01	.96	.97	.94	.88	.92	.91	1.00	.92	.85
Nonwhite.................	1.06	.84	.87	.93	1.08	.98	1.14	1.04	1.33	1.11	1.36	1.29	1.04	.89
Youth:														
White....................	.71	.62	.71	.70	.81	.75	.79	.76	.73	.75	.73	.86	.74	.69
Nonwhite.................	.94	.74	.80	.83	.95	.84	1.01	.87	1.17	.99	1.15	1.19	.95	.81
Old age:														
White....................	.18	.17	.21	.17	.21	.21	.18	.19	.15	.17	.18	.15	.19	.16
Nonwhite.................	.13	.10	.08	.09	.13	.15	.13	.17	.16	.12	.21	.11	.09	.09
SEX RATIO														
White, all ages...........	97.3	95.0	95.9	97.1	99.0	97.1	100.0	97.1	97.4	97.9	98.1	102.2	101.3	99.2
Under 15 years...........	104.1	104.1	104.1	104.2	104.2	104.3	104.2	104.1	104.1	103.7	104.1	103.9	104.1	103.8
15 to 19 years...........	102.1	99.9	99.7	104.2	100.1	99.5	106.2	102.8	106.2	106.2	104.3	103.1	101.5	109.4
20 to 24 years...........	96.6	95.9	93.8	97.4	89.8	91.9	98.4	97.7	103.4	98.5	102.2	98.5	106.7	107.4
25 to 34 years...........	97.3	96.1	96.0	97.0	98.7	97.8	98.6	94.0	96.1	96.0	97.1	100.2	101.3	102.1
35 to 44 years...........	95.9	93.4	94.7	95.5	97.7	99.4	99.4	94.3	96.4	96.6	96.6	100.0	99.6	98.1
45 to 64 years...........	95.2	92.2	94.3	97.0	98.4	95.8	99.0	94.6	92.7	92.7	95.2	105.0	101.8	96.1
65 years and over.......	81.6	75.9	79.0	84.4	90.6	81.4	87.8	84.5	76.4	87.8	82.6	96.7	90.6	77.2
Nonwhite, all ages........	94.5	91.7	106.3	94.6	109.4	95.7	99.9	92.5	92.5	94.6	93.0	102.5	111.4	105.1
Under 15 years...........	100.5	100.0	101.3	99.7	105.1	99.0	100.1	100.2	100.6	100.2	101.3	99.3	103.0	102.6
15 to 19 years...........	98.6	92.1	110.3	90.4	105.4	94.5	98.1	98.1	101.5	99.9	101.4	106.1	104.4	103.8
20 to 24 years...........	89.7	82.4	106.5	76.7	109.5	94.3	116.0	87.7	93.2	92.3	90.5	107.3	132.0	100.4
25 to 34 years...........	86.2	84.9	109.0	86.1	118.1	93.0	88.6	83.1	81.4	89.3	78.3	94.0	101.5	94.7
35 to 44 years...........	89.0	88.2	110.2	94.1	124.8	93.1	95.7	85.9	82.7	87.9	78.6	102.9	110.5	101.1
45 to 64 years...........	94.4	91.1	111.4	102.0	105.4	95.9	89.4	89.4	86.2	92.8	88.3	113.0	138.2	127.1
65 years and over.......	89.2	85.1	101.1	91.8	106.1	93.0	100.8	91.1	82.3	84.8	94.3	118.8	129.2	112.1

Table 15-16A (Continued)

Subject	U.S. Total	Regions 1	2	3	4	5	6	7	8	9	10	11	12	13
AVERAGE POPULATION PER HOUSEHOLD														
Total..................................	3.29	3.20	3.28	3.33	3.37	3.20	3.24	3.37	3.64	3.37	3.30	3.44	3.11	3.10
White.................................	3.23	3.16	3.27	3.29	3.37	3.19	3.22	3.35	3.39	3.28	3.17	3.39	3.08	3.05
Nonwhite..............................	3.85	3.57	3.72	3.72	4.04	3.59	3.87	3.59	4.34	3.85	3.89	4.51	3.92	3.63
MOBILITY STATUS														
White.................................	100.0	100.0	100.0	100.0	100.0	100.0	100.0	100.0	100.0	100.0	100.0	100.0	100.0	100.0
Same house in 1955 and 1960..........	50.9	56.4	59.4	54.7	56.8	52.8	47.8	52.3	48.1	42.0	44.7	43.3	44.2	37.7
Same county..........................	29.3	25.4	27.7	32.2	26.0	29.6	26.8	31.0	31.2	28.9	31.1	27.7	29.5	33.4
Different county:														
Same State........................	7.2	8.7	6.8	6.4	10.6	9.7	11.6	8.5	10.3	8.7	13.9	11.0	10.8	10.3
Different State or abroad.........	10.7	9.5	6.2	6.7	6.7	7.9	13.9	8.1	10.4	20.4	10.3	18.0	15.5	18.6
Not reported......................	1.4	1.7	1.2	1.3	1.0	1.3	1.1	1.3	1.0	1.8	1.3	1.0	1.1	2.1
Nonwhite..............................	100.0	100.0	100.0	100.0	100.0	100.0	100.0	100.0	100.0	100.0	100.0	100.0	100.0	100.0
Same house in 1955 to 1960...........	49.3	48.8	36.0	40.1	42.7	45.0	41.0	51.3	55.0	53.3	53.4	50.2	40.2	41.2
Same county..........................	38.7	36.9	40.7	50.3	32.4	40.5	35.1	39.5	37.2	35.8	36.0	29.7	33.1	38.6
Different county:														
Same State........................	4.8	4.8	7.4	1.7	9.1	3.7	7.4	3.6	5.1	4.9	7.2	5.7	6.9	5.6
Different State or abroad.........	7.2	9.5	15.9	8.0	15.7	10.8	16.5	5.6	2.8	6.0	3.4	14.4	19.8	14.6
Not reported......................	2.7	3.9	4.8	4.7	2.8	3.6	2.7	2.8	1.0	2.4	1.2	1.9	3.4	2.9
Standardized:														
White:														
Same house in 1955 and 1960.......		56.0	58.7	54.7	56.5	52.5	48.2	52.3	49.3	42.7	45.0	44.6	44.2	38.4
Same county.......................		25.5	28.0	32.1	26.1	29.7	26.6	31.0	30.7	28.5	31.0	27.1	29.5	33.1
Different county or abroad........		18.5	13.3	13.1	17.4	17.9	25.3	16.7	20.0	28.7	24.1	28.3	26.3	28.5
Nonwhite:														
Same house in 1955 and 1960.......		52.5	40.1	42.8	45.4	46.6	43.8	51.7	56.3	55.5	53.6	54.3	44.0	44.3
Same county.......................		35.7	38.9	49.0	31.2	39.7	33.9	39.3	36.6	34.8	35.9	27.9	31.4	37.1
Different county or abroad........		12.9	21.0	8.3	23.3	13.6	22.3	9.0	7.2	9.7	10.5	17.8	24.6	18.6
Unstandardized, percent migrant:														
Total................................	19.0	17.8	13.2	12.8	17.3	17.6	25.4	16.1	16.8	25.7	21.5	28.6	26.3	28.1
White................................	19.8	18.2	12.9	13.1	17.2	17.7	25.5	16.7	20.7	29.1	24.2	29.0	26.3	28.9
Nonwhite.............................	12.0	14.3	23.3	9.7	24.8	14.5	23.9	9.2	7.9	10.9	10.6	20.1	26.7	20.2
Ratio of migration to total mobility:														
Total................................	.385	.401	.321	.275	.399	.371	.484	.337	.337	.460	.402	.507	.470	.454
White................................	.403	.407	.318	.289	.398	.375	.489	.350	.399	.502	.438	.511	.471	.464
Nonwhite.............................	.237	.279	.364	.162	.433	.264	.405	.189	.176	.233	.227	.404	.446	.344
COUNTRY OF ORIGIN														
Total foreign stock..................	100.0	100.0	100.0	100.0	100.0	100.0	100.0	100.0	100.0	100.0	100.0	100.0	100.0	100.0
English-speaking Europe and Canada...	23.0	24.8	37.5	19.5	15.1	17.8	18.5	19.7	28.0	17.4	15.8	24.1	33.5	20.6
Scandinavian-German-French portion of Europe....	25.4	17.3	18.4	25.6	59.2	56.2	44.7	42.3	27.4	19.1	28.9	28.0	40.4	14.9
Eastern Europe.......................	23.5	26.9	22.0	36.0	19.6	13.8	22.6	19.4	16.3	13.1	14.5	7.0	12.7	12.7
Southern Europe......................	16.7	25.2	19.4	14.3	4.2	7.6	12.3	14.1	4.4	10.4	7.1	8.0	6.0	12.8
Spanish America......................	6.8	2.7	0.6	2.1	0.5	2.2	5.5	1.7	4.4	36.1	27.2	28.2	2.0	19.8
Asia.................................	3.4	2.1	1.3	1.6	0.8	1.4	2.1	3.0	7.2	2.2	4.3	2.9	4.3	12.5
All other............................	0.4	0.3	1.3	0.2	0.2	0.3	0.5	0.3	1.2	0.4	0.6	0.7	0.7	0.7
Not reported.........................	0.4	0.3	0.3	0.2	0.2	0.4	0.5	0.5	1.2	0.4	0.6	0.7	0.7	1.0
	0.7	0.6	0.7	0.8	0.4	0.6	0.9	1.1	1.3	1.3	1.6	1.0	0.3	0.8

Table 15-16A (Continued)

Subject	U.S. Total	Regions												
		1	2	3	4	5	6	7	8	9	10	11	12	13
STATE OF BIRTH														
Percent born in State of 1960 residence:														
Total	66.5	62.8	77.2	68.1	78.5	73.9	60.1	78.1	82.6	58.8	75.6	56.5	46.2	40.1
White	66.5	64.4	78.0	71.1	78.7	74.9	60.1	79.0	78.9	54.7	72.4	55.7	45.9	39.2
Nonwhite	66.6	50.1	42.0	41.1	58.2	50.6	59.4	66.9	90.6	75.7	87.7	71.6	51.8	47.8
YEAR MOVED INTO PRESENT HOUSE														
Total	100.0	100.0	100.0	100.0	100.0	100.0	100.0	100.0	100.0	100.0	100.0	100.0	100.0	100.0
1959 to 1960	25.4	20.3	19.9	21.8	20.6	24.5	29.3	25.2	27.5	31.1	31.1	32.6	30.4	34.4
1957 to 1958	18.7	18.6	17.2	19.0	17.5	18.4	18.2	18.3	18.3	19.7	18.1	18.9	19.3	20.7
1950 to 1956	29.8	32.7	29.5	32.6	29.6	28.8	27.0	28.2	27.1	28.1	26.8	25.8	29.2	29.1
Before 1950	26.1	28.4	33.5	26.7	32.4	28.4	25.6	28.3	27.0	21.1	23.9	22.8	21.1	15.8
CHILDREN EVER BORN														
Children ever born per 1,000 women ever married:														
White, 15 to 44 years old	2253	2057	2328	2268	2620	2354	2417	2345	2162	2292	2241	2590	2351	2154
Standardized for age	2254	2014	2302	2246	2613	2375	2449	2378	2208	2316	2295	2642	2361	2155
15 to 24 years old	1236	1098	1272	1249	1345	1281	1321	1243	1143	1286	1242	1407	1323	1260
25 to 34 years old	2379	2119	2424	2390	2730	2525	2589	2426	2255	2468	2411	2778	2561	2331
35 to 44 years old	2575	2310	2633	2542	3050	2706	2804	2820	2622	2618	2641	3046	2624	2379
Nonwhite, 15 to 44 years old	2788	2285	2456	2480	2951	2590	2867	2755	3381	2952	3469	3215	2761	2398
Standardized for age	2798	2275	2472	2466	3027	2595	2931	2751	3419	2992	3537	3371	2798	2386
15 to 24 years old	1820	16	1731	1811	1714	1831	1783	1873	1943	1886	1989	1867	1641	1588
25 to 34 years old	2963	2473	2684	2749	3017	2841	2975	3009	3526	3214	3637	3342	2855	2479
35 to 44 years old	3067	2356	2597	2490	3597	2699	3382	2893	3953	3264	4108	4041	3242	2643
Ratio of nonwhite to white fertility in same area:														
15 to 24 years old	1.472	1.518	1.361	1.450	1.274	1.429	1.350	1.507	1.700	1.407	1.601	1.327	1.240	1.260
25 to 34 years old	1.245	1.167	1.107	1.150	1.105	1.125	1.149	1.240	1.564	1.302	1.509	1.203	1.115	1.063
35 to 44 years old	1.191	1.020	.986	.980	1.179	.997	1.205	1.026	1.508	1.247	1.555	1.327	1.236	1.111
Ratio of area to U.S. white[1]	1.242	1.010	1.097	1.095	1.344	1.152	1.301	1.221	1.518	1.328	1.570	1.496	1.242	1.059
Ratio of white area fertility rates to U.S. rate:														
15 to 24 years old	1.000	.888	1.029	1.011	1.088	1.036	1.069	1.006	.925	1.040	1.005	1.138	1.070	1.019
25 to 34 years old	1.000	.891	1.019	1.005	1.148	1.061	1.088	1.020	.948	1.037	1.013	1.168	1.077	.980
35 to 44 years old	1.000	.897	1.023	.987	1.184	1.051	1.089	1.095	1.018	1.017	1.026	1.183	1.019	.924
Total (standardized)[1]	1.000	.894	1.022	.997	1.160	1.054	1.087	1.055	.980	1.028	1.019	1.173	1.048	.957
SCHOOL ENROLLMENT														
Percent enrolled, total	52.0	49.9	53.0	51.5	56.1	53.0	53.9	51.8	52.5	50.6	53.8	55.1	55.1	51.3
7 to 13 years old	97.5	97.5	97.9	98.0	98.4	98.0	97.8	96.6	96.7	97.2	97.0	97.6	98.4	98.2
14 and 15 years old	94.1	94.4	95.0	95.3	96.8	95.3	95.4	90.6	91.2	92.9	92.6	95.0	96.8	96.0
16 and 17 years old	80.9	80.3	82.7	83.7	88.5	83.6	85.2	74.9	75.1	77.0	79.0	85.1	89.0	83.0
18 and 19 years old	42.1	40.0	47.2	40.0	47.8	44.7	46.1	39.7	41.5	37.3	45.8	48.1	48.6	40.6
20 and 21 years old	21.1	21.8	24.6	19.1	24.8	22.9	22.5	19.3	19.8	15.2	23.8	21.5	24.9	21.3
22 to 24 years old	10.2	11.1	9.4	9.2	11.8	9.9	10.9	8.9	8.7	7.7	10.8	12.3	12.1	12.2
25 to 34 years old	4.6	5.1	3.4	3.8	4.4	3.7	5.3	3.8	4.0	4.0	4.7	6.3	5.4	6.5

Table 15-16A (Continued)

Subject	U.S. Total	Regions 1	2	3	4	5	6	7	8	9	10	11	12	13
SCHOOL ENROLLMENT--(Con't.)														
Ratio of actual to potential enrollment:														
White:														
Kindergarten	.991	1.107	1.343	1.307	1.359	1.190	1.021	.446	.307	.535	.336	.714	.972	1.446
Elementary school	.998	.956	1.025	1.015	1.049	1.014	1.017	1.033	.982	1.020	.991	1.052	1.027	.968
High school	.999	1.008	1.014	.995	1.112	.999	1.072	.946	.957	.901	.992	1.071	1.095	1.003
College	1.002	1.141	1.059	.872	1.054	1.048	1.018	.826	.913	.626	1.134	.975	1.113	1.185
Nonwhite:														
Kindergarten	.801	1.042	1.550	1.652	1.364	1.505	1.148	.605	.196	.528	.238	.774	.956	1.523
Elementary school	1.107	.964	.927	1.058	1.014	1.003	1.046	1.114	1.242	1.124	1.263	1.109	1.039	.989
High school	.853	.792	.646	.790	.818	.834	.810	.896	.879	.847	.893	.777	.759	1.008
College	.490	.449	.481	.414	1.170	.708	.491	.643	.389	.389	.337	.388	.892	1.049
Percent nonwhite ratio to white:														
Kindergarten	80.8	94.1	115.1	126.4	100.4	126.5	112.4	135.7	63.8	98.7	70.8	108.4	98.4	105.3
Elementary school	110.9	100.8	90.4	104.2	96.7	98.9	102.9	107.8	126.5	110.2	127.4	105.4	101.2	102.2
High school	85.4	78.6	63.7	79.4	73.6	83.5	75.6	94.7	91.8	94.0	90.0	72.5	69.3	100.5
College	48.9	39.4	45.4	47.5	111.0	67.6	48.2	77.8	42.6	62.1	29.7	39.8	80.1	88.5
YEARS OF SCHOOL COMPLETED STANDARDIZED FOR AGE														
Male														
White		100.0	100.0	100.0	100.0	100.0	100.0	100.0	100.0	100.0	100.0	100.0	100.0	100.0
Elementary: Less than 5 years	7.1	6.7	5.9	6.3	5.7	4.4	5.5	12.7	13.1	11.5	11.5	7.5	3.9	6.6
5 to 7 years	13.2	11.5	14.1	12.7	13.0	12.3	11.4	19.7	22.0	15.1	17.6	10.7	9.6	9.7
8 years	17.6	18.0	20.5	20.2	20.2	24.3	23.0	22.2	12.1	18.2	13.6	17.3	19.6	14.8
High school: 1 to 3 years	19.9	19.5	21.3	20.4	15.2	17.3	16.1	15.1	18.6	18.2	18.6	19.3	19.2	19.0
4 years	20.8	20.8	22.6	22.6	23.1	25.5	24.0	16.8	17.8	21.3	19.2	23.5	19.2	23.4
College: 1 to 3 years	8.7	8.2	7.1	8.4	7.9	7.8	10.0	6.5	7.9	10.3	9.7	11.3	10.8	13.6
4 years or more	12.9	12.9	8.7	9.6	8.6	8.4	9.9	7.1	8.7	10.6	9.6	10.4	10.9	13.6
Median years of school completed	12.1	11.1	10.3	10.6	10.0	10.6	10.9	8.8	9.5	10.7	10.2	11.3	11.6	12.0
Nonwhite	100.0	100.0	100.0	100.0	100.0	100.0	100.0	100.0	100.0	100.0	100.0	100.0	100.0	100.0
Elementary: Less than 5 years	28.4	18.4	19.3	17.4	13.1	16.5	14.6	26.7	44.5	36.8	41.9	33.9	20.4	17.7
5 to 7 years	23.8	23.9	24.8	22.0	20.0	20.6	20.2	24.1	27.4	26.8	24.1	17.8	17.4	16.4
8 years	13.4	16.2	19.3	17.9	21.1	18.0	17.3	15.1	11.5	11.5	8.8	13.4	16.2	14.0
High school: 1 to 3 years	16.5	20.5	20.2	22.2	19.0	21.7	20.6	16.6	10.3	13.5	12.1	15.5	16.3	18.4
4 years	10.5	12.5	9.2	12.4	11.2	14.1	16.0	10.3	5.3	6.6	7.9	12.4	16.1	19.2
College: 1 to 3 years	4.2	4.6	3.8	5.2	6.2	5.4	6.9	4.1	1.9	2.6	2.8	4.3	7.1	8.4
4 years or more	3.2	3.9	3.6	2.9	9.3	3.8	4.6	3.1	2.1	2.1	2.5	2.8	6.4	5.9
Median years of school completed	7.7	8.5	8.3	8.6	8.8	8.7	8.9	7.9	5.6	6.5	6.0	7.7	8.8	9.3
Female														
White		100.0	100.0	100.0	100.0	100.0	100.0	100.0	100.0	100.0	100.0	100.0	100.0	100.0
Elementary: Less than 5 years	5.0	4.8	5.5	3.8	2.7	3.9	3.9	8.4	8.8	9.6	7.6	6.4	2.4	5.0
5 to 7 years	11.0	11.4	11.5	10.6	9.5	9.1	8.6	18.1	19.6	13.6	15.3	9.0	6.9	8.1
8 years	14.5	18.0	19.0	18.1	19.2	21.6	19.0	22.8	11.4	12.6	12.7	14.5	16.1	13.8
High school: 1 to 3 years	20.4	18.0	21.2	20.7	23.3	18.5	19.0	17.3	20.8	19.9	21.6	20.4	16.1	20.2
4 years	30.5	29.5	30.1	30.2	30.8	32.8	31.2	22.0	24.5	28.3	26.3	30.5	34.2	31.9
College: 1 to 3 years	9.1	8.3	8.3	8.0	5.5	10.0	5.3	6.9	6.1	9.9	6.4	6.7	12.6	13.5
4 years or more	9.5	6.5	5.5	11.0	11.1	5.9	13.2	6.7	7.2	6.2	6.4	7.2	7.2	7.7
Median years of school completed	12.1	11.1	11.1	11.0	11.1	11.7	12.0	9.1	10.5	11.1	11.0	12.0	12.1	12.1
Nonwhite	100.0	100.0	100.0	100.0	100.0	100.0	100.0	100.0	100.0	100.0	100.0	100.0	100.0	100.0
Elementary: Less than 5 years	20.4	13.4	13.8	12.2	9.5	10.9	11.0	18.3	29.9	27.3	29.5	35.0	18.0	13.1
5 to 7 years	24.5	22.3	23.7	20.2	19.2	18.4	18.7	23.6	31.3	27.8	27.8	18.0	17.1	16.2
8 years	14.6	14.6	19.1	18.1	19.6	17.9	17.3	17.2	11.1	12.8	11.5	13.2	16.6	15.3
High school: 1 to 3 years	19.7	22.9	23.4	25.0	23.1	25.0	23.4	20.4	15.0	17.4	16.1	16.1	18.5	19.6
4 years	13.3	17.0	14.3	16.5	17.4	15.8	19.0	13.2	7.3	8.7	8.9	12.0	19.5	22.9
College: 1 to 3 years	4.1	4.5	3.5	5.7	5.4	5.9	6.9	4.1	2.1	2.7	3.6	3.6	6.8	8.5
4 years or more	3.3	3.4	2.3	2.5	4.7	3.1	3.6	3.3	2.1	3.1	3.4	2.1	3.5	4.5
Median years of school completed	8.3	8.9	8.7	9.0	9.1	9.3	9.4	8.5	6.9	7.4	7.2	7.5	8.9	9.8

Table 15-16A (Continued)

Subject	U.S. Total	\- Regions - 1	2	3	4	5	6	7	8	9	10	11	12	13
YEARS OF SCHOOL COMPLETED, STANDARDIZED FOR AGE--(Con't.)														
Functional illiterate (0 to 4 grades):														
Percent nonwhite of total................	27.9	19.4	5.2	18.9	2.2	12.0	7.9	14.8	56.2	38.6	44.5	17.5	16.0	21.3
Percent white male of white total........	53.6	47.1	51.6	51.7	57.5	57.7	57.3	57.9	57.5	52.5	58.0	54.4	60.0	54.9
Percent nonwhite male of nonwhite total..	55.9	55.4	61.3	58.4	61.4	58.8	56.3	56.3	55.5	54.8	54.9	50.4	57.7	60.5
Superior education (high school+):														
Ratio nonwhite to white:														
Male......................	.052	.063	.012	.056	.009	.023	.022	.046	.096	.064	.060	.021	.025	.079
Female....................	.058	.074	.011	.064	.006	.024	.021	.054	.128	.080	.077	.018	.020	.074
Ratio female to male:														
White.....................	1.152	1.133	1.224	1.121	1.230	1.212	1.182	1.171	1.216	1.114	1.159	1.083	1.137	1.099
Nonwhite..................	1.284	1.323	1.070	1.273	.884	1.263	1.150	1.380	1.610	1.377	1.485	.937	.904	1.024
PERCENT OF CIVILIAN LABOR FORCE UNEMPLOYED														
White: Male........................	4.6	3.8	6.2	5.1	5.0	3.8	3.9	5.6	3.3	4.7	3.8	5.5	6.2	5.3
Female......................	4.9	4.6	6.1	5.1	4.3	3.9	4.3	4.9	4.6	4.6	4.4	5.9	6.7	6.2
Nonwhite: Male........................	8.8	8.1	14.0	13.3	15.8	10.0	12.1	9.4	6.2	8.5	7.9	13.6	15.7	8.4
Female......................	8.5	7.9	12.0	12.9	9.2	8.5	7.9	7.5	7.6	7.4	8.4	10.6	13.3	8.6
Ratio of nonwhite male to white male......	---	---	---	---	---	---	---	---	---	---	---	---	---	---
RATIO OF UNEMPLOYED TO EMPLOYED IN LOW SES OCCUPATIONS														
White: Male........................	7.5	5.9	9.6	8.0	8.5	6.6	7.4	9.3	5.2	7.3	6.7	9.8	10.4	8.5
Female......................	7.9	7.8	9.3	8.8	6.6	6.1	5.9	7.6	6.7	7.3	6.5	8.9	11.1	10.8
Nonwhite: Male........................	10.2	9.3	16.9	15.9	24.6	11.8	16.2	10.3	7.1	9.4	9.2	18.9	24.0	11.4
Female......................	9.2	8.7	13.6	13.4	11.3	8.8	8.4	7.3	8.4	7.8	9.5	12.2	16.6	10.8
Difference, nonwhite minus white:														
Male........................	2.7	3.4	7.3	7.9	16.1	5.2	8.8	1.0	1.9	2.1	2.5	9.1	13.6	2.9
Female......................	1.3	.9	4.3	4.6	4.7	2.7	2.5	.3	1.7	.5	3.0	3.3	5.5	---
LABOR FORCE PARTICIPATION RATE OF WOMEN														
White......................	33.6	36.3	34.9	33.2	33.6	32.8	32.3	28.9	35.3	30.6	30.4	32.6	34.2	35.4
Married, husband present:														
With children under 6............	18.0	15.2	18.9	14.8	17.5	18.4	18.0	17.6	27.7	17.6	19.8	19.3	19.4	19.0
No children under 6..............	35.3	37.4	37.7	33.5	35.2	34.8	34.6	30.8	39.5	31.9	33.4	36.1	37.5	37.7
Other marital status:														
With children under 6............	46.2	41.9	42.6	48.8	40.0	51.3	47.2	38.6	50.0	50.7	48.7	46.5	45.8	49.2
No children under 6..............	40.3	45.4	40.2	43.7	42.0	38.8	38.9	32.8	34.1	36.7	32.5	38.1	38.7	41.5
Nonwhite...................	41.8	48.3	39.3	39.0	33.3	43.4	36.1	40.1	38.9	44.5	36.1	29.1	34.3	43.7
Married, husband present:														
With children under 6............	31.0	31.1	26.1	26.7	21.2	34.3	26.6	29.5	32.1	36.4	30.8	20.7	21.3	31.2
No children under 6..............	46.7	52.0	45.6	42.3	38.1	48.5	42.7	44.7	44.7	49.6	40.5	35.6	43.6	52.1
Other marital status:														
With children under 6............	46.0	41.8	35.2	32.8	26.4	43.9	32.4	41.6	53.9	61.6	51.1	34.3	35.1	38.5
No children under 6..............	42.4	52.7	42.1	43.0	36.9	43.5	37.2	40.2	36.5	42.7	33.4	30.2	36.3	44.6
Ratio of rate for total nonwhite female to rate for total white female.............	124.4	133.1	112.6	117.5	99.1	132.3	111.8	138.8	110.2	145.4	118.8	89.3	100.3	123.4

493

Table 15-16A (Continued)

Subject	U.S. Total	Regions 1	2	3	4	5	6	7	8	9	10	11	12	13
RATIO OF LABOR FORCE PARTICIPATION RATE TO U.S. RATE														
Male, 14 & over (standardized)	1.000	1.010	.986	1.012	1.013	1.021	1.032	.954	.977	.977	.983	1.016	1.006	1.009
14 to 17 years	1.000	.864	.943	.981	1.264	1.238	1.309	.781	.974	.943	.974	1.208	1.125	1.094
18 to 24 years	1.000	1.004	.935	1.014	.986	1.006	1.026	.941	.974	1.030	.964	1.007	1.025	1.062
25 to 34 years	1.000	1.002	.997	1.011	1.004	1.005	1.014	.979	.983	1.002	.993	1.003	1.004	1.002
35 to 44 years	1.000	1.006	.999	1.009	1.006	1.007	1.012	.972	.980	.997	.988	1.005	1.005	1.006
45 to 64 years	1.000	1.019	.997	1.026	1.017	1.017	1.018	.951	.966	.956	.978	1.007	1.000	1.001
65 years and over	1.000	1.108	.964	.961	.957	1.085	1.141	.921	1.026	.790	1.000	1.095	.921	.911
Female, 14 & over (standardized)	1.000	1.083	1.031	.968	.984	.981	.948	.873	1.052	.954	.925	.935	.997	1.039
14 to 17 years	1.000	1.057	1.014	1.043	1.450	1.236	1.414	.671	.764	.793	.729	1.271	1.279	.936
18 to 24 years	1.000	1.174	1.031	1.060	1.079	.982	.887	.876	.943	.898	.812	.832	.918	.985
25 to 34 years	1.000	1.051	.977	.918	.856	.915	.861	.938	1.241	1.040	1.000	.878	.918	1.054
35 to 44 years	1.000	1.040	1.026	.930	.904	.960	.927	.895	1.138	1.016	.984	.930	.991	1.063
45 to 64 years	1.000	1.084	1.058	.964	1.005	.990	.974	.846	.993	.923	.925	.969	1.041	1.060
65 years and over	1.000	1.117	1.087	.971	1.087	1.087	1.078	.845	.883	.816	.845	1.058	1.078	.961
WEEKS WORKED IN 1959														
Total labor force	100.0	100.0	100.0	100.0	100.0	100.0	100.0	100.0	100.0	100.0	100.0	100.0	100.0	100.0
50 to 52 weeks	56.8	61.3	56.5	55.4	57.6	59.0	58.9	53.9	52.9	55.6	52.8	55.5	53.1	56.4
40 to 49 weeks	14.5	14.5	14.4	16.0	12.1	13.1	11.5	15.3	15.4	14.5	13.9	12.0	13.5	15.4
27 to 39 weeks	9.3	8.0	8.9	10.3	9.4	8.7	9.1	10.4	10.5	9.9	10.2	10.0	9.4	8.6
26 weeks or less	19.4	16.2	20.1	18.3	20.8	19.3	20.6	20.4	21.2	19.9	23.1	22.5	24.0	19.6
CLASS OF WORKER														
Male	100.0	100.0	100.0	100.0	100.0	100.0	100.0	100.0	100.0	100.0	100.0	100.0	100.0	100.0
Agricultural workers:														
Self-employed	5.6	0.9	3.9	1.6	11.3	14.2	16.0	2.9	10.0	2.6	9.1	7.6	4.2	2.1
Wage and salary or government	2.9	0.9	2.3	0.8	2.6	2.9	4.5	2.9	5.3	4.6	7.1	5.1	3.2	4.3
Unpaid family worker	0.4	0.1	0.3	0.1	1.2	0.8	0.9	0.5	0.9	0.1	0.4	0.4	0.2	0.1
Nonagricultural workers:														
Private wage and salary and unpaid family worker	70.3	75.3	72.3	81.5	65.0	63.0	56.6	68.2	64.9	70.0	60.6	61.0	67.2	69.8
Government worker	10.7	12.1	10.9	7.5	9.6	9.3	11.2	9.5	10.1	11.2	11.3	15.3	13.7	13.1
Self-employed	10.1	10.6	10.2	8.4	10.3	9.8	10.9	9.9	8.9	11.4	11.6	10.6	11.6	10.7
Female	100.0	100.0	100.0	100.0	100.0	100.0	100.0	100.0	100.0	100.0	100.0	100.0	100.0	100.0
Agricultural workers:														
Self-employed	0.6	0.1	0.5	0.2	1.4	1.1	1.2	0.9	1.2	0.4	0.9	0.8	0.7	0.3
Wage and salary or government	0.8	0.2	0.5	0.3	0.6	0.5	0.6	0.4	2.0	2.0	1.8	0.9	1.3	0.8
Unpaid family worker	0.6	0.1	0.5	0.2	3.0	1.5	1.4	0.6	1.2	0.2	0.6	0.7	0.5	0.2
Nonagricultural workers:														
Private wage and salary and unpaid family worker	78.6	82.6	79.2	83.7	75.9	75.7	71.3	78.0	76.8	76.8	73.5	69.4	72.9	76.7
Government worker	15.0	13.6	15.0	12.1	14.9	16.3	19.0	15.3	14.8	15.0	16.8	21.5	18.7	16.7
Self-employed	4.5	3.3	4.4	3.6	4.2	4.8	6.5	4.8	3.9	5.7	6.4	6.7	6.0	5.2

Table 15-16A (*Continued*)

Subject	U.S. Total	Regions 1	2	3	4	5	6	7	8	9	10	11	12	13
OCCUPATION														
Male, employed	100.0	100.0	100.0	100.0	100.0	100.0	100.0	100.0	100.0	100.0	100.0	100.0	100.0	100.0
Prof., tech., and kindred workers	10.3	12.4	10.4	10.4	9.5	8.6	9.8	8.2	6.9	9.2	8.8	10.8	11.4	13.4
Engineers, technical	2.0	2.3	2.0	2.3	1.5	1.4	1.7	1.4	1.1	1.6	1.4	1.8	2.4	3.2
Medical and other health workers:														
Salaried	0.5	0.6	0.5	0.5	0.5	0.4	0.4	0.4	0.4	0.5	0.4	0.6	0.5	0.6
Self-employed	0.7	0.8	0.7	0.7	0.7	0.7	0.7	0.6	0.5	0.6	0.6	0.6	0.8	0.8
Teachers, elem. & second, schools	1.0	0.9	1.0	0.9	1.1	1.0	1.2	1.0	0.8	0.9	1.0	1.4	1.4	1.1
Other profes'l, etc.: Salaried	5.4	6.6	5.4	5.3	5.1	4.5	5.1	4.2	3.7	4.9	4.7	5.8	5.6	6.7
Self-employed	0.8	1.1	0.8	0.7	0.7	0.6	0.8	0.6	0.5	0.9	0.7	0.7	0.8	1.0
Farmers and farm managers	5.5	0.9	3.9	1.6	11.2	14.1	15.8	8.8	9.9	2.4	8.7	7.5	4.0	1.9
Mgrs., off'ls, & propr's, exc. farm	10.7	11.3	9.6	9.3	10.3	9.7	11.8	9.4	9.6	12.7	11.5	12.4	12.2	11.9
Salaried	6.7	7.7	6.0	6.3	6.3	6.0	6.9	5.5	5.7	7.5	6.3	7.2	7.3	7.5
Self-employed: Retail trade	1.9	1.7	1.9	1.5	2.0	1.7	2.4	2.1	2.1	2.5	2.3	2.3	2.1	1.8
Other than retail	2.1	2.0	1.6	1.6	1.9	1.7	2.5	1.8	1.8	2.9	2.7	2.8	2.8	2.6
Clerical and kindred workers	6.9	9.2	6.7	7.6	6.0	5.9	5.7	6.0	5.2	7.1	5.6	5.4	5.7	7.0
Sales workers	6.9	7.5	6.5	6.8	6.4	6.4	6.2	6.4	6.5	7.1	6.6	5.4	7.0	7.7
Retail trade	2.9	3.1	3.0	2.5	2.5	2.8	2.7	3.0	3.0	2.9	2.9	2.5	2.7	3.0
Other than retail trade	4.0	4.4	3.5	4.2	4.0	3.6	3.5	3.4	3.5	4.2	3.6	2.9	4.2	4.7
Craftsmen, foremen, & kindred workers	19.5	19.9	20.9	22.1	18.5	17.9	17.6	18.6	17.2	19.9	17.6	19.3	20.4	20.3
Construction craftsmen	5.5	5.3	5.3	4.8	5.2	4.8	5.5	5.9	5.8	7.2	6.0	6.4	6.1	6.0
Foremen (n.e.c.)	2.5	2.6	2.9	3.2	2.3	2.4	2.0	2.4	2.3	2.2	1.9	2.5	2.4	2.3
Mechanics and repairmen	5.1	4.9	5.4	5.2	4.9	4.9	5.1	4.9	4.6	5.5	5.1	5.3	5.4	5.4
Metal craftsmen, except mechanics	2.5	2.7	3.0	4.5	2.4	2.6	1.4	1.9	1.3	1.5	1.1	1.2	2.2	2.7
Other craftsmen	3.9	4.4	4.2	4.4	3.7	3.3	3.6	3.4	3.1	3.6	3.5	4.0	4.3	3.9
Operatives and kindred workers	19.9	19.2	22.5	23.9	20.1	19.1	14.4	22.5	21.7	17.3	18.5	17.3	17.9	16.2
Drivers and deliverymen	5.2	5.0	5.1	4.8	4.1	4.9	4.8	5.9	6.0	6.0	6.9	5.3	5.2	4.5
Other operatives, etc.:														
Durable goods manufacturing	6.3	5.8	7.9	12.2	6.3	7.4	2.3	6.0	4.4	2.2	3.2	2.5	6.2	5.1
Nondurable goods manufacturing	3.7	4.6	5.4	2.7	4.0	2.9	1.7	4.2	7.1	3.1	2.1	2.2	2.2	2.0
Nonmanufacturing industries	4.6	3.7	4.1	4.1	4.7	3.9	5.6	6.4	4.2	6.1	6.3	8.3	4.3	4.7
Private household workers	0.1	0.1	0.1	0.1	0.1	0.1	0.1	0.1	0.2	0.2	0.2	0.1	0.1	0.1
Service wkrs., exc. priv. household	6.0	7.5	5.9	5.7	5.2	5.0	4.9	5.0	5.1	6.4	5.2	6.3	5.6	6.4
Protective service workers	1.5	2.1	1.6	1.6	1.1	1.1	1.0	1.2	1.2	1.5	1.2	1.4	1.4	1.6
Waiters, bartenders, cooks, etc.	1.2	1.7	1.2	1.0	1.2	0.8	0.9	0.8	0.7	1.3	0.8	1.2	1.1	1.4
Other service workers	3.3	3.7	3.1	3.1	3.0	3.0	3.0	3.0	3.2	3.6	3.3	3.7	3.2	3.4
Farm laborers and farm foremen	2.8	1.4	2.3	0.7	3.5	3.4	4.9	3.1	3.6	3.8	3.7	4.8	2.9	3.7
Laborers, except farm and mine	6.9	5.7	6.9	7.0	6.0	5.9	5.8	7.4	8.7	9.5	7.6	7.7	9.7	6.1
Construction	1.5	1.4	1.5	1.0	1.2	1.3	1.6	1.7	1.8	2.3	2.0	1.9	1.2	1.4
Manufacturing	2.3	1.5	2.8	3.4	2.2	1.9	0.9	2.8	3.5	2.0	2.0	2.0	4.4	1.1
Other industries	3.1	2.8	2.6	2.6	2.6	2.7	3.2	2.9	3.3	5.2	3.6	3.8	4.1	3.6
Occupation not reported	4.6	5.5	4.5	4.9	3.3	3.9	3.0	4.5	3.5	5.3	4.1	3.2	3.2	5.2

Table 15-16A (*Continued*)

Subject	U.S. Total							Regions						
		1	2	3	4	5	6	7	8	9	10	11	12	13
OCCUPATION (Con't.)														
Females, employed..........	100.0	100.0	100.0	100.0	100.0	100.0	100.0	100.0	100.0	100.0	100.0	100.0	100.0	100.0
	13.0	12.5	13.8	12.7	14.1	13.5	15.2	12.7	11.2	12.6	12.9	14.9	14.7	14.0
Prof., tech., and kindred workers:														
Medical and other health workers:														
Salaried................	3.4	3.4	4.0	3.6	4.1	3.4	3.7	3.0	2.5	3.0	2.8	3.4	4.0	3.8
Self-employed..........	0.3	0.4	0.4	0.3	0.2	0.3	0.3	0.2	0.3	0.4	0.3	0.2	0.2	0.4
Teachers, elem. & second. schools..	5.2	4.1	5.4	5.0	5.7	5.8	6.6	6.1	5.6	5.7	6.1	6.7	5.5	4.6
Other profes'l, etc.: Salaried.....	3.6	4.0	3.6	3.4	3.6	3.4	3.6	3.1	2.5	3.0	3.2	3.7	4.1	4.4
Self-employed.	0.5	0.5	0.4	0.4	0.5	0.5	0.9	0.4	0.4	0.5	0.6	0.9	0.8	0.7
Farmers and farm managers........	0.6	0.1	0.4	0.2	1.4	1.1	1.1	0.9	1.2	0.3	0.9	0.8	0.7	0.3
Mgrs., off'ls & propr's exc. farm...	3.7	3.2	3.2	3.1	3.4	3.4	4.9	3.6	3.0	4.9	4.5	5.6	4.9	4.8
Salaried....	2.3	2.3	1.9	2.0	2.0	2.1	2.7	2.0	1.8	2.7	2.4	3.1	2.7	3.1
Self-employed: Retail trade.....	0.9	0.6	0.9	0.7	0.9	0.9	1.2	1.1	0.9	1.3	1.4	1.4	1.2	0.9
Other than retail...	0.5	0.3	0.4	0.3	0.5	0.5	0.5	0.5	0.3	0.9	0.7	1.1	1.0	0.8
Clerical and kindred workers........	29.7	33.3	26.5	33.1	28.3	29.0	29.6	25.0	20.0	27.1	26.2	29.8	32.3	34.7
Secretaries, stenographers, and typists..	10.3	12.6	8.9	11.0	9.0	9.3	9.6	8.6	6.9	9.4	8.9	9.9	10.1	11.9
Other clerical workers....	19.4	20.7	17.6	22.1	19.3	19.7	20.0	16.4	13.2	17.6	17.3	19.9	22.1	22.8
Sales workers....	7.8	6.9	7.5	9.0	8.5	8.3	8.8	8.3	6.5	8.2	8.3	8.3	8.5	8.1
Retail trade.....	6.8	5.9	6.7	7.9	7.6	7.4	7.9	7.5	5.9	7.3	7.3	7.3	7.2	6.5
Other than retail trade....	1.0	1.0	0.8	1.1	0.9	0.9	1.0	0.8	0.6	1.2	1.0	1.0	1.3	1.6
Craftsmen, foremen, & kindred workers...	1.2	1.3	1.4	1.3	1.1	1.2	1.1	1.2	1.0	0.9	1.0	1.0	1.1	1.2
Operatives and kindred workers.....	15.4	19.1	22.0	14.5	11.8	13.3	6.9	18.2	22.3	8.9	9.8	6.9	8.1	11.6
Durable goods manufacturing.....	4.0	5.1	5.6	7.3	3.7	5.4	0.9	3.4	1.5	0.7	1.4	0.4	1.2	3.6
Nondurable goods manufacturing.....	8.2	11.4	13.9	4.4	5.2	4.9	1.6	11.8	17.6	3.9	4.4	2.5	3.3	4.4
Nonmanufacturing industries......	3.1	2.6	5.1	2.8	3.0	3.1	3.7	3.0	3.1	4.2	3.9	4.0	3.7	3.6
Private household workers......	7.9	5.9	5.1	5.2	6.2	6.4	7.6	8.0	16.1	13.4	13.3	7.5	7.1	6.2
Service wkrs., exc. priv. household..	13.4	10.4	13.3	13.9	16.9	16.3	18.9	14.4	11.0	15.3	15.5	19.2	16.5	12.1
Waiters, bartenders, cooks, etc...	5.7	3.7	5.4	5.7	7.7	7.6	8.9	6.6	4.3	6.5	6.9	9.2	7.6	5.5
Other service workers..........	7.7	6.7	7.9	8.2	9.1	8.7	9.9	7.8	6.7	8.8	8.6	10.0	8.9	6.7
Farm laborers and farm foremen.........	1.1	0.2	0.8	0.3	3.4	1.8	1.7	0.8	3.0	1.8	2.1	1.1	1.4	0.7
Laborers, except farm and mine......	0.5	0.4	0.6	0.6	0.5	0.6	0.3	0.6	0.6	0.4	0.4	0.5	0.5	0.4
Occupation not reported.........	5.7	6.7	5.4	6.0	4.5	5.2	4.7	6.3	4.1	6.0	5.1	4.5	4.2	5.8
Nonwhite														
Percent of emp. nonwhites.....	60.4	57.5	62.5	63.8	63.9	59.5	61.2	58.5	60.8	59.1	61.3	65.7	65.6	63.8
Percent of all employed males.....	9.2	9.5	1.7	7.8	0.8	3.2	2.5	6.5	25.4	17.2	15.6	3.0	2.6	9.5
Prof., tech., and kindred workers.....	3.5	3.4	0.9	2.7	0.9	1.6	1.4	0.9	9.2	4.9	5.2	1.6	2.1	5.3
Engineers, technical..........	1.4	1.5	0.5	0.9	0.4	0.7	0.7	0.5	0.6	0.6	0.5	0.6	2.2	3.5
Medical and other health workers:														
Salaried.................	7.3	9.7	3.5	8.4	3.4	3.8	3.0	7.5	7.3	5.7	4.6	2.6	3.4	10.1
Self-employed.............	2.6	2.2	0.4	2.7	0.3	1.5	1.3	2.3	4.4	2.7	2.7	0.7	2.3	6.0
Teachers, elem. & second. schools.....	7.3	5.4	0.5	4.0	0.2	1.4	1.4	5.8	35.5	18.7	18.3	1.2	2.3	5.9
Other profes'l, etc.: Salaried.....	3.5	3.6	1.0	2.6	1.1	1.8	1.7	2.9	7.3	4.4	4.3	2.1	2.3	5.9
self-employed.	2.5	2.1	0.4	3.0	0.3	1.2	0.8	2.8	6.9	2.8	3.8	0.6	1.2	3.8

Table 15-16A (Continued)

	U.S. Total	Regions 1	2	3	4	5	6	7	8	9	10	11	12	13
OCCUPATION (Con't.)														
Nonwhite														
Farmers and farm managers	7.4	4.4	0.2	0.3	0.1	0.1	0.8	1.8	31.5	12.1	13.1	3.0	1.9	17.4
Mgrs., off'ls, & propr's exc. farm	2.0	2.4	0.2	1.6	0.3	0.7	0.7	1.2	3.0	2.5	2.0	0.8	1.3	4.3
Salaried	1.5	2.2	0.2	1.1	0.4	0.5	0.5	0.8	1.6	1.4	1.1	0.6	0.8	3.3
Self-employed: Retail trade	2.8	2.4	0.3	2.1	0.4	0.7	1.0	1.4	4.8	5.3	3.7	1.5	2.1	7.8
Other than retail	2.7	3.1	0.4	2.8	0.3	1.1	0.7	2.0	5.0	3.1	2.3	0.7	1.7	4.9
Clerical and kindred workers	6.7	9.3	0.9	7.0	0.7	3.3	2.1	4.8	8.7	7.5	4.5	1.5	2.5	9.9
Sales workers	2.0	2.4	0.3	2.0	0.1	0.6	0.6	1.2	3.0	2.4	2.0	0.8	0.7	6.0
Retail trade	2.8	3.9	0.4	2.6	0.1	0.7	0.7	1.5	3.6	3.4	2.7	1.1	0.9	4.3
Other than retail trade	1.5	1.4	0.3	1.5	0.1	0.6	0.5	0.9	2.9	1.7	1.5	0.5	0.6	3.3
Craftsmen, foremen, & kindred workers	4.8	5.3	1.0	4.1	0.4	2.0	1.5	3.0	11.8	8.0	6.6	1.4	1.4	7.1
Construction craftsmen	6.2	5.9	0.9	3.6	0.4	1.9	1.6	3.4	18.4	11.1	8.7	1.9	4.9	8.6
Foremen (n.e.c.)	1.8	2.8	0.4	1.5	0.2	0.8	0.7	1.0	1.6	2.5	1.5	1.0	1.3	4.3
Mechanics and repairmen	6.0	7.2	1.3	6.0	0.6	2.8	2.0	4.2	12.0	8.3	8.1	2.0	0.8	8.9
Metal craftsmen, except mechanics	3.5	3.6	1.5	4.3	0.4	2.4	1.2	2.8	7.1	3.9	3.7	0.9	2.0	4.6
Other craftsmen	3.5	4.9	0.9	4.0	0.4	1.5	1.3	2.3	8.7	6.3	4.4	2.1	1.2	5.7
Operatives and kindred workers	10.9	12.5	2.0	10.2	0.7	3.9	2.8	6.2	26.4	22.4	18.3	3.0	2.3	10.2
Drivers and deliverymen	13.5	14.7	1.5	8.9	0.5	3.5	2.6	7.5	35.9	31.0	24.0	2.6	1.4	10.2
Other operatives, etc.:														
Durable goods manufacturing	9.4	9.7	3.0	10.8	1.0	3.6	3.1	5.2	30.5	19.8	16.9	3.2	2.3	8.2
Nondurable goods manufacturing	9.3	10.4	1.3	11.5	0.6	5.2	3.9	5.2	13.7	16.0	16.9	2.1	2.1	11.9
Nonmanufacturing industries	11.2	16.4	1.8	9.5	0.6	4.0	2.4	6.8	30.1	18.3	13.2	3.4	3.3	11.6
Private household workers	48.3	47.8	5.3	37.2	2.9	29.2	21.8	60.2	85.8	65.1	74.8	12.7	9.4	39.4
Service wkrs., exc. priv. household	21.1	19.8	3.7	17.8	3.0	12.9	10.6	27.1	50.5	35.9	36.6	7.6	8.0	19.3
Protective service workers	4.3	6.1	0.6	4.8	0.4	2.2	2.2	3.7	4.3	3.1	3.1	2.5	1.0	5.4
Waiters, bartenders, cooks, etc.	19.6	18.6	3.9	15.1	3.8	10.0	11.1	24.4	54.3	33.6	38.1	7.9	13.3	21.2
Other service workers	29.4	28.2	5.3	25.4	3.5	17.5	13.2	37.5	67.4	50.1	47.9	9.5	9.3	25.1
Farm laborers and farm foremen	23.8	21.3	2.0	2.2	0.4	1.2	3.5	8.7	65.1	37.8	47.7	4.1	3.5	16.3
Laborers, except farm and mine	25.9	26.8	5.3	18.9	2.0	9.8	6.8	18.2	63.9	51.8	43.1	7.9	4.9	19.3
Construction	27.0	29.4	5.8	20.6	1.6	10.3	7.2	17.6	60.7	51.1	36.0	11.4	6.3	32.5
Manufacturing	25.1	26.8	6.3	19.1	2.3	9.1	5.8	13.6	63.1	60.3	51.4	5.4	3.2	15.8
Other industries	26.0	26.4	3.8	18.0	1.9	9.9	7.0	23.1	66.5	48.9	42.5	7.4	6.2	19.1
Occupation not reported	16.9	19.4	4.8	20.6	2.6	9.4	7.3	13.7	29.3	24.5	19.4	6.8	8.2	14.3
Percent fem. of emp. nonwhites	39.6	42.5	37.5	36.2	36.1	40.5	38.8	41.5	39.2	40.9	38.7	34.3	34.4	36.2
Percent of all employed females	12.4	13.3	2.0	9.8	0.9	4.8	3.6	10.3	30.4	24.2	21.2	3.7	3.0	10.9
Prof., tech., and kindred workers	7.1	7.7	0.9	5.5	0.7	2.2	1.9	6.1	21.0	13.0	12.6	2.1	1.5	7.3
Medical and other health workers:														
Salaried	7.0	10.5	1.3	6.9	1.1	2.9	2.4	6.4	10.8	8.4	6.3	2.7	2.2	9.3
Self-employed	4.2	6.4	0.4	4.8	0.3	1.1	2.3	4.3	5.8	2.2	4.2	1.6	1.0	5.1
Teachers, elem. & second. schools	9.1	7.3	0.5	5.4	1.1	1.8	1.5	6.8	31.4	19.7	19.5	1.5	0.9	7.4
Other profess'l, etc.: Salaried	5.5	6.6	1.0	5.4	1.1	2.6	2.2	5.0	12.0	7.2	7.2	2.7	1.7	6.3
Self-employed	2.2	2.9	0.6	2.3	0.3	0.8	0.3	2.1	3.3	2.9	2.5	0.8	1.1	3.1
Farmers and farm managers	14.5	3.6	0.2	0.6	0.4	0.	1.0	1.4	46.2	17.1	29.6	11.8	3.3	29.0
Mgrs., off'ls, & propr's, exc. farm	3.9	4.1	0.5	3.7	0.4	1.5	1.2	3.0	8.0	6.2	5.6	0.9	1.7	5.5
Salaried	2.9	3.0	0.4	3.2	0.3	1.4	1.1	2.3	4.9	3.6	2.9	0.6	1.3	4.1
Self-employed: Retail trade	6.4	5.1	0.6	4.4	0.4	1.6	1.5	4.2	14.5	13.0	11.0	1.3	2.8	6.1
Other than retail	4.0	4.5	0.6	5.4	0.5	2.0	1.4	2.9	6.3	3.9	4.2	1.3	2.8	6.1
Clerical and kindred workers	3.5	5.3	0.6	4.1	0.4	1.9	1.3	2.0	2.7	2.1	1.5	1.2	1.4	6.6
Secretaries, steno's, & typists	3.1	4.2	0.6	3.1	0.5	1.8	1.3	1.8	2.6	1.7	1.4	1.3	1.6	6.6
Other clerical workers	3.8	5.9	0.7	4.6	0.5	1.9	1.2	2.0	2.8	2.3	1.5	1.1	1.3	6.6
Sales workers	2.8	3.9	0.5	2.7	0.3	0.9	0.7	1.5	3.9	3.3	2.8	1.0	1.0	5.7
Retail trade	2.6	4.1	0.5	2.6	0.3	0.8	0.7	1.3	3.5	3.0	2.4	1.0	1.1	5.8
Other than trade	3.4	3.1	0.5	3.2	0.2	1.0	0.8	3.4	8.2	5.3	5.2	1.3	0.6	5.3

Table 15-16A (Continued)

Subject	U.S. Total	1	2	3	4	5	Regions 6	7	8	9	10	11	12	13
OCCUPATION (Con't.)														
Nonwhite														
Craftsmen, foremen, & kindred wkrs........	7.0	9.1	1.3	7.9	0.5	2.8	2.4	4.1	12.1	11.0	6.1	5.0	2.6	9.4
Operatives and kindred workers..........	10.3	13.5	1.7	11.7	1.2	3.7	3.7	4.9	12.2	23.5	12.3	3.4	5.1	14.3
Durable goods manufacturing..........	6.0	9.5	1.9	6.1	1.0	1.9	2.7	1.9	15.4	8.5	3.6	2.3	2.5	5.6
Nondurable goods manufacturing........	7.8	11.8	0.9	11.8	1.1	2.5	2.2	2.3	4.8	14.0	5.3	2.3	5.6	19.8
Nonmanufacturing industries..........	22.8	28.8	5.8	26.4	1.6	8.7	4.7	18.5	51.7	35.0	23.5	4.2	5.6	16.4
Private household workers.............	54.1	57.6	8.6	36.3	2.2	19.9	15.6	51.2	91.0	79.4	77.7	12.4	6.8	32.3
Service wkrs., exc. priv. household....	19.1	23.7	4.4	16.6	1.6	8.6	5.3	18.7	49.1	36.8	28.5	5.9	4.6	15.4
Waiters, bartenders, cooks, etc.......	12.0	13.5	1.8	7.5	0.7	4.2	2.7	11.2	43.1	25.9	23.0	3.3	2.4	9.0
Other service workers................	24.3	29.5	6.2	22.9	2.4	12.5	7.7	25.0	53.0	44.9	32.9	8.4	6.6	20.6
Farm laborers and farm foremen........	31.1	22.7	1.4	2.9	0.1	0.2	0.9	3.1	71.0	56.9	58.6	4.4	4.8	26.6
Laborers, except farm and mine........	22.8	25.5	3.9	21.2	2.1	10.1	10.2	18.0	46.3	44.2	30.6	11.4	5.7	24.0
Occupation not reported..............	17.7	21.7	4.5	20.6	2.2	10.0	7.2	14.7	29.0	25.6	20.3	7.4	7.6	14.7
Employed Females as Percent of Total Employed														
Total................................	32.8	34.7	33.6	31.2	31.5	31.4	30.4	31.1	35.0	33.0	31.7	30.0	31.8	33.1
Prof., tech., and kindred workers.....	38.1	34.8	40.3	35.8	40.5	41.8	40.3	41.3	46.6	40.1	40.5	37.3	37.7	34.1
Medical and other health workers......	60.2	58.1	65.1	60.1	62.7	61.1	61.3	58.8	63.2	60.8	59.7	58.7	61.0	59.1
Teachers, elem. & second. schools.....	72.5	71.6	73.2	72.6	71.2	73.0	70.9	74.0	79.7	76.2	73.7	67.1	64.9	67.5
Farmers and farm managers............	4.7	6.5	5.4	5.7	5.5	3.3	3.0	4.4	6.1	6.6	4.6	4.2	7.7	6.8
Mgrs., off'ls, & propr's, exc. farm...	14.4	13.1	14.5	13.0	13.1	13.8	15.3	14.7	14.5	16.0	15.4	16.3	15.7	16.8
Salaried.............................	14.2	13.8	13.7	12.8	12.7	13.5	14.6	14.0	14.3	14.8	14.9	15.5	14.9	17.0
Self-employed: Retail trade..........	18.3	15.0	18.2	17.5	16.9	16.8	18.7	19.1	22.3	22.3	20.6	20.2	21.0	19.6
Other than retail....	11.1	8.3	12.3	8.8	10.0	11.4	13.6	11.1	9.1	13.4	11.0	14.8	13.9	13.9
Clerical and kindred workers..........	67.6	65.8	66.8	66.4	68.5	69.1	69.4	65.3	67.7	68.1	68.7	70.9	72.6	71.0
Sales workers........................	35.8	32.8	36.9	37.7	37.7	37.3	38.4	37.1	34.8	36.4	37.0	40.0	36.4	34.3
Retail trade.........................	53.7	50.2	53.5	58.6	58.5	55.1	55.8	53.3	50.9	54.3	53.7	55.9	55.1	52.1
Other than retail trade..............	11.0	10.6	9.9	10.8	9.3	10.3	11.0	9.9	8.4	12.8	12.8	13.0	12.8	14.1
Craftsmen, foremen, & kindred wkrs....	2.9	3.4	3.2	2.6	2.7	3.0	2.7	2.7	3.0	2.2	2.5	2.1	2.4	2.9
Operatives and kindred workers........	27.4	34.6	33.1	21.6	21.3	24.2	15.7	26.8	35.6	20.1	19.6	14.6	17.5	26.1
Durable goods manufacturing..........	23.7	31.5	26.5	21.4	21.3	24.9	13.9	20.3	15.8	14.3	17.2	6.8	8.2	26.3
Nondurable goods manufacturing........	52.3	56.7	56.6	42.4	37.2	43.9	29.5	55.8	57.2	38.3	49.4	48.1	41.0	51.7
Nonmanufacturing industries..........	24.6	27.5	23.6	23.5	22.6	26.2	22.2	17.6	28.9	25.4	22.4	17.0	28.5	27.5
Private household workers.............	96.5	94.8	95.0	96.4	96.0	97.4	97.3	96.1	97.6	97.1	97.6	96.7	97.1	95.4
Service wkrs., exc. priv. household...	52.3	42.5	53.4	52.4	59.8	60.1	62.6	56.3	53.9	54.1	57.9	56.7	57.8	48.3
Waiters, bartenders, cooks, etc.......	70.4	53.2	70.2	71.5	75.2	80.3	81.6	79.2	77.1	71.7	80.6	76.9	77.2	65.5
Farm laborers and farm foremen........	16.8	14.7	14.4	18.0	30.8	19.7	13.5	10.7	19.2	14.4	9.2	2.7	17.9	9.0
Laborers, except farm and mine........	3.5	3.9	4.1	4.0	4.4	4.4	2.4	3.5	3.5	2.8	2.3	2.7	2.5	3.3
Occupation not reported..............	37.6	39.1	38.2	35.8	38.5	37.7	40.3	38.4	38.6	36.0	36.6	37.1	37.7	35.5
INDUSTRY														
Total employed......................	100.0	100.0	100.0	100.0	100.0	100.0	100.0	100.0	100.0	100.0	100.0	100.0	100.0	100.0
Agriculture.........................	6.6	1.4	4.9	1.9	11.9	13.3	15.8	9.1	2.0	5.8	12.4	9.9	5.9	4.8
Forestry and fisheries..............	0.1	0.1	0.1	...	0.2	...	...	0.1	0.2	0.4	0.1	0.5	0.6	0.1
Mining..............................	1.0	0.1	0.8	0.8	1.5	0.5	2.4	2.7	0.5	1.7	2.9	4.4	0.2	0.6
Construction........................	5.9	5.2	5.5	4.6	5.6	5.3	6.8	6.2	6.3	8.3	7.3	7.9	6.6	6.5

Table 15-16A (*Continued*)

Subject	U.S. Total	\[Regions\] 1	2	3	4	5	6	7	8	9	10	11	12	13
INDUSTRY (Con't.)														
Manufacturing...........	27.1	30.8	34.4	37.8	24.9	25.1	12.9	26.7	27.5	16.0	15.5	12.0	24.1	23.2
Furniture & lumber & wood prod...	1.7	0.7	1.8	0.9	2.0	0.8	0.3	2.8	3.9	1.2	2.2	2.9	8.1	0.9
Primary metal industries (including	1.9	1.6	2.1	6.0	0.7	1.4	0.7	1.3	1.1	0.5	0.5	1.1	0.9	0.9
not specified metal)..........	2.0	2.1	1.6	3.6	2.0	2.0	1.4	1.5	0.8	1.2	0.8	0.8	0.8	3.0
Machinery, except electrical.....	2.4	2.4	3.8	4.6	3.6	4.1	1.1	1.4	0.8	0.9	1.1	0.4	0.9	1.7
Elect. mach., equip., & supplies...	2.3	3.2	3.6	3.5	1.4	3.1	0.4	1.8	0.9	0.5	0.8	0.2	0.5	2.5
Motor vehicles & motor veh. equip.	1.3	0.5	1.2	5.5	0.9	1.5	0.1	0.8	0.3	0.1	0.2	0.1	0.2	0.5
Trans. equip., exc. motor vehicle.	1.5	1.9	1.1	0.9	0.5	0.8	2.0	1.0	0.5	1.0	1.5	0.5	4.3	3.8
Other durable goods..........	2.1	3.1	3.4	2.9	2.5	1.8	0.9	2.0	1.0	1.0	1.1	0.9	3.2	1.7
Food and kindred products......	2.8	2.6	2.7	2.6	4.2	3.9	2.3	3.0	2.4	2.8	2.3	2.2	2.8	3.1
Textile mill products.........	1.5	1.6	2.1	0.2	0.3	0.1	0.1	1.7	8.6	0.3	0.3	0.1	0.2	0.1
Apparel & oth. fab'd textile prod.	1.8	3.7	2.8	0.7	0.7	0.6	0.2	2.2	2.9	0.7	1.1	0.4	0.4	1.0
Print., publishing, & allied prod.	1.3	2.4	1.7	2.2	1.9	1.8	1.3	1.5	0.9	1.0	1.1	1.1	1.4	1.7
Chemical and allied products....	1.3	1.8	1.2	1.5	0.5	0.9	0.6	2.8	1.0	1.7	0.6	0.5	0.8	0.8
Other nondurable goods (including not specified manufacturing)...	2.7	3.3	5.1	2.7	3.7	2.1	1.7	2.8	2.2	3.2	1.9	0.8	1.9	1.7
Railroad & railway express service.	1.5	1.0	1.8	1.8	1.9	1.8	2.1	2.0	1.1	1.2	1.2	2.6	1.6	1.0
Trucking service and warehousing..	1.4	1.2	1.4	1.6	1.5	1.6	1.6	1.6	1.3	2.6	1.5	1.5	1.5	1.0
Other transportation..........	1.4	2.1	0.8	1.0	1.0	0.7	1.1	1.0	0.9	2.6	1.2	0.8	1.9	1.3
Communications............	1.3	1.5	1.2	1.8	1.1	1.2	1.3	1.1	0.9	1.6	1.1	1.4	1.4	1.6
Utilities and sanitary services....	1.4	1.3	1.3	1.4	1.3	1.3	1.6	1.4	1.4	1.6	1.7	1.9	1.4	1.4
Wholesale trade............	3.4	3.7	2.6	3.2	3.4	3.2	3.8	2.9	2.9	4.1	3.6	3.2	4.2	3.8
Food and dairy products stores...	2.6	2.7	2.7	2.6	2.6	2.4	2.5	2.7	2.6	3.0	2.9	2.5	2.5	2.4
Eating and drinking places.....	2.8	2.7	2.5	2.7	3.2	2.9	3.3	2.5	1.9	2.8	2.8	3.6	3.2	3.1
Other retail trade...........	9.4	8.4	8.8	9.2	9.5	9.9	10.8	9.4	9.3	10.8	10.8	10.3	9.9	9.6
Finance, insurance, & real estate.	4.2	5.6	3.0	3.8	3.5	3.6	3.7	3.1	3.1	4.6	3.7	3.3	4.2	5.1
Business services...........	1.2	1.8	0.7	1.2	0.8	0.7	0.7	0.7	0.5	1.6	0.7	1.4	1.0	1.9
Repair services............	1.3	1.3	1.2	1.1	1.3	1.3	1.6	1.4	1.3	1.6	1.7	1.5	1.5	1.5
Private households..........	3.0	2.4	2.0	1.8	2.2	2.3	2.6	2.9	6.2	5.0	4.9	2.6	2.7	2.5
Other personal services.......	3.0	2.8	2.8	2.6	2.6	2.6	3.3	2.9	2.9	4.3	3.6	4.5	3.0	3.2
Entertainment & recreation services.	0.8	0.8	0.6	0.7	0.7	0.6	0.7	0.6	0.5	0.9	0.7	1.3	0.8	1.4
Educational services:														
Government..............	3.9	3.0	4.2	3.3	4.3	4.5	5.1	4.1	4.2	3.7	4.8	5.3	5.2	4.4
Private................	1.3	1.7	1.7	1.3	1.4	1.3	1.2	1.2	1.0	1.2	1.1	1.2	1.1	1.1
Welfare, religious, and nonprofit membership organizations......	1.3	1.4	1.4	1.4	1.5	1.5	1.5	1.3	1.0	1.1	1.4	1.2	1.5	1.2
Hospitals...............	2.6	2.8	3.1	2.7	3.3	2.7	2.9	2.6	2.1	2.2	2.1	2.4	2.6	2.5
Other profess'l & related services.	2.5	2.3	2.4	2.4	2.8	2.2	2.4	1.9	1.7	2.5	2.1	2.6	3.0	3.3
Public administration........	5.0	6.3	4.4	3.5	3.8	4.1	5.1	3.9	4.1	5.5	4.8	7.4	5.5	6.3
Industry not reported........	4.0	5.1	3.7	4.2	2.8	3.4	2.9	3.9	2.8	4.7	3.5	2.8	3.0	4.7
PLACE OF WORK OF THE WORKERS														
Worked outside county of residence:														
White................	15.1	30.2	10.5	11.2	12.1	11.3	10.0	16.9	15.4	7.2	8.3	6.8	8.3	7.4
Nonwhite..............	9.3	20.5	5.8	3.6	10.4	7.1	5.4	8.3	8.0	4.7	5.6	5.5	4.1	4.2
Place of work not reported:														
White................	4.1	4.8	3.9	3.8	3.2	4.0	3.7	4.2	3.2	4.4	3.9	3.3	3.1	4.4
Nonwhite..............	7.5	10.2	10.0	11.2	9.9	9.7	8.0	8.2	4.0	6.4	5.0	8.3	8.6	6.7

Table 15-16A (*Continued*)

Subject	U.S. Total	\[Regions\] 1	2	3	4	5	6	7	8	9	10	11	12	13
MEANS OF TRANSPORTATION TO WORK														
Private automobile or car pool	66.9	55.1	69.2	68.4	64.8	67.9	67.4	69.5	72.5	72.6	72.3	72.3	73.4	76.8
Railway, subway, or elevated	4.0	15.7	0.2	3.6	0.1	0.1	0.1	0.1	0.1	0.1	0.1	0.1	0.1	0.3
Bus or streetcar	8.6	13.0	7.0	13.4	5.8	4.6	3.0	7.4	5.6	8.5	3.9	3.4	6.2	7.7
Walked to work	10.4	10.1	14.5	9.5	13.1	11.0	12.0	10.2	12.9	8.6	9.9	12.3	9.4	6.6
Other means	2.6	2.0	2.1	1.6	1.9	2.5	2.9	2.7	4.0	4.7	4.2	3.2	2.4	2.5
Worked at home	7.5	4.1	6.9	3.5	14.3	13.9	14.7	10.1	9.8	5.6	9.3	8.7	8.5	6.1
Not reported	4.3	5.3	4.0	4.5	3.2	3.9	3.2	4.3	3.3	4.7	3.8	3.0	3.2	4.7
MEDIAN EARNINGS BY OCCUPATION (DOLLARS)														
Male, total	4595	5009	4443	5310	4534	4455	4323	3797	2985	3915	3470	4540	5187	5427
Prof., managerial, and kindred wkrs	6640	7103	6292	7311	6371	6288	6126	5926	5588	6055	5834	6276	6742	7440
Farmers and farm managers	2136	2621	2450	2401	2179	2439	3093	1380	1069	2061	1890	3185	3368	4042
Craftsmen, foremen, & kindred wkrs	5240	5393	4950	5877	5176	5179	4931	4570	3805	4585	4231	5243	5645	5967
Operatives and kindred workers	4282	4415	4215	4988	4454	4569	4226	3658	2819	3392	3178	4271	4972	4974
Farm laborers, except unpaid	1107	1635	1377	1028	928	1222	1584	805	687	1190	830	1673	1465	1943
Laborers, except farm and mine	2940	3512	3172	3803	3159	3235	2800	2342	1703	2223	1883	3020	4007	3608
Female, total	2230	2592	2237	2526	2021	2071	1838	1971	1613	1662	1518	1842	2273	2741
Clerical and kindred workers	3015	3240	2817	3180	2593	2668	2622	2699	2652	2723	2634	2603	3055	3385
Operatives and kindred workers	2270	2352	2293	2808	2301	2415	1728	2125	2109	1514	1708	1485	2068	2352
Ratio to United States Median														
Male, total	1.00	1.09	.97	1.16	.99	.97	.94	.83	.65	.85	.76	.99	1.13	1.18
Prof., managerial, and kindred wkrs	1.00	1.07	.95	1.10	.96	.95	.92	.89	.84	.91	.88	.95	1.02	1.12
Farmers and farm managers	1.00	1.23	1.15	1.12	1.02	1.14	1.45	.65	.50	.96	.88	1.49	1.58	1.89
Craftsmen, foremen, & kindred wkrs	1.00	1.03	.94	1.12	.99	.99	.94	.87	.73	.88	.81	1.00	1.08	1.14
Operatives and kindred workers	1.00	1.03	.98	1.16	1.04	1.07	.99	.85	.66	.79	.74	1.00	1.16	1.16
Farm laborers, except unpaid	1.00	1.48	1.24	.93	.84	1.10	1.43	.73	.62	1.07	.75	1.51	1.32	1.76
Laborers, except farm and mine	1.00	1.19	1.08	1.29	1.07	1.10	.95	.80	.58	.76	.64	1.03	1.36	1.23
Female, total	1.00	1.16	1.00	1.13	.91	.93	.82	.88	.72	.75	.68	.83	1.02	1.23
Clerical and kindred workers	1.00	1.07	.93	1.05	.86	.88	.87	.90	.88	.90	.87	.86	1.01	1.12
Operatives and kindred workers	1.00	1.04	1.01	1.24	1.01	1.06	.76	.94	.93	.67	.75	.65	.91	1.04
FAMILY INCOME														
White families	100.0	100.0	100.0	100.0	100.0	100.0	100.0	100.0	100.0	100.0	100.0	100.0	100.0	100.0
Under $1,000 (incl. none or loss)	4.5	2.7	3.7	2.9	4.3	5.4	4.7	9.3	7.5	5.7	6.9	4.1	3.1	3.1
$1,000 to $2,999	14.1	8.9	13.7	9.5	15.6	16.5	17.0	22.2	20.1	17.9	21.7	15.4	12.3	10.4
$3,000 to $3,999	9.1	7.3	10.4	6.5	9.7	10.1	11.7	11.1	12.4	11.0	11.6	10.3	7.8	7.1
$4,000 to $4,999	10.9	10.2	12.9	9.6	12.1	11.9	12.5	11.4	12.4	11.5	12.3	12.3	10.7	8.8
$5,000 to $5,999	12.7	13.1	14.1	13.3	14.0	13.2	13.1	11.5	12.0	12.0	11.7	13.4	13.8	11.2
$6,000 to $6,999	11.2	12.0	11.7	12.5	11.8	11.0	10.8	9.2	9.6	10.3	9.3	11.4	12.4	11.6
$7,000 to $9,999	21.2	24.4	20.6	25.6	20.1	19.4	18.2	15.4	16.0	18.3	15.8	19.7	23.4	25.3
$10,000 and over	16.2	21.6	13.0	20.1	12.5	12.6	12.4	9.8	10.1	13.3	11.2	13.3	16.4	22.5
Nonwhite families	100.0	100.0	100.0	100.0	100.0	100.0	100.0	100.0	100.0	100.0	100.0	100.0	100.0	100.0
Under $1,000 (incl. none or loss)	15.4	7.7	8.8	8.7	10.7	9.3	11.1	15.8	26.8	14.7	26.3	23.8	8.8	5.8
$1,000 to $2,999	32.5	22.6	25.1	21.5	28.1	25.7	32.7	36.2	44.3	40.8	46.8	26.6	23.2	16.9
$3,000 to $3,999	13.5	15.6	14.9	11.8	14.2	13.9	15.7	14.7	14.0	16.8	11.2	12.5	12.8	11.9
$4,000 to $4,999	11.4	14.6	14.9	14.8	13.2	14.4	13.3	12.2	7.0	11.5	6.8	11.4	12.8	12.7
$5,000 to $5,999	8.6	11.7	12.1	13.5	10.2	12.0	9.6	8.0	4.0	6.5	3.7	8.2	11.0	12.5
$6,000 to $6,999	5.7	8.3	8.2	8.9	8.2	8.1	5.7	4.7	2.8	3.7	1.9	5.4	9.0	10.1
$7,000 to $9,999	8.7	13.2	11.6	14.1	11.4	11.9	8.1	6.2	2.8	4.3	2.5	8.2	14.5	17.9
$10,000 and over	4.2	6.3	4.5	6.8	4.9	4.6	3.7	2.3	0.9	1.6	0.9	4.1	7.8	12.1

subtropical climate, dense urban settlement, intensive irrigated agriculture, rapid industrial expansion, and expanding commerce are the forces that have made this the most rapidly growing region in the nation. (It increased by 53 percent between 1950 and 1960.) The phenomenal development of Southern and Central California is too well known to require repetition here. It is perhaps less well known, however, that this type of development also includes Southern Arizona (Phoenix and Tucson) and Hawaii, which are part of this region.

15.7. Interregional and Intraregional Diversity

Regional differences of the type that have just been described would be of interest to students of population only if there are important demographic differences correlated with them. Such differences do exist, and are very substantial.

Table 15-16B

Characteristic	Highest value		Lowest value		Ratio of highest to lowest value
	Value	Region	Value	Region	
Percent foreign stock	22	1	1	8	22.0
Percent nonwhite	31	8	1	4	31.0
Percent 65 years or older, white	11	5	7	11	1.6
Percent 65 years or older, nonwhite	9	10	4	2	2.2
Sex ratio, white	102	11	95	1	1.1
Sex ratio, nonwhite	111	12	92	1	1.2
Average size of household	3.64	8	3.10	13	1.2
Percent of population migrants, white	29	9	13	2	2.2
Percent of population migrants, nonwhite	27	12	8	8	3.4
Median years of school completed, white	12.0	13	8.8	7	1.4
Median years of school completed, nonwhite	9.3	13	5.6	8	1.7
Percent male labor force in "white-collar" jobs	40	13	28	8	1.4
Median earnings, male	5427	13	2985	8	1.8
Median earnings, female	2741	13	1518	10	1.8
Family income, white (percent under $3000)	43	7	19	1	2.3
Family income, nonwhite (percent under $3000)	73	10	22	13	3.3
Fertility—children ever born, white	2642	11	2014	1	1.3
Fertility—children ever born, nonwhite	3537	10	2275	1	1.5

Table 15-16A presents a great array of demographic data for the 13 economic regions. One has only to read across the lines, comparing the statistics for the individual regions with the corresponding statistics for the nation, to appreciate just how much the populations of the regions differ from each other. This table illustrates well the principle that overall demographic statistics for a nation actually typify only a small fraction of the population, for they are an average of several diverse populations.

In order to become more familiar with this diversity, let us select a few categories of population traits and note the range of values, as shown in Table 15-16B.

Clearly, where the range is as great as indicated in the right-hand column of the table, regional variation is an aspect of population distribution that cannot easily be neglected. For most major demographic traits, the highest regional value is 40 percent or more greater than the lowest regional value. In considering this variation, we must keep in mind that this is only the first of several levels of range of variation; within each region there is subregional variation, and within the subregions there is variation among the economic areas. And within the economic areas there is variation among the individual countries and individual communities.

Regionalism versus Urban-Rural Composition. A critical reader may declare that this regional effect is simply urban-rural differences expressed in another form. Some regions (such as Regions 6 and 7) are much more rural than others (such as Regions 1 and 13). This would cause the regions to have unlike population compositions because of the urban-rural differences reviewed earlier in this chapter. Like so many hypotheses in demography, this claim is partially valid; the interregional differences diminish in size when we hold constant urban and rural residence, *but they still persist and are substantial.* To illustrate this effect, Tables 15-17 to 15-19 are presented. These tables show the interregional variation in 28 selected demographic variables for the urban, rural-nonfarm, and rural-farm populations separately. To save space, the five economic provinces (combinations of the 13 economic regions) are

Table 15-17 Average Values of Selected Demographic Measures of the Urban Population in the Subregions of Each of Five Economic Provinces, United States: 1960

Demographic measure	United States	Economic Provinces				
		Atlantic metropolitan belt Province	Great Lakes and Northeastern Province	Midwest Province	Southern Province	Western Province
Percent foreign born..	3	7	6	3	2	5
Percent nonwhite..	12	11	4	3	20	9
Dependency ratio--white.......................................	90	81	90	97	87	98
Dependency ratio--nonwhite....................................	103	91	80	114	109	99
Sex ratio--white...	95	95	93	94	95	99
Sex ratio--nonwhite...	98	93	118	102	89	101
Migration rate--age standardized--white..................	23	19	15	24	24	31
Migration rate--age standardized--nonwhite..............	18	13	25	25	11	26
Ratio of migration to total mobility--white..............	41	40	32	42	42	51
Ratio of migration to total mobility--nonwhite..........	32	26	42	40	23	45
Percent born in state of residence--white..............	68	65	76	67	72	45
Percent born in state of residence--nonwhite..........	64	52	46	56	80	48
Percent moved into house before 1950.....................	24	28	30	23	23	18
Children ever born--standardized--white................	221	202	228	234	212	233
Children ever born--standardized--nonwhite............	266	243	220	277	282	261
Ratio actual potential elementary enrollment--white.......	99	98	102	100	97	102
Ratio actual potential elementary enrollment--nonwhite.....	108	104	91	107	116	107
Percent white males completed < 8 year school standardized.	21	20	19	15	26	17
Percent white males completed college--standardized........	22	20	18	22	22	25
Percent nonwhite males completed < 8 years school--stand...	45	42	34	33	56	37
Percent nonwhite males completed college--standardized.....	9	8	10	11	7	13
Functionally illiterate--percent nonwhite.................	26	21	8	9	43	18
Functionally illiterate--percent male of white............	53	48	51	55	54	55
Percent of civilian labor force unemployed--white male.....	5	4	6	5	4	6
Percent of civilian labor force unemployed--nonwhite male..	10	9	12	10	8	12
Labor force participation rate of women--white............	36	37	36	37	36	37
Labor force participation rate of women--nonwhite.........	43	46	35	40	46	42
Family income--percent under $3,000--white................	18	12	15	17	22	16
Family income--percent over $7,000--white.................	35	44	38	34	32	42
Family income--percent under $3,000--nonwhite.............	45	32	30	37	60	31
Family income--percent over $7,000--nonwhite.............	11	17	14	12	6	22

Table 15-18 Average Values of Selected Demographic Measures of the Rural-Nonfarm Population in the Subregions of Each of Five Economic Provinces, United States: 1960

Demographic measure	United States	Economic Provinces				
		Atlantic metropolitan belt Province	Great Lakes and Northeastern Province	Midwest Province	Southern Province	Western Province
Percent foreign born	2	4	4	2	1	4
Percent nonwhite	11	7	1	3	19	11
Dependency ratio--white	101	89	102	108	100	102
Dependency ratio--nonwhite	118	94	98	114	131	108
Sex ratio--white	105	102	101	101	104	120
Sex ratio--nonwhite	117	117	138	119	104	130
Migration rate--age standardized--white	23	23	17	22	22	38
Migration rate--age standardized--nonwhite	23	27	31	31	14	30
Ratio of migration to total mobility--white	43	47	37	42	41	58
Ratio of migration to total mobility--nonwhite	44	56	60	54	31	51
Percent born in state of residence--white	72	68	80	71	78	46
Percent born in state of residence--nonwhite	69	57	54	59	84	60
Percent moved into house before 1950	26	26	30	27	26	19
Children ever born--age standardized--white	255	221	225	263	254	262
Children ever born--age standardized--nonwhite	313	272	302	241	353	321
Actual/potential elementary school enrollment--white	99	96	103	101	98	94
Actual/potential elementary school enrollment--nonwhite	99	89	88	83	113	94
Percent white males completed $<$ 8 years school--age stand..	30	25	21	20	40	22
Percent white males completed college--age standardized	13	18	12	14	11	18
Percent nonwhite males completed $<$ 8 yrs school--age stand.	53	50	42	37	66	45
Percent nonwhite males completed college--age standardized.	6	6	7	7	4	7
Functionally illiterate--percent of total nonwhite	20	18	4	5	32	24
Functionally illiterate--percent of white male	59	57	58	58	59	64
Percent civilian labor force unemployed--white male	6	3	7	6	6	6
Percent civilian labor force unemployed--nonwhite male	12	8	18	13	9	15
Female labor force participation rate--white	28	32	30	29	27	28
Female labor force participation rate--nonwhite	28	38	26	23	30	24
Family income--percent under $3,000--white	29	13	20	28	37	20
Family income--percent over $7,000--white	23	40	29	21	17	31
Family income--percent under $3,000--nonwhite	54	35	43	40	71	44
Family income--percent over $7,000--nonwhite	8	18	13	8	3	12

Table 15-19 Average Values of Selected Demographic Measures of the Rural-Farm Population in the Subregions of Each of Five Economic Provinces, United States: 1960

Demographic measure	United States	Economic Provinces				
		Atlantic metropolitan belt Province	Great Lakes and Northeastern Province	Midwest Province	Southern Province	Western Province
Percent foreign born	2	6	4	2	1	5
Percent nonwhite	11	5	...	1	19	12
Dependency ratio--white	99	94	105	100	97	104
Dependency ratio--nonwhite	109	...	...	...	140	106
Sex ratio--white	108	106	110	111	105	110
Sex ratio--nonwhite	89	...	...	...	100	103
Migration rate--age standardized--white	11	11	9	10	10	17
Migration rate--age standardized--nonwhite	13	...	...	...	9	13
Ratio of migration to total mobility--white	35	39	37	36	30	43
Ratio of migration to total mobility--nonwhite	34	...	...	...	25	33
Percent born in state of residence--white	81	75	85	82	86	60
Percent born in state of residence--nonwhite	73	...	...	...	90	73
Percent moved into house before 1950	47	50	55	51	45	36
Children ever born--age standardized--white	276	251	288	278	272	285
Children ever born--age standardized--nonwhite	221	...	...	...	351	217
Actual/potential elementary school enrollment--white	100	96	100	100	100	101
Actual/potential elementary school enrollment--nonwhite	82	...	...	...	108	92
Percent white males completed $<$ 8 yrs. school--age stand.	31	27	21	17	44	23
Percent white males completed college--age standardized	9	14	8	7	7	14
Percent nonwhite males completed $<$ 8 yrs. school--age stand	47	...	...	...	71	35
Percent nonwhite males completed college--age standardized.	3	...	...	...	3	6
Functionally illiterate--percent of total nonwhite	17	...	...	...	29	21
Functionally illiterate--percent of white male	64	58	63	67	64	61
Percent civilian labor force unemployed--white male	3	1	3	2	3	3
Percent civilian labor force unemployed--nonwhite male	4	...	...	...	4	6
Female labor force participation rate--white	23	31	27	20	22	24
Female labor force participation rate--nonwhite	21	...	...	...	25	21
Family income--percent under $3,000--white	42	27	35	42	51	27
Family income--percent over $7,000--white	18	31	21	17	13	30
Family income--percent under $3,000--nonwhite	48	...	...	...	74	30
Family income--percent over $7,000--nonwhite	5	...	...	...	2	15

used for this purpose. This has the effect of understating interregional differences. The values reported are the average values for the subregions within the province. Three principles emerge clearly from a study of these tables:

1. *There are very substantial differences between the five provinces, even when urban-rural residence is held constant.* For example, the proportion of white males who have completed less than 8 years of schooling, when the proportions have been standardized for age, is substantially higher in the Southern Province than in any of the other provinces. This is true for the urban, the rural-nonfarm, and the rural-farm populations separately.

2. *Although the urban-rural differences described for the nation are generally found in each region, there are substantial interregional differences in the urban-rural differences.* For the nation the urban-rural difference in proportions of white males completing less than 8 years of school, standardized for age, by provinces, is as follows:

United States total 10
Atlantic Metropolitan Province 7
Great Lakes–Northern Province 3
Midwest Province 2
Southern Province 18
Western Province 6

3. *The composition of the urban and the rural populations themselves differ greatly among the regions.* Continuing the same example, it may be seen that the rural populations in the Midwest Province have a comparative scarcity of people with very little education and of persons with a college education. This implies a heavy concentration of persons with high school training only. The Atlantic Metropolitan Belt and the Western Province, on the other hand, have much higher proportions in both extremes. The rural farm portion of the Southern Province has a greater concentration of low-education people, with no compensating higher educational group.

To portray in full detail the nature of the urban-rural differences, by economic region, Tables 15-20 and 15-21 are presented. To prepare Table 15-20, two tables similar to Table

15-16 were drawn up, one for the urban population of each region and one for the rural-farm; then the values for the rural-farm population were subtracted from the values for the urban population. A minus sign for any trait, therefore, means that the urban population is deficient in this trait in comparison with the rural-farm, and a plus value indicates that this trait is more prevalent in the urban population than in the rural-farm population. For example, there is a relative scarcity of native white population of native parentage among the urban population and a surplus of foreign-born. *If there were no interregional diversity* in urban-rural composition, each region would have the same value as the "U.S. total" column. That this is not the case for almost every line of this table is most evident. Take the matter of age composition of the white population, for example. In all regions, urban areas have a comparative surplus of younger persons (ages 20 to 44) than rural-farm areas. However, this differential is much stronger in Regions 3, 7, 8, 9, and 10 than in the other regions. In these regions, the exodus of young persons from farms to cities is especially heavy. Continuing, we may note that although the differential between urban and rural fertility (children ever born) shows lower urban than rural-farm fertility in every region, the difference for the white population vary from minus 445 in Region 11 to minus 671 (50 percent greater) in Region 3. For nonwhite fertility the contrast is much greater: from plus 55 in Region 2 to minus 2022 in Region 10. For every other trait similar diversity may be noted in this table.

Interregional Differences between Urban and Rural-Nonfarm Populations. That the rural-non-farm population resembles the urban population more than does the rural-farm population has already been demonstrated. The exact nature of these differentials may be noted by comparing Tables 15-20 and 15-21. (Table 15-21 was prepared in the same way as Table 15-20, except that rural-nonfarm population was used instead of the rural-farm.) Table 15-21 demonstrates also that there are very substantial interregional differences between the urban and rural-nonfarm populations. In the more urbanized regions, the rural-nonfarm

Table 15-20 Differences in Social and Economic Characteristics Between Urban and Rural Farm Populations, by Economic Regions, United States: 1960

Subject	U.S. Total	Region												
		1	2	3	4	5	6	7	8	9	10	11	12	13
Total population														
White:														
Native of native parentage	-12.7	-26.3	-16.3	-24.2	-4.0	-5.8	3.4	-15.6	8.7	7.4	8.4	-.3	-2.6	2.4
Native of foreign or mixed parentage	7.9	15.7	10.4	8.3	1.1	1.1	-6.6	3.9	1.5	.6	.6	2.7	1.4	-2.4
Foreign born	4.9	7.0	3.2	4.6	2.0	1.1	.4	1.3	.6	1.7	.6	1.9	1.4	.7
Nonwhite	0.0	3.7	2.7	11.3	1.0	6.1	2.7	10.5	-10.8	5.1	-9.2	-4.2	1.5	.6
AGE														
White, all ages														
Under 15 years	-1.7	-2.2	-3.3	-.8	-3.3	-2.1	-2.5	.1	1.4	.3	1.5	.9	-1.3	-1.7
15 to 19 years	-2.1	-2.0	-1.7	-2.5	-2.1	-1.1	-1.0	-2.4	-2.6	-2.6	-2.1	-1.2	-1.7	-1.6
20 to 24 years	-1.9	-1.1	-1.3	-1.3	-2.5	-2.7	-2.7	-2.0	-2.7	-2.6	-3.5	-2.9	-2.8	-2.1
25 to 34 years	-3.9	-3.1	-2.3	-4.3	-3.3	-3.3	-3.2	-4.5	-5.8	-4.7	-5.7	-3.7	-3.5	-3.7
35 to 44 years	-1.3	-1.5	-1.3	-1.9	0.0	-.1	-.1	-1.3	-1.6	-1.5	-1.2	-.1	-.5	.1
45 to 64 years	-3.2	-.6	.5	-1.8	-2.4	-3.8	-4.1	-4.3	-6.2	-4.5	-8.2	-5.5	-4.8	-3.8
65 years and over	-.3	-1.1	.5	-2.4	1.8	1.2	1.6	-1.1	-2.8	.1	-1.6	.7	1.1	0.0
Nonwhite, all ages														
Under 15 years	-8.3	-3.6	4.1	6.6	9.9	5.2	-3.2	.2	8.0	-4.3	-7.8	-5.5	-4.1	0.0
15 to 19 years	-4.6	-3.3	-1.6	-3.4	-6.7	-2.0	-1.8	-2.8	-4.2	-3.9	-3.4	-4.0	-1.1	-1.9
20 to 24 years	1.2	.8	.8	2.0	5.8	2.6	-1.4	.9	.9	1.1	1.2	1.4	2.5	-2.5
25 to 34 years	6.4	6.3	6.0	7.2	12.1	5.9	4.3	3.8	4.3	5.4	5.0	4.6	7.0	5.1
35 to 44 years	4.5	4.1	-2.0	3.9	5.9	3.0	1.0	3.0	3.0	4.0	2.6	2.0	-.4	-.8
45 to 64 years	1.4	-1.2	-4.7	-12.1	-8.4	-9.7	-1.1	3.0	2.7	.6	.9	1.8	-2.0	-3.2
65 years and over	.5	-2.9	-2.9	-4.2	1.0	-5.0	.6	-1.1	1.2	-1.7	1.6	.2	-2.5	-3.4
DEPENDENCY RATIO														
Total:														
White	-.14	-.18	-.16	-.21	-.14	-.08	-.07	-.13	-.14	-.12	-.08	-.04	-.08	.12
Nonwhite	-.70	-.39	-.02	-.03	-.78	-.08	-.27	.16	.63	.52	.57	.50	.34	.21
Youth:														
White	-.13	-.14	-.16	-.15	-.17	-.09	-.09	-.09	.07	-.11	-.04	-.03	-.09	.11
Nonwhite	-.64	-.32	-.04	-.05	-.77	-.03	-.24	-.13	-.61	-.45	-.56	-.48	-.27	-.13
Old Age:														
White	-.01	-.04	-.01	-.07	-.03	-.01	-.02	-.04	-.06	-.01	-.03	-.02	-.30	.01
Nonwhite	-.05	-.09	-.06	-.08	-.01	-.11	-.03	-.04	-.01	-.07	-.01	-.03	-.08	-.08
SEX RATIO														
White, all ages	-13.6	-11.6	-18.1	-12.9	-20.2	-15.3	-17.5	-14.5	-11.8	-11.0	-12.2	-13.1	-15.0	-11.4
Under 15 years	-3.2	-3.0	-3.1	-4.5	-2.7	-2.9	-2.6	-4.3	-3.2	-3.9	-4.0	-2.4	-4.6	-3.2
15 to 19 years	-26.4	-17.6	-34.6	-27.6	-37.0	-30.7	-30.6	-30.1	-31.5	-17.0	-29.1	-26.0	-33.0	-11.9
20 to 24 years	-29.8	-18.8	-31.6	-36.4	-52.1	-27.8	-28.4	-33.9	-43.0	-24.6	-21.5	-29.1	-37.3	-9.0
25 to 34 years	-1.9	-1.3	-9.9	-2.9	-1.9	-2.9	-7.8	-2.7	.2	1.7	5.8	5.0	8.6	7.9
35 to 44 years	-2.5	-4.2	-2.5	-2.5	-6.8	-4.4	-7.8	-2.7	3.8	-.2	5.0	-3.3	-1.9	-1.7
45 to 64 years	-19.3	-17.1	-23.6	-14.6	-34.8	-23.0	-32.2	-17.2	-15.2	-20.0	-18.3	-20.5	-17.3	-20.5
65 years and over	-42.4	-30.3	-43.3	-36.0	-57.1	-46.8	-60.0	-45.9	-37.7	-26.8	-47.4	-52.5	-64.1	-53.0

505

Table 15-20 (Continued)

Subject	U.S. Total	Region												
		1	2	3	4	5	6	7	8	9	10	11	12	13
Nonwhite, all ages...........	-10.1	-22.6	-18.4	-15.8	16.7	- 5.4	-12.5	-19.8	-14.4	-13.5	-12.1	.8	- 1.6	-19.6
Under 15 years.............	- 3.2	-10.0	-11.9	-11.8	4.4	1.7	2.0	-10.8	- 3.8	- 4.9	- 2.0	3.3	3.3	-11.7
15 to 19 years.............	-17.5	-30.6	...	-23.2	-25.7	9.6	-19.2	-12.7	-18.1	-16.3	-14.9	-10.6	-34.7	-14.9
20 to 24 years.............	-28.5	-51.0	...	- 3.7	...	-69.0	-22.9	-43.4	-29.8	-36.6	-20.8	- 4.7	11.4	-22.5
25 to 34 years.............	.6	-17.7	16.5	- 3.7	91.0	11.5	-14.6	-12.1	- 4.9	- 8.9	- 2.0	1.4	32.8	- 8.7
35 to 44 years.............	3.2	-12.5	- 8.8	18.2	23.1	17.9	-22.1	- 2.2	- 5.2	- 2.8	- 0.0	2.2	- 6.0	- 2.6
45 to 64 years.............	-13.9	-31.2	-23.3	-36.6	...	-15.0	-23.0	-27.2	-23.1	-14.6	-22.7	2.0	-21.0	-43.9
65 years and over...........	-31.3	-39.4	...	- 6.0	...	-23.8	-30.0	-51.4	-37.0	-42.4	-37.6	-29.2	15.0	-49.8
AVERAGE POPULATION PER HOUSEHOLD														
Total.......................	.59	.60	.65	.41	.77	.44	.56	.46	.88	.56	.57	.35	.49	.45
White.......................	- .50	- .57	- .67	- .46	- .76	- .46	- .56	- .50	- .44	- .51	- .32	- .27	- .48	- .44
Nonwhite....................	-1.67	-1.25	- .38	- .03	-4.03	.68	-1.41	- .83	-1.77	-1.26	-1.45	-1.62	-1.16	.53
MOBILITY STATUS														
White														
Same house in 1955 and 1960...	-24.1	-18.9	-19.6	-24.8	-28.7	-28.6	-35.6	-24.7	-26.4	-28.5	-26.1	-25.6	-22.7	-20.3
Same county................	13.0	10.6	15.4	19.8	17.6	17.7	15.2	14.2	9.9	10.1	10.7	12.2	11.9	10.5
Different county:														
Same state................	2.8	3.2	.9	.2	5.8	3.4	7.0	4.5	6.5	1.6	6.3	1.4	3.6	- 1.2
Different state or abroad...	8.3	5.1	3.2	5.1	5.3	7.5	13.4	6.0	10.1	16.8	9.0	12.0	7.2	11.0
Not reported..............	1.2	1.1	.8	1.0	.8	1.2	1.0	1.3	1.0	1.2	1.2	.6	.6	1.1
Nonwhite														
Same house in 1955 and 1960...	-13.3	-21.1	- 9.3	-18.1	-31.3	-25.8	-23.5	-19.1	- 5.6	-25.7	- 6.1	-22.2	-30.6	-25.3
Same county................	8.1	15.8	25.5	36.1	19.2	26.3	14.4	18.3	3.8	20.5	3.4	- 5.3	17.0	15.3
Different county:														
Same state................	- 1.1	.4	- 5.5	- 6.9	- 3.6	- 4.7	- 3.9	- 1.9	.2	.8	.7	5.4	- 2.0	- 1.0
Different state or abroad...	6.4	4.8	-10.9	-11.1	15.8	4.3	13.0	2.8	2.0	4.5	2.0	22.1	15.6	11.1
Not reported..............	2.7	3.0	1.9	3.0	.2	2.5	2.8	2.4	1.0	1.7	1.7	.5	1.2	1.7
Standardized:														
White:														
Same house in 1955 and 1960...	-22.9	-17.5	-18.9	-22.6	-27.2	-26.6	-33.7	-22.1	-22.5	-26.1	-21.9	-22.6	-20.5	-18.2
Same county................	12.2	10.0	15.1	18.9	17.1	17.1	14.5	13.1	8.2	9.1	9.0	11.0	11.1	9.7
Different county or abroad...	9.7	7.6	3.8	3.7	10.1	9.7	19.3	9.0	14.3	16.9	12.9	11.6	9.4	8.6
Nonwhite:														
Same house in 1955 and 1960...	-11.7	-18.5	- 5.8	-12.5	-25.6	-20.5	-21.7	-17.4	- 5.2	-23.6	- 5.1	-20.9	-27.2	-21.9
Same county................	7.3	14.5	23.9	33.6	17.0	23.9	13.6	17.4	3.7	19.5	3.0	- 5.8	15.6	13.9
Different county or abroad...	4.4	3.8	-18.4	-21.1	8.7	- 3.3	8.0	0.0	1.6	4.1	2.2	26.7	11.5	8.0
Unstandardized, percent migrant:														
Total.......................	10.4	8.0	4.3	4.4	11.2	10.5	20.1	9.2	12.4	15.6	13.4	14.1	10.9	9.8
White.....................	11.0	8.4	4.3	4.9	11.1	10.9	20.5	10.5	16.5	18.3	15.3	13.4	10.8	9.9
Nonwhite..................	5.3	5.2	-16.4	-18.0	12.2	.3	9.1	.8	1.8	5.3	2.8	27.5	13.6	10.0
Ratio of migration to total mobility:														
Total.......................	.061	.018	-.066	-.108	-.007	.004	.106	.037	.157	.111	.115	.048	.019	.018
White.....................	.052	.028	-.060	-.087	-.004	.013	.112	.060	.174	.143	.104	.021	.019	.020
Nonwhite..................	.055	-.015	-.344	-.492	-.042	-.212	-.006	-.066	.021	-.013	.031	.398	.013	.047

Table 15-20 (Continued)

Subject	U.S. Total	Region 1	2	3	4	5	6	7	8	9	10	11	12	13
COUNTRY OF ORIGIN														
Total foreign stock														
English-speaking Europe and Canada	7.1	1.2	-10.6	- 2.9	7.0	8.2	9.2	1.7	- 2.1	11.2	12.5	.9	10.1	12.4
Scandinavian-German-French portion of Europe	-29.0	- 9.5	-10.2	-16.0	-11.0	-27.1	-14.1	-21.3	9.6	- 5.2	-14.2	-12.0	- 9.4	.3
Eastern Europe	7.2	- 5.5	4.7	7.1	1.1	6.8	- 7.9	10.7	2.7	- .1	-10.2	- 1.1	1.1	6.2
Southern Europe	12.0	10.3	15.4	9.0	3.5	7.3	5.1	6.7	4.3	4.6	3.7	.6	2.4	-12.5
Spanish America	1.0	2.1	.2	1.4	.5	2.6	4.5	.9	.7	-12.8	3.0	13.2	3.8	- 2.5
Asia	1.4	1.1	1.0	1.4	1.0	1.6	2.3	1.6	4.2	1.6	4.6	- 1.8	1.6	- 3.9
All other	.2	.1	0.0	.1	.1	.2	.4	.1	.1	...	.3	.2	.4	.5
Not reported	.1	- .2	- .2	0.0	.1	.3	.6	.1	.2	.3	.2	0.0	0.0	.3
STATE OF BIRTH														
Percent born in State of 1960 residence:														
Total	-23.3	-17.1	- 9.5	-20.0	-11.7	-18.2	-24.1	-17.2	-17.6	-26.7	-13.5	-14.5	-11.7	-17.3
White	-21.8	-14.8	- 8.5	-16.9	-11.3	-17.0	-23.9	-15.9	-20.2	-29.0	-14.4	-12.6	-11.2	-16.9
Nonwhite	-34.7	-36.2	- 1.1	2.2	-32.2	-20.5	-34.0	-27.0	-10.3	-20.2	- 5.3	-43.7	-32.3	-22.1
YEAR MOVED INTO PRESENT HOUSE														
Total														
1959 to 1960	12.0	8.6	10.4	13.1	14.5	15.9	20.7	13.9	11.3	16.7	14.0	16.1	15.1	12.6
1957 to 1958	6.9	7.0	6.5	8.9	9.0	8.3	9.4	7.1	5.2	7.5	5.3	5.2	5.6	4.8
1950 to 1956	4.3	5.7	4.5	5.8	8.0	2.2	3.6	3.5	2.6	1.7	.2	- 1.0	- .5	- .6
Before 1950	-23.2	-21.3	-21.4	-27.9	-31.5	-26.4	-33.7	-24.6	-19.1	-25.9	-18.9	-20.3	-20.1	-16.9
CHILDREN EVER BORN														
Children ever born per 1,000 women ever married:														
White, 15 to 44 years old	- 718	- 625	- 676	- 755	- 854	- 599	- 697	- 683	- 752	- 773	- 792	- 585	- 653	- 660
Standardized for age	- 640	- 582	- 632	- 671	- 713	- 482	- 593	- 588	- 627	- 694	- 663	- 445	- 530	- 608
15 to 24 years old	- 230	- 241	- 304	- 202	- 312	- 214	- 269	- 160	- 182	- 261	- 277	- 223	- 304	- 333
25 to 34 years old	- 598	- 539	- 653	- 659	- 693	- 474	- 573	- 469	- 500	- 649	- 578	- 462	- 526	- 632
35 to 44 years old	- 854	- 769	- 752	- 881	- 902	- 602	- 748	- 879	- 933	- 922	- 906	- 525	- 632	- 704
Nonwhite, 15 to 44 years old	-1914	-1249	- 1	- 713	- 554	- 577	- 945	- 876	-1398	-1521	-1946	-1284	- 713	- 732
Standardized for age	-1951	-1264	55	- 534	- 466	- 454	- 967	- 906	-1716	-1569	-2022	-1292	- 665	- 601
15 to 24 years old	- 318	- 260	177	- 628	- 536	- 417	- 17	- 116	- 198	- 340	- 426	- 267	- 8	- 10
25 to 34 years old	-1692	-1175	- 949	- 716	- 379	- 65	- 807	- 707	-1442	-1302	-1807	-1084	- 729	- 459
35 to 44 years old	-2883	-1776	- 807	- 867	- 973	-1179	-1519	-1423	-2614	-2337	-2900	-1920	- 888	- 982
Ratio of nonwhite to white fertility in same area:														
15 to 24 years old	.018	.084	.419	.667	.588	.520	.236	.112	.098	.031	.006	.007	.240	.263
25 to 34 years old	-.339	-.208	.581	.022	.093	.173	-.054	-.033	-.276	-.156	-.352	-.195	-.065	-.926
35 to 44 years old	-.596	-.330	-.013	.007	-.022	-.174	-.210	-.136	-.428	-.361	-.507	-.404	-.068	-.069
Ratio of area to U.S. white*	-.866	-.561	.025	-.237	-.207	-.202	-.429	-.402	.239	-.697	.102	-.573	-.296	-.267

507

Table 15-20 (Continued)

Subject	U.S. Total	Region												
		1	2	3	4	5	6	7	8	9	10	11	12	13
Ratio of white area fert. rates to U.S. rate:														
15 to 24 years old	-.186	-.195	-.246	-.164	.252	-.174	-.218	-.129	-.147	-.211	-.224	-.181	-.246	-.269
25 to 34 years old	-.251	-.227	-.275	-.277	-.291	-.200	-.240	-.197	-.210	-.273	-.243	-.195	-.221	-.266
35 to 44 years old	-.332	-.299	-.292	-.342	-.351	-.233	-.291	-.341	-.362	-.358	-.352	-.204	-.246	-.274
Total (standardized)*	-.284	-.258	-.281	-.298	-.316	-.214	-.263	-.261	-.279	-.308	-.294	-.198	-.235	-.270
SCHOOL ENROLLMENT														
Percent enrolled, total	- 9.9	- 6.3	- 6.1	-10.0	- 9.5	- 9.6	- 9.5	- 6.6	-10.6	-11.5	-12.7	- 8.5	-11.2	- 9.6
7 to 13 years old	.6	- .1	.6	.1	0.0	- .3	.1	1.5	1.4	.8	1.1	1.5	.1	.3
14 and 15 years old	1.9	3.6	.2	.3	0.0	- 1.2	0.0	4.8	2.8	.3	2.0	.7	.7	.5
16 and 17 years old	.2	5.6	1.2	- 1.3	.7	- 6.8	5.6	6.2	2.7	- 1.3	- 1.5	- 4.7	- 1.7	- 1.7
18 and 19 years old	6.3	10.5	17.8	5.1	15.6	12.0	5.9	16.3	9.5	- 5.5	4.4	.7	2.6	4.6
20 and 21 years old	14.8	15.0	23.1	11.8	25.1	21.5	17.0	18.8	16.5	4.3	16.4	12.6	16.5	6.8
22 to 24 years old	7.2	8.0	8.2	6.3	11.4	9.0	6.6	8.4	6.8	2.7	7.2	7.3	8.0	5.2
25 to 34 years old	2.3	3.5	2.5	2.5	2.7	2.3	1.7	2.5	1.4	.4	1.2	2.9	1.6	3.9
Ratio of actual to potential enrollment:														
White: Kindergarten	-.027	-.058	-1.029	-.784	.446	-.683	.308	.494	.273	.239	-.228	-.059	-.067	-1.134
Elementary school	-.005	.016	.021	.031	-.018	-.018	-.008	-.001	-.041	.010	-.053	.031	-.021	.014
High school	-.004	.162	.093	-.009	-.064	-.093	-.030	.016	-.105	-.018	-.174	-.050	-.046	.055
College	.060	-.139	.328	-.310	.618	.417	.064	.328	.394	-.613	.199	-.367	-.544	-1.443
Nonwhite: Kindergarten	.721	.620	-2.145	.041	1.080	.618	.712	.477	.254	.391	.188	-.267	-.841	-1.476
Elementary school	-.122	.003	-.018	.065	-.431	.055	-.035	.103	-.037	-.032	-.110	.049	-.129	.015
High school	.161	.088	-.020	-.301	-.167	-.189	.075	.143	.198	.002	.231	.373	.061	.039
College	.114	.087	-.081	-.358	. . .	-.591	.080	.292	.272	-.139	.131	-.074	.857	-1.988
Percent nonwhite ratio to white:														
Kindergarten	72.3	64.0	-41.8	48.5	55.5	73.9	42.8	4.6	26.0	46.2	2.2	-26.5	-75.6	-11.6
Elementary school	-11.6	- 1.4	- 3.9	3.2	-39.9	7.4	- 2.7	10.5	1.4	- 4.1	- 4.5	1.7	70.3	.1
High school	16.4	- 4.2	- 8.3	-28.7	-10.7	-10.3	9.9	13.9	29.2	2.0	37.7	38.4	8.5	- 1.5
College	9.1	12.6	-24.0	-21.0	. . .	-94.4	4.8	14.5	10.2	16.8	6.5	11.6	79.5	-29.2
YEARS OF SCHOOL COMPLETED, STANDARDIZED FOR AGE														
Male														
White														
Elementary: Less than 5 years	- 3.5	- 1.8	2.3	1.6	- 2.3	1.4	0.0	- 9.9	- 9.2	-14.8	8.0	.2	- .7	7.4
5 to 7 years	- 6.4	- 8.8	- 1.5	- 2.6	- 9.0	- .8	- 3.8	- 9.3	-11.9	9.7	- 9.3	- 1.3	2.8	4.0
8 years	-10.2	- 4.7	-10.4	-13.0	-20.0	-14.5	-16.6	- 6.3	- 1.5	.9	- 3.9	- 7.8	- 7.5	5.1
High school: 1 to 3 years	4.1	1.4	.1	4.6	4.1	- 4.1	.5	- 5.6	- 1.5	3.0	- 1.9	- 1.9	.8	2.0
4 years	1.2	1.4	1.9	- 2.0	7.9	- 3.6	.5	5.3	4.6	.6	3.9	1.5	1.6	2.2
College: 1 to 3 years	5.4	2.8	1.9	4.2	7.1	4.7	6.5	5.6	7.2	6.2	7.6	4.2	3.5	4.8
4 years or more	9.4	6.2	5.9	7.5	10.9	8.4	10.6	8.8	10.8	8.3	10.4	8.2	8.3	7.5
Median years of school completed	2.4	2.0	1.3	1.9	2.9	2.3	3.1	1.9	2.9	3.0	2.8	1.6	1.5	2.4

Table 15-20 (*Continued*)

Subject	U.S. Total	Region 1	2	3	4	5	6	7	8	9	10	11	12	13
Nonwhite														
Elementary: Less than 5 years	-29.6	-28.5	-11.0	- 8.5	- 6.4	- 5.3	- 2.9	-17.8	-17.9	-26.7	-22.5	-34.5	- 2.7	-12.1
5 to 7 years	- 4.0	- 9.2	- 7.7	1.1	- 2.4	2.7	7.1	- 5.2	- 1.8	3.5	4.5	5.2	.5	1.2
8 years	7.8	11.2	5.4	- 3.2	-20.4	3.3	2.7	2.4	3.7	7.5	8.6	5.4	1.6	.6
High school: 1 to 3 years	11.8	12.3	5.8	6.3	10.7	6.7	1.3	11.5	7.2	9.6	8.6	11.3	1.1	4.9
4 years	7.1	7.9	5.7	.7	.8	.4	1.5	4.0	4.0	2.8	4.3	4.6	9.1	- 3.5
College: 1 to 3 years	3.9	3.5	1.1	3.2	4.4	1.7	4.7	3.1	2.1	1.8	2.8	3.8	3.7	4.7
4 years or more	3.2	2.9	1.1	1.6	13.3	2.4	5.0	1.2	2.7	1.4	2.6	3.9	4.9	4.2
Median years of school completed	3.5	3.2	1.4	.4	1.2	.5	.9	2.5	1.9	2.8	2.6	4.1	.1	1.1
Female														
Elementary: Less than 5 years	.6	1.5	2.5	2.3	- 1.2	1.1	.2	- 4.4	- 3.5	- 9.4	- 4.1	2.5	- .4	- 4.1
5 to 7 years	- 4.3	- 5.4	2.6	.2	- 4.4	1.6	.6	- 8.6	-10.6	- 9.5	8.0	.8	.6	3.1
8 years	- 7.1	- 3.4	5.5	8.6	-16.1	- 8.6	9.8	- 8.0	- 2.9	.4	5.2	- 2.9	- 3.3	4.1
High school: 1 to 3 years	2.6	3.2	.7	3.8	3.4	4.1	2.4	4.7	- 1.3	1.9	1.8	- 1.9	.2	- .8
4 years	4.2	4.0	- .1	.2	9.4	1.7	2.5	9.1	- 1.3	.7	.7	- .2	.2	.7
College: 1 to 3 years	1.7	.9	1.6	2.2	3.2	...	.6	3.6	.3	1.7	6.3	.2	1.7	2.3
4 years or more	3.4	1.1	1.1	.6	5.7	3.6	.6	3.4	4.9	4.5	2.5	2.5	1.7	1.8
Median years of school completed	1.6	.8	...	.6	3.2	.4	.8	2.0	2.5	2.7	2.5	.1	.1	.1
White														
Elementary: Less than 5 years	-16.1	-13.1	-11.0	- 3.7	- .8	.5	- .3	- 7.5	- 6.0	-16.8	-13.9	-45.5	- 4.6	- 9.1
5 to 7 years	-12.5	-16.3	- 6.4	- 3.2	- 5.7	- 1.8	- 5.6	- 5.1	- 9.9	- 5.0	- 8.0	7.9	- 3.4	- 1.7
8 years	10.1	10.5	5.5	6.5	3.6	6.5	6.9	4.8	.2	4.6	8.1	4.7	1.7	1.0
High school: 1 to 3 years	9.6	7.3	5.0	8.7	2.6	10.7	6.8	8.8	5.8	9.6	7.4	9.0	3.6	6.4
4 years	3.4	1.5	.8	.3	1.2	2.1	1.5	2.0	5.1	5.0	2.4	4.3	3.0	1.5
College: 1 to 3 years	2.2	2.0	.1	3.1	1.4	.9	1.9	2.0	1.7	1.7	2.9	2.7	1.0	4.1
4 years or more	2.2	2.0	.5	2.0	7.0	.1	2.8	1.8	2.9	.7	2.4	4.8	4.5	2.7
Median years of school completed	2.2	2.0	.5	.6	1.1	.6	1.1	.9	1.1	2.0	1.9	4.8	.9	1.4
Functional illit. (0 to 4 grades):														
Percent nonwhite of total	- 5.1	- 7.3	3.6	19.2	1.7	16.0	5.7	24.8	4.6	16.2	- 1.6	-29.3	4.3	2.8
Percent white male of white total	-13.9	-15.9	-12.9	-11.5	-13.1	-13.5	-12.3	-11.6	-10.8	- 8.7	- 8.2	-17.4	-10.4	-11.2
Percent nonwhite male of nonwhite total	- 6.5	-12.4	-15.8	- 6.0	...	- 9.3	- 9.1	-10.8	- 9.9	- 5.8	- 6.4	8.9	4.3	- 5.6
Superior education (high school+):														
Ratio nonwhite to white: Male	.042	.052	.015	.064	.009	.034	.017	.054	.028	.041	.018	-.008	.011	-.010
Female	.044	.056	.012	.074	.005	.035	.019	.064	.020	.050	.026	-.001	.011	.004
Ratio female to male: White	-.175	-.136	-.088	-.170	-.289	-.110	-.145	-.192	-.227	-.127	-.135	-.127	-.048	-.033
Nonwhite	-.394	-.600	-.088	.012	...	-.785	-.069	-.417	-.668	-.240	-.114	.188	.070	.140
PERCENT OF CIVILIAN LABOR FORCE UNEMPLOYED														
White: Male	2.1	2.3	3.3	1.4	1.6	2.8	2.6	.6	.8	2.0	1.0	3.1	2.1	2.7
Female	.4	1.6	1.1	.3	.6	.4	.1	.6	.2	.1	1.1	.6	1.1	.9
Nonwhite: Male	5.9	4.2	6.9	5.5	9.3	2.1	.5	5.3	5.2	3.2	4.8	3.5	4.4	4.3
Female	.7	2.1	3.0	7.2	3.9	2.1	3.2	2.4	.4	2.3	3.9	2.3	1.3	4.9
Ratio of nonwhite male to white male		- 2.1	- 3.0						+ .4	+ 2.3				

Table 15-20 (*Continued*)

Subject	U.S. Total	Region 1	2	3	4	5	6	7	8	9	10	11	12	13
RATIO OF UNEMPLOYED TO EMPLOYED IN LOW SES OCCUPATIONS														
White: Male	2.3	3.5	4.9	1.5	1.5	3.2	3.2	—	1.0	3.6	1.5	5.2	2.8	4.4
Female	2.2	4.3	2.5	1.7	1.1	2.1	1.4	.4	.9	1.0	.2	2.0	-1.3	-1.4
Nonwhite: Male	6.0	4.7	9.3	3.9	...	1.2	2.0	4.5	4.6	1.9	5.2	-12.9	3.4	4.2
Female	...	-2.7	-4.8	5.2	...	5.4	6.8	2.6	.2	2.4	6.0	-4.3	-5.0	5.5
Difference, nonwhite minus white: Male	3.3	1.2	4.4	2.4	...	-4.4	-5.2	.9	2.6	-1.7	3.7	-18.1	.6	-.2
Female	-2.2	-7.0	-7.3	3.5	...	2.1	-8.2	-1.6	.7	.6	-6.2	-6.3	-3.7	6.5
LABOR FORCE PARTICIPATION RATE OF WOMEN														
White	13.5	7.3	8.6	10.0	10.4	16.2	18.2	14.6	14.6	11.3	17.1	12.4	10.4	12.0
Married, husband present: With children under 6	2.5	-3.6	.8	1.1	-2.1	7.0	8.7	4.1	4.1	4.5	9.9	5.7	4.1	5.2
No children under 6	13.6	7.5	8.1	10.3	8.8	17.5	19.8	15.2	16.8	10.8	18.3	13.4	10.6	12.2
Other marital status: With children under 6	13.8	.8	6.1	9.4	7.2	14.4	14.7	20.8	21.1	13.0	24.2	15.6	5.4	10.8
No children under 6	19.0	11.3	11.6	14.6	18.9	17.9	20.7	19.6	18.7	16.5	21.5	16.7	14.8	15.1
Nonwhite	21.4	9.3	4.8	8.9	15.8	23.1	27.4	12.2	22.7	22.1	26.8	29.5	18.6	9.0
Married, with husband present: With children under 6	11.5	1.7	.9	8.9	...	23.1	15.7	11.1	16.2	14.2	23.0	21.3	14.4	1.3
No children under 6	23.0	7.9	9.2	8.9	9.4	23.6	32.4	13.3	26.6	22.1	30.8	30.1	26.8	9.4
Other marital status: With children under 6	8.0	-6.2	...	...	...	...	...	20.4	18.5	22.3	26.3	30.2	...	1.6
No children under 6	25.1	14.7	4.8	13.3	26.6	25.1	31.1	11.8	22.6	24.8	25.0	31.9	14.3	16.0
Ratio of rate for total nonwhite females to rate for total white females	19.0	-1.3	-16.3	-9.8	13.6	16.8	33.3	-27.5	20.8	26.0	23.7	57.8	25.3	-24.2
RATIO OF LABOR FORCE PARTICIPATION RATE TO U.S. RATE														
Male, 14 & over (standardized)	-.045	-.075	-.105	-.046	-.090	-.075	-.079	-.020	-.027	-.031	-.018	-.059	-.070	-.054
14 to 17 years	-.178	-.536	-.509	-.219	-.400	-.166	-.023	-.008	-.030	-.007	-.166	-.045	-.086	-.083
18 to 24 years	-.020	-.091	-.186	-.044	-.140	-.112	-.068	-.030	-.047	-.052	-.004	-.013	-.048	.020
25 to 34 years	-.003	-.016	-.029	-.004	-.026	-.023	-.015	.011	.008	.014	.006	.004	-.018	-.015
35 to 44 years	...	-.014	-.015	-.005	-.013	-.014	-.013	.013	.005	.007	.004	.003	-.012	-.010
45 to 64 years	-.016	-.027	-.048	-.005	-.032	-.041	-.053	.008	-.009	-.030	-.010	-.035	-.039	-.035
65 years and over	-.663	-.636	-.829	-.613	-.856	-.718	-.964	-.505	-.420	-.682	-.475	.941	-.886	-.791
Female, 14 & over (standardized)	.390	.190	.238	.225	.287	.476	.543	.406	.428	.359	.517	.374	.322	.332
14 to 17 years	.371	.093	.229	.235	.679	.521	.671	.421	.314	.350	.450	.493	.407	.143
18 to 24 years	.302	.139	.161	.064	.254	.251	.415	.238	.267	.260	.401	.324	.275	.301
25 to 34 years	.346	.133	.235	.218	.164	.456	.536	.308	.371	.402	.505	.382	.363	.405
35 to 44 years	.370	.174	.253	.277	.220	.476	.527	.396	.424	.396	.524	.360	.296	.323
45 to 64 years	.474	.282	.279	.350	.387	.577	.618	.529	.538	.382	.589	.390	.371	.375
65 years and over	.359	.059	.136	.213	.165	.563	.428	.505	.496	.145	.437	.320	...	-.020
WEEKS WORKED IN 1959														
Total labor force	1.3	-2.7	-7.9	-2.9	-12.6	-11.9	-10.6	7.8	16.7	.7	15.1	-3.4	3.2	1.9
50 to 52 weeks	1.3	2.5	4.0	3.5	5.5	5.5	4.0	-2.6	-6.1	-.8	-4.5	-2.5	1.5	2.1
40 to 49 weeks	1.2	.7	2.0	.7	2.7	2.7	2.6	-2.6	-2.9	...	-2.9	2.4	.3	.9
27 to 39 weeks	-.3	...	.7	...	...	...	...	...	...	...	...	...	...	...
26 weeks or less	-2.5	.6	1.9	1.2	4.4	3.6	3.9	-7.4	-7.4	-1.9	-7.8	-1.4	...	-4.9

Table 15-20 (Continued)

Subject	U.S. Total	Region 1	2	3	4	5	6	7	8	9	10	11	12	13
CLASS OF WORKER														
Male:														
Agricultural workers:														
Self-employed..........	-52.4	-40.4	-47.4	-41.3	-57.6	-65.2	-61.2	-48.1	-45.9	-39.0	-45.7	-49.5	-42.6	-38.2
Wage and salary or government.........	-11.8	-15.1	-13.2	-7.6	-8.2	-6.9	-10.9	-8.9	-13.6	-18.8	-21.5	-16.9	-14.0	-29.5
Unpaid family worker.........														
Nonagricultural workers:														
Private wage and salary and unpaid family worker....	54.2	47.3	53.2	45.0	56.0	60.1	62.2	50.0	50.9	48.6	52.5	50.5	43.9	54.3
Government worker....	7.1	6.5	6.0	3.6	9.0	8.6	10.0	4.1	7.1	5.1	7.6	11.4	8.5	8.6
Self-employed....	6.6	4.7	5.6	4.0	7.2	7.5	9.9	5.2	6.0	6.6	9.3	7.6	6.0	6.4
Female:														
Agricultural workers:														
Self-employed.........	-9.5	...	...	...	-12.3	-9.6	-12.2	...	-8.9	-9.7	-9.7	-9.5	-12.4	-11.1
Wage and salary or government.........	-4.7	-4.6	-3.6	-2.7	-2.8	-1.9	-3.2	-1.8	-8.2	-6.4	-10.2	-5.2	-7.2	-8.4
Unpaid family worker.........	...	...	...	...	-27.1	...	...	...	...	...	...	...	-8.3	-8.6
Nonagricultural workers:														
Private wage and salary and unpaid family worker....	27.2	24.6	26.9	26.2	37.7	26.7	32.0	20.6	23.0	27.2	26.8	24.3	28.1	29.4
Government worker....	-2.3	-2.8	-3.5	-6.8	-2.8	-1.8	-3.0	-5.3	2.6	-4.3	-.6	-1.3	-1.1	-2.0
Self-employed....	.8	-1.3	.9	.4	2.0	1.2	2.4	.8	1.1	.6	1.5	.8	1.0	.7
OCCUPATION														
Male, employed														
Prof., tech., and kindred workers.....	10.3	8.7	9.6	8.6	11.8	10.0	12.2	9.0	8.5	7.8	10.2	11.3	11.2	11.5
Engineers, technical....	2.2	1.7	1.9	2.1	2.1	1.8	2.4	2.0	1.6	1.4	2.0	2.3	2.7	3.0
Medical and other health workers:														
Salaried....	...	.6	.5	.4	...	...	...	...	.7	.6	...	.5	.5	.6
Self-employed....	.7	.7	.8	.6	...	.6	.9	.7	.7	.6	.7	.7	.7	.6
Teachers, elem. & second. schools....	.5	.3	.5	.2	.9	.6	.9	.1	.5	.3	.5	.7	.8	.6
Other profess'l, etc.: Salaried....	5.5	4.9	5.1	4.6	6.5	5.4	6.4	4.9	4.5	4.1	5.7	6.3	5.6	6.0
Self-employed....	.9	.7	.7	.6	.8	.7	.7	.6	.4	.6	.7	.7	.7	.7
Farmers and farm managers.....	-52.6	-41.1	-47.7	-41.5	-57.7	-65.3	-67.4	-48.3	-46.2	-39.7	-45.8	-49.9	-42.8	-38.8
Mgrs., off'ls, & propr's, exc. farm....	9.2	6.4	7.1	6.3	10.9	10.0	12.9	8.8	10.4	8.8	11.8	11.7	9.8	8.0
Salaried.....	6.5	5.0	5.1	4.8	7.6	6.8	8.2	6.4	7.3	6.1	7.1	7.6	7.0	5.7
Self-employed: Retail trade....	1.3	.8	1.6	.9	1.7	1.6	2.1	1.3	1.5	1.2	2.0	1.8	1.5	1.1
Other than retail....	1.5	.6	.7	.7	1.5	1.5	2.6	1.2	1.6	1.5	2.7	2.3	1.3	1.2
Clerical and kindred workers.....	6.7	7.5	6.4	5.9	7.0	6.4	6.7	6.1	5.2	5.0	5.6	5.5	5.2	6.0
Sales workers....	6.4	5.1	5.1	5.5	7.0	7.2	7.9	6.5	7.0	6.0	7.2	5.8	6.9	6.4
Retail trade....	2.2	1.8	2.6	1.7	2.5	2.7	3.1	2.2	2.2	2.0	2.5	5.8	2.3	2.3
Other than retail trade....	4.2	3.3	3.5	3.7	5.2	4.9	4.8	4.3	4.8	4.0	4.7	3.5	4.6	4.0
Craftsmen, foremen, & kindred wkrs....	13.2	10.2	13.2	9.6	14.6	15.2	16.9	10.7	11.0	11.1	12.1	14.4	11.4	13.8
Construction craftsmen....	2.5	1.4	2.3	1.0	2.6	3.1	4.4	1.2	2.0	3.2	2.9	4.2	2.6	3.5
Foremen (n.e.c.)....	2.0	1.6	2.3	1.8	3.4	2.5	2.2	2.0	1.5	1.2	1.7	1.8	1.4	1.6
Mechanics and repairmen....	3.2	2.6	2.8	1.9	3.5	3.8	4.8	2.9	3.1	3.2	3.9	3.7	3.0	3.1
Metal craftsmen, except mechanics....	2.1	1.7	2.1	2.1	2.2	2.3	1.6	1.6	1.0	.9	.9	1.1	1.4	2.5
Other craftsmen....	3.3	3.1	3.6	2.7	4.0	3.5	3.8	1.6	2.9	2.5	2.7	3.6	3.0	3.2
Operatives and kindred workers....	9.6	9.3	11.9	6.4	10.6	14.0	12.4	7.5	9.6	6.0	5.8	9.1	5.8	9.5
Drivers and deliverymen....	1.7	1.4	1.4	1.0	2.2	3.1	3.7	1.6	2.4	1.0	.7	2.4	1.2	.8
Other operatives, etc.:														
Durable goods manufacturing....	3.7	3.2	6.6	3.8	2.8	5.6	2.4	2.4	1.3	1.1	1.6	1.0	1.5	4.7
Nondurable goods manufacturing....	1.8	2.6	3.7	.7	2.1	2.6	1.8	1.8	3.1	1.5	1.1	.7	.8	1.3
Nonmanufacturing industries....	2.5	2.0	2.4	.9	3.3	3.1	4.5	1.8	2.8	2.4	3.7	5.1	2.4	2.7

Table 15-20 (Continued)

Subject	U.S. Total	1	2	3	4	5	6	7	8	9	10	11	12	13
Private household workers	5.8	—	...	...	...	...	...	...	.2	.1	.1	...	...	...
Service wkrs., exc. priv. household	5.8	6.6	5.5	4.5	5.5	5.8	5.8	5.4	5.7	5.7	5.5	6.4	4.8	5.2
Protective service workers	1.5	1.7	1.6	1.3	1.2	1.6	1.3	1.3	1.2	1.1	1.1	1.3	1.0	1.3
Waiters, bartenders, cooks, etc.	1.3	1.7	1.2	.9	1.1	1.0	1.0	1.0	.8	1.3	1.0	1.2	1.0	1.2
Other service workers	3.1	3.1	2.6	2.2	3.1	3.4	3.6	3.2	3.7	3.5	3.5	3.9	2.7	2.8
Farm laborers and farm foremen	-14.5	-16.5	-16.5	-10.6	-14.2	-10.6	-14.6	-10.7	-17.4	-18.6	-19.4	18.7	-15.0	-27.6
Laborers, except farm and mine	2.7	1.1	1.8	2.1	2.2	4.3	4.6	1.4	3.2	4.0	3.7	2.9	.9	3.3
Construction	.4	.1	.1	—	.1	.6	.9	.2	.6	1.0	.9	.6	.8	.7
Manufacturing	.3	.1	.6	1.0	—	1.4	.8	.1	.1	.3	.3	.1	.1	.5
Other industries	2.1	1.1	1.1	1.4	2.1	2.4	2.8	1.9	2.6	3.0	2.6	2.2	2.2	2.1
Occupation not reported	3.1	2.9	2.5	2.9	2.0	3.0	2.3	3.2	2.6	3.3	3.1	1.5	1.9	2.5
Female, employed														
Prof., tech., and kindred workers	1.2	.6	.5	2.0	6.6	.4	.2	.1	3.9	.7	2.4	.9	2.5	2.2
Medical and other health workers:														
Salaried	1.7	1.1	1.5	.8	3.3	1.5	2.2	2.1	2.2	1.4	1.4	1.5	2.2	1.5
Self-employed	.3	.2	.2	.1	.3	.1	.2	.2	.2	.3	.1	—	—	.3
Teachers, elem., & second. schools	3.1	2.5	2.3	4.6	.4	3.8	4.3	4.6	.9	2.5	1.6	2.0	2.0	1.7
Other profess'l, etc.: Salaried	2.2	1.6	1.2	1.6	3.2	1.9	2.2	1.9	2.0	1.5	2.1	1.6	2.2	2.1
Self-empl.	.1	.1	...	...	.3	.1	.3	.2	.3	.1	.3	.2	.2	—
Farmers and farm managers	-9.4	...	...	...	...	-9.5	-12.0	...	-8.9	-9.5	-9.5	-9.2	-12.2	-10.7
Mgrs., off'ls, & propr's, exc. farm	1.6	.7	.7	1.1	2.3	2.0	2.7	1.0	1.5	1.0	1.8	1.9	1.9	1.6
Salaried	1.3	1.0	.6	.9	1.6	1.3	1.6	.7	1.2	.7	1.2	1.4	1.5	1.7
Self-employed: Retail trade	.2	—	.2	.2	.4	.4	.5	.1	.1	.1	.1	.4	.1	.1
Other than retail	.1	.2	.2	.1	.3	.3	.7	.2	.2	.3	.4	.1	.4	.6
Clerical and kindred workers	16.9	14.4	11.3	13.2	19.6	13.2	18.1	15.4	14.4	11.8	15.9	14.0	15.7	13.5
Secretaries, stenographers, and typists	6.7	5.5	3.7	4.8	7.1	5.0	7.5	6.2	5.7	4.7	7.0	6.0	6.5	5.7
Other clerical workers	10.2	8.9	7.6	8.4	12.5	8.3	10.6	9.2	8.7	7.2	8.8	8.0	9.2	7.9
Sales workers	2.4	1.9	4.3	3.0	5.5	3.0	3.5	1.8	1.4	1.4	1.5	1.9	2.8	2.4
Retail trade	1.8	1.7	3.3	2.6	4.8	2.4	2.7	1.2	.8	.8	.8	1.6	2.4	1.9
Other than retail trade	.6	.2	.3	.5	.7	.6	.7	.6	.4	.6	.7	.4	.5	.6
Craftsmen, foreman, & kindred wkrs	.4	.4	.7	.2	.6	.3	.5	.4	.4	.4	.2	.4	.4	.4
Operatives and kindred workers	.6	1.9	5.8	1.2	1.5	3.1	2.2	8.9	4.8	3.3	2.1	1.9	1.8	3.2
Durable goods manufacturing	1.5	2.3	1.0	.4	.3	1.2	.5	.1	.1	.3	.3	.2	.1	3.4
Nondurable goods manufacturing	2.6	.4	4.6	.4	.2	.6	.6	9.9	6.0	3.2	3.5	1.1	.1	—
Nonmanufacturing industries	.4	.1	.2	.6	1.1	1.2	1.2	1.1	1.2	.4	1.1	.9	2.2	1.0
Private household workers	-1.3	-4.2	3.9	2.1	.4	.3	.3	1.5	2.9	2.3	1.9	4.5	.7	2.1
Service wkrs., exc. priv. household	2.9	1.7	2.4	1.9	5.4	4.0	4.2	3.9	6.2	5.6	4.4	4.5	5.0	1.7
Waiters, bartenders, cooks, etc.	.2	.1	1.7	.3	1.6	.7	.7	1.9	1.9	4.2	3.7	3.8	3.0	1.6
Other service workers	2.8	1.7	1.7	1.6	3.8	3.3	4.3	3.9	4.3	4.4	3.7	3.8	3.0	2.0
Farm laborers and farm foremen	-15.3	-12.2	-14.0	-10.4	-29.8	-16.1	-18.0	-7.1	-17.4	-12.1	-17.0	-12.1	-14.3	-13.6
Laborers, except farm and mine	.2	.1	.7	.2	.1	.3	.2	.2	.7	.6	.6	.2	.2	.2
Occupation not reported	1.3	2.3	1.3	2.0	1.1	.3	1.1	1.1	.7	1.8	.6	.7	.9	1.5
Nonwhite														
Percent male of emp. nonwhites	-17.1	-13.6	-12.8	-7.7	1.1	-17.0	-25.0	-15.2	-20.8	-16.3	-24.5	-17.8	-15.5	10.2
Percent of all employed males	1.2	2.9	2.1	9.0	.9	5.1	2.2	8.0	-9.4	6.1	-6.2	-1.2	1.4	.3
Prof., tech., and kindred workers	.6	1.8	.6	2.5	...	1.8	.6	2.7	-2.6	2.1	-1.8	2.9	1.7	1.9
Engineers, technical	1.1	...	...	...	...	...	...	...	-1.1	...	...	...	1.5	1.3
Medical and other health workers:														
Salaried	4.8	...	-1.2	6.4	...	.7	.7	5.5	-1.1	...	5.5	.7	-15.5	-10.9
Self-employed	1.4	.9	.1	...	...	...	5.2	1.3	16.6	12.3	8.1	.9	.9	3.4
Teachers, elem. & second. schools	1.9	.7	.7	...	...	1.8	.5	9.3	16.6	3.1	.5	6.7	1.4	2.4
Other profess'l, etc.: Salaried	1.2	2.0	.7	2.2	...	1.8	.6	2.4	6.6	6.4	.5	6.7	1.4	2.5
Self-empl.	1.3	1.5	.1	2.6	.1	.7	.6	3.2	-7.0	6.4	4.1	1.1	5.6	20.7

Table 15-20 (Continued)

Subject	U.S. Total	Region 1	2	3	4	5	6	7	8	9	10	11	12	13
Farmers and farm managers	6.2	1.5	.1	2.6	.1	.7	.6	3.2	- 7.0	6.4	- 4.1	1.1	5.6	20.7
Mgrs., off'ls, & propr's, exc. farm	1.1	1.8	...	1.6	...	.8	.1	1.3	.1	.5	.3	...	1.0	.1
Salaried	1.0	2.0	...	1.2	...	...	.4	1.0	...	.8	.4	.7	...	.8
Self-employed: Retail trade	1.9	1.1	...	2.1	...	.8	...	1.6	2.4	2.1	2.5	1.2	2.8	2.9
Other than retail	1.6	2.3	...	3.0	...	...	.6	2.5	.3	...	.5	.3	1.9	.9
Clerical and kindred workers	5.7	6.7	...	7.6	.7	3.9	1.2	6.0	6.4	6.6	2.4	2.8	.7	- 2.4
Sales workers	.8	...	.2	2.1	.1	.7	.4	1.0	1.0	.4	.6	2.3	.7	.6
Retail trade	1.5	.5	...	...	.2	.9	.4	1.6	1.5	.2	.5	3.5	.9	2.8
Other than retail trade	.7	...	.1	1.6	...	.5	...	.7	.7	.1	.2	.3	.6	1.6
Craftsmen, foremen, & kindred wkrs	2.2	2.6	1.2	4.7	.3	2.6	1.2	3.7	3.5	3.9	.7	- 1.0	.4	.7
Construction craftsmen	2.7	1.2	.8	4.3	...	2.7	.9	4.8	10.9	6.4	2.9	- 1.1	.3	.7
Foremen (n.e.c.)	1.3	2.0	...	1.7	...	4.1	...	1.1	.6	.4	.1	- 2.6	.5	1.4
Mechanics and repairmen	3.7	5.2	1.7	7.1	.7	4.1	1.8	5.3	3.3	4.2	.9	.9	.8	.5
Metal craftsmen, except mechanics	2.8	2.5	2.0	4.8	.2	2.8	1.2	3.9	3.1	2.2	2.7	- 1.0	...	.3
Other craftsmen	2.2	2.2	...	4.6	.7	1.6	1.2	2.4	2.2	2.9	1.5	- 2.7	1.4	2.0
Operatives and kindred workers	4.5	- 4.5	2.7	12.2	.4	5.6	2.4	9.0	9.0	10.6	- 4.5	.5	.2	2.8
Drivers and deliverymen	1.9	3.8	1.8	10.8	.4	5.2	1.5	10.5	9.6	16.0	-10.9	.5	...	2.5
Other operatives, etc.:														
Durable goods manufacturing	5.2	4.8	4.4	12.4	1.0	5.1	3.2	7.5	7.7	.6	3.0	- 1.3	2.5	2.5
Nondurable goods manufacturing	6.2	3.1	1.6	13.7	...	7.3	4.1	7.6	8.8	8.2	4.1	1.2	.9	3.4
Nonmanufacturing industries	7.2	8.3	2.2	12.1	...	5.7	2.2	10.3	12.0	11.8	5.6	- 6.7	1.7	4.6
Private household workers	14.7	10.4	4.3	32.6	...	24.2	2.2	41.5	9.6	11.8	13.2	-12.7	10.9	41.1
Service wkrs., exc. priv. household	11.4	8.8	...	18.7	.8	15.5	9.4	27.7	19.7	23.9	22.2	.5	8.7	11.6
Protective service workers	2.7	5.8	...	...	...	4.9	...	3.7	...	2.1	2.6	- 9.9	15.7	3.2
Waiters, bartenders, cooks, etc.	9.0	3.1	...	...	.3	10.8	13.3	23.5	16.8	17.4	26.6	.1	9.6	8.0
Other service workers	16.4	11.9	...	27.0	.7	21.5	13.2	38.3	22.6	30.4	27.0	4.6	9.6	16.7
Farm laborers and foremen	.5	- 2.3	1.2	- 6.3	.7	3.1	2.1	15.4	2.6	25.9	- 6.3	- .4	2.1	5.1
Laborers, except farm and mine	10.6	5.2	8.1	22.6	1.5	14.2	6.5	29.8	16.8	20.3	15.9	- 9.3	3.9	8.5
Construction	16.8	10.8	9.8	...	1.9	17.1	8.3	33.1	21.2	29.4	22.2	-22.3	7.4	8.9
Manufacturing	6.9	1.6	10.8	22.9	1.0	13.4	4.3	27.1	14.7	10.0	16.8	1.4	3.2	3.2
Other industries	10.6	4.1	4.4	20.5	2.0	13.6	6.3	28.7	15.9	23.9	12.4	- 8.9	2.0	10.2
Occupation not reported	9.7	10.1	5.4	22.0	...	11.5	5.0	15.9	- 1.5	13.0	2.3	- 7.1	6.3	4.7
Percent fem. of emp. nonwhites	17.1	13.6	12.8	7.7	1.1	17.0	25.0	15.2	20.8	16.3	24.5	17.8	15.5	10.2
Percent of all employed females	2.5	5.3	2.2	10.6	.9	6.4	3.3	10.8	- 2.8	9.5	- 2.5	- 1.6	1.8	- 1.6
Prof., tech., and kindred workers	3.0	4.5	1.0	6.1	.8	2.8	1.5	7.1	1.4	3.6	.5	.2	1.5	2.6
Medical and other health workers:														
Salaried	6.1	10.7	...	7.5	...	3.2	1.2	6.8	4.8	6.5	3.9	.8	2.5	3.5
Self-employed	3.0	1.7	...	...	.3	2.6	1.6	9.3	9.6	8.0	1.5	.8	1.0	5.3
Teachers, elem, & second, schools	3.6	5.3	.9	5.0	...	3.0	.7	5.1	3.8	2.1	4.5	- 1.7	.9	2.9
Other profess'l, etc.: Salaried	2.0	...	...	...	...	...	...	...	.8	...	...	.8	.9	1.7
Self-employed	3.2	3.7	1.5	3.4	...	3.0	.6	4.9	-14.7	3.4	-14.7	- 5.7	8.1	10.3
Farmers and farm managers	1.9	.6	...	3.6	...	1.5	...	1.8	1.8	5.4	2.6	1.6	1.6	.1
Mgrs., off'ls, & propr's, exc. farm	2.1	...	...	...	...	.7	.6	2.8	2.0	...	1.6	.5	1.1	.2
Salaried	2.6	- 8.4	...	3.9	...	...	.6	4.2	6.0	10.6	1.6	.5	2.9	.2
Self-employed:Retail trade	3.1	5.2	.7	3.7	.4	...	1.8	3.3	4.6	...	.6	4.5	2.0	4.5
Other than retail	2.4	4.4	.6	3.3	...	2.3	.8	2.2	1.9	1.6	.7	- 1.1	.7	.9
Clerical and kindred workers	3.3	5.2	...	4.3	.4	2.3	.3	1.6	1.3	.8	.3	- 1.5	1.4	- 3.5
Secretaries, steno's & typists	2.4	5.7	.7	4.8	.4	2.4	1.0	2.5	2.2	1.9	.9	- 1.3	1.4	2.7
Other clerical workers	3.7	3.2	.4	4.8	...	1.1	.5	1.8	.7	1.1	.5	- 1.3	.7	- 2.0
Sales workers	1.6	.4	.4	2.9	...	1.1	.5	1.6	.3	.5	.3	1.7	1.1	1.7
Retail trade	1.6	3.1	...	...	...	.6	...	...	2.1	...	.6	1.5	1.2	- 3.1
Other than retail trade	1.7	...	...	...	...	...	...	...	...	...	...	...	...	...

Table 15-20 (*Continued*)

| Subject | U.S. Total | \<13>Region | | | | | | | | | | | | |
		1	2	3	4	5	6	7	8	9	10	11	12	13
Craftsmen, foremen, & kindred wkrs.	5.8	5.8	...	8.5	...	3.2	...	4.6	8.7	9.7	4.7	4.4	2.9	1.7
Operatives and kindred workers	9.3	8.4	1.7	13.1	1.3	4.9	3.1	7.9	12.2	17.8	9.9	-2.5	4.2	3.6
Durable goods manufacturing	5.9	7.5	1.9	6.7	.9	2.5	-1.7	2.5	18.0	...	1.9	1.2	3.0	-26.2
Nondurable goods manufacturing	7.7	7.4	...	13.2	1.2	3.0	...	4.0	4.4	10.5	4.5	1.2	2.9	12.9
Nonmanufacturing industries	15.5	16.9	4.8	28.6	2.2	11.5	4.5	21.7	23.1	24.3	14.6	1.0	5.8	5.6
Private household workers	14.3	18.0	11.2	41.1	6.7	27.2	16.0	34.1	-4.9	26.1	6.5	7.4	6.0	19.6
Service wkrs., exc. priv. household	14.1	12.7	5.6	18.5	1.2	12.0	5.7	22.4	17.6	23.1	18.7	.8	4.8	8.9
Waiters, bartenders, cooks, etc.	7.3	3.5	2.1	8.6	.5	6.0	2.4	14.2	13.7	12.6	13.4	.4	1.3	4.0
Other service workers	18.2	17.4	7.7	24.9	1.8	16.6	8.2	27.2	19.6	30.0	22.1	.2	7.7	12.2
Farm laborers and farm foremen	17.7	10.1	2.1	7.3	...	1.9	1.8	11.9	16.7	40.2	9.5	2.3	6.0	.4
Laborers, except farm and mine	11.6	13.6	...	...	...	...	6.1	22.5	9.2	...	5.7	-32.6	4.6	14.2
Occupation not reported	12.0	15.4	5.2	21.8	1.2	12.4	6.1	18.4	5.3	13.3	6.1	-3.5	4.2	3.8
Employed Females as Percent of Total Employed														
Total	13.9	9.6	12.5	10.0	13.8	16.8	19.0	14.6	14.6	13.4	16.8	13.4	12.6	12.4
Prof., tech., and kindred workers	-27.5	-6.1	-24.8	-26.9	-32.3	-31.0	-37.2	-22.2	-20.7	-17.2	-24.1	-26.0	-22.6	21.2
Medical and other health workers	-18.9	-15.4	-19.8	-18.0	-25.6	-21.3	-24.1	-13.9	-15.6	-15.2	-21.1	-12.1	-7.0	-6.1
Teachers, elem. & second schools	-9.3	-8.2	-9.1	-9.0	-18.1	-12.6	-15.9	.1	-3.0	-2.0	-2.4	-8.1	-13.8	-10.3
Farmers and farm managers	2.0	4.0	1.3	4.1	.4	.3	...	1.4	8.4	2.2	-2.4	1.0	2.0	-.4
Mgrs., off'ls, & propr's exc. farm	-2.8	-1.4	-3.8	-2.8	-3.2	-1.5	-4.3	-3.9	-3.4	-1.9	-4.7	-6.4	-1.7	.4
Salaried	-4.6	.9	-5.3	-6.7	...	...	-7.0	-8.4	-3.5	-2.4	.6	...	-2.4	-1.5
Self-employed: Retail trade	-4.0	5.4	-5.4	2.0	-4.2	.2	6.3	3.0	3.5	3.9	5.8	-11.8	9.6	2.3
Other than retail	-3.8	-1.5	.7	.8	2.4	2.7	3.9	3.0	5.1	...	1.6	.2	-3.4	1.2
Clerical and kindred workers	-3.8	9.6	9.2	-5.4	-7.6	-6.6	-5.6	2.1	5.1	12.8	2.5	-8.0	-3.4	-9.2
Sales workers	-13.7	7.2	6.3	-12.0	-14.2	-15.1	-23.1	-11.2	-14.0	-12.3	-17.9	-18.2	-13.7	-12.4
Retail trade	-5.1	-1.6	2.6	-4.1	-4.9	-8.7	-14.1	-1.2	-2.3	-5.2	-10.2	-10.2	-5.3	-8.8
Other than retail trade	-5.4	7.2	6.4	7.4	-6.0	-4.6	-11.0	-2.4	5.0	6.4	6.3	-13.4	-12.3	8.7
Craftsmen, foremen, & kindred wkrs.	.1	.3	.6	.6	.2	-.5	-.4	-4.1	.3	.7	4.2	-.1	.1	.1
Operatives and kindred workers	.3	-2.4	3.8	4.5	2.3	1.0	1.4	4.1	3.8	1.7	4.2	-4.6	-.1	1.8
Durable goods manufacturing	5.6	5.3	.5	3.2	3.5	1.3	...	3.3	3.1	6.9	5.7	4.6	5.6	11.1
Nondurable goods manufacturing	-7.7	-6.9	-.6	6.4	.8	-4.3	6.0	-13.9	3.8	10.5	-13.7	4.6	3.8	6.1
Nonmanufacturing industries	2.5	-7.1	-3.6	8.2	.8	2.7	1.4	11.0	-1.2	1.0	5.3	8.8	-14.9	-12.0
Private household workers	-1.0	-3.2	.5	-.7	-1.5	-1.3	.9	-2.1	.8	.3	1.2	1.2	-.7	-1.6
Service wkrs., exc. priv. household	-19.6	-24.8	-16.3	-15.1	-17.0	-20.0	-22.4	-12.9	-7.2	-10.9	-12.6	-19.7	-7.5	-17.6
Waiters, bartenders, cooks, etc.	-23.8	-36.5	-21.2	-20.5	-14.5	-16.0	-16.0	-18.3	-11.5	-16.7	-13.5	-17.0	-12.8	-17.3
Farm laborers and farm foremen	-7.3	-6.9	-10.3	-4.1	-23.0	-16.3	9.9	-7.9	4.6	9.6	-5.9	6.5	-3.3	-1.1
Laborers, except farm and mine	.4	-1.6	...	-.6	.7	.6	.2	.6	1.2	.3	1.4	.8	-.1	2.1
Occupation not reported	.4	3.7	3.6	2.8	5.2	1.1	4.0	1.3	.7	3.4	1.4	.3	2.3	6.2
INDUSTRY														
Total employed	-59.2	-69.1	-55.2	-45.0	-65.9	-66.7	-74.6	-50.4	-54.8	-52.8	-62.0	-61.0	-51.9	-60.7
Agriculture	-.1	-.2	-.2	...	-.5	...	1.8	-.8	.2	.5	1.6	2.5	.1	...
Forestry and fisheries	-.1	-.1	.2	...	.7	...	...	.1	.1	.2	...	...	.1	..
Mining	1.8	.4	1.0	.2	2.6	2.8	4.6	.1	1.7	3.1	3.0	3.9	2.1	3.2
Manufacturing	16.2	15.4	21.0	16.1	15.4	19.5	13.9	11.9	10.2	7.1	9.1	6.5	8.1	18.3
Furniture & lumber & wood prod.	.9	.7	.9	-.3	-.5	.4	.9	-1.7	.8	.3	.6	.8	.3	.3
Primary metal industries	1.6	.7	1.7	3.5	.5	1.0	.9	.9	1.2	.3	.1	1.0	.5	.9
Fabricated metal industries (including not specified metal)	1.6	1.3	1.1	1.6	1.5	1.8	1.8	1.3	.6	.9	.5	.9	.7	2.8
Machinery, except electrical	1.7	1.3	2.0	1.9	2.7	3.3	1.0	1.4	.6	.7	1.0	.4	.7	1.4
Elect. mach., equip., & supplies	1.9	2.3	2.9	2.1	.9	2.3	.4	1.1	.5	...	.8	...	.4	2.5

Table 15-20 *(Continued)*

Subject	U.S. Total	1	2	3	4	5	6	7	8	9	10	11	12	13
Motor vehicles & motor veh. equip...	.9	.2	.9	1.9	.5	1.0	...	.7	.2	...	.2	...	.2	.4
Trans. equip., exc. motor vehicle...	1.3	1.1	.7	.1	—	.5	2.2	1.1	.4	.5	1.6	.4	4.3	3.7
Other durable goods...	1.5	1.9	2.4	.7	2.3	1.3	.9	1.1	.7	.7	.8	.6	.5	1.5
Food and kindred products...	1.3	.9	1.3	1.0	1.5	3.1	2.3	1.8	1.5	1.1	1.8	.6	.5	.1
Textile mill products...	.2	.6	1.3	.1	.2	.1	...	.1	3.7	.1	.1	.1	.2	...
Apparel & oth. fab'd textile prod...	.4	1.9	1.9	.3	.4	.3	.2	1.2	1.4	.2	.1	.5	.4	1.0
Print., publishing & allied prod...	1.8	2.1	1.7	2.0	2.4	2.0	1.5	1.8	1.1	1.0	1.3	1.1	1.3	1.5
Chemical and allied products...	1.0	.9	1.0	.5	.4	.7	.5	2.2	.8	1.0	.4	.4	.6	.6
Other nondurable goods(including not specified manufacturing)...	1.7	1.5	3.4	1.0	2.5	1.7	1.9	1.4	1.5	1.7	.9	.8	1.0	1.5
Railroad & railway express service...	1.2	.7	1.6	1.2	2.1	1.9	2.0	1.9	1.1	.9	1.1	2.2	1.3	.8
Trucking service and warehousing...	1.0	.4	.4	.4	.7	.9	1.4	.9	1.0	.8	.8	.8	.5	.5
Other transportation...	1.0	1.4	.2	.9	.8	.5	1.0	.1	.2	1.6	.3	.3	1.2	.8
Communications...	1.1	.8	1.4	.9	1.2	1.1	1.5	1.1	1.1	1.0	1.2	1.5	1.3	1.3
Utilities and sanitary services...	1.1	.8	1.0	.8	1.2	1.3	1.5	1.1	1.1	.9	1.4	.9	.8	.5
Wholesale trade...	2.7	2.5	1.9	2.0	3.5	2.5	3.5	2.7	2.9	2.9	3.3	2.2	2.8	2.2
Food and dairy products stores...	1.5	1.4	1.4	1.4	2.1	1.9	2.1	1.3	1.1	1.2	1.4	2.0	1.6	1.3
Eating and drinking places...	2.1	1.7	1.8	1.6	2.1	2.2	2.6	2.0	1.9	2.6	2.3	2.6	2.3	2.1
Other retail trade...	6.5	4.0	6.2	5.0	8.4	8.1	10.1	6.5	7.3	7.0	8.7	8.1	7.2	6.1
Finance, insurance, & real estate...	3.9	4.1	2.3	2.9	3.9	3.5	4.2	4.2	3.8	4.0	4.0	3.8	3.8	3.8
Business services...	1.2	1.6	.6	1.2	1.0	.8	.9	.8	.7	1.1	.9	1.6	.9	1.7
Repair services...	.7	.6	.5	.5	.9	.9	1.3	.6	.6	1.0	1.2	1.1	.9	.9
Private household...	1.0	— .8	— .3	.1	.9	1.2	1.6	1.8	3.5	2.5	2.8	1.3	.9	.5
Other personal services...	2.6	2.2	2.0	2.1	2.4	2.7	3.6	2.7	3.0	3.7	3.4	4.0	2.4	2.2
Entertainment & recreation services...	.7	.5	.5	.4	.6	.6	.8	.6	.6	.8	.7	1.4	.7	1.2
Educational services:														
Government...	1.1	.1	—	.3	2.9	2.1	2.7	.3	2.0	.5	2.3	2.5	2.2	1.4
Private...	1.1	1.0	1.3	.9	1.4	1.0	1.0	1.1	1.0	.9	1.0	.8	.7	.9
Welfare, religious, and nonprofit membership organizations...	1.1	.9	1.1	.9	1.5	1.3	1.4	1.3	1.2	.8	1.3	1.0	1.2	.8
Hospitals...	2.0	1.8	2.2	1.4	3.1	2.4	2.8	2.5	2.2	1.6	1.9	1.9	2.1	1.6
Other profess'l & related services...	2.3	1.8	1.8	1.5	2.3	2.1	2.7	2.0	2.0	2.1	2.2	2.4	2.3	2.3
Public administration...	3.6	3.5	2.9	2.1	3.5	3.4	4.2	2.3	3.1	3.0	3.5	5.4	3.3	3.9
Industry not reported...	2.4	2.6	1.7	2.4	1.3	1.8	1.4	2.3	1.7	2.5	2.1	.6	1.4	2.0
PLACE OF WORK OF THE WORKERS														
Worked outside county of residence:														
White...	5.1	17.8	— 1.5	— 5.9	3.8	.6	7.4	3.3	— 1.4	3.2	2.4	.9	.3	2.9
Nonwhite...	2.2	5.6	— 4.2	-13.7	— 5.4	— 5.6	1.0	.8	— 1.4	— 6.6	.1	— 3.5	— 2.8	2.0
Place of work not reported:														
White...	.8	1.0	.6	.2	.2	.9	.5	.4	.4	1.2	.2	.4	...	.9
Nonwhite...	4.2	5.5	3.1	3.2	9.1	3.6	.8	4.0	.7	1.9	1.3	6.4	2.3	2.8
MEANS OF TRANSPORTATION TO WORK														
Private automobile or car pool...	29.2	6.7	27.2	15.7	41.1	44.6	54.0	27.3	30.5	26.1	39.2	39.7	29.2	28.7
Railway, subway, or elevated...	5.3	17.4	.1	4.0	.1	.1	...	11.3	9.2	9.6	5.3	4.3	8.3	8.3
Bus or streetcar...	10.9	13.7	9.9	15.5	8.9	7.2	4.5	6.1	1.4	2.6	1.5	4.3	2.9	2.0
Walked to work...	4.5	4.9	13.2	7.6	12.6	10.2	5.5	4.0	2.6	1.4	1.7	1.5	1.1	1.5
Other means...	-.4	-.8	-.2	.9	.9	1.5	-1.2	-1.3	-1.3	-2.0	-1.7	-1.5	-1.1	-1.5
Worked at home...	-49.6	-41.8	-50.6	-42.2	-63.6	-63.1	-63.9	-44.9	-41.0	-31.2	-41.2	-45.5	-40.3	-34.0
Not reported...	1.4	1.8	.9	1.5	.6	1.2	1.0	1.1	.7	1.7	.8	.5	.4	1.1

Table 15-20 (Continued)

Subject	U.S. Total	Region												
		1	2	3	4	5	6	7	8	9	10	11	12	13
MEDIAN EARNINGS BY OCCUPATION (DOLLARS)														
Male, total............	2,728	2,106	1,909	2,066	2,796	2,390	2,096	2,749	2,341	2,049	2,455	1,869	1,160	1,920
Prof., managerial, and kindred wkrs.....	1,977	587	1,187	1,659	2,205	1,261	1,616	2,453	2,196	1,621	1,789	1,121	764	730
Farmers and farm managers............	1,252	720	538	866	902	580	1,375	662	760	1,301	1,375	1,210	197	044
Craftsmen, foremen, & kindred wkrs.....	1,562	1,064	830	899	1,481	1,020	1,296	1,859	1,150	825	1,245	737	538	976
Operatives and kindred workers.........	1,382	867	537	639	1,074	772	1,183	1,446	815	1,076	1,561	672	391	1,215
Farm laborers, except unpaid..........	302	7	446	643	485	75	- 415	175	134	- 139	511	- 665	- 466	-1,083
Laborers, except farm and mine........	1,120	1,215	612	734	797	366	398	1,013	674	718	511	- 191	- 118	629
Female, total...........	1,002	853	553	791	912	714	896	555	729	611	828	846	1,107	1,226
Clerical and kindred workers..........	874	626	494	712	686	627	988	659	511	582	663	821	703	821
Operatives and kindred workers........	451	350	237	492	634	456	774	330	172	231	242	642	1,076	1,163
Ratio to United States Median														
Male, total............	.59	.46	.42	.45	.61	.52	.46	.60	.51	.44	.53	.40	.37	.42
Prof., managerial, and kindred wkrs.....	.29	.09	.18	.25	.33	.13	.24	.37	.33	.24	.27	.17	.11	.11
Farmers and farm managers............	.59	.34	.25	.40	.42	.27	.64	.31	.36	.16	.64	.56	.10	.02
Craftsmen, foremen, & kindred wkrs.....	.30	.20	.16	.17	.28	.20	.25	.36	.22	.16	.24	.14	.10	.19
Operatives and kindred workers.........	.33	.21	.13	.15	.25	.18	.28	.34	.19	.25	.36	.15	.10	.28
Farm laborers, except unpaid..........	.27	.69	.41	.58	.44	.06	.37	.16	.13	.12	.02	.60	- .42	.98
Laborers, except farm and mine........	.38	.42	.21	.25	.27	.12	.14	.34	.23	.24	.18	.07	- .04	.21
Female, total...........	.45	.38	.25	.35	.41	.32	.40	.25	.33	.27	.37	.38	.49	.55
Clerical and kindred workers..........	.29	.20	.16	.23	.23	.21	.32	.22	.17	.19	.22	.27	.24	.27
Operatives and kindred workers........	.20	.16	.11	.22	.28	.18	.34	.14	.08	.10	.11	.29	.48	.51
FAMILY INCOME														
White families..........														
Under $1,00 (incl. none or loss)......	- 9.9	- 5.7	- 5.5	- 5.7	- 7.4	- 9.6	- 6.6	-13.7	-14.8	- 9.4	-10.5	- 3.6	- 3.5	- 3.8
$1,000 to $2,999.......	-20.2	-13.4	-13.7	-14.7	-21.8	-19.1	-16.0	-22.9	-21.6	-15.5	-21.0	-12.4	- 8.2	- 7.4
$3,000 to $3,999.......	- 5.5	- 5.4	- 4.2	- 5.9	- 7.2	- 5.6	- 5.4	- 3.3	- 2.0	- 1.4	- 2.0	- 5.3	- 4.9	- 6.6
$4,000 to $4,999.......	.7	- 1.7	.3	- 2.8	- 1.3	.1	.2	1.6	2.1	2.0	2.2	- 1.5	- 3.0	- 3.3
$5,000 to $5,999.......	4.1	2.9	4.0	1.3	5.5	5.3	...	6.1	5.6	3.7	5.1	2.7	1.1	.6
$6,000 to $6,999.......	5.8	4.4	4.7	4.1	7.1	6.5	5.7	6.7	6.2	4.5	5.7	4.3	3.0	3.6
$7,000 to $9,999.......	14.3	11.0	9.7	12.3	14.9	13.8	11.9	14.5	13.7	10.1	12.2	9.6	9.6	11.2
$10,000 and over.......	11.9	7.9	4.9	11.3	10.1	8.8	6.4	11.0	10.8	6.1	8.3	6.2	5.7	5.8
Nonwhite families.......														
Under $1,000 (incl. none or loss)......	-32.0	- 9.1	- 7.1	- 5.5	-10.3	- 6.1	- 5.7	-17.5	-29.5	-20.4	-27.8	-33.7	- 3.8	- 3.4
$1,000 to $2,999.......	-12.4	-22.7	-18.8	-12.5	-27.2	-13.4	-11.1	-13.0	3.2	- 8.8	1.1	1.6	- 9.1	- 7.4
$3,000 to $3,999.......	8.5	2.8	5.1	1.5	2.8	.3	2.4	6.6	10.0	9.9	10.6	7.6	1.9	2.6
$4,000 to $4,999.......	9.3	6.4	.7	.4	2.4	5.0	6.2	8.1	6.3	8.1	6.9	7.8	6.3	2.1
$5,000 to $5,999.......	7.9	5.9	6.0	5.7	9.6	4.6	4.1	5.2	3.9	4.2	3.8	6.3	.2	3.2
$6,000 to $6,999.......	5.5	4.9	5.5	.4	6.4	4.1	1.8	3.5	2.1	1.8	2.0	4.0	.4	3.1
$7,000 to $9,999.......	8.9	8.4	1.7	8.5	...	5.6	2.5	5.1	2.9	3.4	2.7	5.5	4.8	6.5
$10,000 and over.......	4.3	3.3	.9	1.5	5.4	1.7	.1	2.0	1.1	1.1	.8	.8	2.9	.4

Table 15-21 Differences in Social and Economic Characteristics between Urban and Rural Non-Farm Populations, by Economic Regions, United States: 1960

Subject	U.S. Total	Region 1	2	3	4	5	6	7	8	9	10	11	12	13
White:														
Native of native parentage	-13.6	-20.9	-14.7	-22.6	-1.4	-6.2	2.8	-13.2	-1.8	-6.0	5.7	.7	-4.8	-6.0
Native of for. or mixed parentage	7.6	10.2	9.1	7.9	1.3	.4	-2.4	3.5	.9	4.0	1.6	3.1	3.9	3.9
Foreign born	4.2	6.8	3.6	4.6	.7	.7	-.4	1.0	.4	2.2	.6	1.9	2.2	1.9
Nonwhite	1.8	4.0	2.0	10.2	.5	5.2	-.1	8.7	.4	.1	-7.9	-5.7	-1.5	.2
AGE														
White, all ages:														
Under 15 years	-3.7	-5.3	-4.4	-4.8	-2.0	-2.3	.4	-4.9	-2.8	-3.6	.8	...	-3.5	-2.1
15 to 19 years	-.8	.3	-.1	.8	.3	.1	.9	-1.5	-1.2	.8	.8	.1	.6	-1.8
20 to 24 years	-.2	.9	.4	.1	1.3	1.0	.9	.2	.4	.8	1.3	.5	.3	-1.9
25 to 34 years	.2	.1	.7	.7	1.1	.7	1.8	.7	1.3	.3	2.6	.6	.3	.2
35 to 44 years	1.1	1.1	.7	3.7	.2	.7	1.5	1.2	2.2	1.5	1.8	.6	.5	1.3
45 to 64 years	2.7	4.5	2.6	1.2	1.8	1.2	-.9	3.2	.3	2.6	-1.8	-1.1	2.0	1.6
65 years and over	.4	1.9	1.3	1.2	-1.8	-1.3	-2.5	1.3	.3	1.6	-3.1	-.6	2.3	1.6
Nonwhite, all ages:														
Under 15 years	-4.4	-3.3	8.7	5.7	7.1	9.1	-4.8	.9	-5.3	-3.1	-3.2	-5.9	-5.8	2.0
15 to 19 years	-2.4	-2.3	-3.6	-2.6	-1.7	-3.3	-1.9	-2.0	-1.8	1.8	-1.9	-2.1	-2.9	2.0
20 to 24 years	.1	.3	-2.1	-.2	2.1	-2.9	-1.8	.4	.1	.2	.8	...	-2.2	-1.4
25 to 34 years	3.1	2.4	-1.1	1.2	5.7	-.6	-.6	1.1	1.6	2.0	3.3	2.1	.7	1.6
35 to 44 years	3.4	2.8	.1	1.4	3.9	.7	2.5	1.7	2.1	2.5	2.3	2.8	4.7	3.3
45 to 64 years	2.0	2.0	-.2	-2.9	-.1	1.1	3.4	1.6	3.4	1.6	.6	3.0	4.6	-2.6
65 years and over	1.7	-1.3	-1.8	-2.6	-2.7	-2.0	1.0	1.2	.3	-1.4	-1.8	.1	1.0	-.9
DEPENDENCY RATIO														
Total: White	-.15	-.12	-.11	-.16	-.14	-.14	-.13	-.20	-.13	-.11	-.15	-.03	-.07	-.08
Total: Nonwhite	-.39	-.26	.11	.02	-.53	.14	-.27	-.18	-.38	-.30	-.39	-.39	-.33	-.04
Youth: White	-.14	-.15	-.12	-.17	-.09	-.09	-.06	-.20	-.12	-.13	-.07	-.01	-.11	-.10
Old Age: White	...	.03	.01	.01	-.05	-.05	-.07	...	...	.02	-.07	-.02	.04	.02
Old Age: Nonwhite	-.06	-.04	-.03	-.05	-.09	-.03	.01	-.04	-.04	-.05	-.08	-.02	...	-.02
SEX RATIO														
White, all ages	-8.9	-8.3	-8.4	-5.8	-8.9	-6.6	-8.8	-10.2	-11.9	-10.9	-7.9	-11.1	-15.1	-23.8
Under 15 years	-1.8	-1.7	-1.7	-2.1	-2.0	-1.1	-2.3	-2.0	-1.6	-2.5	-2.0	2.8	-2.8	-3.5
15 to 19 years	-18.4	-16.1	-12.3	-7.9	-15.9	-14.6	-21.7	-20.7	-33.1	-17.1	-25.9	-20.5	-30.6	-54.2
20 to 24 years	-21.9	-16.0	-6.2	-4.5	-5.2	-6.9	-30.0	-21.7	-40.2	-24.9	-30.8	-27.6	-55.6	-97.4
25 to 34 years	-2.1	-1.6	-2.7	2.7	-2.4	-.8	-2.3	.4	-5.0	-8.6	.1	8.3	-5.0	-18.8
35 to 44 years	-7.4	-9.2	-8.1	-4.7	-4.1	-6.9	-6.0	-6.5	-8.0	-9.9	2.7	-6.9	-10.2	-18.5
45 to 64 years	-11.0	-11.6	-13.3	-10.4	-12.8	-10.3	-9.4	-12.3	-10.4	-12.2	7.7	-15.5	-17.7	-20.4
65 years and over	-18.4	-10.6	-16.6	-17.0	-28.1	-14.4	-19.3	-25.1	-20.2	-24.0	-19.9	-26.6	-32.6	-38.0

517

Table 15-21 (*Continued*)

Subject	U.S. Total	Region												
		1	2	3	4	5	6	7	8	9	10	11	12	13
Nonwhite, all ages..............	-11.3	-19.5	-51.8	-37.3	1.2	-36.9	-18.0	-17.0	-10.1	-11.7	- 8.0	- 8.2	-16.0	-39.4
Under 15 years..............	- 1.9	- 2.3	- 4.8	- 8.9	...	- 2.6	- 3.3	- 1.3	- 2.3	- .8	- 1.8	- 3.4	- 2.5	- .9
15 to 19 years..............	-23.7	-31.6	-178.2	-64.7	-26.8	-37.1	-42.9	-35.5	-17.5	-15.4	-14.9	-29.8	-36.8	-60.8
20 to 24 years..............	-41.9	-49.8	-155.3	-116.4	4.9	-156.1	-94.4	-59.0	-24.2	-39.9	-24.4	-22.7	-109.2	-124.7
25 to 34 years..............	-16.9	-27.8	-68.4	-77.0	- 3.0	-91.2	-19.2	-25.3	-11.8	-27.1	- 6.9	-10.7	-26.9	-40.2
35 to 44 years..............	-10.8	-25.1	-64.1	-41.7	23.4	-42.9	-22.0	-19.1	-10.2	-17.8	- 4.6	- 8.1	-38.2	-34.8
45 to 64 years..............	- 7.4	-24.3	-41.4	-23.4	5.9	-24.8	- 7.4	-13.5	- 8.6	- 7.6	- 5.1	- 4.4	7.6	-94.2
65 years and over..........	-11.0	-20.7	- 6.5	-43.8	-20.2	-21.8	-14.5	-24.1	-12.1	-11.6	-14.3	3.7	30.7	-49.1
AVERAGE POPULATION PER HOUSEHOLD														
Total................	-.32	-.35	-.26	-.31	-.13	-.12	-.11	-.42	-.41	-.36	-.23	-.11	-.39	-.35
White................	-.30	-.34	-.28	-.36	-.11	-.15	-.08	-.46	-.31	-.33	-.11	-.04	-.35	-.35
Nonwhite.............	-.78	-.74	-.27	-.21	-1.16	-.18	-1.36	-.47	-.77	-.54	-.50	-1.02	-1.58	-.35
MOBILITY STATUS														
White:														
Same house in 1955 and 1960.........	.4	5.8	.7	- 2.1	- 3.5	2.7	- 6.2	- 3.5	- 1.4	3.5	- 6.4	- 1.8	3.7	8.8
Same county.........	1.4	.1	3.2	5.2	3.5	2.6	2.6	1.9	- 1.3	1.4	2.1	4.4	2.6	5.7
Different County:														
Different State.........	- 2.5	- 2.6	- 2.9	- 4.7	- 1.8	2.5	.4	.5	1.1	- 3.0	1.1	- .1	- .2	- .9
Different State or abroad.........	.6	- 3.1	- 1.0	1.5	1.8	2.6	3.2	1.1	1.7	- 1.9	3.1	- 4.5	- 2.4	- 8.8
Not reported.........	.3	- .1	.1	.3	.2	.3	.4	.6	.4	- .1	.5	1.9	- 4.0	5.7
Nonwhite:														
Same house in 1955 and 1960.........	9.1	-10.8	- 6.4	-13.3	-24.9	- 3.1	.7	-12.9	- 1.1	-11.9	- 7.0	-19.7	- 5.5	- 6.8
Same county.........	9.5	13.6	27.0	29.2	12.9	23.5	2.2	19.3	1.7	12.7	5.3	4.2	5.6	11.8
Different County:														
Different State.........	- 2.6	- 2.7	-16.1	-14.7	.2	-13.2	- 1.3	- 3.4	- 1.0	- 1.3	.7	2.6	- 2.4	- 4.4
Different State or abroad.........	2.3	- 1.1	- 4.6	- 1.2	12.2	- 7.2	- 2.9	- 2.9	.4	.6	1.0	12.9	2.3	.6
Not reported.........	1.1	.5	4.2	2.0	2.3	3.7	2.0	.8	.2	.5	1.0	.6	.3	.6
Standardized:														
White:														
Same house in 1955 and 1960.........	.1	4.3	.2	- 3.1	- 2.5	- 2.1	- 4.8	- 4.3	- 1.9	2.3	- 4.3	- 1.1	2.5	7.3
Same county.........	1.8	.6	3.6	5.7	3.1	2.5	1.9	2.3	1.1	1.9	1.2	4.1	3.2	6.2
Different county or abroad.........	- 1.6	- 4.9	- 3.4	2.7	.7	.2	2.9	2.0	3.0	4.2	3.1	3.0	5.8	-13.7
Nonwhite:														
Same house in 1955 and 1960.........	- 8.4	-10.5	- 6.7	-11.8	-22.3	- 3.3	- 1.9	-12.7	- 1.3	-11.4	- 5.6	-19.9	- 7.5	- 6.1
Same county.........	9.1	13.3	26.8	28.4	11.8	23.2	2.6	19.1	1.8	12.4	4.7	4.3	6.2	11.4
Different county or abroad.........	.7	- 2.8	-20.3	-16.6	-10.4	-19.9	.7	- 6.4	.6	- 1.0	1.1	15.6	1.1	- 5.2
Unstandardized, percent migrant:														
Total................	- 1.8	- 5.6	- 3.9	- 3.7	.2	.5	3.4	.4	1.7	- 4.0	4.8	- 1.4	- 6.1	-13.6
White................	- 1.8	- 5.7	- 3.8	- 3.2	.1	.1	3.7	1.6	2.7	- 4.9	4.2	- 2.6	- 6.4	-14.6
Nonwhite.............	- .3	- 2.7	-20.7	-15.9	12.0	-20.3	- 1.5	- 6.4	.7	.7	1.8	15.5	- .1	- 5.0
Ratio of migration to total mobility:														
Total................	-.040	-.082	-.091	-.104	-.028	-.030	-.008	-.018	.024	-.066	.034	-.051	-.077	-.151
White................	-.032	-.068	-.085	-.085	-.032	-.017	.011	.007	.038	-.052	.025	-.060	-.080	-.151
Nonwhite.............	-.054	-.135	-.385	-.381	.025	-.402	-.030	-.216	-.019	-.087	.003	.128	-.043	-.136

Table 15-21 *(Continued)*

Subject	U.S. Total	1	2	3	4	5	6	7	8	9	10	11	12	13
								Region						
COUNTRY OR ORIGIN														
Total foreign stock..........	- 4.1	-12.2	-10.5	- 2.7	.2	2.7	4.0	- 4.2	- 4.3	- 2.5	2.9	3.4	1.7	4.1
English-speaking Europe and Canada......	-10.5	- 5.1	- 5.9	5.1	.1	-13.8	- 8.3	.2	- 2.4	- 4.4	- 6.0	- 5.3	- 2.8	2.1
Scandinavian-German-French portion of Europe......	6.6	7.3	6.3	4.2	3.0	4.3	3.2	5.2	5.3	3.5	2.1	1.4	.1	7.1
Eastern Europe......	7.5	8.3	10.1	1.7		4.6	3.1	3.1	2.9	3.2	1.1	1.7	1.4	1.9
Southern Europe......	.2	1.5		1.0	.4	1.1	2.0	.4	1.1	.2	2.5	11.4	1.9	9.5
Spanish America......	.5	.4	.1	.9	.7	1.0	1.5	.8	.2	.4	1.8	.2	1.7	5.4
Asia......	.1	.3				.1	.3	.1	.5	.2	.1	.1	.2	.1
All other......	- .1	- .1				.1	.5	.2		.2	.1	.2	.1	.2
Not reported......	- .1	- .1				.1	.5	.2		.2	.1	.2		.2
STATE OF BIRTH														
Percent born in State of 1960 residence:														
Total......	-11.8	- 6.5	- 3.6	-13.1	- 4.5	- 7.9	- 8.5	- 9.8	- 8.7	- 7.2	- 8.3	- 4.4	- 1.6	- 2.1
White......	-10.1	- 4.3	- 2.7	-10.3	- 4.1	- 6.8	- 7.9	- 8.8	- 9.5	- 6.3	- 7.9	- 2.0	- .1	- 1.1
Nonwhite......	-15.5	-24.5	- 7.4	- 6.0	-36.3	- 4.2	-25.0	-13.9	- 6.9	-10.4	- 4.4	-35.4	-33.9	-10.9
YEAR MOVED INTO PRESENT HOUSE														
Total......	- 1.0	- 2.9	.3	1.8	1.7	2.1	2.6	.6	.1	2.0	4.4	.8	- 4.0	- 9.5
1959 to 1960......	.2	1.2	.6	.5	.4	.1	1.2	1.2	.4	.2	1.4	.2	.5	...
1957 to 1958......	2.9	1.1	.1	1.1	2.3	.3	2.9	2.5	2.3	5.4	1.3	2.4	3.4	7.3
1950 to 1956......														
Before 1950......	2.1	3.1	.5	3.5	4.4	2.3	6.8	4.3	2.6	3.0	7.0	3.4	1.1	2.2
CHILDREN EVER BORN														
Children ever born per 1,000 women ever married:														
White, 15 to 44 years old......	- 337	- 219	- 237	- 325	- 304	- 274	- 375	- 487	- 324	- 320	- 478	- 237	- 350	- 344
Standardized for age......	- 372	- 239	- 264	- 346	- 334	- 281	- 376	- 527	- 357	- 384	- 479	- 236	- 358	- 377
15 to 24 years old......	- 196	- 182	- 195	- 233	- 250	- 168	- 182	- 210	- 186	- 187	- 207	- 193	- 254	- 207
25 to 34 years old......	- 321	- 254	- 249	- 316	- 300	- 253	- 331	- 390	- 272	- 329	- 405	- 218	- 362	- 346
35 to 44 years old......	- 494	- 352	- 306	- 420	- 100	- 354	- 498	- 787	- 507	- 520	- 662	- 269	- 399	- 478
Nonwhite, 15 to 44 years old......	-1090	- 729	- 124	- 492	-1622	- 237	-1156	- 667	- 931	- 978	-1103	-1063	-1125	- 631
Standardized for age......	-1162	- 754	- 155	- 466	-1758	- 205	-1286	- 669	-1002	-1043	-1150	-1224	-1376	- 682
15 to 24 years old......	- 270	- 346	49	75	- 590	186	- 131	15	- 198	- 270	- 280	- 328	- 265	- 284
25 to 34 years old......	-1001	- 708	65	- 426	-1644	50	- 881	- 435	- 856	- 926	-1040	- 992	-1038	- 448
35 to 44 years old......	-1689	- 970	- 440	- 671	-2362	- 512	-2148	-1172	-1480	-1479	-1622	-1820	-2160	-1064
Ratio of nonwhite to white fert. in same area:														
15 to 24 years old......	.017	- .053	.243	.194	- .192	.320	.086	.265	.103	.005	.033	.057	.034	- .015
25 to 34 years old......	- .237	- .176	.140	- .019	- .470	.094	- .184	.030	- .195	- .187	- .178	- .265	- .240	- .030
35 to 44 years old......	- .395	- .284	- .046	- .086	- .612	- .048	- .521	- .098	- .288	- .284	- .237	- .486	- .604	- .193
Ratio of area to U.S. white [1]......	- .516	- .334	- .069	- .206	- .780	- .091	- .571	- .297	- .449	- .463	- .511	- .543	- .611	- .303
Ratio of white area fert. rates to U.S. rate:														
15 to 20 years old......	- .158	- .147	- .158	- .189	- .202	- .136	- .147	- .170	- .150	- .151	- .168	- .156	- .206	- .167
25 to 34 years old......	- .135	- .007	- .105	- .132	- .128	- .107	- .139	- .164	- .114	- .138	- .171	- .092	- .153	- .146
35 to 44 years old......	- .192	- .098	- .119	- .163	- .156	- .137	- .194	- .305	- .196	- .202	- .257	- .105	- .155	- .186
Total (standardized)[1]......	- .165	- .106	- .117	- .154	- .148	- .125	- .167	- .234	- .159	- .170	- .213	- .105	- .159	- .167

Table 15-21 (Continued)

Subject	U.S. Total	Region 1	2	3	4	5	6	7	8	9	10	11	12	13
SCHOOL ENROLLMENT														
Percent enrolled, total.............	-.3	.5	.4	-1.5	-.5	.7	-2.2	.1	.8	.3	-4.4	1.6	2.4	4.2
7 to 13 years old.............	.7	.1	.7	1.0	.7	.3	.5	1.4	1.0	.5	.9	1.9	1.3	1.1
14 and 15 years old...........	2.3	1.5	.7	1.3	.7	.1	-.1	4.9	2.9	1.2	1.8	2.7	-.1	1.8
16 and 17 years old...........	4.2	2.4	2.2	1.3	+1.7	-1.2	-2.2	9.6	6.7	4.9	.5	-.8	2.8	9.1
18 and 19 years old...........	11.3	9.4	13.6	7.4	12.3	12.7	9.8	16.7	17.7	8.5	10.9	11.6	20.3	15.2
20 and 21 years old...........	13.1	9.7	15.8	10.4	19.4	17.6	13.8	16.7	16.8	7.2	17.3	14.8	21.0	11.5
22 to 24 years old............	6.2	6.2	5.4	5.8	9.9	7.1	4.5	7.8	6.3	3.5	6.8	6.5	8.7	5.8
25 to 34 years old............	1.9	2.5	1.6	2.1	1.9	1.7	.7	2.0	1.1	.8	.7	2.0	2.2	2.1
Ratio of actual to potential enrollment:														
White: Kindergarten..........	.029	-.254	-.557	-.136	-.082	-.123	.120	.383	.165	.165	.191	-.267	-.172	-.552
Elementary school........	.001	.009	-.003	-.008	-.014	-.020	-.004	-.043	.013	.046	-.053	.054	-.024	-.106
High school.............	-.001	.094	.017	-.001	-.134	-.110	-.203	.009	.005	.054	.256	-.112	-.038	.065
College................	-.016	-.258	-.084	-.051	.345	.169	-.214	.268	.184	.056	.479	.196	.326	.407
Nonwhite: Kindergarten.......	.551	.446	-.049	.171	.841	.387	.581	.345	.229	.335	.186	-.243	-.244	-.505
Elementary school........	-.070	.018	.285	.181	-.151	.272	-.022	.050	-.044	-.043	-.108	.059	.017	.121
High school.............	-.025	.005	-.091	-.102	-.096	-.148	.063	.067	-.044	-.040	-.098	.171	.171	.138
College................	-.067	-.373	-.499	-.310	1.338	-3.448	.111	.150	.208	-.366	-.074	.331	.748	-.141
Percent nonwhite ratio to white:														
Kindergarten..............	53.8	56.6	33.5	24.4	59.7	39.6	43.4	-6.5	39.1	47.9	11.4	7.8	-6.9	-4.2
Elementary school.........	-7.1	.9	28.2	18.3	-13.3	29.3	-1.8	9.7	-6.3	-9.3	-4.3	-5.4	-.7	1.4
High school...............	-2.3	-7.1	-9.9	-10.0	-4.6	-4.6	19.9	8.2	4.3	-10.2	13.5	13.3	17.8	20.7
College...................	-7.6	-22.5	-38.6	-34.4	103.4	335.3	16.5	.4	12.0	75.0	-30.4	24.0	50.2	15.7
YEARS OF SCHOOL COMPLETED, STANDARDIZED FOR AGE														
Male														
White.........................	-3.6	-.4	1.4	.4	-2.6	.8	-2.6	-10.1	-7.8	-6.4	-7.6	-1.3	-1.0	-6.6
Elementary: Less than 5 years.....	-5.4	-4.1	.5	-3.9	-4.6	-2.3	-3.2	-8.6	-8.7	-5.1	-7.5	-2.2	-3.0	-3.3
5 to 7 years........	-3.7	-1.2	-5.4	-5.7	-6.6	-5.4	-6.9	-2.0	-1.8	-1.2	-2.4	-4.6	-5.0	-2.4
8 years.............	-1.3	-1.4	.4	.7	.9	.7	1.1	3.4	-.1	-.1	.5	.1	-2.1	+
High school: 1 to 3 years......	2.2	1.0	.7	.6	3.1	.2	1.1	5.7	4.9	3.5	3.8	2.3	2.1	3.5
4 years............	3.9	1.0	1.3	3.6	3.1	3.3	1.6	4.6	5.7	4.4	6.5	4.2	4.0	4.0
College: 1 to 3 years..........	3.4	1.9	2.4	4.9	6.1	4.7	5.2	6.8	7.9	5.5	8.0	5.3	5.9	4.2
4 years or more........	2.0	1.9	.6	1.5	2.5	1.4	2.2	1.8	1.8	2.1	2.6	1.5	1.5	1.8
Median years of school completed....	2.5	.6	.6	1.5	2.5	1.4	2.2	1.8	2.5	2.1	2.6	1.5	1.5	1.8
Nonwhite:														
Elementary: Less than 5 years.....	-20.8	-14.8	-2.3	-4.8	-8.1	-3.4	-2.5	-9.8	-14.2	-18.5	-16.5	-22.6	-15.7	-17.0
5 to 7 years........	-2.6	-7.9	1.0	-1.7	-8.6	-1.5	-5.6	.9	.5	.4	.7	3.0	-5.3	.5
8 years.............	4.8	5.3	5.4	5.3	-5.3	1.7	4.3	1.3	2.5	3.9	3.8	2.0	-1.2	.2
High school: 1 to 3 years......	7.4	7.3	1.0	.3	2.4	.8	1.5	4.5	4.8	6.6	5.8	3.1	1.8	2.0
4 years............	5.8	5.6	2.9	2.9	1.6	2.9	4.2	1.7	3.6	4.3	2.6	7.0	8.1	5.6
College: 1 to 3 years..........	3.2	2.9	1.8	1.8	6.6	1.9	3.1	1.6	1.8	2.0	2.2	4.0	4.4	5.8
4 years or more........	2.2	1.8	.2	1.8	11.3	.9	3.3	1.8	1.8	1.4	1.6	3.3	7.5	4.5
Median years of school completed....	2.5	1.8	.6	.4	1.3	.4	.8	1.1	1.6	2.1	2.1	2.2	1.9	1.6

520

Table 15-21 (Continued)

Subject	U.S. Total	Region												
		1	2	3	4	5	6	7	8	9	10	11	12	13
YEARS OF SCHOOL COMPLETED, STANDARDIZED FOR AGE--(Con't.)														
Female														
White														
Elementary: Less than 5 years	- 1.4	2.2	1.9	.3	- 1.6	.1	- 1.9	- 7.0	- 4.7	- 3.6	- 4.5		.9	- 2.3
5 to 7 years	- 4.5	2.0	1.4	- 2.1	- 3.2	- 1.2	- 2.1	- 9.0	- 8.6	- 5.5	- 7.7	.9	- 2.3	- 3.1
8 years	- 3.0		- 3.0	- 3.9	- 5.5	- 4.6	- 5.6	- 2.6	- 2.4	- 1.7	- 3.0	- 2.7	- 3.5	- 2.2
High school: 1 to 3 years	.2	.9	.2	.8	.6	.4	.3	2.7	1.1	1.4	1.8	3.2	3.0	.7
4 years	4.1		.2	1.0	5.1	1.4	4.1	8.7	6.9	5.9	7.2	2.0	3.4	4.5
College: 1 to 3 years	2.2	- 1.1	.5	1.7	2.3	1.7	2.1	3.9	5.7	3.7	5.9	2.2	3.2	2.2
4 years or more	2.4	.2	.7	2.2	3.4	2.6	2.1	3.2	4.2	2.6	3.9	2.5	3.1	1.3
Median years of school completed	1.2	.1		.8	1.6	.9	.9	2.0	2.3	1.7	2.3	.8	.6	.7
Nonwhite														
Elementary: Less than 5 years	-15.0	- 9.3	- 3.4	3.4	- 5.8	4.1	4.2	5.6	7.2	-16.1	-11.1	-30.2	-20.5	9.5
5 to 7 years	- 7.6	-10.1	2.2	2.9	-11.6	.5	9.1	2.5	5.6	3.1	- 4.1	3.4	- 6.3	- 3.8
8 years	3.6	4.5	1.8	.6	5.6	2.5	.6	4.5	1.5	3.9	2.0	3.0	1.0	- 2.2
High school: 1 to 3 years	7.5	6.4	6.0	3.6	3.3	5.2	3.3	1.3	4.2	7.3	5.8	9.0	6.0	2.7
4 years	7.3	6.1	.8	.5	8.7	1.1	7.7	1.7	3.8	4.8	4.1	9.7	11.7	5.3
College: 1 to 3 years	2.8	2.0	- 1.3	1.9	5.3	.5	3.1	1.4	1.4	1.7	1.5	3.1	3.9	5.0
4 years or more	1.4	.6	- 1.2	.8	5.9	...	3.0	.5	1.9	1.5	2.0	2.1	3.8	2.5
Median years of school completed	1.9	1.2	.1	.4	1.7	.6	1.4	.5	1.0	1.9	1.5	3.1	2.5	1.6
Functional illit. (0 to 4 grades):														
Percent nonwhite of total	- 1.7	- 8.4	1.7	16.0	- 1.1	13.4	3.3	22.1	10.6	- 1.9	- 2.2	-22.4	-13.1	- 3.5
Percent white male of white total	- 9.0	-10.7	- 8.7	- 7.4	- 6.9	- 5.8	- 2.5	- 5.5	- 6.3	- 8.2	- 4.4	- 8.5	- 7.2	-16.3
Percent nonwhite male of nonwhite total	- 3.1	- 7.7	- 5.5	- 8.0	1.2	- 5.0	- 1.5	- 6.5	- 5.0	2.2	2.9	7.4	6.7	-13.5
Superior education (high school+):														
Ratio nonwhite to white:														
Male	.032	.041	.009	.057	.004	.027	.004	.038	.030	.026	-.009	-.014	.005	.016
Female	.037	.052	.009	.068	.002	.031	.010	.049	.034	.035	-.010	-.010	.006	.022
Ratio female to male:														
White	-.016	-.019	-.027	-.084	-.014	.001	-.003	.002	.007	.076	-.039	.017	.086	.115
Nonwhite	.054	.119	.293	.268	-.061	.324	.296	.148	-.071	.147	-.026	.119	.146	.219
PERCENT OF CIVILIAN LABOR FORCE UNEMPLOYED														
White: Male	- 1.4	.4	.7	- 2.6	- 3.3	- 6.1	- 1.2	- 3.8	.8	.3	- 1.7	- 2.2	- 1.8	- .8
Female	- 1.0		.9	- 1.9	- 2.0	- .5	- .3	- 1.7	1.1	.8	- 1.1	- 1.5	- 2.5	- 2.3
Nonwhite: Male	1.0	.7	- 1.2	- 1.9	-19.8	- 3.3	-18.1	- 1.9	1.6	.7	.8	- 9.8	-10.4	.7
Female	.2	- 2.1	.2	.3	- 4.9	1.2	- 5.2	.9	.1	1.2	- 1.7	- 6.3	- 6.1	- 3.1
Ratio of nonwhite male to white male														
RATIO OF UNEMPLOYED TO EMPLOYED IN LOW SES OCCUPATIONS														
White: Male	- 1.7	1.1	.5	3.6	- 4.3	.5	- 1.8	- 4.8	.1	.9	- 1.3	- 2.8	- 1.4	.6
Female	.5	1.2	- 1.3	2.0	- 2.7	.3	.3	- 1.3	.3	.2	- 1.4	- 2.7	- 3.9	- 4.4
Nonwhite: Male	1.0	.9	- 3.4	3.2	-36.6	- 4.1	-35.4	- 2.5	1.5	- 1.2	1.2	-15.4	-20.7	1.6
Female	.4	- 2.7	- 2.3		- 8.9	1.8	- 8.1	1.1		1.2	- 2.2	- 8.3	-15.4	- 4.7
Difference, nonwhite minus white:														
Male	2.7	- 2.0	2.9	.4	-32.3	- 3.6	-33.6	2.3	1.6	- 2.1	2.5	-12.6	-19.3	- 2.2
Female	.1	.6	- 1.0	2.0	- 6.2	2.1	- 8.4	- 1.8	.3	- 1.0	.8	- 5.6	-11.5	- .3

521

Table 15-21 (Continued)

Subject	U.S. Total	Region 1	2	3	4	5	6	7	8	9	10	11	12	13
LABOR FORCE PARTICIPATION RATE OF WOMEN														
White..........	7.7	4.4	5.3	8.4	9.5	7.6	7.8	11.3	6.8	7.6	12.3	7.7	8.7	8.4
Married, husband present:														
With children under 6......	-.1	2.7	.5	.7	1.5	2.2	3.0	2.3	-.1	2.4	5.9	4.2	3.4	2.9
No children under 6.......	4.1	-1.6	.7	4.8	5.7	4.2	6.2	8.6	5.0	5.0	11.8	6.1	6.9	6.2
Other marital status:														
With children under 6......	11.8	1.1	5.2	11.4	8.0	12.0	11.5	22.6	14.2	12.0	20.9	12.4	10.4	10.6
No children under 6.......	14.9	11.5	10.8	15.0	17.4	13.7	12.8	13.2	13.2	11.9	17.6	11.7	12.6	12.4
Nonwhite.........	14.3	8.6	10.1	18.0	27.4	19.3	22.2	13.5	13.7	13.7	20.7	26.2	22.1	15.0
Married, husband present:														
With children under 6......	6.6	-2.7	11.1	10.7	20.0	14.1	15.8	9.6	9.9	8.1	17.3	16.1	15.4	8.4
No children under 6.......	12.6	3.4	4.5	17.4	28.6	15.4	24.6	12.2	13.5	10.6	23.1	30.0	27.2	13.1
Other marital status:														
With children under 6......	4.1	-4.2	1.2	12.3	14.5	11.2	19.5	13.0	12.4	12.5	20.9	31.4	13.1	14.2
No children under 6.......	18.8	17.0	13.5	22.9	31.3	23.5	23.2	15.7	14.7	17.5	20.1	27.8	20.0	20.5
Ratio of rate for total nonwhite fem. to rate for total white fem.	16.0	8.5	13.5	32.1	58.5	34.1	45.2	-1.2	16.9	10.2	19.7	57.8	42.9	16.3
RATIO OF LABOR FORCE PARTICIPATION RATE TO U.S. RATE														
Male, 14 & over (standardized)...	.044	.021	.014	.052	.038	.030	.026	.073	.025	.038	.061	.041	.009	.059
14 to 17 years......	.117	-.053	-.132	.234	.309	.173	.219	.237	.034	-.007	.283	.257	.178	-.064
18 to 24 years......	-.032	-.049	-.072	.028	-.053	-.048	-.053	.025	-.116	-.034	-.051	-.048	-.128	-.026
25 to 34 years......	.023	.015	-.008	.021	-.001	.016	.014	-.029	-.010	-.031	.039	.027	-.006	.065
35 to 44 years......	.032	.021	.015	.021	.022	.023	.018	.047	-.027	.033	.046	.034	.011	.056
45 to 64 years......	.064	.037	.029	.051	.063	.045	.043	.107	.055	.061	.074	.054	.035	.084
65 years and over....	.227	.184	.082	.315	.195	.138	.099	.350	.266	.158	.315	.147	.141	.190
Female, 14 & over (standardized)...	.228	.145	.153	.249	.258	.207	.216	.338	.231	.244	.350	.236	.278	.261
14 to 17 years......	.286	.136	.093	.350	.550	.321	.229	.400	.207	.143	.408	.350	.314	.107
18 to 24 years......	.283	.241	.210	.261	.450	.251	.236	.291	.145	.267	.315	.324	.379	.309
25 to 34 years......	.218	.187	.190	.249	.201	.221	.247	.291	.201	.283	.349	.252	.278	.312
35 to 44 years......	.169	.089	.108	.214	.124	.146	.173	.298	.183	.216	.300	.201	.211	.222
45 to 64 years......	.229	.109	.118	.245	.245	.192	.198	.382	.293	.233	.375	.185	.265	.250
65 years and over....	.349	.233	.204	.359	.389	.359	.311	.534	.457	.320	.524	.330	.349	.281
WEEKS WORKED IN 1959														
Total labor force.....	6.3	2.8	3.1	6.1	6.3	2.6	4.2	10.5	7.9	4.7	11.9	5.6	5.8	5.0
50 to 52 weeks......	.6	-.6	.2	.4	.1	.1	.1	-2.9	-3.0	.7	-2.8	-1.3	-1.2	.7
40 to 49 weeks......	-.6	.6	.7	-.4	-.6	-.1	.1	-3.5	-1.5	-1.2	-2.9	-1.3	-1.1	-.7
27 to 39 weeks......	-1.8	-.7	-.7	-2.2	-2.6	-1.1	-1.3	-3.5	-3.5	-1.2	-2.9	-1.4	-1.1	-1.2
26 weeks or less....	-3.9	-2.4	-2.3	-3.3	-3.9	-1.4	-2.8	-4.6	-3.4	-3.0	-6.3	-2.8	-3.5	-4.5
CLASS OF WORKER														
Male..........														
Agricultural workers:														
Self-employed......	-3.1	-1.3	-1.4	-1.1	-2.3	-4.4	-7.4	-3.4	-4.4	-2.3	-5.4	-3.5	-1.8	-0.0
Wage and salary or government....	-4.9	-3.1	-2.5	-1.6	-2.1	-3.1	-5.3	-3.3	-6.1	-9.7	-11.3	-5.8	-3.8	-17.1
Unpaid family worker.....	...	...	...	...	...	...	...	...	...	...	...	...	...	...
Nonagricultural workers:														
Private wage and salary and unpaid family worker....	8.9	5.0	6.3	3.1	9.8	11.1	18.4	7.1	8.2	10.7	14.7	9.4	6.7	19.2
Government worker.....	.7	.4	.5	1.1	.8	.9	-1.9	.8	2.2	.7	1.2	.8	.3	.3
Self-employed......	-1.3	-.9	-1.7	-1.3	-5.9	-4.2	-3.5	-1.0	-.7	.7	.9	.8	.7	.4

Table 15-21 (Continued)

Subject	U.S. Total	1	2	3	4	5	6	7	8	9	10	11	12	13
Female..........	-.4		.5		.3	.3	.4		.7	.5	.9	.5	.5	.6
Agricultural workers:														
Self-employed...........	-1.5	.9	.5	.7	-.5	-.6	-.4	-.4	-2.8	-4.9	-3.7	-1.0	-2.2	-3.5
Wage and salary or government.....														.2
Unpaid family worker.........														
Nonagricultural workers:														
Private wage and salary and unpaid family worker..........	7.2	6.2	6.3	6.9	7.8	6.4	11.6	5.7	2.0	9.1	9.8	9.1	9.4	12.7
Government worker........	-3.2	-3.7	-3.9	-4.3	-2.9	-2.8	-6.9	-3.3	1.9	-2.2	-2.8	-4.2	-4.2	-6.0
Self-employed..........	-1.8	-1.2	-1.5	-1.7	-3.8	-2.4	-3.5	-1.5	.1	-1.3	-2.1	-3.2	-2.4	-2.4
OCCUPATION														
Male, employed.........	4.2	1.1	2.3	3.7	4.7	3.3	4.3	5.0	4.9	3.6	6.0	4.8	5.3	4.5
Prof., tech., and kindred workers.....	1.1	.5	.4	.9	1.4	1.0	1.7	1.3	1.1	.6	1.7	1.4	1.9	1.5
Engineers, technical....														.1
Medical and other health workers:														
Salaried..........	.3	.3	.3	.3	.5	.3	.4	.5	.4	.3	.3	.2	.2	.3
Self-employed.........	.3	.3	.4	.3	.2	.1	.2	.4	.5	.4	.5	.3	.4	.1
Teachers, elem. & second. schools...	.4	.2	.3	.3	.5	.8	1.2	.3	.1		.6	.5	.5	2.4
Other profess'l, etc.: Salaried....	2.4	.8	1.3	2.2	3.0	2.3	2.7	2.9	2.5	1.7	3.5	2.8	2.7	.3
Self-empl.	.5	.4	.2	.3	.3	.2	.4	.3	.4	.6	.6	.4	.5	2.1
Farmers and farm managers........	-3.1	-1.3	-1.4	-1.1	-2.2	-4.3	-7.3	-3.5	-4.5	-2.4	-5.6	-3.5	-1.8	-2.1
Mgrs., off'ls, & propr's, exc. farm....	2.2	.6	.8	1.4	.5	.9	.8	3.6	5.3	3.5	5.3	3.5	3.7	2.5
Salaried.........	2.7	.9	1.3	1.9	2.7	2.3	2.4	3.7	4.6	3.2	4.4	3.6	3.7	2.7
Self-employed: Retail trade.....	.6				-1.5	-1.2	-1.6	-.4	.3	.4	1.3	.3	.2	.2
Other than retail....	.1	.1	.1	.1	.7	.2		.2	.7	.4	.4	.1	.1	
Clerical and kindred workers......	3.7	4.5	3.0	3.3	3.5	2.7	2.8	3.7	2.8	3.3	3.6	3.3	3.1	3.9
Sales workers.........	2.9	1.6	2.4	2.4	3.3	2.6	3.8	3.5	3.8	3.6	4.4	3.7	4.6	3.6
Retail trade.........	.6	.6	.3	.3	.2	.4	.6	.6	.6	.9	.8	1.2	1.2	1.1
Other than retail trade......	2.3	1.0	1.7	1.9	3.0	2.2	3.1	2.9	3.2	2.6	3.6	2.5	3.3	2.5
Craftsmen, foremen, & kindred wkrs....	2.1	5.2	2.9	4.3	1.7	1.7	.1	2.1	2.1	1.9	1.5	1.4	1.8	1.4
Construction craftsmen.......	2.3	3.5	2.6	2.4	2.5	2.1	1.1	2.5	2.2	2.2	1.4	1.0	1.5	1.1
Foremen (n.e.c.).........	.6	.5		.3	.4	.6	.4	.2	.7	.7	.3	.3	.2	.3
Mechanics and repairmen......	1.0	1.6	1.5	1.7	1.3	1.2	.5	.9	.1	.7	.3	.1	.5	1.5
Metal craftsmen, except mechanics...	.4	.5	.4	.6	.1	.9	.5	.7	.6	.5	.2	.4	.2	1.0
Other craftsmen.........	.7	.7	.8	1.0	1.1	1.6	1.1	.7	.8	.5	.6	.6	.5	1.2
Operatives and kindred workers.....	4.8	1.1	1.9	6.1	5.1	2.9	1.1	9.4	6.2	3.8	5.9	4.4	5.1	1.0
Drivers and deliverymen.......	1.4	.5	1.6	1.1	2.0	1.6	1.1	1.6	1.6	1.0	2.9	.7	1.3	1.0
Other operatives, etc.:														
Durable goods manufacturing.....	.5	.7	.1	1.6	.8	1.0	.5	1.0	2.1	.3	1.1	.4	3.6	3.1
Nondurable goods manufacturing....	.9	.1	.2	3.2	1.5	.3	2.0	.9	3.2	.8	1.5	.2	.2	1.1
Nonmanufacturing industries.....	1.8	.1	.4		1.5	.6	1.6	5.8	1.6	1.6	2.8	2.3	1.1	
Private household workers......	.1	3.2	.1	2.3	.1	2.2	1.6	.1	.1	.3	.1	.2	.3	1.8
Service wkrs., exc. priv. household...	2.6	.9	2.2	.8	1.3	.7	.5	3.0	3.1	3.1	2.8	2.1	2.0	.3
Protective service workers.....	.7	1.0	.8	.5	.6	.3	.2	.8	.5	.3	.5	.3	.3	.3
Waiters, bartenders, cooks, etc....	.7	1.4	.5	1.0	.8	1.2	1.1	1.6	.5	.8	.7	.2	.4	.4
Other service workers.......	1.3	2.1	2.4	1.9	2.0	3.1	5.2	3.2	2.0	2.1	1.6	1.6	1.2	1.1
Farm laborers and farm foremen....	4.5	2.7	2.6	1.5	2.7	1.2	1.2	2.8	6.1	8.4	8.8	5.4	3.6	-15.5
Laborers, except farm and mine....	2.6	2.1	2.9	1.9	1.9	.7	.8	.9	2.4	2.1	3.3	3.9	6.6	.3
Construction.........	.7	.7	1.3	.7	.1	.2	.4	1.1	2.5	1.6	3.9	1.0	.5	.3
Manufacturing........	1.8	.9	1.2	1.3	1.1	.1	.4	.1	.4	1.2	.5	2.1	6.0	.6
Other industries.......	.2	.4	.4	.1	.7	.1	1.2	1.1	1.3	1.6	2.8	.4	.1	.1
Occupation not reported......	1.4	1.3	.6	1.9	.7	1.3		1.8		1.5	1.9		.4	.6

Table 15-21 (Continued)

Subject	U.S. Total	1	2	3	4	5	6	7	8	9	10	11	12	13
								Region						
Female, employed...........	.8	.5	.1	.1	1.6	.3	.7	1.0	3.8	2.2	1.0	.1	.8	- .5
Prof., tech., and kindred workers	.9	...	.8	.4	2.1	1.5	1.7	1.3	1.5	1.0	.8	.4	1.3	- .2
Medical and other health workers	.2	...	.1	.1	.1	.1	.1	.1	.3	.3	.8	.1	.1	.1
Salaried..............	- 1.6	- 1.1	- 1.4	- 1.6	- 2.1	- 2.2	- 3.4	- 2.0	.3	1.0	- 1.9	- 1.2	- 1.7	- .9
Self-employed.........	1.3	.6	.7	1.0	1.4	1.1	1.2	1.4	1.5	1.0	1.6	1.0	1.1	.6
Teachers, elem. & second. schools: Salaried.......	.3	.1	.1	...	...	.2	.3	.1	.2	.4	.8	.5	.4	.1
Other profess'l, etc.: Salaried.............	.5	.1	1.0	.6	1.6	.6	1.8	.7	.5	.3	.7	2.2	.9	1.1
Self-empl.............	.4	.5	.2	.3	.1	.4	.3	.2	.4	.3	.4	.3	.4	.5
Farmers and farm managers......	.7	.4	.5	.7	1.2	.8	1.3	.9	.4	1.0	1.2	1.2	.9	1.1
Mgrs., off'ls, & propr's, exc. farm......	- .2	- .2	- .1	- .2	- .6	- .8	- 1.3	- .4	- .4	- 1.0	- 1.2	- .6	- .9	- 1.1
Salaried.............	10.3	8.2	5.8	8.6	10.5	6.8	10.9	10.2	8.5	7.0	12.0	9.1	9.1	9.0
Self-employed: Retail trade.....	4.6	3.6	3.2	3.4	5.0	3.7	5.9	4.4	3.9	3.1	5.6	4.6	4.4	4.1
Other than retail.....	5.7	4.5	3.7	5.2	5.5	3.2	5.0	5.8	4.7	4.0	6.3	4.5	4.6	5.0
Clerical and kindred workers......	.1	.5	1.6	.5	.2	.4	.8	.4	.6	.4	1.0	.2	.2	.1
Secretaries, stenographers, and typists..	.3	.4	1.4	.7	.5	.6	1.4	.8	.4	.4	.4	.3	.4	.2
Other clerical workers.....	.4	.7	.1	.3	.3	.2	.4	.8	.3	.4	.4	.2	.3	.1
Craftsmen, foremen, & kindred wkrs....	.1	.5	.2	.5	.6	.1	.8	.1	...	.3	.2	.3	.1	.3
Operatives and kindred workers......	- 4.9	- 4.4	- 2.2	- 3.6	- 1.8	- 2.1	.8	- 9.2	- 12.8	- 3.3	- 2.5	1.0	- 1.1	2.2
Durable goods manufacturing.....	.2	.7	1.3	2.7	1.0	1.7	.4	.7	.7	.2	.5	.1	.3	2.5
Nondurable goods manufacturing....	- 4.7	- 3.8	- 1.2	- 1.2	- .5	- .5	- .1	- 9.0	- 13.0	- 2.5	- 2.5	.9	...	- .9
Nonmanufacturing industries........	.3	.3	.3	.3	.3	.1	.5	.5	.8	.6	.7	.3	.7	- 1.1
Private household workers........	- 2.3	- 1.7	- 2.1	- 1.4	- 2.0	- 1.0	- 1.6	- .2	- .6	- .6	- 3.9	- .8	- 1.5	- 2.4
Service wkrs., exc. priv. household...	- 2.6	- 2.5	- 1.8	- 3.2	- 5.7	- 3.0	- 6.6	- 1.2	- 2.9	- .9	- 1.5	- 5.2	- 3.2	- 4.5
Waiters, bartenders, cooks, etc...	- 2.5	- 2.0	- 1.6	- 2.8	- 4.8	- 3.2	- 5.5	- 2.4	- .5	- 2.3	- 2.3	- 4.1	- 3.1	- 3.1
Other service workers......	- 1.5	- .6	- .2	.3	.9	.6	1.0	1.2	2.5	1.4	.8	- 1.2	- 3.1	- 1.4
Farm laborers and farm foremen.......	.7	.7	.4	.5	.6	.6	.6	.4	3.1	4.5	3.6	.8	1.9	- 2.8
Laborers, except farm and mine......	.3	.3	.3	.3	.3	.1	.1	.2	.3	.3	.3	.8	.3	.6
Occupation not reported........	1.2	1.7	.3	1.6	.5	.9	.6	.9	.8	1.1	1.0	.5	.3	.6
Nonwhite														
Percent male of emp. nonwhites.......	- 7.3	- 6.1	- 1.3	- 7.1	- 10.3	- 4.4	- 8.3	- 6.5	- 9.7	- 8.7	- 13.4	- 11.9	- 7.9	- 13.0
Percent of all employed males.....	- 2.3	- 3.8	- 1.9	- 8.5	- .2	- 4.6	- 1.3	- 7.0	- .3	- .4	- 6.1	- 2.1	- .6	- .4
Prof., tech., and kindred workers.......	1.4	1.9	.6	2.7	.7	1.5	.2	2.4	.6	.8	2.6	- 1.8	1.0	1.7
Engineers, technical........	1.0	1.2	.5	.9	.1	.1	.1	.3	.4	.3	.1	- 1.1	1.7	1.6
Medical and other health workers:														
Salaried............	4.7	3.8	2.6	7.8	3.5	2.8	1.9	6.0	.6	3.1	.8	.4	3.1	8.4
Self-employed.........	1.9	1.3	.1	2.4	.2	1.2	.9	2.1	2.9	1.5	1.2	- 1.4	2.1	2.0
Teachers, elem. & second. schools....	3.1	1.8	.2	4.9	.8	2.2	1.3	8.0	17.0	8.5	5.5	.9	.4	1.8
Other profess'l, etc.: Salaried......	1.5	2.1	.5	2.6	.8	2.5	.4	2.2	1.6	.7	- 1.0	- 2.6	- .4	- 1.8
Self-empl............	- .2	- 1.3	.1	3.0	.1	1.6	.7	3.0	.7	- 1.2	- 1.2	.2	1.2	.7
Farmers and farm managers........	.2	2.9	.2	2.2	.1	.5	.5	2.0	- 15.2	2.8	12.5	1.8	4.4	17.9

524

Table 15-21 (Continued)

Subject	U.S. Total	1	2	3	4	5	6	7	8	9	10	11	12	13
								Region						
Mgrs., off'ls, & propr's, exc. farm....	1.2	1.8	.2	1.6	.1	.7	.2	1.2	.5	.5	-.2	.2	.4	.7
Salaried........	1.0	1.9	.1	1.2	.1	.5	.1	.8	.4	.2	-.5	-.6	.6	-.3
Self-employed: Retail trade......	2.0	1.3	.2	2.3	.5	.9	.9	1.6	.8	2.1	1.8	...	1.1	2.3
Other than retail....	1.8	2.0	.3	3.0	.4	1.4	.4	2.6	.8	1.1	.6	...	1.5	2.3
Clerical and kindred workers....	5.4	7.6	.9	2.0	...	3.9	.5	5.3	5.5	4.5	-1.4	-1.4	.2	2.7
Sales workers.........	1.2	1.9	.3	2.9	.1	.7	.2	1.1	1.0	.3	-1.2	-1.2	.4	.8
Retail trade..........	.9	2.9	.4	2.0	...	.9	.5	1.7	.6	.6	.8	.8	.1	.2
Other than retail trade....	1.9	1.2	...	1.5	.1	.6	.1	.7	1.1	.4	1.1	.4		.9
Craftsmen, foremen, & kindred wkrs....	2.7	3.3	1.2	4.5	...	2.5	.7	3.4	5.3	3.1	1.5	1.1	.4	.9
Construction craftsmen....	3.1	3.2	.8	4.1	.5	2.6	.5	4.3	11.6	5.1	.1	1.7	1.5	-1.5
Foremen (n.e.c.)......	1.2	2.1	.5	1.7	.4	.8	.1	1.1	1.6	.7	.6	1.0	.2	2.5
Mechanics and repairmen....	4.0	4.7	1.5	7.0	.5	+3.9	1.5	4.8	4.8	3.4	.4	.5	1.3	-1.2
Metal craftsmen, except mechanics...	2.9	3.3	1.9	4.0	.1	2.8	1.0	3.6	4.3	2.0	.4	.4	.9	.2
Other craftsmen....	2.3	3.4	.9	4.2	...	1.6	.5	2.3	4.0	2.5	1.3	1.4	.2	-1.3
Operatives and kindred workers....	5.2	6.3	2.5	11.4	.9	5.3	1.8	7.5	10.9	6.0	7.5	-2.3	.5	1.7
Drivers and deliverymen....	4.0	6.2	1.9	10.0	.3	4.9	1.3	9.5	9.9	5.9		2.2		
Other operatives, etc:														
Durable goods manufacturing....	5.0	6.3	4.0	11.8	.1	5.0	1.8	6.7	7.2	.4	5.0	1.1	1.9	4.3
Nondurable goods manufacturing....	5.6	5.6	1.2	13.5	.3	7.0	1.5	7.0	11.0	3.3	8.6	1.7	1.8	-12.6
Nonmanufacturing industries....	6.9	9.3	2.0	10.7	.3	5.1	3.5	7.7	11.5	9.1	4.8	2.7	-	5.5
Private household workers....	20.4	27.0	4.6	34.1	3.0	26.3	19.1	32.6	10.3	12.9	12.1	2.3	4.2	13.5
Service wkrs., exc. priv. household....	10.9	7.7	3.8	4.4	3.0	14.7	9.6	9.6	18.4	15.9	15.6	2.5	5.0	8.6
Protective service workers....	2.3	4.2	.6	4.4	...	3.0	1.5	3.5	.2	5.4	1.5	3.7	1.3	1.8
Waiters, bartenders, cooks, etc....	11.3	8.5	3.2	14.6	5.4	11.4	12.0	17.2	19.3	12.0	5.8	5.8	10.3	9.8
Other service workers....	15.5	10.0	6.0	24.6	3.3	20.4	12.7	31.0	21.5	18.5	21.0	3.3	5.7	12.5
Farm laborers and farm foremen....	-8.2	-14.8	.3	3.3	.6	1.7	4.2	11.9	-2.3	11.4	-16.6	3.7	2.0	2.9
Laborers, except farm and mine....	8.7	6.0	7.8	21.1	1.0	13.4	5.4	25.6	15.4	20.5	11.8	-10.4	1.3	4.6
Construction....	14.7	8.8	9.2	25.0	2.3	16.7	3.2	29.1	19.4	20.5	11.8	11.8	4.1	11.4
Manufacturing....	5.9	3.3	10.2	21.6	1.2	12.7	4.0	26.1	14.1	14.1	2.4	3.5	1.3	2.4
Other industries....	8.2	6.2	4.9	19.1	1.0	12.5	5.1	23.4	14.3	15.1	-	5.1	1.7	4.2
Occupation not reported....	10.0	10.7	4.9	21.6	...	10.7	8.3	15.3	5.7	5.0	13.4	2.2	-	5.4
Percent fem. of emp. nonwhites....	-7.3	6.1	1.3	7.1	10.3	4.4	2.1	6.5	9.7	8.7	4.3	11.9	7.9	13.0
Percent of all employed females....	3.5	5.8	1.9	10.1	.5	5.8	.8	9.3	3.9	1.5	3.6	1.7	.7	2.0
Prof., tech., and kindred workers....	2.5	4.2	.8	5.8	.7	2.5	.1	5.7	1.4	2.2	-	2.6	.6	2.3
Medical and other health workers:														
Salaried....	5.1	8.5	1.0	7.3	...	2.8	.1	6.3	3.7	6.3	1.8	3.4	1.2	4.7
Self-employed....	2.6	4.0	.4	4.5	.2	...	...	3.5	1.1	1.6	1.7	3.3	...	4.2
Teachers, elem. & second. schools....	2.3	1.4	.4	5.5	.2	2.5	1.0	7.4	6.3	3.5	1.4	1.8	.6	1.1
Other profess'l etc: Salaried....	2.6	4.2	.9	5.2	.4	2.1	.1	4.1	1.4	1.6	1.4	4.7	...	2.3
Self-empl....	1.5	2.9	1.0	1.8	...	2.8	...	2.6	1.3	1.7	4.7	.2		1.0
Farmers and farm managers....	-13.1	1.4	.6	2.9	.3	1.8	5.9	1.7	-32.9	1.1	-39.4	-20.7	9.2	7.8
Mgrs., off'ls, & propr's, exc. farm....	1.8	1.7	.3	3.9	.3	1.3	.5	2.9	1.7	1.6	.2	.3	.8	-1.1
Salaried....	1.6	2.0		3.2	.2	2.2	.6	2.1	1.2	4.1	.3	.5	1.0	1.1
Self-employed: Retail trade....	3.5	.8	.6	5.5	.4	2.9	1.2	5.0	6.9	1.6	2.2	1.7	2.3	2.7
Other than retail....	3.5	4.4	.4	5.6	.3	2.9	.1	3.9	2.3	1.2	2.4	3.0	3.5	3.6
Clerical and kindred workers....	3.0	4.7	.6	4.3	.2	2.0	1.1	2.1	1.7	1.4	-1.0	.2	.3	1.6
Secretaries, steno's & typists....	2.2	5.4	.4	3.2	...	1.7	.1	1.7	1.0	.6	3.0	.3	.5	1.1
Other clerical workers....	2.4	3.5	.4	4.9	.1	2.2	.1	2.3	2.0	1.0	.4	.7	.6	1.7
Sales workers....	1.8	3.6	.2	3.0	.1	1.0	.1	1.6	1.2	1.7	.1	...	.1	-1.2
Retail trade....	1.7	3.5	...	2.9	...	1.0	.1	1.5	.7	.7	.4	...	.1	1.6
Other than retail trade....	2.0	2.6	-	3.3	...	.8	.9	2.5	3.4	2.5	2.6	...	.3	.4

525

Table 15-21 (*Continued*)

Subject	U.S. Total	Region												
		1	2	3	4	5	6	7	8	9	10	11	12	13
Craftsmen, foremen, & kindred workers	5.3	7.4	1.5	8.4	.2	3.6	1.6	4.9	7.6	4.7	2.8	4.0	1.1	- .3
Operatives and kindred workers	8.3	7.9	1.6	13.4	.7	4.7	- .4	7.3	11.8	10.0	5.4	.6	1.2	1.7
Durable goods manufacturing	5.8	8.1	2.2	7.0	.6	2.5	- 4.0	2.3	15.9	1.4	.4	- 2.6	1.9	.4
Nondurable goods manufacturing	6.8	5.4	.5	13.6	.8	2.9	1.4	3.9	4.5	2.5	3.1	1.3	2.8	2.2
Nonmanufacturing industries	12.8	17.8	6.0	28.4	1.2	10.8	.8	18.4	15.6	16.1	6.1	3.5	2.6	6.2
Private household workers	10.1	17.8	10.1	36.7	.9	24.5	15.5	31.1	3.8	14.9	10.7	.7	2.8	13.2
Service wkrs., exc. priv. household	12.3	13.8	5.2	17.5	.8	11.3	4.2	20.0	15.6	5.6	6.2	1.5	2.9	6.8
Waiters, bartenders, cooks, etc	6.6	7.7	2.1	8.1	.4	5.6	1.9	12.3	13.7	9.4	13.2	1.5	1.1	4.2
Other service workers	15.2	15.9	7.0	23.2	1.0	15.6	5.6	24.6	16.1	16.2	13.2	- .7	4.1	7.8
Farm laborers and farm foremen	-14.6	-27.5	- 1.5	5.4	...	1.6	- .2	7.0	- 2.6	12.1	-22.4	-16.1	4.7	7.7
Laborers, except farm and mine	11.1	7.3	5.3	23.5	.2	13.1	4.2	18.7	15.6	12.1	- 2.8	.2	3.2	6.3
Occupation not reported	10.5	12.6	3.7	20.7	.4	10.8	3.8	15.9	6.4	7.8	3.1	5.6	2.6	6.7
Employed Females as Percent of Total Employed														
Total	5.7	4.4	5.2	6.0	6.7	5.8	5.2	8.0	6.4	7.1	8.2	6.2	7.7	7.7
Prof., tech., and kindred workers	- 2.5	1.6	.7	- 2.6	- 1.2	- 1.3	- 4.7	- 3.7	- 1.0	2.0	- 6.3	3.1	- 1.7	- 1.2
Medical and other health workers	- 1.5	- 6.8	- 3.4	- 4.5	8.7	9.9	6.7	.3	- 3.8	- 5.5	- 6.1	- 1.9	2.7	2.8
Teachers, elem. & second. schools	6.4	4.2	5.5	7.2	6.8	9.4	10.6	7.8	5.4	6.9	11.8	10.1	8.6	6.1
Farmers and farm managers	.9	2.8	2.0	.8	.8	3.6	- 1.8	2.3	- .5	1.8	.5	- 1.2	1.5	- 1.0
Mgrs., off'ls, & propr's, exc. farm	.9	1.2	- 1.7	.4	- 1.6	.4	- 1.2	- 2.4	.8	- 1.7	- 3.1	- 4.8	- 1.7	- 1.8
Salaried	.3	2.9	.9	1.1	.3	.9	.6	2.0	1.1	1.7	2.2	4.4	- .3	1.8
Self-employed: Retail trade	2.7	3.2	2.3	3.1	1.6	.7	.6	2.6	2.5	4.4	2.9	5.8	4.1	7.0
Other than retail	1.1	- 1.0	- .1	- 1.6	- 3.4	- .2	- 2.2	- 1.2	.8	- .2	1.0	3.3	- 1.5	- 1.4
Clerical and kindred workers	1.1	3.0	.2	1.6	3.3	1.8	3.7	4.0	4.4	.2	4.8	-10.8	1.0	1.3
Sales workers	- 4.2	- .9	1.5	- 3.4	4.3	- 3.5	-10.6	- 5.0	- 4.3	- 4.9	-10.7	- 5.6	- 9.6	5.0
Retail trade	.9	2.0	5.0	1.9	4.4	1.9	- 4.1	- 1.8	- 3.2	.6	- 1.8	- 5.6	4.5	2.1
Other than retail trade	.2	- .1	- .5	.5	.7	- .5	- 1.3	.2	...	.5	3.2	6.5	- 4.5	3.6
Craftsmen, foremen, & kindred wkrs	1.2	1.3	1.5	1.1	.8	1.0	.9	1.4	.9	1.2	1.3	1.1	6.7	1.3
Operatives and kindred workers	3.6	1.0	4.7	4.8	6.2	4.4	5.4	5.0	.1	3.1	6.5	7.6	6.7	8.6
Durable goods manufacturing	5.0	3.8	.7	1.5	2.9	1.4	3.3	5.1	4.5	3.5	8.7	6.2	6.1	9.5
Nondurable goods manufacturing	- .4	- 2.6	2.7	3.1	9.0	2.0	4.8	- 4.0	- .5	+	2.2	13.0	7.5	12.7
Nonmanufacturing industries	10.7	4.2	7.0	15.3	7.9	8.1	8.9	18.1	10.9	7.8	9.5	7.0	3.8	5.4
Private household workers	.3	3.4	2.9	.2	1.2	.5	.4	.6	.4	.7	.2	1.6	.5	- .5
Service wkrs., exc. priv. household	- 9.7	-13.8	- 6.7	- 9.2	- 4.9	- 7.5	- 8.5	- 7.0	- .7	- 6.9	- 5.9	- 6.8	- 4.3	- 7.0
Waiters, bartenders, cooks, etc	-14.6	-23.5	-10.9	-13.1	1.9	- 7.4	- 7.3	-11.9	- 6.5	-12.7	-11.2	- 4.3	- 7.0	- 9.5
Farm laborers and farm foremen	2.4	2.3	3.2	6.6	2.1	1.5	3.2	- 7.0	...	.4	2.3	1.4	1.8	4.3
Laborers, except farm and mine	.6	...	.1	.4	.7	1.0	.3	1.6	.8	.4	.6	.4	.5	.4
Occupation not reported	3.9	5.4	4.0	3.3	5.4	3.4	1.0	3.3	3.1	5.0	2.8	1.6	4.1	12.4
INDUSTRY														
Total employed	- 6.6	- 3.5	- 3.1	- 2.3	- 3.7	- 5.8	- 9.6	- 5.3	- 8.6	-10.5	-13.8	- 7.5	- 5.0	-15.4
Agriculture	- .3	.6	.3	.1	.3	...	...	...	.3	- 1.2	...	.7	.9	.2
Forestry and fisheries	2.0	.3	.6	3.4	2.0	.7	1.2	6.2	.5	1.5	1.2	3.0	.4	1.3
Mining	2.7	3.7	3.1	2.7	2.9	2.3	1.9	2.9	2.0	2.4	1.7	1.9	1.8	1.7
Construction														

Table 15-21 (*Continued*)

Subject	U.S. Total	1	2	3	4	5	6	7	8	9	10	11	12	13
Manufacturing	-.5	-2.6	1.0	-1.3	.6	1.6	6.9	-.9	-8.7	-2.5	-1.0	-1.1	-7.0	9.3
Furniture & lumber & wood prod	-2.8	.9	2.4	-.6	-2.3	-.4	.1	-3.5	-4.3	-2.1	-3.9	-4.9	-12.1	-.2
Primary metal industries	.3	-.4	.8	-1.3	.1	.2	.6	...	.6	...	.4	.4	.2	.4
Fabricated metal industries (including not specified metal)	.6	.3	.2	...	.5	.4	1.2	.8	.2	.1	...	.5	.4	1.2
Machinery, except electrical	.7	.7	.8	.1	.6	.4	.5	.8	.1	.4	.5	.2	.2	1.1
Elect. mach., equip., & supplies	.7	.3	.8	.8	.2	.1	.3	.4	...	.1	.6	.2	.2	2.0
Motor vehicles & motor veh. equip	.3	...	.6	.9	...	.3	1.2	.3	.1	...	.2	...	.2	-.4
Trans. equip., exc. motor vehicle	.5	.7	...	...	.3	.1	1.3	.7	...	.3	1.1	.3	2.1	2.6
Other durable goods	.1	.2	.5	-1.9	1.1	.3	.4	.2	.1	...	.1	.2	...	.5
Food and kindred products	.1	.5	...	.7	.7	.8	1.0	.9	.4	.6	.9	.6	.1	-1.5
Textile mill products	-1.6	.7	...	.1	.1	...	...	-1.7	-4.8	.3	...	.1	.1	.2
Apparel & oth. fab'd textile prod	.1	.9	.4	...	.3	...	.7	1.1	-2.3	...	.1	.5	.3	.9
Print., publishing, & allied prod	1.1	1.1	.8	1.2	1.3	.9	.7	1.2	.7	.6	.9	.6	.7	.9
Chemical and allied products	...	1.2	.3	.2	.1	.1	.1	.3	.1	.2	...	.1	.4	.2
Other nondurable goods (including not specified manufacturing)	-.1	.5	.3	.4	.1	.3	1.1	.1	.4	.2	.7	.4	.3	.9
Railroad & railway express service	.2	.2	.4	...	.8	.5	.1	.6	.5	.3	.3	.4	.4	.2
Trucking service and warehousing	.2	.2	.5	.3	.4	.7	.1	.1	.2	1.1	.2	.1	...	...
Other transportation	.7	1.2	.1	.4	.4	.2	.5	...	.3	.2	.2	.5	.5	.7
Communications	.6	.3	.4	.4	.4	.3	.3	.6	.7	.8	.8	.9	.6	.7
Utilities and sanitary services	.1	...	.2	...	.2	.3	.3	.1	.5	.2	.2	.5	.1	.4
Wholesale trade	1.3	1.3	.7	1.1	1.7	.3	.9	1.6	1.6	1.4	2.1	1.4	2.2	1.4
Food and dairy products stores	.2	.4	.3	.2	.3	.3	1.0	.4	.3	.2	.7	.3	...	.1
Eating and drinking places	.2	.5	.3	.1	1.5	.3	.5	.4	.9	.4	.5	.5	...	.1
Other retail trade	1.0	.4	1.3	.6	.5	.2	.7	1.5	2.7	2.9	2.8	2.8	2.8	1.9
Finance, insurance, & real estate	2.5	2.6	1.1	1.9	2.3	1.7	2.2	2.4	2.6	2.6	2.9	2.4	2.8	2.6
Business services	.9	.4	.2	.8	.7	.5	.7	.6	.5	.7	.7	1.3	.6	1.0
Repair services	.4	.4	.6	.4	.9	.7	.6	.5	.3	.1	.2	.2	...	.1
Private households	-.3	.6	.6	.4	.2	.1	.1	.8	1.1	.6	.1	.2	.1	-.4
Other personal services	.9	1.0	.3	1.0	...	1.0	-.9	1.0	1.7	1.9	1.6	.8	.9	.4
Entertainment & recreation services	.3	.2	.2	.1	.2	.3	.1	.3	.3	.3	.3	.4	.3	.6
Educational services:														
Government	.7	1.0	1.1	.8	.1	.8	1.8	.5	.8	...	.2	.1	.1	...
Private	.4	.1	.3	.4	.4	.3	.1	.6	.6	.6	.6	.5	.5	.2
Welfare, religious, and nonprofit membership organizations	.2	.2	.3	.2	.2	...	.2	.5	.5	.3	.4	.3	.4	.1
Hospitals	.9	.4	1.0	.7	1.8	1.5	1.3	1.5	1.4	.9	1.1	.7	1.1	.2
Other profess'l & related services	1.1	.5	.6	.8	.9	.8	1.4	1.3	1.4	1.5	1.6	1.3	1.3	1.1
Public administration	1.3	1.0	1.0	1.4	.7	1.0	.1	1.2	1.5	1.1	1.7	1.5	.5	-.4
Industry not reported	1.5	1.6	.5	1.9	.6	1.0	.8	1.0	1.2	1.4	1.5	.8	.2	.3
PLACE OF WORK OF THE WORKERS														
Worked outside county residence:														
White	-2.9	-6.6	-9.7	-13.6	-4.7	-10.0	2.5	-4.3	-7.0	-5.9	-7.8	-2.2	-2.8	.5
Nonwhite	-3.8	-1.8	-10.9	-20.5	-5.5	-8.4	-2.4	-6.7	-8.2	-7.0	-4.9	-4.4	.6	1.6
Place of work not reported:														
White	.7	.9	.5	.6	.1	.4	.7	-.6	.7	.8	.3	.8	.3	-.2
Nonwhite	3.8	3.7	.5	4.5	1.7	-1.0	4.0	3.9	.6	1.7	1.9	...	1.4	2.7

Table 15-21 (Continued)

Subject	U.S. Total	Region												
		1	2	3	4	5	6	7	8	9	10	11	12	13
MEANS OF TRANSPORTATION TO WORK														
Private automobile or car pool	-7.8	-27.8	-11.7	-17.3	-1.2	.4	12.6	-4.4	-1.1	.7	9.6	9.0	3.3	9.0
Railway, subway, or elevated	5.0	16.2	-.1	3.5	-8.5	6.9	4.3	10.5	8.6	8.8	...	...	...	...
Bus or streetcar	10.1	12.8	8.9	14.3	8.5	6.9	-8.3	-3.5	-3.6	2.6	5.0	3.6	7.4	7.1
Walked to work	-1.0	3.3	6.5	2.6	.7	-1.6	-1.0	.3	-1.1	-3.5	-2.1	-1.3	-1.2	-2.3
Other means	-1.5	-1.2	.6	.9	-.6	-.8	-1.1	.8	-1.1	-3.5	-2.1	-1.3	-1.2	-2.3
Worked at home	-4.9	-3.3	-3.0	-2.0	-6.1	-4.0	-7.5	-5.6	-6.5	-3.4	-7.9	-4.3	-9.2	-11.2
Not reported	1.1	1.0	.4	1.6	.5	.8	1.1	1.0	.9	1.3	.9	.2	.4	.2
MEDIAN EARNINGS BY OCCUPATION (DOLLARS)														
Male, total	999	297	403	517	939	631	953	1288	911	883	1448	629	483	1152
Prof., managerial, and kindred wkrs	1173	93	533	1016	1378	1070	1402	1649	1453	1051	1774	976	781	725
Farmers and farm managers	1463	679	544	974	1005	601	1095	944	954	1348	1590	1247	207	108
Craftsmen, foremen, & kindred wkrs	785	309	415	519	881	576	790	1054	565	419	788	221	165	448
Operatives and kindred workers	643	172	229	361	564	275	504	938	251	247	665	-018	130	587
Farm laborers, except unpaid	260	678	74	635	183	12	-180	264	133	-011	106	-288	-327	-175
Laborers, except farm and mine	766	860	285	456	714	101	195	826	417	458	323	-358	-216	477
Female, total	631	455	249	566	636	454	722	448	242	552	717	484	741	919
Clerical and kindred workers	593	400	295	595	515	420	679	495	312	423	554	377	502	456
Operatives and kindred workers	250	158	160	414	442	236	688	240	...	287	227	449	851	964
Ratio to United States Median														
Male, total	.22	.06	.09	.11	.20	.13	.21	.28	.20	.19	.31	.14	.11	.25
Prof., managerial, and kindred wkrs	.17	.01	.08	.16	.21	.17	.21	.25	.22	.16	.27	.15	.11	.11
Farmers and farm managers	.69	.32	.25	.45	.47	.28	.51	.44	.45	.63	.74	.58	.10	.05
Craftsmen, foremen, & kindred wkrs	.15	.06	.08	.10	.17	.11	.15	.20	.11	.08	.15	.04	.03	.09
Operatives and kindred workers	.15	.04	.06	.08	.13	.07	.12	.22	.06	.06	.15	.01	.03	.13
Farm laborers, except unpaid	.24	.61	.07	.57	.17	.01	.16	.24	.12	.01	.09	.26	.29	.04
Laborers, except farm and mine	.26	.30	.10	.15	.25	.03	.07	.28	.15	.15	.11	.12	.07	.16
Female, total	.28	.28	.11	.25	.29	.20	.32	.20	.11	.25	.32	.21	.33	.42
Clerical and kindred workers	.20	.13	.09	.19	.17	.16	.22	.16	.11	.14	.18	.13	.17	.15
Operatives and kindred workers	.11	.07	.17	.18	.20	.11	.30	.10	...	.12	.10	.20	.38	.43
FAMILY INCOME														
White families														
Under $1,000 (incl. none or loss)	-3.6	-.6	-1.1	-2.0	-3.0	-2.6	-2.7	-8.5	-5.2	-2.6	-6.1	-1.6	-1.1	-1.2
$1,000 to $2,999	-8.3	-1.7	-3.2	-5.0	-9.2	-6.6	-8.5	-13.0	-9.4	-6.6	-14.5	-4.5	-3.2	-5.8
$3,000 to $3,999	-3.8	-1.7	-2.5	-3.2	-4.8	-3.1	-4.2	-3.5	-3.6	-3.0	-3.0	-2.4	-2.2	-3.8
$4,000 to $4,999	-2.8	-1.8	-1.8	-4.0	-3.8	-2.3	-2.6	-.7	-1.8	-1.8	1.8	-1.4	-2.6	-3.2
$5,000 to $5,999	-.4	6.8	-.2	2.4	.3	.1	.1	2.3	.8	.1	3.2	.6	2.4	-.9
$6,000 to $6,999	1.7	-1.8	1.0	6.3	2.6	2.0	2.4	3.8	2.2	1.3			.5	.7
$7,000 to $9,999	7.5	1.8	3.6	6.3	9.5	6.5	8.4	10.1	7.9	5.6	9.7	5.0	5.0	6.1
$10,000 and over	9.5	4.6	4.5	10.0	8.3	6.0	7.3	9.5	8.9	6.9	9.3	6.7	7.0	8.2

Table 15-21 *(Continued)*

Subject	U.S. Total	Region 1	2	3	4	5	6	7	8	9	10	11	12	13
Nonwhites families...............														
Under $1,000 (incl. none or loss).......	-16.2	- 6.6	- 3.3	- 5.6	- 9.4	- 6.9	8.5	- 8.1	-14.8	-10.5	-16.7	-24.1	- 8.7	- 2.7
$1,000 to $2,999...............	-14.4	-12.4	- 2.2	- 7.4	-20.6	- 7.9	7.8	7.6	- 2.4	-10.6	- 3.3	1.0	-10.6	- 7.2
$3,000 to $3,999...............	3.5	- .4	- 1.1	- 1.2	...	1.6	1.7	1.7	5.6	5.8	7.6	6.5	- 2.4	- 5.7
$4,000 to $4,999...............	5.7	2.5	.9	- .9	2.4	2.1	3.5	3.8	4.1	5.6	5.1	4.0	2.2	2.1
$5,000 to $5,999...............	5.9	3.7	4.1	1.9	6.2	4.4	3.2	2.5	2.9	3.8	3.1	3.7	3.3	1.8
$6,000 to $6,999...............	4.4	3.5	1.1	3.1	5.8	2.5	2.8	2.1	1.5	2.3	1.6	2.7	4.6	2.9
$7,000 to $9,999...............	7.3	6.6	1.8	6.4	11.2	3.0	3.4	3.9	2.1	2.6	2.1	3.1	7.1	6.5
$10,000 and over...............	3.8	3.2	- 1.4	3.6	4.3	1.2	1.8	1.7	.8	1.0	.6	2.9	4.4	6.4

529

population is of a suburban character, whereas in the more rural regions it is more of a small-town character. For this reason, Regions 7 and 8 (the more rural regions) tend to show differences of a quite different pattern than do Regions 1, 3, and 13—the more urbanized regions. For example, the differences for such traits as proportion of persons with a college education and proportion of persons earning $10,000 or more are much smaller for urbanized than for more rural regions. Thus we have shown that the composition of the urban, rural-nonfarm, and rural-farm populations varies from region to region and, in addition, that the *differences* between them have substantial interregional variations too. *Thus a complete distributional analysis of a population requires the simultaneous use of the regional and the urban-rural classification.*

It is so essential that the student comprehend that urban-rural and interregional differences exist simultaneously that we present one further example (Tables 15-22 and 15-23): educational attainment of three selected age groups of males, by urban-rural residence, color, and region (South and non-South). It is clearly evident that there are substantial regional differences in educational attainment between the South and the rest of the nation. When we control race and age, these differences are reduced substantially. When we control also urban-rural residence, they are reduced still more. However, even at this level the interregional differences persist and are meaningful; it is for this reason that the regional, subregional, and local units are an essential aspect of the study of population distribution.

15.8. Metropolitan Areas

Thus far the urban population of a nation has been treated as if it were a fully homogeneous entity. This, however, is an oversimplification; individual cities differ substantially in demographic, social, and economic characteristics. These differences can be very sharp indeed. Consider, for example, the differences between London and Liverpool; Tokyo and Yokohama; Washington, D.C., and Detroit; Cairo and Port Said.

A city tends to have a distinctive combination of industries by which it earns its living. It produces a surplus of some goods or services and exchanges them with other communities for the goods and services in which its own production is deficient. The industries that produce a surplus are sometimes called the "economic base" of the community. In addition, because it may be inhabited by persons disproportionately of a particular national origin, race, religion, or culture, a community may have a distinctive "personality," or "social climate." It may have a reputation for traditionalism as Boston, for amoral modernism as New York, crime as Chicago, or hedonism as Los Angeles. Both the "economic base" and the "social climate" phenomena are important research topics, with great practical as well as theoretical implications. Research into these phenomena require that data be available that pertain to individual places. This need has been acknowledged by the world of statistics and population research. In addition to publishing summary data for urban population generally, censuses collect and publish data for individual urban places. The larger the urban place, the greater the interest in having specific information concerning it. The very large cities in a nation usually are larger in size than many of the smaller provinces or states, and the need for factual information about these giant agglomerations is fully as urgent as the need for provincial or regional data. City planners must have information; advertisers and retailers must know the characteristics of their market; manufacturers must have information about potential consumption of their products at particular sites before they establish new plants or expand old ones. For these reasons, there is a great deal of population research that is focused on the *individual community*, usually a major city. The national statistical system is obligated to collect and report such information, and demographers are asked to analyze it. A population forecast that predicts the amount of growth, the pattern of distribution, and the change in population composition that probably will take place in a metropolis over the next decade is one item that is much in demand.

The publication of data for these largest

Table 15-22 Years of School Completed by White Males, by Urban-Rural Residence, for Young and Older Age Groups, South and Remainder of United States: 1960

Age and educational attainment	Northeast, North Center, West				South			
	Total	Urban	Rural nonfarm	Rural farm	Total	Urban	Rural nonfarm	Rural farm
Age: 25 to 29 years	100.0	100.0	100.0	100.0	100.0	100.0	100.0	100.0
Elementary: less than 5 years.....	1.8	1.6	2.2	3.1	4.5	2.8	6.5	11.4
5 to 7 years..........	4.7	4.3	5.9	5.6	10.8	7.7	15.5	17.9
High school: 1 to 3 years.........	20.0	20.0	21.1	15.7	19.3	18.4	21.2	18.3
4 years..............	34.9	33.2	38.2	47.7	29.7	29.9	29.3	29.3
College: 1 to 3 years..........	14.1	15.6	9.8	7.6	12.5	15.5	8.0	6.1
4 years or more.......	16.0	18.1	11.2	3.6	14.4	18.5	8.4	4.2
Age: 40 to 44 years	100.0	100.0	100.0	100.0	100.0	100.0	100.0	100.0
Elementary: less than 5 years	2.1	1.9	2.7	2.3	8.3	5.1	12.6	15.0
5 to 7 years..........	7.5	6.8	9.6	9.0	16.5	11.9	22.4	25.6
8 years..............	15.7	13.1	20.1	32.5	11.9	9.9	14.2	16.9
High school: 1 to 3 years..........	22.5	23.3	21.3	16.2	19.6	20.0	19.2	18.2
4 years..............	31.3	31.5	30.3	31.3	24.1	27.4	19.7	17.4
College: 1 to 3 years..........	10.1	11.1	7.8	5.5	9.3	11.9	6.1	4.0
4 years or more.......	10.8	12.2	8.0	3.2	10.3	13.8	5.9	2.9
Age: 60 to 64 years	100.0	100.0	100.0	100.0	100.0	100.0	100.0	100.0
Elementary: less than 5 years.....	9.6	10.0	9.1	7.3	17.7	13.0	24.3	22.4
5 to 7 years..........	20.1	19.3	22.3	22.7	24.6	20.7	28.4	31.6
8 years..............	30.4	28.2	33.7	43.7	19.7	19.1	19.7	21.9
High school: 1 to 3 years..........	15.7	16.2	15.2	12.5	15.0	16.6	12.9	13.4
4 years..............	11.5	12.3	9.8	7.6	10.4	13.3	7.2	5.4
College: 1 to 3 years..........	6.5	7.1	5.3	4.1	6.9	9.1	4.3	3.5
4 years or more.......	6.1	7.0	4.5	2.0	5.7	8.0	3.3	1.8

Source: U.S. Census of Population: 1960, Detailed Characteristics, United States Summary, Table 241.

urban sites is complicated by the fact that most of them are extremely large agglomerations that have overflowed their legal boundaries to sprawl over the countryside and encompass hundreds or even thousands of smaller cities, towns, villages, and even unincorporated territory. This phenomenon usually is expressed by using the term "metropolitan." "Metropolitan New York" (or "Greater New York"), for example, encompasses not only the boroughs of New York City itself, but a broad expanse of contiguous area in Connecticut, New York, and New Jersey. This portion outside the central city but inside the metropolitan area is termed the "metropolitan ring." Thus a metropolitan area consists of its central city and surrounding metropolitan ring.

Definition of Metropolitan Areas in the United States. The concept of metropolitanism is much broader than that of urbanism. Rural as well as urban populations may properly be said to be within the orbit of influence of a metropolis. For this reason, it is difficult to identify the boundaries of the great city. Indeed, the influence of the city is probably a more or less continuous variable that declines with increasing distance, so that there is no

critical point at which one may mark the change from metropolitan to nonmetropolitan conditions. For this reason, whole counties or (in New England) whole townships are used in delimiting the metropolitan areas of the United States.

For the 1960 census, 212 larger cities were designated as standard metropolitan statistical areas (SMSA's) for which special additional statistical tabulations would be provided. Following is a quotation of the rules that governed the selection and delimitation of areas that were defined as SMSA's:

"The definition of an individual SMSA involves two considerations: First, a city or cities of specified population to constitute the central city and to identify the county in which it is located as the central county; and, second, economic and social relationships with contiguous counties which are metropolitan in character, so that the periphery of the specific metropolitan area may be determined. SMSA's may cross State lines.

"*Population Criteria.* The criteria for population relate to a city or cities of specified size according to the 1960 census of population.

Table 15-23 Years of School Completed by Nonwhite Males, by Urban-Rural Residence, for Young and Older Age Groups, South and Remainder of United States: 1960

Age and educational attainment	Northeast, North Center, West				South			
	Total	Urban	Rural nonfarm	Rural farm	Total	Urban	Rural nonfarm	Rural farm
Age: 25 to 29 years	100.0	100.1	100.1	100.0	100.0	100.0	100.0	100.1
Elementary: less than 5 years.....	4.6	3.7	10.8	22.1	14.9	9.6	21.7	31.6
5 to 7 years..........	9.6	9.4	11.5	14.5	22.6	18.8	28.0	32.4
8 years..............	10.2	10.0	12.0	14.2	10.8	10.6	11.3	10.7
High school: 1 to 3 years..........	30.5	30.7	29.6	17.4	24.7	27.9	20.4	15.4
4 years..............	28.1	28.5	25.1	24.4	17.2	20.4	12.9	7.6
College: 1 to 3 years..........	10.4	10.9	6.9	5.1	5.8	7.6	3.2	1.4
4 years or more.......	6.6	6.9	4.2	2.2	4.0	5.0	2.5	1.0
Age: 40 to 44 years	100.0	100.0	100.0	100.1	100.0	100.0	100.0	100.0
Elementary: less than 5 years.....	11.3	10.6	18.6	21.4	32.2	24.7	42.4	50.7
5 to 7 years..........	19.6	19.5	20.9	15.4	29.3	28.3	30.9	31.6
8 years..............	16.1	16.1	16.4	14.2	10.8	12.1	8.9	7.5
High school: 1 to 3 years..........	23.5	23.8	21.3	14.8	14.1	17.2	9.9	6.6
4 years..............	18.9	19.1	15.6	26.4	8.1	10.6	4.7	2.1
College: 1 to 3 years..........	6.1	6.3	4.5	4.9	2.6	3.4	1.5	0.8
4 years or more.......	4.4	4.5	2.7	3.0	2.8	3.7	1.7	0.6
Age: 60 to 64 years	100.0	100.0	100.0	100.0	100.0	100.0	100.0	100.0
Elementary: less than 5 years.....	32.4	30.9	45.0	45.6	56.4	50.3	65.0	64.1
5 to 7 years..........	27.0	27.4	24.1	23.9	24.9	26.0	22.4	24.8
8 years..............	17.8	18.0	15.9	15.2	7.8	9.2	6.0	5.7
High school: 1 to 3 years..........	10.4	10.6	8.5	8.7	5.4	6.8	3.4	2.9
4 years..............	6.7	7.0	4.0	3.8	2.7	3.6	1.7	1.1
College: 1 to 3 years..........	3.2	3.5	1.4	1.6	1.5	2.1	0.7	0.5
4 years or more.......	2.4	2.6	1.1	1.1	1.4	2.0	0.8	0.3

Source: U.S. Census of Population: 1960, Detailed Characteristics, United States Summary, Table 241.

"1. Each SMSA must include at least:

a. One city with 50,000 inhabitants or more, or

b. Two cities having contiguous boundaries and constituting, for general economic and social purposes, a single community with a combined population of at least 50,000, the smaller of which must have a population of at least 15,000.

"2. If two or more adjacent counties each have a city of 50,000 inhabitants or more (or twin cities under 1b) and the cities are within 20 miles of each other (city limits to city limits), they will be included in the same area unless there is definite evidence that the two cities are not economically and socially integrated.

"Criteria of Metropolitan Character. The criteria of metropolitan character relate primarily to the attributes of the contiguous county as a place of work or as a home for a concentration of non-agricultural workers.

"3. At least 75 percent of the labor force of the county must be in the non-agricultural labor force.

"4. In addition to criterion 3, the county must meet at least one of the following conditions:

a. It must have 50 percent or more of its population living in contiguous minor civil divisions with a density of at least 150 persons per square mile, in an unbroken chain of minor civil divisions with such density radiating from a central city in the area.

b. The number of nonagricultural workers employed in the county must equal at least 10 percent of the number of nonagricultural workers employed in the county containing the largest city in the area, or the county must be place of employment of 10,000 nonagricultural workers.

c. The nonagricultural labor force living in the county must equal at least 10 percent of the number of the nonagricultural labor force living in the county containing the largest city in the area, or the county must be the place of residence of a nonagricultural labor force of 10,000.

"5. In New England, the city and town are administratively more important than the county, and data are compiled locally for such minor civil divisions. Here, towns and cities are the units used in defining standard metropolitan statistical areas. In New England, because smaller units are used and more restricted areas result, a population density criterion of at least 100 persons per square mile is used as the measure of metropolitan character.

"*Criteria of Integration.* The criteria of integration relate primarily to the extent of economic and social communication between the outlying counties and central county.

"6. A county is regarded as integrated with the county or counties containing the central cities of the area if either of the following criteria is met:

> *a.* 15 percent of the workers living in the county work in the county or counties containing central cities of the area, or
>
> *b.* 25 percent of those working in the county live in the county or counties containing central cities of the area.

"Only where data for criteria 6*a* and 6*b* are not conclusive are other related types of information used as necessary. This information includes such items as average telephone calls per subscriber per month from the county to the county containing central cities of the area; percent of the population in the county located in the central city telephone exchange area; newspaper circulation reports prepared by the Audit Bureau of Circulation; analysis of charge accounts in retail stores of central cities to determine the extent of their use by residents of the contiguous county; delivery service practices of retail stores in central cities; official traffic counts; the extent of public transportation facilities in operation between central cities and communities in the contiguous county; and the extent to which local planning groups and other civic organizations operate jointly.

"*Criteria for Titles.* The criteria for titles relate primarily to the size and number of central cities.

"7. The complete title of an SMSA identifies the central city or cities and the State or States in which the SMSA is located:

> *a.* The name of the standard metropoli-

tan statistical area is that of the largest city.

> *b.* The addition of up to two city names may be made in the area title, on the basis and in the order of the following criteria:
>
> > (1) The additional city has at least 250,000 inhabitants.
> >
> > (2) The additional city has a population of one-third or more of that of the largest city and a minimum population of 25,000, except that both city names are used in those instances where cities qualify under criterion 1*b*. (A city which qualified as a secondary central city in 1950 but which does not qualify in 1960 has been temporarily retained as a central city.)
>
> *c.* In addition to city names, the area titles will contain the name of the State in which the area is located." [4]

Metropolitanization of the Population. One of the major distributional changes of the present century has been the progressive concentration of the population into metropolitan areas. In 1960 the 212 SMSA's contained 63 percent of the nation's population (Table 15-24). In 1900 only 42 percent of the total population lived in the places that were metropolitan in 1960, and at that time most of these 212 areas contained too few inhabitants to be classified as metropolitan. Elsewhere it has been estimated that in 1900 only about 32 percent of the nation's population lived in areas that would be classified as SMSA's by current definitions.[5] Whereas two thirds of the population was nonmetropolitan only six decades ago, now only one third of the population lives outside metropolitan areas.

---

[4] U. S. Census of Population, 1960, *Detailed Characteristics. United States Summary,* "Standard Metropolitan Areas," pp. ix–x in the Introduction (Washington, D. C.: Government Printing Office, 1963).

[5] Leo F. Schnore, "Urban Structure and Suburban Selectivity," *Demography,* **1** (1964), 164–176.

Table 15-24   Population Trends and Compositional Differences between Metropolitan and Nonmetropolitan Areas and between Central Cities and Rings, United States: 1900 to 1960

Characteristics	Metropolitan vs. nonmetropolitan			Central city vs. metropolitan ring		
	All SMSA's population	Nonmetro-politan population	Ratio nonmetro to metro	Central city population	Ring population	Ratio nonmetro to metro
	A	B	C=B/A	D	E	F=E/D
Population (thousands)						
1960	112385	66079	.588	57710	54675	.947
1950	88964	61733	.964	52138	36826	.706
1940	72576	59093	.814	45473	27103	.596
1930	66712	56063	.840	43070	23642	.549
1920	52508	53203	1.013	34641	17866	.516
1910	42012	49960	1.189	27122	14890	.549
1900	31836	44159	1.387	19786	12051	.609
Percent of total population						
1960	63.0	37.0	.588	51.4	48.6	.947
1950	59.0	41.0	.694	58.6	41.4	.706
1940	55.1	44.9	.814	62.7	37.3	.596
1900	41.9	58.1	1.387	62.1	37.9	.609
Percent of change						
1950 to 1960	26.3	7.0	.266	10.7	48.5	4.533
1940 to 1950	22.6	4.5	.199	14.7	35.9	2.442
1930 to 1940	8.8	5.4	.614	5.6	14.6	2.607
1920 to 1930	27.1	5.4	.199	24.3	32.3	1.329
1910 to 1920	25.0	6.5	.260	27.7	20.0	.722
1900 to 1910	32.0	13.1	.409	37.1	23.6	.636
Racial composition (percent Negro)						
1960	10.8	10.1	0.935	16.8	4.6	.274
1950	9.4	10.8	1.149	12.4	5.2	.419
1900	7.4	14.7	1.986	6.5	8.9	1.369
Percent change in Negro population						
1940-60	108.8	-5.1	-.469	122.7	68.0	.554
1920 to 1940	64.6	1.6	.025	83.0	27.2	.328
1900 to 1920	50.8	6.7	.132	85.9	8.8	.102

Between 1950 and 1960 the 212 SMSA's outgrew the nonmetropolitan areas by a fantastic proportion. They gained 23.4 million persons, growing at the rate of 26.3 percent. The vast nonmetropolitan area, on the other hand, grew by only 7.0 percent in the decade. The pull of the big city upon migrants has been the outstanding cause of this trend; fertility in the metropolitan areas is lower than in metropolitan areas.

Depopulation of Rural Areas. The simultaneous urbanization and metropolitanization of the population has led to massive depopulation of rural areas. Between 1950 and 1960 a total of 1536 counties actually lost population at a time when the nation was growing rapidly. At the other extreme, about 575 counties grew at above-average rates. Most of these were metropolitan counties and a few were nonmetropolitan counties with rapidly growing urban populations. The greatest depopulation took place in the nonmetropolitan portions of the following economic regions:

Region 4—Upper Great Lakes Region
Region 5—North Center (Corn Belt) Region
Region 6—Central Plains Region
Region 7—Central and Eastern Upland Region
Region 8—Southeast Coastal Plain Region
Region 9—Atlantic Flatwoods and Gulf Coast and Atlantic Flatwoods Region
Region 10—South Center and Southwest Plains Region

In other words, The Atlantic Metropolitan Belt, the Gold Coast, and the Pacific Coast and Rocky Mountain regions grew in both metropolitan and nonmetropolitan population, while the interior of the nation grew almost entirely at metropolitan locations.

Suburbanization of the Population. A preponderant share of the recent metropolitan growth occurred in the metropolitan rings, and not in the central cities of the SMSA's. The growth rates of the internal parts of the SMSA's between 1950 and 1960 were as follows:

Central cities .... 10.7 percent
Metropolitan rings .... 48.5 percent

Table 15-24 (*Continued*)

Racial composition in South (percent Negro)						
1960	19.6	n.a	n.a	25.8	11.5	.446
1950	20.4	n.a	n.a	24.3	14.3	.588
1900	30.7	n.a	n.a	29.6	31.7	1.071
Percent change in Negro population (South)						
1940-60	61.1	n.a	n.a	73.2	33.4	.456
1920-40	40.5	n.a	n.a	59.9	10.2	.170
1900-20	30.9	n.a	n.a	61.5	0.8	.013
Proportion of white women who have ever married						
White women, total 15 to 44 years old	75.8	76.3	1.007	72.5	78.7	1.086
15 to 24 years old	40.8	43.3	1.061	40.2	41.5	1.032
25 to 34 years old	90.9	93.9	1.033	87.4	93.7	1.072
35 to 44 years old	93.5	95.0	1.016	91.2	95.5	1.047
Percentage of nonwhite women ever married						
All Negro women 15 to 44 years old	74.2	66.7	.899	74.7	72.2	.967
15 to 24 years old	41.9	33.3	.795	43.0	37.8	.879
25 to 34 years old	87.3	87.6	1.003	87.0	88.2	1.014
35 to 44 years old	93.0	92.9	.999	92.8	94.1	1.014
Percentage of nonwhite women ever married (South only)						
All Negro women 15 to 44 years old	73.1	65.8	.900	74.0	70.0	.946
15 to 24 years old	40.9	32.6	.797	42.4	36.5	.861
25 to 34 years old	87.9	86.7	.986	87.9	87.9	1.00
35 to 44 years old	93.6	92.8	.991	93.3	94.5	1.013
Children ever born per 1000 ever married women						
All white women 15 to 44 years old	2149	2441	1.136	2037	2242	1.101
15 to 24 years old	1193	1303	1.092	1139	1247	1.095
25 to 34 years old	2277	2564	1.126	2184	2350	1.096
35 to 44 years old	2413	2881	1.194	2303	2504	1.087
All nonwhite women 15 to 44 years old	2468	3564	1.444	2381	2833	1.190
15 to 24 years old	1730	2033	1.195	1700	1856	1.092
25 to 34 years old	2694	3660	1.359	2624	2988	1.139
35 to 44 years old	2574	4228	1.643	2443	3121	1.278

Even this is misleading, however, because much of the population growth of central cities was accomplished by annexation. If the 1950 boundaries are used, to control annexation, the comparative growth of central cities and metropolitan rings were as follows:

Central cities .... 1.5 percent
Metropolitan rings .... 61.7 percent

Thus the central cities of the SMSA's were in somewhat the same situation as the rural portions of the nonmetropolitan areas—they were either losing population or growing very slowly.

There is great regional variation in the metropolitanization process, and even within regions there is much variation from one SMSA to another in the rate of growth and in the growth of the central city in comparison with the metropolitan ring. The study of these differences, and their explanation, lies more in the realm of human ecology than in the realm of demography.

Compositional Differences between Metropolitan and Nonmetropolitan Areas. There are consistent compositional differences between metropolitan and nonmetropolitan populations. Some of these are illustrated in Table 15-24. In comparison with metropolitan populations, the nonmetropolitan population is more inclined to be married, to be fertile, to be employed at blue-collar work, to be poorly educated, and to have a low income. This pattern of difference is similar to the urban-rural pattern of differences, but tends to persist even when the urban and rural parts of metropolitan and nonmetropolitan areas are compared, holding regional factors constant.

Compositional Differences between Central Cities and Metropolitan Rings. In Table 15-24 the three right-hand columns compare the central city population with the population of the metropolitan rings in terms of basic demographic characteristics. From this table, the following differences emerge:

1. The central cities tend to have a much higher proportion of Negro population than do

Table 15-24 (Continued)

All Negro women (South only) 15 to 45 years old	2701	3628	1.343	2551	3216	1.261
15 to 24 years old	1825	2019	1.106	1777	1986	1.118
25 to 34 years old	2948	3769	1.278	2818	3397	1.205
35 to 44 years old	2884	4306	1.493	2659	3659	1.376
Occupational composition percent "white collar"						
White males	29.7	18.1	.609	30.5	28.8	.944
White females	59.2	45.0	.760	59.7	58.9	.987
Negro males	12.6	5.8	.460	13.4	9.8	.731
Negro females	19.6	26.9	1.372	20.8	15.3	.736
Educational attainment, population 25 and older						
White population, 25 years and older:						
Elementary: 0 to 8 years	33.7	44.3	1.314	36.5	30.9	.847
High school: 1 to 4 years	46.9	41.9	.893	45.1	48.6	1.078
College: 1 to 3 years	10.0	7.9	.790	9.7	10.4	1.072
College: 4 years or more	9.4	5.9	.628	8.7	10.0	1.149
Nonwhite population, 25 years and older:						
Elementary: 0 to 8 years	52.6	75.1	1.428	51.4	57.8	1.125
High school: 1 to 4 years	38.0	20.2	.532	39.1	33.6	.859
College: 1 to 3 years	5.5	2.1	.382	5.6	4.8	.857
College: 4 years or more	3.9	2.6	.667	4.0	3.8	.950
Family income, white families						
Under $3,000	12.8	n.a	n.a	14.4	11.4	.972
$3,000 to $9,999	66.9	n.a	n.a	67.1	66.7	.994
$10,000 or more	20.3	n.a	n.a	18.5	21.9	1.183
Family income of nonwhite families						
Under $3,000	36.7	n.a	n.a	35.8	40.4	1.128
$3,000 to $9,999	58.1	n.a	n.a	59.0	54.3	.920
$10,000 or more	5.3	n.a	n.a	5.2	5.3	1.019
Family income of nonwhites families (South only)						
Under $3,000	48.2	n.a	n.a	46.1	54.9	1.190
$3,000 to $9,999	49.0	n.a	n.a	50.8	43.0	.846
$10,000 or more	2.9	n.a	n.a	3.1	2.1	.677

the rings. In fact, one of the major motives for the "flight to the suburbs" at the present time is believed to be the desire of white families to escape from the necessity of living in the same neighborhoods as Negroes, and of sending their children to integrated schools. However, in the recent past, the Negro population has begun to "invade" the suburbs also. With federal laws that prohibit discrimination in most spheres of social and economic life, it may be expected that this process will accelerate rapidly as Negroes rise in the economic scale and can afford to purchase suburban housing and commute to work.

2. Unmarried women tend to congregate in the central cities, while suburban women tend to be married. This is particularly true of the white population. In other words, the metropolitan rings are predominantly family communities, while the center of social life for older unmarried persons is the central city.

3. Fertility rates are higher in the metropolitan rings than in the central cities, even when marital condition is held constant. This is especially true for the white population; some of the Negro population in the suburbs are domestic servants and may have unusual fertility histories.

4. The population of the central city tends to be lower in the social and economic scale than the population of the metropolitan rings. The average level of educational attainment is lower, the average family income is smaller, and the proportion of persons employed as upper-level white-collar workers (professional, etc.) is smaller. However, it would be very easy to exaggerate the metropolitan ring as a zone of residence for the elite and the central city as a zone of residence for the middle and working classes. This topic has been intensively studied by Leo F. Schnore, who has demonstrated that aggregative statistics, such as those presented in Table 15-24, are heavily weighted with the data for the bigger industrial cities of the North (New York, Philadelphia, Chicago, Detroit, etc.). In many of the smaller and new-

er SMSA's, he finds the central city has a higher socioeconomic status than the suburban ring and in the larger and older SMSA's there is a strong tendency toward the dilution of the ring population with working-class people. As a result, the differentials will probably diminish in future decades. Schnore also emphasizes that the size of the differential between central cities and suburbs is greatly affected by the manner of delimiting the central city.

15.9. The Ecological Correlation

Demonstrating that there is substantial inter-area diversity of population density, composition, or rates is only the first step in population distribution research, however. The second step is to *explain* this diversity—to develop theories or principles that *account for* it. One way in which this can be done is by the case-study approach. If a great many facts about how one area differs from another, about the economy of each, and about the changes that are taking place in each are known, the observed population events may be linked to the factors that most plausibly account for them. For example, the exodus of population from Subregion 11, the Pennsylvania Anthracite Subregion, could be linked with the decline in the demand for anthracite coal as an industrial fuel, the mechanization of mining, and the comparative inability of the entire region to attract new industries in competition with other regions. The process involved is informal but straightforward: population facts for an area are linked with economic, social, or other facts for the same area. It is a form of subjective correlation.

This same calculation can be performed by an explicit formal procedure, using conventional statistical techniques, with much less risk of error in judgment concerning whether a relationship does or does not exist. A set of areas (regions, subregions, economic areas, or individual communities) may be adopted as units of observation. The phenomenon of population distribution is accepted as the dependent variable (Y) and the environmental or other observation for the same area is accepted as the independent variable (X). If we take observations concerning both X and Y for each area, we obtain a series of pairs of observations for

Table 15-25 Net Migration Rate and Proportion of Employed Males Who Earned Less Than $3,000 in 1959, by Geographic Divisions

Division	Net migration rate 1950-60	Percent of males earning less than $3,000
New England............	+ 0.3	32.3
Middle Atlantic........	+ 1.0	29.5
East North Central....	+ 2.3	30.5
West North Central....	- 5.8	41.5
South Atlantic........	+ 3.1	47.6
East South Central....	-12.8	55.7
West South Central....	- 4.0	47.6
Mountain..............	+11.0	36.5
Pacific...............	+21.8	31.0

Source: "Estimates of the Components of Population Change by Color, for States: 1950-60" Current Population Reports, Series P,25, No. 247, April, 1962; Table 1. 1960 Census of Population, United States Summary, Table 138.

the dependent and the independent variable. We may use conventional methods of statistical analysis, such as correlation and regression, to find out whether the two sets of observations do indeed tend to covary in a nonrandom way. Table 15-25, for example, presents statistics showing the interrelationships between net migration, 1950-1960, and the percentage of male workers earning less than $3000 in 1959 for the nine geographic divisions. It is evident that during the 1950-1960 decade the flow of migration was not random and undirected, but tended to remove persons from divisions where income was low and to deposit them in areas where income was higher. The correlation coefficient r has a very useful meaning: when squared, it states what proportion of the total variance in the dependent variable has been accounted for by its association with the independent variable.

This correlation-regression procedure may be used to search for interrelationships between a very great many demographic and environmental variables. Although perhaps misnamed, it is popularly called the "ecological correlation" method of research. The ecological correlation is identical to correlation as it is generally understood, except that *aggregates, populations,* or *areas* are used as units of observation instead of individual persons. The conclusions reached, therefore, are in terms of populations, aggregates, or areas and do not necessarily refer to the behavior of individual members of the populations, although the ecological correlation is not without statistical implications for the behavior of individuals. The ecological correlation, in some form, is the basic research procedure in the explanation of population distribution and redistribution. The term should be construed very broadly to include all forms of analysis of variance or accounting for interarea variation.

It should be emphasized that the ecological correlation cannot establish causal relationships; it is no more than a statistical test to determine whether or not a relationship exists, and the nature of the relationship. The imputation of cause, as an explanation, is one that must be done more or less subjectively by the analyst. Thus there is no way of proving that the prospect of gaining a higher income was a major motivating factor to produce the pattern of net-internal migration for 1950-1960 that was observed. This is a presumption or inference that the researcher makes on the basis of the nature of the variables and his inability to account for the observed relationships with any alternative explanation.

The ecological correlation method is useful for studying phenomena that otherwise would be difficult to study for lack of data. In many cases, the ideal set of data would be statistics for individuals, cross-classified by each other for the population of each geographic division (a table of population showing income in 1955 cross-classified by the geographic region of residence in 1960). In the absence of such detailed data for persons, the method of ecological correlation is adopted as the only way of getting at least an approximate explanation. In other cases, the ecological correlation is exactly the measure needed to test an hypothesis, and no other research plan would be as adequate. For example, the explanatory analysis of all phenomena that pertain to communities as entire communities, or to other areal or population units, can be accomplished best in no other way. "What forces are associated with the ability of communities to attract migrants?" "To have an imbalanced sex ratio in favor of females?" "To have extraordinarily high rates of unemployment?" "To have a concentration of lower-echelon white-collar workers?" "To contain disproportionately large concentrations of persons who are divorced or separated?"—investigation of population data for individuals cannot answer these questions, because the unit of analysis is a population.

Often the ecological correlation method is used to discover the extent to which and the way in which two demographic or two environmental variables covary, with no necessary inference concerning cause. This may be done simply to discover the extent to which two different measures are really measuring essentially the same thing. For example, we might correlate birthrates obtained from vital statistics registers with birthrates for the same areas estimated from census data on age.

To illustrate the possibilities for use of ecological correlation, we present Table 15-26. This table undertakes to explain the phenomenon of poverty among white families, from a population distribution point of view, by reporting a series of factors that are significantly correlated with poverty. The units of observation are the 121 subregions of the United States. Poverty is defined as the proportion of white families with incomes below $3000. In order to assure that the factor of urban-rural residence is controlled, the correlations were prepared separately three times—once for the urban, once for the rural-nonfarm, and once for the rural-farm population. Thus from this table we may generalize concerning the socioeconomic correlates of urban and rural poverty among the white population. The following inferences emerge from an analysis of this material:

1. White poverty is inversely related to the proportion foreign-born; the foreign-born population is concentrated in subregions where incomes are above average.

2. Poverty is negatively associated with mobility and positively associated with immobility. In the poorer subregions the rates of in-migration are lowest and proportions of persons living in their state of birth is highest.

3. Fertility is positively associated with poverty. Birthrates tend to be highest among populations where poverty is greatest.

4. Educational attainment among the adult

Table 15-26   Zero-Order Correlations between Proportion of White Families with Incomes of Less Than $3,000 in 1959 and Selected Other Demographic Measures, 121 Economic Subregions; Urban, Rural-Nonfarm, and Rural-Farm Population: 1960

Variable	Urban	Rural nonfarm	Rural farm
Percent foreign born..	- .26	- .31	- .59
Percent nonwhite...	.....	.....	.22
Sex ratio--white..	.....	.....	.....
Migration rate--age standardized--white...................	.....	- .26	- .25
Migration rate--age standardized--nonwhite................	.....	- .25	- .32
Percent born in state of 1960 residence--white............	.27	- .35	- .33
Percent born in state of 1960 residence--nonwhite.........	.46	.38	.55
Children ever born--age standardized--white...............	.18	.45	.52
Percent of white males with less than 8 years of education--age standardized......................................	.54	.40	.....
Percent of white males college graduates--age standardized........	- .25	.64	.59
Percent of nonwhite males with less than 8 years education--age standardized......................................	.25	- .65	- .69
Percent of civilian labor force unemployed--white.........	.....	.28	.38
Labor force participation rate of women--white............	- .32	.21	.....
Percent of employed males which are farmers or farm managers......	.46	- .49	- .47
Percent of the subregion population that is urban.........	- .48	.48	.21
Percent of families with income over $7,000--white........	- .86	- .55	- .62
Percent of families with income under $3,000--nonwhite....	.60	- .90	- .91
Percent of families with incomes over $7,000--nonwhite....	- .61	.50	.45
		- .75	- .44

Note: All correlations reported are significant at 5 percent level or beyond. Correlations too low to be significant at this level are not reported.

population is negatively associated with poverty. Where educational attainment is highest, poverty is lowest.

5. Where women are employed in greater proportions, family income is highest.

6. Employment in agriculture is positively associated with poverty. Where the proportion of employed persons classed as farmers or farm managers is greatest, the proportion of families classed as poor is also greatest.

7. The more urban the population of a subregion, the smaller proportion of its population that is poor. This effect extends to the rural-nonfarm and the rural-farm population; the more urban a subregion, the more prosperous is its rural-farm and its rural-nonfarm population.

8. Poverty among the white population is positively correlated with poverty among the nonwhite population. Where there is a concentration of poor nonwhite families, there tends also to be a concentration of poor white families. This is true for urban, rural-nonfarm, and rural-farm areas.

9. In rural areas, poverty is associated with a low sex ratio; where the proportion of women is highest, the proportion of families with low incomes is greatest.

10. In 1960 the correlation between the proportion of white families that are poor and the proportion of the population that is non-white was nearly zero, except in rural-farm areas where there was a positive correlation. It has sometimes been held that where Negroes concentrate the white families are able to enjoy a higher standard of living. There is no evidence in these data to support this hypothesis. As was pointed out in (8) above, where Negroes are poor, whites tend to be poor also.

The use of correlation and regression procedures in the study of population distribution is not confined to simple two-variable analysis. Multiple and partial correlation and multiple regression techniques, as well as the formal analysis of variance and covariance, are all appropriate. In fact, it is a very useful and powerful approach to the study of multiple variables at the group level. This technique of ecological correlation and regression will be used in later chapters to analyze in more detail the dynamics of population—fertility, nuptiality, mortality, and migration.

CONCLUSION

The overall demographic statistics for a nation are simply the weighted averages for a number of distinctive regions, subregions, and individual communities of which the nation is comprised. The study of population distribution undertakes to reveal this pattern of internal diversity and to explain it. One of the most useful strategies in demographic research is to subdivide the population into subpopulations and to determine whether a given relationship persists, disappears, or changes when it is sought in each group individually. Another equally useful research strategy is to subdivide the population, note the variation among the subpopulations in a demographic phenomenon, and undertake to account for or explain this variation. These two procedures provide the foundation for the subdiscipline of population distribution research.

In addition to being a research strategy, this branch of population study is of immense prac- tical use within a nation. By focusing on the population of a particular region, community, or even neighborhood within a community, and by examining its composition, change, and problems intensively—relating demographic measurements with other measurements for the same locality—it is possible to clarify many practical problems of immense local concern. The "population problem" of a nation is in reality several different problems, each with a particular locale and a unique set of aspects. If demographic analysis remains forever at the national level, it will be able to make only superficial and rather unhelpful statements about these problems.

QUESTIONS AND EXERCISES

1. Select five national censuses, one on each of the major continents of Europe, Asia, Africa, South America, and North America (Canada or Mexico). Make a comparative study of the treatment given population distribution in these censuses, in terms of:

> Urban rural classification
> Regional classification
> Metropolitan areas and tabulations for major places

How adequate are the data (both in terms of numbers of variables tabulated and the degree of cross-classification and area detail) in view of the discussion in this chapter?

2. From the *United Nations Demographic Yearbook* and other sources obtain data on the age and sex composition of the urban and ru- ral populations of a number of nations on vari- ous continents. Analyze the differences in age and sex composition for these countries and write an essay that describes and attempts to explain these differences.

3. Repeat Exercise 2, except obtain data for the capital city and the major industrial cen- ters of the nations and contrast them with cor- responding data for the most rural provinces in the nation.

4. Select some social or economic trait, such as educational attainment, occupation, fertility, or school attendance, and repeat either exercise 2 or 3 with it.

5. Take any social or economic or demo- graphic characteristic listed in Table 15-16 and undertake to find what other characteristics in the table are meaningfully related to it, using the scattergram method. Repeat the procedure for urban-rural differences using Tables 15-20 and 15-21.

6. Analyze Table 15-24 more fully than was done in the text. Do a little supplementary reading selected from the bibliography and write a report on recent trends in metropolitan and nonmetropolitan growth. If you can, bring regional variations into your analysis.

7. One aspect of population distribution not discussed in this chapter is the value of data for individual places as a tool of historical demog- raphy. Although reliable data for a nation may be available for only a short period, sometimes it is possible to have very useful information for a particular community that runs back over many decades. The historical demography movement in Europe makes great use of this procedure. Write a short essay on the value and limitations of studies of individual places for historical demography.

8. Another type of distributional unit not discussed fully in this chapter is the broad metropolitan region, including the "hinter- land" of a metropolis. Almost no data for such units are available, except those generated by individual researchers who add together data for smaller units of territory. Construct a list of hypotheses that could be tested if data were available for units of this type and specify how the data must be tabulated in order to test these hypotheses.

9. Another branch of population distribution that we have not explored in this chapter is the internal variation within metropolitan areas. For such studies the Bureau of the Census has prepared census tract data. Read the introduction to one of these reports and write an essay on the demographic research opportunities these data make possible.

10. Some observers contend that there is more variation between neighborhoods in the suburbs of a metropolis than in the central city. Using census tract data for a moderate size city, see if you can test this hypothesis.

11. Certain cities of the world have attained great size while having only a moderate amount of industrialization. Review the data for occupation and industry for some of these places and write an essay comparing their industrial base with that of more industrialized places such as Rotterdam, London, Tokyo, and Hamburg. Here are some places to consider:

Rio de Janeiro
Caracas
Bangkok
Abadan
Cairo
Jerusalem

Calcutta
Karachi
Manila
Mexico City
Washington, D. C.

Do you think there are unique demographic traits that distinguish a "preindustrial" from a "nonindustrial" city?

12. From the bibliography, select some of the readings on regionalism written by geographers. Write an essay on the role geography can play in the study of population distribution.

13. The text was able to report only a fraction of the information contained in Tables 15-22 and 15-23. Write an essay on color differentials in educational attainment in the United States, from the distributional point of view. Compute these same tables for 1950 and report what change has taken place.

14. From the census find five cities and five rural areas that lost population between 1950 and 1960. Match them with five similar places in the same region that gained population during this time. Write an essay on the characteristics of growing and declining populations, pointing out the similarities and differences between urban and rural examples.

BIBLIOGRAPHY

I. POPULATION DISTRIBUTION: GENERAL THEORY AND METHODS

Arensberg, Conrad M. "The Community Study Method," *American Journal of Sociology*, **60** (1954), 109–124.

Beshers, James M. "Delineation of Demographic Areas and the Contiguity Ratio," in American Statistical Association. *Proceedings of the Social Statistics Section*. Papers presented at the annual meeting of the American Statistical Association, Chicago, Ill., December 27-30, 1958. Under the sponsorship of the Social Statistics Section, Washington, D.C., 1959.

Beshers, James M. "Statistical Inferences from Small Area Data," *Social Forces*, **38** (4) (May 1960), 341–348.

Bogue, Donald J. "Micro-demography," in Population Association of America. Donald J. Bogue (ed.). *Applications of Demography; The Population Situation in the United States in 1975*. Scripps Foundation Studies in Population Distribution, No. 13. Oxford, Ohio: Shoestring Press, 1957.

Bogue, Donald J. "Population Distribution," Chapter 17 in Philip M. Hauser and Otis Dudley Duncan (eds.). *The Study of Population*. Chicago: University of Chicago Press, 1959.

Burgess, Ernest W. "The Growth of the City," in Robert E. Park, Ernest W. Burgess, and R. D. McKenzie. *The City*. Chicago: University of Chicago Press, 1925.

Duncan, Otis Dudley. "Human Ecology and Population Studies," Chapter 28 in Philip M. Hauser and Otis Dudley Duncan (eds.). *The Study of Population*. Chicago: University of Chicago Press, 1959. Part IV. Population Studies in Various Disciplines.

Duncan, Otis Dudley. "The Measurement of Population Distribution," *Population Studies*, **11** (1) (July 1957), 27–45.

Duncan, Otis Dudley, and Beverly Duncan. "An Alternative to Ecological Correlation," *American Sociological Review*, **18** (6) (1953), 665–666.

Duncan, Otis Dudley, and Beverly Duncan. "A Methodological Analysis of Segregation Indexes," *American Sociological Review*, **20** (2) (April 1955), 210–217.

Duncan, Otis Dudley, and Leo F. Schnore. "Cultural, Behavioral and Ecological Perspectives in the Study of Social Organization," *Ameri-*

can Journal of Sociology, 64 (September 1959), 132–146.

Gibbs, Jack P. Urban Research Methods. Princeton, N. J.: D. Van Nostrand Company, 1961.

Goodman, Leo A. "Ecological Regression and the Behavior of Individuals," American Sociological Review, 18 (6) (1953), 663–664.

Goodman, Leo A. "Some Alternatives to Ecological Correlation," American Journal of Sociology, 64 (1959), 610–625.

Halbwachs, Maurice. Population and Society; Introduction to Social Morphology. Translated by Otis Dudley Duncan and Harold W. Pfautz. Glencoe, Ill.: Free Press, 1960.

Hatt, Paul K., and Albert J. Reiss, Jr. (eds.). Reader in Urban Sociology. Glencoe, Ill.: The Free Press, 1956.

Hauser, Philip M. "Demography and Ecology," Annals of the American Academy of Political and Social Science, 362 (November 1965), 129–138.

Hoover, Edgar M. The Location of Economic Activity. New York: McGraw-Hill, 1948.

Isard, Walter. Methods of Regional Analysis. Cambridge, Mass.: published jointly by the Technology Press of the Massachusetts Institute of Technology; New York: John Wiley and Sons, 1960.

Keyfitz, Nathan. "Analysis of Variance Procedures in the Study of Ecological Phenomena," in Ernest W. Burgess and Donald J. Bogue (eds.). Contributions to Urban Sociology. Chicago: University of Chicago Press, 1964.

Menzel, Herbert. "Comment on Robinson's 'Ecological Correlations and the Behavior of In-dividuals,'" American Sociological Review, 15 (October 1959), 674.

Neyman, Jerzy, and Elizabeth L. Scott. "On a Mathematical Theory of Populations Conceived as Conglomerations of Clusters," pp. 109–120 in Cold Spring Harbor Symposia on Quantitative Biology, Vol. 22, 1957.

Robinson, W. S. "Ecological Correlations and the Behavior of Individuals," American Sociological Review, 15 (3) (1950), 351–357.

Schmid, Calvin F., and Kiyoshi Tagashira. "Ecological and Demographic Indices: a Methodological Analysis," Demography, 1 (1) (1964), 211.

Schmid, Calvin F., et al. "The Ecology of the American City; Further Comparison and Validation of Generalizations," American Sociological Review, 23 (4) (August 1958), 392–401.

Schnore, Leo F. The Urban Scene: Human Ecology and Demography. New York: The Free Press; London: Collier-Macmillan, 1965.

Stewart, John Q. "Empirical Mathematical Rules Concerning the Distribution and Equilibrium of Population," Geographical Review, 37 (1947), 461–485.

Stewart, John Q., and William Warntz. "The Field Theory of Population Influence," pp. 62–70 in International Union for the Study of Population. (Session) 7. Miscellaneous topics. International Population Conference, New York 1961 (Proceedings). Vol. 2. London, 1963, pp. 7–80. French and English summaries.

Theodorson, George A. (ed.). Studies in Human Ecology. Evanston, Ill.: Row Petersen and Company, 1961.

II. URBAN-RURAL RESIDENCE AND URBANIZATION

Ahlberg, Gösta. Population Trends and Urbanization in Sweden, 1911–1950. Lund, Sweden, Royal University, Department of Geography, Lund Studies in Geography, Series B, Human Geography, No. 16. Lund: G. W. K. Gleerup, 1956.

Awad, Hasan. "Morocco's Expanding Towns," Geographical Journal, 130 (1) (March 1964), 49–64.

Beale, Calvin. "Rural Depopulation in the United States," Demography, 1 (1964), 264–272.

Berry, Brian J. L. "City Size Distributions and Economic Development," Economic Development and Cultural Change, 9 (4, pt. 1) (July 1961), 573–588.

Berry, Brian J. L. "The Impact of Expanding Metropolitan Communities upon the Central Place Hierarchy," Annals of the Association of American Geographers, 50 (2) (June 1960), 112–116.

Bloom, Len. "Some Problems of Urbanization in South Africa," Phylon, 25 (4) (Winter 1964), 347–361.

Bogue, Donald J. "Population Distribution: Urban-Rural Residence," Chapter 2 in Population of the United States. Glencoe, Ill.: The Free Press, 1959.

Burgess, Ernest W., and Donald J. Bogue (eds.). Contributions to Urban Sociology. Chicago: The University of Chicago Press, 1964.

Clark, Colin. "What Constitutes Rural Over-Population?," Proceedings of the World Population Conference: 1954. New York, 1955. Vol. V.

Davidovich, V. G. "Urban Agglomerations in the USSR," Soviet Geography: Review and Translation, 5 (9) (November 1964), 34–44. Translation of paper presented at the symposium on economic geography of the USSR at the fourth Congress of the Geographical Society of the USSR.

Dewey, Richard. "The Rural-urban Continuum: Real but Relatively Unimportant," American

Journal of Sociology, 66 (1) (July 1960), 60–66.

Duncan, Otis Dudley. "Note on Farm Tenancy and Urbanization," *Journal of Farm Economics,* 38 (4) (November 1956), 1043–1047.

Duncan, Otis Dudley, and Albert J. Reiss, Jr. *Social Characteristics of Urban and Rural Communities,* 1950. New York: John Wiley and Sons, 1956.

Durand, John D., and César A. Peláez. *Patterns of Urbanization in Latin America,* pp. 166–191 in Clyde V. Kiser (ed.). *Components of Population Change in Latin America.* Proceedings of the sixtieth anniversary conference of the Milbank Memorial Fund, held at the Savoy Plaza Hotel, New York City, April 5 to 7, 1965. *Milbank Memorial Fund Quarterly,* 43 (4, Part 2) (October 1965), 1–384.

Fuguitt, Glenn V. "The Growth and Decline of Small Towns as a Probability Process," *American Sociological Review,* 30 (3) (June 1965), 403–411.

Fuguitt, Glenn V. "Trends in Unincorporated Places, 1950–60," *Demography,* 2 (1965), 363–371.

Fuguitt, Glenn V., and Donald W. Thomas. "Small Town Growth in the United States: An Analysis by Size, Class and by Place," *Demography,* 3 (2) (1966), 513–527.

Gibbs, Jack P., and Walter T. Martin. "Urbanization, Technology, and the Division of Labor: International Patterns," *American Sociological Review,* 27 (5) (October 1962), 667–677.

Goldstein, Sidney. *Rural-Suburban-Urban Population Redistribution in Denmark.* Paper contributed for the United Nations World Population Conference, August 30-September 10, 1965.

Gutman, Robert, and David Popenoe. (eds.). "Urban Studies; Present Trends and Future Prospects in an Emerging Academic Field," *American Behavioral Scientist,* 6 (6) (February 1963), 4–63.

Harris, Chauncy D. "A Functional Classification of Cities in the United States," *Geographical Review,* 33 (1943), 86–99.

Harris, Chauncy D., and Edward L. Ullman. "The Nature of Cities," *Annals of the American Academy of Political and Social Science* (242), 7–17.

Hauser, Philip M. and Leo F. Schnore (eds.). *The Study of Urbanization.* New York: John Wiley and Sons, 1965.

Hawley, Amos H. "World Urbanization: Trends and Prospects," in Ronald Freedman (ed.). *Population:* The Vital Revolution. Garden City, N.Y.: Anchor Books, Doubleday, 1964, pp. 70–83.

Hoyt, Homer. "Changing Patterns of Urban Growth: 1959–1965," *Urban Land,* 18 (April 1965).

Hoyt, Homer. *The Structure and Growth of Residential Neighborhoods in American Cities.* Washington, D. C.: U. S. Government Printing Office, 1951.

Johnson, D. Gale. "An Appraisal of the Data for Farm Families," in National Bureau of Economic Research. *An Appraisal of the 1950 Census Income Data.* Studies in Income and Wealth, Vol. 23, by the Conference on Research in Income and Wealth. A report of the National Bureau of Economic Research, New York. Princeton, N.J.: Princeton University Press, 1958.

Kuper, Hilda (ed.). *Urbanization and Migration in West Africa.* Berkeley and Los Angeles; University of California Press; London; Cambridge University Press, 1965.

Kuznets, Simon, and Dorothy S. Thomas (eds.). Vol. III. *Demographic Analyses and Interrelations.* By Hope T. Eldridge and Dorothy S. Thomas. Memoirs of the American Philosophical Society, Vol. 61, 1964, in *Population Redistribution and Economic Growth: United States, 1870–1950.* In 3 vols. Philadelphia: American Philosophical Society, 1957–1964.

Lund Studies in Geography, No. 3. *Studies in Rural-Urban Interaction.* In Lund University, Department of Geography. Lund, 1951. The English summaries of four papers at a meeting held under the direction of the Swedish Social Science Research Council, Uppsala, 1950.

Mayer, Harold M. "Urban Geography," in P. E. James and C. F. Jones (eds.). *American Geography: Inventory and Prospect.* Syracuse, N. Y.: Association of American Geographers, 1954.

Mols, Roger. (*Introduction à la Démographie Historique des Villes d'Europe de XIVe au XVIIIe Siècle* (*Introduction to the Historical Demography of the Cities of Europe from the Fourteenth to the Eighteenth Centuries*). Gembloux, Belgium: J. Duculot, 1956. In 3 vols.

Nelson, Howard J. "Some Characteristics of the Population in Cities in Similar Service Classifications," *Economic Geography,* 33 (2) (April 1957), 95–108.

Ogburn, William F., and Otis Dudley Duncan. "City Size as a Sociological Variable," pp. 129–147 in Ernest W. Burgess, and Donald J. Bogue (eds.). *Contributions to Urban Sociology.* Chicago: University of Chicago Press, 1964.

Park, Robert E., Ernest W. Burgess, and R. D. McKenzie. *The City.* Chicago: University of Chicago Press, 1925.

Powelson, John P., and Anatole A. Solow. "Urban and Rural Development in Latin America," in James C. Charlesworth (ed.). *Latin America Tomorrow.* (A group of 12 articles). *Annals of the American Academy of Political and Social Science,* 360 (July 1965), 1–138.

Reissman, Leonard. *The Urban Process: Cities in Industrial Societies.* New York: Free Press of Glencoe; London: Collier-Macmillan, 1964.

Rodwin, Lloyd. "The British New Towns Policy," *Harvard City Planning Studies,* XVI. Cambridge, Mass.: Harvard University Press, 1956.

Royal Tropical Institute. Amsterdam. *The Indonesian Town: Studies in Urban Sociology.* Selected studies in Indonesia, Vol. 4. The Hague and Bandung, W. van Hoeve, Ltd., 1958.

Schnore, Leo F. "Some Correlates of Urban Size: A Replication," *American Journal of Sociology,* 69 (2) (September 1963), 185–193.

Schnore, Leo F. "The Statistical Measurement of Urbanization and Economic Development," *Land Economics,* 37 (3) (August 1961), 229–245.

Schnore, Leo F. "Urbanization and Economic Development: the Demographic Contribution," *American Journal of Economics and Sociology,* 23 (1) (January 1964), 37–48.

Schwirian, Kent P., and Prehn, John W. "An Axiomatic Theory of Urbanization," *American Sociological Review,* 27 (6) (December 1962), 812–825.

Scientific American. Cities. New York; Knopf, 1965. [Articles originally published in the September 1965 issue of *Scientific American,* 213 (3).]

Seck, Assane. "Introduction à l'Etude des Villes Tropicales" ("Introduction to the Study of Tropical Cities"), *Tiers-Monde* (Paris), 6 (21) (January-March 1965), 171–204.

Shabad, Theodore. "The Population of China's Cities," *Geographical Review,* 49 (1) (January 1959), 32–42.

Simms, Ruth P. *Urbanization in West Africa: A Review of Current Literature.* Evanston, Ill.: Northwestern University Press, 1965.

Smith, T. Lynn. "The Rural Community with Special Reference to Latin America," *Rural Sociology,* 23 (1) (March 1958), 52–67.

Tarver, James D. "Ecological Patterns of Land Tenure, Farm Land Uses, and Farm Population Characteristics," *Rural Sociology,* (June 1963), 138–145.

Taeuber, Karl E., and Alma F. Taeuber. *Negroes in Cities: Residential Segregation and Neighborhood Change.* (In series.) Population Research and Training Center Monographs. Chicago: Aldine Publishing Co., 1965.

Ullman, E. L. "A Theory of Location for Cities," *American Journal of Sociology,* 46 (1941), 853–864.

United Nations Educational, Scientific, and Cultural Organization. Research Centre on Social and Economic Development in Southern Asia. *Report on Urban-rural Differences in Southern Asia;* Some Aspects and Methods of Analysis. Regional Seminar, Dehli, 1962. Delhi, 1964.

United Nations Educational, Scientific and Cultural Organization. Research Centre on the Social Implications of Industrialization in Southern Asia. *Urbanization in Asia and the Far East;* Proceedings of the Joint UN/UNESCO Seminar (in cooperation with the International Labour Office) on Urbanization in the ECAFE Region, Bangkok, 8–18 August, 1956. Philip M. Hauser (ed.). Calcutta, 1957.

U. S. Bureau of the Census and Department of Agriculture. Economic Research Service. *Estimates of the Farm Population of the United States;* 1964. June 4, 1965. *Current Population Reports.* Series Census-ERS P-27. Farm Population. No. 1-. Washington, D. C., 1954-.

U. S. Department of Agriculture. Economic Research Service. Resource Development Economics Division. Alan R. Bird, *Poverty in Rural Areas of the United States.* Agricultural Economic Report 63. Washington, D. C., November 1964.

University of Edinburgh. Centre of African Studies. *Urbanization in African Social Change.* Proceedings of the inaugural seminar held in the Centre of African Studies, 5th-7th January 1963. Edinburgh, 1963.

Weaver, Robert C. "Human Values and City Building," in American Institute of Planners. *Proceedings of the Forty-fourth Annual Conference.* Detroit, November 26–30, 1961. Washington, D. C., June 1962.

Whitney, Vincent H. "Changes in the Rural-nonfarm Population, 1930-1950," *American Sociological Review,* 25 (3) (June 1960), 363–368.

Wolfe, Marshall. *Some Implications of Recent Changes in Urban and Rural Settlement Patterns in Latin America.* Paper contributed for the United Nations World Population Conference, August 30-September 10, 1965.

Zenteno, Benitez. "La Población Rural y Urbana en Mexico" ("The Rural and Urban Population of Mexico"), *Revista Mexicana de Sociología* (Mexico, D. F.), 24 (3) (September-December 1962), 689–703.

III. METROPOLITAN-NONMETROPOLITAN RESIDENCE AND INTRAMETROPOLITAN DISTRIBUTION

Berry, Brian J. L., et al. "Urban Population Densities: Structure and Change," *Geographical Review,* 53 (3) (July 1963), 389–405.

Beshers, James M., et al. "Ethnic Congregation-segregation, Assimilation, and Stratification, *Social Forces,* 42 (4) (May 1964), 482–489.

Bogue, Donald J. "Population Distribution: Residence in Metropolitan and Nonmetropolitan Areas," Chapter 3 in *The Population of the United States*. Glencoe, Ill.: The Free Press, 1959.

Bogue, Donald J. *Population Growth in Standard Metropolitan Areas, 1900-1950*. Washington, D. C.: Housing and Home Finance Agency, 1953.

Bogue, Donald J. *The Structure of the Metropolitan Community*. Ann Arbor, Mich.: University of Michigan Press, 1949.

Duncan, Beverly. "Variables in Urban Morphology," in Ernest W. Burgess and Donald J. Bogue (eds.). *Contributions to Urban Sociology*. Chicago; University of Chicago Press, 1964.

Duncan, Beverly, et al. "*Patterns of City Growth*," *American Journal of Sociology*, **67** (1962), 418–429.

Duncan, Otis Dudley. "Research on Metropolitan Population: Evaluation of Data," *Journal of the American Statistical Association*, **51** (276) (December 1956), 591–596.

Duncan, Otis Dudley. "Residential Segregation and Social Differentiation," pp. 571–577 in *Proceedings of the International Union for the Scientific Study of Population. Vienna*, 1959.

Duncan, Otis Dudley, et al. *Metropolis and Region. Baltimore*, published for Resources for the Future, Inc., by the Johns Hopkins Press, 1960.

Duncan, Otis Dudley, and Beverly Duncan. "Residential Distribution and Occupational Stratification," *American Journal of Sociology*, **60** (March 1955), 493–503.

Feldt, Allan G. "The Metropolitan Area Concept: an Evaluation of the 1950 SMA's," *Journal of the American Statistical Association*, **60** (310) (June 1965), 617–636.

Foley, Donald. "An Approach to Metropolitan Spatial Structure," in Melvin M. Webber, et al. (eds.). *Explorations in Urban Structure*. Philadelphia: University of Pennsylvania Press, 1964.

France. Institut National de la Statistique et des Etudes Economiques. Direction Régionale de Paris. *La Population des Quartiers de Paris et son Évolution Récente (The Population of the Districts of Paris and Recent Changes)*. Bulletin Régional de Statistique, No. 4. 1962, pp. 11–13. Summary of results of the census of March 1962 (Préfécture de la Seine, Bulletin Bibliographique Mensuel 7 (3–4)).

Freedman, Ronald. "Cityward Migration, Urban Ecology, and Social Theory (1950)," pp. 178–200 in Ernest W. Burgess and Donald J. Bogue (eds.). *Contributions to Urban Sociology*. Chicago: University of Chicago Press, 1964.

Germany. Berlin. Statistisches Landesamt. *100 Jahre Berliner Statistik, 1862-1962. Festschrift zum Hundertjährigen Bestehen des Berliner Statistischen Amtes (One Hundred Years of Berlin Statistics, 1862-1962. Publication in Honor of the Century Year of the Berlin Statistical Office)*. Berlin-Schöneberg, 1962.

Gibbs, Jack P., and Kingsley Davis. "Conventional versus Metropolitan Data in the International Study of Urbanization." *American Sociological Review*, **23** (5) (October 1958), 504–513.

Goldsmith, Harold F., and James H. Copp. "Metropolitan Dominance and Agriculture," *Rural Sociology*, **29** (4) (December 1964), 385–395.

Government Affairs Foundation, New York. *Metropolitan Surveys; A Digest*. Chicago, Public Administration Service, 1958. Includes bibliographical references.

Hashmi, Sultan S. *The People of Karachi: Demographic Characteristics*. Pakistan Institue of Development Economics, Monographs in the Economics of Development, 13, Karachi, January 1965.

Hoyt, Homer. "The Residential and Retail Patterns of Leading Latin American Cities," *Land Economics*, **39** (4) (November 1963), 449–454.

Hoyt, Homer, and Jerome P. Pickard. "The World's Million-population Metropolises," *Urban Land*, **23** (8) (September 1964), 2, 7–10.

International Statistical Institute. *Annuaire de Statistique Internationale des Grandes Villes (International Statistical Yearbook of Large Towns)*. Vol. 1. 1961. The Hague, 1962. XXXVI. Duplicate text in English and French.

International Statistical Institute. *Economic Data of Large Towns 1950-1954*. International Statistics of Large Towns, Series C, No. 1. The Hague, 1958. XV.

International Statistical Institute. *Population and Vital Statistics of Large Towns, 1946-1951. (Statistiques Démographiques des Grandes Villes, 1946-1951)* Series A Population, No. 1. The Hague, 1954.

Kono, Shigemi. "Some Characteristics of the Megalopolitan Development in Japan: Migration Velocity Analysis," *Jinko Mondai Kenkyu (Journal of Population Problems)* [Tokyo], (95) (July 1965), 11–20. In Japanese with English summary.

Kuroda, Toshio. Demographic Approach to Megalopolis in Japan: Migration Behavior in Megalopolis. *Jinko Mondai Kenkyu (Journal of Population Problems)* (Tokyo), (95) (July 1965), 1–10.

Lieberson, Stanley. *Ethnic Patterns in American Cities*. New York: Free Press of Glencoe, 1963.

McKenzie, R. D. *The Metropolitan Community*. New York: McGraw-Hill, 1933.

Niedercorn, John H. "An Econometric Model of Metropolitan Employment and Population Growth," *Memorandum RM-3758-RC*. Santa Monica: Rand Corporation, October 1963.

Niedercorn, John H., and John F. Kain. "An Econometric Model of Metropolitan Development," pp. 123–143. *Papers and Proceedings*, Vol. 11, 1963. Philadelphia, Regional Science Association, 1964.

Ogburn, William F. "Inventions of Local Transportation and the Patterns of Cities," *Social Forces*, 24 (May 1946), 373–379.

Palen, J. John, and Leo F. Schnore. "Color Composition and City-suburban Status Differences: A Replication and Extension," *Land Economics*, 41 (1) (February 1965), 87–91.

Pethe, Vasant P. "Economic Functions of the Cities of India," *Sociological Bulletin* (Bombay), March 1965, pp. 1–12.

Pourcher, Guy. *Le Peuplement de Paris*. Origines Régionales. Composition Sociale. Attitudes et Motivations *(The Population of Paris*. Regional Sources. Social Characteristics. Attitudes and Motives). Institut National d'Etudes Demographiques, Travaux et Documents, Cahier 43. Paris: Presses Universitaires de France, 1963.

Redick, Richard W. "A Demographic and Ecological Study of Rangoon, Burma, 1953," pp. 31–41 in Ernest W. Burgess and Donald J. Bogue (eds.). *Contributions to Urban Sociology*. Chicago: University of Chicago Press, 1964.

Robinson, Warren C. "Changes in the Rural Population of the United States by Metropolitan and Nonmetropolitan Status, 1900 to 1960," *Rural Sociology*, 30 (2) (June 1965), 166–183.

Schmid, Calvin F. "Generalizations Concerning the Ecology of the American City," *American Sociological Review*, 15 (2) (1950), 610–625.

Schnore, Leo F. "The Socio-economic Status of Cities and Suburbs," *American Sociological Review*, 28 (1) (February 1963), 76–85.

Schnore, Leo F. "Urban Structure and Suburban Selectivity," *Demography*, 1 (1) (1964), 164–176.

Schnore, Leo F., and Harry Sharp. "Racial Changes in Metropolitan Areas, 1950-1960," *Social Forces*, 41 (3) (March 1963), 247–253.

Sheldon, Henry D., and Siegfried A. Hoermann. "Metropolitan Structure and Commutation," *Demography*, 1 (1) (1964), 186–193.

University of Pennsylvania. Population Studies Center. Technical Papers. No. 1. Philadelphia, November 1961. Processed. I. *Population in 1960 of Areas Annexed to Large Cities of the United States between 1950 and 1960 by Age, Sex, and Color*. By Ann R. Miller and Bension Varon. November 1961.

Zander, Mildred, and Harold Goldblatt. *Trends in the Concentration and Dispersal of White and Nonwhite Residents of New York City, 1950-1960* in New York City. Commission on Human Rights. Research Unit. Research Reports. No. 1. New York, 1961.

IV. REGIONAL DISTRIBUTION AND REGIONALISM

Ackerman, Edward A. "Geography and Demography," Chapter 29 in Philip M. Hauser and Otis Dudley Duncan. *The Study of Population*. Chicago: University of Chicago Press, 1959.

Bogue, Donald J. "Nodal Versus Homogeneous Regions and Statistical Techniques for Measuring the Influence of Each," *Proceedings of the Conference of the International Statistical Institute*, Rio de Janeiro, 1955.

Bogue, Donald J. "Population Distribution: States, Regions, and Geographic Divisions," Chapter 4 in *Population of the United States*. Glencoe, Ill.: The Free Press, 1959.

Bogue, Donald J., and Calvin L. Beale. *Economic Areas of the United States*. Glencoe, Ill.: The Free Press, 1961.

Chatterjee, S. P. "Regional Patterns of the Density and Distribution of Population in India," *Geographical Review of India* (Calcutta), 24 (2) (June 1962), 1–28.

Dickinson, Robert E. *City and Region: A Geographical Interpretation*. International Library of Sociology and Social Reconstruction. London: Routledge and Kegan Paul; New York: Humanities Press, 1964.

Dickinson, Robert E. *City, Region, and Regionalism*. London: Routledge and Kegan Paul, 1947.

Eblen, Jack E. "An Analysis of Nineteenth-century Frontier Populations," *Demography*, 2 (1965), 399–413.

Isard, Walter. *Location and Space Economy*. New York: John Wiley and Sons, 1954.

James, P. E. "The Geographic Study of Population," in P. E. James and C. F. Jones (eds.). *American Geography: Inventory and Prospect*. Syracuse, N. Y.: Association of American Geographers, 1954.

Krotov, V. A. "The Economic Geography of Siberia and the Far East in its Present Stage," *Soviet Geography: Review and Translation*, 5 (5) (May 1964), 56–64. English translation of Russian text in *Doklady Instituta Geografii Sibiri i Dal'nego Vostoka* (4) (1963), 33–41.

Lee, Everett S., et al. *Population Redistribution and Economic Growth, United States, 1870-1950. I. Methodological Considerations and Reference Tables*. American Philosophical Society Memoirs, Vol. 45. Philadelphia, 1957.

Manor, Stella P. "Geographic Changes in U. S. Employment from 1950 to 1960," *Monthly Labor Review*, 86 (1) (January 1963), 1–10.

Myklebost, Hallstein. "Population and Settlements North of the Arctic Circle," in Ornulv Vorren (ed.). *Norway North of 65.* Oslo: University of Oslo Press, and London: Allen and Unwin, 1960.

Nicholls, William H. "The South as a Developing Area," *Journal of Politics,* **26** (1) (February 1964), 22–40.

Roof, Michael K., and Frederick A. Leedy. "Population Redistribution in the Soviet Union," *Geographical Review,* **49** (2) (April 1959), 208–221.

Schnore, Leo F. "City-suburban Income Differentials in Metropolitan Areas," *American Sociological Review,* **27** (2) (April 1962), 252–555.

Stewart, John Q., and William Warntz. "Macrogeography and Social Science," *Geographical Review,* **48** (2) (April 1958), 167–184.

Trewartha, Glen T. "The Case for Population Geography," *Annals of the Association of American Geographers,* **44** (1954), 135–162.

Vining, Rudledge. "On the Delimitation of Economic Areas," *Journal of the American Statistical Association,* 1961.

Wade, Richard C. *The Urban Frontier: The Rise of Western Cities, 1790-1830.* Harvard Historical Monographs, 41. Cambridge, Mass.: Harvard University Press, 1959.

Warntz, William. "A New Map of the Surface of Population Potentials for the United States, 1960," *Geographical Review,* **54** (2) (April 1964), 170–184.

Whittlesey, D. "The Regional Concept and the Regional Method," in P. E. James and C. F. Jones (eds.). *American Geography: Inventory and Prospect.* Syracuse, N. Y.: Association of American Geographers, 1954.

CHAPTER 16

Demographic Aspects of Mortality

16.1. Introduction: Mortality as a Sociodemographic Force

With this chapter we shift from the study of demographic structure to the study of the demographic processes. Here the focus will be on dynamics and *occurrence of events over time* rather than *status of persons* at particular instants of time. Although many different processes are of interest and concern to demographers, only four are considered to lie primarily within the field of demography. These are the study of mortality, marriage, fertility, and residential mobility. They are the processes that are most directly involved in the phenomenon of growth and that determine the total size of a particular population or subpopulation. This and the next three chapters are devoted to the study of these four components of population dynamics. The final chapter on reproduction and population forecasts considers how these forces work together to bring about population change.

There are several other dynamic forces that are of interest to particular branches of demography, which cannot be fully considered here. Among them are occupational mobility, household and family formation, family dissolution from divorce and widowhood, entrance into employment and departure from employment, shifting of workers from one industry to another, change in income level of persons, social mobility, and changes in citizenship. The reader who is especially interested in one of these topics should consult the *Population Index* to obtain a list of pertinent references.

The first of the demographic processes to be considered is mortality. A knowledge of its effects is required for the study of the other processes. Also, the concepts and models developed for mortality analysis are needed to build the systems for the analysis of marriage, fertility, and migration. Demographers are exercising more than just a morbid curiosity when they accept the responsibility for making systematic studies of mortality and its effects on the population.

As has already been described in earlier chapters, data for the study of mortality are obtained from tabulations of death certificates, issued at the time of death, which are required by law in most countries before burial or other disposal of the corpse is permitted. These certificates contain information concerning the sex, age, race, and other characteristics of the individual and, hopefully, a correct assessment of the cause of death. By tabulating these data and relating them to information from a census, it is possible to compute death rates. The crude death rate, defined and used extensively in Chapters 2 and 3, is simply the total number of deaths that occur during one year among a population per 1000 total population as of the middle of the year:

$$\text{CDR} = \frac{\text{total deaths}}{\text{midyear population}} \times 1000$$

It is the purpose of this chapter to present more refined measures of mortality and to use them to trace trends in mortality and differences in the impact of mortality among the various segments of the population.

Mortality is a continuous force of attrition, tending to reduce population but having its effect countervailed by the force of fertility. It is the negative component in the balance of the vital processes. The speed with which a population grows is determined by the level of the death rate conjointly with the level of the birthrate. We have already described, in Chapters 2 and 3, how the decline in death rates between 1650 and 1900 led to a burgeoning of the European and American populations. Also, we noted how the extension of death control to the nations of Asia, Africa, and Latin America is currently leading to an even more dramatic upsurge of growth there. Man has tampered with the vital processes of both fertility and mortality and has attempted to regulate them. He has been conspicuously successful in the instance of mortality, and as a consequence has created a situation of disequilibrium, which, observers agree, cannot long continue, but which can be corrected only by a reduction of fertility or a return of mortality toward a higher level. Thus a comparative *lack* of mortality can create great pressures on the social system where birthrates are high.

But mortality has effects in addition to those associated only with population size. It is an inexorable force for social change and for change in population composition. Because of it, no social system can ever be said to be truly stable, or safe from change. As generations grow old and die, they must be replaced. The resulting turnover in leadership inevitably gives opportunities for a fundamental redirection of efforts. It can be one way in which a society can cleanse itself of corruption, tyranny, incompetent leadership, or bigotry and give itself another opportunity to make progress toward attaining its aspirations. Or it can precipitate a retrogression or diversion that can be corrected only by another cycle of aging and death. Also, the process by which one generation succeeds another, filling all of the statuses and roles with a new set of faces, can lead to fundamental changes in population composition and attitude, as well as in the rate of growth.

Cultures are not immortal; they reside in the minds and hearts of individuals, and each death erases from existence a quantum of knowledge, experience, conviction, and social influence. The role that the deceased individual played is taken over by a new person who must be acculturated afresh. Only if the replacement is identical with the deceased is there no social change. Perhaps the most dramatic of these changes taking place at the present time is the dying off of older generations in the developing nations of Asia, Latin America, and Africa and their replacement with a new generation of citizens that is better educated and imbued with the ideals of progress and improvement.

Mortality analysis has been greatly simplified and systematized by a set of concepts, models, and measures that demographers have developed. Instead of launching directly into the presentation of factual material, we shall digress in the next two sections, to equip ourselves. It is especially essential that the age curve of mortality, the life table, and the stationary population model be understood and appreciated. To his pleasant surprise, the reader who takes time to master these ideas will not only find the entire subject easy to grasp, but he will also find these ideas highly useful in other branches of social research.

16.2. The Age Curve of Mortality

In Chapters 2 and 3 we studied mortality in terms of the crude death rate. With this simple measure we arrived at the all-important lessons that mortality exerts a much greater force on some populations than on others and that its force may change quickly over time. To explore these ideas in more detail and to understand more clearly the sociodemographic implications of mortality, we must recognize that mortality has a very unequal impact on the various age groups. It strikes very hard at the very youngest and the very oldest members of the population. Among young adults it strikes so lightly as to be almost no threat at all in many nations. This commonplace fact is so familiar that it is easy to overlook its many implications. If a child dies the day it is born, its death has far greater demographic implications than does the death of an elderly person. Had it lived, the child would very probably have survived to go through school, enter the labor force, marry, and bear children. The infant death represents the loss not only of one person, but of the many descendants who could be traced to him had he lived. Contrast this with the death of an elderly person; his demise represents a subtraction of one from the population, with few further implications for the nation at large except that whatever income he may have had from accumulated wealth is redistributed to others and whatever positions of status and power he may have occupied must now pass to others. The implication for future population growth of the death of any person who has passed beyond the years of reproduction is, of course, zero.

We may consider briefly an all-too-frequent example: the case of a young college senior killed in an automobile accident on the way back to school from his Christmas holiday. This is an annual news item on New Year's Day. Such a person would have spent most of his 20 years or so as a dependent. Society at large, partially through the media of his family, would have invested perhaps as much as $50,-000 in him by this age—in the form of food, clothing, shelter, and other goods he has consumed, in education, and in expenditure for his protection and health. Meanwhile, aside from minor part-time employment, such a person would have produced comparatively little. His death, therefore, represents a tremendous financial loss to the society. Had he lived, he would soon have begun to earn and reproduce. After about five years or so he would have repaid society for the cost of his upbringing and would then represent a net surplus in productivity that would be invested in his own children or the children of others. If he had survived to retirement age, he would have produced a very large "profit" on the investment made in him.

These examples underscore the general principle that the amount of loss to a society, in terms both of potential population growth and of financial loss, is determined to a great extent by the age at which death takes place. Thus we must begin the intensive study of mortality by learning its age pattern.

Age-Specific Mortality Rates. Most intensive studies of the age pattern of mortality begin by computing age-specific mortality rates. This is simply a crude death rate computed for each age group individually. For much demographic analysis a grouping of ages into five-year intervals is employed. The age-specific death

rate for ages 10 to 14, for example, is the number of deaths per year to persons ages 10 to 14 at the time of death divided by the midyear population aged 10 to 14. These age-specific rates form a distinctive curve, as illustrated in Figure 16-1. Every human population exhibits a curve of this type, showing the incidence of mortality by age.

Mortality is high in the first year of life; it declines rapidly in the second and third years until by age 9 it is very low. It remains low until the mid-thirties, when it gradually begins to increase at an accelerating rate. Thereafter, it rises at an ever increasing pace until by age 60 it becomes high and by age 70 extremely high. Figure 16-1 contrasts the age-specific mortality rates of Sweden and India, two nations where death rates are low and high respectively. Table 16-1 compares the schedule of rates for these two nations. Note that the relative differences between these populations are greatest at the youngest ages; at the older ages the absolute as well as relative differences are reasonably small. Thus the low death rates of Sweden and the high death rates of India are due primarily to differences in their mortality rates before age 45. Table 16-1 illustrates the advantage of comparing whole schedules of age-specific rates over the comparison of crude rates; it shows where along the age curve the mortality levels of two or more populations differ most.

Standardized Death Rates. For comparison of mortality between different nations or subpopulations of a given nation, age composition may be controlled by the process of direct or indirect standardization described in Chapter 5. Table 16-2 illustrates the use of this process. Note that standardization increases the disparity between mortality levels in India and Sweden, for the younger age composition of the world population taken as standard tends to minimize Sweden's mortality when measured by the standardized death rate. Sweden's older age composition tends to maximize its mortality as measured by CDR (crude death rate). The advantage of the standardized death rates is that they express in a single summary measure the level of mortality within a population in such a way that it can be compared with a

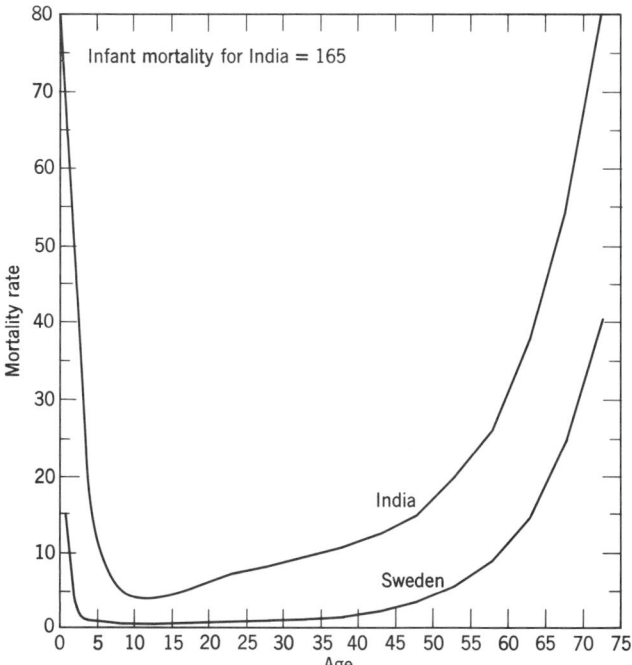

Figure 16-1 Age Pattern of Mortality, India and Sweden: 1960–61.

similar measure computed for other populations, with assurance that differences between them cannot be due to age composition. Such rates cannot reveal, of course, the age pattern of the difference; this must be done by a procedure similar to that already illustrated in Table 16-1. (Indirect standardization is not illustrated in Table 16-2 because a valid set of age-specific death rates for the world, needed as a standard, is not available.)

This summary is only a quick introduction to the study of age patterns in mortality and of the technique for controlling the effect of age on summary measures of mortality. The several additional measures that demographers have developed for special types of problems, including indirect standardization, are described and their meanings explained, in the *Manual of Demographic Research Techniques*.

16.3. The Life Table

The life table is a mathematical model that portrays mortality conditions at a particular time among a population and provides a basis for measuring longevity. It also reveals several other implications of the current mortality situation which would not otherwise be evident. It is based on age-specific mortality rates observed for a population for a particular year or other short span of time. It sets up an "hypothetical cohort" of 100,000 persons and assumes that this cohort is subjected throughout the lifetime of its members to the probabilities of dying that were observed in the actual population during the particular period. For example, the life table for United States males for 1964, reproduced in Table 16-3, takes a hypothetical cohort of 100,000 males and shows how many would die at each age and how many would survive to each age if they were exposed to the probabilities of death at each age that were observed for United States males in the year 1964. The life table thus defined is known as a "cross-sectional" life table, because it provides a picture of the mortality situation as of a given time. With a current life table one can determine:

1. The probability of dying within one year of persons at each age.

Table 16-1 Comparison of Age-Specific Mortality Rates of India and Sweden, and Age Distribution of Deceased Persons: 1960–61

Age	Age-specific death rates			Percentage distribution of deaths		
	India (A)	Sweden (B)	Difference (A)-(B)	India (D)	Sweden (E)	Difference (D)-(E)
Total.....	18.5	9.7	....	100.0	100.0	....
Under 1 year.....	164.9	15.3	149.6	32.6	2.1	30.5
1-4 years........	23.1	1.0	22.1	15.1	0.6	14.5
5-9 years........	5.0	0.5	4.5	3.4	0.4	3.0
10-14 years......	3.8	0.3	3.5	2.2	0.2	2.0
15-19 years......	5.3	0.6	4.7	2.7	0.4	2.3
20-24 years......	7.1	0.8	6.3	3.2	0.5	2.7
25-29 years......	7.9	0.9	7.0	3.2	0.5	2.7
30-34 years......	9.1	1.0	8.1	3.3	0.6	2.7
35-39 years......	10.4	1.4	9.0	3.1	1.0	2.1
40-44 years......	12.2	2.1	10.1	3.1	1.5	1.6
45-49 years......	14.5	3.3	11.2	3.1	2.4	0.7
50-54 years......	19.5	5.3	14.2	3.4	3.7	- 0.3
55-59 years......	25.8	8.6	17.2	3.5	5.3	- 1.8
60-64 years......	37.7	14.5	23.2	3.8	7.6	- 3.8
65-69 years......	53.8	24.5	29.3	3.6	10.6	- 7.0
70-74 years......	80.1	42.4	37.7	3.4	14.3	-10.9
75-79 years......	120.1	73.7	46.4	2.0	16.7	-14.7
80 years and over	221.3	167.5	53.8	5.3	31.6	-26.3

2. The average number of years a newborn infant can expect to live.

3. The average number of years of life remaining to a person of any age.

4. The probability of surviving from any given age to any other given age.

5. The probability of surviving for any given number of years, for persons at any age.

Equally important, the life table provides all of the items of information needed for an analysis of mortality under conditions of the *stationary population* discussed below. This set of concepts furnishes valuable insights into the demographic equilibrium that develops when the numbers of births and deaths are equal.

In addition, the life table has many applications in situations where the force of mortality must be estimated because an actual

Table 16-2 Illustration of Procedure for Standardizing Death Rates for India and Sweden, Using Composition of the World as Standard

Age	Standard population (world in mid-1960)	Age-specific death rates		Expected deaths in standard population	
		India	Sweden	India	Sweden
	A	B	C	AxB=D	AxC=E
Under 1 year.....	30	164.9	15.3	4.947	.459
1-4 years........	111	23.1	1.0	2.564	.111
5-14 years.......	226	4.4	0.4	.994	.090
15-24 years......	181	6.2	0.7	1.122	.127
25-44 years......	261	9.8	1.3	2.558	.339
45-64 years......	146	23.3	7.7	3.402	1.124
65-74 years.....	32	64.8	32.7	2.074	1.046
75 years and over	13	159.6	119.9	2.075	1.559
Total........	1000	.....	.....	19.736	4.835

Standardized rate: India = $\frac{\Sigma D}{1,000}$ =19.7 x Sweden = $\frac{\Sigma E}{1,000}$ = 4.9

Source: Standard population reported by United Nations in Population Bulletin No. 6. Rates from table 16-1.

Table 16-3 Abridged Life Table for the Total Population of the United States: 1964

Age interval	Proportion of 100,000 born			Stationary population		Average remaining lifetime
	Dying	Alive				
Period of life between two exact ages stated in years	Proportion of persons alive at beginning of age interval dying during interval	Number living at beginning of age interval	Number dying during age interval	In the age interval	In this and all subsequent age intervals	Average number of years of life remaining at beginning of age interval
(1)	(2)	(3)	(4)	(5)	(6)	(7)
x to x+n	$_n q_x$	l_x	$_n d_x$	$_n L_x$	T_x	e_x
0-1.............	.0247	100,000	2474	97811	7015291	70.2
1-5.............	.0038	97526	374	389209	6917480	70.9
5-10............	.0022	97152	216	485177	6528271	67.2
10-15...........	.0021	96936	203	484222	6043094	62.3
15-20...........	.0047	96733	453	482626	5558872	57.5
20-25...........	.0063	96280	609	479905	5076246	52.7
25-30...........	.0066	95671	634	476793	4596341	48.0
30-35...........	.0085	95037	807	473261	4119548	43.3
35-40...........	.0120	94230	1134	468503	3646287	38.7
40-45...........	.0183	93096	1700	461534	3177784	34.1
45-50...........	.0284	91396	2600	450953	2716250	29.7
50-55...........	.0447	88796	3972	434637	2265297	25.5
55-60...........	.0669	84824	5672	410722	1830660	21.6
60-65...........	.0985	79152	7794	377213	1419938	17.9
65-70...........	.1464	71358	10448	331660	1042725	14.6
70-75...........	.2044	60910	12449	274326	711065	11.7
75-80...........	.2910	48461	14100	207654	436739	9.0
80-85...........	.4220	34361	14500	134820	229085	6.7
85 and over.......	1.0000	19861	19861	94265	94265	4.7

Source: Vital Statistics of the United States, 1964. Vol. II, Section 5, Life Tables, Tables 5-1.

count of deaths has not been made. It is also an ingredient in building mathematical models that measure nuptiality, fertility, migration, and reproduction in a population.

It is an essential part of the training of every demographer to learn how to compute such tables, to interpret them, and to use them to derive measures that express attrition and survivorship in a variety of ways. The life table is also important in evaluating various causes of death and the part they play in bringing about a particular level of mortality. This section is only a quick introduction to this important topic; for details the reader is referred to the *Manual* or to one of the other sources cited at the end of the chapter.

The life table can best be explained by defining its parts and showing how they form a complete whole. As illustrated in Table 16-3, life tables have seven columns. The life table may be published in one of two ways: as a "com-

plete" life table, which deals with mortality in terms of single years of age, or as an "abridged" life table, which deals with mortality in terms of groupings of age, usually 5 years. The column headings are the same for the complete and abridged tables, except that for the abridged tables the symbols all have a subscript prefix *n*, which refers to the number of years of the age grouping involved. In complete life tables the value of *n* is 1, and is not shown.

The presentation that follows is little more than a paraphrasing of a classic presentation made by Thomas N. E. Greville in conjunction with the publication of the *United States Life Tables* for 1939-1941.[1] Inasmuch as the examples are drawn from an abridged life table for 1964, the intervals refer to groupings of

[1] *Sixteenth Census of the United States: 1940. United States Life Tables and Actuarial Tables, 1939-41,* by Thomas N. E. Greville (U.S. Government Printing Office, 1946).

age. The reader should keep in mind that in a complete life table the corresponding items refer to a single year of age. A complete life table is much more flexible and can therefore have a much greater variety of uses than the abridged tables. If only abridged tables are available, by the procedures of interpolation described in the *Manual* it is possible to estimate the equivalent of a complete life table from an abridged life table.

Column 1. Age interval (x to x + n). The age interval shown in column 1 is the interval between two birthdays. In the symbolic notation for this column and all other columns, *x* denotes the age at the birthday beginning the age interval. For instance, "5-10" indicates the interval between the fifth and the tenth birthday. This column, in other words, indicates the years of life to which each line in the life table refers. In complete life tables the age intervals refer to single-year intervals.

Column 2. Proportion dying ($_nq_x$) or mortality rate (1000_nq_x). This column shows the proportion of the cohort who were alive at the birthday indicating the start of age interval who will die before reaching the end of that age interval. For example, in Table 16-3 in the age interval 20-25, the proportion dying is 0.0063. Often this proportion is multiplied by 1000, and called the life table mortality rate. In this form, the above example indicates that of every 1000 white males who reached their twentieth birthday, 63 will die before reaching age 25.

The $_nq_x$ values are carefully computed *probabilities* that persons who are alive at the beginning of a specific age interval will die before reaching the beginning of the next age interval. They are very similar to, but not exactly the same as, age-specific mortality rates. These probabilities are calculated from death registration statistics and/or census data after making careful corrections for all known deficiencies of the data. The life table is valid or invalid depending on how well these probabilities fit the actual facts. All of the other columns of the life table are derived from the $_nq_x$ values. The procedures for computing these probabilities are described in full in the *Manual* or in the references to Greville, Spiegelman, or Wolfenden in Section VI of the Bibliography at the end of this chapter. This column is the "heart" of the life table.

Column 3. Number surviving (l_x or s_x). This column shows the number of persons who would survive to the exact age marking the beginning of each age interval out of a cohort of 100,000 live births, subject throughout life to the rates of mortality shown in column 2. Thus Table 16-3 shows that out of 100,000 infants born alive, 97,526 will survive to celebrate their birthday at age 1. The l_x values are computed from the $_nq_x$ values. Column 3 for any age is the difference between column 3 and column 4 of the preceding age. For example, the volume of 48,461 reported for age 75-80 represents the difference between the 60,910 who entered age 70 and the 12,449 who died during the interval from 70 to 75. The original cohort of 100,000 (or other number) is termed the *radix* of the life table.

Column 4. Number dying ($_nd_x$). This column shows the number dying in each successive set of ages out of the original cohort of 100,000 live births. For example, out of 100,000 births, according to the 1964 schedule of mortality, 2474 would die in the first year of life, 3972 between 50 and 55, and 14,500 between 80 and 85. Column 4 is the product of the entry in column 2 multiplied by the entry in column 3 of the same line.

Columns 5 and 6. Stationary population. Suppose that a group of 100,000 individuals such as that assumed in columns 3 and 4 is born every year, each such group being subject throughout life to the rates of mortality shown in column 2. If there were no immigration and if the births were evenly distributed over the calendar year, the survivors of these births would make up what is called a "stationary" population because in such a population the number of persons living in any age group would never change. When an individual left the group, either by death or by growing older and entering the next higher age group, his place would immediately be taken by someone entering from the next lower age group. Thus a census taken at any time in such a stationary community would always show the same total population and the same numerical distribution of that population among the various ages. In such a stationary population, column 3 shows the number of persons who, each year, would reach the birthday indicated in column 1, while column 4 shows the number who would die each year in the indicated age interval.

Column 5 ($_nL_x$) shows the number of persons in the stationary population in the indicated age interval. For example, the figure given for the age interval 45-50 is 450,953. This means that in a stationary population of Americans supported by 100,000 annual births and subject always to the rates of mortality shown in column 2, a census taken on any date would show 450,953 persons between 45 and 50 years old.

Column 6 (T_x) shows the total number of persons in the stationary population (column 5) in the indicated age interval and all subsequent age intervals. For example, in the stationary population of white males referred to in the last illustration, column 6 shows that there would be at any given moment a total of 2,716,250 persons who have passed their forty-fifth birthday. The population at all ages 0 and above (in other words, the total population of the stationary community) would be 7,015,291.

Column 7. Average future lifetime ($\overset{\circ}{e}_x$). The average future lifetime (also called the complete expectation of life) at any age is the average number of years remaining to be lived by those surviving to that age on the basis of a given set of mortality rates. It is obtained by dividing each figure in column 6 by the figure on the corresponding line in column 3.

The values in columns 5 and 6 can also be interpreted in terms of a single life table cohort, without introducing the concept of the stationary population. From this point of view, each figure in column 5 represents the total time (in years) lived between the indicated birthdays of 100,000 live births. Thus the figure for the year of life 45-50 is the total number of years that will be lived between 45 and 50 by the 91,396 persons (column 3) who reach their forty-fifth birthday out of 100,000 born alive. The corresponding figure in column 6 (2,716,250) is the total number of years that will be lived after attaining age 45 by the 91,396 reaching that age. This number of years divided by the number of persons (2,716,250

divided by 91,396) gives 29.7 as the average future lifetime at age 45, under the schedule of mortality in effect in 1964. The fact that the "expectation of life" at birth is always greater for one group of persons than for another should not lead one to conclude that the oldest ages reached by the first group of persons necessarily exceed those attained by the most long-lived among the second group. The difference in the average length of life usually is due to the fact that a greater proportion of the higher-mortality group die before reaching old age. For example, in the United States the number surviving to age 65 out of 100,000 born alive is far greater among whites than among Negroes; yet the average length of life remaining at age 65 is practically the same for both races.

To provide the student with a better appreciation of the life table functions, four of them are graphed in Figure 16-2, for a developing country (Peru) and an industrialized country (United States). This figure emphasizes that although the level of mortality may differ greatly, the general shape of the curves remains similar.

16.4. Uses of the Life Table

Life tables have several uses of importance in demographic analysis.

Expectation of Life at Birth ($\overset{\circ}{e}_0$). This is perhaps the most cited figure from a life table. It states the average number of years of life a newborn infant may be expected to live under the schedule of age-specific mortality currently in effect. This is widely accepted as a superior measure of the overall impact of mortality on a population. For this reason it is used in international and other comparisons. It may be used in place of the age-standardized death rate for such comparisons.

The Stationary Population Model. As described in the preceding section, the L_x and T_x columns of the life table may be looked upon as a community or population that would develop if the schedule of mortality indicated in the $_nq_x$ column were to continue indefinitely and if there were exactly 100,000 births and 100,000 deaths each year. The *percent distributions* of these columns give corresponding

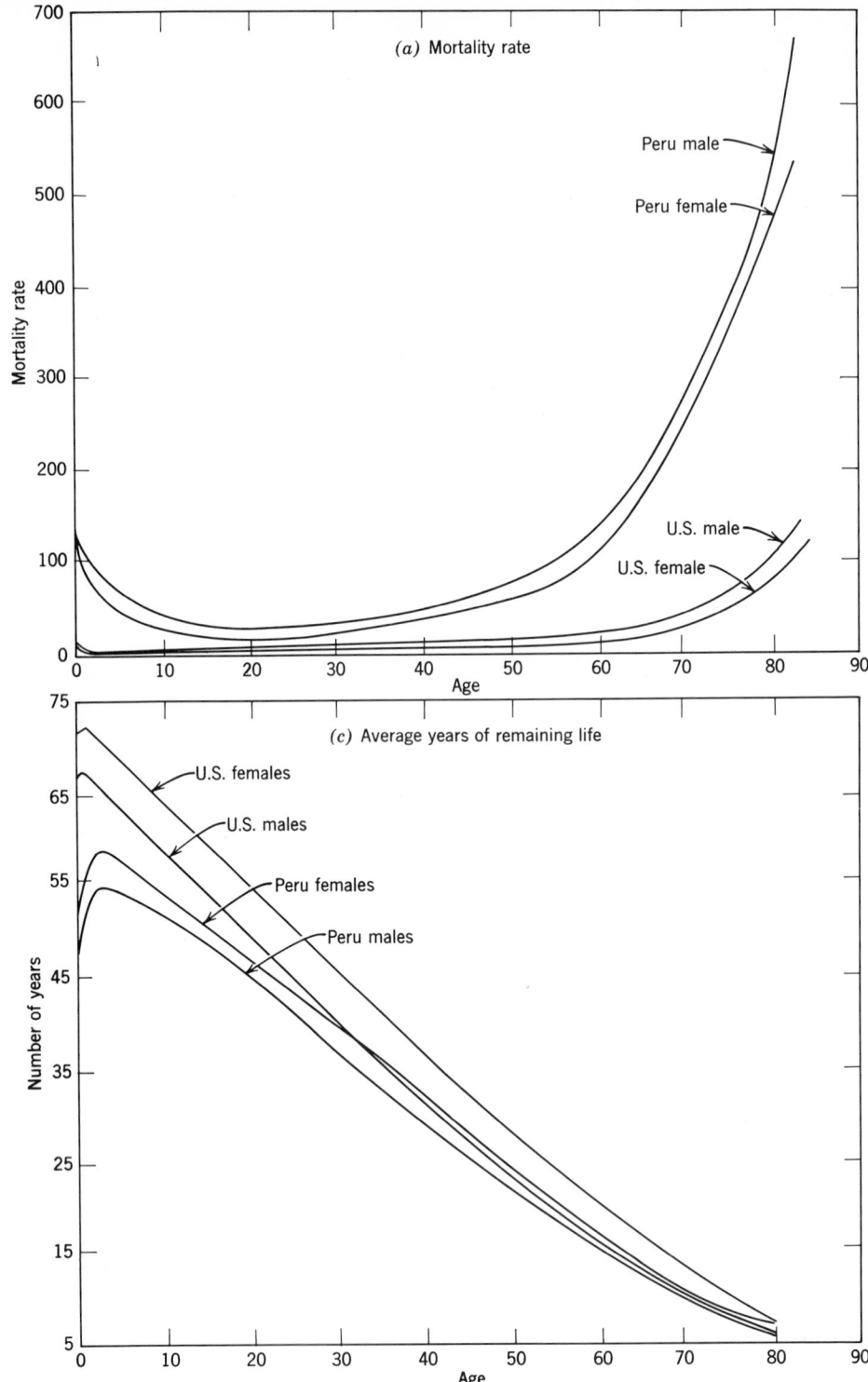

Figure 16-2 Comparison of Life Table Functions for the United States and Peru.

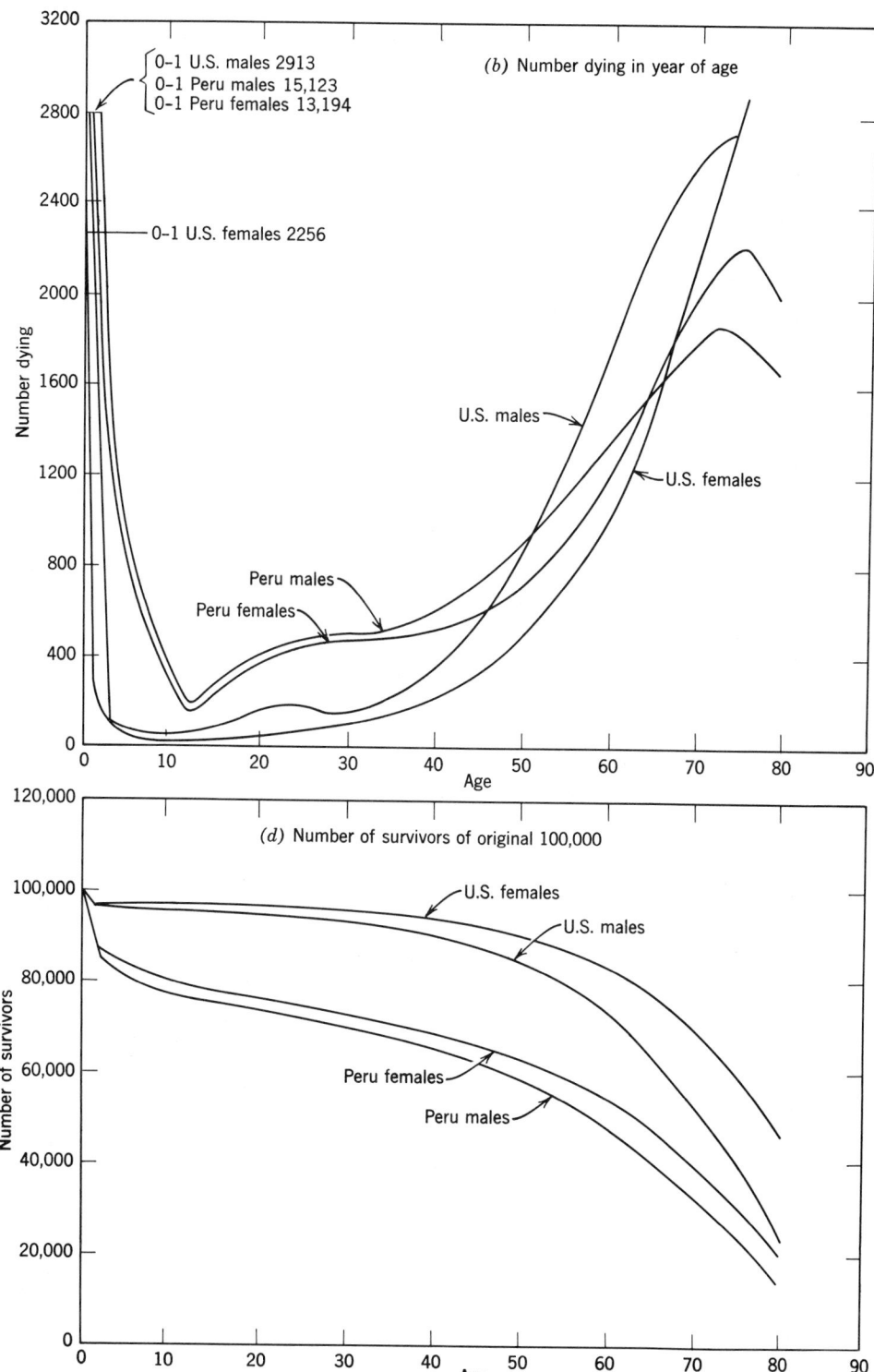

(b) Number dying in year of age

0–1 U.S. males 2913
0–1 Peru males 15,123
0–1 Peru females 13,194

0–1 U.S. females 2256

U.S. males

U.S. females

Peru males

Peru females

Age

Number dying

(d) Number of survivors of original 100,000

U.S. females

U.S. males

Peru females

Peru males

Number of survivors

Age

557

estimates of the composition that could be expected in any real population where fertility and mortality were equal for a prolonged time and where the mortality condition specified by $_nq_x$ were in effect for a long time.

Of particular interest to demographers are the compositional traits of the stationary population for populations such as that of Table 16-3, where death rates have been brought to very low levels. These are taken as indications of the age composition to which the whole world's population will trend at some future date when the demographic transition is completed.

The Life Table Death Rate. This is the crude death rate among the stationary population. It is the total number of deaths in the stationary population (the value of l_0 divided by T_0). In Table 16-3 this is 100,000 divided by 7,-015,291 or 14.3 per thousand. Note that the life table death rate is simply the reciprocal of the expectation of life at birth.

Survival Ratios. By making use of the L_x column of a life table it is possible to calculate what proportion of an age group would survive 5 years, 10 years, and so on. For example, the probability of surviving for exactly 15 years from being in age group 10-15 to being in age group 25-30 is 476,793 divided by 484,222, or .985.

With an abridged life table we are limited to computing survival ratios for 5-year age groups over 5-year intervals of time, but with a complete life table we can compute survival ratios for any combination of ages for any span of time, including fractions of years. Survival ratios are highly useful for estimating how much mortality has occurred among a population for which no death statistics are available. If one can validly assume that the mortality conditions in that population are approximately the same as those represented by the life table, by computing survival ratios that express survival for the span of years and for the age groups desired, it is possible to estimate how many of an earlier cohort will still be alive at a later date, after allowance for mortality.

Distinction between Mortality Rates and Mortality Probabilities. Death rates where the midyear population is used as the denominator are called "central death rates" and are usually identified by the symbol m. Thus, $_5m_x$ is the general identification for age-specific death rates grouped by five-year intervals.

Mortality probabilities are computed with the population aged x at the time of their birthday (start of the year of life) as the denominator. The difference between m_x and q_x may be easily stated in life table terms:

$$q_x = \frac{d_x}{l_x} \; ; \quad m_x = \frac{d_x}{L_x}$$

Comparison of Age Patterns of Mortality. If life tables have been calculated for two populations, a highly precise way of comparing their age patterns of mortality is to compare their values of $_nq_x$, in the manner of comparing death rates illustrated in Table 16-1. Also, we can compare the values of $\overset{\circ}{e}_x$ for selected ages, to assess the cumulative effects of mortality that lie beyond each age.

Pattern of Age at Death. In some forms of advanced demographic analysis, demographers study the pattern of age at death reported in actual populations and compare them with the patterns of age at death (d_x column) of life tables. From these patterns, it is said, one can infer the general level of mortality, even though the data may be incomplete.

Weights for Summarizing Rates. Where we have a schedule of age-specific rates, it often is desired to compute a weighted average for all ages combined. This requires a set of weights to be assigned to each of the various ages. For theoretical as well as practical reasons, the values of $_nL_x$ often provide an ideal set of weights for this purpose. This will be illustrated in the section on cause of death. Most of the uses to which life tables are put fall into one of the above categories, or some combination of categories. Demographers exercise great ingenuity in the use of life tables. Perhaps one of the most imaginative of these is a set of "model life tables" developed by the United Nations for use in circumstances where one can make a rough guess at the level of mortality, but where reliable data with which to compute actual death probabilities are unavailable. For making population projections, computing reproduction rates, and several other important tasks, these model life tables are sufficiently precise and accurate to be useful.[2]

16.5. The Special Significance of the Infant Mortality Rate

Beyond any doubt, the single most influential element of any life table is the infant mortality rate, q_0. This is the probability of dying during the first year of life. In populations that are growing more or less uniformly it may be estimated rather closely by the infant death rate, which is obtained by dividing the number of infants who die during a year before attaining their first birthday by the total number of live births in that year:

$$\text{IMR} = \frac{d_0}{\text{births}} \times 1000$$

Very often it is expressed as the number of infant deaths per 1000 live births, in which case the fraction is multiplied by 1000. For more precise methods of calculating q_0 see the *Manual* or references in Section VII of the Bibliography. In societies where standards of health and medical care are very low, as in preliterate and illiterate societies that are without benefit of modern public health and medicine, infant death rates may rise as high as 500 per thousand. This means that one-half of all live-born children may die within one year of birth. Infant mortality rates of 250 (one-fourth dying within one year) are quite common in the poorest districts of large cities in Asia, Africa, and possibly Latin America and in the most poverty-stricken and backward of the rural areas. This high level of mortality is followed by much lower rates of mortality at ages 1, 2, 3, and so on. In fact, it is not until about age 65 or above that mortality again reaches the high level of infant mortality. Inasmuch as death rates above age 65 have a much smaller

effect upon $\overset{\circ}{e}_0$ than the IMR, it is clear that the number of deaths that occur during the first year of life will affect strongly the expectation of life at birth.

Great success has been achieved in reducing infant mortality by means of public health and medical discoveries. Rates as low as 25 per thousand (one twentieth of the high rate of 500 mentioned above) or even lower are now common in nations of Europe, Northern America, and Oceania. These low rates of IMR are one of the major reasons that values of $\overset{\circ}{e}_0 = 70$ years or more are possible.

Not only are infant mortality rates over-influential in determining the outcome of a life table and in causing a given population to be characterized as having "high," "medium," or "low" overall mortality, but also they are the least predictable of the mortality rates. If a professional demographer or actuary is given the value of q_x for any given age between 5 and 35, by referring to the United Nations model life tables he can do a surprisingly good job of guessing what the rest of the life table for that country is like—except for infant mortality. He can make a guess about infant mortality, but his average error will be larger. For this reason, it is of special importance that the infant mortality rate of a population be measured and known.

Unfortunately, it is even more difficult to obtain valid statistics on infant mortality than on adult mortality. In many societies the death of a newborn infant is not regarded as worthy of official note. In fact, it even appears absurd to go through the double procedure of making out a birth certificate and then following it with a death certificate for an infant who lived less than one hour and who is already deceased when the paperwork is to be done. Often custom does not even consider such infants to be persons yet, hence does not require the usual burial or other death ceremonies, and the body may be disposed of privately by the midwife or a relative. In some nations the custom is to wait a given number of days—perhaps a week or two—and then register the surviving live births. This results in an understatement both of the birthrate and of the infant death rate.

---

[2] United Nations, *Age and Sex Pattern of Mortality, Model Life Tables for Underdeveloped Countries* (1955). An alternative system of life tables has been prepared by Ansley J. Coale and Paul Demeny, *Regional Model Life Tables and Stable Populations* (Princeton, Princeton University Press, 1966).

The infant mortality rate is divided into two parts by physicians and medical researchers: (a) the *neonatal* phase—the first 4 weeks of life—and (b) the *post neonatal* phase—the remaining 48 weeks of life before the first birthday. When the level of medical care is low, a major share of infant deaths takes place in the post-neonatal stage. The newborn infant is fed on his mother's milk and is otherwise protected from the environment during his first days of life. It is when he begins to eat food prepared by human hands, to move about, and to come into contact more intimately and directly with his environment that lack of cleanliness, sanitation, and good health practices cause death. On the other hand, a very large fraction of neonatal deaths are caused by physiological and organic weaknesses in the newborn infant, such as those associated with prematurity. In societies where medical care has achieved low death rates, it is the post-neonatal deaths that have been reduced the most, with the result that a majority of all infant deaths are neonatal. Later sections will provide more details concerning each of these types of infant mortality.

16.6. Mortality Conditions and Trends around the World

In 1963 the United Nations published a special report entitled *The Situation and Recent Trends of Mortality in the World.*[3] In introducing its materials, the United Nations reports estimates of the expectation of life at birth for regions of the world of 1955-1958:

	$\overset{\circ}{e}_0$
World total	50-60 years
Northern America	70 years
Oceania	68 years
Europe	68 years
USSR	68 years
Latin America	50-55 years
Asia (excluding USSR)	40-50 years
Africa	Probably less than 40 years

Figure 16-3 illustrates graphically these differences in the average force of mortality around the world.

[3] United Nations, *The Situation and Recent Trends of Mortality in the World,* Population Bulletin No. 6.

The findings of this report have been integrated with materials subsequently published in the Demographic Yearbooks in the form of a set of notes on each of the world's regions.

Table 16-7 reports the expectation of life at birth for all nations for which a reasonably reliable life table could be constructed. These are the best estimates available of the force of mortality around the world. This is a general reference table that brings together in one place a summary of current levels and recent trends in mortality around the world. The reader should use this table as a general reference for the remainder of this chapter.

Mortality Trends in Europe. At the present time the death rates of all European nations are very low in comparison with the average situation for the world. Although some European countries have higher rates of mortality than do others, the differences are very minor in comparison with the less developed regions of the world. This near uniformity was only recently achieved, however. Before World War II the countries of Southern and Eastern Europe had death rates that were substantially higher than those of Northwestern Europe, where the industrial revolution had acted earliest to raise the standard of living and improve health conditions. Table 16-4 shows the trend in crude death rates for four groups of European countries over the last half century. It may quickly be seen that at the turn of the century Southern and Eastern Europe had death rates moderately high (above 20), the Scandinavian countries and England and Wales had death rates only somewhat higher than at the present time, and the remainder of Western Europe fell in intermediate positions. This differential persisted, despite declining death rates in all European countries, until about 1940. Since then the differential has almost completely disappeared, as all nations have fallen in the interval between 9 and 12 per thousand. During this half century the countries of Southern and Eastern Europe have performed the amazing feat of cutting their death rate by between 50 and 60 percent.

High rates of infant mortality were primarily responsible for the high crude death rate of prewar Southern and Eastern Europe. Since World War II these infant mortality rates have

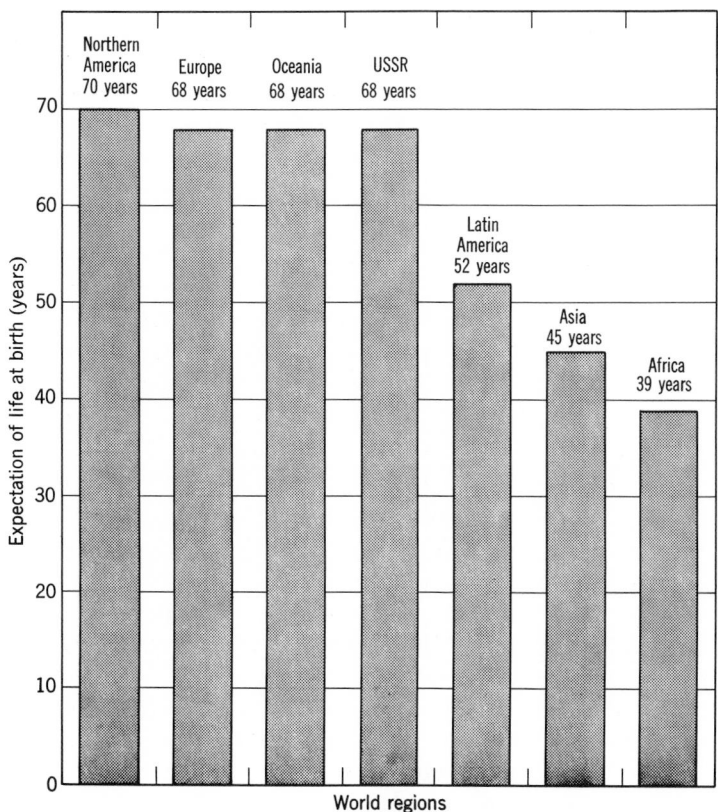

Figure 16-3 Expectation of Life at Birth for World Regions: 1955-58

dropped precipitously, and this movement has helped to create the low level of death rates in these nations. Meanwhile, the infant mortality rate has declined also in the other countries, so that in the Netherlands, Scandinavia, Switzerland, England, and Wales the average infant mortality rates are very low. Figure 16-4, showing the trend of infant mortality in Sweden, is illustrative of the pattern of decline in infant mortality. Sweden holds the world's record of only 15 infant deaths per 1000 births. Although infant mortality is more than twice as high in

Table 16-4   Trend in Crude Death Rates for Four Groups of Nations of Europe: 1906 to 1958

National grouping	1906–1910	1935–1938	1945–1948	1955–1958
Denmark, England and Wales, Netherlands, Norway, Sweden..........................	14.1	10.7	10.3	9.3
Remainder of western Europe (Austria, Belgium, Luxembourg, Northern Ireland, Scotland, Switzerland)...................	17.7	13.3	13.0	11.3
Southern Europe (Portugal, Spain, Italy, Greece)...............................	21.7	15.6	12.7	9.4
Eastern Europe (Albania, Bulgaria, Czechoslovakia, Hungary, Poland, Romania, Yugoslavia).............................	24.5	15.7	14.5	10.0

Source: United Nations: Population Bulletin No. 6, The Situation and Recent Trends of Mortality in the World, page 19.

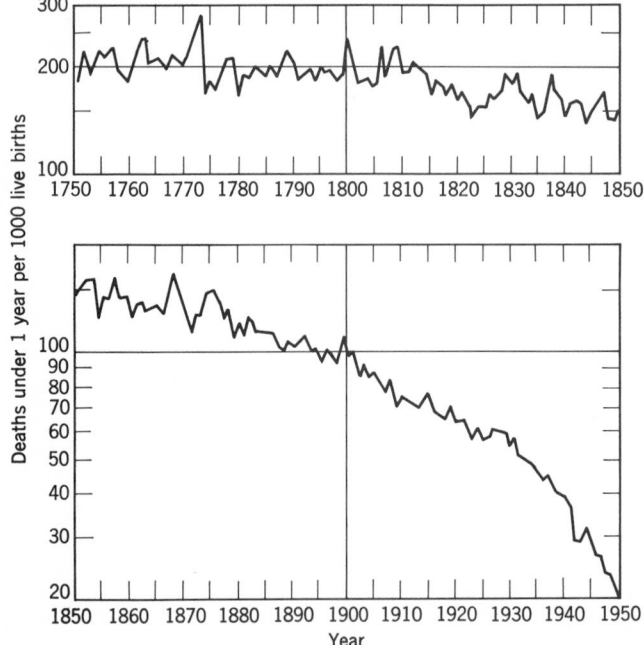

Figure 16-4 Infant Mortality in Sweden: 1750 to 1950.

SOURCE: Sweden, Statistiska Centralbyrån, *Statistisk Årsbok för Sverige 1951* (1951); United Nations, *Foetal, Infant and Early Childhood Mortality,* Volume I (New York: United Nations, 1954).

Southern and in several Eastern European countries, the gap has narrowed substantially and apparently is continuing to narrow.

As a result of its very low level of mortality, the average expectation of life at birth is higher in Europe than in almost any other section of the world. For example, in Sweden the average expectation of life for females is now nearly 76 years and in Norway and in the Netherlands it is equally high. This represents very large gains in expectation of life over the past half century. In most countries the gain in $\overset{\circ}{e}_0$ has been 20 years or more, and in a few nations life expectancy at birth has been increased by as much as 30 years. All countries in Europe now have an expectation of life greater than 60 years.

The United Nations has classified the nations into three categories according to the estimated level of the expectation of life at birth with reference to the period 1955-1958 as follows:

Group 1: $\overset{\circ}{e}_0$ 60-64 years

Albania
Greece
Poland
Portugal
Romania
Spain
Yugoslavia

Group 2: $\overset{\circ}{e}_0$ 65-69 years

Austria
Belgium
Bulgaria
Czechoslovakia
Finland
Germany
Hungary
Ireland
Italy
Luxembourg
United Kingdom: Northern Ireland, Scotland

Group 3: $\overset{\circ}{e}_0$ 70-74 years

Denmark
France
Netherlands
Norway
Sweden
United Kingdom: England and Wales

As a study of Table 16-7 will show, the above classification was still valid for most of the nations in groups 2 and 3 in the 1960-1965 period. Albania, Greece, Poland, Romania, and Spain appear to have moved from group 1 to group 2; as of 1968 there probably is no nation of Europe left in the group 1 category. Many of those in the group 2 category are at the top of it and soon will move into group 3.

In general this ranking is still quite correct. The countries of Northern and Western Europe still lead the rest of Europe in the conquest of mortality and the nations that have the lowest life expectation are still those of Southern and Eastern Europe. As has already been pointed out, however, the range between high and low has narrowed substantially; as economic development and the standard of living increase in these higher mortality nations, there is every expectation that the international differences will be further reduced.

Mortality Trends in Northern America and Oceania. Australia and New Zealand, which together comprise above 90 percent of the population of Oceania, have mortality trends very similar to those in Northern America (United States and Canada), and for this reason the two regions are considered together. It must be kept in mind, however, that the mortality trends of the indigenous populations of the smaller Pacific islands are more similar to those of the less developed regions of the world than to those of Australia and New Zealand.

The mortality condition of these two regions at the present time is extremely favorable. In all four of the leading nations the crude death rate is below 10 per thousand. In all of these countries there is a highly developed system of social security and health insurance, which helps to bolster the ability of the older population to obtain medical care when it is most needed. In addition, the level of income is such that malnutrition is almost nonexistent and medical care is not only available but within the financial means of almost everyone. Everywhere there is a highly developed system of sanitation and public health that makes the outbreak of epidemics almost unheard of.

As nearly as can be determined from the available data, death rates have been moderately low throughout this century. For example, in the United States the crude death rate is estimated to have been 16 in 1900, and in Australia it was 12. In both nations it has declined more or less continuously until it is now only about two-thirds its level 60 years ago. In all of these countries the infant mortality rate has been reduced to a very low point, matching that of the lowest mortality levels in Europe. An exception to this picture are the Maoris of New Zealand, who still have infant mortality rates near 50, although the crude death rate for this group has now declined to a moderately low level.

The expectation of life in all four of the nations is roughly 70 or above. New Zealand is the leader, with an expectation of 72 years, and the United States has the lowest expectation, with 69.5. In all of the nations the expectation of life has increased substantially since 1900.

Thus the nations of Northern America and Oceania fall in the low-mortality category with Europe, and the trends in their death rate have been similar to those in Europe.

Mortality Trends in the USSR. Since the time of the Revolution of 1917 the USSR has made a remarkable transition from a condition of high mortality to one of moderately low mortality, although it is difficult to document this with exact statistical facts. Before the Revolution the death rate was above 30 per thousand; in 1960 it was approximately 8 per thousand. The infant mortality rate had declined to around 40 per thousand. The average expectation of life at birth as of 1962 is almost exactly equal to that of the United States, namely 69 years. As late as 1938 the expectation of life in the USSR was estimated to be only 47. Thus in only twenty years the expectation of life is reported to have increased twenty years, or one year of life per year of time. Few other nations in the world appear to have yet matched this record of sustained mortality decline.

Mortality Trends in Latin America. Mortality conditions in the Latin American nations are highly diverse. At one extreme lie Argentina and Uruguay, where the death rates are comparable to those of Europe and Northern America and Oceania. At the other extreme are nations such as Guatemala, Haiti, and Honduras, where death rates of 20 per thousand or above are registered or estimated. Despite this diversity it can be said that on the average the nations of Latin America occupy an intermediate place between the low-mortality nations and the high-mortality nations. Most of the countries fall in the interval where death rates are 10 to 20 per thousand. Much of the variation is to be explained by differences in level of living. Within most of these countries there are equally striking differences between the urban and rural sections. It is not uncommon to find very low death rates in cities, comparable to those of Europe, especially in the more prosperous sections of the city, while the slums and open countryside show the high death rates found in the high-mortality regions of the world. Much of the Latin American population lives without adequate medical care, with a very low level of public health service, and under conditions of extreme poverty and chronic malnutrition.

Despite this rather pessimistic picture, there have been substantial improvements in mortality in Latin America. Death registration is too incomplete in most countries to yield valid measures of mortality. The best estimates of mortality levels and of recent change in mortality levels that are available from demographic analysis show that since 1940 there have been phenomenal declines in mortality in several of the countries and substantial declines in all for which there are data. Mexico, Venezuela, El Salvador, Costa Rica, Chile, and the Caribbean Islands have had especially large mortality declines during this time. By 1965 all nations had crude death rates below 20 except Guatemala, Bolivia, Dominican Republic, Haiti, Honduras, and Peru. In all of these except the first, death registration is so incomplete that the level of mortality is only estimated,

and it is quite possible that it has fallen below 20 in several of these higher-mortality nations.

It is not unlikely that by 1970 no nation in Latin America will have mortality rates as high as 20. Where life tables are available, they suggest that the improvement in mortality since 1940 has tended to be nearly at the rate of one year of life expectancy added annually. This is a very high rate of increase, which matches the accomplishment of the USSR mentioned above. It is believed that Costa Rica, Mexico, Barbados, and certain urban areas in Brazil have improved at nearly this rate in recent times.

The United Nations has undertaken to group the countries of Latin America into four groups according to the estimated expectation of life at birth:

Group 1: 45-54 years of life
Guatemala
Brazil
Colombia
Ecuador
Peru
Bolivia
Haiti
Honduras

Group 2: 55-59 years
Chile
Cuba
Dominican Republic
El Salvador
Mexico
Panama
Venezuela

Group 3: 60-64 years
Costa Rica
Barbados
Jamaica
Trinidad and Tobago
Argentina
Uruguay

Group 4: 65 years and over
Puerto Rico

Unfortunately, there are too few data in Table 16-7 to evaluate recent changes in classification.

At the United Nations Population Conference in Belgrade, experts from Latin America reported that perhaps the easier part of the mortality reduction phase in Latin America has been largely completed and that further reductions are coming more slowly and with greater effort, but nevertheless are taking place.[4]

Mortality Trends in Asia. Although Asia must still be regarded as a high-mortality region of the world, phenomenal improvement in mortality conditions have taken place in the last decade or so. Three Asian countries—Japan, Ryukyu Islands, and Israel—have mortality rates that are as low as those of Europe and Northern America. All are nations that have progressed far along the road of industrialization and have a much higher level of medical care and public health than their Asian neighbors. In some of the smaller nations, very significant improvements in mortality have taken place as a result of recent health and medical programs. Probably the most outstanding example is Ceylon, which had a recorded death rate of 24.5 for the period 1935–1939 but 9.7 in 1958, a decrease of more than one-half. This truly amazing accomplishment must be attributed to a very intensive campaign of modernization of health and medical services in the country, which included one of the first successful campaigns against malaria. The Federation of Malaya, Hong Kong, Singapore, and Taiwan, have also shown similar dramatic drops in mortality since 1940. In every case systematic programs to eradicate the major infectious killers— smallpox, cholera, malaria, typhoid, and plague —have accounted for much of this decline.

Nevertheless, poverty and malnutrition appear to be major obstacles to the accomplishment of a really low level of mortality in the overcrowded nations of China, India, Indonesia, Pakistan, and the Middle East. In response to a very great increase in investment in health and medical care, death rates are responding, but much more slowly in these areas. Diseases of the respiratory and digestive systems (tuber-

[4] Jorge L. Somoza, "Niveles y tendencias de la mortalidad en América Latina, expresados en función de la edad," and Hugo Behm, "Estructura de las causas de defunción y nivel de mortalidad: une experiencia en América Latina," papers submitted to the United Nations World Population Conference, Belgrade, September 1965.

culosis, pneumonia, dysentery), smallpox, and cholera still infect a substantial percentage of the population and cause many deaths. In these high death rate nations the mortality level is falling, but probably cannot be expected to reach the lower levels attained in Latin America until a substantial improvement in level of living takes place.

The largest single component of the very high mortality rate that has prevailed in Asia has been the infant mortality rate. At the turn of the century it was normal for one infant out of four to die during the first year of life. The United Nations estimates that in 1958 the infant mortality rate was still above 100 in Cambodia, Indonesia, and Thailand and that in British Borneo, Burma, India, Laos, and Pakistan it was above 200. A great deal of the improvement in mortality rates has consisted of reducing infant mortality. For example, in Singapore the infant mortality rate fell from 155 in 1935-1939 to 44 in 1955-1958 and in Taiwan it fell from 144 in the earlier period to 34 in the later period.

During the era of high mortality that prevailed at the turn of the century, the expectation of life at birth was only about 25 to 30 years. Crude life tables for India and Ceylon constructed as late as 1920 still show mortality levels at this expectation. The most recent life table for India, that for 1961, shows an increase to 42 years. The United Nations has categorized the nations into life expectancy groups as of 1955-1958:

Expectations of life	Nation
70-74 years	Cyprus, Israel
65-69 years	Japan, Ryukyu Islands
60-64 years	China, Taiwan, Singapore
55-59 years	Ceylon
50-54 years	Federation of Malaya
45-49 years	Philippine Islands, Thailand
35-44 years	Burma, Cambodia, India

It is not unlikely that by 1970 nearly every nation will have climbed into the group immediately above that now reported for it.

For Mainland China, Indonesia, Pakistan, and North Vietnam almost no mortality data are available. The United Nations estimates that the expectation of life in Mainland China is between 50 and 55 years and that for the other three it is about 40 years or even below.

Mortality Trends in Africa. The average level of mortality in Africa at present is probably higher than the average for any other region of the world. Data concerning deaths are so fragmentary for this region, however, that it is difficult to document even this statement. In urban as well as rural areas of most of Africa, health and medical services for the indigenous population are extremely poor. Housing is badly overcrowded, sanitation is of a very low order. This is coupled with very low income, widespread unemployment, and a great deal of migratory, temporary labor in mines or other extractive industries.

Nevertheless, substantial progress has been made in controlling the major communicable diseases such as tuberculosis, malaria, plague, cholera, yellow fever, smallpox, and typhus. The scattered shreds of evidence available suggest that death rates are 25 per thousand or higher in most of the nations of Africa but that the mortality rates have been falling in recent years as they have in Asia. There are examples of dramatic improvements in mortality, as in Mauritius and in the smaller island territories where it has been possible to carry out more effective programs of public health.

As in Asia, it is becoming apparent that decline in mortality in Africa must rely heavily on improved economic conditions. DDT spraying and the wholesale use of antibiotics are reducing deaths from many causes, but are unable to do the whole job.

Summary of World Trends. The region-by-region review of mortality trends throughout the world leads us to make the following points: (1) Every industrialized nation of the world now is in the low-mortality category. Recent improvements in mortality have been only very small. Further improvement can also be expected to be very minor and gradual. (2) Very great reductions in mortality have been effected in Asia, Africa, and Latin America through the use of antiepidemic campaigns against infectious diseases, especially malaria, smallpox, cholera, and plague. As of 1965, substantial success in conquering these diseases has

been achieved and they are diminishing as major causes of death. Where this conquest has been accompanied by a rising level of living, the result has been a very sharp decline in mortality, as in Singapore, Taiwan, and Mexico. (3) Malnutrition, poverty, and illiteracy are proving to be a major barrier to quick reduction of mortality in large segments of the population in South Asia, the Middle East, and Africa. Although we may look forward to a continued decline in mortality in these areas, it is becoming increasingly evident that further reductions will come somewhat more gradually and more in proportion to socioeconomic improvements in these areas than has been true in the 1945–65 period.

16.7. Historic Trends in Mortality

Although data are fragmentary, it is reasonably certain that throughout the long span of history prior to about 1650 the average expectation of life was 25 years or less. This meant that the infant mortality rate was about 30 percent and that even during the vigorous years of young adulthood 2 to 4 percent of the population died annually.[5] By about 1840, when the first reliable life tables for Northwestern Europe are available, life expectancy appears to have risen to about 41 years. In order to trace the long-range decline in mortality since that date, the United Nations has computed the expectation of life at birth for six European countries and the state of Massachusetts combined. This is shown as Table 16-5. From 1840 to about 1890 the upward trend in life expectancy was very slow indeed, averaging less than about one year of expectation for every ten calendar years. From 1890 to 1930, the pace quickened appreciably and began to average between 0.3 and 0.4 years of expectation for each calendar year. During

[5] See footnote on page 53 of United Nations, Bulletin Number 6, *op. cit.* Durand, after reviewing the various efforts to estimate life expectations from the data of Roman tombstones, concludes that "a range of about twenty to thirty years is indicated for the average expectation of life in the Roman Empire as a whole." John Durand, "Mortality Estimates from Roman Tombstone Inscriptions," *American Journal of Sociology,* 65 (4) (January 1960), 365–373.

Table 16-5 Expectation of Life at Birth for Six European Countries and Massachusetts in the United States: 1840 to 1955

Year	Expectation of life at birth	Average annual increase in e_o
1840..........	41.0	....
1850..........	41.5	0.05
1860..........	42.2	0.07
1870..........	43.5	0.13
1880..........	45.2	0.17
1890..........	47.1	0.20
1900..........	50.5	0.34
1910..........	54.3	0.38
1920..........	58.3	0.40
1930..........	61.7	0.34
1940..........	64.6	0.29
1955..........	71.0	0.43

Source: United Nations, Population Bulletin No. 6, Table IV.1, 1962

the economic depression of 1930–1940, there was a slackening of improvement in mortality, but progress was renewed in about 1940 with the introduction of antibiotic drugs and other life-saving techniques. In very recent years,

since 1955, the gain in life expectancy has slackened again, as the industrialized countries appear to be reaching an upper limit until a new breakthrough is made in the avoidance of death from certain chronic diseases.

In observing this historic trend it is important to note that at no time during this long period did the increase in life expectancy reach as much as one-half year of expectation per calendar year. This stands in very sharp contrast to the annual gains of one year or even one and a half years per calendar year that have been made over short periods by certain developing nations such as Ceylon and Mexico. Thus the conquest of mortality is progressing at a much more rapid rate in the developing nations than during the historic mortality decline in Europe and America. This fact is brought out clearly in Figure 16-5, which is a reproduction of a chart drawn by the United Nations. The curved line in this chart shows the historic trend in mortality in Sweden for the 200 years 1760-1960. The

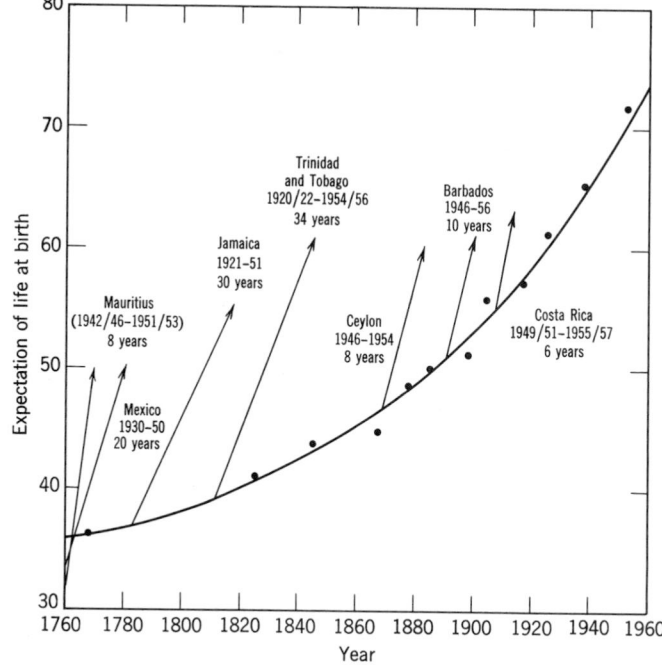

Figure 16-5 Recent Mortality Trends in Various Underdeveloped Countries Compared with the Secular Mortality Trend in Sweden.

SOURCE: United Nations, *The Situation and Recent Trends of Mortality in the World*, Population Bulletin No. 5, 1963, 50.

Table 16-6 Sweden—Percent Increase or Decrease in Average
Age-Specific Death Rates for Both Sexes between Successive Periods:
1751–1800 to 1946–1957

Age (years)	1751–1800 to 1801–1850	1801–1850 to 1851–1900	1851–1900 to 1901–1945	1901–1945 to 1946–1957	1751–1800 to 1946–1957
Under 1 [1/].....	−14.6	−27.9	−53.8	−63.9	−89.7
1–4.............	−27.5	−15.6	−74.5	−81.0	−97.0
5–14............	−29.1	−10.1	−65.6	−75.5	−94.6
15–24..........	−11.5	−17.9	−26.5	−74.9	−86.5
25–44..........	− 5.5	−29.4	−39.7	−64.0	−85.5
45–64..........	+ 5.9	−31.9	−35.2	−26.6	−65.7
65 and over.....	+ 7.1	−21.5	−19.0	− 6.5	−36.3

[1/] Percentage based on death rates per 1,000 live births.

Sources: The Determinants and Consequences of Population Trends(United
Nations publication, Sales No.: 53 XIII.3), p.55. Sweden,
Statistika Centralbyran, Statistisk Arsbok for Sverige, 1959.

arrows in this chart show the slope of the increase in life expectancy in selected developing countries. The fact that the slope for all arrows is steeper than the slope for the line for Sweden shows how much sharper the decline in mortality has been in these countries than was true in Europe. This is another way of demonstrating that modern technology has brought lifesaving practices within a very few years to the developing countries, whereas many decades were required to accomplish this in the nations that invented them. For example, Trinidad and Tobago were able to attain a level of death control in 34 years that required 110 years in Sweden.

The above tracing of mortality in terms of expectation of life fails to reveal the change in age differences in mortality that has taken place. Studies of changes in age-specific death rates over long periods of time for the countries of Northwestern Europe and the United States all reveal that the major declines in mortality occurred at the youngest ages, especially ages under 15. Substantial gains were also made in the intermediate ages between 15 and 55, but much smaller changes have been attained for the older ages, 65 and over. This may be seen from Table 16-6 for Sweden. Gains of reduction in mortality of 90 percent or more have been made in the past two centuries for death rates at ages under 15, and reductions of 85 percent or more have been accomplished for ages under 44, whereas only reductions of slightly more than one third have been attained for ages 65 and over. Studies by

Stolnitz and others reveal that this pattern is present in almost all or in all nations of Europe, America, and Oceania for which data are available.[6]

In the developing nations the recent changes in the pattern of age-specific mortality is similar to but not exactly the same as that of the trend in Europe and the industrialized countries. The gains in mortality have been spread over all ages from infancy through middle age, with the pattern of smaller declines at the oldest ages. Thus the large-scale use of antibiotics, vaccinations, and pesticides and the introduction of public health measures into the environment have brought lifesaving practices to large segments of the population almost simultaneously, so that adults up to middle age have shared the benefits almost equally with children.

A new trend that has developed in age-specific mortality in recent years has been a reversal of the historic decline in mortality for males. In Norway, the Netherlands, and several other European countries the rates of male mortality for ages above 55 have been increasing since about 1950-1953. In some cases the extent of this increase is very substantial. The

[6] France, Statistique générale, *Evolution de la mortalité en Europe depuis l'origine des statistiques de l'état civil*, Études démographiques, No. 2, Paris, 1941; George Stolnitz, "A Century of International Mortality Trends," *Population Studies*, **9** (1) (July 1955) and **10** (1) (July 1956) (in two parts). See other references in Section II of Bibliography at end of the chapter.

possible causes of this reversal will be discussed in the section on causes of death.

Inasmuch as the death rates at the upper ages in the developing countries are only moderately higher than those in the industrialized countries and inasmuch as only modest reductions have been achieved at these older ages in the industrialized countries, it may be concluded that the developing countries are rapidly approaching the point where further declines in mortality will be achieved only with much greater effort. The major avenue for improvement lies in the much higher rate of infant mortality that still persists in the developing countries in comparison with the industrialized nations.

The following statistics for England and Wales probably summarize succinctly the age pattern of the mortality revolution in the developed nations, and adumbrates what will happen in the developing nations as they pass through it.

Age and Sex	Rate per 100,000 population		Index: 1901–10
	1901–10	1956–57	= 100
5–24 years			
Males	318	67	21
Females	305	39	13
45–64 years			
Males	2233	1359	61
Females	1748	757	43
65–74 years			
Males	6485	5412	83
Females	5393	3136	58

Source: United Nations. *Population Bulletin*, Number 6, Table V-6, p. 78.

16.8. Sex Differences in Mortality

It has been noted several times in preceding chapters that males typically have higher age-specific death rates than females. There are certain exceptions to this pattern in sections of Africa, Asia, and Latin America. Most of the instances of higher female death rates occur at the younger ages. Until very recently in

India death rates for females appeared to be higher than for males at almost all ages. This has been thought to be associated with the neglect of females when they become ill and the concentration of medical care on male members of the family. Almost everywhere else life expectation at birth is substantially higher for females than for males. The extent of this superiority of females over males in surviving the force of mortality is moderately small under conditions of high death rates, but as death rates decline, the sex differential widens until in the low-mortality populations females tend to live several years longer than males. Table 16-7, showing the expectation of life at birth for males and females for a selected group of industrialized and developing countries, emphasizes this point. Under current conditions the typical female in industrialized countries may look forward to several years of widowhood even if she marries a husband of her own age. Some demographic wags have pointed out that American girls marrying at the age of 18 would be forced to marry a boy only 12 years old in order to assure that she would not spend time as a widow.

The exact reasons for this large and widening sex differential are not known. The explanations that have been advanced vary from sex differences in metabolism and body chemistry to sex differences in living habits, tension, and self-care. As we will see, when death is traced to specific causes, females survive all forms of disease better than males.

A study of Table 16-7 will reveal that the sex differential is small or reversed in only the following nations for which life tables are available.

Small	Reversed
Rhodesia	Upper Volta
Dominican Republic	Guatemala
Bolivia	Cambodia
Peru	Ceylon
	India
	Pakistan

In all of the other countries, both developed and developing, females have 2 to 8 years' greater life expectancy at birth than males.

Table 16-7   Mortality Trends and Levels in Nations for Which Data Are Available

Nation	Year	Expectation of life at birth--e_o				Infant mortality rate (
		Both sexes	Male	Female	Ratio male to female	
AFRICA						
Algeria (Europeans)	1954	63	....	....	...	37.8
(Muslim)	1948	35	....	....	...	155
Angola	1940	35	....	....	...	17.2
Burundi	1965	....	35.0	38.5	.91	....
Cameroon, West	1964-65	....	34.3	37.2	.92	137.2
Central African Republic	1959-60	35	33	36	.92	....
Chad	1963-64	31	....	....	...	....
Congo (Brazzaville)	1960-61	37	....	....	...	200
Congo (Leopoldville)	1950-52	....	37.6	40.0	.94	144
Dahomey	1961	37.3	....	....	...	....
Gabon	1960-61	32	25	45	.56	....
Ghana	1948	38	....	....	...	155
Guinea (Rural)	1954-55	30.5	26.0	....	...	....
(Urban)	1954-55	35.8	....	....	...	....
	1955	....	26	28	.93	220
Ivory Coast	1957-58	35	....	....	...	164
Kenya	1962	40-45	....	....	...	170
Lesotho	1955-56	....	40	42	.95	....
Mali	1957	27	....	....	...	....
Mauritania	1961-62	40	....	....	...	....
Mauritius	1961-63	....	58.7	61.9	.95	64.1
	1951-53	....	49.8	52.3	.95	....
	1942-46	33.0	32.2	33.8	.95	....
Morocco	1960	49.6	....	....	...	....
Mozambique	1940	45	....	....	...	83.8
Niger	1959-60	37	....	....	...	....
Reunion	1951-55	....	47.5	53.4	.89	101
Senegal	1957	37	....	....	...	....
Seychelles	1960	....	60.8	65.9	.92	....
South Africa (White)	1950-52	....	64.6	70.1	.92	27.3
	1945	66.0	63.8	68.3	.93	....
	1935-37	61.0	59.0	63.1	.93	....
	1925-27	59.6	57.8	61.5	.94	....
	1920-22	57.4	55.6	59.2	.94	....
(Asiatic)	1950-52	....	55.8	54.8	1.02	60.7
	1945-47	....	50.7	49.8	1.02	....
(Colored)	1950-52	....	44.8	47.8	.94	140
	1945-47	....	41.7	44.0	.95	....
Southern Rhodesia (Europeans)	1961-63	....	66.9	74.0	.90	23.0
	1935-37	....	58.5	62.6	.93	....
(African)	1962	50	....	....	...	.....
	1953-55	....	48	49	.98	....
Swaziland	1946	48	....	....	...	220
Togo	1961	....	31.6	38.5	.82	193
United Arab Republic	1960	....	51.6	53.8	.96	118.6
	1946-49	....	41.4	47.0	.88	....
United Rep. of Tanzanica	1957	35-40	....	....	...	14.0
Zanzibar	1958	42.8	....	....	...	....
(Pemba)	1958	40.3	....	....	...	157
Upper Volta	1960-61	....	32.1	31.1	1.03	174
Zambia (Europeans)						18.7
NORTH AMERICA						
Antigua	1959-61	....	60.5	64.3	...	45.4
	1946	....	....	....	...	....
Barbados	1959-61	....	62.7	67.4	...	39.5
	1950-52	....	53.4	58.0	...	....
	1945-47	....	49.2	52.9	.93	....
British Honduras	1944-48	....	45.0	49.0	.92	52.3
Canada	1960-62	....	68.4	74.2	...	23.6
	1955-57	....	67.6	72.9	...	....
	1951	68.6	66.3	70.8	.94	....
	1947	67.1	65.2	69.0	.94	....
	1945	....	64.7	68.0	.95	....
	1940-42	64.6	63.0	66.3	.95	....
	1930-32	61.0	60.0	62.1	.97	....

Table 16-7   (*Continued*)

Nation	Year	Expectation of life at birth--e₀				Infant mortality rate (
		Both sexes	Male	Female	Ratio male to female	
NORTH AMERICAN (contined)						
Costa Rica...................	1962-64	....	61.9	64.8	...	65.2
	1955-57	62.0	....	....	...	....
	1949-51	....	54.6	57.0	.96	....
Dominica.....................	1958-62	....	57.0	59.2	...	107.2
Dominican Republic...........	1959-61	....	57.2	58.6	...	101
El Salvador..................	1960-61	....	56.6	60.4	.94	67.7
	1951-61	....	44.7	47.4	.94	....
	1949-51	....	49.9	52.4	.95	....
Greenland....................	1952-59	....	51.4	53.6	.96	83
	1946-51	....	32.2	37.5	.86	....
	1921	28.2	....	....	...	....
Grenada......................	1959-61	....	60.1	65.6	.92	71
	1945-47	....	47.2	52.5	.90	....
Guadeloupe & Martinique.......	1951-55	....	55.4	59.2	.94	....
Guadeloupe.......		....	....	....	...	49
Martinique.......		....	....	....	...	52
Guatemala....................	1949-51	....	43.8	43.5	1.01	87.9
	1939-41	36.5	36.0	37.1	.97	....
Haiti........................	1950	32.6	....	....	...	....
Jamaica......................	1959-61	....	62.6	66.6	.94	59
	1950-52	....	55.7	58.9	.95	....
	1945-47	52.9	51.2	54.6	.94	....
	1920-22	37.0	35.9	38.2	.94	....
	1910-12	40.2	39.0	41.4	.94	....
Leeward Islands..............	1946	....	49.5	54.8	.90	....
Mexico.......................	1956	....	55.1	57.9	.95	71.0
	1951	....	46.5	49.6	.94	....
	1940	38.8	37.9	39.8	.95	....
	1930	33.2	32.4	34.1	.95	....
Panama.......................	1960-61	....	57.6	60.9	.95	42.8
	1960	....	63.9	66.8	.96	....
	1952-54	....	60.4	63.1	.96	....
	1941-43	....	50.5	53.5	.95	....
Puerto Rico..................	1959-61	....	67.1	71.9	.93	51.6
	1954-56	....	66.0	69.6	.95	....
	1945-47	....	49.2	52.9	.93	....
	1939-41	....	45.1	46.9	.96	....
	1934-36	....	43.1	45.1	.96	....
	1929-31	....	40.8	42.2	.97	....
	1919-21	38.5	....	....	...	....
	1909-11	38.4	....	....	...	....
St. Kitts-Nevis-Anguilla.....	1959-61	....	58.0	61.9	...	98
	1946	....	....	....	...	....
St. Lucia....................	1959-61	....	55.1	58.5	.94	105
	1960	....	54.8	58.4	.94	....
St. Vincent..................	1959-61	....	58.5	59.7	.98	121
Trinidad & Tobago............	1959-61	....	62.2	66.3	.94	35.3
	1957	....	59.9	63.4	.95	....
	1954-56	....	59.8	63.1	.95	....
	1954	....	59.6	62.3	.96	....
	1952-54	....	57.6	59.9	.96	....
	1952	....	56.3	58.4	.96	....
	1945-47	....	53.0	56.0	.95	....
	1946	....	49.5	54.8	.90	....
	1930-32	....	44.5	47.0	.95	....
	1920-22	....	37.6	40.1	.94	....
	1910-12	....	39.0	41.0	.95	....
	1900-03	....	36.7	38.8	.95	....

Table 16-7   (*Continued*)

Nation	Year	Expectation of life at birth--e_o				Infant mortality rate (
		Both sexes	Male	Female	Ratio male to female	
United States.............	1965	....	66.8	73.7	...	24.8
	1963	....	66.6	73.4	.91	....
	1958	....	66.4	72.7	.91	....
	1957	....	66.3	72.5	...	....
	1954-56	....	66.6	72.7	.92	....
	1953	....	65.9	67.0	.98	....
	1952	....	65.7	66.9	.98	....
	1949-51	....	65.5	66.7	.98	....
	1948	....	64.6	69.9	.92	....
	1939-41	63.7	61.6	65.9	.93	....
	1929-31	59.4	57.7	61.0	.95	....
	1919-21	56.4	55.5	57.4	.97	....
	1909-11	51.6	49.9	53.2	.94	....
	1900-02	49.3	47.9	50.7	.94	....
Virgin Islands.............		....	....	....	...	28.4
SOUTH AMERICA						
Argentina..................	1959-61	....	63.1	68.9	.92	55.1
	1957	....	61.4	66.9	.92	....
	1947	59.2	56.9	61.4	.93	....
	1914	46.4	45.2	47.5	.95	....
Bolivia....................	1949-51	....	49.7	49.7	1.00	155
Brazil.....................	1949-51	52.9	49.8	56.0	.89	70.0
	1940-50	....	39.3	45.5	.86	....
	1920	37.4	....	....	...	....
	1890-1920	39.2	....	....	...	....
Chile......................	1952	....	49.8	53.9	.92	114.2
	1940	38.8	40.9	43.2	.95	....
	1930	36.6	35.4	37.7	.94	....
Colombia...................	1950-52	....	44.2	46.0	.96	105
Guyana.....................	1959-61	....	59.0	63.0	.94	48.9
	1950-52	....	53.2	56.3	.94	....
	1945-47	50.7	49.3	52.0	.95	....
	1930-31	41.4	40.3	42.6	.95	....
	1920-22	34.6	33.5	35.8	.94	....
	1910-12	31.2	29.9	32.4	.92	....
Peru.......................	1961	....	51.9	53.6	.97	105
ASIA						
Burma......................	1954	....	40.8	43.8	.93	170
	1921-31	....	30.6	31.0	.99	....
Cambodia...................	1958-59	....	44.2	43.3	1.02	145
Ceylon.....................	1962	....	61.9	61.4	1.01	52.8
	1954	....	60.3	59.4	1.02	....
	1952	....	57.6	55.5	1.04	....
	1950	55.6	56.4	54.8	1.03	....
	1949	....	56.1	54.8	1.02	....
	1948	....	54.9	53.3	1.03	....
	1945-47	45.8	46.8	44.7	1.05	....
	1920-22	31.7	32.7	30.7	1.07	....
China (Taiwan).............	1961	....	62.4	67.1	.93	....
	1959-60	....	61.3	65.6	.93	....
	1956-58	....	60.2	64.2	.94	....
	1936-40	43.4	41.1	45.7	.90	....
	1926-31	....	38.7	43.1	.90	....
Cyprus.....................	1948-50	66.2	63.6	68.8	.92	31
	1931-46	....	57.3	59.3	.97	....
Hong Kong..................	1961	....	63.6	70.5	.90	23.7
India......................	1951-60	....	41.9	40.6	1.03	72.8
	1957-58	....	45.2	46.6	.97	....
	1941-50	32.0	32.4	31.7	1.02	....
	1921-31	26.7	26.9	26.6	1.01	....
	1901-11	23.0	22.6	23.3	.97	....
	1891-1901	23.8	23.6	24.0	.99	....

Table 16-7 *(Continued)*

Nation	Year	Expectation of life at birth--e₀				Infant mortality rate (
		Both sexes	Male	Female	Ratio male to female	
Israel (Jewish population)...	1965	....	70.5	73.2	.96	27.4
	1963	....	70.9	73.0	.97	....
	1962	....	70.8	72.8	.97	....
	1960	....	70.7	73.5	.96	....
	1958	....	69.5	72.4	.96	....
	1956	....	67.9	70.9	.96	....
	1954	....	67.5	70.5	.96	....
	1952	....	66.7	69.8	.96	....
	1950	67.9	66.3	69.5	.95	....
	1942-44	....	....	....	...	....
	1936-38	....	....	....	...	....
Japan......................	1965	....	67.7	73.0	.93	20.4
	1963	....	67.2	72.3	.93	....
	1962	....	66.2	71.2	.93	....
	1959-60	....	65.3	70.2	.93	....
	1959	....	65.2	69.9	.93	....
	1958	....	65.0	69.6	.93	....
	1956	....	63.6	67.5	.94	....
	1955	....	63.9	68.4	.93	....
	1954	....	63.4	67.7	.94	....
	1953	....	61.9	65.7	.94	....
	1952	....	61.9	65.5	.95	....
	1949-50	56.4	56.2	56.6	.99	....
	1948	....	55.6	59.4	.94	....
	1947	52.0	50.1	54.0	.93	....
	1946	....	42.6	51.1	.83	....
	1945	....	23.9	37.5	.64	....
	1935-36	48.3	46.9	49.6	.95	....
	1926-30	45.7	44.8	46.5	.96	....
	1921-25	42.6	42.1	43.2	.97	....
	1909-13	44.5	44.2	44.7	.99	....
	1899-1903	44.4	44.0	44.8	.98	....
Korea......................	1955-60	....	51.1	53.7	.95	120
	1938	....	47.2	50.6	.93	....
Republic of Korea...........	1955-60	....	51.1	53.7	...	....
Malaysia (West Malaysia).....	1956-58	....	55.8	58.2	.96	76
Pakistan....................	1962	....	53.7	48.8	1.10	170
East Pakistan........	1962	....	51.2	47.9	1.07	....
West Pakistan........	1962	....	50.8	47.8	1.06	....
Philippines.................	1946-49	....	48.8	53.4	.91	110
	1938	....	44.8	47.7	.94	....
Ryukyu Islands..............	1960	....	68.0	74.6	.91	10.1
	1955-57	....	65.8	72.0	.91	....
Thailand....................	1960	....	53.6	58.7	.91	145
	1947-48	50.3	48.7	51.9	.94	....
Turkey (Provincial capitals).	1950-51	....	46.0	50.4	.91	165
EUROPE						
Albania.....................	1960-61	....	63.7	66.0	.97	104
	1955-56	....	57.2	58.6	.98	....
Austria.....................	1959-61	....	65.6	72.0	.91	28.3
	1960	....	65.0	71.0	.92	....
	1949-51	64.4	61.9	67.0	.92	....
	1930-33	56.5	54.5	58.5	.93	....
	1901-05	40.1	39.1	41.1	.95	....
Belgium.....................	1959-63	....	67.7	73.5	.95	25.3
	1960	....	66.8	72.8	.92	....
	1946-49	64.6	62.0	67.3	.92	....
	1928-32	57.9	56.0	59.8	.94	....
	1891-1900	47.1	45.4	48.8	.93	....
Bulgaria....................	1960-62	....	67.8	71.4	...	30.8
	1956-57	....	64.2	67.6	.95	....
	1925-28	46.3	45.9	46.6	.98	....
	1899-1902	40.2	40.0	40.3	.99	....

Table 16-7 *(Continued)*

Nation	Year	Expectation of life at birth--e_o				Infant mortality rate
		Both sexes	Male	Female	Ratio male to female	
Czechoslovakia.............	1964	....	67.8	73.6	.92	21.4
	1962	....	67.2	72.8	.92	....
	1960-61	....	67.6	73.1	.93	....
	1958	....	67.2	72.3	.93	....
	1956	....	66.6	66.0	1.01	....
	1955	....	66.2	71.2	.93	....
	1949-51	....	60.9	65.5	.93	....
	1929-32	53.6	51.9	55.2	.94	....
	1899-1902	40.3	38.9	41.7	.93	....
Denmark....................	1963-64	....	70.3	74.6	.94	18.7
	1960	....	70.6	74.1	.95	....
	1956-60	....	70.4	73.8	.95	....
	1946-50	69.0	67.8	70.1	.97	....
	1941-45	66.7	65.6	67.7	.97	....
	1936-40	....	63.5	65.8	.97	....
	1931-35	62.9	62.0	63.8	.97	....
	1926-30	....	60.9	62.6	.97	....
	1921-25	61.1	60.3	61.9	.97	....
	1916-20	....	55.8	58.1	.96	....
	1911-15	57.7	56.2	59.2	.95	....
	1901-05	54.6	52.9	56.2	.94	....
Finland....................	1956-60	....	64.9	71.6	.91	17.6
	1960	....	65.6	72.6	.90	....
	1951-55	....	63.4	69.8	.91	....
	1946-50	....	58.6	65.9	.89	....
	1941-45	57.9	54.6	61.1	.89	....
	1936-40	....	54.3	59.5	.91	....
	1931-40	57.0	54.4	59.6	.91	....
	1921-30	52.9	50.7	55.1	.92	....
	1911-20	46.3	43.4	49.1	.88	....
	1901-10	46.7	45.3	48.1	.94	....
France.....................	1964	....	68.0	75.1	.91	19.4
	1962	....	67.3	74.1	.91	....
	1960	....	67.2	73.8	.91	....
	1959	....	67.0	73.6	.91	....
	1958	....	67.0	73.4	.91	....
	1957	....	65.7	72.4	.91	....
	1952-56	....	65.0	71.2	.91	....
	1951-55	....	63.4	69.8	.91	....
	1950-51	66.4	63.6	69.3	.92	....
	1946-49	64.6	61.9	67.4	.92	....
	1933-38	58.8	55.9	61.6	.91	....
	1928-33	56.7	54.3	59.0	.92	....
	1920-23	54.1	52.2	56.1	.93	....
	1908-13	50.4	48.5	52.4	.93	....
	1898-1903	47.0	45.3	48.7	.93	....
Germany (Eastern Germany)....	1963-64	....	68.3	73.3	.93	31.4
	1960-61	....	67.3	72.2	.93	....
	1955-58	....	66.1	70.7	.94	....
	1956-57	....	66.3	71.0	.93	....
	1955-56	....	66.3	70.6	.94	....
	1954-55	....	66.2	70.1	.94	....
	1952-53	....	65.1	69.1	.94	....
Federal Republic of Germany..	1964-65	....	67.6	73.4	.92	23.9
	1960-62	....	66.9	72.4	.92	....
	1959-60	....	66.7	71.9	.93	....
	1958-59	....	66.8	71.9	.93	....
	1949-51	66.6	64.6	68.5	.94	....
	1946-47	....	57.7	63.4	.91	....

Table 16-7 (*Continued*)

| Nation | Year | Expectation of life at birth--e$_o$ | | | | Infant mortality rate |
		Both sexes	Male	Female	Ratio male to female	
EUROPE (continued)						
Germany......................	1932-34	61.3	59.9	62.8	.95	....
	1924-26	57.4	56.0	58.8	.95	....
	1910-11	49.0	47.4	50.7	.94	....
	1901-10	46.6	44.8	48.3	.93	....
Berlin	1947	....	51.0	60.0	.85	....
(East Berlin)...........	....	....	....	....	...	28.2
(West Berlin)...........	1949-51	....	63.7	68.4	.93	28.3
Greece......................	1960-62	....	67.5	70.7	.95	55
	1955-59	....	66.4	69.7	.95	....
	1940	54.9	53.0	56.9	.93	....
	1926-30	50.0	49.1	50.9	.96	....
	1920	44.7	42.9	46.5	.92	....
Hungary.....................	1964	....	67.0	71.8	.93	38.8
	1961	....	66.8	71.3	.94	....
	1959-60	....	65.2	69.6	.94	....
	1958	....	65.1	69.4	.94	....
	1954	....	63.5	67.3	.94	....
	1948-49	....	58.8	63.2	.93	....
	1941	56.6	54.9	58.2	.94	....
	1930-31					
	1920-21	....	40.4	42.6	.95	....
	1900-01	....	37.1	37.9	.98	....
Iceland.....................	1951-60	....	70.7	75.0	.94	15.0
	1941-50	....	66.1	70.3	.94	....
	1931-40	63.2	60.9	65.6	.93	....
	1921-30	58.6	56.2	61.0	.92	....
	1911-20	55.4	52.7	58.0	.91	....
	1901-10	50.7	48.3	53.1	.91	....
Ireland.....................	1960-62	....	68.1	71.9	.95	25.2
	1956	....	67.4	70.6	.95	....
	1950-52	....	64.5	67.1	.96	....
	1945-47	61.4	60.5	62.4	.97	....
	1940-42	60.0	59.0	61.0	.97	....
	1935-37	58.9	58.2	59.6	.98	....
	1925-27	57.6	57.4	57.9	.99	....
	1910-12	....	53.6	54.1	.99	....
	1900-02	....	49.3	49.6	.99	....
Italy.......................	1960-62	....	67.2	72.3	.93	36.1
	1960	....	66.7	71.7	.93	....
	1954-57	....	65.8	70.0	.94	....
	1950-53	....	63.8	67.2	.95	....
	1930-32	54.9	53.8	56.0	.96	....
	1921-22	50.0	49.3	50.8	.97	....
	1901-11	44.5	44.2	44.8	.99	....
Luxembourg..................	1959	....	67.3	71.5	.94	24.0
	1946-48	63.7	61.7	65.8	.94	....
Malta.......................	1963-65	....	67.1	71.0	.95	34.8
	1961-63	....	67.0	70.6	.95	....
Malta & Gozo (U.K.)........	1960-62	....	67.0	70.7	.95	....
	1957-59	....	66.3	70.3	.94	....
	1955-57	....	65.7	68.9	.95	....
	1948	56.7	55.7	57.7	.96	....
Netherlands.................	1961-65	....	71.1	75.9	.94	14.4
	1961	....	71.6	76.0	.94	....
	1956-60	....	71.4	74.8	.95	....
	1953-55	....	71.0	73.9	.96	....
	1951-55	....	70.9	73.5	.96	....
	1950-52	....	70.6	72.9	.97	....
	1947-49	70.4	69.4	71.5	.97	....
	1931-40	66.2	65.7	67.2	.98	....
	1921-30	62.7	61.9	63.5	.97	....
	1910-20	56.1	55.1	57.1	.96	....
	1900-09	52.2	51.0	53.4	.96	....

Table 16-7 (Continued)

Nation	Year	Expectation of life at birth--e$_0$				Infant mortality rate (
		Both sexes	Male	Female	Ratio male to female	
EUROPE (continued)	1960	....	71.3	75.8	.94	16.4
Norway....................	1956-60	....	71.3	75.6	.94	....
	1951-55	....	71.1	74.7	.95	....
	1946-50	....	69.2	72.6	.95	....
	1945-48	69.8	67.8	71.7	.95	....
1931/32-	1940/41	65.8	64.1	67.6	.95	....
1921/22-	1930/31	62.4	61.0	63.8	.96	....
1911/12-	1920/21	57.2	55.6	58.7	.95	....
1901/02-	1910/11	56.3	54.8	57.7	.95	....
Poland....................	1960-61	....	64.8	70.5	.92	47.7
	1958	....	62.8	68.9	.91	....
	1957	....	61.9	68.0	.91	....
	1956	....	62.4	67.8	.92	....
	1955-56	....	61.8	67.8	.91	....
	1952-53	....	58.6	64.2	.91	....
	1948	59.0	55.6	62.5	.89	....
	1931-32	49.8	48.2	51.4	.94	....
Portugal..................	1959-62	....	60.7	66.4	.92	64.9
	1957-58	....	59.8	65.0	.92	....
	1955-56	....	58.8	63.8	.92	....
	1949-52	58.0	55.5	60.5	.92	....
	1939-42	50.7	48.6	52.8	.92	....
Romania...................	1963	....	65.4	70.2	.93	44.1
	1956	....	61.5	65.0	.95	....
Spain.....................	1960	....	67.3	71.9	.94	41.6
	1950	....	58.8	63.5	.93	....
	1940	50.2	47.1	53.2	.89	....
	1930	50.0	48.4	51.6	.94	....
	1920	41.2	40.3	42.1	.96	....
	1910	41.8	40.9	42.6	.96	....
	1900	34.8	33.9	35.7	.95	....
Sweden....................	1962	....	71.3	75.4	.95	13.3
	1961-65	....	71.6	75.7	.95	....
	1961	....	71.6	75.4	.95	....
	1959	....	71.7	75.2	.95	....
	1957	....	70.8	74.3	.95	....
	1956-60	....	71.2	74.7	.95	....
	1951-55	....	70.5	73.4	.96	....
	1946-50	70.3	69.0	71.6	.96	....
	1941-45	68.4	67.1	69.7	.96	....
	1936-40	....	64.3	66.9	.96	....
	1931-40	65.2	63.8	66.1	.96	....
	1921-30	62.1	61.0	63.2	.97	....
	1911-20	57.0	55.6	58.4	.95	....
	1901-10	55.8	54.5	57.0	.96	....
Switzerland...............	1959-61	....	69.5	74.8	.93	19.0
	1958-63	....	68.7	74.1	.93	....
	1948-53	....	66.4	70.8	.94	....
	1939-44	64.8	62.7	67.0	.94	....
	1933-37	62.6	60.7	64.6	.94	....
	1931-41	....	60.9	64.8	.94	....
	1929-32	61.1	59.2	63.0	.94	....
	1920-21	56.0	54.5	57.5	.95	....
	1910-11	52.3	50.6	53.9	.94	....
	1901-10	....	49.2	52.2	.94	....
United Kingdom=England & Wales	1963-65	....	68.3	74.4	.92	19.0
	1961-63	....	68.0	73.9	.92	....
	1958-60	....	68.1	73.9	.92	....
	1956-58	....	67.8	73.5	.92	....
	1955-57	....	67.7	73.3	.92	....
	1953-55	....	67.5	72.9	.93	....
	1950-52	....	66.4	71.5	.93	....
	1950	68.8	66.5	71.2	.93	....
	1930-32	60.8	58.7	62.9	.93	....
	1920-22	57.6	55.6	59.7	.93	....
	1910-12	53.4	51.5	55.4	.93	....
	1901-10	50.4	48.5	52.4	.93	....

Table 16-7   *(Continued)*

Nation	Year	Expectation of life at birth--e$_o$				Infant mortality rate (
		Both sexes	Male	Female	Ratio male to female	
EUROPE (continued)	1963-65	....	67.8	72.9	.93	25.1
Northern Ireland............	1961-63	....	67.6	72.5	.93	....
	1958-60	....	67.5	71.9	.94	....
	1956-58	....	67.6	71.8	.94	....
	1954-56	....	67.4	71.0	.95	....
	1950-52	....	65.5	68.8	.95	....
	1936-38	....	57.8	59.2	.98	....
	1926	....	55.3	56.1	.99	....
	1925-27	55.8	55.4	56.1	.99	....
	1911	....	50.7	51.0	.99	....
	1901	....	47.1	46.7	1.01	....
Scotland..................	1963-65	....	66.3	72.4	.92	24.0
	1960	....	66.4	71.9	.92	....
	1957-59	....	66.0	71.4	.93	....
	1955-57	....	65.9	71.1	.93	....
	1954	....	65.5	70.5	.93	....
	1953	....	65.7	70.7	.93	....
	1950-52	....	64.4	68.7	.94	....
	1950	66.4	64.5	68.3	.94	....
	1949	....	64.0	67.6	.95	....
	1948	....	63.8	67.6	.94	....
	1930-32	57.8	56.0	59.5	.94	....
	1920-22	54.7	53.1	56.4	.94	....
Yugoslavia.................	1962	....	62.2	65.2	.95	75.8
	1961-62	....	62.4	65.6	.95	....
	1958-59	....	61.6	64.4	.96	....
	1952-54	....	56.9	59.3	.96	....
OCEANIA						
Australia.................	1960-62	....	67.9	74.2	.92	18.5
	1960	....	67.9	73.9	.92	....
	1953-55	....	67.1	72.8	.92	....
	1946-48	68.4	66.1	70.6	.94	....
	1932-34	65.3	63.5	67.1	.95	....
	1920-22	61.2	59.2	63.3	.93	....
	1901-10	57.0	55.2	58.8	.94	....
Gilbert & Ellice Islands.....	1958-62	....	56.9	59.0	.96	....
New Zealand................	1960-62	....	68.4	73.8	.93	19.5
(Europeans).......	1960	....	69.5	74.6	.93	....
	1955-57	....	68.2	73.0	.93	....
	1951-52	70.4	68.3	72.4	.94	....
(Maori)..........	1950-52	....	54.0	55.9	.97	....
	1934-38	67.0	65.5	68.4	.96	....
	1911-15	62.2	61.0	63.5	.96	....
	1901-05	59.3	58.1	60.6	.96	....
USSR......................	1964-65	70	66	54	1.22	41
	1960-61	70	....	....	...	....
	1958-59	....	64.4	71.7	.90	....
	1957-58	....	64	71	.90	....
	1955-56	....	63	69	.91	....
	1954-55	....	61	67	.91	....
	1926-27	44.4	41.9	46.8	.90	....
	1896-97	32.4	31.4	33.4	.94	....
Ukrainian SSR................	1963-64	....	68	74	.92	....
	1958-59	....	66	73	.90	....

United Nations Demographic Yearbook 1966.

16.9. Causes of Death

Beyond a certain level of study, it is superficial to treat death as a single unitary force as has been done in the preceding section. In reality death is an event brought about by one or a combination of a great variety of *causes*, or diseases, and a full understanding of mortality requires an understanding of the trends in each of the major causes of death. Analysis of statistical data for deaths classified according to cause is a major branch of biostatistics, but it also has such profound demographic implications that it is worthwhile for students of population to have at least a general familiarity with this field of study.

In order to provide a uniform framework within which the scientific study of cause of death can proceed, the World Health Organization has sponsored research that resulted in the two-volume *International Classification of Diseases, Injuries, and Causes of Death*. This work sets up 1000 groups of diseases and gives each a code. Specific diseases that are to be classified in each of the 1000 categories are spelled out in detail and full instructions for using the code are provided. This level of detail usually is far too great for most statistical purposes, so that for general presentation the 1000 categories are grouped into 50 causes of death. Almost all of the nations where cause-of-death statistics now are collected make use of this system and slowly a body of international experience is accumulating.

Unfortunately, a great number of difficulties arise in the analysis of cause-of-death statistics, which makes it necessary to interpret them with great caution. First, deaths from some causes appear to be registered with much more regularity than deaths from other causes, with the result that incomplete registration is suspected of having a built-in cause-of-death bias. Second, many times death occurs when a physician is not in attendance and has not seen the patient before death. The only basis that can be used for defining the cause of death in such cases is postmortem examination and evaluation of the symptoms reported by relatives or observers. Not infrequently death occurs with no one present to report even the symptoms. In populations where literacy is low it is very common to get such answers as "fever," "pain," and "digestive upset," which could refer to a great variety of specific diseases. Even where a physician has been in attendance, there is no assurance that cause of death will be reported uniformly. Physicians differ widely in their ability to diagnose, and there are even international differences in the practice of physicians in making and reporting particular combinations of disorders. Moreover, there has been much improvement in diagnosis over the years, especially since the introduction of laboratory testing equipment. This very progress may cause an apparent increase in the incidence of hard-to-diagnose causes, with the result that trends in cause of death for many diseases may not be reliable even where physicians are in attendance in a high proportion of cases. A third set of difficulties arises in the handling of the problems of multiple causes of death. Not infrequently death results from a chain of events involving two or more causes and the task of assigning death to one cause is difficult. Physicians and national medical systems have differed widely in their practice in this regard.

A fourth difficulty with cause-of-death statistics is that not infrequently there is falsification of the record in order to hide death from a cause that is socially disapproved such as suicide, syphilis, alcoholism, or even cancer or tuberculosis. Finally, a fifth major difficulty is the extent to which recorders make use of a "catchall" category, such as deaths "from unknown and ill-defined causes" or deaths attributed to "senility." Where such categories are used in a high percentage of cases, it automatically means that deaths that should have been placed in other categories are missing, hence the rates for these causes are lower than they should be.

The United Nations has reviewed carefully the quality of the cause-of-death statistics for the world and finds that for long historical trend studies only two countries, England and Wales and the United States, qualify and that these are also seriously deficient even for the recent past. Nevertheless the changing pattern of cause of death that is observed in these countries is thought to be fairly typical of that

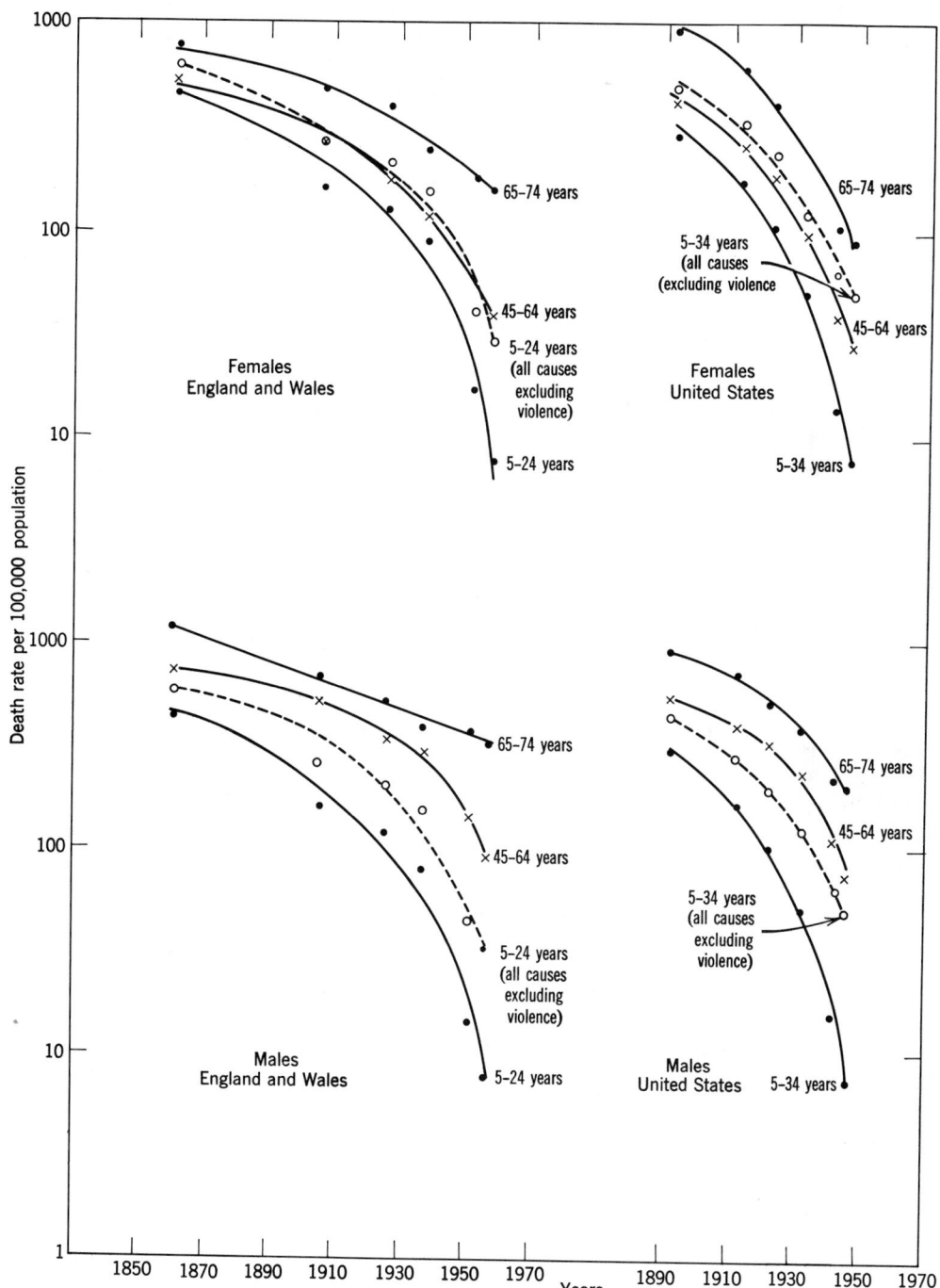

Figure 16-6 Trend of Mortality from Group I Diseases (Infectious and Parasitic Diseases, Influenza and Pneumonia, and Bronchitis below the Age of 5 Years), By Sex and Age Groups. England and Wales from 1848–1872 to 1956–1957 and United States from 1900–1904 to 1956–1957.

SOURCE: United Nations, *Recent Trends of Mortality in the World,* Population Bulletin, No. 6, 1962.

which takes place as mortality falls in the countries around the world.[7]

For the study of long-term trends in cause of death the 50-category summary is too detailed; the United Nations has therefore grouped all causes of death into 5 major types according to their responsiveness to public health programs and medical care.[8]

Group 1: Infectious, parasitic, and respiratory diseases.
Group 2: Cancer.
Group 3: Diseases of the circulatory system.
Group 4: Deaths from violence.
Group 5: Other, including gastrointestinal diseases, diabetes mellitus, birth injuries, and diseases peculiar to the first few weeks of life.

Group 1 Causes of Death. Figure 16-6 shows the long-term trend of mortality from group 1 diseases in England and Wales and in the United States. The dashed line represents general mortality, from all causes for the age group 5 to 34 years. It is clear that the decline in the group 1 diseases has been substantially sharper than in all other disease categories. This means that a disproportionately large share of the decline in general mortality has been due to the conquest of infectious, parasitic, and respiratory diseases. This chart also shows the trend in the group 1 diseases for three age groups. The decline has been very sharp for the young age group 5 to 34 years of age, substantial but less sharp for the age group 45 to 64, and much more moderate for the age group 65 to 74 years. The age difference in progress is greater for England and Wales than for the United States. In both countries essentially the same progress has been made for males and females.

The United Nations has tried to study the progress of deaths from group 1 diseases in several countries of the world, including a few

developing nations, to note the trends. On the basis of their review they conclude that *the rapid decline in mortality being witnessed around the world today in most of the developing countries is due to the fall in the group 1 diseases: infectious, parasitic, or respiratory diseases.* It is supposed that this fall is following an age-differential pattern similar to that for England and Wales and for the United States, although there is very little evidence to support it or to contradict it.[9]

The United Nations finds that the cause-of-death statistics for 13 of the low-mortality nations are sufficiently reliable for the period since about 1940 to permit limited comparison of recent trends. They find that the pattern described for England and Wales and the United States holds generally, except that there are substantial differences between the 13 nations in the proportion of all deaths that are due to group 1 causes. In all of these nations, however, it has been found that the reduction in mortality has come first and primarily from the conquest of group 1 diseases.[10] Table 16-8 summarizes the percentage decrease in mortality from all causes and in mortality from group 1 diseases for these 13 nations for the span of time from 1936 to 1956. When it is remembered that a decrease of 100 percent means complete disappearance, this table shows just how nearly complete has been the conquest of these diseases in a surprisingly short period of time. The smallest decrease at all ages is 56 percent and the greatest decrease is 81 percent, and this refers only to progress in a 20-year period, excluding the very substantial progress made between 1890 and 1935. In the age group 5 to 34, declines as large as 94 percent are registered. Clearly, the lion's share of mortality reduction around the world has been brought about by the reduction of these group 1 diseases.

When the experts search for an explanation of *how* the conquest of group 1 diseases was brought about, it turns out to be a highly complex and intricate problem. The quick and easy answer would be, of course, "improved public

[7] The U.S. National Center for Health Statistics has published a superior analysis of mortality trends in each of these nations, by classes of cause of death. See U.S. Public Health Service, National Center for Health Statistics, *Analytical Studies*, Series 3, Numbers 1 and 3, "The Change in Mortality Trends in the United States" and "Changes in Mortality Trends in England and Wales," 1964 and 1965, respectively.
[8] Population Bulletin No. 6, *op. cit.*, pp. 73–75.

[9] *Ibid.*, pp. 76–78.
[10] *Ibid.*, p. 81.

Table 16-8 Percentage Decrease in Mortality and in Mortality from Group I Diseases, by Sex and for Several Age Groups, 13 Low-Mortality Countries: 1936–1938 to 1954–1956

Country and sex	All ages		5-34 years		45-64 years		65-74 years	
	All causes	Group I causes	All causes except violence	Group I causes	All causes	Group I causes	All causes	Group I causes
MALES								
Denmark............	14	80	73	94	19	78	16	73
Norway.............	15	73	77	94	20	77	13	70
United States......	12	75	70	90	18	77	8	65
Canada.............	11	71	70	90	7	74	5	65
Netherlands........	8	72	64	90	12	73	18	66
England and Wales..	5	62	73	90	14	66	2	24
France.............	23	58	76	90	27	58	20	17
Scotland...........	8	72	67	88	4	66	2	47
New Zealand........	0	62	61	87	9	76	+ 3	44
Japan..............	52	75	79	85	39	51	8	41
Italy..............	34	75	73	84	20	68	17	72
Switzerland........	11	63	74	84	25	68	17	53
Australia..........	4	60	58	84	5	67	+ 5	44
FEMALES								
Denmark............	19	81	65	94	36	83	26	78
Norway.............	17	72	79	95	39	87	21	78
United States......	21	79	75	91	38	84	27	78
Canada.............	26	77	77	91	32	81	26	79
Netherlands........	16	74	69	91	38	81	27	72
England and Wales..	6	60	75	90	33	69	23	46
France.............	19	56	78	91	39	69	31	46
Scotland...........	12	72	69	85	27	74	17	64
New Zealand........	4	59	73	90	25	72	20	55
Japan..............	56	79	80	86	39	60	37	52
Italy..............	36	79	73	88	36	82	24	79
Switzerland........	12	66	75	88	32	76	26	64
Australia..........	4	63	68	88	20	73	20	55

Note: A plus sign indicates an increase in mortality.

Source: United Nations. Population Bulletin Number 6. Table V.9, page 81.

health and medical care," but some of the facts fail to support this as a complete explanation. The more carefully one studies the situation, the more one realizes that almost every major accomplishment of "industrialization" helps to bring about a reduction in mortality. Extension of transportation and roads into remote areas promotes trade and commerce and brings about a rise in level of living that is reflected in improved nutritional levels and a more balanced diet for the population, thereby increasing their resistance to infectious diseases. Some observers have therefore seriously declared that transportation improvements have been the major cause of mortality decline. Others have insisted that one of the major factors was the mere introduction of soap into remote areas, resulting in increased bodily cleanliness and cleanliness in the preparation of food, thereby greatly reducing the hazard of infection from disease. Others have cited improved

housing, lessening of crowding in existing housing, improved techniques for heating housing, improvements in water supply and waste disposal, and rising literacy as important ingredients in the mortality decline. In fact, those who hold extreme views would maintain that physicians and hospitals have had comparatively little to do with the historic decline in mortality and that perhaps one of the major forces has been simply health education—helping people become aware of the germ theory of disease and of the need for cleanliness in body and in preparation of food, for care in the disposal of wastes of all kinds, and for avoiding contamination of food and water supplies. Certainly, it is true that conquest of these diseases requires a total transformation of the environment and of the health habits of the population.

This interpretation is an obvious exaggeration, however. Too many fully documented cases of the immediate and dramatic effect on

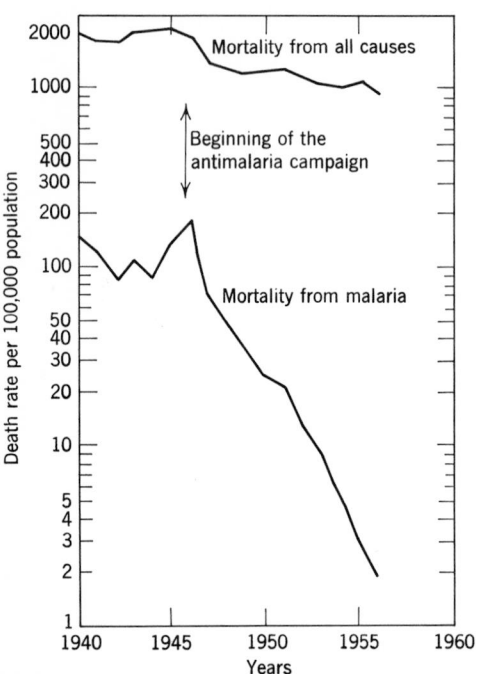

Figure 16-7 Ceylon, 1940 to 1957. Mortality from All Causes and from Malaria (Crude Death Rate per 100,000 Population, Logarithmic Scale).

SOURCE: United Nations, *Recent Trends of Mortality in the World,* Population Bulletin, No. 6, 1962.

mortality of the introduction of new medical discoveries are on record to permit their easy dismissal. In Ceylon, for example, the malaria death rate dropped from 125 per 100,000 population in 1940-1946 to 2 per 100,000 population in 1956. This followed a 10-year antimalaria campaign. Figure 16-7 charts the trend of the malaria death rate for Ceylon. Perhaps somewhat less dramatic but equally potent results have been achieved by penicillin, sulfa drugs, and injections for smallpox. Several major killers in the developing countries—malaria, smallpox, typhoid, and tuberculosis—owe their sharp and abrupt decline in recent years to the mass use of modern drugs rather than to general environmental improvement. In fact, death rates have tumbled in many areas *despite* continued unfavorable environmental conditions.

Today the group 1 diseases in the industrialized nations have declined to a point where they are of only minor significance for all ages

except the very oldest, among whom pneumonia and influenza are still leading causes of death. As economic development brings about total environmental change plus improved public health and medical care, a similar situation may be expected to develop around the world.

Group 2 Causes of Death—Cancer. At the present time, cancer causes about 18 percent of all deaths in developed nations, if the experience of England and the United States can be used as a guide. This represents a dramatic rise from almost negligible rates of death from cancer reported at the turn of the century. However, this rapid rise is largely illusory. Since cancer is primarily a disease of older adulthood, deaths from this cause have increased as populations have grown older. Moreover, as advances have been made both in cancer detection and in diagnosing cause of death, underregistration of death from cancer in earlier years has been gradually corrected. The most appropriate hypothesis at the present time is that the age-specific rates for cancer, taken as a class, have remained unchanged during the span of time in which other forms of disease have declined. By definition, as deaths from group 1 causes have plummeted, deaths from cancer have risen in importance. Cancers of the lung and bronchus appear unmistakably to be on the increase and are associated with cigarette smoking and air pollution. Mortality from cancer of the cervix appears to be on the decline, because of improved methods of detection and early treatment. Figure 16-8 indicates that for the United States population, at least, malignant neoplasms are an increasing cause of death among males 55 to 64 and a decreasing cause among females of the same age group. One of the major unknowns at the present time is the trend in the *incidence* of cancer. Some experts believe that progress is being made in the treatment of cancer, but that death rates from cancer remain unchanged or even increase because the incidence is increasing. Intensive scientific studies, many of them highly sophisticated and imaginative, have been and are being undertaken. Demographers must await their findings before the impact of this group of causes on mortality can be assessed.

In most of the developing countries cancer

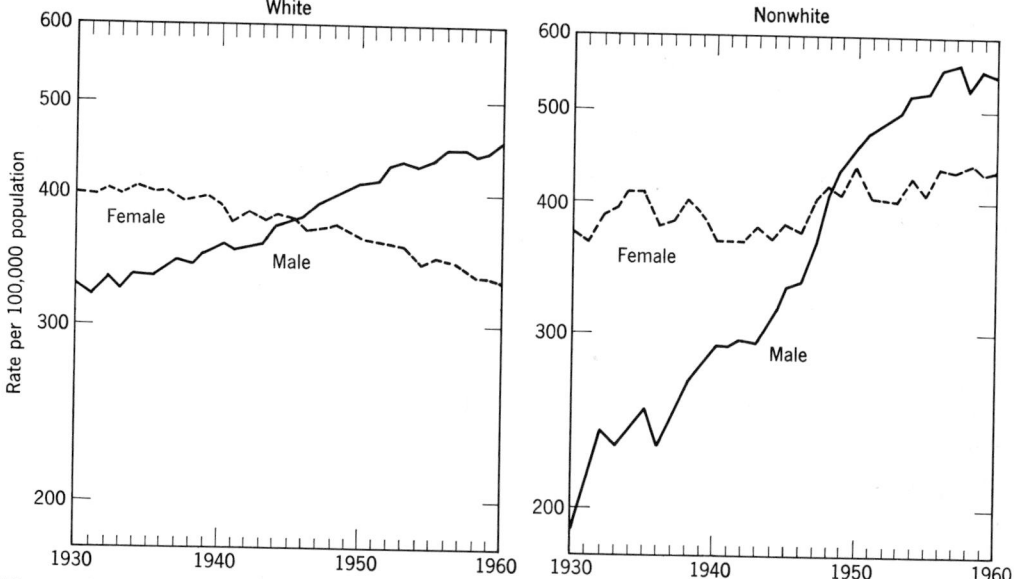

Figure 16-8 Death Rates for Malignant Neoplasms, 55–64 Year Age Group, by Color and Sex, United States: 1930 to 1960.

SOURCE: Iwao M. Moriyama, *The Change in Mortality Trend in the United States,* National Center for Health Statistics, Analytical Studies, Series 3, Number 1, U. S. Department of Health, Education, and Welfare, 1964.

is a comparatively minor cause of death, because the populations have a young age composition. As fertility rates decline and the age composition moves toward older ages, cancer may be expected to assume increasing importance. One of the major improvements in these countries is to help the population survive to an age where its members can enjoy the privilege of being eligible to have cancer.

Group 3 Causes of Death—Cardiovascular Diseases and Bronchitis at Older Ages. Cardiovascular diseases are degenerative diseases and are heavily concentrated at the older ages. As is true of cancer, only modest improvement in anticipation and treatment of these disorders has been made, so that the death rates at each older age have failed to follow the general downward trend of the mortality curve. Sharp declines have been made for this group of diseases for children below 20 years of age, but the incidence of these diseases at these ages is comparatively minor. At ages above 45 years, the rates for males are completely level or somewhat rising, while those for females are completely level or slightly declining. As in the case of cancer, this lack of change may reflect

either a condition of stagnation in medical and health technology or a substantial progress that is being offset by a rising incidence of this class of disorder. An important aspect of this group of diseases is that they can seldom be "cured," as can infective diseases. The disorder remains; the physician merely attempts to postpone death. The United Nations has explained this phenomenon as follows:

"By curing a person aged *a* years of an infectious disease, the mortality rate for the same disease ten years later for persons aged *a* + 10 years is not increased. The effect of a treatment which postpones death is quite different. By reducing mortality from cardiovascular diseases in the 65-74 year age group, the proportion of persons of ages 75-84 years who suffer from the same disease is increased. Because at these ages, as at all advanced ages, physiological stress is greater and treatment which merely postpones death is less effective, the result is an increase in the mortality rates."[11]

There is a sharp sex differential in the inci-

[11] *Ibid.,* p. 95.

dence of cardiovascular diseases; males suffer much more than females. In fact, more than three-fourths of the total sex differential in mortality in developed nations is due to this class of disorder.

Group 4 Causes of Death—Violence: Accidents, Suicide, and Homicide. Deaths from violence have declined since 1900. (This excludes, of course, war deaths.) Deaths from accidents at work and in the home have definitely declined in England and the United States, at each age and sex group. In addition, medical science is now able to prevent death resulting from serious accidental injuries better than in the past. Homicide appears to be declining, although suicide remains almost constant. Deaths from motor vehicle accidents are on the increase or remain almost unchanged; improvements in the safety features of highways and automobiles are offset by the increased volume of exposure to risk. Thus, as a group, these types of cause have contributed almost nothing to the decline of the death rate. Because other causes of death that affect young adults have been greatly reduced, violence is the leading cause of death between ages 15 and 30. This results also because youths tend to be more prone to automobile mishaps and incur risks of violent death that older adults do not.

Group 5 Causes of Death: Other Causes. This group is a diverse set of causes, which includes diabetes, gastritis and enteritis, cirrhosis of the liver, diseases and conditions peculiar to early infancy, and "senility." This is a rather meaningless grouping, and only one general principle can be drawn from it. The trend over time for the group is downward, primarily because of progress in neonatal infant mortality control and because of improved medical techniques for controlling diabetes, gastritis and enteritis, appendicitis, and ulcer of the stomach. Thus declines in this group reflect improved medical technology perhaps more than they reflect general improvement in the environment. The downward trend is very similar to the group 1 diseases.

Synthesis. The United Nations has undertaken to demonstrate how the pattern of cause-of-death changes with change in life expectancy.

By using cause-of-death data for developing countries where reliable data are available and for developed nations for earlier dates when life expectancy was less, a "model" of cause of death in relation to life expectancy has been built up, holding constant the factor of changing age composition. The result is reported in Figure 16-9. In interpreting it, the United Nations states:

"It represents a pattern in the distribution of deaths by causes which might be observed in a country having an age structure identical to the estimated age structure of the world population in 1960 and an expectation of life at birth that progressively rises from 40 to 75 years. The initial stage of such a pattern corresponds to the present situation in many underdeveloped countries. Three general phases may be distinguished:

"1. When the expectation of life at birth increases from 40 to 60 years, the proportion of deaths due to group I diseases (infectious and parasitic diseases, influenza, pneumonia) *declines*. The proportion of deaths due to group II diseases (cancer) and group III diseases (cardiovascular diseases and bronchitis above the age of 5 years) *increases*. The proportion of deaths due to group V diseases (other diseases) increases slightly.

"2. When the expectation of life at birth increases from 60 to 70 years, the proportion of group I diseases continues to decline, and that of group II and group III diseases continues to increase, but *the increase is more rapid*. The proportion of group V diseases remains practically unchanged.

"3. When the expectation of life increases beyond 70 years, the trends previously observed for group I, II, and III diseases continue, while the proportion of deaths due to group V diseases *rapidly declines*." [12]

16.10.   Trends in Infant Mortality

Although infant mortality tends to decrease when general mortality decreases, there are good reasons for giving it separate treatment. (1) In high-mortality populations it is the

[12] *Ibid.*, pp. 109–111.

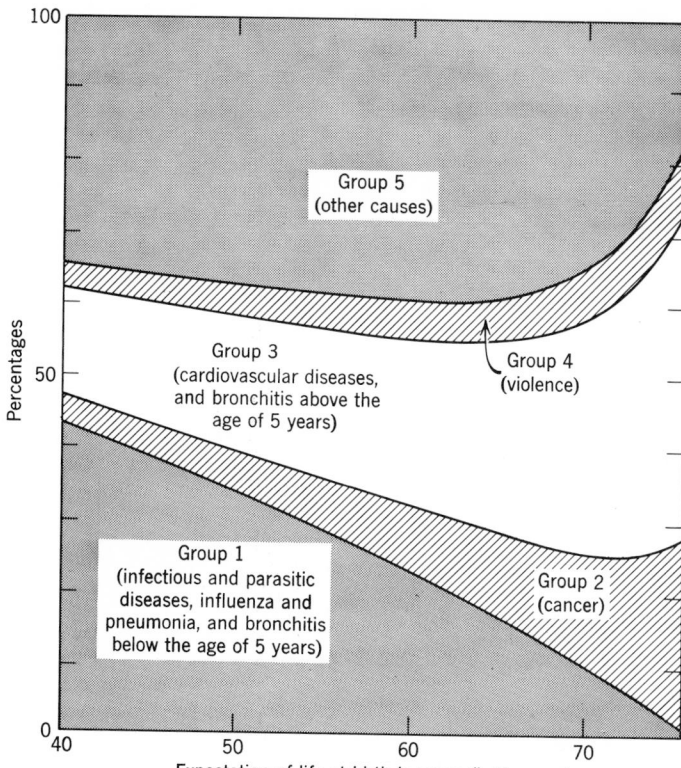

Figure 16-9 Distribution, in a Standard Population, of Deaths
(All Ages and Both Sexes) by Cause-of-Death Groups for
Different Levels of Expectation of Life at Birth Ranging from
40 to 76 Years.

SOURCE: United Nations, *Recent Trends of Mortality in the
World,* Population Bulletin, No. 6, 1962 (New York: United
Nations, 1964).

largest single age category of mortality: a
larger number of persons die during the first
year of life than at any other age. Even in low-
mortality populations it is one of the largest
single categories. It wields a strong influence
in determining the life table values of expectation of life. (2) Deaths at this young age are
due to a peculiar set of diseases and conditions
to which the adult population is less exposed
or less vulnerable. (3) Infant mortality may be
affected rather quickly and directly by specific
health programs, hence may change more rapidly than the general death rate. The infant mortality rate tends to vary more independently of
mortality rates at older ages than the rates at
older ages vary among themselves.

Earlier in this chapter, definitions were given
of the infant mortality rate (IMR) and its two

components, neonatal mortality and post-neonatal mortality. These definitions are rather
widely accepted and used around the world.
Unfortunately, many registration systems are
too deficient to provide reliable data.

In the high-mortality situation, infant mortality rates may be astoundingly high: as high
as 200 per 1000 live births and even higher in
particularly unfavorable village or slum circumstances. In a situation where one live born
infant in five dies during the first year of life,
which is followed by high death rates at adult
ages, it requires high fertility to keep the population replacing itself. It is quite probable that
cultures of high fertility have been strongly re-
inforced by this very direct link between birth
and infant deaths.

As reported earlier, the world leader in low

Table 16-9   Registered Infant Mortality Rates for 43
Countries: 1936–1938, 1946–1948, 1956–1958, and
1963–1964

Country	1936-38	1946-48	1956-58	1963
Chile..............	242.9	155.8	120.1	111.0
Yugoslavia.........	139.1	110.3	95.3	77.5
Portugal...........	142.8	109.0	86.6	73.1
Costa Rica.........	138.8	92.7	85.1	77.6
El Salvador........	123.6	103.3	82.0	67.7
Romania............	178.4	168.5	78.0	55.2
Malaya.............	148.6	94.5	76.8	56.7
Mexico.............	129.9	102.6	77.3	67.7
Poland.............	139.0	109.5	73.5	49.1
Mauritius..........	153.1	148.4	69.5	59.3
British Guiana.....	135.8	82.6	65.7	55.0
Bulgaria...........	146.0	124.3	63.5	35.7
Trinidad and Tobago	105.2	78.4	61.0	38.5
Hungary............	134.6	104.4	60.0	42.9
Jamaica............	126.2	89.5	57.2	52.2
Puerto Rico........	129.0	77.8	53.1	44.6
Spain..............	124.3	79.5	50.7	40.5
Italy..............	105.2	81.7	49.0	39.5
Germany, Eastern...	63.5	111.5	45.4	31.4
U.S.S.R............	184.0	81.0	44.3	30.9
Austria............	88.4	78.6	42.7	31.3
Singapore..........	161.9	85.9	42.3	27.9
Japan..............	112.8	69.2	38.4	23.2
Germany, Western...	63.5	80.7	37.0	26.9
Belgium............	83.4	67.5	35.2	27.2
Ireland............	71.2	60.9	34.7	26.6
China: Taiwan......	145.4	67.0	34.6	26.4
France.............	66.0	63.3	33.8	25.4
Israel, Jews.......	61.5	32.6	33.4	27.5
Czechoslovakia.....	114.6	93.7	31.5	22.0
Canada.............	69.7	46.0	31.0	26.3
Union of South				
Africa: White....	55.8	35.4	30.0	29.0
Scotland...........	77.7	51.4	28.3	25.6
United States......	54.2	32.7	26.4	25.2
Finland............	67.4	55.5	25.9	18.2
Denmark............	64.0	40.5	24.2	19.1
Switzerland........	45.3	38.1	23.6	20.5
England and Wales..	56.3	39.1	23.1	21.1
Australia..........	39.2	28.4	21.2	19.5
Norway.............	40.4	32.9	20.9	17.7
New Zealand........	32.6	24.3	19.6	19.6
Netherlands........	37.8	33.8	17.8	15.8
Sweden.............	43.7	25.0	17.0	15.4

Source: United Nations, Population Bulletin No. 6, Table
          IV. 8, and Demographic Yearbook, Table 19,

infant mortality is Sweden, which currently has
a rate of only 15 per 1000 live births. Figure
16-4 charts the trend by which this was accomplished, starting from a plateau of about 200
which was maintained from 1750 to 1810. Because this chart is drawn on a semilogarithmic
scale, it obscures somewhat the fact that the
IMR dropped by 50 points from 1800 to 1850
and by another 50 points between 1850 and
1900. This must be attributed to general improvements in living conditions and in infant
care, rather than to medical innovations as
such. Between 1900 and 1950 IMR dropped 70
points. Overall, during the 150 years from 1800
to 1950 the Swedish IMR declined by 180

points, or an average of 1.2 points of decline
per year.

Contrast this with changes in IMR in some of
the developing countries today. Chile, for example, reduced its IMR from 243 to 120 in the
20 years between 1937 and 1957, for an average decline of 6 points per year (see Table 16-
9). Taiwan reduced its rate by 110 points for
an average of 3.5 per year. Mexico reduced its
rate by 2.6 points per year. Thus the pace of
decline in the IMR of many of the developing
countries has been very rapid in recent years.
Table 16-9 provides data on IMR for 43 nations
for which reliable data are available. It shows
that steady and rapid progress is being made to

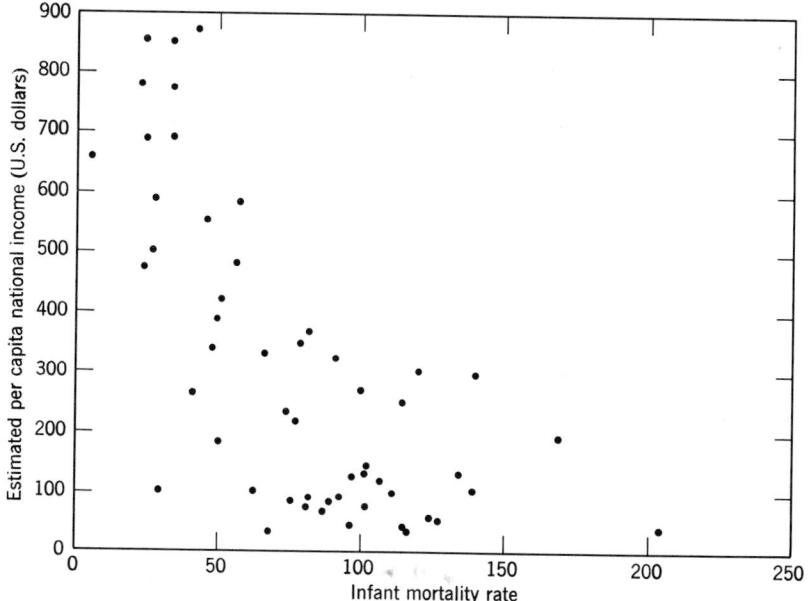

Figure 16-10 Estimated Per Capita National Income and Infant Mortality (Excluding United States).

SOURCE: United Nations, *Foetal, Infant, and Early Childhood Mortality,* Volume II, *Biological, Social, and Economic Factors* (New York: United Nations, 1954).

bring about a convergence. Nations such as British Guiana, Malaya, and Mauritius, which only three decades ago had an IMR of about 150, now all have rates only one-third this large. Although the evidence is not complete, it is possible to assert with a great deal of confidence that the infant mortality rate is one of the first components of mortality to respond to general improvement in the environment and in public health or medical care, and that it responds more flexibly and by a greater amount than the mortality rate among the adult population. The somewhat diffuse, but nevertheless unmistakable, relationship between economic well-being of the population and the infant mortality rate is portrayed in Figure 16-10.

Reliable data on infant mortality are not available for most of the developing nations. Recently the Community and Family Study Center inventoried the available information on this subject and prepared estimates as of 1960 for all nations where rates are not available or appear to be defective. This compilation and estimation was prepared by Dr. Lee-Jay Cho. Table 16-10 presents estimated rates for the

developing countries, grouped into four categories: "very high," "high," "moderately high," and "intermediate." Although the rates are only crude guesses (based on the relationship of IMR to gross national product in nations where data are available) it is quite probable that all but a few are correct within plus or minus 10 percent and that almost every nation is placed in the correct category. This classification puts all of the major developing nations of the world (Mainland China, India, Pakistan, Indonesia, Brazil, etc.) in the "very high" or "high" group. However, it can be said with some confidence that almost all of them are experiencing declining infant mortality at a rate more rapid than prevailed at any time in Europe or America. Some of the nations of Africa may be making less progress than this statement implies, but the generalization applies with full force to Asia and Latin America. It is quite possible that by 1980 only a small handful of nations will remain in the "very high" category and that almost every nation will be found at least one category or more lower in the scale than in 1960. It is quite probable that by

Table 16-10   Estimated and Registered Infant Mortality Rates for Developing
Countries: 1960

VERY HIGH (above 150)		HIGH (100-149)		MODERATELY HIGH (75-99)		INTERMEDIATE (50-74)	
Country	IMR	Country	IMR	Country	IMR	Country	IMR
Guinea	220	India	146	Guatemala	96	Poland	72
Switzerland	220	Cambodia	145	Yugoslavia	96	Mauritius	68
Congo (Brazzaville)	200	Thailand	145	Iran	95	British Guiana	64
Togo	190	Viet-Nam, South	140	Cuba	90	Ceylon	64
Basutoland	181	Congo (Leopoldville)	144	Barbados	89	Bulgaria	62
Upper Volta	174	Brazil	140	Portugal	86	Argentina	61
Afghanistan	170	Union of South Africa	140	Iraq	85	Trinidad and Tobago	60
Kenya	170	Mongolia	135	Greenland	83	Venezuela	60
Burma	170	Tunisia	131	El Salvador	80	Bermuda	59
Pakistan	170	Madagascar	125	Fiji Islands	80	Jamaica	59
Tanganyika	170	Chile	120	Nicaragua	80	Panama	57
Nigeria	165	Paraguay	115	Romania	78	Honduras	55
Turkey	165	Philippines	110	Costa Rica	77	Greece	55
Ivory Coast	164	North Borneo	110	Mexico	77	Puerto Rico	51
Uganda	160	Haiti	110	Malaya	76	Western Samoa	50
Sudan	160	United Arab Republic	110	Virgin Islands	75		
Zanzibar and Pemba	157	Ecuador	107				
Indonesia	155	Colombia	105				
Bolivia	155	Peru	105				
Algeria	155	Albania	104				
Ghana	155	Dominican Republic	101				
China (Mainland)	150	South Korea	100				

Source: Lee Jay Cho, "Estimated Refined Measures of Fertility for All Major Countries of the World", *Demography*, Vol. I, Appendix
Table A.

the year 2000 there will be no nation with an IMR above 75, and the great majority of them should be below 50.

Neonatal versus Post-Neonatal Mortality. Demographers have been inclined to regard neonatal mortality as being dominated by "endogenous" natal and antenatal factors such as birth injuries and congenital disorders. In contrast, they have viewed the post-neonatal period from 4 to 52 weeks as being dominated by "exogenous" or environmental factors. It has been thought that infant mortality during the later phase is more amenable to control by medical, nutritional, and child-care improvements. This has led to the inference that post-neonatal mortality should be expected to decline much more rapidly than neonatal mortality. In fact, this is exactly what happened in Sweden, the Northwestern European nations, and the United States. Figure 16-11 presents data for the United States, however, that alters the picture somewhat. Instead of dividing the first year into two parts, in this figure it is divided into smaller time intervals, such as "less than one day" or "1-2 days." The trend for deaths during the first day is almost level and shows almost no improvement, except dur-

ing the 1940-1950 decade, after which it has leveled off again. The rate for days 1 and 2 has declined, but only slowly. In sharp contrast, the rate for days 3 to 27 has declined very sharply—almost as sharply as the rate for 1 to 5 months. This leads one to suspect that *the endogenous factors dominate infant mortality only for the first three or possibly four days, and that during the remainder of the first month exogenous factors are just as important as during the last 11 months.* In fact, they may be even more responsive to improvements in care, feeding, and handling. Instructions that a doctor, a nurse, or a health educator might give to a new mother could influence greatly the amount of mortality that takes place between days 4 to 27, and approximately one fifth of all infant mortality takes place during this interval. This distinction has important implications for interpreting the trends in the developing nations. It has been observed in at least one nation, Chile, that neonatal mortality has declined somewhat more rapidly than post-neonatal mortality.[13] Figure 16-12 graphs this

[13] Hugo Behm, *Mortalidad infantil y nivel de vida.* Santiago, Chile: Ediciones de la Universidad de Chile, 1962.

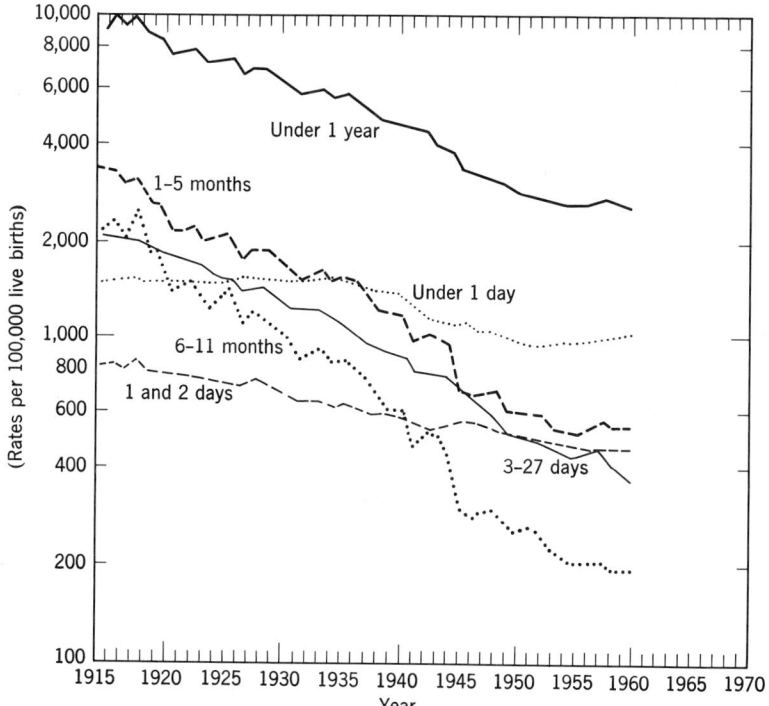

Figure 16-11 Infant Mortality Rates by Age at Death: Birth Registration States of the United States: 1915–1960.

SOURCE: *Vital Statistics of the United States: 1960,* U. S. Department of Health, Education, and Welfare, 1963.

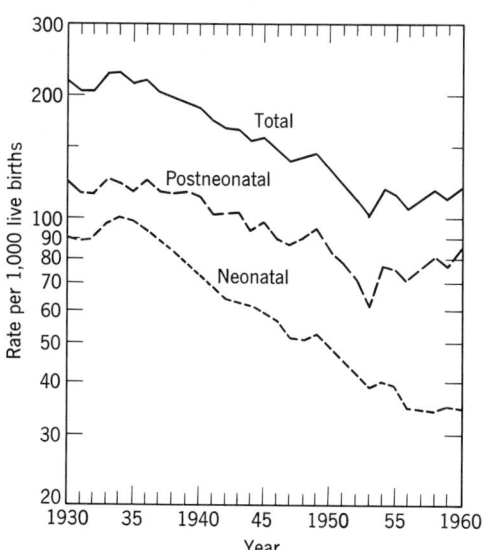

Figure 16-12 Infant Mortality Rates, Chile: 1930 to 1960.

SOURCE: Hugo Behm, *Recent Mortality Trends in Chile,* National Center for Health Statistics, Department of Health, Education, and Welfare, Analytical Studies, Series 3, Number 2, 1964.

surprising discovery of Dr. Hugo Behm. A plausible explanation is that recently most of the developing nations have developed intensive programs of maternal and child health care. Greater emphasis is placed on this than on most other aspects of health. As a result, the proportion of women who are counseled by a health worker during their pregnancy has increased dramatically. It is quite possible that these workers are effecting a sharp drop in neonatal mortality that may parallel or even at times surpass the work of health and medical services in lowering mortality during the remaining 11 months of the first year.

A recent report on infant mortality in the United States also finds that the neonatal death rate of nonwhite children is declining at the same pace as the post-neonatal rate.[14] These two bits of evidence lead us to conclude that

[14] U.S. National Center for Health Statistics, *Infant Mortality Trends,* Series 20, Number 1, Figure 2, p. 2.

in developing nations, where the decline is being forced by medical care, sanitation, and educational programs, there will be only minor differences in the trend of the neonatal and post-neonatal rates, as they currently are defined. This possibly has its obverse side in the fact that improved medical care is running far ahead of improvements in environmental conditions, so that malnutrition and the infective diseases are able to prey on older infants despite improved medical care. It is also interesting to note that in the United States all components of IMR have leveled off except deaths between 6 and 27 days, where the rate is still declining.

Causes of Infant Deaths. The causes of infant deaths can be divided into the endogenous and exogenous types mentioned above. The leading endogenous factors include:

immaturity (weight of less than 2500 grams at
 birth)
congenital malformations
birth injuries
postnatal asphyxia
nutritional maladjustment in early infancy

The endogenous factors include:

pneumonia
gastritis, duodenitis, enteritis, diarrhea
accidents
infective and parasitic diseases

As has been indicated, a high proportion of infants with the first class of disorder die very shortly after birth. Malnutrition, poor environmental conditions, and improper care are underlying causes in the second group of disorders. Inadequate feeding or improper diet renders children vulnerable to gastritis, pneumonia, and infective and parasitic diseases. Modern medicine often is able to save a baby who is badly dehydrated from prolonged diarrhea or is suffering from pneumonia as a result of insufficient resistance to common respiratory infections, but progress in reducing infant mortality comes from *preventing* the occurrence of such episodes, rather than in *curing* them once they have occurred. Luckily, the degree of material well-being, the level of living necessary to achieve a minimum balanced diet, and the amount of knowledge and skill required by a mother to control the environment of an in-

fant to insure his continued health are quite modest. Significant progress toward their achievement can be induced rather quickly, even among low-education and very poor populations. Their full achievement, including adequate diet, requires fundamental and extensive changes in the environment. It is for this reason that expensive economic development will be required before Sweden's accomplishments can be equaled by the developing nations.

16.11. Mortality in the United States: Termination of the Downward Trend?

Mortality trends in the United States are very similar to those outlined above for the industrialized nations generally. Instead of repeating the same findings, this section only attempts to amplify and add details to the general picture. Table 16-11 and Figure 16-13 document the systematic downward drift of the death rate from 1900 to 1967. The central panel of the table presents crude death rates, while the upper panel reports index numbers of mortality which are based on age-standardized death rates, using the 1940 population as standard. The upper panel is a precise measurement of the change in the force of mortality, holding age constant, while the central panel is an historical record of actual rates, not holding constant changing age composition. By either one of these time series, it is clear that mortality has been more than halved since the turn of the century. The overall impact of mortality on the population is only about 40 percent as great as it was at the turn of the century.

Figure 16-13 shows that since 1952 the crude death rate has been rising slightly and irregularly. The increase is due to the older age composition, and if birthrates remain low, it may be expected to continue.

The reader will not fail to note that the index numbers based on standardized rates indicate a larger decline in mortality than do the unstandardized rates. This is shown directly in the bottom panel of Table 16-11, where the ratio of the crude rates to the age-adjusted rates is reported. This panel shows that the age-adjusted rates for 1964 are 27 percent great-

Table 16-11 Trends in Mortality in the United States, by Sex and Color: 1900 to 1964

Type of rate and year	Total population			White population			Nonwhite population		
	Both sexes	Male	Female	Both sexes	Male	Female	Both sexes	Male	Female
Age-adjusted rates (ratio to 1940 base)									
1964.................	69	78	61	70	78	60	63	69	57
1960.................	70	79	63	72	79	64	64	69	59
1955.................	71	77	65	72	78	65	64	68	61
1950.................	78	83	73	78	83	74	75	77	73
1945.................	88	92	85	89	92	85	80	82	79
1940.................	100	100	100	100	100	100	100	100	100
1935.................	107	107	111	109	106	111	106	105	107
1930.................	116	112	120	115	110	120	123	119	128
1920.................	131	121	147	134	122	149	126	116	140
1910.................	146	140	155	153	144	164	148	141	155
1900.................	165	154	181	172	152	191	171	163	181
Percent change, 1900 to 1964........	-58	-49	-66	-59	-51	-68	-63	-58	-68
Crude death rates									
1964.................	9.4	10.8	8.0	9.4	10.8	8.0	9.7	11.2	8.3
1960.................	9.5	11.0	8.1	9.5	11.0	8.0	10.1	11.5	8.7
1955.................	9.3	10.8	7.9	9.2	10.7	7.8	10.0	11.3	8.8
1950.................	9.6	11.1	8.2	9.5	10.9	8.0	11.2	12.5	9.9
1945.................	10.6	12.6	8.8	10.4	12.5	8.6	11.9	13.5	10.5
1940.................	10.8	12.0	9.5	10.4	11.6	9.2	13.8	15.1	12.6
1935.................	10.9	12.0	9.9	10.6	11.6	9.5	14.3	15.6	13.0
1932.................	11.3	12.3	10.4	10.8	11.7	9.8	16.3	17.4	15.3
1920.................	13.0	13.4	12.6	12.6	13.0	12.1	17.7	17.8	17.5
1910.................	14.7	15.6	13.7	14.5	15.4	13.6	21.7	22.3	21.0
1900.................	17.2	17.9	16.5	17.0	17.7	16.3	25.0	25.7	24.4
Percent change, 1900 to 1964........									
Ratio crude to age-adjusted rates									
1964.................	1.27	1.15	1.40	1.32	1.20	1.51	0.94	0.92	0.96
1960.................	1.25	1.16	1.37	1.30	1.20	1.43	0.97	0.95	0.98
1955.................	1.21	1.16	1.30	1.24	1.18	1.37	0.96	0.95	0.97
1950.................	1.14	1.11	1.19	1.19	1.14	1.23	0.91	0.92	0.91
1945.................	1.12	1.14	1.10	1.14	1.17	1.15	0.91	0.93	0.88
1940.................	1.00	0.99	1.01	1.02	1.00	1.04	0.85	0.86	0.84
1935.................	0.94	0.93	0.95	0.95	0.94	0.97	0.83	0.84	0.81
1930.................	0.90	0.91	0.92	0.92	0.91	0.92	0.81	0.83	0.80
1920.................	0.92	0.91	0.91	0.92	0.92	0.92	0.86	0.87	0.83
1910.................	0.93	0.92	0.94	0.93	0.92	0.94	0.90	0.90	0.90
1900.................	0.97	0.96	0.97	0.97	0.96	0.97	0.90	0.90	0.90
Percent change, 1900 to 1964........	31	20	44	36	25	56	4	2	7

Source: Public Health Service. Vital Statistics of the United States: 1964, Tables 1.1 and 1.2. Data for 1900 to 1930 are for death registration States.

er than the crude rates, whereas the corresponding ratio for 1900 was only 0.97. Thus changing age composition tends to hide the true magnitude of mortality decline. The crude death rates suggest only a 46 percent decline in mortality since 1900, whereas the age-adjusted rates suggest a 59 percent decline. The difference of 13 percentage points is attributable to the effect of age composition.

A very important finding of Table 16-11 is that *there has been almost no progress in lowering death rates during the last decade.* The crude death rates for 1964 are almost exactly the same as for 1955, and the age-adjusted death rate shows only very little change. In

fact, when we examine the time series closely, it can be noted that progress in lowering death rates has been rather uneven; periods of great progress have alternated with periods of comparative stagnation, and currently we are in a period of stagnation. This may appear surprising in view of the tremendous expansion of medical services in recent years.

Trends in the mortality of each age group are reported in Table 16-12. When the rates for 1964 are compared with the rates for a decade earlier, it is discovered that, aside from a drop of 4 points in the infant mortality rate and a small decline for ages 1 to 4 and 75 to 84, the two schedules of rates are nearly identical. Thus

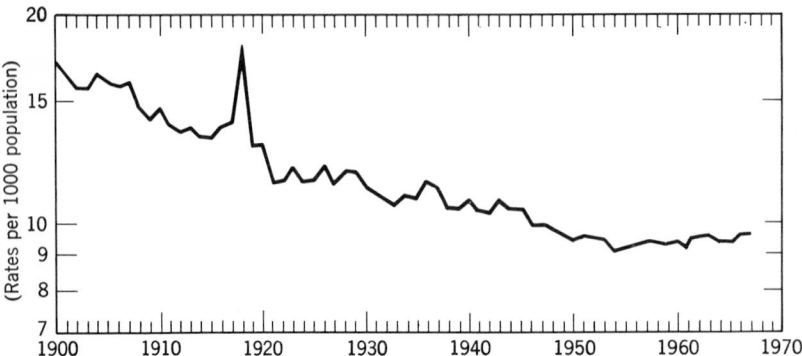

Figure 16-13 Crude Death Rates, Death Registration States of the United States: 1900 to 1967.

the current stagnation in death control extends to all ages.

This recent development has drawn the following comment from Dr. Iwao M. Moriyama, a leading expert in mortality analysis:

"The failure to experience a decline in mortality during this period is unexpected in view of the intensified attack on medical problems in the postwar years. There has been a growth in the volume and scope of health services, in prevention, diagnosis, medical and surgical therapy, and rehabilitation and also an improvement in their quality. The rapid growth of health insurance plans has made high quality medical care readily accessible to ever increasing numbers of people. The rising level of living has resulted in improvement of work and home environment, quality and variety of food, educational attainment, and facilities for recreation. Developments in medicine arising from the exigencies of a global war have become readily available for application to civilian health problems. At no time in the history of the country have conditions appeared so favorable for health progress.

"In this setting, it would seem reasonable to expect further reductions in mortality. On the other hand, the possible adverse effects on mortality of radioactive fall-out, air pollution, and other man made hazards cannot be completely ignored.

"Another consideration is the nature of mortality trends. It is obviously impossible for the death rate to decline indefinitely. At some point

in time, the mortality rate must level off as it reaches the irreducible minimum. Also, with an aging population, the crude death rate may be expected to increase even if no change in age-specific death rates occurs.

"However, the nature of the recent changes in mortality trends does not appear to be consistent with either of these possibilities.

"It is possible that the leveling off of the death rate is due to an artifact, i.e. to changes in the completeness of death registration, errors in intercensal population estimates, and errors in the statement of age in the census enumeration and on death certificates. Because of the consistency in occurrence of the phenomenon in various parts of the world, the recent changes in mortality trends do not appear to be artifacts arising from death registration improvement or errors in population estimation." [15]

Should we conclude from this that death rates have now reached the lowest point possible and that we can look forward to little further progress ever? This is a distinct possibility. If we study Table 16-13 more closely, we note that between 1900 and 1940 there was great progress in reducing death rates at ages under 45, with comparatively little progress in reducing mortality at ages above 55. This was the phase of conquest of the infectious diseases. Between 1940 and 1954 there were substantial re-

[15] Iwao M. Moriyama, *The Change in Mortality Trends in the United States,* National Center for Health Statistics, Analytical Studies, Series 3, Number 1. Washington, D.C., March 1964, pp. 1–2, 37.

Table 16-12 Age-Specific Death Rates, by Sex and Color: 1900 to 1964

Year and age grouping	Total population			White population			Nonwhite population		
	Both sexes	Male	Female	Both sexes	Male	Female	Both sexes	Male	Female
1964, All ages..	9.4	10.8	8.0	9.4	10.8	8.0	9.7	11.2	8.3
Under 1 year....	24.7	27.8	21.5	21.5	24.4	18.5	40.9	45.5	36.3
1-4 years.......	1.0	1.0	0.9	0.8	0.9	0.8	1.6	1.7	1.5
5-14 years......	0.4	0.5	0.3	0.4	0.5	0.3	0.6	0.7	0.5
15-24 years.....	1.1	1.6	0.6	1.0	1.5	0.6	1.6	2.1	1.0
23-34 years.....	1.5	2.0	1.1	1.3	1.7	0.9	3.3	4.3	2.5
35-44 years.....	3.1	3.8	2.3	2.6	3.4	1.9	6.6	8.0	5.3
45-54 years.....	7.4	9.6	5.2	6.8	9.0	4.6	13.2	15.7	10.8
55-64 years.....	17.0	22.9	11.4	15.9	22.1	10.3	27.1	31.4	23.1
65-74 years.....	37.8	49.9	27.8	36.7	48.9	26.7	50.6	61.4	41.3
75-84 years.....	81.8	97.4	70.3	82.8	98.9	70.9	69.9	79.6	61.3
1954, All ages..	9.2	10.7	7.8	9.1	10.6	7.6	10.1	11.4	8.8
Under 1 year....	29.3	33.1	25.3	26.1	29.7	22.4	49.4	55.0	43.8
1-4 years.......	1.2	1.3	1.1	1.1	1.1	1.0	2.0	2.2	1.9
5-14 years......	0.5	0.6	0.4	0.5	0.6	0.4	0.7	0.8	0.6
15-24 years.....	1.1	1.6	0.7	1.0	1.5	0.6	1.9	2.5	1.4
25-34 years.....	1.5	2.0	1.1	1.3	1.7	0.9	3.5	4.3	2.9
35-44 years.....	3.0	3.8	2.4	2.7	3.4	2.0	6.6	7.2	6.0
45-54 years.....	7.8	9.9	5.7	7.0	9.2	4.9	15.1	16.6	13.7
55-64 years.....	17.4	22.5	12.4	16.5	21.7	11.4	28.3	32.3	24.3
65-74 years.....	37.9	46.7	29.8	37.4	46.5	29.2	43.3	50.1	37.0
75-84 years.....	86.0	98.0	76.3	87.1	99.4	77.2	71.1	79.9	62.2
1940, All ages..	10.8	12.0	9.5	10.4	11.6	9.2	13.8	15.1	12.6
Under 1 year....	54.9	61.9	47.7	50.3	56.7	43.6	89.2	101.2	77.4
1-4 years.......	2.9	3.1	2.7	2.6	2.8	2.4	4.8	5.3	4.4
5-14 years......	1.0	1.2	0.9	1.0	1.1	0.8	1.5	1.6	1.4
15-24 years.....	2.0	2.3	1.8	1.7	2.0	1.4	5.0	5.0	5.0
25-34 years.....	3.1	3.4	2.7	2.5	2.8	2.2	7.9	8.5	7.4
35-44 years.....	5.2	5.9	4.5	4.4	5.1	3.7	12.4	13.2	11.7
45-54 years.....	10.6	12.5	8.6	9.5	11.4	7.5	22.9	24.5	21.1
55-64 years.....	22.3	26.2	18.1	21.1	25.2	16.8	37.7	39.5	35.7
65-74 years.....	48.0	54.2	41.9	47.7	54.0	41.5	51.6	56.5	46.3
75-84 years.....	112.0	121.3	103.7	113.0	122.0	104.8	96.1	108.8	84.1
1920, All ages..	13.0	13.4	12.6	12.6	13.0	12.1	17.7	17.8	17.5
Under 1 year....	92.3	103.6	80.7	87.3	98.1	76.1	149.2	167.7	131.1
1-4 years.......	9.9	10.3	9.5	9.4	9.8	9.0	14.6	15.0	14.2
5-14 years......	2.6	2.8	2.5	2.5	2.7	2.3	3.8	3.7	3.9
15-24 years.....	4.9	4.8	5.0	4.3	4.2	4.3	10.4	9.9	10.8
25-34 years.....	6.8	6.4	7.1	6.2	5.9	6.5	12.8	12.2	13.5
35-44 years.....	8.1	8.2	8.0	7.5	7.7	7.3	15.2	14.4	16.0
45-54 years.....	12.2	12.6	11.7	11.5	12.0	10.9	21.5	20.1	23.4
55-64 years.....	23.6	24.6	22.4	23.0	24.2	21.7	33.2	31.1	35.8
65-74 years.....	52.5	54.5	50.5	52.1	54.2	49.9	60.2	60.2	60.4
75-84 years.....	118.9	122.1	115.9	119.3	122.5	116.4	111.2	116.0	106.4
1900, All ages..	17.2	17.9	16.5	17.0	17.7	16.3	25.0	25.7	24.4
Under 1 year....	162.4	179.1	145.4	159.4	175.9	142.6	333.9	369.3	299.5
1-4 years.......	19.8	20.5	19.1	19.4	20.2	18.7	43.5	43.4	43.5
5-14 years......	3.9	3.8	3.9	3.8	3.8	3.8	9.0	7.8	10.1
15-24 years.....	5.9	5.9	5.8	5.7	5.8	5.6	11.5	11.8	11.2
25-34 years.....	8.2	8.2	8.2	8.1	8.1	8.1	12.1	12.5	11.7
35-44 years.....	10.2	10.7	9.8	10.1	10.6	9.6	14.8	14.2	15.6
45-54 years.....	15.0	15.7	14.2	14.8	15.5	14.0	24.3	24.7	23.9
55-64 years.....	27.2	28.7	25.8	27.0	28.5	25.5	42.1	42.1	42.1
65-74 years.....	56.4	59.3	53.6	56.2	59.1	53.4	68.9	71.6	66.4
75-84 years.....	123.3	128.3	118.8	123.3	128.2	118.9	120.9	131.4	113.2

Source: U.S. Public Health Service. Vital Statistics of the United States, reports 1964, 1960, 1950 and earlier decennial census years. 1940, 1920, 1900-1950 Vital Statistics, 1950, Vol. I, Table 8.40

ductions in the mortality rates at these older ages. When we remember that progress in medical science is not one of "saving" lives, but instead is one of death postponement, it can be appreciated that perhaps past progress has accumulated such a mass of impaired lives by the time age 55 is reached that it takes all of our medical skill and technology to "hold the line"

Table 16-13   Trends in Sex and Color Differentials in Mortality, United States: 1900 to 1964 (Based on Age-Standardized Death rates)

Year	SEX DIFFERENTIAL (ratio male to female rate)			COLOR DIFFERENTIAL (ratio nonwhite to white rate)		
	Total population	White	Nonwhite	Both sexes	Male	Female
1964............	1.65	1.70	1.42	1.45	1.36	1.62
1960............	1.61	1.64	1.36	1.42	1.32	1.59
1955............	1.52	1.60	1.31	1.41	1.31	1.60
1950............	1.45	1.48	1.25	1.54	1.42	1.68
1945............	1.39	1.43	1.22	1.44	1.36	1.59
1940............	1.29	1.32	1.17	1.60	1.52	1.70
1930............	1.19	1.21	1.09	1.72	1.64	1.81
1920............	1.06	1.08	0.97	1.50	1.44	1.60
1910............	1.16	1.16	1.07	1.54	1.48	1.61
1900............	1.09	1.10	1.06	1.58	1.56	1.61
Percent change 1900 to 1964...	51	54	34	− 8	−13	+ 1

Note: The above ratios were based upon age standardized death rates age composition of 1940 used as standard.

Source: Computed from Public Health Service, Vital Statistics of the United States; 1964, Table 1.2. Data for 1900 to 1930 are for death registration states.

and to allow this group of persons to enjoy a degree of survivorship that is no worse than in the past.

Yet this is probably an overpessimistic interpretation. It is quite plausible that people arriving at age 55 today are just as healthy, on an average, as those who survived to this age in the past. Moreover, it is certainly known that there is much room for improvement in personal health care. Americans are too fat; they exercise too little; they drink and smoke too much; they lead lives that often are stressful; many of them do not make adequate use of the preventive and curative medical facilities available. Moreover, there is substantial hope that great progress soon will be made in discovering improved methods of treating the major killers—heart disease, cancer, and others.

Clearly, little further progress can be made in reducing mortality between the ages of 1 and 44, because these rates are already nearly zero. Future progress must come in lowering the rates at ages 45 and above. A reasonable prediction might be that there *will* be further progress, but it will come in small increments and slowly. Although we have not exhausted the possibilities in death control, it will require greater and greater inputs of effort to achieve gains, and these gains will progressively apply to the diseases of old age.

Sex Differential in Mortality. Tables 16-11 and 16-12 report death rates separately for males and females and for white and nonwhite population. Tables 16-13 and 16-14 present ratios based on these rates that bring out clearly the sex and color differentials in mortality. The sex differential in mortality is now very large; death rates among men are 65 percent higher than among women. This is a development of very recent origin; in 1900 there was a sex differential, but it was quite small. The differential has arisen, of course, because there has been greater progress in reducing death among females than among males. Table 16-11 reports that whereas age-adjusted death rates declined 66 percent among females between 1900 and 1964, they declined by only 49 percent among males. The differential has increased during the past decade, because what little improvement there has been in death control has almost all accrued to females.

Table 16-14 portrays the sex differential for each age group. It is seen to reach two peaks, one at 15 to 24 years and another at 55 to 64 years. However, death rates for males are 50 percent or more higher than for females at every age from 5 to 74. The nearest approach to equality is attained in the age group 1 to 4 years.

Color Differential in Death Rates. Table 16-

Table 16-14 Trends in Sex and Color Differentials in Mortality, by Age Groups, United States: 1900 to 1964

Year and age group	Sex differential (Ratio male rate to female rate)			Color differential (Ratio nonwhite rate to white rate)		
	Total population	White	Nonwhite	Both sexes	Male	Female
1964 All ages....	1.35	1.35	1.35	1.03	1.04	1.04
Under 1 year.....	1.29	1.32	1.25	1.90	1.86	1.96
1-4 years........	1.11	1.12	1.13	2.00	1.89	1.88
5-14 years.......	1.67	1.67	1.40	1.50	1.40	1.67
15-24 years......	2.67	2.50	2.10	1.60	1.40	1.67
25-34 years......	1.82	1.89	1.72	2.54	2.53	2.78
35-44 years......	1.65	1.79	1.51	2.54	2.35	2.79
45-54 years......	1.85	1.96	1.45	1.94	1.74	2.35
55-64 years......	2.01	2.15	1.36	1.70	1.42	2.24
65-74 years......	1.79	1.83	1.49	1.38	1.26	1.55
75-84 years......	1.39	1.39	1.30	0.84	0.80	0.86
1954 All ages....	1.37	1.39	1.29	1.11	1.08	1.16
Under 1 year.....	1.31	1.32	1.26	1.89	1.85	1.96
1-4 years........	1.18	1.10	1.16	1.82	2.00	1.90
5-14 years.......	1.50	1.50	1.33	1.40	1.33	1.50
15-24 years......	2.29	2.50	1.79	1.90	1.67	2.33
25-34 years......	1.82	1.89	1.48	2.69	2.53	3.22
35-44 years......	1.58	1.70	1.20	2.44	2.12	3.00
45-54 years......	1.74	1.88	1.21	2.16	1.80	2.80
55-64 years......	1.18	1.90	1.33	1.72	1.49	2.13
65-74 years......	1.57	1.59	1.35	1.16	1.08	1.27
75-84 years......	1.28	1.29	1.28	0.82	0.80	0.81
1900 All ages....	1.08	1.08	1.05	1.47	1.45	1.50
Under 1 year.....	1.23	1.23	1.23	2.09	2.10	2.10
1-4 years........	1.07	1.08	1.00	2.24	2.15	2.33
5-14 years.......	0.97	1.00	0.77	2.37	2.05	2.66
15-24 years......	1.02	1.04	1.05	2.02	2.03	2.00
25-34 years......	1.00	1.00	1.07	1.49	1.54	1.44
35-44 years......	1.09	1.10	0.91	1.47	1.34	1.62
45-54 years......	1.10	1.11	1.03	1.64	1.59	1.71
55-64 years......	1.11	1.12	1.00	1.56	1.48	1.65
65-74 years......	1.11	1.11	1.08	1.23	1.21	1.24
75-84 years......	1.08	1.08	1.16	0.98	1.02	0.95

Source: Same as Table 16-12

13 shows that death rates among the nonwhite population are 45 percent higher than among the white population, and that this differential has existed since 1900 (and probably since the days of slavery). Over the past 60 years there has been only a small decline in the color differential. In other words, the death rates of white and nonwhite populations have fallen at about the same relative pace, with the rates for nonwhites always being continuously substantially greater. However, between 1935 and 1945 there was a significant reduction in this differential. But apparently there has been no further progress since 1945. Inasmuch as there is very little reason to believe that Negroes are biologically less fit than whites in their capacity to survive, the 45 percent differential taken as a direct measure may be declared to be a measure of unnecessarily high mortality. Lack of medical care and failure to observe basic principles for preserving health probably are both involved. Figure 16-14 illustrates the sex and race differentials that existed at each age in 1960.

The large color differential in mortality has failed to receive the full degree of attention it deserves because it is hidden. If the crude death rates of Table 16-11 are examined, it will be observed that at the present time the white and nonwhite populations appear to have almost identical death rates. However, because of higher birthrates, Negroes have a younger age composition, and this tends to mask mortality. It is only when we standardize for age, or examine the differentials by individual age groups (as is done in Table 16-14), that the full impact of this social injustice emerges. Infant mortality is 90 percent higher among nonwhites than among whites. Death rates to young adults 25 to 44 years of age is 150 percent greater. It is only at the ages above 70 years that the differential tends to disappear. In other words, *throughout almost all of the ages where great progress in death control has*

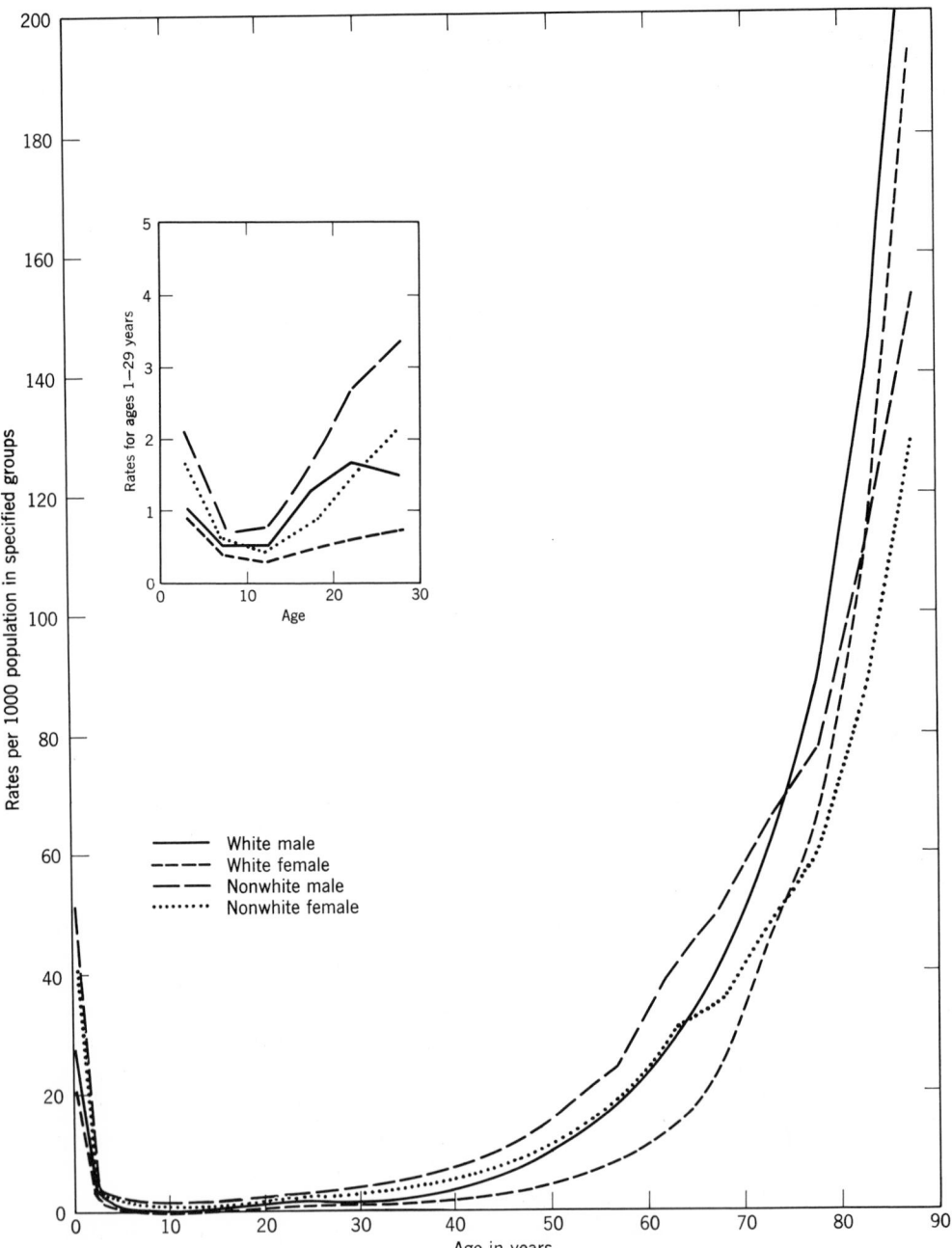

Figure 16-14   Death Rates by Age, Color, and Sex, United States: 1960.

SOURCE: *Vital Statistics of the United States, 1960*

been accomplished, death rates for Negroes are about double those of whites. Moreover, there has been almost no recent progress (during the last decade) in the reduction of this differential.

The color differential is greater for Negro females than for Negro males. As a consequence, the sex differential in mortality is smaller for the nonwhite than for the white population. It appears that Negro women are

Table 16-15 Mortality from 15 Leading Causes of Death; United States: 1963
(Refers only to deaths occurring within the United States; excludes fetal deaths. Rates
per 100,000 estimated midyear population. Ranked on the basis of the "List of 60
Selected Causes of Death." Numbers after causes of death are category numbers of the
Seventh Revision of the International List, 1955)

Rank order	Cause of death	Rate	Percent of total deaths
	All causes................................	961.9	100.0
1	Diseases of heart............................ 400-402,410-443	375.4	39.0
2	Malignant neoplasms, including neoplasms of lymphatic and hematopoetic tissues.............................. 410-205	151.4	15.7
3	Vascular lesions affecting central nervous system....... 330-334	106.7	11.1
4	Accidents.. E800-E962	53.4	5.6
...	Motor vehicle accidents.......................... E810-E835	23.1	2.4
...	Other accidents........................ E800-E802,E840-E962	30.3	3.1
5	Influenza and pneumonia, except pneumonia of newborn.... 480-493	37.5	3.9
6	Certain diseases of early infancy...................... 760-776	33.3	3.5
7	General arteriosclerosis................................ 450	19.9	2.1
8	Diabetes mellitus...................................... 260	17.2	1.8
9	Other diseases of circulatory system.................... 451-468	12.9	1.3
10	Other bronchopulmonic diseases........................ 525-527	12.3	1.3
11	Cirrhosis of liver...................................... 581	11.9	1.2
12	Suicide... E963,E970-E979	11.0	1.1
13	Congenital malformation............................... 750-759	11.0	1.1
14	Other hypertensive diseases............................ 444-447	6.7	0.7
15	Ulcer or stomach and duodenum........................ 540,541	6.5	0.7
...	All other causes...................................... Residual	94.8	9.9

Source: U.S. Public Health Service. Vital Statistics of the United States, Report for 1963,
Table 1-6.

able to achieve a smaller share of the death control that is technologically possible for their sex than is the case for Negro men.

Clearly, one avenue for future progress in death control is the elimination of differentials based on race. Several of the items in Section V of the Bibliography at the end of the chapter deal with this race differential and provide further details concerning it.

This discussion should not be allowed to obscure the fact that Negro death rates are low, *in an absolute sense.* In comparison with mortality levels in Asia, Africa, and Latin America, the Negro population is in a very privileged position and only a few small steps behind the white majority. In fact, only Canada, Oceania, and the wealthier nations of Europe are in a better position. It is only the *relative* differential that is large; the absolute differential is small.

Causes of Death. Heart diseases account for about 40 percent of all deaths, and cancer claims an additional 15 percent, so that together these two leading causes of death account for more than one-half of all deaths. Table 16-15 reports the rate of mortality from each of the 15 leading causes and shows the proportion of all deaths that is attributable to each cause. Except for accidents and suicide, the leading causes of death are of the chronic or degenerative type. Death from infectious diseases has been reduced to nearly zero.

More detail on causes of death is provided by Table 16-16, where 60 leading causes of death are reported by sex and color. The largest single category is arteriosclerotic heart disease, including coronary diseases; the rate of 285 per 1000 population is more than one-fourth of the total death rate. All of the infective and parasitic diseases have rates that are either zero or very nearly so.

Table 16-16 Death Rates for 60 Selected Causes, by Sex and Color: 1964

Cause of death	1964												
	Total population			White population			Nonwhite population			Sex differential		Color differential	
	Both sexes	Male	Female	Both sexes	Male	Female	Both sexes	Male	Female	White	Nonwhite	Male	Female
ALL CAUSES	939.7	1083.1	801.1	935.5	1079.1	796.5	971.6	1116.6	835.0	1.35	1.34	1.03	1.05
Tuberculosis, all forms..........	4.3	6.4	2.3	3.6	5.5	1.8	9.8	13.9	5.9	3.06	2.36	2.53	3.28
Tuberculosis of respiratory system......	4.0	6.0	2.0	3.4	5.2	1.7	8.6	12.5	4.8	3.06	2.60	2.40	2.82
Tuberculosis, other forms.........	0.3	0.4	0.3	0.2	0.3	0.2	1.2	1.4	1.0	1.	1.40	4.67	5.00
Syphilis and its sequelae.........	1.4	1.9	0.8	1.1	1.6	0.6	3.2	4.4	2.1	2.67	2.10	2.75	3.50
Dysentery, all forms.............	0.1	0.2	0.1	0.1	0.1	0.1	0.6	0.6	0.5	1.00	1.20	6.00	5.00
Scarlet fever and streptococcal sore throat	0.0	0.1	0.0	0.0	0.1	0.0	0.1	0.1	0.0	....	....	1.00	....
Diptheria........................	0.0	0.0	0.0	0.0	0.0	0.0	0.1	0.1	0.1	....	0.00	....	....
Whooping cough...................	0.0	0.0	0.1	0.0	0.0	0.0	0.3	0.3	0.3	....	1.00	....	....
Meningococcal infections.........	0.4	0.5	0.3	0.3	0.4	0.3	0.7	0.9	0.6	1.33	1.50	2.25	2.00
Acute poliomyelitis..............	0.0	0.0	0.0	0.0	0.0	0.0	....	....	....	....	....	....	....
Measles..........................	0.2	0.2	0.2	0.2	0.2	0.2	0.4	0.4	0.4	1.00	1.00	2.00	2.00
Other infective and parasitic diseases......	3.1	3.4	2.8	2.8	3.1	2.5	5.3	5.8	4.8	1.24	1.21	1.87	1.92
Malignant neoplasms, all forms.........	151.3	167.0	136.2	154.9	170.3	140.0	124.8	142.3	108.4	1.22	1.31	0.84	0.77
Buccal cavity and pharynx.........	3.4	5.3	1.6	3.5	5.3	1.7	3.2	5.1	1.4	3.12	3.64	0.96	0.82
Digestive organs and peritoneum........	48.7	54.0	43.6	49.6	54.3	45.1	41.7	51.4	32.7	1.20	1.57	0.95	0.72
Respiratory system...............	25.7	44.4	7.7	26.5	45.7	7.9	19.6	34.1	5.9	5.78	5.78	0.75	0.75
Breast...........................	13.7	0.2	26.6	14.2	0.2	27.8	9.5	0.3	18.1	0.01	0.02	0.50	0.65
Genital organs...................	20.9	17.6	24.0	20.5	17.3	23.6	23.8	19.8	27.5	0.73	0.72	1.14	1.16
Urinary organs...................	7.1	9.6	4.6	7.4	10.1	4.8	4.6	5.7	3.5	2.10	1.63	0.56	0.73
Other and unspecified sites.......	17.2	18.9	15.5	17.7	19.5	15.9	13.2	14.3	12.2	1.23	1.17	0.73	0.77
Leukemia and aleukemia...........	7.0	8.2	5.9	7.4	8.7	6.2	4.2	5.1	3.4	1.40	1.50	0.59	0.55
Lymphosarcoma, other neoplasms of lymphatic and haematopoietic tissues....	7.7	8.8	6.6	8.1	9.1	7.0	5.1	6.5	3.8	1.30	1.71	0.71	0.54
Benign neoplasms and neoplasms of unspecified nature.....	2.6	2.5	2.7	2.5	2.5	2.5	3.1	2.6	3.6	1.00	0.72	1.04	1.44
Asthma...........................	2.3	2.8	1.9	2.2	2.7	1.8	3.1	3.7	2.6	1.50	1.42	1.37	1.44
Diabetes mellitus................	16.9	14.1	19.6	16.4	14.0	18.8	20.1	14.6	25.3	0.74	0.58	1.04	1.35
Anemias..........................	1.8	1.8	1.9	1.7	1.6	1.7	3.0	3.1	3.6	0.94	0.86	1.94	2.12
Meningitis, except meningococcal and tuberculous....................	1.3	1.5	1.1	1.0	1.2	0.8	3.4	3.9	3.0	1.50	1.30	3.25	3.75

Table 16-16 (Continued)

Cause of death	1964 Total population Both sexes	Total Male	Total Female	White population Both sexes	White Male	White Female	Nonwhite population Both sexes	Nonwhite Male	Nonwhite Female	Sex differential White	Sex differential Nonwhite	Color differential Male	Color differential Female
Major cardiovascular-renal diseases	514.4	578.0	453.1	523.7	591.1	458.6	444.8	478.9	412.6	1.29	1.16	0.81	0.90
Diseases of cardiovascular system	508.6	571.5	448.0	518.7	585.3	454.2	433.6	466.8	402.3	1.29	1.16	0.80	0.89
Vascular lesions, affecting central nervous system	103.6	98.5	108.5	102.3	96.8	107.6	113.4	111.6	115.2	0.90	0.97	1.15	1.07
Diseases of heart	365.8	432.1	301.8	376.7	447.3	308.4	284.3	317.1	253.3	1.45	1.25	0.71	0.82
Rheumatic fever and chronic rheumatic heart disease	8.3	7.6	9.1	8.6	7.8	9.4	6.0	5.7	6.4	0.83	0.89	0.73	0.68
Arteriosclerotic heart disease, including coronary	285.1	354.2	218.5	300.1	373.9	228.7	173.4	204.9	143.7	1.63	1.42	0.55	0.63
Nonrheumatic endocarditis, myocardial degeneration	27.8	27.8	27.9	28.2	28.0	28.4	25.2	26.5	24.0	1.00	1.10	0.95	0.84
Other diseases of the heart	14.5	16.4	12.6	13.6	15.4	11.9	21.1	24.3	18.1	1.29	1.34	1.58	0.84
Hypertensive heart disease	30.0	26.1	33.8	26.2	22.2	30.0	58.6	55.8	61.2	0.74	0.91	2.51	2.04
Other hypertensive diseases	6.4	6.6	6.2	5.8	5.9	5.7	10.9	11.8	10.0	1.04	1.18	2.00	1.75
General arteriosclerosis	19.4	17.8	21.0	20.4	18.5	22.2	12.2	12.3	12.1	0.83	1.02	0.66	0.54
Other diseases of circulatory system	13.5	16.6	10.4	13.6	16.9	10.3	12.7	13.9	11.6	1.64	1.20	0.82	1.13
Chronic and unspecified nephritis, other renal sclerosis	5.8	6.5	5.1	5.1	5.8	4.4	11.2	12.2	10.3	1.32	1.18	2.10	2.34
Influenza and pneumonia, excluding of newborn	31.1	35.7	26.6	29.1	33.2	25.2	45.8	55.1	37.0	1.32	1.49	1.66	1.47
Influenza	0.9	0.9	0.9	0.8	0.8	0.8	1.2	1.3	1.2	1.00	1.08	1.62	1.50
Pneumonia, except pneumonia of newborn	30.2	34.9	25.7	28.3	32.4	24.3	44.5	53.8	35.8	1.33	1.50	1.66	1.47
Bronchitis	2.8	4.2	1.5	2.9	4.4	1.5	2.1	2.8	1.5	2.93	1.87	0.64	1.00
Other bronchopulmonic diseases	12.2	19.9	4.8	12.8	21.0	4.9	7.8	11.6	4.2	4.29	2.76	0.55	0.86
Ulcer of stomach and duodenum	5.7	8.3	3.2	5.9	8.6	3.3	4.3	6.2	2.6	2.61	2.38	0.72	0.79
Appendicitis	0.9	1.2	0.7	0.9	1.1	0.6	1.3	1.7	1.0	1.83	1.70	1.54	1.67
Hernia and intestinal obstruction	5.2	5.0	5.4	5.2	4.9	5.5	5.1	5.6	4.5	0.89	1.24	1.14	0.82
Gastritis, duodenitis, enteritis, colitis	4.3	4.2	4.3	3.8	3.3	4.0	7.6	8.5	6.9	0.82	1.23	2.58	1.72
Cirrhosis of liver	12.1	16.0	8.4	12.1	16.0	8.2	12.5	15.7	9.5	1.95	1.65	0.98	1.16
Cholelithiasis, cholecystitis, and cholangitis	2.4	2.0	2.8	2.6	2.2	3.0	1.0	0.7	1.3	0.73	0.54	0.32	0.43
Acute nephritis, and nephritis with edema, nephrosis	0.7	0.8	0.6	0.6	0.7	0.5	1.2	1.3	1.2	1.40	1.08	1.86	2.40
Infections of kidney	5.2	5.1	5.2	4.8	4.7	4.9	8.0	8.0	7.9	0.96	1.01	1.70	1.61
Hyperplasia of prostate	2.0	4.1	....	2.0	4.0	....	2.3	4.8	....	....	....	1.20	....
Deliveries and complications of pregnancy, childbirth	0.7	....	1.4	0.4	....	0.9	2.6	....	5.1	....	....	....	5.67
Abortion	0.1	....	0.3	0.1	....	0.1	0.6	....	1.1	....	....	....	11.00
Other complications of pregnancy, childbirth, puerperium	0.6	....	1.1	0.4	....	0.7	2.0	....	4.0	....	....	....	5.71

Table 16-16 (*Continued*)

Cause of death	1964												
	Total population			White population			Nonwhite population			Sex differential		Color differential	
	Both sexes	Male	Female	Both sexes	Male	Female	Both sexes	Male	Female	White	Nonwhite	Male	Female
Congenital malformation.................	10.6	11.5	9.7	10.4	11.2	9.5	12.4	14.0	10.9	1.18	1.28	1.25	1.15
Certain diseases of early infancy........	31.5	37.6	25.7	26.4	31.9	21.2	69.5	80.8	58.9	1.50	1.37	2.53	2.78
Birth injuries, postnatal asphyxia, atelactasis.................	13.2	16.0	10.5	11.6	14.2	9.1	25.1	29.6	20.8	1.56	1.42	2.08	2.29
Infections of newborn..............	2.3	2.7	1.9	1.6	1.9	1.3	7.6	8.8	6.5	1.46	1.35	4.63	5.00
Other diseases peculiar to early infancy, immaturity.................	16.1	18.9	13.3	13.3	15.8	10.8	36.9	42.5	31.6	1.46	1.34	2.69	2.93
Symptoms, senility, and ill-defined conditions.................	13.2	16.1	10.5	9.9	12.3	7.6	37.8	44.2	31.7	1.62	1.39	3.59	4.17
All other diseases..................	28.5	31.8	25.4	27.7	30.8	24.8	34.5	39.7	29.5	1.24	1.35	1.29	1.19
Accidents.................	54.3	75.6	33.8	52.8	72.9	33.4	65.2	95.5	36.6	2.18	2.61	1.31	1.10
Motor vehicle accidents.............	24.5	36.0	13.5	24.5	35.7	13.7	24.4	38.0	11.6	2.60	3.28	1.06	0.85
Other accidents..................	29.7	39.6	20.3	28.3	37.2	19.6	40.8	57.5	25.1	1.90	2.29	1.54	1.20
Suicide..................	10.8	16.1	5.6	11.6	17.2	6.1	4.6	7.2	2.2	2.82	3.27	0.42	0.36
Homicide..................	5.1	7.8	2.5	2.7	3.9	1.6	22.9	37.5	9.2	2.44	4.08	9.62	5.75

Specific causes of death where males are at an especial disadvantage are the following:

tuberculosis
malignancies of the buccal cavity and pharynx
malignancies of the respiratory system
malignancies of the urinary organs
ulcer of stomach and duodenum
bronchopulmonic diseases, including bronchitis
accidents
suicide
homicide

Specific causes of death where nonwhites are at an especial disadvantage in comparison with whites are the following:

tuberculosis
syphilis
dysentery
all infective and parasitic diseases
meningitis
hypertensive heart disease
nephritis, other renal sclerosis
gastritis, duodenitis, enteritis, colitis
birth injuries
infections of newborn
other diseases of early infancy
symptoms, senility, ill-defined
homicide

Almost all of these causes of death respond readily to medical treatment. The conclusion that the race differential in mortality is a simple function of differential medical care and differential use of health preservation practices is almost inescapable.

Can the United States Death Rate Be Lowered Further? To conclude this section, let us return to Dr. Moriyama. After reviewing the available evidence for the trend in rate for each of the leading causes of death he concludes:

"This study indicates that the leveling off of the death rates can be accounted for by the combination of two sets of factors. The first is the dramatic drop in death rate for the diseases of infectious origin with the successive introduction and application of pneumonia serum therapy, the sulfa drugs, and the antibiotics. The accelerated decline started about 1938 and then lost its impetus in the 1950's. By that time, the mortality from diseases of infectious origin had reached a level where it no longer contributed in a major way to the total number of deaths. Even if the trend of the death rates for the in-fective and parasitic diseases, including pneumonia and influenza, had continued downward without interruption, this would not have accounted for all of the leveling off of the total death rate.

"However, the long-term decline in mortality from the infectious diseases resulted in a major realignment of the principal causes of death which uncovered a second set of factors. These factors involve the trends of mortality from the presently numerically important causes of death, namely, malignant neoplasms and cardiovascular-renal diseases at all ages, congenital malformations through the childhood years, accidents and other violence from childhood through middle age, cirrhosis of the liver in middle age, and diabetes mellitus from middle age into old age. None of the trends for these causes of death exhibits the same rate of decline as the trend for the infective diseases. In fact, many of the trends are rising by different degrees. The combined effect of these various trends is to slow down the rate of decline of the total death rate. These diseases and conditions constitute the hard core for which prevention of deaths is more difficult.

"Further reductions in total mortality in the United States are possible, but any substantial decreases must come from the lowering of the death rates for the chronic noninfective diseases and for accidents and other violence. Large increases in longevity will result, not as a consequence of the solution of any single disease process, but as the result of a general breakthrough on the whole front of aging. The elimination of certain causes of death such as the infective and parasitic diseases, malignant neoplasms, diabetes, and accidents would result only in small increases in the average life expectancy. The largest increment would come from the elimination of cardiovascular diseases as a cause of death. It seems certain that the trends for malignant neoplasms and accidents and other violence will also play an important part in shaping the future course of the rate for certain population subgroups. These are problems of long-standing importance. However, new problems may emerge. Cirrhosis of the liver has already come to the forefront as one of the five principal causes of death in the age groups 35-54 years, and the death rate for this disease is still increasing rapidly. The death rate for diabetes in the 45-54 year age groups which had been declining is now leveling off for females and turning upward for males. In the 55-64 year age group, the diabetes death rate for the nonwhite population is increasing rapidly after a period of flat trend. In the groups over 65 years of age, the trends of diabetes mortality for the white population do not appear to be unusual, whereas for the nonwhite the trends are definitely upward.

"Another striking change in trend is presented by the death rates for diseases of the respiratory system other than influenza and pneumonia. These are, for the most part, the chronic obstructive lung diseases such as emphysema, bronchiectasis, and chronic bronchitis. The death rate for these chronic obstructive lung diseases is still at a relatively low level but it has been increasing rapidly especially among males over 45 years of age. The rapidly rising death rate for cancer of the lung and bronchus, another important chronic bronchopulmonary disease, has been well-recognized. An interesting and important question is why the rate of decline of the pneumonia death rate changed during the past decade after a period of impressive decrease. Actually, the pneumonia death rate is now increasing for the older age groups, indicating the possibility of antibiotic-resistant organisms playing an increasing role in older pneumonia patients.

"With regard to the total death rate, examination of the death rates by cause of death indicates that further declines are possible. Also, comparison of death rates by age and sex for the various countries of low mortality for the years 1959 and 1960 shows that the structure of the death rate for the United States is far from the lowest. By taking the lowest death rate recorded by any country of low mortality for each age-sex group and applying these rates to the population of the United States for 1960, the expected number of deaths was obtained. The difference between these numbers and the recorded number may be considered the excess number of deaths in the United States. If the lowest age-sex specific death rate achieved by any country of low mortality in 1959 and 1960

had been obtained in the United States in 1960, there would have been about 397,000 fewer deaths in the United States. This means that the crude death rate for the United States would have been 7.3 per 1,000 population as compared with the recorded death rate of 9.5 per 1,000 population.

"As may be seen from [Figure 16-15], mortality in the U. S. population is favorable, compared with conditions in other countries, only in extreme old age. At other ages, there is considerable difference between the rates for the United States and for countries with the lowest death rates. This is especially true of mortality among the male population in the United States. These differences show that the death rates in the United States have not yet reached the levels that have been attained elsewhere.

"It is difficult to say what the biological irreducible minimum is. However, it is obvious that the death rates in the United States are far above the low levels established in the Scandinavian countries and in the Netherlands. Further decreases may be recorded in the future, but it seems unlikely that the death rate for the United States will soon approach the levels already attained by various other countries."[16]

16.12. Differential Mortality

It is plausible to expect that there would be significant mortality differentials among various subgroups of the population. Some groups have greater access to modern health and medical facilities than others. Some groups live in much less favorable environmental surroundings than others. Some groups live under situations of greater personal stress and strain than others. Some groups have customs and practices that are debilitating to health, while other groups have practices that are conducive to preservation of health. Demographers as well as medical researchers would like to measure the extent of these differentials and study their change over time.

Unluckily, it is very difficult to test most of these ideas unambiguously. The problem is simple enough: a rate requires a numerator and a denominator, and in this case the numerator must come from death certificates and

[16] *Ibid.,* pp. 37–41.

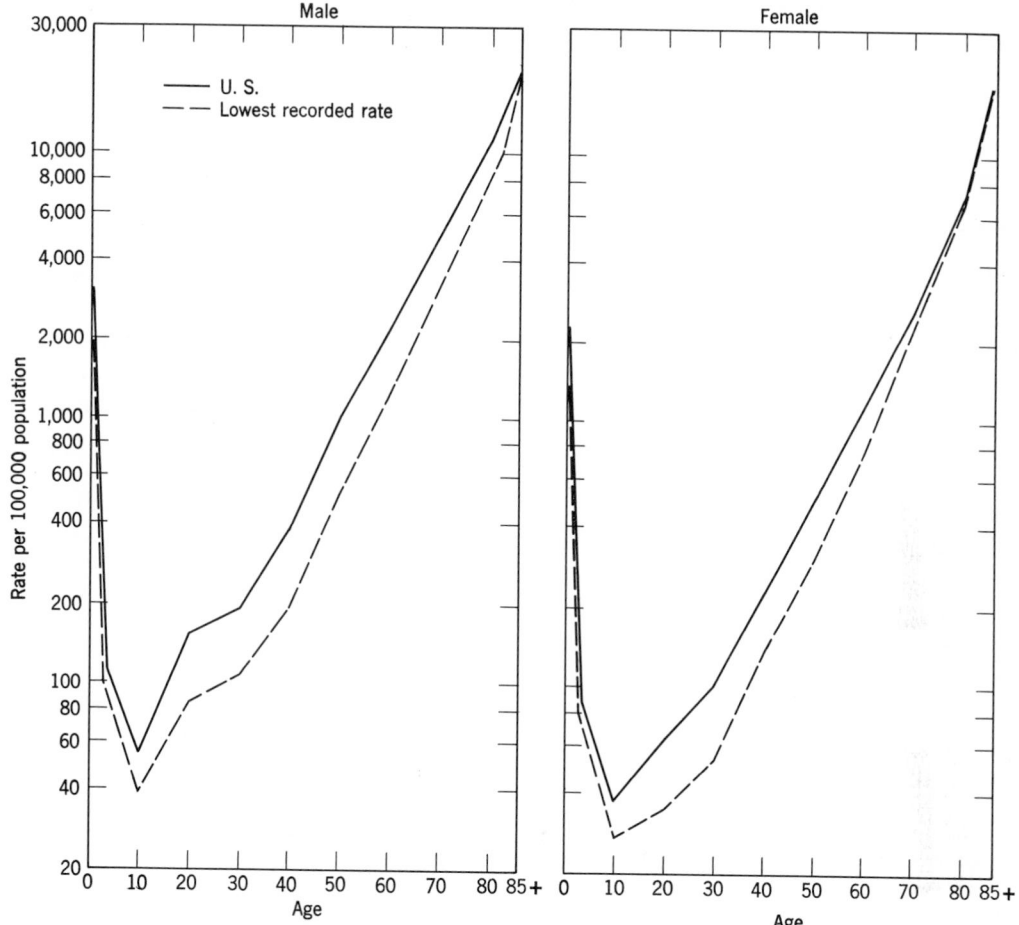

Figure 16-15 Death Rates for the United States and Lowest Recorded Death Rates for Countries of Low Mortality, by Age and Sex: 1959 to 1960.

SOURCE: Iwao M. Moriyama, *The Change in Mortality Trend in the United States*, U. S. National Center for Health Statistics, Analytical Studies, Series 3, Number 2, 1964, Figure 21.

the denominator from census data. The death certificate often does not contain information for the characteristics desired, and the census often is collected by different definitions from those used in filling out the certificate. Also, there often is a problem of the exact date at which a person held a given characteristic. (For example, is the occupation recorded on the death certificate the one that the man held just prior to his death?) Despite these obstacles, researchers make repeated efforts to study differential mortality.

Socioeconomic Differentials. High socioeconomic status is definitely associated with below-average mortality, and low socioeconomic

status is definitely associated with above-average mortality. This has been demonstrated in a variety of ways.[17] Lillian Guralnick has computed standardized mortality ratios (ratio of actual mortality to the mortality that would be expected if the age-specific rates for the general population were to apply) for workers who died between the ages of 25 and 59 years, for five occupational categories, with the following results:[18]

[17] See the various references to class differentials in mortality in Section V of the Bibliography at the end of the chapter.

[18] Lillian Guralnick, *Mortality by Occupation Level and Cause of Death*, Vital Statistics, Special Reports, Vol. 53, No. 5, September 1963.

Occupational class	Total	White	Nonwhite
All occupations	100	92	182
Professional workers	79	. . .	. . .
Technical, administrative, managerial workers	83	81	144
Clerical, sales, and skilled workers	94	93	126
Semiskilled workers	101	97	132
Laborers, except farm	167	127	261
Agricultural laborers	96	81	196

This summary confirms anew the socioeconomic-status hypothesis and reaffirms afresh the very sharp racial differential discussed in the preceding section. Data are not available, but it is very probable that equally strong or even stronger differentials would be found associated with status differences in educational attainment or income.

The Guralnick study refines the socioeconomic analysis in two directions. It examines the data in terms of cause of death, and it examines death statistics for more detailed classification of occupations. There is no paucity of significant differences, but it is not always easy to interpret them. For example, professional workers have excess mortality from:

malignant neoplasm of intestines
malignant neoplasm of the brain and other
    parts of nervous system
leukemia and aleukemia
lymphosarcoma and other neoplasms of lym-
    phatic and hematopoietic tissue
arteriosclerotic heart disease
congenital malformations

Laborers, in contrast, have excess mortality from:

tuberculosis
syphilis
malignant neoplasms of esophagus
malignant neoplasms of stomach
malignant neoplasms of larynx
alcoholism
hypertension with heart disease
other myocardial degeneration
influenza and pneumonia
hernia
cirrhosis of liver
hyperplasia of prostate
accidents
homicide

These causes of death associated with particular statuses and occupations merit repeated study, for from them may come hypotheses that can lead to new programs of preventive medical care and public health.

The study of occupational mortality has often been undertaken with the hope of detecting health-impairing factors in the nature of the work performed. W.P.D. Logan concludes, on the basis of extensive study of occupations, that with the exception of certain highly specific occupations such as sandblasting, mortality is influenced more by the conditions of life implied than by direct, occupational risks entailed.[19] However, he notes (as the Guralnick study demonstrates) that the causes of death are quite different for different occupational groups and believes that this can be of value in guiding further studies of the incidence of particular diseases.

Industry Differentials. Guralnick also has prepared data on mortality by industry, with the results shown in the tabulation on page 605.[20]

For many of these groupings, valuable clues that would explain the differentials are available in the cause-of-death statistics. Examples are accidents in manufacturing, construction, and transportation, cirrhosis of liver among entertainers, tuberculosis and respiratory ailments in mining, and suicide in business and repair services.

Marital Status Differentials. It often is noted that persons who are single, widowed, or divorced have higher death rates than persons who are married and living with a spouse. For example, a study in England by Young and associates finds that the tendency for a widower to die within six months after the death of a spouse occurs with a frequency greater than

[19] W. P. D. Logan, "Social Class Variations in Mortality," *Public Health Reports,* **69** (12) (December 1954), 1217–1223.
[20] Lillian Guralnick, *Mortality by Industry and Cause of Death,* Vital Statistics, Special Reports, Vol. 53, No. 4, September 1963.

Industry	Standardized mortality ratio
Agriculture, forestry, fishing	97
Mining	125
Construction	119
Manufacturing	92
Transportation, communication	124
Wholesale and retail trade	99
Finance, insurance, real estate	94
Business and repair services	110
Personal services	122
Entertainment and recreation services	135
Professional and related services	83
Public administration	93

that which would be associated with chance alone. He proposes various explanations for this phenomenon: (1) homogamy: the tendency for fit persons to marry the fit and for unfit persons to marry the unfit; (2) infection: both spouses may die of the same infectious disease; (3) joint unfavorable environment: an environment that brings about the death of one spouse may do the same for the other; (4) loss of care bestowed by the departed spouse; and (5) grief precipitated by the death of the spouse.[21]

The extent to which each of these is operative and the relative weights of each are not known.

In a more comprehensive study, Shurtleff

found that among both men and women at every age the married have lower death rates than the single, widowed, or divorced. (See Figure 16-16 for a summary of his results.) When allowances are made for variation in age, the mortality of bachelors is nearly two thirds greater than that of husbands and the mortality of widowed and divorced men is about double that of husbands. The differences are smaller for women. The available data do not afford an interpretation of the nature of selection of persons into the marital group and effect of marriage itself on divorce rates.[22]

Joseph Berkson, who has been a perennial

[21] Michael Young *et al.*, The Mortality of Widowers, *Lancet*, **7305** (August 31, 1963), 454–456.

[22] Dewey Shurtleff, "Mortality and Marital Status," *Public Health Reports*, **70** (3) (March 1955), 248–252.

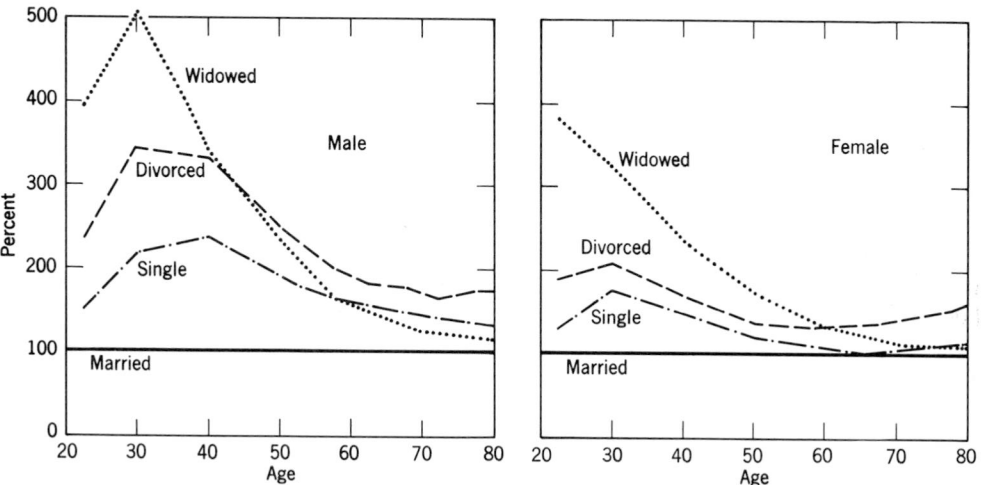

Figure 16-16 Age-Specific Death Rates for Each Marital-Sex Class as Percentages of Death Rates for Married Persons of Corresponding Age and Sex, United States, 3-Year Average: 1949 to 1951.

SOURCE: Dewey Shurtleff, "Mortality and Marital Status," *Public Health Reports* **70**(3) (March 1955), 248–252, p. 251.

critic of the statistics studies of the relationship between smoking and lung cancer, applies his line of reasoning to the marital status differential in mortality. He examines a long list of diseases that might theoretically be related to marital status and finds that they do not all show patterns that lead to sensible hypotheses. On the other hand, he finds marked marital status differentiality that is hard to justify on marital status grounds, such as lung cancer itself. He concludes that the long-established observation of differential mortality by marital status is yet to be explained.[23]

Urban-Rural Differentials. Strong arguments can be made extolling the wholesomeness of the rural environment and the unhealthful conditions in urban areas. Equally strong arguments can be made extolling the modern health facilities, the greater sanitation, and the smaller exposure to the elements that urbanites enjoy in comparison with rural dwellers. The question is a very difficult one because of migration. There is a strong possibility that rural residents when they become seriously ill tend to migrate to the city to seek medical care. If they actually forsake their rural residence, their death is attributed to the city. Migration data show some evidence that this is the case, so that rural-urban tabulations of death certificates can be misleading.

Nevertheless, efforts to study this differential continue. David Glass has shown that in 1841 the expectation of life in London for males was 35, whereas it was 40.2 for the nation as a whole. By 1950-1952 the situation had been reversed: the expectation of life was 67.3 in London and 66.4 in the country as a whole. A similar reversal had taken place for females. At the present time Glass finds a slight differential in favor of rural areas as one progresses from rural districts to other urban districts to county boroughs. However, he finds that large capital cities such as London are especially favored among the urban group. The very high death rate and low expectation of life associated with

the industrial revolution should not be attributed primarily to London, but to Liverpool, Manchester, and other industrial cities, where the expectation of life in 1841 was as low as 24 or 25 for men and only 27 for females.[24]

The urban environment appears to foster high infant mortality. The U.S. Children's Bureau has pointed out that only one of the eleven largest cities in the United States (Los Angeles) has an infant mortality rate lower than the national average rate.[25] Instead of being healthful sites for infants to be born, many neighborhoods in cities are slums where low socioeconomic status is conducive to high infant mortality. A part, but possibly not all, of this is due to the differential medical services given to Negroes living in slums and the care that Negro mothers give their infants.[26]

16.13. Mortality in Relation to Health and Morbidity

Death usually follows an episode of illness. It is logical to extend the study of mortality from death records to records that portray the health of the population, the episodes of illness, the incidence of hospitalization and consultation with physicians, and the amount of time spent in bed or away from work as a result of illness. Despite its close relevance, this is a large and rather complex field of study. International data are almost nonexistent, because national systems for registering or inventorying episodes of illness or the incidence of conditions are not well organized. In the United States, the National Center for Health Statistics of the Department of Health, Education and Welfare maintains a National Health Survey that is systematically producing a large body of in-

---

[23] Joseph Berkson, "Mortality and Marital Status: Reflections on the Derivation of Ediology from Statistics," *American Journal of Public Health and the Nation's Health,* **52** (8) (August 1962), 1318–1329.

[24] David V. Glass, "Some Indicators of Differences Between Urban and Rural Mortality in England and Wales and Scotland," *Population Studies,* **17** (3) (March 1964), 263–267.

[25] U.S. Children's Bureau, "Geography of Infant Mortality in the U.S.," *Public Health Reports,* **78** (3) (March 1963).

[26] Eleanor P. Hunt and Stanley M. Goldstein, "Trends in Infant and Childhood Mortality," U.S. Children's Bureau, Statistical Series, No. 76, Washington, 1964. See also "Geography of Infant Mortality," in *Public Health Reports,* **78** (3) (March 1963), 270–271.

formation on morbidity, health, hospitalization, visits to physicians, and other matters relating to health, morbidity, and medical care. The results of these surveys are reported in series of publications, and interested students should consult these sources. As an additional help, the bibliography at the end of this chapter lists a few key references in this field.

16.14. Conclusion: The Future Trend of World Mortality

It is important for demographers to appreciate that the phenomenon of almost no progress in lowering death rates, found for the last decade in the United States, is characteristic of most of the industrialized nations. Figure 16-17 gives data for England and Wales, Norway, Sweden, Denmark, and Netherlands, and Japan to illustrate this situation. In all of these nations, the crude death rate is either remaining stationary or rising slowly after a long downward trend. Consider the following data from the *United Nations Yearbook*, reporting the crude death rate in 1960 and in 1964:

Nation	1960	1964	Change
Austria	12.7	12.3	−0.4
Belgium	12.4	12.6	+0.2
Bulgaria	8.1	7.9	−0.3
Czechoslovakia	9.2	9.6	+0.4
Denmark	9.6	9.9	+0.3
Finland	9.0	9.3	+0.3
France	11.4	10.7	−0.7
West Germany	11.4	11.0	−0.4
Hungary	10.2	9.9	−0.3
Ireland	11.5	11.4	−0.1
Italy	9.7	9.6	−0.1
Luxembourg	11.8	11.9	−0.1
Netherlands	7.7	7.7	0.0
Norway	9.1	10.0	+0.9
Poland	7.5	7.6	+0.1
Portugal	10.8	10.2	−0.6
Spain	8.8	8.7	−0.1
Sweden	10.0	10.0	0.0
Romania	8.7	8.0	−0.7
Switzerland	9.7	9.2	−0.5
England and Wales	11.5	11.3	−0.3
Scotland	11.9	11.7	−0.2
Yugoslavia	9.9	9.4	−0.5
Australia	8.6	9.0	+0.4
New Zealand	8.8	8.8	0.0
USSR	7.1	7.2	+0.1
United States	9.5	9.4	−0.1
Canada	7.8	7.6	−0.2

Even in nations that recently had been enjoying large declines in mortality the change now is very small if not actually reversed. Moreover, these rates are all so low that they are only a point or two away from what most physiologists would consider the irreducible biological minimum under medical science as it is known today. We are led to conclude, therefore, that the major industrialized nations of the world have completed the mortality transition from high to low mortality and can look forward to no further substantial reductions in mortality. True, there may be a reduction of 20 percent over the next years, but this will only represent a saving of about two deaths per thousand population, and will have a negligible effect on growth. As birthrates decline, the age composition will shift toward the older ages, and the result will be a rise in crude death rates. *In the future crude death rates will rise, therefore, instead of declining, as age-specific death rates will remain almost stationary.*

The mortality component of the demographic transition may be said to be fully completed when the life table death rate for both sexes is 14 per thousand or smaller. This is the point at which the average expectation of life at birth attains the proverbial three score years and ten. As crude birth rates drift down to about 14 to 15 per thousand, the crude death rate will gradually rise to meet them.

What about the developing nations? Will they continue the rapid decline in mortality that they enjoyed between 1945 and 1965? Because data for most of these countries are lacking, this question cannot be answered except on the basis of subjective impressions. It is doubtful whether the recent rapid declines in mortality can be continued into the future. The reason is that most of the "easy" conquest of mortality has been accomplished. Spraying with DDT, mass use of antibiotics, injections, and other lifesaving procedures that can be performed *for* people without their sustained cooperation or informed awareness of the need for preventive action have been accomplished by special campaigns. Even in the developing countries, the tasks that remain are the more difficult ones. Millions of persons must be

Figure 16-17 Crude Death Rates: Specified Countries: 1930 to 1960.

SOURCE: Iwao M. Moriyama, *The Change in Mortality Trend in the United States*, National Center for Health Statistics, Analytical Studies, Series 3, Number 1, U. S. Department of Health, Education, and Welfare, 1964.

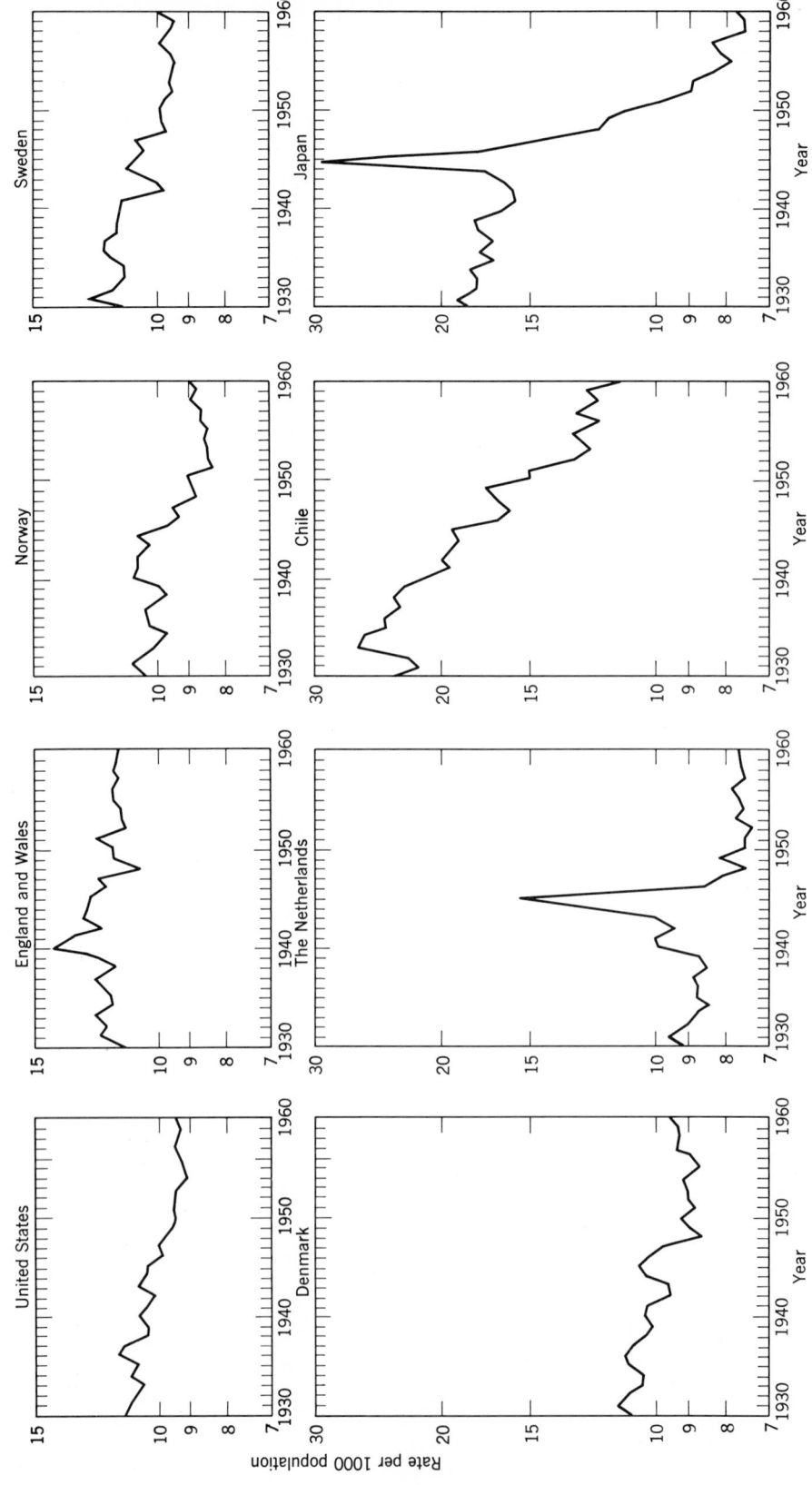

taught the lessons of balanced diet, cleanliness in handling food and drinking water, proper care and feeding of infants, proper disposal of human waste, and all of the other health lore and behavior that are a part of the culture of the developed nations. The environment must be changed by the people themselves; it cannot be done for them by special campaigns. Although educational levels are rising throughout the world, it is doubtful whether the death rates can or will fall as much in any future decade as they have in the past.

Moreover, in many of the developing countries death rates have already been brought very near to the low level common in European nations. This is usually partially fictitious and a result of the young age composition of the population. Nevertheless, the mortality transition is well advanced in almost all nations of the world; further progress will require greater expenditures of manpower and money and will come more slowly.

It may be concluded, therefore, that *the future trend of world mortality will be one of convergence toward a crude death rate which, when standardized, will represent the current mortality levels of Sweden and other nations excelling in death control.* Many nations are now at that point, and will hover around it. Those nations that have not attained it will gradually do so. The pace at which they will accomplish this will be faster than the historic trend of the developed nations, but slower than their own amazing progress in the past 25 years.

QUESTIONS AND EXERCISES

1. Using the data of Table 16-7, compute the average annual increase in life expectancy in Sweden, United States, France, England, and Australia, 1900 to 1950, by decades. Which nation made the largest gain in each decade? Why do you think the pattern of interdecade changes is as it is? What part did medical advance and what part improving environment play in this transition?

2. Using Table 16-7, compute the average annual increase in life expectancy between 1950 and 1960 for all nations for which data are available. Classify the nations according to the amount of progress made during this decade. Develop as many hypotheses as you can to account for this variation. Describe a procedure for testing these hypotheses and actually perform a test for all for which you can obtain data. Is there any evidence that the rate was slower for nations that earlier had just made a very substantial improvement between 1940 and 1950?

3. Using Table 16-7, take the column "ratio of male to female life expectancy" as a dependent variable. Make a scattergram of this variable against average life expectancy for both sexes combined, for (*a*) industrialized and (*b*) developing countries. How close is the relationship? Fit a trend line through the values; is the slope the same in developing as in industrialized nations?

4. Repeat the process of Question 3 for a group of industrialized countries for which there are at least four decades of data. Make a scattergram of the ratio against year. Interpret the results.

5. If you study Table 16-8 closely, you will note that group I diseases declined much less for ages 76-74 than for younger ages and less for ages 45-64 than for ages 5-34. What caused this? In which countries was the age differential the greatest? the least? What would you conclude about the possibilities of eventually achieving complete conquest of the group I diseases, even at advanced ages?

6. Suppose that the age composition of the world, shown in Table 16-2, had been used in-instead of the United States population as of 1940 to standardize the mortality rates whose ratios are shown in the top panel of Table 16-12. What would then be the relationship between the age-adjusted rates and the crude death rates, and the pattern of ratios in the bottom panel of Table 16-11? Explain how you arrive at this conclusion.

7. Using the statistical materials contained in the tables of this chapter, and supplementing them with selected reading from the Bibliography, write an essay on "Similarities and Differences in the Transition from High to Low Mortality in the United States in Comparison with the Nations of Northwestern Europe."

8. Study the materials in the two Guralnick publications [*Vital Statistics Special Reports, 53* (4 and 5) (1963)] and construct a list of preventative medical or health care practices that members of each occupation group should more thoroughly adopt in order to reduce mortality. Repeat for the major industries.

9. Study intensively the trend of infant mortality in the United States. Using the published data, compare the trend in the United States with the trend in Sweden. In what respects is the United States able to equal or surpass the components of the Swedish infant mortality,

and in what respects are we lagging? What do you think are the cause of the lag, and the possibilities of making them up?

10. Consult the latest data from the *Demographic Yearbook* and write an essay on "World Developments in Mortality Control since 1965."

11. Obtain the latest data on the age-color rates of mortality for the United States and write an essay on current status and recent trends on the "Absolute and Relative Differential between White and Nonwhite Mortality Rates in the World Context." Use the life tables that have been constructed for each color group.

BIBLIOGRAPHY

I. GENERAL

Bogue, Donald J. "Mortality and Causes of Death," Chapter 9 in *Population of the United States.* New York: Free Press, 1959.

Dorn, Harold F. "The Effect of Public Health Developments Upon Population Growth," *Annals of the New York Academy of Sciences,* **54** (1952), 742–749.

Dorn, Harold F. "Mortality," pp. 437–471 in Philip M. Hauser and Otis Dudley Duncan (eds.). *The Study of Population: An Inventory and Appraisal.* Chicago: University of Chicago Press, 1959.

Dorn, Harold F. "Prospects for Further Decline in Mortality Rates," *Human Biology,* **24** (4) (December 1952), 235–261.

Dorn, Harold F. "Some Problems for Research in Mortality and Morbidity," *Public Health Reports,* **71** (1) (January 1956), 1–5.

Dublin, L. I., A. J. Lotka, and M. Spiegelman. *Length of Life* (rev. ed.). New York: Ronald Press, 1949.

Haycocks, H. W., and W. Perks. *Mortality and other Investigations.* Cambridge, England: Published for the Institute of Actuaries and the Faculty of Actuaries at the University Press, 1955, Vol. I.

Ledermann, Sully, and Jean Breas. "Les Dimensions de la Mortalité" ("The Dimensions of Mortality"), *Population* (Paris), **14** (4) (October-December 1959), 637–682.

Milbank Memorial Fund. *Trends and Differentials in Mortality.* Papers presented at the 1955 annual conference of the Milbank Memorial Fund. New York: Milbank Memorial Fund, 1956.

Myers, Robert J. *The Effect of Declining Mortality on Old-Age Pension Systems.* Paper contributed for the United Nations World Population Conference, August 30-September 10, 1965.

Myers, Robert J. "Factors in Interpreting Mortality After Retirement," *Journal of the American Statistical Association,* **49** (267) (September 1954), 499–509.

Pedoe, Arthur. "Factors in the Trend of Mortality," *Journal of the Institute of Actuaries,* **88** (I, 378) (1962), 1–48.

Rosenswaike, Ira. "Seasonal Variation of Deaths in the United States, 1951–60," *Journal of the American Statistical Association,* **61** (315) (September 1966), 706–719.

Spiegelman, Mortimer. "Measures of Mortality," Chapter 4 in *Introduction to Demography.* Chicago: Society of Actuaries, 1955.

Spiegelman, Mortimer. "Mortality Trends and Prospects and their Implications," *Annals of the American Academy of Political and Social Science,* **316** (March 1958), 25–33.

Stolnitz, George J. "A Century of International Mortality Trends" (in two parts), *Population Studies,* **9** (1) (July 1955) and **10** (1) (July 1956).

Taeuber, Conrad, and Irene B. Taeuber. "Mortality," Chapter 14 in *The Changing Population of the United States.* New York: John Wiley and Sons, 1958.

Thompson, Warren S., and David T. Lewis. "Mortality" and "Some Environmental Influences on the Death Rate," Chapters 12 and 13 in *Population Problems* (5th ed.). New York: McGraw-Hill, 1965.

United Nations. *The Situation and Recent Trends of Mortality in the World,* Population Bulletin of the United Nations, No. 6. New York, 1963.

Valaoras, Vasilios G. "Standard Age and Sex Patterns of Mortality," pp. 133–149 in Milbank Memorial Fund. *Trends and Differentials in Mortality.* New York, 1956.

II. MORTALITY TRENDS AROUND THE WORLD

Abdel-Aty, S. H., Life-tables Functions for Egypt Based on Model Life-tables and Quasi-stable Population Theory," *Milbank Memorial Fund Quarterly*, **39** (2) (April 1961), 350–377.

Aromin, Basilio B. "The Trend of Mortality in the Philippines, 1903-1960," *Statistical Reporter* (Manila), **5** (3) (July 1961), 1–7.

Barkhuus, Arne. "Non-European General and Infant Mortality in the Non-selfgoverning Territories in Africa South of the Sahara," *Proceedings of the World Population Conference: 1954*. New York, 1955, Vol. I.

Behm, Hugo. *Recent Mortality Trends in Chile*. U.S. Department of Health, Education and Welfare, U.S. National Center for Health Statistics, Analytical Studies Series 3, Number 2, 1964.

Bourgeois-Pichat, Jean, and Chia-Lin, Pan. "Trends and Determinants of Mortality in Underdeveloped Areas," pp. 11–25 in Milbank Memorial Fund. *Trends and Differentials in Mortality*. New York, 1956.

Campbell, Hubert. *Changes in Mortality Trends: England and Wales*. U.S. Department of Health, Education and Welfare, U.S. National Center for Health Statistics Analytical Studies Series 3, Number 3, 1965.

Case, R. A. M., et al. (compilers). *The Chester Beatty Research Institute Serial Abridged Life Tables, England and Wales 1841-1960*. London: Chester Beatty Research Institute, Institute of Cancer Research, Royal Cancer Hospital, 1962.

Chiassino, Giuseppe. "Sull'andamento della Mortalità in Italia dal 1881 al 1951" ("The Death-rate Trend in Italy from 1881 to 1951"), *Rivista Internazionale di Scienze Economica e Commerciali* (Milan), **8** (8) (August 1961), 770–789. With English summary.

Delaporte, Pierre J. N. "Changes in Mortality Trends in Europe During and After the Second World War," *Proceedings of the World Population Conference: 1954*. New York, 1955, Vol. I.

Dorn, Harold F. "Prospective Mortality Trends in Areas of Lower Death Rates," *Proceedings of the World Population Conference: 1954*. New York, 1955, Vol. I.

France. Institut National d'Études Démographiques. "Evolution de la Mortalité en Inde" ("Mortality Change in India"). By L. H., *Population*, **19** (5) (October-December 1964), 972–973.

France, Statistique Générale. *Evolution de la Mortalité en Europe depuis l'Origine des Statistiques de l'État Civil*. Etudes Démographiques Number 2. Paris, 1941.

Fritzwell, Yngve. "Överlevsetabeller för Sverige för 1751–1815" ("Life Tables for Sweden, 1751–1815"), *Statistisk Tidskrift N.F.*, **2** (10) (October 1953), 406–410.

Gille, H. "The Demographic History of the Northern European Countries in the Eighteenth Century," *Population Studies*, **3** (1950) 3–65.

Hartman, Tor. "Suomen ja Ruotsin Kuolleisuussuhteiden Vertailua. Finlands Dödlighetsförhällanden Jämförda med Sveriges" ("Comparative Study of Mortality in Finland and Sweden"), *Tilastokasauksia* (Helsinki), **32** (8) (August 1957), 44–50. With English summary.

Jacobson, Paul H. "An Estimate of the Expectation of Life in the United States in 1850," *Milbank Memorial Fund Quarterly*, **35** (2) (April 1957), 197–201.

Jain, S. P. "Mortality Trends in India," *Proceedings of the World Population Conference: 1954*. New York, 1955, Vol. I.

Jungalwalla, M. "Mortality Trends in Indonesia," *Proceedings of the World Population Conference: 1954*. New York, 1955, Vol. I.

Keyfitz, Nathan, and Edmund M. Murphy. *Comparative Demographic Computations*. Chicago: Population Research and Training Center, University of Chicago, June 1964.

Kiser, Clyde V. "Population Trends and Public Health in Latin America," *Milbank Memorial Fund Quarterly*, **45** (1) (January 1967), 43–59.

Lancaster, H. O. "Generation Life Tables for Australia," *Australia Journal of Statistics* (Sydney), **1** (1) (April 1959), 19–33.

Larsson, Tage. "The Development of Mortality in Sweden and its Medical and Biological Aspects," pp. 691–701 in *International Union for the Study of Population*; Proceedings of International Population Conference, New York, 1961. Vol. I, London, 1963. International Population Conference, New York, 1961. (Proceedings) Vol. I. London, 1963.

Légaré, Jacques. *La Mortalité à 45 ans et Plus: Son Evolution Récente en Norvège et dans d'Autres Pays à Faible Niveau de Mortalité*. Paper contributed for the United Nations World Population Conference, August 30-September 10, 1965.

McKeown, Thomas, and R. G. Record. "Reasons for the Decline of Mortality in England and Wales During the Nineteenth Century," *Population Studies*, **16** (2) (November 1962), 94–122.

Metropolitan Life Insurance Company. "Increase in Survivorship since 1840," pp. 1–3 in Metropolitan Life Insurance Company. *Statistical Bulletin*, **45** (1964).

Michalup, Erich. *La Tendencia de la Mortalidad en Venezuela Durante los Ultimos 20 Años*. Paper contributed for the United Nations

World Population Conference, August 30-September 10, 1965.

Moriyama, Iwao M. *The Change in Mortality Trend in the United States.* U.S. National Center for Health Statistics Analytical Studies Series 3, Number 1, 1964.

Moriyama, Iwao M. "Recent Mortality Trends in Areas of Low Mortality," *Proceedings of the World Population Conference: 1954.* New York, 1955.

Mortara, Giorgio. "A Mortalidade na América Latina" ("Mortality in Latin America"), *Revista Brasileira de Estatística* (Rio de Janeiro), **23** (91–92) (July-December 1962), 105–135.

Newman, Peter. *Malaria Eradication and Population Growth, with Special Reference to Ceylon and British Guiana.* (Bureau of Public Health Economics, Research Series, 10.) Ann Arbor, Mich.: University of Michigan, School of Public Health, 1965.

Norway. Statistisk Sentralbyrå. "Dφdeligheten og den Årsaker i Norge 1856–1955" ("Trend of Mortality and Causes of Death in Norway, 1856–1955"), *Samfunss konomiske Studier,* No. 10. (Oslo, 1961). With English summary.

Pressat, Roland. "Survey of French Mortality since the War" ("Vues Générales sur la Mortalité Française depuis la Guerre"), *Population,* **9** (3) (July-September 1954), 477–506.

Recchini, Zulma L. *Tabla Abreviada de Mortalidad, República de México, 1959–1961. (Abridged Life Table, Republic of Mexico, 1959–1961).* Centro Latinoamericano de Demografía, Serie C. Santiago, Chile, 1963.

Sarhan, A. E. *Mortality Trends in the United Arab Republic.* Paper contributed for the United Nations World Population Conference, August 30-September 10, 1965.

Soda, Takemune, M. D. *Trends of Mortality in Asia and the Far East.* Paper contributed for the United Nations World Population Conference, August 30-September 10, 1965.

Somoza, Jorge L. *Niveles y Tendencias de la Mortalidad en America Latina, Expresados en Funcion de la Edad.* Paper contributed for the United Nations World Population Conference, August 30-September 10, 1965.

Somoza, Jorge. "Trends of Mortality and Expectation of Life in Latin America." Pp. 219–233, discussion pp. 233–241, in Clyde V. Kiser (ed.). *Components of Population Change in Latin America.* Proceedings of the sixtieth anniversary conference of the Milbank Memorial Fund. *Milbank Memorial Fund Quarterly,* **43** (4, Part 2) (October 1965).

Spiegelman, Mortimer. "Mortality Trends and Prospects and their Implications," *The Annals of the American Academy of Political and Social Science,* **316** (March 1958), 25–33.

Spiegelman, Mortimer. *Recent Mortality in Countries of Traditionally Low Mortality.* Paper contributed for the United Nations World Population Conference, August 30-September 10, 1965.

Speigelman, Mortimer. "Recent Trends in Mortality at the Older Ages in Countries of Low Mortality," pp. 760–767 in *International Union for the Study of Population.* International Population Conference, New York, 1961. (Proceedings). Vol. I. (London, 1963).

Stolnitz, George J. "A Century of International Mortality Trends," Part I, *Population Studies,* **9** (1) (July 1955), 24–55.

Stolnitz, George J. "A Century of International Mortality Trends," Part II, *Population Studies,* **10** (1) (July 1956), 17–42.

Stolnitz, George J. "Comparison between some Recent Mortality Trends in Underdeveloped Areas and Historical Trends in the West," pp. 26–34 in Milbank Memorial Fund. *Trends and Differentials in Mortality.* New York, 1956.

Stolnitz, George J. "Recent Mortality Trends in Latin America, Asia and Africa," *Population Studies,* **19** (2) (November 1965), 117–138.

Stolnitz, George J. "The Revolution in Death Control in Non-industrial Countries," *The Annals of the American Academy of Political and Social Science,* **316** (March 1958), 94–101.

Trinidad and Tobago. Central Statistical Office. *Life Tables for British Caribbean Countries 1959-61.* (Census Research Programme, Publication 9.) Kingston, Jamaica: University of the West Indies, 1966.

United Nations. *The Situation and Recent Trends of Mortality in the World.* Population Bulletin of the United Nations, No. 6. New York, 1963.

U.S. National Center for Health Statistics. *Life Tables for the Geographic Divisions of the United States: 1959–61.* Public Health Service Publication, 1252. Vol. I. (May 1965). Life Tables: 1959–61. No.1-.Washington, 1964-.

III. FETAL, INFANT, AND CHILD MORTALITY

Abhayaratne, O. E. R. "Infant Mortality in Ceylon," *Ceylon Medical Journal* (Colombo), **4** (3) (1958), 129–150.

Béhar, Moises. "Death and Disease in Infants and Toddlers of Preindustrial Countries," *American Journal of Public Health and Nation's Health,* **54** (7) (July 1964), 1100–1105.

Behm, Hugo. *Mortalidad Infantil y Nivel de Vida (Infant Mortality and Level of Living).* Santiago: Universidad de Chile, 1962.

Behm, Hugo. "Needed Research on Latin American Mortality in Relation to Public Health. Pp. 338–369, discussion, pp. 369–371, in Clyde V. Kiser (ed.). *Components of Population Change in Latin America.* Proceedings of the sixtieth anniversary conference of the Milbank Memorial Fund. *Milbank Memorial Fund Quarterly,* **43** (4, Part 2) (October 1965).

Biraben, Jean-Noël, and Louis Henry. "La Mortalité des Jeunes Enfants dans les Pays Méditerranéens" ("Mortality of Young Children in Mediterranean Countries"), *Population* (Paris), **12** (4) (October-December 1957), 615–644.

Bourgeois-Pichat, Jean. "Evolution Récente de la Mortalité Infantile" ("Recent Changes in Infant Mortality"), *Population* (Paris), **19** (3) (June-July 1964), 417–438. With Spanish and English summaries.

Brass, W. "Differentials in Child Mortality by the Marriage Experience of the Mothers in Six African Communities," pp. 384–395 in *International Union for the Scientific Study of Population.* Vienna, 1959.

Camacho, L. G., and J. Vildósola. "Algunos Aspectos de la Mortalidad Infantil en el Ecuador" ("Various Aspects of Infant Mortality in Ecuador"), *Boletín de la Oficina Sanitaria Panamericana* (Washington), **45** (1) (July 1958), 1–16.

Canada. Ontario. Department of Health. Division of Medical Statistics. "Infant, Neonatal and Perinatal Mortality and Stillbirths: Ontario, 1925–1960," *Special Report 20.* Toronto, 1963.

Chandrasekhar, S. "Infant Mortality in India, 1901–1951," *Proceedings of the World Population Conference: 1954.* New York, 1955, Vol. I.

Chase, Helen C. *The Relationship of Certain Biologic and Socio-economic Factors to Fetal, Infant, and Early Childhood Mortality.* 3 vols. Albany: New York State Department of Health, 1961–1963.

Corbisier, J. G. "Contribution to the Study of Infant Mortality in Belgium in Relation to Other European Countries," *Courrier* (Paris), **12** (September 1962), 533–548.

Curbelo, Arbelo A. *La Mortalidad de la Infancia en España, 1901-1950 (Infant Mortality in Spain, 1901-1950).* Madrid: Instituto Balmes de Sociología y Dirección General de Sanidad, 1962.

Curbelo, Arbelo A. "La Mortalidad Postneonatal en España. Fallecidos de 1 a 11 Meses Edad. Decenio 1941-1950. Conclusión ("Post-neonatal Mortality in Spain. Deaths from one to eleven Months of Age, Decade of 1941-1950"), *Revista Internacional de Sociologiá* (Madrid), **11** (43) (July-September 1953), 105–130.

Czermak, Hans, and Harald Hanslwuka. "Infant Mortality in Austria," *British Journal of Preventive and Social Medicine,* **16** (4) (October 1962), 196–202.

Febvay, Maurice, and Marcel Croze. "New Data on Infant Mortality: The Influence of the Region and of the Social Setting" ("Nouvelles Données sur la Mortalité Infantile: Influence de la Région et du Milieu Social"), *Population,* **9** (3) (July-September 1954), 387–424.

Federici, Nora. "Aspetti Sociali della Mortalità Infantile a Roma" ("Social Aspects of Infant Mortality in Rome"), *Statistica* (Bologna), **24** (1) (January-March 1964), 79–94.

Freedman, Ronald, et al. "Social Correlates of Fetal Mortality," *Milbank Memorial Fund Quarterly,* **44** (3, Part 1) (July 1966), 327–344.

Freudenberg, Karl. "Regionale Unterschiede der Säuglingssterblichkeit" ("Regional Differentials in Infant Mortality"), *Raumforschung und Raumordnung* (Bad Godesberg and Hanover), **17** (4) (1959), 198–205.

Gamble, David P. "Infant Mortality Rates in a Sierra Leone Urban Community (Lunsar)," *Journal of Tropical Medicine and Hygiene,* **64** (8) (August 1961), 192–199.

Gardiner, C. E. "Maori Infant Mortality," *New Zealand Medical Journal,* **58** (June 1959), 321–340.

Girard, Alain, et al. *Facteurs Sociaux et Culturels de la Mortalité Infantile. Une Enquête sur le Comportement des Familles dans le Nord et le Pas-de-Calais (Social and Cultural Factors in Infant Mortality. A Survey of Family Behavior in the Nord and Pas-de-Calais Departments).* Institut National d'Études Démographiques, Cahiers de Travaux et Documents, No. 36. Paris: Presses Universitaires de France, 1960.

Hammoud, Esmat. "I. Studies in Fetal and Infant Mortality. II. Differentials in Mortality by Sex and Race," *American Journal of Public Health and the Nation's Health,* **55** (8) (August 1965), 1152–1163.

Hansluwka, Harald. "Biological and Socio-economic Factors in Infant Mortality in Austria," pp. 658–666 in *International Union for the Study of Population.* International Population Conference. New York, 1961. (Proceedings). Vol. I (London, 1963).

Heady, J. A., and M. A. Heasman. *Social and Biological Factors in Infant Mortality.* Great Britain. General Register Office, England and Wales. Studies on Medical and Population Subjects, No. 15. London: H. M. Stationery Office, 1959.

Holzer, Jerzy. *The Evolution of Infant Mortality in Poland.* Paper contributed for the United Nations World Population Conference, August 30-September 10, 1965.

Hunt, Eleanor P., and Stanley M. Goldstein. *Trends in Infant and Childhood Mortality, 1961.* U.S. Children's Bureau, Statistical Series, No. 76. Washington, D.C.: Government Printing Office, 1964.

Hunt, Eleanor P., and Earl E. Huyck. "Mortality

of White and Nonwhite Infants in Major U.S. Cities," *Health, Education, and Welfare Indicators* (January 1966).

Kucera, Milan. "Infant and Perinatal Mortality in Czechoslovakia," pp. 675–684 in *International Union for the Study of Population*. International Population Conference, New York, 1961. (Proceedings). Vol. I. (London, 1963).

Martinez, Pedro Daniel, et al. "Mortalidad de la niñez en México" ("Child Mortality in Mexico"), *Boletín de la Oficina Sanitaria Panamericana* (Washington), **47** (2) (August 1959), 101–117. With English summary.

Morris, J. N., J. A. Heady and C. Daly. "Social and Biological Factors in Infant Mortality—England and Wales, 1949-1950," *Proceedings of the World Population Conference: 1954*. New York, 1955. Vol. I.

Morris, J. N., et al. "Social and Biological Factors in Infant Mortality," in 5 parts: *Lancet*, **268** (6859), 343–349; (6860), 395–397; (6861), 445–448; (6862), 499–503; (6863), 554–560 (February 12, 1955 through March 12, 1955).

Moriyama, Iwao M. *Infant Mortality in Certain Countries of Low Mortality*. Paper contributed for the United Nations World Population Conference, August 30-September 10, 1965.

Moriyama, Iwao M. "Recent Changes in Infant Mortality Trends," *Public Health Reports*, **75** (May 1960), 391–405.

Norway. Statistisk Sentralbyro. *Dødelighet blant spedbarn i Norge, 1901-1963 (Infant Mortality in Norway, 1901-1963.)* By Julie E. Backer and Øystein Aagenaes. Samfunnsøkonomiske Studier, 17. Oslo, 1966.

Phillips, Harry T. "An Inter-racial Study in Social Conditions and Infant Mortality in Cape Town," *Milbank Memorial Fund Quarterly*, **35** (1) (January 1957), 7–28.

Pineda, Virginia Gutiérrez de. "Causas Culturas de la Mortalidad Infantil" ("Cultural Causes of Infant Mortality"), *Revista Colombiana de Antropología* (Bogotá), **4** (1955), 11–82.

Rose, R. J. *Infant and Foetal Loss in New Zealand*. New Zealand Department of Health Medical Statistics Branch, Special Report 17. Wellington: Government Printer, 1964.

Sarrouy, Ch., and S. Farouz. "L'Évolution de la Mortalité Infantile en Algérie" ("Development of Infantile Mortality in Algeria"), *Algérie Médicale* (Algiers), **65** (August 1961), 617–669.

Shapiro, S., et al. *Infant and Perinatal Mortality in the United States*. U.S. National Center for Health Statistics, Analytical Studies No. 4, 1965.

Shapiro, Sam, and Iwao M. Moriyama. "International Trends in Infant Mortality and their Implications for the United States," *American Journal of Public Health and the Nation's Health*, **53** (5) (May 1963), 747–760.

Stockwell, Edward G. "Infant Mortality and Socio-economic Status: A Changing Relationship," *Milbank Memorial Fund Quarterly*, **40** (1) (January 1962), 101–111.

Swaroop, Satya. "On Infant and Childhood Mortality in Areas of Higher Deathrates: Levels and Trends: Influence of Changes on Expectation of Life," *Proceedings of the World Population Conference: 1954*. New York, 1955. Vol. I.

Szabady, Egon. "A Csecsemöhalandóságot Befolyásoló Társadalmi és Biológiai Tényezök Magyarországon" ("Social and Biological Factors Affecting Infant Mortality in Hungary"), *Demográfia* (Budapest), **4** (4) (1961), 440–449. With Russian and English summaries.

Tayback, Mathew, and J. S. Prince. "Infant Mortality and Fertility in Five Towns of Ethiopia," *Ethiopian Medical Journal* (Addis Ababa), **9** (1) (1965), 11–17. Report on estimated rates. *Medical Gynaecology and Sociology* **1** (2).

Taylor, Wallis. "Current Differential Infantile Mortality, England and Wales," *British Journal of Preventive and Social Medicine*, **8** (4) (October 1954), 157–161.

Tietze, Christopher, and Clyde E. Martin. "Foetal Deaths, Spontaneous and Induced, in the Urban White Population of the United States," *Population Studies*, **11** (2) (November 1957), 170–176.

United Nations. Population Branch. *Age and Sex Patterns of Mortality. Model Life-tables for Underdeveloped Countries*. Population Studies, No. 22 ST/SOA. Series A/22. December, 1955. Sales No.: 1955. XIII. 9. New York, 1955.

United Nations. *Foetal, Infant, and Early Childhood Mortality*. In 2 vols. Vol. I. *The Statistics;* Vol. II. *Biological, Social, and Economic Factors*. Population Studies, No. 13. New York, 1955.

United Nations. *The Situation and Recent Trends of Mortality in the World*. Population Bulletin of the United Nations, No. 6. New York, 1963.

U.S. National Center for Health Statistics. *Infant Mortality Trends: United States and Each State, 1930-64*. U.S. Department of Health, Education and Welfare, 1965.

U.S. Children's Bureau. U.S. Public Health Service. "Geography of Infant Mortality," *Public Health Reports*, **78** (3) (March 1963), 270–271.

Uttley, K. H. "Infant and Early Childhood Death Rates Over the Last Hundred Years in the Negro Population of Antigua, British West Indies," *British Journal of Preventive and So-*

Health Service Publication 1113. Washington, D.C.: Government Printing Office, 1964.

U.S. Public Health Service. "Lung Cancer Mortality, 1949-51. Supplemental Tables," *Public Health Reports,* **77** (4) (April 1962), 324–328.

U.S. Public Health Service. *Smoking and Health.* Report of the Advisory Committee (on Smoking and Health) to the Surgeon General of the (U.S.) Public Health Service. Public Health Service Publication 1103. Washington, D.C: Government Printing Office, 1963.

Weiss, Hilda P. "Durkheim, Denmark, and Suicide: A Sociological Interpretation," *Acta Sociologica* (Copenhagen), **7** (4) (1964), 264–278.

Widén, Lars. "The Development of Mortality Within Different Groups of Causes of Death in Sweden 1951-1960," *Statistisk Tidskrift* (Stockholm), **11** (1) (January 1962), 3–14.

World Health Organization. "Causes of Death. Deaths Due to Abortion" ("Causes de Deces. La Mortalité due à l'Avortement"), *Epidemiological and Vital Statistics Report* (Geneva), **11** (11) (1958), 558–577.

World Health Organization. "Epidemiological and Statistical Information. Leading Causes of Death," *World Health Organization Bulletin* (Geneva), **18** (11) (November 1964), 425–428.

World Health Organization. *Manual of the International Statistical Classification of Diseases, Injuries, and Causes of Death,* 1957. Vol. I. Geneva, 1958. Also available in French and Spanish.

V. DIFFERENTIAL MORTALITY

Berkson, Joseph. "Mortality and Marital Status. Reflections on the Derivation of Etiology from Statistics," *American Journal of Public Health and the Nation's Health,* **52** (8) (August 1962), 1318–1329.

Calot, G., and M. Febvay. "La Mortalité Différentielle Suivant le Milieu Social. Présentation d'une Méthode Expérimentée en France sur la Période 1955-1960 Premiers Résultats," *Études et Conjoncture* (Paris), **20** (11) (November 1965), 75–159.

Chase, Helen C. "White-nonwhite Mortality Differentials in the United States," *Health, Education and Welfare Indicators* (June 1965), 27–36.

Conrad, Frederick A. "Sex Roles as Factors in Longevity," *Sociology and Social Research,* **46** (1) (January 1962), 195–202.

Cousens, S. H. "Regional Death Rates in Ireland During the Great Famine, from 1846 to 1851," *Population Studies,* **14** (1) (July 1960), 55–74.

Cox, P. R., and J. R. Ford. "The Mortality of Widows, Shortly after Widowhood," *Lancet,* **7325** (January 1964), 163–164.

Daw, R. H. "The Comparison of Male and Female Mortality Rates," *Journal of the Royal Statistical Society,* Series A, **124** (1) (1961), 20–35. Discussion pp. 35–43.

Ellis, John M. "Mortality Differentials for a Spanish Surname Population Group," *Southwestern Social Science Quarterly,* **39** (4) (March 1959), 314–329.

Ellis, John M. "Socio-economic Differentials in Mortality from Chronic Diseases," *Social Problems,* **5** (July 1957), 30–36.

France. Institut National de la Statistique et des Études Économiques. "La Mortalité par Catégorie Socio-professionnelle," *Études Statistiques,* Supplément Trimestriel du Bulletin Mensuel de Statistique, No. 3 (July-September 1957), 39–44.

Glass, D. V. "Some Indicators of Differences Between Urban and Rural Mortality in England and Wales and Scotland," *Population Studies,* **17** (3) (March 1964), 263–267.

Gordon, Tavia. "Mortality Experience Among the Japanese in the United States, Hawaii, and Japan," *Public Health Reports,* **72** (6) (June 1957), 543–553.

Great Britain. General Register Office, England and Wales. "Area Mortality," *The Registrar General's Decennial Supplement, England and Wales, 1951.* London: H. M. Stationery Office, 1958.

Great Britain. General Register Office, England and Wales. "Mortality According to Marital Status," *The Registrar General's Statistical Review of England and Wales for the Year 1959.* Part III. Commentary. London: H. M. Stationery Office, 1961.

Great Britain. General Register Office, England and Wales. "Occupational Mortality, Part I," *The Registrar General's Decennial Supplement, England and Wales, 1951.* London: H. M. Stationery Office, 1954.

Guralnick, Lillian. *Mortality by Industry and Cause of Death.* Vital Statistics—Special Reports 53 (4), U.S. Department of Health, Education, and Welfare. (September 1963).

Guralnick, Lillian. *Mortality by Occupation and Industry Among Men 20 to 64 Years of Age.* United States 1950. U.S. Public Health Service. National Vital Statistics Division. (September 1962.)

Hamilton, C. Horace. "Ecological and Social Factors in Mortality Variation," *Eugenics Quarterly,* **2** (4) (December 1955), 212–223.

Hingson, R. A. "Comparative Negro and White Mortality During Anesthesia, Obstetrics and

Surgery," *Journal of the National Medical Association,* **49** (4) (July 1957), 203–211.

Hofstee, E. W. "Regionale Sterfte-verschillen" ("Regional Differences in Mortality"), in *International Union for the Scientific Investigation of Population Problems.* Netherland National Committee.

Jacobson, Paul H. "Mortality of Native and Foreign Born Population in the United States," pp. 667–674 in *International Union for the Study of Population.* International Population Conference, New York, 1961. (Proceedings). Vol. I. London, 1963.

Kilpatrick, S. J. "Occupational Mortality Indices," *Population Studies,* **16** (2) (November 1962), 175–187.

Koller, Siegfried. "The Development of Excess Male Mortality," pp. 675–684 in *International Union for the Study of Population.* International Population Conference, New York, 1961. (Proceedings). Vol. I. London, 1963.

Kusukawa, Akira. *Social and Economic Factors in Mortality in Developing Countries.* Paper contributed for the United Nations World Population Conference, August 30-September 10, 1965.

Liddell, F. D. "The Measurement of Occupational Mortality," *British Journal of Industrial Medicine,* **17** (July 1960), 228–233.

Logan, W. P. D. "Social Class Variations in Mortality," *Proceedings of the World Population Conference: 1954.* New York, 1955. Vol. I.

Logan, W. P. D. "Social Class Variations in Mortality," *Public Health Reports,* **59** (12) (December 1954), 1217–1223.

Madigan, Francis C. "Are Sex Mortality Differentials Biologically Caused?" *Milbank Memorial Fund Quarterly,* **35** (2) (April 1957), 202–223.

Madigan, Francis C. "Role Satisfactions and Length of Life in a Closed Population," *American Journal of Sociology,* **77** (6) (May 1962), 640–649.

Metropolitan Life Insurance Company. "Mortality and Social Class," *Statistical Bulletin,* **40** (October 1959), 9–10.

Moriyama, Iwao M., and Lillian Guralnick. "Occupational Social Class Differences in Mortality," pp. 61–73 in Milbank Memorial Fund. *Trends and Differentials in Mortality.* New York, 1956.

Netherland National Committee. "Differentiele Sterfte" ("Differential Mortality"). (A group of articles) in *International Union for the Scientific Investigation of Population Problems.* The Hague: Die Vereniging voor Demografie, 1958. With English summaries.

Oginio, Shimako. "An Analysis of Mortality Structure by Occupation in Japan," pp. 19–24; English summary pp. 81–82 in Japan. Welfare Ministry. *Annual Reports of the Institute of Population Problems,* No. 4. Tokyo, 1959.

Pallos, Emil. "Magyarország Falusi és Városi Népességének Halandósági Viszonyai az 1959/60—As Evekben" ("Comparison of Mortality of Hungarian Rural and Urban Populations in 1959/60"), *Demografia* (Budapest), **5** (4) (1962), 509–515. With Russian and English summaries.

Parkhurst, Elizabeth. "Differential Mortality in New York State, Exclusive of New York City, by Sex, Age, and Cause of Death, According to Degree of Urbanization," *American Journal of Public Health and the Nation's Health,* **46** (8) (August 1956), 959–965.

Patno, Mary Ellen. "Mortality and Economic Level in an Urban Area," *Public Health Reports,* **75** (9) (September 1960), 841–851.

Pedoe, Arthur. "Occupation, Social Class and Mortality," Society of Actuaries, *Transactions,* **12** (4) (May 1960), 227–242; discussion 243–257.

Quinney, Richard. "Mortality Differentials in a Metropolitan Area," *Social Forces,* **43** (2) (December 1964), 222–230.

Saw Swee Hock. "State Differential Mortality in Malaya," *Population Review (Madras),* **10** (1) (January 1966), 65–67.

Seidman, Herbert, et al. "Death Rates in New York City by Socio-economic Class and Religious Group and by the Country of Birth, 1949-1951," *Jewish Journal of Sociology,* **4** (2) (December 1962), 254–273.

Sheps, Mindel C. "Marriage and Mortality," *American Journal of Public Health,* **51** (4) (April 1961), 547–555.

Shurtleff, Dewey. "Mortality Among the Married," *Journal of the American Geriatrics Society,* **4** (7) (July 1956), 654–666.

Shurtleff, Dewey. "Mortality and Marital Status," *Public Health Reports,* **70** (3) (March 1955), 248–252.

Stevenson, T. H. C. "The Vital Statistics of Wealth and Poverty," *Journal of the Royal Statistical Society,* **91** (1928), 207–220.

Sweden. Statistiska Centralbyrån. "Dödligheten i de Aktiva Åldrarna i Skilda Yrkesgrupper 1961" ("Mortality in the Active Ages in Various Occupational Groups"). By Lars Widén. *Statistiska Meddelanden B,* **11** (1964). (Stockholm, May 13, 1964). With English summary.

Tabah, Léon. "Social Mortality: A New Study in England" ("La Mortalité Sociale: Enquête Nouvelle en Angleterre"), *Population,* **10** (1) (January-March 1955), 47–78.

U.S. Public Health Service. Division of Special Health Services. *Comparative Mortality Among Metropolitan Areas of the United States, 1949–51.* By Nicholas E. Manos. Public Health Service Publication No. 562. Washington, D.C.: Government Printing Office, 1957.

Upchurch, Harley M. "A Tentative Approach to the Study of Mortality Differentials Between Educational Strata in the United States," *Rural Sociology,* **17** (2) (June 1962), 213–217.

Wolff, P. de, and J. Meerdink. "Mortality Rates in Amsterdam According to Profession," *Pro-*

ceedings of the World Population Conference: 1954. New York, 1955. Vol. I.

Yeracaris, Constantine A. "Differential Mortality, General and Cause-specific in Buffalo, 1939–41," *Journal of the American Statistical Association,* **50** (272) (December 1955), 1235–1247.

Young, Michael, et al. "The Mortality of Widowers," *Lancet,* **7305** (August 31, 1963), 454–456.

VI. METHODOLOGY OF MORTALITY ANALYSIS

Barclay, George W. *Techniques of Population Analysis.* New York: John Wiley and Sons, 1958.

Barnett, H. A. R. "The Components of Mortality," *Journal of the Institute of Actuaries,* **81** (358, Part II) (1955), 105–149.

Benjamin, B. "Actuarial Method of Mortality Analysis: Adaptation to Changes in the Age and Cause Pattern," pp. 38–54; discussion pp. 54–65 in Royal Society of London. A Discussion on Demography. Arranged by P. B. Medawar and D. V. Glass. *Proceedings of the Royal Society of London. Series B. Biological Sciences,* **159** (974) (March 17, 1964), 1–255.

Berkson, Joseph. "Maximum Likelihood Estimate of the Mortal Effect of Smoking, with Particular Reference to Published Statistical Studies of Smoking and Lung Cancer," *Bulletin de l'Institut International de Statistique* (Tokyo), **38** (3) (1961), 91–96.

Bourgeois-Pichat, Jean. "Application of Factor Analysis to the Study of Mortality," pp. 194–229 in Milbank Memorial Fund. *Emerging Techniques in Population Research.* New York, 1963.

Brass, W. "The Construction of Life Tables from Child Survivorship Ratios," pp. 294–301 in *International Union for the Study of Population.* International Population Conference, New York 1961. (Proceedings). Vol. I. London, 1963.

Caffin, S. W. "Construction of Mortality Tables from Population Data," *Transactions of the Actuarial Society of Australasia* (Sydney), **8** (1953), 73–94.

Campbell, Arthur A. "A Method of Projecting Mortality Rates Based on Postwar International Experience," *International Population Reports.* Series P-91. No. 5. Washington: U.S. Bureau of the Census, 1953.

Carrier, N. H. "A Note on the Estimation of Mortality and Other Population Characteristics Given Deaths by Age," *Population Studies,* **12** (2) (November 1958), 149–163.

Case, R. A. M. "Cohort Analysis of Mortality Rates as an Historical or Narrative Technique," *British Journal of Preventive and Social Medicine,* **10** (4) (October 1956), 159–171.

Chiang, Chin Long. "An Application of Stochastic Processes to Life Tables and Standard Error of Age Adjustment Rates," *Biometrics,* **14** (1) (March 1958), 133–134.

Chiang, Chin Long. "A Stochastic Study of the Life Table and its Applications: II. Sample Variance of the Observed Expectation of Life and Other Biometric Functions," *Human Biology,* **32** (3) (September 1960), 221–238.

Chiang, Chin Long. "A Stochastic Study of the Life Table and its Applications: I. Probability Distributions of the Biometric Functions," *Biometrics,* **16** (4) (December 1960), 618–635.

Coale, Ansley J. "The Effect of Declines in Mortality on Age Distribution," pp. 125–132 in Milbank Memorial Fund. *Trends and Differentials in Mortality.* New York, 1956.

Coale, Ansley J., *Regional Model Life Tables and Stable Populations* (Princeton, Princeton University Press, 1966).

Cox, Peter R. "Methods of Comparing Mortality Experiences," Chapter 6 in *Demography.* Cambridge: Cambridge University Press, 1959.

Delaporte, Pierre J. "Sur les Tables de Mortalité de Générations: Effects de la Seconde Guerre Mondiale et des Antibiotiques" ("On Generation Life Tables: Effects of the Second World War and of Antibiotics"), *Bulletin de l'Institut International de Statistique* (Rio de Janeiro), **35** (3) (1957), 445–454. With English summary.

Durand, John D. "Mortality Estimates from Roman Tombstone Inscriptions," *American Journal of Sociology,* **65** (4) (January 1960), 365–373.

Ederer, Fred. "The Effect of Adjusting for Competing Mortality Risks," *American Journal of Public Health and the Nation's Health,* **54** (7) (July 1964), 1129–1133.

Elveback, Lila. "Estimation of Survivorship in Chronic Disease; the "Actuarial Method,"" *Journal of the American Statistical Association,* **53** (282) (June 1958), 420–440.

Freudenberg, Karl. "Nouvel Calcul de la Durée de Vie Normale" (New Computation of the Length of Normal Life), pp. 640–649 in *International Union for the Study of Popula-*

tion. International Population Conference, New York, 1961 (Proceedings). Vol I. (London, 1963). With French and English summaries.

Gabriel, K. R., and Ilana Ronen. "Estimates of Mortality from Infant Mortality Rates," *Population Studies,* **12** (2) (November 1958), 164–169.

Gershenson, Harry. *Measurement of Mortality.* Chicago: Society of Actuaries, 1961.

Gregory, Ian. "Retrospective Estimates of Orphanhood from Generation Life Tables," *Milbank Memorial Fund Quarterly,* **43** (3) (July 1965), 323–348.

Greville, Thomas N. E. "On the Formula for the L-function in a Special Mortality Table Eliminating a Given Cause of Death," *Society of Actuaries Transactions,* **6** (14) (April 1954), 1–5.

Guralnick, Lillian, and Edward D. Winter. "A Note on Cohort Infant Mortality Rates," *Public Health Reports,* **80** (8) (August 1965), 692–694.

Guralnick, Lillian. *Multiple Causes of Death, United States, 1955.* Paper contributed for the United Nations World Population Conference, August 30-September 10, 1965.

Henry, Louis. "L'Age au Décès d'Après les Inscriptions Funéraires" ("Age at Death According to Tomb Inscriptions"), *Population* (Paris), **14** (2) (April-June 1959), 327–329.

Henry, Louis. "Evolution de la Mortalité en Inde" ("Mortality Change in India"), *Population* (Paris), **19** (5) (October-December 1964), 972–973.

Hill, A. Bradford. *Principles of Medical Statistics.* New York: Oxford University Press, 1955.

Hooker, P. F., and H. Longley-Cook. *Life and Other Contingencies.* Vol. II. Cambridge: Cambridge University Press, 1957.

Jacobson, Paul H. "Cohort Survival for Generations since 1840," *Milbank Memorial Fund Quarterly,* **42** (3, Part I) (July 1964), 36–53.

Kannisto, Vaino. "The Value of Certain Refinements of the Infant-mortality Rate," *Bulletin of the World Health Organization* (Geneva), **16** (4) (1957), 763–782.

Keyfitz, Nathan. "A Life Table that Fits the Data," *Journal of the American Statistical Association* (June 1966).

Ledermann, Sully. "Estimation de l'Ésperance de Vie à la Naissance par Catégorie Professionnelle en France" ("Estimated Expectation of Life at Birth by Occupational Class in France" *Population* (Paris), **15** (1) (January-March 1960), 127–131.

Ledermann, Sully, and Jean Breas. "Les Dimensiones de la Mortalité," *Population* (Paris), **14** (4) (October-December 1959), 637–682.

Leser, C. E. V. "Variations in Mortality and Life

Expectation," *Population Studies,* **9** (1) (July 1955), 67–71.

Logan, W. P. D. "The Measurement of Infant Mortality," *Population Bulletin of the United Nations,* (3) (October 1953), 30–55.

MacMahon, B., and W. D. Terry. "Application of Cohort Analysis to the Study of Time Trends in Neoplastic Disease," *Journal of Chronic Diseases,* **7** (1) (January 1, 1958), 24–35.

Miller, C. R., et al. "Latent Class Analysis and Differential Mortality," *Journal of the American Statistical Association,* **57** (298) (June 1962), 430–438.

Mitra, K. N., and A. K. Gayen. "On the Advantages of Longitudinal Survey for the Determination of Infantile Mortality Rates in India," *Bulletin of the International Statistical Institute,* **33** (4) (1954), 105–112.

Moriyama, Iwao M. "Mortality in the United States and in Other Countries of Low Mortality," *Journal of the American Geriatrics Society,* **3** (11) (November 1955), 893–901.

Moriyama, Iwao M., and Thomas N. E. Greville. "Effect of Changing Birth Rates upon Infant Mortality Rates," *Vital Statistics—Special Reports,* **19** (21) (November 10, 1944).

Moriyama, Iwao M., et al. "Inquiry into Diagnostic Evidence Supporting Medical Certifications of Death," *American Journal of Public Health and the Nation's Health,* **48** (10) (October 1958), 1376–1387.

Myers, Robert J. "An Instance of the Pitfalls Prevalent in Graveyard Research," *Biometrics,* **19** (4) (December 1963), 638–650.

Myers, Robert J., and Francisco Bayo. "United States Life Tables for 1959–61," *Transactions of the Society of Actuaries,* **16** (46) (November 1964), 436–451.

Petersen, William. "Morbidity and Mortality," Chapter 10 in *Population.* New York: Macmillan Company, 1961.

Pressat, Roland. *L'Analyse Démographique.* Paris: Presses Universitaires, 1961.

Pressat, Roland. "Mesure de la Mortalité et de la Fécondité en Pays Sous-développé," *Population* (Paris), **12** (4) (October-December 1957), 718–724.

Shapiro, Sam, et al. "A Life Table of Pregnancy Terminations and Correlates of Fetal Loss," *Milbank Memorial Fund Quarterly,* **40** (1) (January 1962), 7–45.

Silcock, H. "The Comparison of Occupational Mortality Rates," *Population Studies,* **13** (2) (November 1959), 183–192.

Sirken, Monroe G. *Comparison of Two Methods of Constructing Abridged Life Tables by Reference to a "Standard" Table: Comparison of the Revised and the Prior Method of Constructing the Abridged Life Tables for the United States.* U.S. National Center for Health

Statistics, Vital and Health Statistics Series 2, No. 4. Public Health Service Publication 1000, Series 2, No. 4. Washington, D.C.: U.S. Public Health Service, 1964.

Spiegelman, Mortimer. *Introduction to Demography.* Chicago: Society of Actuaries, 1955.

Stolnitz, George J. *Life Tables from Limited Data: A Demographic Approach.* Princeton, N.J.: Office of Population Research, 1956).

Stolnitz, George J. "Mortality Declines and Age Distribution," *Milbank Memorial Fund Quarterly,* **34** (2) (April 1956), 178–215.

Tarver, James D. "Projections of Mortality in the United States to 1970," *Milbank Memorial Fund Quarterly,* **37** (2) (April 1959), 132–143.

Tomasson, R. F. "Bias in Estimates of the U.S. Nonwhite Population as Indicated by Trends in Death Rates," *Journal of the American Statistical Association,* **56** (March 1961), 44–51.

United Nations. Population Branch. *Age and Sex Patterns of Mortality. Model Life-Tables for Under-developed Countries.* Population Studies, No. 22. New York, 1955.

United Nations. "Factor Analysis of Sex-Age-Specific Death Rates," *Population Bulletin of the United Nations,* (6) (1963), 149–201.

United Nations. Population Division, Department of Economic and Social Affairs. *Methods of Estimating Basic Demographic Measures from Incomplete Data,* Population Studies, No. 42. New York, 1967.

U.S. National Center for Health Statistics. *An Index of Health: Mathematical Models.* Washington, D.C., May, 1965. Public Health Service Publication No. 1000. Series 2. No. 5.

Winkler, Wilhelm. "Once More the Standardized Death Rate," pp. 475–481 in International Statistical Institute. Institut International de Statistique. Demography. (Joint meeting with the International Union for the Scientific Study of Population.) *Bulletin de l'Institut International de Statistique* (Toronto), **40** (1) (1964), 473–494.

Winkler, Wilhelm. "Relations Between Crude and Life Table Death Rates," *Journal of the Royal Statistical Society,* Series A, **127** (4) (1964), 534–543.

Wolfenden, Hugh H. *Population Statistics and their Compilation.* Chicago: University of Chicago Press, 1954.

VII. MORBIDITY AND HEALTH IN RELATION TO DEMOGRAPHIC ASPECTS OF MORTALITY

Benjamin, B. "The Measurement of Morbidity," *Journal of the Institute of Actuaries,* **83** (III, 365) (1957), 225–248; discussion 249–267.

Burnight, Robert G. "Chronic Morbidity and the Socio-economic Characteristics of Older Urban Males," *Milbank Memorial Fund Quarterly,* **43** (3) (July 1965), 311–322.

Canada. Dominion Bureau of Statistics. Health and Welfare Division. *The Statistical Measurement of Morbidity Frequency: A Technical Working Document.* Ottawa, 1957.

Dorn, Harold F. "A Classification System for Morbidity Concepts," *Public Health Reports,* **72** (12) (December 1957), 1043–1048.

Dorn. Harold F., and Sidney J. Cutler. *Morbidity from Cancer in the United States.* Part I. Variations in Incidence by Age, Sex, Race, Marital Status and Geographic Region. Part II. Trend in Morbidity Association with Income and Stage at Diagnosis. Public Health Monograph No. 56. Public Health Service Publication No. 590. Washington, D.C.: Government Printing Office, 1959.

Feldman, Jacob J. "Barriers to the Use of Health Survey Data in Demographic Analysis," *Milbank Memorial Fund Quarterly,* **36** (July 1958).

Ferguson, T. "Public Health in Britain in the Climate of the Nineteenth Century," *Population Studies,* **17** (3) (March 1964), 213–224.

Great Britain. General Register Office, England and Wales. Registrar General's Advisory Committee on Medical Nomenclature and Statistics. *Measurement of Morbidity; A Report of the Statistics Subcommittee.* Studies on Medical and Population Subjects, No. 8. London: H.M. Stationery Office, 1954.

Great Britain. General Register Office, England and Wales. "Survey of Sickness," Part I, pp. 1–58 in *The Registrar General's Statistical Review of England and Wales for the Ten Years 1940–1951, Supplement on General Morbidity, Cancer and Mental Health.* London: H.M. Stationery Office, 1955.

Lancet. "Health and Social Class," *Lancet,* **1** (7667) (February 7, 1959), 303–305.

Linder, Forrest E. "Health as a Demographic Variable," pp. 489–497 in *International Union for the Scientific Study of Population.* Vienna, 1959.

Locke, Ben Z., and Henrietta J. Duvall. "Migration and Mental Illness," *Eugenics Quarterly,* **11** (4) (December 1964), 216–221.

Logan, W. P. D. "National Morbidity Statistic in England and Wales," pp. 513–518 in *International Union for the Scientific Study of Population.* Vienna, 1959.

MacMahon, Brian, et al. *Epidemiologic Methods.* Boston: Little, Brown, 1960.

Mancuso, Thomas F., and Elizabeth J. Coulter. "Methods of Studying the Relation of Employment and Long-term Illness—Cohort Analysis," *American Journal of Public Health and the Nation's Health,* **49** (11) (November 1959), 1525–1536.

Metropolitan Life Insurance Company. "Health Trends in Canada," *Statistical Bulletin,* **42** (August 1961), 9.

Odoroff, Maurice E., and Leslie M. Abbe. "Use of General Hospitals: Demographic and Ecological Factors," *Public Health Reports,* **72** (5) (May 1957), 397–404.

Rogers, Edward S. *Human Ecology and Health. An Introduction for Administrators.* New York: Macmillan, 1960.

Saunders, Lyle. *Cultural Difference and Medical Care: The Case of the Spanish-speaking People of the Southwest.* New York: Russell Sage Foundation, 1954.

Shanas, Ethel. *The Health of Older People: A Social Survey.* Cambridge, Mass.: Harvard University Press, 1962.

Smith, Alwyn. *The Social Implications of Morbidity in the United Kingdom.* Paper contributed for the United Nations World Population Conference, August 30–September 10, 1965.

Spiegelman, Mortimer. "Morbidity Statistics," Chapter 7 in *Introduction to Demography.* Chicago: Society of Actuaries, 1955.

Swaroop, S., and K. Uemura. "Proportional Mortality of 50 Years and Above: A Suggested Indicator of the Component 'Health Including Demographic Conditions' in the Measurement of Levels of Living," *Bulletin of the World Health Organization* (Geneva), **17** (3) (1957), 439–482.

Thomlinson, Ralph. "Health and Mortality Differentials," Chapter 7 in *Population Dynamics.* New York: Random House, 1965.

U.S. Army. Office of the Surgeon General. *Results of the Examination of Youths for Military Service, 1965.* By Bernard D. Karpinos. Supplement to Health of the Army, Vol. 21. Washington, D.C., July 1966.

U.S. Public Health Service. *The Extent of Cancer Illness in the United States.* By the Biometry Branch of the U.S. National Cancer Institute. U.S. Public Health Service, Publication No. 547. Washington: U.S. Department of Health, Education, and Welfare, Public Health Service, National Institutes of Health, 1958.

U.S. National Health Survey. *Selected Health Characteristics by Area, Geographic Regions and Urban-rural Residence, United States, July 1957-June 1959.* Health Statistics from the U.S. National Health Survey, Series C, No. 5. Washington, D.C.: March 1961.

U.S. National Center for Health Statistics. *Data from the National Health Survey.* U.S. Department of Health, Education, and Welfare National Center for Health Statistics Series 10, Nos. 1-.

Woolsey, Theodore D. *Classification of Population in Terms of Disability.* Paper contributed to United Nations World Population Conference, August 30-September 10, 1965.

World Health Organization. *Measurement of Levels of Health. Report of a Study Group.* World Health Organization, Technical Report Series, No. 137. Geneva, 1957.

CHAPTER 17

*Marriage and Marital Dissolution**

17.1. Marriage and Marital Dissolution as Dynamic Demographic Forces

Marriage, separation, divorce, and widowhood are demographic events that influence the course of population growth. They influence fertility and migration directly, and mortality indirectly. Their effect on marital status composition has already been analyzed in Chapter 11. The present chapter concentrates on them as active events taking place among the population—as components of population dynamics. The rate at which these events occur, trends in their rates, and differentials in these rates between various socioeconomic groups are the topics considered here.

From the demographic point of view, marriage should be looked upon as a continuous force of attrition, exerting its effect on the population of persons who are not currently married. As a result of its operation, the population of not-married persons is progressively reduced. A never-married person can never again occupy that status after marriage. Simultaneously the bachelor population is continuously being replenished by the arrival at nubile ages of younger generations. If age 15 can be taken as the minimum nubile age for most cultures, we may think of each oncoming cohort being "born" as bachelors or spinsters at this age, but immediately being subjected to a force of attrition in the form of marriage. In this sense, marriage acts like mortality to remove persons from a particular (nonmarried) population. It is unlike mortality, of course, in that it only changes their status and places them in a different category of population.

* The materials representing new research for this chapter were prepared as part of a research program, "Basic Demographic Research," under a grant from the Rockefeller Foundation.

Each wedding represents the "death" of a bachelor and spinster and the "birth" of a family.

The population of families created by the event of marriage is itself subject to two forces of attrition: dissolution of marriage due to incompatibility (separation and divorce) or to death of one spouse (widowhood). Each of these events irrevocably changes the status of married persons; never again can they be once-married persons, with spouse present. Thus the frequency with which divorce and widowhood occur depends in part on the supply of couples.

Ideally, the statistics for the study of marriage, widowhood, and divorce are tabulated from a well-maintained system of vital registration. In actual fact, records of these events are kept in most countries with even less care and uniformity than are data for births and deaths, and are tabulated in much less detail. There are several reasons for this. A different set of institutions—courts, churches, and political organizations rather than medical establishments—is involved. There is less public welfare involved in assembling and tabulating marriage and divorce statistics than in the case of births and deaths (for detection of epidemics, measurement of infant mortality, etc.). The impact that these variables have on demographic processes is not negligible, but usually tends to be stable over time and to change slowly, so that for many types of demographic analysis it can be taken as a constant. As has already been explained in Chapter 11, the topic of nuptiality is currently of heightened demographic interest because of the very fact that it has become more volatile, as evidenced by the dramatic increase in the popularity of being married that took place between 1940 and 1955.

17.2. Marriage Rates and Nuptiality Rates

The incidence of marriage may be expressed at various levels of precision. Following is a description of the measures currently in use.

Crude Marriage Rates. This is the number of marriages per year per 1000 total population.

$$CMR = \frac{\text{number of marriages within one year}}{\text{midyear total population}} \times 1000$$

Even though it is widely used, it is a very unsatisfactory and potentially misleading rate. Because the denominator of this rate is comprised primarily of population that is not eligible to marry (either already married or too young to marry), it fails by a very wide margin to meet the specification that a good demographic rate should express events as a ratio of the population "exposed" to the occurrence of these events. Fluctuations in birthrates, changes in age composition, and even fluctuations in marriage rates for preceding years can affect this rate. Action needs to be taken at some international meeting of demographers to abolish this measure as being an internationally unacceptable mode of presenting marriage statistics. Its continued use is sometimes justified on the grounds that for some nations there is no information about the current marital status of the population. On the contrary, marital status statistics are available from censuses for more nations than have accurate marriage and divorce data. Although some population estimating may be required to calculate the appropriate denominator needed in order to present rates in one of the more refined forms described below for years between censuses, the results will invariably be more precise and interpretable than the crude marriage rate.

Nubile and General Marriage Rates. The population that is "exposed" to the likelihood of marrying during a given year is the average number of persons that are eligible to marry. In a strict legal sense, this is the single (never-married) population that has passed the mini-

mum nubile age, the widowed, and the divorced. (The lower age limit for this rate may be set at age 15 in most nations.) The nubile marriage rate is the ratio of marriages to this not-married group:

$$NMR = \frac{\text{number of marriages within one year}}{\begin{array}{c}\text{number of single} + \text{widowed} + \text{divorced} \\ \text{(females) (males) 15 years of age or over} \\ \text{at midyear}\end{array}}$$

$$\times 1000$$

This measure is far more sensitive than the crude marriage rate to changes in the incidence of marriage and is only slightly more difficult to compute. For intercensal periods, the denominator can be estimated with only slightly less precision than the total population. This rate, and all those that follow, should be computed separately for each sex, or else the denominator should be divided by 2, inasmuch as each event in the numerator represents two persons. Age-specific marriage rates must be computed separately for each sex, because the numbers of males and females at each age are almost never equal and because the two sexes have different patterns of age at marriage.

A rate that is superior even to the nubile marriage rate is the *general marriage rate* (GMR) which is the number of marriages per 1000 unmarried persons at the prime nubile ages (preferably 15 to 49 or 54 for women). This rate recognizes that comparatively few marriages occur after age 49 or 54 and that the rather large unmarried population aged 50 or 55 and over (primarily widowed persons) is not "exposed" in the same way as the unmarried population 15 to 49 or 54. The rate is more appropriate when computed for women than for men, because more men than women marry at the older ages. In the United States this rate is computed for ages 15 to 49 or 54; for first marriages this is clearly superior. In some situations, especially where both sexes are considered, a rate based on ages 15 to 59 may be preferable. This rate is analogous to the general fertility rate, as defined in the preceding chapter.

The nubile marriage rate has two subtypes:

1. *First-marriage rate:* the rate of getting married for the first time. It is the ratio of first marriages to the single (never-married) population.

$$\text{FMR} = \frac{\text{Number of first marriages to (males) (females)}}{\substack{\text{number of single (never-married) (females)} \\ \text{(males) 15 years of age or over}}} \times 1000$$

2. *Remarriage rate:* the rate of once-married persons getting married for a second, third, and so on, time.

$$\text{RMR} = \frac{\substack{\text{number of marriages of persons (females)} \\ \text{(males) previously married}}}{\substack{\text{number of widowed or divorced (females)} \\ \text{(males) at midyear}}} \times 1000$$

This definition is valid, of course, only in nations where monogamy is the only accepted form of marriage. In many nations of the world the married population could well be added to the denominator of the above rate, or an additional special rate could be employed:

$$\text{Rate of polygamy} = \frac{\substack{\text{number of marriages involving (males)} \\ \text{(females) already currently married}}}{\text{number of married persons of this sex}}$$

The Nuptiality Rate. This rate expresses the probability that an unmarried person will marry within exactly one year. Its principal use is in calculating nuptiality tables and building mathematical models of demographic processes. In demographic terms, marriage rates are "central rates" based on midyear populations, whereas nuptiality rates are based on an abstract estimate of a cohort of persons of exactly the same age. The distinction is analogous to that made between death rates and mortality rates (m_x versus q_x) in the preceding chapter. The next section is devoted to nuptiality rates and nuptiality tables.

17.3. The Age Curve of Nuptiality

Nuptiality is far more sensitive to changes in age and differences in age than any of the other demographic variables. It has a distinctive curve whose characteristics are not as yet adequately known or appreciated. Figure 17-1 is a graph of such a curve for the United States population by sex and color for 1950-1960. It is based on the formula:

$$n_x = \frac{\substack{\text{number of marriages of persons (of specified} \\ \text{sex and race) in } x \text{ year of age}}}{\substack{\text{number of single, widowed, or divorced persons} \\ \text{of } x \text{ years of age of the sex and race specified}}} \times 1000$$

This rate is obviously nothing more than the nubile marriage rate calculated separately for each age. It is also possible to have primary and remarriage rates that are specific for age.

The curve of n_x for the United States has an extraordinary shape: it begins at zero at about age 15 and then sweeps upward almost vertically to reach a peak of great intensity within 8 to 12 years. Almost immediately it begins nearly as swift a descent to a low level at about age 35. After this age the rate of marriage gradually descends toward zero, which is nearly reached at ages 60 to 65. The curve for females rises to a higher and sharper peak than does that for males. Also, the curve for females is advanced along the age scale about two years earlier than is that for males. Because it ascends more swiftly and reaches a higher peak,

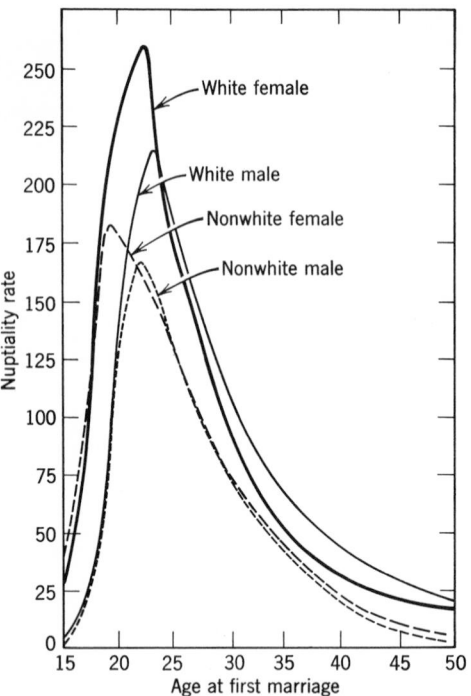

Figure 17-1 Probability of First Marriage at Each Age, United States Population by Sex and Color: 1950 to 1960.

the curve for females falls even more swiftly and approximates zero at an earlier age.

The nuptiality rate for the nonwhite population is significantly different from that for the white population. Although the rates are slightly higher than those for the white population at the early teen years, after about age 18 the rates for the nonwhite population are uniformly lower at every age and sink to nearly zero by age 50.

17.4. The Nuptiality Table

There is need for a procedure for showing the lifetime implications of the nuptiality rates that exist at a particular time. The nuptiality table is a demographic model that accomplishes this. It is analogous to the life table, described in the preceding chapter. Instead of an hypothetical cohort of living persons exposed to an age schedule of probabilities of dying, we have an hypothetical cohort of never-married persons exposed to an age schedule of probabilities of marrying for the first time. Thus instead of q_x,

the mortality rate, the generating function of the nuptiality table is n_x, the nuptiality rate. An hypothetical cohort of 100,000 never-married persons enter their fifteenth year of life simultaneously (in countries with child marriage the nuptiality table can be started at an earlier age) and thereafter are exposed to attrition from nuptiality with an intensity expressed by a set of age-specific nuptiality probabilities that represent the current force of nuptiality. They pass from one age to the next, marrying at the rate specified for each particular year of age. Those who marry are transferred from the ranks of the single to the ranks of the married. Tables 17-1 to 17-4 are approximate nuptiality tables for the United States, for males and females, by color. These tables represent an average of the annual rates for the 1950-1960 decade and are restricted to that segment of the population that marries before age 50. The fraction that marries after this age is too tiny to estimate from the available data. Each table has nine columns, whose definitions are given below. The reader who wishes to study nuptiality tables in more detail should begin with the articles by Mertens and Grabill. (see Bibliography.) A detailed discussion of methodology of construction of nuptiality tables will be found in the *Manual*.

Column 1. Nuptiality rate (n_x). This is a statement of the probability that a person who is single at birthday x will marry before attaining birthday $x + 1$. It is a pure measure of the force of nuptiality, for it is independent of mortality. (It assumes that there are no deaths among the single population; it refers to the attrition of single persons who survive mortality.) For purposes of comparing nuptiality among several populations, a table of this type is superior to a "net" nuptiality table that takes mortality into account, for the differences between the net nuptiality tables may be due to differences either in mortality or in nuptiality or to an unknown mixture of both.

Column 2. Never married at age x (N_x). The number of the original cohort of 100,000 never-married persons who survive the attrition of nuptiality and attain age x without marrying. At age 15, it is the size of the hypothetical cohort, usually 100,000.

Table 17-1 Nuptiality Table for White Males, United States: 1950 to 1960

Age	n_x	N_x	M_x	ML_x	EVM_x	S_x	NEV_x	pM_x	e^n_x
15.............	.0050	100000	500	95441	500	99750	1006495	95.4	10.065
16.............	.0085	99500	846	94941	1346	99077	906745	95.4	9.113
17.............	.0225	98654	2220	94095	3566	97544	807668	95.4	8.187
18.............	.0410	96434	3954	91875	7520	94457	710124	95.3	7.364
19.............	.0725	92480	6704	87921	14225	89128	615667	95.1	6.657
20.............	.1450	85775	12437	81217	26662	79556	526539	94.7	6.139
21.............	.1800	73338	13201	68780	39863	66738	446983	93.8	6.095
22.............	.2025	60137	12178	55579	52041	54048	380245	92.4	6.323
23.............	.2150	47959	10311	43401	62352	42904	326197	90.5	6.802
24.............	.1975	37648	7435	33090	69787	33930	283393	87.9	7.527
25.............	.1775	30213	5363	25655	75150	27532	249463	84.9	8.257
26.............	.1610	24850	4001	20292	79151	22850	221931	81.6	8.931
27.............	.1450	20849	3023	16291	82174	19338	199081	78.1	9.549
28.............	.1320	17826	2353	13268	84527	16650	179743	74.4	10.083
29.............	.1185	15473	1834	10915	86361	14556	163093	70.5	10.540
30.............	.1075	13639	1466	9081	87827	12906	148537	66.6	10.891
31.............	.0975	12173	1187	7615	89014	11580	135631	62.6	11.142
32.............	.0875	10986	961	6428	89975	10506	124051	58.5	11.292
33.............	.0800	10025	802	5467	90777	9624	113545	54.5	11.326
34.............	.0730	9223	673	4665	91450	8886	103921	50.6	11.268
35.............	.0650	8550	556	3992	92006	8272	95035	46.7	11.115
36.............	.0620	7994	496	3436	92502	7746	86763	43.0	10.854
37.............	.0560	7498	420	2940	92922	7288	79017	39.2	10.538
38.............	.0520	7078	368	2520	93290	6894	71729	35.6	10.134
39.............	.0475	6710	319	2152	93609	6550	64835	32.1	9.662
40.............	.0425	6391	272	1833	93881	6255	58285	28.7	9.120
41.............	.0400	6119	245	1561	94126	5996	52030	25.5	8.503
42.............	.0370	5874	217	1316	94343	5766	46034	22.4	7.837
43.............	.0340	5657	192	1099	94535	5561	40268	19.4	7.118
44.............	.0320	5465	175	907	94710	5378	34707	16.6	6.351
45.............	.0290	5290	153	732	94863	5214	29329	13.8	5.544
46.............	.0280	5137	144	579	95007	5065	24115	11.3	4.694
47.............	.0250	4993	125	435	95132	4930	19050	8.7	3.815
48.............	.0230	4868	112	310	95244	4812	14120	6.4	2.901
49.............	.0220	4756	105	198	95349	4704	9308	4.2	1.957
50.............	.0200	4651	93	93	95442	4604	4604	2.0	.990

Column 3. Number marrying at age x (M_x). The number of members of the cohort who marry between the time they attain age x and the time they attain age $x + 1$. It is calculated by multiplying the value in column 1 by the value in column 2.

Column 4. Number ever marrying (ML_x). The number of persons who, when they attain age x, will marry during the next year or some future year. It is calculated by cumulating column 3 from the foot of the table upward.

Column 5. Number of ever-married persons (EVM_x). The cumulative number of persons who have married in previous years, hence enter age x in the status of having previously married. It is calculated by cumulating column 3 downward.

Column 6. Person-years in never-married status in year of age (S_x). If we assume marriages to be evenly distributed over the year, the number of persons who are still single di-minishes continuously, so that the number of person-years spent in single status is smaller than the number of persons who began the year. The number of person-years for S_x is estimated by averaging the values of N_x and N_{x+1}.

Column 7. Cumulative single person-years (NEV_x). This column measures the total number of person-years that will be spent in the never-married status by the cohort during year of age x and all subsequent years. It is computed by cumulating column 6 from the foot of the table upward.

Column 8. Percentage ever marrying (pM_x). The probability that a person who attains age x will marry sometime during his lifetime before age 50 is expressed by this column. It is computed by dividing the entry in column 4 by the entry in column 2. For ages after 15, it represents the proportion of the population which, if single at birthday x, will marry before attaining age 50.

Table 17-2   Nuptiality Table for White Females, United States: 1950 to 1960

Age	n_x	N_x	M_x	ML_x	EVM_x	S_x	NEV_x	p^M_x	e^n_x
15.............	.0280	100000	2800	97141	2800	98600	695010	97.14	6.950
16.............	.0500	97200	4860	94341	7660	94770	596410	97.06	6.136
17.............	.1000	92340	9234	89481	16894	87723	501640	96.90	5.433
18.............	.1750	83106	14544	80247	31438	75834	413917	96.56	4.981
19.............	.2130	68562	14604	65703	46042	61260	338083	95.83	4.931
20.............	.2370	53958	12788	51099	58830	47564	276823	94.70	5.130
21.............	.2500	41170	10293	38311	69123	36024	229259	93.06	5.569
22.............	.2580	30877	7966	28018	77089	26894	193235	90.74	6.258
23.............	.2275	22911	5212	20052	82301	20305	166341	87.52	7.260
24.............	.2000	17699	3540	14840	85841	15929	146036	83.84	8.251
25.............	.1775	14159	2513	11300	88354	12902	130107	79.81	9.189
26.............	.1550	11646	1805	8787	90159	10743	117205	75.45	10.064
27.............	.1370	9841	1348	6982	91507	9167	106462	70.95	10.818
28.............	.1200	8493	1019	5634	92526	7984	97295	66.34	11.456
29.............	.1070	7474	800	4615	93326	7074	89311	61.74	11.950
30.............	.0950	6674	634	3815	93960	6357	82237	57.16	12.322
31.............	.0840	6040	507	3181	94467	5786	75880	52.66	12.563
32.............	.0745	5533	412	2674	94879	5327	70094	48.33	12.668
33.............	.0655	5121	335	2262	95214	4954	64767	44.17	12.647
34.............	.0575	4786	275	1927	95489	4648	59813	40.26	12.497
35.............	.0500	4511	226	1652	95715	4398	55165	36.62	12.229
36.............	.0455	4285	195	1426	95910	4188	50767	33.28	11.848
37.............	.0410	4090	168	1231	96078	4006	46579	30.10	11.389
38.............	.0375	3922	147	1063	96225	3849	42573	27.10	10.855
39.............	.0350	3775	132	916	96357	3709	38724	24.16	10.258
40.............	.0310	3643	113	784	96470	3587	35015	21.52	9.612
41.............	.0290	3530	102	671	96572	3479	31428	19.01	8.903
42.............	.0260	3428	89	569	96661	3384	27949	16.60	8.153
43.............	.0245	3339	82	480	96743	3298	24565	14.38	7.357
44.............	.0225	3257	73	398	96816	3220	21267	12.22	6.530
45.............	.0210	3184	67	325	96883	3150	18047	10.20	5.668
46.............	.0195	3117	61	258	96944	3087	14897	8.28	4.779
47.............	.0180	3056	55	197	96999	3028	11810	6.44	3.865
48.............	.0170	3001	51	142	97050	2975	8782	4.73	2.926
49.............	.0160	2950	47	91	97097	2926	5807	3.08	1.968
50.............	.0150	2903	44	44	97141	2881	2881	0.00	.000

Column 9. Average years before marriage (e^n_x). The average number of years that a person will spend as a bachelor or spinster before first marriage is specified by this column. It is derived by dividing the entry in column 7 by the entry in column 2.

Thus the nuptiality table spells out the full lifetime implications of a particular current schedule of nuptiality rates. The last entry in the S_x column estimates the number of persons (and the proportion of the original cohort) who remain single throughout their lives (or are still single at age 50).

The distribution of entries in column 3 is the age pattern at which first marriages will occur. *It should be noted that the age of greatest number of marriages is not necessarily the age of greatest intensity of marriage.* It is a typical feature of most nuptiality tables for the age of peak intensity to fall two or more years after the age of modal number of marriages.

With the S_x column it is possible to compute the probability of remaining single over any specified number of years.

The probability of escaping attrition for any specified number of years i is equal to

$$_iP_x = \frac{S_{x+1}}{S_x}.$$

For example, the probability that a woman aged 21 (graduating from college) will marry by age 50, beyond the childbearing period, is S_{50}/S_{21}. On the other hand, the probability that a woman aged 40 will marry by age 50 is much less, $S_{50}/_{40}$.

The EVM_x column is extremely useful, because it shows the age distribution of women exposed to childbearing. It can provide a basis for nuptiality-specific fertility rates, to be discussed in the next chapter.

Columns 2 and 5 together show the marital status of the cohort at each age, in terms of never-married and ever-married, respectively.

Table 17-3   Nuptiality Table for Nonwhite Males, United States: 1950 to 1960

Age	n_x	N_x	M_x	ML_x	EVM_x	S_x	NEV_x	p^M_x	e^n_x
15.............	.0050	100000	500	88441	500	99750	1191461	88.4	11.915
16.............	.0100	99500	995	87941	1495	99003	1091711	88.4	10.972
17.............	.0220	98505	2167	86946	3662	97422	992708	88.3	10.078
18.............	.0510	96338	4913	84779	8575	93882	875286	88.0	9.293
19.............	.0990	91425	9051	79866	17626	86900	801404	87.1	8.766
20.............	.1300	82374	10709	70815	28335	77020	714504	86.0	8.674
21.............	.1525	71665	10929	60106	39264	66201	637484	83.9	8.895
22.............	.1665	60736	10113	49177	49377	55680	571283	81.0	9.406
23.............	.1605	50623	8125	39064	57502	46560	515603	77.2	10.185
24.............	.1475	42498	6268	30939	63770	39364	469043	72.8	11.037
25.............	.1325	36230	4800	24671	68570	33830	429679	68.1	11.860
26.............	.1150	31430	3614	19871	72184	29623	395849	63.2	12.595
27.............	.1025	27816	2851	16257	75035	26391	366226	58.4	13.166
28.............	.0900	24965	2247	13406	77282	23842	339835	53.7	13.612
29.............	.0800	22718	1817	11159	79099	21810	315993	49.1	13.909
30.............	.0715	20901	1494	9342	80593	20154	294183	44.7	14.075
31.............	.0630	19407	1223	7848	81816	18796	274029	40.4	14.120
32.............	.0560	18184	1018	6625	82834	17675	255233	36.4	14.036
33.............	.0510	17166	875	5607	83709	16728	237558	32.7	13.839
34.............	.0460	16291	749	4723	84458	15916	220830	29.9	13.555
35.............	.0405	15542	629	3983	85087	15227	204914	25.6	13.185
36.............	.0360	14913	537	3354	85624	14644	189687	22.5	12.720
37.............	.0320	14376	460	2817	86084	14146	175943	19.6	12.176
38.............	.0280	13916	390	2357	86474	13721	160897	16.9	11.562
39.............	.0245	13526	331	1967	86805	13360	147176	14.5	10.881
40.............	.0215	13195	284	1636	87089	13053	133816	12.4	10.141
41.............	.0185	12911	239	1352	87328	12792	120763	10.5	9.353
42.............	.0165	12672	209	1113	87537	12568	107971	8.8	8.520
43.............	.0140	12463	174	904	87711	12376	95403	7.3	7.655
44.............	.0125	12289	154	730	87865	12212	83027	5.9	6.756
45.............	.0115	12135	140	576	88005	12065	70815	4.7	5.836
46.............	.0100	11995	119	436	88124	11936	58750	3.6	4.898
47.............	.0080	11876	95	317	88219	11828	46814	2.7	3.942
48.............	.0075	11781	88	222	88307	11737	34986	1.9	2.970
49.............	.0060	11693	70	134	88377	11658	23249	1.1	1.988
50.............	.0055	11623	64	64	88441	11591	11591	.6	.977

The sum of EVM_x and N_{x+1} is equal to 100,000, the size of the original cohort.

Column 7 permits us to calculate what portion of a person's reproductive life will be spent in a state of nonexposure to childbearing.

Column 9 provides an estimate of the average time a single person must wait before being married. Thus if $e^n_x = 10.1$ at age 15, it indicates that under the current schedule of age-specific marriage rates the average waiting time before marriage for persons entering their fifteenth year is 12.4 years. This statistic is also useful for calculating what portion of a woman's reproductive life will be spent in a state of nonexposure to childbearing. For example, a girl at age 15 may be expected to have a reproductive life of 35 years. If the average number of years before marriage is 7 years at age 15, we may conclude that women are spending 20 percent of their reproductive life in a state of nonexposure to childbearing. (This assumes,

of course, that all childbearing occurs within marriage.)

It is possible to modify the nuptiality table to include the effects of mortality. Such nuptiality tables are termed "net nuptiality tables." They lead to estimates of the average number of years remaining to a single person before death or marriage. Such tables are useful in the study of reproduction, but for the study of nuptiality patterns the nuptiality tables (which do not confound mortality differences with marriage differences) are to be preferred.

We now make use of these demographic tools to explore marriage patterns around the world.

17.5.   Rate of First Marriage and of Marital Dissolution Computed from Census Data

Data for marriages, tabulated by age of bride and bridegroom, are available for only a few nations of the world—and mostly for recent

Table 17-4 Nuptiality Table for Nonwhite Females, United States: 1950 to 1960

Age	n_x	N_x	M_x	ML_x	EVM_x	S_x	NEV_x	$\frac{M}{p}_x$	$\frac{n}{e}_x$
15.............	.0400	100000	400	92144	400	99800	905820	92.14	9.058
16.............	.0580	99600	5777	91744	6177	96712	806020	92.11	8.093
17.............	.0975	93823	9148	85967	15325	89249	709308	91.62	7.560
18.............	.1560	84675	13209	76819	28534	78070	620059	90.72	7.323
19.............	.1820	71466	13007	63610	41541	64962	541989	89.00	7.584
20.............	.1760	58459	10289	50603	51830	53314	477027	86.56	8.160
21.............	.1700	48170	8189	40314	60019	44075	423713	83.69	8.796
22.............	.1610	39981	6437	32125	66456	36762	379638	80.35	9.495
23.............	.1520	33544	5099	25688	71555	30995	342876	76.58	10.222
24.............	.1400	28445	3982	20589	75537	26454	311881	72.38	10.964
25.............	.1300	24463	3180	16607	78717	22873	285427	67.88	11.668
26.............	.1175	21283	2501	13427	81218	20032	262554	63.08	12.336
27.............	.1075	18782	2019	10926	83237	17772	242522	58.17	12.912
28.............	.0960	16763	1609	8907	84846	15958	224750	53.13	13.410
29.............	.0855	15154	1296	7298	86142	14506	208792	48.16	13.778
30.............	.0775	13858	1074	6002	87216	13321	194286	43.31	14.020
31.............	.0680	12784	869	4928	88085	12350	180965	38.55	14.156
32.............	.0600	11915	715	4059	88800	11558	168615	34.16	14.151
33.............	.0525	11200	588	3344	89388	10906	157057	29.86	14.023
34.............	.0460	10612	488	2756	89876	10368	146151	25.97	13.772
35.............	.0400	10124	405	2268	90281	9922	135783	22.40	13.412
36.............	.0350	9719	340	1863	90621	9549	125861	19.16	12.950
37.............	.0310	9379	291	1523	90912	9233	116312	16.24	12.401
38.............	.0260	9088	236	1232	91148	8970	107079	13.56	11.782
39.............	.0225	8852	199	996	91347	8752	98109	11.25	11.083
40.............	.0190	8653	164	797	91511	8571	89357	9.21	10.327
41.............	.0155	8489	132	633	91643	8423	80786	7.46	9.517
42.............	.0125	8357	104	501	91747	8305	72363	5.99	8.659
43.............	.0110	8253	91	397	91838	8208	64058	4.81	7.762
44.............	.0085	8162	69	306	91907	8128	55850	3.74	6.843
45.............	.0075	8093	61	237	91968	8062	47722	2.92	5.897
46.............	.0060	8032	48	176	92016	8008	39660	2.19	4.938
47.............	.0050	7984	40	128	92056	7964	31652	1.60	3.964
48.............	.0045	7944	36	88	92092	7926	23688	1.11	2.982
49.............	.0035	7908	28	52	92120	7894	15762	0.66	1.993
50.............	.0030	7880	24	24	92144	7868	7868	0.30	.998

years. If demographers are to make a study of marriage patterns, in most nations they must rely on other procedures. Fortunately, an approximate but nevertheless highly useful technique for estimating rates of first marriage from census data is available. It is expressed by the very simple equation

$$n_{x+0.5} = \frac{p_x - p_{x+1}}{p_x}$$

where n_x is the nuptiality rate as defined above for the nuptiality table and p is the proportion of the population single at ages x and $x + 1$, respectively, computed from a single census or a survey.

The argument by which this equation is a valid estimate of first-marriage rates (under assumption of equal mortality rates among single and married populations) has recently been summarized and greatly refined by Professor Walter Mertens.[1] An adjustment by in-

terpolation may be made to move the rate back one-half year so that it matches ages as they usually are computed.

An even more valid version of this procedure is to make use of two successive censuses and interpolate between them.

The equation then becomes

$$n_{x+0.5} = \frac{p_x^z - p_{x+1}^{z+1}}{p_x^z}$$

where z and $z + 1$ represent two successive censuses and ages x and $x + 1$ are obtained by interpolating 0.5 years before and 0.5 years after the midpoint between the two censuses. By making use of two censuses, the results tend to be more stable and intergenerational changes in the pattern of age at marriage are held constant. The resulting rates represent an average

[1] Walter Mertens, "Methodological Aspects of the Construction of Nuptiality Tables," *Demography*, **2** (1965), 349–362.

Table 17-5 A Comparison of First-Marriage Rates of India, Japan, and Ireland

Age	India 1951-61		Japan 1955-60		Ireland 1951-61		Ireland 1926-36	
	Male	Female	Male	Female	Male	Female	Male	Female
10..............	13	55	....	....	....	....	....	....
11..............	18	77	....	....	....	....	....	....
12..............	23	100	....	....	....	....	....	....
13..............	30	121	....	....	....	....	....	....
14..............	37	142	....	....	....	....	....	....
15..............	47	165	....	1	....	1	....	....
16..............	57	186	....	4	....	3	....	2
17..............	70	203	1	10	1	8	....	6
18..............	85	224	3	25	3	18	2	13
19..............	99	265	3	45	6	34	4	23
20..............	112	329	5	67	10	49	6	31
21..............	125	360	22	92	18	63	11	38
22..............	134	362	60	11	33	81	19	46
23..............	145	330	100	151	50	99	27	55
24..............	157	187	126	188	62	110	32	63
25..............	187	148	150	256	69	113	36	67
26..............	199	132	167	301	72	112	38	71
27..............	192	116	185	225	72	108	42	72
28..............	180	102	200	155	72	104	45	72
29..............	167	90	220	118	72	100	47	72
30..............	154	82	284	97	71	95	50	70
31..............	140	73	358	85	71	90	51	67
32..............	108	66	378	77	70	82	51	62
33..............	100	60	267	71	67	75	50	57
34..............	91	54	170	66	65	67	50	52
35..............	77	47	132	61	62	69	59	48
36..............	65	43	110	57	59	53	49	44
37..............	55	37	89	53	56	48	48	39
38..............	46	32	74	49	52	43	47	35
39..............	37	27	62	46	48	39	45	30

Note: Rates for India, single years from 10 to 14 are as follows:
Source: Computed from census data and smoothed.

of the rates that prevailed during the interval between the censuses.

This procedure has been followed in computing the rates for the international comparison in the next section, even for nations where registration data are available. In this way, comparability between the statistics for many different places and dates has been preserved.

Again it must be emphasized that values of n_x computed from census data are only approximate. Small differences must therefore be ignored, and only differences of substantial magnitude should be regarded as indicative of genuine international differences in marriage patterns.

17.6. International Comparison of Marriage Patterns

Using the procedures described in the preceding section, rates of first marriage have been computed for selected nations in each of the world's continents. Wherever possible, rates

are presented for two dates—one early in the century and one for the 1950-1960 period. Tables 17-5 to 17-9 present the statistics, some of which are also presented graphically in Figures 17-2 to 17-10. The analysis is intended to be only illustrative rather than comprehensive. Two points are illustrated: (a) there is wide diversity over the world in age patterns of marriage rates and (b) all over the world the age patterns of marriage are changing—nations with young ages at marriage are tending toward an older pattern, and many nations with older ages at marriage are tending toward a younger pattern.

By contrasting the nuptiality rates for India, Japan, and Ireland, Table 17-5 and Figure 17-2 illustrate the great diversity in patterns of marriage rates that exists in the world today. India typifies the culture of female child marriage. Japan, in contrast, represents delayed marriage but in a cultural context where eventually almost all of the population marries. Ireland

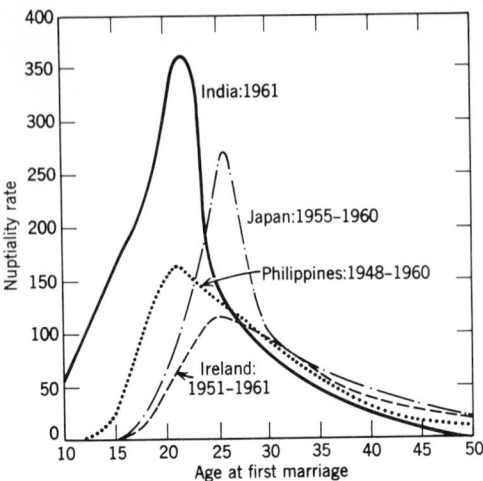

Figure 17-2 Diversity of Nuptiality Patterns in the World: Female Nuptiality Rates for Four Nations.

portrays in extreme form the European pattern of delayed marriage coupled with a high level of lifelong bachelorhood and spinsterhood. Figure 17-2 also graphs nuptiality rates for Philippines to show that not all developing nations have a pattern of child marriage. There can be no question that nation-to-nation variation in nuptiality is as great or greater than variation in mortality and fertility. The illustration above suggests the following hypoth-

esis: Nonindustrialized nations tend to have marriage rates that are high for females and reach a sharp peak in the age span 15 to 20 and then fall rapidly toward zero. Industrialized nations, in contrast, tend to have marriage rates that are low before age 17, reach a moderately high level in the mid-20's, and fall way more slowly. Our review of selected nations will tend to support this generalization, but will emphasize that many developing nations have nuptiality patterns surprisingly similar to those of the industrialized nations.

Given this hypothesis, the interesting question arises: did Europe once have child marriage as a part of its preindustrial culture? In other words, is abandonment of child marriage a normal or expected part of economic development? Fortunately, data are available for one nation that permit us to discuss this idea. Table 17-6 traces the trend of nuptiality in Sweden over one and one-half centuries, from 1800 to 1960. *The nuptiality pattern of Sweden in 1800 portrays later marriage and lower marriage rates than any of the European nations today.* (Compare with Table 17-8.) If child marriage were a part of the cultural pattern of preindustrial Sweden, it must have been well before this date. If these data can be taken as even crudely representative of marriage trends

Table 17-6 Nuptiality Rates for Sweden: 1800 to 1960

Age	1950-60 Male	1950-60 Female	1900-10 Male	1900-10 Female	1900 Male	1900 Female	1850 Male	1850 Female	1800 Male	1800 Female
15.............	0	1	0	0	0	0	0	0	0	0
16.............	0	6	0	2	0	4	0	2	0	2
17.............	1	23	0	8	1	9	0	8	1	9
18.............	10	52	2	21	3	18	1	16	9	17
19.............	29	84	6	40	7	29	6	26	18	27
20.............	40	113	11	49	13	41	14	38	42	39
21.............	52	148	25	57	28	56	24	54	50	55
22.............	71	174	48	65	56	70	37	71	66	72
23.............	102	187	66	78	74	82	55	86	80	85
24.............	130	192	82	90	84	91	75	101	92	96
25.............	151	190	90	99	92	98	93	112	100	104
26.............	164	174	93	100	97	102	108	122	107	110
27.............	149	160	97	91	101	96	122	122	112	108
28.............	133	144	99	85	104	89	135	118	116	104
29.............	122	131	102	78	107	82	146	113	119	99
30.............	111	117	104	72	103	76	155	107	121	95
31.............	100	101	104	66	99	70	163	101	122	90
32.............	90	82	95	62	95	64	122	95	123	86
33.............	82	63	83	57	91	58	110	88	122	82
34.............	73	56	74	52	86	53	102	81	121	77
35.............	65	50	70	46	81	48	97	74	119	73
36.............	58	47	66	40	76	44	94	67	115	69
37.............	52	44	60	34	70	40	93	59	110	64
38.............	46	43	55	29	65	36	92	52	104	60
39.............	40	39	51	26	59	32	91	45	89	55

Source: Computed from census data and smoothed.

in Europe since the early years of the industrial revolution, it must be inferred that the pattern of delaying marriage until age 18 or older among females and age 21 or older among males was firmly established in Northwest Europe before the industrial revolution reached major proportions. It is incorrect, therefore, to attribute this characteristic to urbanization, modernization, and the decline of feudalism.

Nevertheless, it is true that in Sweden there was a trend toward the greater postponement of marriage to even later dates and toward low marriage rates at all ages. This trend may indeed have been a product of the industrial revolution and may have represented an adjustment to changed social and economic conditions. It is important that this be seen only as an intensification of an already existing pattern, however. The movement toward marriage postponement reached its culmination in the late nineteenth century, and by 1900 a reversal had clearly set in among the younger generation. By the 1950-1960 decade, Sweden was enjoying a "marriage boom" at ages 19 to 25 that was unprecedented in its recorded statistical history. Figures 17-3 and 17-4 illustrate graphically the remarkable changes in the pattern of nuptiality rates that have taken place in Sweden since 1900. If we may generalize from these data, we may say that late marriage has been an integral part of the culture of industrialized nations even in their preindustrial

phase, but that throughout the nineteenth century marriage postponement was intensified, only to be reversed in the twentieth century. In the second half of the twentieth century there has been a dramatic shift toward earlier marriage. The shift is not toward true child marriage, but toward accepting ages 18 to 20 as the normal time for females to marry and ages 20 to 22 as the normal time for males to marry.

Selected nations of Asia. Pakistan is shown, in Table 17-7 and Figure 17-5, to have the same (or even greater) tendency toward female child marriage as India. In noting this, it should be kept in mind that there is much less child marriage for males; child brides are married to substantially older bridegrooms. It should also be noted that marriage rates for males remain high, both in India and Pakistan, throughout age 35.

Ceylon also has tendencies toward child marriage. The rates at the youngest ages are substantially lower than those for India and Pakistan, however. The data for the period 1901-1921 suggest that there has been a significant shift in Ceylon toward later marriage (Figure 17-6).

Philippines. Marriage rates in the Philippines are later and lower than in India and Pakistan, yet they are higher at young ages

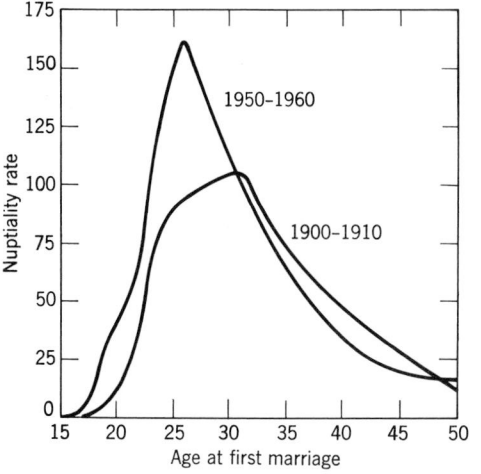

Figure 17-3 Change in Nuptiality Rates for Males in Sweden: 1900 to 1960.

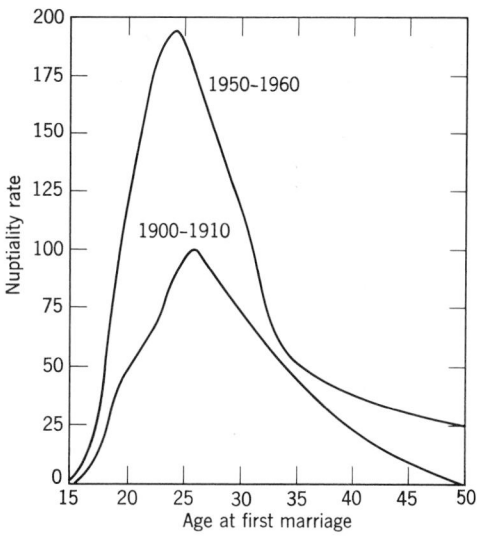

Figure 17-4 Change in Nuptiality Rates for Females in Sweden: 1900 to 1960.

Table 17-7   Age-Specific First-Marriage Rates for Selected Nations of Asia (Ceylon, Pakistan, Philippines)

Age	Ceylon				Pakistan		Philippines	
	1946–53		1901–21		1961		1948–60	
	Male	Female	Male	Female	Male	Female	Male	Female
15............	0	83	0	63	32	245	2	28
16............	3	109	6	177	42	260	7	52
17............	8	130	14	187	55	265	20	81
18............	16	147	27	186	80	262	46	113
19............	27	162	42	179	95	260	77	137
20............	37	177	53	170	110	253	95	154
21............	52	187	65	161	123	242	104	164
22............	67	182	76	147	136	215	114	154
23............	87	169	86	130	147	177	135	145
24............	111	156	95	108	162	145	159	139
25............	125	143	104	90	175	127	188	132
26............	134	131	111	79	186	110	208	125
27............	136	118	115	71	185	96	191	116
28............	136	108	114	65	175	82	164	109
29............	136	95	110	59	163	73	151	103
30............	134	85	105	54	157	63	147	95
31............	132	73	99	49	146	52	135	87
32............	128	63	92	45	135	45	128	79
33............	123	56	86	41	123	37	123	71
34............	116	49	78	37	109	30	116	62
35............	110	43	71	33	90	23	111	57
36............	100	37	63	28	82	18	106	50
37............	91	32	55	24	67	15	100	44
38............	81	27	49	20	57	12	94	38
39............	73	22	43	17	45	9	87	33

Note: Rates for Pakistan, single years form 10 to 14 are as follows:
      Male: 12, 13, 15, 19, 24.
      Females: 70, 80, 110, 158, 203.

than for Europe. Thus it is a clear intermediate type of moderately early and almost universal marriage.

Selected nations of Europe. Data for the recent past and for an earlier date near the turn of the century are presented for several nations of Europe in Table 17-8. In all cases the overall pattern is the same: an earlier condition of low nuptiality followed by a recent "marriage

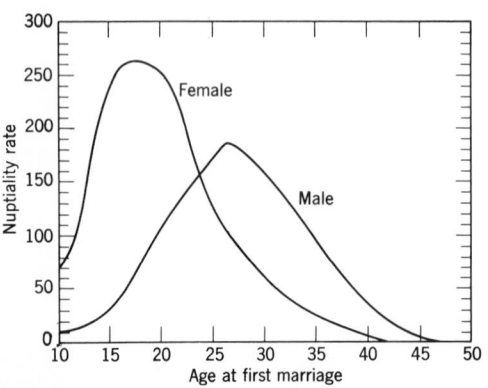

Figure 17-5   Nuptiality Rates for Pakistan: 1961.

boom." Yet there are substantial nation-to-nation variations and differences. England and Wales manifest the greatest tendency toward earlier marriage, followed in order by France, Germany, and Austria. (Figures 17-7, 17-8, and 17-9 illustrate this trend for females.) Ireland has by far the lowest and latest marriage rate, but a very dramatic "marriage boom" has taken place here also, as the data of Table 17-5 and Figure 17-10 demonstrate.

Australia presents a pattern of nuptiality similar to that of England and Wales (Table 17-9). Like the mother nation, she is experiencing a rise in rates and a shift toward earlier marriage since 1911-1921. Both today and earlier, Australians seem to have been more inclined to postpone marriage than have been the English.

Africa: Egypt. Lack of census data make it difficult to measure marriage rates for African nations. However, data for Egypt are presented in Table 17-9. Egypt has a pattern of moderately early marriage for females and of unusually late marriage for males.

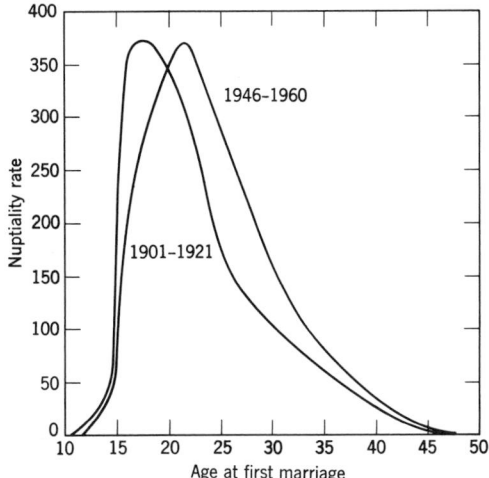

Figure 17-6 Change in Nuptiality Rates for Females in Ceylon: 1900 to 1960.

Latin America. The technique of estimating nuptiality rates from census age data used here yields ambiguous results when applied to most nations of Latin America. This results from the phenomenon of "conviviente" or consensual union, not recognized as true marriage in many censuses. For this reason, no attempt has been made here to study nuptiality in Latin America.

Although the evidence is far from complete, there is much reason to suspect that the marriage patterns of the world are converging. Developing nations with a pattern of child or

Table 17-8 Nuptiality Rates for Selected Nations of Europe (Austria and England): Current and Recent Changes

Age	Austria				England and Wales			
	1900–10		1951–61		1911–21		1961	
	Male	Female	Male	Female	Male	Female	Male	Female
15.............	0	1	0	4	0	0	0	3
16.............	0	3	1	13	0	3	5	16
16.............	0	7	2	31	1	10	12	43
18.............	1	19	12	58	10	29	25	97
19.............	2	32	25	88	24	49	43	148
20.............	2	41	37	110	38	63	85	212
21.............	6	51	49	124	52	77	125	227
22.............	27	63	73	134	70	92	148	228
23.............	55	77	106	144	93	105	167	222
24.............	73	92	134	156	121	115	173	200
25.............	81	103	158	170	138	128	172	175
26.............	87	109	166	176	148	133	160	138
27.............	91	104	168	175	146	119	133	106
28.............	94	99	162	161	141	105	117	85
29.............	100	92	157	149	134	95	105	70
30.............	110	85	150	113	125	84	97	60
31.............	116	77	145	84	116	76	87	53
32.............	106	69	139	70	107	69	80	45
33.............	91	61	132	62	98	62	72	38
34.............	81	52	125	56	85	55	65	32
35.............	76	43	117	50	75	49	58	27
36.............	71	37	108	45	68	44	52	24
37.............	68	33	102	41	60	39	48	19
38.............	62	29	97	37	55	36	43	15
39.............	56	25	88	34	51	31	34	12

Table 17-8   *(Continued)*

Age	France 1954-62 Male	France 1954-62 Female	France 1901-11 Male	France 1901-11 Female	Germany 1950-61 Male	Germany 1950-61 Female	Germany 1900-10 Male	Germany 1900-10 Female
15.............	0	6	1	9	0	2	0	0
16.............	0	17	1	21	0	9	0	4
17.............	0	40	2	41	1	25	0	10
18.............	2	77	3	70	11	54	2	30
19.............	6	126	3	101	25	93	5	55
20.............	12	165	4	120	40	123	9	75
21.............	27	185	6	128	57	138	25	93
22.............	45	190	9	134	77	148	57	107
23.............	77	186	25	139	100	157	96	120
24.............	132	179	69	144	132	169	130	145
25.............	172	172	113	148	164	187	143	169
26.............	165	162	143	151	172	200	151	177
27.............	155	150	170	135	176	195	153	158
28.............	147	128	182	110	180	157	154	132
29.............	135	106	164	93	182	130	152	118
30.............	125	88	149	82	185	110	150	105
31.............	112	73	135	73	187	95	143	95
32.............	100	60	122	65	184	82	132	82
33.............	81	52	109	57	176	73	115	70
34.............	73	45	99	50	162	64	95	58
35.............	64	37	88	44	147	56	77	49
36.............	56	32	78	39	135	48	72	43
37.............	50	27	69	35	123	43	66	37
38.............	45	25	61	30	112	35	61	34
39.............	42	22	53	27	104	29	55	30

very early marriage are drifting toward a pattern of later marriage. This is an adjustment that is a part of a huge overall effort to lessen fertility and improve the level of living. Industrialized nations that have had a tradition of late marriage have shifted toward much earlier marriage—both because their economies can now "afford" this type of luxury and because modern methods of contraception permit earlier marriage without the necessity of early onset of childbearing. However, despite the fact that the range of variation in marriage pat-

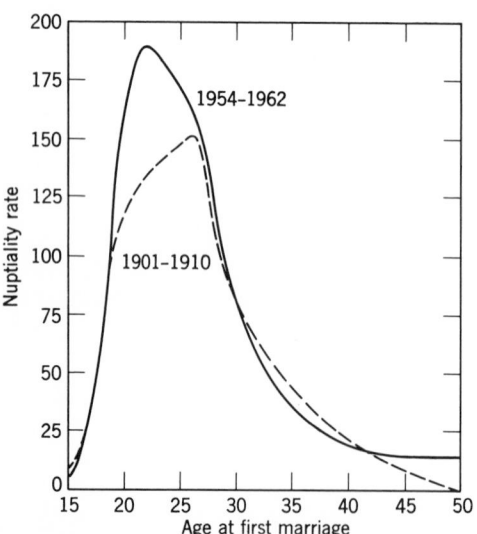

Figure 17-7 Change in Nuptiality Rates for Females in France: 1901 to 1962.

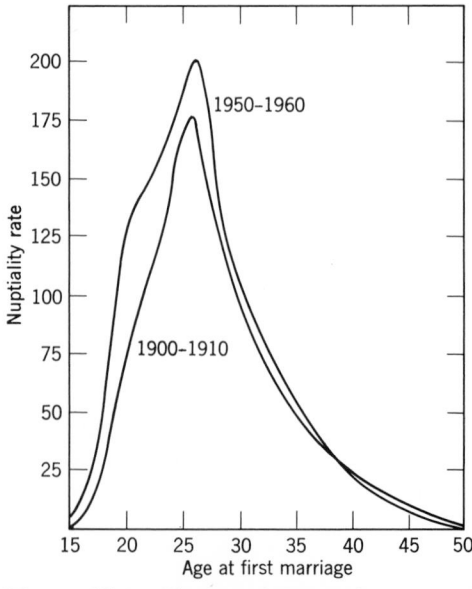

Figure 17-8 Change in Nuptiality Rates for Females in Germany: 1900 to 1960.

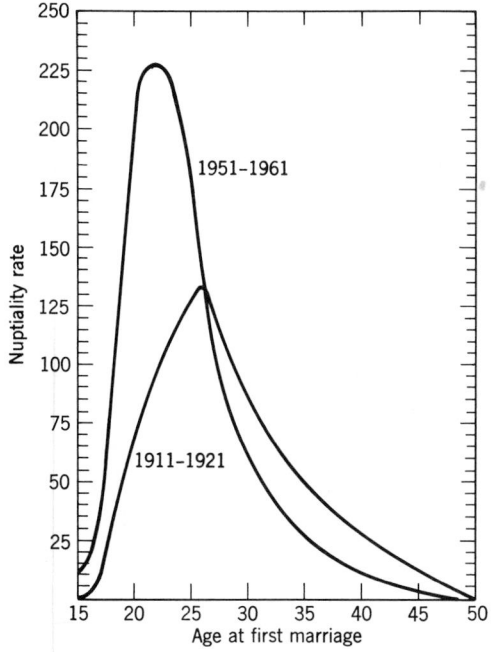

Figure 17-9 Change in Nuptiality Rates for Females in England and Wales: 1911 to 1961.

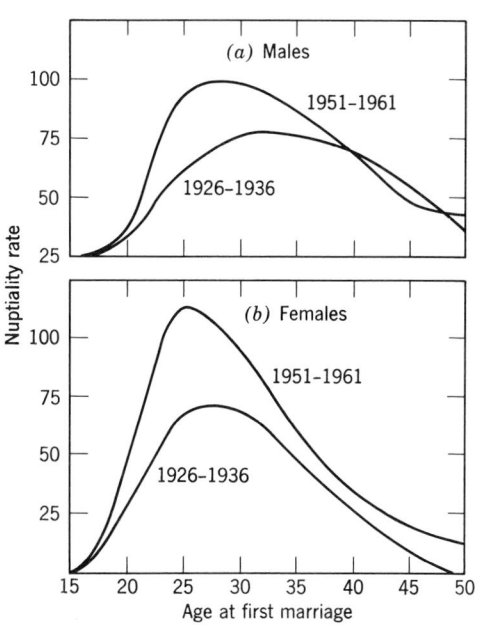

Figure 17-10 Change in Nuptiality Rates in Ireland: 1926 to 1961.

Table 17-9 Age-Specific First-Marriage Rates for Egypt and Australia

Age	Egypt		Australia			
	1947-60		1911-21		1954-61	
	Male	Female	Male	Female	Male	Female
15.............	0	0	0	2	1	7
16.............	1	21	1	11	2	22
17.............	2	72	2	27	5	51
18.............	6	142	9	46	20	91
19.............	15	192	19	70	56	145
20.............	25	204	28	82	77	201
21.............	38	207	39	92	87	241
22.............	53	206	55	101	95	252
23.............	67	203	78	110	123	241
24.............	84	196	95	118	150	238
25.............	107	189	107	128	176	205
26.............	133	181	110	132	189	176
27.............	152	173	110	118	167	150
28.............	165	164	108	104	136	129
29.............	174	155	104	96	112	113
30.............	180	146	102	89	101	104
31.............	184	138	98	83	93	97
32.............	187	130	94	76	86	86
33.............	189	123	89	70	78	71
34.............	187	115	83	65	71	59
35.............	177	107	77	58	64	55
36.............	167	99	72	52	59	54
37.............	155	91	65	47	54	51
38.............	142	83	61	42	50	47
39.............	130	75	56	37	46	45

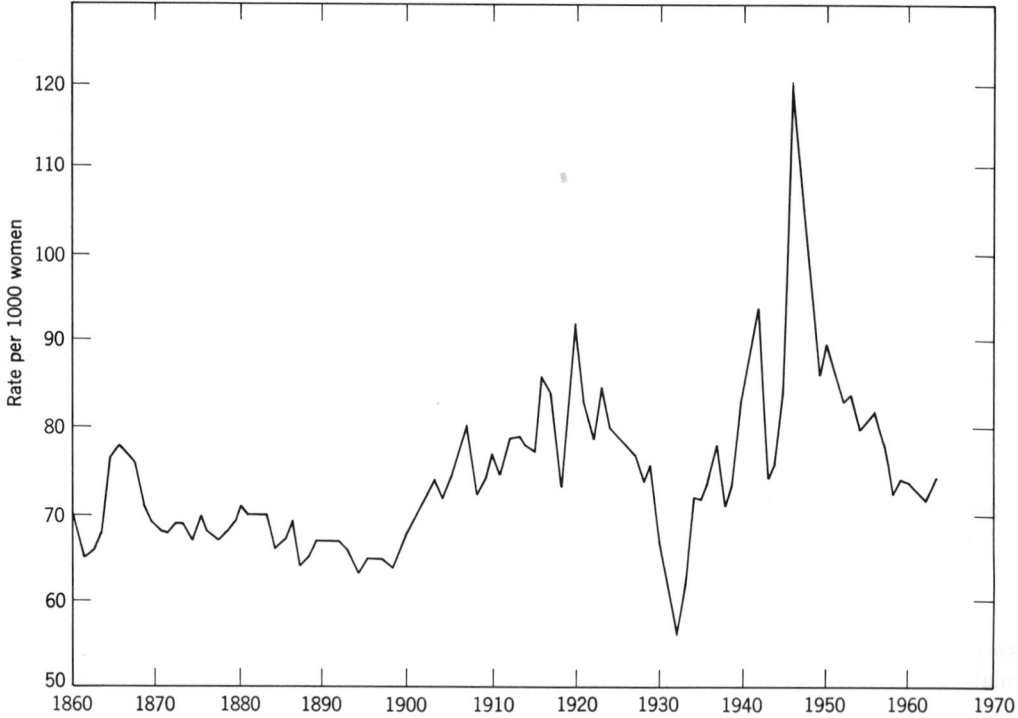

Figure 17-11   Estimated Nubile Marriage Rate per 1000 Unmarried Women 15 Years of Age and Over; United States: 1860 to 1963.

terns is diminishing, there is little reason to suspect that such variation will disappear entirely. The comparative international study of marriage patterns, and explanations for those patterns, will remain a major field of demographic endeavor for many years.

17.7. Nuptiality in the United States

Figure 17-11 shows the trend in the nubile marriage rate in the United States during the century from 1860 to 1960, and on until 1963. It is immediately apparent that the marriage rate is quite volatile; it fluctuates from year to year—apparently in response to changing environmental conditions. When conditions for marriage are favorable, a higher proportion of the eligible bachelors and bachelorettes venture into matrimony, but when conditions are unfavorable, they postpone marriage. If we follow these data through, year by year, it may readily be seen that wars and economic depressions both leave a very strong impress on

the marriage rate. But it is equally clear that these alone are not enough to explain the fluctuations; there is in addition a steady upward secular trend in the propensity to marry, especially since 1932. It is quite possible that there is a special social factor, a "marriage climate" that operates to affect the propensity to marry—independently of economic and political conditions. If it exists, this climate would take the form of attitudes about how appropriate it is for a girl to marry before age 20 and whether or not college students should postpone marriage until after graduation. Jacobson,[2] who has made a special study of marriage trends, believes that changing social and economic conditions affect especially the ability of divorced and widowed persons to remarry.

He has constructed estimates of marriages per 1000 unmarried population for each year between 1860 and 1920, when the vital statis-

[2] Paul H. Jacobson and Pauline F. Jacobson, *American Marriage and Divorce* (New York: Rinehart and Company, 1959), pp. 23–24.

tics series begins. The following 10-year summary reveals the trends in broad outline:

Marriages per 1000 unmarried females over 15

1960-63	72.6
1950-59	81.1
1940-49	92.1
1930-39	68.8
1920-29	80.3
1910-19	78.5
1900-09	73.4
1890-99	65.5
1880-89	67.9
1870-79	68.3
1860-69	72.2

Apparently, after the Civil War there was a slow decline in marriage rates that reached a climax in the 1890 period. Beginning in this century, there was a gradual rise in marriage rates that reached a peak in the period of prosperity following World War I. The decade of the 1930s was one of great economic depression, and marriage rates fell back to the low level of 1870-1879. During and immediately after World War II, however, the marriage reached an all-time high—partially to compensate for the postponement of marriage during the economic depression. The 1950s exhibited rates that were reminiscent of the 1920s. However, in 1957 the rate again began to decline and has declined slowly but rather steadily since then.

The exact meaning of the recent decline is not fully clear yet. On the one hand, large numbers of persons began entering the 15 to 17 age category about 1960, and this has the tendency to inflate the denominator of the rate with persons who are not yet truly eligible to marry. Moreover, the rate must slacken eventually because the median age at first marriage has stopped declining (Chapter 11). The fact that the median age at first marriage has risen since 1960 suggests that there has been a genuine decline in the propensity to marry. In 1965 marriage rates were at such a low level that one must go back to the early 1900s to find comparably low rates during times of economic prosperity. It may be, however, that conditions will stabilize at about the 1965 level, on an age-specific basis.

Wars also affect marriage rates. In 1940 and 1941, when it became apparent that the United States would intervene in the European conflict, marriage rates rose quickly. As large numbers of men were shipped overseas for combat duty in 1942-1944, the rates sank. But they rose to an all-time high in 1945 and throughout 1946 and 1947 as demobilization was accomplished. The Korean War stimulated a similar though smaller cycle.

To give greater detail to the history of nuptiality in the United States, age-specific nuptiality rates have been calculated for each decade 1920 to 1960, by sex and color. These were derived from census data by the same procedure used to develop Tables 17-5 to 17-9. The results are reported in Tables 17-10 and 17-11. For an interpretation, the reader is referred to Exercise 5 at the end of the chapter.

Table 17-12 reports the nubile marriage rate and the general marriage rate for the United States 1940 to 1963. The right-hand column of this table shows the ratio of one rate to the other; the fact that it does not remain constant over time demonstrates the superiority of the GMR over the NMR. Whereas the NMR indicates that the propensity to marry is lower in the 1960s than in the early 1940s, the GMR indicates exactly the opposite. What has happened is that the increasing longevity of women has led to the accumulation of large numbers of widows at the older ages, who enter into the denominator of NMR but are excluded from the GMR.

17.8. Teenage Marriage

One aspect of the declining average age at marriage has been the rapid rise in "teenage marriages," which family experts tend to identify as marriages where either the bride, the bridegroom, or both are 19 years of age or younger at time of marriage. For a variety of reasons, such marriages are regarded as socially undesirable, especially if the bride is 17 years of age or younger. It has been found repeatedly in studies, both in Europe and in the United States, that in such marriages the divorce rate is much higher, the level of marital satisfaction and happiness with the spouse is lower, and a

Table 17-10   Age-Specific First-Marriage Rates for the United States White
Population: 1920 to 1960

Age	1950-60		1940-50		1930-40		1920-30	
	Male	Female	Male	Female	Male	Female	Male	Female
15............	5	28	0	23	0	17	0	18
16............	9	50	7	39	4	30	4	39
17............	23	100	18	70	12	58	9	78
18............	43	176	36	145	22	98	17	108
19............	73	213	72	174	38	121	35	124
20............	145	237	108	193	60	136	74	131
21............	180	250	136	204	86	147	93	137
22............	203	258	154	212	104	156	108	141
23............	215	228	168	215	119	155	118	142
24............	198	200	179	210	130	150	125	141
25............	178	178	187	204	139	142	128	137
26............	161	155	184	195	139	128	131	134
27............	145	137	178	188	136	104	130	128
28............	132	120	170	155	132	84	127	121
29............	118	107	157	130	126	70	120	112
30............	108	95	131	120	117	60	112	102
31............	97	84	118	95	104	51	101	92
32............	88	75	106	84	86	45	91	82
33............	80	65	96	74	72	40	82	74
34............	73	57	88	67	62	36	75	66
35............	67	50	82	61	54	32	67	58
36............	62	46	77	55	48	29	62	51
37............	56	41	73	48	43	27	57	45
38............	52	38	69	43	39	25	53	39
39............	48	35	65	37	36	24	49	34
40............	43	31	...	...	...	...	...	...
41............	40	29	...	...	...	...	...	...
42............	37	26	...	...	...	...	...	...
43............	34	24	...	...	...	...	...	...
44............	32	22	...	...	...	...	...	...
45............	29	21	...	...	...	...	...	...
46............	28	20	...	...	...	...	...	...
47............	25	18	...	...	...	...	...	...
48............	23	17	...	...	...	...	...	...
49............	22	16	...	...	...	...	...	...

higher proportion of couples regret having chosen the mate they did than in marriages contracted at a later date.[3]

One of the leading concerns of family research now is to study this phenomenon of "child marriage" in industrially advanced societies in an effort to explain it. The demographic characteristics of the persons who enter such marriages are of interest. Burchinall has reported the following traits of young marriages:

1. A high proportion of young brides have

[3] J. Joel Moss, "Teen-age Marriage: Cross-National Trends and Sociological Factors in the Decision of When to Marry," *Marriage and Family Living,* **27** (May 1965), 230–241. Lee G. Burchinal, "Trends and Prospects for Young Marriages in the United States," *Marriage and Family Living,* **27** (May 1965), 243–262. Thomas P. Monohan, "Does Age at Marriage Matter in Divorce?" *Social Forces,* **32** (October 1963), 81–87.

an older husband; the difference in age is substantially greater than for adult marriages.

2. One-third to one-half of all young marriages involve premarital pregnancies. (In adult marriages, about 20 percent of United States brides are pregnant at the time of marriage.)

3. Both the bride and her husband are below average in educational level. Teenage marriages are especially prevalent among school dropouts. There appears to be a reciprocal relationship between dropping out and early marriage.

4. A disproportionately large share of teenage marriages involve children whose parents are from the lower working class.

5. The occupation of the bridegroom also tends to be low in the socioeconomic scale—unskilled or semiskilled work and a low income.

6. An above-average proportion of such

Table 17-11 Age-Specific First-Marriage Rates for the United States Nonwhite
Population: 1920 to 1960

Age	1950-60		1940-50		1930-40		1920-30	
	Male	Female	Male	Female	Male	Female	Male	Female
15............	3	40	2	43	2	40	2	41
16............	7	58	7	66	5	72	5	81
17............	22	97	20	136	15	131	20	145
18............	52	156	44	162	30	157	47	185
19............	96	182	110	176	80	164	107	192
20............	132	176	142	186	116	162	124	180
21............	153	170	157	187	134	157	130	170
22............	166	161	164	184	145	148	131	160
23............	160	152	161	173	144	138	127	152
24............	145	140	154	163	138	125	118	144
25............	132	130	147	152	128	112	110	137
26............	117	117	140	141	116	99	102	130
27............	102	107	134	132	104	86	93	122
28............	90	96	126	123	93	75	85	115
29............	80	85	120	115	83	65	80	109
30............	71	77	114	107	74	57	75	102
31............	63	68	108	100	64	50	70	96
32............	57	60	103	94	57	44	66	90
33............	52	52	97	88	50	38	61	83
34............	46	46	93	82	44	34	57	77
35............	41	40	88	77	39	30	53	71
36............	36	35	84	73	34	26	48	67
37............	32	31	80	69	30	24	45	60
38............	28	26	77	66	27	21	42	55
39............	24	23	74	63	24	19	39	50
40............	22	19	...	...	...	...	...	...
41............	19	16	...	...	...	...	...	...
42............	17	13	...	...	...	...	...	...
43............	14	11	...	...	...	...	...	...
44............	13	9	...	...	...	...	...	...
45............	12	8	...	...	...	...	...	...
46............	10	6	...	...	...	...	...	...
47............	8	5	...	...	...	...	...	...
48............	8	5	...	...	...	...	...	...
49............	6	4	...	...	...	...	...	...

couples begin their married life living in the household of one of their parents.

However, these differences probably all existed before the recent upswing in teenage marriage; it is entirely possible that teenage marriage simply has affected all demographic strata alike while preserving old differentials. Intensive demographic research into change in these differentials is needed. Also, theories explaining why youths of all classes are more prone to marry at an earlier age now than only two decades ago need to be formulated and tested. Moss presents a list of sociological hypotheses derived from the changing nature of modern culture and social organization, while Burchinal presents a list of more psychological hypotheses.[4] Both avenues of study need to be explored, based on a solid demographic

foundation of facts about differential changes in teenage marriage. Premarital pregnancy is undoubtedly one of the major reasons for marrying especially among the very young. Yet vital statistics are unavailable in most countries. Nieminen traced the proportion of new marriages in which children were born less then 8 months after the day of marriage in Finland from 1939 to 1961.[5] He discovered an overall rate of about 36 percent for the postwar years. During the 1940s premarital rates were more common in rural than in urban areas, but since then the rates have tended to become equal. His statistics show that premarital pregnancy is concentrated among younger women and that 40 percent of all marriages of women under 25 years of age involve premarital pregnancy. In a very high proportion of cases,

[4] Moss, op. cit., and Burchinal, op. cit.

[5] Armas Nieminen, "Premarital Pregnancy in Finland," Acta Sociologica (1964), 225–264.

Table 17-12 Nubile Marriage Rate and
General Marriage Rate for the United States:
1940 to 1963

Year	Nubile marriage rate A	General marriage rate B	Ratio B/A
1963.........	73.4	143.3	1.95
1962.........	71.2	138.4	1.94
1961.........	72.2	145.4	2.01
1960.........	73.5	148.0	2.01
1959.........	73.6	149.8	2.04
1958.........	72.0	146.3	2.03
1957.........	78.0	157.4	2.02
1956.........	82.4	165.6	2.01
1955.........	80.9	161.1	1.99
1954.........	79.8	154.3	1.93
1953.........	83.7	163.3	1.95
1952.........	83.2	159.9	1.92
1951.........	86.6	164.9	1.90
1950.........	90.2	166.4	1.84
1949.........	86.7	158.0	1.82
1948.........	98.5	174.7	1.77
1947.........	106.2	182.7	1.72
1946.........	118.1	199.0	1.69
1945.........	83.6	138.2	1.65
1944.........	76.5	124.5	1.63
1943.........	83.0	133.5	1.61
1942.........	93.0	147.6	1.59
1941.........	88.5	138.4	1.56
1940.........	82.8	127.4	1.53

marriages have occurred between 5 and 6 months before delivery. Thus it can be seen that the desire to legitimize the unborn child is a very strong reason for getting married. These statistics reveal that, in Finnish society at least, the frequency of intercourse before marriage is high; the quantity of such intercourse involving the use of contraceptives and induced abortion is unknown. It is also very clear that in modern industrial society the childbearing function is a very powerful force in family formation. The idea that the child needs both parents and that the parents should live together to form a family is an integral part of the culture and probably is as strong now as at any previous date. This is a fact that "companionship" theories of modern marriage may overlook. It may very well be that the family is the center of gravity of marriage, rather than the reverse.

17.9. Differentials in Marriage Patterns

It is well known that some socioeconomic groups within a population tend to marry much earlier than others. These differentials are difficult to measure, however, because the method of using census data fails when applied to particular subgroupings other than age, ethnic groups, race, or any traits that the individual is not free to change as he grows older. An alternative source of differential marriage data are special surveys in which the characteristics of recently married persons are compared with the characteristics of the general population. In particular, it is possible to ask persons to report retrospectively their age at the time of their first marriage.

Occupational Differentials. It has been found almost universally that persons standing high in the socioeconomic scale marry at a later age than persons in other socioeconomic strata. This is due, in part, to the necessity of remaining in school for a longer term of years in order to qualify for a profession. This differential is of long standing. For example, E. Grebenik and Griselda Rowntree extracted from the 1884-1885 report of the Registrar General of Great Britain the average age at marriage in the years 1884-1885 for occupational groups, as reported in Table 17-13.[6] The difference in average age at marriage between blue-collar workers and white-collar (especially professional) workers is substantial. Also, this table establishes that in England, as in Sweden and Switzerland, late marriage was characteristic in the middle of the nineteenth century.

Grebenick and Rowntree also examined data from a marriage survey taken in 1959-1960. They found that interclass differences of the same type still persist, although they are reduced. They also found that when marriages occur between members of different social classes the age at marriage is affected. The lower-status party tends to marry at an older age and the higher-status party at a younger age than if either had married within his own group. This differential was much more pronounced among marriages contracted before 1940 than among those contracted since. However, they find that the oldest age at marriage continues to be for persons from white-collar families marrying someone from another

[6] E. Grebenik and Griselda Rowntree, "Factors Associated with the Age at Marriage in Britain," *Proceedings of the Royal Society of London*, Series B, *Biological Sciences*, **159** (97) (1964), 178–197.

Table 17-13 Average Age at Marriage in Britain of Bachelors and Spinsters Marrying in 1884 to 1885 Classified by Occupation of the Groom

Occupation of groom	Spinsters	Bachelors	Age difference
Miners............................	22.46	24.06	1.60
Textile hands......................	23.43	24.38	.95
Shoemakers and tailors.............	24.31	24.92	.61
Artisans...........................	23.70	25.35	1.65
Labourers..........................	23.66	25.56	1.90
Commercial clerks..................	24.43	26.25	1.82
Shopkeepers, shopmen...............	24.42	26.67	2.25
Farmers and sons...................	26.91	29.23	2.32
Professional and independent.......	26.40	31.22	4.82

Source: E. Grebenik and Griselda Rowntree, "Factors Associated with the Age at Marriage in Britain." Proceedings of the Royal Society of London, Vol. 159, Series B. Biological Sciences, No. 974, 19 December, 1963, p. 182.

white-collar household and where in addition the bridegroom himself is a white-collar worker.

Data similar to those for England were collected collaboratively by the National Center for Health Statistics and the U.S. Bureau of the Census. In the June 1958 Current Population Survey a sample of recently married persons were asked to report their age at the time of their marriage. The results, tabulated by occupation, are reported in Table 17-14. The differentials are similar to those of England in 1885. The earliest marriages occur among the agricultural population, laborers, and operatives. Professional and managerial workers have the latest age at marriage. The differentials between the upper blue-collar and lower white-collar strata are small and inconsistent. Contrary to what would be expected in a straightforward social class theory, craft workers tend to marry later than clerical workers. Table 17-14 reports only marriages where the wife is not in the labor force. Where the wife is in the labor force, the differentials in age at marriage are reduced almost to zero.

Educational Attainment Differentials. Christopher Tietze and Patience Lauriat calculated the mean age at marriage for the white population of the United States, 1940 and 1950, after adjusting the younger age groups for eventual educational attainment. They found a significantly later average age at marriage for high school graduates and persons who had attended college than for persons of less education. An exception was found for the very small group (less than 2 percent of the total) who had not completed one year of school; this group has an unusually high average age at mar-

Table 17-14 Median Age at Marriage by Major Occupation Group of Husband at Date of Survey for Persons Married between January 1955 and June 1958 (Wife Not in Labor Force at Time of Survey)

Occupation of husband	Husband	Wife	Difference
All occupations groups..............	23.1	19.8	3.3
Professional, technical, and kindred workers.........	24.0	21.3	2.7
Farmers and farm laborers...........................	21.2	18.4	2.8
Managers, officials, and proprietors, except farm....	24.0	20.6	3.4
Clerical and kindred workers........................	22.8	19.8	3.0
Sales workers.......................................	24.3	20.8	3.5
Craftsmen, foremen, and kindred workers.............	23.8	20.1	3.7
Operatives and kindred workers......................	22.4	18.9	3.5
Service workers.....................................	23.6	20.0	3.6
Laborers, except farm and mine.....................	22.2	19.1	3.1

Source: National Center for Health Statistics, "Demographic Characteristics of Persons Married Between January 1955 and June 1958; United States;" Series 21, No. 2, April, 1965, Table K.

riage. The sudden drop in the age at marriage that took place during the 1940-1950 decade affected all educational levels, but was more pronounced among the upper educational groups, so that the educational differential was smaller in 1950 than it had been in 1940.

Income Differentials. The U. S. Bureau of the Census obtained information in 1948 concerning the median age at first marriage among men who had been married less than 5 years. When these data were classified by the current income of the husband, it was found that men whose current income was low had married at a much younger age and men whose earnings were large had married at a much older age. Thus the men who postponed their marriage were able, on the average, to enjoy a larger income during the early years of their marriage. John Hajnal has studied the changing marriage patterns of Sweden, Switzerland, and Australia by socioeconomic groups for the years of the "marriage boom"–1935-1950.[7] He finds that the following generalizations apply to the industrialized nations of the world.

1. The upswing in marriage rates has been greater in urban than in rural areas.

2. The upswing in marriage rates has been greater among the more educated than among the less educated.

3. The upswing in marriage rates has been greater among employers than among employees.

He finds the greatest changes in exactly those groups that previously had been most inclined to postpone marriage.

17.10.   Interethnic and Interracial Marriages

Interracial marriages in the United States are comparatively rare, with the exception of Hawaii. Moreover, it is exceedingly difficult to obtain information concerning them. One of the most informative studies is that of John H. Burma, who searched more than 375,000 marriage licenses for Los Angeles County for the

period 1948-1959, where a rather careful record of the race of bride and bridegroom had been recorded. He found only 3150 instances in which persons of different race had applied for a marriage certificate. The rate of intermarriage in 1959 was only 16 per thousand marriages, but had risen from 6 per thousand in 1950-1951. The largest number of these marriages were between whites and Negroes, but the highest rates of interracial marriage were among Japanese, Chinese, Filipino, and American Indian groups. White females were more inclined to contract interracial marriages than white males. For Negroes this was reversed: the probability that a Negro male would enter into an interracial marriage was found to be roughly four times that for a Negro female. Intermarried couples were found to be somewhat older on the average than persons intramarrying. Except for white persons, a disproportionately large share of the intermarrying persons had been previously married and divorced.

It is known that there are very wide differences between countries in the rate of interracial marriage. In Brazil, for example, marriage is said to take place with little reference to race or ethnic origin, whereas in South Africa the reverse situation prevails. In the United States, until recently many of the states had laws banning interracial marriage, and these were dissolved only because of federal legislation forbidding them. Hawaii, which has long been a "melting pot", has much racial intermarriage. Schmitt reports a long-term increase in the rate of intermarriage from 11.5 percent in 1916 to 38.5 percent in 1963.[8] He found that interracial marriages tended to occur between persons who were below 20 years of age and between those in middle age. There is a very strong inverse relationship between socioeconomic status and intermarriage: those lowest in status have the highest rates of intermarriage. Schmitt concludes that the rate of intermarriage is affected by the availability of marriage partners (races with a heavy sex imbalance must cross racial lines to find a mate),

---

[7] John Hajnal, "Analysis of Changes in the marriage Pattern by Economic Groups," *American Sociological Review,* **19** (1954), 295–302; John Hajnal, "Differential Changes in Marriage Patterns," *American Sociological Review,* **19** (April 1954), 148–154.

[8] Robert C. Schmitt, "Demographic Correlates of Interracial Marriages in Hawaii," *Demography,* **2** (1965), 466.

the relative size of the racial groups, and the level of racial prejudice and residential segregation.

The conditions that favor racial intermarriage are clearly on the increase in the United States. Segregation is on the decline and propinquity among those of nubile ages is rising; the races are thrown together informally at school, at work, and in places of public recreation as never before. Racial differences in educational level, income level, and occupation are diminishing. Public sensitivity to differences in color is being dulled. There is an increasing shortage of marriageable men, which increases the incentive for white women to cross the race lines. It is difficult to predict how high the rate of racial intermarriage will rise, but it is now so low that it can move only in one direction.

17.11. Interreligous Marriages

Just as there tends to be racial and social-class homogamy, so there also tends to be religious homogamy. In March 1957 the U.S. Bureau of the Census asked a question on religious affiliation for a sample of 35,000 households. By comparing the religious affiliation of the wife with that of the husband, it was possible to learn the prevalence of mixed marriages. In terms of the three major religious groups—Catholic, Protestant, and Jewish—it was found that 94 percent of the married partners belong to the same religion. Contrasting what actually occurred with what potentially could have occurred if mating had taken place on a random basis, Glick found the following ratios of actual to possible expected intermarriage:[9]

Catholics intermarrying with other religions—
    26 percent of possible
Protestant intermarrying with non-Protestant—
    19 percent of possible
Jewish intermarrying with non-Jewish—7 percent of possible

Thus he concludes that religious intermarriage is much less frequent than is possible. If people had married without regard to religion, only

56 percent would have had a spouse of the same religion. Persons of Jewish faith are by far the more endogamous of the religious groups, with Catholics being a little more prone than the Protestants to marry outside their faith.

In a study of interreligious marriages in the state of Iowa from 1953 to 1957, Burchinal and Chancelor found that the rate of religious intermarriage was highest for couples where the bride was unusually young and for couples where the status of the bridegroom was unusually low. Thus the highest rate of religious intermarriage was found among the youngest and lowest-status couples, and the lowest rates of intermarriage were observed among high-status couples where both spouses were older than 20 years of age.[10]

Sociologists have noted that interethnic marriages are more frequent than interreligious marriages and have spoken of the multiple "melting pot" hypothesis.[11] Implicit in this hypothesis is the notion that the population is more willing to marry across ethnic lines than across religious lines. As yet this assertion is ambiguous, except for the Jewish population. Because Protestant and Catholic categories are much larger than ethnic groups, even on the basis of random mating there would be a higher proportion of intrafaith marriages. Moreover, recent studies of religious homogamous marriages have shown that where interfaith marriages do occur, one partner or the other is converted to a different religion in a substantial proportion of cases.[12] Both of these factors operate to exaggerate or produce an inflated picture of religious homogamy of marriage. In a study of intermarriage in Detroit, Besanceney found that about 60 percent of interreligious

---

[9] Paul C. Glick, "Intermarriage and Fertility Patterns Among Persons of Major Religious Groups, *Eugenics Quarterly*, **7** (March 1960), 31–38.

[10] Lee Burchinal and Loren E. Chancelor, "Ages at Marriage, Occupations of Grooms, and Interreligious Marriage Rate, *Social Forces*, **40** (1961), 348.

[11] Ruby Jo Reeves Kennedy, "Single or Triple Melting Pot? Intermarriage Trends in New Haven, 1870–1940," *American Journal of Sociology*, **49** (1944), 331–339.

[12] Gerhard Lenski, *The Religious Factor: A Sociological Study of Religion's Impact on Politics, Economics, and Family Life* (Garden City, N. J.: Doubleday and Co., 1961), 49.

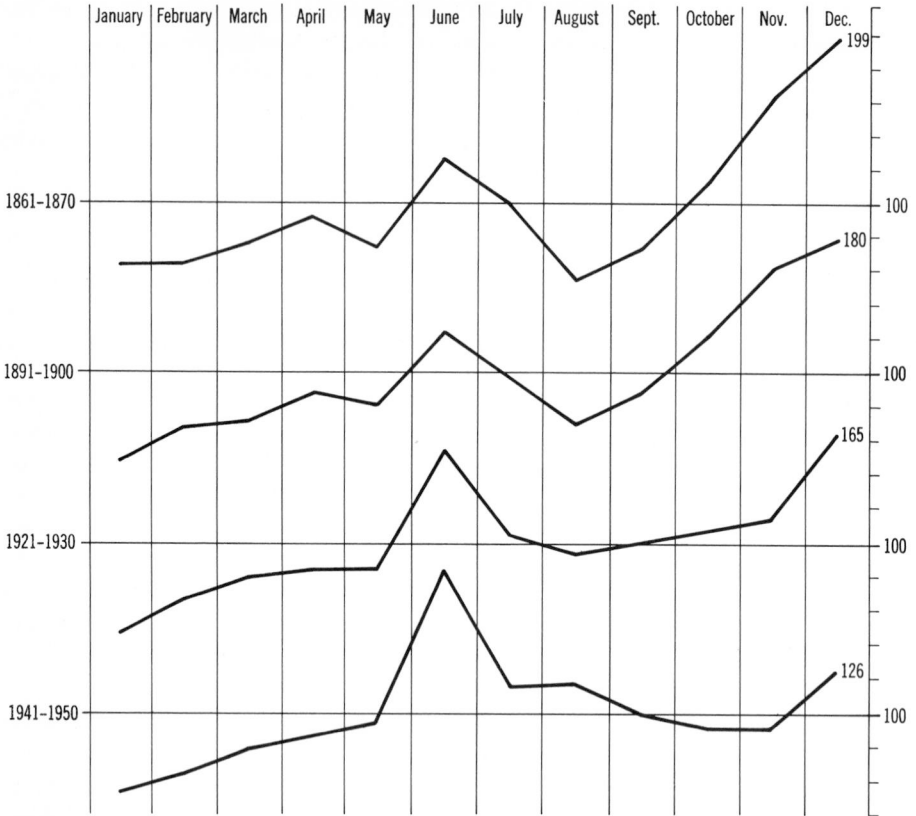

Figure 17-12   Relative Distribution of Marriages by Month in Finland: 1861 to 1950.

SOURCE: Rollin Chambliss, "Contributions of the Vital Statistics of Finland to the Study of Factors That Induce Marriage," *American Sociological Review*, **22** (February 1957), 38–48.

marriages had been made homogamous by conversion of one partner or the other.[13]

17.12.   Seasonality of Marriage

The season of marriage has been traced in Finland for a period of 90 years by Chambliss.[14] His data, adjusted for number of days in the month and converted to an index summarizing ten years of experience, are shown in Figure 17-12. A century ago in Finland, November and December were the favorite months for marriage, with a secondary emphasis on June. May, August, and September (months of

[13] Paul H. Besanceney, "On Reporting Rates of Intermarriage," *American Journal of Sociology*, **70** (May 1965), 721.

[14] Rollin Chambliss, "Contributions of the Vital Statistics of Finland to the Study of Factors that Induce Marriage," *American Sociological Review*, **22** (February 1957), 38–48.

planting and harvesting) were months of low marriage rates. Gradually the summer months have gained popularity so that June is by far the favored month, followed by other summer months and by December. Chambliss attributes the change to urbanization. In the rural economy, the farm population tended to marry after the harvest was in and before regular work in the forests began in January. Urbanization has brought with it the custom of marriage and honeymoon during the summer vacation, when the climate is most favorable. In both cases, the season of marriage is determined by a common factor—respite from work. Thus marriage tends to occur in that season of the year when the routine of living permits free time for it (see Figure 17-12).

In the United States, June is by far the most favored month. Marriage very often follows immediately after graduation of either the bride or bridegroom (or both) from high school or college. January, February, and March are the least favored months. There is a much stronger seasonal aspect to first marriages than to remarriages. Following is a set of indexes of seasonality, based on the five years 1959-1963. These indexes show by what percent the average monthly rate for these years fell above or below the five-year average rate for each calendar month:

January	−27	July	2
February	−17	August	18
March	−25	September	15
April	−10	October	− 5
May	− 8	November	− 3
June	60	December	− 1

17.13. Remarriage of Persons Widowed or Divorced

Many cultures of the world have taboos against the remarriage of widows. In others, divorces are forbidden, so that marrying a divorced person is equivalent to committing adultery. Consequently, once a marriage was broken, it was presupposed that remarriage would not take place.

One of the outstanding indexes of modernization all over the world is the weakening of this cultural prohibition and the increased freedom of widowed or divorced persons to remarry—irrespective of age. It is considered a symptom of good mental health and a well-adjusted personality for a widowed or divorced person to remarry after an appropriate interval, instead of leading a miserable life of loneliness.

The phenomenon of remarriage is apparently increasing rapidly in the United States. Of the 1.5 million marriages that occurred in 1960, 24.7 percent were remarriages. Of the remarriages that occurred, 75 percent represented the remarriage of persons who had been divorced and 25 percent represented the remarriage of widowed persons.[15] Carter calculates the rates of remarriage, by age and previous marital status, as shown in Table 17-15. Three important findings may be derived

[15] Hugh Carter, "Recent Changes in Remarriages of Women of Childbearing Age in the United States," Paper submitted to the World Population Conference, 1965.

Table 17-15 Remarriage Rates of Females under 34 Years of Age by Previous Marital Status: 1960

Age	Remarriages per 1000 divorced or widowed		
	Total	Divorced	Widowed
Less than 25 years...	467	508	142
25-29 years..........	332	396	
30-34 years..........	196	239	84
35-34 years..........	111	156	55

Source: Hugh Carter. Recent Changes in Remarriages of Women of Childbearing Age in the United States. Paper submitted at the United Nations World Population Conference, Belgrade, 1965

from this table. (1) The younger the person at the time of divorce or widowhood, the greater the likelihood that remarriage will take place. (2) Divorced persons are much more inclined to remarry than are widowed persons. (3) The level of remarriage is very high: if the population of persons with a broken marriage is subjected to an annual attrition of one fourth or one fifth, as suggested by these rates, almost all of them will have remarried within a period of five or six years. This table suggests that marriage takes place rather promptly after marital dissolution and that all but a small fraction of persons who suffer a broken marriage remarry at some time during their lives.

In reporting his results, Carter compares these rates with similar rates for 1953 calculated by Glick from the data of a sample survey. He concludes that the rates of remarriage appear to have increased since 1953.

The remarriage of widows is a topic of especial interest to insurance companies and pension systems. The U.S. Social Security Administration maintains a continuing research interest in this subject. In 1962 it released a report on this subject, the highlights of which are reported in Table 17-16. This table, based on rather careful analysis and adjustment of data from vital statistics and insurance systems, suggests that the remarriage of widows has increased remarkably, especially since 1940.[16] Comparing the remarriage rates of widows de-

[16] John P. Jones, "Remarriage Tables Based on Experience Under OASDI and US Employees Compensation Systems," *Social Security Administration Actuarial Study*, No. 55, U.S. Department of Health, Education, and Welfare, 1962.

Table 17-16 Estimated Remarriage Rates, for Widowed Females (Rates per Thousand)

Central age	Limited population study, U.S.		U.S. employees compensation system. Duration of widowed 0-4 years	
	1940	1950	1925-30	1950-55
22 years.........	208	143	75	103
27 years.........	138	139	48	71
32 years.........	79	104	29	47
37 years.........	46	72	17	29
42 years.........	30	47	11	16
47 years.........	20	32	7	9
52 years.........	12	19	4	5
57 years.........	7	13	..	...
62 years.........	3	7	..	...
67 years.........		4	..	...

Source: John P. Jones, "Remarriage Tables Based on Experience under OASDI and U.S. Employees Compensations Systems. U.S. Social Security Administration, Actuarial Study No. 55, December, 1962

rived from Social Security data with the estimated rates for the general population suggests that remarriage rates for widows covered by Social Security are not greatly different from those in the general population. This would mean that the termination of the widow's benefit upon remarriage (the child's benefit does not terminate on remarriage of the widow) does not deter remarriage. There is some evidence that young widows with children (for whom monthly benefits will continue until age

hood. This proportion holds approximately for all ages.

17.14. Marital Dissolution

Once formed, marriages are subject to dissolution from divorce and widowhood. Also, many marriages are dissolved by separation, without benefit of divorce. The rates that are appropriate for measuring dissolution of marriage are analogous to those described for marriage:

$$\text{General marital dissolution rate} = \frac{\text{number of marriages dissolved within the year}}{\text{number of marriages spouse present, midyear}} \times 1000$$

$$\text{General divorce rate} = \frac{\text{number of divorces during the year}}{\text{midyear number of married couples}} \times 1000$$

$$\text{General widowhood rate} = \frac{\text{number of marriages dissolved by death of one spouse during the year}}{\text{midyear number of married couples}} \times 1000$$

18) are matrimonial prizes, for their remarriage rates appear to be especially high. The Social Security study emphasizes that there is a distinctive age pattern in the remarriage of widows. It states: "Under all studies of re-marriages of widows, the rates by duration are quite low for the first year but reach a peak after about 2 or 3 years, after which there is a gradual decline." In general, the average rate for the interval five to nine years after widowhood is only about one-half as high as the average rate for the first five years after widow-

In theory, each of these rates may be calculated specific for age. However, they are often computed specific for duration of marriage instead. An additional measure, the "crude divorce rate"—number of divorces per 1000 total population—is widely used, but is of comparatively little value for purposes of measuring the comparative force of marital dissolution.

As yet, the demographic analysis of marital dissolution is very underresearched and under-appreciated. A preceding chapter has pre-

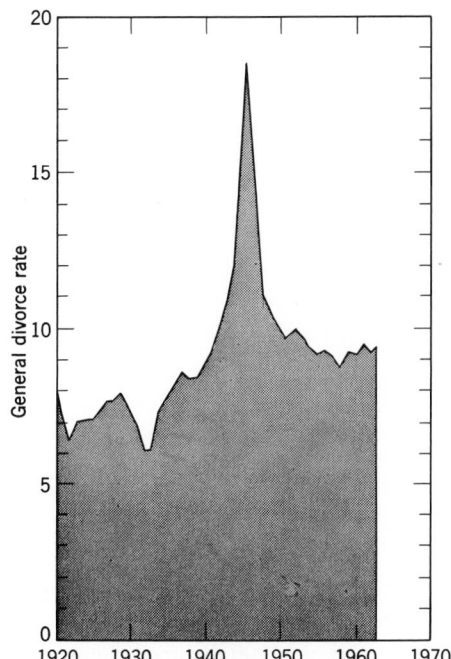

Figure 17-13 Number of Divorces per 1000 Married Women 15 Years of Age or Older, United States: 1920 to 1963.

sented data on the prevalence of divorce, and little information can be added by data from registration systems. Data about divorce decrees are collected with even less precision and completeness than are those about marriages, and less information is collected about the persons involved. There is no systematic procedure for collecting information about the person who becomes widowed during the course of a year. It is important for demographers to incorporate divorce and widowhood into their calculations, for each person-year spent in this status by persons of childbearing age represents a decreased propensity to bear children. Marital dissolution may be regarded as a major depressant of birthrates.

Figure 17-13 shows the trend since 1920 of the divorce rate per 1000 married females 15 years of age and over in the United States. Contrary to popular belief, the divorce rate has fallen in recent years. During World War II and immediately following, it was more than 1 percent per year, and in 1946 it reached almost 2 percent. In the mid-1950s it subsided somewhat and has remained nearly constant at about 0.9 percent per year. It is evident that if a cohort of couples were subjected to this rate of attrition year after year from the time of marriage until the remaining undivorced couples were separated by death, roughly one-fourth of the marriages would be dissolved by divorce.

By far the most dramatic epidemic of divorces took place in 1945-1947, when many marriages hastily entered during and immediately after the war were broken. A similar, though much smaller, episode followed World War I. During the 1920s the divorce rate climbed slowly, but sank sharply during the economic depression days of the 1930s. It returned to its former level in the late 1930s. After World War II it has never returned to the level of the 1920s or 1930s, but has tended to remain about 20 percent higher. In comparison with many other nations, the United States is a high-divorce-rate nation.

Divorces tend to be concentrated in the younger ages and in the early years of marriage. However, it is incorrect to assume that most broken marriages take place shortly after the wedding. In fact, the United States data for 1960 revealed an average duration of 7.2 years, with a duration-of-marriage distribution as follows: [17]

Duration of marriage at time of divorce	Percent of divorces
Under 1 year	6.2
1 year	8.1
2 years	8.1
3 years	7.9
4 years	7.3
5 years	6.4
6 years	5.0
7 years	4.9
8 years	4.3
9 years	3.9
10-14 years	17.0
15-19 years	8.9
20 years and over	12.0

Fully one marriage in five that breaks is broken only after 15 years or more of married life.

[17] U.S. Department of Health, Education, and Welfare, *Vital Statistics of the United States: 1960*, Volume III, *Marriage and Divorce*, Table 3E.

Such a distribution of marriage duration shows that divorces occur at all ages. In the United States in 1960 the median age of husband at time of divorce was 34 years and of wife 31. Nearly 60 percent of divorces involved children.

Japan is one of the few modernizing nations of the world that has had a falling divorce rate. Kawashima and Steiner [18] report a rather steady decline in divorce in Japan from 1833 to 1943:

Year	Divorces per 1000 population
1883	3.39
1893	2.82
1903	1.40
1913	1.12
1923	0.87
1933	0.73
1943	0.66

They conclude: ". . . since these were years of increasing industrialization and urbanization, the case of Japan fails to confirm the hypotheses of a positive correlation between industrialization and divorce rates."

These authors also show that the divorce rate declined between 1947 and 1957, although the rates are higher than they were before World War II. They point out that in traditional Japan it was considered acceptable for the husband to repudiate a wife who was sterile or who was otherwise unsatisfactory. Industrialization gradually weakened the traditional family customs of Japan and made divorce of this type less popular. As women gained in social status and marriage became more of an individual matter, divorce rates fell. In present-day Japan marriage and divorce rates of the traditional type and of the industrial type exist side by side. The trend is toward a gradual adoption of the pattern of divorce that is prevalent in industrial societies and an abandonment of the traditional type of divorce.

Remarriage. The phenomenon of remarriage is a very important aspect of modern nuptiality.

[18] Takeyoshi Kawashima and Kurt Steiner, "Modernization and Divorce Rate Trend in Japan," *Economic Development and Cultural Change*, 9 (1) (1960–1961), 213–239.

In the United States, nearly 30 percent of all marriages are remarriages for one partner or the other. The following distribution of previous marital status of brides and bridegrooms, by color, was as follows in 1960:

All couples	White couples	Nonwhite couples
Single bride		
Single bridegroom 73.2		71.7
Widowed bridegroom .. 1.0		1.8
Divorced bridegroom .. 5.0		6.3
Widowed bride		
Single bridegroom 1.3		1.8
Widowed bridegroom .. 2.5		2.9
Divorced bridegroom ... 1.7		1.6
Divorced bride		
Single bridegroom 5.9		5.7
Widowed bridegroom .. 1.4		2.3
Divorced bridegroom .. 8.1		6.0

Divorced persons are very prone to remarry. In 1960 the rate among divorced persons was 122 remarriages per 1000 divorced women and 168 per 1000 divorced men.

Remarriage is much more frequent at younger than at older ages. The following table summarizes the rates by age and previous marital status for United States women in 1960:

Age	Single	Divorced	Widowed
All ages	88	122	10
14-24 years	109	433	
25-29 years	104		105
30-34 years	76	252	
35-44 years	33	115	47
45-64 years	9	45	15
65+ years	1	9	2

When the factor of age is held constant, it is clearly evident that at ages beyond 35 both widowed and divorced women are more prone to marry than are single women, and the rate for divorced women is especially high.

Remarriage of previously married persons appears to be more acceptable in the developing nations also. For example, in a study of six rural communities in Western India, Dandekar found that 26 percent of women who were widowed later remarried.[19] She found that the

[19] Kumunidi Dandekar, "Widow Remarriage in Six Rural Communities in Western India," *Proceedings of the International Population Union Conference*, New York, 1961.

tendency to remarry was strongly related to age: a high proportion of young widows tend to remarry, while older widows tend to remain widows. She also found that the tendency to remarry is inversely related to caste status. Whereas only 10 percent of the high-status Hindus remarried, fully 41 percent of the scheduled-caste (formerly untouchable) persons remarried.

Socioeconomic Status and Divorce. Reliable data on rates of divorce by socioeconomic status are difficult to obtain. Using data for Iowa in 1953, Monahan has demonstrated that the rate of divorce is inversely related to socioeconomic status.[20] Following is a summary of his findings, which show divorces per 1000 employed males by occupational classification.

	Rate
Professionals	4.4
Owners-officials	2.9
Clerks	4.5
Salesmen	6.9
Craftsmen	7.8
Operatives	8.3
Service workers	5.9
Laborers	26.9
Farm owners	1.7
Farm laborers	0.9

On the basis of these results, Monahan infers that "Divorce is much more characteristic today

[20] Thomas P. Monahan, "Divorce by Occupational Level," *Marriage and Family Living,* **21** (2) (November 1959).

of the lower socio-economic groups in our society and much less prevalent than the average in the upper occupational levels. The considerable publicity given to divorces of leading citizens and professional entertainers (and the repetitive divorces of some of them), among other things, has kept us from seeing the true condition." In the light of the laboring man's marital and other frustrations, the idyllic portrayals of his home need reappraisal and, because of social concerns for the victims of divorce, redirection.

SUMMARY

This chapter is more an argument that there needs to be a systematic development of the demographic aspects of nuptiality than it is a comprehensive exposition of an already developed discipline. It has demonstrated that it is possible to extract marriage patterns from available sources, but that refined studies must await improvement in registration systems or in the use of special sample studies. Because divorce is frequent among persons in the childbearing years, it has a nonnegligible effect on fertility. The phenomenon of remarriage, and its impact on fertility, is also worthy of intensive study. Demographers owe a professional obligation to other branches of social science to undertake intensive studies of special topics such as teenage marriage and divorce, ethnic and religious intermarriage and divorce, and differentials in marriage and divorce rates.

QUESTIONS AND EXERCISES

1. Obtain the latest information concerning marriage and divorce rates and write a short essay on "Trends in Marriage and Divorce in the United States Since 1965." Develop hypotheses to explain the changes that have taken place.

2. Explore some censuses of Latin America and attempt to calculate first-marriage rates by the procedure outlined in this chapter. Look through recent issues of *Population Index* for references to nuptiality research in Latin America. Assemble what information you can

and write an essay on "Nuptiality Patterns in Latin America."

3. Repeat Exercise 2 for Africa.

4. From the vital statistics reports for Sweden, France, England, and Australia (one or all) calculate the age-specific marriage rate for the year of the census reported in Table 17-8. Compare the nuptiality rates from registration data with the rates obtained from census data, adjusting for age. Make one nuptiality table using the registration-derived rates and one from the census-derived rates. How dif-

ferent are the median age at marriage and average elapsed time before first marriage in the two tables? What factors other than errors in the basic data could account for these differences?

5. Tables 17-10 and 17-11 were intentionally inserted without interpretation in order to provide the student an opportunity to write an essay "Comparative Trends in White-Nonwhite Nuptiality in the U.S., 1920-60." Write such an essay and develop hypotheses to explain the observed racial differentials. Bring the account up to a later date if possible.

6. Do you think that the Negro family is more unstable today than it was in 1920 or 1930? If so, will it become even more unstable in the future? Summarize the evidence you have for each side of this question.

7. Compile a bibliography on differential nuptiality in rural and urban areas. From census data compute a nuptiality table for each type of area. Prepare a research paper on this subject.

8. From the data in this chapter and from the *Demographic Yearbooks*, assemble data on "A Comparative International Study of Discrepancies between the Ages of Brides and Grooms at Time of Marriage." Test the hypotheses:

(a) These discrepancies are greater in developing than in industrializing nations.

(b) These discrepancies are diminishing—both in developing and in industrializing nations.

9. Theoretically, it should be possible to construct a "life table" for marriages to show what proportion would "survive divorce." Neglecting the factor of mortality, try to construct such a table for the United States. What proportion of United States marriages may be expected to go 25 years without divorce?

10. Read intensively on the subject of remarriage and write an essay on it.

BIBLIOGRAPHY

Agarwala, S. N. "Effect of a Rise in Female Marriage Age on Birth Rate in India," Paper contributed to the United Nations World Population Conference, Belgrade, 1965.

Allardt, Erik. "The Influence of Different Systems of Social Norms on Divorce Rates in Finland," *Marriage and Family Living*, **17** (November 1955), 325–331.

Barron, Milton H. "Research on Intermarriage: A Survey of Accomplishments and Prospects," *American Journal of Sociology*, **57** (3) November 1951), 249–255.

Beale, Calvin L. "Increased Divorce Rates Among Separated Persons as a Factor in Divorce Since 1940," *Social Forces*, **19** (1) (October 1950), 72–74.

Besanceney, Paul H. "On Reporting Rates of Intermarriage," *American Journal of Sociology*, **70** (May 1965), 721–730.

Barnett, Larry D. "Research on International and Interracial Marriages," *Marriage and Family Living*, **24** (February 1963), 105–107.

Burchinal, Lee G. "Trends and Prospects for Young Marriages in the United States," *Marriage and Family Living*, **17** (May 1965), 243–262.

Burchinal, Lee G., and Loren E. Chancellor. "Ages at Marriage, Occupation of Grooms, and Interreligious Marriage Rate," *Social Forces*, **40** (1961), 348.

Burma, John H. "Interethnic Marriage in Los Angeles, 1948-1959," *Social Forces*, **42** (2) (December 1963), 156–165.

Cannon, Kenneth L., and Ruby Gingles. "Social Factors Related to Divorce Rates for Urban Counties in Nebraska," *Rural Sociology*, **21** (1) (March 1956), 34–40.

Carter, Hugh. "Recent Changes in Remarriages of Women of Childbearing Age in the United States," Paper contributed to the United Nations World Population Conference, Belgrade, 1965.

Carter, Hugh, and Alexander Plateris. "Trends in Divorce and Family Disruption," *Health, Education and Welfare Indicators* (August 1963).

Centers, Richard. "Marital Selection and Occupational Strata," *American Journal of Sociology*, **54** (May 1949), 530–535.

Chambliss, Rollin. "Contributions of the Vital Statistics of Finland to the Study of Factors that Induce Marriage," *American Sociological Review*, **22** (February 1957), 33–48.

Chancellor, Loren E., and Thomas P. Monahan. "Religious Preference and Interreligious Mixtures in Marriages and Divorces in Iowa," *American Journal of Sociology*, **61** (November 1955), 233–239.

Charles, Enid. "The Nuptiality Problem with Special Reference to Canadian Marriage Statistics," *Canadian Journal of Economics and Political Science*, **7** (August 1941), 447.

Christensen, Harold T. "Timing of First Pregnancy as a Factor in Divorce; A Cross-Cultural Analysis," *Eugenics Quarterly*, **10** (3) (September 1963), 119–130.

Dandekar, Kuminidi. "Widow Remarriage in Six

Rural Communities in Western India," *Proceedings of the International Population Conference.* New York, 1961.

Davis, Kingsley. "Statistical Perspective on Marriage and Divorce," *Annals of the American Academy of Political and Social Science,* **272** (November 1950), 12–15.

Day, L. H. "A Note on the Measurement of Divorce, with Special Reference to Australian Data," *Australian Journal of Statistics,* 5 (3) (November 1963), 133–142.

Fitzpatrick, Joseph P. "Intermarriage of Puerto Ricans in New York City," *American Journal of Sociology,* 71 (January 1966), 395–406.

Frazier, E. Franklin. *The Negro Family in the United States.* New York: The Dryden Press, 1948.

Glick, Paul C. *American Families.* New York: John Wiley and Sons, 1947.

Glick, Paul C. "Intermarriage and Fertility Patterns Among Persons in Major Religious Groups," *Eugenics Quarterly,* 7 (1) (March 1960), 31–38.

Glick, Paul C. "Marriage Instability Variations by Size of Place and Region, *Milbank Memorial Fund Quarterly,* 41 (1) (January 1963), 43–55.

Glick, Paul C., and Emanuel Landau. "Age as a Factor in Marriage," *American Sociological Review,* 15 (August 1950), 517–529.

Glick, Paul C., and Robert Parke, Jr. "New Approaches in Studying the Life Cycle of the Family," *Demography,* 2 (1965), 187–203.

Goode, William J. "Economic Factors and Marital Stability," *American Sociological Review,* 16 (December 1951), 802–812.

Goode, William J. "Marital Satisfaction and Instability: A Cross-Cultural Class Analysis of Divorce Rates," *International Social Science Journal,* 14 (1962), 506–507.

Grabill, Wilson H. "Attrition Life Tables for the Single Population," *Journal of American Statistical Association,* 40 (September 1945), 364–375.

Grebenik, E., and Griselda Rowntree. "Factors Associated with the Age at Marriage in Britain," *Proceedings of the Royal Society of London,* Series B, *Biological Sciences,* 159 (97) (1964), 178–197.

Hajnal, John. "Age at Marriage and Proportions Marrying," *Population Studies,* 7 (November 1953), 111.

Hajnal, John. "Analysis of Changes in the Marriage Pattern by Economic Groups," *American Sociological Review,* 19 (1954), 295–303.

Hajnal, John. "Aspects of Recent Trends in Marriage in England and Wales," *Population Studies,* 1 (June 1947), 72–98.

Hajnal, John. "Differential Changes in Marriage Patterns," *American Sociological Review,* 19 (April 1954), 148–154.

Hajnal, John. "The Marriage Boom," *Population Index,* 19 (April 1953), 80.

Henry, Louis. "Mesure de la Fréquence des Divorces," *Population,* 2 (April-June 1952).

Hill, George W., and James D. Tarver. "Marriage and Divorce Trends in Wisconsin, 1915-1945," *Milbank Memorial Fund Quarterly,* 30 (January 1952), 5–17.

Hillman, Karen G. "Marital Instability and Its Relation to Education, Income and Occupation: An Analysis Based on Census Data," pp. 603–608 in Robert F. McGinnis and Herbert R. Barringer (eds.). *Selected Studies in Marriage and the Family.* New York: Holt, Rinehart and Winston, 1962.

Hollingshead, August B. "Class Differences in Family Stability," *Annals of the American Academy of Political and Social Science,* 272 (November 1950), 39–46.

Jacobson, Paul H. *American Marriage and Divorce.* New York: Rinehart and Company, 1959.

Jacobson, Paul H. "Differentials in Divorce by Duration of Marriage and Size of Family," *American Sociological Review,* 15 (April 1950), 235–244.

Jacobson, Paul H. "Total Marital Dissolutions in the United States: Relative Importance of Mortality and Divorce," in George F. Mair (ed.). *Studies in Population.* Princeton, N. J.: Princeton University Press, 1949.

Jones, John P. *Remarriage Tables Based on Experience Under OASI and U.S. Employee Compensation Systems.* Social Security Administration Actuarial Study No. 55. U.S. Department of Health, Education, and Welfare, 1962.

Karmel, P. H. "The Relations Between Male and Female Nuptiality in a Stable Population," *Population Studies,* 1 (March 1948), 352–387.

Kawashima, Takeyoshi, and Kurt Steiner. "Modernization and Divorce Rate Trend in Japan," *Economic Development and Cultural Change,* 9 (1) (1960-1961), 213–239.

Kennedy, Ruby Jo Reeves. "Single or Triple Melting Pot, Intermarriage Trends in New Haven, 1870–1940," *American Journal of Sociology,* 49 (1944), 331–339.

Kephart, William M. "Occupation Level and Marital Disruption," *American Sociological Review,* 20 (4) (August 1955), 456–465.

Korson, J. Henry. "Age and Social Status at Marriage: Karachi, 1961-64," *Pakistan Development Review* (Karachi), 5 (4) (Winter 1965), 586–600.

Lenski, Gerhard. *The Religious Factor: A Sociological Study of Religion's Impact on Politics, Economics and Family Life.* Garden City, N. Y.: Doubleday and Company, 1961.

Matras, Judah. "Social Strategies of Family Formation: Data for British Female Cohorts Born

1831–1906." *Population Studies,* **19** (2) (November 1965), 167–181.

Mertens, Walter. "Methodological Aspects of the Construction of Nuptiality Tables," *Demography,* **2** (1965), 317–348.

Monahan, Thomas P. "Divorce by Occupational Level," *Marriage and Family Living,* **21** (2) (November 1959).

Monahan, Thomas P. "Does Age at Marriage Matter in Divorce?" *Social Forces,* **32** (October 1963), 81–87.

Monahan, Thomas P. "The Duration of Marriage to Divorce: Second Marriages and Migratory Types," *Marriage and Family Living,* **21** (2) (May 1959), 134–138.

Monahan, Thomas P. "One Hundred Years of Marriages in Massachusetts," *American Journal of Sociology,* **56** (May 1951), 534–545.

Monahan, Thomas P. *The Pattern of Age at Marriage in the United States.* 2 vols. Philadelphia: Stephenson Brothers, 1951.

Monahan, Thomas P. "When Married Couples Part: Statistical Trends and Relationships in Divorce," *American Sociological Review,* **27** (5) (October 1962), 625–633.

Monahan, Thomas P., and Loren E. Chancellor. "Statistical Aspects of Marriage and Divorce by Religious Denomination in Iowa," *Eugenics Quarterly,* **2** (September 1955), 166–167.

Moss, J. Joel. "Teen-Age Marriage: Cross-National Trends and Sociological Factors in the Decision of When to Marry," *Marriage and Family Living* (May 1965), 230–421.

Myers, Robert J. "Statistical Measures in the Marital Life Cycles of Men and Women," *Proceedings of the International Union for the Scientific Study of Population. Vienna,* 1959.

Nieminen, Armas. "Premarital Pregnancy in Finland," *Acta Sociologica* (1964), 225–264.

Notestein, Frank W. "Differential Age at Marriage According to Social Class," *American Journal of Sociology,* **38** (1) (July 1931), 22–49.

Ogle, William. "On Marriage Rates and Marriage Ages with Special Reference to the Growth of Population," *Journal of the Royal Statistical Society,* **53** (2) (1890), 274.

Okazaki, Ayanori. "Marital Dissolutions by Divorce in Japan," *Bulletin de l'Institut International de Statistique* (Stockholm), **36** (2) (1958), 316–323.

Ortmeyer, Carl E. "Educational Attainment as a Selective Factor in Marital Status Transitions in the United States," *Demography,* **4** (1967), 108–125.

Pollard, Robert S. W. *The Problem of Divorce.* London: Watts, 1958.

Pressat, Roland. "Le Remariage des Veufs et des Veuves" ("The Remarriage of Widowers and Widows"), *Population* (Paris), **11** (1) (January-March 1956), 47–56.

Rele, J. R. "Some Correlates of the Age at Marriage in the United States," *Eugenics Quarterly,* **12** (March 1965), 1–6.

Rowntree, Griselda. "Some Aspects of Marriage Breakdown in Britain During the Last Thirty Years," *Population Studies,* **18** (2) (November 1964), 147–163.

Rowntree, Griselda, and Norman H. Carrier. "The Resort to Divorce in England and Wales, 1858–1957," *Population Studies,* **11** (3) (March 1958), 188–233.

Ryder, Norman B. "Measure of Recent Nuptiality in the Western World." Paper No. 80, *Proceedings of the Union for the Scientific Study of Population.* New York, 1961.

Ryder, Norman B. "Measure of Recent Nuptiality in the Western World." Paper contributed to the United Nations World Population Conference, 1965.

Schmitt, Robert C. "Demographic Correlates of Interracial Marriage in Hawaii," *Demography,* **2** (1965), 463–473.

Stouffer, Samuel A., and Lyle M. Spencer. "Marriage and Divorce in Recent Years," *Annals of the American Academy of Political and Social Science,* **188** (November 1936), 63–64.

Thomas, John L. "The Factor of Religion in the Selection of Marriage Mates," *American Sociological Review,* **16** (August 1951), 487–491.

Tietze, Christopher, and Patience Lauriat. "Age at Marriage and Educational Attainment in the United States," *Population Studies,* **9** (2) (November 1955), 159–166.

U.S. Bureau of the Census. *Census of Population, 1950.* Vol. IV. Special Reports: Duration of Current Marital Status, 1955.

U.S. Bureau of the Census. U.S. Census of Population: 1960. Final Reports. Series PC (2)-D. Subject reports. Washington, 1963. 4D. *Age at First Marriage: Data on Duration of Marriage, Times Married, Difference in Age between Husband and Wife, Ethnic Origin, Education, Earnings, etc.* May 1966.

U.S. Department of Health, Education, and Welfare: National Vital Statistics Division. "Marriage and Divorce," Vol. III of *Vital Statistics of the United States.* Washington, D.C.: Government Printing Office, annual publication.

U.S. National Center for Health Statistics. *Demographic Characteristics of Persons Married Between January, 1955 and June, 1958.* Series 21, No. 2 (April 1965).

U.S. National Center for Health Statistics. *Divorce Statistics Analysis, 1962.* Series 21, Number 7. By Alexander A. Broel-Plateris.

U.S. National Center for Health Statistics. Vital and Health Statistics. Series 21.. Washington, *Marriage Statistics Analysis,* No. 10. United States, 1962. By Carol E. Ortmeyer and Elizabeth F. Whiteman. January 1967 (vi).

Walle, Etienne van de. "La Nuptialité en Belgique de 1846 a 1930 et sa Relation avec le Déclin de la fécondité" ("Nuptiality in Belgium from 1846 to 1930 and Its Relation to the Decline in Fertility"), *Population et Famille—Bevolking en Gezin* (Brussels), (6-7) (December 1965), 37–56.

Wilcox, Walter F. *The Divorce Problem, A Study in Statistics.* New York: Columbia University Studies, 1891.

Wünsch, Guillaume. "Les Méthodes d'analyse de la Nuptialité: Leur Application au Cas de la Belgique," *Recherches Economiques de Louvain.* Louvain, Belgique: Université Catholique de Louvain Centre de Recherches Economiques, 1965.

CHAPTER 18

Human Natality

18.1. Introduction: Fertility as a Sociodemographic Force

"There is no event in personal history more significant for the future than becoming a parent, and there is no pattern of behavior more essential for societal survival than adequate fertility. . . . The individual and social importance of proper knowledge of this vital activity cannot be overstated. The network of familial relationships, the pattern of familial activities, and the structure of familial rights and responsibilities are transformed by the entrance of a baby. On the aggregate level, although the law of large numbers prohibits such a dramatic parallel, changes in procreative behavior are influential accompaniments of virtually every variation in the fortunes of society. A disturbance of the rate of production of new members portends for the population successive modifications in the numbers of consumers in each higher age group, the demands imposed on the educational structure, the flow of young adults into the labor force, the housing requirements of newlyweds, and so on throughout the life span to the ages beyond retirement when the old seek to derive financial if not psychological security from their savings, their progeny, and their government. It is thus not surprising that the policy-makers in business and in government are avid consumers of those data concerning past, present, and future births which it is the obligation of the fertility analyst to understand." [1]

This quotation, from one of the world's lead-

[1] Norman B. Ryder, "Fertility," Chapter 18 in P. M. Hauser, and O. D. Duncan. *The Study of Population* (Chicago: University of Chicago Press, 1959), p. 400.

ing authorities on fertility analysis, clearly reveals the reverence that demographers have for childbearing. They see fertility as the positive force in the vital process—continuously replenishing the population to combat the attrition of mortality. If the replenishment is either seriously insufficient or excessive, social problems result. Professor Ryder describes well the tremendous social and social-psychological force that fertility constitutes.

American demographers use the term "fertility" to refer to the actual bearing of children and the term "fecundity" to refer to the capacity to bear children (absence of sterility). This is somewhat at variance with the use of these terms in biological sciences, and also is not consistent with international usage. For this reason, the world "natality" is preferable as the term for childbearing; it is not ambiguous. In this chapter, the American usage of the term "fertility" is followed, but it is accompanied by generous use of "natality" as a synonym.

Earlier chapters have already provided a great deal of background for the study of fertility as a component of growth. Using a simple measure, the crude birthrate, Chapter 3 undertook to give a general picture of the natality situation throughout the world. The historic decline of fertility in the industrialized nations was traced, the inverse correlation between fertility and national wealth was pointed out, and the proposition that fertility control apparently must go hand in hand with programs of economic development if long-range gains are to be made was stated. Chapters 4 and 5 described how fertility data are collected and tabulated, and the computation of a second basic measure of fertility—the age-specific fertility rate—was illustrated.

The present chapter undertakes to go beyond this overview and make a much more intensive and detailed analysis, ending with a synthesis of present demographic knowledge about human fertility. As in the preceding chapters on mortality and nuptiality, the reader is asked to prepare himself for the task by first gaining a full set of concepts with which to think about the problems to be discussed. Also, as before, he will find that they are straightforward, logical, and not difficult to grasp. With them we can arrive at principles and insights that otherwise would remain hazy and vague.

Fertility, of course, is an event that occurs over time. We must measure it, therefore, in terms of *incidence*, or the *comparative frequency* with which the event of childbearing occurs. From Chapter 5 we know that this calls for the development of *rates*, which specify the relative frequency of childbearing. As is true for the other vital processes, we have two major avenues of inquiry. (1) *Fertility trends:* what are the changes in the level of fertility rates over time? (2) *Differential fertility:* what are the differences in fertility rates between populations or subgroups of a population at a given time? Both inquiries are pursued through the anaylsis of schedules of fertility rates. In both cases, the final goal is not only to detect and measure changes and differentials, but also to explain them, to develop theories of why they occur.

The replenishment of population through childbearing is a complex phenomenon which is a topic for research in many disciplines. A comprehensive explanation of the factors and forces involved requires theories taken from physiology, sociology, economics, psychology, political science, anthropology, and medicine. An organismic interpretation of fertility—that pregnancy is simply a "natural" result of the human animal expressing its sex drive—is contradicted by a vast amount of anthropological, psychoanalytic, and other social science findings. They show that perhaps no aspect of human behavior is more regulated by cultural prescriptions, more subject to idealization, more conditioned by the process of socialization, and

more subject to inhibition of animal drives by human personality than is sexual behavior—and especially childbearing. In line with the theory of "demographic regulation" stated in Chapter 3, *a more consistently social science perspective on fertility would be to regard a population's birthrate anywhere and everywhere primarily as a social artifact and to presume for purposes of research that the forces that determine the level of the birthrate are primarily social and economic.* Our very elaborate social science theories that extol man as the most adaptable creature on earth, one capable of controlling current behavior to achieve abstract ends that may lie in the future, should be the first to challenge the organismic view that human fertility is simply a biological consequence of breeding, motivated by the same uncomplicated factors as in other animals. Instead, let us begin our more detailed study of human fertility with the view that when we study birthrates, we are investigating a major phase of man's social and economic adjustment. In this view, birth statistics are sociological and economic as well as biological data. Moreover, we should also regard the birthrate as a rather sensitive adjustment to the *current* life situation and expect changes rather promptly when the current functional basis for its level is altered. Let us be prepared to challenge the theory that "cultural lag" will permit birthrates to maintain a given pattern for generations after they have become highly dysfunctional.

The study of birthrates has been a central concern of demographers. Since other social scientists have neglected this field—and since many of the earliest demographers were drawn from the fields of biology, medicine, public health, and actuarial science—until recently much of the research has been done from a more or less organismic point of view, following scientific procedures common in these disciplines. The result has been that (*a*) a rigorous and coherent set of basic concepts and workable definitions has been established for measuring fertility, (*b*) a great quantity of general descriptive and historical information about fertility changes over time and differences between parts of the population around the world has been accumulated, and (*c*) some

Table 18-1 Illustration of Procedures for Computing Six Basic Measures of Fertility, for United States: 1960

Age of woman	Number of women of specified age	Number of births to women of specified age	Age specified birth rate per 1000 women	Standard population (world)	Expected births	Cumulative fertility rate
	(1)	(2)	(3)	(4)	(5)	(6)
Total.........	41,647,349	4,251,070	102	1,000,000	117,128	3640
Under 15 years....						
15–19 years.......	6,588,602	586,966	89	195,827	17,429	445
20–24 years.......	5,519,937	1,426,912	258	174,139	44,928	1735
25–29 years.......	5,537,104	1,092,816	197	153,801	30,299	2770
30–34 years.......	6,111,422	687,722	112	139,763	15,653	3280
35–39 years.......	6,418,536	359,908	56	125,761	7,043	3560
40–44 years.......	5,917,805	91,564	15	111,878	1,678	3635
45–49 years.......	5,553,943	5,182	1	198,231	98	3640

Crude birth rate = Total births divided by total U.S. population = (4,251,070/179,323,798)
       1000 = 23.7
General fertility rate= (4,251,070/41,647,349) 1000 = 102
Age specific fertility rates = entries of column 2 divided by entries of column 1
       multiplied by 1000 for each age
Total fertility rate = sum of ASFR times interval = 728 times 5 = 3,640
Cumulative fertility rate = ASFR times 5, cumulated by age: See Column 6.
Standardized General Fertility Rate = sum of column 5 divided by sum of column 4 =
       (117,128/1,000.000)1000 = 117

ingenious mathematical models capable of simulating fertility processes with a high degree of fidelity have been developed. The major shortcoming in fertility study at the present time is a comparative scarcity of basic *explanations of* fertility changes and differentials. Much of our model-building is no more than curve-fitting to parameters which we do not yet understand and whose variations remain largely unexplained. This, however, is not a unique situation in social science. In fact, fertility study is one of the more sophisticated and advanced branches of study in the social sciences.

18.2. Basic Natality Measures

The "rate" of childbearing may be usefully expressed in six principal forms. Each of these forms is closely related to the other. As will be explained later, several of them can be refined and varied to facilitate the attainment of particular research objectives. The six basic forms of fertility measurement are as follows:

crude birthrate (CBR)
general fertility rate (GFR)
age-specific fertility rate (ASFR)
total fertility rate (TFR)
cumulative fertility rate (CFR)
standardized fertility rates

The mode of calculation of each is illustrated in Table 18-1.

1. *The crude birthrate* (CBR), already defined in Chapter 2, is the number of births per 1000 total population. It is highly useful in expressing current fertility in a form that indicates its effect on population growth. When the crude death rate is subtracted from the crude birthrate, the net residual is the current annual rate of growth, exclusive of migration. As a refined measure of fertility, the crude birthrate is inadequate because the denominator includes a large mass of children and the substantial number of adults past childbearing age who are not "exposed" to childbearing.

It has been shown in the chapter on age composition that the proportion of the population that lies outside the childbearing ages is not constant from one population to another, but varies according to the level of fertility and mortality. Also, since women do the childbearing, it is the supply of females rather than the supply of males that is the truly "exposed" population. Where males are extraordinarily plentiful (or females extraordinarily scarce), as in many areas of in-migration, the crude birthrate can yield artificially low measures of fertility. For these reasons, the crude birthrate is used only to indicate the general magnitude

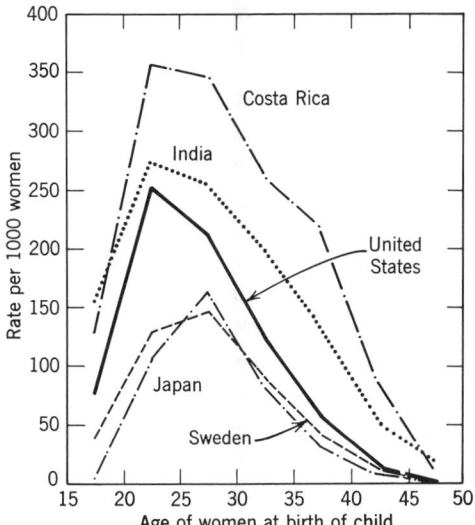

Figure 18-1 Age-Specific Fertility Rates for Selected Nations of the World: 1960.

of the fertility level and to study current growth.

2. *The general fertility rate* (GFR) is the number of births that occur in a year per 1000 women of childbearing age. It is superior to the crude birthrate in that the denominator is more nearly restricted to those actually "exposed" to the risk of childbearing. The age range that is specified as bracketing the childbearing years varies from nation to nation, but usually is defined as ages 15 to 44 or ages 15 to 49, although the interval 10 to 49 has been used by the United Nations and some countries.

3. *The age-specific fertility rate* (ASFR) is the number of births per year to 1000 women of a particular age. In other words, it is a general fertility rate for a particular age group.

An ASFR can be computed for each single year of age, from age 15 to age 49, if desired. Figure 18-1 illustrates the typical curve that represents the pattern of age-specific fertility for all ages in a population. Demographers usually find that adequate precision can be obtained by grouping the data into five-year age groups. The ASFR is useful for three purposes: (1) the rate of childbearing is not uniform throughout all ages, and the ASFR reveals the pattern and extent of this age differential; (2) it permits the study of fertility in terms of real cohorts of women, tracing out

their fertility behavior as they pass through life (see Section 18.13); and (3) it is the raw material from which two of the remaining six basic fertility measures are computed. For these reasons, it is essential that a schedule of age-specific fertility rates, encompassing the entire fertility span, be established and maintained on an annual basis if at all possible. Until it is possible to measure or estimate a schedule of ASFR for a population at least once a decade, it is difficult to make a precise analysis of changes in fertility.

4. *The total fertility rate* (TFR) is an estimate of the number of children a cohort of 1000 women would bear if they all went through their reproductive years exposed to the age-specific fertility rates in effect at a particular time. It is computed simply by summing the age-specific fertility rates for all ages and multiplying by the interval into which the ages are grouped. This rate is generally regarded as the best single cross-sectional measure of fertility, because it is rather closely restricted to the childbearing population and is not influenced by differences in the age composition between childbearing populations. Also, because it assumes that all women survive from birth to the end of the childbearing period, it is independent of mortality. This is the measure that demographers generally regard as the most sensitive, and yet meaningful, with which to measure fertility. Its meaning is very clear: if the TFR is 2, the parents are very nearly replacing themselves but are not contributing to population growth. (However, a population with a TFR of exactly 2 would eventually decline because not all females born survive to the end of the childbearing period and because slightly more than one half of the babies born are males. The net reproduction rate, discussed in Chapter 21, extends the basic definition of the TFR to include the effects of attrition of mortality on the childbearers and on the sex ratio at birth.)

5. *The cumulative fertility rate (CFR): completed and incomplete fertility.* The cumulative birthrate is similar to the TFR, except that it reports the number of children a cohort of 1000 women would bear from the time they begin childbearing until they reach a specified

age, if they were exposed to the schedule of age-specific fertility rates in effect at a given time. Thus cumulative fertility may be computed up to any age. For ages 45 to 49 and over, it refers to *completed fertility*, for beyond this age there is no more childbearing. This statistic of completed cumulative fertility is of unusual importance, because it states the average size of family (including deceased children) that would result from a given schedule of age-specific fertility rates. In other words, it states the number of children that a woman would have ever borne by the time she attained menopause if she had conformed to the average age-specific fertility pattern that is in effect for a current year. The reader is asked to study Table 18-1 carefully, while rereading the definitions given above. If this is done, the discussion in the remainder of this chapter can present no difficulty.

Standardized Fertility Rates. As Figure 18-1 illustrates, the rate of childbearing varies markedly with age. Fertility is comparatively low before age 20 and after age 35, with a peak at about 25 to 29. If two populations were to differ radically in the way their female population is distributed between ages 15 and 49, it would affect the general fertility rate; the population with the greatest proportion in the ages 20 to 29 would tend to have a higher GFR. As was illustrated in Chapter 5, it is possible to control differences in age composition of the female population of childbearing age by the process of direct or indirect standardization. Thus the GFR may be standardized for age or for age plus some other variables such as race, educational attainment, income, and/or occupation of husband. This is illustrated in Table 18-1.

The total fertility rate is also a standardized rate, because it is referred to a constant base of 1000 women at each age group. Therefore, all TFR have the same age composition and therefore are not affected by differences in age composition. In the study of differential fertility, it is desirable to use either TFR or age-standardized GFR. Such standardized rates may also be nuptiality-specific rates (see next paragraph). The ideal measure for the study of differential fertility is a nuptial TFR or nuptial standardized GFR.

Nuptiality Rates. The alert reader will have already argued to himself that age-specific rates do not fully restrict the denominator precisely to persons who are truly "exposed" to childbearing, for they include the unmarried population. Many researchers find it useful to compute the rates on the basis of the currently married or the ever-married (sum of married, widowed, and divorced) population. For precise results, the births should be restricted to legitimate (within wedlock) births, although if the amount of illegitimacy is low, all births can be related to married women without damage. It is possible, therefore, to compute GFR, ASFR, TFR, and CFR for the currently married or for the ever-married female population. However, because all women do not marry at age 15, nuptial TFR must be computed by a more complex procedure, and standardized GFR requires a standard population with the age composition of ever-married or currently married women, rather than all women. For details, see *The Manual of Demographic Research Techniques.* Such rates are especially useful when studying differential fertility, because they eliminate any differences between populations that may arise as a result of differences in marital status. For studying growth and reproduction within a particular population the value of the additional refinement added by these rates is sometimes debatable.

Male Fertility Rates. There is no logical reason why GFR, ASFR, TFR, and CFR cannot be computed for males as well as females. Male rates generally are considered to be inferior because the span of fertile years is longer and more ambiguous for males than for females and introduces the additional variable of difference in age between spouses. It can be reasonably safely presumed that couple fecundity (ability to conceive) is more or less unaffected by the age of the husband on the presumption that almost all ever-fertile wives reach menopause before their ever-fertile husbands become sterile. Thus there seem to be no clear-cut advantages and some disadvantages to computing male fertility rates. Demographers have noted, however, that certain inconsistencies of importance arise when fertility is measured in terms of males instead of females.

Interrelationships between the Measures. We

Table 18-2 Linear Correlations between the Direct Fertility Measures: 50 Nations for Which Reliable Statistics Were Available for the Period 1955 to 1960

Direct fertility measures	CBR	GFR	GFR-- dir.std	GFR-- ind.std	TFR	ASFR, 15-19	ASFR, 20-24	ASFR, 25-29	ASFR, 30-34	ASFR, 35-39	ASFR, 40-44	ASFR, 44-49
						Linear correlations with:						
CBR.......................	1.000	0.992	0.980	0.982	0.982	0.803	0.854	0.919	0.913	0.903	0.824	0.751
GFR.......................	0.992	1.000	0.994	0.996	0.996	0.793	0.877	0.944	0.928	0.910	0.827	0.722
GFR--dir. std.............	0.980	0.994	1.000	0.999	0.998	0.816	0.909	0.947	0.914	0.883	0.791	0.689
GFR--ind. std.............	0.982	0.996	0.999	1.000	0.998	0.806	0.895	0.949	0.924	0.897	0.803	0.695
TFR.......................	0.982	0.996	0.998	0.998	1.000	0.780	0.882	0.957	0.938	0.912	0.826	0.711
ASFR, 15-19..............	0.803	0.793	0.816	0.806	0.780	1.000	0.871	0.627	0.573	0.529	0.425	0.448
ASFR, 20-24..............	0.854	0.877	0.909	0.895	0.882	0.871	1.000	0.811	0.676	0.635	0.526	0.483
ASFR, 25-29..............	0.919	0.944	0.947	0.949	0.957	0.627	0.811	1.000	0.931	0.887	0.787	0.699
ASFR, 30-34..............	0.913	0.928	0.914	0.924	0.938	0.573	0.676	0.931	1.000	0.970	0.910	0.734
ASFR, 35-39..............	0.903	0.910	0.883	0.897	0.912	0.529	0.635	0.887	0.970	1.000	0.949	0.748
ASFR, 40-44..............	0.824	0.827	0.791	0.803	0.826	0.425	0.526	0.787	0.910	0.949	1.000	0.692
ASFR, 45-49..............	0.751	0.722	0.689	0.695	0.711	0.448	0.483	0.699	0.734	0.748	0.692	1.000

Source: Donald J. Bogue and James A. Palmore, "Some Empirical and Analytic Relations Among Demographic Fertility Measures, with Regression Models for Fertility Estimation," *Demography*, Vol. I, (1964) pp 319

should not begin to use these different summary measures of fertility until we have indicated how closely they are interrelated with each other. Although each of the rates is designed to accomplish a particular type of measurement, they are all measures of the same phenomenon and tend to vary together. To illustrate this, let us see how highly they are correlated with each other. In 1963 Bogue and Palmore selected 50 nations for which both vital registration and census data were thought to be reasonably reliable and computed each of the measures for each population.[2] They then computed a coefficient of correlation between each of the measures and between every other measure. The intercorrelations between CBR, GFR, and TFR are indicated in Table 18-2.

In a situation where 1.000 represents perfect association, none of the correlations falls below .982—and even much of this small variation could be due to small defects in the data for particular nations. Clearly, the five basic measures are essentially different ways of expressing a common phenomenon. Table 18-2 shows that, surprisingly, even the individual age-specific birthrates are highly correlated with CBR, GFR, and TFR.

In fact, if we know only one measure, we can convert it to any other by simple substitution in the appropriate simple equation:

[2] Donald J. Bogue and James A. Palmore, "Some Empirical and Analytic Relations Among Demographic Fertility Measures, with Regression Models for Fertility Estimation," *Demography*, 1 (1964), 316–338.

$$GFR = 4.5952\ CBR - 8.5945$$
$$TFR = 137.94\ CBR + 106.16$$
$$CBR = 0.2141\ GFR + 2.2903$$
$$TFR = 30.195\ GFR + 343.28$$
$$CBR = 0.0070\ TFR + 0.2453$$
$$GFR = 0.0328\ TFR - 10.305$$

One use to which we may immediately put these equations is to develop a table for estimating one fertility measure from another, so that if we are given a rate expressed in terms of one measure, by consulting the table we can read off the implied approximate values for the other measures. Table 18-3 is such a table. For example, if someone tells us that a nation has a crude birthrate of 45 per thousand, we can use this table to learn that this implies an average complete family size (TFR) of 6.3 children. On the other hand, if someone tells us that for some population of Africa the average size of completed family, carefully gleaned from fertility histories of a representative group of women past the age of childbearing, is 7.5 children per woman, we can estimate that this implies a crude birthrate of about 54 per thousand. In making use of Table 18-3, the following points should be kept in mind: (1) The interrelationships are *approximate* (say within 5 percent) and the greatest errors of estimate would be at the extreme values. (2) The table was constructed from data deemed to be correct. When using defective data, it is necessary to correct them for estimated deficiencies before substituting in this table. (3) These are *not* the best estimates that can be made. By using multiple regression equations, it is possible to make estimates that are substantially

Table 18-3   Table of Equivalent Values of Crude Birthrate,
General Fertility Rate, and Total Fertility Rate Based on Empirical
Relationships among them in Populations for Which Reliable Data
Are Available

Crude birth rate	General fertility rate	Total fertility rate	Crude birth rate	General fertility rate	Total fertility rate
10.............	37	1490	40.............	175	5620
11.............	42	1620	41.............	180	5760
12.............	47	1760	42.............	184	5900
13.............	51	1900	43.............	189	6040
14.............	56	2040	44.............	194	6180
15.............	60	2180	45.............	198	6310
16.............	65	2320	46.............	203	6450
17.............	70	2450	47.............	207	5690
18.............	74	2590	48.............	212	6730
19.............	79	2730	49.............	217	6870
20.............	83	2860	50.............	221	7000
21.............	88	3000	51.............	226	7140
22.............	92	3140	52.............	230	7280
23.............	97	3280	53.............	235	7420
24.............	102	3420	54.............	240	7550
25.............	106	3550	55.............	244	7690
26.............	111	3690	56.............	249	7830
27.............	115	3830	57.............	253	7970
28.............	120	3970	58.............	258	8110
29.............	125	4110	59.............	263	8240
30.............	129	4240	60.............	267	8380
31.............	134	4380	61.............	272	8520
32.............	138	4520	62.............	276	8660
33.............	143	4660	63.............	281	8800
34.............	148	4800	64.............	285	8930
35.............	152	4930	65.............	290	9070
36.............	157	5070			
37.............	161	5210			
38.............	166	5350			
39.............	171	5490			

Source: Derived from equations developed in Donald J. Bogue and James A.
Palmore, "Some Empirical and Analytic Relations Among Demographic
Fertility Measures, with Regression Models for Fertility Estima-
tion," Demography, Vol. I, 1964, p. 219

more precise. (4) These are empirical estimates based on fitted curves; they can change
over time and can be altered by the addition
of the experience of additional nations. Even
with these restrictions, however, these equations can help substantially in integrating and
unifying the varied array of contemporary fertility research.

In making use of these equations, please
keep in mind that GFR here refers to women
15 to 49 years of age, as defined by the United
Nations. In the United States, published GFR
refer to women 15 to 44, hence must be re-
calculated if these equations are to be used.

***Estimating Fertility through Data Derived
from Censuses.*** The five measures described
above and illustrated in Table 18-1 are considered to be basic because they are direct mea-

sures of fertility, derived from registration data.
In addition to these basic measures, it is possible to develop *indexes* of fertility, derived
from census data. Although these indexes are
not themselves direct measures of fertility rates,
they vary proportionately with the direct
measures.

One of the best known and most widely used
of such measures is the *child-woman ratio*. It
is the number of children 0 to 4 years of age
per 1000 women of childbearing age, usually
defined as women 15 to 44 or 15 to 49 years of
age. This index does not take into account infant mortality, hence implicitly assumes that it
is equal for all groups being compared. Another
rough but often usable index of fertility is simply the percentage of the total population that
is 0 to 14 years of age. Surprising as it may

seem, this measure has a correlation coefficient of .930 with the CBR.

By a process of "reverse survival" the children 0 to 4 can be converted to estimates of actual live births in the five years preceding the census, and the women 15 to 49 can be also "reverse-survived" to obtain estimates of the women of childbearing age who must have borne the infants. With such data it is then possible to compute CBR and GFR. This procedure is widely used for developing estimates of fertility where reasonably accurate census data but no registration data are available. (For details of the procedure, see the *Manual.*) Not infrequently it is found that the age group 5 to 9 or even 0 to 9 provides more reliable results than do ages 0 to 4. Reverse survival, of course, presupposes the availability of an estimate of the mortality rates at the ages being considered. If no other choice is available, a life table from another nation, thought to represent the current mortality condition, may be used for the reverse survival.

An alternative way of estimating fertility directly from census data has been developed by Bogue and Palmore.[3] They used data for nations for which reliable data were available and made use of information for five variables:

1. Child-woman ratio.

2. Median age at first marriage.

3. Age composition within the range 15 to 49 years.

4. Infant mortality rate.

5. Percent of women marrying by ages 15 to 19, 20 to 24, and 45 to 49.

From these data they developed multiple-regression equations that were able to reproduce rather closely the values of CBR, GFR, ASFR, and CFR. The unique accomplishment of these estimates is their ability to generate a set of age-specific fertility rates as well as the summary measures.

18.3.   Review of World Fertility with Refined Measures

Table 18-4 presents estimates of the basic fertility measures for almost all nations of the world. These estimates were prepared by Lee

[3] *Ibid.*

Jay Cho and reported in an article, "Estimated Refined Measures of Fertility for all Major Countries of the World."[4] Dr. Cho made use of reliable fertility data from registration systems where they were available. For the remaining nations he made estimates, using multiple-regression equations developed by Bogue and Palmore and described in the preceding section. For each major nation of the world Dr. Cho prepared estimates of

crude birthrate
general fertility rate
total fertility rate
age-specific fertility rates for each 5 year-age
    group, 15 to 49 inclusive
age-standardized general fertility rate

This table provides a wealth of information about world fertility that hitherto has not been available. Although subject to errors of estimation, it is believed to reveal the details of the fertility picture rather accurately.

Using the standardized general fertility rate as a very good overall comparative measure of fertility level, let us identify the 15 nations of the world with the lowest fertility. Ranked in order of standardized GFR, they are as follows:

Rank	CBR	TFR	GFR
1. Japan	16.8	1978	62.2
2. Luxembourg	15.9	2206	65.6
3. Sweden	14.4	2296	61.1
4. Greece	19.3	2365	73.7
5. West Germany	17.0	2336	67.2
6. Switzerland	17.5	2319	70.0
7. Italy	18.2	2362	71.2
8. Hungary	17.3	2367	69.1
9. Bulgaria	18.6	2412	72.9
10. England and Wales	16.1	2506	68.9
11. Denmark	16.8	2577	70.8
12. Austria	17.2	2558	69.9
13. Belgium	17.0	2565	75.3
14. Czechoslovakia	18.0	2692	76.7
15. Romania	22.3	2668	82.6

From this list we can learn several things.

[4] Lee Jay Cho, "Estimated Refined Measures of Fertility for All Major Countries of the World," *Demography,* 1 (1964), 359–374.

Table 18-4 Estimated Fertility Rates for Countries of the World, 1955 to 1960, and Percent of Demographic Transition Completed

Country	Class of estimate	Summary fertility measures				Age-specific fertility rates							Percent of demographic transition completed
		CBR	GFR	Ind. Std. GFR	TFR	15-19	20-24	25-29	30-34	35-39	40-44	45-49	
NORTHERN AFRICA													
Algeria 1/.................	II	46.5	195.0	191.1	6317	93.1	234.8	316.2	278.4	215.0	102.3	23.7	22.6
Sudan.....................	III	H 54.9	234.8	228.9	7496	136.6	315.4	371.7	309.3	234.6	105.2	26.4	6.9
		L 50.9	212.2	206.5	6751	126.1	291.0	329.9	275.3	209.2	94.9	23.9	
Tunisia...................	II	46.0	195.0	191.9	6244	132.2	305.2	301.6	240.1	174.8	76.1	18.6	23.3
United Arab Republic......	II	42.3	180.7	177.7	5824	113.6	281.7	299.6	228.2	157.9	67.3	16.6	31.3
TROPICAL & SOUTH AFRICA													
Basutoland................	II	49.5	206.1	203.0	6697	88.7	235.1	333.2	299.6	239.2	115.8	27.7	15.8
Congo (Brazzaville).......	IV	H 47.7	189.7	182.4	5955	121.5	250.1	284.6	238.9	182.7	87.9	25.5	28.2
		L 46.9	186.9	179.5	5896	111.3	229.9	291.2	244.8	185.6	90.2	26.3	
Congo (Leopoldville)......	III	42.8	189.6	187.1	6077	132.3	290.0	300.9	233.7	165.8	72.8	20.0	26.4
Ghana.....................	III	H 53.5	224.1	209.9	6860	155.6	306.9	336.3	270.6	194.8	84.7	23.1	14.2
		L 48.6	207.4	194.1	6297	165.3	338.4	306.6	227.1	150.0	57.4	14.6	
Guinea....................	II	54.3	216.4	204.2	6605	187.1	315.8	292.7	239.3	177.6	81.9	26.6	13.8
Kenya.....................	IV	49.7	205.7	198.5	6500	109.8	267.1	322.1	270.9	208.2	97.1	24.9	17.8
Ivory Coast...............	III	49.1	219.4	215.2	6987	167.5	324.1	333.5	268.7	195.2	84.9	23.6	9.3
Madagascar................	III	42.8	178.5	170.7	5612	85.3	243.6	286.5	234.8	174.1	79.7	18.3	34.0
Mauritius.................	I	40.8	185.6	183.0	5907	131.7	301.4	295.4	231.0	154.7	59.3	7.8	29.1
Nigeria...................	IV	H 50.7	209.4	200.5	6510	156.9	308.0	305.2	247.8	181.7	80.3	22.1	19.5
		L 47.9	199.7	191.2	6213	154.8	311.3	300.2	230.3	159.8	67.2	19.0	
Reunion...................	III	47.1	202.4	197.4	6831	62.9	251.2	341.8	329.6	240.1	124.5	16.1	15.6
Seychelles................	II	H 40.0	172.0	168.3	5499	72.6	203.7	282.3	253.3	191.3	83.1	13.6	28.5
		L 38.8	167.7	164.2	5364	71.9	206.0	278.0	245.2	182.1	77.5	12.0	
St. Helena................	II	H 38.4	170.7	178.4	5786	94.1	269.9	299.6	239.6	171.9	69.4	12.7	37.5
		L 35.5	160.8	168.9	5469	92.5	275.2	289.4	220.7	150.6	56.5	8.9	
Swaziland.................	IV	H 54.1	219.7	212.8	6970	110.3	255.2	323.1	301.3	249.5	123.6	30.8	15.7
		L 47.9	198.4	192.3	6290	107.0	266.4	301.1	261.0	203.9	96.0	22.7	
Togo......................	IV	50.0	200.6	188.3	6156	103.1	261.4	293.3	250.8	199.5	97.5	25.7	22.5
Tanganyika................	II	47.7	194.8	187.6	6117	110.5	258.1	299.3	257.6	192.0	89.2	23.4	24.5
Uganda....................	II	47.5	195.9	188.6	6174	99.4	256.7	309.6	250.8	196.9	91.6	23.2	23.7
Union of South Africa 2/..	II	H 48.8	207.7	201.0	6636	89.5	253.0	338.6	292.5	225.4	104.7	23.4	17.4
		L 47.3	202.8	196.2	6478	88.7	255.7	333.5	283.1	214.8	98.3	21.5	
Upper Volta...............	III	49.0	198.8	188.5	6128	142.1	287.2	289.2	233.9	172.4	78.3	22.4	23.3
Zanzibar and Pemba........	III	42.0	167.9	161.4	5232	130.2	266.3	248.6	190.5	133.1	59.6	18.1	40.6
NORTHERN AMERICA													
Bermuda...................	II	29.0	121.4	120.9	3932	68.2	213.3	210.8	153.0	96.9	38.0	6.2	66.1
Canada....................	I	27.8	119.4	124.6	4075	66.7	232.7	242.3	159.4	91.1	30.1	2.7	65.3
Greenland.................	II	40.9	177.7	171.4	5690	72.7	225.7	301.0	254.5	185.9	83.0	15.2	33.4
St. Pierre and Miquelon...	II	29.7	121.5	123.5	4096	42.0	167.1	226.5	182.1	128.3	60.4	12.7	64.5
United States (white).....	I	23.5	101.7	110.9	3674	76.8	252.1	211.5	121.4	57.0	15.2	0.9	74.2
United States (non-white).	I	34.3	145.4	151.3	4861	171.0	314.0	236.7	147.1	78.4	23.0	1.9	50.5

Table 18-4 (Continued)

Country	Class of estimate	Summary fertility measures				Age-specific fertility rates							Percent of demographic transition completed
		CBR	GFR	Ind. Std. GFR	TFR	15-19	20-24	25-29	30-34	35-39	40-44	45-49	
MIDDLE AMERICA													
Barbados	II	31.4	125.8	130.0	4171	124.6	201.9	194.2	171.0	104.3	34.9	3.2	62.6
Costa Rica	I	49.7	223.8	215.2	7068	128.2	355.9	345.4	259.9	218.1	91.4	14.4	7.3
Cuba	III	33.9	139.2	137.4	4412	86.6	245.1	217.3	163.4	113.5	46.9	9.5	58.1
Dominica	II	32.4	133.5	131.7	4253	74.1	227.4	219.0	163.8	111.6	45.9	8.8	11.5
Dominican Republic	III	47.0	212.1	214.5	6975	128.2	346.7	374.0	265.2	161.2	117.6	2.0	27.7
	H	44.8	192.4	185.8	6085	100.5	260.8	307.8	257.8	190.6	82.9	16.7	
	L	42.6	185.0	178.7	5847	99.3	264.7	300.1	243.6	174.6	73.2	13.8	
El Salvador	I	46.5	199.7	193.3	6232	141.6	306.4	318.5	234.3	170.4	56.5	18.8	22.0
Guadeloupe	III	38.5	168.0	168.1	5662	69.7	208.5	278.3	265.0	187.5	93.9	9.8	36.5
Guatemala	I	49.5	204.3	197.0	6510	145.6	272.3	305.4	287.2	189.8	76.9	24.8	18.1
Grenada	II	45.7	204.3	204.3	6394	161.1	325.1	302.9	275.8	159.3	46.3	8.3	19.2
Haiti	II	42.7	175.5	167.4	5576	49.7	153.4	287.3	275.6	219.3	107.7	22.0	35.2
Honduras	II	50.8	220.9	215.7	6962	139.0	328.1	341.0	277.9	205.6	83.2	17.5	9.1
Jamaica	II	42.7	169.8	169.7	5494	148.0	316.2	284.1	190.5	111.4	41.7	6.8	37.6
Martinique	III	39.6	170.7	169.5	5746	62.7	212.0	246.8	291.9	192.8	100.2	12.2	34.9
Mexico	I	45.0	196.7	189.7	6268	104.6	293.3	312.0	257.4	192.2	94.2	0.0	22.6
Montserrat	III	43.4	190.9	200.6	6555	106.5	268.7	321.0	282.4	216.7	96.6	18.1	21.5
Netherlands Antilles	III	39.4	173.8	173.5	5660	108.6	284.1	282.1	224.8	157.5	64.1	13.1	34.8
Nicaragua	I	44.8	194.3	190.2	6127	124.0	298.4	300.4	243.5	176.2	69.8	10.8	24.6
Panama	III	40.9	182.5	181.7	5667	147.6	319.8	304.9	190.9	126.3	36.0	7.9	32.3
Puerto Rico	III	33.7	148.4	153.0	4855	97.6	288.0	240.8	164.5	120.0	50.5	9.7	49.7
St. Kitts-Nevis and Anguilla	II	49.8	224.5	230.4	7531	127.2	326.5	383.8	315.7	234.0	98.4	20.6	2.7
St. Lucia	II	42.8	175.9	181.9	5809	134.0	280.1	283.0	235.4	165.8	53.8	9.7	32.8
St. Vincent	I	49.8	212.0	211.4	6594	182.3	343.7	278.6	241.4	151.8	81.0	9.9	15.1
Trinidad and Tobago	III	39.5	173.0	175.9	5536	139.3	303.1	281.7	211.3	126.5	39.9	5.3	36.2
Virgin Islands (U.S.)	I	35.2	163.4	169.5	5348	153.7	323.7	251.4	192.8	101.1	40.2	6.7	40.8
Virgin Islands (U.K.)	III	50.1	226.2	227.1	7385	147.1	342.5	353.2	301.3	224.8	92.4	15.7	3.6
SOUTH AMERICA													
Argentina	I	23.2	89.9	90.3	2962	59.3	132.6	180.8	116.3	70.5	26.3	6.7	84.3
Bolivia	H	43.6	177.8	170.6	5629	74.7	202.9	281.3	252.2	197.3	95.6	21.8	36.1
	L	41.5	170.7	163.8	5403	73.6	206.7	274.0	238.7	182.0	86.4	19.1	
Brazil	II	44.6	183.7	176.7	5768	91.9	231.5	284.5	247.7	190.7	87.7	19.7	31.0
British Guiana	II	43.2	197.6	196.2	6174	164.0	349.0	303.9	229.2	136.6	48.5	3.6	23.2
Chile	I	35.4	138.8	135.4	4537	76.2	178.7	243.8	204.5	124.0	64.5	15.6	55.4
Colombia	III	42.1	178.7	174.5	5681	108.3	269.5	275.9	227.9	167.1	72.7	14.9	33.2
Ecuador	II	45.2	208.8	233.3	7598	133.5	329.4	382.7	316.7	236.3	99.7	21.4	6.6
Paraguay	II	39.8	162.5	158.5	5077	96.2	230.4	241.7	207.8	157.5	67.9	13.9	43.6
Peru	H	45.9	198.6	196.0	6392	111.2	276.4	316.1	268.6	201.4	87.2	17.4	21.9
	L	44.8	195.1	192.6	6279	110.6	278.3	312.5	261.9	193.8	82.6	16.1	
Venezuela	II	45.8	199.7	194.8	6211	121.1	275.4	292.9	263.1	200.7	78.3	10.6	22.2

Table 18-4 (Continued)

Country	Class of estimate	Est.	Summary fertility measures — CBR	GFR	Ind. Std. GFR	TFR	Age-specific fertility rates — 15-19	20-24	25-29	30-34	35-39	40-44	45-49	Percent of demographic transition completed
SOUTH WEST ASIA														
Cyprus	II		25.8	105.3	104.9	3481	37.4	195.0	207.6	131.6	85.9	31.9	6.8	75.0
Iran	III	H	45.5	195.6	186.6	6083	133.6	315.7	300.3	229.3	158.4	64.7	14.5	27.8
		L	42.4	184.6	175.9	5755	120.3	300.8	296.6	219.6	145.1	56.8	11.8	
Iraq	II	H	50.6	226.3	221.2	7243	145.8	347.8	366.8	286.9	202.0	81.7	17.5	7.5
		L	48.0	217.4	212.7	6960	144.4	352.6	357.7	270.1	182.9	70.2	14.1	
Israel	I		27.9	121.0	126.1	4101	59.9	247.3	236.4	163.2	79.3	27.7	6.4	64.6
Kuwait	III		40.3	174.2	159.0	5207	115.2	294.0	272.4	191.3	117.7	42.7	8.1	39.0
Turkey	II	H	48.2	197.2	186.1	6098	114.4	266.0	301.0	245.9	183.9	85.5	22.8	29.6
		L	44.6	178.4	167.3	5482	105.1	245.0	270.5	217.8	160.9	75.9	21.0	
SOUTH CENTRAL ASIA														
Afghanistan	IV	H	51.7	215.3	208.4	6789	159.4	314.5	324.1	260.9	190.6	84.6	23.8	18.1
		L	45.9	195.4	189.1	6178	144.7	304.3	311.3	234.4	158.2	65.2	17.7	
Ceylon	I		40.0	172.0	168.5	5494	67.8	272.2	315.9	220.3	158.8	42.6	21.0	36.9
India	I		41.0	172.5	168.4	5424	151.6	273.7	255.5	197.0	133.8	51.9	19.2	37.4
Pakistan 3/	II	H	50.8	209.0	201.6	6520	184.6	337.7	298.6	230.5	162.1	69.1	21.4	18.0
		L	49.1	204.5	197.3	6377	184.7	344.3	295.4	220.9	150.0	61.2	18.9	
SOUTH EAST ASIA														
Brunei	II		53.2	234.4	226.3	7391	152.0	354.0	369.5	290.7	207.8	85.0	19.1	1.2
Burma	III		43.0	171.4	163.6	5357	90.9	227.1	262.5	220.0	168.0	81.4	21.5	38.4
Cambodia	III		49.7	213.1	209.1	6895	98.6	267.5	350.6	300.3	230.9	106.6	24.5	12.0
Indonesia	III		47.9	197.3	187.3	6115	123.3	281.4	295.0	240.8	179.4	81.9	21.1	27.7
Federation of Malaya	II		44.0	184.1	174.6	5704	120.5	286.6	286.4	216.6	149.9	64.2	16.6	24.4
North Borneo	II		43.6	192.6	189.6	6195	128.0	320.4	324.2	236.1	156.2	60.2	14.0	23.7
	II		46.4	199.3	192.0	6288	123.2	301.0	322.3	247.3	173.0	72.9	17.8	
Philippines 3/ 4/	II	H	44.3	192.2	185.1	6061	122.1	304.8	315.0	233.9	157.8	63.6	15.1	21.3
		L	48.5	206.2	200.0	6650	99.1	274.7	342.9	285.4	213.6	94.2	20.1	
Sarawak	II	H	44.4	189.5	184.8	6091	90.8	255.7	315.3	260.3	192.1	85.6	18.4	23.4
		L	47.0	200.2	195.7	6409	121.0	290.2	323.3	258.0	187.1	82.0	20.3	
Singapore	I		36.6	189.6	185.5	6070	119.3	295.9	312.3	237.8	164.2	68.2	16.2	37.4
Thailand	I		45.5	168.7	166.2	5541	64.0	257.9	295.9	253.0	161.1	66.6	9.7	27.6
South Viet-Nam	IV		45.0	189.0	181.4	5963	96.5	254.2	296.3	248.4	188.3	88.1	20.9	30.7
	IV		43.0	180.3	172.7	5680	89.4	249.7	290.9	236.3	173.3	78.6	17.9	
EAST ASIA														
China (Mainland) 5/	IV	H	39.3	156.6	149.1	4926	74.6	206.7	247.8	206.6	155.2	75.4	18.8	48.4
		L	37.5	150.2	143.3	4753	59.5	187.5	253.7	206.6	151.2	73.3	18.5	
China (Taiwan)	I		39.5	179.7	172.1	5809	47.1	247.9	327.1	259.9	180.4	85.1	14.3	31.8
Hong Kong	II		35.6	159.4	158.1	5211	71.0	252.8	292.9	216.5	143.0	56.4	9.8	43.2
Japan	II		16.8	62.2	61.5	1978	4.3	102.7	162.3	85.0	32.4	8.4	.5	100.0
South Korea 6/	II		40.6	169.8	167.1	5509	81.7	248.0	292.5	226.4	162.1	73.2	18.0	33.0
South Korea 7/	III		42.0	185.2	180.7	5987	71.2	261.5	330.9	256.8	182.0	78.5	16.5	58.8
Macau	III		30.0	129.5	134.1	4457	43.5	181.9	251.9	201.4	139.5	61.9	11.2	49.7
Mongolia	III	H	37.0	150.1	151.6	4920	98.1	248.3	236.4	187.2	136.0	62.4	15.7	
		L	35.9	146.9	148.7	4795	109.2	270.8	225.5	170.0	118.8	51.9	13.0	
Ryukyu Islands	I		25.8	110.8	105.9	3600	12.7	127.4	201.0	179.5	135.7	56.5	7.2	72.3
U.S.S.R. 8/	II		23.9	99.1	96.5	3182	60.1	202.4	178.1	114.0	58.3	21.2	2.3	79.6

Table 18-4 (Continued)

Country	Class of estimate	CBR	GFR	Ind. Std. GFR	TFR	15-19	20-24	25-29	30-34	35-39	40-44	45-49	Percent of demographic transition completed
NORTHERN AND WESTERN EUROPE													
Belgium	I	17.0	75.3	78.3	2565	24.8	151.2	164.8	103.7	47.3	19.9	1.3	92.2
Denmark	I	16.8	70.8	78.2	2577	36.8	165.8	159.9	95.9	43.3	12.8	0.9	93.4
Faeroe Islands	III	25.5	112.0	115.9	3796	49.1	202.2	221.9	155.2	93.1	33.8	4.0	70.1
Finland	I	19.6	80.5	85.5	2810	28.4	155.2	167.0	111.4	66.5	30.5	3.0	88.4
France	I	18.4	83.9	85.7	2797	21.7	168.6	181.6	112.1	53.2	20.5	1.8	87.5
Iceland	I	28.1	127.0	130.8	4256	77.4	248.3	220.3	156.7	104.6	40.7	3.2	61.5
Ireland	I	21.1	95.5	103.8	3432	9.1	92.8	185.0	197.1	143.9	54.2	4.2	78.2
Luxembourg	I	15.9	65.6	67.7	2206	22.1	138.1	142.1	88.4	37.5	12.2	0.7	98.3
Netherlands	I	21.2	91.1	95.8	3174	15.0	116.2	210.2	162.0	91.6	36.6	3.0	81.9
Norway	I	18.0	78.9	89.1	2961	24.7	156.5	183.6	129.6	70.1	25.3	2.4	87.4
Scotland	I	19.0	80.5	86.4	2832	29.2	167.8	181.8	113.3	56.8	16.5	0.9	88.2
Sweden	I	14.4	61.1	69.1	2296	31.8	128.5	145.8	93.9	44.8	13.4	1.0	98.8
England and Wales	I	16.1	68.9	75.7	2506	28.3	151.2	164.5	98.3	44.6	13.5	0.8	94.6
CENTRAL EUROPE													
Austria	I	17.2	69.9	77.2	2558	38.6	154.1	149.2	101.4	47.9	19.2	1.1	93.8
Czechoslovakia	I	18.0	76.7	80.7	2692	44.1	210.4	150.8	83.2	33.7	15.3	1.0	90.6
West Germany	I	17.0	67.2	71.0	2336	23.1	113.8	154.2	107.5	49.2	18.0	1.3	96.7
Hungary	I	17.3	69.1	72.3	2367	51.9	176.5	127.8	72.7	30.2	13.4	0.8	95.8
Poland	I	26.3	103.1	102.5	3324	44.0	204.8	185.2	123.2	78.7	20.0	2.9	77.1
Switzerland	I	17.5	70.0	71.4	2319	13.9	118.5	150.7	104.8	54.4	19.9	1.5	96.0
SOUTHERN EUROPE													
Albania	III	42.2	182.6	181.1	5967	83.9	248.4	321.5	256.5	184.4	80.4	18.3	29.4
Bulgaria	I	18.6	72.9	72.8	2412	68.2	200.0	124.9	57.9	20.7	9.2	1.4	94.3
Gibraltar	II	16.9	70.2	78.0	2519	39.6	171.6	152.6	90.5	39.6	9.9	0.0	94.1
Greece	II	19.3	73.7	69.7	2365	15.6	109.8	148.8	107.9	59.6	28.0	3.4	94.5
Italy	I	18.2	71.2	72.2	2362	21.2	103.8	150.3	111.6	56.4	27.1	2.0	95.3
Malta and Gozo	I	25.6	107.9	107.5	3559	22.2	192.0	195.0	149.4	106.9	41.4	4.9	73.5
Portugal	I	23.5	91.2	91.2	3020	27.1	145.2	162.1	127.4	89.2	48.0	4.9	83.3
Romania	I	22.3	82.6	83.1	2668	50.1	173.5	141.8	89.1	62.5	14.4	2.3	89.1
Spain	I	21.5	83.9	85.7	2796	9.1	115.3	184.1	138.9	77.7	30.2	3.9	87.5
Yugoslavia	I	24.6	97.9	92.9	3022	51.5	198.9	169.6	96.7	49.9	30.6	7.2	81.4
OCEANIA													
American Samoa	I	40.6	189.4	185.4	6267	44.0	290.2	381.7	260.2	180.2	76.1	21.0	24.7
Australia	II	22.6	97.6	105.2	3485	41.0	210.4	228.2	132.7	63.2	20.1	1.4	77.1
British Solomon Islands	II	41.2	179.5	172.6	5678	103.1	280.1	299.0	225.6	152.3	62.4	13.0	33.0
Cook Islands	II	53.0	230.1	226.8	7503	99.2	272.2	383.8	335.7	261.2	121.2	27.4	1.4
Fiji Islands	I	45.2	199.6	194.9	6386	122.7	313.7	331.5	251.7	172.8	69.6	15.1	20.6
Guam	III	35.2	191.4	177.6	5790	106.2	344.2	285.6	210.5	138.6	65.9	6.2	28.6
New Caledonia	II	35.2	150.2	150.7	4901	92.0	250.3	253.4	191.5	129.6	52.8	10.8	48.7
New Zealand	II	26.3	118.0	128.0	4239	39.4	249.4	285.6	166.8	81.8	23.1	1.7	64.2
Niue	H	48.7	221.4	214.9	7180	92.6	275.4	380.7	324.6	238.8	105.2	18.6	9.5
	L	46.1	212.6	206.4	6897	91.2	280.1	371.5	307.8	219.8	93.7	15.2	
Pacific Islands	H	45.9	195.0	196.0	6418	106.8	322.6	349.8	256.9	171.8	64.2	11.7	21.6
	L	43.9	196.9	193.0	6291	99.1	292.7	350.7	274.3	194.7	77.4	13.9	
Tokelau Islands	II	43.8	203.7	199.5	6506	98.0	289.1	343.8	261.5	180.2	68.6	15.9	20.3
Tonga Islands	H	42.3	184.1	175.8	5840	90.3	237.6	296.2	256.6	188.0	84.6	14.8	31.9
	L	40.7	178.4	170.3	5659	89.4	240.6	290.3	245.8	175.9	77.2	15.0	
Western Samoa	H	48.6	222.4	216.5	7127	120.3	339.5	379.3	290.7	201.2	79.6	15.0	9.2
	L	46.5	215.2	209.7	6901	119.1	343.3	372.0	277.2	186.0	70.3	12.3	

Table 18-4 (*Continued*)

Definitions:
Class I   -   Countries with good census data and vital statistics, and published fertility measures.
Class II   -   Countries with a relatively accurate census, but poor vital registration. Fertility measures presented are estimated except those of the few countries having published data of satisfactory quality.
Class III   -   Countries having data only on age composition. Fertility measures were estimated from available age data and supplementary indices.
Class IV   -   Countries with neither census data or vital statistics. Fertility measures were based on estimated demographic characteristics. Estimated fertility measures in this class are most likely to be in error and therefore are presented an approximate range.

Footnotes:
1/   For Moslem population only.
2/   For colored population only.
3/   Based on population statistics by age groups and marital status of poor or uncertain quality.
4/   Age data without supplementary indices were used to estimate the total fertility rate and the other rates were obtained in the regular way.
5/   Based on age composition estimated by the UN and on other estimated of supplementary indices.
6/   Based on 1955 Korean census.
7/   Based on 1960 Korean census.
8/   Based on recently published 1959 U.S.S.R. census.

668

Table 18-5 Comparison of Average Demographic, Social, and
Economic Characteristics of Nations Having the Highest and the
Lowest Birthrates: 1960

Characteristics	15 nations having:		
	Highest birth rates in world	Lowest birth rates in world	Difference
Percent of demographic transition completed....	9.5	94.9	85.4
Median age at first marriage...................	19.4	22.2	2.8
Percent of childbearing occuring at ages 20-29.	47.8	61.3	13.47
Infant mortality rate.........................	117	41	- 76
Dependency ratio: children....................	146.1	71.8	- 74.3
Percentage of Population 15 yrs + illiterate...	57.4	9.7	- 47.7
Per Capita gross national product.............	211	1149	-938
Percent of labor force employed in agriculture.	56	29	- 27
Percent of population rural...................	74.4	48.7	25.7
Percent of women ever-married by age 45-49.....	88.2	88.7	0.5

Source: United Nations Demographic Yearbooks, Compendium of Social Statistics, and
National Accounts Statistics.

The various measures of fertility by no means rank the nations in exactly the same way, although they usually differ only by a position or two. Even the standardized and unstandardized GFR do not rank the nations exactly alike. (Some of the difference is due to peculiarities of age composition caused by war.)

2. *The nations with the lowest fertility are not necessarily those that are the most industrialized or the most urbanized, have the highest per capita wealth, or have the highest level of educational attainment.* Certainly, when we note that Japan, Greece, Italy, Hungary, Bulgaria, Czechoslovakia, and Romania are on the list and recall that France, the Netherlands, Norway, and Scotland are *not* on the list, it causes us to revise somewhat our interpretation of the prerequisites for attaining complete fertility control. *Greece, Bulgaria, and Romania all report more than 10 percent of their population illiterate at the last census.* We conclude, therefore, that *any nation can attain full demographic equilibrium without having to be luxuriously wealthy, highly urbanized, or completely educated.*

Using the same procedure, let us rank in order the 15 nations having the highest standardized general fertility rate.

Rank	CBR	TFR	GFR
Ecuador	45.2	7598	208.8
St. Kitts	49.8	7531	224.5
Sudan	54.9	7496	234.8
Brunei	53.2	7391	234.8
Iraq	50.6	7243	226.3
Western Samoa ..	48.6	7127	222.4
Honduras	50.8	6962	220.9
Costa Rica	49.7	7068	223.8
Ivory Coast	49.1	6987	219.4
Dominica	47.0	6975	212.1
Swaziland	54.1	6970	219.7
St. Vincent	49.8	6594	212.0
Ghana	53.5	6860	224.1
Cambodia	49.7	6895	213.1
Guinea	54.3	6605	216.4

This tabulation shows even more inconsistencies among the measures than did the low-fertility nations. Inadequate census data and the necessity of making rough guesses about the level of infant mortality and age at marriage account for much of this. In Table 18-5 we compare certain selected characteristics of the nations having the highest and the lowest levels of fertility. This comparison of extremes leads to several important findings:

1. The highest levels of fertility found anywhere in the world show a CBR of about 55, a GFR of about 235, and a TFR of about 7500. These may be taken as the parameters of a population whose fertility is at a biological

near capacity, given factors of nutrition, health, and marriage as they exist around the world today.

2. In the low-fertility nations marriage occurs almost five years later on an average than in the high-fertility nations. Thus postponement of marriage appears to be an important part of fertility limitation. However, this postponement is more than merely the elimination of child marriage as it exists in parts of Asia, but is rather the movement of the average from about age 18 to about age 24 years.

3. In the low-fertility nations childbearing is concentrated in the ages 20 to 29, with rates almost zero at ages beyond 40. In the high-fertility nations the rates are moderately high at all fertile ages, and only the onset of sterility and menopause appears to cause fertility declines.

4. High-fertility populations still have extraordinarily high rates of infant mortality. Possibly this reinforces high-fertility attitudes of the couples.

5. In the high-fertility populations the dependency load for children is extremely high. An average of 44 percent of the population is under 15 years of age.

6. The average high-fertility population is indeed more poorly educated, economically poorer, more rural, more agricultural, and less "economically advanced" generally than the average low-fertility population. Also, the nutrition situation is below the level needed to maintain good health and vitality. The high-fertility nations are making slower progress in their efforts to attain economic development. However, the averages for the two groups hide a great deal of internal variation, which suggests that these are not simple cause-and-effect factors but are parts of a complex total situation. This will be explored more fully in the next section.

18.4. Measuring Progress in Making the Demographic Transition

If we can assume that the countries with the highest fertility today represent maximum possible fertility without fertility control, we can have a base line against which to measure the progress of nations toward demographic transition. We noted earlier that a total fertility rate of 7500 and/or a general fertility rate of 235 represent this maximum. From our earlier analysis we can conclude that the corresponding values for low fertility are a TFR of 2200 and a GFR of 60. Thus *the progress of a nation in making the transition from high to low fertility may be measured by tracing its movement between these two extremes.* In fact, by simple statistical manipulation we can construct an index showing the *percent of demographic transition that has already been completed by a population.* The formula for computing such a measure can be developed as follows:

1. Progressing through the demographic transition involves change in the GFR and the TFR:

Stage of transition	TFR	GFR
Start	7500	235
Complete	2200	60
Total change during transition	−5500	−175

2. If we assume that every population begins the transition at the point indicated by "start" above, we can measure how far it has progressed by taking the difference between its *present* GFR and TFR and the values for "start."

3. Since the "total change during transition" states the total amount of change that must be made to accomplish the demographic transition, a good way of estimating the percent of progress that has been made is to express the difference, obtained in (2), as a percent of the total change during transition.

4. It is possible to perform this process twice, separately for GFR and TFR. Because we are not certain of our data and the estimating process is only approximate, we can accept a simple average of the two answers as our best estimate of what percentage of the demographic transition has been completed.

Table 18-6 Percentage of the Population at Each Decile of the Demographic Transition, World and Regions: 1960

Region	Percent of demographic transition completed										Total
	0–9 percent	10–19 percent	20–29 percent	30–39 percent	40–49 percent	50–59 percent	60–69 percent	70–79 percent	80–89 percent	90–100 percent	
World total.......	1.3	7.1	13.6	23.0	22.0	0.5	0.9	9.3	11.0	11.3	100.0
Developed regions.....	...	0.2	0.3	....	....	...	2.7	32.4	35.9	28.5	100.0
Europe..............	...	...	0.4	....	....	...	...	7.8	34.6	57.2	100.0
Northern America....	...	...	....	....	....	10.4	9.1	80.5	....	....	100.0
U.S.S.R.............	...	...	....	....	....	...	...	100.0	....	....	100.0
Oceania.............	0.8	9.0	7.7	1.2	0.5	...	15.2	65.6	....	....	100.0
Developing regions....	1.9	9.9	18.9	32.1	30.8	0.7	0.1	0.1	1.1	4.4	100.0
Africa..............	9.2	25.4	50.9	14.4	0.1	...	...	...	....	....	100.0
Asia................	0.4	8.4	12.3	33.4	39.6	...	0.1	0.1	....	5.7	100.0
Middle America......	5.1	6.7	62.5	11.7	3.6	10.1	0.3	...	....	....	100.0
South America.......	3.0	...	13.2	61.6	1.2	5.1	...	...	15.9	....	100.0

The proposed index arrived at by this line of reasoning, expressed simply in symbols, is as follows:

$$\text{PCT-DEM-TRANS-COMP} = \frac{1}{2}\left(\frac{235 - \text{GFR}}{175} + \frac{7500 - \text{TFR}}{5300}\right)$$

With this formula we can compute an index of progress toward fertility control for every nation of the world. This has been done and is reported in the right-hand column of Table 18-4.

Now let us use the results of this computation to review the world situation with respect to fertility, by regions and continents.

Table 18-6 breaks the total process of mak-

ing the demographic transition into 10 parts, each representing 10 percent of the distance to be traveled. In other words, it establishes 10 stages or steps and shows how much of the population now has arrived at each stage. This is shown for the world as a whole, for each continent, and for each region. Small nations for which data are not available have been arbitrarily assigned to the same position as the nations that they most resemble. Figure 18-2 illustrates how the world's population is distributed among the 10 steps toward full fertility control. Both the table and the figure are only approximate, of course, because we must put all of a nation's population in the same step, whereas there obviously is a wide distribution within each nation. If we compute a median

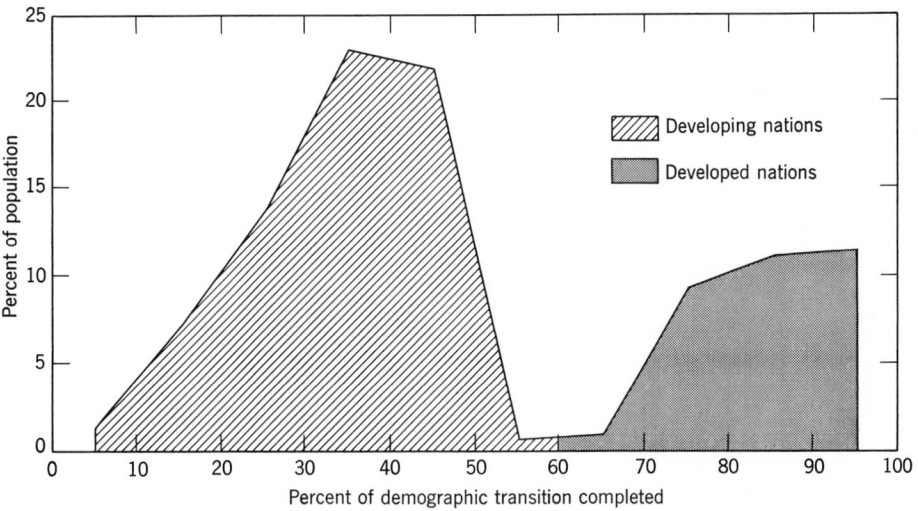

Figure 18-2 Percentage of Demographic Transition Completed by the World Population: 1960.

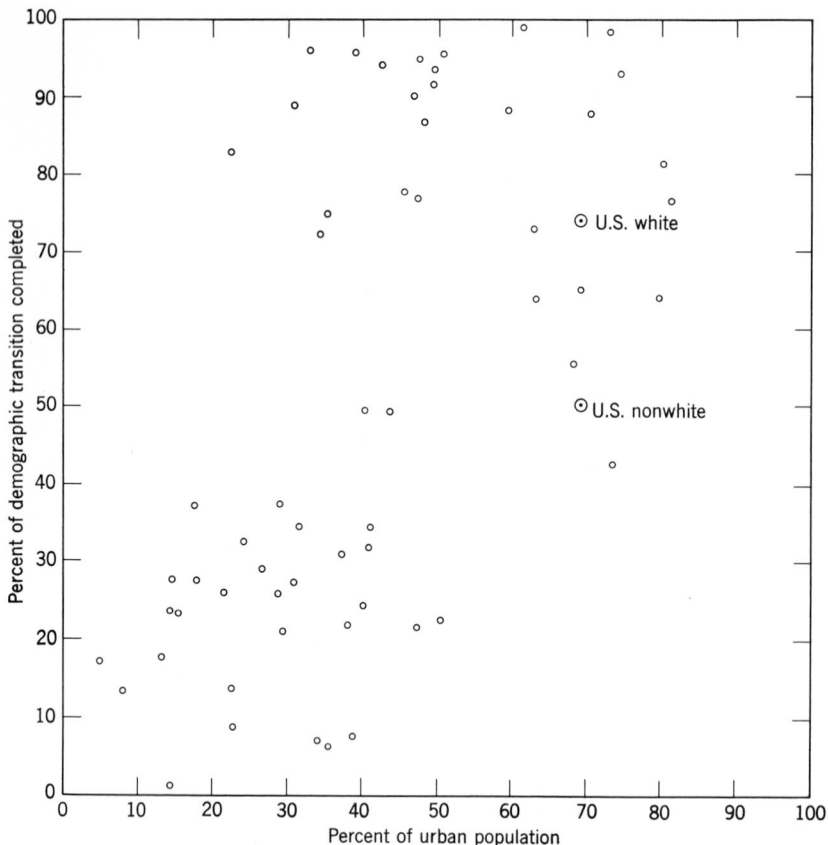

Figure 18-3 Scattergram of Percent of Urban Population Plotted against Percent of Demographic Transition Completed; Nations for Which Data Are Available: 1960.

point for each continent (the step at which 50 percent of the population lies above on the way to the demographic transition), we gain the following results:

Median percent completed

World	43.5
Africa	19.9
America, Northern	79.0
America, Middle	26.3
America, South	35.4
Asia	39.3
Europe	91.4
USSR	80-90

These represent the situation as of 1960; some nations, including the United States, have since made substantial moves toward completing the transition.

These data give us the statistical support needed to justify the somewhat aggressive position taken in Chapter 3 that *the entire world is in the process of demographic regulation.* Only a tiny fraction has failed to move at least 20 percent of the way toward reestablishing demographic equilibrium. *In our thinking about the problem of world population pressure it is important for us to realize that all of the major so-called "underdeveloped nations" have already made 20 to 50 percent of the progress needed to achieve full fertility control. Any view on the part of foreigners undertaking to provide technical assistance in this area that these nations have been indifferent to the problem and have made no attempt to adjust is completely erroneous.* Moreover, any notion outsiders may have that fertility control is not an integral part of the culture and that the desire to avoid pregnancy is a new idea to the "natives" is naïve and reflects our fundamental ignorance about the attitudes of our

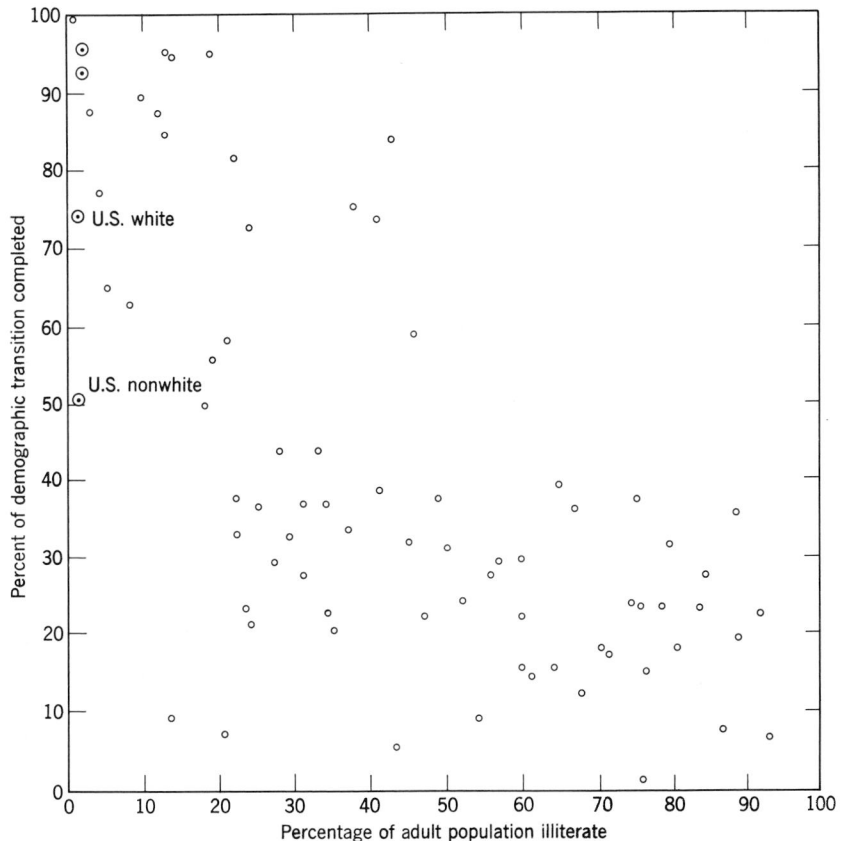

Figure 18-4 Scattergram of Percent of Population Illiterate Plotted against Percent of Demographic Transition Completed; Nations for Which Data Are Available: 1960.

fellowmen around the world. Clearly, all efforts to help bring fertility control to developing nations should be in the spirit of accelerating a movement that is already inherently a part of the values and life goals of the people. What is comparatively new are the *methods, the procedures, and the explicit sustained planned effort through community institutions,* but even these are not absolutely unique in any nation of the world. In summary: our review of the fertility situation around the world reveals that the world's people appear to be at least partially aroused to the dangers of overpopulation and are making adaptive efforts to adjust. Almost everywhere some progress has been made, and total progress is much greater than we customarily permit ourselves to realize. On the other hand, many nations who have completed

only 20 to 50 percent of the task find themselves in a precarious position because they have already accomplished almost 80 to 90 percent of the task of lowering the death rates and are growing at a very rapid rate as a result. Only a major special effort on a nationwide basis can reestablish a reasonable demographic equilibrium in many of these nations.

18.5. Correlates of Progress in Making the Demographic Transition

Let us use the estimates of percent of the demographic transition completed by each of the nations of the world to learn just how closely some of the widely claimed essentials for fertility control are associated with progress in making the demographic transition. Our preliminary explorations in the preceding section

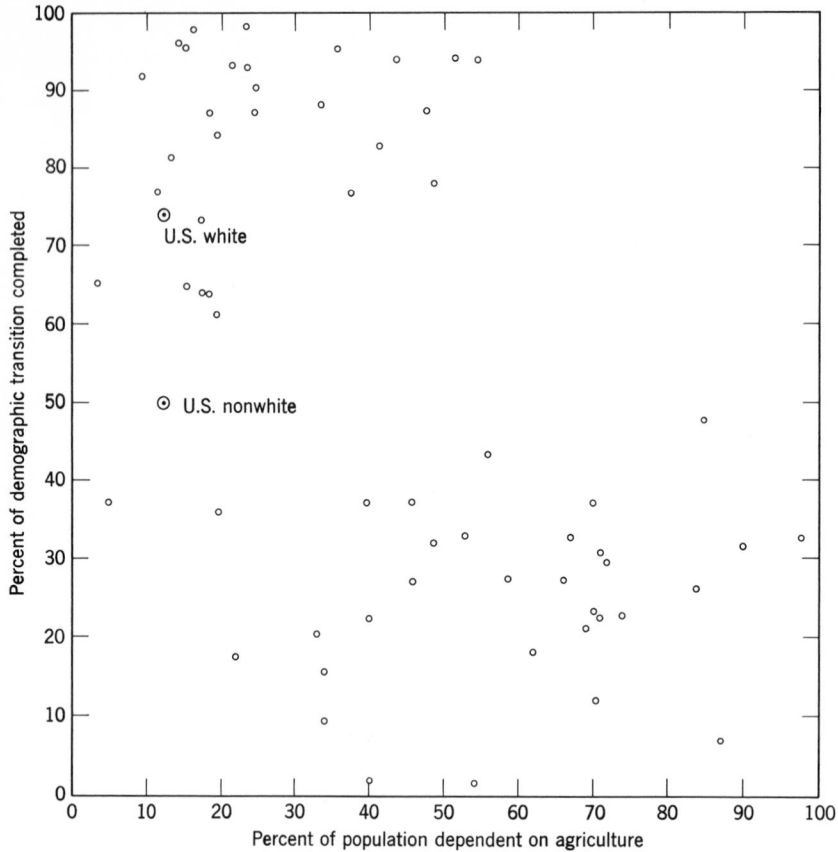

Figure 18-5 Scattergram of Percent of Population Dependent on Agriculture Plotted against Percent of Demographic Transition Completed; Nations for Which Data Are Available: 1960.

lead us to doubt that these relationships are as close as many might have us believe. In a series of scattergrams we have plotted the percentage of completeness of the demographic transition against each of the following variables:

These scattergrams all possess two traits in common: (1) they show that there is an unmistakable relationship between the trait and progress along the scale of demographic transition, but (2) they also show that this relationship is far from perfect and that the deviation of nations away from the general trend line is very large. In fact, the deviations are so pronounced that it would be difficult to consider seriously any one of them, or any combination of them, to be a "cause" of declining fertility.

To formalize the data of these charts somewhat, a coefficient of correlation was computed between these variables and the percent of

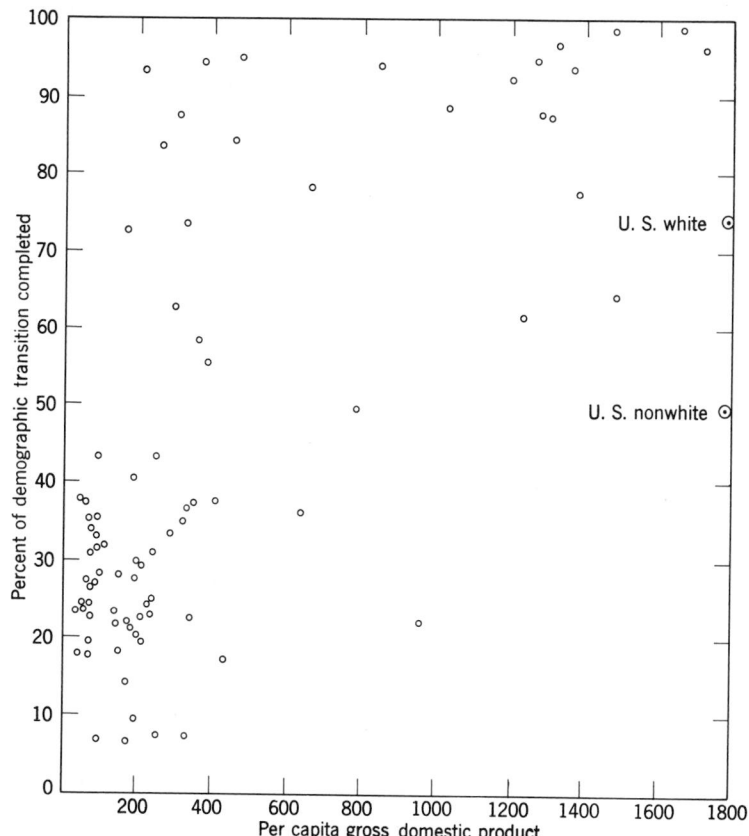

Figure 18-6 Scattergram of Per Capita Gross Domestic Product Plotted against Percent of Demographic Transition Completed; Nation for Which Data Are Available: 1960.

demographic transition completed. These correlations were as shown in the left-hand column below:

Variable	Correlation with percent of demographic transition completed	Controlling percent at educational level 1 or higher
Percent urban	+.55	−.10
Percent of population illiterate	−.77	−.13
Percent of population in agriculture	−.67	−.10
Per capita gross domestic product (dollars)	+.64	+.19
Infant mortality rate	−.69	+.18
Percent educated at level 1 or higher	+.75	—
Percent in school	+.79	+.31
Median age at marriage	+.62	+.23
Expectation of life at birth	+.71	.20

The highest correlations are with variables that reflect educational level and literacy. The lowest ones are those that reflect urbanization and changing levels of living. Of course, there are numerous intercorrelations among the variables themselves. In an effort to learn how the rest would behave if the factor of educational attainment were controlled, a partial correlation coefficient was computed for each, holding constant the educational variable. The results are shown in the right-hand column above. The correlations for urbanization and per capita

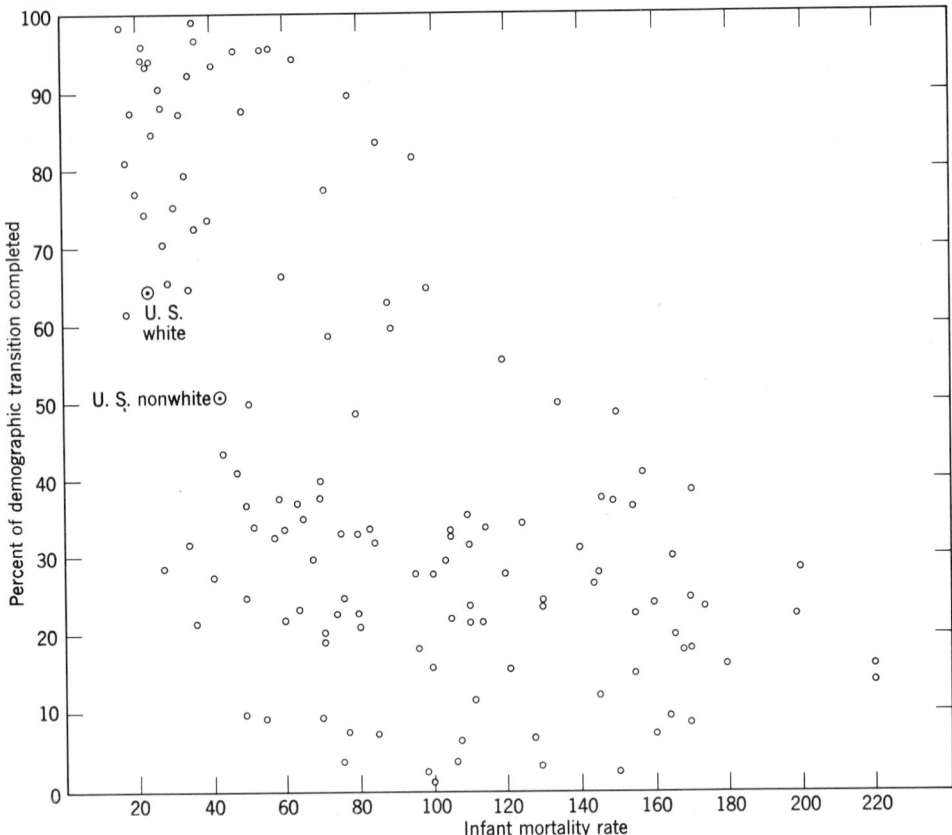

Figure 18-7 Scattergram of Infant Mortality Rate Plotted against Percent of Demographic Transition Completed; Nations for Which Data Are Available: 1960.

gross domestic product decline to a very low level. Although these results are very crude, they suggest that rising educational levels, increased school attendance, and elimination of early marriage are much more powerful in promoting fertility reduction than simple urbanization and rising levels of living. A major driving force behind fertility control appears to be education.

It is also noteworthy that educational level alone accounted for 56 percent of the total variance in demographic transition. Adding all the other variables managed to account for an additional 16 percent beyond this. Taken together, these variables account for 70 percent of the variance in progress toward the demographic transition, leaving 30 percent unexplained and presumably due to other factors. In this, urbanization accounted for only a negligible amount of variance.

It is important to emphasize that differences in fecundity, or physiological capacity to bear children, seem to be almost equal among the world's population and are not a major factor in accounting for international differences in the world's birthrates. The major underlying causes are differential exposure to sex relations and differential use of contraception (see Section 18-9).

The preceding analysis has two important implications. (1) It calls into question the set of "driving forces" that lie behind the demographic transition, as they have been formulated. Perhaps the historical decline of the birthrate has been more a simple function of rising educational attainment than of urbanization and economic and technological development. (2) If this is true, *it should be comparatively easy to discover what aspect of rising literacy and educational attainment is most intimately related to lower fertility and then to "mass-produce" it on a large scale to hasten*

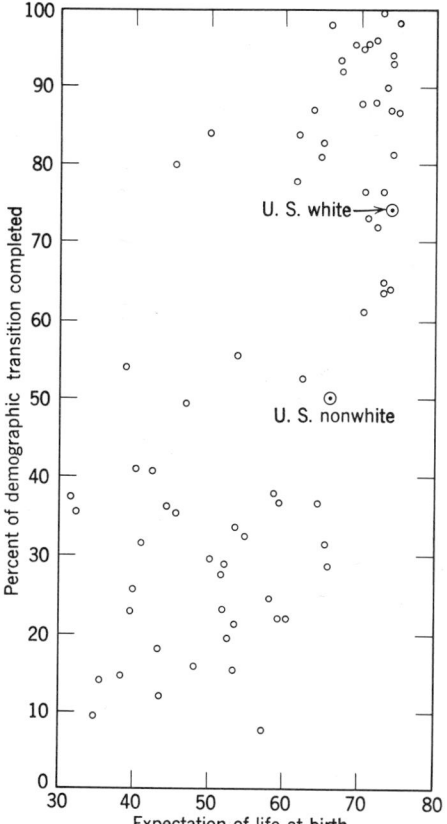

Figure 18-8 Scattergram of Expectation of Life at Birth (Females) Plotted against Percent of Demographic Transition Completed; Nations for Which Data Are Available: 1960.

fertility decline in advance of other aspects of educational attainment. In other words, these findings offer much more hope for a rapid curbing of high fertility than the older urbanization and level-of-living hypothesis.

A multiple-variable approach to the comparative study of international fertility differences has been taken by several recent writers. The procedure they have followed has been to use the statistical techniques of multiple and partial correlation and regression to try to explain international differences in birthrates. Of special concern have been the following variables:

per capita income
level of educational attainment
density of population settlement
degree of urbanization
infant mortality rate

contact with industrialized nations
degree of modernization
progress in economic development
religion
social position of women
cultural heterogeneity
family structure

By using published statistical data, indexes that undertake to measure each of the variables are constructed. The results obtained have varied according to the indexes devised, the number and combination of variables employed, and the procedure followed in computing the regressions and correlations (holding several variables constant). For example, Weintraub,[5] Adelman,[6] and Heer[7] all found a *positive* relationship between per capita income and fertility and a *negative* relationship between level of educational attainment and fertility. This is a surprising result, since educational attainment and per capita income are positively correlated with each other.

Friedlander and Silver[8] have thrown some light on this anomaly by performing a similar analysis in three separate parts: for developed industrialized nations, for intermediate nations, and for underdeveloped nations. They performed such an analysis for 41 different variables, attempting to quantify all of the variables listed above. They discovered that correlations that appeared to be sizeable when all nations were considered together tended to become small and nonsignificant when the three-part analysis was performed. Very often the regressions were of opposite signs for the industrialized and the underdeveloped countries. For example, in the developed nations per capita income was found to be positively associated with fertility, while in the underdeveloped nations it was negatively associated.

[5] Robert Weintraub, "The Birth Rate and Economic Development: An Empirical Study," *Econometrica,* **40** (4) (October 1962), 812–817.
[6] Irma Adelman, "An Econometric Analysis of Population Growth," *American Economic Review* (3) (June 1963), 314–339.
[7] David M. Heer, "Economic Development and Fertility," *Demography,* 3 (2) (1966), 423–444.
[8] Stanley Friedlander and Morris Silver, "A Quantitative Study of the Determinants of Fertility Behavior," *Demography,* 4 (1) (1967), 30–70.

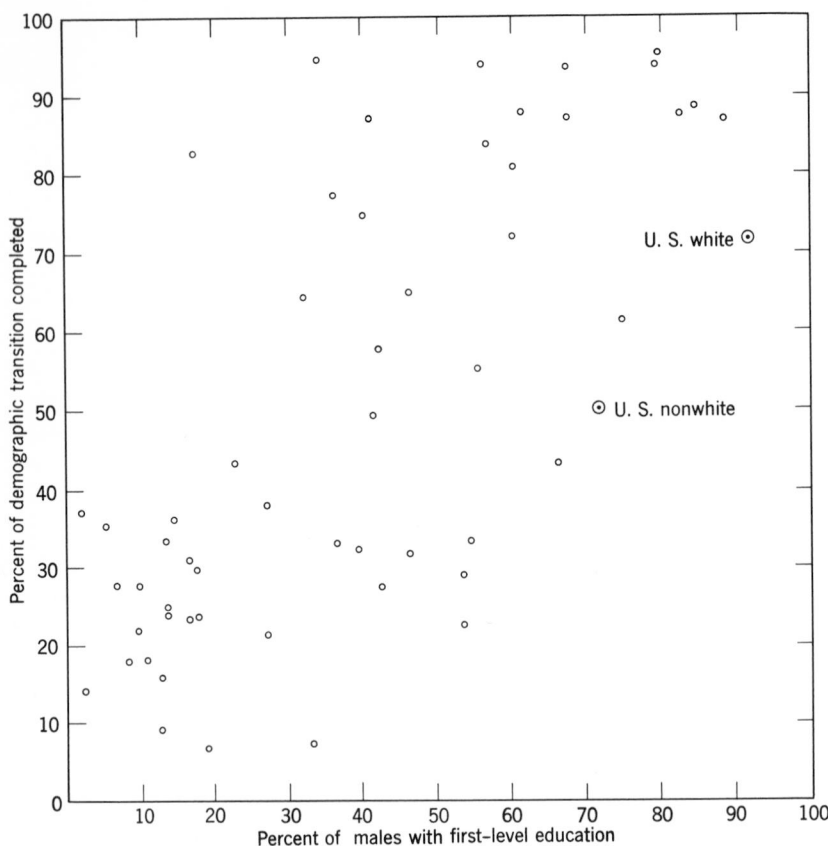

Figure 18-9   Scattergram of Percent of Male Population with First-Level Education Plotted against Percent of Demographic Transition Completed; Nations for Which Data Are Available: 1960.

They conclude that almost all of the variables lost most of their explanatory effect when calculated in this manner, but from the pattern of small associations they develop the general hypothesis that economic factors strongly affect the birthrate, even in the developing nations. This hypothesis had been advanced earlier by Becker,[9] who maintained that the decision to have an additional child is, among other things, a major economic decision and is subject to the same principles of economic analysis that influence other economic activities of persons and groups. Friedlander and Silver believe that there is evidence that parents in developing countries also exercise rational economic choice in bearing or not bearing additional children;

[9] Gary S. Becker, "An Economic Analysis of Fertility," in *Demographic and Economic Change in Developed Countries* (Princeton: Princeton University Press, 1960, 209–40.

the costs of children and their estimated economic value at a later date are consciously or unconsciously components of having additional pregnancies. They assert that ". . . the well-known differences between urban and rural fertility may be explained by the relatively high costs of rearing children in urban areas and not by differences between the two areas in cultural factors or levels of contraceptive knowledge." In a similar vein, they interpret some patterns of regression to suggest that social reforms, in the nature of social security, lessen the economic dependence of parents on their children for support in old age and thereby reduce fertility.

All of the studies cited above suffer from several deficiencies: they are based on very small and not-too-typical samples of data for the underdeveloped countries; the measures of fertility used are crude and are not corrected for

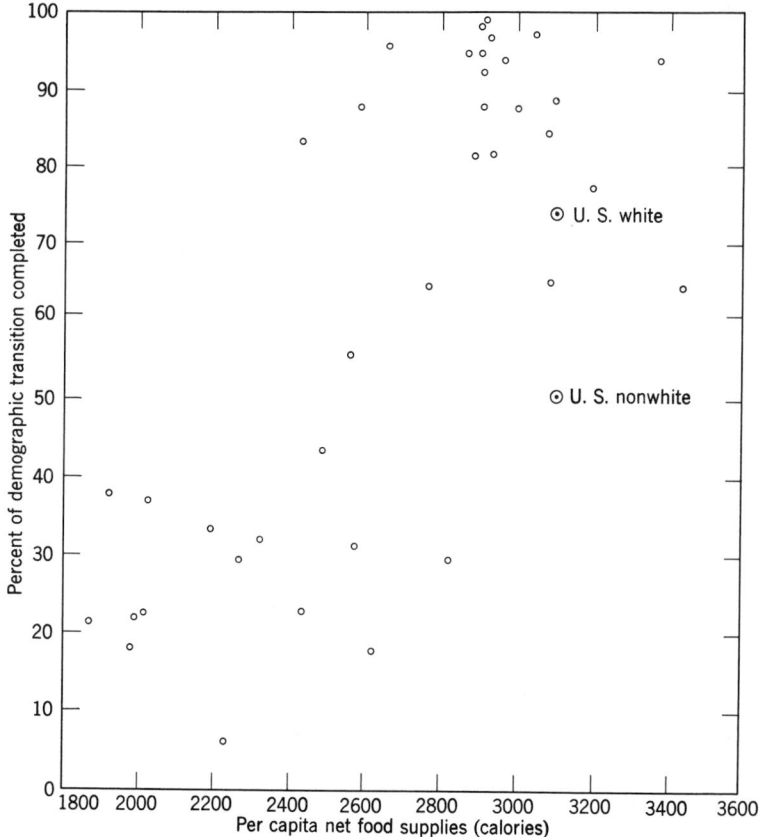

Figure 18-10 Scattergram of Net Food Supplies Per Capita (Calories) Plotted against Percent of Demographic Transition Completed; Nations for Which Data Are Available: 1960.

known biases; the explanatory variables employed are also very crude and often are based on data of highly dubious quality. Finally, the interpretations made of the results are highly subjective, for the various indexes are based on data collected for other purposes, and the validity of these indexes to measure the latent variables the authors read into them is not known. We must conclude *that we do not know why some nations have high birthrates and others low birthrates*. However, many of the analysts who have tackled this problem of explaining international differences in fertility by multiple variables emerge with the very strong impression that the older theory of "cultural inertia" of the masses in the underdeveloped nations cannot be supported by empirical evidence. The only valid explanation we have for international differences in fertility is the extent to which contraceptive practices have been adopted. But it is lack of a valid theory of *why* some nations practice contraception and others do not that concerns us.

18.6. Natality in the United States

Overall Trends. Chapter 6 reviewed the natality trends in the United States in terms of crude birthrates. Refined measures of natality are not available for dates before 1905, and it is not until 1940 that a complete set of precise measures is available. Table 18-7 summarizes the refined measures, separately for the white and nonwhite population. According to these statistics, the average childbearing by white couples in the United States in 1965 was at a level that would produce about 2.8 children per female during the total reproductive cycle. The comparable figure for the nonwhite population was 3.9. This represents a significant decline from a peak in 1957 of 3.6 children

Table 18-7   Measures of Natality in the United States, by Color: 1800 to 1965

Year	White population			Nonwhite population			Ratio of nonwhite to white
	Total fertility rate	General fertility rate	Crude birth rates	Total fertility rate	General fertility rate	Crude birth rates	
1965.........	2790	91.4	18.3	3891	133.9	27.6	1.46
1964.........	3074	99.9	20.0	4153	141.7	29.1	1.42
1963.........	3201	103.7	20.7	4269	144.9	29.7	1.40
1962.........	3348	107.5	21.4	4396	148.8	30.5	1.38
1961.........	3502	112.2	22.2	4532	153.5	31.6	1.37
1960.........	3533	113.2	22.7	4522	153.6	32.1	1.36
1959.........	3567	114.6	23.1	4774	162.2	34.2	1.42
1958.........	3560	114.9	23.3	4727	160.5	34.3	1.40
1957.........	3625	117.7	24.0	4798	163.0	35.3	1.38
1956.........	3546	116.0	24.0	4730	160.9	35.4	1.39
1955.........	3446	113.8	23.8	4550	155.3	34.7	1.36
1954.........	3415	113.6	24.2	4474	153.2	34.9	1.35
1953.........	3306	111.0	24.0	4283	147.3	34.1	1.33
1952.........	3250	110.1	24.1	4147	143.3	33.6	1.30
1951.........	3157	107.7	23.9	4091	142.1	33.8	1.32
1950.........	2977	102.3	23.0	3928	137.3	33.3	1.34
1949.........	3009	103.6	23.6	3855	135.1	33.0	1.30
1948.........	3022	104.3	24.0	3742	131.6	32.4	1.26
1947.........	3230	111.8	26.1	3575	125.9	31.2	1.13
1946.........	2901	100.4	23.6	3238	113.9	28.4	1.13
1945.........	2421	83.4	19.7	3017	106.0	26.5	1.27
1944.........	2501	86.3	20.5	3075	108.5	27.4	1.26
1943.........	2664	92.3	22.1	3128	111.0	28.3	1.20
1942.........	2577	89.5	21.5	3022	107.6	27.7	1.20
1941.........	2328	80.7	19.5	2956	105.4	27.3	1.31
1940.........	2229	77.1	18.6	2870	102.4	26.7	1.33
1939.........		74.8	18.0		100.1	26.1	1.34
1938.........		76.5	18.4		100.5	26.3	1.31
1937.........	2182	74.4	17.9	2868	99.4	26.0	1.34
1936.........		73.3	17.6		95.9	25.1	1.31
1935.........		74.5	17.9		98.4	25.8	1.32
1934.........		75.8	18.1		100.4	26.3	1.32
1933.........		73.7	17.6		97.3	25.5	1.32
1932.........	2225	79.0	18.7	2712	103.0	26.9	1.30
1931.........		82.4	19.5		102.1	26.6	1.24
1930.........		87.1	20.6		105.9	27.5	1.22
1929.........		87.3	20.5		106.1	27.3	1.22
1928.........		91.7	21.5		111.0	28.5	1.21
1927.........	....	97.1	22.7	....	121.7	31.1	1.25
1926.........		99.2	23.1		130.3	33.4	1.31
1925.........		103.3	24.1		134.0	34.2	1.30
1924.........		107.8	25.1		135.6	34.6	1.26
1923.........		108.0	25.2		130.5	33.2	1.21
1922.........		108.8	25.4		130.8	33.2	1.20
1921.........		117.2	27.3		140.8	35.8	1.20
1920.........		115.4	26.9		137.5	35.0	1.19
1915-1919....	....	122.5	27.6	....	.....	....	-
1910-1914....	....	123.5	29.1	....	.....	....	-
1905-1909....	3584	123.6	29.7	4547	.....	....	-
190..........	....	....	30.1	....	.....	....	-
1890.........	....	....	31.5	....	.....	....	-
1880.........	....	....	35.2	....	.....	....	-
1870.........	....	....	38.3	....	.....	....	-
1860.........	....	....	41.4	....	.....	....	-
1850.........	....	....	43.3	....	.....	....	-
1840.........	....	....	48.3	....	.....	....	-
1830.........	....	....	51.4	....	.....	....	-
1820.........	....	....	52.8	....	.....	....	-
1810.........	....	....	54.3	....	.....	....	-
1800.........	....	....	55.0	....	.....	....	-

Source: Vital Statistics of the United States: 1965, Tables 1-2 and 1-6; U.S. Bureau of Census, Historical Statistics of the United States, Table B 19-30.

per white female and 4.8 per nonwhite female. Thus, to the extent that a "cross-sectional" measure can be trusted, the American population definitely appeared to be on a rapid retreat from the high-fertility spree in which it had engaged from 1946 to 1957.

Provisional statistics for early 1968 (March) indicated that the crude birthrate had declined further to about 16.5 per thousand; the GFR had decreased to 80; and the average size of family implied by the TFR was about 2.4 children per woman. As of this date the rate was still declining.

The most precise overview of the recent natality history in the United States may be gained by studying the columns for "general fertility rate." These are available for each year since 1905. In 1910 this rate was about 123.5. Throughout the 1920s it declined steadily, despite a very high level of prosperity in the nation. It declined even more during the 1930s and for the white population reached the unprecedented low of 73 to 74 in 1933 and again in 1936-1938. This represented a decline of nearly 40 percent. During the years of the economic depression, the total fertility rate was only slightly above 2 children per completed family—not quite enough to maintain population growth on a long-range basis.

Between 1935 and 1940 the fertility rates remained low, but started to climb gradually during the early years of 1940s as the economy recovered. Some irregularities occur in 1944-1945 as a result of the fact that many millions of men were overseas. The "baby boom" started abruptly in 1946, as a result of demobilization of military forces, with a sudden jump in the white general fertility rate from 83 to 100 within a single year and a subsequent jump to 112 in 1947. This sudden "baby boom" brought the total fertility rate to a point well above 3 children per completed family—sufficient for moderately rapid growth.

Many observers have failed to appreciate the fact that the high rate that prevailed in the days following demobilization in 1946 and 1947 did *not* represent the peak fertility of the "baby boom." These rates were at about the same level that prevailed immediately after World War I. The really surprising aspect of the "baby boom" has been that in the 1950s the *rate* con-

tinued to climb to amazing heights, reaching a peak in 1957-1958. As we have seen, an average completed family size of 3.6 is highly atypical for industrialized nations. Yet this rate was achieved in 1957-1959, 11 to 13 years after military demobilization and the other dislocations associated with World War II. Two factors have operated to obscure this upsurge of the 1950s from public view: (1) the published crude birthrates mask it because the large number of infants born during the earlier phase of the "baby boom" (1946-1955) enlarged the denominator of the crude birthrate, hence tended to minimize the rates in subsequent years; (2) the women who became mothers in 1952-1962 were comprised, to a very great extent, of the small cohorts born during the depression in 1930-1939. In other words, although the *rates* were unusually high during the 1950s, they applied to an extraordinary *small group of childbearers* in comparison with the groups of childbearers that preceded them and those that are scheduled to follow. Figure 18-11 illustrates this pattern. Only when we use refined fertility measures that restrict the rate to those actually exposed and eliminate the effect of age composition can we detect the true pattern of fertility rate.

The effect of the "baby boom" on fertility can be more fully appreciated when it is realized that the total fertility rates for 1957 were 63 percent above those that prevailed in 1940, only 17 years earlier! The timing of this fertility peak to concide with the small cohort can be appreciated if we perform the following arithmetic:

year of peak fertility—1957
peak age of childbearing—22-24
year of birth of peak childbearers—1933-1935

The decline since the peak fertility of 1957 is substantial. As of March 1968 the GFR was fully 31 percent below the peak level of 1957 and apparently still falling. The trend, on a refined basis, is toward the same low level of fertility, leading to the almost stationary growth that prevailed during the 1930s. This time, however, it has occurred under conditions of unprecedented economic prosperity.

Our review of fertility trends in Europe and the awareness of the low level of fertility that

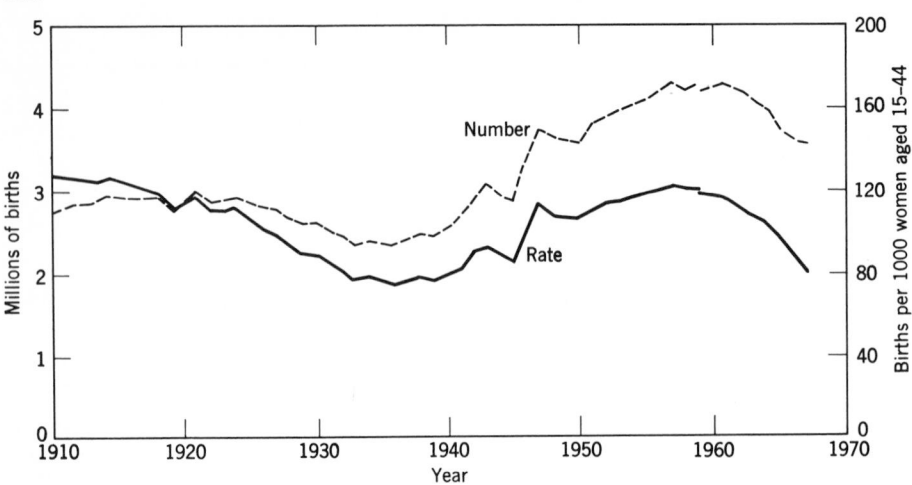

Figure 18-11   Live Births and Fertility Rates, United States: 1910 to 1967.
(Beginning 1959 Trend Lines Are Based on Registered Live Births; Trend Lines for
1910 to 1959 Are Based on Live Births Adjusted for Underregistration.)

SOURCE: U. S. Department of Health, Education, and Welfare, Final Natality
Statistics, 1965, *Monthly Vital Statistics Report*, February 1967, Figure 1.

prevails there lead us to predict that the fertility rate of the United States will continue its
downward trend until it is more or less comparable with those of Northwest Europe. In
other words, after a diversionary fluctuation of
nearly 20 years' duration, the population may
be expected to return to its former course and
to continue on to complete the demographic
transition. The "driving force" behind this is
the mounting dysfunction of higher fertility
for social and individual well-being.

Fertility of the Nonwhite Population. Much
has been written about the high-fertility rates
of the nonwhite population in recent years.
When we examine the data for the nonwhite
population shown in Table 18-7, we discover
that the rates for the nonwhite population have
followed rather closely the general pattern for
the total population. Negro fertility had been
declining steadily, as had white fertility, for
many years prior to the "baby boom," and during the depression years of the mid-1930s it
had become quite low. The only difference has
been that Negro fertility rates were about 30
percent greater than the rates for the corresponding measure for the white population.
For example, the general fertility rates for the
nonwhite group reached a low of 95.9 in 1936,
gradually recovered, and then in 1946-1947 ex-

perienced the same sudden increase that has
already been described for the total population. In fact, the amount of change was almost
identical for the two populations. For example,
the increase in the rate from 74 to 112 between
1937 to 1947 for the white population presented an increase of 38 points, whereas the
jump from 99 to 126 for the nonwhite population represented an increase of only 27 points.
Thus, *during the first phase of the "baby
boom," increase in nonwhite fertility was
absolutely and relatively smaller than that in
white fertility.* However, the chain of events for
the years after 1946 is quite different for the
nonwhite and the white populations. As had already been described, after the sudden upsurge
in 1946-1947 the GFR for the white population
remained at about the same level and then increased somewhat in the 1950s. This was not
the case for the nonwhite population. With the
onset of the "baby boom" in 1946, the rise in
the level of fertility of the nonwhite population
rose year by year and attained a level in 1957
that *it had never before exhibited in the recorded statistical history of the United States.*
The peak fertility of 4.8 children in completed
family size reported for 1957, however, is not
very much out of line with the *relative* position
that had prevailed before. If we examine the

ratios in the right-hand column of Table 18-7, we see that this is true; the ratio of nonwhite to white birthrates was about 1.33 in 1935-1939 and 1.33 in 1950-1955. These ratios suggest that the response of the nonwhite population to the "baby boom" situation was merely delayed. It lagged behind the response of the white population by about six to eight years, but when it did come it reached its peak and occurred in about the overall proportion as could have been expected on the basis of its previous ratio to the white population.

The peak of fertility among the nonwhite population was attained in 1957—the same year as for the white—and since that time has declined nearly as rapidly as has the white population. In fact, the fertility decline among the nonwhite population has been impressively swift since 1959. In the eight-year period between 1957 and 1965, the general fertility rate dropped from 163 to 134—a total of 29 points. In the same period of time the general fertility rate for the white population declined from 118 to 91 by 27 points. *Thus the "baby boom" appears to have struck the nonwhite population somewhat belatedly and to have taken the form of a very sharp, upward swing in the 1950s, which has been followed by a very prompt and sharp downward trend.* Again, we cannot predict the course of future events with certainty, but it appears that the fertility rates of the nonwhite population will continue to decline rapidly and undoubtedly will proceed to complete the demographic transition within a much shorter time than it has taken the white population to accomplish the same change. Meanwhile, because the rate for the white population has declined *relatively* somewhat more rapidly than the rate for the nonwhite population, the ratio in the right-hand column of Table 18-7 has risen rather steadily since 1952.

Reynolds Farley has analyzed intensively the fertility trends of the nonwhite population.[10] He notes that the sudden rise in Negro fertility occurred at a time when there was explosive urbanization of Negroes as they migrated from

[10] Reynolds Farley, "Recent Changes in Negro Fertility," *Population,* 3 (1) (1966), 188–203.

their traditional homes in the rural South. During the same years the educational level of the Negro population has risen sharply, as educational opportunities have been made less unequal. Meanwhile, Negro workers have been entering upper-level occupations in larger numbers, as antidiscrimination legislation has broken the color barriers in hiring practices. All of this seems very anomalous and in contradiction to the theory of demographic transition. Farley and others have attributed the sudden rise in Negro fertility to an improvement in Negro fecundity, resulting from decrease in sterility associated with venereal infection. This hypothesis will be explored more fully in our discussion of childlessness. In view of the recent downward trend of the Negro birthrate, it is difficult to consider improved fecundity as the single force. There is much evidence that the Negro population is rapidly following the white population in the adoption of contraception.

Pattern of Age-Specific Fertility Rates since 1940. The pattern of age-specific fertility rates, by color, for the United States population for selected years from 1940 to 1965 are reported in Table 18-8. Figure 18-12 graphs the ASFR data for the entire population for each year during this interim. From these sources we can gain the following important items of information:

1. The greatest recent changes in childbearing have been in ages 15 to 19, 20 to 24, and 25 to 29 years. The trend has been sharply downward.

2. The "baby boom" was accompanied by almost a doubling of the rates for ages 15 to 19 for whites and an increase of 40 percent for nonwhites. The sudden drop in the age at marriage, described in the preceding chapter, contributed substantially to the sudden rise in natality. Since 1960 the fertility level of this group has declined greatly, suggesting that there is a growing tendency in the teen ages to separate marriage from pregnancy.

3. There was a temporary tendency to increase childbearing beyond age 35, which has been reversed. Between 1938 and 1957 the age-specific rates at ages 35 to 39 and 40 to 44 were higher than in previous years, but since

Table 18-8 Comparison of Age-Specific Fertility Rates of the
White and Nonwhite Population for Selected Dates: 1940 to 1965

Color and age	Year			Change	
	1940	1957	1965	1940-1957	1957-1965
White population					
TFR	2229.1	3625.2	2790.3	1396.1	-834.9
10-14 years.........	0.2	0.5	0.3	0.3	- 0.3
15-19 years.........	45.3	85.2	60.7	39.9	- 24.5
20-24 years.........	131.4	253.8	189.8	122.4	- 64.0
25-29 years.........	123.6	195.8	158.8	72.2	- 37.0
30-34 years.........	83.4	115.9	91.7	32.5	- 24.2
35-39 years.........	45.3	57.4	44.1	12.1	- 13.3
40-44 years.........	15.0	15.4	12.0	0.4	- 3.4
45-49 years.........	1.6	0.8	0.7	- 0.8	- 0.1
Nonwhite population					
TFR	2870.2	4797.8	3891.4	1927.6	-906.4
10-14 years.........	3.7	5.6	4.0	1.9	- 1.6
15-19 years.........	121.7	172.8	136.1	51.1	- 36.7
20-24 years.........	168.5	307.0	247.3	138.5	- 59.7
25-29 years.........	116.3	228.1	188.1	111.8	- 40.0
30-34 years.........	83.5	143.5	118.3	60.0	- 25.2
35-39 years.........	53.7	78.7	63.8	25.0	- 14.9
40-44 years.........	21.5	23.5	19.2	2.0	- 4.3
45-49 years.........	5.2	2.0	1.5	- 3.2	- 0.5

Source: National Center for Health Statistics. *Vital Statistics of the United States: 1965.* Table 1-6

1958-1960 they have receded to their previous level or below. It has been claimed that this phenomenon was due to the efforts of couples who had curtailed their fertility during the economic depression to "make up" for lost births and to attain the size of family they really desired. It may in part also have been due to the efforts of the very substantial number of persons who married for the first time at ages past 25 (the "marriage boom" described in the previous chapter) to have children before they passed out of the childbearing ages. In other words, the culture pattern or suspending childbearing between ages 30 to 35, established during the first half of the twentieth century, has not been abandoned. Instead, there has been a tendency since 1960 to confine the bearing of children to even younger ages.

4. The net result of this change in pattern has been to push the onset of childbearing forward to earlier years and to have it rise to heights of greater intensity during the period of ages 20 to 30.

5. The retreat toward the pattern of later childbearing among young adults that existed in 1940, which reverses the changes of the 1940-1957 period, spans all ages under 25 and is very substantial. The change for the nonwhite population is as large or larger than that for the white population. Especially noteworthy is the drastic cutback in the fertility of teenage girls. In 1968 the level of United States fertility dropped very close to the level of bare replacement, when measured on a cross-sectional basis. Childbearing after age 39 had reached unprecedentedly low levels. Young women were postponing or avoiding childbearing as they had not done since before World War II. Some demographers were expecting these younger cohorts to "make up" for this at a later date. Others, who remembered the outcome of the depression cohorts, were doubting whether this would occur.

Natality and Live-Birth Order. A very informative way in which to investigate the changing pattern of natality is to classify births by their order and to calculate a GFR for each order: the number of first births per 1000 women 15 to 44, and so on. Table 18-9 reports such rates for the white and nonwhite population for selected years 1940-1966. Table 18-13 illustrates these trends. The reader should note that the total of this table is the GFR and that the rates for the various orders add to this total. Thus the order-specific birthrates divide the GFR into parts and show what part of the GFR is due to births of low, intermediate, or high order.

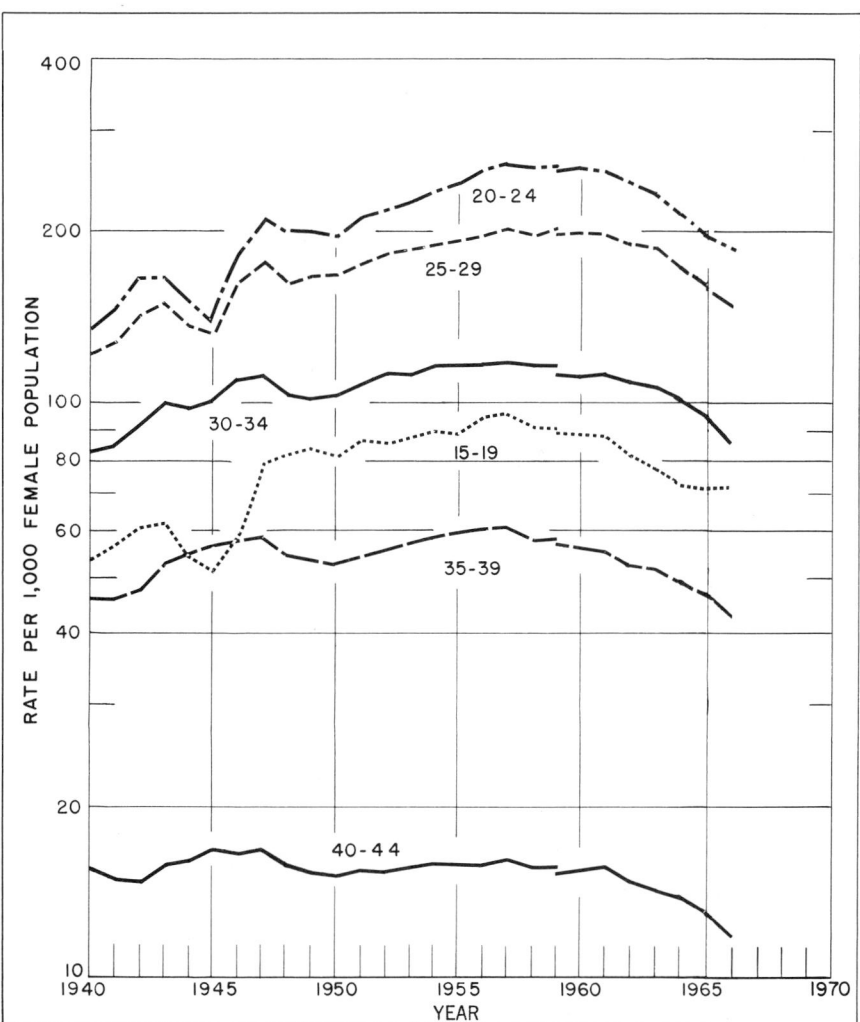

Figure 18-12 Birthrates by Age of Mother, United States: 1940 to 1966. (Beginning 1959 Trend Lines Are Based on Registered Live Births; Trend Lines for 1940-1959 Are Based on Live Births Adjusted for Underregistration.)

A striking feature of Table 18-9 is that the "baby boom" was very clearly a concentration on having 2 to 4 children; the rates for 5 children and over among the general population rose slightly, but not enough to greatly influence fertility.

The recession in births since 1957 is strongly concentrated in the early birth orders (first, second, third) as well as in the higher orders. This suggests that couples are *delaying* having their first, second, third, child in comparison with the practice of only a few years ago. (It

may be due in part to the increasing number of persons who have already had one, two, three children; a more exact analysis will be made in a later section.)

The data for 1947 reveal just how heavily concentrated the onset of the "baby boom" was in having the first child. Once the first child was born, the emphasis by 1950 shifted to having the second and by 1957 to having the third child. Instead of this emphasis passing on to the fourth child by 1965, the rate was lower than in 1957. This suggests that a very substan-

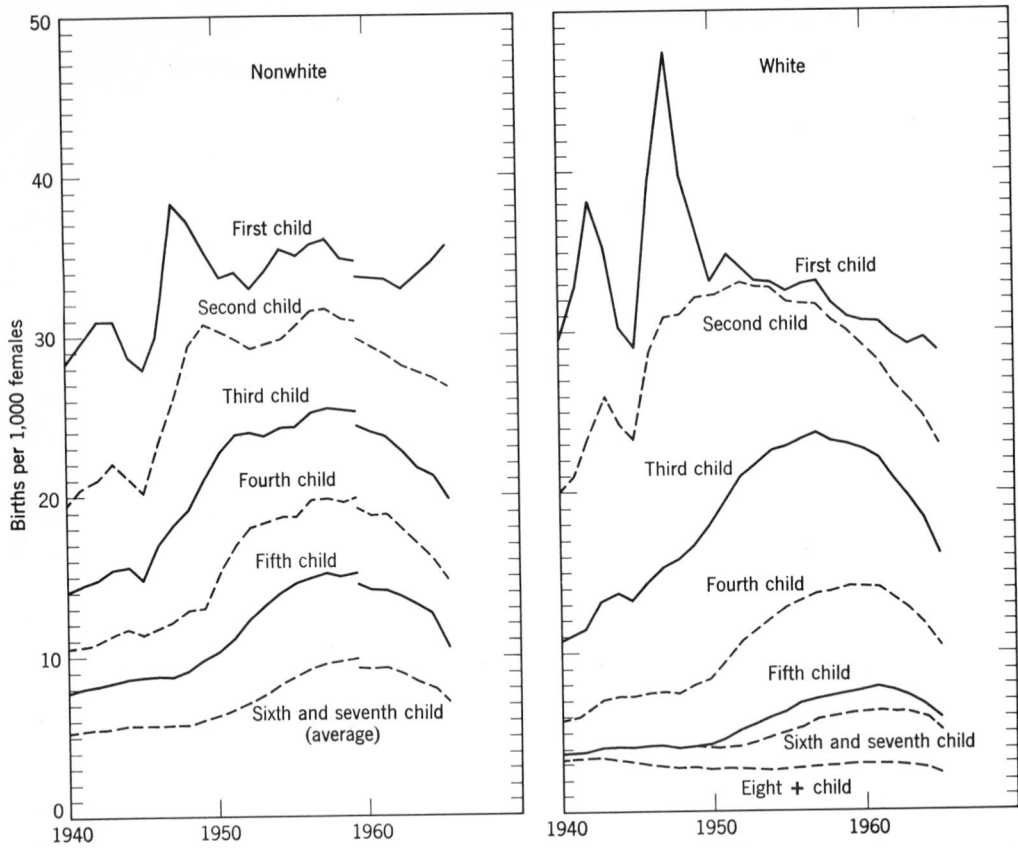

Figure 18-13 Birthrates by Birth Order, United States: 1940 to 1966.

tial fraction were stopping childbearing after the third child.

A very striking feature of Table 18-9 is the continuing high rates for high-order births among the nonwhite population. Whereas the white population has shown only a slight tendency to a rise in births at orders 5 and above, the nonwhite population (which began with a

Table 18-9 Birthrates by Live-Birth Order and Color, United States: 1940 to 1965 (Births per 1000 Women Aged 15-44)

Year and color	Total	Live-birth order						
		1	2	3	4	5	6 & 7	8 & over
Total population								
1965.............	96.6	29.8	23.4	16.6	10.7	6.4	6.0	3.7
1957.............	122.9	33.7	31.7	23.9	14.4	7.9	7.1	4.2
1950.............	106.2	33.3	32.1	18.4	9.2	4.8	4.7	3.6
1947.............	113.3	46.7	30.3	15.6	7.9	4.5	4.6	3.7
1940.............	79.9	29.3	20.0	10.9	6.4	4.1	4.8	4.3
White population								
1965.............	91.4	28.9	23.0	16.2	10.2	5.8	5.0	2.4
1957.............	117.7	33.4	31.7	23.7	13.7	7.0	5.6	2.7
1950.............	102.3	33.3	32.3	17.9	8.4	4.1	3.7	2.5
1947.............	111.8	47.8	30.8	15.3	7.4	4.0	3.8	2.7
1940.............	77.1	29.4	20.0	10.5	5.9	3.6	4.1	3.5
Nonwhite population								
1965.............	133.9	35.8	26.6	19.6	14.6	10.8	13.8	12.6
1957.............	163.0	36.1	31.6	25.7	19.8	15.3	19.0	15.6
1950.............	137.3	33.8	30.3	22.9	15.3	10.4	12.6	12.0
1947.............	125.9	38.4	26.2	17.3	12.1	8.8	11.4	11.6
1940.............	102.4	28.6	19.6	14.1	10.5	7.8	10.4	11.3

Source: Vital Statistics of the United States, 1965, Table 1-9

Table 18-10 Sex Ratio of Births by Color: 1940 to 1965 (Males per 1000 Females)

Year	Total	White	Nonwhite
1965............	1051	1056	1028
1964............	1047	1052	1022
1963............	1053	1057	1030
1962............	1048	1052	1024
1961............	1050	1055	1023
1960............	1049	1055	1018
1959............	1049	1054	1023
1958............	1050	1054	1022
1957............	1050	1055	1025
1956............	1052	1056	1028
1955............	1051	1056	1020
1954............	1051	1056	1020
1953............	1053	1058	1025
1952............	1051	1057	1011
1951............	1054	1058	1025
1950............	1054	1058	1025
1949............	1054	1059	1022
1948............	1054	1058	1028
1947............	1055	1060	1025
1946............	1058	1063	1024
1945............	1055	1061	1020
1944............	1055	1060	1023
1943............	1055	1059	1028
1942............	1058	1062	1033
1941............	1053	1058	1027
1940............	1054	1060	1019

Source: National Center for Health Statistics. Vital Statistics of the United States: 1965: Table 1-19

much higher rate for these orders) has experienced substantial increases. Very sharp declines in the rates for these higher-order births were registered for 1965 and have declined even more since.

As of 1965, the percentage distribution of live births by live-birth order was as follows:

Live-birth order	White	Nonwhite
Total	100.0	100.0
First child	31.6	26.7
Second child	25.1	19.1
Third child	17.7	14.6
Fourth child	11.1	10.9
Fifth child	6.3	8.1
Sixth to seventh child ..	5.4	10.3
Eighth child	2.7	9.4

Sex Ratio at Birth. There seems to be a persistent differential between the white and nonwhite population in the United States in the sex ratio at birth (Table 18-10). For the 25-year period from 1940 to 1965 there was an average of 105.7 male births for each 100 female births among the white population. The

corresponding figure for the nonwhite population was 102.3. It is known that the sex ratio of all pregnancies is quite high and that miscarriage and stillbirth rates are higher for male than for female fetuses. The causes for this difference in sex ratio at conception are not fully known. One theory of differences in sex ratio at birth between the white and nonwhite populations cites the poorer health status and the higher rate of pregnancy loss (miscarriage and stillbirths) among the nonwhite population as leading to a lower sex ratio. If this were the case, one would have expected a rather dramatic rise in the sex ratio at birth among the nonwhite population in the period 1940-1965, during which the health status of the population has improved remarkably. As Table 18-10 shows, no such development has taken place. Another theory is that there is a difference in completeness of registration. It is difficult to adduce a reason why female infants would be more completely registered than male infants among the nonwhite population; on the contrary, neglecting to register female births is thought to be the more common practice (the high sex ratios at birth for some nations in Asia are said to be due to neglect to register female births). Also, the lower sex ratio of the nonwhite population is apparent in census counts for very young children, so that it appears to be a genuine difference.

Median Age of Mother at Birth of Children. The typical mother in the United States is 25 or 26 years old (see Table 18-11). Despite the fact that the average age at marriage has declined sharply since 1940 and the level of fertility has risen sharply, the median age at childbearing has declined by about one year for the white population and almost not at all for the nonwhite.

The typical age at childbearing varies with the birth order. For example, the median age of mothers at the birth of their first child was 22.2 years (white) and 20.2 years (nonwhite) in 1965. For the second birth, the median age was about two and one-half years later and for the third and fourth child about two years later.

In all cases, the median age of bearing children of a given order is higher for the white

Table 18-11   Median Age of Mother, by Live-Birth
Order and Color, United States: 1940 to 1965

Color and live birth order	1965	1960	1950	1940
White				
Total..............	25.9	25.5	26.1	26.9
First child...........	22.2	22.0	22.8	23.6
Second child..........	24.4	24.2	25.7	26.1
Third child...........	27.3	27.0	28.1	28.0
Fourth child..........	29.2	28.9	29.9	29.6
Fifth child...........	31.0	30.6	31.6	31.5
Sixth-seventh child....	32.7	32.4	33.3	33.7
Eighth + child........	35.9	35.9	37.2	37.7
Nonwhite				
Total..............	25.0	24.9	24.6	24.8
First child...........	20.2	19.9	19.8	19.4
Second child..........	22.8	22.5	22.5	22.2
Third child...........	24.4	24.1	24.1	23.9
Fourth child..........	26.4	25.9	26.2	26.2
Fifth child...........	27.9	27.6	28.1	28.4
Sixth-seventh child....	29.8	29.6	30.5	31.0
Eighth + child........	34.2	34.2	35.6	36.4

Source: National Center for Health Statistics.   Vital Statistics
of the United States: 1965, Table 1-12

population than for the nonwhite population.
Among the white population the median age
for first and second births declined sharply between 1940 and 1960, but has since tended to
rise. Among the nonwhite population the age
at bearing the first child has risen since 1940.

Illegitimacy. There has been a very large
and disturbing rise in the rate of illegitimacy in
the United States since 1940 (see Table 18-
12). The rate of illegitimacy is defined as the
number of illegitimate children born per 1000
unmarried women. In 1940 the rate was 7.1 per
thousand. At that time it was highest among
women 20 to 24 years of age and was very
low at ages above 35. During the next 10 years
(by 1950) the rate had more than doubled.

Table 18-12   Estimated Illegitimacy Rates,
by Age of Mother, United States: 1940 to
1965 (Illegitimate Live Births per 1000
Unmarried Women in Specified Group)

Age of mother	1965	1960	1950	1940
Total 15-44 years	23.4	21.8	14.1	7.1
10-14 years....	0.7	0.6	0.6	0.4
15-19 years....	16.7	15.7	12.6	7.4
20-24 years....	38.8	40.3	21.3	9.5
25-29 years....	50.4	42.0	19.9	7.2
30-34 years....	37.1	27.5	13.3	5.1
35-39 years....	17.0	13.9	7.2	3.4
40-44 years....	4.4	3.6	2.0	1.2

Source: Center for Health Statistics.   Vital Statistics
of the United States: 1965, Table 1-26

Although there was a substantial increase in
the illegitimacy rates for girls 15 to 19, the
largest increases both absolutely and relatively
took place for ages 20 to 34. The overall rate increased by 50 percent between the years 1950
and 1960, with very great increases taking place
for years 20 to 29. In 1965 the rate was somewhat higher than in 1960, with significant increases having been registered for the years 25
to 29. On an overall basis, the illegitimacy rate
has more than tripled since 1940. It must be
emphasized, however, that in terms of *rates* it is
not confined to teenage girls. The greatest increase has been in ages 20 and above.

Unfortunately, it is true that a major share of
illegitimate children are born to girls in their
late teens, because at these ages the proportion
unmarried is very high. Although the rate is
lower than for ages 20 to 29, at ages 15 to 19
the rate applies to a very large number of
unmarried girls.

Table 18-13 reports the ratio of illegitimate
births per 1000 total live births by color, 1940-
1965. One nonwhite birth in four was illegitimate in 1965. This represented a very substantial rise from 1940, when one nonwhite birth
in six was illegitimate. From the viewpoint of
the dominant system of morals, this represents a high level of family demoralization. The
rate for the white population has also increased

Table 18-13 Estimated Ratio of Illegitimate to Total Live Births, by Color: 1940 to 1965 (Illegitimate Births per 1000 Live Births)

Year	Total	White	Nonwhite
1965...........	77.4	39.6	263.2
1964...........	68.5	33.9	245.0
1963...........	63.3	30.7	235.9
1962...........	58.8	27.3	228.7
1961...........	56.3	25.3	223.4
1960...........	52.7	22.9	215.8
1955...........	45.3	18.6	202.4
1950...........	39.8	17.5	179.6
1945...........	42.9	23.6	179.3
1940...........	37.9	19.5	168.3

Source: Center for Health Statistics. Vital Statistics of the United States: 1965 Table 1-25

Table 18-14 Estimated Ratio of Illegitimate to Total Live Births, by Age and Color: 1965 (Illegitimate Births per 1000 Live Births)

Age	Total	White	Nonwhite
Total.......	77.4	39.6	263.2
Under 15 years...	785.3	572.8	864.0
15-17 years......	327.1	173.0	625.1
18-19 years......	152.6	91.4	388.7
20-24 years......	67.8	38.4	229.9
25-29 years......	39.8	18.8	162.8
30-34 years......	37.0	16.1	149.0
35-39 years......	40.3	19.0	148.8
40-49 years......	42.9	22.0	140.1

Source: Center for Health Statistics. Vital Statistics of the United States 1965, Table 1-27

substantially since 1940. This trend may be due in part to the tendency of married women to use contraception successfully while unmarried women continue to have sex relations without contraception. Table 18-14 reports these rates by age and color for 1965. Among girls under 15 who become mothers, more than three fourths of the births are illegitimate, while for girls 15 to 17 nearly one third are illegitimate. Even among women 20 to 24, one child in fifteen is illegitimate. Above age 25 the proportion is about 3 percent. These statistics refer only to children whose fathers failed to marry their mothers before they were born. Many more first children are conceived before marriage and then are legitimatized by a wedding ceremony.

Illegitimacy is 6.6 times as prevalent among the nonwhite as among the white population. Table 18-14 shows that in 1965, 26 percent of all nonwhite infants born were illegitimate. For ages under 15 years the proportion is 86 percent, but even above age 25 not less than 14 percent of the children are born out of wedlock. High rates of illegitimacy are a cultural trait of long standing among the Negro population, dating back to the days of slavery and the incomplete family system that was imposed by the slavery system. However, there is clear evidence that the rise in the rates of illegitimacy that has occurred since 1940 has been phenomenally rapid among the nonwhite popu-

lation. The exact explanation of this change has not been adequately studied by sociologists. It may be a concomitant of the social disorganization that has accompanied the rapid urbanization of the Negro population. Many social workers believe that it is partly fictitious and results from the way in which the federal funds providing Aid to Dependent Children are administered. If a Negro father has a large family that he cannot support, by apparently abandoning his wife he makes the mother and children eligible for Aid to Dependent Children. The husband may surreptitiously continue to live with his wife and bear children by her, but in order to retain status on the aid rolls it is necessary to refuse to admit that he is the father. Thus, for the sake of statistical consistency, offspring are declared to be illegitimate. On the other hand, there are those who maintain that the way in which the Aid to Dependent Children program is administered has tended to subsidize genuine illegitimacy and that this has been a factor in its rise. The basic premise of this contention is that the economic penalty for childbearing has been removed or greatly lessened and that this comparative absence of moral imperatives has resulted in an increase in fatherless children.

The entire subject of the sudden increase of illegitimacy both among the nonwhite and the white population is one that deserves more intensive study.

18.7.   Differential Natality in the United States: Cumulative Fertility

The national rates of fertility conceal a great deal of variation in childbearing propensity within the population. Some social, economic, or ethnic subgroups tend to have above-average fertility and others tend to have below-average fertility. Demographers are keenly interested in this phenomenon of *differential* natality between various social and economic subgroups. This section and the next explore the topic, using data for the United States as an example. A similar analysis has been made or can be made for most nations that have taken comprehensive censuses or fertility surveys.

If two subpopulations, A and B, manifest different levels of fertility, the demographer is faced with two tasks: (*a*) to measure the size of this differential and describe it and (*b*) to develop an explanation of why the differential exists and what forces create and maintain it. Unfortunately, with the limited data available it is possible to do a much better job at the first than at the second of these tasks. For this reason, studies of differential natality tend to be more descriptive than explicative.

There are two alternative approaches to the study of differential natality: *cumulative* natality and *current* natality. Cumulative differential natality refers to comparative differences in the average number of children that a group of women with a particular set of characteristics have borne from the onset of childbearing to the time they are contacted by a census or fertility survey. Current differential natality refers to the average number of children that a group of women with a particular set of characteristics have borne in the past year, in the past five years, or during some other definite span of time. Both approaches are valid and highly useful, and a comprehensive study of differential natality should include both.

Cumulative differential fertility is measured by data on "children ever born," tabulated for subgroups of the population from a national census. Demographers have discovered that they can get periodic approximate measures of cohort fertility by having a census ask the following question about ever-married women in a representative sample of households: "How many babies has she ever had not counting stillbirths?" In response to this question, women are expected to report the total number of children they have ever borne who were alive at the time of birth, irrespective of whether or not they have since died. (Especial care must be taken to record a zero for women who have had no children.) By adding up the total number of children that the women have ever borne and dividing by the total number of women of that age, it is possible to obtain an age-specific measure—"children ever born for 1000 women for age X." Table 18-15 illustrates this procedure from the 1960 census of the United States. In Table 18-15, the children are related to ever-married women; they may also be related to all women (including never-married women). Also, the tabulation of both children and women sometimes is confined to women married once and living with husband at the time of the census. This eliminates differences in marital status and family integrity in making comparisons.

Ratios of children ever born to women have two deficiencies, which must be considered in interpreting them. (1) They refer only to *surviving* children and therefore do not take into account differences between groups in infant mortality. (2) Women *underreport* the number of children they have borne; there is an especially strong tendency to omit children who were born several years before the census and who lived only for a short time. This tendency to forget to report such infants may be much greater for some subgroups of the population than for others. When comparing children-ever-born ratios, there is the implicit assumption that infant mortality rates and the degree of underreporting are identical for the groups being compared.

It must be kept in mind that children-ever-born data refer to indefinite spans of time. They do not adequately portray current differentials in fertility, but report only recent differentials in fertility. Table 18-15 provides basic parameters of these data for the United States and illustrates the process of cumulative fertility. This table shows that as women become progressively older, the number of chil-

Table 18-15   Number of Children Ever Born per 1000 Ever-Married Women
15 Years Old and Over, By Color and Age of Woman, United States: 1960

Age and marital status	White women			Nonwhite women		
	Number of women (000)	Number of children ever born (000)	Children per 1000 women	Number of women (000)	Number of children ever born (000)	Children per 1000 women
All ever-married:						
15-19 years..........	928	673	725	133	166	1274
20-24 years..........	3,490	4,783	1,370	444	888	1,999
25-29 years..........	4,364	9,474	2,171	592	1,641	2,771
30-34 yeras..........	5,023	12,881	2,564	658	2,075	3,155
35-39 years..........	5,396	14,165	2,625	653	2,047	3,138
40-44 years..........	4,959	12,472	2,515	578	1,725	2,984
45-49 years..........	4,667	10,987	2,354	534	1,504	2,818
50-54 years..........	4,107	9,515	2,317	446	1,223	2,742
55-59 years..........	3,646	8,934	2,450	397	1,153	2,904
60-64 years..........	3,140	8,401	2,676	292	908	3,109

Source: U.S. Census of Population: 1960, Women by Number of Children Ever Born, Subject
Report PC(2)-3A, Table 1

dren they have borne increases, starting with a small number at ages 15 to 19 and rising steadily until the ages 40 to 44 of completed fertility. For ages 45 and beyond these tables represent completed fertility for older real cohorts of women. Thus the age distribution of Table 18-15 permits us to do two things: (1) by examining the data for women 15 to 44, we can study the process for incomplete fertility and the pattern of childbearing with age in recent years; and (2) at ages 45 and beyond, we can study completed fertility for cohorts that are beyond the childbearing age.

By preparing such data for subgroups of the population, we can study differential fertility.

For many of the variables that affect fertility, the children-ever-born or cumulative fertility approach is superior to current fertility measures to be discussed in the next section. This arises from the fact that these variables exert their effect in a sustained manner over several years. The effect in any one year may be too small to be observable in annual rates or it may be confounded by differences in age at marriage or in other variables. But after the variable has exerted its force on couples who have lived together for several years, its effect may be more readily observable as a significantly greater or lesser number of children born.

Marital Status. One factor that creates differences between groups is, of course, differences in exposure to the risk of childbearing. Socioeconomic groups that have a tendency to

marry late or not marry at all may be expected to have a low overall level of fertility. Conversely, groups that tend to marry early and where a high percentage tend to marry may be expected to have unusually high fertility. In other words, marital status or differences in marital status are a factor of substantial importance in the study of differential fertility. It is a factor, if possible, that should be controlled before attempting to examine the effect of other variables such as education, income, or occupation. Marital status may be controlled, in part, by basing the rates on ever-married women (married, widowed, and divorced), but this does not control fully all of the effects of marital status on fertility. Table 18-16, which reports rates of children ever born by marital status, shows that fertility rates are uniformly *higher* among women married only once and living with their husbands than for women who are separated, widowed, or divorced. The difference is 10 percent or more at ages above 30 for both the white and the nonwhite populations. Broken marriage tends to have a greater effect in depressing Negro fertility than it does in depressing white fertility. For this reason, the often heard stereotyped conclusion that the high-fertility rates of Negroes are due to promiscuity and unconventional family life is absolutely false. The highest fertility among the Negro, as among the white population, is found among couples who are leading a conventional family life—married only once and living with spouse. This is consistent with the

Table 18-16   Number of Children Ever Born per 1000 Women, by Marital Status, Color, and Age of Woman, For the United States, by Types of Residence: 1960

Age of woman and type of residence	White women				Nonwhite women			
	All white women	Ever married women			All nonwhite women	Ever married women		
		Total	Married once husband present	Other ever married		Total	Married once husband present	Other ever married
UNITED STATES								
Total, 15-44 Years	1,712	2,254	2,270	2,178	2,004	2,794	2,901	2,623
15-19 years.....	117	725	709	800	202	1,247	1,235	1,275
20-24 years.....	993	1,370	1,361	1,430	1,288	1,999	2,016	1,957
25-29 years.....	1,960	2,171	2,176	2,144	2,333	2,771	2,807	2,699
30-34 years.....	2,398	2,564	2,598	2,406	2,852	3,155	3,307	2,919
35-39 years.....	2,471	2,625	2,680	2,414	2,902	3,138	3,401	2,798
40-44 years.....	2,362	2,515	2,583	2,294	2,792	2,984	3,320	2,610
45-49 years.....	2,200	2,354	2,420	2,178	2,657	2,818	3,162	2,500
50-54 years.....	2,136	2,317	2,377	2,188	2,582	2,742	3,149	2,440
URBANIZED AREAS								
Total, 15-44 years	1,578	2,102	2,123	2,013	1,810	2,432	2,484	2,354
15-19 years.....	103	708	694	773	217	1,243	1,222	1,293
20-24 years.....	857	1,261	1,244	1,367	1,212	1,859	1,848	1,885
25-29 years.....	1,781	2,024	2,027	2,007	2,146	2,534	2,542	2,517
30-34 years.....	1,220	2,410	2,450	2,232	2,496	2,762	2,859	2,620
35-39 years.....	2,256	2,427	2,493	2,194	2,443	2,647	2,799	2,467
40-44 years.....	2,103	2,270	2,342	2,058	2,207	2,361	2,526	2,197
45-49 years.....	1,905	2,066	2,122	1,930	2,057	2,190	2,344	2,062
50-54 years.....	1,800	1,978	2,016	1,905	2,028	2,159	2,348	2,034
OTHER URBAN								
Total, 15-44 years	1,689	2,229	2,218	2,275	2,098	2,961	3,026	2,875
15-19 years.....	129	692	662	839	204	1,209	1,203	1,221
20-24 years.....	1,015	1,377	1,360	1,485	1,377	2,101	2,107	2,089
25-29 years.....	2,024	2,204	2,195	2,249	2,423	2,930	2,928	2,932
30-34 years.....	2,435	2,585	2,606	2,492	3,100	3,406	3,558	3,209
35-39 years.....	2,491	2,636	2,659	2,558	3,100	3,328	3,550	3,091
40-44 years.....	2,379	2,523	2,550	2,443	3,023	3,223	3,505	2,949
45-49 years.....	2,213	2,365	2,383	2,321	2,710	2,872	3,100	2,686
50-54 years.....	2,190	2,386	2,376	2,405	2,656	2,795	3,020	2,657
RURAL NONFARM								
Total, 15-44 years	1,956	2,468	2,462	2,499	2,409	3,599	3,688	3,411
15-19 years.....	148	768	756	827	190	1,254	1,260	1,235
20-24 years.....	1,277	1,546	1,546	1,545	1,440	2,278	2,370	2,021
25-29 years.....	2,246	2,383	2,380	2,399	2,836	3,363	3,412	3,234
30-34 years.....	2,668	2,780	2,783	2,761	3,701	4,107	4,214	3,881
35-39 years.....	2,814	2,925	2,946	2,833	3,987	4,319	4,581	3,879
40-44 years.....	2,767	2,880	2,913	2,763	4,034	4,333	4,659	3,840
45-49 years.....	2,660	2,784	2,826	2,665	3,863	4,080	4,458	3,659
50-54 years.....	2,665	2,821	2,868	2,714	3,632	3,879	4,329	3,463
RURAL FARM								
Total, 15-44 years	2,073	2,851	2,890	2,523	2,674	4,496	4,704	3,898
15-19 years.....	85	777	780	764	155	1,325	1,317	1,347
20-24 years.....	1,182	1,618	1,647	1,399	1,457	2,569	2,650	2,344
25-29 years.....	2,350	2,570	2,595	2,305	3,061	3,809	3,934	3,406
30-34 years.....	2,945	3,094	3,127	2,762	4,539	5,034	5,202	4,532
35-39 years.....	3,148	3,261	3,291	3,007	5,160	5,508	5,808	4,598
40-44 years.....	3,165	3,270	3,301	3,011	5,357	5,618	6,005	4,656
45-49 years.....	3,051	3,168	3,216	2,841	5,097	5,300	5,659	4,495
50-54 years.....	3,022	3,157	3,216	2,842	4,707	4,926	5,429	3,997

Source: U.S. Bureau of the Census, U.S. Census of Population: 1960: Number of Children Ever Born, Report PC(2)-3A, table 1.

Table 18-17   Number of Children Ever Born per 1000 Ever-Married Women, by Years of School Completed, Age, and Color, for the United States: 1960

| Age and color | Total | No school years completed | Elementary school | | | High school | | College | | |
			1 to 4 years	5 to 7 years	8 years	1 to 3 years	4 years	1 to 3 years	4 years	5 or more years
WHITE										
15-19 years......	725	1,368	1,212	1,067	965	799	470	383	.....	.....
20-24 years......	1,370	2,208	2,101	1,976	1,891	1,779	1,202	890	573	458
25-29 years......	2,171	3,236	2,978	2,765	2,563	2,479	2,064	1,872	1,445	1,039
30-34 years......	2,564	4,009	3,650	3,112	2,829	2,679	2,435	2,405	2,244	1,798
35-39 years......	2,625	4,148	3,836	3,259	2,892	2,685	2,450	2,450	2,445	2,072
40-44 years......	2,515	4,326	3,856	3,155	2,769	2,539	2,275	2,279	2,278	1,969
45-49 years......	2,354	4,121	3,810	3,014	2,601	2,332	2,013	1,970	1,900	1,652
50 years and over	2,753	4,396	4,136	3,369	2,855	2,387	1,966	1,873	1,686	1,370
NONWHITE										
15-19 years......	1,247	1,536	1,636	1,481	1,368	1,232	917	790	.....	.....
20-24 years......	1,999	2,408	2,573	2,603	2,451	2,257	1,530	1,177	738	746
25-29 years......	2,771	3,253	3,546	3,537	3,311	3,050	2,249	1,883	1,284	974
30-34 years......	3,155	3,829	4,031	3,939	3,468	3,256	2,574	2,359	1,691	1,400
35-39 years......	3,138	4,149	4,021	3,844	3,271	3,128	2,457	2,204	1,877	1,461
40-44 years......	2,984	3,799	3,674	3,529	3,004	2,842	2,252	2,077	1,733	1,267
45-49 years......	2,818	3,492	3,332	3,212	2,767	2,628	2,021	1,833	1,394	988
50 years and over	3,197	3,953	3,554	3,353	2,919	2,714	2,277	1,930	1,479	1,235

Source: U.S. Bureau of the Census, U.S. Census of Population: 1960. Number of Children Ever Born, Report PC(2)-3A, table 25.

findings of fertility research all over the world; lax morals and frequent changing of marriage partners tend to depress fertility by lessening the percentage of the population in the reproductive span that is exposed to the likelihood of getting pregnant. One reasonable explanation for the high fertility of the Negro population in recent years is that the family life is becoming *more* conventional and there is less promiscuity and switching of marriage partners than previously and that this greater consistency of exposure is leading to higher fertility rates.

Parenthetically, we should note in Table 18-16 that women who were only 30 to 34 years of age in 1960 already had borne more children than the group of women 50 to 54 years of age who had already entered menopause. This is positive proof that completed fertility of the younger generation of women who launched the baby boom will be substantially higher than that of older women whose fertility was suppressed during the economic depression of the 1930s.

Educational Attainment. Throughout the world there appears to be a strong inverse correlation between the amount of educational attainment and the level of fertility. This differential exists also in the United States. Table 18-17 shows that for each age group of the population the number of children ever born decreases with increasing education. The highest levels of fertility are found among women who have completed no years of schooling, and the lowest levels of fertility are found among women who have completed a college education. Among the nonwhite population an identical pattern exists. This educational differential is the most striking and important differential in fertility that exists in the United States population today. *A comparison of the white and nonwhite races in Table 18-17 reveals that a very large share of the higher fertility of the nonwhite population in comparison with white appears to be due to differences in educational attainment.* When age and education are both controlled simultaneously, the rates for nonwhite population at age 30 and above are little if any higher than those for the white population. This is especially true for all educational levels of high school and above.

Figure 18-14 has been constructed to bring out some of the details of the educational differential. Its four panels show the age pattern for four educational attainment groups, by color. There is a steady progressive lowering of the level of fertility from one educational category to the next. The rates for the nonwhite population tend to be higher than for the white

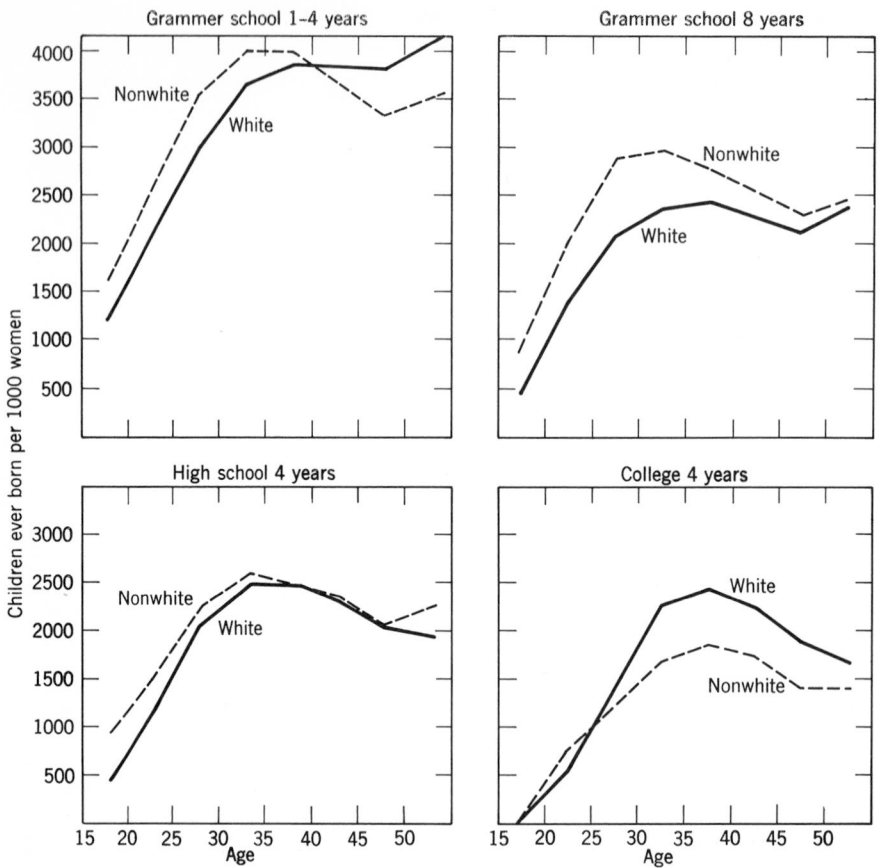

Figure 18-14　Children Ever Born to White and Nonwhite Women, Four Educational Attainment Groups by Age: 1960.

at the younger ages, but at the intermediate and older ages they tend to be either very close to the rates for whites or even *lower*. Finally, the "humped" shape of these curves illustrates graphically the impact of the "baby boom." Women who were aged 35 in 1960 had already borne more children than the older cohorts of women who were 40 years of age or over. Thus the ascending side of these curves represents the incomplete fertility of younger postwar cohorts, the peaks of the "humps" represent the near-complete fertility of the first generation of women who created the "baby boom," and the right-hand sides of the curves represent the fertility of women who did most of their childbearing during the economic depression.

It might be claimed that a major part of the fertility differences attributed to educational attainment could be due to differences in marital statuses. Tables 18-18 and 18-19 controlled the

factor of marital status by presenting data on children ever born per 1000 women ages 35 to 44 by precise marital status of mother. (Table 18-18 is for white women in this age group; Table 18-19 is for nonwhite women.) If we look at line 5 of each table we find that the number of children ever born to women married once, husband present, declines consistently with increasing levels of education. This inverse correlation is even greater among the nonwhite population than among the white. However, it must be pointed out that among the nonwhite population the group that is married once, living with husband, has substantially higher fertility than the corresponding educational group among the white population. The only exception to this is that Negro women with a college education have lower cumulative fertility than the corresponding group among the white population. Thus we must ad-

Table 18-18 Years of School Completed by Marital Status—Number of Children Ever Born per 1000 White Women 35 to 44 Years of Age, for the United States: 1960

Marital status	Total	Educational attainment					
		Elementary		High school		College	
		0 to 7 years	8 years	1 to 3 years	4 years	1 to 3 years	4+ years
Total...............	2,419	3,101	2,686	2,511	2,244	2,219	1,952
Ever married.....................	2,572	3,368	2,823	2,613	2,373	2,373	2,277
Married once...............	2,595	3,412	2,843	2,634	2,405	2,418	2,314
Married more than once........	2,436	3,171	2,718	2,523	2,142	2,046	1,814
Married husband present..........	2,610	3,407	2,859	2,650	2,415	2,435	2,345
Wife married once..............	2,634	3,457	2,878	2,672	2,448	2,479	2,380
Wife married more than once....	2,456	3,163	2,749	2,549	2.166	2,097	1,880
Married, husband absent..........	2,517	3,312	2,747	2,524	2,174	2,123	1,801
Wife married once..............	2,502	3,286	2,747	2,515	2,174	2,136	1,841
Wife married more than once....	2,566	3,387	2,747	2,545	2,172	2,079	1,555
Separated......................	2,540	3,365	2,770	2,503	2,110	2,035	1,605
Married once...................	2,499	3,287	2,762	2,487	2,082	1,991	1,643
Married more than once........	2,655	3,577	2,794	2,539	2,205	2,148	.....
Other..........................	2,494	3,240	2,720	2,549	2,227	2,184	1,916
Married once...................	2,504	3,285	2,731	2,547	2,247	2,226	1,955
Married more than once........	2,454	3,087	2,675	2,554	2,135	2,013	1,662
Widowed........................	2,357	3,284	2,613	2,366	2,013	1,924	1,661
Married once...................	2,357	3,255	2,668	2,373	2,018	1,947	1,689
Married more than once........	2,359	3,428	2,326	2,337	1,980	1,764	1,385
Divorced.......................	1,878	2,683	2,232	2,073	1,644	1,498	1,307
Married once...................	1,798	2,619	2,144	1,990	1,582	1,476	1,291
Married more than once........	2,114	2,835	2,468	2,259	1,856	1,576	1,396

Source: U.S. Bureau of the Census, U.S. Census of Population: 1960. Number of Children Ever Born, Report PC(2)-3A, table 28.

mit that among the cohorts that are now completing their fertility educational attainment explains a large portion of the difference between the white and nonwhite population, but not all of it. Figure 18-15 illustrates the magnitude of the educational differential. It shows that among the younger generation the difference in fertility level between

Table 18-19 Years of School Completed by Marital Status—Number of Children Ever Born per 1000 Nonwhite Women 35 to 44 Years of Age for the United States: 1960

Marital status	Total	Educational attainment					
		Elementary		High school		College	
		0 to 7 years	8 years	1 to 3 years	4 years	1 to 3 years	4+ years
Total..................	2,850	3,454	2,938	2,824	2,217	1,992	1,456
Ever married.....................	3,065	3,738	3,137	3,002	2,376	2,149	1,651
Married once...................	3,160	3,902	3,241	3,094	2,431	2,214	1,685
Married more than once........	2,718	3,172	2,768	2,689	2,139	1,887	1,452
Married husband present...........	3,233	4,028	3,346	3,163	2,477	2,263	1,736
Wife married once..............	3,364	4,265	3,497	3,292	2,549	2,344	1,773
Wife married more than once....	2,753	3,220	2,826	2,743	2,161	1,913	1,494
Married, husband absent...........	2,730	3,072	2,728	2,765	2,189	2,103	1,481
Wife married once..............	2,726	3,079	2,697	2,789	2,182	2,064	1,477
Wife married more than once....	2,745	3,049	2,844	2,667	2,221	2,271	.....
Separated......................	2,734	3,050	2,678	2,759	2,149	2,210	1,520
Married once...................	2,721	3,044	2,625	2,792	2,119	2,160	1,490
Married more than once........	2,787	3,070	2,886	2,620	2,274	.....	.....
Other..........................	2,713	3,165	2,914	2,784	2,301	1,885	1,444
Married once...................	2,741	3,225	2,977	2,778	2,354	1,864	1,465
Married more than once........	2,614	2,964	2,699	2,804	2,069	.....	.....
Widowed........................	3,036	3,481	2,896	2,944	2,262	1,752	1,420
Married once...................	3,078	3,522	2,986	3,006	2,320	1,672	1,405
Married more than once........	2,864	3,318	2,536	2,703	1,984	.....	.....
Divorced.......................	2,130	2,715	2,209	2,164	1,795	1,416	1,130
Married once...................	2,116	2,706	2,212	2,145	1,773	1,471	1,119
Married more than once........	2,173	2,740	2,200	2,223	1,879	1,284	.....

Source: U.S. Bureau of the Census, U.S. Census of Population: 1960. Number of Children Ever Born, Report PC(2)-3A, table 29

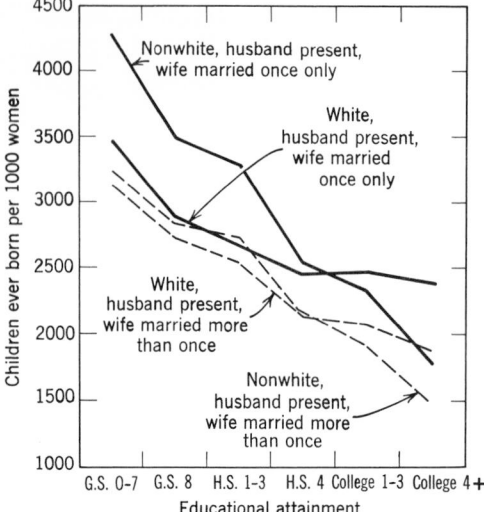

Figure 18-15 Educational Differential in Fertility; Women 35 to 44 Years of Age by Color and Marital Status: 1960.

whites and nonwhites is confined almost exclusively to women who have not graduated from high school. It also demonstrates the principle, noted above, that interruption of marriage has a depressing effect on fertility; the rates for women who have been married previously are much lower than the rates for women married only once, because the color differential is much greater among the marriages that have not been interrupted than among marriages where the wife has been married before. Tables 18-18 and 18-19 also provide data for other types of marital interruption.

Tables 18-18 and 18-19 are important fertility tables because they refer to an age group in which childbearing is 90 percent or more complete. Also, they refer to the cohorts of women who were at peak childbearing (ages 20 to 30) when the "baby boom" began. Hence they refer to the "new" rather than to "prewar" patterns of childbearing. There can be no doubt that among the new cohorts educational attainment differences have a very strong effect on completed fertility, even when marital status and race are fully controlled. This suggests that we may anticipate further rapid and drastic reductions in the fertility of the nonwhite population in the immediate future. This will be true because in future years

the large numbers of women with only an elementary school education will diminish. Instead there will be a growing proportion of nonwhite women who have attended or graduated from high school. Since fertility levels at this point in educational attainment are substantially lower than they are when only elementary school education has been attained, we may expect lower nonwhite fertility rates. Moreover, it is very likely that in the next few years, the age-education-specific pattern for nonwhite women will very nearly approach even closer to that of white women.

Nativity and Parentage. Substantial differences in fertility have existed among the various race, nativity, and parentage groups in the population, and they still exist today. Table 18-20 summarizes the statistical information available on this subject. Until quite recently one of the most fertile subgroups of the population was the foreign-born white population. It consisted mostly of migrants from rural areas of Eastern and Southern Europe, of Roman Catholic faith, who tended to be more fertile than the native-born population. This pattern no longer exists. If we examine the age data of rows 2 and 4 of Table 18-20, we see that the foreign-born white population ever married has lower fertility than the native-born for all ages under 55 years. Only the oldest age groups, 65 and over, reflect the remnants of differential fertility that existed in preceding generations. We have already seen that in Europe the pattern of fertility is one of having fewer children than is common in the United States. Apparently, recent migrants to the United States are bringing this European pattern with them.

Sociologists are often fond of making the claim that second-generation Americans (the children of migrants from overseas) tend to be "marginal men." One of the symptoms that they have taken as proof of this is the tendency for the second generation to have lower fertility. Thus native white women whose parents were foreign-born have tended to have lower fertility than native white women of native parentage. In many cases, however, this has been due less to fertility differences within marriage than to failure of many second-gen-

Table 18-20 Nativity and Parentage—Number of Children Ever Born per 1000 Ever-Married Women 15 Years Old and Over, by Age, for the United States (with Region of Residence for the Foreign-Born and Negroes): 1960

Race and parentage	Age							
	15 to 19 years	20 to 24 years	25 to 29 years	30 to 34 years	35 to 39 years	40 to 44 years	45 to 49 years	50 to 54 years
United States........	791	1,441	2,243	2,633	2,680	2,564	2,402	2,359
Native white...............	724	1,376	2,189	2,584	2,643	2,525	2,365	2,326
Native parentage..........	718	1,388	2,214	2,618	2,690	2,589	2,438	2,406
Foreign or mixed parentage.	838	1,262	2,038	2,440	2,476	2,342	2,168	2,096
Foreign-born white..........	815	1,177	1,706	2,149	2,298	2,285	2,191	2,229
Northeast.................	930	990	1,499	2,004	2,155	2,096	2,024	2,085
North Central.............	747	1,185	1,731	2,174	2,334	2,267	2,204	2,266
South.....................	819	1,402	1,919	2,404	2,510	2,679	2,691	2,801
West......................	739	1,256	1,852	2,185	2,403	2,451	2,371	2,357
Negro......................	1,258	2,030	2,835	3,190	3,139	2,949	2,761	2,696
Northeast.................	1,230	1,709	2,340	2,481	2,439	2,103	2,059	2,006
North Central.............	1,288	1,985	2,726	2,939	2,698	2,396	2,134	2,131
South.....................	1,267	2,172	3,082	3,604	3,639	3,487	3,236	3,128
West.....................	1,137	1,820	2,590	2,709	2,562	2,273	1,983	2,030
American Indian.............	1,092	1,952	3,170	4,238	4,402	4,733	4,709	3,910
Japanese....................	.....	940	1,469	1,968	2,379	2,625	3,013	3,359
Chinese....................	.....	1,151	1,688	2,578	2,547	2,836	2,875	2,963
Other races................	992	1,756	2,526	3,206	3,652	3,974	3,884	3,793

Source: U.S. Bureau of the Census, U.S. Census of Population: 1960. Women by Number of Children Ever Born, Report PC(2)-3A, Table 8.

eration persons to marry at all. Table 18-20, row 3, shows that the native-born of foreign or mixed parentage have rates of fertility that are intermediate between those of the foreign-born and of the native-born. In other words, there is very little evidence of current or recent restriction of fertility because of ethnic cultural factors.

A note needs to be made about row 8 of Table 18-20. The South appears to be an exception to the rule that foreign-born white populations have low fertility. It should be remembered that the United States classifies persons of Mexican ancestry as being white; inasmuch as Spanish-Americans uniformly have high fertility, this explains the difference between the South and the other regions.

The Negro population of the South has substantially higher fertility than the Negro population generally. This is true for older cohorts of completed fertility as well as for the younger cohorts whose fertility has not yet been completed. This regional differential among the Negro population is especially marked for the cohorts aged 30 to 44 years in 1960. This could mean that women of lower fertility or couples of lower fertility have managed to migrate to other regions, whereas couples who

have more children, hence, are less mobile, have been forced to remain in the South.

American Indians appear to be the most fertile single ethnic group in the United States. The average size of completed family of this group is reported to be 4.7 children. As has already been noted, the data for the American Indian population is deficient, but is reliable enough to suggest that among the older generation, at least, fertility has been extremely high. Table 18-20 suggests that the younger generations of Indians under 25 years of age may be more nearly conforming to the fertility pattern of the nation. The older generations of Japanese and Chinese women were also among the most fertile in the nation. This may be seen by looking at the rates of children ever born for age groups 50 to 54 years, in the last column of Table 18-20. However, recent cohorts have tended to show a much more moderate rate of fertility. In fact, they show rates that correspond very closely to those for the native white population. The number of children ever born per thousand women is substantially lower among the Chinese and Japanese population for ages under 30 than for the white population.

Table 18-21 examines the fertility and child-

Table 18-21 Country of Origin of the Foreign Stock—Number of Children
Ever Born to Ever-Married Women 25 to 54 Years Old by Age of Woman,
for the United States: 1960

Country of origin	Foreign born			Foreign or mixed parentage		
	25 to 34 years	35 to 44 years	45 to 54 years	25 to 34 years	35 to 44 years	45 to 54 years
Total foreign stock........	1,949	2,296	2,226	2,280	2,412	2,143
United Kingdom..............	2,023	2,249	1,850	2,304	2,467	2,023
Ireland....................	1,997	2,539	2,539	2,410	2,749	2,223
Norway.....................	1,589	2,167	1,774	2,489	2,627	2,330
Sweden.....................	1,509	2,094	1,718	2,328	2,447	1,942
Germany....................	1,613	1,815	1,565	2,299	2,490	2,121
Poland.....................	1,946	2,015	1,972	2,123	2,269	2,107
Czechoslovakia.............	1,890	1,953	2,073	2,173	2,341	2,194
Austria....................	1,623	1,746	1,781	2,077	2,166	1,959
U.S.S.R....................	2,144	2,011	1,850	2,055	2,163	1,886
Italy......................	1,893	2,317	2,554	2,036	2,225	2,145
Canada.....................	2,159	2,415	2,127	2,477	2,640	2,271
Mexico.....................	3,150	3,982	4,631	3,311	4,221	4,508
Other countries............	1,763	2,157	2,121	2,199	2,368	2,124

Source: U.S. Bureau of the Census, U.S. Census of Population: 1960. Women by Number of
         Children Ever Born Report PC(2)-3A, Table 9.

bearing experience of women according to their parentage. The stub of this table lists the major nations from which migration to the United States has occurred. The table then shows the number of children ever born per thousand ever-married women for selected ages among the foreign-born or those of foreign and mixed parentage for each of these nationality groups. In making this effort to determine if there are differences in fertility according to nationality and country of origin of the foreign-born or foreign-stock, it is important to control the factor of age, because people from various countries enter the United States at different epochs of time and have unlike age compositions. From this table it may be seen that the lowest fertility may be found among women of Scandinavian, Austrian, and German ancestry in the foreign-born class. In contrast, people who have migrated from Puerto Rico or Mexico, or are of other Spanish-American ancestry, have extraordinarily high fertility. The data for women 35 to 44 years of age are especially interesting. These represent younger women who are nearing the completion of childbearing, but who have done most of their childbearing during the postwar "baby boom" years. The differentials among the various ethnic groups are very small except for Puerto Ricans and Mexi-

cans. *The fertility level of Italians, Poles, Czechs, and Irish (customarily thought to be high-fertility populations) actually are below the average for the United States as a whole.* Only the Irish and the Canadians (French Canadians) have unusually high fertility compared with the national level, aside from the Spanish-speaking groups. When we undertake to reexamine the differentials of fertility for the younger age groups of foreign or mixed parentage, those 25 to 34 years of age, we are absolutely unable to perceive any differential that would suggest that persons of Italian, Polish, or other Eastern or Southern European ancestry have higher fertility than do other groups. In fact, they appear to have lower fertility than children of immigrants from Scandinavia and the United Kingdom.

Table 18-21 is also highly important for the fact that it points out that the younger age groups of foreign-born population of each nationality group have lower fertility than the native-born population of foreign-born or mixed ancestry from the same nationality. Thus one of the civilizing influences of Europe on the United States in recent years has been to lend technical assistance, by migration, in helping Uncle Sam with his problem of irresponsible paternity.

Table 18-22 Number of Children Ever Born per 1000 Ever-Married Women 15 Years of Age and Over, by Color, Age, and Urban-Rural Residence: 1960

Region and age	White women					Nonwhite women				
	Total	Urban-ized areas	Other urban areas	Rural non-farm areas	Rural farm areas	Total	Urban-ized areas	Other urban areas	Rural non-farm areas	Rural farm areas
U.S. Total........	2458	2209	2493	2810	3200	2929	2449	3080	3899	4789
15-44 years.......	2254	2102	2229	2468	2851	2794	2432	2961	3599	4496
15-19 years...........	725	708	692	768	777	1247	1243	1209	1254	1325
20-24 years...........	1370	1261	1377	1546	1618	1999	1859	2101	2278	2569
25-29 years...........	2171	2024	2204	2383	2570	2771	2534	2930	3363	3809
30-34 years...........	2564	2410	2585	2780	3094	3155	2762	3406	4107	5034
35-39 years...........	2625	2427	2636	2925	3261	3138	2647	3328	4319	5508
40-44 years...........	2515	2270	2523	2880	3270	2984	2361	3223	4333	5618
45-49 years...........	2354	2066	2365	2784	3168	2818	2190	2872	4080	5300
50-54 years...........	2317	1978	2386	2821	3157	2742	2159	2795	3879	4926
55-59 years...........	2450	2083	2530	3011	3326	2904	2347	2916	4018	4809
60-64 years...........	2676	2313	2773	3260	3494	3109	2510	3269	4107	5010
65 years and over.....	3172	2804	3234	3751	4045	3741	3101	3811	4638	5222

Source: U.S. Census of population, 1960. Women by Number of Children Ever Born, Report PC(2)-3A, Table 1

Urban-Rural Residence. A strong and very consistent inverse relationship between urbanity and cumulative natality runs throughout all age groups of both the white and nonwhite populations. Table 18-22 and Figure 18-16 summarize the evidence concerning this. Metropolitan like agglomerations (urbanized areas) have a level of fertility that for some of the older generations was below replacement levels. The rural-farm population, in contrast, has manifested fertility levels that are as much as 50 percent higher than this. "Other urban places" (primarily cities of less than 25,000 inhabitants have higher birthrates than do the urbanized areas, while the rural-nonfarm population (villages) have even higher rates; both are below the rural-farm population, however.

The fact that these differences between natality in urban and rural areas are present for even the oldest cohorts of women, those 65 and over, demonstrates that it is a fertility differential of long standing. As we shall show, a substantial part of this differential (but not all) is a reflection of differences in educational attainment between urban and rural areas.

Region of Residence. Natality levels have been slightly lower in the Northeast than in the other three regions for many years. Both white and nonwhite women show this differential. It undoubtedly is a reflection of the urban-residence effect described above. The North Central region, being more rural and agricultural, has tended to have higher birthrates. Traditionally, the South has been reputed to have very fertile populations, both white and nonwhite. Table 18-23 demonstrates that this was once true, but is no longer valid for white women. In 1960 the CEB (children ever born) rates for white Southern women were lower at ages 15 to 39 for "new generations" of white

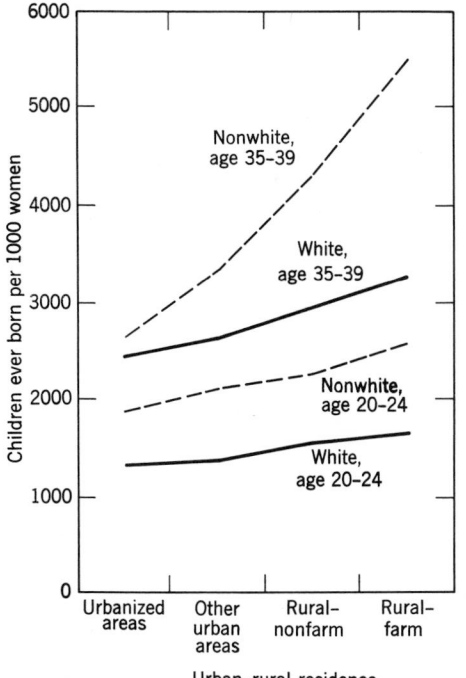

Figure 18-16 Urban-Rural Differentials in Fertility, Selected Age Groups, by Color: 1960.

Table 18-23   Number of Children Ever Born per 1000 Ever-Married Women 15 Years of Age and Over, by Color, Age, and Region of Residence: 1960

Age	White women					Negro nonwhite women				
	Total	North-east	North central	South	West	Total	North-east	North central	South	West
15-44 years...	2254	2141	2351	2241	2271	2794	2220	2550	3147	2514
15-19..........	725	754	713	711	750	1247	1220	1274	1263	1129
20-24..........	1370	1230	1406	1383	1457	1999	1694	1963	2162	1744
25-29..........	2171	1979	2272	2163	2280	2771	2307	2693	3060	2409
30-34..........	2564	2389	2705	2550	2613	3155	2469	2945	3588	2774
35-39..........	2625	2454	2743	2665	2624	3138	2448	2718	3637	2827
40-44..........	2515	2343	2611	2628	2442	2984	2112	2444	3494	2812
45-49.........	2354	2164	2417	2557	2229	2818	2066	2191	3250	2720
50-54.........	2317	2097	2340	2615	2151	2742	2016	2184	3137	2675
55-59.........	2450	2219	2444	2817	2244	2904	2219	2281	3252	3179
60-64.........	2676	2479	2667	3065	2414	3109	2362	2498	3410	3683
65 +.........	3172	2961	3109	3709	2802	3741	2858	2960	4066	4079

Source: U.S. Census of Population, 1960.   Women by number of children   ever born, Report PC(2)-3A, Table 1.

Southerners than for the white women of other regions. In fact, white Southerners are proving to be among the least fertile in the nation. The new development can probably be traced to a variety of factors: rapid urbanization of the South, a dominance of Protestant religious belief, and rising educational levels in the South.

Nonwhite natality in the South was much higher than in any other region in 1960. This may be attributed in large part to the much more rural residence of Negroes in the South. The very rapid urbanization of the Negro population since 1950 (even in the South) portends rapid declines in the fertility level of this group, for it gives this group equal access to family planning services.

Occupation of Husband. Natality appears to be definitely linked to occupational status and even to specific occupations. Yet the relationship is not simply one of socioeconomic status; the occupations with lowest natality are in the lower white-collar group, while upper white-collar families occupy a middle position. Table 18-24 presents children-ever-born data for women aged 35 to 44, married and husband present, classified by occupation of husband. The table therefore portrays primarily the fertility of unbroken marriages that are nearing completion of childbearing, with most of the childbearing having taken place after World War II. The fertility ranking of the major occupations is as follows (ranked in order for the white population):

Occupation of husband	*White*	*Nonwhite*
Private household	2290	2188
Clerical	2302	2340
Sales	2354	2613
Professional, technical	2417	2198
Managers, officials	2431	2567
Service workers	2484	2719
Craftsmen	2607	3001
Operatives	2730	3156
Laborers, except farm	3008	3458
Farmers and farm managers	3170	5572
Farm laborers and foremen ...	3988	5078

Differences in educational attainment of the holders of each occupation account for much of this variation. Within each of the major occupation categories, some specific occupations have natality that is significantly higher or lower than the average for the category. For example, among the white professionals the following are outstanding for having comparatively high fertility:

Physicians	2922
Clergymen	2790
Engineers, electrical	2511
Dentists	2503

The following, in contrast, have unusually low fertility in comparison with the group:

Medical and dental technicians	2121
Authors, editors, reporters	2144
Artists and art teachers	2161
Social scientists	2169
Musicians and music teachers	2170
Accountants and auditors	2182

Table 18-24 Occupation of Employed Husbands—Number of Children Ever Born per 1000 Women and Percent Childless; Women 35 to 44 Years Old, Married, and Husband Present, United States: 1960

Occupation	Children ever born per 1000 women		Percent childless	
	White	Nonwhite	White	Nonwhite
Total...............................	2596	3216	10.7	20.1
Professional, Technical and Kindred workers...............	2417	2198	11.2	19.6
Accountants and auditors..................................	2182	1937	14.6	23.9
Architects...	2416	....	13.1	....
Artists and art teachers.................................	2161	....	15.4	....
Authors, editors, & reporters............................	2144	....	14.0	....
Chemists...	2411	....	10.7	....
Clergymen..	2790	2780	7.5	23.0
College Pres, prof'rs & instr's (nec)....................	2462	1760	11.8	15.5
Dentists...	2503	....	9.8	....
Designers and Draftsmen..................................	2266	....	13.6	....
Engineers: Aeronautical.................................	2306	....	11.7	....
Civil..	2382	....	12.1	....
Electrical...	2511	....	10.1	....
Mechanical...	2427	....	9.5	....
Other technical engineers................................	2428	....	10.7	....
Lawyers and judges.......................................	2466	....	11.3	....
Musicians and music teachers.............................	2170	....	15.5	....
Natural Scientists (n.e.c.)..............................	2460	....	10.6	....
Pharmacists..	2238	....	12.4	....
Physicians and surgeons..................................	2922	2044	7.6	18.0
Social Scientists.......................................	2169	....	13.5	....
Social, Welfare, & Recreation Workers....................	2398	2169	11.7	26.7
Teachers: Elementary School............................	2382	1980	10.7	23.9
Secondary School..........................	2422	1951	10.0	21.8
Teachers (N.E.C.).......................................	2337	....	12.6	....
Technicians: Medical and Dental.........................	2121	....	13.9	....
Electrical and Electronic..................	2357	....	11.7	....
Other Profess'l Techn'l & Kindred workers................	2424	2208	10.6	15.3
Farmers and Farm managers...............................	3170	5572	7.8	9.1
Managers, Offs. & Propr's, exc. farm....................	2431	2567	10.4	19.5
Officials & Insp's State & Local Admin..................	2342	....	11.9	....
Other specified managers & officials....................	2364	2493	11.3	17.2
Managers officials and proprietors (n.e.c.) Salaried......	2417	2459	10.2	17.1
Manufacturing...	2483	....	9.0	....
Wholesale & retail trade..............................	2379	2317	10.6	18.0
Finance, Insurance & Real Estate......................	2314	....	11.2	....
Other industries (incl. not reported).................	2428	2575	10.6	15.1
Mangers, officials and propr's (n.e.c.) Self-employed......	2479	2657	10.2	21.9
Constrution..	2696	2440	8.5	25.8
Manufacturing..	2585	....	8.5	....
Wholesale Trade.......................................	2558	3063	8.6	27.3
Eating and Drinking Places............................	2319	2081	12.6	32.8
Retail Trade, exc. eating and drinking places..........	2417	2705	10.4	13.2
Other industries (incl. not reported).................	2416	2588	11.7	25.3
Clerical and Kindred workers............................	2302	2340	13.1	23.8
Bookkeepers..	2196	....	14.2	...
Mail carriers...	2433	2098	10.8	28.2
Other clerical and kindred workers......................	2292	2384	13.3	22.9
Sales workers...	2354	2613	11.4	18.2
Insurance agents, brokers, & underwriters...............	2448	1993	10.1	24.2
Real estate agents & brokers............................	2368	....	12.8	....
Other specified sales workers...........................	2462	....	11.2	....
Salesmen and sales clerks (n.e.c)......................	2333	2784	11.5	16.8
Manufacturing..	2363	....	10.7	....
Wholesale trade......................................	2294	3033	11.2	7.3
Retail trade...	2332	2819	11.9	18.5
Other industries (incl. not reported).................	2400	....	12.4	....

Similarly, managers engaged in manufacturing, construction, and wholesale trade tend to have higher fertility than managers engaged in finance, retail trade, and operating eating and drinking places. Among clerical workers, bookkeepers have unusually low fertility, while mail carriers are above average. Operatives who work as checkers, assemblers, and meat cutters or who are employed in apparel and fabricated textile, electrical equipment, and aircraft manufacturing plants also have lower fertility than operatives in other types of work.

Table 18-24   (Continued)

Occupation	Children ever born per 1000 women		Percent childless	
	White	Nonwhite	White	Nonwhite
Craftsmen, foremen, & Kindred workers......................	2607	3001	10.0	20.0
Bakers...	2424	3230	11.5	14.8
Blacksmiths, forgemen, & hammermen...........................	2798	....	7.5	....
Boilermakers.......................................	2718	....	10.0	....
Cabinetmakers & patternmakers...........................	2572	....	11.2	....
Carpenters..	2877	3640	9.5	15.1
Compositors & typesetters...............................	2243	....	12.5	....
Cranemen, derrickmen, & hoistmen...........................	2800	2900	7.6	22.2
Electricians......................................	2572	2877	9.5	14.3
Foremen 9n.e.c.)...................................	2500	2645	9.5	16.4
Manufacturing, durable goods........................	2483	2686	8.9	16.7
Mfg. nondurable goods (incl. not specified mfg.).........	2422	2832	9.9	14.0
Nonmanufacturing indus. (incl. not reported).............	2574	2570	10.0	17.1
Linemen & servicemen, telegraph, telephone, and power.......	2488	3179	10.0	17.5
Locomotive engineers.................................	2512	....	8.9	....
Locomotive firemen..................................	2634	....	8.6	....
Machinists and job setters.............................	2509	2453	10.1	23.6
Masons, tile setters, & stone cutters......................	2748	3313	10.1	20.4
Mechanists & Repairmen: airplane.........................	2370	2335	11.4	23.2
Automobile.....................................	2704	3105	9.9	19.9
Radio and TV...................................	2536	3165	11.9	18.3
Other mechanists & repairman & loom fixers................	2603	2784	10.1	23.3
Millwrights.......................................	2624	....	10.1	....
Molders, metal....................................	2920	3076	10.1	21.6
Painters (const.) paperhangers, & glaziers................	2722	2925	10.8	24.0
Plasters & Cement finishers............................	2969	2848	9.0	24.1
Plumbers and pipe fitters..............................	2637	3386	9.2	16.0
Printing craft., exc. compos & typesetters..............	2322	....	11.8	....
Shoemakers & repairers, except factory...................	2249	....	13.9	....
Stationary engineers.................................	2544	2879	10.6	21.5
Structural metal workers..............................	2639	....	10.4	....
Tailors and furriers................................	2034	....	12.9	....
Tinsmiths, coppersmiths, & sheet metal workers.............	2591	....	10.7	....
Toolmakers, and die makers and setters..................	2479	....	9.4	....
Other craftsmen and kindred workers......................	2664	3132	10.4	15.9
Operatives and kindred workers(n.e.c.)..................	2730	3156	10.2	20.3
Apprentices......................................	2667	....	12.8	....
Assemblers.......................................	2490	2559	12.4	25.9
Attendants, auto service and parking.....................	2679	3134	11.9	21.8
Brakemen and switchmen, railroad.......................	2683	2872	8.2	11.5
Bus drivers......................................	2686	3204	10.4	18.9
Checkers, examiners, & inspectors, mfg...................	2370	2816	12.6	20.9
Filers, grinders, & polishers, metal....................	2655	2876	9.6	18.7
Furnacemen, sheltermen, & heaters......................	2849	3165	8.7	21.5
Laundry and dry cleaning operatives.....................	2294	2455	14.9	21.7
Meat cutters, exc. slaughter & packing house..............	2500	3221	9.1	16.7
Mine operatives and laborers (n.e.c.)....................	3391	4422	7.0	13.0
Coal mines.....................................	3723	4736	6.1	9.9
Other...	3092	4054	7.8	16.6
Packers and wrappers (n.e.c.).........................	2761	3028	12.2	27.1
Painters exc. construction and maintenance...............	2811	3171	9.9	21.1
Power station operators..............................	2712	....	8.5	....
Sailors and deck hands...............................	2673	....	11.8	....
Sawyers...	3412	4591	9.3	12.0
Spinners and weavers, textile..........................	2660	....	9.2	....
Stationary firemen..................................	2755	3369	11.8	16.4
Taxicab drivers and chauffeurs.........................	2520	2311	11.5	30.8
Truck drivers and deliverymen..........................	2819	3405	9.8	20.2
Welders and flame-cutters.............................	2770	2901	9.2	21.0
Other spec. operatives and kindred workers................	2754	3165	8.6	22.4
Operatives and kindred workers (n.e.c.)..................	2678	3100	10.5	19.2
Manufacturing....................................	2656	3127	10.6	19.0
Durable goods...................................	2664	3112	10.7	18.8
Saw & planing mills, & misc. wood prod..............	3157	4226	8.3	12.7
Furniture and fixtures............................	2788	3379	9.7	18.1
Stone, clay, and glass products.....................	2841	3234	10.4	20.6
Primary metal industries..........................	2744	3131	8.8	16.4
Fabric'd metal ind. (incl. not spec.).................	2542	2620	12.7	20.3
Machinery, exc. electrical.........................	2618	3056	10.0	17.3
Electrical mach'y, equip., & supplies.................	2471	2479	12.6	17.2

Table 18-24 (Continued)

Occupation	Children ever born per 1000 women		Percent childless	
	White	Nonwhite	White	Nonwhite
Operatives - Continued				
Opeartives and kindred workers (n.e.c.) (Mfg; durable)				
Motor vehicles, & motor vehicle equipment...........	2778	2787	10.7	24.6
Transp. equip., exc. motor vehicles.................	2517	3172	10.5	21.2
Other durable goods................................	2388	2219	13.0	27.0
Nondurable goods.....................................	2645	3153	10.4	19.2
Food and kindred products.........................	2776	3178	10.0	18.9
Yarn, thread, and fabric mills....................	2842	3689	10.4	15.9
Knitting, & other text. mill products.............	2695	....	8.2	....
Apparel & other fab'd textile products............	2124	2369	11.5	30.4
Paper and allied products.........................	2811	3441	9.9	19.2
Chemicals and allied products.....................	2648	3438	9.5	15.7
Other nondurable goods............................	2519	2750	11.7	21.8
Not specified manufacturing industries.............	....	....	....	....
Nonmanufacturing industries (incl. not reported).....	2820	3008	10.1	20.0
Transport., commun., & other public utility.........	2774	2936	11.2	18.6
Wholesale and retail trade..........................	2790	3049	9.8	19.3
Other industries (incl. not reported)...............	2869	3022	9.5	21.0
Private household workers........,..................	2290	2188	18.8	32.4
Service workers, exc. private household.............	2484	2719	12.6	23.9
Barbers...	2334	2416	12.8	24.6
Janitors, and porters...............................	2817	2877	12.5	25.2
Cooks, except private household.....................	2450	2527	14.9	20.8
Elevator operators..................................	2177	2368	19.7	25.5
Firemen, fire protection............................	2521	....	9.1	....
Gurads and watchmen.................................	2585	2689	12.5	20.2
Policemen, sheriffs, and marshals...................	2468	2385	9.5	17.7
Waiters, bartenders, and counter workers............	2192	2310	14.4	25.8
Other service workers exc. private household........	2366	2703	16.9	23.9
Farm Laborers and Foremen...........................	3988	5078	8.3	13.4
Farm laborers: unpiad family workers................	3161	....	7.1	....
exc. unpiad, & farm foremen.........................	4002	5063	8.3	13.5
Laborers, except Farm and mine......................	3008	3458	10.6	19.7
Fishermen and oystermen.............................	3139	....	9.2	....
Longshoremen and stevedores.........................	2603	3137	12.5	20.9
Lumbermen, raftsmen, and woodchoppers...............	3998	5092	6.1	10.8
Other specified laborers............................	2747	3163	13.3	20.4
Laborers (n.e.c.)...................................	3011	3435	10.3	20.0
Manufacturing......................................	2907	3552	10.4	18.6
Durable goods.....................................	2919	3500	10.6	19.1
Furniture, saw & planing mills & misc. wood prodt's..	3408	4305	8.7	13.8
Stone, clay, and glass products...................	2919	3992	11.9	14.0
Primary metal industries..........................	2884	3179	10.9	21.6
Fabric'd metal ind. (incl. not spec.).............	2750	3401	7.7	21.6
Machinery, including electrical...................	2548	2886	13.1	21.5
Transportation equipment..........................	2805	2957	11.9	23.2
Other durable goods...............................	3018	....	5.8	....
Nondurable goods..................................	2885	3654	10.0	17.3
Food and kindred products.........................	3145	3566	7.7	19.3
Textile mill products and apparel.................	2699	3660	13.6	17.0
Chemicals and allied products.....................	2619	3890	13.9	16.5
Other nondurable goods............................	2816	3605	9.1	16.1
Not specified manufacturing industries.............	....	....	....	....
Nonmanufacturing indus. (incl. not reported)........	3079	3365	10.3	20.8
Construction......................................	3103	3530	10.2	19.4
Railroads and railway express service.............	3321	3705	9.5	16.8
Transportation, except railroad...................	2849	2559	10.2	29.1
Commun., & util., & sanitary service..............	2953	3293	9.5	21.5
Wholesale and retail trade........................	3075	3318	8.7	17.9
Other industries (incl. not reported).............	3015	3015	13.0	26.0
Occupation not reported.............................	2406	2582	15.2	25.8

Source: U.S. Census of Population 1960. Women by Number of Children Ever Born, Report PC(2)-3A, Table 33,34.

Among the service workers, barbers, waiters, and bartenders have unusually low fertility, while janitors and porters have above-average fertility for the group. Laborers in textile, machinery, and electrical manufacturing industries have birthrates below the average for all laborers, as do stevedores and longshoremen. In all of these comparisons, educational attainment undoubtedly is one component in accounting for a part of the differences.

Table 18-25   Income of Husband in 1959—Number of Children
Ever Born per 1000 Women and Percent Childless; Women
35 to 39 Years Old, Married and Husband Present, United
States: 1960

Income of husband	Number of children ever born per 1000		Percent of childless	
	White	Nonwhite	White	Nonwhite
Total..........	2664	3299	9.6	18.4
None.................	2905	3472	12.9	21.5
$1,000 - $1,999 or loss	3097	4195	12.7	17.0
$2,000 - $2,999........	2947	3408	12.1	20.0
$3,000 - $3,999........	2755	3099	10.6	18.9
$4,000 - $4,999........	2619	2846	10.7	20.5
$5,000 - $6,999........	2576	2803	9.3	17.3
$7,000 - $9,999........	2583	2830	8.3	13.5
$10,000 - $14,999......	2601	2425	8.2	13.2
$15,000 and over.......	2733	2673	7.1	9.0

Source: U.S. Census of Population, 1960. Women by Number of Children
           Ever Born, Report PC(2)-3A, Table 37

Income of Husband. Children-ever-born
data reveal a slightly U-shaped pattern of differential fertility. The extremely poor and the
wealthy have higher fertility levels, while the
middle classes tend to have the lowest fertility. Among the nonwhite population, the pattern is one of rather strong inverse relationship,
with only a hint that very wealthy Negroes are
more fertile than middle-class Negroes. Table
18-25 and Figure 18-17 illustrate these income
differentials.

Income of husband is a direct measure of the
capacity of families to support children and of
the willingness of various income groups to
bear children as one of several possible economic alternative ways of expending income.
Traditionally, the relationship has been inverse: the poorer the family, the greater the
number of children it tended to have. Since
1945 there seems to have occurred a marked
change in this pattern. With modern birth control readily available to all, the poor and the
middle class seem to be curtailing their fertility and leaving the bearing of larger families
to the group that can afford it best—the rich.
Inasmuch as this pattern is comparatively new,

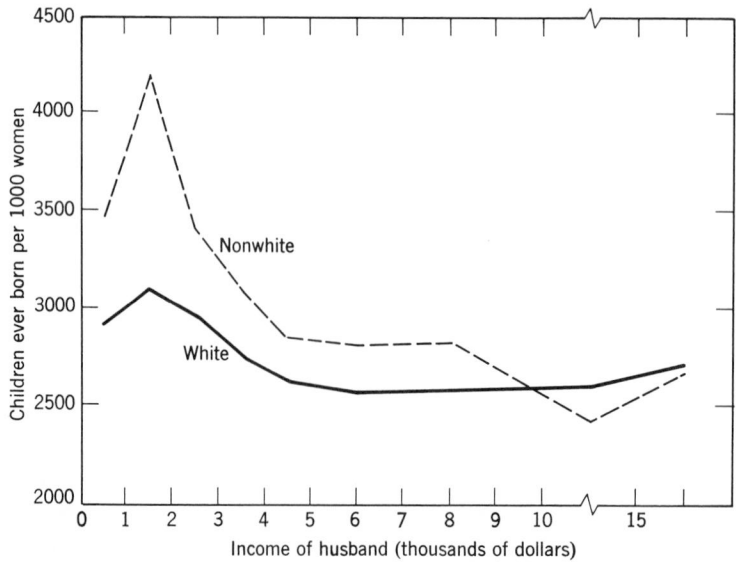

Figure 18-17   Income Differentials in Fertility, by Color: 1960.

it is not readily visible in the cumulative data of Table 18-25. More incisive information will be presented in the next section, using current fertility measures. More conclusive data must await the 1970 census.

Occupation, Income, and Education of Husband. The preceding analysis has shown that occupation, income, and education are all related to differential cumulative natality. The questions arise: How are these three factors interrelated? Does each have an independent effect? Does the factor of education account for both occupation and income? Does the factor of income account for both occupation and education? Does the factor of occupation account for both education and income? Table 18-26 presents data for CEB for women 35 to 44 years of age, cross-classified by the three variables simultaneously. The tabulation is confined to women married once and with husband present, so that the factor of marital dissolution

has been controlled. Also, the factor of age at marriage is controlled by tabulation in two groups—those who married before age 22 and those who married at age 22 and beyond. Data are presented separately for white and nonwhite wives. This table enables us to study intensively the independent effect of each of the three variables.

Independent Effect of Education. Education appears to have a powerful explanatory effect for the nonwhite population at all levels and for the white population among women who married young. However, among white women who married at age 22 and above it has little if any such effect, except in the farmer and laborer category. For example, take the income group $4000 to $6999 and trace it through each combination of occupation and education. The following data, for women with husbands in operative occupations, illustrates the effect.

Education	Married early		Married late	
	White	Nonwhite	White	Nonwhite
No high school	3262	3736	2217	2355
High school 1-4 years	2842	3450	2153	2016
College 1+ years	2771	3338	2189	1915

Among all women who married before age 22, those who did not attend high school have much higher fertility than those who did. Among white wives who married late there is much variation by educational level. But among Negroes the educational differential is very sharp.

Thus the high fertility of white women with low educational attainment (failure to attend high school) appears to be linked to the greater length of exposure to childbearing caused by early marriage and possibly to premarital preg-

nancy, which selectively removed them from the category of those who could afford to wait until a more mature age to marry.

Independent Effect of Occupation. When educational attainment, income, and age at marriage are held constant, most of the occupational differences disappear or become small and ambiguous except for farmers and laborers. Take, for example, the average group of persons who earned $4000 to $6999 and had completed 1 to 4 years of high school:

Occupation	Married early		Married late	
	White	Nonwhite	White	Nonwhite
Professional, technical, etc.	2610	. . .	2003	1785
Managers, officials, etc.	2641	3079	2100	2066
Clerical, sales	2567	2840	2052	1977
Craftsmen	2791	3500	2165	2174
Operatives	2842	3450	2153	2016
Service workers	2793	3079	2163	2047
Laborers, except farm	2989	3545	2173	2141
Farmers, farm managers	3331	5823	2922	2141

Table 18-26 Occupation, by Education by Income—Number of Children Ever Born per 1000 Women 35 to 44 Years Old, Married Once and Husband Present, United States: 1960

Occupation and income of husband	Wives married at age 14 to 21 years						Wives married age 22 or over					
	White wives 35-44 years			Nonwhite wives			White wives			Nonwhite wives		
	No high school	High school 1-4 years	College 1+ years	No high school	High shool 1-4 years	College 1+ years	No high school	High school 1-4 years	College 1+ years	No high school	High school 1-4 years	College 1+ years
Total........	3058	2621	2701	....	3328	2712	2083	2106	2367	....	1824	1886
Professional, Technical wkr.	....	....	....	....	....	....	....	....	....	....	....	....
$1 to $1,999 or loss	....	2780	2792	....	....	....	....	1939	1930	....	....	....
$2,000 to $3,999	3274	2925	2583	....	....	2753	2112	1834	2017	....	....	1770
$4,000 to $6,999	2924	2610	2614	....	....	2418	2126	2003	2153	....	1785	1698
$7,000 to $9,999	2775	2592	2667	....	....	....	2224	2217	2292	....	....	2131
$10,000 and over	....	2595	2780	....	....	....	....	2214	2589	....	....	2129
Managers, Officials, Propr's	2869	2640	2684	3893	3220	2645	2175	2169	2371	2138	1956	2054
$1 to $1,999	3102	2485	2629	4309	....	....	1973	1857	2182	....	....	....
$2,000 to $3,999	2840	2574	2685	....	3079	....	2239	1922	2054	1975	2066	2192
$4,000 to $6,999	2894	2641	2556	....	....	....	2195	2100	2188	....	....	....
$7,000 to $9,999	2877	2657	2661	....	....	....	2157	2246	2322	....	....	....
$10,000 and over	2693	2669	2746	....	....	....	2212	2315	2504	....	....	....
Clerical, Sales, and Kindred Work	2805	2569	2617	3889	2992	2756	2040	2096	2253	2210	1974	1872
$1 to $1,999	2995	2659	2617	3951	3121	....	1919	1754	1918	2515	1980	....
$2,000 to $3,999	2943	2561	2434	3761	2840	2856	1927	1765	1845	1889	1977	1787
$4,000 to $6,999	2707	2567	2562	....	....	....	2073	2052	2131	....	....	....
$7,000 to $9,999	2831	2567	2623	....	....	....	2056	2298	2317	....	....	....
$10,000 and over	2866	2577	2754	....	....	....	2222	2346	2495	....	....	....
Craftsmen, formen and Kindred Work	3207	2798	2736	4206	3491	3248	2219	2204	2276	2359	2144	2046
$1 to $1,999	3684	2902	3139	4737	4122	....	2194	1824	2211	2754	2129	....
$2,000 to $3,999	3490	2897	2690	4268	3502	....	2257	1967	1966	2382	2174	2106
$4,000 to $6,999	3125	2791	2757	3797	3500	2856	2188	2165	2181	2244	2042	....
$7,000 to $9,999	2974	2770	2638	....	3052	....	2257	2349	2292	....	....	....
$10,000 and over	2974	2786	2878	....	....	....	2403	2330	2502	....	....	....
Operatives and Kindred Wkrs.	3405	2884	2820	4294	3572	3356	2259	2167	2193	2633	2070	1864
$1 to $1,999	4315	3254	....	5236	4109	....	2492	1957	....	3240	2207	....
$2,000 to $3,999	3558	2984	2748	4302	3624	3338	2236	2016	1654	2618	2086	1915
$4,000 to $6,999	3262	2842	2771	3736	3450	....	2217	2153	2189	2355	2016	....
$7,000 to $9,999	3110	2885	2897	3883	3701	....	2413	2337	2383	2065	2290	....
$10,000 and over	3158	2968	2857	....	....	....	2361	2388	2453	....	....	....

Table 18-26 (Continued)

Occupation and income of husband	Wives married at age 14 to 21 years						Wives married age 22 or over					
	White wives 35-44 years			Nonwhite wives			White wives			Nonwhite wives		
	No high school	High school 1-4 years	College 1+ years	No high school	High school 1-4 years	College 1+ years	No high school	High school 1-4 years	College 1+ years	No high school	High school 1-4 years	College 1+ years
Service Workers, Inc.												
Private house..........	3205	2771	2744	3916	3319	3037	2044	2123	2209	2022	1911	2101
$1 to $1,999............	3711	2993	....	3859	3346	....	1926	1600	....	2040	1957	....
$2,000 to $3,999........	3376	2694	2763	3896	3368	....	1989	1868	2003	2010	1826	2097
$4,000 to $6,999........	2986	2793	2750	4068	3079	....	2084	2163	2237	2051	2047	....
$7,000 to $9,999........	2737	2732	2767	....	....	....	2246	2452	2406	....	....	....
$10,000 and over........	2840	2748	2906	....	....	....	....	2305	2438	....	....	....
Laborers, exc. Farm & Mine...	3842	3096	3107	4682	4056	....	2365	2174	2123	2732	2178	2093
$1 to $1,999 or less.....	4547	3373	....	5550	4567	....	2664	1827	....	2995	2817	....
$2,000 to $3,999.........	3990	3271	3115	4451	4495	....	2488	2109	2150	2739	1962	....
$4,000 to $6,999.........	3538	2989	....	4159	3545	....	2217	2173	....	2430	2141	....
$7,000 to $9,999.........	3216	3195	....	....	....	....	2492	2410	....	....	....	....
$10,000 and over.........	3403	2911	....	....	....	....	....	....	....	....	....	....
Farmers, Farm Managers, Farm Laborers, & Farm Foremen...	3960	3173	3083	6632	5126	....	2949	2626	2705	3937	3252	2093
$1 to $1,999 or less.....	4014	3032	2951	6681	5971	....	2760	2257	2567	2995	2881	....
$2,000 to $3,999.........	3974	3183	3156	6484	....	....	2954	2630	2596	2739	3193	....
$4,000 to $6,999.........	3906	3331	3312	5823	....	....	3186	2922	2777	2430	2985	....
$7,000 to $9,999.........	3664	3050	2798	....	....	....	3392	2734	2873	....	....	....
$10,000 and over.........	3862	3154	2837	....	....	....	3072	2766	2842	....	....	....

Source: U.S. Census of Population, 1960: Women by Number of Children Ever Born, Report PC(2)-3A, Table 39-40.

Both farmers and laborers have a high level of fertility that cannot be accounted for entirely by their low income and low-education position.

Independent Effect of Income. Among those who marry early, income has a comparatively small effect, which tends to be U-shaped. But among those who marry late it has a powerful effect, in the direction of promoting fertility. In the latter group, the higher the income, the greater the fertility tends to be. However, the effect is not to promote above-average fertility, but simply to help make it possible for the fertility level to more nearly "catch up" with the fertility of those who married early. We take the high school group of persons employed as operatives and observe the income effect:

Income	Married early White	Married early Nonwhite	Married late White	Married late Nonwhite
$1 to $1999 or less	3254	4109	1957	2207
$2000 to $3999	2984	3624	2016	2086
$4000 to $6999	2842	3450	2153	2016
$7000 to $9999	2885	3701	2337	2290
$10,000 and over	2968	....	2388	....

In studying Table 18-26, the reader should remember to place greater emphasis upon the "normal" or usual combinations of education, occupation, and income and to de-emphasize the bizarre or highly unusual combinations. In fact, the complete interpretation of this table would require a return to the original source to note the comparative size of the population in each cell.

Summary of the Independent Effects. The above is a greatly oversimplified analysis of Table 18-26, which is a highly fundamental one in the study of differential fertility. This table demonstrates that *age at marriage is a more powerful factor in affecting cumulative fertility at ages 35 to 44 than is education, income, or occupation.* When this factor is controlled, the variation of the other three diminishes sharply. However, each exerts an independent effect. Among the nonwhite population, education is a sharp differentiator at all levels independently of the effect of the other variables. Income promotes higher fertility among those who marry late. Education is inversely related to fertility among those who marry early. Persons engaged in agricultural and proletarian occupations have higher fertility, even when age at marriage, income, and education are controlled. There are important interactions among these variables. For example, persons with much education, large income, and high-prestige occupations tended to have especially high fertility. On the other hand, the highest fertility rates are found among persons who had no high school education, had less than $2000 income, and worked as laborers—either farm or nonfarm.

Occupation of Employed Women. Table 18-27 reports differential fertility associated with the occupations that employed women hold. The data refer to ever-married women aged 35 to 44. Occupations with unusually low fertility are:

Social scientists	1354
Accountants and auditors	1458
Designers and draftsmen	1498
College professors and instructors	1507
Lawyers and judges	1582

In addition, the following occupations have below-average fertility for the groups in which they fall:

Secretaries	1611
Stenographers	1629
Foremen	1762
Hairdressers	1779
Operatives, assemblers	2142
Operatives, apparel	2142

Above-average fertility (in comparison with major occupational category) is manifest in the tabulation shown on page 710.

Table 18-27 Occupation of Employed Women—Number of Children Ever Born per 1000 Women and Percent Childless; Women 35 to 44 Years Old and Ever Married, United States: 1960

Occupation of woman	Children ever born per 1000 women		Percent childless	
	White	Nonwhite	White	Nonwhite
Professional, Technical and kindred workers..................	1973	1627	18.3	30.0
Accountants and Auditors...................................	1458	....	30.1	....
Actors, Dancers, and Entertainers (N.E.C.).................	1789	....	16.0	....
Artists and Art Teachers...................................	1866	....	19.7	....
Authors, Editors, and Reporters...........................	2009	....	21.0	....
College President, Proffesors and Instruters (N.E.C.)......	1507	....	33.1	....
Designers and Draftsmen....................................	1498	....	29.1	....
Dietitians and Nutritionists..............................	1797	....	21.4	....
Lawyers and Judges...	1582	....	26.2	....
Librarians..	1685	....	26.8	....
Musicians and Music Teachers..............................	2312	....	12.7	....
Natural Scientists..	1831	....	23.4	....
Nurses Professional.......................................	2147	1833	16.2	29.8
Nurses, Student Professional..............................	....	....	....	....
Physicians and Surgeons...................................	1796	....	24.2	....
Social Scientists...	1354	....	36.1	....
Social Welfare and Recreation Workers.....................	1796	1560	23.7	28.8
Teachers, Elementary School...............................	2033	1523	14.8	31.0
Secondary School.................	1904	1437	17.1	31.0
Teachers (N.E.C.)...	2109	1456	12.3	33.2
Technicians, Medical and Dental...........................	1818	1941	22.6	18.5
Therapists and Healers (N.E.C.)...........................	1632	....	32.6	....
Other Professional Technical, and Kindred Workers..........	1782	1758	24.3	29.7
Farmers and Farm Managers.................................	3017	5296	12.0	9.1
Managers, Offs. Propr's except Farm......................	1879	1897	21.2	27.9
Specified Managers and Officials..........................	1777	1510	21.8	27.2
Managers, Offs. and Propr's (N.E.C.) Salaried.............	1742	1656	24.2	28.6
Wholesale and Retail Trade.............................	1879	1761	21.1	18.9
Other Industries (Incl. Not reported)...................	1657	1597	26.1	34.0
Managers Officials, Proprietors (N.E.C.) Self Employed.......	2112	2162	16.9	27.6
Easting and Drinking places..............................	2254	2018	15.0	30.8
Wholesale and Retail Trade, Except eat and Drink...........	2060	2527	17.5	21.2
Other Industries (Incl. Not reported)....................	2059	....	17.9	....
Clerical and Kindred Workers..............................	1787	1747	21.2	27.8
Bookkeepers...	1772	1545	20.7	28.8
Cashiers..	2139	1898	14.0	29.8
Office Machine Operators..................................	1707	1566	22.7	34.0
Secretaries...	1611	1678	25.2	23.3
Stenographers...	1629	1495	24.3	19.1
Telephone Operators.......................................	1766	1599	22.6	35.4
Typists...	1840	1682	19.1	29.5
Other Clerical and Kindred workers........................	1841	1812	20.3	27.5
Sales Workers...	2206	2111	12.1	26.0
Insurance and Real Estate Agents and Brokers..............	2064	2097	16.6	29.6
Other Specified Sales Workers.............................	2646	....	8.0	....
Salesmen and Sales Clerks (N.E.C.) Retail Trade...........	2191	2074	11.9	26.0
Salesmen and Sales Clerks (N.E.C.) Except Retail Trade.....	2171	....	14.5	....
Craftsmen, Foremen and Kindred Workers....................	1959	1884	20.5	30.1
Foremen (N.E.C.)..	1762	....	23.7	....
Other Craftsmen and Kindred Workers.......................	2067	1878	18.7	30.9
Operatives and Kindred Workers............................	2309	2161	14.8	26.5
Assemblers..	2142	1692	16.7	32.4
Checkers, Examiners, and Inspectors, Manufacturing........	2055	1800	17.5	30.5
Dressmakers and Seamstresses, Except Factory..............	2307	2170	13.4	20.9
Laundry and Dry Cleaning Operatives.......................	2616	2206	14.6	29.2
Spinners and Weavers, Textile.............................	2544	....	9.9	....
Other Sepc. Opearatives and Kindred Workers...............	2367	2121	13.7	25.4
Operatives and Kindred Workers (N.E.C.)...................	2304	2219	15.1	24.3
Manufacturing...	2292	2198	15.2	24.8
Durable Goods.......................................	2194	2032	16.3	28.0
Machinery, Including Electrical...................	2157	1644	16.1	28.5
Other Durable goods..............................	2225	2198	16.5	27.8
Nondurable Goods....................................	2646	2261	14.5	23.6
Food and Kindred Products........................	2704	2927	11.4	20.3
Textile Mill Products............................	2501	2355	12.8	22.1
Apparel and Other Fabric'd Test. Products........	2304	1940	14.5	26.3
Other Nondurable Goods (Incl. Not Specified Manufacturing..	2147	2118	16.9	22.2
Nonmanufacturing Indus. (Inc. Not Reported)................	2494	2388	13.4	20.1

Table 18-27 (*Continued*)

Occupation of woman	Children ever born per 1000 women		Percent childless	
	White	Nonwhite	White	Nonwhite
Private household workers....................................	2836	2864	12.8	24.6
Private household workers--Living in...................	1817	1352	31.6	39.9
Private household workers--Living out.....................	2906	2913	11.6	24.1
Service workers, except private household..................	2545	2567	12.0	24.6
Attendants, Hospital and other...........................	2900	2494	10.2	24.3
Charwomen, janitors and porters..........................	2882	2716	9.5	22.3
Cooks, except private household..........................	2994	3181	6.5	19.2
Hairdressers and Cosmetologists..........................	1779	1479	19.3	39.5
Housekeepers and stewards, except private household........	2303	2389	14.3	26.7
Practical nurses and midwives............................	2672	2347	11.5	22.5
Waiters, bartenders, and counter workers..................	2508	2384	12.3	24.1
Other service workers, except private household...........	2663	2627	10.6	24.4
Farm laborers and foremen.................................	3165	5001	10.0	12.0
Farm laborers and unpaid family workers...................	3026	5000	9.6	9.7
Except Unpaid and farm foremen...........................	3538	5001	11.0	12.6
Labor except farm and mine...............................	2496	2584	13.4	25.7
Occupation not reported	2190	2131	20.5	31.0

Authors, editors, reporters	2009
Teachers, elementary	2033
Clerical—cashiers	2139
Nurses, professional	2147
Managers, eating places	2254
Musicians and music teachers	2312
Operatives—laundry and dry cleaning	2616
Operatives—food and kindred products	2704
Charwomen, janitors	2882
Attendants, hospital	2900
Private household workers, living out	2906
Cooks, except private	2994
Farm laborers	3538

Many of the occupations in this list represent positions that permit women with small children to work at home, to work only a part of each week, or to engage in seasonal work. Women who have small children may be selectively attracted to them, just as women who have larger numbers of children may be selectively rejected by the low-fertility occupations.

18.8. Differential Natality in the United States: Current Fertility

Vital registers do not collect detailed data on socioeconomic characteristics of women, and their spouses, who bear children. For this reason, it has been difficult to obtain data with which to measure current differential fertility. Two strategies for correcting this situation have been devised: the postregistration follow-up survey and the "own children under 5" re-

tabulation of census data. In the first of these procedures, parents who have registered a birth in a specified year are contacted in their homes and interviewed to obtain a variety of personal, social, and economic data not available on the birth certificate. This is a new technique, initiated in the United States only in the mid-1960s, and has as yet produced only a limited amount of information.

The "own children under 5 years" system for measuring current fertility was developed by Dr. Wilson H. Grabill of the U.S. Bureau of Census. This procedure reviews and recodes the census schedules, and links into one tabulation record each child under 5 years of age, his mother and father in the household, and the characteristics of the parents and the household. By retabulating the information thus obtained, it is possible to compute ratios of own children under 5 years to women or couples of all socioeconomic characteristics for which the census collects data. In collaboration with Dr. Lee Jay Cho, Grabill developed techniques for converting these ratios to unbiased calculations of ASR, GFR, and TFR.[11] Grabill, Cho, and Bogue jointly have sponsored a retabulation of the 1960 census data on own children. These

[11] Wilson H. Grabill and Lee Jay Cho, "Methodology for the Measurement of Current Fertility from Population Data on Young Children," *Demography*, **2** (1) (1965), 49–73.

Table 18-28   Legitimate Live Births per 1000 Married Women, Husband Present, by Age and Years of School Completed—United States: 1963

| Age of woman | Total | Elementary: 8 years or less | High school | | College | | |
			1 - 3 years	4 years	Total	1 - 3 years	4 years or more
Total, 15-44 yrs.	153	150	167	140	171	179	
15-19 years.....	525	529	588	449	...	...	...
20-24 years.....	342	319	322	324	439	432	456
25-29 years.....	219	321	205	200	231	222	243
30-34 years.....	121	162	112	97	163	169	155
35-39 years.....	59	74	57	49	73	67	80
40-44 years.....	16	22	14	17	10	12	6

Source: Gordon F. Sutton and Gooloo S. Wunderlich, "Estimating Marital Fertility Rates by Educational Attainment Using a Survey of New Mothers", Demography, Vol. 4, (1967) p 141

tabulations provide a mass of detailed information about differential fertility in the United States that previously has not been available. Not only is a much wider range of characteristics reviewed for the differential fertility associated with them, but elaborate multiple-variable cross-tabulations permit the holding constant of one or more variables while studying the differential fertility associated with another variable. A monograph that digests this information, links it to information available in earlier censuses, and makes available in one convenient place all of the pertinent statistics on differential fertility in the United States is now in press.[12] Most of the materials in this section are drawn from the tabulations for this report. It is a brief and incomplete overview, intended only to demonstrate three points:

1. Current differentials are not necessarily identical with cumulative differentials. In fact, at some moments of drastic demographic change they can give contrary indications.

2. A wide variety of factors are apparently linked to differential fertility. Some of these are demographic, but many point directly to rather sophisticated sociological and psychological hypotheses.

3. In order to study the impact of secondary differentials, the very great impact of two powerful differentials—age and educational attainment of women—must be controlled. Many dif-

[12] Lee Jay Cho, Wilson Grabill, and Donald J. Bogue, *Differential Fertility in the United States* (Chicago: Community and Family Study Center, in press).

ferentials that superficially look very sharp disappear when this is done, because they are themselves highly correlated with age and/or education.

Educational Attainment and Current Fertility. Table 18-28, derived by the follow-up technique described above, presents data on the natality of various educational groups. According to this table, the lowest levels of fertility are found among the mass of middle-class women who graduate from high school and do not go on to college. Groups with more education and those with less education are both more fertile. Women with less than a high school education tend to be highly fertile during their teens (if they are married) and also during their twenties, but tend to curtail fertility in their thirties. College women, on the other hand, postpone childbearing until they have completed schooling. They make up for this by extraordinarily high rates of fertility at ages up to age 30. From the data of Table 18-28, one could conclude that after age 35 childbearing is done primarily by college women and girls who did not go to high school (mostly Negro). We learned in the preceding section that there is a strongly inverse correlation between fertility and educational attainment. This is an example of the contradictions that can exist between current fertility and cumulative fertility. Table 18-28 apparently represents a new pattern, which ultimately may be reflected in cumulative fertility a decade or two hence. Despite these higher rates, it may still develop that because of their later age at

Table 18-29 Own Children Under 5 Years Old per 1000 Total Women; Ratio to National Average for Selected Characteristics Standardized for Age and Education: 1960

Differential	United States Population									Rural Farm Population					
	Native white			Foreign born white			Negro			Native white			Negro		
	Unstandardized	Age standardized	Age education standardized	Unstandardized	Age standardized	Age education standardized	Unstandardized	Age standardized	Age education standardized	Unstandardized	Age standardized	Age education standardized	Unstandardized	Age standardized	Age education standardized
Total, all........	0.98	0.98	0.98	0.84	0.95	0.93	1.35	1.30	1.25	0.92	1.07	1.07	1.75	1.93	1.73
Metropolitan status															
Inside an SMSA.......	0.97	0.97	0.98	0.81	0.93	0.91	1.26	1.19	1.17	0.92	1.09	1.09	1.53	1.90	1.72
Outside an SMSA......	0.99	0.98	0.98	1.01	1.06	1.03	1.57	1.56	1.45	0.91	1.07	1.07	1.76	1.93	1.73
Nativity															
Native, of native parentage........	1.02	0.97	0.97	....	....	....	....	....	....	0.92	1.06	1.06	....	....	....
Country of origin															
United Kingdom.......	0.82	1.00	1.01	0.84	0.91	0.92	....	....	....	0.71	1.17	1.17	....	....	....
Ireland.............	1.02	1.28	1.30	1.04	1.32	1.32	....	....	....	0.89	1.26	1.31	....	....	....
Norway..............	0.72	1.02	1.04	0.75	0.95	0.95	....	....	....	0.67	1.23	1.25	....	....	....
Sweden..............	0.68	1.00	1.01	0.62	0.81	0.84	....	....	....	0.62	1.06	1.07	....	....	....
Germany.............	0.70	1.00	1.02	0.86	0.81	0.81	....	....	....	0.67	1.26	1.28	....	....	....
Austria.............	0.64	0.92	0.94	0.57	0.75	0.75	....	....	....	0.89	1.31	1.35	....	....	....
Czechoslovakia......	0.74	1.02	1.04	0.66	0.84	0.84	....	....	....	0.77	1.28	1.31	....	....	....
Poland..............	0.67	0.97	1.00	0.49	0.75	0.72	....	....	....	0.83	1.39	1.41	....	....	....
U.S.S.R.............	0.66	0.87	0.88	0.41	0.79	0.74	....	....	....	0.87	1.22	1.23	....	....	....
Italy...............	0.81	0.98	1.00	0.71	0.90	0.83	....	....	....	0.74	1.02	1.04	....	....	....
Canada..............	1.03	1.07	1.08	0.84	1.06	1.07	....	....	....	0.95	1.22	1.24	....	....	....
Mexico..............	1.69	1.40	1.31	1.47	1.47	1.29	....	....	....	1.90	1.68	1.44	....	....	....
Other Northern European	0.82	1.04	1.05	0.96	0.93	0.93	....	....	....	0.97	1.31	1.34	....	....	....
East, south-east Europe	0.74	0.95	0.96	0.71	0.83	0.80	....	....	....	0.70	1.05	1.08	....	....	....
Latin America.......	1.09	1.00	1.01	0.95	0.85	0.83	....	....	....	0.98	1.06	1.14	....	....	....
Other, including Asia.	1.07	1.06	1.08	0.93	0.93	0.93	....	....	....	1.03	1.21	1.20	....	....	....
Not reported........	0.96	1.08	1.08	0.93	0.99	0.96	....	....	....	0.70	1.03	1.03	....	....	....
Selected ethnic groups															
Spanish speaking....	1.58	1.35	1.26	1.45	1.47	1.29	....	....	....	1.70	1.56	1.37	....	....	....
Puerto Rican........	1.34	1.06	0.97	....	....	....	....	....	....	1.16	1.05	0.90	....	....	....
American Indian.....	1.66	1.49	1.40	....	....	....	....	....	....	1.62	1.64	1.45	....	....	....
Chinese.............	1.12	1.07	1.02	....	....	....	....	....	....	1.00	1.36	1.35	....	....	....
Japanese............	1.09	0.99	1.00	....	....	....	....	....	....	1.12	1.29	1.30	....	....	....
Region of birth															
Northeast...........	0.96	1.00	1.02	....	....	....	1.30	1.10	1.10	0.99	1.14	1.15	1.67	1.57	1.49
North Central.......	1.02	1.03	1.05	....	....	....	1.40	1.18	1.18	1.01	1.17	1.19	1.75	1.71	1.64
South...............	0.92	0.90	0.89	....	....	....	1.37	1.35	1.30	0.77	0.94	0.91	1.75	1.93	1.73
West................	1.08	1.01	1.02	....	....	....	1.39	1.14	1.14	1.01	1.10	1.10	1.88	1.71	1.66
Residence in 1955															
Same house..........	0.61	0.90	0.91	0.49	0.90	0.88	1.03	1.30	1.26	0.69	1.03	1.03	1.46	1.94	1.78
Different house same county......	1.19	1.01	1.01	0.95	1.04	1.01	1.58	1.34	1.29	1.26	1.11	1.10	2.10	1.95	1.74
Different county, same state........	1.27	1.01	1.02	1.07	1.11	1.10	1.68	1.30	1.25	1.36	1.13	1.13	1.90	1.68	1.51
Different state......	1.28	1.00	1.00	1.10	0.88	0.87	1.66	1.15	1.13	1.44	1.15	1.14	1.94	1.73	1.58
Residence not reported	0.99	0.89	0.89	1.14	1.03	0.99	1.24	1.04	1.02	1.30	1.23	1.18	0.52	0.60	0.54

Table 18-29 (Continued)

Differential	United States Population									Rural Farm Population					
	Native white			Foreign born white			Negro			Native white			Negro		
	Unstan-dardized	Age stan-dardized	Age edu-cation stan-dardized	Unstan-dardized	Age stan-dardized	Age edu-cation stan-dardized	Unstan-dardized	Age stan-dardized	Age edu-cation stan-dardized	Unstan-dardized	Age stan-dardized	Age edu-cation stan-dardized	Unstan-dardized	Age stan-dardized	Age edu-cation stan-dardized
Labor Force Status of Woman															
Employed, worked 35+wks	0.39	0.42	0.44	0.29	0.36	0.36	0.74	0.76	0.75	0.40	0.53	0.54	0.94	1.26	1.15
Employed, worked less than 35 weeks	0.62	0.70	0.71	0.48	0.63	0.62	0.97	1.03	0.98	0.61	0.79	0.79	1.34	1.55	1.39
Not in labor force	1.22	1.17	1.16	1.09	1.17	1.15	1.76	1.58	1.52	1.06	1.20	1.19	1.94	2.07	1.87
Occupation of employed Women															
Professional-technical	0.53	0.56	0.59	0.51	0.58	0.58	0.69	0.70	0.67	0.44	0.64	0.63	0.71	0.99	0.92
Managers, officials, proprietors	0.28	0.44	0.45	0.26	0.45	0.45	0.48	0.72	0.71	0.24	0.44	0.45	0.83	1.15	1.02
Clerical	0.42	0.41	0.43	0.28	0.32	0.33	0.74	0.64	0.65	0.44	0.47	0.48	0.16	0.22	0.22
Sales	0.36	0.50	0.52	0.30	0.45	0.46	0.65	0.71	0.72	0.34	0.53	0.54	....	....	....
Craftsmen, foremen, etc	0.30	0.41	0.42	0.29	0.39	0.39	0.65	0.72	0.72	0.30	0.44	0.46	....	....	....
Operatives	0.47	0.55	0.55	0.35	0.44	0.42	0.76	0.77	0.76	0.42	0.52	0.52	0.83	0.96	0.93
Service workers	0.51	0.63	0.64	0.39	0.53	0.52	0.81	0.86	0.86	0.38	0.60	0.61	0.72	0.96	0.94
Private household wks	0.55	0.67	0.66	0.47	0.60	0.58	0.77	0.93	0.88	0.38	0.59	0.58	0.88	1.14	1.04
Occupation not reported	0.59	0.65	0.66	0.42	0.53	0.51	0.95	0.94	0.92	0.69	0.92	0.92	1.30	1.48	1.36
Income of employed women															
Under $1000	0.73	0.79	0.80	0.61	0.72	0.71	1.04	1.09	1.04	0.66	0.86	0.86	1.25	1.52	1.37
$1000-1,999	0.49	0.55	0.57	0.38	0.48	0.48	0.69	0.75	0.74	0.38	0.51	0.52	0.50	0.70	0.67
$2000-2,999	0.36	0.40	0.41	0.25	0.33	0.32	0.56	0.59	0.59	0.29	0.37	0.38	0.74	0.95	0.88
$3000-3,999	0.29	0.31	0.32	0.21	0.26	0.26	0.55	0.58	0.58	0.26	0.35	0.35	0.75	0.98	0.92
$4000-4,999	0.23	0.27	0.28	0.18	0.23	0.24	0.49	0.54	0.53	0.20	0.32	0.31	0.68	0.98	0.92
$5000-6,999	0.20	0.28	0.28	0.16	0.26	0.26	0.45	0.58	0.53	0.19	0.33	0.33	0.33	0.41	0.39
$7000-9,999	0.22	0.37	0.36	0.24	0.48	0.45	0.37	0.55	0.50	0.23	0.39	0.38	....	....	....
$10,000 and over	0.32	0.55	0.53	0.19	0.36	0.34	0.70	0.80	0.76	0.14	0.36	0.35	....	....	....

Source: Lee Jay Cho, Wilson Grabill and Donald J. Bogue. Differential Fertility in the United States, Chicago: Community and Family Study Center, 1968

713

Table 18-30 Differential Current Fertility in the United States: Own Children Under 5 Years Old per 1000 Married Women with Husband Present; Standardized for Age and Education; Ratio to National Average for Selected Characteristics

| Differential | United States Population | | | | | | | | | Rural Farm Population | | | | | |
| | Native white | | | Foreign born white | | | Negro | | | Native white | | | Negro | | |
	Unstan-dardized	Age stan-dardized	Age edu-cation stan-dardized	Unstan-dardized	Age stan-dardized	Age edu-cation stan-dardized	Unstan-dardized	Age stan-dardized	Age edu-cation stan-dardized	Unstan-dardized	Age stan-dardized	Age edu-cation stan-dardized	Unstan-dardized	Age stan-dardized	Age edu-cation stan-dardized
Age at first Marriage															
Under 17 years	1.10	0.98	0.92	0.87	0.98	0.90	1.62	1.47	1.36	0.95	0.99	0.94	2.03	2.02	1.77
17 years	1.10	0.95	0.94	0.93	0.93	0.89	1.66	1.44	1.37	0.97	0.97	0.96	2.09	2.02	1.84
18 years	1.10	0.93	0.95	0.90	0.86	0.83	1.61	1.36	1.31	1.04	1.00	1.02	1.95	2.00	1.82
19 years	1.06	0.91	0.93	0.91	0.85	0.84	1.50	1.29	1.25	0.97	1.00	1.01	1.77	1.83	1.68
20 years	1.03	0.92	0.95	0.91	0.86	0.85	1.45	1.24	1.23	0.96	1.06	1.07	1.62	1.72	1.60
21 years	0.98	0.96	0.98	0.91	0.89	0.89	1.33	1.19	1.17	0.90	1.11	1.12	1.66	1.84	1.67
22 years	0.94	0.99	1.01	0.87	0.91	0.91	1.22	1.13	1.12	0.84	1.17	1.16	1.61	1.98	1.80
23-24 years	0.87	1.06	1.05	0.82	0.94	0.93	1.12	1.13	1.12	0.81	1.26	1.25	1.37	1.82	1.66
25-29 years	0.76	1.18	1.16	0.80	1.08	1.06	0.92	1.17	1.13	0.75	1.46	1.43	1.15	1.79	1.64
30 and over	0.55	1.45	1.42	0.61	1.48	1.40	0.54	1.26	1.19	0.58	1.87	1.81	0.66	1.68	1.35
Age of husband in relation to age of wife															
Husband younger than wife:															
5 years or more	0.79	1.38	1.36	0.82	1.31	1.28	0.94	1.40	1.36	0.67	1.53	1.48	1.04	1.35	1.25
3 or 4 years	0.88	1.23	1.22	1.04	1.32	1.30	1.07	1.22	1.20	0.82	1.45	1.42	1.30	1.57	1.45
1 or 2 years	1.00	1.09	1.10	0.97	1.10	1.08	1.35	1.30	1.29	0.88	1.22	1.22	1.73	1.95	1.79
Husband and wife same	1.08	1.03	1.04	0.94	1.03	1.02	1.41	1.30	1.26	1.01	1.17	1.17	1.84	1.99	1.82
Husband older than wife:															
1 or 2 years	1.10	1.00	1.01	0.90	0.96	0.94	1.60	1.36	1.33	1.02	1.11	1.11	1.90	1.96	1.80
3 or 4 years	1.05	0.97	0.98	0.95	0.97	0.96	1.60	1.36	1.30	0.96	1.05	1.05	1.96	1.95	1.76
5 to 9 years	0.96	0.94	0.94	0.82	0.89	0.87	1.48	1.34	1.29	0.90	1.04	1.03	1.84	1.96	1.77
10 years or more	0.75	0.84	0.83	0.69	0.82	0.78	1.20	1.19	1.12	0.74	0.92	0.90	1.63	1.79	1.58
Migration status of husband and wife															
Husband a migrant:															
Wife a migrant	1.34	1.04	1.05	1.14	0.95	0.93	1.58	1.01	0.98	1.43	1.21	1.19	2.17	1.94	1.76
Wife not a migrant	1.40	0.86	0.88	1.11	0.76	0.75	1.40	1.36	1.30	1.63	1.01	1.02	1.77	1.30	1.17
Husband not a migrant:															
Wife a migrant	1.32	0.82	0.85	1.15	0.78	0.75	2.02	1.14	1.15	1.53	0.96	0.99	1.44	0.97	0.87
Wife not a migrant	0.90	0.98	0.98	0.71	1.00	0.98	1.57	1.10	1.06	0.84	1.06	1.06	1.78	1.95	1.77
Employment status of husband															
Employed	1.01	0.99	0.99	0.85	0.96	0.94	1.46	1.31	1.28	0.94	1.08	1.08	1.84	1.94	1.75
Unemployed	1.06	1.00	0.99	0.91	1.02	0.96	1.53	1.35	1.30	0.98	1.09	1.07	1.96	1.88	1.71
Armed forces	1.34	0.96	0.99	1.46	1.01	1.00	1.87	1.18	1.19	1.30	0.92	0.94	0.58	0.38	0.38
Not in the labor force	0.69	0.80	0.83	0.58	0.76	0.73	1.17	1.33	1.26	0.63	0.96	0.93	1.26	1.66	1.49

Table 18-30 (Continued)

| | United States Population | | | | | | | | | Rural Farm Population | | | | | |
| | Native white | | | Foreign born white | | | Negro | | | Native white | | | Negro | | |
Differential	Unstandardized	Age standardized	Age education standardized	Unstandardized	Age standardized	Age education standardized	Unstandardized	Age standardized	Age education standardized	Unstandardized	Age standardized	Age education standardized	Unstandardized	Age standardized	Age education standardized
Major occupation group of husband															
Professional & technical	1.17	1.05	1.06	1.01	0.98	0.98	1.14	1.01	0.99	0.93	1.05	1.04	1.33	1.33	1.28
Farmers & farm managers	0.91	1.08	1.08	0.91	1.26	1.23	1.66	2.04	1.84	0.91	1.10	1.11	1.69	2.11	1.90
Managers, officials, proprietors	0.83	0.97	0.97	0.69	0.94	0.94	0.98	1.08	1.06	0.69	0.96	0.96	0.72	1.03	1.04
Clerical	1.01	0.94	0.96	0.81	0.88	0.88	1.33	1.12	1.12	0.92	1.01	1.02	1.33	1.37	1.40
Sales	1.00	0.97	0.98	0.74	0.90	0.91	1.13	1.06	1.06	0.75	0.88	0.88	0.83	1.55	1.33
Craftsmen, foremen	0.97	0.99	0.98	0.81	0.92	0.91	1.34	1.25	1.23	0.86	1.02	1.02	1.25	1.47	1.40
Operatives	1.07	0.99	0.98	0.84	0.94	0.90	1.51	1.33	1.29	1.00	1.04	1.04	1.91	1.73	1.58
Service, private house.	0.93	0.96	0.97	0.75	0.91	0.88	1.29	1.20	1.17	0.72	0.96	0.97	1.40	1.37	1.33
Farm laborers	1.32	1.16	1.10	1.64	1.59	1.35	1.95	1.78	1.58	1.33	1.16	1.11	2.12	1.94	1.72
Laborers exc. farm	1.14	1.03	1.01	1.01	1.10	1.02	1.57	1.42	1.35	0.98	1.09	1.08	1.94	1.91	1.76
Occupation not reported	0.96	0.90	0.90	0.91	0.93	0.90	1.30	1.12	1.08	0.82	0.97	0.97	1.41	1.36	1.24
Selected Detailed Occupations of Husband															
Professional-Technical															
Accountants	1.07	1.01	1.02	0.92	0.96	0.97	1.06	1.06	1.04	1.01	1.00	1.00	.....	.....	.....
Clergymen	1.09	1.05	1.06	0.92	1.17	1.17	0.72	1.08	1.06	0.77	0.83	0.88	2.52	1.57	1.63
College Pres. prof'rs	1.12	1.07	1.06	1.09	1.05	1.04	1.10	1.07	1.02	1.35	1.57	1.50	3.34	1.74	1.69
Natural scientists	1.29	1.11	1.10	1.08	0.96	0.94	1.15	0.93	0.94	1.07	1.10	1.10	.....	.....	.....
Electrical engineers	1.33	1.13	1.14	1.08	0.97	0.97	1.51	1.17	1.14	1.29	1.27	1.26	.....	.....	.....
Mechanical engineers	1.18	1.09	1.10	0.97	0.93	0.94	1.09	0.92	0.93	1.38	1.70	1.63	.....	.....	.....
Technical engineers	1.16	1.04	1.05	1.06	1.06	1.06	1.30	1.06	1.04	0.55	0.66	0.68	2.56	1.94	1.68
Lawyers, judges	1.10	1.17	1.14	0.79	0.96	0.99	1.14	1.07	1.01	0.50	0.87	0.83	.....	.....	.....
Physicians	1.23	1.31	1.27	1.15	1.12	1.11	1.08	1.09	1.03	0.86	1.59	1.53	.....	.....	.....
Techers, Elementary & Secondary	1.20	1.00	1.03	1.15	1.10	1.08	1.09	0.94	0.93	0.96	1.10	1.08	1.40	1.48	1.44
Architects	1.29	0.99	1.02	0.99	0.92	0.93	1.22	0.92	0.95	1.06	1.03	1.05	.....	.....	.....
Artists, authors	1.12	1.00	1.01	0.76	0.78	0.79	0.96	0.88	0.87	0.40	0.54	0.52	.....	.....	.....
Managers, officials:															
Salaried--mafg. Indus.	0.85	1.03	1.02	0.70	0.94	0.95	1.30	1.21	1.19	0.75	1.03	1.02	.....	.....	.....
Self employed--mafg.	0.70	0.98	0.97	0.58	0.91	0.92	1.56	1.37	1.31	0.84	1.15	1.13	1.03	1.83	1.60
Salaried-wholesale & retail	0.95	0.96	0.96	0.73	0.85	0.85	1.04	0.95	0.94	0.74	0.86	0.86	0.86	0.55	0.54
Self employed wholesale & retail	0.67	0.91	0.91	0.53	0.88	0.86	0.75	0.98	0.95	0.63	0.93	0.93	0.65	1.01	1.04
Self employed-construction	0.85	1.01	1.02	0.95	1.25	1.25	0.95	1.17	1.15	0.60	0.98	1.00	1.75	2.26	1.89
Salaried-finance	0.99	0.97	0.98	0.69	0.80	0.81	1.24	1.22	1.14	0.96	1.09	1.06	.....	.....	.....
Self-employed finance	0.63	0.91	0.90	0.41	0.66	0.67	0.81	1.42	1.33	0.88	1.80	1.66	.....	.....	.....
Administration--State local.	0.73	0.98	0.98	0.84	0.94	0.95	1.04	0.99	0.96	0.52	0.81	0.80	.....	.....	.....
Salaried, other managers and officials	0.88	0.98	0.99	0.77	0.99	0.99	1.14	1.14	1.12	0.76	0.97	0.98	.....	.....	.....
Self-employed, other managers and officials	0.70	0.94	0.94	0.71	1.03	1.02	0.86	1.06	1.06	0.61	0.92	0.91	.....	.....	.....

Table 18-30 (Continued)

Differential	United States Population									Rural Farm Population					
	Native white			Foreign born white			Negro			Native white			Negro		
	Unstandardized	Age standardized	Age education standardized	Unstandardized	Age standardized	Age education standardized	Unstandardized	Age standardized	Age education standardized	Unstandardized	Age standardized	Age education standardized	Unstandardized	Age standardized	Age education standardized
Clerical															
Bookkeepers	1.03	0.91	0.94	0.73	0.81	0.81	1.49	1.28	1.23	0.88	0.98	0.98	1.66	1.06	0.96
Mail carriers	0.98	1.01	1.03	0.86	1.03	1.01	1.30	1.14	1.14	0.99	1.20	1.20	....	....	....
Sales															
Manufacturing industries	1.06	1.01	1.02	0.75	0.87	0.88	1.23	0.98	1.02	0.79	0.90	0.92	....	....	....
Wholesale trade	1.00	0.99	1.00	0.73	0.90	0.91	1.17	1.20	1.21	0.91	1.02	1.01	....	....	....
Retail trade	0.93	0.91	0.93	0.72	0.88	0.89	1.28	1.15	1.14	0.74	0.83	0.84	1.42	2.25	1.94
Insurance agents	1.13	1.04	1.05	0.85	0.99	0.96	1.10	1.01	1.03	0.71	0.86	0.86	....	....	....
Craftsmen															
Carpenters	0.97	0.99	1.00	0.83	0.93	0.90	1.42	1.49	1.42	0.76	1.01	1.00	1.30	1.88	1.69
Electricians	1.01	0.97	0.98	0.87	0.95	0.96	1.34	1.17	1.14	0.95	1.09	1.10	....	....	....
Foremen--Mafg. Indus.	0.75	0.93	0.95	0.66	0.93	0.95	0.94	0.98	0.98	0.76	1.01	1.03	....	....	....
Foremen--other indus.	0.77	0.93	0.94	0.59	0.85	0.84	1.12	1.15	1.17	0.72	1.03	1.06	....	....	....
Linemen, telephone & telegraph	1.34	1.00	1.02	1.19	0.98	0.97	1.53	1.28	1.24	1.09	0.92	0.92	2.48	1.33	1.22
Mechanists	0.91	0.95	0.96	0.70	0.81	0.80	1.21	1.07	1.08	0.93	1.12	1.14	....	....	....
Auto mechanics	1.04	0.95	0.95	0.96	0.94	0.93	1.44	1.29	1.25	1.01	1.00	1.00	1.14	1.03	1.04
Painters	0.98	1.01	1.00	0.79	0.95	0.92	1.33	1.30	1.28	0.84	0.98	0.98	0.32	0.61	0.59
Plumbers	0.96	0.98	0.99	0.79	0.96	0.96	1.35	130	1.26	0.82	0.94	0.94	3.25	2.03	2.09
Printers	1.06	0.99	1.00	0.94	0.97	0.97	1.69	1.30	1.30	0.94	0.85	0.85	....	....	....
Stationary engineers	0.91	0.98	0.99	0.88	0.99	0.99	1.26	1.21	1.19	0.71	0.91	0.92	2.49	3.12	3.13
Toolmakers	0.94	1.01	1.03	0.89	0.90	0.91	1.31	1.23	1.20	0.85	1.07	1.10	....	....	....
Masons, tile setters	1.24	1.05	1.05	0.99	1.02	0.97	1.51	1.29	1.26	1.07	1.06	1.06	1.44	1.48	1.48
Operatives															
Assemblers	1.08	0.95	0.96	0.84	0.85	0.81	1.35	1.17	1.15	1.00	0.98	0.99	2.00	2.50	2.23
Bus drivers	0.72	0.89	0.90	0.73	1.06	1.09	1.25	1.14	1.12	0.60	0.91	0.91	1.21	1.77	1.58
Checkers--Mafg.	0.96	0.93	0.94	0.81	0.96	0.96	1.30	1.13	1.13	0.84	0.90	0.91	....	....	....
Meat cutters	1.00	0.97	0.99	0.73	0.93	0.90	1.46	1.25	1.22	0.82	0.96	0.97	....	....	....
Mine laborers	1.09	1.03	1.01	0.70	0.89	0.84	1.49	1.58	1.55	1.01	1.18	1.17	1.91	1.80	1.84
Taxi drivers	0.87	0.98	0.99	0.80	1.11	1.08	1.08	1.06	1.06	1.14	1.36	1.33	1.21	1.79	1.62
Truck drivers	1.15	1.01	1.01	1.03	1.10	1.07	1.66	1.40	1.34	1.08	1.06	1.04	2.17	1.30	1.26
Welders	0.98	0.96	0.97	0.87	0.98	0.91	1.39	1.22	1.22	0.95	1.00	1.00	1.66	2.01	1.85
Mafg.--Stone	1.13	1.01	1.00	0.87	0.95	0.91	1.66	1.41	1.35	1.10	1.17	1.18	2.26	1.06	1.02
Mafg.--primary metals	1.03	1.00	0.99	0.86	1.02	0.96	1.37	1.25	1.23	0.95	1.21	1.18	0.99	1.30	1.33
Mafg.--fabricated metals	1.15	1.03	1.02	0.90	0.95	0.89	1.44	1.21	1.19	0.99	1.11	1.14	1.66	1.89	1.80
Mafg.--other durable	1.08	0.99	0.99	0.80	0.88	0.84	1.50	1.34	1.30	1.03	1.03	1.03	1.91	1.25	1.20
Mafg.--food	1.14	1.02	1.02	0.92	0.99	0.94	1.64	1.41	1.39	1.06	1.02	1.03	1.49	1.09	1.10
Mafg.--apparel	0.85	0.84	0.83	0.55	0.66	0.62	1.24	1.04	1.03	0.77	0.70	0.71	1.12	1.49	1.36
Mafg.--other nondurable	1.03	0.93	0.93	0.73	0.84	0.81	1.42	1.29	1.25	0.99	1.00	0.99	1.60	1.67	1.57
Nonmanufacturing	1.08	0.98	0.98	0.83	0.92	0.89	1.49	1.31	1.28	1.01	1.06	1.05	1.82		

Table 18-30 (Continued)

United States Population / Rural Farm Population

Differential	Native white (U.S.) Unstandardized	Age standardized	Age education standardized	Foreign born white Unstandardized	Age standardized	Age education standardized	Negro (U.S.) Unstandardized	Age standardized	Age education standardized	Native white (Rural) Unstandardized	Age standardized	Age education standardized	Negro (Rural) Unstandardized	Age standardized	Age education standardized
Service workers															
Barbers	0.88	0.93	0.94	0.68	0.94	0.90	0.95	0.96	0.95	0.66	1.02	1.04	2.77	1.84	1.82
Janitors	0.77	0.99	0.98	0.68	0.93	0.87	1.28	1.25	1.23	0.75	1.10	1.12	1.51	1.51	1.48
Cooks exc. private household	0.95	1.00	0.99	0.75	0.88	0.83	1.28	1.14	1.12	1.00	1.24	1.25	....	....	....
Waiters, bartenders	0.79	0.89	0.91	0.80	0.93	0.91	1.21	1.03	1.03	0.82	1.14	1.16	....	....	....
Policemen	1.12	0.99	1.01	0.96	1.02	1.03	1.29	1.06	1.07	0.68	0.79	0.78	....	....	....
Laborers															
Fishermen, lumbermen	1.24	1.12	1.08	0.94	1.12	1.09	1.98	1.71	1.55	1.14	1.18	1.13	2.14	1.99	1.84
Mafg.--durable goods	1.17	1.02	1.00	0.91	1.01	0.93	1.58	1.41	1.36	1.07	1.11	1.11	1.55	1.66	1.57
Mafg.--Nondurable goods	1.17	1.01	0.99	1.05	1.14	1.09	1.58	1.46	1.40	1.08	1.11	1.12	2.31	2.15	2.02
Construction	1.15	1.06	1.04	1.12	1.13	1.01	1.58	1.41	1.34	0.89	1.08	1.07	2.02	1.94	1.78
Income of husband															
Under $1,000	0.81	0.87	0.86	0.79	0.86	0.81	1.49	1.48	1.36	0.83	1.03	1.00	1.79	1.95	1.74
$1,000	0.93	0.86	0.86	0.96	0.96	0.89	1.63	1.46	1.37	0.89	1.04	1.02	1.96	1.98	1.80
$2,000	1.05	0.92	0.92	1.01	0.94	0.90	1.57	1.35	1.30	0.97	1.07	1.06	1.71	1.76	1.64
$3,000	1.07	0.94	0.94	0.93	0.93	0.89	1.44	1.25	1.23	0.99	1.09	1.09	1.45	1.63	1.57
$4,000	1.07	0.96	0.97	0.87	0.96	0.90	1.30	1.20	1.19	0.98	1.10	1.11	1.50	1.66	1.61
$5,000	1.06	1.01	1.02	0.85	1.02	0.96	1.24	1.18	1.18	0.96	1.11	1.12	1.07	1.47	1.40
$7,000	0.99	1.06	1.06	0.76	1.03	1.02	1.15	1.20	1.18	0.90	1.09	1.10	1.78	2.48	2.37
$10,000	0.87	1.09	1.07	0.66	1.07	1.01	1.10	1.19	1.15	0.89	1.11	1.11	1.67	1.73	1.82
$15,000 and over	0.75	1.10	1.05			1.04	1.01	1.20	1.13	0.83	1.11	1.11	2.49	4.03	3.60
Family income, wife in labor force															
Under $1,000	0.61	0.71	0.71	0.46	0.56	0.53	1.09	1.23	1.12	0.72	0.93	0.92	1.40	1.74	1.52
$1,000	0.62	0.66	0.67	0.72	0.73	0.70	1.04	1.13	1.06	0.60	0.80	0.79	1.30	1.50	1.35
$2,000	0.65	0.65	0.67	0.62	0.61	0.60	1.06	1.07	1.02	0.54	0.70	0.70	1.12	1.52	1.39
$3,000	0.69	0.66	0.68	0.54	0.60	0.55	0.90	0.92	0.90	0.55	0.69	0.70	0.74	1.04	1.02
$4,000	0.68	0.64	0.66	0.55		0.58	0.86	0.87	0.86	0.48	0.62	0.63	0.88	1.36	1.28
$5,000	0.59	0.59	0.61	0.45	0.53	0.52	0.74	0.76	0.76	0.45	0.59	0.60	0.68	1.13	1.08
$7,000	0.38	0.43	0.44	0.28	0.37	0.37	0.59	0.65	0.64	0.35	0.51	0.52	0.74	1.12	1.02
$10,000	0.24	0.35	0.35	0.19	0.30	0.30	0.48	0.60	0.58	0.30	0.52	0.52	0.37	0.75	0.63
$15,000 and over	0.26	0.47	0.46	0.24	0.46	0.45	0.49	0.69	0.66	0.34	0.58	0.59	....	....	....
Family income, wife not in labor force															
Under $1,000	1.12	1.17	1.11	1.15	1.17	1.09	1.84	1.83	1.66	1.04	1.23	1.19	2.02	2.17	1.94
$1,000	1.22	1.18	1.13	1.32	1.28	1.16	1.96	1.78	1.66	1.06	1.22	1.18	2.11	2.25	2.02
$2,000	1.35	1.18	1.15	1.41	1.23	1.15	1.96	1.67	1.60	1.14	1.23	1.22	1.84	2.06	1.90
$3,000	1.40	1.19	1.17	1.32	1.21	1.16	1.85	1.60	1.56	1.14	1.23	1.23	1.66	2.05	1.90
$4,000	1.33	1.19	1.19	1.25	1.22	1.19	1.66	1.53	1.51	1.11	1.24	1.25	1.49	2.30	2.14
$5,000	1.12	1.19	1.20	1.13	1.18	1.17	1.53	1.47	1.46	1.04	1.21	1.22	1.51	2.44	2.23
$7,000		1.14	1.15	0.98	1.15	1.15	1.28	1.39	1.37	0.91	1.18	1.19	1.24	2.18	2.01
$10,000	0.89	1.12	1.11	0.80	1.13	1.11	1.12	1.29	1.26	0.84	1.15	1.16	1.58	1.84	1.77
$15,000 and over	0.77	1.14	1.10	0.66	1.10	1.07	1.09	1.39	1.34	0.85	1.17	1.17	3.31	4.58	4.12

marriage (hence shorter exposure to childbearing) college-educated women will bear no more children than women with less education.

Tables 18-29 and 18-30 summarize data from the Cho-Grabill-Bogue report cited above. In the stubs of these tables are the categories that represent differentials to be measured. The columns list data on these differentials for five groups of population:

native white
foreign-born white
Negro
rural-farm native white
rural-farm Negro

For each of these groups three measures of current differential fertility are provided:

1. An *unstandardized* measure, with no intervening variables controlled.

2. An *age-standardized* measure, which holds constant the differences in age composition among the groups being compared.

3. An *age-education-standardized* measure, which holds constant differences in both age composition and educational attainment among the groups being compared.

To facilitate comparison, all data are expressed simply as ratios to the national average. In other words, the average fertility of the total United States population, 1955-1960, has an index value of 1. A value below this represents below-average fertility, and a value above it represents above-average fertility. By multiplying the deviation form 1 by 100 and then subtracting 100 from the result, it is possible to state directly the percentage by which the fertility of a particular group exceeds or falls short of the national average.

In reviewing these differentials, please keep in mind that they refer to the years 1955-1960, the time of peak fertility rates. It is to be hoped that a matching analysis will be made as a part of the 1970 Census in order that the recent dramatic drop in fertility may be traced to the particular subgroups of the population that were most responsible for it.

Race. A part of the higher fertility level of Negroes in comparison with whites is attributable to differences in age and education. However, when both of these factors are controlled,

Negroes still have a level of natality that is 25 percent above the national average.

Urban-Rural Residence. Rural-farm population tends to be more fertile than urban. For the white population, the difference is now quite small, but among the Negro the rural-farm group is 38 percent more fertile than the general Negro population, even after both age and educational attainment are controlled.

Nativity. Foreign-born white population tends to be slightly less fertile than the total population. (On a crude unstandardized basis it appears to be very infertile, but this is because of its older age composition.) This is a reversal of one of the nation's strongest differentials; only three decades ago the foreign-born white population was substantially more fertile than the native-born.

Country of Origin. When controls for age and education are applied, women with ethnic origin in one of the following nations emerge as having above-average fertility:

Mexico
Ireland
Canada
Czechoslovakia
Norway
Germany

Surprisingly, this list does not contain nationality groups that previously had high fertility rates—Italy and the other countries of Southern and Eastern Europe. Of equal interest is the discovery that native-born women with foreign-born parents often are more fertile than the foreign-born population of the same nationality. Clearly, recent immigrants to the United States tend to be no more fertile, if not less fertile, than the natives. This is consistent with our previous findings for the nations of Europe in Table 18-4, and the data on cumulative fertility presented in Tables 18-20 and 18-21.

American Indians, Spanish-Speaking Persons and Puerto Ricans. Three ethnic groups, all "native" to the United States, have been reputed to have high fertility, but data with which to measure this fertility have been lacking. Aside from Negroes, American Indians appear to be the most fertile ethnic group in the population today, with a birthrate more than 40 percent above the national average. Persons of Spanish ancestry in the Southwest are also highly fertile. It has been thought that Puerto Ricans are also very fertile, but the data fail to show this. When the facts of the young age composition and the low educational attainment of this group are controlled, Puerto Ricans show a birthrate slightly below average.

Region of Birth. Whites born in the North Central and the West regions tend to be somewhat more fertile than average, while those born in the South appear to have extraordinarily low fertility. This apparent low fertility of Southern whites is surprising, for it is found in the rural-farm as well as the total population.

Labor Force Status of Women. Whether as cause or effect, women who are employed full-time have very low fertility rates, while those who are not in the labor force have above-average rates. Women who work part-time (less than 35 hours a week per year) have an intermediate fertility level. Employment appears to be less of an obstacle to the fertility of Negro women than for white women.

Occupation of Employed Women. Although all employed white women tend to have low fertility, those who hold extremely high-status and extremely low-status jobs tend to be the most fertile. It is the great mass of clerical and the fewer skilled workers who have the lowest fertility. Among Negroes, the pattern is quite different: the higher the occupational level of the woman, the lower her fertility tends to be.

Income. As suggested by the occupational data, the most highly paid and the most poorly paid white women tend to be the most fertile, while those with intermediate incomes tend to have the lowest fertility. Among Negroes the relationship between income and fertility tends to be a simple inverse one.

Table 18-30 refers only to married women with husband present. It excludes broken marriages, but permits a study of fertility according to characteristics of the husband, as well as of the wife.

Age at First Marriage. On a crude basis, persons who are married at an unusually young age tend to have above-average fertility. When standardized for age, white women in this category have unusually low fertility and those married at later ages have high current fertility. Undoubtedly, at least two factors are operating here. Couples who have been married a long time have already had the number of children they desire and are practicing contraception. Couples who have married late are trying to take advantage of the years of fertility that remain to have the families they desire. There appears to be no comparable effect among Negroes, where early marriage is correlated with high current fertility.

Age of Husband. Among white couples, where the husband is older than the wife by five years or more, fertility tends to be below average, but where the husband is younger than the wife, fertility is above average. A similar effect is discernible among Negroes, but only when the disparity between the ages of husband and wife is more extreme.

Migration Status of Husband and Wife. Migrants *appear* to be extraordinarily fertile on a crude basis. For example, in Table 18-29 migrant women had a fertility measure as high as 28 percent above the average. Similar ratios are reported in Table 18-30 for the migration status of the couple. However, this is an illusion resulting primarily from the fact that migrants tend to be young and of prime childbearing age. When standardized for age, the fertility indexes for migrant white women sink to 1 or only very slightly above. When both husband and wife are migrant, the age-education-standardize index is only 1.05. Thus white migrants appear at most to be only 5 percent more fertile than nonmigrants when age is controlled. Among Negroes, there is no systematic pattern. Nonmigrant Negroes tend to be just as fertile, if not more so, than migrant Negroes. Several factors may help to account for this. Nonmigrant Negroes are concentrated in the rural South, where birthrates are high. Moreover, Negroes migrate at a wider range of ages. An odd differential does emerge, however: "mixed" Negro marriages, where one partner is a migrant and the other is not a migrant, tend to have low fertility levels. Since fertility and migration status both refer to the five years preceding the census, many of the "mixed" marriages have been

very recent, and the couple has not been exposed to childbearing for a full five years.

Employment Status of Husband. White families where the husband is not in the labor force
tend to be below-average in fertility. This
probably is an indication of disability or poor
health, or some other contraindication for fertility. Negro males, for whom the status of being unemployed unfortunately is more of a
"normal" state of affairs, show no similar differential.

Occupation of Husband. White husbands
who hold unusually high status positions tend
to have above-average fertility. White husbands who hold unusually low status positions
tend also to have above-average fertility. Lowest fertility is exhibited among those who do
clerical work. Among Negroes, there is a rather
consistent inverse relationship between occupational status and fertility.

**Detailed Occupational Classification of Hus-
band.** Table 18-30 presents fertility measures
for a selected list of detailed occupations. It is
readily apparent that there is a substantial
amount of variation among detailed occupations. The following are occupations with
above-average current fertility:

	Ratio
Physicians	1.27
Lawyers, judges	1.14
Electrical engineers	1.14
Mechanical engineers	1.10
Natural scientists	1.10
College professors, presidents	1.06
Fishermen, oystermen	1.08
Clergymen	1.06
Insurance agents	1.05

Occupations associated with unusually low fertility are:

	Ratio
Operatives—apparel industries	.83
Bus drivers	.90
Managers—self-employed, finance	.90
Managers—self-employed, retail, and wholesale	.90
Sales—retail trade	.93
Foremen, nonmanufacturing industries	.94
Checkers, manufacturing industries	.94
Operatives, nondurable manufacturing	.93

Income of Husband. The income of the husband represents the capacity of the family to
support the bearing of children without having
the wife work. The data of Table 18-30 demonstrate rather conclusively that the lower the
husband's income, the lower the fertility tends
to be, when age and education are controlled.
Thus there is some evidence here for the "economic interpretation of fertility," which regards
children as economic goods that are "purchased" when the family can afford them.
Clearly, the white population that finds itself
in the poverty range was constricting its fertility between 1955-1960.

A similar result is not found among Negroes.
Because the great mass of Negroes are in the
poverty range, the typical higher Negro birthrate is concentrated toward the lower end of
the income scale. Negroes with higher incomes
definitely have lower fertility.

Summary. This rapid review of current fertility differentials reveals that race and socioeconomic status are two of the most powerful
factors affecting fertility levels and that the
patterns of differentials are often dissimilar in
the racial groups. Among the white population,
fertility differentials appear to be rapidly working toward a *direct* association between fertility and socioeconomic status. If this is true, the
dream of the eugenicists—that the most successful and the best educated will bear the most
children while the least successful and those
least able to support children will bear the fewest—will have been realized. This situation is
not yet adumbrated among the Negro population. For Negroes the older "social mobility"
hypothesis seems more applicable, for there
seems to be a simple inverse relationship between fertility and status: the poorest and least
educated are bearing the fewest. At least this
was the situation in the 1955-1960 period.

As has already been demonstrated, the birthrates of Negroes and whites alike have plummeted since the dates to which these data refer.
It may safely be presumed that the declines
have been across the board, but it may nevertheless be true that some groups have reduced
their fertility more rapidly than others. It is
quite possible that as contraceptive service and
information become more widely and more eas-

ily available to lower-status Negroes, the differentials observed here will gradually reverse themselves and parallel those of the white population.

18.9. Contraception: The Explanation for Fertility Differentials

In the two preceding sections it has been clearly demonstrated that some subgroups of a population may be much more fertile than others. This calls for an explanation. At least four possible sets of factors may account for such differentials:

1. *Differential fecundity.* Some subgroups of the population may have greater difficulty in conceiving, or the prevalance of sterility may be higher.

2. *Differential nuptiality.* Some subgroups may delay marriage to a much later age and thereby have a much shorter duration of exposure to childbearing.

3. *Differential sexual activity.* Some subgroups may have sex relations less frequently, and some may abstain for long periods of time for religious, cultural, or personal reasons.

4. *Differential practice of contraception.* Some subgroups may have a much better knowledge of contraception, may have more ready access to medical or other services needed to practice contraception, and may have the income with which to purchase the necessary drugs or appliances.

All four of these hypotheses are valid; each has the capacity to influence the level of natality. For example, after childbirth ovulation does not begin for a few weeks; this is known as post-partum amenorrhea. This period of sterility tends to be lengthened by breast-feeding the infant. In cultures where children are not weaned until they are 1 year or even older, the average fecundity of the population may be substantially lower than in a population where children are weaned at six months or even bottle fed immediately.[13] The postponement of marriage may have a very strong influence on birthrates, because complete abstinence is the safest and most certain form of birth control. Although couples who delay marriage may try to "make up for lost time" in childbearing, certainly they cannot possibly bear as many children as they otherwise would have been able.[14] Research on the relationship between sexual activity and the ease of conception is incomplete, but it is fairly well established that most human groups engage in sexual intercourse with sufficient frequency to maintain a very high birthrate unless some form of contraception is practiced.[15] The male sperm are able to survive for many hours in the female, so that intercourse need not take place exactly at the moment of ovulation. It has been calculated that a single act of uncontracepted coitus, occurring randomly during the menstrual cycle, has about a one-in-five chance of producing a pregnancy. Westoff and his associates found that couples who deliberately increased the frequency of coitus at the estimated time of ovulation in order to hasten conception typically met with only modest success because the correlation between coital frequency and the length of time required to conceive is only moderately inversely correlated.[16] Despite the fact that differential fecundity, differential nuptiality, and differential sexual activity may influence and help to create differentials in natality, *by far the greatest factor is differential use of contraception.*

This principle has been firmly established by careful research. One of the most comprehensive of these studies states its finding simply:

[13] Robert G. Potter, Mary L. New, John B. Wyon, and John E. Gordon, "Lactation and its Effects Upon Birth Intervals in Eleven Punjab Villages, India," in Mindel C. Sheps and Jeanne Clare Ridley (eds.), *Public Health and Population Change* (Pittsburgh, Pa.: University of Pittsburgh, 1965).

[14] Christopher Tietze, "Impact of Age at Marriage on Various Measures of Fertility," *Proceedings of the World Population Conference*, 1954.

[15] Robert G. Potter, Jr., P. Sagi, and Charles Westoff, "Knowledge of the Ovulatory Cycle and Coital Frequency as Factors Affecting Conception and Contraception," *Milbank Memorial Fund Quarterly*, 40 (January 1962), 46–58.

[16] Charles F. Westoff, Robert G. Potter, and Philip C. Sagi, "Voluntary Factors in the Speed of Conception," Chapter 3 in *The Third Child* (Princeton, N.J.: Princeton University Press, 1963); Christopher Tietze, "Probability of Pregnancy Resulting from a Single Unprotected Coitus," *Fertility and Sterility*, 11 (September-October 1960), 485–488.

"The major force keeping American families relatively small is contraception. . . ." [17]

Thanks to a series of fertility studies of representative samples of the United States population, a great deal is known of the attitude of the American public toward contraception and its comparative willingness to use it.

Attitude toward Fertility Control. In a 1960 survey of a representative cross section of American couples of childbearing age, Whelpton and associates found an overwhelmingly favorable attitude toward the practice of family planning, both among Catholic and Protestant couples. Following is a summary of their results.[18]

	Percent favoring fertility control		
Education	*Total*	*Catholic*	*Protestant*
Total	80	52	91
College	86	39	96
High school	82	55	93
High school 1-3	80	58	88
Grade school	68	46	79

This summary excludes 13 percent of the population (5 percent of Protestants and 33 percent of Catholics) who approved of the use of the rhythm method though not of other methods. If we include rhythm as a method of fertility control, 96 percent of Protestants and 85 percent of Catholics approve of some kind of fertility control. And even among the tiny minority that would not approve of contraception for themselves, all but a small fraction (1 percent of Protestants and 5 percent of Catholics) would permit its use by others for social or economic reasons. Although the less well-educated segments of the population were less favorable, in all cases the dissenting group was only a minor fraction of the total. It can correctly be said, therefore, that control of fertility for social and economic reasons is an integral part of the American culture and embraces all socioeconomic and religious groups

[17] Ronald Freedman, Pascal K. Whelpton, and Arthur A. Campbell, "Sterility and Fecundity of American Families," Chapter 2 in *Family Planning Sterility and Population Growth* (New York: McGraw-Hill, 1959), p. 55.

[18] Whelpton, Freedman, and Campbell, *op. cit.*, p. 177.

with a far greater unanimity than do many other social issues.

The Use of Contraceptives. The same survey also asked the couple whether they had ever practiced contraception. Because many of the couples had not yet borne a child or had fewer children than they hoped to have, they were asked if they expected to use contraceptives at a later date. The percentage of persons who said they had already used contraceptives was 81, and an additional 7 percent said they expected to do so later. Among couples who had already borne two or more children the percentage of users was 89, with 3 percent expecting to do so later. The practice of contraception is very widespread among all socioeconomic groups, as the table illustrates:[19]

Characteristic	*Percent have used*	*Percent have used or will use*
Total	81	87
Wife's religion		
Protestant	84	98
Catholic	70	80
Jewish	95	95
Wife's education		
College	88	93
High school 4	83	90
High school 1-3	78	85
Grade school	66	72
Husband's income		
$10,000 or more	89	91
$5,000 to $5,999	80	88
$3,000 to $3,999	77	85
Under $3,000	70	82
Wife's age		
Under 14 years	78	92
25-29	84	91
30-34	83	88
35-39	77	80
Race		
White	81	87
Nonwhite	59	76
Number of births		
0	55	72
1	89	93
3	89	92
4	87	90
5	80	84
6 or more	76	78

[19] *Ibid.*, pp. 184–185.

Not only is the practice of contraception considered to be a positive value by the population, but it is also an established custom and an integral part of conjugal life. Those who have not used contraceptives are primarily couples with fewer than two children or older couples who are passing out of the childbearing years. Even among those couples who are least educated or most poverty-stricken, two thirds or more have used contraceptives.

Methods of Contraception. Contrary to what may be popular opinion, the majority of contraception in the American population is accomplished by use of methods that require no medical prescription but only materials that can be purchased at the corner drugstore. The percentage of white users of contraception, classified by the methods they have most recently used, is as follows:[20]

	1965	1955
Oral pills	27	0
Condom	21	28
Rhythm	13	22
Diaphragm	10	25
Douche	8	10
Withdrawal	5	7
Jelly alone	2	4
Combinations of methods	8	2

Oral contraceptives became available between 1955 and 1965, and enjoyed a phenomenally rapid acceptance. Westoff and Ryder estimate that by October 1964, 18 percent of all married women (husband present) were using the pill.

Contraception among the Nonwhite Population. The nonwhite population approves of contraception just as strongly as the white population, although it apparently has until recently lagged behind the white population in active use of birth control methods. In a survey of Negroes in Chicago, Annie O. Blair[21] found that the attitudes of the white and nonwhite populations toward family planing were as follows:

Attitude	White	Nonwhite
Approves strongly	32	48
Approves moderately	47	39
Neutral	4	2
Disapproves moderately	12	9
Disapproves strongly	5	2

Whelpton and associates found that only 59 percent of nonwhite couples had ever used contraceptives, although 76 percent said they now used or intended to use them at a later date. Thus the very large differential in natality between the races appears to result from differential use; not only is the prevalance of use lower among the nonwhite population, but apparently they wait until a larger number of children have been born before starting to use contraceptives. The studies of Negro family planning attitudes and behavior conducted in Chicago suggest that this situation is changing swiftly with the result that the differential will decline in future years.[22]

Attitudes toward Family Size. The United States population approves of fertility control; it knows how to practice fertility control; the majority of couples now practice fertility control when they have reached the size of family they desire. Under such conditions, it clearly is evident that a major factor determining the level of natality is the number of children that couples wish to have. They may be expected to practice fertility control primarily for spacing births until they have reached the desired family size and then to practice fertility control for family limitation beyond this point. Numerous studies have been undertaken to measure "ideal" family size. For example, Whelpton and associates asked their sample of respondents in 1960 what they considered to be the ideal number of children for the average American family. The results obtained were as follows:[23]

[20] Charles F. Westoff and Norman B. Ryder, "United States: Methods of Fertility Control, 1955, 1960 and 1965," *Studies in Family Planning,* **17** (February 1967), 1–5.

[21] Annie O. Blair, "A Comparison of Negro and White Fertility Attitudes," Chapter 1 in Donald J. Bogue (ed.), *Sociological Contributions to Family Planning Research* (Chicago: Community and Family Study Center, 1967), p. 21.

[22] Donald J. Bogue, *op. cit.* See also Donald J. Bogue, *The Rural South Fertility Experiments* (Chicago: Community and Family Study Center, 1966), for reports of similar results in rural poverty-stricken counties of Central Alabama.

[23] Ronald Freedman, Pascal K. Whelpton, and Arthur A. Campbell. *Family Planning, Sterility and Population Growth* (New York: McGraw-Hill Book Company, 1959).

Number of children	White	Nonwhite
0	0	0
1	0	1
2	18	22
3	28	19
4	43	39
5	5	7
6 or more	6	13
Average	3.5	3.8

These data make it clear that almost no couples wish to be childless or to have only one child, but only a small fraction of couples wish to have more than four children. Thus the current level of fertility in the United States—the average size of completed family (TFR) in 1960 was 3.5 for whites and 4.5 for nonwhites—suggests that the fertility expectations of the white population were being approximately realized, while the nonwhite appeared to be bearing a substantially larger number of children than they desired. Differential access to family planning, rather than lack of desire to control fertility, may underly the very large fertility differentials between the races noted in preceding sections.

Too great a reliance should not be placed on ideal family size data, however, as predictors of the future. (a) These attitudes are subject to change on rather short notice. (b) There is no assurance that oncoming generations will share the attitudes of their parents toward childbearing. (c) Finally, because of the intervention of circumstances, in a well-contracepted society many couples will not achieve their ideal, while fewer will exceed it.

18.10. Childlessness

A surprisingly large proportion of the female adult population is childless, even at the end of the childbearing period. Part of it is due to spinsterhood, but much of it is due to involuntary or voluntary sterility. Table 18-31 reports data, tabulated by age, for a few nations of the world for which recent valid statistics are available. The highest degree of childlessness reliably reported for women of completed fertility is in the United States and Hungary—18 percent, for ages 45 to 49 years. Even in nations where almost 100 percent of the popula-

tion marries and where fertility rates are high and fertility control is very weak, about one woman in fifteen (6 to 8 percent) reaches menopause without bearing a child. Examples are Fiji, Samoa, Puerto Rico, Malaya, and Guinea. Childlessness is very high, of course, before age 20, but there are very great variations among the populations in childlessness at these earlier ages—due to differences in age at marriage. Despite its very high fertility, more than 90 percent of the women 15 to 19 years of age in Western Samoa are childless, whereas only 44 percent of United States ever-married girls in their late teens are childless. There is a marked tendency for nations with lower fertility rates to have a high percentage of childlessness at ages 35 and above and for nations with high fertility to have low proportions of childlessness. However, this relationship is only very approximate and needs to be interpreted. The low level of living that prevails in many nations does not appear to affect the fecundity of couples. It might have been supposed that inadequate diet, frequent illness, and poor general health may predispose couples toward involuntary sterility. Where health conditions are poor and the bearing of children is itself a risk to the mother's life, it might easily have been expected that a disproportionately large percentage of sterile women would survive to reach age 40 and would therefore comprise a larger proportion of all women aged 40. If this were ever true, it appears to be true no longer, because, as has already been observed, the proportion of childlessness among most high-fertility populations is quite low. Voluntary lifelong sterility is not a necessary ingredient in obtaining a state of demographic equilibrium.

If we study the adjustment of Japan, which has one of the world's lowest fertility rates, we find a low rate of childlessness in comparison with most nations of the world. In other words, Japan has managed to complete its demographic transition while maintaining a level of childlessness that is very nearly the same as that of the high-fertility nations. Where it exists, childlessness obviously helps to keep birthrates lower, but it is clearly not a necessary or important consideration among most populations

Table 18-31 Proportion of Women Aged 40 or Over Who Have Borne No Children, Selected Nations of the World

Nation	Age group	Percent childless	Nation	Age group	Percent childless
AFRICA			ASIA (continued)		
Central African Republic....	45–49	18.7	Malaya.....................	45–49	8.2
Congo (Brazzaville).........	45–49	15.5	Sabah......................	45–49	9.0
Gabon......................	45–49	32.1	Sarawak....................	45–49	9.7
Guinea.....................	45–49	5.7	Ryukyu Islands.............	45–49	5.9
Kenya......................	45–49	5.4	Thailand...................	45–49	6.5
Niger......................	45–49	7.2			
Senegal....................	45–49	5.6	EUROPE		
South Africa...............	45–49	6.0	Czechoslovakia.............	45–49	15.4
Sudan......................	50 & over	9.6	Hungary....................	45–49	18.7
Togo.......................	45–49	....	Ireland...................	45–49	12.5
Zanzibar...................	46 & over	23.7	Monaco.....................	45–49	36.2
			Netherlands................	45–49	14.2
NORTH AMERICA			Norway.....................	45–49	12.0
Baham	45–54	20.8	Portugal...................	45–49	12.0
Barbados...................	45–64	24.6	Switzerland................	45–49	19.7
Bermuda....................	45–49	26.8	United Kingdom.............	45–49	12.6
British Honduras...........	45–49	19.7	OCEANIA		
Canada.....................	45–49	13.1	American Samoa.............	45–49	12.6
Jamaica....................	45–54	19.8	British Solomons...........	45–49	11.3
Mexico.....................	40–49	21.8	Fiji Islands..............	45–49	8.8
Nicaragua..................	45–54	12.7			
Panama.....................	50 & over	11.7			
Puerto Rico................	45–49	11.5			
Trinidad and Tabogo........	45–64	22.0			
United States.............	45–49	18.1			
Virgin Islands.............	45–54	2.1			
SOUTH AMERICA					
British Guinea.............	45–64	16.8			
Chile......................	45–49	24.7			
Peru.......................	45–49	11.8			
ASIA					
Brunei.....................	45–49	6.8			
Cyprus.....................	45–49	10.2			
Israel.....................	45–49	9.2			
Japan......................	45–49	8.1			
Jordan.....................	45–49	5.3			
Korea......................	45–49	3.7			
Kuwait.....................	50 & over	16.0			
Macau......................	45–49	11.6			

Source: United Nations Demographic Yearbook, 1965, Table 9.

in the modern world. Far more important is the ability of the population to avoid bearing more than 2 or 3 children per couple.

From the data in Table 18-31, together with the evidence of medical and biological research, we may conclude tentatively that not less than 5 percent of all couples around the world are physiologically unable to bear children and will remain sterile throughout their lives as a result. Unless hitherto undiscovered methods of promoting fertility are developed, it is valid to presume that one couple in 20 is sterile at the time of marriage or else will go throughout its marriage childless for physiological reasons. In addition, childlessness may be an incidental by-product of disruption of marriage by separation and divorce, late marriage, surgery, and psychological factors that make it impossible for a couple to have a child. Together these factors appear to be able to raise the proportion of childlessness among couples in particular populations by an additional 5 percent to a total of 10 percent. Sterility increases steadily with age and often occurs well before the normal time of menopause. It may be surprising to learn that Whelpton, Freedman, and Campbell[24] found that in the United States 10 percent of all white couples with wife aged 18 to 39 years had been rendered surgically sterile. Of this, 4 percent had had "remedial" surgery performed to remove a threat to life: removal of a cancerous growth or correction of a disorder of the reproductive system. Surgery in the remaining 6 percent had been performed for contraceptive reasons.

[24] *Ibid.*, p. 134–138.

Table 18-32 Percent Childless among Ever-Married Women, by Color, Age, and Educational Attainment, for the United States: 1960

Educational attainment and color	Age							
	15 to 19 years	20 to 24 years	25 to 29 years	30 to 34 years	35 to 39 years	40 to 44 years	45 to 49 years	50 years and over
WHITE WOMEN, Total..........	46.4	25.0	12.3	9.6	10.2	13.0	17.1	18.3
No school years completed.......	38.5	15.5	12.4	11.0	10.3	11.5	14.6	10.0
Elementary: 1 to 4 years.......	35.1	15.5	9.6	8.8	10.2	12.1	14.4	12.2
5 to 7 years.......	34.3	14.3	9.5	9.2	9.8	12.5	14.6	14.9
8 years...........	34.7	14.8	9.5	9.4	10.1	12.3	15.2	16.6
High school: 1 to 3 years.......	40.3	14.2	8.7	8.1	9.1	11.7	16.4	19.7
4 years...........	60.4	26.8	12.1	9.7	10.4	13.6	18.7	23.0
College: 1 to 3 years.......	71.7	39.6	15.5	10.5	10.9	13.8	19.3	24.1
4 years...........	....	57.6	23.0	11.7	11.0	13.7	19.9	26.8
5+ years..........	....	67.4	38.8	20.3	18.8	20.0	26.3	36.2
NONWHITE WOMEN, Total.......	25.6	17.4	14.5	15.5	19.3	23.7	27.0	24.7
No school years completed.......	29.7	15.7	14.9	12.4	16.3	19.3	23.7	18.6
Elementary: 1 to 4 years.......	20.0	17.0	12.5	14.9	18.1	21.3	23.5	22.0
5 to 7 years.......	22.1	14.5	12.0	13.8	17.7	21.7	24.7	23.7
8 years...........	20.9	12.9	12.7	15.3	19.4	24.4	27.3	26.7
High school: 1 to 3 years.......	24.2	12.7	11.7	14.6	18.5	23.7	26.9	27.5
4 years...........	36.0	21.0	16.2	16.7	20.8	25.1	31.6	30.0
College: 1 to 3 years.......	43.2	29.7	19.5	16.6	22.3	30.9	34.8	36.8
4 years...........	....	49.0	27.1	20.7	20.7	28.3	40.6	42.8
5+ years..........	....	46.4	39.4	27.6	30.1	36.8	48.4	48.1

Source: U.S. Bureau of the Census, U.S. Census of Population: 1960. Number of Children Ever Born, Report PC(2)-3A, table 25

When childlessness rises above 10 percent in couples, we may infer that it is either primarily voluntary childlessness resulting from the use of contraceptives or else a result of very irregular exposure to childbearing. In the United States the very large amount of childlessness at ages 45 to 49 shown in Table 18-32 appears to have been caused by an adjustment to the economic depression of the 1930s and by the social maladjustment of large numbers if immigrants. In 1960 the proportion of childlessness among younger generations 30 to 34 years of age was only 10 percent or about one-half as great. This sudden transformation was brought about by earlier marriage, economic prosperity, and an apparent decline in voluntary childlessness.

Tables 18-32, 18-33, and 18-34 pursue the matter of childlessness among the United States population more deeply. Table 18-32 shows the proportion of ever-married women who are childless by age, educational attainment, and color at the 1960 census. These statistics allow us to conclude that childlessness is very closely related to the level of educational attainment. Among women who have had 4 years or more of college, childlessness is substantially higher than among women who have had less schooling. This is particularly true of older women. It

is also true of women younger than 30 years of age. At the younger ages we cannot be certain to what extent this greater childlessness is due to voluntary sterility and to the fact that the women have been in college, have only recently married, and have had less chance of becoming pregnant than have women who stopped schooling at a younger age.

This table also shows that at ages beyond 25 childlessness is more pronounced among the nonwhite population than among the white. Some people have claimed that the greater rate of childlessness among nonwhite populations is caused by a higher prevalence of venereal infections that cause sterility. This is not a completely valid explanation. Inasmuch as venereal infection tends to be higher among low-education groups than among more highly educated groups, this explanation, if it were valid, should lead to higher rates of childlessness among nonwhite populations of low educational status and to lower rates of childlessness among nonwhite populations of higher educational status. *The exact situation in reverse is true*: at all age groups, childlessness is higher among the more educated nonwhite than among the less educated nonwhite couples. It is clear that the nonwhite population seems to be responding to the

Table 18-33   Percent Childless among Ever-Married White Women Aged 35 to 44, by Marital Status and Educational Attainment, for the United States: 1960

Marital status	Total	Educational attainment					
		Elementary		High school		College	
		0 to 7 years	8 years	1 to 3 years	4 years	1 to 3 years	4+ years
Total..................	16.8	18.3	15.7	13.9	16.6	17.9	26.4
Ever married.....................	11.6	11.3	11.4	10.4	11.8	12.2	14.1
Married once..................	11.0	10.7	10.8	9.7	11.2	11.5	13.5
Married more than once.........	15.0	13.9	14.3	13.0	16.2	17.7	21.5
Married, husband present..........	10.9	10.9	10.9	9.8	11.1	11.3	12.8
Wife married once..............	10.3	10.2	10.3	9.2	10.5	10.5	12.2
Wife married more than once.....	14.9	14.2	14.1	12.9	16.1	17.0	20.2
Married, husband absent...........	15.0	13.3	14.6	13.3	15.7	16.9	24.5
Wife married once..............	15.2	13.2	14.5	13.5	16.2	16.1	24.3
Wife married more than once.....	14.5	13.8	14.9	13.0	14.0	19.3	25.7
Separated.......................	14.5	12.2	13.1	13.2	16.2	17.9	24.5
Married once..................	14.8	12.0	13.0	13.8	16.7	17.7	23.1
Married more than once.........	13.6	12.6	13.7	11.7	14.2	18.4	....
Other...........................	15.6	14.8	16.3	13.6	15.3	16.2	24.6
Married once..................	15.6	14.6	16.2	13.1	15.7	15.2	25.1
Married more than once.........	15.6	15.7	16.7	14.8	13.7	20.1	21.2
Widowed.........................	15.3	12.0	13.7	13.7	16.9	16.8	24.5
Married once..................	15.2	12.5	12.9	13.3	16.9	16.9	24.2
Married more than once.........	15.6	9.7	17.8	15.5	17.0	16.0	28.2
Divorced........................	21.3	15.8	17.3	16.6	23.3	26.5	33.5
Married once..................	22.7	17.1	18.4	17.9	24.7	27.2	33.9
Married more than once.........	17.1	12.8	14.5	13.8	18.6	24.2	31.3

Source: U.S. Bureau of the Census, U.S. Census of Population: 1960. Number of Children Ever Born, Report PC(2)-3A, table 28

same forces that promote childlessness as is the white population and that these forces are closely linked to the amount of educational attainment.

Some additional light on the problem of childlessness is provided by Tables 18-33 and 18-34. In these tables we have taken one age group of women (35 to 44 years of age) who have been ever married and have subjected them to detailed cross-tabulation according to their educational attainment as well as their current marital status. When we examine the rates of childlessness for all of the women irrespective of their educational attainment, we discover that childlessness is lower among women who have been married only once and whose husbands are still present in the house. Every form of disruption to marriage appears to promote childlessness among the white population: separation, widowhood, and divorce. Among women who are currently married, childlessness is greater if they have been married one or more times before, and among women who are widowed or divorced and who have been married more than once childlessness is very high. These findings do not hold completely true for the group of women who

are "separated" or "husband absent." The separation or desertion not infrequently was caused by the existence of an oversized family that the husband himself helped to procreate. Table 18-34, which pertains to nonwhite women, shows that exactly the same pattern of differences in childlessness exists among the nonwhite population. In every instance married disruption appears to be conducive to greater childlessness. In fact, the differences not infrequently are sharper for the nonwhite than for the white population. When we compare Tables 18-33 and 18-34, line by line, we still observe the rise in childlessness with increasing educational attainment. (An exception is the group of women who completed 1 to 3 years of high school. It is plausible that a major explanation for the failure of this group of women to complete high school is that they became pregnant and were forced to drop out. This would tend to select women of proved fertility into this educational category.) An example will help emphasize the general principle: if we examine line 5 for women who have been married only once and are still living with their husband, we discover that childlessness is about 10 percent among all white

Table 18-34 Percent Childless among Ever-Married Nonwhite Women Aged 35 to 44 Years, by Marital Status and Educational Attainment, for the United States: 1960

Marital status	Total	Educational attainment					
		Elementary		High school		College	
		0 to 7 years	8 years	1 to 3 years	4 years	1 to 3 years	4+ years
Total.................	26.9	25.8	26.8	25.5	27.7	31.4	36.0
Ever married...................	21.4	19.7	21.9	20.8	22.5	26.0	27.4
Married once...............	20.8	19.1	21.5	20.4	21.8	24.6	26.5
Married more than once......	23.4	21.8	23.2	22.0	25.3	31.7	32.9
Married, husband present........	20.5	18.9	21.1	19.9	21.5	24.1	25.8
Wife married once...........	19.7	17.8	20.6	19.3	20.6	22.2	24.8
Wife married more than once..	23.6	22.3	23.1	22.0	25.8	32.1	32.3
Married, husband absent..........	22.6	21.9	22.7	21.3	24.3	27.7	27.9
Wife married once...........	22.8	21.8	23.2	21.4	25.1	29.3	26.1
Wife married more than once..	21.7	22.2	20.7	20.9	20.8	21.0	....
Separated......................	22.7	22.3	22.1	21.9	24.2	27.0	24.9
Married once...............	22.9	22.3	22.9	21.9	25.0	28.6	24.1
Married more than once.......	21.6	22.3	18.7	22.2	21.0	....	....
Other..........................	22.4	20.1	25.0	18.8	24.6	29.2	30.7
Married once...............	22.4	19.7	24.3	19.3	25.6	30.6	28.0
Married more than once.......	22.2	21.7	27.3	17.2	20.1	....	....
Widowed........................	21.5	19.3	22.4	21.8	23.3	33.5	34.8
Married once...............	21.4	19.7	22.2	21.4	22.0	30.0	38.5
Married more than once.......	21.8	17.8	23.0	23.4	30.0	....	....
Divorced.......................	27.7	24.5	27.8	26.6	27.4	36.7	39.8
Married once...............	28.2	25.7	27.0	27.4	27.8	37.7	39.8
Married more than once.......	25.9	21.1	30.1	23.9	25.8	34.3	....

Source: U.S. Bureau of the Census, U.S. Census of Population: 1960. Number of Children Ever Born. Report PC(2)-3A, Table 29

women who have had less than a high school education. It is about 10.5 percent among high school graduates and women who have attended 1 to 3 years of college and is much higher—12.2 percent—among women who are college graduates. If we examine line 5 in Table 18-30 we find the same pattern, with an even sharper differential with educational attainment, for nonwhite women. We can conclude, therefore, that *two of the major factors influencing childlessness both among white and nonwhite couples is the amount of educational attainment and marital disruption.*

We have already discounted the theory that venereal infection is the sole explanation of the very large difference in childlessness between the white and nonwhite population. Yet Tables 18-33 and 18-34 leave us without an adequate alternative explanation. If we compare these two tables cell by cell, we discover that although differences in educational attainment and in marriage disruption explain much of the difference in childlessness between the white and nonwhite populations, childlessness nevertheless persists substantially higher among the nonwhite than among the corresponding

cell for the white population. Thus even when allowance is made for the fact that educational attainment and marital disruption both exert a stronger force on the nonwhite than on the white population, a substantial excess of childlessness still persists among the nonwhite population.

One theory that has been advanced to explain the differences is that in some instances nonwhite women have borne children out of wedlock or by previous marriage whom they do not report at the time of the census. In other words, they will report themselves as being childless if they have borne an illegitimate child and have not as yet borne a child to the man with whom they are currently living. Another explanation may be that while white women may report infants who were born alive but lived only a few days as a "child ever born," nonwhite women tend to forget such events and not report them. Also, there may be some validity to the theory of venereal infection. The phenomenon of childlessness is worthy of much more intensive study than it has received so far.

It is a very impressive fact that although the

Table 18-35 Duration of Marriage: Number of Children Ever Born per 1000 Women 15 Years Old and Over, Ever Married, by Color

Years since first marriage	White women	Nonwhite women
Under 1 year....	372	996
1..............	764	1,258
2..............	1,090	1,560
3..............	1,387	1,824
4..............	1,661	2,063
5..............	1,878	2,285
6..............	2,059	2,448
7..............	2,173	2,565
8..............	2,294	2,713
9..............	2,368	2,792
10..............	2,452	3,002
11..............	2,472	3,073
12..............	2,511	3,062
13..............	2,519	3,102
14..............	2,492	3,021
15..............	2,546	3,068
16..............	2,493	2,973
17..............	2,454	2,959
18..............	2,476	3,070
19..............	2,461	3,107
20..............	2,499	3,274

Source: U.S. Bureau of the Census, U.S. Census of Population: 1960, Number of Children Ever Born, Report PC(2)-3A, Table 20.

average level of fertility among the nonwhite population in 1960 was 30 percent above that among the white population, the proportion of nonwhite women who were childless was more than twice that of the white population. This shows in yet another way that childlessness may be an accompaniment of low fertility but is not a necessary ingredient of fertility control.

18.11. Fertility and Duration of Marriage

Some demographers have claimed that age is less important in influencing the level of fertility than is the duration of marriage. It is held that the tendency is to begin childbearing immediately after marriage and to bear children until the number desired has been attained, after which fertility slackens. Therefore, the typical age-specific fertility curve that we have observed is in reality only an indirect reflection of the duration of marriages. Those who are most enthusiastic about this phenomenon assert that in fertility analysis we can dispense with the variable of age and substitute the variable of duration of marriages. Table 18-35 tends to support this view. Each row of this table represents a duration-of-marriage span; that is, the first line represents the marriages that have lasted less than one year, the second line lists marriages of one year's duration, and so on. There is a separate line for each year of duration up to and including marriages that have lasted 30 years or more. It can be seen that for each additional year's duration of marriage the number of children ever born increases: couples who have been married for 10 years have more children than those who have been married 9 years, and so forth. Similar patterns exist for white and nonwhite women. At ages beyond 20 years, however, the pattern is not fully consistent. This represents almost a maximum range of duration of marriage during the fertile ages and at ages older than this tends to reflect cohort differences in fertility. It is clear that to a very great extent the use of age-specific fertility rates or of duration-of-marriage-specific fertility rates are alternative ways of representing the pattern of childbearing. Whichever variable is used as the *explicit* criterion of classification, the alternate criterion is also used *implicitly*. Which one is used will probably depend on the data available. However, there is not a perfect correspondence between the two. The 1960 census of the United States provided an excellent opportunity to test the comparative influences of age and duration of marriage on fertility, for it produced a very large statistical table showing the number of children ever born to ever-married women, by age, by single years of marriage duration, and by color. By applying the rates of duration of marriage shown in Table 18-35 to the various age groupings of the population, it was possible to estimate what the expected number of children ever born would be if there were only a duration-of-marriage effect but no age effect. These expected values were then divided by the actual values to obtain a ratio of actual to expected. Table 18-36 shows the results. If duration of marriage were the only factor involved, all of the ratios in the two right-hand columns of this table would have been 1. However, it is clear that at almost no age is the ratio of 1 achieved. At the ages of heavy childbearing the ratio tends to be above 1 and to sink below 1 as childbearing slackens. This re-

Table 18-36 Ratio of Births
Expected on the Basis of Duration of
Marriage to Actual Births Classified
by Age of Mother, United States:
1960

Age of mother	Color	
	White	Nonwhite
20 years.........	1.01	1.04
21 years.........	1.02	1.05
22 years.........	1.02	1.07
23 years.........	1.04	1.08
24 years.........	1.04	1.12
25 years.........	1.05	1.11
26 years.........	1.07	1.12
27 years.........	1.07	1.13
28 years.........	1.08	1.13
29 years.........	1.08	1.14
30 years.........	1.09	1.12
31 years.........	1.08	1.11
32 years.........	1.09	1.15
33 years.........	1.09	1.13
34 years.........	1.08	1.08
35 years.........	1.08	1.06
36 years.........	1.07	1.07
37 years.........	1.06	1.02
38 years.........	.92	.95
39 years.........	1.00	.92
40 years.........	.97	.86
41 years.........	.93	.79
42 years.........	.88	.74
43 years.........	.83	.70
44 years.........	.78	.64

Source: U.S. Bureau of the Census, U.S.
Census of Population: 1960
Report PC(2)-3A, Table 20,21,22.

veals that the duration-of-marriage effect is not the only factor involved, but that there is an independent age factor as well. Childbearing at ages younger than about 30 to 35 is greater than what would be expected on the basis of duration-of-marriage rates alone; at ages older than this, childbearing is less than would be expected. There are several explanations for this. (1) At the youngest ages, many marriages are contracted because the woman is already pregnant. (2) Young couples are highly fecund and become pregnant more easily than older couples. (3) Young couples may be less disposed to practicing family planning than older couples. This may include the factor of less frequent sexual intercourse after age 35. (4) At ages beyond 35, involuntary sterility begins to set in and removes a larger and larger proportion of women from the risk of childbearing; hence the low ratios reported at advanced ages are due in part to involuntary sterility as well as to a desire on the part of older couples not to have children even though they may have married only recently.

The pattern of ratios for the nonwhite population in Table 18-36 is not fully consistent with those for the white population. This is possibly due to the fact that a high percentage of the nonwhite population has been married more than once and has reported duration of *current* marriage rather than duration of *first* marriage as was requested in the census inquiry. It may also be due to the fact that teenage nonwhite girls do not report all of the children they have ever borne, as already discussed. From this brief test we conclude that fertility data tabulated by duration of marriage will usually show the same general pattern as fertility data tabulated by age, except for persons married at extremely young or extremely old ages. It is believed that nuptiality rates, specific by age, are preferable to nuptiality rates, specific by duration, for most demographic analysis.

18.12. Parity and Fertility

Another factor that influences the birthrate of a population is *parity*, or the number of children women have already borne. Referring back to the theory of probability, it should be clear that only women who have borne three children are "exposed" to the possibility of bearing a fourth child, and that only women who have borne no children (zero-parity women) are exposed to the probability of bearing a first child. Table 18-37 reports parity-age-specific rates for selected years, 1940-1965. These rates are true birth probabilities in that they express the probability that a woman of a given parity will bear a child of next higher order during a one-year period.

When we examine these rates row by row, we arrive at the surprising discovery that parity-specific rates for any particular age group *increase* with increasing parity. Thus the rate of a third-parity woman aged 30 to 34 bearing a fourth child is substantially higher than the probability that a zero-parity woman aged 30 to 34 will bear a first child. Although this may seem strange at first, on reflection we see that it is only what we would expect: women who are high-fertility childbearers must have babies

Table 18-37 Birth Probabilities for Women, by Parity, by Exact Age, United States: 1940, 1950, 1960, and 1965

Exact age of mother as of January 1	Parity							
	0	1	2	3	4	5	6	7 or higher
15-19 years:								
1965...................	57	291	306	...	...	...	...	...
1960...................	67	357	365	397	...	...	...	...
1957...................	75	354	355	398	...	...	...	...
1950...................	60	322	320	337	...	...	...	...
1940...................	41	257	360	...	...	...	...	...
20-24 years:								
1965...................	146	269	207	216	259	...	...	...
1960...................	187	341	281	300	350	406	444	...
1957...................	195	338	276	296	348	414	449	...
1950...................	142	257	237	284	354	403	...	...
1940...................	92	191	221	299	373	506	...	...
25-29 years:								
1965...................	135	216	147	140	154	186	218	276
1960...................	140	252	181	184	208	258	303	352
1957...................	139	254	179	184	217	267	318	385
1950...................	130	194	144	168	213	274	322	364
1940...................	83	126	122	170	215	276	308	391
30-34 years:								
1965...................	67	112	80	81	92	116	143	205
1960...................	61	120	95	105	124	162	201	282
1957...................	68	123	101	112	135	178	219	296
1950...................	65	114	87	98	120	163	205	291
1940...................	48	72	65	87	115	167	200	287
35-39 years:								
1965...................	24	37	31	37	48	66	83	148
1960...................	27	40	38	52	68	94	120	195
1957...................	29	44	44	58	75	102	127	207
1950...................	25	44	41	52	66	93	119	215
1940...................	19	27	28	40	58	89	109	209
40-44 years:								
1965...................	5	7	6	9	15	21	28	60
1960...................	5	7	8	14	21	31	39	77
1957...................	5	8	9	15	21	32	41	81
1950...................	5	8	8	13	18	27	34	80
1940...................	4	5	6	10	14	23	31	78

Source: Vital Statistics of the United States, 1965, Table 1-14.

at a rapid rate in order to complete a large family size before the completion of the child-bearing period. Therefore, a significant proportion of those who have attained any parity will proceed to bear children in the following year.

However, the major use of the parity-specific birth probabilities of Table 18-37 is not to compare the lines horizontally but to compare them *vertically*, to detect changes over time in the propensity to bear children. Demographers believe that changes in fertility patterns can be detected rather sensitively by studying changes in the parity-age specific probabilities between one year and the next.

When we examine the data of Table 18-37 in this fashion, we see that from 1940 to 1960 there were dramatic increases in the rates for zero, one-, and two-parity women at all ages. There were moderate increases in the proba-

bility of bearing a third or a fourth child among women aged 30 or over and for bearing a fifth or higher-order child among women older than this. (The reader should note that third parity is not usually achieved in most women before ages 25 to 29 and fourth parity not before ages 30 to 34, so that the rates for higher parities for younger ages are somewhat atypical and refer to rather small groups of women in the population.) The age group 35 to 44 represents near completion of childbearing. It is interesting to note that the parity-specific rates for these age groups have risen from 1940 to 1960 for all parities up to and including the sixth, although the rates are small. This means that among these cohorts of women there was a slight return to larger families.

A very important finding in Table 18-37, however, is that since 1960 *there has been a*

*definite turndown in the birth probability at
every age and at every combination of age and
parity. This signals a fundamental change in
the pattern of fertility in the American population.* Together, these rates clearly indicate
that the peak of childbearing in the "baby
boom" years has been reached and that the
trend is now again toward lower fertility rates.
This downward trend is not due to changing
age composition of the population or to changing size of the childbearing cohorts. These
rates mean that fewer women of a given age
who had one child in 1965 were proceeding
to have a second child than was the case in
1960. A similar conclusion can be made for
having a second, third, fourth, and so on, child.
This means that all cohorts of women of all
sizes of families are bearing children at a significantly lower rate than they were only two
years previously. The sharpest declines both
relatively and absolutely are for women 25 to
29, 30 to 34, and 35 to 39 years of age who are
of parities three and above (who have already
borne three or more children). This suggests
that cohorts that had high fertility when they
were younger are now curtailing their fertility
sharply in order to avoid having truly large
families. This is in line with a hypothesis of
the basic change in the age pattern of childbearing due to earlier marriage. According to
the hypothesis, younger generations marry
earlier and complete their childbearing earlier
than did the generations that preceded them.

But this is not the whole story of recent
changes in birth probabilities. *The generation
that is just now starting to bear children is having the first child at a slower rate than did the
preceding generation and is having a second
and third child at an even slower pace.* Thus
it appears that the 1957-1959 period was a distinctive turning point away from the "baby
boom" and that we can look forward to a
genuine decrease in the average size of completed family in future generations. By 1965 it
appeared that the "baby boom" was definitely
over. In 1965 the probability of having a third
child or a child of higher order was much lower,
for each age, than it had been in 1940. Some
demographers still point with dismay to the very
large cohorts who will enter childbearing each

year between 1965 and 1975 and who, even
with lower birthrates, can still produce a true
population "explosion." If these birth probabilities continue their recent downward trend for
even another five years, this danger will be
largely obviated. Demographers must study the
birth probabilities for each age-parity group
carefully for the next several years in order to
evaluate the fertility outlook for the nation.

18.13.   Longitudinal or Real Cohort Fertility

The summary measures of fertility as we have
presented them so far are all "cross-sectional"
or "static" measures of fertility because they
refer to the rate of childbearing in a single
year. To arrive at a summary overall measure
such as GFR or TFR, it is necessary to visualize an imaginary cohort of women going
through life exposed to the fertility conditions
that happen to be in effect in a single year.
The cohorts thus constructed are "hypothetical cohorts" and do not necessarily refer to the
actual behavior of real cohorts of women. Demographers have done a very impressive
amount of research which shows that this cross-
sectional approach using hypothetical cohorts
does not tell the whole truth and is sometimes
misleading. Instead, they recommend the use
of a longitudinal approach, which follows sets
of real cohorts of women through their childbearing years and studies their actual childbearing behavior.

Unfortunately, fertility experts have tended
to overemphasize one of these approaches at
the expense of neglecting the other. The student should appreciate the strengths and weaknesses of each and should understand what
each can do that the other cannot. Many of
the advantages claimed for each actually are
common to both. For a balanced view, it is
necessary to understand what knowledge or
information each can yield. A little prior explanation is necessary before presenting fertility data for real cohorts.[25]

---

[25] The name of Pascal K. Whelpton is internationally linked to the promotion of the longitudinal study of fertility. His book, *Cohort Fertility*
(Princeton, N.J.: Princeton University Press,
1954), is a systematic treatise on the subject.

There are two hypotheses concerning the cohort effect or generation effect that justify its usefulness. (1) Childbearing in a particular year is not simply a response to conditions of that year or the preceding year, but rather a response of the total past experience of the couple up to this point. Thus a couple where the wife is 32 years of age and has had no children because the husband has been in medical, law, or other graduate school is more likely to have a child during her thirty-third year than a couple where the wife is of the same age but where there are three children already and the prospects of increasing income in future years are quite modest. Thus the experience of the couple in its entire childbearing life up to a given moment (as well as the situation that exists at that particular moment) enters into a decision of whether or not the couple should have an additional child. (2) The attitude toward childbearing may differ from one generation to another and is influenced by the conditions and "culture" in which a generation grows up. For example, one generation may have a very strong desire to improve its level of living, to obtain more education, or to rise higher in the occupational scale and may postpone and curtail childbearing for these reasons. Another generation may be more reckless in its outlook; "let's live our lives today, for tomorrow we may all be dead because of the bomb" may be its prevailing philosophy, which may be accompanied by an attitude favorable to early marriage and early childbearing. These "cohort responses" are manifest in unusually low or unusually high rates of natality for the cohort at particular ages in comparison with cohorts that precede or follow. As has been reported earlier in this chapter, couples do have attitudes about what constitutes the appropriate number of children to bear, and their family-size attitudes change over time. The attitudes appear to be reflected (at least in part) in actual behavior.

If cross-sectional data on fertility are assembled and tabulated by single years of age for a succession of calendar years, we can develop measures of longitudinal fertility for various cohorts of women. Such data are presented in Table 18-38. Column 1 of this table

shows the total fertility rates for each year. It takes only a moment's reflection to appreciate that the diagonal cells of Table 18-38 represent the behavior of real generations traveling through the reproductive span. For example, women who were of age 31 in 1922 are one year older or 32 in 1923. By reading the *diagonals* of this table—studying fertility by single years of age for each single year of time—we can trace the actual fertility performance of real cohorts of women. By adding the rates for the various ages of a cohort, we can compute a total fertility rate for each cohort beyond age 49 and the cumulative fertility for cohorts younger than this. The bottom line and the right-hand column of Table 18-38 contain these diagonal sums. The right-hand column represents the *completed* fertility of cohorts that had passed through the childbearing years. (The totals include estimates, prepared by P. K. Whelpton, for ages and years not included in our table. The bottom line represents the *incomplete* fertility of cohorts still in the childbearing years, up through the year 1965. To summarize: we may compute the total and cumulative fertility rates in either of two ways. First, cross-sectional rate —annual fertility rates for hypothetical cohorts. Second, longitudinal fertility rates—generational fertility rates for real cohorts. Here are two alternative ways of analyzing the same set of empirical facts. We can use either or both sets of these measures to try to comprehend a major change in fertility. The set of facts that the data of Table 18-38 summarize is a very interesting and significant one. It is the historical record of the long-term trend of fertility in the United States, spelled out in such a way that it may be studied simultaneously in terms of both cross-sectional and longitudinal fertility analysis.

Before we can analyze the data in Table 18-38, we must decide how to identify the longitudinal measures according to the generation to which they refer. Demographers identify real cohorts in terms of the year of birth of the women. At first this would seem somewhat awkward, since the onset of childbearing falls 15 years after the date of birth, the period of highest fertility is reached 25 to 35 years after

Table 18-38 Age-Specific Birth Probabilities for Single Years of Age, Cumulative Cohort Fertility, and Total Fertility Rates: Calendar Years 1917 to 1965

Year	Total fertility rate	Single years of age																
		14	15	16	17	18	19	20	21	22	23	24	25	26	27	28	29	30
Average....	2925.8	3.7	10.3	28.8	58.7	99.7	138.3	160.6	173.3	181.5	186.7	184.9	171.0	163.5	152.5	148.8	134.0	127.0
1917........	3331.0	2.8	7.3	22.1	47.7	88.8	122.6	154.9	163.9	174.9	183.1	200.0	164.5	170.2	167.2	180.6	161.2	155.1
1918........	3310.9	4.2	7.1	21.7	47.6	85.6	122.7	155.3	164.4	175.4	183.9	199.8	165.0	169.4	165.5	178.1	161.2	154.6
1919........	3076.3	2.7	6.1	18.7	41.8	77.1	106.4	133.1	141.4	153.4	163.1	179.4	153.5	156.9	153.4	165.9	150.2	148.9
1920........	3270.1	3.0	7.6	23.5	52.2	94.9	129.1	155.1	164.5	171.7	181.4	194.9	166.0	167.2	160.6	171.5	154.6	149.8
1921........	3348.9	3.3	8.0	25.0	55.8	102.6	141.1	155.0	159.5	177.1	181.4	197.2	171.1	172.6	165.3	175.1	157.3	152.4
1922........	3124.5	2.9	7.1	22.2	50.1	93.5	130.3	144.1	152.2	158.6	173.4	183.6	160.8	162.7	155.6	163.8	145.5	143.4
1923........	3116.3	3.0	7.0	21.9	49.4	92.8	131.5	142.8	153.1	163.9	167.6	191.4	159.5	161.5	155.1	163.9	145.0	142.6
1924........	3144.0	3.2	7.6	23.7	52.8	97.5	136.1	145.5	157.2	169.5	177.4	187.1	164.1	160.1	153.8	162.4	143.9	144.3
1925........	3026.5	3.2	7.6	23.6	53.4	95.2	130.9	138.8	151.7	166.2	176.0	176.0	161.7	155.0	146.7	153.5	139.4	139.0
1926........	2909.5	3.4	7.5	23.4	50.9	90.4	127.1	135.1	146.8	161.4	170.1	166.7	151.7	153.1	140.8	147.1	132.4	134.0
1927........	2826.4	3.4	8.6	25.2	52.1	86.8	122.2	136.0	143.8	154.8	163.7	163.7	148.6	146.3	142.1	141.5	125.3	127.9
1928........	2656.1	3.0	8.0	23.9	49.7	83.4	114.4	130.9	136.7	147.0	151.9	154.5	144.2	135.2	129.4	137.2	118.4	120.2
1929........	2524.1	2.8	7.9	23.5	48.9	84.9	107.9	124.5	133.0	142.1	145.4	146.7	139.3	132.5	121.2	127.2	115.8	115.8
1930........	2508.7	3.0	8.0	23.5	49.4	78.6	109.7	125.0	130.5	142.7	145.0	146.0	138.5	132.8	122.9	123.8	114.2	115.8
1931........	2375.9	2.6	7.6	21.7	45.5	75.0	104.4	118.2	125.1	133.1	138.9	137.1	132.5	127.1	119.6	119.9	106.4	107.7
1932........	2288.1	2.5	7.4	21.0	42.9	68.9	100.8	115.1	121.7	129.2	131.5	133.9	126.4	122.3	115.1	116.2	104.1	99.8
1933........	2148.9	2.7	7.2	20.0	40.7	73.5	93.2	108.2	114.5	122.1	125.7	123.1	120.2	115.4	107.9	110.1	98.1	96.4
1934........	2204.9	2.8	8.0	21.2	43.3	73.5	95.8	112.1	120.3	127.0	129.5	130.1	120.6	120.0	111.0	112.2	101.5	99.6
1935........	2162.6	2.9	8.6	22.9	43.6	74.1	97.2	110.1	118.6	127.1	129.6	127.1	121.1	114.1	110.1	110.0	98.5	97.5
1936........	2118.5	2.8	7.9	23.0	44.6	73.3	96.4	110.0	117.6	123.8	129.5	127.5	120.9	115.6	105.7	107.8	96.5	94.4
1937........	2147.3	3.0	8.4	23.5	48.8	79.1	99.8	113.5	120.9	126.1	132.2	130.7	123.8	118.1	110.7	106.5	98.7	94.0
1938........	2200.2	3.1	8.3	24.0	49.0	83.6	105.9	118.1	125.0	130.6	134.1	133.7	128.3	122.7	114.5	112.9	98.9	97.1
1939........	2154.2	3.1	8.2	22.5	46.8	79.0	106.1	117.1	122.9	128.0	132.1	128.1	125.6	121.5	112.9	110.8	100.0	94.6
1940........	2214.0	3.0	8.3	22.7	46.1	79.1	106.6	124.9	129.5	133.4	137.4	134.4	127.9	124.8	118.2	114.9	105.4	98.9
1941........	2313.9	3.3	8.8	24.5	48.5	81.4	112.0	128.3	143.3	145.0	148.1	143.5	136.3	130.2	123.5	121.3	109.4	102.8
1942........	2532.4	3.4	9.6	27.0	52.3	85.6	119.5	149.1	158.7	160.6	174.1	159.6	155.0	147.5	134.5	130.5	118.7	112.6
1943........	2616.0	3.7	9.7	26.2	51.6	86.2	120.5	139.6	147.5	161.3	174.7	173.8	155.7	154.1	140.4	133.4	126.3	116.2
1944........	2466.4	3.5	8.9	23.1	45.0	77.0	105.6	126.1	137.2	149.4	156.7	158.1	148.4	141.3	131.1	126.0	116.1	111.8
1945........	2391.4	3.5	8.9	22.7	43.6	71.2	99.1	116.1	125.4	133.3	143.3	141.9	141.6	136.3	129.2	124.5	116.8	111.7
1946........	2829.0	3.3	8.7	23.6	47.1	84.1	119.7	147.0	166.8	177.9	189.7	186.4	178.4	175.0	156.1	148.5	133.9	125.1
1947........	3157.9	4.3	12.1	31.5	66.6	112.7	156.6	182.0	198.3	205.3	212.0	206.2	196.4	188.2	176.6	162.2	144.5	131.5
1948........	3013.4	4.7	13.7	35.4	70.4	116.4	156.4	179.6	190.7	196.0	200.4	195.9	183.7	174.7	162.4	156.8	135.8	124.4
1949........	3030.4	4.7	14.0	37.5	72.5	115.8	158.4	180.6	193.8	197.3	200.7	197.3	186.2	176.0	163.2	154.9	142.1	127.1
1950........	3029.6	4.7	14.0	37.8	73.2	115.4	153.9	179.3	191.5	197.7	200.7	195.2	188.0	176.0	163.5	155.8	141.3	132.3
1951........	3209.1	4.8	14.6	39.0	78.0	126.2	168.7	191.8	208.7	212.1	215.6	207.3	197.2	187.5	172.2	162.9	147.1	134.9
1952........	3306.6	4.5	13.7	38.4	76.3	123.0	171.6	197.5	212.0	220.6	222.5	215.3	201.4	194.1	180.1	167.0	152.6	141.3
1953........	3377.7	4.7	14.1	39.2	79.2	129.5	177.7	209.6	227.1	222.5	231.5	221.5	209.0	194.5	182.1	168.5	152.7	141.8
1954........	3500.8	5.4	15.0	40.5	79.9	131.4	184.3	216.3	236.0	237.4	237.0	217.9	214.2	200.6	185.9	172.1	157.7	145.5
1955........	3520.5	5.1	15.2	40.2	80.1	130.3	185.7	219.1	240.4	246.5	244.0	231.7	220.0	201.9	186.1	172.2	155.1	144.1
1956........	3634.3	5.0	15.4	43.5	84.0	138.7	195.9	229.8	251.7	258.7	259.4	243.0	225.1	209.7	186.6	177.0	155.3	145.6
1957........	3723.6	4.8	15.4	43.9	87.1	141.6	200.7	235.2	259.2	267.4	268.8	255.3	232.4	211.7	196.1	177.8	160.8	145.9
1958........	3653.7	4.6	13.9	39.8	83.4	137.7	195.4	230.4	251.4	262.0	264.3	252.3	234.4	212.2	192.7	177.6	158.3	146.2
1959........	3668.7	4.9	14.7	38.3	79.1	136.7	197.3	234.7	253.5	257.7	264.5	253.2	236.1	218.9	194.9	178.0	161.9	147.4
1960........	3654.9	4.0	14.5	38.6	75.5	129.9	195.6	235.2	256.8	266.4	268.1	259.2	234.4	216.9	196.3	177.5	158.2	145.4
1961........	3619.5	4.0	14.7	38.9	76.2	123.2	190.1	231.9	254.3	260.8	264.0	254.1	233.0	214.7	196.3	180.0	159.4	142.5
1962........	3475.8	4.3	11.7	37.7	73.5	123.0	173.8	218.8	247.1	253.9	252.8	242.5	226.1	209.6	190.8	173.8	155.6	135.9
1963........	3330.6	4.3	12.5	31.6	74.2	118.8	173.5	203.7	227.1	239.2	240.0	220.8	216.6	200.8	184.3	168.0	150.9	135.4
1964........	3197.2	4.7	12.2	33.2	62.4	118.4	166.7	191.3	212.1	223.8	229.1	220.5	205.2	190.7	177.8	162.9	147.1	132.6
1965........	2922.4	4.3	12.6	32.4	63.3	99.4	159.2	174.6	191.0	199.8	204.8	200.1	189.4	173.4	161.9	148.6	133.5	120.9

Cohort cumulative fertility		14	15	16	17	18	19	20	21	22	23	24	25	26	27	28	29	30
Year of birth		1951	1950	1949	1948	1947	1946	1945	1944	1943	1942	1941	1940	1939	1938	1937	1936	1935
Rate		4	17	49	113	209	409		813	1045	1335	1627	1880	2092	2305	2484	2652	2779

Table 18-38 (Continued)

Year	Single years of age																			Cohort cumulative fertility	
	31	32	33	34	35	36	37	38	39	40	41	42	43	44	45	46	47	48	49	Year	Rate
Average	104.1	103.9	91.6	83.9	77.6	69.0	58.8	56.7	44.1	36.0	23.1	20.5	13.4	8.2	6.0	3.0	1.4	0.7	0.6	....	....
1917	118.7	131.6	117.2	111.0	109.9	103.0	88.8	96.0	73.7	64.4	38.1	38.2	25.9	16.7	14.4	6.8	3.4	2.1	1.6	....	....
1918	118.5	131.7	117.2	110.3	108.4	101.2	87.0	93.9	72.6	63.4	38.1	37.6	25.5	16.4	14.2	6.7	3.3	2.1	1.5	....	....
1919	115.1	128.4	114.5	107.8	107.8	99.5	85.2	92.0	71.0	61.5	37.1	36.9	24.7	15.9	13.7	6.5	3.2	2.0	1.5	....	....
1920	115.7	129.5	115.7	108.9	108.9	100.2	84.8	91.1	70.3	61.3	37.2	37.1	25.2	16.0	13.9	6.6	3.3	2.1	1.6	....	....
1921	117.7	132.2	119.2	112.9	111.4	102.3	86.2	91.6	70.4	61.3	37.3	37.4	25.3	16.3	13.9	6.7	3.3	2.1	1.5	....	....
1922	110.5	123.7	111.4	106.1	104.6	96.1	81.0	85.9	65.2	57.0	34.7	34.7	23.6	15.3	12.5	6.2	3.1	1.9	1.5	....	....
1923	109.4	122.6	110.5	105.5	103.9	96.0	81.1	85.8	64.8	55.5	33.6	33.7	22.9	14.9	12.0	5.9	3.0	1.8	1.4	....	....
1924	109.4	121.8	109.4	104.4	102.8	95.3	80.8	85.4	64.8	55.9	33.3	33.4	22.7	14.7	11.6	5.9	3.0	1.8	1.4	....	....
1925	106.0	117.4	106.2	97.8	89.1	80.4	78.8	80.4	62.5	52.9	32.9	32.1	21.3	13.7	11.5	5.5	2.8	1.7	1.3	1876	3743
1926	104.3	111.1	101.1	93.9	91.9	86.3	72.9	79.1	58.2	50.4	30.9	30.7	19.8	12.5	10.6	5.4	2.4	1.5	1.2	1877	3686
1927	100.8	108.5	97.5	91.0	81.0	73.3	73.3	73.8	57.9	48.4	30.6	29.2	17.7	12.1	9.5	4.7	2.3	1.4	1.0	1878	3630
1928	92.2	102.1	91.5	84.3	82.8	75.1	64.9	70.2	52.5	46.3	27.6	27.8	17.7	11.5	9.0	4.5	2.2	1.4	1.1	1879	3585
1929	88.0	94.7	85.6	79.8	78.2	70.0	60.0	62.7	50.3	41.9	26.6	24.9	16.3	10.4	8.2	4.3	2.2	1.0	0.9	1880	3533
1930	89.9	92.8	82.8	79.5	76.8	68.1	59.2	61.6	48.8	41.1	25.4	25.1	16.1	10.2	7.9	3.9	1.8	1.0	1.0	1881	3485
1931	89.6	88.8	77.9	72.6	71.7	65.2	56.4	57.3	45.2	37.9	24.6	23.1	15.4	9.5	7.5	3.8	1.7	1.0	0.7	1882	3436
1932	82.0	82.7	75.7	70.6	70.6	63.1	54.4	54.8	42.1	36.1	22.7	22.7	14.2	9.4	7.1	3.3	1.6	1.1	0.7	1883	3382
1933	74.0	82.9	76.2	67.0	62.8	56.9	50.4	51.3	40.5	33.8	21.6	20.7	14.2	8.8	6.8	3.3	1.7	1.1	0.5	1884	3342
1934	77.5	80.7	74.4	72.7	67.7	56.8	49.2	50.9	40.4	33.8	21.3	20.6	13.2	8.8	6.3	3.3	1.6	1.1	0.6	1885	3308
1935	76.8	79.4	67.9	67.7	65.5	55.8	46.8	47.5	38.2	31.6	19.9	19.2	12.7	7.9	6.1	3.0	1.7	0.9	0.7	1886	3270
1936	75.0	77.5	68.2	62.2	60.0	56.8	45.9	43.9	35.2	29.5	18.9	17.7	11.8	7.4	5.5	2.5	1.3	0.8	0.6	1887	3243
1937	76.4	77.5	67.8	62.9	56.3	45.9	47.5	43.4	33.9	27.5	18.4	16.7	10.8	6.9	5.0	2.4	1.4	0.6	0.6	1888	3224
1938	77.9	78.5	68.0	63.9	57.2	46.0	44.6	44.6	34.5	27.4	17.7	16.5	10.8	6.7	5.1	2.4	1.2	0.7	0.5	1889	3173
1939	78.8	77.6	66.9	62.5	56.8	50.2	42.1	41.9	33.5	26.7	17.0	15.0	9.4	6.5	4.5	2.0	1.1	0.5	0.3	1890	3132
1940	80.0	80.4	69.5	63.1	57.4	50.7	42.7	42.7	33.4	25.8	17.6	14.7	9.4	6.0	4.2	2.0	1.0	0.5	0.3	1891	3064
1941	85.0	80.6	71.6	63.8	57.9	51.2	43.1	40.4	31.1	25.3	17.7	14.3	9.0	5.3	3.8	1.8	0.9	0.3	0.3	1892	3008
1942	94.1	86.7	76.5	67.2	60.9	53.4	44.4	42.1	32.1	26.6	18.6	14.0	9.7	5.3	3.6	1.8	0.9	0.3	0.2	1893	2970
1943	99.6	96.1	85.2	78.4	65.0	58.2	49.8	45.5	35.4	26.6	17.7	14.9	9.2	5.3	3.6	1.9	0.5	0.2	0.2	1894	2914
1944	97.4	95.2	85.7	77.5	67.7	60.2	51.3	46.4	36.0	28.7	18.4	15.2	10.2	6.0	3.7	1.8	0.6	0.2	0.2	1895	2859
1945	98.6	97.8	87.1	80.2	72.5	61.5	53.5	47.4	37.0	28.7	19.0	15.9	10.1	5.9	3.8	2.3	0.7	0.3	0.2	1896	2802
1946	107.3	104.3	93.9	84.6	76.1	66.1	53.1	49.2	37.9	28.6	19.1	15.4	9.8	5.6	3.8	1.8	0.7	0.2	0.2	1897	2718
1947	111.4	105.6	94.6	86.4	80.8	67.7	53.1	48.0	38.0	29.1	19.3	15.5	9.1	5.7	3.4	1.5	0.9	0.3	0.2	1898	2654
1948	104.2	97.7	85.8	79.9	71.1	61.7	53.0	47.1	35.3	27.5	18.2	14.6	9.1	5.2	3.0	1.5	0.6	0.3	0.2	1899	2622
1949	106.3	97.2	85.3	76.9	69.5	60.6	51.4	46.7	36.2	26.7	17.8	14.1	8.8	5.2	3.0	1.4	0.5	0.2	0.2	1900	2580
1950	109.2	99.7	85.7	77.6	68.0	59.8	51.2	45.3	37.2	27.2	17.1	14.2	8.5	4.7	2.9	1.4	0.5	0.2	0.2	1901	2511
1951	119.8	106.1	90.7	79.9	70.4	60.8	52.0	45.8	36.3	28.0	18.5	13.7	8.7	5.0	2.8	1.4	0.3	0.2	0.1	1902	2435
1952	121.7	115.8	97.4	84.8	72.1	62.5	54.0	46.6	38.0	28.0	18.7	14.6	8.6	5.1	2.8	1.4	0.5	0.2	0.1	1903	2425
1953	121.3	114.5	102.1	87.6	75.3	63.6	54.0	46.3	36.6	28.7	19.1	14.6	9.3	5.0	2.7	1.3	0.5	0.1	0.1	1904	2392
1954	124.3	116.7	103.1	94.1	78.8	67.4	55.3	47.7	37.5	28.7	20.0	15.2	9.3	5.3	2.7	1.4	0.5	0.1	0.1	1905	2343
1955	123.2	115.3	101.4	90.9	82.0	67.3	55.5	47.4	37.6	28.2	19.3	14.7	9.3	5.1	2.8	1.2	0.4	0.1	0.2	1906	2306
1956	124.8	116.4	101.9	90.7	80.5	70.7	57.3	50.1	35.6	29.0	19.4	14.4	9.1	5.3	2.6	1.3	0.4	0.1	0.1	1907	2282
1957	125.7	117.3	103.4	91.7	80.8	69.6	57.3	49.8	38.1	29.0	19.4	14.4	9.1	5.2	2.8	1.3	0.4	0.1	0.1	1908	2279
1958	122.6	113.9	100.1	89.3	78.5	67.2	57.5	51.0	37.6	28.6	19.0	13.7	8.6	4.9	2.6	1.2	0.6	0.1	0.1	1909	2230
1959	124.7	112.8	99.2	88.2	76.9	66.9	56.8	49.1	40.2	29.1	19.5	14.0	8.6	5.0	2.7	1.3	0.5	0.1	0.1	1910	2268
1960	122.9	111.5	95.9	85.9	76.4	65.7	55.5	47.8	39.7	29.7	20.0	14.1	8.8	4.7	2.4	1.2	0.5	0.1	0.1	1911	2285
1961	125.9	111.0	97.4	84.1	71.3	65.5	54.7	47.2	37.5	28.9	20.7	14.6	8.7	4.8	2.7	1.1	0.4	0.1	0.1	1912	2303
1962	118.4	108.9	92.0	81.6	62.0	62.0	52.9	44.4	34.5	27.5	19.0	13.7	8.4	4.5	2.5	1.1	0.5	0.1	0.1	1913	2328
1963	114.8	105.4	91.6	78.6	70.8	58.8	50.1	43.0	33.7	26.2	18.2	13.2	8.3	4.4	2.5	1.0	0.3	0.1	0.1	1914	2334
1964	112.3	103.2	88.8	79.4	68.2	56.8	48.7	41.4	33.3	25.9	17.7	13.1	8.3	4.6	2.3	0.9	0.4	0.1	0.0	1915	2331
1965	103.6	96.3	81.6	71.5	64.2	53.5	45.2	38.2	30.8	24.4	16.4	12.1	7.7	4.1	2.4	0.9	0.2	0.1	0.0	1916	2387
Year of birth	1934	1933	1932	1931	1930	1929	1928	1927	1926	1925	1924	1923	1922	1921	1920	1919	1918	1917	1916	1917	
Rate	2884	2963	2962	2972	3030	2989	2991	2941	2936	2917	2877	2833	2814	2775	2776	2639	2521	2442	2387		

this date, and the end of childbearing occurs 45 to 50 years after birth. For example, in 1965 the cohort of 1950 just reached age 15 and started to bear children. At the same time the cohorts of 1935-1945 were at peak childbearing, and the cohorts of 1915-1925 were just completing their childbearing. In the cohort summaries of Table 18-38 the individual cohorts are identified by the year of their birth.

In 1965 the first wave of babies born in the "baby boom" of 1946-1950 were just getting married and starting their families. The demographic events in the next decade will be determined largely by whether they continue the high-fertility pattern of their parents or resort to the lower-fertility patterns that prevailed before 1940. Unfortunately, we do not yet have full information to determine which of these courses will materialize, but there is a substantial amount of evidence to support the belief that the fertility trend is resuming its historic downward march after being interrupted by the "baby boom" following World War II among populations where the knowledge of birth control is universal. With this hypothesis, let us now proceed to examine the data in Table 18-38.

We have before us the full facts of the low fertility of the 1930s and the "baby boom" of 1940-1957. For 1932, the lowest rate for the period shows that the total fertility rate is only 2100, or 2.1 children per couple. This is itself based on a hypothetical cohort. The persons who were most influenced by the depression were those who were 20 years of age and at the peak of childbearing at the time of the economic collapse in 1929. This unlucky cohort was forced to spend the next ten years—the years that normally have highest age-specific fertility rates—in a state of economic depression, with high unemployment, low income, and a bleak outlook for the future. Its men were within the shadow of the military draft during World War II. Many couples in this group postponed having children because of the depression and then the war. When prosperous and secure times finally came, the women were 37 years old, too old to make up all of the postponement. This cohort produced only 2.23 children per woman.

Contrast this cohort with the cohort of women who were of age 35 in 1965. These women were 15 years of age in 1945, hence had spent their entire reproductive life during the postwar era of early marriage, high level of prosperity and the pronatal attitude climate of the "baby boom." By 1965 they had borne an average of 3.03 children per woman. Since this group married at a very young age and there is evidence that they are curtailing further fertility sharply, we may presume that in 1965 their fertility was about 95 percent completed (a conservative estimate). Under this assumption, they will bear an average of 3.2 children apiece by the time they complete childbearing. Thus this "crest of the baby boom" cohort will bear almost exactly 1 child per woman (45 percent) more than the "trough of the depression" cohort. Yet they will have born significantly *fewer* children than the high TFR of 1954-59 would have predicted.

From this example it should be clearly apparent that the chance of any real cohort bearing exactly the number of children indicated by the TFR during its childbearing years is very small, because the TFR itself can fluctuate rather widely between the time of onset of childbearing and the time of end of childbearing.

18.14.   Which is Greater: The Annual or The Generational Effect?

A careful comparison of the cross-sectional (annual) and the longitudinal (cohort) totals in Table 18-38 reveal one fact very clearly: there appear to be two possible components of variation in fertility rates.

An Annual Component. Just as farmers have good and bad years for their crops, some years appear to be highly favorable for producing babies, while others are unfavorable. This fluctuation in the "growing conditions" for offspring may be expected to manifest itself as a single constant force affecting all age groups of the population with the same relative intensity. Although these year-to-year variations may go in cycles, we assume that the strength of the force facilitating or inhibiting childbearing is potentially independent from year to year. We also assume that this annual component in no way affects the age pattern of childbearing, but only its level.

A Longitudinal or Real-Cohort Component. Some generations (cohorts) of women—and their spouses—manifest a different age pattern and a different level of childbearing than did the generations that preceded them. If all generations bore children exactly according to the same age pattern, there would be no longitudinal component. But if some generations marry unusually early or bear children at older ages when other cohorts have ceased, the longitudinal or real-cohort component will measure the amount of fertility that can be attributed to this deviation from the average age pattern. Similarly, a cohort that marries unusually late in life or ceases childbearing unusually early will stand out as a cohort with below-average completed fertility, and the cohort component should be able to measure this. Also, if any particular age groups stand out as being extraordinarily above or below the average level of fertility for the year, we may suspect a cohort effect.

One of the important research questions in demography is, "How important is each of these two components?" If the annual component is zero, we may expect all changes in fertility to take place as a generational phenomenon. If, in contrast, the cohort component is zero, we may presume that all changes in fertility take place as an across-all-age groups secular trend in which no particular generation plays an outstanding role. Actually, there is much reason to expect that both components are present and are acting simultaneously. This raises the basic questions of how big each of these two components is and how much of the change in fertility that takes place is due to one component and how much to the other. These questions have important practical implications and underlie a great deal of recent controversy. Specifically, the TFR as a summary measure of natality can be validly used to study trends only if the cohort effect is presumed to be zero or negligible (if all changes in fertility can be attributed to annual across-all-ages fluctuations in fertility levels). On the other hand, recent criticism of the use of the TFR may have committed the opposite error and presumed that fer-

tility change takes place only in terms of the cohort component. If the cohort component is negligibly small, these criticisms are rather pointless. The following analysis undertakes to divide total fertility change into these two components and to measure the comparative influence of each.

We may divide fertility change into its annual and cohort components as follows:

1. Calculate the total change in age-specific rates from year to year. This is done by subtracting the average (first line of Table 18-38) from each line individually.

2. Estimate what the age-specific fertility rate would have been in each year if the TFR had been equal to the average TFR shown in Table 18-38, but the age pattern had been that of the particular year. This is obtained by multiplying each row of Table 18-38 by a constant factor (average TFR/TFR for the year).

3. Estimate the difference-in-age pattern of fertility for each year. This is done in two steps:

   (*a*) Subtract the average ASFR from the results of (1).

   (*b*) Divide the set of differences by the factor (average TFR/TFR for the year).

4. Estimate the annual difference in fertility levels. This is done by subtracting the results of (3*b*) from the result (1).

The difference-in-age pattern, derived in (3), contains the data with which to measure the independent cohort effect. It is a table of differences (not shown here) in exactly the same format as Table 18-38, in which the rows and columns all add to zero, but the internal cells show annual fluctuations in the age pattern of childbearing independently of the average level of fertility for the year. These are expressed as deviations from the average pattern for the period.

The estimates of annual differences in fertility levels, obtained in (4), are also tabulated in a table (not shown here) of exactly the same format as Table 18-38, in which the columns add to zero (because there is zero average deviation from the average age pattern of fertility) but the rows add to the difference between the actual TFR for each year and the average TFR for all years. The dif-

Table 18-39　Cohort and Annual Components in the Fertility of the "Depression" Cohort of 1907

Age	Year	Age-specific rates				Cumulated rates			
		Total	Difference from average	Cohort component	Annual component	Total	Difference from average	Cohort component	Annual component
14.............	1921	3.3	− 0.4	− 0.9	0.5	0	− 1	− 1	1
15.............	1922	7.1	− 3.2	− 3.9	0.7	3	− 4	− 5	1
16.............	1923	21.9	− 6.9	− 8.7	1.9	10	− 10	− 14	3
17.............	1924	52.8	− 5.9	−10.3	4.4	32	− 16	− 24	7
18.............	1925	95.2	− 4.5	− 8.0	3.4	85	− 21	− 32	11
19.............	1926	127.1	−11.2	−10.4	− 0.8	180	− 32	− 42	10
20.............	1927	136.0	−24.6	−19.1	− 5.5	307	− 57	− 61	5
21.............	1928	136.7	−36.6	−20.6	−16.0	443	− 93	− 82	− 11
22.............	1929	142.1	−39.4	−14.4	−24.9	580	−133	− 96	− 36
23.............	1930	145.0	−41.7	−15.1	−26.6	722	−174	−111	− 63
24.............	1931	137.1	−47.8	−13.1	−34.8	867	−222	−124	− 98
25.............	1932	126.4	−44.6	− 7.4	−37.3	1004	−267	−132	−135
26.............	1933	115.4	−48.1	− 4.7	−43.4	1131	−315	−137	−178
27.............	1934	111.0	−41.5	− 3.9	−37.6	1246	−356	−140	−216
28.............	1935	110.0	−38.8	0.0	−38.8	1357	−395	−140	−255
29.............	1936	96.5	−37.5	− 0.5	−37.0	1467	−433	−141	−292
30.............	1937	94.0	−33.0	0.8	−33.8	1564	−466	−140	−325
31.............	1938	77.9	−26.2	− 0.4	−25.8	1658	−492	−141	−351
32.............	1939	77.6	−26.3	1.1	−27.4	1735	−518	−139	−379
33.............	1940	69.5	−22.1	0.2	−22.3	1813	−540	−139	−401
34.............	1941	63.8	−20.1	− 2.5	−17.5	1883	−560	−142	−418
35.............	1942	60.9	−16.7	− 6.3	−10.4	1946	−577	−148	−429
36.............	1943	58.2	−10.8	− 3.5	− 7.3	2007	−588	−152	−436
37.............	1944	51.3	− 7.5	1.7	− 9.2	2065	−595	−150	−445
38.............	1945	47.7	− 9.0	1.3	−10.3	2117	−604	−149	−456
39.............	1946	37.9	− 6.2	− 4.8	− 1.5	2164	−611	−153	−457
40.............	1947	29.1	− 6.9	− 9.7	2.9	2202	−617	−163	−454
41.............	1948	18.2	− 4.9	− 5.6	0.7	2231	−622	−169	−454
42.............	1949	14.1	− 6.4	− 7.1	0.7	2250	−629	−176	−453
43.............	1950	8.5	− 4.9	− 5.4	0.5	2264	−634	−181	−453
44.............	1951	5.0	− 3.2	− 4.0	0.8	2272	−637	−185	−452
45.............	1952	2.8	− 3.2	− 4.0	0.8	2277	−640	−189	−451
46.............	1953	1.3	− 1.7	− 2.1	0.5	2280	−642	−191	−450
47.............	1954	0.5	− 0.9	− 1.1	0.3	2281	−643	−192	−450
48.............	1955	0.1	− 0.6	− 0.8	0.2	2282	−643	−193	−450
49.............	1956	0.1	− 0.5	− 0.6	0.1	2282	−644	−194	−450
50.............	1957	.....	.....	.....	.....	2282	−644	−194	−450

ferences are also expressed as deviations from the average pattern for the period. These data provide information with which to measure the independent annual effect.

The test for the cohort effect is made by cumulating the differences of (1), (3), and (4) along the diagonals, from upper left to lower right, to obtain cohort totals. If the cumulative total of (3) is significantly different from zero, we must presume that there is a real-cohort effect, and the extent of the deviation from zero is a measure of that effect.

Annual fluctuations in birthrates tend to occur in cycles; the rates will rise across all age groups for a series of consecutive years and then will decline for several consecutive years. Deep recession in births during the 1930s, followed by the rapid rise in the 1947-1957 period, illustrates this tendency. The effect of this cyclical tendency is to create a "pseudo-cohort" effect. This pseudo-cohort effect (which is really the impact of the year-to-year fluctuations on successive generations) may be measured by cumulating the computations of (4) along the diagonals. This is, in fact, the measurement of the impact of a series of consecutive annual (secular) fluctuations on the respective cohorts.

Space does not permit a publication of the full results of these computations. We must summarize the data in order to bring out their major implications.

Table 18-39 illustrates the complete set of computations for one real cohort—the cohort of 1907 that reached peak childbearing at the depth of the economic depression in 1933.

Table 18-40 Cohort and Annual Components in the Fertility of the Postwar "Baby Boom" Cohort of 1936

Age	Age-specific rates				Cumulated rates			
	Total	Difer-ence from average	Cohort com-ponent	Annual com-ponent	Total	Difer-ence from average	Cohort com-ponent	Annual com-ponent
Total.......	4.7	1.0	0.9	0.1	5	1	1	0
15.............	14.6	4.3	3.3	1.0	19	5	4	1
16.............	38.4	9.6	5.9	3.7	58	15	10	5
17.............	79.2	20.5	11.4	9.1	137	35	22	14
18.............	131.4	31.7	12.1	19.6	268	67	34	34
19.............	185.7	47.4	19.3	28.1	454	115	53	62
20.............	229.8	69.2	30.4	38.9	648	184	83	101
21.............	259.2	85.9	38.7	47.2	943	270	122	148
22.............	262.0	80.5	35.4	45.1	1205	350	157	198
23.............	264.5	77.8	30.4	47.4	1469	428	188	240
24.............	259.2	74.3	28.2	46.1	1729	502	216	286
25.............	233.0	62.0	21.4	40.5	1962	564	237	327
26.............	209.6	46.1	15.3	30.7	2171	610	253	358
27.............	184.3	31.8	10.7	21.1	2356	642	263	379
28.............	162.9	14.1	0.3	13.8	2518	656	264	393
29.............	133.5	- 0.5	- 0.3	- 0.2	2652	656	263	392

The cohort effect is dominant during the younger years, as the couples postponed child-bearing. Between ages 22 and 38 the secular (annual) component is predominant, but at age 39 the cohort component again becomes dominant, as the women followed the long-standing trend to curtail the bearing of children at old ages. During the same years the annual component is positive—but small—showing that prosperous times tended to boost the fertility of the cohort a little, but had arrived too late to be of much help. When we compare the two right-hand cumulative columns, we see that from age 25 on the annual component becomes the larger, and by the time age 50 had been reached only 30 percent of the total deviation of the cohort from the average age pattern could be traced to independent cohort effects, so that 70 percent must be attributed to across-all-ages cyclical fluctuations in fertility levels.

Table 18-40 is similar to Table 18-39, except that it refers to a postwar cohort, the cohort of 1936. This is one of the cohorts that married unusually early and had done all of its childbearing during the "baby boom." The cohort differences here are large and positive, as are the annual differences. In this case, the cohort effects are 40 percent and the annual effects are 60 percent by age 30.

By this age the cohort component had become negative, and it will probably remain negative throughout the remaining years as these women curtail their fertility to compensate for their extraordinary early age at childbearing. This means that the annual component probably will dominate the reproductive behavior of this group even more in future years.

Table 18-41 shows the deviation of the cumulative fertility of each real cohort from the average and divides this deviation into its annual and real-cohort components. The extreme right-hand column shows what proportion of the total deviation may be attributed to real-cohort changes. This table shows several interesting relationships:

1. During the early 1920s the cohort component was very large; the decline in births during this period was being accomplished primarily by cohort changes, but in the late 1920s the secular changes took over and dominated the picture.

2. Cohort changes comprise 20 to 35 percent of all changes during the economic depression, and annual changes comprise 65 to 80 percent.

3. During the three years 1946-1948, 100 percent of the changes in fertility were cohort changes.

4. Between 1948 and 1954 the cohort and

Table 18-41 Cohort and Annual Components of Fertility Differences

Age in 1965	Year born	Base matrix	Cumulative cohort diference	Annual diference	Total diference	Percent cohort diference
18...............	1947	209	- 4	12	8	- 50
19...............	1946	409	44	26	70	63
20...............	1945	592	44	48	92	48
21...............	1944	813	62	77	140	44
22...............	1943	1045	77	113	190	41
23...............	1942	1335	139	154	293	47
24...............	1941	1627	203	198	401	51
25...............	1940	1880	239	244	483	49
26...............	1939	2092	244	288	532	46
27...............	1938	2305	263	328	591	44
28...............	1937	2484	258	364	621	42
29...............	1936	2652	263	392	656	40
30...............	1935	2779	242	414	656	37
31...............	1934	2884	229	428	657	35
32...............	1933	2963	200	432	632	32
33...............	1932	2962	110	429	539	20
34...............	1931	2972	46	419	465	10
35...............	1930	3030	42	404	446	9
36...............	1929	2989	- 46	382	336	0
37...............	1928	2991	- 72	351	279	0
38...............	1927	2941	-139	311	172	0
39...............	1926	2936	-141	265	123	0
40...............	1925	2917	-141	215	68	0
41...............	1924	2877	-157	161	5	0
42...............	1923	2838	-155	101	- 54	100
43...............	1922	2814	-128	36	- 92	100
44...............	1921	2775	-108	- 32	-140	77
45...............	1920	2776	- 46	- 99	-144	32
46...............	1919	2639	-120	-164	-284	42
47...............	1918	2521	-174	-230	-403	43
48...............	1917	2442	-191	-292	-483	40
49...............	1916	2387	-190	-349	-539	35
50...............	1915	2331	-196	-398	-595	33
51...............	1914	2334	-153	-439	-592	26
52...............	1913	2328	-126	-472	-598	21
53...............	1912	2303	-128	-494	-623	21
54...............	1911	2285	-134	-507	-640	21
55...............	1910	2268	-150	-508	-658	23
56...............	1909	2230	-198	-498	-696	28
57...............	1908	2279	-169	-478	-647	26
58...............	1907	2282	-194	-450	-644	30
59...............	1906	2306	-206	-414	-619	33
60...............	1905	2343	-211	-371	-583	36
61...............	1904	2392	-210	-324	-534	39
62...............	1903	2425	-225	-275	-500	45
63...............	1092	2431	-267	-224	-491	54
64...............	1901	2500	-237	-175	-412	58
65...............	1900	2545	-210	-128	-338	62
66...............	1999	2534	-205	- 85	-290	71
67...............	1898	2468	-208	- 49	-256	81
68...............	1897	2419	-148	- 20	-167	89

the annual components were of opposite sign; on a cohort basis women were still below average because of the depression and the war, but the rates were soaring because of across-all-ages changes.

5. The cumulative cohort effect of the earlier pattern of marriage had made itself felt by 1955, and the real-cohort effect soared to a peak in 1963, after which it has declined.

But throughout this time the annual component was considerably larger than the cohort component.

6. The "baby boom" thus appears to be comprised of two parts. First, an across-all-ages rise in births due to the annual component that dominated the picture from 1949 until 1954. The second part, from 1955 to 1965 has been one in which the cohort and the an-

nual components have both been substantial, with the annual component being greater. (Inasmuch as the data for these years are for incomplete cohorts, it is probable that the annual component will dominate them in future years.

Summary and Comments. It is possible to subdivide annual changes in fertility into a real-cohort component and an annual component. For most completed cohorts for which data are available, the annual component is greater than the real-cohort component; it is usually 65 to 80 percent of the variation. This leads us to conclude that *there has been a tendency to exaggerate the size of the real-cohort effect by interpreting all changes as cohort changes.* What we have been witnessing have been genuine but violent fluctuations in fertility patterns, and these fluctuations have been primarily in the form of simultaneous across-all-age-groups movements up and down. Moreover, earlier age at marriage has comprised the greater part of recent cohort changes. This adjustment is now completed. *We may look forward, therefore, to an era in which the annual component dominates fertility patterns even more than previously and the real-cohort component declines in magnitude, both relatively and absolutely.* The only possible basis for a revival of the cohort component would be a sudden return to delayed marriage or the adoption of a "prolonged honeymoon" tendency to postpone having the first child.

This division of birth changes into realcohort and annual components is not above criticism. The results depend in part on the schedule of average rates used as "normal," or the basis for measuring deviation. The fact that this standard of comparison is itself a cross-sectional rather than a longitudinal measure affects the results. Had the average been for a longer or a shorter set of years, the results would also have been somewhat different. Many would quarrel with the specific mode of making the division between annual and cohort effect; it is only a rough approximation aimed at stimulating further refined study, rather than a serious methodological solution to a complex problem. However, it is believed that none of these limitations is sufficiently great to alter the conclusion that in the recent past and in the foreseeable future the annual across-all-ages fluctuations in fertility have and will dominate fertility trends and that the cohort component will decrease in importance as time passes.

18.15. Conclusion

This synthesis of the available information concerning fertility throughout the world tends, we believe, toward an outlook concerning the future which is quite different from that which has been held by conventional demography. Although the situation is fully as acute and serious as the demographers have reported, the prospects for "doing something about it" are much brighter than previous demographic theory may have led us to think. (1) Fertility decline in the modern world can take place with far greater rapidity than was true only a few decades ago. (2) Rapid fertility decline can take place spontaneously among populations with only a moderate level of education, urbanization, industrialization, level of living, and so on. The experience of Japan, Eastern Europe, and Southern Europe shows this clearly. (3) As Chapter 20 will document, leaders of governments all over the world and intellectual leaders in many walks of life—medicine, economics, public health, business, political science—have manifested a sensitivity and awareness of the implications of the runaway population growth that surpass all previous expectations. (4) Chapter 20 will also argue that custom and tradition are proving to be far less important as barriers to population readjustment than expected. (5) There is a strong expectation that the skillful application of modern principles of social science, mass communication, and motivation will be able to accelerate greatly the adoption of fertility control practices, even among illiterate populations living in preindustrial environments. (6) Fertility declines need not be a generational real-cohort phenomena, but can take place suddenly as an across-all-age groups phenomena that bring about drastic reductions in fertility at all ages and all parities.

Taken in conjunction with one another, these points represent a radical departure from the inferences that have been drawn from the work of

Raymond Perl, who watched the multiplication of fruit flies to the starvation point in a confined and fixed environment. We seriously doubt that the world can look forward to a similar experience among human populations. It is also contrary to the viewpoint of those who have attempted to defend Malthus and to rationalize his writing into a foundation for "modern population theory." It is a departure from the viewpoint of those anthropologists (white European or American) who have tended to view the high-fertility people of the world as being too tradition-ridden to be capable of adjusting to modern conditions in any short time. It is also a radical departure from the thinking of those who have claimed that economic development must precede fertility control—that it is only *after* a process of economic development has

created a situation of literacy, urbanism, and rising standards of living that fertility control programs can be successful. *The findings made here suggest that fertility control may very well be a first step in economic development rather than one of the last.* And, finally, it is a departure from the judgments of those who tend to regard fertility trends as an evolutional-generational matter, rather than a cross-sectional volitional response to change in the economic, social, and psychological climate. It is believed that the latter view is much more appropriate for the modern world, where the trend is toward universal knowledge, universal acceptance, and universal availability of the means to control fertility—which are felt simultaneously by all age groups as a secular trend rather than selectively as a cohort trend.

QUESTIONS AND EXERCISES

1. Consult the most recent issue of the *Demographic Yearbook* and obtain the latest refined rates of natality for all developing nations for which they are available. Compare these rates with the corresponding rates (*a*) five and (*b*) ten years ago. Search for recent reports on fertility trends in developing nations not represented in the *Demographic Yearbook*. Write an essay on the apparent trends of natality in the developing nations represented by your data.

2. Repeat Exercise 1 for the nations of Europe.

3. From the latest report of *Vital Statistics of the United States,* update all tables in Section 18-6 of this chapter and write an essay on "Changes in U. S. Fertility since 1965."

4. Make an intensive study of the demographic transition in Japan and write a report on the "Implications of Japan's Demographic Transition for the Developing Nations."

5. Make a trait-by-trait comparison of differentials in cumulative fertility and differentials in current fertility from the statistics presented in this chapter. Classify each pair as "consistent" or "inconsistent." For each inconsistency, develop a theory of why it exists. Predict what the pattern of differential fertility in the United States will be at the 1970 census and the 1980 census.

6. Write an essay on the subject, "When Will White-Negro Fertility Differentials Disappear?" After you have catalogued the conditions that must exist for this to happen, search to see if there is a county or a community in the United States where these conditions already exist. If possible, test your theory by comparing white-nonwhite fertility differences and the social and economic conditions of each race in these places.

7. Read all you can about the fertility of women in the labor force in the United States and analyze the published census data on this subject. Write an essay on "Female Employment: Cause or Effect of Low Fertility?"

8. Repeat Exercise 7 for one or more developing countries.

9. Obtain a set of age-specific nuptial fertility rates for a nation, such as the rates presented here for the United States. Calculate what the nuptial fertility rate would be in that country if the age composition were (*a*) that of India and (*b*) that of England. When we compare the GFR for two countries, what assumptions are we making about nuptiality?

10. Some demographers have hypothesized that couples' intentions with respect to the number of children they would eventually bear could be used to predict future (short-run) changes in birthrates. Whelpton, Freedman, and Campbell collected such data in 1960, which are published in Chapters 1 and 2 of their monograph, *Fertility and Family Planning in the United States.* Study these materials carefully and compare the expectations of the couples in 1960 with what actually took place 1960-1965. Study the materials on family-size attitudes listed in the Bibliography. Write an essay on the subject, "Predicting Fertility Changes from Family Size Attitudes and Expectations."

11. Read as much as you can about abortion as a method of controlling fertility, especially in Japan and Eastern Europe. Write an essay on the topic, "Should the Developing Nations Legalize Abortion in Order to Help Solve Their Population Problems?"

12. Update the table on birth probabilities by birth order presented in this chapter. Write an essay on the implications of recent trends in these probabilities for future fertility trends. If the data are available, make this analysis for the nonwhite as well as the white population.

13. In this chapter we have presented data on attitudes toward knowledge and use of contraceptives for the United States population only. Consult the references in the bibliography and more recent research reports for one or more of the developing nations and write an essay comparing the two sets of data.

14. From the most recent reports of the *Vital Statistics of the United States,* update Table 18-38 and write an essay concerning recent cohort fertility trends in the United States. Use the 1917-1965 averages to divide the differences into their component parts. Test the assertion that after 1965 the annual component will greatly surpass the cohort

component by an even wider margin than in the period 1960-1965.

15. As United States birthrates fall, the phenomenon of childlessness may increase. Search recent sample survey reports of the U.S. Bureau of Census to determine whether this has, in fact, taken place. If it has, try to find what subpopulations are most affected.

16. Throughout the United States there is a tremendous drive to bring family planning service to the poverty population. Study the income differentials in fertility from the latest sample surveys. Attempt to evaluate whether the relationship between fertility and income is becoming positive instead of U-shaped.

17. Read as much as you can about Catholicism, Mohammedanism, Hinduism, and fertility in Europe, America, and the developing countries. Write an essay on religion and its relationship to fertility, as established in factual surveys.

18. What other variables do you think underlie the following fertility differentials:

Educational attainment
Urban-rural residence
Occupation
Marital status

19. Critically evaluate the procedure used in this chapter to divide fertility change into annual and cohort components. Develop an improved procedure for doing this.

20. It has been noted that in industrialized nations actual fertility performance tends to be *less* than the size of family that couples, as data indicated, consider ideal. In developing nations the reverse is true. How do you account for both?

BIBLIOGRAPHY

Acsadi, Gyorgy. "Demographic Variables as a Source of Differences in the Fertility of Low Fertility Countries." A paper contributed for the United Nations World Population Conference. Belgrade, 1965.

Adelman, Irma. "An Econometric Analysis of Population Growth," *American Economic Review,* **53** (June 1963), 314–339.

Adelman, Irma, and Cynthia T. Morris. "A Quantitative Study of Social and Political Determinants of Fertility," *Economic Development and Cultural Change,* **14** (2) (January 1966), 129–157.

Axelrod, Morris, et al. "Fertility Expectations of the United States Population: A Time Series," *Population Index,* **29** (1) (January 1963), 25–31.

Bacci, Massimo Livi. "Il Declino della Fecondità della Popolazione Italiana Nell'ultimó Secolo" ("The Decline in Fertility of the Population of Italy in the Past Century"), *Statistica* (Bologna), **52** (3) (July-September 1965), 359–426.

Badenhorst, L. T. "Family Limitation and Methods of Contraception in an Urban Population," *Population Studies,* **16** (3) (March 1963).

Baird, Dugald. "Variations in Fertility Associated with Changes in Health Status." Pp. 353-376 in Mindel C. Sheps and Jeanne C. Ridley (eds.). *Public Health and Population Change: Current Research Issues.* Pittsburgh, Pa.: University of Pittsburgh Press, 1965.

Bash, Wendell H. "Changing Birth Rates in Developing America: New York State 1840-1875," *Milbank Memorial Fund Quarterly,* 41 (2) (April 1963), 161–182.

Becker, Gary S. "An Economic Analysis of Fertility," pp. 209–231 in *Demographic and Economic Change in Developed Countries.* Princeton, N. J.: Princeton University Press, 1960.

Berent, Jerzy. "Fertility and Social Mobility," *Population Studies,* 5 (3) (1950), 244–260.

Biraben, Jean-Noel. "Evolution Récente de la Fécondité des Mariages dans les pays Occidentaux" (Recent Change in Marital Fertility in Western Countries), *Population,* 16 (1) (January-March 1961), 49–70.

Biraben, Jean-Noel. "Situation Présente de la Fécondité et ses Causes en Europe Occidentale" (Prevailing Fertility Situation and Its Causes in Western Europe). A paper contributed for the United Nations World Population Conference, August 30-September 10, 1965.

Blake, Judith. "Ideal Family Size Among White Americans: A Quarter of a Century's Evidence," *Demography,* 3 (1) (1966), 154–173.

Bogue, Donald J., and James A. Palmore. "Some Empirical and Analytic Relations Among Demographic Fertility Measures, with Regression Models for Fertility Estimation," *Demography,* 1 (1) (1964), 316–338.

Borgatta, Edgar F., and Charles F. Westoff. "Social and Psychological Factors Affecting Fertility: The Prediction of Total Fertility," *The Milbank Memorial Fund Quarterly,* 32 (4) (October 1954), 383–419.

Bourgeois-Pichat, Jean. "Les facteurs de la fécondité non dirigée" (Factors of Uncontrolled Fertility), *Population* (Paris), 20 (30) (May-June 1965), 383–424.

Bourgeois-Pichat, Jean. "Measurement of the Fertility of Human Populations," *Proceedings of the World Population Conference: 1955* IV. New York, 1955.

Brass, W. "The Estimation of Total Fertility Rates from Data for Primitive Communities," *Proceedings of the World Population Conference: 1954* IV. New York, 1955.

Brebant, V. "Fertility Trends in the Belgian Congo," *Proceedings of the World Population Conference: 1954,* I. New York, 1955.

Burch, Thomas K. "The Fertility of North American Catholics: A Comparative Overview," *Demography,* 3 (1) (1966), 174–187.

Caldwell, John C. "Fertility Attitudes in Three Economically Contrasting Rural Regions of Ghana," *Economic Development and Cultural Change,* 15 (2, Part 1) (January 1967), 217–238.

Campbell, Arthur A. "Fertility and Family Planning Among Nonwhite Married Couples in the United States," *Eugenics Quarterly,* 12 (3) (1965), 124–131.

Campbell, Arthur A. "Recent Fertility Trends in the United States and Canada." A paper contributed to the United Nations World Population Conference, 1965.

Carleton, Robert O. "Fertility Trends and Differentials in Latin America," pp. 15–31 in Clyde V. Kiser (ed.). *Components of Population Change in Latin America. Milbank Memorial Fund Quarterly,* 43 (4, Part 2) (October 1965).

Carleton, Robert O. "The Effect of Educational Improvement on Fertility Trends in Latin America." A paper contributed for the United Nations World Population Conference. Belgrade, 1965.

Carlsson, G. "The Decline of Fertility: Innovation or Adjustment Process," *Population Studies,* 20 (1) (1966), 149–173.

Carrier, N. H. "An Examination of Generation Fertility in England and Wales," *Population Studies,* 9 (1) (July 1955), 3–23.

Charles, Enid. *The Changing Size of the Family in Canada.* Census Monograph No. 1, Dominion Bureau of Statistics. Ottawa, 1948.

Chandrasekaran, C. "Fertility Trends in India," *Proceedings of the World Population Conference: 1954,* I. New York, 1955.

Chasteland, J. C., and Louis Henry. "Disparités Régionales de la Fécondité des Mariages." (Regional Disparities in Marital Fertility), *Population* (Paris), 11 (4) (October-December 1956), 653–672.

Cho, Lee Jay. "Estimated Refined Measures of Fertility for all Major Countries of the World," *Demography,* 1 (1) (1964), 359–374.

Christensen, Harold T. "Child Spacing Analysis via Record Linkage: New Data Plus a Summing Up From Earlier Reports," *Marriage and Family Living,* 25 (3) (August 1963), 272–280.

Coale, Ansley J. "Factors Associated with the Development of Low Fertility: An Historic Summary." A paper contributed for the United Nations World Population Conference. Belgrade, 1965.

Coale, Ansley J. and Melvin Zelnik. *New Estimates of Fertility and Population in the United States.* Princeton, N. J.: Princeton University Press, 1963.

Coale, Ansley J., and C. Y. Tye. "The Significance of Age-Patterns of Fertility in High Fertility Populations," *Milbank Memorial Fund Quarterly*, **39** (4) (October 1961), 631–646.

Collver, Andrew. *Birth Rates in Latin America*. Berkeley, Calif.: Institute of International Studies, 1965.

Coontz, Sydney. "The Economics of High Fertility in Densely Populated Underdeveloped Areas," pp. 83–91 in *International Union for the Scientific Study of Population*. Vienna, 1959.

Dandekar, Kumudini. "Effect of Education on Fertility." A paper contributed for the United Nations World Population Conference, August 30-September 10, 1965.

Davis, Kingsly, and Judith Blake. "Social Structure and Fertility: an Analytic Framework," *Economic Development and Cultural Change*, **4** (3) (April 1956), 211–235.

Day, Lincoln H. "Age of Women at Completion of Childbearing," *Public Health Reports*, **73** (6) (June 1958), 525–532.

Day, Lincoln H. "Fertility Differentials Among Catholics in Australia," *Milbank Memorial Fund Quarterly*, **42** (Part I, 2) (April 1964), 57–83.

Day, Lincoln H. "Catholic Teaching and Catholic Fertility." A paper contributed for the United Nations World Population Conference. Belgrade, 1965.

Denmark Statistical Department. "Differential Fertility in Denmark," *Statistiske Undersogelser* (Copenhagen) (1965), 1–41.

Driver, E. D. *Differential Fertility in Central India*. Princeton, N.J.: Princeton University Press, 1963.

Duncan, Otis Dudley. "Farm Background and Differential Fertility," *Demography*, **2** (1965), 240–249.

Dykstra, John W. "Pro-natal Influences in American Culture," *Sociology and Social Research*, **44** (2) (November-December 1959), 79–84.

Dzieno, Kazimierz. "Changes in the Fertility Level of Women in Poland," *Studia Demograficzne* (Warsaw), **3** (7) (1965), 79–92.

Easterline, Richard A. "On the Relation of Economic Factors to Recent and Projected Fertility Changes," *Demography*, **3** (1) (1966), 131–153.

Easterline, Richard A. "The American Baby Boom in Historical Perspective," *American Economic Review*, **51** (December 1961), 869–911.

El-Badry, M. A. "Some Aspects of Fertility in Egypt," *Milbank Memorial Fund Quarterly*, **34** (1) (January 1956), 22–43.

El-Badry, M. A., and Hanna Rizk. "Regional Fertility Differences Between Socio-Economic Groups in the UAR." A paper contributed for the United Nations World Population Conference. Belgrade, 1965.

Farley, Reynolds. "Recent Changes in Negro Fertility," *Demography*, **3** (1), 188–203.

Febvay, Maurice L. "Are the Existing Fertility Differentials Between the Various Population Groups Tending to be Reduced?" *Proceedings of the World Population Conference: 1954*, I. New York, 1955.

Febvay, Maurice I. "Niveau et Evolution de la Fécondité par Catégorie Socio-professionnelle en France" (The Level and Trend of Fertility by Occupational Class in France), *Population* (Paris), **14** (4) (October-December 1959), 729–739.

Ford, Thomas R., and Gordon F. DeJong. "The Decline of Fertility in the Southern Appalachian Mountain Region," *Social Forces*, **42** (1) (October 1963), 89–96.

Freedman, Deborah S., et al. "Size of Family and Preference for Children of Each Sex," *American Journal of Sociology*, **66** (2) (September 1960), 141–146.

Freedman, Deborah. "The Relation of Economic Status to Fertility," *American Economic Review*, **53** (3) (June 1963), 414–426.

Freedman, Ronald, et al. "Current Fertility Expectations of Married Couples in the United States," *Population Index*, **29** (4) (October 1963), 366–391.

Freedman, Ronald, and Lolagene Coombs. "Economic Considerations in Family Growth Decisions," *Population Studies*, **20** (2) (1966), 197–222.

Freedman, Ronald. "American Studies of Factors Affecting Fertility," *Proceedings of International Population Conference: 1961*, I. (London: 1963), pp. 67–76.

Freedman, Ronald, et al. "Expected Family size and Family Size Values in West Germany," *Population Studies*, **13** (2) (November 1959), 136–150.

Freedman, Ronald, et al. "Fertility Expectations in the United States: 1963," *Population Index*, **30** (2) (April 1964), 171–175.

Freedman, Ronald, and Doris P. Slesinger. "Fertility Differentials for the Indigenous Non-farm Population of the United States," *Population Studies*, **15** (2) (November 1961), 161–173.

Freedman, Ronald, and Joanna Muller. "The Continuing Fertility Decline in Taiwan: 1965," *Population Index*, **33** (1) (January-March 1967), 3–17.

Freedman, Ronald, and Larry Bumpass. "Fertility Expectations in the United States: 1962–64," *Population Index*, **32** (2) (1966), 181–197.

Freedman, Ronald, et al. "Fertility Trends in Taiwan: Tradition and Change," *Population Studies,* 16 (3) (March 1963), 219–236.

Freedman, Ronald. "Socio-economic Factors in Religious Differentials in Fertility," *American Sociological Review,* 26 (August, 1961), 608–614.

Friedlander, Stanley, and Morris Silver. "A Quantitative Study of the Determinants of Fertility Behavior," *Demography,* IV (1) (1967), 30–70.

Gebhard, Paul H., et al. "Pregnancy, Birth and Abortion," University of Indiana Institute for Sex Research. New York: Harper, 1958.

Gendell, Murray. "Fertility and Development in Brazil," *Demography,* 4 (1967), 143–157.

Gille, Halvor. "Recent Fertility Trends in Countries with Low Fertility," *Proceedings of the World Population Conference,* 1954, I. New York, 1955.

Gille, Halvor. "An International Survey of Recent Fertility Trends," National Bureau of Economic Research. Princeton, 1960.

Girard, Alain, and Louis Henry. "Les Attitudes et le Conjoncture Démographique: Natalité, Structure Familiale et Limites de la Vie Active" (Attitudes and the Demographic Situation: Natality, Family Structure, and the Limits of Active Life), *Population* (Paris), 11 (10) (January-March 1956), 105–141.

Glass, D. V., and E. Grēbenik. "The Trend and Pattern of Fertility in Great Britain: A Report on the Family Census of 1946." Papers of the Royal Commission on Population. Part I, report; Part II, tables. London: H. M. Stationery Office, 1954.

Glick, Paul C. "Marriage and Family Variables Related to Fertility." A paper contributed to United Nations World Population Conference. Belgrade, 1965.

Goldberg, David. "Another Look at the Indianapolis Fertility Data," *Milbank Memorial Fund Quarterly,* 38 (1) (January 1960), 23–36.

Goldberg, David. "Fertility and Fertility Differentials: Some Observations on Recent Changes in the United States," pp. 119–142 in Mindel C. Sheps and Jeanne C. Ridley (eds.). *Public Health and Population Change: Current Research Issues.* Pittsburgh, Pa.: University of Pittsburgh Press, 1965.

Goldberg, David. "The Fertility of Two-Generation Urbanites," *Population Studies,* 12 (3) (March 1959), 214–222.

Goldberg, David, et al. "The Stability and Reliability of Expected Family Size," *Milbank Memorial Fund Quarterly,* 37 (4) (October 1959), 369–385.

Goldscheider, Calvin. "Fertility of the Jews," *Demography,* 4 (1967), 196–209.

Goldscheider, Calvin. "Socio-Economic Status and Jewish Fertility," *Jewish Journal of Sociology,*

7 (2) (December 1965), 221–237.

Good, Dorothy. "Some Aspects of Fertility Change in Hungary," *Population Index,* 30 (2) (April 1964), 137–171.

Grabill, Wilson H., and Paul C. Glick. "Demographic and Social Aspects of Childlessness: Census Data," *Milbank Memorial Fund Quarterly,* 37 (1) (January 1959), 60–86.

Grabill, Wilson H. "Fertility," Chapter 10 in Donald J. Bogue, *Population of the United States.* Glencoe, Ill.: Free Press, 1960.

Grabill, Wilson H., Clyde V. Kiser, and P. K. Whelpton. *The Fertility of American Women.* Published for the Social Science Research Council in Cooperation with the U. S. Department of Commerce, Bureau of the Census, XVI, New York: John Wiley and Sons, 1958.

Grabill, Wilson H., and Lee Jay Cho. "Methodology for the Measurement of Current Fertility from Population Data on Young Children," *Demography,* 2 (1965), 50–73.

Groenman, Sjoerd. "Women's Opinion About Size of Family in the Netherlands: Attempts to Measure Desired Size of Family," *Eugenics Quarterly,* 2 (4) (December 1955), 224–228.

Hair, P. E. H. "Bridal Pregnancy in Rural England in Earlier Centuries," *Population Studies,* 20 (2) (November 1966), 233–243.

Hajnal, John. "The Study of Fertility and Reproduction: A Survey of Thirty Years," *Proceedings of the Milbank Memorial Fund* (New York, 1958), 11–37.

Hashmi, Sultan H. "Factors in Urban Fertility Differences in the United States," Ernest W. Burgess, and Donald J. Bogue (eds.), in *Contributions to Urban Sociology,* XI. Chicago: University of Chicago Press, 1964, pp. 42–58.

Hatt, Paul K. *Backgrounds of Human Fertility in Puerto Rico.* Princeton, N.J.: Princeton University Press, 1952.

Hawley, Amos H. "Rural Fertility in Central Luzon," *American Sociological Review,* 20 (1) (February 1955), 21–27.

Heer, David M., and Elsa S. Turner. "Areal Differences in Latin American Fertility," *Population Studies,* 18 (March 1965).

Heer, David M. "Economic Development and Fertility," *Demography,* 3 (2) (1966), 423–444.

Heer, David M. "Fertility Differences between Indian and Spanish-speaking Parts of Andean Countries," *Population Studies,* 18 (July 1964), 71–84.

Henin, Roushdi A. "Some Aspects of the Effects of Economic Development on Fertility in the Sudan." A paper contributed for the United Nations World Population Conference. Belgrade, 1965.

Henry, Louis. "Aspects Mathématiques de l'Étude de la Fécondité et de la Famaille" (Research on Fertility and Family: Mathematical Aspects), *Bulletin de l'Institute International de Statistique*, (Stockholm), **36** (2) (1958), 137–146.

Henry, Louis, and Roland Pressat. "Evolution de la Fécondité en Italie" (Fertility Evolution in Italy), *Population* (Paris), **10** (3) (July-September 1955), 501–528.

Henry, Louis. "Fécondité et Famille: Modèles Mathématiques (II)" (Fertility and Family: Mathematical Models (II)), *Population* (Paris, **16** (1) (January-March 1961). Also in *Population* (Paris), **16** (2) (April-June 1961), 261–282.

Henry, Louis. *Fécondité des mariages: Nouvelle méthode de mesure.* Paris: Presses Universitaires de France, 1954.

Henry, Louis. "Fécondité et Natalite en Regime Naturel" (Fertility and Natality in Natural Conditions), *Bulletin of the International Statistical Institute,* **34** (3) (1954), 11–16.

Henry, Louis. "Le Fécondité Naturelle: Observation, Théorie, Résultats" (Natural Fertility: Observation, Theory, Findings), *Population* (Paris), **16** (4) (October-December 1961), 625–636.

Henry, Louis. "Fondements Théoriques des Mesures de la Fécondité Naturelle" (Theoretical Foundations for Measures of Natural Fertility), *Review of the International Statistics Institute,* **21** (3) (1953), 135–151.

Henry, Louis. "Mesure de Temps Mort en Fécondité Naturelle" (Measurement of the Null Period in Natural Fertility), *Population* (Paris), **19** (3) (June-July 1964), 485–514.

Henton, Comradge L. "A Comparative Study of the Onset of Menarche Among Negro and White Children," *Journal of Psychology,* **46** (1958), 65–73.

Hofsten, Erland V. "Fertility for Birth Cohorts of Swedish Women 1870-71-," *Statistisk Tidskrift* (Stockholm), n.s., **4** (4) (1966), 295–309.

Horstmann, Kurt. "Schwangerschaft und Eheschliessung" (Pregnancy and Marriage), *International Union for the Scientific Study of Population.* Vienna: 1959.

Horstmann, Kurt, and F. Hage. "Age Specific or Duration Specific Marital Fertility Rates," *Proceedings of the World Population Conference: 1954,* IV. New York, 1955.

Huyck, Earl. "Differential Fertility in Ceylon," *Population Bulletin of the United Nations,* **13** (4) (December 1954), 40.

Hyrenius, H. "Fertility and Reproduction in a Swedish Population Group Without Family Limitation," *Population Studies,* **12** (2) (November 1958), 121–130.

Hyrenius, H., and Ingemar Adolfsson. "A Fertility Simulation Model." Two reports of the Demographic Institute, University of Göteburg, III.

Stockholm: Almquist and Wiksell, 1964, p. 31.

Indra, R. Raja. "Fertility Trends in Ceylon," *Proceedings of the World Population Conference: 1954.* New York, 1955.

International Sociological Association and United Nations Educational, Scientific, and Cultural Organization, "The Sociology of Human Fertility: A Trend Report and Bibliography," *Current Sociology,* **10–11** (2) (1961–1962), 35–121.

Jain, S. P. "Indian Fertility: Trends and Patterns," *Proceedings of the World Population Conference: 1954.* New York, 1955.

James, W. H. "Estimates of Fecundability," *Population Studies* (London), **17** (1) (July 1963), 57–65.

Johnson, Gwendolyn Z. "Differential Fertility in European Countries," *National Bureau of Economic Research.* Princeton, 1960, pp. 36–76.

Jurecek, Zdenek. "Female Fertility Indices in the Light of Population Census Results," *Demografie* (Prague), **8** (1) (1966), 1–16.

Karmel, P. H. "Cohort Fertility," *Milbank Memorial Fund Quarterly,* **33** (3) (July 1955), 317–322.

Kirk, Dudley. "The Influence of Business Cycles on Marriage and Birth Rates," *National Bureau of Economic Research.* Princeton, 1960, pp. 241–260.

Kiser, Clyde V. "Current Mating and Fertility Patterns and Their Demographic Significance," *Eugenics Quarterly,* **6** (2) (June 1959), 65–82.

Kiser, Clyde V. "Differential Fertility in the United States," *National Bureau of Economic Research.* Princeton: 1960, pp. 77–116.

Kiser, Clyde V. "Fertility Rates by Residence and Migration," *International Union for the Scientific Study of Population.* Vienna, 1959, pp. 273–286.

Kiser, Clyde V. "Fertility Trends and Differentials Among Nonwhites in the United States," *Milbank Memorial Fund Quarterly,* **36** (2) (April 1958), 149–197.

Kiser, Clyde V. "Fertility Trends and Differentials in the United States," *Journal of the American Statistical Association,* **47** (March 1952).

Kiser, Clyde V. "Social, Economic and Religious Factors in the Differential Fertility of Low Fertility Countries." A paper contributed for the United Nations World Population Conference, August 30-September 10, 1965.

Kiser, Clyde V., and P. K. Whelpton. "Social and Psychological Factors Affecting Fertility," *Milbank Memorial Fund Quarterly,* **36** (3) (July 1958), 282–319.

Kiser, Clyde V. "Voluntary and Involuntary Aspects of Childlessness," *The Milbank Memorial Fund Quarterly,* **17** (January 1939), 50.

Klinger, Andras. "Trends of Differential Fertility

by Social Strata in Hungary," *Proceedings of the International Population Conference: 1961,* I. London: 1963, pp. 87–96.

Korea. Institute of Population Problems. *The Fertility of Korean Women.* By Kap Suk Koh. A volume in the 1960 Census Monograph Series. Seoul, 1966.

Kuczynski, Robert R. *The Balance of Births and Deaths.* New York: The Macmillan Co., 1928–1931.

Kuroda, Toshio, "Fertility Differentials in Japan," *Proceedings of the International Population Conference: 1961,* I. London, 1963, pp. 97–195.

Kuroda, Toshio. "Migration and Fertility," *Annual Reports of the Institute of Population Problems* (Tokyo), 7 (1962).

Kuroda, Toshio. "An Analysis of the Change of Fertility in Postwar Japan." Pp. 24–40 in *Archives of the Population Association of Japan,* No. 4. English edition. Tokyo, 1963.

Lorimer, Frank, et al. "Culture and Human Fertility: A Study of the Relation of Cultural Conditions to Fertility in Non-Industrial and Transitional Societies," *Population and Culture.* Paris: International Union for the Scientific Study of Population and UNESCO, July 1954, p. 504.

Lorimer, Frank. "Notes on Human Fertility in Central Africa," *The Interrelations of Demographic, Economic and Social Problems in Selected Underdeveloped Areas.* New York: Milbank Memorial Fund, 1954.

Lunde, Anders S. "Some Problem Aspects of Differential Fertility Measurement in the United States." A paper contributed for the United Nations World Population Conference. Belgrade, 1965.

Lunde, Anders S. "White-nonwhite Fertility Differentials in the United States," *Health, Education and Welfare Indicators* (September 1965).

Madigan, Francis C., S.J., and Rosalia Avancena. "Philippine Fertility and Mortality with Special Reference to the North Mindanao Region: A Critique of Recent Estimates," *Philippine Sociological Review* (Quezon City), 12 (1-2) (January-April 1964), 35–53.

Martz, Helen E. "Illegitimacy and Dependency," *Health, Education and Welfare Indicators* (September 1963), 15–30.

Matras, Judah. "Differential Fertility, Integenerational Occupational Mobility, and Change in the Occupational Distribution: Some Elementary Interrelationships," *Population Studies,* 15 (2) (November 1961), 187–197.

McCarthy, M. D. "Irish Fertility Statistics, 1841–1046," *Proceedings of the World Population Conference: 1954,* I. New York, 1955.

McGinnis, Robert. "Similarity in Background Characteristics and Differential Fertility," *Social Forces,* 34 (1) (October 1955), 67–72.

Muhsam, H. V. "The Fertility of Polygamous Marriages," *Population Studies,* 10 (1) (July 1956), 3–16.

Muhsam, H. V., and Clyde V. Kiser. "Social and Psychological Factors Affecting Fertility," *Milbank Memorial Fund Quarterly,* 34 (3) (July 1956), 287–312.

Myers, Robert J. "The Effect of Age of Mother and Birth Order on Sex Ratio at Birth," *Milbank Memorial Fund Quarterly,* 32 (3) (July 1954), 275–281.

Nag, Moni. *Factors Affecting Human Fertility in Nonindustrial Societies: A Cross-Cultural Study.* New Haven, Conn.: Yale University Publications in Anthropology, 1962.

Norway. Statistisk Sentralbyra. *Ekteskap, fodsler og vandringer i Norge 1856-1960 (Marriages, Births and Migration in Norway 1856-1960),* by Julie E. Backer. Samfunnsøkonomiske Studier, 13. Oslo, 1965.

Okazaki, Yoichi. "Analysis of the Decline of Birth Rate in Japan," *Jinko Mondai Kenkyu (Journal of Population Problems)* (Tokyo), 89 (November 1963), 1–14.

Okun, Bernard. *Trends in Birth Rates in the United States Since 1870.* Baltimore: The Johns Hopkins Press, 1958.

Pan, Chia-Lin. "An Estimate of the Long-term Crude Birth Rate of the Agricultural Population of China," *Demography,* 3 (1) (1966), 204–208.

Pearl, Raymond. *The Natural History of Population.* London: Oxford University Press, 1939.

Potter, Robert G., et al. "A Case Study of Birth Interval Dynamics," *Population Studies,* 19 (1) (1965), 81–96.

Potter, Robert G. "Some Comments on the Evidence Pertaining to Family Limitation in the United States," *Population Studies,* 14 (1) (July 1960), 40–54.

Potter, Robert G. "Some Physical Correlates of Fertility Control in the United States," *Proceedings of the International Population Conference: 1961* I. London, 1963, pp. 106–116.

Pressat, Roland. "Tendances Récentes de la Fécondité en Europe Occidentale" (Recent Trends in Fertility in Western Europe), *Proceedings of the International Population Conference: 1961,* I. London, 1963, pp. 117–127.

Quensel, C. T. E. "The Interrelations of Marital Status, Fertility, Family Size and Intelligence Test Scores," *Population Studies,* 11 (3) (March 1958), 234–250.

Rele, J. R. "Fertility Differentials in India: Evidence From a Rural Background," *Milbank Memorial Fund Quarterly,* 41 (2) (April 1963), 183–199.

Renkonen, K. O., et al. "The Time Interval From the Wedding to the Birth of the First Child," *Annales Medicinae Experimentalis et Biologiae Fenniae* (Helsinki), **41** (1963), 560–564.

Ridley, Jeanne C. "Number of Children Expected in Relation to Non-familial Activities of the Wife," *Milbank Memorial Fund Quarterly,* **37** (3) (July 1959), 277–296.

Ridley, Jeanne C. "Recent Natality Trends in Underdeveloped Countries," in Mindel C. Sheps, and Jeanne Clare Ridley, *Public Health and Population Change.* Pittsburgh: University of Pittsburgh Press, 1965.

Rizk, Hanna. "Social and Psychological Factors Affecting Fertility in the United Arab Republic," *Marriage and Family Living,* **25** (1) (February 1963), 69–73.

Roberts, G. W., and Lloyd Braithwaite. "Fertility Differentials by Family Type in Trinidad," *Annals of the New York Academy of Sciences,* **84** (17) (December 1960), 963–980.

Roberts, G. W. "Cultural Factors in Fertility in the British Caribbean," *Proceedings of the World Population Conference: 1954,* I. New York, 1955.

Roberts, G. W. "Some Aspects of Mating and Fertility in the West Indies," *Population Studies,* **8** (3) (March 1955), 199–227.

Robinson, Warren C. "Urbanization and Fertility: The Non-Western Experience," *Milbank Memorial Fund Quarterly,* **41** (3) (July 1963), 291–308.

Rodman, Hyman. "Illegitimacy in the Caribbean Social Structure: A Reconsideration," *American Sociological Review,* **31** (5) (October 1966), 673–683.

Rosenthal, Erich. "Jewish Fertility in the United States," *American Jewish Yearbook: 1961,* **62** (10) (New York and Philadelphia, 1961), 514.

Roth, Danield B. "The Frequency of Spontaneous Abortion," *International Journal of Fertility,* **8** (1) (January-March 1963), 419, 431–34.

Ryder, Norman B. "The Conceptualization of the Transition in Fertility," *Cold Spring Harbor Symposia on Quantitative Biology,* **22** (1957), 91–96.

Ryder, Norman B. "Fertility in Developed Countries During the Twentieth Century." A paper contributed for the United Nations World Population Conference, August 30-September 10, 1965.

Ryder, Norman B. "Fertility," in Philip M. Hauser and O. D. Duncan (eds.), *The Study of Population: An Inventory and Appraisal.* Chicago: University of Chicago Press, 1959.

Ryder, Norman B. "La Mesure des Variations de la Fécondité au Cours du Temps" (The Measurement of Variations in Fertility Over Time), *Population* (Paris), **11** (1) (January-March 1956), 29–46.

Ryder, Norman B. "Problems of Trend Determination During a Transition in Fertility," *Milbank Memorial Fund Quarterly,* **34** (1) (January 1956), 5–21.

Schachter, Joseph, and Wilson H. Grabill. "Child Spacing as Measured from the Ages of Children in the Household," *Milbank Memorial Fund Quarterly,* **36** (1) (January 1958), 74–85.

Schachter, Joseph, and Mary McCarthy. "Illegitimate Births: United States 1938–57," *Vital Statistics—Special Reports,* U.S. National Office of Vital Statistics, **47** (8) (Washington, September 1960), 221–270.

Scott, Joseph W. "Sources of Social Change in Community, Family and Fertility in a Puerto Rican Town," *American Journal of Sociology,* **72** (5) (March 1967), 520–530.

Sheps, Mindel C. "Effects on Family Size and Sex Ratio of Preferences Regarding the Sex of Children," *Population Studies* (London), **17** (1) (July 1963), 66–72.

Sheps, Mindel C. "Pregnancy Wastage as a Factor in the Analysis of Fertility Data," *Demography,* **1** (1) (1964), 111–118.

Silver, Morris. "Births, Marriages, and Income Fluctuations in the United Kingdom and Japan," *Economic Development and Cultural Change,* **14** (3) (April 1966), 302–315.

Sinha, J. N. "Differential Fertility and Family Limitation in an Urban Community of Uttar Pradesh," *Population Studies,* **11** (2) (November 1957), 157–169.

Spengler, Joseph J. "Values and Fertility Analysis," *Demography,* **3** (1) (1966), 109–130.

Spiegelman, Mortimer. "Fertility and Reproduction," Chapter 9 in *Introduction to Demography.* Chicago: The Society of Actuaries, 1955.

Stycos, J. Mayone. "Culture and Differential Fertility in Peru," *Population Studies,* **16** (3) (March 1963), 257–270.

Stycos, J. Mayone. "Education and Fertility in Puerto Rico." A paper contributed to United Nations World Population Conference, August 30-September 10, 1965.

Stycos, J. Mayone. *Family and Fertility in Puerto Rico: A Study of the Lower Income Group.* XV. New York: Columbia University Press, 1955.

Stycos, J. Mayone, and Robert H. Weller. "Female Working Roles and Fertility," *Demography,* **4** (1967), 210–217.

Stycos, J. Mayone. "Needed Research on Latin American Fertility: Urbanization and Fertility." Pp. 299–315 in Clyde V. Kiser (ed.). *Components of Population Change in Latin America. Milbank Memorial Fund Quarterly,* **43** (4, Part 2) (October 1965).

Sutton, Gordon F., and Gooloo S. Wunderlich. "Estimating Marital Fertility Rates by Educational Attainment Using a Survey of New Mothers," *Demography*, 4 (1967), 135–142.

Sutter, Jean, and Francis Morin. "Attitudes Devant La Maternité: Une Enquête à Paris en Service Hospitalier" (Attitudes Toward Maternity: A Survey in Paris in Hospital Departments), *Population* (Paris), 15 (2) (April-May 1960), 223–244.

Sydenstricker, Edgar, and Frank W. Notestein. "Differential Fertility According to Social Class," *American Statistical Association Publications*, 25 (1930), 9–32.

Taeuber, Conrad, and Irene B. Taeuber. "Fertility," Chapter 14 in *The Changing Population of the United States*. New York: John Wiley and Sons, 1958.

Thompson, W. S., and P. K. Whelpton. *Population Trends in the United States*. New York: McGraw-Hill, 1933.

Thompson, Warren S. *Ratio of Children to Women: 1920*. Census Monograph XI, U.S. Bureau of the Census, Washington, 1931.

Tien, H. Yuan. "A Demographic Aspect of Interstate Variations in American Fertility: 1800-1860," *Milbank Memorial Fund Quarterly*, 37 (1) (January 1959), 49–59.

Teitze, Christopher, and Wilson H. Grabill. "Differential Fertility by Duration of Marriage," *Eugenics Quarterly*, 4 (1) (March 1957), 3–7.

Tietze, Christopher. "Impact of Age at Marriage on Various Measures of Fertility," *Proceedings of the World Population Conference: 1954*, IV. New York, 1955.

Tietze, Christopher. "Pregnancy Rates and Birth Rates," *Population Studies*, 16 (1) (July 1962), 31–37.

United Nations. "Fertility," *Population Bulletin*, Number 7. New York, 1963.

United Nations. Department of Economics and Social Affairs (Population Branch). "Recent Trends in Fertility in Industrialized Countries," *Population Studies*, No. 27, 13 (2) (New York, 1958), 182.

U.S. Bureau of Census. *1940 Census of Population: Differential Fertility, 1940 and 1910*. 1945.

U.S. Department of Health, Education, and Welfare, Public Health Service, National Center for Health Statistics. *Natality Statistics Analysis: United States: 1962*. Series 21 No. 1. Washington, 1964.

U.S. National Center for Health Statistics. Vital and Health Statistics. Series 11. *Age at Menopause, United States, 1960-62*. By Brian MacMahon and Jane Worcester, October 1966.

U.S. National Center for Health Statistics. Series 21, No. 11. Washington, 1964-. *Natality Statistics Analysis*, United States, 1964. By Arthur

A. Campbell, et al. February 1967.

Vávra, Z. "Plodnost a Živorodnost v Československu v Letech 1880-1959" (Fertility and Live Births in Czechoslovakia in the Period 1880-1959), *Demografie*, 3 (3) (Prague, 1961), 273–274.

Veilrose, Egon. "Age-Specific Fertility Rates in Poland." A paper contributed for the United Nations World Population Conference, August 30-September 10, 1965.

Vogt, Johan. "En Undersøkelse Over Generasjonenes Fruktbarhet i Norge" (A Study of Generation Fertility in Norway), *Statsøkonomisk Tidsskrift* (Oslo), 70 (3), (September 1956), 181–204.

Walle, Etienne van de. "An Approach to the Study of Fertility in Nigeria" *Population Studies*, 19 (1) (1965); 5–16.

Weintraub, Robert. "The Birth Rate and Economic Development: An Empirical Study," *Econometrica*, 15 (October 1962), 182–217.

Westoff, Charles F. "Differential Fertility Trends in the United States Since 1900," *Proceedings of the World Population Conference: 1954*, I. New York, 1955.

Westoff, Charles F. "Differential Fertility in the United States: 1900-52," *American Sociological Review*, 19 (5) (October 1954), 549–561.

Westoff, Charles F., Robert G. Potter, Jr., Philip C. Sagi, and Elliot G. Mishler. *Family Growth in Metropolitan America*. Princeton, N. J.: Princeton University Press, 1961.

Westoff, Charles F., and Raymond H. Potvin. Higher Education, Religion and Women's Family-Size Orientations," *American Sociological Review*, 31 (4) (August 1966), 489–496.

Westoff, Charles F., Robert G. Potter, and Philip Sagi. "Some Selected Findings of the Princeton Fertility Study: 1963," *Demography*, 1 (1), 130–135.

Westoff, Charles F., et al. "Preferences in Size of Family and Eventual Fertility Twenty Years After," *American Journal of Sociology*, 62 (5) (March 1957), 491–497.

Westoff, Charles F., Robert G. Potter, Jr., and Philip C. Sagi. *The Third Child*. Princeton, N. J.: Princeton University Press, 1963.

Westoff, Charles F., and Raymond H. Potvin. *College Women and Fertility Values*. Princeton, N. J.: Princeton University Press, 1967.

Whelpton, Pascal K. *Cohort Fertility: Native White Women in the United States*. Princeton, N. J.: Princeton University Press, 1954.

Whelpton, P. K., Arthur A. Campbell, and John E. Patterson. *Fertility and Family Planning in The United States*. Princeton, N. J.: Princeton University Press, 1966.

Whelpton, P. K., and Arthur A. Campbell. "Fertility Tables for Birth Cohorts of American

Women, Part 1," National Office of Vital Statistics, *Vital Statistics—Special Reports,* **51** (1) (January 1960).

Whelpton, P. K., and Clyde V. Kiser (eds.). "Social and Psychological Factors Affecting Fertility," *Milbank Memorial Fund Quarterly,* 5 volumes (New York, 1946, 1950, 1952, 1954, and 1958).

Whelpton, P. K. "Trends and Differentials in the Spacing of Births," *Demography,* **1** (1) (1964), 83–93.

Wicksell, S. D. "Nuptiality, Fertility and Reproductivity," *Skandinavisk Aktuarietidskrift,* 1931.

Yaukey, David. *Fertility Differences in a Modernizing Country: A Survey of Lebanese Couples.* Princeton, N. J.: Princeton University Press, 1961.

Zarate, Alvan O. "Fertility in Urban Areas of Mexico: Implications for the Theory of the Demographic Transition," *Demography,* **4** (1967), 363–374.

Zia-Ud-Din, Mohammed. "Relation Between Fertility and Economic Conditions in the Punjam Province, Pakistan," *Proceedings of the World Population Conference: 1954,* I. New York, 1955.

Zikry, Abdel-Khalik M. "Fertility Differentials of the U.A.R. Women." A paper contributed for the United Nations World Population Conference, August 30-September 10, 1965.

Zimmer, Basil, and Calvin Goldscheider. "A Further Look at Catholic Fertility," *Demography,* 3 (2) (1966), 462–469.

CHAPTER 19

Migration:

Internal and International

19.1. The Movement of Population and Its Significance

A population may gain in size by experiencing an influx of migrants and it may diminish in size by an exodus of some of its members to join another population. If this in-migration or out-migration is selective of people with particular demographic, social, or economic characteristics, it will affect not only the size but also the composition of the population. Thus the movement of people from one residence to another is a component of population growth and change in composition, and the study of residential mobility is one of the major branches of demography.

Some of the most acute social problems of the world today are associated with migration. If the problem of human fertility were not so critical at the present time, it is almost certain that human migration and the plight of migrants (especially in the developing nations) would be listed as a top-priority problem for research and action.

Residential mobility is defined as any change of usual residence that involves movement from one structure (house, apartment, hotel, barracks, dormitory, etc.) to another. Demographers classify this mobility into two classes:

1. *Local movement*—change of residence within the same community.

2. *Migration*—change of residence involving movement between communities.

Local movement is a component of growth for *parts* of a community, such as census tracts or the townships of a county. However, the study of differential population changes among the parts of a community is a rather specialized aspect of "microdemography" that is usually of primary interest to human ecology rather than to demography. Migration, on the other hand, is a component of growth of whole communities, regions, and nations; it is of central interest to demographers.

The phenomenon of movement from one community to another has the effect of decreasing the population in the community of origin and increasing the population in the community of destination. It has, therefore, a double-barreled effect on population distribution, as well as on interarea differences in rates of population growth.

It is conventional to divide the field of migration study into two parts:

1. *Internal migration,* or the migration of persons *within* a nation.

2. *International migration,* or the movement of people *between* nations.

That practice is followed in this chapter; a section is devoted to each. Throughout most of the world, international migration now plays only a modest role as a component of growth of nations and there is comparatively little redistribution of population between nations. The opposite is true of internal migration. It is the most important single factor that explains why some communities grow faster than others. Differences in birthrates and death rates between communities of the same nation often are rather small in comparison with differences between communities in migration rates. As a result, the principal mechanism for redistributing the population within a nation is internal migration. Not infrequently, migration can cause a population to redistribute itself by a pattern opposite to that resulting from the balance of birth and deaths. For example, in urban places birthrates tend to be low, while in rural areas they are higher, with death rates being approximately equal in rural and urban areas. As a result, urban places tend to grow more slowly from reproductive change than do rural areas. Yet in actual fact they are growing much more rapidly than rural areas. In the case of urbanization, therefore, migration not only accounts for all the shift of persons from rural to urban areas (and for above-average rates of urban growth) but also offsets a counter-effect toward ruralization created by lower urban fertility.

As will be shown later, migration tends to be selective of persons with particular characteristics (the young, the better educated, the unmarried, etc.). Selective migration, therefore, helps to determine the spatial pattern of differences between communities in population composition and in the change in population composition that communities undergo.

Migration as an Adjustment to Economic and Social Change. Births and deaths are phenomena that involve physiologic as well as socioeconomic processes. This leads, as we have seen, to a certain uniformity over time. Reproductive change tends to be gradual and orderly as a result. Migration, however, has no physiological component; it is a response of human organisms to economic, social, and demographic forces in the environment. The action of human beings, it has been said, is motivated by the desire to satisfy needs or to avoid discomfort or pain. Moreover, it is said that the human organism tends to remain at rest until impelled to action by some unsatisfied need or by the threat of discomfort. Such a theory certainly appears plausible as an explanation of migration. A person tends to remain in the same community so long as his needs are satisfied and he is adjusted. In fact, there tends to be an identification of the self with the locale in which one has resided for a prolonged time, and some emotional strain is involved in separating oneself from this locale and from family, friends, and colleagues

for a strange new environment. Migration research begins, therefore, with the premise that every departure for a new community (migratory movement) is either a response to some impelling need that the person believes he cannot satisfy in his present residence or a flight from a situation that for some reason has become undesirable, unpleasant, or intolerable.

There is a positive and a negative aspect to the migration-provoking situation. Migration may occur as a search for an opportunity to improve one's lot in life. In this case the community of destination exerts a "pull" on the migrant. Migration can also occur as a flight from undesired social or economic situations. These situations constitute an expulsive "push" by the community. This "push-pull" theory is an abstraction which is made in order to classify the specific forces at work. In each case of migration, several variables of both types may be operating and interacting, so that the move cannot be attributed wholly either to "push" or to "pull" factors alone. Moreover, the particular "mix" of push and pull factors that leads to migration in one person may be very different from that which leads to the migration of another. By examining data for large numbers of persons, the common stimulants to movement may be established.

A corollary of this set of premises is that whenever we observe population flowing out of one particular area into others, we should suspect that some major economic or social change is taking place and that people are making an adjustment to it. Examples of such changes are:

A. *"Push" factors:*

1. *Decline in a national resource* or in the prices paid for it; decreased demand for a particular product or the services of a particular industry; exhaustion of mines, timber, or agricultural resources.

2. *Loss of employment* resulting from being discharged for incompetence, from a decline in need for a particular activity, or from mechanization or automation of tasks previously performed by more labor-intensive procedures.

3. *Oppressive or repressive discriminatory*

treatment because of political, religious, or ethnic origins or membership.

4. *Alienation* from a community because one no longer subscribes to prevailing beliefs, customs, or mode of behavior—either within one's family or within the community.

5. *Retreat* from a community because it offers few or no opportunities for personal development: employment or marriage.

6. *Retreat* from a community because of catastrophe—flood, fire, drought, earthquake, or epidemic.

B. "Pull" factors:

1. *Superior opportunities for employment* in one's occupation or opportunities to enter a preferred occupation.

2. *Opportunities to earn a larger income.*

3. *Opportunities to obtain desired specialized education or training,* such as a college education.

4. *Preferable environment and living conditions*—climate, housing, schools, other community facilities.

5. *Dependency*—movement of other persons to whom one is related or betrothed, such as the movement of dependents with a breadwinner or migration of a bride to join her husband.

6. *Lure of new or different activities, environments, or people,* such as the cultural, intellectual, or recreational activities of a large metropolis for rural and small-town residents.

Some of these forces represent impersonal conditions in the environment, while others represent the mental states of individuals. Ultimately, all migration (if it is voluntary) results from a subjective response to two subjectively perceived and subjectively interpreted socio-economic environments—the one presently occupied and another one that is a possible alternative. This is not equivalent to saying that a migrant always knows "why" he is moving. The reasons for moving given by migrants are their personal reactions to what may be fundamental changes in the environment, which they may not understand or correctly interpret.

There are situations in which a migration flow from one area to another persists for many years because of a prolonged disequilibrium of

a particular type. The flow of migrants from the South to the North and from the East to the West in the United States and that from Southern Europe and Eastern Europe to Northwestern Europe are examples of this. We assume that migration will continue to flow in a particular way as long as the disequilibrium exists and will cease when it disappears.

It is incorrect to assume that wherever the flow of migration is zero or small all of the needs of the population are being met and that there are equally satisfactory conditions in all communities. A variety of forces can operate to suppress migration, even in the face of very high levels of unrest and discontent. Migration requires a practicable alternative. Many illiterate villagers in India, Pakistan, Ceylon, Malaya, and other countres of Asia and in many parts of Latin America and Africa find themselves unable to escape from a very uncomfortable setting that threatens them with starvation, because they lack skills and opportunities for other employment in another setting. This is why neither the "push" nor the "pull" factors alone are able to account for the migration that actually takes place.

Intervening Factors. It is incorrect to assume that the flow of migration between places is a simple calculus of the comparative advantages and disadvantages of the place of origin and potential places of destination alone. As Everett S. Lee has emphasized, there are *intervening obstacles* to migration.[1] He states:

"Between every two points there stands a set of intervening obstacles which may be slight in some instances and insurmountable in others. The most studied of these obstacles is distance, which, while omni-present, is by no means the most important. Actual physical barriers like the Berlin Wall may be interposed, or immigration laws may restrict the movement. Different people are, of course, affected in different ways by the same set of obstacles. What may be trivial to some people—the cost of transporting household goods, for example—may be prohibitive to others. The effect of a given set of obstacles depends also upon the

[1] Everett S. Lee, "A Theory of Migration," *Demography,* 3 (1966), 47–57.

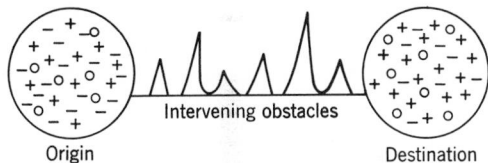

Figure 19-1 Origin and Destination Factors and Intervening Obstacles in Migration: The "Push-Pull-Obstacles" model.

SOURCE: Everett S. Lee, "A Theory of Migration," *Demography,* **3** (1966), 48.

impedimenta with which the migrant is encumbered. For some migrants these are relatively unimportant and the difficulty of surmounting the intervening obstacles is consequently minimal; but for others, making the same move, the impediment, among which we must reckon children and other dependents, greatly increase the difficulties posed by intervening obstacles."

Lee diagrammed his view of the migration context as shown in Figure 19-1. At both the origin and the destination there are positive and negative factors (the zeros inside the circles indicate factors of no consequence, to which the potential migrant is indifferent). He sees the set of pluses and minuses differently defined for every migrant or prospective migrant.

This hypothesis of obstacles has long been recognized, but has been expressed less directly. Zipf defined the obstacles as a simple inverse function of distance[2] and proposed that the attractiveness of two places for the flow of population between them be expressed by the equation

$$\text{attraction} = \frac{P_o P_d}{D}$$

where

P_o = population at the place of origin,
P_d = population at the place of destination, and D is the distance separating origin and destination.

[2] George K. Zipf, "The P_1P_2/D Hypothesis: in the Intercity Movement of Persons, *American Sociological Review,* **11** (1946), 677–686.

Stouffer viewed the problem of obstacles in a positive, rather than negative, way and formulated the hypothesis of *intervening opportunities.* According to this hypothesis, the flow of migrants between two places is inversely related to the number of opportunities for the migrants to satisfy their needs (employment, housing, etc.) that intervene between them.[3] Underlying this theory is the premise that migration is costly and that the mobile person will cease moving as soon as he encounters an appropriate opportunity.

Thus Lee's formulation and diagram summarize nicely the migration "model" that has guided researchers for many years: migration is a resultant of "pushes" and "pulls" or "attractions" and "repulsions" at both origin and destination, balanced in the context of the relative effort or cost of overcoming the obstacles that lie between the individual and potential alternative sites, on the presumption that the individual will try to minimize these costs, whatever they are and however they are measured.

There is also another, and much older, model in the study of migration, which attempts to formulate generalizations that describe the movement of people at all times and at all places. Whereas the "push-pull-obstacles" model is highly situation-oriented, this model undertakes to develop "principles" that are either independent of situations or cover all of them. This tradition dates back to E. G. Ravenstein who, in 1885, published an article "The Laws of Migration."[4] Ravenstein arrived at seven such "laws" or "generalizations" on the basis of the study of data for England and several other nations:[5]

1. *Migration and distance*—most migrants go

[3] Samuel A. Stouffer, "Intervening Opportunities: A Theory Relating Mobility and Distance," and "Intervening Opportunities and Competing Migrants," reprinted in his *Research to Test Ideas* (Chicago: University of Chicago Press, 1963).

[4] E. G. Ravenstein, "The Laws of Migration," *Journal of the Royal Statistical Society,* **48** (Part 2) (June 1885), 167–277, and "The Laws of Migration," *Journal of the Royal Statistical Society,* **52** (June 1889), 241–301.

[5] The seven points listed here follow the exposition of Everett S. Lee, *op. cit.*

only a short distance. As the distance from a certain place increases, there are fewer migrants who have moved from that place.

2. *Migration by stages*—persons living near large cities migrate when economic expansion occurs. The opportunities they forsake at home are filled up by migrants from more remote points in the hinterland. As a result, the expansion of the city exerts an impact, step by step, that reaches to the outer limits of the hinterland.

3. *Streams and counterstreams*—to every stream of migration there is a counterstream.

4. *Urban-rural differences in propensity to migrate*—urban populations are less migratory than are rural populations.

5. *Predominance of females among short-distance migrants*—in short-distance migrations, females tend to outnumber males.

6. *Technology and migration*—technological development tends to promote greater rates of migration.

7. *Dominance of the economic motive*—Although a variety of forces can produce migration, the desire of the masses to improve their economic condition is by far the most potent force.

As a comparison of the materials to be presented later in this chapter will demonstrate, there is still a surprising amount of validity in these statements after more than 80 years. However, they are not inflexible "laws" without exceptions, and to explain the exceptions it is necessary to import the situational model. Several years ago an important study that was undertaken from this viewpoint concluded that despite voluminous research, almost no generalizations of this type could be supported by empirical evidence.[6] As is true for most of social science, migration research findings are not timeless.

I. INTERNAL MIGRATION

19.2. Basic Concepts and Operational Definitions

Migration researchers have gradually built up a standard set of concepts, which are defined in

[6] Dorothy S. Thomas, *Research Memorandum on Migration Differentials*, Bulletin 43 (New York: Social Science Research Council, 1938).

terms that facilitate the collection of data and the testing of hypotheses. Acquiring this vocabulary with its underlying viewpoint is a prerequisite to a systematic review of migration principles.

Migration-Defining Boundaries. In most nations the boundaries of individual communities are not delimited or else are delimited very imprecisely. Only rarely are the legal boundaries coterminous with the functional boundaries. Suburbanization, the scattered residential pattern of rural population, and the tendency to use the automobile to patronize a variety of different service centers make it difficult to determine exactly where the boundaries of a particular community lie. Even if they could be delimited precisely, these boundaries could not be reflected in the data available for the study of migration. For this reason, the definition of migration as intercommunity movement cannot be employed with precise community boundaries. Instead, some existing set of well-established and universally familiar boundaries must be used as an approximation. Units of area that correspond most nearly to the average size of a community are the most desirable. Counties, communes, municipios, and similar areas most nearly match the definition and are practicable. In the United States, for example, it is customary to define migration as intercounty mobility. Any change of residence across a county line therefore constitutes migration, even though it may be only a move across a county-line road or street. In some instances, major cities have been declared to be "quasi-counties," hence movement across their boundaries has also been defined as migration. These conventions are not ideal, but they permit the researcher to do research instead of merely speculate. Frequent use is made of the boundaries of much larger units of area to define migration, such as the boundaries of states or regions. Then the focus of attention no longer is movement from the local community setting, but the longer-distance exchange of persons between major population masses.

It is evident that the number and proportion of persons who are declared to be migrants will be influenced by the size and shape of the areas employed. The larger the average size of

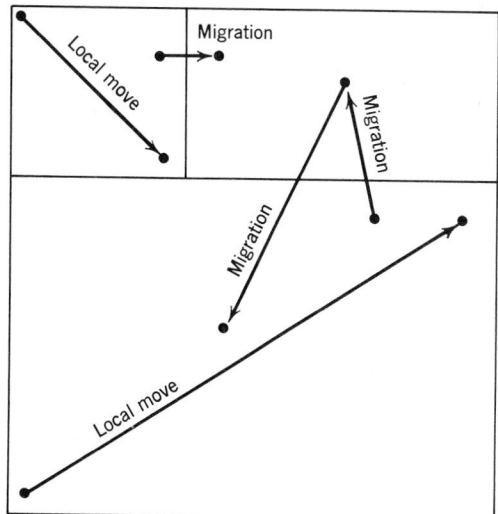

Figure 19-2 The Size and Shape of Migration-Defining Areas and the Distribution of Population within Them Affect Directly the Proportion of Residentially Mobile Persons That Are Classified as Migrants.

the area, the fewer movers who will be defined as migrants (see Figure 19-2). The following summary of mobility from the 1960 U.S. Census illustrates this point:

	Number (000)	Percent of all mobile persons
Total residentially mobile persons	75,186	100.0
Within-county mobility (local movers)	47,387	63.0
Between-county mobility (migration)	27,799	37.0
Between-state migration	14,141	18.8
Between-region migration	7,724	10.3

When states are used as migration-defining areas, the number of migrants is reduced by one-half. When four regions are used instead of states, the number is reduced by nearly one-half again.

The distribution of the population within the parcels also affects migration. Where the population is concentrated near the migration-defining boundary, migration rates will tend to be high and rates of local movement will tend to be low. Conversely, where the population is concentrated near the geographic center of the area, migration rates will tend to be low and rates of local movement high.

The Migration Interval. Migration is an event that occurs in time. It is necessary to specify the interval of time over which migra-

tion is to be observed. Intervals of one, five, or ten years have been used. The larger the length of the interval, the smaller the size of the average annual number of migrants, because a significant proportion of persons who migrate return rather promptly to the place from which they started. Two or more sets of migration statistics that have been collected for unequal intervals of time are therefore not fully comparable, even though they have been reduced to an average annual basis.

Migration Streams. Migrants who depart from a common area of origin and arrive at a common area of destination during a particular migration interval constitute a "migration stream."

Area of Origin and Area of Destination. The area from which a migrant departs is termed the "area of origin." The area at which he arrives is termed the "area of destination."

In-Migration and Out-Migration. Each change of residence involves two events: a departure and an arrival. Departure from the community of origin is termed "out-migration." Arrival at the community of destination is termed "in-migration." (The corresponding terms for international migration are "emigration" and "immigration"; see part II of this chapter.)

Net Migration. Any particular area may simultaneously be receiving migrants from some areas and losing migrants to other areas. The net balance between arrivals and departures is termed "net migration." Net migration is considered to be negative if departures exceed arrivals.

Gross Migration. The sum of the arrivals and departures is "gross migration." It is a measure of the total volume of population turnover that a community is experiencing.

Migration Rates. Migration rates state the relative frequency with which the event of migration occurs. It is a probability number. It is the number of migratory events divided by the population exposed to the possibility of migration. We may define four such rates:

Out-migration rate: $\dfrac{O}{P} \times k$ (1)

In-migration rate: $\dfrac{I}{P} \times k$ (2)

Net-migration rate: $\dfrac{I - O}{P} \times k$ (3)

Gross-migration rate: $\dfrac{I + O}{P} \times k$ (4)

where O is the number of out-migrants from an area, I is the number of in-migrants to an area, P is the average or midinterval population of the area, and k is a constant, usually 100 or 1000.

With reference to population growth, in-migration rate is analogous to the birthrate and out-migration rate is analogous to the death rate. The rate of net migration is analogous to the rate of reproductive change ("natural increase").

All of these migration rates may be computed as "specific" rates—where both the numerator and the denominator refer to the same particular subgroup of the population. Thus there may be rates that are specific for sex, age, marital status, educational attainment, occupation, income, and so on.

Differential Migration. The study of differences in the rate of migration between various demographic, economic, and social groups of the population is termed "differential migration." The term is also applied to the study of differences in population composition between migration streams. Thus the study of differential migration is equivalent to the study of *migration selectivity*—the tendency for persons with particular traits or residency in particular environments to be more migratory than is the general population.

19.3. Procedures for Obtaining Migration Data

There are two procedures for obtaining migration data: *direct* methods and *indirect* methods. To obtain migration data by the direct method, it is necessary to get a count of per-

sons who change their residence across migration-defining boundaries within a particular migration interval. If there is a system of national registration whereby each person who makes a change of parish, commune, municipality, or county of residency is required to report the fact to a municipal office or to the police, direct migration data can be derived by tabulating the data for those who have reported themselves as migrants. The Scandinavian nations, for example, have excellent migration data of this type. Most nations, however, lack a national system for registering changes of residence. Data that measure migration directly may be obtained at the time of the national census by inserting a question, "Where was this person living x years ago?" By comparing the place of enumeration with the place of residence x years ago, it is possible to identify the persons who have been residentially mobile and those who have been migratory. If it is assumed that each migrant moved directly to his present residence from his residence x years ago, it is possible to tabulate streams of in- and out-migration for particular places. The method has limitations: it relies on the memory of respondents and it fails to identify migrants who have returned to their place of origin. Measurement can be made only once each decade, at the time of the census. This approach to migration measurement can be made between censuses by means of sample surveys, but such surveys usually do not provide enough cases for extensive tabulations of migration streams and the characteristics of migrants. Nevertheless, this is a most valuable technique, and much of what is now known about modern internal migration is derived from census data of this type. The census schedule provides a full range of characteristics of persons who are identified as migrants, so that highly detailed studies of differential migration are possible. By cross-classifying area of origin with area of destination, quite detailed studies of the flow of migration streams between regions, states, and urban-rural residence are possible.

There are three *indirect* methods of measuring internal migration: the "vital statistics" method, the "survival ratio" method, and the "place of birth" method. A brief description of each is presented here. For full details see the *Manual of Demographic Research Techniques.*

The Vital Statistics Method. Where reliable statistics of birth and death are available, it is possible to use the data for two successive censuses to estimate net migration. This is done by using the "bookkeeping equation," introduced in Chapter 2:

$$P_t = P_o + B - D + M, \qquad (5)$$

where P_t is the population at the end of an intercensal period (last census), P_o is the population at the beginning of an intercensal period (previous census), B is the number of births during the intercensal period, D is the number of deaths during the intercensal period, and M is the net migration during the intercensal period. For purposes of estimating net migration, this equation is rearranged as follows:

$$M = (P_t - P_o) - (B - D).$$

In other words, net migration is obtained by subtracting reproductive population change from total change.

The Survival Ratio Method. This method estimates how many people from a preceding census would be alive and living in the same place at the time of the next census if there were no migration. It subtracts this expected number of survivors from the actual census count at the second census, and the difference is accepted as an estimate of the net number of migrants. The estimate of survivors is obtained by multiplying each age group of the original census by a "survival ratio," which estimates the proportion of persons of that age who will survive to be counted at the next census:

$$M_i = P_t - P_o s, \qquad (6)$$

where P_t and P_o are as defined above, except that they refer to age groups, and s is an estimate of the proportion of the age group who will survive from one census to another. In this estimate allowance must be made for the

fact that the survivors grow older during the intercensal period and at the second census are counted in different age groups than at the first census.

Place of Birth Statistics. Almost all censuses of the world record the state, province, or commune of birth. By comparing the place of birth with the residence of the person at the time of enumeration, it is possible to separate the population into migrants and nonmigrants. This method usually is confined to large units of area. It cannot be determined exactly when the migration took place. Return migration to the place of birth is not detected. Despite these shortcomings, place of birth statistics can provide useful indications of the direction of migration flows and in many nations are the only source of migration information. They can be tabulated in such a way as to provide data for migration streams as well as for differential migration.

The indirect measures of migration are invaluable, even where direct data are available. For example, estimates of net migration obtained by the vital statistics method probably are fully as accurate, if not more so, than estimates of net migration tabulated from a migration registration system, and they are almost certainly more accurate than estimates of net migration obtained from a census tabulation of residence x years ago.

Perhaps more than any other branch of demography, the study of internal migration is provincial or national in its outlook. It does have its international aspects, but these perhaps are best considered after an intensive study of internal migration in one country. For this reason, this chapter reverses the order of presentation of other chapters, and considers the United States national scene before discussing international migration.

19.4.   Recent Internal Migration in the United States

The 1960 census of the United States contained an inquiry concerning the place of residence five years earlier—April 1, 1955. Table 19-1 summarizes the mobility data derived from the responses to this question. Almost exactly one half of the population (50.1 percent) had

Table 19·1   Mobility Status of the United States Population 5 Years Old and Over, by Sex, Urban and Rural Residence: 1960

Type of residence and sex	Total population 5 years old and over	Same house (non-movers)	Different house in U.S. (movers)								Abroad in 1955	Moved, place of residence in 1955 not reported
			Total	Same county	Different county (migrants)						
					Total	Same state	Different state				
							Total	Contiguous	Non-contiguous		
					Number of persons (thousands)						
Total.........	159,004	79,331	75,186	47,387	27,799	13,657	14,141	4,849	9,293	2,003	2,484
Male...........	77,964	38,293	37,079	22,967	14,113	6,742	7,371	2,428	4,943	1,151	1,440
Female.........	81,040	41,038	38,106	24,420	13,686	6,915	6,771	2,421	4,350	852	1,044
Urban.........	111,222	53,316	54,333	34,715	19,618	9,124	10,493	3,439	7,054	1,630	1,943
Male...........	53,571	25,228	26,345	16,606	9,739	4,423	5,316	1,687	3,628	906	1,092
Female.........	57,650	28,088	27,987	18,108	9,879	4,701	5,178	1,752	3,426	725	851
Rural nonfarm	35,640	17,367	17,458	10,341	7,117	3,813	3,304	1,227	2,077	332	484
Male...........	18,087	8,571	8,994	5,162	3,832	1,956	1,876	674	1,229	214	309
Female.........	17,554	8,796	8,464	5,179	3,285	1,857	1,427	580	847	119	175
Rural farm	12,142	8,649	3,395	2,331	1,064	720	322	182	162	040	058
Male...........	6,306	4,495	1,740	1,198	542	363	179	093	086	031	039
Female.........	5,836	4,154	1,655	1,133	523	357	165	089	077	009	018
					Males per 100 females						
Total.........	96.2	93.3	97.3	94.0	103.1	97.5	108.9	100.3	113.6	135.1	138.0
Urban.........	92.9	89.8	94.1	91.7	98.6	94.1	102.7	96.3	105.9	125.0	128.4
Rural nonfarm...	103.0	97.4	106.3	99.7	116.7	105.3	131.4	111.6	145.0	180.0	176.4
Rural farm......	108.1	108.2	105.1	105.8	103.7	101.5	108.2	105.2	111.7	363.4	215.4
					Percent distribution						
Total.........	100.0	49.9	47.3	29.8	17.5	8.6	8.9	3.0	5.8	1.3	1.6
Male...........	100.0	49.1	47.6	29.5	18.1	8.6	9.5	3.1	6.3	1.5	1.8
Female.........	100.0	50.6	47.0	30.1	16.9	8.5	8.4	3.0	5.4	1.1	1.3
Urban.........	100.0	47.9	48.9	31.2	17.6	8.2	9.4	3.1	6.3	1.5	1.7
Male...........	100.0	47.1	49.2	31.0	18.2	8.3	9.9	3.1	6.8	1.7	2.0
Female.........	100.0	48.7	48.5	31.4	17.1	8.2	9.0	3.0	5.9	1.3	1.5
Rural nonfarm.	100.0	48.7	49.0	29.0	20.0	10.7	9.3	3.4	5.8	1.9	1.4
Male...........	100.0	47.4	49.7	28.5	21.2	10.8	10.4	3.6	6.8	1.2	1.7
Female.........	100.0	50.1	48.2	29.5	18.7	10.6	8.1	3.3	4.8	.7	1.0
Rural farm....	100.0	71.2	28.0	19.2	8.8	5.9	2.8	1.5	1.3	.3	.5
Male...........	100.0	71.3	27.6	19.0	8.6	5.8	2.8	1.5	1.4	.5	.6
Female.........	100.0	71.2	28.4	19.4	9.0	6.1	2.8	1.5	1.3	.1	.3

Source: U.S. Census of Population: 1960. Mobility for States and State Economic Areas, Table 1.

changed residence during the five years. Thus a total of 79.7 million persons moved from one dwelling to another between 1955 and 1960. The number of moves was even larger, for many of these persons moved several times.

However, nearly two thirds of this residential mobility was local movement (movement within the same county). Nevertheless, a very substantial share of the population was migratory —17.5 percent, or 27.8 million persons, were classified as migrants because they crossed a county boundary in the process of moving. About one half of these migrants relocated themselves within the same state, and the other one half moved between states. Of the between-states migration, about one third was between contiguous states and two thirds between noncontiguous states. Only 1.3 percent of the population reported itself as having lived outside the United States in 1955.

Table 19-1 portrays the United States population as one that is residentially very mobile and prone to migrate freely from one part of

the nation to another. In addition, this table establishes two basic differentials:

Sex. Males and females are equally residentially mobile, but males appear to be slightly more migratory than females and to be more inclined to migrate over long distances (between noncontiguous states). These differences are small, however. The second panel of Table 19-1 presents sex ratios that reveal the sex differences clearly.

Residence. Urban and rural-nonfarm populations both are more mobile than rural-farm population.

Annual Mobility Rates. It must be kept in mind that Table 19-1 represents mobility over a five-year interval. To have annual mobility rates, it is necessary to collect data for a one-year interval. Luckily, the U. S. Bureau of Census conducts an annual survey of migration, with a one-year interval, as part of its famous Current Population Survey. Table 19-2 presents data for mobility between March 1964 and March 1965. The tremendous effect of re-

Table 19-2 Differential Mobility of the United States Population by Sex, Age and Color, Single-Year Interval: 1964 to 1965

Characteristics	Total mobility			Migration			Local movement		
	Both sexes	Male	Female	Both sexes	Male	Female	Both sexes	Male	Female
Total..........	20.1	20.4	19.9	6.8	7.0	6.6	13.4	13.4	13.3
White..........	19.5	19.7	19.2	7.1	7.3	6.9	12.4	12.5	12.3
Negro..........	25.4	25.6	25.2	4.2	4.4	4.0	21.2	21.2	21.2
Other races.......	24.6	23.2	26.0	8.1	7.3	8.8	16.5	15.9	17.2
Age............	20.1	20.4	19.9	6.8	7.0	6.6	13.4	13.4	13.3
1 to 4 years......	30.7	31.0	30.5	11.3	11.2	11.4	19.4	19.8	19.0
5 and 6 years.....	23.1	23.3	22.9	8.1	8.0	8.1	15.1	15.3	14.8
7 to 13 years.....	18.0	17.8	18.2	5.8	5.8	5.8	12.2	12.0	12.5
14 to 17 years....	15.1	14.3	15.8	4.4	4.3	4.4	10.7	10.0	11.4
18 to 19 years....	27.2	21.6	32.2	9.9	8.1	11.6	17.3	13.5	20.6
20 to 21 years....	42.7	38.2	46.8	14.2	13.6	14.8	28.5	24.6	32.0
22 to 24 years....	46.7	48.6	45.0	17.8	18.3	17.3	28.9	30.3	27.7
25 to 29 years....	35.8	39.1	32.7	13.1	13.9	12.3	22.7	25.2	20.3
30 to 34 years....	24.3	26.8	21.9	8.8	10.0	7.6	15.5	16.8	14.2
35 to 44 years....	15.9	16.8	15.1	4.8	5.3	4.4	11.1	11.5	10.7
45 to 64 years....	11.0	11.3	10.7	3.2	3.5	3.0	7.8	7.8	7.7
65 to 74 years....	9.7	8.9	10.3	3.0	2.7	3.2	6.7	6.1	7.1
75 years and over.	9.8	8.9	10.5	2.6	2.5	2.6	7.2	6.3	7.8
Median age.......	22.9	23.1	22.7	22.6	22.9	22.3	23.1	23.3	22.9

Source: Current Population Reports: Population Characteristics, Series P-20, No. 150, U.S. Bureau of Census, "Mobility of the Population of the United States, March 1964 to March, 1965", Tables 1 and 4.

peated mobility is immediately apparent by comparing Tables 19-1 and 19-2. If there were no duplication of mobility, the rates of Table 19-1 would be roughly five times those of Table 19-2, assuming the same level of mobility throughout.

Table 19-2 informs us that one person in five changed residence during 1964-1965. Figure 19-3, which summarizes the results of annual surveys since 1948, assures us that this has been the normal situation for 17 successive surveys. If there were no duplication of mobility, within five years 100 percent of the population would change residence. Instead, only one half this proportion was residentially mobile, as reported in the 1960 census. Thus, fully one half

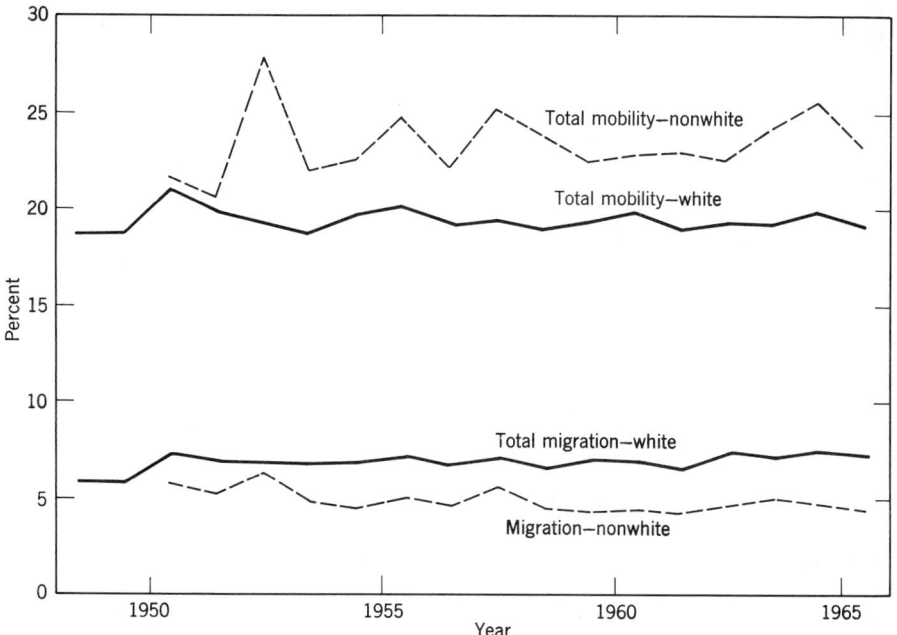

Figure 19-3 Trend in Mobility Rates in the United States, by Color: 1948 to 1966.

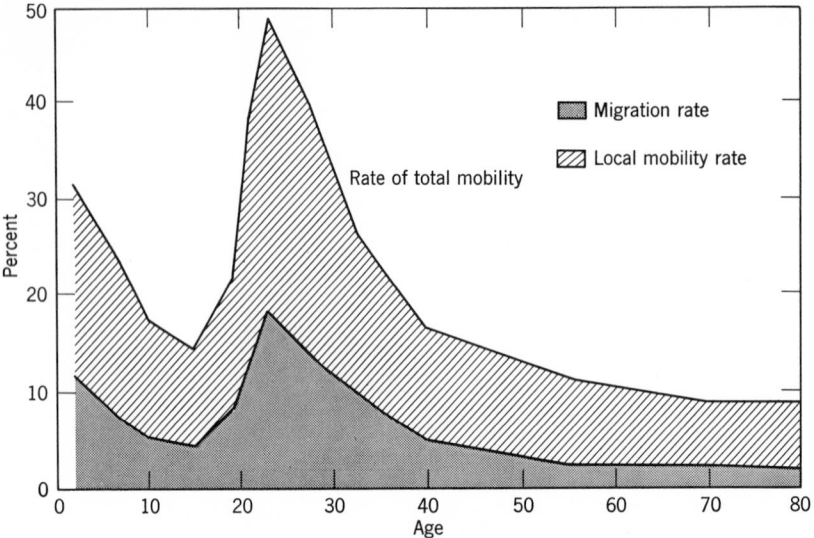

Figure 19-4   Age Pattern of Mobility, United States: 1964 to 1965.

of the residential mobility that took place between 1955 and 1960 was additional moves by persons who had already moved once during the interval.

Continuing this comparison for migration, we see that 6.8 percent of the population (1 person in 16) migrates each year and that this condition has been normal for the 17 successive

surveys. Yet the migration reported in Table 19-1 is not $5 \times 6.8 = 34$ percent, but only 17.5 percent, or one-half as much. A similar comparison for local movement (changing house within same county) produces a similar finding, except that multiple moving appears to be even more common than multiple migration.

Thus we see that the United States popula-

Table 19-3   Migration Rates of the United States Population, by Sex, Color, and Age: 1955 to 1960

Age	Total	Sex		Color	
		Male	Female	White	Nonwhite
Total, all ages.	17.5	18.1	16.9	18.3	10.8
0 – 9............	19.7	19.8	19.6	21.3	10.0
10 – 14...........	15.3	15.3	15.2	16.3	8.4
15 – 19...........	19.7	20.1	19.3	20.7	12.8
20 – 24...........	34.9	35.4	34.4	36.4	23.8
25 – 29...........	31.2	32.3	30.0	32.9	17.7
30 – 34...........	23.3	25.1	21.7	24.6	13.3
35 – 39...........	18.4	19.7	17.1	19.3	10.3
40 – 44...........	14.3	15.5	13.1	15.0	8.2
45 – 49...........	11.5	12.3	10.8	12.0	7.0
50 – 54...........	10.1	10.5	9.7	10.5	6.2
55 – 59...........	9.1	9.1	9.0	9.5	5.5
60 – 64...........	8.6	8.3	8.9	9.0	5.0
65 – 69...........	9.2	9.3	9.0	9.6	4.8
70 – 74...........	8.5	8.4	8.5	8.7	4.9
75 years over.....		8.0	8.9	8.3	5.3
Median age........	26.8	26.9	26.8	27.0	24.7

Source: U.S. Census of Population: 1960. Detailed Characteristics, Table 164.

Table 19-4 Region of Residence in 1960 of Migrants by Region of Residence in 1955, by Color (Thousands)

Region of residence in 1960	U.S. Total	Region of residence in 1955			
		North-east	North Central	South	West
TOTAL...............	27,799	5,853	7,767	9,244	4,935
Northeast............	5,214	4,170	314	569	161
North Central........	6,924	354	5,222	967	382
South................	9,299	883	1,089	6,809	519
West.................	6,361	447	1,142	899	3,874
WHITE...............	25,915	5,585	7,523	8,080	4,726
Northeast............	4,851	3,980	298	419	154
North Central........	6,610	340	5,088	816	367
South................	8,414	835	1,038	6,047	494
West.................	6,040	431	1,100	798	3,711
NONWHITE...........	1,884	268	244	1,164	209
Northeast............	363	190	16	150	7
North Central........	315	14	135	151	14
South................	885	48	50	762	25
West.................	322	16	42	101	163

Source: U.S. Census of Population: 1960. Mobility for States and State Economic Areas, Table 14.

tion, although highly mobile when viewed in a five-year interval, is twice as mobile when viewed annually.

Table 19-2 provides data on two important differentials: age and color.

The Age Pattern of Mobility. The propensity to change residences varies markedly with age. Peak mobility takes place as adulthood is attained. The median age of mobile persons was 22.9 years in 1964-1965. Assuming that mobility had occurred on the average six months earlier, we can infer that the median age of mobile persons at the time of movement is about 22.3 years. For migrants it is roughly one-fourth year younger and for local movers it is roughly the same amount older. But the median can be a very misleading statistic; the rates are high between ages 18 and 34, indicating that residential mobility is high throughout the time of young adulthood. Figure 19-4 illustrates the age pattern of local mobility and migration.

The age pattern is quite similar for the two sexes. In the ages beyond 25 to 45, males are substantially more mobile and migratory than females, although at the oldest ages this tends to be reversed. The comparatively high rate of mobility for persons under 6 years of age indicates that there is a substantial movement of whole families.

The Color Differential. The nonwhite populations are substantially more mobile than the white populations. For Negroes, however, this mobility is heavily concentrated in the form of local movement; the rate of migration of Negroes is only 60 percent as great as the migration of whites. In view of the much-discussed exodus of Negroes from the South, this may seem surprising. The fact is that by 1964 a very substantial majority of the Negro population had already exited from rural areas of the South. Once they arrived at a metropolitan destination, especially in the North, Negroes appeared to have little inclination to migrate further. This stands in rather sharp contrast to the situation that prevailed during and immediately before World War II, when rates for whites and nonwhites were nearly equal. The situation portrayed in Table 19-2 and Figure 19-3 will not necessarily be permanent, however. After a period of assimilation in their metropolitan destinations, Negroes will undoubtedly begin to suburbanize and to flow from one metropolitan area to another in much the same fashion as the white population. Both types of movements involve crossing county boundaries, hence are defined as migration. The high rates of local residential turnover among Negroes possibly reflect their struggle to find adequate housing.

Table 19-3 reports five-year migration rates by age, sex, and color. This table reveals that five-year intervals distort and hide the details of the age pattern, so that all but the largest age differentials tend to be lost. It also shows that the migration of the nonwhite population is more compressed into the years of young adulthood than is that of the white population.

Regional Flows of Migration. The redistributive effect of migration on population can best be understood in terms of migration streams. Streams are portrayed statistically by cross-tabulating place of origin by place of destination. Table 19-4 is such a tabulation, showing the streams of flow between the four major regions of the United States. Of the nearly 28 million migrants, 7.7 million (28 percent) were interregional migrants. This is

another way of showing that the great bulk of internal migration is short-distance—between counties of the same state or between states of the same region. Yet the fact that one migrant in four crossed a major regional boundary is testimony that a substantial fraction of migratory journeys are long-distance ones.

If these migratory journeys were purely circulatory with no redistributive effect, each region would receive as many migrants as it sends. That this was not the case is shown by the following summary obtained by subtracting the total out-migrants from each region from the total in-migrants to the same region:

	Net migration (000)		
Region	*Total*	*White*	*Nonwhite*
Northeast	− 640	− 735	+ 95
North Central	− 842	− 913	+ 71
South	+ 55	+ 334	−279
West	+1427	+1314	+113

On the over-all basis, the Northeast and North Central lost a substantial number of migrants, the South made a small net gain, and the West made a huge gain: it received almost all of the migrants that were lost by the other regions. The South's near equilibrium was achieved by exporting large numbers of nonwhite migrants and replacing them with white migrants. The South lost a large number of nonwhite migrants to all other regions. These migrants

flowed both northward and westward. The Northeast and North Center regions therefore recouped a part of their large net loss to the West by gaining a substantial number of nonwhite migrants from the South.

Sex Ratio of Migrants in Interregional Streams. It has often been noted that females tend to travel short distances, whereas males tend to constitute a disproportionately large part of the total of long-distance migrants.

Table 19-5   Sex Ratio of Migrants by Region and Color

Region of residence in 1960	U.S. Total	Region of residence in 1955			
		North-east	North Central	South	West
TOTAL...........	103.1	101.4	102.0	103.0	107.0
Northeast........	98.8	96.5	113.9	104.0	115.4
North central.....	99.9	111.4	97.5	105.1	110.4
South............	105.3	118.6	115.4	101.1	121.1
West.............	107.3	110.6	108.4	116.0	104.6
WHITE..........	103.2	101.3	101.6	104.1	106.5
Northeast........	99.4	96.3	114.2	114.7	114.6
North central.....	99.8	111.5	97.1	108.5	110.2
South............	105.5	118.6	115.0	101.2	120.4
West.............	106.9	110.2	108.1	117.5	104.0
NONWHITE.......	102.4	104.5	116.4	96.2	121.2
Northeast........	91.5	99.8	107.3	79.0	135.2
North central.....	100.7	108.7	114.0	88.4	115.8
South............	103.5	118.3	125.4	100.5	135.1
West.............	114.6	121.3	117.8	105.3	119.2

Source: U.S. Census of Population: 1960. Mobility for States and State Economic Areas, Table 14.

Table 19-6   Rate of Out-Migration from Each Region to the Urban and Rural Areas of Other Regions: 1955 to 1960

Destination: Region and urban-rural residence	Rate of out-migration from region:				
	Total U.S	North-east	North Central	South	West
All regions.............	198.1	157.6	187.6	226.2	241.5
To urban areas............	139.3	121.9	127.5	151.1	173.6
To rural-nonfarm areas.....	51.4	34.0	50.1	65.4	59.7
To rural-farm areas........	7.4	1.7	10.0	9.7	8.2
Northeast region.........	37.1	112.3	7.4	11.7	7.9
To urban areas............	28.3	85.9	5.6	8.7	5.9
To rural-nonfarm areas.....	8.4	25.0	1.7	2.9	1.9
To rural-farm areas........	0.4	1.4	0.1	0.1	0.1
North Central region.....	50.6	9.6	126.8	22.8	18.8
To urban areas............	33.9	7.9	82.0	17.0	13.3
To rural-nonfarm areas.....	13.6	1.6	36.1	5.1	4.4
To rural-farm areas........	3.1	0.1	8.7	0.7	1.1
South region.............	64.3	23.6	25.8	169.3	25.3
To urban areas............	42.3	17.6	17.3	108.6	17.3
To rural-nonfarm areas.....	19.3	5.8	7.7	52.3	7.2
To rural-farm areas........	2.7	0.2	0.8	8.4	0.8
West region.............	46.2	12.5	27.4	22.3	189.6
To urban areas............	34.9	0.5	22.6	16.8	137.1
To rural-nonfarm areas.....	10.1	1.6	4.5	5.1	46.2
To rural-farm areas......	1.2	0.4	0.3	0.4	6.3

Note: Rates based on average of 1950 and 1960 populations aged 5 years and over.

Source: U.S. Census Population: 1960. Mobility for States and State Economic Areas, Table 14.

Table 19-5 illustrates that this is generally valid. There are exceptions, however. In the rather long trek from the South to the North, nonwhite women greatly outnumber men. Perhaps the theory is more valid if modified as follows: Where migration may be accomplished cheaply and with security, and especially where channels are well-established and large numbers of former migrants at the place of destination are available to provide aid, the sex ratio of migrants tends to be near 1 or to have a feminine balance. Where the movement is extraordinary (not in a popular migration channel), of a "pioneering," "invasion," or "new stream establishment" nature, or involves unusual risks, hardships, or insecurities, male migrants tend to outnumber females. The results of Table 19-5 conform rather well to this generalization. For example, the migration of nonwhite population to the West is rather new. Moreover, the movement of nonwhite population from one region to another outside the South is new. Of special importance is the flow back into the South of more than 120,000 nonwhite residents of the North and West. In all of these new or unusual moves, the sex ratio is well above the average.

Reverse Flow. Another well-established principle of migration is that "for every migration stream there is a corresponding counterstream flowing in the opposite direction." The counterstream may be made up of migration "failures"—people who failed to adjust at the place of destination and are returning to their former home. Also, they may be people returning home to retire or to bring back new skills and capital to invest in their native region. Alternatively, the reverse stream may be made up of persons with completely different characteristics, coming in to fill needs that the outgoing migrants could not fill or to take advantage of opportunities that the out-migrants forsook. For example, a large part of the net gain of white population in the South is related to the mild winter climate, the rapid expansion of industry along the Gulf Coast, and large and active military establishments.

Urban-Rural Residence. When migrants in the United States depart from one region for another at the present time, all but a tiny fraction arrive at an urban or suburban destination. By far the greatest share arrive in urban areas.

Table 19-6, however, leaves little doubt

Table 19-7   Urban-Rural Residence of White Migrants at Destination in Comparison with the Urban-Rural Residence of the Population in the Geographic Division of Origin: 1960
(Each Figure Represents Percent)

Geographic division of residence in 1960	U.S. total	Geographic division of residence in 1955								
		New England	Middle Atlantic	East North Central	West North Central	South Atlantic	East South Central	West South Central	Mountain	Pacific
URBAN										
New England...........	- 6.9	- 7.5	- 5.2	- 4.7	- 4.4	- 6.8	-10.1	- 8.6	- 6.9	- 7.9
Middle Atlantic.......	- 1.6	- 1.1	- 1.4	- 3.1	- 2.2	- 3.9	- 5.7	- 2.7	- 5.4	- 0.0
East North Central....	- 2.4	12.2	13.3	- 6.6	4.3	6.4	6.6	3.9	3.6	6.3
West North Central....	7.0	16.4	17.0	13.9	5.2	12.3	10.9	9.8	6.4	8.5
South Atlantic........	8.2	17.3	18.2	12.2	11.2	4.8	6.3	7.5	7.6	9.4
East South Central....	7.3	12.1	11.2	1.0	15.6	14.3	5.3	14.9	11.7	11.2
West South Central....	4.0	10.1	12.0	6.7	6.2	12.9	9.8	2.2	5.8	3.4
Mountain.............	3.6	10.0	12.1	14.3	8.5	5.5	4.8	3.0	- 0.5	2.0
Pacific..............	- 3.7	6.0	7.7	5.1	1.2	- 2.4	- 2.6	- 6.4	- 3.7	- 7.4
RURAL NONFARM										
New England...........	7.6	8.0	6.2	6.1	5.6	7.4	11.1	10.0	7.8	9.2
Middle Atlantic.......	2.7	2.3	2.4	4.4	3.6	4.8	6.7	4.3	6.3	1.5
East North Central....	5.6	- 5.7	- 6.4	8.9	- 0.7	- 0.6	- 1.6	- 1.1	- 0.6	- 1.4
West North Central....	3.3	0.6	0.2	1.0	3.7	2.7	3.1	3.3	4.2	2.5
South Atlantic........	- 2.8	- 9.8	-11.1	- 5.3	- 4.1	- 0.5	- 0.1	- 0.5	- 0.7	- 2.3
East South Central....	1.0	2.3	3.7	6.4	- 2.6	- 1.8	0.8	- 2.7	1.9	1.2
West South Central....	0.3	- 1.6	- 3.5	- 0.9	- 1.1	- 4.8	- 3.1	1.3	1.5	1.4
Mountain.............	0.5	- 2.4	- 4.7	- 7.1	- 3.2	1.5	2.0	1.0	2.8	2.1
Pacific..............	5.0	- 3.0	- 4.7	- 2.4	0.7	5.2	5.2	7.0	4.9	8.0
RURAL FARM										
New England...........	- 0.7	- 0.5	- 1.0	- 1.4	- 1.2	- 1.0	- 1.0	- 1.4	- 0.9	- 1.3
Middle Atlantic.......	- 1.1	- 1.2	- 1.0	- 1.3	- 1.4	- 0.9	- 1.0	- 1.6	- 0.9	- 1.5
East North Central....	- 3.2	- 6.5	- 6.9	- 2.3	- 3.6	- 5.8	- 5.0	- 5.0	- 4.2	- 4.9
West North Central....	-10.3	-17.0	-17.2	-14.9	- 8.9	-15.0	-14.0	-13.1	-10.6	-11.0
South Atlantic........	- 5.4	- 7.5	- 7.1	- 6.9	- 7.1	- 4.3	- 6.2	- 7.0	- 6.9	- 7.1
East South Central....	- 8.3	-14.4	-14.9	- 7.4	-13.0	-12.5	- 6.1	-12.2	-13.6	-12.4
West South Central....	- 4.3	- 8.5	- 8.5	- 5.8	- 5.1	- 8.1	- 6.7	- 3.5	- 4.3	- 4.8
Mountain.............	- 4.1	- 7.6	- 7.4	- 7.2	- 5.3	- 7.0	- 6.8	- 4.0	- 2.3	- 4.1
Pacific..............	- 1.3	- 3.0	- 3.0	- 2.7	- 1.9	- 2.8	- 2.6	- 0.6	- 1.2	- 0.6

Note: Each cell of the above table represents the proportion of migrants to each destination region who were residing in an urban, rural nonfarm, or rural farm area in 1960 minus the corresponding proportion of the population in the region of origin living in the same type of residence in 1960.

Source: U.S. Census of Population: 1960. Mobility for States and State Economic Areas, Table 15.

about the validity of this generalization. It reports the rate of out-migration from each region to urban and rural residences in 1960 in every region. Of every 100 out-migrants, the pattern of settlement was as follows:

70 went to urban areas
26 went to rural-nonfarm areas
 4 went to farm residences

The same pattern dominated the flow from every region to every other region and even the flow within the same region. Further insight into the urbanizing effects of migration is given in Table 19-7, which reports the urban-rural residence in 1960 of white migrants in comparison with the urban-rural distribution of the population in the regions from which they came. A plus sign denotes that the migrants are concentrated in the particular class of residence. Clearly, migrants appear to be highly urban-oriented. This table also shows that in some divisions there was a strong tendency for white migrants to settle in rural-non-farm areas. This occurred in regions having

large and numerous metropolises and is evidence of the suburban movement rather than of massive settlement in small towns in the open country.

These comparisons are with respect to the place of origin. It is also of interest to learn the extent to which the various residential types were receiving new members through migration. This is shown, by color and regions, in Table 19-8. This table shows that although migrants were flowing in greatest numbers to cities, the rate of in-migration was higher for rural-nonfarm than for urban areas. This must be attributed to suburbanization. (The very high rates of suburbanization shown for the nonwhite population are partially fictitious; the numerator and denominator of these rates are both quite small. The rates represent a great relative increase, but small absolute increase.) Table 19-8 emphasizes that cities in the South received white migrants at a very substantial rate and that the rate of receiving nonwhite migrants was greatest in cities of the West and Northeast.

Table 19-8 Rate of In-Migration (in-migrants per 100 residents) to Urban and Rural Areas, by Color; Regions: 1955 to 1960

Region	Total	White			Total	Nonwhite		
		Urban	Rural nonfarm	Rural farm		Urban	Rural nonfarm	Rural farm
U.S. Total....	18.3	18.5	21.0	8.9	10.8	11.2	11.9	7.1
Northeast.......	13.0	12.5	16.0	7.1	13.2	12.7	25.0	24.1
North Center....	15.5	15.6	19.1	8.3	10.2	9.3	25.6	18.6
South..........	21.7	24.4	21.0	8.7	9.1	9.4	9.5	6.7
West...........	26.4	25.6	32.5	14.6	16.9	17.0	15.0	0.5

Source: U.S. Census of Population: 1960. U.S. Summary, Tables 164, 237 and Mobility for States and State Economic Areas, Table 15.

Migration from Farms. Because the nation now is predominantly urban, there is a tendency to view the rural-urban migration phenomenon from the destination point of view. However, the impact on rural areas probably has been greater than on urban areas. Calvin L. Beale has described recent events as follows:

". . . the effect of World War II was electrifying. Five million people of labor force age alone left the farm in four years (April 1940 to April 1944), the majority for civilian work rather than for military service. The policy of federal encouragement of subsistence farming ceased and agriculture began an accelerated progress toward use of advanced techniques and specialized production for the commercial market. . . . It is estimated that net migration from farms amounted to about 11,390,000 in the 1940's and 10,130,000 in the 1950's. . . . The annual average net migration from farms is estimated at 4.4 percent in the 1940's and 5.5 percent in the 1950's. In the three years since 1960, the rate appears to have risen to 6.3 per 100 annually.

"The factors permitting such a reduction in farm population are numerous and reasonably well known. Mechanization, improved seeds, better breeds and animal nutrition, good management, and advances in fertilizer, pest control, and weed control have all combined to raise productivity and reduce manpower. In addition, the generally high operating level of the nonfarm economy, the ease of physical access to cities, and the dominant stylistic position of metropolitan life have attracted people away from farming areas. Some federal agricultural programs such as acreage restrictions and

conservation reserves (the "soil bank") also have tended to reduce manpower needs in agriculture. In addition to agricultural outmigration, other factors lowered the level of rural population, such as the decline in coal mining employment.

"Although some established young or middle-aged farmers have sold out and moved away in the past decade, most of the reduction in farm population is taking place through the heavy outmovement of young people who have decided not to enter agriculture. Thus, as many older farmers die or retire, their manpower is not replaced, although their land may be absorbed by another farm. Gladys K. Bowles has estimated that of all net migrants from farms in the 1950's, at least 60 percent was less than 20 years old or reached age 20 sometime during the decade. By contrast, it can be shown that decade outmigration rates for middle-aged groups seldom exceed 10 percent even in rapidly declining counties.

". . . in areas where the total rural population has declined by as little as 5 to 10 percent in a decade, the net outmigration of young adults is typically more than 50 percent in the decade. There were about 1,500 counties in the United States in 1960 where this was true. . . . The pertinent research question in such cases would seem to be "Who has remained?" rather than "Who has left?" [7]

Migration and Marital Status. When interviewed in 1960, a higher proportion of married population was found to be comprised of mi-

[7] Calvin L. Beale, "Rural Depopulation in the United States: Some Demographic Consequences of Agricultural Adjustments," *Demography,* **1,** (1964), 264–272.

Table 19-9 Rate of Mobility of the United States Population 18 to 34 Years of Age by Marital Status, Sex, and Color: 1960

Age, marital status and color	Male				Female			
	Rate per 1000 population			Percent of all migrants	Rate per 1000 population			Percent of all migrants
	Within county	Between counties	Between non-contiguous states		Within county	Between counties	Between non-contiguous states	
White population............	279.5	185.3	66.9	100.0	287.6	170.6	53.9	100.0
Single, 14 & over........	220.9	208.7	83.7		238.1	168.7	45.9	
18 and 19 years...	195.8	327.1	137.4	10.9	226.0	282.5	59.9	6.8
20 to 24 years....	175.7	355.3	165.1	15.2	217.8	305.1	74.8	6.8
25 to 29 years....	199.0	235.1	109.4	3.9	249.6	208.3	75.0	1.6
30 to 34 years....	225.6	182.3	76.3	1.9	242.7	154.9	57.1	.9
Married spouse present, 14 & over..............	300.4	175.5	60.0		303.7	181.0	59.1	
18 and 19 years...	570.9	307.9	102.6	.8	555.2	353.0	106.0	3.5
20 to 24 years....	512.3	365.0	138.0	12.8	516.2	386.2	124.4	20.5
25 to 29 years....	452.6	358.8	143.4	22.3	445.0	327.3	113.7	22.1
30 to 34 years....	413.3	264.7	85.9	20.3	367.6	228.7	74.2	17.8
Married spouse absent, 14 & over..............	267.6	279.7	116.7		338.0	214.3	77.3	
18 and 19 years...	204.6	488.5	292.0	.3	391.7	251.6	94.0	.3
20 to 24 years....	195.6	502.0	283.6	1.5	405.0	284.0	106.1	1.1
25 to 29 years....	256.1	372.3	184.4	1.0	393.9	325.4	141.9	.9
30 to 34 years....	291.2	319.6	143.1	.9	374.7	278.8	117.8	.8
Widowed..................	251.9	112.4	31.0	3.6	246.5	105.9	30.9	12.2
Divorced.................	345.5	215.6	80.0	4.4	373.8	174.4	60.7	4.7
Nonwhite population........	359.9	114.5	48.9	100.0	372.1	101.2	43.6	100.0
Single, 14 & over........	312.0	139.4	60.7		335.5	119.1	48.5	
18 and 19 years...	303.0	186.8	86.3	10.6	317.1	169.5	62.6	7.5
20 to 24 years....	271.9	240.4	127.9	19.1	319.0	209.3	93.8	10.9
25 to 29 years....	278.9	174.7	86.0	6.5	366.3	138.3	67.0	3.3
30 to 34 years....	308.9	136.4	53.3	3.3	382.1	96.1	44.1	1.4
Married spouse present, 14 & over..............	389.4	91.9	40.3		390.1	99.0	43.3	
18 and 19 years...	631.0	145.7	51.8	.5	611.6	207.0	90.3	3.0
20 to 24 years....	569.8	226.9	121.2	10.7	576.4	242.9	121.4	16.9
25 to 29 years....	546.3	196.8	104.6	15.8	527.5	170.2	84.6	15.7
30 to 34 years....	510.2	128.9	58.9	12.0	453.0	110.4	48.1	11.1
Married spouse absent, 14 & over..............	359.6	176.3	69.9		431.3	120.1	56.1	
18 and 19 years...	332.9	289.7	123.8	.4	461.8	158.0	59.1	.7
20 to 24 years....	316.4	323.0	167.1	3.8	469.2	187.4	88.8	3.9
25 to 29 years....	348.2	252.9	122.3	4.0	497.6	151.9	78.7	3.8
30 to 34 years....	355.8	215.7	87.1	3.9	481.1	134.6	64.2	3.6
Widowed..................	315.5	76.7	23.1	5.0	306.1	64.3	24.3	13.0
Divorced.................	389.7	126.5	53.1	4.4	409.3	99.4	48.5	5.2

Source: U.S. Census of Population: 1960. Mobility for States and State Economic Areas, Table 7.

grants than was the single population. This is a surprising finding. Traditionally, the popular stereotype has been the migrant as a single person setting off alone from the farm or small town to seek his fortunes in the big city. There are two possible explanations for the results of Table 19-9: either (a) the traditional view is wrong and whole families now are equally migratory (or even more migratory) as single persons or (b) migrants who arrive at their destinations as single persons tend to marry very promptly and at an earlier age than do the resident nonmigrants. With the data at hand, it is difficult to tell which of these hypotheses is correct. It is quite possible that both are correct simultaneously, for they are not incompatible hypotheses and both are highly plau-

sible. As the population becomes better educated and occupations become more specialized and technical, there is a rising tendency for corporations to move workers from one point to another and for heads of families to search farther afield for opportunities for better employment. This would indicate a greater emphasis on the movement of whole families than previously. On the other hand, the lone migrant who arrives in the city having just left his parental household may be stimulated by loneliness to marry and establish his own family. This would indicate a tendency for migrants to marry at an earlier age than do nonmigrants. This phenomenon is stronger for females than for males. Thus females may be impelled to migrate by a double-barreled set of forces—

Table 19-10 Rate of Mobility of the United States Population 25 to 34 Years of Age, by Educational Attainment, Sex, and Color: 1960

Educational attainment	Male				Female			
	Rate per 1000 population			Percent of all migrants	Rate per 1000 population			Percent of all migrants
	Within county	Between counties	Between non-contiguous states		Within county	Between counties	Between non-contiguous states	
WHITE POPULATION..............	390.0	293.4	81.9	100.0	391.3	267.6	91.8	100.0
No school years completed........	286.3	137.7	32.9	.3	313.1	122.5	26.7	.2
Elementary school, less than 5....	440.4	181.1	46.5	1.3	430.1	156.3	40.9	.9
Grade school 5-to 8 years........	438.8	218.6	67.6	12.5	429.2	197.1	58.9	9.6
High school 1 to 3 years.........	430.9	236.5	84.0	17.1	420.1	227.2	73.4	18.4
High school 4 years..............	404.3	258.8	99.2	27.5	395.0	254.5	84.9	41.3
College 1 to 3 years.............	357.7	346.6	135.3	14.6	339.8	369.2	140.6	15.7
College 4 years or more..........	276.7	500.1	213.0	26.7	299.2	455.2	180.3	13.4
NONWHITE POPULATION	449.3	169.7	111.3	100.0	474.3	137.0	65.4	100.0
No school years completed........	402.2	122.3	29.3	1.3	378.2	94.0	18.6	.9
Grade school less than 5 years....	471.6	141.7	46.1	7.9	465.5	113.2	31.4	4.0
Grade school 5 to 8 years........	475.0	145.1	55.2	24.8	486.8	114.7	47.9	21.9
High school 1 to 3 years.........	470.9	161.5	77.3	25.4	504.8	121.8	60.1	26.5
High school 4 years..............	431.6	176.6	106.3	21.1	464.2	141.1	76.7	26.8
College 1 to 3 years.............:	404.2	229.8	125.7	9.8	443.6	195.0	102.7	9.5
College 4 years or more..........	309.4	299.1	167.1	9.7	358.6	274.4	123.9	10.4

Source: U.S. Census of Population: 1960. Mobility for States and State Economic Areas, Table 6.

their proclivity to migrate as single persons and their migration after marriage to accompany husbands who migrate. The phenomenon is also more common among white than among the nonwhite population.

Educational Attainment and Migration. The semiilliterate migrant of the *Grapes of Wrath* type has all but disappeared from the American scene. Table 19-10 reports rates of migration for educational attainment groups, by sex and color. Among both white and nonwhite populations, and for both males and females, the rate of migration tends to vary directly with the level of educational attainment. (In order to control the effects of age and of school attendance, the age group 25 to 34 has been taken for analysis.) The average white college graduate of this age is two to three times as migratory as the person who did not graduate from grammar school. Between these extremes, each increment of education is accompanied by a higher rate of migration. Figure 19-5 illustrates this differential. Among the nonwhite population there are equally consistent but somewhat less dramatic differences in migration rates. The average white migrant is a high school graduate with some college training. The average nonwhite migrant is a person who has completed three years or more of high school. Less than 2 percent of white migrants

of this age are functionally illiterate (have less than 5 years of grammar school). As yet, about 7 percent of the nonwhite migrants fall in this category. Thus as the poorly educated person becomes more scarce in this age of rising technology and improving educational attainment, he is also less mobile than his better educated brother. As the length of the migratory journey increases, these differentials become even sharper.

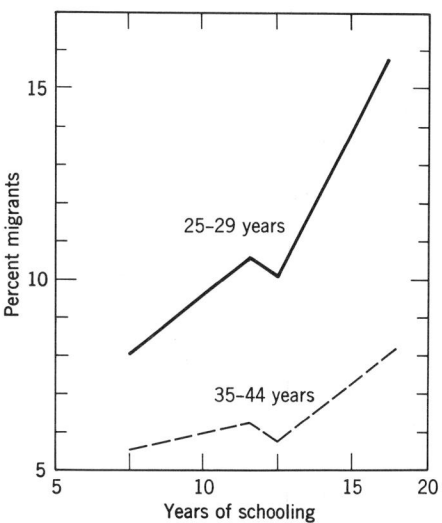

Figure 19-5 Migration Rates, by Educational Attainment, Two Age Groups, United States: 1965 to 1966.

Table 19-11   Rate of Mobility of United States Population 25 to 34 Years of Age, by Occupation, and Labor Force Status, by Sex and Color: 1960

Occupation and color	Male				Female			
	Rate per 1000 population			Percent of all migrants	Rate per 1000 population			Percent of all migrants
	Within county	Between counties	Between non-contiguous states		Within county	Between counties	Between non-contiguous states	
White population.............	390.0	293.4	111.3	100.0	391.3	267.6	91.8	100.0
Total employed...................	412.0	278.4	94.1	83.5	398.0	239.4	83.1	28.3
Professional, technical and kindred workers..............	314.5	463.4	183.3	22.0	326.9	381.6	135.4	7.2
Farmers and farm managers........	296.8	138.5	33.0	1.4	231.2	144.1	20.6	.1
Mgr., off., & prop., exc. farm....	402.6	329.0	103.8	8.9	408.3	244.6	86.6	.8
Clerical & kindred workers........	428.4	259.8	89.7	5.8	413.0	234.8	121.5	10.6
Sales workers....................	416.0	325.2	109.6	6.9	398.2	217.4	76.3	1.5
Crafts., foremen, & kind. workers.	453.8	241.5	77.7	15.2	419.1	177.1	61.2	.2
Operatives & kindred workers......	480.9	222.6	65.4	14.4	468.6	156.1	43.8	3.2
Serv. wkrs., exc. priv. hshld.....	469.0	225.5	78.3	2.6	422.6	259.8	95.2	3.8
Farm laborers & foremen..........	330.9	243.2	62.0	1.3	255.3	142.3	38.5	.1
Laborers, exc. farm & mine........	468.1	215.2	65.7	3.2	429.2	164.2	58.1	.1
Occupation not reported..........	201.7	147.5	59.2	1.8	223.9	122.5	46.0	.7
Unemployed.......................	400.1	244.9	95.3	2.9	422.6	256.3	90.8	1.7
Armed forces.....................	82.4	649.7	499.6	9.1	58.0	760.3	602.6	.1
Not in labor force...............	227.0	301.0	107.2	4.5	387.6	281.0	95.6	69.9
Nonwhite population..........	449.3	169.7	81.4	100.0	474.3	137.0	65.4	100.0
Total employed...................	488.9	145.2	69.0	66.2	477.8	136.0	64.9	43.7
Professional, technical and kindred workers..............	386.1	301.4	152.8	8.3	416.9	229.8	92.5	7.8
Farmers and farm managers........	434.9	98.4	20.1	0.9	338.1	76.8	....	.1
Mgr., off., & prop. exc. farm......	495.6	172.2	82.9	1.3	415.5	138.6	42.2	.4
Clerical & kindred workers........	518.8	141.8	88.9	4.3	510.4	138.8	77.0	5.4
Sales workers....................	506.5	138.0	70.7	0.9	472.3	94.9	65.6	.5
Crafts., foremen, & kindred wkrs..	532.7	143.7	69.7	6.9	519.8	58.9	21.1	.1
Operatives & kindred workers......	551.2	128.8	60.9	15.7	525.8	115.1	68.9	5.5
Serv. wkrs. exc. priv. hshld......	508.4	165.5	89.3	9.0	511.4	135.8	62.8	20.8
Farm laborers & foremen.........	431.7	145.9	30.4	3.4	445.5	146.2	43.4	1.1
Laborers, exc. farm & mine........	528.3	143.6	60.3	12.4	467.4	107.5	67.0	.3
Occupation not reported..........	230.2	76.0	42.2	3.1	243.8	66.1	31.1	1.7
Unemployed.......................	481.7	143.3	76.5	6.0	514.2	157.0	84.4	5.2
Armed forces.....................	114.2	518.3	382.8	12.0	67.5	617.2	551.4	.2
Not in labor force...............	277.1	232.2	65.2	15.8	468.2	135.6	63.8	50.9

Source: U.S. Census of Population: 1960.   Mobility for States and State Economic Areas, Table 9.

C. Horace Hamilton, who has made intensive studies of the educational selectivity of migration from rural to urban areas, has found two different patterns. He finds that at the younger ages, rural-to-urban migration is selective of the better educated. At the older ages, however, he finds the reverse to be true: older migrants who leave rural areas tend to be the less well educated. The volume of the first type of migration is several times greater than the second. He found that despite the selectivity of better educated rural youth for migration, migrants nevertheless were less well educated than the urban populations that they joined. Rural-to-urban migration therefore has the mild tendency to dilute the urban population with less well educated persons. The fear that is sometimes expressed that rural-to-urban migration will inundate the city with masses of semi-literates is unwarranted in American communities.

Occupation and Migration. As the educational differentials would lead us to suspect, the rates of migration are far higher for white-collar workers than for blue-collar workers. Table 19-11 reports migration rates by occupation for the age group 25 to 34, by sex and color. Professional workers are more migratory by far than any other occupational group. Second position is held by the managerial-proprietary occupations. Laborers (nonfarm) tend to be the least mobile group. Sales workers have moderately high migration rates among white males. Service workers have moderately high rates among nonwhite males. These differentials are even more pronounced for longer-distance migration between noncontiguous states.

Persons not in the labor force, both male and female, have surprisingly high mobility. These may be persons who have recently been in school, have recently married, have recently

Table 19-12 Rate of Mobility of United States Family Head, 25 to 34 Years of Age, by Family Income

Age and family income	Rate per 1000 population			Percent of all families migrated
	Within county	Between counties	Between non-contiguous states	
WHITE				
All family heads 25-34 years old.	432.9	306.0	112.2	100.0
Under $ 1,000..................	416.9	284.6	110.1	2.7
$ 1,000 to $ 1,999............	449.3	281.2	101.5	3.0
$ 2,000 to $ 2,999............	423.3	305.2	123.0	5.8
$ 3,000 to $ 3,999............	419.7	309.8	130.9	9.7
$ 4,000 to $ 4,999............	439.7	301.5	114.5	13.4
$ 5,000 to $ 5,999............	446.2	290.2	98.7	16.3
$ 6,000 to $ 6,999............	437.7	301.4	101.6	14.5
$ 7,000 to $ 9,999............	428.8	319.5	114.3	24.2
$ 10,000 to $ 14,999..........	417.2	332.4	126.6	8.3
$ 15,000 and over.............	429.8	304.8	108.7	2.1
NONWHITE				
All family heads 25-34 years old.	542.2	150.3	75.4	100.0
Under $ 1,000..................	560.0	126.1	48.7	10.7
$ 1,000 to $ 1,999............	567.3	128.5	50.9	12.9
$ 2,000 to $ 2,999............	540.6	153.0	72.6	17.5
$ 3,000 to $ 3,999............	526.5	164.4	84.3	16.9
$ 4,000 to $ 4,999............	525.6	166.3	93.4	13.8
$ 5,000 to $ 5,999............	526.6	159.8	93.7	10.2
$ 6,000 to $ 6,999............	546.5	151.5	93.4	6.0
$ 7,000 to $ 9,999............	554.1	156.6	84.0	8.9
$ 10,000 to $ 14,999..........	523.7	154.4	82.8	2.6
$ 15,000 and over.............	417.3	176.8	115.0	0.5

Source: U.S. Census of Population: 1960. Mobility for States and State Economic Areas, Table 10.

been divorced, or who are in poor health and seeking medical care. The occupational differentials emphasize that at the present time the unskilled jobs tend to be filled locally by non-migrant residents at the site, while the more technical and skilled jobs tend to be filled on the basis of regionwide or even nationwide competition and recruitment. Unless mobility is required as a part of his employment or unless he is expelled from a territory because of catastrophic economic or other conditions, the nonfarm laborer tends to be immobile. Although he may find few employment opportunities at home, there are few employment opportunities waiting for him anywhere, so that there is little incentive to migrate. This is one of the complicating phenomena of poverty; little can be gained by migration without retraining to change occupations.

Income and Migration. Migration rates are highest among family heads earning $7000 per year or more and least among those earning less than $2000 per year. Table 19-12 reports rates for income groups of family heads, by color. The income differentials are sharper among the white population than among the nonwhite. Also, the income differentials are much less consistent and sharp than the education and occupation differentials. This may result from a tendency for migrants to enter the lower echelons of the occupation categories, where salaries are lower. It may also reflect the failure to receive income during the time required to change communities and seek new employment. When enumerated in 1960, the average migrant household head was in the $6000 income category, while the average nonwhite migrant was in the $3800 income category. However, both the white and nonwhite population in the highest income category had below-average mobility.

19.5. Internal Migration in Industrialized Nations

From the theoretical orientation stated at the beginning of this chapter, it is clear that the size, direction, and composition of internal migration streams may vary greatly from one country to another, depending on the particular pattern of circumstances that prevails. If the same general patterns are observed for several nations, they will be explained by a claim that there are similar underlying factors and forces. This similarity does exist, for there are substantial similarities (as well as differences) to be observed both in industrialized and developing nations. This section presents a few examples for industrialized nations, whereas the next section will do the same for developing nations.

Sweden. In a study, "Regional Aspects of Internal Migration and Mobility in Sweden: 1946-50," Bertil Wendell finds that more than one half of the parishes in Sweden suffered a net migration loss of 5 percent or more during the period 1946-1950. In contrast, the flow was highly focused on a few urban places. He found that 20 of the 2483 parishes in Sweden attracted nearly one half of the net migration gain. Of these, approximately one third were either within Stockholm itself or in the Stockholm suburbs, and the remainder consisted of other large cities and towns or their immediate environs. The Stockholm area alone received 24 percent of the net migration gain.

Japan. Dr. Minoru Tachi reports that according to the results of the 1960 population census, 26 out of the 46 prefectures of Japan had experienced depopulation during the interval between the 1955 and 1960 censuses.[8] Similar depopulation was also reported for approximately three-fourths of all municipalities, the smallest civil divisions. Yet the same census revealed that the national total population increased by 4,143,000 between 1955 and 1960. This increase was claimed almost entirely by the extraordinary growth of the four metropolitan areas, which have developed around the nuclear cities of Tokyo, Osaka, Nagoya, and Fuouoka. In none of these areas of population decline was the birthrate below the death rate. Therefore, the depopulation that took place over such a major portion of Japan must be attributed to out-migration. Similarly, the birthrates in the major cities are not sufficiently high to account for their unusual growth. These major metropolitan centers were the destination of the out-migrants from the nonmetropolitan areas.

Federal Republic of Germany. Since 1962 the large cities having 100,000 or more inhabitants have had a negative net migration balance, but their suburbs have been growing rapidly. Rural areas, outside metropolitan areas that temporarily housed many thousands of refugees immediately after World War II, have lost population steadily. Thus large cities appear to be undergoing a process of decongestion and the remote rural areas are losing population to the large metropolitan areas.[9]

Italy. There has been a very dramatic urbanization of Italy. The rural municipalities are losing population at a very rapid rate, and the large industrial triangle of Torino-Milano-Genova and Rome are gaining at extraordinarily rapid rates. There is an especially great movement from Sicily, Southern Italy, Middle Italy, and Eastern North Italy into these expanding centers of employment.[10]

France. Between 1954 and 1962 there was an increase of 18.4 percent in the zones of industrial or urban population and a decrease of 5.6 percent in the rural municipalities outside of these zones. There was a net out-migration rate of 10 percent in these rural areas. This deficit increased with decreasing size, so that the rate of migration loss in the least populated areas was very severe. Although the city of Paris itself lost population slightly during this time, the population increased by 30.2 percent in the urban fringe and by 65.3 percent in the suburban fringe. More than 50 percent of Paris' population has been born in rural municipalities.[11]

Belgium. The Brussels metropolitan area, which is comprised of 19 municipalities, has made a steady and rapid growth, despite the fact that it has long had extraordinarily low birthrates and a negative reproductive change. "The population increase within the Brussels area is exclusively ascribable to a continuous

---

[8] Minoru Tachi, "Regional Income Disparity and Internal Migration of Population in Japan," *Economic Development and Cultural Change,* **12** (January 1964), 186–204.

[9] Kurt Horstmann, "Rural-Urban Migration in the European Economic Community," paper read at the United Nations World Population Conference, Belgrade, Yugoslavia, 1965.

[10] Ibid.

[11] Ibid.

stream of immigrants which settled down in the capital. Without these inwardmovers the growth of the capital would have been impossible." [12]

Yugoslavia. Since World War II there has been a rapid urbanization and industrialization of the population, which has led to a massive transfer of workers from the country to the city. Between 1953 and 1961 the growth of the urban population was more than equivalent to the total growth in the national population. In other words, the entire reproductive increase of the rural areas was drained off into the cities by migration. [13]

Hungary. The Budapest metropolitan area has grown substantially faster than the nation between 1949 and 1960, the date of the last census. This population increase has resulted primarily from the migration of persons from the surrounding rural zones into the metropolis. Nearly two thirds of the migration is the movement of persons directly from rural villages into the metropolis, while the remainder is movement from smaller towns. The rate of migration is higher than for most of the larger European cities. [14]

These examples lead us to the conclusion that industrialized nations all over the world are experiencing two major migratory movements:

1. A massive exodus of persons from low-income rural and economically depressed areas toward the great metropolises where new employment opportunities and new economic growth are concentrated.

2. A massive exodus of persons from the core of the metropolitan center to the periphery. Modern metropolises all over the world seem to be suburbanizing rapidly while population densities at their center are declining.

19.6. Internal Migration in Developing Countries

In developing countries internal migration may be of two types: (1) movement to settle new lands or exploit new resources and (2) movement in response to industrialization. Both types have taken place. The following quotation from a United Nations report illustrates the first type of movement for South-East Asia.

"Movement of peasants to new farming areas has occurred in most countries of South-East Asia, with important results. Thus, Burma became an exporter of rice when, at the turn of this century, large numbers of peasants from Upper Burma settled in the irrigated deltas of Lower Burma. During several decades, a similar movement from north to south took place in Viet-Nam: subsistence farmers of the crowded Tonkin Delta moved to Cochinchina, where they entered the cash crop economy. In Ceylon, Indonesia, and the Philippines, the Governments have rendered systematic assistance to the transfer of rural families from densely settled areas to lands of greater opportunity: in Ceylon, the movement of colonists has been from the irrigated south-west to the island's dry zone; in Indonesia, both before and since the Second World War, migrants have been leaving the island of Java for settlement in Sumatra and, in smaller numbers, Borneo; a great part of the movement in the Philippines has been from the island of Luzon and the Visayas to the island of Mindanao. In Malaya, 500,000 rural families have recently been resettled in compact villages, partly for security reasons. Recent warfare has caused an influx of 800,000 refugees into the Republic of Viet-Nam, and the Government is actively engaged in their reintegration in the rural economy, while also undertaking a scheme for land settlement in the country's hilly regions. Plans for the regulation of the Mekong river may some day set in motion a movement of settlers to the river valley in Cambodia, Laos, and Thailand." [15]

[12] Frans van Mechelen, "Qualitative Aspects Associated with Inward and Outward Migration towards and from a Large Urbanized Area," paper presented at the United Nations World Population Conference, Belgrade, 1965.

[13] Sava Obradovic, "Influence du Développement Economique sur les Mouvements Migratoires en Yougoslavie," paper submitted to the United Nations World Population Conference, Belgrade, 1965.

[14] Kalman Tekse, "On Some Interrelationships Between Occupational Mobility and Migration to Budapest," paper submitted to the United Nations World Population Conference, Belgrade, 1965.

[15] United Nations, *The Population of South-East Asia,* 1950–80. New York, 1954.

The building of dams to irrigate arid areas, the drainage of swampy lands, the modernization of tropical farming, the freeing of districts from malaria or other diseases that have prevented settlement, and the movement to semi-arid areas, to subarctic regions, and to tropical islands that thus far have not been densely settled are taking place in many nations—often with international aid. This will produce further migration to new lands. However, this has not been and is not now the dominant form of migration. Instead, even in those developing nations with frontiers yet to exploit the migration streams have also turned toward the metropolis.

Chile. In 1962 the United Nations Demographic Center in Santiago conducted a survey of migration to Greater Santiago.[16] The study found that there has been a large and steady stream of in-migrants. Two thirds of these migrants came from smaller urban centers. It is presumed that much of this migration has taken place in stages—the rural migrants arriving first in small district cities and then later continuing on to the metropolis. When the housing, employment, and other condition of the migrants are compared with those of the general population it is discovered that migrants are disadvantaged. They live in poorer housing with greater crowding and fewer amenities. In comparison with natives, migrants tend to have higher unemployment rates and a lower occupational status, hence, a lower level of income.

India. K.C. Zachariah has estimated that the net rural-urban migration in India during the 1941-1951 decade was 8.2 million, while it was only 5.2 million during the decade 1951-1961.[17] This comparatively low level of urbanward migration in recent years has been attributed to the slow pace of industrial and commercial expansion in the nation, and to the fact that masses of urban proletarians were already present in the expanding areas. Ashish Bose has identified what he calls the "urban push-back" factor: "In India and Pakistan, the urban labour force is sizable and the urban unemployment rates are high and there already exist pools of underemployed and unemployed population in the labour force, pools which act as deterrents to fresh flows of migration from rural areas to urban areas. . . . There is also another type of urban push. In the absence of social security measures, there is a constant push factor in urban areas which operates whenever a migrant in a city falls sick, is unemployed or retires from service. This is especially true of the migrant who comes to the city in the expectation of a job but fails to get it. He is inevitably pushed back to his village or to some other city in search of a job." [18]

Puerto Rico. This developing country has had extensive migration, both in the form of movement to mainland United States and of exodus from rural areas to the cities. Both types of migration originated primarily in rural areas, and there is a correlation of .70 between the rates of out-migration to the United States and out-migration to large urban centers. San Juan has been the principal destination of internal migrants. In recent years, external migration has tended to slacken, but rural-to-urban migration is continuing apace.[19]

Pakistan. In Karachi, of a population of 1,800,000 persons in 1959, only 200,000 were natives. The balance were refugees from India and in-migrants from other districts of Pakistan. Most of this migration occurred in conjunction with partition, and rural-to-urban migration appears to have slackened substantially in the period 1955-1959. The housing, employment, occupational, and income position of migrants is inferior to that of natives.[20]

[16] Juan C. Elizaga, "A Study of Migration to Greater Santiago (Chile)," *Demography*, 3 (2) (1966), 352–378.

[17] K. C. Zachariah, "Population Redistribution in India," Research Report of United Nations Demographic Research and Training Center, Bombay, 1964.

[18] Ashish Bose, "Internal Migration in India, Pakistan and Ceylon," paper presented to the United Nations World Population Conference, Belgrade, Yugoslavia, 1965.

[19] George C. Myers, "Migration and Modernization: The Case of Puerto Rico, 1950–1960," paper presented to the United Nations World Population Conference, Belgrade, 1965.

[20] Sultan S. Hashmi, Masihur Rahman Khan, and Karol J. Krotki, *The People of Karachi*, The Pakistan Institute of Development Economics, 1964.

Ceylon. The apparent pattern of internal movement in Ceylon during the period 1946-1954 was not one of distinctly rural-urbanward movement. Aside from modest gains of Colombo, internal migration showed little response to industrial change. Much of the movement was to reclaim agricultural lands and in response to other rural programs. The intense urbanization that has been observed in other contexts was comparatively lacking.[21]

Mainland China. Informal reports from a variety of sources indicate that migrants are flocking into the major cities from the countryside in large numbers. There have been special campaigns to induce them to remain in the rural areas or to force them to return home. Forcible exportation has been employed at times since 1952, when the policy of retention of rural population through intensive use of manpower in agriculture, afforestation, irrigation, village road repairs, and handicrafts became an explicit part of the national plan. In 1955 a program of organized population transfers was initiated. This has been described by Tien.[22] The objectives of this program were not only to remove to rural areas large numbers of in-migrants to the cities, but also to relocate in rural areas a substantial number of urban residents. To prevent further outflow from the villages, food rationing in cities, centralized hiring, and police checking at railway stops were enlisted to turn back unauthorized out-migrants from the villages. The removal to rural areas of in-migrants to the cities created serious problems, for the rural population itself is having difficulty absorbing its own reproductive change. To resolve the problem, in 1955 the government began a program of organized population transfers to areas of low population density in Manchuria, Inner Mongolia, Kansu, and Sinkiang. Projects were instituted to reclaim wasteland and improve the areas under cultivation. According to the analysis of Tien,

the capital investment required to accomplish the program is impossibly high and at the present rates of transfer would take many years. Meanwhile, the population of China continues to grow rapidly. Tien concludes: "In the demographic context, population transfers in connection with land reclamation work in Communist China in recent years have been of little significance. Whatever their political, military, social and economic returns are, the conclusion is inescapable that the solutions to the Chinese population question must be found in programs other than land reclamation and organized population transfers."[23] From the above, it is clear that the spontaneous migration pressures in China are identical with those elsewhere in the world.

Unfortunately, internal migration has not been the subject of rigorous and sustained study for many of the developing nations as yet. Consequently, comprehensive generalizations cannot be made. The following tentative generalizations, however, appear to be valid.

1. In most of the developing nations, the largest principal political, commercial, and industrial centers are enjoying moderate to rapid growth, both as a result of high fertility and of net in-migration. However, wholesale exodus from rural areas to provincial urban centers has not materialized.

2. An amazingly high proportion of the rapidly accumulating "surplus population" in the developing nations appears to be staying in the rural village areas and is struggling to exist through more intensive cultivation of the land.

3. Whenever significant industrial and commercial expansion does take place, an immediate stream of migration ensues. Much of this migration results in failure and in return to the place of origin.

The evidence thus far suggests that modernization generates tremendous pressures for urbanward migration and that it is lack of industrialization and the rural-retention-of-population programs that is keeping Asia from hav-

---

[21] S. Vamathevan, *Internal Migration in Ceylon, 1946–54,* Department of Census and Statistics, Monograph No. 13, Colombo, 1961.

[22] H. Yuan Tien, "The Demographic Significance of Organized Population Transfers in Communist China," *Demography,* 1 (1964), 220–226.

[23] *Ibid.,* 226.

ing an even more sweeping urbanward movement. It is quite possible that governments
that are consuming precious time and capital
in fighting migration through uneconomic
make-work or submarginal land reclamation
projects or cottage industry are traveling a
path that cannot succeed in the long run and
only worsens the situation by permitting the
surplus population in rural areas to get larger.
This phenomenon deserves much more systematic and intensive sociodemographic research. Population retention, population transfers, and subsidized rural handicrafts have high
(and possibly invalid) priorities in the national
plans of several large nations with serious
population problems—Philippines, Indonesia,
Brazil, and India, for example.

19.7. Migration as a Component of
Internal Population Growth

In Chapter 2 the growth of population was
discussed in terms of two components: reproductive change and net migration. As will
be demonstrated later, at the present time the
migration component is of almost negligible importance in studying the growth of nations; to
all intents and purposes the national populations of nations are "closed" to immigration and
emigration. International differences in growth
rates are therefore explained largely by their
differences in reproductive change—the balance
between birthrates and death rates. For the explanation of internal pattern of population
growth, however, the exact opposite situation
prevails. Within a nation the levels of mortality
and fertility tend to be similar everywhere, with
the result that the rate of natural increase does
not differ a great deal from one place to another. (There are differentials, of course, but
they tend to be smaller than the actually observed differences in population growth.) *The
major factor accounting for differences in rates
of population growth within a country is net
internal migration; the pattern of internal migration is therefore the leading component
in accounting for differential population
growth.*

It follows that one of the major tasks of

migration research is to subdivide the growth
of parts of the nation into their components
and to portray the spatial pattern of each. The
two components then become the raw data for
research into the phenomenon of *population
redistribution.* An understanding of the broad
movements of population distribution and redistribution within a nation, region, or community is greatly facilitated by subdividing
total population change into its two components. If this is not done, the phenomenon
of population change may be misunderstood
and misinterpreted.

The study of population components of
population growth has long been performed
for the major units of nations: states. However,
the detailed analysis of growth in terms of particular communities dates only from the 1950s.
One of the first research undertakings to perform such an analysis for an entire nation, in
terms of its detailed parts, was Bogue's *Components of Population Change, 1940-50: Estimates of Net Migration and Natural Increase
for Each Standard Metropolitan Area and State
Economic Area.*[24] This study made estimates of
net migration and reproductive change for
each state economic area, economic subregion,
and economic region. Figure 19-6 illustrates
the results. There was a very large gain from
migration in the two Pacific regions and in the
Gulf Coast region, and small gains in the Atlantic Metropolitan Belt and the Lower Great
Lakes regions. All of the other regions of the
nation suffered a net migration loss. A negative
correlation ($-.25$) was found between the rate
of net migration and the rate of reproductive
change: regions of high fertility were regions
of net out-migration. A correlation analysis was
undertaken to attempt to explain net migration
differences for the nonmetropolitan areas. On
page 778 is a summary of the results:

[24] Donald J. Bogue, *Components of Population
Change, 1940–50: Estimates of Net Migration and
Natural Increase for Each Standard Metropolitan
Area and State Economic Area.* Ohio: Scripps
Foundation for Research in Population Problems,
Studies in Population Distribution No. 12 (Ox-
ford, Ohio: Miami University, 1957).

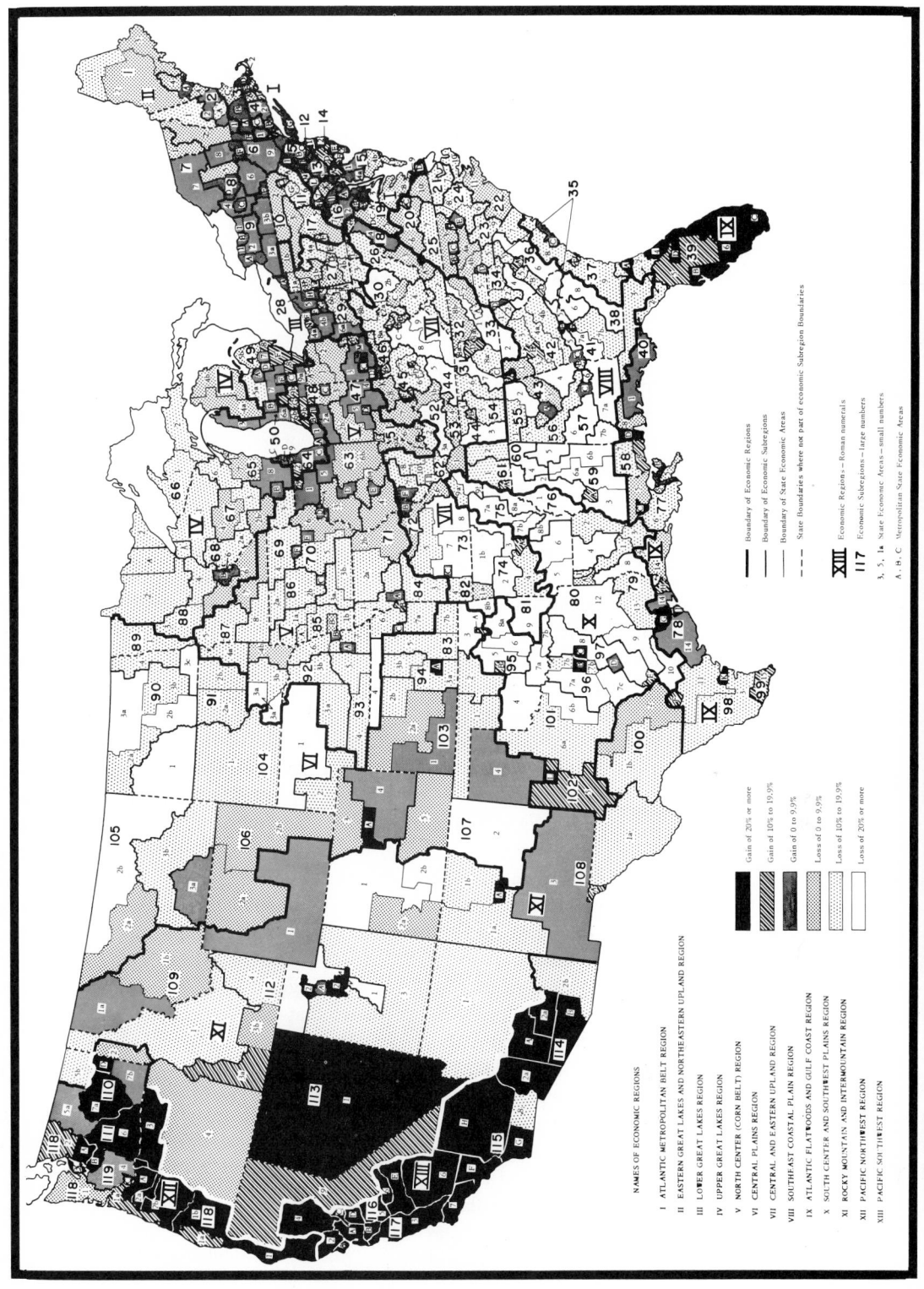

SOURCE: Donald J. Bogue, *Components of Population Change, 1940–50* (Oxford, Ohio: Scripps Foundation for Research in Population Problems, Miami University, 1957).

Factor	Correlation
Percent change, total population	.917°
Percent change, rural-nonfarm population	.548°
Percent change rural-farm population	.488°
Percent in agriculture, 1950	−.519°
Percent nonwhite, 1950	−.286°
Percent change nonwhite, 1940-1950	.393°
Percent in manufacturing, 1950	.279°
Median income, 1949	.645°
Farm operator level of living index	.584°
Rural-nonfarm level of living index	.533°
Percent change in retail sales, 1939-1948	.198°
Percent change in manufacturing, 1939-1947	.082
Infant mortality rate, 1939-1940	−.162°

°Significant at the 95 per cent confidence level.

Because the nonmetropolitan areas were areas of net migration loss for the most part, the above correlations are factors that tend to explain *exodus*. Out-migration was occurring from the more agricultural areas of low level of living or with large concentrations of nonwhite population. Exodus was less from nonmetropolitan areas with some manufacturing, but there was so little manufacturing growth in the nonmetropolitan areas that change in manufacturing had no effect on retarding the outflow. That migration far overshadows reproductive change in accounting for interarea differences in population growth is indicated by the correlation of .917 between percent change in total population, 1940-1950, and net migration rate, 1940-1950.

The same study estimated the net migration and reproductive change components of the central city and suburban ring of each of the standard metropolitan areas individually. The net migration component for each of these areas was broken down by age and color. It was found that central cities as a whole suffered a net migration loss; such growth as did occur in these places was accomplished entirely by reproductive change and annexation. The suburbs, in contrast, grew very rapidly because they enjoyed both reproductive increase and large net migration gains. The net migration loss to the central city was made up of a moderately large net gain of nonwhite population (moving primarily from nonmetropolitan areas of the South) and an even larger net loss of white population (moving primarily to the suburbs).

After the 1960 census, this set of estimates was repeated by the U.S. Bureau of the Census. The Census presented the components in even more detail—for each individual county as well as for economic areas.[25] Essentially the same pattern was found as for the 1940-1950 decade. However, the actual volume of migration differed substantially in the two periods, and individual areas became relatively less and more attractive to migration. Figure 19-7 maps the net migration pattern of the nation, 1950-1960, by county. The Census Bureau did not make the detailed estimates of net migration for the central city and suburban parts of individual metropolitan areas, by age, but this was performed for 45 of the largest standard metropolitan areas by Ann Ratner Miller.[26] In fact, she incorporated Bogue's estimates and extended the computations back even one decade further, to 1930-1940. Moreover, her estimates were made by age and sex for the white and Negro population, with the white population subdivided into foreign-born and native-born for the 1930-1940 and 1940-1950 decades. Figure 19-8, taken from her report, shows that during the 1950-1960 decade the net loss of white population to central cities through net migration became even more

[25] U. S. Bureau of the Census, *Components of Population Change, 1950 to 1960, for Counties, Standard Metropolitan Statistical Areas, State Economic Areas, and Economic Subregions,* Current Population Reports, Series P-23, No. 7, November 1962.

[26] Ann Ratner Miller, *"Net Intercensal Migration to Large Urban Areas of the United States: 1930–40, 1940–50, 1950–60* (Philadelphia: University of Pennsylvania Population Studies Center, 1964).

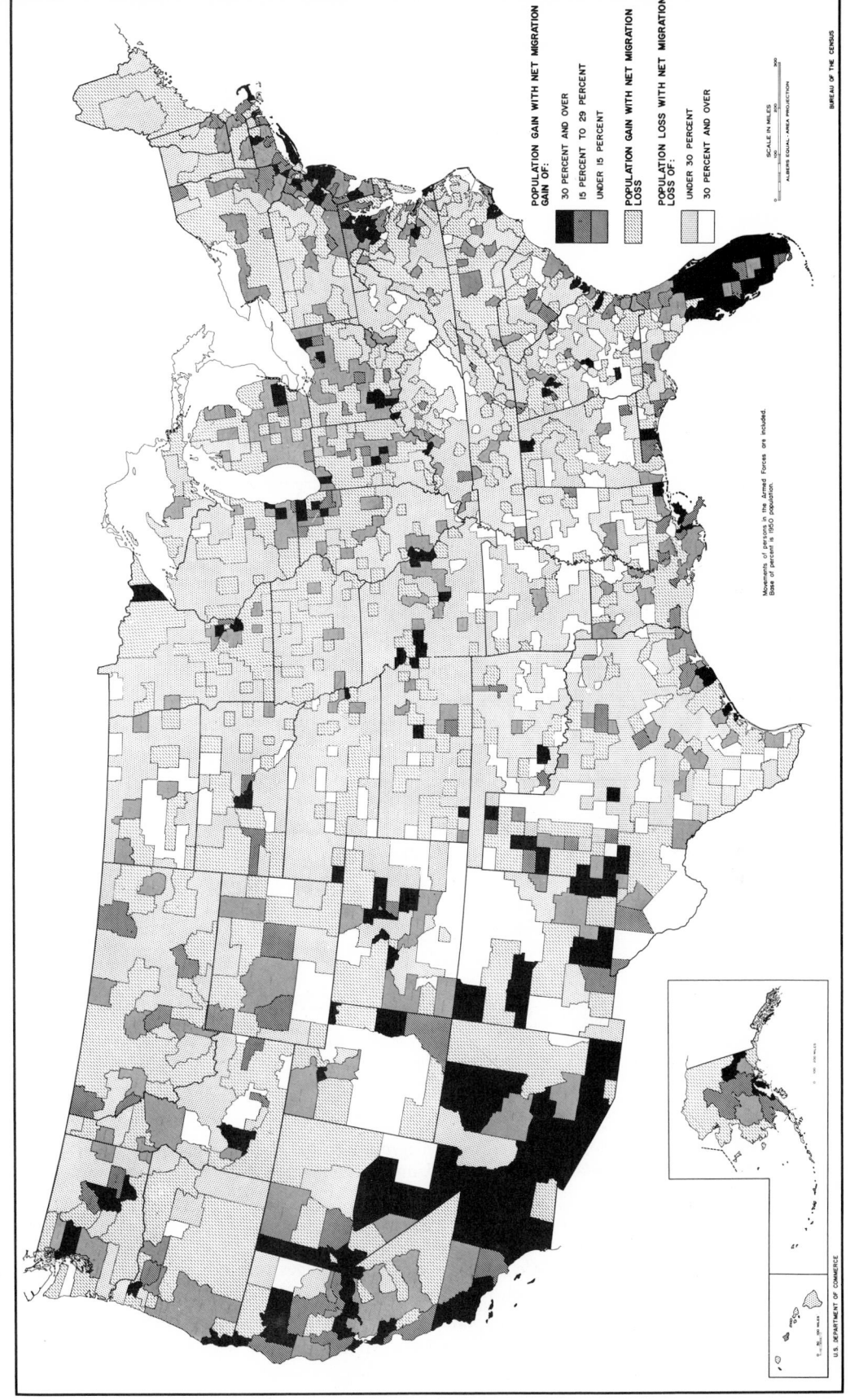

Figure 19-7 Net Migration by Counties: 1950 to 1960.

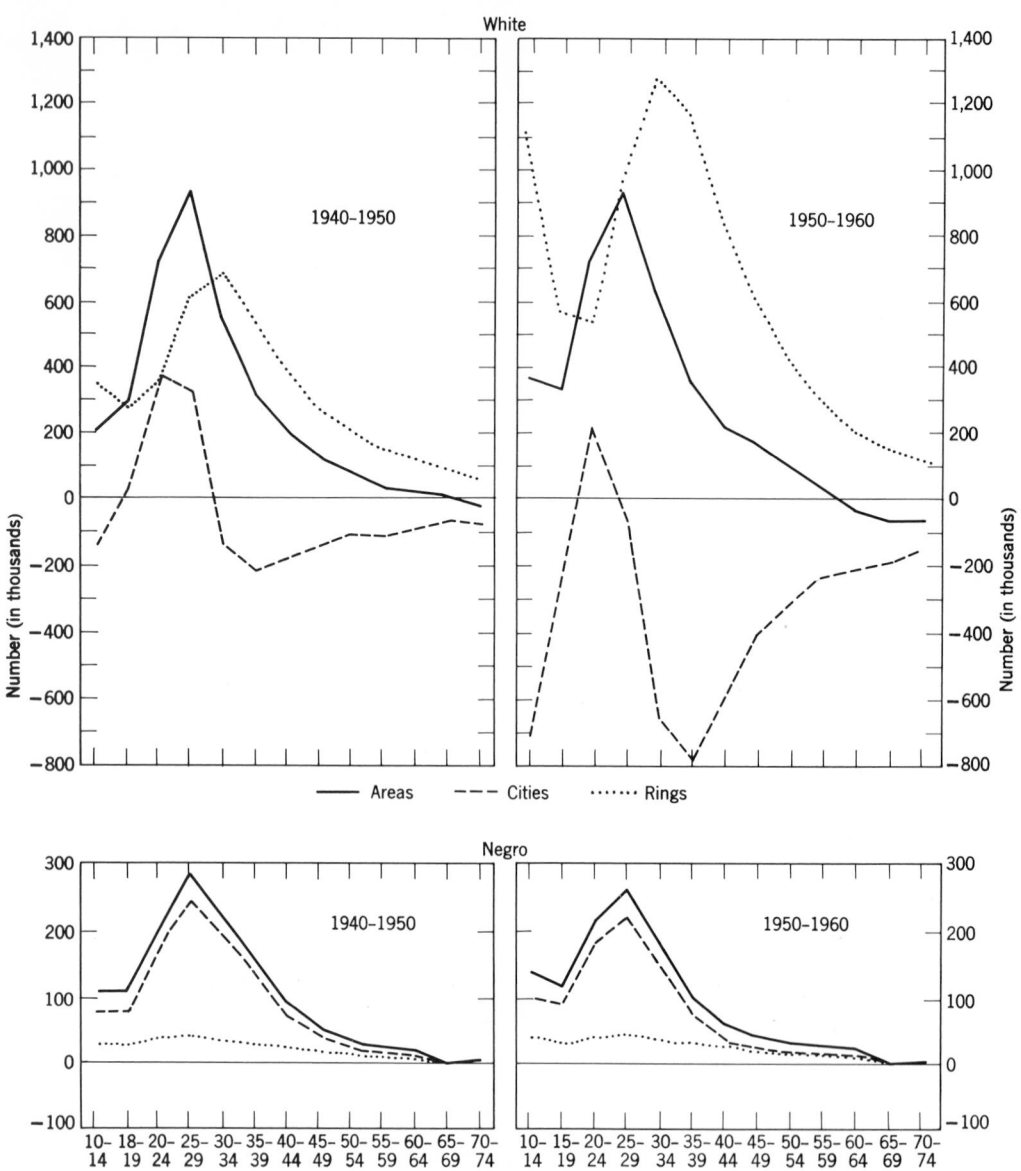

Figure 19-8 Net Intercensal Migration to Cities of 250,000 Population or Over in 1960, Their Standard Metropolitan Areas and Their Suburban Rings, by Age and Color: 1940 to 1950 and 1950 to 1960.

SOURCE: Ann Ratner Miller, *Net Intercensal Migration to Large Urban Areas of the United States, 1930–40, 1940–50, 1950–60* (Philadelphia: University of Pennsylvania Population Studies Center, 1964), p. 37.

severe and that the suburban areas gained very heavily from the net gain of white migrants.

The branch of migration research that deals with the components of growth is comparatively new and underdeveloped. The techniques for making the migration estimates are now well established. However, there is still a shortage of research efforts to explain or account for the differences that are observed. It is hoped that future censuses will continue to provide full information on the components of growth and that demographers will undertake fuller explanations of the migration component particularly.

19.8. History of Regional Internal Migration in the United States

The direction of flow of internal migration from the landing of the Pilgrims until the turn of the twentieth century is almost too well-known to require statistical documentation. As the pioneers and then the frontiersmen pushed westward, recruits were drained from the eastern areas of settlement (and from overseas) and shipped westward to settle the land and establish new towns. However, systematic study of internal migration in the United States extends backward only to about 1870. By this date the frontier had been pushed to the Pacific Ocean, and thereafter a process of economic consolidation and development began. The carving up of the territories to form states was largely completed by 1900.

Migration history in the United States has been researched by three major studies: Goodrich et al.,[27] Thomas-Kuznets[28] et al., and Henry Shryock, Jr.[29]

In 1936 the remarkable monograph *Migration and Economic Opportunity*, edited by Carter Goodrich of the University of Pennsylvania, appeared. It was the thesis of this book that the flow of internal migration is highly responsive to economic opportunities, with large outflows from areas of economic hardship and submarginal economic income. Among the contributors to this volume was C. Warren Thornthwaite, whose monograph *Internal Migration in the United States* was the first systematic attempt to assemble a migration history for the nation.[30] Another monograph in the series, *Migration and Planes of Living*, documented the tendency for populations to desert areas of low level of living in favor of areas of higher levels of living.[31] This program of migration research influenced greatly much economic planning and governmental policies during the economic depression and after. Today, after 35 years, these reports still are filled with insights into migration problems that beset us now.

In the years 1954-1964 the University of Pennsylvania again sponsored a major migration research program entitled "Population Redistribution and Economic Growth in the United States, 1870-1950," under the joint direction of Dorothy Swaine Thomas and Simon Kuznets, an eminent sociologist and an eminent economist, respectively. The results of this second cycle of studies are reported in three volumes, with the bulk of the analysis and interpretation occurring in Volumes II and III.[32] Everett S. Lee, the senior author of the first volume, was primarily responsible for the intricate task of using demographic techniques to estimate net interstate migration, by nativity, sex, age, and color for each state 1790-1950. Volume I, which contains these estimates, is a "gold mine" of information about the historical record of migration in the United States.

In conjunction with the 1950 Census of the United States, Henry S. Shryock, Jr., Assistant Chief of the Population Division and one of the demographers who has been primarily responsible for the planning and conduct of the splendid program of migration statistics from U.S. Census since 1940, prepared a monograph entitled *Population Mobility Within the United States*.[33] This volume also includes a study of

---

[27] Carter Goodrich and Associates, *Migration and Economic Opportunity* (Philadelphia: University of Pennsylvania Press, 1936).

[28] Dorothy S. Thomas, Simon Kuznets, et al., *Population Redistribution and Economic Growth in the United States,* 3 vols. (Philadelphia: The American Philosophical Society, 1957, 1960, 1964).

[29] Henry S. Shryock, Jr., *Population Mobility Within the United States* (Chicago: Community and Family Study Center, 1964).

[30] C. Warren Thornthwaite, *Internal Migration in the United States* (Philadelphia: University of Pennsylvania Press, 1934).

[31] Daniel C. Creamer, *Migration and Planes of Living* (Philadelphia: University of Pennsylvania Press).

[32] The three volumes in this set are, Everett S. Lee, Ann Ratner Miller, Richard A. Easterline, and Carol P. Brainerd, *Methodological Considerations and Reference Tables* (1957); Ann Ratner Miller, Richard A. Easterline, and Simon Kuznets, *Economic Series Analyses of Economic Change* (1960); and Hope T. Eldridge and Dorothy Swaine Thomas, *Demographic Analyses and Interrelations* (1964). All three volumes were published by the American Philosophical Society of Philadelphia.

[33] *Op. cit.,* especially Chapter 5, "The Historical Record of Mobility within the United States," and Chapter 6, "Geographic Variations in Mobility Rates."

Table 19-13 Estimated Intercensal Net Migration for Geographic Divisions, by Color: 1870 to 1960

Color	1950 to 1960	1940 to 1950	1930 to 1940	1920 to 1930	1910 to 1920	1900 to 1910	1890 to 1900	1880 to 1890	1870 to 1880
(NATIVE) WHITE									
New England.........	- 47	-105	- 23	-190	- 53	- 84	21	- 33	- 67
Middle Atlantic......	-159	-714	-139	- 59	-205	-182	- 37	-207	-282
East North Central...	+178	-218	-102	283	-303	-487	- 46	-483	-440
West North Central...	-857	-932	-568	-708	-444	-475	-374	408	471
South Atlantic.......	1,189	465	282	-158	51	-101	- 86	-106	- 21
East South Central...	-845	-571	-241	-391	-374	-342	-213	-211	-155
West South Central...	-292	-397	-335	10	- 63	437	431	104	275
Mountain............	549	70	37	-153	156	364	120	187	116
Pacific..............	2,970	2,402	1,090	1,274	629	869	184	300	102
NONWHITE									
New England.........	70	25	5	7	12	8	14	7	4
Middle Atlantic......	472	387	166	342	170	87	91	39	19
East North Central...	521	494	108	324	201	46	39	16	21
West North Central...	37	35	20	41	44	10	24	8	5
South Atlantic.......	-542	-424	-175	-509	-162	-110	-182	- 73	- 49
East South Central....	-620	-485	-122	-181	-248	-110	- 43	- 60	- 56
West South Central...	-295	-336	- 50	- 61	- 46	50	57	- 61	45
Mountain............	8	20	6	- 1	10	5	...	...	...
Pacific..............	324	284	43	37	18	14	,..	...	...

Source: Data for 1870 to 1950 summarized from data reported in Population Redistribution and Economic Growth, Vol. I, by Everett S. Lee, Ann Ratner Miller, Carol P. Brainerd and Richard A. Easterline,(Philadelphia: The American Philisophical Society, 1957) Tables 1.11 and 1.14. Data for 1950 to 1960 from U.S. Bureau of the Census. Current Population Reports: Population Estimates, Series P-25, No. 247, 162

historical trends of mobility and migration in the United States, especially for the 1930-1950 period.

Space permits here only a brief summary of the highlights of these studies. In general, the period since 1870, for which migration esti-mates may most validly be made, was an era of economic intensification and urbanization, rather than of initial invasion of new territo-ries. During this developmental phase, large amounts of population moved westward to homestead the land, to go into business, or to become wage earners in the enterprises of oth-ers. This process, in general, drew population from east of the Mississippi River and deposited it west of the Mississippi. Table 19-13 sum-marizes the estimated net intercensal migration for the nine geographic divisions, from 1870 to 1950.[34] The data for 1870-1960 demonstrate the final phase of westward movement to settle the newly gained lands.

The rush to settle the prairie lands apparent-ly resulted in oversettlement, or else the mod-ernization of agriculture that came with power

[34] A very comprehensive statement of the his-torical pattern of migration in the United States and its role in redistributing the population has been Hope T. Eldridge, "Demographic Analyses of Population Redistribution," Part I of Eldridge and Thomas, *op. cit.*

farming made dense settlement unprofitable. In any event, beginning in 1900 the North Cen-tral and the South Central states began to suf-fer higher net out-migration, which was largely associated with retreat from the land and mi-gration to cities. Since 1910 there has been a steady trend toward the consolidation of farms into fewer but larger units and a consequent out-migration of farmers from the Middle West and Southwest. Meanwhile, the flow of migra-tion toward the Pacific coast and the Mountain division continued.

After World War I, there was a sharp turn in the tide of internal migration. Instead of population flowing to occupy the land more in-tensively and to establish new towns, it began to flow toward the larger metropolitan centers and centers of expanding industrial employ-ment. This might be called the phase of "met-ropolitanization" of the population. This phase has continued and accelerated. Table 19-13 shows that during the World War II years and thereafter the standard metropolitan areas of each region made substantial migra-tion gains. However, most of this gain went to the suburban portions of the central cities be-cause the central cities were already fully settled and were in a process of deconcentra-tion.

The metropolitanization phase drew off large

numbers of Negroes from rural communities in the South and deposited them in the leading metropolitan centers of the Northeast and North Central divisions. Between 1940 and 1950 the wartime shortage of manpower also attracted Negroes to the West in large numbers. This trend grew between 1950 and 1960 and presumably is one of the dominant features of migration during the 1960s. This outflowing of Negro population from the South to other regions has been overwhelmingly a movement toward urban and especially metropolitan centers. Table 19-13 shows just how great this interregional flow was during the 1950-1960 period—the standard metropolitan areas of the United States gained 1.6 million nonwhites by migration. Since the South lost 1.2 million nonwhite population by net outmigration during this period, it is clear that almost all of the interregional movement of Negroes was to metropolitan centers. Even within the South there was a very heavy movement from rural to metropolitan areas.

This exodus of the Negro has been given a broad overview and interpretation by C. Horace Hamilton in a classic article, "The Negro Leaves the South."[35] He finds that the forces underlying this tremendous shift of people lie both in the South and in the other regions. It is not only the lure of higher pay that induces this movement, but the lack of opportunities for young Negroes in the South. Despite special programs of assistance, farm ownership by Negroes has been insignificant. Because of refusal to sell and inability to buy farmland, it has been almost impossible for the Negro sharecropper to climb the social ladder into the status of owner-operator. Hamilton shows that the rate of loss is highest for better-educated Negroes and lowest for the "functionally illiterate"— those with less than 5 years of schooling. He points out that the South is itself industrializing and urbanizing rapidly, but that Negroes are unable to obtain their proportionate share. Refusal to hire, even when qualified, has replaced refusal to sell land. With the agricultural economy of the South drastically altered through mechanization and the conversion

from cotton to other types of farming, employment even as sharecropper and unskilled laborer is scarce. Under these conditions there are few alternatives but to move North or West.

The Thomas-Kuznets study is especially noteworthy for its effort to arrive at general principles and theories as a result of studying the record of interstate migration over the 80-year period 1870 to 1950. They discovered a fluctuating pattern of migration, with alternate decades of high and low interstate redistribution of population as a result of migration. Thomas undertook to study the relationship between these fluctuations and the business cycles.[36] Estimates of gross national product were prepared for each year, which were summarized into decade measures and related to the migration fluctuations. Figure 19-9 illustrates the correspondence between the migration measures and the fluctuation of gross national product. There is perfect conformity in the direction of the swings between migration and gross national product. Also, there is a high degree of similarity in the relative amplitude of deviation from the trend. It is concluded that the changing level of economic activity, as symptomized by gross national product, explains or accounts for a substantial share of the fluctuations in the level of migration.

Another important finding of this study is that over the decades there has been a distinctive movement toward convergence among the various states of the nation in the level of their incomes. The deviation of the richest and the poorest states from the national average has tended to decrease over time. The interregional flow of migration appears to have played a part in this development, because there have been consistent net flows from areas of low income toward areas of higher income.

Shryock focused his attention primarily on migration during the period 1935-1950.[37] He made a very careful region-by-region analysis of migration flows during this period of time.

---

[35] Hamilton, C. Horace, "The Negro Leaves the South," Demography 1 (1964), 273–295.

[36] Dorothy S. Thomas, "Temporal Interrelations: Decadal Swings," Part II in Volume III of Hope T. Eldridge and Dorothy Swaine Thomas, op. cit.

[37] Henry S. Shryock, Jr., op. cit.

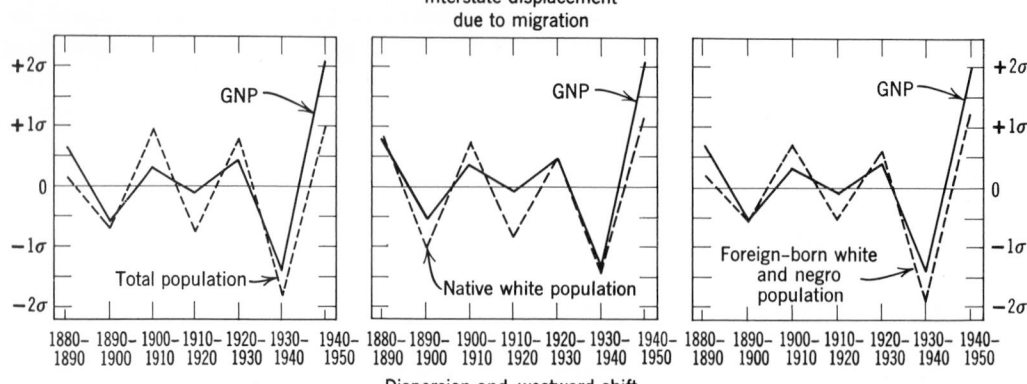

Figure 19-9 Deviations from Trend of Gross National Product and of Indexes of Population Redistribution: 1880 to 1950.

SOURCE: Dorothy S. Thomas, "Temporal Interrelations: Decadel Swings," in Hope T. Eldridge and Dorothy Swaine Thomas, *Population Redistribution and Economic Growth, United States 1860–1950*, Volume III.

His general finding was that there were very consistent flows toward those sections of the country that were undergoing economic expansion and metropolitan growth and away from those sections where the economy (either non-metropolitan or metropolitan) was "mature" or declining. He also identified special sites of migration such as counties containing military posts or atomic energy installations. He found that the migration pattern was similar in the 1940s and 1950s, though the level was different.

One of Shryock's principal concerns was with the "effectiveness" of migration—the ratio of net migration to total mobility turnover (sum of in-migration and out-migration). In "effective" migration there is very little milling about, but rather a clear preponderance of either in-migration or out-migration for each area. He found that effectiveness can differ a great deal from one part of the United States to another and can fluctuate over time. High negative effectiveness seems to characterize the areas of greatest economic hardship and high positive effectiveness is found in areas of greatest economic expansion. Effectiveness appears to have been much higher during the period before World War II than since. The passing of the frontier, the gradual draining of surplus populations from marginal farming activities, the removal of Negroes from the South to bet-

ter employment and income-earning positions in the North, and the rather complete exploitation of the Gulf and the Pacific coasts have succeeded in reducing the inequality of economic opportunity among the different regions of the country. Thus, Shryock hypothesizes, as interregional differences in economic opportunity decrease the effectiveness of migration also decreases. He emphasizes that much of the "milling about" that characterizes present-day migration may be highly effective in achieving the aspirations and goals of individual persons, even though it appears to have much less potent effects than formerly in redistributing population or affecting its composition.

Net Migration in the 1950-1960 Decade. Two studies have calculated estimates of net migration.[38] The study by Bowles and Tarver summarized the principal findings in a set of charts, which are reproduced here. Figure 19-10 demonstrates the continued transfer of non-

[38] Gladys K. Bowles and James D. Tarver, *Net Migration of the Population, 1950–60, by Age, Sex, and Color*, 2 vols. Economic Research Service, U. S. Department of Agriculture in Cooperation with Research Foundation Oklahoma State University (Washington: U. S. Government Printing Office, 1966). Hope T. Eldridge, *Net Intercensal Migration for States and Geographic Divisions of the United States, 1940–60* (Philadelphia: Population Studies Center, University of Pennsylvania, Report No. 5, 1965).

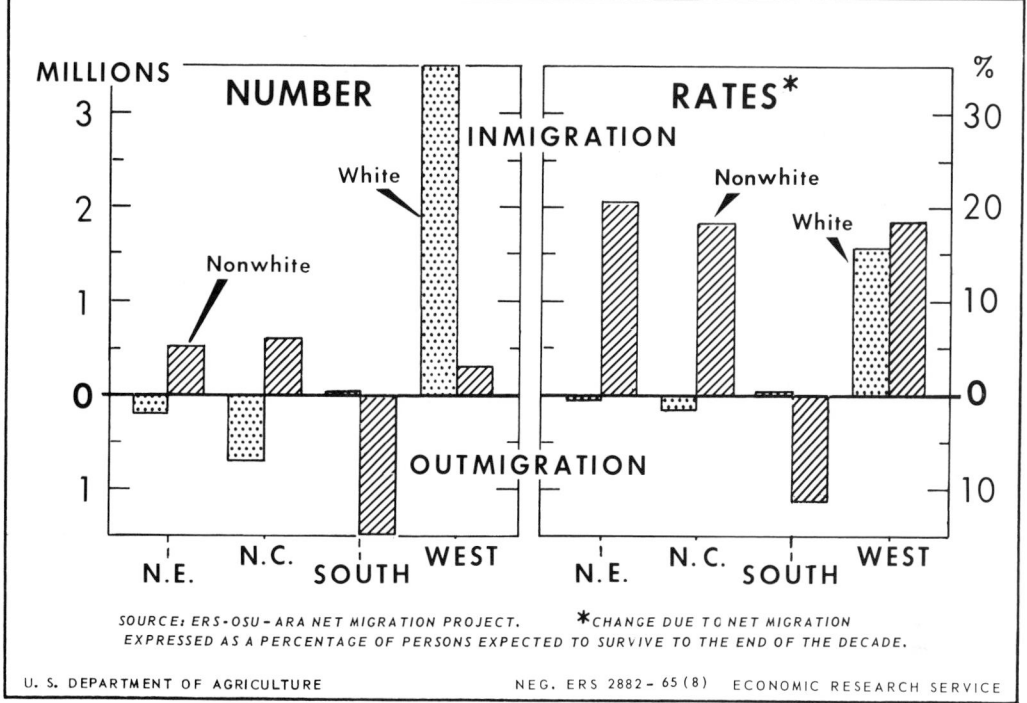

Figure 19-10   Net Migration: 1950 to 1960 (Regions by Color).

SOURCE: Gladys K. Bowles and James D. Tarver, *Net Migration of the Population, 1950–60, by Age, Sex and Color* (U. S. Department of Agriculture and Oklahoma State University, 1965), p. vii.

white population from the South to the Northeast, North Central, and West, and the continued westward flow of white population, with a net loss to the Northeast and North Central. Figure 19-11 reports the amounts of population gained by the receiving states and lost by the sending states. The continued large gain of both white and nonwhite population in metropolitan areas and loss from nonmetropolitan areas is graphed in Figure 19-12. The rates for metropolitan and nonmetropolitan areas are reported in Figure 19-13. This figure shows that the rates are approximately equal for males and females at most ages, with females migrating a little earlier. Figure 19-14 shows the migration pattern for counties grouped by degree of urbanism. As a whole, counties that were less than 50 percent urban lost population, with very severe losses for completely rural or only slightly urbanized counties. Figure 19-15 shows that there was heavy exodus from counties where the median family income was lowest and that the highest in-migration occurred where family in-

come was greatest. This income pattern held for both white and nonwhite populations. The authors also reported migration rates for counties grouped according to their eligibility to receive federal assistance under the Area Redevelopment Act for improving conditions in depressed and poverty-stricken areas. The areas officially designated as "poverty areas" experienced severe net out-migration, while the more prosperous (not eligible) areas had migration gains. Both white and nonwhite populations reacted to the poverty situation by flight. For the nonwhite population the rates were substantial even beyond the usual migration ages 20 to 34, signifying that, in addition to young people who refuse to remain in such places once their schooling is finished, older persons also were being removed from the depressed areas through migration.

19.9.   Subregional Migration

A completely unambiguous explanation of a migration stream can be made if the migrants

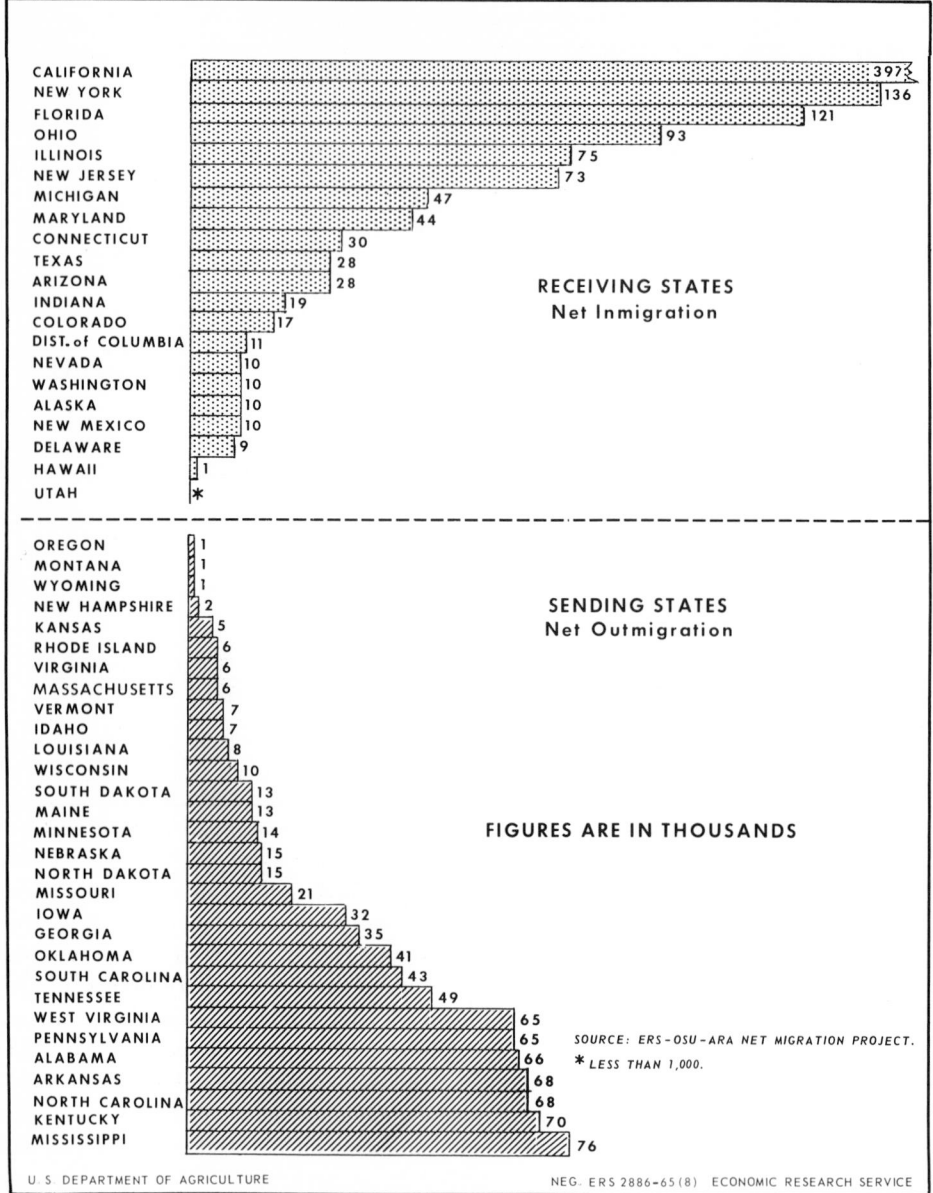

Figure 19-11 Volume of Young Migrants (25 to 29 Years of Age) Gained and Lost by the Individual States: 1950 to 1960.

SOURCE: Gladys K. Bowles and James D. Tarver, *Net Migration of the Population, 1950–60, by Age, Sex and Color* (U. S. Department of Agriculture and Oklahoma State University, 1965), p. viii.

who depart from a given place for another particular destination are all alike in their characteristics and have all been stimulated by the same force or combination of forces. For this to be true, both the place of origin and the place of destination would have to be com-

pletely homogeneous in character and the populations of both would have to be of a uniform composition. This is an ideal that cannot be found in real life; the physical environment is too diverse, community populations are never comprised of individuals with identical charac-

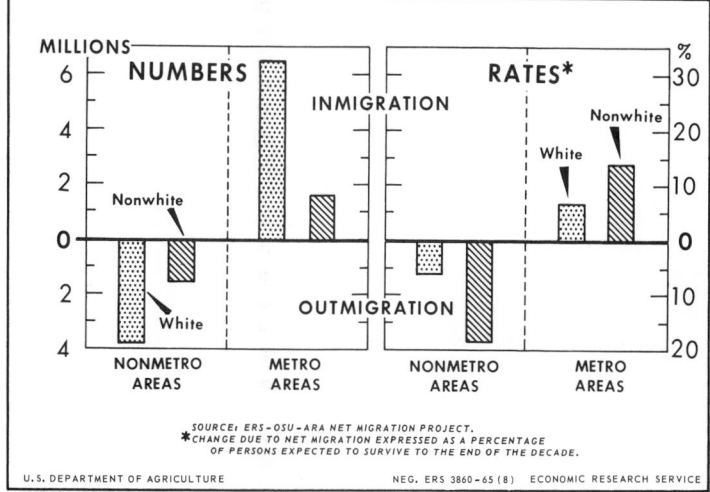

Figure 19-12 Migration Balance of Metropolitan and Nonmetropolitan Areas: 1950 to 1960.

SOURCE: Gladys K. Bowles and James D. Tarver, *Net Migration of the Population, 1950–60, by Age, Sex and Color* (U. S. Department of Agriculture and Oklahoma State University, 1965), p. ix.

teristics, and human adjustments to a given set of conditions are too varied for this to be true. Nevertheless, the scientific study of migration streams requires that this ideal be approached as nearly as possible. In other words, *for meaningful analysis of migration streams the areas of origin and areas of destination should be as homogeneous as possible, both in terms of the environment and the population.* The homogeneity of the population can be height-

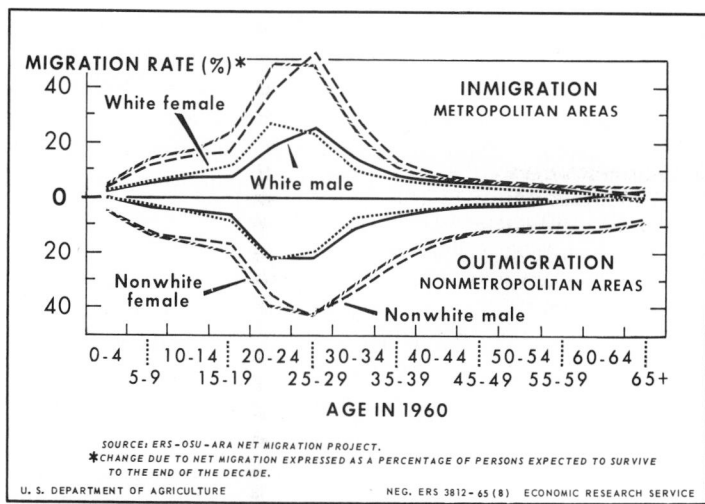

Figure 19-13 Age Pattern of Net Migration Rates to Metropolitan Areas and from Nonmetropolitan Areas: 1950 to 1960.

SOURCE: Gladys K. Bowles and James D. Tarver, *Net Migrations of the Population, 1950–60, by Age, Sex and Color* (U. S. Department of Agriculture and Oklahoma State University, 1965), p. ix.

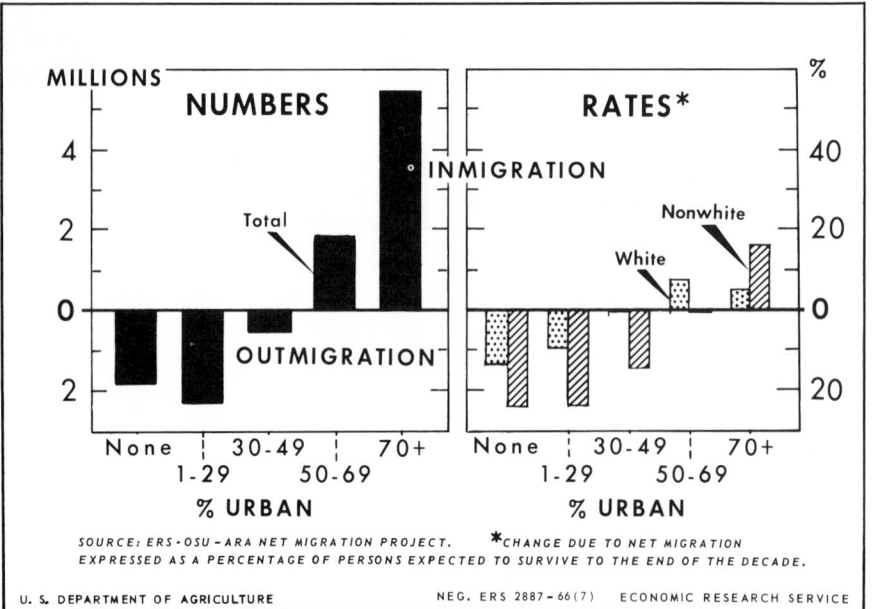

Figure 19-14   Migration Rates for Counties Classified according to Degree of Urbanization: 1950 to 1960.

SOURCE: Gladys K. Bowles and James D. Tarver, *Net Migration of the Population, 1950–60, by Age, Sex and Color* (U. S. Department of Agriculture and Oklahoma State University, 1965), p. x.

ened, as illustrated above, by carrying out a separate analysis for each of several subgroups, such as white and nonwhite populations, or sex, age, occupations, or other groups. The homogeneity of the environment may also be controlled further by making a separate analysis for parcels of territory that have maximum homogeneity.

It is obvious that the 50 states are very heterogeneous units of area. Within each state there are numerous and wide variations in economic and social conditions, so that it is difficult to attach an unambiguous meaning to the flow of migrants from one state to another. Moreover, it is not proper to assume that all parts of a state lose or gain migrants at the same rate; some parts of a state may be suffering very severe loss of migrants while other parts of the same state may be enjoying a migration boom. Hence the state is a comparatively gross unit of area for the measurement and explanation of migration streams. A solution to this problem is to abandon the state as the unit for specifying migration streams and to adopt smaller units that are more homogeneous.

At each of the three censuses for which the U.S. Bureau of Census has collected migration statistics—1940, 1950, and 1960—this principle has been recognized, and the data have been reported for units of area smaller than states. In 1940 these units were state subregions and in 1950 and 1960 they were the system of economic areas, described in Chapter 15. It is possible here to give only a brief account of this program and to summarize some of the major research findings that have emerged from it.

Since migration statistics in the United States are collected in terms of county units, it is necessary that the more homogeneous units consist of one or more whole counties. For the first census tabulations of streams of internal migration for the census of 1940, a set of 328 state subregions (subdivisions of states arrived at by grouping counties) were delimited by Dr. O. E. Baker acting as a consultant to the Census Bureau. Two broad types of sub-

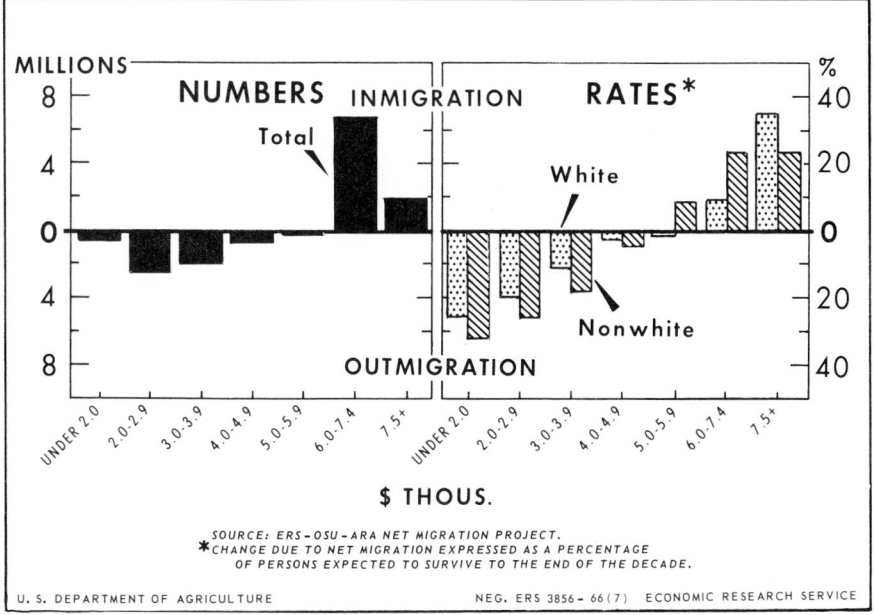

Figure 19-15 Migration Rates for Counties Classified according to Level of Family Income: 1950 to 1960.

SOURCE: Gladys K. Bowles and James D. Tarver, *Net Migration of the Population, 1950–60, by Age, Sex and Color* (U. S. Department of Agriculture and Oklahoma State University, 1965), p. x.

regions were defined: metropolitan and nonmetropolitan. The metropolitan subregions were counties that contained the largest urban agglomerations. The nonmetropolitan subregions subdivided the remainder of the state on the basis of climate, topography, type of rural economy, level of living, and racial and ethnic composition. The origin and destination of each of the 15.7 million migrants who were reported as living in a different county in 1935 than in 1940 were identified in terms of these 328 subregions. For a variety of reasons (many of them having to do with emergencies created by World War II) it proved to be impossible for the Bureau of the Census to carry out its original plan to tabulate the streams of migration from each state subregion to every other state subregion as a part of the official 1940 census. However, such tabulations were made as a special joint project of the Scripps Foundation for Research in Population Problems and the Bureau of the Census during 1940 and 1950. During these years the Scripps Foundation was conducting a study of population distribution and redistribution under the direction of Donald J. Bogue, and a substantial share of the resources of this project was spent in completing the subregional migration tabulations of the 1940 census and in analyzing them. A two-volume report entitled *Subregional Migration in the United States, 1935-40* was published.[39] Volume I of this report tabulated the flow of migration from each subregion to every other subregion in the nation. For summary purposes, the subregions were grouped into the nearest equivalent of the 13 economic regions as delimited in Chapter 15. The following pages summarize the major findings of this study. Unfortunately, as yet an equally intensive analysis of migration streams and differentials has not been undertaken for a more recent interval of time.

[39] Donald J. Bogue, Henry S. Shryock, Jr., and Siegfried A. Hoermann, Volume I, *Streams of Migration Between Subregions;* Volume II, Donald J. Bogue, Margaret Jarman Hagood and Gladys K. Bowles, *Differential Migration in the Corn and Cotton Belts.* Both volumes published by Scripps Foundation for Research in Population Problems, Miami University, Oxford, Ohio, 1953 and 1957.

Figure 19-16 Rate of Net Migration for Each Population Subregion of the United States: 1935 to 1940.

SOURCE: Donald J. Bogue, Henry S. Shryock, Jr., and Siegfried A. Hoermann, *Streams of Migration Between Subregions* (Oxford, Ohio: Scripps Foundation for Research in Population Problems, Miami University, 1957), p. 40.

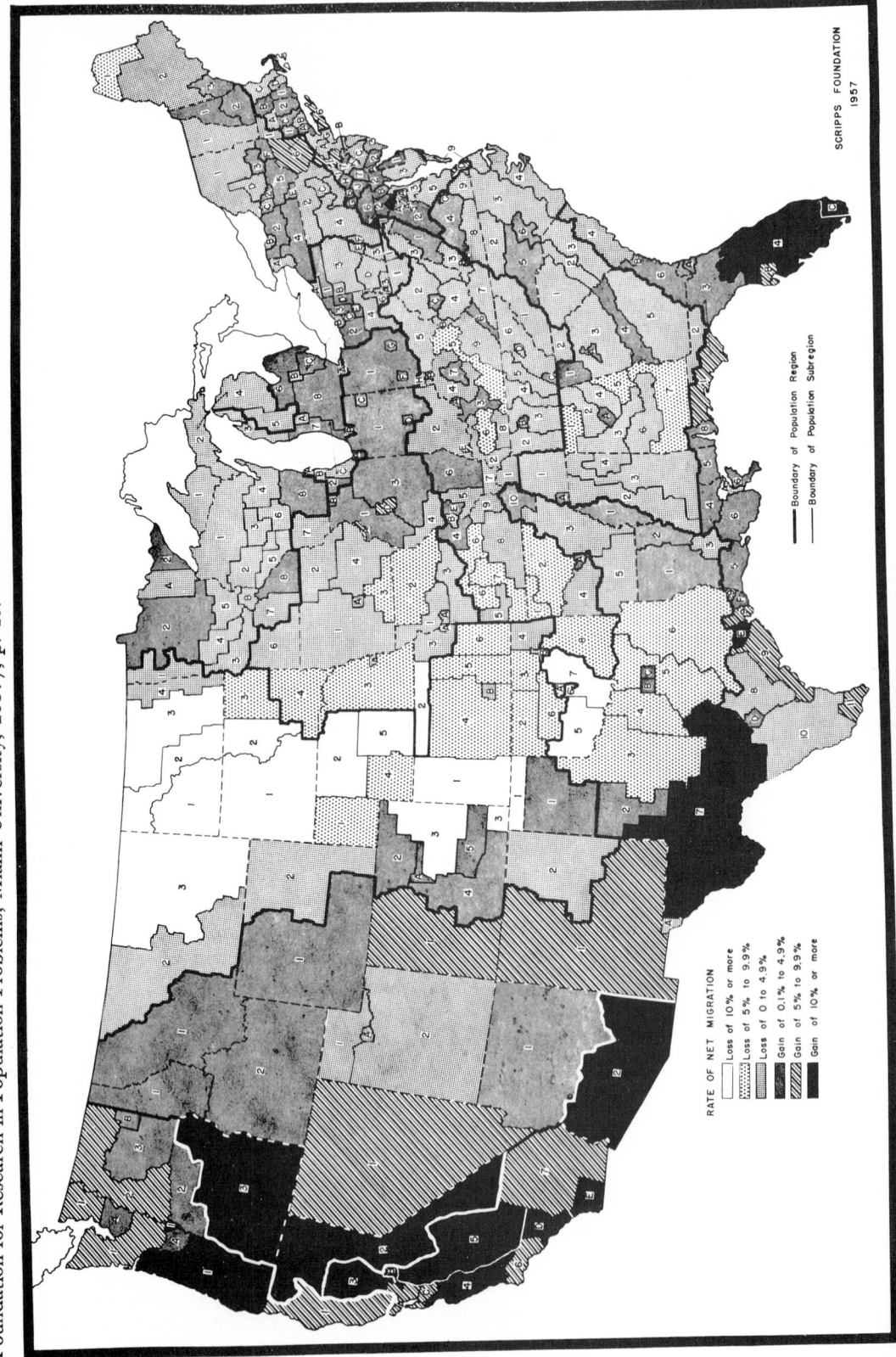

The study found that within every state there were very wide variations in the rate of in-, out-, and net migration. (Figure 19-16 is a map showing the level of net migration for each population subregion. The intrastate variation in migration patterns is clearly evident.) In general, the metropolitan and more urbanized portions received comparatively large streams of in-migrants from nonmetropolitan subregions—both inside and outside the state. The nonmetropolitan portion, in contrast, tended to lose migrants unless it was a subregion with a new expansion of nonagricultural industry or a subregion experiencing spillover from an adjoining metropolitan area. Each subregion tended to have a typical area pattern of migration—it gained migrants from particular subregions and exported migrants to the same or other particular subregions. The tendency for migrants to flow out of areas of economic hardship and toward areas of greater economic expansion and growth was very evident on the subregional level. Moreover, the well-known differentials in migration characteristics tended to vary according to the type of subregional flow. For example, the tendency for migrants to be very young was found to be typical primarily of flows from rural and nonmetropolitan subregions to urban and metropolitan areas; migrants from city to city and from rural-farm to rural-farm areas tended to have an age composition that was much more similar to that of the area of origin.

Urban-Rural Migration Streams. The migration census of 1940 was unique in that it identified the origin of each migrant not only in terms of subregions, but also by urban and rural residence within that subregion. Following are some of the major findings of the analysis of these data:

1. The largest single type of migration was not the flow of migrants from rural to urban areas, as may be supposed. Instead, it was the flow of migrants between one city and another.

2. The volume of migration from rural to urban areas was comparatively small. This appears to be due both to the fact that the population of the nation had become predominantly urban and to the tendency of the economic depression to suppress the cityward flow of rural youths.

3. One of the most common forms of migration was the "circulation" of migrants among communities of the same type: city to city, farm to farm, and rural-nonfarm to rural-nonfarm.

4. Migration probably contributed less to city growth during the 1935-1940 period than did the natural increase of the cities themselves. Net migration to cities accounted for not more than one fourth of the total urban growth during the period.

5. The urban population appeared to be definitely less mobile than the rural population. Once they arrive in cities, people tend to become immobile. When they do leave, they appear to do so only to go to another city or to a suburb.

6. The rates of in- and out-migration from all urban-rural residences tended to rise with increasing educational attainment. This is conclusive evidence that migration tended to involve better educated persons at a higher rate than less educated persons. The net effect of urban-rural migration was to remove from rural-farm areas a disproportionately large share of high school graduates and persons who attended a college and to deposit them in rural-nonfarm (probably suburban) areas and in cities.

7. The in-migrants to urban areas did not appear to have been swelling the ranks of the unemployed or public emergency workers any faster than they were swelling the ranks of the employed. They appeared to have found employment about as readily as the population already residing there. Migrants were less unemployed than the populations from which they came. It appears that unemployed persons remained comparatively immobile (or that those who did migrate and did not find work returned to their place of origin).

8. In-migrants to urban places from other urban places tended to be in professional and other white-collar occupations; migrants from rural-farm areas to cities tended to be more concentrated in operative, service, and laborer occupations. Migrants into rural areas from urban areas tended *not* to be in agricultural occupations; this movement was small and appeared to be a form of suburbanization from cities of all sizes.

Explanation of Migration. The rates of in-, out-, and net migration in 1935-1940 for each population subregion were correlated with each other and with a variety of social and economic traits in an effort to identify some of the major characteristics of subregional migration streams and of the forces associated with them. It was found that there was a strong positive correlation between the rate of in-migration and the rate of out-migration from the same subregion for all types of combinations of subregions: high rates of in-migration tended to be accompanied by high rates of out-migration. This appeared to be the return flow of migrants who were disappointed with the movement or who had failed to adjust in the new environment. Several factors, hypothesized as being explanations of migration streams and for which data were available, were correlated with the rate of net migration for the subregions. Multiple-regression procedures were employed to try to assess the independent effect of each factor. The following quotations from the report summarize the findings:

"1. Differences in employment between the place of origin and possible destinations emerged clearly as one of the driving and guiding forces behind migration. Metropolitan areas that had high rates of unemployment also had high rates of out-migration and low rates of in-migration with a consequent tendency toward negative net migration. Nonmetropolitan areas that had high rates of unemployment had high rates of out-migration to metropolitan areas, low rates of in-migration from all other areas, and a tendency to suffer severe net migration losses. This pattern does not necessarily imply that migrants have foreknowledge of the relative opportunities to be had at all possible destinations and that they choose the most promising one. The results observed for 1935-40 could occur under a great variety of conditions. Even if migrants arrived at places by random selection, at areas of high opportunity the migrant would tend to remain; migrants arriving at areas of low employment opportunity would tend to move on in search of a job—and to continue moving until a satis-

factory place was found. A satisfactory place would probably be an area of greater employment opportunity. Thus, the observed pattern could occur on the basis of pure trial-and-error search of jobs. Many migrants move in response to jobs already contracted for before the move is made. Areas of low job expansion would contract with few migrants, while rapidly expanding places would tend to recruit widely and make commitments to many. Also, information about good and bad areas for employment may be gleaned from newspapers, hiring agencies, trade unions, and by letters from relatives and friends. Undoubtedly, these and other mechanisms operate to locate migrants at points where they can obtain employment and to steer them away from communities where they would incur hardship or enjoy no improvement in their situation. Thus, the analysis has merely demonstrated that differences in opportunity to work are effective in guiding the flow of migrants (probably, especially the young workers first entering the labor force, or unemployed or mal-employed workers who desire to change jobs). The study was not designed to specify exactly how this guidance was accomplished, however.

"2. Another set of forces that unmistakably guided the direction and flow of migration streams were the basic shifts in the regional and territorial balance of the economy. At least five such distributional shifts could be detected for the 1935-40 period: (*a*) the drift toward metropolitan and urban centers from rural and nonmetropolitan areas; (*b*) the westward movement, especially from the midwest; (*c*) the northward movement (especially Negroes) from the south; (*d*) the movement from central cities toward suburbs and the outer edges of metropolitan area; and (*e*) a patterned exchange between large and small, new and old, and expanding and stable metropolitan areas. Migration streams are merely one set of activities by which these changes are carried out. Behind this apparent attractiveness of areas with particular locations there undoubtedly lie shifts in capital investment, changing locations of job opportunities, change in technology, resources, and markets, and changes in levels and standards of living for various segments of the population. The fundamental discovery here is that the flow of migration streams during any particular interval of time is conditioned by the fundamental changes that are taking place in the regional division of labor, technology, and status in the national economy at that particular time. In fact, changes in migration streams possibly are one of the most sensitive indicators of change in the structure of the national economy.

"3. Two factors that seem to contribute most to the mobility of the population at the present time are above-average educational attainment and employment in white collar occupations. Whether as cause or as effect, both persons and communities that have these characteristics tend to be more mobile than those with less education or characterized by blue collar employment. Thus, the high mobility rates in the United States may not be a simple wanderlust, but may result from the present increased emphasis upon tertiary industries and the greater educational level of the population, which increases its knowledge of alternatives and its ability to adjust to a variety of alternative opportunities.

"4. At no point should it be inferred that economic factors and the spatial adjustments being made by the economy are the only forces at work to determine the direction, size, and composition of migration streams. Many of the factors that have been employed here (such as educational attainment) are not completely economic variables. Any theory of economic determinism in migration is inclined to be incomplete. A great variety of conditions, of which the economic may or may not comprise an important set of considerations, can lead to migration, and cause persons to join the particular migration streams they do." [40]

Differentials in Subregional Migration. Volume II of *Subregional Migration in the United States, 1935-40* concentrated on the analysis of migration differentials, holding constant type of origin, type of destination, age, and a variety of other factors. This analysis was limited to two major economic regions: the Midwest (Corn Belt) and the Old South (Cotton Belt) eco-

nomic regions. Following are quotations and summaries of findings from this report.

1. *Age differentials.* The age differential (concentration at young ages) was universal in all subregions. It varied in intensity with type of community of origin and type of community of destination. It was greatest when the difference in degree of urbanism between the sending and the receiving communities was large, and was smallest when the difference in degree of urbanism between the sending and receiving communities was small. Apparently, when migration involves a major change in the type of community of residence, it tends to be undertaken by the more adaptive (younger) members or by those who are faced with the necessity of readjustment but who have few alternatives other than to migrate.

2. *Household status.* A large share of adult migrants moved as individuals rather than as members of families. Nevertheless, there was a large family element in this migration. Migrants tended to make living arrangements that would provide family life; only one migrant in twelve was found to be living in a quasi household. The remaining 11/12 were residing in private households either as lodgers, relatives, or servants or as heads or wives of heads. The concept of the lonely migrant in the big city, living in a single room in a large rooming house and slowly suffering personality deterioration because of isolation, could apply to only a very small part of the population and probably to a rather select part. The much more usual pattern appears to be that the lone migrant to the city sets up his own household at a younger age than nonmigrants of his own age—both at the place of origin and at the place of destination. This often takes the form of early marriage. Rural youths may choose a particular destination because they have relatives living there rather than because it offers the most opportunities. Farm girls may become servants in private households because they do not know what other types of employment are available to them and because their parents will consent to migration under these conditions but no others.

3. *Educational attainment.* Migration to cities selected those persons who were better

[40] Bogue, Shryock, and Hoermann, *op. cit.* chapters 6 and 7

educated than persons of the same age at the place of origin. In many streams the educational level of the migrants is higher than that of the population of the same age at the place of destination. Migrants from rural areas tend to be among the best educated persons in the communities of origin, but their level of education tends to be only average or slightly below average in the urban communities at which they arrive. Migration from the South, possibly because of major social and economic changes under way, contained disproportionately large numbers of the least well educated as well as the better educated.

4. *Employment status.* Migrants were found to have among their ranks a lower percentage of unemployed and a higher percentage of employed than was found among either the origin or destination populations of the same age. It cannot be determined from these data how much of this differential is due to the fact that the migrants who succeeded in obtaining jobs remained in a city while those who did not obtain employment returned to the place of origin. Migrants became wage and salary workers, rather than self-employed workers, in higher proportions than the destination population.

5. *Occupation.* The occupation reported at the time of the census is not necessarily the first job the migrant obtained after moving, but it may be. In comparison with the urban population to which they migrated, migrants from farms were somewhat concentrated in the laborer and manual-work occupations. Male migrants between cities were selected for white-collar occupations. Women migrants were selected for professional and semiprofessional jobs and for service occupations. Nonwhite male migrants were selected for professional and laborer occupations.

Among migrants to cities from rural-nonfarm and other urban areas there was a disproportionately small number of unskilled laborers, male service workers, and factory operatives in comparison with both the sending and receiving population. There are several possible explanations for this set of findings. One explanation would point out that migrants to cities fared much better than those who remained behind, and that they found more satisfactory employment than those who refused to migrate. Another explanation would point out that during these years the cities had a great oversupply of factory operatives and other manual workers and that it was difficult if not almost impossible for migrants with this background to find employment. Therefore, manual workers in nonfarm areas either remained fixed (knowing that it was useless to move), or else moved, failed to find work, and returned home or changed occupations.

6. *Income.* Migration to cities was found to be differentially selective of workers who had earned incomes somewhat larger than the incomes of the population from which migration had taken place. It was not the lowest-paid workers who migrated, but those who had received near-average pay. Young male white migrants received average incomes that compared favorably with the incomes received by residents their own age in the destination city. Older migrants, female migrants, and nonwhite migrants were much lower in the income scale than the destination populations of their own age.

7. *Summary: an approach to a theory of differential migration.* When the results of this analysis are considered in their entirety and in their relations to each other, over-all fundamental implications for a theory of migration selectivity emerge.

Generalization 1. Migration was found to be markedly selective in some way with respect to every factor considered in the study. Therefore, in future studies of internal migration in this country it should be presumed as a working hypothesis that internal migration is highly selective in many different ways. These specific differentials (income, occupation, marital status, etc.) are not independent of each other, but are highly interrelated. Therefore, *in any particular subregion and at any particular moment in time, internal migration is selective of persons with particular combinations of traits.* By this view, all migration should be treated as differential migration until proved otherwise.

Generalization 2. Any assumption that there exists a particular set of permanent basic migration differentials that need only be "discovered" is unfounded. The data presented here indicate clearly that *migration can be highly selective with respect to a given characteristic in one area and be selective to only a mild degree, or not at all, in another area.* If the selectivity of migration can vary in both pattern and intensity between different places, it is equally plausible that it can vary between different periods of time. Hence *it is fruitless to seek permanent inflexible differentials in migration that will not vary, to some degree at least, in pattern and intensity with time and place. The search for migration differentials, then, should be an effort to discover in what ways and why migration was selective of persons with particular characteristics or combinations of characteristics under varying combinations of conditions at origin and conditions at destination.*

If the selectivity of migration varies with time and place, then migration differentials should be regarded as a class of events that is itself subject to scientific research and explanation. By this view, *migration differentials are not an ultimate end of migration research. Rather, they are a class of events, a form of population behavior, about which hypotheses may be formulated, data gathered, and a scientific explanation developed.* Because many of the factors and forces that give rise to differential migration are undoubtedly among the most basic and most enduring aspects of the social and economic system, it would be unwise to emphasize the variability of differentials too strongly. Particular differentials may persist for long periods of time. Those that appear to be the most stable and enduring as well as the most important are especially good candidates for further intensive research.

Generalization 3. The pattern and intensity of migration selectivity was frequently different when measured with respect to the population at the place of origin than when measured with respect to the population at the place of destination. These differences were evident for urban and rural areas of origin within each region, and for size of city of destination. Therefore, *variation in the*

selectivity of migration should not be explained solely in terms either of the situation at the place of origin or the situation at the place of destination, but in terms of the combination of conditions and the type of population residing at the place of origin and the place of destination. By this view, the explanation for the selectivity of a particular type of migration is to be found neither in the "pull" of the destination area nor in the "push" of the area of origin, but in the combination of factors present in both areas. Also, the fact that areas of potential out-migration contain population that has certain unique characteristics increases the probability that, in comparison with the population at the destination, migration will be selective of persons with these characteristics. Similarly, the fact that areas of potential in-migration offer employment and other opportunities of a particular type will increase the probability that, in comparison with the population at the place of origin, migrants will be found to be concentrated in these categories when enumerated at a later date. Hence the unique characteristics of any body of migrants result in part both from the unique characteristics of the population at the place of origin and from the unique opportunities at the place of destination. They also result in part from unique social and economic conditions at the place of origin that make particular categories of population available for migration.

As an extreme illustration of this principle, the migration differentials that existed during the eighteenth and nineteenth centuries and that selected the frontiersmen and settlers who peopled the territory west of the Alleghenies undoubtedly differed strikingly from those that existed in 1935-1940. Those differences may be interpreted in terms of the characteristics of the respective populations at the point of origin and the respective types of social and economic organization at the destinations at these two dates.

Generalization 4. *Under modern conditions, the migrants who leave farms for cities are not greatly handicapped in adjusting to city life if they come from prosperous agricultural communities that have made available to them a good secondary school education, if their families are able to subsidize them temporarily while they get started and if there are no other factors discriminating against them.* The data for native white migrants from farms in the Corn Belt to cities in the same area demonstrate conclusively that even during the 1935-1940 period of slow recovery from a depression, when unemployment was still a serious problem, young migrants from farms succeeded in obtaining jobs in a slightly higher proportion of instances and in about the same occupational pattern as the city youth their own age. Their average salary was nearly equal to that of the city youth. Thus, when they migrate to cities, farm youth are not necessarily relegated to the bottom of the economic ladder and pressed into the more menial jobs. The present study suggests that the adjustment of farm youth to city living may be surprisingly easy and that one factor behind the large stream of farm-to-city migration may be that farm youth can compete effectively and achieve the rewards that the city has to offer with essentially the same degree of success as their city cousins.

Generalization 5. Under modern conditions, farm-to-city migration tends to select those who obtain the most education. Intercity migration tends to select those who are better educated, who hold more responsible positions, and who can earn larger salaries than other city residents their own age. Thus *one major driving force behind internal migration to cities and among cities appears to be the need to distribute and redistribute the potential and actual specialists, experts, and managers to places where their abilities can be used most profitably in the economy.* The data of the present study suggest that even in the absence of high birthrates in rural areas, the modern urbanized economy would still require a great deal of rural-urban and urban-urban migration to satisfy the needs for distributing properly the specialized and trained personnel and those who aspire to become specialized and trained personnel.

Generalization 6. The selective nature of internal migration also emphasizes clearly that *factors other than "economic opportunity"* underlie much movement of population. Failing health and old age appear to bring many migrants into institutions located in the city. Being unable to work brings adults from farms into the city. A death in a family can send children to an orphanage and an older adult to live with one of his or her children. Crime motivates migration to escape punishment, and the punishment of criminals by imprisonment makes migrants of many offenders. Many girls migrate at the time of marriage, and after marriage their migration is conditioned by their husbands' situations more than by their own. Divorce is conducive to migration in at least some areas. These "noneconomic" differentials do not deny that much migration is motivated by efforts to take advantage of economic opportunities; in many areas lack of sufficient opportunities at home is a stimulus to out-migration, but for some elements of the population it may be of secondary importance.

Generalization 7. *In periods of great social change that involve a spatial redistribution of population, the pattern of migration differentials may be unlike those that precede or follow the change.* In the 1935-1940 period, for example, the South was urbanizing rapidly and the traditional rural "sharecropper" economy was breaking up. This fact may help to account for the finding that migration to Southern cities from other areas in the same state contained a concentration of the least well educated as well as of the better educated persons. Social change can cause migration differentials to vary in content, intensity, and direction over time. A study of such variations would be one way of observing social change.

Generalization 8. A large body of evidence was accumulated in the present study to show that *selectivity changes with the age of migrants.* Young migrants, many of whom are just beginning their careers in the labor force or are trying to establish themselves in what they hope will be their permanent line of employment, appear to be selected primarily with respect to factors that involve adjustment to gaining a livelihood and assuming adult roles. Many older migrants, on the other hand, appear to migrate as a result of failure, poor health, disaster, technological change, and many other factors that may not influence the migration of younger people as much. This would lead to the conclusion that, in general, *young migrants are selected primarily along the lines of long-run basic differences and imbalances in the social and economic organization, whereas adults are selected, in addition and to a greater extent, with respect to current personal and social problems and current social changes.* As an example, the movement of young persons from farms to cities may properly be interpreted as a long-run differential arising from differential birthrates and differential rates of economic growth in rural and urban areas. The movement of large proportions of mature adults from farms to cities betokens some extraordinary circumstance such as drought, rapid farm consolidation and mechanization, or loss of markets for a given agricultural commodity.

Generalization 9. The pattern of migration selectivity exhibited in 1935-1940 was such that it would lead to the tentative conclusion that *in future depressions unguided migration should not be relied upon to equalize the hardship between areas or to alleviate unemployment and underemployment in the hardest-hit communities.* In this study it was found that the unemployed who had been without work for the longest periods of time, the unemployed whose last occupation was of a type that was most overcrowded, workers with the lowest incomes, and employed workers in the most unskilled and overcrowded occupations were selected for out-migration less than the types of persons who were under less severe economic duress. If differential migration is to minimize economic distress, the origin differentials should be most intense, rather than least intense, for these categories that contain the persons who are suffering most from a depression.

19.10. Longitudinal (Cohort) Migration

During the 1960s migration specialists have turned their attention to the study of migration in the context of the total life of the individual. George Wilbur pointed out in 1963 that inasmuch as age-specific migration rates were in-

dependent probabilities, they could be summed across all age groups to obtain estimates of the total lifetime mobility the average person would experience. He calculated that the average person would migrate 4 times and change residence 13 times during his lifetime, given the schedule of age-specific migration rates then prevailing.[41]

The argument and the procedure for making these calculations are identical to those for computing the net reproduction rate (explained in Chapter 18.):

$$TMR = \sum_0^{100} \left(ASMR_x \cdot L_x \right)$$

where TMR is the total lifetime migration rate, $ASMR_x$ is the age-specific migration rates for a particular interval of time, and L_x is the survivorship column of a life table.

This measure reports the number of moves 1000 people would make during their lifetime if they were exposed, from birth to death, to the rates of migration in effect at a particular time. Such a measure is a cross-sectional one and is based on the principle of hypothetical cohorts. The argument is eminently logical: even more than fertility, migration is a volitional phenomenon and sensitive to environmental conditions. While it is true that there is no culture-based desire to migrate comparable to the desire for children, as we have seen there are migration-stimulating conditions in the environment to which the person reacts according to his situation and his attitudes and values. Thus one cohort of persons may have a very different migration experience from another, depending on the economic, political, and social conditions that prevail during their lifetime. It should be possible to break time fluctuations in migration rates into their longitudinal (cohort) and their annual (cross-sectional) components, as was done for fertility in Chapter 18.

The question of longitudinal study of migration was opened up by Eldridge in 1964 in a

[41] George Wilbur, "Migration Expectancy in the United States," *Journal of the American Statistical Association* (June 1963), 444–453.

provocative article, "A Cohort Approach to the Analysis of Migration Differentials."[42] As a colleague of Dorothy S. Thomas, she had observed that conventional procedures for correlating age-specific migration rates with time series of economic activity did not give a completely adequate explanation. She raised the question of whether or not a cohort approach to the analysis of time series might yield further insight into association between economic fluctuations and rates of migration. She classified the cohorts into two groups, according to the type of economic conditions that had prevailed during the decade in which they were 25 to 29 years of age. Those who had passed through a period of prosperity during these years were placed in one group and those who had passed through a period of recession were placed in the other. She found that the level of migration and the age pattern were very different for the two groups. Those who had experienced prosperity had higher migration rates and their peak migration rate occurred at ages 20 to 24. Those who had experienced depression had lower rates and the age of peak migration rate was 25 to 29. Whereas the rates had seemed inconsistent in their relationship to the time series before, when arranged in this fashion, they became quite consistent. She concludes that economic conditions tend to affect the age rates of migration streams. If a cohort of youngsters reach age 20 to 24 during a decade of economic recession, they tend to migrate at a lower rate than during prosperity. However, when prosperity returns, a part of this migration loss is apparently made up by above-average movement at a slightly older age. Eldridge concludes that "while cohort analysis of migration may not prove to be so fruitful as cohort analysis of fertility or mortality data, it shows promise as another way of looking at migration data. It does seem to make some relations clearer and to promise further insight into migration differentials."

In 1965 Henry S. Shryock reacted to Eldridge's suggestion by making a longitudinal analysis of data for partial residential histo-

ries.[43] He notes that since the measurement of migration is a comparison of place of residence at two different instants of time, it is inherently longitudinal. If residential history data are used in conjunction with longitudinal data on employment, occupation, marital status, and other sociodemographic statuses, it is possible to measure the association between changes of residence and changes in these other statuses more precisely. As yet data to fill out the complete system he proposes are not available, and Shryock illustrates the utility of his view by special tabulations of existing Census Bureau partial residential histories and data from the National Cancer Survey. He calculates that the average lifetime migration is not less than 3.15 migratory moves. He also finds that for more than one-half of the population lifetime mobility is completely within the same general residence type (urban-urban, nonfarm-nonfarm, farm-farm). He found only comparatively minor net lifetime movement from urban to rural-farm areas, but a considerable amount in the opposite direction. He also found a comparatively small amount of "circular" movement (from farm to urban and back to farm). Shryock also shows that there is wide variation among the population in the number of residences lived in. Following, for example, is the distribution of persons 45 to 54, for the year 1958:

Number of residences	Percent of population
1 residence	22.4
2 residences	27.7
3 residences	19.2
4 residences	11.7
5 residences	7.6
6 residences or more	11.4
Total	100.0

He speculates that if key events in the life cycle such as taking a job, marriage, or retirement tend to stimulate migration, there may be a typical "quota" of moves for the average person. He points out, as did Eldridge in an-

---

[42] Hope T. Eldridge, "A Cohort Approach to the Analysis of Migration Differentials," *Demography*, 1 (1964), 212–219.

[43] Henry S. Shryock and Elizabeth A. Larmon, "Some Longitudinal Data on Internal Migration," *Demography*, 2 (1965), 579–592.

other context, that the cohort approach allows the more precise study of the phenomenon of return migration and of "migration by stages." [44] From longitudinal data Shryock is able to report that about one quarter of the United States adult population were born on a farm, although all but a small fraction have moved to nonfarm residences. On the other hand, about one third of the United States population have lived in a nonfarm home all of their lives. His longitudinal data suggest that unemployed men are more likely to migrate than the employed and that the unemployed who migrate are more likely to find jobs (this contrasts sharply with the findings for the economic depression period). It is his conclusion, after reviewing the data available, that "the longitudinal data recently analyzed have unlocked a number of doors." Karl Taeuber has explored the problem of longitudinal migration in a prospectus for a major research undertaking, "Cohort Migration and the Urbanization of the United States." [45] He concludes that the cohort approach is an invaluable one and that its full benefits will be realized only when demographers are able to analyze residential histories in their full complexity. He suggests that the resolution of this class of problem can lead to a direct contribution to the wider sociological problem of analysis of life histories.

It is not possible, at this time, to present a well-rounded evaluation of the comparative role of cross-sectional versus longitudinal approaches to the study of migration. The purpose here has been primarily to alert the reader to the problem and to sensitize him to further research reports on this topic that may be expected to emerge in quantity in future years.

19.11. Migration and Mental Disorders

"The cowards never started and the weak died on the way" is an old frontier saying that one still often hears in the Midwest and the Far West, where few of even the most elite can trace their ancestry to the Mayflower or to one of the royal families of Europe. If there is a factual basis to this implied selectivity of migration, one would expect the communities that are built up primarily from migrants to exhibit extraordinarily great physical and mental vigor. In 1932 O. Odegaard reported statistics to show that the exact reverse may be true. He demonstrated that Norwegian emigrants overseas were subject to higher rates of hospitalization for mental disorders than were Norwegians who had remained in Norway. [46] In 1956 Benjamin Malzberg and Everett Lee reported similar findings with respect to internal migrants; in New York State the rate of first admission to mental hospitals was substantially higher for migrants from other states than for native-born New Yorkers. [47] Since these pioneering studies there has been a strong interest in the relationship between mental health and spatial mobility. Although the evidence is not unequivocal, it is now a fairly well established fact that in certain contexts there is a positive association between migration and the incidence of mental disease. [48] In some contexts, migrants are more prone to suffer from mental disease (particularly schizophrenia) than nonmigrants.

At least four equally plausible hypotheses can be adduced to explain this phenomenon, if it exists.

1. The process of migration and readjustment to a new community creates mental stress and a certain amount of personal maladjustment, which lead to mental disorder in a significant percentage of migrants. Because they suffer less stress, nonmigrants have lower rates of mental disorder.

2. Persons who are in a state of mental distress and are seriously maladjusted tend to have a flight reaction and attempt to escape from the scene of their problems. As a result,

[44] Hope T. Eldridge, "Primary, Secondary and Return Migration," Demography, 2 (1965), 444–455.

[45] Karl E. Taeuber, "Cohort Migration," Demography, 3 (1966), 416–422.

[46] O. Odegaard, "Emigration and Insanity," Acta Psychiatrica et Neurologia, Suppl. 4, 1932.

[47] B. Malzberg and E. S. Lee, Migration and Mental Disease (New York: Social Science Research Council, 1956).

[48] Mildred B. Kantor (ed.), Mobility and Mental Health (Springfield, Ill.: Charles C. Thomas, 1963). See especially "Migration and the Major Mental Disorder: A Reappraisal" by H. B. M. Murphy.

persons who are emotionally unstable and prone to mental disorder are positively selected for migration.

3. If the rates of mental disorder were equal among migrants and nonmigrants, the fact that a substantial share of migrants are family-less and without anyone to shelter them would tend to lead to their more immediate detection and hospitalization. The nonmigrant neurotic, on the other hand, may be hidden and protected by his family and his illness may be detected early and treatment undertaken by a psychiatrist or simply by family support without hospitalization.

4. The onset of some of the mental illnesses (especially schizophrenia) tends to be linked to the younger ages at which migration takes place. It also tends to be concentrated in certain classes of the population, some of which are highly mobile. Crude rates of first admissions to mental hospitals that do not control for age and possibly socioeconomic status can be misleading.

As yet the problem is unresolved and remains a highly intriguing research topic. A review of the evidence in 1963 led to the conclusion that in some situations migration appears to be linked in a rather direct functional way with mental illness, while in other situations no such relationship seems to exist. This leads to the more sophisticated view that it is not migration as such but some concomitant of migration that may lead to mental disorder.[49] It is not difficult to formulate hypotheses in this vein:

1. Lack of a supportive receiving population that favors rapid and easy social adjustment leads to mental stress and disorder. When the migrant enters a family situation or an ethnic community where he is given personal nurture, rates of mental illness are low. Migrants to the very largest metropolitan areas may be more exposed to mental breakdown than migrants from one small town to another, for example.

2. Aggravated hostility, prejudice, and highly inconsistent behavior on the part of the receiving community may be conducive to men-

[49] For a penetrating discussion at the psychological level, see "Social Mobility as Social Learning" by William E. Henry, in Kantor, *op. cit.*

tal disorders. For example, Negroes who leave the South and enter the competitive situation of the North—with its great differentials in income, its discrimination in employment, its segregation of residence, and its assertion nonetheless that such treatment is wrong and does not really exist—may suffer more mental torture than Negroes who remain in the South and "know where they stand" with respect to the prejudiced majority.

3. In some situations migrants leave their homeland gladly and without great mental stress, but in others their movement is forced by tragic circumstances, so that the separation is a very traumatic one. "Joyful" migration in anticipation of accomplishing high personal ambitions may promote mental health, whereas "tragic" migration made in despair and defeat may have the reverse effect. Thus the victims of war, political revolution, or persecution suffer mental torture and trauma that may be linked to the fact that they are migrants, but not to the act of migration itself.

4. In some instances migration involves comparatively little change for the migrant; he simply continues his former pattern of life in a similar but different place. Other forms of migration may involve a dramatic transition that requires a complete reorganization of the personality. The peasant migrating from a feudal subsistence economy of Eastern Europe to urban America in the 1900s was forced to change language, customs, values, and attitudes. In such cases the stress can be very great.

The above may be overly elaborate ways of stating what may be the obvious: the mental health of migrants is a function of the amount of stress they must undergo in the process of separating themselves from the community of origin and of gaining the status of being accepted members of the community of destination. It is also very plausible that persons in a state of deep anxiety and stress will seek to migrate in an effort to resolve their problems. Certainly, it is well known that criminals and persons given to deviant behavior are often highly migratory—both to escape the consequences of past mistakes and to seek new arenas in which to make new ones.

II. INTERNATIONAL MIGRATION

19.12.   World International Migration Since 1960

The movement of population between nations is the most dramatic form of migration. In this age of nationalism, changing one's citizenship is almost tantamount to changing one's identity. Yet in all recorded history (and apparently before) there has always been an ample supply of persons making this change. In a high proportion of such moves the person not only changes his national loyalties, but also forsakes his native language, his cultural heritage and customs, his relatives and lifelong friends, and his occupation. So drastic is the change that many adults never make a complete adjustment in their lifetime, and it is only their children or grandchildren who are fully integrated into the receiving society.

Most demographic treatments of world migration begin with the prehistoric wanderings from the cradles of civilization and the dawn-of-history movements of Phoenicians, Aryans, Greeks, Polynesians, and the tribesmen from Central Asia. We shall not do that here; instead we shall undertake first to understand international migration as a component of contemporary national growth around the world. We shall explore immigration history for only one nation—the United States. The Bibliography at the end of the chapter lists historical materials for other regions and nations of the world.

An important element in the international flow of migration today is the existence of legal restrictions to movement. Most nations regulate the flow of migrants across their borders, either by establishing quotas or by establishing qualifications that potential immigrants must possess, or both. The most severe of these restrictions have been imposed by industrialized and wealthy nations, for the purpose of avoiding an invasion by citizens from underprivileged nations.

Because of these restrictions, international migration since about 1960 has been at low ebb. At almost no moment in recorded history has the *rate* of out-movement or in-movement to or from nations been lower. Even the volume (number of international migrants) has been comparatively small. As a result, the consideration of international migration as a component of growth has one significant generalization: *almost everywhere in the world, since 1960 international migration is a comparatively insignificant component in population growth or change in population composition.*

Table 19-14 summarizes the world migration situation as of about 1960. Although for many nations data are not available, a high percentage of the nations for which data are lacking are also nations that have no immigration. From this table and from general information about the legal enactments concerning immigration and emigration emerge the following highlights that seem to characterize international migration during the "quiescent" period:

1. Only a few nations—United States, Canada, Brazil, Israel, New Zealand, Australia and Hong Kong—are receiving migrants in significantly large numbers for permanent settlement.

2. The developing nations which have the most severe problems of population pressure and the lowest levels of living—China, India, Pakistan, Indonesia, Philippines, and Egypt—all have zero emigration and near-zero or even positive immigration. Some nations that previously have received immigrants from these areas are forcing them to return to their homeland if possible. Such pressures are being placed especially against the Chinese and Indian minorities. Thus emigration is outside the realm of discussion as even a temporary solution to the population problems of these countries.

3. A partial exception is the sizeable inflow of workers from Algeria into France, of Negroes from the Caribbean into England, of some Indonesians into the Netherlands, and of Puerto Ricans into the United States.

4. In nations with Communist governments, net international migration is either zero or strongly negative. This situation persists despite the fact that these nations tend to welcome skilled manpower. The "Berlin Wall," the mass exodus into Hong Kong, and the strict rules preventing citizens from leaving these coun-

Table 19-14   Number of Immigrants and Emigrants, Selected Nations: 1960

Nation	Number of immigrants	Number of emigrants	Nation	Number of immigrants	Number of emigrants
Africa			Europe		
Gambia....................	60	93	Austria..................	1,012	4,325
Mauritius.................	321	158	Belgium..................	42,248	32,189
Morocco...................	1,757	27,687	Bulgaria.................	20	181
Mozambique................	8,250	1,440	Czechoslovakia...........	1,341	2,900
Rhodesia..................	10,807	9,706	Denmark..................	26,638	23,647
			Finland..................	965	1,844
America, North & Central			France...................	56,038	58,270
Bahama Islands............	23,719	11,719	Ireland..................	1,365	2,047
Bermuda...................	8,886	...	Netherlands..............	33,073	48,885
British Honduras..........	237	6	Poland...................	747	24,050
Canada....................	104,928	...	Portugal.................	1,860	32,318
Costa Rica................	3,454	...	Spain....................	23,114	33,242
Mexico....................	3,628	1,862	Sweden...................	26,143	15,138
Panama....................	624	...	United Kingdom...........	84,740	93,178
Trinidad and Tobago.......	1,096	1,484	Germany..................	...	259,880
United States............	272,238	...			
			Oceania		
America, South			Australia................	39,371	46,595
Argentina.................	8,818	...	New Zealand..............	21,424	14,848
Brazil....................	40,507	...			
Chile.....................	240	....			
Colombia..................	6,530	19,327			
Venezuela.................	6,735	4,906			
Asia					
Hong Kong.................	35,055	...			
Israel....................	23,644	7,206			
Japan.....................	21,175	68,356			
Philippines...............	272	...			
Thailand..................	1,850	...			
Turkey....................	35	265			

Source: United Nations, Demographic Yearbook, 1962, Table 26.

tries serve to keep a net migration balance of zero or a net loss.

5. Several nations of Europe are experiencing a labor shortage because of rapid economic growth and low birthrates. They are admitting temporary workers from Italy, Greece, Turkey, and other nations with lower levels of living. Some of these temporary immigrants are becoming permanent residents. Switzerland, Belgium, France, the Netherlands, and Sweden are among these nations.

6. Despite the fact that Africa has been proclaimed a territory with great untapped resources and in need of skilled manpower and entrepreneurs, the in-movement of Europeans has apparently come to a complete halt. As a result of political and racial unrest, the net international migration balance of Africa at the present time is probably strongly negative and is probably selective of the best educated and most skilled manpower, both white and black.

7. South America, which also has been regarded as a land of immigration opportunity, has lost much of its appeal to potential immigrants. This has happened because almost all lands that can easily be claimed have already been settled. Further settlement requires large investments of capital and great engineering enterprises with skilled manpower. The rural lands now are either fully settled to the capacity of present technology to support population or oversettled. There is a large-scale retreat from the frontiers and the rural agricultural lands into the cities. As a result, the cities of Latin America offer few employment opportunities to most foreigners.

8. There is little prospect that new immigration opportunities will open up anywhere in the world. In fact, the flow into Australia, Hong Kong, and Israel already shows signs of saturation, and there is little likelihood that Canada, the United States, and Brazil will attempt to increase the flow by drastic liberalization of present restrictions. Thus there is a long-term prospect for a continuation of this quiescent situation, unless events such as those described in the next section recur.

19.13.   World International Migration between 1935 and 1960

The present period of quiescence, however, follows on the heels of one of the most wildly tumultuous and cruel periods of international migration in world history. The stormy phase that preceded the present calm and lasted from about 1935 to 1960 may best be characterized as one of *expulsion* and *flight,* based on political and ethnic considerations. The terms "forced migration," "population transfers," and "repatriation" have been used to describe it. Its main characteristic has been its primarily involuntary nature; the migrants have moved out of necessity, for fear of their lives, or because of loss of opportunity of earning a living. These movements have been a consequence of war or of internal political upheavals in which particular groups of citizens were declared unwelcome and were ordered to leave or in which individuals with divergent political beliefs or ethnic backgrounds fled to escape living under a new regime. A recitation of the primary migration episodes of this era will illustrate the nature of the movement.

1. During Hilter's rise to power in Germany in the 1930s millions of Jews and political refugees fled to America and other countries of Europe to escape extermination.

2. During and immediately after World War II large numbers of military and civilian "political prisoners" from defeated nations were conscripted and shipped to labor camps in Asian USSR.

3. After the end of World War II in the Pacific about 3 million Japanese were returned by decree to Japan from Manchuria, Korea, Taiwan, and islands in the Western Pacific.[50]

4. At the time of partition of India and Pakistan, more than 7 million Muslims fled from India to Pakistan, and more than 8.5 Hindus fled from Pakistan to India.[50]

5. Five million Germans living in East Germany have fled to the Allied sector of Berlin or to West Germany.[51]

6. Indonesia has expelled much of its Chinese population.

7. More than 1 million Chinese soldiers and civilians fled to Formosa when Mainland China became Communist.[51]

8. Arabs were displaced or fled from the territory that now is Israel during the upheavals of World War II, and until 1967 a million of them and their offspring lived on the border of Israel as refugees under the United Nations protection.

9. An undetermined number of Russians have been transferred into Eastern Germany and other nations of Eastern Europe.

10. As the nations of Eastern Europe changed to a Communistic form of government, many thousands of political and religious refugees poured into Western Europe, the Americas, and Australia.

11. The number of refugees from Mainland China to Hong Kong is not known, but it almost certainly is in excess of 2 million.[51]

12. Nearly a million North Koreans have fled to South Korea as refugees during and after the Korean war.[51]

13. By 1955 nearly a million Vietnamese had fled from North to South Vietnam during the political upheavals that accompanied the partition of that country, and since then the number has undoubtedly increased.[51]

14. As political independence has come to territories that formerly were colonies, European businessmen and colonial administrators, and other persons of European ancestry living abroad, have returned to England, Holland, Belgium, Spain, Portugal, and Italy. They have been displaced by natives or their businesses or professions could not prosper under the regulations of the new regimes.

15. Several thousands of Turks have been returned to Turkey from Bulgaria.[51]

In reviewing this movement for the period 1946-1955, Robert Cook has estimated that roughly 50 million people migrated from their homelands in search of political and economic stability. If we add to this the movement between 1935 and 1946 and the forced migrations since 1955, the total is quite possibly in excess of 60 million. To comprehend the magnitude

[50] Warren S. Thompson and David Lewis, *Population Problems,* 5th ed. (New York: McGraw-Hill, 1960), pp. 474–501.

[51] Robert C. Cook, "World Migration, 1946–55," *Population Bulletin,* 13 (August 1957), 77–94.

of this movement, it might be noted that the total number of immigrants to the United States from all nations of the world during the 145 years from 1820 to 1965 was about 43 million. The amount of human suffering that has accompanied this expulsive migration staggers the imagination. The vast majority of these migrants were forced to leave on short notice, to sell their property at a fraction of its true value (often converting it to a form that could be smuggled past customs officials), and to arrive in almost any land that would consent to receive them. Without prior arrangements for housing, employment, schooling, and community services the displaced person has been subject to intense economic privation and personal humiliation, for even while showing mercy and giving aid, the receiving countries have exhibited a certain amount of hostility and resentment at being burdened with the outcasts. The great bulk of these victims of world upheaval are now middle-aged or approaching retirement and are being replaced by generations that were not exposed to these horrors.

Meanwhile, the process continues on a smaller scale. Refugees have been arriving in the United States from Cuba, Africa, Yugoslavia, Poland, Greece, China, and other nations, from which persons still are being expelled or are fleeing to avoid persecution. In addition, there are still some tense situations that could break out into new expulsions. For example, expulsion of Chinese and Asian Indians from Africa, Malaya, Burma, Cambodia, and the Philippines are possibilities. Political turmoils in the Middle East have led to the creation of new thousands of homeless persons from Jordan, Syria, and the Sinai Peninsula. The Vietnam conflict created a large displaced population in the

1960s. It is not possible, therefore, to claim that international migration has fully returned to a phase of voluntary movement of individuals seeking to improve their lot in life. We must remember also that pre-World War II international migration was not without its expulsive episodes and population transfers.

Much peaceful and voluntary migration from Europe to Australia, Canada, the United States, and South America took place during the postwar years 1945-1960. Before prosperity returned to Europe many citizens of England, Germany, Italy, Greece, and other nations voluntarily moved to Australia, Canada, South America and the United States. The "expulsion and flight" phenomenon was superimposed upon and overshadowed it.

19.14. Immigration into the United States

The United States is one of the few nations that are still absorbing immigrants in large numbers. Each year more than one-quarter million immigrants enter the country for the purpose of establishing permanent residence. In the course of a decade a population of the size of present-day Ireland is absorbed. This fact surprises many, because it is not widely understood that United States immigration regulations have only reduced the size of inflow from abroad to the extent that it is a sizeable river and not a flood. No other nation of the world has such a volume of immigration.

Where do these migrants come from? Table 19-15 lists the number of immigrants in 1966 according to the last country of permanent residence. This table also shows the long-term source of immigrants to the United States, for purposes of comparison. The current pattern of recent migration can be simplified by categorizing the sources as follows:

	Percent
Europe	37.0
Mexico, South and Central America, and the Caribbean	36.8
Canada	17.5
Asia	7.2
Africa, Oceania, other	1.5
Total	100.0

Table 19-15 Immigration to the United States, Immigration Quotas and Nonquota Immigrants: 1966

Country	Total immi- gration	Quota	Non- quota	Percent nonquota	Legal quota	Percent of legal quota
Total.................	323,040	126,207	48,535	....	158,261	....
NORTHWEST AND CENTRAL EUROPE.....	57,059	53,538	8,205	....	127,036	....
Belgium........................	797	784	13	1.6	1,297	60.4
Denmark........................	1,137	901	236	20.8	1,175	76.7
Finland........................	519	377	142	27.4	566	66.6
France.........................	3,175	2,283	892	28.1	3,069	74.4
Great Britain..................	21,441	23,721	2,280	....	65,361	36.3
Germany........................	18,239	14,461	3,778	20.7	25,814	56.0
Austria........................	1,197	905	292	24.4	1,405	64.4
Ireland........................	3,241	3,068	173	5.3	17,756	17.3
Luxembourg.....................	....	62	......	....	....	.....
Netherlands....................	2,275	2,242	33	1.5	3,136	71.5
Norway.........................	1,676	1,584	92	5.5	2,364	67.0
Sweden.........................	1,807	1,778	29	1.6	3,295	54.0
Switzerland....................	1,555	1,310	245	15.8	1,698	77.1
Ireland........................	....	62	......	....	100	....
EASTERN EUROPE.................	20,477	14,889	5,734	....	14,240	....
Bulgaria.......................	291	221	70	24.1	100	221.0
Czechoslovakia.................	1,463	1,415	48	3.3	2,859	49.5
Estonia, Latvia, Lith..........	626	....	......	....	....	....
Hungary........................	1,665	942	723	43.4	865	108.9
Poland.........................	9,404	7,103	2,301	24.5	6,488	109.5
Yugoslavia.....................	3,728	2,370	1,358	36.4	942	251.6
Romania........................	1,938	1,090	848	43.8	289	377.2
U.S.S.R........................	1,362	1,748	386	....	2,697	64.8
SOUTHERN EUROPE	45,086	32,678	13,080	....	6,887	....
Greece.........................	8,265	4,906	3,359	40.6	308	1592.9
Italy..........................	25,154	18,955	6,199	24.6	5,666	334.5
Portugal.......................	8,713	7,163	1,550	17.8	438	1635.4
Spain..........................	2,954	982	1,972	66.8	250	392.8
Turkey in Europe...............	....	672	......	....	225	298.7
Other Europe...................	2,401	1,092	1,309	54.5	1,534	71.2
ASIA..........................	39,878	21,644	18,234	45.7	3,590	602.9
China..........................	13,736	....	......	....	....	....
Japan..........................	3,394	....	......	....	....	....
Turkey in Asia.................	....	....	......	....	....	....
Other Asia.....................	22,748	....	......	....	....	....
America: Canada................	28,358	....	......	....	....	....
America: Latin.................	124,818	....	......	....	....	....
Mexico.........................	45,163	....	......	....	....	....
Central America................	9,658	....	......	....	....	....
South America..................	25,836	....	......	....	....	....
West Indies....................	43,804	....	......	....	....	....
Other America..................	357	....	......	....	....	....
AFRICA.........................	3,137	1,658	1,479	47.1	4,274	38.8
Australia and New Zealand......	1,202	708	494	41.1	700	101.1
Other Oceania..................	....	....	....	....	....	....
All Other countries...........	624	127	....	....	....	....

Source: Statistical Abstract o₁ the U.S. 1967

Thus about one third of our immigrants are Spanish-speaking, about 55 percent are of European origin, either direct or through Canada, and less than 10 percent come from Asia and Africa.

The leading countries from which these migrants are coming, ranked in order of number of immigrants, are as follows:

Thousands

Mexico	45.2
West Indies	43.8
Canada	28.4
South America	25.8
Italy	25.1
Great Britain	21.4
Germany	18.2
China	13.7
Poland	9.4
Portugal	8.7
Greece	8.3

It would be completely incorrect to conclude that this pattern of immigration represents some "natural" population balance between the United States and other countries. It is entirely a product of a combination of laws and policies limiting the number of migrants from each country. There is one basic immigration law, the Immigration and Nationality Act. This law establishes a quota of a flat one-sixth of 1 percent of the population of that nationality present in the United States in the 1920 census. This has been modified by Presidential proclamations and special acts of Congress to admit refugees. The most recent quotas are reported in Table 19-15. The total of the quota is only 158,000.

Because of its policy of hemisphere solidarity, quotas have not been imposed on immigrants born in Canada, Mexico, Cuba, Haiti, the Dominican Republic, the Canal Zone, and countries of Central and South America. Citizens of these nations are admitted as nonquota immigrants, as are their spouses and children under 21. It is this that accounts for the very substantial Latin American component in present migration.

Change over the Years. There have been dramatic changes in the sources from which the United States has drawn its migrants and in the volume of migration. The history of this movement is outlined, as limited by available data, in Table 19-16. The major phases can be identified as follows:

1. Before 1850, all but a small fraction of immigrants came from England, Ireland, other countries of Northwest Europe, Germany, and Canada.

2. Slaves were imported from Africa until about 1810. This provided today's Negro component of the population.

3. From 1850 to 1885 there was a big influx of Chinese, who came to work on the construction of railroads.

4. In about 1870 a substantial flow of immigrants from Poland, USSR, Eastern Europe, Italy, Greece, and other Southern European nations began. Simultaneously there began an influx of Japanese and Turks.

5. From 1880 to 1915 the volume of immigration reached very high levels. It averaged 1 million persons per year from 1905 to 1915. This flow was drawn very heavily from the countries of Southern and Eastern Europe.

6. Immigration quotas were imposed in 1921. Prior to this date, only qualitative restrictions were imposed. The effect was to diminish the size of the flow and to favor immigration from Northwest Europe and Germany, while discouraging immigration from Southern and Eastern Europe, China, Japan, and Turkey. As quickly as this flow was curtailed, immigration from Mexico shot up rapidly.

7. The economic depression of the 1930s discouraged migration from all sources.

8. During and following World War II large numbers of displaced persons and refugees entered the country, especially persons born in Germany, the USSR, the Baltic States, and Eastern Europe. Also following World War II, prohibitions against Orientals were relaxed, especially to permit returning veterans to bring wives whom they had married in Japan and Korea.

Since 1950 the influx of persons of Latin American ancestry has assumed a larger importance and is now a dominant characteristic.

Characteristics of Immigrants. The characteristics of immigrants for selected intervals of time are shown in Table 19-17.

1. Immigrants are predominantly female. This seems to result from the fact that in addition to the incentives that overseas males have for migrating, a large number of females have also the incentive (and opportunity) to enter as nonquota wives of military servicemen.

2. A very large proportion of immigrants are adults aged 16 to 45 years, with few elderly people and few children.

3. Immigrants tend to be professional people, other white-collar workers, or craftsmen. Instead of being an in-movement of proletarians, modern United States immigration has more of the characteristics of a "brain drain," robbing Europe and many developing countries of their elite intelligentsia and talented leaders.

19.15. Migration and Economic Growth

Overseas migration has received a considerable amount of attention from economists, for the outflowing of population may be regarded as

Table 19-16 Number of Immigrants to the United States, by Continent, Region, and Nation of Origin: 1820 to 1964

Continent, region, country	Decade														
	1960–1964	1950–1959	1940–1949	1930–1939	1920–1929	1910–1919	1900–1909	1890–1899	1880–1889	1870–1879	1860–1869	1850–1859	1840–1849	1830–1839	1820–1829
All countries.............	1417375	2299762	856608	699375	4295510	6347380	8202388	3694294	5248568	2742137	2081261	2814554	1427337	538381	128502
Europe, total............	547188	1485134	473043	445273	2576710	5056560	7634425	3579958	4640057	2252197	1877853	2619774	1369304	422779	99291
Northwest Europe.........	231726	536927	244106	139047	887269	938411	1482834	1246825	2357541	1327183	1128129	1623325	979516	292255	90192
Great Britain...........	105218	285402	124995	54235	337669	371878	469518	328759	810900	578447	532956	445322	218572	74350	26336
Ireland.................	29575	56256	22500	35773	206737	166445	344940	405710	674061	422264	427419	1029486	656145	170672	51617
Scandinavia.............	22997	49147	22500	16945	204735	238275	488208	390729	671783	208101	96490	25429	13060	2076	264
Other northwestern......	73936	146122	74111	32094	138128	161813	180168	121627	200797	118371	71234	123088	91739	45157	11975
Germany.................	125965	566905	119506	119107	386634	174227	328722	579072	1445181	751769	723734	976072	385434	124726	5753
Central and Eastern Europe..	54032	130765	38589	79252	610010	2373620	3656506	1102360	547617	106639	7028	1604	670	654	124
Poland..................	30012	6465	7577	25555	223316	...	...	107793	42910	11016	1886	1087	105	366	19
U.S.S.R. & Baltic States....	1619	1684	4679	9275	88402	1106998	1501301	450101	182698	35177	1670	423	520	280	86
Austria, Hungary, Other..	22401	122616	26333	44422	298292	1266622	2155205	544466	322009	60446	3472	94	45	8	19
Southern Europe..........	135465	250537	70842	107867	692797	1570302	2166363	651701	289718	66606	18962	18773	3684	5144	3222
Italy...................	81388	184576	50509	85053	528133	1229916	1930475	603761	267660	46296	9853	8643	1476	2225	430
Other...................	54077	65961	20333	22814	164464	340386	235888	47940	22058	20310	9109	10130	2208	2919	2792
Asia....................	107223	131250	29914	17966	110370	198587	237980	57738	69771	133809	54281	35986	76	47	15
Turkey..................	2792	2301	212	439	24080	89568	66143	23963	1098	63	2	...	...	...	...
China...................	7925	9557	16072	5874	30648	20916	19884	15268	65797	133139	54028	35933	32	8	3
Japan...................	22164	40651	1557	2683	42057	77125	139712	13998	1583	193	138	...	...	...	...
Other...................	74342	78741	12073	8970	13585	10978	12241	4509	1293	414	113	53	44	39	12
America, total...........	743386	642578	328435	230319	1591278	1070539	277809	37350	524826	345010	130292	84145	50516	31905	9655
Canada & Newfoundland....	240033	353169	160911	162703	949286	708715	123067	3098	492865	324310	117978	64171	34285	11875	2297
Mexico..................	220423	273847	56158	32709	498945	185334	31188	734	2405	5133	1957	3446	3069	7187	3835
Other...................	282930	15562	111366	34907	143047	176490	123554	33518	29556	15567	10357	16528	13162	12843	3523
Africa, total...........	9607	13016	6720	2120	6362	8867	6326	432	763	371	407	84	61	50	15
Australia & New Zealand...	8284	10074	13552	3050	9339	11280	11191	3225	7271	8669	...	...	...	...	...
Other Oceania...........	1603	5236	710	190	521	1059	1164	1479	5090	1027	...	...	...	...	...
All other countries.....	84	12474	4234	457	930	488	33493	14112	790	754	18428	74565	7380	83600	19526

Source: Historical Statistics of the United States: 1789–1945, Table B-304 and Statistical Abstract of the United States, 1967

Table 19-17   Selected Characteristics of Immigrants

Characteristic	Years		
	1941– 1950	1951– 1960	1961– 1965
Sex: percent male................	40.4	45.9	52.6
Age: percent under 16 years......	15.6	22.9	23.8
percent 45 years & over.....	18.4	13.6	12.4
Occupational composition:			
Professional, technical, etc......	7.9	7.3	9.0
Farmers, farm managers...........	3.6	2.0	0.7
Managers, officials, proprietors..	3.8	2.1	2.1
Clerical, sales..................	7.9	7.8	9.6
Craftsmen, foremen...............	7.3	7.8	6.1
Operatives.......................	6.0	6.7	4.8
Private household................	3.4	3.7	3.2
Service workers..................	2.3	2.8	3.3
Farm laborers....................	0.7	1.7	2.2
Laborers, exc. farm.............	2.4	5.3	4.6

Source: Statistical Abstracts of the United States, 1958, 1966
        Table 127

loss of the trained manpower that represents a substantial national investment in education and upbringing. On the other hand, colonization of new lands could increase the market for products of the home country and gave relief from overpopulation. Debates on the economic consequences to national economic growth and welfare of emigration and immigration have been waged since the eighteenth century. A scholarly work that reviews these debates and then proceeds to set up a modern theory of migration and economic growth is *Migration and Economic Growth* by Brinley Thomas, a British economist.[52] He reviews the arguments concerning international migration contained in the writings of each of the "schools" of thought from the mercantilist era to the present.

One empirical fact of international migration became very clear once the statistics were available and were subjected to analysis: the volume of migration flow is very markedly influenced by economic conditions in the receiving country. This thesis was demonstrated more than four decades ago by Harry Jerome, who found that the rather wide fluctuations of the volume of immigration to the United States were correlated with the phase of the business

cycle in this country.[53] It was later verified with Swedish data by Dorothy Swaine Thomas.[54] Brinley Thomas regards this as a one-sided and highly partial view. He asserts: "What is needed is a concept of economic development which stresses the widening of markets, the dynamic of increasing returns, and the international mobility of labour and capital as a medium through which an international economy grows and changes its character. Viewed as an essential part of the process of economic expansion, migration not only induces but is itself partly determined by changes in the structure of the international community." He then proceeds to view the nations on both sides of the Atlantic as a single evolving economy, in which there is a flow of labor, capital, and commodities from one to the other. In this context he sets up the following model:

"We take an old country (A) and a new country (B): the former we assume to be split into two classes, workers and entrepreneurs, with an impassable barrier between them, whereas the new country has complete social mobility and equality of opportunity. A is thickly populated, with a well-established industrial sector and a high propensity to save.

[52] Brinley Thomas, *Migration and Economic Growth* (Cambridge, England: The University Press, 1954).

[53] Harry Jerome, *Migration and Business Cycles* (New York: National Bureau of Economic Research 1926).

[54] *Op. cit.*, pp. 30–34.

B is large in area, rich in fertile land and natural resources, but short of labour and capital. Free trade is assumed, so that A tends to specialize in manufactured goods and B in food and raw materials.

"It is natural that labour and capital should flow from A to B; a wave of technical progress in A will accentuate emigration, for the workers displaced are uncompensated and there is no means by which the ablest of them can cross over into the capitalist camp and displace the weaker entrepreneurs. Of course, not all of the emigration is of this kind; some of it is an outflow which is complementary to capital exports. Indeed there is a sense in which the whole of the migration is an indispensable accompaniment of expanding trade. The rapid development of country B brings about a rise in the price of land, much of which, as a result of previous borrowings, will belong to absentee owners in A. Now, if country B continues its free trade policy and concentrates on producing agricultural produce to sell to A in exchange for manufactured goods, the share of the national income going to rent will increase and much of it will leave the country as annual tribute payable to A. Obviously it is in the national interest of country B to impose a tariff on A's manufactures so as to reduce the scope of agriculture, encourage resources to flow into home industry and thus cut down the slice of the social product taken by landlords.

"A stage will be reached in the evolution of country B when its population will have appropriated all the good land and natural resources. With growing competition for scarce land its value rises rapidly and complete social mobility is no longer possible. More and more workers in the new country remain permanently in the ranks of the wage-earners; the social structure begins to become rigid; no longer are immigrants welcomed as co-operant factors in the conquest for new space. The last frontier has disappeared. This turning point in the evolution of B may be marked also by the achievement of a rate of saving high enough to release the country from further dependence on A's capital market and to reverse the direction of the flow of loanable funds. Moreover, with the transition to industrialism in B, the

trade between A and B will no longer be merely an exchange of manufactured goods for foodstuffs and raw materials.

"Up to the time when the overseas territory reaches maturity as an industrial nation, the influx of immigrants is accompanied by imports of capital, and there is therefore a tendency for periods of relatively rapid increase in population to be associated with upswings in imports of capital and merchandise. On the other hand, the old country experiences its own cycle of booms in emigration and foreign investment followed by booms in home construction. A model of an international economy might be set up consisting of an old country (A) and a new country (B), each divided into two sectors, home construction and export. When emigration and the export of capital from A are booming, the level of activity in that country is governed mainly by the inducement of investment in the export sector, that is, by the marginal efficiency of investment in country B; during this phase the volume of A's exports rises and that of A's imports falls relatively to trend. Modern cycle theory in "real" terms may be invoked to explain why the investment boom in B must result in a crisis and a downturn. This leads immediately to a sharp fall in immigration and inflow of capital; income generated by home investment in B declines and the factors tend to move into the export trades. Meanwhile, the rate of growth of population and the supply of loanable funds in A rise, resources move from the export sector to home construction, and the level of activity responds to the marginal efficiency of internal investment. The volume of imports (i.e., B's exports) now rises and that of exports (i.e., B's imports) falls relatively to trend; a part of these imports constitutes income on previous loans to B. If we assume a gold standard, it is clear that this upswing in home construction in A may well be brought to an end by a crisis in the balance of payments before full employment is reached. In any case, the "real" determinants make a downturn inevitable; it is the signal for the beginning of another round of foreign investment and emigration."

Thomas proceeds to test this model by studying the correlates of the flows of migrants from the United Kingdom to the United States during the period up to World War I. He carefully reconciles the migration statistics of Great Britain and the United States to arrive at estimates of the true flow of migrants. It has a definitely cyclical or fluctuating pattern. In the period before the Civil War these cycles are highly correlated with railroad building. In a very real sense, the economic expansion in America during these years took on the aspect of an undertaking in which the capital, the machinery, and even the labor were imports from Europe, especially from Britain. A careful study of the cycle of foreign investment by Britain and investment within Britain leads to a verification of the model: when Britain was in the phase of a domestic boom with much investment of capital at home, migration to America was slack, but when there was a wave of investment of British capital in America instead of at home, there was an upsurge of migration to America. This is exactly what the model would predict during that phase when the developing country is in an agricultural and raw-material phase. After the Civil War this pattern receives less verification, and Thomas attributes this to the transition of the United States to a mature industrial economy in which protective tariffs and domestic capital accumulation replace investment from abroad. Gradually Great Britain lost her dominant role in the Atlantic Community; this role was assumed by the United States. Fluctuations in supply of capital for foreign investment began to be concentrated in New York instead of London, but in a context in which the nations are all much more "mature" than during the period of British dominance, so that the flow of migrant population following waves of investment is less evident. Thus Thomas's economic model even accounts for the setting up of migration barriers and the gradual diminution of international migration flows (other than forced migration for political, ethnic, or religious reasons). If this model is correct, we may look forward to further diminution of international migration as the developing nations gradually industrialize and generate their own capital supply and as all of the world's frontiers disappear.

19.16. Conclusion: The Future Course of Internal and International Migration

The future course of international migration depends almost exclusively on the nature of legal restrictions imposed by the various nations. For example, if the United States were to manifest the same sympathy for the Arab refugees as it showed for the victims of war in Europe, it would be possible for Congress to pass legislation admitting 50,000 persons each year for 10 years as a special program (as was done in the case of refugees from Eastern Europe). A similar program sponsored by the nations of Latin America and Europe would greatly alleviate this problem or resolve it entirely. Humanitarian motives and political acuity therefore seem to be the major components of future international migration flows. Behind these, of course, lie the traditional ones of potential for economic advancement: the flows tend to go in the direction of greatest opportunity.

Internal migration seems to be guided by the heavy hand of differential economic conditions. Economic expansion and new job opportunities are highly concentrated in metropolitan areas —all over the world. So long as this persists— and there is strong evidence that it will—we can look forward to a sustained urbanization and metropolitanization of the population of each nation. Even the developing nations with fantastically large populations, such as India, China, Pakistan, and Indonesia, must anticipate large-scale movements off the land and into the cities.

As more and more nations complete the demographic transition and approach a condition of zero growth, sudden economic developments that require considerable amounts of additional manpower may force the innovating nation to import manpower from other nations that have a temporary surplus of labor. Under these conditions, both internal and international migration flows may reflect the spatial pattern of economic expansion and capital investment of a type of the model of Brinley Thomas. It is to be hoped that for the study of both internal and international migration, each nation will be divided into homogeneous regions and subregions analogous to the Economic Area system.

QUESTIONS AND EXERCISES

1. Compare Lee's model of migration illustrated in Figure 19-1 with the following quotation from Brinley Thomas: "All sorts of promptings may lie behind the decision of an individual or family to leave one country in order to live in another. History shows the influence of the threat of starvation, political oppression, religious persecution, eviction, avoidance of military service, a sense of adventure, an urge to make a fortune, a desire to join relatives abroad or to get away from those at home, or perhaps just a flight from boredom. It is not by making a catalogue of such 'reasons' that one can hope to understand the phenomenon of migration any more than an attempt to describe the manifold motives leading people to want to buy a commodity would constitute analysis of demand. Nothing is easier than to draw up a list of factors labelled 'push' and 'pull' and then write a descriptive account in terms of these two sets of influences. Such an approach, however, will not throw much light on the deeper problems posed by migration as part of the process of economic expansion" (*Migration and Economic Growth,* p. 26). From what viewpoints is the "push-pull-obstacles" model useful and not useful?

2. How can we obtain valid data on the "push" and "pull" factors? Does a migrant or a potential migrant really know "why" he is leaving one community and going to another or is he perhaps the least objective observer possible, hence the one person least capable of making a valid assessment? What are some of the ways in which data on these factors could be obtained?

3. The greatest difficulty with the use of the Stouffer hypothesis of "intervening opportunities" is the quantification of the variable "opportunity." How would you go about developing statistics that would measure opportunities that intervene between a place of origin and alternative destination? Read Stouffer's second article and discuss whether you agree or disagree with his procedure.

4. Read the materials of this chapter carefully, studying all of the statistical tables in the light of the seven "Laws of Migration" of Ravenstein. Write an essay on the extent to which Ravenstein's generalizations are still valid today and the extent to which they are invalid.

5. In what respects would the reverse flow of migrants (counter to the mainstream) differ from the mainstream—in terms of social, economic, and demographic traits? Write as many hypotheses about this as you can. The migration tabulations of the U.S. Census of 1960 provide some data with which to test these hypotheses. Select at least one of your hypotheses and check it against the data. Read Eldridge's article on "Primary, Secondary, and Return Migration" (see Bibliography) for guidance in how to make this test.

6. Consult the references in the Bibliography and summarize all of the findings you can about the migration component of central city growth. On the basis of your analysis, what would you expect to be the pattern in 1970 in the United States? In 1980?

7. It has often been said that the large metropolitan areas are now so overcrowded and so ridden with slums, air pollution, crime, and other problems that there should be a massive decentralization movement to spread the population more evenly throughout the land, say in communities of not more than 100,000 persons. From what you have learned about planned efforts to control migration, do you think this is feasible?

8. Read about rural depopulation in some other nation—France, Germany, Brazil, South Africa. Try to find out what are some of the social and economic impacts on the communities from which there is mass migration exodus.

9. At periodic intervals the U.S. Bureau of Census puts out estimates of the current population of states, with estimates of components of change since the last census. Look up the latest such report and compare the pattern for the postcensal period with the pattern that prevailed between the two preceding censuses. What changes in the regional pattern of migration do you perceive?

10. Demographers routinely compute the components of population growth for metropolitan areas in much more detail than has been done in this chapter. How would you go about calculating net migration by educational attainment, occupation, income, or other socioeconomic traits? What do you think you would find?

11. Select one developing and one industrialized nation for which substantially detailed internal migration studies have been made. Read these reports and list hypotheses that were not mentioned in Sections 19-5 and 19-6.

12. Most of the estimates of net migration for small areas (Bogue, Ratner, U.S. Census Bureau) were performed before the advent of electronic computers. As a result, an amazing amount of factual data have been published with very little analysis. The *City and County Data Book* of the U.S. Census contains a wide range of data to correlate against the estimates of net migration for individual standard metropolitan areas. Select 10 of the indexes that represent useful hypotheses and, using a packaged computer program, make a regression analysis to test your ideas.

13. Repeat Exercise 12 for a sample of nonmetropolitan counties, using the data of the Census Bureau's report, "Components of Population Change, 1950 to 1960, for Counties, Standard Metropolitan Statistical Areas, State Economic Areas and Economic Subregions" (Series P-23, No. 7, November 1962).

14. Read the monographs on migration by Goodrich et al., and Dorothy S. Thomas et al., in their entirety and write an essay comparing them.

15. Compare the analysis of the economic forces in internal migration given by Kuznets in the Introduction to Volume III of the Thomas-Kuznets monographs (see text and Bibliography) with the model of Brinley Thomas. In what respects are the two sets of generalizations identical and in what respects are they different? Do you think there is a single "economic theory of migration"? Or must there be a separate one for internal and international migration?

16. Read the article "The Negro Leaves the South" by Horace Hamilton. Search for the most recent data available and see if his predictions are materializing. Will they materialize? If not, which ones do you think will not happen and why?

17. Immigration has been blamed for a part of the problems Negroes are having in rising in the socioeconomic scale. Read as much as you can about the actual application of current United States immigration policy and write an essay on "Is Our Present Immigration Policy Making it Difficult for Negroes to Rise Socioeconomically?"

18. There is a substantial amount of international migration among the nations of Africa. Explore the literature to find out as much as you can about this. What are the forces that cause this movement? Is it increasing or decreasing? What relationship does it have to trends in the flow of Europeans and Americans with respect to Africa? Repeat for South America, with respect to Spain and Portugal.

19. Read carefully the four articles on longitudinal (cohort) migration cited here and any others that may have appeared. Write an essay on "How Useful Is the Idea of Real Cohorts in the Study of Migration?" Consider it both from the point of view of internal and international migration.

20. Immediately after World War 11 Australia underwent a period of rapid immigration. Read as much as you can about the ethnic composition of this movement and explain how it happened that there were comparatively few migrants from Australia's overpopulated neighbors—Indonesia, Philippines, Ceylon, Pakistan, and India. What ethnic minorities were admitted and with what social effects?

21. Many people have feared that as England loses her colonies and ceases to be the dominant nation in the Atlantic Community, it will be impossible for her to support all of her present population and it will be necessary for millions to migrate overseas. The last chapter of Brinley Thomas's book deals with this problem (see Bibliography). Read this chapter and discuss it. Do you think this applies to the United States 100 years from now? To all of Europe when the underdeveloped countries become industrialized?

22. Some question has been raised whether the flow of migration is really large enough to have an effect in equalizing socioeconomic conditions among regions. Read as much as you can on this topic and write an essay "Does Migration Really Cure Anything or Only Keep the Kettle from Exploding?"

23. Study the reports of international migration and write an essay on "Emigration from the United States."

24. Write a report on "Social and Economic Characteristics of Areas of Large-Scale Out-Migration in Europe and North America."

BIBLIOGRAPHY

Abramson, J. H. "Emotional Disorder, Status Inconsistency and Migration," *Milbank Memorial Fund Quarterly,* **44** (1) (January 1966), 23–48.

American Academy of Political and Social Science. "The New Immigration." Edward P. Hutchinson (ed.) (A group of 15 articles.). *Annals of the American Academy of Political and Social Science,* **367** (September 1966), 1–149.

Anderson, Theodore R. "Intermetropolitan Migration: Comparison of the Hypotheses of Zipf and Stouffer," *American Sociological Review,* **20** (3) (January 1955), 287–291.

Anderson, Theodore R. "Intermetropolitan Migration: A Correlation Analysis," *American Journal of Sociology,* **61** (5) (March 1956), 459–462.

Appleyard, R. T. "The Economic Absorption of Dutch and Italian Immigrants into Western Australia, Part 1," *R.E.M.P. Bulletin* (The Hague), **4** (3) (July-September 1956), 45–54.

Avila, Fernando Bastos de, S. J. "Immigration in Latin America: A Study Made with the Co-operation of the Inter-governmental Committee for European Migration," Washington: Pan American Union, **18** (1964).

Avila, Fernando Bastos de, S. J. "La Inmigración en América Latina" ("Immigration in Latin America"), *Revista Interamericana de Ciencias Sociales* (Washington), 3 **15**, Número especial (1964).

Baali, Raud. "Social Factors in Iraqi Rural-Urban Migration," *American Journal of Economics and Sociology,* **25** (4) (October 1966), 359–364.

Bachmura, Frank T. "Man-Land Equalization Through Migration," *American Economic Review,* **49** (5) (December 1959), 1004–1017.

Beale, Calvin L. "Rural Depopulation in the United States: Some Demographic Consequences of Agricultural Readjustments," *Demography,* **1** (1) (1964), 264–272.

Beegle, Allan, et al. "Selected Factors Related to Country Migration Patterns in the North Central States, 1940-50 and 1950-60," *Quarterly Bulletin: Reports on Research from the Michigan State University,* Agricultural Experimental Station, **46** (2) (November 1963), 206–241.

Beijer, G. "Overseas Migration of European Agriculturalists, 1918-1940 and 1946-1956," *R.E.M.P. Bulletin* (The Hague), **6** (3/4) (July-December 1958), 63–74.

Beijer, G. "Characteristics of Overseas Migrants," *The Hague,* Government Printing and Publishing Office, **15** (1961).

Beijer, G. *Rural Migrants in Urban Setting: An Analysis of the Literature on the Problem Consequent on the Internal Migration from Rural to Urban Areas in Twelve European Countries, 1945–61,* published under the auspices of the Netherlands Ministry of Social Work and the European Society for Rural Sociology, XIV. The Hague: Martinus Nijhoff, 1963.

Beijer, G. "Demographic, Social and Economic Aspects of Internal Migration in Some European Countries," a paper contributed for the United Nations World Population Conference, August 30-September 10, 1965.

Besterman, W. "Immigration as a Means of Obtaining Needed Skills and Stimulating Economic and Social Advancement," a paper contributed for the United Nations World Population Conference, August 30-September 10, 1965. WPC/WP/277 (B. 9/v/E/277).

Bogue, Donald J. *A Methodological Study of Migration and Labor Mobility in Michigan and Ohio in 1947.* Scripps Foundation Studies in Population Distribution, No. 4. Oxford, Ohio: Miami University, 1952.

Bogue, Donald J. and Warren S. Thompson. "Migration and Distance," *American Sociological Review,* **14,** 236–244.

Bogue, Donald J. *An Exploratory Study of Migration and Labor Mobility Using Social Security Data.* Scripps Foundation Studies in Population Distribution No. 1. Oxford, Ohio: Miami University, June 1950.

Bogue, Donald J. *Components of Population Change: 1940–50: Estimates of Net Migration and Natural Increase for Each Standard Metropolitan Area and State Economic Area.* Scripps Foundation Studies in Population Distribution, No. 12. Oxford, Ohio: Miami University, 1957.

Bogue, Donald J. "Internal Migration," in Philip M. Hauser and Otis Dudley Duncan (eds.), *The Study of Population: An Inventory and Appraisal,* pp. 486–509 (1959).

Bogue, Donald J., Margaret Jarman Hagood, and Gladys K. Bowles. "Subregional Migration in the United States, 1935-40," Vol. II, *Differential Migration in the Corn and Cotton Belts.* Oxford, Ohio: Miami University, 1957.

Bogue, Donald J., Henry S. Shryock, and Siegfried A. Hoermann. "Subregional Migration in the United States, 1935-40," Vol. I, *Streams of Migration between Subregions.* Oxford, Ohio: Miami University, 1953.

Bogue, Donald J. and K. C. Zachariah. "Urbanization and Migration in India," in Roy Turner (ed.). *India's Urban Future.* Selected studies from an international conference sponsored by Kingsley Davis, Richard L. Park, and Catherine Bauer Wurster, IX. Berkeley and

Los Angeles: University of California Press, 1962.

Borrei, W. D., and J. Zubrzycki. "Employment of Post-war Immigrants in Australia," *International Labour Review* (Geneva), **77** (3) (March 1958), 239–253.

Borrie, W. D., et al. "The Cultural Integration of Immigrants: A Survey Based upon the Papers and Proceedings of the UNESCO Conference Held in Havana, April, 1956," *Population and Culture Series 4*. Paris: United Nations Educational, Scientific and Cultural Organization, 1959.

Bouscaren, Anthony T. *International Migrations since 1945*, New York: Praeger, 1963.

Bowles, Gladys K. "Migration Patterns of the Rural-Farm Population, Thirteen Economic Regions of the United States, 1940-50," *Rural Sociology*, **22** (1) (March 1957, 1–11.

Bowles, Gladys K. "Farm Population: Net Migration from the Rural-Farm Population, 1940-50," United States Agricultural Marketing Service, Statistical Bulletin No. 176, II. Washington, D. C., 1956.

Bowles, Gladys K. *Adjustment Processes Associated with Migration, with Special Reference to Population Redistribution in the Great Plains between 1950-60*, II. Washington, D. C.: United States Department of Agriculture, Farm Population Branch, 1962. Reprinted from *Proceedings of the Great Plains Agricultural Council Meeting*. Fort Collins, Colo., August 1962.

Bowles, Gladys K., and James D. Tarver. *Net Migration of the Population, 1950-60, by Age, Sex and Color*, 2 vols. Economic Research Service, United States Department of Agriculture in cooperation with Research Foundation, Oklahoma State University. Washington, D.C.: U.S. Government Printing Office, 1966.

Bowles, Gladys K., and James D. Tarver. "The Composition of Net Migration among Counties in the United States, 1950-60," *Agricultural Economics Research*, **18** (1) (January 1966), 13–19.

Buckley, Kenneth. "Historical Estimates of Internal Migration in Canada," in E. F. Beach and J. C. Weldon (eds.). *Canadian Political Science Association Conference on Statistics, 1960: Papers*. Toronto: University of Toronto Press, 1962, pp. 1–37.

Burnight, Robert G. "Estimates of Net Migration, Mexico, 1930-50," *Proceedings of the International Population Conference: 1961*, I. London, 1963, pp. 412–419.

Centre European d'Etudes de Population. "Chapitre III, Migration; Adaption, Problèmes Sociaux" ("Chapter III, Migration: Adaption, Assimilation, and Social Problems"), *Etudes Européennes de Population* (Paris)

(1954), 335–370.

Choe, Ehn Hyun. "A Study of Internal Migration in Korea, 1955-60," *Monthly Statistics of Korea* (Seoul), **6** (1-2) (1964), 5–23.

Coe, Paul E. "Nonwhite Population Increases in Metropolitan Areas," *Journal of the American Statistical Association*, **50** (June 1955), 283–308.

Coe, Paul E. "The Nonwhite Population Surge to Our Cities," *Land Economics*, **35** (3), (August 1959), 195–210.

Concepcion, Mercedes B. "Migration Differentials in the Visayas, 1960," *Philippine Sociological Review* (Quezon City), **11** (1–2) (January-April 1963), 66–75.

Cook, Robert C. "World Migration, 1946-55," *Population Bulletin*, **13** (5) (August 1957), 77–95.

Cousens, S. H. "The Regional Pattern of Emigration During the Great Irish Famine, 1846–51," *Institute of British Geographers: Transactions and Papers, 1960*, Publication 28.

Cousens, S. H. "Emigration and Demographic Change in Ireland, 1851–1861," *Economic History Review, 2nd series*, **14** (2) (December 1961), 175–288.

Cowan, Helen I. "British Emigration to British North America: The First Hundred Years," Toronto: University of Toronto Press, 1961, XIV.

Creamer, Daniel C. *Migration and Planes of Living*. Philadelphia: University of Pennsylvania Press, 1935.

Crowley, F. K. "The British Contribution to the Australian Population: 1860–1919," *University Studies in History and Economics* (Fremantle, Australia), **2** (2) (July 1954), 55–88.

Dandekar, D. P. "Internal Migration in Some Countries of the East," *Proceedings of the International Population Conference: 1961*, I. London, 1963, pp. 420–427.

Daragan, M. V. "Economic Development and Internal Migration," a paper contributed for the United Nations World Population Conference, August 30-September 10, 1965.

Das Gupta, Ajit. "Types and Measures of Internal Migration." International Union for the Scientific Study of Population. Vienna, 1959, pp. 619–624.

Davis, Kingsley. "Internal Migration and Urbanization in Relation to Economic Development." Proceedings of the World Population Conference, Vol. 11, United Nations, 1964.

Davison, Robert B. "West Indian Migrants: The Social and Economic Facts of Migration from the British West Indies," *Institute of Race Relationships* (Paperbacks). London and New York: Oxford University Press, 1962.

Davison, Robert B. *Black British: Immigrants to*

England. London: Oxford University Press, for the Institute of Race Relations, 1966.

Delf, George. "Asians in East Africa," *Institute of Race Relations*. London: Oxford University Press, 1963.

Ducoff, Louis J. "The Migration Population of a Metropolitan Area in a Developing Country: A Preliminary Report on a Case Study of San Salvador," *Proceedings of the International Population Conference: 1961*, I. London, 1963, pp. 428–436.

Ducoff, Louis J. "The Role of Migration in the Demographic Development of Latin America," pp. 197–210 in Clyde V. Kiser (ed.). *Components of Population Change in Latin America*. Proceedings of the sixtieth anniversary conference of the Milbank Memorial Fund, April 5–7, 1965. *Milbank Memorial Fund Quarterly*, **43** (4, Part 2) (October 1965).

Duncan, Otis D. "The Theory and Consequences of Mobility of Farm Population," in O. D. Duncan and Joseph J. Spengler (eds.). *Population Theory and Policy*. Glencoe, Ill.: Free Press, 1956, pp. 417–434.

Easterlin, Richard A. "Influences in European Overseas Migration before World War I," *Economic Development and Cultural Change*, **9** (3) (April 1960), 331–351.

Eckerson, Helen F. "United States and Canada: Magnets for Immigration," *The Annals of The American Academy of Political and Social Science*, **316** (March 1958), 34–42.

Economic Council of Canada. Staff Study. No. 1-. Ottawa, 1965-. (Series of technical studies prepared as background papers for the Economic Council of Canada, -I.L.R. 92(3), 13. *Internal Migration in Canada, 1921-1961*. By Isabel B. Anderson. March 1966.

Eisenstadt, S. N. "Sociological Aspects of the Economic Adaptation of Oriental Immigrants in Israel: A Case Study in the Problem of Modernization," *Economic Development and Cultural Change*, **4** (3) (April 1956), 269–278.

Eldridge, Hope T. "A Cohort Approach to the Analysis of Migration Differentials," *Demography*, **1** (1), (1964), 212–219.

Eldridge, Hope T. "Primary, Secondary, and Return Migration in the United States, 1955-60," *Demography*, **2**, 444–455.

Eldridge, Hope T. "The Influence of Return Migration upon Rates of Net Migration," *Bulletin: International Statistical Bureau*, (Toronto), **40** (1) (1964), 321–349.

Eldridge, Hope T. *Net Intercensal Migration for States and Geographic Divisions of the United States, 1940-1960*. Philadelphia: Population Studies Center, University of Pennsylvania, Report No. 5, 1965.

Eldridge, Hope T. "Patterns of Dominance in In-

ternal Migration, United States, 1955-60," a paper contributed for the United Nations World Population Conference, August 30-September 10, 1965.

Eldridge, Hope T., and Dorothy Swaine Thomas. "Population Redistribution and Economic Growth, United States: 1870-1950," *Demographic Analyses and Interrelations*. Philadelphia: The American Philosophical Society, 1964.

Elizaga, Juan C. "A Study of Migration to Greater Santiago (Chile)," *Demography*, **3** (1966), 352–377.

Elizaga, Juan C. "Migración Diferencial en Algunas Regiones y Ciudades de la América Latina, 1940-50" ("Differential Migration in Some Regions and Cities of Latin America in the Period 1940-50"). Santiago: Centro Latinoamericano de Demografía Publicaciones, Serie A, 1962.

Elizaga, Juan C. "Internal Migrations in Latin America," pp. 144–161. in Clyde V. Kiser (ed.). *Components of Population Change in Latin America*. Proceedings of the sixtieth anniversary conference of the Milbank Memorial Fund, New York City, April 4-7, 1965. *Milbank Memorial Fund Quarterly*, **43** (4, Part 2) (October 1965).

Engmann, E. V. T. "Population Movements in Ghana: A Study of Internal Migration and Its Implications for the Planner," *Bulletin of the Ghana Geographical Association* (Legon), **10** (1) (January 1965), 41–65.

Fleisher, B. M. "Some Economic Aspects of Puerto Rican Migration to the United States," *Review of Economics and Statistics*, **45** (3) (August 1963), 221–230.

Folger, John K. "Models in Migration," *Proceedings of the Milbank Memorial Fund Conference: 1957*, Part III. New York, 1958.

Freedman, Ronald. "Cityward Migration, Urban Ecology, and Social Theory," in Ernest W. Burgess and Donald J. Bogue (eds.). *Contributions to Urban Sociology*. Chicago: University of Chicago Press, 1964, pp. 178–200.

Fretz, J. W. *Immigrant Group Settlements in Paraguay: A Study in the Sociology of Colonization*. North Newton, Kansas: Bethel College, 1962.

Friedlander, D., and J. Roshier. "A Study of Internal Migration in England and Wales: Part I," *Population Studies*, **19** (3) (March 1966); 239–279.

Friedlander, D., and J. Roshier. "A Study of Internal Migration in England and Wales. Part II. Recent Internal Migrants—Their Movements and Characteristics," *Population Studies*, **20**(1) (December 1966), 45–59.

Fujii, Yukio, and T. Lynn Smith. "The Acculturation of the Japanese Immigrants in Brazil: A

Case-Study," *Latin American Monograph Series*, No. 8. University of Florida, School of Inter-American Studies: Gainesville, 1959.

Galle, Omer R., and Karl E. Taeuber. "Metropolitan Migration and Intervening Opportunities," *American Sociological Review*, 31(1) (February 1966), 5–13.

George Washington University. *Reports on World Population Migrations as Related to the United States of America*. Washington, D.C.: George Washington University, 1956.

Germani, Gino. "Asimilacion de Immigrantes en el Médio Urbano: Notas Methodológicas ("Assimilation of In-Migrants in the Urban Environment: Methodological Notes"), *Revista Latino-Americana de Sociología* (Buenos Aires), 1(2) (July 1965), 158–177.

Geschwind, Henrik. "Inrikes Omflyttning, 1951-55" ("Internal Migration, 1951-55,"), *Statistick Tidskrift*, (Stockholm) 6(11) (November 1957), 607–614.

Gini, Corrado. "La Teoría de la Migrazioni Adaptative" ("The Theory of Adaptive Migration"), *Statistica*, 14 (3) (July-September 1954), 325–337. Also in *Revista Internacional de Sociología*, 12(46) (April-June 1954), 259–271.

Gini, Corrado. "Internation Migrations" ("Delle Migrazioni intenazionali"), *Rivista di Politica Economica*, 45 (3) (March 1955), 173–186; 21 (4), 4276; 45 (1–2) (January-February 1955), 1–13.

Goldstein, Sidney. *Patterns of Mobility, 1910-50: The Norristown Study*. Philadelphia: University of Pennsylvania Press, 1958.

Goodrich, Carter. *Migration and Economic Opportunity*. Philadelphia: University of Pennsylvania Press, 1936.

Grubel, Herbert G., and Anthony D. Scott. "The International Flow of Human Capital," *American Economic Review*, 56 (2) (May 1966), 268–274.

Haenzel, William. "Concept, Measurement, and Data in Migration Analysis," *Demography*, 4 (1967), 253–261.

Hägerstrand, Torsten. "Geographic Measurements of Migration: Swedish Data," *Monaco Colloquia in Human Science: 1962*. Jean Sutter (ed.), XVI. Paris: Hachette, 1963, pp. 61–83.

Hamilton, C. Horace. "Educational Selectivity of Net Migration from the South," *Social Forces*, 38 (1) (October 1959), 33–42.

Hamilton, C. Horace. "Educational Selectivity of Rural-Urban Migration: Preliminary Results of a North Carolina Study," *Proceedings: Annual Milbank Memorial Fund Conference: 1957*, Part III. New York, 1958.

Hamilton, C. Horace. "Effect of Census Errors on the Measurement of Net Migration," *Demography*, 3 (1966), 393–415.

Hamilton, C. Horace. "Practical and Mathematical Considerations in the Formulation and Selection of Migration Rates," *Demography*, 2 (1965), 429–443.

Hamilton, C. Horace. "The Negro Leaves the South," *Demography*, 1 (1), (1964), 273–295.

Handlin, Oscar. "Cultural Adjustment in the United States, 1945-52," *Proceedings of the World Population Conference: 1954*, II. New York, 1955.

Handlin, Oscar (ed.). *Immigration as a Factor in American History*. Englewood Cliffs, N.J.: Prentice-Hall, 1959.

Hannerberg, David, et al. (eds.). "Migration in Sweden: A Symposium," *Lund Studies in Geography*, Series B, No. 13. Lund, Sweden: C.W.K. Gleerup, 1957.

Hawley, Amos H. "Interstate Migration in Michigan: 1935-40," Michigan Governmental Studies No. 25. Ann Arbor, Mich.: University of Michigan Press, 1953.

Heberle, Rudolph. "Migration Mobility: Theoretical Aspects and Problems of Measurement," *Proceedings of the World Population Conference: 1954*, II. New York, 1955.

Heberle, Rudolph. "Theorie der Wanderungen: Soziologische Betrachtungen" ("The Theory of Migration: Sociological Considerations"), *Schmollers Jahrbuch für Gesetzgebung, Verwaltung und Volkswirtschaft (Small Yearbook for Population, Voting, and Economy)*, 75 (1) (1955), 1–23.

Heiss, J. "Residential Segregation and the Assimilation of Italians in an Australian City," *International Migration* (Geneva), 4(3/4) (1966), 165–171.

Hernández Alvarez, José. "A Demographic Profile of the Mexican Immigration to the United States, 1910-1950," *Journal of Inter-American Studies*, 8(3) (July 1966), 471–496.

Herrick, Bruce H. *Urban Migration and Economic Development in Chile*. M.I.T. Monographs in Economics, 6. Cambridge, Mass.: M.I.T. Press, 1966.

Herrick, Bruce H. *Rural-Urban Migration in the European Economic Community*, a paper contributed to United Nations World Population Conference, (August 30-September 10, 1965.

Hitt, Homer L. "Migration Between the South and Other Regions," *Social Forces*, 36 (1) (October 1957), 9–16.

Hock, Saw Swee. "Trends and Differentials in International Migration in Malaya," *Ekonomi, Journal of the Economic Society, University of Malaya*, IV, 1. Singapore (December 1963), 87–113.

Horstmann, Kurt. "Die Berufliche Eingliederung der Vertriebenen 1954/55: Ergebnisse der Statischen Auswertung der Antragsformulare zum Bundesvertriebenenaus Weis" ("The Occupational Integration of the Expelles, 1954/55: Results of the Statistical Evaluation of the Applications for Federal Expellee Certificates"), *Wirtschaft und Statistik* (Stuttgart), **10** (4) (April 1958), 207–212, 184–185.

Horstmann, Kurt. "Internal Migration in the Federal Republic of Germany," *Proceedings of the World Population Conference: 1954,* II. New York, 1955.

Hutchinson, Bertram, "Structural and Exchange Mobility in the Assimilation of Immigrants to Brazil," *Population Studies,* **12** (2) (November 1958), 111–120.

Hutchinson, E. P. "The Changing Composition of the Foreign-Born Population of the United States, 1920-1950," *Proceedings of the World Population Conference: 1954,* II. New York, 1955.

Iklé, Fred C. "Comment on Theodore R. Anderson's Intermetropolitan Migration: A Comparison of the Hypotheses of Zipf and Stouffer," *American Sociological Review,* **20**(6) (December 1955), 713–714.

Illsley, Raymond, et al. "The Motivation and Characteristics of Internal Migrants: A Socio-Medical Study of Young Migrants in Scotland, (Part II: Other Characteristics of Migrants)," *Milbank Memorial Fund Quarterly,* **41**(3) (July 1963), 217–248.

International Catholic Migration Commission. "Brazil: Post-war Immigration (1946-1961)," *Migration Facts and Figures,* (Geneva) (31) (September-October 1963).

International Catholic Migration Commission. Reports from the Third International Catholic Migration Congress, Assisi, 1957. Information Center of the International Catholic Migration Commission, Geneva, 1957.

International Labour Office. "International Migration 1945-57," *Studies and Reports,* New Series, XIV, No. 54, Geneva: 1959.

International Labour Office, "Inter-Territorial Migrations of Africans South of the Sahara," *International Labour Review,* **76** (3) (September 1957), 292–310.

International Labour Office. "The Occupational Selection of Migrants," *International Labour Review,* **72** (5) (November 1955), 406–420.

International Labour Office. "Free Movement of Workers within the European Economic Community," *International Labour Review* (Geneva), **85** (2 and 3) (February and March 1962).

International Sociological Association and the International Economic Association. "The Positive Contribution by Immigrants," *Population and Culture Series,* a symposium prepared for

the United Nations Educational, Scientific, and Cultural Organization, Paris, 1955.

International Statistical Institute. "Internal Migration, II." (Joint meeting with the International Union for the Scientific Study of Population.) *Bulletin of the International Statistical Institute,* (Toronto) **40** (1) (1964), 421–472.

International Union for the Study of Population. Session 4. "Differential Migration: Influence of Age, Sex and Marital Status, Occupation, Educational Level, etc.," *Proceedings of the International Population Conference: 1961.* I, London, 1963, pp. 375–535.

Jones, Maldwyn A. "American Immigration," *Chicago History of American Civilization.* University of Chicago Press; Cambridge University Press; University of Toronto Press, 1960.

Jorge, Arias B. "Internal Migration in Guatemala," *Proceedings of the International Population Conference: 1961,* I. London, 1963, pp. 375–535.

Junior, Manuel Díegues. "Migrations Internes au Brésil" ("Internal Migration in Brazil"), a paper contributed for the United Nations World Population Conference, August 30-September 10, 1965.

Katzen, L. "South-African Immigration and Emigration in the Post-War Period," *International Migration* (Geneva) **1** (3) (1963), 183–191.

Keyfitz, Nathan. "L'Exode Rural Dans la Province de Québec, 1951-61" ("The Rural Exodus in Quebec Province, 1951-61"), *Recherches Sociographiques,* (Montreal) **3** (3) (September-December 1962), 303–316.

Kirchner, Walther, "Emigration: Some Eighteenth-Century Considerations," *Comparative Studies in Society and History* (The Hague), **5** (3) (April 1963), 346–356.

Kirk, Dudley. "Major Migrations since World War II," proceedings of the thirty-fourth annual conference of the Milbank Memorial Fund, October 30-31, 1957, at the New York Academy of Medicine. New York, 1958.

Kono, Shigemi, and Mitsuru Shio. *Inter-Prefectural Migration in Japan, 1956 and 1961: Migration Stream Analysis,* VI. Bombay: Demographic Training and Research Centre, 1963.

Kono, Shigemi, and Mitsuru Shio. "Stream Analysis of Inter-Prefectural Migration in Japan, 1956 and 1961," *Jinko Mondai Kenkyu (Journal of Population Problems),* (Tokyo) **88** (July 1963), 24–51.

Korea. Economic Planning Board. Bureau of Statistics. *Population Distribution and Internal Migration in Korea.* By Ehn Hyun Choe. A volume in the 1960 Census Monograph Series. Seoul, 1966.

Kosa, John. "A Century of Hungarian Emigration, 1850-1950," *American Slavic and East Eu-*

ropean Review, **16** (December 1957), 501–514.

Krotki, Karol J. "Temporariness of Urban Migration Estimated from Age Distributions in Large and Small Towns of East and West Pakistan," *Proceedings of the Pakistan Statistical Association,* **2** (1963), 115–126.

Kulldorf, Gunnar. "Migration Probabilities," *Lund Studies in Geography: Human Geography,* Series B, 14. Lund, Sweden: University of Lund Department of Geography and Statistics, and C.W.K. Gleerup, 1955.

Kuroda, Toshio. "Internal Migration," a paper contributed for the United Nations World Population Conference, August 30-September 10, 1965.

Kuznets, Simon, and Ernest Rubin. "Immigration and the Foreign Born," *National Bureau of Economic Research,* Occasional Paper 46. New York: National Bureau of Economic Research, XII, 1954.

Kuzents, Simon, and Dorothy S. Thomas. "Internal Migration and Economic Growth," *Proceedings of the Thirty-fourth Annual Conference of the Milbank Memorial Fund: 1957.* Part III, New York, 1958.

Ladinsky, Jack. "Sources of Geographic Mobility among Professional Workers: A Multivariate Analysis," *Demography,* **4** (1967), 293–310.

Lee, Everett S. "Negro Intelligence and Selective Migration: A Philadelphia Test of the Klineberg Hypothesis," in J. J. Spengler and O. D. Duncan (eds.). *Demographic Analysis,* Glencoe, Ill.: Free Press, 1951.

Lee, Everett S. "Migration and Mental Disease: New York State, 1949-51," *Proceedings of the Thirty-fourth Annual Conference of the Milbank Memorial Fund: 1957,* Part III. New York, 1958.

Lee, Everett S. "Migration Differentials by State of Birth in the United States," *Proceedings of the International Population Conference: 1961,* Session 4, I. London, 1963, pp. 375–535.

Lee, Everett S. "A Theory of Migration," *Demography,* **3** (1966), 47–57.

Lee, Everett S., and Anne S. Lee. "Internal Migration Statistics for the United States," *Journal of the American Statistical Association,* **55** (292) (December 1960), 664–697.

Lee, Everett S., Ann Ratner Miller, Richard A. Easterline, and Carol P. Brainerd. *Population Redistribution and Economic Growth, United States: 1870-1950.* Vol. I, *Methodological Considerations and Reference Tables.* Philadelphia: The American Philosophical Society, 1957.

Lee, Rose Hum. "The Chinese Abroad," *Phylon,* **17** (3) (1956), 257–270; **23** (3), 3230.

Lee, Rose Hum. "Chinese Immigration since 1940," *Sociology and Social Research,* **41** (3) (January-February 1957), 195–202.

Lipset, Seymour M. "Social Mobility and Urbanization," *Rural Sociology,* **20** (3–4) (September-December 1955), 220–228.

Lively, C. E., and C. Taeuber. *Rural Migration in the United States,* Research Monography XIX. Washington, D.C.: Government Printing Office, Division of Works Progress Administration, 1939.

Macura, Milos. "Locality in Internal Migration Statistics and Analyses," *Bulletin of the International Statistical Institute,* (Toronto) **40** (1) (1964), 421–472.

Makower, H., J. Marschak, and H. W. Robinson. Studies in Mobility of Labour," Oxford Economic Papers I, 1938, pp. 83–123.

Martinson, Floyd M. "Personal Adjustment and Rural-Urban Migration," *Rural Sociology,* **20** (2) (June 1955), 102–110.

Masham, H. V. "Toward a Formal Theory of Internal Migration," *Proceedings of the International Population Conference, 1961,* I. London, 1963, pp. 285–373.

Mayer, Kurt B. "The Impact of Postwar Immigration on the Demographic and Social Structure of Switzerland," *Demography,* 3 (1966), 68–89.

Mayer, Kurt B. "The Impact of Postwar Immigration on the Demographic and Social Structure of Switzerland," *Demography,* 3 (1) (1966), 68–89.

Mayer, Kurt B. "Postwar Migration from Italy to Switzerland," a paper contributed for the United Nations World Population Conference, August 30-September 10, 1965. WPC/WP/16 (B.9/V/E/16).

McDonald, J. S. "Some Socio-Economic Emigration Differentials in Rural Italy, 1902-13," *Economic Development and Cultural Change,* **7** (1) (October 1958), 55–72.

McDougall, Duncan M. "Immigration into Canada, 1851-1920," *"Canadian Journal of Economics and Political Science,* **27** (2) (May 1969), 162–175.

McGinnis, Robert, et al. "Internal Migration as a Stochastic Process," *Bulletin of the International Statistical Institute,* (Toronto) **40** (1), (1964), 421–472.

Meerdink, J. "Internal Migration in Amsterdam," *Bulletin of the International Statistical Institute,* (Paris) **39** (4) (1962), 183–193.

Mellor, George R. "Emigration from the British Isles to the New World 1765-1775," *History,* **40** (138–139) (February-June 1955), 68–83.

Milbank Memorial Fund. "Selected Studies of Migration since World War II," *Proceedings of the Thirty-fourth Annual Conference of the Milbank Memorial Fund, 1957,* Part III, New York, 1958.

Miller, Ann R. *Migration Differentials among Oc-*

cupation Groups: United States, 1960, a paper contributed for the United Nations World Population Conference, August 30-September 10, 1965.

Miller, Ann R. "Migration Differentials in Labor Force Participation: United States, 1960," Demography, 3 (1966) pp. 58–67.

Miller, Ann R. "Net Intercensal Migration to Large Urban Areas of the United States, 1930-40, 1940-50, 1950-60," Analytical and Technical Reports, VIII (4). Philadelphia: Population Studies Center, University of Pennsylania, May 1964.

Miller, Ann R., Richard A. Easterline, and Simon Kuznets. Population Redistribution and Economic Growth, United States: 1870-1951, Vol. II, Economic Series Analyses of Economic Change. Philadelphia: The American Philosophical Society, 1960.

McQuade, G. D. "Trends in Canadian Immigration," International Migration (Geneva), 2 (3) (1964), 221–234.

Mitchell, J. Clyde. "Migrant Labour in Africa South of the Sahara: The Causes of Labour Migration," Bulletin, Inter-African Labour Institute (Brazzaville, London), 6 (1) (January 1959), 8–47.

Mitchlee, J. C. "Factors Motivating Migration from Rural Areas," Proceedings of the Eleventh Conference of the Rhodes-Livingstone Institute for Social Research, 1958. R. J. Apthorpe (ed.), XXX, February 1958, p. 176.

Mortara, Giorgio. "Cento Anni de Emigrazione Italiana per Il Brasile: Nota Statistica" ("A Hundred Years of Italian Emigration to Brazil: Statistical Note"), Geornale Degli Economisti e Annali di Economia (Padua), 21 (9–10) (September-October 1962), 573–581.

Mortara, Giorgio. "Factors Affecting Rural-Urban Migration in Latin America: Influence of Economic and Social Conditions in These Two Areas," a paper contributed for the United Nations World Population Conference, (August 30-September 10, 1965.

Müller, K. V. "The Selective Effects of Internal Migration," Proceedings of the World Population Conference, 1954, II. New York, 1955.

Myburgh, C. A. L. "Migration in Relationship to the Economic Development of Rhodesia, Zambia, and Malawi," a paper contributed for the United Nations World Population Conference, August 30-September 10, 1965.

Myers, George C. "Migration and Modernization: The Case of Puerto Rico, 1950-60," a paper contributed for the United Nations World Population Conference, August 30-September 10, 1965.

Myers, George C., and Earl W. Morris. "Migration and Fertility in Puerto Rico," Population Stud-

ies, 20(1) (July 1966), 85–96.

Neiva, Artur Hehl. "International Migrations Affecting Latin America." Pp. 69–94 in Clyde V. Kiser (ed.) Components of Population Change in Latin America. Milbank Memorial Fund Quarterly, 43 (4, Part 2) (October 1965).

Newton, Mary P., and J. R. Jeffery. "Internal Migration, Some Aspects of Population Movements within England and Wales," General Register Office, Studies on Medical and Population Subjects, No. 5. London: H. M. Stationery Office, 1951.

Neymark, Ejnar. "Migration Differentials in Education, Intelligence, and Social Background: Analyses of a Cohort of Swedish Males," Bulletin of the International Statistical Institute, (Toronto) 40 (1) (1964), 319–417.

Oblath, Attilio. "L'Evolution Récente et les Perspectives des Migrations en Europe" ("Recent Evolution of and Perspectives on Migrations in Europe"), a paper contributed for the United Nations World Population Conference (August 30-September 10, 1965. Geneve: Bureau International du Travail. WPC/WP/67 (A.4/V/F/67).

Okazaki, Yiochi. "Migration in Relation to Future Growth of Population and Its Distribution: Internal Migration and Population Distribution, Japan," a paper contributed for the United Nations World Population Conference, August 30-September 10, 1965.

Oliver, F. R. "Interregional Migration and Unemployment, 1951-61," Journal of the Royal Statistical Society, Series A, 127 (a) (1964), 42–69.

Orleans, Leo A. "The Recent Growth of China's Urban Population," Geographical Review, '9 (1) (January 1959), 43–57.

Ozok, Kemal. "Urbanization and Internal Migration in Turkey," a paper contributed for the United Nations World Population Conference, August 30-September 10, 1965.

Paikert, G. C. "The German Exodus: A Selective Study on the Post-War II Expulsion of German Populations and Its Effects," Publications of the Research Group for European Migration Problems, 12 (The Hague). Martinus Nijhoff, 1962.

Pan American Union. Causes y Efectos del Exodo Rural en Venezuela (Causes and Effects of the Rural Exodus in Venezuela). Consejo Inter-Americano Economico y Social, Organización de los Estados Americanos (Interamerican Economic and Social Council, Organization of American States) XII. Washington, 1955.

Patterson, Sheila. Dark Strangers: A Sociological Study of the Absorption of A Recent West Indian Migrant Group in Brixton, South London. London: Tavistock Publication, XVI, 1963.

Perevedentsev, V. I. "The Interrelation between the Population Migration and the Ethnic Mixing of Peoples under Present Conditions in the USSR," a paper contributed for the United Nations World Population Conference, August 30-September 10, 1965.

Petersen, William, "The Ideological Background to Canada's Immigration," in Bernard R. Blishen et al. (eds.). *Canadian Society: Sociological Perspectives*. Toronto: Macmillan Co. of Canada, Ltd., XV, 1961.

Petersen, William. "Planned Migration: The Social Determinants of the Dutch-Canadian Movement," *University of California Publications in Sociology and Social Institutions*, 2 (10). Berkeley and Los Angeles: University of California Press, 1955.

Petersen, William. "A General Typology of Migration," *American Sociological Review*, 23 (3) (June 1958), 256–265.

Petersen, William. "Internal Migration and Economic Development in Northern America," *The Annals of the American Academy of Political and Social Science*, 316 (March 1958), 52–59.

Phillips, Doris G. "Rural-to-Urban Migration in Iraq," *Economic Development and Cultural Change*, 7 (4) (July 1959), 405–421.

Population Reference Bureau. "Population Growth and Immigration Policy" (in 2 parts.), *Population Bulletin*, 18 (7 and 8) (November-December 1962), 137–159, 161–179.

Pressat, Roland. "L'attraction dans les Migration Interieures" ("Attraction in Internal Migration"), *Bulletin of the International Statistical Institute*, (Toronto) 40 (1) (1964), 421–472.

Price, Charles A. "The Effects of Postwar Immigration on the Growth of Population, Ethnic Composition, and Religious Structure of Australia," *Australian Quarterly*, 29 (4) December 1957), 28–40.

Price, Charles A. *Southern Europeans in Australia*, in association with the Australian National University, Melbourne: Oxford University Press, XVI, 1963.

Price, Daniel O. "Distance and Direction as Vectors of Internal Migration, 1935 to 1940," *Social Forces*, 27 (1948), 48–53.

Price, Daniel O. "Some Socio-economic Factors in Internal Migration," *Social Forces*, 29 (1941), 409–415.

Price, Daniel O. "Nonwhite Migrants to and from Selected Cities," *American Journal of Sociology*, 54 (1948), 196–201.

Price, Daniel O. "Examination of Two Sources of Error in the Estimation of Net Internal Migration," *Journal of the American Statistical Association*, 50 (271) (September 1955), 689–700.

Prothero, R. Mansell. "Characteristics of Rural-Urban Migration and the Effects of Their Movements upon the Composition of Population in Rural and Urban Areas in Sub-Saharan Africa," a paper contributed for the United Nations World Population Conference, August 30-September 10, 1965.

Proudfoot, Malcolm J. "European Refugees; 1939-52. A Study in Forced Population Movement," *Social Science Series*, No. 10, Northwestern University Studies. Evanston, Ill.: Northwestern University Press, 1956.

Raimon, Robert L. "Interstate Migration and Wage Theory," *Review of Economics and Statistics*, 44 (4) (November 1962), 428–438.

Ravenstein, E. G. "The Laws of Migration," *Journal of the Royal Statistical Society*, 48 (Part 2) (June 1885), 167–227.

Ravenstein, E. G. *Journal of the Royal Statistical Society*, (June 1889), 241–301.

Richardson, Alan. "Some Psycho-social Aspects of British Emigration to Australia," *British Journal of Sociology*, 10 (4) (December 1959), 327–337.

Robbins, Richard. "Myth and Realities of International Migration into Latin America," *Annals of the American Academy of Political and Social Science*, 316 (March 1958), 102–110.

Roberts, G. W., and D. O. Mills. "Study of External Migration Affecting Jamaica: 1953–1955," a supplement to Vol. 7, No. 2, *Social and Economic Studies*. Mona, Jamaica (June, 1958), viii, 126, xvi.

Roof, Michael K. "Recent Trends in Soviet Internal Migration Policies," *R.E.M.P. Bulletin*, (The Hague) 8 (1), (January-March 1960), 1–18.

Rose, A. J. "The Geographical Pattern of European Immigration in Australia," *Geographical Review*, 48 (4) (October 1958), 512–527.

Rossi, Peter H. "Why Families Move: A Study in the Social Psychology of Urban Residential Mobility," joint sponsorship by *Bureau of Applied Social Research and the Institute for Urban Land Use and Housing Studies of Columbia University*, X. Glencoe, Ill.: Free Press, 1955.

Rowntree, John A. "Internal Migration: A Study of the Frequency of Movement of Migrants," *General Register Office Studies on Medical and Population Subjects* (11). London: H. M. Stationery Office, 1957.

Saville, John. "Internal Migration in England and Wales during the Past Hundred Years," in Jean Sutter (ed.). *Monaco Colloquia in Human Science*, XVI. Paris: Hachette, 1963.

Sauvy, Alfred, and Claude Moindrot. "Le Renversement du Courant d'Immigration Seculaire" ("The Reversal of the Long-term Trend in Immigration), *Population*. (Paris), 17 (1) January-March, 1962), 51–64 (in two parts).

Schechtman, Joseph B., *Postwar Population Trans-*

fers in Europe 1945-1955. Philadelphia: University of Pennsylvania Press; London: Oxford University Press, 1962.

Schechtman, Joseph B. The Refugee in the World: Displacement and Integration. New York: Barnes; London: Yoseloff, 1963.

Schnore, Leo F. "Components of Population Change in Large Metropolitan Suburbs," American Sociological Review, 23 (5) (October 1958), 570–573.

Schrier, Arnold. Ireland and the American Emigration, 1850-1910. Minneapolis: University of Minnesota Press, 1958.

Schwarz, Karl, and James D. Tarver. "Masszählen in der Wanderungsstatistik" ("Indices in Migration Statistics"), Allgemeines Statistisches Archiv (General Statistical Archive), 43 (1). Munich, 1959, 17–34.

Schwarzweller, Harry K. Sociocultural Origins and Migration Patterns of Young Men from Eastern Kentucky. University of Kentucky, Agricultural Experiment Station Bulletin 685. Prepared in cooperation with Farm Population Branch, Economic and Statistical Analysis Division, Economic Research Service, U.S. Department of Agriculture, December 1963.

Schwarzweller, Harry K., and James S. Brown. "Social Class Origins, Rural-Urban Migration, and Economic Life Chances: A Case Study," Rural Sociology, 32(1) (March 1967), 5–19.

Scott, Franklin D. "The Study of the Effects of Emigration," Scandinavian Economic History Review, (Uppsala, Sweden) 8 (2). (1960), 161–174.

Semmingsen, Ingrid. "Norwegian Emigration in the Nineteenth Century," Scandinavian Economic History Review (Uppsala), 8 (2) (1960), 150–160.

Senior, Clarence. "Integration Problems of Recent Rural Migrants to United States Cities," a paper contributed for the United Nations World Population Conference, August 30-September 10, 1965.

Servicio Informazioni, Italy. "L'Emigrazione Italiana nel Corso di un Secolo" ("Italian Emigration during a Century"), Documenti de Vita Italiana, 12 (123) (February 1962).

Shryock, H. S. "The Efficiency of Internal Migration in the United States," International Union for the Scientific Study of Population (Vienna) (1959), 685–694.

Shryock, H. S. Population Mobility within the United States. Chicago: Community and Family Study Center, 1964.

Shryock, H. S., and Hope T. Eldridge. "Internal Migration in Peace and War," American Sociological Review, 12, 17–39.

Shryock, H. S., and Elizabeth A. Larmon. "Some Longitudinal Data on Internal Migration," Demography, 2 (1965), 579–592.

Sicron, M. "Immigration to Israel, 1948–1953," Falk Project for Economic Research in Israel and Central Bureau of Statistics, Special Series No. 60. Jerusalem: The Falk Project for Economic Research in Israel, XIX, 1957.

Simoniya, N. A. "Overseas Chinese in Southeast Asia: a Russian Study," U.S. Joint Publications Research. Washington: (June 28, 1960), a,b, 1–160.

Skinner, William G. "Overseas Chinese in Southeast Asia," Annals of the American Academy of Political and Social Science, 321 (January 1959), 136–147.

Smith, T. Lynn. "Un Analisis Comparativo de la Migración Rural-Urbana en Latinoamerica" ("A Comparative Analysis of Rural-Urban Migration in Latin America"), Estadistica, Washington) 16 (61) (December 1958), 436–453.

Smith, T. Lynn. "The Role of Internal Migration in Population Redistribution in Brazil," a paper contributed for the United Nations World Population Conference, August 30-September 10, 1965.

Smith, T. Lynn. "Migration from One Latin American Country to Another," International Union for the Scientific Study of Population. (Vienna), 27 (1) (1959).

Sovani, N. V. "Internal Migration and the Future Trend of Population in India," a paper contributed for the United Nations World Population Conference, August 30-September 10, 1965.

Spengler, Joseph J. "The Economic Effects of Migration," Proceedings of the Thirty-fourth Annual Conference of the Milbank Memorial Fund: 1957, Part III. New York, (1958).

Spengler, Joseph J. "Issues and Interests in American Immigration Policy," The Annals of the American Academy of Political and Social Science, 316 (March 1958), 43–51.

Steglich, W. G. "Some Characteristics of Long-vs. Short-Distance Migrants," Proceedings of the Southwestern Sociological Association, 14 (March 1964), 20–25.

Stewart, Charles T., Jr. "Migration as a Function of Population and Distance," American Sociological Review, 25 (3) (June 1960), 347–356.

Stone, Leroy O. "Net Migration and Sex-Age Composition of Puerto Rico, 1950-60," Canadian Review of Sociology and Anthropology, 2(20) (May 1965), 108–116.

Stouffer, Samuel A. "Intervening Opportunities: A Theory Relating Mobility and Distance," American Sociological Review, 5 (December 1940), 845–867.

Stouffer, Samuel A. "Intervening Opportunities and Competing Migration," Journal of Regional Science, 2 (1960), 1–26. Reprinted in the author's *Research to Text Ideas*. Chicago: University of Chicago Press, 1963.

Tachi, Minoru. "Regional Income Disparity and Internal Migration of Population in Japan," *Economic Development and Cultural Change,* **12** (2) (January 1964), 186–209.

Taeuber, Conrad. "Migration and Rural Population Adjustment, *Rural Sociology,* **5,** 399–401.

Taeuber, Irene B. "Continuities in Internal Migration in Japan," *Proceedings of the Thirty-fourth Annual Conference of the Milbank Memorial Fund: 1957,* Part III. New York, 1953.

Taeuber, Karl E. "Cohort Migration," *Demography* (3), 416–422.

Taeuber, Karl E. "Duration-of-Residence Analysis of Internal Migration in the United States," *Milbank Memorial Fund Quarterly,* **39** (1) (January 1961), 116–131.

Taeuber, Karl E. "White Migration and Socio-Economic Differences Between Cities and Suburbs," *American Sociological Review,* **29** (5) (October 1964), 718–729.

Taeuber, Karl E. The Residential Redistribution of Farm-Born Cohorts, *Rural Sociology,* **32**(1) (March 1967), 20–36.

Taeuber, Karl E., and Alma F. Taeuber. "The Negro as an Immigrant Group: Recent Trends in Racial and Ethnic Segregation in Chicago," *American Journal of Sociology,* **69** (4) (January 1964), 374–382.

Taft, Donald R., and Richard Robbins. *International Migrations. The Immigrant in the Modern World.* New York: Ronald, VIII, 1955.

Tarver, James D. "Bureau of the Census Data on the Selectivity of Migration from Farms," *Rural Sociology,* **22** (2) (June 1957), 162–163.

Tarver, James D. "Predicting Migration," *Social Forces,* **39** (3) (March 1961), 207–213.

Tarver, James D. "Interstate Migration Differentials," *American Sociological Review,* **27** (3) (June 1963), 448–451.

Tarver, James D., William R. Gurley, and Patrick M. Skees, "Vector Representations of Migration Streams Among Selected State Economic Areas During 1955 to 1960," *Demography* (4) (1967), 1–18.

Tarver, James, and William R. Gurley. "A Stochastic Analysis of Geographic Mobility and Population Projections of the Census Division in the United States," *Demography* (2) (1965), 134–139.

Thistlethwaite, F. "Migration from Europe Overseas in the Nineteenth and Twentieth Centuries," a paper in *International Congress in History,* 1961. Stockholm: Eleventh, 1960, Vol. 5.

Thomas, Brinley. *Migration and Economic Growth.* Cambridge, England: Cambridge University Press, 1954.

Thomas, Brinley. "The Changing Pattern of Internal Migration in Great Britain, 1921-51," *Proceedings of the World Population Conference, 1954,* Vol. II New York: United Nations, 1955.

Thomas, Brinley (ed.). "Economics of International Migration," the proceedings of a conference held by the *International Economic Association.* London: Macmillan, 1958, XIV.

Thomas, Brinley. "International Migration and Economic Development: A Trend Report and Bibliography," *Population and Culture Series.* Paris: United Nations Educational, Scientific, and Cultural Organization, 1961.

Thomas, Brinley. "The Economic Resurgence of Western Europe and Its Bearing on Oversea Emigration," *Migration.* (Geneva), **2** (3–4) (July-December 1962), 79–83.

Thomas, Brinley. "Long Swings in Internal Migration and Capital Formation," *Bulletin of the International Statistical Institute,* (Toronto) **40** (1) (1964), 319–417.

Thomas, Dorothy. "Research Memorandum on Migration Differentials," *Bulletin 43.* New York: Social Science Research Council, 1938.

Thomas, Dorothy. *Social and Economic Aspects of Swedish Population Movements, 1750–1933.* New York: Macmillan Co., 1941.

Thomas, Dorothy. "Age and Economic Differentials in Interstate Migration," *Population Index,* **24** (4) (October 1958), 313–325.

Thomas, Dorothy. "International Migration," in Philip M. Hauser (ed.). *Population and World Politics.* Glencoe, Ill.: Free Press, 1958.

Thomas, Dorothy. "Some Observations on Migration and Economic Opportuntiy," *Proceedings of the Annual Meeting of the American Statistical Association: 1958.* Washington, D.C., 1959.

Thomas, Dorothy. "Age and Economic Differentials in Internal Migration in the United States: Structure and Distance," *International Union for the Scientific Study of Population* (Vienna) (1959), 714–721.

Thomas, Dorothy. "Internal Migration in the United States: 1870-1960," a paper contributed for the United Nations World Population Conference, August 30-September 10, 1965.

Thomas, Dorothy S., and K. C. Zachariah. "Some Temporal Variations in Internal Migration and in Economic Activity, United States, 1880–1950," *Proceedings of the International Population Conference: 1961,* I. London, 1963, pp. 375–535.

Thomlinson, Ralph. "A Model for Migration Analysis," *Journal of the American Statistical As-*

sociation, **56** (295) (September 1961), 675–686.

Thompson, Warren S. "Research Memorandum on Internal Migration in the Depression," *Bulletin No. 30*. New York: Social Science Research Council, 1937.

Thornthwaite, C. Warren. "Internal Migration in the United States," Philadelphia: University of Pennsylvania Press, 1934.

Ueda, Masao. "*A Study on Internal Migration and Age Structure of Migrants*," pp. 105–129 in *Archives of the Population Association of Japan*, No. 4. English edition. Tokyo, 1963.

United Nations Educational, Scientific and Cultural Organization, "The Positive Contribution by Immigrants," *Population Culture Series*. Paris: The International Sociological Association and the International Economic Association, 1955.

United Nations Educational, Scientific and Cultural Organization. *Flight and Resettlement*. New York: Columbia University Press, 1955.

United Nations Population Division. "*Elements of Immigration Policy*. New York, 1954, Vol. 21, No. 1.

U. S. Bureau of Census, "Components of Population Change, 1950 to 1960 for Counties, Standard Metropolitan Statistical Areas and Economic Subregions," *Current Population Reports, Series P-23*, No. 7 (November 1962).

U.S. Congress, House, Committee on the Judiciary, Subcommittee 1, "Study of Population and Immigration Problems," transcripts of the hearings, Special Series, No. 1. Washington, 1962. Comment by Robert C. Cook, *Population Reference Bureau: Population Bulletin*, **19** (7) (November 1963), 169–195.

U.S. Congress, House, Committee on the Judiciary. Subcommittee to Investigate Problems Connected with Refugees and Escapees, "World Refugee Problems," a hearing before the Subcommittee, Eighty-seventh Congress, first session, July 12–14, 1961. Washington, D.C.: Government Printing Office, 1961, IV.

U.S. Congress, Senate, Committee on Labor and Public Welfare, Subcommittee on Migratory Labor, "The Migratory Farm Labor Problem in the United States," *Report No. 934, 88th Congress, 2nd Session*, X. Washington, D.C.: U.S. Government Printing Office, 1964.

U.S. Social Security Administration. "Geographic Labor Mobility in the United States: Recent Findings," *Social Security Bulletin*, **30** (3) (March 1967), 14–20, 55.

Vance, Rupert B. "Research Memorandum on Population Redistribution within the United States," *Bulletin 42*. New York: Social Science Research Council, 1936.

Velikonja, Joseph. "Postwar Population Movements in Europe," *Annals of the Association of American Geographers*, **48** (4) (December 1958), 458–472.

Velikonia, Joseph. "Postwar Population Movements in Europe," *Annals of the Association of American Geographers*, **48** (4) (December 1958), 458–472.

Whetten, Nathan L., and Robert G. Burnight. "Internal Migration in Mexico," *Rural Sociology*, **21** (2) (June 1956), 140–151.

Wilbur, George. "Migration Expectancy in the United States," *Journal of the American Statistical Association* (June 1963), 444–453.

Willms, A. M. "The Brethren Known as Hutterians," *Canadian Journal of Economics and Political Science*, **24** (3) (August 1958), 391–405.

Wilson, Everett K. "Mobility and the Maverick," *Antioch Review: Population Problems—East and West*, Everett K. Wilson (ed.), **17** (1) (March 1957), 3–71.

Zachariah, K. C. *Historical Study of Internal Migration in the Indian Sub-Continent, 1901–1931*. Bombay: Demographic Training and Research Center, 1962.

Zachariah, K. C. "Internal Migration in India from the Historical Standpoint," *Bulletin of the International Statistical Institute*, (Toronto) **40** (1) (1964), 319–417.

Zachariah, K. C. "Bombay Migration Study: A Pilot Analysis of Migration to an Asian Metropolis," *Demography* (3) (1966), 378–392.

Zubrzycki, Jerzy. "Immigrants in Australia," a demographic survey based on the 1954 census, assisted by Nancy Kuskie, *Social Science Monographs*, No. 17. Melbourne University Press on behalf of the Australian National University, XVII, 1960.

Zubrzycki, Jerzy. "Sociological Methods for the Study of Immigrant Adjustment," *Migration* (Geneva), **1** (4) (October-December 1961), 51–62.

CHAPTER 20

The World Movement toward Fertility Control

20.1. Optimism versus Pessimism over Future Population Trends

Among demographers two contrasting moods can be found today. One group is highly pessimistic and foresees only a long and painful future for the developing nations before a population adjustment is reached—if ever. Another group, many of whom are not demographers at all but professionals in other fields who have joined fertility reduction programs, are cautiously optimistic. The position taken in this chapter falls along this continuum at almost the extreme of the optimistic side. To introduce the topic, two papers that at the time of their presentation were distinctly controversial are reprinted. It is hoped (and expected) that the events of coming years will validate them. They advance the thesis that a gigantic effort to reduce fertility quickly is under way throughout the world. This effort is one of the great social movements of history, and it is a complement to the equally momentous program whereby industrialized nations voluntarily assist in the economic development of poorer nations.

The plan of this chapter is to provide a quick but nevertheless moderately comprehensive review of the programs now under way around the world to achieve a demographic readjustment. This is intended both to provide information that is important to all students of demography and to document more fully the optimistic note on which the introductory papers are written. The fertility control movement is moving so rapidly, however, that this documentation will be quickly outdated. The introductory papers, therefore, will hopefully be the more enduring portion.

THE DEMOGRAPHIC BREAKTHROUGH: FROM PROJECTION TO CONTROL[*]

The years 1963-1964 very probably will go down in demographic history as one of the great landmarks of social science research progress. In the 12 months from June 1963 to June 1964 researchers in fertility control began to get a string of successes that leave no doubt that by planned intervention they had induced a downward change in the birthrate in high fertility populations. Experiences in Taiwan and Ceylon now are quite well documented. Other research, for which the data are only

[*]Donald J. Bogue. Presidential Address, Population Association of America, San Francisco, June 1964.

now being assembled, give every evidence of showing similar results. The work of the Family Planning Institute in Marauli Block near New Delhi; the Gandhigram experiment in South India; the experiments of the University of California School of Public Health at Dacca, East Pakistan; the experiments of the Johns Hopkins School of Public Health at Lahore, West Pakistan; and the research of the Population Council in Korea are among these "successes." In addition, ongoing fertility control programs, for which formal evaluation research has not been made, nevertheless show informal results that strongly suggest success at Comilla,

East Pakistan, Singapore, Malaya, and Hong Kong and Puerto Rico. To this list could be added the experiments on high fertility American populations carried out at the University of Chicago.

Another development, equally portentous but which we cannot take time to elaborate here, is the impressively long list of governments which either have made an outright declaration that slackening of population growth is now a part of their national program of economic development, or have asked for international aid in getting research underway that would explore the necessity of such action. Korea, Turkey, Ceylon, Thailand, Malaya, Egypt, Mainland China and Taiwan now are in this status, and there is a strong likelihood that most or all will join India and Pakistan in having a formal national program of fertility control. This may be operated through the government directly or by private agencies with government sanction and subsidy. In Latin America there is evidence that a similar process is at work.

It would be easy to disparage the "successes" as being too little in their impact, and too costly to be of practical use. In no case yet, with the exception of Taiwan, can it be clearly demonstrated that the birth rate of population of major size in an underdeveloped nation has been genuinely slackened by a fertility control program. (Let me add that there are several cases where such a decline probably has taken place; we merely lack the methodology to measure it quickly.)

Also, it would be easy to depreciate the public and private support for family planning around the world. It could be pointed out that some governments have endorsed the program but have done very little to implement it.

Even if we were to accept this minimization of the accomplishments of the past 12 to 18 months (and to admit that actual support for fertility control is smaller than the nominal support), it would still permit us to declare that a truly tremendous demographic "breakthrough" has taken place. Only two or three years ago demographers tended to hold the gloomy view that only a small miracle could save many nations from disaster because of rapid population growth. The picture is now completely different. If we make generous use of the word "if" we can now find a basis for a cautious optimism.

The smallness of the impact in these first few successes should not deceive us into thinking that this is all that is to come. The history of science shows that a first "breakthrough" success tends to be crude and clumsy. Once the basic principles necessary for success are learned, progress and refinement come rapidly. There is much reason to expect that this will happen with the new discovery of fertility control. This discovery, and the refinements that will be made in the next five to ten years, may well lead to social engineering work that will have as great impact upon the course of human history as any of the great major inventions or discoveries in the physical sciences.

It would seem that these events should cause demographers of the world to set two major tasks for themselves.

(*a*) To distill and summarize their findings until they are general statements of theory or principle, to express the essence of the successful programs.

(*b*) To review the entire field of their work, to appreciate what implications the demographic breakthrough has for other branches of demography.

Both of these tasks will consume many professional hours in the next few years. It is only to help get the task started that I will try to say a few words about each of these tasks.

THE PRINCIPLES (INGREDIENTS) OF SUCCESSFUL FAMILY PLANNING PROGRAMS

One of the peculiarities of recent research in fertility control is that nobody is failing—everyone is getting success to some degree. As population growth has continued, the alchemy of social change has pervaded even the more remote rural areas, so that populations now are "sensitized" that only a few years ago were thought to be inert and unpromising prospects. If we are going to look for basic ingredients or principles from the experience to date, we must look beyond the recipe of particular programs to search for the elements common in all of them. Unless we do this, there is a danger that we will confuse techniques for theories. Also, we must maintain a clear distinction between successes in a particular local group—say the single village—and getting success among a broader population, such as a whole nation, a state, or a city.

During February and March of this year I was privileged to spend several weeks in Asia, visiting most of the major research programs on fertility control. This provided me with an opportunity to interview the researchers in charge, to learn what they were learning, to try to see the problems as they see them now. In addition, I was privileged to sit in on discussions with experts intimately engaged in fertility control action. Since returning from Asia I have tried to summarize what I saw and heard. It seems to me now that all of these successful family planning programs have six fundamental ingredients. Without any one of them a program of fertility control will languish. With all of them, I think, a program cannot fail. In other words, for purposes of discussion I would like to assert that six ingredients are the necessary and sufficient conditions to intervene in the high fertility situation and bring about a fall in the birth rate. I will list them, and then explain briefly each one.

1. Awareness of the possibility and benefits of family planning.

2. Knowledge on how to implement family planning.

3. Impersonalization, desexualization, and public discussion of family planning.

4. Legitimation of family planning, primarily through private informal personal interaction.

5. Self-involvement in family planning.

6. Supplies through convenient and non-punative channels.

1. *Awareness of the Possibilities and Benefits.* This is a necessary prerequisite upon which all of the other ingredients rest. Within any population there seems to be a great variation in readiness and sensitivity with respect to fertility control. The population may be classified into four categories: "Unaware," "aware-and-neutral," "aware-and-positive," "aware-and-negative." This principle is that a program should try to reduce the proportion of the population that is "unaware" and "aware-and-neutral" and move as many as possible into the "aware-and-positive" camp. Bernard Berelson argues, and quite effectively, I think, that very little time or energy should be devoted to trying to convert the aware-and-negative group. Disbelievers should be left to be persuaded gradually by their own colleagues.

2. *Knowledge of How to Implement Family Planning.* Those who are aware and positive in their reaction must know what to do in order to achieve the benefits. At a minimum they must know where to go, whom to see, what to ask for, what it will cost them, and how to use what they are given. For best results they should know some alternative methods and the reputed advantages and disadvantages of each, so they may match their individual desires and preferences with a suitable method. It is quite plausible that for each increment of information provided by the program a certain increment of adoption would result. If this is the case, at some point the information providing principle would be subject to the law of diminishing returns. It is possible to waste time, money, and personnel in over-informing people just as in trying to convert those with negative attitudes.

3. *Massive Impersonalization, Desexualization and Public Attention.* Before the onset of mass fertility control awareness, the subject of family planning is closely linked to sex. Discussion of it tends to evoke feelings of shyness and shame because it is highly personalized. As the topic becomes an item for public discussion, it becomes separated from sex and depersonalized. The strategy of action should be to bring fertility control as rapidly as possible into the scope of public attention and public discussion, without increasing the level of negative awareness.

4. *Legitimization and Social Reinforcement.* Research has shown that only a comparatively few can be persuaded to try out a new idea on the basis of cold logical arguments of the potential benefits alone. In addition the members of the great masses need to have the endorsement or personal recommendation of persons they trust. This endorsement may need to

be from several sources—from a medical authority, from a religious authority, or from some high status person. But almost certainly there is also needed the endorsement of a respected colleague—someone from their own social stratum. Once they adopt, there is a need for social reinforcement—the feeling that they are not alone, that they are not being immoral or unnatural. The program must somehow generate this legitimization and social reinforcement.

5. *Self-Involvement.* In order to get action in family planning, informed persons with a positive attitude must apply what they know to their own life situation and realize that they personally need to take action. This awareness can come by process of individual reflection but seems to be greatly hastened by involving the person in a situation where he is led to consider the possibility of making a commitment. Where others are making a decision or discussing the possibility of making a decision, it causes the person to apply the argument to himself. This self-involvement cannot be manufactured directly but must be induced as a by-product of informing the public.

6. *Convenient and Nonpunative Provision of Supplies and Services.* Those who adopt family planning need a certain amount of help to get started and a continuing source of supplies and service. The type of organization that is set up to serve the masses can facilitate or hinder according to the amount of inconvenience and punishment it hands out. Some systems punish by forcing people to wait for a long time, by giving them supplies for only a few days, by making them walk or travel long distances to get supplies. Others punish them by forcing them into social situations where at the source of supply or service they are embarrassed, lose face, degraded in status, or otherwise humiliated. Recent experience suggests that supplies and services should be divided into two categories: those requiring medical or other clinical help to use and those that are nonclinical. The first group should be provided through conveniently located clinics operated in accordance with the best principles of human persuasion. The nonclinical supplies and services should be treated as convenience

goods, dispersed widely throughout the population and as readily available to eligible persons as tea, rice, or tobacco. Parenthetically, the clinical methods should be furnished with the best possible level of medical service. The individual patient, who has only one body and is highly nervous about the potential effect upon health, is completely unsympathetic with the statistical argument about "the greatest good for the greatest number." Tragic results are communicated quickly among the population and cause all of the five principles cited above to quickly go into reverse, to the detriment of the program.

CONCLUSION

It is my impression that if we utilized fully the knowledge we now have and used only the methods we now have, and made use of all of the personnel that could readily be recruited and trained, it would be possible to bring the birth rate of almost any rural village in Asia to about 25 per thousand within 10 years, and with appropriate organization I believe the birth rate of a nation could be lowered to this level in 15 years. On the other hand, until all six of these ingredients are combined into an experiment or a national program it is my opinion that comparatively little will happen to the birth rate.

It should be emphasized that there are a great many ways of applying these six principles. Some ways probably are better than others. Undoubtedly the most efficient way of creating the desired effect has not yet been discovered. A mountain of research remains.

Yet enough is known now to launch an effective program. If this assertion is true the plague of high fertility is no more insuperable than was malaria or other infectious diseases that now are all but forgotten. The timetable for the eradication of runaway population growth is about the same as for the conquest of these other diseases.

Bringing about an elimination of the population problem now is a matter of combining research with administration and wisdom. It may be that many of our plans built up over the recent years are in need of drastic revision.

Instead of a long-range program of institution-building for decades, in which the functions of education and training are postulated to require a lifetime, we may need an emergency organization to work five or ten years at a frantic pace to bring about the first five of the principles in operations. It may then be followed by a maintenance organization to carry out the ongoing function of providing supplies and service.

The above presentation is not meant to declare that the world population crisis is any less serious than it has been diagnosed to be. Quite the contrary. It is meant only as an assertion that we can now do more than just stand around wringing our hands.

IMPLICATIONS

One of the slogans that we often recite to undergraduate students is that the goal of all science is "prediction" and "control." Demography has been among the first of the social sciences to develop models for making demographic predictions, or projections as we diffidently term them. The demographic breakthrough is permitting us again to be a pacesetter in the social sciences, and in a few years I expect us to define the accomplishments of demography using both terms of the classic definition.

Some demographers seem to be apprehensive that the demographic breakthrough is causing many more familiar lines of research to lose their importance, or that our fraternity will be invaded by some new species of professional person from whom they would prefer to be segregated. This fear of integration, if it exists, is wholly unfounded in my opinion. The great responsibility of demography is still one of scientific research. The demographic breakthrough has merely opened up a great new research field—that of evaluation research. The net long run result, I would predict, will simply be to add another group of researchers to what already is a many branched and very sturdy tree.

THE PROSPECTS FOR WORLD POPULATION CONTROL*

I. THESIS:
POPULATION EQUILIBRIUM IN OUR DAY

Recent developments in the worldwide movement to bring runaway birth rates under control are such that it now is possible to assert with considerable confidence that the prospects for rapid fertility control are excellent. In fact, it is quite reasonable to assume that the world population crisis is a phenomenon of the 20th century, and will be largely if not entirely a matter of history when humanity moves into the 21st century. No doubt there will be isolated pockets of population hardship in the year 2000, but the outlook is that they will be confined to a few nations that were too prejudiced, too bureaucratic, or too disorganized to take action sooner, or will be confined to small regions within some nations where particular ethnic, economic, or religious groups will not yet have received adequate fertility control services and information for a sufficient span of time to complete the demographic transition to lower fertility. With the exception of such isolated remnants (which may be neutralized by areas of growth at less-than-replacement), it is not at all unreasonable to assume that by the year 2000 each of the major world regions will have a growth rate that either is zero or easily within the capacity of its expanding economy to support.

The implications of these assertions for the production of food are obvious. Given the present capacity of the earth for food production, and the potential for additional food production if modern technology were more fully employed, the human race clearly has within its grasp the capacity to chase hunger from the earth—within a matter of a decade or two. Furthermore, it is doubtful whether a total net food shortage for the entire earth will ever develop. If such a deficit does develop, it will

* Donald J. Bogue, revision of a paper presented at Conference on World Food Resources, Ames, Iowa, November 1966; and published in *The Public Interest,* Spring, 1967.

be mild and only of short duration. The really critical problem of food will continue to be one of maldistribution among the world's regions.

These optimistic assertions are not intended to detract from the seriousness of the present population situation. Some years of acute crisis lie immediately ahead for India, Mainland China, the Philippines, Indonesia, Pakistan, Mexico, Brazil, Egypt, and other nations. Severe famines quite probably will develop within local areas of some of these nations unless emergency international measures are taken to lend assistance. The intent here is to emphasize that the engineers and the agricultural technicians striving to increase the output of material goods in these nations are not working alone. Paralleling their activity is a very ambitious international fertility control program which is just starting to "pay off."

Also, these remarks are not intended to cause the participants in this international fertility control program to relax their efforts and be lulled into complacency. The successful outcome anticipated above is not one that will come automatically, but only as the result of a continued all-out "crash program" to make the widest and most intensive use possible of the medical, sociological and psychological knowledge now available and the practical experience that has recently emerged from experimental family planning programs. It also anticipates a continued flow of new research findings and enriched practical experience that is promptly fed back into programs of fertility reduction.

This view is knowingly at variance with the established view of many population experts. For more than a century demographers have terrorized themselves, each other, and the public at large with the essential hopelessness, inevitability, and morale-breaking pessimism of the "population explosion" via exponential growth. Their prophecies have all been dependent upon one premise: "If recent trends continue. . . ." It is an ancient statistical fallacy to perform extrapolations upon this premise when in fact the premise is invalid. It is the major point of this paper that *recent trends have not continued, nor will they be likely to do so.* Instead, there have been some new and re-

cent developments that make it plausible to expect a much more rapid pace in fertility control. These developments are so new and so very different from the past that population trends before 1960 are largely irrelevant in predicting what will happen in the future. Demographers who continue to try to foresee the future of world population growth right now by carefully fitting curves to time series or seek the roots of matrices summarizing masses of age-specific historical information in the search for hidden indicators of the future are making extrapolations from invalid premises.

In times of social revolution it often is fruitless to forecast the future on the basis of past experience. Instead, it is better to abandon time series analysis and study the phenomenon of change itself, seeking to understnd it and to learn in which direction and how rapidly it is moving. If enough can be learned about the social movement that is bringing about the change, there is a hope that its eventual outcome can be predicted. With this intervening information one can then return to the original problem and make a rough prediction. This procedure is followed here. The result is subjective and crude, but is believed to be nearer the future course of demographic history than the official population projections now on record.

II. EVIDENCE

Limitations of space permit only a listing of the major social developments which give rise to the position taken above and to outline briefly the argument supporting the validity of each.[1]

1. Grass Roots Approval.[2] All over the world wherever surveys of the attitudes of the public with respect to fertility have been taken it

[1] Fuller justification of these points was presented in August 1966, in a paper presented to the Pacific Science Congress in Tokyo, "Recent Developments in Family Planning that Promise Hope in Coping with the Population Crisis in Asia and Throughout the World."

[2] For a fuller documentation of this point see Bernard Berelson (ed.), *Family Planning and Population Programs* (Chicago: The University of Chicago Press, 1966).

has uniformly been found that a majority of couples with three living children wish to have no more. Of these, a very large proportion approve of family planning in principle and declare they would like to have more information about it. They also approve of nationwide health service that includes family planning. In other words, active objection among the masses on cultural, moral, or religious grounds are minor rather than major obstacles. This is true both in Asia and Latin America, and seems to be developing rapidly in Africa. Thus, at the "grass roots" level, the attitudinal and cultural conditions are highly favorable. Previously, it had been feared that traditionalism and religious attitudes would prove to be almost insuperable blocks to rapid fertility control. The more sociologists study the situation the more they accept as correct the generalization that in most places where there is a population problem, the attitudes toward family planning among the masses are strongly positive. Moreover, by intensive information programs it is possible to greatly intensify this tendency—this approval—even among rural and illiterate populations.

2. Aroused Political Leadership.[2] Whereas fertility control was regarded as a subversive, immoral and sinful program during the 150 years of fertility decline in Europe and the United States, in the nations with a population problem today the national political leadership has become informed of the problem and openly accepts family planning as a moral and rational solution. Heads of state in India, Pakistan, Korea, Mainland China, Egypt, Chile, Turkey, and Colombia, for example, have made fertility control an integral part of the national plan for economic development. In this, they have followed the lead of Japan. The national ministers of health and welfare not only are permitted but expected to provide family planning services to the masses. National health services are adding family planning to their clinic services, financed by public tax funds. The mass media are increasingly carrying announcements of official public endorsement and encouragement, and specific information.

3. Accelerated Professional and Research Activity. Professional groups in the developing countries (as well as in the rest of the world) are rapidly losing whatever antipathy or prejudice against family planning they may have had. Everywhere, the medical profession is rapidly giving a solid endorsement—even in nations where there have been problems of religious objection. They are being joined by social workers, educators, economists, and lawyers. Within religious groups where there formerly was a hard inflexible prohibition against the use of chemical or mechanical contraceptive appliances there is now a great deal of difference of opinion. Gradually, the laity is reaching the belief that the control of natality is a matter for the individual conscience, or a medical matter to be discussed with a physician—but not with the priest. Physicians and priests alike tend to accept this interpretation without forthright challenge.

Universities, both in the United States and abroad, have undertaken large-scale and sustained research activities in the fields of family planning. Their activities cover the entire range of topics—medical, sociological, and psychological. Most of the nations with a national family planning program are sponsoring a national research-in-family-planning component. This includes not only projects to discover new and improved ways of promoting fertility control, but also the evaluation of present programs. These activities are not amorphous, but within a remarkably short time have been coordinated. The process of integration was greatly facilitated by the holding in Geneva in 1965 of an International Conference on Family Planning Programs.

Much of the credit for the development described above is due to the activities of not-for-profit organizations that have taken population control as a focus of their activities: Ford Foundation, Rockefeller Foundation, Population Council, and International Planned Parenthood are leaders in this support. The Swedish Government, the Milbank Memorial Fund, the Planned Parenthood Association of America, and the Pathfinder Fund have also been highly important sponsors of these activities. These organizations have provided unprecedented financial and technical support. They are now being joined, with massive resources, by the United States Agency for International Development (A.I.D.)

4. The Slackening of Progress in Death Control.[3] Immediately after World War II the industrialized nations of the world realized that there was a series of public health and medical activities that could be accomplished quickly and cheaply to bring about a reduction in mortality. These have been largely carried out—there have been campaigns against malaria, smallpox, cholera, yellow fever, and other diseases that can be brought under control with an injection, a semiannual house spraying, etc. The results have been dramatic, and death rates have tumbled. However, further progress in death control is much more slow, because the remaining problems are those for which a solution is more difficult or is as yet unknown. For example, the death rate in Latin America stands at about 14 per thousand now. Modern medicine could bring it, at best, only to about 8 per thousand—a fall of only 6 points. A very much greater investment must be made, and over a considerably longer span of time, to achieve these 6 points than was required to obtain the preceding six points. In Asia the death rate still stands at about 20, even after the application of the majority of the "miracle drugs" and the mass-innoculation and mass-treatment programs. It may be expected to drift lower, but at an even slower pace than before.

This slackening of death control has a most important implication—a decline in the birth rate would be more directly reflected in a decline in the rate of population growth. During the past two decades, if birth rates were declining, death rates were declining even faster, so that the growth rate increased. That situation now appears to be reaching the end of a cycle: the reverse situation appears to be taking over.

5. A Variety of Sociological and Psychological Phenomena, Previously Unknown or Underappreciated, Are Promoting the Rapid Adop-

tion of Family Planning by the Masses.[4] Here we can only list them, without explanation.

(a) Privation is itself a powerful motivating force for fertility control.

(b) Private communication about family planning is far greater than had been thought, and can be easily stimulated to attain flood proportions.

(c) "Opinion leaders"—indigenous members of the masses who are knowledgeable about birth control and freely undertake to influence others to adopt it—can be mass-produced cheaply and very rapidly by means of mass media and other action programs. Thus, in this area just as in economic development, there is a "multiplier effect" which, if capitalized upon, can greatly hasten "takeoff" into rapidly declining fertility.

(d) Fathers are very nearly equally as interested and responsible in controlling fertility as are wives. Programs aimed at couples, instead of at females, are highly effective.

(e) Illiterate rural populations will make use of the traditional methods of family planning—condom, suppositories, etc., as readily as urban populations after a brief period of information and trial. They will also adopt the newer methods equally or even more readily.

6. Improved Technology in Contraception Promotes Massive Adoption by Uneducated People at a Rapid Pace, and Permits Their Continued Use of Family Planning.[4] Oral contraceptives and the intrauterine devices have both proved to be highly acceptable with only short periods of instruction and familiarity. Even illiterate rural villagers make sustained use of these methods where they have been given unprejudiced trial. These developments are only half-a-decade old, yet already they have had a profound impact upon fertility control programs and plans. As yet there is still a great deal of prejudice against the oral compounds in Asia, so that the advantages of a two-method

---

[3] For fuller documentation of this point see United Nations Population Bulletin No. 6, *Recent Trends of Morality in the World* (New York: United Nations, 1963).

[4] For a fuller documentation of this point see Donald J. Bogue, *The Rural South Fertility Experiments*, Report No. 1 (1966), and Donald J. Bogue (ed.), *Sociological Contributions to Family Planning* (in press). Both published by the Community and Family Study Center, University of Chicago.

assault have not as yet been realized there. In Latin American experiments where the "pills" and intrauterine devices are used side-by-side as alternative methods, the effect is highly impressive.

We are repeatedly being told by the physiologists, however, that our so-called "modern" methods of contraception are crude and barbarous—each with unpleasant side-effects and unsuitable for as much as ¼ of the population or more. They insist that much superior methods are on the horizon—that soon there will be dramatic improvements, that costs will be cheaper, and that the need for "sustained motivation" to practice contraception will be greatly reduced. Millions of dollars are being poured into experimental research on this front each year. This activity is taking place both in the public and the private sector. The giants of the drug industry know that huge markets can be gained by improving upon present contraceptive technology—and that huge markets will be lost if a competitor discovers and markets a superior product. As a result, all of the leading motives that bring about frenzied activity for progress among scientists are harnessed and at work in behalf of improving contraceptive technology—prestige, economic gain, anxiety, compassion.

III. AN EXAMPLE: KOREA

In order to illustrate the above points, a few facts about one of the current family planning programs may be cited. In 1962 the Republic of Korea formally adopted family planning as one of its national policies. In 1965 a National Survey of Family Planning was conducted. Following are some points from that survey:[5]

1. 89 per cent of the wives and 79 per cent of the husbands approved of family planning.

2. The rate of approval was only slightly lower in the rural than in the urban areas (88 per cent for rural women and 77 per cent for rural men).

[5] Ministry of Health and Social Affairs, Republic of Korea, *The Findings of the National Survey on Family Planning*, 1965. Published by the Planned Parenthood Federation of Korea, 1966.

3. Of the minority who disapproved, only 8 per cent mentioned religion or morals. Traditional resistance was as low in rural as in urban areas.

4. Inability to read was no barrier; 81 per cent of those unable to read nevertheless approved of family planning.

5. On the verbal level, the population declared itself willing to practice family planning if given services. 77 per cent of the urban women and 71 per cent of the rural women made such a declaration. Among husbands, 71 per cent of the urban and 65 per cent of the rural made such a declaration.

6. Unwillingness to practice family planning was concentrated primarily among young couples who had not yet had the number of children they desired and older couples (past 40 years of age) who were approaching the end of their childbearing. Couples in the years of prime importance for birth control, 25-40, were most positive. Moreover, the greater the number of living children the greater the willingness to practice.

7. As a result of the national information program, 85 per cent of the urban and 83 per cent of the rural population had heard of family planning. Moreover, 67 per cent of the urban and 64 per cent of the rural population had knowledge of at least one contraceptive method. Even among the illiterate, 51 per cent knew of one method or more. Knowledge of the more reliable methods—oral pill, IUCD, condom, was only very slightly less widespread in rural than in urban areas.

8. At the time of the interview, 21 per cent of the urban and 14 per cent of the rural couples were practicing family planning. Even among the illiterate population, 10 per cent were currently practicing family planning. Although small, these percentages very obviously had sprung from a condition of near-zero within a span of three years. If only 2 per cent are added each year, within 35 years birth rates would be near zero. Actually, standard adoption curves would predict a faster pace than this, at least in the next few years.

9. The methods used by rural families were equal to or superior to those of the urban population in terms of reliability:

Method	Per cent of those using a method	
	Urban	Rural
Condom	51.1	61.1
IUCD	18.4	27.0
Oral pill	8.5	3.5
Foam tablet	34.5	42.2

Note: Figures add to more than 100 because some couples employed more than one contraceptive.

10. In April of 1965 there were 2207 field workers in the national family planning service, stationed in the health centers or in local offices. This is only the first wave of a rapid build-up to a point where there will be one field worker for each 10,000 population. The medical and social science departments of Seoul National University are actively engaged in research, evaluation, and participation in the national program. A private organization, Planned Parenthood Federation of Korea, has a branch in each province and is providing service and information through its office. Yonsel Medical College is conducting special experiments in rural areas, with assistance from the Population Council.

11. The progress of the national program in giving family planning services is most impressive. The progress that results when a well-designed family planning program is carried out in a population of low education is illustrated by the Sungdong Gu Action-Research Project on Family Planning, conducted by Seoul National University School of Public Health under the sponsorship of the Population Council. This program started in July, 1964. It included the use of mass media (T.V., radio, newspaper, posters, pamphlets, leaflets), group meetings, and home visiting. During the first 15 months of the program, of a total of 44,900 eligible (married women in the ages 20-44), 9,809 visited the family planning station for family planning information. About 85 per cent of these visitors (19 per cent of all the eligible women) accepted a method of family planning. Acceptance was divided roughly equally between condoms and other traditional methods and the IUCD's. Within the period, a total of 5,722 insertions (13 per cent of the

eligible women) were made.[6] Even when allowance is made for the fact that the first year's experience would "skim off" the accumulated set of already-motivated people, the fact that one-fifth of the fertile population could be induced to adopt family planning within such short time is most impressive. It suggests the potential progress that can be made when a well-balanced program of information and service is provided, making use both of the mass media and personal contact.

The above brief notes on the progress of fertility control in Korea are not isolated instances. A report just received from the Pakistan Family Planning Programme for July, 1966, suggests that more than one million families in that nation of 100 million (about 5 per cent of the eligible population) now are currently contracepted through this program alone. In India, more than a million insertions of IUCD's are being made annually—in addition to rising use of other methods of contraception. In Colombia in Latin America the oral pills and the IUCD both are being accepted at phenomenal rates; it is estimated that more than 120,000 couples in this nation of 18 million persons are using the oral pills alone; this is roughly 3 per cent of the eligible population. In addition, large quantities of other methods are known to be used. In Santiago, Chile, the IUCD is so well known and widely used that it is a part of the medical service throughout the metropolitan area.

To summarize: Wherever one looks in the underdeveloped segments of the world, one finds evidence of firmly established and flourishing family planning activity. By whatever crude estimates it is possible to make, it is quite clear that a sufficiently large share of the population already is making use of modern contraceptives to have a depressing effect upon the birthrate. Even conservative evaluation of the prospects for growth suggests that instead of a "population explosion" the world is on the threshold of a "contraception adoption explosion." Because of lack of adequate vital statistics, these effects will not be readily mea-

[6] Seoul National University, School of Public Health, *Sungdong Gu Action-Research Project on Family Planning:* Progress Report, April 1966.

surable for a few years, but they almost certainly exist over much of the overpopulated portion of the earth's surface, will start to manifest themselves in the censuses of 1970, and will be most unmistakable in 1980.

IV. IMPLICATIONS FOR THE FUTURE

Given the situation that has just been described, what can be said concerning the future population of the world? If we insist on extrapolating past trends, we are making the unrealistic assertion that conditions have remained unchanged and will continue to do so. If we predict a slow change of the type that was typical of Europe and Northern America before 1960 we are implicitly asserting that the current programs are having zero effect, and that "history will take its course" despite all efforts. This also seems unduly unreal and pessimistic. The course taken here is to try to comprehend the nature of the change that is taking place, and to predict its probable course and speed, so that its impact may be guessed. As crude and subjective as this procedure is, it appears to offer more valid predictions than more conventional population projections. In this section an effort is made to do this.

Looking at the developments listed above, realizing that they are only 5 years old or less, knowing that accomplishments in this area are cumulative and grow by exponential curves, and appreciating that new discoveries and improvements will accrue promptly along all fronts—medical, social, and psychological—both from basic research and from accumulating experience and evaluation, the following generalizations appear to be justified:

The trend of the worldwide movement toward fertility control has already reached a state where declines in death rates are being surpassed by declines in birthrates. Because progress in death control is slackening and progress in birth control is accelerating, the world has already entered a situation where the pace of population growth has begun to slacken. The exact time at which this "switchover" took place cannot be known exactly, but we estimate it to have occurred about 1965. From 1965 onward, therefore, the rate of world population growth will slacken at such a pace that it will be zero or near zero at about the year 2000, so that population growth will not be regarded as a major social problem except in isolated and small "retarded" areas.

This projection has been scheduled out, by world regions, in Table 20-1. This table was constructed as follows: It was assumed that the growth rate of each world region began in 1965 to decline linearly at such a pace that it would reach zero in the year 2000. The population estimates of the United Nations were used as the basis of the estimates.[7] The population that would be expected on the basis of these assumptions was then calculated in 5-year cycles, using an average growth rate for each cycle that corresponded to the assumptions. Had the compounding been done annually instead of in 5-year cycles, the amount would have been somewhat greater. Also, it is quite possible that the decline of the growth rate may follow a logistic rather than a linear pattern, and this also would tend to boost the estimates somewhat. Finally, the age composition of the developing nations is a very young one; hence, even if rates were to fall drastically, the potential for growth remains greater than that envisaged by our linear model. To allow for these and other contingencies, and to summarize the position taken above, the following prediction is submitted for consideration:

It is now technologically possible and operationally plausible that the world population growth will slacken at a pace such that it will equal about 5 billion persons in the year 2000, and when this point is reached growth rates in all of the major world regions will have declined to zero or so very nearly so that there will be little anxiety about a population crisis.

No effort has been made to adjust the individual world regions to conform to known or suspected differences in their inclination to accept family planning programs promptly. It is

[7] United Nations, *Demographic Yearbook*, 1964, Table 2.

Table 20-1 Estimates of Future Growth of World Population by Regions, 1965 to 2000, Assuming Condition of Linear Decline of Growth Rate to Zero by 2000 (All Figures in Millions)

Continent and World region	1965	1970	1980	1990	2000
AFRICA	309	345	409	455	473
Western Africa	98	111	134	150	157
Eastern Africa	84	93	108	119	123
Northern Africa	76	86	104	117	122
Middle Africa	31	33	37	40	41
Southern Africa	20	22	26	29	30
AMERICA	458	505	591	651	674
North America	215	231	259	277	284
Latin America	244	274	332	374	388
Tropical South America	130	148	181	205	213
Middle America	54	62	77	88	92
Temperate South America	36	39	45	49	50
Caribbean	23	25	29	32	33
ASIA	1,814	1,979	2,262	2,456	2,524
East Asia	851	910	1,006	1,070	1,091
Mainland	701	747	823	873	890
Japan	98	103	110	115	116
Other East Asia	53	60	73	82	85
South Asia	964	1,069	1,256	1,386	1,433
Middle South Asia	650	719	842	927	958
South East Asia	248	277	328	364	377
South West Asia	66	73	86	95	98
EUROPE	445	465	497	518	525
Western Europe	144	153	168	178	182
Southern Europe	122	127	134	139	140
Eastern Europe	100	103	108	111	112
Northern Europe	79	82	87	90	91
OCEANIA	17.5	19.3	22.6	24.9	25.6
Australia & North Zealand	14.0	15.3	17.7	19.3	19.8
Melanesia	2.4	2.7	3.2	3.6	3.7
Polynesia & Micronesia	1.1	1.3	1.7	2.0	2.1
U.S.S.R.	232	249	279	298	305
World Total	3,276	3,562	4,061	4,403	4,527

Source: Basic data from Demographic Yearbook, (New York: United Nations, 1964), p. 111.

quite plausible that growth in Africa will surpass these estimates substantially. On the other hand, it is equally plausible that extraordinary successes in other parts of the world may counterbalance this, to maintain an approximate correctness for the world totals.

CONCLUSION

In evaluating this report, it must be kept in mind that the topic is a deadly serious one, and the penalties for misjudgment may be very great. There is one set of penalties that results from over-optimism. But there is another set of penalties that results from over-pessimism. It is quite possible that nothing has sapped the morale of family planning workers in the developing countries more than the Malthusian pessimism that has been radiated by many demographic reports. It is like assuring soldiers going into battle that they are almost certain to be defeated. If the comments made here should be so fortunate as to fall into the hands of these same family planning workers, it is hoped that those who read them will appreciate just how close they actually are to success. They have it within their grasp to improve dramatically their countries' fortunes. Coupled with the companion programs of industrialization and modernization, the effects will appear almost miraculous as they unfold in the 1970's and 1980's.

All too often the present generation is passing on to the next grave problems that are snarled up worse than when they were received from Grandfather. This need not, and very probably will not be the case with respect to the World Population Problem.

20.2. The Methods Available for Fertility Control

No assessment of the prospects for fertility control can be realistic if it does not take into account the dramatic advances that have recently been made in contraceptive technology. Technical details of the methods for fertility control need not be presented here; it is sufficient merely to enumerate the methods and describe their utility for bringing down birthrates in developing nations with high fertility.

Hormonal Control of Ovulation: "Pills" and Injections. Research in the 1950s led to the discovery that ovulation in the female could be completely suppressed by administering hormones that induce a chemical balance in the human body that is normal during pregnancy. These hormones may be administered either by mouth in the form of "birth control pills" or in the form of injections. The form most widely used at the present time is a system whereby a woman who desires not to become pregnant takes one pill each day for 20 or 21 days (depending on the brand) beginning shortly after the onset of menstruation. Pill-taking is then suspended for seven or eight days, during which menstruation takes place. The process is then repeated. Other systems provide for an injection of the hormones prepared in such a way that the drug becomes available to the body progressively, so that an injection is required only every three months or even less frequently.

The acceptability of this form of fertility control is amazingly high. It separates contraception from direct interference with the sex act. Early fears that uneducated people (and many educated ones) would not be able to remember to take the pills daily or to return on schedule for their "shot" have proved to be unfounded. As of 1967, an estimated 12 million couples in the United States are making use of this method, and this class of contraception is gaining steadily. In Europe, Australia, and Canada there has been a similar pattern.

When first introduced, the costs of production were high; couples were required to pay $10 or even more per month. Competition among the corporations producing these compounds and rising volume of use has lowered the cost. It has been found that much smaller dosages of hormones are required than were originally prescribed. It has proved possible to synthesize the hormones, instead of extracting them from plants. By mid-1967 manufacturers were offering to supply huge potential customers such as the governments of India and Pakistan for a cost of only 14 to 17 cents per cycle. Inasmuch as there are 13 cycles per year, the cost per woman for a year of protection is only about $2. This brings the method within the purchasing power of even the poorest family, for nowhere in the world can a child be supported for so little. It also brings it within the power of any developing nation to provide free contraception to its citizenry as part of national economic development. At these prices, no money input known has a larger "payoff" than investment in family planning, where the goal is to raise per capita income.

When used correctly and absolutely on schedule, this method provides almost 100 percent protection from pregnancy. A few women find that even with the newer low-dosage compounds they experience unpleasant side effects in the form of nausea, dizziness, or occasional menstrual bleeding outside the established cycle. These symptoms usually disappear after one or two months of use, but for some they persist. Physicians advise against prescribing these drugs to women who have experienced certain circulatory or other disorders. This method is applicable to about 90 to 95 percent of women in the reproductive ages and has a record of high sustained use among European and American populations.

Only limited experience has been gained with the use of this method of contraception by populations of nations with critical population problems. In Latin America use by the upper social strata is very extensive, and seems to be descending rapidly into the middle and lower strata. In India and Pakistan, early field trials were disappointing, but some believe that more positive results can be achieved when full medical endorsement and massive public education are provided as a foundation. Family planning workers in these countries are especially hopeful for the success of injections that provide longer-term protection and "once-a-month" pills, once they are developed. They report repeated requests for such methods by illiterate women coming to their clinics for family planning assistance. Pills are being used successfully in Ceylon, Hong Kong, Singapore, and Malaysia among Hindu and Chinese populations.

Control of conception by chemical means is still in its infancy, claim most of the scientists who are doing research in this area. They are almost unanimous in predicting newer, more acceptable, and inexpensive systems that provide full protection for much longer periods of time. They predict the development of a "morning-after" pill to be taken after intercourse, and of control of male as well as female fertility. It is easily within the realm of expectation that by 1980 contraception by control of body chemistry will be available in such a multiplicity of forms and with such high reliability, low side effects, and low cost that it will be easily within the power of any government on earth to provide free fertility control service to its citizens as a part of its national economic development program. Moreover, all but a tiny fraction of the citizenry will have available a method that it finds acceptable, from a medical or use point of view.

Intrauterine Contraceptive Devices: The Plastic Coil or Loop (IUCD). It has long been known that if a metal ring or other similar foreign body is inserted inside the uterus, conception will not take place. Such intrauterine contraceptive devices were originally made in the form of gold or other metallic rings. Later it was discovered that the same result could be accomplished by small rings made of silk or nylon thread. Experiments with the use of plastic "coils" or "loops" proved that highly effective contraception could be achieved by this technique. Extensive laboratory research led to the medical verdict that no harmful long-term effect results from the practice of this mode of contraception. As yet, physiologists are not certain what causes this contraceptive effect. Some believe that the IUCD hastens the passage of the ovum through the Fallopian tubes, so that the fine timing required for fertilization is thrown off. Others hold that it prevents the fixation of a fertilized ovum to the wall of the

uterus, so that even though fertilization may occur, pregnancy does not.

The virtue of this method is that once the device is in place, no further action is needed. The device is simply left in place until the couple desires to have another child. It is then removed, and pregnancy follows after the normal interval. It is cheap; under conditions of mass production, the cost of the IUCD and the materials required for its insertion is only about 10 to 15 cents per woman.

When plastic IUCD's were first introduced, this method was believed to be ideal for developing countries. Insertion involves only a simple and quick procedure that can be taught to practical nurses with no previous medical training; sustained action is not required, and failure of this method is very low (about 2 births per 100 woman-years of protection).

Use of this method is complicated by the fact that immediately following insertion many if not most women experience some physical discomfort in the form of cramps and pain. Usually there is some bleeding, and the menstrual flows tends to be heavier than before. For a majority of women these symptoms disappear within a few days or weeks, and after three months there are few further complications. In about 10 percent of the cases, these symptoms persist, and it is necessary to remove the device and prescribe some other form of contraception. The IUCD is not always retained; in a few cases it is spontaneously expelled by the uterus and must be reinserted.

Among illiterate populations the 10 percent of users who cannot use the device but experience prolonged discomfort tend to create fear and apprehension among those who are in the process of considering the adoption of family planning. As a result, the rate of adoption of this method has been less than was hoped. However, it has been so clearly superior to the "conventional" methods that it has had a most revolutionary effect on the outlook for rapid control of the world's population problem. Entire nations have adopted it as a major vehicle for family planning—Korea, India, Pakistan, Chile, for example. It has given the hope and optimism needed to make a determined and long-range program of national family planning. Teams of family planning educators have been trained to motivate the population, and corps of IUCD inserters have been trained and posted to remote rural areas. As a result, there has been swift and thorough sensitization of the population for family planning.

Improved medical follow-up, more adequate instruction of the clients beforehand about the nature of the side effects and their temporary nature, and prompt attention to the needs of those who must have the IUCD removed are being emphasized to heighten the acceptability of this method.

The long-term place of this method of family planning is difficult to assess. It is quite likely that contraception by chemical means soon will be so inexpensive, so cheap, and so convenient (long-term protection) that the emphasis on the IUCD will diminish. Even if this should occur, the tremendous role that this method has played in giving momentum to the world movement toward fertility control should not be forgotten. Meanwhile, during the 1960s, it is bearing much of the weight of the program.

"Conventional" Contraceptives. The term "conventional contraceptives" is widely used to denote those methods that require action at the time of sexual intercourse. Among the methods are (ranked in order of use-reliability):

diaphragm and jelly
condoms
aerosol foam
spermicidal jellies and cremes
vaginal suppositories (spermicidal)
foaming tablets (vaginal)
douche

Except for the first and last, all of these items are now in extensive use by populations of developing countries, and their acceptability is rising. The diaphragm and jelly and the douche are not appropriate for use under the living conditions that prevail in most rural villages. In addition, the reliability of the douche is so low that family planning organizations consider it worthless. Condoms are especially enjoying a steadily growing acceptance in developing nations. Vaginal foaming tablets, originally developed because they are cheap and

can be manufactured within the developing nation itself, have also played an important part in getting family planning started at the village level. As newer, more reliable, and aesthetically more pleasing methods are developed, the use of these techniques will decrease. Probably the decrease will be inversely related to the order ranked above.

"Rhythm Method" and Withdrawal (coitus interruptus). Two methods of contraception—periodic abstinence during those days of the month during which fertilization could take place, and coitus interruptus—require no drugs or appliances. The use-effectiveness of both methods is quite low, and a high proportion of couples find them unacceptable. Nevertheless, both have had a powerful effect in lowering the birthrate in the countries of Europe and America, and it may be expected that they will exert a substantial effect in the developing countries. In Latin America, the rhythm method is used extensively, because its use is not condemned by the Roman Catholic religion. Once a couple has been sensitized for family planning, withdrawal is a method that can be used when other services are not available. A small but nevertheless significant and possibly growing number of couples in developing nations will resort to this method (as did the populace of Northwest Europe during the nineteenth century when other methods were unavailable).

Abortion. Whenever abortion has been legalized and allowed as a legitimate medical activity under hospital conditions, there has been a swift and substantial decline in the birthrate. This has been demonstrated in Japan and the several countries of Eastern Europe where abortion for social and economic as well as medical reasons is approved. When abortion is offered under such conditions, the physiological effects appear to be little more adverse than carrying the child to term and the natural complications of childbirth. However, this method of contraception is so highly condemned by the Hindu, Muslim, and Christian religions that it is not seriously considered as a family planning method. In fact, family planning is being accepted by many religious leaders as a way of fighting illegal abortion, which has reached alarmingly high rates in Latin American capitals and other places where modernization is taking place but modern family planning is unavailable.

There is a growing movement to legalize abortion. The lower socioeconomic classes appear to make ready use of legal abortions when the service is available. Many experts believe that it is only a matter of a few years before the United States and many other nations will permit use of this method, with controls over who may have an abortion and over the social, economic, medical, and health conditions under which it may be legally performed.

Sterilization. Surgical sterilization, both of males and females, has contributed substantially to fertility control in particular cultures. The operation can be performed on women at time of childbirth to take advantage of hospitalization and is very popular. Sterilization of the male is only a minor operation that does not require hospitalization. Except for India and East Pakistan, however, it has not been popular. Sterilization can supplement, but cannot be a leading method of fertility control. Since it is irreversible, it usually is not performed until 3 or 4 children have been born. This is too large an average family size to solve the problem. Yet as an interim measure that solves the problem for some couples, it is useful.

Abstinence. Complete abstinence or abstinence for prolonged periods of time is widely practiced in India and other developing countries. This most often occurs toward the end of the childbearing period. When a woman becomes a grandmother (which often happens by age 30) it is often considered a joke if she bears children simultaneously with her own daughter. The solution to the problem is to avoid sexual contact with the husband. Often when a woman bears a child she resides with her parents for a full year and does not have sexual relations with her husband during this time. Also, abstinence is prescribed on many religious or holy days. Students of family planning, especially in India, often say that Western minds cannot appreciate the extent to which abstinence has helped to depress the birthrates and keep them well below the biologically possible maximum. Modernization, by

relaxing these prescriptions, can act as a stimulant to the birthrate.

20.3. Motivation for and against Fertility Control

It is a sociological mistake to consider a high birthrate the result either of the "natural" operation of uninhibited biological drives or of a "high-fertility culture" that may be expected to persist stubbornly without reference to current changes in environmental circumstances. Instead, we should regard a high birthrate as an effort of a population and its individual members to satisfy certain needs that they experience. In a similar vein, we should regard a low birthrate as an effort to satisfy certain other needs. Thus need satisfaction may be postulated as the explanation, or "social cause," of the birthrate. These needs, or motives, are the social and psychological reasons why birthrates are high, intermediate, or low at a particular time and place. When the needs change, the birthrate may be expected to change.

A first step in accomplishing rapid fertility control is to inventory the needs that couples are seeking to satisfy by bearing children. Also, we must know what needs they are seeking to satisfy when they practice contraception. This is a very important point for all "action programs" aimed at reducing fertility quickly.

One of the objectives of an action program is to bring about an awareness that fertility control is possible and that it will help the population to attain many of the goals (satisfy the needs) for which it is striving. The initial reaction to such a program may be favorable or hostile, but in either event *an irreversible change in the situation is thereby created.* Once this awareness has been established, high fertility can be maintained only by refusing to use knowledge and rejecting services that they know to be available. In other words, modern action programs establish quickly a situation that never before has existed in human history and has gradually developed only over decades by a slow process of institutional change. Persistent high fertility under the conditions imposed by a well-designed action program can be maintained only out of motivation to satisfy certain high-fertility needs. It cannot be maintained out of mere cultural inertia for more than a very short time, apart from contemporary need satisfaction.

An inventory has been made of the motives that promote high fertility and those that promote low fertility around the world. This is reproduced below in two lists. The first list inventories the high-fertility motives and the second inventories the low-fertility motives. The lists are not lengthy. This signifies that the phenomenon of fertility is much less complex than perhaps has been thought.

The major hypothesis of this chapter is that most populations of the world subscribe to a great many of the low-fertility motives and that this adherence is rapidly on the increase. Adherence to the high-fertility motives is everywhere steadily declining—irrespective of educational or economic status. If they are given a free choice, if they are fully aware that contraception is possible, and if they have available convenient service with acceptable methods and adequate information on how to practice family planning, human beings follow the age-old tendency to adjust their behavior to conform to need satisfaction.

INTERNATIONAL LIST OF HIGH-FERTILITY MOTIVES

HEALTH
> *Children often die.* It is necessary to have large families in order to make sure you get living children who grow to adulthood.

ECONOMIC CONDITION
> *Children are an economic advantage.* They are needed or are useful in helping the family earn a living. They pay for themselves by working as they grow.
> *Social security in old age.* If you have many children, one will be able to take care of you in old age.

FAMILY WELFARE
> *Can help with work around house.* Older children help the younger.
> *Big families are happy families.* Family life is more enjoyable; they have a good time together.
> *Children from big families have better personalities.* They are better adjusted, better able to get along with other people, not so spoiled or egotistical.
> *Continue the family name.* It is necessary to have many children to be sure to have a son to carry on the family name.
> *Strength of the clan.* The family is stronger; sons can help you fight your battles; family rights can be upheld.

MARRIAGE ADJUSTMENT
> *Large families promote good marriage adjustment.* Couples get along with each other better, marriage is happier.

PERSONALITY NEEDS
> *Ego support.* A demonstration of virility, manliness.
> *Companionship.* It is good to have a child around the house; a parent needs to have little children to love.

COMMUNITY AND NATIONAL WELFARE
> *Large families are good for the community or nation.* They promote population growth, make the nation strong.

MORAL AND CULTURAL
> *Large families are God's will.* It is against religious beliefs to limit fertility.
> *Large families promote morality.* Help prevent divorce or infidelity.
> *Tradition.* The community, village, family, or clan expects large families.
> *You have high status in the community.* If you have a big family, you are more important, are looked up to.

DISLIKE FOR CONTRACEPTION
> *Dislikes use of contraception* for aesthetic or health reasons or because it interferes with sex.

INTERNATIONAL LIST OF LOW-FERTILITY MOTIVES

HEALTH
> *Preserve health of mother.*
> *Assure healthy children.*

Lessen worry and overwork on the part of father and mother, because less work is needed to support a small than a large family.

ECONOMIC CONDITION

Everyday, general expenses are less.

Avoid worsening present (poor) economic condition.

Gain a higher standard of living, more comfort, afford better house.

Permit saving for future, for retirement.

Desire to avoid subdividing property or savings among many children.

Family able to have money for recreation, vacation.

FAMILY WELFARE

Improve children's lot in life, give them good education, help get started in a career.

Happier family life, more companionship, less tension.

Opportunity to do a better job of rearing children; able to devote more time to each, better able to socialize with child.

Avoid overcrowding of house; more opportunity for individual expression.

More peace and quiet in the home.

Easier to find a more desirable house or apartment.

MARRIAGE ADJUSTMENT

Provides husbands and wives more leisure, opportunity to enjoy each other's companionship.

Improves the sexual adjustment by eliminating or reducing fear of unwanted pregnancy.

PERSONALITY NEEDS

Facilitates realization of ambitions. Permits either husband or wife or both to pursue occupational or vocational objectives.

Facilitates self development. Permits an intelligent or talented wife to express herself outside the home, yet have a normal family and married life.

Facilitates realization of social needs. Permits the person (especially wife) to have contacts and friendships outside the home and to participate in neighborhood activities.

Reduces worry of the future. Avoids danger of childbearing when one is really too old—danger of dying and leaving behind orphan children.

COMMUNITY AND NATIONAL WELFARE

Helps avoid overpopulation, overcrowding.

Helps community meet demands for education, other community services.

Helps nations with economic development, avoids eating up technical progress with more mouths to feed.

Helps keep down delinquency, social problems of youth.

Helps reduce welfare burden on the community.

These lists are not long. From the motivational point of view the problem may be much less complex than it has been advertised to be.

20.4. Attitude of the Public toward Family Planning

"Would you like to have at least one more child or do you already have as many children as you want?" is a question the answer to which is of critical importance for the assessment of the prospects for fertility control around the world. Surveys of attitudes toward fertility and family planning have been taken in many nations, both developed and underdeveloped. Table 20-2 reproduces the results of several studies completed in 1964 or before. One generalization emerges clearly from this table: almost everywhere in the world the desire to have five children or more is very small.

Once a family has three children, it usually wishes to have no more, and as the number of children rises beyond three, the desire for cessation of childbearing increases. Results similar to those of Table 20-2 have been obtained repeatedly in many different surveys. There is not on record a single major study conducted with precision for a representative cross-section of a community where strong support for the six-child family has been found. *Yet the six-child and the seven-child family are the average size of completed family in high-fertility nations.* Thus there is a substantial inconsistency between attitude and actual behavior, with the attitudes favoring a substantially lower level of fertility than actually exists.

Observers differ on the cause of this discrepancy. Some regard it as a measure of the unreliability of social surveys, while others regard

Table 20-2 Percentage Not Wanting More Children, by Number of Children, Selected Nations of the World

Country	Number of children					
	0	1	2	3	4	5 or more
Ceylon...............	2	8	29	57	69	88
India................	2	7	25	43	74	88
Pakistan.............	4	5	25	42	67	74
Taiwan...............	0	1	24	54	76	88
Thailand.............	12	30	48	71	85	96
Turkey...............	19	34	58	68	67	76
Philippines..........	3	24	42	56	68	85
Korea................	1	8	28	65	81	94
Tunisia..............	1	9	26	44	68	87
Brazil...............	21	53	85	95	93	93
Colombia.............	15	45	55	67	79	93
Costa Rica...........	20	45	60	67	78	86
Mexico...............	16	30	48	64	76	86
Panama...............	11	35	51	70	86	94
United States........	8	20	57	62	81	74

Source: Bernard Berelson, "KAP Studies on Fertility," in Bernard Berelson, et al Family Planning and Population Programs, University of Chicago Press, 1965, p. 662.

it as a measure of the potential for rapid fertility decline. The latter group attributes the discrepancy to lack of adequate knowledge, lack of adequate family planning service and supplies, and lack of a major national program of sustained encouragement for fertility control. They assert that a well designed action program could capitalize on this apparently favorable climate and bring about a dramatically rapid reduction in fertility.

Fortunately, the question posed by this discrepancy will not long go unresolved. National family planning programs that do meet the specifications for good action programs are now under way in several countries. They will need to be in operation for only a decade or so before an unambiguous answer will be forthcoming; if fertility rates do not fall within this time, and by a substantial amount, it can be presumed that attitudes have not been reliably measured. If people will systematically report small-family ideals to interviewers while secretly holding large-family motives, no change in the birthrate will occur. If birthrates fall, however, this may be taken as validation of the principle that the people of developing nations really desire to limit their fertility and will do so rather promptly when offered knowledge and service in a context where they trust those offering this help.

Another question that frequently is asked in fertility surveys is "What do you regard as the ideal size of family?" When responses to this

inquiry are compared with the actual size of completed family, it has almost universally been found that the ideal size of family is smaller than the actual size of completed family in developing countries. (This is true despite the universal tendency for some persons with big families to rationalize their past behavior by stating the number of children they actually have as their ideal.) Table 20-3 reports the results of surveys from a variety of countries. It is clear that according to their verbal reports, the citizens of developing countries appear to desire a family that is not less than 25 percent smaller than the families they are actually producing.

Many demographers are concerned that the ideal expressed in many developing societies is still very high—four children or more. They insist that even if birthrates were brought to the level of four children per family, the population would still grow very rapidly. Perhaps this is an unfounded worry. As fertility falls and the gains from fertility limitation become more clearly visible to the entire population, ideals may be expected to decline further. The ideals reported in these surveys are simply the "natural resources" with which family planning programs may begin—the action program may be expected to generate further shifts in attitudes toward lower fertility.

Limited experiments have shown that there is a strong correlation between attitude and behavior with respect to family planning. Those

Table 20-3   Completed and "Ideal" Family Size
(Approximate)

Country	Completed family size	"Ideal" family size	"Ideal" of completed (percent)
Ghana (urban)..........	7.0	5.3	76
Tunisia (national).....	5.9	4.3	73
Korea (national).......	5.4	4.2	78
Taiwan (urban).........	5.5	3.9	71
Thailand (rural).......	5.2	3.8	73
Turkey (national)......	5.8	3.5	60
Colombia (urban).......	4.8	3.6	75
Venezuela (urban)......	4.3	3.5	81
Mexico (urban).........	5.0	4.2	84
Panama (urban).........	3.8	3.5	92
Brazil (urban).........	3.3	2.7	82
Costa Rica (urban).....	4.3	3.6	83

Source: Bernard Berelson, "KAP Studies on Fertility, " in
Bernard Berelson, et al <u>Family Planning and Population
Programs</u>, University of Chicago Press, 1965, p. 658.

who have low-fertility motives and those who
have attitudes that are favorable to family
planning are much more likely to be found
practicing contraception than those who do not
have these traits. Moreover, knowledge itself
seems to promote the adoption of family planning, for couples with the greatest knowledge
of contraception tend to be adopters of family
planning, whereas those with little knowledge
tend to have only limited adoption. Data to
support these generalizations are reported in
Table 20-4. For this table, a small but representative sample of slum residents were classified into four categories of adoption:

Pretrial—persons who had never practiced family planning
Trial—persons who had practiced family planning but were not practicing it at the time
  they were interviewed
Quasi adoption—persons who were practicing
  family planning, but not regularly ("taking chances"), or were using only methods
  known to be unreliable (douche, withdrawal)
Adoption—regular use of a reliable method of
  family planning without taking chances

The members of each group were further classified according to their level of knowledge, the
nature of their motivation, their attitudes to-

ward family planning, and their desire for more
children. As Table 20-4 demonstrates, the statistical relationships are very strong and in the
direction that supports the psychological theory
that there is a strong pressure for behavior to
be consistent with attitudes.

20.5.   Experiments to Promote Fertility Control among Illiterate Populations

Since 1960 there have been a series of experiments to induce rapid fertility decline among
illiterate villagers of developing nations. The
results have been very encouraging. Beyond a
doubt, two family planning experiments that
have profoundly affected the thinking of population specialists are those conducted in Comilla, East Pakistan, and in Pho-tharam, Thailand. Both were conducted with highly rural
agricultural populations. Both succeeded in
getting a very significant proportion of the
population to adopt family planning. In both
cases it was found that *it was not the more educated and urbane villager who was the first to
accept contraception, but that the lowest stratum of illiterate and landless laborers were
equally if not more disposed to accept and persist.*

The Comilla Experiment. The Pakistan Academy for Rural Development at Comilla, East

Table 20-4 Relationship of Motives and Attitudes to Use of Contraception, 118 Male Respondents, Slums of Chicago

Motive or attitude	Total	Adoption classification			
		Pre-trial	Trial	Quasi-adopter	Adopter
Motivation					
Expresses motives for small family..........	100.0	13.4	23.9	25.4	37.3
Expresses motives that are ambivalent.......	100.0	13.8	27.6	34.5	24.1
Expresses motives for large family..........	100.0	25.0	12.5	27.5	25.0
Desire for more children					
Wants no more children.....................	100.0	9.6	21.9	31.5	37.0
Wants more children........................	100.0	25.8	29.0	22.6	22.6
Attitude toward birth control					
Approves...................................	100.0	8.5	19.5	31.7	40.2
Disapproves................................	100.0	36.4	40.9	18.2	4.5
Knowledge of contraception					
Good.......................................	100.0	12.8	23.1	28.2	35.9
Fair.......................................	100.0	11.3	22.6	32.1	34.0
Poor.......................................	100.0	33.3	33.3	16.7	16.7

Source: Fertility Inventory of Chicago Low Income-Low Education population, 1963.

Pakistan, launched a pilot project for family planning in nine rural villages in 1960, under the guidance of and according to a plan developed by Dr. Akhtar Hameed Khan, director of the Academy, with assistance from Dr. A. Majeed Khan, a sociologist. The members of the village councils were approached by the sponsors of the experiment and told about family planning. They were asked to join a program and to select a local woman from their own village to be an "organizer" for the village. The organizers were trained at the Academy and began working in their respective villages. They taught family planning, sold supplies, and visited those who had shown interest in family planning. At the end of one year, 146 out of 880 eligible women had tried family planning. After two years, 324 (37 percent) of the eligible women had joined. After two years, 51 percent of those who had tried family planning were continuing to practice it.[8]

The impressive aspect of this experiment was that the methods used were the "conventional" ones—condom and vaginal foaming tablet. Moreover, these materials were sold to the poverty-stricken villagers—not given away. (The price was subsidized to the point of being almost free—$0.025 per dozen condoms and $0.038 per dozen foaming tablets.) A second

[8] A. Majeed Khan and Harvey M. Choldin, "New Family Planners in Rural East Pakistan," *Demography*, **2** (1965), 1–7.

impressive aspect of the "Comilla approach" is that the innovation of family planning was introduced to the village by a person chosen by the villagers themselves from their midst, rather than by highly trained and well educated family planning specialists who tend to be treated as outsiders.

After two years, the characteristics of family planning were compared with the population characteristics survey of five villages in the same area that were considered to have no significant economic or population differences from those where the family planning action program was under way. A comparison of the adopters of family planning and of the general village population yields the following astounding findings:

1. There was no apparent difference in the education level between the general village populations and those who tried family planning. About one-half of the adopters were wholly illiterate; illiteracy was slightly more prevalent among the adopters than among the general population.

2. Landless couples were more prone to adopt family planning than the general population. *Whereas 19 percent of the families in the general population had no land, 40 percent of those who adopted family planning were landless.*

3. The illiterate and the landless adopted just as readily (were among those first to

adopt) and persisted just as well as those with education and land.

The authors concluded from their experiment that "The data indicate that under certain rural conditions—(1) extreme poverty, (2) extreme population density, and (3) little expansion of economic opportunities for the lowest classes—the poorest and least educated may nevertheless be induced to adopt fertility control practices. Moreover, they may be as likely to adopt family planning as others more educated and prosperous."[9]

The Pho-tharam Experiment. In 1964 an action program providing family planning advice and appliances was initiated in the Pho-tharam District of Thailand, 85 kilometers west of Bangkok. The district is predominantly rural with 60 percent of the household heads engaged in agriculture. A fertility survey inventorying the attitudes, knowledge, and practice of family planning was taken immediately before the action program was begun. A second survey was taken a year later, after the program had been in operation eight months. These surveys revealed that the educational level of this population was quite low; only 12 percent of the husbands and 3 percent of the wives had completed 5 years of schooling or more, and about 20 percent of the adult population was illiterate. Of those who could read, fewer than 10 percent actually read printed materials.

When asked about their ideal number of children, 66 percent of the women of childbearing age declared that they wished to have no more than four children. The actual fertility level was such as to lead to an average size of completed family of six children or more.[10]

The second survey sought to assess the impact of the program on the people. The program was known to 86 percent of the women at the second interview.

The program created a great deal of discussion among the people. More than 60 percent of the women who knew of the program had learned of it from friends, and 86 percent of the women reported having discussed it in informal conversations in their respective villages. Over half of the women said they had talked about it with their husbands. The impression of the program was so favorable that more than 90 percent of the women felt that a similar program should be extended to all of Thailand. The program succeeded in increasing the level of motivation. The ranking of the population on a motivational scale between the first and second surveys was as follows:

	First survey	*Second survey*
Definitely motivated	65.9	66.1
Ambivalent or moderately positively motivated	9.9	26.9
Not motivated	24.2	7.0

It appeared that even within this short time the hard core of resistance to family planning (not large to begin with) had been almost completely neutralized and that the great mass of people had moved toward a moderately positive position.

At the first survey, 66 percent of the women interviewed had absolutely no knowledge about methods of contraception, but in 1965 only 12 percent were still in this class. For those who were "informed" in the first survey, knowledge consisted primarily of sterilization. At the second survey 50 percent of the women had either heard about or knew how to use the IUCD or the oral pills. This dramatic increase in knowledge occurred at all educational levels, but was greater among the more than among the less educated.

Less than 1 percent of the women reported that they were practicing contraception at the time of the first survey, and less than 2 percent said that they had ever practiced contraception. After only eight months of operation in the dis-

[9] *Ibid.*, p. 7.

[10] Amos H. Hawley and Visid Prachuabmoh, "Family Growth and Family Planning: Responses to a Family Planning Action Program in a Rural District of Thailand," *Demography*, **3** (1966), 319–331.

trict, 21 percent of all eligible women in the sample were currently practicing some form of contraception. ("Eligible women" were defined as married women who were not sterilized, had borne a child within five years of the survey, and were not pregnant at the time of the interview.) This dramatic adoption of family planning was concentrated in the intermediate ages —25 to 39 years. The adoption was greatest among those who had borne four children. Many of the women reported that they wished to practice contraception after having one or two more children. A total of 62 percent of the women claimed either to be currently practicing contraception or to have the intention to practice if after they had attained the size of family they regarded as ideal.

In order to learn the sources of support for family planning, Prachuabmoh cross-tabulated the responses concerning desire for more children according to a variety of social, economic, and demographic characteristics.[11] The results were similar to those for Comilla: the desire to have no more children was highest among the landless or those with only small holdings, among those who possessed the least amount of farming tools and other wealth, and among the least educated. Moreover, he found that the desire to end childbearing was less among those who are more modernized and in frequent contact with the outside world by means of travel, who attend to the mass media, and who reside in larger population concentrations than it was among the more provincial, rural, and isolated families who never read newspapers or magazines, never listen to the radio, and have no personal contacts with large urban centers. In making these tests, he controlled for number of children already born. A typical table reporting his data is reproduced as Table 20-5.

On the basis of his findings, Prachuabmoh concludes: ". . . This study found that the desire for having no more children was very prevalent among all strata of a rural Thailand population and was strongest among the least

Table 20-5 Percent of Rural Thai Women Who Want More Children, by Number of Living Children and Index of Family Wealth; Photharam District, Thailand: 1964

Number of living children	Total	Index of family wealth		
		Low	Medium	High
Total.......	29.1	25.7	28.0	35.0
0-1 child......	75.6	65.5	69.2	90.6
2 children.....	50.3	57.2	46.0	48.1
3 children.....	30.7	28.1	29.4	33.9
4 children.....	17.8	17.6	16.2	22.2
5 children.....	6.2	3.0	6.0	10.9
6 children.....	4.4	1.3	6.5	5.2

Source: Visid Prachuabmoh, "Factors affecting Desire or Lack of Desire for Additional Progeny in Rural Thailand," Ch. VIII in Donald J. Bogue, editor, Sociological Contributions to Family Planning Research, Chicago: University of Chicago Community and Family Study Center, 1967, pp386.

urbanized and modernized segments. . . . The most important finding is that low economic status and deprivation seem to be the most important factors discouraging women from having additional children. It is found in the studies in Western societies that urbanization and economic status are inversely associated with fertility. Therefore, one might anticipate the inverse association between urbanization and economic status and desire for additional children in Thailand, but the finding in this study is contrary to this anticipation. It is found that desire for additional children is directly associated with economic status, urbanization and modernization."

Prachuabmoh points out that his findings contradict the following view, widely held by many demographers: "As in earlier days, poverty and deprivation alone are not likely to generate a slowdown of the birth rate. But personal aspirations are. The agrarian peoples of the backward countries now look to the industralized, affluent fourth of the world. They nourish aspirations that come directly from New York, Paris and Moscow. No more inclined to be satisfied with a bare subsistence than their wealthier fellows would be, they are demanding more goods, education, opportunity and influence. And they are beginning to see that many of their desires are incompatible with enlarged families that low mortality and customary reproduction are giving them."[12]

[11] Visid Prachuabmoh, "Factors Affecting Desire or Lack of Desire for Additional Progeny in Rural Thailand," Part VIII of D. J. Bogue (ed.), *Sociological Contributions to Family Planning Research* (Chicago: Community and Family Study Center, 1967).

[12] Kingsley Davis, "Population," *Scientific American*, **209** (3) (1963), 71.

While admitting that this "revolution of rising expectations" may be a strong force promoting the adoption of family planning, Prachuabmoh challenges Davis' theory and flatly asserts that *deprivation* is a force of equal or greater power in gaining adoption of contraception in developing nations.

Both the Comilla and the Pho-tharum experiments demonstrate conclusively that when rural populations sink to the brink of starvation and malnutrition, one of their reactions is to accept readily and promptly one avenue of remedy—fertility reduction. This is consistent with the hypothesis of demographic readjustment that was advanced in Chapter 3 and succeeding discussions. According to this theory, population pressure brings its own antidote once the facts of contraception are known and family planning service is available. Put simply, most people would prefer to take birth control pills, wear an IUCD, or use condoms than go hungry or eat algae, and even the most illiterate and isolated rural villager can appreciate the significance of this choice, once he realizes that he has a choice.

Changes in Birthrates. Programs of the type described above did not exist before 1960. Until 1964, the programs that did exist were only small experiments covering a district or a few villages. In 1964-1966 several very large programs covering large populations began to operate (see next section). Inasmuch as no tangible results can be expected until nine months after the start of a program and since the registration of births is very deficient in the areas where these programs are being carried out, as of 1968 it was not possible to give clear scientific proof that birthrates had actually fallen in direct response to the program. It will require an accumulation over three to five years, reflected in changed age composition at a census, to validate the claim that a genuine decline in births has set in. Such a test will become possible in the 1970 censuses. If these programs are indeed having the desired effect, the 1970 census will show a decrease in the proportion of all population under 5 years of age in comparison with the 1960 census in the districts where the programs have been conducted.

Meanwhile, indirect evidence that fertility is being lowered is accumulating. Stoeckel recently evaluated the fertility of couples who had practiced contraception in the Comilla experiment and concluded that their fertility over a three-year period was only about 25 percent what it would have been had they not practiced contraception.[13] It must be admitted that during the first few years of these programs a substantial share of rural populations use the methods incorrectly and irregularly, with the result that many accidental pregnancies occur. However, that the veil of ignorance can be lifted so quickly, that resistance is so small and evaporates in such a short time, that acceptance of contraception in principle sweeps through even the most rural and illiterate populations within a matter of months under the conditions created by a well-designed and well-executed program are most encouraging. That such significant proportions of the populace actually come forward and make an attempt to use contraceptives must be taken as evidence that there a potential is being created for very rapid fertility decline. An IUCD that is properly in place, oral pills taken even reasonably correctly, and condoms or spermicidals used with even 80 percent regularity can have only one effect on the birthrate. It is this evidence and this inference that have led to the optimistic position taken in the papers reproduced above and to the prediction that the 1970 rounds of censuses will provide limited but unmistakable proof that birthrates are falling in the areas where vigorous family planning programs have been in operation for three years or more under a well-designed and well-administered program and that by 1980 there will be widespread evidence of very extensive fertility declines in a great many if not most of the developing nations of the world. When to this is added the prospect for even simpler, cheaper, and more acceptable methods of contraception that will be widely available within a decade or so, the temptation to reach the conclusion that by the year 2000 the world's population problem will be largely if not entirely resolved is difficult to resist. Certainly, tangible evidence that this is an unrea-

[13] John Stoeckel, "Social and Demographic Correlates of Contraceptive Adoption in a Rural Area of East Pakistan," *Demography*, 5 (1968)

sonable expectation is scarce and of dubious validity—especially in the light of the massive efforts now being made by all but a few of the developing nations, described in the section that follows.

20.6. An Inventory of Family Planning Action Programs around the World

Since 1960 there has been a worldwide movement to establish nationwide family planning programs in the developing nations. Starting from a position of indifference or even a negative policy, some of the most powerful international organizations now have family planning as one of their top-priority programs. Among these may be listed the United Nations, World Health Organization, United States Agency for International Development, United States Department of Health, Education, and Welfare, Pan American Health Organization, the Peace Corps, and the governments of several European nations that are actively sponsoring modernization of developing nations. Within the developing nations, powerful political, economic, medical, and educational leaders are throwing their full weight behind national family planning programs. The result has been a remarkable mobilization of world opinion, talent, and finances for bringing a quick end to the population problem.

Space forbids a detailed description of the events that are occurring in each individual nation. Moreover, progress is currently so rapid that such accounts are out of date within a few months. The brief set of notes presented here is intended only to illustrate the scope, enthusiasm, and intelligent action being taken around the globe.

I. LATIN AMERICA

Colombia. The nation's seven medical schools, through their professional association, have established a Population Division, which is spearheading the development of a national program. This organization is training physicians throughout the nation in techniques of contraception. It is providing a steady stream of information to all Latin America about the population problem and the need for urgent action. All of the member universities are operating family planning programs through their hospitals and outlying clinics and are conducting research on the medical, social, and psychological aspects of fertility and family planning. The government is favorably disposed, and a national family planning program is being born, despite the fact that in Colombia the Roman Catholic Church has long been a powerful force in the political and economic life of the nation.

Chile. Under the leadership of the University of Chile's Medical School, large-scale action programs have been undertaken throughout Santiago metropolitan area, using the IUCD as the principal means of contraception. The program was touched off by research showing that illegal abortion had reached alarming proportions and had become a major threat to health and family integrity. Research and experimental action programs in low-income districts of Santiago and in outlying areas have been undertaken, with universally encouraging results. A national family planning program has been formulated and is now in process of implementation. It is a part of the material and child health program of the National Health Service. Research leadership is being provided by the United Nations Demographic Center at Santiago. This Center has sponsored fertility and family planning surveys in nine metropolitan areas of Latin America and is now sponsoring rural fertility surveys in six Latin American nations. All of the survey results obtained to date reveal a strong sentiment in favor of fertility control and a steadily increasing trend toward the use of contraception.

Cuba. A national family planning program has been initiated. All methods of contraception are being offered within the limits of obtaining overseas supplies. Technical assistance is being given by a number of Latin American experts in other Latin American nations.

Jamaica. A national family planning program has been established within the Ministry of Health, with assistance from U.S. A.I.D. A strong Planned Parenthood program is offering services in both rural and urban areas.

Brazil. Although there is no government program, there is a very large and very active private family planning program (BEMFAM) with clinics operating in every state of the nation. Family planning clinics are numerous and active in all of the leading cities.

Argentina. Because of greater European influence, birthrates have long been low here because of family planning action using conventional contraceptives and also because of massive reliance on illegal abortion. Recently newer action programs of private agencies have developed, which concentrate on serving the poor who lack access to service. The Argentinian Association for the Protection of the Family operates several family planning centers located in district and regional centers.

Costa Rica. Demographic and fertility surveys have been completed, a family planning program has been organized, and service is available in nearly 100 health centers throughout the country. In additions, U.S. A.I.D. is providing technical help.

Venezuela. A Center for the study of Population has been established. The very large Municipal Maternity Hospital in Caracas provides services to a large clientele. The Ministry of Health is sponsoring a pilot family planning project in its health centers.

Puerto Rico. A national program and a private program are both in existence, but are not well financed, hence are not as active as in previous years. Nevertheless, birthrates appear to be definitely declining, even when allowance is made for out-migration of childbearing population to the mainland United States.

Panama. A private family planning organization is very active.

Burmuda. A national family planning program is in effect.

Barbados. A national family planning program is in effect.

Honduras. A national family planning program is providing service in health centers, including rural areas. There is also an active private family planning organization.

Guatemala. A private family planning organization (Family Welfare Association) is active. The national Social Security System provides family planning service in its clinics.

Bolivia. A private family planning program

has had excellent success in working with Indian populations.

Ecuador. A private family planning program was established in 1965-1966. It operates centers in all regions of the country.

Paraguay. A pilot family planning center was opened in 1967.

Uruguay. The Uruguayan Family Planning Association has an active program in Montevideo and is extending its activities to the cities.

Mexico. Private family planning organizations are active in Mexico City. Interest is rising in the medical schools, and several major research studies of fertility attitudes have been undertaken. These studies all reveal strong public support for fertility control.

Peru. The Population and Development Center in Lima has established a pilot family planning program in the Lima metropolitan area. Other private organizations offer family planning services on a limited scale.

Dominican Republic. A small IUCD program is being carried out through the Dominican Family Welfare Association, established in 1966.

El Salvador. Nearly a dozen family planning clinics, generated by the Salvadorian Demographic Association, are providing family planning service.

Haiti. A small private family planning program was launched in 1966.

Honduras. A nationwide family planning is now a part of the Ministry of Health. More than 80 clinics are operated throughout the country.

Nicaragua. A family planning association was established in 1966.

Trinidad and Tobago. The Trinidad and Tobago Family Planning Association operates clinics in Port-of-Spain and San Fernando.

Note. The International Planned Parenthood Federation is sponsoring and giving financial support to some private family planning activity in almost every nation of Latin America. Supplemented by contributions from local interested citizens, all but two or three nations of Latin America now have a substantial and very rapidly growing family planning movement, with clinic services openly available. In several nations these private organizations have unofficial approval and cooperation of the national health services and medical schools. In addition, all methods of contraception including oral pills are available without prescription in pharmacies. As a result, the oral pills are enjoying a phenomenal rise in adoption, independently of planned action programs. The Population Reference Bureau has established a Latin American office in Bogota, which is a center of diffusion of information about population and family planning to all of Latin America, with materials prepared in Spanish and Portuguese. International Conferences on Population and Family Planning have been held in Colombia and Chile, with attendance from all of the Latin American nations. Training courses in family planning for physicians of other Latin American nations are being offered at the University of Chile. The Pan American Health Organization has established a major population program and is promoting the study of Latin America's population problems, introduction of population study and family planning into the curriculum of medical schools, and in lending technical assistance to individual nations that request help in setting up programs of fertility control.

II. ASIA

Japan. The Ministry of Health introduced national family planning in 1952, by establishing a nationwide network of clinics that are highly effective. By a combination of contraception and legalized abortion, the Japanese birthrate has been reduced to the point of neutralizing population growth. Japan is the prototype for emulation by developing nations.

India. A national family planning program was launched in 1954, which was revised for the third five-year plan. The IUCD, foaming tablets, and condoms are offered through family planning units established at 8000 national health centers. A well-planned organization for family planning education and service personnel has been established in each state. The system works through the health centers of the local districts. There has been a steady increase in acceptance of the idea of contraception, although problems of side effects with

IUCD and accidental pregnancies with foaming tablets have created some negative attitudes toward the service. In 1966 more than 1 million IUCD's were inserted. Increase in sales of conventional contraceptives was steady. In 1966 the University of Chicago trained a group of 55 Peace Corps workers who went to Maharashtra State for family planning education works.

Pakistan. A national family planning program was launched in 1960, which was drastically revised in 1965. The organization is operated as a separate civil entity, in which physicians act as technical consultants and subcontractors for service. Strong reliance on native village midwives (one midwife for each three villages) brings family planning action to the grassroots level. The IUCD and conventional contraceptives are offered at clinics located at district and subdistrict centers. Midwives sell condoms and foaming tablets at subsidized prices and are allowed to keep three-fourths of the proceeds for their efforts. Midwives receive 50 cents for each woman they persuade to accept the IUCD, as part of their salary. In mid-1967, nearly 1 million IUCD's had been inserted, and new insertions were proceeding at the rate of 60,000 per month. Use of condoms was steadily increasing. Family planning was third largest employer in the nation: 90,000 workers, the great majority of whom were midwives.

Mainland China. Information is incomplete, but a strongly supported national family planning program seems definitely to be in existence, backed by publicity campaigns and campaigns through worker groups. Quite possibly, it is one of the most effective programs anywhere.

Taiwan. One of the most successful family planning programs in the world is in operation in Taiwan. It is organized along lines developed from a highly successful program in Taichung City. It uses IUCD with great success. By reason of an excellent research and evaluation program, much information that has been useful in starting programs in other nations has come from this "model" program.

South Korea. A national program was begun in 1964, and very rapid strides have been made since then. Extensive use has been made of mass communication to inform the public. Strong reliance is being placed on IUCD, condom, and foaming tablets. Some of the details of the progress have already been presented in Section 20-1.

Thailand. As yet there is no national program, although very strong interest is shown by the medical schools, which offer family planning services in their clinics. The dramatic success of a pilot project at Pho-tharum has already been described.

Malaysia. A new national program of family planning was started in 1965. The phase of a survey of attitudes, knowledge, and practice has been followed by greatly expanded services in urban areas, later to be extended to rural areas. For five years preceding this development, Malaysia had been the site of one of the most successful Planned Parenthood programs in a developing nation. The strikingly successful performance of this private group led to the national program.

Singapore. For many years Singapore has had a very active and successful family planning program. A program of education through radio, public displays, mass mailings, and family planning instruction in maternity wards of hospitals aroused public acceptance, and birthrates have been declining steadily for several years. International Planned Parenthood has established a regional training center. In 1966 the government nationalized the program, which trains family planning workers for the entire Southeast Asia region.

Hong Kong. Like Singapore, Hong Kong was one of the earliest and most active of the Planned Parenthood movements in behalf of an underdeveloped population. Through more than 50 clinics scattered throughout the territory, all methods of family planning are provided to all economic classes: pills, IUCD, and conventional contraceptives. The birthrate has been falling for several years.

Ceylon. An active Planned Parenthood movement sponsors family planning in Colombo and several outlying places. A number of pilot projects are under way. The best known and probably most successful of these is that sponsored by the Swedish Economic Development As-sociation. In 1965 a national family planning program was begun.

Turkey. Much interest in family planning has developed since 1963. An ancient law prohibiting sale of contraceptives was repealed, and the Ministry of Health is working with foreign advisers to make plans for a national program.

Iran. In 1965 the Ministry of Health made family planning an official part of the government's maternal and child health services.

Israel. Family planning is available through medical facilities in much the same way as in Europe and North America.

Indonesia. From 1957 to 1960 a strong interest in the population problem was shown by the government. Advisers from United Nations promoted demographic research, while private groups established a Planned Parenthood movement. This promising development suffered severe setbacks between 1963 and 1967, during a phase of radicalism in government. In 1967, with a new government, there is good prospect of not only returning to the former state but of launching even larger programs of action. Family planning clients have increased rapidly since 1966, and all methods are being rapidly accepted. Pilot fertility studies and plans for a national program are being made.

Philippines. Because of resistance by the Catholic Church, family planning is strictly forbidden as an official national program. However, a number of vigorous private groups are thriving and expanding, and there is a nationalized program. Many of these are Protestant groups—especially church-sponsored hospitals. There is official national concern about population matters. A very active Population Center is at the University of Manila. This center has conducted surveys of the attitudes of the public toward fertility and family planning. Many physicians are beginning to support fertility control. Meanwhile, conventional contraceptives are being used on an expanding scale in urban centers. The Philippine Reconstruction Movement supports family planning works in rural areas.

Vietnam. Family planning service is being offered by private groups striving to help in the reconstruction of wartorn villages and in the modernization of the nation.

Jordan. In 1963 the Jordan Family Planning Association was established. It now operates clinics in the principal cities.

Nepal. Family planning is a part of the National Health Service.

III. AFRICA

Kenya. A Family Planning Association was organized in 1961. It now operates about 50 clinics.

Egypt. A national program was announced in 1964 and was launched in 1965. Strong reliance was placed on oral pills as well as conventional contraceptives. The program was conducted through health centers. After some problems of developing a service organization, the program appeared to be making good progress when the war with Israel in 1967 began.

Algeria. Official interest in establishing a national family planning program has been expressed.

Ethiopia. Although the government has shown little official interest, a Planned Parenthood unit (Family Guidance Association) is operating in the capital with apparent success.

Zambia. A Family Planning Association is active.

Ghana. Strong interest has been shown in the problem of population. Foreign advisors are in residence to explore the possibilities of helping to develop a program. A Family Planning Association is offering service.

Morocco. A Family Planning Program was launched by the Ministry of Health in 1966.

Uganda. A Family Planning Association is expanding its services.

Mauritius. A strong Planned Parenthood movement is in operation on the island, despite resistance from religious authorities.

Liberia. A Family Planning Association is offering service in Monrovia.

Nigeria. The University of Lagos has a very active population study program for physicians, and family planning is taught in the medical schools. At Abadan a population study center is exploring the social and economic implications of rapid population growth. In Lagos, planned parenthood clinics operated through the municipal health centers have a substantial clientele. It has now been established that the cultures of Africa do not preclude the adoption of family planning when the need for it is made clear to the people in terms of maternal health and child welfare.

Sierra Leone. Family planning service is offered through medical facilities, and by a Family Planning Association.

South Africa. Planned Parenthood units offer family planning service in the major urban centers through more than 100 clinics.

Rhodesia. A Family Planning Association has been established and operates clinics in several cities.

Tunisia. A national program has been announced. Foreign consultants are assisting with the development of a program.

Tanzania. A Family Planning Association is offering service.

Note. A special issue of *Demography* (Vol. 5, No. 2) is devoted to the topic "Progress and Problems of Fertility Control around the World." More than 40 on-the-spot reports are made from all over the world by leading researchers. The interested reader is referred to this source to supplement the materials above.

IV. INTERNATIONAL AGENCIES

Almost all of the international agencies with a strong interest in promoting social and economic progress have thrown their weight behind the world movement for fertility control. Among those having extensive action programs are:

Economic Commission on Asia and the Far East
Ford Foundation
International branches of the U. S. Department of Health, Education, and Welfare
International Population Union
Milbank Memorial Fund
Pan American Health Organization
Pathfinder Fund
Population Council
Population Division of United Nations
Rockefeller Foundation
Swedish Economic Development Association
U.S. A.I.D.
World Bank
World Health Organization

20.7. Conclusion: The Future Course of Population Growth and the Future Condition of the World's Peoples

The review of nation-by-nation developments in fertility control provides a factual basis for the contention of this chapter that almost everywhere in the world where a severe population problem exists there is widespread awareness of its dangers and an aggressive movement (either national or private) to bring fertility under control. Moreover, *the more severe the pressure of population, the more comprehensive and aggressive this program has become.* Of the large nations of the world with high fertility and low per capita income, only the Philippines and Indonesia now lack a comprehensive national program to reduce fertility, and there are hopeful signs that they too will join the other developing nations of the world within a short time. (These two nations are not among the group with family planning programs for religious or political reasons only; both have large unsettled spaces of outer islands, and an influential leadership in each has [probably mistakenly] insisted that resettlement of population from the overpopulated central islands to the undersettled ones would solve the population problem. As the invalidity of this view is proved by experience, public opinion is swinging in support of a program to reduce birth rates.) It is now clearly established that illiterate rural people who are in a population crisis dilemma will adopt modern family planning when high-quality service is offered by a system that enjoys their confidence and is concerned for the well-being of individuals as well as of the masses. The educational and administrative techniques for accomplishing this have been sensed only since 1960, and they are still undergoing revision and improvement. Nowhere in the world is there massive resistance to fertility control as a principle. Objections have come mostly from conservative religious and political bureaucrats; this resistance is being rapidly dissolved as national leaderships are threatened by being out of step with the desires of their constituents. *This condition of aroused national leadership with an official national plan to reduce fertility is a new ingredient in demography; it had never existed before in history, until initiated by Japan.*

The revolutionary developments in the medical technology of contraception have also created a favorable set of conditions for quick adoption of fertility control that had never previously existed. The peasants of Europe and America were forced to migrate to the city to get birth control information, or else the information seeped gradually into the countryside from urban centers. They were forced to pay comparatively high prices for family planning services and materials. In contrast, today this information is being brought directly to the countryside by especially designed programs, and service is either free or so cheap that most if not all can easily afford it. Inasmuch as even the IUCD and the oral pills that now are so widely in use are due to be replaced in the near future by procedures that are even simpler, longer-lasting, and with fewer undesirable side effects, we can look forward to even more favorable conditions for rapid adoption of family planning.

For centuries the thinking of population specialists has been dominated by a study of the implications of exponential population growth. The compound interest formula, with population growth as the compounding entity, has led scholars to foresee only gloom and doom. Now a new set of exponential curves has emerged—the curves of adoption. These also function according to the compound interest formula, with the rates of net adoption as the compounding entity. If we apply this class of formulas, using current data from the programs for developing nations, and project into the future the size of the population that will be practicing contraception, a picture of near-universal practice of contraception within an amazingly short time emerges. Thus *today two sets of exponential curves are counterposed: the population growth curve and the contraception adoption curve. Both cannot be valid simultaneously in the future.* Either the rates of current adoption of contraception are a temporary condition that will quickly subside or current rates of population growth will sink more rapidly in the near future than they have in the past as a result of massive use of contraception.

In a world that has seen a steady improvement in the lot of mankind through adjustment to changing conditions and use of new technologies, and in a world where every underdeveloped nation is striving mightily to undergo social change in order to achieve a better level of life, it is much more consistent with the broad sweep of history to predict that the compounding of fertility control instead of the compounding of population through persistent high birthrates will soon emerge as the dominant way of viewing the world's population problem.

Two important implications of this optimistic position need to be emphasized. First, current official predictions of the growth of world population not only specify growth to astronomical numbers, but also are scheduling fertility decline to proceed at such a slow pace that by the year 2000 the population would still be growing at an alarming rate that could lead only to disaster. The prediction made here is that by the year 2000 not only can the size of the world's population be smaller than official predictions indicate, but also that by that time the growth rate can be nearly zero. If it is not zero, then it is very likely that by that date the population throughout the world will be highly sensitized to the need for fertility control, will be well informed, and will have available adequate service. Under these conditions, these nations that persist in population growth will do so only because (unlike at present) national leadership sees no cause for alarm—possibly because of unforeseen technological developments in food production.

The second implication concerns the pattern of population distribution and composition that may be anticipated. The culturologists of demography have predicted that intensive urbanization and industrialization must precede fertility decline. The perspective that now emerges is that *fertility control may precede and lead the way in modernization.* Hence it is possible for a nation with a highly rural economy and with only very limited resources for industrial development nevertheless to pass from a condition of dangerously rapid growth and universal misery to a state of stationary population and a comfortable level of living based primarily on a twin program of family planning and the modernization of its agriculture, without having first to develop a large component of manufacturing and services. Thus the painful process of impossibly high rates of forced saving and capital accumulation necessary for "economic takeoff" may be greatly mitigated by programs of intensive family planning and modernization of farming. Industrialization may follow at a more modest pace than that currently envisaged as a prerequisite for achieving "the good life." This may appear to be Maoist thinking applied to demography; research and experience in recent years justify it.

The movement for fertility control should thus be viewed as linked to the process of economic development, but not wholly dependent on it. Instead, as a semiautonomous aspect of modernization it appears to be a new force, which has emerged as a human readjustment to help rescue the world's hopes for a cessation of hunger, misery, and war. The prospects for a rapid decline in population growth everywhere such decline is needed to achieve these goals—accompanied or followed by a rising level of living through economic development—now appear to be excellent.

QUESTIONS AND EXERCISES

1. Select one particular developing country that had a high birthrate in 1960. Read as many of the selections pertaining to this country as you can from the bibliography at the end of this chapter. Supplement this with more recent reports. From the *Demographic Yearbook* chart the recent trend in the birthrate. Write a comprehensive essay about the effort at fertility control in this country, the trend in the birthrate, and the prospect for stationary growth within the foreseeable future.

2. From *Demography*, Volume 4, Number 1 (1967), read the book review article, "Family Planning and Population Programs" by Philip

M. Hauser. Also read the article on "Can Population Control Programs Succeed?" by Kingsley Davis in *Science*, November 17, 1967. Contrast the position taken in these two articles with the position that has been taken in this chapter. Write an essay concerning what you believe to be the valid and invalid points of both positions.

3. The entire issue of *Demography*, Volume 5, Number 2 (1968), is devoted to the topic "Problems and Progress of Fertility Control." Read all of the articles in this issue that pertain to a particular continent, such as Asia. Contrast the tone of these articles with the tone of the materials presented in this chapter for Korea and Thailand. Also, contrast the degree of optimism among demographers with the degree of optimism shown by "action groups."

4. Suppose that it is a valid principle that, because of the threat of starvation, the poorest and most desperate members of the population will be among the first to adopt fertility control. Will they as soon as economic development removes this threat, revert to the old fertility patterns and abandon contraceptive practices? Upon what theoretical principles do you base your answer?

5. Write an essay on "Abortion as a Method of Fertility Control." Some experts have made the blunt assertion that the developing nations cannot master their population problem until they follow the example of Japan and legalize abortion. This attitude is held especially about some illiterate populations. Evaluate this proposition in the light of the reading you do and the evaluations that have been made of who accepts abortion and who does not.

6. Many persons have blamed the Roman Catholic Church for high birthrates in Latin America and have maintained that religious beliefs are the major barrier to rapid fertility decline in Latin America. Read as much as you can about:

(*a*) The attitudes of Latin American publics toward fertility and fertility control—and the extent of resistance based on religious belief.

(*b*) The actions of the Church to obstruct or prevent provision of modern family planning services and the dissemination of information.

(*c*) The actions that have been taken by governments, physicians, medical societies, and private businesses to circumvent or evade these obstructions.

Considering all of these items together, write an essay about how much of an obstruction religion has been and is now to fertility decline in Latin America. Discuss the hypothesis that birthrates in Latin America may reach low levels of slow growth in only two-thirds the time it will take in most nations of Asia.

7. Read as much as you can about the use-effectiveness of the rhythm method as a form of fertility control. Do you think this method is reliable enough to be taken seriously by physicians? Differentiate between methods that make use of body measurements, such as temperature, and those that make use only of the calendar.

8. One of the "mysteries" of fertility control is that the oral contraceptives have had amazingly rapid adoption by persons of all socioeconomic levels. But this success has been limited as yet to Europe, North America and Latin America, Japan, and possibly Egypt. The first trials in India, Pakistan, and other Asian and African populations seemed to be disappointing. Some observers blame this on cultural differences and others blame it on the prejudices of the persons conducting these early tests. Read as much as you can about recent experiments in this field and write an essay concerning the basis of resistance to oral contraception in Asia and/or Africa.

9. Read as much as you can about "the male as a factor in fertility control." Because the male is a dominant figure in most family systems in the developing nations, his attitude and behavior should be of critical importance. What empirical evidence is there to support the following hypotheses:

(*a*) Most resistance and failure to adopt fertility control can be traced to male dominance, male ignorance, and male traditionalism.

(*b*) As the group that is much more literate, much more in contact with the outside world, and much more sensitive to the economic implications of family planning, males are no less reluctant than females to adopt family planning.

10. Those who are most pessimistic about the prospects for inducing fertility control by democratic methods sometimes recommend more drastic measures, such as enforced sterilization after the third child, removal of benefits to parents who have large families, increased taxes on those who have large families, and so on. Evaluate these ideas from a sociological point of view, invoking theories of social control, social change, and the basis of conformity. Repeat the same evaluation for the group of recommendations that would reward people for practicing family planning, such as paying x dollars bonus for each year that a couple spends free of childbearing.

BIBLIOGRAPHY

Agarwala, S. N. "Abortion Rate Among a Section of Delhi's Population," *Medical Digest,* **30** (January 1962).

Agarwala, S. N. *Attitudes Toward Family Planning in India.* Institute of Economic Growth Occasional Papers, No. 5, Vol. IX. Bombay: Asia Publishing House, 1962.

Ahmed, Mohiuddin. "Male Attitudes Towards Family Limitation in East Pakistan." Paper contributed to United Nations World Population Conference, 1965.

Aird, John S. "Population, Planning, and Economic Development in Mainland China in a Decade of Crisis," *Population Bulletin,* **19** (August 1963), 114–135.

American Association for Public Opinion Research. "Sample Surveys and Population Control," *Public Opinion Quarterly,* **28** (1964), 361–394.

American International Association for Economic and Social Development. Programa Interamericano de Información Popular. *A Survey of Attitudes Related to Costa Rican Population Dynamics.* By F. B. Waisanen et al. San José, 1966.

American Medical Association. Committee on Human Reproduction. "The Control of Fertility," *Journal of the American Medical Association,* **194**(4) (October 25, 1965), 230–470.

American Public Health Association. Program Area Committee on Population and Public Health. Public health programs in family planning. (A group of 15 papers.) *American Journal of Public Health and the Nation's Health,* **56** (1, Part 2) (January 1966).

Anand, K. "Opinion and Attitude Towards Family Planning in Chandigarh," *Journal of Family Welfare* (Bombay), **10** (June 1964), 60–65.

Angulo-Arvelo, L. A. "Actitudes ante la Fecundidad en General y Particularmente en Venezuela" ("Attitudes toward Fertility in General and in Venezuela Particularly"), *Asuntos Sociales (Caracas),* **2**(7) (June 1966), 31–79.

Aren, Per. "On Legal Abortion in Sweden: Tentative Evaluation of Justification of Frequency During Last Decade," *Acta Obstetricia et Gynecologica Scandinavica,* translated by L. James Brown, **37** (1958).

Bachi, Roberto, and Judah Matras. "Contraception and Induced Abortions Among Jewish Maternity Cases in Israel," *Milbank Memorial Fund Quarterly,* **40** (April 1962), 207–229.

Back, Kurt W. "A Model of Family Planning Experiments: The Lessons of the Puerto Rican and Jamaican Studies," *Marriage and Family Living,* **25** (February 1963), 14–19.

Badenhorst, L. T. "Family Limitation and Methods of Contraception in an Urban Population," *Population Studies,* **16** (March 1963), 286–301.

Bain, Ian. "The Development of Family Planning in Canada," *Canadian Journal of Public Health,* **55** (August 1964), 334–340.

Balfour, M. C. "Family Planning in Asia," *Population Studies,* **15** (November 1961), 102–109.

Bang, Sook. *A Survey of Fertility and Attitude Toward Family Planning in Rural Korea,* 1963.

Banks, Joseph A., and Olive Banks. *Feminism and Family Planning in Victorian England.* Studies in Sociology. New York: Shocken Books, 1964.

Basu, R. N. "Experiences with a Poorly Effective Oral Contraceptive in an Indian Village," *Demography,* **1** (1964), 106–110.

Basu, R. N. "Some Findings on the Family Planning Programme," *Journal of Family Welfare* (Bombay), **9** (September 1962), 16–24.

Beasley, Joseph D., et al. "Attitudes and Knowledge Relevant to Family Planning among New Orleans Negro Women." Pp. 1847–57. *American Journal of Public Health* and *Nation's Health,* **56** (11) (November 1966).

Bebarta, Prafulla C. "Problems of Planned Parenthood in Village India," *AICC Economic Review* (New Delhi), **11** (June 15, 1959), 27–30, 33.

Berelson, Bernard. "On Family Planning Communication," *Demography,* **1** (1964), 94–105.

Berelson, Bernard. "Turkey: National Survey on Population," *Population Council Studies in Family Planning* (New York), No. 5 (December 1964), 1–5.

Berelson, Bernard. "National Family Planning Programs: A Guide," *Population Council Studies in Family Planning* (New York), No. 5 (December 1964).

Berelson, Bernard. "A Review of Major Governmental Programs." Paper contributed for the United Nations World Population Conference, 1965.

Berelson, Bernard. "Communication, Communication Research, and Family Planning," *Emerg-*

ing Techniques in Population Research. New York: Milbank Memorial Fund.

Berelson, Bernard, and Ronald Freedman. "A Study in Fertility Control," *Scientific American,* **210** (May 1964), 29–37.

Berelson, Bernard, Richmond K. Anderson, Oscar Harkavy, John Maier, W. Parker Mauldin, and Sheldon J. Segal (eds.). *Family Planning and Population Programs.* Chicago: University of Chicago Press, 1966.

Bergues, Helene, et al. *La Prevention des Naissances Dans la Famille. Ses Origines Dans les Temps Modernes.* Institut National d'Etudes Démographiques, Cahiers de Travaux et Documents, No. 35. Paris: Presses Universitaires de France, 1959.

Bhatia, Brajesh, et al. "A Study in Family Planning Communication—Direct Mailing," *Demography,* **3**(2) (1966), 343–351.

Blacker, C. P. "The Rhythm Method: Two Indian Experiments," *Eugenics Review,* **47** (July 1955), 93–105.

Blacker, C. P. "Voluntary Sterilization: Transitions Throughout the World," *Eugenics Review,* **54** (October 1962), 143–162.

Blair, Annie O. "A Comparison of Negro and White Fertility Attitudes," in Donald J. Bogue (ed.), *Sociological Contributions to Family Planning Research.* Chicago: Community and Family Study Center, 1967, pp. 1–35.

Blake, Judith. *Family Structure in Jamaica: The Social Context of Reproduction.* Glencoe, Ill.: The Free Press of Glencoe, 1961.

Blake, Judith. "The Americanization of Catholic Reproductive Ideals," *Population Studies* (July 1966), 27–43.

Blake, Judith. "Demographic Science and the Redirection of Population Policy." Pp. 41–69 in Mindel C. Sheps and Jeanne C. Ridley (eds.). Pittsburgh, Pa.: University of Pittsburgh Press, 1965.

Blake, Judith. "Parental Control, Delayed Marriage, and Population Policy." Paper contributed for the United Nations World Population Conference, 1965.

Blake, Judith, and Kingsley Davis. "Population and Public Opinion—The Need for Basic Research." University of California, Institute of International Studies, General Series, Reprint 105. Berkeley, 1963. Reprinted from *The American Behavioral Scientist* (May 1963), 24–29.

Bogue, Donald J. "Some Tentative Recommendations for a 'Sociologically Correct' Family Planning Communication and Motivation Program in India," in Clyde V. Kiser (ed.), *Research in Family Planning.* Princeton, N.J.: Princeton University Press, 1962, pp. 503–538.

Bogue, Donald J. (ed.). *Mass Communication and Motivation for Family Planning.* Chicago: Community and Family Study Center, 1967.

Bogue, Donald J. (ed.). *Sociological Contributions to Family Planning Research.* Chicago: Community and Family Study Center, 1967.

Bogue, Donald J. (ed.). *The Rural South Fertility Experiments, Report Number 1.* Chicago: Community and Family Study Center, 1966.

Bogue, Donald J., and Veronica S. Heiskanan. *How To Improve Written Communication for Birth Control.* Chicago: Community and Family Study Center, 1963.

Bose, Ashish. "The Population Puzzle in India," *Economic Development and Cultural Change,* **7** (April 1959), 230–248.

Brackett, James W., and Earl Huyck. "The Objectives of Government Policies on Fertility Control in Eastern Europe," *Population Studies,* **16** (November 1962), 134–146.

Brown, George, and Amor Daly. "Evaluation du Programme de Planning Familial de Tunisie." Paper contributed for the United Nations World Population Conference, 1965.

Burman, Roy. "Problem of Family Planning Among the Scheduled Tribes of West Bengal," *Vanyajati* (Delhi), **6** (October 1958), 160–164.

Byrne, Joycelin. "A Fertility Survey in Barbados," *Social and Economic Studies* (Jamaica), **15** (4) (December 1966), 368–378.

Cadbury, George W. "Population Planning: Some Suggestions for Emphasis in Future Research." Paper contributed for the United Nations World Population Conference, 1965.

Calderone, Mary S. (ed.). *Abortion in the United States.* New York: Hoeber-Harper, 1958.

Campbell, Arthur A. "Fertility and Family Planning among Non-White Married Couples in the United States," *Eugenics Quarterly,* **12**(3) (September 1965), 124–131.

Carlsson, Gösta. "The Decline of Fertility: Innovation or Adjustment Process," *Population Studies,* **20**(2) (November 1966), 149–174.

Carrasco, Eugenio. *Control de la Natalidad en México y América Latina* (Birth Control in Mexico and Latin America). México, D.F.: Librería de Manuel Porrúa, 1965.

Champion, Phyllis. "A Pilot Study of the Success or Failure of Low-Income Negro Families in the Use of Birth Control," in Donald J. Bogue (ed.), *Sociological Contributions to Family Planning Research.* Chicago: Community and Family Study Center, 1967, pp. 112–128.

Chandrasekaran, C. "Survey of Family Planning Clinics in Greater Bombay," *Journal of Family Welfare,* **60** (March 1963), 1–90.

Chandrasekaran, C. "Indian Fertility in a Changing Economic and Social Setting," *Family Planning News* (New Delhi), **3** (October 1962), 228–236.

Chandrasekaran, C., and P. C. Bebarta. "The Relative Role of Information Sources in the Dissemination of Knowledge of Family Planning Methods in Bombay City," *Journal of Family Welfare* (Bombay), 9 (June 1963), 5–14.

Chandrasekaran, C., and Moye W. Freymann. "Evaluating Community Family Planning Programs." Pp. 266–86 in Mindel C. Sheps and Jeanne C. Ridley (eds.). *Public Health and Population Change: Current Research Issues.* Pittsburgh, Pa.: University of Pittsburgh Press, 1965.

Chandrasekaran, C., and Katherine Kuder. *Family Planning Through Clinics.* Demographic Training and Research Centre, Bombay, Research monograph 2. Bombay: Allied Publishers, 1965.

Chandrasekhar, Sripati. "Cultural Barriers to Family Planning in Underdeveloped Countries," *Population Review* (Madras), 1 (April 1957), 44–56.

Chesser, Eustace, et al. *The Sexual, Marital and Family Relationships of the English Woman.* London: Hutchinson's Medical Publications, 1956; New York: Roy Publishers, 1957.

Chow, L. P. "A Programme to Control Fertility in Taiwan: Settling, Accomplishment and Evaluation," *Population Studies,* 19(2) (November 1965), 155–166.

Christensen, Harold T. "Selected Aspects of Child Spacing in Denmark," *Acta Sociologica* (Copenhagen), 4 (1959), 35–45.

Clark, Colin. "Population and Progress. The Problem of Birth Control," *Queen's Quarterly* (Kingston, Ontario), 62 (Autumn 1955), 411–422.

Coale, Ansley J. "The Economic Effects of Fertility Control in Underdeveloped Areas," *Human Fertility and Population Problems.* Cambridge: Schenkman Publishing Co., 1963, pp. 143–161.

Cook, Robert C. "India: High Cost of High Fertility," *Population Bulletin,* 14 (December 1958), 153–171.

Coughlin, Richard J., and Margaret M. Coughlin. "Fertility and Birth Control Among Low Income Chinese Families in Hong Kong," *Marriage and Family Living,* 25 (May 1963), 171–177.

Croley, H. T., S. Z. Haider, Sultana Begum, and Harold Gustafson. "Characteristics and Utilization of Midwives in a Selected Area of East Pakistan," *Demography,* 3 (1966), 578–581.

Cummins, G. T. M., et al. "Population Control in Barbados," *American Journal of Public Health and the Nation's Health,* 55 (10) (October 1965), 1600–1608.

Dandekar, Kumudini. "Family Planning Studies Conducted by the Gokhale Institute of Politics and Economics, Poona," in Clyde V. Kiser (ed.). *Research in Family Planning.* Princeton, N.J.: Princeton University Press, 1962, pp. 3–16.

Dandekar, Kumudini. "Possible Targets and Their Attainment in the Field of Family Planning In India during 1966–76," *Artha Vijñana* (Poona), 8(3) (September 1966), 239–249.

Dandekar, Kumudini. "Promotion of Family Planning in Rural Areas: A Field Experiment," *Artha Vijñana* (Poona), 3 (March 1961), 24–37.

Dandekar, Kumudini. "Vital Rates and the Efforts at Family Planning in the Various States of India," *Artha Vijñana* (Poona), 6 (December 1964), 290–301.

Dandekar, V. M., and Kumudini Dandekar. *Survey of Fertility and Mortality in Poona District.* Gokhale Institute of Politics and Economics, Publication No. 27, 1953.

Davis, Kingsley. "Fertility Control and the Demographic Transition in India," *The Interrelations of Demographic, Economic and Social Problems in Selected Underdeveloped Areas.* New York: Milbank Memorial Fund, 1954, pp. 66–89.

De Lestapis, Stanislas. *Family Planning and Modern Problems: A Catholic Analysis.* New York: Heder and Herder, 1961.

Devereux, George. *A Study of Abortion in Primitive Societies.* New York: Julian Press, 1955.

Dingle, Janet T., and Christopher Tietze. *Comparative Study of Three Contraceptive Methods: Vaginal Foam Tablets, Jelly Alone, and Diaphragm with Jelly or Cream.* National Committee on Maternal Health, Inc., Publication No. 17, New York.

Dowse, Robert E., and John Peel. "The Politics of Birth-Control," *Political Studies,* 13(2) (June 1965), 179–197.

Duke University School of Law. "[A Symposium on] Population Control," *Law and Contemporary Problems,* 25 (Summer 1960), 377–629.

Eldridge, Hope T. *Population Policies: A Survey of Recent Developments.* Washington, D.C.: The International Union for the Scientific Study of Population, 1954.

Elkan, Edward. "Sexual Hygiene in Sweden," *International Journal of Sexology,* 6 (February 1953), 155–160.

Enke, Stephen. "The Economics of Government Payments to Limit Population," *Economic Development and Cultural Change,* 8 (July 1960), 339–348.

Enke, Stephen. "The Gains to India From Population Control: Some Money Control: Some Money Measures and Incentive Schemes," *Review of Economics and Statistics,* 42 (May 1960), 175–181.

Enke, Stephen. *The Worth of Population Control*

to India: Some Money Measures and Incentive Schemes. Rand Corporation Series P-1649. Santa Barbara, 1959.

Ericksen, E. Gordon. The West Indies Population Problem: Dimensions for Action. Lawrence, Kansas: University of Kansas Publications, 1962.

Erskine, Hazel G. "The Polls: The Population Explosion, Birth Control, and Sex Education," Public Opinion Quarterly, 30(3) (Fall 1966), 490–501.

Fagley, Richard M. "Doctrines and Attitudes of Major Religions in Regard to Fertility." Paper contributed for the United Nations World Population Conference, 1965.

Family Planning Association. Abortion in Britain. Proceedings of a conference held by the Family Planning Association at the University of London Union on April 22, 1966. London: Pitman Medical Publishing Co., 1966.

Frank, Richard. "Clinical Evaluation of a Simple Jelly-Alone Method of Contraception," Fertility and Sterility, 13 (September-October 1962), 458–464.

Freeberne, Michael. "Birth Control in China," Population Studies, 18 (July 1964), 5–16.

Freedman, Ronald. "American Studies of Family Planning and Fertility: A Review of Major Trends and Issues," in Clyde V. Kiser (ed.), Research in Family Planning. Princeton, N.J.: Princeton University Press, 1962, pp. 211–227.

Freedman, Ronald. "Fecundity and Family Planning in the White Population of the United States: 1955," Thirty Years of Research in Human Fertility: Retrospect and Prospect. New York: Milbank Memorial Fund, 1958, pp. 61–73.

Freedman, Ronald. "Next Steps in Research on Problems of Motivation and Communication in Relation to Family Planning," in Clyde V. Kiser (ed.). Research in Family Planning, Princeton, N.J.: Princeton University Press, 1962, pp. 593–604.

Freedman, Ronald, et al. "Current Fertility Expectations of Married Couples in the United States: 1963," Population Index, 31 (January 1965), 3–20.

Freedman, Ronald, et al. Family Planning, Sterility and Population Growth. New York: McGraw-Hill, 1959.

Freedman, Ronald, et al. "Fertility and Family Planning in Taiwan: A Case Study of the Demographic Transition," American Journal of Sociology, 70 (July 1964), 16–27.

Freedman, Ronald, et al. "Stability and Change in Expectations About Family Size: A Longitudinal Study," Demography, 2 (1965), 250–275.

Freedman, Ronald, and Lolagene Coombs. "Childspacing and Family Economic Position," American Sociological Review, 31(5) (October 1966), 631–648.

Freedman, Ronald, and Lolagene Coombs. "Economic Considerations in Family Growth Decisions," Population Studies, 20(2) (November 1966), 197–222.

Freedman, Ronald, and John Y. Takeshita. "Studies of Fertility and Family Limitation in Taiwan." Pp. 174–197 in Mindel C. Sheps and Jeanne C. Ridley (eds.). Public Health and Population Change: Current Research Issues. Pittsburgh, Pa.: University of Pittsburgh Press, 1965.

Freymann, Moye W. "Population Control in India," Marriage and Family Living, 25 (February 1963), 53–61.

Freymann, Moye W., and Herbert F. Lionberger. "A Model for Family Planning Action-Research," in Clyde V. Kiser (ed.). Research in Family Planning. Princeton, N.J.: Princeton University Press, 1962, pp. 443–461.

Fryer, Peter. The Birth Controllers. London: Secker and Warburg, 1965; New York: Stein and Day, 1966.

Gandotra, M. M. "Factors Affecting Indian Fertility in a Changing Set-up," Journal of Family Welfare (Bombay), 12(4) (June 1966), 30–37.

Gilbert, Robert I. The Acceptance, Knowledge, and Use of Family-Planning Techniques as Related to Social-Class Membership in the White Population of a Southern Community. Ann Arbor, Mich.: University Microfilms, 1957.

Girard, Alain. Psychological Aspects of Demographic Investigation. Proceedings of the World Population Conference: 1954, Vol. VI. New York, 1955.

Glass, David V. "Family Planning Programmes and Action in Western Europe," Population Studies, 19(3) (March 1966), 221–238.

Glass, D. V. "Fertility and Birth Control in Developed Societies, and Some Questions of Policy for Less Developed Societies," Journal of Family Welfare, 9 (March 1963), 6–18.

Glass, D. V. "Family Limitation in Europe: A Survey of Recent Studies," in Clyde V. Kiser (ed.). Research in Family Planning. Princeton, N.J.: Princeton University Press, 1962, pp. 231–261.

Glass, David V. Population Growth and Population Policy. Pp. 3–24 in Mindel C. Sheps and Jeanne C. Ridley (eds.). Public Health and Population Change: Current Research Issues. Pittsburgh, Pa.: University of Pittsburgh Press, 1965.

Goodhart, C. B. "The Frequency of Illegal Abortion," Eugenics Review, 55 (January 1964), 197–200.

Goodman, L. A. "Some Possible Effects of Birth

Control on the Sex Ratio," *Annals of Human Genetics,* **25** (May 1961), 75–81.

Goodman, Leo A. "Some Possible Effects of Birth Control on the Incidence of Disorders and on the Influence of Birth Control," *Annals of Human Genetics,* **27** (August 1963), 41–52.

Gore, Sushila. "Review of Abortion as a Method of Population Control," *Maharashtra Medical Journal* (Poona) (April-May 1964), 245–253.

Goyal, R. P. "Attitude Studies Relating to Family Planning in India." Paper contributed for the United Nations World Population Conference, 1965.

Gray, Naomi T. "Family Planning and Agricultural Migrant Workers: A Case Study," *Journal of Family Welfare,* **9** (March 1963), 46–55.

Green, Lawrence W., and Yasmin A. Jan. "Family-Planning Knowledge and Attitude Surveys in Pakistan." *Pakistan Development Review* (Karachi), **4** (Summer 1964), 332–355.

Griffiths, William, Beryl J. Roberts, and Raisunnessa Huq. "Application of Learning Theory to a Family Planning Program in Dacca, East Pakistan." Paper contributed for the United Nations World Population Conference, 1965.

Guha, Uma. "Attitude of U.P. Village Women on Planned Parenthood," *Bulletin of the Department of Anthropology* (Calcutta), **4** (January 1955), 41–50.

Gustafson, Harold G., H. T. Croley, William Griffiths, and Beryl J. Roberts. "Educational Efforts in the Implementation of Rural Family Planning Programs in East Pakistan," *Demography,* **4**(1) (1967), 81–89.

Guttmacher, Alan F., et al. *The Complete Book of Birth Control.* New York: Ballantine Books, 1961.

Hall, Francoise. "Birth Control in Lima, Peru: Attitudes and Practises," *Milbank Memorial Fund Quarterly,* **43**(4, Part 2) (October 1965), 409–438.

Hall, Francoise. "Family Planning in Lima, Peru," Pp. 100–112, discussion pp. 112–116, in Clyde V. Kiser (ed.). *Components of Population Change in Latin America. Milbank Memorial Fund Quarterly,* **43** (4, Part 2) (October 1965).

Hanhart, Dieter. "Der Zürcher Arbeiter und sein Leitbild von der Idealen Familiengroesse," *Schweizerische Zeitschrift fuer Volkswirtschaft und Statistik* (Bern), **99** (December 1963), 482–492.

Hauser, Philip M. "Family Planning and Population Programs," *Demography,* **4** (1) (1967), 397–414.

Hauser, Philip M. "Some Observations on Method and Study Design," *Current Research in Human Fertility.* New York: Milbank Memorial Fund, 1955, pp. 151–162.

Hawley, Amos H., and Visid Prachuabmoh. "Family Growth and Family Planning: Responses to a Family Planning Action Program in a Rural District of Thailand," *Demography,* **3** (1966), 319–331.

Heer, David M. "Abortion, Contraception, and Population Policy in the Soviet Union," *Demography,* **2** (1965), 531–539.

Heiskanen, Veronica. "A Cross-Cultural Content Analysis of Family Planning Publications," in Donald J. Bogue (ed.), *Sociological Contributions to Family Planning Research.* Chicago: Community and Family Study Center, 1967, pp. 71-111.

Hill, Reuben et al. "Intra-Family Communication and Fertility Planning in Puerto Rico," *Rural Sociology,* **20** (September-December 1955), 258–271.

Hill, Reuben, J. Mayone Stycos, and Kurt W. Back. *The Family and Population Control: A Puerto Rican Experiment in Social Change.* Chapel Hill, N.C.: The University of North Carolina Press, 1959.

Himelhoch, Jerome, and Sylvia F. Fava (eds.). *Sexual Behavior in American Society: An Appraisal of the First Two Kinsey Reports.* New York: Norton, 1955.

Himes, Norman E. *Medical History of Contraception.* New York: Gamut Press, 1963.

Houghton, Vera. "International Planned Parenthood Federation (I.P.P.F.): Its History and Influence," *Eugenics Review,* **53** (January 1962), 201–207.

Husain, A. F. A. *Human and Social Impact of Technological Change in Pakistan.* 2 vols. Oxford University Press, 1956.

Husein, Hasan M. "Evaluation of Progress in Fertility Control in U.A.R." Paper contributed for the United Nations World Population Conference, 1965.

Inayatullah, Attiya. "Impact of Culture on Fertility in Pakistan." Paper for the Seventh International Conference on Planned Parenthood, Singapore, 1963.

India, Directorate General of Health Services. *Studies in Family Planning.* New Delhi, 1960.

India, Kerala, Demographic Research Centre, Trivandrum. *Attitude to Family Planning,* Part 1. Trivandrum: Government Press, 1961.

India, Madras, Government. *Report on a Survey of Attitudes of Married Couples Toward Family Planning in the Pudupakkam Area of the City of Madras, 1958.* Madras, 1959.

India, Ministry of Health. *Report of the Family Planning Third Five-Year Plan Committee.* Delhi, 1960.

Inghe, Gunnar. *The Characteristics of the Abortion Clientele. Proceedings of the World Population Conference: 1954,* Vol. II. New York, 1955.

Institut National d'Etudes Démographiques, France. "La Limitation de Naissances en France," *Population*, 11 (April-June 1956), 209–234.

International Planned Parenthood Federation. *Proceedings of the Seventh Conference of the International Planned Parenthood Federation, Singapore, February 10–16, 1963.* Excerpta Medical Foundation, International Congress Series, 72. Amsterdam, 1964.

Iutaka, Sugiyama. "Inter-Generational Mobility and Family Planning in Urban Brazil." Paper contributed for the United Nations World Population Conference, 1965.

Johnson, Virginia E., and William H. Masters. "Intravaginal Contraceptive Study," *Journal of Surgery, Obstetrics, and Gynecology* (July-August 1962), 202–207.

Jürgens, Hans W. "The Planning of the Family Size in the Different Social Classes According to the Results of Investigations in Schleswig-Holstein, Federal Republic of Germany." Paper contributed for the United Nations World Population Conference, 1965.

Kahl, Joseph A. "Los Valores Modernos y los Ideales de Fecundidad en Brasil y México" ("Modern Values and Ideal Fertility in Brazil and Mexico"), *Améruia Latina* (Rio de Janeiro), 9(2) (April-June 1966), 22–40.

Kantner, John F., and J. Mayone Stycos. "A Non-Clinical Approach to Contraception: Preliminary Report on the Program of the Family Planning Association of Puerto Rico," in Clyde V. Kiser (ed.). *Research in Family Planning.* Princeton, N.J.: Princeton University Press, 1962, pp. 573–590.

Károly, Mitenyi. "Z Születéskorlátozás Szociális es Lélektani Háttere" ("Social and Psychological Background of Birth Control"), Russian and English titles and summaries, *Demografia* (Budapest), 5 (1962), 33–72.

Khan, Akhter H. "Islamic Opinions on Contraception" Comilla: Pakistan Academy for Village Development, 1960. Reprinted from *Journal of the East Pakistan Academy for Village Development,* 1 (August and October 1960).

Khan, A. Majeed. *Rural Pilot Family Planning Action Programme: First Annual Report, March 1961-May 1962.* Comilla: Pakistan Academy for Rural Development.

Khan, A., and Harvey M. Choldin. "New Family Planners in Rural East Pakistan," *Demography,* 2 (1965), 1–7.

Kinch, Arne. "A Preliminary Report from the Sweden-Ceylon Family Planning Pilot Project," in Clyde V. Kiser (ed.), *Research in Family Planning.* Princeton, N.J.: Princeton University Press, 1962, pp. 85–102.

Kinch, Arne. "Family Planning in the Context of Community Health Services in Rural Ceylon." Paper contributed for the United Nations World Population Conference, 1965.

Kirk, Dudley, and Dorothy Nortman. "Population Policies in Developing Countries," *Economic Development and Cultural Change,* 15(2, Part 1) (January 1967), 129–142.

Kirtikar, Mandakini R., and Katayan D. Virkar. "Socio-Economic Study of Women Attending an Urban Clinic and Their Attitude toward Oral Contraceptives," *Journal of Family Welfare* (Bombay), 13(2) (December 1966), 22–27.

Kiser, Clyde V. "The Indianapolis Study of Social and Psychological Factors Affecting Fertility," in Clyde V. Kiser (ed.), *Research in Family Planning.* Princeton, N.J.: Princeton University Press, 1962, pp. 149–166.

Kiser, Clyde (ed.). *Research in Family Planning.* Princeton, N.J.: Princeton University Press, 1962.

Koya, Yoshio. "Does the Effect of a Family Planning Program Continue?" *Eugenics Quarterly,* 11 (September 1964), 141–147.

Koya, Yoshio. "Family Planning Among Japanese on Public Relief," *Eugenics Quarterly,* 4 (March 1957), 17–23.

Koya, Yoshio. "A Family Planning Program in a Large Population Group: The Case of the Japanese National Railways," *Milbank Memorial Fund Quarterly,* 40 (July 1962), 319–327.

Koya, Yoshio. "A Family Planning Program in a Large Population Group." *Archives of the Population Association of Japan,* No. 4. English edition. Tokyo, 1963 (iii), 164 pp. Pp. 18–23.

Koya, Yoshio. "Five-Year Experiment on Family Planning Among Coal Miners in Joban, Japan," *Population Studies,* 13 (November 1959), 157–163.

Koya, Yoshio. "Some Essential Factors for Fertility Control in Japan," Paper contributed for the United Nations World Population Conference, 1965.

Koya, Yoshio. *Pioneering in Family Planning: A Collection of Papers on the Family Planning Programs and Research Conducted in Japan.* Tokyo: Japan Medical Publishers, 1963.

Kronus, Sidney. "Fertility Control in the Rural South: A Pretest," in Donald J. Bogue (ed.), *Sociological Contributions to Family Planning Research.* Chicago: Community and Family Study Center, 1967, pp. 129–160.

Kubo, Hidebumi, et al. *Family Planning in Japan.* Tokyo: Asia Family Planning Association, 1961.

Kurup, R. S., and T. K. Mathen. "Sterilization as a Method of Family Limitation in Kerala State," *Population Review* (Madras), 10(2) (July 1966), 61–68.

Lal, A. "Age at Marriage and Fertility," *Maharashtra Medical Journal* (Poona) (April-May 1964), 85–92.

Lieberman, E. James. "Preventive Psychiatry and Family Planning," *Journal of Marriage and the Family,* **26**(4) (November 1964), 471–477.

Lindstrom, Ulla. "On Technical Assistance in the Field of Family Planning." Paper contributed for the United Nations World Population Conference, 1965.

Mahn, Erna H. "Septic Abortion Problems in Chile," *Journal of the American Medical Women's Association,* **12** (April 1957), 99–104.

Mandagere, S. P. Rukmini. "Opinion and Attitude Toward Family Planning in Rural Madras," *Journal of Family Welfare* (Bombay), **10** (September 1963), 32–37.

Mathen, K. K. "Preliminary Lessons Learned from the Rural Population Control Study of Singur," in Clyde V. Kiser (ed.), *Research in Family Planning.* Princeton, N.J.: Princeton University Press, 1962, 33–49.

Mathen, K. K., and Muktha Sen. "The Singur Population Study as an Action Research Model for Family Planning," *Journal of Family Welfare* (Bombay), **10** (June 1964), 4–15.

Mauldin, W. Parker. "Fertility Studies: Knowledge, Attitude, and Practice," *Studies on Family Planning,* No. 7. New York: Population Council, June 1965, pp. 1–10.

Mauldin, W. Parker. "Population and Population Policy in Pakistan," *Marriage and Family Living,* **25** (February 1963), 62–68.

Mehlan, Karl-Heinz. *Die Problematik der Schwangerschafts-Unterbrechung auf Grund der Sozialen Indikation: Statische Auswertung des Materials der Schangerschaftsunterbre Hungskommissionen aus den Jahren 1949/1950.* Institut fur Sozialhygiene der Humboldt Universitat zu Berlin.

Mehlan, Karl-Heinz (ed.). *Internationale Abortsituation, Abortbekampfung, Antikonzeption.* Leipzig: VEB George Thieme, 1961.

Meier, Gitta. "The Effect of Unwanted Pregnancies on a Relief Load: An Exploratory Study," *Eugenics Quarterly,* **8** (September 1961), 142–153.

Meier, Gitta. "Research and Action Programs in Human Fertility Control: A Review of Literature," *Social Work: Journal of the National Association of Social Workers,* **11**(3) (July 1966), 40–55.

Mendoza, Ofelia. "Population Growth and Family Planning in Latin America," *Journal of Sex Research,* **1**(2) (July 1965), 161–173.

Mendoza, Ofelia. "What Are the Factors in Latin American Culture that Might Stimulate or Discourage Fertility Control?" *Journal of Family Welfare,* **9** (March 1963), 19–29.

Milbank Memorial Fund. *Thirty Years of Research in Human Fertility: Retrospect and Prospect.* New York: Milbank Memorial Fund, 1958.

Misra, B. D. "Correlates of Male's Attitudes Toward Family Planning," in Donald J. Bogue (ed.), *Sociological Contributions to Family Planning.* Chicago: Community and Family Study Center, 1967, pp. 161–271.

Mitra, K. N. "Action-Research in One-Time Family Planning Methods Outline of a Plan for West Bengal." Paper contributed for the United Nations World Population Conference, 1965.

Morrison, William A. "Attitudes of Female Toward Family Planning in a Mahrashtrian Village," *Milbank Memorial Fund Quarterly,* **35** (January 1957), 67–81.

Morrison, William A. "Attitudes of Males Toward Family Planning in a Western Indian Village," *Milbank Memorial Fund Quarterly,* **34** (July 1956), 262–286.

Morrison, William A. *The Relationship of Family Size and Socio-Cultural Variables to Attitudes Toward Family Planning in a Village of India.* Ann Arbor, Mich.: University Microfilms (Publication No. 23,109), 1957.

Morrison, William A. "Family Planning Attitudes of Industrial Workers of Ambarnath, a City of Western India: A Comparative Analysis," *Population Studies,* **14** (March 1961), 235–243.

Morrison, William A. "Some Thoughts and Proposals Relating to Educational Programme for Population Control in India," *Indian Journal of Social Work* (Bombay), **21** (March 1961), 321–336.

Muramatsu, Minoru. "Effect of Induced Abortion on the Reduction of Births in Japan," *Milbank Memorial Fund Quarterly,* (April 1960), 152–166.

Muramatsu, Minoru. "Some Observations on the Recent Trends in Family Planning Promotion Activities in Japan." Paper for Seventh International Conference on Planned Parenthood. Singapore, February 1963.

Muramatsu, Minoru. "Policy Measures and Social Changes for Fertility Decline in Japan," Paper contributed for the United Nations World Population Conference, 1965.

Muramatsu, Minoru, and Paul A. Harper (eds.). *Population Dynamics: International Action and Training Programs.* Baltimore: The Johns Hopkins Press, 1965.

Namboodiri, N. Krishnan. "The Wife's Work Experience and Child Spacing," *Milbank Memorial Fund Quarterly,* **42** (July 1964), 65–77.

Noda, Minoru. "Contraception in Japan: Problems of Motivation and Communication," in Clyde V. Kiser (ed.), *Research in Family Planning.* Princeton, N.J.: Princeton University Press, 1962, pp. 551–572.

Noonan, John T., Jr. *Contraception: A History of Its Treatment by the Catholic Theologians and Canonists.* Cambridge, Mass.: Belknap Press of Harvard University Press, 1965.

Norton, J. W. R. "Twenty-one Years' Experience with a Public Health Contraceptive Service," *Journal of Public Health and the Nation's Health,* 49 (August 1959), 993–1000.

Ogburn, William F., and Russell Middleton. "Fertility Control in Underdeveloped Areas: An Experimental Design," *Indian Journal of Economics* (Allahabad), 40 (July 1959), 73–82.

Opler, Morris E. "Cultural Context and Population Control Programs in Village India," in Earl W. Count and Gordon T. Bowles (eds.). *Fact and Theory in Social Science.* Syracuse, N. Y.: Syracuse University Press, 1964, pp. 202–221.

Pacheco, Antonio, and Trinidad Osteria. "Some Findings on the Attitudes toward Family Size Preferences and Family Limitation," *Statistical Reporter* (Manila), 20(3) (July-September 1966), 1–8.

Palmore, James. "The Chicago Snowball: A Study of the Flow of Influence and Diffusion of Family Planning Information," in Donald J. Bogue (ed.), *Sociological Contributions to Family Planning Research.* Chicago: Community and Family Study Center, 1967, pp. 272–363.

Pascual, Elvira, "Socio-Economic Correlates of Attitudes Toward Family Size," in Donald J. Bogue (ed.), *Sociological Contributions to Family Planning Research.* Chicago: Community and Family Study Center, 1967, pp. 36–70.

Patel, H. G. "Resisting Factors to Motivation toward Sterilization—A Method of Family Planning," *Indian Journal of Social Work* (Bombay), 27(1) (April 1966), 71–74.

Patel, Tara. "Some Reflections on the Attitude of Married Couples Toward Family Planning in Ahmedabad," *Sociological Bulletin* (Bombay), 12 (September 1963), 1–13.

Peel, John. "Birth Control and the British Working Class Movement," *Bulletin of the Society for the Study of Labour History,* (7) (Autumn 1963), 16–22.

Peel, John. "Contraception and the Medical Profession," *Population Studies,* 18 (November 1964), 133–145.

Peel, John. "The Manufacture and Retailing of Contraceptives in England," *Population Studies,* 17 (November 1963), 113–125.

Pethe, Vasant P. "Practice of Contraception and Attitudes Towards Family Planning," *Economic Review* (Delhi) (January 4, 1962).

Pierce, Rachel M. "The Extent of Family Planning in Britain," *Family Planning,* 41 (April 1961), 3–5.

Pierce, Rachel M., and Griselda Rowntree. "Birth Control in Britain: Contraceptive Methods Used by Couples Married in the Last Thirty Years," *Population Studies,* 15 (November 1961), 121–160.

Pincus, Gregory. *The Control of Fertility.* New York: Academic Press, 1965.

Poffenberger, Thomas, and Haribhai G. Patel. "The Effect of Local Beliefs on Attitudes Toward Vasectomy in Two Indian Villages in Gujarat State," *Population Review* (Madras), 8 (July 1964), 37–44.

Pohlman, Edward. "Mobilizing Social Pressures toward Small Families," *Eugenics Quarterly,* 13(2) (June 1966), 122–127.

Ponniah, S., et al. "A Report After Two Years' Work on a Rural Family Planning Project," *Journal of Family Welfare* (Bombay), 5 (June 1959), 15–21.

Population Council. *Studies in Family Planning.* (No. 1). New York, July 1963.

Population Council. "National Seminar on Population Problems of Thailand: Conclusions of the Seminar," *Studies in Family Planning.* (No. 4). New York, August 1964, pp. 5–10.

Population Council. "Pakistan: The Medical Social Research Project at Lulliani," *Studies in Family Planning.* (No. 4). New York, August 1964, pp. 5–10.

Population Council. *Studies in Family Planning.* (No. 6). New York, March 1965.

Population Council. *Second International Conference on Intra-Uterine Contraception, New York, October 2-3, 1964.* New York, 1964.

Population Problems Research Council. *Sixth Opinion Survey on Family Planning and Birth Control: A Preliminary Report.* Population Problems Series, No. 18. Tokyo: The Mainichi Newspapers, 1962.

Potter, Robert G., Jr. "Contraceptive Practice and Birth Intervals Among Two-Child White Couples in Metropolitan America," *Thirty Years of Research in Human Fertility: Retrospect and Prospect.* New York: Milbank Memorial Fund, 1958, pp. 74–92.

Potter, Robert G., Jr., Philip C. Sagi, and Charles F. Westoff. "Improvement of Contraception During the Course of Marriage," *Population Studies* (November 1962), 160–174.

Potter, Robert G., Jr., Philip C. Sagi, and Charles F. Westoff. "Rhythm Method," *Science,* 143 (March 27, 1964).

Prachuabmoh, Visid. "Factors Affecting Desire or Lack of Desire for Additional Progeny in Thailand," in Donald J. Bogue (ed.), *Sociological Contributions to Family Planning Research.* Chicago: Community and Family Study Center, 1967, pp. 364–409.

Pyke, Margaret. "Family Planning: An Assessment," *Eugenics Review*, **55** (July 1963), 71–79.

Pyke, Margaret. "Population Planning in Great Britain," *Eugenics Quarterly*, **3** (September 1956), 148–151.

Raina, B. L. *Family Planning Programme: Report for 1962-63*. New Delhi, 1963.

Rainwater, Lee. *And the Poor Get Children: Sex, Contraception, and Family Planning in the Working Class*. Chicago: Quadrangle Books, 1960.

Rainwater, Lee. *Family Design: Marital Sexuality, Family Size, and Contraception*. Social Research Studies in Contemporary Life. Chicago: Aldine Publishing Co., 1965.

Raman, M. V. "A Study of Current Attitudes Toward Family Planning," *Journal of Family Welfare* (Bombay), **9** (June 1963), 18–29.

Raman, M. V. "Attitudes Toward Family Size and Fertility Control in India—An Assessment." Paper contributed for the United Nations World Population Conference, 1965.

Ranadive, K. T., et al. "A Socio-Economic Survey of a Population-Group in Relation to Family Planning," *Population Review* (Madras), **5** (January 1961), 27–38.

Reeder, Leo G., and Goteti B. Krishnamurty. "Family Planning in Rural India: A Problem in Social Change," *Social Problems*, **12** (Fall 1964), 212–223.

Requena, B. Mariano. "Social and Economic Correlates of Induced Abortion in Santiago, Chile," *Demography*, **2** (1965), 33–49.

Rice-Wray, Edris. "The Provoked Abortion—A Major Public Health Problem," *American Journal of Public Health and the Nation's Health*, **54** (February 1964), 313–321.

Riemer, Ruth, and Clyde V. Kiser. "Social and Psychological Factors Affecting Fertility: Economic Tension and Social Mobility in Relation to Fertility Planning and Size of Planned Family," *Milbank Memorial Fund Quarterly*, **32** (April 1954), 167–231.

Riemer, Ruth, and P. K. Whelton. "Social and Psychological Factors Affecting Fertility: Attitudes Toward Restriction of Personal Freedom in Relation to Fertility Planning and Fertility," *Milbank Memorial Fund Quarterly*, **33** (January 1955), 63–111.

Roberts, Beryl J., et al. "Family Planning Survey in Dacca, East Pakistan," *Demography*, **2** (1965), 74–96.

Robinson, Warren C. "Pakistan's New National Family Planning Experiment." *Eugenics Quarterly*, **13**(4) (December 1966), 316–325.

Rock, John. *The Time Has Come: A Catholic Doctor's Proposals To End the Battle Over Birth Control*. New York: Knopf, 1963.

Rowntree, Griselda, and Rachel M. Pierce. "Birth Control in Britain: Attitudes and Practices

among Persons Married Since the First World War," *Population Studies*, **15** (July 1961), 3–31.

Roy, Jyotirmoy. "Population Control in the Rural Sector," *Indian Journal of Economics* (Allahabad), **37** (January 1957), 291–297.

Sagi, Philip C., et al. "Contraceptive Effectiveness as a Function of Desired Family Size," *Population Studies*, **15** (March 1962), 291–296.

Salunkhe, G. R. "Family Planning as Understood and Practiced in the City of Indore," *Indian Sociologist* (Indore), **1** (March 1959), 59–65.

Samuel, T. J. "Culture and Human Fertility in India," *AICC Economic Review* (New Delhi), **14** (March 1, 1963), 19–22.

Samuel, T. J. "The Strengthening of the Motivation for Family Limitation in India," *Journal of Family Welfare* (Bombay), **13**(2) (December 1966), 1–16.

Satterthwaite, Adaline P. "Experience with Oral and Intrauterine Contraception in Rural Puerto Rico." Pp. 474–80 in Mindel C. Sheps and Jeanne C. Ridley (eds.). *Public Health and Population Change: Current Research Issues*. Pittsburgh, Pa.: University of Pittsburgh Press, 1965.

Saxena, R. N., et al. "Follow-Up of Vasectomy," *Journal of Family Welfare* (Bombay), **11** (March 1965), 1–12.

Schorr, Alvin L. "Income Maintenance and the Birth Rate," *Social Security Bulletin*, **28**(12) (December 1965), 22–30.

Sharma, R., and V. C. Jain. "Attitude Toward Family Planning: A Survey in Jaipur City," *Journal of the Indian Medical Association* (Calcutta), **36** (May 16, 1961), 452–459.

Sheridan, Pamela. "Birth Control Behind the Curtain," *Journal of Family Welfare*, **9** (December 1962), 63–66.

Singh, Amrit W., and Suman B. Gunde. "Analysis of Couples Following Family Planning on Advice of Regional Family Planning Training Centre, Poona," *Journal of Family Welfare* (Bombay), **9** (December 1962), 6–19.

Singh, Baljit. *Five Years of Family Planning in the Countryside*. J. K. Institute Monograph, No. 6. Lucknow: Lucknow University, J. K. Institute of Sociology and Human Relations, 1958.

Skinner, G. William. "Cultural Values, Social Structure, and Population Growth," *Population Bulletin of the United Nations*, No. 5 (July 1956), 5–12.

Smith, M. Brewster. *Motivation, Communications Research, and Family Planning*. Pp. 70–89 in Mindel C. Sheps and Jeanne C. Ridley (eds.). *Public Health and Population Change: Current Research Issue*. Pittsburgh, Pa.: University of Pittsburgh Press, 1965.

Song, Jun-Yong. "Effect of the National Family Planning Program on the Reduction of Births in Korea, *Journal of Population Studies* (Seoul), (1) (1965), 28–38.

Spivack, Sydney S. "The Doctor's Role in Family Planning," *Journal of the American Medical Association*, **188** (April 13, 1964), 152–156.

Srb, Vladimir, et al. "Une Enquête Sur la Prevention de Naissances et le Plan Familial en Tchecoslovaquie" ("A Survey of Birth Control and Family Planning in Czechoslovakia"), Spanish and English summaries, *Population* (Paris), **19** (January-March 1964), 79–94.

Srb, Vladimir, et al. "Pruzkum Manzelstvi, Antikoncepce a Potratu," Part 4 ("Investigation of Marriage, Birth Prevention, and Abortion") Russian and English summaries, *Demografie* (Prague), **3** (1961), 311–330.

Srb, Vladimir, and Milan Kuccera. "Potratovost v Ceskoslovensku v Letech 1958-1962" ("The Abortion Rate in Czechoslovakia in the Period 1958-1962"), Russian and English summaries, *Demografie* (Prague), **5** (1963), 289–307.

Stone, Abraham. *Present Day Family Planning Techniques. Proceedings of the World Population Conference: 1954*, Vol. I. New York, 1955.

Stycos, Mayone J. "Opinions of Latin-American Intellectuals on Population Problems and Birth Control," in James C. Charleswirth (ed.). *Latin America tomorrow*. (A group of 12 articles.) *Annals of the American Academy of Political and Social Science*, **360** (July 1965), 11–26.

Stycos, J. Mayone. "The Pattern of Birth Control in Puerto Rico," *Eugenics Quarterly*, **1** (September 1954), 176–181.

Stycos, J. Mayone. "Contraception and Catholicism in Jamaica," *Eugenics Quarterly*, **5** (December 1958), 216–220.

Stycos, J. Mayone. "Female Sterilization in Puerto Rico," *Eugenics Quarterly*, **1** (June 1954), 3–9.

Stycos, J. Mayone. "Haitian Attitudes Toward Family Size," *Human Organization*, **23** (Spring 1964), 42–47.

Stycos, J. Mayone. "Some Directions for Research on Fertility Control," *Milbank Memorial Fund Quarterly*, **36** (April 1958), 126–148.

Stycos, J. Mayone. (ed.). "Family Planning in Modernizing Societies," *Marriage and Family Living*, **25** (February 1963), 5–80.

Stycos, J. Mayone. "Obstacles to Programs of Population Control—Facts and Fancies," *Marriage and Family Living*, **25** (February 1963), 5–13.

Stycos, J. Mayone. "Social Class and Preferred Family Size in Peru," *American Journal of Sociology*, **70** (May 1965), 651–658.

Stycos, J. Mayone. "Experiments in Social Change: The Caribbean Fertility Studies," in Clyde V. Kiser (ed.). *Research in Family Planning*.

Princeton, N. J.: Princeton University Press, 1962.

Stycos, J. Mayone. "A Critique of the Traditional Planned Parenthood Approach in Underdeveloped Areas," *Research in Family Planning*, Clyde V. Kiser (ed.). Princeton, N. J.: Princeton University Press, 1962, pp. 477–501.

Stycos, J. Mayone. "Population and Family-Planning Programs in Newly Developing Countries," in Ronald Freedman (ed.). *Population: The Vital Revolution*. Garden City, N. Y.: Anchor Books, Doubleday, 1964, pp. 166–177.

Stycos, J. Mayone. "Birth Control Clinics in Crowded Puerto Rico," in Benjamin D. Paul (ed.). *Health, Culture, and Community: Case Studies of Public Reactions to Health Programs*. New York: Russell Sage Foundation, 1955, pp. 189–210.

Stycos, J. Mayone. "Cultural Checks on Birth Control Use in Puerto Rico," *The Interrelations of Demographic, Economic, and Social Problems in Selected Underdeveloped Areas*. New York: Milbank Memorial Fund, 1954.

Stycos, J. Mayone, and Kurt W. Back. *The Control of Human Fertility in Jamaica*. Ithaca, N. Y.: Cornell University Press, 1964.

Stycos, J. Mayone, Kurt Back, and Reuben Hill. *Problems of Communication Between Mates on Matters Relating to Family Limitation. Proceedings of the World Population Conference: 1954*, Vol. VI. New York, 1955.

Sung-bong Hong, and Joong-hi Yoon. "Male Attitudes Toward Family Planning on the Island of Kangwha-Gun, Korea," *Milbank Memorial Fund Quarterly*, **40** (October 1962), 443–452.

Sutter, Jean. "Inquiry into the Possibility of Spreading the Ogino Method in India," *Population*, **10** (April-June 1955), 361–365.

Sutter, Jean. "The World Movement on Behalf of Limitation of Families, 1945-1954," *Population*, **10** (April-June 1955), 277–294.

Sutter, Jean, and Helene Berques. "Facteurs Sociaux et Psychologiques Influencant le Controle de la Fecondité en Europe." Paper contributed for the United Nations World Population Conference, 1965.

Szabady, Egon, and András Klinger. "Az 1965-66. évi termékenységi, családtervezési és születésszabályozási vizsgálat" ("The 1965-66 Hungarian Study on Fertility, Family Planning and Birth Control"), *Demográfia* (Budapest), **9**(2), 135–161.

Tabah, Leon. "A Study of Fertility in Santiago, Chile," *Marriage and Family Living*, **25** (February 1963), 20–26.

Tabah, Leon, and Samuel Raul. "Preliminary Findings of a Survey on a Fertility and Attitudes Toward Family Formation in Santiago, Chile," in Clyde V. Kiser (ed.). *Research in Family*

Planning. Princeton, N. J.: Princeton University Press, 1962, pp. 263–304.

Taik, Il Kim. "Review of the Korean Family Planning Action Program." Paper contributed for the United Nations World Population Conference, 1965.

Takeshita, John Y. "Population Control in Japan: A Miracle or Secular Trend?" *Marriage and Family Living,* 25 (February 1963), 44–52.

Thapar, Savitri. "Family Planning in India," *Population Studies* (London), 17 (July 1963), 4–19.

Tien, H. Yuan. "Induced Abortion and Population Control in Mainland China," *Marriage and Family Living,* 25 (February 1963), 35–43.

Tien, H. Yuan. "Birth Control in Mainland China: Ideology and Politics," *Milbank Memorial Fund Quarterly,* 41 (July 1963), 269–290.

Tietze, Christopher. *Intra-Uterine Contraceptive Rings: History and Statistical Appraisal.* New York: National Committee on Maternal Health, Inc., 1962.

Tietze, Christopher (ed.). *Surbical Sterilization of Men and Women: A Selected Bibliography.* New York: National Committee on Maternal Health, Inc., 1962.

Tietze, Christopher (ed.). *Selected Bibliography of Contraception: 1940-1960.* New York: National Committee on Maternal Health, Inc., 1960.

Tietze, Christopher. "The Condom as a Contraceptive," in Hugo G. Biegel (ed.). *Advances in Sex Research.* New York: Hoeber Medical Division, Harper and Row, 1963, pp. 88–102.

Tietze, Christopher. "The Current Status of Contraceptive Practice in the United States," *Proceedings of the Rudolph Virchow Medical Society in the City of New York* (New York and Basel, Switzerland), 19 (1960), 28–41.

Tietze, Christopher. "The Current Status of Fertility Control," *Law and Contemporary Problems,* (Summer 1960), 426–444.

Tietze, Christopher. "The Demographic Significance of Legal Abortion in Eastern Europe," *Demography,* 1 (1964), 119–125.

Tietze, Christopher. "Effectiveness, Acceptability, and Safety of Modern Contraceptive Methods." Paper contributed for the United Nations World Population Conference, 1965.

Tietze, Christopher. "The Use-Effectiveness of Contraceptive Methods," in Clyde V. Kiser (ed.). *Research in Family Planning.* Princeton, N. J.: Princeton University Press, 1962, pp. 357–369.

Tietze, Christopher, and Charles Alleyne. "A Family Planning Service in the West Indies," *Fertility and Sterility,* 10 (May-June 1959), 259–271.

Tietze, Christopher, and Hans Lehfeldt. "Legal Abortion in Eastern Europe," *Journal of the American Medical Association,* 175 (April 1, 1961), 1149–1154.

Tietze, Christopher, and Sarah Lewit. *Intra-Uterine Contraceptive Devices.* Amsterdam: Excerpta Medica Foundation, 1962.

Tietze, Christopher. "Effectiveness and Acceptability of Intrauterine Contraceptive Devices," *Journal of Public Health and the Nation's Health,* 55 (12) (December 1965), 1874–1879.

Tietze, Christopher. "History and Statistical Evaluation of Intrauterine Contraceptive Devices." Pp. 432–449 in Mindel C. Sheps and Jeanne C. Ridley (eds.). *Public Health and Population Change: Current Research Issues.* Pittsburgh, Pa.: University of Pittsburgh Press, 1965.

Tietze, Christopher. "Induced Abortion and Sterilization as Methods of Fertility Control. Pp. 400–416 in Mindel C. Sheps and Jeanne C. Ridley (eds.). *Public Health and Population Change: Current Research Issues.* Pittsburgh, Pa.: University of Pittsburgh Press, 1965.

Toynbee, Arnold J. "The Menace of Overpopulation," in Fairfield Osborn (ed.). *Our Crowded Planet: Essays on the Pressures of Population.* Garden City, N. Y.: Doubleday, 1962.

United Nations, Department of Economics and Social Affairs. *The Mysore Population Study: Report of a Field Survey Carried Out in Selected Areas of Mysore State, India.* Population Studies, No. 34, 1961.

United Nations, Economic Commission for Asia and the Far East. "Population and Food Supplies in Asia and the Far East," *Economic Bulletin for Asia and the Far East,* 7 (May 1956), 1–10.

United Nations, Technical Assistance Administration. *The Effectiveness of the Family Planning Service in Barbados.* New York, 1958.

United Nations Programme of Technical Assistance. *Report on the Family Planning Programme in India,* prepared for the Government of India by a United Nations Advisory Mission. Report No. TAO/IND/48. New York: United Nations, 1966.

U.S. Agency for International Development. Population Branch. Health Service. *Assistance for Family Planning Programs in Developing Countries.* Washington, January 1967.

U.S. Public Health Service, National Institutes of Health. *A Survey of Research on Reproduction Related to Birth and Population Control* (as of December, 1962). Washington, D.C.

Urner, John B. *Fertility Reduction and Economic Growth in Underdeveloped Countries: Some General Considerations and Special Case Studies.* Chicago: Department of Photoduplication, University of Chicago Library, 1953.

Velayudhan, G. "Post Partum Sterilisation as a Method of Family Planning," *Journal of Family Welfare*, 9 (December 1962), 41–45.

Von Hofsten, Erland. *The Cost of a Child: Alternative Solutions. Proceedings of the World Population Conference: 1954*, Vol. VI. New York, 1955.

Wadia, Avabai B. "Some Thoughts on the Educational Programme for Family Planning," *Journal of Family Welfare* (Bombay), 11 (March 1965), 13–18.

Warburton, Dorothy, and F. Clark Fraser. "Spontaneous Abortion Risks in Man: Data From Reproductive Histories Collected in a Medical Genetics Unit," *American Journal of Human Genetics*, 16 (March 1964), 1–25.

Westoff, Charles F. "Fertility Control in the United States." Paper contributed for the United Nations World Population Conference, 1965.

Westoff, Charles F., and Edgar F. Borgatta. "Social and Psychological Factors Affecting Fertility: The Prediction of Planned Fertility," *Milbank Memorial Fund Quarterly*, 33 (January 1955), 50–62.

Westoff, Charles F., et al. *The Third Child: A Study in the Prediction of Fertility*. Princeton, N.J.: Princeton University Press, 1963.

Westoff, Charles F., and Robert G. Potter, Jr. *Family Growth in Metropolitan America*, Princeton, N. J.: Princeton University Press, 1961.

Westoff, Charles F., and Raymond H. Potvin. "Higher Education, Religion and Women's Family-size Orientations," *American Sociological Review*, 31(4) (August 1966), 489–496.

Whelpton, P. K., and Ronald Freedman. "A Study of the Growth of American Families," *American Journal of Sociology*, 61 (May 1956), 595–601.

White, P. E., A. Rasheed Ghazi, and Paul A. Harper. "Use of the Intra-Uterine Contraceptive Device in Rural West Pakistan," *Demography*, 3 (1966), 332–342.

Wichmann, A. A. "Burma: Agriculture, Population, and Buddhism," *American Journal of Economics and Sociology*, 24 (January 1965), 71–83.

Wishik, Samuel M. "Community Programs to Modify Family Size: Indications for Organization and Planning." Pp. 198–218 in Mindel C. Sheps and Jeanne C. Ridley (eds.). Pittsburgh, Pa.: University of Pittsburgh Press, 1965.

Wishik, Samuel M. "Designs for Family Planning Programs and Research in Developing Countries," *American Journal of Public Health and the Nation's Health*, 57 (1) (January 1967), 15–21.

World Health Organization, *Final Report on Pilot Studies in Family Planning*. New Delhi: W.H.O. Regional Office for South East Asia, 1954.

Wrigley, E. A. "Family Limitation in Pre-Industrial England," *Economic History Review*, 2nd series, 19(1) (April 1966), 82–109.

Yang, Jae Mo, et al. "Fertility and Family Planning in Rural Korea," *Population Studies*, 18 (March 1965), 237–250.

Yaukey, David. "Some Immediate Determinants of Fertility Differences in Lebanon," *Marriage and Family Living*, 25 (February 1963), 5–80.

Yerushalmy, J. "Religious, Educational, and Socio-Economic Factors Associated With Different Methods of Fertility Control." Paper contributed for the United Nations World Population Conference, 1965.

Yoneda, Akiko. "Trends in Artificial Termination of Pregnancy as Seen from the Results Obtained from the Questionnaire on Childbirth." Annual reports of the Institute of Population Problems, Tokyo, 1964.

Zaidi, W. H. "Attitude of Rural Population Towards Family Planning," *Journal of the Eastern Pakistan Academy of Village Development*, 1, 36–42.

Zalduondo, Celestina. "A Family Planning Program Using Volunteers as Health Indicators," *American Journal of Public Health and the Nation's Health*, 54 (February 1964), 301–307.

CHAPTER 21

Reproduction and Forecasts
of Future Population Growth

21.1. Introduction: Reproduction as a Synthesis of Growth Components

Preceding chapters (Chapters 16, 18, and 19) have been devoted to each of the components of population growth: mortality, fertility, and migration. The purpose of this chapter is to synthesize the principles developed there into a more refined and insightful understanding of the process of population growth. With these principles, the all-important topic of future growth is discussed. The principles are then used to study demography's most intricate problem: predicting the future course of population growth for the world, for individual nations, and for individual communities and localities within nations.

Chapter 3 introduced the topic of growth on an elementary level by uniting the three components of growth in one equation:

$$\text{increase} = \text{births} - \text{deaths} + \text{in-migrants} - \text{out-migrants}$$
$$= \text{reproductive change} + \text{net migration} \qquad (1)$$

This equation summarizes the amount of growth that results from the action of the components. The obvious next step is to calculate the rate of growth. This yields the familiar "demographic bookkeeping equation" introduced in Chapter 3:

$$\text{rate of increase} = \text{crude birthrate} - \text{crude death rate} + \text{in-}$$
$$\text{migration rate} - \text{out-migration rate} \qquad (2)$$
$$= \text{rate of reproductive change} + \text{rate of net}$$
$$\text{migration}$$

This equality holds when the rates are "crude rates" (rates per 1000 total population), because the denominators of the four rates are identical—the population at the midpoint of the span of time for which the rates are computed.

It would be easy to underestimate the utility and power of these simple rates. They may be used to give an exact summary of growth and growth rates that actually occur during a particular year or an intercensal period. In other words, they state what actually has happened to population size during an interval of time.

For refined analysis, however, these formulas are inadequate. It has been emphasized in the individual chapters on mortality, fertility, and migration that the rates for each of these events vary widely according to age. It has also been shown that populations differ widely in their age composition, or that the age composition of a particular population can fluctuate or evolve over time. Under these conditions, the crude growth may be very misleading. For example, a newly established frontier community or a newly built suburban subdivision on the edge of a metropolis may have very high crude birthrates and very low crude death rates because of young age composition—plus high rates of in-migration. On the other hand, a community such as Tampa, Florida, where the population is concentrated at the ages of retirement and beyond, may be expected to have very low crude birthrates, very high crude death rates, and a negligible rate of reproductive change. If we wish to compare the growth rates of a suburb and a retirement community, it is clear that in some way we should take account of differences in age composition. But it is clear that we cannot resolve this problem simply by substituting age-specific rates in Equation 2. Instead, it is necessary to construct models of population growth that simultaneously include all of the components. These more sophisticated models are the subject matter of this chapter.

21.2. The Net Reproduction Rate (NRR)

Let us establish an hypothetical cohort of 1000 newborn female infants and imagine that throughout their lives the members will be exposed to the mortality rates that are observed in the population for a particular year. Let us also assume that those who survive will bear children at the fertility rate observed for the population in the same year as that for which the death rates are observed. We then count the number of female infants borne by this cohort and express it as a ratio of the original cohort.[1]

If the ratio is 1, the population is exactly replacing itself. If the ratio is greater than 1, the population is growing. If the ratio is less than 1, the population is not replacing itself.

Thus the net reproduction rate, as this ratio is named, shows the long-term growth implications of present schedules of fertility and mortality rates. It combines into one figure the results of the simultaneous action of current age-specific fertility rates and age-specific mortality rates. It has a meaning that is simple and clear: it shows the relative size of a generation in relation to the generation that preceded it. Therefore, it is an intergenerational reproduction rate. The gross reproduction rate is the

net reproduction rate without the mortality component. It is a fertility measure only.

Table 21-1 presents net reproduction rates for various nations of the world for which estimates have been prepared. It is easily seen that there is wide variation between countries. For example, Japan (with a rate of 0.92) appears not to be reproducing itself. At the other extreme, Costa Rica has a rate of 3.34 (which calls for a trebling of population in each generation). It is the latter phenomenon that recently has caused such fright among demographers. One searches in vain the past reproductive history of European nations for such fantastically high reproductive rates. Yet rates of this magnitude are almost typical of most developing nations. Data of sufficient precision with which to calculate net reproduction rates for the developing nations are lacking. Yet if such rates could be calculated, they would almost certainly be concentrated between 2 and 3.5—which are in the zone of "explosive growth."

The net reproduction rate has a characteristic that has subjected it to criticism by many demographers: it tends to fluctuate widely over time within the same population.[2] For example, in Austria in 1931-1932 the NRR was only 0.89, whereas in 1960-1964 it was 1.35 in the same population. In Hungary in 1948-1949 the NRR was 1.08, in 1952-1954 it was 1.20, and then sank back to 1.07 in the next five years. Fluctuations such as these are due to three causes: (1) genuine fluctuation in fertility levels from year to year by populations that have it within their power to control fertility, (2) intergenerational changes in the age pattern of childbearing, and (3) variations in the coverage and quality of the basic data. The second of these is of especial concern, for theoretical reasons. If there is a lowering of the age at marriage, there is a resulting tendency for the NRR to rise because the birthrates for persons aged 15 to 19 and 20 to 24 will tend to rise. Even though those who marry early and bear children early may later curtail their fertility, this is not reflected immediately in the

---

[1] *The Manual of Demographic Research Techniques* describes the computational procedure and illustrates it.

[2] George J. Stolnitz and Norman B. Ryder, "Recent Discussions of the Net Reproduction Rate," *Population Index,* 15 (1949), 114–128.

Table 21-1 Measures of Fertility, Mortality, and Reproduction of Female Populations, Selected Nations of the World

Country	Years	Reproduction rate Gross	Reproduction rate Net	Mean age of fertility	Expectation of life at birth	Intrinsic r	Intrinsic b	Intrinsic d	Crude b	Crude d
North America										
Barbados..................	1956	1.97	-	-	-	-	-	-	-	-
	1957	2.01	-	-	-	-	-	-	-	-
	1958	2.0	-	-	-	-	-	-	-	-
	1960-64	1.93	-	-	-	-	-	-	-	-
Canada	1930-34	1.48	1.28	30.0	62.5	8.1	21.2	13.1	22.9	10.0
	1935-39	1.31	1.16	29.8	64.6	4.8	18.4	13.6	21.1	9.5
	1946-49	1.69	1.57	28.8	69.2	15.8	24.7	8.9	28.0	8.5
	1950-54	1.76	1.67	28.4	71.3	18.3	26.0	7.7	27.5	7.5
	1955-59	1.89	1.81	28.1	73.2	21.6	28.1	6.4	27.6	6.9
	1960	1.89	1.83	27.9	74.0	22.0	28.2	6.2	26.5	6.6
	1961	1.87	1.81	27.8	74.2	21.6	27.8	6.2	25.6	6.5
	1962	1.84	1.77	27.8	74.2	20.9	27.3	6.4	24.9	6.5
	1963	1.80	-	-	-	-	-	-	-	-
Costa Rica	1954	3.14	-	-	-	-	-	-	-	-
	1956	3.17	-	-	-	-	-	-	-	-
	1957	3.04	-	-	-	-	-	-	-	-
	1958	*3.05	-	-	-	-	-	-	-	-
	1959	3.38	-	-	-	-	-	-	-	-
	1960	3.58	-	-	-	-	-	-	-	-
	1962	3.32	-	-	-	-	-	-	-	-
	1963	3.53	-	-	-	-	-	-	-	-
	1964	3.34	-	-	-	-	-	-	-	-
Honduras..................	1955	2.78	-	-	-	-	-	-	-	-
	1956	2.67	-	-	-	-	-	-	-	-
	1957	2.77	-	-	-	-	-	-	-	-
Jamaica (ex. dep.).........	1949	1.87	-	-	-	-	-	-	-	-
	1950-54	2.04	-	-	-	-	-	-	-	-
	1955	2.23	-	-	-	-	-	-	-	-
Panama	1952	2.29	-	-	-	-	-	-	-	-
	1953	2.42	-	-	-	-	-	-	-	-
	1954	2.48	-	-	-	-	-	-	-	-
	1955-59	2.52	-	-	-	-	-	-	-	-
	1960-64	2.78	-	-	-	-	-	-	-	-
Trinidad and Tobago	1931	1.66	1.21	-	-	-	-	-	-	-
	1946	2.36	1.95	-	-	-	-	-	-	-
	1954	2.83	-	-	-	-	-	-	-	-
	1955-59	2.61	-	-	-	-	-	-	-	-
U.S., Continental	1946-49	1.51	1.42		69.9	13.5	22.8	9.4	24.2	8.5
	1950-54	1.63	1.55	-	71.7	16.8	24.7	7.9	24.0	8.1
	1955-59	1.80	1.73	-	72.8	21.1	27.7	6.6	23.9	8.0
	1960	1.78	1.72	-	73.1	20.8	27.4	6.6	22.8	8.1
	1961	1.77	1.70	-	73.6	20.5	27.1	6.6	22.4	7.9
	1962	1.70	1.63	-	73.4	18.8	25.8	7.0	21.5	8.1
	1963	1.62	1.56	-	73.4	17.1	24.6	7.5	20.8	8.2
Whites...................	1946-49	1.48	1.40	-	70.9	12.7	22.0	9.2	23.5	8.4
	1950-54	1.56	1.50	-	72.8	15.4	23.5	8.0	22.9	7.9
	1955-59	1.73	1.67	-	73.7	19.5	26.3	6.8	22.7	7.9
	1960	1.72	1.66	-	74.1	19.5	26.2	6.7	21.7	8.0
	1961	1.70	1.65	-	74.5	19.1	25.8	6.7	21.3	7.8
	1962	1.63	1.58	-	74.4	17.4	24.6	7.1	20.6	8.0
	1963	1.56	1.51	-	74.4	15.6	23.2	7.7	19.8	8.1
Nonwhites................	1946-49	1.78	1.54	-	62.0	18.8	29.0	10.2	30.4	10.1
	1950-54	2.07	1.84	-	64.0	25.7	33.8	8.1	32.8	9.5
	1955-59	2.33	2.11	-	65.8	30.7	37.6	6.8	33.4	8.9
	1960	2.24	2.04	-	66.3	29.2	36.1	6.9	30.8	8.7
	1961	2.24	2.10	-	67.0	29.2	35.9	6.7	30.4	8.4
	1962	2.17	2.03	-	66.8	27.9	34.8	6.9	29.3	8.5
	1963	2.10	1.97	-	66.5	26.7	33.8	7.1	28.4	8.7
South America										
British Guiana............ (excl. Amerindians)........	1954	2.83	-	-	-	-	-	-	-	-
	1955	2.89	-	-	-	-	-	-	-	-
Chile....................	1930-34	2.14	-	-	-	-	-	-	-	-
	1936-39	2.03	-	-	-	-	-	-	-	-
	1940-43	2.04	-	-	-	-	-	-	-	-
	1952	2.07	-	-	-	-	-	-	-	-
	1959	2.16	-	-	-	-	-	-	-	-
	1960-64	2.25	-	-	-	-	-	-	-	-

Table 21-1   (*Continued*)

Country	Years	Reproduction rate		Mean age of fertility	Expectation of life at birth	Vital rates of female population				
						Intrinsic			Crude	
		Gross	Net			r	b	d	b	d
Venezuela..................	1959	3.11	-	-	-	-	-	-	-	-
	1960	3.14	-	-	-	-	-	-	-	-
	1961	3.12	-	-	-	-	-	-	-	-
	1962	3.00	-	-	-	-	-	-	-	-
	1963	3.04	-	-	-	-	-	-	-	-
Europe										
Austria....................	1931-32	0.89	0.74	-	-	-	-	-	-	-
	1951	0.99	-	-	-	-	-	-	-	-
	1952	0.99	-	-	-	-	-	-	-	-
	1953	1.01	-	-	-	-	-	-	-	-
	1954	1.02	-	-	-	-	-	-	-	-
	1955-59	1.19	-	-	-	-	-	-	-	-
	1960-64	1.35	-	-	-	-	-	-	-	-
Belgium....................	1939	1.02	0.90	28.9	63.6	-3.9	13.6	17.5	15.0	13.0
	1946-49	1.19	1.08	29.0	67.3	2.6	16.5	13.8	16.9	12.0
	1950-54	1.13	1.06	28.7	69.1	1.9	15.5	13.7	15.9	11.3
	1955-59	1.20	1.14	28.2	71.4	4.6	16.6	12.0	16.2	10.9
	1960	1.24	1.20	28.0	73.0	6.3	17.3	11.0	16.1	11.3
	1961	1.28	1.24	28.0	73.5	7.7	18.1	10.4	16.4	10.6
	1962	1.26	-	-	-	-	-	-	-	-
	1963	1.30	-	-	-	-	-	-	-	-
Bulgaria..................	1956-57	1.12	1.01	-	-	-	-	-	-	-
	1960-64	1.09	-	-	-	-	-	-	-	-
Czechoslovakia.............	1950-54	1.43	1.32	27.4	67.8	9.1	20.4	11.3	20.7	10.8
	1955-59	1.30	1.23	26.7	71.1	7.9	18.7	10.8	17.5	9.0
	1960	1.16	1.12	26.0	73.1	4.1	16.0	11.9	15.1	8.5
	1961	1.16	1.11	26.0	73.1	4.0	16.0	12.0	15.1	8.5
	1962	1.14	1.09	25.9	72.8	3.3	15.7	12.3	14.9	9.3
	1963	1.22	-	-	-	-	-	-	-	-
Denmark....................	1930-34	1.06	0.93	29.4	63.6	-2.7	14.3	17.0	17.2	10.9
	1935-39	1.04	0.93	28.8	65.4	-2.5	14.0	16.5	17.0	10.5
	1946-49	1.36	1.27	28.4	70.0	8.4	19.4	11.0	20.3	9.1
	1950-54	1.24	1.18	27.6	72.0	6.0	17.3	11.4	17.2	8.8
	1955-59	1.24	1.19	27.1	73.5	6.5	17.3	10.8	16.2	8.5
	1960	1.24	1.20	27.0	73.8	6.7	17.4	10.7	16.1	8.9
	1961	1.24	1.20	27.0	74.4	6.9	17.4	10.5	16.0	8.7
	1962	1.24	1.20	29.6	74.4	7.0	17.4	10.5	16.2	9.0
	1963	1.28	1.24	26.9	74.4	8.2	18.2	10.0	17.0	9.0
Estonia....................	1931-34	0.96	0.77	-	-	-	-	-	-	-
Finland....................	1936-39	1.19	0.99	30.4	60.0	-0.2	16.6	16.8	19.3	12.6
	1946-49	1.66	1. 8	29.6	65.4	13.5	24.1	10.6	25.3	10.3
	1950-54	1.47	1.37	29.3	69.0	10.7	21.1	10.4	21.3	9.0
	1955-59	1.38	1.31	28.7	71.2	9.5	19.7	10.2	18.7	8.5
	1960	1.32	1.26	28.4	71.6	8.1	18.7	10.6	17.5	8.3
France....................	1935-37	1.00	0.87	-	-	-5.0	-	-	-	14.3
	1946-50	1.45	1.32	-	-	9.8	-	-	-	-
	1951-55	1.33	1.25	-	-	8.1	-	-	-	-
	1956-60	1.32	1.27	-	-	8.6	-	-	-	-
	1960	1.33	1.29	-	73.8	9.2	-	-	-	-
	1961	1.38	1.33	-	74.5	10.4	-	-	-	-
	1962	1.36	1.31	-	74.1	10.0	-	-	-	10.9
	1963	1.41	1.36	-	74.1	11.4	-	-	-	11.0
	1964	1.42	1.37	-	75.1	11.7	-	-	-	10.1
Germany....................	1933	-	0.71	-	-	-11.6	10.4	22.0	-	-
Democratic Rep.............	1952-54	1.15	1.07	26.8	69.3	2.2	15.8	13.6	14.3	11.0
(incl. East Berlin)........	1955	1.13	1.06	26.4	70.3	1.9	15.4	13.4	14.3	11.0
Federal Rep................	1947-49	-	0.90	-	-	-3.4	13.7	17.1	-	-
	1950-54	-	-	-	-	-2.4	13.7	16.1	-	-
	1955	-	-	-	-	-1.7	14.1	15.8	-	-
	1956	-	-	-	-	-0.1	15.0	15.1	-	-
	1957	-	1.07	-	-	2.4	16.0	13.6	-	-
	1958	-	1.07	-	-	2.3	15.8	13.5	-	-
	1959	-	1.11	-	-	3.5	16.4	12.9	-	-
	1960	-	1.11	-	-	3.8	16.5	12.8	-	-
	1961	-	-	-	-	4.5	16.9	12.5	-	-
	1962	-	1.13	-	-	5.6	17.6	12.0	-	-
	1963	-	-	-	-	-	-	-	-	-
Greece....................	1931-32	1.87	1.25	-	-	-	-	-	-	-

Table 21-1   (*Continued*)

Country	Years	Reproduction rate Gross	Reproduction rate Net	Mean age of fertility	Expectation of life at birth	Intrinsic r	Intrinsic b	Intrinsic d	Crude b	Crude d
Hungary	1930-31	1.38	1.03	27.0	51.8	1.1	20.2	19.0	23.3	15.2
	1948-49	1.24	1.08	27.3	63.2	2.7	17.4	14.8	19.3	10.6
	1952-54	1.32	1.20	27.0	67.1	6.6	19.0	12.4	20.0	10.7
	1955-59	1.15	1.07	26.2	69.2	2.3	15.9	13.6	16.6	9.7
	1960	0.98	0.91	25.6	69.6	-3.9	12.4	16.4	13.7	9.6
	1961	0.94	0.88	25.8	70.2	-5.1	11.7	16.8	13.1	9.1
	1962	0.87	-	-	-	-	-	-	-	-
	1963	0.88	-	-	-	-	-	-	-	-
Ireland	1935-37	1.43	1.19	-	-	-	-	-	-	-
	1940-42	1.41	1.20	-	-	-	-	-	-	-
	1945-47	1.63	1.40	-	-	-	-	-	-	-
	1950-52	1.60	1.47	-	-	-	-	-	-	-
	1955	1.59	-	-	-	-	-	-	-	-
	1960	1.86	-	-	-	-	-	-	-	-
	1961	1.83	-	-	-	-	-	-	-	-
	1962	1.90	-	-	-	-	-	-	-	-
	1963	1.90	-	-	-	-	-	-	-	-
Italy	1936-39	1.46	1.17	29.8	57.8	5.3	20.9	15.6	22.5	13.5
	1946-49	1.36	1.14	29.7	61.3	4.5	19.2	14.7	21.0	10.8
	1950-54	1.16	1.02	29.3	64.6	0.4	15.8	15.4	17.3	9.2
	1959	1.14	-	-	-	-	-	-	-	-
	1960	1.15	1.10	29.2	72.7	3.2	15.7	12.4	17.3	8.8
	1961	1.18	1.13	29.2	72.9	4.0	16.0	12.0	17.5	8.4
	1962	1.20	1.15	29.1	73.4	4.7	16.3	11.6	17.6	9.2
	1963	1.23	1.18	29.0	73.4	5.6	16.8	11.2	17.8	9.2
Latvia	1929-31	1.09	0.89	-	-	-	-	-	-	-
	1934-36	1.01	0.84	-	-	-	-	-	-	-
Netherlands	1930-34	1.37	1.22	31.2	65.9	6.4	19.1	12.7	20.5	8.7
	1935-39	1.26	1.15	31.0	67.7	4.5	17.4	12.9	19.3	8.4
	1946-49	1.73	1.63	31.2	71.3	15.8	24.1	8.3	25.7	7.7
	1950-54	1.49	1.43	30.8	73.2	11.7	20.8	9.1	21.4	7.2
	1955-59	1.50	1.45	30.2	74.6	12.5	21.0	8.5	20.6	7.0
	1960	1.52	1.47	29.8	74.8	13.3	21.4	8.1	20.1	7.0
	1961	1.56	1.52	29.7	75.2	14.3	22.1	7.8	20.6	6.9
	1962	1.55	1.51	29.6	75.7	14.0	21.8	7.8	20.2	7.1
	1963	1.55	1.51	29.4	75.7	14.3	22.0	7.7	20.2	7.1
Norway	1930-34	0.97	0.85	31.2	66.2	-5.2	12.3	17.6	14.9	10.3
	1935-39	0.90	0.80	30.6	68.2	-7.4	11.0	18.4	14.3	10.1
	1946-49	1.26	1.19	30.4	72.4	5.7	17.1	11.4	20.1	9.1
	1950-54	1.24	1.18	29.4	74.3	5.8	16.8	11.0	18.0	8.5
	1955-59	1.37	1.32	28.6	75.4	9.6	19.0	9.4	17.6	8.4
	1960	1.38	1.33	28.4	75.6	10.2	19.3	9.1	16.8	8.6
	1961	1.40	1.36	28.0	75.6	11.0	19.8	8.8	16.7	8.6
Poland	1932-34	1.58	1.15	30.4	51.4	4.6	22.7	18.2	-	14.3
	1950-54	1.77	1.54	28.8	63.9	15.3	26.1	10.8	27.9	9.9
	1955-59	1.66	1.53	28.1	69.0	15.3	24.5	9.2	25.2	8.4
	1960	1.44	1.35	27.6	70.5	10.9	20.9	10.0	20.8	7.0
	1961	1.36	1.28	27.4	70.5	8.9	19.6	10.7	19.6	7.0
	1962	1.30	-	-	-	-	-	-	-	-
	1963	1.30	-	-	-	-	-	-	-	-
Portugal	1930-33	1.87	1.29	30.8	49.5	8.4	26.6	18.3	27.5	16.0
	1935, 1938-39	1.70	1.21	30.8	51.3	6.1	24.0	17.9	25.1	14.9
	1946-49	1.57	1.24	30.4	58.2	7.1	22.0	15.0	23.6	13.1
	1950-54	1.49	1.23	30.2	61.6	6.9	20.8	13.9	22.4	11.2
	1955-59	1.43	1.23	30.1	64.7	7.0	19.9	12.9	22.5	10.9
	1960	1.52	1.33	29.6	66.4	9.8	21.4	11.6	22.4	10.1
Spain	1922	2.01	-	-	-	-	-	-	-	-
	1932	1.79	-	-	-	-	-	-	-	-
	1937	1.44	-	-	-	-	-	-	-	-
	1940-41	1.42	-	-	-	-	-	-	-	-
	1943	1.43	-	-	-	-	-	-	-	-
Sweden	1930-34	0.87	0.77	30.0	65.1	-8.8	11.0	19.7	13.8	11.8
	1935-39	0.86	0.78	29.5	66.8	-8.8	10.6	19.4	14.0	11.8
	1946-49	1.20	1.14	28.6	71.4	4.4	16.6	12.2	17.9	10.2
	1950-54	1.08	1.03	27.9	73.1	1.1	14.4	13.2	14.9	9.5
	1955-59	1.09	1.06	27.6	74.3	1.8	14.7	12.9	13.9	9.2
	1960	1.06	1.03	27.6	74.9	0.8	14.2	13.4	13.3	9.5
	1961	1.07	1.05	27.5	75.4	1.4	14.1	12.7	13.4	9.2
	1962	1.09	1.07	27.3	75.6	2.3	14.5	12.2	13.8	9.5
	1963	1.13	1.10	27.3	75.8	3.5	15.1	11.6	14.3	9.4
	1964	1.21	1.18	27.2	75.9	6.1	16.6	10.5	15.6	9.3

Table 21-1 *(Continued)*

Country	Years	Reproduction rate		Mean age of fertility	Expectation of life at birth	Vital rates of female population				
		Gross	Net			Intrinsic			Crude	
						r	b	d	b	d
Switzerland...............	1932	0.96	0.84	30.5	63.6	-5.9	12.6	18.5	15.7	11.7
	1936-39	0.87	0.77	30.1	65.4	-8.7	10.9	19.6	11.5	8.8
	1946-49	1.28	1.18	29.7	69.1	5.7	17.8	12.1	18.1	10.6
	1950-54	1.14	1.08	29.4	71.6	2.3	15.4	13.1	16.4	9.6
	1955-59	1.13	1.09	29.0	73.4	2.7	15.2	12.5	16.5	9.2
	1960	1.19	1.15	28.7	74.1	4.8	16.2	11.4	16.7	9.1
	1961	1.21	1.18	28.6	74.1	5.6	16.7	11.0	17.4	8.6
	1962	1.20	1.16	28.6	74.1	5.3	16.5	11.2	17.5	9.0
United Kingdom										
England and Wales..........	1930-34	0.89	0.78	29.9	63.4	-8.7	11.3	20.0	14.4	11.3
	1935-39	0.88	0.78	29.2	65.5	-8.6	10.9	19.6	13.9	11.3
	1946-49	1.19	1.12	28.6	70.6	3.9	16.4	12.5	17.4	10.8
	1950-54	1.06	1.01	28.0	72.0	0.2	14.1	13.9	14.5	10.9
	1955-59	1.17	1.13	27.7	73.5	4.3	16.1	11.8	14.9	10.9
	1960	1.29	1.25	27.5	74.1	8.0	18.2	10.2	16.1	10.9
	1961	1.35	1.30	27.4	73.8	9.7	19.3	9.6	16.9	11.3
	1962	1.38	1.33	27.4	73.9	10.6	19.8	9.2	16.9	11.3
	1963	1.39	1.34	27.4	74.0	10.9	20.0	9.1	17.2	11.6
Scotland....................	1935-39	1.06	0.91	29.0	62.4	-3.2	14.3	17.5	16.6	12.5
	1946-49	1.35	1.23	29.0	67.3	7.1	19.2	12.1	18.8	11.8
	1950-54	1.20	1.12	28.6	69.5	3.7	16.6	12.9	16.6	11.5
	1955-59	1.31	1.24	28.0	71.2	7.6	18.6	11.0	17.6	11.2
	1960	1.40	1.34	27.8	71.9	10.4	20.2	9.8	18.3	11.1
	1961	1.42	1.35	27.8	71.9	10.8	20.5	9.7	18.2	11.5
	1962	1.45	1.38	27.7	71.9	11.9	21.2	9.3	18.8	11.3
	1963	1.47	1.40	27.7	71.9	12.3	21.5	9.1	18.5	11.6
	1964	1.49	1.43	27.7	72.8	13.1	21.8	8.7	18.7	10.8
Yugoslavia.................	1949	2.00	1.61	29.4	57.8	16.5	29.4	12.9	28.0	12.3
	1950-54	1.88	1.54	28.9	58.8	15.1	27.8	12.7	27.1	11.9
	1955-59	1.40	1.21	28.0	63.1	6.8	20.2	13.4	23.3	10.2
	1960	1.36	1.21	27.6	65.3	6.8	19.6	12.8	22.3	9.7
	1961	1.33	1.18	27.4	65.3	6.0	19.1	13.1	21.6	8.8
	1962	1.30	1.16	27.3	65.6	5.5	18.6	13.1	20.8	.9.7
Asia										
Cyprus.....................	1948-50	1.99	1.84	30.3	68.8	20.5	28.4	7.9	29.0	7.9
	1951-53	1.78	-	-	-	-	-	-	-	-
	1955-59	1.69	-	-	-	-	-	-	-	-
	1960-64	1.66	-	-	-	-	-	-	-	-
Hong Kong..................	1956	2.31	-	-	-	-	-	-	-	-
	1957	2.23	-	-	-	-	-	-	-	-
	1958	2.37	-	-	-	-	-	-	-	-
	1959	2.33	-	-	-	-	-	-	-	-
	1960	2.49	-	-	-	-	-	-	-	-
	1961	2.46	-	-	-	-	-	-	-	-
	1962	2.46	-	-	-	-	-	-	-	-
Israel, Total population.....	1955-59	1.89	-	-	-	-	-	-	-	-
	1960	1.91	-	-	-	-	-	-	-	-
	1961	1.84	-	-	-	-	-	-	-	-
	1962	2.36	-	-	-	-	-	-	-	-
	1963	2.08	-	-	-	-	-	-	-	-
Jews......................	1949	1.66	-	-	-	-	-	-	-	-
	1950-54	1.88	-	-	-	-	-	-	-	-
	1955-59	1.73	-	-	-	-	-	-	-	-
	1960	1.69	1.62	-	-	-	-	-	-	-
	1961	1.63	1.58	-	-	-	-	-	-	-
	1962	1.60	1.54	-	-	-	-	-	-	-
	1963	1.63	1.57	-	-	-	-	-	-	-
Japan.....................	1930-34	2.32	1.62	30.4	48.2	16.2	33.7	17.5	31.7	17.7
	1935-39	2.08	1.49	30.6	49.8	13.2	30.2	17.0	30.0	16.4
	1947-49	2.13	1.72	30.2	57.8	18.4	30.7	12.4	32.0	11.9
	1950-54	1.46	1.30	29.4	65.1	8.9	21.0	12.1	22.5	8.8
	1955-59	1.04	0.96	28.5	68.6	-1.7	13.7	15.4	17.3	7.2
	1960	0.96	0.90	27.9	70.3	-3.8	12.3	16.1	16.4	6.9
	1961	0.94	0.89	27.8	70.8	-4.4	11.9	16.3	16.1	6.7
	1962	0.95	0.90	27.8	71.2	-4.0	12.1	16.0	16.2	6.8
	1963	0.96	0.92	27.8	72.3	-3.0	12.3	15.3	16.6	6.4
Thailand..................	1947-49	1.74	1.30	-	-	-	-	-	-	-
	1950-54	2.06	-	-	-	-	-	-	-	-

Table 21-1   (Continued)

Country	Years	Reproduction rate		Mean age of fertility	Expectation of life at birth	Vital rates of female population				
		Gross	Net			Intrinsic			Crude	
						r	b	d	b	d
Africa										
Algeria										
Non-Algerian population...	1948-49	1.40	-	-	-	-	-	-	-	-
	1950	1.34	-	-	-	-	-	-	-	-
	1951	....	-	-	-	-	-	-	-	-
	1952	1.30	-	-	-	-	-	-	-	-
	1953	1.24	-	-	-	-	-	-	-	-
Mauritius.................	1952	3.12	2.38	-	-	-	-	-	-	-
	1955	2.80	-	-	-	-	-	-	-	-
South Africa										
Coloureds.................	1945-49	3.14	-	-	-	-	-	-	-	-
	1950-54	3.18	-	-	-	-	-	-	-	-
	1955-59	3.10	-	-	-	-	-	-	-	-
Whites....................	1945-49	1.65	-	-	-	-	-	-	-	-
	1950-54	1.64	-	-	-	-	-	-	-	-
	1955-59	1.70	-	-	-	-	-	-	-	-
Southern Rhodesia										
European Population........	1951	1.77	-	-	-	-	-	-	-	-
Indigenous Population......	1954	2.9	-	-	-	-	-	-	-	-
South West Africa										
Coloureds.................	1960	3.28	-	-	-	-	-	-	-	-
Whites....................	1960	1.95	-	-	-	-	-	-	-	-
United Arab Rep.										
Egypt.....................	1937	3.11	1.44	-	-	-	-	-	-	-
Oceania										
Australia.................	1930-34	1.11	1.02	28.8	66.9	0.2	15.3	15.0	17.4	7.9
	1935-39	1.06	0.98	28.4	67.9	-1.0	14.2	15.3	17.0	8.5
	1946-49	1.46	1.38	28.3	70.8	11.5	21.2	9.7	22.8	8.7
	1950-54	1.53	1.46	28.1	72.1	13.5	22.3	8.8	22.7	8.3
	1955-59	1.64	1.57	27.9	72.8	16.4	24.3	7.8	22.3	7.8
	1960	1.68	1.62	27.5	74.2	17.9	24.9	7.0	22.2	7.7
	1961	1.72	1.67	27.5	74.2	19.0	25.7	6.8	22.7	7.5
	1962	1.66	1.61	27.5	74.2	17.5	24.6	7.1	21.9	7.8
	1963	1.62	1.57	27.5	74.2	16.6	24.0	7.4	21.4	7.8
Fiji Islands										
Fiji population............	1949	2.08	-	-	-	-	-	-	-	-
	1950-54	2.15	-	-	-	-	-	-	-	-
	1955-59	2.22	-	-	-	-	-	-	-	-
	1960-64	2.35	-	-	-	-	-	-	-	-
Indian population..........	1949	3.03	-	-	-	-	--	-	-	-
	1950-54	3.00	-	-	-	-	-	-	-	-
	1955-59	3.13	-	-	-	-	-	-	-	-
	1960-64	2.77	-	-	-	-	-	-	-	-
New Zealand...............	1930-34	1.10	1.01	29.6	68.0	0.1	14.8	14.8	-	-
	1935-39	1.07	0.99	29.2	68.7	-0.6	14.3	14.9	-	-
	1946-49	1.64	1.55	29.0	71.5	15.2	23.6	8.4	24.9	8.4
	1950-54	1.69	1.62	28.3	72.7	17.3	24.9	7.6	23.9	8.3
	1955-59	1.89	1.82	27.9	73.9	21.9	28.1	6.2	24.3	8.1
	1960	1.97	1.91	27.7	74.5	23.8	29.4	5.6	24.4	7.9
	1961	2.03	-	-	-	-	-	-	-	-
	1962	2.00	1.94	27.5	73.8	24.5	30.1	5.6	25.7	8.0
	1963	-	-	-	-	-	-	-	-	-
	1964	1.83	1.77	27.4	73.8	21.2	27.5	6.3	23.4	7.9

This table presents female reproduction rates, the mean age of the female fertility schedule, the female expectation of life at birth, intrinsic vital rates, and crude vital rates for the female population, for dates since 1930. In calculating intrinsic rates, fertility and mortality schedules for the same period have been employed, so that these rates often differ from those published earlier. The intrinsic rates are based on model stable populations, and the required data are the gross reproduction rate, the mean age of the fertility schedule, and the expectation of life at birth. Where necessary, the mean age of fertility and expectation of life at birth have been estimated by interpolation between published values for nearby years. For a decription of the method of calculation see the Current Item note, in Population Index, Vol. 31, No. 2., April 1965, pp. 139-140. Sources are listed on pp. 304 to 309, below. For countries for which these calculations have not as yet been made we show the gross reproduction rates collected by the United Nations Statistical Office, with their associated net rates if these pertain to the same year as the life table used in their computation.

NRR, because it is computed from cross-sectional data. Conversely, a postponement of marriage to a later age can cause the NRR to slow or show a decline, although those who marry late may space their children closer together and continue childbearing to a later age. Thus the basic assumption that a given year's birthrates may be taken as typical of the fertility behavior of a whole life-span of a real cohort is challenged by many.

It would be shortsighted to reject the NRR completely as a demographic tool. Once its weaknesses and biases are known, it is possible to evaluate its fluctuations more adequately. The following points are worthy of consideration.

1. For most developing nations that have experienced prolonged high birthrates there are no major fertility fluctuations and no distorted age distributions, with the result that the NRR tends to yield the same value year after year, unless there is a genuine decline in fertility or mortality or both.

2. In many developing nations there is a tendency to postpone marriage. This would tend to cause the NRR to decline, at least temporarily. In other nations (especially in Latin America) there is a tendency for marriage to be regularized into more permanent unions. This would tend to cause a rise in NRR.

3. In most industrialized nations, marriage age has declined in recent years. This would tend to cause a temporary rise in NRR by increasing fertility rates at the younger ages.

4. The cohort changes that distort the NRR occur primarily at ages under 20 and over 35. These ages exert only a modest effect on the value of NRR, and it is possible to calculate NRR with a variety of values of these rates, adjusted for presumed intergenerational effects. If there is a net raising or lowering of fertility among women aged 20 to 34, it is likely to signal a genuine change in fertility level.

21.3. The Stable Population and Intrinsic Rates

The NRR suffers from another deficiency that often has been noted—it is expressed as an intergenerational rate that is not a fixed time span. In some populations the interval of time that represents a generation may be much longer than in other populations. The mean age of the mother at the time of childbearing is a measure of the length of a generation. This measure is reported for selected countries in Table 21-1. It is clear that there is substantial country-to-country variation, ranging from 25.8 years in Hungary to 29 in Italy. If data were available for India and Pakistan, the range would undoubtedly be much larger. One way to correct for this variation in the length of a generation is to express growth on an annual basis, instead of a per generation basis. The intrinsic rates, described below, do this.

Another drawback of the NRR is that it presumes an age composition of the population specified by a current life table. Actually, the life table age composition is that of a stationary population where the death rate equals the birthrate. Where the population is growing very rapidly or declining rapidly, this is an inappropriate assumption. Instead, it would appear more realistic to use an age composition that is consistent with the schedule of birth and death rates being used.

In an article that is perhaps the most famous single bit of demographic writing Alfred J. Lotka proposed a model that employed an age composition that is consistent with the vital rates and expressed reproductive change on an annual instead of a generational basis.[3] This model is the "stable population" or "intrinsic rates" model. Lotka demonstrated that if a given combination of birth and death rates were to remain in effect for a sustained period of time, a population with a characteristic age composition would emerge, and that this age composition would remain unchanged (stable) indefinitely so long as the rates remained unchanged. This stable age composition is the basis for estimating the number of women of childbearing age in the population for calculating the intrinsic rate of increase. The Lotka model also calculates the mean length of a generation and uses this value to express reproduction on an annual rather than a per generation basis. As a result, the intrinsic or "true"

[3] Alfred J. Lotka, "On the True Rate of Natural Increase," *Journal of the American Statistical Association*, **20** (1925), 305–339.

rate is theoretically free of the two major computational limitations of the NRR.

However, the intrinsic rate of increase is subject to all of the other limitations and biases of the NRR—its tendency to be affected by intercohort changes in age pattern of childbearing and changes in age at marriage. It fluctuates as widely over time as the NRR, and for the same reasons.

The stable population model provides not only a measure of intrinsic rate of increase, but also an intrinsic birthrate and an intrinsic death rate. These are the crude birth and death rates that would result if a given combination of schedules of birth and death were to persist in a population until the condition of stable age composition had evolved. Table 20-1 presents these rates for selected nations. A comparison of the actual current crude birthrate and death rate with the intrinsic rates shows that they can be very unlike in some instances. For example, Japan shows the following discrepancy:

	Crude rates	*Intrinsic rates*
Birthrate	16.6	12.3
Death rate	6.4	15.3
Reproduction rate	10.2	−3.0

Although Japan was growing at the rate of 1 percent per year in 1965, the stable population analysis indicated that on the long-term basis it was not reproducing itself, but would eventually undergo a population decline if current fertility and mortality rates persisted.

Despite the criticisms that have been made of the NRR and the intrinsic rates, these are highly useful techniques for synthesizing into summary measures current schedules of age-specific fertility and mortality rates and showing their implications for population growth. The facts that demographic conditions are changing and that the use of age-specific rates to represent a hypothetical cohort is only a crude way of looking at reproductive behavior should counsel caution in use but not abandonment. These techniques are not intended to be interpreted as predictions of what *will* happen, but as indicators of what *would* happen *if* a particular set of conditions were to continue.

There has been a tendency to overlook the fact that the rather violent fluctuations that these rates have shown in recent decades have been a genuine reflection of the markedly erratic reproductive behavior of the industrialized nations. The amplitude of the swings may be exaggerated somewhat by these measures, but the timing and direction of the swings tend to be valid.

21.4. Population Projections: Components-of-Growth Method

One of the highest ambitions of demographers long has been to be able to predict with precision what the population of a nation, state, or city will be at some specified future date. The need for such estimates is felt by a wide variety of "practical" persons: market analysts, economists, planners, public administrators, and other professional persons whose decisions are affected by the rate of population growth and the size of the population. When population growth is viewed as a single entity and is expressed as a single rate, the only type of forecast that is available is the extrapolation of this growth rate or some assumed change in the growth rate to the future.

When growth is subdivided into its components, however, the door is opened for much more elaborate and much more detailed forecasts. Various combinations of assumptions may be made about the future course of birth, death, and migration rates separately, and the implications may be scheduled out. The procedure for doing this was first developed in detail by P. K. Whelpton.[4]

The details for forecasting population by the components procedure are described in the *Manual of Demographic Research Techniques*. The subject is not a complicated one, but involves a series of steps that need only be listed here without technical details.

1. Establish a base population as of the date for which the forecast begins.

2. Establish a schedule of vital rates that are estimated to be in effect at the date to which

[4] P. K. Whelpton, "An Empirical Method of Calculating Future Population," *Journal of the American Statistical Association,* 1936.

the base population refers—birth, death, migration rates.

3. Establish an estimating cycle (usually 5 years) and provide an estimated schedule of age-specific birth, death, and migration rates that will be expected to apply during the next cycle period following the base date.

4. Multiply the rates by the base population. This yields estimates of the number of births, deaths, and migrants that will occur during the next cycle period.

5. Add (or subtract) these components to the base population, using the demographic bookkeeping equation. In doing this keep in mind that the population ages as the cycle progresses, so that persons aged x at the beginning of the cycle are aged x plus 5 at the end of the cycle. This yields an estimate of what the population will be at the end of the cycle.

Steps 1 through 5 may be repeated for as many cycles as desired, to reach the estimated population as of some future date.

The validity of these estimates, of course, depends entirely on how successfully the estimator is able to anticipate future changes in mortality, fertility, and migration rates. In most instances it is easier to forecast the future course of mortality rates than that of fertility rates. In making forecasts for an entire nation, migration tends to be only a small component of growth. This means that the critical element in national forecasts is the fertility rate. In making forecasts for states, provinces, metropolitan areas, or local communities the component of migration also becomes highly important and often outweighs fertility in importance. For this reason, it is much more difficult to obtain precision in making local forecasts than in making national ones.

Because demographers are seldom confident that they can specify a single most likely schedule of future rates, they are inclined to "bracket" the future course of growth by making three estimates: a "high," a "low," and an "intermediate" estimate. In general, it is presumed that the future course of growth will not be greater than the high estimate nor lower than the low estimate and that the intermediate estimate is the "best guess" of what actually will happen.

21.5.   Estimates of Future Growth of World Population

One of the greatest demographic achievements of the Population Division of the United Nations has been to prepare forecasts of the future growth of the world's population, by major regions. When it was first launched in the early 1950s, this task appeared to many to be impossible to accomplish, for the United Nations proposed to use the refined components method rather than simple arithmetic extrapolation. At that time the components of population growth were unknown for most of the world's nations. Not only were birth and death data lacking, but the censuses for most developing nations were seriously deficient. Before it could undertake the task, the United Nations was forced to work out procedures for estimating the components of growth from highly inadequate and fragmentary data. With great patience, by skillful work and new techniques developed especially for the purpose, the first major set of worldwide projections using the components method was prepared. These were published in a report, "The Past and Future Growth of World Population —A Long View," in 1952.[5] The findings literally "shook the world," for they indicated that by almost any reasonable set of assumptions the world was in a state of runaway population growth. Chapter 3 has already presented some of the information from this and later projections, and in Chapter 1 we quoted from the United Nations report to show how alarming the prospects for future growth appeared at that time. These projections indicated that the world's population would double, from 3 to 6 billion persons, between 1965 and 2000. Thus within the short span of 35 years it would add 3 billion inhabitants—the number that it had taken millions of years to accumulate thus far.

The world population conference of 1954, held in Rome, took these results as its central theme. Somewhat refined and revised, these estimates were published in full detail in a

[5] United Nations, "The Past and Future Growth of World Population—A Long View," *Population Bulletin of the United Nations*, No. 1, New York, 1952.

Table 21-2   United Nations Population Projections or World Population by "High", "Medium" and "Low" Assumptions, 1957 and 1966 Estimates

Date and level	1960	1970	1980	1990	2000
		Population (Millions)			
1966 report:					
"High".............	2,998	3,659	4,551	5,690	6,994
"Medium"..........	2,998	3,592	4,330	5,188	6,130
"Low"..............	2,998	3,545	4,147	4,783	5,449
1957 projections:					
"High".............	2,920	3,500	4,280	5,360	6,900
"Medium"..........	2,910	3,480	4,220	5,140	6,280
"Low".............	2,900	3,350	3,850	4,370	4,880
		Decennial increase (Percent)			
1966 report:					
"High".............		22	24	25	23
"Medium"..........		20	21	20	18
"Low"..............		18	17	15	14
1957 projections:					
"High".............		20	22	25	29
"Medium"..........		20	21	22	22
"Low"..............		16	15	14	12

Source: United Nations. World Population Prospects, Department of Economic and Social Affairs, Population Studies, No. 41., New York, 1966, pp 15.

report, *The Future Growth of World Population*.[6] Actually this report was a synthesis of a series of monographic reports that estimated the future population growth of the major world regions.[7]

This report anticipated a total population of 6.3 billion by the year 2000, which represented a doubling of the population in the 40 years from 1960 to the end of the century. (A set of "high" estimates that called for more than 7 billion persons by the year 2000 were also reported. Also, a "low" set of population projections were made, which anticipated a population of 4.9 billion by the year 2000. The "high" assumptions anticipated comparatively little fertility decline, while the "low" assumptions anticipated a substantial fertility decline toward the end of this century.) Estimated

future population in 1975 was reported for each individual nation.

It would be difficult to exaggerate the impact that these population projections and the international meetings and conferences that they precipitated have had on world opinion and international planning. For the first time, man was able to see the implications for his own welfare of a combination of highly controlled mortality and uncontrolled fertility. This advanced warning called into being vast action programs to deal with the problem. These have been described in Chapter 20.

A new round of censuses were taken in many nations of the world in 1960-1961. To incorporate the new information that these censuses provided and to correct known errors of estimation that continued study had revealed in the earlier projections, the United Nations published, in 1966, a new set of world population projections in a report entitled *World Population Prospects*.[8] As of 1968, these

[6] United Nations, *The Future Growth of World Population*, New York, 1958.

[7] United Nations, *The Population of Central America (including Mexico), 1950-1980* (1954); *The Population of South America, 1950-1980* (1955); *The Population of South-East Asia (including Ceylon and China), 1950-1980* (1959); *The Population of Asia and the Far East, 1950-1980* (1959).

[8] United Nations, *World Population Prospects, as Assessed in 1963*, Department of Economic and Social Affairs, Population Studies, No. 41, New York, 1966.

Table 21-3   World Population in 1960, Estimated Increase, 1920 to 1960; and Increases Expected According to the "Medium" Variant, 1960 to 2000, in More and Less Developed Regions

Area	Population 1960	Estimated increase		Projected increase	
		1920–1940	1940–1960	1960–1980	1980–2000
		Number millions			
World total..............	2,998	433	702	1,332	1,799
More developed regions.................	978	146	155	217	247
Europe...............................	425	53	45	55	48
USSR................................	214	40	19	63	75
Northern America.....................	199	28	54	63	92
Japan................................	93	16	22	18	11
Temperate South America..............	33	7	11	13	14
Australia and New Zealand............	12.7	2	4	5	7
Less developed regions.................	2,021	287	547	1,115	1,552
South Asia...........................	865	140	255	555	750
East Asia, excluding Japan...........	701	65	138	229	235
Africa...............................	273	48	81	176	319
Latin America, excluding Temperate South America......................	179	33	72	153	245
Melanesia, Polynesia ans Micronesia...	3.0	0.5	0.7	1.8	3
Percent of world total........	100.0	100.0	100.0	100.0	100.0
More developed regions.................	32.6	33.9	22.0	16.3	13.7
Europe...............................	14.2	12.3	6.4	4.1	2.6
USSR................................	7.2	9.1	2.8	4.8	4.2
Northern America.....................	6.6	6.6	7.7	4.7	5.1
Japan................................	3.1	3.7	3.1	1.3	0.6
Temperate South America..............	1.1	1.7	1.5	1.0	0.8
Australia and New Zealand............	0.4	0.5	0.6	0.4	0.4
Less developed regions.................	67.4	66.1	78.0	83.7	86.3
South Asia...........................	28.8	32.3	36.4	41.7	41.7
East Asia, excluding Japan...........	23.4	15.0	19.6	17.2	13.1
Africa...............................	9.1	11.2	11.6	13.2	17.1
Latin America, excluding Temperate South America......................	6.0	7.6	10.3	11.5	13.6
Melanesia, Polynesia and Micronesia....	0.1	0.1	0.1	0.1	0.2

estimates stand as the best official estimate available of the probable course of future population growth. Table 21-2 summarizes these projections and permits a comparison with the earlier 1957 projections. Figure 21-1 illustrates them, with alternatives discussed below. Table 21-3 provides similar information for the world regions. For information concerning the United Nations population projections for individual nations, see Chapter 3.

The revised "medium" population projections are quite similar to the medium projections of 1957: a total population of 6.1 billion persons is anticipated for the year 2000. The "high" figure was raised slightly. Surprisingly, the "low" estimate was raised sharply, from 4.9 to 5.5 billion.

The crude birthrates that the United Nations anticipates and the rates of reproductive change (natural increase) for the world as a whole and for each major world region are shown in Tables 21-4 and 21-5. In the 1995-2000 period the United Nations anticipates a birthrate of 25.7 per thousand, a death rate of 9.3, and a natural increase rate of 16.4 per thousand for the world as a whole.

21.6.   Are the United Nations Population Projections Too Pessimistic?

The optimistic position taken in Chapter 20 concerning the prospects for fertility control throughout the world is inconsistent with the population projections of the United Nations. Both cannot be correct. In Chapter 20 it was stated that it would be possible to attain a rate of zero growth by the year 2000; the United Nations projections expect a rate of growth only 10 percent lower than that at present by 2000. It is the opinion of the writer that the United Nations estimates seriously underrate

Table 21-4 Crude Birthrates Implied in "Medium" Variant for the World, More or Less Developed Regions, Major Areas and Regions, 1960 to 2000, No Adjustment Being Made in Respect of Migration (per 1,000 Population)

Area	1960-1965	1965-1970	1970-1975	1975-1980	1980-1985	1985-1990	1990-1995	1995-2000
World Total a/	33.9	32.9	32.4	31.6	29.9	28.5	26.9	25.7
(a) More developed....................	20.0	18.5	18.7	19.4	19.3	19.0	18.5	18.3
(b) Less developed a/................	40.4	39.4	38.2	36.5	33.9	31.8	29.7	28.0
A. East Asia b/......................	32.6	30.7	29.3	27.3	24.8	22.9	21.3	19.9
(1) Mainland region c/..........	34.3	32.3	30.6	28.2	25.7	23.8	22.0	20.4
(2) Japan......................	17.0	15.6	16.7	16.8	15.2	13.6	13.0	13.2
(3) Other East Asia d/..........	40.0	37.5	34.6	31.8	29.2	26.5	24.2	23.3
B. South Asia e/.....................	43.0	42.1	40.8	38.6	35.0	32.3	29.3	26.9
(4) Middle South Asia...........	43.6	43.1	42.0	39.2	34.5	31.2	27.7	25.0
(5) South-East Asia.............	41.9	39.5	37.5	36.7	35.8	34.4	32.5	30.4
(6) South-West Asia e/..........	41.2	41.4	41.0	39.6	37.3	34.7	31.9	29.9
C. Europe.............................	17.8	16.6	16.3	16.4	16.5	16.4	16.1	15.9
(7) Western Europe..............	17.1	16.0	15.7	15.8	16.1	16.3	16.2	16.0
(8) Southern Europe.............	19.0	17.7	17.0	16.8	16.7	16.5	16.2	16.0
(9) Eastern Europe..............	18.2	16.9	16.8	17.2	17.2	16.8	16.2	15.9
(10) Northern Europe.............	16.6	15.7	15.6	15.9	16.0	15.9	15.8	15.8
D. (11) USSR........................	22.1	19.4	19.0	19.9	21.0	20.7	20.0	19.3
E. Africa.............................	45.5	45.4	45.1	44.6	43.4	42.2	41.1	40.0
(12) Western Africa..............	52.0	51.0	49.9	49.0	48.2	48.3	48.2	47.8
(13) Eastern Africa..............	41.7	42.3	42.8	43.0	42.6	41.8	41.4	41.4
(14) Middle Africa..............	40.0	40.7	41.1	41.4	41.2	40.9	40.9	41.1
(15) Northern Africa.............	44.1	43.9	43.5	42.1	39.0	35.4	32.1	28.8
(16) Southern Africa.............	42.8	42.7	42.5	42.3	42.1	41.0	38.0	34.4
F. (17) Northern America f/.........	22.6	21.3	22.6	22.6	23.4	23.0	22.4	22.2
G. Latin America......................	39.6	39.0	38.2	37.2	35.3	33.6	31.9	30.3
(18) Tropical South America......	41.9	41.2	40.1	38.8	37.2	35.2	33.2	31.0
(19) Middle America (mainland)....	43.6	42.8	41.8	40.8	39.3	36.9	34.7	32.6
(20) Temperate South America......	26.4	25.5	24.4	23.5	22.4	21.2	20.9	21.0
(21) Caribbean...................	38.3	38.2	37.4	36.1	34.4	32.4	30.4	28.4
H. Oceania g/........................	25.0	24.4	24.7	25.5	25.7	25.4	25.2	25.3
(22) Australia and New Zealand....	22.3	21.5	21.8	22.8	22.9	22.6	22.1	22.1
(23) Melanesia h/................	40.0	40.7	41.1	41.4	41.2	40.9	40.9	41.1

a/ Not including areas listed in footnotes b, e, and g.
b/ Not including Hong Kong, Mongolia, Macao, and Ryukyu Islands.
c/ Mainland China only.
d/ Not including Ryukyu Islands.

e/ Not including Israel and Cyprus.
f/ Corresponding to immigration assumption made in original projections.
g/ Not including Polynesia and Micronesia.
h/ Assumed same as Middle Africa.

Source: United Nations. World Population Prospects. New York. United Nations, 1966, Table 7.1.

the impact of the current efforts at fertility control and fail to make allowance for the even more intensive and dramatic developments that very probably will take place in the next 35 years. If this is correct, the United Nations estimates are too pessimistic and the estimates of future population and future growth rates are too high.

As of 1968, there was very little data with which to test which of these two positions—the optimistic or the pessimistic—would eventually prove to be correct. The full range of available information, including that presented in Chapter 20, was reviewed by the United Nations in late 1967, at which time the 1966 estimates were reaffirmed. The inconsistency, therefore, is one of different interpretation and different weighting of the many unmeasured and presently unmeasurable new developments and anticipated developments. Some hopeful signs appeared in Korea, where a new census indi-

cated that growth rates had dropped slightly, and in Pakistan, where estimates indicated that as many as 2 million births had been prevented by the current family planning program in the first three years of operation. On the pessimistic side is the suspicion of many that the size of Mainland China's population and its current rate of growth are substantially larger than the United Nations estimates. Not until the 1970-1971 round of censuses is taken will the first indications of a slackening of growth, if one has occurred, become demonstrable. But the crucial test of whether the optimistic or the pessimistic position is proving to be correct will not be made until the 1980-1981 round of censuses. According to the United Nations estimates, the annual rate of population growth throughout the world will be identical to that at present, if not a little higher. The position taken in Chapter 20 and reiterated here is that by this date there should be unmistakable signs

Table 21-5 Rates of Natural Increase Implied in "Medium" Variant for the World, More and Less Developed Regions, Major Areas and Regions, 1960 to 2000, No Adjustment Being Made in Respect of Migration (per 1,000 Population)

Area	1960–1965	1965–1970	1970–1975	1975–1980	1980–1985	1985–1990	1990–1995	1995–2000
World Total.a/	18.0	18.5	18.8	18.8	18.4	17.8	17.0	16.4
(a) More developed regions	11.5	10.0	10.1	10.4	10.2	9.7	9.1	8.8
(b) Less developed regions	21.2	22.1	22.5	22.1	21.4	20.6	19.7	18.8
A. East Asia	13.7	13.6	13.6	13.0	11.8	10.9	10.0	9.4
(1) Mainland region	13.3	13.2	13.1	12.4	11.3	10.6	9.9	9.2
(2) Japan	9.0	7.9	9.0	9.0	7.3	5.3	3.8	3.0
(3) Other East Asia	29.0	28.0	26.4	24.8	23.1	21.0	19.0	18.3
B. South Asia	24.1	25.1	25.3	24.5	23.4	22.1	20.4	19.0
(4) Middle South Asia	23.3	24.7	25.1	23.7	22.0	20.1	18.0	16.5
(5) South-East Asia	26.0	25.5	25.0	25.5	25.9	25.9	25.1	24.0
(6) South-West Asia	25.4	27.4	28.7	28.8	27.9	26.2	24.5	23.1
C. Europe	7.8	6.7	6.2	6.0	5.8	5.4	5.0	4.7
(7) Western Europe	6.4	5.2	4.7	4.3	4.2	4.2	4.3	4.4
(8) Southern Europe	9.3	8.2	7.6	7.6	7.4	6.6	5.9	5.2
(9) Eastern Europe	9.3	7.7	7.5	7.7	7.2	6.6	5.9	5.2
(10) Northern Europe	6.1	5.4	4.7	4.4	4.1	3.7	3.5	3.7
D. (11) USSR	14.9	12.3	11.9	12.6	13.2	12.6	11.5	10.6
E. Africa	23.0	24.4	25.6	26.5	26.7	26.8	26.9	26.9
(12) Western Africa	26.9	27.5	28.1	28.6	29.2	30.4	31.8	32.1
(13) Eastern Africa	17.7	19.6	21.2	22.6	23.5	23.8	24.6	25.6
(14) Middle Africa	15.3	17.2	19.1	20.5	21.6	22.5	23.7	24.9
(15) Northern Africa	26.6	28.1	29.3	29.5	28.1	26.1	24.2	21.9
(16) Southern Africa	24.9	25.6	26.3	26.8	27.8	28.3	27.0	25.0
F. (17) Northern America	13.4	11.9	13.2	14.4	15.4	15.0	14.5	14.3
G. Latin America	28.4	29.1	29.1	28.8	28.1	26.7	25.5	24.1
(18) Tropical South America	31.0	31.6	31.2	30.6	29.6	28.2	26.6	25.0
(19) Middle America (mainland)	32.0	33.0	33.7	34.0	33.1	31.2	29.5	27.6
(20) Temperate South America	17.2	16.5	15.5	14.7	14.0	12.5	12.1	12.5
(21) Caribbean	23.4	24.3	24.5	24.2	23.5	22.5	21.4	20.0
H. Oceania	14.2	14.4	15.2	16.0	16.2	15.9	15.5	15.7
(22) Australia and New Zealand	13.8	13.7	14.4	15.4	15.2	14.6	14.0	13.9
(23) Melanesia	15.3	17.2	19.1	20.5	21.7	22.5	23.6	24.9

a/ For qualifying observations, see footnotes to table 21-4.

Source: United Nations. World Population Prospects, New York. United Nations, 1966 Table 7.3.

of fertility decline and slackening growth rates almost everywhere. Unfortunately, in the absence of reliable vital registration in the developing countries, there is little that can be done except to note the incompatibility of the two positions and wait for history to unfold.

Meanwhile, there are some shreds of evidence that the United Nations estimates are indeed too pessimistic. This evidence comes from the current birth statistics of the United Nations. As has been stated repeatedly, they are highly incomplete. The trend they take must therefore be interpreted with caution. A "rising" birthrate may signify nothing more than that registration is becoming more complete, while a "declining" birthrate may indicate only that the system is deteriorating. The United Nations attempts to separate its data into three classes: those that are reliable, those that are unreliable, and those for which reliability is unknown. We have summarized these birthrates into 5-year intervals, 1955-1959 and 1960-1964, to see if there is any recent change.

Table 21-6 presents a summary of these data for world regions, and Table 21-7 presents a country-by-country report.

The overall picture seems to be that on almost every continent birthrates are falling. Moreover, they appear to be falling faster than death rates. Thus what little evidence we have, and as crude as it is, suggests that the peak has been passed; the growth of world population may be decelerating. Latin America appears to be the only exception to this trend, and even here improved birth registration rather than rising birthrates may explain the trend.

The United Nations forecast of the future trend of fertility was made according to a particular model that may be described as follows. Starting at the date at which a definite decline in fertility begins, we may expect a reduction of 50 percent in fertility over a period of the next 30 years, with the following ratios of fertility to the initial level at the midpoints of the 5-year periods: 97.5, 90, 80, 70, 60, and 57.25, respectively. Figure 21-2 contrasts this model

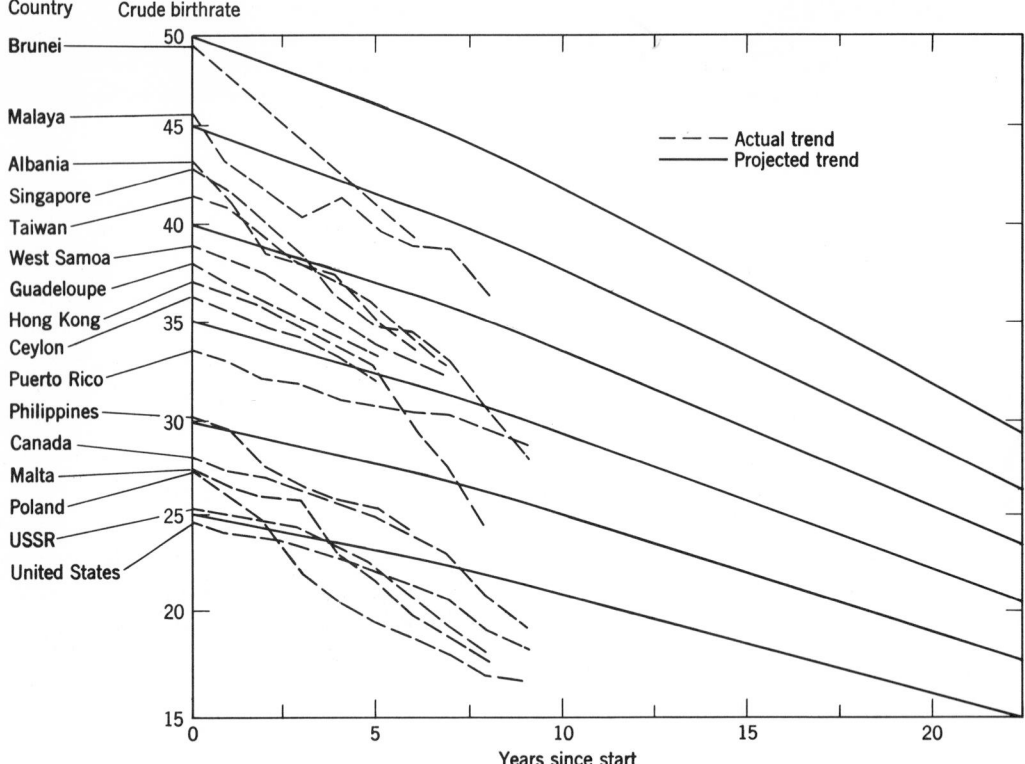

Figure 21-1

with the actual behavior of several recent national trends in several underdeveloped and developed nations. The heavy black lines depict the expected course of births according to the United Nations model. The broken lines portray the actual trend of births in selected nations in recent years. If the birthrates of the various nations were behaving in accordance with the United Nations model, they would be traveling down the paths parallel to the heavy

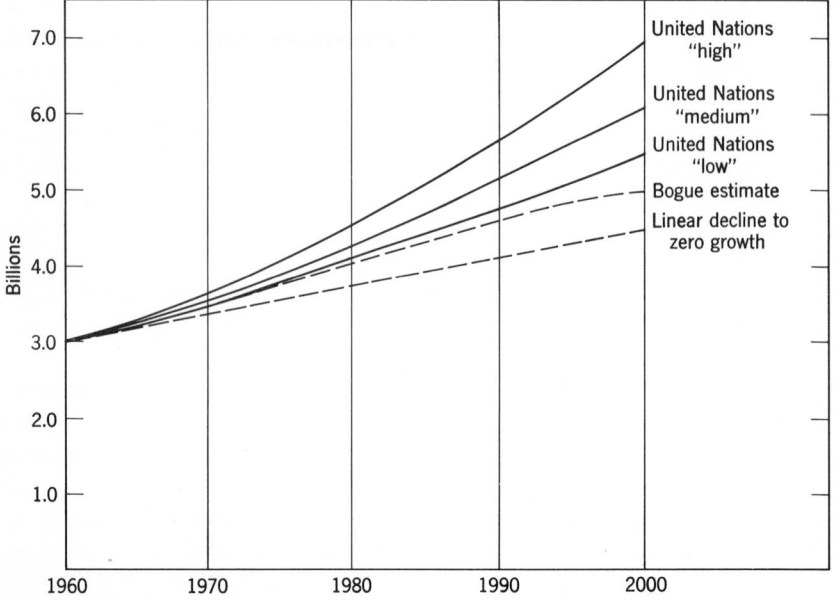

Figure 21-2

black lines. Actually, in almost every case they are declining at a much more rapid pace than that anticipated by the model. The slopes of these lines indicate a halving of the birthrate in 10 to 15 years, instead of 30 as the United Nations model specifies. Please note that the base line of this graph is a crude birthrate of 15 per thousand—which is approximately the level of zero growth. The slopes of these lines are such that they all lead to zero growth within less than 20 years.

Admittedly, these are selected nations. Admittedly, many of the data are suspect. However, they do indicate that the United Nations model is being violated by not just a few, but by almost all nations for which we have reliable data and by many for which the data are unreliable. In fact, a careful consideration of the nations involved leads plausibly to the conclusion that the United Nations model is unduly pessimistic on three points:

1. It places the start of fertility decline for many developing nations too far into the future.

2. It anticipates much too slow a decline in fertility once the decline starts.

3. It fails to allow for acceleration in fertility decline toward the end of this century, because of the cumulative impact of the fertility control programs.

The combined result of these possible errors could be a substantial overestimate of the world population by the year 2000. Even worse, it could result in a serious overestimate of the rate of growth of population at the year 2000.

On the basis of the argument presented in Chapter 20, supported by the somewhat tenuous statistics concerning current trends and the failure of events to conform to the demographic model of the United Nations, we feel justified in reaffirming the earlier thesis that growth rates could well be zero almost everywhere by the year 2000. If this materializes, as of that date, the total population of the world could well be below the "low" estimate predicted by the United Nations.

There is not sufficient information in support of the optimistic position to undertake to develop an alternative set of projections to compete with those of the United Nations. In Chapter 20 a set of statistics was submitted to show what the world population would be if it were to decline linearly to zero growth by the year 2000. These statistics are almost certainly too low to be treated seriously as population projections, because the current young age composition of the world's population would require negative net reproduction rates for some years to accomplish this. A more realistic estimate would be about 5 billion persons.

To summarize, there is fragmentary empirical evidence and possibly much more circumstantial evidence that the United Nations population projections are too pessimistic. *What is of critical importance is not the projected size of the world's population by the year 2000, but the projected rate of growth as of that date.* If the decennial rate of increase of 18 percent between 1990 and 2000 projected by the United Nations is even half this large by the year 2000 (1.0 percent per year), the demographic dread that has been foretold by the apprehensive demographers will indeed beset us. We seriously doubt that growth rates will be this high by the year 2000. We also believe that modern technology can feed a growth to 5 billion if during that time we do succeed in conquering the growth rate.

21.7. The Future Growth of the United States Population

A casual observer might be tempted to expect that the United States, with its impressive array of technical demographers, its high quality of vital registration, and its tradition of accurate and detailed decennial censuses, should be in a position to predict its future population with great precision. Unluckily, this has not been the case thus far. In fact, demographers in several of the developing nations of Latin America and Asia have had greater success in predicting future growth of their national populations than have American demographers. The major difficulty has been the highly volatile birthrates that have characterized the United States. Before 1965, there was a tendency to make predictions that were too low; after 1960 there seems to have developed the opposite tendency to anticipate more population growth than eventually takes place.

Table 21-6 Summary of Recent Changes in World Birthrates, by Continent: 1955 to 1959 and 1960 to 1964. Selected Nations for Which Data are Available

Components and growth	World (available)	Continent and Nation							
		Asia	Africa	Europe	U.S.S.R.	United States	North America	South America	Oceania
All nations for which data are published									
Birth rate: 1955-59......	31.8	33.5	34.7	20.2	25.3	24.6	38.8	36.0	33.9
1960-64......	30.5	32.6	33.9	19.6	22.4	22.4	36.7	35.9	30.4
1965......	29.9	32.0	32.5	19.0	18.4	19.4	35.8	38.4	29.1
Death rate: 1955-59......	10.0	8.6	10.3	10.4	7.7	9.4	10.4	11.1	8.7
1960-64......	9.1	8.0	9.4	10.3	7.2	9.5	8.9	10.1	6.7
1965......	8.8	6.2	9.1	10.4	7.3	9.4	9.5	9.0	6.8
Rate of reproductive change (natural increase)									
1955-59......	21.6	24.9	24.4	9.8	17.6	15.2	28.2	23.8	25.2
1960-64......	21.2	24.6	24.4	9.3	15.2	12.9	27.5	24.7	23.8
1965......	19.5	25.0	23.2	8.6	11.1	10.0	25.6	13.5	22.3
Change in growth components --1955-1965									
Births rate......	-1.6	-0.9	-1.0	-0.5	-2.9	-2.2	-2.1	-0.2	-3.5
Death rate......	-0.9	-0.7	-0.9	+0.1	-0.5	+0.1	-1.4	-1.0	-2.0
Rate of reproductive change..	-0.6	-1.0	-0.1	-0.6	-2.4	-2.3	-0.7	+0.9	-1.4

Note: These are unweighted averages of rates as published by United Nations, without regard to quality of the data or size of the nation.

Source: Compiled from United Nations Demographic Yearbook: 1967

Table 21-7 Recent Changes in Components of Population Growth, Nations for Which Data are Available

Nation	Reliability	Births			Deaths			Reproductive change			Change 1955–64		
		1955–59	1960–64	1965	1955–59	1960–64	1965	1955–59	1960–64	1965	Births	Deaths	Change
ASIA													
Aden................	C	28.3	34.7	38.4	10.6	8.8	8.2	17.7	25.9	30.2	6.4	− 1.8	8.2
Brunei..............	C	54.0	44.3	41.5	13.1	7.6	6.6	40.9	36.7	34.9	− 9.7	− 5.5	− 4.2
Ceylon..............	U	36.6	35.1	32.7	9.9	8.5	8.1	26.7	26.6	24.6	− 1.5	− 1.4	− 0.1
China (Taiwan)......	C	42.8	37.1	32.7	8.0	6.4	5.5	34.8	30.7	27.2	− 5.7	− 1.6	− 4.1
Cyprus..............	C	25.7	25.0	24.4	6.1	6.0	6.1	19.6	19.0	18.3	− 0.7	− 0.1	− 0.6
Hong Kong...........	C	36.3	33.2	27.7	7.2	5.7	4.8	29.1	27.5	22.9	− 3.1	− 1.5	− 1.6
Indonesia...........	U	45	38.4	48	12.6	10.7	...	32.4	27.7	...	− 6.6	− 1.9	− 4.7
Israel..............	C	27.9	25.5	25.8	6.2	6.0	6.3	21.7	19.5	19.5	− 2.4	− 0.2	− 2.2
Japan...............	C	18.2	17.2	18.6	7.8	7.3	7.1	10.4	9.9	11.5	− 1.0	− 0.5	− 0.5
Jordan..............	U	40.1	45.9	46.5	8.1	15.9	5.4	32.0	30.0	41.1	5.8	7.8	− 2.0
Kuwait..............	..	33.8	43.5	46.2	...	6.3	5.2	...	37.2	41.0	9.7	...	...
Lebanon.............	U	28.6	31.8	32.3	4.3	4.5	3.9	24.3	27.3	28.4	3.2	0.2	3.0
East Malaysia:													
Sabah..............	U	33.4	33.4	35.7	8.9	6.6	5.6	24.5	26.8	30.1	0.0	− 2.3	2.3
Sarawak............	U	23.8	26.6	28.0	6.1	5.3	5.0	17.7	21.3	23.0	2.8	− 0.8	3.6
West Malaysia......	C	44.4	40.3	36.7	11.3	9.0	7.9	33.1	31.3	28.8	− 4.1	− 2.3	− 1.8
Philippines........	U	30.5	27.4	24.6	8.7	7.3	7.3	21.8	20.1	17.3	− 3.1	− 1.4	− 1.7
Portuguese Timor...	U	23.5	21.8	19.1	17.2	12.5	10.0	6.3	9.3	9.1	− 1.7	− 4.7	3.0
Ryukyu Islands.....	C	29.2	23.9	21.7	5.4	5.4	5.3	23.8	18.5	16.4	− 5.3	0.0	− 5.3
Singapore..........	C	42.8	35.6	31.1	7.3	5.9	5.6	35.5	29.7	25.5	− 7.2	− 1.4	− 5.8
Syria..............	U	24.5	28.6	33.2	5.3	5.0	4.6	19.2	23.6	28.6	4.1	− 0.3	4.4
Viet-Nam, (Rep.)...	U	34.1	35	27.7	7.0	18	6.4	27.1	17.0	21.3	0.9	11.0	− 10.1
AFRICA													
Angola..............	U	20.5	20.2	22.2	6.3	3.2	1.7	14.2	17.0	20.5	− 0.3	− 3.1	+ 2.8
Cape Verde Islands.	C	46.8	43.8	42.9	13.0	13.0	10.6	33.8	30.8	32.3	− 3.0	...	− 3.0
Equatorial Guinea..	U	13.2	27.2	22.8	7.1	7.0	14.0	6.1	20.2	8.8	+14.0	− 0.1	+14.1
Gambia-Bathurst....	C	43.5	45.4	48.5	17.5	14.1	14.1	26.0	31.3	34.4	+ 1.9	− 3.4	+ 5.3
Kenya (Non-African)	..	34.3	29.9	26.8	5.4	6.0	4.8	28.9	23.9	22.0	− 4.4	+ 0.6	− 5.0
Madagascar.........	U	34.9	33.4	32.5	13.3	13.3	10.5	21.6	20.1	22.0	− 1.5	...	− 1.5
Mauritius ex.dep...	C	41.0	38.9	35.4	11.9	9.7	8.6	29.1	29.2	26.8	− 2.1	− 2.2	+ 0.1
Rodrigues..........	C	47.3	49.0	46.6	12.8	12.3	15.3	34.5	36.7	31.3	+ 1.7	− 0.5	+ 2.2
Reunion............	C	46.7	44.0	42.6	14.1	11.1	9.3	32.6	32.9	33.3	− 2.7	− 3.0	+ 0.3
St. Helena ex.dep..	..	27.6	27.5	24.6	10.2	9.9	9.2	17.4	17.6	15.4	− 0.1	− 0.3	+ 0.2
Sao Tome & Princepe	C	48.9	49.6	53.1	25.1	19.0	15.8	23.8	30.6	37.3	+ 0.7	− 6.1	+ 6.8
Seychelles.........	..	38.4	40.7	37.4	11.4	11.5	11.9	27.0	29.2	25.5	+ 2.3	+ 0.1	+ 2.2

Table 21-7 (*Continued*)

Nation	Reliability	Births			Deaths			Reproductive change			Change 1955-64		
		1955-59	1960-64	1965	1955-59	1960-64	1965	1955-59	1960-64	1965	Births	Deaths	Change
SOUTH AFRICA													
Asiatic.............	C	31.5	30.7	34.4	8.3	7.5	8.1	23.2	23.2	26.3	- 0.8	- 0.8	0.0
White.............	C	24.9	24.0	22.8	8.6	8.9	9.1	16.3	15.1	13.7	- 0.9	+ 0.3	- 1.2
Colored.............	C	45.6	46.4	46.1	16.1	15.2	15.8	29.5	31.2	30.3	+ 0.8	- 0.9	+ 1.7
Southern Rhodesia:													
Asiatic.............	C	37.6	35.2	32.6	6.7	6.9	5.1	30.9	28.3	27.5	- 2.4	+ 0.2	- 2.6
European.............	C	26.5	22.4	18.3	6.2	6.3	6.3	20.3	16.1	12.0	- 4.1	+ 0.1	- 4.2
Spanish North Africa													
Ceuta.............	C	21.1	21.1	18.1	7.5	7.0	6.4	13.6	14.1	11.7	...	- 0.5	+ 0.5
Melilla.............	C	21.7	19.2	17.6	7.4	6.9	7.2	14.3	12.3	10.4	- 2.5	- 0.5	- 2.0
Spanish Sahara.......	U	9.0	10.6	14.0	4.1	4.7	4.0	4.9	5.9	10.0	+ 1.6	+ 0.6	+ 1.0
Togo-African.........	U	27.7	22.8	29.4	9.4	5.8	6.5	18.3	17.0	22.9	- 4.9	- 3.6	- 1.3
Tunisia.............	C	39.8	44.2	43.5	8.9	10.6	11.7	30.9	33.6	31.8	+ 4.4	+ 1.7	+ 2.7
United Arab Rep.....	U	40.6	42.3	41.6	16.9	16.5	14.8	23.7	25.8	26.8	+ 1.7	- 0.4	+ 2.1
Zambia:													
Asiatic.............	..	67.1	51.9	35.3	5.6	4.3	3.7	61.5	47.6	31.6	-15.2	- 1.3	-13.9
European.............	C	31.7	26.9	22.6	4.3	4.3	4.1	27.4	22.6	18.5	- 4.8	...	- 4.8
EUROPE													
Albania.............	C	41.8	40.1	35.2	11.4	9.8	9.0	30.4	30.3	26.2	- 1.7	- 1.6	- 0.1
Austria.............	C	16.8	18.5	17.9	12.5	12.5	13.0	4.3	6.0	4.9	+ 1.7	0.0	+ 1.7
Belgium.............	C	17.0	17.0	16.4	11.9	12.1	12.1	5.1	4.9	4.3	0.0	+ 0.2	- 0.2
Bulgaria.............	C	18.7	16.9	15.3	8.9	8.2	8.2	9.8	8.7	7.1	- 1.8	- 0.7	- 1.1
Channel Islands.....	C	14.6	17.9	17.8	11.6	12.1	12.0	3.0	5.8	5.8	+ 3.3	+ 0.5	+ 2.8
Czechoslovakia.......	C	18.5	16.3	16.4	9.7	9.5	10.0	8.8	6.8	6.4	- 2.2	- 0.2	- 2.0
Denmark.............	C	16.8	17.0	18.0	9.1	9.7	10.1	7.7	7.3	7.9	+ 0.2	+ 0.6	- 0.4
Faeroe Islands.......	..	23.9	23.0	24.0	7.2	6.9	7.1	16.7	16.1	16.9	- 0.9	- 0.3	- 0.6
Finland.............	C	19.9	18.1	16.9	9.1	9.2	9.6	10.8	8.9	7.3	- 1.8	+ 0.1	- 1.9
France.............	..	18.4	18.0	17.7	11.8	11.2	...	6.6	6.8	...	- 0.4	- 0.6	+ 0.2
Germany:													
Eastern.............	C	16.3	17.5	16.5	12.4	13.1	13.4	3.9	4.4	3.1	+ 1.2	+ 0.7	+ 0.5
Federal Rep.........	C	16.9	18.3	17.9	11.0	11.1	11.2	5.9	7.2	6.7	+ 1.4	+ 0.1	+ 1.3
West Berlin.........	C	8.3	11.1	11.8	14.9	16.9	18.0	- 6.6	- 5.8	- 6.2	+ 2.8	+ 2.0	+ 0.8
Gibraltar.............	C	23.6	24.9	27.3	9.6	8.9	9.8	14.0	16.0	17.5	+ 1.3	- 0.7	+ 2.0
Greece.............	C	19.3	18.1	17.7	7.3	7.8	7.9	12.0	10.3	9.8	- 1.2	+ 0.5	- 1.7
Hungary.............	C	17.8	13.6	13.1	10.3	10.1	10.7	7.5	3.5	2.4	- 4.2	- 0.2	- 4.0
Iceland.............	C	28.3	26.1	24.7	7.1	6.9	6.7	21.2	19.2	18.0	- 2.2	- 0.2	- 2.0
Ireland.............	C	21.1	21.9	22.1	12.0	11.8	11.5	9.1	10.1	10.6	+ 0.8	- 0.2	+ 1.0
Isle of Man.........	C	12.6	14.2	14.9	15.2	17.0	17.7	- 2.6	- 2.8	- 2.8	+ 1.6	+ 1.8	- 0.2
Italy.............	C	18.0	18.9	19.2	9.6	9.8	10.0	8.4	9.1	9.2	+ 0.9	+ 0.2	+ 0.7

Table 21-7 (Continued)

Nation	Reliability	Births 1955-59	Births 1960-64	Births 1965	Deaths 1955-59	Deaths 1960-64	Deaths 1965	Reproductive change 1955-59	Reproductive change 1960-64	Reproductive change 1965	Change 1955-64 Births	Change 1955-64 Deaths	Change 1955-64 Change
EUROPE (continued)													
Liechtenstein	...	22.1	21.7	20.5	8.6	8.2	8.1	13.5	13.5	12.4	- 0.4	- 0.4	0.0
Luxembourg	C	15.9	16.0	16.0	11.8	11.9	12.3	4.1	4.1	3.7	+ 0.1	+ 0.1	0.0
Malta	C	26.9	22.5	17.6	8.8	8.7	9.4	18.1	13.8	8.2	- 4.4	- 0.1	- 4.3
Monaco	...	19.2	19.4	20.5	13.1	15.5	16.0	6.1	3.9	4.5	+ 0.2	+ 2.4	- 2.2
Netherlands	C	21.3	20.9	19.9	7.6	7.8	8.1	13.7	13.1	11.8	- 0.4	+ 0.2	- 0.6
Norway	C	18.1	17.3	17.5	8.8	9.5	9.1	9.3	7.8	8.4	- 0.8	+ 0.7	- 1.5
Poland	C	27.1	20.0	17.3	9.0	7.6	7.4	18.1	12.4	9.9	- 7.1	- 1.4	- 5.7
Portugal	C	24.2	24.1	22.9	11.5	10.8	10.3	12.7	13.3	12.6	- 0.1	- 0.7	+ 0.6
Romania	C	22.9	16.7	14.6	9.7	8.6	8.6	13.2	8.1	6.0	- 6.2	- 1.1	- 5.1
Spain	C	21.3	21.6	21.3	9.4	8.8	8.7	11.9	12.8	12.6	+ 0.3	- 0.6	+ 0.9
Sweden	C	14.5	14.5	15.9	9.6	10.0	10.1	4.9	4.5	5.8	0.0	+ 0.4	- 0.4
Switzerland	C	17.5	18.5	18.8	9.9	9.5	9.3	7.6	9.0	9.5	+ 1.0	- 0.4	+ 1.4
United Kingdom:													
England and Wales	C	15.9	17.9	18.1	11.6	11.8	11.5	4.3	6.1	6.6	+ 2.0	+ 0.2	+ 1.8
Northern Ireland	C	21.4	22.9	23.1	10.9	10.8	10.6	10.5	12.1	12.5	+ 1.5	- 0.1	+ 1.6
Scotland	C	18.9	19.8	19.3	12.1	12.1	12.1	6.8	7.7	7.2	+ 0.9	0.0	+ 0.9
Yugoslavia	C	24.8	22.0	20.9	10.5	9.4	8.7	14.3	12.6	12.2	- 2.8	- 1.1	- 1.7
USSR	C	25.3	22.4	18.4	7.7	7.2	7.3	17.6	15.2	11.1	- 2.9	- 0.5	- 2.4
NORTH AMERICA													
Antigua	C	35.4	31.5	30.4	10.0	8.7	8.4	25.4	22.8	22.0	- 3.9	- 1.3	- 2.6
Bahamas	C	31.1	31.4	32.7	9.2	7.5	6.4	21.9	23.9	26.3	+ 0.3	- 1.7	+ 2.0
Barbados	C	31.8	29.5	29/32	10.7	9.2	9.1	21.1	20.3	21.5	- 2.3	- 1.5	- 0.8
Bermuda	C	26.2	26.0	23.1	8.3	7.4	7.4	17.9	18.6	15.7	- 0.2	- 0.9	+ 0.7
British Honduras	U	45.2	45.7	46.2	9.9	7.7	....	35.3	38.0	....	+ 0.5	- 2.2	+ 2.7
Canada	C	27.8	25.2	21.4	8.1	7.7	7.6	19.7	17.5	13.8	- 2.6	- 0.4	- 2.2
Cayman Islands	U	32.1	32.1	26.9	7.8	7.2	7.0	24.3	24.9	19.9	0.0	- 0.6	+ 0.6
Costa Rica	U	49.5	45.4	44/46	9.6	8.5	8/9	39.9	36.9	36.5	- 4.1	- 1.1	- 3.0
Cuba	C	29.9	34.7	34/36	6.5	6.6	8/9	23.4	28.1	26.5	+ 4.8	+ 0.1	+ 4.7
Dominica	C	44.4	42.6	42.7	15.1	12.3	8.9	29.3	30.3	33.8	- 1.8	- 2.8	+ 1.0
Dominican Republic	U	40.4	33.4	45/48	9.1	7.4	14/16	31.3	26.0	31.5	- 7.0	- 1.7	- 5.3
El Salvador	C	49.3	48.7	47/49	13.7	11.1	14/16	35.6	37.6	33.0	- 0.6	- 2.6	+ 2.0
Grenada	C	47.3	39.2	30.9	11.9	9.9	8.6	35.4	29.3	22.3	- 8.1	- 2.0	- 6.1
Guadeloupe	C	38.5	36.3	33.7	10.3	8.4	8.1	28.2	27.9	25.6	- 2.2	- 1.9	- 0.3
Guatemala	C	48.7	47.6	46/48	19.7	16.7	18/20	29.0	30.9	28.0	- 1.1	- 3.0	+ 1.9
Haiti	.	45/50	45/50	45/48	....	....	20/24	....	....	25.5	....	....	....
Honduras	U	42.4	43.9	47/50	10.5	9.1	15/17	31.9	34.8	32.5	+ 1.5	- 1.4	+ 2.9
Jamaica	C	39.2	39.9	39/40	9.8	8.5	8/9	29.4	31.4	31.0	+ 0.7	- 1.3	+ 2.0
Martinique	C	39.4	35.3	32.7	9.9	8.5	7.3	29.5	26.8	25.4	- 4.1	- 1.4	- 2.7
Mexico	C	44.9	44.4	44/45	12.2	10.4	10/11	32.7	34.0	34.0	- 0.5	- 1.8	+ 1.3

Table 21-7 (Continued)

Nation	Reliability	Births			Deaths			Reproductive change			Change 1955–64		
		1955–59	1960–64	1965	1955–59	1960–64	1965	1955–59	1960–64	1965	Births	Deaths	Change
NORTH AMERICA (cont.)													
Montserrat............	C	31.2	26.8	27.4	13.6	9.9	8.6	17.6	16.9	18.8	− 4.4	− 3.7	− 0.7
Netherlands Antilles..	U	34.5	32.2	27.3	5.2	5.0	5.0	29.3	27.2	22.3	− 2.3	− 0.2	− 2.1
Nicaragua.............	U	44.0	43.8	47/50	9.1	8.0	14/16	34.9	35.8	33.5	− 0.2	− 1.1	+ 0.9
Panama................	C	39.8	40.6	41/42	9.1	7.8	10/11	30.7	32.8	31.0	+ 0.8	− 1.3	+ 2.1
Canal Zone............	C	27.5	15.5	12.8	3.0	2.8	2.9	24.5	12.7	9.9	−12.0	− 0.2	−11.8
Puerto Rico...........	C	33.7	31.2	30.2	7.1	6.9	6.7	26.6	24.3	23.5	− 2.5	− 0.2	− 2.3
St.Kitts–Nevis........	C	46.5	35.6	31.0	12.9	10.8	9.3	33.6	24.8	21.7	−10.9	− 2.1	− 8.8
St. Lucia.............	C	42.3	42.2	42.4	13.3	12.4	8.9	29.0	29.8	33.5	− 0.1	− 0.9	+ 0.8
St. Vincent...........	C	51.2	45.9	41.2	14.2	12.1	9.0	37.0	33.8	32.2	− 5.3	− 2.1	− 3.2
Trinidad & Tobago.....	C	38.3	37.0	37/39	9.6	7.3	8.0	28.7	29.7	30.0	− 1.3	− 2.3	+ 1.0
Turks & Caicos Isl....	...	40.3	39.3	23.2	11.3	10.7	10.4	29.0	28.6	12.8	− 1.0	− 0.6	− 0.4
United States........	C	24.6	22.4	19.4	9.4	9.5	9.4	15.2	12.9	10.0	− 2.2	+ 0.1	− 2.3
Virgin Islands(US)...	C	35.3	38.7	46.0	11.3	9.4	9.6	24.0	29.3	36.4	+ 3.4	− 1.9	+ 5.3
SOUTH AMERICA													
Argentina.............	C	24.1	22.6	22/23	8.6	8.5	8/9	15.5	14.1	14.0	− 1.5	− 0.1	− 1.4
Bolivia...............	U	30.5	25.2	43/45	9.1	7.6	20/22	21.4	17.6	23.0	− 5.3	− 1.5	− 3.8
Brazil................	...	41/43	41/43	41/43	...	...	11/12	...	...	...	0.0	...	...
Chile.................	C	35.9	34.9	34/36	12.5	11.8	12/14	23.4	23.1	23.5	− 1.0	− 0.7	− 0.3
Colombia..............	U	40.0	39.1	41/44	12.2	10.8	12/14	27.8	28.3	29.5	− 0.9	− 1.4	+ 0.5
Ecuador...............	U	45.6	52.9	47/50	14.7	14.7	13/15	30.9	38.2	34.5	+ 7.3	0.0	+ 7.3
Falkland Islands......	...	19.9	22.3	24.9	9.9	11.2	8.6	10.0	11.1	16.3	+ 2.4	+ 1.3	+ 1.1
French Guiana.........	U	32.5	32.1	32.4	13.9	12.9	11.2	18.6	19.2	21.1	− 0.4	− 1.0	+ 0.6
Guyana................	U	43.6	41.6	40/41	11.0	8.5	9/10	32.6	33.1	31.0	− 2.0	− 2.5	+ 0.5
Amerindian............	U	46.0	42.6	45.8	12.1	8.6	6.5	33.9	34.0	39.3	− 3.4	− 3.5	+ 0.1
Paraguay..............	.	42/45	42/45	42/45	...	...	12/14	...	...	30.5	0.0	...	...
Peru..................	U	36.1	35.2	44/45	11.8	10.3	12/14	24.3	24.9	31.5	− 0.9	− 1.5	+ 0.6
Uruguay...............	U	20.8	24.6	24/25	8.8	8.8	9	12.0	15.8	15.5	+ 3.8	0.0	+ 3.8
Venezuela.............	U	44.1	44.2	46/48	9.0	7.2	9/10	35.1	37.0	37.5	+ 0.1	− 1.8	+ 1.9
OCEANIA													
Australia.............	C	22.6	21.9	19.6	8.8	8.7	8.8	13.8	13.2	10.8	− 0.7	− 0.1	− 0.6
Christmas Island......	C	41.4	28.0	19.2	4.6	3.6	1.8	36.8	24.4	17.4	−13.4	− 1.0	−12.4
Cook Islands..........	C	47.1	46.1	40.8	14.1	9.0	7.0	33.0	37.1	33.8	− 1.0	− 5.1	+ 4.1
Fiji Islands..........	C	40.7	39.2	35.9	7.6	6.2	5.1	33.1	33.0	30.8	− 1.5	− 1.4	− 0.1
Gilbert & Ellice Isl..	U	34.0	33.4	22.8	16.9	8.7	7.1	17.1	24.7	15.7	− 0.6	− 8.2	+ 7.6
Guam..................	C	33.9	37.6	33.0	4.0	4.9	4.4	29.9	32.7	28.6	+ 3.7	+ 0.9	+ 2.8
Nauru.................	C	32.0	31.6	41.9	6.2	4.8	7.6	25.8	26.8	34.3	− 0.4	− 1.4	+ 1.0
New Caledonia.........	...	34.0	32.4	29.3	10.1	8.5	7.3	23.9	23.9	22.0	− 1.6	− 1.6	0.0
New Guinea (non-indigenous).......	C	28.8	30.8	32.2	4.4	3.3	4.6	24.4	27.5	27.6	+ 2.0	− 1.1	+ 3.1
New Zealand...........	C	26.3	25.8	22.8	9.1	8.9	8.7	17.2	16.9	14.1	− 0.5	− 0.2	− 0.3

Table 21-7 (*Continued*)

Nation	Reliability	Births 1955–59	Births 1960–64	Births 1965	Deaths 1955–59	Deaths 1960–64	Deaths 1965	Reproductive change 1955–59	Reproductive change 1960–64	Reproductive change 1965	Change 1955–64 Births	Change 1955–64 Deaths	Change 1955–64 Change
OCEANIA (cont.)													
Niue..............	...	45.0	44.5	38.1	9.5	7.6	8.9	35.5	36.9	29.2	- 0.5	- 1.9	1.4
Norfolk Island......	C	18.9	11.9	17.3	16.0	13.1	15.3	2.9	- 1.2	- 2.0	- 7.0	- 2.9	- 3.2
Pacific Island......	U	31.8	33.9	33.1	5.3	5.4	5.8	26.5	28.5	27.3	2.0	0.1	2.0
Papua non-indigenous.....	C	30.0	27.8	32.1	3.9	2.5	2.2	26.1	25.3	29.9	- 2.2	- 1.4	- 0.8
Pitcairn............	...	34.4	5.0	11.2	13.8	9.9	11.2	20.6	- 4.9	0.0	-29.4	- 3.9	-25.5
Tonga..............	...	36.5	33.4	34.6	7.1	4.3	3.6	29.4	29.1	31.0	- 3.1	- 2.8	- 0.3
Western Samoa.......	U	38.9	33.0	30.7	5.9	4.3	5.8	33.0	28.7	24.9	- 5.9	- 1.6	- 4.3

Note: Reliability symbols: C= reliable; U = unreliable; ... = reliability unknown.

Source: United Nations. Demographic Yearbook. 1967.

Table 21-8 Projections of the Total
Population of the United States: 1970 to 2000

Year	Millions of persons			
	Series A (High)	Series B	Series C	Series D (Low)
1970..........	209	207	206	205
1975..........	230	224	219	215
1980..........	250	243	235	228
1985..........	275	265	253	242
1990..........	300	287	271	256
1995..........	361	310	289	269
2000..........	398	336	308	283

Source: U.S. Bureau of Census. Current Population
Reports, Population Estimates, Series P-25,
No. 359, 1967, Table A.

Table 21-8 presents the official projections of the U. S. Bureau of Census published in 1967. There are four series of projections, A, B, C, and D—ranging from high to low. By these projections the United States can look forward to a maximum population of 361 million and a minimum of 283 million by the year 2000. The usual practice in making population projections, to attempt to "bracket" the probable range of future growth, is usually accompanied by a central estimate that would most nearly represent the "probable" trend. The Series B and C projections, calling for a population from 307 to 335 million by 2000, could be given this interpretation. The Census Bureau is very explicit in stating that the person who uses the projections must select his own best estimate:

"In view of the many uncertainties in predicting future fertility, the Bureau of the Census does not recommend any one series as the "best" series. Furthermore, Series A and Series D are not regarded as probable upper and lower limits. . . . Long-term projections, such as those for 1995 to 2015 are necessarily subject to the possibility of considerable error, inasmuch as they require the projection of births, deaths and net immigration up to a half century ahead." [9]

Despite this disclaimer, the only possible utility to the general public of such official re-

[9] U. S. Bureau of the Census, "Projections of the Population of the United States by Age, Sex, and Color to 1990, with Extensions of Total Population to 2015," *Current Population Reports, Population Estimates,* Series P-25, No. 359, February 20, 1967.

ports could be in their guidance in ascertaining probable future population trends, and this is the use to which they are put by those who study them.

Death rates are now so low and immigration is such a small part of total national growth that foreseeable fluctuations in neither can affect the projected total for the nation by more than just a few million. It is, therefore, evident that one's estimate of the future size of the United States population is determined largely by his estimate of the future course of fertility. To interpret the projections of Table 21-8, we need to study the underlying assumptions concerning anticipated trends in natality. Table 21-9 summarizes the fertility pattern anticipated by these projections. The following explanation of the Census Bureau accompanies this table:

"The projected average number of children per 1,000 women at the end of childbearing (average size of completed family) for all races would gradually move towards the following terminal levels: Series A, 3350 approximately the level of the calendar-year total fertility rate in 1963; Series B, 3, 100, about the level of the average of the calendar-year rates in 1964 and 1965; Series C, 2775, corresponding to the calendar-year rate of

Table 21-9 Total Fertility Rates Assumed
for Population Projections of the United States:
1966 Estimates

Year and series	All classes	White	Nonwhite
1963 to 1966 [1]/......	3,104	2,962	4,120
1975			
Series A.............	3,458	3,310	4,483
Series B.............	3,111	2,973	3,987
Series C.............	2,715	2,582	3,425
Series D.............	2,343	2,208	2,916
1990			
Series A.............	3,370	3,235	4,260
Series B.............	3,117	2,989	3,825
Series C.............	2,787	2,693	3,287
Series D.............	2,457	2,406	2,809
2000			
Series A.............	3,351	3,228	4,160
Series B.............	3,102	2,995	3,694
Series C.............	2,777	2,711	3,126
Series D.............	2,451	2,423	2,641

[1]/ Average for 3-year period extending from July 1,
1963, to June 30, 1966.
Source: U.S. Bureau of Census. Current Population
Reports Population Estimates, Series P-25,
No. 359, 1967, Table C

1966; and Series D, 2, 450, last observed as a calendar-year rate in the early forties.

"Fertility of whites and nonwhites was assumed to follow the general trend postulated for all races during the projection period but with partial convergence between white and nonwhite levels. . . . The projections of nonwhite fertility were derived on the basis of an assumed relation . . . between the age-specific birth rates for nonwhite and the age-specific birth rates for all races. Specifically, the relative difference between the age-specific birth rates for the nonwhite population and those for all races observed in the year 1965 would be reduced by the year 2,000 as follows: 25 percent for Series A, 40 percent for Series B, 60 percent for Series C, and 75 percent for Series D."

With this information, we may proceed to evaluate these projections. As of spring 1968, fertility levels were already well below those implied by Series A and B, had recently passed below the level implied by Series C, and were approaching the level implied by Series D. If this is a fundamental trend (and we think it is), we would be justified in dismissing Series A and B as being implausibly high and focus our attention on Series C and D.

The total fertility rates of 2775 and 2450 of Series C and D represent moderately high fertility levels for a developed country, and as cross-section (hypothetical cohort) measures of fertility they are quite high. In comparison with Japan and the various nations of Europe they are high indeed. In the history of the United States (the mid 1930s) and in the contemporary situation in Europe, fertility levels lower than this are common. In fact, total fertility rates below replacement level have occurred rather frequently in the past. As we have seen, the tendency toward earlier marriage has stabilized, so that the boost to the total fertility rate that came from earlier onset of childbearing and the tendency to bear children early in the marriage has now been fully realized. There may be some postponement of childbearing because of military service, however, which may temporarily depress fertility. Yet military service alone cannot ac-

count for the sharp and ubiquitous decline noted in Chapter 18 for all age levels and all birth orders. The conclusion that America is in retreat from the "baby boom" to substantially lower levels of fertility is inescapable. What is not known is at what point the decline will level off.

It is difficult to understand why the "low" level of projected United States fertility should not call for at least a lowering to the level of Sweden, Japan, and other low-fertility nations by the end of this century. In other words, it could reasonably be expected that the demographic transition could be completed in this century. In fact, it could reasonably be expected to be completed within a decade if the proper fertility "attitude climate" were to develop.

It is also difficult to comprehend why the differential in fertility between the white and the nonwhite population should not be wholly dissipated by the turn of the century. As of that date, the nonwhite population in the fertile ages will consist largely of third-generation urbanites; the educational differential that has long separated these two populations will have almost wholly disappeared; many if not most of the present income differentials will have been removed. Presumably, both populations will be equally well informed of family planning and will have equally easy access to contraceptive services. A "low" projection series should include this possibility.

To summarize, it does not seem implausible to anticipate a situation in the United States population where the net reproduction rate could fall below unity by 1975 if not before and the completed fertility of cohorts just starting their childbearing could be at the replacement level. Moreover, it is not difficult to visualize a situation in which the cohorts that have been so very fertile during the "baby boom" could literally cease to bear children during the remainder of their fertile years, if they find it advantageous or desirable to do so. Finally, it does not seem implausible to anticipate a complete elimination of the race differential in fertility within 20 years. As the white population approaches replacement while the non-white population continues to learn contraception, this gap could close rapidly. This combination of circumstances is within the realm of possibility. Indeed, it is a development of about this type that the present writer expects to take place. The full impact of the "baby boom" has not yet impressed itself upon the economy and the social life of the nation. As it does so, the dysfunctional side effects of high fertility could easily cause the "average size of desired family" to sink to two children. This could occur well before the year 2000. Such a course is no less improbable than the extraordinarily high Series A of the Census.

The writer would tend to regard the U. S. Bureau of Census Series C as a "high" estimate of the future course of population growth in this country. Series D could be accepted as a "medium" estimate until 1975, with the expectation that thereafter it might be too high. In the historical context of an industrialized nation with an already low age at marriage, this would appear to represent near-maximum fertility that could be expected.

Because of their extreme volatility and because the entire population of reproductive age knows of contraception and all but a tiny fraction is not adverse to using it, it would be wise in future population projections to maintain a "low" series that represents a sudden and drastic curtailment of fertility. A curtailment of this type occurred during the period 1930-1937; it is only an historical accident perhaps that it took place in response to an economic depression. A similar curtailment—equally drastic and even more complete—could occur nowadays in response to a wide variety of situations or a combination of situations: inflation, poverty, economic recession, desire to give children a college education, antiwar feeling, or rational comprehension of the implications of the third child for national long-run welfare. A "low" prediction that the crude birthrate of the United States could be at the level of 14 or 15 per thousand population by the year 2000 is not absurd.

In interpreting long-run birth trends, it should be kept in mind that in about 1985 the supply of women of prime childbearing age will level off and start to decline, at least temporarily, because of the curtailment of births that began in 1957. The population size for the nation that is achieved very shortly after that date could very well be the population size at about which a stationary population could be achieved. If recent fertility declines continue, this point could be reached at as low a figure as 220 million, but more plausibly might take place at between 250 and 330 million. An overall "medium" estimate for the United States population in the year 2000 is regarded by the writer to be a population of roughly 245 million, with near-zero growth thereafter. A "low" estimate would be 220 million and a "high" would be the 282 million specified by Series D.

This critical review of current official population projections for the United States is admittedly made from the "optimistic" viewpoint concerning the possibility for rapid achievement of fertility control. It is based on the theory that one of the commandments of the new set of international morals is a condemnation of uncontrolled childbearing; both individuals and families have a moral obligation, already elevated to a semi-sacred status, to conform or be ostracized.

Future Racial Composition. The Series D projections, regarded as least unreliably predicting the future composition of the population, indicate an increase in the nonwhite population to 35 million in 1990 and a rise from 11.4 to 13.7 percent of the total. Whereas one person in 9 was nonwhite in 1960, by 1990 one person in 7 or 8 will be nonwhite. It is possible that the percentage nonwhite may eventually stabilize at about 13 or 14 percent of the total population. Because nonwhite fertility may well decline below the levels anticipated by Series D, these estimates may be somewhat high.

Future Age Composition. Age composition is highly sensitive to changes in fertility. For this reason, the Series D estimates are able to predict future age composition only if the fertility schedule that they assume materializes. If they do predict the future course of fertility, there will be a sudden decline in the proportion of the population under 15. This is developing now, and will be fully developed by 1975. Thereafter, about one fourth of the population (instead of nearly one third as in 1960) will be under 15. Conversely, there will be a gradual

Table 21-10 Estimated Sex and Color Composition of the United States Population: 1970 to 1990 (Based on Series D Projections)

Year	Nonwhite population		Sex ratio	Percent under 15	Percent 65 and over
	Millions	Percent			
1960...........	20.7	11.4	97.8	31.0	9.2
1970...........	25.1	12.3	94.9	28.7	9.6
1975...........	27.2	12.6	91.1	26.4	9.8
1980...........	29.5	13.0	87.6	25.1	10.1
1985...........	32.3	13.4	84.9	25.9	10.3
1990...........	35.2	13.7	82.5	26.6	12.0

Source: U.S. Bureau of Census. Current Population Reports, Population Estimates, Series P-25, No. 359, 1967 Tables 1, 2, 3, 4, 5, 6.

aging of the population. By 1990 about one person in 8 would be of retirement age, whereas in 1960 only one person in 11 was this old. Whether the population continues to get progressively older will depend on whether or not fertility levels continue to fall, especially after 1975.

Future Sex Composition. The sex composition of the population is scheduled to undergo a sharp decline, from 97.8 in 1960 to 82.5 in 1990. This is associated primarily with the aging of the population and differential mortality.

21.8 Short-Range Projections of United States Population Composition

Despite their poor record of making long-range population projections, United States demographers have an excellent record for making short-range projections of a highly specific nature. For example, it is possible to make 10- or 15-year projections for such topics as the following:

age and sex composition (see Table 21-10)
school enrollments (see Table 21-11)
number of households and families (see Table 21-12)
size of labor force (see Table 21-13)
educational attainment of the adult population (see Table 21-14)

These topics refer primarily to adults. Inasmuch as the future trend of mortality is quite predictable within reasonably narrow limits and inasmuch as mortality does not affect population size very much until age 55 or beyond, it is possible to specify quite accurately for a

10- or 15-year period the number of adults who will be available for each of these activities—to be in the labor force, to live in households, and so on. This is true because the adults will already have been born at the time the projection is made. The precision of these specialized short-range projections depends on how accurately the estimator can anticipate the "participation rate" of adults in a particular activity in future years. (Examples are labor force participation rates, school attendance rates, and marriage rates.) In general, these participation rates either are very regular from year to year or have been changing by a rather steady secular trend, so that it has not proved difficult to anticipate what they will be 10 or 15 years hence. The short-range projections have been most useful for planning and administrative use. For example, they help to anticipate the needs in the near future for houses, jobs, schools, hospitals, automobiles, telephones, and a wide variety of products consumed by the public.

The short-range projections are also needed for local areas (individual metropolitan areas or even a neighborhood within a city). Because of the added complexity of migration, it is more difficult to prepare estimates of this type. However, despite the fact that they are prone to be wide of the mark by a substantial amount, even crude projections if made with full evaluation of the potential for future reproductive growth and migration are likely to be better than the uneducated guess of a nondemographer who is faced with the necessity of making a decision.

Table 21-11   Projections of School Enrollment, United States: 1966 to 1985

Years	Both sexes				Male				Female			
	Total enrolled	Elem. or kinder.	High school	College	Total enrolled	Elem. or kinder.	High school	College	Total enrolled	Elem. or kinder.	High school	College
1966........	55070	35624	13364	6085	28733	18197	6791	3749	26337	17425	6574	2337
Projections												
B - 1												
1970........	58899	36471	15005	7424	30910	18743	7566	4601	27989	17729	7438	2822
1975........	61858	36088	16310	9459	32714	18592	8262	5860	29144	17496	8048	3599
1980........	67572	40684	15706	11181	35879	20922	8017	6940	31694	19763	7689	4241
1985........	76867	47675	17345	11846	40680	24519	8815	7346	36187	23157	8530	4501
B - 2												
1970........	58228	36419	14762	7047	30542	18739	7417	4386	27686	17679	7344	2662
1975........	60433	35965	15903	8565	31923	18555	8022	5346	28510	17410	7882	3219
1980........	65381	40451	15212	9718	34652	20827	7728	6097	30729	19624	7484	3621
1985........	74040	47361	16751	9927	39100	24392	8466	6242	34940	22969	8285	3686
D - 1												
1970........	58899	36471	15005	7424	30910	18743	7566	4601	27989	17729	7438	2822
1975........	59428	33659	16310	9459	31473	17351	8262	5860	27955	16308	8048	3599
1980........	59156	32381	15593	11181	31584	16679	7964	6940	27572	15702	7629	4241
1985........	61498	35632	14278	11588	32812	18335	7274	7203	28686	17299	7003	4385
D - 2												
1970........	58228	36419	14762	7047	30542	18739	7417	4386	27686	17679	7344	2662
1975........	58041	33573	15903	8564	30702	17333	8022	5346	27339	16239	7882	3219
1980........	57050	32233	15099	9718	30402	16628	7677	6097	26648	15605	7422	3621
1985........	58880	35404	13781	9695	31344	18243	6985	6115	27536	17160	6796	3580

Notes : All figures in 00's
    Series B (enrollment rates) assumes
      1 - Net immigration of 400,000 per year as slightly decreasing mortality
      2 - TFR = 1965-6 2888
            1985   3129
    Series D (enrollment rates) assumes
      1 - Same as B
         TFR = 1965-6 2888
              1985   2435
    Series 1 & 2 (population projections) were combined with B & D to produce above 4 projections

Source: Current Population Report, Series P, 25 No. 365, 5-5-67 Bureau of the Census

Table 21-12 Projections of the Number of Households and Families, United States: 1966 to 1985

Type of household	Year				
	1966	1970	1975	1980	1985
A. All households					
Series 1....................	58092	63300	70001	77308	84421
Series 2....................	58092	62425	68229	74728	81207
B. Primary families					
Husband-wife families					
Series 1....................	42060	45556	50020	54957	59790
Series 2....................	42060	45053	49087	53702	58443
Other families, male head					
Series 1....................	1165	1135	1106	1126	1192
Series 2	1165	1182	1186	1229	1305
Female head					
Series 1....................	4944	5380	5938	6581	7224
Series 2....................	4944	5281	5772	6331	6858
C. Primary individuals					
Male					
Series 1....................	3292	3698	4280	4909	5590
Series 2....................	3292	3573	3991	4451	4930
Females					
Series 1....................	6631	7532	8657	9734	10626
Series 2....................	6631	7335	8193	9014	9671

Notes: 1 - All figures in thousands, reference date July 1, except 1966, which is March 1.

2 - Definitions -

Series 1 The trends of 1957-64 (1957-65) for primary individuals were used to establish projected proportions for age-sex-marital status groups in 1985. Proportions for intervening years were obtained by fitting a curve to the observations of 1957 and 1964 and projections of 1985. For primary individuals the data of 1957 and 1965 were used together with 1985

Series 2 This was produced by overaging series 1 and current levels

Source: Current Population Report, Series p-25, No. 360, 2-20-67, Bureau of the Census

21.9. Conclusion: The Future of Demography

Demographically speaking, the remainder of the twentieth century will be one of the most interesting and intellectually challenging epochs in history. There will be need to evaluate and reevaluate population trends and projections as the fertility control programs make their respective claims for success. The composition of the population will begin to change rapidly as fertility decline and economic development combine to bring about a change in the socioeconomic status of underdeveloped nations. There will also be dramatic changes in population distribution, with serious problems of concentrations in urban areas of migrants who need to be assimilated. There will be a steady growth of generalizations and theories to explain demographic events, to substitute for the more or less empirical extrapolative bent that is characteristic

today. The quantity and quality of census and vital statistics data will increase. More and more special surveys of increasingly improved design and execution will add to knowledge concerning facets that have not been made the subject of inquiry at the time of the census. This mountain of data will be increasingly released on punched cards or magnetic tape in order that it can be subjected to analysis by electronic computers.

These developments are all now under way. Among the social sciences, demography has been one of the first to promote empirical quantitative research of a high order. There is every reason to anticipate that it will continue to play this role.

Long ago, Carr-Saunders predicted that when the world had finally resolved its problem of numbers, it would quickly turn to the consideration of population quality. This is still an insightful prediction. The science of genet-

Table 21-13   Labor Force—Total, and Participation Rates, by Age and Sex: 1960 and 1965, and Projections 1970 to 1980

Sex and age	Total labor force					Participation rates (percent)				
	1960[1]	1965	1970	1975	1980	1960[1]	1965	1970	1975	1980
Total..............	73,081	78,357	85,999	93,646	101,408	57.4	56.7	57.5	57.8	58.3
Male................	49,563	51,705	55,844	60,281	64,981	79.7	76.9	77.0	76.9	77.2
14 to 19 years........	3,792	4,591	5,164	5,589	5,744	46.3	43.8	44.4	44.4	44.8
14 to 17 years......	1,952	2,336	2,574	2,717	2,716	34.4	32.6	32.3	32.1	32.0
18 to 19 years......	1,840	2,254	2,590	2,872	3,028	73.1	68.3	70.3	69.8	70.2
20 to 24 years........	4,939	5,926	7,466	8,331	9,064	88.9	86.2	86.6	86.7	87.2
25 to 34 years........	10,940	10,653	12,063	14,966	17,590	96.4	96.0	96.2	90.2	96.2
35 to 44 years........	11,454	11,504	10,930	10,703	12,084	96.4	96.2	96.7	96.7	96.7
45 to 54 years........	9,568	10,131	10,725	10,810	10,219	94.3	94.3	95.0	95.0	95.0
55 to 64 years........	6,445	6,768	7,388	7,795	8,184	85.2	83.2	84.3	83.9	83.7
65 years and over.....	2,425	2,131	2,108	2,087	2,096	32.2	26.9	25.1	23.4	21.8
Female..............	23,518	26,653	30,155	33,365	36,427	36.1	37.5	39.1	39.9	40.6
14 to 19 years........	2,408	2,940	3,406	3,739	3,832	30.1	28.9	30.1	30.6	31.0
14 to 17 years......	1,148	1,375	1,594	1,711	1,711	20.8	19.8	20.7	20.8	20.9
18 to 19 years......	1,260	1,565	1,812	2,028	2,121	51.0	48.6	50.6	50.6	50.8
20 to 24 years........	2,558	3,375	4,267	4,865	5,380	46.1	49.7	50.3	51.5	52.6
25 to 34 years........	4,159	4,336	4,894	6,124	7,347	35.8	38.5	38.6	39.3	40.3
35 to 44 years........	5,325	5,724	5,555	5,582	6,386	43.1	45.9	47.5	49.0	50.0
45 to 54 years........	5,150	5,714	6,675	7,024	6,805	49.3	50.5	55.3	57.6	59.5
55 to 64 years........	2,964	3,587	4,267	4,826	5,337	36.7	40.6	43.8	45.7	47.3
65 years and over....	954	976	1,091	1,205	1,340	10.5	9.5	9.8	9.8	9.9

[1]   Based on revised population estimates; differ from figures in Tables 307 and 308.

Source: Dept. of Labor, Bureau of Labor Statistics; Projections of the Labor Force, 1970-80, Special Labor Force Report, No. 49.

ics is progressing steadily, and the social sciences are learning more and more about the socialization process. It is quite possible that empirical research will be able to combine these fields, in the name of scientific demography, to derive some theoretical and policy principles that might lead to populations better adapted to the environment of the twenty-first century.

QUESTIONS AND EXERCISES

1. From the United Nations *Demographic Yearbook* transcribe onto one large table the following information for each of the developing nations of the world for which information is available:

Crude birthrate in 1965 and each year thereafter

Crude death rate in 1965 and each year thereafter

Crude rate of reproductive change in 1965 and each year thereafter

Compute the change, from 1965 to latest date at which information is available, in each of the three measures. Note the United Nations ratings of the reliability of the data. Write an essay concerning the apparent trend of births, deaths, and reproductive change in the developing nations. Contrast your findings with the basic assertions of Chapter 20.

2. Obtain the U. S. Census reports where the official projections are given for labor force, school attendance, number of families, and age composition for 1960, made during the 1950s. Compare the projected totals (medium) with the actual counts that were made by the decennial census. Calculate the errors of estimation. By studying the premises on which the projections were made, arrive at an explanation of how and why the errors occurred.

3. Repeat Exercise 2 for the total population projections for states, made during the 1950's. Compare with the actual census count and determine whether it was fertility, mortality, or migration that caused the discrepancies.

4. From the most recent issue of the *Demographic Yearbook,* compare the current estimate of world population, rate of growth, and birth and death rates by regions with the projections that were made in *World Population Prospects* by the United Nations. Note the differences for each world continent, in birthrates, death rates, and rates of reproductive change

Table 21-14 Percent of High School and College Graduates, by Sex, in the Population 25 Years Old and Over, for the United States: 1950 and 1960, and Projections to 1985
(Projections for 1970 to 1985 Based on Series B)

Year and sex	Both sexes		Male		Female	
	High school graduates[1]	College graduates[2]	High school graduates[1]	College graduates[2]	High school graduates[1]	College graduates[2]
1950.........	34.3	6.2	32.6	7.3	36.0	5.2
1960.........	41.1	7.7	39.5	9.7	42.5	5.8
1965.........	44.8	8.8	43.5	11.4	46.0	6.4
1970.........	49.0	10.1	48.0	13.4	50.0	7.2
1975.........	53.7	11.5	52.9	15.4	54.5	8.0
1980.........	58.3	12.9	57.5	17.5	58.9	8.8
1985.........	62.5	14.3	61.9	19.4	63.1	9.7

[1] Persons who completed 4 years of high school or beyond.
[2] Persons who completed 4 or more years of college.

between the projections and current estimates. Write an essay on the implication of these differences for future population estimates of the world.

5. Nothing has been said in the present chapter about the problem of predicting future population composition of small areas. Read as much as you can about this topic and write an essay on it. For example, discuss the problem of forecasting the future educational, ethnic, marital status, occupational, or income status of a suburban city.

6. Make an intensive study of famines, past and recent. Learn to what extent each famine was due to an absolute net shortage of food in the entire nation at the time and to what extent it was due to failures of emergency remedial action. Test the hypothesis that every famine that has taken place in the twentieth century could have been greatly mitigated by fairly simple administrative actions. Discuss the plausibility of a major famine now developing anywhere in the world as long as the U. S. has a net surplus of food production.

7. Make an intensive study of the net food balance of developing nations, and of the potential for improving the net food balance. Make a list of the changes that must take place—social, technical, and organizational—to achieve these gains. Write an essay evaluating the possibility of making these changes speedily in order to avert famines. Discuss the prop-

osition that with only moderate social progress almost every nation of the world could maintain a food balance such that it could support its population at a minimum level, even if population growth remained at the "high" level projected by the United Nations, at least until the year 2000.

8. Make a special study of the trend of death rates in the developing countries—especially in countries where birthrates are also remaining high. Is the death rate tending to remain high also—perhaps for the same reasons that are preventing fertility declines? What implications does this have for future growth of population?

9. Study the impact of delayed marriage on fertility. Read as much as you can about marriage trends in developing countries. Evaluate the proposition that rising age at marriage alone could account for most of the decline in fertility anticipated by the United Nations in its "medium" population projections.

10. Suppose that you are asked to prepare an estimate of the future population of the United States, given the birth, death, and migration rates that have been in force since 1960—and the changes that have taken place in each. Prepare what would be your best guess of age-specific fertility, mortality, and immigration rates to predict the population as of 1975 and 1980. Compare your results with those of the most recent official census projections.

BIBLIOGRAPHY

Aird, John S. "The Present and Prospective Population of Mainland China," in *Population Trends in Eastern Europe, the U.S.S.R. and Mainland China.* New York: The Milbank Memorial Fund, 1960.

American Society of Agronomy. *World Population and Food Supplies, 1980: A Symposium Sponsored by the American Society of Agronomy.* Matthias Stelly (ed.). ASA Special Publication 6. Madison, Wis., 1965.

Donald J. Bogue, "Recent Developments in Family Planning that Promise Hope in Coping with the Population Crisis and Throughout the World," *Proceedings of the Pacific Science Congress,* Tokyo, 1966.

Boulding, Kenneth E. *The Meaning of the Twentieth Century: The Great Transition.* New York: Harper and Row, 1964; London: Allen and Unwin, 1965.

Centro Latinoamericano de Demografia. *Proyección de la Poblacion de los Paises de Latinoamericano.* Santiago: Centro Latinoamericano de Demografia, Series C. 1960–68.

Coale, Ansley J., and Edgar M. Hoover. *Population Growth and Economic Development in Low Income Countries.* Princeton, N. J.: Princeton University Press, 1958.

Dorn, Harold F. "Pitfalls in Population Forecasts and Projections," *Journal of the American Statistical Association,* 45 (September 1950), 311.

Easterline, Richard A. "Economic-Demographic Interactions and Long Swings in Economic Growth." *American Economic Review,* 56 (5) (December 1966), 1063–1104.

Grauman, John V. "Population Estimates and Projections," Chapter 23 in P.M. Hauser and O. D. Duncan (eds.). *The Study of Population.* Chicago: University of Chicago Press, 1959.

Hagood, Margaret J., and J. S. Siegel. "Projections of the Regional Distribution of the Population of the United States to 1975," *Agricultural Economics Research,* 3 (1951), 41–52.

Hajnal, J. "The Prospects for Population Forecasts," *Journal of the American Statistical Association,* 50 (June 1955), 309–322.

Holzer, Jerzy. *Urodzenia i Zgony a Struktura Ludności Polski 1950-2000 (Births and Deaths and the Population Structure of Poland, 1950-2000).* Warsaw, Pánstwowe Wydawnictwo Ekonomiczne, 1964.

Hoover, Edgar M. "Economic Consequences of Population Growth," *Indian Journal of Economics* (Allahabad), 47 (184) (July 1966), 1–11.

Hoover, Edgar M. *Measuring Aspects of Economic Development. McGraw-Hill Series in Economic Development.* New York: McGraw-Hill, 1966.

Hyrenius, H. "Reproduction and Replacement," *Population Studies,* 4 (1951), 421–431.

Karmel, P. H. "The Relations between Male and Female Reproduction Rates," *Population Studies,* 1 (1947), 249–274.

Keyfitz, Nathan. *World Population.* Chicago: University of Chicago Press, 1968.

Kuczynski, R. R. *The Balance of Births and Deaths.* Vol. I—New York: Macmillan Co. (1928); Vol. II—Washington, D.C.: The Brookings Institution, 1931.

Kuczynski, R. R. *Fertility and Reproduction.* New York: Falcon Press, 1932.

Lotka, A. J. "The Geographical Distribution of Intrinsic Natural Increase in the United States, and an Examination of the Relations between Several Measures of Net Reproductivity," *Journal of the American Statistical Association,* 31 (1936), 273–294.

Lotka, A. J. "On the True Rate of Natural Increase," *Journal of the American Statistical Association,* 20 (September 1925), 305–339.

Lotka, A. J. "The Place of the Intrinsic Rate of Natural Increase in Population Analysis," *Proceedings of the Eighth American Scientific Congress,* 8 (1940), 247–255.

Lowry, Ira S. *Metropolitan Populations to 1985: Trial Projections.* Santa Monica, Calif.: Rand Corporation Memorandum RM-4125-RC, September 1964.

Notestein, F. W., et al. *The Future Population of Europe and the Soviet Union.* Geneva: League of Nations, 1944.

Organization for Economic Cooperation and Development. *Demographic Trends 1965-80 in Western Europe and North America.* Paris: Organization for Economic Cooperation and Development, 1966.

Shorter, Frederic C. "The Application of Development Hypotheses in Middle Eastern Studies," *Economic Development and Cultural Change,* 14(3) (October 1966), 340–354.

Shryock, Henry S. "Projections of Total Population and of Age-Sex Structure." Background Paper for the World Population Conference, Belgrade, 1965.

Siegel, J. S. "Forecasting the Population of Small Areas," *Land Economics,* 29 (1953), 72–88.

Spengler, J. J. The Economist and the Population Question. *American Economic Review,* 56(1) (March 1966), 1–24.

Spiegelman, Mortimer. "Fertility and Reproduction," Chapter 9 in *Introduction to Demography.* Chicago: The Society of Actuaries, 1959.

Spiegelman, Mortimer. "Population Estimates and Projections," Chapter 12 in *Introduction to Demography.* Chicago: The Society of Actuaries, 1959.

Stockwell, Edward G. "Some Demographic Correlates of Economic Development," *Rural Sociology*, 31(2) (June 1966), 216–224.

Stolnitz, George, and Norman B. Ryder. "Recent Discussion of the Net Reproduction Rate," *Population Index*, 15 (1949), 114.

Tachi, Minoru, and Yoichi Okazaki. "Economic Development and Population Growth—with Special Reference to Southeast Asia," *The Developing Economies* (Tokyo), 3(4) (December 1965), 497–515.

Thompson, Warren S. *Ratio of Children to Women: 1920*. (Census Monograph XI). Washington, D.C.: Government Printing Office, 1931.

United Nations. Department of Economic and Social Affairs. *World Population prospects as assessed in 1963*. Population Studies, No. 41. New York: United Nations, 1966.

United Nations. *The Future Growth of World Population*. New York: United Nations, 1958.

United Nations. *Methods for Population Projections by Sex and Age*. Manual III, Population Studies, No. 25, 1956. New York: United Nations.

U.S. Bureau of Census. "Illustrative Projections of the Population of States: 1970 to 1985." *Current Population Reports, Population Estimates*, Series P-25, March 1967.

U.S. Bureau of the Census. Foreign Demographic Analysis Division. "Projections of the Population of the Communist Countries of Eastern Europe, by Age and Sex: 1965-1985." By James L. Scott. *International Population Reports*, Series P-91, No. 13. Washington, D.C., 1965.

U.S. Bureau of the Census. "Projections of the White and Nonwhite Population of the United States, by Age and Sex, to 1985." *Current Population Reports*, Series P-25, No. 345, July 1966.

U.S. Bureau of Census. "Projections of School and College Enrollment in the United States to 1985." *Current Population Reports*, Series P-25, No. 338, May 31, 1966.

U.S. Bureau of the Census. "Projections of the Population of the United States, by Age and Sex: 1964 to 1985." By Jacob S. Siegel, Meyer Zitter, and Donald S. Akers. *Current Population Reports. Population Estimates*, Series P. 25, No. 286, July 1964.

U. S. Bureau of the Census. "Projections of the Population of the United States, by Age, Sex and Color to 1990, with Extensions of Total Population to 2015. Advance Figures." *Current Population Reports, Population Estimates*, Series P-25, No. 359, February 1967.

U.S. Bureau of Census. "Projections of the Number of Households and Families, 1967 to 1985." *Current Population Reports, Population Estimates*, Series P-25, February 1967.

U.S. Bureau of Labor Statistics. "Labor Force Projections, by Color, 1970-80." By Sophia Cooper and Denis F. Johnston. *Special Labor Force Reports*, No. 73, September 1966.

U.S. Bureau of Labor Statistics. "Labor Force Projections by State, 1970-80." By Denis F. Johnston and George R. Methee. *Special Labor Force Reports*, No. 74, October 1966.

Wander, Hilde. "Die Beziehungen zwischen Bevölkerungs und Wirtschaftsentwicklung dargestellt am Beispiel Indonesiens" ("The Relationship between Population Growth and Economic Growth as Exemplified by Indonesia"), *Kieler Studien*, Vol. 70. Tübingen, J. C. B. Mohr (Paul Siebeck), 1965.

Whelpton, P. K. "An Empirical Method of Calculating Future Population," *Journal of the American Statistical Association*, 49 (1954), 480–498.

Whelpton, P. K. "Reproduction Rates Adjusted for Age, Parity, Fecundity and Marriage," *Journal of the American Statistical Association*, 41 (1946), 501–516.

Wicksell, S. D. "Nuptiality, Fertility and Reproductivity," *Skandinavisk Aktuarietidskrift* (1931).

Yamaguchi, Kiichi. *Trends of Population Reproductivity in Japan*. Institute of Population Problems, Research Series, No. 172, December 1966.

Index

Abortion, fertility control and, 838
Abstinence, fertility control and, 839
Accidents, trends in deaths from, 584
Achievement, socioeconomic, defined, 428; *see also* Socioeconomic achievement
ADELMAN, IRMA, 677
Africa, family planning in, 852
  mortality trends in, 566
  population growth of, North, tropical, and South, 70
Age, of bride, color of household head and, 375
  marital status and disparity with age of groom, 329
  marital status and number of children-ever-born, effect on labor force participation rates, 229–231
  children-ever-born and, 692
  by economic regions, 491
  United States, 693
  color and, educational attainment in childlessness, United States, 726
  illegitimacy, 688
  sex and income, United States, 403
  composition, cohort principle, 150
  defined, 147
  of detailed occupations, 292
  developed *versus* underdeveloped nations, 148
  fertility and, 148
  life cycle and, 149
  long-term trends in, 164
  nations of the world, 154, 156
  regional differences in, 164
  statistics for, principles of interpretation, 153
  of United States population, 162
  future, 892
  life cycle and, 163
  urban-rural differences, 164, 472
  world population, 154, 156
  curve of nuptiality, 625
  at death, 558
  divorce proportions and, 340
  educational attainment by, by sex and color, 491–492
  in United States, 197
  at first marriage, 625
  current, and fertility, 719
  by occupation, 362
  of groom, disparity with age of bride and marital status, 329
  of household head, 374
  family size and, family income adjusted for, 418
  nonwhites and, 420
  race and, 406
  in internal migration, United States, 762
  labor force and, in participation rates, United States, 217, 224
  in status of urban-rural population, United States, 476
  marital status and, 314

Age (*cont.*)
  color and type of residence for children-ever-born and, 692
  educational attainment in childlessness and, 727
  at marriage, median, United States, marital status, 347
  recent changes in developing nations, 338
  median years of school completed and, United States urban and rural population, 474, 477
  proportion under 15 and, by per capita gross domestic product, 396
  race composition and, United States, by economic region, 489
  unemployment and, 235
  school enrollment and, 193, 199
  sex and, color and income, United States, 403
  color and unemployment, 236
  residence and internal migration, United States, 760
  sex differentials and, color differentials in internal migration, 761
  in trends in income, United States, 404
  sex ratio of United States population for economic regions by, 489
  structure, differentials in industrial composition, 263
  unemployment by, 233
  United States population, urban and rural and, living arrangements, 475
  marital status, 475
  school attendance, 473
  weeks worked by, economic regions, 495
Aged, poverty among, 415
Age-specific death rates, 119
  by sex and color, United States, trends, 593
Age-specific fertility, by color, 684
  pattern, United States, 683
  rates, 119
  method for computing, 120
Age-specific migration rates, 760
Agglomeration, urban, 7
Agriculture, dependence on, relation to fertility, 674
  work force participation rates, 221
American Indians, current fertility and, 718
  marital status of, 358
Ancient world, population growth, 53
ANDIC, S., 399
Annual rate of growth, defined, 34
  procedure for computing, 124
Area classification, systems of, 464
ARGENGAUD, ANDRE, 54
Asia, family planning in, 850
  marriage patterns in, 631, 633
  mortality trends in, 565
  population growth in, East, 69
  Middle South, 68
  Southwest, 70